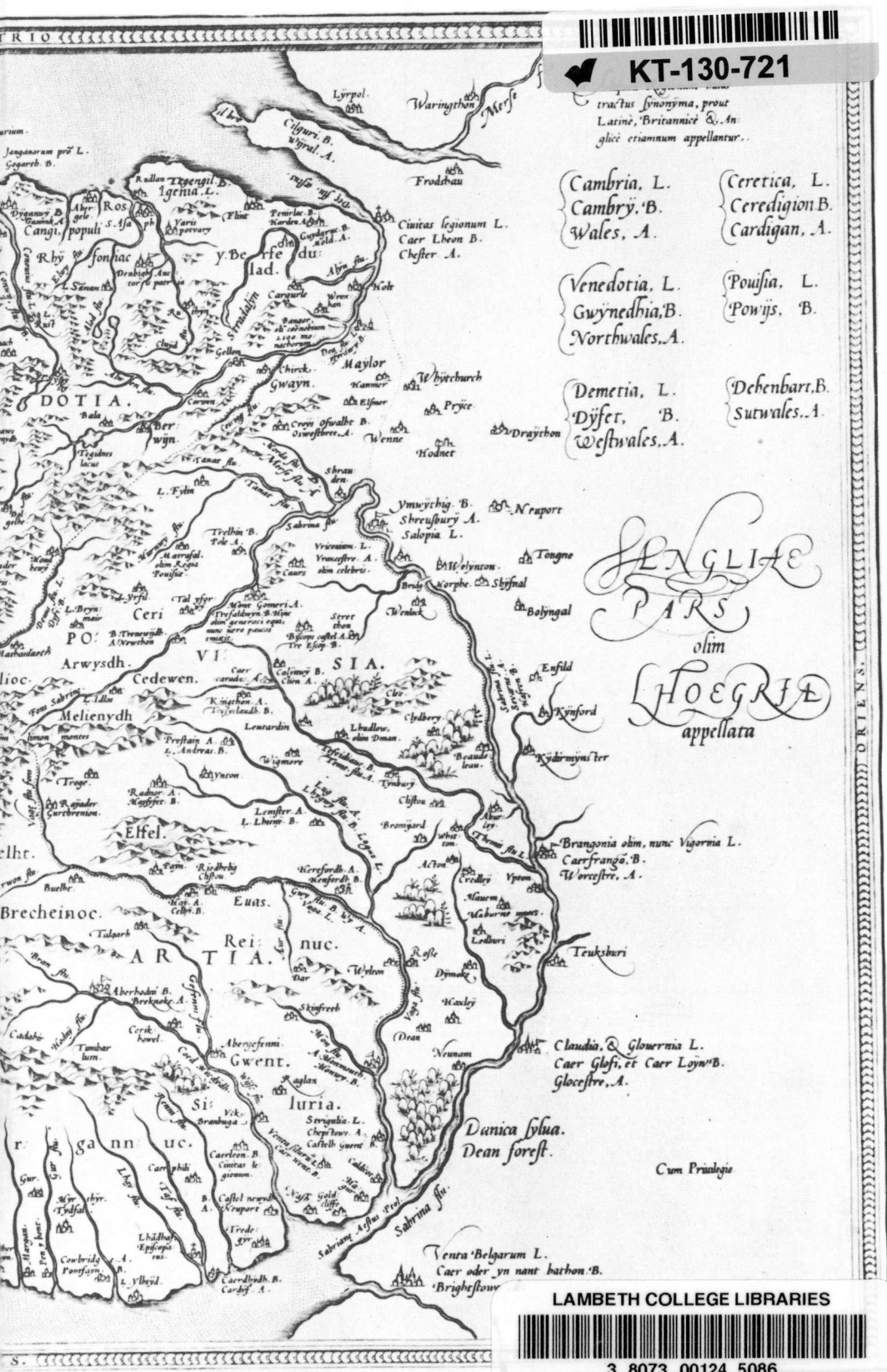

THE
OXFORD COMPANION
TO THE
LITERATURE OF WALES

The Oxford Companion to the Literature of Wales

Compiled and edited by
MEIC STEPHENS

**NOT TO BE
TAKEN AWAY**

Oxford New York
OXFORD UNIVERSITY PRESS
1986

Oxford University Press, Walton Street, Oxford OX2 6DP

Oxford New York Toronto
Delhi Bombay Calcutta Madras Karachi
Kuala Lumpur Singapore Hong Kong Tokyo
Nairobi Dar es Salaam Cape Town
Melbourne Auckland
and associated companies in
Beirut Berlin Ibadan Nicosia

OXFORD is a trade mark of Oxford University Press

This book, commissioned by Yr Academi Gymreig (The Welsh Academy),
is published with the financial assistance of the
Welsh Arts Council and the Arts Council of Great Britain

British Library Cataloguing in Publication Data
The Oxford companion to the literature of Wales.
1. Welsh literature—History and criticism—
Dictionaries
I. Stephens, Meic   II. Academi Gymreig
891.6'6'0321   PB2206
ISBN 0–19–211586–3

Library of Congress Cataloging in Publication Data
The Oxford companion to the literature of Wales.
1. Welsh literature.   2. Welsh literature—
Translations into English.   3. English literature—
Translations from Welsh.   4. English literature
Welsh authors.   I. Stephens, Meic.   II. Welsh Academy.
PB2361.094   1986   891.6'6'03   85–7095
ISBN 0–19–211586–3

Map of Wales by Edward Lluyd reproduced by
kind permission of the National Library of Wales

Set by Wyvern Typesetting Ltd
Printed in Great Britain by
Richard Clay (The Chaucer Press) Ltd
Bungay, Suffolk

EDITOR'S PREFACE

This book is intended to be a general introduction or useful guide to one of the oldest vernacular literatures in Europe. It spans the period from the sixth century, when the poets Aneirin and Taliesin flourished in the north of Britain, down to the present day. Among the finest achievements of writing in Welsh, the historic language of Wales, are the poems of eulogy and elegy associated with the independent Princes, the medieval prose-masterpiece known as *The Mabinogion*, the bright flowering of Dafydd ap Gwilym's genius, the scholarship produced by Renaissance Humanism, the powerful hymns of the Methodist Revival and, in Victorian times, the fruits of that predominantly literary culture which was maintained by the common people under the aegis of the Eisteddfod. During the twentieth century this long and rich tradition has continued to find vigorous expression through the medium of Welsh, while in English there has emerged a body of writing which, like that in the senior language, is informed not only by a sense of nationhood but also by a concern with the broader issues of the modern world.

All these aspects of the Welsh heritage, and much else besides, are treated here under a single alphabet and with a system of cross-references devised to help the reader, whether layman or student, over what may be unfamiliar ground. Some 2,825 entries have been included, of which nearly twelve hundred, the core of the work, deal with authors. Most of the authors listed are writers in the Welsh language, but also included is a selection of those Welsh men and women who have written in English, Latin and, in at least two instances, dialects of Norman French. Besides the poets, short-story writers, novelists, dramatists, hymn-writers and other men of letters whose writing forms the corpus of the country's literature, there are entries for some of the most important antiquaries, lexicographers, almanackers, balladeers, scholars, historians, journalists, editors, translators, critics, and writers on miscellaneous subjects such as topography, religion, philosophy and politics, who have made their own significant contributions. I have borne it in mind that, in the case of many, this book will be bringing them to the attention of a wider public for the first time, and so I have ensured that biographical and bibliographical details take precedence over critical discussion. The very fact of a writer's inclusion usually implies literary merit, unless there is a statement to the contrary, but I have tried to avoid giving the impression that all my geese are swans. While the length of an entry must be determined largely by its subject's importance, several considerations such as a writer's life-span and the sum of his or her work have sometimes upset the application of exact standards. Some entries, I hope, will arouse rather than satisfy the reader's curiosity, while others may reveal new facets of previously familiar topics.

All periods are represented and I have tried to strike a balance in my selection of writers for inclusion. With regard to Welsh writers in English, the canon of whose work has never been fully established, I have tended to be somewhat less than stringent for the reason that many are not to be found in any other work of reference. I have been rather more selective in the case of Welsh-language poets whose verse exists only in manuscript or in periodicals. Perhaps, too, I have been a trifle severe on certain Welsh poets of the late nineteenth century who wrote, usually for competition at eisteddfodau, verse of which the length now seems more remarkable than the quality, and more generally on English-language writers who, despite birth or domicile in Wales, cannot be said to have shown in their work any awareness of the history, landscape or people of this country. On the other hand, it seemed germane to the book's purpose that entries should be included for some of those wholly English writers such as Matthew Arnold, George Borrow, Gerard Manley Hopkins, Francis Kilvert and Thomas Love Peacock whose work has touched on Wales and the Welsh. As for living writers, they are so numerous and contemporary judgement so tentative that I could have wished it had been possible to exclude them as a matter of principle, but I decided instead to make a selection, however invidious it proved in some instances. No writer, whether in Welsh or English, has been included who was born after 1950, a terminal date necessary and yet unfortunate in that it excludes some younger people who have earned literary reputations, but in this, as in most other respects, I have followed the example of the series to which the book belongs. Entries for writers born during the 1940s have been kept as brief as possible. All writers who were alive during the period of the book's compilation were offered the opportunity of checking the drafts of their entries and the information given about them was up to date at the end of 1984. A few details pertaining to the first half of 1985 were added to the galley proofs. Only one writer refused to to be included, on grounds of confidentiality which I have respected. It was at the prompting of the Board responsible for supervising the work that I included an entry on myself, a breach of editorial etiquette for which I ask the reader's indulgence.

The next largest category is that which comprises entries for prosody, the literary genres, motifs, manuscripts, periodicals, serial publications, anthologies, novels and collections of short stories and verse. The English edition differs from the Welsh in that the technical complexities of *Cerdd Dafod* (the traditional rules of poetic art) are treated here in less detail and under fewer heads, though such unique features as *cynghanedd* and native forms like the *awdl*, the *cywydd* and the *englyn* have entries to themselves. Entries for the genres common to most European literatures have been limited to those such as biography and the epic to which a peculiar Welsh dimension is discernible. The selection of books requiring a separate entry was a particularly thorny problem. In some cases it seemed more appropriate to deal with them under the author-entry, so that *Dail Pren* (to take a conspicuous example), the only book published by Waldo Williams, has been subsumed in the entry for the poet. A few famous poems have their own entries, as do a representative number of the most popular folk-songs and hymns, though I cannot hope to have made a selection which will satisfy the reader whose interest is primarily musical. Some fictitious characters and places will be found by means of cross-references to books or authors, but many such from the treasury of Welsh myth, legend and folklore appear in their own right.

Although literature is its principal concern, this book is much more than a gazetteer of writers and their works, for it takes into account the impingement of history on the literature of Wales, its historical span exceeding its literary scope by several hundred years. A chronology of the history of Wales is printed as an appendix to the book, so there is no need to go into detail here. Suffice it to say that, although the net has been less widely cast, I have included entries for a substantial number of saints, kings, princes, gentry, patrons, philanthropists, martyrs, patriots, landowners, villains, soldiers, preachers, reformers, industrialists, politicians, publishers, painters, musicians, sportsmen and eccentrics, a motley company who share with the writers an undeniable place in the Welsh patrimony. The main principle of selection, which has been applied only to the dead, was not so much that these historical figures should have some intrinsic interest (although that is usually evident) as that the salient facts of their lives, however eminent or obscure, might be expected to enrich the reader's understanding of literary allusions to them, a nice consideration which sometimes produced surprising results. For the same reason I have admitted entries for events both historical and pseudo-historical, for buildings with cultural associations and for the ancient territories of Wales, especially if they may be said to feed the Welshman's imagination or to have a resonance requiring an elucidatory note. The inclusion of entries for national symbols, folk customs, societies, institutions and movements, completes my attempt to throw light, albeit selectively, on the social background to the country's literature.

In such a compilation as the one I have described an editor must rely on the goodwill and co-operation of many friends, colleagues and others known to him only from their publications and by correspondence. They are too numerous to mention by name but I should like to acknowledge here the assistance of those on whom I have depended most.

This book was commissioned by the Welsh Academy, the English-language section of *Yr Academi Gymreig*, the national society of writers in Wales. First of all, I have to thank the Academy for inviting me to undertake the editorship and thereby affording me the means of learning more about my country's history and literature. I am especially grateful to the Board which was charged with responsibility for overseeing the work on the Academy's behalf. This committee held its first meeting early in 1978 under the chairmanship of Professor Gwyn Jones. It discussed such matters as the book's size, content and arrangement and laid down general principles for the Editor's guidance but, the kindest of taskmasters, it allowed me a free hand at every subsequent stage of the work. In April 1981, though he remained a Board member thereafter, Professor Jones was succeeded by Dr R. Brinley Jones who served as Chairman until the work's completion in late 1985. Both Chairmen were staunch champions of the project from first to last and I am very thankful for their support. The other members of the Board were Dr Roland Mathias (1978–85), Dr R. Geraint Gruffydd (1978–

85), Mr Sam Adams (1978–85), Dr Pennar Davies (1978–81) and Mr Harri
Webb (1978–81); Dr G. O. Jones (Chairman of the Academy, 1978–81)
attended meetings in an *ex officio* capacity. The Oxford University Press was
represented on the Board by Mrs Dorothy Eagle and the University of
Wales Press, the publisher of the Welsh edition, by Professor Ceri W. Lewis.
The Academy's officers during the period in question were Mrs Sue Harries
(1978–83) and Mrs Ceri George (1983–85).

During the eight years that the work was in preparation the project was
funded annually by the Welsh Arts Council and the books are published now
with the aid of a grant provided by the Arts Council of Great Britain. I thank
the Council, as enlightened an employer as it is a patron, for allowing me to
accept the editorship in addition to my responsibilities as the Welsh Arts
Council's Literature Director, and for providing me with office facilities.

I was very fortunate in having, as my editorial team, three colleagues
whose services proved indispensable to the progress of the work and its
punctual conclusion. On the expertise of Mrs Nan Griffiths, one of the
Welsh Arts Council's Literature Officers, who took up her duties as Assistant Editor in June 1982, I relied heavily for the accuracy of the final Welsh
text. The Editorial Assistants, employed by the Academy in an administrative capacity, were Mrs Christine James (1978–81) and Miss Anne L.
Howells (1981–85), the second of whom was also engaged in seeing the
Welsh text through the press. All three were meticulous, resolute and
cheerful in their devotion to the work.

Next I should like to record my indebtedness to several experts whose
professional interest helped me in the shaping of the book. By courtesy of
Professors R. M. Jones and Bedwyr Lewis Jones respectively, the list of
entries was examined by the staff of the Welsh Departments at the University College of Wales, Aberystwyth, and the University College of North
Wales, Bangor, and by this means some lacunae were filled. A particularly
helpful analysis of the work's composition was made by Mr Dafydd Glyn
Jones of Bangor. Among others who suggested additions to the entry-lists
were Professor J. E. Caerwyn Williams of the University College of Wales,
Aberystwyth, and Dr Kenneth O. Morgan of The Queen's College, Oxford.
Unfortunately, the exigencies of space did not allow the inclusion of entries
for all the topics suggested during the later stages of the book's preparation
and the final choice, difficult as it sometimes was, had to be mine. I shall
therefore have to disappoint the reader who expects completeness or absolute consistency, though I remain confident that the book has its own
balance within the limits prescribed.

It was hardly feasible that *The Oxford Companion to the Literature of Wales*
could have been written by any one author, so wide is its purview. The
venture depended, as a matter of fact, on the collaboration of as many as 222
contributors. It was agreed at the outset that their names would be listed
separately at the head of the work, rather than under the entries. I am
grateful to all the contributors, many of whom are among the most
distinguished in their fields, but five deserve my special thanks for writing
much more extensively than the rest, namely Dr Roland Mathias, Professor
A. O. H. Jarman, Mr Robin Gwyndaf, Dr Pennar Davies and Dr Rachel
Bromwich. About a seventh part of the whole was written by the Editor.

The right to alter, reduce, rewrite, discard and recommission contributions according to my own discretion was another of the responsibilities entrusted to me by the Board, especially since it was part of my function to ensure concision and a measure of stylistic uniformity in material written by so many hands. The book's debt to *The Dictionary of Welsh Biography down to 1940* (prepared under the auspices of the Honourable Society of Cymmrodorion and published in a Welsh edition in 1953 and in English six years later) is evident in so far as many contributors drew on the information contained in that excellent compendium, but in several other respects the present work breaks new ground.

The process of emendation was sometimes made even more necessary by the fact that many entries were received only in one language, either Welsh or English, and had to be translated for the purposes of a book intended for publication in both. Among those who helped most with the task of translation were Mr Bryan Martin Davies and Mrs Mair Elvet Thomas. The cost of translation was partly defrayed by small grants received from Gwynedd County Council, Gwent County Council and the Catherine and Lady Grace James Foundation.

The texts were read in draft by twelve specialists. Dr Glyn Jones, Professor A. O. H. Jarman, Dr John Gwynfor Jones, Professor Brynley F. Roberts, Professor Bedwyr Lewis Jones, Professor Gwyn Thomas, Dr Derec Llwyd Morgan, Mrs Branwen Jarvis, Dr Gruffydd Aled Williams and Dr R. Brinley Jones read large parts of the work at various stages of its preparation and to them I offer warm thanks for their advice and assistance. My greatest obligation, however, is to the late Sir Thomas Parry and Dr Roland Mathias, who were particularly generous of their time and erudition, and whose close scrutiny of the complete texts, in Welsh and English respectively, ensured that many an error was avoided.

With the book's publishers I had the most cordial relations at all times. I found the guidance of Mrs Dorothy Eagle in matters relating to house-style and the aesthetics of reference books to be an enormous boon; she also helped me to read the proofs of the English edition. The patience of Mr Bruce L. Phillips of the Oxford University Press was matched by that of Mr John Rhys, the Director of the University of Wales Press, both of whom exercised their prerogatives very lightly.

The texts were typed by Mrs Nansi Jones, assisted by Miss Nia Rhosier, Mrs Anne Baik, Mrs Mair Williams and Miss Angela Howells. The typing of correspondence was undertaken by Mrs Gwenith Morgan and Mrs Mari Wyn Williams, while Mrs Gwyneth Evans helped with administrative chores.

For any errors which remain the Editor has to accept responsibility, of course. It is my earnest hope that the reader who finds them, or notes any serious omissions, will bring them to my attention so that they can be considered in time for any further edition which may appear.

Lastly, but as a matter of priority, there is one debt of gratitude which can be discharged only in the most personal terms. Although it was deemed to be part of my professional duties, my work on *The Oxford Companion to the Literature of Wales* was carried out mostly at home and in my own time. Each of the two texts went through four main drafts before it was ready for the printers. The eight-year task of compiling and editing them would have proved too daunting had I not been able to count on the support of a sympathetic family. My most heartfelt thanks are therefore due to my wife Ruth for her forbearance, encouragement and practical assistance, and to my children Lowri, Heledd, Brengain and Huw who played an important part by often diverting me from too zealous a commitment to the work.

MEIC STEPHENS
Whitchurch, Cardiff
September, 1985

CONTRIBUTORS

Sam Adams
Siôn Aled
Cary Archard
Glyn M. Ashton

Douglas A. Bassett
Angela Bennett
Gareth A. Bevan
Tony Bianchi
D. J. Bowen
Geraint Bowen
Rachel Bromwich
M. T. Burdett-Jones

A. D. Carr
Glenda Carr
Harold Carter
Idris Cox
Kathryn Curtis

Marged Dafydd
Don Dale-Jones
Iestyn Daniel
Wayne David
B. L. Davies
Brian Davies
Cennard Davies
Gwyn Davies
Helen Davies
John Davies
John Williams Davies
Pennar Davies
Philip Wyn Davies
Walford Davies
W. Beynon Davies
Wendy Davies
Moira Dearnley
Barbara Dennis
Armel Diverres

Aled Eames
Marion Eames
D. Islwyn Edwards
Hywel Teifi Edwards
Jane Edwards
Keri Edwards

Siân A. Edwards
Islwyn Ffowc Elis
Mary Ellis
John Emyr
Huw Ethall
D. Ellis Evans
D. Simon Evans
Eifion Evans
Emrys Evans
J. Wynne Evans
Lindsay Evans
Meredydd Evans
Rebecca Evans
R. Wallis Evans

Hywel Francis

Noel Gibbard
Gwyn Griffiths
J. Gwyn Griffiths
Llion Griffiths
Nan Griffiths
Robert Griffiths
T. Elwyn Griffiths
T. Gwynfor Griffiths
R. Geraint Gruffydd
Arfon Gwilym
Robin Gwyndaf

Marged Haycock
Elissa Henken
Greg Hill
Rhisiart Hincks
Graeme Holmes
Jeremy Hooker
David Howell
Anne L. Howells
Brian Howells
Glyn Tegai Hughes
Mathonwy Hughes
Belinda Humfrey
Gwilym Huws
Richard Huws

Dafydd Ifans
Rhiannon Ifans

Carolyn Iorwerth

Allan James
Christine James
E. Wyn James
A. O. H. Jarman
Eldra Jarman
Branwen Jarvis
Dafydd Jenkins
David Jenkins
Elfyn Jenkins
Geraint H. Jenkins
Bedwyr Lewis Jones
Bobi Jones
Bryn Jones
E. D. Jones
Emrys Jones
Glyn Jones
G. O. Jones
Gwerfyl Pierce Jones
Gwilym R. Jones
Gwyn Jones
Harri Pritchard Jones
Hugh D. Jones
Ieuan Gwynedd Jones
John Gwynfor Jones
Llewelyn Jones
Philip H. Jones
R. Brinley Jones
R. Gerallt Jones
Richard L. Jones
R. Merfyn Jones
Roger Stephens Jones
R. Tudur Jones
Sally Roberts Jones
Tecwyn Vaughan Jones
Tegwyn Jones
Watcyn Jones
W. J. Jones

D. P. Kirby

W. R. Lambert
Aneirin Lewis
D. Geraint Lewis

Peter Elfed Lewis
William Gwyn Lewis
D. Myrddin Lloyd†
D. Tecwyn Lloyd
Nesta Lloyd
Ceridwen Lloyd-Morgan
Alan Llwyd
Alun Llywelyn-Williams

D. F. Marks
Roland Mathias
R. W. McDonald
D. Parry M. Michael
E. G. Millward
Donald Moore
Derec Llwyd Morgan
Kenneth O. Morgan
Prys Morgan
T. J. Morgan
Brian Morris

W. Rhys Nicholas

John Ormond
D. Huw Owen
Gerallt Lloyd Owen
Goronwy Prys Owen
Goronwy Wyn Owen
Morfydd E. Owen
Trefor M. Owen
B. G. Owens

Thomas Parry†
Dewi Z. Phillips
Douglas Phillips
Richard Phillips†

John Pikoulis
Richard Poole
Nia Powell
W. Eifion Powell
Cecil J. Price
Emyr Price
A. G. Prys-Jones

Helen Ramage
D. Ben Rees
Ioan Bowen Rees
Brinley Richards†
W. Leslie Richards
Brynley F. Roberts
D. Hywel E. Roberts
Gomer M. Roberts
Hywel D. Roberts
W. M. Rogers
Jenny Rowland
Eurys Rowlands
John Rowlands
Gilbert Ruddock

D. Roy Saer
Elfyn Scourfield
David Smith
J. Beverley Smith
Peter Stead
Elan Closs Stephens
Meic Stephens
Catrin Stevens

D. O. Thomas
Graham Thomas

Gwyn Thomas
Isaac Thomas
Mair Elvet Thomas
Ned Thomas
R. L. Thomson
David A. Thorne
S. Minwel Tibbott
Geraint Tudur

Huw Walters
Meurig Walters
J. P. Ward
Gareth Watts
Harri Webb
Urien Wiliam
Gareth W. Williams
Glanmor Williams
Glyn Williams
Gruffydd Aled Williams
Gwyn A. Williams
Harri Williams†
Huw Williams
Ifan Wyn Williams
Iwan Llwyd Williams
J. E. Caerwyn Williams
J. Gwynn Williams
Patricia Williams
R. Bryn Williams†
Rita Williams
Roger Jones Williams
T. Arfon Williams
Trefor Williams
W. D. Williams†
Linda Wyn

NOTE TO THE READER

THE entries are arranged alphabetically in word-by-word order and according to the English alphabet. The names of authors from the modern period, when they form headwords, are printed in bold capitals, e.g. **JONES, DAVID**, the surname taking precedence. Authors from earlier times whose names are formed according to the patronymic principle appear thus, **DAFYDD AB EDMWND**. Names formed with the particle *ab* ('son of', before a vowel) precede those with *ap* (before a consonant or consonantal i) in the word-order. The Welsh penchant for bardic names, pseudonyms, sobriquets, nicknames, hypocoristic and other alternative forms accounts for the high incidence of one-line cross-references, by means of which the reader will find that many authors can be traced, e.g. **Iolo Morganwg**, see WILLIAMS, EDWARD (1747–1826).

The titles of literary works are printed in bold italics, e.g. *How Green was my Valley*, as are the titles of magazines and newspapers. The definite and indefinite articles have been discounted for the purpose of deciding the word-order, e.g. *Anglo-Welsh Review, The*. Except in the titles of books and periodicals, when these form headwords, modern orthography has usually been employed, as in quotations from the Welsh.

The headwords of all other entries are set in bold roman type, e.g. **Englyn**, **Harlech** and **Wassailing**. This style is also used for historical persons other than authors, e.g. **Bevan, Aneurin** and **Owain Glyndŵr**. Such persons are listed under their real names, when these are known, alternative forms appearing as one-line cross-references. Fictitious and legendary characters, whose names form an indissoluble whole, are listed according to the first element, e.g. **Polly Garter** and **Lleu Llawgyffes**. Persons bearing exactly the same names are arranged in chronological order. For persons with more than one first name, only the name or names by which they are commonly known will be found here. In the formulation of headwords the recourse to inversion has been kept to a minimum but in some instances, e.g. **Bosworth, The Battle of**, it was unavoidable.

An asterisk, representing *quod videm*, indicates that a separate entry will be found for the subject thus denoted.

The bibliographical information which appears at the foot of many entries is not meant to be exhaustive but refers, rather, to printed sources where more detailed discussion of the subject is to be found. The reader who requires more than is given here is advised to consult the bibliography of Welsh literature edited by Thomas Parry and Merfyn Morgan, *Llyfryddiaeth Llenyddiaeth Gymraeg* (1976); unfortunately, there is not yet any equivalent bibliography of Anglo-Welsh literature.

For the spelling of place-names the work relies on *A Gazetteer of Welsh*

Place-names (ed. Elwyn Davies, 1957). The names of the former counties of Wales, as they existed between 1284 and the reorganization of local government in 1974, have been preferred to their present counterparts which, in historical and literary terms, are of too recent provenance to have acquired their own significance.

THE PRONUNCIATION OF WELSH

WELSH is a language which is not so difficult to pronounce as many people seem to assume on first encountering it. Once the elements are mastered, the process is relatively straightforward because the language is largely phonetic, its sounds as represented by letters being, on the whole, fairly consistent. The following advice may help readers who wish to grasp the rudiments of Welsh pronunciation, especially if they bear in mind that the language, although euphonious, has an essentially robust character and is not one which can be spoken mincingly or through pursed lips.

There are twenty-eight letters in the Welsh alphabet: *a, b, c, ch, d, dd, e, f, ff, g, ng, h, i, l, ll, m, n, o, p, ph, r, rh, s, t, th, u, w, y*; the letters *j, k, q, v, x* and *z* occur only in words borrowed from other languages and, in the case of *k* and *v*, in archaic orthography.

The consonants, of which there are twenty-one, usually have the same sound-values as in English, but with the following exceptions: *c* is always pronounced as in 'cap', never as in 'centre'; *ch* as in 'loch', not as in 'chorus' or 'chat'; *dd* as in 'this'; *f* as in 'of'; *ff* as in 'off'; *g* as in 'god', not as in 'gin'; *ng* as in 'singing' but sometimes as in 'finger'; *h* is always aspirated as in 'house', never silent; *ll*, the voiceless fricative lateral, has no equivalent in English but is similar to the sound in 'antler' and can be reproduced, if not by imitation, by pronouncing *tl* rapidly, as if it were a single consonant and with a strong emission of the breath; *ph*, like *ff*, is as in 'phone'; *r* is always trilled as in 'horrid'; *rh*, an aspirated, voiceless, trilled *r*, is rarely heard in English; *s* is always sibilant as in 'son', never as in 'cousin', *si* representing *sh* as in 'shoe'; *th* is always as in '*think*'.

The seven vowels are *a, e, i, o, u, w* and *y*, all of which represent pure vowel-sounds and not diphthongs as in English. Unlike the consonants, they have two values, long and short, and a circumflex accent is sometimes used to distinguish between the two. As this difference is not always shown in writing, it should be remembered that, in general, vowels are short when followed by two or more consonants or by *c, ng, m, p, t*, and long when followed by *b, ch, d, dd, f, ff, g, s, th*. The vowel-sounds are as follows: *a* can be long as in 'palm' or short and flat as in French *à la*, but has nothing to do with the *æ* sound so often given to *a* in English, as in 'cake'; *e* is a pure half-close front vowel rarely heard in southern England but, when long, it is similar to *a* in 'face' as pronounced in the north of England (and south Wales) or to the sound in the French word *très*, and when short it is as in 'pen'; *i* can be vocalic and long as in 'feed' or short as in 'lip', or consonantal as in 'young'; *o* is pronounced long as in 'door' (a pure half-close back vowel) or short as in 'not'; *u* is like long and short *i* in south Wales while in the north-west it resembles the close, centralized vowel in the French pronoun *tu*, but is not rounded; *w* can be long as in 'school' or short as in 'cook' but is sometimes consonantal as in 'war'; *y*, in monosyllables and final syllables, is usually clear like the long or short vocalic *i*, but in non-final syllables it is usually the obscure sound which, when long, is like *u* in 'further', and when short as in 'gun'.

Welsh in its written form has sixteen diphthongs, in all of which the principal vowel comes first. In the Welsh of south Wales they fall into two groups. Those ending on a close front vowel are *ae, ai, au* as in 'aye, aye', *ei, eu, ey* as in 'day', *oe, oi, ou* as in 'boy', and *wy* which has no English equivalent but is pronounced 'oo + ee'; the diphthongs ending on a back rounded vowel are *aw* as in 'miaow', *iw, uw, yw* as in 'yew', *ew* which is the short *e* followed by 'oo', and *ow* as in 'cow'. In the Welsh of north Wales the diphthongs *ae, au, eu, ey, oe, ou, wy*, end on a close central vowel.

The main accent usually falls on the penultimate syllable: *Dáfydd, cynghánedd, Llanfairféchan, hunanlywódraeth, camgymeriádau*.

Further details about the pronunciation of the language will be found in the introduction to H. Meurig Evans, *The Dictionary of Modern Welsh* (1981). Also set out there are the rules governing the soft, nasal and spirant mutation of initial consonants and the aspiration of vowels, a feature which Welsh has in common with other Celtic languages.

ABBREVIATIONS

AD	*anno Domini* (in the year of our Lord)	HTV	Harlech Television
		L.	Latin
ang.	*anglice* (Anglicized)	lit.	literally
Ang.	Anglesey	MA	*Magister Artium* (Master of Arts)
b.	born		
BBC	British Broadcasting Company	Mer.	Merioneth
		Mon.	Monmouthshire
BC	before Christ	Mont.	Montgomeryshire
BL	British Library	MS(S)	manuscript(s)
Brecs.	Breconshire	n.d.	no date
c.	*circa* (about)	NLW	National Library of Wales
Caerns.	Caernarfonshire	no.	number
Cards.	Cardiganshire	Pembs.	Pembrokeshire
Carms.	Carmarthenshire	pl.	plural
cent.	century	Rads.	Radnorshire
cf.	*confer* (compare)	RAF	Royal Air Force
Ches.	Cheshire	Salop	Shropshire
d.	died	St.	Saint
Denbs.	Denbighshire	trans.	translator, translation
E.	English	TWW	Television Wales and the West
ed.	edited by, editor		
edn.	edition	UCW	University College of Wales
et al.	*et alii* (and others)		
F.	French	UCNW	University College of North Wales
fl.	*floruit* (flourished)		
Flints.	Flintshire	UNESCO	United Nations Educational, Scientific, and Cultural Organization
G.	German		
gen.	genitive		
Glam.	Glamorgan		
Glos.	Gloucestershire	USA	United States of America
Herefs.	Herefordshire	vol.	volume
HMSO	Her Majesty's Stationery Office	W.	Welsh

A

'A oes heddwch?' (lit. 'Is there peace?'), the cry of the Archdruid in the ceremonies of *Gorsedd Beirdd Ynys Prydain*, was devised by Edward *Williams (Iolo Morganwg). At the third challenge and the audience's final response of 'Heddwch!', the Great Sword—partly drawn from its scabbard—is sheathed, in symbolic acknowledgement that 'the Bards of the Isle of Britain are men of peace and bear no naked weapon against anyone'.

AARON, RICHARD ITHAMAR (1901–   ), writer on philosophical subjects. Born at Blaen Dulais, Glam., and educated at Oriel College, Oxford, he was Professor of Philosophy at the University College of Wales, Aberystwyth, from 1932 to 1969. Among the honorary offices he has held are the Vice-Chairmanship of *Coleg Harlech*, the Presidency of the Mind Association and the Chairmanship of the Council for Wales. His published works include *The Nature of Knowing* (1930), *Hanes Athroniaeth* (1932), *John Locke* (1937), *The Theory of Universals* (1952) and *Knowing and the Function of Reason* (1971). From 1938 to 1968 he was the editor of the journal *Efrydiau Athronyddol*, of which a special number (vol. 32, 1969) was published in his honour on the occasion of his retirement.

Ab Ithel, see WILLIAMS, JOHN (1811–62).

Aber Alaw, see under BRANWEN.

Aber Henfelen, see under GWALES.

Aberbechan, a mansion in the parish of Llanllwchaearn, Mont., which played an important part in maintaining bardic patronage in the county. Morys ab Owain (d. 1568), like his father before him, welcomed poets to his home but the most noteworthy patron was his son Rhys, who extended both the house and its traditions. The poets *Huw Arwystli and Sir Ieuan of Carno (*fl.* 1530–70) competed for the patronage of Aberbechan which was continued by Thomas, the next heir, and by his daughter Gwen (d. 1639), the wife of Sir Richard Price (d. 1651) of *Gogerddan.

Aberconwy, an abbey affiliated to the *Cistercian Order, was founded about 1186 as a daughter-house of *Strata Florida. First established at Rhedynog Felen, near Caernarfon,

the community moved to Aberconwy in 1192 under the patronage of *Llywelyn ap Iorwerth (Llywelyn Fawr) and, like his sons Gruffudd and Dafydd, the Prince was buried there. In 1282, or perhaps in the following year, the abbey was moved once again, to Maenan, up the Conwy valley, because Edward I wanted the Aberconwy site for his new castle. The monks kept a short register which includes a list of the possessions of Aberconwy and Strata Florida, together with charters, legal documents and a chronicle of events from the seventh century down to 1283.

From about 1490 to 1513 the abbot was Dafydd ab Owain who was also, in his time, abbot of *Strata Marcella and of Strata Florida; he later became Bishop of *St. Asaph. The poets Wiliam Egwad, Rhys Pennardd (*fl.* 1480), *Lewys Môn, *Tudur Aled and *Owain ap Llywelyn ab y Moel, among others, were unstinting in their praise of Dafydd's godliness and hospitality. They also emphasized his good pedigree from the Dolobran family of Powys, his great learning from Oxford, his contribution towards the cost of restoring the abbey's fabric and his support for the cause of Henry *Tudor. Altogether eighteen poems addressed to him during his prosperous years at Maenan have survived but, oddly enough, no elegy. Tudur Aled sang in praise of Dafydd's successor, Sieffre Cyffin (*c.*1513–*c.*1527), and abbot Sieffre Johns (*c.*1528–*c.*1536) was one of those from whom the poet Huw *Llwyd requested oxen. The abbey was dissolved in 1536.

For further details see Rhys W. Hays, *The History of the Abbey of Aberconwy* (1963).

Aberconwy, The Battle of (1194), marked a crucial phase in the military fortunes of *Llywelyn ap Iorwerth (Llywelyn Fawr). Assisted by his cousins Gruffudd and Maredudd ap Cynan, he defeated the forces of his uncle *Dafydd ab Owain Gwynedd at the mouth of the river Conwy. By 1202 Llywelyn was established as the sole ruler of *Gwynedd between the Dee and the Dyfi. His victory at Aberconwy was celebrated by the court poets *Cynddelw Brydydd Mawr and *Llywarch ap Llywelyn (Prydydd y Moch).

Aberconwy, The Treaty of (1277), was concluded between Edward I and *Llywelyn ap Gruffudd after the English victory in the first

*War of Welsh Independence (1276–77). Llywelyn kept the title of Prince of Wales but henceforth only five Welsh lords were to render homage to him. He was required to release his elder brother, *Owain Goch ap Gruffudd, whose long captivity had been deplored by the poet *Hywel Foel ap Griffri ap Pwyll Wyddel. Another brother, Dafydd, was granted the cantrefi of *Rhufoniog and Dyffryn Clwyd in the *Perfeddwlad, between the Conwy and the Dee. Two other cantrefi, *Rhos and *Englefield (Tegeingl), were placed in the custody of Reginald de Grey, Justice of Chester. Llywelyn was deprived of the territorial gains conferred on him by the Treaty of *Montgomery (1267). Differences in the interpretation of certain clauses in the Treaty of Aberconwy were to lead to further friction which contributed to the outbreak of the second War of Welsh Independence in 1282.

For further details see J. E. Lloyd, *A History of Wales* (1911) and J. Conway Davies (ed.), *The Welsh Assize Roll 1277–1284* (1940).

Abercuawg, presumed to be an early name for the mouth of the river Dulas which flows into the Dyfi some two miles east of Machynlleth, Mont. The earliest reference to it occurs in '*Claf Abercuawg*', a sequence of *englynion* in *'Canu Llywarch Hen*', where a lame man, complaining that he cannot go to war, speaks of a cuckoo calling at Abercuawg. Edward *Thomas used a translation of the verses in his book, *Beautiful Wales* (1905), in order to articulate his response to 'the magic of Wales', and R. S. *Thomas invoked the place in his lecture, *Abercuawg* (1977), which attempts an imaginative realization of a quintessential Wales.

Aberfan, a village near Merthyr Tydfil, Glam., where part of a coal-tip slid into the valley, crushing houses and burying the Pant-glas Junior School, on 21 October 1966. In all, 116 children and twenty-eight adults lost their lives in the disaster.

Aberffraw, a village in the south-west of Anglesey. In the Second Branch of *Pedair Cainc y Mabinogi*, the wedding-feast of *Matholwch and *Branwen is held at Aberffraw and the Princes of *Gwynedd had their chief court there during the Middle Ages. After 1230 *Llywelyn ap Iorwerth (Llywelyn Fawr) began to use the title 'Tywysog Aberffraw ac Arglwydd Eryri' ('Prince of Aberffraw and Lord of Snowdonia'). In the famous elegy by *Gruffudd ab yr Ynad Coch for *Llywelyn ap Gruffudd, the last independent Prince of Wales, he is described as '*frenin, dderwin ddôr, Aberffraw*' ('the king, the oaken door, of Aberffraw').

Abergele Martyrs, The, two members of the clandestine Nationalist group *Mudiad Amddiffyn Cymru*, by name William Alwyn Jones and George Francis Taylor, of Abergele, Denbs., were killed when the explosives they were carrying were accidentally detonated on 1 July 1969, the day of the investiture of the Prince of Wales. Their deaths were commemorated by several poets, including Euros *Bowen and Bobi Jones (Robert Maynard *Jones), and their graves have become the focus for an annual ceremony.

Aberglasne, see under GRONGAR HILL (1726).

Abergwili, the residence of the Bishops of *St. David's, is situated near Carmarthen. Henry Gower, Bishop between 1328 and 1347, had a palace built at St. David's, Pembs., but William Barlow, Bishop from 1536 to 1548, who stripped the roof of its lead to provide for his daughters' marriages, tried to have the see moved to Carmarthen. Only the palace at Abergwili was ever completed.

Since many of the Bishops were not Welshmen, or even of Welsh sympathies, the tradition of offering patronage to poets was intermittent. During the episcopacy of Richard *Davies (1501?–81), however, the poets enjoyed generous hospitality at Abergwili. The poet Gruffudd ab Ieuan ap Llywelyn Fychan was a cousin of the bishop's mother and *Gruffudd Hiraethog may have been his bardic teacher, so he had literary as well as ecclesiastical interests. Furthermore, the work of translating the New Testament into Welsh was begun there under Davies's supervision. Many poems composed by poets and minor gentry who had received his patronage have survived, testifying to the part played by Abergwili as a centre of learning. Some of Davies's successors maintained the tradition, but none to the same extent, into the early years of the seventeenth century.

For further details see Glanmor Williams, *Bywyd ac Amserau'r Esgob Richard Davies* (1953), *Welsh Reformation Essays* (1967) and *Grym Tafodau Tân* (1984).

Aberlleiniog, The Battle of (1094), see under GELLAN (11th–12th cent.).

Aberpergwm, a mansion in the parish of Nedd Uchaf, Glam., was once famous for its bardic patronage and its library of manuscripts. The house was the principal resort for the county's poets and the poetry devoted to the family which lived there testifies to the literary activities of at least four generations. Rhys ap Siancyn (*fl.* 1430–50) was the first known patron and his great-grandson, also named Rhys, the most notable. The poet most frequently associated with Aberpergwm is *Iorwerth Fynglwyd.

In the eighteenth century Aberpergwm was the home of Rees Williams (d. 1812), believed to have been the last in Wales to employ a household poet, in the person of Dafydd *Nicolas. A daughter of his, Maria Jane Williams (Llinos; 1795–1873), was a renowned singer and collector of folk-songs. The version of the Chronicle of the Princes (*Brut y Tywysogyon) which is known as Brut Aberpergwm was made, it is claimed, by Edward *Williams (Iolo Morganwg) from a text copied in 1764 by Thomas Richards from a manuscript belonging to George Williams, a member of this family. It records events from the year 660 down to 1196 and was published in The Myvyrian Archaiology of Wales (1801) at the expense of Owen *Jones (Owain Myfyr).

Aberthged, see BLODEUGED.

'Aberystwyth', a well-known hymn-tune by Joseph *Parry, was composed in 1877. There are several spurious stories about the circumstances of its composition. First published in Ail Lyfr Tonau ac Emynau (ed. Stephen and Jones, 1879), with the words 'Beth sydd imi yn y byd?' by Morgan *Rhys, it has subsequently been included in many collections of hymns in Wales and England. It is often sung to the English words 'Jesu, Lover of my Soul', by Charles Wesley.

Aberystwyth Studies, a journal of which fourteen numbers appeared at irregular intervals between 1912 and 1936. The original aim, to produce 'an annual publication which should consist of contributions to learning—more especially in the Humanities—made by past and present members of the College' (the UCW, Aberystwyth), was realized to a large extent: of some hundred articles, only a dozen are on scientific subjects. However, only a few deal with topics of specifically Welsh interest and, almost without exception, the contents are in English. The most significant volume is the tenth (1928), which is devoted to the celebration of the millenium of *Hywel Dda and in which may be found important contributions to the study of the Welsh Laws by such scholars as J. E. *Lloyd, T. H. *Parry-Williams and Timothy *Lewis.

Ablett, Noah (1883–1935), miners' leader. Born in the *Rhondda Valley, he first came to prominence when he persuaded the *South Wales Miners' Federation to transfer scholarships from Ruskin College, Oxford, to a new Central Labour College which dispensed Marxist teachings to a generation of leaders, including Aneurin *Bevan, James *Griffiths and Lewis *Jones (1897–1939). It was Ablett who inspired the writing of The Miners' Next Step (1912) by A. J. *Cook and the mixture of *Marxism and Syndicalism in that pamphlet is typical of his thinking, which was categorically opposed to the conciliatory attitudes of the older miners' leaders such as William *Abraham (Mabon).

Abraham, William (**Mabon**; 1842–1922), miners' agent, Member of Parliament for the

*Rhondda and first President of the *South Wales Miners' Federation, was a native of Cwmafan, Glam. He began his parliamentary career in 1885 as a Radical with the Liberals until the Labour Party emerged as an independent party in 1906. A keen eisteddfodwr, of burly physique and powerful tenor voice, he was fond of leading audiences in the singing of Welsh hymns. He was also an advocate of the Welsh language and had a hand in the formation of the first *Cymdeithas yr Iaith Gymraeg (1885). On one famous occasion in 1892 he ventured to speak Welsh in the House of Commons, at which some members broke into laughter, only to be informed by Mabon that he had been reciting the Lord's Prayer. During the 1890s the miners of south Wales did not work on the first Monday of each month, in order to limit production and maintain wages, and this day was popularly known as 'Mabon's Monday'. Towards the end of his career, Abraham was often charged with 'Lib-Labbery' by a new generation of more militant Socialists in the coalfield of south Wales, but as a champion of the miners he was widely respected.

For an account of his life and work see E. W. Evans, Mabon, a Study in Trade Union Leadership (1959).

ABSE, DANNIE (1923–), poet, dramatist and novelist, was born and grew up in Cardiff. He studied at the Welsh National School of Medicine before moving, in 1943, to London where he continued his medical studies at King's College and Westminster Hospital. Qualifying as a doctor in 1950, he maintained close contact with the family home but has lived since then in London where he works part-time in a chest clinic.

The political and social events of the 1930s are central to Dannie Abse's writing. As a schoolboy he discussed *Socialism with his brother Leo, who was later to become the Labour Member of Parliament for Pontypool (now Torfaen), and was deeply moved by the Spanish Civil War, about which he wrote in his autobiography, A Poet in the Family (1974). He also became aware of new ideas in psychiatry through conversations with another brother, Wilfred, who became a psychoanalyst. A Cardiff upbringing, the bitter-sweet quality of Jewish family life and the real and imaginary worlds of childhood were evoked in his first novel, *Ash on a Young Man's Sleeve (1954). It was followed by Some Corner of an English Field (1956), which draws on his experiences in the RAF to depict unromantic, drab, post-war England losing its way among decaying customs and conformities, and by O. Jones, O. Jones (1970), a novel about a medical student's picaresque adventures in London.

It is as a poet, especially as a reader in public, that Dannie Abse is best known, however. He has published seven volumes of poetry: After Every Green Thing (1948), Walking Under Water

(1952), *Tenants of the House* (1957), *Poems, Golders Green* (1962), *A Small Desperation* (1968), *Funland* (1973) and *Way Out in the Centre* (1981); his *Selected Poems* appeared in 1970 and his *Collected Poems 1948–76* in 1977.

At the heart of his poetry lies a concern for the unusual and eccentric in human nature. He believes the most dangerous forces of the twentieth century to have been towards uniformity and he identifies with those who have not obeyed or who have suffered as a result of mass obedience. The tension of much of his work has come from his sense of belonging to two minorities, the Welsh and the Jews. Although he is primarily a lyricist, his characteristic forms are parables which allow him to deal with issues deeper than the narrowly personal. A transcendental poet haunted by forgotten tunes and unfocused voices, his melancholy invites comparison with that of Philip Larkin but he is never as cynical or as self-indulgent. A stronger sense of Jewishness has deepened his gloom and his humanity since the early 1960s and his images have become more original and more opposed to their contexts.

Also a dramatist, Dannie Abse has published seven plays: *Fire in Heaven* (1956), *The Eccentric* (1961), *Three Questor Plays* (1967), *The Dogs of Pavlov* (1972) and *Pythagoras* (1979), most of which deal experimentally with contemporary themes. A selection of his occasional writings, including a short story, a diary and a one-act play, has been published in the volume *Miscellany One* (1981) and a further volume of autobiography under the title *A Strong Dose of Myself* (1983); he has also edited the anthologies *Wales in Verse* (1983) and *Doctors and Patients* (1984).

For a critical discussion see *The Poetry of Dannie Abse* (ed. Joseph Cohen, 1983); see also the essays by Roland Mathias in *The Anglo-Welsh Review* (vol. 16, no. 38, 1967) and by John Pikoulis in *Poetry Wales* (vol. 13, no. 2, 1977), and the booklet *Under the Influence of* (The Gwyn Jones Lecture, 1984). There is a monograph on Dannie Abse by Tony Curtis in the *Writers of Wales* series (1985).

Ac Eto Nid Myfi (lit. 'And yet not me'; 1976), a play by John Gwilym *Jones. The title is taken from a couplet in the poem '*Dryswch*' by T. H. *Parry-Williams:

> *Mae amryw byd ohonom yn fy nghlai.*
> *Myfi ŷnt oll,—ac eto nid myfi.*

('There are various elements in my clay. They are all me,—and yet not me'). If this suggests that there are autobiographical aspects to the work, it should not be interpreted as being literally true. The play revolves around Alis's refusal to marry Huw, the chief character, even though she is carrying his child. The reason she gives him is, '*Am mai chi ydach chi*' ('Because you are you'). The influences which made Huw what he is are then traced in a series of short, episodic scenes in which he appears as a child, an adolescent and a young man. In his relationships with his parents, his grandmother, his best friend and with Alis, he is portrayed as extremely sensitive, emotional and keenly aware of the dichotomy of life, of its pain and its joy. The play shares a basic theme with all John Gwilym Jones's work: Man is a captive being, created by his inheritance and environment, with which he must eventually come to terms.

Academi Gymreig, Yr (lit. 'The Welsh Academy'), the national society of writers in Wales, was founded in 1959 on the basis of conversations between Bobi Jones (Robert Maynard *Jones) and Waldo *Williams, writers in Welsh who chose the adjective '*Cymreig*' (rather than '*Cymraeg*') to allow the subsequent inclusion of writers in English, and other artists. The creation of an English-language section in 1968 was the result of an initiative by Meic *Stephens, in his capacity as Literature Director of the *Welsh Arts Council, in association with members of the Guild of Welsh Writers, a group based mainly in London.

The society exists to promote literature in Wales and to assist in maintaining its standards by providing a forum for writers, about a hundred and thirty of whom make up its elected membership. With funds mostly provided by the Welsh Arts Council, it has been constitutionally independent since 1978 and has its own offices in Cardiff. Among the publications sponsored by the Welsh-language section are an English-Welsh Dictionary, translations into Welsh of modern foreign poetry and prose, a series of Welsh classics and the literary journal *Taliesin*. The present *Companion* was compiled under the aegis of the English-language section, which also organizes a variety of literary events, such as writers' work-shops, competitions, public readings and an annual conference.

For details about the establishment of *Yr Academi Gymreig* see the account by D. Gwenallt Jones in *Taliesin* (vol. 1, 1961) and the lecture by Bobi Jones in the volume *Dathlu* (ed. R. Gerallt Jones, 1985); the inaugural meeting of the English-language section was described by Meic Stephens in *Poetry Wales* (vol. 4, no. 2, Winter, 1968).

Ace, Maggie (b. 1854) and **Jessie** (b. 1861), daughters of the lighthouse keeper at the Mumbles, a resort near Swansea, won fame during the shipwreck there, on 27 January 1883, of a German vessel, the *Prinz Adalbert*. The sisters saved a member of the lifeboat's crew from drowning by wading into the stormy sea and pulling him to safety with their scarves. This act of bravery was celebrated in a stirring (but inaccurate) ballad by Clement Scott (1841–1904), 'The Women of Mumbles Head', which immediately captured the public's imagination and became a favourite piece for recitation in school and music-hall.

The ballad and further details will be found in Carl

Smith, *The Men of the Mumbles Head* (1977) and P. H. Rees, *Gower Shipwrecks* (1978).

Acid Drop, The, see WILLIAMS, THOMAS MARCHANT (1845–1914).

Acre of Land, An (1952), R. S. *Thomas's second volume of verse, contains thirty-one poems written between 1946 and 1951 while the poet was rector of Manafon, Mont. The publisher, Marcele Karczewski, who also published Thomas's *The *Minister* (1953), was a Polish refugee. After receiving an enthusiastic review by Alan Pryce-Jones on BBC radio, the first impression of the book sold out and a second appeared later in the same year. The volume includes such famous poems as 'Depopulation of the Hills', 'Cynddylan on a Tractor' and 'Death of a Peasant'; six poems were never reprinted.

Acts of Union, The (1536 and 1543), two acts of Parliament which provided for the political annexation of Wales to England. Henry VIII, determined to divorce his first wife, Catherine of Aragon, had rejected Papal power within his realm. With the assistance of Thomas Cromwell, his chief administrator, and through the agency of the Reformation Parliament (1529–36), he set about creating a new, independent, sovereign kingdom with himself as head of both Church and State. In order to strengthen his hold over Wales and the Marches, and well aware of the disorder which existed, especially in the borderlands, Cromwell decided to abolish the Marcher lordships and annex them, together with the *Principality, to England.

Under these Acts the Welsh were granted equality of status before the law and English law became official. All legal and commercial encumbrances which had previously affected relations between England and Wales were withdrawn. Five new counties were created in the March (see under SHIRING OF WALES) and all the Welsh counties were given parliamentary representation. A system of higher courts, known as Great Sessions, was established and the Council in the Marches given statutory authority. The preamble to the Act of 1536 referred to the Welsh language (for the first time in any statute) thus: 'the people of the same dominion have and do daily use a speche nothing like ne consonaunt to the naturall mother tonge used within this Realme'. It went on to announce its intention 'utterly to extirpe alle and singular the sinister usages and customs' of Wales which differed from those of England. It was also stipulated (in Clause 20), in the interests of uniformity, that only the English language was to be used in law and administration throughout Wales and that no Welshman who did not speak English could hold public office. Although it is possible to argue that the Acts did not expressly prohibit the Welsh language, it is clear that they intended the government of Wales to be entrusted thereafter to a minority, some five per cent of the population, who knew English. Welsh poets of the time did not refer directly to these Acts but their eulogies show that they did not disapprove of the acquisition of lands and offices by their patrons.

For further discussion of the Acts see W. O. Williams, *Tudor Gwynedd* (1958), J. G. Edwards, *The Principality of Wales* (1972), and G. H. Jenkins, *Hanes Cymru yn y Cyfnod Modern Cynnar* (1983); see also W. Ogwen Williams, 'The Survival of the Welsh Language after the Union of England and Wales: the first phase, 1536–1642', in *The Welsh History Review* (vol. 2, no. 1, 1964); and P. R. Roberts, 'The Act of Union in Welsh History' in the *Transactions* of the Honourable Society of Cymmrodorion (1972–73).

ADAM OF USK (1352?–1430), chronicler. By favour of Edmund Mortimer, Earl of March, who had acquired the lordship of Usk, he was able to study law at Oxford where he later became a tutor. In the armed skirmishes at the University in 1388 and 1389 the Welshman sided with the Southerners against the Northerners. While serving in the courts of the Archbishop of Canterbury, he was among those who examined Walter *Brute in 1390. Refused the bishopric of Hereford by Henry IV, he spent two years as a lawyer in France and Flanders. Although in touch with the allies of *Owain Glyndŵr, he kept out of danger and after his return to Wales in 1408 became a chaplain in Welshpool under the patronage of Edward Charlton, Lord of Powys. He wrote a valuable chronicle of the events of his age, *Chronicon Adae de Usk*, which includes an account of Glyndŵr's rising.

The chronicle was edited by E. Maunde Thompson, *Chronicon Adae de Usk* (2nd edn., 1904); for further details see the article by W. Llewelyn Williams in *Y Cymmrodor* (vol. XXXI, 1921) and Glanmor Williams, *The Welsh Church from Conquest to Reformation* (1962).

ADAMS, DAVID (1845–1923), theological writer, a native of Tal-y-bont, Cards. After a period as a schoolmaster he became a minister with the Independents at Hawen (Rhydlewis) and Bryngwenith, Cards., and later held pastorates at Bethesda, Caerns., and in Liverpool. While at Hawen, he incurred the hatred of the young Caradoc Evans (David *Evans) who, as conservative in religion as in other matters, was bitterly opposed to the political *Liberalism and theological Modernism for which Adams stood. The chief spokesman in Wales for the New Theology which had originated in Germany, Adams published two works of theology, namely *Paul yng Ngoleuni'r Iesu* (1897) and *Yr Eglwys a Gwareiddiad Diweddar* (1914).

The biography of David Adams was written by E. Keri Evans and W. Pari Huws (1924); see also the article by W. Eifion Powell in *Y Traethodydd* (July, 1979).

ADAMS, SAM (1934–), poet, critic and editor. Born at Gilfach Goch, Glam., he was educated at the University College of Wales, Aberystwyth, and was a Lecturer in English at Caerleon College of Education until his appointment to Her Majesty's Inspectorate of Schools in 1974. He joined the editorial board of *Poetry Wales in 1970 and, succeeding Meic *Stephens, was its editor from 1973 to 1975. Among the anthologies he has edited are The Shining Pyramid (with Roland *Mathias, 1970) and Ten Anglo-Welsh Poets (1974). He also contributed a volume of poems, The Boy Inside (1973), to the Triskel Poets series and an essay on Geraint *Goodwin to the *Writers of Wales series (1975).

Adar Llwch Gwin, legendary birds, probably the equivalent of griffins. In a contest (recorded in Mostyn MS 146) between *Arthur and Drudwas ap Tryffin, the latter owns three of these birds and orders them to kill the first protagonist to reach the battlefield. Arthur is delayed by his adversary's sister, so that Drudwas, the first to arrive, is torn to pieces by his own birds. The *Poets of the Gentry used the phrase as a synonym for hawks or falcons and as a metaphor for a strong or brave man.

ADDA FRAS (1240?–1320?), a poet to whom much vaticinatory verse has been attributed, though none with any certainty; he is associated with Is-Conwy and is said to have been buried in the abbey of Maenan (*Aberconwy).

Addaon, the son of Taliesin, is named in the Triads, in *Englynion y Clyweit and in *Breuddwyd Rhonabwy, as 'the most eloquent and wisest young man to be found in this Island'.

Adfer (lit. 'To restore'), a Nationalist group founded by Emyr Llywelyn in 1971. Having broken away from *Cymdeithas yr Iaith Gymraeg, it is dedicated to the achievement of monolingualism, especially in those districts which it considers to be Y Fro Gymraeg, the Welsh-speaking heartlands of north and west Wales.

Adolygydd, Yr (lit. 'The reviewer'), a quarterly magazine of which thirteen numbers appeared between 1850 and 1853. Established by Independents in south Wales, its aim was 'to place religion above the chief joy of the Welsh'; the editor and contributors were not named. The periodical carried substantial articles on religious, political and scientific subjects, including agriculture and mining, together with a number of long poems.

Aedd Mawr, the father of Prydain, the legendary founder of the Isle of *Britain; the Britons or Welsh were sometimes known as 'hil Aedd Mawr' ('the progeny of Aedd Mawr').

Aeddan ap Gafran, see under FAITHFUL AND FAITHLESS WAR-BANDS.

Aeddon, see under ECHRYS YNYS (c.1050–1100).

Afallach, the son of Aflech fab *Beli Mawr, according to the royal genealogies. There is a traditional belief that he was the father of *Modron, the mother of *Owain ab Urien. Ynys Afallach was the original name of the ideal country to which *Arthur was taken to recover from his wounds; *Ynys Afallon (The Isle of Avalon) is a later form.

'*Afallennau, Yr*' (lit. 'The apple-trees'), a series of vaticinatory stanzas which are ascribed to *Myrddin (Merlin). In the oldest text, found in The *Black Book of Carmarthen (c.1250), there are ten stanzas and in a text preserved in *Peniarth Manuscript 3 (c.1300) there are sixteen. Texts found in later manuscripts and printed in The Myvyrian Archaiology of Wales (2nd edn., 1870) and Thomas *Stephens's The Literature of the Kymry (1849) contain respectively twenty-two and twenty-three stanzas. Each stanza opens with the formula 'Afallen beren' ('Sweet apple-tree') and usually contains from six to twelve rhyming lines of nine to eleven syllables, four of which are stressed.

The content of the stanzas is concerned with two separate matters, namely the early Welsh legend of Myrddin, the wild man who was said to have fled from the battle of Arfderydd in AD 573 to live in the Caledonian Forest, and vaticinations prophesying the failures and successes of the Welsh in their struggles against their enemies, which are ascribed to Myrddin. The gift of prophecy granted to him in his madness provides the link between the two layers of subject-matter. Myrddin speaks in the first person in each stanza and in his addresses to the apple-tree, which sustains him with its sweet fruit, he attributes to it remarkable powers such as the ability to protect him from his pursuers, *Rhydderch Hael and his men. He declares that he was a gold-torqued warrior in the battle of Arfderydd, but since the death of his lord *Gwenddolau he has endured sickness and grief in the Forest of Celyddon for fifty years. The wild man also states that he has been guilty of the death of the son of Gwenddydd (who is referred to as his sister in other texts) and he complains because she does not visit him.

Some of the references to the legendary material are obscure but it is certain that the stanzas in which they occur contain the earliest nucleus of the Myrddin legend. It has been suggested that they could date from the ninth or tenth century. The vaticinations in the Afallennau are later and deal with the Norman period: the first stanza in the Black Book text, for example, refers to the battle of Machafwy in Elfael, fought on 12 August 1198, while other stanzas prophesy the return of Cynan and *Cadwaladr to lead the Welsh.

For further details see A. O. H. Jarman, Llyfr Du

Caerfyrddin (1982) and 'The Welsh Myrddin Poems' in *Arthurian Literature in the Middle Ages, a Collaborative History* (ed. R. S. Loomis, 1959).

Afallon, see YNYS AFALLON.

Afan, a cantref of *Morgannwg. After the collapse of the kingdom of Glamorgan, it was held by the descendants of Morgan ap Caradog, the grandson of Iestyn ap Gwrgant, the last King of Glamorgan, and was later a centre of resistance to Norman rule. Lleision ap Morgan Fychan adopted the surname de Avene but, on the death of his grandson Thomas about 1350, Afan was wholly absorbed into the lordship of Glamorgan.

AFAN FERDDIG (7th cent.?), a poet whose memory survived among the *Gogynfeirdd* as having been one of the *Cynfeirdd. According to a Triad he was the poet of *Cadwallon ap Cadfan of *Gwynedd and he may have been the author of the poem *'Moliant Cadwallon'.

Afanc, an aquatic monster in early Welsh legend. *Hu Gadarn, in the Triads, helps to drag it from Llyn Llion in order to prevent the lake from overflowing a second time. From the waters of Llyn yr Afanc, Caerns., it is said to have been hauled by the *Horned Oxen. In the romance of Peredur (see under TAIR RHAMANT) the beast shoots poisoned darts at anyone who tries to enter its cave. These traditions may derive from folk-memory of floods caused by the bursting of beavers' dams.

Afarwy, the son of Lludd, King of Britain, according to *Geoffrey of Monmouth's *Historia Regum Britanniae* (1136), where the name occurs as Androgeus. On the death of his father Afarwy was not old enough to succeed to the throne and so *Caswallon, Lludd's brother, was made king in his stead. Strife was caused between uncle and nephew when Hirelgas, Caswallon's son, was killed by Cuhelyn, the son of Afarwy. In the ensuing battle Afarwy had the support of Julius Caesar and together they defeated Caswallon's army. The latter was released by Afarwy who then accompanied Caesar to Rome. There may well be no historical basis for this legend and Afarwy is not mentioned in Caesar's *De Bello Gallico*.

'After the Funeral', an elegy written by Dylan *Thomas in 1938 'in memory of Ann Jones', his mother's sister. She had died in 1933, when the first attempt at the poem had been very different in tone and attitude. With her husband, Ann Jones had farmed *Fern Hill near Llangain, Carms., where the poet had spent childhood holidays. Unlike the later poems which celebrated the place, this celebration of the person is a deep response to the Welsh-speaking society which she represented. The character-istic features of the Welsh front-parlour such as the stuffed fox and the potted fern are, for the poet, stale emblems which belie the spontaneous generosity behind his aunt's austerity. This is a central *Anglo-Welsh poem in the very duality of its response, seeking a relationship of love beyond the natural tendency to caricature the customs and ceremony of a world to which the poet is related without belonging.

Age of the Saints, The, a period extending from the fourth to the eighth century during which Wales was converted to Christianity by itinerant monks and missionaries, later known as 'saints'. Early memorial stones record the impact on Wales of a missionary drive which was directed from Gaul and influenced by the teachings of St. Martin of Tours and others. Traditions surviving from the Roman period may explain the early growth of Christianity in south-east Wales. *Dyfrig (Dubricius) was active in the borderland of *Gwent while *Cadog and *Illtud founded monasteries, renowned as centres of learning, at *Llancarfan and *Llanilltud Fawr (Llantwit Major). *Dewi Sant and *Teilo, saints associated with south-west Wales, were popular preachers and evangelists in the sixth century. *Beuno led the ascetic movement in north Wales which had already felt the influence of saints travelling along the western seaways and which had close contact with northern Britain. See also CELTIC CHURCH and LIVES OF THE SAINTS.

The most authoritative accounts of the Age of the Saints are E. G. Bowen's books, *The Settlements of the Celtic Saints in Wales* (1954) and *Saints, Seaways and Settlements* (1969).

Agricultural Societies, formed in Wales on a county basis in the mid-eighteenth century, encouraged the improvement of rural life by awarding prizes for the planting of trees, the excellence of livestock and traditional craftsmanship, the maintenance of roads and the good behaviour of farm servants. Lewis *Morris, the antiquary, who had read Jethro Tull's classic work, *The Horse Hoing Husbandry* (1733), was among the enlightened Welshmen who supported the formation of these societies. The first, and one of the earliest in Britain, was that of Breconshire, which was founded in 1755 by Howel *Harris and others, mainly on the initiative of Charles Powell of Castell Madoc. It was followed by counterparts in Glamorgan (1772) and Cardiganshire (1784), until by 1815 the societies existed in most parts of Wales, becoming the channel through which the Agricultural Revolution reached the country.

Alafon, see OWEN, OWEN GRIFFITH (1847–1916).

Alan Fyrgan, see under FAITHFUL AND FAITHLESS WAR-BANDS.

Alba Landa, see WHITLAND.

Alban Hefin, see under ST. JOHN'S DAY.

Albanactus, see under CAMBER.

Albion, see under HISTORIA REGUM BRITANNIAE (c. 1136).

ALEXANDER, EWART (1931–   ), dramatist, was born at Cwmgiedd, Ystradgynlais, Brecs., and educated at the University College, Swansea. Formerly a teacher, he became a full-time writer who, although Welsh-speaking, writes in English. He is the author of more than forty plays for the stage, radio and, most notably, for television. A critical appreciation of his work is hampered by the fact that his best stage-plays, *Buzz Buzz Critch Critch* (1969), *The Rose-tinted Pelicans* (1972) and *White Plains* (1976), remain unpublished. One of his television plays, *Omri's Burning* (1968), was chosen for the National Film Archives.

There is an autobiographical essay by Ewart Alexander in the volume *Artists in Wales* (ed. Meic Stephens, 1973).

Alice Rowena (mid-5th cent.), the daughter of Hengist. According to early tradition, *Vortigern, leader of the Britons in the mid-fifth century, fell in love with her at a banquet and, as his wife, she encouraged the spread of Saxon rule over southern Britain. In some versions the girl's name was preserved as Alys or Alice, in others as Rhonwen, and misremembered sometimes as Rowena. *Nennius referred to the tradition in the *Historia Brittonum*, without mentioning Alice by name, but it was given wider currency by *Geoffrey of Monmouth. Welsh poets of the later Middle Ages often referred to the English as 'cyff Rhonwen' ('Rowena's stem') or 'plant Alys' ('the children of Alice') and such expressions were not uncommon as late as the nineteenth century. See also TREACHERY OF THE LONG KNIVES.

ALIS (fl. 1545), poet, was the daughter of *Gruffudd ab Ieuan ap Llywelyn Fychan, a gentleman-poet of Lleweni Fychan, Denbs. The little of her work which has been preserved includes a series of *englynion* on the kind of husband she wanted, another on her father's second marriage and a *cywydd* of reconciliation. It is probable that *Catrin (fl. 1545), author of an *awdl* to God and the world, was her sister.

All Things Betray Thee (1949), a historical novel by Gwyn *Thomas (1913–81) about industrial unrest in Moonlea, a fictitious town in south Wales, during the nineteenth century. Some of the events relate the narrative to the *Merthyr Rising of 1831 and the execution of Dic Penderyn (Richard Lewis). The book's title is taken from a line in Francis Thompson's 'The Hound of Heaven' (1893): 'All things betray thee, who betrayest Me'. John Simon Adams, the hero, organizes the workers in a protest march against furnace closures and the unarmed men are attacked by the soldiers of Lord Plimmon; Adams is arrested and sentenced to be hanged. The novel, explicitly radical, is among the author's most successful and its theme resembles that of his play, *Jackie the Jumper* (1963).

Alleluia Victory, The, see under GARMON (c. 378–448).

ALLEN, JOHN ROMILLY (1847–1907), archaeologist, was born in London into a family whose roots were in Pembrokeshire. After joining the *Cambrian Archaeological Association in 1875, he abandoned his career as a civil engineer in favour of archaeology, to the study of which he devoted the rest of his life. He became editor of the journal *Archaeologia Cambrensis* in 1891 and of *The Reliquary* two years later. Besides collaborating with Sir John *Rhys in a survey of the early inscribed stones of Wales, he published a number of books which include *Early Christian Symbolism in Great Britain and Ireland* (The Rhind Lectures, 1887), *The Monumental History of the Early British Church* (1889) and *Celtic Art in Pagan and Christian Times* (1904).

Alltud Eifion, see JONES, ROBERT ISAAC (1815–1905).

Almanac, a publication in the form of a cheap, paper-covered booklet. Among its contents were found the current calendar, weather predictions, astrology, notices of fairs and festivals, advertisements for books and so on. In the Welsh context it was also substantially literary: carols and songs composed to English and Welsh airs, *englynion* and longer poems, together with instruction in the art of *cynghanedd and the strict metres, appeared regularly in these publications.

The first to be published in Welsh was that of Thomas *Jones (1648–1713) in 1681. After the Government's decision in 1698 not to renew the Licensing Act which restricted printing to specific centres such as London, he began publishing his almanacs in Shrewsbury and that town remained the main centre for compilers and sellers of Welsh almanacs until at least 1793. These men included John Rogers (d. 1738), Siôn Rhydderch (John *Roderick), Evan Davies (Philomath; fl. 1720–50), John Prys (Philomath; 1739?–86?), Gwilym Howell (1705–75) and Cain Jones (fl. 1738?–95). The first almanac published in Wales was that of Siôn Rhydderch (1733) whose example was followed by Mathew Williams (1732–1819) and several others.

The almanackers also held eisteddfodau, the

first of which was the one organized by Thomas Jones at Machynlleth in 1701; there were others at Llandegla in 1719, at Dolgellau in 1734, at Cymer in 1735 and at Bala in 1738. These events took place in taverns: no medal or prize-money was awarded but the custom was for the winner's health to be drunk by his fellow-poets.

The importance of the almanacs should not be under-estimated for they were a medium of communication and information among the common people in an age of superstition and ignorance. They also represented a revival of the literary tradition which had lapsed after the *Caerwys Eisteddfodau (1523, 1567) and provided the poets of the period, who had very little learning, with an opportunity of reclaiming some part of what had become, for them, a lost heritage.

For further details about the eisteddfodau see the articles by Bob Owen in Y Genedl Gymreig (7 Jan. – 8 April, 1929); see also Hywel Teifi Edwards, Yr Eisteddfod (1976) and Geraint H. Jenkins, Thomas Jones yr Almanaciwr (1980) and 'The Sweating Astrologer' in Welsh Society and Nationhood (ed. R. R. Davies et al., 1984).

Alone to the Alone, The (1947), a comic novel by Gwyn *Thomas (1913–81), is set in the Terraces, part of a mining town in south Wales, during the *Depression of the years between the World Wars. Four groups of characters are involved: Rollo, a Fascist bus-conductor, and his family; Eurona and Morris, her chronically unemployed father; Shadrach Sims, a chain-store owner; and four young miners whose attempts to promote Eurona's love-life form the basis of the plot. The novel is remarkable for the steady flow of the author's typical humour.

Alun, see BLACKWELL, JOHN (1797–1841).

Alun Cilie, see JONES, ALUN JEREMIAH (1897–1975).

'Alun Mabon', a poem by John Ceiriog *Hughes with which he won the prize for a pastoral poem at the National Eisteddfod of 1861, was published in his volume Oriau'r Bore (1862). The eponymous hero is a farmer and the simple story of his courtship and married life is the substance of the poem. It consists of twenty-three songs and three recitations, many of which are still popular, such as 'Cân yr Arad Goch', 'Bugail Aberdyfi' and the famous 'Aros Mae'r Mynyddau Mawr', one of the best lyrical poems in Welsh. The poem is noteworthy for the portrait it presents of the ideal Victorian marriage, marked by virtue and propriety, which Ceiriog intended as a refutation of the allegations made by the *Blue Books (1847) concerning the immorality of the Welsh people.

Amaethon, one of the children of *Dôn, is regarded in Welsh tradition as the god of agri-culture. In the tale of *Culhwch and Olwen, Ysbaddaden Bencawr sets the hero the task of enlisting the god's services in cultivating the land in order to provide food and drink for Olwen's wedding-feast.

AMBROSE, WILLIAM (Emrys; 1813–73), poet. A native of Bangor, Caerns., he spent most of his life as a minister with the Independents at Porthmadog, where he became a man of great influence in the community. Besides editing the periodical, Y Dysgedydd, he wrote much verse, mostly for eisteddfodau, three volumes of which were published posthumously: Gweithiau y Parch. W. Ambrose (1875), Gweithiau Rhyddieithol y Parch. William Ambrose (1876) and Ceinion Emrys (1876); the last two were edited by William *Rees (Gwilym Hiraethog). His awdl 'Y Greadigaeth' was denied a prize at the Eisteddfod held at Aberffraw in 1849: two of the adjudicators (both Churchmen) disagreed with the third, Eben Fardd (Ebenezer *Thomas), and awarded the Chair to Nicander (Morris *Williams), the vicar of Amlwch, thus causing one of the most bitter literary controversies of the nineteenth century. Emrys is no longer highly regarded as a poet, although he could write memorably, as in the poem 'Y Blodeuyn Olaf'. His weakness was one shared by most of his contemporaries, namely the failure to distinguish between dignity and pomposity. A selection of his poems was published by Owen M. *Edwards in the series *Cyfres y Fil (1916).

Ambrosius, see EMRYS WLEDIG (fl. 430 or 475).

Amlyn and Amig, The Friendship of, a very popular tale in the Middle Ages, occurs in some form in nearly every European country from Italy to Iceland, including Wales.

Two friends, identical in appearance, are born on the same day and (in some versions) are baptized together by the Pope at St. Peter's in Rome. On reaching manhood they go to the court of the king (or duke) where they are held in high esteem until the chief steward, who is jealous of their success, discovers that Amlyn is in love with the daughter of his feudal overlord, and betrays him. To defend his honour, Amlyn is obliged to fight a duel with the steward, but because of the medieval belief that a guilty man could not win in a trial by combat, he persuades Amig to fight in his stead and the steward is defeated. In the meantime, Amlyn goes to Amig's court and sleeps with his friend's wife, but places a naked sword between them. Some time later, stricken with leprosy and an outcast, Amig goes to Amlyn's court where he is warmly received. One night an angel tells Amig that he will be healed if washed in the blood of Amlyn's sons. Such is Amlyn's affection for his friend that he sacrifices his children and effects a cure for Amig by bathing him in their blood, whereupon the boys are miraculously restored to life. The friends die on the same day and are buried together in the same place.

Some versions have an epilogue which portrays the two heroes as Christian soldiers fighting a holy war against the King of Lombardy. They are killed in battle and buried in two separate churches at Mortara in northern Italy. The following morning their bodies are found side by side in the same tomb. It is thought that the earliest form of the tale was pagan but that it became Christianized in order to provide entertainment for pilgrims and to entice them to Mortara on their way to Rome.

The different versions of the tale can be divided into two groups, the romantic and the hagiographic, a distinction more convenient than accurate since Christian elements intrude into the romantic versions and pagan elements survive in the hagiographic. The oldest extant version belongs to the romantic group, a Latin poem in hexameter verse written about 1090 by Radulphus Tortarius, a monk of Fleury. The immediate source of all the hagiographic versions is the twelfth-century Latin prose tale, *Vita Sanctorum Amici et Amelii*.

The Welsh version, preserved in *The *Red Book of Hergest*, was edited by J. Gwenogvryn *Evans under the title *Kymdeithas Amlyn ac Amic* in 1909. A prose adaptation of the Latin text, the work seems in its language and orthography to date from the early fourteenth century. The tale is the basis of Saunders *Lewis's verse-play for radio, *Amlyn ac Amig* (1940). The proposition that a man's salvation (as well as his honour) may depend on a seemingly irrational and abhorrent act is one which held a deep fascination for the playwright and it finds powerful expression in this, perhaps his first great play. An English translation by Joseph *Clancy was published in 1985 under the title *The Vow*.

For further details see Patricia Williams, *Kedymdeithas Amlyn ac Amic* (1982).

Amnon, see JONES, REES (1797–1844).

Amoret, a name for the beloved used by Henry *Vaughan. In *Poems, with the tenth Satyre of Iuvenal Englished* (1646) he included at least five poems to his Amoret, almost certainly his first wife, Catherine Wise of Gylsdon Hall, Coleshill, Warwicks. Borrowing from William Habington's *Castara* (1634) the manner of his titles and his anti-Petrarchan determination to celebrate his betrothed rather than some courtesan, Vaughan writes of 'some predestin'd sympathie' between himself and Amoret.

Amserau, Yr (lit. 'The times'), a newspaper founded by William *Rees (Gwilym Hiraethog) in 1843. A fortnightly, it was strongly Nonconformist and Radical, becoming popular when Rees began to publish his *'Llythurau 'Rhen Ffermwr'* in its pages. As the circulation increased, John Lloyd, publisher of *Cronicl yr Oes*, was employed as its publisher and in 1848 his family purchased the newspaper. Gwilym Hiraethog was succeeded as editor by John *Roberts (Ieuan Gwyllt) in 1852. The sales fell sharply as a result of the newspaper's pro-Russian line during the Crimean War and it offended many readers by printing attacks on the former editor. Vulnerable to competition from new weeklies founded after the abolition of newspaper stamp-duty in 1855, it was bought by Thomas *Gee in 1859 and merged with his *Baner Cymru* to form *Baner ac Amserau Cymru* (later to be known as *Y Faner*).

Anarawd ap Rhodri (d. 916), the eldest son of *Rhodri Mawr. After his father's death he ruled Anglesey and parts of *Gwynedd, avenging his father's defeat by the Mercians in a battle on the banks of the Conwy in 881. According to *Asser, he swore allegiance to Alfred of Wessex and it was with English help in 895 that he plundered *Ceredigion and *Ystrad Tywi, the territories of his brother Cadell. From Anarawd were descended the later rulers of Gwynedd, as those of *Deheubarth were sprung from Cadell.

Anathémata, The (1952), a poem of epic proportions by David *Jones. Divided into eight named parts, with nine illustrations and a long preface by the author, it is at once devotional and commemorative, a celebration of Christian mysteries and a recalling of the making—both geological and cultural—of Britain. Its central symbol is the ship, vessel of both 'the argosy or voyage of the Redeemer', and of voyages which from pre-historic times have brought shaping influences to the culture of the British Isles. The poem draws its material mainly from Celtic, Latin and Teutonic 'deposits' underlying London and Wales, and from English literature. This *Matter of Britain requires many explanatory footnotes, but the difficulties acknowledged by the poem's sub-title, 'fragments of an attempted writing', are also inherent in the modern crisis of the validity of sacrament and symbol which *The Anathémata* confronts. In combining poetry and prose, it achieves even greater verbal richness and rhythmic flexibility than the author's *In Parenthesis* (1937). David Jones felt that of all his writings it was 'the one that really matters' and W. H. Auden called it 'probably the finest long poem in English in this century'.

For a detailed discussion of the poem see René Hague, *A Commentary on The Anathémata of David Jones* (1977) and Neil Corcoran's study, *The Song of Deeds* (1982).

'Anatiomaros' (1925), a long poem by T. Gwynn *Jones, describes the rituals practised by *Plant y Cedyrn* ('Children of the Mighty'), a tribe who live in Gwernyfed, on their return from summer quarters in the mountains to their winter home in the valley. Gathering around an ancient oak-tree under the guidance of the elders, the wise men and the ★Druids of the tribe, they listen to their teacher, the patriarch Anatiomaros ('Great Soul'), who narrates the history and feats of their forefathers. As blue smoke rises from the altar and the young people dance around the tree, the maidens collect torches and from hearth to hearth is rekindled 'the unquenchable fire of the gods', cleansing the tribe of all evil and pestilence. At dawn, when Anatiomaros is found dead before the altar, his body is placed in a barge carved in the shape of a swan which, with fiery embers on the bier, glides downstream towards the sea. The poem is richly descriptive and a memorable expression of the poet's awareness of the value of national traditions.

For critical discussion see the article by Annie Owen and Stephen J. Williams in *Yr Athro* (April, 1934), that by H. Meurig Evans in *Barn* (no. 13, 1963) and another by Wenna Williams in *Ysgrifau Beirniadol* (ed. J. E. Caerwyn Williams, 1969).

Ancestors, The Cult of, a feature of pagan Celtic religion. According to Caesar's *De Bello Gallico*, the Gauls believed that they were all descended from Dis Pater, in Roman terms the god of ★Annwn, the Otherworld, a statement which corroborates the belief that descent from a common ancestor-deity was pan-Celtic. In Welsh tradition the name of ★Beli Mawr fab Manogan may be regarded as the universal ancestor deity commemorated by the Brythonic Celts. See also MOTHER GODDESSES.

Ancient Britons, The Most Honourable and Loyal Society of, the first official Welsh society in London, was founded in 1715 with the twofold object of demonstrating the loyalty of the ★London Welsh to the House of Hanover and of dispensing charity to boys of poor Welsh parents. The Society met annually on St. David's Day (1 March), the birthday of the Princess of Wales, for a sermon and a dinner, and in 1718 it established a Welsh Charity School which is known today as St. David's School, Ashford. See also CYMMRODORION, CYMREIGYDDION and GWYNEDDIGION.

Andronicus, see JONES, JOHN WILLIAM (1842–95).

ANEIRIN or **NEIRIN** (*fl.* the latter part of the 6th cent.), one of the famous ★*Cynfeirdd* who is named with ★Taliesin in the ★*Historia Brittonum* (*c.*830) of ★Nennius as having flourished in the ★Old North. He is commemorated in the Triads as '*Aneirin Gwawdrydd Mechdeyrn Beirdd*' ('Aneirin of flowing verse, prince of poets') and to him is ascribed the composition of '*Y* ★*Gododdin*'.

Aneirin ap Talfan, see DAVIES, ANEIRIN TALFAN (1909–80).

Angels of Mons, The, see under BOWMEN OF AGINCOURT.

Anglia Transwallina (lit. 'England beyond Wales'), a term first applied to Pembrokeshire in the late sixteenth century by the English antiquary, William Camden. George ★Owen, the historian, in his *Description of Penbrockshire* (1603), claimed that the southern part of the county was usually called 'Little England beyond Wales' because, soon after the ★Norman Conquest, it had been settled by Flemings and English. Later writers with an eye for the picturesque have stressed the differences between the largely Welsh-speaking districts to the north of the *landsker* (a line running from about Newgale to Laugharne, Carms.) and the English-speaking parts to the south. The term may give offence if used to imply that the present-day inhabitants are not Welsh.

Anglicanism, a doctrinal system originating in the reign of Elizabeth I and intended to represent a middle road between the teachings of Rome and Geneva. Its formularies, which remain substantially unchanged, date from the same period, as does the Book of Common Prayer. The sanction of Anglicanism lay in the joint testimony of Scripture and ecclesiastical authority deriving from the traditions of the first four centuries: Bishop Richard ★Davies, in his ★*Epistol at y Cembru* which prefaces the Welsh translation of the New Testament of 1567, recalled the purity of the early Church. The two basic teachings of Anglicanism were the sacraments of baptism and holy communion. It witnessed its golden age in England in the seventeenth century and declined somewhat in the face of secular learning in the eighteenth century.

For the whole of the seventeenth century the priests and laymen of the Anglican Church such as Robert ★Holland, Rowland ★Vaughan (*c.*1587–1667) and John ★Davies (*c.*1567–1644), were very active in the writing of books in Welsh, almost all being translations of works of piety and instruction, and its priests such as Ellis ★Wynne, Edward ★Samuel and Theophilus ★Evans were among the great masters of Welsh prose well into the eighteenth century. There were, nevertheless, widespread abuses among the clergy, including pluralism, absenteeism and illiteracy, about which Erasmus ★Saunders complained in 1721.

The influence of the Anglican Church was at its lowest ebb in Wales during the eighteenth and early nineteenth centuries, by which time Anglicans had become associated with the landowners, the Tories and those who spoke English. It was against this background of alienation from the common people that ★Methodism had its early successes in Wales. Nevertheless, Welsh culture was served with devotion by Yr ★*Hen Bersoniaid Llengar* ('The old literary clerics') who were among those who helped to revive the *National Eisteddfod and other institutions.

The nineteenth century saw the conflict in England between the Tractarian and Evangelical Movements, the former seeking to re-shape Anglicanism in a Catholic mould and the latter placing emphasis on the experience of conversion, the doctrine of atonement and the primacy of Scripture. The Welsh writers who were influenced by the *Oxford Movement included Morris *Williams (Nicander) and John *Williams (Ab Ithel).

An Act of 1914 disestablished the Welsh Church and a separate province of Wales within the Anglican communion was created in 1920 (see under DISESTABLISHMENT). Among writers who have served as priests of the Church in Wales are Euros *Bowen and R. S. *Thomas, while Aneirin Talfan *Davies was one of its most distinguished laymen.

For further details see *A History of the Church in Wales* (ed. David Walker, 1976) and *The Oxford Dictionary of the Christian Church* (ed. F. L. Cross, 1978).

Anglo-Welsh, a literary term denoting a writer Welsh by birth or association who, for a variety of reasons, writes not in Welsh but in English, also describes the work of such a writer and the whole genre of such writing. First used with a literary connotation by H. Idris *Bell in 1922 (but apparently not widely accepted by 1926 when Lewis Davies contributed an article to The *Welsh Outlook on 'The Anglo-Cymric School of Poets'), it came into general use towards the end of the 1930s with the advent of the magazines *Wales* and The *Welsh Review.

By the present day, except that it continues to acknowledge the existence of a literature in the Welsh language, the term has become less meaningful because it necessarily has reference to such a wide field. For this reason some critics prefer to apply it only to writers who, while using English as their medium, are concerned to link their writing to the Welsh cultural tradition, whether their emphasis is on the Welsh language or the literary and historical traditions of Wales. This limitation of the term creates an inner-circle of 'Anglo-Welshness' (both for writers and their works) which is regarded as the sum of what is worth categorizing, the wider application having rapidly become no more than a description of origin in English-speaking parts of Wales.

Several English-language writers, including Gwyn *Williams, Emyr *Humphreys and Vernon *Watkins, have objected to the term as misleading because it seems to imply mixed blood or 'half-and-halfery' (cf. Anglo-Irish or Anglo-Indian) but it has not so far been replaced by any alternative which is not too cumbersome for continuous use. The epithet 'Welsh', although applicable to the person (whose nationality is not in question, for there is no such creature as an 'Anglo-Welshman') is not entirely satisfactory as a description of what is written in English. This particular difficulty does not arise in Welsh which has two forms for the adjective 'Welsh', namely '*Cymreig*' (as in the title of Yr *Academi Gymreig, where it pertains to Wales, the country) and '*Cymraeg*' which refers specifically to the Welsh language.

There has been much discussion in literary journals concerning the validity and use of the term 'Anglo-Welsh', some would say *ad nauseam*. Welsh-language writers who have addressed themselves to this question, with varying degrees of sympathy for the English-speaking Welsh, include Waldo *Williams, Ioan Bowen *Rees, John Gwilym *Jones, D. Tecwyn *Lloyd, Jac L. *Williams, Aneirin Talfan *Davies and Bobi Jones (R. M. *Jones), the last-named in a stimulating article published in the magazine *Planet* (no. 16, 1973).

Among the most important statements on the subject are Saunders Lewis's pamphlet, *Is there an Anglo-Welsh Literature?* (1939), Gwyn Jones's lectures *The First Forty Years* (1957) and *Being and Belonging* (1977), Glyn Jones's *The Dragon has Two Tongues* (1968), Raymond Garlick's essay in the *Writers of Wales* series, *An Introduction to Anglo-Welsh Literature* (1970), the introduction by Roland Mathias to the anthology *Green Horse* (ed. Meic Stephens and Peter Finch, 1978) and (with Raymond Garlick) to the anthology *Anglo-Welsh Poetry 1480–1980* (1984); see also *A Bibliography of Anglo-Welsh Literature 1900–1965* (1970) by Brynmor Jones.

Anglo-Welsh Review, The, a magazine originally entitled *Dock Leaves* which was founded in 1949 by a small literary circle in Pembroke Dock, among whom Raymond *Garlick, its first editor, and Roland *Mathias, the editor from 1961 to 1976, were the most prominent; the title was changed in 1957, four years after the editor had moved to Blaenau Ffestiniog, Mer. Under Raymond Garlick's editorship, the magazine – the only English-language literary journal in Wales at the time – took as its aim the closing of the breach between Welsh and Anglo-Welsh writers. From the outset it published translations and articles about Welsh literature, together with poems, stories and reviews in English.

After Raymond Garlick's departure for the Netherlands in 1960 the editorial policy remained unchanged but Roland Mathias, living in England and having fewer contacts with Welsh-language writers, chose to develop the magazine as a journal of the arts in Wales, publishing studies of Welsh composers and painters as well as scholarly articles about aspects of Anglo-Welsh literature which had not, until then, received much critical attention. With no specific political commitment, he sought to strengthen the attachment of English-language writers and readers in Wales to the national heritage. His professional interest in history was clearly reflected in the magazine's contents, notably in the substantial reviews section where his aim was to provide a forum dealing with books about all aspects of Welsh life and by authors born or living in Wales. In particular, Roland Mathias's own articles, reviews and editorials were wide-ranging and authoritative.

By 1976, when he resigned from the editorship in order to concentrate more on his own writing, *The Anglo-Welsh Review* had had a longer continuous existence than any other English-language literary magazine in Britain, except for *Outposts*. Since then, it has appeared three times a year under the editorship of Gillian *Clarke in association, at different times, with Tony Bianchi, John *Davies and Greg Hill; the last-named became editor in 1984. The magazine is still published by the Five Arches Press (H. G. Walters Ltd.) of Tenby, the printer from its third number.

The early years of *Dock Leaves* were described by Raymond Garlick in *Planet* (no. 9, Dec., 1971 /Jan., 1972).

Angry Summer, The (1943), 'a poem of 1926' by Idris *Davies. It consists of fifty short, untitled sections, several of which have come to be known by their first lines, such as 'Send out your homing pigeons, Dai'. The poem is a loosely chronological record, with interludes, of the *General Strike, from the high spirits of its beginning to the ignominious return to work. With its main focus on the plight of the ordinary people, especially women, but also on the archetypal Dai as unemployed miner, it presents—besides the starkly political aspect of the crisis—some of the scenes characteristic of that time, such as the rare pleasures of mountain walks, the reading-room, brass bands, the allotment, singing festivals and excursions to the seaside. There is, too, as in *Gwalia Deserta* (1938), the poet's sympathy with his own people and his passionate denunciation of the hardship they suffered. It was for these reasons that the poems of Idris Davies, after his death, drew from T. S. Eliot (who edited his *Selected Poems*, 1953) the tribute, 'They are the best poetic document I know about a particular epoch in a particular place, and I think that they really have a claim to permanence'.

There is an essay on the structure of the poem by Roger Stephens Jones in *Planet* (nos. 37/38, May, 1977).

Ann of Swansea, see HATTON, JULIA ANN (1764–1838).

Anna Beynon, see under DAVIES, DAVID (1817–88).

Annales Cambriae, the name given to three sets of annals edited by John *Williams (Ab Ithel) and published in the Rolls Series in 1860. The editor attempted to prepare a composite text with variant readings but, notwithstanding the similarity between the three texts due to their use of common sources, they are distinct compositions which must be discussed separately so that their evolution over a period of time and in different centres may be traced. The A text (British Library Harleian MS 3859) was written about 1100 and contains annals from the year 445 to 954; it is a *St. David's chronicle composed about 954. The B text, written on the flyleaves of the Breviate Domesday Book and now kept in the Public Record Office, can be dated towards the end of the thirteenth century. It opens with the six ages of the world; British history appears with Julius Caesar, and down to 954 it is similar to the A text; thereafter to 1202 St. David's annals are the main source. A chronicler at *Strata Florida, using material from his own abbey and from *Whitland and *Cwm-hir, took the chronicle to 1263, and between 1189 and 1263 the annals 'speak with the voice of independent Wales'. This aspect is replaced by a more English tone in the final part of the chronicle to 1286 which uses English material and which was written probably at *Neath abbey. The C text (British Library Cotton Domitian i) which was written in 1288, is a St. David's chronicle based on the earlier set of annals. The opening section has been rewritten to conform with *Geoffrey of Monmouth's *Historia Regum Britanniae and the annals continue to the scribe's day. A fourth set of annals (1190–1266), called *Cronica de Wallia, was discovered in the twentieth century in Exeter Cathedral Library. It resembles text B in some respects and was probably written at Whitland in the thirteenth century.

These annals represent the basic material of the lost Latin chronicle which was translated as *Brut y Tywysogyon. Together they are evidence of the vigour of historical activity in both Welsh and Latin in the *Cistercian houses of Wales in the twelfth century and throughout the thirteenth century, and they are the prime sources for Welsh history in the Middle Ages.

For further details see Kathleen Hughes, 'The Welsh Latin Chronicles: *Annales Cambriae* and related texts' (The Sir John Rhŷs Lecture, in the *Proceedings* of the British Academy, 1973).

Annwn or **Annwfn**, a Welsh name for the Celtic Otherworld. In Welsh, as in Irish, mythology the Otherworld was believed to exist in two distinct forms, either as an island or islands somewhere in the western ocean (see YNYS AFALLON) or else it was situated under the earth in a *sidh* or fairy-mound. Ifor *Williams explained the name as being composed of the elements *dwfn* ('world') with a prefix *an* meaning 'in'. The poem *'Preiddiau Annwfn' alludes to an overseas raid made by *Arthur upon a number of *caerau* or fortresses, of which one is named Caer Siddi. Yet the concept of Annwfn as situated beneath the earth rather than across the sea is the one found most frequently in early poetry, as in a poem in The *Book of Taliesin which contrasts '*yn annwfyn is eluyd*' ('below the world') with '*yn awyr uch eluyd*' ('in the air above the world'). So also *Dafydd ap Gwilym who, in speaking of the fox's lair, wrote, '*Nid hawdd imi ddilid hwn*' /*A'i dy annedd hyd annwn*' ('It is not easy for me to follow him / since his home is afar, in Annwfn'); in another poem he speaks of Summer as retreating to Annwfn when Winter comes. In both Irish and Welsh sources the inhabitants of the Otherworld are in certain stories portrayed as engaged in warfare with each other, as are *Arawn and Hafgan in the story of *Pwyll, and their contest can be resolved only by the intervention of a mortal hero, that is Pwyll himself (cf. the Irish tale of Cú Chulainn's Sickbed).

The Celtic Otherworld is never represented as being the home of the dead, but rather as a place of everlasting joy and happiness. But under the influence of Christianity the name of Annwn came to be used as the Welsh equivalent of Hell, and its inhabitants regarded as demons. Hence the folklore associated with *Gwyn ap Nudd, the legendary king of the *Tylwyth Teg, and his sinister hell-hounds, who hunt the souls of the departed and whose barking forebodes death (see Dogs of Annwfn). Ellis *Wynne, in his *Gweledigaetheu y Bardd Cwsc (1703), described Annwn as '*Ufferneitha, cartre'r Cythreuliaid*' ('the lowest or uttermost Hell, the home of the devils').

For further details see John Rhŷs, *Celtic Folklore* (1901), Ifor Williams, *Pedeir Keinc y Mabinogi* (1930), and T. Gwynn Jones, *Welsh Folklore and Folk Custom* (1979).

Anoethau (lit. 'Tasks'), the seemingly impossible tasks set *Culhwch by Ysbaddaden Bencawr as conditions for the winning of the giant's daughter, Olwen. Interwoven with the account of how the hero accomplishes these feats are several international and popular motifs such as the Grateful Animal, the *Oldest Animals and the Wondrous Helpers.

Anthropos, see ROWLAND, ROBERT DAVID (1853?–1944).

Antiquarianism, an interest in Man's past and the things he has made, is not synonymous with archaeology, but represents an earlier and less scientific development. The ideas about historical evidence on which it was based – the literal validity of the Book of Genesis as an account of the First Men, the unique importance of the civilizations of Greece and Rome, and the reliability of written sources for Britain's early history—have now been discarded.

An active interest in British antiquity emerged in *Tudor times, embracing sites, monuments, ruins and artefacts as well as genealogies, traditions and language. John Leland recorded antiquarian and contemporary information and William Camden wrote an ambitious work, *Magna Britannia* (1586), partly topographical and partly historical. Interest in Wales itself was considerable. David *Powel published *A Historie of Cambria now called Wales* (1584) and Humphrey *Lhuyd prepared a map of Wales, *Cambriae Typus* (1573), itself an antiquarian exercise representing the Wales of a much earlier period. Two important county antiquaries were Rice *Merrick and George *Owen of Henllys. The former compiled *A Booke of Glamorganshire Antiquities* (1578) dealing with genealogy, history, tradition and topography; for him the word 'antiquities' included oral and literary traditions, as it did for many later scholars. George Owen, in his *Description of Penbrockshire* (1603), produced a comprehensive account of the natural and human history of his county. Drawings of churches, castles, houses and memorials in Wales were made by the English antiquary Thomas Dinely, while he was accompanying the Duke of Beaufort on a progress through Wales and the Marches in 1684. Edward *Lhuyd became Keeper of the Ashmolean Museum at Oxford and achieved distinction in many fields of learning, including antiquities, geology, botany and Celtic languages, although only parts of his researches were published in his lifetime.

Interest continued throughout the eighteenth century. Henry *Rowlands published an account of ancient Anglesey, *Mona Antiqua Restaurata (1723). The druidomania of Rowlands and other antiquaries led to the erroneous belief that the ancient burial chambers known as cromlechs and the circles of standing stones were druidical monuments. They were linked to the Welsh bardic tradition by Edward *Williams (Iolo Morganwg) in his successful attempt to 're-establish' *Gorsedd Beirdd Ynys Prydain. Some antiquaries, such as Richard *Fenton, excavated ancient sites, usually in a desultory and sometimes irresponsible way, while others made private collections of antiquities. Among topographical illustrators, the brothers Samuel and Nathaniel Buck published views of castles, abbeys, churches, mansions and towns in Wales, during the 1740s. Many artists made paintings and drawings of antiquarian interest and books of tours by such writers as Thomas *Pennant, Benjamin Heath *Malkin and William *Coxe, became popular (see under Tours of Wales).

During the nineteenth century, however, discoveries in biology and geology showed that the origins of Man went back much further than 4004 BC, the date calculated by Archbishop Ussher from Genesis. Excavations disclosed ancient civilizations in the Mediterranean and the Middle East other than those of Greece and Rome. For British antiquity an important advance was the adoption of the model of Stone, Bronze and Iron Ages, enunciated in 1836 by Christian J. Thomsen in Denmark, a new perspective extended by finds of earlier artefacts in France. The 'Three Ages' chronology was introduced in 1849 to the readers of *Archaeologia Cambrensis*, the journal of the *Cambrian Archaeological Association, and the adjective 'prehistoric', coined in 1851, was used in the same journal in 1855. Antiquarianism was then gradually superseded by archaeology.

For a full account of Antiquarianism in Wales see T. D. Kendrick, *British Antiquity* (1950) and Donald Moore's chapter, 'Cambrian Antiquity: Precursors of the Prehistorians', in *Welsh Antiquity* (ed. George C. Boon and J. M. Lewis, 1976).

ANWYL, EDWARD (1866–1914), Celtic scholar. Born in Chester, he was educated at Oriel and Mansfield Colleges, Oxford, where he was a founder member of *Cymdeithas Dafydd ap Gwilym*. He was appointed Professor of Welsh at the University College of Wales, Aberystwyth, in 1892 and in 1905 became Professor of Comparative Philology also, but died before taking up his appointment as the first Principal of the Monmouthshire Training College, Caerleon.

He published *A Welsh Grammar for Schools* (1897–99), an important work in its day, *Celtic Religion in Pre-Christian Times* (1906), a revised edition of *The Poetry of the Gogynfeirdd from the Myvyrian Archaiology of Wales* (1909), with a succinct but useful introduction, *Llyfr y Proffwyd Hosea* (1911), as well as numerous articles on early Welsh literature and on Celtic religion and legend. For many years a leader of Welsh cultural life, he was knighted in 1911.

His brother, **John Bodfan Anwyl** (1875–1949), was the author of a volume of *englynion* (1933), edited revised editions of *Drych y Prif Oesoedd* (1716) and *Gweledigaetheu y Bardd Cwsc* (1703), and prepared various editions of William *Spurrell's Dictionary. He was the secretary of the University of Wales Dictionary project from 1921 until his retirement in 1935.

A biography of Edward Anwyl has been written by Llywelyn C. Huws (1972); see also the monograph by Brynley F. Roberts in the *Transactions* of the Honourable Society of Cymmrodorion (1968).

AP GWILYM, GWYN (1950–   ), poet, was born at Bangor, Caerns., and brought up at Machynlleth, Mont. Educated at the University College of North Wales, Bangor, where he graduated in Welsh, and at the University College of Ireland in Galway, he was appointed Lecturer in Old Irish and Middle Irish at the College of the University of Ireland at Cork in 1975. He returned to Wales in 1977 to take up an appointment as secretary of the Welsh section of Yr *Academi Gymreig*, but he remained in that post only for a short while. He has published two volumes of poems, *Y Winllan Werdd* (1977) and *Gwales* (1983), a novel, *Da o Ddwy Ynys* (1979), and a translation of some of the stories of Patrick Pearse (1980). He has edited *Y Flodeugerdd Delynegion* (1980), a collection of Saunders *Lewis's literary essays entitled *Meistri a'u Crefft*

(1981) and a volume of critical essays on the work of T. Gwynn *Jones in the *Cyfres y Meistri* series (1982). He was joint editor of the magazine *Barn* from 1979 to 1981 and since 1982 he has been chairman of *Cymdeithas Cerdd Dafod.

Ap Vychan, see THOMAS, ROBERT (1809–80).

Apostle of Carmarthenshire, The, see HUGHES, STEPHEN (1622–88).

Apostle of Liberty, The, see PRICE, RICHARD (1723–91).

Apostle of Peace, The, see RICHARD, HENRY (1812–88).

APPERLEY, CHARLES JAMES (Nimrod; 1779–1843), sporting writer, was born at Plas Gronow, near Wrexham, Denbs., and educated at Rugby. After serving in Ireland with Sir Watkin Williams Wynn's Ancient British Light Dragoons, he married a *Wynn of Peniarth in 1801 and became a landowner in various parts of England. In 1813, having exhausted his capital, he returned to Wales as agent to the Wynn estates, living at Llanbeblig, near Caernarfon.

No 'gentleman' ever wrote for a sporting paper, but in 1822, under the pseudonym Nimrod, he began to contribute regularly to *The Sporting Magazine*, receiving a liberal salary and a stud of hunters in recognition of his part in trebling the paper's circulation. But in 1830, with the journal in difficulties and his debts mounting, he was obliged to leave England for Calais, eventually regaining solvency as a staff member of *The Sporting Review*. Literary recognition came in 1835 when J. G. Lockhart asked him to contribute articles to *The Quarterly Review* and these appeared in book form in 1837. A fine horseman and an all-round sportsman of unusual scholarship, Apperley put together ten books, of which the most important are *Nimrod's Hunting Tours* (1835), *Memoirs of the Life of John Mytton* (1837), *The Life of a Sportsman* (1842) and *Hunting Reminiscences* (1843).

For further details see Apperley's autobiography, *My Life and Times* (ed. E. D. Cuming, 1927), and E. W. Bovill, *The England of Nimrod and Surtees* (1959).

'Ar Hyd y Nos' (lit. 'All through the night'), a popular harp-tune first published by Edward *Jones (Bardd y Brenin) in his *Musical and Poetical Relicks of the Welsh Bards* (1784). The words '*Holl amrantau'r sêr ddywedant*', which are commonly associated with the tune in Wales, are by John Ceiriog *Hughes.

Arawn, the king of *Annwfn in the First Branch of *Pedair Cainc y Mabinogi*. *Pwyll insults him by allowing his own hounds to feed on a stag killed by Arawn's. In order to compensate Pwyll for this discourtesy, they agree to change places and appearance for a year, after which Pwyll wages battle with Hafgan, Arawn's enemy in Annwfn, and defeats him. On his return to his kingdom Arawn learns, as he lies with his wife in bed, that Pwyll has not had sexual intercourse with her, although she had been unaware that he was not her husband. With honour restored, the two kings remain friends thereafter. Arawn is not found outside the *Mabinogi*, but there is a traditional tale in which a voice is heard saying, '*Hir yw'r dydd a hir yw'r nos a hir yw aros Arawn*' ('Long is the day and long is the night and long is the wait for Arawn').

Arberth, a place in *Dyfed where, in the First and Third Branches of *Pedair Cainc y Mabinogi, *Pwyll's chief court is situated. Near by is Gorsedd Arberth, one of those hillocks where, according to Welsh tradition, the human world and *Annwfn meet. Whatever lord or nobleman sits upon it would either suffer a wound or behold a marvel, and when Pwyll sits there he sees *Rhiannon riding past. *Pryderi and *Manawydan, returning from the attack on Ireland, come at last to Arberth where a feast is prepared for them by Rhiannon and Cigfa. After the four have sat on Gorsedd Arberth, a spell falls on Dyfed, leaving the court empty and desolate. Arberth remains the focal point of the story until the end of the Third Branch.

Arbor Vitae, see JOHN OF WALES (d. *c.*1285).

Arcade, a fortnightly magazine launched in October 1980 by a group which included John *Osmond as editor and Ned Thomas (Edward Morley *Thomas), David *Smith, Robin Reeves and Nigel *Jenkins as members of the editorial board. A number of associates had responsibility for coverage of the arts, politics, education, sport and other aspects of life in Wales. The magazine's contribution in literary terms was not substantial but the work of several new writers first appeared in its pages and it carried lively comment on the cultural scene. Despite its declared aim of increasing its circulation, however, the magazine failed to keep its readers after the initial phase and the *Welsh Arts Council's grant-aid, on which it depended heavily, was withdrawn after the appearance of its thirty-fourth number in March 1982.

Archaeologia Britannica (lit. 'The archaeology of Britain'; vol. I, *Glossography*, 1707), is all that was published of a gigantic survey of the philology, antiquities, folklore, natural history and geology of the Celtic countries undertaken by Edward *Lhuyd. The volume contains *Comparative Etymology, or Remarks on the Alteration of Languages: A Comparative Vocabulary of the original Languages of Britain and Ireland*, arranged alphabetically by the Latin equivalents; a translation by Moses *Williams of a Breton grammar and vocabulary by Julien Maunoir; an alphabetical list of *Some Welsh Words Omitted in Dr. Davies's Dictionary*; *A Cornish Grammar* (containing also an alphabetical list of *Some Obsolete or less known Welsh Words*); a catalogue (in Latin) of Welsh manuscripts; a *British Etymologicon* by David Parry (1682?–1714), Lhuyd's Underkeeper at the Ashmolean Museum; *A Brief Introduction to the Irish or Ancient Scottish Language*; *An Irish-English Dictionary*; and *A Catalogue of Irish Manuscripts*.

This book was the first important work in Celtic Philology. Almost all its sections are the earliest of their kind, at least in English, and the Cornish Grammar in particular is one of the most important sources of information about Modern Cornish. Lhuyd's method of comparing cognates to seek 'correspondencies', resulting from the 'alteration of languages', anticipated to a considerable extent the methods of Comparative Philology in the nineteenth century.

Archaeologia Cambrensis, see under CAMBRIAN ARCHAEOLOGICAL ASSOCIATION.

Archfardd Cocysaidd Tywysogol, see EVANS, JOHN (1827?–95).

Ardudwy, a cantref lying between the rivers Glaslyn and Mawddach which, with *Eifionydd, formed the early kingdom of *Dunoding. The story of *Branwen in *Pedair Cainc y Mabinogi opens with a description of the court of Bendigeidfran (*Brân) at Harlech in Ardudwy.

Areithiau Pros, Yr (lit. 'The prose orations'), the work of fledgeling poets in their attempts to acquaint themselves with the language, rhetorical exercises and the *declamationes* of novices in the bardic schools. Several versions have been published; the title was given to a collection which included, among other texts, *Araith Iolo Goch, Araith Wgon* and *Araith Ieuan Brydydd Hir*. A distinction can be drawn, however, between the first three *areithiau* in this volume, namely *Araith Wgon, Araith Iolo Goch* and *Breuddwyd Gruffudd ap Adda ap Dafydd*, and the remainder of the texts. The first three resemble folk-tales, except that they use techniques and formulae derived from the literary tales of the Middle Ages. It is possible that they show more affinity with the oral stage of such literary compositions as are found in the great codices, The *White Book of Rhydderch and The *Red Book of Hergest. Certainly, they are more than the exercises of apprentice poets multiplying clichés or parodying *Pedair Cainc y Mabinogi.

For further details see the collection of *areithiau* edited by D. Gwenallt Jones (1934) in which particular attention is paid to the rhetorical figures found in these exercises.

Arfon, a cantref on the mainland facing Anglesey, was the heartland of the kingdom of

*Gwynedd, and had its centre at *Caernarfon.

'Argoed', a poem in four cantos by T. Gwynn *Jones in a metre similar to that of *'*Anatiomaros*' (1925) and *'*Broséliawnd*' (1922), was written in 1926 and 1927. According to the poet, Argoed was a remote part of Gaul occupied by the Arofan tribe. Like their forefathers, they lived a pastoral life, wanting no luxuries, wishing no violence and fearing no enemy, but honouring their ancient history, their heroes and their wise men. In the secret places of the forest the people of Argoed do not realize, however, that Gaul has already been conquered by Rome, that the splendour of its cities is no more and that its language and customs are being destroyed under a foreign yoke. One night a poet belonging to this tribe visits the court of Alesia where he sings a song in his mother-tongue, only to discover that there is none present who understands his language or appreciates his skill. His only acknowledgement is the grinning of his servile compatriots with their pidgin Latin. Disgusted by their boorish laughter, he walks out into the cold mist. Shortly afterwards, Rome imposes a tax on the men of Argoed and is thrice refused. The tribe prefers to sacrifice its independence by setting the forest on fire rather than surrender to the foe.

For critical discussion of this poem see the articles by E. Prosser Rhys in *Baner ac Amserau Cymru* (31 Jan., 1928) and H. Meurig Evans in *Barn* (no. 14, 1963).

Argoed Llwyfein, The Battle of (late 6th cent.), a British victory, commemorated in an *awdl* by *Taliesin, which was fought by Urien ap Cynfarch (*Urien Rheged) and his son *Owain ab Urien against an Anglian attacker nicknamed Fflamddwyn. The battle is believed to have taken place in the valley of the Eden in Westmorland, within the confines of Urien's kingdom of Rheged.

Arianrhod, the sister of *Gwydion and mother of *Lleu Llawgyffes, in the Fourth Branch of *Pedair Cainc y Mabinogi*. In greeting *Math, Gwydion refers to her as 'Arianrhod daughter of Dôn, your niece, your sister's daughter'; according to one of the Triads, *Beli was her father. After Goewin is raped by Gilfaethwy, Math asks Gwydion to advise him in the choice of a virgin to succeed her as his *troedog* ('foot-holder'). Gwydion names Arianrhod and when Math asks whether she is a virgin she affirms that she is. Math decides to test her virginity, however, by making her step over a magic wand; she then gives birth to two sons, *Dylan Ail Ton and Lleu Llawgyffes (as he was known later). Lleu is brought up by Gwydion, and when the two go to visit Arianrhod she asks Gwydion why he pursues her with her shame. She then swears three oaths against her son: that he should have no name unless she gives him one, that he should never bear arms unless she equips him with

them, and that he should never find a wife among mortal women. By means of trickery, wit and magic, Gwydion causes her to give her son a name, to equip him with arms, and Math and Gwydion make for him a wife of flowers, *Blodeuwedd.

Arianrhod is not mentioned thereafter and references to her outside the *Mabinogi* are scarce. The poem, 'Cadair Cyrridfen', in The *Book of Taliesin*, mentions her beauty and the phrase *Carchar Arianrhod* ('Arianrhod's prison') occurs in later texts. A *cywydd* by *Lewys Môn states that Math fab Mathonwy could not live without her and, according to a *cywydd* by *Tudur Aled, she was watched and imprisoned by her husband and parents. It therefore seems likely that, besides the one preserved in the *Mabinogi*, there once existed other stories about Arianrhod which have been lost.

For further details see W. J. Gruffydd, *Math vab Mathonwy* (1928), Ifor Williams, *Pedeir Keinc y Mabinogi* (1964) and Rachel Bromwich, *Trioedd Ynys Prydein* (1961).

Arllechwedd, a cantref lying between the rivers Ogwen and Conwy, of which the centre at Aber was one of the favourite residences of the Princes of *Gwynedd.

Arloeswr, Yr (lit. 'The pioneer'), a magazine published in Bangor between 1957 and 1960. Of its eight numbers the first six were edited by R. Gerallt *Jones and Bedwyr Lewis *Jones and the last two by the latter alone. Although the visual arts, music and the theatre received some attention, the magazine's interests were primarily literary and one of its objectives was to provide a platform for new poets such as Gwyn *Thomas (1936–) and Bobi Jones (Robert Maynard *Jones). Most numbers carried an interview with a well-known writer, together with an example of his or her unpublished work and, in this way, remarkable first chapters of novels (which remain unpublished) by John Gwilym *Jones and Kate *Roberts found their way into print. Brief though its life-span was, the magazine had an important role in the interval between the end of Y *Llenor and the advent of *Taliesin (1961).

'Armes Dydd Brawd' (lit. 'The prophecy of Domesday'), a vaticinatory poem the earliest text of which is found in The *Book of Taliesin.

'Armes Prydein' (lit. 'The prophecy of Britain'), a poem in The *Book of Taliesin*, is by far the most sustained and coherent example of early *vatication in verse. It has a clearly recognizable political motivation: the insistent theme over its two hundred lines is that the Welsh, in concert with their Celtic cousins in Cornwall, Ireland, Brittany and the *Old North, and aided by the Scandinavians of Dublin, will arise to drive the English from the

Isle of Britain, thereby reclaiming the whole realm, 'from Manaw Gododdin to Brittany, from Dyfed to Thanet'.

The occasion for the exposition of this powerful myth was the expansion of Wessex under Athelstan, who succeeded to the throne in 924 and defeated a combination of Scandinavian, Scottish and British forces at the battle of Brunanburh (937). The poem expresses seething rancour at the levies imposed on the Welsh princes and if these references are to the tributes exacted by Athelstan at the Council of Hereford (c.926–30) it may be that it was composed soon afterwards. By 937 Athelstan's unassailable position as *imperator* had put an end to British hopes of recovering possession of the Island.

The poet's familiarity with the politics of the day and his knowledge of learned traditions found also in the *Historia Brittonum (c.830) imply that he was a monk, probably from south Wales. He declares that victory will be achieved through the intercession of *Dewi and the saints as well as with the help of the traditional heroes, Cynan and *Cadwaladr. If the poet was a subject of *Hywel Dda, he may well have been speaking for a faction in the kingdom who abhorred Hywel's policy of appeasement towards the advancing Saxons.

This highly polemical poem is printed, with full notes and translations, in *Armes Prydein* (ed. Ifor Williams, 1955); an English version has been edited by Rachel Bromwich (1972).

ARNOLD, MATTHEW (1822–88), English poet and critic, was the son of Thomas Arnold, headmaster of Rugby. Educated at his father's school and at Balliol College, Oxford, he was elected to a Fellowship of Oriel College in 1845. Except for ten years as Professor of Poetry at Oxford (1857–67), his career from 1851 was spent as an Inspector of Schools, a post in which he earned a distinguished reputation as an educationist and an uncompromising critic of the social, religious and political ethos of Victorian England. Among his best-known poems are 'Tristram and Iseult' (1852), 'The Scholar Gypsy' (1853), 'Sohrab and Rustum' (1853) and 'Dover Beach' (1867), but he abandoned the writing of poetry at the age of forty-five in favour of literary and social criticism. Arnold was appalled by the vulgarity of the times in which he lived but believed that culture, which he saw as classless and universal, could save society from the materialism which was threatening to destroy it. The most crucial of his writings are to be found in the volumes *Culture and Anarchy* (1869) and *Friendship's Garland* (1871) but his *Essays in Criticism* (1865) and *Literature and Dogma* (1875) are among his other major works.

Matthew Arnold is noted here on account of his 'Lectures on Celtic Literature' which he delivered at Oxford in 1865 and the following year in his capacity as Professor of Poetry. First published in *The Cornhill Magazine* in 1866, the *Lectures* appeared in book form in 1867 and were reprinted in 1891. Arnold could read none of the Celtic languages but had made a sympathetic study of such literary texts as were available to him; he drew heavily on the Ossian poems (1760) of James Macpherson and had studied the French translations of Hersaut de la *Villemarqué, in particular his *Barzaz Breiz* (1839) and *Les Bardes Bretons du Sixième Siècle* (1850), as well as Lady Charlotte *Guest's *Mabinogion* (1849), Thomas *Stephens's *The Literature of the Kymry* (1849) and Eugene O'Curry's *Manuscript Materials of Ancient Irish History* (1861). From this study Arnold deduced three characteristics as belonging to the early literatures of Wales, Ireland, Brittany and Scotland: 'Celtic magic', 'Celtic melancholy' and a gift for style—not for large-scale design which he denied to the Celt, but for that found at its most perfect in small units of poetry, in illuminated manuscripts and in stone-carving. However hotly these claims have been disputed since Arnold's day, his definitions continue to be quoted and discussed, often by scholars with a more profound and extensive knowledge of the early Celtic literatures than he possessed. With his friend Ernest *Renan, whose *Essai sur la Poésie des Races Celtiques* (1854) had an influence on him, Arnold was a pioneer in the comparative study of the Celtic literatures.

Unfortunately, the *Lectures* also contain much which is less commendable. The writing is often diffuse and at times hardly relevant, the author's attempts to dissect English literature into its Celtic, Norman and Teutonic strains is at best purely hypothetical, while his confident assertion of national characteristics may now strike the reader as highly dubious. Furthermore, Arnold has been criticized for concentrating his sympathy on the early medieval masterpieces in Welsh and Irish, while at the same time expressing antipathy towards the continuity of these traditions in the living Celtic languages of his own day. The most moving message of the *Lectures* springs from his genuine and passionate concern that England should show respect and sympathy for the different cultural traditions of its Celtic neighbours, thereby avoiding misunderstandings and injustice on all sides. More curiously, he damns the *Eisteddfod with faint praise and asserts that 'if a Welshman has anything of real importance to say he must say it in English'. Nevertheless, Arnold deserves to be considered in the context of the time in which he was writing. He could not have foreseen the momentous developments in the cultural and political consciousness of the Celtic peoples which were to take place in the century after his death. The *Lectures* gave to the study of the Celtic languages and literatures the prestige of an academic discipline and their influence led directly to the foundation in 1877 of the Chair of Celtic at Jesus College, Oxford, of which the first incumbent was John *Rhŷs, a member of the first audience which had listened to the lectures. They also helped in the foundation of professorships in Welsh and Celtic Studies in the *University of Wales.

For further discussion see A. Nutt (ed.), *Arnold's Lectures on Celtic Literature* (1910), R. H. Super (ed.), *Matthew Arnold's Lectures and Essays in Criticism* (1962), F. J. W. Harding, 'Matthew Arnold and Wales' in the *Transactions* of the Honourable Society of Cymmrodorion (1963) and Rachel Bromwich, *Matthew Arnold and Celtic Literature: a Retrospect 1865–1965* (The O'Donnell Lecture, Oxford, 1965).

AROFAN (7th cent.), is named in a Triad as the poet of *Selyf ap Cynan Garwyn, Prince of *Powys.

Arofan tribe, see under ARGOED (1927).

Arthur (late 5th cent.–early 6th cent.), a British chieftain or military leader who had developed by the Middle Ages, in folk-memory and in the imagination of story-tellers and writers, into the focus of a large body of tales and romances. The historical evidence for his existence is meagre, but there is probably sufficient to make it acceptable. His name may be derived from the Latin *Artorius* and it has been suggested that he was a member of a family which sought to sustain and continue Roman military traditions in southern Britain in the fifth century. He is not named in the *De Excidio Britanniae*, probably composed by *Gildas shortly before AD 547, notwithstanding the fact that this author refers to a great victory gained by the Britons over the Saxons, about the year 519, at the battle of the Badonic Hill. In later ages it was generally believed that the victorious commander in this battle was Arthur and that the golden age of his reign succeeded it. The *Annales Cambriae, a chronicle regarded as reliable and deriving its material from early sources, records the battle of Mount Badon as having occurred in the year 516 and adds that in the battle Arthur bore the Cross of Our Lord Jesus Christ on his shoulders for three days and three nights and that the Britons were the victors. These details may be interpreted as reflecting an incipient ecclesiastical saga but the entry for the year 537 gives a brief reference to 'the battle of *Camlan in which Arthur and Medrawd (*Medrod) fell'. It is conceivable that this is the most authentic of the early Arthurian references and it should be noted that the wording does not indicate whether the two warriors were enemies or allies.

In the *Historia Brittonum, a work associated with *Nennius and composed in the early ninth century, but based on earlier sources, Arthur is described as 'a leader of battles' ('*dux bellorum*') and credited with having fought the Saxons in twelve victorious engagements. The final battle was that of Mount Badon, but since the names of several of the battles form rhymes (*Dulas/Basas* and *Celyddon/Gwynnion/Lleon/Baddon*) there is good reason to believe that they are derived from an early Welsh poem celebrating Arthur's victories, so that their value as historical evidence is dubious. Arthur's historicity, however, is supported by the occurrence of records of four rulers bearing his name in the sixth and seventh centuries, one in Dyfed and three in Scotland. This fact may reasonably be taken as a reflection of the fame of a genuine historical figure of an earlier generation. On the other hand, it must be admitted that Arthur does not appear in the early genealogies. Some scholars, on the basis of references to him of northern provenance, have claimed him as one of the 'Men of the North', but others place him in a more Roman setting in southern England and think that the location of the battle of Badon was at one of the several Badburys in that region.

Literary references to Arthur begin with the two early poems, 'Y *Gododdin' and '*Marwnad Cynddylan', in which he is named as a paragon of valour and ferocity. If it were certain that the texts of these poems are exactly as they existed in the seventh century these references would constitute historical evidence of the highest order, but unfortunately this certainty cannot be claimed. A number of poems preserved in *The *Black Book of Carmarthen* (c.1250) and *The Book of Taliesin* (c.1275) contain references to Arthur which show that by the time of their composition (c.900–c.1100) he had developed in popular memory into a folk-hero and a figure of legend. In a series of *englynion* he is described as 'emperor, ruler of battle' and brought into association with *Geraint, who was actually a king of Devon three-quarters of a century later than the Arthurian period. In a poem entitled '*Pa Ŵr yw'r Porthor?*' ('What man is the gate-keeper?') Arthur arrives at the entrance of a fortress and seeks admittance for himself and his band of followers, among whom are *Cai, *Bedwyr, *Manawydan son of Llŷr and *Mabon son of Modron. Here we are in the marvellous world portrayed in the tale of *Culhwch and Olwen and a third of the poem is devoted to an account of the feats performed by Cai. In the poem *'Preiddiau Annwfn' Arthur has entered the world of the *Mabinogi and he is described leading an expedition overseas in his ship, Prydwen, against *Annwfn or Caer Siddi (the Celtic Otherworld) in order to seize its greatest treasure, the cauldron of the king of Annwfn. In a single *englyn* in *Englynion y Beddau the memory of Arthur is linked to the tradition of the *Mab Darogan* ('Son of Prophecy') and the statement made that his grave will not be found until the Day of Judgement. A religious poem, *'Ymddiddan Arthur a'r Eryr', composed somewhat later than the others mentioned (c.1150?), gives a primitive portrayal of Arthur, describing him as 'head of the hosts of Cornwall' and as a semi-pagan king who would wish to 'contend with God'.

In Welsh prose the principal composition on an Arthurian theme is the tale of Culhwch and Olwen, which in its present form may be dated around 1100 and is thus the earliest Arthurian tale in any language. Here Arthur presides in his court at Celli-wig in Cornwall over a fantastic world of magic and enchantment, his authority extending over southern Wales and southern Ireland, Brittany, Somerset, Devon and Cornwall. Culhwch comes to his court to seek aid in the search for Olwen, daughter of Ysbaddaden Bencawr. Arthur and his men assist him readily and the climax of the tale is the account of the hunting of the *Twrch Trwyth. Some references to Arthur deriving from early Welsh tradition are also found in the Triads but in 1136, in his *Historia Regum Britanniae, *Geoffrey of Monmouth presented a very different portrait of Arthur. The court was now moved from Celli-wig to Caerleon on the river Usk and its ruler depicted as a medieval feudal emperor who conquered the armies of Rome but fell as a consequence of Medrod's treachery. Geoffrey was also the first to state, both in the Historia and in the Vita Merlini, that Arthur, having been wounded at Camlan, was carried away to *Ynys Afallon to heal his wounds. The Round Table was first mentioned in Wace's Norman-French adaptation of Geoffrey's Historia, the Roman de Brut (1155).

Geoffrey's portrayal of Arthur became widely known in Wales through the medium of the translations of his work entitled *Brut y Brenhinedd. In the Welsh romances of Owain, Historia Peredur and Geraint fab Erbin (see under TAIR RHAMANT), which correspond respectively to the Yvain, the Perceval and the Erec of Chrétien de Troyes, Arthur again appears as a king holding splendid court at Caerleon and no doubt the influence of Geoffrey can here be discerned. In these romances, however, Arthur has become a background figure and the tales they tell of the adventures of some of his knights were derived from sources totally unconnected with Geoffrey. A fairly prominent place is given to Arthur also in the satirical tale *Breuddwyd Rhonabwy, in which he is associated with Cornwall and is made to play *Gwyddbwyll (a medieval board-game) against *Owain ab Urien while his men fight Owain's ravens. Some of the *Lives of the Saints of the Celtic Church which were composed in Wales, in particular those of *Cadog, *Padarn, *Carannog and Gildas, contain a portrait of Arthur which differs greatly from the more common heroic one. Their authors view him from an ecclesiastical standpoint and delineate him as a proud and foolish local tyrant and an oppressor of the saints. Invariably, through divine intervention, he is brought to repentance for his evil deeds and thereupon he extends his patronage to the Church.

This is not the place to attempt an account of Arthur's career in literatures other than that of Wales. In the Renaissance the validity of Geoffrey's portrayal of him was the subject of much debate and English authors such as Leland, the antiquary, in his Assertio inclytissimi Arturii Regis Britanniae (1544), as well as the Welshman Sir John *Price in his Historiae Brytannicae Defensio (1573), are found defending the Historia Regum Britanniae against the criticism of the historian Polydore Vergil in his Anglica Historia (1534). Theophilus *Evans gave Arthur an honourable place in his Drych y Prif Oesoedd (1740), although he rejected certain 'old fables' related of him, such as the tale of the sword in the stone, and he did not follow Geoffrey in claiming for him the conquest of a host of other kingdoms. During the nineteenth century a new romantic interest in Arthur developed and received expression in Welsh in T. Gwynn *Jones's *'Ymdawiad Arthur' (1902), a poem which clothes some of the ideals of the poet's own period in archaic diction and medieval dress.

R. S. Loomis's Arthurian Literature in the Middle Ages, A Collaborative History (1959), gives a conspectus of the entire field of Arthurian literature; the Welsh material is surveyed by Thomas Jones in 'The Early Evolution of the Legend of Arthur' in Nottingham Medieval Studies. The relevant Latin sources and texts may be found in E. K. Chambers, Arthur of Britain (1966); see also Arthur's Britain (1971) by Leslie Alcock and The Age of Arthur (1973) by John Morris.

Arthur's Cave, the subject of a folk-tale based on the international theme of the hero who sleeps until called upon to lead his country. In the most common Welsh version a young drover carrying a hazel-stick meets on London Bridge a wizard who asks to be taken to the spot where the stick was cut. When, in Wales, they discover a cave in which *Arthur and his men are sleeping, the youth tries to steal the knights' treasure but accidentally strikes a bell which awakens the sleepers. 'Has the day come?', they ask and he replies, 'No, not yet, sleep on'. At the third attempt the youth forgets to reply, is beaten by the knights and thereafter can no longer locate the cave.

The tale is associated with caves in Pontneddfechan, Llantrisant and Ystradyfodwg, Glam., in Dyffryn Tywi, Carms., and in Llanllyfni, Caerns. In several versions such as those associated with Troed-yr-Aur, Cards., and Llandybie, Carms., it is Owain Lawgoch (*Owain ap Thomas ap Rhodri), and not Arthur, who is asleep in the cave, while in some Glamorgan versions the cave is connected with *Owain Glyndŵr. The theme was the subject of an awdl for which William *Morris was awarded the *Chair at the National Eisteddfod of 1934.

Arvonius, see ROBERTS, THOMAS (1765/6–1841).

Arwest Glan Geirionydd, see under ROBERTS, WILLIAM JOHN (1828–1904).

Arwystli, a cantref comprising the upper reaches of the valley of the Severn. The dispute between the rulers of *Gwynedd and *Powys over this territory was one of the factors which exacerbated relations between *Llywelyn ap Gruffudd and the English Crown in the years from 1277 to 1282.

Ash on a Young Man's Sleeve (1954), an autobiographical novel by Dannie *Abse in which the adolescence of a Jewish boy growing up in Cardiff during the 1930s is evoked with sensitivity, lyricism and humour. It is set against a background of *Socialism in south Wales and the rise of Fascism, at first remote but then close at hand as the narrator's friend is killed in an air-raid. The book, which ends on a note of lost innocence, takes its title from an adaptation of a line in T. S. Eliot's poem, 'Little Gidding':

> Ash on an old man's sleeve
> Is all the ash burnt roses leave.
> Dust in the air suspended
> Marks the place where a story ended.

ASHTON, CHARLES (1848–99), bibliophile and literary historian, was born at Llawr-y-glyn, Mont. An illegitimate child, he received little formal education and was put to work at the age of twelve in the lead-mines of Dylife. Eventually, after much hardship, he joined the police force, serving at Dinas Mawddwy, Mer. A voracious reader and researcher in the libraries of Cardiff, Oxford and London, he published several books on historical and literary topics, the most important of which is *Hanes Llenyddiaeth Gymreig o 1651 hyd 1850* (1893). Towards the end of his life he suffered from mental illness but continued to work on his bibliography, *Llyfryddiaeth y 19fed Ganrif*, of which only one volume was published in 1908. He also published a study of the life and times of Bishop William *Morgan (1891) and edited the works of *Iolo Goch (1896). Some of his work has been corrected by later research but his contribution to Welsh bibliographical studies was substantial.

For further details see the article by Glyn M. Ashton in *Y Genhinen* (vol. 10, no. 3, 1960).

ASHTON, GLYN MILLS (Wil Cwch Angau; 1910–), scholar, critic and satirical writer. Born in Barry, Glam., and educated at University College, Cardiff, he was Welsh master at St. Illtyd's College, Cardiff, for more than twenty years, then Curator of the Salesbury Library at University College, Cardiff. He is the author of a number of humorous novels, including *Tipyn o Annwyd* (1960), *Y Pendefig Pygddu* (1961), *Doctor! Doctor!* (1964), *Canmol dy Wlad* (1966) and *Angau yn y Crochan* (1969), all written under his pseudonym; he has also edited the

autobiography and letters (1948) of Twm o'r Nant (Thomas *Edwards), *Drych yr Amseroedd* (1958) and two volumes in the series of autobiographical essays, *Atgofion* (1972).

ASPDEN, BRYAN (1933–), poet, was born in Blackburn, Lancs., and educated at the University of Durham. He moved to Wales in 1965 and now lives at Conwy, Caerns., where he works in local government. He has learned Welsh and writes in the language. With his first collection of poems, *News of the Changes* (1984), he won the *Welsh Arts Council's New Poets Competition.

Asser (d. 909), scholar, bishop and counsellor to Alfred the Great, King of Wessex. He spent his youth in the monastic community at *St. David's where he belonged to the family of the bishop, Nobis. Becoming head of the *clas*, he gained fame as a scholar and was invited to serve Alfred, thereafter dividing his time between St. David's and the King's court, an early example of a Welshman finding a career in England. Alfred became more and more dependent on his judgement and he was made Bishop of Sherborne shortly before the King died in 901. To Asser is attributed (although his authorship has been doubted) the unfinished mixture of chronicle and personal memoir of the reign of Alfred known as *Annales rerum gestarum Alfredi Magni*.

For further details see D. P. Kirby, 'Asser and his Life of King Alfred' in *Studia Celtica* (vol. VI, 1971). The Life of King Alfred was edited by W. H. Stevenson in 1904; a Welsh translation was made by J. O. Jones, *O Lygad y Ffynnon* (1899), and an English version by L. C. Jane in 1926.

'Asyn a fu farw, Yr' (lit. 'The ass which died'), a very popular ballad, was immortalized by the singing of Bob Roberts (Robert *Roberts, 1870–1951) of Tai'r Felin; the authorship of the words and tune is uncertain. The sham lamenting in the song is similar to that in 'Y *Mochyn Du' and, although it was 'while carrying coal to Flint' that the ass died, the ballad is as well known in south Wales as it is in the north.

Aubrey, William (The Great Civilian; c.1529–95), lawyer, was born at Cantref, near Brecon. At Oxford he read Law, obtained his doctorate in 1554 and became a Fellow of Jesus and All Souls Colleges and Principal of New Inn Hall. Although appointed Reader in Civil Law by Queen Mary, his career lay outside Oxford, where his practice in the prerogative and ecclesiastical courts brought him the offices of Master in Chancery (c.1555), Master of Requests (1590), Advocate in the Court of the Arches and Judge of Audience in the Court of Canterbury (c.1592). Early involved with political issues, he was Judge Advocate with the Earl of Pembroke's expedition to France in 1557 and a member of Archbishop Parker's commission which declared the marriage of the Earl of Hertford and Lady Catherine Grey illegal in 1562.

An anti-Puritan and a kind of all-purpose legal expert (he was one of those who condemned his distant cousin John *Penry in 1593), he was much concerned with the reform of the Church courts of the Province of Canterbury, of which he became joint Administrator in 1577, and sole Vicar-General five years later, both during Archbishop Grindal's suspension and after the appointment of Whitgift. Retained as counsel by a variety of organizations, he made himself particularly indispensable after 1590, when Burghley and the Privy Council referred to him, as Master of Requests, various difficult constitutional issues and petitions. Having both bought land in Wales and received grants of it, Aubrey was said to have died worth more than two thousand pounds a year, by contemporary standards an enormous sum.

His great-grandson, **John Aubrey** (1626–97), was of wholly English birth and upbringing. He learned about Wales by having to visit it during the 1650s in vain attempts to defeat the chicanery in which the inheritance of 'The Great Civilian' had become involved. He is remembered chiefly for his *Brief Lives* (1813), a book notable for its many portraits of people from Herefordshire and Breconshire, but his interest in his Welsh ancestry drove him to write the unpublished *Interpretation of Villare Anglicanum* for 'the honour of Wales'. He was also the first to investigate Avebury and to associate the *Druids with Stonehenge, where the 'aubrey-holes' were named after him.

For further details see Theophilus Jones, *History of Brecknock* (1805), and a new edition of *Brief Lives* edited by Richard Barber (1975); see also Michael Hunter, *John Aubrey and the Realm of Learning* (1975).

Augustinian Canons, a monastic order founded by a community of clerics in northern Italy and southern France during the eleventh century. The Papal Synods of 1059 and 1063 gave official blessing to the order and by the beginning of the twelfth century the communities had adopted the Rule of St. Augustine of Hippo. The monks were also called Black Canons because of the colour of their habit. They were subject to the authority of local bishops and could undertake parochial responsibilities. In Wales, priories were established at Llanthony Prima in 1103, at *Carmarthen in 1148 and at Haverfordwest in 1200; the old monasteries at *Penmon, *Bardsey and Beddgelert joined the order about 1200. The priories developed close links with the native population and promoted Welsh culture by copying manuscripts and patronizing the poets. All six Augustinian priories in Wales were dissolved between 1536 and 1539.

For further details see D. Knowles, *The Religious Orders in England* (1948–59), and J. C. Dickinson, *The Origins of the Austin Canons and their Introduction into England* (1950).

Autobiography of a Super-Tramp, The (1908), by W. H. *Davies, although from its first sentence factually unreliable, gives a vivid account of the vicissitudes of the author's early life. Only the first two chapters are set in his home town of Newport, Mon., the others take the reader on the roads of England, America and Canada. The book presents with humour and deep humanity the author's adventures in the company of unskilled workers on both sides of the Atlantic, among whom Brum, New Haven Baldy, Australian Red, Three-Fingered Jack and Scotty Bill are the most memorable. It also describes how the writer lost a foot while trying to jump a freight-train in America in 1899. The book's preface by G. B. Shaw praising its direct, unaffected style did much to help establish W. H. Davies's literary reputation. His subsequent attempts at re-working the same field in *Beggars* (1909), *The True Traveller* (1912) and *Later Days* (1925) were less successful, but in the last-named there is the added interest of his acquaintance with Rupert Brooke, Joseph Conrad, Walter de la Mare, Ralph Hodgson, John Masefield and other English writers, to whom he was introduced by Edward *Thomas.

Avalon, see YNYS AFALLON.

Awdl, a long poem in the traditional metres. The words '*awdl*' and '*odl*' ('rhyme') were originally synonymous and the essence of an *awdl* was that it was in monorhyme, as in 'Y *Gododd-in*', for example. Similarly, to the *Gogynfeirdd an *awdl* was a poem in monorhyme of between twenty and forty lines, two or three being sometimes linked to make one long poem. The usual metres were *cyhydedd nawban*, *cyhydedd hir*, *toddaid* and *byr-a-thoddaid*, and the poem ended with an *englyn. By the time of the *Poets of the Gentry a fixed pattern had become established: a number of *englynion* were linked by a word from the last line of one *englyn* being repeated in the first line of the next; a number of stanzas in another metre in monorhyme then followed, ending with a link as before between the last line and the first in the poem, the whole making between sixty and a hundred lines. Some poets in the fifteenth century, such as *Dafydd Nanmor, *Gwilym Tew and Lewys Morgannwg (*Llywelyn ap Rhisiart), wrote *awdlau* consisting of one example of each of the *Twenty-four Metres, but this was never regarded as the standard pattern.

By the beginning of the eighteenth century it was assumed that an *awdl* should contain all the metres and there are six such poems in the Grammar (1728) of Siôn Rhydderch (John *Roderick). Such too were the poems submitted at the first eisteddfod held by the *Gwyneddigion Society at Bala in 1789, but the competitors were persuaded to limit the number of metres. As a result, only four or five metres appeared in the many hundreds of long *awdlau* composed during the nineteenth century. Those written since 1900 are much shorter, with the metres more functionally arranged. Only one metre, the *hir-a-thoddaid*, is used in T. H. *Parry-Williams's 'Eryri'* (1915) but Geraint *Bowen in his 'Moliant i'r Amaethwr'* (1946) has emulated the Poets of the Gentry by using them all. Among the innovations introduced in the twentieth century were the use by Cynan (Albert *Evans-Jones) of the *tri-thrawiad* metre in '*I'r Duw nid adweinir*', and the use by Gwyndaf (Evan Gwyndaf *Evans) of *cynghanedd* in *vers libre* in '*Magdalen*' (1935). For the last two hundred years few poets have written *awdlau* except for competition purposes, but by this means a number of excellent poems have been produced, including (besides those already named) '*Yr Haf*' (1910) by R. Williams *Parry, '*Min y Môr*' (1921) by Robert John *Rowlands (Meuryn), '*Y Glöwr*' (1950) by Gwilym R. *Tilsley and '*Y Cynhaeaf*' (1966) by Dic Jones (Richard Lewis *Jones). See also CHAIR.

A selection of prize-winning *awdlau* is to be found in the volume *Awdlau Cadeiriol Detholedig 1926–50* (ed. Thomas Parry, 1953).

Awdl-Bryddest, a long poem consisting of stanzas in both the strict and the free metres. Competitions for such a poem were sometimes set at eisteddfodau during the last quarter of the nineteenth century but the form was never popular.

Awdl-Gywydd, one of the *Twenty-four Metres, a metrical unit of two seven-syllable lines linked together not by terminal rhyme but by means of an *odl gyrch*. Popular with the minstrel poets, it was adopted in the fifteenth century by professional poets who introduced *cynghanedd* into it and ruled that the accents of the final syllables in each of the two lines had to vary. The metrical unit was seldom used on its own and is usually found incorporated in the metrical forms known as *Englyn Cyrch* and *Cyrch a Chwta*. The *Awdl-Gywydd* without *cynghanedd* continued to be used in *cwndidau* and harp-stanzas.

Awenydd, a term with two meanings: it can be used as a synonym for a poet or one who has the muse (*awen*) or it can denote the muse or poetical inspiration itself. *Gerald de Barri (Giraldus Cambrensis), in his *Descriptio Kambriae* (1193), gives a vivid account of *awenyddion*, by which he meant sooth-sayers. Iolo Morganwg (Edward *Williams) used the word in his manuscripts for a bardic pupil.

B

Bachegraig, a house in Tremeirchion, Flints., built in 1567 for Sir Richard Clough (d. 1570), the second husband of *Catrin of Berain. The first house in Wales to be made from bricks, it was built so quickly that it was said to be the work of the Devil: if the builders lacked materials, a fresh supply would await them each morning beside a brook known to this day as Nant-y-Cythraul ('The Devil's Brook'). Local tradition has it that Sir Richard used to study the stars and commune with the Devil in an attic room and that, one night, his wife discovering them, the Devil escaped through the walls with the master in his arms. The house was demolished at the beginning of the nineteenth century by order of its new owners, Hester Lynch *Piozzi and her husband.

BACHELLERY, EDOUARD (1907–), Celtic scholar, of French birth, graduated in English at the Sorbonne in 1938, but took up Celtic Studies as a pupil of Joseph *Vendryes. Elected Director of Celtic Studies at the *École des Hautes Études* in 1941, he was the editor of the journal *Études Celtiques* from 1948, when it reappeared after the war, until 1977. His study of *Gutun Owain, L'Œuvre Poétique de Gutun Owain* (2 vols., 1950, 1951), with introduction, detailed notes and a French translation of the poems, is an important contribution to Welsh scholarship. He is one of the editors of the Dictionary of Old Irish for which Vendryes collected the material, and which continues to be published in parts.

Bachymbyd, a house in the parish of Llanynys, near Ruthin, Denbs., the home of a branch of the *Salesbury family of Lleweni who played an important part in the tradition of bardic patronage during the sixteenth century. The branch was established by Piers Salusbury who had married Margaret Wen, the heiress of Ieuan ap Hywel ap Rhys of Y *Rug, Mer., and the literary associations of Bachymbyd are very closely linked with those of the family's principal home.

Bacon, Anthony (1718–86), an English iron-master who leased virgin mineral land in the valley of the Taff near Merthyr Tydfil, Glam., in 1765. He owned the Cyfarthfa and Plymouth works and acquired rights at Hirwaun in 1780. During the War of American Independence (1775–83) he made huge profits by supplying the British Government with iron for guns and cannon ball. It was he who was mainly responsible for developing Merthyr Tydfil, formerly a hamlet, into an iron-smelting centre with the largest population of any town in Wales.

BADDY, THOMAS (d. 1729), translator and hymn-writer, one of the early Dissenting ministers, had charge of the Independent congregation in Denbigh from 1693 until his death. He published a translation of a religious work by Thomas Doolittle, *Pasc y Christion* (1703), and a volume of hymns, *Caniad Solomon* (1725). Few of his compositions have proved popular in public worship but they are noteworthy for being among the first attempts at hymnody by Dissenters in Wales.

Badon, The Battle of (c.519), see under ARTHUR (late 5th cent.–early 6th cent.).

Baglan (6th cent.), a saint who came from Brittany as a young man to be educated by *Illtud at *Llanilltud Fawr (Llantwit Major). It was said that he carried fire in his cloak to warm his teacher and that Illtud gave him a magic staff with a brass crook (*bagl*) from which he took his name. Advised to follow the staff until it brought him to a place where grew a tree bearing three kinds of fruit, he was to build a church and live there for the rest of his life. When Baglan reached the tree he saw a herd of swine grazing beneath it, a swarm of bees on its trunk and a flock of crows nesting in its branches, and these creatures were the saint's companions ever after. The saint is commemorated in the name of Baglan, a district of Port Talbot, Glam.

Bailey, Crawshay (1789–1872), iron-master of Nant-y-glo, Mon., was a nephew of Richard *Crawshay of Cyfarthfa, Merthyr Tydfil, Glam. He is remembered on account of 'Cosher Bailey's Engine', an anonymous song with innumerable verses which are sung impromptu to the tune of 'Y *Mochyn Du' and with the refrain, 'Did you ever see (thrice) such a funny thing before?'. He was a great promoter of railways, for which his works provided the iron, and served as the Conservative Member for Monmouth from 1852 to 1868.

Baker, Augustine (1575–1641), see BAKER, DAVID (1575–1641).

Baker, Charles, see LEWIS, DAVID (1617–79).

BAKER, DAVID (Augustine Baker; 1575–1641), scholar and mystic, was born at Abergavenny, Mon., to parents who, although privately Catholic, conformed in public. At the age of twelve he was sent to Christ's Hospital with a view to his learning English, which was but little spoken in his home town at that time, and three years later he entered Broadgates Hall (now Pembroke College), Oxford. His studies were completed at Clifford's Inn and the Inner Temple. The young man's dissolute life-style was severely shaken by a religious conversion in 1600 and three years later he was received into the Catholic Church. Attracted to the religious life, he joined the Cassinese Benedictine community of St. Justinian at Padua in 1605 and was given the name Augustine. Ordained as a priest at Rheims in 1613, he spent much of his time in England and in Wales, returning often to Abergavenny and persuading many of his relatives and neighbours to the Catholic faith. After a short period at Douai, he became spiritual director to a community of Benedictine nuns at Cambrai in 1624.

At his death by plague Baker left unpublished several treatises on ecclesiastical history and English law, together with many volumes of mystical and theological works of which excerpts were published at Douai under the title *Sancta Sophia* (1657). This book, re-titled *Holy Wisdom*, remained part of Benedictine life until the latter part of the nineteenth century, as did his English and Latin rhymes embodying religious and moral teaching. He also wrote much of the history of the English Benedictines which was later collated by his friend John *Jones (Leander). His *Holy Practices* (1657) and *Confessions* (1922), with his autobiography (written 1637–38) complete the list of Baker's works outside manuscript. A Life was published by his *socius*, Leander Prichard, in 1643 and there have been two more since then. He was described by William Llewelyn *Williams as 'the last Welsh Catholic who played a large part in the history of Catholicism in England'.

For further details see R. Baker Gabb, *Families of Baker and Baker Gabb* (1903) and Joseph Bradney, *The History of Monmouthshire* (1904); see also the article by Frances Meredith marking the quatercentenary of Baker's birth in *The Anglo-Welsh Review* (vol. 25, no. 55, 1975).

Ballad, a narrative poem usually on a topical subject and intended to be sung. Huw *Morys and Edward *Morris wrote poems in ballad form during the seventeenth century. Ballads were published in broadsheet form and sold at fairs by pedlars, who were usually their authors. Most Welsh ballads were set to popular English melodies but there are numerous examples in the *Triban* and *Tri Thrawiad* measures, some of the earlier ones embellished with *cynghanedd. Balladeers flourished in the Vales of Clwyd, Dee and Conwy in the eighteenth century and their songs were mostly printed in Shrewsbury, Chester and Trefriw. The most famous were Elis *Roberts, Huw Jones (1700?–82) of Llangwm, Dafydd Jones (1708?–85) of Trefriw, Owen Griffith of Llanystumdwy and Twm o'r Nant (Thomas *Edwards). During the nineteenth century the ballad came into its own in the industrial parts of south Wales, although many more were written in Welsh than in English. Dafydd *Jones (Dewi Dywyll or Deio'r Cantwr), Abel *Jones (Bardd Crwst), Owen *Griffith (Ywain Meirion or Owen Gospiol), Richard Williams (Dic Dywyll or Bardd Gwagedd) and Levi *Gibbon were among the best-known exponents of the form.

The balladeer's role was to provide the common people with entertainment which found its subjects in folk-tales and contemporary events. Some ballads treated of love and patriotism or had religious themes, especially morality and *Temperance, but most described murders and such disasters as pit-explosions, strikes and shipwrecks. The ballads of I. D. *Hooson, despite their immense popularity, do not belong to this folk tradition but their lyrical language is typical of the literary revival of the ballad form in the twentieth century.

For discussion of the ballad form in Welsh, together with examples, see Thomas Parry, *Baledi'r Ddeunawfed Ganrif* (1935) and Ben Bowen Thomas, *Baledi Morgannwg* (1951) and *Drych y Baledwr* (1958); see also John Humphreys Davies, *A Bibliography of Welsh Ballads printed in the Eighteenth Century* (1909) and *Hen Faledi'r Ffair* (ed. Tegwyn Jones, 1971).

Ballad of the Mari Lwyd (1941), the first volume of poetry to be published by Vernon *Watkins. While not achieving the uniformly high standard of his later work, it nevertheless includes poems which show the development of the poet's thought from the initial platforms of his 'grief'. It opens with that much misunderstood and perhaps ultimately obscure poem, 'The Collier'. Other early poems meriting inclusion in any select canon of Vernon Watkins's work are 'Prime Colours', 'Griefs of the Sea', 'Sycamore', 'Portrait of a Friend', 'A Prayer against Time', 'Thames Forest' and 'Stone Footing'.

The title poem was suggested by a radio broadcast (heard by the poet on New Year's Eve, 1938) of the *Mari Lwyd ritual in his father's home village of Taff's Well, Glam., and its six hundred lines were completed during the following winter. The poet associated the tradition with the 'crack in time' at the year-change and he makes the Dead much more versatile and cunning than the Living. That they are not admitted to the House of the Living, the greed and terror of its occupants being too strong, is his implicit indictment of the mythless and materialistic modern world: there is a god outside, but no God within.

The fullest discussion of the poem and the folk-practice is to be found in Dora Polk, *Vernon Watkins and the Spring of Vision* (1977).

BALLINGER, JOHN (1860–1933), the first Librarian of the *National Library of Wales, was born at Pontnewynydd, Mon. Orphaned, he left Canton School, Cardiff, when he was fourteen years old and found work as an assistant in the Cardiff Free Library, rising to become Chief Librarian in 1885. Well known in the profession for his prodigious energy, administrative ability and progressive views on librarianship, he refrained from taking sides in the debate over the location of the proposed National Library of Wales, with the result that, in 1908, he alone was considered for the post of Librarian. There were many furious quarrels between him and his staff during the early years, but Ballinger was resolute and soon had the young institution firmly under his control.

He set great store on technical librarianship and published a large number of articles on the subject. With Ifano *Jones he was responsible for the valuable *Cardiff Free Library Catalogue* (1898) and *The Bible in Wales* (1906). He edited new editions of *Rhann o Psalmau Dafydd Broffwyd* (1603), *Basilikon Doron* (1604), *Y Llyfr Plygain* (1612), *Yr Ymarfer o Dduwioldeb* (1630) and *The History of the Gwydir Family* (1770), but his work as editor of Welsh texts was not satisfactory because he had only a scant knowledge of the language; he was the author of *Gleanings from a Printer's File* (1928) and 'Katheryn of Berain' (in *Y Cymmrodor*, vol. XI).

Among the honorary posts in which he served with distinction were those of secretary to *Cymdeithas Llên Cymru (The Welsh Literary Society), editor of *The Journal of the Welsh Bibliographical Society* and Chairman of the University of Wales Press Board. In 1922 he was elected President of the Library Association of Great Britain in recognition of his great and untiring service to the profession and he was knighted in 1930. The Medal of the Honourable Society of *Cymmrodorion was presented to him in 1932 for his contribution to the study of the literature and bibliography of Wales.

For further details see the book by W. Ll. Davies, *The National Library of Wales* (1937).

Banbury, The Battle of (1469), at which William *Herbert of Raglan, Earl of Pembroke and a staunch Yorkist, was defeated and many Welshmen killed, evoked an immediate response from Welsh poets. *Guto'r Glyn, who had earlier warned the Earl not to trust the English in a *cywydd* composed at Raglan, described the battle in detail in his elegy for Herbert. *Lewys Glyn Cothi (Llywelyn y Glyn), in an elegy for *Thomas ap Roger Vaughan of

Hergest, the grandson of Sir *Dafydd Gam, referred to his widow's grief and the desire of his three sons for revenge. Both poets regarded the Yorkist success at the battle of Barnet (1471), when the Earl of Warwick was slain, as retribution for the defeat suffered at Banbury.

Nevertheless, despite their nominal affiliations, the work of some other Welsh poets reveals indifference to the issues of the Wars of the Roses. For example, *Dafydd Llwyd of Mathafarn, a Yorkist, called on Henry *Tudor to avenge the deaths of the Herberts at Banbury, although he belonged to the other side: the nationality of the fallen Welshmen was more important to him than the colours under which they had fought.

Banc y Ddafad Ddu and **Banc yr Eidion Du**, see under DROVERS.

Bancroft, William John (1870–1959), rugby-player, appeared for Wales in the full-back position on thirty-three consecutive occasions between 1890 and 1901, a record in the annals of the game. Captain of Wales a dozen times and the first Welshman twice to be included in a side which won the Triple Crown, Billy Bancroft was audacious, cunning and renowned for his daring runs and superb kicking.

Band of Hope, The, a society for children and adolescents, devoted to the ideal of *Temperance. The name was first used about 1847 and the Band of Hope Union was formed in England eight years later. The movement, which had more than three million members by the 1930s, founded the *Boy's Own Paper* in 1892. Branches were formed in Wales under the aegis of Nonconformist chapels, but after the Second World War they lost much of their original emphasis and became more like other youth clubs, although still keeping their religious affiliations.

Bando, a game similar to hockey or hurley which, until the end of the nineteenth century, was popular throughout Wales. John *Elias, the preacher, was a keen player in his younger days, as was David *Lloyd George. The game was especially popular in the Vale of Glamorgan, where villages and parishes competed against each other. The 'Margam Bando Boys' were immortalized in a famous ballad with that title. The rules were never standardized, but varied from parish to parish and would often be agreed immediately before the start of the game. It was played on a flat pitch, sometimes on beaches, and the aim was to drive a small wooden ball between two posts which served as goals at both ends. A clubbed stick known as a '*bando*' was used to hit the ball and the teams, with sometimes as many as thirty players in each, wore the coloured ribbons of their side. There have been local revivals of the game during the present century, most notably in the industrial valleys of Glamorgan.

For descriptions of the game see Charles Redwood, *Vale of Glamorgan* (1839), Henry Lewis (ed.), *Morgannwg Matthews Ewenni* (1953), G. J. Williams, 'Glamorgan Customs in the Eighteenth Century' in *Gwerin* (vol. 1, 1956–57), and Howard Lloyd, '*Tri o Hen Chwaraeon Cymru*' in the *Transactions* of the Honourable Society of Cymmrodorion (1960).

Baner ac Amserau Cymru (lit. 'The banner and times of Wales'), a newspaper, also known as **Y Faner**, was launched in 1859 when Thomas *Gee merged Yr *Amserau* with another weekly, *Baner Cymru*. The new periodical's first editor was William *Rees (Gwilym Hiraethog), assisted by John Hughes and Thomas Jones (Glan Alun), but Thomas Gee was its guiding spirit from the outset and he soon took control of it. Under his editorship the newspaper exerted a powerful influence on the religious, political and literary life of Wales throughout the latter half of the nineteenth century. It was staunchly Liberal in outlook, defending *Nonconformity against the Established Church and supporting the common people in Radical causes such as *Temperance and *Land Reform. Literary and cultural matters were given much attention in its columns and it regularly carried reviews of English books. By the time of Thomas Gee's death in 1898 the newspaper claimed a weekly readership of 50,000 and it enjoyed a reputation unrivalled by that of any other Welsh-language journal of its day.

The newspaper's fortunes declined during the first two decades of the twentieth century but improved in 1923 when E. Prosser *Rhys was appointed to the editorship, a post in which he was to remain until his death in 1945. The publishing company *Gwasg Gee* was bought by Kate *Roberts and her husband in 1935 and many of the writer's articles and reviews appeared thereafter in *Y Faner*'s pages. During the Second World War the newspaper was avidly read for the column *Cwrs y Byd* in which Saunders *Lewis wrote about world affairs. After the war, with Gwilym R. *Jones as its editor, the newspaper changed its proprietor twice and in 1958 it was bought by *Gwasg y Sir*, Bala. During the 1960s and 1970s its circulation dwindled and it was in danger of having to cease publication until, in 1977, with the financial support of the *Welsh Arts Council, it changed its format to that of a weekly magazine. Since then it has had three editors, namely Geraint *Bowen (March 1977 – December 1978), Jennie Eirian Davies (January 1979 – May 1982) and Emyr Price, who took up his duties in January 1983. With a circulation of about three thousand, *Y Faner* continues to play an important role as one of the two national weekly journals in Welsh. Aiming at a balance between news coverage and features, it provides a forum for all shades of public opinion but is still capable of expressing the Radical viewpoint for which, in its heyday under Thomas Gee, it was highly respected and widely read.

For further details see T. Gwynn Jones, *Cofiant Thomas Gee* (1913) and Gwilym R. Jones, *Rhodd Enbyd* (1983).

Bangor, a cathedral and diocese in Caernarfonshire. The word '*bangor*' was originally used to denote the wattled hedge around a monastery. This particular Bangor was known in medieval times as *Y Bangor Fawr yn Arfon* ('The Great Bangor in Arfon') to distinguish it from Bangor Is-y-Coed, Flints., and Bangor Teifi, Cards. In *Annales Cambriae* the date 584 is given for the death of *Deiniol who, according to tradition, founded a monastery at Bangor. Some manuscripts of the Gwynedd version of the Welsh Laws refer to Bangor and Clynnog Fawr as guarantors of the 'Privileges of the Men of Arfon'. The Danes devastated the cathedral in 1073. The present building was begun in the time of *Gruffudd ap Cynan who, like his son *Owain Gwynedd, was buried near the high altar.

The poet *Gwalchmai ap Meilyr described Bangor as '*bangeibr oleuad*' ('a bright church') in his elegy for *Madog ap Maredudd (1160) and a number of its bishops and canons were praised by the poets, including Madog ab Iorwerth (Matthew of Englefield, bishop, 1328–57) by Goronwy Gyriog and Hywel ap Goronwy (dean, 1371) by *Dafydd ap Gwilym. The last-named described the cathedral as '*tŷ geirwgalch, teg ei organ*' ('a house white-washed as white as foam, fair is its organ'), and observed a girl listening to a psalm in the choir there. Anian Sais (bishop, 1309?–28) was rebuked by Iorwerth Beli for neglecting poets in favour of musicians. *Dafydd Trefor (d. 1528), in his *cywydd* to Deiniol, refers to Thomas Skevington (bishop, 1509–33) who paid for the restoration of the cathedral's nave and the erection of a tower.

Bangor Is-coed, see under CHESTER, THE BATTLE OF (c.615).

Bangu, a hand-bell once kept in the church at Glascwm, Rads., which was said to have been brought there by magic oxen as a gift from *Dewi Sant (St. David). According to local tradition, a woman took it to the town of Rhayader in the belief that her husband, a prisoner in the castle, would be released by the sound of its chiming, but the relic was seized by the guards and she was turned away. That night the town was destroyed by fire, except for the wall on which the bell had been hung. The story is related by *Gerald de Barri (Giraldus Cambrensis) in his *Descriptio Kambriae* (1193).

Banks of Wye, The (1811), a long poem in four

books by the English writer Robert Bloomfield (1766–1823), agricultural labourer, shoemaker and author of *The Farmer's Boy* (1800). It describes a journey made in 1807 by boat from Ross to Chepstow, Mon., on horseback from Raglan to Brecon, and back by way of Hay and Hereford. The poem, in the author's words, 'exhibits the language and feeling of a man who had never before seen a mountainous country'. On the climbing of the Sugar Loaf, with Blorenge and the Skirrid in view, he exclaims, 'These are Alps to me', a common response among English visitors to Wales during the early nineteenth century. There are four poems inset: 'The Gleaner's Song' (near Bicknor), 'The Maid of Landoga' (Llandogo), 'Morris of Persfield' (Piercefield) and 'Mary's Grave' (Hay).

Baptists, a Christian denomination emphasizing the baptism, by immersion in water, of those who make a personal profession of faith in Jesus Christ as Saviour and Lord, belong to one of the largest Nonconformist groups in the world. They claim that baptism was the practice of the Early Church which was rediscovered by the Continental Anabaptists in the wake of the *Reformation. The first Baptist church in England was founded in 1612.

There may have been Baptists at Olchon on the Herefordshire border in 1633 and among the congregation at Llanfaches, Mon., the first Nonconformist church in Wales (1638). It is known for certain that there were some in the church at Llanigon, Brecs., formed during the Commonwealth by the Watkins family of Penyrwrlod. Vavasor *Powell was baptized in 1655 but it was John *Miles, founder of a church at Ilston, Glam., in 1649, who was responsible for establishing the Baptist cause in Wales. The influence of *Methodism provided further stimulus and by the 1770s a mission to north Wales had been launched. It has been estimated that in 1800 the Baptists had some nine thousand members in Wales and more than a hundred thousand by the end of the nineteenth century. The *Religious Census of 1851 revealed that the Baptists were the third largest of the Nonconformist denominations, a calculation based on the number of their chapels.

The Welsh Baptists practised strict communion and only baptized persons were admitted to membership of their 'gathered churches' to which worshippers often came from long distances and which sometimes moved from place to place in order to meet their needs. A trend towards more centralization became apparent, however, with the formation of Assemblies and, in 1866, of a Baptist Union. There was, too, a change in theology: with but few exceptions, Welsh Baptists had been Calvinists from the outset but by the end of the eighteenth century some had embraced *Unitarianism and, during the latter half of the nineteenth century, a

greater emphasis was placed upon biblical criticism. Radical tendencies, as in the preaching of Morgan John *Rhys, were also to be found among them and, although less revolutionary in character, these also lay behind the denomination's later support for political *Liberalism.

The literary output of the Baptists is mainly theological in nature but some of their writings have an important place in the history of Welsh literature. Joshua Thomas's *Hanes y Bedyddwyr* (1778) and *Hanes y Bedyddwyr yng Nghymru* (1892–1907) by James Spinther *James are significant works of historiography, while *Y *Cylchgrawn Cymraeg*, *Y *Greal* and *Seren Gomer* have made valuable contributions to the periodical press. The Baptist contribution to hymnology is modest in comparison with that of some other denominations. Benjamin *Francis and Joseph *Harris (Gomer) were perhaps their best hymn-writers, although John and Morgan *Dafydd and Dafydd *Wiliam, all former Methodists, should not be overlooked. Among other prominent Baptists who were also writers may be mentioned Titus *Lewis, Christmas *Evans, Robert *Ellis (Cynddelw), John *Jones (Mathetes), William Roberts (Nefydd; 1813–72), John *Jenkins (Gwili) and Ben *Bowen.

The standard work on the denomination, besides those mentioned above, is T. M. Bassett, *The Welsh Baptists* (1977); the *Transactions* of *Cymdeithas Hanes Bedyddwyr Cymru* (The Historical Society of the Baptists of Wales) should also be consulted.

'Barbara Miltwn, Marwnad' (lit. 'Elegy for Barbara Middleton'), by Huw *Morys, was written for the wife of Richard Middleton of Plas Newydd, Llansilin, Denbs., who died from smallpox in 1695 at the age of twenty-three. The traditional serenade took the form of a dialogue between a young woman, usually locked in her bedroom, and her ardent lover standing beneath her window, but this poem gives the ritual a new interpretation in a dialogue between the living and the dead. One of the finest elegies in the Welsh language, it is a powerful expression of grief, relieved only by Christian faith, and a moving celebration of love between husband and wife.

Bard, a term which in English was originally only a word borrowed from Welsh ('*bardd*', a poet) but which, under the influence of classical writers, came to be adopted as a synonym for 'poet'. The Latin author, Lucan, referred to the '*bardi*' of Gaul and Britain, and Caesar held that they were a class among the *Druids. In William *Owen Pughe's dictionary (1826), 'priest' and 'philosopher' are given as equivalents of 'bard'. Antiquarian interest during the early eighteenth century created an image of 'the Celtic bard', as in the Pindaric ode by Thomas Gray, 'The Bard' (1757), which is now recognized as foreign to the Welsh tradition. The word is preserved in the

English designation of *Gorsedd Beirdd Ynys Prydain ('The Gorsedd of Bards of the Isle of Britain'), which was the creation of Iolo Morganwg (Edward *Williams). It was he who carried the idealization of the bard to its extreme form, partly under the influence of Goronwy *Owen and Evan *Evans (Ieuan Brydydd Hir) and partly because he suffered from a persecution complex which demanded that the bard, whom he saw as druid, scholar and historian, should occupy a central place in the history and literature of Wales. The word is now seldom used in Wales as a noun meaning 'poet', except pretentiously and in journalese. See also MASS-ACRE OF THE BARDS.

Bard of Liberty, The, see WILLIAMS, EDWARD (1747–1826).

Bard of Snowdon, The, see LLWYD, RICHARD (1752–1835).

Bardd a'r Cerddor, Y (lit. 'The poet and the musician'; 1863), a manual by John Ceiriog *Hughes which offers advice to poets in the writing of songs and words for music, and of traditional tales, together with a catalogue of Welsh melodies. One section includes an apologia for laughter and a few satirical songs written under the author's pseudonym, Syr Meurig Grynswth. Intended for a Victorian audience, the book reflects contemporary taste and illustrates Ceiriog's talent as a poet of popular appeal. The title was also given to a comedy (1895) by Robert Arthur *Griffith (Elphin).

Bardd Bach, Y (**Rhys Fardd**; *fl.* 1460–80), see under CWTA CYFARWYDD (*c*.1425–*c*.1456).

Bardd Bol Clawdd, Bardd Pen Pastwn, Bardd y Blawd, Bardd Ysbaddad, see BARDD TALCEN SLIP.

Bardd Coch o Fôn, Y, see HUGHES, HUGH (1693–1776).

Bardd Cocos, Y, see EVANS, JOHN (1827–88).

Bardd Crwst, Y, see JONES, ABEL (1830–1901).

BARDD CWSG, Y (12th–13th cent.?), a vaticinatory poet of whom nothing is known except that his poems express great hatred of the English. See also GWELEDIGAETHEU Y BARDD CWSC (1703).

Bardd Cwsg (**Rhys Fardd**; *fl.* 1460–80), see under CWTA CYFARWYDD (*c*.1425–*c*.1456).

BARDD GLAS, Y (*c*.1350?), a vaticinatory poet of whom nothing is known. There are references to him in the work of later poets such as *Dafydd Llwyd ap Llywelyn ap Gruffudd and *Dafydd Gorlech among others.

Bardd Gwagedd, see WILLIAMS, RICHARD (*c*.1790–1862?).

Bardd Gwlad (lit. 'Country poet'), a term often applied to a poet with little or no secondary education whose verse extols his own locality and celebrates its communal life. A master of the traditional metres and the intricacies of *cynghanedd, the *bardd gwlad* fulfils a social function by recording such occasions as births, marriages and deaths or by recounting incidents in the life of the neighbourhood. The proliferation of local newspapers and eisteddfodau in the nineteenth century allowed the *beirdd gwlad* to see their work in print and many of their *englynion* were cut on gravestones. These poets now contribute verse to *papurau bro and compete with others on a local or regional basis. Some communities, such as Ffair Rhos and Llangrannog, Cards., Mynytho, Caerns., and Penllyn, Mer., are renowned for the numbers of *beirdd gwlad* still to be found in their vicinities. Perhaps the most famous are those associated with the *Cilie family. Dic Jones (Richard Lewis *Jones), for example, is a poet who, although enjoying a national reputation as a consummate craftsman, takes seriously his role as a *bardd gwlad* in his own community.

The work of some contemporary *beirdd gwlad* is contained in the series *Beirdd Bro*. The anthologies *Llais y Meini* (ed. G. T. Roberts, 1979) and *Englynion Beddau Ceredigion* (ed. M. Euronwy James, 1983) are collections of *englynion* found on gravestones. There is an essay on the *bardd gwlad*, entitled *The Folk Poets*, by W. Rhys Nicholas in the *Writers of Wales* series (1978).

Bardd Nantglyn, see DAVIES, ROBERT (1769–1835).

Bardd Newydd, Y (lit. 'The new poet'), the name given to a school of poets who dominated the competitions at the *National Eisteddfod during the years from 1890 to 1901. Prominent among them were Iolo Carnarvon (John John *Roberts) and Ben *Davies; Gwili (John *Jenkins) and Ben *Bowen were also associated. The group's work was a reaction against the superficiality of John Ceiriog *Hughes and the over-long descriptions of much eisteddfodic verse of the time. Its members, for the most part, were Nonconformist ministers who shared similar views about the function of poetry. Religion and the preaching of the Word were their prime concerns and they held that the poet should deal with 'the Truth' rather than with any external beauty. Admirers of Lewis *Edwards's philosophical poem, 'Cysgod a Sylwedd', and of the work of Islwyn (William *Thomas), they considered most contemporary verse to be lacking in seriousness. For them poetic form was unimportant and they believed that the strict metres were unsuitable for the expression of great thoughts; it was the message and the sublimity of the content that mattered. Alas, the message of the New Poet was often far from clear: his work was vitiated by verbosity and empty rhetoric, by which means he sought to ask unanswerable questions about the meaning of Life and the essence of the Universe.

It was inevitable that there would be a reaction against this kind of verse in due course: in two scathing articles in Y *Geninen, Robert Arthur *Griffith (Elphin) mocked these poets, condemning them for their obscurity and lack of poetic sensibility, while John *Morris-Jones demolished all they represented in Y *Traethodydd after the National Eisteddfod of 1902. Gwili attempted a rearguard action on behalf of the New Poet's ideas in Y Geninen, but the opening years of the twentieth century saw the end of one of the most disastrous periods in the history of Welsh poetry.

There is a chapter on Y Bardd Newydd by Alun Llywelyn-Williams in Gwŷr Llên y Bedwaredd Ganrif ar Bymtheg (ed. Dyfnallt Morgan, 1968); see also the article by D. Tecwyn Lloyd in Ysgrifau Beirniadol III (ed. J. E. Caerwyn Williams, 1967).

Bardd Talcen Slip (lit. 'Poet of the receding forehead'), a term first used in the mid-nineteenth century by Talhaiarn (John *Jones) to denote a composer of rhymes which are of little or no substance or which are shoddily made. The musician Robert Griffith (1847–1911), in his Llyfr Cerdd Dannau (1893), claimed that Talhaiarn borrowed the phrase from a verse by a local poet, Huwcyn y Cowper, describing a ramshackle old house in Llanddoged, Denbs. Phrases with similar meanings are Bardd Bol Clawdd, Bardd Cocos, Bardd Pen Pastwn, Bardd y Blawd, Bardd Ysbyddad and Crach Fardd.

Bardd Teulu, see under BARDIC ORDER.

Bardd y Brenin, see JONES, EDWARD (1752–1824).

Bardd yr Haf, see PARRY, ROBERT WILLIAMS (1884–1956).

Barddas (lit. 'Bardic lore'; 2 vols., 1862, 1874), writings on devotional and moral subjects which were extracted by John *Williams (Ab Ithel) from the manuscripts of Iolo Morganwg (Edward *Williams), who had fathered them on the ancient poets and *Druids. The books had a considerable influence on many Welsh poets during the latter part of the nineteenth century and contributed to the spread of 'druidic fever'. The title also belongs to the magazine of *Cymdeithas Cerdd Dafod.

Barddoniadur Cymmreig, Y (lit. 'The Welsh poetic dictionary'; 2 vols., 1855, 1857), by William *Williams (Creuddynfab), was described by Saunders *Lewis as one of the few important contributions to Welsh literary criticism

between the time of Goronwy *Owen and that of Emrys ap Iwan (Robert Ambrose *Jones). The author took issue with Caledfryn (William *Williams), flatly rejecting his neo-classical standards and arguing in favour of a poetry unimpeded by the demands of common sense and a slavish adherence to grammar. He insisted on the poet's right to use figurative language and emphasized the Romantic elements in literature—sublimity, pathos, invention and imagination—as opposed to reason and moderation. Under the influence of the Scottish School of Philosophy, he hoped to create a new literary criticism, psychologically orientated, which would reveal the essential nature of poetry. Although he did not succeed, his Barddoniadur is important for an understanding of the critical background to the *epic, the *pryddest and the lyric in the second half of the nineteenth century.

Bardhoniaeth neu Brydydhiaeth (lit. 'Poetry or poesy'; 1593), an elementary treatise by William *Midleton (Gwilym Ganoldref) on the technicalities of Welsh prosody, was intended for the cultured gentleman rather than the professional poet or scholar. The latter was served by the grammar of Siôn Dafydd *Rhys whom Midleton helped and to whom he was indebted. The essay deals only with the traditional strict metres and reflects, in true humanist fashion, the amateur's interest in its subject. The work was re-issued, with some changes, at the end of *Flores Poetarum Britannicorum (ed. Dafydd Lewys, 1710).

The first edition was reproduced in 1930 with an introduction by Griffith John Williams and appendices of Midleton's poetical works.

Bardic Controversy, a debate between poets on matters related to their craft and status. Some contentions were frivolous or scurrilous in the flyting tradition but others, such as that between *Rhys Goch Eryri and *Siôn Cent and another between *Guto'r Glyn and Hywel Dafi, amounted to serious discussions of such topics as the origin of poetic inspiration and the nature of eulogistic poetry. One of the earliest for which evidence has survived is the controversy between *Gruffudd Gryg and *Dafydd ap Gwilym. Gruffudd initiated the debate, attacking Dafydd in verse on account of his frequent complaints about love's spears and arrows. Replying, Dafydd ridiculed Gruffudd's poetic talent and castigated him for being imitative, a charge angrily denied with spirited invective: like the two seven-day wonders, a wooden hobby-horse and a new organ at Bangor, Dafydd's cywydd was no longer a novelty in Gwynedd, retorted Gruffudd. Despite an element of jest, the debate was significant in that Gruffudd attacked those features of Dafydd's poetry which derived from *courtly love, his view reflecting an adherence to conservative literary standards.

A longer and more important controversy took place between Edmund *Prys and Wiliam *Cynwal during the years between 1581 and 1587. After each poet had exchanged seven poems, both wrote sequences of three and nine *cywyddau*. Prys sent Cynwal a letter in which he criticized his adversary's work, then returned to the medium of verse. When Cynwal died, before the sixteenth *cywydd* was completed, his fellow-poet mourned him in an elegy. There are more than five thousand lines in the fifty-four *cywyddau* produced by this contention and the letter from Prys to Cynwal has been called 'the first review' in the Welsh language.

The *cywyddau* by Edmund Prys are the nearest equivalent in Welsh to a humanist *Ars Poetica*. Criticising Cynwal, and similar professional poets, for the exaggeration of their praise-poems, he also deplored their lack of erudition, specifically the new humanistic learning which entailed knowledge of languages and the arts. He urged the poets to widen the horizon of Welsh poetry by composing scientific poetry of the kind then being written in other countries. But Cynwal's response was wholly negative: he insisted that Prys was unqualified to judge in bardic matters for he was a clergyman, not a poet. Their debate is important for its evidence of the differences between the literary values of the humanists and those of more conservative professional poets. Cynwal's intransigence partly explains the failure of men such as Prys to promote in Welsh the equivalent of the humanistically inspired literature which was developed in other vernaculars during the same period.

For further details see A. T. E. Matonis, 'Later Medieval Poetics and some Welsh Bardic Debates' in *The Bulletin of the Board of Celtic Studies* (vol. XXIX, 1982) and 'Barddoneg a rhai Ymrysonau Barddol Cymraeg yr Oesoedd Canol Diweddar' in *Ysgrifau Beirniadol XII* (ed. J. E. Caerwyn Williams, 1982); for the debate between Edmund Prys and Wiliam Cynwal see the article by Gruffydd Aled Williams in *Ysgrifau Beirniadol VIII* (ed. J. E. Caerwyn Williams, 1974).

Bardic Order, The, existed in Wales for more than a thousand years. From earliest times poets were associated with kings and princes, forming a distinct section of society with its own privileges. According to the law books, the *Bardd Teulu* ('Household Poet' or 'Poet of the Retinue') was one of the Twenty-four Officers of the King's Court. The *Pencerdd* ('Chief of Song') was an officer not of the court but of the king's domain, though he had his own chair at court and his status was higher than that of the *Bardd Teulu*. The third class of poet was the *Cerddor* (L. *joculatores*), who came under the jurisdiction of the *Pencerdd* and whose business it was to provide entertainment with jests and satire. It is not clear to what precise period these categories belong (but they certainly flourished between the middle of the tenth century and the end of the twelfth) nor is it known to what extent they reflect actual practice.

The large amount of poetry which has survived from the Age of the Princes (11th–14th cents.) suggests that there were three stages in the later development of the Bardic Order. First, the old classification of poetry had begun to break down: *Cynddelw Brydydd Mawr, for example, who wrote two elegies to *Madog ap Maredudd, Prince of Powys, one an *awdl* and the other a series of *englynion*, may have been acting as a *Pencerdd* in composing the former and, in the latter case, as a *Bardd Teulu*. Secondly, a poet might be associated with more than one court: Cynddelw began his career as the court poet of Madog ap Maredudd, but after Madog's death he sang to *Owain Gwynedd and to the princes of *Deheubarth. Thirdly, the poets sang the praises of men who were of noble stock but not ruling princes, like Cynddelw to Rhirid Flaidd (fl. 1160). It was on this class, the *uchelwyr*, that the poets had to rely after the death of *Llywelyn ap Gruffudd in 1282, when they were deprived of princely patronage and legal recognition, and when bardic circuits became a necessity.

From the fourteenth century onwards there were two types of bardic practitioner: one was the professional poet supported by the patronage of the nobility and the other comprised those *uchelwyr*, such as *Dafydd ap Gwilym and *Dafydd ab Edmwnd, who had mastered the poetic craft. The chief occupation of all these poets was to compose elegies and eulogies, poems to solicit gifts and thank the donor, as well as love-songs, religious songs and flyting poems. During the sixteenth century some poets became famous as heralds.

All practitioners of the bardic craft regarded themselves as belonging to a corporate body or guild. Much importance was attached to mastery of the traditional metres and the *cynganeddion*, and to familiarity with the grammars, archaic vocabulary, the history of the nation and its myths and legends. As with other crafts, instruction was imparted orally by teachers, recognized masters of the craft. When the pupil had achieved a certain competence, he was awarded a certificate or licence and authorized to visit the *uchelwyr* and to write poems in their honour for suitable reward. *Gruffudd Hiraethog's licence, granted in 1545 and signed by his teacher, Lewis Morgannwg (*Llywelyn ap Rhisiart), and by two *uchelwyr*, is still extant, as is *Simwnt Fychan's licence as a *Pencerdd*, for which he qualified in 1567. Only a small part of the instruction given to poets was committed to writing. Such is the grammar composed by *Einion Offeiriad in the fourteenth century which contains linguistic material, definitions of the *Twenty-four Metres (but not of the *cynganeddion*) and directions as to the writing of praise-poems. Simwnt Fychan's *Pum Llyfr Cerddwriaeth*, written in the second half of the sixteenth century, is a similar compendium but much more detailed. The poets kept the details of their craft a secret from all except those *uchelwyr* and clerics who were anxious to learn and they never made use of the printing-press to disseminate their teaching or their poems, an attitude for which they were reprimanded by Siôn Dafydd *Rhys and other humanists in the sixteenth century. In spite of its conservatism and the rigidity of its regulations, change did take place in the Bardic Order, however. Between 1350 and 1550 there were modifications in the structure of the *cywydd*, the favourite metre of the poets, and the great masters, such as *Guto'r Glyn and *Tudur Aled, developed their own personal styles.

The aims of the Bardic Order were to maintain the prestige of the craft, to encourage excellence and to safeguard the livelihood of the professional poets by preventing unskilled rhymesters from going on bardic itineraries to the annoyance of patrons. It was to this end that certain metrical regulations were reinforced at the *Carmarthen Eisteddfod held about the year 1450 and at the two Eisteddfodau held at *Caerwys in 1523 and 1567. In the document associated with the first of these, known as the Statute of *Gruffudd ap Cynan (though that prince had nothing to do with it) there are rules governing the relationship between teacher and pupil, the grades of pupils, the conditions of bardic circuits, payment for poems and even advice about the behaviour of poets when they visited their patrons. It is unlikely that these rules were strictly observed and they probably represent an ideal arrangement rather than common practice.

A request was made in 1594 for a commission to hold another Eisteddfod similar to those held at Caerwys, but without result. The Bardic Order was by then in decline and the need to safeguard the interests of the professional poets was diminishing. Although some poets wrote for noble families in the sixteenth century and later, and were occasionally paid for their labours, hardly any made a living out of it. Siôn Dafydd Las (John *Davies) is said to have been a family poet at *Nannau and he sang the praises of the noble families of Arfon and Meirionydd. Owen *Gruffydd of Llanystumdwy wrote poems in the traditional manner to local gentry, and received gifts of money in return, but he was a weaver by trade. By his day the Bardic Order as a social institution was dead.

For further details see T. Gwynn Jones, 'Bardism and Romance' in the *Transactions of the Honourable Society of Cymmrodorion* (1913–14), G. J. Williams and E. J. Jones, *Gramadegau'r Penceirddiaid* (1934), Thomas Parry, '*Statud Gruffydd ap Cynan*' in the *Bulletin of the Board of Celtic Studies* (vol. V, 1930) and Gwyn Thomas, *Eisteddfodau Caerwys*, in the *St. David's Day* series (1968).

Bardsey or **Ynys Enlli**, a small island about two miles off the extreme tip of the Llŷn peninsula, Caerns., on which a monastery was founded in the sixth century. Cadfan and Lleuddad, believed to have been the first abbots, are mentioned as custodians of the island by the poet *Llywelyn Fardd (*c*.1150). According to tradition, some twenty thousand saints—including *Beuno, *Dyfrig and *Padarn—are buried on this holy island. They were eulogized in poems by *Lewys Glyn Cothi (Llywelyn y Glyn) and *Hywel ap Rheinallt, among others. In the thirteenth century the monks adopted the rule of the order of *Augustinian Canons. During the Middle Ages pilgrims thronged to Bardsey. The dangerous boat journey is described in a poem by Rhys Llwyd. Others, such as Llywelyn ap Gutun ap Ieuan Lydan in the late fifteenth century, sought the abbot's hospitality but were disappointed by the frugality of his welcome, the poet *Deio ab Ieuan Ddu complaining that he was given only bread, cheese and buttermilk.

The abbey was dissolved about 1537 but the island's religious associations have continued to inspire Welsh poets such as T. Gwynn *Jones and R. S. *Thomas. Among writers who have lived there in recent times were Dilys *Cadwaladr, who was a teacher there, and Brenda *Chamberlain; the island is now a bird sanctuary. The last 'King of Enlli', elected by the islanders to settle disputes, was Love Pritchard and he left the island, with his family, in 1926.

For further details see Glanmor Williams, *The Welsh Church from Conquest to Reformation* (1962) and G. Hartwell Jones, *Celtic Britain and the Pilgrim Movement* (1912).

Barn (lit. 'Opinion'), a monthly magazine founded in 1962 and published by *Llyfrau'r Dryw (later Christopher Davies Ltd.) of Llandybie and Swansea. Its first editor was Emlyn Evans, the company's manager at that time, and it was he who established the magazine as a major journal of current affairs. From the outset it carried articles on the arts, politics, broadcasting, education and religion as well as poetry, essays, short stories and book reviews. The magazine's second editor, Aneirin Talfan *Davies, was succeeded in 1966 by Alwyn D. *Rees who saw it through its most noteworthy phase, one of the most exciting periods in the history of any Welsh periodical. It was during the years of his editorship that *Cymdeithas yr Iaith Gymraeg was at its most active, *Plaid Cymru was making electoral progress and various campaigns were being waged on behalf of the Welsh language in law, education and public administration. The magazine became the mouthpiece for the Welsh Nationalist movement, challenging the law and calling for reform in the face of indifference and obstinacy on the part of the Government and other authorities. In his editorials Alwyn D. Rees displayed a sharp, analytical mind, a broad cultural background and a witty prose style, continuing to enliven the cultural and political scene in this way until his death in December 1974. It is generally acknowledged that the gains made by campaigners on the Welsh language's behalf during the late 1960s and early 1970s were partly the result of arguments first formulated in the pages of *Barn*, mostly by the editor.

Gwyn Erfyl (Gwyn Erfyl *Jones), who was the magazine's editor from May 1975 to March 1979, was followed by an editorial board which included Gwynn *ap Gwilym and Alan *Llwyd; Rhydwen *Williams was appointed editor in 1981.

Baron Hill, see under BULKELEY FAMILY.

BARRINGTON, DAINES (1727–1800), antiquary. An Englishman, the son of John Shute, the first Viscount Barrington, he was from about 1757 a judge on the Merioneth, Caernarfon and Anglesey circuit of the Court of Great Sessions, a post which he held for more than twenty years. During his frequent visits to north Wales he acquired a considerable knowledge of 'British antiquities'. It was he who first published Sir John *Wynn's *History of the Gwydir Family* (1770), later included in his *Miscellanies* (1781), and he also helped to bring the work of Ieuan Brydydd Hir (Evan *Evans) on early Welsh literature to the attention of Thomas Gray and Samuel Johnson.

For further details see W. R. Williams, *History of the Great Sessions in Wales together with the Lives of the Welsh Judges* (1899).

Barry Island, a seaside resort near Cardiff, much enjoyed by the people of the valleys of south Wales, especially on excursions organized by the chapels and trade unions during the years between the World Wars. In the section of Idris *Davies's poem *Gwalia Deserta* (1938) which begins 'Let's go to Barry Island, Maggie fach', the archetypal mother escapes the monotony and troubles of the *General Strike for a day out by the sea.

Barti Ddu or **Black Bart**, see ROBERTS, BARTHOLOMEW (1682?–1722).

BARTRUM, PETER CLEMENT (1907–   ), genealogist, was born in Hampstead, London, and educated at Queen's College, Oxford. An Englishman who worked as a meteorologist in the Colonial Service between 1932 and 1955, he learned to read Welsh during the course of his study of genealogical manuscripts and the legends associated with *Arthur and the Dark Ages in Britain. Besides numerous contributions to Welsh periodicals, he has published *Early Welsh Genealogical Tracts* (1966), *Welsh Genealogies AD 300–1400* (1974) and *Welsh Genealogies AD 1400–1500* (1983).

Basingwerk, a monastery in Flintshire founded by Ranulf II, Earl of Chester, in 1131, was originally affiliated to the Order of Savigny but joined the *Cistercians in 1147. It has been suggested that *The Book of Aneirin* (see under GODODDIN) was copied there during the second half of the thirteenth century. *The Black Book of Basingwerk*, containing *Ystoria Dared*, a version of *Historia Regum Britanniae* and *Brut y Saeson* down to 1461, was probably written at the abbey. The first part of the manuscript belongs to the fourteenth century but the rest is written in the hand of *Gutun Owain. Like *Tudur Aled and *Siôn ap Hywel ap Llywelyn Fychan, he wrote eulogies to the abbot, Tomas ap Dafydd Pennant (*c.*1480–*c.*1515/22). *Huw Pennant, poet and priest, the translator of the *Legenda Aurea* (a Life of Saint Ursula) into Welsh, was this abbot's brother. The abbey appropriated the shrine of St. Winifred (*Gwenffrewi) at Holywell, Flints., the healing powers of which drew tributes from *Iolo Goch, Ieuan Brydydd Hir (Evan *Evans), Tudur Aled and Siôn ap Hywel.

For further details see the article by E. Owen in the *Flintshire Historical Society Journal* (vol. VII, 1920), and by A. Jones in *Essays presented to James Tait* (ed. J. G. Edwards, V. H. Galbraith and E. F. Jacob, 1933).

BAYLY, LEWIS (d. 1631), devotional writer and Bishop of Bangor, is believed to have been a native of Carmarthen. Appointed bishop in 1616, he challenged Sir John *Wynn of Gwydir, the most influential layman in the diocese, but later became one of his closest friends, lending his support to Sir John's son in his endeavours to become the Member of Parliament for Caernarfonshire. Bayly's book, *The Practice of Piety* (1611), which revealed some Puritan influences, proved immensely popular; it was translated into Welsh by Rowland *Vaughan of Caer-gai under the title *Yr Ymarfer o Dduwioldeb* (1630) and had run to seventy-one editions by 1792. Bayly's son, Thomas (1608–*c.*1657), had a career both as Protestant and Roman Catholic, and was the author of several books, including the contemplative work, *Herba Parietis* (1650). The grandson of Lewis Bayly, Edward Bayly, succeeded to the estate of Plas Newydd, Anglesey, and it was his grandson, Henry Bayly (1744–1812), who took the name and arms of Paget (as 9th Baron) and was the father of the first Marquis of Anglesey.

For further details see the article by J. Gwynfor Jones, 'Bishop Lewis Bayly and the Wynns of Gwydir, 1616–27' in *The Welsh History Review* (vol. 6, no. 4, 1973).

BBC Wales Annual Lecture, The, a series begun in 1938 and broadcast on radio (with an interregnum during the years from 1940 to 1950) down to the present. Delivered alternately in Welsh and English, the lectures have included several on topics relating to Welsh and Anglo-Welsh literature, for example, *Ceiriog* (1939) by

W. J. *Gruffydd, *Henry Vaughan* (1953) by Edward Williamson, *Ymhel â Phrydyddu* (1958) by T. H. *Parry-Williams, *Iolo Morganwg* (1963) by Griffith John *Williams, *David Jones, Artist and Writer* (1965) by Harman Grisewood, *Y Llenor a'i Gymdeithas* (1966) by Alun *Llywelyn-Williams and *Being and Belonging* (1977) by Gwyn *Jones. Others have dealt with the religious, political, scientific and artistic aspects of Welsh life. It was the lecture for 1962, *Tynged yr Iaith* by Saunders *Lewis, that inspired the creation of *Cymdeithas yr Iaith Gymraeg.

BEALE, ANNE (1816–1900), novelist, was an Englishwoman who lived for many years at or near Llandeilo, Carms. Among the novels of hers which have Welsh settings are *Rose Mervyn of Whitelake* (1879), a story about the *Rebecca Riots, *Gladys of Harlech* (1858), a historical romance, and *Gladys the Reaper* (1881); she also published a volume entitled *Poems* (1842). Her most important work, *The Vale of Towey* (1844), republished as *Traits and Stories of the Welsh Peasantry* (1849), is partly a travel-book about an English girl settling in Wales and partly a collection of short stories in embryonic form. With only one location, they make a continuous narrative and may be considered, in the Welsh context, as marking a significant stage in the development of the *novel in English.

Bear-baiting, a sport in which several dogs were encouraged to attack a bear tied to a stake and often blindfolded. The onlookers would bet on the dogs' resistance to the wrath of the bound animal under continuous onslaught. The bear and its owner sometimes toured the countryside to advertise forthcoming contests and to bid the populace to bring their dogs, to bet, or merely to witness the bloody event. The sport was given royal patronage in the *Tudor period when the post of Master of Bears was created to promote it, and it was not declared illegal until 1835.

Beau Nash, see NASH, RICHARD (1674–1761).

Beaumaris, a castle on the Menai Straits, was built by order of Edward I near the port of Llanfaes, Ang., between 1295 and 1298, after the *Welsh Revolt led by Madog ap Llywelyn in which Sir Roger Pilsden, the Sheriff of Anglesey, had been killed. The town of Llanfaes, destroyed after the rebellion, was finally dismantled, the stones of its houses being used to build Newborough, to which place the Welsh burgesses were obliged to move. The castle, used as a prison during the fourteenth century, was occupied by Welsh forces during the rising of *Owain Glyndŵr. The property of the *Bulkeley family thereafter, it was captured by the Parliamentary army in 1646. *Lewys Glyn Cothi (Llewelyn y Glyn) and *Lewys Môn were among the poets who wrote elegies for Joan, the

daughter of William Bulkeley and the wife of Huw Lewis of Presaeddfed. An eisteddfod was held in the castle's courtyard in 1832. Beaumaris remained in the hands of the Bulkeleys until 1925.

For further details see the account of Beaumaris published by the Ministry of Works in 1949, A. J. Taylor, *The King's Works in Wales 1277–1330* (1974), and A. D. Carr, *Medieval Anglesey* (1982).

BEBB, WILLIAM AMBROSE (1894–1955), writer and historian. Born at Goginan, Cards., and educated at the University College of Wales, Aberystwyth, he joined the staff of the History Department at the Normal College, Bangor, in 1925 and later became its Head. During the four years he spent in Paris as a student and lecturer at the Sorbonne, he became, under the influence of Charles Maurras and the *Action Française*, a fervent Francophile, publishing his reflections on European civilization in a book, *Crwydro'r Cyfandir* (1936). He was also well acquainted with Brittany and the three volumes *Llydaw* (1929), *Dyddlyfr Pythefnos* (1939) and *Pererindodau* (1941) give an account of his involvement with the national movement in that country. On the history of Wales he wrote a sequence of five books: *Ein Hen, Hen Hanes* (1932), *Llywodraeth y Cestyll* (1934), *Cyfnod y Tuduriaid* (1939), *Machlud y Mynachlogydd* (1937) and *Machlud yr Oesoedd Canol* (1950). With Saunders *Lewis and Griffith John *Williams he was a founder of *Y Mudiad Cymreig* in 1924, a group which a year later grew into *Plaid Genedlaethol Cymru* (The Welsh Nationalist Party), and he was among the party's most diligent workers up to the Second World War. Towards the end of his life, however, his political zeal diminished and he came to place more emphasis on Christian principles, as in his last book, published posthumously, *Yr Argyfwng* (1955).

For a discussion of Ambrose Bebb's political convictions see the chapter by Gareth Miles in *Adnabod Deg* (ed. Derec Llwyd Morgan, 1977), the same author's article in *Planet* (nos. 37/38, 1977) and D. Hywel Davies, *The Welsh Nationalist Party 1925–1945* (1983). A bibliography of his writings has been compiled by Rhidian Griffiths (1982).

Bedloe, William (1650–80), criminal. A native of Chepstow, Mon., he was a thief, a swindler and an informer who, during the aftermath of the Popish Plot of 1678, misused his powers of imagination and fluency of speech in the denunciation of Roman Catholic priests.

BEDO AEDDREN (*fl.* 1500), poet, may have been a native of Llanfor, Mer., but he took his name from Aeddren, near Llangwm, Denbs. More than forty poems are attributed to him, most of which are *cywyddau* on traditional themes, although some have also been ascribed to other poets, particularly *Bedo Brwynllys.

His main theme is love-sickness and reflected in his poetry, much influenced by *Dafydd ap Gwilym, are many of the clichés of the *courtly love tradition.

A volume of the love-poems of Bedo Aeddren, together with those of Bedo Brwynllys and Bedo Phylip Bach, has been published under the title *Cywyddau Serch y Tri Bedo* (ed. Patrick Donovan, 1982).

BEDO BRWYNLLYS (*fl.* 1460), poet, was a native of Breconshire, but almost nothing else is known about him. His work, preserved in manuscript, includes many love-poems, some religious *cywyddau*, a few *awdlau* and several epitaphs. One of these, his epitaph to Sir Richard Herbert of Coldbrook, can be dated 1469 and he also addressed satirical poems to *Ieuan Deulwyn and Hywel Dafi (Hywel ap Dafydd ap Ieuan ap Rhys). It may be that he and *Bedo Phylip Bach were the same man; if not, they were certainly contemporaries and belonged to the same district.

His love-poems are to be found in the volume *Cywyddau Serch y Tri Bedo* (ed. Patrick Donovan, 1982).

BEDO HAFESB (*fl.* 1567–85), poet, a native of Montgomery who held the office of Sergeant of Newtown; very little else is known about him. Of the few *cywyddau* of his which are extant, most were composed in honour of Powys gentry, such as John Games of Newton, Brecon. He wrote some satirical poems, was engaged in a bardic contention with Ieuan Tew and is believed to have been a famous poet in his day because he graduated at the second *Caerwys Eisteddfod (1567).

BEDO PHYLIP BACH (*fl.* 1480), poet, a native of Breconshire, may have been the same man as *Bedo Brwynllys, although there is no evidence to prove it. Eleven *cywyddau* are attributed to him, some of which are included in the volume *Cywyddau Serch y Tri Bedo* (ed. Patrick Donovan, 1982).

'Bedwenni Y' (lit. 'The birches'), three stanzas in The *Black Book of Carmarthen* which immediately precede the series known as 'Yr *Afallennau'. They were attributed in the Middle Ages to *Myrddin (Merlin) but do not allude specifically to the legend about him. Each stanza opens with the words 'Gwyn ei byd y fedwen' ('Blessed is the birch') and refers to the trees in the Wye valley, on Pumlumon and at the summit of Dinwythwy. The verses also mention battles in Ardudwy, Dygannwy and Edrywy, Frenchmen bearing shields, monks often becoming knights and the building of bridges over the rivers Taff, Tafwy and Wye. Better times are prophesied 'in the time of Cadwaladr', a *vaticination believed to be a reference to *Cadwaladr Fendigaid.

For further details see M. E. Griffiths, *Early Vaticination in Welsh* (1937) and A. O. H. Jarman, *Llyfr Du Caerfyrddin* (1982).

Bedwyr, the son of Pedrawg, a mythical hero who is the second of the men of *Arthur's court listed in the tale of *Culhwch and Olwen. There he throws a spear back at Ysbaddaden Bencawr, helps *Cai to free *Mabon from prison and to pluck *Dillus Farfog's beard, and takes part in the hunting of *Twrch Trwyth. It is said that he would accompany Cai on any expedition and that he was more handsome than any man in the Island except for Arthur and Drych, the descendant of Cibddar. Although he had only one hand, three soldiers could not strike more quickly than Bedwyr. Before the gate of *Wrnach the Giant, the head of his spear draws blood from the wind before returning to its shaft. In the poem 'Pa ŵr yw'r Porthor?' (10th/11th cent.) he is praised for his prowess and is said to fight his enemies by the hundred. In *Geoffrey of Monmouth's *Historia Regum Britanniae* Bedwyr helps Arthur to combat the giant at Mynydd Mihangel (Mont Saint Michel). He is known in English as Bedivere.

For further details see Rachel Bromwich, *Trioedd Ynys Prydein* (1961).

Beibl Bach and ***Beibl Coron***, see under BIBLE.

Beirdd Coleg (lit. 'College poets'), a term of abuse for the writers who took part in the renaissance of Welsh letters during the early years of the twentieth century. The phrase was applied in particular to the pupils of John *Morris-Jones who displayed their University training in their use of language, their choice of style and forms, and in their efforts to widen their experience and the horizons of Welsh poetry. Their work was criticized with special spleen by some critics who claimed to represent the self-taught poets of the common people.

Beirdd y Niwl (lit. 'Poets of the mist'), a term applied to some poets, such as T. Gwynn *Jones and W. J. *Gruffydd, but more specifically to their imitators, during the first decade of the twentieth century, because they were so fond of using the words 'niwl' ('mist') and 'tarth' ('haze') in images conveying mystery.

Alun Llywelyn-Williams has written a study of these poets' work under the title *Y Nos, y Niwl a'r Ynys* (1960).

Beirdd yr Uchelwyr, see POETS OF THE GENTRY.

Beirniad, Y (lit. 'The critic'), a periodical of which eighty-two numbers were published between 1859 and 1879. Edited by John Davies (1823–74) of Aberaman and William Roberts (1828–72) of the Brecon Memorial College, and after their deaths by John Bowen Jones (1829–1905), the magazine carried articles on religion, history, literature, geology, physics and agriculture, as well as bitter criticism of *Roman Catholicism, the *Oxford Movement and the

Church Rate; it also supported the education and emancipation of women and opposed capital punishment. Most of its contributors were anonymous but, with *Y* *Traethodydd*, it was one of the two most influential and learned Welsh periodicals of the nineteenth century. See also the next entry.

Beirniad, Y (lit. 'The critic'), a quarterly magazine edited by John *Morris-Jones which appeared regularly from 1911 until 1917 but thereafter intermittently until its demise in 1920, was published under the auspices of the Welsh Societies of the three constituent colleges of the *University of Wales. Its main achievement was the consolidation of the reform in Welsh linguistic and literary standards initiated by the editor. John Morris-Jones's own contributions, more profuse in the earlier issues, were in the form of book-reviews, articles and notes on the fictitious origins of *Gorsedd Beirdd Ynys Prydain and on common errors of Welsh orthography and syntax. A no less prolific contributor was his former student, Ifor *Williams, whose articles included the initial results of his exhaustive analysis of '*Y* *Gododdin' in *The Book of Aneirin*. Among other distinguished scholars who contributed the fruits of their research were J. E. *Lloyd and R. T. *Jenkins. The magazine also published two major poems, *'Madog' by T. Gwynn *Jones and *'Ynys yr Hud' by W. J. *Gruffydd, as well as a wealth of verse and prose by such devotees of the new learning as R. Dewi *Williams, E. Tegla *Davies, J. J. *Williams, R. G. *Berry, R. Williams *Parry and T. H. *Parry-Williams. Far from confining the magazine's purview to language and literature, however, the editor welcomed contributions on any subject of national interest and *Y Beirniad* became the most influential Welsh periodical of its day. See also the previous entry.

Bela, Belene or **Penloi**, see PENELOPE.

Beli Mawr, the son of Manogan and King of the Britons in the time of Julius Caesar, according to *Nennius. His existence may have been mythical: the traditions associated with him have been lost but he is mentioned at the beginning of *Cyfranc Lludd a Llefelys and in The *Book of Taliesin. In *Breuddwyd Macsen*, *Macsen Wledig is said to have taken the Isle of Britain from Beli but this claim is obviously without foundation. The early heraldry shows that eminent families in Wales and the *Old North, such as those of *Cunedda and *Coel Hen, claimed descent from Beli Mawr.

BELL, HAROLD IDRIS (1879–1967), scholar and translator. He was born at Epworth, Lincs., of a Welsh mother, and educated at Oriel College, Oxford, studying later at universities in Germany and France. Appointed to the staff of

the British Museum in 1903, he held the post of Keeper of Manuscripts and Egerton Librarian from 1929 until his retirement in 1944; he left London to live in Aberystwyth two years later. During his distinguished career his most important work was done in the field of papyrology and classical scholarship, in recognition of which several universities, including the *University of Wales, conferred honorary degrees upon him. In 1946 he was knighted and awarded the Medal of the Honourable Society of *Cymmrodorion for his services to Welsh literature.

Having learnt Welsh, he had begun to contribute critical articles and translations of Welsh poetry to such magazines as The *Welsh Outlook, *Wales and The *Nationalist. He subsequently published two volumes of his translations, *Poems from the Welsh* (1913) and *Welsh Poems of the Twentieth Century in English Verse* (1925), to both of which his father, Charles Christopher Bell, also contributed. These books were followed by *The Development of Welsh Poetry* (1936), a short survey from the *Gogynfeirdd to the twentieth century, and *Dafydd ap Gwilym: Fifty Poems* (1942); his son, David Bell (1916–59), was co-translator of the latter. Among his other publications were *Thoughts on Translation* (1943; reprinted from the *Transactions* of the Honourable Society of Cymmrodorion, 1941) and *The Nature of Poetry as conceived by the Welsh Bards* (The Taylorian Lecture, 1955). He was also the translator of Thomas *Parry's *Hanes Llenyddiaeth Gymraeg hyd 1900* (1944), published as *A History of Welsh Literature* (1955), to which he wrote an appendix on the twentieth century.

As a translator of Welsh poetry who was content with 'the humbler role of interpreter', as he put it, Sir Idris Bell was important chiefly on account of his scholarship. Like those of his predecessors, Edmund O. *Jones and Alfred Percival Graves (see under WELSH POETRY OLD AND NEW), his translations of Welsh poetry may now seem flowery and archaic in comparison with the later work of Gwyn *Williams, Anthony *Conran and Joseph P. *Clancy, but for a quarter of a century they were unsurpassed.

There is an obituary of H. Idris Bell by C. H. Roberts in the *Proceedings* of the British Academy (vol. LIII, 1967).

'Bells of Aberdovey, The', see CLYCHAU ABERDYFI.

Bendigeidfran, see BRÂN.

Bendith y Mamau, see under MOTHER GODDESSES.

Benlli Gawr, a giant to whom numerous fleeting references are made in the poetry of the *Gogynfeirdd. The *Historia Brittonum of *Nennius presents him as a tyrannical ruler in *Powys whose citadel was destroyed by fire from heaven as a punishment for his oppression of St. Germanus (*Garmon). This tradition may have been confused with that of *Vortigern of whom it was said that he suffered the same fate and for the same reason.

BENNETT, AGNES MARIA (d. 1808), novelist, the year and place of whose birth are uncertain, has been identified as Anna Maria Evans of Merthyr Tydfil, Glam., who married a tanner from Brecon. Her early circumstances appear to have been humble but she rose to become matron of a workhouse in London. She published four popular novels: *Anna, or Memoirs of a Welch Heiress* (1785), *Juvenile Indiscretions* (1786), *Ellen, Countess of Castle Howell* (1794) and *The Beggar Girl and her Benefactors* (1794).

BENNETT, RICHARD (1860–1937), historian, was born at Llanbrynmair, Mont. A farmer until 1914, he gave up the land because of deafness and went to live first in Bangor, Caerns., and later at Caersws, Mont. His main interest was in the history of his community, which he researched in a most professional manner. He specialized in the study of Howel *Harris's visits to Montgomeryshire and his most important work was *Blynyddoedd Cyntaf Methodistiaeth* (1909), a detailed account of Harris's life up to 1738; it was translated by Gomer M. *Roberts as *The Early Life of Howell Harris* (1962) and the author's *Methodistiaeth Trefaldwyn Uchaf* (1929) is a continuation of that work. Bennett also wrote three booklets, *Methodistiaeth Trefeglwys* (1933), *Methodistiaeth y Cemaes* (1934) and *Early Calvinistic Methodism in Caersws* (1938). An excellent example of the self-educated local historian, he made a valuable contribution to the study of his subject.

BERDDIG (11th cent.), a poet who, according to Domesday Book, held duty-free lands in Gwent by virtue of his office as *joculator regis* ('king's jester') to *Gruffudd ap Llywelyn.

Bere, Y, a castle occupying a strategic site near *Cadair Idris, Mer., and guarding the southern boundary of *Gwynedd, was probably built by order of *Llywelyn ap Iorwerth (Llywelyn Fawr) in the early thirteenth century and reinforced by his grandson, *Llywelyn ap Gruffudd. After the latter's death in the second *War of Welsh Independence (1282–83), his brother *Dafydd ap Gruffudd made it the centre of his resistance. In the early summer of 1283 the castle was besieged and eventually surrendered to English forces. Bere was then repaired and in 1285 a borough was established near by. During the *Welsh Revolt (1294–95) the castle was attacked by the Welsh but it was soon relieved. It may have been temporarily occupied during the Wars of the Roses, for *Lewys Glyn Cothi (Llywelyn y Glyn) sang in praise of Dafydd Gough who used it as a base for a campaign against his Yorkist enemies.

BERGAM, Y (12th or 14th cent.), a vaticinatory poet many of whose poems have been preserved in manuscript, may have been a native of *Maelor.

BERRY, ROBERT GRIFFITH (1869–1945), playwright and short-story writer, was a native of Llanrwst, Denbs. Educated at the University College of North Wales, Bangor, and at Bala-Bangor College, he spent the rest of his life as an Independent minister at Gwaelod-y-Garth, Glam. He wrote plays to be performed by amateurs in the chapel vestry, some of which were of remarkable literary merit. They include *Ar y Groesffordd* (1914), *Noson o Farrug* (1915), *Asgre Lan* (1916), *Y Ddraenen Wen* (1922), *Dwywaith yn Blentyn* (1924) and *Yr Hen Anian* (1929). Like his short stories, collected in the volume *Y Llawr Dyrnu* (1930), R. G. Berry's plays have a strong element of satire.

There is an article about him by T. J. Morgan in *Ysgrifau Beirniadol I* (ed. J. E. Caerwyn Williams, 1965); see also the article by T. Robin Chapman in *Taliesin* (vol. 44, July, 1982) and Ifor Rees (ed.), *Ar Glawr* (1983). For a full account see the biography of R. G. Berry by Huw Ethall (1985).

BERRY, RON (1920–), novelist, was born at Blaen-cwm in the *Rhondda Valley, Glam., where he still lives. He left school at the age of fourteen and worked as a miner until the outbreak of the Second World War, during which he served in both the army and the merchant navy. After spending a year at *Coleg Harlech (1954–55) he began writing novels, five of which have been published: *Hunters and Hunted* (1960), *Travelling Loaded* (1963), *The Full-Time Amateur* (1966), *Flame and Slag* (1968) and *So Long, Hector Bebb* (1970). He has also written short stories, as yet uncollected, and plays for radio and television. The Rhondda of his novels is very different from that of Rhys *Davies or Gwyn *Thomas (1913–81): it is economically more prosperous and its people more sophisticated, more hedonistic, less concerned with politics and religion, and what Ron Berry involves them in is comedy, much of it sexual.

Berth-Lwyd, a mansion near Llanidloes, Mont., which was once an important destination for itinerant poets. A good deal of poetry addressed to members of the family has survived in manuscript. The first and most notable patron was Dafydd Llwyd ap Siencyn (d. 1587), a cultured man whose patronage was commensurate with his status and influence in the county. Not much verse addressed to his son, Jenkyn Lloyd (d. 1627), has survived, but his grandsons Oliver and Edward maintained the tradition until the middle years of the seventeenth century.

Bessi of Llansantffraid, see under DIC SIÔN DAFYDD.

Bessie Bighead, the cow-herd at Salt Lake Farm in Dylan *Thomas's *Under Milk Wood (1954), puts daisies on the grave of Gomer Owen 'who kissed her once when she wasn't looking and never kissed her again although she was looking all the time'.

Best of Friends, The (1978), a novel by Emyr *Humphreys, follows *Flesh and Blood (1974) in narrative sequence. Amy and Enid go together to university, where the former takes a leading part in a Nationalist campaign against Anglicization. Later, Enid pairs off with John Cilydd More, a young solicitor who is also a poet, and Amy with Val Gwyn, an idealistic student leader. But Val dies of tuberculosis and Amy, in the post-university world, falls prey to Pen Lewis, Communist and opportunist; Enid also dies. In this section of the narrative, Amy loses her way: the props provided by other people's ideals and visions of society (the Communist one proving to be just another exploitation of women) having been removed, she is empty of purpose.

Beti Jones y Ceunant, a mother who, exasperated by the finicky preferences of her twenty-five children, each for a different kind of food, taught them a lesson one supper-time by preparing the dishes of their choice, mixing them in a baking-pan and then standing over her brood with a porridge-stick until they had eaten the mess. The famous cure, described by Hugh *Evans in his Cwm Eithin (1931), became a warning to children for generations afterwards.

Beuno (5th–6th cent.), a saint who is associated mainly with Clynnog Fawr, Caerns., although there is evidence of his cult elsewhere in north Wales, especially in Anglesey and Llŷn. His name occurs in the north more frequently than that of any other saint and his mission there was comparable with that of *Dewi Sant in the south; his feast-day is 21 April. The earliest copy of Beuno's Life is found in The *Book of the Anchorite, a Welsh version probably based on a lost Latin original, in which it is stated that he was born on the banks of the Severn in *Powys, that he was educated in Caer-went and that he belonged to the royal family of Glamorgan. Leaving Powys to escape oppression from English invaders, he and his disciples arrived in *Gwynedd and converted the king, *Cadfan, to the Christian faith. The saint was reputed to have performed many miracles, even after his death; for example, it was said that he brought *Gwenffrewi and Digiwg back to life after they had been beheaded by their persecutors, and that children washed in a well dedicated to Beuno would be restored to health overnight, a belief persisting in the late eighteenth century.

A traditional tale relates how Beuno's book of sermons was saved from the sea by a curlew. The saint is said to have dropped it as he walked across the sands of the Menai Straits on his way from preaching in Anglesey. On reaching his cell at Clynnog Fawr, he found the book there in the care of a curlew. He prayed for God's protection of the bird and that is why, so the story goes, the curlew's eggs are so difficult to find, their colours having been made to match those of the ground on which they are laid.

Bevan, Aneurin (1897–1960), politician, was the Labour Member of Parliament for Ebbw Vale, Mon., from 1929 to 1960. He was brought up to attend chapel and local eisteddfod and was named after the poet Aneurin Fardd (Aneurin Jones; 1822–1904), but he was always ambivalent in his attitude towards Welsh culture. As a miner in his native Tredegar, though much influenced by Syndicalist thinking, he veered away from direct action after the *General Strike of 1926 to seek power at Westminster. The 1930s brought him an international reputation for scathing oratorical wit and passionate left-wing politics. He was the founder and editor (1942–45) of Tribune, the journal of the British Left, and the author of In Place of Fear (1952). Appointed Minister of Health in 1945, he proved a creative administrator by his establishment of the National Health Service, which many consider to be his memorial, but his resignation from the Cabinet in 1951 resurrected charges of wrecking. In retrospect he appears to have been the most dazzling exponent of democratic *Socialism ever produced in Wales.

His biography was written by Michael Foot (2 vols., 1962, 1973); see also Jennie Lee, My Life with Nye (1980), Aneurin Bevan, 'The Claim of Wales—a statement', in Wales (Spring, 1947), and the article by Robert Griffiths, 'The Other Aneurin Bevan' in Planet (no. 41, 1978).

Bevan, Bridget (1698–1779), see under JONES, GRIFFITH (1683–1761).

BEVAN, HUGH (1911–79), critic, was born at Saron, Carms., a miner's son. He was a Senior Lecturer in Welsh at University College, Swansea, and the author of two volumes of literary criticism, Morgan Llwyd y Llenor (1954) and Dychymyg Islwyn (1965), and of an autobiography, Morwr Cefn Gwlad (1971). A collection of his literary articles has been edited by Brynley F. *Roberts (1982).

BEYNON, TOM (1886–1961), historian. Born near Kidwelly (Cydweli), Carms., he was educated at Bala Theological College and ordained minister in 1916, serving at Blaengwynfi (1917–33) and near Aberystwyth (1933–51). A popular public lecturer, he won a reputation for his research into the history of Calvinistic *Methodism and edited his denomination's history magazine for many years. Besides writing numerous articles, he edited the diaries of Howel *Harris in three volumes: *Howel Harris, Reformer and Soldier* (1958), *Howell Harris's Visits to London* (1960) and *Howell Harris's Visits to Pembrokeshire* (1966). He also published two volumes of reminiscences about his native district, *Allt Cunedda* (1935) and *Cwmsêl a Chefn Sidan* (1946), both written in a lively style.

Bible, The. The earliest examples of Scriptural translation into Welsh are those passages found in the religious literature of the Middle Ages. Translations not of the original Hebrew and Greek but of the Latin version known as the Vulgate, they are neither numerous nor extensive. The following passages are found as stated: Genesis 1:1–2; 2:21–3 in *Y Bibyl Ynghymraec* (*c.*1350–1400), an anonymous prose translation of *Promptuarium Bibliae* by Petrus Pictaviensis; twenty-eight Psalms and a few verses from the New Testament and the Apocrypha in *Gwassanaeth Meir* (*c.*1400); the Lord's Prayer, the Beatitudes, John's Prologue, the Ten Commandments, and 150 verses from the Old Testament and the New Testament in the various tracts collected in *The *Book of the Anchorite* of Llanddewi Brefi; Matthew 26:1–28:7 in *Y Groglith*; and a few parables and verses from the New Testament in *Y Seint Greal*. It is unlikely that any of these was ever used as a lectionary. The only Scriptures of the Latin Church in Wales, as in Western Europe generally, were those of the Latin Vulgate.

With the Renaissance and the Protestant *Reformation there was a great change. The original texts of the Bible were recovered and printed, a series of new Latin translations was published and the entire Bible was translated into several Western European languages. Wales was fortunate in having scholars competent to undertake a vernacular version and foremost among them was William *Salesbury. His translations of the Epistles and Gospels of the Book of Common Prayer were published under the title *Kynniver llith a ban* (1551). His general principles of translation were fidelity to the original without bondage to its exact wording, dignity of diction achieved by archaic and latinized phraseology, and diversity of expression; the idiosyncratic orthography was meant to emphasize the last two of these principles.

Because of the limitations on the use of Welsh imposed by the *Act of Union (1536), *Kynniver llith a ban* could not be used in the churches and Wales had to wait another twenty-seven years before Parliament was persuaded to authorize a Welsh translation of the complete Bible. The Welsh Prayer Book and the New Testament appeared in 1567. Salesbury was the translator of the Prayer Book, including the Psalter, and of all the books of the New Testament except five Epistles, which were translated by Bishop

Richard *Davies, and Revelation, which was the responsibility of Thomas Huet (d. 1591). Clarity was Huet's aim and he ventured to translate into the Demetian (Dyfed) dialect of Welsh. Salesbury kept to the principles and literary devices of *Kynniver llith a ban*, except that, following the Geneva Bible, he now gave more weight to literal fidelity. Davies also aimed at fidelity, but he had hardly any of Salesbury's literary embellishments. Salesbury was a Renaissance man, Davies a Protestant missionary, and this difference probably accounted for their failure to complete the translation of the whole Bible.

The work begun by Salesbury and Davies was completed by William *Morgan whose Welsh Bible (1588) is the foundation stone on which modern Welsh literature has been based. His particular merits as a translator were his skilled and scholarly handling of the original texts of the Scriptures, his elimination of the archaisms and oddities used by Salesbury, his presentation of the Welsh language in an intelligent, sensitive, up-to-date, consistent fashion and his superb gifts as a writer which enabled him to incorporate into his translation the strength, correctness, purity and majesty of the classical idiom of the poets. His achievement was all the more important because it came at a time when the *Bardic Order, hitherto the guardian of the literary language, was already in decay.

The Welsh Bible of 1620, *Y Bibl Cyssegr-lan*, was a revised edition inspired by the publication of the English Authorised Version of 1611. By now copies of William Morgan's Bible had become scarce and its language needed revision because, in particular, he had kept closely to Hebrew idiom. The revision was the work of Bishop Richard *Parry of St. Asaph. Unfortunately, Parry's attitude was arrogant and unscholarly: in his dedication of the work to James I he explained that he had retained some of Morgan's translation but had changed so much that it was difficult to decide whose work it really was. He did not acknowledge any assistance but, according to bardic testimony, John *Davies of Mallwyd, Parry's brother-in-law and one of the greatest scholars of his age, had standardized the language and done much of the revision.

The Welsh Bible of 1630 is a reprint of the revised version of 1620, its only remarkable feature being its size. It was called *Y Beibl Bach* ('The Small Bible') or *Y Beibl Coron* ('The Five-Shilling Bible') and was published at the expense of a group of wealthy Welshmen in London, including Sir Thomas *Middleton and Rowland *Heilyn. This was the first family Bible in Welsh and bound with it were the Book of Common Prayer, the Psalms and Edmund *Prys's *Salmau Cân*.

For further details see Charles Ashton, *Bywyd ac Amserau'r Esgob William Morgan* (1891), John Ballinger,

The Bible in Wales (1906), W. J. Gruffydd, *Llenyddiaeth Cymru: Rhyddiaith o 1540 hyd 1660* (1926). Thomas Parry, *Hanes Llenyddiaeth Gymraeg hyd 1900* (1944), Glanmor Williams, *Bywyd ac Amserau yr Esgob Richard Davies* (1953) and Geraint Bowen (ed.), *Y Traddodiad Rhyddiaith* (1970).

Bid Ale or **Cwrw Bach**, a gathering at which money was raised by the sale of cakes and beer, was a custom forbidden by law in 1534 because it led to extortionate practices. Sometimes, in order to avoid breaking the law, the cakes were sold at an inflated price and the beer was given away. Singing and dancing were part of the entertainment provided in the house and for that reason the custom was popular among young people, especially courting couples. It was often observed in order to help a neighbour who was ill or who had fallen on hard times. The *pastai* held in taverns in the Swansea Valley during the nineteenth century was another form of the tradition. Later, it was the practice in some parts to give a tea-party for the same purpose.

Bidden to the Feast (1938), a novel by Jack *Jones about working-class life in Merthyr Tydfil, Glam., between 1865 and 1900. It goes into great detail about social conditions and the town's development as an industrial centre but the fortunes of the family of Rhys Davies, a miner, are the novel's principal theme. Two sons emigrate to America, another becomes a ship-owner in Cardiff and a daughter finds success as an opera-singer; Megan, the unmarried daughter, grows up to be the loving but unsentimental head of the family.

Bidding or **Neithior**, a folk-custom associated with the wedding-feast. Among gentry families in the sixteenth century it had literary significance as a gathering at which poets were present, the apprentices of the *Penceirddiaid* ('chief poets') often being admitted to their grades on such an occasion. For example, at the wedding-feast of Ieuan ap Dafydd ap Ithel Fychan of Northop, Flints., *Tudur Aled was awarded his first grade and *Gruffudd Hiraethog received his at that of Huw Lewis of Harpton, Rads., in 1546. By the eighteenth century the wedding-feast had become popular among the common people, providing an opportunity of helping young couples to set up house. A 'bidder' was employed to announce details of the wedding and to invite as many people as possible to attend the feast. He wore a white apron, flowers and ribbons, carried a staff and recited verses which were often composed by local poets. The guests were expected to repay their 'bidding debts', that is, the gifts of money which they had previously received from the families of the bride and groom at their own weddings. A vivid description of the custom, which flourished mainly in Dyfed and the western parts of Glamorgan and Breconshire, is given in T. J.

Llewelyn *Prichard's *The Adventures and Vagaries of *Twm Shôn Catti* (1828).

BIDGOOD, RUTH (1922–), poet, was born at Seven Sisters, near Neath, Glam., and went to school in Port Talbot where her father was the vicar. After reading English at Oxford, she served as a coder with the Women's Royal Naval Service in Alexandria and later worked for *Chambers's Encyclopaedia* in London. She began writing after her return to Wales during the 1960s when she settled at Abergwesyn, near Llanwrtyd, Brecs. Besides numerous articles on the history of Breconshire and Radnorshire, she has published three volumes of poetry, *The Given Time* (1972), *Not Without Homage* (1975) and *The Print of Miracle* (1978), all of which are concerned with the people, landscape and seasons of mid-Wales. A volume of her selected poems has appeared under the title *Lighting Candles* (1982).

BIELSKI, ALISON (1925–), poet. Born in Newport, Mon., she worked as a secretary with various industrial companies and with the British Red Cross in Cardiff. Among her volumes of poetry are *Twentieth Century Flood* (1964), *Across the Burning Sand* (1970), *Monogrampoems* (1971), *Eve* (1973), *Mermaid Poems* (1974), *The Lovetree* (1974), *Seth* (1980), *Night Sequence* (1981) and *Eagles* (1983). Much of her work draws on Welsh folklore and mythology and some of it, being experimental and combining words with graphic images, has been exhibited in Wales and abroad. She has also published several booklets of local history, including *Flower Legends of Wales* (1974) and *Tales and Traditions of Tenby* (1981). From 1969 to 1974 she was, with Sally Roberts (later Sally Roberts *Jones), the honorary joint secretary of the English-language section of Yr *Academi Gymreig.

BINGLEY, WILLIAM (1774–1823), see under TOUR ROUND NORTH WALES (1800).

Biography, as a literary form, did not appear in Welsh until the nineteenth century, if the *Lives of the Saints and the *Historia Gruffudd vab Kenan* are discounted. The first to be published, in 1816, was the biography of Thomas *Charles of Bala which was translated from the English by Thomas *Jones of Denbigh and included the author's autobiography up to his marriage in 1783. To the same period belong the autobiographies of Twm o'r Nant (Thomas *Edwards) and of Thomas Jones himself, the one fresh and individualistic, the other heavily pious. They were followed throughout the century by several hundred biographies, mostly of preachers great and small. The most important on several counts is the huge *Cofiant* of John *Jones of Tal-y-sarn by Owen *Thomas, which touches on theology and preaching in Wales as well as giving a portrait of its subject.

These works developed a pattern of their own: a record of the man's life would usually be followed by an appreciation of him as Christian and minister, a selection of his sermons and letters, ending with tributes by friends and an elegy. The details of his life were often idealized or paid a good deal of uncritical attention, and much emphasis was laid on the intervention of Divine Providence in his career. David *Owen (Brutus), disgusted by what he called 'this biographical nonsense', parodied the form by writing the Lives of fictitious characters, the best known being *Wil Brydydd y Coed (1863–65), as well as serious biographies of the great preachers, John *Elias and Christmas *Evans.

It was not until the twentieth century that Welsh biography achieved literary excellence, and then only sporadically. Among the earliest were those by T. Gwynn *Jones of Emrys ap Iwan (Robert Ambrose *Jones) and Thomas *Gee and one of the finest that of Owen M. *Edwards by W. J. *Gruffydd. The most distinguished autobiographies of the twentieth century include those of W. J. Gruffydd, E. Tegla *Davies, D. J. *Williams, Kate *Roberts, R. T. *Jenkins and Alun *Llywelyn-Williams. Since the 1950s volumes of reminiscences have been popular and some, such as those by D. J. Williams, Ifan *Gruffydd and J. G. *Williams, have already become minor classics. Among Anglo-Welsh writers of the twentieth century who have written autobiographies are Dannie *Abse, W. H. *Davies, Llewelyn Wyn *Griffith, Glyn *Jones, Jack *Jones, Goronwy *Rees, Emlyn *Williams and Gwyn *Williams.

For a discussion of biography as a literary form in Welsh see the chapters by Emyr Gwynne Jones in Gwŷr Llên y Bedwaredd Ganrif ar Bymtheg (ed. Dyfnallt Morgan, 1968), by Alun Llywelyn-Williams in Ysgrifennu Creadigol (ed. Geraint Bowen, 1972), by Saunders Lewis in Meistri'r Canrifoedd (ed. R. Geraint Gruffydd, 1973), by Bedwyr Lewis Jones in Y Traddodiad Rhyddiaith yn yr Ugeinfed Ganrif (ed. Geraint Bowen, 1976) and by John Gwilym Jones in Swyddogaeth Beirniadaeth (1977).

Black Affray of Beaumaris, The, see under Dafydd ab Ieuan (d. c.1440).

Black Book of Basingwerk, The, see under Basingwerk.

Black Book of Carmarthen, The or *Llyfr Du Caerfyrddin*, has been generally regarded as the oldest manuscript in the Welsh language. The opinion of J. Gwenogvryn *Evans in 1899 was that it had been written by several hands in the twelfth and early thirteenth centuries and this dating was accepted during the first half of the twentieth century. The expert view now, however, is that it belongs to a later period: in the opinion of E. D. *Jones, the probability is

that no part of the manuscript was written much earlier than 1250 and that the work continued for some time after that date. While the handwriting is large at the beginning of the manuscript, it becomes smaller, but this does not necessarily mean that two different hands are to be discerned. The Book is thought to be the work of one scribe, possibly (though not certainly) a member of the Priory of St. John the Evangelist and St. Teulyddog at *Carmarthen, written during various phases of his life. Gaps occur in the text (between pp. 8/9, 28/29 and 96/97) and one page (p. 80), now illegible, was written by a different hand; some (such as pp. 8, 9 and 96) are more soiled than the rest. The Book, therefore, may be a collection of different manuscripts or parts of manuscripts which have been bound together.

The contents (108 pp. in all) consist almost entirely of poetry but there is none from the early period. They belong to the two, three or perhaps four centuries preceding the writing of the manuscript and may be classified as follows: fourteen poems on religious subjects; prophecies and poems containing elements of the *Myrddin (Merlin) legend; half a dozen poems of panegyric and elegy; poems in the englyn metre including *'Englynion y Beddau' ('The Stanzas of the Graves') and englynion from *'Canu Llywarch Hen'; eight poems on legendary subjects, including some on *Arthurian themes; and a few occasional pieces.

Nothing is known of the history of the manuscript before it came into the possession of Sir John *Price during his period as Commissioner for the Dissolution of the Monasteries. In the seventeenth century it was in the library of Hengwrt, where Robert *Vaughan made a complete copy of it (Peniarth 107). From Hengwrt it went to Peniarth in 1859 and to the *National Library of Wales in 1909.

The text was published by W. F. Skene in his *Four Ancient Books of Wales* (1868) and by J. Gwenogvryn Evans in facsimile (1888) and in a diplomatic edition (1906/7). The manuscript has also been edited with an introduction, textual notes and a full glossary by A. O. H. Jarman (1982).

Black Book of Chirk, The or *Llyfr Du o'r Waun*, includes the oldest Welsh text of the *Laws of Hywel Dda, a *Llyfr Iorwerth* version. The manuscript, written on parchment in Gwynedd, dates from the mid-thirteenth century and the orthography suggests that the transcriber was unfamiliar with the Welsh language. Later additions include an elegy to *Llywelyn ap Gruffudd, a list of proverbs and marginalia by Sir Thomas *Wiliems dated 1608. The manuscript was owned by John Edwards of Chirk at the beginning of the seventeenth century.

A photographic facsimile of the manuscript was produced by J. Gwenogvryn Evans in 1909.

Black Book of St. David's, The or *Llyfr Du Ty Ddewi*, a survey of the bishop's lands in the diocese of *St. David's. The original manuscript no longer exists but its contents are known from a transcript made in 1516 by order of Bishop Vaughan; another, dating from the seventeenth century, is kept at the *National Library of Wales. The Book, in recording details of land tenure, reflects the influence of both English law and traditional Welsh practice. Rents and services are listed, as are the sums due to the bishop from fairs, markets and courts. The survey was carried out in 1326, during David Martin's episcopacy, by David Francis, Chancellor of St. David's.

Black Canons, see AUGUSTINIAN CANONS,

Black Chair of Birkenhead, The, see under EVANS, ELLIS HUMPHREY (1887–1917).

Black Death, The, the plague in pneumonic and bubonic forms which devastated much of western Europe in the mid-fourteenth century. About a third of Britain's population was killed by the bacillus which was carried by the fleas on rats at the rate of a mile a day. In Wales, where it arrived in 1348, the lands of free tribesmen, who died in large numbers, were seized by lords or acquired by neighbours who had survived, with the result that a society began to emerge in which social rank was based not on birth or blood relationships, as formerly, but on the ownership of land. The epidemic thus helped the process of the villein's emancipation from service on his lord's land as the great open fields on lowland manors were divided into farmsteads, each cultivated by its tenant, and the manor ceased to function as a collective organization, slowly giving way to the pattern of farming characteristic of modern times. The 'Great Pestilence' also affected the fortunes of the Church in Wales and the economic dislocation which it caused led to the widespread discontent which was partly responsible for the rising of *Owain Glyndŵr.

Black Domain, The, see under SCOTCH CATTLE.

Black Friars, see DOMINICANS.

Black Friday (15 April 1921), the day on which it was decided by representatives of workers in other industries to refuse to support a strike by the miners of Britain. In the coalfield of south Wales it was widely believed—the strike having lasted for ninety-four days—that the miners' cause had been betrayed by the leadership of the trades union movement.

Black Gentiles, Black Host, Black Pagans, see VIKING RAIDS.

Black Knight of the Fountain, The, a charac-

ter in *Iarlles y Ffynnon*, one of the three Welsh Arthurian romances known as Y *Tair Rhamant*. Owain, inspired by the account of Cynon's encounter with a Black Knight who guards a fountain within *Arthur's dominions, sets off on a quest for him. Like Cynon, he is directed by a discourteous black man to follow a path through a valley until he comes to a fountain under a green tree. Finding near by a marble slab on which stands a silver bowl, he dashes water over the slab whereupon there is a peal of thunder and a cloudburst which strip the tree of its foliage. A flock of birds then settles on the bare branches and its enchanting song announces the arrival of a knight clad in black silk and riding on a black horse. Owain strikes him a terrible blow and the knight flees towards a great shining city. Pursuing him, the hero is trapped between the city's gates and his horse cut in two by the portcullis. He is rescued by *Luned who helps him win the Black Knight's widow as his wife. This tale was very popular in medieval Europe, the best known versions being the *Yvain* of Chrétien de Troyes and Hartmann von der Aue's *Iwein*.

The text has been edited by R. L. Thomson, *Owein or Chwedyl Iarlles y Ffynnon* (1968).

Black Parade (1935), a novel by Jack *Jones. Set in Merthyr Tydfil, Glam., it opens about the year 1880, deals with four generations of a mining family and ends in the early 1930s. Among events occurring during this period and reflected in the novel are the South African or Boer War (1880–81, 1899–1902), the religious revival of 1905 (see under ROBERTS, EVAN), the *Senghenydd Explosion (1913) and the *General Strike of 1926. The book contains much action and a gallery of colourful characters, including Harry the mountain fighter, Steppwr the public-house entertainer, Davies M.A., the public elocutionist, and Saran, the matriarchal figure who was based on the author's own mother.

Black Spot, The, an international folk-tale based on the motif of parents who unknowingly murder their own son. In Wales the story is associated with the heir of Cae'r Bwla, Llanerfyl, Mont., who came home after many years spent abroad and was robbed and killed by his parents who recognized him, too late, by a black spot on his arm. The story was made popular by the ballad 'Y Blotyn Du' which dates from the early seventeenth century and is based on the English ballad 'Newes from Perin in Cornwall'. See also under UNITARIANISM.

Black Venus, The (1944), a novel by Rhys *Davies, is set in and around the fictitious village of Ayron in south-west Wales. Its theme is *Courting in Bed, a custom practised with decorum by the heroine, the beautiful and opinionated Olwen Powell, a rich farmer's daughter, until she becomes pregnant by

Rhisiart Hughes, the local squire's illegitimate son. The novel, a fantasy about life in rural Wales during Edwardian times, has suspense and style but some aspects of its plot and dialogue are incredible.

Black Witch, The, a character in the tale of *Culhwch and Olwen. The final task accomplished before the hero wins Olwen's hand is the obtaining of the Black Witch's blood from the Valley of Grief in the Uplands of Hell. The blood, which must still be warm, is to be used for the shaving of Ysbaddaden Bencawr's beard. *Arthur, with his companions, finds the witch's cave and, throwing his knife, Carnwennan, he splits her in two; the blood is collected by Caw o Brydyn.

Blackbird of Cilgwri, The, see under OLDEST ANIMALS.

BLACKMORE, RICHARD DODDRIDGE (1825–1900), novelist, was born at Longworth, Oxon., but spent much of his childhood at Nottage Court, Glam. He trained as a lawyer but poor health prevented him from practising law and a legacy from his uncle, who was vicar of Neath, enabled him to take up authorship instead.

Although for most readers R. D. Blackmore is known only as the author of the famous *Lorna Doone* (1869), he wrote fourteen other novels set in various parts of England and Wales, as well as several books of verse and a volume of short stories. His Welsh connections are evident in his earliest novels, *Clara Vaughan* (1864) and *Cradock Nowell* (1866), and even in *Lorna Doone*, but they are reflected most vividly in *The Maid of Sker* (1872), perhaps his best work. Although set mainly in Glamorgan, this novel makes no reference to the traditional tale of Elizabeth *Williams (The Maid of Sker). It is, rather, a knowledgeable and patriotic portrait of Welsh life in the latter part of the eighteenth century. Blackmore's other books include *Alice Lorraine* (1875), *Cripps the Carrier* (1876), *Christowell* (1882), *Springhaven* (1887) and *Tales from the Telling House* (1896). He was primarily a storyteller and his writing, especially in the earlier novels, has both vigour and wit.

Biographies of R. D. Blackmore have been written by Q. G. Burris (1930), W. H. Dunn (1956) and K. Budd (1960); see also the article by Sally Jones in *The Anglo-Welsh Review* (no. 55, Autumn, 1975).

BLACKWELL, JOHN (**Alun**; 1797–1841), poet, was born near Mold, Flints. As a child he received little formal instruction but, apprenticed to a shoemaker, he followed his master's example and took an interest in Welsh and English literature. His poems and essays brought him to the notice of local gentry and clergymen who subscribed to a fund which provided him with an education under Thomas

Richards (1785–1855) of Berriw, and he entered Jesus College, Oxford, in 1824. At the eisteddfod held at Denbigh in 1828 he won a prize for his best-known poem, an elegy for Bishop Heber. He was ordained curate at Holywell in 1829 and, four years later, was preferred to the rectory of Manordeifi, Pembs., where he remained until his death.

Although Alun's verse in the strict metres is competent and devoid of pomposity, it is inferior to his delightful lyrical poems in the free metres which show English influences and for which alone he is remembered. Some of the most famous are '*Doli*', '*Cân Gwraig y Pysgotwr*' and '*Abaty Tintern*'. No volume of his poems was published during his lifetime but *Ceinion Alun* (1851) was edited by Griffith Edwards (Gutyn Padarn; 1812–93) ten years after his death; a number of Blackwell's letters in both Welsh and English, included in this volume, are redolent of a leisurely age in which letter-writing was one of the social arts.

For further details see a selection of Alun's verse edited by Isaac Foulkes in 1879 and by Owen M. Edwards in the series, *Cyfres y Fil* (1909); see also the article by D. Gwenallt Jones in *Llên Cymru* (1951).

'*Blaenwern*', the only well-known hymn-tune composed by William Penfro Rowlands (1860–1937), first appeared in the collection *Cân a Moliant* (ed. H. Haydn Jones, 1916). Later sung to the words 'Love divine, all loves excelling' by Charles Wesley, it became popular in England.

Blanchland, see WHITLAND.

Bleddyn ap Cynfyn (*fl.* 1063–75), King of *Gwynedd and *Powys, is said to have revised the *Laws of Hywel Dda and was remembered as a good ruler. The royal House of Powys was descended from him and one of his sons was *Cadwgan ap Bleddyn.

BLEDDYN FARDD (*fl.* 1268–83), one of the Poets of the Princes, lamented the fall of all the House of *Gwynedd in *awdlau* and *englynion* on the deaths of *Llywelyn ap Gruffudd, *Owain Goch ap Gruffudd and *Dafydd ap Gruffudd, the sons of Gruffudd ap Llywelyn. The greatest of all these poems is his *awdl* in memory of Llywelyn ap Gruffudd in 1282. Unlike the famous elegy by *Gruffudd ab yr Ynad Coch, the most poignant expression of utter dismay in the Welsh language, Bleddyn's poem is an appeal for steadfastness: '*A bortho gofid bid bwyllocaf*' ('Who suffers grief let him be the calmest'). He praises Llywelyn for not having taken the path of least resistance against the English king and for having given his life for his country. The Prince's fate is likened to that of Priam, a comparison the significance of which was that, for the Welsh, with their belief in the nation's Trojan origins, the fall of Troy was not only an end but also a beginning. Bleddyn addressed other poems in the conventional manner of his time to gentry families in Anglesey, the Vale of Towy, Edeirnion and elsewhere. He had, unlike many of the earlier *Gogynfeirdd, a direct and simple style which is often found in the poetry written towards the close of the period of Welsh independence.

BLEDRI AP CYDIFOR (*fl.* early 12th cent.), magnate, interpreter and tale-teller, is believed to have been responsible for introducing Welsh myth and legend to the Normans and so into the literature of Europe. His home was in the district of Carmarthen and, although delighting in the Welsh cultural heritage, he was nevertheless on friendly terms with his Norman neighbours and, in 1116, when some of the Welsh were in rebellion, Bledri was put in charge of the castle of Robert Courtemayn. Able to speak both Welsh and French, he was described as '*latemeri*' ('latimer' or 'interpreter') in Latin documents which record his patronage of the priory at *Carmarthen.

The name Bledericus Walensis, found in a legal document of 1130, identifies him with the Bledhericus mentioned by *Gerald de Barri (Giraldus Cambrensis) as a renowned master of romance who had died not long before. Another form of his name, Bleherus, was used in an allusion to the seizing of Bledri's daughter by brothers from Pencader. It can be assumed that he was the Bleheris who, according to a statement in the second continuation of the *Conte de Graal*, had been the author of an early form of the Perceval story. *Thomas, the author of *Tristan*, speaks of Breri as the only true authority on that ancient tale. This reference seems to be to Bledri and it is possible that his account of the story was available in written form. If all this is so, Bledri ap Cydifor is the man who, out of the rich store of Welsh legend, gave to the world two of its most famous stories, the tale of *Tristan and Iseult and the tale of the Quest for the Holy *Grail.

For further details see C. Bullock-Davies, *Professional Interpreters and the Matter of Britain* (1966).

Bleeding Yew, The, in the churchyard at Nanhyfer (Nevern), Pembs., is known for the red resin which oozes from its trunk. It is said that a man, perhaps a monk, about to be hanged on this tree, swore that it would bleed thereafter as testimony to his innocence.

Blegywryd, see under LAWS OF HYWEL DDA.

Bleiddud or **Bladud** (*fl.* 9th cent.), the son of Rhun, said to have succeeded his father as king of north Britain. According to the *Historia Regum Britanniae* of *Geoffrey of Monmouth, the city of Bath was built by his order. It is also said that he practised necromancy and fell to his death while at-tempting to fly. See also EDMYG DINBYCH.

Blind Harpist, The, see PARRY, JOHN (1710?–82).

Blodau Dyfed (lit. 'The flowers of Dyfed'; 1824), an anthology edited by John Howell (Ioan ab Hywel, Ioan Glandyfroedd; 1774–1830) after the Carmarthen Eisteddfod of 1819. The editor, a prominent Churchman, dedicated his collection to Thomas Beynon (1744–1833), Archdeacon of Cardigan and president of the *Cymreigyddion Society of Carmarthen. The poets represented in the anthology, all Anglicans, include Ieuan Brydydd Hir (Evan *Evans), Eliezer *Williams, Daniel Ddu o Geredigion (Daniel Evans; 1792–1846), Iaco ab Dewi (James *Davies), Edward *Richard and Ioan Siengcin (John *Jenkins). The book's significance is that it was the first attempt to anthologize Welsh poets on a regional basis.

Blodeuged, formerly **Aberthged**, a sheaf of corn entwined with wild flowers which is presented to the Archdruid by a young woman in the ceremonies of *Gorsedd Beirdd Ynys Prydain. The custom, devised in the late nineteenth century, is intended to symbolize, together with the Flower Dance, introduced in 1936, the desire of Welsh youth to offer the flower of its talent to the *National Eisteddfod.

Blodeugerdd o'r Ddeunawfed Ganrif (lit. 'An anthology of the eighteenth century'; 1936), edited by Gwenallt (David James *Jones), was intended to present readers with a wider experience of the classical poetry of the eighteenth century than is usual in a consideration of Goronwy *Owen alone. The poets represented include Hugh *Hughes (Huw ap Huw), Lewis *Morris, Edward *Richard, Goronwy Owen, Ieuan Brydydd Hir (Evan *Evans) and Iolo Morganwg (Edward *Williams). In the fourth edition (1947) some poems were removed and the work of other poets— Owen *Gruffydd, Edward *Samuel, Rhys *Jones and Thomas *Jones of Denbigh—was added.

Blodeuwedd, the beautiful and unfaithful wife of *Lleu Llawgyffes in the Fourth Branch of *Pedair Cainc y Mabinogi. When *Arianrhod swears a destiny upon Lleu that he shall never have a mortal wife, *Math and Gwydion conjure her from the flowers of the oak, the broom and the meadowsweet. It is uncertain whether the original form of her name was Blodeuwedd ('Flower Face') or Blodeu-fedd ('Queen of the Flowers') or Blodeu-edd ('Flowers'), but it is by the first of these that she is usually known.

One day during Lleu's absence from the court, his wife receives a visit from Gronw Pebr, the lord of Penllyn. They fall in love, spend the night together and conspire to kill Blodeuwedd's husband. Lleu does not die, however, but turns into an eagle and Gronw then occupies his court. Later, on Lleu's return to Ardudwy, Blodeuwedd and her maids flee over the river Cynfael but she is captured by Gwydion who transforms her into an owl. Ordered never to show her face in daylight, she is fated to become the eternal enemy of all other birds and for this reason, the story-teller explains, the owl was known thereafter by the name of Blodeuwedd.

By means of this powerful fable Saunders *Lewis, in his play *Blodeuwedd* (1948), explored such themes as the nature of tradition, the perils of unbridled *eros* and the limits of science. Both Gronw and Blodeuwedd, in their different ways, are among the most memorable of his characters.

For further details see W. J. Gruffydd, *Math vab Mathonwy* (1928) and Ifor Williams, *Pedeir Keinc y Mabinogi* (1964). There is a discussion of Saunders Lewis's play by Dafydd Glyn Jones in *Ysgrifau Beirniadol VII* (ed. J. E. Caerwyn Williams, 1971). The play was published in an English translation by Joseph Clancy in 1985, under the title *The Woman made of Flowers*.

Blodwen, the first Welsh opera, of which the music was composed by Joseph *Parry and the libretto by Richard *Davies (Mynyddog). It was given its première in a concert conducted by Parry at Aberystwyth in 1878 and was first staged in Aberdare in the following year. Set in the Wales of the fourteenth century, the opera was immediately popular with choral societies and by 1896 it had been performed more than five hundred times. Seldom heard since the early 1930s, by now only parts of the work, such as the duets 'Hywel a Blodwen' and 'Mae Cymru'n barod', are at all well known, but the opera's centenary was celebrated by a concert perform-ance of the complete orchestral version at the Menai Music Festival in 1978.

BLOOMFIELD, ROBERT (1766–1823), see under BANKS OF WYE (1811).

Blue Bed, The (1937), Glyn *Jones's first collec-tion of short stories, brought him renown by virtue of its unusually lyrical tone and its loving concern for language. If these qualities often inflate the narrative line beyond what it will bear, they also take the story beyond mood into a new dimension. Almost half the book is taken up with 'I was born in the Ystrad Valley', a tale about a failed revolution. The most memorable stories are those of the comic-supernatural, such as 'Wil Thomas' and 'Eben Isaac', but the perfec-tion of the title-story and some others is marred by heavy symbolism.

Blue Books, The (3 vols., 1847), reports published by the Government on the state of education in Wales, caused religious controversy and an upsurge in patriotic sentiment which were to have lasting effects on the cultural and political life of Wales. After a motion proposed by William *Williams, Member of Parliament for Coventry, that an inquiry be conducted into the state of education in Wales, 'especially into the means afforded to the labouring classes of acquiring a knowledge of the English tongue', three lawyers named Lingen, Symons and John-son were appointed to conduct the survey. Able though they were, the selection of these young, inexperienced Anglicans, who had no specialist knowledge of education and no Welsh, to investigate the state of education in a country which was mainly Nonconformist and Welsh-speaking, did not augur well for a perceptive report. Nevertheless, with no intention of being unjust, they set about the task with great enthusiasm and produced a detailed report in three volumes which, bound in blue covers, were known thereafter as *The Blue Books*.

The Commissioners lamented the lack and the deplorable condition of schools, the poor equip-ment, the absence of textbooks, the untrained teachers and the irregular attendance or absen-teeism of the children. Equally critical were their comments on the teaching methods, the harsh discipline and the inability of the staff to teach English to monoglot Welsh children. It is unlikely that their condemnation of the schools was wide of the mark, but the reasons offered for this sorry state of affairs were widely irrespon-sible and amounted to a travesty. Misled by the bias of Anglican informants, the Commissioners reported that the common people were dirty, lazy, ignorant, superstitious, deceitful, promis-cuous and immoral, and they blamed all this on *Nonconformity and the *Welsh language.

The *Blue Books* met with bitter and wide-spread resentment among Nonconformists and Anglicans alike, and the controversy rever-berated for many years. Those Welshmen who had given evidence before the Commissioners were satirized by R. J. *Derfel in a play entitled *Brad y Llyfrau Gleision* (lit. 'The treachery of the Blue Books'; 1854), its title echoing the *Treachery of the Long Knives, one of the favourite patriotic stories of the period, and the word 'treachery' has been inseparably attached to the *Blue Books* ever since.

The effects of the *Blue Books* on Welsh society were profound but paradoxical. On the one hand, they made the Welsh more anglophobe and, on the other, more ready to refute the commissioners' criticism by becoming more like the English by emulating the practical, hard-headed aspects of their national character. The reports also caused new divisions and new alliances, contributing especially to the growing dichotomy between such cultural leaders as *Yr *Hen Bersoniaid Llengar* ('The Old Literary Clerics') and the common people.

For accounts of the controversy caused by the *Blue Books* see David Salmon, 'The Story of a Welsh Education Commission' in *Y Cymmrodor* (vol. XXIV) and Ieuan D. Thomas, *Addysg yng Nghymru yn y Bedwaredd Ganrif ar Bymtheg* (1972); see also the articles by Prys Morgan in *Y Traethodydd* (April, 1982) and in *Welsh Society and Nationhood* (ed. R. R. Davies et al., 1984).

BLWCHFARDD (*fl.* 6th cent.), poet, is mentioned in the *Historia Brittonum* of *Nennius as one of the British poets who flourished in the *Old North, but none of his work has survived.

BOADEN, JAMES (1762–1839), see under CAMBRO-BRITONS (1798).

Boadicea, see BOUDICA (1st cent.).

Board of Celtic Studies, The, established by the *University of Wales in 1919, was one of the consequences of the Report of the Royal Commission on University Education in Wales (1918). Although the Commission was not unmindful of the excellent philological work already accomplished, it hoped that the Board would also stimulate wider studies relating to the life, thought and culture of the Welsh nation, thus nourishing the education provided in secondary schools and colleges. Three Committees of the Board were at once set up: Language and Literature, History and Law, Archaeology and Art, and a fourth in 1969, the Social Science Committee.

The duties of the Board are to encourage and to organize Celtic Studies in Wales, to employ researchers, to publish regularly the fruits of research and to report annually to the University Council, its main financial source. Most of its members are drawn from the academic staffs of the University Colleges. Among the Board's numerous publications are books on archaeology, texts in Welsh for the use of schools and colleges, substantial volumes of sources of Welsh history, bibliographies and scholarly monographs as well as the journals *Studia Celtica*, The *Welsh History Review* and *Llên Cymru*. Since 1921 it has published a *Bulletin*, the editors of which have been Ifor *Williams (1921–48), Henry *Lewis (1948–64) and Thomas *Jones (1964–72); D. Ellis *Evans was appointed editor in 1972. The Board also has two principal projects in train, the Welsh Dictionary which is expected to be completed before the end of the century, and the standard Atlas of Wales.

The progress of Celtic Studies in Wales since 1920 may be largely attributed to the activities of the Board. Like the University of Wales Press, which publishes on its behalf, it is an excellent example of inter-College co-operation within the University.

Bob Tai'r Felin, see ROBERTS, ROBERT (1870–1951).

Bodeon, a mansion in the parish of Llangad-waladr, Ang., the home of a family which contributed generously to bardic patronage on the island. They were descended from the Presaeddfed family and Meurig (d. *c.*1489), the son of Llywelyn ap Hwlcyn (d. 1475), was the first known patron; his brothers settled at *Bodychen and *Chwaen Wen. At least three generations of Meurig's descendants maintained the tradition at Bodeon until after 1625.

Bodfel, the home in the parish of Llannor, Caerns., of a family noted for its patronage of poets. Huw Bodfel (d. 1605) was the most outstanding but the tradition was maintained down to the time of his grandson, when the family's fortunes began to wane.

Bodidris, the home of the Lloyd family in the parish of Llandegla, Denbs., and a famous resort for itinerant poets. The family achieved status and wealth mainly by its adherence to the *Tudors and by propitious marriages at the end of the fifteenth century. It extended patronage to many poets, including *Tudur Aled, almost without interruption into the seventeenth century, when Lewys *Dwnn and Tomos *Prys of Plas Iolyn eulogized Sir John Lloyd (d. 1606).

Bodleian Manuscript 572 (10th cent.), a composite Latin manuscript now in the Bodleian Library, Oxford. Termed '*codex Oxoniensis posterior*' by Zeuss in his *Grammatica Celtica*, it has since then been commonly known by that name, often abbreviated as *Ox.2*. It contains the *Missa S. Germani*, a treatise on the Mass, the Book of Tobit, two epistles of St. Augustine, Latin colloquies and Anglo-Saxon prayers. The provenance of the work is unknown but several parts have definite Cornish connections. The section comprising a series of colloquies contains important glosses (both interlinear and incorporated in the text) which have been variously claimed as Old Welsh and Old Cornish, an indication in part of the difficulty in distinguishing between these two languages at an early period. Most of the glosses may be Welsh in origin with an occasional indication of intrusive Cornish features; they are best described as hybrid Welsh-Cornish. The whole codex, with its extensive use of Carolingian script from the middle of the tenth century, reflects a common insular (Welsh–Cornish–English) milieu with especially clear Cornish connections and influences.

Bodwrda, a mansion in the parish of Aberdaron, Caerns., the home of a family noted as bardic patrons over four generations in the sixteenth century. The most significant periods were those of Hugh and his son John Wyn (*fl.* 1585), both of them poets, and of the latter's son Hugh (d. 1622), when the family's political influence was at its height. The patronage tradition was maintained into the seventeenth century by John Bodwrda (d. 1648?) whose brother, William Bodwrda (1593–1670), was a transcriber of manuscripts. The tradition ended with John's grandson, Hugh Bodwrda (d. 1694).

Bodychen, a mansion in the parish of Bodwrog, Ang., where the family kept a welcome for itinerant poets. The earliest patron was Llywelyn ap Hwlcyn (d. 1475) of Presaeddfed. Another, Rhys ap Llywelyn (d. c.1503/04), employed *Lewys Môn as his household poet. The tradition was honourably maintained by his son Siôn Wyn (d. 1559), and by three more generations until the death of Siôn Bodychen in 1639. *Gruffudd Hiraethog, *Siôn Brwynog and Wiliam *Cynwal were among the poets received at Bodychen.

Book of Aneirin, The, see under GODODDIN (c.600).

Book of Llandâv, The, see under LLANDAF.

Book of St. Chad, The, also known as **The Lichfield Gospels** and **The Book of Teilo**, is a Latin manuscript containing texts of the Gospels of St. Matthew and St. Mark and part of that of St. Luke. Probably written during the first half of the eighth century, it is in Insular script and its very fine illumination includes portraits of the Evangelists Mark and Luke. There are four large coloured initials and smaller initial letters are also decorated, while on some pages decorative borders frame the text. The illumination, similar to that in *The Book of Lindisfarne*, suggests Northumbrian influence on this manuscript. Its precise origins are not known for certain, but some early Latin entries mention St. *Teilo and these references, together with the evidence of placenames, suggest that the manuscript, early in its history, was probably at *Llandeilo Fawr, Carms. One entry notes that it was given to 'God and St. Teilo on the altar' by Gelhi son of Arihtiud, who had bought it for the price of his best horse. The Book was in the possession of the Church at Lichfield by the end of the tenth century and is now kept in the Cathedral library there.

The manuscript contains several important additional entries, one of which is known as the *Surexit Memorandum* from its initial word. This short memorandum of some sixty-four words, written in Old Welsh with a light sprinkling of Latin words or phrases, may be the earliest extant passage of written Welsh. The text records the dispossession of a person by law of his entitlement to land in a lawsuit between Tutbulc son of Liuit and Elcu son of Gelhig. The disposition and primacy of this memorandum in relation to another additional entry (in Latin) on the same page have been the subject of much scholarly disagreement. It is supported by a list of witnesses at the foot of the page and the first name is that of Teilo. Especially interesting for students of palaeography, language and law, it is in a peculiar script (a small, rather crude majuscule in process of becoming a minuscule), which has been assigned to the eighth century and its language is distinctly conservative and archaic. The entry reveals the use made of written Welsh at least as early as the eighth century to record the settling of legal disputes (not unusual in a gospel-book of that time) and shows the adoption of an especially formal kind of language for this purpose; at the same time, the status of Latin is evident. However, it is impossible to say to what extent this entry indicates a comparatively early shift from an oral to a written transmission in the realm of law.

There is a thorough discussion of the Welsh marginalia in the Lichfield Gospels by Dafydd Jenkins and Morfydd E. Owen in *Cambridge Medieval Celtic Studies* (1983, 1984).

Book of Taliesin, The or **Llyfr Taliesin**, a plain manuscript (N.L.W. MS Peniarth 2), with sober red and blue initials, belongs to a group of five written by a practised scribe in a south or mid-Wales scriptorium in the early fourteenth century. The entire manuscript, copied by John *Davies of Mallwyd between 1631 and 1634, was in Robert *Vaughan's collection at Hengwrt before 1655.

Although its title was not a medieval designation, the manuscript may well have been intended as a compendium of poems, some believed to have been composed by *Taliesin and others pertaining, by reason of their exotic or arcane nature, to the darker shamanistic side of Welsh poetry of which the Taliesin-persona came to be the chief representative. There is a strong case for attributing to the historical Taliesin a core of eight praise-poems to *Urien Rheged and a lament for his son, *Owain ab Urien. Far less certain is the authorship of three other contemporary poems, two to another North British leader, *Gwallog, and one to *Cynan Garwyn of Powys. Two further poems, *'Edmyg Dinbych', a panegyric to the fort at Tenby (c.875–900) and a lament (c.1000–1050) for an Anglesey nobleman, Cynaethwy, testify to the continuity of the formal bardic tradition of laud and lament in the later period.

The remainder of the manuscript consists of poems based on the Taliesin legend, others on religious or biblical subjects, several about heroes of the ancient world such as Alexander and Hercules, together with a number of elegies and prophecies of which the best known is *'Armes Prydein' (c.930). See also HANES TALIESIN.

The manuscript was reproduced with a diplomatic text in J. Gwenogvryn Evans, *Facsimile and Text of the Book of Taliesin* (1910). The poems of the historical Taliesin were edited by Ifor Williams (1960); there is also an

English version, *The Poems of Taliesin* (ed. Ifor Williams and J. E. Caerwyn Williams, 1968), which has a useful survey, with full references, of the manuscript as a whole.

Book of Teilo, The see under BOOK OF ST. CHAD (8th cent.) and TEILO (6th cent.).

Book of the Anchorite, The or *Llyfr Ancr Llanddewibrefi*, a manuscript now kept in the Bodleian Library, Oxford (Jesus College MS CXIX), is the earliest and most extensive collection of Middle Welsh religious texts, having been written on parchment in 1346. Its title is derived from a note by the writer after the preface to the first text which says that it was made, at the request of Llywelyn ap Phylip ap Trahaearn of Cantref Mawr, a nobleman with a love of literature who lived at Rhydodyn, near Llansawel, Carms., by an anchorite of Llanddewibrefi, Cards. In fact, what the anchorite did was to transcribe and compile, not to compose and translate the work. Of the Book's seventeen texts all except one are religious in content.

The manuscript remained for a very long time in the keeping of the Rhydodyn family, for it belonged to Dafydd ap Morgan Fychan, the great-great-grandson of the Dafydd who was *Gruffudd ap Llywelyn's brother. Between 1684 and 1697 it was donated to Jesus College, Oxford, by Thomas Wilkins of Llan-fair in the Vale of Glamorgan. In 1781 it was in the possession of Griffith Roberts of Penmorfa, Eifionydd, who appears to have received it from Richard Thomas of Ynyscynhaearn, Caerns., who had been an under-librarian at Jesus College. In 1800 Owen *Jones (Owain Myfyr) and William *Owen Pughe bought the manuscript from Griffith Roberts and returned it six years later to the College.

The text was edited by John Morris-Jones and John Rhys, *The Eluciarium and Other Tracts in Welsh from Llyvyr Agkyr Llandewivrevi* (1894); see also the article by Idris Foster in the *Proceedings* of the British Academy (vol. XXXVI, 1949) and Thomas Jones in the *Transactions* of the Cardiganshire Antiquarian Society (vol. XII, 1937).

Book of the Vicar of Woking, The or *Llyfr Bicar Woking*, a manuscript (Cardiff 7) of poetry from the period of the *Poets of the Gentry, includes in its 963 pages a total of seventy-four *cywyddau* by *Dafydd ap Gwilym as well as poems by many other poets. An introduction states that the Book was made at the court of Rowland Meyrick (1505–66), Bishop of Bangor, on 3 February 1565 and that its owner was the vicar of Woking, Sir Richard Gruffudd.

Book of Wales, A (1953), an anthology of prose and verse, edited by D. Myrddin *Lloyd and his wife, E. M. Lloyd, for the Collins National Anthologies series. It included, in translation, a miscellany of excerpts from Welsh literature of all periods, from Anglo-Welsh literature and from English writing about Wales and the Welsh, thematically arranged. Expertly compiled, generously illustrated, reasonably priced and the only book of its kind, it proved very popular and ran to many editions for more than twenty-five years.

BOORE, WALTER HUGH (1904–), author. Born and educated in Cardiff, he lived in Birmingham until his retirement, after which he settled in New Quay, Cards. He has published two volumes of verse, *Winter Seas* (1953) and *Eternity is Swift* (1958), seven novels, *The Valley and the Shadow* (1963), *Flower after Rain* (1964), *A Window in High Terrace* (1966), *The Old Hand* (1966), *Cry on the Wind* (1968), *Riot of Riches* (1969) and *Ship to Shore* (1970), and a collection of short stories, *The Odyssey of Dai Lewis* (1983), most of which are set in Wales, as well as a work of philosophy, *First Light: a Study in Belief* (1973).

His son, **Roger Boore** (1938–), the owner of the publishing company *Gwasg y Dref Wen*, is the author of a volume of short stories, *Ymerodraeth y Cymry* (1973), and of several books in Welsh for children.

Bord Gron Ceridwen (lit. 'Ceridwen's round table'), a group of anonymous male writers who, pretending to be women, took the side of the new school of poets, such as T. Gwynn *Jones, W. J. *Gruffydd and R. Silyn *Roberts, against the supporters of the older generation of Dyfed (Evan *Rees) and Pedrog (John Owen *Williams) in the years from 1910 to 1912. The debate began after the appearance in Y *Brython (25 Aug. 1910) of an article entitled 'Y beirdd newydd yn beirniadu'r hen' ('The new poets criticising the old') which raised three questions: the antiquity of *Gorsedd Beirdd Ynys Prydain, the quality of John *Morris-Jones's poetry (which had been attacked by T. Marchant *Williams in The *Nationalist) and the literary standards of the newcomers; the last soon emerged as the principal bone of contention. The controversy, which was an important episode in the renaissance of Welsh letters at the beginning of the twentieth century, was carried on in Y Brython until November 1912 and continued sporadically thereafter. It was re-fired by another anonymous group, supporters of the new school, who called themselves Y Macwyaid ('The Young Lords'), and among whom were E. Tegla *Davies (Y Macwy Hir), Ifor *Williams (Macwy'r Llwyn), R. Williams *Parry (Macwy'r Tes), W. Hughes *Jones and, under the pseudonym Oxoniensis, T. H. *Parry-Williams.

For further details see the article by the editor of *Ysgrifau Beirniadol IX* (ed. J. E. Caerwyn Williams, 1976).

Border Country (1960), the first in a trilogy of novels by Raymond *Williams. Matthew Price, a university lecturer in London, who is its central character, returns to the village of his childhood on the Welsh border to visit his dying father, a railway signalman. The story consists of a series of flashbacks recalling his early days, especially the *General Strike of 1926 and the consequent ironical evolution of one worker, Morgan Rosser, into a small but successful wholesale food entrepreneur whose offer of a job in his new factory Matthew declines. The book is notable for its highly delicate style and the evocation of a rural way of life in the years between the World Wars.

The second novel in the trilogy, *Second Generation* (1964), is set in an old university city where there is also a major car plant. Harold Owen is a union official and his wife Kate a teacher with radical political beliefs. Their son, Peter, is a student at the university where his tutor is Robert Lane, a man of somewhat ineffectual liberal conscience. Less successful than the other two, this novel nonetheless presents characters and incidents of vital interest and has a deeply questioning central attitude.

The third novel, *The Fight for Manod* (1979), begun soon after the first two but laid aside for several years, is a powerful climax to the trilogy, bringing the chief characters together and containing much drama and intrigue. Matthew, now well into middle age by the 1970s, is appointed by Whitehall to study the feasibility of a New Town development in mid-Wales, Peter Owen is his assistant and Robert Lane, now a civil servant, his immediate superior. Matthew's investigations into the project gradually reveal monied interests and machinations with far-reaching consequences.

BORROW, GEORGE (1803–81), English writer, was born at East Dereham, Norfolk, the son of a recruiting officer. Educated mainly in Edinburgh, he was articled at the age of seventeen to a solicitor in Norwich. Studies in philology with William Taylor, Robert Southey's friend, revealed the young man's extraordinary talent for languages and by 1826 he had already published two translations, *Faustus* (from Klinger's German) and *Romantic Ballads* (from the Danish). His book, *Targum* (1835), contained translations from as many as thirty languages. Encouraged by Taylor to think of a literary career, Borrow moved to London after his father's death, only to find himself obliged to earn a living by hackwork under Sir Richard Phillips. To escape from this drudgery, he began to travel, first throughout Britain and then elsewhere in Europe.

His experiences as a colporteur in Spain not merely created in him a virulent anti-Romanism but brought him to write *The Bible in Spain* (1843), his first literary success, though it was preceded by *Gipsies in Spain* (1841), a subject of less general interest. Borrow's affinity with gypsies led him to purchase an estate at Oulton Broad in Norfolk and allow his Romany friends to pitch their tents there. By now enjoying public recognition as an author, he wrote two more books, *Lavengro* (1851) and *Romany Rye* (1857), which were less an account of his earlier travels than an idealization of a way of life hostile to that of the contemporary Establishment. His praise for ale and boxing, his insistence on robust physique and physical prowess (which he possessed himself), his familiarity with gypsies and his railing against the kid-glove writing of Lytton and Disraeli, brought him an exaggerated notoriety as the high priest of the vulgar taste. Zest for the manly tradition and his scorn of genteel humbug cost him thereafter a great part of the readership he had earned, and his subsequent works, from *Wild Wales* (1862) onwards, were not widely read; his book, *Romano-Lavo-Lil: Word-Book of the Romany* (1872), for example, was both esoteric and disregarded. He was, nevertheless, unabashed: Low Church, anti-Romanist and ale-drinking, he remained the enthusiastic traveller so long as his health permitted. His linguistic powers were exercised most unusually, perhaps, in translating the New Testament into Manchu.

Borrow's interest in Welsh, which he had developed in conversations with a Welsh-speaking groom in Norwich long years before, was further demonstrated by his publication of *The Sleeping Bard . . . from the Cambrian-British* (1860), a translation of Ellis *Wynne's *Gweledigaetheu y Bardd Cwsc* (1703). A collection of translations from the Welsh was edited by Ernest *Rhys in *Welsh Poems and Ballads* (1915), and his prose work on the history and literature of Wales by Herbert G. Wright in *Celtic Bards, Chiefs and Kings* (1928).

Biographies of the writer have been published by M. D. Armstrong (1950), B. Vesey-Fitzgerald (1953) and R. R. Myers (1966); see also David Williams, *A World of his Own: The Double Life of George Borrow* (1982) and Michael Collie, *George Borrow, Eccentric* (1982).

BOSSE-GRIFFITHS, KATE (1910–), novelist and scholar, was born in Wittenburg (Lutherstadt), Germany. After studying the Classics and Egyptology, she had a distinguished career in universities and museums in Germany, England and Wales, and since her retirement she has been the Honorary Curator of the Wellcome Museum, Swansea. She has published two novels, *Anesmwyth Hoen* (1941) and *Mae'r Galon wrth y Llyw* (1957), and a collection of stories, *Fy Chwaer Efa* (1944), which are remarkable chiefly on account of their frank discussion of sexual topics. Something of the political philosophy of the group known as *Cylch Cadwgan* (she is the wife of J. Gwyn *Griffiths) is expressed in her non-fiction books,

Mudiadau Heddwch yn yr Almaen (1943), *Bwlch yn y Llen Haearn* (1951), her travel-book, *Trem ar Rwsia a Berlin* (1962) and *Tywysennau o'r Aifft* (1970). Her most recent work is a study of the occult, *Byd y Dyn Hysbys* (1977).

Bosworth, The Battle of, the final battle of the Wars of the Roses, was fought on 22 August 1485. Henry *Tudor, the only surviving Lancastrian claimant to the English throne, having failed in a previous invasion attempt in 1483, landed at Dale, near Milford Haven, Pembs., on 7 August with a force of some two thousand men. Avoiding the Yorkist territory between Milford and London, Henry marched north-eastwards to summon support from Lancastrian north Wales, but had reached the Long Mountain, near Welshpool, before he received any significant additions to his force. At that point there came in, not merely William *Griffith of Penrhyn but Rhys ap Thomas of west Wales (who had followed him cautiously thus far, half a day behind) and, more surprisingly, the Herbert levies from Gwent and Glamorgan. Even so, at Shrewsbury Henry Tudor had no more than five thousand men at his back. King Richard III, surprised that Lord Stanley and his brother Sir William, assigned the duty of guarding the Welsh border, had not engaged the invader, belatedly moved from Nottingham to Leicester. But Lord Stanley, Henry Tudor's stepfather, refused the King's summons to attend him, keeping his force some miles off on the flank of the armies as they met two miles south of Market Bosworth, Leics.

Richard had twice as many troops as Henry and the advantage of the high ground of Ambien Hill, occupied on the morning of the battle. The Earl of Oxford, commanding for Henry Tudor, advanced uphill but was assailed by the Duke of Norfolk coming down from the brow: Oxford was beaten back, but Norfolk was killed. Richard, appraised of this and sighting Henry on the slope of the next hill westwards, risked a charge from the northern end of his battle line in the hope of engaging him before Oxford could recover. The violence of his attack almost reached Henry's person: the Tudor standard fell but was recovered and the Welshmen closed ranks. Richard's advance, meanwhile, had carried him across Sir William Stanley's front and the latter, judging his moment, attacked the King from the flank. Richard and most of his bodyguard were killed and the remainder fled. According to popular tradition, Henry found the crown under a hawthorn bush, which is no more than to say that he rules most safely whose opponent is dead.

Henry Tudor, though a Lancastrian, was also a realist who had engaged himself to marry Elizabeth of York if he won the throne. Although Yorkist attacks continued, Henry's good sense and moderation commended themselves to a country sick of strife and, never a faction-leader, he allowed the wounds to heal. Bosworth's importance is that it established a dynasty, perhaps the most impressive in Britain's ascertainable history, which was to last more than a hundred years. For Wales its significance, though immediately proud, was ultimately less happy. The expectation of a second *Arthur, known in Welsh *vaticination as *Y Mab Darogan* ('The Son of Prophecy') who would reconquer Britain for the Welsh, was doomed to disappointment. Arthur, Henry VII's son, died at the age of fifteen, and Welsh sentiment at court was gradually defeated by the necessity of governing the country from London. The court's attraction, and the grants of lands in England to Welshmen who had fought at Bosworth, drew from Wales many of its native gentry. A generation thus lost its natural leaders and the appointment in Wales of a few Welsh-speaking bishops and Welsh-born sheriffs proved inadequate protection against the centralizing tendencies which appeared in the reign of Henry VIII.

For further details see the article by W. T. Williams, 'Henry Richmond's Itinerary to Bosworth', in *Y Cymmrodor* (vol. XXIX, 1919), the article by S. B. Chrimes, 'The landing place of Henry of Richmond, 1485', in *Welsh History Review* (vol. 2, 1964), A. L. Rowse, *Bosworth Field and the Wars of the Roses* (1966), and Emyr Wyn Jones, *Bosworth Field: a Welsh Retrospect* (1984).

Botryddan, a mansion on the border of the parishes of Rhuddlan and Diserth, Flints., the home of the Conways, an immigrant family who maintained the tradition of bardic patronage, especially after 1475. *Tudur Aled was probably among the first poets to visit the house during the time of John Conway (Siôn Aer Ifanc; 1457?–1523/24); the tradition was continued for a further five generations until the death of Sir John Conway in 1641. Other branches of the family patronized poets at Sychtyn and Llaneurgain.

Boudica or **Boadicea** (1st cent.), Queen of the Iceni, a Belgic tribe living south of the Wash, is known in Welsh tradition as Buddug (E. Victoria). The death of her husband, Prasutagas, about AD 59, presented the corrupt Roman Procurator Catus with an opportunity of despoiling the Iceni. In AD 61, after Boudica had been flogged and her two daughters raped, the tribe rose, seeking vengeance. They defeated the IXth Legion, sacked the Roman capital of Colchester (Camelodunum) and the port of London (Londinium), and went on to take St. Albans (Verulamium), capital of the Catuvellauni, who were now the Iceni's allies. The Roman governor, Suetonius Paulinus, who had been quelling the last British resistance in Anglesey, was too late to save Londinium but, retiring, awaited Boudica's forces near High Cross on Watling Street. There, although outnumbered by ten to one, the disciplined Romans cut the unruly, booty-laden Iceni to pieces. Boudica, red of hair and huge of frame, fled home to die before Paulinus began to ravage her tribal territory.

For further details see Ian Andrews, *Boudicca's Revolt* (1972), G. Webster, *Boudicca: the British Revolt against Rome* (1978) and Charles Kightly, *Folk Heroes of Britain* (1982).

BOWEN, BEN (1878–1903), poet. A native of Treorci, Rhondda, Glam., he began work in the local colliery when he was twelve years old, by which time he was said to be a competent *englynwr*. Five years later he won the *Chair at the National Eisteddfod held in Penrhiw-ceibr, the youngest poet ever to do so. He went on to study in the Academy at Pontypridd and then at University College, Cardiff, where he mastered the classical languages and German. His long *pryddest* to William *Williams (Pantycelyn) was placed second in the National Eisteddfod of 1900. After a period of ill-health, he went in 1901 to South Africa to recuperate, a public fund having been organized on his behalf. The theological articles which he published on his return in 1902 caused controversy because of their unorthodoxy and he was expelled from his chapel, Moriah, Pentre. His health then deteriorated rapidly and he died before fulfilling his early promise as a poet.

He is usually linked with the *Bardd Newydd* and the hyper-philosophical tendencies of that school marred some of his work. One volume of his poems, *Durtur y Deffro* (1897), was published during his lifetime; others, prepared for publication by his brother David Bowen (Myfyr Hefin) and published posthumously, include *Rhyddiaith Ben Bowen* (1909), *Blagur Awen Ben Bowen* (1915), *Ben Bowen yn Neheudir Affrica* (1928) and *Ben Bowen i'r Ifanc* (1928).

For further details see David Bowen (Myfyr Hefin), *Cofiant a Barddoniaeth Ben Bowen* (1904).

BOWEN, DAVID JAMES (1925–), scholar. A native of Dinas, Pembs., he was educated at the University College of Wales, Aberystwyth, and joined the staff of the Welsh Department there in 1953; he was given a personal chair in 1980. The chief historian of Welsh poetry between the fourteenth and sixteenth centuries, he has written specifically about the two great poets of that period, *Dafydd ap Gwilym and *Gruffudd Hiraethog, in a series of substantial articles which are most important contribution to Welsh scholarship. He has also published *Barddoniaeth yr Uchelwyr* (1956) and *Gruffudd Hiraethog a'i Oes* (1958).

BOWEN, EDWARD ERNEST (1836–1901), poet. Born near Chepstow, Mon., where his father was a curate, he became a master at Harrow in 1859 and spent the rest of his career at the school. He is remembered as the author of the Harrow School Song, 'Forty Years On', written in 1872, which is to be found in his only book, *Harrow Songs and Other Verses* (1886).

BOWEN, EMRYS GEORGE (1900–83), geographer, was born at Carmarthen and held the Gregynog Chair of Geography and Anthropology at the University College of Wales, Aberystwyth, from 1946 until his retirement in 1968. The main focus of his interest was Historical Geography and his first published book was *Wales, A Study in Geography and History* (1941). His concern with settlement studies led him into extensive work on the *Age of the Saints, best represented by his two books, *The Settlements of the Celtic Saints in Wales* (1954) and *Saints, Seaways and Settlements* (1969). This theme was developed in both time and space by his *Britain and the Western Seaways* (1972); he also wrote an account of the life of *Dewi Sant (1981). He was a scholar of the broadest interests, his writings ranging over aspects of the geography, archaeology, history (especially the proto-history of the Dark Ages), culture and society of Wales.

The volume *Geography, Culture and Habitat* (ed. H. Carter and W. K. D. Davies, 1976), which brought together a number of his shorter works in honour of his seventy-fifth birthday, includes an outline of E. G. Bowen's polymathic career, an appreciation of his work and a complete bibliography to 1975.

BOWEN, EUROS (1904–), poet, was born at Treorci in the Rhondda Valley, the son of a Nonconformist minister; Geraint *Bowen is his brother. Intending to enter the ministry with the Independents, he was educated at the Presbyterian College, Carmarthen, at the University College of Wales, Aberystwyth, at University College, Swansea, and at Mansfield and St. Catherine's Colleges, Oxford, but he completed his education at St. David's College, Lampeter, before taking up his duties as a parish priest of the Church in Wales. After a curacy at Wrexham, Denbs., he became rector of Llangywair and Llanuwchllyn, near Bala, Mer. On his retirement in 1973 he returned to live in Wrexham.

He began to write poetry in earnest during the winter of 1947 in the snow-bound vicarage of Llangywair, at the same time as he founded the magazine *Y *Fflam*. In the following year he won the *Crown at the National Eisteddfod with his *pryddest*, 'O'r Dwyrain', repeating his success in 1950 with another *pryddest* in *cynghanedd* entitled 'Difodiant'. In 1963 the *awdl* entitled 'Genesis' which he entered for the *Chair competition proved to be too abstruse for two of the adjudicators. Since then he has been one of the most prolific of contemporary Welsh poets, publishing the following volumes of poetry: *Cerddi* (1957), *Cerddi Rhydd* (1961), *Myfyrion* (1963), *Cylch o Gerddi* (1970), *Achlysuron* (1970), *Elfennau* (1972), *Cynullion* (1976), *O'r Corn Aur* (1977), *Amrywion* (1980), *Dan Groes y Deau* (1980), *Masg*

Minos (1981), *Gwynt yn y Canghennau* (1982), *O Bridd i Bridd* (1983) and *Detholion* (1984). He has also translated from Greek into Welsh the two Oedipus plays of Sophocles under the titles *Oidipos Frenin* (1972) and *Oidipos yn Colonos* (1979), as well as *Electra* (1984) and Athanasius's theological classic on the Incarnation of the Word (1977). From Latin he has translated Virgil's *Eclogues* (1975) and from the French a selection from the work of the Symbolists, *Beirdd Simbolaidd Ffrainc* (1980).

Euros Bowen has always been concerned with experimentation in both language and prosody, and in his attempts to combine *cynghanedd* with new modes of expression many critics have seen him as an heir to T. Gwynn *Jones. But he has a more stable religious faith than his great predecessor and, with his knowledge of languages both classical and modern, he is more open to influences from other literatures and other arts. A number of the poems in *Cerddi* (1957) are in the form of a metrical unit which he calls an *ugeined*, his own invention. In *Cerddi Rhydd* (1961) he dispensed even with the line and wrote in rhythmical paragraphs. Although some have detected the influence of the French Symbolists on his poems, he considers himself a Sacramentalist rather than a Symbolist because to him words are more important than images. In the poems in *Myfyrion* (1963) the rhythm is effectively engaged with the old *cynghanedd* metres and in *Cylch o Gerddi* (1970) typographical devices are employed. The principal medium in his later volumes is free verse and for some readers they are the ones more easily understood, but for this highly self-conscious poet the attraction of *cynghanedd* remains. The volumes, *O'r Corn Aur*, *Dan Groes y Deau* and *Masg Minos* record impressions of the poet's visits to Asia Minor, Istanbul, Australia and Crete respectively.

He claims to have rejected from the beginning the tradition of 'photographic poetry' and the customary use of images as ornamentation, preferring to use them as the very medium of expression. Furthermore, in spite of his association with the group known as *Cylch Cadwgan, he came to feel that poetry should not be regarded as a vehicle for the communication of ideas and that poets who give lyrical expression to their feelings about the natural world should not for that reason be disregarded. Against the tendency to exalt the poet as prophet or teacher he argues in favour of the principle that the poet has a priestly or sacramental role. On the other hand, he does not always succeed in concealing his own Christian convictions and it cannot be said that he delights in nature for its own sake. For him, nature is a treasury of images, although his method of 'imaging thought' causes some readers to find his work difficult or even obscure.

For a critical appreciation of this poet's work see *Barddoniaeth Euros Bowen* (1977) by Alan Llwyd, a study to which he responded in a forthright manner in his volume *Trin Cerddi* (1978). A selection of Euros Bowen's poems in his own English versions was published in 1974. There is an essay on the poet by R. Gerallt Jones in *Ansawdd y Seiliau* (1972). See also an interview given to the magazine *Mabon* (ed. Gwyn Thomas, 1969), an article by Dafydd Elis Thomas in *Poetry Wales* (vol. 5, no. 3, Spring, 1970), the article by Gwyn Thomas in *Dyrnaid o Awduron Cyfoes* (ed. D. Ben Rees, 1975) and a note on the poet by John Rowlands in *Profiles* (1980).

BOWEN, GERAINT (1915–   ), poet, critic and editor. Born at Llanelli, Carms., a brother of Euros *Bowen, he was educated at University College, Cardiff, and became a schoolmaster and later a member of Her Majesty's Inspectorate of Schools. At the National Eisteddfod in 1946 he won the *Chair with his *awdl*, 'Moliant i'r Amaethwr', a poem of remarkable craftsmanship which demonstrated his mastery of the strict metres. He has also edited four volumes of literary criticism, *Y Traddodiad Rhyddiaith* (1970), *Y Traddodiad Rhyddiaith yn yr Oesau Canol* (1974), *Y Traddodiad Rhyddiaith yn yr Ugeinfed Ganrif* (1976) and *Ysgrifennu Creadigol* (1972). As editor of *Y Faner* (*Baner ac Amserau Cymru*) from 1977 to 1978 and as Archdruid from 1979 to 1981, he won a reputation as an outspoken and uncompromising Nationalist. Among his other publications are an index to John *Morris-Jones's *Cerdd Dafod* (1947), as well as *Gwasanaeth y Gwŷr Newydd* (1970), *Atlas Meirionydd* (1973) and *Bwyd Llwy o Badell Awen* (1977). A selection of his poems is to be found in the volume *Cerddi* (1984).

Bowmen of Agincourt, The, the Welsh archers whose part in the battle of Agincourt (1415) secured a victory for Henry V against the French. In his story 'The Bowmen', first published in *The London Evening News* (29 Sept. 1914), Arthur Machen (Arthur *Jones) used this historical fact in a fictional account of how, at the battle of Mons in August of that year, the archers' ghosts had come to the aid of a British company by discharging their arrows against the German positions. They were described as 'a long line of shapes, with a shining about them' and their arrows were said to kill without leaving visible wounds. Within a week, Machen's bowmen had been transformed in the popular imagination into 'The Angels of Mons' and, much to his distress, what he had written as palpable fiction had been credited as fact, especially by some jingoists who suggested that it was unpatriotic to doubt it.

Boyce, Max (1943–   ), folk-singer, was born in Glyn Neath, Glam., where he later worked as a miner and where he still lives. He won a local reputation during the early 1970s with his songs and ballads about *rugby, coal-mining and the industrial valleys of south Wales. His fame as one of the most popular entertainers in contemporary Wales is attributable not only to his many records and television appearances, but also to his zeal for the game of rugby, which grows even more partisan when Wales plays against England. Some critics regard him as a caricature of a certain type of Welshman, a 'rugby-fool', but this is too harsh a view: Welsh-speaking and a patriot, Max Boyce is the manifestation of a cultural phenomenon which requires more careful analysis. His best songs, such as 'The Pontypool Front Row', 'Duw, it's Hard', 'Hymns and Arias', 'The Devil's Marking me' and 'Rhondda Grey', share with the verse of Idris *Davies (whose poems he sometimes sings), the authentic quality of modern folk-song. Others are very funny and only a few are over-sentimental. The fact remains that many are widely sung, especially among those for whom Max Boyce has become a troubadour of their own place and experience.

BOYER, HYDWEDD (1912–70), novelist, a native of Allt-wen, Pontardawe, Glam. He travelled widely as a military cartographer during the Second World War and was the author of three novels, *Ym Mhoethder y Tywod* (1960), *Pryfed ar Wydr* (1965) and *Ffarwel Ha'* (1974), and of two books for children, *Anturiaethwyr y Ganrif Hon* (1963) and *I'r Ynysoedd* (1967).

Brackenbury, Augustus (d. 1874), see under RHYFEL Y SAIS BACH (1820–26).

Brad (lit. 'Betrayal'; 1958), a 'historical tragedy' by Saunders *Lewis, is based on events in France during the German army officers' plot to kill Hitler (20 July 1944). Kaisar von Hofacker, a Protestant, convinced that Hitler is an agent of the Devil and that European civilization is about to be engulfed by the Communist incursion from the East, attempts to persuade von Kluge, German Supreme Commander in the West, to join the plot and arrange a truce with the Allies so that they can reach Berlin before the Red Army. The plot fails and von Kluge, bound to Hitler by a personal debt, hands the conspirators over to the Gestapo. Else, von Hofacker's mistress, attempts to save him by giving herself to a Gestapo officer, but von Hofacker rebukes her bitterly for betraying their love, thus completing the circuit of treachery, and goes bravely to his death. In this play Saunders Lewis is concerned to show that an individual can influence the course of history by his or her action or inaction, and that the hopelessness of a cause is no reason for its abandonment.

For a discussion of the play's merits and historical background see the articles by Dafydd Glyn Jones in *Barn* (no. 68, June, 1968) and Prys Morgan in *Ysgrifau Beirniadol V* (ed. J. E. Caerwyn Williams, 1970). An English translation of the play by Joseph Clancy was published in 1985 under the title *Treason*.

BRADFORD, SIÔN or **JOHN** (1706–85), poet, of Betws, *Tir Iarll, Glam., was one of a small circle of literary men in that district during the early part of the eighteenth century. A weaver, fuller and dyer, he belonged to a family which had moved from Bradford-on-Avon in the previous century. As a young man he studied the bardic tradition and collected Welsh manuscripts. His own verse is not important, but Iolo Morganwg (Edward *Williams), who received instruction from him, claimed him as an heir to the druidic and bardic system which, Iolo insisted, had persisted over the centuries in Tir Iarll, maintaining that it was in Bradford's manuscripts he had found much of the material which was later shown to be of his own invention.

For further details see G. J. Williams, *Traddodiad Llenyddol Morgannwg* (1948) and Ceri W. Lewis, 'The Literary History of Glamorgan from 1550 to 1770' in *Glamorgan County History* (vol. IV, ed. Glanmor Williams, 1974).

BRADNEY, JOSEPH ALFRED (1859–1933), county historian, was an Englishman whose contribution to the public life of Wales, including services to the *National Library and the *National Museum, were recognized when he was knighted in 1924. Among his publications were *The Diary of Walter Powell* (1907), *Acts of the Bishop of Llandaff* (1908), *Llyfr Baglan* (1910) and *A Dissertation on Three Books* (1923). He learned Welsh and wrote verse in Latin, publishing *Carmina Jocosa* (1916) and *Carmen* (1923), but his most important work was undoubtedly the monumental history of his adopted county, *The History of Monmouthshire* (1904, 1932).

Braint Hir (early 7th cent.), the nephew of *Cadwallon ap Cadfan, king of north Wales. According to *Brut y Brenhinedd, he joined forces with his uncle to oppose attempts by Edwin of Northumbria to share the kingship. In the ensuing war, they tried to flee to Brittany, only to be shipwrecked on the island of Garneria. Such was Cadwallon's distress that he would neither eat nor drink for three days. At last his appetite was whetted by the thought of meat, but Braint failed to kill any game. In desperation, Braint cut off a slice of his own thigh and the king, after eating it, recovered.

Braint Teilo (lit. 'Teilo's privilege'), a passage of Old Welsh or Early Middle Welsh in *The Book of Llandâv* (see under LLANDAF) concerning the ancient charter accorded to the church of *Teilo by the kings of Glamorgan, its rights before the law and the authority of the state; of its two sections the second is the earlier, dating from between 950 and 1090. It is a written example of the idea of privilege which is found not only in the Welsh Laws but also in ancient poetry. The first section (*c.* 1110–29) belongs to the Norman period and represents the reaction of the community of Llandaf to political developments early in the twelfth century and their threat to the strength, profit and independence of the Church.

The passage is discussed in an article by Wendy Davies in the *Bulletin* of the Board of Celtic Studies (vol. XXVI, 1975).

Brân or **Bendigeidfran**, the son of *Llŷr, is described in the Second Branch of *Pedair Cainc y Mabinogi* as 'the crowned king of the Isle of Britain'. He was of gigantic build and, on his way to Ireland to avenge the wrong done to his sister *Branwen, he waded through the sea alongside his fleet. From the incident in which he lay across the river Llinon, his men using his body as a pontoon, is derived the famous proverb '*A fo ben bid bont*' ('Let he who is leader be a bridge'). After the slaughter in Ireland the seven survivors brought his head to the White Mount in London for burial, having spent years feasting at Harlech and on the island of *Gwales.

It has been suggested that Brân was a half-human form of one of the ancient Celtic gods. The Old Irish legend known in English as *The Voyage of Brân* tells how King Brân sails from Ireland to the Islands of the Otherworld. The two Brâns may be one and the same or, at least, it may be that some elements from the Irish legend went to the making of the Second Branch of the *Mabinogi*. There is also a strong tendency in the Irish legend to Christianize the old pagan material, which could be the source of the adjective *Bendigaid* ('Blessed') as ascribed to Brân in Wales. Most scholars believe that the Welsh traditions about Brân are the source for the medieval French romances of Bron the Fisher King.

For further references see Rachel Bromwich, *Trioedd Ynys Prydein* (1961) and P. Mac Cana, *Branwen Daughter of Llŷr* (1958).

Brangwyn, Frank (1867–1956), painter, was born in Bruges of Welsh parentage. He began his career in the workshops of William Morris and became famous as a painter of large landscapes and scenes from mythology and history, of which the British Empire Panels, commissioned in 1925 and hung in the Guildhall, Swansea, are typical examples.

Branwen, the daughter of *Llŷr and the wife of *Matholwch, King of Ireland, in the Second Branch of *Pedair Cainc y Mabinogi*. During the first year of her reign she bears a son, named Gwern, but her happiness is shattered when *Efnysien, half-brother to Brân and herself, insults the Irish by maiming their horses, thus causing war between Ireland and Wales. As a consequence, Branwen is put to work in the kitchen of the Irish court but, after three years of this humiliation, she manages to send a message to Wales by means of a tame starling. Brân, her brother, then invades Ireland and she tries, without success, to reconcile the two sides, lest they destroy each other. Defeated in the subsequent conflict, only seven of the Welsh return from Ireland, but Branwen is with them. They land at Aber Alaw in Anglesey where the Queen, with a deep sigh, declares that two good islands have been laid waste because of her: she dies, heart-broken, and is buried on the banks of the river Alaw.

The story of Branwen was the subject of a television play by Saunders *Lewis which was first broadcast in 1971 and published in the volume *Dramau'r Parlwr* (1975). The play is not so much a retelling of the tale, however, as an exploration of Efnysien's nihilism which, despite Branwen's sense of responsibility, destroys her and much else besides. The playwright discusses this interpretation in an essay in *Ysgrifau Beirniadol V* (ed. J. E. Caerwyn Williams, 1970).

For further details see P. Mac Cana, *Branwen Daughter of Llŷr* (1958), Derick S. Thomson, *Branwen Verch Lyr* (1961) and Rachel Bromwich, *Trioedd Ynys Prydein* (1961).

Braslun o Hanes Llenyddiaeth Gymraeg (lit. 'An outline of the history of Welsh literature'), a projected series of monographs by Saunders *Lewis. Only the first volume was published (1932), dealing with its subject down to 1535, although it may be assumed that the substance of others was incorporated elsewhere in the author's work. The book has chapters on *Taliesin, the *Gogynfeirdd, the *Poets of the Gentry, *Dafydd ap Gwilym, 'the Oxford School' (*Siôn Cent and others) and *Y Ganrif Fawr* ('The Great Century', 1435–1535). They are remarkable for their attempt to place medieval Welsh literature, particularly the poetry of the late medieval period, within the context of evolving European thought. Some of the theories of the first two chapters, such as the attempts to explain the *englynion* of *Canu Llywarch Hen* as bardic exercises and to connect the poetry of the *Gogynfeirdd* with *la poésie pure*, have been largely abandoned by scholars. But the emphasis of the last four chapters on the neo-Platonic and neo-Aristotelian elements underlying the poetics of the period have, in more or less modified form, become part of the received orthodoxy of Welsh literary history. The book is full of fresh, penetrating insights and is quite brilliantly written. See also MEISTRI'R CANRIF-OEDD (1973).

Brawd Llwyd, Y (lit. 'The grey brother'), a Franciscan monk who, in a *traethodl* by *Dafydd ap Gwilym, rebukes the poet in the confessional for his pre-occupation with the love of girls and with composing *cywyddau* in their praise. Dafydd, advised to pray for the good of his soul, defends himself on the grounds that God is less severe than the Friar, that there is a time for everything and that his kind of poetry, like that of the psalmist David, is as necessary for human well-being as prayer and hymns.

Bredwardine or **Brodorddyn**, a village and castle in Herefordshire near the borders of the old counties of Breconshire and Radnorshire, was the home of the main branch of the Vaughan family. The castle was built by order of Walter Seys who married the heiress of Sir Walter Bredwardine and added to his wealth, land and influence by currying royal favour under Edward III. In the time of his grandson, Roger, who is believed to have died at Agincourt (1415), Brodorddyn became a famous resort for itinerant poets. By his marriage to Gwladus, the daughter of *Dafydd Gam, two further branches of the family were established at *Hergest and Tre-tŵr (Tretower). Welsh poets were given patronage for three more generations at Brodorddyn and when the main branch of the family removed to *Dunraven, Glam., the tradition continued there. Some poetry survives to the family who took their place at Brodorddyn, the Vaughans of *Porthamal. Francis *Kilvert, the diarist, who was vicar of Bredwardine for the last two years of his life, is buried in the churchyard there.

BRERETON, JANE (**Melissa**; 1685–1740), poet. Born at Mold, Flints., she married the English dramatist Thomas Brereton in 1711 and, after his death in 1722, settled in Wrexham, Denbs. Under her pseudonym she contributed verse to *The Gentleman's Magazine*. A volume of her work was published posthumously under the title *Poems on Several Occasions* (1744).

Breuddwyd Pabydd wrth ei Ewyllys (lit. 'A Papist's dream as he would have it be'; early 1890s), a series of essays by Emrys ap Iwan (Robert Ambrose *Jones) which was first published in the periodical Y *Geninen. The author imagines that he is listening to a lecture on 'The Cause of the Fall of Protestantism in Wales' by a Jesuit priest, Father Morgan, in the year 2012. The country has returned to *Roman Catholicism, the faith of a Church more concerned with Welsh culture than are the Nonconformist denominations, and the language flourishes among the common people as their national respect is restored and their horizons widened. The deliberate exaggeration of the essays was intended to pierce the complacency of the author's countrymen in matters affecting Wales and its language, and as such they are among his most trenchant writings. The essays were republished in the series *Llyfrau'r Ford Gron* (1931).

Breuddwyd Pawl Ebostol (lit. 'The vision of the apostle Paul'), a religious work (earliest text in Peniarth MS 3, c.1300) comprising three different, anonymous, prose translations of *Visio*

Sancti Pauli, an apocryphal work of unknown authorship and early Christian origin about St. Paul's visions when swept up into the third heaven (2 Cor. 12: 2–3); it was very popular in medieval Wales.

Breuddwyd Rhonabwy (lit. 'Rhonabwy's dream'), a native Arthurian tale, the only medieval copy of which is found in The *Red Book of Hergest*. Various dates for its origin have been suggested, ranging from the mid-twelfth century to the late thirteenth. The tale is set in *Powys during the reign of *Madog ap Maredudd. While searching for the prince's brother, Rhonabwy spends a night at the hall of Heilyn Goch, the son of Cadwgan ab Iddon. As he sleeps he has a splendid dream in which he is transported to *Arthur's encampment on an island in the river Severn. The complex narrative, related in a highly polished style, contains several unrelated scenes and characters from different periods in Welsh history, as well as much social and literary satire contrasting the great men of Arthurian times with those of the author's own day. The story is the first example of the use of the dream-motif as a framework for a story in Welsh literature. The same motif appears in the tale of *Brutus in *Brut y Brenhinedd* and in Geoffrey Keating's history of Ireland, *Forus Feasna Érenn* (1900).

The text of *Breuddwyd Rhonabwy*, with introduction and notes, was edited by Melville Richards (1948); see also the article by Dafydd Glyn Jones in *Y Traddodiad Rhyddiaith yn yr Oesau Canol* (ed. Geraint Bowen, 1974).

Breviary of Britayne, The (1575), see under Commentarioli Descriptionis Britannicae Fragmentum (1572).

'Briodas, Y' (lit. 'The marriage'; 1927), a *pryddest* by Caradog *Prichard with which he won the *Crown at the National Eisteddfod in 1927. It consists of a series of dramatic lyrics recited by five characters: the woman, the mountain, the river, the yew and the spirit. The woman is a widow but still feels an unbreakable attachment to her dead husband. In the first part she swears to be faithful to him for ever and in the third, some twenty years later, she dances maniacally in the delusion that he has returned to remarry her. In 'Penyd', a poem which may be seen as a sequel to 'Y Briodas', the woman is in an asylum. Like much of the author's work, these poems are based on the fate of his own mother and are all the more moving for that reason.

There is an essay on the poem by Saunders Lewis in his *Meistri a'u Crefft* (1981); see also the article by Dafydd Glyn Jones in *Dyrnaid o Awduron Cyfoes* (ed. D. Ben Rees, 1975).

Briog (c.440–c.530), a saint who laboured in more than one of the Celtic lands; his name also occurs in the form Briomaglus. Educated in

Paris by Germanus (not the saint who came to Britain in the second quarter of the 5th cent.), he spent his life partly in Wales and partly in Cornwall and Brittany where he is commemorated in several place-names, such as St. Brieuc. His Life was first composed in the eleventh century by a cleric of Angers, where the saint's remains rested from the ninth century to the French Revolution (1789). Briog, on account of his generosity, is the patron saint of bag-makers and his feast-day is 1 May.

Britain, the name of the Island once inhabited by the Brythonic *Celts and now applied to the modern State. The concept of Britishness has played a vital part in the history of Wales over the centuries. The word 'Prydain' is found very frequently in early Welsh literature as meaning the Isle of Britain and 'Prydain Fawr' ('Great Britain') was used to distinguish it from Brittany; the Picts of Scotland were known as 'Prydyn'. Caesar referred to 'Britannia' and to its people as 'Britanni'.

The confusion and ambiguity inherent in the name can be traced to medieval times. Although the Welsh, as the descendants of the Brythoniaid or Ancient Britons, had a prior claim to call themselves British, and still regarded Britain as their birthright, they later began to use the words 'Cymry' and *'Cymru' as applying to themselves and their territory. From the *Tudor period onwards, even as late as the nineteenth century, the word 'British' was sometimes used to mean Welsh and sometimes applied to the State of Great Britain. For example, Thomas *Jones's (1648?–1713) Welsh dictionary of 1688 is entitled The British Language in its Lustre. In English, the word 'British' gradually came to be used in the political sense after the union of England and Scotland in 1603 and even more after 1707. Some of the Welsh took to calling themselves 'Cambro-Britons' at that time.

Since then, as if aware that the word 'British' originally referred to the Britons or Welsh, the English have been reluctant to use it with any consistency. In current English usage the word 'England' can refer to the United Kingdom or to that part of it which excludes Wales, Scotland and Northern Ireland, while the word 'Britain' is often used, especially in wartime, to denote the political State which is dominated by the largest partner, England. The terms 'England' and 'Britain' are, for many English people, interchangeable but 'Britain' and 'British' are no longer applied solely to Wales and the Welsh.

A philosophical and political study of the question, in particular the concept of a British State in which the national identity of the Welsh and Scots is submerged or denied by an English hegemony, was made by J. R. Jones in his pamphlet Prydeindod (1966).

Britannia (1586), an account by the English writer William Camden (1551–1623) of his antiquarian tours through Britain in search of Roman remains. Six Latin editions appeared during his lifetime, the last translated into English by Philemon Holland in 1610. Camden, who had learned Welsh, presented Britain, first of all, within the frame of the divisions into the Celtic tribal areas recorded by the classical geographers. Wales, which he visited between 1589 and 1596, is considered as the land of three peoples, the *Silures, the *Demetae and the *Ordovices, before it is observed as thirteen shires. Some of Camden's material was taken from Leland. For Wales his main medieval sources were *Gerald de Barri (Giraldus Cambrensis) and William of Malmesbury but for later information, for example on *Owain Glyndŵr's conflict with Sir *Dafydd Gam, he went to historians such as Robert *Vaughan of Hengwrt. The best of its kind for two centuries, Britannia was subject to two major revisions with copious additions, the first by Edmund Gibson (1695) and the second (1789), more pious than radical, by the topographical collector, Richard Gough, who was helped in the Welsh section by Thomas *Pennant.

A facsimile of Edmund Gibson's edition of Britannia was published in 1971 with an introduction by Stuart Piggott; those parts of the work dealing with Wales were reprinted under the editorship of Gwyn Walters in 1984.

British and Foreign School Society, The, founded in 1814 for the purpose of establishing elementary schools on a non-denominational basis, had to operate prior to 1833 without financial support from the Government. It paid scant attention to Wales during its early years, only two schools being established in the north and about eight in the south. In 1833 the Society shared with the *National Society a Government grant of £20,000 and although it was to receive some fifty thousand pounds from the Government between 1833 and 1844, no more than two thousand pounds was spent on schools in Wales. This neglect was the consequence of a lack of leadership in Wales and widespread suspicion of the Government's intentions. Another factor was the poverty of the common people who were expected to collect money on a pound-for-pound basis before they became eligible for a Government grant. It was this state of affairs which spurred Hugh *Owen (1804–81) to write a famous letter to his compatriots in 1843, exhorting them to establish British Schools, as a result of which the Society appointed John Phillips (1810–67), a Calvinistic Methodist minister, as its agent in north Wales. Despite many obstacles, Phillips slowly succeeded in arousing the interest of the people; more than a hundred British Schools had been built by 1854.

In south Wales the Voluntaryists, who rejected all financial aid from the Government, were so influential that the Society refrained from appointing an agent for a while. Between 1845 and 1853 the Voluntaryists opened between three hundred and four hundred schools in the south without Government aid, as well as a Training College for teachers at Brecon in 1846. By 1853, however, Voluntaryism was on the decline in south Wales: in that year it was conceded by David *Rees, and others, that the acceptance of Government aid was inevitable and the Society appointed William Roberts (Nefydd) as agent for south Wales. By the time of the Education Act of 1870, more than three hundred British Schools had been opened in Wales with the assistance of Government grants. Unlike the National or Church Schools, the British Schools were entirely non-denominational and were therefore attended by children of Nonconformist families, the majority of the population. Unfortunately, like all other schools in the nineteenth century, these schools attempted to teach monoglot Welsh children through the medium of English, with the direst consequences.

For an account of the Society's work see the chapter by A. L. Trott in The History of Education in Wales (ed. Jac L. Williams and Gwilym Rees Hughes, 1978), and Idwal Jones, 'The Voluntary System at Work: a history of the British School Society' in the Transactions of the Honourable Society of Cymmrodorion (1931–32); see also J. R. Webster, 'Dyheadau'r Bedwaredd Ganrif ar Bymtheg' in Ysgrifau ar Addysg (vol. IV, ed. Jac L. Williams, 1966) and Ieuan D. Thomas, Addysg yng Nghymru yn y Bedwaredd Ganrif ar Bymtheg (1972).

British Martial, The, see OWEN, JOHN (1564?–1628?).

Brogynin, see under DAFYDD AP GWILYM (fl. 1320–70).

Brogyntyn, a manor and estate (also known as **Porkington**) in the parish of Selatyn, near Oswestry, Salop., which grew through marriage settlements over the centuries to be one of the great houses of north Wales. Its importance was first established by the marriage of Sir William Maurice, the heir of Clenennau, to the heiress of John Wyn Lacon of Brogyntyn and Llanddyn, in the sixteenth century. The surname Maurice gave way to Owen with the marriage of the family heiress to John Owen of Bodsilin and the house belonged to Owens for eight generations thereafter. On the marriages of William Owen to the heiress of the Anwyl family of Parc in 1648, and of his son, Sir Robert Owen, to the heiress of Glyn, Talsarnau and Ystumcegid, Llanfihangel y Pennant, the Owen family's wealth was substantially increased. By today the family's home is at Glyn, Talsarnau, Mer. The Owen name came to an end in 1777 with the marriage of an heiress to Owen Ormsby. In 1815 their daughter married William Gore who adopted the surname Ormsby-Gore and the son of that marriage was the first Lord Harlech.

The Brogyntyn estate consisted not only of land but also of valuable collections of books, manuscripts and other documents which are now housed (with the exception of the printed books) in the National Library of Wales. In 1934 the third Lord Harlech gave a generous selection of Welsh and other manuscripts (described by A. J. Horwood in the report of the Historical Manuscripts Commission, 1871) to the National Library. Further gifts were made in 1945 by the fourth Lord Harlech and his son, the Lord Harlech who died in 1985, the greater part of which reflects the family's interest in the literature and culture of Wales over four centuries.

The family's connections are traced in an article by the fourth Lord Harlech on the printed treasures of Brogyntyn in the Journal of the National Library of Wales (vol. V, 1948); for details about the contents of the manuscripts see the series of articles by E. D. Jones in the same magazine (vols. V-VIII, 1948–53).

BROMWICH, RACHEL (1915–   ), scholar. Born in Brighton, Sussex, she was brought up in Egypt until the age of ten and afterwards in Cumbria. After graduating in English at Cambridge University in 1938, she studied Welsh in Bangor under Sir Ifor *Williams and Irish at Queen's University, Belfast. She returned to Cambridge as a lecturer in 1945 and in 1973 was appointed Reader in Celtic Languages and Literatures; she retired in 1976 and now lives in Aberystwyth.

Her principal work is the edited text of *Trioedd Ynys Prydein (1961), an invaluable dictionary of the traditional characters of Welsh legend. She has published other important studies on aspects of early Welsh literature, including the Celtic sources of the Arthurian legend, the poems of *Dafydd ap Gwilym, the legend of *Tristan and Iseult and Matthew *Arnold's interpretation of the Celtic literatures. In all her work she combines a broad interest in the history and culture of the Celtic countries with a sympathetic knowledge of the Welsh texts. Her most recent book, a bilingual edition of the poems of Dafydd ap Gwilym (1982), is much admired.

A full list of her publications will be found in Ysgrifau Beirniadol XIII (ed. J. E. Caerwyn Williams, 1985), a volume of essays published in her honour.

Bron the Fisher King, see under BRÂN.

Bron yr Erw, The Battle of (1075), took place near Clynnog Fawr, Caerns., between the forces of *Gruffudd ap Cynan and *Trahaearn ap Caradog. Despite the great bravery of Gruffudd's men, he was defeated and had to flee to Ireland. The battle was commemorated more than a century later in the poetry of *Cynddelw Brydydd Mawr and *Llywarch ap Llywelyn (Prydydd y Moch) who praised *Llywelyn ap Iorwerth for restoring his grandfather's kingdom to its former glory.

BROOKS, JEREMY (Clive Meikle; 1926–   ), novelist and playwright, was born in Southampton, educated at Llandudno, Caerns., and has lived in Llanfrothen, Mer., since 1952. A prolific writer for the stage, radio, television and the cinema, he has adapted many Russian plays for the English stage and worked as a journalist, most recently for *The Sunday Times*. He joined the Royal Shakespeare Company as its literature manager in 1962 and has been a script adviser since 1969. He has published four novels and three novellas; *Jampot Smith* (1960) and *I'll Fight You* (1962) are both set in Llandudno, *The Water Carnival* (1957) is a satire loosely based on Portmeirion (the creation of Clough *Williams-Ellis) and *Henry's War* (1962), a pacifist fable, is also partly set in north Wales. His latest work, in collaboration with Adrian Mitchell, is 'a play with songs' (1982) based on Dylan *Thomas's story, 'A Child's Christmas in Wales'.

'Broséliâwnd', an unrhymed *awdl* with *cynghanedd* by T. Gwynn *Jones, was written in 1922. According to Breton tradition, the forest of Brociliande (Brecilien), which may be identified with the Forest of Paimpont between Rennes and Plöermel, was the cradle of magic. The well of Barenton was located in the forest and *Myrddin (Merlin) was endowed with magical powers because he had drunk its waters. In T. Gwynn Jones's poem, Myrddin wanders until he comes 'to the magical valley of his enchanting dreams' when an eternal passion for natural beauty is awakened in him. As he contemplates the scene, he sees an ancient forest in the oblivion of which he might escape from his distress. But magic, he discovers, offers no more than a deceptive peace and he leaves the forest, only to learn that its bewitchment is preferable to the garish halls of the restless world. He returns to Broséliâwnd and, secure in its carefree peace, is seen no more. The poem is a masterly expression of the poet's mystical intimacy with nature and may be read as a powerful indictment of European civilization during the years following immediately after the First World War.

The poem is discussed in an essay by Wenna Williams in *Ysgrifau Beirniadol VII* (ed. J. E. Caerwyn Williams, 1972).

Brother Eliodorus, see ELIDYR.

BROUGHTON, RHODA (1840–1920), novelist, was born near Denbigh but grew up at Broughton, Staffs., where her father had been presented to the family living. Her life was without great incident. In 1864 she went to live with her married sister at Upper Eyarth, near Ruthin, Denbs., where all her early writing was done, and in 1878 removed from there to Oxford, where her vitality and wit soon opened many doors for her. A move to Richmond in 1890 was followed four years later by a return to Headington Hill,

Oxford, where she spent the rest of her life.

Her first novel, *Cometh up as a Flower* (1867), made Rhoda Broughton a name for audacity. Its frank emotions, fresh dialogue and mocking humour, all of them even more apparent in *Not Wisely But Too Well* (1867), anticipated the freer expression of the century's later decades. Of many books which followed, *Good-bye, Sweetheart* (1872), *Nancy* (1873), *Joan* (1876), *Doctor Cupid* (1886), *Foes-in-Law* (1900) and *A Waif's Progress* (1905) are perhaps the best. Her extraordinary freedom of speech disguised a conservative outlook and enabled her to satirize much of what fashion thought new and wonderful. As popular in her day as Mrs. Henry Wood or Wilkie Collins—Mount Rhoda in the Antarctic was named after her—she was also a writer of quality whose reputation has suffered an undeserved eclipse.

Brut Aberpergwm, see under ABERPERGWM.

Brut Gruffudd ab Arthur, Brut Tysilio, Brut y Brytaniaid, see under BRUT Y BRENHINEDD (13th–15th cents.).

Brut Ieuan Brechfa, see under BRUT Y TYWYSOGYON.

Brut y Brenhinedd (lit. 'The chronicle of the kings'; 13th–15th cents.), the title of a collection of various Middle Welsh and Early Modern Welsh texts which originated from the *Historia Regum Britanniae* of *Geoffrey of Monmouth. There are more than sixty of these manuscripts, whether translations or adaptations, some of which are also known by such titles as *Brut y Brytaniaid* ('The Chronicle of the Britons') and *Chronicl y Brenhinoedd* ('The Chronicle of the Kings').

The earliest translations belong to the thirteenth century but a few can be dated in the fourteenth and fifteenth centuries. Altogether, there are six or seven versions, some corresponding very closely to the Latin and others which curtail the material or add to it. By the end of the seventeenth century and in the eighteenth century it was believed that some of the Welsh versions represented the 'old book' which Geoffrey claimed was the main source of the *Historia*, but no such work has come to light and the view is without substance. Scholars refer to the translations of Geoffrey's Latin texts as 'long texts' and to the simpler originals as 'short texts'. When the *Myvyrian Archaiology of Wales* (1801) was published, however, the term *Brut Gruffudd ab Arthur* (L. *Galfridus Arthurus*) was used to refer to the former and the latter was called *Brut Tysilio*, in the belief that *Tysilio was the author of the original. In fact, *Brut Gruffudd ab Arthur* is a late combination of about five manuscripts and *Brut Tysilio* consists of two earlier translations put together before the fifteenth century.

Selections from one version of *Brut y Brenhinedd* have been edited by Brynley F. Roberts (1971); the full text of another was edited by Henry Lewis (1942); see also the articles by Brynley F. Roberts in *Studia Celtica* (vols. XII/XIII, 1977–78) and *Y Traddodiad Rhyddiaith yn yr Oesau Canol* (ed. Geraint Bowen, 1974).

Brut y Tywysogyon (lit. 'The chronicle of the princes'), the major achievement of historiography in independent Wales, is found in two versions which are translations of a lost Latin text, *Cronica Principum Wallie*, written as a continuation of *Geoffrey of Monmouth's *Historia Regum Britanniae*. The *Brut*, which begins with the death of *Cadwaladr Fendigaid in 682 and ends with the death of *Llywelyn ap Gruffudd in 1282, is based on the *annales* which had been kept by churchmen and monks since the eighth century. Those models were brief and unadorned but the *Cronica* was composed in an elegant style which becomes rhetorical in places. The author adhered to historical facts, but they were incorporated into a work of creative literature. It is not known for certain where it was composed but the work may have been carried out at *Strata Florida and at least one of the translations into Welsh may have originated from the same monastery. The version of the chronicle known as *Brut Ieuan Brechfa* is said to have been based on a copy made by Rhys Thomas (1720?–90), a printer of Cowbridge, Glam.

The texts of *Brut y Tywysogyon* were edited by Thomas Jones (1941, 1952, 1955). For discussion of the text see the lecture by Thomas Jones, *Brut y Tywysogyon* (1953) and the article 'Historical Writing in Medieval Welsh' in *Scottish Studies* (vol. 12, 1968); see also Brynley F. Roberts, '*Testunau Hanes Cymraeg Canol*' in *Y Traddodiad Rhyddiaith yn yr Oesau Canol* (ed. Geraint Bowen, 1974).

Brute, Walter (*fl.* 1390–1402), a layman who held beliefs which showed the influence of John Wyclif and the Lollards but which expressed hope of an entirely Welsh nature and went further in the direction of the basic conviction of *Protestantism. Standing trial before John Trefnant, the Bishop of Hereford, in 1390–91, he defended himself by declaring the authority of Christ and the Scriptures and affirming the superiority of the Gospel to the Law and the value of faith as the means of justification. He was proud to be a Brythonic Christian for the reason that the Britons, from whom the Welsh were descended, had originally received Christianity not from Rome but from the East. Condemning the cupidity and lechery of priests and the superstition associated with indulgences, he ventured to identify the Pope with Antichrist and to accuse the Papacy of fomenting wars which were contrary to Christ's will. He added that he believed it to be God's plan, with the help of the Welsh, to overthrow Antichrist, an idea which combined biblical apocalypticism with the Welsh *vaticinatory tradition. The result of Brute's testimony was that he was released by

the bishop without making a full recantation.

For further details see W. W. Capes (ed.), *Registrum Johannis Trefnant* (1916) and Glanmor Williams, *The Welsh Church from Conquest to Reformation* (1962).

Brutus, the legendary progenitor of the British people. According to the *Historia Regum Britanniae* he was a son of Silvius, the son of Ascanius. It was foretold that he would be the cause of his parents' deaths and, after his father was killed in a hunting accident, he was banished from Italy. In Greece he won acclaim as a soldier, married Ignoge and became the leader of the Trojans. On the island of Leogetia he dreamed in the temple of Diana that he would discover a land beyond the setting sun, and this dream was realized when he and his companions landed at Totnes in Britain. Having defeated the giant Gogmagog, Brutus built a capital city and introduced a code of laws to the land which was named after him, Britain (*Prydain*). The word '*brut*' was originally used to denote the history of Brutus but it later came to mean a chronicle of the history of the Britons.

Brutus, see OWEN, DAVID (1795–1866).

Brwes, a traditional dish consisting of a thick layer of crushed oatbread steeped in boiling meat-stock to which a second layer is added before serving. Popular in the rural areas of north Wales, it used to be prepared as a breakfast dish, especially for farm servants. See also LLYMRU and SIOT.

BRYAN, ROBERT (1858–1920), poet, was born at Llanarmon yn Iâl, Denbs. Educated at the Normal College, Bangor, the University College of Wales, Aberystwyth, and at Oxford, he was a man of wide culture in both letters and music. His lyrics, collected in *Odlau Cân* (1901), are marred by rhetorical questions, but the words he wrote for music have lasting merit. Having lived for a time in Egypt, he wrote about that country for Owen M. *Edwards's periodicals, particularly *Y *Llenor* (1895). His second volume, *Tua'r Wawr* (1921), appeared posthumously.

Brychan (5th cent.), saint and king. Most of what is believed about him is doubtful and there must have been confusion between several men with the same name. There is some substance, however, in the two traditions that he was of Irish stock and that he was connected with *Brycheiniog, later known in English as Breconshire. Both agree with evidence that there were Irish settlements at the head of the valley of the Nedd around Ystradfellte. Brychan was said to be the son of Marchell, daughter of Tewdrig, the King of Garthmadrun, who went to Ireland at her father's request and there married Anlach, son of Coronac, an Irish prince, by whom she bore a child. The journey, during which some three hundred men died from the severe cold, was described in a manuscript dated about 900 and printed by W. J. *Rees in his *Lives of the Cambro-British Saints* (1853). They returned to Wales and Brychan succeeded his father as the king of Garthmadrun, the name of which was then changed to Brycheiniog. According to another tradition, Brychan fathered twenty-four children, most of whom became saints of the *Celtic Church; they are considered to be one of the three tribes of the saints of Wales, the other two being the families of *Cunedda and Caw. The distribution of churches bearing Brychan's name and those of his progeny suggests a missionary movement originating in Brycheiniog in the fifth and sixth centuries and proceeding along some of the old Roman roads. The date of his feast-day is 5 April.

Brychan, see DAVIES, JOHN (1784?–1864).

Brycheiniog, a kingdom centred upon the Usk Valley, was founded according to tradition by *Brychan, a chieftain of Irish stock. Earlier the kingdom of Garthmadrun, somewhat smaller in extent, had been ruled by Tewdrig from a centre at Llanfaes, across the Usk from Brecon. Brycheiniog's line came to an end about 940 when Brycheiniog was drawn into the orbit of *Deheubarth. The territory was conquered in 1093 by the Norman, Bernard of Neufmarché, who established his centre at Brecon. The lordship of Brecon, one of the largest and richest of the lordships of the March, was held by Bernard's descendants until 1521.

Bryfdir, see JONES, HUMPHREY (1867–1947).

'Bryn Calfaria' (lit. 'Calvary Hill'), a popular hymn-tune by William Owen (1813–93) of Prysgol, Caerns., which first appeared to the words *'Gwaed y Groes'* by William *Williams (Pantycelyn) in Owen's collection, *Y Perl Cerddorol* (1852). It is said that the tune was composed as he was on his way to work at Dorothea Slate Quarry and that it was first written on a piece of slate. The arrangement of the tune for male voices by Daniel *Protheroe under the title *Laudamus* has great power.

Bryn-celli-ddu, a burial-chamber near Llanfair, Ang., which, with Barclodiad-y-Gawres near Aberffraw, is among the most important Bronze Age monuments in Wales.

Bryn Derwin, The Battle of (1255), which took place on the boundary between *Arfon and *Eifionydd, established the authority of *Llywelyn ap Gruffudd over the whole of *Gwynedd to the west of the river Conwy. After the death of *Dafydd ap Llywelyn in 1246, the two sons of Gruffudd ap Llywelyn, Owain and Llywelyn, had shared the kingdom between

them, this arrangement being confirmed by Henry III at the Treaty of Woodstock (1247). By 1253, a third brother, Dafydd ap Gruffudd, was laying claim to his share. The English king supported him, as did his brother Owain, and it was they who made the first approach to Llywelyn to yield in Dafydd's favour. But it was Llywelyn who was victorious at Bryn Derwin. Defeated, Owain and Dafydd were imprisoned and only the latter was released in 1256. By overthrowing his brothers, Llywelyn restored the whole of Gwynedd as it had been in the time of *Llywelyn ap Iorwerth (Llywelyn Fawr) and *Owain Gwynedd, thus winning the title of Prince of Wales.

Bryn Glas, The Battle of, see PILLETH, THE BATTLE OF (1402).

Bryn Mawr, see under ELLIS, ROWLAND (1650–1731).

Brynach or **Byrnach** (late 5th cent. – early 6th cent.), saint, is also known as Brynach Wyddel ('the Irishman') and it is possible that, like *Brychan, he was of Irish stock; the two may have been related by marriage. From a Life of Brynach written in the twelfth century, it seems that he was a native of Cemaes in what is now north Pembrokeshire. He went on a pilgrimage to Rome and spent some years in Brittany, but returned to Wales and settled in the ascetic life where the village of Nanhyfer (Nevern) stands today. Brynach's cult is found mainly in that district but there are also villages called Llanfrynach in Breconshire and Glamorgan and a Llanfyrnach in Pembrokeshire. It is said that the cuckoo, on arriving in Wales, used to sing its first song from a cross in the churchyard at Nanhyfer on the saint's feast-day, 7 April.

Brynaich a Deifr, the men of Bernicia and Deira, two Anglian kingdoms united by Ethelfrith in 604 to form Northumbria, were the enemies of the *Gododdin in the time of *Aneirin. By the period of the *Gogynfeirdd (12th–14th cents.) the terms were used generically to denote the English. *Gruffudd ap Maredudd ap Dafydd refers to the city of Chester as being at the extremity of the land held by the Deifr. Although the kingdoms had ceased to exist by the time of *Dafydd Benfras, he wrote that in his own day 'the Brynaich ravaged over *Offa's Dyke', as a way of implying that the Welsh were still struggling against their old enemy.

Brynfab, see WILLIAMS, THOMAS (1848–1927).

Brython, Y (lit. 'The Briton'), a weekly newspaper established in 1906 by Hugh *Evans for the Welsh community in *Liverpool, but which extended its circulation to the whole of

Wales. John Herbert Jones (J. H.; 1860–1934), the first editor, did much to ensure the paper's success and among its contributors were some of the foremost writers of the day. He was succeeded in 1931 by Gwilym R. *Jones who gave the paper a more political colouring and remained editor until it ceased publication in 1939. For details of the earlier magazine of the same name (1858–63) see JONES, ROBERT ISAAC (1815–1905).

Brython Association, The, see under JONES, MICHAEL DANIEL (1822–98).

Buchedd Garmon (1937), see under GARMON (c.378–448).

Buddug, see BOUDICA (1st cent.) and under PRYSE, ROBERT JOHN (1807–89).

Buellt, a cantref on the right bank of the upper Wye, was linked dynastically with the commot of *Gwrtheyrnion in southern *Powys, where the ruling house claimed descent from Gwrtheyrn (*Vortigern). Buellt was conquered about 1095 by Philip de Breos but it returned to Welsh rule in 1229 after the marriage of *Dafydd ap Llywelyn to Isabella de Breos. Captured for the English Crown in 1241, it eventually became part of the patrimony of the Mortimers, the earls of March. *Llywelyn ap Gruffudd's campaign in Buellt led to his death at Cilmeri in 1282 and ever after the jibe '*bradwyr Buellt*' ('the traitors of Buellt') was used against the people of the district. See also LLYWELYN'S CAVE.

'*Builth*', a powerful and popular hymn-tune by David Jenkins (1848–1915), probably composed in 1890. It appeared under the title '*Buallt*' in *Y Salmydd* (1892) and later under the title 'Builth' in the composer's *Tunes, Chants, and Anthems with Supplement* (1883). The tune is usually associated with the hymn '*Rhagluniaeth fawr y nef*' by David *Charles.

Bulkeley family, The, originally from Cheshire, had settled at Beaumaris, Ang., by 1450. A branch through marriage was established in the borough of Conwy and extended its influence over the neighbouring commot of *Arllechwedd Isaf. By their trading activities and business acumen, the Bulkeleys built up large estates in Anglesey and Caernarfonshire at a time when landed estates were emerging as the dominant feature of the Welsh landscape. The most prominent was Sir Richard Bulkeley III, head of the family from 1572 to 1621 and the founder of Baron Hill, the main family seat near Beaumaris, in 1618. Other Bulkeleys were prominent in public life, particularly parliamentary affairs, until the death of the seventh and last Viscount in 1822. A vivid picture of life in the commot of Talybolion was given by William

Bulkeley (1691–1760), the squire of Brynddu in Llanfechell, Ang., who belonged to a cadet branch of the family. His diary, for the periods 1734–43 and 1747–60, was edited by Barbara *Dew Roberts under the title *Mr. Bulkeley and the Pirate* (1936).

For further details see A. D. Carr, *Medieval Anglesey* (1982) and the article on the Bulkeley family by D. C. Jones in the *Transactions* of the Anglesey Antiquarian and Field Society (1961).

Bundling, see COURTING IN BED.

Bunyan of Wales, The, see SHADRACH, AZARIAH (1774–1844).

Burden of Thorns, a symbol of woe. According to a traditional belief, the Man in the Moon bore a burden of thorns or withes, for the gathering of which on a Sunday he had been imprisoned for eternity. The image is found in *cywyddau* of reconciliation, in elegies and in love-poems written during the period of the *Poets of the Gentry.

Burgess, Thomas (1756–1837), Bishop of *St. David's from 1803 to 1825, was an Englishman who took a keen interest in the ecclesiastical and literary traditions of Wales. He took part, with Iolo Morganwg (Edward *Williams), in the eisteddfod held at Carmarthen in 1819 and was the founder of St. David's College, Lampeter, three years later.

Burton, Richard (1925–84), actor, was born at Pontrhydyfen, near Port Talbot, Glam., into a mining family named Jenkins. He later adopted the surname of Philip Burton, a teacher who had fired in him a passion for the stage. Given his first chance as an actor at the age of eighteen in *The *Druid's Rest*, a play by Emlyn *Williams, he studied English briefly at Exeter College, Oxford, before embarking on a career which led to international stardom both in the theatre and in films. As an actor he was endowed with intelligence, a powerful physical presence and a ringing voice which won him acclaim in many heroic and tragic parts, most notably in plays by Shakespeare. His five marriages, particularly to the American actress Elizabeth Taylor (whom he married twice), and his rumbustious life-style, were widely reported but, from the mid-1970s, his career was threatened by a serious drinking problem and he seemed to lose his way, his great gifts unfulfilled. Welsh-speaking and generous in his support of patriotic causes, he was popular in his native country and, despite the luxury of his life in America and Switzerland, he never lost touch with the village of Pontrhydyfen.

For further details see the biographies of Richard Burton by Paul Ferris (1981, 1984) and Fergus Cashin (1982).

BUSH, DUNCAN (1946–   ), poet, was born

in Cardiff and educated at Warwick University and Wadham College, Oxford. With Nigel *Jenkins and Tony *Curtis, he won the *Welsh Arts Council's Young Poets Competition in 1974 and some of his work is to be found in the volume, *Three Young Anglo-Welsh Poets* (1974). Since then he has published three more collections of poems, *Nostos* (1980), *Aquarium* (1983) and *Salt* (1985). His verse is technically versatile, its imagery precise, and even in his most personal work there is an awareness of social and political forces.

Bush, Percy (1879–1955), rugby-player, was capped for Wales eight times between 1905 and 1910 in a career marked by erratic genius rather than consistent skill. He toured New Zealand in 1904 and played against the All Blacks, who had cause to fear his wily attacks, in the famous game at the Cardiff Arms Park in 1905.

Butcher Beynon, in Dylan *Thomas's *Under Milk Wood* (1954), delights in frightening his wife by pretending that he sells the meat of cats and *corgis.

Bute family, The, 'the creators of modern Cardiff', were descended from Robert II of Scotland and were established as landowners on the Isle of Bute in the fourteenth century. In 1766, Lord Mountstuart (1744–1814), son of the third Earl of Bute, George III's Prime Minister, married Charlotte Windsor, heiress of Lord Windsor, owner of the *Cardiff Castle estate in Glamorgan, which had come into existence through grants from the Crown to Lord Windsor's ancestor, William Herbert, Earl of Pembroke, in the sixteenth century. Mountstuart, who became the first Marquess of Bute in 1796, began the restoration of Cardiff Castle but played only a modest role in the life of Glamorgan. He was succeeded by his grandson, John Crichton Stuart (1793–1848), whose property included not only the Bute and Cardiff estates, but also the Luton Hoo estate in Bedfordshire and land in County Durham as well as the extensive possessions of his maternal grandfather, the Earl of Dumfries.

The second Marquess proved indefatigable in his efforts to develop his estates and to extend their influence. He dominated the politics and administration of Glamorgan, controlled the Corporation of Cardiff, supported a wide range of charities and took the lead in the establishment of the county police force. The owner of vast tracts of mineral land, he pursued a policy with regard to mineral leases which went far to set the pattern and the pace of the exploitation of the south Wales coalfield. As landlord of the Dowlais Ironworks, he was in frequent conflict with his tenant, Sir John *Guest, and uncertainty over the renewal of the lease which expired in 1848 caused widespread anxiety. Owner of much of the land upon which Cardiff was built, he was partly instrumental in establishing the ninety-nine-year lease as a predominant form of tenure in urban south Wales. In 1830 he obtained an Act of Parliament authorizing him to build a dock at Cardiff at his own expense. Opened in 1839, it was the first of a series built by the Bute family, an enterprise which facilitated the growth of Cardiff as the world's leading port for the exporting of coal.

The third Marquess (1847–1900), a convert to Roman Catholicism and the hero of Disraeli's novel, *Lothair* (1870), enjoyed immense wealth, some of which he used upon the magnificent refurbishing of Cardiff Castle and the reconstruction of *Castell Coch. During the marquessate of his son, the fourth Marquess (1881–1947), the Bute Docks were taken over by the Great Western Railway Company, the mineral reserves of the family were nationalized and their urban leaseholds sold. The fifth Marquess (1907–56) presented the Castle and its park to the city of Cardiff in 1947.

For a full account of the Bute family see John Davies, *Cardiff and the Marquesses of Bute* (1981).

Butler family, see under DUNRAVEN.

Butler, Eleanor (1739–1829) and **Ponsonby, Sarah** (1755–1831), were known as 'The Ladies of Llangollen'. Two eccentrics of aristocratic Irish connection, they eloped to escape the conventions of provincial life in Ireland and set up a ménage, together with their faithful maid Mary Carryll, at Plas Newydd, in Llangollen, Denbs., a cottage which they gothicized into a picturesque, over-timbered house that is now a tourist attraction. For nearly half a century after their arrival in 1780 the place became a mecca for many distinguished visitors to north Wales, including Wellington, Burke, Castlereagh, Shelley, Byron and Scott. Most fulfilled their hosts' expectation that they should leave a tribute, preferably some curio in carved oak. Wordsworth, who offered a sonnet in 1824, made the mistake of referring to the house as 'a low-roofed cott', and was never invited again. The Ladies' life at the Plas was spent in gardening, reading, writing, conversing, playing backgammon and in dominating the life of Llangollen, a village at that time. Unfortunately, despite the wide circle of their acquaintances, their journals are quite dull.

A fictional biography, *The Chase of the Wild Goose* (1936), was written by Mary Gordon who commissioned the memorial to the Ladies in the parish church of St. Collen, but the most authoritative account is *The Ladies of Llangollen: a Study in Romantic Friendship* (1971) by Elizabeth Mavor; see also *Life with the Ladies of Llangollen* (ed. Elizabeth Mavor, 1984).

Buttercup Field, The (1945), Gwyn *Jones's first collection of short stories, includes a few which were originally published in the late

1930s. Although there are light-hearted and lyrical tales among them and at least one, 'Shacki Thomas', set in the industrial valleys, which treats of married love with sympathy and insight, the most powerful of these highly wrought narratives are concerned with passionate triangular relationships in which rivalry, vengeance and violence are common elements, often set in contrast with a pastoral background.

Bwa Bach, Y, see under MORFUDD.

Bwci Bo, a bogey-man invoked as a means of frightening children into good behaviour, often mentioned in rhymes and folk-tales; regional variants include *Bwci Bol*, *Bo Lol* and *Bolelo*. See also LADI WEN, FRAN WEN and JAC Y LANTERN.

Byddin Ymreolaeth Cymru, see under JONES, HUGH ROBERT (1894–1930).

Byr-a-thoddaid, see under TWENTY-FOUR METRES.

Byw sy'n Cysgu, Y (lit. 'The living who are asleep'; 1956), a novel by Kate *Roberts. Lora Ffenig, having taken her marriage for granted, is astounded to discover that her husband has left her for a Mrs. Amred. Slowly she begins to awaken to an understanding of herself and her relationship with other people. The novel includes extracts from Lora's diary which show that the book is closely related to *Stryd y Glep (1949) and, like that novel, it ends on a fairly hopeful note.

For a critical discussion of the novel see the essay by John Gwilym Jones in *Cyfrol Deyrnged Kate Roberts* (ed. Bobi Jones, 1969). A translation by Ll. Wyn Griffith has been published under the title *The Living Sleep* (1978).

Bywyd a Marwolaeth Theomemphus (lit. 'The life and death of Theomemphus'; 1764), a long poem of some six thousand lines by William *Williams (Pantycelyn). The author chose to describe it as a dramatic poem and it deploys more than two dozen characters. His intention was to portray the spiritual pilgrimage of one of the converts of the Methodist Revival or, as he would have claimed, that of any true Christian. Theomemphus is depicted as a young man indulging in gross sins, being brought under conviction of sin, experiencing forgiveness, back-sliding (when he is tempted to marry Philomela), being restored and enduring to the end through all manner of afflictions. The design of the poem is superbly ambitious and it has many very fine passages but, in general, the author lacked the craftsmanship which would have enabled him to maintain a consistently high standard in such a long poem as this.

For critical discussion see the articles by W. J. Gruffydd in *Y Llenor* (1922), T. Williams in *Y Traethodydd* (1959) and D. Gwenallt Jones in *Gwŷr Llên y Ddeunawfed Ganrif* (ed. Dyfnallt Morgan, 1966).

C

Cacamwri, a comical character in the story of *Culhwch and Olwen. He shows such enthusiasm while threshing in a barn with an iron flail that he reduces the rafters to splinters. Almost drowned in the Severn as he takes part in the hunt for *Twrch Trwyth, he is hauled from the river and survives to help *Arthur in his attack upon the *Black Witch.

Cad Goddau, see under FUTILE BATTLES.

Cadair Idris, a mountain situated between the rivers Mawddach and Dysynni, named perhaps after a giant, marks the boundary between the old kingdoms of *Gwynedd and *Powys. It is said that whoever spends a night alone on the summit will come down mad, blind or endowed with poetical powers. This local tradition was given wider currency by Felicia *Hemans in a poem, 'The Rocks of Cader Idris', which was published in her *Welsh Melodies* (1832). The tune 'Cader Idris', also known as 'Jenny Jones', was composed by John Parry (Bardd Alaw; 1776–1851) in 1804.

Cadfan (mid-6th cent.), a saint who was traditionally said to be the son of Gwen Teirbron, the daughter of Emyr Llydaw. He came to Wales from Brittany as a missionary and his first settlement may have been at Tywyn, where the church has a memorial stone which bears two inscriptions from the eighth century, the earliest surviving examples of Old Welsh, but his cult spread as far as Llangadfan in Powys, where medicinal qualities were attributed to the waters of a well dedicated to him. Cadfan's name is also associated with the island of *Bardsey which, with Tywyn, claims his grave. The saint's feast-day is 1 November.

Cadi Haf, a traditional character who took part in the festivities associated with *May Day in north-east Wales when the Summer Branch, a version of the Maypole, was carried from house to house by dancers. He collected money in a ladle while the revellers performed and he entertained the spectators with buffoonery. Also known as *Yr Hen Gadi*, the role was sometimes played by a man who, with blackened face, wore a man's coat and a woman's petticoat, an example of the half-male, half-female figures typical of such customs as found throughout Europe. See also SUMMER BIRCH.

The custom is described by Trefor M. Owen in *Welsh Folk Customs* (1959); see also the same author's article in *Gwerin* (vol. 3, 1961).

Cadog (mid-5th cent.), a saint who was one of the foremost religious leaders of his time. His Life was composed by Lifris early in the twelfth century and revised a little later by *Caradog of Llancarfan. It is said that Cadog's father was *Gwynllyw, a chieftain of Gwynllwg, and his mother Gwladus, a daughter of *Brychan. Tradition has it that he was carried on a cloud to Beneventana in northern Italy, where he was made a bishop, that he was killed there as he celebrated mass and that miracles were performed after his death. Besides the churches bearing the saint's name in south-east Wales, such as those at Gelli-gaer and Caerleon, Mon., there are others in Anglesey, Cornwall, Brittany and Scotland which are dedicated to him, but the best-known are those at Llangadog, Carms., and Llangattock, Brecs. The monastery founded by Cadog at *Llancarfan in the Vale of Glamorgan was famous as a centre of learning.

Cadrawd, see EVANS, THOMAS CHRISTOPHER (1846–1918).

Cadriaith, a character in the tale known as *Breuddwyd Rhonabwy*, of whom it is said that no man in Britain could give sounder advice than he, despite his youth. When poets come to recite in the presence of *Arthur, only Cadriaith is able to understand their poem, although it is thought to praise the King, and on the young man's recommendation the poets are paid. His name means 'one of powerful or splendid language' and the incident may have been intended as a satire on obscurity in the work of the court poets.

Cadvan, see DAVIES, JOHN CADVAN (1846–1923).

Cadwaladr (d. 664), prince, the son of *Cadwallon ap Cadfan, the King of Gwynedd whose death in Rome is the starting-point of the chronicle known as *Brut y Tywysogyon*. In the Triads it is said that he was killed by a blow from Golyddan Fardd. Little is known about him except that, with Cynan, he is mentioned in vaticinatory poems as a hero who is expected to deliver the Welsh from the English (see under VATICINATION). Gentle and generous, he was reputed to have enjoyed a peaceful reign. Henry VII, who claimed him as an ancestor, carried the *Red Dragon to the battle of *Bosworth in 1485 in the belief that it was the banner of Cadwaladr. The prince, sometimes called Cadwaladr Fendigaid ('the Blessed') may also have been the saint who is commemorated in Llangadwaladr, Ang., and at other places in north-east and south-east Wales.

Cadwaladr, Beti, see DAVIES, ELIZABETH (1789–1860).

CADWALADR, DILYS (1902–79), poet and short-story writer, was a native of Four Crosses, Caerns. During the 1940s she lived on the island of *Bardsey (Ynys Enlli), farming and teaching. She published only one volume of stories (1936), but examples of her work may be found in the periodical Y *Llenor and English translations in G. K. Chesterton's Miscellany of Prose 1900–34 (1935). As a poet, she is remembered as the first woman to win the *Crown at the National Eisteddfod, a feat which she accomplished in 1953 with a pryddest entitled 'Y Llen'.

For further details see Merch yr Oriau Mawr (ed. Eigra Lewis Roberts, 1982), which includes four of her short stories and a number of her poems, and a biographical essay in Atgofion (vol. 2, 1972).

CADWALADR, RHYS (fl. 1666–90), poet, a native of Conwy, Denbs., and vicar of Llanfairfechan, Caerns., wrote verse for his own pleasure, adapting selections from Horace and Seneca to traditional Welsh metres. He also addressed poems to the *Mostyn family and there was a light-hearted exchange of verse between him and Thomas *Jones (1648?–1713), the almanacker.

CADWALADR, SIÔN or **JOHN KADWALADR** (fl. 1760), balladeer and writer of interludes. A native of Llanycil, Mer., he was transported to America in his youth and spent seven years there as punishment for having stolen half-a-crown. On his return to Wales he began writing interludes, two of which remain in manuscript, Einion a Gwenllian (c.1756) and Gaulove a Clarinda (c.1756–62); a third, which he wrote with Huw Jones (1700?–82) of Llangwm, Brenin Dafydd a Gwraig Urias (c.1765), was published in Chester. They are livelier than most of those written in his day and as witty as the best.

Cadwallon ap Cadfan (d. 633), King of *Gwynedd, was the only British king of historic times to overthrow an Anglian dynasty. Edwin of Northumbria, conqueror of the British kingdom of Elmet (Elfed), led the first English invasion of Wales. In alliance with Penda of the royal house of heathen Mercia, Cadwallon killed Edwin in a battle believed to have been fought at Heathfield (probably Hatfield Chase, Yorks.),

near Doncaster, in 632. This was the first recorded occasion on which a British and an English ruler had made common cause in arms. Northumbria fell apart and Cadwallon's triumph, a victory known in Welsh tradition as the battle of Meigen, briefly raised British hopes that the Island might yet be saved from the Teutonic invaders. He proved unable to exploit his advantage, however, and in the following year he was killed near Hexham (Cantscaul or Hefenfelth) by the forces of Oswald of Bernicia. In later centuries, a defender of the freedom of Wales was sometimes hailed as a new Cadwallon. See also MOLIANT CADWALLON.

Cadwedigaeth yr Iaith Gymraeg (lit. 'The preservation of the Welsh language'; 1808), a short treatise on the grammar and syntax of Welsh by William *Owen Pughe. First published in the author's own esoteric orthography, it proved of little worth because it was quite unreadable. Nevertheless, Thomas *Charles of Bala took the view that its contents merited republication in the standard orthography and, in new editions appearing in the same year, the work became a popular primer for *Sunday Schools. Based on Owen Pughe's Grammar of the Welsh Language, but substituting more homely examples for the numerous quotations from early poetry in that book, the treatise must nevertheless have struck many readers as curious, if not downright bogus.

Cadwgan ap Bleddyn (d. 1111), prince, the second son of *Bleddyn ap Cynfyn of *Powys, fought for many years against Rhys ap Tewdwr of *Deheubarth before warring against the Normans. Married for diplomatic reasons to the daughter of his neighbour, Picot de Sai, lord of Clun, he played a prominent part in the Welsh campaigns during the reign of William Rufus, aiding *Gruffudd ap Cynan in his defence of Anglesey at the battle of Coed Yspwys (1094) and fleeing with him to Ireland four years later. On his return from exile in 1099 his lands in Powys and Ceredigion were restored to him in vassalage. During his last years he was engaged in strife with his own kinsmen and it was his nephew, Madog ap Rhirid, who killed Cadwgan at Welshpool while he was preparing to build a castle there.

CADWGAN OF BANGOR (d. 1241), abbot and bishop. The son of a Welsh mother by an eloquent, Welsh-speaking priest of Irish origin, he joined the *Cistercian Order and became abbot of *Strata Florida and subsequently of *Whitland. By favour of *Llywelyn ap Iorwerth (Llywelyn Fawr) he was consecrated Bishop of Bangor in 1215. *Gerald de Barri (Giraldus Cambrensis), writing with animus in Speculum Ecclesiae, claimed that Cadwgan had been promoted by dint of his own ambition and cunning.

During a famine in 1234 he provided corn for his stricken people and, two years later, retired to the abbey of Dore, Herefs., where soon afterwards he was reprimanded for neglecting discipline. Of his theological writings only three short examples have survived: *De modo confitendi*, a *Tractatus* on a verse from the Psalms and his *Orationes*, of which the style and the alliteration reflect the influence of the Welsh bardic tradition.

Cadwr, one of *Arthur's allies, is called '*dux Cornubie*' ('earl of Cornwall') in *Geoffrey of Monmouth's *Historia Regum Britanniae*. There it is recorded (without historical basis) that when the king's surrender was demanded by Rome, Cadwr expressed joy at an opportunity for the Britons to relinquish the comforts of court life at *Caerleon and to revive their military skills. Arthur's wife, *Gwenhwyfar, was fostered by Cadwr and it was his son, Custennin, who inherited the Crown of the Isle of Britain after the king's defeat at *Camlan (*c*.539). The earl also appears in *Breuddwyd Rhonabwy* where these details recur in somewhat embroidered form.

Cadwynfyr, see under TWENTY-FOUR METRES.

Caeo, a commot of *Cantref Mawr, was the heartland of the resistance by the rulers of *Deheubarth against the incursions of the Normans.

Caer Dathl, see under MATH FAB MATHONWY.

Caer Siddi, see under ANNWN.

Caerfallwch, see EDWARDS, THOMAS (1779–1858).

Caerhun Manuscripts, The, see under MAURICE, HUGH (1755?–1825).

Caerleon or **Caerllion ar Wysg**, the site of a Roman encampment known as Isca which was founded by Julius Frontinus about AD 75 near the estuary of the river Usk. In his *Historia Regum Britanniae* *Geoffrey of Monmouth located *Arthur's court there and under his influence so did the romances of Peredur, Owain and Geraint (see under TAIR RHAMANT). In the native Welsh tradition, however, as the legend of *Culhwch and Olwen illustrates, the site of the court was always given as *Celli-wig in Cornwall. Towards the end of the twelfth century *Gerald de Barri (Giraldus Cambrensis) testified that Roman walls still stood at Caerleon and they may have commended the spot to Geoffrey, who was a native of the district. In *Brut y Brenhinedd*, which describes Arthur's coronation, Caerleon is said to have been 'the second city to Rome in the beauty of her houses, her wealth of gold and silver, and her pride'. It is listed among the Twenty-eight Cities of Britain in *Nennius's *Historia Brittonum* and in the legend of *Macsen the fortification is reputed to have been built at the same time as that of *Carmarthen.

Caernarfon, a castle built by order of Earl Hugh of Chester on a site controlling the south-western approach to the Menai Straits and near the Roman auxiliary fort of Segontium. After the Norman withdrawal from north-west Wales in the early twelfth century, the castle was used as a residence by the Princes of *Gwynedd. The site is associated with the tales centred on *Elen Luyddog in the legend of *Macsen and on *Branwen in *Pedair Cainc y Mabinogi*.

At the collapse of the feudal *Principality, Edward I embarked upon the construction of a new fortress which, with the newly-established borough, was to form the administrative centre for both the shire of Caernarfon and the Crown lands in north-west Wales. Between 1283 and 1327 a sum of about twenty-seven thousand pounds was spent on castle and borough, of which more than twenty thousands went on the castle alone; it was thus the most expensive of Edward's royal fortresses, costing almost half as much again as *Conwy. Extensive damage was caused during the *Welsh Revolt (1294–95) but, despite two sieges in 1402 and 1403, *Owain Glyndŵr's forces failed to capture the castle. Although forbidden from acquiring property in this garrison town, Welshmen had established themselves there by the fifteenth century. The poet *Rhys Goch Eryri compared the castle unfavourably in his *cywydd* to the court of Gwilym ap Gruffudd of Penrhyn and *Tudur Penllyn sang in praise of William Gruffudd, alderman of Caernarfon in 1468 and Chamberlain of North Wales in 1483. The castle was held by the Royalists during the first *Civil War, but was taken by Mytton in 1646. Two years later, in the second Civil War, the Parliamentarian garrison successfully beat off a renewed Royalist attack. The Eisteddfod of 1821 was held in the castle under the auspices of the *Cymmrodorion Society of Gwynedd.

Outside the castle there stands today a statue of David *Lloyd George who held the office of Constable of Caernarfon Castle. It was in the castle's grounds in July 1969 that Charles, the Queen's eldest son, was invested as Prince of Wales, a setting in which many, including poets, saw political significance (see under PRINCIPALITY). Near by, but outside the castle's walls, stands a memorial to *Llywelyn ap Gruffudd, the last Prince of independent Wales, which was erected by Gwynedd County Council in 1982, the seventh centenary of his death.

For further details see Alun Llywelyn-Williams, *Crwydro Arfon* (1959), A. J. Taylor, *The King's Works in Wales 1277–1330* (1974), and the chapter by K. Williams-

Jones in *Boroughs of Mediaeval Wales* (ed. R. A. Griffiths, 1978); see also the account published by the Ministry of Works in 1953.

Caernarvon Herald (1831), a weekly newspaper which first appeared as the *Caernarvon Herald and North Wales Advertiser*, a title changed in 1837 to *Caernarvon and Denbigh Herald and North and South Wales Independent*. James Rees was its publisher until 1871 and among its editors were William Powers Smith, John Evan Jones, Alfred Austin and Daniel Rees. The newspaper was owned by Tom Jones in the 1940s and, on his death in 1953, became the property of his son, John Morus Jones; its editor until his retirement in 1983 was the poet John Tudor *Jones (John Eilian).

Caerphilly, a castle built on an old Roman site by order of Gilbert de Clare, the powerful Lord of Glamorgan, about 1271, for the defence of his territory against attack by *Llywelyn ap Gruffudd. The largest fortification ever built in Wales, and the second most extensive in Britain after Windsor, the castle was protected by a concentric system of land and water defences which made it, with *Beaumaris, one of the most redoubtable of Norman strongholds. It was attacked by Welsh forces during the revolt of *Llywelyn ap Gruffudd (Llywelyn Bren) in 1316, by dissident barons in 1321 and again during the rising of *Owain Glyndŵr. Lewis ap Richard, a member of one of the most prominent Welsh families in the lordship of *Senghennydd, was Constable of Caerphilly in the early sixteenth century and his hospitality was praised by the poet Rhys Brychan (*c.*1500). His son, Edward Lewis, lived at Y *Fan in the vicinity of the castle which was a ruin when John Leland visited the district in 1536. The castle is famous for its leaning tower, some eighty feet in height and thirteen feet out of the perpendicular, which was damaged and left thus during the *Civil Wars. The work of clearing the houses which once stood under the castle's walls was begun by the third Marquess of *Bute in the late nineteenth century.

For further details see William Rees, *Caerphilly Castle, a history and description* (1937) and H. P. Richards, *A History of Caerphilly* (1975).

Caerwys Eisteddfodau, The (1523 and 1567), two gatherings of poets and others with an interest in poetry, were not *eisteddfodau in the modern sense but rather assemblies which met to decide upon the rules governing the crafts of the poet and the musician. Their aim, in particular, was to protect the professional poet's status in society against infiltration by inferior practitioners. It is probable that they were held under the patronage of the *Mostyn family of Flintshire, the heads of which were Rhisiart ap Howel ab Ieuan Fychan in 1523 and Wiliam Mostyn in 1567. The first Eisteddfod took place on 2 July 1523 'with the personal counsel of Gruffudd ab Ieuan ap Llywelyn Fychan and *Tudur Aled . . . so as to bring order and government to the craftsmen in poetic art (*Cerdd Dafod) according to the Statute of *Gruffudd ap Cynan', as the Roll explains. This was the occasion with which the pseudo-antique Statute of Gruffudd ap Cynan is associated. Although the Statute stipulated that an Eisteddfod should be held every three years, the second did not take place until 1567. The last of its kind, the Eisteddfod of that year marked the end of the *Bardic Order and when the eisteddfod was revived in the eighteenth century it was quite a different institution.

For further details see Gwyn Thomas, *The Caerwys Eisteddfodau* (1968) and Hywel Teifi Edwards, *Yr Eisteddfod* (1971).

Cafall, see under MIRABILIA BRITANNIAE.

Cafflogion, a commot of the cantref of *Llŷn, also known as Afloegion, is said to have been named after Abloyc, one of the sons of *Cunedda.

Cai, the son of Cynyr, a character in the tale of *Culhwch and Olwen, is foremost among the men of *Arthur's court in their quest for Olwen. He undertakes the first task set by Ysbaddaden Bencawr, that of securing the sword of *Wrnach, and succeeds in cutting off the giant's head. With *Bedwyr, he sits astride the Salmon of Llyn Llyw as it swims up the river Severn to the fort at Gloucester where *Mabon fab Modron is held prisoner. From the beard of *Dillus Farfog he makes a leash for the hunting dog Drudwyn but because he strikes the sleeping giant Arthur composes an *englyn* casting suspicion on his valour, at which Cai takes offence and refuses to be of further assistance. At two points in the tale some of Cai's attributes are listed. For example, he is able to go without sleep or hold his breath under water for nine days and nights; no doctor can heal the wound caused by his sword; he is able to grow at will, as tall as the highest tree; so great is his natural heat that whatever he holds in his hand remains dry, even in the heaviest rain; and any load he carries is rendered invisible. These were among the traditional feats of the Celtic hero and they are also attributed to Cú Chulainn (Cuchulain) in the Irish sagas. Cai also appears in the poem '*Pa ŵr yw'r Porthor?*' (10th or 11th cent.), which belongs to the same world as the tale of Culhwch and Olwen, and in Y *Tair Rhamant and *Breuddwyd Rhonabwy. He continued to be a prominent character in Arthurian legend and is known in English and French literature as Keu or Kay and by other forms of his name.

Caldey (Ynys Bŷr), see under PYR (6th cent.).

Caledfryn, see WILLIAMS, WILLIAM (1801–69).

Caledfwlch, the sword of King *Arthur. It is listed in the tale of *Culhwch and Olwen as one of the King's most cherished possessions and is used by Llenlleawg Wyddel to kill *Diwrnach Wyddel and his men. In the Welsh versions of *Geoffrey of Monmouth's *Historia Regum Britanniae the weapon is described as the best sword ever made in Ynys *Afallach and Arthur wields it against the giant on Mynydd Mihangel (Mont Saint Michel) in Brittany. In Irish the name *Caladbolg* is given to a flashing sword, which suggests that the Welsh is either a borrowing from the Irish or cognate with it. The form used by Geoffrey is *Caliburnus*, from which the English name Excalibur is derived.

Calennig, a small gift presented on New Year's Day (*Dydd Calan*). In some districts of south-west Wales an apple or orange decorated with holly and oats, and mounted on three wooden skewers, was carried from house to house. References to this tradition occur in *cywyddau* of the medieval period when a similar practice was known in England, but most of the Welsh evidence belongs to the nineteenth century. By then the custom was upheld only by children, especially those of the poor, who sang or recited verses and were given apples or new pennies, but on the understanding that they had only until noon to solicit these gifts. The rhymes associated with the *calennig*, many of which have survived, usually offered good wishes to the household for the coming year, asked for the gift of money or some bread and cheese, and referred to the cold weather. Another version of the custom was 'the bringing of New Year's water' which was carried in a bowl and sprinkled over members of the family.

For further details see Trefor M. Owen, *Welsh Folk Customs* (1959).

'Calon Lân' (lit. 'A pure heart'), a hymn-tune written by John Hughes (1872–1914) of Landore, Swansea. Included in *Seren yr Ysgol Sul* (1899) and subsequently in many singing-festival programmes, it became very popular during the religious revival led by Evan *Roberts in 1904. The tune is almost inseparably linked with the words '*Nid wy'n gofyn bywyd moethus*' by Daniel *James (Gwyrosydd) which are still sung on public occasions, not all religious.

Calumniated Wife, The, a motif in folk-literature, also known as the Mother Wrongly Accused, Patient Griselda and the Suffering Queen. A woman, accused of some misdeed, is punished and serves her penance until her innocence is eventually proved, after which she is restored to her rightful status. The theme, represented in English by the story of Grissel in Chaucer's *The Clerk's Tale*, is found in the tales of *Rhiannon, *Branwen and Enid.

Calvinistic Methodists, see under METHODISM.

Camber, one of the three sons of *Brutus. With his brothers, Locrinus and Albanactus, he was one of the eponymous founders of the three countries of the Isle of Britain, according to *Geoffrey of Monmouth. After the death of Brutus the kingdom was divided into three parts: to Locrinus was given the land named Loegria (England), to Camber was given Cambria (Wales), and the third son, Albanactus, was given Albania (Scotland). These names are onomastic and are derived from the Welsh place-names *Lloegr* (England), *Cymru* (Wales) and *Yr Alban* (Scotland). Little is said of Camber and Albanactus in the *Historia Regum Britanniae*, but through Locrinus Geoffrey traced the lineage of the Kings of England. Although Locrinus fell in love with Estrildis, the exiled daughter of the king of Scotland, and had a child by her, he was forced to marry Gwendolen, the daughter of Corineus. Their son was Maddan, who ruled after Locrinus had been murdered by Gwendolen because he had returned to Estrildis. See also CYMRU, DOLFORWYN and WALES.

Cambria, see under previous entry, CYMRU and RHYS, MORGAN JOHN (1760–1804).

Cambrian, The, the first weekly newspaper to be founded in Wales. It was established in 1804, as a means of fostering the commercial growth of Swansea, by George Haynes and L. W. Dillwyn, and published by Thomas Jenkins until 1822. Sold to the Cambrian Newspaper Company in 1891, it was merged with *The Herald of Wales* in 1930.

Cambrian Archaeological Association, The, a society founded in 1846 for the study and preservation of the antiquities of Wales. Its promoters were Henry Longueville Jones and John *Williams (Ab Ithel), who became its first secretaries and the editors of its journal, *Archaeologia Cambrensis*, launched in the previous year. From its inception, the society has held annual meetings at centres of antiquarian interest in Wales and elsewhere. Its journal, written in English, reflects the Association's wide-ranging interests and has included much valuable material on the manuscripts, genealogy, heraldry, toponymy, folklore and literature of Wales, as well as reports on the society's numerous excavations. See also CAMBRIAN INSTITUTE.

For further details see the Association's centenary volume, *A Hundred Years of Welsh Archaeology 1846–1946* (1946).

Cambrian Institute, The, a society originally known as the Historic Institute of Wales, was founded in 1853 by John *Williams (Ab Ithel) in an attempt to break away from the *Cambrian Archaeological Association. Its objects were 'the promotion of Celtic and Welsh literature and the advancement of the arts and sciences', but no meetings were held, except by the London branch. Between 1854 and 1864 the society published *The Cambrian Journal*, a quarterly intended as 'a publication of a truly national character, being devoted, not only to the illustration of our ancient literature, but also to the development of the natural resources of the country and the advancement of such arts and sciences as influence the duties, and promote the comfort and happiness, of domestic or social life'. The magazine carried essays on philology, topography, botany, biography, music and literary history, as well as poetry, reviews and news. Among its contributors were Eben Fardd (Ebenezer *Thomas), Thomas *Stephens, William *Owen Pughe and D. Silvan *Evans. The editor, until his death in 1862, was Ab Ithel whose uncritical acceptance of the claims of Iolo Morganwg (Edward *Williams) vitiated the magazine's worth. Its demise was caused by a falling away in the Institute's membership and indifference on the part of its readership.

Cambrian Quarterly Magazine and Celtic Repertory, The, published in London between 1829 and 1833, was founded by Rice Pryce Buckley Williams who was also its first editor. Almost entirely in English, the magazine aimed to preserve 'native lore' for posterity and to win 'the incurious and indifferent into an interest for Wales'. It carried passages translated from early and medieval Welsh literature and articles on historical, topographical and biographical subjects. Despite its antiquarian bias, it also published a little poetry and reviews of recent books on Celtic subjects as well as 'London and Provincial News'. Among its contributors were William *Owen Pughe, Walter *Davies (Gwallter Mechain) and Samuel Rush *Meyrick.

Cambrian Register, The, a periodical of which three volumes were published under the editorship of William *Owen Pughe in 1795, 1796 and 1818. In the preface to the first volume, Pughe described the wealth of material hidden in the ancient manuscripts and oral traditions of Wales, adding that the primary purpose of his journal was 'to investigate this hidden repository, and to bring to light whatever may be deemed most rare and valuable'. It carried selections from early and medieval Welsh literature, together with English translations, and articles on biographical, topographical and historical subjects. Pughe also published some of the correspondence of Lewis *Morris, John *Davies of Mallwyd, Edward *Lhuyd and Edward *Williams (Iolo Morganwg), as well as poetry, bookreviews and news. Chiefly under the patronage of the *Gwyneddigion Society, the magazine counted Walter *Davies (Gwallter Mechain) and David *Samwell among its contributors. Nevertheless, the nature of its contents, its high price and the fact that it was written in English, put this periodical beyond the reach of most Welshmen and, on the editor's own admission, the chief reason for its demise was 'want of support'.

Cambrian Shakespeare, The, see EDWARDS, THOMAS (1738–1810).

Cambrian Strike, The (1910–11), see under TONYPANDY RIOTS.

Cambrian Visitor, The, see under WARING, ELIJAH (c.1788–1857).

Cambriol, see under VAUGHAN, WILLIAM (1575–1641).

Cambro-Briton and General Celtic Repository, The, a periodical published in London by its founder and editor, John Humffreys *Parry, who had originally planned a fortnightly 'devoted exclusively to the interests of Wales'. The magazine began, however, as a monthly in September 1819 and continued thus, with one break between July and October 1821, until its demise in June 1822, the occasion of a bitter circular from Parry to the 'Editors of the Provincial Papers' in which he denounced the apathy of his countrymen to the cause of their national literature. Reflecting the editor's antiquarian tastes, the magazine carried articles on the Triads, the Welsh language, the wisdom of *Catwg Ddoeth, Welsh proverbs, Welsh music and the like, but very little original creative work in Welsh or English, and none of lasting value. Welsh verses were usually accompanied by English translations and all articles, though expressing support for the Welsh language and its culture, often explicitly, were entirely in English. The only concessions to contemporaneity were reviews, an attempt by the editor to introduce a revised Welsh alphabet, and a series which consisted largely of notices of eisteddfodau and meetings of Welsh societies; the editorial style, like that of most contributors, was pedantic and circumlocutory. Despite, or perhaps because of, their quaintness, the three volumes of the periodical remain of interest to students of the period.

Cambro-Britons, The (1798), a historical drama by the English writer James Boaden (1762–1839). Based on the wars between *Llywelyn ap Gruffudd and Edward I, it is remarkable for the author's concern to present Llywelyn less as a rebel against the English king than as 'a great patriot . . . who seeks to sustain the independence of his country', and for the sympathetic way in which many of the characters are endowed with qualities for long denied Welshmen in English literature, such as courage, fidelity and honour.

CAMDEN, WILLIAM (1551–1623), see under BRITANNIA (1586).

Camlan, The Battle of (*c.*539), in which, according to *Annales Cambriae*, *Arthur and *Medrod (Medrawd) were killed, has been variously identified as having taken place at Camelford in Cornwall, in Somerset, by Malory near Salisbury, and more recently at Camboglanna, the fort now called Birdoswald on Hadrian's Wall. Camlan was known to early Welsh poets as a terrible or futile slaughter and the word '*cadgamlan*' came to mean 'a rout' or 'a rabble'. See also FUTILE BATTLES.

'Cân yr Henwr', see under CANU LLYWARCH HEN (9th or 10th cent.).

CANAWAY, WILLIAM HAMILTON (**William Hamilton**; 1925–), novelist. Born in Altrincham, Ches., of partly Welsh parentage, and educated at the University College of North Wales, Bangor, he lectured at technical colleges in England until 1964 when he settled in Deiniolen, Caerns.; since 1976 he has lived in Derbyshire. Among his fourteen novels the best-known is *Sammy Going South* (1961), which was made into a film, but those who have read the whole *œuvre* may be likely to prefer some of his other work, such as *The Ring-Givers* (1958), *The Seal* (1959), *The Hunter and the Horns* (1962), *Crows in a Green Tree* (1965), *The Grey Seas of Jutland* (1966), *The Mules of Borgo San Marco* (1967), *Harry Doing Good* (1973) and *The Glory of the Sea* (1974). A common theme of these novels is some quest, chase or trial in which the chief character, who is usually ordinary, is tested through extraordinary and sometimes violent circumstances. There is, too, a sense of spiritual adventure in this author's work, which is why he can be considered as more than merely a writer of exciting stories. Several of his novels are set in Wales: *My Feet upon a Rock* (1963) is the story of a boy growing up in the slate-quarrying districts of Caernarfonshire, while in *A Declaration of Independence* (1971), also set among the quarries, an old lady looks back from her daughter's home in Los Angeles on her life in north Wales towards the end of the nineteenth century. W. H. Canaway was also the author of the screen-play *The Ipcress File* (1965).

Candlemas Singing, a folk-custom. In the Church calendar six feasts were associated with the Virgin Mary and one of these, the Feast of Mary at the Beginning of Spring or Mary's Festival of the Candles (2 Feb.), was connected with the custom of *wassailing which was popular in the eighteenth century. The feast celebrated the purification of Mary but in Wales the Christian festival was grafted on to a much older tradition associated with the beginning of Spring in the Celtic year. It is this fact which accounts for the frequent emphasis in Candlemas Singing on wishing success to crops and animals during the coming year. The custom involved a contest in verse, the singers outside the house making frequent reference to the cold weather, a welcome on the hearth, the drink and the young women inside from whom they hoped to receive kisses. It has been suggested that this last detail, couched in terms of the holly and the ivy, is an echo of ancient rivalry between the sexes. In north-west Wales a 'chair carol' was sung after the singers had entered the house, a young girl with a child on her knee representing Mary and the child Jesus. A carol of thanks was also sung before the visitors' departure. Some of the carols associated with the festival were sung to tunes which bore English names.

Many examples of Candlemas Singing in Anglesey were recorded by Richard Morris, one of the *Morris Brothers, in the eighteenth century and edited by T. H. *Parry-Williams in *Llawysgrif Richard Morris o Gerddi* (1931). This important collection includes a number of cumulative songs and feat-songs which were part of the competition at the door on Candlemas Eve.

For further details see the article by Trefor M. Owen in the *Transactions* of the Caernarvonshire Historical Society (1964); see also Rhiannon Ifans, *Sêrs a Rybana* (1983).

Caniadau Cymru (lit. 'Songs of Wales'; 2 vols., 1897), an anthology edited by William Lewis Jones (1866–1922) with notes by Ifor *Williams, is the most satisfactory anthology made in the nineteenth century of verse in the free metres from about 1450 until the time of John Ceiriog *Hughes. The editor was Professor of English (1897–1919) at the University College of North Wales, Bangor, but he also had a wide knowledge of Welsh literature. An attempt to emulate Palgrave's *Golden Treasury* (1861), his anthology was primarily intended for schools and colleges, but the general reader may still derive pleasure from it. The most important among the poets represented in the first volume are Edward *Morris, Huw *Morys, Edward *Richard, Thomas *Edwards (Twm o'r Nant), Robert *Davies (Bardd Nantglyn), David *Thomas (Dafydd Ddu Eryri), John *Blackwell (Alun), and Evan *Evans (Ieuan Glan Geirionydd), and in the second William Ellis *Jones (Cawrdaf), Ebenezer *Thomas (Eben Fardd), William *Williams (Caledfryn), John *Jones (Talhaiarn), Evan *Jones (Ieuan Gwynedd), Owen Wynne *Jones (Glasynys), William *Thomas (Islwyn), Richard *Davies (Mynyddog) and John Ceiriog Hughes (Ceiriog).

Caniadau y rhai sydd ar y Môr o Wydr (lit. 'The songs of those who are on the sea of glass'; 1761/62), the fourth collection of hymns by William *Williams (Pantycelyn), was written when the poet was at the height of his powers and contains some of his finest work. Several of the hymns, on metres not used by him previously and emphasizing the complex nature of the Christian's experience, were responsible for setting in motion the religious Revival of 1762 which was led by Daniel *Rowland of Llangeitho, Cards.

Canlyn Arthur (lit. 'Following Arthur'; 1938), a volume of political essays by Saunders *Lewis; all except one, on the function of Art, were first published in *Y Ddraig Goch* (1926–36), the newspaper of *Plaid Cymru*. They set out cogently and memorably the author's political philosophy which may be broadly described as Catholic distributivism, as opposed to *laissez-faire* Capitalism on the one hand and *Marxism on the other. The book contains essays on economic matters, on the Welsh language, on the Fire in Llŷn (see PENYBERTH) and on a trio of highly diverse political figures: H. R. *Jones, David *Lloyd George and Thomas Masaryk. The title is taken from a speech by *Cai in *Breuddwyd Rhonabwy: 'Whoever wishes to follow Arthur let him be with him in Cornwall tonight. And whoever does not so wish, let him be against Arthur'.

Canthrig Bwt, a giantess who was reputed to eat children. According to local tradition, she lived under a cromlech near Llanberis, Caerns., until one day she was enticed into the open and beheaded with an axe.

Cantref, an administrative and territorial unit of medieval Wales, consisted in theory of a hundred townships. Reliable information on the boundaries of cantrefi is rarely available before the thirteenth century but it is reasonable to assume that the cantref was a unit of which the roots were contemporaneous with the origin of the Welsh kingdoms. Some early kingdoms, such as *Rhos in *Perfeddwlad, were absorbed into wider *gwledydd* and then demoted to the status of a cantref. The cantref pattern could thus represent the remnants of the network of statelets which may have emerged in post-Roman Wales. Perhaps as early as the eleventh century, cantrefi were divided into commots. In some areas of Wales, *Ceredigion for example, the commots became the sole unit of local government and all traces of the ancient cantrefi were lost. In regions such as the Vale of Glamorgan, where Norman settlement was both early and intensive, the older administrative units were overlaid by manorial organization, causing any statements about the boundaries of the cantrefi and commots to be, at best, tentative. The counties of Anglesey, Caernarfon, Merioneth, Cardigan and Carmarthen, established in the wake of the Edwardian Conquest of Wales, were divided into hundreds, as were the counties established under the *Act

of Union of 1536. These hundreds were generally based upon the cantrefi but sometimes their names and boundaries bear little relationship to the older pattern.

For further details see J. E. Lloyd, *A History of Wales* (1911), William Rees, *An Historical Atlas of Wales* (1951) and Melville Richards, *Welsh Administrative and Territorial Units* (1969).

Cantref Bychan, a cantref lying between *Brycheiniog and the river Tywi. From about 1116 the Normans sought to bring it under the control of their castle at Llandovery but from 1162 until 1277 it was held by the rulers of *Deheubarth. Thereafter, its two northern commots became the lordship of Llanymddyfri (Llandovery) and the southernmost commot eventually passed to the estates of the Duchy of Lancaster. The castle known as *Carreg Cennen was the chief stronghold of the Welsh in Cantref Bychan.

Cantref Gwarthaf, a cantref comprising most of eastern Dyfed and consisting of eight commots. Within it lay *Whitland, traditionally associated with the promulgation of the *Laws of Hywel Dda.

Cantref Mawr, a cantref lying to the north of the river Tywi and consisting of seven commots. Within it lay *Dinefwr, the traditional seat of the rulers of *Deheubarth. The cantref provided a base for the restoration of Welsh rule over Deheubarth under *Rhys ap Gruffudd (The Lord Rhys) but his descendants were dispossessed in 1277 when the territory was attached to the county of Carmarthen.

Cantre'r Gwaelod (lit. 'The lowland hundred'), the land of *Gwyddno Garanhir which, according to legend, was drowned beneath what is today Cardigan Bay. The traditional belief is thought to have its origins in folk-memory from a time in the Neolithic or the Iron Age when the sea between Wales and Ireland was still rising, but in its earliest written form it dates from the thirteenth century and is to be found in a series of *englynion* in The *Black Book of Carmarthen. It was given a wider currency by T. J. Ll. *Prichard's poem 'The Land beneath the Sea', and the song *'Clychau Aberdyfi'. The land, known as Maes Gwyddno, is said to have been submerged when a well-maiden named Mererid neglected her duties. According to a better known version of the legend, which is about three hundred years old and derives from similar stories in the Low Countries, Gwyddno's kingdom had sixteen noble cities and was defended from the sea by an embankment with sluices. The drunken Seithenyn, keeper of the dyke, was responsible for letting in the water which drowned all the inhabitants save the king himself. On calm evenings, it is claimed, the church bells of Cantre'r Gwaelod can be heard ringing beneath the waves of Cardigan Bay.

The tradition is also associated with other parts of the Welsh coast, such as Tyno Helyg, Caerns., and with places in other countries such as Brittany, where the legend of Ker Ys inspired Debussy's 'La Cathédrale Engloutie'. See also MISFORTUNES OF ELPHIN (1829).

For discussion of the legend see John Rhŷs, *Celtic Folklore* (1901) and F. J. North, *Sunken Cities* (1957); see also Rachel Bromwich, 'Cantre'r Gwaelod and Ker-Is' in *The Early Cultures of North-West Europe* (ed. Cyril Fox and Bruce Dickens, 1950).

Cantscaul, The Battle of (633), see under CADWALLON AP CADFAN (d. 633).

'Canu Bychan, Y' (lit. 'The short song'), a poem of exultation by ★Llywarch ap Llywelyn (Prydydd y Moch) addressed to ★Llywelyn ap Iorwerth (Llywelyn Fawr) in the Prince's heyday. It consists of fifteen quatrains with the same main rhyme and all except the last two lines, each of nine syllables, are formed of highly ornamented couplets of nineteen syllables mostly of the *Cyhydedd Hir* pattern with three internal rhymes and alliteration, varied occasionally by means of a *Toddaid*. The poem has a surge or onrush which is evocative of the irresistible power of Llywelyn: the names of places associated with his successes throughout Wales are listed in rapid juxtaposition and the Prince is hailed as the embodiment of the ancient ★vaticinations in a mixture of historical fact and patriotic fervour. See also CANU MAWR.

'Canu Heledd' (lit. 'The song of Heledd'; 9th or 10th cent.), one of the longest and most unified cycles of saga *englynion*. The main character and narrator is Heledd, the last surviving member of the royal House of ★Powys, who laments the loss of her home, the destruction of the surrounding countryside and the deaths of her brothers, particularly that of the king, Cynddylan, who ruled in the early seventh century. The anonymous poet seems to have used the dimly-remembered historical past to reflect the suffering of contemporary Powys in the ninth or tenth century. The lost narrative may have been more complex than that which can be deduced from the verses; for instance, there is probably some reason of plot why Heledd blames herself for the fall of Cynddylan's court. The cycle is sufficiently clear, however, for an appreciation of the poetry which is intensely emotional, tragic and well wrought.

The choice of Heledd as the narrator may also be determined, if only subconsciously, by the ancient Celtic myth which held the land to be personified by a goddess. Heledd's lamentation can be compared with other reflections on this theme in which the loss of the rightful king brings desolation upon the land and destitution to the goddess. This thematic element of the passing of a kingdom and the destruction of a culture still has great immediacy and there have been several modern Welsh adaptations of the central poem in the cycle, 'Stafell Cynddylan' ('Cynddylan's hall').

The text was published with notes in *Canu Llywarch Hen* (ed. Ifor Williams, 1935).

'Canu Llywarch Hen' (lit. 'The song of Llywarch the Old'), a cycle of *englynion* about an old man and his sons, was written in the ninth or tenth century. It was Ifor ★Williams who demonstrated that they were not composed by Llywarch, as had been previously believed, but that they are poems about him. The cycle now consists of dialogues and monologues which dramatize emotional peaks in a saga of which the narrative has not survived. The poems may originally have been combined with prose to tell a continuous story, or they could have illustrated certain incidents while depending on the audience's familiarity with the story. It is unlikely that the extant poems come from a single prose–verse saga since they vary considerably in style and date, but recognition of their narrative background is essential to their understanding.

At the heart of the cycle is the presentation of Llywarch as a cantankerous old man in 'Cân yr Henwr' ('The song of the old man'), a poem which portrays him musing upon old age and adversity. His circumstances are very different from those of his youth, when he was merry, daring and handsome; now, in his own words, '*Wyf cefngrwm, wyf trwm, wyf truan*' ('I am hunchbacked, I am weary, I am wretched'). In times gone by he enjoyed the company of others but now his only companion is a wooden crutch. Aware of his inescapable fate, he identifies himself with a leaf blown hither and thither by the wind: '*Gwae hi o'i thynged. Hi hen, eleni ganed*' ('Woe is her fate. Old, born this year').

The old man's desire for vicarious glory causes him to make unreasonable demands on his twenty-four warrior sons which ultimately lead to their deaths in battle. His typical taunting is seen in a poem to Maen and more fully in a dialogue with his last surviving son, Gwên. Only with the latter's death does he become aware of what he has done, expressing his grief in a moving lament. Miscellaneous verses to other sons have primarily antiquarian interest, listing their names or their burial places, and one poem tells how Llywarch travelled to northern Britain to seek the assistance of his cousin, ★Urien Rheged. See also ENGLYNION GERAINT.

An annotated version of the text of the Llywarch Hen cycle has been published in *Canu Llywarch Hen* (ed. Ifor Williams, 1935), and a translation of the poem in *The Poems of Llywarch Hen* (ed. Patrick K. Ford, 1974); for further details see *The Saga of Llywarch the Old* (1955) by Glyn Jones, T. J. Morgan and Ifor Williams; the essay by Ifor Williams in *The Beginnings of Welsh Poetry* (ed. Rachel Bromwich, 1972), the essay on '*Cân yr Henwr*' by Gwyn Thomas in *Astudiaethau ar yr Hengerdd* (ed. Rachel Bromwich and R. Brinley Jones, 1978) and Eurys Rolant, *Llywarch Hen a'i Feibion* (1984).

'Canu Mawr, Y' (lit. 'The long song'), a poem by *Llywarch ap Llywelyn (Prydydd y Moch), the chief poet at the court of *Llywelyn ap Iorwerth (Llywelyn Fawr) during the first half of that Prince's reign. A strong supporter of the policy of expansion pursued by the House of *Gwynedd, the poet exults in Llywelyn's progress from the achievements of his youth to his mastery of all Gwynedd and *Powys. The poem consists of four mono-rhyming *laisses* of respectively sixty-six, thirty-six, forty-two and sixty-four lines, each of eight syllables, with some groups of sixteen syllables forming their own metrical patterns. Opening with an invocation to '*Lywiawdr llu daear a nef*' ('Ruler of the hosts of heaven and earth') for inspiration to extol his Prince, the poet follows Llywelyn's early career on his way eastward to the limits of Chester and then southward to Welshpool. The splendour of this second *Arthur, he who loved not hoarding gold or silver, is also praised. To those who disapproved of Llywelyn's war-making, the poet's answer is, '*Llwrw gwelwch neud heddwch heno*' ('Wherever you look tonight there is peace'). The poem is an appeal to Powys to accept Llywelyn, a generous Welshman who is preferable to any Norman. See also CANU BYCHAN.

'Canu y Byd Bychan' (lit. 'The small song of the world'), a poem which follows its partner, *'Canu y Byd Mawr', in The *Book of Taliesin. It deals briefly (in 21 short lines) with a problem which exercised early medieval thinkers and those such as Bede who wrote commentaries on the Book of Genesis: exactly how is the Earth suspended or supported in space? Written at some time between the ninth and twelfth centuries, the poem takes the form of a volley of questions addressed, not (as in other poems in the manuscript) to the learned ecclesiastical orders, but to 'the poets of the world'. It concludes with the Christian orthodoxy that the Earth is maintained by the grace of the Holy Spirit as manifested in the figures of the Four Evangelists. The poem is of interest primarily because it points to a degree of interface between nature poetry and the more popular elements of received learning in medieval times.

'Canu y Byd Mawr' (lit. 'The great song of the world'), a poem in The *Book of Taliesin incorporating several cosmographical ideas in common currency during the early Middle Ages which had circulated since classical times, namely, the five zones of the Earth, the tripartite divisions of the oceans and the land, and the seven firmaments with their respective planets. More idiosyncratic is the listing of seven rather than the traditional five senses, and seven rather than the four elements which constitute both Earth and Man, the latter being regarded as the former's microcosm. Like its partner, *'Canu y Byd Bychan', the poem shows how the received learning of medieval times was being assimilated into the Welsh poetic canon, in this case to bear out the boasts of the omniscient *Taliesin-persona.

'Canu y Gwynt' (lit. 'Song to the wind'), a poem of some sixty lines preserved in The *Book of Taliesin as well as in Hanes Taliesin. It has not been dated, but belongs to the class of imaginative poetry found in Old English and Norse and may be placed among those poems on various subjects which were composed towards the end of the period of the *Cynfeirdd (6th–9th cents.). Considered to be a forerunner of *Dafydd ap Gwilym's famous cywydd to the wind, the poem opens with the words '*Dychymyg pwy yw*' ('Imagination who is it') and goes on to give a vivid description of the wind, but without naming it.

Canwyll y Cymru (lit. 'The candle of the Welsh'; 1659–72), a collection of didactic verses by Rhys *Prichard, vicar of Llandovery, Carms., was first published in parts by Stephen *Hughes, an ejected Puritan minister, and was given this title in an edition of 1681. The verses, clearly reflecting the influence of the *Bible, the Book of Common Prayer and the Protestant *cwndidau, immediately became very popular and remained so for nearly two hundred years. They include Nativity and biblical verses, together with homilies for moral and domestic purposes, most of which were composed between 1615 and 1635. Although sometimes pedestrian, these verses often have a certain charm. The author's aim was to set rural life within the framework of the Articles of Faith of the Established Church, emphasizing that to please God was to work hard, honour the Church and obey the King and all authority.

The text was edited by R. Rees in 1862.

Cap Coch (1730–1820), a murderer who kept a tavern known as the New Inn between Merthyr Mawr and Bridgend, Glam. His crimes remained undetected until some eighteen years after his death when, in the tavern's ruins and the fields around, the remains of his numerous victims were discovered. The publican's real name is no longer remembered but it is said that he acquired his sobriquet from the red cap which he wore as a sign of support for the French Revolution of 1789.

Capel Celyn, see under TRYWERYN.

Captain Cat, the blind sailor in Dylan *Thomas's *Under Milk Wood (1954) who dreams about his drowned shipmates and identifies the inhabitants of Llareggub by their voices, thus sharing the narrator's role of the First and Second Voices.

Captain Trefor, see under ENOC HUWS (1891).

Caradawg or **Caradoc**, see CARATACUS (1st cent.).

Caradog, the son of *Brân, according to the Second Branch of *Pedair Cainc y Mabinogi, was put in charge of the six Principal Officers who were left by Bendigeidfran to guard the Island of Britain while he went on the expedition to Ireland. When *Caswallon, the son of Beli, wearing a magic cloak which made him invisible, killed all six of them, Caradog was terrified to death. There is no early evidence for the traditional belief that he was the same man as *Caratacus, the leader of the Britons in the first century.

Caradog Freichfras, a hero of the Arthurian cycle, appears in French legends and romances of the Middle Ages such as Lai du Cor, Le Manteau Mautaillié and Livre de Caradoc. In these works his name occurs in such forms as the French Karadues Briebraz and the Breton Karadoc Brech Bras; the adjective 'Briebraz', meant to convey 'short-armed', shows a confusion between the Welsh adjective 'bras' ('stout') and the French noun 'bras' ('arm').

Undoubtedly, Caradog was of Welsh origin, and he is often mentioned in Welsh sources, but far less evidence exists for him in Welsh than in French. In one of the Triads he is called the son of Llŷr Merini and is said to have cast the wonderful spell of love on *Tegau Eurfron, the daughter of Nudd Llawhael, King of North Britain. According to another Triad, he was one of the Three Battle-Horsemen of the Isle of Britain and his horse was called Lluagor. He is described in *Breuddwyd Rhonabwy as a virtuous, proud man, an eloquent and bold speaker, the chief counsellor and cousin of *Arthur. In the Life of *Collen it is said that he injured his arm at the battle of Hiraddug and the Life of *Padarn records a tradition which associates him with the settlement of the Britons in Brittany. There exist French legends about Caradog's relationship with Tegau, of which no Welsh version has survived, but references to him in cywyddau of the medieval period suggest that they were known in Wales.

For further details see Rachel Bromwich, Trioedd Ynys Prydein (1961).

CARADOG OF LLANCARFAN (fl. 1135), the author of several *Lives of the Saints. The little that is known about him is based on two references, one at the end of *Historia Regum Britanniae by *Geoffrey of Monmouth and the other in his own work. Geoffrey stated that he was leaving the Kings of the Welsh as a subject to Caradog of Llancarfan, just as he left the Kings of the English to William of Malmesbury and Henry of Huntingdon, and referred to Caradog as 'contemporare meo'. The precise meaning of this expression is not clear, but it may suggest a degree of intimacy between Geoffrey and Caradog and that they had an interest in the same field, the early history of Wales.

The second reference to Caradog is found in a Latin couplet at the end of the Life of Saint *Cadog which he revised from the more famous version by Lifris. These lines, which attribute the work to Caradog, is evidence of his industry in honour of the founder of *Llancarfan. They recur, together with the same attribution to Nancarbanesis . . . Caratoci, at the end of the Life of *Gildas. The Latin preserves an older and more correct form of the place-name, Nant Carfan, which became Llancarfan by concord, but without mutation. One of the sources of the Life of Gildas was the history of Saint Cadog and it shows a good deal of respect for him and the learning of his house, as was expected of an author who claimed allegiance to a monastery founded by him. But the chief purpose of the Life of Gildas was to claim him for the monastery of Glastonbury, so Caradog may have been one of the many authors who strove to increase the honour of that house and to show its unique place in the early history of British Christianity.

It is possible that Caradog was the author of other Lives, including those of Cyngar and *Illtud, and that he was a writer of such works by profession. Some have suggested that he was also the author of The Book of Llandâv and of *Brut y Tywysogyon. The latter begins in the exact place where Geoffrey's Historia ends and it contains the material which Geoffrey left to his 'contemporary'. Nevertheless, the first to suggest Caradog's authorship of the Brut was David *Powel in his English version of that work, The History of Wales . . . written originally in British by Caradoc of Lhancarvan (1584), an ascription which cannot be correct since the Brut is a chronicle from many centres and periods and it is written not in 'British' but in Latin.

For further details see the article by J. S. P. Tatlock in Speculum (vol. 13, 1938) and that by Christopher Brooke in N. K. Chadwick (ed.), Studies in the Early British Church (1958).

Caradogion, Y, an offshoot of the *Gwyneddigion Society, had English-speaking as well as Welsh-speaking members and its weekly debates were held in English. It met during the 1790s at the Bull's Head, a tavern in Walbrook, which was a favourite haunt of *London Welshmen who knew it as 'Y Crindy' ('The thatched house'). In the turmoil caused by the French Revolution of 1789 some of the society's members were suspected of sedition and its books were confiscated.

Carannog (mid-6th cent.), a saint who is commemorated in many parts of Wales, in Ireland, in south-west England and in Brittany. He may have been a native of a coastal district in what later became Cardiganshire and he may have been associated with Llangrannog. A short Life of Carannog was composed in the twelfth century, possibly by Lifris, the author of the Life of *Cadog. If he was a son of Ceredig, the son of *Cunedda, he would have been an uncle of *Dewi Sant. His feast-day is 16 May.

Caratacus or **Caradawg** or **Caradoc** (1st cent.), the son of Cunobelin (Shakespeare's Cymbeline) who was King of the Catuvellauni. After the defeat of his people by the Roman army under Aulus Plautius at the Battle of the Medway (AD 43), he fled to the battle-hardy *Silures in south-east Wales to avoid the probable treachery of the Trinovantes whom his father had subjugated. From AD 47 when the Romans established the line of forts known as the Fosse Way, he made a series of daring forays, putting Roman convoys and the lands of the conquered Dobunni to fire and sword. The establishment of a new forward fort at Kingsholm (Gloucester), however, restricted his movements and an attempt to link his forces with those of the *Ordovices of north Wales was miscalculated. A hard-fought battle on a hill in mid-Wales (probably not one of the several called Caer Caradoc), was followed by his flight to Cartimandua, Queen of the Brigantes. She, having given sureties to the Romans for the good behaviour of her tribe, surrendered him to his enemies. Taken in chains to Rome, Caratacus was spared a savage and public death by challenging the Emperor Claudius to let him live in the city as a free man on condition that he gave his word not to escape, this bond being kept on both sides. Caradawg's fame in later generations rested on his pan-Celticism as well as his bravery.

For further details see S. C. Stanford, *The Archaeology of the Welsh Marches* (1980), Graham Webster, *Rome against Caratacus: the Roman Campaigns in Britain AD 48–58* (1981) and Charles Kightly, *Folk Heroes of Britain* (1982).

Cardi, a nickname for a native of the former county of Cardiganshire, is sometimes applied more generally to any person who is tight-fisted with money. The reputation of Cardiganshire people for thriftiness is thought to be derived from the business acumen of the county's hill-farmers, a hardy breed, some of whom became wealthy dairymen in London. There are many jokes which depend on the Cardi's alleged parsimony but the nickname is not necessarily considered pejorative, for it is often used with pride by Cardis about themselves. See also the next entry.

Cardi, Y, a magazine first published by *Cym-*

deithas Ceredigion ('The Cardiganshire society') in 1966. Among its editors have been Donald *Evans, Dafydd *Jones (1907–) and Dic Jones (Richard Lewis *Jones); Roy Stephens was appointed editor in 1983. The contents are mostly of regional interest but include a good deal of verse and prose by eminent writers associated with the former county. Commemorative numbers have been published in honour of Gwenallt (David James *Jones), Dafydd *Jones (Isfoel), T. E. *Nicholas, T. J. *Thomas (Sarnicol), E. Prosser *Rhys and Alun *Jones (Alun Cilie).

Cardiff castle, an early Norman fortification built by order of Robert Fitz Hamon, Earl of Gloucester, on the site of a Roman fort, in the late eleventh century. The motte and bailey structure, rebuilt in stone in the twelfth century, became the centre of the feudal lordship of Glamorgan. In the Middle Ages the castle was owned by various Norman families such as de Clare, Despenser and Beauchamp. It was attacked by Ifor Bach (*Ifor ap Cadifor) in 1158, by Llywelyn Bren (*Llywelyn ap Gruffudd) in 1316 and by *Owain Glyndŵr in 1403. During the fifteenth century it belonged to Richard Beauchamp, Earl of Warwick, who ordered the erection of the octagonal tower about 1425. In 1766 the castle became the centre of the *Bute estate and parts were rebuilt under the direction of the first Marquess in 1796. The nineteenth century saw the restoration of the clock-tower and the west wing, to the design of the architect, William Burges (1827–81), who added new rooms and embellished them with ornate carvings and vaulted ceilings. The castle and grounds were presented to the City of Cardiff by the *Bute family in 1947.

For further details see William Rees, *Cardiff, a History of the City* (2nd edn., 1969) and S. Williams (ed.), *South Glamorgan: a County History* (1975).

Cardigan castle, built by order of Roger de Montgomery, Earl of Shrewsbury, during his occupation of *Ceredigion in 1093, was fought over by Norman and Welsh families throughout the first half of the twelfth century. A second fortress was erected in 1110 by order of Gilbert Fitz Richard de Clare.

The castle was captured in 1165 by *Rhys ap Gruffudd (The Lord Rhys) who rebuilt it in stone and mortar; it was there at Christmas 1176 that he presided over an assembly of poets and musicians which is sometimes said to have been the earliest recorded eisteddfod. In *Brut y Tywysogyon* it is stated that the assembly had been proclaimed a year in advance throughout Wales, England, Scotland and Ireland, and that two chairs were offered as prizes. The Lord's personal harpist was victorious and in the bardic contests the men of Gwynedd were supreme.

Hospitality was provided at the castle for

Archbishop Baldwin and *Gerald de Barri (Giraldus Cambrensis) during their itinerary of Wales in 1188. The stronghold, described in the *Brut* as '*clo a chadwedigaeth holl Gymru*' ('the lock and stay of all Wales'), was sold to the English king in 1199 but was recaptured by *Llywelyn ap Iorwerth (Llywelyn Fawr) in 1215 and again in 1231. The administration for the new county of Cardiganshire was housed there from 1277 and, throughout the later Middle Ages, Cardigan served in a subordinate administrative capacity to *Carmarthen in relation to the Crown lands in south Wales. *Dafydd Nanmor composed an *awdl* in praise of Dafydd ap Thomas ap Dafydd, Constable of Cardigan castle and a supporter of the Yorkist cause in the Wars of the Roses. The castle was attacked by Parliamentary forces during the *Civil War.

For further details see the article on the early history of Cardiganshire and Carmarthenshire by J. G. Edwards in *The English Historical Review* (vol. XXXI, 1916); J. E. Lloyd, *The Story of Cardigan 400–1277* (1937) and the article by D. J. C. King on the castles of Cardiganshire in *Ceredigion* (vol. 3, 1956).

Carew castle, built during the last decade of the eleventh century and in the early stages of the *Norman Conquest of west Wales, belonged to Gerald de Windsor, custodian of Pembroke castle and the grandfather of *Gerald de Barri (Giraldus Cambrensis). Rebuilt in the thirteenth century and renovated in the late fifteenth century, it became the residence of Sir Rhys ap Thomas (1449–1525), Chamberlain and Justiciar of South Wales, a renowned bardic patron, under whom it became an important centre of literary life. His court poet, *Rhys Nanmor, sang his praises as did *Tudur Aled, *Lewys Môn, Ieuan Brechfa and Lewys Morgannwg (*Llywelyn ap Rhisiart). In 1507 Sir Rhys held a great tournament to celebrate his admission to the Order of the Garter which was attended by many of the most eminent families in Wales. The last major phase of reconstruction began after the castle had been granted to Sir John *Perrot, the Elizabethan politician and Lord Deputy of Ireland. Originally a Royalist stronghold in the *Civil War, the garrison surrendered to Parliamentary forces in April 1645. The accusation that he had used the castle's revenues to pay his men caused John *Poyer to declare for the King and thus set the Second Civil War in motion.

For further details see W. G. Spurrell, *The History of Carew* (1921), the article by R. F. Walker in *Archaeologia Cambrensis* (1956) and E. Llwyd Williams, *Crwydro Sir Benfro* (vol. I, 1958).

Carmarthen castle, built by order of Henry I before 1109, stood on a site overlooking a strategic crossing of the river Tywi. Attacked, burned and taken by Welsh insurgents over more than a hundred years, it became a formidable royal military stronghold in south-west

Wales during the thirteenth century. Despite its capture by *Owain Glyndŵr's forces in 1403, and again in 1405, the castle was the administrative centre of south Wales in the later Middle Ages, thus contributing to the growth of the town.

An eisteddfod was held in the castle about the year 1451 under the patronage of Gruffudd ap Nicolas of Dinefwr, the first assembly to have been held during the time of the *Poets of the Gentry. The date usually given for this event derives from one of the manuscripts of Iolo Morganwg (Edward *Williams) and is therefore unreliable, but it may have been held after the renovation of the castle in 1452–53. Both poets and musicians took part, the adjudicator being Gruffudd ap Nicolas, and a miniature silver chair was won by *Dafydd ab Edmwnd, whose subsequent reform of the *Twenty-four Metres was the chief significance of this occasion.

The grandson of Gruffudd ap Nicolas, Sir Rhys ap Thomas (1449–1525), also of Dinefwr, built a 'newe place' within the castle soon after 1485; his praises were sung by *Lewys Glyn Cothi (Llywelyn y Glyn), Lewys Morgannwg (*Llywelyn ap Rhisiart) and *Tudur Aled. The castle was twice captured by Parliamentary forces during the *Civil War but subsequently fell into desuetude. At the end of the eighteenth century the site was occupied by a gaol and the offices of Dyfed County Council were situated there in 1974.

For further details see the article by J. G. Edwards on the early history of Carmarthenshire and Cardiganshire in *The English Historical Review* (vol. XXXI, 1916), J. E. Lloyd (ed.), *A History of Carmarthenshire* (1935, 1939) and the chapter by R. A. Griffiths in *Boroughs of Mediaeval Wales* (ed. R. A. Griffiths, 1978). Details of the Carmarthen Eisteddfod will be found in Hywel Teifi Edwards, *Yr Eisteddfod* (1971), and in the article by D. J. Bowen in *Barn* (no. 142, August, 1974).

Carmarthen Journal, The (1810), the oldest surviving newspaper in Wales, was launched by a number of Whigs and minor gentry but turned Tory during the 1820s and took the side of the Established Church. The Liberal newspaper, *The *Welshman*, was established in 1832 to counteract its influence and there was often friction between them. The *Journal* thereafter became more local in its coverage of news and more popular on account of its Welsh columns and the space it devoted to poetry. Among its editors were D. Archard Williams, Henry and Lewis Giles, H. Tobit Evans and Emlyn Thomas. By the 1980s the paper had become almost wholly confined to news of the town and the former county of Carmarthen.

Carmarthen priory, believed to have been founded about 1127 as a Benedictine cell and daughter-house of the great abbey of Battle, had been transferred by 1148 to the Order of *Augustinian Canons and was dedicated to St.

John the Evangelist. A long religious poem in Anglo-Norman French by *Simon of Carmarthen, a canon at the priory during the thirteenth century, has survived. It has been suggested that *The *Black Book of Carmarthen* was written there between 1170 and 1230. *Lewys Glyn Cothi (Llywelyn y Glyn) wrote a eulogy to the prior, Morgan ab Owain ab Einion (c.1450–c.1464).

The friary at Carmarthen, affiliated to the *Franciscan Order, was founded by Edward I about 1284. William Egwad sang its praises and, according to tradition, *Rhys Nanmor and *Tudur Aled were buried in its grounds. It was dissolved in 1538, two years after the priory.

Carnelian (**Coslett Coslett**; 1834–1910), see under CLIC Y BONT.

Carnhuanawc, see PRICE, THOMAS (1787–1848).

Carnwennan, see under BLACK WITCH.

Carnwyllion, a commot on the right bank of the river Llwchwr, was always associated with *Kidwelly and, from the early twelfth century, constituted the eastern part of the Norman lordship of that name.

Carol, a form of verse intended to be sung. In the sixteenth and seventeenth centuries carols were composed in Welsh in a complex alliterative style which retained regular accentuation. Many were examples of the festal and seasonal song associated with Epiphany, *Candlemas, *Easter and *May Day, but not all were Christian in origin. The *carol wirod* ('liquor carol'), *carol dan bared* ('carol under the wall') and the *carol yn drws* ('doorway carol'), for example, belonged to the pagan tradition of *wassailing. When that custom began to die out during the eighteenth century, the term 'carol' was confined to the festal song of church and chapel and by the nineteenth century it referred almost exclusively to the songs of the Christmas Nativity. See also CWNDID.

For further details see the article by David Jenkins, 'Carolau Haf a Nadolig' in *Llên Cymru* (vol. II, 1952–3).

Carr, Glyn, see STYLES, FRANK SHOWELL (1908–).

Carreg Cennen, a castle situated on a rock above the river Cennen near Llandeilo, Carms. The ancient stronghold was held by the Lord Rhys of Dinefwr (*Rhys ap Gruffudd) and by his descendants in the twelfth and thirteenth centuries. It was captured by the King's forces during the first *War of Welsh Independence (1276–77) and, although briefly occupied by the Welsh during the War of 1282–83, it was afterwards granted to John Giffard who ordered it to be rebuilt. Extensive damage was caused during

the rising of *Owain Glyndŵr, when a prolonged siege was mounted, and again during the Wars of the Roses. After the defences had been reinforced by Gruffudd ap Nicolas of Dinefwr, the garrison surrendered to Sir Richard Herbert of Raglan. The castle was granted by Henry VII to Sir Rhys ap Thomas (1449–1525) of Dinefwr and later held by the Vaughan and Cawdor families of Golden Grove.

For further details see J. E. Lloyd (ed.), *A History of Carmarthenshire* (1935, 1939) and J. M. Lewis, *Carreg Cennen Castle* (1960).

CARTER, DANIEL (fl. 1840–63), poet, possibly a native of Herefordshire, claimed to have travelled widely in Europe before settling to his life's work as Master of the Foundation Grammar School at Rhayader, Rads. His long descriptive poem in English, *Rhaiadr Gwy* (1863), was written in 1840 when he was living in the town but was published only after he had become blind and infirm. Taking Robert Bloomfield's *The Farmer's Boy* (1800) as model, it is technically competent, resolutely antiquarian in tone and celebrates the poet's personal friendships. Carter was the author of six other works, all undated, of which *The Legend of Devil's Bridge* and *The Rose of Pont Vathew* are the most remarkable.

Carter, Isaac (d. 1741), a printer whose press, established in 1718 at Atpar (Trefhedyn) in the parish of Llandyfrïog, Newcastle Emlyn, Carms., was the first permanent printing-press to be founded in Wales. He began by printing the ballad by Alban Thomas, 'Cân o Senn i'w hen Feistr Tobacco' (1718), and went on to produce three larger works, *Eglurhad o Gatechism Byrraf y Gymanfa* (1719), *Dwysfawr Rym Buchedd Grefyddol* (1722) and *Y Christion Cyffredin* (1724). The press was transferred about 1725 to Carmarthen, where Carter continued to print books of a religious nature.

Cartrefi Cymru (lit. 'The homes of Wales'; 1896), a volume of essays by Owen M. *Edwards which, with one exception, first appeared in his magazine *Cymru* between 1891 and 1895. The book describes the author's visits to the homes of a number of major figures in Welsh history, including Dolwar Fach (Ann *Griffiths), Tŷ Coch (Robert *Thomas, Ap Vychan), Y Gerddibluog (Edmund *Prys), Pantycelyn (William *Williams), Bryntynoriad (Evan *Jones, Ieuan Gwynedd), Trefeca (Howel *Harris), Caer Gai (Rowland *Vaughan), Cefnbrith (John *Penry), Y Glasynys (Elis *Wynne), Tŷ'r Ficer (Rhys *Prichard), Y Garreg Wen (David *Owen) and St. David's (*Dewi Sant). Like much of the author's work, these essays were written with the express intention of arousing the common people's interest in the history and geography of Wales. Very popular in its day, the volume is still entertaining, not least for its historical romanticism and sensitive response to natural beauty.

The book was translated into English by T. E. Jones as *Homes of Wales* (1931).

Carw Coch (William Williams; 1808–72), see under CYMREIGYDDION Y CARW COCH.

Caseg Broadsheets, The, see under CHAMBERLAIN, BRENDA (1912–71).

Casglwr, Y, see under CYMDEITHAS BOB OWEN.

CASNODYN (*fl.* 1320–40), the earliest poet of Glamorgan whose work has survived. His elegiac *awdl* to Madog Fychan of Coetref, Llangynwyd, steward of *Tir Iarll, is the first extant panegyric to a native of that district. It seems from verses by *Hywel Ystorm that the poet came from Kilvey, near Swansea, and that his real name may have been Gruffudd. There are references in his work to the contemporary dialects of Gwynedd and Gwent but his verses are in the style of the *Gogynfeirdd*. In a poem to Ieuan ap Gruffudd of Ceredigion he states that it was from him that he learned to compose a 'perfect poem' in contradistinction to 'the rubbishy language' of some poets of his day. Casnodyn, in a time of rapid change, held to the ancient literary standards and admired the old type of Welsh landowner who knew no English. Yet despite its archaic diction, his work represents an advance in the development of *cynghanedd*.

His themes vary from praise of a lady and elegies for patrons in Ceredigion and Glamorgan to a sequence of twelve mono-rhyming *awdlau* to the Trinity. The best-known line of his occurs in an *awdl* to Gwenllian, the wife of Sir Gruffudd Llwyd and daughter of Cynan ap Maredudd, whose husband held high office in north Wales during the reigns of Edward I and Edward II: '*Main firain riain gain Gymraeg*' ('A slender, exquisite lady of beautiful Welsh speech'). He is at his best not so much in his lurid descriptions of Hell's torments as in passages of intense religious devotion where he demonstrates his mastery of a richly ornate metrical art. This scholarly exponent of an ancient tradition frequently inveighed against the low standards of the poetasters, making it clear that he would not be counted among their number.

Castell Coch, a castle built in 1872 to the design of William Burges (1827–81) for the third Marquess of *Bute. It stands in a wood above Tongwynlais, to the north of Cardiff, on the site of a fort built for Gilbert de Clare, Lord of Glamorgan, in the thirteenth century. An extravaganza of Victorian Romantic styles, it has conical towers, a drawbridge and portcullis in working order, and a richly ornamented interior. In medieval times an earlier castle on the site was the stronghold of Ifor Bach (*Ifor ap Cadifor) whose treasure is said to be buried in a vault, guarded by three eagles, at the head of a tunnel leading from *Cardiff castle.

Caswallon, the son of Beli, a character in the Second and Third Branches of *Pedair Cainc y Mabinogi*, of whom it is said that he had conquered the Island of the Mighty while *Brân (Bendigeidfran) was in Ireland and that he was crowned king in London. Coming upon the youths who had been left to guard the Island and wearing a magic mantle which made him invisible, he killed six of them but spared the seventh, *Caradog son of Brân, because he had seen his cousin's son. Nevertheless, Caradog died of fear when he saw the sword killing his comrades. At the beginning of the Third Branch, *Manawydan refers to Caswallon as his cousin but says that he is loath to share the same house with anyone except Bendigeidfran, his brother. Later, *Pryderi goes to Oxford to swear allegiance to Caswallon.

It is likely that the name Caswallon retains a memory of Cassivellaunus, the king of the Catuvellauni and leader of the Britons against Julius Caesar in 54 BC. No Roman connections are attributed to him in the *Mabinogi* but according to the Triad of the Three Levies he went 'across the sea in pursuit of the men of Caesar'. In other Triads he is given as one of the Three Lovers in references behind which there must have been a lost story about Caswallon, Fflur and Caesar. Welsh traditions concerning Caswallon appear to derive from an extensive body of narrative, only fragmentarily preserved, concerning the domination over Britain of *Beli Mawr and his sons.

For further details see W. J. Gruffydd, *Rhiannon* (1953), I. Williams, *Pedeir Keinc y Mabinogi* (1977) and Rachel Bromwich, *Trioedd Ynys Prydein* (1961).

Catheiniog, a commot of *Cantref Mawr, had its centre at Dryslwyn.

Catraeth, The Battle of, see under GODODDIN (*c.*600).

CATRIN (*fl.* 1545), poet, the daughter of *Gruffudd ab Ieuan ap Llywelyn Fychan, belonged to a family living in the Vale of Clwyd, Denbs. A good deal of her father's work has survived, together with a few poems by *Alis, who was probably her sister, but only two by Catrin. They are an *awdl* to God and the world and a series of *englynion* to Christ, but these poems are sometimes attributed to another Catrin, the daughter of Gruffudd ap Hywel, who is the subject of the next entry.

CATRIN (*fl.* 1555), poet, the daughter of Gruffudd ap Hywel of Llanddaniel-fab, Ang., wrote poems in strict metres including *englynion* to God and the cold summer of 1555, some of which have survived in manuscript. To her are sometimes attributed the two extant poems of Catrin, the daughter of Gruffudd ab Ieuan ap Llywelyn Fychan, who is the subject of the previous entry.

Catrin of Berain (1534/5–91), was connected by descent and marriage with many of the leading families of north Wales and her numerous descendants formed an intricate web of family connections, for which reason she has been called 'The Mother of Wales'. The granddaughter of an illegitimate son of Henry VII, Catrin (or Katheryn) was the owner of the ★Tudor family home at Penmynydd in Anglesey. She was married four times: her first husband was John ★Salusbury (d. 1566) of Llewenni, Denbs.; her second was Sir Richard Clough (d. 1570) of Denbigh, a successful merchant whose business interests took them to Antwerp, Hamburg and Spain; by her marriage to Maurice Wynn (d. 1580) she became the stepmother of Sir John ★Wynn of Gwydir; her fourth husband was Edward Thelwall (d. 1610) of Plas-y-Ward, Denbs. Thomas ★Pennant claimed that Maurice Wynn proposed marriage to her as he escorted her from church at the funeral of John Salusbury. She refused him 'with great civility', as she had already accepted a proposal from Sir Richard Clough on whose arm she had entered, but she promised that he might depend on being her third husband. It was Pennant who also recorded the tradition that in the famous portrait of Catrin by Lucas de Heere she is wearing a locket in which she kept a lock of hair which had belonged to Sir Richard Clough. She had children by her first three husbands and marriages took place between her children and her stepchildren. The matrimonial affairs of Catrin reflect a movement from Catholicism to Protestantism although Thomas Salusbury, the elder son of her first marriage, remained a Catholic and was executed for his involvement in the Babington Plot (1586). Among the poets who sang in her praise was Wiliam ★Cynwal who addressed her as '*Catrin wych, wawr ddistrych wedd / Cain ei llun, cannwyll Wynedd*' ('Splendid Catrin, like the brightness of foam / Fine her aspect, the candle of Gwynedd').

For further details see the article on Catrin by John Ballinger in *Y Cymmrodor* (vol. XL, 1929) and those on Sir Richard Clough in the *Transactions* of the Denbighshire Historical Society (vol. XIX, 1970; vol. XX, 1971) by Robin Gwyndaf. Three novels based on the life and times of this remarkable woman have been written by R. Cyril Hughes: *Catrin o Ferain* (1975), *Dinas Ddihenydd* (1976) and *Castell Cyfaddawd* (1984).

Catwg Ddoeth, one of the fabrications of Iolo Morganwg (Edward ★Williams). The medieval Welsh treatise entitled *Cynghoreu Catwn*, a father's exhortations to his son, translated from a Latin work, *Catonis Disticha*, was known to Iolo. Having identified the author, the Welsh form of

whose name was Cadw or Cadwn, with the patron saint of Llangatwg, Glam., he composed an immense body of 'wisdom' literature which he attributed to Catwg Ddoeth ('The Wise') and published it in *The Myvyrian Archaiology* (1801).

Cauldron of Inspiration and Knowledge, The, is described in the folk-tale known as *Hanes Taliesin*. Ceridwen, wife of Tegid, has a son called Afagddu, who is proverbial for his ugliness. To compensate him for this misfortune, his mother plans to endow him with exceptional knowledge by placing on the fire the Cauldron of Inspiration and Knowledge, which has to be kept boiling for a year and a day. Gwion Bach is appointed to stir the cauldron, while Ceridwen collects herbs and plants for her magic brew. At the end of the year three drops of the magic potion, intended for Afagddu, splash on to Gwion's finger, which he puts into his mouth. Immediately he becomes the most knowledgeable man in the world and has to flee to escape Ceridwen's wrath. After a series of metamorphoses Gwion is eventually re-born as the poet ★Taliesin.

Cauldron of Plenty, The, see under DIWRNACH WYDDEL.

Cauldron of Rebirth, The, plays a vital part in the story of ★Branwen, daughter of Llŷr, in the Second Branch of ★*Pedair Cainc y Mabinogi*. It is presented to ★Brân (Bendigeidfran) by Llassar Llaes Gyfnewid in return for his protection, after the latter's escape from the Iron House. Brân subsequently gives it to ★Matholwch as part of his reparation for ★Efnysien's mutilation of the king's horses. The chief characteristic of this cauldron is that, if a dead warrior is thrown into it, he will be restored to life next day but without the power of speech. Several years later, when Brân wages war against Matholwch in an attempt to avenge the insult to his sister Branwen, it is the Cauldron of Rebirth which, ironically, causes the destruction of the men of Britain, for it restores the dead Irish warriors to life.

CAVE, JANE (*fl.* 1770–96), poet, was born at Brecon, the daughter of an exciseman from Dorset who, while stationed at Talgarth, was converted by Howel ★Harris. Precocious and Methodistical, she may have taken employment in Winchester for her volume, *Poems on Various Subjects, Entertaining, Elegiac and Religious* (1783), was first published there. After marriage to a man named Winscom, she lived in Bristol where she persuaded some fifteen hundred persons, many of them titled, to subscribe to later editions of her book (1789, 1796) from which, however, several of her poems on Welsh subjects, one on the death of Harris among them, were excluded.

Caw o Brydyn, see under BLACK WITCH and
SAINTLY LINEAGES.

Cawrdaf, see JONES, WILLIAM ELLIS (1795–
1848).

Cedewain, a commot of *Powys between the
rivers Rhiw and Severn, within which lay
*Dolforwyn, a stronghold built by *Llywelyn
ap Gruffudd in 1273. The commot was granted
to Roger Mortimer by Edward I in 1279.

Ceffyl Pren, Y (lit. 'The wooden horse'), a folk
custom in which a man suspected of mis-
demeanour was carried on a pole or ladder,
whether in person or effigy, for the purpose of
public derision. It may have been derived from
the riding of the hobby-horse in ancient revelry
and the phallic significance of the victim's posture was generally associated with marital
infidelity. The 'horse-play' usually took place
during the hours of darkness, the mob blackened
their faces, the men wore women's clothes, a
mock-trial was held and the procession was
accompanied by the beating of drums and the
firing of guns. Such incidents took place prior to
the *Rebecca Riots and the attacks on toll-gates
in west Wales grew out of the practice. The
custom as practised in England, where it was
known as the Skimmington (or the skimmity
ride), was described by Thomas Hardy in *The
Mayor of Casterbridge* (1886).
For further details see David Williams, *The Rebecca
Riots* (1955).

Cefnamwlch, a mansion in the parish of Tud-
weiliog, Caerns., was the home of the Griffith
family which was famous for its patronage of
poets over ten generations down to the end of
the seventeenth century. The most notable
patron was John Griffith (d. 1585), for whom
many poets composed verse.

Cefnllanfair, a house in the parish of
Llanbedrog, Caerns., where patronage was
given to poets over five generations during the
sixteenth and seventeenth centuries. Huw ap
Rhisiart ap Dafydd (d. 1590) was the first head of
the family to welcome poets and the tradition
was maintained by his son, Gruffudd Huws, and
his grandson Huw; some poetry addressed to
their descendants at the beginning of the
eighteenth century has also survived. One of
Huw ap Rhisiart's sons was Richard *Hughes (d.
1618), a soldier and officer at the court of
Elizabeth I, who wrote a number of love-poems
in the free metres which were included by T. H.
*Parry-Williams in the volume *Canu Rhydd
Cynnar* (1932).

Cefnllys, a mansion, formerly a castle, in the
parish of the same name in Radnorshire, was the
site of a victory won by *Llywelyn ap Gruffudd

over Roger Mortimer. By the fifteenth century
the house had become famous for its patronage
of poets in the county. The most notable patron
was Ieuan ap Phylip (*fl.* 1450) and *Lewys Glyn
Cothi (Llywelyn y Glyn) was among the poets
whom he welcomed.

Ceingaled, see under GWALCHMAI FAB GWYAR
and TRIOEDD Y MEIRCH.

Ceinion Llenyddiaeth Gymreig (lit. 'Gems of
Welsh literature'; 1876), an anthology edited by
Owen *Jones (Meudwy Môn) whose purpose
was 'to provide the inhabitants of the
Principality with an entertaining and instructive
body of literature'. The book contains a selection
of verse from the time of the great *cywyddwyr*
down to the nineteenth century, and of prose
from the classical Welsh tales. The weakest parts
are those extracts in which the Victorian spirit is
seen at its worst, in excessive sentiment and in
pompous, unidiomatic language.

Ceinmeirch, a commot of the cantref of *Rhufoniog, lying to the west of the river Clwyd,
became part of the honour of Denbigh in 1282.

Ceiriog, see HUGHES, JOHN CEIRIOG (1832–87).

Celli-wig, in Cornwall, the court of King
*Arthur in the tale of *Culhwch and Olwen,
where he rests after major campaigns such as
those against Ysgithrwyn Ben Beidd and the
*Twrch Trwyth. It was *Geoffrey of Monmouth
who claimed that the court had been situated in
*Caerleon. The site of Celli-wig is unknown but
among locations suggested are Callington,
Gweek Wood near Helston, Calliwith near Bod-
min, and Kelly near Egloshayle.

Celt, see HUMPHREYS, EDWARD MORGAN
(1882–1955).

Celt, Y (lit. 'The Celt'; 1878), a weekly
newspaper which first appeared under the
editorship of Samuel *Roberts of Llanbrynmair.
It had a troubled history and was subsequently
published in various parts of Wales, including
Caernarfon (1879–81), Bangor (1882–94),
Aberafan (1894–95) and Llanelli (1896–1900).
Having become *Y Celt Newydd* in 1903, it was
amalgamated with Y *Tyst three years later.
Published under the auspices of the Independents, the newspaper was supported by
followers of Michael D. *Jones in opposition to
Y Tyst a'r Dydd. Among its editors were Evan
Pan *Jones, D. Stephen Davies, William
(Keinion) Thomas and D. Silvan *Evans. It
weathered many storms, especially during the
editorship of Pan Jones (1881–84), when *Land
Reform, landlordism and Home Rule for Ireland
were the major issues of the day, and the editor
was prosecuted for libel on more than one
occasion.

Celtic Anthology, A (1927), edited by Grace Rhys, contains poems from Ireland, Scotland and Wales. From the Welsh there are translations of poetry from all periods, mostly the work of Ernest *Rhys, the compiler's husband, and H. Idris *Bell. The contemporary period of Welsh poetry is represented by T. Gwynn *Jones, Eifion Wyn (Eliseus *Williams) and R. Williams *Parry among others. The Anglo-Welsh contributors include George *Herbert, Henry *Vaughan, Felicia *Hemans, Wil Ifan (William *Evans), Huw Menai (Huw Owen *Williams), A. G. *Prys-Jones, W. H. *Davies and Richard *Hughes. Like *Lyra Celtica (1896), the anthology was intended to present the poetry of the Celtic countries to the English reader, and was largely a product of 'the Celtic Twilight' of the late nineteenth century. The editor's choice was inevitably restricted to the English versions available in her day, many of which lacked scholarship and were couched in archaic language, so that her anthology now has more interest for students of the period than for the intrinsic merit of its translations.

Celtic Church, The, the Christian societies among the Celtic peoples of Britain and Ireland, lasted from the fourth down to the end of the eighth century. It is recorded that representatives from Britain were present at the Councils of Arles (314) and Rimini (359). The Christian faith had taken root in Britain during the last quarter of the third century yet missionaries were still seeking to convert the inhabitants in the fifth and sixth centuries. *Patrick went to Ireland from somewhere in western Britain in the fifth century and there was a great deal of missionary activity in Wales during this period, for which reason it is sometimes called the *Age of the Saints. Columba left Ireland in 563 and settled in Iona from where, about 635, Aidan came to Northumbria and settled on Lindisfarne. The Celtic Church, as it became recognizable, thus belonged to the north and west of Britain, and to Ireland. From these parts, especially from Ireland, there was missionary activity from the seventh century on, northwards as far as Iceland, south to Switzerland and Italy and eastwards as far as Kiev. When Augustine came to Britain from Rome in 597, the Britons were reluctant to acknowledge his authority, their Church having developed its own characteristics which they were to defend over the next two centuries.

Monasticism, a system more suited to the organization of the tribe than that of town or city, was the system adopted by the Celtic Church and the head of the monastery was the abbot. The authority and influence of the monastery could extend over a number of institutions in other places which had been founded from it. Ecclesiastics were not forbidden to marry and raise families, so that position

and honour could be handed down from father to son.

Little is known about the practices and beliefs of the Celtic Church, except what can be deduced from the work of such authors as Patrick, *Gildas, Bede and *Nennius, from *Lives of the Saints, from poems and chronicles, and later from oral tradition. It appears that the Pelagian heresy, which maintained that the individual had a part to play in salvation, always had some influence among the Celts. There was an emphasis on asceticism and self-denial and, during the seventh and eighth centuries, an ardent eremitical movement, especially in Ireland. The importance of Scripture was stressed, whereas the influence of the Early Fathers seems to have been slight; the Old Latin versions, more than the Vulgate, seem to have been followed. The most prominent divergences from the Roman Church were the method used for fixing the date of Easter and the cut of the tonsure. These differences were, in general, indicative of a reluctance on the part of the Celts to recognize the authority of Rome and were developed during the period of their separation from the rest of Europe, especially after incursions by the barbarians.

The Celtic Church was never a separate organization and never had a central authority, which probably explains why it eventually lost its identity and became part of the Roman Church during the seventh and eighth centuries. Southern Ireland was the first to conform, about 632, then Northumbria after the Synod of Whitby in 664; northern Ireland followed about 695 and Scotland about 717, although some Christians there retained their independence until the second quarter of the twelfth century. The British of Cornwall, Devon and Somerset conformed about 768 and the Welsh under *Elfodd the Bishop of Bangor, yielded about the year 777. But in Wales the Church generally preserved its own character, more especially in centres such as *Llanbadarn and *St. David's, until the end of the eleventh century.

For further details see H. Williams, *Christianity in Early Britain* (1912), L. Gougaud, *Christianity in Celtic Lands* (1932), Nora K. Chadwick, *The Age of Saints in the Early Celtic Church* (1961) and C. Thomas, *Britain and Ireland in Early Christian Times* (1971).

Celtic Congress, The, a society which seeks to foster the languages, cultures and national ideals of the six Celtic peoples. It was at the National Eisteddfod of 1900 that plans were laid to call a Pan-Celtic Congress in Dublin in the following year. Held again in Caernarfon in 1904 and in Edinburgh in 1907, the society was re-established in 1917 by E. T. *John and renamed the Celtic Congress. Between the World Wars there were branches in every Celtic country except Cornwall and since 1947 meetings have been held regularly in all six countries. The society is non-political and should not be confused with the more recently founded Celtic League, a forum for Nationalist movements which publishes a magazine entitled *Carn*, nor with the International Congress of Celtic Studies which exists for the fostering of academic study.

Celtic Davies, see DAVIES, EDWARD (1756–1831).

Celtic League, The, see under CELTIC CONGRESS.

Celtic Miscellany, A (1951), a volume of translations by Kenneth Hurlstone *Jackson. The literatures of all six Celtic countries, both prose and poetry, and of all periods down to the nineteenth century, are represented, the space devoted to Welsh and Irish literature exceeding that occupied by Scottish Gaelic, Breton, Cornish and Manx. All the translations are the work of the compiler and are, for the most part, prose versions in plain but elegant English which aim at being 'exact and accurate, though not slavish', and which avoid the flowery paraphrase which nineteenth-century taste usually preferred. Unlike earlier compilations such as *Lyra Celtica* (1896) and A *Celtic Anthology* (1927), which tended to rely on translations already available, the volume includes a large number of poems and prose extracts never before rendered into English, by a scholar who is familiar with all six Celtic languages. Discussing in his preface the misconceptions nurtured by 'the Celtic Twilight' of the nineteenth century, the translator concludes, 'In fact, the Celtic literatures are about as little given to mysticism and sentimentality as it is possible to be; their most outstanding characteristic is rather their astonishing power of imagination'. The volume may be regarded as the first successful scholarly attempt to translate the literatures of the Celtic peoples into modern English.

Celtic Twilight, The, see under CELTIC ANTHOLOGY (1927), CELTIC MISCELLANY (1951) and RHYS, ERNEST (1859–1946).

Celts, The, a confederation of peoples who at the zenith of their civilization were among the most cultured and influential in the history of Europe, have their ultimate origins in a period before written records began, so their earliest development can be traced only by means of archaeology. Even so, the evidence of the spade can be used with certainty for this purpose only when material of a definably Celtic nature occurs: all remains from earlier strata can only be considered as Celtic, or proto-Celtic, by assumption. Nevertheless, because place-names have been shown to date back to times much earlier than those of the records in which they appear, onomastic evidence can be used to indicate the distribution of Celtic peoples in areas where their former presence might not otherwise have been ascertainable. For example, a document from the sixth century BC, no longer extant but known as the *Massiliote Periplus*, referred to Ireland and Britain as *Ierné* and *Albion*, evidence that these islands were occupied by Celtic peoples before the date of that record. In the same way the names of the Iberian tribes *Celtae* and *Celtiberi* indicate that these people recognized themselves as forming part of the great Celtic confederation.

Little for certain is known about the very earliest migrations of Celtic peoples, though archaeologists and linguists have their ever-changing theories. The Celts become distinguishable perhaps for the first time at Hallstatt, in the Upper Austrian Salzkammergut, where from about the eighth century BC their use of iron made their civilization wealthy and dominant. They were able to expand trade in many directions, notably with Etruria and Greece, while more distant enterprises are indicated by the presence of Chinese silks in the tombs of this period. Wars took the Celts to the sack of Rome in 387 BC and the invasion of Greece in the late fourth century BC, and they founded colonies in Ankara and other distant places.

While the Hallstatt culture was still producing wealth, a fresh and possibly more decorative life-style developed farther west, typified by the material discovered in the votive deposits at La Tène, near the head of Lake Neuchâtel in what is now Switzerland. Celtic artificers, supported apparently by princely or chieftainly wealth, had developed the manufacture of wide ranges of artefacts: gold, silver, bronze and iron were beaten and cast into forms combining great beauty with utility, while the making of glass, enamelling, ceramics and work in wood and wool all developed in excellence. The Celts at this time were the most imaginative craftsmen of Europe and their art, which contrasts vitally with the realism and strong sense of formal balance of the Greeks and Romans, has had an important effect on artistic conceptions in the twentieth century. For such written documents as were thought to be necessary for commercial transactions and calendars, Greek and Roman letters and numerals were used. Laws and the dogmas of religion were, according to tradition, recorded strictly by memory, apparently to keep them away from profane eyes.

From Iron Age evidence, both material and written, it is possible to recognize much of the everyday life of the Celts, particularly the feasting and fasting, farming and warfare, trading and domestic economy, religion and laws, the last-named revealing a striking affinity with the Sanskrit code. Celtic society was highly aristocratic, comprising three tiers: the priest, who combined religious with secular leadership, the aristocrat and the freeman; the third tier could rise to the state of aristocrats if they became wealthy and powerful enough. It should not be concluded that there were no native slaves, but the servant, though poor, may have been free in social terms and protected by law.

A clearer picture is gradually being reconstructed of the emergence of the Celtic languages both in the ancient world and in the new Celtic realms of the early Middle Ages. Variants of Celtic are attested from the fourth to the third centuries BC in Ancient Gaul, Celtiberia and the region of the North Italian lakes, although the Celtic speech extended far beyond these areas in Central and Eastern Europe and into Asia Minor. Celtic languages or dialects were eventually superseded by other languages on mainland Europe, but Breton may be in part an exception if there is any firm basis for the view that it reflects something of Old Celtic. Insular Celtic shows a major cleavage between the parent language of Irish, Scottish Gaelic and Manx on the one hand and the parent language of *Welsh, Cornish and Breton on the other; these two parent languages are usually termed Goidelic and British (or Brittonic) respectively.

Politically, the Celtic tribes are believed to have formed a loose confederation and to have dominated the greater part of Europe, including the areas now known as France, Germany west of the Rhine, central and southern Spain, Switzerland and northern Italy, the Adriatic coast, Bohemia and the Danube Valley, perhaps to the Black Sea until the Romans attacked north of the Alps late in the second century BC. To the north and west of them were the related Germanic tribes, also Indo-European in origin. Opinions about proto-Celtic history have varied greatly in the last fifty years, not least as to the date at which the Celts arrived in Britain and Ireland. It now seems very unlikely that the Beaker Folk, who crossed the Channel before and after 1900 BC were in any sense Celtic. Much of the argument in recent years has claimed that Celtic peoples reached Britain and Ireland through a cumulative process during the latter part of the first millennium BC. A wave of arrivals, who practised La Tène culture, it seems, came earlier than 200 BC, the date previously suggested. Cart-graves and other relics of the culture found at Cowlam and elsewhere in east Yorkshire are now dated to the fifth century BC, and evidence both of movement and of social change in the Marne valley in north-east France confirms the expansionism of this 'Arras culture'. It is likely, too, that the Catuvellauni farther south (possibly to be identified with the Catalauni of the Marne) entered Britain in a related movement. Their chariot tactics and woad-painting, as described by Julius Caesar, may suggest that they had left the continent before the classical historians of Roman military practitioners had knowledge of them.

Invasions of Hallstatt-culture peoples which more clearly affect the borders of Wales have been identified in recent decades. Rectangular buildings of a suggested date in the seventh century BC were succeeded about 470 BC by square ones at sites at Croft Ambrey, Herefs., Ffridd Faldwyn, Mont., and Moel Hiraddug, Flints., suggesting that two separate waves of invaders landed west of the Wye and advanced northward up what is now the Welsh Border. The *Silures, who came in by the same route about 200 BC (though perhaps by way of Cornwall), advanced scarcely at all until times more historical: their material culture differed very little, it appears, from that of the Dobunni east of Severn. For the last identifiably Celtic invaders there is documentary evidence. Julius Caesar states that the Belgae, part of a large grouping of tribes, two-thirds of whom remained on the continent near the mouth of the Rhine, had been in Britain about forty years when he landed on its shores in 55 BC. These people occupied the south-east and south, pushing the Catuvellauni northwards at their first arrival but developing, a hundred years later, a cautious and pro-Roman attitude. Much of our knowledge of the disposition of the Celtic tribes in Britain is owed to the second-century Egyptian geographer, Ptolemy. See also ROMAN CONQUEST.

For further details see Paul Jacobsthal, *Early Celtic Art* (1944), Alwyn and Brinley Rees, *Celtic Heritage* (1961), Myles Dillon and Nora Chadwick, *The Celtic Realms* (1967), Proinsias Mac Cana, *Celtic Mythology* (1970), Jan Filip, *Celtic Civilization and its Heritage* (1977), T. G. E. Powell, *The Celts* (1979), Barry Cunliffe, *The Celtic World* (1979) and Geraint Bowen (ed.), *Y Gwareiddiad Celtaidd* (1985).

Cemais, a cantref of *Dyfed between the rivers Teifi and Gwaun. Robert Fitzmartin seized it about 1115 and it remained the property of his descendants until it was sold to William, the father of George *Owen of Henllys, in 1543. The name also belonged to a cantref of Anglesey which consisted of the commots of Talybolion and Twrcelyn.

Cerdd Dafod (lit. 'Tongue art') or **Cerddwriaeth**, the art of writing Welsh prosody. The word 'cerdd', now meaning 'a poem', originally meant 'a craft' or 'an art'. Later, the term *Cerdd Dafod* came to denote the art of composing poetry in the traditional metres. John *Morris-Jones was the first in modern times to classify the rules of Welsh prosody, in his book *Cerdd Dafod* (1925). See also CERDD DANT, CYMDEITHAS CERDD DAFOD, CYNGHANEDD and TWENTY-FOUR METRES.

For discussion of the art as practised in contemporary Wales see Alan Llwyd (ed.), *Trafod Cerdd Dafod y Dydd* (1984).

Cerdd Dant (lit. 'String art'), the musician's art as distinct from *Cerdd Dafod. There is evidence in medieval manuscripts that Welsh poets recited their work to musical accompaniment but no precise details exist as to how this was done. Today *Cerd Dant* consists of the singing of a counter-melody to a tune played on the *harp. Poetry in both the strict and free metres is often sung in this way and a society known as *Cymdeithas Cerdd Dant*, founded in 1934, exists to promote the art.

For further details see Aled Lloyd Davies, *Cerdd Dant, Llawlyfr Gosod* (1983) and *Hud a Hanes Cerdd Dannau* (1984).

Cerddor, see under BARDIC ORDER.

Cerddwriaeth, see CERDD DAFOD.

Ceredigion, an ancient kingdom traditionally claimed to have been established by Ceretic, one of the alleged sons of *Cunedda. Seisyll ap Clydog, King of Ceredigion, created the kingdom of Seisyllwg about 730 by adding *Ystrad Tywi to his dominions and his descendant, *Hywel Dda, added *Dyfed and *Brycheiniog, thereby creating the kingdom of *Deheubarth. Ceredigion was invaded in 1093 by the Norman Roger de Montgomery, who set about building a castle at *Cardigan at the mouth of the Teifi. But before it was completed *Cadwgan ap Bleddyn of Powys returned from exile in Ireland and, since Earl Roger's son and successor, Robert of Bellême, was less interested in Ceredigion than in more ambitious schemes in England, Cadwgan obtained from him a grant of the castle and the whole western sea-region. After many vicissitudes the territory of Ceredigion was restored to the House of Deheubarth in 1165. The borough of Cardigan, and part of the commot of Iscoed, which were held at intervals for the English Crown after 1200, became the county of Cardigan in 1241.

Ceri, a commot of *Powys lying to the south of the loop of the upper Severn. In 1176 *Gerald de Barri (Giraldus Cambrensis) successfully insisted that it was part of the diocese of *St. David's. Hubert de Burgh sought to bring the commot under the authority of the castle of *Montgomery, an attempt foiled by *Llywelyn ap Iorwerth's campaign of 1228. Captured by Edward I in 1276, it became part of the Mortimer inheritance.

Ceridwen, see under TALIESIN (*fl.* 6th cent.).

Ceridwen Peris, see JONES, ALICE GRAY (1852–1943).

Cewydd ap Caw (6th cent.), a saint who was associated with the belief that if it rained on his feast-day (1 July) it would rain for forty days afterwards; he was also known as Cewydd y Glaw ('Cewydd of the Rain'). The tradition seems to have been strongest in south Wales for his name is associated with churches at Llangewydd, Glam., and at Aberedw and Diserth, Rads. *Lewys Glyn Cothi (Llywelyn y Glyn) refers to Cewydd in an elegy for Morgan ap Dafydd Gam. The superstition was later transferred to Saint Swithin, whose feast-day is 15 July.

CHADWICK, NORA KERSHAW (1891–1972), Celtic scholar, was born at Great Lever near Bolton, Lancs., the daughter of a cotton industrialist. After studying at Newnham College, Cambridge, she became a Lecturer in English at St. Andrew's University but resigned in 1919 and returned to Cambridge, devoting all her time thereafter to the study of early Germanic literature. In 1950 she was appointed to a special lectureship in Cambridge on the history and culture of early Britain. Her career was at first devoted to the study of Old English, Norse and Russian, and she published several books on these subjects. She then worked with her husband, H. M. Chadwick, in the production of *The Growth of Literature* (3 vols., 1932, 1936, 1940), an attempt to define the common features of early literature in various languages.

Subsequently she concentrated her interest on the history and literature of the lands of Britain, especially the Celtic countries, between the Roman and the Norman periods. She made her most important contribution in this field, in volumes such as *Poetry and Letters in Early Christian Gaul* (1955) and in her studies of the cultural life of Wales in the early Middle Ages. Among the books she edited, and to which she contributed, are *Studies in Early British History* (1954), *Studies in the Early British Church* (1958) and *Celt and Saxon* (1963). In her last years she wrote several more popular books on Celtic subjects, including *The Celts* (1970) and, with Myles Dillon, *The Celtic Realms* (1967).

For further details see the essay by Morfydd E. Owen in *Studia Celtica* (vols. VIII/IX, 1973–74) and J. Henderson, *A Published List of the Writings of H. M. and N. K. Chadwick* (1971); see also the obituary by Kenneth Jackson in the *Proceedings* of the British Academy (vol. LVIII, 1972).

Chair, The, a traditional prize for Welsh poets, the award of which was an ancient custom in the time of *Hywel Dda. The *Laws testify that a seat was reserved for the *Pencerdd* ('Chief Poet') in the prince's hall and that the honour of sitting in it was won by bardic contest. The same status was indicated among the *Poets of the Gentry by a silver medal, fashioned in the shape of a chair and worn on the left shoulder. It is stated in the manuscripts that silver chairs were won at the *Carmarthen Eisteddfod held about 1451 and at the *Caerwys Eisteddfodau of 1523 and 1567. The custom lapsed at the eisteddfodau held in taverns during the eighteenth century and at the provincial eisteddfodau of the early nineteenth century the prize was often only a medal, although it was sometimes engraved with the image of a chair.

From 1887 it became usual at the *National Eisteddfod for a wooden Chair to be presented for the winning *awdl*, a silver *Crown being awarded for the poem (*pryddest*) in the free metres. This practice has continued, with an interregnum during the Second World War, down to the present. The Chairing ceremony, which is held under the auspices of *Gorsedd Beirdd Ynys Prydain*, is the most impressive event in the pageantry of the National Eisteddfod. Among poets of the twentieth century who have won the Chair twice (the maximum now allowed) have been T. Gwynn *Jones (1902, 1909), T. H. *Parry-Williams (1912, 1915), Gwenallt (David James *Jones, 1926, 1931), Alan *Llwyd (1973, 1976) and Gerallt Lloyd *Owen (1975, 1982). The prize, which includes a monetary award, has been withheld, there being no worthy winner, on ten occasions since 1900.

CHAMBERLAIN, BRENDA (1912–71), writer and painter, was born at Bangor, Caerns., where she was educated privately. In 1931 she went to London to train as a painter in the Royal Academy Schools and five years later, after marrying John Petts, the artist-craftsman, she settled in Llanllechid, near Bethesda, Caerns. During the Second World War she temporarily gave up painting in favour of poetry and worked, with her husband, on the production of the *Caseg Broadsheets*, a series of six which included poems by Dylan *Thomas, Alun *Lewis, Lynette *Roberts and herself as well as translations of early Welsh poems by H. Idris *Bell. The story of this venture is told in the volume *Alun Lewis and the Making of the Caseg Broadsheets* (1969) which also contains letters from the poet. In 1946, her marriage ended, she visited Germany to stay with Karl von Laer, the friend to whom she dedicated *The Green Heart* (1958), her first collection of poems. The following year she went to live on *Bardsey where she remained until 1961, writing and again painting, with the islanders as her subjects. In 1961 she moved to the Greek island of Ydra, an experience described in a journal, *A Rope of Vines* (1965). The colonels' coup of 1967, however, interrupted democracy in Greece and she returned to Bangor, depressed and with financial problems; it was there she died.

Her volume *The Green Heart* consists mainly of lyrics, many about life among mountain-dwellers and fishermen, together with a cycle of love-poems with a German background; some also appear in *Poems with Drawings* (1969). The prose work *Tide Race* (1962), perhaps her most important, is an account of the austerities and excitements of her life on Bardsey; it has a constant awareness of the sea and the small community's politics, its superstitions and tensions, its physical and mental health, are treated with a vividness which has been described as both 'close to poetry' and 'nightmarish'. In *The Water Castle* (1964), her only novel, which is a six weeks' journal of love and discord in post-war Germany, she appears to have drawn on her visit to that country in 1946.

There is an autobiographical essay by Brenda Chamberlain in *Artists in Wales* (ed. Meic Stephens, 1971) and a chapter on her writings in Anthony Conran, *The Cost of Strangeness* (1982).

Change of Heart, A (1951), the third novel of Emyr *Humphreys, was the first to reveal his concept of the 'Protestant' novel, concerned to examine the means whereby 'good' is transmitted in society and moral and spiritual progress continues. Howell Morris, Professor of English at a University College in Wales, is the 'good man' only in part: he fails either to animate or define the 'good' he represents and is concerned almost solely with the welfare of his former student and former brother-in-law, Frank Davies, who stands in, psychologically, for his estranged dead wife. The denouement, with Howell's ironic 'escape' from the University, confirms the limitation of his 'good' and leaves his critics unimpressed; Frank is his sole victory.

CHAPPELL, EDGAR LEYSHON (1879–1949), civil servant and author. A native of Ystalyfera, Glam., he was a specialist in the housing and industrial problems of south Wales. Besides editing *The *Welsh Outlook*, he published numerous articles and pamphlets dealing with social questions, including *The Government of Wales* (1943) and *Wake Up, Wales!* (1943), as well as several works of local history, among which *Old Whitchurch* (1945) is the most highly regarded.

Charity Schools, see under SOCIETY FOR PROMOTING CHRISTIAN KNOWLEDGE.

CHARLES, DAVID (1762–1834), hymnwriter, was born at Llanfihangel Abercywyn, Carms., a brother of Thomas *Charles. He had very little formal education and was apprenticed as a rope-maker in a factory of which he later became the owner. Converted at the age of fifteen after reading the sermons of Ralph Erskine, he began preaching in 1807 and was ordained a minister with the Calvinistic Methodists in 1811. He was not a preacher of popular appeal but he is now regarded as one of the greatest of his time on account of his theological erudition and epigrammatic style. Collections of his sermons were published in 1840 and 1860, and some in English translation in 1846. He was among those involved in the work of compiling the Methodist constitution and Confession of Faith (1823). The best-known of his hymns are 'O fryniau Caersalem ceir gweled', 'Rhagluniaeth fawr y nef', 'O! Iesu mawr, rho'th anian bur' and the translation 'Diolch i Ti, yr Hollalluog Dduw'.

His son, also named **David Charles** (1803–80), was ordained in 1851 and became prominent among the Calvinistic Methodists. In 1823 he began publishing a small monthly, Yr Addysgydd, and he was the chief editor of the collection of hymns published by the South Wales Methodists in 1841. He composed and translated many hymns, some of which are still popular, such as 'Mor beraidd i'r credadun gwan', 'O! Salem, fy annwyl gartrefle' and 'Tydi sy deilwng oll o'm cân'.

A complete collection of hymns by father and son has been edited by Goronwy Prys Owen under the title Ffrydiau Gorfoledd (1977).

CHARLES, EDWARD (Siamas Gwynedd; 1757–1828), controversialist, was born at Clocaenog, Denbs. He went to London as a young man and joined the *Gwyneddigion Society. One of the services he performed was to copy a large number of old Welsh manuscripts on behalf of Owain Myfyr (Owen *Jones); another was to preserve every letter received by him and his friends, a collection which is now a valuable source of information about the *London Welsh in his day. In 1796 in Y *Geirgrawn, a magazine published at Holywell, he adversely criticized Seren tan Gwmwl, the work of his friend, Jac Glan-y-gors (John *Jones), and in Morgan John *Rhys's *Cylchgrawn Cynmraeg he fiercely attacked *Methodism. His Epistolau Cymraeg at y Cymry (1797), on the same subject, was answered by Thomas *Roberts of Llwyn'rhudol under the pseudonym Arvonius in Amddiffyniad i'r Methodistiaid (1806).

CHARLES, THOMAS (1755–1814), leader of the second generation of Welsh Methodists, was born at Llanfihangel Abercywyn, Carms., a brother of the David *Charles who later became a hymn-writer, and he was educated at Llanddowror, Carms., and Oxford. He served the Anglican Church in Somerset for five years before marrying Sally Jones of Bala, Mer., in 1783 and settling in that town. Joining the Methodists in the following year, he soon became prominent among them and devoted the rest of his life to the work of the Connexion.

His literary endeavours sprang from his educational work. Convinced of the importance of the catechism, he began by publishing Crynodeb o Egwyddorion Crefydd, neu Gatecism Byrr i Blant ac Eraill i'w Ddysgu (1789), a book later revised and published under the title Catecism Byr (1799) and translated as A Short Evangelical Catechism (1801). It was followed by Hyfforddwr yn Egwyddorion y Grefydd Gristnogol (1807), the fruit of twenty years' work among children and a clear statement of his theological position. In the ferment caused by the religious revivals of his day, Charles came to the fore as an able apologist with his Welsh Methodists Vindicated (1802; Welsh

trans. by Henry Hughes, 1892), his response to anonymous pamphlets which had been written from the standpoint of the Established Church. His magnum opus is his *Geiriadur Ysgrythyrawl (4 vols., 1805, 1808, 1810, 1811), a Scriptural dictionary which presented new learning about the history and geography of Bible lands, together with polished theological discussion of important biblical concepts.

As an editor, Charles's principal achievement was the standardization of the text of the first Welsh Bible to be published by the British and Foreign Bible Society which he had done so much to establish. He was asked to work on the edition prepared under the auspices of the *Society for Promoting Christian Knowledge (1749, 1799) but without altering the orthography. This task was begun in 1804, with the assistance of Robert *Jones of Rhos-lan and Thomas *Jones of Denbigh. When the New Testament appeared in 1806 Charles could say that its accuracy surpassed any previous Welsh publication, an assertion which was to be the measure of his disappointment in 1807 when the Bible appeared without Judges 8 as the result of carelessness on the part of the proof-reader, William *Owen Pughe. Charles's last editorial feat was the Welsh Bible of 1814, one of the most accurate editions ever produced and the fruit of ten years' diligent study of every previous edition.

Biographies of Thomas Charles have been written by D. E. Jenkins, The Life of the Rev. Thomas Charles B.A., of Bala (3 vols., 1908) and R. Tudur Jones, Thomas Charles o'r Bala, Gwas y Gair a Chyfaill Cenedl (1979); see also the article by R. Tudur Jones in Ysgrifau Beirniadol IV (ed. J. E. Caerwyn Williams, 1969).

Charles y Telynor (fl. mid-18th cent.), a harpist from the district of Llanycil, Mer., who was reputed to have persistently ridiculed the early Nonconformists. It is said that he sold his soul to the *Devil by feeding communion bread to dogs and that, on his way home one evening from playing at the palace of Fach Ddeiliog, he drowned while crossing Llyn Tegid, a column of smoke rising from the water at the spot where he perished.

Charmer, see DYN HYSBYS.

Charms, for the protection of human life and property, reflected in early Celtic society a strong belief in the supernatural and the efficacy of traditional remedies to ward off bad luck, disease and evil. Many were connected with the safeguarding of the home and the family. During the construction of a house the bones of animals were placed in the foundations and a horse's skull in the walls and, when it was finished, trees with religious significance such as the oak, the ash, the holly and the rowan would be planted around it.

In later times the doorstep and the hearthstones were painted white, salt thrown in the fire and a horseshoe nailed to the stable door. Fertility was ensured by the carving of phallic symbols and the hanging of corn dollies on door-posts. Herbs bearing the name of Christ were often grown in gardens. Other talismans brought into the house included witches' sticks, four-leafed clover, scarlet thread and 'stone mesh'—beads thought to have been formed from the skin and saliva of snakes. The ancient belief in the magical properties of iron demanded that an object such as a poker should be placed across the cradle of an unbaptized baby, against the child's being stolen by the *Tylwyth Teg. There were many spells for keeping the *Devil away and for the healing of sick persons and animals which were often recommended by the sooth-sayer or *Dyn Hysbys. Some of these superstitions, and others, have persisted to the present day.

For further details see Evan Isaac, Coelion Cymru (1938) and Brynley F. Roberts, 'Rhai Swynion Cymraeg' in the Bulletin of the Board of Celtic Studies (1965).

Chartism, a mass movement in favour of social and political *Reform during the nineteenth century. In the years between 1837 and 1844 disappointment over the limited Reform Act of 1832, and the fury at the New Poor Law of 1834, were fused with the desperation born of economic depression. There were two kinds of Chartists: the 'Moral Force' Chartists and the 'Physical Force' Chartists. The crisis year was 1839 when the Chartist Convention met in London, with Wales represented by Hugh *Williams (1796–1874), Charles Jones and John Frost (1784–1877). The six points of the Charter were universal male suffrage, equal electoral districts, annual parliaments, vote by ballot, abolition of the property qualification for election to Parliament and payment for Members of Parliament. The Chartist Petition, which carried more than a million and a quarter signatures, was rejected by Parliament in July 1839.

In Wales, after a number of huge open-air meetings had been held, representatives of the 'Physical Force' Chartists began to arm and there were several clashes with the authorities, most notably at Llanidloes, Mont., in April 1839. The Government then cracked down: Henry Vincent (1813–78), the most brilliant Chartist orator in south Wales and the west of England, was arrested in May, and others soon afterwards. The Convention debated 'ulterior measures' but, convinced of its inability to act effectively against the Government, dissolved itself on 6 September 1839. Leadership then passed to more determined men and it is possible that the events in south Wales, with activists such as John Frost, Zephaniah Williams (1795–1874) of Nantyglo and John Rees (Jack the Fifer) of Tredegar pressing for revolutionary policy, were intended to signal a general rising. On the morning of 4 November 1839 a crowd of perhaps twenty thousand, many armed, marched down Stow Hill into Newport, Mon. After a confused verbal exchange with the authorities inside the Westgate Hotel, fighting began in the street outside and troops opened fire, killing at least twenty-two and wounding about fifty demonstrators. For their part in the incident, John Frost, Zephaniah Williams and William Jones (1809–73) of Pontypool were condemned to death, but the sentences were commuted to transportation for life to Van Diemen's Land.

The débacle at Newport did not mark the end of Chartism. A general strike involving ironworkers was attempted at Merthyr Tydfil in the summer of 1842 and, a year later, Chartists were recruiting for the Miners' Association in the town. Economic revival removed mass support but individual Chartists continued to be active into the 1860s, mostly as Liberals.

For further details see the chapter by David Williams entitled 'Chartism in Wales' in Chartist Studies (ed. Asa Briggs, 1959) and John Frost; a study in Chartism (1939) by the same author; see also Dorothy Thompson, The Chartists (1984), Ivor Wilks, South Wales and the Rising of 1839 (1984), Angela V. John, 'The Chartist Endurance: Industrial South Wales 1840–1868', in Morgannwg (1971); D. J. V. Jones, 'Chartism in Welsh communities' in The Welsh History Review (vol. 6, no. 3) and O. R. Ashton, 'Chartism in mid-Wales' in the Montgomeryshire Collections (LXII). The events of 1839 are described by David J. V. Jones in The Last Rising (1985).

Chaste Brother or **Chaste Friend, The**, a popular motif in folk literature. A man goes in search of his lost twin brother and, because of their identical appearance, is taken for his brother by everyone including the brother's wife whose chastity he respects by placing a naked sword between them in bed. The theme is found in the tale of the friendship of *Amlyn and Amig and in that of Alexander and Lodwig; the tale of *Pwyll, Prince of Dyfed, contains a variation of it.

Chepstow or **Casgwent**, a lordship of the March, also known as **Strigoil**, perhaps a corruption of Ystrad Cul. William Fitz Osbern, Earl of Hereford, had, by the time of his death in 1071, erected a castle at the mouth of the Wye in Gwent Is Coed, the centre of which became the lordship of Strigoil. About 1115 Henry I granted the lordship to Walter Fitz Richard of Clare and it passed from the Clares, in turn, to the families of Marshall, Bigod, Plantagenet and Mowbray. In the 1460s William Herbert of Raglan became administrator of the lordship and his hold over it tightened after the extinction of the Mowbray family, in the male line, in 1476. In 1507 Strigoil passed to Charles Somerset, later Earl of Worcester and the husband of Elizabeth Herbert, and his son's rights as a lord of the March were specifically protected by the *Act of Union of 1536.

Chess, see under GWYDDBWYLL.

Chester, The Battle of (*c*.615), at which King Aethelfrith of Northumbria won a victory over *Selyf ap Cynan Garwyn, King of Powys, was preceded (according to Bede) by the slaughter of some twelve hundred of the monks of Bangor Is-coed, an incident which came to be known in Welsh tradition as the Massacre of the Saints. After this defeat the Britons of Wales were cut off from their countrymen in Cumbria.

Children's Literature, The history of the printed word in Welsh from the sixteenth to the nineteenth century is dominated by the religious movements of the period. For nearly four hundred years the child, like his elders, was seen primarily as a soul to be saved, by means of exhortation and admonishment. Besides the *Bible, the most popular works for children were the verses of *Cannwyll y Cymru (1659–72) by Rhys *Prichard and Welsh versions of Bunyan's *Pilgrim's Progress* (1684). It was not until 1758 that the first translations of the children's hymns of Isaac Watts appeared in Peter *Williams's hymnal, *Blodau i Blant*, and another hundred years were to pass before the Nonconformist endeavour to save children's souls reached its peak in the burgeoning of the Welsh periodical press. Foremost among the early magazines aimed specifically at children were *Y Winllan* (1848), *Yr Oenig* (1854), *Telyn y Plant* (1859) and, the most successful of all, *Trysorfa y Plant* (1862), which sold about forty thousand copies a month under the indefatigable editorship of Thomas *Levi.

By the beginning of the twentieth century this religious zeal had given way to a new awareness of the need for education in the Welsh language. It was fostered by one man, namely Owen M. *Edwards, whose vision and energy were largely devoted to the creation of a system of education in which the Welsh language would have its rightful place. Among the magazines he founded was *Cymru'r Plant* (1891), a periodical intended for children in which the work of many writers was first published. A new spirit of writing for Welsh children now emerged, much of it emulating what was available in English, but in the work of some writers, such as E. Tegla *Davies and Elizabeth Watkin *Jones, dealing with aspects of Welsh history and contemporary Wales in fresh, exciting ways. The influence of Owen M. Edwards was not confined to Welsh-speaking Wales but only in the writing of Owen Rhoscomyl (Robert Scourfield *Mills) did it help to produce books in English of a patriotic nature.

Since the Second World War the number of Welsh books for children has increased steadily and by the 1980s there were about two hundred titles published every year. The most prolific and popular Welsh children's writer is undoubtedly T. Llew *Jones, whose narrative gifts are admired as much by adults as by the younger readers for whom his books are intended. But a number of new writers have emerged, many of whom have produced work of good standard. They include Dafydd *Parri, J. Selwyn *Lloyd, Irma *Chilton and Gweneth *Lilly. The emergence of a corpus of children's literature in Welsh has been encouraged since the 1970s by public bodies such as the *Welsh Joint Education Committee, the *Welsh Arts Council and the *Welsh Books Council. With the support of these bodies, and in response to growing public interest, the *Welsh National Centre for Children's Literature was founded in 1979 and the Tir na n-Óg Prizes are awarded annually for children's books in Welsh and English. It is a cause for regret, however, that while Wales has provided inspiration for many English and American children's writers, notably Alan Garner, Susan Cooper and Nancy Bond, the publication of children's books in English by Welsh writers continues to be sporadic.

Details about children's writers in Welsh will be found in Mairwen and Gwynn Jones (ed.), *Dewiniaid Difyr* (1983); the Welsh National Centre for Children's Literature publishes two magazines devoted to the genre, *Pori* and *Dragon's Tale*. See also the *Proceedings* of the 16th International Seminar on Children's Literature (1983).

Chiliasm, see FIFTH MONARCHISM.

CHILTON, IRMA (1930–   ), children's writer, was born at Pengelli, Glam., and educated at the University College of Swansea before becoming a teacher. She writes in both Welsh and English and her books for children cover a wide age-range, from *Yr Iâr Goch* (1980), stories for reading to nursery children, to *Y Llong* (1979), a novel for adolescents which won the Tir na n-Og Prize in 1980. Among her books in English are *Flash* (1981) and *The Prize* (1983). Her subjects, too, are unusually varied, from country life and ancient Egypt to space travel and the time-slip theme which appears in several of her books, such as *The Time Button* (1970). A collection of her short stories was published in 1978; she has also written two novels for adults, *Cusannau* (1968) and *Rhwng Cwsg ac Effro* (1975), and a volume of short stories, *Y Cwlwm Gwaed* (1981).

Chirk or **Swydd y Waun**, a cantref of *Powys Fadog. As the lordship of Chirk and Chirkland, it was held from 1282 to 1322 by the Mortimers of Chirk, a cadet line of the Mortimers of Wigmore. From 1359 to the early fifteenth century it was one of the numerous lordships held by the Fitz Alan family in the north-eastern borderlands of Wales. It was granted to William Stanley in 1475 but became a Crown lordship in 1495 after his execution. From 1536 it was part of the county of Denbigh and since 1974 it has been part of the Wrexham-Maelor district of the county of Clwyd.

Chivalry (F. '*la chevalerie*', lit. 'the art of mastering horses') was an ideal code of behaviour for medieval knights. It probably developed during the ninth and tenth centuries, encouraged by the Church as part of its efforts to control the almost constant violence which had plagued western Europe during the Dark Ages. The knight was expected to be a fearless fighter against all odds and a true master of his arms. When dubbed, he swore to perform without fail certain religious and social duties, including the defence of the Church and the protection of his lord, his vassals and the weak. He was also expected to act courteously both in battle and, at least from the beginning of the twelfth century, towards ladies. At this time Chivalry received an impetus from the Crusades, and from then onwards the element of spectacle increased in importance with the tournament and heraldry. In literature, the knight was depicted as an individualist engaged in a life of adventure, winning glory by his prowess in single combat in order to prove himself worthy of his lady's love (see under COURTLY LOVE).

The tales of *Arthur and his knights illustrate this literary conception of Chivalry, but there is no evidence of a chivalrous Arthur before *Geoffrey of Monmouth. On the other hand, it can be argued that some of Chivalry's features sprang from Welsh or British mythology. The rescue of a captive lady is a theme in the tale of *Branwen, for example. Courtly Love is adumbrated in the story of *Tristan and knight-errantry in the tales of *Culhwch and Peredur (see under TAIR RHAMANT), although the first author fully to adapt the Tristan story to the ideal of Courtly Love was the man who wrote the mid-twelfth century French version, now lost, and in comparison with which the Welsh versions are little more than folk-tales. The counsel of Peredur's mother summarizes the knightly privileges and duties. Some scholars are of the opinion that the source of the *Grail romances is to be discerned in the primitive myth of the wounded god *Brân (Bendigeidfran).

For further details see Robert Richards, *Cymru'r Oesau Canol* (1933), Grant Uden, *A Dictionary of Chivalry* (1968) and R. W. Barber, *The Reign of Chivalry* (1980).

CHÖTZEN, THEODOR MAX (1901–45), Celtic scholar, was born of Dutch Jewish parents and educated at Leyden and Utrecht. He was appointed Librarian of the Peace Library at The Hague in 1931 and enlisted in the Dutch Army at the beginning of the Second World War. After the collapse of the Netherlands he returned, as best he could, to his scholarly pursuits but, towards the end of the War, he was arrested by the Germans and died in prison.

His main research interest was in late medieval Welsh poetry and its continental parallels. In his doctoral thesis, *Recherches sur la Poésie de Dafydd ap Gwilym* (1927), he examined the similarities between *Dafydd ap Gwilym's poetry and that of the troubadours and *clerici vagantes* and looked at possible channels of transmission; the second part is a discussion of the poet's themes. Although written before Thomas *Parry established the canon of Dafydd ap Gwilym's poetry, the book is still a useful guide to the European context of medieval Welsh lyric poetry. It was followed by a number of articles by Chotzen on related topics, such as '*Débats goliardiques en gallois*' and '*La querelle des femmes au Pays de Galles*'. He also published a number of early Modern Welsh texts, an attempt at classifying the Welsh texts of *Geoffrey of Monmouth and various articles on Cambro-Dutch relations.

Christopher Davies, see under LLYFRAU'R DRYW.

Chronicle of the Kings, The, see BRUT Y BRENHINEDD (13th–15th cents.).

Chronicle of the Princes, The, see BRUT Y TYWYSOGYON.

CHURCHEY, WALTER (1747–1805), poet, a native of Brecon and a solicitor by profession, was a friend of John Wesley and one of the earliest pillars of Wesleyan *Methodism in that town. A prolific writer of religious verse, including an epic poem entitled 'The Life of Joseph', he published several volumes of which the most notable were *Poems and Imitations* (1789) and *An Apology by W. Churchey for his Public Appearance as a Poet* (1805).

CHURCHYARD, THOMAS (*c*.1520–1604), see under WORTHINES OF WALES (1587).

Chwaen Wen, a mansion in the parish of Llantrisant, Ang., the home of a branch of the Presaeddfed family which maintained the tradition of bardic patronage. The first known patron was Siôn Lewys (*c*.1528–1573/4) and Wiliam *Cynwal was a frequent visitor to the house during his time. Siôn's heir, Wiliam (1553–1630/1), had a similar interest in poetry and music, as well as wealth and influence. After his death, branches of the family continued the tradition at other homes in the county.

Chwalfa (lit. 'Dispersal'; 1946), a novel by T. Rowland *Hughes, is perhaps his finest work. The story is set against the background of the *Penrhyn Lock-outs (1900–03) and the social disruption they caused, in particular to the family of Edward Ifans. Of his sons, Idris leaves for south Wales in search of work, Dan turns to journalism and alcohol, Llew goes to sea and the youngest son, Gwyn, dies after being beaten and thrown into a river by a blackleg's son. The source of the father's greatest grief is that his son-in-law, Ifor, is one of the '*bradwyr*' ('traitors'), those who returned to work in the quarries despite the Union's stand. The theme of the novel is the suffering and courage of the faithful few who adhered to their principles despite great adversity.

The novel was translated by Richard Ruck under the title *Out of their Night* (1954). For discussion of the novel's background see the articles by E. Hywel Owen in the magazine *Lleufer* (vol. 13, no. 4; vol. 14, no. 3; vol. 19, no. 2) and R. Merfyn Jones, *The North Wales Quarrymen 1874–1922* (1982); see also the articles by Eurys Rolant in *Y Genhinen* (Autumn, 1966) and by T. Emrys Parry in *Barn* (nos. 36–40, Oct., 1965 – August, 1966).

Chwedlau Odo (lit. 'The legends of Odo'; late 14th cent.), a translation into Welsh (Llanstephan MS 4) of a Latin text entitled *Narraciones* or *Parabole* by Odo of Cheriton (d. 1247). A volume of Latin sermons, completed in 1219, the work contains an abundance of anecdotes or *exempla* and copies are to be found in England, France, Spain and Italy. Odo's stories are different from most of their kind in that his characters are all animals: he found his material, according to Ifor *Williams, who edited the text in 1926, in Aesop's *Fables*, in the *Roman de Renard* and in the *Bwystoriau*.

Chwedlau Saith Ddoethion Rhufain (lit. 'Tales of the seven sages of Rome'), a collection of fabliaux on the theme of how the Emperor's son is saved from his *Jealous Stepmother. The earliest version in Welsh is attributed to Llywelyn Offeiriad and is thought to have been composed about the middle of the fourteenth century. It is not a translation, for it includes two tales not found in other versions and its narrative style is characterized by the stereotypes of native Welsh tales. Some sections echo parts of the tales of *Culhwch and Olwen, Owain and *Macsen Wledig. A later version, probably produced in Glamorgan, is extant in the hand of *Llywelyn Siôn, a copyist in whose collection is also to be found the story of Alexander and Lodwig.

The tales have been edited by Henry Lewis (1925).

CIAN, a poet listed by *Nennius in the *Historia Brittonum* as one who flourished in the sixth century. The words '*Gueinth Guaut*' (*recte* '*Guenith Guaut*', probably 'Wheat of Song') are appended to his name. He is also mentioned in a poem in *The *Book of Taliesin*, but none of his work has survived.

Cibwr, the southernmost commot of the cantref of *Senghennydd, is now occupied by the northern part of the city of Cardiff which lies between the rivers Taff and Rhymni, including the suburbs of Rhiwbina and Whitchurch.

Cigfa, see under PRYDERI.

Cilgerran, a castle on the border between Pembrokeshire and Cardiganshire, was built on a site above the river Teifi by order of either Roger de Montgomery (*c*.1093) or Gilbert fitz Richard de Clare (*c*.1100). The fortress may have been the scene of the abduction of *Nest, the wife of Gerald de Windsor, by *Owain ap Cadwgan in 1109. It was seized by *Rhys ap Gruffudd (The Lord Rhys) in 1165. According to tradition, it was while Rhys was entertaining Henry II at Cilgerran that a poet prophesied the discovery of the bodies of *Arthur and his queen at Glastonbury. The castle was captured in 1204 by the forces of William Marshall, Earl of Pembroke, and by those of *Llywelyn ap Iorwerth (Llywelyn Fawr) in 1215. The latter granted Cilgerran to Maelgwn, the son of Rhys, in the following year. The castle, which fell into desuetude about 1223, was owned during the fifteenth century by William *Herbert, Earl of Pembroke. The ruins were visited by Benjamin Heath *Malkin, Richard *Fenton and John *Blackwell (Alun), and painted by Turner.

For further details see J. R. Phillips, *History of Cilgerran* (1867) and O. E. Craster, *Cilgerran Castle* (1957).

Cilie family, The, or **Bois y Cilie**, a family of poets whose home was the farm known as Y Cilie, near Llangrannog, Cards. The father, **Jeremiah Jones** (1855–1902), a popular *bardd gwlad* ('country poet'), had been a blacksmith before becoming a farmer and it was at the smithy in nearby Blaencelyn that his wife Mary bore their first eight children; the other four were born at Y Cilie. Of their seven sons, six vied with each other in bardic competition from an early age. The eldest, **Fred Jones** (1877–1948), an Independent minister and one of the earliest members of *Plaid Cymru, was the father of Gerallt *Jones and the grandfather of Dafydd *Iwan. The second child, Margaret, was the mother of Fred *Williams, the fourth child was Dafydd *Jones (Isfoel) and the fifth was **John Jones** (Tydu; 1883–1968) who emigrated to Canada as a young man; an English couplet of his is carved on the Memorial Arch on the Ottawa Peace Tower. Esther, the seventh child, was the mother of **John (Jac) Alun Jones** (1908–82) and the tenth child was **Evan George Jones** (Sioronwy; 1892–1953), also a poet. Simon Bartholomew *Jones was the eleventh child and Alun Jeremiah *Jones (Alun Cilie) the twelfth. The literary talent of this extraordinary family persists in the second and third generation.

The brothers' light verse was collected in *Awen Ysgafn y Cilie* (ed. Gerallt Jones, 1976) and the family-tree is to be found in *Cerddi Pentalar* (ed. T. Llew Jones, 1976); for further details see the article by Gerallt Jones in *Deri o'n Daear Ni* (ed. D. J. Goronwy Evans, 1984).

Cilmeri, see under LLYWELYN AP GRUFFUDD (c. 1225–1282).

Circle of the White Rose, The, see under JACOBITISM.

Circulating Schools, see under JONES, GRIFFITH (1683–1761).

Cistercians, The, a monastic order established as a reformed branch of the Benedictines at Cîteaux in 1098. Known as White Friars from the colour of their habit, they stressed simplicity, poverty and solitude. Under the leadership of St. Bernard of Clairvaux (1090–1153), the order grew rapidly and in 1131 the first house was founded in Wales, at *Tintern. In 1147 abbeys were established at *Margam and *Neath, while *Basingwerrk joined the Cistercians from the Savigniac Order.

The Cistercians made little impact in Wales, however, until a group of monks established themselves at *Whitland between 1140 and 1157. This abbey became the mother-house of the order in Wales. Others were founded at *Strata Florida in 1164, at *Strata Marcella in 1170, at *Cwm-hir in 1176, at *Llantarnam in 1179, at *Llanllŷr about 1180 and at *Aberconwy about 1186. The order was generously patronized by the Welsh Princes and the monks, in turn, supported many of their political aspirations. The Cistercians contributed to the native culture by writing chronicles and registers, preserving and copying manuscripts, and patronizing the poets, especially towards the end of the Middle Ages during a relatively prosperous period in their history. All the Cistercian abbeys in Wales were dissolved between 1535 and 1539.

For further details see D. H. Williams, *The Welsh Cistercians* (1969).

Civil Wars, The (1642–48), between the armies of King Charles I and the Parliament, were fought on issues which appeared largely irrelevant to Wales. *Puritanism had penetrated no farther than the southern March and the Welsh squirearchy, having participated scarcely at all either in the mercantile development or the constitutional dispute characteristic of their counterparts in southern England, were initially loyal to the King, mainly because the habit of loyalty to the former *Tudor monarchy was not yet dead. In north Wales, however, the Middletons of *Chirk, though at first absentee, were Parliamentarian, and in Pembrokeshire fears of Popery and of an attack from the King's army in Ireland enabled John *Poyer to motivate the small mercantile class based on Pembroke and Tenby. In this county the Royalists, though greatly in the majority, were poorly led and Rowland *Laugharne, who became the local leader for the Parliament, was able, with intermittent help from Parliamentarian ships, to subdue all resistance in west Wales by 1646. In north Wales Royalist commanders like Sir John Owen (1600–66) of Clenennau and William Salusbury gave a much better account of themselves and the conflict on the northern borders was ultimately resolved as much by the Parliament's superiority in organization and finance as by valour on the ground. Also crucial, however, were the disregard of the advice of the moderate Archbishop John *Williams and his subsequent defection to the Parliament in 1645.

The importance of Wales in the Second Civil War is unquestionable. Late in 1647, because of the ingratitude shown by the Parliament in London towards Laugharne and Poyer, and the increase in sectarian pressure upon their stance as moderates, the latter broke into revolt, taking many officers and men of the west Wales army with him. Laugharne joined Poyer and an approach was made to the Royalist headquarters in Paris. This war, generated in Wales, was ended there only when Oliver Cromwell compelled the garrison of Pembroke Castle to surrender, after a six weeks' siege, on 10 July 1648.

For further details see J. F. Rees, *Studies in Welsh History* (1947), N. Tucker, *North Wales in the Civil War* (1958), A. L. Leach, *The History of the Civil War in Pembrokeshire* (1937) and, for a comprehensive account, J. R. Phillips, *Memoirs of the Civil War in Wales and the Marches* (2 vols., 1874).

CLANCY, JOSEPH PATRICK (1928–   ), American poet and translator. Born in New York City, of Irish and French descent, he became a Lecturer in English at Marymount Manhattan College, New York City, in 1948 and is now Professor there. He discovered an interest in Welsh literature after reading *An Introduction to Welsh Poetry* (1953) by Gwyn *Williams. Having published *The Odes and Epodes of Horace* (1960), he spent several years acquiring a knowledge of the Welsh language and paid two long visits to Wales while preparing his first volume of translations from the Welsh, *Medieval Welsh Lyrics* (1965). This highly accomplished work was followed, after further visits to Wales, by a companion volume, *The Earliest Welsh Poetry* (1970), and by *Twentieth Century Welsh Poems* (1982). It is on these three books that Joseph P. Clancy's reputation as one of the most successful translators of Welsh poetry into English rests. He has also translated some of the plays of Saunders *Lewis, John Gwilym *Jones and Gwenlyn *Parry, and a selection of the poems of Gwyn *Thomas published under the title *Living a Life* (1982). His original works are *Pendragon* (1971), a book for children about King *Arthur, and a volume of poems, *The Significance of Flesh* (1980; enlarged edn., 1984), many of which are based on traditional Welsh metres.

CLANVOW, JOHN (1341–91), poet, belonged to a family, prominent in the political life of the Border counties, which was descended from Hywel ap Meurig, a supporter of Edward I and the Marcher Lords. The sons of Hywel ap Meurig, Rhys and Philip ap Hywel, held administrative power under Edward II. It was their nephew, Philip de Clanvow, who adopted the name by which the family was subsequently known and which may have been derived from that of Vowchurch, Herefs. The family acquired lands in the lordships which later formed parts of Radnorshire, Breconshire and Herefordshire, among them the estate of *Hergest; there may have been a branch of it, too, at Gladestry, Rads. Sir John Clanvow, who was the grandson of Philip de Clanvow, followed a career in the service of Richard II and died while on a diplomatic mission to Constantinople. To him is now attributed the poem known as 'The Cuckoo and the Nightingale', more correctly entitled 'The Boke of Cupid, God of Love', which was once thought to be the work of Chaucer. This poem, composed in the dream-vision form, tells of the cuckoo which scoffs at love and of the nightingale's praise of it. Whether Clanvow spoke Welsh is uncertain but of his Welsh descent there is no doubt. That being so, he may be regarded as predating by almost a hundred years *Ieuan ap Hywel Swrdwal, sometimes said to have been the first Welshman to write verse in English. His connections with the Lollards are reflected in a religious essay of his which is preserved in the library of University College, Oxford.

For further details see V. J. Scattergood (ed.), *The Works of Sir John Clanvowe* (1975), K. B. McFarlane, *Lancastrian Kings and Lollard Knights* (1972), and the article by J. Beverley Smith, 'Edward I and the Allegiance of Wales' in *The Welsh History Review* (no. 8, 1976).

CLARK, GEORGE THOMAS (1809–98), antiquary, was an Englishman and, by profession, an engineer who worked under Brunel on the Great Western Railway, to which he published a guide. From 1852 until 1897 he was controller of the ironworks at Dowlais, near Merthyr Tydfil, Glam., where he took a prominent role in public life. He helped to found the society which later became the Royal Archaeological Institute and was an active member of the *Cambrian Archaeological Association for most of his life. His studies of Welsh castles were collected in the volume *Medieval Military Architecture* (1884) while his six volumes of the Glamorgan charters, *Cartae et Alia Munimenta quae ad Dominium de Glamorganicia pertinent . . .* (1910), were the basis for his *Land of Morgan* (1883). He also published a volume of Glamorgan pedigrees, *Limbus Patrum Morganiae et Glamorganiae* (1886), which in its meticulous detail is typical of all his work.

CLARKE, GILLIAN (1937–), poet. Born in Cardiff, she read English at University College, Cardiff, and worked with the BBC in London before returning to her native city in 1960. Since 1975 she has been a part-time lecturer in poetry in the Faculty of Art and Design at the Gwent College of Higher Education and a free-lance writer. Her poems were first published by Meic *Stephens in *Poetry Wales in 1970 and, as part of the Triskel Poets series, in the pamphlet *Snow on the Mountain* (1971). She has since published two collections of poetry, *The Sundial* (1978) and *Letter from a Far Country* (1982). A volume of her *Selected Poems* appeared in 1985. Many of her poems are concerned with the rhythms of the seasons, rural life and landscape, while others are set in suburbia or reflect her experiences as a mother. She became assistant editor of *The *Anglo-Welsh Review* in 1971 and was its editor from 1976 to 1984.

For further details see Gillian Clarke's contribution to *Common Ground: Poets in a Welsh Landscape* (ed. Susan Butler, 1985).

Classicism, a term often used to mean the adherence, in literature and the other arts, to recognized canons and patterns of composition, and the subjection of the artist's vision and mode of utterance to a perceptible relationship with the acknowledged masterpieces of the past, especially the Greek and Roman. In western Europe, particularly France and Germany, Classicism made for orderliness, clarity, rationality and wit, but with the Romantic Revival some found it stultifying.

The heyday of Classicism in England, often called the Augustan Age, influenced Welsh poets of the eighteenth century such as *Goronwy Owen and Ieuan Fardd (Evan *Evans; 1731–88) but with an important difference: in their work there was an attempt to revive the tradition of ancient and medieval Welsh poetry. This tradition is now regarded as a vigorous example of a sustained native 'classicism' in poetic craft, a view which owes much to John *Morris-Jones in exposition and to Saunders *Lewis in theory. The philosophical foundation of this bardic classicism was not so much Aristotelian and Horatian as Platonic and Augustinian, and it was bound up with the social pattern of medieval Welsh cultural life.

For a discussion of Classicism in Welsh see Saunders Lewis, *A School of Welsh Augustans* (1924), *Williams Pantycelyn* (1927) and *Braslun o Hanes Llenyddiaeth Gymraeg* (1932).

CLEMENT OF LLANTHONY or **GLOUCESTER** (d. 1190?), prior and theologian. Educated at Llanthony Prima, he became prior of the *Augustinian Canons there in 1150. His scriptural and theological commentaries, including a work on the Gospels, *Concordia Quattuor Evangelistarum*, were widely used.

Clêr, a term with two distinct meanings: it can denote poets in general or, more pejoratively, an inferior class of poets. *Iolo Goch used it in its first sense when he referred to the house of Penmynydd, Ang., as the refuge of poets, as did *Dafydd ap Gwilym in describing the abundance of wine given to poets by one of his noble friends. The verb '*clera*' implies the honourable custom of poets visiting their patrons, entertaining them with their poems and being paid for their work. *Guto'r Glyn in the late fifteenth century used it thus to describe his journeys in Anglesey, Gwynedd and Gwent.

The word's second meaning, referring to an inferior class of poets, including probably minstrels and other entertainers, was uppermost in the mind of *Gruffudd Llwyd when, in maintaining his right to accept gifts from his noble patrons, he wrote that he was not one of the dissolute *clêr*. The derivative form '*clerwr*' also has this second meaning: in *Einion Offeiriad's Grammar it is said that there were three classes of poets, of which the lowest was the *clerwr*. The business of the *clerwr* was to satirize, to mock, to cause disgrace and ignominy. No rules governed his verse, because it was essentially unruly, for which reason the serious poet was advised to eschew it. In the Statute of *Gruffudd ap Cynan, the document associated with the first *Caerwys Eisteddfod (1523), to the *clerwr* were attributed mimicry, bickering, discourtesy, ribaldry and derision. It is very unlikely, however, that there was any consistent validity in such statements: they were part of the professional poet's insistence on literary standards and mastery of his traditional craft.

Clerk versus Knight, a popular medieval theme, is found for example in a poem by *Dafydd ap Gwilym, '*Merch yn Edliw ei Lyfrdra*'. In response to a girl's rebuke about his cowardice, Dafydd defends himself by contrasting the merits of the poet and the soldier as lovers. He may not be brave on the battlefield, but at least he would cherish and protect her, the poet argues. Furthermore, a soldier's restless nature would take him to France or Scotland at the first rumour of war and there was always the danger that he would return covered with scars. The clerkly Dafydd, on the other hand, if accepted as her lover, would never leave her side.

Clic y Bont (lit. 'The bridge clique'), a circle of poets and musicians associated with the district of Pontypridd, Glam. It included such men as Evan *Davies (Myfyr Morganwg), William *Thomas (Glanffrwd), Thomas Essile Davies (Dewi Wyn o Esyllt; 1820–91), David Evans (Dewi Haran; 1812–85), Coslett Coslett (Carnelian; 1834–1910) and Thomas *Williams (Brynfab). None of these was of any great distinction as a poet but their coterie was typical of the many bardic circles which flourished in the industrial parts of south-east Wales during the nineteenth century.

Clogyrnach, see under TWENTY-FOUR METRES.

Clough, Richard (d. 1570), see under BACHEGRAIG and CATRIN OF BERAIN (1534/5–91).

Clwb Awen a Chân (lit. 'The muse and song club'), a literary and cultural society established at Caernarfon in 1908. Among its founders were T. Gwynn *Jones, E. Morgan *Humphreys and O. Llewelyn *Owain. The club flourished, attracting some four hundred members, but its success depended to a large extent on the remarkable personality of R. D. *Rowland (Anthropos), whose ill health led to its demise in 1932.

Clwydfardd (**David Griffiths**; 1800–94), see under GORSEDD BEIRDD YNYS PRYDAIN.

Clych Atgof (lit. 'Bells of memory'; 1906), a volume of autobiographical essays by Owen M. *Edwards, parts of which first appeared in the magazine *Cymru*, was published in book form in the series *Llyfrau Ab Owen*. It consists mainly of the author's memoirs of his childhood and youth, especially the years when he was a pupil at a Church school (which he detested) in Llanuwchllyn, Mer., and a student at the University College of Wales, Aberystwyth, and at Jesus College, Oxford. But it also includes memorable portraits of his father and, more generally, of the Welsh-speaking, Nonconformist community in which he was brought up. The essence of Owen M. Edwards's prose-style, rich in idiom and charming in its intimacy, was derived from the language of his home and in these respects the essays were to have a profound influence on the work of later writers such as E. Morgan *Humphreys, R. T. *Jenkins and W. J. *Gruffydd. A second edition of the book appeared in the series *Cyfres Gwerin Cymru* (ed. Ifan ab Owen Edwards, 1921) and Ifor *Williams edited a limited edition for the *Gregynog Press in 1935.

For a discussion of the book's merits see the articles by D. Tecwyn Lloyd in *Barn* (nos. 101–104, 1971) and the essay by R. Gerallt Jones in *Ansawdd y Seiliau* (1972).

'Clychau Aberdyfi' (lit. 'The bells of Aberdyfi'), a folk-song first published in a Welsh collection by Maria Jane Williams (Llinos; 1795–1873), namely *Ancient National Airs of Gwent and Morgannwg* (1844), with the words '*Os wyt ti'n fy ngharu i*'. Because the tune had appeared in several English collections before 1844, it has been wrongly described as being of English derivation and ascribed to Charles Dibdin. Some have maintained that the song's original title was '*Clychau Abertawe*' ('The bells of Swansea'). The song is sometimes connected in the popular mind with the legend of *Cantre'r Gwaelod because it imitates the chiming of underwater bells.

'Clydach Vale Lock-out, The', an anonymous

ballad to the tune 'Just Before the Battle, Mother' was written by an unemployed miner at Clydach, near Swansea, Glam., during a lock-out which began there in August 1921.

CLYNNOG, MORYS (1525–81), Catholic refugee and author. A native of Llŷn or Eifionydd, Caerns., he was educated at Christ Church, Oxford. He lectured on Civil Law for six years and then studied Law for eight years at Louvain, Bologna and Padua. After the Rising in the West (1554) he was obliged by command of Queen Mary to live in Padua as a companion to Edward Courtenay, the Earl of Devon, and he was exiled to Louvain at the accession of Elizabeth I. Ordained priest in 1555, he was preferred to several livings, including those of Corwen and St. Asaph, and later became Bishop of Bangor, a position which he renounced at the passing of the Act of Supremacy in 1559. He spent the remainder of his life assisting other Catholic refugees abroad. As Principal of the English College in Rome, he was alleged to have favoured Welsh students, a charge which led to the expulsion of the Welsh and the control of the College by the Jesuits. Some historians believe this fact to have been crucial in turning the Welsh against the agents of the *Counter-Reformation, the Jesuit missionaries in their midst. Clynnog published a short Welsh catechism, entitled *Athravaeth Gristnogavl* (1568), which was seen through the press in Milan by his friend, Gruffydd *Robert. The work was an adaptation of a catechism written by the Spaniard, Ioannes Polanco (d. 1574), the first secretary of the Society of Jesus. The Welsh volume was distributed in Wales but only one copy, now kept in the Newberry Library, Chicago, has survived.

For further details see the article by T. J. Hopkins and Geraint Bowen in *The Journal of the National Library of Wales* (vol. XIV, 1965) and that by Geraint Bowen in the *Transactions* of the Caernarvonshire Historical Society (vol. XXVII, 1966).

Cnapan, a game which was popular in south-west Wales until the middle of the nineteenth century, was played on Sundays and feast-days between the men of neighbouring parishes. The object was to deliver a small ball to a goal, sometimes the church porch, in the parish of the rival team. There were no rules, the players moved on foot or horseback and the game was usually the occasion for fisticuffs and bloodshed. There is a vivid description of the custom as it was upheld during the sixteenth century in George *Owen's *The Description of Penbrockshire* (1603). See also BANDO.

Coch Bach y Bala, see JONES, JOHN (1854–1913).

Cock-fighting, one of the most popular entertainments in both town and country until 1849 when it was made illegal, survived clandestinely in Wales for long after that date. In the version known as Welsh Main, spurred cocks were paired and set to fight to the death, the winners of each round being pitted against each other until only a single bird survived. An important element in cock-fighting, which was patronized by all classes, was the wager. In the countryside it was usually held in a pit in the open-air, but in the towns of north-east Wales there were special buildings for this purpose, often attached to taverns.

Cocosfardd y De, see JONES, ELIAS (fl. 1897).

Codex Oxoniensis Posterior, see BODLEIAN MANUSCRIPT 572 (10th cent.).

Coed Glyn Cynon, a wood of oak and birch which, in the sixteenth century, filled the valley of the Cynon from Penderyn to Abercynon, Glam. The felling of the trees by English industrialists for the purpose of obtaining charcoal, used in the smelting of iron before the discovery of coal, was bitterly lamented by an anonymous poet of the time.

Coed Yspwys, The Battle of (1094), see under CADWGAN AP BLEDDYN (d. 1111).

Coel Hen (early 5th cent.), probably the last *dux* of the Roman army in northern Britain, his name deriving from the Latinized Coelius or Coelestius, was an older contemporary of *Vortigern. He successfully held the region from the Pennines to Hadrian's Wall against intermittent attack from Angles and Saxons. Most of the later Celtic dynasties of that territory, such as those of *Urien Rheged, *Gwallog and Peredur of York (d. 580), afterwards the Perceval of Arthurian legend (see under TAIR RHAMANT), claimed descent from Coel. This fact may mean either that Coel made himself a king or that his army commanders, after his death, held on to their fragmented power in the name of the last *dux* to have full Roman sanction. Medieval fantasy turned Coel into Old King Cole and associated him, quite erroneously, with Colchester.

For further details see Charles Kightly, *Folk Heroes of Britain* (1982).

Coelbren y Beirdd (lit. 'Sign-board of the poets'), a spurious alphabet which Edward *Williams (Iolo Morganwg) ascribed to the ancient Britons. Its letters, based on the mystic sign /|\, were cut for display on a wooden frame, which was similar to an abacus. Iolo claimed that it formed part of the Welsh poet's armamentarium and had survived only in his beloved Glamorgan. Several examples dating from the nineteenth century have been preserved and the alphabet is sometimes found as part of the ornamental carving on chairs presented as prizes to poets at eisteddfodau.

Coety, a mesne lordship of the honour of *Glamorgan in which the Turberville family was established by the early twelfth century. Pain de Turberville's despotic administration of Glamorgan after the death of Gilbert de Clare in 1315 led to the rising of *Llewelyn ap Gruffudd (Llywelyn Bren) a year later.

Coffin, Walter (1784–1867), colliery pioneer, was a native of Bridgend, Glam. In 1807 he bought Dinas Rhondda farm and opened there the first coal-level in the *Rhondda valleys. He later became a director of the Taff Vale Railway and was the Liberal Member of Parliament for Cardiff between 1852 and 1857.

Cofion Cymru, see under UNDEB CYMRU FYDD.

Cofiwn (lit. 'Let us remember'), a patriotic group devoted to the commemoration of events and heroes of national significance, was formed in 1977. Its emblem is an ivy-leaf and it was among those organizations which marked the seventh centenary of the death of *Llywelyn ap Gruffudd, the last Prince of independent Wales, in 1982.

Coke, Thomas (1747–1814), evangelist, was born at Brecon, the son of an apothecary, and educated at Christ College there. In August 1763 he heard John Wesley preach in his native town and was stirred. Graduating from Jesus College, Oxford, in 1768, he entered the Church but in 1777 was removed from the curacy of South Petherton, Som., on account of his Methodist sympathies. An avowed Methodist evangelist thereafter, he became the organizer of the cause, Wesley's chief aide and superintendent of the Methodist Episcopal Church of America. Coke's interest in evangelizing overseas made him the 'father' of the Methodist mission: he was on his way to India to establish one there when he died. Probably the most important Welsh 'Wesleyan' after the death of Howel *Harris and the secession of the Calvinists, he was aware that his cause was disadvantaged in much of Wales for the lack of Welsh-speaking missioners. In 1800 he persuaded the Methodist Conference to send two such preachers to Ruthin and the Wesleyan cause in consequence gained a foothold in the north-east.

Coleg Harlech, an independent residential college for adult students at Harlech, Mer., was founded at the instigation of Thomas *Jones (1870–1955) in 1927. It was born out of his commitment to the cause of adult education and his belief that it would produce a new generation of leaders in Wales drawn from the working-class. The first Warden of the College, of which the motto is '*A fo ben bid bont*' (see under BRÂN),

was Ben Bowen Thomas (1899–1977). Its teaching staff has included the writers T. Rowland *Hughes, D. Tecwyn *Lloyd, Gwyn Erfyl *Jones and Richard *Poole, while Bryn *Griffiths, Ron *Berry and Gloria *Evans Davies are among its former students. Today the College has places for about a hundred and twenty students, most of whom go on to receive university education, for which reason it is popularly known as 'The College of the Second Chance'.

For further details see the monograph by Eirene White, *Thomas Jones, Founder of Coleg Harlech* (1978) and Peter Stead, *Coleg Harlech, the First Fifty Years* (1977). A selection of verse and prose by writers associated with the College was published in the volume *A Harlech Anthology* (ed. R. Wallis Evans, John Selwyn Davies and Graham Allen, 1976).

Coleshill, a commot of the cantref of Tegeingl (*Englefield) lying along the estuary of the Dee. Henry II narrowly avoided being ambushed by *Owain Gwynedd ap Gruffudd (Owain Fawr) in the woods of Coleshill in 1157.

Coll ap Collfrewi, see under POWERFUL SWINEHERDS.

Collen (late 6th cent.), a saint whose feast-day is 21 May. According to his Life, which is preserved in two manuscripts of the sixteenth century, his mother was Ethni Wyddeles, the daughter of an Irish chieftain named Matholwch. From Llangollen, probably his chief settlement, Collen's cult spread throughout the commot of Nanheudwy as far as Ruabon, and he was also known in Cornwall and Brittany.

COLLINS, WILLIAM JOHN TOWNSEND (Dromio; 1868–1952), journalist, local historian and poet, was born at Stratford-upon-Avon but settled in Newport, Mon., after joining the staff of the *South Wales Argus* when it was launched in 1892; he was that newspaper's editor from 1917 until his retirement in 1939. Well known for his authoritative coverage of *rugby, written under his pseudonym, he published a book about the game, *Rugby Recollections* (1948). His books and pamphlets, which were all published in Newport, a town he served in many capacities, include two volumes of biography about Monmouthshire writers (1945, 1948), a life of the etcher Fred Richards, *Artist-Venturer* (1948), and books about the history of free-masonry in the county. He published several volumes of lyrics as well as topical, humorous verse on local subjects, including *West Ward Rhymes* (1898), *In Gold and Purple* (1931), *Autumn Sunshine* (1934) and *Pilgrimage* (1944). Ephemeral as his comic verse undoubtedly is, it is more lively and engaging than the rather facile Romanticism of his other work. He also wrote two slim volumes of imaginative prose in the pseudo-medieval manner of the late-Victorian prose romance, *Tales from the New Mabinogion*

(1923) and *The Romance of the Echoing Wood* (1937).

Commentarioli Descriptionis Britannicae Fragmentum (lit. 'A fragment of a short treatise on the description of Britain'; 1572), a Latin treatise by Humphrey *Llwyd which was presented, together with one map of Wales and two of England and Wales, to his friend Abraham Ortelius, an Antwerp cartographer, in 1568. It contained notes on the history of Britain and, like the *De Mona Druidium Insulâ*, which he had also sent to Ortelius earlier in the same year, it attacked historians such as William of Newburgh, Boethius and Polydore Vergil for repudiating *Geoffrey of Monmouth's interpretation of early British history. The work, published in Cologne and dedicated to Ortelius, also appeared in an English translation by Thomas Twyne entitled *The Breuiary of Britayne* (1575). The map of Wales and one of the two showing both England and Wales were included in an appendix to Ortelius's atlas, *Theatrum Orbis Terrarum* (1573). Humphrey Llwyd, a true Renaissance scholar and antiquary, was concerned to defend the traditional view of British history. In this work, the first attempt to compile a *chorographia* for Britain, he attacked Polydore Vergil, defended the Galfridian myth of the glorious origins of the Britons, and expressed fervent belief in the apostolic purity of the early British Church. See also MYTH OF DESCENT.

Communism, see under MARXISM.

'Computus Fragment, The', a passage consisting of twenty-three lines of Old Welsh prose (Cambridge Univ. Lib. MS/Add.4543). Its source is not known, but it seems to be related to Bede's *De Temporum Ratione* which discusses methods of recording the moon's course through the signs of the Zodiac. A computator, writing in Welsh, is concerned here with explaining apparent difficulties in the two methods of computing, for calendrical purposes, according to the two tables of the moon's course described by Bede in the *Annalis Libellus* and the *Pagina Regularis*. The dating of the fragment is uncertain but on palaeographical grounds, and because of its subject-matter and some other associated but dubious evidence, it has been assigned to the beginning of the tenth century. The *Computus* is a particularly important fragment of Old Welsh prose, illustrating the effective practical use made of the language for discussing complex and abstruse topics. The linguistic evidence preserved in this fragment is of great value, especially for use in conjunction with that of other sources.

CONDRY, WILLIAM MORETON (1918–), naturalist and author, was born in Birmingham but he has lived most of his adult life in Wales,

working as a teacher and warden on a wild bird reserve. His numerous books on natural history include a standard work in *Collins's New Naturalist* series on the *Snowdonia National Park* (1966), *Exploring Wales* (1970), *The World of a Mountain* (1977) and *The Natural History of Wales* (1981). For many years he has contributed to the 'Country Diary' column in *The Guardian*.

Congregationalism, see INDEPENDENCY.

Conjuror, see DYN HYSBYS.

CONRAN, ANTHONY (1931–), poet, translator and critic, was born in India where his father was a railway engineer. The family had connections with north Wales and he was educated from the age of eight at Colwyn Bay and at the University College of North Wales, Bangor. By 1953 he was already known as a poet but the death of Dylan *Thomas in that year turned his attention to Anglo-Welsh poetry and a reading at about the same time of Gwyn *Williams's English translations of Welsh poetry aroused in him an interest in Welsh literature also. He returned to Bangor in 1957 to become Research Fellow and Tutor in the Department of English at the University College, a post from which he retired in 1982.

The discovery of Welsh literature was a crucial event in his literary career. The first book he produced after this new beginning, *Formal Poems* (1960), included dramatic monologues by Llywarch Hen (see under CANU LLYWARCH HEN), *Dafydd ap Gwilym, *Gruffudd ab yr Ynad Coch and Huw *Morys. He learned the rules of *cynghanedd and wrote poems in English which were based on Welsh metres, often on the occasion of births, marriages and deaths, in the manner of the *Bardd Gwlad. The most substantial of his collections of verse are *Spirit Level* (1974) and *Life Fund* (1979), but he has also published a large number of pamphlets. His collected poems, which appeared in four volumes between 1965 and 1967, and as one volume entitled *Poems 1951–67* in 1974, are written in a great variety of metres and styles and on a wide variety of topics.

As a translator Anthony Conran is best known for his *Penguin Book of Welsh Verse* (1967), an anthology which established his reputation as one of the most distinguished in this field. It has a long introduction which describes his view of the poet's role in Welsh society. He has also published a volume of critical essays about Anglo-Welsh poetry, *The Cost of Strangeness* (1982), which is among the most informed and stimulating studies of its subject.

There is an autobiographical essay by Anthony Conran in the volume *Artists in Wales* (ed. Meic Stephens, 1973). For critical discussion of Anthony Conran's writing see the articles by Gwyn Thomas in *Poetry Wales* (vol. 3, no. 1, 1967) and Jeremy Hooker in *The Anglo-Welsh Review* (vol. 18, no. 3, 1983); see also the note on the poet by Glyn Jones in *Profiles* (1980).

CONWAY, JOHN (d. 1606), translator, was a son of John Conwy II, a descendant of the family of that name which had settled in west Flintshire in the late thirteenth century and which was eventually established at *Botryddan, near Rhuddlan. He translated two treatises into Welsh, John Case's *Apologia Musices* (1588) under the title *Klod Kerdd Dafod a'i Dechryad* (1609), and Leonard Wright's *A Summons for Sleepers* (1589), an attack on *Puritanism, as *Definiad i Hennadirion* (*c.*1593). They are not very accurate as translations and it may be that he merely wished to follow the example of his kinsman, Sir John Conway, the author of three religious books. A number of poets, including *Sion Tudur and *Simwnt Fychan, sang his praises and he was among those who signed a petition requesting that an eisteddfod be held in 1594.

Conwy castle, built by order of Edward I after his military successes in the second *War of Welsh Independence (1282–83), stands on the former site of the Cistercian abbey of *Aberconwy which was moved to Maenan in order to make room for it. During the *Welsh Revolt (1294–95) the English king was besieged inside the castle and the capture of Conwy in 1401 by the brothers Gwilym and Rhys ap Tudur was a significant stage in the rising of *Owain Glyndŵr. The castle and borough were attacked during the Wars of the Roses. John Williams, Archbishop of York and a native of Conwy, held the castle for the King during the *Civil Wars but, after a dispute with the royalist commander, Sir John Owen (1600–66) of Clenennau, he assisted Parliamentary forces to gain control of it. The castle was dismantled in 1665.

For further details see R. Williams, *History and Antiquities of the Town of Aberconway* (1835); A. J. Taylor, *Conway Castle and Town Walls* (1956) and *The King's Works in Wales 1277–1330* (1974); see also Alun Llywelyn-Williams, *Crwydro Arfon* (1959).

Cook, Arthur James (1884–1931), miners' leader. Born in Somerset, he found work at a colliery in the *Rhondda Valley in 1903 and, as national secretary of the Miners' Federation of Great Britain, played a prominent role in the *General Strike of 1926. He it was who coined the slogan 'Not a penny off the pay, not a second on the day' which became a rallying-cry throughout the coalfields of Great Britain. A. J. Cook was also the author of *The Miners' Next Step* (1912), in the writing of which he was influenced by Noah *Ablett.

COOMBES, BERT LEWIS (1894–1974), author. Born on a small farm at Madley, Herefs., he went to work as a collier in Resolven, Glam., at the age of eighteen and there he married a local girl, learned Welsh and lived for the rest of his life.

His first book, *These Poor Hands: the autobiography of a miner working in south Wales* (1939), was acclaimed by English critics like J. B. Priestley and Cyril Connolly. Generally considered to be among the most authentically vivid accounts ever written about mining, it describes with a moving simplicity the harsh conditions in which he and his comrades worked and lived, and the bond which existed among them in the face of poverty, hunger, danger and death. The book also deals with the author's experiences while unemployed during the lock-outs and strikes of 1921 and 1926, when he taught himself to play the violin, trained to be an ambulance man, became active with the *South Wales Miners' Federation, and began to write.

Encouraged by John Lehmann, to whom his autobiography was dedicated, B. L. Coombes published several essays and short stories in *Penguin New Writing* and other magazines between 1937 and 1942. Two more books followed, namely *Those Clouded Hills* (1944) and the documentary, *Miners' Day* (1945). All three books are consistent in their theme, philosophy, style and integrity, and they are written with a scrupulous lack of sentimentality but with immense sympathy for the miners' lot, its hardship and humour. As a result of their success, B. L. Coombes became a frequent broadcaster on the subject of how society should be reorganized after the Second World War, publishing his *Plan for Britain* in the magazine *Picture Post* in 1945, but he continued to work underground as before. Disappointed that the Labour Government's nationalization of the mining industry in 1947 did not bring about the changes for which he had always argued, he disappeared from public view during the 1950s and died shortly before the re-publication of *These Poor Hands* in 1974.

For further details see the articles by David Smith in *The Anglo-Welsh Review* (vol. 24, no. 53, 1974) and by Beata Lipman in *Planet* (no. 23, 1974).

Coracle, a small, nearly square, flat-bottomed boat made from wicker-work which was originally covered with animal skin but later by canvas or calico water-proofed with pitch. The first clear description of a coracle was given by *Gerald de Barri (Giraldus Cambrensis) in 1188, although similar craft are mentioned in 'Y *Gododdin', and there are references to the boat in the work of Pliny and Caesar. Once commonly in use on the rivers and lakes of Wales and the Marches, the coracle is now used only for salmon fishing on the rivers Teifi, Tywi and Taf in Dyfed, but even there its numbers are rapidly diminishing.

Coraniaid, see under CYFRANC LLUDD A LLE-

FELYS (*c*.1200) and OPPRESSIONS WHICH CAME TO THIS ISLAND.

Cordell, Alexander, see GRABER, GEORGE ALEXANDER (1914–   ).

Corgi, a small, short-legged dog native to Wales, has been used for centuries as a house-guard and working dog, especially for the herding of cattle. There are references to the corgi in *The *Red Book of Hergest* and it was later known as a 'cur-dog'. Two breeds were recognized by the Kennel Club in 1934: the short-tailed Pembroke and the larger, long-tailed Cardigan; both are rough-haired, brown and white in colour and much given to yapping.

Corineus, the legendary leader of the second company of Trojans whom *Brutus met beyond the Pillars of Hercules. He is described in *Historia Regum Britanniae* as a genial, brave man renowned for his good advice and his ability to slay giants. When offered his choice of any British territory he chose Cornwall (*Cernyw*), which was named after him, because there were so many giants in that part of the Island.

Corn Dollies, see under CHARMS.

Corn is Green, The, a comedy in three acts by Emlyn *Williams, was first produced in London on 24 September 1938. The author's most successful play, it is based on his experience at Holywell County School and on his relationship with his teacher, Sarah Grace Cooke. It tells how Morgan Evans, a young Welsh miner, becomes an Oxford scholar under the coaching of Miss Moffat, an English bluestocking, and is a study of the emotional stress and alienation caused by academic ability in a working-class boy. Morgan's rebellion against the impersonality of his teacher leads him to seek solace with the slut, Bessie Watty. Impelled by instinctive or conventional morality to marry Bessie when her pregnancy is discovered, he decides to abandon his scholarship but is persuaded to change his mind by the selfless devotion of Miss Moffat, who offers to adopt the child. Glan Sarno, the play's fictitious setting and the author's first dramatic recreation of a rural community, Welsh-speaking but dominated by an English squirearchy, is based on his home village of Pen-y-maes, Flints.

Corpse Bird, a premonition of death in the form of an owl, hedge-sparrow or robin, tapping on a window or door. The name is also given to a person who habitually brings bad tidings or fears the worst. See also CORPSE CANDLE and CYHYRAETH.

Corpse Candle, a premonition of death in the form of a light which was said to appear in a house shortly before a bereavement and travel slowly along the funeral route to the churchyard, where it would vanish. To interfere with the candle, or touch its flame, was believed to result in death. See also CORPSE BIRD and CYHYRAETH.

Cors Fochno, an extensive bog between Aberystwyth and Tre Taliesin, Cards., was formerly believed to be the home of Yr Hen Wrach ('The Old Witch'), a woman more than seven feet tall who, appearing on foggy nights, would breathe on people in their houses, inflicting the ague. The sickness may have had to do with the burning of peat in the district for with the advent of coal it became less prevalent.

Corsygedol, a mansion in the parish of Llan-ddwywe-is-y-graig, Mer., one of the most popular centres of bardic patronage in the county for more than three centuries. Poetry dedicated to Gruffudd Fychan ap Gruffudd ab Einion (d. *c*.1483) has survived but a welcome was extended to poets before his time. The evidence is more plentiful for the period of his grandson, Rhys Fychan and his wife, Gwen, and their son Richard Vaughan (d. 1584), and his son, Griffith (d. 1616). A further three generations maintained the tradition and the family was later linked by marriage to the *Nannau family. The most distinguished member of the Vaughan family was William Vaughan (1707–75), who represented Merionethshire in Parliament for many years, served as President of the Honourable Society of *Cymmrodorion and was a friend of the *Morris Brothers.

Cory family, a prominent family of colliery owners and coal freighters in Glamorgan during the nineteenth century. Richard Cory I (1799–1882), a native of Devon, began a ship chandlery at Cardiff Docks in 1842. In 1856, with his sons John (1828–1910) and Richard Cory II (1830–1914), he established the firm of Richard Cory and Sons, brokers, shipowners and coal exporters. Renamed Messrs. Cory Brothers and Company after the retirement of Richard Cory I in 1859, the firm became the world's largest supplier of coal to ships, the Corys establishing some eighty bunkering stations on international shipping lanes. The family also became colliery proprietors, owning pits in the valleys of the Rhondda, the Ogwr, the Neath and the Cynon.

John Cory, a leading advocate of the Barry Dock scheme, was active in Liberal politics in the county and was reputed to donate £50,000 a year to charitable causes, especially those concerned with *Temperance, education and *Nonconformity. The brothers divided over the issue of Irish Home Rule, Richard's more rigid Protestantism—he was a munificent patron of the Salvation Army—causing him to see no merit in Gladstone's proposals. Cory Hall, once a popular centre for meetings in Cardiff, was a gift of the brothers to the city. John Cory's second son, Clifford John Cory (d. 1941), was president of the Monmouthshire and South Wales Coalowners' Association in 1906 and his youngest son, Reginald Cory (d. 1934), was responsible for the design of the splendid gardens at the family home of Dyffryn in the Vale of Glamorgan.

There is no detailed study of the Cory family but references will be found in A. H. John and Glanmor Williams (ed.), *Glamorgan County History* (vol. V, 1980).

'Cosher Bailey's Engine', see under BAILEY, CRAWSHAY (1789–1872).

COSLETT, COSLETT (Carnelian; 1834–1910), see under CLIC Y BONT.

Council for the Welsh Language, The, see under WELSH OFFICE.

Council of Hereford, The (c.926–30), see under ARMES PRYDEIN.

Counter-Reformation, The, the Catholic response to the Protestant Reformation in England and Wales. Under the Acts of Supremacy and Uniformity of Elizabeth I's first Parliament (1559), the Protestant Church inaugurated by Henry VIII was established by law and *Roman Catholicism was proscribed. The Catholics struck back: Elizabeth was excommunicated by Papal Bull in 1570 and, from 1574, missionary priests crossed to England from seminaries on the Continent. The resistance was both defensive and offensive, for the missionary efforts of the *Society of Jesus were directed to the reversal or cancellation of the Reformation, while many laymen and secular priests adhered to the old faith and refused to conform to the Elizabethan settlement. The Penal Laws became increasingly severe: from 1581 a Catholic layman refusing to go to church could be obliged to pay £260 a year in fines and, from 1586, merely to be a Catholic priest was deemed high treason. Some held fast to their Catholic profession in spite of persecution and, in Wales, Recusancy (the refusal to attend the parish church) flourished most in the north-east and south-east, especially in Flintshire and Monmouthshire.

The movement produced a good deal of prose writing in Welsh. Popular catechisms were translated by Morys *Clynnog (1568), Roger *Smyth (1609–11), Richard *Vaughan of Bodeiliog (1618), John Hughes (1615–86), the son of Hugh *Owen (1575?–1642), and Gwilym *Puw. Three controversial works dealing with the points at issue between Catholics and Protestants were written by the pioneer missionary priest Robert *Gwyn of *Penyberth, but none was published. Gwyn also wrote the first, and possibly the second, of the eight devotional or didactic works produced by the Welsh Recusants, namely *Y Drych Cristianogawl*, a treatise on the commandments of God and the Church, an anonymous translation of Stephen Brinkley's *A Manual of Meditation*, a translation by Hugh Owen of Robert Parsons's *Christian Directory*, Owen's translation of Thomas à Kempis's *De Imitatione Christi*, John Hughes's *Allwydd Paradwys* and translations by Gwilym Puw of Richard Whitford's *Jesus Psalter* and the *Golden Litany*. At least fourteen other works are known to have been lost. Among the relatively small number of books which have been preserved, those by Gwyn stand out by virtue of their ambitious scope and plain style.

The Recusants also had their poets, including *Tomas ab Ieuan ap Rhys, the two martyrs Richard *Gwyn and William *Davies, and *Siôn Brwynog, the author of the famous *cywydd*, 'I Dduw ydd wyf weddïwr'. Two *awdlau* noteworthy for their spirited invective are those by Edward Turberville (c.1648–81) of Pen-llin, Glam., and Edward *Dafydd (*fl.* early 17th cent.).

Although Recusancy produced no classic, with the possible exception of *Y Drych Cristianogawl*, it contributed towards the variety and interest of Welsh literature during the latter half of the sixteenth century and throughout the seventeenth century.

For further details see Emyr Gwynne Jones, *Cymru a'r Hen Ffydd* (1951) and D. Aneurin Thomas, *The Welsh Elizabethan Catholic Martyrs* (1971).

Country Poet, see BARDD GWLAD.

Courting in Bed, a custom among the Welsh peasantry which caught the attention of many an English traveller in the eighteenth and nineteenth centuries. Maidservants, denied the use of the parlour, were sometimes allowed to receive their sweethearts in their own rooms. As a rule, the young people were expected to remove only their shoes and to spend the evening in conversation while reclining on, rather than in, the bed which was often the only furniture in the room. The custom, known in other countries as bundling, came to be frowned upon in the nineteenth century and attempts were made to suppress it. See also BLACK VENUS (1944).

The custom is described by Alwyn D. Rees in *Life in a Welsh Countryside* (1950) and by Catrin Stevens in *Arferion Caru* (1977).

Courtly Love, a type of romantic love which was celebrated in poetry and romance and cultivated in the courts of kings and nobles during the Middle Ages. Formerly known as *amour courtois* (a term invented by the French scholar Gaston Paris in 1883), the phenomenon has come to be denoted by the medieval Provençal term *fin'amor*. It was an elaboration and idealization of courtship leading to dalliance and occasionally the satisfaction of sexual passion between a knight and a married lady, sometimes in the absence of her lord. For the wooing knight it may have been a refining diversion from the brutalities of the warrior's life, while for the lady it could mean a delectable relationship in an age when marriage was largely an economic transaction and a wife's liberty severely limited. The tendency was to regard love and marriage as incompatible and the knight had to keep the name of his beloved secret in order to protect her reputation and to suffer much because she was beyond his reach.

It is often said that Courtly Love began among the troubadours of Provence in the twelfth century and owed much to Ovid and a little to the love-poetry of the Moors. But there is something similar in the poems of *Hywel ab Owain Gwynedd and *Gwalchmai ap Meilyr in Wales in the same century, and the Celtic theme of tragic love between the king's nephew and the king's wife (as in the Irish tales of Deirdre and of Diarmuid and Gráinne) began to make its impact on Europe through the story of *Tristan and Iseult. It may also be suggested that the comparative freedom of women under the old Welsh *Laws would have lent itself to a kind of romantic love. Associated with gentle wooing and chastity as commended in the tale of *Pwyll, this tradition, when transported into different social conditions, could have evolved into the more conventionalized fin'amor, with the Tristan story providing a more sombre motif which was developed in the love of Lancelot for Guinevere.

Later continental developments in the literature of Courtly Love undoubtedly influenced Wales. The theme was treated allegorically by Guillaume de Lorris in his Le Roman de la Rose (finished with satirical cynicism by Jean de Meun) and Llywelyn Bren (*Llywelyn ap Gruffudd) was reputed to have owned a manuscript of this work. But the more playful treatment of love by the clerici vagantes was the more likely influence on *Dafydd ap Gwilym, who may have inherited the aubade ('dawn song'), the serenade ('evening song'), as well as the dream motif, from the troubadours and the trouvères. See also CHIVALRY.

For further details see C. S. Lewis, The Allegory of Love (1936), Moshe Lazar, Amour courtois et fin'amor dans la littérature du XIIe siècle (1964), John Lawlor (ed.), Patterns of Love and Courtesy (1966) and Douglas Kelly, Medieval Imagination (1978).

Covertside, Naunton, see DAVIES, NAUNTON WINGFIELD (1852–1925).

Cowper, Y, see ROBERTS, ELIS (d. 1789).

COX, LEONARD (fl. 1524–72), grammarian and rhetorician. Born at Monmouth, he began his career as headmaster of Reading Grammar School, taught for several years at Caerleon, Mon., and in 1572 became headmaster of Coventry Grammar School; he also travelled widely in Europe and was a friend of Erasmus

and Melanchthon. Cox published The Art and Crafte of Rhethoryke (1524) and Commentaries upon Will. Lily's Construction of the Eight Parts of Speech (1540); among his translations was an English version of Erasmus's Paraphrase of the Epistle to Titus (1549).

COXE, WILLIAM (1747–1828), archdeacon and historian, was born in Piccadilly, London, and educated at Eton and King's College, Cambridge. Although ordained deacon, he abandoned his first curacy to become a travelling tutor to the sons of the Duke of Marlborough and the Earl of Pembroke in turn, and by 1794 he had been to Switzerland, Russia and Hungary. Preferred to Kingston-on-Thames in 1786, he began a more settled way of life when the Earl of Pembroke presented him in 1788 to the living of Bemerton, Wilts., from which he never permanently moved.

His main interest was in publishing accounts of his travels and in working on the family papers of his noble patrons. It was his friend and patron, Sir Richard Colt Hoare of Stourhead, translator of *Gerald de Barri (Giraldus Cambrensis) and patron, amongst others, of Richard *Llwyd, who persuaded him to accompany him on a tour of Monmouthshire in the autumn of 1789. Hoare, who had made a number of drawings, some sixty of which subsequently appeared in Coxe's Tour, encouraged him to return to Monmouthshire twice during 1799 to interview countless gentry and amplify his notes. The author declared that he spent five months in the county and travelled some fifteen hundred miles. The result of his enquiries, An Historical Tour of Monmouthshire (1801), although disclaiming any pretension to being a history of the county and despite its plodding style, is much fuller and more valuable (granted its socially stratified sources of information) than the accounts of most other travellers in Wales during the late eighteenth century.

For further details see M. W. Thompson (ed.), The Journeys of Sir Richard Colt Hoare 1793–1810 (1983).

Crach Fardd, see BARDD TALCEN SLIP.

Cradock, Walter (1610?–59), Puritan preacher, was a native of Llangwm, Mon. Although well travelled, the main sphere of his labour was Monmouthshire and William *Wroth, from the same county, was one of the chief influences on his life. Cradock became curate to William *Erbery at St. Mary's Church, Cardiff, until he was forced to move to Wrexham on account of his Puritan tendencies, and he was present at Wroth's church in Llanfaches when the first Independent cause was formed in 1639. He refused to read The Book of Sports (1633) from the pulpit, as Puritan ministers were required to do on the King's order for the instruction of the people on how to keep the Sabbath, because that work allowed for the playing of certain games on a Sunday. After wandering to Wrexham, Shrewsbury, London and Brampton Bryan, he returned to his native county. An itinerant preacher, he was the principal supporter of Cromwell in Wales and an Approver under the Act for the *Propagation of the Gospel (1650). He expressed his evangelistic zeal in sermons which are remarkable for their simple vocabulary and homely imagery. Together with 'The saints fulnesse of joy in their Fellowship with God', which Cradock preached to the House of Commons in July 1646, his sermons were edited by Thomas *Charles and Philip Oliver in 1799.

Craigfryn, see HUGHES, ISAAC (1852–1928).

Cranogwen, see REES, SARAH JANE (1839–1916).

Crawshay family, The, of Cyfarthfa, Merthyr Tydfil, Glam., the foremost iron kings of south Wales. Richard Crawshay (1739–1810), who came of Yorkshire farming stock, obtained an interest in Anthony *Bacon's ironworks at Cyfarthfa in 1786, soon becoming the sole owner, and by 1800 the works were the largest of their kind in the world. He was the main instigator of the Glamorgan Canal Company which, in 1794, linked Merthyr to Cardiff by water, and he was among the first industrialists to leave a fortune of more than a million pounds.

His son, William Crawshay I (1764–1834), spent little of his time at Merthyr, being more concerned, when not in dispute with his father or his son, with the Cyfarthfa Iron Company's business in London, but his son, William Crawshay II (1788–1867), was the very epitome of an iron king. Manager of Cyfarthfa in 1813, it was he who ordered the building of the extravagant, mock-gothic Cyfarthfa Castle in 1825. He was given to a flamboyant radicalism and the *Merthyr Rising of 1831 proved an embarrassment to him. Cyfarthfa was expanded in his day and, although the rival works at Dowlais proved more flexible in adapting to technological change, he was among the first ironmasters to see the possibilities of the coal trade. He also developed the family's ironworks at Hirwaun and bought works at Treforest and in the Forest of Dean. After his purchase of Caversham Park, Oxon., his links with Merthyr became more intermittent and Cyfarthfa was left to his son, Robert Thompson Crawshay (1817–79), who is chiefly remembered for his tomb in the churchyard at Faenor, near Merthyr, with its inscription, 'God forgive me'.

The Cyfarthfa works continued under the management of Robert's sons until they were absorbed by *Guest, Keen and Nettlefold in 1902. The Crawshay family was closely related to the Baileys of Nantyglo and Glanusk, and to the Halls of Hensol and Llanover. Descendants of the Crawshays, particularly Captain Geoffrey Crawshay (1892–1954) and Sir William Crawshay (1920–   ), have played prominent parts in the social and cultural life of Wales in the twentieth century.

Further details will be found in John P. Addis, *The Crawshay Dynasty* (1957) and Margaret Stewart Taylor, *The Crawshays of Cyfarthfa Castle* (1967).

CRAWSHAY-WILLIAMS, ELIOT (1879–1962), poet and novelist, was a grandson of Robert Thompson Crawshay (see under CRAWSHAY FAMILY). Educated at Eton and Trinity College, Oxford, he began his career in secretarial posts with Winston Churchill and David *Loyd George and, from 1910 to 1913, was the Liberal Member of Parliament for Leicester. After the First World War, in which he served as lieutenant-colonel, he returned to live at the family home, Coed-y-Mwstwr, Bridgend, Glam. Among his numerous books were the volumes of verse *Songs on Service* (1917), *The Gutter and the Stars* (1918), *No one wants Poetry* (1938), *Barrage* (1944) and *Flak* (1944). Those of his novels with Welsh settings were *Speckled Virtue* (1940), *The Wolf from the West* (1947) and *Rough Passage* (1950); his plays included *Five Grand Guignol Plays* (1924). He also wrote two volumes of autobiography, *Leaves from an Officer's Notebook* (1918) and *Simple Story* (1935).

Crécy, The Battle of, fought on 26 August 1346, was one of the decisive engagements in the Hundred Years War (1337–1459) between England and France. The English, under Edward III and the Black Prince, had at their command a paid and well-equipped army the infantry of which included many Welshmen who had served the Crown at Flanders (1297) and Falkirk (1298) and were experts with the longbow. Distinguished by coats and hats of green and white cloth (sometimes said to be the first military uniform), approximately five thousand Welshmen were in the army which crossed the Seine and met the feudal forces of the French king on a hill near Crécy. Their leaders were Rhys ap Gruffudd and *Hywel ap Gruffudd (Hywel y Fwyall), both of whom were knighted on the field of battle after the defeat of the French. The poet *Iolo Goch, in a *cywydd* addressed to Edward III, celebrated the victory.

For further details see the article by D. L. Evans, 'Some notes on the history of the Principality in the time of the Black Prince' in the *Transactions* of the Honourable Society of Cymmrodorion (1925–26) and the article by A. D. Carr, 'Welshmen in the Hundred Years War', in *The Welsh History Review* (vol. 4, 1968).

Creiddylad, the daughter of Lludd Llaweraint, is described in the story of *Culhwch and Olwen as 'the maiden of most majesty that was ever in the Isle of Britain and its three adjacent islands'. She is fought over by Gwythyr ap Greidawl and

*Gwyn ap Nudd until *Arthur intervenes with the judgement that they shall compete for her on the first day of May until Doomsday, and that the victor on that day shall have her. The contest has been interpreted as corresponding to the struggle between summer and winter.

Creuddyn, a commot of the cantref of *Rhos, lies on the peninsula now dominated by the town of Llandudno, Caerns. The fort at *Degannwy was probably the seat of the rulers of the ancient kingdom of Rhos. Creuddyn was separated from the rest of Rhos in 1284 and attached to the county of Caernarfon, presumably in order to strengthen English control over the approach to the castle at Conwy. The name was also given to the southernmost commot of the cantref of *Penweddig in Ceredigion.

Creuddynfab, see WILLIAMS, WILLIAM (1814–69).

Crindy, Y, see under CARADOGION.

Crogen, The Battle of (1165), fought in Dyffryn Ceiriog between the forces of *Owain ap Gruffudd (Owain Gwynedd) and Henry II, resulted in a great victory for the Welsh. The slaughter is remembered in several place-names in the district, including those of the farms known as Plas Crogen and Melin Crogen. It is said of a field at Crogen Wladus that the corpses of the men and horses killed in the battle were buried there and that it must not be ploughed, lest their bones should be disturbed.

Cronica de Wallia (lit. 'Chronicle of Wales'), a text in Latin consisting of material dating from the period 1190 to 1260, with a number of lacunae. It was compiled under political pressure which influenced the chronicler's point of view and his choice of the material available to him. The most interesting feature of the text is that it resembles, both in content and style, the lost Latin text which provided the basis for *Brut y Tywysogyon. It may have been compiled at the monastery of *Whitland. See also ANNALES CAMBRIAE.

For further details see Thomas Jones, 'Cronica de Wallia and other Documents from Exeter Cathedral MS3514' in the *Bulletin* of the Board of Celtic Studies (vol. XII, 1946–48), J. Beverley Smith, 'The Cronica de Wallia and the Dynasty of Dinefwr', in the *Bulletin* of the Board of Celtic Studies (vol. XX, 1962–64) and Kathleen Hughes, 'The Welsh Latin Chronicles: Annales Cambriae and related Texts' in the *Proceedings* of the British Academy (vol. LIX, 1973).

Cronica Principum Wallie, see BRUT Y TYWYSOGYON.

Cronical Glyndŵr (lit. 'Chronicle of Glyndŵr'; c.1422), an annalistic chronicle of the rising of *Owain Glyndŵr from its beginning in 1400 to his disappearance in 1415. It first appears, as part of a longer chronicle, in the hand of *Gruffudd Hiraethog, which extends from the arrival of *Brutus in Britain to the death of Henry V and the coronation of his infant son in 1422, and it seems to have been composed soon after that date. The section concerning Glyndŵr is found in two other manuscripts, one deriving from a book by Lewys Morgannwg (*Llywelyn ap Rhisiart), and it is also inserted into another popular chronology, *Blwyddyn o eisiau deucant*, in one of *Wiliam Llŷn's books. These longer chronicles have no value but *Cronical Glyndŵr* is important because it is the earliest record of the Welsh view of the rising, a mere generation after the event. The chronicle's closing entry (in English translation) says of Glyndŵr: 'Owen went into hiding on St. Matthew's Day in Harvest, and thereafter his hiding-place was unknown. Very many say that he died, the seers maintain that he did not'.

The text was published, with an English translation, by J. E. Lloyd in *Owen Glendower* (1931).

Cronicl Cymru (lit. 'Chronicle of Wales'), a weekly newspaper established by J. K. Douglas of Shrewsbury in 1866; John Davies (Gwyneddon; 1832–1904) was its editor for the first two years. Although established as an independent newspaper, it supported the Conservatives during the election campaign of 1868 and continued in that role until its demise in 1872. Morris *Williams (Nicander) was another of the paper's editors and among the most regular contributors were John *Williams (Ab Ithel), Owen Wynne *Jones (Glasynys) and Richard Parry (Gwalchmai; 1803–97).

Crown, The, one of the traditional prizes awarded to poets at the *National Eisteddfod. It was first presented in 1867 for a *pryddest* (a poem in the free metres), the older ceremony of the *Chair being reserved for an *awdl* (a poem in the strict metres). This custom has continued to the present and the Crown ceremony, held under the auspices of *Gorsedd Beirdd Ynys Prydain, has become one of the high moments in the pageantry of the National Eisteddfod.

Among the poets who have won the Crown more than once during the twentieth century have been T. H. *Parry-Williams (1912, 1915), Cynan (Albert *Evans-Jones; 1921, 1923, 1931), Caradog *Prichard (1927, 1928, 1929), Rhydwen *Williams (1946, 1964), Euros *Bowen (1948, 1950), Dafydd *Rowlands (1969, 1972), Bryan Martin *Davies (1970, 1971), Alan *Llwyd (1973, 1976) and Donald *Evans (1977, 1980). The prize (which includes a monetary award) has been withheld, for lack of a worthy winner, on five occasions since 1900.

Crown, see NINE MEN'S MORRIS.

Crown of Britain, The, see under VATICINATION.

Crwth or **Crowd**, a traditional musical instrument belonging to the lyre family but played with a bow. During the period of the *Poets of the Gentry it was the only instrument other than the *harp which was recognized within the official organization of Welsh minstrelsy. There are references to the *crwth* in the *Laws of Hywel Dda and it remained in vogue until the eighteenth century, when it was supplanted by the fiddle; by then both were folk-instruments only. Daines *Barrington reported to the Society of Antiquaries in 1770 that the last Welsh crowder was alive in Anglesey but that he had no successors. To the eighteenth century belong the three earliest specimens still extant, all of which have six strings, including two open strings running diagonally to one side of the fingerboard. See also PIBGORN.

For further details see Otto Anderson, *The Bowed-Harp* (1930) and A. O. H. Jarman, '*Telyn a Chrwth*' in *Llên Cymru* (vol. VI, 1960–61).

Crwys, see WILLIAMS, WILLIAM CRWYS (1875–1968).

Cuhelyn, see under AFARWY.

CUHELYN FARDD (early 12th cent.), poet, the son of Gwynfardd Dyfed and father of Gwrwared Gerdd Gemell, was an ancestor of *Dafydd ap Gwilym. The fact that the names of these three poets occur together among Dafydd's earliest recorded forebears seems to indicate that he was descended from men who both practised and patronized poetry in the role of gifted amateurs. A praise-poem addressed to Cuhelyn Fardd is preserved in The *Black Book of Carmarthen* and a later legend, recorded by George *Owen of Henllys, portrays Cuhelyn as prophet and story-teller as well as poet.

Culhwch and Olwen, the chief characters in one of the most ancient tales in the Welsh language, the text of which has been dated about 1100 and is preserved in The *White Book of Rhydderch* and The *Red Book of Hergest*, together with the collection of tales commonly called The *Mabinogion*.

The subject of the tale is the attempt by the young hero, Culhwch, to win Olwen, the daughter of the giant Ysbaddaden Bencawr, his stepmother having sworn on him a destiny to love and marry Olwen alone. Culhwch is advised by his father to go to *Arthur's court in order to seek assistance in the winning of Olwen. Refused admittance by the gate-keeper, *Glewlwyd Gafaelfawr, because the feast has already begun, he succeeds in entering the court without dismounting from his horse. He is warmly received by Arthur who agrees to help and then Culhwch, *Cai, *Bedwyr and others set out on the search. They are received at Custennin Heusor's house by his wife, Culhwch's aunt, who warns him of the perils involved in the quest for Olwen: no contender for her has ever escaped alive from her father's wrath. Culhwch is not daunted, however, and when he chances to meet Olwen, he declares his love for her. There follows an onomastic tale about how Olwen ('ol wen', 'white foot-prints') received her name: four white trefoils had sprung up where she had trodden. Advised by Olwen to accept and fulfil any condition set by her father, Culhwch appears three times before the giant who, on each occasion, defers an answer and draws the meeting to a close by hurling a poisoned spear at him. On the third occasion, Culhwch catches the spear and throws it back, piercing the giant's eye-ball. Then, next day, Ysbaddaden lists forty seemingly impossible tasks (*anoethau) as conditions to be fulfilled before Olwen may be won, to which Culhwch replies that each will be easy to accomplish. The hero is not mentioned again until the last sentences of the story, because most of the tasks are carried out on his behalf by Arthur and his men. Eventually, *Gorau fab Custennin cuts off Ysbaddaden's head and Culhwch marries his Olwen.

The tale is important as one of the few surviving examples of the craft of the *Cyfarwydd, or traditional story-teller, which interweaves the themes of the Giant's Daughter and the *Jealous Stepmother. The text poses several difficult problems, however. Its style and narrative techniques are very close to those of oral tradition and some scholars have concluded that the redactor followed too many marginal strands before returning to the main narrative of how Olwen was won. Others have complained that the long lists of knights at Arthur's court, no doubt intended to entertain the tale's first audiences who would have been familiar with the story associated with each character, tend to slow the pace of the narrative. Nevertheless, the tale provides many examples of ancient story-telling skills such as the portrait of Olwen as Culhwch sees her for the first time and the hunting of the *Twrch Trwyth. It is also a rich storehouse of native traditions. Not only does it employ narrative motifs characteristic of the folk-tale but it also includes passages corresponding to passages of old Welsh poetry, such as the conversation between Culhwch and the gate-keeper, Glewlwyd. Moreover, the tale reflects native traditions about King Arthur and his knights: in particular, and in contrast to the continental tradition, Arthur himself takes an active role in the adventures, although there is an element of burlesque in the portrayal. Cai, who has not yet acquired his surly character, is seen here as warrior and leader. The tale's importance, then, is of European dimensions, in as much as this is one of the few Arthurian texts predating *Geoffrey of Monmouth's *Historia Regum Britanniae, and therefore not influenced by that work.

For discussion of the tale see the chapters by Idris Foster in *Arthurian Literature in the Middle Ages* (ed. R. S. Loomis, 1959) and in *Y Traddodiad Rhyddiaith yn yr Oesau Canol* (ed. Geraint Bowen, 1974); see also the essay by the editor in *Ysgrifau Beirniadol VII* (ed. J. E. Caerwyn Williams, 1972).

Cumbria, see under OLD NORTH.

Cumulative Tale, a story which cumulates from clause to clause or from sentence to sentence in a repeated pattern. Examples in Welsh are '*Yr Hen Wraig Fach a'r Oen*' ('The Little Old Woman and the Lamb') and '*Y Frân Fawr a'r Frân Fach a aeth i'r Coed i Gnoia*' ('The Big Raven and the Little Raven which went to the woods to gobble'). Similar in form to folk-rhymes and songs such as '*Y Pren ar y Bryn*' ('The Tree on the Hill') and '*Y Deuddeg Dydd o'r Gwyliau*' ('The Twelve Days of Christmas'), it relies on memory and speech-skills for its effects.

Cunedda (*fl.* 400 or 450), a chieftain of the *Gododdin tribe who, according to *Nennius, was brought south to expel the Irish from what is now Wales. Argument centres chiefly on the date of Cunedda's move and the possible authority for it. One theory is that the command came from the Roman general Stilicho who was attempting to re-establish Roman authority in north Wales in the decade before 400. More favoured recently is the possibility that Cunedda may have been brought south about 450, on the authority of *Vortigern. The fact that Cunedda had a father and grandfather with Roman names, together with the later pedigrees (*Maelgwn Gwynedd is believed to have been his great-grandson), suggests a date in the mid-fifth century. The success of the mission to expel the Irish seems to have been less than complete, despite the tradition that Cadwallon Lawhir, Maelgwn's father, finally defeated them at Trefdraeth in Anglesey.

The eight sons of Cunedda, who accompanied him, are each said to have established a dynasty in Wales (e.g. Ceredig in *Ceredigion) and medieval pedigrees sedulously derive many of the princely houses of Wales from them. It is more likely, however, that the names of Cunedda's sons are eponymous—that is to say, Rhufon was invented for *Rhufoniog, and Edeyrn for *Edeyrnion, and so on—and that the only credible dynasty was that which had its seat at *Aberffraw and, in Maelgwn's day, at *Degannwy.

The coming of Cunedda, now generally though not universally accepted by historians, may well explain the lineal and cultural link with 'the Men of the North', which helped to transmit the poetry of *Aneirin, and perhaps *Taliesin, to Wales after the military defeat of the British in the northern kingdoms. For further details see M. P. Charlesworth, *The Lost Province* (The Gregynog Lectures, 1948, 1949) and Rachel Bromwich, *Trioedd Ynys Prydein* (2nd edn., 1978).

Curig (mid-6th cent.), a saint who may be connected with such places as Llangurig, Mont., and Capel Curig, Caerns. What is known about him is of doubtful authenticity, mainly because he was confused with Cyriacus, the child from Asia Minor who was killed with his mother Julitta (Ilid) during the persecution of Diocletian about 304. This confusion resulted from the Norman policy of replacing the Celtic saints with others of Roman origin. Curig is often mentioned by medieval poets who called him Curig Lwyd ('the Blessed') and sometimes Curig Farchog ('The Knight').

CURTIS, TONY (1946–   ), poet, was born at Carmarthen and educated at University College, Swansea, and Goddard College, Vermont. A Senior Lecturer in English at the Polytechnic of Wales, he has edited *Madog*, an arts magazine, and a volume of critical essays, *The Art of Seamus Heaney* (1982). Some of his early poems, together with those of Nigel *Jenkins and Duncan *Bush, are to be found in the volume *Three Young Anglo-Welsh Poets* (1974). Since then he has published three more volumes of verse, *Album* (1974), *Preparations* (1980) and *Letting Go* (1983), and a collection of prose-poems and short stories, *Out of the Dark Wood* (1977). He addresses everyday subjects, frequently concerned with family or place, in a voice which is poised, compassionate and quietly celebratory. In 1984 he was elected Chairman of the English-language section of Yr *Academi Gymreig. Tony Curtis won the National Poetry Competition organized by the Poetry Society and BBC Radio 3 in 1984. He is also the author of a monograph on Dannie *Abse in the *Writers of Wales* series (1985).

Curwen, The, see under LLANBADARN FAWR.

Custennin Heusor, see under CULHWCH AND OLWEN.

Cwm Glo (lit. 'Coal valley'; 1935), a play by J. Kitchener *Davies, shocked its first audiences by its frank treatment of sexual behaviour and its realistic portrayal of working-class life. Dai Dafis, a lazy and selfish collier, is sacked by Morgan Lewis, the pit's manager. Lewis is blackmailed by Dai on account of his lust for the collier's daughter, Marged, whose aim in life is to walk the streets of Cardiff as a prostitute, and she seduces Idris who is courting Morgan's sister, Bet. In the last act the secrets of this imbroglio are revealed and, struck by Lewis, Dai falls dead. The play, intended by its author to demonstrate the material and moral crisis of the industrial valleys of south Wales during the 1930s, was a milestone in the development of Welsh *drama and it has some memorable scenes.

Cwm-hir, an abbey near Rhayader, Rads., was established by the *Cistercian Order as a daughter-house of *Whitland under the patronage of Cadwallon ap Madog, prince of Maelienydd, in 1176. The monks supported the Welsh cause during the thirteenth century and tradition claims that the headless body of *Llywelyn ap Gruffudd was secretly buried there in 1282. During the rising of *Owain Glyndŵr the abbey was devastated, after which its religious life never fully recovered.

At the abbey's dissolution in 1536, the lands went to the Turner family and, in the seventeenth century, belonged to the Fowlers. The well-known rhyme, thought to be the lament of a commissioner sent to collect fines from Royalists during the Commonwealth, refers to the latter owners:

> Radnorsheer, poor Radnorsheer,
> Never a park and never a deer,
> Never a squire of five hundred a year
> But Richard Fowler of Abbey Cwmhir.

For further details see the accounts of Cwm-hir by W. J. Rees in *Archaeologia Cambrensis* (1849) and S. W. Williams in *Radnorshire Transactions* (1894–95); see also Glanmor Williams, *The Welsh Church from Conquest to Reformation* (1962) and F. G. Cowley, *The Monastic Order in South Wales 1066–1349* (1977).

'Cwm Rhondda' (lit. 'The Rhondda Valley'), a very popular hymn-tune by John Hughes (1873–1932) of Llanilltud Faerdref (Llantwit Fardre), Glam. Written for a Baptist singing festival at Pontypridd in 1905, it was originally entitled '*Rhondda*' and is reputed to have been sung in over five thousand festivals during the composer's lifetime. It has been included in many collections of hymns, not only in Wales where it is usually sung to the words '*Wele'n sefyll rhwng y myrtwydd*' by Ann *Griffiths, but also in England, set to the words 'Guide me, O Thou great Jehovah' by William *Williams (Pantycelyn). In both versions it is perhaps the best known of all Welsh hymn-tunes and certainly it is one of the most powerful.

Cwmsgwt, the nickname for any derelict place, especially in Glamorgan. According to William *Thomas (Glanffrwd) in his *Plwyf Llanwynno* (1888), it was originally given to the land around Pwllhywel, a farm between Pontypridd and Ynys-y-bwl, which was over-worked, despoiled and then deserted by coal-prospectors. The name has acquired comic associations and is often used, albeit imprecisely, to denote a place which is remote, obscure or undistinguished. See also DAI LOSSIN.

Cwndid, a form of *carol, popular with

minstrels in Glamorgan and Gwent between the sixteenth and early eighteenth centuries, was written without *cynghanedd in metres such as *Awdl-Gywydd, *Cywydd Deuair Hirion and *Triban (Englyn Unodl Cyrch). The word is derived from the English 'condut' (L. conductus), a sort of motet sung while the priest was proceeding to the altar. Religious cwndidau, sung on saints' days, were intended for moral instruction and it was to this end that biblical parables were set to verse. Among exponents of the form were *Llywelyn Siôn, Edward *Dafydd of Margam, Edward *Evan of Pen-y-fai and Lewis *Hopkin.

A collection was edited by L. J. H. James and T. C. Evans under the title *Hen Gwndidau, carolau a chywyddau* (1910); see also the two articles by Glanmor Williams in *Grym Tafodau Tân* (1984).

Cwrtmawr Manuscripts, The, see under DAVIES, JOHN HUMPHREYS (1871–1926).

Cwrw Bach, see BID ALE.

Cwta Cyfarwydd, Y (lit. 'The short guide'), the name given to a number of manuscripts (the most important and famous is Peniarth MS 50 in the NLW), containing a miscellany of poetry and prose in Welsh, Latin and English, much of which is vaticinatory in nature. Dates within the prophecies ranging between 1425 and 1456, together with the evidence of the hands found in the manuscript, suggest that it belongs to the first half of the fifteenth century. This evidence, in turn, tends to disprove the assertion made at the beginning of the manuscript which states that it was written by *Gwilym Tew. It is more likely that the manuscript was transcribed by a certain Dafydd who was, possibly, a monk at the abbey of *Neath. A great deal of vaticinatory verse, fiercely anti-English, by Rhys Fardd (Y Bardd Bach or Bardd Cwsg; *fl.* 1460–80) is contained in the volume, which is said to have once belonged to Sir Thomas Morgan of Ruperra, Mon.

The manuscript is described in J. Gwenogvryn Evans, *Report on Manuscripts in the Welsh Language* (vol. 1, part 2, 1899).

Cybi (mid-6th cent.), a saint who lived in Wales and Cornwall. Two versions of his Life have survived from the twelfth century. He may have been the son of a Cornish nobleman but, according to the genealogies, his father was Selyf, son of *Geraint fab Erbin. His chief settlement was at Holyhead (Caergybi) in Anglesey, a place renowned as a collegiate church throughout the Middle Ages, but he is also commemorated in other place-names such as Llangybi, Caerns., where a well near the church was said to cure disease.

For further details see the article by A. D. Carr in *Gwŷr Môn* (ed. Bedwyr Lewis Jones, 1979).

Cybi o Eifion, see THOMAS, EBENEZER (1802–63).

Cyfaill yr Aelwyd (lit. 'The friend of the hearth'), a monthly journal founded in 1881 and edited by Beriah Gwynfe *Evans until 1894 when it ceased publication. Carrying poetry, reviews and articles on musical, literary, scientific, antiquarian and topical subjects, it is believed to have provided Owen M. *Edwards with a model when he launched his magazine *Cymru in 1891.

Cyfarthfa, see under CRAWSHAY FAMILY.

Cyfarwydd, the name given in medieval Welsh society to the story-teller. Only one such, *Bledri ap Cydifor, is known by name. The craft, or art, of the Cyfarwydd is demonstrated at its richest in *Pedair Cainc y Mabinogi, in the last of which his function is described thus: 'And that night he entertained the court with pleasant tales and story-telling till he was praised by every one, and it was a pleasure for *Pryderi to converse with him'. The Cyfarwydd, in his relationship with his patron, fulfilled the obligations of Pencerdd ('Chief Poet') and Bardd Teulu ('Household Poet') but he used verse only under certain conditions. In saga-cycles, for example, he employed verse mainly of the *englyn type for monologue and dialogue, but prose for narrative and description, sometimes exclusively. For all his gifts, he belonged to a lower echelon in the *Bardic Order and a distinction was made between the beirdd, of whom he was one, and the Penceirddiaid. He relied on material other than that of his own imagination, taken from the repertory of other storytellers or from written sources. Qualities essential for his success were a formidable memory, great physical stamina and an unerring dramatic instinct.

For further details see the article by Patrick Ford, 'The Poet as Cyfarwydd in Early Welsh Tradition', in Studia Celtica (vol. X/XI, 1975-76).

Cyfeiliog, a commot of *Powys comprising the basin of the Dyfi. With the break-up of his kingdom after the death of *Madog ap Maredudd in 1160, it came into the possession of Madog's nephew, Owain Cyfeiliog (*Owain ap Gruffudd ap Maredudd), one of the most accomplished of the *Gogynfeirdd.

CYFFIN, ROGER (fl. 1587-1609), a poet who was perhaps a native of Denbighshire. It is said that he left home in order to receive the patronage of John Vaughan of Golden Grove. He composed many poems in free and strict metres for his patrons in both north and south Wales, and engaged in bardic contentions with *Gruffudd Hafren, Richard *Davies, Bishop of St. David's, and Dafydd Llwyd of Dolobran.

Cyfnerth, see under LAWS OF HYWEL DDA.

'Cyfoesi Myrddin a Gwenddydd' (lit. 'The conversation of Myrddin and Gwenddydd'), a long poem in the form of a dialogue which has survived in manuscript (Peniarth MS 3, c.1300), and also in The *Red Book of Hergest. In alternating englynion, Gwenddydd questions and her brother *Myrddin (Merlin) replies, prophesying the names of the kings of Wales and England, and foretelling the eventual supremacy of the Welsh under *Cadwaladr. The poem also contains references to early northern kings, such as *Rhydderch Hen and *Gwenddolau, and to the battle of Arfderydd at which Myrddin lost his reason.

Cyfran, see GAVELKIND.

Cyfranc Lludd a Llefelys (lit. 'The tale of Lludd and Llefelys'), the shortest of the four native tales included in The *Mabinogion. It is found entire in The *Red Book of Hergest and the beginning of it in The *White Book of Rhydderch. Early in the thirteenth century it was inserted into one version of the Welsh translation of *Geoffrey of Monmouth's *Historia Regum Britanniae, in connection with the reign of Lludd. In all copies Geoffrey's account of Lludd, King of Britain shortly before the arrival of Julius Caesar, appears as the introduction to the tale. The story was, therefore, current in its present form about the year 1200 and other references suggest it may be a little older. It is concerned with three oppressions afflicting Britain: a foreign people, the Coraniaid, who could hear anything spoken in the open and so could not be plotted against, a cry every May Eve which produced shock and sterility in humans, beasts and land, and a mysterious disappearance of all surplus food supplies. Lludd consults his brother Llefelys, King of France, is told how to overcome each oppression and, carrying out his instructions successfully, he reigns happily thereafter.

The tale has been interpreted as a popular version of one of the Triads enumerating the invaders of Britain in which folk-tale figures replace those drawn from the traditional account of early British history. Among these the red and white pryfed ('dragons'), whose struggle in the second episode symbolizes the conflict of Briton and Saxon, are also found early in the ninth century in the *Historia Brittonum, in a close Latin rendering of a vernacular tale. The style of the Cyfranc is similar to that of the rest of The Mabinogion but it is not a particularly good example of it, and it is likely that an oral tale has been recorded by a non-professional story-teller to supplement Geoffrey's meagre account of Lludd.

The tale has been edited by Ifor Williams (1910) and by Brynley F. Roberts (1976); for further details see A. O. H. Jarman and Gwilym Rees Hughes (ed.), A Guide to Welsh Literature (1976).

Cyfres Crwydro Cymru (lit. 'The wandering of

Wales series'), a series of travel-books launched by the publishers *Llyfrau'r Dryw in 1952. Each of its eighteen volumes (to 1985) deals with the topography, history and culture of one of the former counties of Wales, or parts of them. Among the authors are T. I. *Ellis, Aneirin Talfan *Davies, Frank Price *Jones, Alun *Llywelyn-Williams, Gomer M. *Roberts, Ffransis G. *Payne and Bobi Jones (Robert Maynard *Jones). The purview of the series, which is generally of a high literary standard, has been extended to include volumes on Cornwall, Brittany, the Outer Hebrides, *Patagonia and London.

Cyfres Gŵyl Dewi (lit. 'The St. David's Day series'), a series of booklets, mostly biographical studies of eminent Welsh people, has been published annually by the University of Wales Press from 1928 (with a gap during the World War) to the present day. The first was an essay on *Hywel Dda by J. E. *Lloyd; it was followed by monographs on *Dafydd ap Gwilym (1935), Daniel *Owen (1936), Goronwy *Owen (1951), John *Morris-Jones (1958), *Geoffrey of Monmouth (1966), William *Salesbury (1967), William *Williams of Pantycelyn (1969) and Edward *Lhuyd (1971), among others. The series also includes essays on such subjects as the Welsh *Bible (1938), the *Rebecca Riots (1961), the Welsh Colony in *Patagonia (1965), the *Caerwys Eisteddfodau (1968), the story of the *harp in Wales (1980) and Henry *Tudor (1985). Attractively produced with a bilingual text, and cheaply priced, the series is primarily intended for use in schools but it also appeals to the general reader.

A full list of the forty-one titles published down to 1980 is to be found in Y Casglwr (March, 1980), the magazine of Cymdeithas Bob Owen.

Cyfres Pobun (lit. 'Everyone's series'), a series of nineteen volumes dealing with social, industrial and cultural issues in Wales and the world during the 1940s, was published by Hugh Evans and Sons, Liverpool, in 1944 and 1945 under the editorship of E. Tegla *Davies. Among the titles of literary interest were those on the Welsh press by E. Morgan *Humphreys, on modern Welsh Literature by Thomas *Parry, on Welsh Drama by Elsbeth Evans and the volume Y Bardd yn ei Weithdy, edited by T. H. *Parry-Williams.

Cyfres y Beirdd Answyddogol, see under LOLFA.

Cyfres y Brifysgol a'r Werin (lit. 'The university and the people series'), a series of twenty-three volumes published by the University of Wales Press between 1928 and 1949. Modelled on the Home University Library, it was primarily intended to meet the needs of adult education classes, some volumes being based on extramural lectures. The more successful authors took a boldly interpretative, rather than a textbook approach, to their subjects and several have proved to be of lasting value, especially Hanes Cymru yn y Ddeunawfed Ganrif (1928) and Hanes Cymru yn y Bedwaredd Ganrif ar Bymtheg (1933) by R. T. *Jenkins, Datblygiad yr Iaith Gymraeg (1946) by Henry *Lewis and *Braslun o Hanes Llenyddiaeth Gymraeg (1932) by Saunders *Lewis.

A full list of titles is to be found in Y Casglwr (March, 1981), the magazine of Cymdeithas Bob Owen.

Cyfres y Fil (lit. 'The thousand series'), a series of books published by Owen M. *Edwards during the years from 1901 to 1916, comprised (with a Welsh dictionary appearing in 1905) a total of thirty-seven volumes. Most were devoted to the life and work of a single author such as *Dafydd ap Gwilym (1901), Islwyn (William *Thomas, 1903), Ann *Griffiths (1905), Iolo Morganwg (Edward *Williams, 1913) and *Iolo Goch (1915). Printed in a small, distinctive format with dark-blue covers, they were cheaply priced but few volumes found the thousand subscribers from whom the series took its name and for whom the editor appealed in his magazine, *Cymru. A similar series in English, and another in Welsh on historical subjects, were announced but, presumably for lack of response, were never published. See also LLYFRAU AB OWEN.

A full list of titles is to be found in Y Casglwr (March, 1977), the magazine of Cymdeithas Bob Owen.

Cyfres y Werin (lit. 'The people's series'), a series of books edited by Ifor Leslie Evans and Henry *Lewis, was published by the Educational Publishing Company, Cardiff, during the years from 1920 to 1927 and by the University of Wales Press from 1950 to 1954. Although it began with Blodeuglwm o Englynion (1920), edited by W. J. *Gruffydd, the intention was to present selections of foreign classics in Welsh translation. Among the fourteen titles published up to 1927 were works by Ibsen, Maupassant, Daudet, Gogol, Molière, Descartes, Goethe, Schiller and Luther. This policy was resumed in 1950 when the series was revived by the University of Wales Press: translations of works by Sophocles, La Fontaine, Boccaccio, Keller and Balzac were the five published before the series was brought to an end in 1954.

A full list of titles is to be found in Y Casglwr (1980), the magazine of Cymdeithas Bob Owen.

Cyfrinach y Beirdd, see under PEDWAR ANSAWDD AR HUGAIN.

Cyhydedd Fer, Cyhydedd Hir and **Cyhydedd Naw Ban**, see under TWENTY-FOUR METRES.

Cyhyraeth (lit. 'Apparition'), a portent of death

in the form of a plaintive or agitated sound in the night. It was believed by some, especially in the Tywi Valley, to be the lament of those about to die, while others connected it with *Gwrach y Rhibyn. There is a vivid description of the phenomenon in Edmund *Jones's A Relation of Apparitions in Wales (1767). See also CORPSE BIRD and CORPSE CANDLE.

Cylch Cadwgan (lit. 'The Cadwgan circle'), a group of writers who met in the home of J. Gwyn *Griffiths and his wife, Kate *Bosse-Griffiths, during the Second World War, was known by the name of their house at Pentre in the Rhondda Valley. Sharing the same pacifist and Nationalist ideals and aesthetic interests, its members included D. R. Griffiths and Gwilym Griffiths (the host's brothers), as well as Pennar *Davies, Rosemarie Wolff, Rhydwen *Williams, Gareth Alban *Davies and the musician John Hughes. The group was significant in that it discussed contemporary trends in European literature and argued in favour of liberating Welsh literature from what it saw as the shackles of *Puritanism. Among the publications which reflect the group's identity are the anthology Cerddi Cadwgan (1953), the novel by Pennar Davies, Meibion Darogan (1968), the novel by Rhydwen Williams, Adar y Gwanwyn (1972), the periodical Y *Fflam and the book I Ganol y Frwydr (1970) by J. Gwyn Griffiths.

For further details see the memoir by Rhydwen Williams in Barddas (no. 60, Feb., 1982).

Cylch-grawn Cynmraeg neu Drysorfa Gwybodaeth, Y (lit. 'The Welsh magazine or treasury of knowledge'), a quarterly journal of which five numbers appeared in 1793 and 1794. Its editor was Morgan John *Rhys but, like most of the contributors, he was not named; among the contributors who can be identified were Edward *Charles (Siamas Gwynedd) and G. Owain o Veirion (i.e. William *Owen Pughe). The magazine's contents were largely religious but also included poetry, biographical notes and reviews, becoming more secular when it began to carry articles on prison conditions, slavery, the French Revolution and the legend of *Madog ab Owain Gwynedd. Some material in the first numbers is in Pughe's 'new orthography', part of his campaign to replace the double letters of Welsh with single symbols.

Cymanfa Ganu (lit. 'Singing festival'), a feature of Nonconformist worship in Wales. Hymn-singing services were held from 1830 on, but festivals became more frequent under the influence of John *Roberts (Ieuan Gwyllt) who led a memorable gathering at Aberdare, Glam., in 1859. The trend developed on denominational lines and was helped by the increasing use of tonic sol-fa among the Welsh. At first the congregational singing was disciplined but it became more sentimental and was often marred by a straining after extraneous, even histrionic, effects. The custom enjoyed a great vogue, however, and although enthusiasm has waned, it still persists in many districts. Much depends on the conductor whether the emphasis is on worship or on a special kind of community hymn-singing.

Cymbeline, see under CARATACUS (1st cent.).

Cymdeithas Bob Owen (lit. 'The Bob Owen society'), a society for bibliophiles, founded in 1976, was named after the genealogist and book-collector, Robert *Owen (1885–1962) of Croesor, Mer. Its chief activity is the publishing of Y Casglwr, a magazine edited by John Roberts *Williams, the contents of which deal with the history and collecting of printed material of all kinds. The society, which encourages the interest of its members in buying second-hand books, has done much to revive the market in Wales and its magazine is an indispensable source of information for collectors.

Cymdeithas Cerdd Dafod (lit. 'The society of tongue art'), a society formed in 1976 by poets whose chief interest is in Welsh poetry in the traditional strict metres. Its programme includes competitions, weekend schools and other events at the *National Eisteddfod. In response to a recent manifestation of public interest, it has successfully defended the ancient rules of Welsh prosody (*Cerdd Dafod) against those who advocated innovation. The society also publishes books and a monthly magazine, Barddas, the first number of which appeared in 1976 under the editorship of Alan *Llwyd and Gerallt Lloyd *Owen. The society acquired its first full-time officer in 1983 when it appointed Alan Llwyd as its organizer.

Cymdeithas Cymru Newydd, a society of writers planned by Pennar *Davies and Keidrych *Rhys early in 1939, was to have been known in English as The New Wales Society. Its aim was 'to substitute energy and responsibility for the dilettantism and provincialism of Welsh life and literature' by bringing together writers in the two languages of Wales for a discussion of the literary and social questions of the day. 'Let us do our best', wrote Keidrych Rhys, 'to make Wales a less dead place, less of an intellectual desert, so that it will be possible for our writers and artists to work at home'. The debate on the need for change was carried on mainly in the newspapers *Baner ac Amserau Cymru and the *Western Mail, and in the magazines *Wales and *Tir Newydd. Among the writers who expressed an interest in joining the society were Jack *Jones, Emlyn *Williams, Idris *Davies, Dylan *Thomas, Waldo *Williams, Emyr *Humphreys and Alun *Lewis. A manifesto was drafted but before it could be published the Second World War was declared and, with the dispersal of most of the younger writers, all plans for the establishment of the society were abandoned. There was no further attempt to found a society for writers in Wales until the creation of *Yr *Academi Gymreig* in 1959.

For details about the New Wales Society see the article by Meic Stephens in *Poetry Wales* (vol. 4, no. 2., Winter, 1968).

Cymdeithas Dafydd ap Gwilym (lit. 'The Dafydd ap Gwilym society'), a society founded by Welsh students at the Colleges of Oxford University in 1886. Its first president was John *Rhŷs and among its earliest members were Owen M. *Edwards, John *Morris-Jones, Edward *Anwyl and J. Puleston *Jones; for this reason the society was described by Thomas *Parry as 'a nursery of giants'. Meeting informally in their rooms to discuss Welsh affairs, the society's members were especially interested in the need for reform of the Welsh language's orthography, attempting to write their own prose in a style based on classical models and rural speech. Their work was at first disparaged as 'Oxford Welsh' but later accepted as an integral part of the renaissance in Welsh letters at about the turn of the century. The society has continued in existence to the present day.

For further details see the articles on the Society by J. E. Caerwyn Williams in *Astudiaethau Amrywiol* (ed. Thomas Jones, 1968) and in *Y Traethodydd* (Oct., 1983).

Cymdeithas Emynau Cymru (lit. 'The hymn society of Wales'), a society formed in 1967 for the purpose of fostering interest in all aspects of Welsh hymnody. An annual lecture delivered during the *National Eisteddfod under the society's auspices is published in its *Bulletin* (ed. E. Wyn James), together with studies of hymn-writers and bibliographical surveys.

Cymdeithas Llên Cymru (lit. 'The literature of Wales society'), a group of six bibliophiles, among whom John *Ballinger and John Humphreys *Davies were prominent, who came together in 1900 for the purpose of publishing Welsh books in fine, limited editions. Over the next fifteen years there appeared, in three series known as *Y Gyfres Las*, *Y Gyfres Goch* and *Y Gyfres Felen*, a total of nine books which included *Carolau gan Richard Hughes* (1900), *Hen Gerddi Gwleidyddol 1588–1660* (1901), *Casgliad o Hen Ganiadau Serch* (1902), *Casgliad o Hanes-gerddi Cymraeg* (1903), *Caniadau yn y mesurau rhyddion* (1905) and *Gwaith Morgan Rhys* (1910).

Cymdeithas yr Iaith Gymraeg (lit. 'The society of the Welsh language'), also known by its English title, **The Society for the Utiliza-tion of the Welsh Language**, was founded in 1885 at the National Eisteddfod in Aberdare. Among its leaders were Dan Isaac *Davies and Isambard Owen (1850–1927) and it had the ear of Henry *Richard. The Government's policy of allowing only English in the schools of Wales throughout the latter half of the nineteenth century was first challenged by this society which campaigned successfully for the introduction of Welsh to the curriculum, both as a subject and as a medium of instruction. See also the next entry.

Cymdeithas yr Iaith Gymraeg (lit. 'The society of the Welsh language'), was formed in 1962, largely out of frustration among young Nationalists at the failure of *Plaid Cymru either to make electoral progress or effectively to defend the interests of Wales (as in the case of *Tryweryn) but also in response to the lecture *Tynged yr Iaith* by Saunders *Lewis. Under the presidency of Huw T. *Edwards, the society launched its first campaign at Trefechan Bridge, Aberystwyth, on 23 February 1963 when some forty members blocked the entrance to the town in an attempt to draw public attention to the inferior legal status of Welsh by deliberately breaking the law and demanding Welsh or bilingual summonses.

The next three years were spent in correspondence with local authorities and Government bodies such as the General Post Office and the Registrar General. The report, *The Legal Status of the Welsh Language* (1965), which recommended that Welsh be granted equal validity with English in law, but not equal official status, was among the first fruits of the society's work. It then adopted a policy of non-violent civil disobedience designed to test the provisions of the Welsh Language Act of 1967, many of its members being fined and imprisoned at this time. The society's activities were given an intellectual basis by the philosopher J. R. *Jones and by Alwyn D. *Rees in his editorials in the magazine *Barn and a wider appeal in the songs of Dafydd *Iwan.

From 1968 there was an increase in militancy, especially prior to the investiture of the Prince of Wales in July 1969, and with the painting out of English road-signs in many parts of the country. Throughout the 1970s, with a membership drawn largely from among young people but enjoying the support of many older Welsh-speakers, including several eminent writers, the society continued to press for the provision of adequate television facilities in Welsh, often courting prosecution for those of its members who took direct action against the property of the broadcasting authorities. The creation of a fourth television channel broadcasting in Welsh was among the society's objectives and this aim was partially achieved with the establishment of *Sianel Pedwar Cymru* (*S4C*) in November 1982. It has also widened its purview in recent years by entering other spheres such as planning, housing and education where proper provision for the Welsh language is considered vital for its survival.

The society publishes a lively newsletter, *Tafod y Ddraig* and from time to time a manifesto (see *Planet*, nos. 26/27, 1974/75). For further details see the chapter by Cynog Davies in *The Welsh Language Today* (ed. Meic Stephens, 1973) and the same author's *Cymdeithaseg Iaith a'r Gymraeg* (1979) and *Mewnlifiad, Iaith a Chymdeithas* (1979). The history of the society from 1962 to 1976 was edited by Aled Eurig, *Tân a Daniwyd* (1976); see also the article by Colin H. Williams, 'Non-violence and the development of the Welsh Language Society 1962–c.1974' in *The Welsh History Review* (vol. 8, no. 4, 1977).

Cymhortha, a form of tax or tribute demanded by a lord in the Middle Ages. Sometimes the payment was in the form of cattle but later it was usually money. The practice deteriorated into a convenient but unpopular means of raising taxes, and a form of oppression. Unsuccessful attempts were made to prohibit it from the middle of the fourteenth century onwards but it is clear that it flourished during the sixteenth century when it was often associated with *Bid Ale. The name was also applied to the custom of social co-operation at such times as shearing, harvesting and threshing.

Cymmrodorion (lit. 'Earliest inhabitants'), **The Honourable Society of**, a cultural and patriotic society founded by Richard Morris (see under MORRIS BROTHERS) in 1751 with the aim of gathering *London Welshmen in 'unity and fraternity' and of supporting the Society of *Ancient Britons; his brother, Lewis *Morris, drew up its ambitious, comprehensive list of objects. The Society, which had corresponding members in Wales, achieved little in its corporate capacity, but it encouraged the endeavours of literary men in Wales and, during the first phase of its history (1751–87), it was regarded as the principal manifestation of Welsh culture. During the second phase (1820–43) the Society was revived largely as a result of the efforts of Yr *Hen Bersoniaid Llengar ('The Old Literary Clerics') who deemed it necessary for the supervision of the provincial eisteddfodau organized by the Cambrian Societies. But there was little co-operation; the Cymmrodorion and the Societies could not agree over matters of finance and the literary clergymen accused the London Welsh of Anglicizing the eisteddfodau and turning them into lavish musical entertainments. The Society, at this time, undertook some publishing and presented medals as prizes for poetry; it also gave prizes to boys who were pupils at grammar schools in Wales.

The third phase, from 1873 to the present, is the most important in the Society's history. Once more it was revived, this time with the objects of directing and co-ordinating the endeavours of the Welsh people in the fields of education and social reform, and of giving patronage to the arts and scholarship. The Society was responsible for forming the *National Eisteddfod Association and ensuring that the festival is held annually; it also stimulated developments in Welsh education such as the Intermediate Education Act (1889) and the *University of Wales (1893). But from its inception its most distinctive work has been the promotion and publishing of scholarly studies. It published the magazine Y *Cymmrodor* from 1877 until 1951, the *Cymmrodorion Record Series* from 1889, and the *Dictionary of Welsh Biography* (1959); its *Transactions* continue to appear annually, under the editorship of Prys *Morgan. The Society's Medal is presented to Welsh people for eminent service to Wales in the fields of literature, the arts and science.

For further details see R. T. Jenkins and Helen Ramage, *A History of the Honourable Society of Cymmrodorion and of the Gwyneddigion and Cymreigyddion Societies, 1751–1951* (1951).

Cymraeg Byw (lit. 'Living Welsh'), a form of Welsh intended to be a standard spoken model acceptable both to Welsh-speakers and to learners of the language. The attempt to agree on a literary means of representing the standard spoken language was prompted by the *BBC Wales Annual Lecture delivered by Ifor *Williams in 1960. His exhortation to teach more spoken forms to schoolchildren resulted in research being carried out in the Faculty of Education at the University College of Wales, Aberystwyth, and in the creation in the Faculty of Education at University College, Swansea, of a committee which published its recommendations in the booklet, *Cymraeg Byw* (1964). The new form was welcomed by teachers engaged in the practical work of teaching Welsh as a second language, but some argued for the uncompromising retention of the literary language alone and others for the use of more dialectal forms. On the whole, the middle way has prevailed. The oralization of written Welsh (though moderate and conservative) has done much to bring dialogue in stories, novels and plays nearer to that which is familiar throughout Wales as a common spoken form.

For further details see the three numbers of the booklet *Cymraeg Byw* (1964, 1967, 1970) and *Cymraeg Cyfoes* (1975); see also the article by G. J. Williams, 'Yr Iaith Lafar a Llenyddiaeth' in *Taliesin* (1967), and that by Ceinwen H. Thomas, 'Y Tafodieithegydd a Chymraeg Cyfoes' in *Llên Cymru* (1980).

Cymreigyddion, Y (lit. 'The Welsh scholars'), the most democratic and bohemian of the *London Welsh societies in the early nineteenth century. Founded in 1794 as a debating society, its primary aim was to foster the Welsh language and to promote good fellowship, but with John *Jones (Jac Glan-y-Gors) and Thomas *Roberts, both radical pamphleteers, among its founders, politics and social reform loomed large in the weekly debates. In its later years it became less bohemian for, although its interest in the welfare of Wales remained, the growth of *Nonconformity among the London Welsh put an end to conviviality and the society's activities ceased in 1855.

A description of the society will be found in R. T. Jenkins and Helen Ramage, *A History of the Honourable Society of Cymmrodorion and of the Gwyneddigion and Cymreigyddion Societies 1751–1951* (1951).

Cymreigyddion y Carw Coch, a literary society founded by William Williams (Carw Coch, 1808–72) at his inn, The Stag (*Y Carw Coch*), in Trecynon, Glam. Formerly a society of 'Free Enquirers', it adopted the bardic name of its founder in 1841, on the occasion of its first eisteddfod. The society flourished for many years and a selection of verse and prose by some of its members was published in the volume *Gardd Aberdâr* (1854).

Cymreigyddion y Fenni, a cultural society established in 1833 by Welsh patriots in the district of Abergavenny, Mon. At first it was similar to many other societies calling themselves *Cymreigyddion, but early in its history it began to hold eisteddfodau, of which there were ten in all, and these became popular and important events in the Welsh cultural calendar. The most prominent members were Thomas *Price (Carnhuanawc) and Lady Augusta *Hall (Gwenynen Gwent). The most significant literary works produced in the society's competitions were undoubtedly the essay by Thomas *Stephens which was later published under the title *The Literature of the Kymry* (1849), and the volume *Ancient National Airs of Gwent and Morganwg* (1844) by Maria Jane Williams (Llinos, 1795?–1873). The *Welsh Manuscripts Society was founded in 1837 by some of the society's members and to the eisteddfod of 1838 came a deputation of Bretons led by Hersart de la *Villemarqué. These events were patronized by friends of Lady Hall, attended by Celtophiles from overseas and were occasions for exuberance and patriotic fervour. The society came to an end very suddenly and without explanation on 14 January 1854.

An account of its history is given in *Afiaith yng Ngwent* (1979) by Mair Elvet Thomas.

Cymro, Y (lit. 'The Welshman'), a weekly newspaper which first appeared in 1932 under the editorship of John Eilian (John Tudor *Jones). It was published by the Woodall Minshall Thomas Company (incorporating *Hughes a'i Fab*) at the Principality Press, Wrexham, and at the Caxton Press, Oswestry. The intention of Rowland Thomas, the proprietor, was to publish a paper which would 'unite Wales and create a Welsh view and opinion on all things

pertaining to Wales and the Welsh'. Among its editors have been Einion Evans, J. R. Lloyd Hughes and Edwin Williams (co-editors, 1939–46), John Roberts *Williams (1946–62), Glyn Griffiths (1962–64), Gwyn Jones (1964–66) and D. Llion Griffiths; the last-named has been editor since 1966. The paper is published today by North Wales Newspapers Limited and continues to play an important role as a weekly newspaper of general interest, reflecting life in Wales in all its aspects.

Cymro Gwyllt, see JONES, RICHARD (1772–1833).

Cymru, the country of Wales, a comparatively modern spelling of the older term *Cymry* (now limited to mean the Welsh people), dates from the middle of the sixteenth century. Although the Welsh, for many centuries after the arrival of the Saxons, thought of themselves as the true Britons ('*Y Gwir Frythoniaid*') and of Great Britain (*Prydain Fawr*) as their birthright, the Welsh word for a Welshman, *Cymro* (pl. *Cymry*), must date from a very early period because it was also used by the people of Cumbria, who were separated from the Welsh of Wales proper by the Saxon victory at the Battle of *Chester (*c.*615). The earliest known example of the forms '*Kymro*' and '*Kymry*' (spelt thus) are apparently those found in the poem *'Armes Prydein'* (*c.*930); these names are derived from the Celtic word '*combrogos*', meaning 'compatriot'. It was *Geoffrey of Monmouth, about 1136, who gave currency to the myth that *Cymru* took its name from an eponymous founder called *Camber, and Britain from *Brutus. The Latinized form of *Cymru*, *Cambria* (adj. Cambrian), was given prestige by classical scholarship during the period of the Renaissance, although it had been used by *Gerald de Barri (Giraldus Cambrensis). The form lost ground to the word 'Welsh' during the later nineteenth century, although for a while it seemed as if the word 'Cymric', based on '*Cymreig*' ('Welsh'), would replace it in some contexts. See also BRITAIN and WALES.

Cymru (lit. 'Wales'), a monthly magazine devoted to the history, literature and culture of Wales, was popularly known as *Y Cymru Coch* ('The Red Wales') from the colour of its cover. Under the editorship of Owen M. *Edwards, the first number appeared in August 1891 and he continued to edit it until his death in 1920; thereafter (July 1920 – June 1927), it was edited by his son, Ifan ab Owen *Edwards.

The magazine's motto was '*Codi'r hen wlad yn ei hôl*' ('To raise the old country to what it once was') and it strove to achieve this aim by steeping its readers in the nation's history and culture and laying special emphasis on its heroes and writers. Part of its appeal was the engaging personality of the editor who published and answered readers' letters in a simple, direct and friendly way, and shared with them his delight in the beauty of Wales by publishing drawings, photographs and maps. Many were stimulated into writing in the hope of having their work published in *Cymru* and among the poets who made their début in its pages were Eifion Wyn (Eliseus *Williams), W. J. *Gruffydd and T. Gwynn *Jones. Other writers, such as John Puleston *Jones, R. T. *Jenkins and E. Tegla *Davies, testified to the influence which the magazine had on the minds of young Welsh people during the three decades of Owen M. Edwards's editorship. It may also be argued that *Cymru*, the editor's greatest success in periodical publishing, was his answer to the failure of the *Cymru Fydd* movement.

An index to the magazine's contents has been compiled by William Phillips (1971).

Cymru Fydd (lit. 'The Wales of the future'), a movement known in English as **Young Wales**, was founded by Welshmen in London in 1886 on the model of Young Ireland. Among its most prominent members were J. E. *Lloyd, Owen M. *Edwards and T. E. *Ellis; its secretary from 1895 was Beriah Gwynfe *Evans, its president Alfred Thomas (1840–1927, later Lord Rhondda), and its many branches were to be found in most parts of Wales. *Home Rule was central to its programme and, for a while, it was intended by Michael D. *Jones and others to oust the Liberal Party and to become an independent national party. This progress was checked in 1892 when T. E. Ellis accepted a junior whip's office in Gladstone's ministry. The movement's star fell from its ascendancy during the years from 1894 to 1896 with an attempt by David *Lloyd George, disillusioned by his failure to win the Government's support for *Disestablishment and other Welsh issues, to take over *Cymru Fydd* and to fuse it with the Liberal Federations of North and South Wales. At a tumultuous meeting in Newport, Mon., in January 1896, the motion to unite the two associations, proposed by the poet Elfed (Howell Elvet *Lewis), was heavily defeated. This catastrophe for the cause of self-government was largely the result of antipathy between delegates from the Anglicized ports of Newport, Cardiff, Barry and Swansea, and those from the rest of Wales. But it also had its roots in the divisions among Welsh Liberals who, after two decades of success within the British political system, were in fact indifferent to the national cause of Wales except in religious terms. Shortly afterwards *Cymru Fydd* collapsed. See also the next entry.

For further details see William George, *Cymru Fydd: Hanes y Mudiad Cenedlaethol Cyntaf* (1945) and K. O. Morgan, *Rebirth of a Nation: Wales 1880–1980* (1981).

Cymru Fydd (lit. 'The Wales of the future';

1967), a tragedy in three acts by Saunders *Lewis. Dewi, a minister's son turned petty criminal, escapes from prison but is persuaded by his girl-friend Bet, who is committed to Welsh causes, to surrender to the police in return for spending the night in her bed. The following morning, he taunts her for her naïve idealism and hurls himself from the top of the house to his death. Dewi has rejected both Christianity and Wales as foci for his life and, realizing that the promises of Communism are incapable of fulfilment in a nuclear age, he attempts to create meaning for his life by pitting himself against society and, ultimately and paradoxically, by suicide. He is the future of Wales, unless there is born of the union between him and Bet a child of more promising substance. The play is noteworthy for its mature and subtle characterization. An unremitting tragedy, it is grouped by the author with two other plays of the 1960s, *Excelsior* (performed in 1962, published in 1980) and *Problemau Prifysgol* (1968), both lighthearted satires on Welsh political and academic life. An English translation by Joseph *Clancy was published in 1985 under the title *Tomorrow's Wales*. See also the previous entry.

Cyn Oeri'r Gwaed (lit. 'Before the blood grows cold'; 1952), a volume of essays by Islwyn Ffowc *Elis, with which he won the *Prose Medal at the National Eisteddfod in 1951. In his introduction to the volume, T. J. *Morgan describes the themes of the essays as 'the fundamental things —those things that are true and that are also truisms; enduring moments; inborn longings; those things that are the Platonic images', and says of the author that he deals with them as experiences and concrete entities, not as 'bearded doctrines'. Apart from the sad, subtle sensitivity of the author's vision, the volume is exceptional for its rich, effortless style, later developed in the narrative of his novels.

For a discussion of the book's merits see the essay by Gwyn Thomas in *Ysgrifau Beirniadol VII* (ed. J. E. Caerwyn Williams, 1972).

Cynaethwy, see under ECHRYS YNYS (*c.*1050–1100).

Cynan, see EVANS-JONES, ALBERT (1895–1970).

Cynan Garwyn (*fl.* second half of the 6th cent.), the son of Brochwel Ysgithrog and father of *Selyf ap Cynan, who fell at the battle of *Chester (*c.*615). The *Book of Taliesin* contains an *awdl* of praise for him entitled 'Trawsganu Cynan Garwyn' which, if accepted as the authentic work of *Taliesin, is probably the earliest extant poem in the Welsh language. Its content is primitive panegyric, consisting principally of praise for the King's prowess in battle, together with a list of his gifts to the poet.

Cynan Meiriadog, one of the traditional founders of Brittany. According to the legend of

*Macsen Wledig, he was the brother of *Elen Luyddog and the son of Eudaf. He was held to be chiefly responsible for having invaded Gaul, and even Rome, on behalf of his brother-in-law, the Emperor Macsen, and as a reward for his services he was granted Armorica (*Brytaen Fechan*). This account is apparently a development of an older tradition in which Macsen led his armies from Britain, never to return. In order to preserve the purity of their language among his exiled people, Cynan had the women's tongues cut out, which is said to account for the Welsh name for Brittany, *Llydaw* ('lled-taw'). In *Geoffrey of Monmouth's version of this legend, *Conanus Meriadocus* (Geoffrey and the chronicles supply the epithet) is a nephew of Octavius (Eudaf) and therefore a cousin of Elen, Macsen's wife; *Arthur himself is of this Breton stock. Cynan, together with *Cadwaladr of Gwynedd, is cited as a hero who will one day return to restore to the Welsh the honour and majesty of governing the Isle of Britain. In the poem *'*Armes Prydein*' this Cynan is not identified but as he returns 'by sea' in the *Vita Merlini* the Breton Cynan is probably the person denoted, thus representing the unification of the Welsh and Bretons.

For further details see N. K. Chadwick, *Early Brittany* (1969), Léon Fleuriot, *Les Origines de la Bretagne* (1980) and Rachel Bromwich, *Trioedd Ynys Prydein* (1978).

Cynddelw, see ELLIS, ROBERT (1812–75).

CYNDDELW BRYDYDD MAWR (*fl.* 1155–1200), the most prolific and important court poet of his century. He was called '*mawr*' ('big') and '*cawr*' ('giant') early in his career, and that by an opponent for the bardic chair of *Madog ap Maredudd, so it was not for the quality of his poetry that he was called '*Brydydd Mawr*' ('Great Poet'). Cynddelw was probably a native of *Powys. In his earliest poems there is a glimpse of Madog ap Maredudd's court in his latter days and later poems of his, in *awdl* and *englyn* form, lament the breaking up of a united Powys at the death of Madog and the killing of Madog's son Llywelyn, to whom Cynddelw had been court poet. He continued to sing to the leaders of divided Powys—Iorwerth Goch, Owain Fychan and *Owain ap Gruffudd ap Maredudd (Owain Cyfeiliog)—to Efa, Madog's daughter, and to her husband, Cadwallawn ap Madog ab Idnerth of Maelienydd, and later to Gwenwynwyn and lesser leaders such as Rhirid Flaidd. He also sang in praise of Meifod, the principal church of Powys, addressed an *awdl* to *Tysilio, one of its patron saints, and other poems to the Privileges and the Tribes of Powys.

But it was not only to Powys that Cynddelw sang, for he was the earliest poet known to have addressed, in their turn, the leaders of the Three Provinces. He composed a series of panegyric *awdlau* and a very extensive elegy to *Owain Gwynedd ap Gruffudd (Owain Fawr) and a long poem to his son, *Hywel ab Owain Gwynedd, who is praised not for his excellence as a poet but as a warrior, prince and patron of poets. Late in his career, Cynddelw sang a fine series of *awdlau* to the Lord Rhys (*Rhys ap Gruffudd), pleading for the restoration of friendship and expressing in a couplet the traditional relationship between poet and patron: '*Ti hebof nid hebu oedd teu / mi hebot ni hebof finnau*' ('Thou without me cannot speak / I without thee have nothing to say'). Among his more personal poems there is a sequence of *awdlau* to God, a death-bed poem and a short love-song, in which (long before *Dafydd ap Gwilym) Gwen shares the bed of *Le Jaloux* (*Jealous Husband). In a different vein three elegiac *englynion* lament with tenderness and intensive grief the death in battle of Dygynnelw, his son. Falsely attributed to Cynddelw is the long sequence of *englynion* entitled '*Cylch Llywelyn*', which traces the career of *Llywelyn ap Iorwerth (Llywelyn Fawr).

The grammarians refer to the *clogyrnach* metre as 'Cynddelw's manner' and poets of the two succeeding centuries acknowledged him as being among the best of poets who wrote in praise of princes. He was strongly influenced by the *awdlau* of *Taliesin and *Aneirin but, on the other hand, the influence of the *englyn* tradition of his own province is often seen in the work of this Powys poet. An exception among the *Gogynfeirdd, he combined elements of both traditions and was the author of verse which was simple and topical as well as formal and technically complex. He can express the horrors of war in the crudest of imagery, as in '*Gwelais wedi cad colud ar drain*' ('I saw, after battle, bowels on thorns'), but he is equally impressive in presenting the traditional role of the princes, to be '*garw wrth arw*' ('rough with the rough'), '*glew wrth lew*' ('bold with the bold') and '*gŵyl wrth ŵyl*' ('gentle with the gentle'). Cynddelw was very proud of his mastery over the poetic art. At a court in south Wales, where his welcome was uncertain, the northerner cried out, '*gosteg feirdd, bardd a glywch*' ('Silence, poets, you are about to hear a poet') and in his poem to Efa he refers to the court ladies crowding at the windows as he passed by.

For further details see the articles by D. Myrddin Lloyd in *Y Llenor* (vol. XI, 1932 and vol. XIII, 1934).

'**Cynddilig**' (1935), a poem by T. Gwynn *Jones which first appeared under the pseudonym Rhufawn in the magazine *Yr Efrydydd*, was later published in the author's collection *Y *Dwymyn* (1944). The chief character in the poem is Cynddilig, one of the sons of Llywarch Hen (see under CANU LLYWARCH HEN), despised by his father on account of his irenic nature. Wandering in a landscape devastated by war, he stumbles upon two bodies, that of Gwên, the last of his brothers, and that of a Mercian soldier. He draws a dagger from Gwên's body and plunges it into his enemy's heart, but realizes how sterile is this act of revenge: after burying the corpses he erects cairns to the memory of both his brother and his foe. The poem ends with Cynddilig's death at the hands of the Mercians after he attempts to protect one of their slaves. Llywarch recognizes his son too late. The poet considered this to be his greatest poem. It reflects more than any other his view of the world in the 1930s, the years of desolation and despair, and is a fervent protest against war and the fear of war which depressed all men of culture. More generally, it is an analysis of the motives of perfect and imperfect men throughout history, and a poem of considerable force.

For a critical discussion of this poem see the article by John Rowlands in *Y Traethodydd* (vol. CXXVI, 1971).

Cynddylan (early 7th cent.), see under CANU HELEDD (*c*.9th or 10th cent.).

Cynfeirdd, Y (lit. 'The early poets'), the name formerly applied only to the poets of the sixth century who were mentioned by *Nennius, namely *Talhaearn, *Aneirin, *Taliesin, *Blwchfardd and *Cian; of these the works of Aneirin and Taliesin alone have survived. A gap was once thought to exist between these poets and the early *Gogynfeirdd of the twelfth century, but modern scholarship has done much to show that this is not so. The names of the other poets of the period are known, for example, *Afan Ferddig, *Arofan, *Dygynnelw and Meigan, but nothing remains of their work. Some anonymous poems have, however, been interpreted, such as the one in praise of *Cadwallon ap Cadfan, King of Gwynedd, killed in a battle near Hexham in 633, and an elegy on Cynddylan, King of Powys, who died about 660, two poems in the Taliesin tradition. Not dissimilar are the poem *'Edmyg Dinbych', written between 875 and 900, and *'Armes Prydein', dated about 930, which is remarkable for its expression of Welsh patriotism and its call for an alliance to drive the English from the land. More abundant, however, are the poems based on sagas and popular tales, of which the best known are those belonging to the cycles of *'Canu Llywarch Hen' and *'Canu Heledd' and those attributed to Taliesin and *Myrddin, written about the middle of the ninth century. The stanzas known as *'Englynion y Beddau', purporting to locate the graves of mythical heroes, probably belong to the ninth or the tenth century. A considerable body of nature poetry and of gnomic, vaticinatory and religious verse is contained in The *Black Book of Carmarthen and The *Red Book of Hergest, all of it anonymous and mostly dated to the period of the *Cynfeirdd.

For a selection of the poetry of the *Cynfeirdd in English translation see Joseph P. Clancy, *The Earliest Welsh Poetry* (1970). The work of these poets is discussed by

A. O. H. Jarman in an essay in the series *Writers of Wales* (1981) and in a chapter in *A Guide to Welsh Literature* (ed. A. O. H. Jarman and Gwilym Rees Hughes, 1976); see also the essay by Ifor Williams in *The Beginnings of Welsh Poetry* (ed. Rachel Bromwich, 1972), the chapter in *Y Traddodiad Barddol* (1976) by Gwyn Thomas and the volume *Astudiaethau ar yr Hengerdd: Studies in Old Welsh Poetry* (ed. Rachel Bromwich and R. Brinley Jones, 1978).

CYNFRIG AP DAFYDD GOCH (*fl.* mid-15th cent.), poet. Preserved in manuscript are two of his eulogies to Wiliam Gruffudd, 'the Old Chamberlain', of Penrhyn, Llandygái, Caerns., an elegy to Llywelyn ap Ieuan of Eiriannell, and a poem requesting a pair of peacocks. It is doubtful whether he was the Cynfrig Goch to whom a love-poem is attributed and a *cywydd* addressed to Tudur ap Iorwerth Sais is wrongly attributed to him. His few surviving poems are worthy examples of their kind: he sustains his imagery skilfully and exploits the technique of *dyfalu with mastery.

Cyngen (d. 855), the son of Cadell, ruler of *Powys. He is remembered for having erected, near the site on which the abbey of *Valle Crucis was later built, a memorial to his great-grandfather, Elise, whom he described as the deliverer of Powys from the English. The inscription on the cross, which is known as Eliseg's Pillar (the 'g' was the engraver's error), is now almost illegible, the stone having been damaged during the *Civil Wars and re-assembled in 1779, but it was recorded by Edward *Lhuyd in 1696. Cyngen ended his days in Rome, the first Welsh prince known to have made the pilgrimage after the submission of Wales to papal authority, and with him the ancient dynasty of Powys came to an end, the territory then passing to *Rhodri Mawr.

Cynghanedd (lit. 'Harmony'), an ancient and intricate system of sound-chiming within a line of verse, is found in primitive form in the earliest extant poetry of the sixth century, and in rich complexity in the poetry of the medieval period. An integral feature of *Cerdd Dafod, codified over the centuries, it is still used to striking effect in modern Welsh poetry, and not only in the traditional strict metres.

The system involves the serial repetition of consonants in precise relationship to the main accents in a line, together with the use of internal rhymes. The four main types may be described and illustrated (albeit artificially) in English as follows:

1. *Cynghanedd Groes*. In this type the line divides into two parts at the caesura, each bearing one main accent. The consonants of the first part are repeated in the second in the same order and in the same relationship to the main accent. There are three main patterns; in the first two the order of the parts may be interchanged if the syntax allows.

i) *Cynghanedd Groes Gytbwys Acennog* (lit. 'balanced, rising'):

A rose blooms / where Isobel walk'd
r z bl - / r z bl-

ii) *Cynghanedd Groes Gytbwys Ddiacen* (lit. 'balanced, falling'):

One víllăge / in a vállĕy
n v-l - / n v-l -

iii) *Cynghanedd Groes Anghytbwys Ddisgynedig* (lit. 'unbalanced, end-falling'):

To revéal / a true válŏur
t r v -l / tr v-l-

A more intricate overlapping form, *Cynghanedd Groes o Gyswllt*, is possible in which the second series of consonants begins before the caesura.

2. *Cynghanedd Draws*. This type is similar to *Cynghanedd Groes* but one consonant or more remains unmatched before the serial assonance is resumed. Again there are three main patterns.

i) *Cynghanedd Draws Gytbwys Acennog* (lit. 'balanced, rising'):

My lass léads / a blameless life
m l s l - / (bl)m l s l-

ii) *Cynghanedd Draws Gytbwys Ddiacen* (lit. 'balanced, falling'):

Lóllĭng / beneath the lílăc
l- l - (b n th) l-l-

iii) *Cynghanedd Draws Anghytbwys Ddisgynedig* (lit. 'unbalanced, end falling'):

A róse / betrays its présĕnce
r-z /(b tr z ts p)r-z -

In both *Cynghanedd Groes* and *Cynghanedd Draws* there is a fourth pattern, *Cynghanedd Anghytbwys Ddyrchafedig* (lit. 'unbalanced, end-rising'), but its use is restricted.

3. *Cynghanedd Sain*. In this type the line divides into three parts. The first two rhyme while the second and third parts carry the same scheme of serial consonantal repetition as in *Cynghanedd Groes* and *Cynghanedd Draws*. Four main patterns are used.

i) *Cynghanedd Sain Gytbwys Acennog* (lit. 'rhymed, balanced, rising'):

By the breeze / the treés / entrańc'd
tr - /(n)tr -

ii) *Cynghanedd Sain Gytbwys Ddiacen* (lit. 'rhymed, balanced, falling'):

His bow / and árrŏw / dáriňg
d -r - / d-r -

iii) *Cynghanedd Sain Anghytbwys Ddisgynedig* (lit. 'rhymed, unbalanced, end-falling'):

The weak / who seék / are súccŏur'd
s- k / (r)s-k -

iv) *Cynghanedd Sain Anghytbwys Ddyrchafedig* (lit. 'rhymed, unbalanced, end-rising'):

Embracĭng / the súrgĭng / séa
s-rj - / s -

Other patterns such as *Cynghanedd Sain Gadwynog* and *Cynghanedd Sain Drosgl* are also possible.

4. *Cynghanedd Lusg*. This type is possible only when the last syllable in a line is unaccented. The penultimate accented syllable rhymes with a word occurring earlier in the line, the first rhyme being accented or unaccented.

The flowers wélcŏme Summer
They come to náught in Autumn

The use of *Cynghanedd* has been attempted with some success in English poetry, notably by William Barnes and Gerard Manley *Hopkins. In Welsh, however, the use of compound words, and particularly of initial mutation, allows a very large number of permutations which enable the master craftsman to produce immaculate lines of great integral beauty and force by exploiting the whole range of possibilities offered by the medium.

For further details see *Cerdd Dafod* (1925) by John Morris-Jones, *Odl a Chynghanedd* (1938) by Dewi Emrys (David Emrys James), *Llawlyfr y Cynganeddion* (1939) by J. J. Evans, *Anghenion y Gynghanedd* (1973) by Alan Llwyd and *Bwyd Llwy o Badell Awen* (1977) by Geraint Bowen; for a discussion in English see the note by Dillwyn Miles in *The Royal National Eisteddfod of Wales* (1977), the articles by Alan Llwyd and Donald Evans in the special number of *Poetry Wales* (vol. 14, no. 1, 1978) which is devoted to Welsh poetry in traditional forms, the chapter by Eurys Rowlands in *A Guide to Welsh Literature* (ed. A. O. H. Jarman and Gwilym Rees Hughes, 1979), and the introduction by Rachel Bromwich to her volume, *Dafydd ap Gwilym: Poems* (1982).

Cyngogion, a series of *englynion* in which the rhyme changes from one stanza to the next, but where the final word of the previous stanza is repeated at the beginning of the following verse to link the *englynion*. The series closes with a repetition of the opening word or words of the first stanza. An early example, ascribed to Elaeth, is found in *The *Black Book of Carmarthen*.

Cynhyrfwr, Y, see REES, DAVID (1801–69).

Cynllaith, a commot of *Powys comprising the basin of the river Ceiriog. After the defeat of the rulers of Powys Fadog in 1282, it became part of the lordship of *Chirk but the line of Powys Fadog succeeded in retaining possession of half of it. This part, called Cynllaith Owain, with its centre at Sycharth, was the main inheritance of *Owain Glyndŵr, and the rest was known as Cynllaith yr Iarll ('The Earl's Cynllaith').

'Cyntefin Ceinaf Amser' (lit. 'Spring is the most beautiful time'), a series of stanzas in *The *Black Book of Carmarthen*. It begins with a description of Spring with its birdsong, green groves and agricultural activity, but ends on a sorrowful note as the poet hears the cuckoo's monotonous call. Ifor *Williams suggested that the constant repetition of '*cw*' (Old Welsh, 'where?') reminded the poet of his kinsmen who had passed away: it is as if the cuckoo is asking, 'Where are they, where have they gone?'. The poet's thoughts then turn to religion and he prays that he may find a way to the Gate of Glory and be happy before Christ's throne.

For further details see the essay by R. Geraint Gruffydd in *Ysgrifau Beirniadol IV* (ed. J. E. Caerwyn Williams, 1969).

CYNWAL, RICHARD or **RHISIART** (d. 1634), a poet who was a native of Capel Garmon, Denbs., and a contemporary of the *Phylip family of Ardudwy, to whose literary circle he belonged. His status as family poet at *Rhiwedog, near Bala, Mer., is confirmed by the bardic controversy between him and Rhisiart Phylip, who also wrote his elegy. He wrote eulogies to Siôn Llwyd of Rhiwedog and Tomos *Prys of Plas Iolyn, as well as elegies for Dafydd Llwyd of Henblas, Ang., and Lewis Gwyn of Dolau-gwyn.

CYNWAL, WILIAM (d. 1587/8), poet, was a native of Ysbyty Ifan, Denbs. Although it has been claimed that he lived at Ty'n-y-berth or Dôl Cynwal, an autographed manuscript shows that Cerrigellgwm was his home in 1567. A pupil of *Gruffudd Hiraethog, he graduated '*disgybl pencerddaidd*' ('apprentice chief poet') at the *Caerwys Eisteddfod of 1567 and was later awarded the premier degree of *Pencerdd* at a wedding-feast. He became an itinerant poet in 1564 and subsequently wandered throughout north Wales singing the praises's of patrons both lay and clerical.

His manuscripts, which contain genealogical and heraldic material together with copies of the poetic grammar and chronicles, show him to have been familiar with all the branches of traditional bardic lore. Like his teacher, he found genealogy and heraldry particularly congenial and his expertise in these fields was praised by his contemporary, *Huw Llŷn. Cynwal is chiefly remembered for his long bardic contention with Edmund *Prys, but the poems belonging to that exchange form only a small part of his output. Of his work almost three hundred *cywyddau*, about fifty-five *awdlau*, nearly five hundred *englynion* and two poems in the free metres are extant. Most, addressed to patrons, are eulogies, elegies and poems of solicitation and thanksgiving, but they also include religious, moral and love poems. A thoroughly conservative poet, he adhered to the conventions of the eulogistic tradition and his poems, on the whole, make somewhat monotonous reading: his eulogies and elegies tend to be stereotyped and often contain much versified genealogy. He is seen at his best in his religious poems which are charac-

terized by intense devotion. Although his poetry lacks the elegance and intellectual vigour of the work of the best poets of his kind, Wiliam Cynwal nevertheless has historical importance not only as the rival of Edmund Prys but as one of the most prolific practitioners of traditional bardism during the second half of the sixteenth century.

For details of the debate between Wiliam Cynwal and Edmund Prys see the works listed under the entry on Bardic Controversy; details about Wiliam Cynwal will be found in the articles by Enid Roberts in the *Transactions* of the Denbighshire Historical Society (XII, 1963), Rhiannon Williams in *Llên Cymru* (vol. VIII, 1965) and G. P. Jones and R. L. Jones in *Llên Cymru* (vol. XI, 1971).

Cyrch-a-chwta, see under TWENTY-FOUR METRES.

Cysgod y Cryman (lit. 'The shadow of the sickle'; 1953), the first novel of Islwyn Ffowc *Elis, was a milestone in the history of the Welsh *novel. By virtue of the modernity of its themes, its flowing style and its sensuous responses to the natural world, it succeeded in attracting a wide and enthusiastic readership, especially among young people, who welcomed its novelty and freshness. The novel centres on the farm of Lleifior, somewhere in Montgomeryshire, and the revolt of the young against the stability of rural tradition forms an important part of its appeal. In its sequel, *Yn ôl i Leifior* (1956), the son Harri Vaughan is leader of the co-operative community which runs the farm. At the outset he has no religious faith but one of the novel's themes is the pilgrimage of his soul towards Christian commitment. Another is concerned with the troubles of Harri's sister, Greta, whose marriage to Paul Rushmere is unhappy. Rejecting his standards, she becomes more consciously Welsh and a supporter of the Welsh Nationalist Party, but after her husband is killed in a road accident she is left with a sense of guilt and is eventually re-united with her first love, the gentle German Karl.

Cystennin, the son of Constance and Elen, *Coel's daughter. According to *Brut Dingestow*, he succeeded his father as King of Britain and with Roman help conquered *Macsen and was received by the Emperor of Rome. In the *Historia Regum Britanniae* the form of his name is Constantinus and, according to *Geoffrey of Monmouth, it was Custennin Fendigaid, a legendary figure based on Cystennin, who came from Brittany to rule Britain after the departure of the Romans and who was the father of *Uthr Bendragon and grandfather of *Arthur. Historically, these stories are seriously confused. There were indeed two Constantines, father and son. The first, usually called Constantius, was the Roman general who re-conquered Britain in AD 296 from the rule of the usurper Carausius and his successor Allectus (hence perhaps the confusion with Macsen, who was governor almost a hundred years later). Constantius afterwards became Roman Emperor. The second was Constantine, who succeeded to the imperial throne immediately on his father's death at York in 306. Welsh interest in these two arose because Helena, who married Constantius, was alleged to have found the True Cross in Jerusalem. Her son became the first Christian Emperor, ruling in both Rome and Constantinople. It was possible to give these facts a British dimension when Helena was later claimed as the daughter of the fictitious King Coel (or Cole) of Colchester.

For further details see Charles Kightly, *Folk-Heroes of Britain* (1982).

Cywydd, one of the major metrical forms of Welsh prosody. *Einion Offeiriad refers in his Grammar (c.1350–1400) to four types, namely the *Awdl-Gywydd, the *Cywydd Deuair Hirion*, the *Cywydd Deuair Fyrion* and the *Cywydd Llosgyrnog*. The term *cywydd* as used today is applied to the most popular of these, the *Cywydd Deuair Hirion*, which consists of a rhyming couplet, each line of seven syllables, written in *cynghanedd*, with the accent falling alternately on the last and penultimate syllable; *Cynghanedd Lusg* is not permitted in the second line of the couplet. It differs from the *Cywydd Deuair Fyrion*, which is seldom used, in one feature only, namely the syllabic length of the line, the latter having only four syllables in each line. Also rarely used is the *Cywydd Llosgyrnog* which consists of lines of two, three or four syllables, together with one of seven (*llosgwrn*), of which the caesura rhymes with the terminal rhyme of the previous lines: the rhyme in this last line is the same as that in the final line of the previous unit. The *cywydd* was the favourite metrical form of the *Poets of the Gentry and is still practised today, most notably in the *Chair competition of the *National Eisteddfod.

A selection of poems in this form is to be found in the anthology, *Y Flodeugerdd o Gywyddau* (ed. Donald Evans, 1981). There is an essay on the style of the *cywydd* by Eurys Rowlands in *Ysgrifau Beirniadol II* (ed. J. E. Caerwyn Williams, 1966).

'Cywydd y Farn Fawr' (lit. 'Cywydd of the great judgement'), one of Goronwy *Owen's earliest and most famous *cywyddau*, was composed at Donnington in the spring of 1752. The subject was a popular one with contemporary English poets but according to the author, 'I was sick with the ague when I began the *cywydd*, and as far as I can remember it was the thought of death which made me choose such a subject'. As Lewis *Morris remarked, the poem is too short to be considered an *epic, but its subject and style are in the epic tradition, and the poem influenced many later poets in their attempts to write an epic in Welsh.

'Cywydd y Gof' (lit. 'Cywydd to the blacksmith'), a poem by William *Rees (Gwilym Hiraethog), is not a complete *cywydd*, but a passage of thirty-two lines in that metre from the long *awdl* on 'Peace' with which he won the Chair at the Royal Madoc Eisteddfod of 1851. With a preface by the poet in English, it describes the blacksmith forging an old sword into a ploughshare. The lively simplicity of its diction, in the middle of a long prosaic poem, helps to make it the only part of the author's verse (except for his hymns) which is still widely known.

D

Daffodil (L. *Narcissus pseudonarcissus*), one of the most common flowers of spring in Wales, shares with the *leek and the *Red Dragon the status of a national symbol. There has been argument as to whether the leek (*Cenhinen*) or the daffodil (*Cenhinen Bedr*, 'Peter's leek') should be worn and displayed on St. David's Day (1 March). The earliest evidence favours the leek but during the nineteenth century the daffodil gained in popularity, particularly among women. The flower's status was enhanced by David *Lloyd George who was fond of sporting it on the patron saint's day. He also caused it to be used in preference to the leek in the ceremonies marking the investiture of the Prince of Wales at Caernarfon in 1911, and on official publications pertaining to Wales. The daffodil is also known in Welsh by a variety of other names which include *Lili Mawrth, Lili'r Grawys, Lili Bengam, Lili Felen, Blodyn mis Mawrth, Croeso'r Gwanwyn, Cennin y Gwinwydd, Twm Dili, Blodyn Gwyddau Bach, Gwayw'r Brenin, Blodau Dewi* and *Cennin Dewi*.

Dafis Castellhywel, see DAVIS, DAVID (1745–1827).

DAFYDD AB EDMWND (*fl.* 1450–97), poet, was a native of Hanmer in *Maelor Saesneg, Flints., where he owned Yr *Owredd and other lands, but he probably lived also at Pwll Gwepra in Northop, his mother's home district. He belonged to a branch of the Hanmers, a gentry family descended from Sir Thomas de Macclesfield, one of Edward I's officials who had settled in north-east Wales. Dafydd's bardic teacher was Maredudd ap Rhys and he in turn instructed *Gutun Owain and *Tudur Aled, each of whom composed an elegy in his memory; the former described him as '*pencerdd a feddai'r holl gelfyddyd*' ('a master who possessed all art') and the latter as '*ewyrth o waed*' ('my uncle by blood').

Dafydd ab Edmwnd was of major significance in the history of the bardic tradition. It was he who won the silver chair at the eisteddfod held in *Carmarthen about the middle of the fifteenth century and who was responsible for the changes then decided in the canonical *Twenty-four Metres. As replacements for the *englyn o'r hen ganiad* and the *englyn milwr* he introduced two highly complicated metres of his own devising, namely the *gorchest beirdd* and the *cadwynfyr*. He also rendered others more difficult, decreeing

that the *cywydd* metres were henceforth to contain full *cynghanedd and prescribing double fore-rhymes in the *rhupunt byr*, the *rhupunt hir* and the *tawddgyrch cadwynog*; he was also responsible for outlawing the primitive *cynghanedd bengoll* and *cynghanedd fraidd gyffwrdd*. These innovations, which reflected the genius of a consummate artist who delighted in technical intricacy, were incorporated in copies of the bardic grammars written by his disciple, Gutun Owain, who accompanied him to Carmarthen. The grammar also included a new translation of Latin material, the *dwned, which was probably the work of Gutun's teacher.

Because of the somewhat restrictive nature of his reforms, Dafydd ab Edmwnd has been criticized in modern times. John *Morris-Jones, for example, maintained that his two new metres were so complicated that 'they engendered nonsense rather than poetry'. It must be remembered, nevertheless, that the display of metrical virtuosity was an essential feature of the art of the high-ranking poets of the fifteenth century. The gathering at Carmarthen had been motivated by the desire to safeguard the privileges and status of the professional poets who believed that more difficult metres would reduce the number of bardic degrees awarded and so increase the opportunities for patronage.

Although Dafydd ab Edmwnd's innovations were not accepted by all his contemporaries—*Dafydd Nanmor and *Gwilym Tew, for example, composed *awdlau* containing the old Twenty-four Metres—they eventually won general acceptance and were regarded by Welsh scholars of the sixteenth and seventeenth centuries as marking a new era in the history of prosody. Dafydd's metrical reforms were the last of their kind: at the *Caerwys Eisteddfodau held in 1523 and 1567 there was no consideration of the metres. Furthermore, the poet's authority was upheld at the *National Eisteddfod where, from 1938 to 1964, the *awdl* or *Chair competition required a poem containing 'any number of the Twenty-four Metres of Dafydd ab Edmwnd'.

Primarily a love-poet (almost two-thirds of his *cywyddau* are addressed to women), Dafydd ab Edmwnd chose themes similar to those found in the *cywyddau* of *Dafydd ap Gwilym: the lover's frustration, his antagonism towards the *Jealous Husband, his serenading of the loved one, his delight in the woodland bower, and so on. But Dafydd ab Edmwnd's poems, much more classical in tone, read like elaborate exercises within a convention: they are highly wrought works of art devoid of the true passion which underlines the work of his greater predecessor. He differs also in his penchant for detailed physical description of women, as in the *cywyddau* to his lady's hair, poems notable for the sensuous beauty of their cumulative imagery. Some of his work displays the art of metrical ornamentation to an extent which caused Saunders ★Lewis to remark, 'The *cywydd*, not the girl, was his first love'.

A gentleman by birth and social status, Dafydd ab Edmwnd did not depend on his poems for a livelihood and there are relatively few eulogies, elegies or request-poems among them. For Rhys ap Llywelyn of Bodffordd, however, he composed *awdlau* and *cywyddau*, one of which urged him not to marry an Englishwoman. He also wrote a number of poems on religious themes and a *cywydd* satirizing ★Guto'r Glyn. Two of his elegies, namely that for ★Siôn Eos, perhaps one of the finest *cywyddau* ever written, and that for ★Dafydd ab Ieuan, are among his most accomplished poems.

Much of Dafydd ab Edmwnd's poetry has been preserved in manuscript and a large part of it was published under the editorship of Thomas Roberts in 1914. For a discussion of the poet's work see the introduction to the volume *Gramadegau'r Penceirddiaid* (1934) by G. J. Williams and E. J. Jones, the article by D. J. Bowen on Dafydd ab Edmwnd and the Carmarthen Eisteddfod in *Barn* (August, 1974) and the essay by Saunders Lewis in *Meistri a'u Crefft* (ed. Gwynn ap Gwilym, 1981).

Dafydd ab Ieuan (d. *c.*1440), a nobleman, of ★Llwydiarth, Ang., died of wounds received during a disturbance between English burgesses and local Welshmen, which is known as the Black Affray of Beaumaris. Shortly before his death his wife Angharad also died, perhaps as a result of hearing the news of her husband's misfortune. ★Dafydd ab Edmwnd, in a famous elegy for them, portrayed the dead man as a debtor summoned to God and described the double funeral at the friary of Llanfaes. The poet asks that the couple be granted heavenly bliss and is consoled by the knowledge that their son Gwilym and his wife will continue Llwydiarth's tradition of hospitality.

Dafydd ab Owain Gwynedd (d. 1203), one of the sons of ★Owain ap Gruffudd (Owain Gwynedd) by his second wife, Cristin. With his brother ★Rhodri he defeated and killed their father's chosen successor, ★Hywel ab Owain Gwynedd, at the battle of Pentraeth in 1170, an event graphically described in the third canto of T. Gwynn ★Jones's poem '*Madog*' (1918). Ruler of all ★Gwynedd by 1174, he was on friendly terms with Henry II, marrying the king's half-sister, Emma of Anjou, in a union which was the

first between members of Welsh and English royal houses. After 1175 Gwynedd was divided between the brothers although Dafydd seems to have inherited the kingship. He ruled north Wales to the east of the river Conwy from his base at ★Rhuddlan where he entertained Archbishop Baldwin and ★Gerald de Barri (Giraldus Cambrensis) in 1188. Attacked by his nephew ★Llywelyn ap Iorwerth (Llywelyn Fawr) in 1194, he spent the rest of his life at Ellesmere, Salop., and Halesowen, Worcs., where he had been granted lands. See also PERYF AP CEDIFOR WYDDEL (*fl.* 1170).

Dafydd ap Gruffudd (d. 1283), a younger brother of ★Llywelyn ap Gruffudd, was for a few months the last Prince of Wales of the line of ★Gwynedd. He proved persistently hostile to his brother, rising against him in 1255, siding with Henry III in 1263, plotting his assassination in 1274 and joining Edward I's attack upon him in 1277. Llywelyn claimed that his reluctance to pay homage to the English King, which led to his humbling in 1277, was caused by Edward's harbouring of Dafydd ap Gruffudd and Gruffudd ap Gwenwynwyn, whom he counted as his enemies. The war of 1282, in which Llywelyn was killed and his Principality destroyed, began when Dafydd, dissatisfied with the rewards bestowed upon him by Edward, attacked the castle of ★Hawarden. Llywelyn, faced with a choice between supporting his unpredictable brother or standing aside and denying the naturally warlike response of his people, elected to fight. After his death in December 1282, Dafydd assumed the title of Prince of Wales and led the Welsh resistance until his capture in June 1283. He was executed as a traitor to the English Crown at Shrewsbury in the following October.

For further details see Ralph Maud, 'David, the last prince' in the *Transactions* of the Honourable Society of Cymmrodorion (1968).

DAFYDD AP GWILYM (*fl.* 1320–70), the most distinguished of medieval Welsh poets and perhaps the greatest Welsh poet of all time. During the century of political and social turmoil which followed the loss of independence he brought innovations to the language, subject-matter and metrical techniques of poetry which gave a new dimension to the poetic art in Wales. He accomplished a bold synthesis by integrating elements from the European concepts of ★Courtly Love into the bardic tradition, thus drawing Welsh poetry, albeit briefly, into the mainstream of European literature.

The poet is said to have been born at Brogynin in the parish of ★Llanbadarn Fawr, a few miles to the north of Aberystwyth, and to have been buried within the precincts of the monastery of ★Strata Florida, both spots now marked by commemorative plaques (but see the entry for TALLEY). His family, which had its origins in

Cemaes, Pembs., had included in earlier generations several officials who had held high office
under the English Crown in south-west Wales
and it claimed descent from a legendary Gwynfardd Dyfed and his son, *Cuhelyn Fardd. It is
tempting to believe that Dafydd may thus have
inherited from his forebears a long tradition of
poetry as practised by gifted amateurs, un-
restricted by the rigid prescriptions of the
*Bardic Order regarding the style, content and
metrical arrangement of their compositions.

This combination of cultural and administrative roles is strikingly exemplified in the person
of Dafydd's uncle, Llywelyn ap Gwilym (d.
1346?), the Constable of Newcastle Emlyn, who
was named as having sworn allegiance to the
Black Prince in 1343. In two *awdlau* which
Dafydd addressed to his uncle he acknowledged
a profound intellectual debt, describing him as a
poet, a linguist and one who possessed 'all
knowledge'. The instruction received from so
eminent a teacher is not likely to have been
limited to a training in indigenous bardic techniques, however, but almost certainly included
an awareness of cultural influences from the
Anglo-Norman world. An acquaintance with
such popular foreign verse-forms as the *alba*,
pastourelle and *serenade*, and with literary works
such as the *Roman de la Rose*, all of which find
echoes in Dafydd ap Gwilym's poetry, must
have been accompanied by more than a passing
knowledge of the French language. The richness
of Dafydd's vocabulary arises from his command not only of an extensive knowledge of
Welsh poetry from previous centuries but from
his ability to draw upon words of French origin
such as were rapidly infiltrating Welsh during
the fourteenth century and which he frequently
employed in a figurative manner. He displayed
perfect artistry in playing on the rich nuances of
his vocabulary and made extensive use of
innuendo and double meaning.

The ostensible theme of Dafydd's most
celebrated verse is his pursuit of love, for he is
invariably depicted as a principal figure in his
poems. He describes himself as 'Ovid's man',
thus acknowledging his allegiance to the poet
who was for the Middle Ages the supreme
authority on all affairs of love. In the tradition of
the continental *fabliau* poems Dafydd flees from
Yr Eiddig, his sweetheart's *Jealous Husband, as
in 'Y Cwt Gwyddau', or is frustrated by a succession of obstacles, as in *'Trafferth mewn
Tafarn'. More characteristically, he presents the
love-theme in an idealized woodland setting
where he imagines himself as building a house of
leaves and branches in which to shelter with
*Morfudd, *Dyddgu, or some other girl, or
where he will retreat with her in the wilderness
in order to escape from conventional society.

But as often as not it is the forest setting itself,
with its animals and birds, which is the poet's
real subject. The thrush, the nightingale and the
skylark are for him Nature's own poets and
priests in whose activities he discerns the implicit
counterparts of his own, since poet and bird are
in unison in singing a paean of praise to God for
the marvels of His Creation. Frequently a bird,
or some other creature, is imagined as being sent
as *llatai* (love-messenger) to the poet's sweetheart and in one of his most famous poems it is
the Wind itself, characteristically personified as a
living being, who is despatched on such an
errand. Such themes were entirely new in Welsh
poetry and on occasion they inspired Dafydd to
flights of imagination which far transcended
anything to be expected in the light poetry of
love's intrigue.

Hardly less novel was the verse-form in which
he enshrined these themes, the seven-syllabled
lines in rhyming couplets of the *cywydd*,
endowed with full *cynghanedd, for whose
increasing popularity over the succeeding centuries, if not for its inception, Dafydd was in
large part responsible. He developed his chosen
metre into a highly flexible medium, varying its
pace as suited his purposes by such devices as
*sangiad and *dyfalu. At times he even contrived
to incorporate passages of racy, colloquial dialogue into his verse-pattern, as in 'Ymgom y
Wawr' or in his imaginary confrontation with Y
*Brawd Llwyd (The Grey Friar). His *cywyddau*
are normally between thirty and sixty lines in
length, rarely longer. Yet he did not entirely
neglect the older bardic metres of *toddaid* and
*englyn, and of these he displayed an equal
mastery, composing in them several eulogies
and elegies, a traditionally vituperative satire
and a small group of poignantly devotional
verses.

Of Dafydd's life virtually nothing is known
beyond the little to be deduced from his poetry.
He described himself as a member of the *clêr,
the equivalents of the *clerici vagantes* (wandering
scholars) of other countries, and he may have
qualified at some period of his life for minor
religious orders. Dafydd appears to have travelled widely throughout Wales and to have been
as familiar with places in Gwynedd such as
*Bangor cathedral and the Norman boroughs at
Caernarfon and Newborough in Anglesey as he
was with his native district and with Dyfed and
Glamorgan. There is no certain evidence that he
ever set foot outside Wales. Acquainted with
other poets among his contemporaries, such as
Madog Benfras, *Gruffudd ap Adda ap Dafydd
and *Gruffudd Gryg, he exchanged several
cywyddau with the last-named in a debate concerning the propriety of the innovations which
Dafydd had made under foreign influences in the
subject-matter of his verse. He addressed a
group of seven poems, both *awdlau* and *cywyddau*, to Ifor Hael (*Ifor ap Llywelyn) of Bassaleg.
These poems of affection for a generous patron
have the added interest of illustrating the
transference of the traditional concepts of praise-

poetry into the new verse-form of the *cywydd*.
The standard edition of the poet's work is that of Thomas Parry, *Gwaith Dafydd ap Gwilym* (1952); see also Alan Llwyd (ed.), *50 o Gywyddau Dafydd ap Gwilym* (1980). Translations of the poems will be found in Joseph P. Clancy, *Medieval Welsh Lyrics* (1965), Anthony Conran, *The Penguin Book of Welsh Verse* (1967), Rachel Bromwich, *Dafydd ap Gwilym: Poems* (1982), and Richard Loomis, *Dafydd ap Gwilym: the Poems, Translation and Commentary* (1982). For general accounts see the essay by Rachel Bromwich in the *Writers of Wales* series (1974) and Gwyn Thomas, *Y Traddodiad Barddol* (1976); the special number of *Poetry Wales*, devoted to the poet (vol. 8, no. 4, Spring, 1973), the critical studies collected in the volume *Dafydd ap Gwilym a Chanu Serch yr Oesau Canol* (ed. John Rowlands, 1975), A. O. H. Jarman and Gwilym Rees Hughes (ed.), *A Guide to Welsh Literature* (vol. 2, 1979) and the special number of *Y Traethodydd* (April, 1978).

Dafydd ap Llywelyn (d. 1246), Prince of *Gwynedd from 1240 until his death, was the younger son of *Llywelyn ap Iorwerth (Llywelyn Fawr) but his father's chosen heir. Much of Llywelyn's diplomacy was aimed at securing his undisputed succession and the consequent disinheritance of his elder brother, Gruffudd, caused friction between the sons. Within a month of his accession Dafydd was forced by Henry III to surrender all the gains granted to his father under the Treaty of Gloucester (1240). In 1244 he attempted to become a papal vassal, a move which, if it had succeeded, would have made him entirely independent of the English Crown. On at least one occasion at about this time Dafydd ap Llywelyn used the title 'Prince of Wales'. His premature death was a disaster for the plans which his father had laid for Gwynedd: had he lived (Henry III being so weak a king) he might have been accepted as Prince but, childless, he left Gwynedd to be divided between the sons of his disinherited brother Gruffudd.

For further details see Michael Richter, 'Dafydd ap Llywelyn, the first Prince of Wales' in *The Welsh History Review* (vol. 5, no. 3, 1971).

DAFYDD AP SIANCYN AP DAFYDD AB Y CRACH (*fl.* second half of the 15th cent.), poet, of Nanconwy, Caerns., was a Lancastrian supporter who lived as an outlaw in Carreg-y-gwalch, Llanrwst, during the reign of Edward IV. Eight *englynion*, some on moralistic themes, are attributed to this poet but he is chiefly remembered because *Tudur Penllyn addressed a *cywydd* to him which vividly portrays the outlaw's life. Ieuan ap Gruffudd Leiaf also praised Dafydd and his companions as '*adar o greim ar dir Grwst*' ('birds of crime in the land of Grwst'). The Dafydd ap Siancyn who wrote three poems for patrons in the Oswestry district in the sixteenth century was almost certainly not the same man.

DAFYDD ALAW (*fl.* 1550), a poet who graduated at the second *Caerwys Eisteddfod (1567), by which time he may be assumed to have been elderly. Only a little of his work has survived and most of it is in praise of patrons in Anglesey such as Rowland Melville, Constable of Beaumaris, William Bulkeley of Llangefni and the family of *Myfyrian.

Dafydd Bach ap Madog Wladaidd, see under SYPYN CYFEILIOG (*fl.* latter half of the 14th cent.).

DAFYDD BENFRAS (*fl.* 1230–60), a court poet who witnessed the triumphs of both *Llywelyn ap Iorwerth (Llywelyn Fawr) and his grandson, *Llywelyn ap Gruffudd. The main source for details about his life is an elegy by *Bleddyn Fardd in which it is said that he was the only son of Llywarch (possibly the poet *Llywarch ap Llywelyn) and that he was killed in battle beyond the borders of *Gwynedd and buried at Llangadog in Dyfed. In his poems to Llywelyn ap Iorwerth Dafydd exults in the Prince's military successes, as in the long *awdl* which praises God, describes the Harrowing of Hell and hails Llywelyn for his scourging of the English. The poet's dismay at the death of Llywelyn is poignantly expressed in three meditative *englynion* in which the earth is seen as a morass sucking the best of men into its depths. Dafydd Benfras was fortunate enough to witness the rise of Llywelyn ap Gruffudd but to be spared the anguish of that Prince's defeat in 1282. As a court poet and soldier, he lived through a crucial period of changing fortunes for the House of Gwynedd and he responded with deep feeling in fine verse to the fate of his country.

DAFYDD BENWYN (*fl.* second half of the 16th cent.), poet, one of the most prominent figures in the literary history of Glamorgan, is believed to have been a native of Llangeinor in *Tir Iarll, as were his bardic teachers Rhisiart Iorwerth (Rhisiart Fynglwyd; *fl.* 1510–70) and Lewys Morgannwg (*Llywelyn ap Rhisiart). The most prolific and widely itinerant of all the county's poets who wrote in the strict metres, he addressed poems to most of the landed families of Glamorgan and Gwent and he was typical of the class of poet who earned a living from the art. Nevertheless, although he received instruction from famous and gifted masters, and was familiar with the work of the *Penceirddiaid*, his own poems are somewhat commonplace in both subject-matter and expression. A study of Dafydd's *awdlau* and *cywyddau*, with those of Lewys Morgannwg or *Iorwerth Fynglwyd, illustrates only too well that the Glamorgan poets of the late sixteenth century no longer had the same command of the bardic craft as had their predecessors. Exceptions among his poems are a fine *cywydd* soliciting the gift of a horse from Rhisiart Tomas ap Gruffudd Goch of *Ynysarwed in the Vale of Neath and elegies for Lleision ap Rhys of Llansawel and Tomos Lewys of Baglan. Dafydd's verse is important for other reasons, however: it contains valuable information about the genealogies of some of the most eminent families in south-east Wales and it provides the Welsh forms of many place-names not found in the official Latin records relating to the period.

A small selection of the poet's work was published by J. Kyrle Fletcher under the title *The Gwentian Poems of Dafydd Benwyn* (1909); see also many references to Dafydd Benwyn in G. J. Williams, *Traddodiad Llenyddol Morgannwg* (1948) and Ceri W. Lewis, 'The Literary History of Glamorgan from 1550 to 1770' in *Glamorgan County History* (vol. IV, ed. Glanmor Williams, 1974).

DAFYDD DDU ATHRO O HIRADDUG

(*fl.* second half of the 14th cent.), poet and scholar, perhaps a *Dominican. His epithet indicates that his home was in the district of Moel Hiraddug in Tegeingl, Flints. According to John *Davies of Mallwyd, he was archdeacon of Diserth and was responsible for the translation from Latin of *Gwasanaeth Meir. Thomas *Wiliems of Trefriw ascribed to him the compilation of a version of the Bardic Grammar. Both attributions are doubtful and rest almost entirely on the authority of the two scholars named. In the section of the Bardic Grammar dealing with the *Twenty-four Metres, the version in *The *Red Book of Hergest attributes the invention of three new metres to *Einion Offeiriad, with whom the compilation of the Grammar is usually associated. The Peniarth 20 version, however, states that these same three metres were invented by Dafydd Ddu. One of these new metres, the *Hir-a-Thoddaid*, is employed in *Gwasanaeth Meir* to translate the hymn 'Ave Maris Stella'. The authorship of these two works therefore remains an undecided question; a possible solution of the second problem is that Dafydd Ddu may have revised a text of the Grammar which had previously been redacted by Einion Offeiriad. The Peniarth 20 version was the one followed by many of the new adapters of the Grammar in the sixteenth century and in this fact there lies perhaps an explanation of why Dafydd Ddu, and not Einion Offeiriad, was the scholar regarded by the poets of later generations as the prime authority on the bardic craft.

A religious *awdl* is attributed to Dafydd Ddu in *The Myvyrian Archaiology* (1801) and there has come down in his name a *cywydd* embodying the Ten Commandments. The choice of the *cywydd* metre for a *paternoster* which is also ascribed to him may suggest that Dafydd Ddu intended his doctrinal adaptations for an unlearned audience. See also EDERN DAFOD AUR.

For further details see G. J. Williams (with E. J. Jones), *Gramadegau'r Penceirddiaid* (1934), G. J. Williams, *Traddodiad Llenyddol Morgannwg* (1948), Brynley F. Roberts (ed.), *Gwasanaeth Meir* (1961) and Glanmor Williams, *The Welsh Church from Conquest to Reformation* (1962).

Dafydd Ddu Eryri, see THOMAS, DAVID (1759–1822).

Dafydd Ddu Feddyg, see SAMWELL, DAVID (1751–98).

Dafydd Gam (d. 1415), soldier, called thus because he squinted or had only one eye, was born of the stock of Einion Sais at Pen-pont, near Brecon. His entry into the King's service was facilitated by the royal possession of the Buckingham lordship of Brecknock and his reputation as a warrior in the King's cause was one of the reasons for *Owain Glyndŵr's failure to win the allegiance of south-east Wales. The latter's defeat at Pwll Melyn, near Usk, in 1405, was decisive in this respect. In 1410, or later, Dafydd fell into Owain's hands and was ransomed by the Seneschal of Brecon. At the battle of Agincourt (1415) he was one of the few killed on the English side but not, so popular legend has it, before he had saved the King's life and been knighted on the field. In Shakespeare's *Henry V* (c.1600) he is named among the fallen but as 'esquire' only. Dafydd's male descendants took the name Games, still to be found in the Usk Valley, and through his daughter Gwladus and her marriage to Sir *Wiliam ap Tomas of Raglan he was the ancestor of all the Herberts, including the Earls of Pembroke.

DAFYDD GORLECH (1410?–90?), a poet of whom nothing is known. His name suggests some connection with the river Gorlech and perhaps with the village of Abergorlech in the parish of Llansawel, Carms. About a dozen vaticinatory *cywyddau* bearing his name have been preserved in manuscript, half of which have also been attributed to *Dafydd Llwyd of Mathafarn, and to other poets. One of the reasons for this dubiety may be the fact that the poet's name sometimes appears as Dafydd Llwyd Gorlech. He made copious use of the ancient Welsh prophecies and his poems contain references to such poets as *Taliesin, *Myrddin and Y *Bardd Glas.

Dafydd Ionawr, see RICHARDS, DAVID (1751–1827).

DAFYDD LLWYD AP LLYWELYN AP GRUFFUDD (c.1395–c.1486), gentleman and poet, of Mathafarn in the parish of Llanwrin, Mont., wrote eulogies and elegies and a small number of love-poems. His poem to Tydecho, patron saint of some of the *Mawddwy churches, is noteworthy as the only surviving source of the traditions concerning the saint. Dafydd Llwyd engaged in a jesting disputation with *Llywelyn ap Gutun, in which each accused the other of reducing the noble art of itinerant minstrelsy to shameless beggary. He is best known, however, as an authority on the old prophetic literature and as the author of *vati-

cinatory poems, of which forty are attributed to him, reflecting anti-English sentiments and foretelling the coming of the saviour of the Welsh people. As in all such prognostications these poems refer to prominent figures of the age under the names of animals and birds, with the result that they are often extremely abstruse. Although valuable for the light they throw on historical events of the day, they lack inspiration. During the Wars of the Roses Dafydd Llwyd favoured the Lancastrian side and there is a tradition that Henry *Tudor spent a night at Mathafarn on his way to the battle of *Bosworth in 1485.

For further details see W. Leslie Richards (ed.), *Gwaith Dafydd Llwyd o Fathafarn* (1964) and Enid P. Roberts, *Dafydd Llwyd o Fathafarn* (1981).

DAFYDD   LLWYD   MATHEW   or **MATHAU** (*fl.* 1601–29), poet and itinerant minstrel, was a native of Cilpyll, Llangeitho, Cards. He sang the praises of patrons in north Pembrokeshire, in particular in an *awdl* for the wife of William *Owen of Henllys, an elegy for the wife of George *Owen, another for William Warren of Tre-wern, a *cywydd* for William Bowen of Pontgynon and *englynion* for George William Griffith of Penybenglog and Thomas ap Risiart of Marloes. Eulogies to families in north Wales and Glamorgan are also attributed to him and it is believed that Llanstephan Manuscript 38 preserves some of the poet's compositions written in his own hand.

Dafydd Morganwg, see JONES, DAVID WATKIN (1832–1905).

DAFYDD NANCONWY (*fl.* 1637), poet, was the son of Tomas Dafydd of Pwllycrochan, Llechwedd Isa, in the Conwy Valley, Denbs. He and Tomos *Prys of Plas Iolyn addressed eulogies to the same families and they shared in their light verses the habit of using English phrases. Dafydd's elegy for William Myddelton (d. 1637) of Gwaenynog is in the *cywydd* tradition.

DAFYDD NANMOR (*fl.* 1450–80), one of the greatest of the *Poets of the Gentry, was a native of Nanmor, Caerns. He was exiled from Gwynedd about 1453 on account of his poems to a married woman whom he had addressed as Gwen o'r Ddôl, and he fled to south Wales, there to spend the rest of his life. The poems which he wrote for the family of Rhys ap Maredudd of Tywyn, Cards., are among his best but he also eulogized Edmund and Jasper *Tudor in both *awdl* and *cywydd*, recalling their Welsh ancestry. In these rhetorical poems there is a *vaticinatory note of the kind which helped to prepare the way for the battle of *Bosworth (1485). One of his best known *awdlau* is that composed for Sir Dafydd ap Tomas, priest of Faenor and Constable of Cardigan. He also wrote a number of religious poems. An educated man who prob-

ably knew Latin, he delighted in bardic feats, composing an exemplary *awdl* and versifying many contemporary ideas about astronomy, weather-signs and herbal remedies. He was an experienced copyist and it is likely that he wrote Peniarth Manuscript 52 which contains poems by *Dafydd ap Gwilym and himself.

He was above all a philosophical poet who, in contrast with Dafydd ap Gwilym, preferred the cultured, luxurious life of noblemen's courts to the lot of a wandering poet. Nature was not the principal source of his inspiration: his images were mostly drawn from the human world, as in the famous *cywydd* to a girl's hair, '*I wallt Llio*'. A good example of his detailed description of indoor scenes is found in his *cywydd* to *Strata Florida. For him the last and greatest honour which could be accorded any nobleman was that he should be buried within the walls of the abbey. For this reason Saunders *Lewis called Dafydd Nanmor 'the poet of *perchentyaeth*', a household poet (*Bardd Teulu*) in a deeper sense than had ever before been given to that term. There is a sacramental quality to the civilized life which he eulogizes: a feast becomes a communion, the privilege of ownership a priesthood and the householder a guardian of civilized life. His philosophy is also seen in his Tywyn poems where he contemplates the history of the nobility and its function in society, praising its conservatism as the essence of civilization and finding its symbol in the oak-tree.

In the work of Dafydd Nanmor there is a consistency of thought, a classical conciseness and an aura of tranquillity which place him among the most distinguished poets of his time, but he was also able to indulge in the hyperbole of the praise-poet when the occasion demanded. His style displays the mastery which the greatest *cywyddwyr* had gained over their craft by the second half of the fifteenth century and some of his opening couplets are especially striking. Although his *awdlau* follow the set pattern of the period, he contributed to the development of the form by introducing into it the simplicity and immediacy which characterize his *cywyddau*, succeeding in rising above literary convention in verse of a powerful dignity.

For further details see *The Poetical Works of Dafydd Nanmor* (ed. Thomas Roberts and Ifor Williams, 1923), the essay on the poet by Saunders Lewis in *Meistri'r Canrifoedd* (ed. R. Geraint Gruffydd, 1973) and the chapter by D. Myrddin Lloyd in *A Guide to Welsh Literature* (ed. A. O. H. Jarman and Gwilym Rees Hughes, 1979); see also the article by Gilbert E. Ruddock in *Llên Cymru* (vol. XIII, nos. 3 and 4, 1980–81).

DAFYDD Y COED (*fl.* late 14th cent.), one of the last of the *Poets of the Gentry, was a native of south Wales, perhaps of Llandovery. He sang the praises of Hopcyn ap Tomas of Kilvey, near Swansea, and of members of the families of Uwch-Aeron and *Gogerddan in Ceredigion. His lampoon about the town of Rhayader (W.

Rhaeadr, 'a water-fall') contains onomatopoeia imitating the noise of falling waters. In his poem to Hopcyn ap Tomas there is a glimpse of his library which included, among other works, copies of the *Lucidarius*, the Grail and the Annals.

Dafydd y Garreg Wen, see OWEN, DAFYDD (1711/2–41).

DAFYDD, EDWARD (*c*.1600–1678?), poet. A native of Margam, he was the most famous of all Glamorgan poets in the seventeenth century and the last important professional poet in the province. He wrote verse for most of the prominent landed gentry, including the Mansels whose home was situated in his parish, but he also travelled beyond the boundaries of Glamorgan. Two persons called Edward David (*sic*) were buried at Margam in 1678 and it is likely that one of them was the poet.

He wrote eulogies and elegies in the traditional manner, his work displaying at its best a quality reminiscent of some of his immediate predecessors such as *Dafydd Benwyn and *Llywelyn Siôn. The latter may have been his bardic tutor. Unfortunately, Edward Dafydd's work lacks the vigour and conciseness of the poets of the fifteenth century and gone is the traditional mastery of the literary language.

According to Iolo Morganwg (Edward *Williams), it was Edward Dafydd who systematized *Dosbarth Morgannwg* ('The Glamorgan Classification' of the traditional metres, also known as the *Twenty-four Metres) as they occur in *Cyfrinach Beirdd Ynys Prydain* (1829). Iolo also maintained, without foundation, that Edward Dafydd was among the *Penceirddiaid* who confirmed the metrical system at the *Gorsedd* reputed to have been held at Beaupré, Glam., in 1681, and he attributed to this poet some of the best of his own compositions.

For further details see G. J. Williams, *Traddodiad Llenyddol Morgannwg* (1948) and Ceri W. Lewis, 'The Literary History of Glamorgan from 1550 to 1770' in *Glamorgan County History* (vol. IV, ed. Glanmor Williams, 1974).

DAFYDD, EDWARD (Edward Bach; *fl.* early 17th cent.), a poet who was a native of Trefethin (Trefddyn), Mon., according to Gwilym *Puw. He is probably the 'Edward David, yeoman', who was presented for recusancy in July 1607. There is a Catholic flavour to several of his poems, most of which are in the free metres. Among his poems in strict metre, of which he was not a master, the most important is '*Awdl Wrthryfelgar*', probably written either on the eve of the Essex rebellion in 1601 or of the subsequent disturbances of 1603 and 1605, which calls on Welsh Catholics to take up arms against Protestants.

DAFYDD, JOHN (1727–83) and **MORGAN** (d. 1762), hymn-writers and brothers, were

shoemakers by trade and lived at Bedw-gleision, Caeo, Carms. The former was a Methodist exhorter for a while, but it is known that both brothers were members of Bethel Baptist Church, Caeo, and attended services at Bwlch-y-rhiw. John later lived at Tirybedw in the parish of Cil-y-cwm and Morgan at Aberbranddu Mill. William *Williams (Pantycelyn) included five of John's hymns and nine of Morgan's in his volume *Aleluia* (1747). John's hymn '*Newyddion braf a ddaeth i'n bro*' and Morgan's '*Yr Iesu'n ddi-lai*' are still sung by Welsh congregations.

DAFYDD, MARGED (**Meg Elis**; 1950–   ), writer, was born at Aberystwyth, Cards., the daughter of T. I. *Ellis, and educated at the University College of North Wales, Bangor. Appointed assistant editor of *Y Faner* (*Baner ac Amserau Cymru*) in 1982, she has published a volume of poetry, *Cysylltiadau* (1973), a novel, *I'r Gad* (1975), and a collection of short stories, *Carchar* (1978), the last two of which draw on her experiences as a militant member of *Cymdeithas yr Iaith Gymraeg*. She won the *Prose Medal at the National Eisteddfod in 1985.

DAFYDD, MEURIG (1510?–95), a professional poet of gentle lineage, born in Llanishen, Cardiff, was an important figure in the literary history of Glamorgan during the second half of the sixteenth century. Although there exists no documentary evidence concerning his family history, it is assumed that he was the gentleman who married Joan Mathau, the granddaughter of Sir Cristor Mathau (Mathew) of Llandaf. He went as an itinerant poet to the homes of most of the landed families of Gwent and Glamorgan, especially the Lewises of Rhiw'r-perrai (Ruperra) and Y *Fan, near Caerphilly. A large part of his poetry, surviving probably in the poet's own hand, belongs to the period between 1580 and 1593. With some exceptions, such as passages in his *cywydd* to Aberafan, his verse is inferior in its craft and inspiration to the work of the great *Penceirddiaid* of the fifteenth century, and for this reason it was seldom copied. Like that of *Dafydd Benwyn, however, his work is of interest to the historian because it preserves details about some of the county's place-names and its old gentry families.

For further details see G. J. Williams, *Traddodiad Llenyddol Morgannwg* (1948) and Ceri W. Lewis, 'The Literary History of Glamorgan from 1550 to 1770' in *Glamorgan County History* (vol. IV, ed. Glanmor Williams, 1974).

DAFYDD, MORGAN (d. 1762), see under DAFYDD, JOHN (1727–83).

DAFYDD, THOMAS (*fl.* 1765–92), hymn-writer and elegist, of Llanegwad, Carms., published five collections of hymns between 1765 and 1766 under the title *Taith y Pererin*, and six others between 1777 and 1784. Although these booklets have become collectors' items, because of their rarity, few of his hymns are still sung.

Dai, see under ANGRY SUMMER (1943), GWALIA DESERTA (1938) and IN PARENTHESIS (1937).

Dai Bread, the baker in Dylan *Thomas's *Under Milk Wood* (1954), has two wives, one large and homely, the other a dark and gaudy fortune-teller, and he is loved by both.

Dai Lossin, a character created by the cartoonist D. Gwilym John for *The South Wales Football Echo* in 1919. As captain of the *Cwmsgwt Football Club, he led a team which included Ianto Full Pelt, Dai Small Coal and Billy Bara Chaws. Dai, who became something of a folk-hero, was famous for the rich dialect in which he commented on the sporting scene in Wales during the years between the World Wars. By today he is remembered only when the name Dai Lossin is used to refer to a droll person or a likeable rogue.

Dai'r Cantwr, see DAVIES, DAVID (1812–74).

Dail Pren (1956), see under WILLIAMS, WALDO (1904–70).

Dalar Hir, Y (1648), a skirmish between the forces of the Royalist commander Sir John Owen of Clenennau and Colonel George Twisleton, Governor of Denbigh, which took place on the flatlands of the Menai Straits between Llandygái and Aber, Caerns. It occurred early in the second *Civil War when Owen was laying siege to *Caernarfon castle (then held for Parliament) in the hope of regaining it for the Crown as a preliminary to a Royalist uprising in north Wales. He was forced to retreat towards Bangor under pressure from the forces of Major-General Mytton who were defending the castle. Wounded and captured during the engagement, Owen was imprisoned at Denbigh and later taken to London to face charges of treason.

For further details see A. H. Dodd, 'Caernarvonshire in the Civil War' in the *Transactions* of the Caernarvonshire Historical Society (1953), and N. Tucker, *North Wales in the Civil War* (1958).

Dame Venedotia, see under HUGHES, HUGH (1790–1863).

Dame Wales, a personification or caricature of the Welsh people, made her first appearance in cartoons published in such periodicals as *Y *Punch Cymraeg* in the mid-nineteenth century, and later in the *Western Mail*. Depicted as a homely old woman dressed in an apron, cloak and tall black hat, she once formed part of what might be called a heraldry of culture but she is now only rarely seen. See also WELSH COSTUME.

Daniel, see JONES, FRANK PRICE (1920–75).

DANIEL AP LLOSGWRN MEW (*fl.* 1170–1200), a court poet of whose work there have survived an elegiac *awdl* to *Owain Gwynedd and, according to *The *Red Book of Hergest* (but not the *Hendregadredd MS), a series of elegiac *englynion* to his grandson, Gruffudd ap Cynan ab Owain Gwynedd. The *awdl* conveys not only the poet's loss of his patron but also the crisis and uncertainty for his country after the death of a strong ruler. Like *Gruffudd ab yr Ynad Coch more than a century later, Daniel is stricken with a grief which is reflected in the natural world and, in a notable example of Titanism, he challenges the divine will which has caused the disaster into which he and his country are plunged.

DANIEL, GLYN EDMUND (Dilwyn Rees; 1914–), archaeologist and writer. Born at Lampeter Velfrey, Pembs., he was brought up at Llantwit Major, Glam., where his father was a schoolmaster, and educated at University College, Cardiff, and St. John's College, Cambridge. He had a distinguished academic career and enjoys an international reputation as an archaeologist. During the 1950s he was a well-known popularizer of his subject on radio and television, particularly as a participant in the programme, *Animal, Vegetable, Mineral?*. His numerous works of pre-history include *The Megalith Builders of Western Europe* (1958), *The Hungry Archaeologist in France* (1963) and *The First Civilisations* (1968); he also edited, with Idris Ll. *Foster, Prehistoric and Early Wales* (1965). Under his pseudonym he has published two detective novels, namely *The Cambridge Murders* (1945) and *Welcome Death* (1954). In the year of his retirement from the Disney Chair of Archaeology at Cambridge he published *A Short History of Archaeology* (1981), the hundredth volume in the series *Ancient People and Places*, of which he is general editor. A collection of essays in his honour, *Antiquity and Man* (ed. John D. Evans, Barry Cunliffe and Colin Renfrew) appeared in the same year.

Daniel Ddu o Geredigion (Daniel Evans; 1792–1846), see under BLODAU DYFED (1824).

Daniel y Pant, see THOMAS, DANIEL (1851–1930).

Darian, Y, see TARIAN Y GWEITHIWR.

Daugleddau, a cantref of *Dyfed lying between the eastern and the western Cleddau rivers, was extensively colonized by Flemings during the early twelfth century. See also ANGLIA TRANSWALLINA.

David, saint, see DEWI SANT (6th cent.).

DAVIES, ANEIRIN TALFAN (Aneirin ap Talfan; 1909–80), critic, poet and broadcaster. Born at Felindre, Henllan, Carms., the son of a Calvinistic Methodist minister, he received his secondary education at Gowerton Grammar School, the family having moved to Gorseinon, Glam., in 1911. He left school at the age of fourteen and was apprenticed to a pharmacist. While working in London, he became interested in literature and theology under the influence of the Welsh Calvinistic Methodist chapel at Charing Cross, and founded the magazine *Heddiw*. He returned to Swansea in 1938 but, three years later, his chemist's shop was destroyed by German bombs, after which he went back to London and started a new career as a broadcaster. At the end of the war he joined the staff of the BBC in Cardiff, becoming Head of Programmes with BBC Wales in 1966. By then he was a member of the Church in Wales and, by virtue of his writing, lay-preaching and committee work, had become one of its leading laymen.

He was the author of a substantial body of literary criticism which reflected a broad range of interests, particularly in English literature and in theology. His books include *Eliot, Pwshcin, Poe* (1942), a study of James Joyce, *Yr Alltud* (1944), *Y Tir Diffaith* (1946), *Sylwadau* (1957), a study of the sermon in the Christian tradition, *Pregethau a Phregethu'r Eglwys* (1957), *Astudio Byd* (1967), *Yr Etifeddiaeth Dda* (1967) and *Gyda Gwawr y Bore* (1970). He also edited anthologies of verse such as *Munudau Gyda'r Beirdd* (1954) and *Englynion a Chywyddau* (1958), and a volume of literary criticism, *Gwŷr Llên* (1948). His critical works in English include *Dylan: Druid of the Broken Body* (1964) and *David Jones: Letters to a Friend* (1979). He also wrote lyrics and libretti in collaboration with the composer Arwel Hughes.

With his brother, Alun Talfan Davies, he founded *Llyfrau'r Dryw* (the publishing house now known as Christopher Davies) and contributed notable volumes to that company's series *Cyfres Crwydro Cymru* on Carmarthenshire and the Vale of Glamorgan. He was also a poet in the free metres, publishing two volumes of verse, *Y Ddau Lais* (with W. H. Reese, 1937) and *Diannerch Erchwyn* (1975). A cultured, sensitive and emotional man whose mind turned often to numinous and philosophic issues, he made many contributions to the life of Wales, not the least of which was his generous patronage of writers in both Welsh and English during his time with the BBC.

DAVIES, BEN (1864–1937), poet, born at Cwmllynfell, Carms., was an Independent minister in Ystalyfera, Glam., from 1891 to 1926. He composed long *pryddestau*, religious and philosophical in tone, in the manner of the *Bardd Newydd*, and he won the *Chair at the National Eisteddfod in 1896.

DAVIES, BRYAN MARTIN (1933–   ), poet. Born at Brynaman, Carms., and educated at the University College of Wales, Aberystwyth, he was a teacher of Welsh at Yale Sixth Form College, Clwyd, until his retirement in 1985. He has published four volumes of poetry, namely *Darluniau ar Gynfas* (1970), *Y Golau Caeth* (1972), *Deuoliaethau* (1976) and *Lleoedd* (1984), and he won the *Crown at the National Eisteddfod in 1970 and 1971. Among the works he has translated into Welsh are Dylan *Thomas's A Child's Christmas in Wales, under the title *Nadolig Plentyn yng Nghymru* (1978), and the Prologue to Chaucer's *The Canterbury Tales* (1983). He is also the author of a critical study of the work of Watcyn Wyn (Watkin Hezekiah *Williams), *Rwy'n gweld o bell* (1980).

Davies, Clara Novello (1861–1943), choirmistress. Born in Cardiff, she was named after the celebrated Italian singer, Clara Anastasia Novello (1818–1908). With her choir, she visited the World Fair in Chicago and toured the USA in 1893, and performed at the Paris Exhibition of 1900. She enjoyed immense popularity in Wales, especially during the First World War when her concerts raised funds for the armed forces. She had one son, Ivor Novello (David Ivor *Davies), and wrote an autobiography entitled *The Life I Have Loved* (1940).

Davies, Dan Isaac (1839–87), teacher and patriot. Born at Llandovery, Carms., he became headmaster of *Ysgol y Comin* (Mill Street School) at Aberdare, Glam., in 1858. There, against the general current of the day, he pioneered the use of Welsh in the class-room by encouraging his staff to speak it with pupils. After joining the schools inspectorate in 1868, he campaigned for the wider teaching of Welsh and won a measure of success when his recommendations to the Royal Commission on Elementary Education in Wales were largely adopted in 1886. He was also one of the founders of *Cymdeithas yr Iaith Gymraeg* (The Society for the Utilization of the Welsh Language) and the author of an influential series of articles which he published in 1885 under the title *Tair Miliwn o Gymry Dwyieithog*.

For further details see the article by Ifano Jones, 'Dan Isaac Davies and the Bilingual Movement' in *Welsh Political and Educational Leaders in the Victorian Era* (ed. J. Vyrnwy Morgan, 1908) and J. Elwyn Hughes, *Arloeswr Dwyieithedd* (1984).

DAVIES, DANIEL JOHN (1885–1969), poet. Born near Crymych, Pembs., and educated at University College, Cardiff, and the Memorial College, Brecon, he was the minister of Capel Als, a Congregational chapel in Llanelli, from 1916 to 1958. The author of several *awdlau*, he won the *Chair at the National Eisteddfod in 1932 and published one volume of verse, which was entitled *Cywyddau a Chaniadau Eraill* (1968).

Davies, David (Dai'r Cantwr; 1812–74), rioter and vagrant, born near Llancarfan, Glam., worked as a labourer but could also preach and sing. With John *Jones (Shoni Sgubor-fawr), he took a prominent part in the demolition of toll-gates during the *Rebecca Riots, for which he was sentenced in 1843 to twenty years' transportation to Van Diemen's Land. His threnody for the scenes of his youth, 'Cân Hiraethlon', shows that he was acquainted with the strict metres. Pardoned in 1854, he returned to Wales, living as a tramp, and was burned to death when the barn in which he was sleeping was set on fire by his pipe.

DAVIES, DAVID (Dewi Emlyn; 1817–88), writer, was born at Cenarth, Carms., but emigrated in 1852 to the USA, where he enjoyed a reputation as a poet. He is remembered as the author of *Llythyrau Anna Beynon* (1870), a volume of letters purportedly written by a young Welsh girl to her sister in America between 1719 and 1727, describing country life with its traditional beliefs and theological wranglings. First published in *Yr Haul* as authentic, the letters were not called into doubt until they appeared in book form and subsequent arguments about their historical accuracy have tended to ignore their considerable literary merit.

Davies, David (Top Sawyer; 1818–90), industrialist, was born at Llandinam, Mont. After leaving school at the age of eleven in order to help his father in the timber trade, he began his career as a contractor in 1846 when he was commissioned to build a bridge over the river Severn in his native village, and went on to undertake the construction of railways. In 1864 he sank the Parc and Maendy pits in the *Rhondda Valley and to these collieries, known as the Ocean Merthyr pits, he added others, forming the Ocean Coal Company in 1887. To handle the output of his mines he built a new dock at Barry, thus contributing to the rapid development of that town. He became a man of great wealth and entered public life as the Liberal Member of Parliament for Cardigan, but he never lost the homelier virtues of his youth, including a robust sense of humour. During his later years he was fond of recalling his prowess at saw-mills where he had worked as 'top sawyer', that is to say, the man who worked in the upper position during the sawing process and thus avoided the saw-dust. Generous towards religious and educational causes, he was a devout Calvinistic Methodist and strict in his observance of Sunday and in his abstinence from strong drink. It was his son, Lord Davies, who established the magazine *The *Welsh Outlook* in 1914, continuing to pay for it until 1927. David Davies's granddaughters, Gwendoline and Margaret Davies, lived at Gregynog, near Newtown, Mont., where they were patrons of the *Gregynog Press.

Biographies of David Davies were written by Goronwy Jones (1913) and by Ivor Thomas, *Top Sawyer* (1938).

DAVIES, DAVID (1849–1926), author. Born at Rhyd-ar-gaeau, Carms., he moved with his parents at the age of nine to live at Treforest, near Pontypridd, Glam., where he later became a pupil-teacher at a National School. After being dismissed from his post for refusing to attend Anglican services, he became a bitter opponent of the Established Church and joined the *Baptists. A friend of the English preacher C. H. Spurgeon, he was a minister at various places in England before returning to Wales in 1908 as pastor at Penarth, Glam. He published three books with the intention of 'presenting a picture of peasant life as it has existed for generations in the heart of Wales', namely *Echoes from the Welsh Hills* (1883), *John Vaughan and his Friends* (1897) and *Reminiscences of my Country and People* (1925), as well as a study of Vavasor *Powell (1896).

DAVIES, DAVID IVOR (Ivor Novello; 1893–1951), composer, actor and playwright. He was born in Cardiff, the son of the choir-mistress Clara Novello *Davies, and educated at Magdalen College School, Oxford. After publishing his first song at the age of fifteen, he won fame during the First World War as the composer of the tune 'Keep the Home Fires Burning', the words of which were written by Lena G. Ford. For the rest of his life he enjoyed almost continuous success as one of the most versatile men of the theatre in his day. His non-musical plays include *The Truth Game* (1928), *A Symphony in Two Flats* (1929), *Party* (1932) and *Proscenium* (1933). But his greatest triumphs were the musical comedies *Glamorous Night* (1935), *Careless Rapture* (1936), *The Dancing Years* (1939), *Perchance to Dream* (1945) and *King's Rhapsody* (1949), for all of which the lyrics were written by Christopher Hassall. Although he acted in his musical plays, he could not sing and never tried to on the stage. He was idolized by many women for his good looks and impeccable manners.

Among the accounts of Ivor Novello's life and work the following are especially recommended: W. Macqueen Pope, *Ivor, the story of an achievement* (1954), Richard Rose, *Perchance to Dream: the world of Ivor Novello* (1974), Peter Noble, *Ivor Novello: man of the theatre* (1975) and Sandy Wilson, *Ivor* (1975). The novel *The Painted King* (1954) by Rhys Davies is based on Ivor Novello's career.

DAVIES, DAVID JAMES (1893–1956), political thinker. Born near Carmel, Carms., he joined his father in the local colliery at the age of twelve but in 1912 emigrated to the USA, where he worked as a prospector, professional boxer and ship's engineer. Discharged from the American Navy in 1919, he returned to Wales and became active with the Labour Party in the Ammanford area. During a visit to Denmark, however, he was deeply influenced by the co-operative principles of the Folk High School Movement and he joined *Plaid Cymru soon after its formation in 1925. Having taken a doc-tor's degree in agricultural economics at the University College of Wales, Aberystwyth, he settled with his wife Noëlle at Pantybeiliau near Gilwern, Brecs., where in 1934/35 they ran a school for the unemployed. He wrote numerous pamphlets on economic and philosophical topics, some of which formed the basis for the early policies of *Plaid Cymru*, and he also waged a relentless press campaign for the official recog-nition of Monmouthshire as a county of Wales. His most important book was *Economic History of South Wales* (1933). A selection of his writings was edited by Ceinwen Thomas in the volume *Towards Welsh Freedom* (1958).

For further details see the chapter on D. J. Davies by Ceinwen Thomas in *Adnabod Deg* (ed. Derec Llwyd Morgan, 1977). There is an account of D. J. Davies's contribution to the early philosophy of *Plaid Cymru* in D. Hywel Davies, *The Welsh Nationalist Party 1925–1945* (1983).

DAVIES, DUDLEY GARNET (1891–1981), poet. Born in Swansea and educated at Lland-overy College and Queen's College, Oxford, he was found unfit for military service and in 1916 joined the Indian Civil Service, becoming a Sessions Judge in Bengal. A recurrence of ill health compelled his resignation in 1928 and, after a year at Wells Theological College, ordination and two curacies, he became rector of parishes in Hertfordshire and Oxfordshire. Known best for his poem 'Carmarthenshire', written in India in 1920 and included in the anthology *They Look at Wales* (1941), he published two volumes of verse, *Poems, Calcutta* (1925) and *Boatrace* (1971).

DAVIES, EBENEZER THOMAS (1903–   ), historian. Born at Pontycymmer, Glam., and educated at the University College, Cardiff, he taught at schools in the Garw Valley and in Cardiff from 1928 to 1936, when he was ordained as a priest in the Church in Wales; thereafter he served in parishes in Monmouth-shire until his retirement. His published works include *The Political Ideas of Richard Hooker* (1946), *A History of the Parish of Mathern* (1950), *An Ecclesiastical History of Monmouthshire* (1953), *Monmouthshire Schools and Education to 1870* (1957), *Religion in the Industrial Revolution in South Wales* (1965) and *Religion and Society in Wales in the Nineteenth Century* (1981).

DAVIES, EDMUND COEDFRYN (1905–

27), poet, was born at Llanstephan, Carms., and worked as a bank-clerk. He published two volumes of rather conventional verse, namely *Woodland Breezes* (1924) and *Passion Flowers* (1927), and died before reaching maturity as a poet.

DAVIES, EDWARD (**Celtic Davies**; 1756–1831), critic, poet and dramatist, was born in the parish of Llanfaredd, Rads. After spending a year at Christ College, Brecon, he followed a career as a schoolmaster and curate, much of it in England, until in 1805 he became rector of Bishopston, Glam., where he remained until his death. He published two volumes of verse, namely *Aphtharte, the Genius of Britain* (1784) and *Vacunalia* (1788), a novel entitled *Eliza Powell or the Trials of Sensibility* (1795), and a discourse on the authenticity of Ossian in 1825. Between 1779 and 1783 he wrote three five-act plays: two comedies, *The Gold Mine* and *The Guardian*, and a tragedy, *Owen or the Fatal Clemency*. It is as the author of two volumes dealing with Welsh and Celtic subjects, *Celtic Researches* (1804) and *The Mythology and Rites of the British Druids* (1809), which earned him his nickname, that he is remembered today. A diligent collector of manuscripts, some of which were used by the editors of *The Myvyrian Archaiology* (1801–07), he had only an imperfect knowledge of Welsh and no qualifications for the task of interpreting the older poetry in which he delighted. On the other hand, despite his profound belief in Druid-ism, he was percipient enough to be among the first to doubt the claims made by Iolo Morganwg (Edward *Williams) on behalf of *Gorsedd Beirdd Ynys Prydain*.

For further details see the memoir by W. J. Rees in *The Cambrian Quarterly Magazine* (1831), the article by Frank R. Lewis in the *Transactions* (1969) of the Rad-norshire Society and that by G. R. Orrin in *Gower* (1980).

DAVIES, EDWARD TEGLA (**Tegla**; 1880–1967), prose-writer, was born at Llandegla-yn-Iâl, Denbs., the son of a quarryman. After seven years as a pupil-teacher he entered Didsbury College, Manchester, and spent the rest of his life as a minister of the Wesleyan Methodist Church. A close friend of T. Gwynn *Jones, Ifor *Williams and other men of letters, he edited the periodicals *Y Winllan* (1920–28) and *Yr Efrydydd* (1931–35), as well as the series *Cyfres Pobun*.

Most of his works were serialized in magazines before appearing in book form. The first, *Hunangofiant Tomi* (1912), was followed by other humorous tales about boys, notably *Nedw* (1922), the space fantasy *Rhys Llwyd y Lleuad* (1925) and *Y Doctor Bach* (1930). Tegla's gift of fantasy first appeared in *Tir y Dyneddon* (1921) but can also be seen, gradually maturing, in *Hen Ffrindiau* (1927), which is about the characters in Welsh nursery-rhymes struggling to free themselves from the eternal bondage of their verses, and in *Stori Sam* (1938). These books have been criticized for their somewhat laboured allegorizing, but they can be enjoyed solely for their rich inventiveness. His only full-length novel, *★Gŵr Pen y Bryn* (1923), describes the spiritual conversion of a well-to-do farmer during the ★Tithe War of the 1880s. His short stories were collected in the volume *Y Llwybr Arian* (1934). Two of the most inventive, '*Yr Epaddyn Rhyfedd*' and '*Samuel Jones yr Hendre yn Diolch am ei Gynhaeaf*', although dismissed by some Welsh critics as sentimental philosophizing, have been acclaimed in English translation.

Between 1946 and 1953 he wrote a weekly column for *Yr ★Herald Cymraeg*. Selections from these articles, some of them fiercely satirical of humbug in the religious and secular life of Wales, others literary sermons written in fine prose, were later published in *Rhyfedd o Fyd* (1950), *Y Foel Faen* (1951) and *Ar Ddisberod* (1954). He also wrote educational books for children and published selections of sermons and radio talks, such as *Yr Hen Gwpan Cymun* (1961), all of which were informed by his powerful intellect and rare imagination. His autobiography appeared under the title *Gyda'r Blynyddoedd* (1952).

For further details see the biography of Tegla by Huw Ethall (1980). A symposium in his honour, *Edward Tegla Davies, Llenor a Phroffwyd* (1956), was edited by Islwyn Ffowc Elis who has also written a study of his work, *Dirgelwch Tegla* (1977). See also the critical study by Pennar Davies in the *Writers of Wales* series (1983) and the essay by Dyddgu Owen in *Dewiniaid Difyr* (ed. Mairwen and Gwynn Jones, 1983).

Davies, Edwin (1859–1919), publisher. Born near Welshpool, Mont., but brought up in Brecon, he was apprenticed to a printer in that town and later acquired his own business there. His contributions to the literature of Wales derived from his passion for county history, especially that of Breconshire and Radnorshire, about which he amassed and preserved a vast collection of material. Among the works he edited and re-issued were *A History of the County of Brecknock* by Theophilus ★Jones, *The History and Antiquities of the County of Cardigan* by Samuel Rush ★Meyrick, *A Historical Tour through Pembroke-shire* by Richard ★Fenton, *An Historical Tour of Monmouthshire* by William ★Coxe and *A General History of the County of Radnor* (1905), the last of which he compiled mainly from the manuscripts of Jonathan Williams (1752?–1829).

Davies or **Cadwaladr, Elizabeth** (**Beti Cadwaladr**; 1789–1860), nurse. Born in Llanycil, near Bala, Mer., a minister's daughter, she ran away from home at the age of fourteen. She worked as a maid-servant for many years, travelling abroad with her employers and, although religious, indulging her taste for the theatre. Her life of adventure, described in an autobiography (2 vols., 1857) compiled by Jane

★Williams (Ysgafell), reached its climax in 1854 when she volunteered (at the age of sixty-five) for nursing service in the Crimea, where she worked with Florence Nightingale. A society for Welsh-speaking nurses, founded in 1970, has been named after her.

For further details see the monograph on Beti Cadwaladr by Meirion Jones in the *St. David's Day* series (1960).

DAVIES, ELWYN (1912–   ), poet. Born in Cardiff, he was a journalist and later a teacher at Pembroke Dock, but in 1957 joined the staff of an International Quaker School in the Netherlands, where he still lives. His two volumes of verse are *Words across the Water* (1970) and *A Lifting of Eyes* (1974).

DAVIES, EMYR (1878–1950), poet, was born at Llannor, Caerns. He won the ★Crown at the National Eisteddfod on two occasions, in 1906 for his *pryddest*, '*Branwen ferch Llŷr*', and in 1908 for '*Owain Glyndŵr*'. A volume of his poetry was published under the title *Llwyn Hudol* (1907).

Davies, Evan (**Eta Delta**; 1794–1855), see under TEMPERANCE.

DAVIES, EVAN (**Myfyr Morganwg**; 1801–88), archdruid, of Pontypridd, Glam., was a watchmaker by trade. Deeply affected by the 'druidic fever' of his day, he claimed to have succeeded to the title of '*Arch Derwydd Beirdd Ynys Prydain*' ('Archdruid of the Bards of the Isle of Britain') after the death of Taliesin ★Williams in 1847. From about 1853 he began conducting quasi-religious ceremonies at the rocking-stone on Pontypridd common and these occasions became the focus for literary competitions. Believing that Christianity was but a Jewish form of Druidism, he expounded his fantastic theories in several books on this subject, including *Gogoniant Hynafol y Cymry* (1865) and *Hynafiaeth Aruthrol* (1875).

DAVIES, GARETH ALBAN (1926–   ), poet and scholar. Born at Ton Pentre in the Rhondda Valley, he was associated with the group known as ★Cylch Cadwgan. He worked as a Bevin Boy in the coal industry between 1944 and 1947. Educated at The Queen's College, Oxford, he was appointed to the Chair of Spanish at Leeds University in 1975. Besides his contributions to Hispanic studies, he has published a volume of verse, *Baled Lewsyn a'r Môr* (1964), a diary, *Dyddiadur America* (1967), and a volume of essays about the Welsh settlement in ★Patagonia, *Tan Tro Nesaf* (1976). He also edited and contributed to the volume of critical essays, *Y Llenor yn Ewrop* (1976) and, with his wife Caryl, has translated Gide's *La Symphonie Pastorale* (1919) into Welsh under the title *Y Deillion* (1965).

Davies, George Maitland Lloyd (1880–1949), advocate of peace, was born in Liverpool, a grandson of John *Jones of Tal-y-sarn. After working with the Bank of Liverpool and with the Welsh Town Planning and Housing Trust, he became a full-time, unpaid worker for the Fellowship of Reconciliation in 1914. Imprisoned several times for his opposition to the First World War and to conscription, he was active in the immediate post-war years as an intermediary in situations of conflict, in particular between David *Lloyd George and De Valera. In 1923 he was elected Member of Parliament for the University of Wales as a Christian Pacifist and joined the Labour group in Parliament, his election providing evidence of growing disillusionment with the Liberal Party among the Welsh intelligentsia. Defeated in the following year, he was ordained in 1926 as a minister of the Calvinistic Methodist Church. Throughout the 1930s George M. Ll. Davies was involved in work with the unemployed, moving to the Quaker settlement at Maes-yr-Haf in the *Rhondda Valley in 1932. He wrote extensively on matters relating to international peace and in *Pererindod Heddwch* (1945) and *Pilgrimage of Peace* (1950) he gave an account of his mission.

For further details see the biography by E. H. Griffiths, *Heddychwyr Mawr Cymru; George M. Ll. Davies* (2 vols., 1967, 1968).

Davies, Gwilym (1879–1955), advocate of international understanding and pioneer of popular peace movements, was born at Bedlinog, Glam. From 1908 to 1922 he was a Baptist minister but, concerned to apply Christian principles to social questions, he became active on behalf of the Welsh School of Social Service. The Honorary Director of the League of Nations Union from 1922 to 1945, he attended every General Assembly of the League at Geneva between 1923 and 1938, and wrote extensively about its work in Welsh periodicals. The constitution of UNESCO was based upon his draft plans for international co-operation in education. Excited by the potential of radio, it was he who, in 1922, inaugurated the Goodwill Message of the Children of Wales, an initiative subsequently organized by *Urdd Gobaith Cymru*, and his talk on St. David's Day in 1923 was the first radio broadcast in Welsh. In a series of articles published in *Y *Traethodydd* in 1942 he claimed that *Plaid Cymru* was inspired by the French right-wing, a charge which brought a vigorous retort from Saunders *Lewis.

DAVIES, IDRIS (1905–53), poet. Born at Rhymney, Mon., into a Welsh-speaking home, he learned English at the local elementary school and, in later life, read widely in Welsh and wrote a little in the language. He left school at the age of fourteen to become a miner in the pit where his father was chief winder-man. A fellow-collier introduced him to the work of Shelley and he quickly perceived that poetry could relate to politics and illuminate the causes of *Socialism and human dignity. Early in 1926 he lost a finger in a colliery accident and had barely restarted work when the long miners' strike, and the subsequent closure of the pit where he had been employed, forced him to consider other ways of earning a living. Having taken a correspondence course, he matriculated and went on to study at Loughborough College and the University of Nottingham, qualifying as a teacher. In 1932 he began teaching at a primary school in the East End of London and, an avid reader of poetry, soon made contact with those Welsh writers who frequented Griff's Bookshop, off the Charing Cross Road.

A few of his poems were published in newspapers and obscure journals in the early 1930s, but his emergence as a poet coincided with the appearance of Keidrych *Rhys's magazine, *Wales*, to which he became a regular contributor. With his first volume, *Gwalia Deserta* (1938), which takes as its theme the desert of industrial south Wales during the 1920s and the Depression, he announced himself as the voice of a generation. At the outbreak of the Second World War his school was evacuated and he accompanied the pupils to Pytchley, Northants., where he contemplated in his journal a number of themes for a long poem, the outcome of which was The *Angry Summer* (1943). Further wartime transfers took him to schools in Hertfordshire, Llandysul, Cards., and Treherbert in the *Rhondda Valley where he completed his third book, *Tonypandy and Other Poems* (1945), a more varied collection gathered from ten years of writing. After many unsuccessful attempts, he obtained a teaching post in the Rhymney Valley in 1947 and returned home but, in 1951, was found to be suffering from cancer. A volume of his selected poems was published shortly before his death.

Early judgements of Idris Davies emphasized his integrity while criticizing the narrow range of his work and its occasional descents to banality. It is now clear, however, that the limitations were self-imposed in order to give finer focus and power to his chosen theme and that he was a writer of considerable sophistication. Within the two sequences which form the substantial core of his *œuvre* there is a subtle juxtaposition of wry humour and passionate social and moral indignation, the whole pervaded by an unfailing humanity. Although several sections have become widely known, often as songs, only recently have *Gwalia Deserta* and *The Angry Summer* been recognized as long and unified dramatic poems.

The *Collected Poems* (1972) of Idris Davies were edited by Islwyn Jenkins who contributed an essay on the poet to the *Writers of Wales* series (1972); see also the essay on the poet by Stephen Wade in *The Anglo-Welsh Review* (vol. 24, no. 53, Winter, 1974), the special number of *Poetry Wales* (vol. 16, no. 4, Spring, 1981) which is devoted to his work, and the essay by Anthony Conran in *The Cost of Strangeness* (1982).

DAVIES, JAMES (Iaco ap Dewi; 1648–1722), copyist and collector of manuscripts, was born at Llandysul, Cards. He was for a while a member of the Independent church at Pencader and he also lived in *Penllyn, Mer., but it was at Llanllawddog, Carms., that he spent most of his life. It appears that he made his living by copying old manuscripts and in this occupation he was heavily influenced by Edward *Lhuyd. In turn, a number of copyists, such as William Bona of Llanpumsaint, David Richards of Llanegwad and Ben *Simon of Abergwili, came under his influence. His manuscripts are noteworthy for the critical attention to which the texts have been subjected and the importance of his work is exemplified by the fact that it preserves (as in Llanstephan MS 133) a number of poems which would be otherwise unrecorded. He assisted Stephen *Hughes in the compilation of the works of Rhys *Prichard and he also collected traditional songs. The few poems of his own composition which have survived are unremarkable except for the evidence they provide about the poverty and melancholy of his life.

For further details see Garfield H. Hughes, *Iaco ab Dewi* (1953).

DAVIES, JAMES CONWAY (1891–1971), historian and palaeographer, was born in Llanelli, Carms., and educated at the University College of Wales, Aberystwyth, at University College, Cardiff, and at Emmanuel College, Cambridge. Employed during the Second World War in the *National Library of Wales as archivist to Monmouthshire County Council, he virtually established the County Record Office in that county and issued two reports on the county records. He was appointed Reader in Palaeography and Diplomatic at the University of Durham in 1948 and became Custodian of Manuscripts at Durham Cathedral. The first editor of the *Journal* of the Society of the Church in Wales, he published extensively on medieval themes, his work displaying a profound knowledge of official muniments. Among the most important of his publications are *The Baronial Opposition to Edward II* (1918), an erudite examination of political intrigue; *The Welsh Assize Roll 1277–1282* (1940), a close analysis of the legal and administrative aspects of the crucial period before the death of *Llywelyn ap Gruffudd; *Episcopal Acts and Cognate Documents relating to Welsh Dioceses, 1066–1272* (2 vols., 1946, 1948); and with E. A. Lewis, *Records of the Court of Augmentations relating to Wales and Monmouthshire* (1954).

DAVIES, JAMES EIRIAN (1918–), poet. Born at Nantgaredig, Carms., he has been a minister with the Calvinistic Methodists all his life, most recently at Mold, Flints. He is the author of three volumes of verse, namely *Awen y Wawr* (1947), *Cân Galed* (1974) and *Cyfrol o Gerddi* (1985), and from 1978 to 1982 was deputy to his wife, Jennie Eirian Davies (1926–82), the editor of *Y Faner* (*Baner ac Amserau Cymru*). The young writer Siôn Eirian (b. 1954) is one of his sons.

DAVIES, JAMES KITCHENER (1902–52), poet and dramatist, was brought up on a small-holding near Cors Caron, Cards., and educated at Tregaron County School and the University College of Wales, Aberystwyth. In 1926 he settled in the *Rhondda Valley and remained there for the rest of his life, teaching Welsh at various schools in the valley and promoting with tireless devotion the cause of *Plaid Cymru.

He first attracted public attention as a dramatist at the National Eisteddfod of 1934 with his three-act play *Cwm Glo* (1935), which deals in plain language with the dire social consequences of the *Depression in the mining valleys of south Wales. The adjudicators recognized the author's talent but took the view that the play was unsuitable to be performed because of its doubtful morality, and the prize was withheld. This decision caused controversy and when the play was published and successfully performed, first in Swansea and then elsewhere in south Wales, the controversy continued in the Welsh and English press.

Apart from *Cwm Glo*, Kitchener Davies's two main achievements were his verse play, *Meini Gwagedd* (1945), which won a prize at the National Eisteddfod of 1944, and above all his pryddest, *'Sŵn y Gwynt sy'n Chwythu'* (1953), broadcast by the BBC while the poet was on his death-bed. The poem is a self-searching, autobiographical work which is widely regarded as one of the finest written in Welsh during the twentieth century.

His widow, Mair I. Davies, has edited a volume of his most important poems and plays (1980). For further details see the note by John Rowlands in *Profiles* (1980) and the special number of *Poetry Wales* (Winter, 1982) which is devoted to the work of Kitchener Davies; see also the articles by Alun Llywelyn-Williams and Dyfnallt Morgan in *Lleufer* (vol. 9, 1953 and vol. 21, 1965) and the study by Ioan Williams in the series *Llên y Llenor* (1984).

DAVIES, JOHN (1565?–1618), poet and writing-master, was the son of Welsh parents who lived in Hereford, a city only four miles from the boundary of the old Welsh kingdom of *Erging. He was known during his lifetime as 'the Welsh poet' and in his poem 'Cambria', which is included in the volume *Microcosmos* (1603), he took it upon himself to speak 'for Wales' to Henry Stuart, the heir of James I and the new Prince of Wales. This poem, with its pan-Celtic overtones, makes the same assumption of

Wales's seniority in the Union (through *Brutus the Trojan, *Arthur and the *Tudor monarchy) as is found in writers such as Morris *Kyffin and James *Howell. Davies, one of three brothers in the profession, practised as a writing-master in Oxford, mainly at Magdalen College, but by 1609 he was practising in Fleet Street, London. Among his pupils were the children of the Earl of Northumberland and Henry, the Prince of Wales, a tribute to Davies's reputation for he was a Catholic and the Prince the focus of Puritan antipathy for the King's policies.

John Davies of Hereford, as he is sometimes called, published several collections of verse during his lifetime, including *Humour's Heav'n on Earth* (1609), which is dedicated to the Northumberland children, *The Scourge of Folly* (1611), containing poems to Bacon and John *Owen the epigrammatist, and *The Muses Teares for the losse of their Hope* (1613) in memory of his royal pupil. The first edition of his book entitled *The Writing-Schoolmaster or The Anatomy of Fair Writing* cannot be dated with certainty, but there were later editions in 1633, 1663 and 1669.

The *Complete Works* of John Davies, characterized, as to the poetry, by a fatal fluency and verbosity, were published by Alexander B. Grosart in 1878 and there is a critique of them by H. E. G. Rope in *The Anglo-Welsh Review* (no. 28, 1961).

DAVIES, JOHN (*c.*1567–1644), one of the greatest Welsh scholars of the later Renaissance period, was born at Llanferres, Denbs., and graduated at Jesus College, Oxford, in 1594. It is probable that he was in close contact with William *Morgan when the latter was Bishop of Llandaf between 1595 and 1601, for in the preamble to his *Grammar* (1621) Davies stated that he had been an unworthy assistant in the translation of the *Bible into Welsh. He was appointed rector of Mallwyd, Mer., in 1604; the rectory of Llanymawddwy, Mer., was added to his living in 1614 and he was appointed prebendary of Llanefydd, Denbs., three years later.

It is believed that Dr. John Davies of Mallwyd (as he is usually called) did most of the work of revising the Welsh Bible for the new version which appeared in 1620 and that he may have revised the Book of Common Prayer which was republished in 1621. In the same year appeared his Welsh grammar in Latin, *Antiquae Linguae Britannicae . . . Rudimenta*, and in 1632 his Welsh-Latin dictionary, together with an abridged version of the Latin-Welsh dictionary of Thomas *Wiliems of Trefriw, the *Dictionarium Duplex*. Davies also published *Llyfr y Resolusion* (1632), a translation of *The First Book of the Christian Exercise appertayning to Resolution* by the Jesuit, Robert Parsons, the intention of which was to introduce Christian truths to his parishioners. He edited *Y Llyfr Plygain a'r Catechisme* (1633) and after his death there

appeared *Yr Articulau* (1664) and *Flores Poetarum Britannicorum* (1710), an anthology of poetry.

He was an industrious collector and copyist of manuscripts and his work in preserving bardic vocabulary established the basis for a scientific study of the Welsh language.

For further details see the article by Rh. Ff. Roberts, 'Dr. John Davies o Fallwyd' in *Llên Cymru* (vol. II, 1952), the chapter by R. Geraint Gruffydd, 'Richard Parry a John Davies', in *Y Traddodiad Rhyddiaith* (ed. Geraint Bowen, 1970) and C. Davies, *Rhagymadroddion a Chyflwyniadau Lladin, 1551–1632* (1980).

DAVIES, JOHN (1627–93), translator, was born at Kidwelly (Cydweli), Carms., and educated at Jesus College, Oxford, and St. John's College, Cambridge, his studies being interrupted by the *Civil Wars. Returning to London about the year 1652 after travels in France, he began his life's work of translating books from French into English on behalf of booksellers. Among the thirty or so titles ascribed to him are *Treatise against the Principles of Descartes* (1654) and *A History of the Civil Wars of Great Britain and Ireland* (1661); he is also believed to have edited *Enchiridion* (1686), the work of his friend Henry Turberville.

DAVIES, JOHN (Siôn Dafydd Las; d. 1694), poet. Little is known about his life, but according to tradition he was born at Llanuwchllyn, Mer., and lived for a while in the district of *Penllyn. He was regarded as the family poet of *Nannau but he wrote for members of other gentry families in north-west Wales, being one of the last to receive such patronage. Like other poets of his day, he made use of the *carol measures and it has been suggested that he was the composer of the tune 'Pant Corlan yr Ŵyn'.

DAVIES, JOHN (Brychan; 1784?–1864), one of the self-taught poets of Gwent and Glamorgan. A native of Llanwrthwl, Brecs., he moved to Tredegar, Mon., to work in a colliery, but later became a bookseller, publisher and promoter of the *Friendly Societies in Wales. He edited four anthologies of the work of his contemporaries, *Llais Awen Gwent a Morgannwg* (1824), *Y Gog* (1825), *Y Llinos* (1827) and *Y Fwyalchen* (1835). Brychan was among those initiated into *Gorsedd Beirdd Ynys Prydain by Iolo Morganwg (Edward *Williams) in 1818.

DAVIES, JOHN (Ossian Gwent; 1839–92), poet. He was born at Cardigan but his parents moved to the Rhymney Valley when he was young and there he learned the carpenter's craft. The author of two volumes of poetry, *Caniadau* (*c.*1873) and *Blodau Gwent* (1898), he was a better poet than many others who were prominent during his lifetime.

DAVIES, JOHN (1944–   ), poet, was born at Cymmer Afan, Glam., and educated at the

University College of Wales, Aberystwyth. A teacher at Prestatyn, Flints., he has published five volumes of verse, namely *Strangers* (1974), *Spring in a Small Town* (1979), *At the Edge of Town* (1981), *The Silence in the Park* (1982) and *The Visitor's Book* (1985). Frequently concerned with the experience of isolation, his work has been praised for its formal precision and for its marriage of delicate lyricism with intellectual toughness. With Mike Jenkins he edited the anthology *The Valleys* (1984).

DAVIES, JOHN CADVAN (Cadvan; 1846–1923), hymn-writer and Methodist minister. Born at Llangadfan, Mont., he was prominent in the eisteddfodau of the period as competitor, adjudicator and, in 1923, as Archdruid. He published *Caneuon Cadvan* (4 vols., 1878, 1883, 1893, 1894), *Dydd Coroniad* (1894) and *Atgof a Phrofiad*, an autobiography which appeared in *Yr *Eurgrawn* (1917).

DAVIES, JOHN GLYN (1870–1953), poet and scholar, was born in Liverpool, a grandson of John *Jones of Tal-y-sarn and a brother to George M. Ll. *Davies. For nearly ten years he campaigned for the establishment of the *National Library of Wales. He became assistant lecturer to Kuno Meyer in the Celtic Department of Liverpool University in 1907 and was Head of the Department from 1920 to 1936. His publications include *Welsh Metrics* (1911), *Yr Ymhonwyr* (1922), a translation of Ibsen's play, *The Pretenders*, a volume of poetry, *Cerddi Edern* (1955), as well as contributions to the study of the history of Welsh gypsies. But he is remembered primarily as the author of the popular verses for children, *Cerddi Huw Puw* (1923), *Cerddi Robin Goch* (1935) and *Cerddi Portinllaen* (1936).

His widow, Hettie Glyn Davies, published a memoir of J. Glyn Davies in 1965.

DAVIES, JOHN HUMPHREYS (1871–1926), scholar and bibliophile, was born at Cwrt Mawr, Llangeitho, Cards. Educated at the University College of Wales, Aberystwyth, and at Lincoln College, Oxford, he took an early interest in public life and held a number of influential posts. Appointed Registrar of the University College of Wales, Aberystwyth, in 1905, he became Principal in 1919. His chief publications, besides many articles in periodicals, include *Rhai o Hen Ddewiniaid Cymru* (1901), *A Bibliography of Welsh Ballads* (1909–11), *The Morris Letters* (2 vols., 1907, 1909) and *The Letters of Goronwy Owen* (1924). His knowledge of Welsh literature, encouraged by friendship with Owen M. *Edwards and T. E. *Ellis, was extensive and he owned a large collection of books and manuscripts, known as the Cwrtmawr Manuscripts.

For further details see the biography of John Humphreys Davies written by T. I. Ellis (1963).

DAVIES, JONATHAN CEREDIG (1859–1932), writer. Born at Llangunllo, Cards., he travelled widely and published three books about his visits to *Patagonia, namely *Darlith ar Batagonia* (1891), *Patagonia: A Description of the Country* (1892) and *Adventures in the Land of Giants: a Patagonia Tale* (1892). He also wrote *Folk-lore of West and Mid-Wales* (1911), *Welsh and Oriental Languages* (1927) and a volume of reminiscences (1927).

DAVIES, LEWIS (1863–1951), children's writer, was a native of Hirwaun, near Aberdare, Glam. A teacher by profession, he was a schoolmaster at Cymmer from 1886 to 1925. He was the author of four adventure novels for young people, namely *Lewsyn yr Heliwr* (1922), *Daff Owen* (1924), *Wat Emwnt* (1928) and *Y Geilwad Bach* (1929). All are set in the industrial areas of the Breconshire-Glamorgan border at the end of the eighteenth or early nineteenth century and they paint a vivid portrait of the society of that district and its many hardships. In each the chief character leaves his native patch and has a series of adventures in distant lands before returning to Wales. Lewis Davies also compiled a volume of romantic stories based on events in Welsh history, *Bargodion Hanes* (1924).

DAVIES, MYLES (1662–1715?), religious propagandist and author. Born in the parish of Whitford, Flints., he was educated at the English Jesuit College in Rome where he was ordained priest in 1688 but, returning to Wales, was converted to *Protestantism, an experience described in his book, *The Recantation of Mr. Pollett, a Roman Priest* (1705). His principal work was *Athenae Britannicae* (6 vols., 1716), in which it was his purpose to record and refute the propaganda of Roman Catholic tracts, mainly by citing their Protestant counterparts. These books provide a valuable source for the bibliography of this kind of literature in his day. The work also includes a Latin play in prose and verse, entitled *Pallas Anglicana*, which has more literary merit than the rest of his writing.

For further details see the article by R. George Thomas in the *Transactions* of the Honourable Society of Cymmrodorion (1963).

DAVIES, NAUNTON WINGFIELD (Naunton Covertside; 1852–1925), novelist and playwright, born in Newport, Mon., into an old Rhondda family, was a doctor by profession and lived for many years at Llantrisant, Glam. He published three novels, namely *The King's Guide* (1901), *The Reverend Jack* (n.d.) and *The Secret of a Hollow Tree* (n.d.), all of which are set in south Wales. He is remembered for the part he played in promoting the amateur *drama movement in Wales during the first decades of the twentieth century, and as a playwright.

Eight of his plays were published: *The Village Wizard* (1913), *The Arrogance of Power* (1920), *The Conversion* (1920), *The Epidemic* (1920), *The Great Experiment* (n.d.), *The Human Factor* (1920), *The Schemer* (1920) and *The Second Son* (1920), most of which are set in Glamorgan.

DAVIES, OLIVER (1881–1960), poet, was born at Greenwich, Kent, the son of a Welsh-speaking builder from Llechryd, Cards. Entering the prison service in 1901, he joined the clerical staff at Dartmoor and worked in turn at various gaols in England. He published five volumes of verse, namely *Between Time Poems* (1909), *Songs at Random* (1912), *Dartmoor Prison Lyrics* (1915), *Songs and Signs* (1920) and *Plain Song* (1949). His poems, while short on observation and never moving far from 'the poetic', have a fragile lyricism which occasionally lifts them above the mediocrity of most writing by Welshmen in English during the first two decades of the twentieth century.

DAVIES, PENNAR (**Davies Aberpennar**; 1911–), poet, novelist and scholar. A coalminer's son, he was born at Mountain Ash (Aberpennar) into a family whose roots on both sides were in Pembrokeshire. His mother's people came from the south of the county and his father's from the Welsh-speaking north, but English was the language of their home. After a distinguished academic career at University College, Cardiff, where he graduated in Latin (1932) and English (1933), and then at Balliol and Mansfield Colleges, Oxford, and at Yale University, he was from 1943 a minister of religion in Cardiff and later a Professor at Bala-Bangor Theological College and the Memorial College, Brecon. In 1952 he was appointed Principal of the Memorial College and continued in that post (after it became the Swansea Memorial College) until his retirement in 1981. In 1943 he married a refugee from Nazi Germany; one of their sons is the poet Meirion ★Pennar.

Pennar Davies's early verse was written in English and Welsh under the name Davies Aberpennar, a pseudonym he relinquished in 1948. He became known to Welsh readers in the 1940s as a member of ★*Cylch Cadwgan* and some of his poems were published in the group's volume, *Cerddi Cadwgan* (1953). Four collections of his verse have appeared since then, namely *Cinio'r Cythraul* (1946), *Naw Wfft* (1957), *Yr Efrydd o Lyn Cynon* (1961) and *Y Tlws yn y Lotws* (1971), all of which include a number of well-wrought love-lyrics and religious poems shot through with passionate imagery.

His creative prose is unusual in its combination of mythical symbolism and personal tenderness. The first of his prose works, *Cudd fy Meiau* (1957), is a spiritual journal containing much uncompromising self-analysis. As he worked his way through from the novel, *Anadl o'r*

Uchelder (1958), a study of the psychology of a religious revivalist, by way of a volume of short stories, *Caregl Nwyf* (1966), to his second novel, *Meibion Darogan* (1968), he moved more and more into an ambiguous symbolic world of complex mythical patterns. The most mature of these books, *Mabinogi Mwys* (1979), examines the marital problems of a sensitive young man within the context of contemporary Wales and its social and political uncertainties. Another volume of his short stories, entitled *Llais y Durtur*, appeared in 1985. A contemplative Christian, and the author of a number of critical and scholarly works, such as *Y Brenin Alltud* (1974), in which studies of Jesus emphasize His practical goodness, and *Rhwng Chwedl a Chredo* (1966), which traces the direction of Welsh religious thought in early times, Pennar Davies is a writer whose chief characteristic is a calm, mystic passion, religious but also deeply personal and human, which illuminates all his work. Some measure of his wide culture, erudition and literary gifts, together with a list of his numerous publications, is to be found in the volume published as a tribute to him under the editorship of Dewi Eurig Davies in 1981.

There is an autobiographical essay by Pennar Davies in the volume *Artists in Wales* (ed. Meic Stephens, 1971) and an essay on the writer by J. Gwyn Griffiths in *Triskel Two* (ed. Sam Adams and Gwilym Rees Hughes, 1973); see also the article by Gareth Alban Davies in *Dyrnaid o Awduron Cyfoes* (ed. D. Ben Rees, 1975), the essay by Siân Megan in *Ysgrifau Beirniadol IX* (ed. J. E. Caerwyn Williams, 1976) and the note by John Rowlands in *Profiles* (1980).

DAVIES, REES (1938–), historian, was born at Llandderfel, Mer., and educated at University College, London, and Merton College, Oxford. Between 1963 and 1973 he was a lecturer at University College, London, and was appointed Professor of History at the University College of Wales, Aberystwyth, in 1976. Besides contributions to journals and symposia, he has published *Lordship and Society in the March of Wales 1282–1400* (1978).

DAVIES, RHYS (1903–78), novelist and short-story writer. Born in Clydach Vale in the ★Rhondda Valley, the son of the village grocer, he attended Porth Intermediate School and, in his early twenties, went to live in London where he became a full-time writer. His first three books, including the novel, *The ★Withered Root*, all appeared in 1927 and the following year he spent in France where he became friendly with D. H. Lawrence, at that time a cult figure for the young. Apart from a period during the Second World War, he lived almost entirely by the writing of novels and short stories, not even undertaking lecturing or literary journalism.

Without higher education, Rhys Davies prepared himself for a writing career by a study of the English and European classics, especially the French masters of the short story and Chekhov, whom he called 'my god'. The influence of Caradoc Evans (David *Evans) and D. H. Lawrence is also discernible on his earlier work. The novel *Rings on her Fingers* (1930) tells of the love of Edgar Roberts for Edith Stevens, one of the dominant women who appear in various guises in Davies's work; *Count your Blessings* (1932) concerns Blodwen Evans and her superior Cardiff brothel; *The Red Hills* (1932) is the story of Iorwerth, one of Davies's 'artist' figures, owner of a small coal-mine, and his love for possessive Ceinwen and for more satisfying Virginia. His next three novels, *Honey and Bread* (1935), *A Time to Laugh* (1937) and *Jubilee Blues* (1938), form a trilogy dealing with the history of an industrial valley in south Wales culminating in the *Depression of the 1930s. *Under the Rose* (1940) is a revenge-murder story set in rural Wales and in *Tomorrow to Fresh Woods* (1941) he draws heavily upon his own experience, for the novel's hero is an artistic boy, the son of a grocer in an industrial town. *The *Black Venus* (1944) is probably Rhys Davies's best-known novel. Two later novels present portraits of famous Welshmen living in London: *The Painted King* (1954) is based on the career of Ivor Novello (David Ivor *Davies), and in *The Perishable Quality* (1957) the gifted, bohemian young poet who is its central character is named, not Dylan *Thomas, but Iolo Hancock. Among his other novels are *The Dark Daughters* (1947), *Marianne* (1951), *Girl Waiting in the Shade* (1960) and *Nobody Answered the Bell* (1971).

He also wrote many short stories, the subject-matter of which is as varied as that of his novels. On the whole, they would appear to be the most successful part of his very considerable output (which is too extensive to list fully here). They are to be found in *The Things Men Do* (1936), *The Trip to London* (1946), *Boy with a Trumpet* (1949), *The Darling of her Heart* (1958), *The Chosen One* (1967) and in his *Collected Stories* (1955). Some of the pictures of Welsh society presented by Rhys Davies in his novels may not strike those who know well the society he portrays as being entirely convincing. But in his short stories the emphasis is less on sociology and more on a small number of characters in some single situation; the stories 'Canute', 'Nightgown', 'The Benefit Concert', 'Revelation', 'Weep not my Wanton' and 'Resurrection' are a few among his many successes in this genre. Unaffected by the gospelling fervour of his early master, D. H. Lawrence, Rhys Davies took the Anglo-Welsh story to its limit in objectivity. With his humour, inventiveness, attention to significant detail, skill in creating moments and situations of high drama, the best of his completely professional works is highly entertaining.

Rhys Davies also wrote a play, *The Maid of Cefn Ydfa*, a successful musical, *Jennie Jones*, as well as the topographical essays, *My Wales* (1937) and *The Story of Wales* (1943), and a volume of autobiography, *Print of a Hare's Foot* (1969).

David Rees contributed an essay on Rhys Davies (with a bibliography) to the *Writers of Wales* series (1975); see also the critical sketches by R. L. Mégroz (1932) and G. F. Adam, *Three Contemporary Anglo-Welsh Novelists* (1948).

DAVIES, RICHARD (1501?–81), bishop and translator. Educated at Oxford, where he came under the influence of the reformers, he stayed there until 1536 at least and, between 1555 and 1558, was an exile for religion in Frankfurt. He returned on Elizabeth's accession and was made Bishop of *St. Asaph and, in 1561, of *St. David's.

With his friend William *Salesbury, Richard Davies is presumed to have persuaded Parliament to pass the Act of 1563 ordering the translation of the *Bible and the Book of Common Prayer into Welsh. To expedite the translation, he invited Salesbury to his household at *Abergwili, although it seems certain that the bishop did not himself have a hand in the work. Richard Davies did, however, translate the Epistles of 1 Timothy, Hebrews, James and 1 and 2 Peter for the New Testament of 1567, his language and style being superior in these epistles to Salesbury's in the rest of the Testament. He also wrote *Epistol at y Cembru* (1567) which prefaced the Testament and which was to exercise so powerful an influence on Welsh historiography. The two men intended to translate the Old Testament but did not do so because, according to Sir John *Wynn, they quarrelled over the meaning of one word. Fragments of Davies's translations were left in the Gwysaneu Manuscripts (see LLANNERCH MANUSCRIPTS). He also translated the books between Joshua and 2 Samuel for the 'Bishop's Bible' (1568) at Archbishop Matthew Parker's request, though it is not a particularly distinguished translation.

It seems that Richard Davies was a member of a group of moderate Puritans and traces of this activity are to be found in Edmund Spenser's *The Shepheardes Calender* (1579). At Abergwili he offered generous hospitality to clerics, poets and other men of culture. He was a good bishop of St. David's, battling against spiritual indifference and defending his diocese against greedy laymen, and also an effective member of the House of Lords, the Council in the Marches and other administrative bodies.

Biographies of Bishop Davies have been published by D. R. Thomas (1902) and Glanmor Williams (1953).

DAVIES, RICHARD (1635–1708), Quaker, of Cloddiau Cochion, Mont. Despite imprisonment and fines, he kept open house for Friends, and accompanied *John ap John on his first mission to south Wales. He was also associated in his imprisonment with the *Lloyds of

Dolobran. His autobiography, *An Account of the Convincement, Exercises, Services and Travels of that Ancient Servant of the Lord, Richard Davies* (1710), is considered to be a classic of Quaker writing.

DAVIES, RICHARD (Mynyddog; 1833–77), poet, was born at Llanbrynmair, Mont. Famous as a conductor and soloist, he published three volumes of verse during his lifetime, namely *Caneuon Mynyddog* (1866), *Yr Ail Gynnig* (1870) and *Y Trydydd Cynnig* (1877); a fourth, *Pedwerydd Llyfr Mynyddog* (1882), appeared posthumously. His verses, sung to popular English melodies, are mostly doggerel on such themes as the folly of false pride and the odiousness of hypocrisy. Few have any lasting merit, but one, namely 'Gwnewch Bopeth yn Gymraeg', is still sung. He is also remembered for having collaborated with Joseph *Parry in the composition of the opera *Blodwen*.

A biography of Mynyddog was written by T. R. Roberts (1909).

DAVIES, ROBERT (Bardd Nantglyn; 1769–1835), poet. Born at Nantglyn, Denbs., he was apprenticed to a tailor and became known for his humorous and topical verses. He published a collection of carols and *englynion* in the volume *Cnewyllyn mewn Gwisg* (1798), and a selection of his work in *Diliau Barddas* (1827). His most famous line is 'Beibl i bawb o bobl y byd' ('A Bible for everyone in the world'), which occurs in his elegy for George III, although it is also attributed to Robert *Williams (1744–1815). He won the *Gwyneddigion Society's prize at the Caerwys Eisteddfod of 1798 with an *awdl*, 'Cariad i'n Gwlad', before moving to London in 1800. Elected the official poet of the Society in 1801, he became its secretary in the following year but returned to Nantglyn in 1804 to be with his family. His Grammar, *Ieithiadur neu Ramadeg Cymraeg* (1808), had a profound influence on poets throughout the century and had run to five editions by 1848.

Davies, Ryan (1937–77), entertainer. Born at Glanaman, Carms., he was educated at the Normal College, Bangor, and the Central School of Drama in London. He taught at an elementary school in Croydon from 1960 until 1966, the year in which he signed a contract with BBC Wales, and thereafter he enjoyed immense popularity as singer, actor and comedian on the stage and on television. Among his many talents was that of mimickry, in which he made brilliant use of his aquiline features, and perhaps his most memorable performances were given in the television series *Fo a Fe*, in which he played the part of Twm Twm, the epitome of the proletarian Welshman. His death while on holiday in Buffalo, New York, robbed Wales of one of its most versatile comic geniuses.

For further details see the memoirs by Rhydderch Jones, *Cofiant Ryan* (1979) and *Ryan* (1980); a selection of Ryan's songs was published in 1983.

DAVIES, THOMAS ESSILE (Dewi Wyn o Esyllt; 1820–91), see under CLIC Y BONT.

DAVIES, THOMAS GLYNNE (1926–), poet and novelist. Born at Llanrwst, Denbs., he was educated at the grammar school there and took his first job in a laboratory. During the Second World War he worked at a colliery in Oakdale, Mon. In 1949, after military service, he turned to journalism, working as a reporter for *The Cambrian News*, *Y Cymro* and *The South Wales Evening Post*. He joined the BBC in 1957 as a news-reporter and became a producer of radio programmes, developing into a talented broadcaster noted for his dry wit and informal manner. His promise as a poet was recognized when he won the *Crown at the National Eisteddfod in 1951 with a *pryddest*, 'Adfeilion', which was widely acclaimed. A kind of caustic nostalgia is the chief characteristic of his two collections of poetry, *Llwybrau Pridd* (1961) and *Hedydd yn yr Haul* (1969). His most ambitious work is the novel *Marged* (1974), one of the most substantial published in Welsh since 1950, in which he traces the history of a Llanrwst family over the span of a hundred years. He has also published a volume of short stories, *Cân Serch* (1954), and another novel, *Haf Creulon* (1960).

There is an autobiographical essay by T. Glynne Davies in the volume *Artists in Wales* (ed. Meic Stephens, 1977); see also the interview he gave to the magazine *Mabon* (ed. Gwyn Thomas, 1972), the article by Philip Wyn Jones in *Dyrnaid o Awduron Cyfoes* (ed. D. Ben Rees, 1975), the article by John Rowlands on *Marged* in *Ysgrifau Beirniadol XI* (ed. J. E. Caerwyn Williams, 1979) and the note by the same writer in *Profiles* (1980).

Davies, Walford (1869–1941), musician. Born at Oswestry, Salop., and educated at the Royal College of Music, he had a distinguished career as an organist and conductor before taking up a double appointment as Director of Music in the University of Wales in 1919 and Professor of Music at the University College of Wales, Aberystwyth. Knighted in 1922, he succeeded Sir Edward Elgar as Master of the King's Musick in 1934. For many years his work was frequently performed at the Three Choirs Festival and he was closely associated with music-making at Gregynog. He was also widely known for his talks and record programmes on radio.

For an account of Walford Davies's association with Gregynog see Ian Parrott, *The Spiritual Pilgrims* (1964).

DAVIES, WALFORD (1940–), literary critic and editor, was born at Pontyberem, Carms., and educated at Keble College, Oxford. A former Lecturer in English at the University College of Wales, Aberystwyth, and a Senior Lecturer at St. Anne's College, Oxford, he has been Director of the Department of Extra-Mural Studies at the University College of Wales, Aberystwyth, since 1976. He contributed an essay on Dylan *Thomas to the *Writers of Wales series (1972) and has edited Thomas's early prose writings (1971), a volume of critical essays on his work (1972) and his selected poems (1974), as well as selected editions of the poetry of Wordsworth (1975), Gerard Manley *Hopkins (1979) and Thomas Hardy (1982). Walford Davies is also the senior literary adviser to the publishers J. M. Dent, with special responsibility for the *Everyman* series.

DAVIES, WALTER (**Gwallter Mechain**; 1761–1849), poet and editor, was born at Llanfechain, Mont. With but little formal education, he delighted as a boy in the company of local poets and wrote *plygain* carols in the traditional style. Educated later at St. Alban's Hall, Oxford, he was ordained in 1795 and held the living of Manafon, Mont., from 1807 to 1837. Sponsored by the Board of Agriculture, he produced *A General View of the Agriculture and Domestic Economy of North Wales* in 1810 and a similar survey of south Wales in 1815.

His most important contribution to Welsh letters was as an adjudicator at provincial eisteddfodau, in which he promoted the literary standards of Goronwy *Owen, and as an editor. One of the founders of the journal *Y *Gwyliedydd* (1822–38), he published *Eos Ceiriog* (1820–23), a volume containing the works of Huw *Morys, culled mostly from the manuscripts of Richard Foulkes of Llansilin, and *Salmau Dafydd* (1827) by William *Midleton. He was co-editor with Tegid (John *Jones) of the works of *Lewys Glyn Cothi (1837) and assisted Samuel Lewis in the writing of his *Topographical Dictionary of Wales* (1833). His several parish histories, published in the English periodicals of the *London Welsh, are still well regarded. Much of his work remains in manuscript, including his weather diaries and his correspondence with others among *Yr *Hen Bersoniaid Llengar* ('The Old Literary Clerics'). His famous *englyn* beginning '*Y nos dywell yn distewi*' is to be found in his *awdl*, '*Cwymp Llywelyn*' (1821).

The work of Gwallter Mechain was edited by D. Silvan Evans (1868); for details of his life and work see Bedwyr Lewis Jones, *Yr Hen Bersoniaid Llengar* (1963) and Glenda Carr, *William Owen Pughe* (1983).

DAVIES, WALTER HAYDN (1903–84), writer. Born at Bedlinog, Glam., he left school at the age of thirteen to work in the local colliery. Having attended evening classes, he took degrees in economics at University College, Cardiff, and became a teacher at various schools in south Wales and finally headmaster of Bargoed Grammar Technical School in 1953. He published three volumes of autobiography,

namely *The Right Place, the Right Time* (1972), *Ups and Downs* (1975) and *The Blithe Ones* (1980). These books present an authentic, humorous and vivid picture of life in a mining community in the early years of the twentieth century and include a great deal of valuable information, including songs, about the folk-culture of industrial south Wales.

Davies, Wilfred Mitford (1895–1966), illustrator of children's books, was born at Menai Bridge, Ang., and brought up at Star, near Llanfairpwll. After serving in the First World War, he trained at the Liverpool School of Art and then worked as a commercial artist in that city. On his return to Wales in 1922 he was invited by Ifan ab Owen *Edwards to illustrate the magazine *Cymru'r Plant* and thus began an association with *Urdd Gobaith Cymru* which lasted for more than forty years. As an illustrator of children's books, he produced work which was a delight to younger readers and is now generally admired.

Davies, William (d. 1593), Catholic martyr, was a native of Croes-yn-Eirias, Caerns., a detached part of Llandrillo-yn-Rhos, Denbs. He became a priest in 1585 and, for part of the following year, lived in Rhiwledyn cave on the Little Orme, Caerns. There, with other Catholics, he was engaged with others in the re-printing of *Y Drych Cristianogawl*, almost certainly the first book to be printed in Wales. Arrested in 1592, he spent a year in prison at Beaumaris, during which he composed a carol. Refusing to recant and declining all offers of escape, he was executed on 27 July 1593.

DAVIES, WILLIAM (**Gwilym Teilo**; 1831–92), poet and local historian. Born near Llandeilo Fawr, Carms., he was an ardent supporter of the *National Eisteddfod at which he won many literary prizes. Among his published works are *Llandilo-Vawr and its Neighbourhood* (1858) and *Traethawd ar Caio a'i Hynafiaethau* (1862), and his best poem is '*Hen Goed y Benlan Fawr*'. His most important work, an essay which was intended as a continuation of Thomas *Stephens's *The Literature of the Kymry* (1849), remains unpublished.

The poems of Gwilym Teilo were collected after his death by P. H. Griffiths.

DAVIES, WILLIAM HENRY (1871–1940), poet. Born in Newport, Mon., the son of an iron-moulder who died in the writer's infancy, he was adopted soon after his mother's second marriage by his father's parents and brought up by them in the dockland public house to which his grandfather, a former sea-captain, had retired. He was educated at local elementary schools where he acquired a love of English poetry and the Bible. After leaving school, he was apprenticed to a picture-framer, absorbing from this work an appreciation of art. Walks in rural Gwent sharpened his interest in nature and friends encouraged him to extend his reading and persevere with his early attempts at composition.

In 1893, with an advance on the small weekly income he received as his grandmother's beneficiary, he set out for America where, unable to find regular employment, he became a tramp, taking occasional farm jobs, begging and wintering in gaols. He returned to Newport in 1898, squandering there and in London the greater part of the accumulated income from his share of his grandmother's estate before setting out for the Klondyke. In Ontario in March 1899, on his way to the goldfields, his right foot was crushed when he fell under the train on which he was trying to steal a ride, and his leg was amputated below the knee.

Fired with ambition to make his mark in the world of literature, he decided to settle in London and applied himself obsessively to the tasks of study and writing, despite continuous hardship and many disappointments. At length, his volume The Soul's Destroyer and Other Poems (1905) was published at his own expense. In large measure a social document, it did not meet with immediate success but recognition of the writer's gifts by George Bernard Shaw was soon followed by a review in The Daily Mail which effectively launched Davies as a poet. In the same year he was befriended by Edward *Thomas who provided him with a home in the cottage which he rented near Elses Farm, Sevenoaks. Davies's second book, New Poems (1906), an uneven collection in which the first glimpses of his mature manner are nevertheless observable, brought favourable reviews but little else. On the other hand, The *Autobiography of a Super-Tramp (1908), written at Edward Thomas's suggestion and revised under his direction, was an immediate critical success and sold steadily.

W. H. Davies was established as a poet with the publication of Nature Poems and others (1908), a collection which, though not lacking in subtlety, achieved its best effects by virtue of directness and simplicity in brief, lyrical forms. Somewhat better off as a result of his literary earnings, he moved in the summer of 1909 into lodgings in Sevenoaks, where he maintained a considerable output of prose and poetry which included Beggars (1909), a sequel to the Autobiography, and another volume of verse, Farewell to Poesy (1910). Anxious to win himself time and the financial security in which to devote himself to poetry, he next attempted a novel, but A Weak Woman (1911) has little to commend it. Songs of Joy (1911) is one of his finest books of verse, however, and it has some of his best-known lyrics, including the frequently anthologized poem, 'Leisure'. Also in 1911, again largely through the efforts of Edward Thomas, he was awarded a Civil List pension. His reputation as a

poet was confirmed by the inclusion of some of his lyrics in each of the five volumes of Georgian Poetry, the first of which appeared in 1912.

Soon after the publication of Foliage: Various Poems (1913), he moved to London where he widened his circle of acquaintance among writers and artists. Though never again so prolific as he had been in his Sevenoaks period, he continued to publish books of poems, including various selected and collected editions, almost annually, interspersed with occasional prose works, among them Later Days (1925), a further volume of reminiscences, and another unsuccessful novel, Dancing Mad (1927). His marriage to Helen Payne in 1923 had brought contentment to his life and a new emphasis to his work: the theme of married love has a significance almost as great as that of the delights of nature in the poems he wrote subsequently. He and his wife lived first in East Grinstead but towards the close of the 1920s they settled in Nailsworth, Glos.

W. H. Davies enjoyed, almost from the outset, a satisfying share of recognition among fellow-writers and from the public at large, official acknowledgement being made in the form of an Honorary Doctorate of the University of Wales in 1929. Keenly aware of his status and role as a poet, and a self-conscious artist, he deliberately focussed on the commonplace and, in contrast to the developing intellectualism in the mainstream of poetry in the 1920s and 1930s, eschewed complexity. Some of his work touches upon social injustice, hardship and pain, but the vast majority of the 636 pieces in The Poems of W. H. Davies (1940), published shortly before his death, express an uncomplicated delight in aspects of the natural world and human companionship. Though they lack intellectual rigour, his finest lyrics have a natural, memorable charm and are rightly praised for their simplicity and their sure control of form.

A study of his work was published by Richard Stonesifer in W. H. Davies: A Critical Biography (1963) and L. W. Hockey contributed an essay on the author in the Writers of Wales series (1971); see also the special number of Poetry Wales (vol. 18, no. 2, 1983) which is devoted to the poet's work, and the autobiographical novel, Young Emma (1980). A volume of W. H. Davies's Selected Poems, edited by Jonathan Barker, was published in 1985.

Davies Aberpennar, see DAVIES, PENNAR (1911–).

DAVIS, DAVID (Dafis Castellhywel; 1745–1827), schoolmaster and poet, was born at Llangybi, Cards., and educated at the College School and the Academy, Carmarthen, which he later recalled in verse. He was influenced there by the principal, Jenkin Jenkins, who held Arian views, but he did not become a Unitarian, although he publicly declared his sympathy with Joseph Priestley in 1770. Another influence upon him was Richard *Price, whose support for the cause of the French Revolution of 1789 is reflected in Davis's verse. At his famous school, opened at Castellhywel, Cards., about 1782, a number of well-known men received a sound classical education. Among his best poems are his *englynion* to the ruined mansion of Peterwell, near Lampeter, Cards., the former home of Herbert *Lloyd. He also translated some of the works of William Cowper, Alexander Pope and Isaac Watts into Welsh, as well as Gray's 'Elegy written in a Country Churchyard' (1750). His poetical works were collected in the volume *Telyn Dewi* (1824).

Ddinas, Y and **Y Ddolen**, see LONDON WELSHMAN.

De Excidio Britanniae (lit. 'On the destruction of Britain'; c.547), a Latin work attributed to *Gildas; another title is **Ormesta Britanniae**, a title in which '*ormesta*' is thought to represent a Welsh word, '*gormes*' or '*armes*'. A kind of open letter to the leaders of the Welsh, it denounces sin, warns of the crisis of the times, expresses a monk's prejudice against princes and parish priests, and a Romanophile's prejudice against promoters of the Brythonic revival and enthusiasts for radical asceticism. In respect of prophetic indignation and the idea that an unworthy nation receives punishment from God, Gildas was indebted to the Old Testament. The letter of the Brythons to Agitius (Aetius) asking for help (c.446) is quoted. *Vortigern is blamed for inviting the Saxons to Britain as mercenary troops and the general Ambrosius Aurelianus (*Emrys Wledig) is praised. The reference to the great victory of Mount Badon (*Mons Badonicus*, c.519) does not mention *Arthur. In illustration of the degeneracy of the Britons there are attacks on five contemporary kings, namely Constantinus (Devon and Cornwall?), Aurelius Caninus (the West Midlands of England?), Voteporix (Dyfed), Cuneglassus (mid-Wales?) and Maglocunus (*Maelgwn Gwynedd).

The work has been translated into English by Hugh Williams (1901) and Michael Winterbottom (1928), and into Welsh by J. O. Jones under the title O *Lygad y Ffynnon* (1899).

Death Bell, The (1954), Vernon *Watkins's third volume of poems, includes a number such as 'Music of Colours: the Blossom Scattered', 'Taliesin in Gower', 'The Turning of the Stars', 'The Heron', 'Woodpecker and Lyre-Bird', 'The Dead Shag' and 'The Shell', which are among his finest work. Others, such as 'Niobe', 'Climbing above the Cave' and most of the eight ballads (many of them early compositions) —especially 'Ballad of the Rough Sea'—are important to the understanding of the sources of poetic energy which Watkins developed from the limbo of 'grief' into which he had fallen as a young man. Less pleasing philosophically, though technically faultless, are the claims for the Muse as an agent of immortality found in the two parts of 'Pledges to Darkness' and 'Art and the Ravens'. The title-poem, 'The Death Bell', is an elegy for the poet's father, one of the more obscure and less effective pieces in the volume.

Deaths and Entrances (1946), Dylan *Thomas's fourth volume of poetry, is substantially dominated by seven poems written in response to the experience of bombing raids on London. They are characterized by an affirmative sense of the resilience of a life-force which is celebrated in elemental, sexual and religious (though not necessarily Christian) terms, an emphasis found in the very titles of the poems, such as 'A Refusal to Mourn the Death, by Fire, of a Child in London' and 'Ceremony after a Fire Raid'. Against the background of that experience of war stand two of Thomas's most famous poems, 'Poem in October' and *'Fern Hill', which explore the adult's memories of childhood in relation to the world of nature and the poetry of place. Possibly in reaction to the moral shock of war, these poems embark on a theme—the nature of innocence, explored in a pastoral idiom —which was intended to be the principal concern of the poems in his next volume, *In Country Sleep* (1952), and of *Under Milk Wood* (1954). Other poems express, both directly and obliquely, the experience and tensions of the poet's marriage. The book illustrates Dylan Thomas's expert control over a widening variety of verse-forms, rhyme-patterns and line-lengths, and it consolidated the gradual move away from what sometimes tended to be rhythmic monotony in his earlier verse. The book was republished in a de luxe edition by the *Gregynog Press in 1984, with an introduction by Walford *Davies.

Declaimer or **Datgeiniad**, a lowly grade of poet in the Middle Ages. He could play the harp or *crwth and declaim a poem, but not his own, to musical accompaniment, or merely sing to the rhythm of a tapping stick. A jack-of-all-trades, he was expected to know the eight parts of speech, the syllables, the rules of *cynghanedd and the main classifications of prosody. In addition, he was employed as a servant by the master-poets, in whose company he had an opportunity of improving his acquaintance with their art.

DEE, JOHN (1527–1608), mathematician, astronomer, philosopher, magician, geographer, antiquary, propagandist and spy, was the magus of his age and the successor to Robert *Recorde as interpreter and popularizer of science. Born at Mortlake, Surrey, of a father from Pilleth, Rads., he claimed descent from Llewelyn Crugeryr and cousinship with Blanche *Parry, John *Lewis of Llynwene and many others in the March. He enrolled at St. John's College, Cambridge, in 1542, and became Fellow of the newly-founded Trinity College four years later; but, dissatisfied with the backwardness of English universities in mathematics and science, he left Cambridge in 1548 and in 1550 was lecturing in Paris to enormous acclaim. Established a year later at Edward VI's court, he barely survived the Marian persecution to become Elizabeth's consultant in State affairs, including the reform of the Julian calendar.

In 1576 Dee worked on a series of *Titles*, now lost, which set out his concept of a British Empire. Based on the work of William Lambard, that of the Venetian Zeno brothers and the polar maps of Dee's friend, Gerard Mercator, the *Titles* claimed not only Scandinavia and the Arctic but islands westward as far as a supposed Estotiland (perhaps Newfoundland) as the conquests of ★Arthur. In his *Title-Royal* presented to the Queen in 1580 Dee, dissatisfied with Mercator's chronology (according to Siôn Dafydd ★Rhys), reinforced his Arthurian claims by bringing the story of ★Madog ab Owain Gwynedd into the northern hemisphere. Whether or not the Queen was impressed, royal patronage of Dee was no more than occasional. His unique reputation was marred in the years after 1582 by his accounts of intercourse with spirits (his partner, Edward Kelley, was revealed as an impostor) and a mysterious invitation to Poland in 1584 kept him abroad until 1589. In 1596 he was given the Wardenship of Christ's College, Manchester.

Dee's treatises, in great number, remain in manuscript but his works on hieroglyphics were published abroad in his lifetime and his diary in England much later. His most accessible writings are his augmentation of Recorde's *The Ground of Artes* (1561), his 'Mathematical Preface' to the English translation of *Euclid* (1570) made by Henry Billingsley of Penhow Castle, and *Memorials pertayining to the Perfect Arte of Navigation* (1577).

For further details see Richard Deacon, *John Dee* (1968), Peter J. French, *John Dee: the World of an Elizabethan Magus* (1972) and O. E. Roberts, *Dr. John Dee* (1980); see also Gwyn A. Williams, *The Welsh in their History* (1982).

Deffrobani, see under GWLAD YR HAF and HU GADARN.

Deffynniad Ffydd Eglwys Loegr (lit. 'A defence of the faith of the Church of England'; 1594), a Welsh translation by Morris ★Kyffin of the first defence of Anglican doctrine, namely *Apologia Ecclesiae Anglicanae* (1562) by Bishop John Jewel. Kyffin's intention was to benefit the language as well as the religion of Wales, so scarce were Welsh printed books, and in his introduction he pleaded for the printing of Welsh books and condemned those who opposed it. Acknow-

ledged to be one of the early masters of Welsh prose, he sought to write smoothly, naturally and intelligibly, and in spite of occasional errors he succeeded remarkably well. Although his book appeared after William ★Morgan's Bible (1588), and notwithstanding his praise of Morgan and chiding of William ★Salesbury, his work is less standardized in accordance with the Bible than might have been expected.

There is an excellent modern edition of his work by W. P. Williams (1908) and a discussion of it in W. J. Gruffydd's *Llenyddiaeth Cymru* (1926).

Degannwy, the traditional seat of the court of ★Maelgwn Gwynedd near Conwy, Caerns. A castle was built on the site by order of Robert of Rhuddlan in the eleventh century and there he met his death at the hands of ★Gruffudd ap Cynan. In the *Oianau* in The ★*Black Book of Carmarthen* reference is made to 'making a strong fortress of Degannwy' against the invasion of north Wales by King John in 1211. The castle changed hands several times and was rebuilt for King Henry III in 1245; in the war of that year an English army was encamped there, suffering terrible privation. After 1282 the castle was superseded by the new one built by order of Edward I at ★Conwy.

Deheubarth, a kingdom founded during the reign of ★Hywel Dda when the Vale of Tywi, ★Ceredigion and ★Dyfed were combined, bringing that part of south-west Wales lying to the west of the rivers Teifi and Tawe under the authority of a royal line which was to rule it, although not without interruption, until Rhys ap Tewdwr was killed in 1093. The Norman lords then extended their power over the territory but in 1136, after the death of Henry I, Gruffudd ap Rhys began a campaign which eventually brought about a restoration of the kingdom. The Normans were never expelled from Dyfed nor from the lordships of the southern reaches of the Tywi, but the remainder of that province, namely ★Cantref Mawr, ★Cantref Bychan and Ceredigion, became a strong kingdom under the rule of the youngest of Gruffudd ap Rhys's sons, ★Rhys ap Gruffudd, who was known as *Yr Arglwydd Rhys* (The Lord Rhys).

With ★Gwynedd and ★Powys, Deheubarth was one of the three kingdoms of Wales in the twelfth century. It was ruled from ★Dinefwr which was listed, together with ★Mathrafal and ★Aberffraw, as one of the three chief courts of Wales. The most reliable evidence for the significance of Deheubarth belongs to this period, when Rhys ap Gruffudd consolidated his family's political gains and established a relationship with the King of England, Henry II, who acknowledged the Welshman's authority over the wider kingdom. The strength of Deheubarth under Rhys ap Gruffudd is reflected in the work of the poets *Cynddelw Brydydd Mawr and *Gwynfardd Brycheiniog and the patronage which Rhys extended to the Cistercian monasteries at *Whitland and *Strata Florida, and to the Premonstratensian monastery at Talyllychau (*Talley), is an indication of the kingdom's importance. It is also certain that the lawyers of Deheubarth during his reign left their mark on the law-books which survive, in Welsh and Latin, from later periods. A notable example of Deheubarth's literary tradition exists in the form of a Latin poem composed on the occasion of Rhys ap Gruffudd's death in 1197.

Towards the end of Rhys's reign there was tension between his sons over who should inherit the kingdom. The succession of the chosen heir, Gruffudd ap Rhys (d. 1201), was opposed by his half-brother, Maelgwn ap Rhys (d. 1236), and other members of the family joined in the dispute. However, none of them succeeded in gaining complete supremacy and eventually it was agreed that the patrimony of Deheubarth should be shared by the sons and grandsons of Rhys ap Gruffudd. The lands were divided in the presence of *Llywelyn ap Iorwerth (Llywelyn Fawr) in 1216, an occasion which reflects the fact that the Prince of Gwynedd had established an authority which formed the basis for the greater power which *Llywelyn ap Gruffudd later wielded in Deheubarth. Some space is given in *Brut y Tywysogyon to the fate of the lords and lands of Deheubarth. The lineage was praised by poets such as *Phylip Brydydd, *Prydydd Bychan, *Llywarch ap Llywelyn (Prydydd y Moch) and *Bleddyn Fardd.

Llywelyn ap Gruffudd maintained his authority over Deheubarth for twenty years, but his authority was shaken in the war of 1277 as Edward I tightened his grip on the province. With the sole exception of Rhys ap Maredudd, the lords of Deheubarth rose in support of Llywelyn ap Gruffudd in 1282. Rhys ap Maredudd benefited from their defeat, but within five years he too rose in rebellion with the result that the line of Deheubarth was destroyed completely and for all time. In establishing the Province of South Wales, Edward I created an administrative unit out of a territory which was similar to the old Deheubarth over which Rhys ap Gruffudd had ruled.

For further details see J. E. Lloyd, A History of Wales (1911), R. A. Griffiths, The Principality of Wales in the Later Middle Ages (vol. 1, 1972) and Wendy Davies, Wales in the Early Middle Ages (1982).

Deian a Loli (1927), a novel by Kate *Roberts, is a short tale about, rather than for, children. The two eponymous characters are twins, a boy and a girl who—although close to each other—have their own unique personalities, and the book describes their emotional development up to the time they leave elementary school. The novel's sequel was Laura Jones (1930).

Deiniol (mid-6th cent.), saint, the founder of *Bangor in Arfon, was also connected with Bangor Is-coed to the east, the most important of the Brythonic monasteries (in Bede's judgement) before its destruction at the Battle of Chester (c.615). According to the genealogies, Deiniol was one of the same stock as *Urien Rheged. His associations are with north-west Wales, particularly Gwynedd, but he is also commemorated by churches in the west and south. He came to be regarded as the first Bishop of Bangor and it was the extent of his cult which largely determined the boundaries of the diocese from the Norman period onwards. According to Liber Landavensis (The Book of *Llandâf), he was consecrated bishop by *Dyfrig (Dubricius) and his name appears in connection with the latter in the Life of *Dewi Sant. Named by *Gerald de Barri (Giraldus Cambrensis) as one of the saints buried on the island of *Bardsey, he was often mentioned in the work of medieval poets, among them *Dafydd ap Gwilym. Deiniol's feast-day is 11 September.

DEIO AB IEUAN DU (fl. 1450–80), poet, whose home was in the parish of Llangynfelyn, Cards., had patrons in Cardiganshire, Merioneth, Denbighshire and Glamorgan. Three of his poems are notable: one is an attempt at reconciling Gruffudd Fychan of *Corsygedol and Rhys ap Maredudd of Tywyn, another is a greeting to Maredudd ap Llywelyn of Genau'r Glyn on his being rescued from a shipwreck in the Dyfi estuary, and the third expresses the poet's thanks to Siôn ap Rhys of Glyn-nedd for the gift of a bull. The last poem contains the well-known line, 'Y ddraig goch ddyry cychwyn' ('The red dragon will show the way'), which is used, together with the *Red Dragon, on the royal badge for Wales.

Deio'r Cantwr, see JONES, DAFYDD (1803–68).

Delw y Byd (lit. 'The form of the world'), a description of men and places throughout the known world, is found in medieval manuscripts, the oldest of which is Peniarth 17 (c.1250). It is a translation of the first part of a treatise entitled Imago Mundi by Honorius Augustodunensis, written presumably about 1122. To that author is also attributed the Elucidarium which appears under the title Hystoria Lucidar in The *Book of the Anchorite.

The translation was edited by Henry Lewis and P. Diverres in 1928.

'Delyn Aur, Y' (lit. 'The golden harp'), a hymn-tune of uncertain origin which is usually sung to the words 'Dechrau canu, dechrau canmol' by William *Williams (Pantycelyn). Although described in most hymn-books as a Welsh tune, it is not included in any of the early collections and was first published in Ail Lyfr Tonau ac Emynau (ed. Stephen and Jones) in 1879. In his *Welsh Church Tune and Chant Book* (1859), Thomas Jones refers to it as a tune of 'trashy character', from which it may be deduced that it was sung during the religious revival of 1859. The tune was arranged for male voices by David Pugh Evans (1866–97) and is still a favourite with the choirs of Wales.

Demetae, The, one of the five principal tribes of pre-Roman and Roman Wales listed by the geographer Ptolemy (2nd cent.), occupied the south-western extremity bounded by the rivers Teifi and Tywi. Little is known of their early history for they seem not to have resisted the Roman advance. The relative absence of Roman forts (cf. the territory of the *Silures) and the apparently peaceful transition, discovered at Walesland Rath, Pembs., from a pre-Roman settlement with round huts to a single rectangular building and Romanized pottery, suggest a settled pastoralism in the area. The substantial Roman fort at Moridunum (Carmarthen), established about AD 75, probably had more to do with an easy land connection for ships guarding the Irish Sea than with control of the lands of the Demetae. Of the other three Roman sites, two—at Castle Flemish on the road from Maenclochog to St. David's and at Cwmbrwyn which commands the Taf valley south of Llanddowror —were no more than small signal stations set up early in the second century. The third, Ptolemy's Luentinum, is more significant: it is usually now identified with the Dolaucothi gold mines near Pumsaint, Carms., probably worked in a small way by the Demetae in pre-Roman times and certainly operated by state monopoly during the Roman period.

The passivity of the Demetae poses a further problem. Towards the end of the fourth century AD the Deisi, a tribe settled on the banks of the river Blackwater in southern Ireland, entered Demetian territory and assumed military dominance. The early Irish epic, *The Expulsion of the Deisi*, which describes a mass migration under a king named Eochaid Allmuir, is now regarded as onomastic and unreliable. It is more likely that a chief and his war-band were planted by the Romans to keep other Irish invaders out of south-west Wales. A list of the Irish kings of Demetia is preserved in both Irish and Welsh sources and includes the sixth-century Voteporix (or *Protector*, the Roman title for a *foederatus*) who was inveighed against by *Gildas. This dynasty may have become aggressive, for one view is that the *llannau* along the Teifi were built (with Breton help) as defences against the Irish. *Dewi Sant, brought up at Hen Fynyw, north of the river, directed his main missionary activity towards the extreme south-west of the peninsula, where he is said to have encountered Irish hostility. The numerical superiority of the Demetae finally ensured the triumph of the

Welsh language over the Irish. Memorial stones in the area, which from the sixth century had been inscribed both in *Ogam and in Latin, ceased to show Ogam by the tenth, a development which perhaps also reflected the end of the Irish dynasty with the death of Llywarch in 892 and the virtual annexation of Demetian territory by *Hywel Dda.

For further details see Barry Cunliffe, *Iron Age Communities in Britain* (1974) and V. E. Nash-Williams, *The Roman Frontier in Wales* (1954).

Denbigh castle, was built by order of Henry de Lacy, Earl of Lincoln, after he had been granted the lordship in 1282. The construction of the castle and the walls of the associated borough was impeded by the attacks launched during the *Welsh Revolt of 1294. During the Wars of the Roses the castle, with its lordship, was one of the main Yorkist bastions in Wales. The right of possession was contested by Jasper *Tudor and William, Lord Herbert of Raglan. Among the members of prominent local families associated with the castle was Roger *Salusbury of Lleweni, constable and porter in 1506, whose praises were sung by *Tudur Aled and *Lewys Môn. In 1563 Denbigh was granted to Robert Dudley, Earl of Leicester, who built near by a new church intended to be the cathedral church of north-east Wales. In the *Civil Wars the castle was held for the King by William Salesbury of Y *Rug but it was captured at last in October 1646, after a siege by Parliamentary forces lasting six months. The castle began to fall into ruins after the Restoration of Charles II in 1660. *The Survey of the Honour of Denbigh*, compiled in 1334 and published under the editorship of P. Vinogredoff and F. M. Morgan in 1914, is the most important single document on the structure of Marcher society.

For further details see the article by W. J. Hemp in *Y Cymmrodor* (vol. XXXVI, 1925), Frank Price Jones, *Crwydro Gorllewin Dinbych* (1969), L. A. S. Butler, *Denbigh Castle, Town Walls and Friary* (1976) and the chapter by D. Huw Owen in *Boroughs of Medieval Wales* (ed. R. A. Griffiths, 1978).

Deorham or **Dyrham, The Battle of** (577), one of the decisive battles, fought near Bath, in the bitter struggle between the British and the Saxons. The victory of the invaders, led by Cuthwine and Ceawlin, marked the first stage in the separation of the early Welsh from their compatriots in south-west Britain: the Severn Valley and the towns of Gloucester, Cirencester and Bath were overrun and land communications between Wales and Devon and Cornwall severed.

Depression, The, a term used to describe the economic failures, social misery and political unrest of the years between the World Wars. This period saw the collapse of all the old heavy industries established in Britain during the

*Industrial Revolution. In Wales there was a decline in the metallurgical and coal industries, as well as a virtual shut-down of the busy export ports along the southern coast. The numbers employed in coalmining alone fell from 270,000 in 1920 to 128,000 by 1939. The population of Wales was drained away to the new industrial areas of England with a total decline (in removals and loss of natural increase) of nearly half a million persons. The standard of living fell, nutritional deficiencies marred the health of more than one generation and a culture of unemployment settled on south Wales, a region of which the rate of long-term, mass unemployment exceeded that for any other part of Britain. The period was punctuated by political militancy and also served to root the Labour Party's collectivist reformism deep into the Welsh psyche as the main practical avenue to social justice in the future.

Among the poets whose work reflected the proletarian ethos of south Wales during the Depression were Gwenallt (David James *Jones), J. Kitchener *Davies and Idris *Davies, while many novels, such as those of Gwyn *Thomas (1913–81) and Lewis *Jones, were set in this period. See also GENERAL STRIKE, HUNGER MARCHES and JAZZ BANDS.

For further details see D. H. Aldcroft, *The Inter-War Economy: Britain 1919–1939)* (1970), W. Branson and M. Heinemann, *Britain in the 1930s* (1971), J. Stevenson and C. Cook, *The Slump: Society and Politics during the Depression* (1977), and Stephen Constantine, *Social Conditions in Britain 1918–1939* (1983).

Derfel Gadarn (6th cent.), saint, was reputed to have been a soldier who had taken part in the battle of *Camlan (*c.*539). At Llandderfel, Mer., there was once a famous wooden statue of him, mounted on a horse and holding a staff. The effigy was removed in 1538 by order of Thomas Cromwell, in order to put a stop to the common people's veneration of it, and then used to feed the bonfire on which a Franciscan friar was executed at Smithfield. Later, a wooden horse placed on the summit of Bryn Derfel commemorated the traditions associated with the saint.

DERFEL, ROBERT JONES (1824–1905), writer and Radical, was born near Llandderfel, Mer. He adopted the name *Derfel as his own surname after moving to Manchester where he was a commercial traveller for most of his life. As a lay-preacher with the *Baptists, he contributed to denominational journals but later came under the influence of Socialist and agnostic ideas, suggesting in a letter to Y *Cymro in 1903 that Robert *Owen should replace *Dewi Sant as the patron saint of Wales. His play *Brad y Llyfrau Gleision* (1854), which is about the Treachery of the *Blue Books, and his volume of essays, *Traethodau ac Areithiau* (1864), show his patriotic zeal. A powerful advocate of *Rad-

icalism, he was still writing articles at the turn of the century in an attempt at integrating Christianity, *Socialism and *Nationalism in a Welsh context.

A selection of R. J. Derfel's prose-works was edited by D. Gwenallt Jones (2 vols., 1945).

Deryn Mawr, Y, see JONES, GRUFFYDD (*fl.* 1880).

'Deryn Pur, Y' (lit. 'The pure bird'), a folk-song first published by Maria Jane Williams (see under ABERPERGWM) in *Ancient National Airs of Gwent and Morganwg* (1844), with words from two verses of the poem '*Y deryn pur a'r adain las*' which are traditionally attributed to Dafydd *Nicolas.

Descriptio Kambriae (lit. 'The description of Wales'; 1193), by *Gerald de Barri (Giraldus Cambrensis), like the *Itinerarium Kambriae (1191), was the fruit of the author's journey through Wales with Archbishop Baldwin in 1181. But whereas the earlier work was a direct reflection of his experiences and thoughts on the journey, the *Descriptio* is a meditation on the nature of Wales and its people. It is a formal composition in two contrasting parts, the one describing the people's virtues and the other their faults. On the one hand he praises their culture, their bravery, their wit, their wiser customs, their warm hospitality and their respect for breeding; on the other, he contrasts their deceit and dishonesty, their lack of respect for boundaries and oaths, and their foolish customs such as those governing the inheritance of land and the fostering of children. The work is of the utmost value to social historians and succeeds in revealing much of the author's own attitudes in what is a consciously literary work. It ends with his advice to the English and Welsh on how to draw the best out of each other. Gerald's attitude is sometimes ambiguous and he cannot be completely impartial, but the book ends with a declaration of faith in the justice of the Welsh cause and the prophecy of the *Old Man of Pencader.

Description of Wales (1584), a work by Humphrey *Llwyd (Lhuyd). The author had translated *Brut y Tywysogyon into English from a lost version which combined the texts of the three extant versions. Its historical record ended in 1270 but Llwyd added an appendix to 1295 and also used material by Matthew Paris, Nicholas Trivet and *Geoffrey of Monmouth, among other sources. The work, entitled *Cronica Walliae*, was written in 1559 and began with the 'Description of Wales', a section written originally by Sir John *Price of Brecon, but translated and extended by Llwyd. He wrote on each Welsh prince or ruler, from *Cadwaladr (late 7th cent.) to Madog ap Llywelyn (late 13th cent.). It was Llwyd who first referred to the legend of *Madog ab Owain Gwynedd and provided the first clear exposition of the theory of the Early British Church. As a Renaissance scholar and antiquary it was Llwyd's aim to make known and popularize the history of medieval Wales and maintain its most cherished traditions. The work was popular in manuscript and, on the request of Sir Henry Sidney, President of the Council in the Marches, it was prepared for publication, with corrections and additions, by David *Powel of Ruabon, and entitled *The Historie of Cambria* (1584).

Devastated Hearth, The, a motif forming part of a series of stanzas in the cycle known as *'Canu Llywarch Hen'*, which are associated with *Urien Rheged. In the first two sections, Llywarch mourns the death of Urien, his cousin, whose body has been left lying on the battlefield, but whose head he has cut off, presumably to prevent it from being desecrated by the enemy. The third section is a lament not only for Urien himself, but for his entire court. The contrast between former splendour and the desolation of the present is more than mere nostalgia for a glorious past: in an age when the hall was synonymous with protection and prosperity, its ruin was the symbol of the destruction of the community which it had served.

Devil, The, is the subject of numerous traditions and tales in Welsh folklore, most of which reflect the age-old battle between Good and Evil. Some tell how the Devil interferes with church bells and services or attempts to prevent the building of churches, but is thwarted by the parson. Because a priest entered a church by the south door, the door in the north wall by which the Devil fled was known as the Devil's Door and it was left open during services to facilitate the departure of Evil. The graveyard on the northern side of the church was where suicides, criminals and unchristened infants were buried.

The Devil was reputed to have built a number of bridges such as Devil's Bridge, Cards., and the popular belief was that he was entitled to the soul of the first person or animal to cross a new bridge. He also had the power to carry people through the air, sometimes with terrible consequences, as is vividly described in the poem by Talhaiarn (John *Jones), 'Sôn am Ysbrydion', an adaptation of Robert Burns's 'Tam O'Shanter' (1790). Those who could raise and subdue spirits were said to have sold their souls to the Devil. There is a traditional belief that the poet *Siôn Cent was among those who contended with the Devil.

In the nineteenth century the playing of cards and travel on the Sabbath were said to attract the Devil, usually in the form of a gentleman with the feet of a goat or horse. He was sometimes seen by sinners in the shape of a horned, black-faced shepherd leading a pack of dogs, or as a small black sow known as *Yr *Hwch Ddu Gota*. Priests, soothsayers and others practised special methods of resisting the Devil's power. The most common names by which the Devil was known in Welsh were *Y Diawl, Y Cythraul, Yr Hen Fachgen, Yr Hen Law, Yr Hen Nic, Y Giaffar, Liwsiffer* and *Andras*.

For further details see Elias Owen, *Welsh Folk-lore* (1896) and T. Gwynn Jones, *Welsh Folklore and Folk Custom* (1930).

Devolution, a term which in its political sense denotes the process by which power is transferred from the centre to the periphery, was used during the 1970s in connection with the British Government's proposals for the creation of elected Assemblies in Wales and Scotland. Largely in response to an increase in support for *Plaid Cymru and the Scottish National Party, but also reflecting a body of opinion within the Labour and Liberal Parties, the Government established a Royal Commission on the Constitution in 1968 which published its findings in 1973 in a document known (after the name of its Chairman, Lord Kilbrandon) as *The Kilbrandon Report*. The general principle of Devolution was accepted by the Government and detailed proposals were set out in the discussion papers entitled *Devolution and Democracy* (1974) and *Our Changing Democracy* (1975; supplementary statement, 1976). After a long debate over the complexities of the issue, the Government's plans were fully revealed in the Wales and Scotland Bill which proposed a legislative Assembly for Scotland and an executive Assembly for Wales. The Bill was fiercely contested in the House of Commons by members on both sides who represented constituencies in England and it was eventually defeated on a time-tabling motion. Two separate Bills were then introduced and the one for Wales passed into law as the Wales Act (1978).

The Act's provision for the transference of some responsibilities of government from London to Cardiff, and for the creation of a new tier of administration in the form of an elected Assembly with limited powers, immediately revealed the fissiparous nature of society in Wales and caused debate which raged for more than a year. All the political parties in Wales, with the exception of the Conservative Party, traditionally centralist, were officially in favour of the principle of Devolution. However, there was opposition towards the Government's proposals on the part of certain Welsh Labour Members of Parliament, notably some of those representing constituencies in industrial south-east Wales such as Leo Abse, the member for Pontypool (now Torfaen), and Neil Kinnock, the member for Bedwellty (now Islwyn). In rebellion against their own party, these members (assisted by several members for English constituencies, both Labour and Conservative) led a campaign at Westminster and in Wales against the Devolution proposals and succeeded in making the implementation of the Act dependent on the result of a referendum in which at least forty per cent of the electorate would be required to vote in favour. The level of the public debate which followed was not high, and the opponents of the Assembly found it easy to expose the weaknesses or ambiguities of the Act, so much so that the electorate soon became confused and dubious. Among the groups and individuals who declared themselves in favour of the Assembly were the Wales Trades Union Council and a number of the most eminent writers of Wales, both Welsh and Anglo-Welsh, who signed an open letter which was published in The *Anglo-Welsh Review (no. 64, 1979). Although officially committed to support for Devolution, the major political parties were lukewarm in their attitude towards the Act, while Plaid Cymru, which considered the provisions as falling far short of what was required for Wales, did not campaign with any enthusiasm.

The referendum campaign culminated on St. David's Day, 1 March 1979, when the vote was taken. A total of 1,199,378 persons (some 58% of the electorate) cast their votes, of whom 243,048 were in favour and 956,330 against the Government's proposals. In Scotland, a small majority voted in favour but the result did not adequately fulfil the conditions laid down. The Wales and Scotland Acts were repealed by the Conservative Government which came to power in May 1979.

The crushing defeat of the Devolution proposals confirmed the apparent lack of enthusiasm in Wales for a small measure of self-government, at least in the form offered, which was as pronounced in 1979 as it had been during the *Cymru Fydd débâcle of 1896. A marked feature of both debates was the lack of common ground between the population in the rural, Welsh-speaking parts of north and west Wales and that in the English-speaking conurbations of the industrial south-east. But even the largely Welsh-speaking county of Gwynedd, which registered the highest percentage of votes in favour, showed a two-to-one majority against the Devolution proposals. The result of the referendum therefore seemed more like the end of an older phase of Welsh national politics rather than the beginning of a new thrust towards self-government. There then followed, against a background of economic crisis and high unemployment, a period of re-assessment by all those concerned with the social and cultural life of Wales. See also HOME RULE and PARLIAMENT FOR WALES CAMPAIGN.

For detailed accounts of the debate over Devolution in Wales see Harry Calvert (ed.), Devolution (1975), John Osmond, The Centralist Enemy (1974) and Creative Conflict (1977), Vernon Bogdanor, Devolution (1979), Kenneth O. Morgan, Rebirth of a Nation: Wales 1880–1980 (1981) and The Welsh Veto (ed. David Foulkes, J. Barry Jones and R. A. Wilford, 1983); see also John Osmond (ed.), The National Question Again (1985).

DEW ROBERTS, BARBARA (1885?–1963), historian and novelist, was born Elizabeth Mary Dew Roberts (or Roberts Dew) at Plas Dinam, Caernarfon. Extremely reticent about her age and personal history, she was brought up by her aunt, educated at Cheltenham Ladies' College and employed during the First World War at the Admiralty and in Salonika. Some of her writing was done at Neuadd Tryfan, Rhostryfan, Caerns., which she owned, but her last years were spent in rooms at Llanfaglan. From 1932 she published historical articles, chiefly about Anglesey, in The *Welsh Outlook, edited the diary of William *Bulkeley of Brynddu under the title Mr. Bulkeley and the Pirate (1936) and wrote Mitre and Musket (1938), a life of John Williams, Archbishop of York under Charles I. She then turned to fiction, publishing the historical novels Still Glides the Stream (1940), Some Trees Stand (1945), The Island Feud (1947) and The Charlie Trees (1951), all of which are set in north Wales.

Dewi Dywyll, see JONES, DAFYDD (1803–68).

Dewi Emlyn, see DAVIES, DAVID (1817–88).

Dewi Emrys, see JAMES, DAVID EMRYS (1881–1952).

Dewi Haran (**David Evans**; 1812–85), see under CLIC Y BONT.

Dewi Havhesp, see ROBERTS, DAVID (1831–84).

Dewi Hefin, see THOMAS, DAVID (1828–1909).

Dewi Medi, see JONES, DAFYDD (1803–68).

Dewi Sant or **St. David** (6th cent.), the patron saint of Wales. Little is known for certain about him. He may have died in the year 589, the date given by *Rhigyfarch who wrote his Life in Latin towards the end of the eleventh century. Although there are some earlier references to Dewi, most of what is believed about him is derived from this Life. There it is said that his mother was *Non and his father Sant, the son of Ceredig, King of *Ceredigion. Educated first at Hen Fynyw (to the south of Aberaeron) and subsequently by Paulinus, perhaps in Llanddeusant, he went on a pilgrimage through parts of south Wales and the west of England, where it is related that he founded important religious centres such as Glastonbury and Croyland. He settled in Glyn Rhosyn (L. Vallis Rosina, i.e. *St. David's) after defeating an Irish chieftain named Boia, and a very detailed account is given of the strict ascetic life required in the community which he established there. With *Teilo and *Padarn, Dewi went on a pilgrimage to Jerusalem, where he was consecrated archbishop. Although many miracles were attributed to him, his greatest feat was his preaching at the Synod of Llanddewibrefi, the ground rising under him so that all could see and hear him, after which he was made archbishop and his city proclaimed as a metropolis of the whole land. It should be remembered, however, that Rhigyfarch's father was *Sulien, Bishop of St. David's, and that the purpose of the Life was to demonstrate Dewi's superiority, in order to defend the independence of St. David's from encroachment by Canterbury and the Normans. It was an appeal to 'history', although credence can hardly be given to the history presented in it. Later, more than one version of the Latin Life was produced, one of them by *Gerald de Barri (Giraldus Cambrensis) and, some time during the first part of the fourteenth century, an unknown author produced an abridged version in Welsh which is preserved in The *Book of the Anchorite.

After the twelfth century Dewi's fame and cult spread rapidly throughout south Wales, to Ireland and to Brittany. There is more than one reference to him in Irish sources from the eighth and ninth centuries and, in a part of Wales like Demetia where there was little Roman influence, the Irish language must have been spoken and contacts with Ireland maintained during his lifetime. In a letter to the Pope written between 1124 and 1130 the chapter of St. David's claimed that Dewi was an archbishop and that he had been consecrated by his predecessor, *Dyfrig (Dubricius). Likewise, *Geoffrey of Monmouth and Gerald de Barri state that the seat of the archbishopric was originally at *Caerleon-on-Usk, in Dyfrig's territory. The cathedral of St. David's became popular as a place of pilgrimage, especially after Dewi had been officially recognized as a saint of the Catholic Church by Pope Callixtus in 1120. In 1398 Archbishop Arundel ordained that Dewi's feast-day be kept by every church in the Province of Canterbury. Already the author of the poem *'Armes Prydein' (c.930) had referred to him as saint and leader of the Welsh, but from the twelfth century on he became prominent in the work of the poets, including *Gwynfardd Brycheiniog, *Dafydd Llwyd ap Llywelyn, *Iolo Goch, Ieuan ap Rhydderch, *Lewys Glyn Cothi (Llywelyn y Glyn) and Rhisiart ap Rhys. The feast of Dewi as a religious festival ceased with the Protestant Reformation in the sixteenth century, but the day of his birth, or perhaps death (1 March), became a national festival among the Welsh during the eighteenth century, and is celebrated today by patriotic and cultural societies and in the schools of Wales.

The Life of Dewi was edited by D. Simon Evans, *Buchedd Dewi* (1959), and studies of the saint's life have been published by E. G. Bowen (1982, 1983): see also the chapter entitled 'The Tradition of St. David in Wales' by Glanmor Williams in *Religion, Language and Nationality in Wales* (1979).

Dewi Wyn o Eifion, see OWEN, DAVID (1784–1841).

Dewi Wyn o Essyllt (**Thomas Essile Davies**; 1820–91), see under CLIC Y BONT.

Dewisland or **Pebidiog**, one of the seven cantrefi of *Dyfed, was ruled by the successors of *Dewi Sant. After the Norman incursions into west Wales, the cantref became Marcher territory with the Bishop of St. *David's enjoying the status of a Lord of the March.

Dewisol Ganiadau yr Oes Hon (lit. 'A selection of poems of this age'; 1759), an anthology edited by Huw Jones of Llangwm, is in two sections, the one consisting of *awdlau*, *cywyddau* and *englynion*, and the other of songs and carols. The authors represented in the first section are William Wynn of Llangynhafal, Goronwy *Owen, Ieuan Brydydd Hir (Evan *Evans), Rhys *Jones of Blaenau, Edward Jones of Bodfari, Edward *Samuel and Hugh *Hughes of Anglesey, all of whom were Churchmen. In the second part there are poems by the editor and by the folk-poets Elis *Roberts, Jonathan *Hughes, Daniel and Thomas Jones of Ruabon, Hugh Jones of Park, and Thomas Edwards. There is more variety in this book than in the editor's other collection, *Dyddanwch Teuluaidd* (1763) and, because it contained works by poets of local repute, it proved very popular and had run to five editions by 1827.

Dewma, see LLANTARNAM.

Dial-a-Poem, a scheme launched by the *Welsh Arts Council in 1970. Each week, over a period of four years, a poet recorded a poem which could be heard by callers on the telephone. The first of its kind in Britain, the service aroused a great deal of public interest, with several hundred calls being made every week. From 1975 to 1979 it continued under the aegis of the South-East Wales Arts Association.

Dialect, the variant spoken forms of the language which have enriched Welsh literature for many centuries. In such early works as *Pedair Cainc y Mabinogi*, in *cywyddau* from the medieval period and even in William *Morgan's *Bible, it is possible to recognize dialect forms. They are even more evident in the works of Morgan *Llwyd, Ellis *Wynne, Theophilus *Evans, William *Williams (Pantycelyn) and especially so in *interludes and *ballads.

There were, however, few deliberate attempts to write in dialect until the nineteenth century. Among the first writers to employ it were William *Rees (Gwilym Hiraethog), David *Owen

(Brutus) and Daniel ★Owen. During the twentieth century the tendency to write dialogue in dialect, whenever appropriate, has increased steadily. Kate ★Roberts, who championed the use of dialect in an article in *Y ★Llenor* in 1931, wrote dialogue in the spoken Welsh of Rhosgadfan, Caerns., her native district. The characters created by D. J. ★Williams speak the dialect of north-east Carmarthenshire, but only in inverse proportion to their sophistication and snobbishness. E. Tegla ★Davies put the speech of Iâl (Yale), Denbs., into the mouths of Tomi and Nedw, just as Islwyn ★Williams used the dialect of the Swansea Valley in his short stories. Among dramatists who have made effective use of dialect are W. S. ★Jones and Gwenlyn ★Parry. The most remarkable novel in which both dialogue and narrative are written in dialect, namely that of Bethesda, Caerns., is ★*Un Nos Ola Leuad* (1961) by Caradog ★Prichard. A number of famous poems have been written in dialect, including '*Anfon y Nico*' by Albert ★Evans-Jones (Cynan), '*Pwll Deri*' by David Emrys ★James (Dewi Emrys) and '*Y Llen*' by Dyfnallt ★Morgan.

Since the 1970s some young authors have written in a new kind of Welsh, not the speech of any particular district but that of a generation educated through the medium of Welsh in Anglicized areas. Branded as corrupt by conservative critics, these forms may have to be accepted as dialect from now on.

The use of dialect in Anglo-Welsh writing has followed a different historical progression, largely confined to the twentieth century. Its first significant appearance, in the short stories of Caradoc Evans (David ★Evans), was in essence a fabrication, for the people about whom he was writing spoke very little English. He therefore produced for his own satirical purposes a speech which was in part a translation from the Welsh, with deliberate excursions towards the outlandish, and in part based on the language of the Book of Genesis. Authors of a generation later, such as Jack ★Jones, made limited and unemphatic use of the English-Welsh speech-forms prevalent in the valleys of south Wales, but many other writers, including Glyn ★Jones, Dylan ★Thomas and Gwyn ★Thomas (1913–81), subordinated the distinctiveness of dialect to a general vivacity of language and a poetic or humorous intention. Perhaps the fuller importance of dialect is best seen in the novels of Alexander Cordell (George Alexander ★Graber), who is not a Welshman. In the north Wales of Emyr ★Humphreys the characters are rarely proletarian and their delineation does not require any emphasis on English dialect, because for much of the time they are presumed to be speaking in Welsh. In the last few decades the gradual disappearance of most of the individuality of the English spoken in Wales has, in any case, robbed writers of the proletarian novel of any very distinctive effects, and most attempts to write 'Anglo-Welsh' dialect now seem to lack authenticity. The use of Welsh words nevertheless persists in the verse and prose written in English by certain Welsh writers.

For a detailed analysis of the six main Welsh dialect regions of Wales see Alan R. Thomas, *A Linguistic Atlas of Wales* (1973). The English dialect forms of Wales have been examined and recorded by students from the English Department at University College, Swansea, under the direction of David Parry who has edited a number of bulletins containing the findings of their survey; see also *The Survey of Anglo-Welsh Dialects* (ed. David Parry, 2 vols., 1979, 1980).

Dic Aberdaron, see JONES, RICHARD ROBERT (1780–1843).

Dic Dywyll, see WILLIAMS, RICHARD (*c.*1790–1862?).

Dic Penderyn (Richard Lewis; 1808–31), see under MERTHYR RISING (1831).

Dic Siôn Dafydd, the eponymous character in a satirical poem by John ★Jones (Jac Glan-y-gors). Illiterate, he succeeds as a haberdasher in London, but pretends to have forgotten his Welsh and refuses to speak the language with his mother. His arrogance and dishonesty cause his ruin and he returns to Wales in poverty and shame. Parry Bach is a cousin of Dic's and another of the same type is Bessi of Llansant-ffraid, a flighty Welshwoman who falls prey to London fashions. The poem about Dic was popular throughout the nineteenth century and inspired the writing of similar poems, including a ballad by Abel ★Jones (Bardd Crwst), and in the twentieth century a famous epigram by Sarnicol (Thomas Jacob ★Thomas). The name Dic Siôn Dafydd is now usually applied to a Welshman who affects the loss of his Welsh or his national identity (cf. the Irish Shauneen).

Dic Tryfan, see WILLIAMS, RICHARD HUGHES (1878?–1919).

Dici Bach Dwl, see under FRANCIS, JOHN OSWALD (1882–1956).

Dillus Farfog, a character in the tale of ★Culhwch and Olwen. One of the tasks which Ysbaddaden Bencawr sets for Culhwch is to make a leash from the beard of Dillus to hold Drudwyn, the whelp of Graid mab Eri, during the hunting of the ★Twrch Trwyth. The giant stipulates that the leash must be snatched from the beard of Dillus while he is still alive. ★Cai and ★Bedwyr catch sight of Dillus from the summit of Pumlumon as he roasts a wild boar and Cai remarks that he was the mightiest warrior who ever fled from ★Arthur. They let him eat his fill, dig a pit under him, push him into it, strike him a mighty blow, pull out his entire beard with wooden tweezers, and then they kill him. Cai makes a leash out of the beard and gives it to Arthur in *Celli-wig, but Arthur recites an *englyn* casting doubt on Cai's bravery which sours their relationship thereafter.

DILLWYN, AMY ELIZABETH (1845–1935), novelist, was born in Swansea and spent most of her life there, becoming a pioneer of women's rights in industrial and public life. After her father's death in 1892 she managed the Dillwyn Spelter Works, her unorthodox views and way of life bringing her a reputation for eccentricity. She was a literary critic of some standing and her review of *Treasure Island* (1883) for *The Spectator* helped to discover the talent of Robert Louis Stevenson. Her first and best novel, *The Rebecca Rioter* (1880), is set in the Swansea area. In her later novels, *Chloe Arguelle* (1881), *A Burglary* (1883), *Jill* (1884), *Jill and Jack* (1887) and *Maggie Steele's Diary* (1892), all of which deal with contemporary society, the Welsh element is less obvious but the author's progressive outlook is always evident.

Dinas Brân, a castle in the commot of *Yale, Denbs., overlooks the river Dee and the town of Llangollen. The hill-fort previously occupying the site was associated with Cadell, ruler of *Powys in the early ninth century, and was later held by *Madog ap Maredudd and his descendants, the lords of Powys Fadog. The castle, probably built by order of Gruffudd ap Madog (d. 1269), was captured by *Dafydd ap Llywelyn in 1282 but, in the same year, it was retaken by English forces and, together with the cantrefi of Bromfield and Yale, granted as a new lordship to John de Warenne, Earl of Surrey. Dinas Brân was then allowed to fall into ruin. According to tradition, a beautiful young woman named Myfanwy lived in the castle in the fourteenth century; her love for the poet Hywel ab Einion is the subject of the poem *'Myfanwy Fychan' by John Ceiriog *Hughes. The castle plays an important part in the early chapters of John Cowper *Powys's novel, *Owen Glendower* (1940).

Dinefwr or **Dynevor**, a castle which was traditionally one of the three major royal seats of Wales, belonged to the rulers of *Deheubarth. Occupying a strategic site on a hillside overlooking the river Tywi near Llandeilo, Carms., it was the home of *Rhys ap Gruffudd (The Lord Rhys) in the twelfth century and was later held by his descendants. The castle was surrendered to English forces during the first *War of Welsh Independence (1276–77) by Rhys Wyndod. The Welsh failed to recapture it, despite a heavy siege in 1282, and again in 1403 during the rising of *Owain Glyndŵr. In the fifteenth century a part of the castle was converted into a mansion which was used as a residence by Gruffudd ap Nicholas, Deputy-Justice and Deputy-Chamberlain of the Principality of South Wales, and also by his grandson, Sir Rhys ap Thomas (1449–1525). Both were patrons of the poets and were associated with *Carmarthen castle. Dinefwr was partially destroyed by fire in the eighteenth century, after which the Dynevor family lived in a modern house near by.

For further details see J. E. Lloyd (ed.), *A History of Carmarthenshire* (1935, 1939).

Dinmael, a commot of the cantref of *Penllyn, in the valley of the Alwen, became part of the honour of Denbigh in 1282.

'Dinystr Jerusalem' (lit. 'The destruction of Jerusalem'; 1824), an *awdl* by Eben Fardd (Ebenezer *Thomas), was based on the model of *'Cywydd y Farn Fawr' by Goronwy *Owen, and was influenced by Dewi Wyn o Eifion (David *Owen), the young poet's mentor, and by English panoramic poetry. The poem has three parts, describing Jerusalem prior to the Roman siege, the city under siege, and after its destruction. The poet found the story in *Holl Waith Flavius Josephus, yr hanesydd Ieuddewig* (1819), a translation by Hugh *Jones of Maesglasau of the work of Flavius Josephus, the Jewish historian. Although the influence of William *Owen Pughe's orthography vitiates the poem, it is generally regarded as the best descriptive *awdl* written in the nineteenth century.

Disestablishment of the Anglican Church in Wales, The, was an issue which caused bitter political and religious controversy during the second half of the nineteenth century. Demands for Disestablishment by Welsh Radicals and Nonconformists did not make any serious headway until the 1840s. The formation of the *Liberation Society in 1844 was a landmark, and by the 1860s all the Nonconformist churches were committed to Disestablishment, including the Calvinistic Methodists. Thomas *Gee and Henry *Richard were among the most zealous advocates of the reform.

The issue first came before the House of Commons in 1870 when a motion by Watkin Williams, the Member for Denbigh District, received only forty-seven votes. Gladstone was out of sympathy and denied that there was any analogy between Wales and Ireland, where the Church had recently been disestablished. The demand, however, continued to gain momentum, fanned by the *Tithe War of the late 1880s, and motions advocating Disestablishment gained greater support in the Commons in 1886, 1891 and 1892. Furthermore, the Liberal Party was now committed to Disestablishment, Gladstone having patently changed his mind. In 1894 the Liberal Government introduced a Welsh Disestablishment Bill, after pressure from young back-benchers such as David *Lloyd

George, and it passed its second reading in 1895. The Bill was described by F. E. Smith as one 'which has shocked the conscience of every Christian community in Europe', a piece of cant which inspired G. K. Chesterton to write his satirical poem 'Antichrist, or the Reunion of Christendom', which ends, 'Chuck it, Smith'.

There then followed ten years of Unionist government, during which no progress was made, but the Liberal ministry, elected in 1906 with Lloyd George a Cabinet minister, re-iterated its commitment to Welsh Church Dis-establishment. After a Royal Commission on the Welsh churches had reported that Noncon-formists still outnumbered Anglicans by three to one, a bill for Welsh Disestablishment passed through the Commons in 1912 and the follow-ing year. In 1914, under the protection of the Parliament Act, it escaped the veto of the Lords and became law. Although the issue was suspended during the First World War, Lloyd George was determined to settle it, while modi-fying the terms of disendowment, after becom-ing Prime Minister. A compromise Bill on endowments was patched up and Welsh Dis-establishment took effect in June 1920. A new ecclesiastical province of Wales was created, fortified by a Treasury grant of a million pounds and with A. G. Edwards as the first Archbishop of Wales. Since then, Disestablishment has been a dead issue, while the income from the secularized property of the Anglican Church has passed to the county councils. See also ANGLICANISM.

The issue of Disestablishment is discussed by Kenneth O. Morgan in *Wales in British Politics 1868–1922* (1963), *Freedom or Sacrilege?* (1966) and *Rebirth of a Nation: Wales 1880–1980* (1981); see also E. T. Davies, *Religion in the Industrial Revolution in South Wales* (1965), Philip Bell, *Irish and Welsh Disestablishment* (1969) and David Walker (ed.), *A History of the Church in Wales* (1976).

Dissent, see under NONCONFORMITY.

Dissenting Academies, educational establish-ments founded by Nonconformist sects, had a great influence in Wales, as in England, during the seventeenth and eighteenth centuries. They sought, primarily, but not exclusively, to pro-vide education for young men who—by reason of their dissenting views—were excluded from the Universities of Oxford and Cambridge. The first in Wales, and the oldest of all the dissenting academies which have an unbroken history down to the twentieth century, was that founded by Samuel *Jones at Brynllywarch, Glam., at some time before 1672. Its location was frequently changed. At Llwyn-llwyd, Brecs., under Vavasor Griffiths (d. 1741) in 1735, it was merged with a school established by Rhys Prydderch and continued by David Price (*fl.* 1700–42). Among those who studied under Price or Griffiths, or both, were Howel *Harris, William *Williams (Pantycelyn) and Richard

*Price, the philosopher.

The academy afterwards settled at Carmar-then where Thomas *Charles and David *Wil-liams were among its students. Theological ten-sions caused schism in 1757 so that—in addition to the Carmarthen institution supported by the Presbyterian Board—there appeared a rival academy assisted by the Congregational Board. The latter was moved from one centre to another in the border counties before settling at Brecon in 1839. Among those associated with these two traditions as tutors or students were Thomas Morgan (1720–99), Josiah Rees (1744–1804), Benjamin Davies (1739?–1817), David *Davis of Castellhywel, Edward Williams (1750–1813), George *Lewis, Michael Jones (1787–1853), Michael D. *Jones, Samuel *Roberts, John Roberts (1804–84) and William *Williams of Wern. The *Baptists set up their own academies, at Trosnant (1734–61) and afterwards at Abergavenny (1807) under Micah Thomas (1778–1853), and at Haverfordwest (1839). From 1839 onwards it becomes more appropri-ate to speak of 'the theological colleges'.

The academies provided *Nonconformity with ministers who honoured knowledge as well as spirituality and, to some extent, they pioneered a more modern type of education than that provided in those days by the Universities of Oxford and Cambridge. Such tutors as Edward Williams and Micah Thomas con-tributed substantially to the movement which adapted Calvinism so as to safeguard human responsibility and promote social progress.

Accounts of the Dissenting Academies will be found in the article by H. P. Roberts in the *Transactions* of the Honourable Society of Cymmrodorion (1928–29), in G. Dyfnallt Owen, *Ysgolion a Cholegau yr Annibynwyr* (1939), R. Tudur Jones, *Hanes Annibynwyr Cymru* (1966), D. Eirug Davies, *Hoff Ddysgedig Nyth* (1976) and T. M. Bassett, *Bedyddwyr Cymru* (1977).

Dissolution of the Monasteries, The, was begun by Henry VIII in 1536. The Norman monasteries of Wales had, in the Middle Ages, been important religious, economic and cultural institutions. Many poets had sung their praise and, in the thirteenth century, some of the most significant manuscripts had been copied and preserved at *Cistercian houses, the most popular in Wales. From the mid-fourteenth cen-tury onwards, however, the monasteries lost much of their importance, chiefly because of the effects of the *Black Death and general weaknes-ses in the Roman Catholic Church. Some of their lands were leased to prosperous land-owners, the number of monks was reduced, their hospitality and patronage declined, their religious and cultural zeal weakened. On the eve of the Protestant Reformation their influence was much reduced and when Henry VIII decided to break with Rome and establish himself at the head of a centralized, sovereign state, those institutions which were seen as obstacles to his ambitions were the first to be dismantled. Commissioners were sent to investigate the condition of the monasteries and the *Valor Ecclesiasticus*, a detailed report of their material value, was drawn up. In 1536 the smaller monasteries were closed, including the forty-eight poor and degenerate Welsh houses, their lands falling to the Crown, which later sold or leased them to local gentry.

For further details see Ambrose Bebb. *Machlud y Mynachlogydd* (1937) and Glanmor Williams, 'The Dissolution of the Monasteries in Glamorgan' in *Welsh Reformation Essays* (1967).

Diwrnach Wyddel, in the tale of *Culhwch and Olwen, is the owner of a cauldron in Ireland. Ysbaddaden Bencawr, the father of Olwen, insists that the cauldron be procured in order to prepare food for the guests at his daughter's wedding-feast. *Arthur enlists the help of Odgar fab Aedd, King of Ireland, but despite his pleading Diwrnach refuses to part with it. After a second attempt to persuade Diwrnach, Arthur's men take it from him by force and return to Wales with the cauldron full of Irish treasure. This incident involves one of the Cauldrons of Plenty which are often found in Irish literature and of which there are parallels in the Second Branch of *Pedair Cainc y Mabinogi and in the poem *'Preiddiau Annwfn'.

Dock Leaves, see ANGLO-WELSH REVIEW.

Doctor Coch, Y, see PRYS, ELIS (1512?–94?).

DODD, ARTHUR HERBERT (1891–1975), historian, was a native of Wrexham, Denbs. Educated at New College, Oxford, he was appointed Lecturer in History at the University College of North Wales, Bangor, in 1919 and succeeded Sir John Edward *Lloyd as Professor in 1930. His teaching in both the History and Extra-Mural Departments, like his publications, were remarkable for vitality as well as profound scholarship. The chapter he contributed to *A History of Wrexham* (1957), a volume which he edited, and his *A History of Caernarvonshire* (1968), reflect his lifelong interest in urban and regional history. An earlier volume, *The Industrial Revolution in North Wales* (1933), is still regarded as a masterpiece of pioneering scholarship. A. H. Dodd's many papers, published in various journals, especially those on Stuart politics and the *Civil War, are valuable for their erudition and historical perspective. They preceded *Studies in Stuart Wales* (1952), his major work on Welsh society and administration in the seventeenth century. It was he who reinterpreted that century and gave it a significance in Welsh social development which had not previously been appreciated. The scope of his writings was broadened with the publication of *The Growth of Responsible Government* (1956) and

Life in Elizabethan England (1961). A useful summary of his work is to be found in the posthumous volume, *A Short History of Wales* (1977).

For further details see the obituary of A. H. Dodd by J. Gwynn Williams in *The Welsh History Review* (vol. 8, no. 1, 1976).

Dogfeiliog, a commot of the cantref of Dyffryn Clwyd; tradition claims that it was named after Docmail, one of the alleged sons of *Cunedda.

Dogs of Annwfn, The, a premonition of death, were said to be seen or heard by those who walked abroad on windy nights. The belief was that they came from the Otherworld to hunt the souls of the living through the air. They terrified ordinary dogs and that is why a dog howling at night was thought to be an ill omen. Described as small and red-grey in colour, they were sometimes led by a black-faced man with horns, perhaps *Gwyn ap Nudd, King of *Annwfn. They were also known as *Cwn Cyrff* ('Corpse Dogs'), *Cwn Wybr* ('Sky Dogs'), *Cwn Toili* ('Toili Dogs') and *Cwn Bendith y Mamau* ('Fairy Dogs'). See also CORPSE BIRD, CORPSE CANDLE and CYHYRAETH.

Dolau-gwyn, a mansion in the parish of Tywyn, Mer., the home of a family which gave patronage to itinerant poets, including Rhisiart *Phylip and Siôn Phylip of Ardudwy. The most notable patron was Lewis Gwynn (d. 1630), a descendant of the Ynysmaengwyn family.

Dolbadarn, a castle built for the Princes of *Gwynedd on a rock overlooking Llyn Padarn, Caerns., at the northern end of the Llanberis Pass and controlling an ancient route from Caernarfon to the upper Conwy Valley, was used as a royal residence during the thirteenth century. After the establishment of *Llywelyn ap Gruffudd as sole ruler of Gwynedd in 1255, his ousted brother Owain was imprisoned at Dolbadarn for some twenty years, his long captivity being deplored by contemporary poets. Captured by the King's forces during the latter stages of the Second *War of Welsh Independence (1282–83), the castle was then dismantled and its timber removed for the construction of the new Edwardian stronghold at *Caernarfon.

For further details see the account of Dolbadarn by C. A. Ralegh-Radford (1948) and R. Avent, *Castles of the Princes of Gwynedd* (1983).

Dolforwyn, a castle the remains of which lie near the village of Abermule, Mont., is associated by local tradition with a story of how the river Severn came to be so called. Locrinus, the eldest son of *Brutus, is reputed to have fallen in love with Estrildis who bore him a daughter. His wife Gwendolen, consumed by jealousy, hurled the child into the river from a spot still known as Dolforwyn ('The maiden's meadow') and thereafter the river was called by the child's name,

Sabrina (W. Hafren, E. Severn). This story, the invention of *Geoffrey of Monmouth, was used by Milton in his masque, *Comus* (1634), where Sabrina is invoked as the goddess of chastity. The castle of Dolforwyn was, in fact, built by order of *Llywelyn ap Gruffudd in 1273.

Dolwar Fach, see under GRIFFITHS, ANN (1776–1805).

Dolwyddelan, a castle towards the head of the Lledr Valley in Caernarfonshire, was first built by order of either *Owain ap Gruffudd (Owain Gwynedd) or of his son, Iorwerth Drwyndwn. According to tradition, the latter's son, *Llywelyn ap Iorwerth (Llywelyn Fawr), was born in the castle. This structure was replaced in the late twelfth or early thirteenth century by a two-storey stone keep and a curtain wall was added by *Llywelyn ap Gruffudd. The site was important to the Welsh because it guarded the route up the Conwy and Lledr Valleys over what is now called the Crimea Pass (Bwlch Gorddinan) into Meirionydd. During the Second *War of Welsh Independence Edward I's forces attacked it and on 24 January 1283, after a siege of no more than three weeks, the castle surrendered. Its loss, significant to the Welsh because of Dolwyddelan's association with Llywelyn Fawr, also made vulnerable the key defensive position at Penmaenmawr and gave the English King control of the west bank of Conwy and the valleys leading into *Eryri.

For further details see Richard Avent, *Castles of the Princes of Gwynedd* (1983).

Dominicans, an order of mendicant friars established by St. Dominic of Castilla in 1215. Known also as Black Friars on account of the colour of their habit, they took vows which stressed obedience, poverty and chastity. Travelling widely to preach in the towns, they won a reputation for scholarship and many were made bishops. They flourished in the thirteenth century during which five friaries were founded in Wales: Cardiff (c.1242), Haverfordwest (c.1246), Bangor (c.1251), Rhuddlan (c.1258) and Brecon (c.1269). The Black Friar *Thomas Wallensis was an eminent scholar and preacher during the first half of the fourteenth century. As the Friars became rich and standards deteriorated, they were criticized by such poets as *Dafydd ap Gwilym and *Madog Benfras. The author of the medieval prose work *Cysegrlan Fuchedd* may have been a Dominican. Towards the end of the Middle Ages poems were composed to the prior and rood at Rhuddlan and to the rood at Bangor. All five Welsh friaries were dissolved in 1538.

For further details see the article by R. C. Easterling in *Archaeologia Cambrensis* (1914), B. Jarrett, *English Dominicans 1221–1921* (1921) and W. Rees, 'The Suppression of the Friaries' in the *South Wales and Monmouth Record Society* (1954).

Dôn, the Welsh name for the Celtic goddess Danu who is also commemorated in the name of the river Donau (Danube). In Ireland her family was known as *Tuatha Dé Danann*. Her sons, *Gwydion and Gilfaethwy, and her daughter *Arianrhod, play a prominent part in the Fourth Branch of *Pedair Cainc y Mabinogi. Gofannon and *Amaethon were other sons of hers and *Math fab Mathonwy was her brother.

Don Ciceto, see under DWYMYN (1944).

Dorcas, a society for women who made clothes for the poor, flourished in the nineteenth century but survived into the twentieth. The name was taken from the Bible (Acts 9:36), in which Dorcas (Tabitha) is said to be 'full of good works and alms deeds'. In the poem by W. J. *Gruffydd, '*Gwladys Rhys*', the Dorcas is part of the monotony of chapel life which burdens the soul of the minister's daughter.

Drafod, Y (lit. 'The discourse'), the newspaper of the Welsh community in *Patagonia. Established in 1891 by Lewis *Jones, one of the first settlers, it was published as a weekly until 1961 and among its editors were Lewis Jones, Eluned *Morgan, W. H. Hughes and Richard Nichols. Welsh was the journal's sole language at the outset, but there was an increase in the amount of English and Spanish after the First World War. It became a fortnightly in the early 1960s and is now published quarterly under the editorship of Irma Hughes de Jones. The newspaper is an indispensable source for the study of the early history of *Y Wladfa*.

Dragon, national emblem, see RED DRAGON.

Dragon, The, also entitled **Y Ddraig**, the magazine of the University College of Wales, Aberystwyth. Founded in 1878, it was run by College staff until 1903 and until the mid-1930s, when it adopted a bilingual title, the contents were mainly in English. The proportion of material in Welsh increased substantially thereafter until 1965, when the Welsh-language magazine *Y Ddraig* was launched. T. H. *Parry-Williams and T. Gwynn *Jones contributed to some of *The Dragon*'s early numbers and among its editors were the writers Iorwerth C. *Peate and Waldo *Williams. Student contributors who later produced more substantial work included J. O. *Francis, Alun *Lewis, Gwyn Erfyl *Jones, Bryan Martin *Davies and Gwynne *Williams. The magazine celebrated the Festival of Wales in 1958 by issuing a special edition which carried poems and stories by well-known Anglo-Welsh writers, among them Roland *Mathias, Gwyn *Thomas (1913–81) and Gwyn *Jones.

Dragon Has Two Tongues, The (1968), a work

of literary history by Glyn *Jones, was also the first detailed account of 'the first flowering' of Anglo-Welsh writing in the twentieth century. It begins with a description of the author's own family background, richly illustrative of his view of other writers, and goes on to deduce from the changing language pattern of the years when he was young that an Anglo-Welsh writer was likely to appear when 'a radical, nonconformist, Welsh-speaking family begins to speak English'. Modestly disclaiming the loftier aspects of literary criticism, the author offers a chapter of introduction each to the writing of poetry and of prose and then deals warmly and in terms of personal acquaintance with Caradoc Evans (David *Evans), Huw Menai (Huw Owen *Williams), Idris *Davies, Jack *Jones, Keidrych *Rhys, Dylan *Thomas and Gwyn *Thomas (1913–81), on all of whom he has much to say which is illuminating and of lasting significance.

Draig Glas, see under PERFIDIOUS WELSHMAN (1910).

Drama. The earliest plays in Welsh, surviving from the medieval period, are Y *Tri Brenin o Gwlen and Y Dioddefaint a'r Atgyfodiad. These two mysteries, a Herod play and a Passion play, are akin to the major English cycles and were probably written in north-east Wales during the second half of the fifteenth century. There is, however, no record of the staging of these works and, since Wales lacked cities to compare with York and Chester, with their influential guild systems, it is thought that the Welsh plays were performed only by travelling players. Nor did Wales share in the flowering of the theatre which was one of the delights of Shakespeare's England. The sixteenth century had seen the collapse of the *Bardic Order and, as the gentry families found new allegiances at the *Tudor court, the patronage and practice of the arts in Wales had declined rapidly. The adaptation by an anonymous author of poems by Henryson and Chaucer entitled *Troelus a Chresyd (c.1600) is not only the first full-length play in Welsh but also the sole dramatic monument to that Renaissance interest in Classical themes which informed the work of the great Welsh Humanists. Wales had to wait until the eighteenth century for the emergence of a popular theatre and even then the most sophisticated form to be produced was only that of the *interlude, of which the most popular exponent was Twm o'r Nant (Thomas *Edwards).

Under the influence of *Methodism in the nineteenth century, the traditions of *Hen Gymru Llawen waned and, in many parts of the country, died out completely. The interlude, like all other entertainments, was discouraged but it survived to some extent in preaching styles and in the ymddiddanion (dramatic dialogues on the virtues of good living) which were presented in the chapels for the edification of the common people. By the 1870s there was growing interest in more secular forms of drama: prizes were awarded for plays at the eisteddfodau held in Llanberis and Trefriw, one of which was a play by Beriah Gwynfe *Evans about *Owain Glyndŵr. But the emergence of this embryonic Welsh drama continued to provoke vehement reactions in Nonconformist circles: in 1887, for example, the Methodist Sessions meeting at Corwen urged the chapels to shun all dramatic performances. It was not for another thirty years that such hostility showed signs of abating. Some respectability was bestowed on the art when David *Lloyd George, at the National Eisteddfod held at Bangor in 1902, called for patronage of Welsh drama and during the first decade of the twentieth century it became fashionable for plays to be performed as a means of raising money for good causes. Nevertheless, the development of drama in Wales continued to be sporadic and without any remarkable results.

The English-speaking theatre has a long history in Wales, beginning with performances to fairground spectators, then to smaller audiences at inns and town halls, and eventually in playhouses. The Kembles, Keans, Macreadys, Sheridan Knowles and Andrew Cherry were among those who entertained the gentry in the towns and villages of Wales with plays from the English classical repertoire. Religious opposition, so powerful in the history of drama in Welsh, was less evident in the English-speaking theatre, though it, too, felt the pinch in the middle of the nineteenth century. From 1875 to 1925, however, theatre in English developed rapidly in Wales and by 1912 there were thirty-four theatres and about as many halls holding dramatic licences. Unfortunately, these theatres were not able to compete with the 'talking pictures' and most of them closed, or became cinemas, in the 1930s.

When the wave of Naturalism broke in Wales it was to break simultaneously in both Welsh and English. The first Welsh playwrights of the twentieth century, mostly University graduates, had read or seen William Archer's translations of Ibsen's plays and they were inspired by the work of the Abbey Theatre in Ireland. They began by writing plays about contemporary Welsh society, especially those aspects which reflected the narrower traits of *Nonconformity. Among their number were W. J. *Gruffydd, J. O. *Francis, Idwal *Jones (1895–1937) and Kitchener *Davies. Most of these writers were helped by the patronage of Lord Howard de Walden (Thomas Evelyn *Scott-Ellis) who, during the 1930s, paid for the work of his own bilingual company at Plas Newydd, Llangollen. The new Welsh drama of the inter-War years was essentially amateur but, with some five hundred companies flourishing in all parts of

Wales, it was lively and genuinely popular. This 'golden age', as it now appears, came to an end during the Second World War and, with the advent of television in the 1950s, it proved no longer possible to revive public interest to the same extent. For this reason it has been remarked that drama in Welsh is unusual in having had the experience of television before that of the professional theatre.

The traditionally amateur base of theatre in Welsh gave way to a new professionalism in the late 1950s and the 1960s. By then there had emerged a number of writers, including Saunders *Lewis, John Gwilym *Jones, Huw Lloyd *Edwards and Gwenlyn *Parry, who were to make important contributions to the literary drama in Welsh, while in English the work of Emlyn *Williams, Gwyn *Thomas (1913–81) and Alun *Richards was being performed in theatres in England. Central to the new situation were the Welsh Theatre Company and its Welsh-language counterpart *Cwmni Theatr Cymru*, which was founded in 1968 under the directorship of Wilbert Lloyd Roberts, and an important factor in its development was the financial support provided on an increasing scale by the *Welsh Arts Council. At the same time a number of gifted Welsh actors, including Richard *Burton, Donald Houston, Rachel Roberts, Hugh Griffiths and Siân Phillips, were making their names on the London stage and in the cinema. Some of these actors joined with others in calling for a National Theatre to be established in Wales and, under the aegis of the St. David's Theatre Trust, there was much discussion of the principles and the practical problems involved. The failure of the campaign for a National Theatre was largely due to the clash of factions.

Some protagonists, notably Raymond Edwards, the first Principal of the Welsh College of Music and Drama in Cardiff, remain convinced that without a National Theatre the drama in Wales will never flourish. Be that as it may, the growth of a network of arts centres in various parts of the country, mostly financed jointly by the University Colleges of Wales, the local authorities and the Welsh Arts Council, has provided an alternative solution to the problems of Welsh theatre which, in its turn, has its own advocates who argue that the very vigour of the contemporary scene is derived from the organic growth of smaller units operating at a community level. If that is the case, there is some irony in the fact that the work of such companies as *Brith Gof, Bara Caws, Moving Being* and *Cardiff Laboratory Theatre* (to name only four of the smaller companies) makes of drama in Wales an activity not unlike that of the travelling players in the eighteenth and nineteenth centuries. But at least it may be noted that in these circumstances there are young writers, actors and producers who find their opportunities and audiences which the mainstream theatre seems unable to provide. See also RADIO AND TELEVISION, WRITING FOR.

For further details see Olive E. Hart, *The Drama in Modern Wales 1905–28* (1928), O. Llew Owain, *Hanes y Ddrama yng Nghymru 1850–1943* (1948) and Cecil Price, *The English Theatre in Wales* (1948) and *The Professional Theatre in Wales* (1984); see also the chapter by Elan Closs Stephens in *The Arts in Wales 1950–75* (ed. Meic Stephens, 1979).

Dramau'r Byd (lit. 'Plays of the World') a series of plays translated from other languages into Welsh, is published by the University of Wales Press on behalf of the *Welsh Arts Council. It was launched in 1969, under the title *Y Ddrama yn Ewrop*, and the first play to appear was *Diwéddgan*, a translation by Gwyn *Thomas (1936–   ), the editor of the series, of Samuel Beckett's *Fin de Partie* (1957). Since then a total of seventeen volumes have appeared, including plays by Sophocles, Terence, Molière, Chekhov, Anouilh, Lorca, Camus, Sartre, Ionesco, Dürrenmatt and Weiss. Among the translators are Saunders *Lewis, Euros *Bowen, R. Bryn *Williams, John Gwilym *Jones, Prys *Morgan and John *Rowlands.

DRAYTON, MICHAEL (1563–1631), see under POLYOLBION (1622).

Dream of Jake Hopkins, The (1954), a verse-play for radio by Glyn *Jones (which provided the title of the author's second volume of poetry) was commissioned by Aneirin Talfan *Davies and broadcast in 1953. Jake, a middle-aged teacher denied promotion by a bombastic head-master, a prey to the malice of his fellows and acutely aware of his own failure, indulges in the bitter-sweet comfort of remembering his childhood and early manhood. This 'radio-ode', which is memorable for its technical virtuosity and brilliant cameos of Jake's pupils and colleagues, may be assumed, like his novel *The Learning Lark* (1960), to draw upon the author's experience as a teacher. Also included in the volume to which the play gave the title is the poem 'Merthyr' and three translations of poems by *Dafydd ap Gwilym.

Dream of Rhonabwy, The, see BREUDDWYD RHONABWY.

Dref Wen, Y (lit. 'The white town'), is celebrated in five stanzas of *'Canu Heledd' which lament the interruption of peaceful, agricultural pursuits by constant warfare and the tragic irony that bloodshed has become more usual than the customs of centuries. The *Gogynfeirdd called Whittington, Salop., '*y dref wen*', but the name means 'Hwita's town', not 'white town'. The Welsh name may be descriptive rather than a specific place-name.

Dreflan, ei Phobl a'i Phethau, Y (lit. 'The

townlet, its people and its affairs'; 1881), Daniel *Owen's first novel, was first published in monthly parts in *Y Drysorfa* in 1879 and 1880. It portrays a small town similar to Mold, Flints., and its central characters are members of the Calvinistic Methodist chapel. The author intended the new minister, Noah Rees, to be its principal character, but the stage is dominated by others who are much more interesting, with the result that the story-line becomes fragmented and loses the unity of a novel. The satire is scathing, especially on the author's own denomination: apart from the genuinely pious Benjamin Prŷs, the church elders are materialistic, hypocritical businessmen and Mr. Smart, the chief elder, exhorts the new minister to 'Remember the motto: "Appearance, appearance"'. The duality in man, appearance and reality, became one of Daniel Owen's main themes, and it is explored in several of the novel's characters such as Mr. Bevan, the rogue Jeremiah Jenkins, Sharp Rogers and even the poor, deluded John Aelod Jones. The most memorable character, however, is the amiable benefactor, Peter Pugh. Despite weaknesses, its gifted characterization and dialogue make *Y Dreflan* a work of importance in the history of the *novel in Welsh.

For discussion of the novel's merits see Saunders Lewis, *Daniel Owen* (1936), D. Gwenallt Jones, 'Nofelau Cylchgronol Daniel Owen' in *Llên Cymru* (vol. IV, 1956–57) and J. Gwilym Jones, *Daniel Owen: Astudiaeth Feirniadol* (1970).

DRESSEL, JON (1934–   ), American poet. Born in Saint Louis, Missouri, USA, the grandson of immigrants from Llanelli, Carms., he was educated at Washington University in Saint Louis and, from 1958 to 1967, ran his family's dairy and food business, as well as writing for newspapers in that town. A former Professor of English at Webster College, Saint Louis, he became Director of the Programme for American Studies at Trinity College, Carmarthen, in 1976. He has published one volume of poetry, *Hard Love and a Country* (1977), in the Triskel Poets series and, with T. James Jones, a sequence of poems, *Cerddi Ianws* (1979), which was deemed worthy of the *Crown at the National Eisteddfod of 1979 but disqualified because of its joint authorship. A third collection of his poems, *Out of Wales*, appeared in 1985.

Driscoll, James (**Peerless Jim**; 1880–1925), boxer, was born in Cardiff of Irish parentage and won the world featherweight championship in 1909. The novel *Peerless Jim* (1984) by Alexander Cordell (George Alexander *Graber) is based on his life and times.

Dromio, see COLLINS, WILLIAM JOHN TOWNSEND (1868–1952).

Drovers, the men whose trade was the driving of large herds of cattle and sheep from Wales to fairs in England. The practice began in the fifteenth century and ended in the late nineteenth century. One of their regular routes, over the Cotswolds into the Thames Valley, became known as 'The Welsh Way'. Their characteristic cry was '*Haiptrw Ho! Haiptrw Ho!*' and their overnight stopping-places were the numerous inns some of which still bear the name of Drover's Arms. Tough, resourceful and courageous, these men also tended to be coarse and dissolute. Among the writers who criticized them as a class were Rhys *Prichard, who exhorted them to avoid excessive drinking, Ellis *Wynne, who imagined their suffering in Hell because they swindled their clients, and Twm o'r Nant (Thomas *Edwards) who satirized them for their knavery. They may also be seen as romantic figures who travelled widely by the standards of the day, bringing back the news, songs and stories they had heard in the towns of England and at fairs such as those at Barnet, Herts., and the St. Bartholomew Fair at Smithfield in London.

Some drovers became prosperous and one, David Jones (d. 1839), who was High Sheriff of Carmarthenshire in 1820, founded *Banc yr Eidion Du* ('The Bank of the Black Ox') at Llandovery in 1799, a firm which remained in the hands of his descendants until 1909 when it was taken over by Lloyds Bank. Another famous drovers' bank was *Banc y Ddafad Ddu* ('The Bank of the Black Sheep') in Aberystwyth and Tregaron. Among drovers who were literary men of note were Edward *Morris and Dafydd *Jones of Caio.

For further details see P. G. Hughes, *Wales and the Drovers* (1947), Richard Colyer, *The Welsh Cattle Drovers* (1976) and *The Drovers' Roads of Wales* (1977) by Fay Godwin and Shirley Toulson.

Drudwas ap Tryffin, see under ADAR LLWCH GWIN.

Druids, an order of priest-philosophers, comparable with the Indian Brahmins, whose existence on the European continent and in Galatia, Asia Minor, was known to classical writers from the second century before Christ. Information about them is most frequently derived from the full and circumstantial account given by Julius Caesar in *De Bello Gallico* (VI) of the functions, status, and privileges of the Gaulish Druids. He states that they had authority over divine worship, officiated at sacrifices (including human sacrifices), exercised supreme power in all judicial and legislative matters, and educated the youth of the nobility together with aspirants to their order. In status Caesar ranks them with the '*equites*' or knights. Their judicial functions were exercised at a yearly meeting in the territory of the Carnutes, considered to be the centre of Gaul. A primate among them had supreme authority over the others for life. Druids paid no taxes and were not required to go to war. The teaching imparted in their schools was oral, their pupils being required to learn by heart a great number of verses and spend as long as twenty years in study. This teaching was concerned with astronomy and natural science. They calculated time by nights instead of days and held that souls do not die but are re-born in a different form. Britain was the centre from which druidic teaching had originally come and to which specialist students resorted to study it.

As evidence for the scientific and astronomical studies of the Druids, there exists a remarkable fragmentary calendar on bronze, found at Coligny and now preserved at Lyons, which dates from the late first century BC, a little after Caesar. This, the oldest extensive example of writing in a Celtic language, gives the names of the months and marks them as either '*MAT*' ('good', i.e. 'auspicious') or '*ANM*' (an abbreviation for '*Anmat*', 'not good'); these words have been perpetuated in Welsh in those Triads which list certain events as '*mad*' ('fortunate') and '*anfad*' ('unfortunate').

It is not, however, believed that Caesar's account rests to any appreciable extent upon direct observation, but that it is based in the main upon the accounts of earlier writers, in particular that of the Greek historian Posidonius, which is no longer extant. His account cannot represent the contemporary status of the Druids in Gaul, but refers rather to the conditions a century or more previously when the Druids were at the height of their power, during the period of Gaulish independence.

While Caesar speaks of the Druids as constituting the single learned caste among the Gauls, his near-contemporaries Strabo and Diodorus Siculus distinguish three learned orders, the '*druides*' (philosophers and theologians), the '*vates*' or '*manteis*' (diviners and seers) and the '*bardi*' who were panegyric poets. It is remarkable that this triple category of learned orders is attested in a clearly-defined form some centuries later in Ireland, whose early medieval sources represent the *disjecta membra* of a tradition of prehistoric antiquity. Here again are found the three classes of Druids, '*druidh*', '*filidh*' ('seers') and '*baird*' (poets) who were praise-poets. No continuity can be proven between these orders and those which existed in Gaul and Ireland is nowhere mentioned in the classical accounts of Druids. Nevertheless, the overall correspondence is striking: in both countries it is difficult to make a clear distinction between the first two classes, while by the seventh century the '*filidh*' had in Ireland effectively taken over the functions and privileges of the Druids, owing to the opposition made by the latter to the introduction of Christianity. Unlike the Druids, the '*filidh*' managed to accommodate themselves to the new religion and in their role of official poets they retained a position of immense power and prestige down to the end of the native Irish cultural order in the seventeenth century.

Irish '*druidh*' (sing. *druí*) is cognate with Latin '*druides*' or '*druidae*'. This word has been explained as derived from an unattested Gaulish compound '*dru-vid*'. The second element is cognate with an Indo-European root '*wid*' ('to know'), preserved in Welsh '*gwybod*'. The first element has been alternatively explained as representing a superlative intensive prefix, giving the meaning 'those who have very great knowledge', or as related to the Greek word '*drùs*' (oak), Welsh '*derw*' and Irish '*daire*', ('those familiar with the oak'). This latter meaning was first advanced by Pliny, who stated that oak-groves were held sacred by the Druids: it would indeed conform well with the Celtic predilection for sacred trees. The Welsh cognate '*dryw*' (-*on*), not to be confused with '*dryw*' ('wren'), came to be equated in the eighteenth century with 'druid', but is earlier attested only in two instances in The *★Book of Taliesin*, in both of which the meaning is doubtful. However, '*derwydd*' (in which the root '*wid*' is combined with two prefixes) is used, with prophetic connotations, in *★'Armes Prydein'*, '*Cad Goddeu*', and other poems in *The Book of Taliesin*. In 1632 John *★*Davies of Mallwyd rendered '*derwyddon*' as '*druides*', '*sapientes*', '*vates*', and favoured the 'oak' derivation.

The most striking account given in classical sources of Druids in Britain is Tacitus's description (*Annals*, xiv) of the ranked Druids of Anglesey, in the year AD 61, hurling imprecations against the troops of Suetonius who were drawn up on the opposite shore of Menai. According to Tacitus, the Druids were subsequently massacred and their sacred groves on the island destroyed. It is not possible to determine how long the druidic order survived in Britain or in Ireland, but the *★*Lives of the Saints contain reverberations of the confrontations which inevitably took place between them and the Druids. '*Magi*' is the Latin word used to denote 'druid', though it is often applied widely and imprecisely for magicians and wizards in general. A significant indication of the survival of druidism into the Dark Ages in Britain is preserved in the episode in the *★Historia Brittonum* in which the divinatory powers of *★*Vortigern's '*magi*' are confuted by the superior powers of the youthful Ambrosius (*★*Myrddin).

However ancient may be the origins of druidism in Britain, it cannot be too strongly emphasized that there is no valid archaeological or literary evidence to associate the Druids with Stonehenge, as was first argued by the antiquaries John Aubrey (see under AUBREY, WILLIAM) and William Stukely in the seventeenth century. Furthermore, any association between the ceremonies of *★Gorsedd Beirdd Ynys Prydain* and ancient druidic tradition should be rejected as the creation of Iolo Morganwg (Edward *Williams) who first convened such a gathering on Primrose Hill, London, in June 1792. It was Iolo who was mainly responsible for the spread of 'druidomania' during the nineteenth century. For further discussion of the Druids see T. D. Kendrick, *The Druids* (1927), A. L. Owen, *The Famous Druids* (1962), N. K. Chadwick, *The Druids* (1966) and Stuart Piggott, *The Druids* (1968).

Druid's Rest, The (1944), a play by Emlyn *Williams set in the fictitious village of Tan-y-Maes, is the author's fullest dramatic re-creation of his home village, Pen-y-Maes, Flints. It presents a selection of typical characters: Lord Ffynnon, the squire, Sarah Jane Jehovah, an evangelist, Issmal Hughes South America, a poetic tramp, and Zachariah Policeman; the Publican, Job Edwards, is based on Emlyn Williams's father. Tommos Edwards, the hero, is a comic portrait of a mischievous, imaginative, bookish boy who, denied access to his books because of the fantasies about local people which they provoke, takes revenge by convincing his family that a visitor is the man responsible for the notorious 'Brides-in-the-Bath' murders.

Drws y Society Profiad (lit. 'The door of the experience society'; 1777), a small book published by William *Williams (Pantycelyn) under the full title (in trans.), *Templum Experientiae Apertum: or, the door of the experience society opened wide . . . in seven dialogues. Taking the form of a conversation between Theophilus and Eusebius.* The fruit of many years' experience of conducting private religious societies, it defends the societies on Scriptural grounds and because of their usefulness, and then stresses the importance of securing competent stewards to lead them. The technique of conducting societies is discussed, including such matters as the treatment of elderly members, and discipline. The work combines profound spirituality with robust common sense and is written in a style at once lucid and strikingly flexible.

Drych, Y (lit. 'The mirror'; 1851), a newspaper for Welsh people in America, was established in New York by John Morgan Jones, a native of Llanidloes, Mont., in 1851; in the following year John Williams Jones of Llanaelhaearn, Caerns., was appointed editor. Between 1855 and 1858 *Y Drych* was merged with *Y* *Gwyliedydd* to form *Y Drych a'r Gwyliedydd*. Bought by the editor, the paper was moved to Utica in 1860 and, subsequently the property of John Mather Jones, it became the principal newspaper for Welsh expatriates in north America. Among its editors were Dafydd Rhys Williams (Index; 1851–1931), Thomas Morris (Gwyneddfardd), John C. Roberts and his son, Arthur M. Roberts. Welsh was the language of *Y Drych* until the early 1930s. The paper was bought by Horace Breece Powell in 1962 and moved from Utica to Milwaukee, Wisconsin, where it is still published.

Drych Barddonol (lit. 'A poetic mirror'; 1839), a volume of literary criticism by William *Williams (Caledfryn). It discusses such topics as the nature of poetry, poetry in the Scriptures, *cynghanedd and the *Twenty-four Metres, hymn-writers, the free metres, common errors, Welsh poets, the Muse and the contribution of the *Eisteddfod to poetry; it also contains three eisteddfod adjudications and the author's prize-winning *awdl* on the wreck of 'The *Rothesay Castle'. Considered to be an important book in its day, it makes many percipient comments (given the state of contemporary scholarship) and emphasizes what Caledfryn held to be the essentials of poetry, namely metre, correctness of language and clarity of meaning.

Drych yr Amseroedd (lit. 'A mirror of the times'; 1820), a history of the Methodist Revival, particularly in Caernarfonshire, by Robert *Jones of Rhos-lan. The author's main source was his close acquaintance with two generations of Methodist leaders, his wife being the granddaughter of the man who first invited Howel *Harris to the county. The work reveals the theological convictions of an ardent Methodist and is written in a style which combines the vernacular of *Eifionydd with the literary Welsh of the *Bible.

Drystan ap Tallwch, see under POWERFUL SWINEHERDS.

Dubricius, see DYFRIG (5th cent.).

Ductor Nuptiarum (1777), a small book by William *Williams of Pantycelyn. Its lengthy title (in trans.) gives an idea of its form and content: *Ductor Nuptiarum: or a guide to marriage, in the form of a dialogue between Martha Pseudogam, and Mary Eugamus, both at first making a profession of Godliness, but the one having lapsed, marrying after the flesh; and the other holding fast to the power of Godliness, marrying in the fear of the Lord. In three Dialogues . . . The first of the depraved mode of courtship and marriage of Martha, and her unhappy life afterwards. The last containing the advice of Mary to Martha to please her husband, and through that to make her marriage happier and more agreeable, and perhaps to win him to the faith. To which has been added a dialogue between Efangelus and Pamphila, concerning the danger of marrying unbelievers.* Inspired by Williams's concern for the spiritual welfare of the converts belonging to the religious societies, the work is noteworthy for its realistic treatment of sex and marriage, within the guidelines clearly laid down in the New Testament teaching on the subject, and its style combines dignity and homeliness to a remarkable degree. See also MONICA (1930).

Duke of the Britains (L. *Dux Britanniarum*), the title given in Roman times (3rd–4th cent. AD) to the commander of the forces of the two sub-provinces of upper Britain, including Wales, whose responsibility was to defend the territory against invaders from Ireland and Scotland. His counterpart in lower Britain was the 'Count of the Saxon Shore' who faced Saxon and other raiders on the south-eastern side.

Dunoding, a cantref of *Gwynedd consisting of the commots of *Ardudwy and *Eifionydd, is said to have been named after Dunaut, one of the alleged sons of *Cunedda.

Dunraven, a castle near St. Bride's Major, Glam., built for the de Londres family in the very early Norman period, was extended under the le Botelers (Butlers) who lived there from the late eleventh to the twelfth century. The Butler line ended with the marriage of an heiress early in the sixteenth century, to Sir Richard Vaughan of *Bredwardine and Tretower, Brecs. Dunraven remained in the Vaughan family's possession until 1642 when it was bought by John Wyndham of Clearwell, Gloucs. His descendant, Thomas Wyndham, Member of Parliament for Glamorgan from 1789 to 1814, restored the castle early in the nineteenth century. A tradition persists about the wrecking activities associated with the last of the Vaughans, which provided the theme of a very popular ballad, '*Brad Dynrafon*' by David Pughe Evans (1866–97). The castle was dismantled in the 1960s.

For further details see W. H. W. Quin, *Dunraven Castle* (1926).

Dwarf, The, see MORGAN, THOMAS (1604–79).

Dwned, a grammatical treatise which was studied in the bardic schools of the fifteenth and sixteenth centuries, was a Latin grammar, partly adapted to suit the Welsh language. The word was borrowed from the English 'donet' in turn was derived from Donatus, a Latin grammarian of the fourth century, whose work was the basis of much of the Welsh *dwned*. By the eighteenth century the word had come to mean 'gossip' or 'idle talk'.

Dwnn, Gruffudd (*c*.1500–*c*.1570), patron, of Ystrad Merthyr, near Kidwelly (Cydweli), Carms., was an assiduous copier and collector of manuscripts and, at one time, owned the *Hendregadredd and parts of the *Peniarth collections. Among the poets who wrote verses in his honour were Harri ap Rhys ap Gwilym, Thomas Fychan, *Wiliam Llŷn, *Huw Llŷn, *Gruffudd Hiraethog and *Owain Gwynedd.

DWNN, LEWYS (Lewys ap Rhys ab Owain;
fl. 1568–1616), poet and genealogist, of Betws Cedewain, Mont. He took the name of Dwnn from his mother, one of the descendants of David Dwnn (Donne) of Kidwelly (Cydweli), Carms., who had fled to Powys after the murder of the mayor of that town. Lewys, a bardic disciple of *Wiliam Llŷn and *Hywel ap Mathew, left two substantial volumes of his poems, surviving in his own elegant hand, which consist of *englynion*, *cywyddau* and odes to patrons from several parts of Wales. His poetry is uninspired but rich in genealogical detail and it is more as a genealogist than as a poet that he is remembered. In recognition of his collections of pedigrees and armorial bearings, and of his proficiency in the Welsh language, he was granted a patent of deputyship for north and south Wales in 1568. He then became a deputy-herald and, after the expiry of the patent, continued to collect pedigrees according to the standards set by the College of Heralds. Two volumes of his genealogical collections in his own hand, together with a few individual charts, have been preserved; one is in the National Library of Wales (Peniarth 268, Gwynedd) and the other in the British Library (Egerton 2585, Dyfed). These, or copies, together with transcripts of other books by Dwnn, were published on behalf of the *Welsh Manuscripts Society in 1846 by William Rees under the editorship of Samuel Rush *Meyrick and entitled *Heraldic Visitations*.

His son, **James Dwnn** (*c*.1570–*c*.1660), was a poet who wrote in the traditional metres for families in Montgomeryshire, Cardiganshire and Merioneth, his work having been preserved in several collections, especially in *The Book of James Dwnn* (Llanstephan MS 53). He enjoyed a long life and his work reflects the continuity of poetic tradition from the Elizabethan age to the time of Oliver Cromwell. Nevertheless, apart from a series of *englynion* which commemorate the burning of Mathafarn in 1644 by the Parliamentarians, there are very few references in his poetry to the political conflicts of the period.

Dwymyn, Y (lit. 'The fever'; 1944), a volume of poems by T. Gwynn *Jones. Having completed his adjudication of the odes on the subject of *Arthur's Cave in the competition for the *Chair at the National Eisteddfod of 1934, the poet entertained himself by writing a satirical ode in free verse and in *cynghanedd* on the same subject, which he published in the magazine *Yr Efrydydd* under the pseudonym Don Ciceto. Amused by the reaction of some critics, he decided to write a poem a month during the following year, and published them in the same periodical in 1934 and 1935 under the *nom de plume* of Rhufawn. Their appearance caused conjecture in literary circles: some saw in the novelty of the metrical form and the realistic treatment of the themes the work of a young poet, while others maintained that the mastery of style and maturity of craftsmanship could belong only to an experienced poet. Instead of the ancient Celtic myths which had pervaded *Caniadau* (1934), T. Gwynn Jones chose modern themes for the majority of these poems. The fever of enmity and violence, and the primitive hatred which worshipped power rather than reason and righteousness, are the basic themes of such poems as 'Y Saig', 'Y Dadannudd', 'Ofn', *'Cynddilig', 'Dynoliaeth', 'Y Duwiau' and 'Dirgelwch'.

The collection (to which a thirteenth poem was added before publication in book form) is discussed by Derec Llwyd Morgan in *Barddoniaeth T. Gwynn Jones* (1972) and in the biography of the poet by David Jenkins, *Cofiant T. Gwynn Jones* (1973).

Dwynwen (5th cent.), the daughter of *Brychan and sister of Cain, is considered in Wales to be the patron saint of lovers and her feast-day is 25 January. A curious account of how she achieved this status was given by Iolo Morganwg (Edward *Williams). In love with a youth named Maelon, she displeased him by rejecting his sexual advances and, despite her love, prayed to God to release her from the liaison. Appearing to her in a dream, God offered her a sweet drink which dispelled her passion and which, when tasted by Maelon, turned him to ice. Dwynwen was then granted three wishes which were to revive Maelon, to become patron saint of lovers and never to marry. The saint is associated mainly with Anglesey, where her name is commemorated in Llanddwyn and Porthddwyn, but also with Glamorgan. There is a spring called Ffynnon Dwynwen (or Ffynnon Fair) near the church of Llanddwyn, in which the fish were said to reveal the fate of the lovesick.

Dydd, Y (lit. 'The day'; 1868), a newspaper launched by Samuel *Roberts of Llanbrynmair shortly after his return from America, was published by William Hughes of Dolgellau; Roberts was assisted in the editorship by Richard *Davies (Mynyddog). In 1871 the paper was merged with *Y Tyst Cymreig* and became known as *Y Tyst a'r Dydd*. This arrangement did not last, however: *Y Tyst a'r Dydd* was moved to Merthyr Tydfil in 1872, while *Y Dydd* continued to be published under its original name at Dolgellau until 1891, when it suspended publication for about a year. Although there was no official connection between *Y Dydd* and the Independents, it was among them that the paper found a readership. William Hughes was its publisher until 1910 and his two sons thereafter. The newspaper was united with the *Corwen Chronicle* to form *Y Dydd a'r Corwen Chronicle* in 1954 and is still published in Dolgellau under that title.

Dyddgu, the dark-haired woman who is the subject of nine *cywyddau* by *Dafydd ap Gwilym, was the daughter of Ieuan ap Gruffudd ap Llywelyn whose home was at Tywyn in south Ceredigion, and she was descended from Tewdwr Mawr ap Cadell. A contrast in every respect to Dafydd's *Morfudd, Dyddgu was aristocratic, remote and virginal, and remained the unattainable object of the poet's affections.

DYER, JOHN (1699–1757), poet and painter, was born at Llanfynydd, Carms., the second son of a solicitor who owned Plas Llangathen. It was not until 1714 that the family moved to Aberglasne, the house with which the poet's name is usually associated. Educated at Westminster School, from which he ran away, he was destined for the law but, on his father's death, went to London as an apprentice to the painter Jonathan Richardson. In 1724 he went to paint in Italy but while there he composed 'The Ruins of Rome' and re-wrote the poem *'Grongar Hill'. After painting at various places in the Marches for a year or two, he farmed in Herefordshire and then at Higham-on-the-Hill, Leics. Established there, he married, published 'The Ruins of Rome' (1740) and in 1742 was inducted as rector of Catthorpe, Leics., where he farmed the glebe. Abandoning work he had done on a commercial map of Britain, he began his longest poem, 'The Fleece', in 1743 and, after many vicissitudes, all four books of it were published in 1757. Meanwhile, he had returned to his commercial map and, at the instance of friends, was in 1751 granted the living of Belchford and Coningsby, Lincs. Unhappy in this 'squalid region', he lauded Siluria in 'The Fleece' (an indication that his Welshness was complicated), though the poem's mastery of the processes of wool production and marketing supports wider allegiances.

A poet who has not yet had his due, Dyer was praised by Wordsworth for his imagination and purity of style, which he thought the best since Milton. An attractive character, the Welshman sought both to 'augment the public good' and to achieve that 'quiet in the soul' which 'Grongar Hill' so simply advocates.'

There is no complete edition of John Dyer's poems; a biography by Ralph M. Williams appeared in 1956 and Belinda Humfrey has contributed an essay on the poet to the *Writers of Wales* series (1980).

Dyfalu, the practice of multiplying fanciful comparisons by using tropes such as metaphors, personifications and autonomasia. The profusion of such figures was considered by the *cywyddwyr* to be a great feat, especially in *cywyddau* of request, and *Dafydd ap Gwilym's poem 'Y Sêr' contains a good example.

Dyfed, the region of west Wales in which the First and Third Branches of *Pedair Cainc y Mabinogi* are set. *Pwyll, *Pendefig Dyfed* ('The ruler of Dyfed'), was lord over its seven cantrefi

—*Cemais, Pebidiog (*Dewisland), *Rhos, Penfro (*Pembroke), *Daugleddau, *Emlyn and *Cantref Gwarthaf. *Manawydan's remark that there were no better seven cantrefi supports the view that the final redactor of the *Mabinogi* was a Dyfed man. Sometimes the Latin form *Demetia* was used to refer to an area greater than the seven cantrefi. The First Branch claims that Pryderi had conquered the three cantrefi of *Ystrad Tywi and the four cantrefi of *Ceredigion and, in the Fourth Branch, the seven hundreds of *Morgannwg are added to his kingdom. It is probable that there was a considerable Irish population living in Dyfed in early times and there is reason to believe that many of the narrative themes in the Four Branches have Irish origins and associations. The old royal dynasty of Dyfed, which continued until the tenth century, traced its ancestry to the Deisi tribe who, it is said, had migrated to Wales from Ireland in the third century. Its last representative was Llywarch ap Hyfaidd who died about 904, after which Dyfed became part of the kingdom of Deheubarth. The modern county of Dyfed (Pembs., Carms. and Cards.), created in 1974, is far more extensive than the ancient kingdom.

Dyfed, see REES, EVAN (1850–1923).

Dyfnallt, see OWEN, JOHN DYFNALLT (1873–1956).

Dyfr, one of the Three Splendid Maidens of *Arthur's court; the other two were Enid, the daughter of Yniwl, and *Tegau Eurfron. She was popular among the *cywyddwyr* as a standard of beauty, especially on account of her golden hair, and it is suggested in the Triads that *Glewlwyd Gafaelfawr was her lover.

Dyfrig or **Dubricius** (second half of the 5th cent.), saint, was one of the earliest and most important religious leaders in Wales. He is associated more particularly with the south-east, and with the south-west of Herefordshire. In the Life of Samson (early 7th cent.), he is depicted as a bishop and connected with *Llanilltud Fawr and the island of Caldey. The subject of three Lives, all written in the twelfth century, the earliest of which is in *The Book of Llandâf*, Dyfrig is reputed to have been the son of Efrddyl, daughter of Peibio, King of *Erging. It was said that he had been born in Matle (Madley, near Hereford) and that the circumstances of his birth were miraculous: when Efrddyl's father learned of his daughter's pregnancy, he tried to kill her, but later the king was cured of sickness by the touch of the infant Dyfrig's hand. The saint was renowned for his wisdom and founded a monastery at Hennlann (Hentland-on-Wye), where he taught his disciples for some seven years before returning to live in the district of his birth at Mochros (Moccas). In his old age, and

with failing health, he retired to *Bardsey and was buried on the island but in 1120 his remains were removed to *Llandaf.

The Life reflects the propaganda of its period. It contains many traditions current at the time and its main purpose was to demonstrate the antiquity and pre-eminence of Llandaf, and its right to the churches of Dyfrig, many of which belonged to the bishopric of Hereford. It is claimed that Dyfrig was the first Bishop of Llandaf, that he was Archbishop of South Britain, and that he consecrated *Deiniol as Bishop of Bangor. The chapter of St. David's, in a letter to the Pope written between 1124 and 1130, asserted that Dyfrig had consecrated *Dewi Sant as archbishop in succession to himself. He is also described as an archbishop by *Geoffrey of Monmouth, Benedict of Gloucester and *Gerald de Barri (Giraldus Cambrensis), and at Caerleon it was he, according to Geoffrey, who crowned *Arthur there. Dyfrig, however, occupies an inferior position to Dewi in the latter's Life: with Deiniol, he was sent to request Dewi's presence at the Synod of Llanddewibrefi. It is unlikely that there is any substance in the tradition which links Dyfrig with Germanus of Auxerre. Among churches dedicated to him are those of Gwenddwr, Brecs., and Porlock, Som., and he is also connected with places in Pembrokeshire and Gower. But it is undoubtedly to Erging that he originally belonged, a district where Christianity had taken root before the end of the Roman era.

DYGYNNELW (6th cent.), poet, is named in a Triad as the poet of *Owain ab Urien; the same name was given by *Cynddelw Brydydd Mawr to his son, whom he mourned in an elegy.

Dylan Ail Ton, the son of *Arianrhod in the Fourth Branch of *Pedair Cainc y Mabinogi*, was born after his mother stepped over *Gwydion's magic wand. Immediately after his baptism he made for the sea and received the sea's nature: he could swim as well as any fish and a wave (W. *ton*) never broke under him. A blow from his uncle, Gofannon fab Dôn, caused his death. Dylan is mentioned in several of the old mythological poems in The *Book of Taliesin, among which is his elegy, and in one instance his name is given as Dylan Ail Mor ('The son or heir of the sea'). It is possible that behind these references there was an independent myth concerning one of the sea-gods which became associated with the traditions concerning *Lleu Llawgyffes and the children of *Dôn. The poet Dylan *Thomas is thought to have been the first in modern times to be given the name.

DYMENT, CLIFFORD (1914–70), poet. Although he was born in Alfreton, Derbs., and lived most of his life in England, he spent several happy years in Caerleon, Mon., and always thought of himself as Welsh. His childhood and sense of belonging to Wales were described in his autobiography, *The Railway Game* (1962), and in the poem, 'Derbyshire Born, Monmouth is my Home', published in the sixth of his seven volumes of verse, *Experiences and Places* (1955). Leaving school in Leicestershire at the age of sixteen, and plagued with ill health, he had a variety of unskilled jobs in Loughborough and London. During the Second World War he was employed in the making of documentary films and became a friend of Dylan *Thomas. After the death in 1968 of Marcella Salzer, the Viennese actress with whom he had lived for some thirty years and to whom his *Collected Poems* (1970) are dedicated, he became more solitary than ever, seeing few of his friends, unnoticed in the literary life of London, but steadfast in his resolve to follow no other calling than the poet's. His early poems, published during the 1930s, were unfashionably plain but well constructed. All his work reflects a highly personal, almost hermetically sealed world which is presented mainly through images and symbols from nature. Like his poems, several passages in his autobiography bear testimony to a life which, in the words of his friend, the Irish writer Robert Greacen, 'had much pain and disappointment in it, yet also its moments of joy and fulfilment'.

Dyn Hysbys (lit. 'Wise man'), the most common name in Wales for a wizard; other names were '*consuriwr*' (conjurer), '*swynwr*' (charmer) and '*dewin*' (magician). Found in many districts, he was said to possess the power of breaking spells by undoing the evil perpetrated by *witches and others. There were three kinds of *Dyn Hysbys*: clerics such as Edmund *Prys and Walter *Davies (Gwallter Mechain); men familiar with medicine and black magic who had learned their craft from books, the most famous of whom were John and Henry *Harries of Cwrtycadno, Carms.; and those who had inherited the power from their families, such as the *Dynion Hysbys* of Llangurig, Mont.

The *Dyn Hysbys* was considered to be a person who knew and could reveal the unknown, especially events in the future pertaining to love and death. Some divination beliefs were associated with *May Day, *St. John's Day and Winter's Eve when it was thought that the world of the spirits came so close to the human world that the spirits' help could be enlisted in foretelling fortunes. Although he took advantage of ignorance and belief in the supernatural, the *Dyn Hysbys* fulfilled a special, and sometimes valuable, role in society. Among his functions were the healing and safeguarding of people and animals. For the latter purpose he used charms consisting of a prayer or blessing in a scarcely decipherable mixture of Latin and English, together with the abracadabra and the signs of the zodiac. Written on a piece of paper, the charm was placed in a bottle which was hidden in the building housing the sick animals. The owner was instructed not to remove the cork, for it was believed that the evil spirit troubling the animals would become encapsulated in the bottle for ever. Several examples of these charms are kept at the National Folk Museum and the National Library of Wales.

For further details see J. H. Davies, *Rhai o Hen Ddewiniaid Cymru* (1901), T. Gwynn Jones, *Welsh Folklore and Folk-custom* (1930), Kate Bosse Griffiths, *Byd y Dyn Hysbys* (1977) and Robin Gwyndaf, '*Dirgel Fyd y Dewin*' in *Barn* (nos. 176, 177, 1977).

'**Dyrfa, Y**' (lit. 'The crowd'), the *pryddest* for which Cynan (Albert *Evans-Jones) won the *Crown at the National Eisteddfod in 1931. It tells the story of John Roberts, a grandson of John John *Roberts (Iolo Caernarvon), who played for Wales on thirteen occasions between 1927 and 1929. The excitement of the spectators and the ecstasy of the player as he experiences '*un foment lachar pan yw clai'n / Anfarwol megis Duw*' ('one blinding moment when clay / becomes immortal, like God') are vividly described. The poem goes on to relate how John Roberts's passion was later channelled into God's service in missionary work in China. The subject was probably suggested to Cynan, who here demonstrates his gifts as balladeer and playwright, by J. C. Squire's poem 'The Rugger Match'.

Dyri, a poem in the free metres, its lines regularly accented and partly or fully in *cynghanedd, was listed by Iolo Morganwg (Edward *Williams) as one of his *Pedwar Ansawdd ar Hugain.

E

Eagle of Gwernabwy, The, see under OLDEST ANIMALS.

Eagle of Pengwern, The, see ERYR PEN-GWERN.

Eagles of Snowdonia, The, birds which were thought in Welsh tradition to be oracles of peace and war. When they circled high in the sky it was said that victory was imminent but that, if they flew low, crying incessantly, they were warning of catastrophe for the Welsh. The white eagle of *Eryri has been adopted as a symbol by clandestine groups such as the *Free Wales Army and *Mudiad Amddiffyn Cymru, and it is to be seen with slogans painted on walls throughout Wales.

EAMES, ALED (1921–), maritime historian, was born at Llandudno, Caerns., and educated at the University College of North Wales, Bangor. Having served in the Royal Navy during the Second World War, he was the British Council's North Wales Representative for two years before becoming a teacher. In 1955 he was appointed to a lectureship in the Education Department at his old College, a post in which he remained until his retirement in 1982. His publications include *Ships and Seamen of Anglesey* (1973), *Porthmadog Ships* (with Emrys Hughes, 1975), *Letters from America* (with Lewis Lloyd and Bryn Parry, 1975), *Llongau a Llongwyr Gwynedd* (1976), *Ships and Seamen of Gwynedd* (1976), *Meistri'r Moroedd* (1978), *O Bwllheli i Bendraw'r Byd* (1979), *Morwyr Môn Gan Mlynedd yn Ôl* (1979), *Shipmaster* (1980), *Rescue, the Story of the Moelfre Lifeboats* (1980), *Machlud Hwyliau'r Cymry* (1984), *Gwraig y Capten* (1984) and *The Twilight of Welsh Sail* (1984). All these books deal with aspects of the maritime history of Wales, to the study of which Aled Eames has made a major contribution.

EAMES, MARION (1921–), novelist, was born of Welsh parents in Birkenhead, but she was brought up and went to school in Dolgellau, Mer. She worked as a librarian, as a regional organizer for *Plaid Cymru and as the editor of a local newspaper before studying the piano and harp at the Guildhall School of Music in London. In 1957, having married the journalist Griffith Williams, she returned to Wales to take up work as a radio producer with BBC Wales in Cardiff, a post in which she remained until her retirement in 1980.

She is the author of four excellent historical novels. The first two of these, *Y Stafell Ddirgel* (1969) and *Y Rhandir Mwyn* (1972), tell the story of Rowland *Ellis the Quaker, a member of the minor gentry of Merioneth, of his emigration to Philadelphia and the creation of the *Welsh Tract there. Her third novel, *I Hela Cnau* (1978), traces a different kind of emigration, namely the depopulation of north Wales to feed the conurbation of Merseyside, and describes life among the *Liverpool Welsh, while *Y Gaeaf sy'n Unig* (1982) is set in the time of *Llywelyn ap Gruffudd. In all four novels Marion Eames makes effective use of her familiarity with specific localities and historical periods, creating a lively, realistic impression of other times and places. Meticulous research and a talent for both narrative and dialogue place her in the front rank of contemporary Welsh novelists. She has also published a novel for children, *Sionyn a Siarli* (1978).

The first two of her novels have been translated under the titles *The Secret Room* (1975) and *Fair Wilderness* (1976). For discussion of her work see the interview which the writer gave to Victor John in *Barn* (no. 122, 1972).

EARLE, JEAN (1909–), poet, was born in Bristol but brought up in the Rhondda Valley and has lived since 1937 in various parts of Wales, latterly at Abergwili, Carms. She has published two volumes of poems, *A Trial of Strength* (1980) and *The Intent Look* (1984).

EARLEY, TOM (1911–), poet. Born at Mountain Ash, Glam., he has spent most of his life in London where he was a teacher of English. A pacifist and anarchist, he has published three collections of poems, namely *Welshman in Bloomsbury* (1966), *The Sad Mountain* (1970) and *Rebel's Progress* (1979), all of which reflect his political convictions and his interest in Welsh affairs.

Eastaway, Edward, see THOMAS, EDWARD (1878–1917).

Easter, the feast of Christ's Resurrection, is celebrated on the first Sunday after the full moon occurring on 21 March or next after that date; if the full moon occurs on a Sunday, the following Sunday is Easter Sunday. On this calculation depends a number of other movable feasts, including the nine Sundays before and the eight Sundays after Easter, as well as Shrovetide and Whitsun. With the coming of Easter the fasting of Lent ceases. In Wales, two foods symbolical of the feast, namely the new season's lamb and eggs collected during the previous week, were eaten on Easter Sunday. Open-air games, including stool-ball and *cock-fighting, were played on Easter Monday. In the towns of north-west Wales the custom of '*stocsio*' took place as part of the merriment of the day; people were 'arrested' in their homes early in the morning and taken by cart to the local stocks. It was the tradition in some districts to rise early on Easter Day and climb a hill to see the sun dancing in celebration of the Resurrection, and sometimes a bowl of water was taken so that the sun's reflection could be seen on its surface. According to Lewis *Morris the antiquary, it was customary in Anglesey to view the sun through wisps of straw on Easter morning, and there is an allusion to the tradition in the poem '*Heulwen y Pasg*' by Gwenallt (David James *Jones).

For further details see Trefor M. Owen, *Welsh Folk Customs* (1959).

Eben Fardd, see THOMAS, EBENEZER (1802–63).

Ecclesiastical and Instructional Literature, an extensive and varied body of religious prose dating from the thirteenth to the sixteenth century, may be considered—by virtue of the homogeneity of its language and its Catholic background—as a specific department of Welsh literature. Most of the texts are translations, usually anonymous and almost always based on Latin originals. Intended for the instruction of laymen and clergymen, they are simple, popular and traditional in content and very different from scholastic discussions of theological and philosophical subjects. The impetus for their composition came from the twelfth Ecumenical Council (or the fourth Lateran Council), held by Pope Innocent III in 1215, which gave birth to a large body of auxiliary literature written in vernacular languages by the clergy. The most important collections of this kind of literature in Welsh are found in manuscripts of the thirteenth and fourteenth centuries. The texts may be classified in six main groups: *Lives of the Saints; Midrash, for example *Ystorya Adda, a translation of *Historia Adam*; Apocrypha and pseudo-epigraphia, for example *Efengyl Nicodemus, a translation of *Evangelius Nicodemi*; vision literature, for example *Purdan Padrig*, a translation of *De Purgatorio S. Patricii*; short biblical passages; and biblical exegesis, for example *Pwyll y Pader o Ddull Hu Sant*, a translation of a section of *Speculum de Mysteriis Ecclesiae*. There are also some isolated works, of which the most noteworthy are the compendium of Christian theology, *Historia Lucidar*, a translation of Honorius

Augustodunensis' *Elucidarium*, an original work by an anonymous Dominican on practical spirituality, *Ymborth yr Enaid*, and the *Penityas*, a work of masterly prose and uncertain derivation.

The language of this literature at its most exalted is one of the glories of the Welsh prose tradition. It also bears witness to the maturity of Welsh prose in the medieval period, for whereas verse was normally employed for translating into the other vernaculars (with the exception of the Irish), the superior, unequivocal medium of prose was employed in this instance. Furthermore, the vocabulary and syntax of this literature provided a sound basis for the New Testament of 1567 and the *Bible of 1588.

For further details see the chapter by J. E. Caerwyn Williams in *Y Traddodiad Rhyddiaith yn yr Oesau Canol* (ed. Geraint Bowen, 1974).

'**Echrys Ynys**' (lit. 'Harm has befallen an island'; *c.*1050–1100), the opening words of an elegy in *The *Book of Taliesin* for a chieftain named Aeddon (or Cynaethwy) of Anglesey. While some of the poem's references are obscure, the poet appears to be complaining that, at some time in the past, his lord had brought home four female slaves after a raid upon 'Gwydion's land', that is to say, *Arfon or *Eryri. The four have now taken possession of the court, the poet laments, and do not accord him the respect and patronage to which he is accustomed.

For a discussion of the elegy see Ifor Williams, 'An Early Anglesey Poem' in *The Beginnings of Welsh Poetry* (ed. R. Bromwich, 1972).

Edeirnion, a commot of the cantref of *Penllyn lying in the valley of the Dee. Tradition claims that it was named after Etern, one of the alleged sons of *Cunedda. The commot, once under the influence of *Powys, was brought within the orbit of *Gwynedd by *Owain Gwynedd ap Gruffudd (Owain Fawr), much to the distress of the poet *Cynddelw Brydydd Mawr. It became part of the county of Merioneth in 1284, although the senior line of Powys Fadog retained a foothold at Glyndyfrdwy, where *Owain Glyndŵr raised the standard of revolt in 1400. Edeirnion, previously a rural district, became part of the district of Glyndwr in the county of Clwyd in 1974.

EDELMAN, MAURICE (1911–75), politician and novelist. Born in Cardiff, he was educated in the city and at Trinity College, Cambridge, where he read Modern Languages. During the Second World War he was a correspondent in North Africa and France. He was the Labour Member of Parliament for Coventry West from 1945 to 1950, and for Coventry North West from 1950 until his death. His career included service as delegate to the Consultative Assembly of the Council of Europe (1949–51), as Vice-chairman of the British Council (1951–

57) and as Chairman of the Socialist Group of the Western European Union (1968–70).

Most of Maurice Edelman's novels have parliamentary settings and are primarily concerned with British political life. They include *A Trial of Love* (1951), *Who Goes Home* (1953) which is partly set in a Welsh constituency, *A Dream of Treason* (1955), *The Happy Ones* (1957), *A Call on Kuprin* (1959), *The Minister* (1961), *The Fratricides* (1963), *The Prime Minister's Daughter* (1964), *Shark Island* (1967), *All on a Summer's Night* (1969) and *Disraeli in Love* (1972). Among the subjects treated are the demise of colonialism and the emergence of new states in Africa and the West Indies, the power of the press, political scandal and the take-over of business interests. The novels' method is to juxtapose the complexities of public issues with those of private needs such as the sexual proclivity of male politicians for women who are usually beautiful, intelligent, rich and sometimes neurotic. Maurice Edelman also wrote plays for television and several works of non-fiction, including a study of the Fourth Republic in France, a biography of David Ben-Gurion and a political history of *The Daily Mirror*.

Edern, the son of Nudd, a character in the romance of *Geraint fab Erbin*. When Edern's dwarf insults *Gwenhwyfar, *Arthur's wife, by lashing her maiden with a whip, Geraint pursues his master to the town of Caerdyf (Cardiff), defeats him in a contest for a sparrow-hawk and sends him to Arthur's court to make amends for the insult. Edern is shown mercy by the king and Morgan Tud, the chief physician, is commanded to heal his wounds. Geraint later allows Edern to join the troop which escorts him to Erbin's court.

EDERN DAFOD AUR (13th cent.?), believed to have been an early grammarian, was credited by Iolo Morganwg (Edward *Williams) with authorship of the bardic grammar usually associated with *Einion Offeiriad and *Dafydd Ddu Athro o Hiraddug. Although this claim was groundless, a text of the grammar entitled *Dosparth Edeyrn Dafod Aur* was published by John *Williams (Ab Ithel) in 1856.

'Edmyg Dinbych' (lit. 'Praise of Tenby'; late 9th cent.), a poem in The *Book of Taliesin* which combines a fine panegyric to the fortress of Tenby, Pembs., with a lament for its lord, *Bleiddudd. It consists of seven stanzas with an anomalous verse describing a battle, also found in The *Black Book of Carmarthen*, appended to it in the manuscript. The poem, which may have been composed for recital at a Calend-tide feast, alludes to the privileges accorded to the poet at court and, more tantalizingly, to 'the writing of Britain' kept in a library in the fortress, or at a nearby ecclesiastical centre, but it is not known to what work this is a reference.

There is a study of the poem by Ifor Williams in *The Beginnings of Welsh Poetry* (ed. Rachel Bromwich, 1972); see also R. Geraint Gruffydd, 'The Early Court Poetry of South West Wales' in *Studia Celtica* (vols. XIV/XV, 1979/80).

Ednyfed Fychan ap Cynwrig (d. 1246), Seneschal of *Gwynedd from 1215 until his death, was the chief counsellor and envoy of *Llywelyn ap Iorwerth (Llywelyn Fawr) and his son *Dafydd ap Llywelyn. Endowed with extensive lands by the Princes of Gwynedd, his sons formed an aristocracy of service in the Wales of the late thirteenth century, two of them serving as Seneschals to *Llywelyn ap Gruffudd. After 1282 their descendants proved adroit in coming to terms with the English Crown and were among the ancestors of most of the landed families of north Wales, including the *Tudor family of Penmynydd.

EDWARD AP ROGER (d. 1587), poet and genealogist, of Bodylling, Denbs., a member of the Euton family who were landowners in the district, was the author of a detailed and comprehensive work of genealogy which is preserved in the *Peniarth Manuscripts. Little of his verse has survived, except for a series of *englynion* written in the year of his death and a few others on subjects such as miserliness and the brevity of life.

Edward Bach, see DAFYDD, EDWARD (*c*.1600–78?).

EDWARD HUW O BENLLYN (*fl.* 1570–90), a poet who was probably a native of Brynllysg in the parish of Llanfor in *Penllyn, Mer. He graduated at the second *Caerwys Eisteddfod in 1567. Most of his work is in praise of the families of *Bodidris, Y Foelas, Lleweni, *Rhiwedog, *Rhiwlas and Werclys.

EDWARD MAELOR (*fl.* 1586–1620), poet and player of the *crwth*, composed *englynion* and elegies for Sir Evan Lloyd of Iâl (d. 1586), for David Powel of Ruabon and his son Samuel (d. 1600), and for *Siôn Tudur (d. 1602). He also engaged in bardic controversies with William *Midleton and Morys Powel.

EDWARDS, ARTHUR TRYSTAN (1884–1973), author, was born in Merthyr Tydfil, Glam., and educated at Clifton College and Hertford College, Oxford. A pioneer of town planning, he wrote a number of books on the philosophy of art and on various architectural topics, including *The Things which are Seen* (1921), *Good and Bad Manners in Architecture* (1924), *A Hundred New Towns for Britain* (1933) and *Towards Tomorrow's Architecture* (1968). He described his experiences as a naval rating in *Three Rows of Tape* (1929) and, after retiring to his native town, published a regional study, *Merthyr Tydfil, Rhondda and the Valleys* (1958). His autobiography, *Second Best Boy* (1970), is a typically witty account of how, mastering a speech impediment, he rose to eminence in his profession.

EDWARDS, CHARLES (1628–91?), writer and editor, was born at Rhydycroesau, Llansilin, Denbs., into a well-to-do family. Although he wrote a brief autobiography towards the end of his life, 'to leave some Account of my Ways', he did not record any details about his career prior to his election as Bible Clerk at All Souls College, Oxford, in 1644. When, after their victory in the first *Civil War (during which Oxford had been the headquarters of the Royalists), the Parliamentarians sent Visitors to the colleges to ask whether or not the members were prepared to submit to the authority of Parliament, they received an unsatisfactory reply from Edwards and he was dismissed from his post. However, he must have submitted subsequently because, in October 1648, he received a scholarship to Jesus College and graduated in the following year. It is not known what brought about this change but in 1650 he was appointed an itinerant preacher.

After the expiry of the term of the Act for the *Propagation of the Gospel in Wales, Edwards was presented to the lucrative living of Llanrhaeadr-ym-Mochnant, Denbs. According to his own testimony, he preached and catechized conscientiously in that parish but many were hostile towards him and he left about 1659 for reasons unknown. Although he took the oath of loyalty to the new king, Charles II, in 1660, his Puritan opinions were obviously widely known because he suffered persecution for the rest of his days. In 1666 armed men entered his house, frightening one of his children to death and taking Edwards away to prison. His family turned against him 'and my wife importuned me to part with her and live asunder'. Much of his time during the next twenty years was spent in Oxford and London. It is not known where exactly he lived in Wales and the Marches, although he was preaching with the Nonconformists in the vicinity of Oswestry in 1672. In 1686, the year of his wife's death, he took a farm in the district, where he suffered further unhappiness, and in 1690 he was described as an ejected minister. Nothing is known of him after 1 July 1691, the date on which his autobiography comes to an end.

Charles Edwards published his first book, *Y *Ffydd Ddi-ffuant* (1667), in Oxford. An enlarged edition appeared in 1671 and a third in 1677 under the fuller title *Y Ffydd Ddi-ffuant, sef Hanes y Ffydd Gristianogol, a'i Rhinwedd*. It was this third edition which became one of the classics of the Welsh language. He also published *Hebraismorum Cambro-Britannicorum Specimen*

(1676) and translations of selections from the works of the Latin fathers of the Church in *Fatherly Instructions* (1686). Among the books he edited were *Dad-seiniad Meibion y Daran* (1671), a reprint of *Deffynniad Ffydd Eglwys Loegr* (1594), and Richard *Davies's *Epistol at y Cembru* (1567). His literary work brought Edwards into contact with Thomas Gouge and Stephen *Hughes and from 1675 until the mid-1680s he was busy editing, translating and overseeing the printing of works for the Welsh Trust. Among the books with which he was associated was an edition of *Ymarfer o Dduwioldeb, Prifannau y Grefydd Gristianogawl* (1675) and *Llwybr Hyffordd i'r Nefoedd* (1682). His last publication was his autobiography, *An Afflicted Man's Testimony concerning his Troubles* (1691), a book which (as its title suggests) shows signs of paranoia.

Charles Edwards made a notable contribution to the work of the Welsh Trust, helping to fulfil the spiritual needs of a nation which he would have liked to have been 'livelier and more fervent in the Christian religion as were some of our ancestors'. But his greatest work is undoubtedly *Y Ffydd Ddi-ffuant*, a book which in 1667 was no more than an uninspired abridgement of John Foxe's *Acts and Monuments* but which grew by the time of its 1677 edition to be a book with its own excellent plan. In the historical sections the general history of the Christian Faith is discussed, then its history in Wales, and in the last part, *Rhinwedd y Ffydd*, 'the order of Christian sanctity through grace' is described. The work is also a model of Welsh prose, full of brilliant figures of speech, especially metaphors.

The best discussion of Charles Edwards's life and work is to be found in G. J. Williams's introduction to his edition of *Y Ffydd Ddi-ffuant* (1936); there are also studies by Saunders Lewis in *Ysgrifau Dydd Mercher* (1945) and by Derec Llwyd Morgan in *Ysgrifau Beirniadol IV* (ed. J. E. Caerwyn Williams, 1969) and in *Y Traddodiad Rhyddiaith* (ed. Geraint Bowen, 1970).

EDWARDS, DAVID MIALL (1873–1941), theologian and author, was born at Llanfyllin, Mont., and educated at Bala-Bangor College and Mansfield College, Oxford. He served as an Independent minister at Blaenau Ffestiniog and Brecon before becoming Professor of Theology and Philosophy of Religion at the Memorial College, Brecon, where he remained from 1909 until his retirement in 1934. A prolific writer on religious subjects, he contributed regularly to the periodical press of his day, edited *Y Dysgedydd* (1916–18) and was the first editor of *Yr Efrydydd* (1920–28). He took a particular interest in the connections between religion and culture, fostering the Liberal view in theology and writing in both English and Welsh in a flowing style. His most important works are *Crefydd a Bywyd* (1915), *Crist a Gwareiddiad* (1921), *Iaith a Diwylliant Cenedl* (1927), *Bannau'r Ffydd* (1929), *Crefydd a Diwylliant* (1934) and his two books in English, *The Philosophy of Religion* (1923) and *Christianity and Philosophy* (1932).

For further details see the article by T. Robin Chapman in *Y Traethodydd* (Oct., 1982).

EDWARDS, DOROTHY (1903–34), prose-writer, was born, a schoolmaster's daughter, in Ogmore Vale, Glam., and educated at Howell's School, Llandaf, and at University College, Cardiff. Well read in several literatures and an accomplished singer in Russian, German and Italian, she spent some time in Vienna, Florence and London but her permanent home was in Cardiff. Her first book, *Rhapsody* (1927), is a collection of ten short stories which are deftly written and full of understated ironies. Her only novel, *Winter Sonata* (1928), like the stories, is reminiscent of Turgenev and Chekhov and was hailed by English critics as one of the best books of its year. Both volumes are the work of a writer with a perceptive mind who was skilled in nuance and atmosphere but who did not live long enough to develop real narrative power. Cultured, reserved and unaffiliated to the homelier mores of the south Wales of the 1920s—though described by those who knew her best as a Socialist and Welsh Nationalist —she seemed a lonely figure among the Anglo-Welsh writers of her day. She put an end to her life by suicide.

For further details see the article by S. Beryl Jones in *The Welsh Review* (vol. 7, no. 3, Autumn, 1948).

EDWARDS, FRANCIS (1852–1927), translator. Born at Llangollen, Denbs., he was the Liberal Member of Parliament for Radnorshire from 1892 to 1918 and was created a baronet in 1907. His sole claim to a literary reputation rests on *Translations from the Welsh* (1913), a volume of Welsh poetry with English versions in parallel text. What makes this book significant in the history of the Englishing of Welsh poetry is that Edwards chose to translate not from the great tradition of medieval poetry but from the work of his contemporaries and immediate predecessors, such as Ceiriog (J. Ceiriog *Hughes), Eifion Wyn (Eliseus *Williams), Elfed (Howell Elvet *Lewis) and John *Morris-Jones. In so doing, he made a noteworthy contribution to the process of making Welsh poetry more accessible to English readers, even though his lyrical translations in a late Romantic idiom may not be much to modern taste.

EDWARDS, HENRY WILLIAM JOHN (1910–   ), author, was born into a Welsh family in London, went to live in Wales at the age of fourteen and settled at Trealaw, in the *Rhondda Valley, his wife's home, in 1947, working as a journalist and later as an accountant. Considering himself to be a Tory in the original, seventeenth-century sense, he supported Franco against the Republic during the Civil War in Spain. A birthright Quaker, he was received into the Roman Catholic Church in 1942, while serving in the army, but after Vatican II he became increasingly critical of the Church and was identified with the traditionalist wing, defending the Latin Mass and attacking all liberal trends in his contributions to such periodicals as *Christian Order*, *Yr Haul* and *Y Llan*. In his writings on Welsh topics he has lent his support to various extreme Nationalist groups. The publications of H. W. J. Edwards include a study of Disraeli, *The Radical Tory* (1937), a book about life in the Rhondda Valley, *The Good Patch* (1938), *Young England* (1939) and *Sons of the Romans: the Tory as Nationalist* (1977).

EDWARDS, HUW LLOYD (1916–75), playwright. Born at Penisa'r-waun, Deiniolen, Caerns., he was educated at St. David's College, Lampeter, and St. Michael's College, Llandaf, with a view to entering the priesthood of the Church in Wales, but his first job was that of statistician with an oil company. Deciding later to train for the teaching profession, he studied at Gaddesden College, Berkhamsted, and after fifteen years as an English master at Dyffryn Nantlle, Caerns., he was appointed Lecturer in the Drama Department at the Normal College, Bangor.

Entertainment was the only concern of his early comedies, *Llwyn Brain* (1954), *Yr Orffiws* (1956), *Y Gŵr Drwg* (1957) and *Y Felin Wynt* (n.d.), but his ethical and humanitarian concerns came to the fore in the short play *Noson o Lety* (1955) and especially in *Ar Ddu a Gwyn* (1956), translated into English as *Salvador*, a play about racial prejudice in South Africa. In *Cyfyng Cyngor* (1958) he dealt with a religious issue and, under Pirandello's influence, made his characters turn in the end to their author. The same didactic and allegorical tendency is found in *Y Gŵr o Gath-Heffer* (1958), which is about Jonah, and *Y Gŵr o Wlad Us* (1960), about Job. Social protest is expressed in *Pros Kairon* (1967), in *Y Llyffantod* (1973) which makes use of Aristophanes and comments on the political life of Wales, and in the posthumous *Y Lefiathan* (1977), where a symbol from the Book of Jonah is made to challenge the modern world.

There is a note by John Rowlands on the work of Huw Lloyd Edwards in *Profiles* (1980); see also J. Ellis Williams, *Tri Dramäydd Cyfoes* (1961).

Edwards, Huw Thomas (1892–1970), a prominent trade unionist and public figure whose political career embraced six years (1959–65) as a member of *Plaid Cymru and the presidency of *Cymdeithas yr Iaith Gymraeg. While Chairman of the Council for Wales he wrote a pamphlet, *What I Want for Wales* (1944). A former quarryman and, for a while, the proprietor of *Baner ac Amserau Cymru, Huw T. Edwards published two volumes of autobiography, *Tros y Tresi* (1956; trans. *Hewn from the Rock*, 1967) and *Troi'r Drol* (1963; trans. *It was my Privilege*, 1962). He also contributed poems to the volume *Ar y Cyd* (1962) with Mathonwy *Hughes, Gwilym R. *Jones and Rhydwen *Williams.

EDWARDS, HYWEL TEIFI (1934–), critic and literary historian. Born at Llanddewi Aber-arth, Cards., and educated at the University College of Wales, Aberystwyth, he became in 1965 a Tutor in Welsh Literature in the Extra-Mural Department of University College, Swansea. He is the author of two histories of the *Eisteddfod, namely *Yr Eisteddfod 1176–1976* (1976) and *Gŵyl Gwalia: Yr Eisteddfod yn Oes Aur Victoria 1858–1868* (1980), both of which are as entertaining as they are authoritative.

Edwards, Ifan ab Owen (1895–1970), patriot and founder of *Urdd Gobaith Cymru (The Welsh League of Youth), was born at Llanuwchllyn, Mer., the son of Owen M. *Edwards, and educated at the University College of Wales, Aberystwyth, where he read History. After serving in the First World War, he began his career as a teacher at Dolgellau but later joined the staff of his old College. It was as editor of the magazine *Cymru'r Plant* that he first announced (in January 1922) his plan to start a movement for the young people of Wales. The *Urdd* was founded in the same year and the rest of his life was devoted to furthering the League's aims. Among the many other initiatives with which he was associated was the opening of the first Welsh-medium primary school at Aberystwyth in 1939. He was knighted in 1947.

There is an account of his life and work by Norah Isaac in the *St. David's Day* series (1972) and an essay in *Cymwynaswyr y Gymraeg* (1978) by Morgan D. Jones; see also the monograph published by *Urdd Gobaith Cymru, Cofio Syr Ifan* (1970).

EDWARDS, JANE (1938–), novelist and short-story writer. Brought up at Newborough, Ang., she studied at the Normal College, Bangor, and in due course became a teacher. Her first novels, *Dechrau Gofidiau* (1962) and *Byd o Gysgodion* (1964), were love-stories presented in a modern idiom which attracted young readers. In *Bara Seguryd* (1969) she examined, in a sub-urban setting, the emotional disappointments of women after marriage. Having found her own sphere of psychological realism, she explored it further in a novel entitled *Epil Cam* (1972), for which the campaigns of *Cymdeithas yr Iaith Gymraeg* provided the background. She also turned to studies of childhood in the short stories of *Tyfu* (1973). In *Dros Fryniau Bro Afallon* (1976) she resumed her exploration of adult relationships. Her novel *Miriam* (1977) relates how a widower's second marriage affects the daughter who was born of the first, while *Hon, debygem, ydoedd Gwlad yr Hafddydd* (1980) depicts the disenchantment of married life and the psychological frustrations of the divorced, the widowed and the unmarried. An eighth novel, *Cadno Rhos y Ffin*, appeared in 1984. Jane Edwards, who is the wife of Derec Llwyd *Morgan, is a frequent broadcaster and has written much for radio and television. She is generally considered to be, with Eigra Lewis *Roberts, among the most distinguished of contemporary women novelists in Welsh.

For further details see the note by John Rowlands in *Profiles* (1980) and the article by Jennie Eirian Davies on the novel *Miriam* in *Taliesin* (vol. 36, 1978); there is a profile of Jane Edwards in *Portreadau'r Faner* (ed. Marged Pritchard; vol. 3, 1976).

EDWARDS, JENKIN MORGAN (1903–78), poet. Born at Llanrhystud, Cards., and educated at Trinity College, Carmarthen, he became a teacher in Barry, Glam., in 1935 and lived there for the rest of his life. He published nine volumes of verse: *Cerddi'r Bore* (1924), *Y Tir Pell* (1933), *Cerddi'r Plant Lleiaf* (1936), *Cerddi Pum Mlynedd* (1938), *Peiriannau* (1947), *Cerddi'r Daith* (1954), *Cerddi Hamdden* (1962), *Cerddi'r Fro* (1970) and *Cerddi Ddoe a Heddiw* (1975). The three main influences on his poetry were the Belgian poet Emile Verhaeren, the American Robert Frost and R. Williams *Parry. Rooted in country life, his writing presents a rich mixture of con-temporary and traditional themes; its techniques are those of the *Bardd Gwlad, but it attempts a scientific, analytic contemplation of the conflict between spiritual and material values, and expresses a deep concern about the influence of industry and technology on modern life. J. M. Edwards, who won the *Crown at the National Eisteddfod in 1937, 1941 and 1944, also pub-lished a volume of essays, *Y Crefftwyr* (1976), and his collected poems appeared posthumously under the title *Y Casgliad Cyflawn* (1980).

For further details see the article by R. M. Jones in *Barn* (no. 50, 1966) and the same author's *Llenyddiaeth Gymraeg 1936–1972* (1975); see also the special number of the magazine *Barddas* (no. 24, Nov., 1978).

EDWARDS, JOHN GORONWY (1891–1976), historian, was born in Manchester to Welsh parents who returned to Pentre Halkyn, Flints., when he was very young. Educated at Holywell Grammar School and Jesus College, Oxford, he became a Fellow and Tutor at his old College and, in 1948, was appointed Director of the Institute of Historical Research and Professor of History in the University of London.

It was Sir John Edward *Lloyd's two volumes on the history of Wales down to 1282 which deepened his interest in medieval Welsh history. His *Calendar of Ancient Correspondence* (1935) is an invaluable collection of administrative and political letters from the early thirteenth century onwards. In his introduction to *Littere Wallie* (1940), the correspondence of the Princes of *Gwynedd, he examined the Principality during the thirteenth century from a constitutional point of view. His Raleigh Lecture (1956) on the structure of the Welsh March and *The Principality of Wales 1267–1967* (1969) were further developments of this theme. He also wrote on the Welsh Laws and on parliamentary petitions in the fourteenth century. Highly respected as a medieval historian of the old school, he held many offices, including the Presidency of the Royal Historical Society (1961–64), and was editor, at various times, of the *English Historical Review*, the *Bulletin* of the Institute of Historical Research and the publications of the Flintshire Historical Society.

For further details see the obituary of J. Goronwy Edwards by J. B. Smith in *The Welsh History Review* (vol. 8, no. 4, 1977).

EDWARDS, JOHN HUGH (1869–1945), biographer and editor. Born at Aberystwyth, Cards., he was the Liberal Member of Parliament for Mid-Glamorgan from 1910 to 1922 and later represented the constituency of Accrington. From 1895 to 1904 he was the editor of *Young Wales*, a magazine published under the aegis of *Cymru Fydd. He published three biographies of David *Lloyd George, namely *From Village Green to Downing Street* (1908), *A Life of David Lloyd George, with a short history of the Welsh people* (4 vols., 1913), and *David Lloyd George, the Man and the Statesman* (2 vols., 1929). The editor and publisher of the magazine *Wales* from 1911 to 1914, he was for many years a regular contributor to English newspapers, especially *The British Weekly* and *The Empire News*. The latter part of his life was spent at Hindhead, Surrey, where he was active with the Free Church Council and where he worked on a new history of Wales which remains unpublished.

EDWARDS, LEWIS (1809–87), essayist and theologian, was born at Pwllcenawon, a farm near Pen-llwyn, Cards. He was recognized as a preacher with the Calvinistic Methodists in 1827 and later attended the college which became part of the University of London. After a period as preacher and schoolmaster at Laugharne, he went to study at Edinburgh University where Thomas Chalmers and John Wilson (Christopher North) had a great influence on him. In 1863 he married a granddaughter of Thomas *Charles and settled in Bala, where, with his brother-in-law, David Charles (1812–78), he founded a school which began to prepare students for the Calvinistic Methodist ministry and which was recognized by the denomination in 1839 as its ministerial college. Edwards worked to raise the educational standards of the ministry and, more generally, brought a new breadth and depth to the perception of Welsh affairs. In his own denomination he favoured an ordered polity of a Presbyterian pattern, with

central funds and an organized ministry. He approved also of 'the English cause' (the development of English-language churches in Wales) and in this he represented a tendency which was forcefully challenged by Emrys ap Iwan (Robert Ambrose *Jones).

Although he enjoyed a high reputation for his gifts as a preacher, Lewis Edwards was also an influential editor and a talented prose-writer. In 1843, with Roger *Edwards, he founded the magazine Y *Traethodydd. His literary essays, collected in the volume *Traethodau Llenyddol* (c.1865), include studies of Homer, Shakespeare, Milton, Kant and Goethe, as well as essays on William *Salesbury, Morgan *Llwyd, Daniel *Rowland, Thomas Charles and Eben Fardd (Ebenezer *Thomas), and on a variety of religious, social and educational topics. Although he displays something of the complacency of his period, there are remarkable insights into Welsh literature in some of these essays, as when Edwards scorns the folly of referring to Twm o'r Nant (Thomas *Edwards) as 'The Cambrian Shakespeare'. A second volume, *Traethodau Duwinyddol* (c.1872), contains long essays on the doctrine of Atonement and the harmony of the Faith, together with discussions of biblical themes and the condition of the churches. One of his basic principles is that 'the true view' on all subjects consists of two opposing truths. In these two substantial volumes, and in his history of Theology which was published posthumously under the title *Hanes Duwinyddiaeth* (1889), the heritage of the evangelical Calvinism of the Methodist Revival in Wales was modified by the humanistic and Romantic movements of Europe, for which reason Edwards has been admired and, in some circles, denounced.

An account of his life and thought will be found in Trebor Lloyd Evans, *Lewis Edwards: ei Fywyd a'i Waith* (1967); see also J. Vyrnwy Morgan, *Welsh Religious Leaders in the Victorian Era* (1905).

EDWARDS, OWEN MORGAN (1858–1920), editor, writer and educationist, was born at Coed-y-pry, near Llanuwchllyn, Mer. His education, begun in the local Church school and described in his volume of essays *Clych Atgof* (1906), was continued at Bala Theological College and then at the University College of Wales, Aberystwyth. After studying for a year at Glasgow University, he became in 1884 a student at Balliol College, Oxford, where he had a brilliant career in the school of Modern History. The next two years were spent wandering in Brittany, Switzerland, Italy and Germany, travels which bore fruit in his books *Tro yn Llydaw* (1888), *Tro yn yr Eidal* (1888) and *O'r Bala i Geneva* (1889). In 1889 he was appointed Fellow and Tutor in History at Lincoln College, Oxford, where he remained until his appointment as Chief Inspector of Schools of the Welsh Board of Education in 1907. From then until his death he lived at Llanuwchllyn in a house which he named Neuadd Wen ('White Hall') after the headquarters of the Board of Education in London.

While at Oxford, where Edward *Thomas was one of his students, O. M. Edwards had played a prominent part—together with such men as John *Morris-Jones, Edward *Anwyl, D. Lleufer Thomas and J. Puleston *Jones—in the establishment of *Cymdeithas Dafydd ap Gwilym, the society which was, to a great extent, the initiator of the renaissance which took place in Welsh scholarship and literature in the early twentieth century. From 1888 he devoted himself to the publishing of Welsh books and magazines of a popular kind, specializing in bringing out such series as *Cyfres y Fil and *Cyfres y Werin. For the Welsh who knew little about the history of their own country he set about writing books such as Hanes Cymru (1895, 1899), *Cartrefi Cymru (1896), Wales (1901), A Short History of Wales (1906) and Ystraeon o Hanes Cymru (1894), as well as numerous articles. As an editor and publisher of magazines, Owen M. Edwards made a contribution to Welsh letters which was comparable to that of Thomas *Gee. He began work in this field as co-editor of *Cymru Fydd (1889–91) but then launched his own monthly, *Cymru (1891–1920), and the even more influential Cymru'r Plant (1892–1920) which in its heyday, in 1900, sold some twelve thousand copies a month. His magazine *Wales, for the English-speaking Welsh, was a failure, however, appearing for only three years, from 1894 to 1897, as were a more substantial quarterly, Y *Llenor (1895–98), and Heddyw (1897–98), a monthly review of current affairs. In the midst of this prodigious activity, O. M. Edwards also wrote books for children, including Llyfr Del (1906), Llyfr Nest (1913) and Hwiangerddi Cymru (1911). The society for children known as Urdd y Delyn which he founded in 1896 was a forerunner of *Urdd Gobaith Cymru which was later established by his son, Ifan ab Owen *Edwards.

Owen M. Edwards's influence on the education system in Wales was profound and permanent. Before his day all education in Wales had been through the medium of English (apart from that dispensed in the *Sunday School), but he pressed for education in Welsh and for recognition of the need to teach children about the traditions of their country. In his magazines he helped more than one generation to become familiar with the classics of Welsh literature from every period. He himself was a pioneer in the writing of a more natural, readable Welsh. Although his motto was 'Codi'r Hen Wlad ar ei hôl' ('To restore the Old Country to its former glory'), he had virtually no interest in politics and did not seek re-election after spending a year (1899–1900) as Member of Parliament for his native county. Some have concluded that the influence of the apolitical 'O.M.' (as he was generally known) led patriots of his generation to over-emphasize the importance of cultural *Nationalism at the expense of economic and political policies. Nevertheless, it is generally agreed that he was one of those who laid the foundations of national consciousness in Wales during the twentieth century.

Accounts of the life and work of O. M. Edwards will be found in Owen Morgan Edwards (1937) by W. J. Gruffydd and Bywyd a Gwaith Owen Morgan Edwards (1958) by Gwilym Arthur Jones.

EDWARDS, ROGER (1811–86), author and editor, was born at Bala, Mer., and brought up in Dolgellau. Ordained by the Calvinistic Methodists in 1842, he became one of the foremost members of his denomination. His hymnal Y Salmydd Cymreig (1840), comprising nearly six hundred hymns, was published as a rival to Grawnsypiau Canaan, the collection made by Robert *Jones of Rhoslan, which had been in use for many years. Appointed co-editor of Y Drysorfa in 1847, he was its sole editor from 1856 until his death and his novel Y Tri Brawd (1866) first appeared in that magazine. Intent on removing the Methodists' prejudice against novels, he invited Daniel *Owen to contribute to Y Drysorfa, publishing Y *Dreflan in its pages. Isaac *Foulkes, the novelist's biographer, was of the view that the greatest literary, moral and religious influence on Daniel Owen was that exerted by Roger Edwards.

Among other periodicals edited by Edwards were Y Pregethwr (1841–42) and Y Dyddiadur Methodistaidd (1843–86); he also published a volume of verse, Caneuon (1855). But his major contribution was the founding of the journal Y *Traethodydd, in association with Lewis *Edwards, in 1845. As the co-editor with Owen *Jones (Meudwy Môn) of Cronicl yr Oes, he incensed those such as John *Elias who represented the conservative wing of the Calvinistic Methodist denomination, and prepared the way for the Liberalism of Gwilym Hiraethog (William *Rees) and Thomas *Gee.

For further details see Cofiant y Parch. Roger Edwards (1908) by T. M. Jones; see also the study by J. E. Caerwyn Williams in Cylchgrawn Cymdeithas Hanes y Methodistiaid Calfinaidd (1980).

EDWARDS, THOMAS (**Twm o'r Nant**; 1738–1810), writer of *interludes. Born at Penparchell Isaf, Llannefydd, Denbs., of peasant stock, he was brought up at Nant Ganol, Henllan, and was known thereafter by his nickname. He attended school for only a few weeks, during which he nevertheless discovered the pleasure of reading, and then joined his father as a farm-labourer. Introduced to the bardic tradition by his fellow-workers during their leisure hours, he started to write and to act in interludes. After his marriage in 1763 he earned a living in Denbigh as a haulier but continued to write during slack periods. He fled to south Wales for a while to avoid his creditors, his family keeping a tavern and a toll-gate at Llandeilo, Carms. During his old age he became friendly with Thomas *Charles, whom he admired greatly. Besides an autobiography published in 1805, Twm o'r Nant wrote a large number of songs, most of which remain in manuscript. A mixture of godliness and grossness, they were printed in booklets and sung by ballad-singers at fairs and markets. A substantial collection of them was published under the title *Gardd o Gerddi* in 1790.

It is as a writer of interludes that Twm o'r Nant is remembered today. Among these works the following are the most significant: *Tri Chydymaith Dyn* (1762), *Y Farddoneg Fabilonaidd* (1768), *Cyfoeth a Thlodi* (1768), *★Pedair Colofn Gwladwriaeth* (1786), *Pleser a Gofid* (1787), *★Tri Chryfion Byd* (1789) and *Bannau y Byd* (1808); another, *Cybydd-dod ac Oferedd* (1870), was discovered after his death. The early interludes are full of ribaldry and are lighter in tone and substance than his later work which reflects a keen intelligence, a fertile imagination and traces of deep meditation. His powerful command of Welsh, and the complementary seriousness and frivolity of his personality, have secured for him a reputation as the most significant figure in the history of Welsh ★Drama between the Middle Ages and the twentieth century. As a consequence of the dearth of drama in Welsh during that period, however, excessive claims have been made on his behalf, such as the view of Twm o'r Nant as 'The Cambrian Shakespeare'. Nevertheless, he earned a lasting reputation as an author who was bold enough to attack the injustices of his day in language which still has a robust charm.

A selection of the work of Twm o'r Nant was included in the series *Cyfres y Fil* (2 vols., 1909 and 1910); his autobiography and letters were edited by Glyn Ashton (1948). For discussion of his work see the monograph by Wyn Griffith in the *St. David's Day* series (1953), the essay by Kate Roberts in *Gwŷr Llên y Ddeunawfed Ganrif* (ed. Dyfnallt Morgan, 1966) and that by Saunders Lewis in *Meistri'r Canrifoedd* (ed. R. Geraint Gruffydd, 1973).

EDWARDS, THOMAS (Caerfallwch; 1779–1858), lexicographer, was born at Caerfallwch, Northop, Flints. Apprenticed to a saddler in Mold, he was self-educated and moved to London in 1803 to work as a clerk. A slavish imitator of William ★Owen Pughe, he set himself the task of completing the latter's Welsh dictionary, publishing lists of neologisms for English industrial, economic and scientific terms. Not all the words he coined were accepted, but among the many examples with which he enriched the language are '*pwyllgor*' ('committee'), '*buddsoddi*' ('to invest'), '*cyngerdd*' ('concert'), '*hirgrwn*' ('oval'), '*nwy*' ('gas') and '*safon*' ('standard'). He also published an *Analysis of Welsh Orthography* (1845) which was republished as *Geirlyfr Saesoneg a Chymraeg, an English and Welsh Dictionary* (1850). His poetic effusion '*Adgofion*' describes his childhood, but his verse has little merit.

For further details see the article by Elwyn L. Jones in *Taliesin* (vol. 22, 1971).

Edwards, Thomas (Yr Hwntw Mawr; d. 1813), murderer, was hanged at Dolgellau, Mer., for the killing of Mary Jones, the maid of Penrhyn Isa, a farm near Penrhyndeudraeth, Mer. His motive was robbery but, surprised by the girl, he assaulted her with a ferocity which brought him widespread notoriety. Despite his sobriquet ('The Big Southerner'), Edwards is believed to have been a Borders man who had found employment under William Alexander ★Madocks in the building of the Cob near Porthmadog, Caerns.

Edwards, William (1719–89), stonemason and Independent pastor of Groes-wen in the parish of Eglwysilan, Glam., was described in his epitaph as 'a builder for both worlds'. He is remembered as the designer of the 'New Bridge' (now called the Old Bridge) over the river Taff at Pontypridd, Glam., which was built for Lord Windsor, a local industrialist, after four previous attempts during the years between 1746 and 1756. The town of Pontypridd which later grew around the bridge was first called Newbridge. The bridge's construction was considered a marvel of engineering and the grace of its single span (some 140 feet in length) was much admired by visitors to south Wales and by artists such as Richard ★Wilson who painted 'The Great Bridge over the Taaffe' within ten years of its completion.

For an account of William Edwards's life see the biography by H. P. Richards (1983).

EDWARDS, WILLIAM (Gwilym Callestr, Wil Ysgeifiog; 1790–1855), poet, was born at Caerwys, Flints. A millwright by trade and a tolerably good poet, he won the prize for an *awdl* at the Eisteddfod held at Beaumaris in 1832. Excessive drinking ruined him and he died in the Denbigh asylum. A collection of his poems, with those of others, was published in the volume *Cell Callestr* (1815).

EDWARDS, WILLIAM THOMAS (Gwilym Deudraeth; 1863–1940), poet, was born at Caernarfon and brought up at Penrhyndeudraeth, Mer. He worked in the Oakley slate quarries at Blaenau Ffestiniog and later on the Ffestiniog railway. He is remembered mainly for the wit of his *englynion* which are to be found in two volumes of his poetry, *Chydig ar Gof a Chadw* (1926) and the posthumous collection *Yr Awen Barod* (1943).

EDWART AP RAFF (*fl.* 1557–1606), poet,

was the son of Raff ap Robert of *Bachymbyd, Denbs. About a hundred and fifty of his *cywyddau* survive in manuscript, many addressed to the gentry of Dyffryn Clwyd and other parts of north Wales, such as the *Salusbury, Thelwall, Goodman and *Middleton families. He composed elegies for *Siôn Tudur and *Simwnt Fychan, as well as *englynion* and *cywyddau* of a religious nature, in one of which he recalled his part in the siege of St. Quentin in 1557.

EDWART URIEN (*c.*1580–1614), poet, is believed to have been a native of Mawddwy, Mer., and to have lived in the parish of Mallwyd. His bardic teacher was *Rhys Cain and he wrote eulogies to families in the valleys of the Dyfi and the Ardudwy. Three of his *awdlau*, some thirty *cywyddau* and two of his *englynion* have survived in manuscript.

Edwinsford, a mansion in the parish of Llansawel, Carms., was the home of one of the most cultured families in the county. Poets were welcomed there during the late fourteenth century when *Madog Dwygraig eulogized his patron, Morgan ap Dafydd, and *Lewys Glyn Cothi was frequently a visitor. Patronage was also extended to religious prose-writers and translators and The *Book of the Anchorite of Llanddewibrefi* was in the family's possession.

At the beginning of the seventeenth century Edwinsford was owned by the Williams family. In 1687, when James II wanted to remove the penal laws against Dissenters, Sir Rice Williams of Edwinsford was the only Justice of the Peace in the county to agree with him, saying that he did not believe the laws were consistent with primitive Christianity. Towards the end of the eighteenth century the estate passed to an Englishman, Sir James Hammet Hamlyn, whose son, Sir James Hamlyn Williams, served as Member of Parliament for the county after 1802. After the death in 1913 of the last owner, Sir James Hamlyn Williams Drummond, the estate had several owners; it is now derelict.

Efangelus and Pamphila, see under DUCTOR NUPTIARUM (1777).

Efengyl Nicodemus (lit. 'The gospel of Nicodemus'), a religious text (in Peniarth MS 5, the part dated 1300–25), which consists of two different translations of the apocryphal gospel, *Evangelium Nicodemi*. This latter work is a conflation made (after the 5th cent.) of two compositions, *Acta Pilati*, concerning Christ's death and resurrection, and *Descensus Christi ad Infernos*, His descent into Hell.

Efnysien, a character in the Second Branch of *Pedair Cainc y Mabinogi*, introduced at the beginning of the tale as the brother of Nisien and half-brother of Bendigeidfran (*Brân) and

*Manawydan, is a trouble-maker who is easily insulted. After Brân agrees to give *Branwen in marriage to *Matholwch, King of Ireland, Efnysien antagonizes the Irish by disfiguring their horses as an act of revenge because she has been given without his consent, thus causing the humiliation of Branwen and the campaign in Ireland by the Welsh. When it appears that Irish attempts to pacify the Welsh are succeeding, he snatches Gwern, the son of Branwen and Matholwch, and throws him into the fire, at which there is further hostility between the two sides. During the subsequent battle, Efnysien performs the unselfish act of shattering the *Cauldron of Rebirth which restores life to the Irish dead, but he destroys himself in so doing. It has been suggested that Efnysien is based on Bricriu Nemthenga in the Irish tale *Fled Bricrenn*, but there is no exact correspondence.

Efrydiau Athronyddol (lit. 'Philosophical studies'), a journal published annually by the University of Wales Press on behalf of the Philosophy Section of the Guild of Graduates of the University, first appeared in 1938 under the editorship of Richard I. *Aaron, who was its editor until 1968. It carries a wide range of articles on philosophical subjects, as well as book-reviews. Contributors to recent numbers have included Hywel D. *Lewis, D. Myrddin *Lloyd, J. R. *Jones (1911–70), Pennar *Davies, R. Tudur *Jones and Gwyn *Thomas (1936–   ).

Eglvryn Phraethineb, sebh Dosparth ar Retoreg (lit. 'The exponent of wit, namely a handbook on rhetoric', 1595), a manual by Henry *Perri on Rhetoric, one of the seven liberal arts taught in medieval schools. Although he used William *Salesbury's earlier treatise (1552), Perri's work was more extensive. Many of his examples of rhetorical terms derive from traditional Welsh poetry but his work must be interpreted against the broader background of Renaissance scholarship in the art of Rhetoric in the England of this period. Perri's aim was to produce in Welsh what scholars had already achieved in English and he was heavily influenced by them. The volume was printed by John Dantes in London at the expense of Sir John *Salusbury of Llewenni, to whom it was dedicated. A second edition was published by Owain Myfyr (Owen *Jones) and William *Owen Pughe in 1807 and a reprint of the 1595 edition, with an introduction by G. J. *Williams, was issued by the University of Wales Press in 1930.

Egryn, a house in the parish of Llanaber, Mer., was the home in the sixteenth century of Wiliam ap Tudur, whose generous hospitality was celebrated by Wiliam *Cynwal, *Lewis Menai and Siôn *Phylip. One of Wiliam's sons, Huw, married Gwen, the daughter of Rhisiart Fychan of *Corsygedol, and for her *Edwart Urien and

*Siôn Cain wrote elegies. William *Owen Pughe grew up in the house after his family moved to live there about 1766.

Ehangwen, see under GWLYDDYN SAER.

Ehedydd Iâl, see JONES, WILLIAM (1815–99).

Eiddilig Gor, a dwarf, one of the Three Enchanters of the Isle of Britain, according to a Triad, who could take any form he wished in order to avoid capture.

Eifion Wyn, see WILLIAMS, ELISEUS (1867–1926).

Eifionydd, a commot in *Gwynedd extending from Pwllheli to the outskirts of Porthmadog, formed part of the early kingdom of *Dunoding. It is renowned for the large number of poets who were born or lived within its boundaries. They include Robert *Williams (Robert ap Gwilym Ddu), David *Owen (Dewi Wyn o Eifion), Ebenezer *Thomas (Eben Fardd), John *Thomas (Siôn Wyn o Eifion), Eliseus *Williams (Eifion Wyn) and William *Jones (1896–1961). Some of these poets are commemorated at 'Capel y Beirdd' ('The poets' chapel'), in the vicinity of Yr Ynys. Among prose-writers associated with Eifionydd are Robert *Jones of Rhos-lan and John *Jones (Myrddin Fardd). One of R. Williams *Parry's most famous poems, 'Eifionydd', refers to the tranquillity of the district, especially of Y *Lôn Goed, the tree-lined road which runs through it.

An account of the commot's literary and cultural associations will be found in Gruffudd Parry, Crwydro Llŷn ac Eifionydd (1960).

Eifionydd, see THOMAS, JOHN (1848–1922).

Eigr, the daughter of Anlawdd Wledig and the most beautiful woman in Britain, according to *Brut y Brenhinedd, was married to Gwrlais, Duke of Cornwall, but *Uthr Bendragon became infatuated with her. When Uthr was transformed by *Myrddin into the shape of Gwrlais, he seduced her and from this union *Arthur was born. After her husband's death, Eigr (known in English as Igraine) became the wife of Uthr.

Einion, Yr, see WELSH ANVIL.

EINION AP GWALCHMAI (fl. 1203–23), poet, belonged to the third generation of a family of poets who lived in Anglesey: his grandfather was *Meilyr ap Gwalchmai, court poet to *Gruffudd ap Cynan; his father, *Gwalchmai ap Meilir, sang to *Owain ap Gruffudd (Owain Gwynedd) and others; *Meilyr ap Gwalchmai was his brother, and so, possibly, was *Elidir Sais. Of Einion's works there have survived a tender elegy for Nest, the daughter of Hywel of

Tywyn, Mer., a few lines of a poem addressed to *Llywelyn ap Iorwerth (Llywelyn Fawr) and, most important of all, three long awdlau to God. He was a master of the single line and had more lyrical intensity than many of the other court poets. In his religious poems he expressed weariness in the service of princes, his loathing of war and his longing for the monastic life. He also praised mead, feasts, the long bright summer, horses and sports, but most of all he sang the glory of God. The poet *Gwilym Ddu o Arfon paid tribute to Einion's lyrical genius when he compared it with a foaming fountain.

Einion was the only poet of his day who became a figure of folklore. It is said that he once leapt fifty feet in his sweetheart's presence. Another traditional tale relates how his wife recognized him, on his return from a long pilgrimage, by his playing of the harp and his production of a half of their wedding-ring, the other half of which had been left with her.

For further details see the article by Tomos Roberts in Gwŷr Môn (ed. Bedwyr Lewis Jones, 1979).

EINION AP GWGAN (fl. 1215), a poet of whose work there has survived only one awdl, a long and resounding paean of praise to *Llywelyn ap Iorwerth (Llywelyn Fawr) at the height of his power. The Prince's valour is hailed, the poet affirms, from the Vale of Tanat and *Offa's Dyke to Carmarthen and Cardigan, the English fleeing before him. In the poem Llywelyn is set in the tradition of the heroes of the *Old North, such as *Rhydderch Hen and *Rhun ap Maelgwn Gwynedd, and Einion pledges his loyalty to the Prince just as his father had done to Iorwerth Drwyndwn, the Prince's father.

EINION AP MADOG AP RHAHAWD (fl. 1237), a poet of whose work only one short awdl has survived. Of historical more than literary interest, it praises Gruffudd ap Llywelyn and was composed after that Prince's release from captivity in 1234 and before his final imprisonment in 1239 by his half-brother, Dafydd ap Llywelyn. During the intervening years Gruffudd had held Llŷn and parts of *Powys. The poet refers to Gruffudd's bravery against 'the French' (the Anglo-Normans) and praises him for holding his lands without homage or tribute.

EINION OFFEIRIAD (fl. 1330), a priest to whom the authorship of a bardic grammar is ascribed. The work was first attributed to him by Thomas *Wiliems who referred to him as Einion Offeiriad of Gwynedd. The texts themselves do not mention Einion as author of the grammar but state that he composed three of the measures contained in it. They belong to the first half of the fourteenth century and may have been written by a native of Caernarfonshire or Cardiganshire.

The grammar, an adaptation of the Latin

grammars attributed to Donatus and Priscianus, deals with letters, syllables, parts of speech, construction, metrics (but not *cynghanedd*), the *Twenty-four Metres and the prohibited faults; three of Einion's own compositions are also included. The work is not an authoritative re-cension of a fixed canon of *Cerdd Dafod. It is, rather, an acknowledgement of new forms and an expression of the author's own viewpoint, and it proved to be an important document in the development of metrics and aesthetics. Part of the work's distinction is its discussion of 'the way all things should be praised', in which are propounded the principles of the master poets' eulogistic art. To Einion Offeiriad must there-fore be attributed the earliest known discussion of the metrical and philosophical principles of Welsh prosody, as well as a clear statement of its social function. See also DAFYDD DDU ATHRO and EDERN DAFOD AUR.

For further details see the article by Thomas Parry, 'The Welsh Metrical Treatise attributed to Einion Offeiriad', in the *Proceedings* of the British Academy (vol. XLVII, 1961), the article by J. Beverley Smith in the *Bulletin* of the Board of Celtic Studies (vol. XXI, 1966), the chapter by Ceri Lewis in *A Guide to Welsh Literature* (ed. A. O. H. Jarman and Gwilym Rees Hughes, 1979) and the article by Rachel Bromwich in *Ysgrifau Beirniadol X* (ed. J. E. Caerwyn Williams, 1977).

EINION WAN (*fl.* 1230–45), a court poet who lived towards the end of the reign of *Llywelyn ap Iorwerth (Llywelyn Fawr). Six of his sequences of *englynion* have survived, including an elegy for Madog ap Gruffudd Maelor, who died in 1236, and poems addressed to Llywelyn and his sons Dafydd and Gruffudd.

Eisteddfod, a word which originally meant a session or assembly of poets, is derived from the Welsh verb '*eistedd*', meaning 'to sit'. It has come to denote a festival which includes not only a literary element but also cultural activity of other kinds, often organized on competitive lines. The tradition can be traced with certainty to the fifteenth century and perhaps to the event held under the patronage of *Rhys ap Gruffudd (The Lord Rhys) at *Cardigan in 1176. The early eisteddfod was a gathering of poets who belonged to the *Bardic Order and its main function was to regulate the affairs of their pro-fession by establishing the metrical rules and granting licences to those who had completed the prescribed stages of their apprenticeship, in order to prevent the proliferation of itinerancy. The most important of these eisteddfodau were held at *Carmarthen about the year 1451 and at *Caerwys in 1523 and 1567.

Thereafter the tradition degenerated but, dur-ing the eighteenth century, literary men still met in taverns for disputation and entertainment in verse, occasions associated with the *Almanac. During this period of decline the neo-druidic

institution known as *Gorsedd Beirdd Ynys Pry-dain* was invented by Iolo Morganwg (Edward *Williams). The eisteddfod was revived on a provincial basis during the nineteenth century by the *Cymreigyddion Society and Yr *Hen Bersoniaid Llengar* ('The Old Literary Clerics'). The movement culminated in the 1860s with the formation of the National Eisteddfod Society under the aegis of the Honourable Society of *Cymmrodorion. The *National Eisteddfod is by now the principal festival of its kind but there are also several regional eisteddfodau, such as those held annually in Powys, Cardigan, Anglesey and Pontrhydfendigaid, which make significant contributions to the culture of Wales by means of competitions and performances, while many towns and villages continue to organize their own local festivals. Among other bodies which organize eisteddfodau are the National Union of Mineworkers and *Urdd Gobaith Cymru. See also LLANGOLLEN INTER-NATIONAL MUSICAL EISTEDDFOD.

For further details see Idris Foster (ed.), *Twf yr Eistedd-fod* (1968) and Hywel Teifi Edwards, *Yr Eisteddfod* (1976) and *Gwyl Gwalia: Yr Eisteddfod yn Oes Aur Victoria 1858–1868* (1980).

Elen Luyddog (lit. 'Elen of the Hosts'; 4th cent.), the heroine of *The Dream of Macsen Wledig*, one of the two historical tales in the *Mabinogion. *Macsen can almost certainly be identified with Magnus Maximus, the Roman Governor of Britain who, in AD 383, frustrated by the weakness of imperial rule, left Britain with his army to conquer Rome and make him-self Emperor. In the *Dream* Macsen was already Emperor when the image of Elen entered his sleeping brain, but this is a romantic misremem-bering. Elen was the daughter of Eudaf, a British chieftain who held Segontium (Caernarfon) for the Romans, and Maximus was very probably married to her before he left, accompanied by Elen and her two brothers, Cynan and Gadeon who, in the *Dream*, re-conquer Rome for him. This part of the story has become markedly less ridiculous since the discovery in the *Notitia Dignitatum* (AD 429) of a legion called the Segon-tientes serving in the Balkans. One of Elen's brothers, *Cynan Meiriadog, is described in the *Dream* as settling on the Continent after the completion of his service for the Emperor and recent research finds it very likely that he settled near Nantes. Elen is therefore historical enough as the wife of Maximus, though her fate after his overthrow in 388 is not known.

The attribution to Elen of the initiative in building roads from one stronghold to another across the island of Britain is plainly an onomastic interpolation caused by the existence for long after the Roman occupation of sections of road (in Cardiganshire, Caernarfonshire, Merioneth and Breconshire) called Sarn Helen, the purpose of which seems to have been to facilitate the removal of metal ores from the hilly heart of Wales. The Helen of Sarn Helen may have originally signified '*elbow*' or '*angle*' (W. '*elin*'), the normally straight Roman roads not being possible in such country, or, with less likelihood, may have been derived from '*Y Lleng*' ('The Legion'). The popular confusion about Sarn Helen was made worse by Welsh writers of the twelfth and thirteenth centuries who were anxious to claim that Elen of Segontium was also Saint Helen, whose association with Britain is in any case fictitious. Saint Helen was said to be the daughter of the eponymous King Cole of Colchester (see under COEL HEN) and married to the Roman Emperor Constantius, to whom she bore Constantine, the first Christian Emperor. She was also alleged to have discovered the True Cross at Jerusalem. This Helen, who was never in Britain, was more than a generation too old to be identified with Elen of the Hosts.

For a discussion of this last confusion see Charles Kightly, *Folk Heroes of Britain* (1982); see also Rachel Bromwich, *Trioedd Ynys Prydein* (2nd edn., 1978).

Elerydd, see GRUFFYDD, WILLIAM JOHN (1916–   ).

Elfael, a cantref of southern *Powys lying to the north-east of the Wye, was ruled by the descendants of Elystan Glodrydd, traditionally said to have been the father of the fifth of the Royal Tribes of Wales. In 1276 the cantref came into the possession of Ralph Tony, from whose descendants it passed to the Earls of Warwick. Its centre at Painscastle was one of the key fortifications in the March.

Elfed, a commot of *Cantref Gwarthaf in Dyfed, was linked in the thirteenth century with the commots of Derllys and *Gwidigada to form the core of what later became the county of Carmarthen.

Elfed, see LEWIS, HOWELL ELVET (1860–1953).

Elffin ap Gwyddno, a character often remembered in poems connected with the legend of *Taliesin, is depicted as a prodigal son who squanders the wealth of his father, *Gwyddno Garanhir, at the court of *Maelgwn Gwynedd in *Deganwy. As Gwyddno's riches diminish, his decides to give his son a chance of improving his circumstances by granting him the first haul of fish from his weir on May Day, when the catch is usually worth a hundred pounds. On this occasion, however, not one fish is caught but the child Taliesin is found in a basket. Elffin takes the child to his father's court and fosters him until he is thirteen years old and, from the day on which Taliesin is rescued, Elffin's fortunes improve steadily. He is later imprisoned at the court of Maelgwn, however, for boasting about his own wife's chastity and for asserting that he has at

home a poet who is superior to those of the king. On Taliesin's advice, Maelgwn's plot to ruin the good name of Elffin's wife is foiled and Taliesin visits the court where he defeats all other poets. Elffin is released and shortly afterwards his horse, again with Taliesin's aid, wins a race against the king's horses. The poet commands Elffin to dig in the earth at the spot where the race has ended and there he finds a cauldron full of gold which Taliesin bids him keep as a reward for saving him from the weir.

Elfynydd, see KENWARD, JAMES (*fl.* 1834–68).

Elfodd (d. 809), the chief Bishop of *Gwynedd, according to the record of his death in *Annales Cambriae*, is believed to have been a member of the monastic community at Caergybi (Holyhead). There is also more dubious evidence that he was elected Bishop of Bangor in 755. Admired by *Nennius, he gave an important lead to Christianity in Wales by accepting the Roman method of dating *Easter, as other branches of the *Celtic Church had already done.

Eli Jenkins, the minister in Dylan *Thomas's *Under Milk Wood* (1954), is a simple, kindly soul for whom life is 'a green-leaved sermon on the innocence of men'. He is moved by the wanton *Polly Garter's singing, particularly about her many lovers, to observe, 'Praise the Lord! We are a musical nation'. Every morning and evening it is his function as the poet of Llareggub to stand at the door of Bethesda's manse and recite his verses. Hymn-stanzas full of old-fashioned diction and benevolent sentiments, they include his 'Sunset Poem' with its famous lines:

> We are not wholly bad or good
> Who live our lives under Milk Wood,
> And Thou, I know, wilt be the first
> To see our best side, not our worst.

Elian's Well, a spring in the parish of Llandrillo-yn-Rhos, Denbs., which was said to have issued from the ground when the saint prayed for water to drink. It became famous throughout Wales in the nineteenth century as a cursing well: the name of the victim was written on a piece of paper or slate which was thrown into the water while the curse was uttered. An end was put to the practice after a local man, one John Evans (d. 1854), had been imprisoned for taking money by means of deception. The well's reputation is remembered in various curses and sayings still to be heard in the district.

ELIAS, JOHN (1774–1841), Calvinistic Methodist minister, the first to be ordained when the Connexion was formed in 1811, was the most famous preacher of his denomination in his day. He was born at Crynllwyn, near Pwllheli, Caerns. Uncompromising in his commitment to High Calvinism and in his belief in the literal truth of the Bible, he embraced the controversial teaching that the Atonement was reserved for the Elect of God. Despite his wide interests, 'the Methodist Pope', as he was commonly known, opposed all political *Radicalism as well as the idea that the voice of the people is the voice of God. His writings include *Traethawd ar y Saboth* (1804), *Golygiad Ysgrythurol ar Gyfiawnhad Pechadur* (1821), a number of essays contributed to the periodical *Y Drysorfa* and an autobiography (1974).

For further details see the article by Harri Williams in *Y Traethodydd* (Oct., 1974) and the autobiography of John Elias which was edited by Goronwy Prys Owen in 1974.

ELIAS, JOHN ROOSE (**Y Thesbiad**; 1819–81), poet and critic. Born at Bryn-du, Ang., a nephew of John *Elias, he was engaged for most of his life in historical research, publishing many articles in Welsh and English on literary, political and social subjects in which he displayed a keen critical faculty. He also wrote verse in both languages, but published only a small selection in the volume *Llais o'r Ogof* (1877).

ELIDIR SAIS (*fl.* 1195–1246), a court poet, perhaps the son of *Gwalchmai ap Meilyr, was critical of *Llywelyn ap Iorwerth's policies and may, for this reason, have had to go into exile in England, thus acquiring the epithet *Sais* ('Englishman'). In a poem of intercession addressed to Llywelyn he warned the Prince of the consequences of his campaign and appealed to him to show more restraint. The poet also risked Llywelyn's displeasure by lamenting the death of *Rhodri ab Owain Gwynedd and comparing his persecution of Dafydd, the Prince's other uncle, with the occupation of Jerusalem by Saladin. Even in the religious poems ascribed to Elidir he is outspoken in his disapproval of Llywelyn's use of force. In one there is a magnificent description of Llywelyn in his ascendancy but it is followed by Elidir's assertion that he, the poet, would prefer tranquil joy and faith to the triumphs of the world. His attitude towards the splendour of princes is made clear in the line '*Bardd fyddaf i Dduw hyd tra fwyf dyn*' ('I will be a poet to God as long as I am a man'). His religious poems are grounded in a profound knowledge of the Scriptures and, in a poem for Lent, while meditating upon the events of Passion Week, he displayed a fervour which was typical of the new emphasis in the devotional life of the period.

Elidir Sais, see JONES, WILLIAM HUGHES (1885–1951).

Elidyr, a character in a folk-tale recorded by *Gerald de Barri (Giraldus Cambrensis). The boy, while playing truant, hides under a river bank and there he meets two little men who lead him to a land full of games and luxuries. When, at last, he finds his way home, he is encouraged by his mother to return to that delightful country and to bring her back gold or jewels. He does her bidding and steals a golden ball, but on his way home once more he accidentally drops the ball and is never able to find the land of the *Tylwyth Teg again. Years later, as the priest Brother Eliodorus, he is said to have described this adventure to Gerald's uncle, Dewi II, the Bishop of *St. David's.

ELIS, ISLWYN FFOWC (1924–   ), novelist. Born at Wrexham, Denbs., but brought up a farmer's son in Dyffryn Ceiriog, he was educated at the University College of North Wales, Bangor, and later served as a Calvinistic Methodist minister at Llanfair Caereinion, Mont., and at Newborough, Ang. He left the ministry in 1956 and went to live in Bangor as a free-lance writer and producer for the BBC. In 1963 he joined the staff of Trinity College, Carmarthen, as a Lecturer in Welsh. From 1968 to 1971 he worked as an editor and translator with the *Welsh Books Council, then returned to Wrexham, living once more as a full-time writer for four years. In 1975 he took up the post of Lecturer in Welsh at St. David's University College, Lampeter, and was appointed Reader in 1984.

He gained recognition as a writer when he won the *Prose Medal at the National Eisteddfod of 1951 for a collection of essays, *Cyn Oeri'r Gwaed* (1952). From then on, despite many difficulties, not least his decision to give up the ministry and earn his living as a writer, he laid solid foundations for the contemporary *novel in Welsh on which other writers were able to build during the 1960s and 1970s. In *Cysgod y Cryman* (1953) he demonstrated not only a mastery of his medium but also a gift for storytelling and the ability to create memorable characters, establishing with that book a new, young and enthusiastic readership for the Welsh novel. With his second novel, *Ffenestri Tua'r Gwyll* (1953), he moved into the less familiar world of the fine arts with a bold portrayal of a rich woman and the painters who enjoy her patronage. But that book was not so well received and he returned in his third novel, *Yn Ôl i Leifior* (1956), to the rural setting he knew best. Other novels followed in quick succession: *Wythnos yng Nghymru Fydd* (1957) is an investigation into the Wales of the future, *Blas y Cynfyd* (1958) a study of tensions between town and country and *Tabyrddau'r Babongo* (1961) a satirical comedy set in Africa. After a silence of a few years, he published three more novels, namely *Y Blaned Dirion* (1968), *Y Gromlech yn yr Haidd* (1971) and *Eira Mawr* (1972), a play about the Methodist Revival, *Harris* (1973), and a selection of short stories, *Marwydos* (1974).

Some critics take the view that Islwyn Ffowc Elis, in his attempts to create a wider audience for the Welsh novel by deliberately making his work more popular in its appeal, has set limits on the literary value of his writing. Nevertheless, while the need to sustain suspense in the narrative sometimes affects adversely the characterization in his books, it is agreed that he has succeeded in giving the Welsh novel contemporary relevance and, in so doing, increased its potential for other writers.

There is an autobiographical essay by Islwyn Ffowc Elis in the volume *Artists in Wales* (ed. Meic Stephens, 1971); see also the interview he gave to the magazine *Mabon* (ed. Gwyn Thomas, 1973) and the note by John Rowlands in *Profiles* (1980).

Elis, Meg, see DAFYDD, MARGED (1950–   ).

Elis o'r Nant, see PIERCE, ELLIS (1841–1912).

Elis Wyn o Wyrfai, see ROBERTS, ELLIS (1827–95).

Eliseg's Pillar, see under CYNGEN (d. 855) and GENEALOGIES.

Ellis, Alice Thomas, see HAYCRAFT, ANNA (1932–   ).

ELLIS, DAVID (1736–95), priest and scholar. Born in the parish of Dolgellau, Mer., and educated at Oxford, he was a curate for most of his life but was preferred to the living of Llanberis, Caerns., in the year before his death. He made Welsh translations of Thomas Wilson's *The Knowledge and Practice of Christianity* (1774), James Merrick's *A Short Manual of Prayers* (1774) and William Smith's *History of the Holy Jesus* (1776). But his most important contribution to Welsh scholarship was made as copyist of a large number of manuscripts now preserved in the National Library of Wales, in the library of the University College of North Wales, Bangor, and in the Cardiff City Library; they include a transcription of *Mona Antiqua Restaurata* by Henry *Rowlands.

ELLIS, ROBERT (**Cynddelw**; 1812–75), poet and editor, born near Pen-y-bont-fawr, Mont., began preaching in 1834 and later became a Baptist minister. Among the works he edited were the second edition of Rhys *Jones's anthology *Gorchestion Beirdd Cymru* (1864), *Geiriadur y Bardd* (n.d.) and *Barddoniaeth Dafydd ap Gwilym* (n.d.). Of his own work he published *Manion Hynafiaethol* (1873) and biographies of his schoolmaster, John Williams (1806–56), and of Dr. Ellis Evans of Cefn Mawr. His poems were collected posthumously in the volume *Barddoniaeth Cynddelw* (1877); his best-known poem is 'Cywydd y Berwyn'. A regular contributor to the Baptist press, he edited the periodicals *Y Tyst Apostolaidd* (1846–50) and *Y *Tyst* (1851), and he was poetry editor of *Y *Greal* and *Seren Gomer* from 1852 until

the year of his death.

For further details see the biography of Robert Ellis by David Williams (1935).

Ellis, Rowland (1650–1731), Quaker leader, of Bryn Mawr near Dolgellau, Mer., was driven by persecution to America and soon after his arrival in 1686 he joined the settlement of William Penn. A man of culture, he became a prominent figure in the community and a representative for Philadelphia on the governing body of the colony. He translated into English the work of a fellow-Quaker, Ellis Pugh, namely *Annerch i'r Cymry* (1721), under the title *A Salutation to the Britains* (1727). The name of his old home is preserved in that of the celebrated Bryn Mawr College for Women in Pennsylvania. The novel *Y Stafell Ddirgel* (1969) and its sequel, *Y Rhandir Mwyn* (1972), by Marion *Eames are based on the life of Rowland Ellis. See also WELSH TRACT.

Ellis, Thomas Edward (1859–99), politician, was born at Cefnddwysarn, near Bala, Mer., the son of a tenant farmer. His education, unusually extensive for a Welsh Nonconformist of the time, included nearly ten years divided between the University College of Wales, Aberystwyth, and New College, Oxford, where he read History. In 1886 he was elected as the Gladstonian Liberal Member for Merioneth on a platform unequivocally advocating *Home Rule for Wales. He proved to be a subtle and extremely conscientious parliamentarian who did much in a practical way to advance Welsh causes, notably education, *Disestablishment and *Land Reform. Having been instrumental in securing the appointment of the Royal Commission on Land in Wales, he was perhaps the most effective witness to appear before that body. There was also in his outlook a vein of idealism like Mazzini's and, for a time, a strong sense of Celtic identity. He was much to the fore in the establishment of the *Cymru Fydd movement in 1886, but his appointment, hesitatingly accepted, to the office of Junior Whip in 1892, and Chief Whip two years later, advanced his parliamentary influence at the expense of his radical appeal. On holiday in Egypt in 1890 he had contracted typhoid and thereafter he suffered from ill health, exacerbated by overwork.

Tom Ellis was a cultured man (he edited a volume of the works of the Puritan writer Morgan *Llwyd) and maintained the closest links with his roots in rural, Nonconformist Wales. He charmed the common people with his attractive personality, becoming the most potent symbol of Welsh aspirations—educational, denominational, cultural and, in varying degrees, political—and his early death canonized him as the lost leader of Victorian Wales.

The *Speeches and Addresses* of T. E. Ellis were published in 1912 and there is a biography in Welsh by his son, T. I. Ellis (2 vols., 1944, 1948); see also Neville Masterman, *The Forerunner: the Dilemmas of Tom Ellis* (1972) and the article by Frank Price Jones in the *Transactions of the Honourable Society of Cymmrodorion* (1960) which was reprinted in his *Radicaliaeth a'r Werin Gymreig yn y Bedwaredd Ganrif ar Bymtheg* (1977).

ELLIS, THOMAS IORWERTH (1899–1970), author, was born in London, the posthumous son of Thomas Edward *Ellis, and educated at the University College of Wales, Aberystwyth, and Jesus College, Oxford. He was a Lecturer in Classics in the University of Wales and, for ten years, Headmaster of the County School at Rhyl, Flints. A prolific contributor to the Welsh periodical press, he wrote six volumes in the series *Cyfres Crwydro Cymru* (1953–59), as well as a biography of his father (2 vols., 1944, 1948), numerous pamphlets on cultural and political topics and a volume of essays, *Ym Mêr fy Esgyrn* (1955). T. I. Ellis's literary work would undoubtedly have been more extensive but for his devotion to the institutions on whose committees he served; these included the *University of Wales, the *National Library and the Church in Wales. His most important contribution was his indefatigable service as secretary of *Undeb Cymru Fydd during the years from 1941 to 1967.

ELLIS, THOMAS PETER (1873–1936), historian, was born in Wrexham, Denbs., and educated at Lincoln College, Oxford, where he read Law. He entered the Indian Civil Service as a legal officer and became a judge in the Punjab. Returning to Wales in 1921, he was converted to Roman Catholicism and lived near Dolgellau, Mer. There he began to study and publish works on medieval Welsh law, including *Welsh Tribal Law and Custom in the Middle Ages* (2 vols., 1926) which, because of its comprehensive treatment of the subject, is still considered valuable. Also important are his books *The First Extent of Bromfield and Yale* (1924), a transcript of and introduction to the land survey made of those territories in 1315, *The Catholic Martyrs of Wales 1535–1680* (1933) and *The Welsh Benedictines of the Terror* (1936).

Elphin, see GRIFFITH, ROBERT ARTHUR (1860–1936).

Emlyn, one of the seven cantrefi of Dyfed, was seized by Gerald de Windsor, Castellan of Pembroke, about 1105. Welsh rule was restored under *Rhys ap Gruffudd (The Lord Rhys) but the western half of the cantref (Emlyn Is Cuch), with the castle of *Cilgerran, fell to the Earls of Pembroke in 1204. The new castle in Emlyn was built by Maredudd, the grandson of Rhys ap Gruffudd, in Emlyn Uwch Cuch about 1240. Uwch Cuch was incorporated into the county of Carmarthen after the revolt of Rhys ap Maredudd in 1287 and Is Cuch became part of the county of Pembroke in 1536.

'Emmanuel' (2 vols., 1861, 1867), a poem in blank verse by William *Rees (Gwilym Hiraethog), consisting of approximately twenty-two thousand lines, is the longest poem in the Welsh language. The first part contains twelve cantos treating of Divinity, Creation, Satan's Revolt and the Fall of Man, and the second a further twelve cantos describing several allegorical visions. Miltonic in inspiration and design, the poem was an attempt at a Christian *Epic, the dream of Welsh poets since the eighteenth century. However, no critic has yet contested the view of Thomas *Parry that 'there is in the whole barren length of the work scarcely one poetic virtue'.

Emral, a mansion in Maelor Saesneg, Flints., was the home of the Pulestons, who maintained the tradition of bardic patronage in the county. The family was descended from Sir Roger de Puleston, granted land by Edward I before 1283, and his great-grandson Richard (c.1350) was probably the first patron. Many poets, such as *Guto'r Glyn, *Gutun Owain and *Lewys Glyn Cothi (Llywelyn y Glyn), were received by Richard's great-grandson Roger, and patronage continued for four generations thereafter until 1587.

Emrys, see AMBROSE, WILLIAM (1813–73).

Emrys Wledig or **Ambrosius** (*fl.* 430 or 475), British commander, was more certainly a historical figure than any Briton of his day except Gwrtheyrn (*Vortigern). *Gildas, in his *De Excidio Britanniae*, names no other leader against the Saxon invaders. It is possible, however, that there were two men of this name who were, perhaps, father and son. The elder Ambrosius was a rival of Vortigern in the decade after 430, while Ambrosius the younger (Ambrosius Aurelianus) began a British resistance to the invaders which Gildas regards as continuous until its successful conclusion in the battle of Badon. If the year 519, the more usual date for this battle, be accepted, then the beginning of the resistance led by Emrys can perhaps be dated 475 or 480. Gildas's history is dubious, however, in that he appears to be writing of the father, or the elder Ambrosius, while his chronology indicates the younger man.

It is certainly the elder Ambrosius who appears in the much later narrative of *Nennius, *Historia Brittonum. In this text, Vortigern, retiring to the frontiers of his kingdom, tries to establish a new fortress in *Gwynedd but is frustrated by the collapse, time after time, of its foundations. His wise men advise him that the blood of 'a fatherless boy' must be sprinkled over the site before the fortress can be built. Such a boy is found playing with a ball in Carmarthen and, when brought before the king, he tells Vortigern that his name is 'Ambros, in British

Embresguletic', and that his father had been a Roman consul. The boy proceeds to confound the wise men with his own wisdom and then reveals that, under the foundations of the fortress, there is a pool in which lurk two dragons, one red and the other white, and that it is their movement which causes the foundations of Vortigern's fortress to collapse. The *red dragon, it is understood, represents the native British and the white dragon the Saxon invaders. Discovered, the beasts engage in a fight to the death, the red dragon proving in the end victorious.

It was *Geoffrey of Monmouth, realizing from the magic elements of the tale that two stories had probably been conflated, who called the boy Ambrosius Merlin and had him prophesy that, while the red dragon would eventually triumph, the red and the white would be locked in combat for centuries. In the tale known as *Cyfranc Lludd a Llefelys, there is a reference to the terrible scream, heard every May Eve, which is said to be made by the native dragon fighting against the dragon of the invaders. Lludd, on his brother's advice, captures both and hides them in a stone coffer at Dinas Emrys. At this site, in Gwynedd, there is archaeological evidence of such a pool as the tale requires, but the narrative may have grown onomastically from that fact. See also FORTUNATE CONCEALMENTS AND UNFORTUNATE DISCLOSURES.

For further details see Leslie Alcock, *Arthur's Britain* (1971), John Morris, *The Age of Arthur* (1973) and A. H. A. Hogg, *Hill-Forts of Britain* (1975).

EMYR, JOHN (1950–   ), novelist and critic, was born at Llanwnda, Caerns. Educated at the University College of Wales, Aberystwyth, he has been the Head of the Welsh Department at Friar's School, Bangor, since 1984. He has published a critical study of the work of Kate *Roberts, *Enaid Clwyfus* (1976), a novel, *Terfysg Haf* (1979), and a volume of short stories, *Mynydd Gwaith* (1984).

Enclosures, a prominent feature of the Welsh landscape from the early modern period onwards. In medieval times, open fields were sometimes fenced or sub-divided by temporary wooden hurdles, but the landscape was for the most part not enclosed. Hedges were introduced as a result of Anglo-Norman settlement: small, enclosed fields were created around manorial centres and hunting parks, while the larger freehold farms were bounded by hedge-banks.

During the sixteenth and early seventeenth centuries, however, the Welsh gentry were extremely active in extending their estates and, wherever possible, they created 'closes', or hedged fields, on their demesnes. Those tenants who held scattered strips in open fields were encouraged to make consolidated holdings by means of voluntary exchanges and the enclosure

of their lands, but this proved a protracted process which, in some counties, took hundreds of years to accomplish. Because of the pressure of a growing population upon land resources, smallholdings were often made out of waste land. Usually such assarts were licensed by manorial authority, but in some districts the practice of erecting 'y tŷ unnos' ('the one-night house') gradually developed. According to this custom, if a man built a cottage overnight on waste land and had smoke issuing from its chimney by morning, he had the right to live in the house and to farm a small parcel of surrounding land.

By the eve of the French Revolutionary Wars, most land—apart from the extensive common wastes of the uplands—had been enclosed and during the years between 1793 and 1815 these too were brought into private ownership and sub-divided by the dry stone walls which remain a feature of the Welsh countryside to this day. These late enclosures caused much hardship for the poorer classes who thus lost common grazing and turbary rights, as Hugh *Evans vividly described in his book *Cwm Eithin* (1931). See also BLACK DEATH.

For further details see Ivor Bowen, *The Great Enclosures of Common Lands in Wales* (1914).

ENDERBIE, PERCY (1601?–70?), historian, was an Englishman who married into the *Morgan family of Llantarnam, Mon.; he lived in Wales for many years, learned Welsh and was an admirer of the nation's history. His chief work, *Cambria Triumphans* (1661), written at Llantarnam, was intended to demonstrate the Welsh descent of the Stuarts.

'Eneth gadd ei Gwrthod, Yr' (lit. 'The girl who was refused'), a *stable-loft song which was popular at the end of the nineteenth century and early in the twentieth. The words, written by John Jones (Llew o'r Wern), refer to the sad fate of Jane Williams, Ty'n-y-caeau, Cynwyd, Mer., who drowned herself in 1868 at the age of twenty-three after being jilted by her sweetheart. The tune is not traditionally Welsh, as is often supposed: it is known in England as 'There's love among the roses'.

Englefield or **Tegeingl**, one of the four cantrefi of *Perfeddwlad. The name is probably derived from that of the Deceangli, the tribe which inhabited the district between the rivers Clwyd and Dee at the time of the Roman invasion. Tegeingl was bisected by *Offa's Dyke but was restored in its entirety to Welsh rule by Gruffudd ap Llywelyn. The Norman Earls of Chester claimed Tegeingl as part of their territory but *Owain ap Gruffudd (Owain Gwynedd) succeeded in maintaining it under his jurisdiction, as did *Llywelyn ap Iorwerth (Llywelyn Fawr) and *Llywelyn ap Gruffudd. From 1277 onwards, however, the cantref was firmly in the possession of the English Crown and under the provisions of the Statute of *Rhuddlan (1284) it became part of the county of Flint. In the *gorhoffedd* of *Hywel ab Owain Gwynedd Tegeingl is described as '*y tir tecach yn elfydd*' ('the fairest land in the world').

Englyn, the oldest recorded Welsh metrical form, dates from at least the ninth century. Several types occur among the *Twenty-four Metres of *Cerdd Dafod, but by far the most popular is the *englyn unodl union*, a four-line monorhyming combination of a *toddaid byr* and a *cywydd couplet. The *toddaid byr*, here called the *paladr*, is presented in two lines, ten syllables in the first and six in the second. The end-rhyme of the verse is announced in the seventh, eighth or ninth syllable of the first line. The remaining syllable or syllables, known as the *cyrch*, form *cynghanedd with the second line, usually with its first part only. The end-rhyme of the first line may be accented or not but that of the second line is almost invariably unaccented. The *cywydd* couplet, here known as the *esgyll*, consists of two seven-syllable lines, the end-rhyme of one being accented and the other unaccented. All four lines, excepting the last part of the second line, must be in full *cynghanedd* but *cynghanedd lusg* is not permitted in the second and fourth lines. Variations on the *englyn unodl union* are the *englyn penfyr*, the *englyn milwr*, the *englyn unodl crwca*, the *englyn cyrch* and the *englyn proest*.

Originally found as a verse in a long poem such as an *awdl, the *englyn* can still be so used. It may also form a link in a chain where the end of one *englyn* is repeated at the beginning of the next and where the end of the last *englyn* matches the start of the first (see CYNGOGION). More commonly, the *englyn* occurs as a single-stanza poem, for which reason it has been compared with the Greek epigram and the Japanese haiku. It can be didactic, elegiac, proverbial, epigrammatic, lyrical or humorous in tone and its brevity and integral intricacy give it a unique intensity. The form also lends itself to impromptu competition, to greeting on occasions such as weddings and to inscription on gravestones.

Here is an example in English by T. Arfon *Williams:

> A bee in your flower bed—I alight
> b' (n   r fl   r)b'   l'
> on the lips full-parted
> (n th) l'
> of your fox-glove, beloved,
> and am freely, fully fed.
>   f'   f'

For further details and discussion of the *englyn* see *Ynglŷn â Chrefft Englyna* (ed. T. Arfon Williams, 1981). The best modern anthology is *Y Flodeugerdd Englynion* (ed. Alan Llwyd, 1978); for a selection of humorous examples see Huw Ceiriog (ed.), *Y Flodeugerdd o Englynion Ysgafn* (1981). There is an article on the form

by R. M. Jones in *Ysgrifau Beirniadol XII* (ed. J. E. Caerwyn Williams, 1982).

'Englynion Dydd Brawd' (lit. 'The stanzas of judgement day'), a series of short poems describing the signs to be expected during the fifteen days before the Day of Judgement. These signs, a knowledge of which was widespread in the medieval period, were thought to have been listed in a lost work by Jerome, *Annales Hebraeorum*. The Welsh poems, which occur in The *White Book of Rhydderch and The *Red Book of Hergest, were published in the volume *Hen Gerddi Crefyddol* (ed. Henry Lewis, 1931).

'Englynion Eiry Mynydd' (lit. 'The stanzas of the mountain snow'), a series of gnomic verses, each opening with the phrase, '*Eiry mynydd*', which are preserved in The *Red Book of Hergest and other manuscripts. There are thirty-six *englynion* in the oldest text, but others have been added in later texts such as that published in *The Myvyrian Archaiology of Wales* (1801). Each *englyn* begins with a reference to the natural world, such as '*gwyn pob tu*' ('it is white all around'), '*hydd ar naid*' ('a leaping hart'), '*pysg yn llyn*' ('fish in the lake') and '*gochwiban gwynt uwch blaen onn*' ('the whistling of the wind above the ash'). There follow such gnomic or proverbial statements as '*ni ddaw da o drachysgu*' ('no good comes from too much sleep'), '*nid ymgêl drwg yn lle y bo*' ('evil does not hide where it is'), '*celfyddyd, celed ei arfaeth*' ('art, let it hide its purpose'), '*lle ni bo dysg ni bydd dawn*' ('where there is no learning there is no gift') and '*bas dwfr myn yd lefair*' ('shallow water will babble'). See also GNOME.

For further details see Kenneth H. Jackson, *Early Welsh Gnomic Poems* (1935) and *Studies in Early Celtic Nature Poetry* (1935).

'Englynion Geraint' (lit. 'The stanzas of Geraint'), a poem consisting of twenty-six *englynion*, is preserved in The *Black Book of Carmarthen and The *Red Book of Hergest. Composed before 1100, possibly as early as the year 900, the poem is a eulogy of *Geraint fab Erbin, King of Devon at the end of the sixth century and the eponymous hero of the medieval romance. It contains a description of the battle of Llongborth (perhaps Langport, Som.) at which *Arthur is said to have been present. This claim is an anachronism, for Arthur belonged to an earlier period, but the reference to him is an early example of the tendency of Arthurian traditions to attract characters from different periods and narrative cycles. It has been suggested that the *englynion* are the metrical remains of a tale which was the basis or background of *'Canu Llywarch Hen'.

For discussion of the poem see Brynley F. Roberts, '*Rhai Cerddi Ymddiddan—Geraint fab Erbin*' in *Astudiaethau ar yr Hengerdd* (ed. R. Bromwich and R. Brinley Jones, 1978) and A. O. H. Jarman, *Llyfr Du Caerfyrddin* (1982).

'**Englynion y Beddau**' (lit. 'The stanzas of the graves'), a collection of poems which name the graves of heroes. The earliest and most extensive text is found in The *Black Book of Carmarthen, another survives only in late copies and some poems are scattered elsewhere, often inserted into other works. The main group probably dates from the ninth or tenth century, but it is a type of verse to which additions could easily have been made. The stanzas combine the lore of place-names with lists of heroes in a typically Celtic fashion, in some the commemoration of the hero being the more important and the location of the grave remaining vague. Many of the identifiable places appear to be ancient burial sites such as cairns or cromlechs and, in such cases, the primary interest is in explaining these puzzling relics of the past. Despite their antiquarian interest, the general effect of the poems is lyrical and elegiac, with the vigour of the hero in life being contrasted with the desolation of his grave.

The stanzas were collected and translated by Thomas Jones in the *Proceedings of the British Academy* (vol. LIII, 1967).

'**Englynion y Bidiau**', a series of *englynion* preserved in The *Red Book of Hergest* and other manuscripts. Each opens with the singular imperative form of the verb '*bod*' ('to be'), namely '*bid*', which here means 'let there be' or 'there is of necessity'. Their content is chiefly gnomic as in, for example, '*Bid goch, crib ceiliog*' ('Red is the cockerel's comb'), '*Bid amlwg marchog*' ('A knight is, of necessity, prominent') and '*Bid grafangog iâr*' ('It is a hen's nature to scratch'), but there are also proverbial touches such as '*Cyfaill blaidd bugail diog*' ('A lazy shepherd is a wolf's friend'). See also GNOME.

For further details see Kenneth H. Jackson, *Early Welsh Gnomic Poems* (1935) and *Studies in Early Celtic Nature Poetry* (1935).

'**Englynion y Clyweit**' (lit. 'The have you heard? stanzas'), the most original of all gnomic poems in Welsh. The invariable opening formula of each is '*A glyweist ti a gant . . . ?*' ('Have you heard what . . . composed?') and the core is a proverbial or gnomic statement in the third line, attributed in the rest of the stanza to a famous hero or saint. The choice of a hero upon whom to foster the statement is based on the rhyme-word although, in a few instances, a personal name proves elusive and the wisdom is then ascribed to an animal. The poems are therefore worthless as evidence about the persons named, but they demonstrate the links between proverbial literature and the antiquarian lore preserved by the poets. See also GNOME.

The poems were edited by T. H. Parry-Williams and Ifor Williams in the *Bulletin of the Board of Celtic Studies* (vol. III, 1927); see also the study by Kenneth

H. Jackson, *Early Welsh Gnomic Poems* (1935).

'**Englynion y Misoedd**' (lit. 'The stanzas of the months'), a gnomic poem found in many late-medieval and early-modern manuscripts. Each stanza begins with a brief description of one of the months of the year and the remainder consists of unconnected gnomic and proverbial sayings. A fairly mechanical technique, it was popular with medieval audiences and is reminiscent of other works from this period which give metrical form to lists such as the Ten Commandments and the Seven Deadly Sins. The poem was usually attributed to an eminent poet of the past such as *Aneirin, *Myrddin or *Taliesin, a further indication of its popularity. See also GNOME.

Kenneth H. Jackson edited the poem in *Early Welsh Gnomic Poems* (1935).

Enid, see under GERAINT FAB ERBIN.

Enoc Huws (1891), Daniel *Owen's third novel, was first published in weekly parts in Y *Cymro in 1890 and 1891. The eponymous hero, an illegitimate child reared in a workhouse, becomes a prosperous grocer and this comedy relates his hopeless love-affair, his grotesque troubles with his housekeeper and the efforts of Captain Trefor to persuade him to invest in the empty lead-mine of Pwll-y-gwynt. The Captain is one of the author's greatest creations, a monstrous rogue who sacrifices everyone and everything, including his family, to satisfy his lust for profit and status. The novel's central mystery is the identity of Enoc's father who is revealed, in the end, to be Captain Trefor, which makes Susi, the Captain's daughter whom Enoc loves, his half-sister. Weak in structure after the first masterly hundred pages or so, the novel lapses into chapters of discussion, largely irrelevant to the plot but not without interest, until the author ties together the loose strands at the denouement. Its satire is keen and, as a study of self-deceit and hypocrisy, it is a work of considerable genius which, in this respect, may be considered as the author's finest novel.

The novel appeared in an unsatisfactory English translation by Claude Vivian in 1895 and in an abridged edition in modern Welsh orthography, edited by T. Gwynn Jones, in 1939. For a critical discussion of the novel see the essay by John Gwilym Jones in *Ysgrifau Beirniadol II* (ed. J. E. Caerwyn Williams, 1966) and *Swyddogaeth Beirniadaeth* (1977), and another by Dafydd Glyn Jones in *Ysgrifau Beirniadol III* (ed. J. E. Caerwyn Williams, 1967); see also the articles by T. J. Morgan in *Y Llenor* (1948) and in the volume devoted to the novelist in *Cyfres y Meistri* (ed. Urien Wiliam, 1983).

Enwau Ynys Prydain (lit. 'The names of the Isle of Britain'), a short tract forming a sub-section in the version of *Trioedd Ynys Prydain* which is found in The *White Book of Rhydderch* and The *Red Book of Hergest*; it also appears in an expanded version in some later manuscripts. It begins (in translation), 'The first Name that this Island bore, before it was taken and settled, *Myrddin's Precinct. And after it was taken and settled, the Island of Honey. And after it was conquered by Prydein son of Aedd the Great it was called the Island of Prydain'. This reference to three early colonizations of the Island presents many problems. It probably derives from a pseudo-learned tradition of successive invasions of Britain which is paralleled in Irish, but which is long anterior to *Geoffrey of Monmouth. The belief gains some support from the fact that the names of *Prydain and *Aedd Mawr are found in certain lists of the prehistoric rulers of *Britain. It is plausible, therefore, to suppose that Geoffrey of Monmouth suppressed this older account in order to give pre-eminence to the rival tradition of the colonization by *Brutus and the Trojan fugitive which he elaborated in his *Historia Regum Britanniae. 'The Island of Honey' ('Y Fêl Ynys') was for the poets a popular pseudonym for Britain, but nothing has survived to account for Myrddin's association with a story of colonization.

The items which follow in the tract are geographical. Britain has Three Adjacent Islands (namely, Anglesey, Man and Wight), Thirty-four Chief Ports, Thirty-three Chief Cities and Thirty-four Chief Marvels. The length of the Island (900 miles) is given from Penrhyn Blathaon (an unidentified place in Scotland) to Penrhyn Penwaedd (Penwith Point) in Cornwall, and its breadth (500 miles) from Crigyll in Anglesey (a river with an estuary near Rhosneigr) to Soram (Sarre) in Kent. The tract continues, 'There should be held in it a Crown and Three Coronets. The Crown should be worn in London, and one of the Coronets at Penrhyn Rhionedd in the North (unidentified), the second at *Aberffraw, and the third in Cornwall'. There are three archbishoprics, one in Mynyw (*St. David's), a second in Kent and a third at York. Lists of the Cities and Marvels of Britain follow in some of the manuscripts, in a form which is an expansion of similar lists to be found in the work of *Gildas and in the *Historia Brittonum.

All these geographical specifications are paralleled elsewhere in early Welsh literature and appear to stem from an ancient, pseudo-learned and widely accepted body of learning. The 'Three Realms of Britain (apparently Cornwall, Wales and the North) and her Three Adjacent Islands' are alluded to in the tale of *Culhwch and Olwen, and the 'adjacent islands' are cited in the Historia Brittonum and elsewhere. Gildas gives the number of the Cities of Britain as twenty-eight and their names are given in Old Welsh orthography in the Historia Brittonum. Traces of the threefold division of Britain and of the measurements of the Island survive even in Geoffrey of Monmouth's Historia Regum Britan-

niae, and it seems possible that he may have derived his knowledge from this tract. The claim of Mynyw (St. David's) to be the leading church of Wales had already been advanced in some quarters in the tenth century, although it was not until the twelfth century that the archi-episcopal status of St. David's became a political issue. Above all, the concept of Britain as a sovereign, united and undivided kingdom whose rightful owners were the Britons (even if temporarily subjugated by the invaders) is one which persists throughout medieval Welsh literature in prose and verse, and it is reiterated in various ways in Trioedd Ynys Prydain. The idea that the sovereignty of the Island was in London accounts both for the description of Bendigeidfran (*Brân) in *Pedair Cainc y Mabinogi as 'exalted with the Crown of London' and for Geoffrey of Monmouth's long lists of the Kings of Britain stretching back into the remotest antiquity.

The text is to be found in The Mabinogion from The Red Book of Hergest (ed. John Rhŷs and J. G. Evans, 1887); see also Rachel Bromwich, Trioedd Ynys Prydein (1961) and Brynley F. Roberts, 'Geoffrey of Monmouth and Welsh Historical Tradition' in Nottingham Mediaeval Studies (vol. XX, 1976).

Eos Ceiriog, see MORYS, HUW (1622–1709).

Eos Eyas, see PARRY, JAMES RHYS (c. 1570–1625?).

Eos Gwynfa or **Eos y Mynydd**, see WILLIAMS, THOMAS (c. 1769–1848).

Epic, a long narrative poem which usually relates a hero's adventures. The form was not used in Wales during the Renaissance period and Gruffydd *Robert was the only Welsh writer to attempt it. In the eighteenth century some poets believed that parts of the works of the *Cynfeirdd and *Gogynfeirdd were in the epic tradition. It was Goronwy *Owen's ambition for a while to write a national epic, but he did no more than discuss the technical problems in his letters and write an exercise in the epic style, namely *'Cywydd y Farn Fawr'. Other poets translated Homer and Milton into Welsh. Milton's fame in Wales was extended with the appearance of William *Owen Pughe's strange translation of Paradise Lost (1667) entitled Coll Gwynfa (1819) and of the more intelligible rendering (1865) by John *Evans (I. D. Ffraid) of the same work. Goronwy Owen's style influenced the heroic awdlau of the first half of the nineteenth century. Some critics have argued that the traditional metres inhibited the writing of true epics in Welsh.

The golden age of the epic in Wales began when the *Chair at the Eisteddfod held at Rhuddlan in 1850 was awarded to Evan *Evans (Ieuan Glan Geirionydd) for his pryddest, 'Yr Adgyfodiad', with the awdl by William *Williams

(Caledfryn) placed second; however, the unsuccessful *pryddest* by Ebenezer *Thomas (Eben Fardd) was the poem with the greatest literary merit in that competition. From then on, epics flowed from the presses and hundreds of poets aspired to be the nation's Virgil or Milton by writing long poems on biblical and historical subjects or about contemporary heroes such as T. E. *Ellis. The epic was satirized by John *Morris-Jones at the end of the century, but the *pryddest* by William Crwys *Williams (Crwys), 'Gwerin Cymru' (1911), was an aspect of the same tradition and a prize for an epic was offered at the National Eisteddfod as late as 1930.

For a discussion of the epic in Welsh see the article by Derwyn Jones in *Gŵyr Llên y Bedwaredd Ganrif ar Bymtheg* (ed. Dyfnallt Morgan, 1968), E. G. Millward, '*Geni'r Epig Gymraeg*' in *Llên Cymru* (vol. IV, 1957) and the article by Saunders Lewis in *Meistri a'u Crefft* (ed. Gwynn ap Gwilym, 1981).

Epic of Hades, The (1877), a long poem by Sir Lewis *Morris and his best-known work, was written mainly on the London Underground while he was commuting to his work as a lawyer. Although it describes a visit to the classical underworld, it is not an epic in the traditional sense, but a series of episodes in which characters such as Tantalus tell their tales, affording the poet an opportunity of adding comment of a moralistic nature. Composed in blank verse, it is heavily influenced by the author's acknowledged master, Tennyson, and combines technical competence with a vague sense of moral uplift. Published in more than twenty editions during the lifetime of Lewis Morris, the work lacks vitality, though some passages may be said to have a delicate beauty.

Epistol at y Cembru (lit. 'An epistle to the Welsh'; 1567), a prefatory letter to the Welsh translation of the New Testament of 1567, in which Richard *Davies sought to appeal to the patriotic pride of the Welsh people in the history of their religion. He tried to show that their Christianity had apostolic origins, having first been brought to them on the initiative of Joseph of Arimathea, that it owed nothing to the Papacy, that it had been maintained for centuries free from Romanist corruptions and that it was firmly based on an allegedly early Welsh version of the Scriptures. He warmly commended the new translation and the Reformation as 'the second flowering of the Gospel' in their midst.

There are discussions of this influential letter by Saunders Lewis in *Efrydiau Catholig II* (1947) and by Glanmor Williams in *Yr Esgob Richard Davies* (1953) and *Welsh Reformation Essays* (1967).

Epistolae Ho-Elianae (lit. 'Familiar letters'; 1645), a book by James *Howell, was the first volume of letters in the history of writing in English addressed to named individuals but intended for publication. The authenticity of the letters has been much challenged, for many of their dates are demonstrably wrong. The detailed observation of the earlier letters in particular, however, makes it barely conceivable that they should be *post hoc* fiction. Probably the explanation is that Howell's papers were confiscated when he was consigned to the Fleet prison in 1642 and that only the copies of letters written before 1622 were returned to him. No dates were assigned to the letters until the edition of 1650 and Howell, an editor in a hurry, took too little trouble and possibly attempted to rewrite from recollection some epistles of which his copies were lost.

The book, whatever its authenticity, is remarkably lively. Its vein of high and fanciful writing is interrupted often by worldly wisdom, scatological jokes and extraordinary stories. Although learned, Howell was an early example of the quality journalist. His essays or pseudo-letters on the history of languages and the analysis of various religions, for example, owe much to Edward Brerewood's *Enquiries touching the Diversity of Languages* (1614) and to *Europae Speculum* (1638) by Sir Edwin Sandys. Howell's account of the prolonged ritual of his personal devotions is one of his more extraordinary inclusions. He spent a lifetime in London and abroad, knowing of Wales only what he remembered from his youth. But he was loyal to the Welsh language and his sentiments in these letters make him the last major exponent of the *Tudor revival of 'The *Matter of Britain'. The work's long popularity—there had been ten editions by 1737—is well understandable for as a compendium of the knowledge and feeling current in anti-Puritan circles in the decades before the *Civil Wars it had no rivals.

The definitive edition is that prepared by Joseph Jacobs, *Epistolae Ho-Elianae, The Familiar Letters of James Howell* (2 vols., 1890, 1892).

Eples (lit. 'Leaven'; 1951), a volume of poems by Gwenallt (David James *Jones). Full of raw, realistic descriptions and striking, original images, these poems spring from his experience of poverty in the industrial areas of south Wales during the *Depression. One of the best-known, '*Y Meirwon*', describes some of his most powerful memories of that period, while others express his disillusionment with *Marxism or portray aspects of his rural background. Among the most significant are such poems as '*Y Draenog*', '*Dyn*' and '*Narcisws*', which diagnose contemporary Man's sickness; others, such as '*Yr Eglwys*', '*Amser*' and '*Y Calendr*', offer the remedy, or leaven, of Christian faith.

Erbery, William (1604–54), one of the four great preachers of the first generation of *Puritanism in Wales, was born at Roath-Dogfield, near Cardiff in which town he was vicar of St. Mary and St. John until compelled to resign by the Court of High Commission in 1635. Chaplain to Skippon's regiment during the *Civil War, he took part in the subsequent Army Debates and preached in Glamorgan under the Act for the *Propagation of the Gospel in Wales (1650); but in 1653 he was required to answer for his heresies to the Committee for Plundered Ministers. A mystic after the belief of Jacob Böhme, he nevertheless became very disputatious in later years. Morgan *Llwyd thought of him as his teacher and Walter *Cradock learned from him while serving as his curate in Cardiff. Richard Baxter in Catholick Communion Defended (1684) accused Vavasor *Powell, Cradock, Llwyd and Erbery of Antinomianism. But an anonymous defender in A Winding-Sheet for Mr. Baxter's dead (1685), while acquitting the first three, admitted that Erbery 'was taken ill of his whimsies', adding that, 'Mr. Erbery's Disease lay in his Head, not in his Heart', a verdict which perusal of his later writings confirms. All Erbery's works, except Apocrypha (1652), are included in The Testimony of William Erbery left upon Record for the Saints of Succeeding Ages (1658).

For further details see Thomas Rees, History of Protestant Nonconformity in Wales (1861) and Geoffrey F. Nuttall, The Welsh Saints 1640–1660 (1957).

Erddig, see under YORKE, PHILIP (1743–1804).

Erging, the district between the rivers Mynwy (Monnow) and Wye, now wholly within the old county of Hereford, was one of the gwledydd (lordships) of early Wales and was probably named after the Roman settlement of Ariconium. The cult of *Dyfrig (Dubricius), who may have been the Bishop of Ariconium, and who was the first of the saints of the *Celtic Church, was centred upon Erging. *Offa's Dyke is wholly absent from its confines because of its dense forests and the natural boundary provided by the wide easterly loop of the Wye. The linguistic boundary, concurrent with the river where Welsh Bicknor fronts English Bicknor across the water, then moves away northwestwards along the heights from Pencraig and Llangarren to Gorsty Common and Clehonger, coming within four miles of Hereford and rejoining the Wye near Bridge Sollers, from which a section of the Dyke runs northwards. It is not unreasonable to see this great eastward loop as the expansionist frontier of the *Silures, the more because English settlements west of it, evident from the eighth century onwards, were re-Celticized. The description of the social structure of Erging in the Domesday Book (1086) is that of an essentially Welsh community. The survival of *gavelkind, when the *Acts of Union (1536 and 1542) had abolished an already disappearing practice in Wales, shows it to have been an intensely conservative one. Distinctive in several respects (the skills of its bowmen and the

separateness of its Welsh tongue are two), Erging clung to *Roman Catholicism until well into the seventeenth century. After the time of Urban, Bishop of Llandaf (1107–33), it was absorbed into the bishopric of Hereford, but Recusancy (see under COUNTER-REFORMATION) played off Llandaf against Hereford in the Monnow valley with continuing success. The Welsh language survived in Erging until after 1700.

For further details see John Duncumb, Collections towards the History and Antiquities of the County of Hereford (4 vols., 1804–92), especially the continuation devoted to the Hundred of Wormelow (1912) by John Hobson Matthews.

'Erof Greulon' (lit. 'Cruel Herod'), a fragment of fifteen lines from a Herod-poem in The *Book of Taliesin. As was usual in the Middle Ages, it conflates Herod the Great with Herod Antipas, the Tetrarch. It refers to Herod's 'betrayal of Jesus' and 'the quaking of the earth', as well as to the carrying off of Herod from his house by the devils 'into the depths of Hell'.

'Eryr Pengwern' (lit. 'The eagle of Pengwern'), a poem belonging to the *'Canu Heledd' cycle in which Heledd describes the screaming birds of prey as they feast on fallen warriors, particularly her brother Cynddylan. Pengwern is elsewhere called the court of Cynddylan. *Gerald de Barri (Giraldus Cambrensis) states in his Itinerarium and *Descriptio Kambriae that Pengwern was in former times one of the three chief courts of Wales and he identifies it with Shrewsbury. The Welsh name for Shrewsbury, however, is Amwythig, and no archaeological evidence for settlement previous to the late Saxon period has come to light in the district. Pengwern was probably situated in what is now Shropshire but it has not been positively identified. It may have been the ancient fort known in Welsh as Din Gwrygon (The Wrekin) or, more probably, Wroxeter, the fourth largest town in Roman Britain, which was in the territory of the Cornovii, to whom Cynddylan is believed to have belonged.

For a discussion of Pengwern's location see John Morris, The Age of Arthur (1973), Melville Richards, 'The Lichfield Gospels' in the Journal of the National Library of Wales (vol. XVIII, 1973), and S. C. Stanford, The Archaeology of the Welsh Marches (1980).

Eryri, the mountainous district in north-west Wales which in the Middle Ages was the heartland of the kingdom of *Gwynedd, was also known by the Latin form of its name, Snowdonia. Its highest point is Yr Wyddfa (alt. 3,560 feet) or Snowdon, which is also the highest mountain in Wales. The title Princeps Northwallie et Dominus Snowdonia ('Prince of Gwynedd and Lord of Eryri') was adopted by *Llywelyn ap Iorwerth in 1230 and his grandson *Llywelyn ap Gruffudd used a similar title in 1258. The name survived the loss of Welsh independence in 1282 and is still in general use, together with Snowdonia, as denoting what is now a National Park. See also EAGLES OF SNOWDONIA and RHITA GAWR.

For further details see the article by Ifor Williams in the *Bulletin* of the Board of Celtic Studies (vol. IV, 1939) and J. E. Lloyd, 'The Mountains in History and Legend', in R. C. Carr and G. A. Lister (ed.), *The Mountains of Snowdonia* (1925).

Esgair Oerfel, see under TWRCH TRWYTH.

Essay, The, a recent form in Welsh literature, has its beginnings in the years immediately after the First World War. Prior to 1918 many articles, sometimes called essays, had been published on abstract and other topics, but their purpose had been primarily didactic, as in the work of Owen M. *Edwards. The pioneer of the modern essay in Welsh was T. H. *Parry-Williams, whose first collection was *Ysgrifau* (1928) but who had published some of his work in *Y *Llenor* in 1922. He was fond of choosing an apparently unpromising subject, such as telegraph poles or drowning a cat, and would treat it lightly and wittily in order to convey some aspect of his own personality. From 1937 the essay became a subject for competition at the *National Eisteddfod where, for many years, the tendency was to adhere (often to the point of pastiche) to the models set by T. H. Parry-Williams. Gradually, however, the definition of the form was widened to include portraits of people, as in the essays of E. Morgan *Humphreys, T. Gwynn *Jones and D. Tecwyn *Lloyd, as well as essays on places by authors such as R. T. *Jenkins. After the Second World War, many essays on foreign travel were published and there was some memorable writing on scientific topics. Among writers who contributed to the further development of the essay form were T. J. *Morgan, J. O. *Williams and Islwyn Ffowc *Elis. By today, the essay in Welsh has matured and discarded the studied, almost affected character it once had, and almost any piece of fine prose now tends to be called an essay, no matter what its subject.

For a selection of essays by contemporary writers see *Ysgrifau Heddiw* (ed. Gwilym Rees Hughes and Islwyn Jones, 1975); there is a discussion of the form by Emrys Parry in *Y Traddodiad Rhyddiaith yn yr Ugeinfed Ganrif* (ed. Geraint Bowen, 1976).

Esther (1960), a play in three acts by Saunders *Lewis, is based on the story of Esther in the Old Testament and the Apocrypha. The Jewish wife of Ahasuerus, King of Persia, she is persuaded by her uncle Mordecai to risk incurring her husband's mortal anger in order to intercede on behalf of the Jews, condemned to extermination by the decree of the villainous Prime Minister, Haman. The plan succeeds, the decree is rescinded, Haman is executed and the future of the Jewish people (and thus of Christianity) assured. The play is a meditation not only upon the central position of the Jews in world history, and thus an antidote against anti-Semitism, but also upon the nature of politics and the role of such elements as opportunism, ruthlessness and blind courage. Another element in the play is a strong awareness of the claims and power of erotic love. In the same volume was published a short but delightful libretto after Molière, *Serch yw'r Doctor*, described by the author as a palinode, presumably because of its generally positive, although not uncynical, attitude towards sexual love as precursor of marriage.

The play was published in an English translation by Joseph Clancy under the title *Esther* in 1985. For discussion of the play's merits see the articles by Bruce Griffiths in *Ffenics* (1963) and Gerald Morgan in *Barn* (no. 41, March, 1966).

Esyllt Fynwen (lit. 'Whiteneck') and **Esyllt Fyngul** (lit. 'Slenderneck'), two ladies of *Arthur's court in the tale of *Culhwch and Olwen. According to the Triads, the former was Culfanawyd Prydain's daughter and one of the Three Defiled Women of the Isle of Britain. It has been suggested that reference to the two Esyllts was a jest (cf. the three Guineveres) and that it may identify the source of the two women of the same name in the French romances of *Tristan and Iseult.

Eta Delta (Evan Davies; 1794–1855), see under TEMPERANCE.

ETHERIDGE, KEN (1911–81), poet, playwright and painter. Born at Ammanford, Carms., he was educated at Swansea College of Art and University College, Cardiff, where he read English. He became art master at Queen Elizabeth Boys' Grammar School, Carmarthen, in 1947. From 1935 he was a producer with the Cymric Players in Ammanford and wrote a number of plays in Welsh and English which include *Underground* (1937), *The Lamp* (1938) and *Birds of Rhiannon* (1941). He also published two volumes of verse, *Songs of Courage* (1940) and *Poems of a Decade* (1958), as well as a history of Welsh folk-costume, two handbooks on stage costume and scenic design for amateurs, and a volume of his *Collected Drawings* (1970).

Études Celtiques (lit. 'Celtic studies'), a magazine launched in 1936 as a replacement for *Revue Celtique*. Its first editor was Joseph *Vendryes, a professor at the Sorbonne, who had assisted in the production of the earlier journal. Initially the magazine's scope was limited to linguistic and literary studies but in recent years it has included important papers on archaeology.

Eugenius Philalethes, see VAUGHAN, THOMAS (1621–66).

Eurgrawn Wesleyaidd, Yr (lit. 'The Wesleyan treasury'), the denominational magazine of the

Wesleyan Methodists in Wales, first appeared in 1809 under the editorship of John Bryan (1770–1856). Among his successors were William *Rowlands (Gwilym Lleyn), John Hughes (Glanystwyth), D. Tecwyn Evans and Gwilym R. *Tilsley. The magazine's original purpose was to instruct members in matters of doctrine and organization, much emphasis being placed on the activities of Wesleyans in England. By the end of the century, however, it had become less denominational and more Welsh in outlook, a trend promoted by D. Tecwyn Evans who developed it into a magazine of more general literary and national appeal. The magazine's title was changed to Yr Eurgrawn in 1933, after the adjective 'Wesleyan' had been dropped by the Connexion, and it was merged with the inter-denominational periodical Cristion (ed. Enid Morgan) in 1983.

EVAN, EDWARD (1716–98), poet. Born near Aberdare, Glam., a cobbler's son, he was apprenticed as a carpenter and glazier to Lewis *Hopkin, but later became a farmer and a Presbyterian minister. His only volume of verse, Caniadau Moesol a Duwiol (1804), was very popular and ran to three more editions under the title Afalau'r Awen.

Evangelicism, an interpretation of the Christian faith which accepts the infallibility of the Scriptures and the doctrines of grace, emphasizing that every Christian must be 'born again'. Within the Anglican Church in Wales during the nineteenth century the Sacramentalist faction was opposed by Evangelical writers such as John Williams, William Howells, John Hughes and David Howell (Llawdden). This Evangelical emphasis was a continuation of the trend found within the Established Church in the eighteenth century and advocated by Daniel *Rowland, Howel *Harris and William *Williams (Pantycelyn) who were, in turn, the heirs of Puritans such as Vavasor *Powell and Morgan *Llwyd.

The term Evangelical may be used for certain earlier groups, such as the *Cistercians and the Celtic saints, found within the medieval Catholic Church. The word 'Methodist' in the term 'Calvinistic Methodist' is concerned with the same emphasis and refers to the experiential aspect of the character of this denomination which withdrew from the Established Church in 1811. Some of the Nonconformist denominations which were revitalized in the Methodist Revival, such as the *Baptists and Independents (*Independency), are also sometimes referred to as Evangelical denominations. The three most important Evangelical revivals in Wales were those associated with David Morgan (1859), Richard Owen (1882–83) and Evan *Roberts (1904), but there were several others. In literary terms the fruit of Evangelical fervour in Wales

may be seen in the number and variety of books on religious subjects published during the nineteenth century and in the nature of the poetry written during that period.

The Evangelical Movement of Wales of the present day grew out of Y Cylchgrawn Efengylaidd, a magazine founded in 1948. Among Welsh writers whose writing has been influenced by their Evangelicism are Bobi Jones (Robert Maynard *Jones), R. Tudur *Jones and D. Martyn *Lloyd-Jones.

For further details see E. Wyn James (ed.), Cwlwm o Dystion (1977), Derec Llwyd Morgan, Y Diwygiad Mawr (1981) and R. Tudur Jones, Ffydd ac Argyfwng Cenedl (2 vols., 1981, 1982).

Evans, Arise, see EVANS, RHYS or RICE (c.1607–post 1660).

EVANS, BERIAH GWYNFE (1848–1927), journalist and author, was born at Nant-y-glo, Mon. He was a schoolmaster at Gwynfe, Carms., when in 1881 he launched the periodical *Cyfaill yr Aelwyd which was to bring him to public notice. In 1887 he took up journalism and subsequently edited several weekly newspapers, mainly in Caernarfon. A keen romantic Nationalist, he was secretary of the *Cymru Fydd movement and the first secretary of *Cymdeithas yr Iaith Gymraeg (1885). He wrote several books, including The Life Romance of Lloyd George (n.d.), of which a Welsh version was published in Utica, New York, and another version in French. His most entertaining book is Dafydd Dafis (1898) which purports to be a Welshman's impressions of life in London, with gossip about some of the young Welsh Members of Parliament of the day. He also wrote several plays on historical subjects but they have little merit.

There is an essay on Beriah Gwynfe Evans by E. Morgan Humphreys in Gwŷr Enwog Gynt (1953) and John Gwilym Jones discusses his plays in the volume Swyddogaeth Beirniadaeth (1977).

EVANS, CHRISTINE (1943–), poet, was born in Yorkshire but came in 1967 to her father's birthplace, Pwllheli, Caerns., to teach English. She has published one collection of poems, Looking Inland (1983), in which she observes the rural communities of Llŷn with a mature perception and profound sympathy.

EVANS, CHRISTMAS (1776–1838), preacher and hymn-writer. Born on Christmas Day in the parish of Llandysul, Cards., the son of a shoemaker, he had no early schooling. He learned to read after becoming a member at Llwynrhydowen Chapel and later attended the school of David *Davis of Castell Hywel. Joining the *Baptists in 1788, he became an itinerant preacher in Llŷn, Caerns., and in 1791 settled in Llangefni, Ang., where he remained for thirty-five years, ministering to the entire county. His fame as a preacher rested on his dramatic presentation and his vivid illustrations from scientific and industrial subjects. He published many pamphlets on theological subjects, the sale of which supplemented his meagre stipend, and he wrote several well-known hymns, including 'Dwy fflam ar ben Calfaria' and ' 'Rhwn sy'n gyrru'r mellt i hedeg'.

The biography of Christmas Evans was written by E. P. Hood (1881) and B. A. Ramsbottom and his allegories were edited by Hugh Bevan (1950).

EVANS, DANIEL (Daniel Ddu o Geredigion; 1792–1846), see under BLODAU DYFED (1824).

EVANS, DANIEL SILVAN (1818–1903), lexicographer and poet. Born at Llanarth, Cards., he was educated briefly at Brecon Independent College. After spending five years as a schoolmaster, he joined the Church of England and, in 1846, entered St. David's College, Lampeter. Ordained priest in 1849, he served in several parishes in north Wales and ended his days at Llanwrin, Mont. He was Professor of Welsh at the University College of Wales, Aberystwyth, from 1875 until 1883.

He published four volumes of verse, including Telynegion (1846), none of which has any special merit. He edited reprints of some of the Welsh prose classics and was editor of Y Brython from 1858 until 1860 and of Archaeologia Cambrensis from 1872 until 1875. Translations of The *Black Book of Carmarthen, The Book of Aneirin and the poetry of The *Red Book of Hergest published in W. F. Skene's The *Four Ancient Books of Wales (1868), were provided by him. Among his other works were his editions of classics, such as Y Bardd Cwsc (1853) and Gwirionedd y Grefydd Gristnogol (1854), numerous articles in Y *Gwyddoniadur Cymreig, and a book on Welsh orthography, Llythyraeth yr Iaith Gymraeg (1856), which is no longer well regarded.

Silvan Evans's most important contribution was as a lexicographer. Having already begun to compile an English-Welsh dictionary, he came into contact with young scholars, such as John *Rhŷs and John Gwenogvryn *Evans, who helped him to reject the fanciful ideas of William *Owen Pughe. His great ambition was to produce a dictionary of the Welsh language comparable with the Oxford English Dictionary. After many years of preparation it began to appear in parts (1887, 1888, 1893, 1896 and, posthumously, 1906). The work, which was never completed (it ends at the word 'enyd'), was an exceedingly ambitious undertaking and Silvan Evans had too many irons in the fire to devote his full time to it, but what was published is proof that he had considerable lexicographical ability.

For a discussion of D. Silvan Evans as a scholar see the essay in Cymwynaswyr y Gymraeg (1978) by Morgan D. Jones and the article by Thomas Parry in the Transactions (1981) of the Honourable Society of Cymmrodorion.

EVANS, DANIEL SIMON (1921–), scholar, was born at Llanfynydd, Carms., and educated at University College, Swansea, the Theological College, Aberystwyth, and Jesus College, Oxford; D. Ellis *Evans is his brother. Formerly Professor of Welsh at University College, Dublin, and Head of the Department of Celtic Studies at Liverpool University, he became Professor of Welsh at St. David's College, Lampeter, in 1974.

He began his career by publishing articles on various aspects of Medieval Welsh syntax in the Bulletin of the *Board of Celtic Studies and *Studia Celtica. In his volume Gramadeg Cymraeg Canol (1951) he set out to describe the phonemes, accidence and syntax of Medieval Welsh, and expanded on this work in the English adaptation, A Grammar of Middle Welsh (1964). In 'Iaith y Gododdin', the third chapter in Astudiaethau ar yr Hengerdd (ed. R. Bromwich and R. Brinley Jones, 1978), he discussed some of the language's forms in its early period and also gave his attention to the problem of the antiquity of 'Y *Gododdin'. He edited Medieval Welsh texts in his two volumes, Buchedd Dewi (1959) and Historia Gruffudd vab Kenan (1977). His interest in the *Lives of the Saints as a literary genre was demonstrated in his chapter 'Y Bucheddau', published in Y Traddodiad Rhyddiaith yn yr Oesau Canol (ed. Geraint Bowen, 1974), and in his editorship of G. H. Doble's Lives of the Welsh Saints (1971). In 'Rhyddiaith Anchwedlonol yn yr Oesoedd Canol', published in Llên Cymru (vol. II, 1971), he cast an interpretative eye over the whole body of medieval prose and in 'Aneirin—Bardd Cristnogol?', published in Ysgrifau Beirniadol X (ed. J. E. Caerwyn Williams, 1977), he discussed an aspect of Early Welsh Poetry in a similar manner.

EVANS, DAVID (Dewi Haran; 1812–85), see under CLIC Y BONT.

EVANS, DAVID (Caradoc Evans; 1878–1945), short-story writer and novelist, was born at Pantycroi, Llanfihangel-ar-Arth, Carms. After the early death of his father, an auctioneer, his mother and her five children moved to Lanlas Uchaf, Rhydlewis, Cards. The details of his childhood are obscure or misrepresented, but it was not over-happy. In 1893 he was apprenticed to a draper in Carmarthen and thereafter he worked as a shop assistant in Barry, Cardiff and London, a phase of his life of which he always spoke with loathing. While in London he attended evening classes in English composition, published some short stories under the name D. Evans-Emmott and, so encouraged, found employment as a journalist in 1906. He became editor of the magazine Ideas in 1915 and was acting editor of Cassell's Weekly and T.P.'s Weekly from 1923 to 1929.

His first collection of short stories, *My People

(1915), brought him immediate notoriety. Two further volumes followed quickly: *Capel Sion* (1916), pursuing the same dark themes of greed, lust and degraded religion in west Wales, and *My Neighbours* (1919), which for good measure also turned a lurid searchlight on the foibles of the *London Welsh. He confirmed his self-appointed role as scourge of the Welsh with a savagely hurtful 'play of Welsh village life in three acts' entitled *Taffy* (1923).

His marriage to Marguerite Hélène, a prolific writer of romantic novels for women under her first married name, Countess Barcynska, and under the pseudonym Oliver Sandys, took place in 1933, his first wife having divorced him in the previous year. In the late 1930s the Evanses were involved in theatrical ventures, both in Wales and England. After the outbreak of war in 1939 they went to live in Aberystwyth and eventually settled at New Cross, Cards., where Caradoc Evans lies buried in the graveyard of Horeb chapel.

It was in the early 1930s, after a longish silence apart from journalism and the sedulous cultivation of his self-defined reputation as 'the best-hated man in Wales', that Caradoc Evans entered upon a new period of authorship. First came four novels: *Nothing to Pay* (1930); *Wasps* (1933), of which there were two versions, one with a libellous portrayal of the novelist Edith *Nepean, withdrawn before publication; *This Way to Heaven* (1934); the 'dangerous and pornographic', but more obviously claustrophobic and tedious, *Kitty Shore's Magic Cake*, appeared under the title *Mother's Marvel* in 1949. He also published a volume of short stories, *Pilgrims in a Foreign Land* (1942), a highly formalized short novel, *Morgan Bible* (1943), and a last gathering of short stories, *The Earth Gives All and Takes All* (1946), published posthumously. His brief and comparatively genial *Journal* for the years 1939 to 1944 was edited by his widow for *The *Welsh Review* (June and September, 1945). A miscellany of his writings is to be found in the volume *Fury Never Leaves Us* (ed. John Harris, 1985).

The best of Caradoc Evans's novels, never a good vehicle for his hooded vision and increasingly aphoristic style, were *Nothing to Pay*, a morbid study of hypocrisy and greed against a squalid background of the 'rag trade' of his days as a shop assistant, and *Morgan Bible*, a comic if contorted extravaganza tightly confined by its foreshortened, epigrammatic prose. The later short stories show an amelioration of mood though not always of style, as if in the end the author's daemon had come to feel as exhausted as his reader.

Despite, or because of, the sharply contradictory views held of his life and work, Caradoc Evans must be regarded as one of the most remarkable Welshmen of his time. His literary reputation rests on the best of his short stories, his legend on the devious assaults made on so many cherished aspects of 'the Welsh way of life', from *Nonconformity and the *Eisteddfod to the integrity and intelligence of the common people. His abiding status depends on his example, and some would say warning, as a founding-father of modern *Anglo-Welsh literature.

There is a sound factual record of Caradoc Evans's life and work by Trevor L. Williams in the *Writers of Wales* series (1970). The memoirs, *Full and Frank* (1941) and *Unbroken Thread* (1948), by Oliver Sandys are unreliable, but the same writer's *Caradoc Evans* (1946) offers hints of a truer, harsher story, and contains useful source material. See also the chapter by Glyn Jones in *The Dragon has two Tongues* (1968) and the article by Trevor Williams on the style of Caradoc Evans's later works in *The Anglo-Welsh Review* (vol. 24, no. 53, 1974).

EVANS, DAVID ELLIS (1930–   ), scholar. Born, like his brother D. Simon *Evans, at Llanfynydd, Carms., he was educated at University College of Wales, Aberystwyth, the University College, Swansea, and Jesus College, Oxford. He was Professor of Welsh Language and Literature at the University College, Swansea, from 1974 to 1978 and is now Professor of Celtic and a Fellow of Jesus College, Oxford. His chief interests lie in early Celtic culture throughout Europe, with special reference to its relationship with that of the classical world, and in the history of the Celtic languages and the early literatures of Wales and Ireland. He is the author of the standard volume *Gaulish Personal Names, a study of some Continental Celtic Formations* (1967) and has published a host of articles in learned journals. The title of his inaugural lecture at University College, Swansea, was *Gorchest y Celtiaid yn yr Hen Fyd* (1975). His contribution to the volume *Studies in Old Welsh Poetry/Astudiaethau ar yr Hengerdd* (ed. R. Bromwich and R. Brinley Jones, 1978) was an introduction to the prosody of 'Y *Gododdin'. Since 1973 D. Ellis Evans has been editor of the Literature and Language Section of the *Bulletin* of the *Board of Celtic Studies and he also edited the volume *Cofiant Agricola* (1975).

EVANS, DAVID EMRYS (1891–1966), scholar and translator, was born at Clydach, Glam., and educated at the University College of North Wales, Bangor, and Jesus College, Oxford. He was Professor of Classics at University College, Swansea, from 1921 to 1927, and afterwards Principal of the University College of North Wales, Bangor, until his retirement in 1958. Besides *Crefydd a Chymdeithas* (1933) and *The University of Wales, a Historical Sketch* (1953), he published a number of Welsh translations of Plato's works, including *Amddiffyniad Socrates* (1936), *Phaedon* (1938), *Ewthaffron: Criton* (1943), *Gorgias* (1946) and *Y Wladwriaeth* (1956). He wrote excellent Welsh, with a touch of old-fashioned refinement which was perhaps incompatible with his subject-matter.

EVANS, DONALD (1940–), poet, was born at Esgair Onwy Fawr, a farm on Banc Siôn Cwilt in Cardiganshire, and now lives at Talgarreg. Educated at the University College of Wales, Aberystwyth, he was a teacher of Welsh in that town until 1984. Emulating the achievement of T. H. *Parry-Williams and Alan *Llwyd, he won both the *Chair and the *Crown at the National Eisteddfodau of 1977 and 1980. He has published seven volumes of verse, namely *Egin* (1976), *Haidd* (1977), *Grawn* (1979), *Eden* (1981), *Gwenoliaid* (1982), *Machlud Canrif* (1983) and *Eisiau Byw* (1984). A prolific poet and a master of *Cerdd Dafod*, he finds inspiration in 'the square mile' of his native place. He has also edited two anthologies, one of *englynion*, *Parsel Persain* (1976), the other of *cywyddau* (1981).

Evans, Edgar (1876–1912), explorer. Born at Rhosili in Gower, Glam., he took part as a petty officer in Captain Scott's Antarctic Expedition which left Cardiff on the '*Terra Nova*' in 1910. Chosen for his immense strength and unfailing good spirits to be among the five who made the final bid for the South Pole, he died on the return journey and was buried at the foot of Beardmore Glacier. The commemorative monument in the church at Rhosili bears the inscription, 'To strive, to seek, to find, and not to yield', a quotation from Tennyson's poem 'Ulysses' (1842).

EVANS, EINION (1926–), poet. Born at Mostyn, Flints., a miner's son and the brother of T. Wilson *Evans, he worked as a miner before becoming a librarian. An accomplished poet in the strict metres and a keen satirist, he has won many prizes at eisteddfodau and has published two volumes of poetry, *Cerddi* (1969) and *Cerddi'r Parlwr* (1978). He won the *Chair at the National Eisteddfod in 1983 for his *awdl*, '*Yr Ynys*', which expresses the grief and loneliness he felt at the death of his daughter Ennis at the age of twenty-nine. A young writer of promise, she was the author of a novel, *Y Gri Unig* (1975), and a volume of short stories, *Pruddiaith* (1981).

EVANS, ELLIS HUMPHREY (Hedd Wyn; 1887–1917), poet, was born near Trawsfynydd, Mer. After leaving school he helped his father on the family farm, Yr Ysgwrn. Poetry was his passion and, from the age of nineteen, he was a frequent competitor at eisteddfodau. He is remembered mainly on account of the circumstances of his death during the First World War. Early in 1917 he enlisted with the 15th Battalion of the Royal Welsh Fusiliers, which left for France in June of that year, and he was killed in the battle for Pilkem Ridge on 31 July. At the National Eisteddfod held at Birkenhead in the following September, his *awdl* was awarded the *Chair. When it was announced that the author

had been killed in action the chair was draped in black, to the great emotion of the audience.

A collection of Hedd Wyn's poems, edited by J. J. *Williams, was published under the title *Cerddi'r Bugail* in 1918. The *awdl* which won 'The Black Chair of Birkenhead', entitled '*Yr Arwr*', relates the myth of Prometheus to Christian symbolism and, with the possible exception of a few of his lyrics, can be claimed as his best poem. The well-known sequence of *englynion* which opens with the words '*Y bardd trwm dan bridd tramor*' was composed by R. Williams *Parry in memory of Hedd Wyn. The bronze statue portraying the poet as a shepherd which stands in his native village of Trawsfynydd was erected in 1923.

A biography of Hedd Wyn was written by William Morris (1969); see also the essay by Derwyn Jones in the volume *Ysgrifau Beirniadol VI* (ed. J. E. Caerwyn Williams, 1971).

EVANS, EVAN (Ieuan Fardd, Ieuan Brydydd Hir; 1731–88), poet and scholar, was born in the parish of Lledrod, Cards. He was educated by Edward *Richard at Ystradmeurig School and later studied at Merton College, Oxford. Ordained priest in 1755, he served for two years as curate of Manafon, Mont., and then for some twenty years, unpreferred, in various parishes in Wales and England. During the last ten years of his life he lived at his mother's home, Cynhawdref, and was supported by annual contributions from well-wishers, including Paul *Panton who paid him a pension in return for his collection of manuscripts. Ieuan's wandering life in the service of the Anglican Church was an epitome of the tension which was almost inevitable for any priest at that time who wished to devote himself to the fostering of Welsh culture. His fondness for strong drink, to which, in the words of Samuel Johnson, he was 'incorrigibly addicted', has been blamed for his lack of preferment, but he had also incurred the wrath of some who might have been his allies by his criticism of the anti-Welsh attitudes of the bishops in the Wales of his day, the '*Esgyb Eingl*' as he scornfully called them in a long essay.

It was Lewis *Morris, settled in Cardiganshire since 1746, who set Ieuan on the road to becoming a poet and scholar by teaching him the rules of prosody and how to copy manuscripts. Thus encouraged, Ieuan spent three months in Oxford copying the old Welsh poetry preserved in *The *Red Book of Hergest* in the library of Jesus College. Although it was his ambition as a poet (and his envy of Goronwy *Owen) which first took him to Oxford, the result was the channelling of his energies into scholarship. Returning to north Wales, where he lived between 1758 and 1766, he discovered a number of important texts such as '*Y *Gododdin*' and the work of *Taliesin. His volume *Some Specimens of the Poetry of the Antient Welsh Bards* (1764) was the first substantial selection of early Welsh poetry to be published and it brought him immediate and lasting fame. It also satisfied the desire of English antiquaries for information on Welsh literature and provided new material for the leaders of the Celtic movement in England at the end of the eighteenth century. Ieuan undertook the work of translation at the request of Thomas Gray, Thomas Percy and Daines *Barrington, at whose expense the work was printed, and for the rest of his career the copying and studying of manuscripts was his chief delight. Unfortunately, his attempts to fulfil the needs of Welsh scholarship as it existed in his day met with little response from his compatriots, except that the editors of *The Myvyrian Archaiology* (1801–07) later made unacknowledged use of his copies.

Throughout this time he wrote poetry, mainly *cywyddau* for his patrons and friends, and between 1751 and 1756 he composed several *awdlau* and *cywyddau* such as 'Teifi', a poem subtitled 'Hiraeth y bardd am ei wlad', written while he was an unhappy curate in Kent. He also published *Rhybudd Cyfr-drist i'r Diofal a'r Difraw* (1773), a short address and a sermon, and a collection of his sermons translated from the English (2 vols., 1776). His English poem 'The Love of our Country' (1772), was an attempt to arouse the pride of educated Welshmen in their national heritage by defending the reputation and history of the Welsh against insinuations by English writers. A diligent writer of *englynion*, he composed the well-known sequence 'Llys Ifor Hael' in 1779 during a visit to the ruins of the court of *Ifor ap Llywelyn at Bassaleg, Mon., in the company of Iolo Morganwg (Edward *Williams).

A collection of Ieuan's work was published by Daniel Silvan Evans in 1876 and a selection was edited by Owen M. Edwards in the series *Cyfres y Fil* (1912). The volume *The Correspondence of Thomas Percy and Evan Evans* (ed. Aneirin Lewis, 1957) contains a short biography and much information regarding his scholarly achievements; see also the essay by John Gwilym Jones in the volume *Gwŷr Llên y Ddeunawfed Ganrif* (ed. Dyfnallt Morgan, 1966) and *Swyddogaeth Beirniadaeth* (1977), the article by D. Myrddin Lloyd in *Y Llenor* (1929), Gerald Morgan in *Y Traethodydd* (April, 1982) and Aneirin Lewis in *Llên Cymru* (vol. I, 1950–51; vol. VII, 1962–63), the *Journal* of the Welsh Bibliographical Society (vol. VIII, 1954–57) and *Ysgrifau Beirniadol X* (ed. J. E. Caerwyn Williams, 1977). There is a lively portrait of Ieuan in Emyr Humphreys, *The Taliesin Tradition* (1983).

EVANS, EVAN (Ieuan Glan Geirionydd; 1795–1855), poet, was born at Trefriw, Caerns., to parents who were among the earliest Calvinistic Methodists in the district. Educated at Llanrwst Free School, where he received instruction in music, he worked for a while on his father's farm before becoming a schoolmaster at Tal-y-bont, Caerns., in 1816. He later lived in Chester, where he was employed as a translator and sub-editor on the monthly periodical

Goleuad Gwynedd. During this period of his life he began winning prizes for poetry at eisteddfodau and was encouraged to become a priest in the Church of England. Ordained in 1826, he held the curacies of parishes in Cheshire until his retirement in 1852, when he returned to his native town.

Ieuan Glan Geirionydd was the most versatile Welsh poet of the nineteenth century. Although some of his *awdlau*, such as 'Gwledd Belsassar' (1828), are in the tradition of Goronwy *Owen, their language adversely affected by the theories of William *Owen Pughe, others such as 'Y Bedd' (1821) are among the greatest poems written in the strict metres during this period. But it was in the free metres that he excelled most consistently, so much so that he and Alun (John *Blackwell) are generally regarded as the pioneers of the lyric in Welsh. His knowledge of traditional forms, together with his musical gifts, gave a certain style to his poetry which consists of a clarity and dignity of language, and a smooth, melodic metre. In such poems as 'Caniad y Gog i Arfon' and 'Cyflafan Morfa Rhuddlan', for example, he imitated the old harpstanzas brilliantly. His two most famous lyrical poems, 'Ysgoldy Rhad Llanrwst' and 'Glan Geirionydd', were original in that they delighted in childhood memories and the poet's communion with nature. Saunders *Lewis has claimed that it was in the poems written by Ieuan in the free metres that he most truly belonged to the tradition of Goronwy Owen, because in them the greatest care was taken over form and language. For Lewis these poems show the paramount spirit and philosophy of the classical tradition in Welsh, namely Stoicism. Ieuan's achievement was crowned by his hymns, which include 'Ar lan Iorddonen ddofn' and 'Mor ddedwydd yw y rhai trwy ffydd', some of which are among the finest ever written in Welsh.

A collection of Ieuan's work, together with biographical notes, was edited by Richard Parry (Gwalchmai) in 1862 and selections were edited by Owen M. Edwards in the series *Cyfres y Fil* (1908) and by Saunders Lewis (1931). See also the articles by G. Gerallt Davies in the *Transactions* of the Caernarfonshire Historical Society (1963), D. Eifion Evans in *Yr Haul* (1947) and T. Hevin Williams in *Y Traethodydd* (1930).

EVANS, EVAN EYNON (1904–), playwright, was born at Nelson, Glam. He worked for many years as a bus-driver and lived in Caerphilly where he helped to found the Tonyfelin Dramatic Society, for which he wrote an annual three-act comedy. His plays include *Affairs of Bryngolau* (1936), *Cold Coal* (1939), *Kith and Kin* (1946), *Half a Loaf* (1950) and *Bless This House* (1954). His best-known work and the play which established him as a professional playwright, *Wishing Well* (1946), was later filmed as *The Happiness of Three Women*, with the author playing one of the leading parts. E. Eynon Evans is not a profound writer, but his plays cast a sharp eye over the more incongruous aspects of life in south Wales and have been very popular. He also published a volume of short stories, *Prize Onions*(1951).

EVANS, EVAN GWYNDAF (1913–), poet, was born at Llanfachreth, Mer. As an undergraduate at the University College of Wales, Aberystwyth, he won the prize at the Inter-College Eisteddfod in 1934 with his *awdl*, '*Deirdre'r Gofidiau*', his first successful attempt to write free verse with *cynghanedd. In the following year he won the *Chair at the *National Eisteddfod with his *awdl*, '*Magdalen*', composed in the same style. He served as a minister in Llanelli from 1938 to 1957 and then as a schoolmaster at Llandovery, becoming Head of Religious Education at Brynrefail School, Caerns., in 1957. A gifted singer of *penillion*, he was Archdruid from 1966 to 1969 and succeeded Cynan (Albert *Evans-Jones) as Recorder of *Gorsedd Beirdd Ynys Prydain in 1970. He has published only one volume of poetry, entitled *Magdalen a Cherddi Eraill* (1962), but has contributed verse to many Welsh periodicals.

EVANS, EVAN KERI (1860–1941), biographer, was born at Pontceri, near Newcastle Emlyn, Carms. Apprenticed to a carpenter before entering the Presbyterian College at Carmarthen, he went on to graduate in Classics and Philosophy at the University of Glasgow in 1888. He had a distinguished career as Professor of Philosophy at the University College of North Wales, Bangor, and at his old College. Deeply affected by the Revival of 1904–05 which was led by Evan *Roberts, he resigned from his post in 1907 in order to devote himself to writing. He published biographies of his brother, D. Emlyn Evans (1919), of Joseph *Parry (1921) and of David *Adams (1924). But perhaps his most remarkable work was his autobiography, *Fy Mhererindod Ysbrydol* (1938), in which he gave an account of his own religious beliefs.

Evans, Evan Vincent (1851–1934), patriot, was born in the parish of Llangelynnin, Mer. He had little formal education but went to London in 1872 and became a very successful accountant and journalist, writing as a lobby correspondent for *The Manchester Guardian*, *Baner ac Amserau Cymru* and other newspapers. In 1881 he was appointed secretary of the *National Eisteddfod Association and five years later the editor of the *Transactions* of the Honourable Society of *Cymmrodorion. He also edited the magazine *Y Cymmrodor* and the *Cymmrodorion Record Series*, about a hundred volumes in all. He used the *London Welsh societies of which he was a zealous officer to promote all kinds of cultural causes and, a lifelong friend of David *Lloyd George, he was knighted in 1909.
There is a chapter on E. Vincent Evans in *Pedwar

Eisteddfotwr (1949) by Daniel Williams; see also the article by E. Morgan Humphreys in *Gwŷr Enwog Gynt* (vol. 1, 1950).

EVANS, FREDERIC (Michael Gareth Llewelyn; 1888–1958), novelist, was born at Llangynwyd, Glam., the son of T. C. *Evans (Cadrawd). Educated at Trinity College, Carmarthen, and at St. Catharine's College, Cambridge, he served as a Lieutenant-Colonel during the First World War. From 1923 to 1928 he was an Inspector of Schools in West Glamorgan and then became Director of Education for Erith, Kent. Besides plays and books for children, he wrote five novels, namely *Sand in the Glass* (1943), *Angharad's Isle* (1944), *The Aleppo Merchant* (1945), *White Wheat* (1947) and *To Fame Unknown* (1949). Largely autobiographical and sometimes crudely didactic, they deal with life in the industrial valleys of Glamorgan during the first decades of the twentieth century. The most satisfactory, *White Wheat*, is based on the tale of Wil Hopcyn and the Maid of Cefn Ydfa (Ann *Maddocks) which the author's father had done much to propagate in his *History of the Parish of Llangynwyd* (1887). Frederic Evans also wrote a history of his native district, *Tir Iarll* (1912).

EVANS, GEORGE EWART (1909–), writer, was born at Abercynon, Glam., and educated at University College, Cardiff, where he read Classics. He began his career as a teacher in Cambridgeshire in 1931 and served with the RAF during the Second World War. In 1948 he became a full-time writer, lecturer and broadcaster and, settling permanently in East Anglia, began to publish a series of books about the oral traditions of that region which are much admired by scholars and lovers of country lore. They are *Ask the Fellows who Cut the Hay* (1956), *The Horse in the Furrow* (1960), *The Pattern under the Plough* (1966), *The Farm and the Village* (1969), *Where Beards Wag All* (1970), *The Leaping Hare* (with David Thomson, 1972), *The Days that We Have Seen* (1975), *From Mouths of Men* (1976) and *Horse Power and Magic* (1979). It is a matter for regret among students of the oral traditions of Wales that George Ewart Evans, a Welsh-speaker, was unable to do for his own country what he has done in so many splendid books for East Anglia.

He is also a novelist and short-story writer, however, and many of his stories are set in Wales. The short novel, *The Voices of the Children* (1947), largely autobiographical, is about a family of eight boys and girls, a grocer's children, in an industrial valley of south Wales during the early years of the twentieth century. It has little plot and the treatment is episodic, but the book is notable for its warmth and charm, especially in the portrait of its gentle and sensitive narrator. The author returned to the same period of his life in a volume of autobiography, *The Strength of the Hills* (1983). The collection of short stories *Let Dogs Delight* (1975) is also about a Welsh mining valley and has the authenticity which comes of deep-rooted knowledge, understanding and affection for the people among whom the author was born and grew up. Among his other books are a gangster-story for young people, *The Fitton Four-Poster* (1953), and a collection of short stories set in Suffolk, *Acky* (1973). It was George Ewart Evans who edited the anthology *Welsh Short Stories* (1959).

EVANS, GWYNFIL (**Arthur Gwynne**, **Barry Western**; 1898–1938), writer of boys' fiction, was born at Porthmadog, Caerns., where his father was a Wesleyan minister, into a family which was related to George Eliot (née Mary Ann Evans). In 1924, after working as a journalist in Egypt, Evans began writing stories about Sexton Blake, the character created by Harry Blythe (the pseudonym of Harold Meredith), and soon became one of the most popular writers of all time in the field of juvenile fiction. His stories, nearly a hundred in all, appeared in serial form in such periodicals as *Union Jack*, *The Sexton Blake Library*, *Detective Weekly*, *Champion* and *Boys' Realm*, and among the characters he created were Splash Page, Mr Mist, Ruff Hanson, Julius Jones and the League of Onion Men. He published twenty-two novels, of which *Hercules Esquire* (1930) was the greatest commercial success. Most were based on his Sexton Blake stories (with the names of the chief characters altered for copyright reasons) but they also include *His Majesty the Crook* (1935), *The Riddle of the Red Dragon* (1935) and *The Mysterious Miss Death* (1937). By all accounts a mercurial personality, Gwynfil Evans became a legend during his own lifetime: it was once said of him that there was no character in his books as remarkable as himself.

EVANS, GWYNFOR (1912–), politician and historian. Born at Barry, Glam., he was educated at the University College of Wales, Aberystwyth, and St. John's College, Oxford. He was trained as a lawyer but chose to become a market-gardener and made his home at Llangadog, Carms. From 1945 until 1981 he was President of *Plaid Cymru* and became the party's first Member of Parliament when he was elected to represent the constituency of Carmarthenshire in 1966; after losing the seat in 1970 he held it again from 1974 to 1979. He has played a leading role in the development of *Plaid Cymru* as a political force and has been to the fore in all Nationalist initiatives since the Second World War. A prominent figure in the public life of Wales, he enjoys a high reputation even among his political adversaries. During the campaign of the 1970s for the creation of a fourth television channel broadcasting in Welsh (see under RADIO AND TELEVISION, WRITING FOR) Gwynfor Evans announced his intention of going on hunger-strike, if necessary to the death, unless the Government carried out its commitment to the provision of such a service.

He is a prolific pamphleteer who has set out his belief in the principles of *Pacifism and *Nationalism in numerous works which include *Cenedlaetholdeb Di-drais* (1973). Among his books on political subjects are *Rhagom i Ryddid* (1964), *Wales Can Win* (1973), *A National Future for Wales* (1975) and *Diwedd Prydeindod* (1981), the last-named a trenchant analysis of the 'Britishness' of the Welsh people. His emphasis on the nation's history and culture is at its most eloquent in his volume *Aros Mae* (1971), a history of Wales which was translated into English as *Land of My Fathers* (1974). As a historian, Gwynfor Evans takes his place with writers such as Theophilus *Evans and Owen M. *Edwards in attempting to nurture in the Welsh people a pride in the glories of their history and literature while drawing on the work of more specialist scholars.

A study of Gwynfor Evans's work and thought was published by Pennar Davies in 1976; a volume of his autobiography has appeared in the series *Cyfres y Cewri* under the title *Bywyd Cymro* (ed. Manon Rhys, 1982).

EVANS, HAROLD MEURIG (1911–), lexicographer, was born at Hendy, Pontarddulais, Glam., and educated at the University College of Wales, Aberystwyth. After working for several years at the *National Library of Wales, he became a schoolmaster and ended his career as Head of the Welsh Department at the Amman Valley Comprehensive School. Besides editing the anthology *Cerddi Diweddar Cymru* (1962), he has published *Y Geiriadur Newydd* (1953), *Y Geiriadur Bach* (1959), *Llwybrau'r Iaith* (1961), *Cymraeg Heddiw* (4 vols., 1965–69), *Sgyrsiau Cymraeg Byw* (1966), *Dilyn Cymraeg Byw* (1974), *Rhodio gyda'r Gymraeg* (1978), *Y Mabinogi Heddiw* (1979) and *Sylfeini'r Gymraeg* (1981). His principal works are the dictionaries *Y Geiriadur Mawr* (1958), done in collaboration with W. O. Thomas, and *The Dictionary of Modern Welsh* (1981).

EVANS, HOWELL THOMAS (1877–1950), historian, was born at Cwmbwrla, near Swansea, and educated at the University College of Wales, Aberystwyth, and St. John's College, Cambridge. Between 1907 and 1917 he taught at the Cardiff High School for Boys and was then appointed headmaster of the County School at Aberaeron, Cards. He published several books on the history of Wales, some of which were used for examination purposes. They include *A History of England and Wales* (1909), *The Making of Modern Wales* (1912), *The Age of Expansion* (1933), *Modern Wales* (1934) and *Mediaeval Wales* (1935). His most important contribution, however, was *Wales and the Wars of the Roses* (1915) which, in spite of its inadequacies by modern standards, is still regarded as a useful manual on the military and political history of Wales in the fifteenth century.

A biography of H. T. Evans, *Portrait of a Pioneer* (1982), was written by his son, Lyn Evans.

EVANS, HUGH (1854–1934), author and publisher. Born at Llangwm, Denbs., he had very little schooling before being set to work as a waggoner on local farms. In 1875 he went to Liverpool where he established a printing press known as *Gwasg y Brython* in 1897. Among the periodicals he founded were Y **Brython* (1906) and Y **Beirniad* (1911). He was the author of several books, including *Camau'r Cysegr* (1926), *Y Tylwyth Teg* (1935) and *Hogyn y Bwthyn Bach To Gwellt* (1935). But the work which won him immediate popular acclaim was *Cwm Eithin* (1931; trans. *Gorse Glen*, 1948), a thesaurus of information about rural life and crafts, which is now regarded as a minor classic.

For further details see the essay by Richard Huws in *Dewiniaid Difyr* (ed. Mairwen and Gwynn Jones, 1983).

Evans, John (1770–99), cartographer and explorer, was born at Waunfawr, Caerns. Recruited by Iolo Morganwg (Edward **Williams) to be his companion on an expedition to America in search of the Welsh Indians (said to be the descendants of **Madog ab Owain Gwynedd), he eventually proceeded alone, reaching Baltimore in October 1792. Five months later he set out on foot for the West and, after many vicissitudes, arrived in St. Louis, only to be imprisoned there by the Spanish Governor. Released, he found a place in 1795 as second-in-command to the Scotsman, James MacKay, on an expedition which the Spanish Missouri Company (created by a half-caste named Jacques Clamorgan) was planning with the intention of establishing forts up the Missouri and clearing a way to the Pacific Ocean. Mackay, compelled to pacify the Omahas and short of supplies, sent Evans on ahead in January 1796 and the latter, though at first forced to flee before the Sioux, got through to the Mandans (the supposed Welsh Indians of his quest) and remained with them throughout the Dakota winter. His influence with them was sufficient to exclude British and Hudson's Bay parties attempting to trade and to foil an attack on his life. The first man to map the Missouri nearly two thousand miles above its confluence with the Mississippi, he was ultimately forced in July 1797 to return to St. Louis. His subsequent report that the Mandans were not, after all, the Welsh Indians was brief and 'rather lame', in the words of Morgan John **Rhys. John Evans, out of employment, slumped into the depression which had begun to assail him and died in New Orleans, still only twenty-nine years old.

For further details see David Williams, *John Evans and the Legend of Madog* (1963) and Gwyn A. Williams, *The Search for Beulah Land* (1980).

EVANS, JOHN (I. D. Ffraid, **Adda Jones**; 1814–75), translator and lexicographer, was born at Llansanffraid Glan Conwy, Denbs. A businessman who was also an ordained minister with the Calvinistic Methodists (although never in charge of a church), he edited and had a hand in writing *Difyrrwch Bechgyn Glan Conwy* (1855). He compiled the dictionary *Geiriadur Saesneg-Cymraeg* (1847), which has a glossary of herb names, and *Pennau Teuluoedd a'r Ysgol Sabothol* (1870). His most accomplished work was *Coll Gwynfa* (1865), a translation of Milton's *Paradise Lost* (1667). He became a superintendent of the Society for the Emancipation of Religion and was the author of some five hundred letters which were published under the title *Llythyrau Adda Jones* in **Baner ac Amserau Cymru* (Jan., 1869–Dec., 1874); he also translated into Welsh a life of the highwayman Dick Turpin (1835).

EVANS, JOHN (Y Bardd Cocos; 1827–88), rhymester, of Menai Bridge, Ang., earned a living by selling cockles and gathering chaff. He became famous for the unintentional humour of his doggerel in which meaning was neglected or abandoned for the sake of rhyme. The title '*Archfardd Cocysaidd Tywysogol*' ('Royal high cockle-poet') was conferred upon him by local wags and he was invested in a long coat and a hat with a crown of coloured beads, in which attire he appeared regularly at the **National Eisteddfod. He used to say that he did not know the year of his birth but that he was sure his name was John Evans because he had heard his mother calling him thus on many occasions. His high opinion of his own verses led him to hope for Queen Victoria's hand in marriage and some of his acquaintances encouraged him by replying to his proposals with letters of their own composition. He had had no schooling and was of the opinion that certain other Welsh poets of his day had had too much. The more kindly of his admirers printed examples of his work in leaflet form, for him to sell at fairs. One of his most famous verses was inspired by the monumental lions on the Britannia Bridge which links Anglesey with the mainland:

> Pedwar llew tew
> Heb ddim blew,
> Dau 'rochor yma
> A dau 'rochor drew.

('Four fat lions/Without any hair/Two on this side/And two over there'.)

John Evans had counterparts in other parts of Wales, such as Anellyd (Arthur Simon Jones) of Abergwili and Elias **Jones (Cocosfardd y De) but he was the most ingenious of them all. A selection of his work was published in 1879 and another, with an introduction by Thomas Roberts (Alaw Cerris), in 1923. The terms '*cocosfardd*', '*cocoswaith*' and '*cocosaidd*' are now used to describe writing of this type.

EVANS, JOHN GWENOGVRYN (1852–1930), paleographer and editor, was born in the parish of Llanybydder, Carms., but his family moved to Llanwenog, Cards., shortly afterwards and it was there he grew up. He was educated at the Presbyterian College in Carmarthen and was ordained the Unitarian minister of Parcyfelfed, Carms., in 1876. After a period of poor health, he studied at Owens College in Manchester and then went to Oxford where he frequented the classes of John *Rhŷs, a connection which was to give a new direction to his academic career.

He began preparing diplomatic editions of some of the principal medieval Welsh manuscripts and published the first volume of a series entitled *Old Welsh Texts*, namely *The Text of the Mabinogion from The *Red Book of Hergest*, in 1887. Like all his editions, this work is valuable for the accuracy of its readings: aiming to show details of the manuscript by means of typography, he set great store on the form and size of letters. It was followed by editions of the *Bruts* (1890), *The Book of Llandâf* (1893), *The *Black Book of Carmarthen* (1906), *The White Book of the Mabinogion* (1907), *The Book of Aneirin* (1908), *The Book of Taliesin* (1910) and the poetry of *The Red Book of Hergest* (1911); he also published several facsimiles. These editions, more correct than any hitherto published, were milestones in the history of publishing in Wales. Towards the end of his career, however, J. Gwenogvryn Evans grew dissatisfied with the mere copying of manuscripts and attempted to edit and translate texts. Unfortunately, he was too ready to alter readings in order to support a particular theory and, as a result, his work on the poems of *Aneirin and *Taliesin was unscholarly.

In 1894 J. Gwenogvryn Evans was appointed Inspector of Welsh Manuscripts on behalf of the Historical Manuscripts Commission. Between 1898 and 1910 he prepared seven reports listing the contents of approximately eight hundred and seventy manuscripts, and attempted to describe and date them. Although the dates need revising in the light of modern scholarship, the knowledge displayed in these volumes, together with the suggestions about hands and sources, make these reports the starting-point for every study of Welsh manuscript literature. He also played a key part in the discussions which led to the purchase of the *Peniarth Manuscripts.

EVANS, JOHN ROBERTS (1914–82), novelist and playwright, was born at Lampeter, Cards., and educated at Trinity College, Carmarthen. He was a teacher in London until 1947 when he returned to Wales to take up an appointment as headmaster of the primary school at Penuwch, Cards. From 1954 until his retirement

in 1976 he was headmaster of the village school at Llanilar in his native county and it is with that place he is usually associated. His published plays include *Broc Môr* (1956), *Chwe Drama Fuddugol* (1960), *Ar Ymyl y Dibyn* (1965), *Cath mewn Cŵd* (1968) and *Brawd am Byth* (1981). But J. R. Evans made his most important contribution as a novelist and short-story writer. Among his best work are *Ar Drothwy'r Nos* (1962), *Y Delfrydwr* (1968), *Yn Dawel gyda'r Nos* (1970) and *Y Cwm Cul* (1980). His short stories were collected in the volumes *Blynyddoedd Coll* (1960), *Diwrnod Poeth* (1963) and *Lleisiau yn y Niwl* (1974). Much of his work draws on his wartime experiences in the Navy.

Evans, Margaret (**Marged uch Ifan**; 1695–1801?), a woman of Amazonian reputation who lived at Penllyn, near Llyn Padarn, Llanberis, Caerns. In his *Tours of Wales* (1778–81) Thomas *Pennant records how he called at her house and was disappointed not to find her at home. He then goes on to relate some of the many tales told about her in the district. She was, he reports, the greatest hunter, shooter and fisher of her time, a champion wrestler, a blacksmith, a boatbuilder, a maker of harps and an excellent fiddler. 'At length', Pennant concludes, 'she gave her hand to the most effeminate of her admirers, as if predetermined to maintain the superiority which nature had bestowed on her'.

There is a chapter on Marged uch Ifan in Eigra Lewis Roberts's book, *Siwgwr a Sbeis* (1975).

Evans, Margiad, see WHISTLER, PEGGY EILEEN (1909–58).

Evans, Philip (1645–79), Catholic martyr. A native of Monmouth, he became a Jesuit in 1665 and, ordained priest ten years later, was sent to his order's mission in south Wales. During the hysteria caused by the disclosures of Titus Oates, the fabricator of the Popish Plot, in 1678, he was arrested and imprisoned in Cardiff Castle with his fellow-martyr, John Lloyd (1630?–79). It is said that the only people who would testify that they had seen him minister as a priest were a poor woman and a dwarf, both of whom had been paid to give evidence against him. According to a contemporary ballad, Evans expressed his joy on hearing the death-sentence by singing to his own accompaniment on the harp and, at his execution, he is reputed to have climbed the ladder to the gallows with the words, 'Sure, this is the best pulpit a man can have to preach in'. He was canonized by Pope Paul VI in 1970 as one of the *Forty Martyrs of England and Wales.

Evans, Rhys or **Rice** (**Arise Evans**; *c*.1607–*post* 1660), magician and soothsayer. He was first called Arise while working as a tailor's apprentice at Wrexham, Denbs., and thereafter he applied to himself every verse in Scripture containing this word. A man of dreams and visions, he went to London in 1629 to warn Charles I of his fate, but was ignored, and in Cromwell's time he foretold the Restoration of the Monarchy. Among his more ridiculous exploits was an attempt to cure a fungoid growth on his nose by rubbing it on the hand of Charles II. His tracts include a work of autobiography entitled *Narration of the Life, Calling and Visions of Arise Evans* (1653).

For further details see the article by Christopher Hill in *Change and Continuity in Seventeenth-Century England* (1974).

EVANS, STUART (1934–), poet and novelist. Born in Swansea and brought up at Ystalyfera, Glam., he read English at Oxford, served in the Royal Navy and then taught at Brunel College of Advanced Technology. Since the mid-1960s he has worked for BBC Radio in London as a producer in the Schools Broadcasting Department.

While still an undergraduate, Stuart Evans won the Newdigate Prize for his long poem *Elegy for the Death of a Clown* (1955). It was followed by *Imaginary Gardens with Real Toads* (1972) and by his first substantial collection of poetry, *The Function of the Fool* (1977). His most serious work as a poet is characterized by its intellectual quality and by the influence of the American poet Wallace Stevens.

It is as a novelist that Stuart Evans has established a reputation since the mid-1970s by publishing seven long, technically complex novels which are more inclined to the philosophical than is usual in modern English fiction. His interest in exploring the processes of narrative was evident in his first novel, *Meritocrats* (1974), in which he employed multiple viewpoints, each with its own style and technique. The form and structure of *The Caves of Alienation* (1977) is even more intricate since the central character, a Welshman and writer named Michael Caradock, is revealed through intercut sources of information, such as samples of his own work, reviews, memoirs, critical studies and interviews. Besides *The Gardens of the Casino* (1976), Stuart Evans has written four other novels, *Centres of Ritual* (1978), *Occupational Debris* (1979), *Temporary Hearths* (1982) and *Houses on the Site* (1984) which are parts of a quintet entitled *The Windmill Hill Sequence*.

EVANS, THEOPHILUS (1693–1767), historian, was born near Newcastle Emlyn, Cards., a grandson of the royalist Evan Griffith Evans, the 'Captain Tory' of the army of Charles I who had been imprisoned in Cardigan by Cromwell. It is not known where he received his formal education but he learned much about history and literature in the company of such men as Samuel *Williams who lived in the locality. Ordained priest in 1718, he served the Church of England

in Breconshire for the rest of his life, except for the period from 1722 to 1728 when he held the living of Llandyfriog, Cards. He began his career as a curate under Moses *Williams at Defynnog and Llanlleonfel (1717–22), was rector of Llanynys with Llanddulas (1728–38) and then moved to the living of Llangammarch (1740–43), which he held with Llanwrtyd Abergwesyn, where William *Williams (Pantycelyn) was his curate. So hostile was Evans towards *Methodism that he refused to support Williams's request to be invested in full orders, whereupon the latter resigned. It was about this time that Theophilus Evans was made family chaplain to Marmaduke Gwynne of Garth, Llanlleonfel, a supporter of Howel *Harris, who was later to become the father-in-law of Charles Wesley. In 1739 he was presented to the living of Llanfaes, Brecon, but he did not resign from Llangammarch until 1763, when the living was given to his son-in-law, Hugh Jones, the father of Theophilus *Jones, the author of *A History of Brecknockshire* (1805, 1809).

Religion is the most important element in Theophilus Evans's books and the characteristics of Anglican thought are evident in many of them. But he was also concerned to uphold the ancient traditions of Wales and the authority of the Established Church. In 1715 he translated and published, one after the other, *Galwedigaeth Ddifrifol i'r Crynwyr i'w gwahawdd hwy ddychwelyd i Gristnogaeth* and *Cydwybod y Cyfaill Gorau ar y Ddaear*, two works dealing with devotion and worship. There followed in 1722 *Prydferthwch Sancteiddrwydd yn y Weddi Gyffredin* and, in 1733, *Pwyll y Pader, neu Eglurhad ar Weddi'r Arglwydd*. Among his other publications are some of his own sermons, *Drych y Dyn Maleisus* (1747?) and *Pregeth yn Dangos beth yw Natur ac Anian Pechod yn erbyn yr Ysbryd Glan* (1760). His contempt for Methodists, whom he accused of being secret Papists, is revealed in his translation, *Llythyr-Addysc Esgob Llundain* (1740), and in *A History of Modern Enthusiasm* (1752), which discusses the heretical sects which had sprung up since the Protestant Reformation. Theophilus Evans would have been truly happy in the company of Elizabethan Anglicans for he took the historians and scholars of this period, such as Camden, Powel and Ussher, and their spiritual descendants, Stillingfleet and Cave in particular, as the pattern for his chief work, *Drych y Prif Oesoedd* (1716, 2nd edn., 1740). This book, a prejudiced but entertaining account of the early history of Wales, is regarded as one of the classics of Welsh prose on account of its robust style and striking metaphors. Furthermore, it presented for the first time in two hundred years a view of Wales as a country with a history distinct from that of England.

For further details see David Thomas (ed.), *Drych y Prif Oesoedd* (1955), Garfield H. Hughes, *Theophilus Evans a Drych y Prif Oesoedd* (1963); see also the articles by R. T.

Jenkins in *Yr Apêl at Hanes* (1930), John Gwilym Jones in *Ysgrifau Beirniadol IV* (ed. J. E. Caerwyn Williams, 1969), Bedwyr Lewis Jones in *Y Traddodiad Rhyddiaith* (ed. Geraint Bowen, 1970) and D. Ellis Evans in *Y Traethodydd* (April, 1973).

EVANS, THOMAS or **THOMAS AB IFAN** (*fl.* 1580–1633), poet and copyist, of Hendreforfudd, near Corwen, Mer. A bardic disciple of *Simwnt Fychan, he was a prolific writer of *englynion*, carols and religious *cywyddau*, and he took part in bardic contentions with Siôn Wiliam and Rheinallt ap Dafydd.

EVANS, THOMAS (**Tomos Glyn Cothi**; 1764–1833), minister and author, was born at Capel Sant Silyn, Gwernogle, Carms. A weaver by trade, he came under the influence of liberal thinkers such as David *Davis of Castellhywel and Joseph Priestley. Having embraced *Unitarianism, he came to be known as 'Priestley Bach'. About 1794 he became the minister of Cwm Cothi Meeting House, the first Unitarian chapel to be built in Wales.

His support for the democratic principles of the French Revolution (1789) led to his imprisonment in Carmarthen from 1802 to 1804. In 1811 he became pastor at the Old Meeting House, Aberdare, Glam., and there he remained until the end of his life. He was a prolific author and a competent poet in both the strict and free metres, attending the *Gorsedd* held on the Garth mountain, near Cardiff, in 1797. His *Amddiffyniad o Bennadwriaeth y Tad* (1792) was the first Unitarian sermon to be published in Welsh. He also edited a collection of hymns (1811) for Unitarian congregations and several pamphlets in which his religious, political and social ideals were expressed.

For further details see the articles by Irene George in the *Journal* of the Welsh Bibliographical Society (vol. IV, 1932), D. Jacob Davies in *Yr Ymofynnydd* (1964), D. Elwyn Davies in *Yr Ymofynnydd* (1964) and the study by Geraint Dyfnallt Owen (1964).

EVANS, THOMAS CHRISTOPHER (**Cadrawd**; 1846–1918), antiquary and folklorist. Born at Llangynwyd, Glam., the parish clerk's son, he was encouraged in his youth by Mary Pendrill Llewelyn (1811–74), the vicar's wife, whose championship of the traditional story of the Maid of Cefn Ydfa (Ann *Maddocks) he was later to defend. A blacksmith by trade, he made a valuable collection of old furniture and farm implements. He was a prolific writer on local history, contributing to such journals as *Cyfaill yr Aelwyd*, *Cymru* (ed. O. M. Edwards) and Cardiff newspapers; he also edited (with L. J. Hopkin Jones) *Hen Gwndidau* (1910), a volume of old religious verse, and a selection from the work of Iolo Morganwg (Edward *Williams) in the series *Cyfres y Fil* (1913). But by far his most valuable work was *The History of the Parish of Llangynwyd*

(1887). One of his sons was Frederic *Evans, who wrote under the pseudonym Michael Gareth Llewelyn.

EVANS, TREBOR LLOYD (1909–79), author, was born near Bala, Mer., and educated at Bala-Bangor College and the University College of North Wales, Bangor. As Independent minister at Pen-y-groes, Caerns., and at Morriston, Glam., he became Secretary of the Union of Welsh Independents in 1964. He was the author of books mainly on religious subjects, including *Damhegion y Deyrnas* (1949), *Detholiad o Adroddiadau* (1950), *Ail Ddetholiad o Adroddiadau* (1952), *Cymeriadau'r Beibl* (2 vols., 1955 and 1958), *Gwyrthiau Galilea* (1960), *Gwerth Cristnogol yr Iaith Gymraeg* (1967), *Y Cathedral Anghydffurfiol Cymraeg* (1972) and *Chwilio'r Ysgrythyrau* (1973). Among his books on literary topics are *Diddordebau Llwyd o'r Bryn* (1966) and *Lewis Edwards, ei Fywyd a'i Waith* (1967). He also translated *Pilgrim's Progress* into Welsh as *Taith y Pererin* (1962), as well as parts of Francis *Kilvert's *Diary* under the title *Cymru Kilvert* (1973).

EVANS, TUDOR WILSON (1928–), novelist. Born at Picton, near Ffynnongroyw, Flints., a brother of Einion *Evans, he was a coal-miner before entering the Normal College, Bangor. Formerly a schoolmaster at Prestatyn, Flints., he is now a full-time writer. Among his best novels are *Rhwng Cyfnos a Gwawr* (1964), *Nos yr Enaid* (1965), *Trais y Caldu Mawr* (1968), *Iwan Tudur* (1969), *Ar Gae'r Brêc* (1971), *Ha' Bach Mihangel* (1972), *Yr Ynys* (1975), *Melinau'r Meddwl* (1975) and *Gilfach Lamorna* (1977). He won the *Prose Medal at the National Eisteddfod in 1983 with his short novel *Y Pabi Coch* (1983).

EVANS, WILLIAM (**Wil Ifan**; 1882–1968), poet, was born at Llanwinio, Carms. He was educated at the University College of North Wales, Bangor, and Mansfield College, Oxford, before entering the Congregational ministry. A prolific writer in both Welsh and English, he won the *Crown at the National Eisteddfod on three occasions (1913, 1917 and 1925) and officiated as Archdruid from 1947 to 1950. He wrote several plays and contributed frequently to periodicals. Two collections of his essays were published under the titles *Y Filltir Deg* (1954) and *Colofnau Wil Ifan* (1962). But it is as a poet that he is chiefly remembered. Among his volumes of poetry are *Dros y Nyth* (1913), *Dail Iorwg* (1919), *Plant y Babell* (1922), *O Ddydd i Ddydd* (1927), *Darnau Adrodd* (1932), *Y Winllan Las* (1936), *Darnau Newydd* (1944), *Unwaith Eto* (1946), *Difer a Dwys* (1960) and *Haul a Glaw* (n.d.). He was a charming lyrical poet and his name is often linked with that of his friend, Crwys (William Crwys *Williams). His volumes of English verse include *A Quire of Rhymes* (1943), *Where I Belong* (1946) and *Here and There* (1953).

EVANS, WILLIAM DOWNING (**Leon**; 1811–97), poet, a native of Caerleon, Mon., who earned his living as Clerk to the Guardians and later as Registrar of Births and Deaths at Newport. He published three volumes of verse, namely *A Tale of a Winter Night* (1838), *The Gwyddonwyson Wreath* (1853) which was an elegy for David Rhys Stephen (Gwyddonwyson; 1807–52), and *Lyra Silurum* (1867).

EVANS DAVIES, GLORIA (1932–   ), poet. Born at Maesteg, Glam., she left school at the age of fourteen and has lived most of her life in Carmarthenshire and Breconshire. She has published two volumes of poems, *Words—for Blodwen* (1962) and *Her Name Like the Hours* (1974).

Evans-Emmott, D., see EVANS, DAVID (1878–1945).

EVANS-JONES, ALBERT (**Cynan**; 1895–1970), poet, playwright and *eisteddfodwr*. A native of Pwllheli, Caerns., he was educated at the University College of North Wales, Bangor. He served in the First World War as a soldier and later as a chaplain, taking part in the campaign in Macedonia. During the 1920s he was a Calvinistic Methodist minister at Penmaenmawr, but in 1931 he became a tutor in the Extra-Mural Department of his old College and remained in that post until his retirement.

He won the *Crown at the National Eisteddfod three times: for *'Mab y Bwthyn'* in 1921, for '*Yr Ynys Unig*' in 1923 and for '*Y *Dyrfa*' in 1931; he also won the *Chair, for '*I'r Duw nid Adweinir*', in 1924. As Archdruid (1950–53) and President of the Eisteddfod Court (1963–65) he played a dominant role in the administration of both the *National Eisteddfod and *Gorsedd Beirdd Ynys Prydain*, in the activities of which his genial and colourful personality was given full expression.

Some of his poems caught the public imagination immediately by virtue of their lyrical charm and dramatic power. They include narrative poems, war poems, lyrics and ballads, some of which are among the best-known Welsh verse of the twentieth century. He published two volumes of verse, *Telyn y Nos* (1921) and *Caniadau* (1927), and his collected poems, *Cerddi Cynan*, appeared in 1959.

Deeply interested in the theatre, both as performer and author, he wrote several pageants, adapted plays by John Masefield and Norman Nicholson, amongst others, and wrote two of his own, *Hywel Harris* (1932) and *Absalom fy Mab* (1957); his only novel was *Ffarwel Weledig* (1946). He was knighted in 1969 for his services to the cultural life of Wales.

Dafydd Owen has contributed an essay on Cynan in the *Writers of Wales* series (1979); see also the memorial number of the magazine *Llwyfan* (no. 5, 1971), the article on Cynan's poetry by Alun Llywelyn-Williams in *Poetry Wales* (vol. 9, no. 1, Summer, 1973), the lecture by Bedwyr Lewis Jones, '*Cynan: y Llanc o Dref Pwllheli*' (1981), and the pictorial account of his life in the series *Bro a Bywyd* (ed. Ifor Rees, 1982).

Evans the Death, the undertaker in Dylan *Thomas's *Under Milk Wood* (1954) who has difficulty in keeping his heart from leaping at the arrival of spring in Llareggub.

Eve of St. John, The (1921), Saunders *Lewis's first play and his only play in English, is 'a comedy of Welsh life' set in the early nineteenth century. The heroine, Megan Morris, acting according to an ancient folk belief, summons the devil to appear to her on *St. John's Eve in the shape of her future husband in order to thwart her mother's wish to marry her off to a pallid but prosperous neighbour. Unfortunately, an old tramp makes his appearance at the critical moment but Megan is prepared to stand by her choice, until the tramp reveals that he is already married. Although the play is chiefly significant for the author's attempt to create an Anglo-Welsh idiom comparable with J. M. Synge's in Ireland, it also foreshadows many of the themes of his mature drama. Saunders Lewis considered the attempt to be a failure and thereafter wrote all his plays in Welsh.

Ewias, a commot embracing some of the valleys of the Black Mountains. Eastern Ewias (Ewias Harold), by the eleventh century a part of Herefordshire, was the property of Harold, the son of Earl Ralph of Hereford. Western Ewias (Ewias Lacy), seized by the Lacy family from the rulers of Gwent, passed through marriage to the Mortimer family in 1292. Most of Ewias Lacy was incorporated into Herefordshire in 1536, although Welsh continued to be spoken there until the nineteenth century. A narrow strip, including the vale of Ewias and the priory of Llanddewi Nant Hoddni (Llanthony), was incorporated into the county of Monmouth.

Excalibur, see under CALEDFWLCH.

F

Faenor, a house at Berriew, Mont., was built for Edward ap Hywel ab Ieuan Llwyd in the mid-fifteenth century. Among the poets who enjoyed its hospitality were *Guto'r Glyn, *Gwilym ab Ieuan Hen and *Owain ap Llywelyn ab y Moel. The old house was replaced by the present building in the seventeenth century.

Fair Princes of the Isle of Britain, Three, a Triad naming *Owain ab Urien, Rhun ap Maelgwn Gwynedd and Rhufawn Befyr ap Dewrarth Wledig. When the poet *Gwalchmai ap Meilyr described his patron, *Owain ap Gruffudd (Owain Gwynedd), as 'Gwyndeyrn Prydain' ('Fair Prince of Britain') it is likely that he was comparing him with the earlier hero Owain ab Urien, not least because that prince and his father, *Urien Rheged, were the patrons of *Taliesin who was for later ages the archetype of all praise-poets.

Fair Womb-burdens of the Isle of Britain, Three, a Triad naming *Urien Rheged and Efrddyl, the children of Cynfarch, who were in the womb of Nefyn, daughter of *Brychan Brycheiniog; secondly, *Owain and Morfudd, the children of Urien Rheged by *Modron, daughter of *Afallach; and thirdly, Gwrgi and Peredur, the sons of Eliffer Gosgorddfawr by Efrddyl. This Triad is preserved in its full form only in two manuscripts of the fifteenth century (Peniarth 47 and 50) which give slightly variant forms of the names. In origin, however, it appears to be ancient, since it is mentioned in a corrupt and abbreviated form in a genealogical document (Jesus MS 20) which lists the saintly descendants of Brychan Brycheiniog. The Triad seems to be a statement about the miraculous fertility of Nefyn, the daughter of Brychan, who gave birth to twins. Her son, Urien Rheged, and her daughter Efrddyl, were also the parents of twins. Peniarth 47 turns each of these sets of twins into triplets and adds to the third item the names of Cornan and Tonllwyd, the horse and cow of the sons of Eliffer, who are known from *Trioedd y Meirch. Their inclusion suggests that a story of congenital animal companions, such as is associated with the births of prominent Celtic heroes, may have been connected also with Gwrgi and Peredur.

Fairies, see under TYLWYTH TEG.

Faithful and Faithless War-bands of the Isle of Britain, Three, an antithetical pair of Triads which name the Faithful War-bands as those of *Cadwallawn ap Cadfan, Aeddan ap Gafran and *Gwenddolau ap Ceidio and the Faithless War-bands as those belonging to Gronw Pebyr of Penllyn, to Gwrgi and Peredur, and to Alan Fyrgan. A brief note attached to each explains the manner in which the war-bands displayed these qualities. The incident relating to Gronw Pebyr is narrated at the end of the story of *Math in *Pedair Cainc y Mabinogi, but all the other allusions are to stories which have not come down. *Cynddelw Brydydd Mawr assumed a familiarity with this Triad on the part of his audience when he complimented the *teulu* (war-band) of *Madog ap Maredudd by describing it in a praise-poem as one of the Three Faithful War-bands, thus proving that the Triad was well known in *Powys in the mid-twelfth century.

Fan, Y, a mansion near Caerphilly, Glam., built for Edward Lewis about 1548, was a well-known resort for itinerant poets, especially during the sixteenth and early seventeenth centuries. Edward's son, Thomas (d. 1593), continued the tradition, as did his son Edward (1560–1628). The family achieved wealth and influence, for which they were praised by the poets, especially *Dafydd Benwyn, the poet most often associated with the family during the time of Thomas Lewis. The Lewises of Y Fan (originally The Van) were, with the *Bulkeleys of Beaumaris and the *Morgans of Tredegar, among the wealthiest gentry in Wales at the time of Leland's journeys through the country (c.1540).

Far Off Things (1922), a volume of autobiography by Arthur Machen (Arthur *Jones). First published as 'The Confessions of a Literary Man' in *The Evening News* during 1915, it contains the quintessence of Machen but does not purport to observe chronological truth. Writing evocatively to please himself, he returns often to his native Monmouthshire, recreating 'impressions of wonder and awe and mystery' by means of reverie. The book's sequel, *Things Near and Far* (1923), lacks the quality of its predecessor, its unity marred by over-long digressions and the narrative sequence broken by Machen's refusal to mention his first wife and her painful death.

FASTIDIUS (*fl*.411), a British bishop to whom

the historian Gennadius attributed a treatise on the Christian life, *De Vita Christiana*. This work is often identified with a Pelagian document of the same title which is wrongly preserved among the works of Augustine of Hippo. An epistle of counsel to a young widow, it rebukes the rich and demands a fair deal for the poor, thus echoing the cry for social justice heard in writings emanating from a radical wing among the followers of Pelagius. It is, nevertheless, not as provocative as the utterances of the *Sicilian Briton.

FAUSTUS OF RIEZ (*c.*408–*c.*490), abbot, bishop and semi-Pelagian theologian, was brought from Britain to Gaul by his mother, became a monk at Lérins and in 433 was made abbot there. Chosen about 459 to be Bishop of Rhegium (Riez) in Provence, he opposed the Arian view of Christ and rejected Augustinian predestinarianism. His book, *De Gratia* (*c.*472), while accepting the transmission of Adam's sin to his posterity, insists on free will as necessary both to receive God's grace and to co-operate with it. Faustus kept in touch with Brythonic Christianity and was twice visited by a fellow-Briton named Riocatus, who brought some of the bishop's books to Britain. Several of the sermons of Faustus have been preserved under a false attribution.

Feat Stone, a smooth, oval stone used in contests of strength. Usually weighing between seventy-five and a hundred pounds, it could be lifted or else lifted and thrown, either by raising it with both hands and hurling it backwards over the head or between the legs. The game, which usually took place in churchyards on Sundays and feast-days, is mentioned in the *Pedair Camp ar Hugain* ('The Twenty-four Feats'), which every gentleman in the Middle Ages was expected to achieve in order to keep his status in society.

Fellowship of Reconciliation, The, see under DAVIES, GEORGE MAITLAND LLOYD (1880–1949).

Fellten, Y (lit. 'The lightning'), a weekly newspaper published by Rees Lewis, a printer, in Merthyr Tydfil, Glam., between 1860 and 1876. Radical in outlook, it circulated in the industrial valleys of south Wales. Among its contributors were Thomas Essile Davies (Dewi Wyn o Essyllt), Ossian Davies and David Watkin *Jones (Dafydd Morgannwg), and the early articles of Beriah Gwynfe *Evans were published in its pages.

FELTON, RONALD OLIVER (Ronald Welch; 1909–82), children's author, was born in Port Talbot, Glam., and educated at Cambridge University. By profession a schoolmaster, he taught history at schools in England, ending his career as headmaster of Okehampton Grammar School, Devon. During the Second World War he served with the Welch Regiment, the name of which he later adopted as his pseudonym. Only one of his books, *The Story of Sker House* (1954), was published under his real name. As Ronald Welch he wrote *The Gauntlet* (1951), a story set in and around the castle of *Carreg Cennen in the fourteenth century, and *Knight Crusader* (1959), the first in a series of novels about the Carey family of Llanstephan, which is set partly in the Palestine of the twelfth century. His particular interest was military history: battles and weaponry are at the heart of his stories. The Carey series continued with the novels *For the King* (1961), *The Hawk* (1967), *Tank Commander* (1972) and *Ensign Carey* (1976), all of which have Welsh characters or locations, while two independent novels, *Sun of York* (1970) and *The Galleon* (1971), are located in the author's native district between Swansea and Kenfig.

Fenni, Y, a lordship consisting of the western part of Gwent Uwch Coed. By the early twelfth century it was in the possession of Miles of Gloucester, the son-in-law of Bernard of Neufmarché. Having passed in marriage to *William de Braose (The Ogre of Abergavenny), it was held in turn by the families of Cantelupe, Hastings, Beauchamp and Nevill. The line of the Nevill lords of Abergavenny is still extant.

FENTON, RICHARD (1747–1821), topographical writer and poet, a native of St. David's, Pembs., was a lawyer by profession but had literary interests. He wrote *A Tour in Quest of Genealogy* (1811) and *Memoirs of an Old Wig* (1815), two witty, anecdotal works which were published anonymously. While living in London he became a friend of William *Owen Pughe and a member of the *Gwyneddigion Society and the Honourable Society of *Cymmrodorion. He is chiefly remembered for his *A Historical Tour through Pembrokeshire* (1810) and his *Tours in Wales 1804–13* (1917), the latter of which John Fisher edited from his manuscripts. He was also the author of a volume of verse, *Poems* (1773), which was republished in two volumes in 1790.

'Ferch o Blwyf Penderyn, Y' (lit. 'The girl from the parish of Penderyn'), a ballad which was very popular in the nineteenth century, is still sung. The music is a version of the tune '*Callyn Serchus*', published by Maria Jane Williams (Llinos; 1795–1873) in her *Ancient National Airs of Gwent and Morganwg* (1844). The words refer to a feud between two families in the parish of Penderyn, Glam.: the young man belongs to one and his sweetheart to the other, and so their love is thwarted for ever.

'Fern Hill', perhaps the most famous of all

Dylan *Thomas's poems, was written in 1945. It is an imaginative recreation of his experiences as a child on holiday at the farm of that name near Llan-gain, Carms., the home of his aunt Anne Jones (1863–1933), in whose memory he wrote *'After the Funeral'. The poem succeeds in combining two levels of consciousness, that of the remembered child absorbed in the original sights and sounds, and that of the remembering adult, aware now that such experience is at the mercy of time. The full effect is not of nostalgia or of simple complaint at loss, for the gusto of the re-enactment is a celebration of the reality of the experience and its accessibility in memory and through art. The visual effects of the poem's language suggest, in the manner of Chagall, a world of movement, wonder and oneness. The fluidity of tone and language hides very carefully achieved patterns of sounds, images, line- or phrase-lengths, as well as multiple syntactic possibilities within a single group of words; without appearing to rhyme, for example, the lines chime according to a strict pattern of assonance. There were more than two hundred work-sheets of the poem and its intricate craftsmanship is characteristic of the poet's later work. The comic-realistic treatment of the same farm in 'The Peaches', the opening story of the autobiographical volume *Portrait of the Artist as a Young Dog (1940), where it is called Gorsehill, contrasts with this visionary poem.

Ferrar, Robert (d. 1555), Protestant martyr, was an Englishman who was made Bishop of *St. David's in 1548, the first to be consecrated in a ceremony performed according to the English form of service. During the Marian persecution he was imprisoned for heresy and, refusing to recant, was burned at the stake in the market square at Carmarthen. The English poet Ted Hughes included a poem on the martyrdom of Bishop Ferrar in his volume The Hawk in the Rain (1957). See also NICHOLL, WILLIAM (d. 1558) and WHITE, RAWLINS (c.1485–1555).

FERRIS, PAUL (1929–), novelist and investigative writer. Born in Swansea, he began his career in 1949 with The South Wales Evening Post but since 1953 he has been a full-time writer and journalist, living in London and writing regularly for The Observer and for television. He is the author of ten novels: A Changed Man (1958), Then We Fall (1960), A Family Affair (1963), The Destroyer (1965), The Dam (1967), Very Personal Problems (1973), The Cure (1974), The Detective (1976), Talk to me about England (1979) and A Distant Country (1983). The fifth of these is about a Welsh Nationalist attempt to blow up a reservoir which is being built to supply water to an English city and the last also explores an expatriate's response to *Nationalism in Wales. His reputation as a writer is based, however, as much on his investigative books as

on his novels. These include The City (1960), The Church of England (1962), The Doctors (1965), The Nameless (1966), Men and Money (1968), The House of Northcliffe (1971), The New Militants (1972) and two biographies of Richard *Burton the actor (1981, 1984). His biography of Dylan *Thomas (1977) presents a fresh perspective and some new information about the poet's life, especially his family background and his early years in Swansea.

Ffair Gaeaf (lit. 'Winter fair'; 1937), Kate *Roberts's third collection of short stories, has several characters who struggle against poverty, as in 'Y Cwilt' and 'Y Taliad Olaf', and against the cruelty of social conditions, as in 'Plant'. There is, too, an unremitting bitterness, as in 'Dwy Storm', and a consciousness of fate's inevitability, as in 'Y Condemniedig'. But the book also reflects her characters' assiduity, perseverance and sometimes their longing to rise above life's wretchedness, as in the title story. Three of the stories, 'Buddugoliaeth Alaw Jim', 'Diwrnod i'r Brenin' and 'Gorymdaith', are located in the industrial valleys of south Wales during the *Depression.

'Ffarwel i Blwy' Llangower' (lit. 'Farewell to the parish of Llangower'), a folk-song which exists in several versions, including 'Ffarwel i Aberystwyth' and others purporting to be sung by soldiers and sailors about to leave home. The best-known version, with the words 'Ffarwel i Blwy' Llangower a'r Bala dirion deg', was given wider currency by Lewis Davies *Jones (Llew Tegid) who first heard it sung in Llanuwchllyn, Mer., and added two verses of his own to the traditional opening.

'Ffarwel Ned Puw' (lit. 'Ned Puw's farewell'), a folk-tune associated with an onomastic tale about a piper, a bugler and a *crwth-player who were drawn to Ogof Ddu, a cave near Cricieth, Caerns., by the sound of beautiful music. The three were never seen again but they were to be heard playing tunes later called 'Ffarwel Dic y Pibydd' and 'Ffarwel Ned Puw'. The cave is sometimes called Ogof y Pibydd Du ('The Cave of the Black Piper'), and the places where the musicians were heard are known as Braich y Bib, Braich y Cornor and Tyddyn y Crythor. The tune only is associated with Twll yr Ogof, Llanymynech, Mont., in another version of the tale.

Ffarwel Weledig (lit. 'Farewell to seen things'; 1763–69), the fifth collection of hymns by William *Williams of Pantycelyn, has as its full title Ffarwel Weledig, Groesaw Anweledig Bethau ('Farewell to seen, welcome to unseen, things'). There are eighty-four hymns in the first part and eighty-five in each of the second and third parts; several new metres are employed and the second part (1766) has a particularly valuable introduction. Some of the hymns form complete sequences and the writer's art comes to full fruition in them.

Ffestivalis, Y (lit. 'The feast-days'; 1575–1600), a work translated from part of John Mirk's *Liber Ffestialis* (early 15th cent.) is a collection of homilies for the Sundays and feast-days of the year. Intended for the use of parish priests, it is of interest mainly because it reflects the flexibility of the spoken Welsh of its period, and it is preserved among the Hafod Manuscripts.

The text was published with an introduction by Henry Lewis as an appendix to the *Transactions* of the Honourable Society of Cymmrodorion (1923–24).

Fflam, Y (lit. 'The flame'), a literary magazine of which eleven numbers were published between 1946 and 1952 under the editorship of Euros *Bowen, assisted by Davies Aberpennar (Pennar *Davies) and J. Gwyn *Griffiths. It was launched partly in response to what the editors considered to be the reactionary views of W. J. *Gruffydd and his journal *Y *Llenor*, but its chief aim was to create a new platform for younger writers. The magazine's watch-words were '*Dynoldeb a Chymreictod*' ('Humanity and Welshness'), the flame of its title signifying light, warmth and beauty. Publishing poems, stories, articles and reviews, it followed the lead given by *Tir Newydd* before the Second World War, sometimes causing controversy with provocative and propagandist items among its contents. Its contributors included several of the most progressive writers of the day, such as Rhydwen *Williams, J. Eirian *Davies, D. Tecwyn *Lloyd, Gareth Alban *Davies and Bobi Jones (Robert Maynard *Jones); there were also several contributions in Welsh by R. S. *Thomas.

Fflamddwyn, see under ARGOED LLWYFEIN, THE BATTLE OF (late 6th cent.).

'Fflat Huw Puw' (lit. 'Huw Puw's deck'), a sea-shanty which became popular after it was published by J. Glyn *Davies with the opening words, '*Mae sŵn ym Mhortinllaen*', in *Cerddi Huw Puw* (1923). The air was first published by John Parry (Bardd Alaw) under the title '*Y dydd cyntaf o Awst*' in *The Welsh Harper* (1848). The words were suggested by a rhyme which the old seamen of Llŷn used to sing.

Ffon Wen (lit. 'White stick'), a hazel rod stripped of its bark, was sent anonymously to a rejected lover on the day of his sweetheart's wedding; sometimes a black ribbon and verses were fastened to it. This malicious custom survived in Montgomeryshire until the 1920s.

Ffordd y Brawd Odrig (lit. 'Brother Odoric's journey'; *c.*1450–1500), a prose translation of a Latin work, *Itinerarium Fratris Odorici*, was made by a priest, Dafydd Bychan of Glamorgan, for Rhys ap Tomos, a brother of Hopcyn ap Tomos. It is a history of the travels of Odoric, a Franciscan, through Asia early in the fourteenth century.

Ffordd yng Nghymru, Y (lit. 'The road in Wales'; 1933), a history book for children by R. T. *Jenkins, tells the story of Wales by tracing the development of its roadways from the mountain tracks of the early Britons to the lowland highways of modern times. There are chapters on the builders and users of the roads: the Romans, the soldiers, the poets, the pilgrims, the friars, the *drovers, and on famous travellers such as *Gerald de Barri (Giraldus Cambrensis), Howel *Harris and Thomas *Pennant. Although one or two chapters tend to be catalogues of place-names, the brilliant teacher in the author, with his graphic comparisons and witty asides, draws memorable pictures throughout the book which have earned for it the status of a minor classic.

Ffraid, I. D., see EVANS, JOHN (1814–75).

Ffydd Ddi-ffuant, Y (lit. 'The sincere faith'; 1667), a prose classic by Charles *Edwards. The first edition was no more than a brief outline of the history of the Christian faith in the world; to the second, published in 1671, was added a section on the history of the Faith among the Welsh, including an abridgement of the *De Excidio Britanniae* of *Gildas. This new section had a specific purpose, namely to present to the Welsh an account of their own history from the viewpoint of an author whose historical philosophy was one with that of the Old Testament prophets. The work also included a section on 'the certainty of the Faith', comprising several 'proofs' of Christian truth. In the third edition, which appeared in 1677, this aspect was developed by a study of the Faith in the life of the Welsh nation and of the individual Welshman, and it is in this edition that the author's genius as a writer is most fully displayed.

For further details see the articles by Derec Llwyd Morgan in *Ysgrifau Beirniadol IV* (ed. J. E. Caerwyn Williams, 1969), Saunders Lewis in *Meistri'r Canrifoedd* (ed. R. Geraint Gruffydd, 1973) and R. M. Jones in his *Llên Cymru a Chrefydd* (1977).

Fifth Monarchism, a belief in the imminence of the personal reign of Christ, the Fifth Monarch, who would rule on earth for a thousand years. The four previous monarchies had been those of Assyria, Persia, Greece and Rome, as stated in the Book of Daniel (chapter 2). The teaching infused radical Puritan eschatology during the Interregnum and became the *raison d'être* of the Fifth Monarchy Men as a separate group whose leader, Major-General Thomas Harrison, was nominated as the President of the Commission for Wales under the *Propagation Act of 1649. In

Wales itself, however, the chief representatives of this literal millenarial belief were Vavasor *Powell and Morgan *Llwyd. The former was the main protagonist but the early writings of the latter reverberate with the paramount convictions of the creed. Although primarily religious in tenor, the ideology of both Powell and Llwyd was politically motivated and both were convinced that the power wielded by the saints in England would prepare the way for Christ's world-wide utopia.

Powell had a hand in nominating some of the Welsh representatives to the Saints' Parliament of 1653. In this assembly the Chiliasts failed to secure the implementation of policies specifically designed to undermine the old order and to establish the political, social and economic superstructure of the impending theocracy. When Cromwell dissolved the Sanhedrin and was proclaimed Lord Protector in 1653, Powell launched a vehement campaign in Wales against the Protectorate, the 'Beast' he believed it was his godly duty to extirpate. His outspoken criticism of Cromwell's rise to power at the expense of Fifth Monarchist expectations crystallized in the form of a petition which he organized in 1655, A Word for God.

Morgan Llwyd's name appears on the list of signatories appended to this petition but he protested his innocence to Colonel John *Jones, emphatically denying that he had signed it. He capitulated to the Cromwellian regime and thenceforth disassociated himself from Powell's Chiliasm. Powell clung to his belief and, though persisting in his fulminations against Cromwell, remained a staunch Parliamentarian. Llwyd, on the other hand, withdrew into the rapturous devotions of the inner life. After his estrangement from Powell, his main concern was for the 'existential' encounter with the Spirit of the Risen Christ in the depths of the heart. Despite modifying in this way his earlier Chiliasm, he remained a Puritan convinced that the coming of Christ was imminent.

For a discussion of this subject see Bernard Capp's The Fifth Monarchy Men (1972); see also the third chapter in Morgan Llwyd (1930) by E. Lewis Evans and the monograph on Llwyd by M. Wynn Thomas in the Writers of Wales series (1984).

FINCH, PETER (1947–), poet and short-story writer, was born in Cardiff and educated at the Glamorgan College of Technology, Treforest. After working in local government, he was appointed in 1973 to the post of manager of the *Welsh Arts Council's Oriel Bookshop in Cardiff. He is the author of seventeen collections of poetry, including The End of the Vision (1971), Connecting Tubes (1980), Blues and Heartbreakers (1981), Visual Texts 1970–1980 (1981) and Some Music and a Little War (1984), and of a volume of short stories, Between 35 and 42 (1982). Much of his work is experimental, involving perform-

ance, improvisation and tapework, and he has exhibited examples of his visual texts in Wales and abroad. The founder of the magazine *Second Aeon in 1966, he was its editor until it ceased publication in 1974. He has also edited the anthology Typewriter Poems (1972) and, with Meic *Stephens, was co-editor of *Green Horse (1978).

FINNEMORE, JOHN (d. 1928), writer, believed to have been a native of East Anglia, took up an appointment as head teacher at Tanygarreg School on Mynydd Bach, Cards., in 1891, his wife being engaged as sewing-mistress. Still in charge there some thirteen years later, he shortly afterwards returned to East Anglia, only to miss Mynydd Bach so much that he reapplied for his old post and served a second term; he was afterwards a farmer at Llanilar. One of the most popular boys' authors of his day, he published several books with a Welsh background, including The Custom of the Country (1898) and The Red Men of the Dusk (1898), wrote The Story of England and Wales (1913) and, with his wife as co-author, Stories from a Welsh Hillside (1928). Untypical of his time and profession, he also edited and published, prior to 1905, a number of Anglo-Welsh Historical Readers for use in the schools of Wales.

FIRBANK, THOMAS (1910–), the Canadian author of I Bought a Mountain (1940); the story of life during the 1930s at Dyffryn Mymbyr, a sheep-farm near Capel Curig, Caerns., it tells how he and his wife strove to make it prosper in the face of many hazards and misadventures. One of the first to write about a newcomer's attempts to farm in Wales, his knowledgeable, sympathetic account of the mountains, the weather, the sheep and his neighbours, proved extremely popular over many years among English and Welsh readers alike. He drew upon the same experiences in writing the novel Bride to the Mountain (1940) and his book Country of Memorable Honour (1953) describes, with many a digression, a journey made through Wales in the manner of George *Borrow. Firbank also published a book about his part in the Second World War, I Bought a Star (1951).

Fire in Llŷn, see under PENYBERTH.

FISHER, GEORGE (1909–70), dramatist, was born at Bargoed, Glam., and educated at University College, Cardiff. Appointed to a post as mathematics master at Llangefni County School, Ang., in 1931, he taught himself Welsh while serving in the Navy during the Second World War. He published three one-act plays, Y Lleoedd Pell, Y Blaidd-Ddyn and Awena, all of which are undated, and a verse play, Y Ferch a'r Dewin (1958). It was through his efforts that Theatr Fach Llangefni opened in 1955 and under his direction this little theatre fostered a talented group of actors and stage technicians. A producer of great originality and sensitivity, his work contributed substantially to the development of *drama in Wales.

For further details of his life and work see the account by Llewelyn Jones (1983).

Fitt, Mary, see FREEMAN, KATHLEEN (1897–1959).

FITZGERALD, JOHN (1927–   ), poet, was born at Ludlow, Salop., of Irish parents. He learned Welsh under Saunders *Lewis in Aberystwyth and, after ordination as a priest of the Catholic Church, returned to live in Wales in 1956. A Lecturer in the Department of Philosophy at the University College of Wales, Aberystwyth, he has published one volume of poetry, *Cadwyn Cenedl* (1969), and edited (with J. I. Daniel) a collection of philosophical essays in Welsh, *Ysgrifau Athronyddol ar Grefydd* (1982).

Fitzwarine, Fulk (d. c.1256), outlaw, belonged to a family of Border barons who were the Lords of Whittington, Salop., for eleven generations between 1150 and 1420. Outlawed by King John, he came to be regarded in local tradition on both sides of the Border as a romantic figure whose exploits were similar to those of Robin Hood, and a wealth of folklore was associated with his name. An Anglo-Norman poem, no longer extant, was composed about his career in the late thirteenth century. On it was based in the early fourteenth century a French prose 'history', *Fouke le fitz Warin*, which has come down in a single copy and in which the hero's patronymic is borrowed from his ancestor, Warin de Metz (d. 1170), the first Lord of Whittington. The work shows a detailed knowledge of north Wales and the Marches and refers to border-warfare with the Princes of *Powys, including Owain Cyfeiliog (*Owain ap Gruffudd ap Maredudd). It is known that Fulk Fitzwarine had been an ally of *Llywelyn ap Iorwerth and afterwards his deadly enemy. He seems also to have been associated with Cardiff and Glamorgan for he appears as Ffowc Ffitswarren in a cautionary tale published by Isaac *Foulkes in his volume *Cymru Fu* (1862–64), but the source of that version is unknown. There is no Welsh translation of the story but 'Syr Ffwg' was mentioned by several Welsh poets, among whom the earliest were *Dafydd ap Gwilym and *Iolo Goch, as a type of redoubtable valour.

For further details see J. Lloyd-Jones, *Geirfa Barddoniaeth Gynnar Gymraeg* (1931–63), Jessie Crosland, *Medieval French Literature* (1956), M. D. Legge, *Anglo-Norman Literature and its Background* (1963), A. Robson, *Fouke le Fitz Warin* (1975), and the article by Rachel Bromwich in *Ysgrifau Beirniadol XII* (ed. J. E. Caerwyn Williams, 1982).

Flame-Bearers of Welsh History (1905), a popular and influential history of Wales, was intended by its author, Robert Scourfield *Mills (Arthur Owen Vaughan or Owen Rhoscomyl) as a textbook for use in schools. With prefaces by John *Rhŷs and Kuno Meyer, it set out to end the deprecation of Welsh history, actual or implied, by stressing its glories and dramas from the earliest times to the Battle of *Bosworth (1485). Subtitled *The Sons of Cunedda*, the book is full of valuable insights but its enthusiasm and lack of caution in matters of detail allowed academic historians to discount it. Histories of Wales in the previous hundred years had sought only to conserve and defend but this book is proud, even aggressive, waiving all excuses. A Nationalist challenge in English by a popular writer, it anticipated and helped to create the wave of excitement which marked David *Lloyd George's first years in the Cabinet.

Flesh and Blood (1974), a novel by Emyr *Humphreys and the first in narrative sequence of the sextet of which *National Winner* (1971) is the last, takes the reader back to a part of north Wales native to the author where the language line is complicated and Welshness is precarious. Amy (not yet Lady Brangor) grows up in the house of her uncle and aunt in the most wretched poverty. Her attendance at the County School and her friendship with Enid, who comes of a middle-class family with Nationalist inclinations, draw her out and leave her poised for university. The novel does not disguise either the narrowness or the male selfishness of Lucas Parry, Amy's uncle, who represents a debilitated form of the Nonconformist tradition: in his world there was only hard work and ineradicable poverty for women. Amy, seen in the last volume, *National Winner*, despite the advantages of education and idealistic companionship, proves true to her childhood, seeing in the money, comfort and status of the Anglicized world what she most desires from life.

FLETCHER, HARRY LUTF VERNE (**John Hereford, John Garden**; 1902–74), novelist and topographical writer. He was born at Christchurch, Hants., but his father was appointed schoolmaster at Amroth, Pembs., in the year of his birth and he was brought up there, attending Narberth County School before going to Goldsmith's College in London. For most of his life he was a teacher and lived at Llandrindod, Rads. Under his own name he published the novels *The Woman's House* (1943), *Miss Agatha* (1943), *Forest Inn* (1946), *The Devil has the Best Tunes* (1947), *The Whip and the Tongue* (1949), *The Rising Sun* (1951) and *The Storm* (1954). As John Hereford he wrote *Shepherd's Tump* (1947), *The May Fair* (1948), *May Harvest* (1949) and *A Day to Remember* (1950), and as John Garden, *Six to Ten* (1947), *All on a Summer's Day* (1949) and

Murder isn't Private (1950). Most of H. L. V. Fletcher's novels are set in the Welsh Border country; those which he wrote under other names are, for the most part, thrillers with no literary pretensions. He also wrote a number of topographical books, including two guide-books in the *Queen's Wales* series, which are perhaps his most distinguished work.

Flint castle, was built by order of Edward I during the first ★War of Welsh Independence (1276–77). The borough established near by was attacked by Welsh forces in 1282. Richard II, on his return from Ireland in 1399, arrived in Flint to await the coming of Henry Bolingbroke, a scene depicted by Shakespeare. In the fifteenth century a poet, possibly ★Tudur Penllyn, attended a wedding-feast at Flint and, disappointed by the response of the guests, bitterly attacked the town and its English inhabitants. Control of the castle fluctuated during the Civil War but it was eventually captured by Parliamentary forces and then dismantled.

For further details see C. R. Williams, *The History of Flintshire* (1961) and A. J. Taylor, *The King's Works in Wales 1277–1330* (1974).

Flores Poetarum Britannicorum (lit. 'An anthology of British poets'; 1710), a collection of extracts and quotations from Welsh poetry made by John ★Davies of Mallwyd during the compilation of his *Dictionarium Duplex* (1632). The manuscript was later owned by Dafydd Lewys (d. 1727), vicar of Llanllawddog, Carms., who made his own additions and published it in Shrewsbury, together with a second edition of William ★Middleton's ★*Bardhoniaeth* (1593), a book on the art of Welsh prosody.

Flower Dance, The, see under BLODEUGED.

Flowering Sunday, the Sunday before ★Easter (i.e. Palm Sunday) when graves are decked with flowers, especially ★daffodils. There are references to this custom as early as the fifteenth century, when it was also an ancient tradition to decorate graves at Christmas and Whitsun. One of the most memorable passages in the diary of Francis ★Kilvert is his description of the dressing of the graves in the churchyard at Clyro, Rads., in 1870. By the beginning of the twentieth century the Easter-tide practice was more popular than ever, particularly in the industrial areas of south Wales, and it is still widely observed.

Fluellen, see under LEEK and WILLIAMS, ROGER (1540?–95).

Fluellyn, see under PERFIDIOUS WELSHMAN (1910).

Flyting, see under BARDIC CONTROVERSY.

Folk Narrative, a branch of oral folklore which includes the tale, the legend and the anecdote, is a rich element in the cultural heritage of the Welsh people. Although Wales has not had its professional story-tellers (see under CYFARWYDD) since the Middle Ages, the Folk Narrative has always had an important place in the everyday life of the common people, whether at work or play. References in the Triads and in ★*Pedair Cainc y Mabinogi* suggest that many early examples have been lost. Story-telling formed a central part of a wider activity, unofficial and informal, which also included gossip, games, dancing, and the reciting of riddles, tongue-twisters, nursery-rhymes, harp-stanzas, folk-songs and ballads. The Folk Narrative was handed down from generation to generation on the hearth in the ★*noson lawen* and the ★knitting night and on certain days of the year such as Winter's Eve, but also in smithy, stable-loft and on occasions of neighbourly co-operation such as sheep-shearing and harvest. The religious revivals of the eighteenth and nineteenth centuries took their toll, many Folk Narratives dying out and others acquiring moral and didactic overtones, but the tradition persists in many districts to the present day.

Welsh Folk Narratives may be distributed into nine main groups: tales about animals with human characteristics (e.g. the ★Oldest Animals); tales of magic relating to mythological characters who live in a timeless world of wonder (e.g. *Pedair Cainc y Mabinogi*); tales of romance about humans who live in the real world, usually based on international motifs (e.g. ★Gelert); formula tales such as the cumulative tale and the story without end; tales of humour about types or actual persons (e.g. ★white-lie tales); local legends about historical or pseudo-historical persons, especially saints and heroes such as ★Arthur and ★Twm Siôn Catti; local legends about historical and pseudo-historical events, such as those associated with ★*Gwylliaid Cochion Mawddwy*; traditions based on place-names and topographical features, many of which are onomastic; and finally those reflecting a belief in the supernatural, such as tales about giants, the ★*Tylwyth Teg*, the ★Devil, ★witches, ghosts, death omens, dragons, and so on.

Although these tales are the product of an oral tradition, many have been written down since the time of ★Nennius, ★Gerald de Barri (Giraldus Cambrensis) and ★Geoffrey of Monmouth, and some are recorded in the ★Lives of the Saints. There are also references to Folk Narratives in the work of poets and scholars such as Rhys Amheurig (Rice ★Merrick) and George ★Owen of Henllys. This antiquarian interest culminated in the great work of Edward ★Lhuyd, the ★Morris Brothers of Anglesey and Iolo Morganwg (Edward ★Williams). With the growth of the folklore movement in the mid-nineteenth century—the term 'folklore' (coined by W. J.

Thoms in 1846) was translated into Welsh as '*llên y werin*' by Daniel Silvan *Evans in *Y Brython* in 1858—several important collections of Folk Narratives were published. They include *Cambrian Popular Antiquities* (1815) by Peter Roberts; *Cambrian Superstitions* (1831) by W. Howells, *Cymru Fu* (1862) by Isaac *Foulkes, *British Goblins* (1880) by Wirt Sikes, *Celtic Fairy Tales* (1892) by Joseph Jacobs, *Ystên Sioned* (1894) by Daniel Silvan Evans and John Jones, *Welsh Folklore* (1896) by Elias *Owen, *Folklore and Folk Stories of Wales* (1909) by Marie Trevelyan, *Folk-Lore of West and Mid-Wales* (1911) by J. Ceredig Davies, and many others.

During the twentieth century the Folk Narratives of Wales have been studied by John Rhŷs in *Celtic Folklore* (1901), T. Gwynn Jones in *Welsh Folklore and Folk Customs* (1930), and by such scholars as W. J. Gruffydd, Ifor Williams, Thomas Jones, Alwyn D. Rees, Brinley Rees and J. E. Caerwyn Williams. The centre for folklore research in Wales is the Welsh Folk Museum at St. Fagans, near Cardiff, where more than fifteen thousand recorded examples of Folk Narratives are now housed.

Folk Poet, see BARDD GWLAD.

Ford Gron, Y (lit. 'The round table'), a monthly magazine which was published by *Hughes a'i Fab* between 1930 and 1935 under the editorship of J. Tudor *Jones and later of Meredydd J. Roberts, was intended primarily as a periodical for Welsh expatriates. It contained poetry, short stories, articles on literary and linguistic topics, travel, fashion, art, the Eisteddfod and famous Welshmen. Many of the leading writers of the 1930s contributed to the magazine, including Waldo *Williams, R. Williams *Parry, W. Ambrose *Bebb, E. Prosser *Rhys, Caradog *Prichard and T. I. *Ellis.

Formula Tale, see under FOLK NARRATIVE.

Fortunate Concealments and Unfortunate Disclosures of the Isle of Britain, Three, a contrasting pair of Triads. The Concealments were the head of Bendigeidfran ap Llŷr (*Brân), which was buried at the White Mount in London, the bones of Gwerthefyr (Vortimer) which were buried in the chief ports of Britain (as recounted in the *Historia Brittonum*) and the dragons buried by Lludd ap Beli in Dinas Emrys (see under CYFRANC LLUDD A LLEFELYS and EMRYS WLEDIG). The Disclosures were made by Gwrtheyrn (*Vortigern) who dug up the bones of his son Gwerthefyr, and who also dug up the dragons, while *Arthur dug up Bendigeidfran's head 'because it did not seem right to him that this Island should be defended by the strength of anyone but his own'.

There are analogies in early Irish literature for the theme of talismanic burial, that is to say the burial of a king's body near the border of his territory as a supernatural defence against his enemies. But they differ from the Welsh examples cited here in that the enemy is within Ireland rather than an invader as in Welsh tradition. A remarkable parallel to all such talismanic burials is found in a folk-tradition recorded in the nineteenth century to the effect that Arthur, after pursuing an unspecified enemy towards the summit of Snowdon (Yr Wyddfa), was slain and buried in a cairn on the summit of the pass known as Bwlch y Saethau above Llyn Llydaw, Caerns., 'so that no enemy might march that way so long as Arthur's dust rested there'. The burial of the dragons in Dinas Emrys is, however, a concealment of an entirely different kind and may be an intrusive element in the Triad.

Forty Martyrs of England and Wales, The, a representative group of Roman Catholics who were martyred between 1535 and 1679, were selected from among two hundred already beatified by earlier Popes. Canonized by Paul VI on 25 October 1970, the forty include six Welshmen who were executed on account of their priesthood or for refusing to take the Oath of Supremacy, namely Philip *Evans, Richard *Gwyn, John *Jones, David *Lewis, John *Lloyd and John *Roberts. The long poem 'Acclamation' by Raymond *Garlick, published in his book *A Sense of Time* (1972), is a celebration of their martyrdom and a statement of its significance in the context of contemporary Wales.

For further details see T. P. Ellis, *The Catholic Martyrs of Wales* (1933), C. Tigar, *The Forty Martyrs of England and Wales* (1961), and D. Aneurin Thomas, *The Welsh Elizabethan Catholic Martyrs* (1971).

FOSTER, IDRIS (1911–84), scholar, a native of Bethesda, Caerns., was educated at the University College of North Wales, Bangor, and later studied in Dublin and Bonn. After a period of teaching at Liverpool University, he was appointed Jesus Professor of Celtic at the University of Oxford in 1947 and he held the Chair until his retirement in 1978; he was knighted in 1977. His main research interest was the tale of *Culhwch and Olwen, but he also wrote about the period and background of early Welsh poetry, as in the volume *Prehistoric and Early Wales* (1965) which he co-edited with Glyn E. *Daniel, his essay on Wales and Northern Britain in *Archaeologia Cambrensis* (1969) and another on the early poetry in *Ysgrifau Beirniadol V* (ed. J. E. Caerwyn Williams 1970). He discussed various aspects of medieval Welsh prose in his contribution to *Y Traddodiad Rhyddiaith* (ed. Geraint Bowen, 1970), and of the tale of Culhwch and Olwen in *Y Traddodiad Rhyddiaith yn yr Oesau Canol* (ed. Geraint Bowen, 1974); two essays of his are to be found in *Arthurian Literature in the Middle Ages* (ed. R. S. Loomis, 1959). A thorough analysis of the contents of one of the Welsh religious manuscripts appears in the Sir John Rhŷs Lecture, *The Book of the Anchorite* (*Proceedings* of the British Academy, XXXVI, 1949–50).

From 1954 to 1977 Idris Foster edited the *Transactions* of the Honourable Society of *Cymmrodorion. With Leslie Alcock, he co-edited the volume *Culture and Environment* (1963). Welsh scholarship is indebted to him for establishing and presiding over *Cylch yr Hengerdd* ('The Ancient Poetry Circle') which met regularly at Jesus College, Oxford, from 1972 until 1978. The members of the circle presented him with the volume *Astudiaethau ar yr Hengerdd / Studies in Old Welsh Poetry* (ed. Rachel Bromwich and R. Brinley Jones, 1978), on the occasion of his retirement.

Fothergill family, The, ironmasters of Sirhowy, Pont-hir and Tredegar, Mon., and of Abernant, near Aberdare, Glam. The first Richard Fothergill (1758–1821), a native of Cumberland who had been attracted to south Wales by its rich mineral resources, became a partner at the Sirhowy ironworks in 1794 and joined Samuel *Homfray at Tredegar in 1800. He had three sons, Richard (1789–1851), Thomas (1791–1858) and Rowland (1794–1871), who were employed as managers of the family's works, the last-named acquiring control of the Llwydcoed ironworks, near Aberdare, in 1846. The second Richard Fothergill's eldest son, also named Richard (1822–1903), supervised the great expansion of Abernant in the 1850s and 1860s and took control of the Plymouth and Penydarren works, near Merthyr Tydfil, in 1862. With Henry *Richard, he was elected to Parliament as one of two members for Merthyr and Aberdare in 1868 but his companies declined after the introduction of the Bessemer process and closed down during the 1870s.

FOULKES, ISAAC (Llyfrbryf; 1836–1904), publisher, journalist and author. Born at Llanfwrog, Denbs., he was a printer by trade and started his own press in 1862. His first important ventures were the anthology *Cymru Fu* (1862–64) and *Enwogion Cymru* (1870); the latter was for many years the best biographical dictionary in Welsh. He edited a few scholarly works, such as *Barddoniaeth Dafydd ab Gwilym* (2nd edn., 1873), *The Royal Tribes of Wales* (1887) by Philip *Yorke and *The Cefn Coch Manuscripts* (ed. John Fisher, 1899), as well as publishing the series *Cyfres y Ceinion* and *Cyfres y Clasuron Cymreig* which included the works of contemporary poets. Among his own works were valuable biographies of J. Ceiriog *Hughes (1887) and Daniel *Owen (1903). He also edited the poetry and letters of Goronwy *Owen (1878) and the works of Twm o'r Nant (Thomas *Edwards). There is little literary merit in his novels, which include *Rheinallt ap Gruffydd* (1874) and *Y Ddau*

Efell (1875). He did excellent work, however, as editor and publisher of the newspaper which was a forerunner of *Y *Cymro* and he did more than any other publisher of his time to make the literature of Wales available to a wider readership.

Four Ancient Books of Wales, The (2 vols., 1868), edited by William Forbes Skene (1809–92), include poetry in Welsh, with an English translation, from four manuscripts, namely *The *Book of Taliesin*, *The *Black Book of Carmarthen*, *The *Red Book of Hergest* and *The Book of Aneirin* (see under GODODDIN), together with the *Juvencus *englynion* and some of the Triads. The first volume presents a survey of early Welsh literature, with special reference to the historical and linguistic context of the texts, the editor claiming that some poems are strictly historical and others mythological or prophetic; while the original texts and the notes are found in the second volume. By modern standards the work is unreliable and has long been superseded by better editions and more accurate translations. But until the advent of J. Gwenogvryn *Evans and Ifor *Williams, this was the only attempt at a translation and it was a brave step forward in the study of the literary history of Wales. Skene, a Scot, was a lawyer by profession but he received philological training and had edited much early Scottish material. Most of the work of translation from the Welsh was done for him by Daniel Silvan *Evans.

Four Branches of the Mabinogi, The, see PEDAIR CAINC Y MABINOGI.

Fox and Geese, a game involving the strategic manoeuvre of pegs fitting into a series of holes in a wooden board. One player's object is to immobilize the 'fox' by moving his thirteen 'geese' to pen him in; the other player, moving alternately, tries to move his 'fox' through the net to the other end of the board. This ancient game is mentioned in the Icelandic *Grettis Saga* (*c*.1300) and was popular in Wales from the fourteenth century onwards. Although there is now a standard version, the form of play known in Wales varied according to locality. See also GWYDDBWYLL.

Fox in the Attic, The (1961), the first volume of Richard *Hughes's incomplete historical novel, *The Human Predicament*. Its action covers a period of three weeks in late 1923 and centres on the Munich Putsch of 9 November in that year. The chasm separating the political and cultural sensibilities of the British upper class and its Bavarian counterpart is explored at length and with no little irony. The fictive and the historical are seamlessly interfused, Hitler emerging as the chief 'fox'. Acclaimed on publication, the novel was compared by some English critics with Tolstoy's *War and Peace* (1864–69).

Augustine Penry-Herbert, the central character, shares with his creator the year of his birth but Hughes always maintained, despite the fact that Augustine goes through some of the author's own experiences, that the book was not autobiographical. Free of the irksome task of earning a living, and disabled by education and temperament from placing an easy faith in the traditional values of his class, Augustine embodies the moral and intellectual uncertainty of his generation. Some critics have complained about his passivity and it is true that this aspect of his personality enables the author continually to point up racial and cultural differences. Augustine, however, is cast very much in the mould of 'the superfluous man' of Russian literature and his restless travels in Europe, Africa and America serve only to bring home to him the bewildering variety of moral perspectives to be found in the world.

The end of the second volume, *The Wooden Shepherdess* (1973), sees Augustine no more committed to a vocation or to another person than he was at the beginning of *The Fox in the Attic*. The unfinished typescript of the third volume leaves him contemplating marriage to Nora, the mill-girl of Slaughterhouse Yard.

For critical discussion of the first two parts of this novel see the monograph by Peter Thomas in the *Writers of Wales* series (1973), the article by Richard Poole, 'Morality and Selfhood in the Novels of Richard Hughes' in *The Anglo-Welsh Review* (no. 55, 1975) and the same author's article 'Fiction as Truth', in *The Anglo-Welsh Review* (no. 57, 1976).

Fran Wen, Y (lit. 'The white crow'), a bird often mentioned in Welsh, usually in jest, in order to avoid revealing a source of information, is also used as a bogey to frighten children.

FRANCIS, BENJAMIN (1734–99), poet and hymn-writer, was born near Newcastle Emlyn, Carms. An orphan, he was brought up in Swansea and educated at the Baptist Academy in Bristol. Although a minister in England for most of his life, he kept in touch with Wales, preaching and writing in Welsh. Some of the hymns in his collections *Aleluia* (1774, 1786) are still sung and several of his English hymns appeared in John Rippon's *Selection* (1787). He also published long poems in English, such as *The Conflagration* (1770) and *The Association* (1790), as well as two satirical poems on the Baptismal controversy.

FRANCIS, JOHN OSWALD (1882–1956), playwright, was born in Merthyr Tydfil, Glam. Educated at the University College of Wales, Aberystwyth, he joined the Civil Service in London but continued to keep in close touch with the amateur dramatic movement in Wales. His play, *Mrs. Howells Intervenes* (later retitled *The Bakehouse*), was performed in London in 1912. It was followed by *Change*, a play based on the railwaymen's strike at Llanelli in 1911, which won a prize offered by Lord Howard de Walden (Thomas Evelyn *Scott-Ellis) for a play 'suitable for a national company'. J. O. Francis, who had taken an active interest in Liberal politics in his early days, also wrote *Cross Currents: a play of Welsh politics* (1923), but it was not, perhaps unfortunately, for this vein of social realism that he was to be remembered.

The one-act rural comedy *The Poacher* (1914) is perhaps his best-known work. Its characters, especially Dici Bach Dwl, were to be revived later for such plays as *The Little Dark People* (1922) and *Birds of a Feather* (1927), comedies in a country setting which was recognizably authentic. As plays, these works are enjoyable, but they lack the dimension which could have transformed a competent playwright into a serious dramatist. There were reasons for this limitation. J. O. Francis, as he remarks in his collection of essays *The Legend of the Welsh* (1924), grew disillusioned with politics and, although the Welsh National Theatre movement continued after the First World War, it was more sporadic and less able to sustain its impetus or sponsor serious work.

Franciscans, The, an Order of Friars Minor founded early in the thirteenth century by St. Francis of Assisi. Its rule, approved by Cardinal Ugolino in 1209, stressed obedience, poverty and chastity, together with preaching and ministry to the sick, and its members were called Grey Friars on account of the colour of their habit. The thirteenth century was the order's golden age and it flourished in Wales because the friars preached in Welsh and recruited from among the native population. Three friaries were founded, at Llan-faes, Ang., in 1245 and at Cardiff and *Carmarthen before 1284. It has been suggested that the poet *Madog ap Gwallter was a member of the order. In the first half of the fourteenth century John Gwent, *Roger of Conway and Laurence Wallensis were eminent Franciscan scholars. William Egwad sang in praise of Carmarthen friary. The friars engaged in fierce disputes with parish priests over issues concerning material possessions and the right to preach and beg, and they were satirized by the poets *Dafydd ap Gwilym and *Iolo Goch. The three Franciscan friaries of Wales were dissolved in 1538.

For further details see A. J. Little, *Studies in English Franciscan History* (1917), W. Rees, 'The Suppression of the Friaries' in *South Wales and Monmouthshire Records Society* (1954) and J. Moorman, *A History of the Franciscan Order from its Origins to the year 1517* (1968).

FRASER, MAXWELL (1902–80), see under PHILLIPS, EDGAR (1889–1962).

Free Wales Army, The, a group of young Welsh Nationalists, perhaps not more than a score in all, among whom the most prominent was Julian 'Cayo' Evans. Their uniforms, drills, weapons and exaggerated claims about the strength of their movement attracted the attention of some of the less scrupulous among English journalists during the years from 1965 to 1969. Brought to trial on 1 July 1969—the day of the investiture of the Prince of Wales—six, including Evans, were sentenced to terms of imprisonment for belonging to a quasi-military organization. See also MEIBION GLYNDŴR and MUDIAD AMDDIFFYN CYMRU.

FREEMAN, KATHLEEN (Mary Fitt; 1897–1959), classical scholar and novelist, was born in Cardiff and became a Lecturer in Greek at the University College there in 1918. After her first publication, *The Work and Life of Solon* (1926), she wrote *The Intruder and Other Stories* (1926) and three novels. From 1929 until the outbreak of the Second World War she wrote nothing more but then, while lecturing for the Ministry of Information, she found time and inspiration to begin again. Among the war-orientated books which followed were *Voices of Freedom* (1943) and *What They Said at the Time: a Survey of the Causes of the Second World War* (1945). In 1946 she became a full-time writer. Works on classical subjects, such as *Greek City-States* (1950) and *God, Man and the State: Greek Concepts* (1952), still appeared over her own name but, as Mary Fitt, she published between 1940 and her death at least twenty-one detective novels. Some of the best-known are *Death and Mary Dazill* (1941), *Clues to Christabel* (1944), *Pity for Pamela* (1950), *Death and the Shortest Day* (1952), *The Nightwatchman's Friend* (1953), *Love from Elizabeth* (1954), *Sweet Poison* (1956), *The Late Uncle Max* (1957) and *Case for the Defence* (1958).

Friendly Societies, the main purpose of which was to provide their members with financial support during sickness or infirmity, were widely established in Wales, as in England, by the end of the eighteenth century; they were also known as sick clubs, or benefit clubs. The first to be founded in Wales were the Wrexham Neighbourly Society (1744), the Old Club at Holywell (1751), Sgubor y Coed Society, Cards. (1760), the Llangollen Club (1763) and the Esgair y Mwyn Society, Cards. (1765); Thomas *Johnes founded the Hafod Friendly Society in 1798. One of the most important at county level was the Anglesey Druidical Society (1772–84), established by squires and clergymen, which used its funds to reward bravery at sea, to help local hospitals and to pay for the apprenticing of poor children.

During their early years some societies were suspected of harbouring trades unionists and, because of the secrecy in which their meetings were usually held, Methodists were forbidden to join. By the middle of the nineteenth century,

however, the societies flourished in most parts of Wales. In rural areas it was common for up to a hundred members to belong to one lodge, but membership in the industrial valleys was sometimes as high as three thousand. Besides holding monthly meetings for the purpose of collecting and distributing their funds, the societies organized annual parades in which members wore regalia and marched behind a band to a place of worship. Among prominent members in Wales were John *Davies (Brychan), who edited a Welsh version of *The Oddfellows' Magazine*, John Jones (Ioan Emlyn), William Thomas (Gwilym Mai), T. E. Watkins (Eiddil Ifor), William Williams (Carw Coch) and J. R. Morgan (Lleurwg).

The societies began forming themselves into Orders early in the nineteenth century. The first to become established in Wales were the Ancient Order of Foresters, the Loyal Order of Ancient Shepherds and the Ancient Order of Druids. The only order indigenous to Wales was the Philanthropic Order of the True Ivorites, founded in Wrexham in 1836 and named after Ifor Hael (*Ifor ap Llywelyn), which added to the societies' usual aims the promotion of the Welsh language and its culture. Other orders, such as the Independent Order of Rechabites and the International Order of Good Templars, placed an emphasis on *Temperance. Many of the smaller orders became defunct during the twentieth century, but the most recent to be established in Wales, the Loyal Order of Moose, which was founded during the 1920s, still exists, as do several of those already named.

For further details see P. H. J. H. Gosden, *The Friendly Societies in England 1815–1875* (1960) and *Self-Help, Voluntary Associations in Nineteenth-century Britain* (1973); see also the article on the Ivorites by B. G. Owens in *Ceredigion* (vol. 3, 1956–59) and that by Elfyn Scourfield on the Ivorites and Oddfellows in *The Carmarthenshire Antiquary* (vol. VII, 1971).

Frivolous Poets of the Isle of Britain, Three, a Triad naming *Arthur, *Cadwallon ap Cadfan and Rhahawd eil Morgant. The term '*oferfardd*' as used here appears to be synonymous with *'cler' and the probable meaning is that these three were amateur poets, rather than praise-poets of professional status. Both satire and all lighter types of verse would have been considered as their proper subject-matter and the naming of Arthur may refer to the fact that mocking and provocative *englynion* are sometimes attributed to him in the native tales.

Fro Gymraeg, Y, see under ADFER.

Frost, John (1784–1877), see under CHARTISM.

FRY, ROSALIE KINGSMILL (1911–), children's author, was born in Vancouver, Canada, but was educated at Swansea and the Central School of Art, London. She served in the Women's Royal Naval Service as a Cypher Officer during the Second World War and settled afterwards near Swansea. Of her three novels with Welsh settings, *The Riddle of the Figurehead* (1963) is a light holiday adventure, but *The Echo Song* (1962) gives an authentic and unstereotyped picture of a semi-industrial community and *Promise of the Rainbow* (1967) is a non-pious but convincing story about religious faith.

FURNIVAL, CHRISTINE (1931–), poet and dramatist, was born in London of partly Welsh parentage, grew up in Gloucestershire, was educated at Cambridge and made her home near Llandovery, Carms., in 1973. She has published four volumes of poetry, namely *A Bare-Fisted Catch* (1968), *Prince of Sapphires* (1976), *The Animals to Orpheus* (1977) and *Towards Praising* (1978). Her plays for radio include *The Flame you Gave me* (1971), *Not Like Home* (1973) and *Hen's Trek* (1978) and she has also written a stage-play about Sarah *Jacob, *The Starving of Sarah* (1980).

Futile Battles of the Isle of Britain, Three, a Triad listing Cad Goddau ('The Battle of the Trees'), 'which was caused by the bitch, the roebuck and the plover', Gwaith Arfderydd, 'which was brought about through the cause of the lark's nest', and *Camlan, 'which was brought about because of a quarrel between *Gwenhwyfar and Gwenhwyfach'. A poem in *The *Book of Taliesin* states that *Lleu and *Gwydion were present at Cad Goddau, which in one account appears to have been fought between trees which had been changed by magic into soldiers. In words which recall the Triad, a fragment in a tale in a manuscript by John *Davies of Mallwyd explains that it was fought 'because of a white roebuck and a greyhound pup which came from Annwfn', and that the opponents were *Arawn, the king of *Annwfn, and *Amaethon fab Dôn. A mythological milieu is therefore suggested, resembling that of *Pedair Cainc y Mabinogi*. The battles of Arfderydd and Camlan are more famous and are both more fully documented. The Triad portrays Camlan (the emphasized third item) as the most futile and disastrous of the three. Each was reputedly fought between rival factions of Britons, rather than against an external enemy, which gives significance to *Tudur Aled's quotation of the Triad (in a rather confused form) in a *cywydd* written to reconcile Hwmffre ap Hywel with his relatives.

FYNES-CLINTON, OSBERT HENRY (1869–1941), scholar, son of the rector of Barlow Moor, near Didsbury, Manchester, was educated at the University of Oxford. He was the Professor of French at the University College of North Wales, Bangor, from 1904 until his retirement in 1937. His book, *The Welsh Vocabulary of the Bangor District* (1913), is a masterpiece and model for the scientific study of *dialect.

G

Galanas, see under LAWS OF HYWEL DDA.

GALLIE, MENNA (1920–), novelist, was born at Ystradgynlais, Brecs. Formerly an English teacher, she has travelled widely in Europe and North America, but has lived at Newport, Pembs., since her husband's retirement from the Chair of Political Science at Cambridge University. Her first novel, *Strike for a Kingdom* (1959), deals with the *General Strike of 1926, her second, *Man's Desiring* (1960), located partly in England and partly in Wales, draws on her knowledge of university life, while *The Small Mine* (1962) returns to an industrial setting in south Wales. She has an exuberant prose-style and an inventive comic flair but, although humorous, she cannot be called a comic writer since comedy tends to go with seriousness and pathos in her work, resulting in a bitter-sweet amalgam. In her two later novels, *Travels with a Duchess* (1968) and *You're Welcome to Ulster!* (1970), she breaks new ground; in the latter she depicts life in Northern Ireland against a background of communal conflict during the late 1960s. Menna Gallie has also written short stories and translated Caradog *Prichard's novel *Un Nos Ola Leuad* (1960) under the title *Full Moon* (1973).

GAMBOLD, WILLIAM (1672–1728), grammarian. Born at Cardigan and educated at Oxford, where he was a friend of Edward *Lhuyd, he was the rector and schoolmaster of Puncheston and Llanychaer, Pembs. From 1707 to 1722 he was engaged in the compilation of a Welsh dictionary but failed to raise the money necessary for its publication; the manuscript is kept in the National Library of Wales. His *Grammar of the Welsh Language* (1727) was the first English book to be printed in Wales. The Moravian bishop John Gambold (1711–71) was William Gambold's son.

Garden, John, see FLETCHER, HARRY LUTF VERNE (1902–74).

GARLICK, RAYMOND (1926–), poet and critic. An Englishman, born in London, he first came to Wales as a schoolboy and lived at Llandudno, Caerns., where his grandparents had settled. As a student reading English at the University College of North Wales, Bangor, he began to acquire a knowledge of Welsh and was received into the Roman Catholic Church. In 1949 he became a teacher at Pembroke Dock, Pembs., where he was a founder and the first editor of *Dock Leaves* (later *The *Anglo-Welsh Review*), and then at Blaenau Ffestiniog, Mer., where he was a neighbour of John Cowper *Powys. During the 1950s he published two volumes of poetry, *Poems from the Mountain-House* (1950) and *The Welsh-Speaking Sea* (1954), and a long poem for radio, *Blaenau Observed* (1957). He left Wales in 1961 to join the staff of an International School in the Netherlands. As editor and critic he has made an important contribution to the study of Anglo-Welsh literature, arguing in numerous essays—most notably in his contribution to the *Writers of Wales* series, *An Introduction to Anglo-Welsh Literature* (1970)— that from the late fifteenth century there was a tradition of writing by Welshmen in the English language which deserves wider recognition, not least in the schools of Wales. He has also edited, with Roland *Mathias, the anthology *Anglo-Welsh Poetry 1480–1980* (1984).

Returning to Wales in 1967, Raymond Garlick took up a post at Trinity College, Carmarthen, where he became Principal Lecturer in the English Department. Since then he has published a trilogy of verse collections: *A Sense of Europe* (1968), *A Sense of Time* (1972) and *Incense* (1976). The unity of these three volumes is apparent not only in their verse-forms, which are often intricately structured, but also in their common themes. These include a Nationalist view of Wales, his adopted country, as an integral part of European civilization, a celebration of people in the praise-tradition of Welsh poetry, a passionate concern for justice and non-violence which reflects his involvement in the campaigns of *Cymdeithas yr Iaith Gymraeg, and a preoccupation with language, especially with English as one of the languages of a fully bilingual Wales. He is no longer a member of the Roman Catholic Church.

There is an autobiographical essay by Raymond Garlick in the volume *Artists in Wales* (ed. Meic Stephens, 1973) and Anthony Conran discusses his work in *The Cost of Strangeness* (1982); see also the note on the poet by Glyn Jones in *Profiles* (1980), the article by John Hill in *The Anglo-Welsh Review* (vol. 21, no. 47, 1972) and the article by Tony Bianchi in *Planet* (no. 40, Nov., 1977).

Garmon or **Germanus** (c.378–448), a powerful civil and military official in Gaul who was elected Bishop of Auxerre in 418. He is recorded as having visited Britain in 429 with Lupus (Bleiddian), Bishop of Troyes, with the intention of suppressing Pelagianism, and he may have made a second visit in 447. According to the Life of Germanus, written about the year 480, he led the Christian Britons to victory over their pagan foes by bidding them shout '*Alleluia!*' at the battle of Maes Garmon in the year 430. His activities in Britain probably had more political than theological significance. It was a time when the stability of the Roman Empire was under threat, not only from invading Picts and Saxons but from resurgent Britons and Pelagian protestors against wealth and privilege.

Saunders *Lewis in his verse-play *Buchedd Garmon* (1937) presents the bishop as a champion of Christian civilization and, by implication, as relevant to the needs of Wales in the 1930s. The play was written for radio while the author was awaiting re-trial for his part in the burning of materials at *Penyberth and by the time of its first broadcast (2 March 1937) he was in prison. Some of the speeches in the play, especially the one beginning '*Gwinllan a roddwyd i'm gofal yw Cymru fy ngwlad*' ('A vineyard placed in my care is Wales my country'), are among the most famous passages in Welsh literature.

For further details see the Life of Garmon by Constantius of Lyon (*c*.480) which was included by Bede in his *Historia Ecclesiastica* (731); see also Hugh Williams, *Christianity in Early Britain* (1912) and Charles Thomas, *Christianity in Roman Britain* (1981).

Garn, a castle situated between Haverfordwest and St. David's, Pembs., was built in the thirteenth century by order of Adam de la Roche. According to local tradition, a high rock was chosen as its site because a witch had prophesied that Adam would die before the end of the year from a snake's poison. He locked himself in the castle, but on the last night before the year's expiry a viper came into his room in a basket of firewood, and he was bitten and died.

Garthmadrun, see under BRYCHAN (5th cent.) and BRYCHEINIOG.

Gavelkind, a method of bequeathing land and property by means of equal distribution among the owner's sons. It was common in some parts of England during the Middle Ages and the term was used by English lawyers of the period to describe a similar practice found in Wales, where it was known as *Cyfran*. The inevitable effect of the custom over several generations was the morcellement of land holdings but this process was checked, to a certain extent, by the settling of some of the heirs on what was formerly common land. Nevertheless, the general tendency of gavelkind was to undermine the stability of society. This long-established form of inheritance, already abandoned in many areas of Wales, was forbidden outright by the *Act of

Union of 1536 and replaced by the English custom of primogeniture, or inheritance by the eldest son. Gavelkind, however, was not prohibited in England (it was, indeed, common practice in Kent) and for that reason the custom continued to flourish in *Erging, most of which, after the Union, became part of Herefordshire.

For further details see T. Jones Pierce, *Medieval Welsh Society* (1972).

Gawain, see GWALCHMAI FAB GWYAR.

Gazooka Bands, see JAZZ BANDS.

Gee, Thomas (1815–98), publisher and editor, was born at Denbigh. Apprenticed at the age of fourteen in his father's printing works, he spent two years learning the trade in London before returning to join the family business in 1838. From 1845 until his death he developed *Gwasg Gee* into an institution of national importance. During this period, 'the golden age of Welsh publishing', a large number of magazines, newspapers, dictionaries, grammars, books of poetry, hymnals, sermons and theological works flowed from his press. At the same time he cultivated the acquaintance of political and religious leaders, thus ensuring that his influence was felt in every sphere of Welsh public life. A fervent Methodist, he preached regularly and was a prominent supporter of the *Sunday Schools. Among the most notable publications produced by *Gwasg Gee* were the magazine *Y *Traethodydd*, the encyclopaedia *Y *Gwyddoniadur Cymreig* and the newspaper *Baner ac Amserau Cymru*. The major issues which Thomas Gee fought on the pages of his newspaper, which was staunchly Liberal and Radical in outlook, included the provision of non-sectarian education for Nonconformists, the widening of electoral suffrage and the *Disestablishment of the Anglican Church in Wales. Although he did not live to see the fruits of all his labours, he succeeded in bringing these causes to the forefront of Welsh politics. His *Radicalism hardly touched the industrial areas of south Wales but his press played a vital role in shaping and leading public opinion in the rural parts for more than half a century.

After Thomas Gee's death the business was carried on until 1903 by his son, John Howel Gee, and remained in the family until 1914. Thereafter the press had several owners, including the Viscountess Rhondda, the Berry brothers (later the Lords Camrose and Kemsley), and the writer Kate *Roberts who, with her husband Morris Williams, continued to publish books of literary merit, a tradition which has continued to the present day.

For further details see the biography of Thomas Gee by T. Gwynn Jones (2 vols., 1913) and the pamphlet by Emyr Price (1977).

Geirgrawn, Y (lit. 'The treasury of words'), a

magazine of which nine numbers were published in 1796 by David Davies (d. 1807) of Holywell, Flints. Claiming that its purpose was to spread 'Knowledge, Justice, Love, and Peace, throughout Wales', it supported *Radicalism, took the colonists' side in the American War of Independence and supported the principles of the French Revolution (1789), one number carrying a Welsh version of 'La Marseillaise'. A famous controversy was caused when this magazine published *Seren Tan Gwmwl* by Jac Glan-y-gors (John *Jones).

Geiriadur Ysgrythyrawl (lit. 'A Scriptural dictionary'; 4 vols., 1801–11), a compendium of the Bible's history, theology and philosophy, and of Scriptural criticism, by Thomas *Charles, was intended for the instruction of converts during the Methodist Revival. The author's scholarship is displayed in his frequent quotations from classical and Christian writers down the centuries, and in his mastery of the biblical languages and exegesis. In these respects his dictionary did much to broaden the intellectual and cultural horizons of the Welsh people. The work is notable for its vivid but balanced treatment of the Bible's themes, its clear explication of difficult passages, and its presentation of scientific, medical, geographical and historical facts. All this was contained within a comprehensive, Calvinistic framework which viewed the whole world as being under the sovereignty of the living God. The influence of this dictionary on the thought and attitudes of the Welsh people was immense: it was one of the most popular books ever published in Welsh and among the greatest achievements of Welsh *Methodism during the early nineteenth century.

Gelert, the favourite hound of *Llywelyn ap Iorwerth (Llywelyn Fawr). According to the folk-tale associated with the village of Beddgelert, Caerns., the Prince, returning from the hunt, found the animal covered with gore and, assuming that it had attacked his infant son, slew it—only to discover that the dog had killed a marauding wolf and that the child was safe. This version of the story, an early form of which is found in *Chwedlau Saith Ddoethion Rhufain*, was unknown in the village before 1784 for it was the fabrication of one David Prichard, landlord of the local inn, the Royal Goat. The cromlech which is said to be Gelert's grave, like the well-known poem by W. R. Spencer which Joseph Haydn set to music, was based on details supplied by Prichard. A more likely explanation of the village's name is that, in the sixth century, it was the site of a priory dedicated to Celert.

GELLAN (d. 1094), a poet who accompanied the forces of *Gruffudd ap Cynan in the battle of Aberlleiniog (1094), Ang., where he was slain; it is presumed that he was Gruffudd's household poet and he may have been Irish.

Genealogies, or family trees, were kept over many centuries by the Welsh poets. *Gerald de Barri (Giraldus Cambrensis), in his *Descriptio Kambriae*, states that the poets, singers and reciters preserved the genealogies of the princes in their 'ancient and authentic books'. From the time of *Taliesin the poets had been concerned to compliment their patrons by emphasizing their ancestry and to recall their noble ancestors as a reminder of the standards of behaviour which society expected from them. The oldest genealogies are those of the native dynasties which ruled in independent Wales and in the *Old North. The earliest inscribed stone bearing a genealogy is the unique monument known as Eliseg's Pillar (9th cent.), near the abbey of *Valle Crucis, which traces the descent of *Cyngen, grandson of Elise(g), from a certain Britu said to have been the son of *Vortigern by a daughter of *Macsen Wledig.

The most important and extensive collection of early dynastic pedigrees is that contained in Harleian Manuscript 3859, written about the year 1100 but derived from a document of the mid-tenth century. This archetype was evidently drawn up in order to illustrate the lines of descent of Owain, the son of *Hywel Dda, and incorporates the main dynasties of *Gwynedd, *Dyfed, *Powys and Strathclyde, together with a number of fragmentary or collateral lines. Other important collections are those in Jesus College Manuscript 20 (14th cent.) and *Bonedd Gwŷr y Gogledd* in Peniarth Manuscript 45 (late 13th cent.), a guide to the northern rulers of the sixth century who came from one or other of two ancestral stocks, those of *Coel Hen and Dyfnwal Hen. The content of these three basic collections overlaps, though there are some discrepancies: the common source of the Harleian and Jesus texts appears to have been drawn up in the ninth century during the reign of *Rhodri Mawr. Oral transmission over many centuries must have preceded the written redaction of the genealogies and it is believed that these are in some instances reliable as far back as the fifth century. Before that date the boundary between history and legend tends to be nebulous. Obvious mythical elements are the descent of several leading dynasties, including that of Gwynedd, from the ancestor-deity *Beli Mawr, and perhaps of others, including that of Dyfed, from Macsen Wledig and *Elen Luyddog.

Genealogies in the *Historia Brittonum* record the claim of the descent of the Britons from *Brutus, the grandson of Aeneas, and add a genealogy traced back to Adam. Early genealogical collections also include the genealogies of the native saints: the many versions of *Bonedd y Saint* give the genealogies of the founding fathers of Christianity in Wales and were drawn up in an ecclesiastical milieu during the twelfth century. Descent is claimed for many saints from royal lines, in particular those of *Cunedda, allegedly the ancestor of *Dewi Sant, and of Macsen Wledig and *Brychan Brycheiniog. The last, by his three wives, is said to have engendered more than thirty (or more traditionally, twenty-four) saintly sons and daughters, and is an outstanding example of the fictional element which inevitably finds a prominent place in these early genealogies.

After the death of *Llywelyn ap Gruffudd in 1282 the dynastic genealogies continued to be copied and retained in popular memory and a number of the gentry families rejoiced in their descent from ancient royal lines. Apart from its prestige value, the correct assessment of descent and of the intricacy of family relationships was essential for legal purposes under the *Laws of Hywel Dda, both in regard to the payment of *sarhaed* and *galanas*, and because of the institution of *Gavelkind, by which all of a man's sons were equally his legal heirs. Descent through female lines was also recorded in *Achau'r Mamau*, and could be of prestige value, since it might lead back to a royal line.

It was after 1282 that genealogy (and later, to some extent, heraldry) came to play an increasing part in the poetry of the *cywyddwyr*, first with *Iolo Goch who traced in a poem the descent of *Owain Glyndŵr over several generations, and subsequently in the verse of *Guto'r Glyn. The period from 1485 to 1600, following the accession of the *Tudors, has been called the golden age of Welsh genealogy. Two poets in particular were famous for their genealogical researches and for the amount of material which they collected and transcribed. *Gutun Owain was a leading member of the commission charged to record the Welsh descent of Henry VII, which he traced back to Brutus, incorporating most of the Welsh royal lines afterwards set out in Lewys *Dwnn's *Heraldic Visitations*. In his manuscripts is to be found the original nucleus of the classification of 'The Five Royal Tribes of Wales' and 'The Fifteen Tribes of Gwynedd'. *Gruffudd Hiraethog compiled a number of genealogical manuscripts and, with his pupils *Wiliam Llŷn, Wiliam *Cynwal, *Simwnt Fychan and others, he formed a school of bardic genealogists who were active until the end of the sixteenth century. Lewys Dwnn, a pupil of Wiliam Llŷn, became deputy herald for Wales, and in his life-work he distilled much of the documentary material of the bardic genealogies of the sixteenth century.

The end of that century also saw the dawn of a new era in which the study and conservation of Welsh genealogy passed from the poets into the hands of educated country squires such as George *Owen, Rice *Merrick, Robert *Vaughan of Hengwrt and John *Jones of Gelli Lyfdy. All these were men motivated by a deep respect for the work of their bardic predecessors and were dedicated to the study and preservation of the traditional corpus of their country's learn-ing, in which they recognized the significant part played by genealogy.

The most authoritative works are those by P. C. Bartrum, *Early Welsh Genealogical Tracts* (1966), *Welsh Genealogies A.D. 300–1400* (1974) and *Welsh Genealogies A.D. 1400–1500* (1983); see also Francis Jones, 'An Approach to Welsh Genealogy' in the *Transactions* of the Honourable Society of Cymmrodorion (1948).

Genedl Gymreig, Y (lit. 'The Welsh nation'; 1877–1937), a Radical weekly newspaper established by Hugh Pugh, Evan Jones, John Davies (Gwyneddon) and W. Cadwaladr Davies in Caernarfon. After 1892 it became more political and several prominent journalists were among its editors, including John Owen Jones (Ap Ffarmwr), Beriah Gwynfe *Evans, John *Thomas (Eifionydd), E. Morgan *Humphreys and O. Llew *Owain. In 1937 the newspaper was merged with *Yr *Herald Cymraeg*.

General Strike, The (4–12 May, 1926), was called after the rejection by the Miners' Federation of Great Britain of an ultimatum by the coal-owners. As a result of the capitulation of the Trades Union Council to Stanley Baldwin's Government, the miners were left to struggle on alone in defence of their already reduced living standards. The Strike was relatively peaceful even in south Wales, although the Government had ensured the nearby presence of armed forces and was, in all respects, better prepared than the strikers whose stance remained defensive. However, the lock-out which followed the Strike was marked over the seven months of its duration by continuous, if localized, clashes with the police (there were eighteen major affrays) and there was great antipathy towards the small minority who, during the summer, began to drift back to work. The miners survived for a few months by bankrupting themselves and their local authorities, by communal feeding in soup-kitchens and by the co-operative endeavours of their Union, but by December they had been starved back to work on worse terms than those which had prevailed before. Many were subjected to victimization, the Union's strength was impaired and no real protection was left against the onset of mass unemployment. This defeat left a legacy of bitterness in the coalfield of south Wales which has still not entirely disappeared. The poem, *The *Angry Summer*, by Idris *Davies, reflects the Strike in most of its aspects. See also DEPRESSION and HUNGER MARCHES.

For further details see P. Renshaw, *The General Strike* (1975), the book of the same title by G. A. Phillips (1976) and another edited by J. Skelley (1976).

Generous Men of the Isle of Britain, Three, a Triad naming Nudd Hael ap Senyllt, Mordaf Hael ap Serwan and *Rhydderch Hael ap Tudwal Tutglyd, all heroes of the *Old North, was the most popular of all the Triads among Welsh poets from the twelfth to the sixteenth centuries.

Many patrons were compared with one or other of the three heroes and the Triad itself was often cited, as in *Dafydd ap Gwilym's bestowal of the epithet *Hael* ('generous') upon his patron *Ifor ap Llywelyn.

Geninen, Y (lit. 'The leek'), a quarterly magazine established in 1883 and edited by John *Thomas (Eifionydd) between that date and 1928. It was primarily intended as a platform for poets associated with the eisteddfodau but, independent and catholic, it also attracted contributions from many prominent writers of other affiliations. Revived by Gomer Press in 1951, the spelling of its title modernized as *Y Genhinen*, it was edited by R. J. *Rowlands (Meuryn) and S. B. *Jones until 1963. Thereafter, under the editorship of W. Rhys *Nicholas and Emlyn Evans, the magazine continued, until its closure in 1980, to reflect the traditional, rural, literary culture of Wales and, at the same time, became one of the liveliest Welsh periodicals of its day.

GEOFFREY OF MONMOUTH (c.1090–1155), Latin writer and pseudo-historian. On account of his name in its Latin form, *Galfridus Monemutensis*, and the knowledge of the district which is shown in his work, it is believed that he was born in the vicinity of Monmouth town. Nothing is known of his family connections more than the possibility that it is his father's name which is preserved in another form of his name, *Galfridus Arturus*, and that there is a suggestion of sympathy with Brittany in his work. Between 1129 and 1151 his name occurs in six charters, all concerned with religious houses in the neighbourhood of Oxford. In two he signed his name as *Magister*, and it is possible that he was a canon in the house of the *Augustinian Canons in St. George's, Oxford. The house came to an end in 1149 and the next reference to Geoffrey's career is a record testifying that he was ordained priest in St. Stephen's in February 1152 and consecrated Bishop of *St. Asaph within a week. There is no evidence that he ever visited his see. He was a witness to the Agreement of St. Stephen between King Stephen and Henry in 1153, and according to *Brut y Tywysogyon he died in 1155. He spent the greater part of his life in Oxford, it appears, although it is obvious that his earlier connections with south-east Wales are significant in his writing.

In his most important work, *Historia Regum Britanniae*, which contains a chapter on the prophecies of *Myrddin, *Prophetiae Merlini, there are suggestions that he had used part of the same material as appears in *The Book of Llandâv*. The latest opinion is that the latter was drafted between 1120 and 1129 and certainly before 1140; if so, it is likely that it was before going to Oxford that Geoffrey was connected with the writers of *The Book of Llandâv* and knew what they were engaged upon. His last known work is a poem entitled *'Vita Merlini'*.

For further details about the life of Geoffrey of Monmouth see the article by Edmond Faral in *Romania* (1927), the article by J. E. Lloyd in the *English Historical Review* (1942) and the chapter in R. S. Loomis, *Arthurian Literature in the Middle Ages* (1959).

GEORGE, WILLIAM RICHARD PHILIP (1912–), poet and biographer. Born at Cricieth, Caerns., where he is a solicitor, he has published four volumes of verse, namely *Dwyfor a Cherddi Eraill* (1948), *Cerddi'r Neraig* (1968), *Grawn Medi* (1974) and *Tân* (1979); the last-named takes its title from the *pryddest* with which he won the *Crown at the National Eisteddfod in 1974. He has also edited a collection of the letters of Eluned *Morgan, *Gyfaill Hoff* (1972), and he has written plays for radio. A nephew of David *Lloyd George, W. R. P. George has published two books about his uncle, *The Making of Lloyd George* (1976) and *Lloyd George, Backbencher* (1983), both of which are studies of Lloyd George's family and social background and of his career down to 1905.

Geraint fab Erbin (b. c.580), the hero of the Arthurian romance *Geraint ac Enid*, was a historical figure associated with Devon. The series of *englynion* to him in *The *Black Book of Carmarthen* and *The *Red Book of Hergest*, which describes his meeting with *Arthur, is an anachronism, for Arthur preceded him by two or three generations, but it is an early example of the tendency for heroes of different periods to be featured in the Arthurian legend. According to the romance, Erbin (Geraint's father) was Arthur's uncle, and Geraint a cousin of his. Geraint first appears as one of the young men at Arthur's court and the romance tells how he defeats *Edern fab Nudd in revenge for that knight's insult to Arthur's wife, *Gwenhwyfar. He then marries Enid, the daughter of *Yniwl Iarll, whom he treats badly after his companions complain that he is ignoring them in favour of his wife. Having succeeded to his father's earldom, Geraint is reconciled with Enid who has remained faithful to him, despite his suspicions of her infidelity.

In the corresponding French poem by Chrétien de Troyes, *Erec et Enide*, the hero's name is a form derived from the Breton, Guerec; it is believed that he was the hero of a Breton legend and that the author of the Welsh version changed his name to Geraint. There are many references to Enid's beauty in the work of the *Gogynfeirdd and the *cywyddwyr but it is unlikely that her name was known before the writing of the romance and its French counterpart, where she is called Enide. It may be that Enid's name is a mis-spelling or misunderstanding of the territorial name Bro Wened in Brittany.

GERALD DE BARRI (Giraldus Cambrensis, Gerald of Wales, Gerald the Welshman; c.1146–1223), one of the greatest Latin writers produced in Wales, was born at Manorbier, Pembs., the son of William de Barri and Angharad, the daughter of Gerald de Windsor and his wife *Nest. The de Barri family had moved from Glamorgan, of which they had appropriated a part during the Conquest, and had settled in Pembrokeshire. Gerald de Windsor's position as keeper of *Pembroke castle had been strengthened when he married Nest, the daughter of Rhys ap Tewdwr, Prince of Deheubarth. The children of Gerald and Nest, sometimes known as the Geraldines, were powerful secular and ecclesiastical lords, and with Nest's other children, the sons she had by Henry I and Stephen, the keeper of *Cardigan castle, they claimed relationship with the family of *Rhys ap Gruffudd (The Lord Rhys). To this privileged position Gerald de Barri was born: son of the lord of Manorbier, nephew of the Bishop of *St. David's, he was proud of his mixed Welsh and Norman lineage.

He was educated at St. Peter's Church School in Gloucester and in Paris, where he remained until about 1175. The mastery of Latin styles which characterizes his writing, and the complete familiarity with the 'authorities' which is so obvious an element in his wide learning, were doubtless learned in Paris. On his return to Wales he was preferred by his uncle to a number of livings, and before long he had shown himself to be an energetic ecclesiastical reformer. Nominated Bishop of St. David's in 1176 on the death of his uncle, he returned to Paris after his name had been rejected by the King. He taught law in France for about three years before returning once more to Britain. While Bishop Peter de Leia was at loggerheads with his chapter, Gerald was the administrator of the bishopric, and for about ten years (1184–94) he was a royal clerk in Henry II's court. He travelled a good deal and his most important writings were the fruit of his journeys, particularly those on which he accompanied Prince John to Ireland in 1185 and Archbishop Baldwin through Wales in 1188. These works are *Expugnatio Hibernica* (*The Conquest of Ireland*), *Topographia Hibernica* (*The Topography of Ireland*), *Itinerarium Kambriae* (*The Story of the Journey through Wales*) and *Descriptio Kambriae* (*A Description of Wales*).

About 1194 he again left the service of the King to study in Lincoln, but the happiness of these years was broken in 1198 when he was nominated for the bishopric of St. David's for the second time, only to have his name rejected by the Archbishop of Canterbury and the King. By now Gerald was convinced of the justice of his cause and of the right of St. David's to its former status as an archiepiscopal church. For the next five years he pleaded the cause of his church and his own right to be consecrated

bishop (or archbishop) before the Pope; he visited Rome three times to present his case. The Pope showed interest in the historical testimony (much of it gathered by Bernard, a former Bishop of St. David's), but the verdict went against Gerald. He lost the support of the chapter of St. David's, although Welsh princes were in favour of him, and Geoffrey de Henlaw was consecrated Bishop of St. David's in 1203. To the end of his life Gerald maintained that it was his sympathy for the Welsh and a fear of the effect his appointment might have had on national politics in Wales which was the main reason for his lack of success. But this consideration was not the most important in the argument; there were in the campaign reformist elements which the Crown could not accept, just as Canterbury could not accept the challenge to its authority. Gerald's ecclesiastical zeal was no doubt as much of an obstacle as his Welshness. Whatever the reason may have been, after this disappointment he spent the rest of his life writing and editing new versions of his books.

Apart from a few *Lives of the Saints, Gerald's writings fall into four categories. He gave the history of his struggle for the privilege of St. David's in his autobiography, *De Rebus a se Gestis* (1208), and in *De Jure et Statu Menevensis Ecclesiae* (1218), both of which are remarkable for the liveliness of their narrative and their dramatic sense. A third book, *De Invectionibus* (1216), is more documentary. In *De Principis Instructione* (1218) there are more philosophic discussions on such subjects as the characteristics of the ideal Prince, together with a detailed history of the reign of the exemplary Henry II. In an attempt to express his disappointment and anger at the unfaithfulness of a nephew, Gerald wrote an essay on ingratitude and the principles of education, *Speculum Duorum* (1216). In *Gemma Ecclesiastica* (1197) and *Speculum Ecclesiae* (1220) the ecclesiastical reformer comes to the fore, criticizing the immorality and gluttony of monks and the ignorance of parish priests. Although these works are characterized by breadth of learning, a mastery of style and the ability to tell a lively story, Gerald's most distinguished writing is to be found in his books on Ireland and Wales. There is praise for his family, depicted as heroes of the Norman Conquest, in *Expugnatio Hibernica* (1188) which reveals his ability to arrange facts and shape a narrative full of memorable portraits. In *Topographia Hibernica* (1188) he gives a description of Ireland and its people which is a fascinating mixture of detailed, realistic observation and completely groundless beliefs. The two books on Wales, *Itinerarium Kambriae* and *Descriptio Kambriae*, are the most important of his compositions, and these, on account of their content and the enthusiasm of the writing, have the greatest appeal for modern readers. Here, as in the autobiographical works, the various facets of the author's engaging personality are most fully revealed: the amusing companion, the conceited conversationalist, the superstitious observer and the learned reformer. There is a Welsh version by Thomas Jones of the two books on Wales, entitled *Hanes y Daith trwy Gymru a'r Disgrifiad o Gymru* (1938) and a bilingual volume by the same author in the *St. David's Day* series (1947). English translations have been made by Sir Richard Colt Hoare (1806, reprinted in *Everyman's Library* in 1908 and reissued in 1976) and by Lewis Thorpe (1978). A survey of the literature on Gerald by Eileen A. Williams is to be found in the *Journal* of the National Library of Wales (1961). See also Michael Richter, *Giraldus Cambrensis and the Growth of the Welsh Nation* (1972), the essay on Gerald by Brynley F. Roberts in the *Writers of Wales* series (1982) and Robert Bartlett, *Gerald of Wales* (1982).

Giant Herdsman, The, see under SACRED ANIMALS, BIRDS AND TREES.

Giant of Gilfach Fargoed, The, a folk-tale which relates how the *Tylwyth Teg* of the Rhymney Valley in Monmouthshire were disturbed by a marauding giant. At last the owl of Pen-coed Fawr shot an arrow through the giant's heart while he was paying court to a witch under an apple-tree. The body was then burned, whereupon the earth around caught fire, and that is how coal was discovered in the valley. It is said that the owls still hoot in Pencoed Fawr on moonlit nights in celebration of the giant's death.

GIBBON, LEVI (1814–70), balladeer. A native of Carmarthenshire who was blinded at the age of twenty-five, he sang in Welsh in the fairs of south Wales which he frequented in the company of his two daughters. Most of his ballads, of which some thirty-five have been preserved, deal with social events such as the coming of the railway, but others describe religious and amatory experiences, sometimes crudely.

GILDAS (*c.*495–*c.*570), Brythonic monk and Latin author. According to the Life written about him by a Breton monk in the ninth century, he was born in Arecluta (now Clydeside in Scotland) and founded a monastery at Ruys in Vannes, Brittany. The Breton associations of Gildas have been doubted by some scholars, but place-names commemorate his family's movements in Wales, Cornwall and Brittany. With *Dewi Sant, Samson and Paul (according to Paul's *Vita*, written in 884), he was educated at *Illtud's school. Famous for the bitter prophetic utterance known as *De Excidio Britanniae*, he represents a tradition of Romano-British Christianity which regarded even the victory of the Britons at the battle of Badon as grievously marred by the usurpation of civil government by military leaders, some of whom, like *Maelgwn Gwynedd, had returned to the trappings of Brythonic kingship. The effect of his polemic was to increase greatly the momentum of the monastic movement, by which 'good men' could withdraw from the corrupt society depicted by Gildas. His colourful and inventive Latin—he calls it *'nostra lingua'*—seems to have pioneered a style which reached an extreme of eccentricity in the *Hisperic literature.

For further details see Hugh Williams (ed.), *Gildae De Excidio Britanniae* (2 vols., 1899, 1901) and the translation by A. W. Wade-Evans, *Coll Prydain* (1950); see also Leslie Alcock, *Arthur's Britain* (1971), *The Ruin of Britain* (ed. Michael Winterbottom, 1978), J. R. Morris, *The Age of Arthur* (1973) and Charles Thomas, *Christianity in Roman Britain* (1981).

Gilfaethwy fab Dôn, see under MATH FAB MATHONWY.

GILPIN, WILLIAM (1724–1804), see under OBSERVATIONS ON THE RIVER WYE (1782).

Giraldus Cambrensis, see GERALD DE BARRI (*c.*1146–1223).

Glamorgan, see MORGANNWG.

Glamorgan Classification, The, see under PEDWAR ANSAWDD AR HUGAIN.

Glan Sarno, see under CORN IS GREEN (1938).

Glanffrwd, see THOMAS, WILLIAM (1843–90).

Glasynys, see JONES, OWEN WYNNE (1828–70).

Glewlwyd Gafaelfawr, the chief door-keeper at the court of *Arthur. In the tale of *Culhwch and Olwen it is said that he serves in this capacity only on New Year's Day, but according to the romance of Owain (see under TAIR RHAMANT) his duties are to receive guests throughout the year and to explain to them the customs of the court. He refuses to allow Culhwch to enter the hall because the feast has begun, but opens the door at last on Arthur's command. In the poem *'Pa ŵr yw'r Porthor?'* in The *Black Book of Carmarthen*, Glewlwyd appears not as Arthur's door-keeper but as keeper of a court to which the king and his retinue seek admission. It has been suggested that there are traces here of an earlier version of a tale about *Cai seeking to enter the court of *Wrnach the Giant. In the *araith* of *Iolo Goch, Glewlwyd is described as *'y gŵr a ddyrchafodd y pair i lawr oddi ar y tân yn ei unllaw . . . a chig llen saith ychen ynddo'* ('the man who raised the cauldron from the fire in one of his hands . . . with the dead flesh of seven oxen in it').

Gloch, Y, see under RHEDEGYDD.

Glyn family, see under GLYNLLIFON.

Glyn Rhosyn, see under DEWI SANT (6th cent.).

Glyndyfrdwy, a lordship within the commot

of *Edeirnion, was granted in 1283 to Gruffudd Fychan of the house of Powys Fadog. It was in Glyndyfrdwy that his great-grandson *Owain Glyndŵr raised the standard of revolt on 16 September 1400.

Glynllifon, a house near Llandwrog, Caerns., was formerly the home of the Glyn family. The Glyns were typical of the new gentry in that they took advantage of the political and social changes which followed the accession of Henry *Tudor in 1485. Wiliam, the eldest son of Iemwnt Llwyd ap Robert, succeeded in weathering the storms of the years from 1540 to 1590 without losing his authority in Arfon. The family differed from most of their contemporaries in combining an acceptance of the new order with support for the bardic tradition. Wiliam, who was a poet, wrote a moving elegy for his first wife, Catrin Mostyn. He served as an adjudicator in the bardic contention between Edmund *Prys and Wiliam *Cynwal and he was also a commissioner in the Eisteddfod held at *Caerwys in 1567. After his death in 1594, Glynllifon was inherited by Tomas Glyn, who was Sheriff of Anglesey in 1584 and 1601. He too was an amateur poet and his elegy was written by his friend, Tomos *Prys of Plas Iolyn. Tomas was succeeded by Wiliam, who served in Ireland and was knighted in Dublin in 1606. His eldest son, Tomas, owned the estate during the Civil War, shifting his allegiance from the Crown to Parliament in 1646. Patronage at Glynllifon was discontinued after the death of Wiliam Glyn in 1648 and the Glyn family became extinct when Siôn, the son of Tomas Glyn, died without an heir in 1666. The house afterwards came into the possession of the Wynns of Bodfean.

For an account of the estate's development see the article by Glyn Roberts in the *Transactions* of the Caernarvonshire Historical Society (1948).

Glynne-Jones, William, see JONES, WILLIAM GLYN (1907–77).

Glynrhondda, a commot of the cantref of Penychen in Glamorgan, was held after the Norman invasion by the line of Cadwallon ap Caradog, the grandson of *Iestyn ap Gwrgant, the last King of *Morgannwg. With the 'second conquest' of Morgannwg in the mid-thirteenth century, it came directly under the rule of the Clare family. The boundaries of the commot were those of the parish of Ystradyfodwg and broadly those of the municipal borough of *Rhondda. The old view of Glynrhondda as 'the tail' of Glamorgan may account for the nickname *Gwŷr y Gloran* as applied to the indigenous population of the Rhondda Valleys before the discovery of coal.

Glywysing, a lordship lying between the rivers Tawe and Usk, is said to have been named after King Glywys. The name is sometimes used as though it were a synonym of *Morgannwg, but that early kingdom also included *Gwent.

Gnome, a concise statement about something which is obviously true. The early Welsh gnomic poems, usually in *englyn form, comprise lyrical descriptions of nature as well as truisms about human behaviour and natural phenomena, of which the purpose, it could be argued, is to emphasize the dependability of daily observations which are necessary presuppositions for every thought or action. What makes a truism appear strange is that it is too obvious, as in the statement '*Bid goch crib ceiliog*' ('The essence of a cock's comb is redness') where the word '*bid*' encompasses frequency of occurrence as well as established condition. Examples of gnomic utterances are found in *'*Englynion Eiry Mynydd*', *'*Englynion y Bidiau*', *'*Englynion y Clyweit*' and *'*Englynion y Misoedd*'. The *Gnodiau* are another well-known series, the word '*gnawd*' meaning 'usual' or 'customary', as in the statement '*Gnawd gŵr gwan godenau*' ('A weak man is usually rather lean'). Several of the series are formed within a framework of the repetition of part of the first line as a link in a chain and usually they tend to employ the construction of the noun sentence.

For further details see Kenneth Jackson, *Early Celtic Nature Poetry* (1935), *Early Welsh Gnomic Poems* (1953) and 'Incremental Repetition in the Early Welsh Englyn' in *Speculum* (vol. 16, 1941).

Goat, an animal still to be seen in its wild state in the mountains of *Eryri (Snowdonia), is considered by some to be a Welsh symbol. Thomas *Pennant used a goat-herd carrying a *pibgorn as the frontispiece to his *Tours of Wales* (1778, 1781) and Lady Llanover (Augusta *Hall) had a wild goat as one of her heraldic supporters. The beast has often been featured in cartoons about Wales and the Welsh, sometimes with satyrical overtones, especially in the hey-day of David *Lloyd George. Some Welsh regiments, such as the Royal Welch Fusiliers, have adopted white goats as mascots. See also DAFFODIL, LEEK and RED DRAGON.

'God Bless the Prince of Wales' (1862), a song of which Brinley Richards (1819–85) composed the tune and J. Ceiriog *Hughes the words beginning '*Ar D'wysog Gwlad y Bryniau*'; the English words beginning 'Among our ancient mountains' were written by G. Linley. It was sung in public for the first time in February 1863 by Sims Reeves, the Swansea tenor, and later in the same year it was heard on the wedding-day of the Prince of Wales. The tune is still widely known and the words have often been parodied.

'Gododdin, Y', a long poem attributed to the poet *Aneirin, commemorates the heroic deeds of a war-band chosen from the Gododdin tribe and its allies who fell in a disastrous assault upon the strategic site of Catraeth (Catterick, Yorks.)

about the year 600. Their tribal territory, part of which was known as Manaw Gododdin, extended along the shores of the Firth of Forth and had as its capital an unidentified Din Eidyn, which may have been the Rock of Edinburgh. The importance of Catraeth was that it lay on the western boundary between the Anglian kingdoms of Bernicia and Deira, not yet joined, and that the Gododdin's attack at this point might have hindered their alliance.

The war-band travelled southwards for about one hundred and fifty miles to reach Catraeth and was defeated in battle by the overwhelmingly superior numbers of the enemy. Variant statements in the poem claim that either one or three men escaped from the engagement, in addition to the poet who survived to commemorate it. The leader of the Britons was Mynyddawg Mwynfawr. He had a *comitatus* or *gosgordd* of three hundred picked warriors, some of whom had joined him from other British kingdoms; they included a contingent from *Gwynedd, a warrior from the little kingdom of Elmet around Leeds (destined to fall to the invaders soon afterwards), and one from as far away as Devon. These were the horse-borne leaders of the British force; the number of foot-soldiers who may have accompanied them is not given. The war-band had been feasted lavishly by Mynyddawg for a year before setting out, a statement which seems to indicate that the expedition had been carefully planned a long time in advance. These bare facts are virtually all that can be elicited from the internal evidence of the poem. No external sources allude to the expedition and there are objections to identifying it with any of the known battles of the sixth and seventh centuries. The capture of Edinburgh by the Angles in 638 provides a *terminus ad quem*, but Ifor *Williams argued on the basis of converging lines of circumstantial evidence that the battle took place some years earlier than this, and the decade from 590 to 600 is usually regarded as the most likely period for it.

The poem, which consists of 1,480 lines, is heroic in that it is concerned with the interests and values of a warrior aristocracy, the main preoccupation of which lay in fighting. Ferocity on the field of battle is praised, as is generosity (especially to poets) in the court when at peace. Fame is coveted above all else and cowardice no less abhorred. Death in battle is acceptable if it is the means of winning deathless fame. Loyalty to his lord is the warrior's supreme virtue: the poem insists that Mynyddawg's war-band 'paid for its mead', willingly giving their lives for the leader who had maintained them. Some eighty warriors are individually praised and lamented by name and it is implied that all were known personally to the poet. Occasionally a stanza is devoted to lamenting the war-band as a whole. The language, metrical forms and general technique of the poem indicate that there lies behind it a long tradition of praise-poetry in the Brythonic language, that is to say in the form of primitive Welsh which was current in Cumbria and southern Scotland.

The 'Gododdin' is preserved in a single manuscript, The Book of Aneirin (Cardiff MS I), which has been dated about 1265. But this text is incomplete and breaks off abruptly, several pages having been cut away at the end. As it stands, it comprises two independent versions of the poem, the so-called A and B texts, written in distinct but contemporary hands. Hand B is the more archaic of the two, preserving orthographical features which point to an exemplar in Old Welsh written between the late eighth and the late eleventh centuries. Hand A, likewise a copy but of a less ancient exemplar, subjoins four *gorchanau* or 'lays' to the poem which consist, in the main, of extended elegies for individual warriors. The differences between the A and B texts are too great to be entirely accounted for by previous miscopying of written sources. It is agreed that before the poem was ever committed to writing there must have been a long period during which it was transmitted orally and that during this time extensive changes took place, interpolations creeping in and the order of the stanzas becoming misplaced and confused. Preservation solely by oral means during the earliest stages of transmission would be consistent with Ifor Williams's arguments for the extreme antiquity of the poem, yet in the last resort such arguments must of necessity be of a historical rather than a linguistic nature since there are no certain means of tracing back the text any earlier than to the date at which it was first committed to writing, and this can hardly have been much before the ninth century. For nearly two hundred years scholars have debated whether the poem can be in its essentials what it purports to be—the composition of the poet Aneirin. Certain interpolations of extraneous matter into the text are clearly identifiable, but there is reason to suspect the existence of a number of less obvious interpolations, so that it is impossible to claim with certainty of any given line that it belongs to the original nucleus of the poem. It may, however, be fairly said that the balance of opinion favours the belief that the original nucleus of the 'Gododdin' was composed shortly after the event to which it refers, a battle fought at Catterick about the year 600.

The 'Gododdin' was edited with an introductory discussion by Ifor Williams in Canu Aneirin (1938). An English translation by Kenneth H. Jackson, entitled The Gododdin: the Oldest Scottish Poem (1969), summarizes Williams's findings and adds further arguments in favour of the poem's authenticity. See also the chapter by Ifor Williams in The Beginnings of Welsh Poetry (ed. R. Bromwich, 1972) and the collection of specialist studies in Astudiaethau ar yr Hengerdd: Studies in Old Welsh Poetry (ed. R. Bromwich and R. Brinley Jones, 1978).

Goeden Bechod, Y (lit. 'The tree of sin'), a thorn bush in the vicinity of Nefyn, Caerns., near which many local people claimed to have had a supernatural experience, such as seeing a phantom horse and carriage, usually as a premonition of death.

Goeden Eirin, Y (lit. 'The plum tree'; 1946), a volume of six short stories by John Gwilym *Jones. Although the tree of the title is real—it grows in the parish of Llandwrog, Caerns.—the stories are not set in any particular district. The book is a milestone in the development of the Welsh *short story in that it uses the technique known as 'stream of consciousness'. In the first story, for example, the thoughts of seven characters at a marriage service are revealed. The author, aware that he was breaking new ground in Welsh and that the stories would perplex some readers, wrote the last story in the collection, 'Cerrig y Rhyd', as an apologia for his method. One character says that she is 'fed up with these stories without a plot' and another proceeds to tell such a story, but one which explains and justifies the technique employed.

For a critical discussion of the book see the article by Derec Llwyd Morgan in *John Gwilym Jones: Cyfrol Deyrnged* (ed. Gwyn Thomas, 1974).

Goewin ferch Pebin, see under MATH FAB MATHONWY.

Gofannon fab Dôn, see under DYLAN AIL TON.

Gogerddan, a mansion in the parish of Trefeurig, Cards., was important in the history of bardic patronage in the county. The first patron, Dafydd Llwyd ap Dafydd ap Rhydderch, was the grandson of *Rhydderch ab Ieuan Llwyd of Glyn Aeron and *Dafydd ap Gwilym was among the poets who received his patronage. The tradition was continued over six more generations and by other branches of the Gogerddan family, of whom Sir Richard Pryse (d. 1651) was the last patron. Despite this continuity, much of the extant poetry associated with the house is mundane and stereotyped. The Pryse family, however, were more remarkable than the poetry written to them: in the seventeenth century they caused turmoil among the silver-lead miners of Cwmsymlog and in the eighteenth they were prominent in the cause of *Jacobitism. Gogerddan is now the site of the Welsh Plant Breeding Station.

The fortunes of the house during the period 1800–1960 are discussed in an article by Richard J. Colyer in *The Welsh History Review* (vol. 9, no. 4, 1979).

Gogynfeirdd, Y (lit. 'The fairly early poets'), a term used more or less synonymously with *Beirdd y Tywysogion* ('The Poets of the Princes') to denote those poets who flourished between the first half of the twelfth century and the second half of the fourteenth century, but excluding those who used the *cywydd* metre.

The earliest was *Meilyr who composed an elegy for *Gruffudd ap Cynan in 1137 and the greatest were *Cynddelw Brydydd Mawr, *Llywarch ap Llywelyn, *Dafydd Benfras and *Bleddyn Fardd. Poetry composed in the style established by these poets continued to be written for long after the death of *Llywelyn ap Gruffudd, however, and for this reason the term *Gogynfeirdd* tends to refer to a mode of composing poetry, while *Beirdd y Tywysogion* is restricted to the function of those who served the Princes up to 1282.

These *Gogynfeirdd* were professional poets who expressed their learning in ancient diction and intricate forms. The poets celebrated their patrons' military feats, often recording the gruesome details of the carnage. Their vocabulary made abundant use of hyperbole, compound nouns, archaic forms and compressed syntax which rendered their work difficult to understand even by their contemporaries. The metres were the various *awdl measures, with occasionally a series of *englynion. The metrical adornment of the line gradually developed from the simple consonance of the earlier poets to the regular *cynghanedd of the later ones. A similar mode of expression is found in the *awdlau* of the early *cywydd* poets such as *Dafydd ap Gwilym and *Iolo Goch.

For general discussion of the *Gogynfeirdd* see the chapter by Ceri Lewis in *A Guide to Welsh Literature* (vol. 1, ed. A. O. H. Jarman and G. R. Hughes, 1976), D. Myrddin Lloyd's *Rhai Agweddau ar Ddysg y Gogynfeirdd* (1976), the chapter by Gwyn Thomas in his *Y Traddodiad Barddol* (1976), and the essay by J. E. Caerwyn Williams in the *Writers of Wales* series, *The Poets of the Welsh Princes* (1978); see also the article by D. Myrddin Lloyd, 'Some Metrical Features in *Gogynfeirdd* Poetry' in *Studia Celtica* (vol. III, 1968) and that by J. E. Caerwyn Williams in *Llên Cymru* (vol. XIII, nos. 1–2, 1974–79).

Gohebiaethau Syr Meurig Grynswth (lit. 'The correspondence of Sir Meurig Grynswth'), a satirical work by John Ceiriog *Hughes which first appeared in the periodicals *Yr Arweinydd* (1856–58) and *Y Punch Cymraeg* (1858), and later in the author's volume *Oriau'r Hwyr* (1860). Untypical of the Victorian Age in its sense of humour, the work represents a brave attempt to legitimize laughter and fiction before Daniel *Owen's time. The most memorable of Sir Meurig's adventures is his trip to the moon in the company of Bywbothfardd, Arthur, Rhys Grythor and Siorti the cat. There, far away from Wales, he is bold enough to satirize some of the most sacred cows of his country's culture, especially the *Eisteddfod. One of the funniest of his jests involves a machine for the making of *cynghanedd.

Gohebydd, Y, see GRIFFITH, JOHN (1821–77).

Golden Shoemakers of the Isle of Britain, Three, are named in a Triad as *Caswallon ap

Beli 'when he went to Rome to seek Fflur', *Manawydan ap Llŷr 'when the enchantment was on Dyfed', and *Lleu Llawgyffes 'when he and Gwydion were seeking a name and arms from his mother Arianrhod'. The Triad is cited twice in *Pedair Cainc y Mabinogi in reference to the relevant incidents in the tales of Manawydan and Math. In quoting it, the redactor implied that the Triad was one with which his audience was familiar. He interpreted 'eur-' in 'eurgrydd' in its literal sense of 'golden', for the shoes made by Manawydan and those made for Lleu Llawgyffes are said to have been gilded. But this is unlikely to have been the original significance of the Triad, since 'eur-' is often employed in poetic compounds in its figurative sense of 'excellent' or 'noble'. The meaning is more likely to have been that these three were all nobly-born shoemakers, men who were obliged for some years to adopt the humble craft of shoemaking, perhaps as a disguise. This interpretation gains support from Cigfa's remark to Manawydan later in the tale to the effect that shoemaking was not 'glanweith' ('cleanly').

Goleuad, Y (lit. 'The torch'), the newspaper of the Calvinistic Methodists, was founded in 1869 as a private venture. Its first editor was John Davies (Gwyneddon), who was followed by John *Roberts (Ieuan Gwyllt) and others. It reflected the interests of its denomination from the outset and was bought by the Union of Calvinistic Methodists in 1911. Since then its editors have included E. Morgan *Humphreys, T. E. Jones, T. Lloyd Jones, G. Wynne Griffith, Harri Parri and Elfed ap Nefydd Roberts. Besides publishing news of the Union's activities, the newspaper strove to promote *Temperance and Radical opinion among Calvinistic Methodists. It no longer carries foreign and national news, concentrating more on local and denominational matters, but it is still a periodical of substance and repute.

'*Golwg ar Deyrnas Crist*' (lit. 'A view of the kingdom of Christ'; 1756), a long poem of some 5,500 lines by William *Williams (Pantycelyn), was revised and republished in 1764 under the title (in trans.) 'A view of the Kingdom of Christ, or Christ all, and in all'. The poem, which has eight sections or chapters, drew heavily for its description of the Creation on such popular scientific works as William Derham's *Physico-theology* (1713) and *Astro-theology* (1715). It is flawed by the author's choice of an unsuitable metre of thirteen syllables per line and by a lack of self-discipline, but it is important as an attempt to write a religious *epic in Welsh comparable with those produced in other languages under the influence of the European Renaissance.

For discussion of the poem's merits see the articles by D. Gwenallt Jones in *Gwŷr Llên y Ddeunawfed Ganrif*

(ed. Dyfnallt Morgan, 1966), Saunders Lewis in *Meistri'r Canrifoedd* (ed. R. Geraint Gruffydd, 1973) and Roger Stephens Jones in *Ysgrifau Beirniadol XI* (ed. J. E. Caerwyn Williams, 1979).

Golyddan (John Robert Pryse; 1840–62), see under PRYSE, ROBERT JOHN (1807–89).

Golyddan Fardd, see under CADWALADR (d. 664).

Gomer, see HARRIS, JOSEPH (1773–1825).

Gomer Press, see under LEWIS, JOHN DAVID (1859–1914).

GOODMAN, GABRIEL (1528–1601), Dean of Westminster and biblical translator. A Churchman who proved adroit in surviving the religious changes of the sixteenth century, he was an associate of the Cecils and served as a link between Wales and the court of Elizabeth I. He was an ardent advocate of the claims of Ruthin, Denbs., his native town, where in 1590 he established Christ's Hospital, a charitable institution for the poor, adding a grammar school to his foundation in 1595. One of the translators into Welsh of the Bishop's Bible of 1568, he also assisted in the publication of William *Morgan's translation of the *Bible.

GOODWIN, GERAINT (1903–41), short-story writer and novelist, was born at Newtown, Mont. His father, a prominent figure in the town, died when he was eight years old and his mother subsequently married a local provisions merchant. After leaving Towyn County School, where he had been a boarder, Goodwin began an apprenticeship with the *Montgomeryshire Express* but later moved to Fleet Street where he soon made his mark as a reporter. His first book, *Conversations with George Moore* (1929), though little more than a modest extension of his journalism, was generally well received. The same year, after a medical examination had revealed that he was suffering from a tubercular condition, he received treatment in a sanatorium and took a long convalescence abroad. He drew upon these and other experiences in the writing of his second book, *Call Back Yesterday* (1934). A contract for two further books from his publisher persuaded him to abandon journalism in order to concentrate on a literary career. He moved, with his wife and daughter, from London to Dagnall, Herts., and there, with the encouragement of his chosen mentor, Edward Garnett, he embarked upon a creative exploitation of the landscape and people he knew best.

The first product of this new approach, a novel entitled *The *Heyday in the Blood* (1936), was an immediate critical success and has remained his best-known work. It was followed by a volume of short stories, *The White Farm*

(1937), and *Watch for the Morning* (1938), his most ambitious novel. These books not only share the same distinctive setting of Goodwin's much loved Welsh Border country, but explore similar themes and recreate similar characters. They focus frequently on contrasts between the squalid mill-town (Newtown-Moreton) and a rural landscape of water-meadows and hills, between strong-willed, passionate women and weak, physically frail men, between a deep-rooted, precious Welsh heritage and a super-ficial, Anglicized culture of little worth. Having thus drawn closer to his Welsh roots in his writing, Goodwin finally decided to make a permanent return to Wales. In 1938 the family moved to a cottage in Corris Uchaf, Mer., where in the following year a second child was born and where his last novel, *Come Michaelmas* (1939), was written. His health deteriorated, however, and he spent almost a year in the sanatorium at Talgarth. He was still far from well when he discharged himself to rejoin his family at their new home in the market town of Montgomery, and it was there he died.

The collected stories of Geraint Goodwin were edited by Sam Adams and Roland Mathias (1976) and Sam Adams has contributed an essay on the writer to the *Writers of Wales* series (1975); see also the correspondence between Geraint Goodwin and Edward Garnett published in *The Anglo-Welsh Review* (vol. 22, nos. 49 and 50, 1973) which reveals how the English writer pressed Goodwin to return to Wales and write about it, and the note by Glyn Jones in *Profiles* (1980).

Gorau, the son of Custennin ap Mynwyedig and herdsman to Ysbaddaden Bencawr in the tale of *Culhwch and Olwen. Because the giant had killed his twenty-three brothers, his mother hid him in a chest in order to save him from the same fate. He takes part in the task of capturing the sword of *Wrnach and is given his name ('the best') in recognition of his valour. It is he who, at the end of the tale, beheads Ysbaddaden. These adventures may be the vestiges of a *mabinogi* which relates how Gorau avenged the death of his brothers. He is also named in *Breuddwyd Rhonabwy*, in the romance of *Geraint and Enid, and in a Triad where he is reputed to have rescued *Arthur, his cousin, from three prisons. Gorau's name may be a corruption of Corneu which is connected with the name Custennin in some versions of the royal lineage of Devon.

Gorchan (lit. 'A song or lay'), a type of poem considerably longer than the compact *awdlau* of 'Y *Gododdin*', to which four examples are appended in the A text of *The Book of Aneirin*. The first, '*Gorchan Tudfwlch*', commemorates Tudfwlch fab Cilydd who is mentioned several times in '*Y Gododdin*' as one of the men of *Gwynedd in Mynyddawg Mwynfawr's war-band at the battle of Catraeth. The second, '*Gorchan Cynfelyn*', is a panegyric also concerned with a Gwynedd warrior, Cynfelyn fab Tegfan.

More baffling is the third, '*Gorchan Maeldderw*', a lament for a warrior lord of that name. The fourth, '*Gorchan Adebon*', which is unlike the other three in having no connections with the defeat at Catraeth, consists of proverbs and gnomes. The inclusion of the fourth poem in the manuscript may imply a tacit attribution to *Aneirin, whose name was sometimes attached to sententious verse from the sixteenth century onwards, but it may have been included by accident.

These obscure poems are discussed and partially translated by Kenneth H. Jackson in *The Gododdin: the Oldest Scottish Poem* (1969); the text may be consulted in *Canu Aneirin* (ed. Ifor Williams, 1970).

Gorchest y Beirdd, see under TWENTY-FOUR METRES.

Gorchestion Beirdd Cymru (lit. 'The triumphs of the poets of Wales'; 1773), an anthology compiled by Rice *Jones of Y Blaenau, Mer., is one of the most important collections ever made of Welsh poetry. The fruit of Jones's deep and intelligent interest in classical poetry, the volume was printed in Shrewsbury by Stafford Prys. The compiler may be forgiven for attributing *'Englynion y Misoedd' to *Aneirin and for the numerous printer's errors: he did not have an opportunity of seeing every manuscript and of collating variant readings to form the best text. Nevertheless, this was a standard anthology for more than a century and it was for long unsurpassed in its presentation of the work of the *cywyddwyr* from *Dafydd ap Gwilym to *Wiliam Llŷn. The book has a preface which is full of optimism about the future of the Welsh language for which, Jones averred, 'Helicon is inexhaustible'. Among the subscribers were Samuel Johnson, Iolo Morganwg (Edward *Williams) and Hester Lynch *Piozzi. A second edition was edited by Robert *Ellis (Cynddelw) in 1864. R. Williams *Parry wrote an amusing poem about how he cherished, more than the masterpieces of the famous, the barely literate signatures of humbler folk who had once owned his copy of the book.

'Gorddodau, Y' (lit. 'Canons of prophecy'), a series of vaticinatory verses, each of which opens with the phrase '*Orddod fron gorfod'. Preserved mainly in Peniarth Manuscript 50, they are attributed to *Taliesin, but a different text is to be found in *The Myvyrian Archaiology of Wales* (1801) which names *Myrddin as their author. The prophecy refers to a noble hero who will arise from his hiding-place to destroy the English.

Gorhoffedd, a boasting-poem which expresses the poet's delight in nature, or his love of a woman, or his martial prowess in the service of his lord, or all of these. Among the finest examples are those of the court poets *Gwalchmai ap Meilyr and *Hywel ab Owain Gwynedd.

Goronva Camlann, see WILLIAMS, ROWLAND (1817–70).

Goronwy Ddu o Fôn, see OWEN, GORONWY (1723–69).

Gorsedd Beirdd Ynys Prydain (lit. 'The throne or assembly of bards of the Isle of Britain'), a society of poets, musicians and other representatives of Welsh culture, was founded by Iolo Morganwg (Edward *Williams) in 1792. Its first meeting was held on Primrose Hill in London under the direction of Iolo Morganwg, assisted by Edward *Jones (Bardd y Brenin), William *Owen Pughe and David *Samwell. London was chosen as the venue because it was, for Iolo, the heart of the old Brythonic world and because he thought it was there he could best demonstrate to the English the antiquity of the druidic civilization from which he claimed Welsh literature had descended in an unbroken tradition.

The first assembly to be held in Wales (discounting Iolo's insistence that there had been one at Beaupré, Glam., in 1681), took place at Bryn Owen (Stalling Down), Glam., in 1795. Thereafter the society was fostered by Iolo as a kind of bardic system intended to uphold the Welsh literary tradition. He encouraged the establishment of a *gorsedd* (his word was '*cadair*', 'chair') in each province of Wales. It was not until 1819, at the Dyfed Provincial Eisteddfod held in the garden of the Ivy Bush tavern at Carmarthen, that Iolo's creation became associated with the *Eisteddfod but, even then, the connection was tenuous. The winning poet on that occasion, Gwallter Mechain (Walter *Davies), was among those initiated by Iolo, who presented the ovates with arm-bands of green, blue and white.

The ceremonies devised by Iolo for his *Gorsedd* became an integral part of the Eisteddfod's pageantry in 1858. At Llangollen in that year the president, Ab Ithel (John *Williams), organized the Eisteddfod on a stage and introduced into the pageantry such features as the *Gorsedd* Prayer which Iolo had described in his manuscripts and which have survived to this day. At the end of the nineteenth century and in the first decades of the twentieth, there was much criticism of the *Gorsedd*, especially by John *Morris-Jones and G. J. *Williams, mainly because of claims concerning its antiquity. By today, however, it is generally acknowledged that the assembly was Iolo's creation and there is no longer any argument on that score.

There have been twenty-one Archdruids, the first of whom was Clwydfardd (David Griffiths; 1800–94) who served from 1876 to 1894. The office was twice held by Cynan (Albert *Evans-Jones) in 1950–54 and in 1963–66, and it was he who, as Recorder, did much to improve the dignity of the ceremonies, introducing such features as the Flower Dance. The Great Sword

and the Horn of Plenty date from the end of the nineteenth century. Among recent Archdruids have been Bryn (R. Bryn *Williams; 1975–78), Geraint (Geraint *Bowen; 1978–81) and Jâms Niclas (James *Nicholas; 1981–84), the last two of whom used their office to speak out boldly on topics of the day.

Membership of the *Gorsedd* has increased from 460 in 1927 to about thirteen hundred at the present time. This number includes those who belong to the Order of Ovate (for which entry is by examination or special acknowledgement), the Order of Poet, Musician and Author (entry to which is by examination only), and the Order of Druid. To the third category are admitted men and women from a wide spectrum of public life who have rendered outstanding service to the Welsh language and its culture. Members of these Orders wear green, blue and white gowns respectively, the colours of the arm-bands used by Iolo Morganwg in 1819.

The activities of *Gorsedd Beirdd Ynys Prydain*, often parodied but bringing a colourful dignity to a people generally deprived of indigenous pageantry, are usually confined to ceremonies pertaining to the *National Eisteddfod, particularly those of the Proclamation, the *Chair and the *Crown, but it held an extraordinary session at Cilmeri in 1982 in commemoration of the seventh centenary of the death of *Llywelyn ap Gruffudd, the last independent Prince of Wales. It also fosters international contacts with the other Celtic countries, especially with Cornwall and Brittany and with the *Mod* and *Oireachtas*, the national festivals of Scotland and Ireland respectively. See also DRUIDS.

For further details see the collection of essays by G. J. Williams, *Agweddau ar Hanes Dysg Gymraeg* (ed. Aneirin Lewis, 1967) and the articles by Geraint Bowen in the magazine *Eisteddfota* (nos. 1, 3, 4, 1983). A list of articles pertaining to the *Gorsedd* will be found in Thomas Parry and Merfyn Morgan (ed.), *Llyfryddiaeth Llenyddiaeth Gymraeg* (1976).

Gough, Mathew or **Mathau Goch** (1386–1450), soldier, was the son of Owain Goch, the bailiff of the manor of Hanmer in the valley of the Dee. He probably went to France in the service of John Talbot, later the Earl of Shrewsbury, who had been brought up by his mother. In the battles of Cravant (1423) and Verneuil (1424) he played a prominent part but he had to yield Beaugency to the forces of Joan of Arc in 1429. He was later made captain of the city-fortresses of Laval, St. Denis, Le Mans, Bellême and Bayeux. In 1432, when he was captured by the French, *Guto'r Glyn was among those who composed poems in his honour. During the truce which followed the Treaty of Tours (1445), Gough led a battalion to fight in Lorraine and Germany under the King of France. By this time Mathago, as the French called him, had become a household name in Normandy. He served Henry VI as ambassador to Gilles de Bretagne and the task of handing over Anjou and Maine to the French in 1448 was entrusted to him and Ffowc Eutun. With his cavalry, he succeeded in escaping from the disastrous battle of Formigny in 1450, at which the English were heavily defeated, but within the month he was forced to surrender Bayeux, the last of his French strongholds. On his return to England he served as captain of the Tower of London. He was killed on London Bridge while defending the city from attack by the rioters of Jack Cade. His death, according to William of Worcester, was the cause of widespread grief in Wales.

Further details will be found in H. T. Evans, *Wales and the Wars of the Roses* (1915).

Gould, Arthur Joseph (1864–1919), a rugby-player who played for Wales as a centre three-quarter on twenty-seven occasions between 1885 and 1897, was famous for his tremendous speed.

Gower, a commot of the cantref of Eginog in *Ystrad Tywi and, with *Kilvey, one of the principal Marcher lordships of medieval Wales, extended from the upper Aman Valley to Worms Head. After the murder in 1106 of its ruler, Hywel ap Gronw, who was of the line of Elystan Glodrydd, it was granted by Henry I to the Earl of Warwick. The Earl built a castle at Swansea to serve as the *caput* of the lordship and encouraged English settlement in the peninsular half of the commot, with the result that Gower became one of the first Englishries in south Wales. Gower was restored to Welsh rule by *Rhys ap Gruffudd (The Lord Rhys) but in 1203 it became the property of the Braose family, from whom it passed in 1331 to the Mowbrays, later the Dukes of Norfolk. In 1464, John, Duke of Norfolk, was induced to convey Gower to William Herbert of Raglan. Herbert's grand-daughter, Margaret, married Charles Somerset and their descendants, the Dukes of Beaufort, still retain certain rights of lordship in Gower. Although the commot, as part of the diocese of *St. David's, had been within the sphere of influence of *Deheubarth, and despite attempts in the fourteenth century to bring it under the authority of the royal administration at Carmarthen, it became part of the county of Glamorgan in 1536. There is now a tendency to restrict the use of the name Gower to the peninsula alone but the constituency of Gower, created in 1885, includes almost the whole of the ancient commot.

GRABER, GEORGE ALEXANDER (Alexander Cordell; 1914–   ), English novelist, was born in Colombo, Ceylon, into a soldiering family. Having spent much of his youth in the Far East, including seven years in the China about which he was to write in some

of his novels, he followed a military career from 1932 to 1936 and during the Second World War he was a major in the Royal Engineers. He came to Wales in 1936 and worked as a quantity surveyor in Monmouthshire until 1963. During the 1970s he moved to Pembrokeshire but later left Wales to live in the Isle of Man.

Although he began to write in 1946 and published his first novel, *A Thought of Honour*, in 1954, Alexander Cordell's first successful work was *Rape of the Fair Country* (1959) which, together with *The Hosts of Rebecca* (1960) and *Song of the Earth* (1969), forms the first trilogy about life in early industrial Wales. These immensely popular novels give romanticized accounts of the fight for trade union rights in the ironworks, of the *Chartist movement and of the *Rebecca Riots. The historical events which form the backgrounds are illuminated by larger-than-life characters acting out their own personal dramas. In *The Fire People* (1972) the *Merthyr Rising of 1831 is brought alive by the telling of the story of Dic Penderyn (Richard Lewis) who was hanged for his alleged part in the disturbances. With *This Sweet and Bitter Earth* (1977) Cordell turned again to a Welsh subject: this novel deals with strikes in the slate-quarries of the north and the *Tonypandy Riots in the south. The novel *Land of my Fathers* (1983) completes his second trilogy set in Wales.

Cordell's other novels include *Race of the Tiger* (1963), about Irish immigrants in America, *The Sinews of Love* (1965), about an orphaned girl in Hong Kong, *The Bright Cantonese* (1967), a spy story set in China and America, *If you Believe the Soldiers* (1972), a novel set in the future, *The Dream and the Destiny* (1975), which is based on 'The Long March' of Mao Tse-tung, *To Slay the Dreamer* (1980), a story of the Spanish Civil War, *Rogue's March* (1981), which portrays the life of a Post-Impressionist artist, and *Peerless Jim* (1984), an account of the fortunes of James *Driscoll, the boxer. Among his other works is a trilogy (1971) for younger readers set against the 1798 Rebellion in Ireland, and *Sea Urchin* (1979), a Manx tale.

Grail Romances, The, a group of texts belonging to the Arthurian cycle which recount the last and highest adventure of the Knights of the Round Table. Some scholars have claimed that the theme derives from Celtic and, perhaps Welsh, sources but no reference to the Grail exists in early indigenous Welsh literature. The only complete texts relevant in this context are *Peredur* and *Y Seint Greal*. The word 'grail' does not occur in *Peredur*, one of *Y *Tair Rhamant corresponding to the *Perceval* composed by Chrétien de Troyes between 1180 and 1190; it is in *Y Seint Greal*, a translation made in the late fourteenth century of two earlier French romances, that the first reference to the Grail as such is found. Among the most influential French versions were two romances from the Vulgate Cycle, the *Estoire del Saint Graal* and *Queste del Saint Graal*, both of which belong to the early thirteenth century.

These last two stories illustrate the main aspects of the legend: the first is concerned with the early history of the Grail and the second with the hero who found the Grail and discovered its meaning. Romances of the first type (which in their present form are later in date than the *Estoire*) tell how the Grail was brought to Britain by Joseph of Arimathea. Some texts suggest that the Grail was the platter used by Christ at the Last Supper, others that it was a vessel (a goblet or a chalice) in which Joseph collected Christ's blood at the Crucifixion. This theme was developed by the monks of Glastonbury Abbey as part of the tradition prevalent in some parts of Somerset and Cornwall that Joseph brought Christianity to Britain. In the second type of text this early history is used as the background to events taking place in the time of *Arthur in order to explain not only how the Grail came to his kingdom but also to prove that the new hero, Perceval or Peredur (or Galahad in the *Queste del Saint Graal*) was descended from the line of Joseph of Arimathea.

Three important themes are linked in the tales of the Grail hero. The first is that of the innocent, foolish boy who gradually matures into an experienced knight. Secondly, there are the adventure and mystery of the Grail Castle or Castle of Wonders, the home of Bron the Fisher King or the Maimed King. In this castle the hero witnesses a strange procession. Two youths enter the hall, carrying an enormous lance with three streams of blood running from it. They are followed by two maidens bearing a huge salver on which there is a man's head in a pool of blood. The company is stricken with grief but no explanation of the spectacle is sought or given. Thirdly, the hero tries to discover the meaning of what he has seen in the Castle of Wonders, in the hope of healing the king and freeing the Waste Land. In the Welsh *Peredur* the adventure in the Grail Castle is linked with the hero's duty to avenge insult and injury done to members of his family (see under QUESTION TEST and VENGEANCE QUEST). All versions stress the importance of the hero as one whose coming has been long prophesied and awaited. Usually he is said to have lost his father as a child and to have been brought up by his mother in the wilderness. In the Welsh tale the quest for the Grail is primarily a personal and family concern for Peredur and in this respect the text has probably retained a feature of the earliest traditions. The French texts, on the other hand, emphasize far more the Arthurian and social context. In the *Queste* especially the adventure involves all the Knights of the Round Table and in the theme of the Grail Quest Arthur's court reaches its zenith, since his knights alone are deemed worthy enough to take part. After the success of Galahad, Perceval and Bort, the court falls into decline. The continental versions also stress the religious aspects of the Grail, which are absent from *Peredur*. Chrétien de Troyes left ambiguous the meaning of the Grail but his successors underlined the links between the Grail, the Crucifixion and the experiences of the first Christians.

There is no single, simple meaning to the Grail. Almost every French redactor suggested a different interpretation, some offering more than one. Others, like Chrétien de Troyes, preferred to leave its significance obscure. The author of the *Queste* maintained that none could comprehend the Grail, for no mortal could live once God had revealed its mystery to him. None the less, the Grail is usually represented as a dish or phial which is carried by a maiden in a procession at the Castle of Wonders. The Maimed King is said to be nourished only by the contents of the Grail, in some versions a host. The sword and lance, often associated with the Grail, are connected with the early history of Christianity. Some romances state that the lance was the one with which the Roman soldier Longinus wounded Jesus on the Cross, thus explaining the blood which Peredur sees running from it. Another theory is that the severed head represents Peredur's father and his lost sovereignty, while the bloody lance suggests how his country was lost and how it might be regained.

Scholars of the nineteenth and twentieth centuries have put forward many hypotheses concerning the sources and evolution of the Grail legend, and much disagreement remains. Some have suggested that it developed from the concept of one of the wonderful vessels, such as the *Cauldron of Rebirth, which are found in tales of *Annwn, the Celtic Otherworld. It is now generally agreed, however, that the traditions were pagan in origin and that they developed down the centuries until they received a new Christian meaning at the hands of French redactors of the twelfth and thirteenth centuries. These later traditions had become popular in Wales by the fourteenth century; hence the numerous references to characters from the French romances both in *Trioedd Ynys Prydain* and in the poetry of the *cywyddwyr*.

For detailed studies of the development of the Grail legend see R. S. Loomis, *The Grail from Celtic Myth to Christian Symbol* (1963) and Glenys Goetinck, *Peredur, a Study of Welsh Tradition in the Grail Legends* (1975).

Grammar Schools, had existed in the Middle Ages under the aegis of cathedrals, collegiate churches, some parish churches and guild priests. The earliest school independent of the Church was probably the one founded in Oswestry about 1407; some of the later schools were re-foundations. The spread of 'secondary' education dates from the reigns of Henry VIII, Edward VI and Elizabeth I, with grammar schools established at Brecon (1541), Abergavenny and Carmarthen (both 1543), Caerleon (perhaps 1550), Bangor (1561), Presteigne (1565), Ruthin (1574) and Cowbridge (1603). Others, like those at Haverfordwest and Cardigan, date from the seventeenth century, when new foundations were most frequent. A notable exception was Ystrad Meurig, founded in 1770.

At these schools, where numbers varied from twenty to one hundred and twenty, places were kept for 'poor scholars' and they provided able boys with the training necessary for entry into the universities and the professions. Some schools, such as those at Bangor and Brecon, offered accommodation but most were attended only by day-boys. The Welsh language had no place in these schools. Instruction was almost exclusively in Latin and Greek, though often, as in the case of Christ College, Brecon, the intention was to perfect the understanding of the pupils in English. On the whole the eighteenth century was a period of decline, but there was reform and reorganization in the nineteenth century, new subjects being added to the classical disciplines.

County Schools, as the first local authority schools were called, were founded under the Education Acts of 1896 and 1902. After the First World War many more schools were established, some of which were known as grammar schools, and entry to them depended on the results of scholarship examinations. In the second half of the twentieth century comprehensive education was introduced, the county of Anglesey, between 1955 and 1958, being the first in Wales to develop all its secondary schools as comprehensives. Grammar schools, with selected entry, began swiftly to disappear thereafter: in 1984 the grammar school at Milford Haven was the only school of this type to have survived.

For further details see L. S. Knight, *Welsh Independent Grammar Schools to 1600* (1926), David Williams, *A History of Modern Wales* (1969), Huw Thomas, *A History of Wales 1485–1660* (1972) and Jac L. Williams and Gwilym Rees Hughes (ed.), *The History of Education in Wales* (1978).

Grateful Lion, The, a common motif in classical and medieval literature. The best-known example is found in the story of Androcles and the Lion by Gellius, a Latin author of the second century. In Welsh literature the motif occurs in the tale of the Lady of the Fountain in *Y *Tair Rhamant*. Owain saves a lion from the power of a serpent and, in gratitude, the beast becomes devoted to him. It helps Owain in the rescue of the earl's two sons by slaying a giant, in freeing Luned by killing the two chamberlains who have imprisoned her, in vanquishing the Black Oppressor and in the release of twenty-four fair ladies from their captivity.

GRAVES, ALFRED PERCEVAL (1843–1931), see under WELSH POETRY OLD AND NEW (1912).

GRAY, THOMAS (1716–71), see under BARD and MASSACRE OF THE BARDS.

Greal, Y (lit. 'The Grail'; 1805–07), a quarterly magazine published in London. The editor was anonymous and only nine numbers appeared. Its contents included occasional letters by Goronwy *Owen, the story of *Madog ab Owain Gwynedd, selections from the Dream of *Macsen Wledig, the autobiography of Twm o'r Nant (Thomas *Edwards), and many poems. Henry *Perri's *Eglvryn Phraethineb* was published in the last number.

Greal neu Eurgrawn: sef Trysorfa Gwybodaeth, see under PRICHARD, EVAN (1769–1832).

Great Civilian, The, see AUBREY, WILLIAM (c. 1529–95).

Great Prisoner, The, see under MODRON.

Great Schism, The, see under HARRIS, HOWEL (1714–73).

Green Horse (1978), an anthology of verse by young poets, edited by Meic *Stephens and Peter *Finch. The forty-six contributors, all of whom were under the age of forty in 1977, included the Anglo-Welsh poets Gillian *Clarke, John *Davies, Alan *Perry, Duncan *Bush, Tony *Curtis, John *Pook and Nigel *Jenkins, as well as English poets living in Wales such as Jeremy *Hooker, J. P. *Ward, Nigel *Wells and Sheenagh *Pugh. The volume's title was taken from that of Pablo Neruda's magazine, *Caballo Verde*, and the Chilean poet's assertion, 'There is plenty of room in the world for horses and poets of all the colours of the rainbow', was used as its epigraph. Roland *Mathias, in his introduction, discussed the development of *Anglo-Welsh poetry since the 1960s, concluding that the anthology offered 'considerable hope for the future, though whether that future will long contain what could meaningfully be called Anglo-Welsh poetry must be open to doubt'.

Gregynog Press, The, a private press founded in 1923, at their home near Tregynon, Mont., by the sisters Gwendoline (1882–1951) and Margaret Davies (1884–1963), the granddaughters of David *Davies of Llandinam. Its chairman and guiding light was Thomas *Jones (1870–1955) but a distinctive, if varying, stamp was given to its books by successive Controllers: Robert Ashwin Maynard, William McCance,

Loyd Haberly and James Wardrop. The early works, beginning with a selection of poems by George *Herbert in 1923, had clear Welsh connections and, of the forty-two titles published, seven were in Welsh with one, T. Gwynn *Jones's translation of *Y Bardd Cwsc, Visions of the Sleeping Bard* (1940), appearing in both Welsh and English. Some productions of the 1930s were either vehicles for gifted illustrators like Blair Hughes Stanton and Agnes Miller Parker, or highly decorative books, such as *The History of St. Louis* (1937). The best Gregynog books, which are now collectors' items, are remarkable for the excellence of their typography, the superb quality of the press-work and the harmony of the whole production. In each case a few copies, generally fifteen, were ornately bound in full leather by George Fisher, but the ordinary bindings are sometimes almost as elaborate. The press was revived as *Gwasg Gregynog* by the University of Wales in 1974 and since then it has published books by R. S. *Thomas, R. Williams *Parry, Kate *Roberts, Francis *Kilvert and Dylan *Thomas, among others.

The history of the press has been written by Thomas Jones (1954) and Dorothy A. Harrop (1980); see also Michael Hutchins, *Printing at Gregynog: Aspects of a Great Private Press* (1976); the history of the house was edited by Glyn Tegai Hughes and others in 1977. A selection of the poems written in honour of Gregynog and its owners between 1450 and 1650, together with a note on the Blaeniau (Blayney) family, was edited by Enid P. Roberts and published by *Gwasg Gregynog* in 1979. For an account of life at Gregynog in the sisters' day see Eirene White, *The Ladies of Gregynog* (1985).

'**Gresford Disaster, The**', an anonymous but widely known ballad, one of the few written in English about Welsh coalmining, commemorates the two hundred and sixty-five workers killed by an explosion and fire in the pit at Gresford, a village near Wrexham, Denbs., on 22 September 1934.

GRESHAM, COLIN ALASTAIR (1913–), historian, was born at Knutsford, Ches., but in 1919 moved to Criccieth, Caerns., where he still lives. After graduating in Archaeology at the University of London in 1935, he began researching into local history and archaeology, initially with W. J. Hemp and Mortimer Wheeler. The author of numerous articles on the history and archaeology of north-west Wales, he was recognized as the chief authority on the family history of the commot of *Eifionydd after the publication of his volume, *Eifionydd: a Study in Landownership* (1973). His other main works are *History of Merioneth* (with E. G. *Bowen, vol. 1, 1967) and *Medieval Stone Carving in North Wales* (1968).

Greville, Charles Francis (1749–1809), creator of the town of Milford Haven, Pembs. He may

be noted first for passing on his mistress, Emma Hart, to his uncle, Sir William Hamilton, who married her; she later became the mistress of Lord Nelson. But Greville's main triumphs, as his uncle's agent, were three: in inducing Quaker whalers from Nantucket, Mass., to use the port of Milford from 1793, in obtaining a Navy Board contract in 1796 for one Jacob of London to build ships there, and in persuading Nelson, with Emma and Sir William in train, to provide favourable publicity for Milford by visiting the town in 1802.

Grey Friars, see FRANCISCANS.

Griffith family, The, of Penrhyn, Caerns., one of the oldest families of *Gwynedd, traced its lineage to *Ednyfed Fychan. During the early phase of the rising of *Owain Glyndŵr the family was on the Welsh side but in 1406 was one of the few that submitted to the King. Gwilym ap Gruffudd, the head of the family, subsequently benefited from the oppression of the Welsh. Nevertheless, the family was popular with the poets: *Rhys Goch Eryri, *Guto'r Glyn, *Lewys Môn, *Tudur Aled and *Tudur Penllyn were among those who sang in its praise. Patronage of poets was maintained until the time of Sir Rhys Gruffudd, one of the deputators at the second *Caerwys Eisteddfod in 1567. Late in the reign of Elizabeth his son, Piers Griffith (1568–1628), was reputed to be a pirate and the latter's friend, Tomos *Prys of Plas Iolyn, addressed a number of *cywyddau* to him and wrote his elegy. The house remained in the possession of this branch of the family until the death of Gruffudd Williams, the last of the line, in 1689.

GRIFFITH, ALEXANDER (1601?–76), cleric and controversialist. Born at Llysfaen, Caerns., he held livings in the diocese of Bangor until his ejection under the Act for the *Propagation of the Gospel in Wales (1650). Much incensed by Vavasor *Powell's treatment of the Anglican clergy, he organized a petition against the Act in 1652 and two years later published a pamphlet in the same vein which he addressed to the new Protector. Also in 1654 he published a tract of typically extreme vituperation entitled *Strena Vavasoriensis* which Powell answered in his *Examen et Purgamen Vavasoris* (1654). At the Restoration Griffith was given the living of Glasbury, Rads.

Griffith, Jasper (d. 1614), the third warden of Ruthin School, was the last to be appointed by its founder, Gabriel *Goodman, Dean of Westminster, who also gave him the living of Hinckley, Leics., in 1600. Griffith owned some of the more important Welsh manuscripts such as *The *Black Book of Carmarthen, Brut Dingestow*, the Life of *Gruffudd ap Cynan, *The *White Book of

Rhydderch and certain of the law manuscripts. He copied some of *Dafydd ap Gwilym's poems and those of other poets (Llanstephan MS 120) and several of his manuscripts came to the library of Hengwrt through Meredith *Lloyd.

GRIFFITH, JOHN (Y Gohebydd; 1821–77), journalist, was born at Barmouth, Mer., where as a youth he was apprenticed to a grocer. From 1847 to 1849 he assisted Hugh *Owen in establishing British Schools in Wales and began writing for *Cronicl Cymru*, the monthly periodical of his uncle, Samuel *Roberts. His most important journalistic work appeared in Thomas *Gee's *Baner Cymru* and he became well known as that newspaper's London correspondent (W. 'gohebydd'), writing to inform his monoglot Welsh readers of British and world affairs. An ardent Liberal, he was among those who re-established the Honourable Society of *Cymmrodorion in 1873; he was also a keen supporter of the *National Eisteddfod and an advocate of higher education for Wales.

For further details see the biography by Richard Griffiths (1905).

GRIFFITH, LLEWELYN WYN (1890–1977), novelist, poet and translator, was born and educated at Dolgellau, Mer. He entered the Civil Service in 1909 and made his career with the Inland Revenue, of which he was Assistant Secretary from 1945 to 1952. His experiences as a captain with the Royal Welch Fusiliers during the First World War, in which he won the *Croix de Guerre*, are recounted in *Up to Mametz* (1931). A second autobiographical work, *Spring of Youth* (1935), describes his boyhood and the quality of the Welsh tradition which sustained him throughout a long life of public service in England. He published two novels, *The Wooden Spoon* (1937) and *The Way Lies West* (1945), as well as a volume of poetry, *The Barren Tree* (1945)—which includes the verse play for radio, *Branwen*—and a book for children, *The Adventures of Pryderi* (1962). Among the books of his which were intended to interpret Welsh culture to the English reader were *The Welsh* (1950) and his translations from the work of Kate *Roberts, *Tea in the Heather* (1968) and *The Living Sleep* (1976). A frequent broadcaster in both Welsh and English, he was for many years a member of the Welsh team in the Round Britain Quiz. He also made a distinguished contribution to Welsh life and was a prominent member of the Honourable Society of *Cymmrodorion, the *Transactions* of which he edited for many years.

There is an essay on Ll. Wyn Griffith by Greg Hill in the *Writers of Wales* series (1984); see also the writer's autobiographical essay in *Y Llwybrau Gynt* (ed. Alun Oldfield-Davies, 1971) and the memorial address by Huw Wheldon in the *Transactions* of the Honourable Society of Cymmrodorion (1978).

Griffith, Moses (1747–1819), water-colourist.

Born at Bryncroes, Caerns., he received no formal training as an artist but, at the age of twenty-two, was discovered by Thomas *Pennant who engaged him during the years 1769 to 1790 to accompany him and provide illustrations for his books.

GRIFFITH, OWEN (Ywain Meirion, Owen Gospiol; 1803–68), balladeer. Famous at fairs in many parts of Wales, especially Glamorgan, he habitually wore a top hat and sang his own compositions, of which about sixty have survived. A selection of his ballads, including a lament for the one hundred and eleven miners who lost their lives in an explosion at the Insole Colliery, near Pontypridd, on 15 July 1856, has been edited by Tegwyn Jones in the volume *Baledi Ywain Meirion* (1980).

Griffith, Peter, see GRUFFYDD, PETER (1935–).

GRIFFITH, ROBERT ARTHUR (Elphin; 1860–1936), poet, a native of Caernarfon, was educated in Liverpool and at the University College of Wales, Aberystwyth. He became a solicitor, a barrister and eventually the Stipendiary Magistrate of Merthyr Tydfil and Aberdare, Glam. Two volumes of his poems were published, *Murmuron Menai* and *O Fôr i Fynydd*, as well as a comedy, *Y Bardd a'r Cerddor*, none of which can be dated with certainty. He also contributed critical and satirical articles to Welsh periodicals, especially *Y *Geninen*. With David Edwards and John Owen Jones he was the co-author of *The Welsh Pulpit: divers notes and opinions, by a Scribe, a Pharisee and a Lawyer* (1894).

For further details see the lecture by T. H. Parry-Williams which was published in the *Transactions* of the Honourable Society of Cymmrodorion (1967).

Griffith, Sidney (d. 1752), see under HARRIS, HOWEL (1714–73).

GRIFFITH, WILLIAM JOHN (1875–1931), short-story writer, was born at Aberffraw, Ang., and brought up near Llansadwrn. After taking a short course in agriculture at the University College of North Wales, Bangor, he farmed Cefn Coch and later Henllys Fawr, Aberffraw, his father's family home. Encouraged by E. Morgan *Humphreys, he began in 1924 to write stories and articles for *Y *Genedl Gymreig* which were collected in the volume *Storïau'r Henllys Fawr* (1938) under the editorship of T. Rowland *Hughes. His stories, the most famous of which is probably 'Yr Hen Siandri', are thought by some to be among the funniest ever written in Welsh; they were successfully adapted for television by Gareth *Miles in 1983.

GRIFFITHS, ANN (1776–1805), hymn-writer, was born at Dolwar Fach in the parish of Llanfihangel-yng-Ngwynfa, Mont., into a family in comfortable circumstances. Her father, John Thomas, a man highly respected in the community, had received some education; he was a *bardd gwlad and an ardent Churchman, and his home was known for its hospitality and the *noson lawen. Ann was a sickly child but intelligent, gregarious and particularly fond of dancing. On her mother's death in 1794 she became, at the age of seventeen, the mistress of the household. Her brother John was the first in the family to experience religious conversion and to join the Methodists but, in their turn, the father and four of his five children did the same. Ann was converted in 1796 during a sermon preached at Llanfyllin by the Independent minister, Benjamin Jones of Pwllheli, and she became a member of the Methodist Fellowship at Pontrobert in the following year, at a time of fervent religious revival in the district. Her subsequent life was one of complete dedication to God and the Methodist cause. Dolwar Fach became a centre of Methodist preaching and was officially registered as a place of worship in 1804. In the same year, after her father's death, Ann married Thomas Griffiths, the son of a prosperous family from the parish of Meifod and an elder with the Methodists in Pontrobert, and they made their home at Dolwar Fach. A daughter was born to them in July 1805 but the child lived for only a fortnight and the mother died shortly afterwards.

Ann Griffiths is remembered on account of her letters and hymns. Of the eight of her letters which have survived, seven are copies made by John *Hughes (1775–1854) of Pontrobert of letters she wrote to him between 1800 and 1804; the eighth, in her own hand, belongs to the same period and was sent to Elizabeth, the sister of Ruth Evans, the maidservant at Dolwar Fach and Ann's companion. They reflect vividly the atmosphere of the Methodist meetings and, as examples of religious prose, are considered to be among the most sublime in the Welsh language. As a hymn-writer, she is regarded as highly as William *Williams (Pantycelyn), despite the fact that only seventy-four of her verses have been preserved. Among the finest and best known of her hymns are 'Er mai cwbl groes i natur . . . ', 'O! am gael ffydd i edrych . . . ', 'Dyma babell y cyfarfod . . . ' and 'Wele'n sefyll rhwng y myrtwydd . . . '. Saunders *Lewis has described her longest hymn, 'Rhyfedd, rhyfedd gan angylion . . . ', as one of the greatest religious poems in any European language. Few of her hymns were ever written down and only one has survived in her own hand. The expression of personal spiritual experiences, they were not intended by their author to be sung by congregations. The versions recorded by John Hughes from the memory of his wife, the illiterate Ruth Evans, are the earliest and probably the best. They were

first published, though with many alterations, in Casgliad o Hymnau (1806), a volume edited by Thomas *Charles of Bala and probably Robert *Jones of Rhos-lan.

The two main facets of Ann Griffiths's religious life were the peculiar depth and intensity of her spiritual experience and a firm grasp of the essential truths of her faith. Also evident in her work are the influences of folk-song and the *plygain carols of her native district, the hymns and sermons of her fellow-Methodists, and the books which she had read, including the Book of Common Prayer and Tragwyddol Orffwysfa'r Saint, a translation of a work by Richard Baxter. But the greatest influence on her thought was the Bible: her work abounds with scriptural references and shows a keen intellectual awareness of Christian theology. She meditates on the revelations of her faith and expresses her awe in clear, memorable images. Her main themes are the person and sacrifice of Jesus Christ, her love for Him, and her longing for sanctity and heaven. Added to her sharp intellect and her deep sensitivity was her ability as a poet who had the gift of clothing abstract ideas in rhythmic, melodious language.

There has been much study of the work of Ann Griffiths. Owing to the unusual intensity of her life, some critics have discerned mystical qualities in her hymns, while others have demonstrated the similarities between her work and that of other religious writers of very different traditions. But a proper understanding of her genius must rely on the fact that she was a poet in the Calvinistic Methodist tradition. Her life and work were characterized by the sturdy, biblical theology learned from such men as John Hughes and Thomas Charles, and they were the products of the vivid spiritual experiences associated with the Methodist Revival in Wales.

The two most important early works on Ann Griffiths are the short biography published by John Hughes in Y Traethodydd in 1846 and the memoir by Morris Davies, Cofiant Ann Griffiths (1865). See also the essay by A. M. Allchin in the Writers of Wales series (1976) and the volume of critical essays edited by Dyfnallt Morgan, Y Ferch o Ddolwar Fach (1977). Her own work is chronicled in the manuscripts of John Hughes, in Gwaith Ann Griffiths (ed. Owen M. Edwards, 1905), Cofio Ann Griffiths (ed. William Morris, 1955) and Gwaith Ann Griffiths (1982) by Siân Megan. English translations of her hymns can be found in A Short Memoir of Ann Griffiths (1916) by Evan Richards, Homage to Ann Griffiths (1976) and The Hymns of Ann Griffiths by John Ryan (1980). The diary Fy Hen Lyfr Cownt (1960) by Rhiannon Davies Jones is based on the hymn-writer's life.

GRIFFITHS, BRYN (1933–   ), poet. Born in Swansea, he left school at the age of fourteen and served for seven years in the Merchant Navy. After a year at *Coleg Harlech, he worked in a variety of jobs in London, where he founded the Guild of Welsh Writers which was later merged with Yr *Academi Gymreig, and in Australia, his wife's country, where he has lived for periods since the 1970s. He has published nine volumes of poetry: *The Mask of Pity* (1966), *The Stones Remember* (1967), *Scars* (1969), *The Survivors* (1971), *At the Airport* (1971), *Starboard Green* (1972), *Beasthoods* (1972), *The Dark Convoys* (1974) and *Love Poems* (1980); he edited the anthology *Welsh Voices* (1967). Bryn Griffiths also writes for radio, television and the theatre.

Griffiths, Ieuan, see WILLIAMS, DAVID MAT-THEW (1900–70).

Griffiths, James (1890–1975), miners' leader and politician. Born at Ammanford, Carms., he was a miners' agent from 1925 to 1936, when he was elected as the Labour Member of Parliament for Llanelli, a seat which he held until his retirement in 1970. Among the offices in which he served at Westminster were those of Minister of National Insurance (1945–50), Chairman of the Labour Party (1948–49) and Secretary of State for the Colonies (1950–51). Welsh-speaking and sympathetic to the principle of *Devolution, he became the first Secretary of State for Wales in 1964.

His career is described in his autobiography, *Pages from Memory* (1969); there is an appreciation of him by J. Beverley Smith in the volume *James Griffiths and his Times* (1977).

GRIFFITHS, JOHN (1907–80), children's author, was born at Treharris, Glam., but after spending many years abroad he settled in Swansea, working as a producer and writer of radio plays and features for the BBC. His novel, *Griff and Tommy* (1956), drew on a childhood in the industrial valleys of south Wales and is among the few children's books to do so in a convincing manner. Its sequel, *Griff and Tommy and the Golden Image* (1964), though a more conventional adventure story and set in rural Wales, has the same quality of authenticity.

GRIFFITHS, JOHN GWYN (1911–), poet, critic and scholar, is a native of Porth, Rhondda, Glam., and was educated at the Universities of Wales, Liverpool and Oxford. He is Emeritus Professor of Classics and Egyptology at University College, Swansea. With his wife, Kate *Bosse-Griffiths, he founded the group known as *Cylch Cadwgan* during the Second World War and contributed to the anthology *Cerddi Cadwgan* (1953); he also co-edited the magazine *Y *Fflam* with Euros *Bowen and Pennar *Davies. As well as scholarly works, he has published four volumes of verse, namely *Yr Efengyl Dywyll* (1944), *Ffroenau'r Ddraig* (1961), *Cerddi Cairo* (1969) and *Cerddi Holl Eneidiau* (1981), and a volume of literary studies, *I Ganol y Frwydr* (1970), which discusses the social and moral obligations of the writer in the modern world. J. Gwyn Griffiths is also the author of a number of political pamphlets, including

Anarchistiaeth (1944) and *Y Patrwm Cydwladol* (1949), and was editor of *Plaid Cymru*'s newspaper *Y Ddraig Goch* from 1948 to 1952. His translation of Aristotle's essay on poetry, in which he discusses the Greek's influence on Welsh literary criticism and particularly on the standards of John *Morris-Jones and Saunders *Lewis, appeared in 1978. A friend of D. J. *Williams, he edited the volume published in that writer's honour in 1965, a collection of his early stories, *Y Gaseg Ddu* (1970), and the volume dealing with his life and work in the *Bro a Bywyd* series (1982). The young writers Robat and Heini Gruffudd are the sons of J. Gwyn Griffiths.

GRIFFITHS, RALPH (1937–), historian, was born at Aberbargoed, Mon., and educated at the University of Bristol. He was employed as Research Assistant with the *Board of Celtic Studies by the University of Wales before his appointment as Lecturer in History at University College, Swansea, in 1964 and he became Professor of Medieval History at the College in 1982. Specializing in the political and administrative history of Wales and England during the later Middle Ages, he has published a number of important works which include *The Principality of Wales in the later Middle Ages: South Wales, 1277–1536* (1972), *Boroughs of Medieval Wales* (1978), *Patronage, the Crown and the Provinces in later Medieval England* (1981) and *The Reign of King Henry VI* (1981).

GRIFFITHS, STEVE (1949–), poet, was born at Trearddur Bay, Ang., and educated at Churchill College, Cambridge. A welfare rights worker in London, he is the author of three collections of verse, namely *A Sting in the Air* (1980), *Anglesey Material* (1980) and *Civilised Airs* (1984), the second of which is a meditation on the people, landscape and history of his native island.

GRIMES, WILLIAM FRANCIS (1905–), archaeologist. A native of Pembroke, he was the Director of the Institute of Archaeology and Professor of Archaeology at the University of London until his retirement in 1973. Educated at the University of Wales, he was Assistant Keeper of Archaeology at the National Museum of Wales from 1926 to 1938, when he became keeper of the London Museum. He has served on many public bodies relating to archaeological studies, notably as Chairman of the Royal Commission on Ancient Monuments in Wales and as President of the Council of the British Archaeological Association. He has published extensively on various aspects of his subject; two of his most important works are *The Prehistory of Wales* (1951) and *The Megalithic Monuments of Wales* (1936). The volume *Archaeological Theory and Practice* (ed. D. E. Strong, 1973) was presented to him on the occasion of his retirement.

'**Grongar Hill**', a descriptive landscape poem by John *Dyer, who first drafted it in 1716 when still living at home at Aberglasne in the parish of Llangathen, Carms. The hill of the title lies less than a mile south-west of Aberglasne, overlooking the valley of the Tywi from the north. The poem was re-written in 1724 and the following year when Dyer was studying painting in Italy, and published in three different versions in 1726 after his return to London: in Richard Savage's *Miscellaneous Poems*, in *A New Miscellany* and in David *Lewis's *Miscellany*. Early as it is in the development of topographical poetry, the poem deserves much more credit for innovation than its inclusion in so inexactly observed a genre might allow. The replacement of the heroic couplets of the 1716 version by freer seven-syllabled lines, together with the inspiration of the painter's eye, create a 'landskip' in language which, towards the poem's end, becomes genuinely memorable.

GRONOW, REES HOWELL (1794–1865), author, was born at Castle Herbert, Neath, Glam. He deserted his regiment in London to join Thomas *Picton on the battlefield of Waterloo, but left the army in 1821 to live, chiefly in Paris, as a man-about-town. He published four volumes of memoirs, *Reminiscences of Captain Gronow* (1862), *Recollections and Anecdotes* (1863), *Celebrities of London and Paris* (1865) and *Last Recollections* (1866), all of which are of interest for the author's knowledge of war and society.

GRONW DDU O FÔN (14th cent.), poet. Nothing is known of his life and only a few of his vaticinatory poems have survived in manuscript, but the numerous copies of a dream-poem attributed to him suggest that it was very popular in its day and among later poets.

Gronw Pebr, see under BLODEUWEDD.

GRUFFUDD AB ADDA AP DAFYDD (*fl.* 1340–70), poet, a native of Powys Wenwynwyn, perhaps of *Arwystli, was commemorated in an elegy by *Dafydd ap Gwilym as '*aur eos garuaidd*' ('an amorous golden nightingale') who was slain by a blow from a kinsman's sword. This account may be fictitious but Gruffudd's reputation as a love-poet is confirmed in the *areithiau pros*. Only two of his *cywyddau* and one *englyn* have been preserved. His *cywydd* to a birch-tree cut down and used as a maypole in the town of Llanidloes has timeless excellence, the tree serving as a poignant symbol of beauty's transience and exile's pain. The *englyn* alludes to '*Cainc Gruffudd ab Adda*', a harp-tune of which the score appears in *The Myvyrian Archaiology of Wales* (1801).

GRUFFUDD AB IEUAN AP LLYWELYN FYCHAN (*c.*1485–1553), gentleman and poet,

of Lleweni Fechan (or Llannerch) near St. Asaph, Flints. A cousin of Bishop Richard *Davies's mother, he was also one of the five Commissioners at the *Caerwys Eisteddfod of 1523. His work as a poet includes love-poems in the traditional style, a few religious and request poems and an elegy for *Tudur Aled. He wrote one rather unusual poem, stating the characteristics of the true poet. Gruffudd ab Ieuan's work is that of the amateur, not of the professional poet, but he had full mastery of *Cerdd Dafod.

A selection of his poems was edited by J. C. Morrice in *Detholiad o Waith Gruffudd ab Ieuan ab Llywelyn Fychan* (1910).

GRUFFUDD AB YR YNAD COCH (*fl.* 1280), poet, belonged to a family associated with Llanddyfnan, Ang., but of his life no other details are known. He was the author of one of the most famous poems in Welsh, an elegy for *Llywelyn ap Gruffudd, the last Prince of independent Wales. The diction of this poem, the most powerful expression of utter dismay in the language, is comparatively simple, and although the usual technique of *Gogynfeirdd poetry—the closely knit pattern of alliteration and rhyme—is scrupulously observed, the effect is quite unique. It is in monorhyme, the woe-laden sound -*aw* being repeated, internally and finally, ninety-four times, with accumulative effect. The style is linear, but with several crescendos of emotion which are sustained by repetition of phrases, such as '*Gwae fi*' ('Woe is me'), '*Poni welwch chwi*' ('Do you not see?') and '*Pen*' ('Head'), vividly conveying the apprehension of the Welsh at the Prince's death.

To Gruffudd is also attributed a number of religious poems, one of which is preserved in *The *Red Book of Hergest*. Doubt has been cast on their authenticity, but their direct style and preoccupation with Christ's suffering on the Cross, and the grimness of the grave, suggest a common authorship.

For further details see the article by Ann Matonis in *Studia Celtica* (vols. XIV-XV, 1979–80) and that by Catherine McKenna in the *Bulletin* of the Board of Celtic Studies (1982).

Gruffudd ap Cynan (*c.*1055–1137), King of *Gwynedd, succeeded in re-establishing the authority of his family, the line of *Cunedda and *Rhodri Mawr. Despite many vicissitudes, including imprisonment and years of exile in Ireland, he had by the end of his reign brought Gwynedd firmly under his control and maintained its integrity against attack by Norman lords and the forces of Henry I. Tradition ascribes to him the introduction of new regulations for the poets and there was certainly a literary renaissance during his reign. His close connection with Ireland, where his father had married the daughter of the Viking ruler of Dublin, may have resulted in the introduction of new poetic forms into Wales. The elegy for

Gruffudd composed by *Meilyr Brydydd, the chief poet of his court, heralded a century-and-a-half of panegyric to the House of Gwynedd down to the loss of Welsh independence in 1282. His son, *Owain ap Gruffudd (Owain Gwynedd), commissioned a Latin life of his father, *Historia Gruffudd ap Cynan*, of which only the Welsh version has survived.

The text of the *Historia* has been edited by D. Simon Evans (1977); see also the monograph on Gruffudd ap Cynan by V. Eirwen Davies in the *St. David's Day* series (1959).

GRUFFUDD AP DAFYDD AP TUDUR (*fl.* 1300), poet. Among the five poems of his which are preserved in *The *Red Book of Hergest* there is a complaint against the indifference of a girl from Aber, Caerns., and an appeal to another from Eyton, Denbs. Of all the poems addressed to women by the *Gogynfeirdd* these are the most similar to the love-poems of *Dafydd ap Gwilym, who included a couplet from one of them in his elegy for his uncle, Llywelyn ap Gwilym.

GRUFFUDD AP DAFYDD FYCHAN (15th cent.), a poet of *Tir Iarll in Glamorgan whose verse is an important source of information about the history of that famous district. He composed several vaticinatory poems, some love-poems and, in 1471, an elegy for Henry VI.

GRUFFUDD AP GWRGENAU (*fl.* late 12th cent.), poet. The only extant examples of his work are a laudatory *awdl* to Gruffudd ap Cynan ab Owain Gwynedd, a monk in the abbey of *Aberconwy, and a series of *englynion* expressing his grief at the death of friends. The *awdl* is unique in that, rather than emphasizing the lineage and generosity of Gruffudd, it takes the form of a humble homily, seeking harmony with God.

Gruffudd ap Huw ab Owain, see GUTUN OWAIN (*fl.* 1450–98).

Gruffudd ap Llywelyn (d. 1063), King of *Gwynedd and *Powys, and briefly from 1055 the King of Wales, was the only native monarch to extend his rule over the whole country. A grandson of Maredudd ab Owain, King of *Deheubarth, and the son of Llywelyn ap Seisyllt who had held Gwynedd from 1018 to 1023, Gruffudd seized Gwynedd and Powys in 1039. By 1055 he was established in Deheubarth, had driven out the local dynasty from *Gwent and *Morgannwg, and won back territory beyond *Offa's Dyke which had been lost to the English. The author of *Brut y Tywysogyon described him as '*pen a tharian ac amddiffynnwr y Brytaniaid*' ('the head and shield and defender of the Britons'). Married to the daughter of his ally Aelfgar, the Earl of Mercia, he wielded great power in Wales but his raids along the Border

and his intervention in English affairs on behalf of his father-in-law led to the invasion of Wales by Harold, Earl of Wessex, and to his death in *Eryri (Snowdonia).

GRUFFUDD AP LLYWELYN FYCHAN (15th cent.), a poet of whose work several *cywyddau* have been preserved. One is a disputation with *Dafydd Llwyd of Mathafarn concerning prophecies and another is in praise of Dafydd ab Owain, abbot of *Strata Marcella.

GRUFFUDD AP MAREDUDD AP DAFYDD (*fl.* 1352–82), the greatest of the *Gogynfeirdd after the death of *Llywelyn ap Gruffudd in 1282, came of Anglesey stock, like his contemporary *Gruffudd Gryg, and was sheriff of Talybolion in 1372. He wrote verse which, for the most part, was addressed to his native island and in praise of one family, the *Tudors of Penmynydd and their kin. The range of reference in his verse is wider than that of any other *gogynfardd* and includes literary traditions, romance, Scripture and much else. Although a contemporary of *Dafydd ap Gwilym and the other masters of the first upsurge of the new school of *cywydd* poets, he held strictly to the older forms of *awdl* and *englyn*. Nevertheless, his verse is very varied and rich in detail, his chief delight being in the beauty of women, in the landscape of Anglesey and in fine clothes. In an age beset by the *Black Death he was much moved by the deaths of the young and beautiful and by the contrast between their joy in life and their bodily putrefaction. His best-known poem, to a girl named Gwenhwyfar, is a masterpiece on this theme, a magnificent elegy composed with all the artistry of the bardic tradition.

He could also praise the Penmynydd family for their prowess in the French Wars and for their support in Wales of the old native way of life and the *Bardic Order. This dual ideal is one of his most common themes; when in 1370 there were hopes that Owain Lawgoch (*Owain ap Thomas ap Rhodri), who was descended from the Princes of Gwynedd, would return to reclaim his inheritance, the patriotism of a poet like Gruffudd came to the fore. He also shared the religious beliefs of his day, particularly the increased contemplation of the Passion of Christ and the cult of Mary who was the inspiration of some of his finest lyrical verse. His long poem to the Cross at Chester reflects the growing importance of crucifixes in the devotional life of his day.

Gruffudd ap Nicolas (*fl.* 1425–56), a nobleman who served the English Crown as steward for the lordship of *Dinefwr, was sheriff of Carmarthen in 1426. He was closely associated with the eisteddfod held at *Carmarthen about the year 1450 when *Dafydd ab Edmwnd won the Chair and when the *Twenty-four Metres of Welsh prosody were agreed. Eulogies were addressed to him by the poets Dafydd ab Edmwnd, *Lewys Glyn Cothi and *Gwilym ab Ieuan Hen.

GRUFFUDD BOLA (*fl.* 1265–82), translator of the Athanasian Creed into Welsh, may have been connected with the abbey of *Strata Florida; the name Bola is a Welsh version of the English surname Bole. His translation was done for Efa, the daughter of Maredudd ap Owain, a descendant of *Rhys ap Gruffudd (The Lord Rhys) and a sister of Gruffudd ap Maredudd.

GRUFFUDD GRYG (*fl.* 1357–70), poet, probably of Tregwehelyth, Llantrisant, Ang., was traditionally regarded as being much younger than *Dafydd ap Gwilym, but recent research suggests that they may have been close contemporaries. He was the beadle of Malltraeth in 1357 and his elegy for Rhys ap *Tudur of Penmynydd (d. 1411/12) may have been composed during the lifetime of Rhys. Of his work some sixteen *cywyddau*, one *awdl* and a number of *englynion* have survived, including love-poems, debate poems, devotional verse and poems addressed to patrons. He took part in a bardic contention with Dafydd ap Gwilym deploring the exaggeration of the latter's love-poetry. A pilgrimage to Santiago de Compostella inspired a fine poem addressed to the moon, which he blamed for the tempestuous sea-journey, and another to a wave which he depicted as a love-messenger from his sweetheart, Goleuddydd. An important pioneer of the *cywydd*, Gruffudd was a gifted poet who employed the new metre successfully for a variety of purposes.

Examples of his work are to be found in the volume *Cywyddau Dafydd ap Gwilym a'i Gyfoeswyr* (ed. Ifor Williams and Thomas Roberts, 1914); see also E. D. Jones, 'Cartref Gruffudd Gryg' in *The National Library of Wales Journal* (vol. X, 1957) and Dafydd Wyn Williams, 'Y Traddodiad Barddol ym Mhlwyf Bodedern, Môn' in the *Transactions* of the Anglesey Antiquarian Society and Field Club (1969–70).

GRUFFUDD HAFREN (*fl.* 1600), poet, was possibly a native of Montgomery. The greater part of his work remains in manuscript, including poems to members of the *Gogerddan and Henllys families. The author of two *cywyddau* in praise of John *Davies of Mallwyd and of elegies for the poets Siôn *Phylip and Thomas Penllyn, he was involved with Rhisiart *Phylip in a bardic contention against Siôn Phylip and Ieuan Tew and in another against Roger *Cyffin.

GRUFFUDD HIRAETHOG (d. 1564), one of the major *cywyddwyr* of the sixteenth century, was a native of Llangollen, Denbs. He may have acquired his second name on account of his close connection with Plas Iolyn, the home of Dr. Elis *Prys, one of his chief patrons, which stands to the south-west of Mynydd Hiraethog. No

eisteddfod was held during Gruffudd's lifetime and so all his bardic degrees were conferred upon him at wedding-feasts, according to the custom of his time. His licence as deputy-*pencerdd*, granted in 1545/6, bears the signature, among others, of Lewys Morgannwg (*Llywelyn ap Rhisiart), his bardic teacher.

The other extant document relating to Gruffudd's career is the list of instructions he received as Deputy-Herald for Wales under the College of Arms. Of his poems there have survived ten *awdlau* and 120 *cywyddau*, and also some occasional *englynion*, most of which were written in praise of the gentry and clerics of north Wales in the traditional manner. His industry as a herald is to be seen in the substantial collection of genealogies and other material found in his manuscripts which also include a Welsh dictionary of his compilation and a miscellany prepared for Welsh expatriates in England.

There was a close connection between Gruffudd and William *Salesbury, who published a collection of proverbs belonging to the poet in *Oll Synnwyr pen Kembero ygyd* (1547). Salesbury also dedicated his *Llyfr Rhetoreg* (1552) to Gruffudd 'and others of his craft', referring to him in the dedication as his chief ally in his effort to save and maintain the Welsh language. Gruffudd Hiraethog's pupils were the most prominent graduates at the *Caerwys Eisteddfod of 1567. The elegy written on his death by one of them, *Wiliam Llŷn, is among the great poems of the Welsh language.

D. J. Bowen has published a study of the poet, *Gruffudd Hiraethog a'i Oes* (1958); see also the same writer's contribution to *Astudiaethau Amrywiol* (ed. Thomas Jones, 1968) and his article, 'Cywyddau Dychan Gruffudd Hiraethog' in *Studia Celtica* (vols. XII/XIII, 1977–78).

GRUFFUDD LLWYD AP DAFYDD AB EINION LLYGLIW (*c.*1380–*c.*1420), poet. A native of Llangadfan, Mont., he was a nephew of *Hywel ab Einion Llygliw and, according to the elegy for him written by *Rhys Goch Eryri, his bardic disciple, a descendant of Einion Yrth. He composed *cywyddau* for *Owain Glyndŵr, Sir David Hanmer, Owain ap Maredudd of Neuadd Wen and Hywel and Meurig Llwyd of *Nannau. Some of his work, which includes love-poems and religious verse, contains references to the Triads and medieval tales about *Uthr Pendragon, *Arthur and *Rhita Gawr.

GRUFFUDD, SIÔN (d. 1586?), a poet of whose work only two poems, both in the free metres, have survived: one is a religious carol and the other the well-known 'Hiraeth am Gaernarfon'. The latter was written when the poet was serving in Flanders as chaplain to William ap Sir Rhys Thomas who was killed at Zutphen in 1586, in which battle the poet is also presumed to have died.

GRUFFYDD, ELIS (The Soldier of Calais;

*c.*1490–*c.*1552), copyist, chronicler and translator, was born in the parish of Llanasa, Flints. Little is known of his early years in Wales, but he later entered the service of the Wingfield family in London and accompanied Sir Robert Wingfield at the Field of the Cloth of Gold, near Calais, in 1520. From 1524 to 1529 he was the Steward of Sir Robert's mansion in London, where he copied a collection of Welsh prose and poetry, now known as the Cardiff Phillipps Manuscripts, which consists mainly of transcripts from earlier manuscripts and contains such items as genealogies of the Saints, *cywyddau*, a few short pseudo-historical texts, a Welsh version of the *Secreta Secretorum*, vaticinatory poems and a Welsh version of *Chwedlau Saith Ddoethion Rhufain*. Gruffydd returned to Calais as a soldier in 1529 and remained there for the rest of his life, copying and translating several manuscripts from the Cwrt Mawr collection. He also wrote a chronicle of the history of the world from the Creation to his own day, which is valuable not only for its details of his life but also because it contains descriptions of contemporary events.

For further details see Thomas Jones, 'A Welsh Chronicler in Tudor England' in *The Welsh History Review* (vol. 1, no. 1, 1960).

GRUFFYDD, IFAN (1896–1971), author, was born at Llangristiolus, Ang., where he spent all his life except for the years he served in the First World War. He was a farm labourer, and later a caretaker in the Council Offices, but he was well known locally as a lay-preacher and as a playwright long before his two volumes of autobiography, *Gŵr o Baradwys* (1963) and *Tân yn y Siambar* (1966), brought him to literary prominence. The *Paradwys* ('Paradise') in the first title is the name of his native district and the autobiography is a colourful portrait of country life there during the period between the turn of the century and the 1930s. As a boy and young man he suffered many disadvantages, but in rich prose, full of anecdotes laced sometimes with Chaplinesque humour, he wrote a masterly memoir of a unique, lost way of life. In 1971, after his death, J. Elwyn Hughes edited the volume *Cribinion*, which includes a selection of Ifan Gruffydd's stories, together with commemorative essays by some of his friends.

GRUFFYDD, OWEN (*c.*1643–1730), genealogist, poet and antiquary, was born at Llanystumdwy, Caerns. A weaver by trade, he became blind but composed poems in the strict metres for local families as well as popular carols, some of which appeared in the anthologies *Carolau a Dyriau Duwiol* (1688) and *Blodeu-Gerdd Cymry* (1759). A selection of his verse was published by Owen M. *Edwards in 1904.

GRUFFYDD, PETER (1935–), poet. Born in Liverpool but brought up in north Wales, to

which his family was evacuated during the war, he was educated at the University College of North Wales, Bangor. He taught English at Llanberis and Rhyl for several years before taking a variety of jobs in England and Germany. As Peter M. Griffith he contributed poems (with Meic *Stephens and Harri *Webb) to the volume *Triad* (1963) and has since published one volume of poems, *The Shivering Seed* (1972).

GRUFFYDD, ROBERT GERAINT (1928–), scholar and critic, was born at Tal-y-bont, Mer.; he was brought up there and at Cwm Ystwyth and Capel Bangor, Cards. Educated at the University College of North Wales, Bangor, and Jesus College, Oxford, he spent two years as an assistant editor on the staff of the University of Wales Dictionary before his appointment to a lectureship in Welsh at Bangor in 1955. He became Professor of Welsh at the University College of Wales, Aberystwyth, in 1970 and was appointed *Librarian of the *National Library of Wales in 1980. He has concentrated in his research on the prose of the Protestant Revival, on the work of the Humanists and on the early Puritans, and he is the author of a large number of booklets and articles. Yet he has not confined himself to these fields: he shows the same meticulous learning and the same mastery of several disciplines in his work on some of *Dafydd ap Gwilym's *cywyddau*, on the *Cynfeirdd and in his literary criticism. He has also edited a collection of essays by Saunders *Lewis, *Meistri'r Canrifoedd* (1973) and a *Festschrift* in honour of J. E. Caerwyn *Williams, *Bardos* (1982). His appointment as Director of the Institute of Advanced Welsh and Celtic Studies was announced in March, 1985.

GRUFFYDD, WILLIAM JOHN (1881–1954), poet, scholar and critic. Born at Bethel in the parish of Llanddeiniolen, Caerns., the eldest son of a quarryman, he was educated at Jesus College, Oxford, where he read Classics and English Literature. At Oxford he came under the influence of John *Rhŷs and, in particular, of Owen M. *Edwards, whom he was to admire profoundly for the rest of his life. He also cultivated his interest in Welsh literature at meetings of *Cymdeithas Dafydd ap Gwilym. In 1906 he was appointed Lecturer in the Celtic Department of University College, Cardiff, and Professor of Celtic (a title later changed to Welsh) in 1918, remaining in that post until his retirement in 1946. From 1922 until it ceased publication in 1951 he edited the quarterly magazine *Y *Llenor*. One of his lifelong interests was the *National Eisteddfod and he was appointed President of its Council in 1945. At a by-election for the University of Wales seat in 1943 he was elected, on a Liberal platform, and held the seat until parliamentary representation of the Universities was abolished in 1950. His opponent in that famous contest was the *Plaid Cymru candidate, Saunders *Lewis: Gruffydd received the support of all the parties of the wartime Coalition and won the seat with 3,098 votes against Lewis's 1,330.

In spite of the English and Classical bent of his education at the Caernarfon County School, W. J. Gruffydd developed an early interest in Welsh poetry. With his friend, R. Silyn *Roberts, he published a volume of lyrical verse, Telynegion (1900), and was introduced to the work of John *Morris-Jones. Although in later years he considered his early poems to be merely the products of his apprenticeship, they demonstrate an endeavour to promote a new conception of poetry in Welsh with an emphasis on colour, feeling and sensitivity as opposed to the didactic, philosophical modes which were fashionable in that period. At Oxford he began reading the works of Thomas Hardy, whose influence served to restrain his Romanticism and to bring terseness and sobriety into his thought and style. These characteristics are to be discerned in all his subsequent volumes of verse, Caneuon a Cherddi (1906), Ynys yr Hud a Chaneuon Eraill (1923) and, in particular, Caniadau (1932), his own selection of his best poems which was published by the *Gregynog Press. He was also an anthologist of high standards, editing Y Flodeugerdd Newydd (1909), Blodeuglwm o Englynion (1920) and Y Flodeugerdd Gymraeg (1931).

As he grew older, W. J. Gruffydd turned increasingly from verse to prose and criticism as a medium of expression and much of his best work is to be found in *Hen Atgofion (1936), in his biography of Owen M. Edwards (1937) and in Y Tro Olaf (1939). In Y Llenor he wrote lively, often scathing, editorials dealing with topics of the day. His important contributions to scholarship include two volumes on the history of Welsh literature, Llenyddiaeth Cymru 1450–1600 (1922) and Llenyddiaeth Cymru 1540–1660 (1926). His principal scholarly interest, however, was in the construction and narrative content of *Pedair Cainc y Mabinogi, a subject to which John Rhŷs's work on the pagan Celtic tradition had first drawn his attention. Among his numerous publications in this field the two volumes Math Vab Mathonwy (1928) and Rhiannon (1953) deserve especial mention. While it may be agreed that much detailed re-examination of his conclusions is needed, his originality and perceptiveness and the essential validity of his basic hypothesis are not in doubt.

W. J. Gruffydd was temperamentally restless and subject to frequent changes of mood. A Nonconformist by conviction, he laid great stress on tolerance and freedom of thought, finding any formalized system of ideas unacceptable. He began his career as a rebel against the standards of the Victorian era but made extensive use of his gifts to praise the simple, hardy, rural folk from whom he had sprung (see GWERIN). His critics saw evidence of inconsistency in the behaviour of a man who attacked the warmongers after the First World War, who lent his support to the Welsh Nationalists who caused the Fire in Llŷn in 1936 (see under PENYBERTH), who called on his compatriots to boycott the Coronation in order to express national anger, but who by 1939 was no less enthusiastically in favour of fighting the Second World War to a victorious conclusion. There can, however, be no doubt that he genuinely believed in the different standpoints which he took and defended from time to time.

For an objective appraisal of W. J. Gruffydd's attitudes, by one who enjoyed a close acquaintance with him, see T. J. Morgan's essay in the Writers of Wales series (1970); see also the essay by Alun Llywelyn-Williams in Gwŷr Llên (ed. Aneirin Talfan Davies, 1948), the memorial number of Y Llenor (1955), the article by John Gwilym Jones in Ysgrifau Beirniadol I (ed. J. E. Caerwyn Williams, 1965), Iorwerth C. Peate's pamphlet on the writer (1966) and the essay by John Gwilym Jones in Swyddogaeth Beirniadaeth (1973).

GRUFFYDD, WILLIAM JOHN (Elerydd;

1916–), poet, novelist and short-story writer, was born at Ffair-rhos, Cards. A Baptist minister, he won the *Crown at the National Eisteddfod in 1955 and 1960 and became Archdruid in 1983. He is the author of three novels, Hers a Cheffyl (1967), Cyffwrdd â'i Esgyrn (1969) and Angel heb Adenydd (1971), two volumes of poems, Ffenestri (1961) and Cerddi'r Llygad (1973), and three collections of stories about Tomos and Marged, the amiable characters who are his most memorable creations.

Guest family, The,

ironmasters of Dowlais, Merthyr Tydfil, Glam., were descended from a line of yeomen farmers of Broseley, Salop. John Guest (1722–85) arrived in Merthyr Tydfil in 1763 and was appointed manager of the ironworks established at Dowlais by Thomas Morgan and others. By the time of his death the annual production at the works was more than a thousand tons. His son, Thomas Guest (d. 1807), succeeded him as manager and greatly expanded the business. Under Thomas's son, Sir Josiah John Guest (1785–1852), Dowlais became the largest ironworks in the world, with more than five thousand employees, and was in the forefront of every technological innovation. It was Sir Josiah, the first Member of Parliament for Merthyr Tydfil, who married Charlotte, the Earl of Lindsey's daughter and the translator of the *Mabinogion into English; she is the subject of the next entry. She encouraged him in his paternalistic rule at Dowlais, but their links with Wales grew weaker after 1845 when they bought Canford Manor in Dorset. The family disposed of its interests in the Dowlais works in 1900 when it became part of Guest, Keen and Company.

For further details see the Journals of Lady Charlotte

Guest (2 vols., 1950, 1952), Glanmor Williams (ed.), *Merthyr Politics: the Making of a Working-class Tradition* (1966) and Gwyn A. Williams, *The Merthyr Rising of 1831* (1978).

GUEST, CHARLOTTE (1812–95), translator and diarist. Born at Uffington, Lincs., the daughter (*née* Bertie) of the Earl of Lindsey, she became interested in the literature and traditions of Wales after her marriage in 1835 to Sir Josiah John Guest (1785–1852), the ironmaster of Dowlais, Glam., whose family is the subject of the previous entry. Between 1838 and 1849, with the help of John *Jones (Tegid) who provided her with a transcript he had made from *The *Red Book of Hergest* in the library of Jesus College, Oxford, she translated the eleven tales now known as *The *Mabinogion*. With these she included the story of *Taliesin, apparently from eighteenth-century manuscript sources, and it may have been in this connection that she was assisted by Thomas *Price (Carnhuanawc) and others. The complete translation was published in three sumptuous volumes in 1846 and a popular edition, in a single volume, appeared in 1877. The extent of Charlotte Guest's labours as a translator is an open question: she was certainly acquainted with Welsh and her children were taught the language, but it seems likely that her part in the venture was the rendering into graceful English of her collaborators' literal translation rather than any close involvement in the basic task of translating the original texts.

A lifelong collector, she also published, as Lady Charlotte Schreiber after her second marriage in 1855, *Fans and Fan Leaves* (1888–90) and *Playing Cards of Various Ages and Countries* (1892–95). One of her sons, Montague Guest, edited *Lady Charlotte Schreiber's Journal 1869–85* (2 vols., 1911) and the Earl of Bessborough edited *Lady Charlotte Guest, Extracts from her Journal 1833–52* (2 vols., 1950, 1952).

For further details see D. Rhys Phillips, *Lady Charlotte Guest and the Mabinogion* (1921) and the article by Leslie Wynne Evans, 'Sir John and Lady Charlotte Guest's Educational Scheme at Dowlais in the Mid-Nineteenth Century', in the *Journal* of the National Library of Wales (vol. IX, no. 3, 1956).

Guild of Welsh Writers, The, see under ACADEMI GYMREIG and LONDON WELSH.

Guinevere, see GWENHWYFAR.

Guto Nyth Brân, see MORGAN, GRIFFITH (1700–37).

GUTO'R GLYN (c.1435–c.1493), poet. It is not known for certain where he was born and brought up but he is usually associated with Glyn Ceiriog, Denbs., where several of his patrons lived. This uncertainty extends to his poetry: some of his early *cywyddau* were attributed to a poet known as Guto ap Siancyn y

Glyn, although some scholars have argued that they were the same man, a view now generally accepted. Some of his patrons, such as Edwart ap Dafydd and his son, Robert Trefor of Bryncunallt, and Siôn Edwart of Plasnewydd, lived in Chirk, while others lived in the vicinity of that town; they included the Pilstons in Welsh Maelor and Sieffre Cyffin, the constable of Oswestry. Further afield, Guto found patrons throughout north Wales and in his famous *cywydd* to the Earl of Pembroke he asked him to protect the nobility of Gwynedd who had patronized the poets. Other poems were written for Dafydd ap Gwilym of *Llwydiarth, Ang., for the *Griffith family of Penrhyn, for members of the Kyffin family and, in Meirionydd, for the families of *Nannau, *Corsygedol and Llangywair. In south Wales he wrote for patrons in Dyfed, Glamorgan and Gwent.

Besides poems in praise of his patrons, Guto'r Glyn wrote verse reflecting his military career on the Yorkist side in the Wars of the Roses. He addressed poems to Edward IV and to two soldiers who distinguished themselves in the war with France, Sir Richard Gethin and Mathew *Gough. In his poems to the Yorkist leader William Herbert, he made it clear that he considered the well-being of Wales more important than that of any faction. His request-poems and poems of thanks include *cywyddau* for the gifts of a pony, a greyhound, an ox, a sallet, a bayonet, a horn, slates, the Book of the Grail and a mantle. Among those with whom he engaged in bardic contentions were *Llywelyn ap Gutun, *Dafydd ab Edmwnd and *Tudur Penllyn; in a contention with Morgan ap Rhosier of Newport he wrote a poem in defence of his function as a praise-poet. Of all the Poets of the Gentry, Guto'r Glyn was second only to *Dafydd ap Gwilym, whose subjects were completely different.

The work of Guto'r Glyn has been edited by J. Ll. Williams and Ifor Williams (1939). The problem of the poet's identity has been discussed by J. Ll. Williams in *Y Llenor* (vol. X, 1931) and by Thomas Roberts in *Y Llenor* (vol. XXVI, 1947). The poet's work is treated in *Guto'r Glyn a'i Gyfnod* (1963) by R. M. Jones, by Saunders Lewis in 'Gyrfa Filwrol Guto'r Glyn' in *Ysgrifau Beirniadol IX* (1976), by Enid Roberts in *Y Beirdd a'u Noddwyr ym Maelor* (1977), and by J. E. Caerwyn Williams in *A Guide to Welsh Literature* (ed. A. O. H. Jarman and Gwilym Rees Hughes, 1979).

GUTUN OWAIN or **GRUFFUDD AP HUW AB OWAIN** (*fl.* 1450–98), poet, came of gentry stock and was a native of Dudleston in the lordship of Oswestry. His earliest poems extant belong to the 1460s, but he may have begun his poetic career earlier, for it is said that he accompanied *Dafydd ab Edmwnd, his bardic teacher, to the *Carmarthen Eisteddfod about the year 1450. Familiar with all the branches of bardic learning, he made copies of the grammars which were the first to incorporate Dafydd ab

Edmwnd's reformation of the *Twenty-four Metres and which became the prototypes of the bardic grammars of the sixteenth century. He also copied the chronicles *Brenhinedd y Saeson* and *Brut Tysilio* from *The Black Book of Basingwerk*. An expert genealogist, he was a member of the commission appointed by Henry VII in 1491 to enquire into the pedigree of his grandfather, Owain Tudor. Although only one of his genealogical manuscripts has survived, there are many references to his books of pedigrees in the work of later genealogists. His copy of the Welsh heraldic treatise, *Llyfr Arfau*, is the earliest surviving work of its kind. There are also, among his manuscripts, religious texts, including *Lives of the Saints, as well as medical and astrological treatises, which demonstrate his scholarly inclinations. His unknown elegist described Gutun as 'Dysgwr, myfyriwr maith' ('A learner, one who studied long') and his erudition is reflected in the rich allusions of his verse.

Gutun Owain's extant poetry consists of fifty-four *cywyddau*, eight *awdlau*, one *awdl-gywydd* and three series of satirical *englynion*. The majority are eulogies and elegies for patrons in north-east Wales, especially Bromfield, Maelor Saesneg and Chirkland, and they reflect the prosperity of the gentry of those districts in his day. From the number of poems addressed to them, fourteen in all, his chief patrons seem to have been two successive abbots of *Valle Crucis, namely Siôn ap Rhisiart and Dafydd ab Ieuan ab Iorwerth. Gutun visited the abbey over a period of about forty years: his *awdlau* and *cywyddau* in praise of the abbots portray the sumptuous feasting, the splendour of worship and the magnificence of the architecture. He also wrote elegies for some of his fellow-poets, including Dafydd ab Edmwnd, his old teacher, and *Guto'r Glyn, who was his frequent companion on feast-days at Valle Crucis.

Gutun Owain's muse was refined and cultivated, his verse polished and highly wrought. His request poems, in which he excelled, are full of delightful *dyfalu* and his metrically intricate *awdlau* are notable for their musicality. The gifts he solicits, be they horses, hounds, bucklers or swords, are imaginatively realized in memorable language. By virtue of his finely attuned ear, his sure poetic taste and the elegant classicism of his poetry, he was a faithful and worthy disciple of Dafydd ab Edmwnd and undoubtedly one of the finest practitioners of late medieval Welsh bardism.

For discussion of the poet's work see *L'Œuvre Poétique de Gutun Owain* (2 vols., 1950, 1951) by Edouard Bachellery, the chapter by J. E. Caerwyn Williams in *A Guide to Welsh Literature* (ed. A. O. H. Jarman and Gwilym Rees Hughes, 1979) and the essay by Saunders Lewis in *Meistri a'u Crefft* (ed. Gwynn ap Gwilym, 1981).

Gutyn Peris, see WILLIAMS, GRIFFITH (1769–1838).

Gwaed Ifanc (lit. 'Young blood'; 1923), a volume of poems produced in collaboration by E. Prosser *Rhys and J. T. *Jones (John Eilian). It was a landmark in the development of modern Welsh poetry because—passionate, experimental and socially aware—it was an attempt to break away from the stereotyped, rhetorical style of the verse written for eisteddfod competitions of the period.

Gwaed yr Uchelwyr (lit. 'Blood of the Gentry'; 1922), Saunders *Lewis's second play and his first in Welsh. The elements of the traditional kitchen-drama—the imperious squire, the lowly but well-descended tenant, the dastardly steward, the love affair between the squire's son and the tenant's daughter—are here pressed into the service of a tragedy in the manner of Corneille. Luned chooses lonely exile with her evicted parents rather than allow Arthur to accompany her to her new home, the happy ending demanded by the conventions of the genre. She does this, as her father explains to her, because her noble blood demands it; personal happiness is of little account when confronted by the claims of honour. The play, although flawed, shows evidence of a powerful dramatic talent and marks the beginning of Saunders Lewis's quest for a standard Welsh suitable for the stage.

GWALCHMAI AP MEILYR (*fl.* 1130–80), a court poet to *Owain ap Gruffudd (Owain Gwynedd), also wrote for his brothers, for Dafydd and Rhodri (two of Owain's sons), and for *Madog ap Maredudd. He was the son of *Meilyr Brydydd and father of the poets *Meilyr ap Gwalchmai and *Einion ap Gwalchmai, and possibly of *Elidir Sais; the family was probably connected with Trewalchmai in Anglesey.

Although composed according to the conventions of *Gogynfeirdd poetry, Gwalchmai's work is original in content, simple in diction, direct and lyrical in style. Unusual in the poetry of this period is his gift for narrative description, such as that found in his *awdl* to Owain Gwynedd which describes a sea-battle off the coast of Anglesey, with the effective hyperbole of an ebb-less Menai caused by the stream of blood. As a rule, the poet's relationship with Owain and his sons was cordial, but it was not always so, as is evident from an intercessionary *awdl* addressed to the prince. Gwalchmai also composed a dream poem and a gnomic poem, but the *awdl* to God ascribed to him by the *Hendregadredd Manuscript is more likely to belong to his son Meilyr, as is recognized in *The *Red Book of Hergest*.

The most famous poem by Gwalchmai is his *Gorhoffedd*, a long boasting-poem, the best of the few of its kind which have been preserved. It consists of nine monorhyming *laisses*, mainly of nine-syllable lines, each interspersed with units of nine or ten syllables with their own metrical patterns. Woven into it are many memorable images reflecting his joy in the natural world, his love of women and his allegiance to Owain Gwynedd. He delights in a May dawn, the song of the birds, the play of seagulls on the face of the water, the blue of the wave on the beach, and in the names of his favourite rivers. This poem is one of the great poems of the Welsh language.

There is an article about Gwalchmai ap Meilyr by Tomos Roberts in *Gwŷr Môn* (ed. Bedwyr Lewis Jones, 1979); see also the pamphlet edited by Iwan Llwyd Williams (1984).

Gwalchmai fab Gwyar, one of *Arthur's knights, is known in French as Gauvain, in English as Gawain and in Latin as Gualguainus. In the tale of *Culhwch and Olwen he is described as a nephew of Arthur and is chosen by the king to accompany Culhwch in his quest. His horse, Ceingaled (F. Guingalet) is named in *The *Black Book of Carmarthen*, and his burial-place is said to be in Peryddon. On the other hand, William of Malmesbury in *De Rebus Gestis Anglorum* (1125), claimed that he ruled in a part of Britain called Walweitha and that he was buried in 'that province of Wales known as Rhos'; there is a commot known as Castell Gwalchmai in the hundred of *Rhos in Dyfed.

In the European romances Gauvain was the essence of courtesy and bravery and in the Triads Gwalchmai is listed as one of the 'three best men with guests and visitors from afar'. Similarly, in *Historia Peredur*, Arthur says of him *'mwy a wna ef o'i eiriau teg na nyni o nerth ein harfau'* ('he achieves more with his fair words than do we from our strength in arms'). In *Y *Tair Rhamant*, Gwalchmai meets the hero after his battles with Arthur's men and in each case he is the means by which reconciliation with the king is achieved. In the *Brut* of *Geoffrey of Monmouth, his military feats are given prominence and it is said that it was while fighting the traitor *Medrod that he was killed.

Gwales or **Grassholm**, an island about eight miles off the western coast of Pembrokeshire. In the Second Branch of *Pedair Cainc y Mabinogi the seven who return from the campaign in Ireland spend eighty years on the island, with the head of Bendigeidfran (*Brân) as company, without ageing or any recollection of their former sorrows, until Heilyn fab Gwyn opens the closed door which faces Aber Henfelen and Cornwall. The memory of the past then returns and they have to leave. Gwales is an example of *Annwfn or the Otherworld which is sited, in this instance, on a magic island beyond the bounds of time. The name Gwales was superseded by that of Grassholm at some time after the end of the tenth century, when Norse seamen, sailing out of Swansea and Haverford, made the island one of their navigational marks.

Gwalia, a name for Wales which first appeared in the later Middle Ages as a half-Latin, half-Welsh neologism deriving from *Wallia*, a Latinized form used in English and Norman documents. It was revived in the Romantic period and had an extraordinary vogue, in both English and Welsh, during the reign of Queen Victoria. Because it has such a period flavour, the name has been used with piquant effect by some modern writers, as in the title of the poem which is the subject of the next entry.

Gwalia Deserta (lit. 'Wales a desert'; 1938), Idris *Davies's first book, consists of a sequence of thirty-six poems, numbered but untitled, presenting the poet's view of south Wales, Rhymney in particular, during the years of the *Depression. All the poems are cast either as short lyrics in the style of A. E. Housman or in the accumulative, long-line form which was to become characteristic of Davies's later work. They include the well-known section, 'Do you remember 1926?', and the poem which was set to music by Pete Seeger and entitled 'The Bells of Rhymney'. The poet's *alter ego*, Dai, makes his first appearance in this volume which, because of its preoccupation with dereliction, both industrial and social, earned for its author (according to the testimony of Islwyn Jenkins, his friend and biographer) the nickname Ap Anialwch ('Son of Desolation').

Gwallog (6th cent.), one of the four British kings who, according to the Saxon Genealogies incorporated in *Nennius's *Historia Brittonum, resisted the Anglian king, Hussa. Two poems to Gwallog are found in The *Book of Taliesin, one praising him and listing his battles, and the other perhaps an elegy for him. On the basis of a reference in one of the poems it has been claimed that he ruled over the kingdom of Elmet in the region of Leeds. It is possible that the poet *Aneirin was the son of his sister Dwywai and a reference in *'Moliant Cadwallon' suggests that he was in some way associated with the battle of Catraeth. Indications of legendary accretions to his name are found in an *englyn* in *'Canu Llywarch Hen' and in certain poems preserved in The *Black Book of Carmarthen.

Gwallter Mechain, see DAVIES, WALTER (1761–1849).

Gwasanaeth Bwrdd, Y (lit. 'The service of tables'; 16th cent.), a text which gives instructions on how the table should be laid and the food prepared for a royal feast. Two versions are extant in sixteenth-century manuscripts, one in the *Llanstephan Manuscripts in the hand of Ieuan ap Dafydd ap Einws and the other in the *Peniarth Manuscripts in the hand of *Gruffudd Hiraethog. It is thought that they are adaptations of English books on the subject of cookery and household management. References in the works of the poets show that cookery books were known in Wales before the sixteenth century and service at table, according to Siôn Dafydd *Rhys, was a part of the duty of the *Declaimer.

Gwasanaeth Mair (lit. 'Mary's service'), a religious work (the earliest text of which is in Shrewsbury School MS XI, c.1400), is an anonymous verse translation of a Dominican version of *Officium Parvum Beatae Mariae Virginis*, a short service in honour of the Virgin Mary. It is the only Middle Welsh translation of an ecclesiastical service; its author was well versed in the poetic craft of his day, both free and strict metres.

The work has been edited by Brynley F. Roberts (1961).

Gwasg Gee, see under GEE, THOMAS (1815–98).

Gwasg Gwynedd, see under OWEN, GERALLT LLOYD (1944–   ).

Gwasg y Brython, see under EVANS, HUGH (1854–1934).

Gwasg y Dref Wen, see under BOORE, WALTER HUGH (1904–   ).

Gwawdodyn and **Gwawdodyn Hir**, see under TWENTY-FOUR METRES.

Gweirydd ap Rhys, see PRYSE, ROBERT JOHN (1807–89).

Gweledigaetheu y Bardd Cwsc (lit. 'The visions of the sleeping poet'; 1703), the prose masterpiece of Ellis *Wynne, was based on free translations by Roger L'Estrange and an author known as 'J.S.' (probably John Stevens) of *Los Suenos* (1627), a work by the Spanish writer, Quevedo. Wynne's version, written from the viewpoint of a Welsh Tory and Churchman, contains three 'visions'—the Vision of the World's Course, the Vision of Death in his Nether Kingdom and the Vision of Hell—and the passing of sinners through life and death to Hell is portrayed satirically under these heads. The book has been highly praised for its powerful Welsh and it had a lasting influence on the development of prose-writing in the language. Annotated versions of the text were edited by John Morris-Jones (1898) and Aneirin Lewis (1960). The work was translated into English by George Borrow (1860), by Robert Gwyneddon Davies (1897) and by T. Gwynn Jones (1940) under the title *The Visions of the Sleeping Bard*. For a discussion of the work's historical background and the author's ideas, see Gwyn Thomas, *Y Bardd Cwsg a'i Gefndir* (1971) and the same author's essay on Ellis Wynne in the *Writers of Wales* series (1984).

Gwên, see under CANU LLYWARCH HEN (9th or 10th cent.).

Gwen o'r Ddôl, see under DAFYDD NANMOR (fl. 1450–80).

Gwen Teirbron, see under CADFAN (mid-6th cent.).

Gwen Tomos (1894), the fourth and last novel of Daniel *Owen, was first published in weekly parts in Y *Cymro in 1893 and the year following. Unlike his other novels, it depicts life in the rural hinterland of Mold, Flints., during the decades before the author's birth. The two narrators are Rheinallt, who marries the eponymous heroine, and the author himself, a device which tends to blur the focus and make for some awkwardness in the development of the plot. The story opens dramatically with a cock-fighting scene, a prelude to the fight between Gwen's brother, Harri, and the squire's son, reflecting the conflict between the old-established *Anglicanism and the uncompromising idealism of the new Methodists. Later, Gwen sees the death of her father and her drunkard brother, Harri. Her marriage to her distant cousin, Rheinallt, causes consternation in the Methodist chapel of which she is a member. Finally, and unwillingly, she emigrates with her husband to America, where she dies of a broken heart. The book contains two famous mysteries: one concerning the murder of Dafydd Ifans, the gamekeeper, and the other the identity of Gwen's parents. It is the best constructed of Owen's novels, but there are some implausible coincidences towards the end. The author's great talent for characterization was not yet spent when he wrote this book: among the most memorable portraits are those of Robert Wynn of Pantybuarth, the colourful Nansi'r Nant and her outlaw son, Twm.

A revised edition of *Gwen Tomos* in modern Welsh orthography was published by Thomas Parry in 1937 and an English translation by T. Ceiriog Williams and E. R. Harries in 1963. The novel is discussed by W. Beynon Davies in *Ysgrifau Beirniadol V* (ed. J. E. Caerwyn Williams, 1970), by D. Tecwyn Lloyd in *Y Traethodydd* (1964) and by R. Gerallt Jones in *Ansawdd y Seiliau* (1972).

Gwenallt, see JONES, DAVID JAMES (1899–1968).

Gwenddolau (6th cent.), a chieftain of the Coeling family in the *Old North who fell at the battle of Arfderydd in 573. His memory may be preserved in the place-name Carwinley (Caer Wenddolau, 'Gwenddolau's fort'), near Longtown, Cumbria. He was mourned by *Myrddin in 'Yr *Afallennau' and 'Yr Oianau' and later developed into a figure of legend. According to one of the Triads, his war-band continued to wage battle for several weeks after its leader's death. In another Triad, more hostile to him, it is stated that he owned two birds, with a yoke of gold on them, which fed upon the corpses of the Britons. *Geoffrey of Monmouth, in his *Vita Merlini*, records him as Guennolous, King of

Scotland, who fought against Peredurus, Merlinus and Rodarchus.

Gwenddydd, see under CYFOESI MYRDDIN A GWENDDYDD (c.1300) and PUM BREUDDWYD GWENDDYDD.

Gwenffrewi or **Gwenfrewy** or **Winefred** (7th cent.), a saint of whom more than one Life was composed, works which contain traditions and folk-beliefs rather than genuine history. Her father was Tevyth, a native of *Englefield (Tegeingl), and according to the saints' genealogies her mother was Gwenlo, the daughter of Insi, King of *Powys. There was some connection between Gwenffrewi and *Beuno, who is described as her uncle in late genealogies. It is said that she was raped and killed by a prince named Caradog, but was later restored to life by Beuno. From the spot where her blood had fallen there sprang a well, the waters of which had healing powers; it is now known as St. Winefred's Well, Holywell, Flints. In other accounts of Gwenffrewi's life she is said to have gone on a pilgrimage to Rome and to have spent her last years with saint Eleri in Gwytherin, Denbs. There she was buried, but it is also claimed that her remains were moved to Shrewsbury in 1138. Many miracles are attributed to Gwenffrewi, but very few churches bear her name. Her renown spread in the later Middle Ages and there are many references to her in the work of Welsh poets. Even after the Protestant Reformation, Holywell (W. Treffynnon) continued to be a popular place of pilgrimage for Roman Catholics. Samuel Johnson saw people washing themselves in the well in 1774 and interest in the place, which is one of the *Seven Wonders of Wales, has persisted to the present day.

Gwenhwyfar, the wife of King *Arthur, is also known by the French form of her name, Guenièvre or Guinevere. Some sources refer to her as the daughter of Ogrfran Gawr. There are traces of a fable concerning Gwenhwyfar, *Cai and *Melwas in the series of ancient *englynion* known as *'Ymddiddan Arthur a Gwenhwyfar'*, now lost and surviving only in a more recent version. The Life of *Gildas by *Caradog of Llancarfan (pre–1136) tells how Melwas abducted her and imprisoned her in Glastonbury for a year. The same fable is found in *Le Chevalier de la Charette* by Chrétien de Troyes. In *Geoffrey of Monmouth's *Historia Regum Britanniae* (1136) it is claimed that Gwenhwyfar was of noble Roman stock and had been brought up in the court of *Cadwr, the Earl of Cornwall, that she committed adultery with *Medrod (Medrawd), Arthur's nephew, and ended her days as a nun in Caerleon. The testimony of *Gerald de Barri (Giraldus Cambrensis), who visited Glastonbury in 1192 and was present at the exhumation of two corpses said to be those of Arthur and Gwenhwyfar, was that a leaden cross was found on which, after the name of Arthur, the words '*cum Wenneveria uxore sua seconda*' were inscribed. This is the only suggestion that Gwenhwyfar was Arthur's second wife. Ralph of Coggeshall and later, John Leland, though they verify the cross and the description of Arthur, make no mention of the addition made by Gerald. According to the Triads, Gwenhwyfar was even less chaste than the 'Three Lewd Women of the Isle of Britain', for she had humiliated the best of men and was the cause of the battle of *Camlan. She is also mentioned in *Y *Tair Rhamant* where her honour is avenged by both Peredur and Geraint. See also HERO'S MARRIAGE WITH SOVEREIGNTY.

Gwenllian (d. 1136), a warrior-lady of *Deheubarth, was the daughter of *Gruffudd ap Cynan, King of *Gwynedd, and the wife of Gruffudd, the son of Rhys ap Tewdwr, the last king of Deheubarth. After the death of Henry I in 1135, a general rising was planned in south Wales against the Norman settlements there. While her husband was in Gwynedd appealing to her father for help, Gwenllian led the forces of Deheubarth against the castle of *Kidwelly, only to be routed and killed by the forces of Maurice de Londres at a spot known thereafter as Maes Gwenllian ('Gwenllian's field').

Gwennan Gorn, see under MADOG (1918).

Gwent, a *gwlad* of south-east Wales, divided by Wentwood into Gwent Uwch Coed and Gwent Is Coed. The Welsh kingdom of Gwent, which had its origins in the administrative system established by the Romans at Caer-went, lasted from the fifth to the eleventh century. Its rulers were also the kings of *Glywysing and from 974, if not from 665, the joint kingdom was known as *Morgannwg. On the eve of the *Norman Conquest, its probable ruler was Caradog ap Gruffudd ap Rhydderch whose descendants were to retain a degree of authority at Caerleon until the thirteenth century. By 1070 the kingdom of Gwent had been overrun by the forces of William Fitz Osbern, Earl of Hereford, and its territory was parcelled out among about a dozen Marcher lordships until 1536. The county of Monmouth, created in that year, consisted of almost the whole of the ancient *gwlad* together with the cantref of *Gwynllŵg. The modern county of Gwent, established in 1974, lost parts of Gwynllŵg but gained Brynmawr and Gilwern from what had been the county of Brecon.

Gwenynen Gwent, see HALL, AUGUSTA WADDINGTON (1802–96).

GWERFUL MECHAIN (fl. 1462–1500), poet. Little is known about her except that she was of

*Mechain in Powys; one of her *cywyddau* suggests that she may have kept a tavern. *Dafydd Llwyd of Mathafarn exchanged poems with her and sent *Llywelyn ap Gutun as a love-messenger on his behalf. She is famous as a writer of salacious verse, although the most accomplished poem of this type attributed to her, namely a *cywydd* describing the male sexual organ, is more probably the work of *Dafydd ap Gwilym. Often technically lax, she nevertheless excels in her poem on Christ's Passion and in another in defence of women which was written in response to a *cywydd* by *Ieuan Dyfi.

Gwerin (lit. 'Folk'), a term meaning either the people in general without reference to social class (probably the original sense) or else the common people in contradistinction to the gentry. The second meaning began to emerge as a result of egalitarian ideas which gained a wider currency in the wake of religious and political events during the eighteenth and nineteenth centuries, when the common people came to be idealized and regarded as the main upholders of Welsh culture. This concept, associated with an emphasis on education, *Temperance and *Radicalism, is to be detected particularly in the work of Owen M. *Edwards, both as writer and publisher, but is also clearly reflected in the work of writers such as William Crwys *Williams, John *Morris-Jones, W. J. *Gruffydd and Iorwerth C. *Peate. The term was used as the title of a political society which is described in the next entry.

Gwerin (lit. 'Folk'), a group founded in 1935 at the University College of North Wales, Bangor, by Goronwy Roberts and others in an attempt to marry the principles of *Socialism and Welsh *Nationalism. Its allegations of Fascist tendencies among the leaders of *Plaid Cymru were brought to a head in 1942 in a St. David's Day speech to the Honourable Society of *Cymmrodorion at Cardiff by Thomas *Jones, the Deputy Secretary to the Cabinet at Westminster, which was later published as a pamphlet, *The Native Never Returns* (1942). An article on similar lines was published by Gwilym *Davies, secretary of the Welsh League of Nations Union, in the magazine *Y *Traethodydd*, to which Saunders *Lewis and J. E. Daniel replied in their pamphlet, *The Party for Wales* (1942). In the following year, during the controversy generated by the campaign on behalf of W. J. *Gruffydd as Liberal candidate for the University of Wales seat in the House of Commons, in opposition to the Nationalist candidate, Saunders Lewis, those associated with *Gwerin*, such as Harri *Gwynn, D. Tecwyn *Lloyd and Iorwerth C. *Peate, were mostly to be found in the Gruffydd camp. The society failed, however, to develop any impetus of its own and did not continue after the Second World War, its members dispersing into

the ranks of *Plaid Cymru* and the Labour Party. Goronwy Roberts became the Labour Member of Parliament for Caernarfon in 1945 and, in 1974, was elevated to the peerage.

Gwernyclepa, see under IFOR AP LLYWELYN (*fl.* 1340–60).

Gwernyfed, see under ANATIOMAROS (1925).

Gwidigada, one of the seven commots of *Cantref Mawr in *Ystrad Tywi, was linked in the thirteenth century with the commots of Derllys and *Elfed to form the core of what later became the county of Carmarthen.

Gwili, see JENKINS, JOHN (1872–1936).

GWILYM AB IEUAN HEN (*fl.* 1440–80), poet. About thirty of his poems have survived in manuscript, although the authorship of some is doubtful. They include religious poems, love-poems, request poems and a number of masterly elegies and eulogies to patrons, many of whom had their homes in *Powys.

GWILYM AP SEFNYN (*fl.* 1408), poet. A supporter of *Owain Glyndŵr, he forfeited his land in Llandyfrydog, Ang., as a result of the rising. Five of his *cywyddau* are addressed to Gwilym ap Gruffudd of Penrhyn, Llandygái. In another he chides the Menai Straits and the river Ogwen, the waters of which prevented him from visiting Cochwillan, the home of Robin ap Gruffudd, Gwilym's brother. His best poems are two *cywyddau* composed in old age, an elegy for his ten children who predeceased him, and a confessional poem. If a vaticinatory poem is correctly attributed to him, he was still alive during the Wars of the Roses.

Gwilym Callestr, see EDWARDS, WILLIAM (1790–1855).

Gwilym Cowlyd, see ROBERTS, WILLIAM JOHN (1828–1904).

Gwilym Cyfeiliog, see WILLIAMS, WILLIAM (1801–76).

GWILYM DDU O ARFON (*fl.* 1280–1320), a poet of the period immediately following the death of *Llywelyn ap Gruffudd, the last Prince of independent Wales, in 1282. Gwilym's poem to his patron, Sir Gruffudd Llwyd, an Arfon man of high degree who was imprisoned in Rhuddlan Castle, and his elegy for the poet *Trahaearn Brydydd Mawr, reflect the plight of the court poets during the crisis and for some while afterwards.

Gwilym Deudraeth, see EDWARDS, WILLIAM THOMAS (1863–1940).

Gwilym Ganoldref, see MIDLETON, WILLIAM (c. 1550–c. 1600).

Gwilym Gellideg, see MORGAN, WILLIAM (1808–78).

Gwilym Hiraethog, see REES, WILLIAM (1802–83).

Gwilym Lleyn, see ROWLANDS, WILLIAM (1802–65).

Gwilym Marles, see THOMAS, WILLIAM (1834–79).

Gwilym Morgannwg, see WILLIAMS, THOMAS (1778–1835).

Gwilym Pant Taf, see PARRY, WILLIAM (1836–1903).

GWILYM RYFEL (*fl.* 1174), poet. From an *englyn* by *Gruffudd ap Gwrgenau in a series lamenting the loss of his friends, it appears that Gwilym was a native of *Powys and that he was killed in battle far from home. All that has survived of his work consists of two rather conventional sequences of intercessionary *englynion* to *Dafydd ab Owain Gwynedd which were composed about 1174 when Dafydd ruled the greater part of *Gwynedd. More than a century later the poet Iorwerth Beli included Gwilym with *Llywarch ap Llywelyn (Prydydd y Moch), *Cynddelw Brydydd Mawr and *Dafydd Benfras among the '*prifeirdd heirdd, hardd weision cuddawn*' ('the splendid chief poets, fine sons of rare talent'). Because he would not have been given this status on the strength of the surviving *englynion*, it seems probable that Gwilym Ryfel was one of those court poets whose work, in large part, has been lost.

A study of his work was published by J. E. Caerwyn Williams in *Ysgrifau Beirniadol X* (1977).

Gwilym Teilo, see DAVIES, WILLIAM (1831–92).

GWILYM TEW (*fl.* 1460–80), poet, of *Tir Iarll, Glam., was either the son of Rhys Brydydd or his brother. He wrote two *awdlau* to the shrine of the Virgin Mary at Penrhys, Rhondda, as well as several love-poems and others in praise of patrons. It is believed that he owned *The Book of Aneirin* (see under GODODDIN) and among his manuscripts is one which includes copies of the Triads, a list of treasures, two vocabularies and a small collection of genealogies.

Gwion Bach, see under TALIESIN (*fl.* 6th cent.).

'Gwir yn erbyn y Byd, Y' (lit. 'The truth against the world'), the motto of *Gorsedd Beirdd Ynys Prydain*, was devised by Iolo Morganwg

(Edward *Williams). Seen on the regalia of the *Gorsedd* and heard during its ceremonies, it is much quoted in other contexts, both religious and political.

Gwlad y Gân (lit. 'The land of song'), a name for Wales dating from about 1876 when Welsh choirs began winning prizes at international music festivals, is one of the commonest clichés in the country's cultural life. That the Welsh had an ability to sing 'in parts, with many modes and phrases' was noted by *Gerald de Barri (Giraldus Cambrensis) in the twelfth century. But it was the vogue for harp-music in the eighteenth century and the growth of the tonic solfa movement in the nineteenth, under the impetus of *Nonconformity, which won for Wales a reputation as 'The Land of Song'. The widespread belief that all Welsh people are endowed with naturally melodious voices gives a special piquancy, in Dylan *Thomas's *Under Milk Wood* (1954), to the comment by the Reverend *Eli Jenkins on the wanton singing of *Polly Garter: 'Praise the Lord! We are a musical nation'. Nevertheless, communal singing is still popular in Wales and is to be heard at its most powerful in chapels and public houses and at rugby-matches. More formally, the tradition is maintained by numerous male voice choirs to a standard of excellence which is widely acknowledged as an integral part of Welsh culture. See also the next entry.

Gwlad y Menig Gwynion (lit. 'Land of the white gloves'), one of the names for Wales which were popular in late Victorian times, refers to the custom of presenting judges with white gloves when there were no cases for them to try. It derived from an idealized view of the country, not unaffected by the accusations of the *Blue Books, which held that the Welsh, in comparison with the English, were a people among whom serious crime was virtually unknown. This view is borne out to some extent by crime statistics for the period, at least by those pertaining to the indigenous inhabitants of rural areas as distinct from the incoming population of industrial south-east Wales. In its exaggerated form it gave rise to a myth of *Cymru lân a Chymru lonydd* ('A clean and peaceful Wales') which was to find one of its last manifestations in Richard Llewellyn's novel, *How Green was my Valley* (1939). For similar reasons, the names '*Gwlad y Breintiau Mawr*' ('Land of great privileges'), '*Gwlad y Cymanfaoedd*' ('Land of religious assemblies') and '*Gwlad y Diwygiadau*' ('Land of revivals') were also applied to Wales. See also the previous entry.

Gwlad yr Haf (lit. 'The land of summer'), the name given by Iolo Morganwg (Edward *Williams) to the original home of the Welsh people, from whence he claimed they had come to

Britain under the leadership of *Hu Gadarn. Iolo derived the name from an allusion in The *Book of Taliesin to 'deproffani ynys' (Deffrobani), which is the 'Taprobanes insula' of Isidore of Seville, that is Ceylon, said to have been the first home of the human race. In his own translation of the Triads, Iolo rendered the name as 'the Summer Country' or 'Summerland', but when he added that it was 'where Constantinople now is' he was misled by his remembrance of *Iolo Goch's 'Cywydd y Llafurwr', with its statement to the effect that Hu Gadarn had been Emperor of Constantinople. The name should not be confused with the Welsh name for Somerset, also Gwlad yr Haf.

Gwladgarwr, Y (lit. 'The patriot'), a monthly periodical of which 102 numbers were published between 1833 and 1841. It was edited by Evan *Evans (Ieuan Glan Geirionydd) and printed in Chester until 1835, after which it was edited by Hugh Jones (Erfyl; 1789–1858) and printed in Liverpool. The magazine's aim was to extend its readers' general knowledge and among its contents were to be found Scriptural exposition, substantial but anonymous articles on astronomy, farming, geography and the rudiments of music, together with biographies and much verse by contemporary poets. This was a periodical with wide interests and it remains a valuable document of the intellectual life of its period. See also the next entry.

Gwladgarwr, Y (lit. 'The patriot'), a weekly newspaper published in Aberdare, Glam., between 1858 and 1884. It was established by some of the most prominent men in the town, including David Williams (Alaw Goch), Abraham Mason and William Williams (Carw Coch). Lewis William *Lewis (Llew Llwyfo) and John *Roberts (Ieuan Gwyllt) were among its editors. The newspaper, which had a wide circulation in the industrial valleys of south Wales, was of Liberal sympathies and supported the cause of the working class and *Nonconformity, but it had scarcely any political influence. It was more important as a literary journal mainly by virtue of its poetry column which was edited by William *Williams (Caledfryn), William *Thomas (Islwyn) and others. Although he was inclined to be harsh in his criticism, Caledfryn gave a number of young poets their first opportunity of seeing their verse in print. See also the previous entry.

Gwladus Ddu (d. 1251), the daughter of *Llywelyn ap Iorwerth (Llywelyn Fawr) who, in furtherance of his policy of alliance with powerful Marcher families, gave her in marriage in 1215 to Reginald de Braose (d. 1228) and in 1230 to Ralph Mortimer (d. 1246). The latter union made the Mortimers, and subsequently the Dukes of York, the direct descendants of

Llywelyn Fawr, enabling David *Powel in the sixteenth century to claim that Queen Elizabeth I, while inheriting England through her grandfather, Henry VII, had inherited Wales through her grandmother, Elizabeth of York, the descendant of Gwladus Ddu. The laconic note on the death of Gwladus Ddu in *Brut y Tywysogyon inspired a poem by Griffith John *Williams.

Gwlyddyn Saer, the builder of Ehangwen, *Arthur's hall, in the tale of *Culhwch and Olwen, is slain by *Twrch Trwyth.

Gŵr Pen y Bryn (lit. 'The master of Pen y Bryn'; 1923), the only full-length novel of E. Tegla *Davies. Its background is the *Tithe Wars of the 1880s, when many Nonconformist farmers refused to pay the tithe towards the upkeep of the Church of England, some suffering for their stand. The hasty heroism of John Williams, the tenant of Pen y Bryn, a large, prosperous farm, crumbles under the threat of eviction and blackmail, and he seeks purification from his shame in spiritual conversion. The first appearance of the novel was well received but, when it was reprinted in 1926, its theme and moralizing were severely criticized and the novel fell under a cloud. By now, however, despite its deficiencies, it is regarded as one of the important pioneering novels in Welsh by virtue of its skilful construction, its sometimes dignified prose, some memorable characters and its perceptive study of a soul in torment.

The book's virtues and defects are discussed by D. Tecwyn Lloyd in Edward Tegla Davies, Llenor a Phroffwyd (ed. Islwyn Ffowc Elis, 1956); an English translation by Nina Watkins appeared under the title The Master of Pen y Bryn in 1975.

Gwrach y Rhibyn, an apparition in the shape of a huge woman said to be a premonition of ill fortune or death; she appeared in foggy weather and was recognizable by her loud and terrible scream. See also CORS FOCHNO.

Gwreiddiau (lit. 'Roots'; 1959), a volume of poetry by Gwenallt (David James *Jones). Although the themes from his earlier works reappear here, the voice of the prophet and satirist is louder than before. The central poem is 'Jezebel ac Elias', a long, allegorical poem which attempts to interpret the crisis in European civilization, but equally significant is a series of englynion satirizing the self-importance of modern, scientific Man. Other poems describe Gwenallt's spiritual pilgrimage, castigating his early agnosticism and humanism, rejecting the Romantic notion of the poet's function and insisting that the Muse must be subject to God.

Gwrhyr Gwalstawd Ieithoedd (lit. 'Gwrhyr interpreter of tongues'), one of *Arthur's men in the tale of *Culhwch and Olwen, is able to speak all languages, including those of the birds and the beasts. He uses his talent on behalf of Culhwch and his friends to address Custennin Heusor and his wife, *Wrnach's door-keeper, the animals in the tale of the *Oldest Animals, *Mabon fab Modron in his prison at Gloucester and *Twrch Trwyth and his seven little pigs.

Gwri, see PRYDERI.

Gwrnerth, see under YMDDIDDAN LLYWELYN A GWRNERTH.

Gwrtheyrn, see VORTIGERN (early 5th cent.).

Gwrtheyrnion or **Gwerthrynion**, a commot of southern *Powys lying between *Buellt and *Maelienydd, of which the ruling house claimed descent from Gwrtheyrn (*Vortigern). The Mortimer family and the descendants of Elystan Glodrydd fought for control of the commot but in 1256 it was seized by *Llywelyn ap Gruffudd, who held it until 1276. Thereafter it was part of the territories of the Mortimer family, becoming a Crown lordship when the Duke of York succeeded to the throne of England in 1460.

Gwyddbwyll (lit. 'Wood-sense'), a game which is identified with chess only in a popular misconception. There are numerous references to board-games in Welsh and Irish literature but little information is given about their precise nature, other than that they were played on lavishly fabricated boards. In the Dream of *Macsen, for example, the hero has a vision in which he sees two auburn-haired youths playing the game with golden pieces on a silver board. The game takes on supernatural qualities in *Y* *Tair Rhamant*: Peredur, in the Castle of Wonders, sees two sets of *gwyddbwyll* playing against each other with no human hand to move them. The set he supports loses the game, the other raises a shout, 'as if they were men', and he hurls the board angrily into a lake. A third reference is that in *Breuddwyd Rhonabwy*: *Arthur and Owain sit before a silver board playing one game of *gwyddbwyll* after another but their play is interrupted by a succession of young men who ask Owain why he allows his ravens to be harassed by the Emperor's men. It has been suggested that this is an allegorical representation of the battle of Mount Badon and it may be compared with the incident in the Icelandic saga in which Frithiof and Bjorn play at *hnefatafl*, a medieval hunt-game. See also FOX AND GEESE.

For further details see Frank Lewis, 'Gwerin Ffristial a Thawlbwrdd' in the *Transactions* of the Honourable Society of Cymmrodorion (1941) and Rachel Bromwich, *Trioedd Ynys Prydein* (1961); see also the note by Glyn M. Ashton in *Llên Cymru* (vol. X, nos. 3 and 4, 1969).

Gwydderig, see WILLIAMS, RICHARD (1842–1917).

Gwyddno Garanhir, a character who belonged to the heroic tradition of the *Old North, is said in *Bonedd Gwŷr y Gogledd* to have been a descendant of Dyfnwal Hen. Early tales about him were connected with maritime traditions, especially the flooding of coastal districts in north and west Wales, the most famous of which is the story of *Cantre'r Gwaelod. The name Caer Wyddno was given to a group of rocks eight miles out to sea from Aberystwyth. The poem 'Seithennin Saf Allan' in The *Black Book of Carmarthen* refers to the sea drowning Maes Gwyddneu, but its location is not given. In the tale of *Culhwch and Olwen, one of the feats imposed on the hero by Ysbaddaden Bencawr is the procuring of Gwyddneu's basket for the wedding-feast, for it is an inexhaustible source of food. An early poem consisting of a discourse between Gwyddneu and *Gwyn ap Nudd tells how the former is defeated in battle but is then given hospitality. In *Hanes Taliesin* the child *Taliesin is discovered by *Elffin, the son of Gwyddno, in a coracle at Gwyddno's weir on the beach between the river Dyfi and Aberystwyth.

Gwyddoniadur Cymreig, Y (lit. 'The Welsh encyclopaedia'; 10 vols., 1854–79), an encyclopaedia published by Thomas *Gee under the general editorship of his brother-in-law, John Parry (1812–74), a lecturer at the Calvinistic Methodist College at Bala. After Parry's death, Gee assumed the editorship and was responsible for the second edition which appeared between 1889 and 1896. A work of nearly nine thousand pages, the longest ever undertaken in Welsh, it includes a substantial core of theological material but also a wealth of information on geographical, scientific, literary, Welsh and Celtic subjects. Its value to the modern reader is mainly as a mirror of thought and scholarship in the nineteenth century but many of the biographical articles on eminent Welshmen are still useful. Among the contributors to the second edition, some two hundred in all, were Owen M. *Edwards and John *Morris-Jones; the latter's article on the Welsh language was the seed from which grew his monumental work, *A Welsh Grammar, Historical and Comparative* (1913).

There is an account of the history of the publishing of the encyclopaedia in *Llên Cymru* (vols. IX, 1967 and XII, 1973) by R. Jones Williams.

Gwydion fab Dôn, a magician, one of the chief characters in the Fourth Branch of *Pedair Cainc y Mabinogi. Astute and aggressive, he attempts to help his brother Gilfaethwy who is in love with Goewin, the virgin who is the foot-holder of *Math fab Mathonwy. Gilfaethwy's passion is hopeless because Math cannot be separated from Goewin except when there is war in the land. Gwydion therefore arranges a conflict between *Gwynedd and *Deheubarth in order to cause Math to leave his court at Caer Dathl.

He visits *Pryderi at Rhuddlan Teifi and deceives him with gifts which prove to be illusory. Pryderi pursues Gwydion to Gwynedd and, by means of magic as well as force, is defeated at Y Felenrhyd. Meanwhile, because Gilfaethwy has raped Goewin, the two brothers are punished by Math who turns them into animals and causes them to have children by one another. Gwydion spends three years in the forms of a stag, a wild sow and a wolf. He is also involved with Math in the creation of *Blodeuwedd as a wife for *Lleu, the son of his sister, Aranrhod. After Blodeuwedd's adultery with Gronw Pebr, Gwydion wanders through Gwynedd and *Powys in search of Lleu, finding him in the guise of an eagle, and it is he who turns Blodeuwedd into an owl.

From references in several poems connected with the tale of *Taliesin, which are consistent with the account in the Fourth Branch, it seems there was once a larger body of literature about Gwydion than that preserved in the *Mabinogi*. The Milky Way is known in Welsh as Caer Gwydion ('Gwydion's fortress').

For further details see Rachel Bromwich, *Trioedd Ynys Prydein* (1978).

Gwydir, see under WYNN FAMILY.

Gwyliedydd, Y (lit. 'The observer'; 1877–1909; *Y Gwyliedydd Newydd*, lit. 'The new observer'; 1910–   ), a newspaper launched by Wesleyans for the propagation of their denomination's viewpoint as opposed to that of *Baner ac Amserau Cymru*, in which they were sometimes criticized. It was edited by ministers, among whom the most prominent were John Hughes (Glanystwyth; 1842–1902), T. R. Marsden, W. Hugh Evans (Gwyllt y Mynydd; 1831–1909), J. Ellis *Williams, E. H. Griffiths (1851–1932) and George Brewer. Like other denominational papers, it carried local and national news during its early years and often attacked Toryism and the Established Church.

Gwylliaid Cochion Mawddwy (lit. 'The red bandits of Mawddwy'), a band of thieves who lived in the Mawddwy and Cwm Dugoed areas of Merioneth in the sixteenth century. The earliest reference to them occurs in Thomas *Pennant's *Tours of Wales* (1778) where it is said that eighty of their number were hanged and buried by order of Judge Lewis Owen (d. 1555) near the farm known as Collfryn. It is a historical fact that the judge, who made determined efforts to uphold the rule of law as Sheriff of Merioneth, was murdered in Dugoed Mawddwy while on his way home to Dolgellau from the assizes at Welshpool. The tale of the bandits has since been richly embroidered in several popular traditions, as several place-names in the district testify, and it is said that the red hair which is a feature of the physical characteristics of many of the inhabitants of north-west Wales was inherited from them.

Gwyn ap Nudd, a mythological figure portrayed in early Welsh literature as king of the *Tylwyth Teg or of *Annwfn, the Otherworld. In his poem '*Y Niwl*', *Dafydd ap Gwilym refers to '*tylwyth Gwyn*' and in *The *Black Book of Carmarthen* it is Gwyn ap Nudd who leads the pack of dogs known in folk literature as *Cŵn Annwn*. In the tale of *Culhwch and Olwen he is condemned by *Arthur to fight with Gwythyr fab Greidawl for the hand of *Creiddylad, the daughter of Lludd Llaw Ereint, on the first day of May every year until the Day of Judgement. It is supposed that Nudd is the Brythonic name of the god Nudons or Nodens whose sanctuary was discovered in Lydney Park, Glos.

For further details see the note by Brynley F. Roberts in *Llên Cymru* (vol. XIII, nos. 3 and 4, 1980–81).

Gwyn Erfyl, see JONES, GWYN ERFYL (1924–   ).

GWYN, DAVID (*fl.* 1580), sailor, spy and versifier. His fancied exploits against the Armada were the subject of a ballad by Sir Lewis *Morris. The Huntington Library has the only known copy of his *Certaine English Verses* (1588), three unctuous paeans to Queen Elizabeth I.

GWYN, RICHARD or **RHISIART**, also known as **RICHARD WHITE** (*c.*1557–84), the first Catholic martyr in Wales. Born at Llanidloes, Mont., of a Protestant family, he left St. John's College, Cambridge, in 1562 to keep school in the district of Wrexham where, under the influence of Father John Bennett, he became a convert to *Roman Catholicism. Fined and imprisoned several times for his refusal to conform, he rattled his chains so loudly, when forcibly taken to church on one occasion, that the preacher could not be heard. After his conviction for refusing to recognize Elizabeth as Head of the Church of England, he spent four years in prison under torture and, on 15 October 1584, he was hanged, drawn and quartered. He was canonized by Pope Paul VI in 1970 as one of the *Forty Martyrs of England and Wales.

The five poems in which he defended his faith were edited by T. H. Parry-Williams, *Carolau Richard White* (1931).

GWYN, ROBERT, also known as **ROBERT JONES, ROBERT WYN** and **ROBERT JOHNS GWYN** (*c.*1540/50–1592/1604), Recusant, was the most prolific Welsh writer of the Elizabethan age. The son of Siôn Wyn ap Thomas Gruffudd of *Penyberth, near Pwllheli, Caerns., and of Catrin the daughter of Siôn ap Robert ap Llywelyn of Castellmarch, he was brought up in a home which had conformed with the Anglican ecclesiastical order. In 1568 he graduated from Corpus Christi College,

Oxford, and was persuaded by Robert Owen of Plas-du, a law student at Douai, to join the exiled Catholic community there in 1571; he graduated in 1575 and was ordained priest.

While at Douai he wrote *Nad oes vn Ffydd onyd yr wir Ffydd* and *Gwasanaeth y Gwŷr Newydd* which together form part of the manuscript known as *Lanter Gristnogawl*. On his return to Wales he was sent on mission to Llŷn, Maelor, the Usk Valley and probably to Glamorgan and Gwent. It is known that he met his co-religionists Robert Persons and Edmund Campion at Uxbridge in 1580 to discuss how best to overcome the legal restrictions on publishing Catholic works, and that he was given refuge at Werngochyn, near Abergavenny, in 1586. He was also associated with Siôn Dafydd *Rhys, the grammarian, in the clandestine printing of books.

He is chiefly remembered as the possible author of *Y Drych Cristionogawl*, a work dealing with 'the Four Last Things', which survives in a manuscript of 1600; part of it was printed in 1586-87 in a cave on the Little Orme, near Llandudno, Caerns. Among other texts which may confidently be attributed to Robert Gwyn are *Coelio'r Saint* (c.1590), *Tretys ar Ddiwinyddiaeth Foesol* and a Welsh translation of an English manual on meditation.

For further details see Geraint Bowen's introduction to his edition of *Gwasanaeth y Gwŷr Newydd* (1970) and the same author's chapter in *Y Traddodiad Rhyddiaith* (1970); the connection between Robert Gwyn and the family of Penyberth was first demonstrated by W. Gerallt Harries in an article in the *Bulletin* of the Board of Celtic Studies (1974).

Gwynedd, a kingdom established in the period after the departure of the Romans from Britain. Although it is clear that this was the first of the early kingdoms, little is known of its beginnings. According to the *Historia Brittonum* of *Nennius, the royal lineage was descended from *Cunedda who, it is said, migrated to Gwynedd from Manaw Gododdin in the *Old North, but the accuracy of this tradition remains uncertain. Nevertheless, it is undisputable that a strong kingdom had been established in north-west Wales by the time of *Maelgwn Gwynedd, who ruled over it in the sixth century. With the island of Anglesey, the mountains of *Eryri (Snowdonia) formed the heart of the kingdom but during those periods when it was ruled in its entirety Gwynedd extended eastwards and included *Perfeddwlad (or Gwynedd-is-Conwy), namely the territory lying between the rivers Conwy and Dee, and Meirionnydd. In the ninth century *Rhodri Mawr, King of Gwynedd, extended his authority over *Powys, *Ceredigion and *Ystrad Tywi. This unity did not last but Gwynedd later came to reaffirm its supremacy over the other Welsh kingdoms.

After a period of exceptional power under the government of *Gruffudd ap Llywelyn (d.

1063), Gwynedd suffered internal divisions and attacks by the Normans which almost overwhelmed the kingdom until *Gruffudd ap Cynan began the work of restoration, which was completed by his son *Owain ap Gruffudd (Owain Gwynedd). The kingdom experienced further internal troubles, but these were solved by *Llywelyn ap Iorwerth (Llywelyn Fawr) who succeeded in re-uniting it. Under Llywelyn's government Gwynedd became the cornerstone of a broader unity in Wales as he led the princes of Powys and *Deheubarth against the presumption of King John, persuading them to accept him as their overlord. It was possibly at this time that the scholars of Gwynedd hatched the theory that the court of Gwynedd, namely *Aberffraw, had supremacy over the other courts of Wales and that the other princes were the vassals of the Princes of Gwynedd. The kingdom was united once more by the grandson of Llywelyn ap Iorwerth, namely *Llywelyn ap Gruffudd, and he succeeded in accomplishing the dual feat of persuading the princes of Wales to accept the supremacy of Gwynedd and of making the King of England, Henry III, recognize the *Principality.

The kings of England acknowledged that they would have to shatter the strength of Gwynedd before they would be able to conquer Wales and it was to this purpose that Edward I directed his forces in 1277 and 1282. After the death of Llywelyn at the end of 1282 and the capture of his brother *Dafydd ap Gruffudd in Eryri in the following year, Edward reinforced his hold on Gwynedd by transferring to his lords the greater part of Perfeddwlad, namely the hundreds of *Rhos, *Rhufoniog and the Vale of Clwyd, in order to create new lordships, while keeping Anglesey, Eryri and *Englefield (Tegeingl) for himself. The most revered symbols of the kingdom of Gwynedd—the Crown of Aberffraw and the *Croes Naid*—became the property of the English king; the latter relic, believed to have been a piece of the true Cross, had been passed down the centuries from ruler to ruler. It appears that Edward's awareness of the political heritage of Gwynedd, which he had destroyed, influenced the architecture of the castle built at *Caernarfon as the centre of a new administrative system which was created in Gwynedd uwch Conwy out of the new counties of Anglesey, Caernarfon and Merioneth. These three counties were amalgamated in 1974 to form the present county of Gwynedd.

The history of Gwynedd is reflected in the work of the twelfth- and thirteenth-century poets of Gwynedd, poems which include the masterpieces of *Gwalchmai ap Meilyr and *Cynddelw Brydydd Mawr, *Llywarch ap Llywelyn (Prydydd y Moch), *Dafydd Benfras, *Llygad Gŵr and *Bleddyn Fardd. Many of the events in the Four Branches of *Pedair Cainc y Mabinogi* are located in Gwynedd and this work, together with *Hanes Gruffudd ap Cynan*, provides a valuable introduction to the heritage and psychology of the kingdom.

For further details see J. E. Morris, *The Welsh Wars of Edward I* (1901), J. E. Lloyd, *A History of Wales* (1911), W. H. Waters, *The Edwardian Settlement of North Wales in its Administrative and Legal Aspects* (1935), T. Jones Pierce, *Medieval Welsh Society* (1972), Wendy Davies, *Wales in the Early Middle Ages* (1982) and David Stephenson, *The Governance of Gwynedd* (1984).

Gwyneddigion, The, a literary and cultural society founded in London in 1770. With the exception of Iolo Morganwg (Edward *Williams), most of its members hailed from north Wales; the ability to speak Welsh fluently and a love of harp-music were conditions of membership. Mainly through the influence and wealth of Owen *Jones (Owain Myfyr), the society succeeded in bringing to fruition some of the aims of the *Cymmrodorion Society (1751–87), such as the publication of manuscripts and periodicals. These included the poetry of *Dafydd ap Gwilym (1789), three volumes of *The Myvyrian Archaiology of Wales* (1801–07), and the magazine *Y *Greal* (1805–07).

In its early years the society held debates and after a famous debate on the alleged discovery of America by *Madog ab Owain Gwynedd it collected money to send John *Evans of Waunfawr in search of the 'Welsh Indians'. It also maintained a correspondence with antiquaries and writers, and poetry was often read at its meetings. In 1789 the society became the patron of eisteddfodau, thus initiating a new phase in the literary life of Wales. Among the most notable eisteddfodau held under its auspices were those at Bala in 1793 and Caerwys in 1798. There is no reference to the society after 1837, by which date it may have been merged with the *Cymreigyddion. A literary society for the *London Welsh was formed in 1978 and bears the name of the Gwyneddigion.

For a full account see R. T. Jenkins and Helen Ramage, *A History of the Honourable Society of Cymmrodorion and of the Gwyneddigion and Cymreigyddion Societies 1751–1951* (1951).

GWYNFARDD BRYCHEINIOG (*fl.* 1176), a poet of whom little is known except that, as his name suggests, he may have been a native of what later became Breconshire. Only two of his poems have survived: his *awdl* to *Dewi Sant (St. David) is a patriotic expression of the renewed pride in the native religious and cultural traditions of Wales while his *awdl* to *Rhys ap Gruffudd (The Lord Rhys) may have been written in the year of the eisteddfod held at *Cardigan.

Gwynllŵg or **Wentloog**, a cantref of *Morgannwg lying between the rivers Rhymni and Usk, was named according to tradition after *Gwynllyw (Woollo). After 1090 it became part of the territories of Robert Fitzhammo, lord of Glamorgan, but, with the division of the inheritance of the Clares, the ultimate heirs of Fitzhammo, in 1314, the lords of Gwynllŵg were to differ from those of Glamorgan. From 1347 the lordship was in the hands of the Stafford family, but when Edward Stafford, Duke of Buckingham, was executed in 1521, the lordship fell into the hands of the Crown. It consisted of manorialized lowlands around Newport and the essentially Welsh lordship of Machen.

Gwynllyw or **Woollo** (5th cent.), saint, was the son of Glywys, the king of *Glywysing, and Gwawr, the daughter of Ceredig, son of *Cunedda; his feast-day is 29 March. There are references to him in the Lives of *Cadog and Tatheus but the main source of information about him is the Life of Gwynllyw, written in the twelfth century. He inherited the land between the rivers Usk and Rhymni, which was called *Gwynllŵg (Wentloog) after him. By his wife Gwladus, the daughter of *Brychan Brycheiniog, he was the father of Cadog, but they later lived apart as hermits. The saint's name is commemorated in the parishes of St. Woollos and Pilgwenlli in Newport, Mon.

GWYNN, HARRI (1913–85), poet. Born in London but brought up at Penrhyndeudraeth, Mer., he was a teacher, a civil servant, a farmer in *Eifionydd, a journalist and a broadcaster. He published two volumes of poetry, *Barddoniaeth* (1955) and *Yng Nghoedwigoedd y Sêr* (1975), and a collection of essays, *Y Fuwch a'i Chynffon* (1954).

Gwynne, Arthur, see EVANS, GWYNFIL (1898–1938).

GWYNNETH, JOHN (1490?–1562?), Catholic divine and musician, was born at Castellmarch, Caerns., and educated at Oxford, where he took a doctor's degree in music in 1531. After his ordination as a priest he was involved in controversy, principally with Bishop Bulkley in the Court of Star Chamber, before being granted in 1541 the sinecure of Clynnog Fawr, which he held until his death. As a composer he was among the most eminent of Tudor times and one of his songs was included in Wynkyn de Worde's collection of 1530. He was also a prominent polemicist on behalf of the Catholic faith: several of his theological works, written in English, were attacks on the Protestant John Frith, Tyndale's friend.

Gwŷr Cwm-y-felin, a secret society of Unitarians which was said by Iolo Morganwg (Edward *Williams) to have met at Cwm-y-felin in Betws, *Tir Iarll, Glam., in the seventeenth century. Iolo, who claimed that *Unitarianism had been the creed of Welsh poets down the centuries, also maintained that the society had flourished during his youth. There is some basis for these assertions: most of his teachers had been Nonconformists—some, such as Edward Evans, had been Arians and Siôn *Bradford was a Deist—but Iolo's attempt to connect the early poets with the district of Tir Iarll in this way should be regarded as almost wholly bogus.

Gwyrosydd, see JAMES, DANIEL (1847–1920).

Gwyrthyeu e Wynvydedic Veir (lit. 'Blessed Mary's miracles'), a religious work (the earliest text is in Peniarth MS 14, *c.*1350), is a collection of thirty-two miracles attributed to the Virgin Mary. The direct source is as yet unknown but the work belongs to a large body of religious literature, Latin and vernacular, which was very popular from the twelfth to the thirteenth century.

Gwysaney Manuscripts, The, see LLANNERCH MANUSCRIPTS.

Gymdeithas Genedlaethol Gymreig, Y (lit. 'The Welsh national society'), one of the groups which contributed to the creation of *Plaid Genedlaethol Cymru*, later known as *Plaid Cymru*. Sometimes called '*Y Tair G*', it was formed in 1922 by a number of young Nationalists, including Lewis Valentine and Moses Griffith, at the University College of North Wales, Bangor; E. T. *John was its president and R.

Williams *Parry its chairman. The members met regularly to discuss the problems of Wales; among their proposals were the nationalization of the mining and quarrying industries, the development of hydro-electric power schemes and the recognition of Welsh as an official language in Wales.

Gymerwch chi Sigaret? (lit. 'Will you have a cigarette?'; 1955), a tragedy in three acts by Saunders *Lewis. Loosely based on an incident in the world of Cold War espionage, it tells how Marc, a young political policeman in an East European State, is commissioned to kill (with a pistol disguised as a cigarette-case) the exiled Phugas, who is directing counter-revolutionary activities from Vienna. Phugas is the godfather of Marc's Catholic wife, Iris, and she swears on her rosary never to see him again if he carries out his orders. Marc goes to Vienna but is prevented from pulling the trigger when he glimpses Iris's rosary which she has concealed in the case. He joins Phugas, knowing that his wife, who is expecting a child, will almost certainly die at the hands of the secret police, but also believing that his soul will be saved by her sacrifice. A metaphysical thriller, the play was graced in its first performance by the acting, in the part of Iris, of the young Siân Phillips.

The play was translated into English by Joseph Clancy under the title *Have a Cigarette?* (1985). For a discussion of the play's merits see the essay by Dafydd Marks in *Ysgrifau Beirniadol X* (ed. J. E. Caerwyn Williams, 1977).

H

Ha! Ha! Among the Trumpets (1945), Alun
*Lewis's second and posthumous collection of
poems, has a foreword by Robert Graves
(whom he had sought as mentor) and contains
forty-eight poems arranged in three sections:
England, the Voyage, and India. The third,
larger than the first two sections combined,
charts the flux of the poet's life and thought
between the English spring of 1942 and the
Indian autumn of 1943. The impact of India and
army life upon his sensibilities, the remnants of
conventional religious belief and the bonds of
love are continuing themes explored in these
lyrical, reflective and allegorical poems. The
volume's title is taken from the Book of Job
39:25: 'He saith among the trumpets, Ha, ha; and
he smelleth the battle afar off, the thunder of the
captains, and the shouting'.

'Haf, Yr' (lit. 'The summer'), the *awdl* with
which Robert Williams *Parry won the *Chair
at the National Eisteddfod in 1910, is one of the
most famous of all Welsh poems written for
competition. Using the same metre as that in T.
Gwynn *Jones's '*Gwlad y Bryniau*', it employs
the image of summer at its zenith, then at its
waning and its lingering in the hope of a new
spring. The poet later rejected the poem's aestheticism and parodied it in '*Yr Hwyaden*', but at
the time of its composition the poem represented
a brave attempt to face Death by a man who was
unable to believe in personal resurrection.
Melodious and verbally rich in the manner of
Keats, the *awdl* gave its title to Williams Parry's
first collection of poems, *Yr Haf a Cherddi Eraill*
(1924) and the poet was known thereafter as
'Bardd yr Haf' ('The Poet of Summer').

Hafgan, see under ARAWN.

Hafod, see under JOHNES, THOMAS (1748–1816).

Hafod a hendre, the practice of moving sheep
and cattle to upland pastures in summer, the
owners accompanying their stock. The *hendre*
('old settlement'), in contrast to the *hafod* ('summer settlement'), was usually situated in one of
the more fertile, sheltered valleys. The custom, a
version of transhumance, was noted by Thomas
*Pennant in Snowdonia during the 1770s,
shortly before it was discontinued. During the
nineteenth century many of the *hafod* settlements
in upland districts became independent farms

which sent their flocks and herds to winter in the
lowlands, and this part of the practice has
survived to the present day.

Hafod Lom, a farmhouse on Mynydd Hiraethog, Denbs., famous for the *Noson Lawen*
held there in the seventeenth and eighteenth
centuries. The well-known folk-verse, '*Mi af
oddi yma i'r Hafod Lom/Er bod hi'n drom o
siwrne. . . .* ', refers to the traditional hospitality
and merry-making enjoyed by the participants.
The house is now under the waters of Llyn
Brenig. The poem by R. S. *Thomas entitled
'Hafod Lom' refers not to this house but to a
remote holding near Llanfair Caereinion, Mont.

Hall, Augusta Waddington (**Lady Llanover,
Gwenynen Gwent**; 1802–96), of Llanover
Court, Mon., was a patron of Welsh folk-
culture, especially music, dance and the *'Welsh
costume'. Although her knowledge of the
language was slight, she was an enthusiast for all
things Welsh and organized her household on
what she believed were traditional lines. Under
the influence of Thomas *Price (Carnhuanawc),
she became an early member of *Cymreigyddion y
Fenni* and also lent her support to the *Welsh
Manuscripts Society. Among her other interests
were the cause of *Temperance and the furtherance of *Protestantism.

Her husband, **Benjamin Hall** (1802–67),
whom she married in 1823, was a champion of
the Welsh people's right to have religious services in their own language and the first industrialist to dissociate himself from the Established
Church. During his term of office as Commissioner of Works the clock of the House
of Commons was named Big Ben after him.
As Member of Parliament for Monmouth
Boroughs, he introduced the Truck Act of 1831
in an attempt to curtail the infamous truck-
system which had been one of the causes of the
*Merthyr Rising.

The collection known as the Llanover Manuscripts, deposited in the National Library of
Wales in 1916, was formed mainly by Edward
*Williams (Iolo Morganwg). It was inherited by
his son, Taliesin *Williams, and subsequently
came into the possession of the Halls. The manuscripts include *cwndidau by *Llywelyn Siôn of
Llangewydd, several medieval prose texts such
as *Owain a Luned*, the only copy of a Welsh
translation of *Gesta Romanorum*, the papers of

Iolo Morganwg, poems by various Glamorgan poets and documents relating to the history of the Cymreigyddion Society of Abergavenny.

For further details about Lord and Lady Llanover see the articles by Maxwell Fraser in the *Journal* of the National Library of Wales (1962, 1966) and in the *Transactions* of the Honourable Society of Cymmrodorion (1968).

HALL, RICHARD (1817–66), poet, kept a pharmacy in Ship Street, Brecon, of which town he was a native. The themes upon which he versified fluently were the joys and pastimes of youth, the glories of angling days on the Usk, home and boyhood friends departed, and Wales unrivalled in beauty and friendship. His one substantial volume, *A Tale of the Past, and Other Poems* (1850), is now best known locally in the quotations made from it by Hall's friend, the Welsh-speaking patriot and *eisteddfodwr* Dr. James Williams, in his *Guide to Brecon and District* (1867).

Halsingod (E. 'hailsing'), carols of a religious or moral nature, were often a feature of services in the churches of north Pembrokeshire, Carmarthenshire and south Cardiganshire during the period between the *Civil War and the Methodist Revival. The twelve manuscripts in which they are preserved attribute the *halsingod* to some fifty authors in all, including Ifan Gruffydd of Y Tŵr Gwyn, Cards., and Daniel *Rowlands of Llangeitho. For the most part, these poems retell Bible stories, interpret Scriptural allegories and emphasize Sabbatarianism, *Temperance and anti-Popery. The only examples ever published appeared in the volume *Pedwar o Ganuau* (1718), believed to be the work of Samuel *Williams.

HAMER, EDWARD (1830?–*post*-1901), local historian, was born at Llanidloes, Mont. After training at Battersea College, he taught in schools at Tal-y-waun and Abersychan, Mon., but in 1878 returned to his native place to work as a book-keeper. In 1867 he published *The Chartist Outbreak at Llanidloes*, of which a centenary edition appeared in 1939. He collaborated with J. Y. W. (The Chevalier) Lloyd in writing *A Parochial Account of Llangurig* (1869) and assisted him in completing his six-volume work *The History of Powys Fadog* (1881–87). Hamer also wrote *A Parochial Account of Llanidloes* (1876) and in 1879 put together most of *A Parochial Account of Trefeglwys* but never finished it. He contributed a number of papers to *Montgomeryshire Collections*, the journal of the Powysland Club, of which he was an original member, and to *Archaeologia Cambrensis*.

Hamilton, William, see CANAWAY, WILLIAM HAMILTON (1925–).

Hanbury family, The, industrialists of Pontypool, Mon., whose association with that town began in 1565 when Capel Hanbury purchased an estate in the district and developed an ironworks there. A later Capel Hanbury (1625–1704) left the estate to his son, John Hanbury (1664–1734). With the assistance of his managers, Thomas Cooke and Edward Allgood, John Hanbury produced rolled iron sheets known as 'blackplate' in the 1690s, on account of which he is generally regarded as the pioneer of the tinplate industry. The satirical writer Charles Hanbury *Williams was his third son.

The history of the Hanbury family has been written by A. A. Locke (1916).

Handball, a game which was very popular in the industrial valleys of Glamorgan until the beginning of the twentieth century. Similar to fives or squash, it was played on a hard court with three walls, an example of which has been preserved in the village of Nelson, Glam. The game, in which two or four players participated, developed from the old custom of hitting a ball against the church wall on Sundays and feast-days. It was practised at a semi-professional level and attracted heavy betting.

Hanes Llywelyn ap Iorwerth a Chynwrig Goch (lit. 'The story of Llywelyn ap Iorwerth and Cynwrig Goch'), a rare example of a medieval Welsh folk-tale, is associated with Trefriw, Denbs. Two versions are extant, one (in Peniarth MS 27) in the hand of *Gutun Owain and the other in Elis *Gruffydd's chronicle (in Mostyn MS 158). The story tells how *Llywelyn ap Iorwerth (Llywelyn Fawr) meets a strange Red Man named Cynwrig Goch who accompanies him to London and defeats the English in a contest at the king's court. Several very common folk-motifs are woven into the tale, the chief of which is a contest in metamorphism between magicians.

Hanes Rhyw Gymro (lit. 'The story of a certain Welshman'; 1964), a play by John Gwilym *Jones, is his only historical drama. The chief character is Morgan *Llwyd, the Puritan writer, but the play's interpretation of his life and religious convictions differs from that of most historians and theologians. Llwyd is here portrayed as an emotional, unstable man who follows one whim after another until, at the end of his life, he rejects all dogma and finds satisfaction in the warm companionship of his wife and children. The play was a milestone in the development of modern Welsh *drama in that it took advantage of the theatrical flexibility associated with the work of Brecht.

For a critical discussion of the play see the article by R. Geraint Gruffydd in *John Gwilym Jones: Cyfrol Deyrnged* (ed. Gwyn Thomas, 1974).

Hanes Taliesin, see under TALIESIN (late 6th cent.).

HANLEY, JAMES (1901–   ), novelist. His father, once a printer in Ireland, took to the sea after moving his family to Liverpool and the young James, born in that city, followed him at the age of fourteen in time to serve in submarines during the First World War. He later jumped ship, joined the Canadian army, saw military action in France, worked on the railways and finally decided to devote himself to writing.

After some years of free-lance journalism, he published his first novel, *Drift* (1930), in the year in which he arrived in Wales. He settled at Tŷ-nant, Mer., but later moved to Llanfechain, Mont., where he lived from 1940 until 1964. Despite his second novel, *Boy* (1932), a study of victimized adolescence at sea, Hanley's early writing was mostly about working-class life in Liverpool, of which perhaps the five books about the Fury family (1935–58) are the epitome. It was not until the period from 1938 to 1943 that he wrote the three novels of the sea which are his best, namely *Hollow Sea* (1938), *The Ocean* (1941) and *Sailor's Song* (1943), and it was probably to these that Henry Green referred in describing him as 'far and away the best writer of the sea and seafaring men since Conrad'.

Hanley's residence in Wales which he still regards as his home, despite residence in London since 1964, evoked four novels with Welsh settings: *Don Quixote Drowned* (1953), one section of which is called '*Anatomy of Llyngyllwch*', *The Welsh Sonata* (1954), *Another World* (1971) and *A Kingdom* (1978). He also wrote three plays, *A Winter Journey* (broadcast 1958–59), *The Inner World of Miss Vaughan* (1964) and *Nones*, the last of which has not yet been performed. Some of his work is experimental: the fusion of fantasy and reality in *Sailor's Song* and *The Welsh Sonata*, for example, belies his categorization as merely a 'realist'.

If he began as 'the well-known proletarian novelist'—John Lehmann's description of him in *New Writing*—he later developed a vision of Man as essentially solitary, obsessed, unable to communicate, the inhabitant of a landscape as bleak as that of Thomas Hardy. The fantasies and nightmare dreads of his characters are often lifted entirely out of the prosaic, however, and through the quality of his writing they communicate at a different level, especially in his novels, *The Closed Harbour* (1953), *Levine* (1956) and *Another World* (1971). Although praised as one of the most important of contemporary writers—who, moreover, has published twenty-four novels and thirteen books of short stories—James Hanley has received relatively little critical notice and remains, in consequence, not widely read.

Hanmer family, see under OWREDD.

Hardie, Keir (1856–1915), miners' leader and founder of the Independent Labour Party which grew in strength in south Wales after the coal-field strike of 1898. A Scot who was elected for the two-member constituency of Merthyr Tydfil in 1900 as the first Socialist Member of Parliament to be returned from Wales, he led the Labour Parliamentary group until his death, winning many admirers in Wales with his fervent *Radicalism, *Pacifism and support for *Home Rule.

His biography has been written by Kenneth O. Morgan (1975).

Harlech, a castle in Merionethshire, which was built by order of Edward I after his military success in the Second *War of Welsh Independence (1282–83). The site, called Harddlech in *Pedair Cainc y Mabinogi, is traditionally regarded as the residence of Bendigeidfran (*Brân) and his sister *Branwen. The garrison survived a siege during the *Welsh Revolt of 1294 but was captured by *Owain Glyndŵr's forces in 1404. Harlech became the capital of Glyndŵr's Principality and a parliament was held there. In 1408, however, the castle was recaptured by English forces and Glyndŵr's wife, Margaret, his daughter and her four children were among the prisoners taken. During the Wars of the Roses the castle was the last Lancastrian stronghold to hold out against Yorkist forces and the gallantry of its defenders was admired by several Welsh poets. *Dafydd Llwyd of Mathafarn emphasized the allegiance of Harlech to the Crown and *Dafydd Nanmor sang in praise of the custodian, Dafydd ab Ifan ab Einion. Much of the castle was in ruins by the sixteenth century. During the *Civil Wars it was held for the King and when it surrendered to Parliamentary forces under Colonel John *Jones in 1647 it was the last Royalist outpost to do so. See also RHYFELGYRCH GWŶR HARLECH.

For further details see the article by W. D. Simpson in *Archaeologia Cambrensis* (1940) and A. J. Taylor, *The King's Works in Wales 1277–1330* (1974); see also the account of Harlech castle published by the Ministry of Works in 1947.

Harp, a traditional musical instrument which is sometimes regarded as the national instrument of Wales. Although it enjoyed a special status in Wales for a thousand years or more, no native harp from earlier than 1700 survives today. Some *cywyddau* of the medieval period, together with other manuscript sources, provide valuable information about the instrument and its music at that time. By the end of the eighteenth century the triple harp—so called because it had three rows of strings, the sharps and flats being played on the middle row—was widely known as the Welsh harp *par excellence* on account of its popularity in Wales. Although generally thought to have been invented in Wales it was, in fact, one of the baroque instruments devised in Italy about a hundred years before. Having lost, by about 1600, the patronage of the major gentry, the native harp was relegated to the homes of lesser families and to taverns where it was used for the accompaniment of folk-singing and dancing and as a solo instrument. Iolo Morganwg (Edward *Williams) claimed that the triple harp had first been made in Wales by Elis Siôn Siamas, harpist to Queen Anne. During the nineteenth century, often in the wake of religious revivals, there was great prejudice against the playing of the harp and its concomitant pleasures but the instrument's popularity revived during the late Victorian period under the patronage of gentry such as Lady Llanover (Augusta *Hall). It is now played in private and public throughout Wales, especially for the purposes of *Cerdd Dant.

For a detailed study see Osian Ellis, *The Story of the Harp in Wales* (1980) and Ann Rosser, *Telyn a Thelynor 1700–1900* (1981).

Harries, John (d. 1839), magician, of Cwrt-ycadno, Carms. It was widely believed that he could cure sickness in man and beast, remove spells, cast out evil spirits, foretell the future and find lost property. His son, Henry, spent a period in London where he studied sorcery under the instruction of the famous Raphael, before joining his father in the practice of the magic arts. John Harries died, according to local tradition, on the day which he had himself prophesied: he stayed in bed that morning to avoid his fate, and was burned to death when his house caught fire. Some of his books and manuscripts, which include medicinal recipes, are preserved in the National Library of Wales. See also DYN HYSBYS.

An account of the life of John Harries will be found in J. H. Davies, *Rhai o Hen Ddewiniaid Cymru* (1901).

HARRIS, ERNEST HOWARD (1876–1961), poet, was born and brought up in Swansea, Glam. Much of his life was spent as a teacher of English at schools in England and he travelled extensively, especially in northern Europe. He translated Finnish poetry into English and wrote books about the literatures of Friesland and Estonia. His own verse, lyrical and nostalgic for the scenes of his youth in Swansea and Gower, was published in the volumes *An Exile's Lute* (1919), *The Harp of Hiraeth* (1922), *Songs in Shotsilk* (1924), *Singing Seas* (1926), *Song Cycle at the Worm* (1934) and *A Swansea Boy* (1959).

Harris, Howel or **Howell** (1714–73), one of the leaders of the Methodist Revival in Wales, was born at Trefeca in the parish of Talgarth, Brecs. In 1735, when he had been for three years schoolmaster at Llangorse, he was converted by hearing the vicar of Talgarth preach and began himself to evangelize in the neighbourhood. Hoping to take Holy Orders, he was entered at St. Mary Hall, Oxford, but stayed there only a few days. Subsequently his irregular preaching (out of doors and in private houses) made the bishop refuse him ordination on four occasions.

Making contact in Wales with other 'enthusiastic' religious leaders like Daniel *Rowland and William *Williams (Pantycelyn) led him to meet George Whitefield and the Wesley brothers in England. It was Howel Harris who emerged as the organizer of the Methodist Revival in Wales by gathering the converts into 'societies' and 'associations'. Harris was influenced theologically by the Moravians and some Patripassian tendencies were heard in his preaching during the 1740s, but a much more important cause of a gradual rift between himself and the Calvinists Rowland and Williams was his prolonged endeavour to keep the doors of Wales open for John Wesley and his refusal to declare against the latter's Arminianism. The tension increased when he began to itinerate in the company of Madam Sidney Griffith (d. 1752), the 'Prophetess' of the Methodist Revival in Wales and the wife of the drunken squire of *Cefn Amwlch, Caerns., and there occurred the division known amongst the Methodists as 'The Great Schism'. Two years later, Harris retired from his public role in the Revival.

At Trefeca he gathered together a 'Family' of converts who came from all parts of Wales to live and work with him, practising their skills to an extent which made them all but self-sufficient. In 1757 Harris started a press at Trefeca at which such printers as David Griffith and Thomas Roberts (1735–1804) learned their craft. Reconciled with his old friends in 1760, he returned to the work of the Revival but did not succeed in making the same contribution as in the early years. Towards the end of his life a college was founded at Trefeca by the Countess of Huntingdon and Harris took a keen interest in the teaching there.

Howel Harris was less gifted as a preacher than Daniel Rowland, but his abounding energy and persuasiveness made him, despite his dictatorial temper, the outstanding figure of the Methodist Revival. Some historians have seen him as the greatest Welshman of his century. His roles as a founder-member of the Brecknock-shire *Agricultural Society (1755) and as a militia captain in charge of a company from 'the Family' add to the impression of an unusual individuality.

A large collection of Harris's personal papers, both letters and diaries, are preserved in the *National Library of Wales. They provide valuable information about various prominent Welshmen of the time, as well as a detailed account of his life from day to day. His journals, written in an untidy, sometimes illegible hand, as a record of God's grace in his life, are attractive in their honesty about himself and others. Since he was primarily a preacher and organizer, Harris left the literary aspect of the Revival to others, but he composed a few hymns and attempted to write an autobiography. His hymns are to be found in *Llyfr o Hymneu o Waith Amryw Awdwyr*

(1740), *Sail, Dibenion, a Rheolau'r Societies* (1742) and *Ychydig Lythyrau . . . Ynghyd a Hymnau* (1782). The Autobiography was published by the 'Family', with an appendix, under the title *A Brief Account of the Life of Howell Harris, Esq., Extracted from Papers written by Himself* (1791).

For further details see M. H. Jones, *The Trevecka Letters* (1932), Geoffrey F. Nuttall, *Howell Harris* (1965) and Gomer M. Roberts, *Portread o Ddiwygiwr* (1969) and *Selected Trevecka Letters 1742–47* (1956).

HARRIS, JOSEPH (**Gomer**; 1773–1825), author. Born at Llantydewi, Pembs., he became a minister in Swansea in 1801. He also kept a day-school and a bookshop there and owned a printing works. He published sermons in Welsh and English, several works defending Trinitarianism, such as *Bwyall Crist yng Nghoed Anghrist* (1804) and *Traethawd ar Briodol Dduwdod ein Harglwydd Iesu Grist* (1816–17), as well as a collection of hymns, *Casgliad o Hymnau o'r Awdur Gorau* (1821), which proved popular. He it was who, in 1814, launched and edited the first weekly newspaper in Welsh, **Seren Gomer*, which became in 1880 the official journal of the Welsh **Baptists* Union.

His biography was written by D. Rhys Stephen (1839). For further details see the article by Glanmor Williams, '*Gomer, sylfaenydd ein llenyddiaeth gyfnodol*', in the *Transactions* of the Honourable Society of Cymmrodorion (1982).

Harrowing of Hell, The, a common theme in medieval literature, is derived from the Apocryphal Gospel of Nicodemus in which Christ descends into Hell to free the souls of the Just. The work of the **Gogynfeirdd* abounds with graphic descriptions of the Day of Judgement and the horrors of Hell. See also ANNWN.

HARRY, GEORGE OWEN, also known as **GEORGE OWEN** (*c.*1553–*c.*1614), antiquary. Born in Gower, he was rector of Whitchurch, near Cemais, and of Llanfihangel Penbedw, Pembs., from 1597 to 1613. A friend for nearly thirty years of George **Owen* of Henllys, he was the author of *The Genealogy of the High and Mighty Monarch, James . . . King of great Brittayne, &c. with his lineall descent from Noah, by divers direct lynes to Brutus* (1604), a work intended to demonstrate how James I was entitled to rule over the whole of Great Britain.

Harry, Miles (1700–76), the outstanding Baptist minister of his time, was born in the parish of Bedwellty, Mon., and ordained in 1729 at Blaenau Gwent, a church which had formerly been a branch of the Particular Baptist cause at Llanwenarth. At first assistant to his brother John, he became in 1731 the first minister of the newly-founded church at Pen-y-garn, Pontypool, of which he remained in charge till his death. Of a lively mind, with unorthodox views about the Trinity and infant baptism, he had to tread a careful path between militant Calvinism and the Arminianism of the original **Baptists*. A strong personality and a powerful preacher, he arranged an itinerary for Howel **Harris* in 1739 and, when the latter was arrested on the charge of causing a riot, Harry was largely instrumental in having him acquitted at the Monmouth Assizes. His co-operation with Harris in establishing the first printing press in the county, at Pontypool, proved less happy. Harry was among those who opened a Baptist Academy at Trosnant in 1734 and his support kept it going until 1761, by which time some forty young men had been trained there. His successor at Pen-y-garn, David Jones (1741–92), wrote his elegy.

For further details see T. M. Bassett, *The Welsh Baptists* (1977).

Harvest Mare, the last sheaf of corn to be left standing in the field. It was formerly the custom in west Wales for farmworkers to vie with one another by hurling their reaping-hooks in an attempt to cut the sheaf. The successful reaper took it to the house, from the doors and windows of which the womenfolk would try to drench him with water, and he was given the place of honour at table during the harvest feast. The custom, or local variations of it, was known throughout Europe and probably reflected the ancient belief that the forces of natural growth remained potent in the last sheaf of the harvest.

For further details see Trefor M. Owen, *Welsh Folk Customs* (1959) and the article by T. Llew Jones in *Taliesin* (vol. 37, 1978).

HATTON, JULIA ANN (**Ann of Swansea**; 1764–1838), poet and novelist. Born at Worcester, the seventh child of the strolling players Roger Kemble and Sarah Ward, she was prevented by lameness from following the family's theatrical tradition, unlike her eldest brother John Kemble and her sister Sarah **Siddons* who achieved fame in the London playhouses of their day. Married, and forsaken, by an adventurer named Curtis before she was nineteen years old, she became the wife of William Hatton in 1792 and, seven years later, after returning from America, they took a lease of Swansea Bathing House. On the death of her second husband in 1806 she moved to Kidwelly, Carms., where she kept a dancing school, but returned to Swansea in 1809 and devoted herself to writing, being maintained by an annuity granted her by her brother and sister. She wrote a play, *Zaffine or the Knight of the Bloody Cross*, in which Edmund Kean acted in Swansea in 1810; she also published two collections of verse, *Poems on Miscellaneous Subjects* (1783) and *Poetic Trifles* (1811), and about a dozen novels, including *Cambrian Pictures* (3 vols., 1810?) and *Chronicles of an Illustrious House* (5 vols., 1814).

For further details see the essay by Ivor J. Bromham in *Glamorgan Historian* (ed. Stewart Williams, 1971).

Hawarden, a castle in Flintshire, built in the late eleventh century during the initial period of Norman settlement in north-east Wales. In the twelfth century it belonged to the lordship of Moldesdale, but control of it fluctuated and a new castle was built on the site about 1276. *Dafydd ap Gruffudd's attack on the castle, on Palm Sunday 1282, was the first engagement in the second *War of Welsh Independence. In 1284 the lordship was excluded from the new shire of Flint and was held over the next two centuries by the *Salesbury and Stanley families. During the *Civil Wars the castle was first held for the King but was surrendered in 1646 to Parliamentary forces; in the following year it was dismantled. The modern edifice, rebuilt near by in the early nineteenth century, was associated with the Gladstone family after the marriage of William Ewart Gladstone and Catherine Glynne at Hawarden church in 1839. The castle now houses St. Deiniol's Hall and Library.

For further details see C. R. Williams, *The History of Flintshire* (1961).

HAYCOCK, MYFANWY (1913–63), poet, was born at Pontnewynydd, Mon., and educated at the Cardiff School of Art. She published four volumes of verse: *Fantasy* (1937), *Poems* (1944), *More Poems* (1945) and the posthumous collection *Mountain over Paddington* (1964), which was compiled during a long period of ill health. They are the work of a compassionate, lively personality imbued with a deep love for the natural scene in her native Gwent and with a deep appreciation of the simple scenes and occasions of ordinary life.

HAYCRAFT, ANNA (Alice Thomas Ellis; 1932–), novelist. Born in Liverpool and brought up at Penmaenmawr, Caerns., she went to school in Bangor and later studied at Liverpool Art College. With her husband, she is now director and fiction editor of the Duckworth publishing house in London. Besides cookery books (written under the name Anna Haycraft), she has published five novels under her pseudonym, namely *The Sin Eater* (1977), *The Birds of the Air* (1980), *The 27th Kingdom* (1982), *The Other Side of the Fire* (1983) and *Unexplained Laughter* (1985).

Heads, The Cult of, a feature of pagan Celtic religion, both insular and continental (see under CELTS). The head, as a symbol of divinity, was the most important part of the body, presumably because it was regarded as the residence of the immortal soul. The cult of the human head is widely attested throughout the entire Celtic world, alike in iconography, in allusions by classical writers, and in vernacular literature and folklore. Representations of warriors holding dismembered heads appear on Gaulish coins and stone heads, sometimes horned, sometimes wearing torques, sometimes with three faces, have been discovered in abundance. References by classical writers to the Celtic practice of head-hunting, and to the embalming of enemy heads, are corroborated both in archaeological finds in France and in the Irish tales, where the head was believed capable of prolonged independent life. Heads adorned with gold or cupped in leather were sometimes used as drinking-vessels or set up on the roof-tree as symbols of the control thought to be exercised by the victor over the vanquished even after death. But undoubtedly the most striking and meaningful account of a dismembered head occurs in the tale of *Branwen in *Pedair Cainc y Mabinogi* where the head of Bendigeidfran (*Bran) presides at the Otherworld feasting at *Harlech and *Gwales. When afterwards buried in London, the head serves as a talisman for the protection of Britain from all threat of foreign invasion.

For further details see Anne Ross, *Pagan Celtic Britain* (1967) and *Everyday Life of the Pagan Celts* (1970); see also the same author's article, 'The Human Head in Insular Pagan Celtic Religion' in the *Proceedings* of the Society of Antiquaries of Scotland (vol. XCI, 1957–58).

Hear and Forgive (1952), the fourth novel of Emyr *Humphreys, which was awarded the Somerset Maugham Prize in 1953, is the best early example of what its author called 'the Protestant novel', concerned as it is with conscience and the transmission of good in society. The narrator of the action is David Flint, a young novelist and teacher of religious knowledge in a London boys' school, who has deserted his wife and is living with Helen, the niece of the chairman of his school's governors. The real focus of attention, however, is upon the Allenside brothers: Edward, the school's headmaster, a man of conscience who seeks justice rather than convenience and refuses personal advancement, and Roger, a ne'er-do-well who is trying to lead his lumpish nephew astray. Edward, the 'good man', is boxed in by life, unlikely to avoid defeat, but his example persuades his friend David to return, if without joy, to his wife. A serious theme is much enlivened by staffroom wit and maladroit politicking.

Heathfield, The Battle of (632), see under CADWALLON AP CADFAN (d. 633) and MEIC MYNGFRAS (6th cent.).

Hedd Wyn, see EVANS, ELLIS HUMPHREY (1887–1917).

Heddiw (lit. 'Today'), a magazine edited by Aneirin ap Talfan (Aneirin Talfan *Davies) and Dafydd *Jenkins. A total of fifty-eight numbers appeared between 1936 and 1942, of which the first four volumes were published by *Gwasg Heddiw*, a partnership consisting of the editors and Alun Talfan Davies, and the remainder by *Gwasg Gee* of Denbigh. Dafydd Jenkins was not named as co-editor after his appointment as Organiser of the Welsh Language Petition in November 1938 but his name alone appeared on the last two numbers after Aneirin Talfan Davies had joined the staff of the BBC.

The magazine was intended by its editors to be a Welsh counterpart to English magazines such as the *New Statesman* but its contents were more literary. Nevertheless, it discussed contemporary politics, especially Welsh *Nationalism, from a left-wing point of view, and its editorials took the Republican side in the Spanish Civil War. Its editorial policy, both before and after the outbreak of the Second World War, was strongly pacifist and it devoted space to pacifist arguments based on the Catholic concept of 'the just war'. Special features were a diary written by various hands, the column '*Cwrs y Byd*' by Cyril P. Cule, and the inclusion of cartoons and caricatures. Besides the editors, the magazine's most regular contributors (often under pseudonyms) were J. Gwyn *Griffiths, Pennar *Davies and Geraint Dyfnallt *Owen; it also carried poems by, among others, R. Williams *Parry, Gwenallt (David James *Jones) and Waldo *Williams.

Hedge of Mist, The, in the romance of Geraint and Enid (see under TAIR RHAMANT), guards a field in which enchanted games are played. None who has penetrated it has ever returned but Geraint insists on entering and, once inside, he sees a head impaled on every stake in the hedge, except two. Beyond, at the entrance to a magnificent pavilion, there is an apple-tree on which is hung a hunting horn, and a maiden is seated near by on a golden chair. Geraint sits beside her but he is immediately challenged by a nameless knight, whose seat he has taken. They fight and the victorious Geraint is granted his wish that the Hedge of Mist and the enchantment be removed: he sounds the horn and, at the first blast, the mist disappears. He then returns in triumph to his own country, which he rules with Enid for many years thereafter.

Hefenfelth, The Battle of (633), see under CADWALLON AP CADFAN (d. 633).

Heilyn, Rowland (1562?–1631), merchant and patron, was descended from the family resident at Pentreheylin, on the Vyrnwy near Llanymynech, Mont. In association with Sir Thomas *Myddleton and others, he used his fortune, made in London, to pay for the publication of Welsh books. Among the works published in this way were the Welsh-Latin dictionary of John *Davies of Mallwyd, the translation by Rowland *Vaughan of Caergai of *The Practice of Piety* by Lewis *Bayly, and the Welsh quarto Bible of 1630 (*Y Beibl Bach*), bound with the Welsh Prayer Book and the psalter of Edmund *Prys.

Heledd (early 7th cent.), see under CANU HELEDD (9th or 10th cent.).

Helen of Wales, The, see NEST (*fl.* 1120).

HELLINGS, PETER (1921–), poet, born in Swansea, Glam., was employed by the Great Western Railway until 1941, when he joined the RAF. Returning to his home town after the War, he took a degree at University College, Swansea, but left Wales in 1952 to become a teacher in England. He has published two collections of poems, *Firework Music* (1950) and *A Swansea Sketchbook* (1983); the latter is part of a verse autobiography.

Helyntion Bywyd Hen Deiliwr (lit. 'The troubles of an old tailor's life'; 1877), a work of fiction by William *Rees (Gwilym Hiraethog), was first published in weekly episodes in the newspaper *Y *Tyst*. Although it is fiction, it can hardly be called a novel: the Old Tailor begins by reminiscing about his days as an apprentice, but goes on to recount the conversion of the Hafod Uchaf family to chapel religion and to describe the course of three love-affairs. Nevertheless, the character of the old man of Hafod Uchaf and the customs of the times are lovingly presented while the dialogue, in the author's own colourful dialect, has considerable charm.

The work was published in a new edition prepared by Dafydd Jenkins in 1940.

HEMANS, FELICIA DOROTHEA (1793–1835), poet, was born in Liverpool but the family moved to Gwrych, near Abergele, Denbs., in 1800. Her formal education was neglected but, a voracious reader, she published her first volume of verse, *Juvenile Poems* (1808), when she was only fifteen years old. Married to a Captain Alfred Hemans in 1812, she bore him five sons before they were separated six years later. From 1809 to 1825, save for a year at Daventry after her marriage, she lived at her mother's house in St. Asaph, Flints., and to this period of her life belongs most of her work, including *The Domestic Affections* (1812), *The Sceptic* (1820), *The Siege of Valencia* (1823), *The Forest Sanctuary* (1825) and *Lays of Many Lands* (1825). Her play *The Vespers of Palermo*, was performed in Covent Garden, London, in 1823 to great acclaim and in Edinburgh the following year it was again a triumph. On her mother's death in 1827 she went to live at Wavertree, near Liverpool, and four years later moved to Ireland where her religious poems were highly esteemed; she died in Dublin.

Her fondness for the scenery of north Wales was doubtless sincere and her extremely popular *Welsh Melodies* (1821) include English versions of a number of Welsh poems. Several of her lyrics were sung at the eisteddfod held in London under the auspices of the Honourable Society of

*Cymmrodorion in 1822, for which occasion she wrote a poem entitled 'The Meeting of the Bards'. Her poems on Welsh themes contributed to the renewal of interest in the traditions of Wales which was a feature of the Romantic movement in England.

Of a tender, amiable nature, Mrs. Hemans counted Wordsworth and Lord Byron among her English admirers. But her work has little permanent value, mainly because she treated fashionably heroic subjects in an inflated manner. Her best-known poem (and one of the most concise) is 'Casabianca' which begins, 'The boy stood on the burning deck'. It was the piety and liberalism of her work which appealed to her contemporaries but her reputation has suffered badly since her death. Only Sir Walter Scott among her friends perceived the vacuity of her verse, commenting of it, 'too many flowers and too little fruit'.

Her collected works, in seven volumes with a memoir by her sister, were published in 1839 and again in 1873, edited by W. M. Rossetti. For further details see A. H. Miles (ed.), *The Poets and Poetry of the Nineteenth Century* (11 vols., 1905–07) and A. T. Ritchie, 'Felicia Felix' in *Blackstick Papers* (1908). There is a monograph on Mrs. Hemans by Peter W. Trinder in the *Writers of Wales* series (1984).

Hen Atgofion (lit. 'Old memories'; 1936), the reminiscences of his childhood and youth by W. J. *Gruffydd (1881–1954), were first published in Y *Llenor, the magazine he edited between 1922 and 1951. The style is intimate, personal and humorous, and there are frequent discursive passages in which the author's views on public matters are trenchantly expressed, and for these reasons the book ranks with his best and most characteristic writing.

It has been translated by D. Myrddin Lloyd under the title *The Years of the Locust* (1976).

Hen Benillion (lit. 'Old stanzas'), traditional verses preserved orally and sung to harp accompaniment, sometimes occur as a short chain of related stanzas, but usually consist of a single brief stanza in free metre. While echoing the literary conventions of more formal verse, their artistry is less conscious and their language more homely. Like the *englyn, they rely for their effect on pithiness and vivid imagery. The products of a rural society, often local in their original appeal but sometimes achieving a wider currency, the best of them are quoted for their philosophical content as if they were proverbs or verses from the Bible. Among the writers who have been attracted to the form are Lewis *Morris the antiquary and Edward *Jones (Bardd y Brenin) and, in modern times, Aneirin Talfan *Davies and Glyn *Jones.

For a substantial collection of these stanzas, together with a full discussion of them, the standard work is T. H. Parry-Williams, *Hen Benillion* (1940). Two selections have been translated by Glyn Jones under the

titles *When the Rosebush Brings Forth Apples* (1981) and *Honeydew on the Wormwood* (1984).

Hen Bersoniaid Llengar, Yr (lit. 'The old literary clerics'), a group of Anglican clergymen who fostered Welsh culture during the years from 1818 to 1858, often in the face of stern opposition from their anti-Welsh superiors within the Established Church. Among the most prominent were Ifor Ceri (John *Jenkins), W. J. *Rees of Cascob, Rads., Gwallter Mechain (Walter *Davies), Ieuan Glan Geirionydd (Evan *Evans), Ab Ithel (John *Williams) and Carnhuanawc (Thomas *Price). Associated with the group were a number of lay-people such as Angharad *Llwyd, Augusta *Hall (Lady Llanover), Charlotte *Guest and Maria Jane Williams of *Aberpergwm.

In many respects these patriots were the guardians of the nation's literary traditions in the period between the foundation of the *Gwyneddigion Society and the new *scholarship of the Universities of Oxford and Wales. It was they, in particular, who transformed the *Eisteddfod from a gathering of poets into a national festival. Somewhat reactionary in politics, they looked back to the Wales of the eighteenth century and sought to defend the Welsh from the growing influence of *Methodism. The means by which they hoped to stem the tide included the *Welsh Manuscripts Society, the *Cambrian Archaeological Association, the public school at Llandovery, Carms., and St. David's College, Lampeter. It was the report of the *Blue Books which caused their authority to be challenged and eventually to be replaced by that of Radicals and Nonconformists who substituted the Anglicans' interest in the remote past with a new image of Welsh culture based on the chapel.

The name by which they are collectively known was bestowed upon them by R. T. Jenkins in *Hanes Cymru yn y Bedwaredd Ganrif ar Bymtheg* (1933) and is the title of an essay by Bedwyr Lewis Jones (1963); see also the latter's essay in *Gwŷr Llên y Bedwaredd Ganrif ar Bymtheg* (ed. Dyfnallt Morgan, 1968).

Hen Broffwyd, Yr, see JONES, EDMUND (1702–93).

Hen Ddosbarth, see PEDWAR ANSAWDD AR HUGAIN.

Hen Dŷ Ffarm (lit. 'The old farmhouse'; 1953), part of an autobiography by D. J. *Williams. As the author explains in a preface, it deals more with his background than with himself. The first six years of his life are covered in this volume, the sequel to which was *Yn Chwech ar Hugain Oed* (1959). It describes the district of Rhydcymerau in north Carmarthenshire, the author's 'square mile'. Despite the enthusiastic devotion colouring the view, there is much objective commentary which makes the book an important sociological document. Gwenallt (David

James *Jones), who also knew the district well, maintained that it gave too rosy a picture of the farmers' economic circumstances. D. J. Williams's chief interest, however, was in the farmers themselves and their families; he was also very fond of their animals, especially the horses.

The volume was translated by Waldo Williams as *The Old Farmhouse* (1961).

Hen Ficer, Yr, see PRICHARD, RHYS (1579–1644).

Hen Gadi, Yr, see CADI HAF.

Hen Gorff, Yr, see under METHODISM.

Hen Gymru Lawen (lit. 'Merry old Wales'), a term used by patriots and folklorists of the Romantic period to refer to the life of the common people before *Puritanism and *Nonconformity brought a new sobriety to Welsh society. Until the seventeenth century the popular culture of Wales had its bastions in such centres of the countryside as the tavern, the fair, the market, the churchyard and the village green. Among the events at which the peasantry gathered were the festivals of the Church, the *Noson Lawen, the wedding and the funeral wake. Entertainment was provided by harpists, fiddlers, ballad-singers, story-tellers and strolling players; there were also games, interludes and dancing. Twm o'r Nant (Thomas *Edwards) may be regarded as a late exemplar of this rural, coarse, superstitious, economically poor but colourful society. As it declined between 1660 and 1850, mainly as a result of industrialization and Methodist teaching, the popular culture of the seventeenth and eighteenth centuries came to be regarded by Robert *Jones of Rhos-lan, for example, as a dark, immoral period in the history of Wales and a new Nonconformist identity began to be fostered among the Welsh people. The social and spiritual amelioration which was brought about by this process cannot be denied but it is now recognized as one which did irreparable harm to the cultural heritage of Wales.

For further details see R. T. Jenkins, *Hanes Cymru yn y Ddeunawfed Ganrif* (1931), Geraint H. Jenkins, *Literature, Religion and Society in Wales 1660–1730* (1978) and *Hanes Cymru yn y Cyfnod Modern Cynnar 1530–1760* (1983), and Prys Morgan, *The Eighteenth Century Renaissance* (1981).

'Hen Wlad fy Nhadau' (lit. 'The old land of my fathers'), the national anthem of the Welsh people. The words were written by Evan *James (Ieuan ap Iago) and the music by his son, James James (Iago ap Ieuan). The latter is said to have composed the tune one Sunday morning in January 1856 while walking near the river Rhondda at Pontypridd, Glam. The three verses were written by his father on the same and the follow-

ing day. The tune was sung in public for the first time in the vestry of Tabor chapel, Maesteg, Glam., in 1856, and the first printed version of the words is dated 1858. The song grew in popularity at the eisteddfodau of the 1860s largely through the influence of John *Owen (Owain Alaw) who included it in the third volume of his collection *Gems of Welsh Melody* (1860–64).

The date of the song's adoption as the national anthem is uncertain. It is known, however, that the tune was given prominence during the National Eisteddfod held at Bangor in 1874 when it was sung by Robert Rees (Eos Morlais), with the choir under the direction of John Richards (Isalaw) joining in the chorus, and from about that time it came to be considered as the song which, more than any other, expressed Welsh national sentiment. Now accorded official status as the national anthem of Wales by general assent, 'Hen Wlad fy Nhadau' is sung on a wide variety of public occasions throughout the country, often with a fervour which matches the high patriotism of its words and the stirring beauty of its music.

A Breton adaptation of 'Hen Wlad fy Nhadau' was published by William Jenkin Jones in *Telen ar C'hristen* (1895); the version which was adopted as the Breton national anthem, *Bro Goz ma Zadou*, in 1902, was made in 1897 by François Jaffrenou (Taldir; 1879–1956).

For further details see the articles by Percy Scholes in the *Journal* of the National Library of Wales (vol. III, 1943) and Tecwyn Ellis in the same journal (vol. VIII, 1953).

Hen Wynebau (lit. 'Old faces'; 1934), a volume of autobiography by D. J. *Williams. Among the characters portrayed there is more than one *rara avis*, such as Dafydd'r Efailfach, an illiterate labourer who is nevertheless a meticulous artist in words with 'the simple philosophy of the healthy, natural pagan'. Towards the end of his life he seeks chapel membership, though he is still 'a witty and happy sinner' who will cause perplexity among the angels. An element of story-telling intrudes into several of the portraits and it was natural for the author to move on to the short story, a form which had attracted him much earlier, as the stories in *Y Gaseg Ddu* (1970) show. Although the character-sketches in *Hen Wynebau* are consistently kind, they have a Flaubertian fidelity to truth, as in the study of Jones y Goetre Fawr, the drink-sodden optimist.

Hendregadredd Manuscript, The, the earlier of the two most important sources of the work of the Poets of the Princes (see under GOGYNFEIRDD). The volume was written on parchment by several hands at the beginning of the fourteenth century. During the 1330s, when the manuscript was in the possession of Ieuan Llwyd ap Ieuan ap Gruffudd Foel of *Parcrhydderch, Llangeitho, a number of poems were added, including some by *Dafydd ap Gwilym and *Gruffudd Gryg. The former had connections with Parcrhydderch (he wrote an elegy for Ieuan's wife Angharad) and it is believed that Dafydd's handwriting is to be seen in the manuscript. It was owned by Gruffudd *Dwnn of Ystrad Merthyr about the middle of the sixteenth century, subsequently by *Wiliam Llŷn, and later passed by way of *Rhys Cain to Robert *Vaughan's library at Hengwrt. It was copied by John *Davies of Mallwyd in 1617 and it was his transcript which was used as a source for *The Myvyrian Archaiology* (1801). Nothing more is known about the manuscript's whereabouts until it belonged, in the early nineteenth century, to Archdeacon Richard Newcome of Ruthin. It was rediscovered in 1910 in a wardrobe at Hendregadredd, a house near Pentre'rfelin, Cricieth, Caerns. Ignatius Williams of Denbigh had purchased it and bequeathed it to his nephew, John Ignatius Williams of Hendregadredd. Auctioned in London in 1923, it was bought by the Davies sisters (see under GREGYNOG PRESS) who presented it to the *National Library of Wales. Among the poets represented in it are *Meilyr Brydydd, *Gwalchmai ap Meilyr, *Bleddyn Fardd, *Cynddelw Brydydd Mawr, *Gwynfardd Brycheiniog, *Llywarch ap Llywelyn (Prydydd y Moch) and *Hywel ab Owain Gwynedd. This manuscript and The *Red Book of Hergest are the principal extant sources for the poetry of the *Gogynfeirdd*.

For further details see the text of the manuscript edited by John Morris-Jones and T. H. Parry-Williams (1933) and the article by Daniel Huws in the *Journal* of the National Library of Wales (vol. XXII, 1981).

Hengerdd, Yr, see under CYNFEIRDD.

Hengwrt, see under VAUGHAN, ROBERT (c.1592–1667).

Henwen, see under POWERFUL SWINEHERDS.

Herald Cymraeg, Yr (lit. 'The Welsh herald'; 1855–), a weekly newspaper established by John Rees in Caernarfon, was launched under the editorship of James Evans. Liberal and staunchly Nonconformist, it also carried verse and other contributions from such writers as Lewis William *Lewis (Llew Llwyfo), T. Gwynn *Jones, Daniel *Rees, R. J. *Rowlands (Meuryn) and Gwilym R. *Jones. By today, however, the paper is one of the *Herald* group, more Conservative in outlook and—although edited until 1983 by the poet John T. *Jones (John Eilian)—it no longer publishes material of any literary significance.

HERBERT, EDWARD (Lord Herbert of Cherbury; 1583–1648), philosopher, writer and ambassador, the eldest of the brothers of the poet George *Herbert, was born at Eyton, Salop, a great-grandson to Sir Richard Herbert of Cold-

brook, Mon. Sent at the age of nine to Edward Thelwall of Plas-y-Ward, Ruthin, to learn Welsh, he spent nine months there suffering from tertian ague and learned little. He was admitted to University College, Oxford, in 1596 and in 1599 married Mary Herbert, six years his senior, sole heiress to Sir William Herbert of St. Julians, Newport, a grandson of the first Earl of Pembroke. His private studies at Oxford were devoted to languages and music but later he spent much time in fencing, mastering 'the great horse' and experimenting with medicines.

After Oxford his time was divided between London and Montgomery Castle until 1608 when, his wife at last pregnant, he made the first of the several journeys to the Continent which he described in his *Life*, a work which reveals a formidable eccentricity. Ridiculously courageous in war, vain about his person and his favour with women, inordinately concerned with his reputation and the punctilios of honour, he visited the French court, fought under the Prince of Orange in the Low Countries, went to Rome, engaged to raise men for the Duke of Savoy and, ultimately, was appointed Ambassador to the French Court by James I in 1619. After five years' service there he was recalled and, although made Lord Herbert of Castle Ireland in 1625 and of Cherbury in 1629, was offered no further Crown appointment. In the later quarrels between King and Parliament he at first supported the former but by 1639 he had changed his allegiance and in effect took no part in the subsequent struggle. His health broke down in 1643 and for his last five years he was a sick man.

Herbert's *Life*, discovered in manuscript in 1737 and published many times subsequently, is fuller of extraordinary incident than much fiction. His *De Veritate* . . . , published in Paris in 1623 and 1624 and in London in 1645, with a French translation in 1639, is profoundly anticlerical and anti-revelatory. Seeking to expound a rational theology by using 'universal consent' as the touchstone of truth, Herbert argues that there is a Supreme Power which is good, wise and deserving of worship, that good conduct is a better worship than ceremonies, that vices and crimes must be expiated and that there are rewards and punishments in an afterlife. This deism, of which he was later said to be the father, was derived from his survey of the world's religions. Herbert also published *De Religione Gentilium* (1645, 1663, Englished in 1700). After his death there appeared *Expeditio Buckinghami Ducis in Ream Insulam* (1656), the much-admired *Life and Reign of Henry the Eighth* (1649, 1672, 1682), for which Thomas Master did much of the research, and *Occasional Verses* (1665) which are as obscure as they are metaphysical.

For further details see *The Autobiography of Edward, Lord Herbert of Cherbury* (ed. Sidney Lee, 1884; 2nd edn., Gregynog Press, 1928). Herbert's *De Veritate*, in which his philosophy is set out, was translated and edited with an introduction by M. H. Carré (1937). There are critical discussions of Herbert's work in B. Willey, *Essays and Studies* (1941), and in M. Bottrall, *Every Man a Phoenix* (1958); see also the article by W. Moelwyn Merchant in the *Transactions* of the Society of Cymmrodorion (1956).

HERBERT, GEORGE (1593–1633), poet, was born either at Eyton, Salop, or in London. Of the mixed Norman and Welsh stock favoured by succeeding English kings, the Herberts had become the foremost of the Border families by the fifteenth century and, before the *Acts of Union, George Herbert's great-grandfather had been the steward of all royal lands in Wales. His father, therefore, was kin to the Earls of Pembroke and his mother daughter to the largest landowner in Shropshire. Given this lineage, it is not surprising to hear of George Herbert's excessive pride, during his early Cambridge years, in 'his parts and parentage'. He may have learned some Welsh in infancy, but this knowledge could hardly have survived into adulthood for, on his father's death in 1596, the family moved first to his mother's parental home, then to Oxford and finally to London, where at the age of twelve he was sent to Westminster School. Three years later, in 1608, he entered Trinity College, Cambridge, from which, on New Year's Day 1610, he addressed two sonnets to his mother (his earliest surviving verse) declaring his intention of dedicating his poetic talents to God's service. Apart from a few complimentary poems in Latin, he stuck to this resolution throughout his life. The covering letter which accompanied these sonnets draws attention to another early manifestation of an important factor in his life, namely his chronic ill health.

Academically gifted, Herbert was appointed a Fellow of Trinity College in 1616 and University Reader in Rhetoric in 1618, when he desired to enter the Anglican priesthood. His successful canvassing for the Public Oratorship at Cambridge, however, indicates a change of intention by 1620, for this was a post which previous holders had found invaluable as a stepping-stone to high office in the royal service. He held the Oratorship until 1627, though he was not often at Cambridge; instead, he spent his time pursuing his hopes of a secular career and serving as a Member of Parliament for Montgomery in 1624–25. He was ordained deacon in 1626, nevertheless, having been encouraged to return to his original vocation by his mother, by the poet John Donne (a close friend of the family), and by the death of several of his Court patrons. Though ordination ruled out the possibility of government service, it was several years before Herbert became a priest. These years of delay were spent in ill health, feelings of personal unworthiness for his calling and lingering ambi-

tions which made acceptance of his lot difficult. On being restored to health in 1629, he married and in the following year accepted the rectorship of Fulston and Bemerton, near Salisbury. His remaining three years of life were spent in devotion to his priestly duties. When not thus engaged he was busy organizing repairs to his churches and rectory, performing music and writing.

Nothing substantial by Herbert was published during his lifetime, though many of his poems had circulated in manuscript for several years. Within a few months of his death, there appeared *The Temple* (1633), a collection of poems, which records 'the many spiritual Conflicts that have past betwixt God and my Soul, before I could subject mine to the will of Jesus my Master'. It is not, however, a strict narrative of these conflicts but, organized around the procession of the feasts of the Church year, concentrates on the theme of God's love for Mankind and reflects the fluctuation in moods of one man in relation to this theme. Lacking the tempestuous drama and death-obsession of Donne's religious verse, Herbert's poems nevertheless have their own quiet agonies, despairs, reliefs and joys, all set in the context of the natural, domestic, ecclesiastical and social world of his age. His language is precise and he is the master of the unexpected *volte face* to conclude a poem; equally impressive is the vast variety of metrical forms he employs with unerring effect. Herbert's influence on Henry *Vaughan and other religious poets of the seventeenth century is well attested. His other substantial work, *A Priest to the Temple*, a prose tract on the duties of a country parson, was first published in Herbert's *Remains* (1652).

The standard edition of Herbert's *œuvre* is *The Works of George Herbert* (ed. F. E. Hutchinson, 1941); popular editions are *The Poems of George Herbert* (1961) with an introduction by Helen Gardner and *A Choice of George Herbert's Verse* (ed. R. S. Thomas, 1967). Izaak Walton's *Lives* is an invaluable, if over-admiring, source for Herbert's biography; critical works of note are M. Bottrall, *George Herbert* (1954), E. Tuve, *A Reading of George Herbert* (1952) and J. H. Summers, *George Herbert: His Religion and Art* (1954).

HERBERT, JOYCE (1923–), poet and short-story writer, was born in the Rhondda Valley and read English at University College, Cardiff; she lives near Cowbridge, Glam. Having given up writing in the 1940s, she began again in 1976 and has published her work in various magazines and anthologies since then, collecting her poems in the volume *Approaching Snow* (1983).

Herbert, William (d. 1469), founder of the extensive Herbert clan, was the leading Welsh supporter of the Yorkists in the Wars of the Roses. The son of William ap Thomas of Raglan, Mon., and Gwladys, the daughter of *Dafydd Gam, his influence at a sensitive point in the

March of Wales made him the object of much manœuvring by both Yorkists and Lancastrians in the 1450s. By 1460 he was one of the Yorkist party and in 1461 he contributed to Edward of York's victory over Owen and Jasper Tudor at the battle of *Mortimer's Cross. Elevated to the peerage as Lord Herbert of Raglan at Edward's coronation in 1461, he attacked the remaining Lancastrian strongholds in Wales, capturing *Harlech and *Pembroke and, temporarily with the latter, the young Henry Tudor. Created Earl of Pembroke in 1468, he was shown by the king a favour which antagonized the Earl of Warwick (the Kingmaker) who defected to the Lancastrians. Herbert's defeat and execution by Warwick at the battle of Banbury in 1469 made possible the brief restoration of the Lancastrian king, Henry VI. Through the marriage of his granddaughter, Herbert's vast estates in Wales passed to the Somerset family, Earls of Worcester and, later, Dukes of Beaufort. His natural son, Richard, was the father of William Herbert (c. 1501–1570), the first Earl of Pembroke of the second creation to whom Gruffydd *Robert dedicated his Welsh Grammar of 1567. To the poets, William Herbert was the epitome of the Welsh hero and *Guto'r Glyn appealed to him to lead a national crusade to free Wales from English rule.

For further details see the article by H. T. Evans in the *Transactions of the Honourable Society of Cymmrodorion* (1909–10) and the same author's *Wales and the Wars of the Roses* (1915).

HERBERT or **HARBERT, WILLIAM** (c. 1583–1628?), poet, was born in Glamorgan and educated at Christ Church, Oxford. Little is known of his life and that he may have died in a debtor's prison in London is no more than speculation. His one major work, *A Prophesie of Cadwallader, last King of the Britaines* (1604), is a diffuse survey of British history in which there are passages of considerable power, including a description of Katherine de Valois, Owen Tudor's bride, which uses imagery normally associated with the Virgin Mary, and some vigorous stanzas about the Wars of the Roses. His last printed verses were in commendation of the publication of William Browne's *Britannia's Pastorals* in 1625. Alexander Grosart, who edited Herbert's *Works* in 1870, described him, with some of the hyperbole of the pioneer, in terms little short of those he used for his other protégé, Henry *Vaughan.

Hereford, John, see FLETCHER, HARRY LUTF VERNE (1902–74).

Hergest, a mansion in the parish of Kington, Herefs., was the home of one of the many branches of the Vaughan family who extended patronage to poets during the fifteenth and early sixteenth centuries. *Thomas ap Roger Vaughan established the Hergest line, his brother, Roger *Vaughan the Tre-twˆr (Tretower) branch and

another brother, Watcyn, the Brodorddyn (*Bredwardine) line. They were the sons of Roger Vaughan of Brodorddyn and his wife, Gwladus. The father was a patron and his son Thomas and his wife, Ellen Gethin, maintained the tradition at Hergest. Many of the foremost poets of the period, such as *Guto'r Glyn and *Lewys Glyn Cothi (Llywelyn y Glyn), visited their home. On the death of Thomas in 1469 his son Watkin inherited both the estate and the family traditions; several poems to him and his family have been preserved. See also RED BOOK OF HERGEST.

Heroic Ideal, The, in Welsh literature, reflects the values of British society in the period following the withdrawal of the Roman legions (c. 450–c. 600) when the social order was dominated by a powerful warrior class. The qualities most highly esteemed in the leaders of this military aristocracy were courage in war and generosity in peace, and they, in turn, expected absolute loyalty from their followers, even if it meant death. *Aneirin's poem, 'Y *Gododdin', is the classic exposition of the ideals of the Heroic Age in Welsh literature. Although it is not a narrative poem, but rather a combination of panegyric and elegy, its tone is essentially heroic: the men who go to Catraeth fail in their mission but they desire, above all else, to die a glorious death and thus to win 'deathless fame'. The Heroic Ideal is also present in modified forms in the work of *Taliesin, the saga poetry of the ninth century associated with *'Canu Llywarch Hen', and in the verse of the *Gogynfeirdd.

For further details see Nora Chadwick, *The British Heroic Age: the Welsh and the Men of the North* (1976).

Hero's Marriage with Sovereignty, The, an important theme in early Welsh mythology, is found especially in Y *Tair Rhamant. Sovereignty is represented as a beautiful woman whose marriage to the hero symbolizes his union with the kingdom. Wearing a golden crown and seated on a magnificent throne, she offers him food and drink; or else she appears as an old hag whose beauty is restored by marriage with the hero. The winning of Sovereignty is often preceded by the hunt of a magic animal, usually a stag or boar. The quest is never easy and, at the moment of triumph, the hero is overcome by calamity which is caused by the powers of *Annwn, the Otherworld. He is put to the test and has to prove himself once more worthy before he can reclaim his status as the rightful ruler. It has been suggested that *Gwenhwyfar, *Arthur's queen, may have been a representation of Sovereignty, which may explain why there are so many abduction tales associated with her.

HESELTINE, NIGEL (1916–), poet and short-story writer. Born at Montgomery, a son of Philip Heseltine (the composer Peter Warlock), he was an associate of Keidrych *Rhys and co-edited some of the early numbers of the magazine *Wales, contributing poems, acerbic editorial comment and short stories. Some of his stories were published in the volume *Tales of the Squirearchy* (1946), which is as malicious towards the gentry of mid-Wales as was Caradoc Evans (David *Evans) in his view of the peasantry. After the Second World War, Heseltine severed all connection with Wales and lived in Ireland and in Africa, latterly as an economic and financial adviser to the President of Madagascar. To his Dublin period belongs a small volume of English versions of poems by *Dafydd ap Gwilym (1944); he also published a collection of poems, *The Four-walled Dream* (1941).

Heyday in the Blood, The (1936), Geraint *Goodwin's best-known and most successful book, is set in Tanygraig, a fictitious village in the borderland between Wales and England. The Red Lion is the natural focus of local life and its landlord, Twmi, is an imposing character endowed with wit and ancestral wisdom. The main narrative thread is the relationship between his daughter Beti and two young men: Llew, her cousin, also a vividly potent figure, and the doomed poet, Evan, heir to a bankrupt mill. The underlying theme of the novel is the threat to Tanygraig's Welsh way of life posed by tourism in league with the local council which plans to drive a new road through the village. Although spiced with broad humour, the book is permeated with an awareness of irreplaceable loss and profound regret. In it Goodwin revealed that, as well as being a gifted landscape artist, he could create character and a range of dramatic effects. More importantly, he realized in this work the potential of the novel form as a vehicle for expressing ideas.

Hir-a-thoddaid, see under TWENTY-FOUR METRES.

Hiraeth, a word with more than one meaning in Welsh and perhaps no exact equivalent in English, is used to denote nostalgia for childhood, youth, native district or country, or else a yearning for an ideal spiritual state or emotional experience in the future, usually beyond place and time. Some critics, such as Ernest *Renan and Matthew *Arnold, have taken *hiraeth* to be characteristic of the Celts in general. The elegiac note has been struck in Welsh literature since the time of the *Cynfeirdd and it is heard so often in *The *Mabinogion*, in *cywyddau* of the medieval period and in folklore, that it may be regarded as a motif as common as the themes of the Otherworld, the Waste Land, the *Devastated Hearth and Lost Time. It has been argued that the military and political defeats of the Welsh

may explain why their literature looks back to past glories and forward to the return of national heroes, as in the legends associated with *Arthur and other forms of the cult of *Y Mab Darogan* (see under VATICINATION). A similar sentiment has been detected in attempts to found a new Wales in America. It was certainly a factor in the experience of those Welsh writers, such as William *Williams (Pantycelyn) and William *Thomas (Islwyn), who yearned for the glory of heaven and those others who, under the late influence of *Romanticism, hoped for a redeemed humanity and a better world. The theme has new complexities in *Anglo-Welsh literature of the twentieth century, especially in the work of those writers who have lamented the loss of the Welsh cultural heritage.

An anthology of verse and prose illustrating this theme has been edited by Dora Polk under the title *A Book Called Hiraeth* (1982).

Hiriell, a hero traditionally associated with *Gwynedd, is said to sleep, like *Arthur, until the time comes when his people are in direst need of him.

Hirlas Horn, The, in the ceremonies of *Gorsedd Beirdd Ynys Prydain*, is offered to the Archdruid by a young woman on behalf of the district in which the *National Eisteddfod is held. See also BLODEUGED.

'Hirlas Owain' (lit. 'Owain's drinking horn'), a poem by Owain Cyfeiliog (*Owain ap Gruffudd ap Maredudd), preserved in *The *Red Book of Hergest*, refers to an expedition by Owain's war-band, in 1155, to rescue his brother Meurig from imprisonment in *Maelor. The setting is Owain's court at night, where the warriors have gathered for a feast after returning triumphantly from the expedition. Owain calls upon the cup-bearer to bring the drinking horn to each warrior in turn. The war-band is compared with that of Mynyddog Mwynfawr whose fate at Catraeth is described in 'Y *Gododdin' and each verse praises the one to whom the drink is offered. An unstereotyped praise-poem, it presents a vivid picture of the relationship between prince and war-band and of their rejoicing and sorrowing after battle.

For discussion of the poem see T. Gwynn Jones, 'Catraeth, and Hirlas Owain', in *Y Cymmrodor* (vol. XXXII, 1922), Rachel Bromwich, 'The date of *Hirlas Owein*' in the *Bulletin* of the Board of Celtic Studies (vol. XVI, 1955) and Gruffydd Aled Williams in the same publication (vol. XXVI, 1974).

Hisperic Literature, a number of Latin works written in or about the seventh century in a style and vocabulary which have been condemned as unclassically bizarre, but which may be regarded as an eccentric development of the 'Western Latin' pioneered by *Gildas. Dismissed by champions of classical Latinity, Gildas has been praised by some for using Latin in an uniquely vital and experimental way. It is agreed that these works are of Celtic origin and the fact that the vocabulary contains Brythonic words (as well as Hebrew, Syriac and Greek) suggests that it developed among the Britons of Wales and Brittany; another theory is that some of the *Druids became Latin *rhetores*. Because the writings make much use of alliteration and assonance and are in verse, with examples of *cynghanedd sain*, it is thought that Hisperic Literature may have influenced and been influenced by developments in *Cerdd Dafod*.

Further details will be found in F. J. H. Jenkinson (ed.), *The Hisperica Famina* (1908), Evan J. Jones, *History of Education in Wales* (1931) and Michael W. Herren (ed.), *The Hisperica Famina* (1974).

Historia Brittonum (lit. 'The history of the Britons'), a source of fundamental importance for the early literature of Wales (however great its deficiencies from a historical point of view), was compiled from a number of disparate sources, both literary-learned and native-oral, and it is this amalgam which gives to the work its disjointed character. The text has come down in a number of manuscripts which fall into four main recensions, of which the one found in Harleian Manuscript 3859 (*c*.1100, but originally redacted *c*.830) is acknowledged to be the best and the most complete. The same manuscript contains the *Annales Cambriae* and a collection of regnal lists of Welsh dynasties, both historical documents unique in value. The attribution of the *Historia* to *Nennius is found in a prologue which appears only in the much later 'Cambridge' recension of the mid-eleventh century. Apart from this Nennian prologue, the Harleian recension is the only one which contains the contents of the *Historia* in their entirety.

The following summary of these contents will serve to indicate to how great an extent the *Historia* is the earliest source for concepts and traditions which retained a primary significance for the Welsh literary heritage throughout the Middle Ages and beyond. The text includes a computation of the world dated from the Flood to the year 831, with a list of the Six Ages of the World; a description of Britain and of the successive invaders of Britain and Ireland, culminating in the arrival of *Brutus, the Trojan fugitive and eponymous ancestor of the Britons; an account of Roman Britain, its emperors and tyrants, the British settlement of Armorica and the departure of the Romans from the Island; the story of *Vortigern (Gwrtheyrn) and his dealings with the Saxons; the arrival of St. Germanus (*Garmon) in Britain; the account of Vortigern's collapsing tower and the intervention of *Emrys Wledig; the death of Vortigern and of his heroic son Vortimer (Gwerthefyr Fendigaid); an account of St. *Patrick; the first reference to *Arthur as *dux bellorum* ('leader of battles') and

his twelve victorious engagements against the nation's enemies; and the so-called 'Saxon Genealogies', which list the rulers of the Anglian settlements in Northumbria and Yorkshire, interspersed with notes of undoubted British provenance which give important information about early north British and Welsh history. This last includes the unique passage about the early poets who flourished in the time of Ida of Northumbria in the latter half of the sixth century, of which the significance is so great as to deserve quotation in full: 'Then *Talhaearn Tad Awen gained renown in poetry, and *(A)neirin and *Taliesin and *Blwchfardd and *Cian who is called *Gwenith Gwawd* gained renown together at the same time in British poetry'. The work ends with a computation, estimating the period of Vortigern's reign against Roman consular dating, followed by a list of the Cities and Marvels of Britain.

The standard edition is that of Thomas Mommsen in volume XIII of *Monumenta Germaniae Historica, Auct. Antiquus* (1894); see also F. Lot, *Nennius et l'Historia Brittonum* (1934), and the translation by A. W. Wade-Evans, *Nennius's History of the Britons* (1938). For discussion of the text see Ifor Williams, '*Hen Chwedlau*', in the *Transactions of the Honourable Society of Cymmrodorion* (1946–47), D. N. Dumville, 'Nennius and the *Historia Brittonum*' in *Studia Celtica* (vols. X/XI, 1975–76), 'Sub-Roman Britain: History and Legend' in *History* (vol. 62, 1977) and 'Celtic-Latin Texts in Northern England *c*.1150–1250' in *Celtica* (vol. XII, 1977).

Historia Regum Britanniae (lit. 'History of the Kings of Britain'; *c*.1136), a spurious chronicle by *Geoffrey of Monmouth, claims to trace the history of the kings of Britain down to *Cadwaladr Fendigaid, the last British king, who lost the sovereignty of Britain to the Saxons. In his preface Geoffrey claims only to have translated 'an ancient book in the British tongue' brought out of 'Britannia' (Brittany is probably meant) by Walter of Oxford.

The *Historia* traces the origins of the Britons to Aeneas and his son Ascanius who escaped after the fall of Troy and settled in Italy, becoming the founder of Rome. The founder of the British line was *Brutus, the grandson of Ascanius, who after much wandering came to the isle of Albion, later renamed Britannia. The chronicle relates the vicissitudes of the Britons, their conquest by Romans and Saxons, the flight of the most noble to Brittany and the brilliance of *Arthur's reign which was the high point of their fortunes. Arthur's resistance stamped his name on history but thereafter the dark night of Saxon domination engulfed the Britons.

Geoffrey's claim regarding 'the ancient book' may reflect the use which he may have made of a Welsh manuscript containing genealogies and other historical information as one source among many others. His assertion cannot be accepted at face value because the skilful use of classical and medieval texts, the careful structuring of the work and the author's contemporary attitudes all point to the *Historia* being a consciously literary composition. It contains, however, some of the main themes of medieval Welsh historiography, such as ideas of British sovereignty, of conquest, of loss of sovereignty and of the eventual restoration to the Britons of their ancient heritage. The *Historia* was a most influential work in that it served as the pattern for the writing of British history from its first appearance down to the Renaissance. Its influence lasted even longer in Wales where it was one of the bases of national consciousness; but by the eighteenth century few gave credence either to the *Historia* or to Geoffrey's claims as to its source. See also MATTER OF BRITAIN and MYTH OF DESCENT.

There is no satisfactory edition of the *Historia* but Acton Griscom published a Latin text in 1929, as did Edmond Faral in his *La Légende Arthurienne* (1929); Jacob Hammer published a variant version in 1951. An English translation by Lewis Thorpe appeared in the *Penguin Classics* series in 1966 and an edition, by Henry Lewis, of one of several Medieval Welsh translations, *Brut Dingestow*, was published in 1942. The most comprehensive study is J. S. P. Tatlock, *The Legendary History of Britain* (1950).

Historiae Britannicae Defensio (lit. 'The defence of British history'; 1573), by Sir John *Price of Brecon. Like other contemporary Welsh scholars and antiquaries, the author was determined to defend *Geoffrey of Monmouth's account of 'The *Matter of Britain' against Polydore Vergil, who in 1534 had attacked Geoffrey's account of the *Brutus legend and its supposed connection with the origins of British and Arthurian traditions. Price set out his arguments in writing but, although he had probably completed this work about the same time as *Yn y lhyvyr hwnn (1547), it was not printed until his son Richard published it several years after his father's death. John Price was probably the first collector of manuscripts relating to Welsh history after the *Dissolution of the Monasteries and the work displays clearly his thorough knowledge of sources. Agreeing with Vergil that some of the extra-insular traditions concerning Brutus and *Arthur were false, he disagreed over their British associations. Price, more than Vergil, relied heavily on his manuscript sources and the *Defensio* is of interest mainly because it is the work of a scholar who, in true Renaissance spirit, sought to revive the study of Welsh antiquity and history by examining the origins of the Britons. See also MYTH OF DESCENT.

For further details see Ceri Davies, *Rhagymadroddion a Chyflwyniadau Lladin 1551–1632* (1980) and *Latin Writers of the Renaissance* in the series *Writers of Wales* (1981).

Historic Institute of Wales, The, see CAMBRIAN INSTITUTE.

'Hob y Deri Dando', a traditional song of which Edward *Jones (Bardd y Brenin) included two versions, a southern style and a northern, in his *Musical and Poetical Relicks of the Welsh Bards* (1794). The air, which has several other titles, became one of the most popular tunes for choruses at the *Noson Lawen. More recently it has become a favourite with mixed choirs, set to the words of 'Brethyn Cartref' by Crwys (William Crwys *Williams).

HODGES, CYRIL (Cyril Hughes; 1915–74), poet. Born in Cardiff, he had little formal education but taught himself to read Welsh poetry of the early and medieval periods. An industrialist in a small way, he was generous in his financial support of young writers and their magazines, and of *Plaid Cymru. He published three volumes of verse: *Seeing Voice Welsh Heart* (1965), a sumptuously produced sequence of poems on Welsh mythical themes, with lithographs by the American artist Paul Jenkins; a booklet, *Remittances* (1971); and his collected poems, *Coming of Age* (1971). Under his pen-name he contributed verse and prose to various magazines and wrote, in collaboration with Cenydd Morus (Kenneth Vennor *Morris), a series of prose translations entitled *China Speaks* (1941).

HOLLAND, HUGH (1569–1633), poet. Born at Denbigh, he was educated at the University of Cambridge, where he was noted for his classical scholarship, and later travelled abroad, visiting Rome, Jerusalem and Constantinople. He published two volumes of his longer poems, *Pancharis: the first Booke* (1603) and *A Cypres Garland* (1625), both of which were dedicated to King James I, as well as a number of commendatory verses which were printed in works by other authors, including Ben Jonson. His chief claim to fame rests on the sonnet of his which was prefixed to the first folio edition of Shakespeare's plays in 1623: the poem is unremarkable in itself but it suggests that Holland was personally acquainted with Shakespeare.

HOLLAND, ROBERT (c. 1556/7–1622?), author and translator. Born at Conwy, Caerns., he was educated at the University of Cambridge and held livings in England and Wales, including that of Llanddowror, Carms. He published at least six books: *The Holie Historie of our Lord* (1592), a metrical paraphrase of the biblical narrative; a dialogue against soothsayers, *Dau Gymro yn Taring yn bell o'u Gwlad* (c. 1595), known only from the reprint in Stephen *Hughes's edition of *Canwyll y Cymru (1681); *Agoriad byrr ar Weddi'r Arglwydd* (reprinted by Stephen Hughes in *Cyfarwydd-deb i'r Anghyfarwydd*, 1677), a translation of the *Exposition of the Lord's Prayer* by William Perkins; *Darmerth, neu Arlwy i Weddi* (1600); *Catechism Mr. Perkins*

(1672), a translation of William Perkins's *The Foundation of Christian Religion*; and *Basilikon Doron* (1604), a translation of the work by King James I, which Holland made with the assistance of George Owen *Harry.

Hollantide, the beginning of winter in the Celtic calendar, was a festival (1 Nov.) associated with the dead. The previous evening, Winter's Eve, was one of three nights when the spirit world came so close to the human that the boundary between the two was obscured. This was the evening when the *Ladi Wen* and the *Hwch Ddu Gota* were reputed to roam the countryside. Other traditions included the belief that those who were going to die during the coming year could be seen through the key-hole of the parish church at midnight. The sowing of hemp by young people at cross-roads, again at midnight, was said to cause their future sweethearts to appear. It was also the practice to light bonfires on Winter's Eve, but by the nineteenth century this custom had become associated with Bonfire Night (5 Nov.), when the failure of the Guy Fawkes Plot was celebrated. The change in the calendar which occurred in 1752 (when eleven days were 'lost') added to the confusion and many fairs were held on the old date. The age-old emphasis on the dead was retained when the Feast of All Saints (1 Nov.) was made a Church festival in the seventh century, the Feast of All Souls being celebrated on the following day. In north Wales it was the occasion to collect food for the messenger of the dead and to go 'souling', that is to collect gifts to pay for prayers for the souls of the dead in Purgatory. By the nineteenth century many of these religious associations had been lost and the feast had become merely a day to go *wassailing.

For further details see Trefor M. Owen, *Welsh Folk Customs* (1959).

Home Rule, a limited degree of self-government for Wales in the form of a domestic parliamentary legislature within a federal, imperial British framework, became a controversial but not the predominant issue in Welsh politics during the years from 1886 to 1896. In the main, the demand came from a small group of young Radical, Nonconformist, Liberal Members of Parliament who were elected to Westminster at the General Election of 1886 and at subsequent by-elections. Advocates of Home Rule were a minority both among Welsh Liberals at Westminster and among the party's supporters in the country. The major spokesmen were T. E. *Ellis and David *Lloyd George, both disciples of Michael D. *Jones, who had been almost alone in calling for Home Rule for Wales since the 1860s. Ellis, influenced by Mazzini and Thomas Davis, the Irish Nationalist, was the leading advocate until he accepted a Government post in Gladstone's third administration of

1892. He foresaw a Welsh legislature emerging as a glowing example of social democracy within a progressive and multi-cultured British Empire. After 1892, despite opposition within his own party, Lloyd George led the campaign for Home Rule during the Liberal Ministries of Gladstone and Rosebery (1892–95) by founding the League known as *Cymru Fydd in 1894 and the journal known as *Young Wales* in 1895 and by rebelling openly against the Government in proposing radical policies for Wales. This rebellion was indirectly responsible for the Government's fall in 1895. The Liberals having lost the General Election of that year, Lloyd George then led a vociferous campaign for Home Rule which ended in débâcle: at a meeting held in Newport, Mon., in January 1896, his proposals were defeated by the South Wales Liberal Federation. In effect this disaster marked the end of the Home Rule movement, although further initiatives were undertaken intermittently by individual Liberals, particularly between 1911 and 1914.

The cause also attracted support from a few other quarters, most notably from Emrys ap Iwan (Robert Ambrose *Jones) who advocated a Welsh Parliament within a federal Britain with far more extensive powers than those envisaged by Home Rulers. It was also supported by some Welsh Socialists such as E. Pan *Jones and R. J. *Derfel who expected of a Welsh legislature (unlike the Imperial Parliament) that it would implement Socialist measures, especially those associated with ownership of the land. Home Rule was not, however, a mass movement: it received no more than token support from most of the emerging leaders of the Labour movement in the 1890s, while from the Liberal Establishment in Wales it met with indifference and eventually hostility. See also DEVOLUTION and PARLIAMENT FOR WALES CAMPAIGN.

The question of Home Rule for Wales is discussed by Reginald Coupland in *Welsh and Scottish Nationalism* (1954), by K. O. Morgan in his article 'Welsh Nationalism: the Historical Background' in the *Journal of Contemporary History* (vol. 6, no. 1, 1971), and by the same author in *Rebirth of a Nation: Wales 1880–1980* (1981).

Homfray family, ironmasters, of Penydarren near Merthyr Tydfil, Glam., and of Ebbw Vale, Mon. In 1782 Francis Homfray (1726–98) leased from Anthony *Bacon a mill at Penydarren for the boring of cannon. His sons, Jeremiah (1759–1833) and Samuel (d. 1822), were frequently in conflict with Bacon, whose larger works at Dowlais were built further upstream on the Morlais brook which supplied both enterprises with water, but they too prospered. Jeremiah Homfray, who was knighted in 1810, started the ironworks at Ebbw Vale in 1789 and his brother that at Tredegar in 1800. Samuel was also one of the chief promoters of the Glamorgan Canal which was built in 1795 to carry iron from

Merthyr Tydfil down the Taff Valley to Cardiff. Francis Homfray, rector of Llanfair Cilgedyn, Mon., whose long poem *Thoughts on Happiness* was published in 1817, was probably a member of this family.

HOMFRAY, FRANCIS ALEXANDER (1854–1928), poet. Born at Court St. Lawrence, Mon., he was ordained as a clergyman but earned his living as a private tutor in Bristol. His poems were published in two volumes, namely *Idylls of Thought* (1898) and *Poems* (1930).

Homiliau (lit. 'Homilies'; 2 vols., 1906, 1909), a collection of sermons by Emrys ap Iwan (Robert Ambrose *Jones). Although the author was not a great preacher in the sense that he had the gift of oratory displayed by the giants of the Welsh pulpit in the nineteenth century, his sermons left their mark on Welsh thought and literature. They reflect a sharply logical mind and emphasize the role of religion on a practical, day-to-day basis, while expressing a passionate love of God (which has been described as Pascalian) in prose which verges at times on the poetic.

Hooker, see JENKINS, JOHN (1770–1829).

HOOKER, JEREMY (1941–   ), English poet and critic. Born at Warsash, Hants., and educated at Southampton University, he became a Lecturer in English at the University College of Wales, Aberystwyth, in 1965. He has published seven volumes of poetry: *The Elements* (1972), *Soliloquies of a Chalk Giant* (1974), *Landscape of the Daylight Moon* (1978), *Solent Shore* (1978), *Englishman's Road* (1980), *Itchen Water* (1982) and his selected poems under the title *A View from the Source* (1982). His verse is concerned, in a highly controlled style at once probing yet reticent, with the historical and mythic associations of landscape and with the poet's attachment to place, both in his native Wessex and, latterly, in Wales. He has elaborated upon these themes in his collection of essays, *Poetry of Place* (1982). His other critical works are an essay on John Cowper *Powys in the *Writers of Wales* series (1973), *David Jones: an exploratory study* (1975) and *John Cowper Powys and David Jones: a comparative study* (1979); he has also edited (with Gweno Lewis) the selected poems of Alun *Lewis (1981). He left Wales in 1984 to live in the Netherlands.

There is an autobiographical essay by Jeremy Hooker, in which he discusses his interest in the literature of Wales, in the volume *Artists in Wales* (ed. Meic Stephens, 1977).

HOOSON, ISAAC DANIEL (1880–1948), poet. Born at Rhosllannerchrugog, Denbs., he was by profession a solicitor and had a practice in Wrexham. He began writing poetry at an early age and was later to claim that it was by contributing to O. M. *Edwards's magazine *Cymru* that he served his apprenticeship. Most of the verse in the only collection he published during his lifetime, *Cerddi a Baledi* (1936), was written between 1930 and 1936. His adaptation of Browning's 'The Pied Piper of Hamelin', was published under the title *Y Fantell Fraith* in 1934. The poems of I. D. Hooson won immediate and lasting popularity, especially for the purposes of recitation in public. Such poems as '*Wil*', '*Barti Ddu*', '*Guto Nyth Brân*' and '*Guto Benfelyn*' are among the best-known poems for children in the Welsh language. For the most part, his poems are charming lyrics in the free metres, his favourite subjects being animals and flowers. Although a note of nostalgia for his childhood and youth is sometimes heard in his earlier work, his pessimism became more apparent in the posthumous volume *Y Gwin a Cherddi Eraill* (1948).

A critical assessment of his work, with an account of his life, was published by W. R. Jones (1954); see also the essays by R. Geraint Gruffydd and Gwilym R. Jones in *Ysgrifau Beirniadol III, VI* (ed. J. E. Caerwyn Williams, 1967, 1971) and by Hugh Bevan in *Beirniadaeth Lenyddol* (ed. B. F. Roberts, 1982).

Hopcyn ap Tomas ab Einion (c.1330–post 1403), see under RED BOOK OF HERGEST.

Hopedale or **Yr Hôb**, a commot, originally of *Powys, was brought under the rule of *Gwynedd in the twelfth century. With Dyffryn Clwyd and *Rhufoniog it was granted to *Dafydd ap Gruffudd in 1277 and under the Statute of *Rhuddlan (1284) it became part of the county of Flint.

HOPKIN, LEWIS (1708–71), poet. Born at Llanbedr-ar-fynydd, Glam., he settled at Hendre-Ifan-Goch in the parish of Llandyfodwg, where his family had its roots. He was one of the Glamorgan Grammarians and is believed to have been bardic tutor to Iolo Morganwg (Edward *Williams) and Edward *Evan. His only volume of verse, *Y Fel Gafod* (1812), is mediocre, but some of his poems in the strict metres, such as his elegy for William Bassett of Bewper (Beaupré), were written out of the rich literary tradition to which he belonged.

HOPKINS, BENJAMIN THOMAS (1897–1981), poet, a native of Lledrod, Cards., spent most of his life farming at Blaenpennal, near Y Mynydd Bach, where he held regular literary workshops with J. M. *Edwards and E. Prosser *Rhys. A frequent adjudicator at the *National Eisteddfod, he is best remembered for his *cywydd*, '*Rhos Helyg*', which praises the beauty of his locality and laments the decay of its traditional way of life. A selection of his verse was published in the volume *Rhos Helyg a Cherddi Eraill* (1976).

HOPKINS, GERARD MANLEY (1844–89), English poet. He was born at Stratford, Essex, and educated at Balliol College, Oxford. Converted to Roman Catholicism while at Oxford, he decided on graduation to become a Jesuit priest and, between 1870 and 1877, underwent three distinct periods of training for the priesthood. The last phase was one of three years of theological study at St. Beuno's College, near St. Asaph, Flints. After his final ordination in 1877, his career up to 1884 included various teaching appointments and periods as priest in England and Scotland. His last years, from 1884 to 1889, were spent in Dublin as Fellow of the Royal University of Ireland and Professor of Greek at University College. Frail and prone to illness, his heavy academic duties added to a sense of physical and spiritual collapse, articulated especially in the so-called 'terrible sonnets' of 1885. He died in Dublin of typhoid fever.

The period spent at St. Beuno's College was crucial for Hopkins. Having destroyed the poems written during his undergraduate days, because he had feared that the writing of poetry was at odds with his calling as a priest, he was prompted to resume the practice by his Rector's wish that someone might write a poem on the fate of five nuns, refugees from the anti-clerical Falk Laws in Germany, who had been drowned in a shipwreck in the mouth of the Thames: the result was the poem 'The Wreck of *The Deutschland*' (1875). It was the first, and fullest, employment of a prosody now known as 'sprung rhythm', which was determined by the number of stresses rather than of syllables in the line. The new poetry also demonstrated ideas formulated in his journals as 'inscape' and 'instress', by which he meant the unique pattern comprising the identity of things, individuals and events, and the energy bringing parts into the relationship of the whole, which Hopkins saw as the dynamic presence of God in the world.

These ideas, much influenced by the medieval philosopher Duns Scotus, were crystallized for the poet by his new location overlooking the valley of the Elwy and facing Snowdon across the Vale of Clwyd. The way in which that landscape fed his particular way of seeing the world is shown in the ten sonnets of his final year (1877) at St. Beuno's, among which were 'The Starlight Night', 'The Windhover' and 'Hurrahing in Harvest'. Likewise, his aim of matching the 'inscape' of things with the 'inscapes' of sound and shape in language itself was greatly influenced by the strict patterning of consonants and vowels in Welsh poetry. He learned Welsh, mastered and employed the rules of *cynghanedd, and even wrote some strict-metre poetry in the language. This interest in what might be called 'poetry of place' in the linguistic as well as the topographical sense, marked his subsequent career. He was to cross several other regional and national boundaries, finding endless delight in local idiom and dialect and in the mobile outsider's advantage in not taking the English language, in any central or standardized sense, for granted. The experience of Wales—'woods, waters, meadows, combes, vales,/All the air things wear that build this world of Wales'—went earliest and deepest towards the making of the mature poet.

Apart from items in a few anthologies, the poetry of Gerard Manley Hopkins was not published until 1918. Though substantially governed by his thinking, his experiences and his responsibilities as a Jesuit priest in Victorian times, his work was technically revolutionary and influential in that it restored a new weight and density, and an abrupt expressiveness, to English verse. The date of its publication, however, ensured that its influence would fall mainly on the second generation of Modernist poets, the generation of W. H. Auden rather than that of T. S. Eliot. Many English poets of the 1930s (Auden himself in his early poems is a notable example) rather self-consciously imitated the hallmarks of Hopkins's style. But it was a Welshman, Dylan *Thomas, who was in a position more deeply to emulate the way in which Hopkins had activated difficult forms with expressive energy. It is likely that Hopkins's poetry was Thomas's closest contact with the stylistic enrichment deriving from a knowledge of Welsh. A natural kinship in terms of poetic temperament meant that Hopkins's influence, unlike that on his English contemporaries, remained constant enough to grow to its finest flowering in Dylan Thomas's later verse.

The most authoritative biographies of Hopkins are those by Bernard Bergonzi (1977) and P. Kitchen (1978); for critical discussion of his work see the studies by W. H. Gardner (2 vols., 1944, 1949) and Geoffrey Grigson in the *Writers and their Work* series (1955), the collection of essays edited by G. H. Hartman (1966) and the essay by N. H. Mackenzie in the *Writers and Critics* series (1968). For a study of the Welsh influences on Hopkins's poetry see the articles by Gweneth Lilly in *Modern Language Review* (vol. XXXVII, July, 1943) and that by A. Thomas in the *Transactions* of the Honourable Society of Cymmrodorion (1965).

Horned Oxen, mythological beasts about which several stories have survived in Welsh literature and folklore. In the tale of *Culhwch and Olwen, for example, the two oxen are named Nynniaw and Peibiaw and the task set for Culhwch is to harness them and use them to plough the land in preparation for Olwen's wedding-feast. Huge and exceptionally strong, they were reputed to have pulled the *Afanc out of the river Conwy and to have hauled a large boulder for use in the building of the church of Llanddewi Brefi, Cards. A piece of horn said to belong to one of the oxen (it may have been that of the primitive Urus) was kept for centuries in that church and is now in the Welsh Folk Museum.

Horner, Arthur Lewis (1894–1968), miners' leader. Although born in Merthyr Tydfil, Glam., he was always associated with Maerdy, Rhondda. As a young man he went to Dublin to join the Citizens' Army of James Connolly and he was imprisoned on his return. A protégé of Noah *Ablett, he remained wedded to the primacy of trade union politics, despite his own stance as a leading British Communist. From 1936, as the first Communist President of the *South Wales Miners' Federation, his influence grew steadily and from 1946 to 1959 he served as General Secretary of the newly created National Union of Mineworkers. Despite many setbacks, political and personal, Horner was among the ablest of all trade union leaders and, with his close friend, A. J. *Cook, he was certainly the best loved by the miners of south Wales.

For further details see Horner's autobiography, *Incorrigible Rebel* (1960).

Household Poet, see under BARDIC ORDER.

How Green Was My Valley (1939), a novel by Richard Llewellyn (Richard Llewellyn *Lloyd), is perhaps the most famous novel ever written by a Welsh writer in English. It depicts an early mining community, innocent, deeply religious and thoroughly Welsh, which is gradually destroyed by an influx of English and Irish workers, by the deterioration of the physical environment, by the divisive philosophy and practice of the Miners' Union, and by the break-up of the Morgan family unit which is central to the narrative, all these resulting from the new practices of strike and confrontation. Although its scenario bears some superficial resemblance to that of life in the valleys of south-east Wales in late Victorian times, perhaps that of the *Rhondda, the novel is much less a historical account than a powerful myth with political connotations, related in its effect to Owen Wister's *The Virginian* (1902) and the American Myth of the Frontier. The hard work and co-operation of the first arrivals are vitiated by exploitation and manipulation: Eden is lost for ever. Powerfully written, with a sustained poetic quality and some memorable scenes and characters, the novel was acclaimed by an English reading public which was unhappy about the direction of politics and society after 1918. Welsh readers, perplexed at first by its lack of correlation with their own experience, were persuaded by its success—it became a best-seller and was filmed in America—to acclaim it too.

The later life and subsequent rise to industrial power of Huw Morgan, the narrator of *How Green Was My Valley* whose boyhood it describes, were the subject of three sequels: *Up, into the Singing Mountain* (1963) and *Down where the Moon is Small* (1966) are set in the Welsh community of *Patagonia, and in *Green, Green my Valley Now* (1975) Huw Morgan returns to present-day Wales. None of these, however, has the undeniable qualities of Richard Llewellyn's first and best novel.

For a critical assessment of this novel see Glyn Tegai Hughes, 'The Mythology of the Mining Valleys', in *Triskel Two* (ed. Sam Adams and Gwilym Rees Hughes, 1973), David Smith, 'Myth and Meaning in the Literature of the South Wales Coalfield—the 1930s' in *The Anglo-Welsh Review* (vol. 25, no. 56, 1976) and the chapter 'Colour Wales Green' in the same author's *Wales! Wales?* (1984).

Howard de Walden, see SCOTT-ELLIS, THOMAS EVELYN (1880–1946).

HOWELL, FLORENCE (1869–1946), short-story writer and playwright. Born at Whalecwm, Cosheston, Pembs., she and her sister Daisy (1864–1904) spent many holidays with their grandparents at Blackpool Mill on the eastern Cleddau. There, together and separately, they wrote short stories, a selection of which was edited by Morwyth Rees and published under the title *Stories at the Mill* (1969). In later life Florence confined her interest to drama, writing *Jane Wogan* (included in *The Best One-Act Plays of 1934*) and *Castle Garth*, a full-length drama. Many of her shorter plays, including *A Woman of Compassion*, *The Thirteenth of March*, *The Sentence* and *Pembroke Castle*, were broadcast, translated into Welsh and frequently performed in both languages by amateur companies.

HOWELL, JAMES (1593–1666), writer, was born at Aber-nant, Carms., the second son of the rector there. Educated at Jesus College, Oxford, he was by 1616 the steward of Sir Robert Mansel's Glass House in Broad Street, London, but preferred thereafter to use his flair for languages by representing the company abroad. Returned in 1623 from extensive travels throughout Europe, and without employment, he was sent to Madrid by merchants of the Turkey Company to seek compensation for a ship seized by the Sardinians, then subject to Spain. While there he had opportunity to comment in detail on the Prince of Wales's courtship of the Infanta, historically the most valuable part of his *Letters*, but the Spaniards' anger at the failure of the intended alliance ruined Howell's mission. In 1626 he was appointed Secretary to the Council for the North and in the following year he was elected Member of Parliament for Richmond, Yorks. The high point of his public service came in 1632, when he accompanied the Earl of Leicester to the Court of Denmark and was able to air the unfailing fluency of his Latin as the mission's public orator. Thereafter his career is difficult to follow: he became an 'intelligencer' or spy for the Earl of Strafford, perhaps as early as 1633, certainly from 1639. At the outbreak of the *Civil Wars the King appointed him Extra Clerk of the Council, but within two months he was clapped into the Fleet prison by the Parliamentarians and there remained until the general amnesty of 1650. The eight years of his incarceration made Howell a writer: at his death he had written some forty books, more than any other of his contemporaries. In 1661 he was appointed Historiographer Royal and lived the rest of his life in Fetter Lane, Holborn.

His poems are often clever and always well-turned: his principal volumes, *Dodona's Grove* (1641), a heavy political allegory, and *England's Teares* (1644), an appeal for peace, were translated into several European languages but left less mark in England. Among his other works were *Lexicon Tetraglotton* (1659–60), an English-French-Italian-Spanish dictionary, and a collection of proverbs from those languages and from Welsh. Howell is remembered chiefly for his *Familiar Letters* (*Epistolae Ho-Elianae*, 1645), but his *Parly of Beasts* (1660) was probably the last unashamed literary defence of Wales to be written in English before the twentieth century.

The fullest consideration of Howell is that by Joseph Jacobs in his edition of *Epistolae Ho-Elianae* (2 vols., 1890, 1892); but see also the commentary in Edwin Poole's *Old Welsh Chips* (1888), the article by G. H. in *The Red Dragon* (Feb., 1883), W. H. Vann, *Notes on the Writings of James Howell* (1924) and the article by Gareth Alban Davies in *Dock Leaves* (vol. 7, no. 20, Winter, 1956).

HOWELL, JOHN (Ioan ab Hywel, Ioan Glandyfroedd; 1774–1830), see under BLODAU DYFED (1824).

Hu Gadarn, a legendary hero described by William *Owen Pughe in his *Cambrian Biography* (1803) as 'the deified progenitor of the Cymry' or Welsh. This laudatory description was inspired by Iolo Morganwg (Edward *Williams) who, in the highly idiosyncratic 'Third Series' of the Triads of the Isle of Britain which he contributed to *The Myvyrian Archaiology of Wales* (1801) with the purpose of outlining Welsh and British prehistory, represented Hu Gadarn as a 'culture hero' who first led the Cymry to Britain from the legendary *Deffrobani* (i.e. Ceylon). According to Iolo, it was Hu Gadarn who established them in the country by peaceful means, introduced the arts of agri-culture and social organization, and instituted oral tradition in poetry by adapting the use of song for the preservation of records. Iolo had obtained the leader's name from *Iolo Goch's poem, 'Cywydd y Llafurwr', which told in an apologue how Hu Gadarn, Emperor of Con-stantinople, guided a plough with his own hands and would eat no bread but what came from his own labour. The original source of this apologue was the translation *Campau Charlymaen* (13th cent.), in which Hu Gadarn ('the strong') renders the name *Hugun le Fort* in the French original. See also GWLAD YR HAF.

Huail fab Caw, one of the sons of Caw o

Brydyn, was brother to *Gildas, and a man about whom a cycle of tales once existed. He is listed in *Trioedd Ynys Prydain* as one of 'the Three Crowned Heads of Battle in the Isle of Britain'. In the tale of *Culhwch and Olwen he stabs his nephew, Gwydre fab Llwydeu, an act which causes ill feeling between him and *Arthur. In the Life of Gildas by *Caradog of Llancarfan it is said that he never submitted to any king, not even Arthur, and that he often led raids from Scotland on Arthur's kingdom, for which Arthur killed him. *Gerald de Barri (Giraldus Cambrensis), in his *Descriptio Kam-briae* (c.1194), repeats the assertion that Arthur killed Huail, adding that Gildas, in mourning for his brother, threw all the fine books which he had written about Arthur's exploits into the sea. These statements were used in later periods to explain the absence of any references to Arthur in the work of Gildas. A sixteenth-century source, the chronicle of Elis *Gruffydd, pro-vides another version of the tale of the enmity between Arthur and Huail, this time located in north-east Wales. It tells of a skirmish between the two, on account of one of Arthur's con-cubines, which leads to the beheading of Huail on the stone known as Maen Huail, Ruthin, Denbs.

For further details of all these tales see the essay by the editor in *Astudiaethau Amrywiol* (ed. Thomas Jones, 1968).

HUCKS, JOSEPH (b. 1772), see under PEDESTRIAN TOUR THROUGH NORTH WALES (1795).

HUDSON-WILLIAMS, THOMAS (1873–1961), scholar and translator. A native of Caernarfon, he was a Lecturer in Greek, Latin, French and Celtic at the University College of North Wales, Bangor, and Professor of Greek from 1904 to 1940. In classical studies his main contribution was his edition of Theognis and other elegiac poets. He translated a good deal into Welsh, especially from Russian; among his publications are *Y Groegiaid Gynt* (1932), *Storïau o'r Rwseg* (1942), *Anfarwol Werin* (1945), *Cerddi o'r Rwseg* (1945), *Ar y Weirglodd* (1946), *Merch y Capten* (1947), *Rwsalca* (1950), *Atgofion am Gaernarfon* (1950), *Bannau Llên Pwyl* (1953), *Straeon Tad Hanes* (1954), *Y Tadau a'r Plant* (1964) and *Pedair Drama Fer o'r Rwseg* (1964).

HUES, IVAN (fl. 1889), poet. Almost nothing is known about him, but he was certainly a Welsh-speaker and may have been a native of Carmarthenshire. The only work ascribed to Hues (*recte* Hughes) is a long allegorical poem entitled *Heart to Heart: the Song of Two Nations* (1889), which is important for an understanding of the Welshman's sense of inferiority in the nineteenth century. It has a double theme: the attraction of writing in English and the wounds caused by English sneers. The foreword is by Sir

Lewis *Morris and the central, probably auto-biographical, figure of Awen Wealh is son to the knight of Dynver Towers. Attracted by the 'loftier' tone of English poetry and dissatisfied with the defensively antiquarian attitudes prevailing at the *Eisteddfod and among Welsh poets, Awen is driven from Wales by the presence of intruders who 'affect sore to despise/ Both land and people'. Rescued from death by Inglissa, a maiden who promises that the sons of Wales shall be among the foremost in 'the glorious, grand/Broadening nationality', he is taken by Credwen, the goddess of poetry, to see Morwyn, enthroned between *Arthur and Merlin (*Myrddin), who gives him to understand that a separate Welsh tradition must pass away and that Awen and Inglissa will be one. The poem has enormous facility, occasionally rising to the memorable, however naïve the sentiments may seem to the modern reader.

For further details see the lecture by Roland Mathias in the volume *Dathlu* (ed. R. Gerallt Jones, 1985).

HUGH OF RHUDDLAN or **HUE DE ROTELANDE** (*fl.* 1180–90), the author of romances in the dialect of Norman French current in Britain in the twelfth century, probably lived at Rhuddlan before settling in the Credenhill district to the west of Hereford. Between 1180 and 1190 he wrote *Ipomedon* and its sequel, *Protheselaus*, for the amusement of Gilbert Fitz-Baderon, lord of Monmouth, the grandson of Gilbert de Clare, Earl of Pembroke. In the first of these works Hugh sought to win the interest of the royal court by setting his story in southern Italy and Sicily, because Henry II's daughter, Joan, had married William the Good, King of Sicily. The poem relates how the adventurous squire Ipomedon becomes the husband of the Duchess of Calabria and King of Apulia. There are references to Walter *Map as the author of a work on Lancelot and to a Welsh king named Ris, perhaps Rhys ap Tewdwr. In the sequel the hero Protheselaus succeeds in overcoming his brother Daunus and in winning the hand of Medea, Queen of Sicily. The plots of both works are of the thinnest but Hugh excels in dialogue, humour and word-play, and his attitude to sexual love is jocularly cynical. Like *Thomas, the author of *Tristan*, he was one of the pioneers of a Norman-French literature which in his day may have been livelier than that of France itself.

For further details see Jessie Crosland, *Medieval French Literature* (1956), M. Dominica Legge, *Anglo-Norman Literature and its Background* (1963) and A. J. Holden (ed.), *Ipomedon* (1975).

HUGHES, ANNIE HARRIET (Gwyneth Vaughan; 1852–1910), novelist. Born at Talsarnau, Mer., a miller's daughter, she received no more than an elementary education, but read widely. Her four novels which are authentic in their descriptions of country manners, appeared as serials in *Y *Cymro* (1903–06) and *Y *Brython* (1907–09) and were developed from material published in *Yr Haul* (1903–04), the main characters being modelled on her parents. In *O Gorlannau y Defaid* (1905) she describes the religious revival of 1859, *Plant y Gorthrwm* (1908) is the story of the elections of 1868, and *Cysgodau y Blynyddoedd Gynt* is set in an earlier period. She also contributed verse and prose to periodicals, such as *Cymru* and *Young Wales*.

Her son, **Arthur Hughes** (1878–1965), was the editor of two anthologies of poetry, *Cywyddau Cymru* (1909) and *Gemau'r Gogynfeirdd* (1910). In 1911 he emigrated to *Patagonia where he pursued his literary interests and contributed to the Welsh periodical press.

There is an article on Gwyneth Vaughan by Thomas Parry in the *Journal* of the Merionethshire Historical and Records Society (vol. VIII, 1980) and another on Arthur Hughes by the same author in *Taliesin* (vol. 38, 1979).

HUGHES, BETI (1926–81), novelist, was born near St. Clears, Carms., and educated at University College, Cardiff. A teacher of Welsh, she became deputy-headmistress of *Ysgol Bro Myrddin*, Carmarthen, in 1978. She was a prolific writer and wrote many popular novels, including *Wyth Esgid Du* (1962), *Dwy Chwaer* (1963), *Adar o'r Unlliw* (1964), *Carchar Hyfryd* (1965), *Wyth Pabell Wen* (1966), *Genethod Abergwylan* (1967), *Hufen Amser* (1968), *Wyth Olwyn Felen* (1969), *Aderyn o Ddyfed* (1971) and *Pontio'r Pellter* (1981).

HUGHES, CLEDWYN (1920–78), novelist and topographical writer, was born at Llansantffraid, Mont., where his family had been gentlemen farmers for centuries. A qualified pharmacist, he gave up his practice to become a full-time writer in 1947 and, for the rest of his life, he lived on his income from writing, which was supplemented by a cosmetics business which he ran from his home at Arthog, Mer. He was the author of twenty-seven books, including the novels *The Different Drummer* (1947), *The Inn Closes for Christmas* (1947), *Wennon* (1948) and *The Civil Strangers* (1949). The last-named, perhaps his most distinguished work, describes the influence of an unscrupulous headmaster upon the lives of three of his pupils, in particular Idris Prys whose adolescence is delicately portrayed. Of the author's topographical books, *A Wanderer in North Wales* (1949) and *Portrait of Snowdonia* (1967) are the most accomplished in literary terms and may even be said to be among his finest writings. Cledwyn Hughes also wrote books for children, including the delightful collection of short stories, *The King who lived on Jelly* (1961).

Hughes, Cyril, see HODGES, CYRIL (1915–74).

Hughes, Gaenor (1745–80), a woman who was

said to have lived for nearly six years on nothing but water from a spring near her home at Bodelith, Llandderfel, Mer. Bedridden, she claimed to have seen visions and, on one occasion, 'The Tree of Life'. Like Sarah *Jacob, she received many visitors, including Thomas *Pennant, and Jonathan *Hughes was among the poets who addressed poems to her.

HUGHES, GWILYM REES (1930–   ), poet and editor. Born at Llanllechid, Caerns., and educated at the University College of North Wales, Bangor, he is a lecturer at the Gwent College of Higher Education. He has co-edited numerous volumes of poetry and prose in both Welsh and English, including *Cerddi Heddiw* (1968), *Storïau* (6 vols., 1968–74), *Cerddi Hir* (1970), *Triskel* (2 vols., 1971, 1973), *Blodeugerdd y Plant* (1971), *Saunders Lewis* (1975), *Dragon's Hoard* (1976) and *A Guide to Welsh Literature* (2 vols., 1976, 1979). A former member of the editorial board of *Poetry Wales, he has published one volume of his own poems, *Cysgod Llygliw* (1972).

HUGHES, GWILYM THOMAS (1895–1978), dramatist. A native of Glyn Ceiriog, Denbs., who was for many years a teacher in London, he was the author of numerous one-act plays which won prizes at the *National Eisteddfod, including *Y Pren Planedig* (1953), *Ei Seren tan Gwmwl* (1955), *Cyfamod* (1960), *Pan Ddêl Mai* (1962) and *Cyffro yn y Cosmos* (1966); he also won the Drama Medal in 1961 and 1963.

HUGHES, HUGH or **HUW AP HUW (Y Bardd Coch o Fôn**; 1693–1776), poet and tutor of poets at his home, Llwydiarth Esgob, Llandyfrydog, Ang., was a friend of Lewis *Morris and a corresponding member of the Honourable Society of *Cymmrodorion. Some of his work was published in *Diddanwch Teuluaidd* (1763) and a few of his religious poems in the free metres in *Diddanwch i'w Feddiannydd* (1773); he also translated moral works into Welsh. His *cywydd* of greeting to Goronwy *Owen inspired that poet's famous response which begins, '*Darllenais awdl dra llawn serch*' and which includes an eloquent tribute to Anglesey. The two poems appear in *Blodeugerdd o'r Ddeunawfed Ganrif* (ed. D. Gwenallt Jones, 1938).

Hughes, Hugh (1790–1863), artist and publisher, was born at Llandudno, Caerns., and trained as a wood-engraver. His best-known work, *The Beauties of Cambria* (1823), which includes some sixty plates, is an account of a tour of Wales made in the years from 1819 to 1821. He also published, at Carmarthen, a number of periodicals, including *Yr Hynafion Cymreig* (1823–24), *Yr Addysgydd* (1823–24) and *Brut y Cymry* (1824). After spending about eight years in London, during which time, as a Radical and

Independent, he was involved in controversy with the Calvinistic Methodists led by John *Elias, he lived at Caernarfon and assisted William *Williams (Caledfryn) in publishing the periodicals *Y Seren Ogleddol* and the short-lived *Papur Newydd Cymreig* (1836). Among his best-known artistic creations is the map entitled 'Dame Venedotia, alias Modryb Gwen' (1845), in which he depicted north Wales as an old lady carrying a burden on her back.

HUGHES, HUGH DERFEL (1816–90), poet and local historian, was born at Llandderfel, Mer., and was by trade a farm labourer and quarryman. It is said that he composed his poem '*Y Cyfamod Disigl*', the last verse of which is the hymn '*Y Gŵr a fu gynt o dan hoelion*', while on his way home over the Berwyn hills after working at the harvest on a farm in Shropshire. After settling at Tre-garth, Caerns., in about 1844, he began studying the history and geology of the district in great detail, publishing his observations in *Hynafiaethau Llandegái a Llanllechid* (1866). He was also the author of two volumes of verse, *Blodau'r Gân* (1844) and *Y Gweithiwr Cariadgar* (1849), which include, as was customary in that period, the poems of his friends. His son, **Hugh Brython Hughes** (1843–1913), translated children's books into Welsh and Ifor *Williams, the scholar, was his grandson.

HUGHES, ISAAC (Craigfryn; 1852–1928), novelist, was born at Quakers Yard, Glam. A coalminer, he was blind for the latter part of his life. Of his six novels the most popular was *Y Ferch o Gefn Ydfa* (1881), a fictionalized version of the story of Ann *Maddocks, which also appeared in an English edition. He tried his hand at writing a thriller in *Y Llofruddiaeth yng Nghoed y Gelli* (1893), but his technique was elementary. Among his other works were *Y Ferch o'r Scer* (1892), the story of Elizabeth *Williams, and *O'r Cryd i'r Amdo* (1903).

Hughes, John (Hugh Owen; 1615–86), see under OWEN, HUGH (1575?–1642).

HUGHES, JOHN (1775–1854), Calvinistic Methodist minister and writer, was born of poor parents in the parish of Llanfihangel-yng-Ngwynfa, Mont., and was apprenticed to a weaver at the age of eleven. Converted in 1795, he became a teacher in Thomas *Charles's circulating schools but settled at Pontrobert in 1805 after his marriage to Ruth Evans, the maidservant at Dolwar Fach, the home of Ann *Griffiths. He began preaching in 1802 and became influential within his denomination. Ordained in 1814, he was one of those who drew up the Confession of Faith adopted by the Calvinistic Methodists in 1823.

A prolific writer of both prose and poetry, John Hughes published about twenty books and often contributed to the magazines of his day, especially *Goleuad Cymru* and *Y Drysorfa*, on a variety of religious topics. His short biographies of some of his fellow-Methodists such as Owen Jones (1787–1828) of Gelli (1830) are particularly valuable. Earlier in his life, after he was converted, he had turned to the writing of hymns, many of them for children, and to the versification of the Psalms; some of his hymns are still popular, especially 'O! Anfon Di yr Ysbryd Glân'. A formative influence on Ann Griffiths, it was he and his wife who were mainly responsible for preserving her hymns and letters, and he wrote a biography of the hymn-writer (1864) which was first published in *Y ★Traethodydd* in 1846.

Of their seven children, two daughters, Jane and Hannah, wrote religious ballads. **Jane Hughes (Deborah Maldwyn**; 1811–80?) took to roaming the countryside after her parents' death, following the Methodist associations and living off the sale of her verses. More than forty booklets of her work were published, some of which were collected under the title *Yr Epha Lawn o Ymborth Ysprydol* (1877), and more of her verse appeared in the volume *Telyn y Cristion* (1877).

Hughes, John (1814–89), a pioneer of the iron industry in Russia, was a native of Merthyr Tydfil, Glam. He began his working life at the Cyfarthfa works but in 1869, at the invitation of the Russian Government, he formed the New Russia Company for the development of the steel and iron industries in that country. The town which grew around his foundries became the centre of the Donetz industrial basin: it was called, after its founder, Yuzovka, and workers from Wales were encouraged to settle there. After the Bolshevik Revolution of October 1917, the company was taken over by the Soviet Government. In 1924 the town's name was changed to Stalino, in honour of a Ukrainian leader, and in 1961 to Donetsk.

For further details see the biographical account by E. G. Bowen in the *St. David's Day* series (1978).

HUGHES, JOHN (1850–1932), Calvinistic Methodist minister and writer, was born in Swansea but brought up at Cwmafan, Glam. Trained at Trefeca and Glasgow University, he served at Dowlais, at Machynlleth and in Liverpool, becoming in 1911 the Moderator of his denomination's General Assembly. His first published work was a volume of verse in English, *Songs in the Night* (1885), but this was followed by a number of theological works, *Rhagluniaeth Duw mewn Anian ac mewn Hanesyddiaeth* (1886), *The Sabbatical Rest of God and Man* (1888), *Gwanwyn Bywyd a'i Ddeffroad* (1899), *Ysgol Jacob* (1899) and *The Christian Consciousness* (The Davies Lecture, 1902). His volume of poetry entitled *Tristiora* (1896) was an extension of the theme of *Songs in the Night* and his last

volume, *Dan y Gwlith* (1911), includes his hymns. A powerful preacher, he impresses less as a poet because although his verse is technically highly competent, he varies his themes, which are unquestioningly religious and fervent, scarcely at all.

HUGHES, JOHN CEIRIOG (Ceiriog; 1832–87), poet. Born at Llanarmon Dyffryn Ceiriog, Denbs., he left school at the age of fifteen and tried his hand at farming and at printing before moving to live with a relation in Manchester in 1848. There he worked as a grocer before finding a job as a clerk in the London Road goods station in 1855. His friendship at this time with men such as R. J. ★Derfel, Creuddynfab (William ★Williams) and Idris Fychan (John Jones; 1825–87) was of crucial significance in his development as a poet. It was Derfel who taught him to appreciate the traditions of Wales and persuaded him to assume the name Ceiriog, while Idris Fychan was largely responsible for firing his interest in Welsh melodies. Creuddynfab's influence on Ceiriog's poetry was the deepest, for he convinced him that it should be simple, natural and full of feeling.

In 1868 Ceiriog returned to Wales to take up the post of stationmaster at Llanidloes, Mont., and two years later he was appointed superintendent of the newly-opened line from Caersws to the Fan. This was an important period in Ceiriog's literary life: he became friendly with some of the leading writers in the district, such as Mynyddog (Richard ★Davies) and Nicholas Bennett (1823–99), by adjudicating at eisteddfodau and frequenting the taverns where they used to meet.

Ceiriog had begun writing poetry before going to Manchester, but his first volume of poems, *Oriau'r Hwyr*, was not published until 1860; there followed *Oriau'r Bore* (1862), *Cant o Ganeuon* (1863) and *Y ★Bardd a'r Cerddor* (1865). These early volumes were his most popular, although he also published *Oriau Eraill* (1868), *Oriau'r Haf* (1870) and *Oriau Olaf* (1888) after returning to Wales. They contain poems which were recited and sung on concert platforms throughout Wales for years afterwards; some, such as 'Nant y Mynydd', 'Dafydd y Garreg Wen' and ★'Alun Mabon', remain popular to this day. Ceiriog's gift was his ability to write words for old Welsh airs and he produced some of the finest lyrics in the Welsh language on such themes as nature, love and patriotism. Although they are often sentimental and even sometimes maudlin by today's standards, they were the popular songs of the Victorian era. In his poetry Ceiriog was the servant of society, satisfying the needs of his time, but in his prose he satirized that society. In ★*Gohebiaethau Syr Meurig Grynswth* (1856–58; ed. Hugh Bevan, 1948) he criticized the eisteddfod and certain of its poets, attacking the pseudo-respectability of Welsh society in general.

For critical accounts of the poet's work see Saunders Lewis, *Yr Artist yn Philistia I: Ceiriog* (1929), and W. J. Gruffydd, *Ceiriog* (1939). A selection of Ceiriog's poems was translated into English by Alfred Perceval Graves (1926).

HUGHES, JOHN GRUFFYDD MOEL-WYN (Moelwyn; 1866–1944), hymn-writer, a native of Tanygrisiau, Blaenau Ffestiniog, Mer., was one of the most prominent ministers among the Calvinistic Methodists. A prolific author, he published a study of William *Williams (Panty-celyn) and four volumes of verse, all of which were entitled *Caniadau* (1893–1914). Two of his hymns are still popular, those beginning '*Pwy a'm dwg i'r ddinas gadarn*' and '*Fy Nhad o'r Nef, O! gwrando 'nghri*'. His later poems were published posthumously under the title *Caneuon Olaf Moelwyn* (1955).

HUGHES, JOHN LEWIS (1938–   ), novelist. Born at Pontypridd, Glam., he has been a teacher at special schools in England and Wales but he also spent a few years as a grocer in his home town. His two novels, *Tom Jones Slept Here* (1971) and *Before the Crying Ends* (1977), written in a colloquial style and almost entirely in the present tense, deal with the poverty and violence of the seamier side of working-class life. John L. Hughes has also written plays, including *The Alphabet* (1968), *Shifts* (1978), *Death in Custody* (1982) and *Total Allergy* (1983).

HUGHES, JONATHAN (1721–1805), poet. A native of Llangollen, Denbs., he began writing verse at an early age and, during the course of a long life, composed an enormous number of poems, most of which remain unpublished. Like his friend Twm o'r Nant (Thomas *Edwards), who composed *englynion* for Hughes's gravestone, he competed in the eisteddfodau organized by the *Gwyneddigion Society and wrote at least one interlude, *Y Dywysoges Genefetha* (1744). He published a volume of poetry during his lifetime, *Bardd a Byrddau* (1778), and shortly after his death the anthology *Gemwaith Awen Beirdd Collen* appeared, the greater part of which is his work. A master of the *carol form, he was typical of the rural poets of his time.

HUGHES, MATHONWY (1901–   ), poet and editor, was born in the parish of Llanllyfni, Caerns., a quarryman's son. Like his uncle R. Silyn *Roberts, he has been associated with the Workers' Education Association as both student and tutor. From 1949 to 1977 he was assistant editor of *Baner ac Amserau Cymru. He won the *Chair at the National Eisteddfod in 1956 and has since published three volumes of poems, *Ambell Gainc* (1957), *Corlannau* (1971) and *Creifion* (1979), four collections of essays, *Myfyrion* (1973), *Dyfalu* (1979), *Gwin y Gweunydd* and *Chwedlau'r Cynfyd* (1983), and a volume of autobiography, *Atgofion Mab y Mynydd* (1982).

HUGHES, RICHARD (d. 1618), poet, of Cefn Llanfair, Caerns., was among the men of his county who fought in the English ranks during the attack on Cadiz in 1596. He spent the rest of his life as a liveried servant in the courts of Elizabeth I and James I. None of his *awdlau* and *cywyddau* have survived but some of his *englynion* have been preserved. It was, however, in the free metres that he wrote his most important verse and his love poems demonstrate by their supple style and lively language how Welsh poetry might have developed at this time if the poets had not chosen to write in the strict metres and the carol form. His elegy was composed by Gruffudd *Phylip (d. 1666) of Ardudwy.

Six of Richard Hughes's poems were published in the volume *Canu Rhydd Cynnar* (ed. T. H. Parry-Williams, 1932).

Hughes, Richard (1794–1871), publisher, a native of Adwy'r Clawdd, Denb., established a printing press at Wrexham in 1820. On his death the business passed to his son, Charles Hughes (1823–86), and became known as *Hughes a'i Fab*. The company's first publications were religious books, such as *Eglwys yn y Tŷ* (1829), and this tradition was continued throughout the nineteenth century with the printing of the enormously popular catechism, *Rhodd Mam* (1879), and other works for the use of the Methodist denominations. Hughes also published the poetry of John Ceiriog *Hughes (to whom he was related) and—in response to the growing tonic sol-fa movement—specialized in the printing of sheet-music. The volume *Sŵn y Jiwbili* (1874), edited by Ieuan Gwyllt (John *Roberts), an arrangement in Welsh of Sankey and Moody hymns, and John *Owen's *Gems of Welsh Melody* (1860) were among the company's most successful publications. The copyright of the works of Daniel *Owen was purchased in 1885. After their father's death, the sons of Charles Hughes ran the business until 1921; thereafter it kept its original name but had several owners who were not connected with the family. Between 1922 and 1952 the press published the periodical *Y *Llenor* and, advised by a panel of writers which included T. Gwynn *Jones, John *Morris-Jones and W. J. *Gruffydd, a large number of books of literary interest. The imprint was bought by Christopher Davies Ltd (*Llyfrau'r Dryw) in 1971 and is now owned by *Sianel Pedwar Cymru*, the fourth television channel in Wales, which has begun to use it for the publishing of children's books.

For further details see the history of *Hughes a'i Fab* by Thomas Bassett (1946).

HUGHES, RICHARD (1900–76), novelist. Although born to English parents at Weybridge, Surrey, he claimed descent through Elystan Glodrydd (c.940–1010) from *Beli Mawr, King of Britain, and so regarded himself as a Welshman, despite the fact that his family had left Wales in *Tudor times. When he arrived at Charterhouse School, Robert Graves was just ending a stormy career there. Hughes's first home in Wales, a cottage he rented at Talsarnau, Mer., while still a schoolboy, was close to Graves's house at Harlech. At Oxford, where Hughes quickly fell under the fascination of T. E. Lawrence, his entry into literary society was rapid: Aldous Huxley and Robert Blunden were there and W. B. Yeats, John Masefield, Robert Bridges and A. E. Coppard had houses in the vicinity. He published poems and stories in a variety of magazines, but it was the critical acclaim accorded to his first play, *The Sisters' Tragedy* (1922), which crowned his university career. While at Oxford he began to travel as a means of countering the strain of creative writing: he went steerage to New York on an immigrant-boat and, within a week of leaving university, dabbled dangerously in Balkan politics. Back in Wales and concentrating on drama, he became a founder-member of the Portmadoc Players. His best play, *A Comedy of Good and Evil* (1924), was written for this company; set in Cylfant, an imaginary village in Snowdonia, it is a witty exploration of the nature of moral values, a theme which haunts Hughes's writings. His play *Danger* (1924), written in a single night for the BBC, became the first play to be broadcast by radio. Hughes then abandoned the drama and cleared his decks with the publication of *Plays* (1924), *Collected Poems* (1926) and a volume of stories, *A Moment in Time* (1926).

He began *A High Wind in Jamaica* (1929) on Capodistria in the Adriatic in 1925 and finished it in Connecticut in 1928. At once a colourful story, a book rich in poetry, and a novel of ideas, this novel appeals on many levels. In it the author explores some of the confusions, paradoxes and absurdities to which conventional assumptions about the nature of Good and Evil may give rise. At the same time, in giving an account of the emergence of personal identity which takes cognizance of the theories of Darwin and Freud, he seeks ironically to explode the Romantic literary tradition of the child as originally innocent which developed in the writings of Rousseau, Blake and Wordsworth, and which had become decadent in the popular Victorian novel. The novel became an immediate best seller, a modern classic, and was filmed.

Withdrawing to Morocco in 1929 to escape the attention which *A High Wind in Jamaica* had brought him, Hughes bought a house in the Kasbah of old Tangier for two donkey-loads of silver. Outside Wales, Morocco was his favourite country, inspiring a number of articles and stories, the best of which were collected after his death under the title *In the Lap of Atlas* (1979). In 1932 he married the painter Frances Bazley and in 1934 they settled in Laugharne castle,

Carms. There Augustus *John was a frequent house-guest, there the young Dylan *Thomas probably met Caitlin Macnamara, his future wife, and there Hughes's second novel was written: *In Hazard* (1938) is the tale of a steamship caught by a hurricane in the Caribbean. Vivid, beautiful, strange, it is nevertheless a true story, for it is based on an actual voyage of the *Phemius* in 1932. Often compared to Joseph Conrad's *Typhoon* (1902), this book is the more complex work, its storm symbolically prefiguring the World War which was about to begin.

From 1940 to 1945 Richard Hughes served as a civilian in the Admiralty and then, in 1946, he moved with his wife and five children to Talsarnau, Mer., where he lived for the rest of his life. In the 1950s he collaborated on a volume of Official War History and wrote a series of screen-plays, mostly for Ealing Studios. Appointed Gresham Professor of Rhetoric at the University of London in 1954, he lectured periodically in London until 1956, resigning the post in order to devote himself to his *magnum opus*, *The Human Predicament*. This *roman fleuve*, conceived as an exploration of the social, political, economic and moral forces which shaped the period from the birth of Nazism to the death of Hitler, was never completed. But *The *Fox in the Attic* (1961) and *The Wooden Shepherdess* (1973), together with twelve chapters of a third volume, are proof of the ambitious nature of the undertaking. The action takes place in a number of countries—Wales, England, Germany, America and Morocco—and historical figures rub shoulders with invented characters; the author's depiction of Hitler is a major triumph. Hughes viewed work on *The Human Predicament* as a race between publisher and undertaker and, if the latter won with regard to the major project, at least *The Wonder Dog* (1977), a collection of children's stories, was completed shortly before his death. Another posthumous volume, *Fiction as Truth* (1983), collects the essays, lectures, broadcasts and reviews of Richard Hughes.

The incompleteness of *The Human Predicament* must complicate any attempt to assess Hughes's achievement as a novelist. Had its projected four volumes been finished, and had the third and fourth maintained the standard of their predecessors, it is likely that it would have come to be regarded as his major contribution, its seriousness and breadth of conception putting the work of such writers as Anthony Powell or C. P. Snow into its shade. As it is, it remains enigmatic, its characters suspended in their lives and its themes not fully worked out. It therefore seems inevitable that Richard Hughes's reputation will rest upon his two pre-war novels. The very readability and surface glitter of these books appear to have contributed to their critical neglect; yet they were written out of a conviction that a novel should aim to please on a variety of levels, from the popular to the intellectual.

There is an essay on Richard Hughes by Peter Thomas in the *Writers of Wales* series (1973); see also Walter Allen, *Tradition and Dream* (1964), the articles by Richard Poole in *The Anglo-Welsh Review* (no. 51, 1974) and *Planet* (nos. 45/46, 1978) and the memoir by the author's daughter, Penelope Hughes, *Richard Hughes, Author, Father* (1984). There is a critical article on Richard Hughes by Belinda Humfrey in *Dictionary of Literary Biography: British Novelists, 1930–1959* (1983).

HUGHES, RICHARD CYRIL (1932–   ), novelist, was born in Anglesey and educated at the University College of Wales, Aberystwyth. He taught Welsh at various schools before becoming a Senior Lecturer at the Normal College, Bangor, and then Senior Language Advisor to Gwynedd County Council. He has published three historical novels, *Catrin o Ferain* (1975), *Dinas Ddihenydd* (1976) and *Castell Cyfaddawd* (1984), all of which deal with the life and times of *Catrin of Berain.

Hughes, Richard Samuel (1855–93), songwriter, was born at Aberystwyth, Cards. He had little formal education as a musician but earned his living as an organist in Bangor and London, and as an accompanist at the *National Eisteddfod, for which work he was famous. Among the well-known songs R. S. Hughes composed are 'Y Golomen Wen', 'Arafa Don' and *'Suo Gân'.

HUGHES, STEPHEN (1622–88), Nonconformist leader, translator and editor, was born at Carmarthen and held the living of Meidrym in the time of Cromwell. After being ejected in 1661, he moved to Swansea where he married into a wealthy family, with whom he supported the Independent cause in that town. It was for his work in his native county, however, that he earned the title 'The Apostle of Carmarthenshire'.

He was indefatigable in the translating and preserving of Puritan works, some of which are to be found in the miscellaneous volume *Catechism Mr. Perkins* (1672), in *Trysor i'r Cymru* (1677) and in *Cyfarwydd-deb i'r Anghyfarwydd* (1677); he also edited *Cynghorion Tad i'w Fab* (1683). Realizing the importance of making the Scriptures readily available in Welsh, he secured the publication of inexpensive translations of the Psalms together with the New Testament in 1672, and of the whole Bible in 1678. He it was who edited the work of Rhys *Prichard, which appeared, originally in parts, complete in 1672 and then under the title *Canwyll y Cymru* in 1681. With three friends, Hughes made the first translation into Welsh of Bunyan's *Pilgrim's Progress*, published as *Taith neu Siwrnai y Pererin* (1688). He contributed substantially to the work of educating the common people, thus paving the way for Griffith *Jones and Thomas *Charles.

For further details see the essay in *Cymwynaswyr y Gymraeg* (1978) by Morgan D. Jones.

HUGHES, THOMAS (*fl.* 1818–65), poet, was the son of **DAVID HUGHES** (*fl.* 1770–1817), Headmaster of Ruthin School, Denbs. The verse of these two Anglican parsons, in Welsh, Latin and English, was published in the volume *Poems by Hughes* (1865). It is, for the most part, conventional in diction and sentiment, often to the point of platitude, but a sequence of light verses written in the form of correspondence between Thomas Hughes and Richard Newcome, Archdeacon of Merioneth and Warden of Ruthin School, succeeds in capturing a formal facetiousness which is rather more attractive.

HUGHES, THOMAS ROWLAND (1903–49), novelist and poet. Born at Llanberis, Caerns., a quarryman's son, he was educated at the University College of North Wales, Bangor, where he read English; he then taught for two years at Aberdare, Glam. After studying for two higher degrees at Bangor and at Jesus College, Oxford, he became in 1930 a Lecturer in English and Welsh at *Coleg Harlech. Four years later he was appointed Warden of the Mary Ward Settlement, an adult education centre in London, where he was also responsible for the Tavistock Little Theatre. Too heavily burdened by the administrative duties there, he returned to Wales in 1935 as a producer of feature programmes for the BBC in Cardiff. The first indications that he was suffering from multiple sclerosis appeared about 1937 but, although increasingly disabled by the illness, he remained in his post until 1945. It was out of admiration for the way he bore his suffering that R. Williams *Parry addressed him, in an *englyn* greeting the novelist on his birthday in 1948 which was later carved on his gravestone, as '*y dewra' o'n hawduron*' ('the bravest of our authors').

T. Rowland Hughes made his literary debut as a poet by winning the *Chair at the National Eisteddfod of 1937 with his poem 'Y Ffin' and again in 1940 (this occasion was broadcast on radio owing to war conditions) with his poem 'Pererinion'. His only volume of verse, *Cân neu Ddwy* (1948), despite some fine individual poems, is not remarkable enough to place him in the front rank as a poet. He also wrote plays, including *Y Ffordd* (1945), which was based on the *Rebecca Riots and published in both Welsh and English, and edited anthologies of short stories. His book *Storïau Mawr y Byd* (1936) consists of retellings of some of the great stories of the world, such as those of Jason, Beowulf, *Arthur, *Branwen and Cuchulain.

But it is as the author of five novels that T. Rowland Hughes finds a permanent place in the history of Welsh literature. They are *O Law i Law* (1943), *William Jones* (1944), *Yr Ogof* (1945), *Chwalfa* (1946) and *Y Cychwyn* (1947). Much of his material was based on his own memories, or those of his relatives and friends, of life in the slate-quarries of his native county, although *William Jones* is partly set in south Wales and *Yr Ogof* has a biblical theme. All his books display their author's gift for telling entertaining stories with flesh-and-blood characters and a rich mixture of sadness and humour. His geniality as a writer may have limited his vision to some extent, causing him to avoid the darker side of human nature, but in his portrayal of the plight of the quarrymen and their families during the *Penrhyn Lockouts, in the novel *Chwalfa*, it is generally agreed that he came close to greatness.

The five novels of T. Rowland Hughes have been translated into English by Richard Ruck: *From Hand to Hand* (1950), *William Jones* (1953), *Out of their Night* (1954), *The Story of Joseph of Arimathea* (1961) and *The Beginning* (1969). A memoir of the author was written in Welsh by Edward Rees (1968) and John Rowlands has contributed an essay on his life and work to the *Writers of Wales* series (1975); see also the essay on the novels of T. Rowland Hughes by Hugh Bevan in *Beirniadaeth Lenyddol* (ed. B. F. Roberts, 1982).

Hughes a'i Fab, see under HUGHES, RICHARD (1794–1871).

HUMPHREYS, EDWARD MORGAN (**Celt**; 1882–1955), journalist and novelist, was born in Dyffryn Ardudwy, Mer. He became a member of the staff of the weekly newspaper *Y *Genedl Gymreig* in 1905 and was appointed editor three years later; he was also editor of *The North Wales Observer* and *Y *Goleuad*. As a weekly columnist and reviewer under the pseudonym Celt in the *Liverpool Daily Post* and the *Manchester Guardian*, he was generally regarded as a journalist of great distinction and his comment was authoritative. Humphreys was one of the first Welsh authors to recognize the need for reading material in the Welsh language for young people, as he mentioned in the preface to his novel *Dirgelwch yr Anialwch* as early as 1911. He made a valiant effort to fulfil this need, with stories set against historical backgrounds, such as *Rhwng Rhyfeloedd* (1924) and *Yr Etifedd Coll* (1924), and detective stories like *Y Llaw Gudd* (1924), *Dirgelwch Gallt y Ffrwd* (1938), *Ceulan y Llyn Du* (1944) and *Llofrudd yn y Chwarel* (1951). The craftsmanship in these tales is of a very high order, which makes them interesting reading for adults as well as young people. Among his other publications are *Y Wasg Gymraeg* (1945), *The Gorse Glen* (1948, a translation of *Cwm Eithin* by Hugh *Evans) and the two volumes *Gwŷr Enwog Gynt* (1950, 1953) which contain articles on Welshmen with whom the author had been acquainted.

For a portrait of E. Morgan Humphreys by one who knew him well see R. T. Jenkins, *Ymyl y Ddalen* (1957); see also the article by Bedwyr Lewis Jones in *Dewiniaid Difyr* (ed. Mairwen and Gwynn Jones, 1983).

HUMPHREYS, EMYR (1919–), novelist, poet and dramatist. He was born at Prestatyn, Flints., brought up in Trelawnyd and educated at the University College of Wales, Aberystwyth, where he read history, threw himself into student politics, learned Welsh and became a Nationalist. Liable for military service in 1940 after an additional year at university, he declared himself a conscientious objector on his twentieth birthday (April, 1939) and was sent to work on the land in Pembrokeshire. In 1944, still subject to call-up, he went as a war relief worker first to the Middle East and then to Italy, where until 1946 he was an official of the Save the Children Fund under the aegis of the United Nations Organization. His marriage, on his return in 1947 to the daughter of a Congregational minister, is significant in the context of his writing: it opened to him the heart and tradition of Welsh *Nonconformity, for Emyr Humphreys, reared in an Anglicized region, had been brought up a Churchman and had intended to enter the priesthood. Demobilized, he taught for three years at Wimbledon Technical College before obtaining a post in 1951 at Pwllheli Grammar School and in 1955 he joined BBC Wales as a drama producer. Ten years in radio and television, however, greatly impeded his writing, already well established, and in 1965 he took up a lectureship in Drama at the University College of North Wales, Bangor. In 1972 he was confident enough of his literary output to resign this post to become a full-time writer. Remarkably successful as a young novelist, he had already won the Somerset Maugham Award for *Hear and Forgive* (1952) and the Hawthornden Prize for *A *Toy Epic* (1958).

Emyr Humphreys has remained true to the realist novel which so many have deserted. Unable as a Christian to accept the novel as life-game or fable, he declared in 1953, 'In our time the novelist's attitude is more crucial than his manner of expression'. His own technical experimentation notwithstanding, the essence of his writing is the moral questioning which arises naturally (if in these days infrequently) from the Nonconformist Wales of the past. The central concern of his novels is an examination of the means by which good is, or is not, passed on from generation to generation. His Christianity presses him to believe that, despite appearances, there *is* progress, however slow, towards the Kingdom of God. 'Many men', he has written, 'are better for the existence of one good man, and one good man is the product of some kind of progress that was both individual and social'. But is it human love that creates such progress, changing lover and loved? Is conscience handed down from parents to children or is it learned from contemporaries, from the experience of living? Or, again, is it all so difficult to discern that divine intervention must be supposed? It was this emphasis on conscience, the executor of the Christian *agape*, that made Emyr Humphreys assert in 1953 that he was attempting to write 'the Protestant novel'. Concern for individuals, apparent in all his work, is subsumed in concern for the future of society, which for him is a vision of a Wales emerging at last from its betrayals.

Complexity of narrative pattern, an ever-enlarging time-scheme, the use of uninterpreted dialogue and severely episodic cutting, together with a surface wit and (in earlier works) a lyrical quality in the writing, have enabled many readers to enjoy Emyr Humphreys's novels without in the least understanding his underlying concerns. Judgement has to be suspended, in any case, on the 'answers' which may emerge from the sextet of novels still in progress.

Besides sixteen novels and a collection of short stories, *Natives* (1968), Emyr Humphreys has published four volumes of verse: *Ancestor Worship* (1970), *Landscapes* (1976), *The Kingdom of Brân* (1979) and *Pwyll a Rhiannon* (1980). The chief quality of the poems (a selection appeared in the *Penguin Modern Poets* series in 1979) is their successful encapsulation of the drama and pathos of human situations and their appeal is more emotional and direct than that of the novels. The latter can be summarily divided into three groups. The first would contain *The *Little Kingdom* (1946), *The Voice of the Stranger* (1949), *A Toy Epic* (1958)—which, despite its date, was his first novelistic writing—and a late American-Welsh version of some of the same preoccupations, namely *The Anchor-Tree* (1980). These are concerned with the vulnerability of idealism and the deceit which attacks it in a leader: the conclusion, that means defeat ends and that the whole leadership-concept is suspect, is pessimistic.

The 'Protestant novel' proper begins with *A Change of Heart* (1951), proceeds through *Hear and Forgive* (1952), the most masterly of the early works, *A Man's Estate* (1955) and *The Italian Wife* (1957) to the most complete of the *schemae* yet available, **Outside the House of Baal* (1965). In these emerge the themes of 'the keeper' as a stopgap for 'the good man', the inability of erotic love to become *agape* and its reverse, the failure of conscience to translate itself into *eros*. In *Outside the House of Baal*, *agape* is not merely deceived by *eros* into false choices but brings about wounds and death, rather than love, and apparently fails in its function to pass that love on. The sextet, collectively entitled *Land of the Living*, which begins thematically with **Flesh and Blood* (1974) and continues so far with *The *Best of Friends* (1978), **National Winner* (1971) and *Salt of the Earth* (1985), examines no less searchingly the working space of three generations. *The Gift* (1963), best described as an entertainment, is in a category of its own, as perhaps is *Jones* (1984), though it displays some of the preoccupation with the acceptance of responsibility which belongs to 'the Protestant novel'.

It can be seen by hindsight that *The Little Kingdom* (1946) was one of the three markers of what may be called the second phase of Anglo-Welsh writing, a phase more patriotic, more scholarly, more concerned with the Welsh heritage than was the first. With David *Jones and R. S. *Thomas (though the emphases of all three were quite dissimilar), Emyr Humphreys inaugurated a new attitude which even now has not worked through. He stands alone, however, in seeking a valid continuity with the Wales of the last two hundred years and in making the quest the subject of his writing.

There is an essay on the work of Emyr Humphreys by Ioan Williams in the *Writers of Wales* series (1980) and an essay on the writer by Derec Llwyd Morgan in *Ysgrifau Beirniadol VII* (ed. J. E. Caerwyn Williams, 1972) and by Roland Mathias in *The Anglo-Welsh Review* (no. 70, 1982). See also the miscellany of the author's stories, poems and essays which appeared in 1981, and his 'selected history' of Wales. *The Taliesin Tradition* (1983), which is important for an understanding of the themes in his novels. Roland Mathias has contributed an article on Emyr Humphreys to *Dictionary of Literary Biography: British Novelists, 1930–1959* (1983).

HUMPHREYS, HUMPHREY (1648–1712), bishop and antiquary, was born at Penrhyndeudraeth, Mer., and educated at Jesus College, Oxford. Ordained in 1670, he was consecrated Bishop of Bangor in 1689 and of Hereford in 1701, in both bishoprics applying himself to administrative reform. Soon after his consecration he published *Ymofynion Iw Hatteb Gan Brocatorion, Wardenied, a Swyddogion ereill* (1690). He was one of the most enthusiastic supporters of the *Society for Promoting Christian Knowledge which, under his patronage, distributed an increasing number of Welsh books. He also encouraged authors such as Edward *Samuel, Samuel *Williams and Ellis *Wynne; the last-named dedicated his *Rheol Buchedd Sanctaidd* to him in 1701. Humphreys was greatly praised by poets and priests alike on account of his support for Welsh learning and his reforming zeal. An experienced antiquary, he was a friend of Edward *Lhuyd who deemed him 'incomparably the best skill'd in our Antiquities of any person in Wales'. He produced many amendments to the volumes of Anthony à Wood, *Athenae Oxonienses* (1691–92), but his notes on Camden's *Britannia* (1586) and on St. Winefred's well (see under GWENFFREWI) have been lost.

HUMPHRIES, ROLFE (1894–1969), American poet and translator. Of Welsh descent, he taught Latin and English at various colleges in the USA, concluding his academic career at Amherst College, Mass. His nine volumes of verse, some of which were republished in his *Collected Poems* (1966), include *Green Armor on Green Ground* (1956), a sequence of poems in the *Twenty-four Metres of Welsh poetry. He discovered an interest in Welsh prosody by reading *An Introduction to Welsh Poetry* by Gwyn *Williams but, on his own admission, paid only token attention to its rules when writing his versions. Similarly, his *Nine Thorny Thickets* (1969) is a volume of poems on themes taken from *Dafydd ap Gwilym but presented as 'new arrangements' of the medieval poet's work. His knowledge of Welsh verse-forms is also to be discerned in the posthumous volume *Coat on a Stick* (1969). Besides his renderings of Welsh poetry, Humphries translated from Lorca and the Latin poets during a long literary career in which his technical skills were widely acclaimed.

Hunangofiant Tomi (lit. 'Tomi's autobiography': 1912), the first book of E. Tegla *Davies, is a series of stories in the form of letters from a dreamy, sometimes mischievous boy who often finds himself in trouble. With only a few exceptions, Tomi's adventures—such as his calamitous attempt to sell chickens—are very funny and have kept their charm. The book's chief merits are the author's sense of humour and his ability to recreate his childhood, although his tendency to moralize spoils the innocence of some stories.

Hunger Marches, in which unemployed workers called on the Government to improve their conditions, were a feature of life in south Wales during the 1920s and 1930s. They began in 1922, the year in which the National Unemployed Workers' Movement was formed, but the first march representing the whole of Wales set off from the *Rhondda Valley on 9 November 1927. With the unemployment figures rising rapidly (there were 1,127,000 out of work in Britain in May 1929 and 2,643,000 in December 1930), many marches were organized in Wales, Scotland and England, but several—sometimes consisting of demonstrators in their tens of thousands—converged on London. The movement's leader in England was Wil Hannington, a former engineer, and Idris Cox, Arthur *Horner and A. J. *Cook took prominent parts in the marches in south Wales. In 1933 Lewis *Jones (1897–1939) led five hundred unemployed men in a march to Newport from the valleys of Monmouthshire which brought out huge crowds in their support. The last march, which took place in 1936, was backed by a united front of Socialists and Communists, who co-operated to an extent without precedent. The marches remain in popular memory as a symbol of the hardship, solidarity and militancy of south Wales during the *Depression of the years between the World Wars. See also GENERAL STRIKE.

Hunting the Wren, a folk-custom found in many parts of western Europe, was once widely observed in Wales. Although the wren is the smallest British bird, it is also held to be the king of birds, and as such it occupied an important place in the celebration of Christmas, especially at Epiphany (6 Jan.). A number of songs in both Welsh and English attest to the popularity of the custom in various parts of Wales, but particularly in Pembrokeshire. The bird, when caught, was carried in a box on an ornate bier from house to house and exhibited in return for money and refreshments. The bearers pretended that there was a heavy burden on their shoulders and their song, in the form of question and answer, referred to the bird as their king. It is believed that the original purpose of the custom, perhaps as early as Neolithic times, was to sacrifice the bird in order to ensure the fertility of land and livestock. Later, the wren may have come to be regarded as the king of birds during the Roman Saturnalia and the reign of the Lord of Misrule, when the normal order was temporarily overturned.

For further details see Trefor M. Owen, *Welsh Folk Customs* (1959).

Huw ap Huw, see HUGHES, HUGH (1693–1776).

HUW ARWYSTLI (*fl.* 1542–78), poet, of Trefeglwys in Arwystli, Mont. Apart from eulogies, elegies and poems of request, his *cywyddau* include contention poems and love-poems, some of which are distinguished by memorable epigrammatic couplets. One of his *awdlau* records that it was while sleeping in St. Llonio's church at Llandinam that he received the gift of poetry. Lewys *Dwnn's elegy for him is dated 1583.

HUW CAE LLWYD (*fl.* 1455–1505), poet, was probably brought up at Llandderfel, Mer., but most of his life was spent in south Wales. Among the patrons for whom he wrote eulogies and elegies were William Fychan of Brecon and Sir Rhys ap Thomas of Dinefwr. He also wrote request poems and religious poems, including one *cywydd* composed while he was on a pilgrimage to Rome and another to the Rood at Brecon. His son, Ieuan, was also a poet but not as accomplished as his father.

The poet's work has been edited by Leslie Harries (1953).

HUW CORNWY (*fl.* 1580–96), poet, possibly a native of Llanfair-yng-nghornwy, Ang., wrote elegies for some of the island's leading families such as the Meyricks of Bodorgan and the Rhydderchs of *Myfyrian, and for Rhys ap Thomas. He was also involved in a bardic controversy with Rhydderch ap Rhisiart of Myfyrian.

HUW LLŶN (*fl.* 1532–94), poet. A native of Llŷn, Caerns., and a brother of *Wiliam Llŷn, he graduated at the second *Caerwys Eisteddfod of 1567. Among poems of his which have survived in manuscript are those to Henry Rowland and Simon Thelwall and others to gentry in south Wales such as Walter Devereux, Thomas Vaughan, Gruffudd *Dwnn, William and

George *Owen, and John Lloyd. He took part in a bardic contention with *Siôn Mawddwy and in another with Wiliam Llŷn, Ieuan Tew Brydydd Ieuanc (*fl.* 1560–90), Siôn *Phylip and Hywel Ceiriog (*fl.* 1560–1600).

Huw Menai, see WILLIAMS, HUW OWEN (1888–1961).

Huw Morgan, see under HOW GREEN WAS MY VALLEY (1939).

HUW PENNANT (*fl.* 1465–1514), poet, a native of Flintshire, some of whose vaticinatory poems have also been attributed to *Dafydd Llwyd of Mathafarn. A small number of his *cywyddau* and elegies to various gentry families in north Wales have survived in manuscript, as well as his translation into Welsh of a Latin *Life* of St. Ursula. This Huw Pennant, who used the clerical title *Syr* ('Sir'), should not be confused with the poet of the same name who is the subject of the next entry.

HUW PENNANT (*fl.* 1565–1619), poet, was a native of Llanfihangel-y-Pennant, Caerns. His bardic teacher was Morys Dwyfech and he graduated at the second *Caerwys Eisteddfod of 1567. Among the *awdlau*, *cywyddau* and *englynion* attributed to him are poems to patrons in Llŷn, Eifionydd and Arfon. His work, which remains in manuscript, compares favourably with that of his better-known contemporaries. This Huw Pennant should not be confused with his namesake who is treated in the previous entry.

Hwch Ddu Gota, Yr (lit. 'The bob-tailed black sow'), an embodiment of the *Devil which was said to appear, especially at Hallowe'en (31 Oct.), from the embers of the bonfire and to catch the last reveller who lingered on his way home. There is a striking reference to the traditional belief at the end of Alun *Llywelyn-Williams's poem 'Cofio'r Tridegau'.

Hwfa Môn, see WILLIAMS, ROWLAND (1823–1905).

Hwmffre ap Hywel ap Siencyn (*fl.* 1480–1520), gentleman, of *Nannau, near Dolgellau, Mer., to whom *Tudur Aled addressed a *cywydd* in an attempt to reconcile him with his kinsmen. The poem, which gives no details about the cause of the feud, is among Tudur Aled's best work because it makes poignant remarks upon the meaning of life and sharply criticizes the morality of the age; the most vivid of its metaphors is found in a description of 'the wheel of society'. The poet, who belonged to the Nannau family, appeals for unity on the grounds that schism among the Welsh is to the advantage of the English.

Hwntw Mawr, Yr, see EDWARDS, THOMAS (d. 1813).

Hyfforddwr, Yr (lit. 'The instructor'; 1807), a catechism by Thomas *Charles. Based on an earlier work, *Crynodeb* (1789), but also indebted to Griffith *Jones and the Westminster Assembly's *Shorter Catechism*, the book was primarily intended to help parents to catechize their children. In this respect it reflected not only the author's personal experience of teaching children but also an important aspect of Calvinistic *Methodism. As a short volume of systematic theology (its full title is the same as that of Calvin's *Institutio*), especially in its conciseness, its simple prose and its theological accuracy, it conveyed the main tenets of Christianity in a masterly fashion. One of the most widely read and influential of all Welsh books published during the Methodist Revival, it had run to more than eighty editions before the end of the nineteenth century.

'Hyfrydol' (lit. 'Melodious'), a popular hymn-tune by Rowland Hugh Pritchard (1811–87), which first appeared in the author's *Cyfaill y Cantorion* (1844). It was later included in several collections of Welsh and English hymns, either to the words 'O! Llefara, addfwyn Iesu' by Wiliam *Williams (Pantycelyn) or 'Love Divine, all loves excelling' by Charles Wesley. The tune was arranged for male voices by Oliver Edwards under the title *Christus Redemptor* and was used by Ralph Vaughan Williams in his *Three Preludes on Welsh Hymn Tunes for Organ* (1920).

Hymn, a song in praise of God to be sung in congregation. No Welsh hymn is older than the twelfth century because the singing in churches at and up to that time was in Latin. The earliest hymn in Welsh is '*Gogonedauc argluit, hepich guell*', a poem in The *Black Book of Carmarthen*, but Henry *Lewis published other similar songs from the period of the *Gogynfeirdd in his *Hen Gerddi Crefyddol* (1931). The hymns in *Gwasanaeth Mair are more elaborate than the psalms, the former representing the strict tradition of the nobility and the latter the freer folk-tradition. The same ecclesiastic–classical quality is found in William *Middleton's attempt to versify the Psalms (1603) and particularly in the work of Edmund *Prys (1621). The work of the latter, together with the moralistic verses of Rhys *Prichard in *Canwyll y Cymru* (1646), constitutes the bulk of the most noteworthy religious poetry of the seventeenth century, with the exception of the lyrics of Morgan *Llwyd. The hymn by Ellis *Wynne, '*Myfi yw'r Atgyfodiad Mawr*', is again ecclesiastic and classical. Early Nonconformists of his time were wont to make hymns out of translations from the English or paraphrases from the Scriptures; they included Thomas *Baddy, James Owen (1654–1706), Dafydd Lewis, John Prichard Prys (*fl.* 1704–21), John Evans and Lewis Thomas. The hymns of Wales up to that point were comparatively unspectacular, but from 1744 there ensued a golden age, with the appearance of the work of such hymn-writers as Morgan *Rhys, Dafydd *William, Thomas *William, John Thomas (1763–1834), John *Williams of St. Athan and, the greatest of them all, William *Williams (Pantycelyn). All these were poets who, with taste and skill, married theology and personal experience. In the nineteenth century the development of hymn-singing moved into *Gwynedd and *Powys with the publication of the work of Edward *Jones of Maes y Plwm, Eben Fardd (Ebenezer *Thomas), Robert ap Gwilym Ddu (Robert *Williams), Pedr Fardd (Peter *Jones), Ieuan Glan Geirionydd (Evan *Evans), Gwilym Hiraethog (William *Rees) and Ehedydd Ial (William *Jones). To some extent the novelty of the experience was lost in the move, the hymns becoming more embellished under the influence of the traditional carols. But the work of Ann *Griffiths and others clearly shows that the experience was still real and the intellect still powerful. By the end of the nineteenth century, intellectual content, the awareness of sin and the thrill of salvation had all diminished. Perhaps the last hymn-writers to retain something of the old fervour were Elfed (Howell Elvet *Lewis), Watcyn Wyn (Watkin Hezekiah *Williams), Nantlais (William Nantlais *Williams), and J. T. *Job.

For a discussion of the Welsh hymn as literature see Saunders Lewis, *Williams Pantycelyn* (1927), Gomer M. Roberts, *Y Pêr Ganiedydd* (1958), John Thickens, *Emynau a'r Hawduriaid* (1961), Bobi Jones, *Pedwar Emynydd* (1970) and the essay by John Gwilym Jones in *Swyddogaeth Beirniadaeth* (1977). A bibliography of Welsh hymnology has been compiled by H. Turner Evans (1977); see also the *Bulletin* of *Cymdeithas Emynau Cymru*.

'Hymn to the Virgin' (c.1470), a poem attributed to *Ieuan ap Hywel Swrdal, is believed to have been composed as a riposte to English contemporaries at Oxford who had baited the Welshman. Consisting of ninety-six lines and thirteen stanzas, the poem is written in English but its orthography is Welsh and it employs four kinds of *cynghanedd*. The fourth and fifth stanzas, for example, read as follows:

Wi sin ddy bricht kwin wyth kwning/and blys,
ddy bloswm ffruwt bering;
ei wowld, as owld as ei sing,
wynn iwr lwf on iwr lofing.

Kwin od off owr God, owr geiding/mwdyr,
maedyn not wythstanding,
hwo wed syts wyth a ryts ring
as God wod ddys gwd weding.

The poem is an address to Christ (through Mary as intermediary) in which the poet prays that he may lead a good life, die a good death and go to heaven. With its images of branch and tree, blossom and fruit, king and queen, it has the naïve charm of many medieval lyrics on the same theme, while its vigour and tight structure derive wholly from its unique prosody. Sometimes said to be the earliest extant example of verse written by a Welshman in English (but see the entry for CLANVOW, JOHN), it is of more than mere curiosity interest because its orthography records English pronunciation before 1500, at least as it struck the ear of a Welsh-speaking Welshman.

For further details see the essay by E. J. Dobson in the *Transactions* of the Honourable Society of Cymmrodorion (1954); see also the introduction by Raymond Garlick to an edition of the poem published by the Gregynog Press in 1985.

Hystoria Gwlat Ieuan Vendigeit (lit. 'A history of Prester John's kingdom'), a secular work (the earliest text is in Jesus College MS 2, 1346) which exists as two different, anonymous, prose translations of *Epistola Presbyteri Johannis*, said to be a letter from Prester John to Frederick I, Holy Roman Emperor. Prester John, or John the Presbyter, was a legendary Christian priest-king who was supposed in medieval times to have reigned over a wonderful country somewhere in the heart of Asia. He appears in *Ariosto's Orlando Furioso* (1516) and is the eponymous hero of a novel by John Buchan (1910).

Hystoria Lucidar (lit. 'A narrative of light'), a religious work (the earliest text is in Jesus College MS 2, 1346), which is an anonymous translation of the *Elucidarium* of the early twelfth-century writer Honorius Augustodunensis. A summary of Christian doctrine in the form of a dialogue between master and pupil, it was very popular in medieval Wales.

The text was edited by John Morris-Jones and John Rhŷs and published in 1894.

HYWEL AB EINION LYGLIW (*fl.* 1330–70), poet. Nothing is known of his life but an Einion Lygliw, possibly his father, was living in the township of Rhiwedog, Llanfor, Mer., in 1292 and was a tax assessor in the commot of Tal-y-bont, Mer., in 1318. Hywel's only extant work is his love-poem to Myfanwy Fychan of *Dinas Bran, Llangollen, which was included in *The Myvyrian Archailogoy* (1801). This poem, or more probably the English version of it published in Thomas *Pennant's *Tours in Wales*, inspired the well-known poem 'Myfanwy Fychan' by John Ceiriog *Hughes.

HYWEL AB OWAIN GWYNEDD (d. 1170), prince and poet, was the illegitimate son of Owain Gwynedd (*Owain ap Gruffudd) and an Irishwoman named Pyfog. Although he referred to himself in his poetry as an enemy of the English, he fought against his own kinsmen in the house of *Gwynedd and against the leaders of south Wales, siding even with the Normans against the Lord Rhys (*Rhys ap Gruffudd) in 1159. Very soon after his father's death he was killed in battle against two of his half-brothers at Pentraeth.

There remain extant only eight of his poems, but he is remembered primarily as a poet of love and nature whose work has sensitivity, tenderness, warmth and a sense of humour. Unlike the professional court poets, he was not confined to traditional subjects and was able to strike a personal note which is rare in Welsh poetry of the period. In his *Gorhoffedd (boasting-poem), for example, he praises the qualities of his beloved Merioneth—its wild and inhabited places and its lovely women. In another poem, after naming eight of his lady-loves, he admits that there are others, but declares that teeth are good for biting the tongue. The rapid association of images—the bright fort proud beside the chattering wave and the maid within like the brightness of the year, and so on—is characteristic of his verse, which is the earliest extant love-poetry in Welsh. As *Taliesin and *Aneirin had formulated the pattern of the prince and the soldier, so Hywel ab Owain Gwynedd established that of the maiden as the object of the poet's affections. In this he was probably influenced by the example of French poetry and he, in turn, was to be imitated by many Welsh poets who came after him.

For further details see T. Gwynn Jones, *Rhieingerddi'r Gogynfeirdd* (1915), Ifor Williams, 'Marwnad Hywel ab Owain Gwynedd' in the *Transactions* of the Anglesey Antiquarian Society (1923) and J. Lloyd-Jones, *The Court Poets of the Welsh Princes* (The Sir John Rhŷs Memorial Lecture, 1928).

HYWEL AP DAFYDD AB IEUAN AP RHYS (Hywel Dafi; *fl.* 1450–80), poet, was a native of Raglan, Mon. Among his religious poems is a cywydd to the twenty thousand saints reputed to have been buried on the island of *Bardsey (Enlli) and two cywyddau to the Virgin Mary; he also wrote a few love-poems. Most of his elegies and eulogies were addressed to the Herberts of Raglan and the descendants of *Dafydd Gam. With the exception of the polemic of poems which he exchanged with *Guto'r Glyn, his work was not popular among the copyists, partly because it did not conform to the conventions of his day. He also took part in bardic contentions with *Bedo Brwynllys and others. According to *Rhys Cain, Hywel Dafi was the author of a history of Britain in Latin and a history of Wales in Welsh but, if that is so, the manuscripts have not survived.

Hywel ap Gruffudd (Hywel y Fwyall; d. 1381?), professional soldier, was an *Eifionydd man descended from *Ednyfed Fychan. As a younger son, he decided to make his career in the French wars of Edward III. At the battle of *Crécy (1346) he led a contingent of Welshmen under the command of the Black Prince and did such great service that he was created knight-banneret on the field. At Poitiers (1356), though

the tradition that he captured the French king is unfounded, his famous battle-axe (W. *bwyall*) caused so much destruction among the French that the Black Prince, half-jokingly, gave it thereafter a place of honour in the royal hall. Food was served before it daily and later distributed to the poor, a tradition which was continued into the reign of Elizabeth I. About 1359 Sir Hywel was appointed Constable of Cricieth castle and probably remained in that office until his death. A poem by *Iolo Goch describes life at the castle in Sir Hywel's day.

HYWEL AP MATHEW (d. 1581), poet and historian, was a native of Llanfair Waterdine, Rads., where his family were landowners and where his father had been parish priest. One of the graduates of the first *Caerwys Eisteddfod (1523), he was said by Lewys *Dwnn to have been a bardic teacher. He addressed eulogies and elegies in the traditional manner to some of the leading figures of his time, including William *Herbert, Earl of Pembroke, and Richard *Davies, the Protestant bishop of St. David's. An accomplished scribe, he made copies of *The Book of Arms* and was a herald bard. His chronicle of British history, written in Welsh, which survives in two copies, follows the style of contemporary historians in England, beginning with the sons of Noah and continuing down to 1556. In it Hywel states that he had been present at the siege of Boulogne in 1544 and some of his comments suggest that he was a devout Catholic. Both Lewys Dwnn and *Dafydd Benwyn wrote elegies for him.

HYWEL AP RHEINALLT or HYWEL RHEINALLT (*fl.* 1461–1506/7), poet, was a native of Llannor, Caerns. Most of his work consists of eulogies and elegies for patrons in *Llŷn and *Eifionydd, but his most famous poem is an elegy for four of his fellow-poets, namely *Dafydd Nanmor, *Deio ab Ieuan Du, *Ieuan Deulwyn and *Tudur Penllyn; he also wrote request-poems, love-poems and devotional poems. His verse, which is chiefly of historical interest, shares some of the anti-English sentiment of his day and more than once expresses the view that Henry *Tudor's accession to the English throne in 1485 had inaugurated a propitious new era for Wales and the Welsh. In his cywyddau to the statue of the Virgin at Pwllheli and to Cawdra Sant and Einion Frenin, the patron saints of Abererch and Llanengan, Caerns., the religious life of Llŷn in the period is clearly reflected.

HYWEL CILAN (*fl.* 1435–70), poet, was a native of Cilan, Llandrillo, Mer. He wrote verse for Gruffudd ap Rhys ab Ieuan of Branas in his native parish, as well as for the gentry families at Y *Rug and Plas yn Iâl, and to other patrons in north-east Wales. Most of his cywyddau are fairly

stereotyped praise-poems, but they are of a good technical standard.

The poet's work has been edited by Islwyn Jones (1963).

Hywel Dafi, see HYWEL AP DAFYDD AB IEUAN AP RHYS (*fl.* 1450–80).

Hywel Dda or **Hywel ap Cadell** (d. 950), king and law-giver, was a grandson of *Rhodri Mawr. He inherited the southern part of his principality, namely *Ceredigion and *Ystrad Tywi and claimed *Dyfed through his marriage to Elen, the daughter of Llywarch ap Hyfaidd, the last of the 'Irish' princes of Dyfed. When Idwal Foel, the Prince of Gwynedd, was killed by the English in the year 942, Hywel took over his territory, thus acquiring authority over most of Wales. More diplomat than warrior, Hywel succeeded in keeping the peace with the English kings by a policy of conciliation. He had a special relationship with Wessex (where *Asser held high office) and his name is frequently found in documents appertaining to that court from the period 931 to 949. It has been suggested that he was following the example of Alfred, King of Wessex, when he went on a pilgrimage to Rome in 928 and when, towards the end of his life, he undertook the reorganization of the laws and customs of his kingdom. He also struck coins bearing his name and was the only Welsh king to do so, as far as is known. A man of rare gifts, Hywel was described in *Brut y Tywysogyon as 'the chief and most praiseworthy of all the Britons' and he is the only king in the history of Wales to have been called *Da* ('The Good'). See also LAWS OF HYWEL DDA.

For a discussion of Hywel Dda's relation with King Alfred, see the article by D. P. Kirby, 'Hywel Dda: Anglophile?' in *The Welsh History Review* (vol. 8, no. 1, 1976).

HYWEL FOEL AP GRIFFRI AP PWYLL WYDDEL (*c.*1240–1300), poet, of whose work only two *awdlau* are extant. Both protest against the long incarceration of *Owain Goch ap Gruffudd by his brother *Llywelyn ap Gruffudd from the battle of Bryn Derwin in 1255 to 1277.

The poems of Hywel Foel are included in *Llawysgrif Hendregadredd* (ed. J. Morris-Jones and T. H. Parry-Williams, 1933); see also the article by Brynley F. Roberts in *Bardos* (ed. R. Geraint Gruffydd, 1982).

Hywel Fychan fab Hywel Goch o Fuellt, see under RED BOOK OF HERGEST.

Hywel Sele (*fl.* early 15th cent.), the lord of *Nannau, Mer., is traditionally believed to have betrayed his cousin, *Owain Glyndŵr. The abbot of Cymer endeavoured to reconcile the two, who had for long been enemies, and Owain was invited to Nannau. One day, while hunting a stag, Hywel shot an arrow at Owain but the latter's life was saved by the chain-mail he was wearing. Hywel was then killed by Owain and his body hidden in old oak which was known thereafter as *Ceubren yr Ellyll* ('The fiend's hollow tree').

HYWEL SWRDWAL (*fl.* 1430–70), poet, may have been descended from Hugh Surdwal, a Norman who had settled in Brycheiniog after the Conquest. During the Wars of the Roses Hywel supported the House of York and was bailiff of Newtown under Richard, Duke of York, from 1454 to 1456; most of his life was spent at Cedewain, Mont. According to tradition, he was one of the poets commissioned by Edward IV in 1460 to trace the genealogy of the Herberts. He is believed to have been the author of historical works in Latin and Welsh, but these have not survived; his son, *Ieuan ap Hywel Swrdal, was also a poet. Hywel addressed eulogies and elegies to patrons in Gwent and Glamorgan, his chief patron being William *Herbert, Earl of Pembroke. After the Earl's execution in 1469 the poet composed an elegy reviling the English whom he called '*Hŵr-swns o Hors a Hensiyst*' ('the whoresons of Horsa and Hengist') for causing the tragedy.

For further details see *Gwaith Barddonol Howel Swrdwal a'i fab Ieuan* (1908) by J. C. Morrice; see also the article by Eurys Rowlands in *Ysgrifau Beirniadol VI* (ed. J. E. Caerwyn Williams, 1971).

Hywel y Fwyall, see HYWEL AP GRUFFUDD (d. 1381?).

HYWEL YSTORM or **HYWEL YSTORYN** (*fl.* early 14th cent.?), a poet who shares with *Madog Dwygraig the reputation of having composed many of the foulest lampoons in the Welsh language. Revelling in coarseness, especially at the expense of human deformity, he refers to places in various parts of Wales, especially taverns, where his kind of verse was popular. The purpose of praise-poetry was to elevate Man by showing forth his finer qualities, but this poet's aim was to debase him.

I

'I Ofyn Cŵn Hela' (lit. 'To ask for hunting dogs'), a *cywydd* by *Gutun Owain and his most famous request-poem, was composed on behalf of *Dafydd ab Ieuan to ask for the gift of two hounds from his uncle, Hywel ap Rhys of Y *Rug, Corwen, one of 'the barons of Edeirnion'. The poem is noteworthy for its description of the dogs and its striking use of the technique of *dyfalu*. The hounds are depicted as '*gweision pennau goisel*' ('servants with heads bowed down') as they follow the scent in pursuit of their quarry, their 'conversation' directed towards *Annwn, and particular attention is paid to their baying which is rendered in musical terms. Apart from its fanciful imagery, the poem also excels in its rhythms which suggest the bustle and excitement of the chase.

Iaco ap Dewi, see DAVIES, JAMES (1648–1722).

Iago ap Ieuan (James James; 1833–1902), see under JAMES, EVAN (1809–78).

Iago Prytherch, see under THOMAS, RONALD STUART (1913–).

Iarll y Cawg, see under OWAIN AB URIEN (6th cent.).

Iarlles y Ffynnon, see under TAIR RHAMANT.

Iceni, see under BOUDICA (1st cent.).

Iestyn ap Gwrgant (*fl.* 1081–93), the last independent King of *Morgannwg. According to tradition, which is inaccurate in its detail, he slew Rhys ap Tewdwr at Penrhys in the valley of the Rhondda. It is said that because he refused the offer of Einion ap Collwyn's daughter in marriage, he was overthrown by Einion's Norman allies, who divided the lowlands among themselves and left only the uplands of Glamorgan to the Welsh. Most of the noble families of south Wales were later to claim descent from Iestyn ap Gwrgant.

IEUAN AP HYWEL SWRDWAL (*fl.* 1430–80), poet. Like his father *Hywel Swrdwal, he was associated with the district of Cedewain, Mont., and perhaps with Machynlleth, for he exchanged poems with *Llawdden, a priest in the parish at that time. Ieuan was a student at Oxford when he wrote the *awdl* known in English as *'Hymn to the Virgin'. As for his other works, there is doubt as to which should be attributed to him and which to his father. Furthermore, both poets were reputed to have written a history of Wales but neither of these works has survived. On Ieuan's death elegies were written for him by *Hywel ap Dafydd ap Ieuan ap Rhys, *Llywelyn Goch y Dant and *Gruffudd ap Dafydd Fychan.

The works of father and son are included in the volume *Gwaith Barddonol Hywel Swrdwal a'i Fab, Ieuan* (ed. J. C. Morrice, 1908).

Ieuan ap Iago, see JAMES, EVAN (1809–78).

IEUAN AP IEUAN AP MADOG (*fl.* 1547–87), copyist, was a native of *Tir Iarll and a member of a family which owned land in the parish of Betws, although he is known to have bought a smallholding in the neighbouring parish of Llangynwyd in 1547. He became a prominent figure in the life of his native district as one of a group of scribes who flourished there towards the end of the sixteenth century. Although some were professional copyists, others, like Ieuan, were literary-minded gentlemen. He made collections of the prose texts and translations of the period, including a Welsh version of 'Y *Marchog Crwydrad* ('The Voyage of the Wandering Knight', Llanstephan MS 178, *c*.1585) and a copy of *Chwedlau Saith Ddoethion Rhufain (Llanstephan MS 171), both works with a didactic or moral purpose.

For further details see G. J. Williams, *Traddodiad Llenyddol Morgannwg* (1948) and Ceri W. Lewis, 'The Literary History of Glamorgan from 1550 to 1770', in *Glamorgan County History* (vol. IV, ed. Glanmor Williams, 1974).

IEUAN AP SULIEN (d. 1137), the author of a Latin poem on the life of his father *Sulien, *Carmen de vita et familia Sulgeni*, written between 1085 and 1091, was a brother to *Rhygyfarch, Arthen and Daniel and an industrious member of the *Llanbadarn school of copyists. His fine work as illuminator can be seen in the manuscripts of Augustine's *De Trinitate* at Corpus Christi College, Cambridge, which contains a Welsh quatrain, and of the Psalter kept in Trinity College, Dublin.

IEUAN AP TUDUR PENLLYN (*fl.* 1465–1500), poet, was probably born at Caer-gai, Llanuwchllyn, Mer. He wrote praise-poems for patrons at Gesailgyfarch and Ystumcegid in Eifionydd, at Ynysmaengwyn and *Nannau, Mer., and also at Abertanad, Mold and Newtown. One of the many poets who wrote for Abbot (later Bishop) Dafydd ab Owain, he composed several *cywyddau* of request and also some satirical poems, including a *cywydd* to the Clwyd estuary, as well as *englynion* addressed to his father, *Tudur Penllyn.

For a discussion of his work see Thomas Roberts, *Gwaith Tudur Penllyn ac Ieuan ap Tudur Penllyn* (1958).

Ieuan Brydydd Hir, see EVANS, EVAN (1731–88).

IEUAN BRYDYDD HIR HYNAF (*fl.* 1450–85), poet, of Ardudwy, Mer., about half of whose extant work consists of religious poems. Besides celebrating the rood at Chester and the well of *Gwenffrewi, he wrote a confessional poem and three *awdlau* praising God, one of which is a continuation of an *awdl* by *Dafydd ap Gwilym. The mock satirical poems which he exchanged with *Tudur Penllyn are evidence of their friendship. His most memorable poem is a *cywydd* to old age which graphically portrays physical decline. Ieuan's name is associated with two of the *Areithiau Pros.

Ieuan Ddu, see THOMAS, JOHN (1795–1871).

IEUAN DEULWYN (*fl.* 1460), poet. A native of Kidwelly, Carms., he wrote religious poems and love-poems, making great use in the latter of the theme of love's affliction. Among his *cywyddau* to patrons in south Wales are a eulogy to Sir Richard Herbert, which was part of a bardic contention with *Bedo Brwynllys, and a number of *cywyddau* of request.

His work was published in an edition prepared by Ifor Williams (1909).

IEUAN DYFI (*fl.* late 15th cent.), poet, was said by John *Davies of Mallwyd to have been a native of Aberdyfi, Mer. Although he addressed an *awdl* to Sir Richard Herbert and a *cywydd* to *Dafydd Llwyd of Mathafarn, he was essentially a love-poet who wrote verse for his sweetheart, Anni Goch. One of his poems, a *cywydd* illustrating the deceit of women down the ages, was very popular among the poets and copyists of the period and it elicited a reply from *Gwerful Mechain.

Ieuan's poems are to be found in *Gwaith Huw Cae Llwyd ac eraill* (ed. Leslie Harries, 1953).

Ieuan Fardd, see EVANS, EVAN (1731–88).

IEUAN GETHIN AP IEUAN AP LLEISION (*fl.* 1437–90), poet and gentleman, of Baglan, Glam., of whose work about ten *cywyddau* and an *awdl* have survived. Two poems to Owain *Tudur deplore his imprisonment in

Newgate in 1437 and lament his execution in 1461. Ieuan wrote an elegiac *awdl* for his daughter and a similar *cywydd* for a son who died of bubonic plague; it was either he or Llywelyn Fychan ap Llywelyn Foelrhon who wrote a celebrated elegy for four children who died of the same disease. Ieuan ap Rhydderch sang his praise, referring to his bardic contention with a poet known as Y Proll, and *Iorwerth Fynglwyd wrote his elegy.

Ieuan Glan Alarch, see MILLS, JOHN (1812–73).

Ieuan Glan Geirionydd, see EVANS, EVAN (1795–1855).

Ieuan Gwyllt, see ROBERTS, JOHN (1822–77).

Ieuan Gwynedd, see JONES, EVAN (1820–52).

Ieuan Llawdden, see LLAWDDEN (*fl.* 1450).

Ieuan Lleyn, see PRICHARD, EVAN (1769–1832).

Ieuan Llwyd (*fl.* 1351), the son of Ieuan Fwyaf, is listed in state documents as *prepositus* of the commot of Perfedd in Uwch Aeron in 1351. He is known principally from an *awdl* addressed to him by *Dafydd ap Gwilym which describes him as a man who loved poetry and as 'un o hil Llawdden' ('of the race of *Llawdden'). His family's home was at Morfa Bychan but he is associated primarily with the commot of Genau'r Glyn, where he subsequently settled.

IFANS, DAFYDD (1949–), novelist, was born at Aberystwyth, Cards. Educated at the University College of North Wales, Bangor, and the University College of Wales, Aberystwyth, he joined the staff of the National Library of Wales in 1972 and was appointed Assistant Keeper of Manuscripts in 1975. With his short novel *Eira Gwyn yn Salmon* (1974), he won the *Prose Medal at the National Eisteddfod, and he has since published another, *Ofn* (1980). He also edited the letters of Eluned *Morgan under the title *Tyred Drosodd* (1977); with his wife Rhiannon he has edited a modern edition (1980) of The *Mabinogion and, with Kathleen Hughes, a part of the *Diary* of Francis *Kilvert (1982).

Ifans, Robert, see ROBERT AB IFAN (*fl.* 1572–1603).

Ifor ap Cadifor (**Ifor Bach**; *fl.* 1158), Lord of *Senghennydd, Glam. Among his exploits was an attack on *Cardiff castle in 1158 during which he captured William, Earl of Gloucester, his wife and son, refusing to release them until the lands stolen from him by the Normans had been restored. The attack was a favourite subject in the competitions of the Eisteddfod during the nineteenth century, perhaps as a result of

Taliesin *Williams's long poem, *Cardiff Castle* (1827).

Ifor ap Llywelyn (Ifor Hael; *fl.* 1340–60), the friend and chief patron of *Dafydd ap Gwilym, may be said to have symbolized for the poet the very ideal of patronage. Dafydd addressed to him four *cywyddau*, a sequence of *englynion*, and two *awdlau* of which the second (of doubtful authenticity) is a combined elegy for Ifor and his wife, Nest. The four *cywyddau* are the supreme example of the combination in Dafydd's poetry of the old with the new, of the blending of the traditional concepts of praise-poetry with imagery of a kind which is elsewhere characteristic of Dafydd's *cywyddau* of love and nature. Their language is relatively simple and unadorned, their style relaxed and personal. At the same time, the heroic concepts which they embody come down in direct descent from the praise-poetry of the *Gogynfeirdd. In words which are reminiscent of *Cynddelw Brydydd Mawr, Dafydd stresses the mutual dependence of poet and patron, alluding in these poems more frequently than elsewhere to the traditional heroes of the *Old North. He envisages himself as another *Taliesin receiving benefits from his patron such as that poet had received from *Urien Rheged.

The fact that the epithet 'Hael' ('the Generous') clung to Ifor in poetic allusions throughout succeeding generations is to be explained by Dafydd's claim to have bestowed on Ifor 'the great name of Rhydderch', a reference to the Triad of the Three *Generous Men, one of whom was *Rhydderch Hael whose generosity to poets was proverbial. The four *cywyddau* praise Ifor and celebrate the delights to be enjoyed in his luxurious house at Bassaleg, Mon. So many references are made to Dafydd's visits to Ifor's home that it seems he was a regular visitor there, although whether early or late in the poet's career it is impossible to say. Dafydd addresses his friend in terms of admiration and affection which verge upon adulation, from which it may be concluded that he was suffering from a reaction against his earlier absorption in poetry written in praise of women.

Ifor Hael was the ancestor of the *Morgan family of Tredegar. The ruins of his home at Gwernyclepa, which lie in the woods about a mile from the present village of Bassaleg, inspired the famous *englynion* known as 'Llys Ifor Hael' by Evan *Evans (Ieuan Brydydd Hir).

For further details see Thomas Parry, *Gwaith Dafydd ap Gwilym* (1951) and Ifor Williams, *Dafydd ap Gwilym a'i Gyfoeswyr* (1935). The controversy over the authenticity of the Ifor Hael poems is traced by R. Geraint Gruffydd in the number of *Poetry Wales* (1973) devoted to Dafydd ap Gwilym. See also the articles by Saunders Lewis in *Llên Cymru* (1952–53), those by D. J. Bowen in *Llên Cymru* (1958–59; 1966), the *Transactions* of the Honourable Society of Cymmrodorion (1969) and *Y*

Traethodydd (vol. CXXXI, 1976) and that by Eurig R. Ll. Davies and Eirian Edwards in *Ysgrifau Beirniadol XI* (ed. J. E. Caerwyn Williams, 1982).

Ifor Bach, see IFOR AP CADIFOR (*fl.* 1158).

Ifor Ceri, see JENKINS, JOHN (1770–1829).

Ifor Hael, see IFOR AP LLYWELYN (*fl.* 1340–60).

Igraine, see EIGR.

Illtud (second half of the 5th cent.), saint, was one of the founders of monasticism in Britain. He belongs more especially to south-east Wales, although he is commemorated also in Llanelltud near Dolgellau, Mer., and in Brittany. The tradition that he founded a school at *Llanilltud Fawr (*ang.* Llantwit Major), and that he instructed there many saints who later achieved renown, is probably true. In the Life of Samson (early 7th cent.) it is said that Eltut (Illtud) was a disciple of Germanus of Auxerre and more emphasis is laid upon his learning, both classical and Christian, than on his practice of the ascetic life. The Life of Illtud, composed in the twelfth century, probably by a monk of Llanilltud, has hardly any historical value. It claims that he came from Letavia (Brittany) and draws on several implausible local traditions. In the Life of *Cadog by Lifris of Llancarfan, Illtud is described as a former soldier.

In Parenthesis (1937), David *Jones's first writing, a 'war book'. Centring on the figure of Private John Ball, it portrays the experience of a group of soldiers belonging to the Royal Welsh Fusiliers, Welshmen and Cockneys in almost equal proportions, during the period from December 1915 to July 1916. Its seven parts present the stages of their movement from the parade ground before embarkation to France and deep into the world of the trenches; the narrative ends with their assault on Mametz Wood where most are wounded or killed. The work combines immediacy with a large temporal perspective. Realistic in its rendering of the chaos of war, and of the humour, companionship and suffering of 'the essential foot-mob', it uses a wealth of historical, mythological and literary allusions—notably to Malory, Shakespeare and 'Y *Gododdin'—to set the war in the context of past wars involving 'representatives of the Island of Britain', and to present the men as makers of an order in which the underlying unity of Britain is re-created. The most-quoted passage is that from Part IV, popularly entitled 'Dai's Boast', in which an old sweat, invisible in the denouement, embodies the Taliesin theme of the spirit immortal and alive in every age by claiming that he was present when Cain murdered Abel, that he was a Roman soldier at Christ's crucifixion, and that he served with *Macsen Wledig and *Arthur.

For critical discussion see the article by William Blissett in *David Jones: Eight Essays on his Work as Writer and Artist* (ed. Roland Mathias, 1976), Samuel Rees, *David Jones* (1978), Thomas Dilworth, *The Liturgical Parenthesis of David Jones* (1979), Colin A. Hughes, *David Jones: The Man who was on the Field* (1979) and Elizabeth Ward, *David Jones Mythmaker* (1983).

In the Green Tree (1948), a posthumous collection of letters and short stories by Alun *Lewis, which includes tributes by other writers to his achievement and promise. Five of the six stories are set in India and draw extensively upon Lewis's experience of landscapes and incidents gathered from training, reconnaissance and hospitalization during 1943. All of them contain studies of officers under pressure, some wounded or dying, or strangely burdened by death, as in 'The Orange Grove', perhaps the writer's finest work of fiction. The tendency to melodrama in some of the stories, which might have been eradicated had Lewis edited the text for the press, is entirely absent from the letters to his wife and his parents. The letters illuminate the stories at many points and are an even more remarkable achievement.

Indeg, the daughter of Garwy Hir, is listed in a Triad as one of the Three Mistresses of *Arthur. No stories about her have survived but the medieval poets often referred to her as a standard of beauty.

Independency or **Congregationalism**, the type of church polity which emphasizes the liberty of the local congregation and the voluntary nature of membership in a fellowship of persons who profess Christ. The Independent principle is also expressed in the term 'gathered Church' and in the doctrine of the priesthood of all believers. The sovereign nature of each democratic church unit, under God, made Independency more attractive to many freer spirits in Wales in the late eighteenth and nineteenth centuries when the first enthusiasm of *Methodism had begun to succumb to organization. The words 'Annibynia' and 'Annibynia Fawr' have been used somewhat jocularly, probably for this reason, in speaking of the Welsh Independents, while allusions to their 'annibendod' ('disorderliness') are made more frequently perhaps by themselves than by others.

The Puritan John *Penry is honoured by Welsh Independents and others, although it was only in the last months of his life that he was a Separatist. In 1639 the Independent Church at Llanfaches, Mon., was established by William *Wroth, William *Erbery and Walter *Cradock, with the assistance of Henry Jessey, on the pattern of 'New England' Independency. About the same time a less organized movement was causing excitement in the Olchon district on the Herefordshire border. Among these early groups there were some who accepted and others who rejected infant baptism as, for instance, in the 'gathered church' which met at Llanigon during the Commonwealth and after the Restoration. But most of the *Baptists, led by John *Miles and others, formed a separate movement in 1649. The stress of persecution changed the outlook of the Nonconformist fellowships and the Independents came to be called 'y Sentars Sychion' ('the Dry Dissenters'), but the Evangelical Revival brought new zeal in the eighteenth century. Welsh Congregationalism, in its English-language form, is now largely contained within the United Reformed Church but in its Welsh-language form it continues in *Undeb Annibynwyr Cymraeg* (The Union of Welsh Independents).

The Independents were prominent in the development of *Radicalism in Wales and they have been busier than most in the activities of the *National Eisteddfod. A full list of theologians, poets, preachers and contributors to the Welsh periodical press would include a goodly number of Independents. A comparison of the denominations in respect of literary achievement—though it should be borne in mind that there is no such thing as creative denominational literature and that there are Independents who deny that their Union is a denomination—could not fail to acknowledge the distinction of the most notable literary figures of the Calvinistic Methodists from William *Williams (Pantycelyn) on, but it can be argued that writers of Independent background are more varied and more versatile, such as Gwilym Hiraethog (William *Rees), Elfed (Howell Elvet *Lewis) and W. J. *Gruffydd. Among living writers whose Independent connections bear some relationship to their literary work are Pennar *Davies, Glyn *Jones, Emyr *Humphreys and Roland *Mathias.

For further details see J. Morgan Jones (*et al.*), *Hanes ac Egwyddorion Annibynwyr Cymru* (1939), G. F. Nuttall, *Visible Saints* (1957) and R. Tudur Jones, *Congregationalism in England* (1962), *Hanes Annibynwyr Cymru* (1966) and *Yr Undeb: Hanes Undeb yr Annibynwyr Cymraeg 1872-1972* (1975).

Index (Dafydd Rhys Williams; 1851–1931), see under Drych.

Industrial Revolution, The, a term usually applied to a complex series of changes which became apparent in Britain in the late eighteenth century. Although there had been phases of rapid industrial and technological advance in other countries and in other ages, the changes initiated in Britain between 1750 and 1800 are considered revolutionary because they set in motion a process of self-sustained industrial growth by means of perpetual technological innovation and social transformation. In consequence, agriculture was displaced as the primary source of employment and wealth, the age-old pattern of domestic production was superseded by the factory system, the power available to industry was vastly augmented by the development of new sources of energy and the urban proletariat came to constitute the majority of the British population.

In Wales the pattern of self-sustained growth first became apparent in the iron-making areas of north Glamorgan and Monmouthshire during the Franco-British Wars (1793–1815). By the end of the eighteenth century, however, industrial production was also transforming communities in the Holywell district of Flintshire, in the Wrexham district of Denbighshire, in Amlwch in Anglesey, in Llanelli in Carmarthenshire and in Swansea in west Glamorgan. At that time almost all parts of Wales were experiencing a quickening of economic growth and it was by no means clear in 1800 where the industrial centre of gravity would eventually lie. The development of the steam-engine, dependent upon coal, and the need for large quantities of coal for the smelting of metal ores, led by the mid-nineteenth century to the concentration of industrial enterprise in the coalfields, particularly in that of south-east Wales, but also, to some extent, in the smaller coalfield of the north-east. In consequence, parts of north-west and mid-Wales may be said to have experienced an Industrial Revolution which failed.

Industrial Wales took little part in the production of consumer goods and had virtually no role in the cotton industry, the pioneer of the factory system. Its experience was almost totally restricted to the production of capital goods, metals, coal and (to a lesser extent) slate, a dependence upon extractive industries which would cause grave problems when Britain's pre-eminence as a producer of capital goods was eroded in the years after the First World War. In the earliest phase of the Industrial Revolution, copper was the most important commodity produced, but from 1790 to 1850 the Welsh industrial economy was dominated by the great iron-works of Merthyr Tydfil where, by 1830, some forty per cent of Britain's pig-iron and a half of its iron exports were manufactured. It was an area which had previously been virtually uninhabited and therefore the industrial communities which developed there lacked civic foundations. The physical shape of the settlements was determined by the contours of the narrow valleys of upland Glamorgan and Monmouthshire, thus creating industrial communities with unique characteristics.

After 1850, the iron industry was replaced by the coal industry as the mainstay of industrial Wales and by the late nineteenth century the south Wales coalfield, the world's most important coal-exporting centre, provided the energy source for transport and industrial undertakings over much of the globe. By 1850 agriculture provided employment for only one-third of the population of Wales. It can therefore be claimed that by then the Industrial Revolution had triumphed, although—as the initiation of perpetual change was the most striking characteristic of that Revolution—any attempt to seek its terminal date must be a futile exercise.

Of the 2,600,000 people living in Wales in 1921, some 1,150,000 lived in the coalfield, 650,000 in the coastal towns of Glamorgan and Monmouthshire and 800,000 in the rest of Wales. Until the later nineteenth century, the majority of those migrating to the coalfield had come from the rural areas of west and mid-Wales and this influx of population into the valleys of Glamorgan and Monmouthshire had strengthened the Welsh character of the communities which had developed there. Between 1881 and 1911, however, the two counties attracted substantially more immigrants from England than from the other counties of Wales, causing the authors of the *Report on Industrial Unrest* to comment in 1917, 'Until some fifteen to twenty years ago, the native inhabitants had, in many respects, shown a marked capacity for stamping their own impress on all newcomers and communicating to them a large measure of their own characteristics; of more recent years the process of assimilation has been unable to keep pace with the continuing influx of immigrants'. On the other hand, it can be argued that, instead of being a threat to the indigenous culture of Wales, industrialization was its salvation, for it provided employment opportunities within Wales for the surplus population of the Welsh-speaking countryside. This process enabled Wales to avoid the disasters which overtook Ireland in the nineteenth century and made possible the development of a Welsh-language culture in an urban environment. Some of the most characteristic manifestations of Welsh-language culture in the nineteenth century—working-class *Nonconformity, for example, or male voice choirs or the growth of a flourishing periodical press—were dependent upon the existence of mass societies and a degree of prosperity, both the consequence of industrialization.

Early Welsh industrial communities, with their marked lack of civic amenities and with their people subject to the unfettered power of the industrialists, were highly turbulent. In the first half of the nineteenth century, industrial Wales was the scene of a remarkable series of commotions, including the activities of the *Scotch Cattle (1820–35), the *Merthyr Rising of 1831, the Newport Rising of 1839 (see under Chartism) and a host of bitter industrial disputes. In the second half of the century, however, the rapid expansion of employment activities, the growth of self-help organizations and the advance of democracy provided increasing opportunities for law-abiding political action. An alliance was formed between the middle classes and the working classes, cemented by Nonconformity and finding expression through the Liberal Party. This alliance was breaking down by the early twentieth century when, with the spread of Socialist and, in particular, of Syndicalist ideas and with the rise of the Independent Labour Party, the concept of the brotherhood of working men became the dominant ideology of industrial Wales. By the eve of the First World War, the South Wales coalfield was proving itself to be among the most dissident areas of the United Kingdom and after the War the coalfield seats emerged as the most solid block of Labour constituencies in the kingdom and the *South Wales Miners Federation as a vanguard of British *Socialism.

The Industrial Revolution totally transformed the life of Wales, not only in those parts of the country which experienced extensive industrialization, but also in those areas which remained wholly rural. Indeed, it has been plausibly asserted that the marriage-rate in remotest Cardiganshire by the late nineteenth century was fluctuating in unison with the fluctuations in the price of coal. The Industrial Revolution gave rise to the central fact of the recent history of Wales, namely the creation of the community of the south Wales coalfield. The Anglicization of much of industrial Wales in the twentieth century has been accompanied by the growth of a consciously Welsh English-language culture and most of the work of Anglo-Welsh writers has been inspired by the experience of the people of the coalfield. See also DEPRESSION.

For further details see J. F. Rees, *Studies in Welsh History* (1947), A. H. John, *The Industrial Development of South Wales, 1750–1850* (1950), A. H. Dodd, *The Industrial Revolution in North Wales* (1971) and A. H. John and G. Williams (ed.), *Glamorgan County History* (vol. V. 1980).

INGLIS-JONES, ELISABETH (1900–   ), biographer and novelist, was born in London but brought up on the family estate of Derry Ormond near Lampeter, Cards. She lived there until her early adulthood and made the district the setting for her first romantic novel, *Starved Fields* (1929). Since then she has published *Crumbling Pageant* (1932), *Pay thy Pleasure* (1939), *The Loving Heart* (1941), *Lightly He Journeyed* (1946) and *Aunt Albina* (1948). The best of these novels are written in a biographical style and it was as a writer of biography that she achieved literary success. The story of Thomas *Johnes and his estate of Hafod is fascinatingly related in her *Peacocks in Paradise* (1950). Perhaps her best-known work outside Wales is *The Great Maria* (1959), a biography of the Anglo-Irish novelist Maria Edgeworth. She is also the author of *The Story of Wales* (1955), a popular history of the country from early medieval times.

Innes, James Dickson (1887–1914), landscape painter. Born at Llanelli, Carms., he trained at Carmarthen School of Art and the Slade School, London. He travelled widely in Europe with artist friends, including Augustus *John, with whom he also spent a period painting in the Arenig Valley near Bala, Mer. His death was caused by the consumptive condition which had dogged him all his life.

Interlude, a type of metrical play, usually on the *triban or *carol measure, but sometimes with *cynghanedd, which was performed by strolling players at fairs and taverns for the entertainment of the common people. The Welsh were familiar with the word '*anterliwt*' as early as the sixteenth century, but the forty-four examples which survive belong to the seventeenth and eighteenth centuries. About seven are attributed to Thomas *Edwards (Twm o'r Nant), the most famous writer of this type of play, and another eight to Elis *Roberts. Other notable writers of interludes include William Roberts, Richard Parry, Huw Jones (1700?–82), Siôn *Cadwaladr, Lodwig Williams and Jonathan *Hughes. The interlude, usually presented by a narrator, provided a medium for attacking social injustice and immorality, and most were dramatizations of well-known stories. Some contain songs and parodies of the outmoded bardic tradition. Landlords, lawyers and negligent clerics were the main butts of the interlude's broad humour, and the sometimes uncouth language and licentious actions of the interlude were among the reasons why they met with the disapproval of religious leaders. The characters were often personifications of human virtues or vices, and some, such as the Miser and the Fool, appeared regularly in the style of *commedia dell'arte*.

For further details see Glyn M. Ashton, *Hunangofiant a Llythyrau Twm o'r Nant* (1948) and the essay by T. Rhys Jones in *Gwŷr Llên y Ddeunawfed Ganrif* (ed. Dyfnallt Morgan, 1966).

Ioan ab Hywel or **Ioan Glandyfroedd (John Howell;** 1774–1830), see under BLODAU DYFED (1824).

Ioan Pedr, see PETER, JOHN (1833–77).

Ioan Siengcin, see JENKIN, JOHN (1716–96).

Ioan Tegid, see JONES, JOHN (1792–1852).

Iolo Carnarvon, see ROBERTS, JOHN JOHN (1840–1914).

IOLO GOCH (*c.*1320–1398), poet, whose home was in the township of Lleweni in the Vale of Clwyd, composed awdlau in the style of the Poets of the Princes, but he is noteworthy as being one of the first to write poems of praise to the gentry and others in the *cywydd metre. One of them is to King Edward III and another to Sir Roger Mortimer, and in both poems he displays detailed knowledge of the wars of the period and of people and places in Ireland, England and France.

His chief patron was Ithel ap Robert of Coedymynydd near Caerwys, but he also wrote poems for patrons much further afield, such as Tudur Fychan and other members of the *Tudor family, and for *Hywel ap Gruffudd (Hywel y Fwyall) of Eifionydd and Sir Rhys ap Gruffudd of Dyfed. He probably visited houses in the Marches and went south to the valleys of Glamorgan and westwards to *Whitland and *Strata Florida. Three of his poems to *Owain Glyndŵr are extant, one of which celebrates the luxury of the court at Sycharth, but he did not live to see Glyndŵr's rising. His elegy for *Llywelyn Goch ap Meurig Hen testifies to a long association between the two poets.

Iolo also composed satirical poems in a jesting bardic contention with *Gruffudd Gryg and two poems attacking the Franciscans and advocating clerical wedlock. The most notable of his poems is the one to 'Y Llafurwr' ('The labourer'), which contains a witty description of the plough in the form of a series of fanciful metaphors as prescribed by the bardic practice of *dyfalu. Only twenty-nine cywyddau can be attributed to Iolo Goch with any degree of certainty, but they are enough to show that he was an accomplished poet.

The cywyddau were edited by Henry Lewis in the volume Cywyddau Iolo Goch ac Eraill (1925, 1937); see also Eurys Rowlands's article in Celtic Studies: Essays in memory of Angus Matheson (ed. James Carney and David Greene, 1968).

Iolo Morganwg, see WILLIAMS, EDWARD (1747–1826).

Ionoron Glan Dwyryd, see WALTER, ROWLAND (1819–84).

Iorwerth, see under LAWS OF HYWEL DDA.

IORWERTH FYNGLWYD (fl. 1485–1527), poet, was born and bred in St. Bride's Major in the Vale of Glamorgan. Apart from his eulogy of Sir Rhys ap Thomas and his elegy for the poet William Egwad, all his extant poems were addressed to patrons in Glamorgan and Gwent, especially the powerful Herbert family. One of his three cywyddau for Rhys ap Siôn of Glynnedd (Glynneath) is among the most striking of all the poems composed during the period of the *Poets of the Gentry. The poet's attachment to Rhys vexed Sir Mathias Cradog, the Deputy-sheriff of Glamorgan, with the result that Iorwerth composed for him a cywydd of reconciliation. Iorwerth also engaged in bardic contentions with his teacher, Rhisiart ap Siôn, and with Siôn ap Hywel Gwyn, and he wrote a satire of the minstrel Siôn Leision of Margam.

Iorwerth Fynglwyd's work has been edited by H. Ll. Jones and E. I. Rowlands (1975) and his place in the bardic tradition is discussed by G. J. Williams in Traddodiad Llenyddol Morgannwg (1948).

Iorwerth Glan Aled, see ROBERTS, EDWARD (1819–67).

Iron House, The, an episode in the Second Branch of *Pedair Cainc y Mabinogi. *Matholwch, King of Ireland, while out hunting one day, is approached by Llasar Llaes Gyfnewid, a large ugly man, and his even larger wife, Cymidei Cymeinfoll, who is soon to give birth to a fully armed warrior. The king gives them his protection but they make themselves hated in his land by molesting his subjects. They are eventually lured into an iron house which is set on fire, but Llasar, by dint of his exceeding strength, succeeds in charging the white-hot wall and escapes with his wife. They come to Wales and present Bendigeidfran (*Brân) with the *Cauldron of Rebirth which plays an important part in the subsequent events of the story. The theme is also to be found in Irish literature and was recorded by the Brothers Grimm.

Isca, see CAERLEON.

Isfoel, see JONES, DAFYDD (1881–1968).

Island of Apples, The (1965), Glyn *Jones's third novel, weaves realism with a strand of fantasy. In a society detailed with the author's usual meticulousness live Dewi Davies, the schoolboy narrator, and his three friends. The enigmatic, older boy called Karl Anthony, first seen floating down the river and last seen floating out to sea, is a proud, brave and secretive individual who, as the story proceeds, becomes a surrogate for the orphaned Dewi in the achievement of a number of feats of daring, finally standing accused of the murder of Growler, the headmaster. The novel's power is based on the skill with which the real and the fantastic are intertwined but there is an insistence at various points in the narrative that Karl is real. This approach to *Ynys Afallon by the adolescent mind makes of the novel the author's greatest success in the genre.

Islwyn, see THOMAS, WILLIAM (1832–78).

Itinerary of John Leland, The (1710), a manuscript which was given to the Bodleian Library by Thomas Burton, the English historian, in 1632, consists of the notes from tours through England and Wales made by John Leland (1506–52) between 1534 and 1543. This extraordinary scholar and collector, librarian to Henry VIII, was in 1533 appointed King's Antiquary, a post without precedent, and commissioned to search for records of antiquities in all cathedrals, abbeys, priories and colleges. The information which he gathered is recorded in the Itinerary, together with his own observations, descriptive of landscape, produce, landowners, towns, buildings, history and occasional 'marvelous tales'. Probably entering Wales from Gloucester, Shrewsbury and Chester, Leland rode through the country between 1536 and 1539, interesting years historically, as the Acts for the suppression of monasteries were passed in 1536 and 1539, and the 'New Act', 'for lawes and justice to be ministered in Wales in like fourme as it is in this realme', in 1536. *The Itinerary in Wales* (1906), edited and published separately by Lucy Toulmin Smith, is valuable as the first such work in English, and was much used by later antiquarians and topographers.

Ivorites, see under FRIENDLY SOCIETIES.

IWAN, DAFYDD (1943–), folk-singer and poet, was born at Brynaman, Carms.; through his father, Gerallt *Jones, he is related to the *Cilie family of poets. Although he graduated from the Welsh School of Architecture, he has never practised in the profession but has made a career as a singer, a director of the Sain recording company and organizer of the housing association, *Cymdeithas Tai Gwynedd*. From 1968 to 1971 he was Chairman of *Cymdeithas yr Iaith Gymraeg* and played a leading part in that movement's campaigns, for which he served a sentence in prison.

His commitment to the cause of Welsh *Nationalism is reflected in many of his songs which, for the most part, make political points about the history, language and present condition of the Welsh people. Some have the quality of topical ballads and are genuinely popular, while others are more lyrical and semi-religious in their themes. The best are those with a satirical aim, such as 'Carlo' and 'Croeso 69', written at the time of the investiture of the Prince of Wales in 1969. Others, such as 'Pam fod eira'n wyn?', 'I'r Gad!' and 'Wrth Feddwl am fy Nghymru', are widely known, especially by young people, and are among the finest in the repertoire of Welsh patriotic music. Besides numerous records, he has published four collections of his songs, including *Y Byd Gwyrdd* (1975) and *Cant o Ganeuon* (1982), both of which have had an influence on the writing of young poets in the Welsh language. The singer announced his retirement as an entertainer in 1982 and since then, mainly as Chairman and Vice-President of *Plaid Cymru, he has devoted his energies to the party's electoral struggle in which his ebullient personality, personal courage and practical gifts have won many admirers.

For details of Dafydd Iwan's career as a folk-singer see his essay in the volume *Artists in Wales* (ed. Meic Stephens, 1977) and his autobiography in the series *Cyfres y Cewri* (ed. Manon Rhys, 1981).

J

Jac Glan-y-gors, see JONES, JOHN (1766–1821).

Jac Llanfor, see JONES, JOHN (1854–1913).

Jack Black, the cobbler in Dylan *Thomas's *Under Milk Wood (1954), dreams of chasing courting couples through the night. His cry of 'Ach y fi! Ach y fi!' is one commonly used in Wales as an expression of disgust.

Jack o'Lantern, a hollow turnip carved in the shape of a human face and lit by a candle from inside, is still used in celebration of Hallowe'en (31 Oct.). The name is also given to the will-o'-the-wisp, the gaseous, phosphorescent glow which sometimes appears on marshy ground. Like the *Corpse Candle, the phenomenon is said to be an omen of death. There is a good description of 'the bogfire' in James *Motley's notes to his poem 'The Canwyll Corph' in Tales of the Cymry (1848).

Jack the Giant-killer, a traditional English nursery tale, was first printed in chapbook form in Glasgow (1695–98) and later in Newcastle (1711). Full of absurd accretions, such as its setting in the days of King *Arthur, it appears to have been in origin a propaganda tale from the early decades after the conquest of Cornwall by the King of Wessex (i.e. after AD 838) when it was important to free Cornwall from pockets of Celtic resistance and to discredit in Cornish eyes their uncouth relatives, the Welsh.

Jack, the son of a Cornish farmer, who appears throughout as an Englishman, kills the giant Cormoran and then travels to Wales, accounting for several other giants on the way. The first Welsh giant he meets demonstrates the traditional Celtic characteristics of hospitality, cunning and inability to resist a challenge. Jack hides some hasty pudding in a bag under his coat and rips it open in the giant's view. The latter, astonished but determined to match the feat, sticks a knife into his own stomach and kills himself. Another Welsh giant turns out to be Jack's uncle, incomprehensibly in the story as told. From him the hero receives the coat of invisibility, the cap of knowledge, the sword of sharpness and the shoes of swiftness. At this point, with Jack helping a prince to win a lady-love, the story partakes of some of the elements of the tale of *Culhwch and Olwen.

Yet another giant encountered by Jack is called Thunderdell and comes from 'the northern dales', thought to be a reference to the Celtic kingdom of Strathclyde which lasted until the early eleventh century. Sensing Jack's approach, despite his invisibility, this giant declaims the famous words,

> Fee, fi, fo, fum!
> I smell the blood of an Englishman!
> Be he alive or be he dead,
> I'll grind his bones to make my bread.

The fact that Jack lures Thunderdell into a moat and kills him is of less importance in the tale than the establishment of a difference of blood.

JACKSON, KENNETH HURLSTONE (1909–   ), Celtic scholar, was born at Wallington, Surrey, and educated at St. John's College, Cambridge, to which he returned in 1934 as a Fellow. From 1939 to 1950 he taught Celtic Studies at Harvard University and in 1950 he was appointed to the Chair of Celtic Languages, Literatures, History and Antiquities at Edinburgh University, remaining in that post until his retirement in 1979.

One of the world's foremost Celtic scholars, Kenneth Jackson has published numerous works of specifically Welsh interest. They include his essays, with texts and translations, Early Welsh Gnomic Poems (1935) and Studies in Early Celtic Nature Poetry (1935). His conclusions regarding the Hengerdd (see under CYNFEIRDD) are set out in his translation and treatise, The Gododdin: the Earliest Scottish Poem (1969). In his magisterial study Language and History in Early Britain (1953) he attempts to date the main phonetic changes in the insular Brythonic languages, while his extensive work on early Irish and Welsh literature is to be found in The International Popular Tale and Early Welsh Tradition (1961). A complete scholar, learned in the archaeology, history, languages and literatures of the Celtic world, he has also published for the layman an excellent volume of translations, A *Celtic Miscellany (1951).

A full list of Kenneth H. Jackson's publications will be found in Studia Celtica (vols. XIV/XV, 1979–80).

Jacob, Sarah (1857–69), also known as The Welsh Fasting Girl, was said by her parents, Evan and Hannah Jacob of Lletherneuadd Uchaf, a farm near Pencader, Carms., to have lived for more than two years without food or drink. This claim aroused widespread curiosity, both popular and medical, but under closer surveillance the child died. Her parents, whose belief that 'The Great Doctor' would take care of Sarah remained apparently unshakeable, had encouraged visitors to give the girl, who lay in bed dressed as a bride, gifts of money. They were subsequently sentenced to terms of hard labour for the crime of manslaughter. The evidence at their trial suggested that Sarah, in her apparent refusal to eat and drink, had either been the willing accomplice of her parents, or else had made them and herself the victims of her own duplicity; she may have been suffering from anorexia nervosa. A post-mortem examination found traces of food in the girl's stomach. Whatever the truth may have been, this macabre case was allowed to proceed towards its inevitable conclusion, with all those involved in it—parents, relatives, neighbours, as well as doctors and clergymen—more interested in seeing for how long the child could survive than in inducing her to take proper sustenance. See also HUGHES, GAENOR (1745–80).

For full details of the incident see John Cule, Wreath on the Crown (1967); Gwenlyn Parry and Christine Furnival have written plays based upon the story of Sarah Jacob, Paul Ferris a documentary television programme and Aled Islwyn a novel, Sarah Arall (1982).

Jacobinism, a Republican creed which came to dominate revolutionary thought in France in 1789. The Jacobin Club, founded in that year, virtually ruled France under Robespierre's leadership between 1792 and 1794, using violence to implement its extreme egalitarian principles. The term 'Jacobin' was often used generically by more conservative elements in society to denote all kinds of radical and democratic ideas, some of which sprang as much from the American Revolution as from the French.

Welshmen such as Richard *Price, David *Williams and Morgan John *Rhys had been preaching republican ideas before 1789, but the first phase of the French Revolution gave them a new relevance. The Welsh societies in London, such as the *Gwyneddigion, the *Cymreigyddion and the *Caradogion, became hotbeds of *Republicanism and John *Jones (Jac Glan-y-gors) spread Tom Paine's ideas in Welsh. In Wales itself they were promoted by Unitarians such as Thomas *Evans (Tomos Glyn Cothi) and Edward *Williams (Iolo Morganwg) who once signed himself 'Bard of Liberty'. The Welsh political periodical was born in this period, in the form of Y *Cylchgrawn Cynmraeg (1793) and Y *Geirgrawn (1796), the latter carrying a Welsh version of 'La Marseillaise'; many pamphlets, too, were published on the subject of Republicanism. In some literatures the movement provided a stimulus to *Romanticism but this cannot be said of its early influence on Welsh literature, except perhaps in the peculiar case of Iolo Morganwg.

Because the Welsh Jacobins were both zealous and articulate their influence can easily be over-emphasized. They had, however, little support from the orthodox religious denominations and the *Methodists were particularly hostile, partly because of the *Unitarian, if not deistic, tendencies of most of the Jacobin leaders. The war between Britain and France, the excesses of the Terror, the landing of the French at Fishguard (see under NICHOLAS, JEMIMA), and the advent of Napoleon, all these resulted in a popular reaction against Jacobinism which has caused some historians to argue that it did more to hinder than to stimulate *Radicalism in Wales. Nevertheless, the tradition did not disappear entirely. Under the leadership of Morgan John Rhys, it led to an attempt to establish a Welsh colony on democratic principles in America, while in Wales it reappeared from time to time, usually in the midst of industrial and political upheavals, as an expression of egalitarian and humanitarian ideals.

For further details see D. Davies, The Influence of the French Revolution on Welsh Life and Literature (1926), J. J. Evans, Dylanwad y Chwyldro Ffrengig ar Lenyddiaeth Cymru (1928) and Gwyn A. Williams, The Search for Beulah Land (1980).

Jacobitism, a movement which supported the right to the throne of England of the Catholic Stuarts, particularly James Edward ('The Old Pretender'), the son of James II, and his son, Charles Edward ('The Young Pretender'). This support, mostly found among Tory gentry, became evident after the dethronement of James II in 1688, continued after the Hanoverian Succession in 1714 and culminated in two abortive Jacobite Rebellions in 1715 and 1745.

In Wales, the Jacobite cause was upheld by such families as the Pryses of *Gogerddan, the Kemeyses of Cefnmabli, the *Philippses of Picton Castle (from 1743) and the *Bulkeleys of Baron Hill. Two Jacobite societies were established—in Denbighshire, The Circle of the White Rose (1710), of which the chief member was Sir Watkin *Williams-Wynne of Wynnstay, and in south-west Wales, The Society of Sea Serjeants, revived in 1725, which was less politically active. The movement, however, was never strong in Wales: it gained little support in 1715 and when 'The Young Pretender', or 'Bonnie Prince Charlie', landed in Scotland in 1745 he met with little response from Wales. The Jacobite cause was crushed on the battlefield of Culloden Moor in Scotland in April of the following year.

For further details see H. M. Vaughan, 'Welsh Jacobitism', in the Transactions of the Honourable Society of Cymmrodorion (1920–21), the article by Donald Nicholas in the Transactions of the Honourable Society of Cymmrodorion (1948) and that by Peter D. G. Thomas in The Welsh History Review (vol. 1, no. 3, 1962); see also G. H. Jenkins, Hanes Cymru yn y Cyfnod Modern Cynnar (1983).

JAMES, DANIEL (Gwyrosydd; 1847–1920), poet, a native of Treboeth, Swansea. On the death of his father he found employment at the Morriston Iron Works. His lyrics, which were very popular as recitation pieces, were collected in the volumes *Caneuon Gwyrosydd* (1892) and *Aeron Awen Gwyrosydd* (1898). It was he who wrote the words beginning '*Nid wy'n gofyn bywyd moethus*' to which the famous hymn ★'*Calon Lân*' is usually sung.

James, David (1887–1967), philanthropist, was the benefactor of numerous good causes and institutions, including the eisteddfod held annually in his native village of Pontrhydfendigaid, Cards. He made a fortune from business interests in London which, since his death, has been administered by The Catherine and Lady Grace James Foundation. He was buried in the churchyard at ★Strata Florida (Ystrad Fflur), not far from the yew-tree which is said to mark the grave of ★Dafydd ap Gwilym.

JAMES, DAVID EMRYS (Dewi Emrys; 1881–1952), poet, was born at New Quay, Cards., but brought up at Rhosycaerau, Pembs. His first job was in journalism but, after studying at the Presbyterian College in Carmarthen, he became a minister with the Independents, holding pastorates at Dowlais, Buckley and Pontypridd, and in London. Returning to journalism in 1918, he led a bohemian life in London but settled at Talgarreg, Cards., in 1940.

He won the ★Crown at the National Eisteddfod in 1926 and the ★Chair in 1929, 1930, 1943 and 1948; some of his prize-winning poems, such as '*Y Gân ni Chanwyd*' (1929), were published in pamphlet form. Two volumes of his verses appeared during his lifetime, *Y Cwm Unig* (1930) and *Cerddi'r Bwthyn* (1950); the commemorative volume *Wedi Storom* (1965) was published posthumously. He also wrote a volume of essays (1937), a textbook of Welsh prosody, *Odl a Chynghanedd* (1937) and, as David Emrys, a volume of poems in English, *Rhymes of the Road* (1928). As the editor of the poetry column '*Y Babell Awen*' in *Y* ★*Cymro* (1936–52), he was an important influence on other poets. A selection of the contributors' work appeared in the volume *Cerddi'r Babell* (1938). Although Dewi Emrys was a prolific writer and a colourful personality, very little of his work has proved to be of permanent value. The most famous of his poems is '*Pwllderi*', written in the Welsh dialect of north Pembrokeshire.

The poet's biography was written by Eluned Phillips, *Cofiant Dewi Emrys* (1971); see also the biographical note by D. Jacob Davies in *Wedi Storom* (1965), the lecture by T. Llew Jones (1981) and the note by Donald Evans in *Deri o'n Daear Ni* (ed. D. J. Goronwy Evans, 1984).

JAMES, EDWARD (1569?–1610?), cleric and translator. A native of Glamorgan, he was edu-cated at Jesus College, Oxford. He was granted the living of Caerleon, Mon., in 1595, but also served at Shirenewton and Llangatwg-juxta-Usk before becoming vicar of Llangatwg Feibion Afel in 1599 and of Llangatwg-juxta-Neath in 1603. Appointed Chancellor of ★Llandaf in 1606, he was one of a small group of cultured clerics associated with that bishopric. It is possible that William ★Morgan, Bishop of Llandaf between 1595 and 1601, urged him to translate *The Book of Homilies*, a work which appeared in a Welsh version by James in 1606. He was not the first to undertake this task, for earlier translations of the Homilies had been included in John Mirk's *Liber Ffestialis*, but he based his versions on the Welsh ★Bible and for that reason the work was of a high standard.

For further details see the article by Glanmor Williams in *Morgannwg* (vol. XXV, 1981).

JAMES, EVAN (Ieuan ap Iago; 1809–78) and **JAMES (Iago ap Ieuan**; 1833–1902), the author and the composer respectively of the national anthem of Wales, ★'*Hen Wlad fy Nhadau*'. The father, a native of Caerphilly and a weaver by trade, became the owner of a wool factory in Pontypridd, Glam., in 1844. His son, who is believed to have composed the tune, assisted his father and, after 1873, kept public houses in Pontypridd and Mountain Ash. A memorial to father and son, the work of Sir Goscombe ★John, was erected in Ynysangharad Park, Pontypridd, in 1930.

For further details about Evan James see the article by Daniel Huws in the *Journal* of the National Library of Wales (vol. XVI, 1970).

JAMES, JAMES SPINTHER (1837–1914), historian, a native of Talybont, Cards., was a shepherd and drover before he became a collier at Aberdare in 1854. Ordained in 1861, he was an eloquent preacher and political orator, and a prolific author. His most important work is *Hanes y Bedyddwyr yng Nghymru* (4 vols., 1892–1907), a history of the Welsh ★Baptists, written in a readable but idiosyncratic style. James also wrote hymns, contributed articles to encyclopaedias and, after the death of Ioan Emlyn (John Emlyn Jones; 1818–73), completed a geographical work entitled *Y Parthsyllydd* (1875).

JAMES, JOHN (1939–), poet. Born in Cardiff, he was educated at the University of Bristol and edited the magazine *R* from 1963 to 1969. He has published numerous collections of verse, including *The Welsh Poems* (1967), *Trägheit* (1968), *Letters from Sarah* (1969), *One for Rolf* (1975) and *Berlin Return* (1983).

JAMES, SIÂN (1932–), novelist, was born near Llandysul, Cards., and educated at the University College of Wales, Aberystwyth. Formerly a teacher, she is the author of six novels: *One Afternoon* (1975), *Yesterday* (1978), *A*

Small Country (1979), *Another Beginning* (1980), *Dragons and Roses* (1983) and *A Dangerous Time* (1984). The third of these, perhaps her most distinguished work so far, is set in a farming community in west Wales at the time of the First World War.

James, Thomas (1593?–1635?), navigator, was brought up at Llanwytherin (Llanvetherine), Mon. He set out from Bristol on board the *Henrietta Maria* in May 1631 in search of the North-west Passage to the Pacific. After reaching James Bay, he gave up the quest and returned to England where he arrived in October 1633. An account of his adventures will be found in *The Strange and Dangerous Voyage* (1633), a work which is supposed to have inspired *The Ancient Mariner* (1798) of S. T. Coleridge.

JARMAN, ALFRED OWEN HUGHES (1911–   ), scholar, a native of Bangor, Caerns., was educated at the University College of North Wales, Bangor, and was a Lecturer attached to the Department of Extra-Mural Studies there before his appointment as a Lecturer in the Welsh Department at the University College of Wales, Cardiff, in 1946. He was Professor of Welsh there from 1957 until his retirement in 1979.

Of all modern Welsh scholars, it is A. O. H. Jarman who has thrown most light on the obscurities of the legend of *Myrddin (Merlin). In his contribution to *Arthurian Literature in the Middle Ages* (ed. R. S. Loomis, 1959), to *Studia Celtica* (vols. X/XI, 1975/76) and to *Astudiaethau ar yr Hengerdd* (ed. R. Bromwich and R. Brinley Jones, 1978), as well as in the volume *The Legend of Merlin* (1960), he has traced the development of the story from its Celtic and Welsh roots to its French versions. He has also edited the texts of *Ymddiddan Myrddin a Thaliesin* (1951) and *The *Black Book of Carmarthen* (1982). An authority on *Geoffrey of Monmouth and the history of the Arthurian legend, A. O. H. Jarman was elected President of the British Branch of the International Arthurian Society in 1980. His interest extends to the *Cynfeirdd, on whom he contributed an essay to the *Writers of Wales* series (1981), to *'Canu Llywarch Hen' and to the *Morris Brothers of Anglesey. With Gwilym Rees *Hughes, he has edited *A Guide to Welsh Literature* (2 vols., 1976, 1979), and with his wife, Eldra Jarman, he is the co-author of a book about Welsh gypsies, *Y Sipsiwn Cymreig* (1979). He has been editor of the periodical *Llên Cymru since 1962.

JARMAN, GERAINT (1950–   ), poet and singer, was born at Denbigh and brought up in Cardiff where he still lives. He is one of the best-known performers in the field of light entertainment in Wales today and the leading exponent of the reggae style in Welsh. Many of his songs reflect his urban background and the influence of modern European poetry has been discerned in some of his work. Besides seven recordings of his music, he has published two collections of poetry, *Eira Cariad* (1970) and *Cerddi Alfred Street* (1976).

Jarvis Valley, The, the fictitious location of most of Dylan *Thomas's early short stories, especially the more arcane and surrealistic which, like the work of Caradoc Evans (David *Evans), draw on a wilfully distorted view of rural Wales. In a letter to Pamela Hansford Johnson (May, 1934) Thomas recorded that he had contemplated including several of the stories, such as 'The Visitor', 'The Tree' and 'The Map of Love', into what he called 'my novel of the Jarvis valley', but that work was never finished.

Jazz Bands or **Gazooka Bands**, manifestations of popular culture in the mining valleys of south-east Wales during the years between the World Wars. Their heyday was the strike-bound summer of 1926, when the industrially dislocated *Rhondda, Aberdare and Merthyr Valleys, in particular, saw a proliferation of groups in fancy-dress with such exotic names as the Gelli Toreadors, the Cwmparc Gondoliers and the Treharris Indians. The gazooka was an instrument made of tin and shaped like a cigar which gave a distinctive, if somewhat monotonous, sound which could be produced by anyone capable of humming a marching tune into it. Viewed with scorn by more orthodox culture-bearers, the bands were not merely a diversion from everyday realities but, like the football clubs and the operatic and choral societies of the *Depression years, they boosted morale and asserted collective values at a time when the very existence of the valley communities was in doubt. Although the tradition is maintained by the drum-majorettes who march in carnival processions in present-day south Wales, the bands were the product of special circumstances and are seen no more. They are celebrated in the radio play *Gazooka* (broadcast 1952) by Gwyn *Thomas (1913–81) and in his collection of short stories which bears the same title (1957).

Jealous Husband, The, a stock character in medieval literature. The two earliest Welsh examples, which date from the twelfth century, occur in a short poem by *Cynddelw Brydydd Mawr and in the *Gorhoffedd (boasting-poem) of *Hywel ap Owain Gwynedd. But the best-known is found in the work of *Dafydd ap Gwilym, for whom *y gŵr eiddig* ('the jealous husband'), also called *y bwa bach* ('the little hunchback'), is the greatest obstacle to the poet's amorous encounters. The theme is not confined to poetry, however. In the romance of Peredur (see under TAIR RHAMANT), the Tent Maiden's husband punishes her because he suspects her of adultery, only to discover that his suspicion is unfounded. Enid, in the tale of *Geraint, warns her husband that he has become unpopular with his peers because he prefers dalliance with her at court to knightly pursuits. The jealous Geraint wrongly suspects that his wife is trying to induce him to leave the court so that she can indulge in a love-affair during his absence, and he punishes her accordingly. The theme also occurs in a modified form in the story of *Amlyn and Amig.

Jealous Stepmother, The, a popular international motif. The most famous example is the story of Snow White in which the King's second wife tries to kill the daughter born of his first marriage. It is also the opening theme of the tale of *Culhwch and Olwen. The hero refuses to marry his stepmother's daughter, with the result that the stepmother swears that he will marry none but Olwen, the daughter of the giant Ysbaddaden. By using the device of this oath, the tale's redactor introduced the motif of the Giant's Daughter and thus united two otherwise independent motifs. The theme of the Jealous Stepmother also forms the framework within which the collection of tales known as *Chwedlau Saith Ddoethion Rhufain* was composed. The Emperor's wife tries to seduce the young prince, her stepson, but the boy resists and, accused of attempted rape, is condemned to death. One of the boy's mentors then tells a story about a woman's deceit in order to persuade the Emperor to put off the day of execution. A reprieve is granted and the six other wise men tell similar tales, all of which are answered by the stepmother, until finally on the eighth night the boy breaks his silence and speaks for himself.

Jeffreys, George (1645–89), judge, was born at Acton, Wrexham, Denbs. As a lawyer he took the side of the Court against the Parliamentarians in the State trials of the 1680s and served as Lord Chancellor to James II. In the Bloody Assizes which followed the Duke of Monmouth's rebellion in 1685, Jeffreys earned a fearsome reputation by sentencing hundreds to be hanged and many more to be exiled. Arrested in the Revolution of 1688, he died a prisoner in the Tower of London. Judge Jeffreys was vilified as a monster by Whig historians such as Lord Macaulay, but other biographers have emphasized his role as a lawyer rather than as a political figure, showing him to be a man of exceptional brilliance and eloquence, flawed perhaps by an unbridled temper.

For further details see the article by G. W. Keeton, 'Judge Jeffreys: towards a Reappraisal' in The Welsh History Review (vol. 1, no. 3, 1962) and the same author's 'George Jeffreys: His Family and Friends' in the Transactions of the Honourable Society of Cymmrodorion (1967).

JENKIN, JOHN (Ioan Siengcin; 1716–96), poet. Born the son of Siencyn Tomas, at Cwm Du, Llechryd, Cards., he was apprenticed to a cobbler and instructed by his father in the art of poetry. In 1754 he became a teacher at Nanhyfer (Nevern), Pembs., under the aegis of Griffith *Jones of Llanddowror, and remained there until about 1793. He composed verse in both the free and strict metres, eulogizing in the traditional manner the gentry of his district, in particular Thomas Lloyd of Cwmglöyn. His poem celebrating the launching of the squire's schooner was praised by Saunders *Lewis for its awareness of the Welsh poetic tradition, the continuity of which, Lewis argued, 'may enable a quite minor poet to write a major poem'. A collection of Ioan Siengcin's work was published under the title Casgliad o Ganiadau Difyr (1823).

Jenkins, Albert (1895–1953), a rugby-player who played in the centre three-quarter position for Llanelli. He was capped for Wales fourteen times between 1920 and 1928 and was famous for his brilliant gifts in handling and running with the ball.

JENKINS, DAFYDD (1911–), critic and historian, was born in London of a Cardiganshire family and educated at Sidney Sussex College, Cambridge. Called to the Bar in 1934, he worked as a barrister in Carmarthen and, in 1938, organized the Welsh Language Petition which called for the legal recognition of Welsh. A committed pacifist, he was a conscientious objector during the Second World War, working on the land. In 1965 he began lecturing in the Law Department at the University College of Wales, Aberystwyth, and from 1975 until his retirement in 1978 he held a personal chair in Legal History and Welsh Law.

He has published books on a variety of subjects, including an account of the burning of the bombing school at *Penyberth, Tân yn Llŷn (1937), a volume of literary criticism, Y Nofel Gymraeg (1948), two travel-books, Ar Wib yn Nenmarc (1952) and Ar Wib yn Sweden (1959), and an essay on D. J. *Williams in the Writers of Wales series (1973). He also co-edited the magazine *Heddiw with Aneirin Talfan *Davies and prepared an edition of *Helyntion Bywyd Hen Deiliwr (1940) by Gwilym Hiraethog (William *Rees). But his most substantial works are his studies of the *Laws of Hywel Dda, in which—by looking at medieval Welsh Law through the eyes of a lawyer—he has set new standards of scholarship. These works include his editions of Llyfr Colan (1963) and Damweiniau Colan (1973), and his general studies, Cyfraith Hywel (1970), Celtic Law Papers (1973), The Welsh Law of Women (with Morfydd E. Owen, 1980) and Hywel Dda and the Law of Medieval Wales (1985).

Jenkins, David (1848–1915), conductor and

composer, was born at Trecastle, Brecs. A poor boy, without education, he was first apprenticed to a tailor, but the spread of the tonic sol-fa movement revealed his musical gifts and, at the age of twenty-five, he enrolled as a student at the University College of Wales, Aberystwyth, under Joseph *Parry. Appointed Lecturer in Music there in 1893 and Professor in 1910, he was very active in eisteddfodau and hymn-singing festivals, both as a popular conductor and as a prolific composer who did much to raise standards. Whatever else of his is forgotten, his tune, 'Penlan', sung to the English words, 'In heavenly love abiding', and the Welsh 'Pa le, pa fodd dechreuaf', is still cherished. Also memorable are his choral works, Arch y Cyfamod, Job, Yr Ystorm and The Psalm of Life, the last of which was written especially for the Cardiff Triennial Festival of 1895. David Jenkins was for many years the editor of Y Cerddor, a magazine devoted to music-making in Wales.

For further details see the memorial volume edited by J. H. Jones (1935).

JENKINS, DAVID (1912–), librarian and scholar, was born at Blaenclydach, Rhondda, and educated at the University College of Wales, Aberystwyth. Appointed to the staff of the *National Library of Wales in 1957, he became Librarian in 1969, a post he held until his retirement in 1979. He is the author of a biography of Thomas Gwynn *Jones (1973) and has edited the literary essays of Kate *Roberts (1978).

JENKINS, GERAINT HUW (1946–), historian. Born at Penparcau, Aberystwyth, Cards., and educated at University College, Swansea, he became a Lecturer in Welsh History at the University College of Wales, Aberystwyth, in 1968 and a Senior Lecturer in 1980. He is the author of three books on historical subjects: Literature, Religion and Society in Wales 1660–1730 (1978), a study of Thomas *Jones the almanacker (1980) and Hanes Cymru yn y Cyfnod Modern Cynnar 1530–1760 (1983); he has also published books about the game of football.

JENKINS, JOHN (Ifor Ceri; 1770–1829), musicologist and antiquary. Born at Cilbronn-au, Llangoedmor, Cards., he was vicar of Ceri (Kerry), Mont., from 1807 until his death. He began collecting folk-songs as a young man, especially ballads, carols, the works of Huw *Morys and Thomas *Edwards (Twm o'r Nant), and the psalm-tunes and hymn-tunes sung during the early days of the Methodist Revival.

Famous for his generosity to other antiquaries, he kept open house for his literary and musical friends, earning the sobriquet Ifor Hael o Geri, in the tradition of *Ifor ap Llywelyn (Ifor Hael) who had been *Dafydd ap Gwilym's patron. It was at his home that the idea of forming Cambrian Societies to collect and publish Welsh manuscripts was first mooted. He was a member of the *Gorsedd held by Iolo Morganwg (Edward *Williams) at the Ivy Bush tavern, Carmarthen, in 1819 and he played a leading role in reforming the Honourable Society of *Cymmrodorion and in the administration of the provincial eisteddfodau, but grew dissatisfied as these occasions tended to become, in his words, 'an Anglo-Italian farce'. His only writings in Welsh are the articles which he contributed to the magazine Y *Gwyliedydd under the pseudonym Hooker. Among the writers and musicians who benefited from his patronage were Alun (John *Blackwell), Ieuan Glan Geirionydd (Evan *Evans), Taliesin *Williams, Cawrdaf (William Ellis *Jones), John Howell and Henry Humphreys, the harper.

Ifor Ceri wrote the parish histories of Ceri and Mochdref which were included anonymously in A Topographical Dictionary of Wales (1811) by Nicholas Carlisle and again in Cathrall's A History of North Wales (1828). Many of the airs collected by Ifor Ceri were published by Maria Jane Williams in her Ancient Welsh Music (1855) and by John Parry (Bardd Alaw) in his Welsh Harper (1839).

For further details see the lecture by Stephen J. Williams, 'Ifor Ceri, noddwr cerdd' (1954), Bedwyr Lewis Jones, Yr Hen Bersoniaid Llengar (1963), Mary Ellis's articles in Cerddoriaeth Cymru (vol. V, no. 1, 1978–79; vol. VI, no. 1, 1979), and the same author's article, 'Rhai o hen bersoniaid llengar Maldwyn' in Maldwyn a'i Chyffiniau (ed. Gwynn ap Gwilym and Richard H. Lewis, 1981).

JENKINS, JOHN (Gwili; 1872–1936), theologian and poet, was born at Hendy, Carms., and educated at the Baptist College, Bangor, and University College, Cardiff. After spending eight years as a teacher at Gwynfryn School, Ammanford, he entered Jesus College, Oxford. He was appointed Professor of New Testament Greek in the Baptist College and a Lecturer at Bangor Theological School in 1923. As a theologian he made his most important contribution as the author of a history of theology in Wales, Hanfod Duw a Pherson Crist (1931). A selection of his sermons and essays was published in the volume Y Ddwy Efengyl a Phethau Eraill (1915). As a poet he belonged to the *Bardd Newydd school. He won the *Crown at the National Eisteddfod of 1901 and served as Archdruid from 1932 to 1936. But he published only one volume of poetry in Welsh, Caniadau (1934), and one, Poems (1920), in English. A jovial man, much liked by his contemporaries, he became a friend of the poet Edward *Thomas in 1897.

For further details see the biography of Gwili by E. Cefni Jones (1937) and the article by J. Beverley Smith in the Transactions of the Honourable Society of Cymmrodorion (1974/75).

JENKINS, JOHN GERAINT (1929–), writer on folk-life subjects. Born at Penbryn,

Cards., and educated at the University Colleges of Swansea and Aberystwyth, he joined the staff of the *Welsh Folk Museum in 1960 and became Keeper of Material Culture in 1969. He was appointed Curator of the *Welsh Industrial and Maritime Museum in 1979. His numerous publications on aspects of folk-life deal particularly with traditional crafts and include *The English Farm Wagon* (1963), *Traditional Country Craftsmen* (1965), *The Welsh Woollen Industry* (1969), *Crefftwyr Gwlad* (1971), *Nets and Coracles* (1974) and *Maritime Heritage* (1982).

JENKINS, JOSEPH (1886–1962), author of stories and plays for children, was a native of Pontrhydygroes, Cards. After leaving school at the age of thirteen, he worked for a while in the local lead-mines, moving later to Aberaeron as pastor of the Calvinistic Methodist Church there. He spent three years at Handsworth College and served as a minister for his denomination in north and mid-Wales. For many years he was the editor of *Y Winllan*, the Methodist children's magazine. One of the most prolific of Welsh children's authors during the first half of the twentieth century, he published about twenty books between 1926 and 1952. Mostly collections of stories about mischievous boys, they include *Dai y Dderwen* (1926), *Robin y Pysgotwr* (1926) and *Ianto ac Ystorïau Eraill* (1929). He was awarded the Owen M. *Edwards Memorial Prize in 1947 in recognition of his important contribution to this branch of Welsh literature.

There is an article on Joseph Jenkins by Gwyn Jones in *Dewiniaid Difyr* (ed. Mairwen and Gwyn Jones, 1983).

Jenkins, Leoline (1625–85), civil lawyer and state servant, was born at Llantrisant, Glam., and educated at Cowbridge School. His studies at Jesus College, Oxford, which he entered in 1641, were soon interrupted by war and he spent the next few years tutoring children, first at Llantrithyd, where he met his future patron, Gilbert Sheldon, then at Oxford and finally—on suspicion of being a Royalist—abroad. At the Restoration, equipped by long study of the Civil Law, he became a Fellow of Jesus College and from 1661 to 1673 was its Principal. But, persuaded by Sheldon, he began to practise as a civil lawyer and after 1665 he was appointed to preside over both the High Court of the Admiralty and the Prerogative Court of Canterbury. At the former, his work on Prize Law was of the first importance: he is recognized as one of the three great founders of that branch of International Law. Subsequently, he began a third career as a state servant and diplomat: from 1675 to 1679 he was principal mediator at the Congress of Nymegen and, from 1680 to 1684, Secretary of State. Elected Member of Parliament for Hythe in 1671, he represented the

University of Oxford in the Parliaments which followed.

A generous benefactor to Jesus College, which he set on its feet after the Restoration, building the library at his own expense, he willed his entire real and personal estate to the College at his death, endowing scholarships for Cowbridge School and adding to the Welshness of its establishment. Modest, shy and deferential, he made a curious impression as a diplomat, for his intelligence and incorruptibility took his contemporaries by surprise. It was he who once answered a French courtier with the Welsh proverb, '*Nid wrth ei big y prynir cyffylog*' ('It is not by its beak you buy a woodcock').

For further details see *The Life of Leoline Jenkins* (1724) by W. Wynne; a less favourable portrait will be found in the second volume of Gilbert Burnet's *History of my Own Time* (1897–1900).

JENKINS, NIGEL (1949–   ), poet, was born in Gower, Glam., and educated at Essex University. A former journalist, he lives in Swansea and is a freelance writer and lecturer. He shared the *Welsh Arts Council's first Young Poet's Prize with Tony *Curtis and Duncan *Bush and some of his early work can be found in the volume *Three Young Anglo-Welsh Poets* (1974). Political themes are prominent in his two collections of poems, *Song and Dance* (1981) and *Practical Dreams* (1983). His play about Dr. William *Price, *Strike a Light!*, was first performed in 1985. He took a leading part in the creation of the *Welsh Union of Writers and was its first Secretary.

JENKINS, ROBERT THOMAS (1881–1969), historian and author, was born in Liverpool but, his parents having died when he was a child, he was brought up by grandparents at Bala, Mer. Educated at the University College of Wales, Aberystwyth, and at Trinity College, Cambridge, he became a teacher in Llandysul, Brecon and Cardiff. He was appointed Independent Lecturer in Welsh History at the University College of North Wales, Bangor, in 1930, and later became Professor. In Cardiff he was a neighbour and close friend of W. J. *Gruffydd and was one of the distinguished group of writers who contributed regularly to the magazine *Y *Llenor*.

R. T. Jenkins collected his early articles in two volumes, *Ffrainc a'i Phobl* (1930) and *Yr Apêl at Hanes* (1930); his *Hanes Cymru yn y Ddeunawfed Ganrif* (1928) and *Hanes Cymru yn y Bedwaredd Ganrif ar Bymtheg* (1933) are notable as works of history for their stimulating prose style. During the Second World War he took the view that there was a need for more popular reading matter in Welsh and, under the pseudonym Idris Thomas, published short stories and a light novel, *Ffynhonnau Elim* (1945). But much more important is his short historical novel *Orinda* (1943), a minor classic of Welsh fiction, which is based on the story of Katherine *Philipps. He also published a delightful book for young readers, Y *Ffordd yng Nghymru (1933), and a volume of essays, Casglu Ffyrdd (1956). It was he who was mainly responsible for editing Y Bywgraffiadur Cymreig / The Dictionary of Welsh Biography (1953) to which he contributed more than six hundred entries. He collaborated with Helen M. Ramage in the writing of the authoritative work, A History of the Honourable Society of Cymmrodorion (1951). R. T. Jenkins was both an inspired teacher and a talented creative writer who could make the abstruse clear and the dull fascinating. He had a gift for portraying people and places in a vivid, memorable way and a vivacious, almost colloquial style which is sometimes idiosyncratic but always compellingly readable.

R. T. Jenkins wrote an autobiography, Edrych yn Ôl (1968). See also the memorial number of Y Traethodydd (April, 1970) and the essays by Prys Morgan in Triskel One (ed. Sam Adams and Gwilym Rees Hughes, 1971), by Alun Llywelyn-Williams in the Writers of Wales series (1977) and by John Gwilym Jones in Swyddogaeth Beirniadaeth (1977); there is an obituary of R. T. Jenkins by E. D. Jones in the Transactions of the Honourable Society of Cymmrodorion (part 2, 1970) and an appreciation of him by Glanmor Williams in Taliesin (1970).

JENKINS, THOMAS (1774–1843), poet. Born at Llandeilo, Carms., he spent much of his life as a solicitor's clerk in Carmarthen, from where he helped to orchestrate the *Rebecca Riots. His political *Radicalism shows in only two of his poems, the rest of which are well-turned but conventional. His sole volume, Miscellaneous Poems (1845), was published posthumously. A son of his, also named **Thomas Jenkins** (1813–71), kept a diary between 1826 and 1870 which, although devoid of literary quality, is valuable for its record of life in the district of Llandeilo and the variety of its author's interests, scientific as well as practical; it was published in 1976.

Jesuits, see under SOCIETY OF JESUS.

JÔB, JOHN THOMAS (1867–1938), poet, was born at Llandybïe, Carms., and educated at Trefeca College. He began to preach in 1887, was ordained by the Calvinistic Methodists in 1894 and later ministered at Aberdare, Carneddi, Bethesda and Fishguard. The winner of the *Chair at the National Eisteddfod on three occasions (1897, 1903 and 1918) and of the *Crown on one (1900), he published a selection of his poems under the title Caniadau Jôb (1929). Some of J. T. Jôb's many hymns, such as 'Cofia'r byd, O! Feddyg da', 'O! Arglwydd grasol, trugarha' and 'Arglwydd nef a daear', are included in contemporary hymn-books.

JOHANNES WALLENSIS or **JOHN WALEYS**, see JOHN OF WALES (d. c.1285).

John ap John (1625?–97), the first *Quaker evangelist in Wales, was born at Trevor Issa, near Ruabon, Denbs. An Independent who was from 1646 to 1648 a minister at Beaumaris, Ang., he came home to join Morgan *Llwyd's congregation at Wrexham and, in 1653, was sent to Swarthmore to meet George Fox and bring back a report on his doctrines. He returned to Wales a convinced Quaker and began his evangelizing by establishing a 'church' at Trevor and then proselytizing southwards along the Border. Richard *Davies of Cloddiau Cochion, who was converted by him in Shrewsbury at Christmas 1657, described him as not perfect in English but very sound and intelligible in Welsh, a judgement which does less than justice to the uproar caused by John ap John's street preaching in many Welsh counties. Frequently imprisoned, he was released several times as a result of intervention by George Fox, whom he accompanied on his tour of Wales in 1657. From 1667 he was consolidating the Quaker movement and remained faithful throughout the increasing persecution after 1681, when many Welsh Quakers fled to Pennsylvania.

For further details see An Account of the Convincement, Exercises, Services and Travels of that Ancient Servant of the Lord Richard Davies (1710) and Norman Penney, John ap John and Early Records of Friends in Wales (1907).

John Ball, see under IN PARENTHESIS (1937).

John Eilian, see JONES, JOHN TUDOR (1904–85).

JOHN OF WALES or **JOHANNES WALLENSIS** or **JOHANNES GALLENSIS** or **JOHN WALEYS** (d. c.1285), medieval humanist. A Franciscan friar, he took a bachelor's degree in theology at Oxford and by 1282 was in charge of his Order's house there. A fellow-Franciscan, John Peckham, Archbishop of Canterbury, who claimed authority over the Welsh Church, sought his help in trying to persuade *Llywelyn ap Gruffudd to accept the humiliating terms demanded by Edward I. Soon afterwards the Welshman was in Paris where, in 1283, he was among the theologians bidden to examine the suspected teachings of the Spiritual Franciscan, Petrus Joannis Olivi. As teacher and author, John was given the honorific title Arbor Vitae ('Tree of Life'). His writings include treatises on ethical principles, such as Monoloquium, Legiloquium, and Breviloquium de sapientia sanctorum, and two works basing Christian morality on teachings culled from classical antiquity, Breviloquium de virtutibus antiquorum principum et philosophorum and Compendiloquium de vitis illustrium philosophorum. A compiler rather than an original thinker, he nevertheless pointed the way to Renaissance humanism in his emphasis on Man's moral responsibility.

The John of Wales who is the subject of this entry should not be confused with that earlier

Johannes Wallensis or **Galensis** (*fl.* 1215) who was an authority on canon law at the University of Bologna.

John, Augustus (1878–1961), painter. Born at Tenby, Pembs., he spent most of his life outside Wales, travelling widely in France and Italy, and won a reputation as a portrait painter whose bohemian life-style was an essential part of his genius. It was he who introduced Dylan *Thomas to his future wife, Caitlin Macnamara, in 1936; the poet parodied him as Hercules Jones in *The Death of the King's Canary* (1976). Two volumes of the artist's autobiography were published, *Chiaroscuro* (1952) and *Finishing Touches* (1964). His sister, **Gwen John** (1876–1939), was also a painter of distinction, but she lived and died in poverty and obscurity. From 1904 until his death in 1917 she was one of the mistresses of the sculptor, Auguste Rodin, who encouraged her art. At her death Augustus John remarked that posterity would remember him only as Gwen John's brother.

The standard biography of Augustus John is that by Michael Holroyd (2 vols., 1975); Gwen John's has been written by Susan Chitty (1981).

John, Edward Thomas (1857–1931), politician. Born at Pontypridd, Glam., he became the owner of an ironworks in Middlesborough but, on his retirement, took up politics and served as Liberal Member of Parliament for East Denbighshire from 1910 to 1918. Throughout his political career he was a keen advocate of *Home Rule for Wales, diligently amassing statistics to support the economic arguments in its favour. A frequent contributor to periodicals such as *Y* *Beirniad and The *Welsh Outlook, E. T. John was the President of the Union of Welsh Societies, and of the Peace Society from 1924 to 1927.

John, Goscombe (1860–1952), sculptor. A native of Cardiff, he received many public commissions, including the designing of medals and regalia for the *National Eisteddfod and the carving of portrait heads of prominent figures such as David *Lloyd George, Sir John *Williams and T. E. *Ellis. One of his works is the memorial to Evan *James and James James, the composers of the Welsh national anthem, which stands in Ynysangharad Park, Pontypridd.

JOHNES, ARTHUR JAMES (1809–71), author, of Garthmyl, Mont., was educated at Oswestry School and University College, London, and was called to the Bar from Lincoln's Inn in 1835. As a young man he was very active on behalf of Welsh culture. He was one of the promoters of the *Cambrian Quarterly Magazine* (1830–33) and published some translations from the work of *Dafydd ap Gwilym (1834). At the age of twenty-one he was pressed by Thomas Richards, the vicar of Llangynyw, to

write *An Essay on the Causes which have produced Dissent from the Established Church in the Principality of Wales* for the Royal Medal to be awarded by the London Cambrian Institution in 1831. The adjudicator, William *Owen Pughe, awarded him the prize and the society published the essay in 1831. Johnes, a Churchman and a patriot, was against *Disestablishment but indicted an alien hierarchy which failed to understand the Welsh character, appointed clergy who knew no Welsh and tolerated clerical absenteeism. In 1838 he was a staunch opponent of the amalgamation of the sees of *St. Asaph and *Bangor and served for many years from 1847 as a County Court judge. The preface to the third edition of his book (1870) is concerned to refute the contemporary theory of the inferiority of the Celtic peoples.

A selection of Johnes's letters was published by Marian Henry Jones in the *Journal* of the National Library of Wales (vol. X, nos. 3 and 4, 1958).

Johnes, Thomas (1748–1816), landowner. Born at Ludlow, he settled in 1783 at Hafod Uchtryd, a mansion in the Ystwyth valley, Cards., and for the next twenty years used his fortune in transforming the house and its estate into a private paradise. Magnificent gardens were laid out, six million trees were planted and experiments made in the breeding of stock. Hafod became a mecca for artists, writers and agriculturalists from England and beyond. Among its visitors was Coleridge who may have had it in mind when writing of Xanadu. The library housed a major collection of Welsh manuscripts, including many which had belonged to Edward *Lhuyd, as well as manuscripts of medieval French chronicles, some of which Johnes translated and published at his own Hafod Press between 1803 and 1810. When, in 1807, the house was badly damaged by fire, most of the books and manuscripts were destroyed. The owner rebuilt it but found that he could not recapture the first enchantment of the place and, after the death of his only child, Mariamne, he lost heart and gave up the attempt. At his death Hafod was sold. The house no longer exists: a new owner stripped the roof and felled the timber in 1946 and the ruin was demolished in 1962.

The history of Hafod became more widely known from the book, *Peacocks in Paradise* (1950) by Elisabeth Inglis-Jones; see also the essay on Thomas Johnes by Dafydd Jenkins in the *St. David's Day* series (1948).

Johnny Onions, the nickname given to the Breton onion-sellers who were a familiar sight in the streets of Wales (and other parts of Britain) until the 1950s. Peasants from the districts around Roscoff and St. Pol de Léon in northwest Brittany, they sold their produce—red onions strung together in a distinctive style—from door to door. They were tough, genial and persistent, living frugally in rented rooms or warehouses throughout the winter months and returning to their farms for the spring and summer. The pioneer of the trade is believed to have been one Henri Olivier, a Santec man, who took a boatload of onions from Roscoff to Plymouth in 1828. The golden age of the Johnny (known as Sioni Nionod in some parts of north Wales and Sioni Wynwns in parts of south Wales) was during the 1920s when some thousand sellers crossed from Brittany every year. But after the Second World War, mainly as a result of import restrictions, the devaluation of sterling and the daunting rigours of the work, their numbers dwindled and by the late 1970s they were to be seen only rarely.

For further details about these men see the article by Sam Adams in The Anglo-Welsh Review (no. 49, Spring, 1973) and Gwyn Griffiths, Y Shonis Olaf (1981).

JOHNS, DAVID (*fl.* 1573–87), copyist, poet and scholar, was born in the district of Tywyn, Mer., and held the living of Llanfair Dyffryn Clwyd, Denbs. He wrote a number of *cywyddau*, made metric versions of some of the Psalms, translated into Latin an *awdl* attributed to *Taliesin and also translated a poem by St. Bernard and a prayer by St. Augustine from Latin into Welsh. Like others among his contemporaries in Dyffryn Clwyd, he was a zealous collector and copyist of Welsh manuscripts, especially those of the *Poets of the Gentry.

For further details see the article by Garfield Hughes in the *Journal* of the National Library of Wales (vol. VI, 1950).

Johns, Thomas, see JONES, THOMAS (*c.* 1530–1609).

JOHNSON, ARTHUR TYSSILIO (d. 1956), see under PERFIDIOUS WELSHMAN (1910).

JONES, ABEL (Y Bardd Crwst; 1830–1901), balladeer. A native of Llanrwst, Denbs., he sang in many parts of Wales but was particularly famous in the fairs of Glamorgan and Gwent. The last of the great ballad-singers, he ended his life, like so many of his kind, dissolute and out of favour, in the workhouse.

Jones, Adda, see EVANS, JOHN (1814–75).

JONES, ALICE GRAY (Ceridwen Peris; 1852–1943), author and editor. Born at Llanllyfni, Caerns., she was a teacher, an early feminist and a founder of the North Wales Women's Temperance League. She wrote several books for use in *Sunday Schools, a number of *Temperance tracts, a pamphlet about the morals of young girls and a volume of poems, Caniadau (1934). From 1896 to 1919 she was the editor of the women's magazine Y Gymraes.

JONES, ALUN (1946–), novelist, was born at Trefor, Caerns., and since 1970 he has been the owner of a bookshop in Pwllheli. He is the author of three novels, namely Ac Yna Clywodd Sŵn y Môr (1979), Pan Ddaw'r Machlud (1981) and Oed Rhyw Addewid (1983), the first of which was awarded the Daniel *Owen Memorial Prize at the National Eisteddfod of 1978.

JONES, ALUN JEREMIAH (Alun Cilie; 1897–1975), poet. The youngest child in the *Cilie household, it was he who remained to work the farm after his brothers had left home, as was the established practice in Cardiganshire and north Pembrokeshire. Having learned the poetic craft in family competition, he wrote englynion, cywyddau and lyrics, chronicling the changing seasons in the countryside and wistfully observing the decay of the rural community around him. In his time Cilie became a centre for a younger generation of poets, mostly members of the family but also including the young farmer, Dic Jones (Richard Lewis *Jones). Towards the end of his life he published a collection of verse, Cerddi Alun Cilie (1964), which confirmed his reputation as a *bardd gwlad of the first water. His neighbour, T. Llew *Jones, his niece's husband, edited the posthumous volume Cerddi Pentalar (1976).

For a note on Alun Cilie as bardd gwlad see that by John Rowlands in Profiles (1980).

Jones, Ann (1863–1933), see under AFTER THE FUNERAL (1938) and FERN HILL (1945).

JONES, ARTHUR (Arthur Machen; 1863–1947), prose-writer, was born at Caerleon, Mon. His father, an impoverished clergyman, added his Scottish wife's surname to his Jones and the boy went to Hereford Cathedral School as Arthur Jones-Machen, but later dropped the Jones. Denied the requisite university training for entry into Anglican orders by his father's bankruptcy, he went to London to learn shorthand in the hope of making a career in journalism. There, barely sustaining himself by a variety of poorly paid jobs, he published The Anatomy of Tobacco (1884), a piece of scholarly hack-work of sufficient promise, despite its youthful flaws, to persuade a publisher to engage him to translate from the French The Heptameron (1886). This early success in turn prompted Machen to attempt a translation of The Memoirs of Jacques Casanova (1894) which is still acknowledged to be among the finest. His first original work of any note, The Chronicle of Clemendy (1888), also purports to be a translation.

Machen had married Amelia Hogg in 1887 and settled first in humble lodgings in Soho, but with the help of a small legacy and gradually increasing earnings from literary journalism, the couple moved to a cottage in the Chilterns. During the 1890s a number of influences—the landscape of his beloved Gwent, his reading of

Poe, Stevenson and other exponents of the gothic and decadent, his profound study of the seventeenth-century Rosicrucians, including the scientist and philosopher Thomas *Vaughan (the twin brother of Henry *Vaughan), his friendship with A. E. Waite, an authority on the occult, and his interest in Arthurian legend and Celtic and pre-Christian religions—combined to inspire a remarkable outpouring of tales of the supernatural. Only a few, notably *The Great God Pan* (1894), appeared at the time; others were published much later in collections such as *The House of Souls* (1906) and *The Shining Pyramid* (1925), which has in its title story, written in 1895, a masterpiece of the genre. His novel *The Hill of Dreams* (1907) also belongs to this period.

After the death of his wife in 1899, Machen suffered an emotional crisis from which he emerged in 1901 to start a new life as an actor with F. R. Benson's touring company. He married the actress Purefoy Hudleston in 1903. Although several books were published during his theatrical career, his only substantial new work was the novel *The Secret Glory* (1922), a curious re-working of the *Grail legend in which the main protagonist, Ambrose Meyrick, like Lucian Taylor of *The Hill of Dreams*, is firmly based on the author's own life and character. Machen left the stage in 1909 and the following year joined the staff of the *London Evening News*. The daily routine of journalism was not greatly to his liking, but his entire literary output of the period from 1910 to 1921 appeared in serial form in that newspaper. 'The Bowmen', a story in which a visionary host of archers is seen fighting alongside the British in the trenches of Mons, so caught the popular imagination that he was subsequently lured into repeating ever weaker versions of the same theme (see under BOWMEN OF AGINCOURT). His novella, *The Great Return* (1915), set in rural Wales, as is the bulk of his fiction, draws once more upon the Grail legend, while *The Terror* (1917) anticipates more recent quasi-scientific fables of animals conspiring to destroy Mankind.

When he left the newspaper, Machen's reputation as a man of letters was at its zenith and he was already a cult figure in America. As a writer of autobiography, particularly in *Far Off Things* (1922), he is invariably elegant and charming, if diffuse and digressive, and as an essayist, for example in *Dreads and Drolls* (1926), his work, though uneven, is marked by an engaging and mellifluous personal style. Settled with his wife in Amersham, Bucks., in 1929, he remained active as a publishers' reader and reviewer but most of the tales in the three collections published in the 1930s, *The Green Round* (1933), *The Cosy Room* (1936) and *The Children of the Pool* (1936), had been written many years before. These stories reveal that Machen's strength was his ability to illuminate within the brief compass of the short story a moment of horror or a vision

of splendour. He made little money out of his writing and, although he was granted a Civil List pension in 1932, enjoyed security in his declining years only through the generosity of friends.

Among biographies and critical studies of Arthur Machen are those by Vincent Starrett (1918), Aidan Reynolds and William Charlton (1963), Wesley D. Sweetser (1964) and D. P. M. Michael in the *Writers of Wales* series (1971); a bibliography of the author's works has been edited by W. D. Sweetser and A. Goldstone (1965).

JONES, BEDWYR LEWIS (1933–), scholar and critic, was born at Wrexham, Denbs., and brought up at Llaneilian, Ang. He was educated at the University College of North Wales, Bangor, and Jesus College, Oxford. As a student he was one of the editors (1957–60) of the magazine *Yr *Arloeswr*. He was appointed Professor of Welsh at Bangor in 1974. Among his publications are a study of the literary clerics, *Yr Hen Bersoniaid Llengar* (1963), an essay on R. Williams *Parry in the *Writers of Wales* series (1972), *Arthur y Cymry / The Welsh Arthur* (1975) and *Iaith Sir Fôn* (1983); he has also edited anthology *Blodeugerdd o'r Bedwaredd Ganrif ar Bymtheg* (1965), a study of the prose of R. Williams Parry (1974), *Gwŷr Môn* (1979), a collection of articles about eminent people of Anglesey, and (with Derec Llwyd *Morgan) *Bro'r Eisteddfod: Ynys Môn* (1983).

JONES, BOBI, see JONES, ROBERT MAYNARD (1929–).

JONES, DAFYDD (1711–77), hymn-writer, was born at Cwm Gogerddan, Caeo, Carms. By trade a *drover, he was converted in the meeting-house at Troedrhiwdalar while on his way home from a cattle-drive into England. He joined the Independent chapel at Crug-y-bar, near his home, and was a member there for the rest of his life. Dafydd Jones o Gaeo, as he was known and is remembered today, had a reputation as a rhymester before his conversion and William *Williams (Pantycelyn) included one of his hymns in the volume *Aleluia* (1747). But his most important work was the translation into Welsh of the hymns and psalms of Isaac Watts, which were published in three volumes, namely *Salmau Dafydd* (1753), *Caniadau Dwyfol* (1771) and *Hymnau a Chaniadau Ysprydol* (1775). A collection of his own hymns appeared under the title *Difyrrwch i'r Pererinion* (3 vols., 1763, 1764, 1770). Although he had little formal education, Dafydd Jones succeeded in rendering Isaac Watts's classic English verse into dignified, powerful, singable Welsh. His translations and hymns, such as *'Pererin wy'n y byd'*, *'Wele cawsom y Meseia'* and *'O Arglwydd, galw eto'*, are still in vogue.

A study of his life and work has been written by Gomer M. Roberts (1948); a selection of his hymns is to be found in *Pedwar Emynydd* (ed. Bobi Jones, 1970).

JONES, DAFYDD (Dewi Dywyll, Deio'r Cantwr, Dewi Medi; 1803–68), a blind balladeer, of Llanybydder, Carms., was well known for his singing throughout south Wales; he was the author of some seventy ballads.

JONES, DAFYDD (Isfoel; 1881–1968), poet, a member of the *Cilie family, was a blacksmith and farmer. A *bardd gwlad equally skilful in the free and strict metres, he enjoyed a reputation for the writing of humorous englynion. His verse has been published in three volumes, namely Cerddi Isfoel (1958), Ail Gerddi Isfoel (1965) and Cyfoeth Awen Isfoel (ed. T. Llew Jones, 1981); a collection of his reminiscences in prose appeared under the title Hen Ŷd y Wlad (1966).

JONES, DAFYDD (1907–   ), poet, was born at Ffair Rhos, Cards., a village known as 'pentref y beirdd' ('the poets' village') because many a *bardd gwlad has been produced in the district. He was a shepherd before he became an official of the Ministry of Agriculture. He won the *Crown at the National Eisteddfod in 1966 for his pryddest, 'Y Clawdd', but he excels as a writer of lyrics. A selection of his work is to be found in his only volume, Yr Arloeswr (1965).

JONES, DAVID (1895–1974), writer and artist, was born at Brockley, Kent. His father, a printer's overseer, had gone to London from Holywell, Flints., about 1885; his mother was English, the daughter of a Thames-side mast-and block-maker. He had little formal education but his love of drawing, firmly established by the age of six, was encouraged and he attended the Camberwell Art School from 1909 to 1914 and the Westminster School of Art in 1919. During the First World War (Dec. 1915–March 1918) he served as a private with the Royal Welsh Fusiliers on the Western Front. This experience was to influence all his writings, either directly or obliquely, but the centre of his life and art was established by his reception into the Roman Catholic Church in 1921. In the same year he met the English artist Eric Gill, joining his community at Ditchling, Sussex, in 1922, and at Capel-y-ffin in the Black Mountains for long periods during the mid-1920s. David Jones had had a strong sense of his Welshness from an early age and his vision of Welsh landscape and culture was now intensified. At the same time, working in a community dedicated through the practice of religion and the arts to living an integrated life helped him to develop his own art and ideas. The late 1920s and early 1930s were for him an intensely creative period and he was now closely involved in friendship and intellectual effort with a circle of Catholics whose wide-ranging discussions of religion, art and history centred on the problems of defining and realizing their ideas of Christian order in the modern world.

David Jones was a master of several arts, notably water-colour painting, wood-engraving and, later, calligraphy, and his reputation as a painter and engraver was established before the publication of his first writing, *In Parenthesis (1937). Begun in 1927, it was virtually complete when, in 1933, he suffered the first of a series of breakdowns in health which were to afflict him periodically for the rest of his life. In 1934 he visited Palestine as a convalescent, gaining impressions which, many years later, contributed to his writings concerned with Roman Jerusalem. Subject to interruptions from ill health, he nevertheless continued his creative work until his death, concentrating, after the publication of In Parenthesis, mainly on his writing, though his lettering and some of his finest paintings also belong to his later years. Based at the parental home at Brockley until his mother's death in 1937, he then lived in Notting Hill and later in Harrow-on-the-Hill, in rooms in which he was surrounded by his paintings and books. With characteristic modesty he would always disclaim any aptitude for scholarship, but he was in fact a scholar-poet whose reading in subjects such as archaeology, history, mythology and anthropology provided much of his material. He did not marry, but with his genius for friendship he was far from being a recluse.

David Jones's long poem The *Anathémata (1952) was followed by Epoch and Artist (1959), a book of essays on subjects which include Wales and the *Matter of Britain, art and artists, and of which the unifying theme is the predicament of Man-the-artist (synonymous with Man in David Jones's philosophy) in a civilization inimical to signs and sacraments. In 1974 The Sleeping Lord was published, The Kensington Mass (unfinished) in 1975 and The Dying Gaul, a largely unrevised collection of essays which continues the themes of Epoch and Artist but includes probably his greatest essay, 'An Introduction to The Rime of the Ancient Mariner', in 1978. The volume The Roman Quarry (1981) was compiled from the large number of manuscripts which were found after the author's death. His letters to friends such as René Hague, which were published in Dai Great-coat (1980), and to Saunders *Lewis, Vernon *Watkins (1976) and Aneirin Talfan *Davies (1980), reveal another form which his rare spirit animated.

His use of modern structures, together with his sense of history and myth, relates David Jones to Eliot, Joyce and Pound, but his was largely an independent development and only Gerard Manley *Hopkins may be fairly cited as a possible influence on his verbal texture and music. His modernism was dedicated to the validation of beliefs which he held to be eternally true. He sought to marry form and content in all his work and his long poems are unified by an underlying mythic structure, the integration of poetry and prose, and an intricate patterning of sounds and motifs. His language ranges widely from the colloquial to the technical and is at once precise, richly sensuous and allusive, invoking traditional associations within a cultural context which he further establishes by the inclusion of Welsh and Latin words. Although his allusiveness, together with his use of more common but now obscured sources, not least the Matter of Britain, makes for initial difficulties, he ultimately restores meanings and revives symbols which a general loss of continuity with the past has impaired. His writings are above all commemorative, recalling and celebrating the makers and champions of cultural diversity in these islands. They are in a special sense distinctively Anglo-Welsh, expressing and deeply reflecting upon the historical connections and tensions of his dual inheritance as a London Welshman. He had a unified vision of the creation of Man as a maker, but also an acute sense of cultural and spiritual crisis caused by centralizing and secularizing forces in the modern world, as represented by the Anglicization of Wales. As a thinker he made a unique contribution to a tradition of concern with Man's plight in a technological civilization descending from Blake, through Ruskin, William Morris and Eric Gill.

A study by David Blamires (1971) and a collection of essays edited by Roland Mathias (1976) consider David Jones as artist and writer. René Hague has written about David Jones in the *Writers of Wales* series (1975) and in *A Commentary on 'The Anathemata' of David Jones* (1977), and there is a book-length essay on the writings by Jeremy Hooker (1975). See also the special numbers of the magazines *Poetry Wales* (Winter, 1972) and *Agenda* (Spring-Summer, 1967 and 1974) which are devoted to the work of David Jones.

JONES, DAVID JAMES (Gwenallt; 1899–1968), poet, critic and scholar, was born in the village of Alltwen, near Pontardawe, in the Swansea Valley. His childhood and adolescence in a Welsh-speaking, chapel-going, industrial community in the shadow of the steel and tin-plate works are vividly evoked in his contribution to the volume of autobiographical essays, *Credaf* (ed. J. E. Meredith, 1943), as is his intellectual and spiritual odyssey. In rebellion against the callousness of industrial capitalism—his father was killed by molten metal in an accident at the works—and against a religion which lacked social commitment, he moved first to Christian Socialism and later to atheistic Marxism. His early background is also treated fictionally in the unfinished novel, *Ffwrneisiau* (1982), published posthumously. But rural Carmarthenshire, as well as industrial Glamorgan, was part of his early experience. Both his parents came from that county and on visits to relatives in the district of Rhydcymerau (D. J. *Williams was a relative) he encountered the traditional culture of the Welsh farming community and the beauty of the countryside.

During the First World War he was a con-scientious objector, imprisoned in Wormwood Scrubs and Dartmoor, and from his novel *Plasau'r Brenin* (1934), which deals with the experience of those years, it can be deduced that elements of Christian pacifism, International Socialism and Welsh national feeling all came together in his refusal of war service. After the War, Gwenallt became a student at the University College of Wales, Aberystwyth, graduating in Welsh and English. This was a period when his cultural horizons were broadened and he embraced, for a while, the principles of aestheticism. After a short period as a teacher in Barry, he became a Lecturer in the Welsh Department of his old College, a post which he held until his retirement. A visit to the Irish *Gaeltacht* deepened his interest in the national tradition of his own country and his persistent reading in philosophy and theology brought him to a religious position within the Calvinistic Methodist Church which was both traditionalist and radical. He rejected the modern theology of the early twentieth century but never ceased to argue for Christian commitment to social justice.

Gwenallt first became known as a poet when his *awdl*, 'Y Mynach', won the *Chair at the National Eisteddfod of 1926. Two years later his unconventional *awdl*, 'Y Sant', was the centre of literary controversy when the Chair was withheld, but he won again in the same competition in 1931. His reputation, however, rests chiefly on a number of shorter poems contained in his five volumes of poetry: *Ysgubau'r Awen* (1939), *Cnoi Cil* (1942), *Eples* (1951), *Gwreiddiau* (1959) and the posthumous *Coed* (1969). He also contributed to scholarship and literary criticism in works such as *Yr Areithiau Pros* (1934), *Blodeugerdd o'r Ddeunawfed Ganrif* (1936), *Detholiad o Ryddiaith Gymraeg R. J. Derfel* (1945) and *Cofiant Idwal Jones* (1958). He was a founder member of Yr *Academi Gymreig and the first editor of its magazine, *Taliesin*.

His earlier poetry contains a rich lyrical strain which has made anthology pieces of such poems as 'Adar Rhiannon' and 'Cymru', but the later and more characteristic styles are sometimes rough and caustic, sometimes rounded and compressed (as when he uses the sonnet form), but always vigorous. Religious and national themes become stripped of sentimentality and Wales becomes 'putain fudr y stryd' ('a dirty street prostitute') and its people wolves 'yn udo am y Gwaed a'n prynodd ni' ('howling for the Blood that redeemed us'). But alongside these rejections of the respectable and the prettified there are powerful assertions in Gwenallt's work. He is a great national poet in the sense that he unifies differing strands in the historical experience of the nation: rural and industrial Wales, Carmarthenshire and Glamorgan, Socialism and Christianity: '*Ac y mae lle i ddwrn Karl Marcs yn Ei Eglwys Ef*' ('And there is a place for the fist of Karl Marx in His

Church'). These are not schematic assertions but spring from his own experience and they are expressed in images which arise from a landscape and tradition with which he was entirely familiar. In his poem 'Colomennod', for example, the pigeons released by miners at the end of the working day from the top ends of gardens behind black industrial terraces circle the valley like symbols of the Holy Ghost in the smoky haze. Besides much anger, bitterness, courage and resolve, Gwenallt shared with Idris *Davies a capacity, especially in Eples, to incorporate in poetry not only an industrial landscape but the whole experience of an industrial community.

For further details see the memorial number of Y Traethodydd (vol. CXXIV, 1969), the monograph by Dyfnallt Morgan in the Writers of Wales series (1972) and J. E. Meredith, Gwenallt, Bardd Crefyddol (1974). An English translation of the essay 'Credaf', under the title 'What I Believe', appeared in Planet (no. 32, 1976) and there is a photographic account of the writer's life in the Bro a Bywyd series (ed. Dafydd Rowlands, 1982). A bibliography of Gwenallt's writings has been compiled by Iestyn Hughes (1983).

JONES, DAVID RICHARD (1832–1916), poet, was born at Dolwyddelan, Caerns., a nephew of John *Jones of Tal-y-sarn. In 1845 he emigrated with his parents to the USA, where he became an architect. He began contributing poems to the periodical Y Drych (Utica) in 1858, some of which caused offence because they showed the influence of Darwinism, and he later published a collection, Yr Ymchwil am y Goleuni (1910). Among those who admired his work was T. Gwynn *Jones, who discussed it in Hanes Llenyddiaeth Gymraeg y Bedwaredd Ganrif ar Bymtheg (1920).

JONES, DAVID WATKIN (Dafydd Morganwg; 1832–1905), historian and poet, was born in Merthyr Tydfil, Glam., where he worked as a miner and agent for a company of prospectors. His two most important works were Hanes Morganwg (1874), a sketchy history of Glamorgan, and Yr Ysgol Farddol (1896). From the latter book many poets obtained their knowledge of the strict metres and it continued to serve as a guide to Welsh prosody until the appearance of David Thomas's Y Cynganeddion Cymreig in 1923.

JONES, DIC, see JONES, RICHARD LEWIS (1934–).

JONES, DYFED GLYN (1939–), novelist, was born at Y Gaerwen, Ang., and educated at Manchester University. He joined the staff of the BBC in London in 1963 and in Wales two years later; since 1974 he has been Head of Children's Programmes. His five novels are Iâr ar y Glaw (1970), Ergyd yn Eden (1971), Lle Crafa'r Iâr (1972), Albert Regina Jones (1973, English version, 1975) and a novel for children, Y Ddraig Werdd (1982).

JONES, EBENEZER (1820–60), poet, was born in Islington, London, the son of a Welsh father, and brought up in a severely Calvinistic home. The family returned to Wales about 1837, but he remained in the counting-house in the City where he had been placed and where the financial trickery served to confirm his view of men and society. Working long hours in uncongenial conditions, he yet found time to write verse, which was published in his only volume, Studies of Sensation and Event (1843), but its unfavourable reception made him abandon poetry for political journalism. He became editor of Fireside Journal, a penny weekly broadsheet, and published Radical pamphlets entitled Kings of Gold and The Land Monopoly. An unhappy marriage and the onset of consumption brought him back to poetry in his last years, but he completed only eight poems for a projected second volume, some of which—such as 'When the World is Burning' and 'Winter Hymn to the Snow'—have been over-praised. Although a Republican and in sympathy with Chartist aims, he wrote not a line about *Chartism, but has nevertheless been confused with Ebenezer Elliott, 'the Corn Law Rhymer', and with Ernest Charles *Jones, who was indeed a Chartist poet.

The only available biographical material is to be found in memorial notices by his brother Sumner Jones and by W. J. Linton, which are included in Richard Herne Shepherd's edition of Studies of Sensation and Event (1879). Articles were published by Theodore Watts in Atheneum (Sept. and Oct., 1878) and by William Bell Scott in Academy (Nov., 1979).

JONES, EDMUND (1702–93), author and Independent minister, known to his contemporaries as 'Yr Hen Broffwyd' ('The Old Prophet') and to later generations as Edmund Jones the Transh, was born in the parish of Aberystruth, near what later became Nant-y-glo, Mon. Ordained in 1734, he built an Independent chapel at the Transh, near Pontypool, and was said by George Whitefield to have sold his collection of books for fifteen pounds in order to complete the work which his congregation, who paid him only three pounds a year, were too poor to afford. His piety and zeal put him on cordial terms with Howel *Harris but he never agreed that Methodist societies should reform the Church of England rather than move towards Dissent. An indefatigable rather than a popular preacher, Edmund Jones wrote An Historical Account of the Parish of Aberystruth (1779), valuable because so early in date, and A Relation of Apparitions in Wales (1780), a work which showed him to be as credulous as he was pious, for it attacked the growing disbelief in magic. An incessant recorder of religious events, Jones kept diaries, some of which were rescued from use as wrapping paper in a Pontypool shop after his death.

For further details see Edgar Phillips, *Edmund Jones, the Old Prophet* (1959).

JONES, EDMUND OSBORNE (1858–1931), translator. Born at Barmouth, Mer., and educated at Merton College, Oxford, he was the vicar of Llanidloes, Mont., from 1891 until 1923, when he moved to a living in England. He published two volumes of translations, *Welsh Lyrics of the Nineteenth Century* (1896) and *Welsh Poets of Today and Yesterday* (1906).

JONES, EDWARD (**Bardd y Brenin**; 1752–1824), antiquary and harpist, was born in the parish of Llandderfel, Mer., and from his youth he delighted in the traditional music of his native district. He went to London about 1775 and such was his success as a musician that he was appointed harpist to the Prince of Wales, later King George IV, which earned him the sobriquet 'The King's Poet'. Although there was later to be bitter enmity between him and Iolo Morganwg (Edward *Williams), Jones was present at the *Gorsedd held by the latter on Primrose Hill in 1792. He was the author of some twenty books on musical subjects, including *Lyric Airs* (1804), a study of ancient Greek music. But his major work was undoubtedly *The Musical and Poetical Relicks of the Welsh Bards* (1784), which was followed by a second volume, *The Bardic Museum* (1802), and a third, *Hen Ganiadau Cymru* (1820). These books contain much valuable information about early Welsh poetry and traditional Welsh music, together with English translations which aroused the interest of antiquaries and writers in England.

For further details see the biography of Edward Jones by Tecwyn Ellis (1957).

JONES, EDWARD (1761–1836), poet and hymn-writer, was born at Llanrhaeadr yng Nghinmeirch, Denbs., but lived from about 1796 at Maes-y-plwm, Denbs., and is usually associated with the latter place. He received an elementary education and was employed as a schoolmaster and farmer. A popular poet in his day, he wrote carols, hymns and elegies which were collected in the volume *Caniadau Maes y Plwm* (1857). In his lifetime he published a collection of hymns, *Hymnau . . . ar Amryw Destynau ac Achosion* (1810; enlarged edns., 1820, 1829), and a satirical poem, *Gwialen i Gefn yr Ynfyd* (1831). Many of his hymns, such as '*Mae'n llond y nefoedd, llond y byd*', '*Cyfamod hedd, cyfamod cadarn Duw*' and '*Pob seraff, pob sant*' are still popular.

A biography, together with his literary remains, was published by his sons in 1839; J. E. Caerwyn Williams has written a study of Jones's life and work (1962).

JONES, EINIR (1950–), poet, was born at Traeth Coch, Ang., and educated at the University College of North Wales, Bangor. She has published two volumes of poetry, namely *Pigo Crachan* (1972) and *Gwellt Medi* (1980).

JONES, ELIAS (**Ffumerydd Jones, Cocosfardd y De**; *fl.* late 19th cent.), rhymester. Very little is known about him and his only published work, *Simleiau'r Cwm* (1897), is of interest merely because it makes of him the south Wales equivalent of *Y Bardd Cocos* (John *Evans). He won prizes at local eisteddfodau, but whether he was serious or frivolous in his intentions is unclear, for his lines are clumsy, his rhymes uncertain and his language ridiculous, although not to the same hilarious extent as those of his more famous counterpart in north Wales.

JONES, ELIAS HENRY (1883–1942), author. Born at Aberystwyth, Cards., the eldest son of Sir Henry *Jones, he was educated at the Universities of Glasgow, Grenoble and Oxford. A lawyer by profession, he became an administrator in Burma in 1905 but returned to Wales in 1922 after serving in the Indian Army during the First World War. He achieved enormous popular success with his book, *The Road to En-dor* (1920), the story of how he and a fellow-officer survived a long forced march and escaped from the Turkish prison-camp at Yozgad by feigning madness and spiritualistic powers. E. H. Jones, who took a keen interest in the international Peace Movement of the 1920s, was editor of the magazine *The Welsh *Outlook* from 1927 to 1933 and, from then until his death, held the post of Registrar at the University College of North Wales, Bangor.

JONES, ELIZABETH MARY (**Moelona**; 1878–1953), novelist, was born at Rhydlewis, Cards. A teacher by profession, she was the author of more than thirty books for children and adults. Much of her work, including her most famous novel, *Teulu Bach Nantoer* (1913), is set in her native county, but she also translated the stories of Alphonse Daudet into Welsh under the title *Y Wers Olaf* (1921). Patriotic and progressive in her views on the social status of women, she championed women's rights in her novel *Cwrs y Lli* (1927) and in '*Alys Morgan*', the first story in her collection, *Dwy Ramant o'r De* (1911). Although her prose style may have lost much of its appeal for the modern reader, her works were extremely popular in their day.

For further details see the essay on Moelona by Roger Jones Williams in *Dewiniaid Difyr* (ed. Mairwen and Gwynn Jones, 1983).

JONES, ELIZABETH WATKIN (1888–1966), children's writer, was born at Nefyn, Caerns., and educated at the Normal College, Bangor. She was a teacher at schools in south Wales before returning to her native town in 1920, there to spend the rest of her life. A prolific writer, she made an important contribution to Welsh children's literature by writing exciting stories in a rich idiom at a time when there was a dearth of such reading material. Her historical novels include *Plant y Mynachdy* (1939), *Luned Bengoch* (1946), *Y Cwlwm Cêl* (1947), *Y Dryslwyn* (1947), *Esyllt* (1951), *Lowri* (1951) and *Lois* (1955). Most are located in the Llŷn peninsula and all but two are set during the *Civil Wars.

There is an essay on Elizabeth Watkin Jones by R. Maldwyn Thomas in *Dewiniaid Difyr* (ed. Mairwen and Gwynn Jones, 1983).

JONES, ELWYN (1923–82), television playwright and documentary writer. Born at Cwmaman, near Aberdare, Glam., and educated at the London School of Economics, he joined the BBC's Television Service in London in 1957, where he worked in Drama and Documentaries, resigning in 1964 to become a full-time writer. From 1975 until his death he lived near Llandysul, Dyfed. His best-known creations were the television series *Softly, Softly*, and the character of Inspector Barlow. He published a number of books based on the latter, including *Barlow in Charge* (1973) and *The Barlow Casebook* (1975), as well as the documentary studies, *The Last Two to Hang* (1966), *The Ripper File* (1975) and *Death Trials* (1981). His translation of Saunders *Lewis's play, *Brad, which he adapted for television, is included in the volume *Presenting Saunders Lewis* (ed. Alun R. Jones and Gwyn Thomas, 1973).

JONES, EMYR (1914–), novelist, was born at Waun-fawr, Caerns. He left school at an early age to work at Dinorwic Quarry but later studied at Cartrefle Training College, Wrexham, becoming first a schoolmaster at Abergele and then a headmaster at Betws-yn-Rhos. His experiences as a quarryman fired his interest in the industry, the history of which he has written in *Canrif y Chwarelwr* (1963) and *Bargen Dinorwig* (1980). He has also published two novels, *Gwaed Gwirion* (1965), written in the first person from the viewpoint of a soldier in the First World War, and *Grym y Lli* (1969) which tells the story of John *Evans of Waun-fawr and his search for the 'Welsh Indians'; the latter won the *Prose Medal at the National Eisteddfod in 1969.

JONES, ERASMUS (1817–1909), novelist. Born in the parish of Llanddeiniolen, Caerns., he emigrated to the USA in 1833 and became a minister of the Methodist Episcopal Church at Remsen, Oneida County, New York State, but he settled eventually in nearby Utica. Among his novels, all of which were published in America, are *The Captive Youths of Judah* (1856), *The Adopted Son of the Princess* (1870) and *Llangobaith: A Story of North Wales* (1886). He was also the author of *The Welsh in America* (1876) and *Gold, Tinsel and Trash* (1890).

JONES, ERNEST (1879–1958), psychoanalyst and biographer. Born at Gowerton, Glam., and educated at Llandovery College and the University Colleges of Cardiff and London, he qualified as a doctor in 1900, by which time he was already interested in the theory of psychoanalysis. He became a friend and disciple of Sigmund Freud after they had met at the first Psychoanalytical Congress, which was held at Salzburg in 1908, shortly before he left London to take up a teaching post at the University of Toronto. His first wife, Morfydd Llwyn *Owen, died in 1918 soon after their marriage and, in the following year, he married again. By his second marriage he had two daughters and two sons of whom the elder is the novelist Mervyn Jones.

In 1919 Ernest Jones founded the International Psycho-Analytical Association, of which he was president over a period of some thirty years. An early member of *Plaid Cymru, he expressed regret in his autobiography, *Free Associations* (1959), that he was unable to speak Welsh fluently but he considered his nationality to be an essential element in his personality, a view with which Freud concurred. Of his visits to meetings of the Psycho-Analytical Society of Vienna he wrote, 'Coming myself from an oppressed race, it was easy for me to identify myself with the Jewish outlook'. A man of immense energies, but unyielding and intolerant of both critics and colleagues, he was devoted to Freud, often quite uncritically. At considerable personal risk he was instrumental in rescuing his master after the Nazi invasion of Austria in 1938 and in having him taken to London. Ernest Jones's most important book is *Sigmund Freud: Life and Work* (3 vols., 1953–57), the culmination of his career as the principal expositor in English of Freudian theory and practice.

T. G. Davies has contributed an essay on Ernest Jones to the *St. David's Day* series (1979); a fuller account of his life and work is to be found in *Ernest Jones, Freud's Alter Ego* by Vincent Brome (1983).

JONES, ERNEST CHARLES (1819–68), novelist and *Chartist poet. The son of a Welsh officer of the 15th Hussars who was the Duke of Cumberland's equerry, he was born in Berlin. Called to the Bar in 1844, he adopted the views of the Chartists in an extreme form two years later, becoming one of their foremost orators. His advocacy of violence led to his imprisonment in 1848 and, on his release from prison, he edited a Chartist newspaper. He later returned to his practice as a barrister and spent the last years of his life in Manchester. Between 1853 and 1855 he published a sensational novel, *The Lass and the Lady*, and a number of tales including *The Maid of Warsaw*, *Woman's Wrongs* and *The Painter of Florence*. He also published three volumes of verse, *The Battle Day* (1855), *The Revolt of Hindostan* (1857) and *Corayda* (1859); some of his lyrics, such as 'Song of the Poorer Classes', are memorable.

JONES, EVAN (**Ieuan Gwynedd**; 1820–52), essayist and pamphleteer, was born near Dolgellau, Mer. He kept schools in various places before entering the Congregational ministry, which he served briefly at Tredegar, Mon. In poor health for most of his life, he edited Radical periodicals, both Welsh and English, in Cardiff and London. He was a champion of the *Temperance movement and of *Nonconformity against both the insinuations and conclusions of the *Blue Books commissioners (1847). His essays, published in the form of pamphlets and booklets, include *A Vindication of the Educational and Moral Condition of Wales* (1848) and *Facts, Figures and Statements in Illustration of the Dissent and Morality of Wales: an Appeal to the English people* (1849); a selection of his prose was edited by Brinley Rees in the series *Llyfrau Deunaw* (1957).

JONES, EVAN DAVID (1903–), scholar, was born at Llangeitho, Cards., and educated at the University College of Wales, Aberystwyth. Appointed to the staff of the *National Library of Wales in 1929, he became Head of the Department of Manuscripts in 1938 and Librarian in 1958, remaining in that post until his retirement in 1969. An authority on the work of *Lewys Glyn Cothi (Llywelyn y Glyn), he has published two standard volumes on the poet, as well as a variety of essays. He edited the Appendix (1941–50) to *Y Bywgraffiadur Cymreig / The Dictionary of Welsh Biography* (1970) and continues to be its general editor. Since 1953 he has been the editor of the *Journal* of the Merionethshire Historical Society.

JONES, EVAN GEORGE (Sioronwy; 1892–1953), see under CILIE FAMILY.

JONES, EVAN PAN (1834–1922), Congregational minister, social reformer and author, was born in the parish of Llandysul, Cards. Educated at denominational Colleges in Wales and at the University of Marburg, he was ordained at Mostyn, Flints., in 1870, and there he remained for the rest of his life. He was a fervent Nonconformist and strove to establish School Boards to counteract the influence of *Anglicanism and *Roman Catholicism on the education of Welsh children. The *Disestablishment of the Anglican Church in Wales was a topic on which he spoke and wrote a great deal. But his main preoccupation was with the relationship between the tenant farmer and his landlord. In 1891 he and four companions spent ten weeks travelling in all parts of Wales and addressing meetings on the nationalization of land. He edited two periodicals, *Y *Celt* and *Cwrs y Byd*, wrote a biography of Samuel *Roberts and his brothers (1892) and of Michael D. *Jones (1903), and contributed to the controversy among Congregationalists concerning the future of their Theological Colleges. It was as part of this controversy that he wrote his fantastic 'play', entitled *Y Dydd Hwn. Annibyniaeth yn symud fel Cranc* (1880). His autobiography, *Oes Gofion* (n.d.), is untidy, but

interesting, and gives a vivid picture of the author's eccentric personality and his age.

Jones, Ffumerydd, see JONES, ELIAS (*fl.* 1897).

JONES, FRANCIS (1908–), historian, was born at Trefin, Pembs. As county archivist of Carmarthenshire, he wrote a short history of the parish of Llangunnor (1966) as well as a more general historical work, *The Holy Wells of Wales* (1954). In his office of Wales Herald Extraordinary, he has published innumerable articles and several books on genealogical subjects, including *The Princes and the Principality of Wales* (1969) and *God Bless the Prince of Wales* (1969). Dedwydd Jones, the playwright, is his son.

JONES, FRANK PRICE (1920–75), historian. A native of Denbigh, he was educated at the University College of North Wales, Bangor, and was a teacher at Ruthin before becoming a Lecturer in Welsh History in the Extra-Mural Department of his old College. He published *The Story of Denbighshire through its Castles* (1951), *Thomas Jones o Ddinbych* (1956), *Crwydro Dwyrain Dinbych* (1961), *Crwydro Gorllewin Dinbych* (1969) and *Radicaliaeth a'r Werin Gymreig* (1975). He also contributed many articles to magazines, including *Baner ac Amserau Cymru*, to which, under the pseudonym Daniel, he was a regular contributor between 1956 and the year of his death.

JONES, FRED (1877–1948), see under CILIE FAMILY.

JONES, GERAINT VAUGHAN (1904–), novelist, was born at Llandudno, Caerns., and educated at Leeds University, at Mansfield College, Oxford, and at Marburg University. A Congregational minister in Halifax until 1949 and in Glasgow until 1974, he has written a number of theological works, including *Christology and Myth in the New Testament* (1956) and *The Art and Truth of the Parables* (1964). His novels include *Y Fro Dirion* (1974), *Y Ffoaduriaid* (1979), *Yr Hen a'r Ifainc* (1983) and *Morwenna* (1983); he has also published a collection of short stories, *Broc Môr* (1979), and a play, *Gofeb* (1983).

JONES, GERALLT (1907–84), poet, was born at Rhymney, Mon., the eldest son of Fred Jones, a member of the *Cilie family of poets. An Independent minister for most of his life, he edited a selection of the essays and verse of his uncle, Simon Bartholomew *Jones (1966), his cousin Fred *Williams's poetry, *Codi'r Wal* (1974), and the light verse of his father, uncles and grandfather in *Awen Ysgafn y Cilie* (1976). His own work consisted of a Welsh translation of Haydn's *Creation* (1952), a volume of poetry, *Ystâd Bardd* (1974), a study of Sarah Jane *Rees,

Cranogwen (1981), and a volume of essays in memory of Jac Alun Jones (1984). The folk-singer Dafydd *Iwan is one of his sons.

JONES, GLYN (1905–), poet, short-story writer and novelist, was born in Merthyr Tydfil, Glam., into a Welsh-speaking family, but a totally English education at Cyfarthfa Castle Grammar School nearly deprived him of his first language. After training at St. Paul's College, Cheltenham, he became a teacher in Cardiff, where the poverty of many of his pupils and his admiration for the work of D. H. Lawrence, whose industrial, Congregational background was so like his own, stimulated his desire to write. His own powers answered Lawrence's imagery and love of words and the poetry of Gerard Manley *Hopkins, discovered a little later, added a new syntactical dimension. It was, however, his return to the reading of the Welsh language after some twenty years' indifference that persuaded him, unlike Lawrence, to remain true to his origins; Merthyr now became his main subject. Although entirely competent in Welsh in adult life he never felt able to use the language creatively, the decisive factor having been—according to his own testimony—that his first appreciation of the power of words, and the first stirring of adolescent imagination, had been through the medium of English. On the other hand, he has translated Welsh poetry into English, most notably in The Saga of Llywarch the Old (in collaboration with T. J. *Morgan, 1955) and in two selections of harp stanzas, When the Rose Bush brings forth Apples (1981) and Honeydew on the Wormwood (1984), both of which were published by the *Gregynog Press.

Glyn Jones's early poems appeared in The Dublin Magazine in 1931 but, although poetry remained his chief love, his output was small. It was The *Blue Bed (1937), a volume of short stories, which made his name. Detailed, rhetorical, full of a poetry of sorrow and distaste, these stories were tapestries of imaginative language in which malformed, gross and feckless humanity revealed a beating heart. A meeting with Dylan *Thomas and admiration for his stories may have confirmed Glyn Jones in his own use of a boy narrator. Certainly The *Water Music (1944) applied the same poetry of word and imagination more uniformly to the memories of childhood. In these stories compassion and praise break through, most of all in the title-story itself, which is almost devoid of narrative. In this volume Glyn Jones's achievement became distinctive, even unique. The work in Poems (1939) is less intuitive because it is early, but the alliteration of some of the poems reveals their author's fascination with poetic disciplines in Welsh. His often dispiriting experience as a teacher in a secondary modern school made possible The *Dream of Jake Hopkins (1944), originally a poem for broadcasting.

The middle of Glyn Jones's writing life was devoted to the novel. His first novel, The *Valley, The City, The Village (1956), is full of character, incident and splendid peripheral description, but its evocations of place and person reveal the natural short-story writer rather than the novelist. The Learning Lark (1960), which sets out to pillory the corruption in teaching appointments at schools in south Wales, is more cohesive in plot, but the ultimate ironies fall too limply from an insufficiently realized narrator. Perhaps the best of his novels, because the boys' world resolves itself outside time, is The *Island of Apples (1965), in which the stranger youth, Karl Anthony, fulfils the narrator's dreams for him.

A change of course was signalled with the appearance of The *Dragon Has Two Tongues (1968), for this book offered nor merely a measure of autobiography but the first critical appreciation of those Anglo-Welsh writers whom Glyn Jones had known, such as Dylan Thomas, Huw Menai (Huw Owen *Williams), Idris *Davies and Jack *Jones. He rendered further service to contemporary literature in Wales as the co-author with John *Rowlands of Profiles (1980), a volume of essays about some of the more important Welsh and Anglo-Welsh writers of the twentieth century, and has also returned to poetry, his Selected Poems (1975) including much new work. His eminence as a short-story writer, too, demanded the publication of his selected short stories (1971), to be followed by a previously unpublished collection, Welsh Heirs (1977).

Glyn Jones was the pioneer of the generation of Anglo-Welsh writers which included Vernon *Watkins, Dylan Thomas and Idris Davies. It was he who experienced the isolation of living and working in Cardiff during the late 1920s. Fascinated with much of contemporary English writing, especially that of D. H. Lawrence, he did not know until he was twenty-five how to use what he had learned in work which would do justice to the Welshness of his religious and family heritage. Having to struggle to publish his poems outside Wales and condemned to write in English, as the language in which his aesthetic consciousness had been nurtured at school, he could nevertheless write in The Dragon Has Two Tongues, 'I have never written (in English) a word about any country other than Wales or any people other than Welsh people'.

This assertion might suggest a kind of claustrophobia, but in fact Glyn Jones's prose as much as his poetry—and with few writers can there have been so little difference in feeling between the two—expresses very clearly that sense of being 'a foreigner' in English which prefigures the lyricism of Dylan Thomas and Gwyn *Thomas (1913–81). His images are fresh and bountiful, the words have a shining newness, as though turned over for the first time, pebbles on an unfamiliar beach. In his poem 'Merthyr', one of the most brilliantly balanced, humorous and evocative in the Anglo-Welsh canon, Glyn Jones wrote, 'I fancy words', and his especial quality as a writer is that through the often peculiar or ridiculous exteriors of his 'lively men', which he delineated as meticulously and as richly as the painter he once thought of becoming, he has sought to make an affirmation of hope and compassion. At less than his best (when the narrative line, for example, does not satisfy), this manner of his has a cloying effect, but his great achievement lies in his power to make of a recollected personal world a series of images and portraits which even the uncommitted reader cannot forget. It is Glyn Jones's gift, of heart as well as of mind, that he has always known how to make of the blemished and unlovable an unexplainable song.

There is an essay on Glyn Jones by Leslie Norris in the *Writers of Wales* series (1973) and an autobiographical essay in *Y Llwybrau Gynt* (ed. Alun Oldfield-Davies, 1971); see also his memoir of literary life in Wales, *Setting Out* (1982) and the articles by Robert Minhinnick and Mercer Simpson in *Poetry Wales* (vol. 19, no. 3, 1984), which also contains a bibliography of Glyn Jones's writings by John and Sylvia Harris.

Jones, Griffith, see JONES, JOHN (1559–98).

Jones, Griffith (1683–1761), the founder of the Welsh Circulating Schools and, in the opinion of many, the greatest Welshman of the eighteenth century, was born at Penboyr, Carms. While employed as a shepherd he had an intense religious experience which was a turning-point in his life. After attending the Carmarthen Grammar School, he was ordained priest in 1708. He enjoyed a reputation as a preacher and, despite incurring the displeasure of his bishops on several occasions, was given the rectory of Llanddowror, Carms., by one of his patrons, Sir John Philipps, in 1716. He remained at Llanddowror for forty-five years and it is with that village he is usually associated.

An active member of the *Society for Promoting Christian Knowledge, he grew dissatisfied with its attempts to teach literacy in the English language and, in 1731, began establishing circulating schools in his native county. Usually held during the winter when farm work would allow, and moving on to some other place after three months, these schools taught children and adults to read the Welsh *Bible and to learn the Catechism of the Anglican Church. They met with immediate success and were an important factor in the spread of literacy in the Welsh language. In the year of Griffith Jones's death, the movement's annual report, *Welch Piety*, was able to record that, during the previous twenty-five years, some three thousand of these schools had been established in 1,600 places throughout Wales. After his death the work was carried on by Madam Bridget Bevan (1698–

1779), who had been the principal patron of the schools.

Griffith Jones has had several biographers, including Henry Phillips (1762), D. Ambrose Jones (1928), R. T. Jenkins (1930), F. A. Cavanagh (1930), and Thomas Kelly (1950); see also Geraint H. Jenkins, *Hen Filwr dros Grist* (1983) and Gwyn Davies, *Griffith Jones, Llanddowror, Athro Cenedl* (1984). For details of the Circulating Schools see M. G. Jones, *The Charity School Movement* (1938) and the chapter entitled 'Religion, Language and the Circulating Schools' in *Religion, Language and Nationality in Wales* (1979) by Glanmor Williams.

JONES, GRIFFITH HARTWELL (1859–1944), historian. Born at Llanrhaeadr-ym-Mochnant, Mont., and educated at Jesus College, Oxford, he spent most of his life as an Anglican cleric in Surrey. Although actively interested in Welsh affairs, most notably as Chairman of the Honourable Society of *Cymmrodorion for more than twenty years, he was denied office in the Church in Wales and in his autobiography, *A Celt Looks at the World* (1946), he made no secret of his disappointment that he was not called upon to fulfil, in his own country, the higher ecclesiastical duties of which he believed himself capable. Among his historical works were *The Dawn of European Civilisation* (1903), *Celtic Britain and the Pilgrim Movement* (1912), *The Celt in Ancient History* (1921) and *Early Celtic Missionaries* (1928).

Jones, Gruffydd (*Y Deryn Mawr*; *fl.* 1880), a witty old man from Bethel, Caerns., who had a great gift for telling *white lie tales. A quarryman, he earned his nickname by the frequent telling of a story about how a large bird (W. *aderyn mawr*) once carried him home from America. There is a cameo portrait of him in W. J. *Gruffydd's *Hen Atgofion* (1936).

JONES, GWILYM GWESYN (1910–78), poet. Born at Caerphilly, Glam., the youngest of a farmer's ten children, he left school at the age of fourteen; the rest of his life was spent in a variety of jobs but mainly in forestry. He published two volumes of verse, *Pacific Poems* (1936) and *The Loom of Love* (1953), both of which reflect his joy in the natural scene and for which A. G. *Prys-Jones wrote a foreword.

JONES, GWILYM MEREDYDD (1920–), short-story writer and novelist, was born at Glanyrafon, Flints., and educated at the Normal College, Bangor. From 1946 until his retirement in 1982 he was a teacher at schools in Toxteth and Broad Green, Liverpool. He has published two collections of stories, *Ochr Arall y Geiniog* (1982) and *Gwerth Grôt* (1983), and two novels, *Dawns yr Ysgubau* (1965) and *Yr Onnen Unig* (1985).

JONES, GWILYM RICHARD (1903–), poet and journalist, was born at Tal-y-sarn,

Caerns. He began working as a reporter on the staff of Yr *Herald Cymraeg in Caernarfon, then became the editor of Herald Môn, Y *Brython and The North Wales Times in turn, before taking up the editorship of *Baner ac Amserau Cymru in 1939, a post he held until his retirement in 1977. As a poet, he is an accomplished craftsman in the strict metres, but he was also one of the first to experiment with vers libre in Welsh, and he has continued to write in both styles. He has published five volumes of verse: Caneuon (1953), Cerddi (1969), Y Syrcas (1975), Y Ddraig (1978) and Eiliadau (1981). With Huw T. *Edwards, Mathonwy *Hughes and Rhydwen *Williams, he contributed poems to the volume Ar y Cyd (1958). He has also written fiction. The effects of poverty and the shadow of the First World War on the quarrying community of Dyffryn Nantlle form the basis of his two short novels, Y Purdan (1942) and Seirff yn Eden (1963). Gwilym R. Jones has won the *Chair (1938), the *Crown (1935) and the *Prose Medal (1941) at the National Eisteddfod.

A study of his poetry is to be found in Awen Gwilym R. (1980) by Mathonwy Hughes; see also Gwilym R. Jones's autobiography, Rhodd Enbyd (1983) and the article by Mathonwy Hughes in Dyrnaid o Awduron Cyfoes (ed. D. Ben Rees, 1975).

JONES, GWYN (1907–), scholar, novelist and short-story writer. He was born in Blackwood, Mon., and educated at University College, Cardiff, where his M.A. thesis on the Icelandic sagas was the first step in a lifetime of distinguished scholarship. In 1929 he became a schoolmaster, first in Wigan and later in Manchester. The first-fruits of his scholarship and creative ability were his translation, Four Icelandic Sagas (1935), and a novel, Richard Savage (1935). The latter, widely acknowledged to be among the outstanding books of its year, contains in its account of the eponymous hero a masterful evocation of life in Augustan England.

Gwyn Jones returned to Wales in 1935 as a Lecturer in the English Department at University College, Cardiff. Three very different novels, *Times Like These (1936), The Nine Days' Wonder (1937) and A Garland of Bays (1938), followed in quick succession. The first of these, a moving account of family life against the background of the *Depression in the valleys of south Wales, is remarkable for its authenticity and restraint; the second, set near Manchester, is a rather sordid tale of low-life, and the last a historical novel about the Elizabethan dramatist, Robert Greene.

In 1939, prompted by a consciousness of the gathering strength of Anglo-Welsh writing, Gwyn Jones founded the magazine, The *Welsh Review, and in the following year he became Professor of English at the University College of Wales, Aberystwyth. The major literary triumph of his years at Aberystwyth was his collaboration with Thomas *Jones in the translation of The *Mabinogion. This work, published by the Golden Cockerel Press in 1948 and in Everyman's Library in 1949, not only satisfied Welsh scholars but also won the admiration of a wide readership on account of its subtle evocation of the spirit of the original and the unfailing elegance of its style. Gwyn Jones was involved as editor and translator of several other fine editions from the Golden Cockerel Press, including Sir Gawain and the Green Knight (1952) and The Metamorphoses of Ovid (1958). His own novella, The Green Island (1946), first published by the Press, was included in the second of three collections of his short stories, The Still Waters (1948). Two novels were published during his time at Aberystwyth, The Flowers Beneath the Scythe (1952), which spans the two World Wars, and The Walk Home (1962), another historical novel, set in industrial south Wales. He also published during this period two more collections of short stories, The *Buttercup Field (1945) and *Shepherd's Hey (1953), a descriptive essay, A Prospect of Wales (1948), and the volume Welsh Legends and Folk Tales (1955); his selected short stories appeared in 1974.

From 1964 until his retirement in 1975, Gwyn Jones held the Chair of English at University College, Cardiff. His research into Viking exploration and conquest was acknowledged during this period by the award of the Order of the Falcon by the President of Iceland in 1963, while the publication of The Norse Atlantic Saga (1964), A History of the Vikings (1968) and Kings, Beasts and Heroes (1972) brought him worldwide recognition.

In his many editorials, articles and lectures, Gwyn Jones has done much to define and promote *Anglo-Welsh literature, a field in which he has been a major figure for nearly fifty years. Among the anthologies of Anglo-Welsh literature which he has edited are Welsh Short Stories (1941), Welsh Short Stories (1956), Twenty-five Welsh Short Stories (with Islwyn Ffowc Elis, 1971) and The Oxford Book of Welsh Verse in English (1977); his principal lectures on Anglo-Welsh literature are The First Forty Years (1957) and Being and Belonging (The BBC Wales Annual Lecture, 1977). He served as Chairman of the Welsh Committee of the Arts Council from 1957 to 1967.

There is an essay by Cecil Price on Gwyn Jones's life and work, with a select bibliography, in the Writers of Wales series (1976). See also the article by Glyn Jones in Dictionary of Literary Biography: British Novelists, 1930–1959 (1983).

JONES, GWYN ERFYL (1924–), poet and editor, was born near Llanerfyl, Mont. After a period spent as a Lecturer in Philosophy and Political Science at *Coleg Harlech, he entered the Congregational ministry and held pastorates at

Trawsfynydd and Glanaman and in Cardiff. Well known since then as a producer and presenter of television programmes in Welsh, he has won several international prizes for his documentary films; he became Head of Documentary and Religious Programmes with HTV Wales in 1980, a post from which he retired in 1985. A selection of his interviews with eminent Welshmen was published in the volume *Dan Sylw* (1971). He has published one volume of poems, *Cerddi* (1970), and was editor of the magazine *★Barn* from 1975 to 1979.

JONES, GWYN OWAIN (1917–), novelist. Born in Cardiff, he was educated at Jesus College, Oxford, and later taught at the University of Sheffield and Queen Mary College, University of London, at the last of which he became Professor of Physics in 1953. He returned to Wales in 1968 on his appointment as Director of the ★National Museum of Wales, a post in which he remained until his retirement in 1977. Besides two books on scientific subjects, G. O. Jones has published three novels, *The Catalyst* (1960), *Personal File* (1962) and *Now* (1965), and a largely autobiographical work, *The Conjuring Show* (1981).

JONES, HARRI PRITCHARD (1933–), short-story writer and novelist. Born in Dudley, Worcs., but brought up at Menai Bridge and Llangefni, Ang., he studied medicine at Trinity College, Dublin. During his ten years in Ireland he became deeply immersed in Irish culture and was converted to the Roman Catholic faith. He works, on a part-time basis, as a doctor in Cardiff. Ireland provided the inspiration for his first volume of short stories, *Troeon* (1966), and his novel *Dychwelyd* (1972) is also partly set in that country. He has published a second volume of short stories, *Pobl* (1978), in which the delicate evocation of place is matched by skilful analysis of human character, and a study of Sigmund Freud in the series *Y ★Meddwl Modern* (1982).

JONES, HENRY (1852–1922), philosopher and author. Born at Llangernyw, Denbs., he was apprenticed at the age of twelve to his father, a shoemaker, but later entered the Normal College, Bangor, and went on to Glasgow University. He became a Lecturer in Philosophy at the University College of Wales, Aberystwyth, in 1882, Professor at the University College of North Wales, Bangor, two years later, and then, moving to Scotland where he lived for the rest of his life, Professor at St. Andrew's University in 1891 and at Glasgow University in 1894.

An outstanding teacher, his doctrine was a version of Hegelian idealism, influenced by the Bible. A Liberal in politics and deeply interested in educational reform, he was a leader of the movement which resulted in the Intermediate Education Act of 1889 and he it was, after the establishment of the ★University of Wales, who devised the plan of a penny rate (sometimes described as 'the pennies of the poor') which was levied by the county councils for the purposes of higher education.

The most important of his numerous philosophical works were *Browning as a Philosophical and Religious Teacher* (1891), *Lotze* (1895) and *A Faith that Enquires* (1922). The last-named is the work for which he is generally remembered today; based on the Gifford Lectures which he delivered in Glasgow, the book reflects many of the theological tendencies in the Wales of his day. Knighted in 1912, he described his struggle for education and his early career in a volume of autobiography, *Old Memories* (1923), which was edited by Thomas ★Jones. Elias Henry ★Jones was his son.

For further details see H. J. W. Hetherington, *The Life and Letters of Sir Henry Jones* (1924).

JONES, HUGH (1749–1825), translator and hymn-writer, was born at Maesglasau, between Dinas Mawddwy and Dolgellau, Mer. As a young man he became prominent with the Calvinistic Methodists and found his chief delight in the production of devotional literature. While living as a schoolteacher in London he wrote *Cydymaith yr Hwsmon* (1774), a volume of religious meditations. Back in Wales by 1786, he kept school in his native county, supplementing his meagre income by working as a translator for various publishers, among whom was Thomas ★Gee. The author or translator of some twenty books, including the work of Josephus, the Jewish historian, he published two volumes of his own poetry, *Gardd y Caniadau* (1776) and *Hymnau Newyddion* (1797). He is remembered especially for his hymn, 'O tyn y gorchudd yn y mynydd hyn', which Owen M. ★Edwards, who edited a selection of his work in 1901, considered to be the finest hymn in the Welsh language.

Jones, Hugh Robert (1894–1930), pioneer of the Welsh Nationalist Party. Born at Ebenezer (he later succeeded in having the village's name changed to Deiniolen), Caerns., he began working in the local quarry at the age of thirteen. The group he founded, known as *Byddin Ymreolaeth Cymru*, joined with others in 1925 to form *Plaid Genedlaethol Cymru* ('The National Party of Wales'), which later became ★*Plaid Cymru*. He served as the party's first Secretary until his death from tuberculosis. H. R. Jones is the hero of the awdl, 'Breuddwyd y Bardd' (1931) by Gwenallt (David James ★Jones), and Caradoc Evans (David ★Evans) is its villain.

For further details see the essay by Saunders Lewis in *Canlyn Arthur* (1938) and the chapter by Gwilym R. Jones in *Adnabod Deg* (ed. Derec Llwyd Morgan, 1977).

JONES, HUMPHREY (Bryfdir; 1867–1947), poet, was born in Cwm Croesor, Mer. Besides winning sixty-four chairs and eight crowns at various eisteddfodau, he published two volumes of poetry, *Telynau'r Wawr* (1899) and *Bro fy Mebyd* (1929), as well as several pamphlet collections.

JONES, IDWAL (1887–1964), author, was born at Blaenau Ffestiniog, Mer., but emigrated with his family to the USA at the age of twelve. After working as a mining prospector and lumberjack, he became a journalist in San Francisco and earned a living by writing about the theatre, gastronomy and the history and folklore of California, and by undertaking historical research for Paramount Film Studios. Although he never lost his Welsh, only two of his dozen novels, *The Splendid Shilling* (1926) and *Whistler's Van* (1936), remember Wales. For the most part, he turned to Californian or cosmopolitan themes, as in such books as *High Bonnet* (1945) and *Vermilion* (1947), a long, colourful novel about quicksilver mining in the Santa Cruz mountains. His most important literary work was *China Boy* (1936), a collection of short stories, the title-story of which was first published in The *Welsh Review* in May, 1939.

JONES, IDWAL (1895–1937), playwright and humorist, was born at Lampeter, Cards. He worked for his father, a coal-merchant, as a clerk in a solicitor's office, and served in East Africa during the First World War before entering the University College of Wales, Aberystwyth, where he graduated in English in 1923. After a period as a schoolmaster at Devil's Bridge, he became an extra-mural lecturer. Something of a legend during his own lifetime, Idwal Jones was famous for his student pranks, but he is also remembered as the author of much light verse which includes parodies, limericks, nonsense poems and a musical comedy about college life, *Yr Eosiaid* (1936). His poems and stories were published in the volumes *Cerddi Digri a Rhai Pethau Eraill* (1934), *Cerddi Digri Newydd a Phethau o'r Fath* (1937) and *Ystoriau a Pharodïau* (1944). He wrote a number of short plays, including *My Piffle*, a bilingual parody of *My People* by Caradoc Evans (David *Evans), but his most important works are *Pobl yr Ymylon* (1927), an argument against respectability, and *Yr Anfarwol Ifan Harris*, the prize-winning play at the National Eisteddfod of 1928. His contribution to light entertainment was made as founder and member of the popular musical group known as *Adar Tregaron* and as a script-writer for radio.

A biography of Idwal Jones was written by D. Gwenallt Jones (1958).

JONES, IEUAN GWYNEDD (1920–), historian, was born in the Rhondda Valley and educated at University College, Swansea, and Peterhouse, Cambridge. Appointed to a lectureship at Swansea in 1953, he was the Sir John Williams Professor of Welsh History at the University College of Wales, Aberystwyth, from 1969 until his retirement in 1984. His main interests are in the parliamentary history of Wales in the seventeenth century and the political life of Victorian Wales. Among his publications are *The Religious Census of 1851* (2 vols., 1976, 1981) and a collection of miscellaneous essays, *Explorations and Explanations* (1981).

JONES, IFANO (1865–1955), bibliographer, was born at Aberdare, Glam. Apprenticed to the printing trade as a boy, he began work in the offices of *Tarian y Gweithiwr* and later became a compositor and proof-reader with the weekly newspaper *Y Gweithiwr Cymraeg*. In 1896 he was appointed to the staff of the Cardiff Free Library to catalogue, with John *Ballinger, the material in the Welsh collection, and he worked in the library's Reference Department until his retirement in 1925. The catalogue was published in 1898 under the title *Cardiff Free Libraries. Catalogue of Printed Literature in the Welsh Department*, with supplements appearing in the periodical *Bibliography of Wales* between 1899 and 1912. Jones went on to compile (again in association with Ballinger) a bibliography of the Welsh *Bible, which appeared in 1906, and to write his *magnum opus*, *A History of Printing and Printers in Wales to 1810* (1925).

For further details see the article by W. W. Price in the *Journal* of the Welsh Bibliographical Society (July, 1955).

Jones, Inigo (1573–1652), the great architect of the early Stuarts, was the son of a Welsh clothworker. A persistent tradition associates his family with Denbighshire and his unusual Christian name may be an attempt to write the old Welsh name Inco. Thomas *Pennant, in his *Tours* (1810), gave a wider currency to the local belief that Jones designed Gwydir chapel in 1633 and the famous bridge at Llanrwst in 1636. The architect's armorial bearings resemble those of the Trevors, for whom he is said to have designed the great house of Plas Teg, Flints.

For further details about the Welsh connections of Inigo Jones see the studies by J. A. Gotch (1928) and J. Summerson (1966).

JONES, JACK (1884–1970), novelist. Born in Merthyr Tydfil, Glam., one of a miner's fifteen children, he began working underground at the age of twelve and joined the army five years later, serving in South Africa and on the North-west Frontier of India. After the First World War, during which he was wounded in Belgium, he became active in left-wing politics and in 1923, while a member of the Communist Party, he was elected miners' agent for the Garw Valley. After five years he left both job and party and, between 1928 and 1932, was a member in turn of the Labour Party, the Liberal Party and Oswald Mosley's New Party. During the 1930s he had a variety of jobs, including those of cinema manager and navvy, and he was frequently unemployed. An experienced platform speaker, he visited America in 1941 and 1942 on behalf of the British Government and again in 1949 under the aegis of the Moral Rearmament Movement.

He took up serious writing during a period of unemployment in 1928, when he was living in Rhiwbina, Cardiff. His first attempt, a novel of some quarter of a million words, entitled *Saran*, was never published, but a much reduced version of it appeared as *Black Parade* (1935). His other novels include *Rhondda Roundabout* (1934), *Bidden to the Feast* (1938), *Off to Philadelphia in the Morning* (1947), *Some Trust in Chariots* (1948), *River out of Eden* (1951), *Lily of the Valley* (1952), *Lucky Lear* (1952), *Time and the Business* (1953), *Choral Symphony* (1955) and *Come, Night; End, Day!* (1956), the last five of which were of inferior quality. Among his finest achievements was *Unfinished Journey* (1937), the first of three volumes of autobiography. The others were *Me and Mine* (1946) and *Give me back my Heart* (1950). He also wrote three plays, *Land of my Fathers* (1937), *Rhondda Roundabout* (1939) and *Transatlantic Episode* (1947), and a biography of David *Lloyd George, *The Man David* (1944).

Jack Jones undertook much research into the histories of the towns which are the backgrounds of his novels and this method resulted sometimes in works of excessive length. He was widely read in modern prose fiction and drama, where his preference was for the naturalism of the earlier American novelists, such as James T. Farrell and John Dos Passos. His strength as a writer lies in his understanding and complete sympathy with working-class life in the industrial valleys of Glamorgan in the late nineteenth century and the beginning of the twentieth, and in his ability to portray that life with warmth and fidelity. Written in an unpretentious style, his best novels have great narrative vigour, much humour and pathos, a wide variety of vivid scenes and a host of vital and bizarre characters, while his autobiographies present a volatile and expansive personality, facing with courage the many sorrows and hardships which beset him.

There is a critique of Jack Jones's novels in *Three Contemporary Anglo-Welsh Novelists* (1948) by G. F. Adam, and Keri Edwards has contributed an essay on his life and work to the *Writers of Wales* series (1974); see also Glyn Jones, *The Dragon Has Two Tongues* (1968).

JONES, JAMES RHYS (Kilsby Jones; 1813–89), eccentric and editor, was born at Llandovery, Carms. An Independent minister in various parts of Wales and England, including Kilsby, Northants., he contributed numerous articles to the Welsh periodical press. But his most important literary work was the editing of a complete collection of the poetry and prose of William *Williams of Pantycelyn (1867). He was considered by his contemporaries to be among the greatest of Welsh eccentrics on account of his dress, manners and style of self-expression, but he was nevertheless a very effective preacher.

The biography of Kilsby Jones, as he was known throughout Wales, was written by Vyrnwy Morgan (n.d.).

Jones, Jenkin (b. 1623), Puritan preacher, was born at Tŷ Mawr, Llanddeti, Brecs., across the Usk Valley from the Newton of Henry and Thomas *Vaughan. Having enrolled at Jesus College, Oxford, in 1639, only a few months after the Vaughan twins, he fought in the *Civil War as a captain on the Parliamentarian side. Becoming a Baptist of the Catabaptist persuasion, he was appointed an Approver in his native county under the Act for the *Propagation of the Gospel in Wales (1650) and was effectively the administrator of its religious practice for a decade, reputedly able to raise a hundred armed men at call. He aroused strenuous objection from ejected clergy like Thomas *Powell and Alexander *Griffith, but continued to preach zealously over a wide area from Merthyr Tydfil to Llantilio Crossenny. According to local legend, he greeted the Restoration by firing three shots into the church door at Llanddeti and riding off westward with his troop, only to be clapped into Carmarthen Gaol. Released, he made fiery speeches and attempted to gather followers, but after a further imprisonment nothing more is known of him.

There is an account of Jenkin Jones in the article by Pennar Davies, 'Episodes in the History of Brecknockshire Dissent', in *Brycheiniog* (vol. III, 1957); see also Frederick Rees, 'Breconshire during the Civil War', in *Brycheiniog* (vol. VIII, 1962).

JONES, JEREMIAH (1855–1902), see under CILIE FAMILY.

Jones, John or **Griffith** (1559–98), Catholic martyr, was born at Clynnog, Caerns. He became a *Franciscan friar in Rome in 1591, taking the name of Brother Godfrey Maurice. On his return to England in disguise, he was arrested in 1594 by the priest-hunter Richard Topcliffe and was hanged at Southwark on 12 July 1598. It is said that there was an hour's delay on the scaffold because the executioner had forgotten to bring a rope. Jones was canonized by Pope Paul VI in 1970 as one of the *Forty Martyrs of England and Wales. His brother William (b. 1574/5) was a leading figure in the Benedictine revival at Douai and founder of the order's convent at Cambrai.

Jones, John (**Leander**; 1575–1635), Catholic divine. Born at Llanfrynach, Brecs., he was converted to the Roman Catholic faith in 1596 and went to study theology with the Jesuits at Valladolid where, three years later, he became a monk of the Benedictine Order, taking the name

Leander a Sancto Marino. A brilliant oriental linguist, he became the first President General of the English Benedictines in 1619 and was sent to England in 1633 to offer a cardinal's hat to Archbishop Laud (whose room-mate he had been at St. John's College, Oxford) if he would bring the English Church back to Rome.

JONES, JOHN (c.1585–1657/8), copyist and collector of manuscripts, was born in the mansion of Gellilyfdy in the parish of Ysgeifiog, Flints. He inherited the passion for collecting from his father, William Jones, and his grandfather, Siôn ap Wiliam, both of whom were patrons of poets whose work they had copied for the family archives. John Jones began as a copyist at an early age, either as a pupil in Shrewsbury School, or while articled in a lawyer's office, using his family's collection of manuscripts from sources in the Vale of Clwyd. In 1612 he was in Cardiff copying and collecting manuscripts which included *The Book of Llandâf* (see under LLANDAF). There followed an interval during which he was involved in litigation with family and neighbours over land and property. All this time he copied little, but the unproductive phase ended in 1632. From then on he found opportunity enough to resume his copying as an inmate of the debtors' prison in the Fleet, London. He was imprisoned there at least three times, serving in all about twelve years, and was also sentenced to imprisonment as a debtor at Ludlow in 1617, and elsewhere. Familiar with all the most eminent Welsh scholars and patrons of his day, he was able to rely on them to lend him their manuscripts which he copied accurately and in a distinctive, decorative style. At the time of his death in the Fleet, there were several manuscripts in his cell but they were rescued by Robert *Vaughan of Hengwrt and added to what became the Peniarth-Hengwrt collection now housed in the *National Library of Wales.

Jones, John (1597?–1660), regicide, came from the old gentry family of Maesygarnedd in Ardudwy, Mer. As a younger son, he entered the Puritan household of Sir Hugh *Myddelton in London. On his marriage to Margaret, the daughter of John Edwards of Stansty, at some time before 1639, he moved to live with her. During the *Civil War he fought for the Parliament and rose rapidly through the ranks, taking part in the sieges of Laugharne (1644) and Chester (1645). In 1646 he was promoted Colonel and, in the following year, became Member of Parliament for his native county. He was also a Commissioner for the *Propagation of the Gospel in Wales (1650), a Commissioner for Ireland (1650) and for North Wales (1655). His second wife was the sister of Oliver Cromwell. Jones, a staunch Puritan, corresponded with the movement's leaders in Wales. He achieved notoriety because he had been present at the trial of Charles I and had been one of the signatories of the King's death-warrant, for which he was executed at the Restoration.

For further details see the article by J. Lloyd in the *Transactions* of the Merioneth Historical and Records Society (vol. II, 1953–54).

JONES, JOHN (Jac Glan-y-gors; 1766–1821), satirical poet, took his *nom de guerre* from the farm in the parish of Cerrigydrudion, Denbs., where he was born. He went to London about 1789, kept a tavern there and became prominent in the Welsh life of the city as the secretary and official poet of the *Gwyneddigion Society and as one of the founders of the *Cymreigyddion. Sharing the views of Thomas Paine on War, the Monarchy, the Church and the Rights of Man, he published them in two pamphlets, *Seren Tan Gwmwl* (1795) and *Toriad y Dydd* (1797), for which he was bitterly denounced by more conservative writers. He was famous in his day, and is still remembered, as the author of lampoons in which he criticized Welsh expatriates in London, especially for their readiness to forsake their native language as their social status improved. The name of *Dic Siôn Dafydd, a character he created, has become synonymous with this kind of Welshman, whether in London or Wales.

A selection of the work of Jac Glan-y-gors, including a number of his lyrics, was edited by Richard Griffith (Carneddog) in the series *Cyfres y Fil* (1905); his two pamphlets were published as one volume in 1923; see also the article by Albert E. Jones (Cynan) in the *Transactions* of the Denbighshire History Society (vol. XVI) and Robin Gwyndaf, '*Traddodiad yr Hen Bennill a'r Rhigwm yn Uwchaled*', in *Allwedd y Tannau* (1976).

JONES, JOHN (1788–1858), poet. Born at Llanasa, Flints., he began work at the age of eight in a cotton-mill at Holywell. After spending some ten years in the Navy, during which he read voraciously, he returned to the mill in 1814. Six years later he went to work in a factory at Stalybridge, Ches., supplementing his meagre wages by printing his own verses and selling them in the local market. Known among his English neighbours as Poet Jones, he published a small selection of his poems, which are mostly of an edifying nature, in a volume entitled *Poems by John Jones* (1856).

JONES, JOHN (Ioan Tegid, Tegid; 1792–1852), poet and orthographer, was born and educated at Bala, Mer. Under the guidance of his mentor, Robert *William of Y Pandy, he mastered traditional Welsh prosody. On his departure for Jesus College, Oxford, in 1814, Siarl Wyn (Charles Saunderson; 1810?–32) complained in a *cywydd* that he had forgotten his native heath, but Tegid's connection with Bala was maintained and his zeal for Welsh culture never waned. Graduating in mathematics in 1818, he was ordained the following year and, having been appointed chaplain and precentor of Christ Church, Oxford, he was presented to the living of St. Thomas, where he established schools for boys and girls.

Deeply interested in the orthography of the Welsh language, Tegid became a disciple of William *Owen Pughe. In reply to John Roberts of Tremeirchion, who opposed Pughe's outlandish theories, he published *A Defence of the Reformed System of Welsh Orthography* (1829) and, in the same year, edited an edition of the New Testament for the *Society for Promoting Christian Knowledge, using his own adaptation of Pughe's orthography already defended in his pamphlet *Traethawd ar gadwedigaeth yr iaith Gymraeg* (1820). The work caused such a furore that the Old Testament was not published in the same orthography. Tegid also wrote a pamphlet entitled *Traethawd ar iawn-lythreniad neu lythyraeth yr iaith Gymraeg* (1830). The new spelling's main antagonist was William Bruce Knight (1785–1845), to whose *Remarks, historical and philological, on the Welsh language* (1830), Tegid made a vigorous response in the following year. Knight then retaliated with *A Critical review of J. Jones's Reply* (1831).

The orthography developed by Tegid was accepted by the Honourable Society of *Cymmrodorion in 1830 but preference was expressed for the use of the letter *v* in place of *f*. In 1833 the Royal Cambrian Institution asked Tegid and Gwallter Mechain (Walter *Davies) to prepare an edition of the works of *Lewys Glyn Cothi (Llywelyn y Glyn) and he immediately set about using the version copied by Owain Myfyr (Owen *Jones) in 1776 as the basis for his own copy, adapting the poems to his own spelling but substituting the *v* for *f*. Gwallter Mechain provided most of the annotations to the work and Tegid copied the text, changing some words which he found incomprehensible to his own idiosyncratic versions. In 1841 his desire to return to Wales was realized when he was given the living of Nanhyfer (Nevern), Pembs., and there he spent the rest of his days. He was one of the translators of the Report of the Commission on Education in Wales (see under BLUE BOOKS), which was published in Welsh in 1848.

A collection of Tegid's poetry, together with a biography by his nephew, Henry Roberts, was published in the volume *Gwaith Barddonawl* (1859); see also the G. J. Williams Memorial Lecture published by E. D. Jones in 1973.

Jones, John (1796–1857), preacher, was a native of Dolwyddelan, Caerns., but is usually associated with Tal-y-sarn where he worked in the Dorothea Quarry, kept a shop and was tutored by Ieuan Glan Geirionydd (Evan *Evans). Ordained in 1829, he introduced among the Calvinistic Methodists a style of preaching which was warmer-hearted and informed by a wider, more positive, ethical interest than had

been evident in that of John *Elias. In this more practical version of Calvinism he bore some relationship to the Independents of the 'New System' and to such *Baptists as were influenced by Andrew Fuller. One of the most powerful preachers ever produced in Wales, he has been revered by many, including his descendant, George M. Ll. *Davies.

The account of his life and times by Owen Thomas, *Cofiant y Parch. John Jones Talysarn* (1874), is a classic of biography, perhaps the best ever written in Welsh, which remains indispensable for students of the religious history of Wales in the early nineteenth century.

JONES, JOHN (Talhaiarn; 1810–69), poet, was born in the Harp Inn, Llanfair Talhaearn, Denbs. Apprenticed as a youth to an architect, he found work with a company of church architects in London and, in 1851, was employed by Sir Joseph Paxton as superintendent of the construction of the Crystal Palace. He became a prominent member of the *Cymreigyddion Society and its President in 1849. He returned to Wales in 1865 suffering from severe arthritis and died by his own hand in the tavern which had been his home.

As a poet, Talhaiarn was often disappointed, not least by his several failures to win the *Chair at the Eisteddfod. At Aberffraw in 1849 he seized the platform to defend his *awdl*, which had been denied the prize, thus making that eisteddfod one of the more memorable of the mid-nineteenth century. Failing yet again at Swansea in 1863, he took the view that as a Churchman he was being victimized by Nonconformist adjudicators. No one enjoyed the thought of being victimized as much as he. Furthermore, in the debate between exponents of the free and strict metres, Talhaiarn was the strident champion of the latter. Yet the public much preferred his lyrics and the words he composed to traditional tunes and fashionable melodies to his verse in *cynghanedd. In constant demand as the author of singable words for concert purposes, he liked to describe himself as 'the favourite writer of songs for the Welsh people'. The subjects which mattered most to him were Wine, War and Women, and he treated them in numerous songs which brought him a great deal of fame. Many were written for airs collected by John *Thomas (Pencerdd Gwalia) and for songs by Brinley *Richards and John *Owen (Owain Alaw); with the last-named he collaborated in the composition of the most popular love-song of his day, 'Mae Robin yn swil'. Talhaiarn might have written more serious poetry if only the wish to please his audience had not been so dominant.

His poems and songs were collected in *Gwaith Talhaiarn* (3 vols., 1855, 1862, 1869) and a selection edited by T. Gwynn Jones was published in 1930.

Jones, John (Shoni Sgubor Fawr; 1811–c.1858), pugilist, took his sobriquet from the name of the farm at Penderyn, near Hirwaun,

Glam., which was his home. A dissolute and violent man, at one time 'emperor' of the notorious China district of Merthyr Tydfil, he was paid for using his immense physical strength in demolishing the toll-gates attacked by *Rebecca rioters in the district of Pontyberem, but he later betrayed a number of his associates to the police. In 1843 he was found guilty of shooting at a man in a public house at Pontyberem and was transported, first to Norfolk Island and then to Van Diemen's Land where he remained until conditionally pardoned in 1858.

JONES, JOHN (**Mathetes**; 1821–78), Baptist minister and author. A native of Newcastle Emlyn, Carms., he went to work in a Dowlais colliery in 1837. He subsequently held eight pastorates, generally brief, from his ordination at Porth-y-rhyd, Carms., in 1846 until his death at Briton Ferry, Glam. Prominent in the public affairs of the *Baptists, especially during his ministry at Rhymney (1862–77), Mon., he was a prolific writer, especially to the magazine *Seren Gomer. His main works were a popular volume of sermons, Areithfa Mathetes (1873), and the well-known Geiriadur Beiblaidd a Duwinyddol (3 vols., 1846, 1849, 1883), a massive biblical and theological dictionary. He was also co-editor of two Baptist periodicals, Y *Greal (1857–59) and Yr Arweinydd (1869–70).

A memoir of Mathetes was published by D. Bowen (Myfyr Hefin) in 1921.

JONES, JOHN (**Myrddin Fardd**; 1836–1921), author and antiquary. Born at Llangïan, Caerns., he received some elementary education and practised the trade of blacksmith, eventually settling at Chwilog where most of his life was spent. A diligent researcher and copyist, he helped many scholars and won prizes for his literary work, including his valuable Enwogion Sir Gaernarfon (1922), published posthumously. He was the author of about a dozen books, amongst which were Adgof uwch Anghof (1883), Gleanings from God's Acre (1903), Cynfeirdd Lleyn (1905), Gwerin-Eiriau Sir Gaernarfon (1907) and Llên Gwerin Sir Gaernarfon (1908). As in the case of many of his contemporaries, his lack of formal education excluded him from the first rank of scholars, but his contribution to Welsh letters was considerable and towards the end of his life he received a Civil List pension in recognition of his services.

For a discussion of Myrddin Fardd's work see the chapter in Ansawdd y Seiliau (1972) by R. Gerallt Jones; see also Y Genhinen (1922).

Jones, John (**Coch Bach y Bala, Jac Llanfor**; 1854–1913), thief and gaolbird, was famous for his exploits in escaping from prison. Known in England by such names as 'The Little Welsh Terror' and 'The Little Turpin', he generally stole only objects of small value. There was

widespread sympathy for him in Wales, especially after he escaped from Ruthin prison in 1913, and public opinion turned to outrage when he was shot by the son of the squire of Euarth, Llanfair Dyffryn Clwyd, and bled to death. He was buried at Llanelidan, Denbs., and in 1963 a commemorative stone was placed on his grave by local people. There are several popular poems about Coch Bach and the story of his life has been told by Ernest Jones (1972).

JONES, JOHN (**Tydu**; 1883–1968), see under CILIE FAMILY.

JONES, JOHN ACKERMAN (1934–   ), critic and poet. Born at Maesteg, Glam., and educated at King's College, London, he was a Senior Lecturer in English at the Glamorgan College of Education, Barry, until his appointment in 1966 to a lectureship at Avery Hill College, London. His critical writings include Dylan Thomas: his Life and Work (1964), an early study of the poet which did much to establish standards in an appreciation of his work. He has also published a volume of his own poetry, The Image and the Dark (1975), and a further critical biography, Welsh Dylan (1979).

Jones, John Aelod, see WILLIAMS, JOHN ROBERTS (1914–   ).

JONES, JOHN ALUN (1908–82), see under CILIE FAMILY.

JONES, JOHN CYNDDYLAN (**Non Con Quill**; 1841–1930), theologian and biblical commentator, was born at Capel Dewi, Cards., and trained for the ministry at Bala and Trefeca. By 1867 he had become a Congregational minister at Pontypool, Mon., but later moved to London where he came under the influence of Owen *Thomas and David Charles Edwards. He returned to Wales in 1875 and settled as minister of the English Presbyterian Church in Frederick Street, Cardiff, also serving as secretary of the Bible Society in south Wales (1877–1909). His theological views, especially his attempt to introduce a form of ritual into church worship, caused dissension and he resigned the pastorate in 1888. He was Moderator of the Presbyterian Province of Wales in 1894 and Chairman of the General Assembly in 1901. Under his pen-name he contributed a series of articles to the *Western Mail in which various institutions and individuals were bitterly criticized. He also wrote The Welsh Pulpit Today (1885) and Eternal Truth in the Eternal City (n. d.), both of which attracted much attention, and numerous expository works in Welsh, including his principal work, Cysondeb y Ffydd (4 vols., 1905–16), which was considered in its day as authoritative.

JONES, JOHN GWILYM (1904–   ), dramatist, short-story writer, novelist and literary critic. Born at Groeslon, Caerns., where he still lives, he entered the University College of North Wales, Bangor, after a year as a pupil teacher. While teaching in London (1926–30), he discovered an interest in the professional theatre and was a frequent visitor to the West End. On his return to Wales he taught in Llandudno (1930–44), Pwllheli (1944–48) and Penygroes (1948–49), before being appointed producer of radio plays with the BBC in Bangor (1949–53). He then accepted a post as Lecturer in Welsh at his old College and was later appointed to a Readership, a post from which he retired in 1971.

John Gwilym Jones's first published play, Y Brodyr (1934), was unusual in that, set in a kind of limbo, it discussed its subject seriously and eschewed all attempts at being merely an amusement. His next play, Diofal yw Dim (1942), deals in a series of nine scenes with the bitterness which springs from too close an adherence to principle. In the two family plays Lle Mynno'r Gwynt a Gŵr Llonydd (1958) he discusses the crisis caused by public and private events. In rebellion against the old-fashioned, kitchen-sink dramas of Welsh theatre, John Gwilym Jones chose in these plays to present intelligent, cultured characters (without endangering for a moment their innate Welshness) who are extremely self-conscious and express their innermost feelings with no reserve.

The plays of his later period are more subtle. Y *Tad a'r Mab (1963) follows only one main theme, namely the obsessional love of a father for his son and its tragic result, but the play experiments with form and technique and makes more cunning use of irony and symbolism. For his next play the author chose what was ostensibly a historical subject, but *Hanes Rhyw Gymro (1964), the story of Morgan *Llwyd, is also contemporary in its preoccupations and interest. The volume Pedair Drama (1971) consists of short works first broadcast on radio and television. As he moved away from naturalistic drama, the success of the Brecht-like effect used in Hanes Rhyw Gymro enabled John Gwilym Jones to venture further both in technique and subject, as may be seen in his three short plays, Rhyfedd y'n Gwnaed (1976), which had a successful run in New York in 1980 in the author's English translation. The quintessence of his philosophy and skill as a dramatist is undoubtedly *Ac Eto Nid Myfi (1976) which is a masterpiece of the modern Welsh theatre. His play Yr Adduned (1979) is also an important work.

It is generally agreed that John Gwilym Jones is one of the two greatest Welsh dramatists of the twentieth century, the other being Saunders *Lewis. His work is in many respects in sharp contrast with that of Saunders Lewis, however, for its basic tenet is that feeling is stronger than reason. Man can come to terms with the restrictions of his existence only by tolerating them, rather than by trying to resist.

John Gwilym Jones has also written two novels, Y Dewis (1942) and Tri Diwrnod ac Angladd (1979), and a volume of short stories, Y *Goeden Eirin (1946). A distinguished literary critic, he left a deep impression on a generation of Bangor students by virtue of his teaching and his work in the theatre. Among his most important critical works are those on William *Williams of Pantycelyn (1969), Daniel *Owen (1970), Crefft y Llenor (1977) and Swyddogaeth Beirniadaeth (1977).

Studies of John Gwilym Jones are to be found in the volume published in his honour (ed. Gwyn Thomas, 1974); see also the essay by John Ellis Williams in Tri Dramaydd Cyfoes (1961), an interview with the writer in the magazine Mabon (ed. Gwyn Thomas, 1970) and the articles by John Rowlands, 'Agweddau ar Waith John Gwilym Jones' in Ysgrifau Beirniadol III (ed. J. E. Caerwyn Williams, 1967) and 'The Humane Existentialist' in Welsh Books and Writers (Autumn, 1980).

JONES, JOHN IDRIS (1938–   ), poet. Born at Llanrhaeadr-ym-Mochnant, Denbs., and educated at the Universities of Keele, Leeds and Cornell, he was a lecturer in the USA and at the City of Cardiff College of Education until 1973 when he became the managing director of his own publishing company, John Jones Cardiff Ltd. He returned to teaching in 1980 and is now an English master at Yale Sixth Form College, Wrexham. Three volumes of his own poetry have been published, namely Way Back to Ruthin (1966), Barry Island (1970) and Football Match and Other Events (1981).

Jones, John Pritchard (**Siôn Ceryn Bach**; d. 1927), quarryman, of Tregarth, Bethesda, Caerns., where he is still remembered for his witty sayings and *white-lie tales. One example of the latter must suffice. He was fond of relating how, in the company of the British Ambassador, he travelled to the USA and was entertained by the President to a meal of thirteen courses at a table so big that he had to use a telescope in order to converse with those who sat opposite him. Heavily embroidered, his tales are typical of the surrealist humour of the quarrying districts and are much admired by aficionados of the genre.

JONES, JOHN PULESTON (1862–1925), essayist, was born at Llanbedr Dyffryn Clwyd, Denbs. Blinded in an accident at the age of eighteen months, he was taught by his mother to fend for himself in all matters. Educated at the Universities of Glasgow and Oxford, he was among the founders of *Cymdeithas Dafydd ap Gwilym in 1886 and became an exponent of the orthographical standards of John *Morris-Jones. He was ordained a Calvinistic Methodist minister in 1888. His sermons were published in the volume Gair y Deyrnas (1924) and his essays in Ysgrifau Puleston (1926). Among the achievements for which he is remembered is a Braille system for the Welsh language, devised by him and still in use today.

For further details see the biography of John Puleston Jones by R. W. Jones (1930).

JONES, JOHN RICHARD (1765–1822), Baptist minister and writer. A native of Llanuwchllyn, Mer., and originally a member of *Yr Hen Gapel*, the Independent chapel there, he joined the *Baptists in 1788 and was ordained minister of Ramoth, Llanfrothen, with which place he is usually associated. During the next ten years he became one of the foremost preachers and leaders of his denomination, but towards the end of 1798, under the influence of Archibald McLean, the Scotsman who emphasized the intellectual side of faith and the simple rites of the Apostolic Church, he left the Particular (or to use his word, the Popular) Baptists and formed a new connexion known as the Scotch Baptists, which still survives in some parts of north Wales. As a result of this division, the Baptist cause in north Wales was permanently impaired. J. R. Jones is also remembered as a scholar, hymn-writer, musician, poet and the teacher of poets. Among his pupils was Robert ap Gwilym Ddu (Robert *Williams), while Robert *Thomas (Ap Vychan) eulogized him as 'the greatest man ever nurtured in Merioneth'.

Biographies of J. R. Jones were written by David Davies (1911), David Williams (1913) and J. I. Jones (1966).

JONES, JOHN RICHARD (1923–   ), poet, was a farmer at Tal-y-bont, Cards., before joining the staff of the *Welsh Books Council in 1967. He has published three volumes of poetry, *Rhwng Cyrn yr Arad* (1962), *Cerddi J. R.* (1970) and *Cerddi Cwm Eleri* (1980), and is a well-known adjudicator and elocutionist.

JONES, JOHN ROBERT (1911–70), philosopher. Born at Pwllheli, Caerns., and educated at the University College of Wales, Aberystwyth, and Balliol College, Oxford, he was a Lecturer in Philosophy at Aberystwyth from 1938 to 1952, when he was appointed to the Chair of Philosophy at University College, Swansea.

His main philosophical interests were the nature of the self and other selves, the nature of religious belief and the nature of a nation. Besides numerous contributions to journals of philosophy, he published four books: an examination of the concept of Britishness in *Prydeindod* (1966), a study of the sociological implications of the Welsh language, *A Raid i'r Iaith ein Gwahanu?* (1967), *Gwaedd yng Nghymru* (1970), and a collection of essays and sermons on the crisis of Wales in the twentieth century, *Ac Onide* (1970), his most substantial work. His Presidential Address to the Aristotelian Society was published in that body's *Proceedings* for 1967. Other papers by J. R. Jones will be found in the journals *Diwinyddiaeth* (vol. XX, 1969), *Philosophy* (April, 1950), and in the symposia,

Saith Ysgrif ar Grefydd (ed. D. Z. Phillips, 1967) and *Religion and Understanding* (ed. D. Z. Phillips, 1967).

After his move to Swansea in 1952, the earlier empiricism of J. R. Jones was modified by the influence of Ludwig Wittgenstein mediated through personal contact with a colleague, Rush Rhees, who taught at the College from 1940 to 1966. This modification made possible a close interaction between J. R. Jones's views in philosophical psychology, the philosophy of religion and political philosophy, and he began to see the identity of the individual in relation to the community. In the case of Wales the community was, for J. R. Jones, the Welsh cultural heritage and essentially the Welsh language. His writings on the subjects of Welsh nationhood and Welsh nationality, especially concerning what he described as 'cydymdreiddiad tir ac iaith' ('the interpenetration of land and language'), made a major contribution to the perception of what is involved in the contemplation of a people's identity and they continue to exercise a powerful influence on the Welsh Nationalist movement, particularly *Cymdeithas yr Iaith Gymraeg and *Plaid Cymru.

There are tributes to J. R. Jones by D. Z. Phillips in *Y Traethodydd* (1970) and by Richard I. Aaron and Pennar Davies in *Efrydiau Athronyddol* (1971). For a discussion of his philosophy see the articles by Saunders Lewis on *Ac Onide* in *Ysgrifau Beirniadol VI* (ed. J. E. Caerwyn Williams, 1971) and *Efrydiau Athronyddol* (1972).

JONES, JOHN TUDOR (John Eilian; 1904–85), poet and editor, was born at Llaneilian, Ang., and educated at the University College of Wales, Aberystwyth, and Jesus College, Oxford. A former journalist on the staff of the *Western Mail, the *Daily Mail*, the *Daily Express* and the BBC, for which he worked in Iraq and Ceylon, he was the first editor of *Y *Cymro* and ended his career as chief editor of the *Herald* newspapers in Caernarfon. He founded the magazine *Y *Ford Gron* in 1930 and edited the series known as *Llyfrau'r Ford Gron*. With E. Prosser *Rhys, he published a volume of poetry, *Gwaed Ifanc* (1923), and went on to win the *Chair and *Crown at the National Eisteddfod in 1941 and 1949 respectively.

JONES, JOHN WILLIAM (Andronicus; 1842–95), essayist, was born at Bala, Mer., and worked as a shop assistant in Manchester until 1884. He is remembered as the author of *Adgofion Andronicus* (1894), a volume of essays which are among the most entertaining of their period. A further selection was published posthumously under the title *Yn y Trên* (1895).

JONES, JONAH (1919–   ), sculptor and novelist, was born in Durham, of Welsh descent on his father's side. After war service with a field ambulance unit in Europe and the Middle East, he joined John Petts and Brenda *Chamberlain at the Caseg Press in 1947 and later settled with his wife, Judith *Maro, near Porthmadog, Caerns., working as a sculptor. From 1974 to 1978 he was Director of the National College of Art and Design in Dublin, but kept his home in Wales. The first in his trilogy of novels about relations between Britain and Ireland from 1916 to the present day has been published under the title *A Tree May Fall* (1980). He has also written a guide-book, *The Lakes of North Wales* (1983).

There is an autobiographical essay by Jonah Jones in *Artists in Wales* (ed. Meic Stephens, 1973).

Jones, Kilsby, see JONES, JAMES RHYS (1813–89).

JONES, LEWIS (1836–1904), pioneer and writer. A native of Caernarfon, he was by trade a printer. With Love Jones-Parry, he went to survey *Patagonia in 1862 and returned with a report which encouraged the emigration of Welsh settlers but which proved, in its too favourable description of conditions there, to be misleading. The only Welshman to be appointed Governor of the Welsh colony, he was imprisoned by the Argentinian authorities for upholding the rights of his compatriots. The town of Trelew was named in his honour. He founded two newspapers to serve the colony, *Ein Breiniad* (1878) and *Y *Drafod* (1891), and published a history of the settlement, *Y Wladfa Gymreig* (1898). One of his daughters was the writer Eluned *Morgan.

JONES, LEWIS (1897–1939), political activist and novelist. Born in Clydach Vale, Rhondda, he was orphaned early in life and brought up by his grandmother. At the age of twelve he went to work underground in the Cambrian Colliery and was married four years later. He joined the Communist Party while at the Central Labour College, London (1923–25), and during the *General Strike of 1926 he spoke publicly on behalf of the *Rhondda miners, having been elected chairman of the Cambrian Lodge in 1918. On the miners' return to work after the strike he was removed—like many other militants—from his job as checkweighman for refusing to work with blackleg labour. He then became an organizer for the National Unemployed Workers' Movement, leading contingents from south Wales in the *hunger marches to London in 1932, 1934 and 1936, and arranging many demonstrations against the Means Test which culminated in the mass movement of 1935. Elected a member of the Welsh Committee of the Communist Party in 1931, he was one of two Communist members of Glamorgan County Council for the last three years of his life. A fiery orator who was imprisoned for his allegedly seditious speeches, he commanded a strong personal following among miners and other industrial workers. He

played a prominent part in the campaign in Wales in favour of the Spanish Republic and died of a heart-attack after addressing some thirty street-meetings in the week that Barcelona fell.

Like others in south Wales during the inter-war years, Lewis Jones was influenced in his thinking by the quasi-syndicalism of *The Miners' Next Step* (1912) but the central fact of his volatile personality, whether expressed in his stormy political career or in his passionate writing, was the *Marxism which he embraced so wholeheartedly. He was remarkable not least because, during a brief, difficult and busy life, he wrote two novels about the mining valleys of south Wales which, flawed though they may be from a strictly literary point of view, were highly authentic and are extremely powerful still. They are *Cwmardy* (1937) and its sequel, *We Live* (1939).

There is an essay by David Smith on Lewis Jones's life and work in the *Writers of Wales* series (1982); see also the article by John Pikoulis in *The Anglo-Welsh Review* (no. 74, 1983).

Jones, Lewis Davies (**Llew Tegid**; 1851–1928), conductor, born near Bala, Mer., was a well-known *eisteddfodwr* in the years between 1902 and 1925, leading audiences with wit and charm. With J. Lloyd Williams, he collected traditional tunes and verses on behalf of the Welsh Folk Song Society and wrote words to many of the airs which were discovered.

Jones, Margam, see JONES, WILLIAM MORGAN (1864–1945).

Jones, Mary (1784–1872), a weaver's daughter of Ty'n-y-ddol, Llanfihangel-y-Pennant, near Abergynolwyn, Mer. As a girl of sixteen in 1800, having learned to read and after saving the sum of three shillings and sixpence over a period of six years, she walked barefoot to Bala, a distance of some twenty-five miles across the mountains, in order to buy a Welsh Bible from Thomas *Charles. Her name became synonymous with the desire among the common people for literary and religious knowledge, and it is believed that her zeal was in Thomas Charles's mind when, five years later, he took part in discussions which resulted in the creation of the British and Foreign Bible Society.

Jones, Michael Daniel (1822–98), minister and patriot, was born at Llanuwchllyn, Mer., the son of the minister who founded and became first Principal of the Independent College at Bala in 1841. Educated at Carmarthen Presbyterian College and Highbury College, London, he went to America in 1847 and was ordained at Cincinnati, where he founded the Brython Association, the immediate object of which was to help Welsh immigrants and out of which there grew his idea of establishing a politically independent second homeland for the Welsh people in north America. His proposal, first outlined in Welsh-American periodicals, was for a society where farmers would own their own land and workers the means of production on a co-operative basis, but Jones later abandoned the notion in favour of locating the homeland in *Patagonia. He had realized that the USA was a melting-pot for the nationalities of its immigrants in which the English language would inevitably be predominant.

On his return to Wales Michael D. Jones succeeded his father as Principal at Bala but his tenure of that post was marred by a quarrel known as 'the Battle of the Two Constitutions'. Jones insisted that the government of the College should be in the hands of its subscribers while others, led by John Thomas of Liverpool, believed it should belong to representatives appointed by the churches in the counties of Wales. The controversy spread throughout Wales and took a more bitter turn when Jones began to play a prominent part in the move to establish a Welsh colony in Patagonia. The appeal of Patagonia for Michael D. Jones was that it was an uncharted region far from any English influence. Of the new Wales beyond the sea he wrote: 'There will be chapel, school and Parliament and the old language will be the medium of worship, of trade, of science, of education and of government. A strong and self-reliant nation will grow in a Welsh homeland'. He contributed a good deal of money to the Patagonian enterprise and was obliged to sell his house to the College authorities who, soon after accepting the New Constitution of his opponents, sacked him. The two sides were eventually reconciled and he was allowed to remain on the College's staff, but he resigned in 1892 in order to facilitate the creation of a new institution to be known as the Bala-Bangor Theological College.

With Emrys ap Iwan (Robert Ambrose *Jones), Michael D. Jones is generally considered to be the father of modern Welsh *Nationalism and it was certainly he who was the first in modern times to offer the Welsh a rational political solution to the question of how best to maintain their identity, whatever the fate of the Patagonian adventure subsequently proved to be. He wrote extensively to the Welsh press on social topics, reserving his most scathing remarks for landlordism and 'the English cause' which encouraged Welsh-speakers to worship in English, and preaching openly on national freedom. Among those who came under his influence were T. E. *Ellis, David *Lloyd George and Owen M. *Edwards; the last-named claimed to have first learned from him about the history and literature of Wales.

The biography of Michael D. Jones was written by E. Pan Jones (1903); see also D. Gwenallt Jones, 'Hanes mudiadau Cymraeg a chenedlaethol y bedwaredd ganrif ar bymtheg' in Seiliau Hanesyddol Cenedlaetholdeb Cymru

(1950) and the same author's contribution to Triwyr Penllyn (ed. Gwynedd Pierce, 1956). The contribution of Michael D. Jones to the movement for the establishment of a Welsh homeland in Patagonia is discussed by R. Bryn Williams in Y Wladfa (1962) and by Alun Davies in the Transactions of the Honourable Society of Cymmrodorion (1966).

JONES, MORUS (Morus Cyfannedd; 1895–1982), poet, born at Blaenau Ffestiniog, Mer., was a farmer for most of his life. He published two volumes of verse, Dros Gors a Gwaun (1969) and the ninth volume in the series Beirdd Bro (1978).

JONES, MOSES GLYN (1913–   ), poet, was born near Mynytho, Caerns. Educated at the University College of North Wales, Bangor, he was a teacher at schools in his native county. He has published three volumes of poetry, namely Y Ffynnon Fyw (1973), Mae'n Ddigon Buan (1977) and Y Sioe (1984). With his awdl, 'Y Dewin', he won the *Chair at the National Eisteddfod in 1974.

JONES, NATHANIEL CYNHAFAL (1832–1905), poet and editor. Born in the parish of Llangynhafal, Denbs., he worked in his youth as a tailor in Angel Jones's workshop in Mold, where he was Daniel *Owen's companion, and began to preach in 1859 with the Calvinistic Methodists. He published five volumes of verse, Fy Awenydd (1859), Elias y Thesbiad (1869), Y Messiah (1895), Y Bibl (1895) and Charles o'r Bala (1898). With Richard Mills, he was co-author of Buchdraeth John Mills (1881). But his chief contribution to Welsh letters was the editing of the works of William *Williams of Pantycelyn (2 vols., 1887, 1897).

JONES, NESTA WYN (1946–   ), poet, was born at Dolgellau, Mer., and educated at the University College of North Wales, Bangor. She has been employed by the Welsh Theatre Company, the Schools Council and the *Welsh Books Council but since 1980 she has worked on her family's farm at Abergeirw, near Dolgellau. Her two volumes of poetry are Cannwyll yn Olau (1969) and Ffenest Ddu (1973); she has also published a travel journal, Dyddiadur Israel (1982).

Jones, Owen (Owain Myfyr; 1741–1814), patron, was born at Llanfihangel Glyn Myfyr, Denbs. As a youth he went to London and took up the skinner's trade, becoming by the age of forty the proprietor of his own business and a wealthy man. His interest in the literature of Wales was encouraged by Richard *Morris and other Welsh expatriates. He joined the Honourable Society of *Cymmrodorion and, with Robert Hughes (Robin Ddu o Fôn), founded the *Gwyneddigion Society in 1770, serving as its benefactor for more than twenty years.

In 1789, with William *Owen Pughe, Owain Myfyr edited and paid for the cost of printing the works of *Dafydd ap Gwilym, intending to publish in due course a series of books based on the old manuscripts. The first and second volumes of *The Myvyrian Archaiology of Wales* appeared in 1801 and the third in 1807. These books were of the greatest value for they included selections from the poetry of the *Cynfeirdd and the *Gogynfeirdd, as well as the *Bruts*, but the second and third volumes contained many forgeries by Iolo Morganwg (Edward *Williams). The grandiose scheme was to have included the publication of The *Mabinogion, the Romances and classics from the sixteenth and seventeenth centuries but, as a result of financial losses incurred by Owain Myfyr's business and Owen Pughe's return to Wales, the series ended with the third volume.

For further details see W. D. Leathart, *The Origin and Progress of the Gwyneddigion Society* (1831), the articles by G. J. Williams in *Y Llenor* (vol. I, 1923) and the *Journal of the Welsh Bibliographical Society* (vol. X, 1966), and R. T. Jenkins and Helen Ramage, *A History of the Honourable Society of Cymmrodorion* (1951).

JONES, OWEN (Meudwy Môn; 1806–89), editor and historian. A native of Llanfihangel Ysgeifiog, Ang., he received some elementary education, was ordained a Calvinistic Methodist minister in 1842 and worked tirelessly in the cause of *Temperance and the Bible Society. His most important literary work was the editing of two volumes, *Cymru, yn Hanesyddol, Parthedegol a Bywgraphyddol* (1875) and *Ceinion Llenyddiaeth Gymreig* (1876), which were devoted to the history and literature of Wales respectively.

Jones, Owen Glynne (1867–99), pioneer of rock-climbing. Born in London of Welsh parents, he later made his home with relatives at Barmouth, Mer., and first took to the rocks, alone, on *Cadair Idris in 1888. His *Rock-Climbing in the English Lake District* (1897) was the first work to grade climbs and to popularize climbing, while much of the Abraham brothers' *Rock-Climbing in North Wales* (1906) was based on his notes. He was killed on the Dent Blanche in the Swiss Alps and was buried at Evolène.

JONES, OWEN WYNNE (Glasynys; 1828–70), antiquary, novelist and poet, was born at Rhostryfan, Caerns. He began work at the age of ten in the local quarry, but later became a teacher at Church of England schools in Clynnog, Llanfachreth and Beddgelert. Ordained deacon in 1860, he served as a curate at Llangristiolus and Llanfaethlu, Ang., and at Pontlotyn, Glam. He found his material, especially for such historical novels as *Dafydd Llwyd neu Ddyddiau Cromwel* (1854), in the pre-Methodist traditions of Wales. Among his collections of verse are the volumes *Fy Oriau Hamddenol* (1854), *Lleucu Llwyd* (1858) and *Yr Wyddfa* (c.1877). He excelled in the depic-

tion of Welsh rural life and in writing versions of ghost stories and fairy-tales, some of which first appeared in periodicals under the pseudonym Salmon Llwyd. A selection of his verse appeared in 1898 and some of his stories, edited by Saunders *Lewis, were published under the title *Straeon Glasynys* (1943).

For a discussion of his work see the essay by Kate Roberts in *Gwŷr Llên y Bedwaredd Ganrif ar Bymtheg* (ed. Dyfnallt Morgan, 1968), and an article by the same writer in *Ysgrifau Beirniadol II* (ed. J. E. Caerwyn Williams, 1966).

JONES, PETER (Pedr Fardd; 1775–1845), hymn-writer and poet, was born in the parish of Garn Dolbenmaen, Caerns., and spent most of his life in Liverpool. By trade a tailor, he also worked as a schoolmaster and shopkeeper, and became prominent with the Calvinistic Methodists. One of the last great hymn-writers of the Methodist revival, he published several collections, including *Hymnau Newyddion* (1825) and *Crynoad o Hymnau* (1830). Among his best-known hymns are 'Cysegrwn flaenffrwyth ddyddiau'n hoes', 'Cyn llunio'r byd, cyn lledu'r nefoedd wen' and 'Mae'r iachawdwriaeth rad'. He was also a master of *cynghanedd, as is demonstrated in the volume *Mêl Awen* (1823).

Jones, Philip (1618–74), Puritan administrator and soldier, was born in the hamlet of Clase in Llangyfelach, Glam. Appointed Governor of Swansea by Parliament in 1645 and a colonel from 1646, he fought in the battle of St. Fagan's (1648). His meeting with Oliver Cromwell was decisive for his career. The Member of Parliament for Breconshire from 1650, he was the leading Welshman in London and for nine years the virtual ruler of south Wales. In 1653 he became a member of the Council of State and in 1657 Comptroller of the Household, a post in which he was responsible for the arrangements for Cromwell's funeral. His enemies sought to impeach him in 1659 as 'an oppressor of his countrey' but the restored Rump Parliament referred the charges to a largely Republican committee. The Restoration intervened and Jones's escape from all punishment was probably due to the leniency with which he had treated Royalists in Wales. He lived out his life at Fonmon Castle in Glamorgan, which he had bought during the Interregnum.

For further details see the article by A. G. Veysey in the *Transactions* of the Honourable Society of Cymmrodorion (1966).

Jones, Philip (1855–1945), one of the most famous Welsh preachers of modern times, was a Calvinistic Methodist who inherited the tradition adorned by Edward *Matthews of Ewenni. Born at Tai-bach, Glam., he was educated at Trefeca and ordained at Aberystwyth in 1887. His fame reached its height during the years of his retirement at Porthcawl: his delicious

Glamorgan dialect, his agile word-play, his charm and wit and ease of utterance, his gift for telling a story often with an unexpected conclusion or application, and his not entirely innocent exploitation of his oddities of appearance and manner, won him a rare popularity among the many who did not look for spiritual rapture or moral challenge.

JONES, REES (Amnon; 1797–1844), poet. Born at Talgarreg, Cards., he was briefly a pupil in the school of David *Davis of Castellhywel before being obliged by his family's poverty to earn a living on the land. His only volume of verse, Crwth Dyffryn Clettwr (1848), published posthumously, gathered together many of his poems which have remained popular to the present day.

JONES, RHIANNON DAVIES (1921–), novelist, was born at Llanbedr, Mer., and educated at the University College of North Wales, Bangor. A teacher of Welsh at Llandudno and Ruthin before her appointment to a lectureship at the Caerleon College of Education, she later became a Senior Lecturer at the Normal College, Bangor. She first came to prominence as a writer by winning the *Prose Medal at the National Eisteddfod with a novel, Fy Hen Lyfr Cownt (1961), which is cast in the form of a diary kept by Ann *Griffiths, the hymn-writer, and she repeated this feat four years later with another novel, Lleian Llanllŷr (1965), set in the thirteenth century. Her later novels also have historical themes: Llys Aberffraw (1977) is set in the time of Owain Gwynedd (*Owain ap Gruffudd) and Eryr Pengwern (1981) in the *Powys of the seventh century, but both have relevance to contemporary Wales. A fifth novel, Dyddiadur Mari Gwyn (1985), deals with the life and times of the Catholic martyr Robert *Gwyn of Penyberth. The prose-style and authenticity of these books have won for Rhiannon Davies Jones an assured place among Welsh historical novelists. She has also published short stories and a collection of original rhymes for children (1971).

The novelist discussed the influences on her writing in Ysgrifau Beirniadol III (ed. J. E. Caerwyn Williams, 1967).

JONES, RHYDDERCH (1935–), dramatist, was born at Aberllefenni, Mer., and educated at the Normal College, Bangor. After a period as a teacher at schools in London and Wales, he joined BBC Wales in 1965 and became a television producer in the Light Entertainment Department in 1973. The producer and co-writer of the comedy series Fo a Fe, he has published a play, Roedd Catarina o Gwmpas Ddoe (1974), a collection of plays for stage, radio and television entitled Mewn Tri Chyfrwng (1979), and Cofiant Ryan (1979), a biography of Ryan *Davies, the entertainer who was his friend.

JONES, RHYS or RICE (1718–1801), poet and editor, of Y Blaenau, Llanfachreth, Mer., was educated for a legal career at Dolgellau and Shrewsbury but, on the death of his father in 1736, he returned home and spent the rest of his life in comfortable circumstances. He is remembered chiefly as the editor of the anthology *Gorchestion Beirdd Cymru (1773), but he was also a poet in his own right. He was steeped in the poetry of the cywyddwyr and most of his poems are in that tradition, on similar themes, and full of wit and bonhomie. His work was collected by his grandson, Rice Jones Owen, and published under the title Gwaith Prydyddawl (1818).

For further details see the article by David Jenkins in the Journal of the Merionethshire History and Records Society (vol. I, 1951).

JONES, RICHARD (Cymro Gwyllt; 1772–1833), hymn-writer, was born at Llanystumdwy, Caerns., but later lived at Y Wern, Llanfrothen, Mer., with which place he is usually associated. Ordained by the Calvinistic Methodists in 1816, he became one of the disciples of David *Thomas (Dafydd Ddu Eryri) and contributed much to the periodical press. He was involved in the theological disputes of his time and his Drych y Dadleuwr (1829) caused a great commotion. John *Elias collected many of his hymns under the title Hymnau a Chaniadau Ysgrythyrol a Duwiol (1836).

JONES, RICHARD (1926–), novelist. Born at Rhydyfelin, near Aberystwyth, Cards., he was educated at the University College of Wales in that town. Formerly a journalist, working with the South Wales Echo, Reuters and the BBC Overseas Service in London, he was appointed to a lectureship at the University of Virginia in 1973. He has published four novels: The Age of Wonder (1967), which is set in mid-Wales during the Edwardian era, The Toy Crusaders (1968), A Way Out (1969) and The Tower is Everywhere (1971), the last of which also has a Welsh setting. All are accomplished social novels, but the second—which deals with the loss of British cultural self-confidence—is perhaps the most brilliant.

JONES, RICHARD GOODMAN (Dic Goodman; 1920–), poet, a native of Mynytho, Caerns., was a teacher at Botwnnog until his retirement in 1985. A poet of ready wit, he has published a collection of poems for children, Caneuon y Gwynt a'r Glaw (1975), and a volume of poems I'r Rhai sy'n Gweld Rhosyn Gwyllt (1979), which includes some of his best englynion.

JONES, RICHARD LEWIS (Dic Jones; 1934–), poet. Born at Tre'r-ddôl, Cards., he farms Yr Hendre, Blaenannerch. He learned the craft of prosody from Alun Jeremiah *Jones

(Alun Cilie) and it was in his home that the young poet's talent was nurtured. After winning the Chair five times at the Eisteddfod of *Urdd Gobaith Cymru, he published his first volume of poetry, Agor Grwn, in 1960. At the National Eisteddfod of 1966 he won the *Chair with a poem, included in his second volume, Caneuon Cynhaeaf (1969), which is generally considered to be among the most accomplished awdlau written in the twentieth century. The awdl which he submitted to the National Eisteddfod of 1976 was judged the best but it was disqualified because it infringed the competition's rules; Alan *Llwyd was awarded the Chair on that occasion, there was controversy in the press and opposing camps emerged. Since then Dic Jones has published a third volume, Storom Awst (1978). A traditional poet, he celebrates his own rural community, the earth's bounty, nature and the seasons, in poems which are masterly in their craftsmanship and suffused with wit and a lyrical delight. See also BARDD GWLAD.

For further details see the review of Storom Awst by Gwynn ap Gwilym in Barddas (no. 23, 1978), the articles by Bobi Jones in Barn (nos. 40 and 41, 1966) and the note by John Rowlands in Profiles (1980).

Jones, Richard Robert (Dic Aberdaron; 1780–1843), polyglot, was a native of Aberdaron, Caerns., where his father was a carpenter. Unschooled, he taught himself Latin at the age of twelve and, during a life of wandering in which he became known for his outlandish appearance and eccentric habits, he developed his extraordinary talent for learning foreign languages, both ancient and modern. With a cat at his side and a ram's horn slung around his neck, he travelled the length and breadth of Wales and was reputed to be able to summon and command devils. He seemed, however, to have no interest in literature, reading the many books which he always carried about his person with little appreciation of their contents. T. H. *Parry-Williams described him in a poem as 'ffŵl gydag ieithoedd' ('a fool with languages'), but concluded, 'Chwarae teg i Dic—nid yw pawb yn gwirioni'r un fath' ('Fair play to Dic—not everyone goes barmy in the same way').

Jones, Robert, see GWYN, ROBERT (c.1540/50–1592/1604).

Jones, Robert (1560–1615), Jesuit scholar and for six years Superior of the Jesuits on the English Mission, was born near Chirk, Flints. Possibly a pupil of the martyr Richard *Gwyn, he entered the English College at Rome in 1582 when the Welsh dissentients there were still active. The only important Welsh Catholic of his time who became a member of the *Society of Jesus, and a distinguished scholar, he was Professor of Philosophy at the Roman College from 1590 until sent on missions to Britain in 1595. Resident at Llantarnam, Mon., and described in

1605 as 'the Fyerbrande of all', he established at The Cwm, Llanrothal, a massing-place which may be suspected of having become in his lifetime the nucleus of the Jesuit College of St. Francis Xavier. The majority of Welsh secular clergy, however, remained hostile to his propaganda, which in 1610 even went as far as to assert that the martyr Roger Cadwaladr (1568–1610) had made his peace with the Jesuits. Despite Jones's efforts, the *Counter-Reformation failed in Wales: Welsh Catholics continued to mistrust Jesuit fanaticism and its willingness to overturn the monarchy at the Pope's behest.

JONES, ROBERT (1745–1829), Calvinistic Methodist exhorter and author. Born at Suntur, Llanystumdwy, Caerns., he was taught to read by a devout mother and attended one of the circulating schools of Griffith *Jones. He is usually associated with Rhos-lan where he lived for some years, having gathered a *Methodist society around him. Among his publications are Ymddiffyn Crist'nogol (1770; 2nd edn. 1776, under the title Lleferydd yr Asyn), a sarcastic description of an attempt by the local vicar to disrupt a Methodist open-air meeting; Drych i'r Anllythyrennog (1788), a spelling primer for Sunday Schools; Grawnsyppiau Canaan (1795), the first hymn-book used by Methodists in north Wales; his most controversial work, Achos Pwysig yn cael ei Ddadleu (c.1799), a translation of a pamphlet by Sir Richard Hill; Llwybr hyffordd i'r anllythrenog i ddysgu darllen Cymraeg (1805); and his masterpiece, *Drych yr Amseroedd (1820). Jones also assisted Thomas *Charles in producing the 1807 edition of the Welsh Bible and had a part in persuading Charles to remain in Wales in 1784.

JONES, ROBERT (1806–96), Baptist minister and author, of Llanllyfni, Caerns., was brought up with the *Methodists, but joined the *Baptists in 1831 and became a keen opponent of infant baptism. Among his books on religious topics, some were controversial works on baptism and *Roman Catholicism; his Gemau Duwinyddol (1865) was particularly popular. He also published Casgliad o Hymnau ar Destynau Efengylaidd (1851), a collection of about a thousand hymns, many of which were his own and of which a few, such as 'O cenwch fawl i'r Arglwydd', are to be found in contemporary hymn-books.

JONES, ROBERT (1810–79), clergyman and editor, a native of Llanfyllin, Mont., was educated at Oswestry Grammar School and at Jesus College, Oxford. While curate of Barmouth (1840–42) he published a volume of psalms and hymns in Welsh, but then moved to a living at Rotherhithe in London. He edited a reprint (1864) of *Flores Poetarum Britannicorum (the work of John *Davies of Mallwyd), two volumes of the poetry and correspondence of

Goronwy *Owen, together with a biography (1876), and the poems of *Iolo Goch (1877). A zealous supporter of the *National Eisteddfod and of the University College of Wales, Aberystwyth, he was from 1876 the editor of the magazine, Y Cymmrodor.

JONES, ROBERT AMBROSE (Emrys ap Iwan; 1851–1906), literary critic and writer on religious and political subjects, was born at Abergele, Denbs. Like his father, he worked as a gardener at Bodelwyddan, and then spent a year in Liverpool as a shop assistant. Later he entered the Calvinistic Methodist Theological College at Bala. In the knowledge that his great-grandmother had been a Frenchwoman, he took pride in his French ancestry and his European interests. A German living near his home had taught him the elements of French and German, and in 1874 Jones went to teach English at a private school near Lausanne in Switzerland. On his return to Wales he began to contribute to Y *Gwyddoniadur Cymreig and to Thomas *Gee's newspaper, *Baner ac Amserau Cymru.

He was very forthright in the expression of his opinions and his caustic criticism of 'the English cause'—the increasing tendency within his own denomination, the Calvinistic Methodists, to establish English-language chapels in order to please immigrants into Welsh-speaking districts—brought forth the venom of such eminent men as Lewis *Edwards. Emrys ap Iwan argued that there was plenty of missionary work to be done among the Welsh-speaking Welsh without expending energy on English immigrants and he was generally opposed to what he called 'English fever'. Although the majority of the Welsh people spoke Welsh, Lewis Edwards was more typical of attitudes prevailing at the time when he maintained that there was no future for the language. Emrys ap Iwan's candidature for ordination was dismissed at the association held in Llanidloes in 1881, but he was accepted two years later at Mold and served as a minister in Ruthin, Trefnant and Rhewl for the rest of his life.

The method used by Emrys ap Iwan for the propagation of his ideas was that of the pamphleteer and the influence of Pascal and Paul-Louis Courier on his thinking was abundantly clear. He satirized, in particular, those Welsh people who feigned English manners and speech and he attempted to restore self-respect among the Welsh-speaking Welsh. At a time when Britain's imperial expansion was at its zenith, it was no easy task to convince the Welsh that they could remain faithful to their cultural heritage. But Emrys ap Iwan preached uncompromising *Nationalism, despite the fact that he had no political ambitions of his own. It was he who coined the word 'ymreolaeth' (a synonym for 'hunan-lywodraeth', 'self-government') and he argued passionately in favour of *Home Rule for

Wales within a federal system on the Swiss model. He was not a practical politician but an ideologist who argued on the grounds of principle. In his writings on language and style there is a classicist's bias, particularly in his plea for form and purity in prose, and in his dislike of ostentation and foreign idiom.

Despite this emphasis, he did not neglect the aesthetic qualities of literature. He published only two books in his lifetime, namely Camrau mewn Gramadeg Cymraeg (1881) and an edition of Ellis *Wynne's Gweledigaetheu y Bardd Cwsc (1898). But his own creative gifts enabled him to devise imaginary situations, as in his famous *Breuddwyd Pabydd wrth ei Ewyllys (1931), which takes the form of a lecture delivered in the year 2012 when Wales has returned to 'the old faith' of Roman Catholicism. His sermons, published in 1927, and his *Homiliau (1906, 1909), have claims to be considered as literary masterpieces. A regular contributor to the Welsh-language press between 1876 and 1903, he used Y Faner and Y *Geninen as his main platforms. Although he is not regarded as a creative writer in the strict sense of that term, and although he went against the ethos of his age in his ideology, he had a widespread influence on later generations. T. Gwynn *Jones's biography of Emrys ap Iwan (1912) did much to enhance his reputation.

For further details see the selection of Emrys ap Iwan's articles and letters made by D. Myrddin Lloyd (3 vols., 1937, 1939, 1940), the essay by Saunders Lewis in Meistri'r Canrifoedd (ed. R. Geraint Gruffydd, 1973), the chapter by Alun Llywelyn-Williams in Y Traddodiad Rhyddiaith yn yr Ugeinfed Ganrif (ed. Geraint Bowen, 1976), the essay by D. Myrddin Lloyd in the Writers of Wales series (1979), the lecture by Enid Morgan, Emrys ap Iwan, Garddwr Geiriau (1980), and the lectures by Ellis Wynne Williams and Gwynfor Evans published by Cymdeithas Emrys ap Iwan in 1983.

JONES, ROBERT GERALLT (1934–), poet, novelist and critic. Born and brought up in Llŷn, Caerns., the son of an Anglican clergyman, he was educated at public schools in England and at the University College of North Wales, Bangor, where he read English. While still a student, he launched and co-edited with Bedwyr Lewis *Jones a literary magazine, Yr *Arloeswr. He has since been an English teacher, a lecturer in Education, the Principal of a new College of Education in Jamaica, the Warden of Llandovery College and a full-time writer. Appointed Senior Tutor in the Department of Extra-Mural Studies at the University College of Wales, Aberystwyth, in 1979, he has written and produced programmes for radio and television, some of which, such as the English journal, Bardsey (1976), and the travel series Pererindota (1979), were subsequently published in book form.

One of the most prolific of contemporary Welsh writers, R. Gerallt Jones has written in a variety of genres from the outset. As a poet, he writes meditative verse from the standpoint of a questioning Christian. His first two collections, *Ymysg y Drain* (1959) and *Cwlwm* (1962), contain lyrical poems on personal themes, but the later verse in *Cysgodion* (1972) and *Dyfal Gerddwyr y Maes* (1981) is more spare and more complex in its social comment. Among the few Welsh poets who also write in English, he has published a sequence of poems entitled *Jamaican Landscape* (1969), one of three books reflecting his experience of the Caribbean islands, as well as a substantial volume of translations, *Poetry of Wales 1930–70* (1974).

He is the author of five novels, all of which deal with contemporary social problems. The first, *Y Foel Fawr* (1960), and its sequel *Nadolig Gwyn* (1962), tell the story of a Welshman who campaigns for the rights of black people in South Africa. In *Triptych* (1977), one of two novels with which he won the *Prose Medal at the National Eisteddfod, he deals with the spiritual disintegration of modern culture as a backcloth to a physical education teacher's slow dying of cancer, while the other, *Cafflogion* (1979), describes a commune in Llŷn in a dark, authoritarian future. The novel *Gwyntyll y Corwynt* (1978) is about Irish terrorists. Exceptional among his prose-work is *Gwared y Gwirion* (1966), a collection of autobiographical short stories about a young boy growing up in Llŷn; it was adapted for television under the title *Joni Jones*.

In his literary criticism, R. Gerallt Jones displays a fundamentally liberal outlook, examining Wales and its culture in a wider context which includes his interest in the Third World. He has published two volumes of essays on literary subjects, *Yn Frawd i'r Eos Druan* (1961) and *Ansawdd y Seiliau* (1972), and has contributed monographs on T. H. *Parry-Williams to the *Writers of Wales series (1978) and on T. S. Eliot to the series *Y *Meddwl Modern* (1982). R. Gerallt Jones was elected Chairman of the Welsh section of *Yr *Academi Gymreig* in 1982.

For further details see the profile of R. Gerallt Jones in Marged Pritchard, *Portreadau'r Faner* (1976), the interview he gave to *Book News / Llais Llyfrau* (Winter, 1977) and the essay on the writer in Glyn Jones and John Rowlands, *Profiles* (1980).

JONES, ROBERT ISAAC (**Alltud Eifion**; 1815–1905), poet and editor, was born at Pentrefelin, near Porthmadog, Caerns., and earned a living as a chemist in that town. His verse has little merit but he did valuable work as a printer and publisher. A zealous *eisteddfodwr*, he made an untidy collection of local antiquities entitled *Y Gestiana* (1892) but his most notable contribution was the publication of *Y Brython*, a literary and antiquarian journal, which he launched in 1858 as a weekly newspaper and which became a quarterly journal before its demise in 1863. Its first editor was D. Silvan *Evans who left his

mark on the magazine by publishing *cywyddau*, medieval tales, old letters and folklore—stories, sayings, and popular verse—material of which the significance had not previously been appreciated. This magazine, one of the most important in its day, should not be confused with the journal, also entitled *Y *Brython*, which was launched by Hugh *Evans in 1906.

JONES, ROBERT LLOYD (1878–1962), author of adventure novels for children, was a native of Minffordd, near Penrhyndeudraeth, Mer., and by profession a teacher at elementary schools in Caernarfonshire. Most of his stories are maritime adventures, among which *Ynys y Trysor* (1926), *Capten* (1928), *Mêt y Mona* (1929) and *Ym Môr y De* (1936) are the best.

JONES, ROBERT MAYNARD (**Bobi Jones**; 1929–), poet, short-story writer, novelist, critic and scholar. Born in Cardiff into an English-speaking home, he took a degree in Welsh at University College, Cardiff, in 1949, having begun to learn the language as a schoolboy. After teaching Welsh at Llanidloes, Mont., and Llangefni, Ang., he lectured at Trinity College, Carmarthen, and in the Education Department at the University College of Wales, Aberystwyth. He joined the staff of the Welsh Department of the College in 1966 and he was appointed Professor of Welsh in 1980.

Bobi Jones, by far the most prolific Welsh writer of the latter half of the twentieth century, began his literary career as a poet with the publication of *Y Gân Gyntaf* (1957). The poems in this first collection are characterized by a daring or insolent innocence both in their themes and style. They are the celebrations of 'a new Adam' who has discovered love, the Welsh language and the natural world. Many are naïve, the songs of one whose vision has not yet been tainted by the ordinariness of things, and they use the Welsh language as if it had never been used for poetry before, spurning common usage and creating a cascade of fresh, often abstruse or incongruous images. Although the book contains some work which lacks discipline, several of Bobi Jones's most thrilling poems are to be found here. After the publication of this, his first collection, he soon enjoyed a reputation as an *enfant terrible*, partly because of his criticism, both implied and explicit, of his elders and partly on account of his imagistic and (for many readers) bewilderingly abstruse style. *Y Gân Gyntaf* was followed by six more volumes of verse: *Rhwng Taf a Thaf* (1960), *Tyred Allan* (1965), *Man Gwyn* (1965), *Yr Wŷl Ifori* (1967), *Allor Wydn* (1971) and *Gwlad Llun* (1976). The themes of his later poetry are still concerned with love, especially love of his wife and family, his land and people, and some refer to the time he has spent outside Wales, notably in Canada, Mexico and Africa. The volume *Allor Wydn* contains a high proportion of autobiographical poems, including some which deal with his family's history and his relationship with one of his grandfathers, a Marxist, while others express a satirical attitude towards contemporary politics and religion in Wales from the viewpoint of a Nationalist and Evangelical Calvinist. In *Rhwng Taf a Thaf* he writes mainly about his wife, their courtship and marriage, in poems which are rich in hyperbole and wit. The volume *Tyred Allan* is remarkable for its references to the poet's religious conversion and for its sonnets and ballads on political themes.

Bobi Jones is also the author of two novels, *Nid yw Dŵr yn Plygu* (1958) and *Bod yn Wraig* (1960), as well as five collections of short stories: *Y Dyn na Ddaeth Adref* (1966), *Ci Wrth y Drws* (1968), *Daw'r Pasg i Bawb* (1969), *Traed Prydferth* (1973) and *Pwy Laddodd Miss Wales?* (1977). Like his poetry, his prose reveals a highly original talent in both content and style. Tightly packed and moving rapidly, it makes few concessions to the reader not familiar with contemporary trends.

During the mid-1960s the work of Bobi Jones underwent a fundamental change. He had first shown his originality as a critic with the publication of the volume, *I'r Arch* (1959). From that point his writing became more and more obviously informed by his Calvinistic faith. His collection of essays on 'historical Christianity', *Sioc o'r Gofod* (1971), was written from a deeply religious viewpoint. It was followed by *Tafod y Llenor* (1974) and *Llên Cymru a Chrefydd* (1977), his most important contributions in the field of literary criticism. The first of these discusses literary forms and structures while the second examines the purpose of literature, especially that of the Welsh Christian tradition, of which it becomes a Calvinist critique. His other works of literary criticism, such as *Pedwar Emynydd* (1970), *Llenyddiaeth Cymru 1936–72* (1975) and *Ann Griffiths: y Cyfrinydd Sylweddol* (1977), should be read in the light of these two volumes.

As a teacher, R. M. Jones has been no less productive. Besides five books for children and several scholarly editions of Welsh poetry and prose, he has published five volumes for students of Welsh: *Y Tair Rhamant* (1960), *Llenyddiaeth Saesneg yn Addysg Cymru* (1961), *Emile* (1963), *Highlights in Welsh Literature* (1969) and *Ysgrifennu Creadigol i Fyfyrwyr Prifysgol* (1974). Having mastered Welsh as a second language and made his discovery of a new world one of the themes of his writing, he has done a great deal to attract and teach others to enter it. In the field of linguistics, where he is particularly erudite, he has published *System in Child Language* (1964) and for teachers and students of Welsh, the textbooks *Cyflwyno'r Gymraeg* (1964) and *Cymraeg i Oedolion* (1965–66); he is co-author of *Cyfeiriadur i'r Athro Iaith* (3 vols., 1974–79).

This prodigious energy—he has been des-

cribed by one critic as hyperactive—shows no sign of abating, despite his declaration that he intends publishing no more books of creative literature for a while. Indeed, such has been the abundance of Bobi Jones's work that there is every reason to conclude that the first line of his poem '*Y Gân Gyntaf*', '*Angau, 'r wyt ti'n fy ofni i*' ('Death, you are afraid of me'), was intended to present, as it were, a challenge to the demise of the Welsh language and its literature; it will certainly serve as an epigraph to his career so far.

For critical discussion of Bobi Jones's work see the articles by Waldo Williams in *Lleufer* (vol. 13, 1957), R. Gerallt Jones in *Yr Arloeswr* (no. 7, 1960), Pennar Davies in *Y Genhinen* (vol. 17, 1967), Bryan Martin Davies in *Poetry Wales* (vol. 8, no. 1, 1972) and Derec Llwyd Morgan in *Barn* (May, 1975); see also the essay by Bobi Jones, 'Why I write in Welsh', in *Planet* (no. 2, Nov., 1970) and the interview in *Ysgrifau Beirniadol IX* (ed. J. E. Caerwyn Williams, 1976).

JONES, ROBERT TUDUR (1921–), church historian, was born at Llanystumdwy, Caerns., and educated at the Universities of Wales, Oxford and Strasbourg. A Congregational minister at Aberystwyth before becoming Professor of Church History and later Principal of Bala-Bangor Theological College, he is a prolific author on both religious and political topics. His most substantial volumes are *Congregationalism in England 1662–1962* (1962), *Hanes Annibynwyr Cymru* (1966), *Vavasor Powell* (1971), *Yr Ysbryd Glân* (1972), *Diwinyddiaeth ym Mangor* (1972), *The Desire of Nations* (1974), *Yr Undeb: Hanes Undeb yr Annibynwyr Cymraeg, 1872–1972* (1975) and *Ffydd ac Argyfwng Cenedl: Cristionogaeth a Diwylliant yng Nghymru 1890–1914* (2 vols., 1981, 1982). He has for many years been a regular contributor to such periodicals as *Y*＊*Cymro*, ＊*Barn*, *Y*＊*Tyst* and *Y Ddraig Goch* and a selection of his articles has been published under the title *Darganfod Harmoni* (1982). In theology R. Tudur Jones is an orthodox Protestant, in politics a fervent Nationalist. His works are characterized by meticulous and wide-ranging scholarship, unambiguous judgement and, particularly in the case of his Welsh writing, a profound sense of the beauty of language.

JONES, ROGER (1903–82), poet, a native of Rhoshirwaun, Caerns., was a Baptist minister until his retirement. He was the author of three volumes of poetry, namely *Awelon Llŷn* (1970), *Haenau Cynghanedd* (1975) and *Ysgubau Medi* (1979), which demonstrate his mastery of the ＊*englyn* and the ＊*cywydd*.

JONES, ROWLAND (1722–74), philologist. Born at Llanbedrog, Caerns., he was admitted to the Inner Temple in 1751 but abandoned his legal training to return to Wales after acquiring an estate known as Y Weirglodd Fawr in the parish of Abererch, Caerns. Regarded in his day as a leading authority on philological matters, he published five books, in one of which, *The Origin of Languages and Nations* (1764), he described his theory that all words were derived from monosyllabic roots and that the primeval language was Celtic. His other works were *Hieroglyphic, or a Grammatical Introduction to an Universal Hieroglyfic Language* . . . (1768), *The Philosophy of Words in two dialogues between the Author and Crito* (1769), *The Circles of Gomer, or an Essay towards an Investigation and Introduction of the English as an Universal Language* (1771) and *The 10 Triads, or the Tenth Muse, wherein the origin, nature, and connection of the Sacred Symbols, Sounds, Words, Ideas are discovered* (1773). These works had a great influence on the linguistic theories of William *Owen Pughe.

JONES, ROWLAND (Rolant o Fôn; 1909–62), poet. Born at Rhostrehwfa, Ang., he spent his life on the island as a solicitor. After coming to prominence as a young poet at provincial eisteddfodau, he won the *Chair at the National Eisteddfod in 1941 with his *awdl*, 'Hydref', and again in 1949 with 'Y Graig'. He edited the poetry column in the newspaper *Herald Môn* for some years and published a volume of his own verse, *Y Brenin a Cherddi Eraill* (1957); a second collection, *Yr Anwylyd* (ed. Huw Ll. Williams, 1963), was published posthumously. A master of *cynghanedd*, with which he experimented, he was at his best when writing on religious themes. He was also well known for his witty participation in bardic contentions.

JONES, SALLY ROBERTS (1935–), poet and publisher. Born in London, of a Welsh father, she moved with her parents at the age of thirteen to live at Llanrwst, Denbs., and later at Llangefni, Ang. She was educated at the University College of North Wales, Bangor. Having trained as a librarian in London, she returned to Wales in 1967 to take up a post as a reference librarian at Port Talbot, Glam. With Alison *Bielski, she was the first honorary secretary of the English-language section of *Yr *Academi Gymreig*. Her four volumes of poetry are *Turning Away* (1969), *Sons and Brothers* (1977), *The Forgotten Country* (1977) and *Relative Values* (1985). Much of her poetry is set in and around Port Talbot, where she has made her home, and is informed by a steely sense of irony and an ability to reveal the darker side of the most mundane circumstances and events. She is also the compiler of a bibliography, *Books of Welsh Interest* (1977), and the author of an essay on Allen Raine (Anne Adaliza Beynon *Puddicombe) in the *Writers of Wales* series (1979). With her husband, she established a publishing business, Alun Books, in 1977 and also owns the imprint known as Barn Owl Press, which specializes in books for children.

Jones, Samuel (1628–97), minister and schoolmaster. A native of Chirk, Denbs., and a Fellow of Jesus College, Oxford, he became vicar of Llangynwyd, Glam., about 1657 but was deprived of his living in 1662 by the Act of Uniformity. Moving to Brynllywarch in the same parish, he opened there a *Dissenting Academy which became famous for the training of young men for the Nonconformist ministry, among whom was Rice Price, the father of Richard *Price, the philosopher.

JONES, SIMON BARTHOLOMEW (1894–1966), poet and editor, was the youngest child but one of the *Cilie family. He went to sea as a young man but, after a serious accident on board ship in Buenos Aires, he returned to Wales and trained for the ministry. A conscientious objector during the First World War, he graduated at the University College of North Wales, Bangor, in 1920 and then held pastorates at Liverpool, Carno and Carmarthen. He won the *Crown at the National Eisteddfod in 1933 for his *pryddest*, 'Rownd yr Horn', and the *Chair for his *awdl*, 'Tyddewi', in 1936. With Meuryn (R. J. *Rowlands) and, later, W. Rhys *Nicholas, he edited *Y *Genhinen* from 1950 until his death. A selection of S. B. Jones's poems and essays was edited by his nephew Gerallt *Jones and published in 1966.

JONES, THEOPHILUS (1759–1812), historian, was born at Brecon, a grandson of Theophilus *Evans, many of whose muniments he inherited. Educated at Christ College in the town, he practised as a lawyer and became Deputy-Registrar of the archdeaconry of Brecon. His *History of the County of Brecknock* (2 vols., 1805, 1809), continues to be the standard work on the county; comprehensive and scholarly, despite some bias, it is the most noteworthy of Welsh county histories. The author also collected manuscripts, was acquainted with the historian Thomas *Price (Carnhuanawc) and contributed many papers to antiquarian journals such as *The *Cambrian Register*. The memorial volume to Theophilus Jones published by Edwin *Davies in 1905 contains his correspondence with his schoolfellow, Edward *Davies (Celtic Davies) and Walter *Davies (Gwallter Mechain).

Jones or **Johns, Thomas** or **Tomas Siôn Dafydd Madoc (Twm Siôn Cati**; c.1530–1609), antiquary and herald, was the illegitimate son of Siôn ap Dafydd ap Madog ap Hywel Moetheu of Porth-y-ffynnon (Fountain Gate), near Tregaron, Cards. His mother, Catherine (Cati), was the illegitimate daughter of Maredudd ab Ieuan ap Robert, the great-grand-father of Sir John *Wynn of Gwydir. The first reference to Thomas Jones dates from 1559 when he was among the hundreds who obtained a pardon in the great amnesty extended by

Elizabeth I in the first year of her reign, but the nature of his offence is not known.

To his contemporaries he was a gentleman and a poet ('*y godidocaf a phennaf a pherffeithiaf . . . yng nghelfyddyd arwyddfarddoniaeth*' ('the most excellent, most impressive and most perfect . . . in the art of genealogical poetry'), wrote Siôn Dafydd *Rhys in his Grammar (1592), and such heraldic experts as Lewys *Dwnn and George *Owen also acknowledged his ability. Several of Thomas Jones's heraldic ancestral rolls on parchment, and other manuscripts, have been preserved. A few *cywyddau* and *englynion* are also attributed to him, but their authenticity is doubtful. It is known, however, that he was on familiar terms with poets of his day because there is extant a *cywydd* by Silas ap Siôn (*fl.* late 16th cent.) which compares the rivalry between Thomas Jones and *Dafydd Benwyn over a girl called Ely to the war caused by Helen of Troy.

The little that is known about Thomas Jones suggests that he often had recourse to the law while serving as steward for the lordship of Caron in 1601. For example, he was involved in a case against a vicar in the Court of Star Chamber, alleging that he had been attacked while holding the local court. At some time after May 1605 he sent a petition to Robert Cecil, Earl of Salisbury, citing their family ties as descendants of Hywel Moetheu, to ask for a case against him to be moved to a court nearer his home on account of his old age. About 1607 Thomas Jones took as his second wife the widow of Thomas Rhys Williams of Ystrad-ffin, the daughter of Sir John *Price of Brecon, and she went to live with him at Porth-y-Ffynnon, but he died two years later.

There are several apocryphal tales associated with the name of Thomas Jones, deriving perhaps from the fact that he was amnestied in 1559, but also because he has been confused with others of the same name who were raiders and highwaymen in the district of Tregaron. Samuel Rush *Meyrick collected a number of these stories in his *History of the County of Cardigan* (1808) and they were embroidered by William Frederick Deacon in his books, *Twm John Catty, the Welsh Robin Hood* (1822) and *The Welsh Rob Roy* (1823). But the fame of Thomas Jones is mainly attributable to T. J. Llewelyn *Prichard's novel, *The Adventures and Vagaries of* *Twm Shon Catti* (1828).

For further details see Lewys Dwnn, *Heraldic Visitations* (1846) and D. C. Rees, *Tregaron: Historical and Antiquarian* (1936).

Jones, Thomas (1648–1713), printer and almanacker, was born at Tre'r-ddôl, near Corwen, Mer. A tailor's son, he went to London in 1666 with a view to plying his father's trade, but was soon established there as a bookseller and compiler of *almanacs. From 1680 until his death he published an annual almanac in the Welsh language which was among the most popular of its kind. While living in London he also published a number of Welsh books, including *Llyfr Plygain* (1683), a Welsh edition of the Book of Common Prayer (1687), the metrical psalms of Edmund *Prys (1688) and a Welsh-English dictionary, *Y Gymraeg yn ei Disgleirdeb* (1688).

Having previously depended on agents in various parts of Wales for the marketing of his books, Thomas Jones moved nearer home to Shrewsbury in 1695 after the passing of the Printing Act which allowed books to be printed in centres other than London. There he continued to print books, among them a Welsh edition of Bunyan's *Pilgrim's Progress* under the title *Taith y Pererin* (1699). Known as Thomas Jones the Stargazer among his English neighbours, he devoted his energies to the compiling of almanacs and the publishing of devotional books and ballads in the Welsh language. He lived in an age of intense political and religious controversy and, a devout Churchman, defended the Established Church by attacking Catholics and Dissenters. His almanacs were intended to entertain as well as to instruct: they included verse by some of the leading Welsh poets of his day and were eagerly bought by those who wished to read material other than religious works. Despite ill health, domestic unhappiness and the vagaries of his publishing business, Thomas Jones persevered for more than thirty years in this important work. He was, nevertheless, considered by certain scholars among his contemporaries as a quack or, at best, a plausible rogue. The kindest reference to him made during his lifetime was that by William *Morris of Anglesey who described him as 'an old fellow who did a lot of good despite his ignorance'. See also PRINTING AND PUBLISHING.

There is an account of Thomas Jones's life and work in Geraint H. Jenkins, *Thomas Jones yr Almanaciwr* (1980); see also the same author's article, 'The Sweating Astrologer', in *Welsh Society and Nationhood* (ed. R. R. Davies, R. A. Griffiths, Ieuan Gwynedd Jones and K. O. Morgan, 1984).

Jones, Thomas (1742–1803), landscape-painter, was born in the parish of Cefnllys, Rads., but is usually associated with the mansion of Pencerrig, Llanelwedd, in the same county, where he was brought up. Intended by his parents to take Holy Orders, he was educated at Jesus College, Oxford, but left in 1761 to devote himself to painting. He became a pupil of Richard *Wilson in London, spent seventeen years as a painter in Italy and finally settled at the family home of Pencerrig in 1789.

For further details see his *Journal* (1960) and *The Family History of Thomas Jones, artist, of Pencerrig* (1970) by R. C. B. Oliver; see also the article by Prys Morgan in the *Transactions* of the Honourable Society of Cymmrodorion (1984).

JONES, THOMAS (1752–1845), cleric and author, was born near Hafod, Cards., and educated at Ystrad Meurig. After ordination, he served the Anglican Church in various parishes in Wales and England, but spent most of his life at Creaton, Northants., and he is usually associated with that place. He corresponded with Thomas *Charles about the establishment of *Sunday Schools and helped him in the creation of the British and Foreign Bible Society. Jones translated a number of religious works into Welsh, including several by Richard Baxter, and was the author of seventeen books in English, of which *The Welsh Looking-glass* (1812), written in protest against the decision by the Calvinistic Methodists to leave the Established Church, is perhaps the most noteworthy.

JONES, THOMAS (1756–1820), Calvinistic Methodist minister and author. Born at Penucha, near Caerwys, Flints., he received a classical education in Holywell but, refusing to prepare for Holy Orders, joined the Methodists and began preaching among them in 1772. He met Thomas *Charles in 1784 and they became firm friends; Jones's religious and social horizons were widened and Charles's literary Welsh was improved thereby. They edited the journal *Trysorfa Ysprydol* together and corresponded regularly. Jones exerted a strong influence on Charles in completing the rift with the Established Church and was one of the first to be ordained a minister of the new Methodist Connexion in 1811. He was thrice married and in comfortable circumstances, but he suffered both physically and mentally because of the Arminian activities of the *Wesleyan newcomers to north-east Wales.

In his published works he presented powerful arguments in favour of moderate Calvinism and may be considered as the foremost thinker among the Calvinistic Methodists of his day. Among his most important theological works are *Y Cristion mewn Cyflawn Arfogaeth* (1796–1820), a translation of William Gurnall's *The Christian in Complete Armour* (1655–62), and his *Hanes Diwygwyr, Merthyron a Chyffeswyr Eglwys Loegr* (1813), a history of the Church of England. With the possible exception of Robert *Jones of Rhos-lan, Jones was the best writer of Welsh in his period. He took a leading part in theological debates, endeavouring to steer his denomination between the extremes of Arminianism and the High Calvinism of the young John *Elias. His most readable works are an autobiography (1814) and his biography of Thomas Charles (1816). Among his best-known hymns are 'Mi wn fod fy Mhrynwr yn fyw', 'A oes obaith am achubiaeth?' and 'O arwain fy enaid i'r dyfroedd'. Jones was also a poet of some distinction: the finest example of his verse is the *cywydd* to the thrush, 'I'r Aderyn Bronfraith' (1773). Most of his work was printed on a press which he set up in

his home at Ruthin in 1804 and sold to Thomas *Gee (the elder) in 1813. Had he applied himself to philology—and his English-Welsh Dictionary (1800) bears out his ability—instead of to theology, Thomas Jones might have counteracted the baneful influence of William *Owen Pughe.

For further details see the biography of Thomas Jones by Frank Price Jones (1956).

JONES, THOMAS (1860–1932), poet, was born at Nantglyn, Denbs., but for the last twenty years of his life lived at Cerrigellgwm, with which place he is usually associated. He wrote ballads, specialized in setting *penillion* to the accompaniment of the harp and published the volumes *Caneuon* (1902), *Beirdd Uwchaled* (1930) and *Pitar Puw a'i Berthynasau* (1932).

JONES, THOMAS (1870–1955), civil servant and author, was born at Rhymney, Mon., and educated at the University College of Wales, Aberystwyth, and at Glasgow University. After a distinguished academic career, he became in 1910 Secretary to the National Health Insurance Commissioners and in 1914 the first editor of The *Welsh Outlook*. David *Lloyd George's acquaintance with his work in the former post brought about his promotion in 1916 to the Deputy-Secretaryship of the Cabinet. He took part in the negotiations for the Anglo-Irish Treaty of 1921 and, in Wales, was a staunch anti-Nationalist propagandist. Prime Ministers from Lloyd George to Baldwin came under his influence and his services were rewarded by the Companionship of Honour in 1929. In later years he became President of *Coleg Harlech*, which he was instrumental in founding, President of the University College of Wales, Aberystwyth, and Chairman of the *Gregynog Press. He was the prime mover in the establishment of the Council for the Encouragement of Music and the Arts, which later became the Arts Council of Great Britain, and was its Vice-Chairman from 1939 to 1942.

Thomas Jones wrote a volume of autobiography, *Rhymney Memories* (1939), an apparently unfinished work valuable for its social documentation, as well as *Leeks and Daffodils* (1942), *Cerrig Milltir* (1942), *The Native Never Returns* (1946), *Lloyd George* (1951), *Welsh Broth* (1951) and *A Diary with Letters 1931–50* (1954); his *Cabinet Diaries* were edited by Keith Middlemas (3 vols., 1970–72).

For further details see *Harlech Studies* (1938), a volume of essays presented to Thomas Jones, and the monographs written by Ben Bowen Thomas (1970) and Thomas Jones's daughter, Eirene White (1978).

JONES, THOMAS (1910–72), scholar, born at Alltwen, Pontardawe, Glam., was Professor of

Welsh at the University College of Wales, Aberystwyth, from 1952 to 1970. He was appointed to the staff of the Welsh Department at that College in 1933 and, apart from military service, spent the rest of his life in Aberystwyth where he played a prominent role in the academic and administrative life of his College and the University.

Thomas Jones was among the most outstanding scholars produced by the *University of Wales. His interests were wide-ranging, for he published translations from Irish and Breton, studies on such subjects as Thomas *Jones the almanacker, Owen M. *Edwards, David *Owen (Brutus), folklore and *Arthurian matters, as well as a little of his own poetry. It was he who drew attention to the work of Elis *Gruffydd. But his main contribution was made as a scholar of Welsh literature in the medieval period. At the beginning of his career he worked on historical texts and developed his research with the publication of Y Bibyl Ynghymraec (1940) and *Brut y Tywysogyon (4 vols., 1941, 1952, 1955, 1971). The latter work introduced the first reliable texts of this chronicle and also contained English translations and discussions of the manuscripts, their chronology and their language. Another aspect of his interest in Latin-Welsh culture was reflected in his translations from the works of *Gerald de Barri (Giraldus Cambrensis). He published the text, a translation and a discussion of *'Englynion y Beddau'.

It was undoubtedly his translation of The *Mabinogion, which he undertook in collaboration with Gwyn *Jones and published in 1948, which was largely responsible for awakening world interest in these tales. It is still the authoritative translation, notable for its combination of meticulous accuracy and a fine literary style.

An obituary of Thomas Jones by J. E. Caerwyn Williams, together with a bibliography of his writings by Brynley F. Roberts, will be found in Studia Celtica (vols. X/XI, 1975–76); see also the article by D. J. Bowen in Y Traethodydd (1973).

Jones, Thomas Artemus (1871–1943), journalist and judge. Born at Denbigh, a stonemason's son, he left school at the age of eleven to work in a newsagent's shop and, four years later, became a reporter with The Denbighshire Free Press. He studied law in his spare time while working for The Daily Telegraph and The Daily News in Manchester and London, and was called to the Bar in 1901. As a result of his success in his own case of libel against Messrs. E. Hutton and Co., for having unwittingly used the name Artemus Jones in an abusive manner in The Sunday Chronicle in 1908, it became the custom for publishers to disclaim any similarity between living persons and characters in novels.

A county court judge in north Wales from 1930 to 1942, he was knighted in 1931 and, from 1939 to 1941, was Chairman of the North Wales Conscientious Objectors' Tribunal. On this body he was identified with the view that objection to military service was not admissible except when couched in religious terms. He contributed numerous articles to the Welsh periodical press, most of which reflected the influence of his humble origins and the *Liberalism of the *Cymru Fydd movement. Among his chief contributions to Welsh life were his attempts to secure the use of Welsh in courts of law. He chose to hear several cases in the language, did much to support the petition which resulted in the Welsh Courts Act of 1942 and always argued in favour of restoring to Wales its own legal system.

A selection of his more important articles, including an account of the trial of Sir Roger Casement, in which he defended the Irishman, was published posthumously in the volume Without my Wig (1944).

JONES, THOMAS GWYNN (1871–1949), poet, scholar, translator, novelist, dramatist, critic and journalist. Born at Gwyndy Uchaf, Betws-yn-rhos, Denbs., he spent his childhood, described in the volume Brithgofion (1944), at Llaneilian-yn-rhos in the same county. He received little formal education but his bent for writing led him into journalism. From 1890 until 1909 he worked on several newspapers, including *Baner ac Amserau Cymru and Yr *Herald Cymraeg. Some of his colleagues, notably Emrys ap Iwan (Robert Ambrose *Jones) and Daniel *Rees, aroused his interest in foreign languages and literature, while scholars such as J. E. *Lloyd inspired him to study medieval Welsh poetry. After a period working as a cataloguer in the *National Library of Wales, he was appointed Lecturer in Welsh at the University College of Wales, Aberystwyth, in 1913. By 1919, when he was appointed to the Gregynog Chair of Welsh Literature at the College, he had already published a work of criticism entitled Bardism and Romance (1914) and written on aspects of the Poetry of the Princes in Rhieingerddi'r Gogynfeirdd (1915). He was also by this time the author of a handbook on medieval Welsh literature, Llenyddiaeth y Cymry (1915). During his early years at Aberystwyth he translated some Ibsen, Goethe's Faust (1922), Von Hofmannsthal, and selections of Greek and Latin epigrams, Blodau o Hen Ardd (1927). He retired in 1937 and in the following year received honorary doctorates from the University of Wales and from the National University of Ireland in recognition of his work in Irish and other Celtic languages.

His versatility as a writer was obvious from the outset. Besides a volume of poems, Dyddiau'r Parchedig Richard Owen (with W. M. Jones, 1890), he wrote a lengthy satire in verse, Gwlad y Gân, published in book form with other poems in 1902, a play about the *Tithe War, *Eglwys y Dyn Tlawd* (1892), and a novel, *Gwedi Brad a Gofid* (1898). He continued to write plays and novels for another quarter of a century—the novels *John Homer* (1923) and *Lona* (1923) are the best-known—and he also wrote excellent biographies of Robert Ambrose *Jones (1912) and of his first employer, Thomas *Gee (1913), which have not been surpassed. From 1919 onwards he published more works of scholarship, including an edition of *Tudur Aled (2 vols., 1926) and *Welsh Folklore and Folk-custom* (1930). Between 1932 and 1937, *Hughes a'i Fab* (see under HUGHES, RICHARD) published a uniform edition of six collections of his works, four of them containing collected essays in meditation and criticism called respectively *Cymeriadau* (1933), *Beirniadaeth a Myfyrdod* (1935), *Astudiaethau* (1936) and *Dyddgwaith* (1937). T. Gwynn Jones also composed a host of lyrics and songs, as well as a translation into English of Ellis *Wynne's *Gweledigaetheu y Bardd Cwsc* (1940), under the title *Visions of the Sleeping Bard* (1940), for the *Gregynog Press, which published a fine edition of a selection of his poems, *Detholiad o Ganiadau*, in 1926.

It was, however, as a poet that he excelled and he was generally recognized as the foremost poet of his generation. In 1902 he won the *Chair at the National Eisteddfod with an *awdl*, *'Ymadawiad Arthur'*, which is a landmark in the history of Welsh poetry in the twentieth century. It is the first of a series of major poems which he wrote in *cynghanedd either in the classical metres or in new, experimental metres based upon traditional prosody. They include 'Gwlad y Bryniau', for which he was awarded the Chair in 1909, *'Tir na n-Og' (1910), *'Madog' (1917), *'Broséliâwnd' (1922), *'Anatiomaros' (1925) and *'Argoed' (1927). All these poems make use of Celtic legends or what the poet called 'the variegated pictures of the imagination of the centuries', structured anew in such a way as to accommodate the great issues of modern Man's tragedy and presented in a style which makes majestic use of classical diction. Their grand themes are the Quest for Paradise and the importance of preserving honour, custom and ancient wisdom in the face of encroaching materialism and philistinism. They contain some of the most brilliantly sustained descriptions of nature and human action that Welsh poetry can boast and their psychology is exquisitely exacting. During 1934 and the following year the poet abandoned this symbolic system to write a series of powerful poems collected in Y *Dwymyn (1944), a volume which portrays the fever of common life under the threat of barbarism.

For further details see the memorial number of *Y Llenor* (vol. XXVII, no. 2, 1949), the special number of *Y Traethodydd* (vol. CXXVI, Jan., 1971), the study by W. Beynon Davies (1962) and the same author's monograph in the *Writers of Wales* series (1970), the biography by David Jenkins, *Cofiant T. Gwynn Jones* (1973) and the same author's photographic account of the poet's life in the *Bro a Bywyd* series (1984); for critical surveys see Derec Llwyd Morgan, *Barddoniaeth T. Gwynn Jones* (1972) and Gwynn ap Gwilym (ed.), *Thomas Gwynn Jones* in the series *Cyfres y Meistri* (1982). A bibliography of the writings of T. Gwynn Jones has been compiled by D. Hywel E. Roberts (1981).

JONES, THOMAS HENRY or **HARRI** (1921–65), poet, was born at Cwm Crogau, near Llanafan Fawr, Brecs. His studies in the English Department at the University College of Wales, Aberystwyth, were interrupted by war service with the Royal Navy, but he returned to complete them in 1947 and, two years later, received his Master's degree. Having obtained a teaching post at the Portsmouth Naval Dockyard Apprentices' School, he became active as a lecturer with the Workers' Education Association.

From early childhood Harri Jones had written poetry and, during the war years, had begun contributing to literary journals, including *The *Welsh Review and *The Dublin Magazine*. His first volume, *The Enemy in the Heart* (1957), containing poems written over the previous decade, showed promise of a new, turbulent talent exploiting the resources of language to explore the tensions between human passions and an atavistic *Puritanism. In 1959, despairing of a university post in Wales or England, he became a Lecturer in English at the University of New South Wales and quickly established contacts with writers and editors there, although for his second volume of poems, *Songs of a Mad Prince* (1960), he drew substantially on poems written before his arrival in Australia. Active and successful in literary and academic circles, with many friends and admirers, he was nevertheless prone to depression and given to heavy drinking. Increasingly, he used poetry as a vehicle for the expression of his personal and emotional problems, discovering in the process a distinctive voice free of the conflicting influences of Dylan *Thomas and R. S. *Thomas which, along with a predilection for metaphysical conceits, had marked much of his earlier writing.

His next volume, *The Beast at the Door* (1963), with its expatriate's evocation of Wales, its incisive portraits and its love-poetry combining dramatic complexity and colloquial ease, is perhaps his most accomplished. The confessional mode of his later writing, and an experiment in the form of a long dramatic monologue, pointed the direction of possible future development which was not to be fulfilled: Harri Jones was found drowned in an old rock bathing-pool near his home. His ashes were returned to Wales and buried in the churchyard of Llanfihangel Brynpabuan, not far from the mouth of Cwm Crogau. A posthumous volume of T. H. Jones's poetry, *The Colour of Cockcrowing*, was published in 1966 and his *Collected Poems* (ed. Julian Croft and Don Dale-Jones) appeared in 1977.

There is an essay on the poet by Julian Croft in the *Writers of Wales* series (1976); see also *The Cost of Strangeness* (1982) by Anthony Conran and the note by Glyn Jones in *Profiles* (1980).

JONES, THOMAS LLEWELYN (1915–), poet and children's writer. Born at Pentrecwrt, Carms., he was a primary school teacher in Cardiganshire before becoming a full-time writer. By marrying into the *Cilie family, he became associated with that famous circle of poets and its leader after the death of Alun Jeremiah *Jones. As a master of the traditional strict metres, he has been President of *Cymdeithas Cerdd Dafod from its inception in 1976, but he is also a lyrical poet in the free metres and his poems for children are especially popular. He won the *Chair at the National Eisteddfod in 1958 and 1959.

T. Llew Jones is among the most prolific of contemporary Welsh writers and is the author of more than fifty books. His collections of verse include *Penillion y Plant* (1965), *Sŵn y Malu* (1967) and *Cerddi Newydd i Blant o Bob Oed* (1973). He has edited several anthologies, including the work of the Cilie poets, and *Cerddi '79* (1979), which caused controversy because its foreword castigated what the editor held to be 'difficult poetry'.

As the author of popular fiction for children he has made an important contribution to the range of writing in Welsh, which was recognized by the *University of Wales in 1977 when an honorary degree was conferred upon him. Some of his novels recount the exploits of such folk-heroes as *Siôn Cwilt, Barti Ddu (Bartholomew *Roberts) and Twm Siôn Cati (Thomas *Jones; *fl.* 1530–1609), and some are detective novels. They include *Trysor Plas y Wernen* (1958), *Trysor y Morladron* (1960), *Y Ffordd Beryglus* (1963), *Ymysg Lladron* (1965), *Dial o'r Diwedd* (1968), *Corn, Pistol a Chwip* (1969), *Yr Ergyd Farwol* (1969), *Y Corff ar y Traeth* (1970), *Barti Ddu* (1973), *Un Noson Dywyll* (1973), *Cri'r Dylluan* (1974), *Cyfrinach y Lludw* (1974), *Arswyd y Byd* (1975), *Tân ar y Comin* (1975), *Ysbryd Plas Nant Esgob* (1976), *Dirgelwch yr Ogof* (1977) and *Lawr ar Lan y Môr* (1977).

For further details see the volume of essays on T. Llew Jones's life and work which was edited by Gwynn ap Gwilym and Richard H. Lewis (1982); a full bibliography is to be found in Siân Teifi's study, *Cyfaredd y Cyfarwydd* (1982).

JONES, TOM PARRI (1905–80), poet and short-story writer. Born in Anglesey, he left school at the age of thirteen to work on his father's farm, but contracted poliomyelitis as a young man and was bedridden for long periods during his last years. Besides winning the

*Chair, the *Crown and the *Prose Medal at the National Eisteddfod, he published two volumes of verse, *Preiddiau Annwn* (1946) and *Cerddi Malltraeth* (1978), and a novel, *Y Ddau Bren* (1976). But his most original writing is to be found in his racy tales of Anglesey life, *Teisennau Berffro* (1958), *Yn Eisiau, Gwraig* (1958), *Traed Moch* (1971) and *Y Felltith* (1977).

JONES, TRISTAN (1924–), sailor and author, was born at sea aboard a British ship off the island of Tristan da Cunha. Brought up by Welsh-speaking parents near Barmouth, Mer., he left school at the age of thirteen and went to sea, serving in the Royal Navy (he was torpedoed three times) and later with the Royal Hydrographic Service. Severely injured when his survey vessel was blown up by guerrillas in Aden in 1952, he was discharged and told by doctors that he would never walk again. Since then he has sailed, mostly single-handed, a record 345,000 miles in small boats, crossing the Atlantic eighteen times under sail, nine times alone.

In his book *The Incredible Voyage* (1977) he describes 'a personal Odyssey' which took him between 1969 and 1975 from New York through the Mediterranean to the Red Sea, around the Cape of Good Hope, across the Atlantic, up the Amazon, around South America, where he hauled his boat over the Andes to sail on Lake Titicaca (the highest lake in the world), through the swamps of the Mato Grosso, and then back across the Atlantic to London. His previous adventures in Arctic waters, remarkable for his physical stamina and delight in the natural world, were related with the same panache in *Ice!* (1978) and *Saga of a Wayward Sailor* (1979), which some critics compared with the writing of Joshua Slocum. He has also written a novel set in the Netherlands of 1940, *Dutch Treat* (1979), and three further volumes of autobiography, *Adrift* (1981), *A Steady Trade* (1982) and *Heart of Oak* (1984).

JONES, WILLIAM (1764–1822), hymn-writer. He was born at Cynwyd, Mer., but spent most of his life at Bala where he worked as a weaver. He published a collection of hymns, *Aberth Moliant neu Ychydig Hymnau* (1819), but is chiefly remembered as the author of the hymn beginning, 'Dyma iachawdwriaeth hyfryd'.

Jones, William (1809–73), see under CHARTISM.

JONES, WILLIAM (Ehedydd Iâl; 1815–99), poet, was born at Derwen, Denbs., and was by occupation a farmer and miller. He is remembered as the author of the famous hymn which begins 'Er nad yw 'nghnawd ond gwellt'. A volume of his poems, *Blodau Iâl* (1898), was edited by John Felix.

JONES, WILLIAM (1896–1961), poet, was born at Trefriw, Caerns., and educated at the

University College of North Wales, Bangor. He became a Calvinistic Methodist minister but left to work as a librarian at Tremadog. He published two volumes of verse, *Adar Rhiannon* (1947) and *Sonedau a Thelynegion* (1950). One of his early lyrics, '*Y Llanc Ifanc o Lŷn*', is still very popular.

JONES, WILLIAM ELLIS (Cawrdaf; 1795–1848), poet, a native of Abererch, Caerns., was by trade a printer. He became acquainted with such poets as Dafydd Ionawr (David *Richards) and Dafydd Ddu Eryri (David *Thomas) while engaged in the printing of their work at Dolgellau. His only success at eisteddfodau was in 1824 when his *awdl* on the regency of George IV won him the *Chair. In his romance, *Y Bardd neu'r Meudwy Cymreig* (1830), there are some graphic descriptions of a storm at sea. Written in a highly moralistic style, it has been described as the first Welsh *novel, but it is hardly recognizable as belonging to that genre. After his death a selection of his verse and prose was published in the volume *Gweithoedd Cawrdaf* (1851).

JONES, WILLIAM GLYN (William Glynne-Jones; 1907–77), novelist, was born at Llanelli, Carms., and worked as a moulder in a steel foundry there until 1943 when he left to become a full-time writer in London. He wrote two novels, *Farewell Innocence* (1950), and its sequel, *Ride the White Stallion* (1950), two volumes of short stories, *He who had Eaten of the Eagle* (1948) and *The Childhood Land* (1960), and a collection of autobiographical stories, *Summer Long Ago* (1954). His subjects are usually childhood and working-class life in Llanelli in the first half of the twentieth century. He also wrote more than a dozen books for children, including *Brecon Adventure* (1945), *Dennis and Co.* (1947), *Pennants on the Main* (1950) and *Legends of the Welsh Hills* (1957).

JONES, WILLIAM HUGHES (Elidir Sais; 1885–1951), literary critic, was born at Rhyl, Flints., and acquired his sobriquet by his habit of speaking English to his Welsh-speaking friends. The author of a book about Welsh poetry, *At the Foot of Eryri* (1912), published while he was a teacher of history at Bethesda, Caerns., he subsequently went to London as private secretary to Ernest *Rhys. In 1935 he took a job with the BBC in Cardiff, but later left Wales again for England. His brother, Tom Elwyn Jones, who was drowned in the Battle of Jutland in the First World War, was '*Y Tom gwylaidd twymgalon*' ('The modest, warm-hearted Tom') of the famous elegy by R. Williams *Parry. Among other books by William Hughes Jones are *What is Happening in Wales?* (1937), *Wales Drops the Pilots* (1937) and *A Challenge to Wales* (1938), all of which were written in favourable response to the fire at *Penyberth in 1936.

JONES, WILLIAM JOHN (1928–), novelist and children's writer, was born at Ystradmeurig, Cards., and educated at the University College of Wales, Aberystwyth. After a period spent as a teacher at Newtown, Mont., and as headmaster at Borth and Ynysgedwyn, he was appointed in 1963 to a lectureship at the Cardiff College of Education, where he later became Head of the Welsh Department. A prolific writer of children's books, he has also published a number of novels including *Rhwng y Sêr* (1957), *Ffoi heb ei Erlid* (1959), *Amser i Faddau* (1964), *Y Cleddyf Aur* (1971) and *Heledd* (1973).

JONES, WILLIAM MORGAN (Margam Jones; 1864–1945), poet and novelist, was born at Margam, Glam., and became a Calvinistic Methodist minister. Some of his time was spent on journalism and some on verse, his collected poems appearing under the titles *The Village Lyre* and *Caniadau'r Pentref* (1934). But his most important works were a volume of essays, *Ysgrifau Byr am Matthews Ewenni* (1939), and his two novels, *Stars of the Revival* (1910) and *Angels in Wales* (1914).

JONES, WILLIAM SAMUEL (1920–), playwright and short-story writer. Born at Llanystumdwy, near Cricieth, Caerns., he had little formal education but kept a garage which became a meeting-place for writers and other cultural activists in the district. He began his literary career by writing humorous verse and stories for competitions at the *National Eisteddfod, then turned to amateur drama and went on to write for radio and television, eventually earning a living as a full-time writer. Some of his best plays were collected in the volume *Dinas Barhaus a Thair Drama Arall* (1968).

W. S. Jones's talent combines slapstick comedy with a verbal ingenuity which exploits the resources of a healthily plebeian version of the Gwynedd dialect not unaffected by the influence of English, sometimes with incongruous results. He has a knack for symbolic devices in which some have detected the characteristics of the Theatre of the Absurd. But his muse is comic rather than tragic. His best-known character, Ifas y Tryc (popularized by actor Stewart Jones), is famous for the horse-sense with which he views the stupidities of contemporary Wales; a selection of his soliloquies was published in the volume *Ifas y Tryc* (1973).

The publications of W. S. Jones include *Tair Drama Fer* (1962), *Pum Drama Fer* (1963), *Tŷ Clap* (1965), *Dau Frawd* (1965), *Y Fainc* (1967), *Mae Rhywbeth Bach* (1969), *Dinas* (with Emyr *Humphreys, 1970) and *Y Sul Hwnnw* (1981). He has also published a lecture, *Y Toblarôn* (1975), and a volume of short stories, *Dyn y Mwnci* (1979).

For further details see the autobiography of W. S. Jones in the series *Cyfres y Cewri* (1985).

Journalism. The first attempt at publishing a Welsh periodical was Lewis *Morris's *Tlysau Hen Oesoedd* in 1735; only one number appeared and from then until 1770 no further attempt was made. From that year until the beginning of the nineteenth century there appeared several short-lived magazines such as *Trysorfa Gwybodaeth* (1770), *Y *Cylchgrawn Cynmraeg* (1793), *Y Drysorfa Gymysgedig* (1795) and *Trysorfa Ysbrydol* (1799). The content of these publications was heavily antiquarian and religious and shows the influence of the Religious Tract Society. Similarly influenced were the first efforts at publishing a magazine for children in Welsh, namely *Yr Addysgydd* (1826) and *Pethau Newydd a Hen* (1826–29).

It was not until 1814 that a Welsh newspaper appeared: *Seren Gomer* (Jan. 1, 1814 – Aug. 9, 1815) was founded and edited by Joseph *Harris (Gomer) of Swansea. He claimed a weekly circulation of 2,000 copies but, owing to the oppressive Government taxation of the day on newsprint, paper and advertisements, only eighty-five numbers appeared. The *Seren* was not the first newspaper in Wales, for English papers such as The *Cambrian* (1804), *The North Wales Chronicle* (1807) and The *Carmarthen Journal* (1810) were already in the field. As a result of the work of the *Sunday School move-ment in Wales, however, a high percentage of the common people could read and when Government taxes were abolished between 1853 and 1861 there was a steady increase in the number of Welsh periodicals. Not that the first half of the century had been barren. In his *Hanes Llenyddiaeth Gymraeg: 1650–1850* (1893) Charles *Ashton showed that between 1735 and 1850 there had been fifteen quarterlies, two bi-monthlies, 107 monthlies, eleven bi-weeklies and four weeklies in the Welsh language; most of these had been short-lived.

The Welsh newspaper and Welsh journalism belong to the second half of the nineteenth century and the first half of the twentieth, especially the period from 1880 to 1914. During this time, as many as forty local, national and denomina-tional weekly papers were published. Most of them were local papers but there were others which, although of local provenance, had a wider appeal. Such, for example, were *Y Cymm-ro* (1890–1907, Liverpool), *Y *Brython* (1906–39, Liverpool), *Yr *Herald Cymraeg* (1854–), Caernarfon), *Gwalia* (1881–1921, Bangor), *Y Celt* (1878–1906, Bala), *Y *Genedl Gymreig* (1879–1937, Caernarfon) and *Tarian y Gweithiwr* (1875–1914, Aberdare). Some weeklies were designed as national papers from the start, for example *Yr *Amserau* (1843–59, Liverpool), *Baner Cymru* (1857; after incorporat-ing *Yr Amserau* in 1859 it became *Baner ac Amserau Cymru*), *Yr *Amseroedd* (1882–83) and *Papur Pawb* (1893–1955). With these may be grouped some weekly denominational papers

such as *Y *Gwyliedydd* (1877–1908), *Y Bedyddiwr Cymreig* (1885–86), *Y Cymro* (1914–31, Dolgell-au), *Y *Goleuad* (1869–), *Y Llan a'r Dywyso-gaeth* (1884–), *Seren Cymru* (1851–), *Y *Tyst* (1867–) and *Ysbryd yr Oes* (1904–07).

Inevitably, in view of this activity, from 1860 onwards journalism in Welsh became a pro-fession. Correspondents, editors and presses were needed and towns like Carmarthen, Caernarfon, Liverpool, Aberdare, Denbigh, Aberystwyth and Merthyr Tydfil became pub-lishing centres of the first importance. Even in America, *Y *Drych* appeared (from 1851) and the Welsh colony of *Patagonia was served by *Y *Drafod* (1891). There arose a group of Welsh-language journalists, among the most eminent of whom were Lewis W. *Lewis (Llew Llwyfo), John *Griffith (Y Gohebydd), Thomas *Gee, William *Rees (Gwilym Hiraethog), Beriah Gwynfe *Evans, Samuel *Roberts, David *Owen (Brutus), David *Rees, Isaac *Foulkes (Llyfrbryf) and Daniel *Rees. The literary con-tent of the Welsh-language press during the nineteenth century was always substantial: many papers published 'novels' in serial form and most had poetry columns.

The First World War marked the end of 'the golden age' of Welsh journalism. A number of newspapers disappeared or were amalgamated under new titles, at the same time as English daily papers were beginning to penetrate the Welsh-speaking areas. Nevertheless, two new Welsh papers were launched in 1932, namely *Y *Cymro* in Oswestry and *Y Cyfnod*, a local weekly published in Bala. A new generation of editors and journalists included such writers as E. Morgan *Humphreys, T. Gwynn *Jones, John Dyfnallt *Owen, R. J. *Rowlands (Meuryn) and E. Prosser *Rhys. This tradition continued after the Second World War, attract-ing many Welsh writers who include Kate *Roberts, Saunders *Lewis, Caradog *Prichard, Gwilym R. *Jones, John Roberts *Williams and T. Glynne *Davies. The general decline in read-ing habits which has taken place since the 1950s, particularly since the advent of television, has had a baneful effect on the Welsh press. No Welsh paper sells more than ten thousand copies a week and only *Y Cymro* and *Y Faner* have claims to be national weeklies with readers in most parts of Wales. An attempt to launch a popular Sunday paper, known as *Sulyn*, foundered in January 1983 after only fourteen issues.

The only daily newspapers to serve Wales have been English ones such as the *Western Mail*, the *South Wales Evening Post* and, in the past, the *Cambria Daily Leader* and the *South Wales Daily News*. There has never been a daily paper in North Wales, although the *Liverpool Daily Post* has a fairly wide circulation there. In the 1980s there were between fifty and sixty local weeklies in English, sixteen of which were established in the nineteenth century. Many of these papers started life as advertising sheets and only gradually became local newspapers. On the whole, their contents and viewpoints are more parochial and limited than those of their counterparts in Welsh. The English press in Wales has very little national consciousness, except perhaps fitfully in the *Western Mail*, and it was in reaction against this deficiency that the *papurau bro* ('neighbourhood papers') were launched in the 1970s, an initiative generally considered to be the most significant in the field of Welsh journalism during the twentieth century. See also PRINTING AND PUBLISHING.

Further details will be found in E. Morgan Humphreys, *Y Wasg Gymraeg* (1945), J. Ellis Williams (ed.), *Berw Bywyd* (1968), and the chapters by D. Tecwyn Lloyd in *The Welsh Language Today* (ed. Meic Stephens, 1973) and *Traddodiad Rhyddiaith yr Ugeinfed Ganrif* (ed. Geraint Bowen, 1976).

J. R. Tryfanwy, see WILLIAMS, JOHN RICHARD (1867–1924).

Juan de Mervinia, see ROBERTS, JOHN (1576–1610).

Jubilee Blues (1938), a novel by Rhys *Davies, the third of a loosely connected trilogy, recounts the decline into bankruptcy of The Jubilee, a public house in a coal-mining valley during the *Depression of the inter-war years. The owner is Cassie Jones, a handsome and religious girl from the country who dominates the plot, and her weak husband, Prosser, who contributes by his gambling to her misfortunes. The conflict between these two is one of the novel's main themes and sex, class and social conditions also find an important place in it.

Jumpers, the name given to some of the converts of the Methodist Revival because of their practice of jumping and dancing as an expression of their spiritual joy. They were first seen in large numbers during the revival at Llangeitho, Cards., in 1762 but similar scenes had occurred before that year. The practice drew many curious spectators to the Revival meetings and continued, despite constant mockery, well into the nineteenth century. Early Methodist leaders did not attempt to discourage the Jumpers and William *Williams (Pantycelyn) published two pamphlets defending them (1762, 1763).

Juvencus Manuscript, The, a complex ninth-century Latin manuscript now in the Cambridge University Library (MS Ff.4.42). It contains a copy of the metrical version of the Gospels by the late Latin Christian poet Juvencus, together with a number of glosses and other additional material in Latin, Welsh and Irish, written by several hands in round minuscule. The work of the main copyist belongs to the ninth century and the scribe may have been named Nuadu, if the colophon is to be believed, an Irishman working perhaps in a Welsh milieu where there was strong Irish influence. The manuscript also contains numerous Latin glosses in an Insular hand of the ninth and tenth centuries, as well as Old Welsh glosses added by several hands in square minuscule during the first half of the tenth century, and others in Old Irish, or hybrid Old Welsh-Old Irish.

Two important series of three-line *englynion in Old Welsh are preserved in the manuscript: three *englynion* similar to the stanzas connected with *'Canu Llywarch Hen' and an incomplete series of nine religious *englynion*. The first series of three (which are not yet fully understood) seem to be stray saga or narrative verses recounting the fate of a lordly warrior who has lost his retinue, perhaps after carnage in battle. The other nine are religious poems celebrating the power of God and urging men to revere the Holy Trinity. Both series were copied by the same scribe and the copies probably belong to the first half of the tenth century or perhaps to the late ninth century; but, as the poems may have been composed earlier than these dates, the Juvencus *englynion* may be said to be the earliest surviving poetry in Welsh. As such they are of great linguistic and literary significance.

For further details see the article by T. Arwyn Watkins in *Bardos* (ed. R. Geraint Gruffydd, 1982).

K

Kadwaladr, John, see CADWALADR, SIÔN (*fl.* 1760).

Kayles, a game formerly played in the open air on greensward as well as in bowling alleys. The object was to throw a metal-edged wooden disc or ball at a number of kayles, or skittles, knocking over as many as possible. By the Middle Ages, despite numerous attempts to prohibit it, the game was widespread and popular among the common people of Wales. During the nineteenth century it was often banned by local magistrates because of the heavy betting which was associated with the game.

KEATING, JOSEPH (1871–1934), novelist. Born at Mountain Ash, Glam., to parents who were Irish immigrants, he left elementary school at the age of twelve and worked for six years at a local colliery. When the mine closed he tried a variety of occupations and, in 1893, found employment in the commercial department of the *Western Mail* in Cardiff but left in 1904 to live in poverty in London.

His first published novel, *Son of Judith* (1901), uses a melodramatic plot to present the industrial, Nonconformist village-life of the Cynon Valley towards the end of the nineteenth century. The best of his novels, *Maurice: the Romance of a Welsh Coalmine* (1905), has features which make it a humble forerunner of some of the novels of Jack *Jones and Rhys *Davies. Of his other novels, *Queen of Swords* (1906), *The Great Appeal* (1909), *The Perfect Wife* (1913), *The Marriage Contract* (1914), *Tipperary Tommy* (1915) and *Flower of the Dark* (1917) have little literary merit, while *The Exploited Woman* (1923), *The Fairfax Mystery* and *A Woman Fascinates* (the last two were published posthumously in 1935) have none at all. But at least three of the stories in *Adventures in the Dark* (1906) are noteworthy and some of their characteristics may be recognized in later stories by Anglo-Welsh authors. His play *Peggy and her Husband* (1914), adapted from his novel *The Perfect Wife*, ran for only three weeks at the Royalty Theatre, London. Parts of his autobiography, *My Struggle for Life* (1916), have moments of genuine pathos.

A supporter of the Irish Nationalist Movement, Keating contributed a section to a book entitled *Irish Heroes of the War* (1917); he also published an English translation of Emile Zola's *Nana* (1926). After the failure of his play, he began to spend more time in Mountain Ash where—embittered and poverty-stricken—he became involved in political life: he was elected as a Labour councillor in 1923 and in 1931 became chairman of the local education committee. As an author, Joseph Keating may be seen as an obscure pioneer, a precursor of those more gifted writers from the valleys of south Wales who began to emerge at the time of his death.

Keenor, Fred (1892–1972), footballer, was captain of the Cardiff City team when it won the English Cup in 1927. He played 369 times for the *Bluebirds in the half-back position and won thirty-two Welsh caps.

KELSALL, JOHN (*fl.* 1683–1743), Quaker and diarist, was an Englishman who settled in Wales in 1702 as a schoolmaster at Dolobran, Mont., where he also worked as a clerk in the ironworks of the *Lloyd family. His extensive diary (now kept in the Friends' House, London) is important for its account of the iron industry and the Quaker faith in north Wales. A selection from Kelsall's diary was published by O. M. *Edwards in his magazine *Wales* (1895).

Kelt, The, see LONDON WELSHMAN.

Kemble, Charles (1775–1854), actor, was born at Brecon, the eleventh child of the itinerant players Roger Kemble and Sarah Ward; Julia Ann *Hatton and Sarah *Siddons were his sisters. Educated at the English College in Douai, he first appeared on the stage in 1792 and made his London début two years later in *Macbeth*. Although not an actor of the fame of his elder brother, John Philip Kemble, or his sister, Mrs. Siddons, he became a well-known figure in the theatre and is credited with the authorship or adaptation of six plays. All three of his children achieved distinction: John Mitchell Kemble (1807–57) was a philologist and historical writer, Adelaide Sartoris (1814?–79) a singer and writer, and Frances Anne Butler (1809–93) an actress and writer.

KENWARD, JAMES (**Elfynydd**; *fl.* 1834–68), an English poet who lived at Smethwick, near Birmingham, was the author of *A Poem of English Sympathy with Wales* (1858) and *For Cambria: themes in Verse and Prose, 1834–68* (1868). The latter, dedicated to the Breton writer La

*Villemarqué, contains a long poem which the author read at the Eisteddfod held at Llangollen in 1858.

Kidwelly or **Cydweli**, a castle or baronial fortress situated on a steep bank above the estuary of the Gwendraeth Fach, Carms., was built by order of Bishop Roger of Salisbury, minister to Henry I. In 1136 the forces of his successor, Maurice de Londres, defeated and slew *Gwenllian, the daughter of *Gruffudd ap Cynan and leader of a Welsh contingent at a battle fought to the north of the castle at a spot still known as Maes Gwenllian. In 1188 Archbishop Baldwin and *Gerald de Barri (Giraldus Cambrensis) stayed overnight at the castle. It was periodically held by Gwenllian's son, *Rhys ap Gruffudd (The Lord Rhys) of Dinefwr, and by his descendants in the late twelfth and early thirteenth century, and it was burned by *Llywelyn ap Iorwerth (Llywelyn Fawr) in 1231; it was rebuilt in stone in the late thirteenth century and early fourteenth century. *Owain Glyndŵr's forces were unable to capture the castle in 1403, despite the fact that one of the leaders of the rebellion was Henry Dwn, steward of Kidwelly and a dominant figure in the locality. *Lewys Glyn Cothi referred to Owain, the son of Gruffudd ap Nicholas of Dinefwr, as governor of the castle in the fifteenth century. It was granted by Henry VII to Sir Rhys ap Thomas of Dinefwr and was later held by the Cawdor family of Golden Grove. Among those who lived in the vicinity of the castle were the poets *Ieuan Deulwyn and Ieuan Tew Ieuanc.

For further details see D. D. Jones, *A History of Kidwelly* (1908), J. E. Lloyd (ed.), *A History of Carmarthenshire* (1935, 1939) and C. A. Ralegh-Radford, *Kidwelly Castle* (1952).

KILVERT, FRANCIS (1840–79), English diarist. Born at Hardenhuish, near Chippenham, Wilts., and educated at Wadham College, Oxford, he first served as curate to his father at Langley Burrell, Wilts., and then, in 1865, went as curate to Clyro, Rads. The seven years spent in Clyro were the genesis and heart of the diary for which he is now famous. Returning to Langley Burrell in 1872, he was soon afterwards preferred to the living of St. Harmon, Rads., only to become in less than a year the incumbent of Bredwardine, Herefs. Two years later, no more than five weeks after his marriage, he died of peritonitis.

The *Diary*, which runs (with gaps) from January 1870 to March in the year of Kilvert's death, originally consisted of between twenty-two and thirty notebooks containing well over a million words. His widow, who died in 1911, is presumed to have destroyed those notebooks referring to herself long before Kilvert's nephew, Perceval Smith, brought the manuscript to William Plomer, who selected about one third of the original for publication in three volumes in 1938, 1939 and 1940. Both Plomer's carbon transcript and the publisher's top copy of the original notebooks were lost or destroyed during the Second World War and in 1958 it was discovered that Essex Hope, Kilvert's niece, had probably destroyed nineteen of the twenty-two notebooks which had come into her possession; only the published selection and three notebooks survived. One of these (for 19 July to 6 August 1874, when Kilvert was on holiday in Cornwall) was deposited under the terms of Plomer's will at the library of the University of Durham in 1974. Another, given to Jeremy Sandford by Essex Hope, was bought by the National Library of Wales in 1979, and a third, for long in the keeping of an unidentified person, was also acquired by the Library in 1985.

This literary tragedy may be explained, perhaps, by the presence in the *Diary* of a strong vein of erotic sensibility which Kilvert's relatives, especially Essex Hope, preferred to keep from public view. Like Lewis Carroll, the diarist was very partial to young girls and, of the more mature beauties he met, few were treated with indifference. His doting used to be thought excessive, but is now recognized as the innocent affection of a young man who longed to be married and to have children of his own. Be that as it may, the special charm of his writing lies in a kind of poetic zest: life was to him 'a curious and wonderful thing' which even in 'a humble and uneventful' pattern, it was a pity not to record. A diligent Churchman, he was made to feel at home both in Hay society and among the poor of Clyro. It is during his Clyro years that his *Diary* is fullest and most vivid, presenting a detailed and often objective picture of everyday life in a remote countryside in mid-Victorian times which was still largely unaffected by the growth of communications. No intellectual himself, Kilvert is often unacceptably sentimental in the eyes of modern intellectuals, but his gift for the right image and the telling detail, his loving evocation of landscape and people, make him one of the great diarists, capable of crowd scenes, conversation pieces and a keen insight into tragedy. He was a keen walker and the accounts of his excursions from Clyro to Aberedw, to Capel-y-ffin to visit Father Ignatius, and to see the Reverend John Price, the eccentric 'solitary' who was vicar of Painscastle, are among the *Diary*'s most memorable passages. An aura of romantic failure, not least in his feelings for Daisy Thomas (1852–1928) of Llanigon, and in his passionate attachment to Ettie Meredith Brown, both of which were thwarted by parental disapproval of his prospects as a poor curate, makes the *Diary* enduringly attractive to a wide variety of readers. Kilvert's poetic spirit, however, was somehow subdued by the requirements of poetry itself: the volume *Musings in Verse* (1882), selected by an unknown friend after his death, offers little more than a conventional piety.

The standard text of *Kilvert's Diary* is that edited by William Plomer (3 vols., 1938, 1939, 1940); the notebook bought by the National Library of Wales, covering the period from 27 April to 10 June 1870, when the diarist was in Clyro, was published in 1982 under the editorship of Kathleen Hughes and Dafydd Ifans. There are only two books about Kilvert's life and writing: A. L. Le Quesne's *After Kilvert* (1978) and Frederick Grice's *The World of Francis Kilvert* (1983). A synopsis of the years Kilvert spent in Wales will be found in the introduction to *The Curate of Clyro* (ed. Meic Stephens, 1983). The Kilvert Society, founded in 1948, has published many booklets and issues a newsletter containing much valuable information about the diarist and related topics.

Kilvey or **Cilfái**, that part of the commot of Nedd which lies on the eastern side of the mouth of the river Tawe. It was linked with the commot of *Gower, probably when Swansea castle was built, thus forming the lordship of Gower and Kilvey.

King and the Bishop, The, an international folk-tale on the theme of an uneducated youth who defeats a learned man. A king commands a bishop, or priest, to answer certain questions or to lose his life. Unbeknown to the king, the questions are answered by the bishop's brother, usually a shepherd or servant, and his life is saved. The characters vary from country to country (in England the theme is found in the ballad 'King John and the Abbot of Canterbury'), but common to all versions are questions in riddle form and cunning replies. For example, the answer to the question 'What is the moon's weight?' is 'A pound, because it consists of four quarters'. In the most popular version known in Wales, one of two brothers whose heart is set on becoming a priest is sent to appear before a bishop and to the question 'What am I thinking?' he replies, 'You think that I am my brother'. In some versions the questions are asked and answered by means of manual gestures. One theory is that the theme originated in the Holy Land, possibly as early as the seventh century, and that it was brought to Europe by the Crusaders.

KNIGHT, BERNARD (**Bernard Picton**; 1931–   ), novelist. Born in Cardiff, he is Professor of Forensic Pathology at the Welsh National School of Medicine, having qualified as both doctor and barrister. He has combined his medical and legal interests in the writing of several crime novels, such as *The Lately Deceased* (1962), *The Thread of Evidence* (1965), *Mistress Murder* (1966), *Policeman's Progress* (1968), *Tiger at Bay* (1970) and *The Expert* (1975), all published under his pseudonym, and has also published a number of historical novels on Welsh subjects which include *Lion Rampant* (1972) and *Madoc, Prince of America* (1977).

KNIGHT, LEONARD ALFRED (1895–1977), novelist. Born near Arundel, Sussex, he saw active service during the First World War and, after demobilization, joined the staff of a petroleum company, first at Bridgend, Glam., and then at Hereford. While at Bridgend in 1921 he submitted six pieces on the countryside to the *Western Mail* and their acceptance created in him an ambition to write novels. The second of these, *Dead Man's Bay* (1929), was an immediate success, and he followed it with *The Pawn* (1931), a spy story of the Peninsular War (1808–14). He made use of a Glamorgan background in *The Creaking Tree Mystery* (1933) and *Rider in the Sky* (1953) is set in mid-Wales. But L. A. Knight became best known for his Pembrokeshire novels, of which *Conqueror's Road* (1945), later serialized on radio and television, *The Dancing Stones* (1946), *The Brazen Head* (1948) and *High Treason* (1954) are probably the most distinguished.

Knight Errantry, see CHIVALRY.

Knitting Night, a folk-custom. During the winter months the inhabitants of upland districts would assemble on each other's hearths to knit stockings and to amuse themselves by recitation and the singing of verses to harp accompaniment. The custom was particularly popular in Merionethshire, where there was an important knitting industry in the eighteenth century. Under the influence of *Methodism, it became a meeting for the exchange of religious experiences. A similar tradition was the *pilnos*, when neighbours gathered to peel rushes for candle-making.

KYFFIN, MORRIS (*c.*1555–98), author and soldier, studied poetry under the direction of *Wiliam Llŷn and was a pupil and friend of John *Dee. He wrote much poetry in English and Welsh, his best-known poem in English being 'The Blessedness of Brytaine' (1587), a loyal effusion to Elizabeth I which was probably prompted by the Babington Plot of the previous year. Many of his Welsh poems remain in manuscript. For some years after 1588 he was an officer in the English army in the Netherlands and in France. On his return to London he published his masterpiece, *Deffyniad Ffydd Eglwys Loegr* (1594), a translation of Bishop John Jewel's classic defence of the faith of the Anglican Church (1562), which was printed by Richard Field. An officer in the army in Ireland for the last two years of his life, he tried to maintain discipline over some of his fellow-officers who were cheating the Government and oppressing the Irish. His brother, **Edward Kyffin** (*c.*1558–

1603), was a priest who composed a number of metrical psalms in Welsh.

For further details see W. P. Williams (ed.), *Deffynniad Ffydd Eglwys Loegr* (1908), W. J. Gruffydd, *Llenyddiaeth Cymru: Rhyddiaith o 1540 hyd 1660* (1926) and Thomas Parry, *A History of Welsh Literature* (1955).

Kynniver Llith a Ban (lit. 'So many lessons and excerpts'; 1551), William *Salesbury's translation into Welsh of the Epistles and Gospels of the First Book of Common Prayer (1549). Dedicating the book to the Bishops of Wales and Hereford, Salesbury urged them to appoint six men from each diocese to examine it and authorize it for public use. It contained the first extensive Welsh translations from the Scriptures to be made directly from the original languages. The quality of many of them was excellent but their usefulness was marred by Salesbury's quirks such as Latinized spellings and neglected mutations. Nevertheless, the work established an invaluable precedent for his later translations and emphasized the need for a Welsh *Bible and *Prayer Book. Copies survived Mary's reign and were used early in Elizabeth's.

For further details see John Fisher's modern edition of the work (1931); see also D. R. Thomas, *The Life of Richard Davies and William Salesbury* (1902), the article by G. T. Roberts in *Yr Eurgrawn* (vol. CXLIII, 1951), Glanmor Williams, *Welsh Reformation Essays* (1967), the chapter by W. Alun Mathias in *Y Traddodiad Rhyddiaith* (ed. Geraint Bowen, 1970) and Isaac Thomas, *Y Testament Newydd Gymraeg 1551–1620* (1976).

L

Labour Voice, see LLAIS LLAFUR.

Ladi Wen, Y (lit. 'The white lady'), an apparition in the form of a woman dressed in white,
one of the most common bogies used to warn
children against the consequences of mis-
behaviour.

Ladies of Llangollen, The, see BUTLER,
ELEANOR (1729–1829) AND PONSONBY, SARAH
(1755–1831).

Lady Llanover, see HALL, AUGUSTA WAD-
DINGTON (1802–96).

Lady with the Unicorn, The (1948), Vernon
*Watkins's second and probably most successful
collection of poems. It opens with 'Music of
Colours—White Blossom', undeniably one of
his finest pieces, and includes 'Returning to
Goleufryn', 'Money for the Market', 'Llywelyn's Chariot' (for Dylan *Thomas's son),
'Sardine-Fishers at Daybreak', 'Swallows over
the Weser', 'Ophelia', 'The Return of Spring',
the superb 'Foal', 'Rhossili', 'The Feather',
'Gravestones', 'The Butterflies' and 'Zacchaeus
in the Leaves'. Of much less impact are the
elegies, which are mostly ornate and obscure.
'The Song of the Good Samaritan' embodies the
poet's highly personal and unorthodox theology
and the title-poem his formal excellence.

'Land of my Fathers', see HEN WLAD FY
NHADAU (1856).

Land of Strange Names, The, an international
folk-tale in which a master tests his servant's
ability by obliging him to learn outlandish
names for ordinary things about the house and
farm. Most of the Welsh versions, some twenty
in all, have been recorded during the twentieth
century. The strange names vary from district to
district and it is usually only the servant's
attempt to memorize them which survives. In
one version a hot coal falls from the fire on to the
cat's tail in the middle of the night and the
servant uses his new vocabulary to awaken his
master, with hilarious results.

Land Reform, a major social question in Wales
during the nineteenth century. Exorbitant rents
and insecurity of tenure were amongst the
grievances which caused the *Rebecca Riots

(1839–43). Many landowners, estranged from
their tenants not only in social status but by
barriers of language, religion and politics, raised
rents on property improved by the occupants,
neglected their estates, were harsh in their application of the hated game-laws and preferred
Churchmen to Nonconformists; their agents
were often even more intransigent. The evic-
tions which followed the elections of 1868 intensified the already strained relations on many
estates. With the onset of agricultural depression
in the 1880s, landowners were further criticized
for failing to give sufficient aid to their tenants.
The charge was also levelled against them that
they had supported the Anglican clergy in the
*Tithe War.

With the movements for Land Reform in
Ireland and the Western Highlands of Scotland
brought to their attention, many tenants in
Wales sought legislation which would have
improved their lot. The Welsh Land Commission established by Gladstone (through the persuasion of T. E. *Ellis) published a voluminous
report in 1896 dealing with various aspects of life
in rural Wales. Most of the Commission's nine
members were in favour of legislation but, with
the advent of a Conservative Government and
an improvement in economic conditions during
the late 1890s, nothing came of the proposals.
While tenants' grievances were real enough on
small estates, which comprised just over half of
the cultivated land in Wales, conditions on the
larger estates tended to be more favourable. That
they were often depicted as otherwise was part
of the Radical campaign to denigrate landlordism in general. By the time the Liberals were
returned to power in 1905 the question of Land
Reform had been replaced in public interest by
that of *Disestablishment of the Anglican
Church. See also LIBERALISM.

For further details see D. W. Howell, *Land and People in
Nineteenth Century Wales* (1978) and J. P. D. Dunbabin,
Rural Discontent in Nineteenth Century Britain (1974).

LANGFORD, JOHN (1640–1715/16), trans-
lator and zealous Anglican, was born at Ruthin,
Denbs., a member of the family which had lived
at Allington (Trefalun, near Gresford) since the
fifteenth century. An ancestor of his, Richard
Langford (d. 1586), had taken a keen interest in
Welsh literature, copying manuscripts. John
Langford's main literary work was *Holl Ddled-*

swydd Dyn (1672), a translation of Richard Allestree's *The Whole Duty of Man*.

Last Inspection, The (1942), a volume of short stories, some little more than sketches, by Alun *Lewis. A handful, written somewhat earlier and set in the mining valleys of south Wales during the 1930s, deal with themes of childhood, hardship and repression in a manner reminiscent of D. H. Lawrence. But most are the direct result of the writer's experience of army life and they reflect his painful adjustment to its routines at a time when, under attack from the air, the civilian population seemed to be in greater peril than the military. Welsh characters, portrayed sympathetically, figure prominently throughout the book, which helped to earn for Alun Lewis a reputation as a prose-writer of promise.

Last Invasion of Britain, The, see under NICHOLAS, JEMIMA (*fl.* 1797).

Laugharne or **Talacharn**, a commot of *Cantref Gwarthaf in *Dyfed. Norman penetration was contained under *Rhys ap Gruffudd (The Lord Rhys) but by the thirteenth century the commot was held by the Bryan family. From the Bryans it passed by marriage in turn to the Scropes, the Lovells and the Butlers. Its lords paid tribute at the court at Carmarthen and therefore, although Laugharne was a Marcher lordship, it was also part of the county of Carmarthen.

Laugharne, Rowland (d. 1676?), Parliamentary commander, of St. Brides, Pembs., was once page to the third Earl of Essex and served under him in the Low Countries. Absent from the county at the outbreak of the first *Civil War, he returned in September 1643 to take over command from John *Poyer, who had stoutly defended *Pembroke, the Parliament's only hold. From January 1644, aided by seamen from a Parliamentary squadron, Laugharne daringly picked off Royalist garrisons one by one, ending with the recapture of Haverfordwest and Tenby. The arrival of part of the professional army from Ireland forced him back on Pembroke and Tenby (a situation in which, after recovery, he was to find himself again) but in August of 1645 he crushed the last Royalist forces at Colby Moor and, in a few months, mastered all west Wales. Like Poyer, however, he was whispered against in high places and was even accused of treating with the King. Disillusioned, he was called to London in 1648 when Poyer and Rice *Powell were moving towards revolt, but on his return he threw in his lot with Powell at the battle of St. Fagans and, after defeat there, held out in Pembroke Castle against Oliver Cromwell until 11 July. Sentenced to death by court martial, he was reprieved by Cromwell and, at the Restoration, was elected Member of Parliament for Pembroke Borough.

The best single source for information about Laugharne is Arthur Leonard Leach, *The History of the Civil War in Pembrokeshire 1642–1649* (1937).

Laverbread (L. *Porphyra umbilicalis*), an edible seaweed which grows on the rocky shores of south Wales to the west of Swansea. The centre of the trade which gathers it, with cockles, is the village of Penclawdd. The plant is washed, boiled, pulped and mixed with oatmeal until it becomes black, glutinous and aromatic. When fried, this traditional food is considered to be a delicacy and is popularly known as 'Welsh caviare'. See also WELSH RABBIT.

Lawrence de Berkerolles (d. 1411), the Norman lord of East Orchard Castle, near St. Athan, Glam. According to Iolo Morganwg (Edward *Williams), who may have found the story in local folk-tradition, a friendship was struck up between him and the disguised *Owain Glyndŵr. When the mysterious stranger, a guest at the castle, revealed his true identity, the Norman was struck dumb for the rest of his life. The tale was used by John *Morris-Jones as the basis for a famous lyric which was published in his volume *Caniadau* (1907).

LAWS, EDWARD (1837–1913), county historian, was descended on his mother's side from the Mathias family of Lamphey Court and Llangwaran, Pembs. Educated at Wadham College, Oxford, he settled in Tenby where he played a prominent part in public life for many years, devoting his leisure to the study of the county's history. His most valuable published work was the volume *Little England Beyond Wales* (1880); the significance of this book's title will be found in the entry for *Anglia Transwallina*.

Laws of Hywel Dda, The, the traditional name for the native laws of Wales which are preserved in about eighty Welsh and Latin manuscripts varying in age between the twelfth and eighteenth centuries. Tradition has it that the Laws were formulated at a convention held at Tŷ Gwyn (Hendy-gwyn or *Whitland, Carms.) under the authority of *Hywel Dda. The earliest references to this convention are to be found in the Law Books themselves, but it is impossible to accept all the details given. The exact nature of Hywel Dda's legislative activity is no longer known. Certainly none of the extant manuscripts are copies of any document which might have been formulated at Tŷ Gwyn, nor do they preserve the laws exactly as they were in the tenth century. It is generally accepted, however, that they contain a nucleus of material compiled during the lifetime of Hywel Dda. The Laws were administered in lawcourts throughout the land, by professionally trained judges in *Gwynedd and *Powys and by amateurs in south Wales. This system persisted (with minor alterations) until the sixteenth century, for the Welsh Laws were not abolished by the Edwardian Conquest, as is often thought; some parts of them were still in force as late as 1540.

About half the law-texts belong to the Middle Ages and they may be contrasted with the medieval narrative tales in two distinct ways. Firstly, more than ten times as many copies have been preserved of the Laws as of the most popular tales. Secondly, whereas the texts of the tales are, as a rule, simple copies, the one of the other, almost every law-book written before the mid-sixteenth century is unique in the exact nature of its content. The reason for these differences is twofold. Hywel's Laws were not static, royal proclamations, but an organic system which developed over the centuries according to political and social needs. Interpreters of the law, rather than 'pure' copyists, were responsible for producing these books. They were the Welsh lawyers' work-books, used daily in the lawcourts, and as the laws changed to meet contemporary requirements, so were the books changed and adapted; their content was reorganized, new material was added and material thought to be redundant was omitted.

A pattern exists beneath the manifold textual variations and it is possible to recognize three classes of Welsh texts. The first person to draw attention to the existence of these classes was Aneurin *Owen (although he was somewhat indebted for his classification to William *Maurice). Owen called them the 'Venedotian Code', the 'Dimetian Code' and the 'Gwentian Code', believing them to represent geographical variations of Hywel's Laws. It has since been realized that the differences between the three groups are to be attributed to the period, not the location, of their development, and they are now classified according to the names of the lawyers mentioned in them, although it is not to be assumed that these men were the authors of the codes. The earliest expression of the Laws is to be found in the Cyfnerth manuscripts ('Gwentian Code'), the Blegywryd manuscripts ('Dimetian Code') reveal an ecclesiastical influence, and the Iorwerth manuscripts ('Venedotian Code') reflect the favourable legislative and social climate created in Gwynedd under the rule of *Llywelyn ap Gruffudd (Llywelyn Fawr).

Almost every law-book opens with a preface relating the story of the Tŷ Gwyn convention. This is usually followed by the Laws of the Court, a section which lists the officers of the king's court—steward, priest, court poet, doctor and so on—and notes their special rights and privileges. There follows a series of sections on various subjects, each with its own peculiar interest, not only from a legal point of view but also as a historical source. Much of the information is purely legal and concerns such matters as witnesses, contract, oath-taking and the rules of inheritance. But there are also to be found lists of equipment for the household, for ploughing and fishing, and of the legal value placed on each, as well as evidence for the geographical distribution of different kinds of trees, for hunting customs, bee-keeping, and many other aspects of agricultural life, all of which is excellent evidence concerning the nature of Welsh society in the Middle Ages.

One of the most interesting sections in this respect is that dealing with 'galanas' which, together with the sections on 'Fire' and 'Theft', forms a vestigial criminal law. The word 'galanas' means 'murder' (or 'manslaughter') and it also means 'the price put on a man's life and paid to his kin (i.e. his family as far as the seventh—or sometimes ninth—generation) by members of the kin of the person who slew him'. The section opens with a list of nine ways in which a person can be an accessory to murder; then follow rules relating to the sharing and paying of the 'galanas-payment' by the king, and the 'galanas-value' of various members of society. The concept of kinship is essential to the law of 'galanas', and reflects one of the social, characteristics of the period, namely, that blood-ties were very important since the individual's activities affected so many of his relatives.

The law-books are invaluable in the interpretation of references in medieval Welsh literature which would otherwise be obscure. The fact that it was the kin to the third (or sometimes the fourth) generation which gave a girl in marriage, throws new light on *Efnysien's wrath when his sister *Branwen is given in marriage to *Matholwch in the Second Branch of *Pedair Cainc y Mabinogi, and explains the satirical reference to the four grandsires and four grand-dames whose permission, it is claimed, had to be sought for *Culhwch's marriage to Olwen. Again in the Second Branch, Matholwch is given (as compensation for the disfigurement of his horses by Efnysien) 'a cover as large as his face'; this reference would be obscure but for the fact that the law-books list such an item as part of the payment made to a king who had been insulted. The story of *Manawydan catching a mouse which he has found stealing corn, in the Third Branch, develops a new dimension when seen in the light of the law of theft and the Triad of the 'Three thieves liable to be hanged'.

Furthermore, Welsh medieval literature is full of technical, legalistic words which can only be properly understood by reference to the law texts. Saunders *Lewis has declared that the Welsh Laws are one of the pinnacles of medieval European culture, not only on account of the body of law they contain but also because they are a literary masterpiece which directly influenced the form and style of Welsh prose. One of the crowning glories of the Welsh language is its technical, legalistic vocabulary, in particular its rich store of abstract nouns, this richness being fused with masterly, scientific definition and logic. The detail of the Laws' definitions depends on flexibility and a highly developed syntax.

For studies of the Laws see J. E. Lloyd, *Hywel Dda 928–1928* (1928), J. Goronwy Edwards, *Hywel Dda and the Welsh Lawbooks* (1929), Melville Richards, *The Laws of Hywel Dda* (1954), the special number of *The Welsh History Review* (1963), Dafydd Jenkins, *Cyfraith Hywel* (1970) and *Hywel Dda and the Law of Medieval Wales* (1985) and Dafydd Jenkins and Morfydd E. Owen, *The Welsh Law of Women* (1980); see also the two chapters by Morfydd E. Owen in *Y Traddodiad Rhyddiaith yn yr Oesau Canol* (ed. Geraint Bowen, 1974).

Leander, see JONES, JOHN (1575–1635).

Lee, Rowland (d. 1543), English bishop and from 1534 the President of the King's Council in the Marches of Wales. Based at Ludlow and faced with a lawlessness which his predecessor had been unable to control, he made capital punishment his regime's main weapon, hanging and harrying up and down the old Marcher lands but having no powers on shire ground. Tradition suggests that it was in his court that Welshmen were first compelled to plead to their names in English form (see under SURNAMES). His opinion of the Welsh gentry was low and the *Act of Union of 1536 which established Justices of the Peace in Wales and made the whole Principality shire ground, brought him to vigorous protest: 'If one thief shall try another, all we have here begun is foredone'. The execution of the Act was probably delayed by his influence until 1541 or later, but he was proven wrong by immediate events: the King needed Welsh support over the *Dissolution of the Monasteries and the gentry of Wales grasped at the legal opportunities of the Act with both hands. Lee was described by one William Gerard as 'not affable to any of the Walshrie, an extreme ponisher of offenders'.

No biography of Rowland Lee has been written but there are useful assessments of his work in David Williams, *A History of Modern Wales* (1950), Penry Williams, *The Council in the Marches of Wales under Elizabeth I* (1958) and Ralph Flenley, *A Calendar of the Register of the Queen's Majesty's Council in the Dominion and Principality of Wales and the Marches* (1916); see also Caroline A. J. Skeel, *The Council in the Marches of Wales* (1903).

Leek (L. *Allium Porrum*), a plant adopted by the Welsh as their national emblem. The custom of wearing the leek on St. David's Day (1 March) is widespread and well-established. The plant was used for centuries by the Welsh as a national badge, the colours of green and white being associated with the independent Princes and used as a primitive military uniform in the fourteenth century. The leek is worn today as a badge-cap by the Welsh Regiment and the eating of the leek by the youngest recruit on St. David's Day is a ceremony which still persists. An early reference to the leek as a Welsh emblem is to be found in the Account Book of Princess Mary Tudor (1536/7) and in his play, *King Henry V*, Shakespeare refers to the custom of wearing the leek as 'ancient tradition'. Fluellen observes that Henry wears the leek upon St. David's Day and the King replies, 'I wear it for a memorable honour, for I am Welsh, you know, good countryman'. The leek was worn at court as late as the eighteenth century and it has been suggested that this practice may have been one of the ways in which the Church of England tried to usurp the memory of the early British Church. The plant formed part of the symbolism of the *Eisteddfod in the early nineteenth century. But when and why exactly the leek was first worn on 1 March is not known.

According to legend, reflected in a reference by the English poet, Michael Drayton, the plant was associated with St. David (*Dewi Sant) because he ordered his soldiers to wear it on their helmets during a battle against the pagan Saxons in a field full of leeks. It is also said that the forces of *Cadwallon ap Cadfan wore it at the battle of Heathfield (Meigen) in the year 633. A more probable explanation, however, is that great importance has been attached to the leek throughout the centuries. Leek soup was a vital part of the Welsh people's diet, especially during Lent, and on social occasions; furthermore, it was believed to have medicinal properties. The manuscripts of the *Myddfai Physicians refer to its use for the prevention of bleeding, for healing bruises, mending broken bones and assisting women in childbirth. The leek also became a symbol of purity and immortality, a means of foretelling the future and protection against lightning. It was thought that rubbing the body with the plant protected soldiers in battle, that the growing of the leek in gardens brought luck and that wearing it kept away evil spirits. There was formerly a custom for young girls on Hallowe'en to place a leek under their pillow in the belief that they would see the apparition of their future husbands. See also DAFFODIL and RED DRAGON.

For further details see Arthur E. Hughes, 'The Welsh National Emblem: Leek or Daffodil', in *Y Cymmrodor* (vol. XXV, 1916).

LELAND, JOHN (1506–52), see under ITINERARY OF JOHN LELAND (1710).

Lent, a period of forty days' fasting which precedes Easter and begins on Ash Wednesday. On the previous day, Shrove Tuesday, there is a last chance to eat the foods prohibited by the Anglican Church during Lent, which is the origin of such customs as *blawta a blonega*, the house-to-house collection of ingredients for the making of pancakes. In the district of Kidwelly, Carms., the Lenten Crock—a turnip or egg-shell containing morsels of food—was placed outside windows after dark on this day. Mothering Sunday, the fourth Sunday in Lent, was the occasion when servants and apprentices returned home with presents for their mothers. It was followed by Pea Sunday, when the importance of peas in the Lenten diet was emphasized by eating them with great ceremony. During the week beginning on *Flowering Sunday it was the practice to 'clap for Easter eggs' in north-west Wales. On Good Friday the more serious significance of the day was emphasized. The inhabitants of Tenby, Pembs., for example, walked barefoot to church and 'Christ's bed' was prepared by making a figure of reed leaves to be laid on a wooden cross and left in a nearby garden, a vestige of the ancient custom of taking down the image of Christ and burying it in the churchyard until Easter morning. In some English-speaking districts of south Wales the baking of 'hot cross buns', believed to possess curative powers for the rest of the year, was popular.

Leon, see EVANS, WILLIAM DOWNING (1811–97).

LEVI, THOMAS (1825–1916), minister and author. Born near Ystradgynlais, Brecs., he received very little schooling and was put to work in the local ironworks at the age of eight. From about 1855 he served as a minister with the Calvinistic Methodists, his last pastorate being that of Tabernacl in Aberystwyth (1876–1901). A prolific author, he wrote some thirty books on religious and historical subjects and translated another sixty from English into Welsh. He composed many hymns, including the well-known '*Rwyf innau'n filwr bychan*' and '*Oleuni Mwyn*', the latter a version of Newman's hymn, 'Lead, kindly light', much more singable than that by John *Morris-Jones. His most important contribution to the cultural life of Wales was his editorship for half a century of *Trysorfa'r Plant* (1862–1911), a magazine for children. Although published under the auspices of the Calvinistic Methodists, it was popular with all Nonconformist denominations and was widely read, achieving a monthly circulation of 44,000.

A short biography of Thomas Levi was written by J. E. Meredith (1962); see also the essay by Nia Roberts in *Dewiniaid Difyr* (ed. Mairwen and Gwynn Jones, 1983).

LEWIS AB EDWARD or **LEWIS MEIRCHION** (*fl.* 1541–67), poet, of Bodfari, Flints., was one of *Gruffudd Hiraethog's pupils and he graduated as *pencerdd* at the *Caerwys Eisteddfod of 1567. Among his manuscripts there are one *awdl*, thirty-eight *cywyddau* and about twenty *englynion*, all of which were addressed to families in north Wales. His elegy for Edmund Llwyd of *Glynllifon (1541) is the earliest example of his work which can be dated and his best-known poem is an elegy for Humphrey *Llwyd.

LEWIS MENAI (*fl.* 1568), poet, lived at Crochancaffo in Llangeinwen, Ang. Very little is known about him but he graduated at the *Caerwys Eisteddfod of 1567. Most of his poems, which are preserved in manuscript, were composed in traditional metres for members of gentry families in north Wales, especially that of *Myfyrian.

Lewis family, see under FAN.

LEWIS, ALUN (1915–44), poet and short-story writer. Born at Cwmaman, near Aberdare, Glam., he was educated at Cowbridge School, the University College of Wales, Aberystwyth, where he read History, and at Manchester University. He showed early promise as a writer, contributing poetry and short stories to school and college magazines, but poems published in *The Observer* and *Time and Tide* in 1937, while he was training at Aberystwyth to be a teacher, launched him on his literary career. In 1938 he joined the staff of the Lewis Boys' School, Pengam, Mon., where he quickly established himself as a gifted teacher. Early in the following year he renewed his acquaintance with Gweno Ellis, whom he had known during their student days at Aberystwyth, and within a few months they were engaged. Alun Lewis had pacifist inclinations and, as the threat of hostilities increased and finally war broke out, his intellectual and emotional life was fraught with tensions. He continued writing, however, and in the winter of 1939 began a novel of 'Welsh Life' which was never finished. Despite his doubts, he resigned from his teaching post in the Spring of 1940 and, on impulse, enlisted in the Royal Engineers.

After a painful period of adjustment to army routine, he began writing once more. The prose and poetry produced at this time revealed his rapid development to maturity as a writer under the stresses of love and separation, of war and its uncertainties. By the summer of 1940 he had sent his fiancée a number of important poems, including 'The Soldier' and 'All day it has rained'. He applied for a commission in the infantry and embarked on an arduous course, first at Gloucester where, in July 1941, he and Gweno Ellis were married and later at Morecambe. By the time his first collection of poems, *Raiders' Dawn* (1942), appeared he had been posted to the 6th Battalion South Wales Borderers at Woodbridge in Suffolk. He found the life-style expected of him as a commissioned officer distasteful and preferred the company of the men, most of them drawn, like himself, from the valleys of south Wales.

He had already won a measure of fame as a soldier-poet: *Raiders' Dawn*, quickly sold out and reprinted, had been well received by reviewers and a public attracted by its combination of tragic vision and passionate lyricism. There followed a steady output of short stories and his volume, *The *Last Inspection* (1942), was published while the regiment was being mechanized at Bovington in Dorset. The stories portray with sympathy, directness and an unmistakable authenticity the vicissitudes of army life in the long period of waiting and training after Dunkirk. In the winter of 1942 the battalion was shipped to India and eventually settled under canvas near Poona. Early in 1943 the poet spent six weeks in hospital after breaking his jaw while playing football and then contracting dysentery, and to this period belongs 'Ward "O" 3B', one of his finest stories. A period of intense creative activity followed as he absorbed the experience of the sub-continent of India, embodying it in poems like 'Karanje Village' and 'The Jungle', and in a number of stories, notably 'The Orange Grove' and 'The Reunion'. The last-named draws upon two days' leave with his brother Glyn in Poona in December 1943. In the following January he revised for publication a new collection of poems to which he gave the ironic title, *Ha! Ha! Among the Trumpets*, and then travelled with his regiment to Chittagong in Burma, where he was to die. Although Intelligence Officer to the unit, he asked permission to join his company in a forward position and, on 5 March, he died of wounds received in an accident with a revolver; he was buried in Taukkyan War Cemetery. After his death there appeared *Ha! Ha! Among the Trumpets* (1945), his uncollected short stories, *In The Green Tree* (1948), and a volume entitled *Letters from India* (1946).

Alun Lewis had only four years of public recognition as a writer and he wrote only four books containing a total of ninety-five poems and twenty-five stories. His was essentially an elegiac outburst forced to early maturity by his involvement in the War. Within the limited scope of the lyric poem and the short story his achievement was substantial, however. Even his sternest critics acknowledge his seriousness, his integrity and his great promise, so tragically prevented from fulfilment.

A selection of Alun Lewis's poetry and prose was made by Ian Hamilton (1966) and a selection of his poems was edited by Jeremy Hooker and Gweno Lewis in 1981. An essay by Alun John on the writer's life and work has appeared in the *Writers of Wales* series (1970); see also the special number of *Poetry Wales* (1982) devoted to his work. Among many articles on the poetry of Alun Lewis the one by Roland Mathias in *The Anglo-Welsh Review* (no. 67, 1980) is specially recommended. A miscellany of Alun Lewis's writings, including previously unpublished poems and prose, has been edited by John Pikoulis (1982), who is also the author of *Alun Lewis, a Life* (1984).

LEWIS, ALUN THOMAS (1905–), short-story writer. Born at Llandudno, Caerns., and educated at the University College of North Wales, Bangor, where he graduated in mathematics, he was a teacher at Llanrwst for some thirty years and ended his career there as Deputy Headmaster. Having confined himself to the medium of the short story, in which genre he is a consummate craftsman, Alun T. Lewis has published five collections: *Corlan Twsog* (1948), *Y Piser Trwm* (1957), *Blwyddyn o Garchar* (1962), *Y Dull Deg* (1973) and *Cesig Eira* (1979).

LEWIS, CERI WILLIAMS (1926–), scholar, is a native of Treorchy in the Rhondda Valley, where he still lives. A miner's son, he became a Bevin Boy in 1944, working underground in Cwmparc for four years, and then took a degree in Welsh (1952) and History (1953) at University College, Cardiff. He was appointed to the staff of the Welsh and History Departments at the College in 1953 and became Lecturer in the Welsh Department four years later. Given a personal chair in the Welsh Department in 1976, he was appointed to the post of Professor of Welsh in 1979.

Some of his contributions to Welsh scholarship are on historical subjects, such as his article on the Treaty of Woodstock (1247) in *The Welsh History Review* (1964) and his appreciation of the work of William *Rees, presented to the historian by the Brecknock Society in 1968. He has discussed the Wales of the Roman period and the early history of the Church in *Llên Cymru*, revealing his interest in the *Celtic Church and the disputes over the bishopric of *Llandaf in the Norman period. The *Bardic Order is the subject of his three chapters in *A Guide to Welsh Literature* (vols. 1 and 2, ed. A. O. H. Jarman and Gwilym Rees Hughes, 1976, 1979). He is the author of two detailed chapters in *The Glamorgan County History* (vol. 3, 1971 and vol. 4, 1974). Among his other interests are philology and grammar: he has contributed substantial chapters on the Welsh language to two collective works, *The Cardiff Region* (1960) and *Rhondda Past and Future* (1975), and on the Celtic languages to various encyclopaedias.

Lewis, David (1617–79), also known as **Charles Baker**, priest and martyr. Born at Abergavenny, Mon., of a Catholic mother, he conformed until his conversion to the Roman faith while on a visit to Paris in his thirteenth year. Ordained priest in 1642, he joined the *Society of Jesus three years later and spent the rest of his life ministering to the Recusant houses of south Wales, most notably to the Morgans of Llantarnam, Mon. He was known in that district as 'Tad y Tlodion' ('Father of the Poor') and, although frequently denounced, was not molested until the Popish Plot caused widespread alarm in 1678. On the orders of John Arnold of Llanfihangel Crucorney, the local Member of Parliament and a fanatical hunter of priests, Lewis was arrested while on his way to mass and executed at Usk on 27 August 1679. It is said that the official hangman refused to carry out his task. A convict who had been offered his freedom for his services was stoned by the crowd. Eventually, a blacksmith was induced to kill Lewis. On the scaffold the priest spoke at length in Welsh, summarizing his beliefs and explaining why he had to suffer for them. He was canonized by Pope Paul VI in 1970 as one of the *Forty Martyrs of England and Wales and his grave at Usk is still visited by pilgrims.

LEWIS, DAVID (1683?–1760), poet. Born at Llanddewi Felffre, Pembs., and educated at Jesus College, Oxford, he published a collection entitled *Miscellaneous Poems by Several Hands* (1726) which included translations from Martial, Horace and Anacreon, together with poems by John *Dyer and Alexander Pope; his own contribution to the volume cannot be identified. He also published *Philip of Macedon* (1726), a tragedy in blank verse dedicated to Pope, and a second *Collection of Miscellany Poems* (1730).

LEWIS, EDWARD ARTHUR (1880–1942), historian, was born at Llangurig, Mont., and educated at the University College of Wales, Aberystwyth, and the London School of Economics. He was appointed Assistant Lecturer in Welsh History at Aberystwyth in 1910, Professor of Economics in 1912, and became the first Sir John Williams Professor of Welsh History at the College in 1930. His prime interests lay in Welsh social and economic history and his early researches into tribal decay in Wales led to the publication in 1903 of a pioneering study on this subject in the *Transactions* of the Honourable Society of *Cymmrodorion. His book, *The Mediaeval Boroughs of Snowdonia* (1912), laid the basis for later studies of the urban history of Wales and is still recognized as the standard work on the subject. The contributions he made to Welsh economic, administrative, legal and commercial history in the Middle Ages were, in their time, considered important but of greater value are his editions of original sources such as *The Welsh Port Books, 1550–1603* (1927), *Early Chancery Proceedings Concerning Wales* (1937) and *Records of the Court of Augmentations Relating to Wales and Monmouthshire* (1950).

LEWIS, EILUNED (1900–79), novelist and poet. Born at Newtown, Mont., she was educated at Westfield College in the University of London, before entering journalism in Fleet Street where from 1931 to 1936 she was assistant to the editor of *The Sunday Times*. Her first novel, *Dew on the Grass* (1934), describes her childhood in Wales, without sentimentality but capturing a dream quality which won praise from English critics and the Gold Medal of the Book Guild as the best novel of its year. She went on to publish two volumes of verse, *December Apples* (1935) and *Morning Songs* (1944), and with her brother, Peter Lewis, a topographical book, *The Land of Wales* (1937). Her novel, *The*

Captain's Wife (1943), is set in Pembrokeshire towards the end of the nineteenth century among the seagoing, farming community from which her mother's people had sprung. It was followed by a collection of essays, *In Country Places* (1951), another novel, *The Leaves of the Tree* (1953), and *Honey Pots and Brandy Bottles* (1954), the record of a countrywoman's year. Eiluned Lewis, who lived in Surrey after her marriage in 1937, also edited the selected letters of Charles Morgan (1967), the husband of Hilda *Vaughan.

LEWIS, ELIS (*fl.* 1640–69), translator, was born at Llanuwchllyn, Mer. His Welsh version of Ralph Winterton's translation of *The Considerations of Drexelius upon Eternitie* (1636, 1646) appeared in 1661. Drexelius, the author of the original Latin text, *De Aeternitate Considerations*, was a Jesuit professor of Greek and Latin at Augsburg and Dillingen, and court preacher to the Elector of Bavaria. Lewis, described in the book's full title as a gentleman, included in the Welsh volume two prayers not found in Drexelius and Winterton, as well as effusions by John *Vaughan, Elis Anwyl, Edward *Morris and William and Gruffydd Phylip.

LEWIS, GEORGE (1763–1822), theologian, was born near Trelech, Carms. A minister at Llanuwchllyn, Mer., for many years, he became head of the Independent Academy at Wrexham in 1812 and, three years later, moved it to Llanfyllin and then to Newtown. It was he who wrote the most balanced Bible commentaries of his time, work distinguished from the mass of contemporary writing on theological subjects by its meticulous scholarship and temperate judgement. His principal achievement was *Drych Ysgrythyrol* (1796), which remained a standard textbook until the end of the nineteenth century.

LEWIS, GEORGE CORNEWALL (1806–63), political writer and statesman, of Harpton Court, Rads., had a distinguished parliamentary career under Lord Palmerston. Member of Parliament for Radnor Boroughs, he was Chancellor of the Exchequer (1855–58), Home Secretary (1859–61) and Secretary for War (1861–63). A scholarly man, who nevertheless displayed great ability in the world of finance, he was also a well-known wit to whom was attributed the remark, 'Life would be tolerable but for its amusements'. His literary interests included the editorship of *The Edinburgh Review* (1852–55). The most important of his numerous publications are *Remarks on the Use and Abuse of some Political Terms* (1832), *The Government of Dependencies* (1841) and his essay *On the Influence of Authority in Matters of Opinion* (1849). His *Letters* were edited by G. F. Lewis in 1870.

LEWIS, HENRY (1889–1968), scholar and first Professor of Welsh at University College,

Swansea, was born at Ynystawe, Glam. Educated at University College, Cardiff, he was appointed Assistant Lecturer there in 1918 and became Professor of Welsh at University College, Swansea, two years later. It was his energy and enthusiasm which were chiefly responsible for the status enjoyed by Celtic Studies at Swansea.

His interests were many and wide: he prepared one of the earliest standard editions of the poetry of the *Gogynfeirdd, Hen Gerddi Crefyddol (1931), as well as a number of medieval prose texts such as *Chwedlau Saith Ddoethion Rufein (1925), *Delw y Byd (1928), Brut Dingestow (1942) and several early modern Welsh texts. He was one of the editors of the volume Cywyddau Iolo Goch ac Eraill (1925), published studies on such varied subjects as Welsh bibliography, Hugh *Jones of Maesglasau and Edward *Matthews (Matthews Ewenni), and made a pioneering contribution to comparative Celtic linguistics and the study of the syntax of the Welsh sentence. Holger Pedersen's Vergleichende Grammatik der keltischen Sprachen (1909, 1913) relied heavily on Henry Lewis's assistance in the preparation of its English epitome, A Concise Comparative Celtic Grammar (1937). In Yr Elfen Ladin yn yr Iaith Gymraeg (1943) Henry Lewis made a comprehensive analysis of the development of Latin phonemes into Welsh and he also set Medieval Breton and Cornish grammar on firm ground by publishing handbooks for those languages in 1922 and 1923.

His other main interest was syntax and in many respects his lecture, The Sentence in Welsh (1943), and his studies of Old Welsh constructions, are the starting-point for modern studies. He succeeded in conveying the complexities of comparative linguistics in a lively way in his volume, Datblygiad yr Iaith Gymraeg (1931). The same gifts are to be seen in his great work in preparing an edition of the *Bible in standard modern Welsh orthography and in his joint-editorship of Beibl y Plant (1929) and the hymnal Y Caniedydd Cynulleidfaol (1959).

A complete list of Henry Lewis's publications, compiled by D. Ellis Evans, will be found in the Journal of the Welsh Bibliographical Society (vol. X); see also the obituary by T. J. Morgan in Studia Celtica (vol. IV, 1969).

LEWIS, HOWELL ELVET (Elfed; 1860–1953)

LEWIS, HOWELL ELVET (Elfed; 1860–1953), minister, poet and hymn-writer, was born at Cynwyl Elfed, Carms. Educated at the Presbyterian College, Carmarthen, he ministered in churches in England and Wales for the greater part of his life, most notably at Tabernacl, King's Cross, London (1898–1940), where his sermons attracted many Welsh expatriates. He won the *Crown at the National Eisteddfod in 1888 and 1891 and the *Chair in 1894; he was Archdruid from 1923 to 1927. An important figure in the history of modern Welsh

poetry in that he spanned the schools of Islwyn (William *Thomas) and John *Morris-Jones, he made his most lasting contribution in his volume of poems, Caniadau (2 vols., 1895, 1901). Although some of his Socialist and patriotic verse brought him fame, his romantic lyrics about the beauty of nature were more popular, particularly the poems 'Gwyn ap Nudd', 'Pan Ddaw'r Nos' and 'Y Ddau Frawd'. With the exception of his hymns, his subsequent poetry is unremarkable.

His hymns, for the most part, are lyrical, devotional meditations, but they bear the hallmarks of wide reading in both Welsh and foreign hymnody. More sensuous than the hymns of his predecessors, they include 'Rho im yr hedd', 'Na foed cydweithwyr Duw', 'Glanha dy Eglwys' and 'Cofia'n Gwlad'; the last-named is so often sung at patriotic gatherings that it has been called 'the second national anthem' of Wales. His English hymns include 'Lamb of God, unblemished', 'Whom oceans part, O Lord, Unite', 'The Light of the morning is breaking' and 'The days that were, the days that are'. He was also the author of Sweet Singers of Wales (c.1890), a study of Welsh hymns and their authors.

Although he shared the weaknesses of the *Bardd Newydd, Elfed's knowledge of the history of Welsh literature was extensive, if lacking in any real analytical power. Besides his studies of Welsh hymnody, he wrote authoritatively on the history of the Welsh sermon, in particular in his volumes Planu Coed (1894) and Lampau'r Hwyr (1945), the content of which is more moral and devotional than theological. Among his collections of verse in English were My Christ and Other Poems (1891), Israel and Other Poems (1930) and Songs of Assisi (1938). He also published studies of the work of J. Ceiriog *Hughes (1899), Ann *Griffiths (1903) and Morgan *Rhys (1910).

A biography of Elfed was written by Emlyn G. Jenkins (1957); see also the critical studies by E. Curig Davies (1954) and Dafydd Owen (1965) and the article by H. Idris Bell in the Transactions of the Honourable Society of Cymmrodorion (1940).

LEWIS, HUGH (1562–1634)

LEWIS, HUGH (1562–1634), cleric and translator, born at Bodellog, near Caernarfon, was educated at All Souls' College, Oxford, where his interest in Welsh literature and Protestant evangelization was deepened. Presented to the living of Llanddeiniolen in 1598, he became Chancellor of Bangor Cathedral in 1608 and in 1623 succeeded Edmund *Prys as rector of Ffestiniog and Maentwrog. His literary reputation rests primarily on his translation, entitled Perl mewn Adfyd (1595), of the third edition (1561) of Miles Coverdale's work, A Spyrytuall and most Precious Pearle, itself a translation of a treatise by Otto Werdmüller of Zürich (1548). The Welsh translation was printed in Oxford by Joseph Barnes, the first Welsh book to be printed there, and was intended to provide the Welsh with spiritual uplift and to foster the use of their language. Occasionally, by summarizing or expanding the original, Lewis demonstrated that, despite some colloquial phrases, he was a scholar conversant with his country's literature. Nevertheless, the quality of the translation does not match that of Morris *Kyffin's *Deffynniad Ffydd Eglwys Loegr* which had appeared some months earlier. It was reprinted in 1929 with an introduction by W. J. *Gruffydd.

LEWIS, HYWEL DAVID (1910–), philosopher and theologian, was born at Llandudno, Caerns., and educated at the University College of North Wales, Bangor, and Jesus College, Oxford. He was Professor of the History and Philosophy of Religion at University College, London, for many years until his retirement in 1975. His publications include *Gweriniaeth* (1940), *Y Wladwriaeth a'i Hawdurdod* (with J. A. Thomas, 1943), *Ebyrth* (1943), *Diogelu Diwylliant* (1945), *Crist a Heddwch* (1947), *Morals and the New Theology* (1947), *Morals and Revelation* (1951), *Dilyn Crist* (1951), *Gwybod am Dduw* (1952), *Our Experience of God* (1959), *Freedom and History* (1962), *World Religions* (with R. L. Slater, 1966), *Dreaming and Experience* (1968), *The Elusive Mind* (1969), *Hen a Newydd* (1972), *The Self and Immortality* (1973), *Persons and Life after Death* (1978) and *Pwy yw Iesu Grist?* (1979).

LEWIS, JOHN (1548?–1616?), historian, of Llynwene, Llanfihangel Nant Melan, Rads., was born at Harpton Court (Tre'r Delyn) in the parish of Old Radnor (Pencraig) and about 1570 was called to the Bar at Lincoln's Inn. His only published work, *The History of Great Britain . . . til the Death of Cadwaladr* (1729), was edited more than a century after his death by the genealogist Hugh Thomas (1673–1720), who himself died before its appearance. Bound with the volume was an English translation by Thomas Twyne of Humphrey *Llwyd's *The Breviary of Britayne*. The *History*, dedicated to James I, was written in refutation of Polydore Vergil, in vindication of *Geoffrey of Monmouth, in defence of the traditional history of Wales and in praise of the House of Stuart. Other works by Lewis are found among the *Peniarth Manuscripts, several of which were in his keeping and which include a part of his 'Ecclesiastical History of the Britains til St. Augustin's Tyme'.

For further details see the *Transactions* of the Radnorshire Society (vol. XXX, 1960) and the essay by Ffransis G. Payne in his volume *Cwysau* (1980).

LEWIS, JOHN (*fl.* 1646–56), Puritan pamphleteer, of Glasgrug, Cards. His first published work, *Contemplations upon these Times* (1646), was a pamphlet written in support of the Presbyterian-dominated Parliament's efforts to reach a compromise with King Charles in order to end the Civil War and silence extremist Puritans

whom the war had brought into prominence. Lewis suggested the founding of colleges in Wales to train ministers, but at a time when some Puritans were seeking the destruction of the English universities he showed his conservative tendencies by making it clear that such colleges should not interfere with the status of Oxford and Cambridge. His appointment as a Commissioner under the Act for the *Propagation of the Gospel in Wales (1650) was a recognition of his willingness to compromise, for most other conservative Presbyterians had turned their backs on politics as a protest against the King's execution in 1649. John Lewis became a Justice of the Peace for Cardiganshire shortly after publishing his pamphlet, *Some Seasonable and Modest Thoughts* (1656), a response to Oliver Cromwell's decision to become Lord Protector of England.

Lewis, John David (1859–1914), printer and publisher, of Llandysul, Cards. He began, as a grocer's son with literary interests, by selling books from his father's shop-counter, and in 1892 he bought machinery and set up as a printer in the village. By 1908 his company had been named Gomerian Press out of his admiration for Joseph *Harris (Gomer). The high printing standards for which the firm is renowned were set by William J. Jones (1883–1955), its first chief printer. After the death of J. D. Lewis, his eldest son David carried on the business, to be joined later by his brothers Edward, Rhys and Emrys who, in their turn, were followed by the cousins J. Huw Lewis and John H. Lewis, the present directors. In 1929 the Gomerian Press (*Gwasg Gomer*) bought the Caxton Hall Press, Lampeter, and in 1945, *Gwasg Aberystwyth*.

The company's reputation as a publisher is based on a list which includes many of the most important Welsh authors of the twentieth century, including T. H. *Parry-Williams, Gwenallt (David James *Jones), D. J. *Williams, Waldo *Williams, T. Rowland *Hughes and Islwyn Ffowc *Elis, and on its major contribution to the development of Welsh book production. It was also the publisher of *Y *Genhinen* from 1950 until the magazine's closure in 1980.

For further details about J. D. Lewis and the early history of the press see the article by J. Tysul Jones in *Ceredigion*, the journal of the Ceredigion Antiquarian Society (1976).

Lewis, Lewis (**Lewsyn yr Heliwr**; 1793–1848), see under MERTHYR RISING (1831).

LEWIS, LEWIS HAYDN (1903–85), poet, born at Aberaeron, Cards., was educated at the University College of Wales, Aberystwyth, and Exeter College, Oxford. A Presbyterian minister at Devil's Bridge, Cards., until 1935 and in Ton Pentre, Rhondda, until his retirement in 1973, he published four volumes of verse: *Cerddi Cyfnod* (1963), *Cerddi Argyfwng* (1966), *Eisin*

(1969) and *Meini ac Olion* (1975). He won the *Crown at the National Eisteddfod in 1961 and 1968.

LEWIS, LEWIS WILLIAM (Llew Llwyfo; 1831–1901), poet, novelist and journalist, was born at Pensarn, Llanwenllwyfo, Ang. As a boy he worked in the copper-mines at Parys, near Amlwch, and as a draper's apprentice in Bangor. From about 1850 he earned a living from journalism, founding or editing a number of Welsh-language newspapers in north and south Wales, in Liverpool and in America. An accomplished soloist and compère, he became one of the most popular public figures at eisteddfodau during the late nineteenth century. In a poem expressing nostalgia for 'the good old times' of his youth, R. Williams *Parry referred to Lewis in the line 'Y Llew oedd ar y llwyfan' ('The Llew (or Lion) was on the platform'). Paralysed at the age of forty-seven, Lewis ended his life in distress and poverty, living for a while in the workhouse at Llangefni.

He was a prolific writer of heroic verse, winning many prizes for his long epics, some of which are to be found in the volumes *Awen Ieuanc* (1851), *Gemau Llwyfo* (1868), *Y Creadur* (1868) and *Buddugoliaeth y Groes* (1880). His novel, *Llewelyn Parri: neu y Meddwyn Diwygiedig* (1855), is hardly more than propaganda for the *Temperance movement but it has some lively scenes. It was followed by other novels, *Huw Huws neu y Llafurwr Cymreig* (1860), *Cyfrinach Cwm Erfin* (n.d.) and *Y Wledd a'r Wyrth* (n.d.). He also edited *Drych y Prif Oesoedd* (1883), the prose classic by Theophilus *Evans, to which he wrote his own introduction, and published a volume of English translations of Welsh verse. D. Tecwyn *Lloyd has described Llew Llwyfo as 'an artist in Philistia', because the materialism and respectability of the times in which he lived all but smothered his vivacious spirit.

For further details see the articles by D. Tecwyn Lloyd in *Barn* (nos. 17 and 18, 1964).

Lewis, Richard (Dic Penderyn; 1808–31), see under MERTHYR RISING (1831).

LEWIS, ROBYN (1929–), prose-writer, was born at Llangollen, Denbs., and educated at the University College of Wales, Aberystwyth. A lawyer by profession, he serves as Assistant Judge in the Crown Court of the Wales and Chester Circuit. He has written much about the legal status of the Welsh language, including the books *Second-class Citizen* (1969), *Y Gymraeg a'r Cyngor* (1972), *Termau Cyfraith: Legal Terms* (1972) and *Trefn Llysoedd Ynadon a'r Iaith Gymraeg* (1974). Among his collections of essays are *Esgid yn Gwasgu* (1980), with which he won the *Prose Medal at the National Eisteddfod, and *Gefynnau Traddodiad* (1983).

LEWIS, SAUNDERS (1893–1985), dramatist, poet, literary historian and critic, is generally regarded as the greatest figure in the Welsh literature of the twentieth century. Born at Wallasey, Ches., to parents who belonged to prominent Calvinistic Methodist families—his father and his maternal grandfather were both ministers—he was educated at the Liscard High School for Boys and at Liverpool University, where he studied English and French. His studies were interrupted by the First World War in which he served as an officer with the South Wales Borderers in France, Italy and Greece. After the War he returned to Liverpool University and graduated with First Class Honours in English, subsequently writing the thesis on English influences on the classical Welsh poetry of the eighteenth century which later formed the basis of his book, *A School of Welsh Augustans* (1924). He worked as a librarian in Glamorgan for a year before joining the Welsh Department of University College, Swansea, in 1922 as a Lecturer.

In 1925 Saunders Lewis was one of the founders of the Welsh Nationalist Party (later *Plaid Cymru) and the following year he became its President. He was received into the Roman Catholic Church, which he had been defending in his writings for some years, in 1932. In 1936, with D. J. *Williams and Lewis Valentine, he committed a token act of arson on building materials assembled for the construction of an RAF bombing school at *Penyberth, Caerns., an incident known as the Fire in Llŷn. After his release from prison and dismissal from his post at Swansea, he supported himself by journalism, teaching, farming and occasional work for His Majesty's Inspectorate of Schools until he was appointed, in 1952, as a Lecturer and later Senior Lecturer in the Welsh Department at University College, Cardiff. During this period he gradually withdrew from most overt political activity. He was a prolific and accomplished political journalist, particularly in *Y Ddraig Goch* (1926–37) and in *Baner ac Amserau Cymru* (1939–51); a number of his essays from the earlier phase were collected in the volume, *Canlyn Arthur* (1938). In 1957 he retired to his home in Penarth, near Cardiff, to devote himself to his writing, although continuing to comment from time to time on the political and spiritual state of the Welsh nation. The most famous of these comments, the BBC Wales Radio Lecture for 1962, *Tynged yr Iaith*, led directly to the formation of *Cymdeithas yr Iaith Gymraeg.

Saunders Lewis's achievement can only be described as astonishing, for he excelled as a scholar and as a creative writer, and in all the genres which he attempted. The present entry will deal only with his creative and critical work. So far, nineteen of his plays have been published: The *Eve of St. John (1921), *Gwaed yr Uchelwyr (1922), *Buchedd Garmon* (1937), *Amlyn ac Amig* (1940), *Blodeuwedd* (1948), *Eisteddfod Bodran*

(1952), *Gan Bwyll (1952), Siwan (1956), *Gymerwch Chi Sigaret? (1956), *Brad (1958), *Esther (1960), Serch yw'r Doctor (1960), Yn y Trên (in Barn, 1965), *Cymru Fydd (1967), Problemau Prifysgol (1968), Branwen (1975), Dwy Briodas Ann (1975), Cell y Grog (in Taliesin, 1975) and Excelsior (1980). His plays Y Cyrnol Chabert (broadcast 1968) and 1938 (broadcast 1978) remain unpublished but his translations of Molière's Le Médecin Malgré Lui and of Samuel Beckett's En Attendant Godot (Waiting for Godot) appeared in 1924 and 1970 respectively.

Two volumes of verse by Saunders Lewis have been published: Byd a Betws (1941) and Siwan a Cherddi Eraill (1956); other poems of his have appeared in periodicals, mostly in Y *Traethodydd. He had also published two novels, *Monica (1930) and *Merch Gwern Hywel (1964). His historical and critical studies of Welsh literature began with A School of Welsh Augustans (1924) and include An Introduction to Contemporary Welsh Literature (1926), Williams Pantycelyn (1927), Ceiriog (1929), Ieuan Glan Geirionydd (1931), *Braslun o Hanes Llenyddiaeth Gymraeg (1932), Straeon Glasynys (1943), Crefft y Stori Fer (1949) and Gramadegau'r Penceirddiaid (1967). His essays on literary topics have been collected in the three volumes, Ysgrifau Dydd Mercher (1945), Meistri'r Canrifoedd (ed. R. Geraint Gruffydd, 1973) and Meistri a'u Crefft (ed. Gwynn ap Gwilym, 1981); the last-named includes hitherto unpublished essays on the poets *Siôn Cent and *Gutun Owain.

The writings of Saunders Lewis are informed by a love of Wales seen in the context of European Catholic Christendom. He had a profound knowledge of Latin, French and Italian literature as well as English and Welsh. Early formative influences included W. B. Yeats and J. M. Synge, Maurice Barrès (in his role as regional novelist) and Emrys ap Iwan (Robert Ambrose *Jones). The masters of his mature works, however, were largely the luminaries of the French Catholic revival of the twentieth century—Paul Claudel, François Mauriac, Etienne Gilson and Jacques Maritain—and also the Italian literary historians and critics, Francesco de Sanctis and Benedetto Croce. Welsh literature has always seemed to Saunders Lewis to be at its greatest during the late Catholic centuries and he did more than any other critic to expound the profundity of thought as well as the mastery of expression displayed by the great cywyddwyr of the fourteenth and fifteenth centuries whose work he saw as a body of praise to the created order unparalleled in European literature. Nor was he unappreciative of post-Reformation Welsh writers, although he regarded the tradition within which they worked as seriously attenuated. Many of his studies of individual poets and prose-writers revealed for the first time their true stature.

His own most important contribution to Welsh literature was as a dramatist. Apart from a handful of comedies in which Welsh institutions are gently but tellingly satirized, his plays explore such weighty and often sombre themes as the imperatives of honour, the responsibilities of leadership, the nature of politics and the conflict between eros and agape. Over much of his greatest work lies the shadow of Pierre Corneille. His delineation of character, particularly that of women, is masterly and his dialogue achieves an unerring balance between classical dignity and colloquial vigour.

Apart from Siwan (1956), which he described as a poem, Saunders Lewis published no more than three dozen poems in all but some of them are undoubtedly among the finest Welsh poems of the twentieth century. They deal, in a variety of metres both traditional and innovatory, with the predicament of Wales, the glory of nature and the call of God. His novel, Monica, is a powerful study of the self-destructive force of lust, whereas Merch Gwern Hywel explores the fusion of the old and the new in the formation of the Methodist élite of the early nineteenth century, the theme also of the delightful late play, Dwy Briodas Ann.

Studies of Saunders Lewis have been edited in Welsh by Pennar Davies, Saunders Lewis: ei feddwl a'i waith (1951), and by D. Tecwyn Lloyd and Gwilym Rees Hughes (1975), and in English by Alun R. Jones and Gwyn Thomas, Presenting Saunders Lewis (1973). There is a monograph on the writer by Bruce Griffiths in the Writers of Wales series (1979); see also J. Ellis Williams, Tri Dramaydd Cyfoes (1961) and Emyr Humphreys, Theatr Saunders Lewis (1979). An account of Saunders Lewis's part in establishing Plaid Cymru will be found in D. Hywel Davies, The Welsh Nationalist Party 1925–1945 (1983). Twelve of Saunders Lewis's plays, translated into English by Joseph Clancy, were published in four volumes in 1985; they include The Vow (Amlyn ac Amig), The Woman made from Flowers (Blodeuwedd), Treason (Brad), Tomorrow's Wales (Cymru Fydd), The Two Marriages of Ann Thomas (Dwy Briodas Ann) and The King of England's Daughter (Siwan).

LEWIS, THOMAS (1759–1842), hymn-writer, was born at Llanwrda, Carms., but later settled as a blacksmith in the village of Talyllychau (Talley), becoming an elder in the Methodist cause at Esgair-nant. He is renowned as the author of one hymn, 'Wrth gofio'i riddfannau'n yr ardd', which is still frequently sung in the service of Holy Communion. First published, according to tradition, in a small catechism on Christ's suffering, it was included in a collection of hymns, Hymnau ar Amryw Destynau (1823), and has been very popular ever since. There is a famous reference to Thomas Lewis in the poem, 'Sir Forgannwg a Sir Gaerfyrddin', by Gwenallt (David James *Jones) in which the work of blacksmith and hymn-writer is memorably compared.

LEWIS, TIMOTHY (1877–1958), scholar, was born at Efail Wen, Carms., but moved to

Cwmaman, Aberdare, Glam., about 1887. Educated at University College, Cardiff, and at the Universities of Dublin, Freiburg and Berlin, he was appointed Assistant Lecturer in Welsh at the University College of Wales, Aberystwyth, in 1910 and soon afterwards published a valuable volume, *A Glossary of Mediaeval Welsh Law* (1913). He was involved in the dispute over the appointment of a Professor of Welsh at Aberystwyth in 1920, which was eventually resolved when T. H. *Parry-Williams was offered the Chair and Lewis was appointed Reader. For several years thereafter Lewis continued to offer unscholarly theories in the fields of philology and the history of literature, the result of which was the publication of his two books, *Beirdd a Beirdd-rin Cymru Fu* (1929) and *Mabinogi Cymru* (1930). His theories, which were based on insufficient evidence, were severely criticized by W. J. *Gruffydd and Ifor *Williams.

LEWIS, TITUS (1822–87), antiquary and poet. A native of Llanelli, Carms., he was engaged in commerce for most of his life and lived at Llanblethian, near Cowbridge, Glam. An enthusiast for Welsh literature, he wrote poems in English, including *The Soldier's Wife, a Tale of Inkerman* (1855), and also translated a number of Welsh hymns and poems into English.

LEWIS, WILLIAM (*fl.* 1786–94), hymn-writer, of Llangloffan, Pembs., was a weaver by trade. He composed many hymns, popular in their day, which were published in the collections, *Galar a Gorfoledd y Saint* (1786, 1788), *Hymnau Newyddion* (1798) and *Y Durtur, sef Ychydig o Hymnau ar Amryw Destynau Efengylaidd* (*c.*1805). His most famous hymn is 'Cof am y cyfiawn Iesu', which is still sung in Communion services.

LEWIS, WILLIAM ROBERT (1948–), playwright, was born at Llangristiolus, Ang., and educated at the University College of North Wales, Bangor. He taught Welsh at St. Asaph and Amlwch before his appointment in 1978 to a lectureship in the Drama Department of his old College. Among his plays for radio and television are *Yn ôl i'r Wlad* (1976), *Kate* (1977), *Y Fuddugoliaeth* (1980) and *Ymylau Byd* (1980). He has also written plays for the stage, including *Dan Flodau'r Gastanwydden* (1974), *Y Gwahoddiad* (1978) and *Tŷ Mawr* (1983) but only one of them, *Geraint Llywelyn* (1976), has been published.

Lewys ap Rhys ab Owain, see DWNN, LEWYS (*fl.* 1568–1616).

LEWYS DARON (*fl.* 1550), poet, was a native of Aberdaron, Caerns. He composed eulogies and elegies to gentry families of north Wales, including those of *Bodeon, Cochwillan and

*Glynllifon. His *cywyddau* include one requesting a horse of Dafydd, the prior of Beddgelert, on behalf of John *Wynn of Gwydir. A bardic contention with *Lewys Môn is attributed to him and he was among the poets who wrote elegies for *Tudur Aled.

A selection of his work was published by Myrddin Fardd (John Jones) in *Cynfeirdd Lleyn* (1905).

LEWYS GLYN COTHI or **LLYWELYN Y GLYN** (*c.*1420–89), one of the greatest Welsh poets of the fifteenth century. The little that is known about him has been gleaned from his work. A couplet in his *awdl* to God states that he was baptized Llywelyn, but he is believed to have taken the bardic name by which he is generally known from the forest of Glyn Cothi near Llanybydder, Carms. Nothing is known of his lineage and it is only speculation that he may have belonged to the families of Dolau Cothi and Rhydodyn. In his *awdl* to Morgan ab Owain, prior of Carmarthen, there is a suggestion that he was, during his youth, in the prior's service and it is possible that he received some education under him.

The absence of facts about Lewys has given rise to traditions for which no foundation exists. In the eighteenth century, for example, it was claimed that he had been a soldier in the army of Jasper Tudor, Earl of Pembroke, and a century later that he had been promoted to the rank of officer. For this reason, on the assumption that his work was a primary source for historians in the period of the Wars of the Roses, the Honourable Society of *Cymmrodorion in 1837 published a selection. The editors, Walter *Davies (Gwallter Mechain) and John *Jones (Tegid), omitted all *cywyddau* which did not support this particular view of the poet's significance. Although there is no evidence that Lewys was an officer in the army, he was probably present with the sons of Gruffudd ap Nicolas in the fateful battle of *Mortimer's Cross (1461), after which he became an outlaw on the eastern slopes of Pumlumon. In another *cywydd* he describes himself as an outlaw with Owain ap Gruffudd in Gwynedd and this could have been as early as 1442. Lewys's support of the Lancastrian cause did not prevent him from composing poetry for patrons who were Yorkists. According to some of his poems, Lewys lived in Chester at one time but was evicted, perhaps under the penal laws which denied Welshmen the right to settle in boroughs; the claim that his offence was in marrying a widow is a fabrication. The *awdl* to Rheinallt ap Gruffudd ap Bleddyn, in which the citizens of Chester are satirized, cannot be accepted as Lewys's authentic work and neither can the *cywydd* to the burgesses of Flint, even though he—like the majority of his fellow-poets at that time—could be very critical of the English.

The first *cywydd* by Lewys Glyn Cothi which

can be dated with any certainty is his elegy to Sir Gruffudd Fychan of Guilsfield, who was executed at Castell Coch in Powys in 1447, and the last is his elegy to the vicar of Llanarthne in the Tywi Valley who died in 1489. His work does not conform strictly to the rules of *Cerdd Dafod but he was familiar with the disciplines of bardic lore. His speciality was in genealogy and heraldry, his patrons' coats of arms sometimes being found worked in colour into his manuscripts. Learned in Latin, he wrote for a cultured society which expected eulogy and elegy from its poets. He also introduced a highly personal note into some of his poems, as in the moving elegy for his son, Siôn y Glyn, who died at the age of five.

There have survived about 230 of Lewys Glyn Cothi's poems, of which 154 were published by the Cymmrodorion Society in 1837. His original work is extant in the *Peniarth Manuscripts, in The *Red Book of Hergest, in The *White Book of Hergest, which is said to have been largely written by him, and in the *Llanstephan Manuscripts. John *Davies of Mallwyd made a complete collection of Lewys's work in 1617 and this copy, with a few missing pages, is kept in the British Library (BL MS 14871).

The work of Lewys Glyn Cothi was edited by E. D. Jones and published in 1953; the same editor produced a further selection which appeared in 1984. See also the chapter by E. D. Jones in *A Guide to Welsh Literature* (ed. A. O. H. Jarman and Gwilym Rees Hughes, 1979) and the same author's article in *Celtica* (vol. V).

LEWYS MÔN (*fl.* 1485–1527), poet, of the commot of Llifon, Ang., is believed to have been a blacksmith by trade but he was also a professional poet. It is probable that he was the *Lodowicus mon* who died in the monastery of *Valle Crucis in 1527. His chief patrons in Anglesey were the descendants of Llywelyn ap Hwlcyn in Presaddfed, *Chwaen Wen, *Bodeon and *Bodychen, but he also wrote poems for many other gentry families in north and south Wales, foremost among whom was the *Griffith family of Penrhyn, Llandygái. He wrote a *cywydd* on the imprisonment of Wiliam Gruffudd, seven others to his son of the same name who was knighted on the field of battle at Thérouanne (1513) in the Netherlands, an elegy to Siân Stradling, Sir Wiliam's first wife, and an *awdl* on the occasion of his patron's second marriage to Jane Puleston. Lewys Môn's poems to the Griffith family are especially powerful and are among the most perfect examples of the art of praise-poetry. He also wrote elegies for the poets *Dafydd ab Edmwnd, *Rhys Nanmor and *Tudur Aled, and six love-poems, but all these are inferior to the poems addressed to his patrons. His elegy was composed by *Dafydd Alaw.

The poems of Lewys Môn have been edited by Eurys Rowlands (1975); see also the same author's articles in

Llên Cymru (vol. IV, nos. 1 and 2, 1956) and *Gwŷr Môn* (ed. Bedwyr Lewis Jones, 1979).

Lewys Morgannwg, see LLYWELYN AP RHISIART (*fl.* 1520–65).

LHUYD, EDWARD (1660?–1709), scientist and philologist, was the illegitimate son of Edward Lloyd of Llanforda, Oswestry, and a distant relation of his, Bridget Pryse of Glanffraid, the home of a branch of the *Gogerddan family, Cards. His ancestors, the Llwyds, were a well-to-do family in the Border counties: his grandfather had been Governor of Oswestry Castle for a short period during the Civil War, loyalty to the King costing him dearly, for the fines imposed on him caused the decline of his estate. Llanforda was sold to William Williams of Glascoed in 1676, although Edward Lloyd continued to live there until his death in 1681. There is no record of Lhuyd's birth (he spelt his name thus after the custom of Humphrey *Llwyd or Lhuyd, but like him he also used the forms Llwyd and Lloyd), but it is believed that he was reared in the parish of Lappington by a nurse named Catherine Bowen. He spent his youth at his father's house, although his mother, who continued to work with Lloyd in his fishing business on the Dyfi, visited him there, and he would also stay with her in Cardiganshire.

Probably educated at Oswestry School, he went after his father's death to Jesus College, Oxford, to read law, but he did not complete his degree course because he had by that time become completely engrossed in experimental scientific work at the Ashmolean Museum, opened in 1683, where he was registrar of the chemistry courses. He was appointed an Assistant Keeper at the Ashmolean in 1687 and Keeper in 1691. Although devoted to the work of the Museum, Lhuyd spent much of his time out of Oxford, especially during the years from 1695 to 1701 when he was engaged in research in the Celtic countries, the first-fruits of which were published in his *Archaeologia Britannica* (vol. 1, *Glossography*, 1707). The University of Oxford conferred an honorary master's degree upon him in 1707; he was elected a Fellow of the Royal Society in 1708 and Senior Divinity Beadle (an administrative post) in 1709. Throughout his life Lhuyd enjoyed good health and it is believed that it was his relentless industry which was partly responsible for his sudden death. He was buried in an unmarked grave in the Welsh Aisle of St. Michael's Church, Oxford.

As a boy at Llanforda, Lhuyd had roamed the fields and kept notebooks of the flowers he saw, so that he was already a keen botanist when he went up to Oxford. He had also seen his father's experiments in chemistry and the scientific books in his library. These interests were encouraged under the guidance of Robert Plot, Professor of Chemistry and the Ashmolean's

first Keeper, and one of Lhuyd's first responsibilities was the collection of shells and fossils.
His catalogue of shells at the Museum was
presented to the Oxford Philosophical Society in
1685 and his catalogue of British fossils,
Lithophylacii Britannici Ichnographia, appeared in
1699.

Although he never forsook his botanical and
geological studies, from about 1693 Lhuyd grew
more and more interested in philology and antiquities. In that year he was invited to write
additional notes on the antiquities of the counties
of Wales for Edmund Gibson's new edition of
William Camden's *Britannia. These notes,
based on personal letters and questionnaires, as
well as field work, were a milestone in the
history of topographical and archaeological
studies in Britain by virtue of their wide scope
and their detailed, balanced descriptions. Lhuyd
built on the foundation of the answers to his
questionnaires by travelling through Wales
(1697–99) and thereafter in Scotland, Ireland,
Cornwall and Brittany (where he was arrested
as a spy), returning to Oxford in 1701.
Throughout the journey he had made detailed
notes, copied manuscripts and corresponded
with a host of learned acquaintances. He spent
the rest of his life at Oxford, preparing for
publication the huge amount of material which
he had collected. By means of subscriptions and
gifts he was able to publish the first volume of his
Archaeologia Britannica in 1707. This work was
the starting-point for the modern study of the
Celtic languages. It contains not only grammars
and dictionaries of those languages but also a
scientific discussion on the nature and conditions
of phonological variations. The scientific
method of dealing with the material and the
descriptive, rather than theoretical, attitude
towards the data, make this book a keystone in
the history of comparative philology, of which
Lhuyd was a pioneer, if not one of the fathers.

Edward Lhuyd died before preparing the
second volume of *Archaeologia Britannica* and he
had no worthy successor who could carry on his
work. The University seized his printed books
in payment for his debts but refused to keep his
manuscripts and they were sold to Sir Thomas
Sebright of Beechwood, Herts., in 1715. The
collection was subsequently divided between
Trinity College, Dublin, and Thomas *Johnes
of Hafod. Some of Lhuyd's manuscripts were
sold to the owners of private libraries, in particular
Sir Watkin *Williams-Wynn of Wynnstay and
Robert *Vaughan of Hengwrt. Unfortunately,
most of these manuscripts were destroyed by
fires. The remainder are now among the Hafod
Manuscripts at Cardiff Public Library, the
Wrexham Manuscripts and the *Peniarth Manuscripts at the National Library of Wales. The
greater part of Lhuyd's correspondence is
preserved at Oxford. Most of his letters were
published by R. T. Gunther, *The Life and Letters*

of Edward Lhuyd (1945) and the replies to his
questionnaires in *Parochial Queries* as three supplements to *Archaeologia Cambrensis* (1909–11),
edited by R. H. Morris.

The best descriptions of Lhuyd's career are by Richard
Ellis in the *Transactions* of the Honourable Society of
Cymmrodorion (1906), Frank Emery's *Edward Lhuyd*
(1971) and *Edward Lhuyd, the Making of a Scientist* (1980)
by Brynley F. Roberts; see also the article by Glyn
Daniel, 'Edward Lhuyd: antiquary and archaeologist'
in *The Welsh History Review* (vol. 3, no. 4, 1967).

Liber Landavensis, see under LLANDAF.

Liberalism, a philosophical, political, economic or theological principle stressing individual freedom rather than authority. The classic
Liberalism, philosophic or economic, of Bentham
or Mill had comparatively little direct influence
in Wales: *Radicalism had its Welsh roots in felt
injustices, particularly in rural areas. In the years
following the Reform Act of 1832 Welsh Dissenters, chiefly the *Baptists and Independents
(see under INDEPENDENCY), took up the old complaints against Church rates, tithes, burial laws,
religious disqualifications and, more generally,
landlordism. These causes found literary expression in the writings of Samuel *Roberts and
Gwilym Hiraethog (William *Rees), notably in
the latter's *Llythurau'r Hen Ffarmwr. The *Blue
Books report on education (1847) and the dispossession of tenants who had voted Liberal in
the 'Great Election' of 1868 crystallized a sense of
national outrage and enlisted widespread support for Radicalism, mainly in the Liberal Party.

The most powerful advocacy of Liberalism
after 1869 was found in Thomas *Gee's
newspaper *Baner ac Amserau Cymru and it had
an incisive publicist in John *Griffith (Y Gohebydd). In the election of 1880, under the protection of the 1872 Ballot Act, the Liberals won
twenty-nine of the thirty-three seats in Wales
and from then on Welsh Liberal members had a
considerable, though ultimately inadequate,
influence on British politics as a whole. An
attempt was made in 1894 and the following year
to form a separate Welsh Liberal Party in the
wake of the *Cymru Fydd movement, but
nothing came of it. The issues of *Land Reform
and *Disestablishment, as well as the improvement of education and the establishment of
institutions, engrossed the new national feeling.
Many of the leading literary figures of Wales,
such as Daniel *Owen, were deeply committed
to these causes, while lesser figures such as
Beriah Gwynfe *Evans were more directly
active in Liberal Party work. With David *Lloyd
George's concentration on British politics, the
rise of the Labour Party (see under SOCIALISM)
and later of *Plaid Cymru, Liberal influence
rapidly declined, though Owen M. *Edwards
and W. J. *Gruffydd were briefly Liberal Members of Parliament, even if to no great effect. At
the General Election of 1950 only five Liberal

Members survived and, after the death of Clement Davies in 1962, only two constituencies, Ceredigion and Montgomery (both of which were to be lost and regained), were still represented by Liberals; this position remained unchanged in 1983, despite the Alliance with the Social Democratic Party but a Liberal candidate was returned at a by-election in Brecon and Radnor in 1985.

In its theological dimension Liberalism substituted personal experience for orthodoxy and historical and scientific enquiry for dogma. After Schleiermacher, its main representatives in the latter part of the nineteenth century were Ritschl and Harnack. It had its greatest influence in Wales in the years after the First World War, with David *Adams, John Morgan Jones (1873–1946), and D. Miall *Edwards among the Independents, and through the volume *Llestri'r Trysor* (1914), edited by the Wesleyan Methodists E. Tegla *Davies and D. Tecwyn Evans (1876–1957). Its new approach to biblical studies is best represented by the Dictionary of the Bible published in three volumes between 1924 and 1926.

For further details about political Liberalism in Wales see R. T. Jenkins, *Hanes Cymru yn y Bedwaredd Ganrif ar Bymtheg* (1933), Cyril Parry, *The Radical Tradition in Welsh Politics: a Study of Liberal and Labour Politics in Gwynedd 1900–1920* (1970), Frank Price Jones, *Radicaliaeth a'r Werin Gymreig yn y Bedwaredd Ganrif ar Bymtheg* (1977), Kenneth O. Morgan, *Rebirth of a Nation: Wales 1880–1980* (1981) and John Osmond (ed.), *The National Question Again* (1985); for Liberalism in its theological dimension see R. Tudur Jones, *Ffydd ac Argyfwng Cenedl: Cristionogaeth a Diwylliant yng Nghymru 1890–1914* (2 vols., 1981, 1982).

Liberation Society, The, or **The Anti-State-Church Association** as it was originally called, was founded in 1844 by the English Congregational minister, Edward Miall. Its purpose was by 'all peaceable and Christian means to accomplish a separation of the church from the state'. The Society's inaugural conference was attended by twenty-two delegates from Wales and by expatriate Welshmen such as James Rhys *Jones (Kilsby Jones). One of its first secretaries was Thomas Rees (1777–1864), the historian and editor of *The Eclectic Review*. It received support from the Welsh Dissenting press in such periodicals as *Y Diwygiwr* and *Seren Gomer*, and from publicists such as Samuel *Roberts who sought to exploit an older, indigenous tradition of disestablishment. In 1847 a London Welshman, John Carvell Williams, was appointed the Society's full-time secretary and in 1853 it changed its name to the Society for the Liberation of Religion from State Patronage and Control.

The new title reflected a change to more radical political aims, to a concentration on constituency politics and the return of Liberationist sympathizers to Parliament. In 1862, Henry *Richard having been elected to its executive committee, the Society turned its attention to Wales as the most promising ground for the realization of its aims. Richard failed to be elected for Cardiganshire in 1865 but was returned on a partly Liberationist platform for Merthyr Tydfil in 1868. The disestablishment of the Irish Church by Gladstone in 1869, though it enhanced the reputation of the Society, also stimulated defence of the Anglican Church, and subsequently there was always tension between the Society, which aimed at 'Disestablishment All Round' and its Welsh supporters, many of whom wished to concentrate on *Disestablishment in Wales.

The Society declined in influence after the Disestablishment of the Anglican Church in Wales in 1920 but survived in an attenuated form until 1971, when it was disbanded. Its influence on the political development of Wales in the nineteenth century was profound, mainly because of its unique blend of religious idealism and political realism.

The role of the Society is discussed by Ieuan Gwynedd Jones in *Explorations and Explanations* (1981).

Lichfield Gospels, The, see BOOK OF ST. CHAD.

Lifris (12th cent.), see under CADOG (mid-5th cent.), CARANNOG (mid-6th cent.) and LLANCARFAN.

LILLY, GWENETH (1920–), writer of novels for children, was born and brought up in Liverpool. Educated at the University in that city, she lectured in English Literature there before being appointed to the staff of St. Mary's College, Bangor, in 1946. Although it was not until she retired prematurely in 1977 that she began writing in earnest, she soon won a reputation as a children's writer. She based her first novel, *Y Drudwy Dewr* (1980), on the Second Branch of *Pedair Cainc y Mabinogi*, treating it from the viewpoint of a boy in Anglesey during the Iron Age. Her subsequent novels include *Gaeaf y Cerrig* (1981), *Y Gragen a'r Drych* (1982) and *'Rwyn Cofio dy Dad* (1982), the last of which was commissioned to mark the seventh centenary of the death of *Llywelyn ap Gruffudd. Supernatural elements are found in some of her more recent books, such as *Hwyl a Helynt Calan Gaeaf* (1981), *Gêm o Guddio* (1980) and *Hogan y Plas* (1983). She has won the Tir na n-Og Prize (see under CHILDREN'S LITERATURE) on two occasions, in 1981 and 1982. Her first novel for adults, *Orpheus*, which is set in Roman Britain, appeared in 1984.

Lilting House, The (1969), an anthology of Anglo-Welsh poetry for the years 1917 to 1967, was edited by John Stuart *Williams and Meic *Stephens. Taking as its title a phrase from the poem *'Fern Hill' by Dylan *Thomas, it was the first authoritative attempt to present representative work by twentieth-century Anglo-Welsh poets in one volume. Beginning with W. H.

*Davies and Edward *Thomas, it includes selections from the work of David *Jones, Idris *Davies, Glyn *Jones, Vernon *Watkins, R. S. *Thomas, Dylan Thomas and Alun *Lewis and traces the course of modern Anglo-Welsh poetry by including such lesser poets as Huw Menai (Huw Owen *Williams), A. G. *Prys-Jones, Ll. Wyn *Griffith, Brenda *Chamberlain and T. H. *Jones. It also includes poems by all the poets who contributed to 'the Second Flowering' of Anglo-Welsh poetry during the 1960s. The anthology's introduction was written by Raymond *Garlick and the book was dedicated to Keidrych *Rhys and the memory of Vernon Watkins.

For a critical discussion of this anthology's significance see the review-article by Jeremy Hooker in *The Anglo-Welsh Review* (vol. 18, no. 42, 1975).

Little England beyond Wales, see ANGLIA TRANSWALLINA.

Little Kingdom, The (1946), the first published novel of Emyr *Humphreys. Like R. S. *Thomas's *The *Stones of the Field* (1945), it was a harbinger of the second phase of modern Anglo-Welsh writing, marking a change of attitude to Wales and the Welsh heritage. Although its title is protective and inward-looking, its theme *Nationalism, the novel is nevertheless the reverse of the unthinkingly partisan. Owen, the leader of Nationalist feeling against the attempt to build an aerodrome on his uncle's land (a plot which echoes the incident at *Penyberth in 1936) is shown as increasingly divorced from conscience, his means becoming violent and deceitful. Rhiannon and Geraint, in their different ways, are misled by 'love', in the latter's case to treachery. The novel's argument is that Wales can only be served by those who share both its legitimate aspirations and its heritage of conscience.

Little Welsh Terror, The, see JONES, JOHN (1854–1913).

Liverpool Welsh, The, a community of expatriates who played a prominent role in Welsh affairs during the nineteenth and early twentieth centuries. Many families from north Wales settled in the city and the adjacent townships, especially Birkenhead, attracted mainly by the opportunity of employment and trade in the cotton and shipping industries. Some parts of the city were built largely on their initiative and the Welsh element in the population was so remarkable that Liverpool was sometimes jocularly said to be 'the capital of north Wales'. There emerged a Welsh-speaking middle class which maintained a wide spectrum of cultural activity, producing its own institutions and leaders around the nuclei of the Nonconformist chapels to which most belonged. The *Temperance movement, as it affected Wales, began among the Liverpool Welsh and the city became a centre of publishing in the Welsh language through the work of such men as Gwilym Hiraethog (William *Rees), Isaac *Foulkes (Llyfrbryf) and Hugh *Evans. The *National Eisteddfod was held in Liverpool in 1884, after the establishment of the Welsh Society in that year, and again in 1900 and 1929. An eisteddfod is still held annually on Merseyside.

The community has produced relatively few writers who were born and brought up in the city; the most brilliant exception is undoubtedly afforded by Saunders *Lewis, whose family belonged to the prosperous middle class. For the peculiar English idiom of Liverpool's inhabitants, whether of Welsh or Irish extraction, the reader must turn to the plays of Alun *Owen. The most accomplished novel of Liverpool Welsh life is *I Hela Cnau* (1978) by Marion *Eames who was born and spent the first four years of her life in Birkenhead. Set in the 1860s, it catches superbly the atmosphere and detail of the place and period, in particular the dilemma of young Welsh people losing their roots in an alien society.

The University of Liverpool no longer has a Celtic Department (it was closed during the 1970s) but for many years the Department made an important contribution to Welsh scholarship, among its heads being J. Glyn *Davies, Idris *Foster, Melville *Richards and D. Simon *Evans. The tradition of Welsh-language publishing in Liverpool is upheld by *Cyhoeddiadau Modern Cymreig*, an imprint run by D. Ben Rees, a native of Cardiganshire who is minister of the Welsh Calvinistic Methodist chapel in the city. The Liverpool Welsh have their own community newspaper, *Yr Angor*, and one of its regular contributors, Gwilym Meredydd *Jones, won the *Prose Medal at the National Eisteddfod in 1982 with a collection of short stories. See also LONDON WELSH.

For further details see the novel by Eleazar Roberts, *Owen Rees* (1899), J. R. Jones, *The Welsh Builder on Merseyside* (1946), J. Hughes Morris, *Hanes Methodistiaeth Lerpwl* (2 vols., 1929 and 1932), D. Ben Rees (ed.), *Pregethwr y Bobl: Bywyd a Gwaith Dr. Owen Thomas* (1979) and *Cymry Lerpwl a'u Crefydd Fethodistaidd Galfinaidd Gymraeg* (1984); see also the articles by Griffith Ellis in *Y Geninen* (1898), Owen Hughes in *Y Drysorfa* (1910) and David Adams in *Y Geninen* (1916).

Lives of the Saints, works which form a substantial body of medieval literature in Latin and Welsh, were composed with the purpose of promoting the interests of the church or churches associated with the name of the saint celebrated. All were first written in Latin and invariably some time after the saint's death. The typical Life contains only a kernel of truth and usually consists of tales which the author considered would serve his purpose. The saint, as hero, is connected with any suitable event already part of the oral tradition and a striking feature of all such works is a lack of invention, for the same themes are used time and again, the same virtues attributed to the subject.

Of the Lives written in honour of the saints of the Church Universal, some—such as those of Catherine, Margaret, Mary Magdalen, Martha and Mary of Egypt—were translated into Welsh during the second half of the twelfth century. Other later Welsh texts are based in the main on the work of Jacobus de Voragine, the *Legenda Aurea*, which belongs to about the middle of the thirteenth century. The earliest Life of a saint with Welsh connections is that of Samson, composed early in the seventh century. Most, however, were written in the twelfth century and formed part of the intense literary activity which blossomed in the wake of the radical movements which occurred at that time.

The two most important are the Life of St. David (*Dewi Sant) by *Rhygyfarch, Bishop of *St. David's, and the Life of *Cadog by Lifris of Llancarfan, the son of Bishop Herewald. A collection of the Lives dating from the twelfth century is to be found in the manuscript *Cotton Vespasian* (*c.*1200), written by the monks of either Brecon or Monmouth. It contains the Lives of *Gwynllyw, Cadog, *Illtud, *Teilo, David (Dewi), Dubricius (*Dyfrig), *Brynach, *Padarn, Clydog, *Cybi, Tatheus and *Carannog. The Lives of *Gwenffrewi and *Collen occur in other manuscripts. The life of *Beuno is found, together with a Welsh version of the Life of Dewi, in *The *Book of the Anchorite of Llanddewibrefi*, a manuscript of religious texts which belongs to about the middle of the fourteenth century. Although the Lives of the Saints (even the Welsh Saints) were originally composed in Latin, some were later translated into Welsh and it is clear from many references in these works that the contents were widely known among poets. See also AGE OF THE SAINTS.

The most authoritative studies of the Lives of the Saints are S. Baring-Gould and John Fisher, *The Lives of the British Saints* (1907), E. G. Bowen, *The Settlements of the Celtic Saints in Wales* (1954) and *Saints, Seaways and Settlements in the Celtic Lands* (1969), and G. H. Doble, *Lives of Welsh Saints* (ed. D. Simon Evans, 1971); see also the chapter by D. Simon Evans in *Y Traddodiad Rhyddiaith yn yr Oesau Canol* (ed. Geraint Bowen, 1974) and the article by J. E. Caerwyn Williams, 'Bucheddau'r Saint', in the *Bulletin* of the Board of Celtic Studies (vol. XI).

Llacheu fab Arthur, a warrior who may have had an important part in early traditions concerning *Arthur, although very little evidence about him has survived. In the poem '*Pa Ŵr yw'r Porthor?*' in *The *Black Book of Carmarthen* there is a reference to a battle between Cai Wyn and Llacheu and in the same manuscript *Gwyddno Garanhir claims that he was present at the place where Llacheu, a man '*rhyfeddol mewn cerddi*' ('remarkable in song'), was killed. He is often mentioned by the *Gogynfeirdd as a model warrior and according to *Bleddyn Fardd he was

killed 'below Llech Ysgar'. Llacheu is also named in the Triad of the Three Fearless Men, the Triad of the Three Well Endowed Men and in *Breuddwyd Rhonabwy*.

Llafur (lit. 'Labour'), the Society for the Study of Welsh Labour History, was established in 1970 with the aim of fostering research into and of teaching the history of the working class in Wales. Under the presidency of Will Paynter, the former miners' leader, the Society played a prominent part in the creation of the South Wales Miners' Library in Swansea. Its magazine, also known as *Llafur*, which was first published in 1972, has made a major contribution to an understanding of the industrial history of Wales.

Llais Llafur (lit. 'The voice of labour'; 1898–1971), a weekly newspaper established by Ebenezer Rees at Ystalyfera, Glam. The founder was prominent in the Labour movement and his paper found a wide circulation among the miners and tin plate workers of west Glamorgan and east Carmarthenshire. When Rees died in 1908 his sons inherited the newspaper and under them its language became more commonly English than Welsh; its title was changed to *Labour Voice* in 1915 and to *South Wales Voice* in 1927. The newspaper provided a platform for Socialists such as R. J. *Derfel, George Greenwood, W. H. Stevenson and others, but its quality declined and its circulation fell after the Second World War. A London journalist, Claude Morris, bought it in 1952 and for a while its fortunes revived as a result of the new owner's policy of aggressive journalism. But he eventually lost the financial support of a number of Swansea businessmen, who used to advertise in the paper's columns, there was a sharp fall in circulation and the last number appeared at the end of 1971.

Llais y Wlad (lit. 'The voice of the country'; 1874–84), a weekly newspaper established by J. K. Douglas, the Anglican owner of *The North Wales Chronicle*. It was edited by Thomas Tudno Jones (1844–96) until 1880, when he left to take Holy Orders, and thereafter by Evan Jones of Llangristiolus. Under the latter's editorship it became a more independent paper; as a result, it lost some Church support and had to close down in 1884.

Llanbadarn Fawr, a church and parish near Aberystwyth, Cards. The church, formerly a monastery, was the centre of a pre-Norman bishopric and the parish was the largest in Wales until the nineteenth century. Traditions about *Padarn which later became the basis of a Life of the saint were preserved at Llanbadarn. There, too, was kept the Curwen, the saint's pastoral staff, which is the subject of an *englyn* written in the margin of a folio of St. Augustine's *De*

Trinitate by *Ieuan ap Sulien for his father, *Sulien. Two decorated crosses (9th–11th cent.) are also preserved in the church.

Frequent references to Llanbadarn and its clerics in *Brut y Tywysogyon* suggest that the lost Latin chronicle underlying that work was kept there in the twelfth century. In 1116, a priory, subordinate to the Benedictine abbey of St. Peter at Gloucester, was established at Llanbadarn, but after 1135/6 Llanbadarn regained its independence and the previous ecclesiastical order was restored. At the time of the visit by *Gerald de Barri (Giraldus Cambrensis) in 1188 the church was headed by a lay abbot whose family served as priests of the altar. Rhys Ieuanc (d. 1222) kept court at Llanbadarn and, according to the *Hendregadredd Manuscript, *Phylip Brydydd composed an *awdl* there against poetasters. Brogynin, once contained within the parish, was the birthplace of *Dafydd ap Gwilym, who wrote a famous *cywydd* in which he claimed that the girls of Llanbadarn distracted him from worship. Within the chancel of the church are buried members of the *Gogerddan and *Nanteos families, as is their opponent, Lewis *Morris, the antiquary.

For further details see the history of Llanbadarn by E. G. Bowen (1979).

Llanbrynmair Tradition, The, see under PEATE, IORWERTH CYFEILIOG (1901–82) and RADICALISM.

Llancarfan, a parish in the Vale of Glamorgan where, according to tradition, *Cadog founded a monastery in the sixth century. There, in the pre-Norman period, the Gospels of *Gildas were kept. Some scholars believe that Llancarfan was the home of a learned clerical family, one of whose members, named Lifris, wrote an immense Latin Life of Cadog at some time between 1061 and 1100. The version of the Life which has survived (in Cotton Vespasian A xiv MS, c.1200) appears to be a composite one, with the additions of a chartulary and administrative documents relating to the monastery and its clerics. A carved stone dating from the ninth or tenth century and bearing an inscription from the eleventh or twelfth is preserved in Llancarfan church, but according to *Annales Cambriae the site of the monastery was destroyed in 988. Llancarfan's independence came to an end about 1100 when the Normans bestowed the church on the abbey of St. Peter, Gloucester. Rhisiart ap Rhys composed two poems in praise of Cadog. Iolo Morganwg (Edward *Williams) was born at Pennon in the parish of Llancarfan, for which he created a brilliant, but totally fictional, past.

Llandaf, a cathedral and diocese in Glamorgan. By the beginning of the twelfth century it had gathered together the traditions, privileges and churches of three saints—*Dyfrig, *Teilo and Euddogwy. The early history of the site is obscure but a cross dating from the tenth or eleventh century, preserved in the cathedral, testifies to the presence of a pre-Norman ecclesiastical institution.

Urban (d. 1134), Bishop of Llandaf, was in dispute with the bishops of Menevia (*St. David's) and Hereford over property and the boundaries of their respective dioceses, especially in the years from 1128 to 1133. The Latin text known as *Liber Landavensis* (*The Book of Llandav*) was compiled between 1120 and 1140 to justify his claims to churches dedicated to the three patron saints of Llandaf which lay outside the diocese. The original, written in nine hands of the twelfth and thirteenth centuries, is a fictional account of the history of the diocese from its foundation by Dyfrig until the death of Herewald in 1104. This material is more than a comment on ecclesiastical politics in the twelfth century, however, for most of the charters are edited and embellished versions of earlier documents and are of unique significance for the pre-Conquest history of south-east Wales. The bishop's efforts were unsuccessful, despite an appeal to the Pope, and he died on his way to Rome. He had built a new church at Llandaf, dedicated to St. Peter and the three Welsh saints, and arranged for Dyfrig's bones to be taken there from *Bardsey. *Gerald de Barri (Giraldus Cambrensis) was offered the bishopric in 1191 but refused it. Llandaf was the home of the Mathew family, some of whom were buried in the cathedral. Two *englynion* by *Dafydd Benwyn to Bishop William Blethyn (1575–90) and his wife survive on a leaf of *The Book of Llandav*. Ieuan Llwyd ap Gwilym wrote a poem in praise of Teilo. William *Morgan was Bishop of Llandaf between 1595 and 1601.

The text of *Liber Landavensis* was reproduced from the *Gwysaney Manuscripts* by J. Gwenogvryn Evans with the co-operation of John Rhŷs and published in a limited edition in 1893; a facsimile edition appeared in 1979. For further details see the article by E. D. Jones in the *Journal* of the National Library of Wales (vol. IV) and Wendy Davies, *The Llandaff Charters* (1979).

Llandeilo Fawr, a church and parish in Carmarthenshire; it was there, according to *The Book of Llandav*, that *Teilo died. The Old Welsh and Latin marginalia in the St. Chad Gospels (*The *Book of St. Chad*) testify that the book was originally intended for use at the altar of the church of Llandeilo Fawr. The same entries reveal that Llandeilo was the centre of the cult and bishopric of Teilo in the eighth and ninth centuries, but it probably lost episcopal status in the latter half of the tenth century. Two decorated cross-heads from the ninth or tenth century survive in the church and Edward *Lhuyd recorded the existence of another which has since been lost. Llandeilo Fawr, unsuccessfully claimed by the diocese of *Llandaf in the twelfth century, was in the possession of the

Praemonstratensian Canons of Talyllychau (★Talley) by 1239. According to *The ★Black Book of St. David's*, both the town and the surrounding countryside had become part of the jurisdiction of the Bishop of ★St. David's by 1326. A close connection existed between the lords of ★Ystrad Tywi and Llandeilo Fawr, their court at ★Dinefwr lying on the outskirts of the town.

'**Llanfair**', a well-known hymn-tune by Robert Williams (1781–1821) of Llanfechell, Ang. Its title is probably derived from Llanfair-yng-Nghornwy, a hamlet in Anglesey, although in a manuscript dated 1817 and in the first published version which appeared in *Peroriaeth Hyfryd* (1837) the tune is entitled '*Bethel*'. It is included in every Welsh congregational hymnal, as well as in *Songs of Praise* and many other English hymn-books, and one of the four official hymns sung at the ★Llangollen International Musical Eisteddfod is sung to this tune.

Llanfair-pwllgwyngyll-gogerychwyrndro-bwyll-llantysiliogogogoch, the longest place-name in Britain, belongs to a village in Anglesey. Usually abbreviated to Llanfair P.G., the name can be rendered in English as 'The church of St. Mary in a hollow of white hazel near the rapid whirlpool and the church of St. Tysilio near a red cave'. According to John ★Morris-Jones, it was concocted by a tailor from Menai Bridge in the mid-nineteenth century. Ever since the name has been something of a joke, mainly for the entertainment of foreign visitors who delight in failing to pronounce it.

Llangeitho Revival, The (1762), see under CANIADAU Y RHAI SYDD AR Y MOR O WYDR (1761/62) and ROWLAND, DANIEL (1713–90).

Llangollen International Musical Eisteddfod, a festival held annually in the small town of Llangollen, Denbs., since 1947. First mooted by Harold Tudor of Coedpoeth, Wrexham, an official of the British Council, the idea for an international folk-festival won the support of W. S. Gwynn Williams, a prominent figure in the musical life of Wales and at that time the ★National Eisteddfod's Music Organiser, and of G. H. Northing, a teacher who was also the Chairman of Llangollen Urban District Council. Among their chief concerns was the wish to help the people of Wales to contribute towards healing the scars of the post-War world. The festival's motto was specially composed by T. Gwynn ★Jones:

> Byd gwyn fydd byd a gano,
> Gwaraidd fydd ei gerddi fo.

('Blessed is a world that sings,/Gentle are its songs'). Represented at the first festival were fourteen nationalities. Since 1947 the Eisteddfod has become world-famous, attracting each year several hundred folk-singers, folk-dancers and instrumentalists, as well as professional artistes of international repute, from more than seventy countries. The week-long event, which is not confined to the main pavilion but spills colourfully, multilingually and confraternally into the streets of Llangollen and the surrounding countryside, was described by Dylan ★Thomas in a radio talk broadcast in 1953 and subsequently published in his *Quite Early One Morning* (1954).

For a full account of the festival's history see Kenneth A. Wright, *Gentle are its Songs* (1973).

Llanilltud Fawr (*ang.* **Llantwit Major**), a church and parish in Glamorgan. The church stands on the site of a former monastery believed to have been founded by ★Illtud. The Life of Samson (d. 565), which dates perhaps from the seventh century, contains the earliest reference to Illtud's monastery. The importance of the place in the ninth century is suggested by the early Christian monuments preserved in the church: one refers to an abbot, another is the gravestone of Ithel, King of Gwent (d. 848), and a third is thought to name Hywel ap Rhys, King of ★Glywysing (d. 886). The rediscovery of Ithel's tombstone was made by Iolo Morganwg (Edward ★Williams) while he was working in the churchyard in 1789 and the inscriptions on these monuments prompted him to invent a glorious past for Llanilltud. About a mile from the modern village of Llantwit Major lie the remains of a Roman villa which was in ruins by the fifth century. Llanilltud was devastated in 988. At some time before 1135, as a consequence of the ★Norman conquest of Glamorgan, the site of the former monastery passed into the possession of Tewkesbury Abbey. The village of Llanilltud was the home of Lewys Morgannwg (★Llywelyn ap Rhisiart), who wrote a poem in praise of Illtud.

Llanllugan, a nunnery in Montgomeryshire affiliated to the ★Cistercian Order, was founded as a daughter-house of ★Strata Marcella by Maredudd ap Robert, Lord of Cedewain, about 1236. ★Dafydd ap Gwilym sent a love-messenger to greet the nuns in verse. The nunnery was dissolved in 1536.

Llanllŷr, a nunnery near Llanfihangel Ystrad, Cards., affiliated to the ★Cistercian Order, was founded as a daughter-house of ★Strata Florida by ★Rhys ap Gruffudd (The Lord Rhys) about 1180. The nunnery's only known literary association is a poem by ★Huw Cae Llwyd, in which he requests the gift of a pet ape from Sir William ★Herbert on behalf of the abbess, Dame Annes. The history of this house, which was dissolved in 1536, inspired the novel *Lleian Llan Llŷr* (1964) by Rhiannon Davies ★Jones.

Llannerch or **Gwysaney Manuscripts, The**, one

of the most important collections ever made in north Wales, was formed mainly by Robert Davies (c.1658–1710), the owner of the Llannerch and Gwysaney estates, near St. Asaph, Denbs. Now housed in the *National Library of Wales, the collection contains many valuable manuscripts in Latin, a copy of *Gesta Alexandri Magni* (13th–15th cent.), homilies and hymns of the thirteenth century, *The Book of Llandaf*, the *Brut Chronicle* (an English MS written in the 15th cent.), a copy of Archbishop Ussher's version of *Nennius's *Historia Brittonum*, three manuscripts belonging to the sixteenth century which contain Welsh poetry of the medieval and Renaissance periods, and two manuscripts of Welsh pedigrees.

Llanstephan Manuscripts, The, a collection of which the nucleus was formed between 1690 and 1742 by Samuel *Williams of Llandyfriog, Cards., and his son, Moses *Williams. Together with manuscripts from the collections of Walter *Davies (Gwallter Mechain), Lewis *Morris, Edward Breese, Sir Thomas Phillips and E. G. B. *Phillimore, they were presented to the *National Library of Wales in 1909 by Sir John *Williams of Llanstephan, Carms. An important source for medieval and Renaissance Welsh literature, the collection contains many manuscripts written by some of the foremost poets and copyists of those periods, including *Gutun Owain, *Siôn Brwynog, Sir Owain ap Gwilym, *Morgan Elfael, *Llywelyn Siôn and Siôn Dafydd *Rhys. A Cornish dictionary in the hand of Edward *Lhuyd is also part of the collection. The most valuable manuscript is *The Red Book of Talgarth*, which was written about 1400 by Hywel Fychan ap Howel Goch of Builth. The collection also contains the work of such poets as *Dafydd ap Gwilym, *Lewys Glyn Cothi, *Guto'r Glyn and *Tudur Aled.

Llantarnam, an abbey near Cwmbran, Mon., affiliated to the *Cistercian Order, was founded on land given by Hywel ab Iorwerth of Caerleon in 1179. A daughter-house of *Strata Florida, the abbey was also known as Caerleon, Nant Teyrnon and Dewma. *Lewys Glyn Cothi sang in praise of the abbot, Siôn ap Rhosier (c.1476), and an unknown poet paid tribute to the image of the Holy Trinity kept in the abbey. Several others, including Llywelyn ab Hywel ab Ieuan, *Huw Cae Llwyd, Lewys Morgannwg (*Llywelyn ap Rhisiart) and *Gwilym Tew, sang eulogies to the healing powers of the image of the Virgin Mary which the abbey appropriated from the chapel of Penrhys in the Rhondda Valley. Llantarnam was dissolved in 1536 and its lands purchased in 1561 by William Morgan, a member of the *Morgan family of Tredegar Park, who encouraged its use as a place of pilgrimage. For further details see Glanmor Williams, *The Welsh Church from Conquest to Reformation* (1962), the article

by D. H. Williams in *The Monmouthshire Antiquary* (vol. 2, part III, 1967) and the same author's *White Monks in Gwent and the Border* (1976); see also F. G. Cowley, *The Monastic Order in South Wales 1066–1349* (1977).

Llareggub, see under UNDER MILK WOOD (1954).

Llatai (lit. 'Love-messenger'), a term associated with the convention by which a poet sends a bird, animal, or more rarely some other creature, with a message or letter to his sweetheart. It appears first in the fourteenth century and is exemplified most fully in the *cywyddau* of *Dafydd ap Gwilym, though parallels are also to be found in the work of his contemporaries, *Gruffudd Gryg, *Llywelyn Goch ap Meurig Hen and *Gruffudd ap Adda ap Dafydd. The convention is thought to be older, however, and the 'horse-messengers' employed by *Cynddelw Brydydd Mawr and *Llywarch ap Llywelyn (Prydydd y Moch) have been associated with it. The earliest occurrence of the word 'llatai' is found in a poem in which Gruffudd ap Dafydd ap Tudur asks his patron for the gift of a bow, which suggests that the convention is to be related to the poem of request, such as was a recognized prerogative of Welsh poets from very early times and which was specifically permitted by the *Laws of Hywel Dda.

Dafydd ap Gwilym's *llatai* poems follow a regular pattern and each contains most or all of the following elements: an initial greeting to the messenger, followed by a descriptive passage in its praise, often in elaborate *dyfalu* and showing a close observation of the creature's characteristics; a request to carry a message of love, a letter, or a kiss; an account of the proposed journey with a warning to avoid its hazards; a brief description of the girl or of her home; and a final blessing on the messenger. The poet's *llateion* are most frequently birds—nightingale, lark, thrush, seagull, or woodcock—but in one *cywydd* he commissions the stag. He also employs the term '*llateion*' for hounds of the chase in his dream-poem and '*llateiaeth*' for the intercession he requests of St. *Dwynwen and for a projected embassy which he claims that he is unwilling to entrust to an old hag. In a famous poem the wind itself is imaginatively employed to carry Dafydd's message. Among the rejected poems in the apocrypha of Dafydd ap Gwilym are *cywyddau llatai* to the eagle, the blackcap (or titmouse), the swan, the blackbird, the cuckoo, the salmon and the trout, some of which may be the work of his contemporaries.

The literatures of medieval France and Provence provide examples of birds—most frequently nightingales—despatched as messengers of love, but these do not have anything comparable with the long passages descriptive of the messenger which are found in Welsh. They may, however, have had some influence on the long persistence of the theme in the sometimes cynical advice given by birds to love-sick poets in Welsh free-metre poetry of the sixteenth century.

For discussions of the *llatai* convention see Saunders Lewis, *Braslun o Hanes Llenyddiaeth Gymraeg* (1932), J. E. Caerwyn Williams, 'Beirdd y Tywysogion: Arolwg' in *Llên Cymru* (vol. II, 1970), the monograph by Rachel Bromwich on Dafydd ap Gwilym in the *Writers of Wales* series (1982) and the same author's *Dafydd ap Gwilym: a Selection of Poems* (1982).

LLAWDDEN or **IEUAN LLAWDDEN** (*fl.* 1450), poet. A native of Llwchwr (Loughor), Glam., who lived at Machynlleth, Mont., he is reputed to have catalogued the strict metres in a work known as *Dosbarth Llawdden*, but this rests on a claim by Iolo Morganwg (Edward *Williams) which may well be false. Prominent at the *Carmarthen Eisteddfod of 1450, Llawdden is also said to have accused *Gruffudd ap Nicolas of accepting a bribe for having awarded the Chair to *Dafydd ab Edmwnd. Most of his poems, written in the strict metres, were in praise of such gentry as Thomas ap Rhosier of *Hergest and Phylip ap Rhys and Maredudd Fychan of Maelienydd.

'Llef' (lit. 'Lament'), a well-known hymn-tune by Griffith H. Jones (Gutyn Arfon; 1849–1919) which first appeared in *Tunes, Chants, and Anthems, with Supplement* (ed. David Jenkins, 1883). Said to have been written in memory of the composer's brother, Dewi Arfon, the tune is almost inseparably linked with the hymn 'O! Iesu mawr, rho'th anian bur' by David *Charles. It was arranged for male voices by Mansel Thomas under the title 'Deus Salutis!'.

Lleision, a traditional hero of *Powys. *Cynddelw Brydydd Mawr referred to *Madog ap Maredudd as the Lleision of his day.

Llên Cymru (lit. 'The literature of Wales'), an annual magazine published for the *Board of Celtic Studies by the University of Wales Press from 1950 to the present; its editor until 1960 was Griffith John *Williams and thereafter A. O. H. *Jarman. Intended as a journal in which scholars of the history of Welsh literature might present the fruits of their research, it publishes work by members of the staff of the University's Welsh Departments, and others, and has thus made an important contribution to Welsh literary *scholarship.

Llenor, Y (lit. 'The writer'), a quarterly magazine edited by Owen M. *Edwards during the years from 1895 to 1898, was a companion to *Cymru but its articles were generally longer and more learned. Although it carried poetry and articles on the work of such poets as David *Owen (Dewi Wyn o Eifion), Islwyn (William *Thomas), Glasynys (Owen Wynne *Jones) and

Robert *Jones of Rhos-lan, the periodical's title was misleading in that it also dealt with subjects other than literature, including history, foreign travel and nature. See also the next entry.

Llenor, Y (lit. 'The writer'; 1922–55), a quarterly magazine established as a successor to *Y *Beirniad* by the initiative of the Welsh Societies of the four Colleges of the *University of Wales. At a meeting convened by Henry *Lewis in 1921, W. J. *Gruffydd was appointed editor. The first seven numbers were produced by the Educational Publishing Company of Cardiff, but thereafter (102 numbers to 1951) the magazine was published by *Hughes a'i Fab* of Wrexham (see under HUGHES, RICHARD, 1794–1871) and later of Cardiff. T. J. *Morgan joined W. J. Gruffydd as co-editor in 1946 and it was he who produced in 1955 a special memorial number for W. J. Gruffydd who had died in the previous year.

Among the outstanding features of *Y Llenor* were the editorial notes which, from the seventeenth issue (Spring, 1926), commented in an outspoken manner, which was typical of W. J. Gruffydd, on controversial matters of public interest. The magazine's aim, from the beginning, was 'the promotion of the highest literary culture' and the 'provision of a place in which Welsh writers may publish their work with only one criterion applied, namely literary merit'. Among the authors who regularly contributed critical and creative work to the magazine were Saunders *Lewis, T. H. *Parry-Williams, G. J. *Williams, R. T. *Jenkins, Ambrose *Bebb, R. G. *Berry, Kate *Roberts, Iorwerth C. *Peate, Ffransis G. *Payne, D. Myrddin *Lloyd, D. Tecwyn *Lloyd and, of course, the editors themselves. In the summer of 1949 an entire number was devoted to the memory of T. Gwynn *Jones. Among contributions of lasting significance which first appeared in *Y Llenor* were Saunders Lewis's seminal article on *Dafydd Nanmor (Autumn, 1925), 'Yr Apêl at Hanes' by R. T. Jenkins (Autumn and Winter, 1924), W. J. Gruffydd's 'Hen Atgofion' (*passim*), many of the essays and poems of T. H. Parry-Williams, the short stories of Kate Roberts and the poems of R. Williams *Parry.

The magazine dominated the literary activity of the thirty years during which it was published and provided a focus for the literary criticism and a large part of the literary *scholarship of the period. While it did not attach itself to any particular school of thought, either literary or philosophical, it maintained the rigorous standards of style and grammatical construction which John *Morris-Jones had advocated and sustained during the early years of the century. See also the previous entry.

An index to *Y Llenor* has been compiled by William Phillips (1973). For further details see the articles by T. J. Morgan in *Y Traethodydd* (Jan., 1982) and by T.

Robin Chapman in the same magazine (April, 1984); see also *Nodiadau W. J. Gruffydd* (ed. R. Chapman, 1985), a selection of editorials from *Y Llenor*.

Lleu Llawgyffes, a central character in the Fourth Branch of *Pedair Cainc y Mabinogi*. He is born of *Arianrhod after *Math fab Mathonwy tests her virginity, but is abducted by *Gwydion, Arianrhod's brother, and it is he who brings up the boy. It may be gathered from certain references in the text that Gwydion was originally his father but that the final redactor of the Branch did not wish to draw attention to the incest in his account of the incident. As he grows up, the boy shows the characteristics of the *Wondrous Child: by his first birthday he is as strong as a child twice his age and by the end of his second year he is able to go to the court by himself.

One day, when Gwydion takes the boy to Caer Arianrhod and tells his sister that he is her son, she turns in wrath against her brother, accusing him of 'pursuing her shame', and swears that the boy shall never have a name unless she gives him one. Gwydion overcomes this destiny by causing the boy and himself to appear as shoemakers in a ship and the boy is given the name Lleu Llawgyffes ('the fair one with the deft hand'). Arianrhod describes him thus without knowing his identity after he has aimed his needle at a wren on board the ship, striking it between the sinew of its leg and the bone. Arianrhod then condemns him to a second fate, namely that he shall never bear arms unless she equips him therewith, but she is again defeated after Lleu and Gwydion are received at Caer Arianrhod in the guise of poets from Glamorgan. The fortress is surrounded by a magic fleet of Gwydion's creation and Arianrhod is deceived by the apparent threat into arming Lleu. The third fate to which she condemns Lleu is that he shall never have a wife 'of the race that is now on this earth', whereupon Math and Gwydion immediately fashion a wife of flowers for him, namely *Blodeuwedd.

The final section of the Branch relates the troubles which befall Lleu as a result of Blodeuwedd's infidelity. Math gives Lleu and his wife a court in which to live, namely Mur Castell in Cantref *Dunoding in the uplands of *Ardudwy, and there, in Lleu's absence, Blodeuwedd extends hospitality to the wandering hunter, Gronw Pebr, Lord of Penllyn, and falls in love with him. The two plot Lleu's death and Blodeuwedd, feigning concern for her husband's welfare, learns how he may be killed. He cannot be slain in a house nor in the open air, on horseback or on foot. The spear with which he may be killed must have been a year in the making and then only during the time of Sunday Mass. Before the blow can be effective, Lleu must be standing with one foot on the back of a goat and the other on the edge of a tub, and under a thatched frame. Lleu is persuaded to put himself into this exact position so that Blodeuwedd may recognize the fatal circumstances and at that moment Gronw Pebr smites him in the side with a spear. Lleu does not die, however, but turns into an eagle and flies away with a terrible scream. Gwydion eventually discovers him on a tree-top in Nantlleu and his human form is restored, but because of his pitiful condition he is taken to the court at Caer Dathyl to recover.

Within the year Lleu is completely restored to health and seeks revenge on Gronw Pebr. Mur Castell is taken by the troops of Gwynedd, Blodeuwedd is punished by being turned into an owl and Gronw flees to *Penllyn. Lleu refuses any reconciliation with him, although Gronw admits his crime and offers land or territory, gold or silver, in recompense for the injury. Rather, Lleu insists that Gronw receive a blow from his spear in exactly the same position as he had received the blow from Gronw's. This is arranged, Gronw is killed and Lleu is re-established in his lordship and thereafter rules over *Gwynedd.

Lleu is portrayed as a capable, righteous, innocent and gullible character, but is somewhat pallid in comparison with his uncle (or father), Gwydion. He may be regarded as Gwynedd's traditional hero, as *Pryderi was the hero of Dyfed, and the above story is his *mabinogi*. One difference between Lleu and Pryderi is that Pryderi's lineage is not known, while Lleu may be associated, if not identified, with the Irish or Goedelic god Lug, as well as the Celtic god Lugus. The latter appears in the first element of the name Lugudunum, a form from which are derived the names of the cities of Lyons, Laon, Leyden and Leignitz; Dinlleu in Wales and Lothian (Lleuddin) in Scotland correspond to these forms. Lug was associated with light (*golau go-leu*, cf. Arianrhod's remark above) and skills in many crafts (cf. *llaw-gyffes*, 'deft hand') were attributed to him. In the episode in which Arianrhod is forced into naming her son, Lleu appears as a shoemaker and he is called 'one of the three golden shoe-makers', an event which may be associated with the commemoration of the Lugoves (pl. of Lugus), the guardian gods of shoemakers, in an inscription at Osma in Spain. Lleu is sometimes called Llew, but there is no basis for such a form, except for the miscopying of *-u* as *-w*.

For further details see W. J. Gruffydd, *Math vab Mathonwy* (1928) and Rachel Bromwich, *Trioedd Ynys Prydein* (1978).

Lleucu Llwyd (*fl.* mid-14th cent.), of Pennal, Mer., the woman loved adulterously by *Llywelyn Goch ap Meurig Hen, whose elegy for her is regarded by many as one of the finest love-poems in the Welsh language. It became famous during the poet's lifetime, for a contemporary, *Iolo Goch, records that wherever young people were assembled it was the first poem to be called for. In it Llywelyn reproaches his dead mistress for having died while he was away on his travels in south Wales, thus breaking their tryst. Gwynedd is now empty for him and he desires to leave it but, facing the fact of her death, he bids her a final farewell in this passionate, moving poem.

For further details see the articles by R. Geraint Gruffudd and Gilbert Ruddock in *Ysgrifau Beirniadol I* and *IX* (ed. J. E. Caerwyn Williams, 1965 and 1976).

Lleufer (lit. 'Light'), the magazine of the Workers' Education Association in Wales, was established in 1944 under the editorship of David *Thomas (1880–1967). Although its main purpose was to record the activities of the Association and provide material for study, the magazine also published articles of general literary interest, as well as poetry, short stories and book reviews. David Thomas was succeeded as editor by Edward Williams, Geraint Wyn Jones and C. R. Williams but with the death of the last-named in 1979 the magazine ceased publication.

Llew Llwyfo, see Lewis, Lewis William (1831–1901).

Llew Tegid, see Jones, Lewis Davies (1851–1928).

LLEWELLYN, ALUN (1903–), novelist. Born in London of parents from Machynlleth, Mont., and educated at St. John's College, Cambridge, he was a barrister specializing in International Law. His novels include *The Deacon* (1934), *The Soul of Cezar Azan* (1938) and *Jubilee John* (1939); his plays, *Ways to Love* (1958) and *Shelley Plain* (1960), like two of the novels previous, are set in mid-Wales; his volume of science fiction, *The Strange Invaders* (1934), was claimed by the English author Brian Aldiss as the impetus for his own writing. Alun Llewellyn is also the author of two political studies, *Confound their Politics* (1934) and *The Tyrant from Below* (1957) and, with Wynford *Vaughan-Thomas, the co-author of *The Shell Guide to Wales* (1969).

Llewellyn, Richard, see Lloyd, Richard Llewellyn (1906–83).

LLEWELYN, GWYN (1942–), author and broadcaster. Brought up in Tynygongl, Ang., he left school at the age of sixteen to join *The North Wales Chronicle* and later worked in Cardiff with the *Western Mail* and the independent television companies before becoming an introducer and news reporter with BBC Wales in 1979. He has published one novel, *Pry'r Gannwyll* (1975), and a book about journalism, *Hel Straeon* (1973), both of which are distinguished by a sophisticated and racy prose-style.

Llewelyn, Michael Gareth, see Evans, Frederic (1888–1958).

Llewelyn Ddu o Fôn, see Morris, Lewis (1701–65).

Llinos (**Maria Jane Williams**; 1795–1873), see under Aberpergwm.

Llinwent, a mansion in the parish of Llanbadarn Fynydd, Rads., which was a resort for itinerant poets in the fourteenth and fifteenth centuries. The family line was established by Phylip Dorddu ap Hywel ap Madog of *Maelienydd, a patron of *Iolo Goch. One of his five sons, Cadwgan, settled at Llinwent and was a patron of poets, as was Cadwgan's son, Dafydd Fychan. *Lewys Glyn Cothi enjoyed the hospitality of Llinwent and the tradition was continued there over the next three generations. Branches of the family were established at Pant-y-garegl, Bugeildy, Maes-mawr and Garddfaelog, at all of which a welcome was kept for poets.

Llongborth, The Battle of, see under Englynion Geraint.

Lloyd family, The, of Dolobran, Meifod, Mont., were Quakers, iron-masters and bankers. The first significant members of the family were the poets Dafydd ap Dafydd Llwyd (b. 1549) and his son, John Lloyd (b. 1575). The latter's grandsons, Charles (b. 1637) and Thomas Lloyd (b. 1640), abandoned their studies at Jesus College, Oxford, because of the persecution of Quakers in the town and university. Both became followers of George Fox in 1662 (see under Quakerism), suffering periods of imprisonment in Welshpool before the Declaration of Indulgence in 1672. The sons of Charles Lloyd, Charles (b. 1662) and Sampson (b. 1664), both entered the iron industry, the former establishing a forge at Dolobran, the latter first farming in north Herefordshire and then setting up as an ironmonger in Birmingham. Meanwhile, Thomas Lloyd, in 1683, had left his home at Maesmawr, near Welshpool, for Pennsylvania, where he became President of the Provincial Council and served as Deputy-Governor for William Penn until 1693, the year before his death. Two of his pamphlets were published, *An Epistle to my Dear and well beloved Friends of Dolobran* (1788) and *A Letter to John Eccles and Wife* (1805).

The Dolobran forge and its successors failed and Charles Lloyd's elder line died out, but the descendants of Sampson Lloyd, who himself set up a town mill and various forges, besides investing in canals, included Charles Lloyd 'the poet' (1775–1839), who was a great-grandson, and Charles Lloyd 'the banker' (1748–1828), a grandson, who developed the partnership in Birmingham's first bank, Taylor's and Lloyd's, established in 1765. The ultimate removal of Lloyd's Bank to London and its survival to the present day as one of the five major clearing-house banks is a story complicated by the re-use of family names such as Sampson and Charles and by the intermarriage of a numerous family with other leading Quaker families such as the Barclays. Sampson Samuel Lloyd repurchased Dolobran and the old Quaker meeting-house there in 1877 and the first Lord Lloyd of Dolobran (1879–1941) was his grandson.

An account of the Lloyds of Dolobran will be found in Humphrey Lloyd, *The Quaker Lloyds in the Industrial Revolution* (1975).

LLOYD, DAVID (1597–1663), author. Born near Llanidloes, Mont., he was educated at Hart Hall, Oxford, and, after serving as rector of various parishes in Anglesey and Flintshire, was promoted at the Restoration to the deanery of *St. Asaph. An ardent Royalist, he was known chiefly as the author of *The Legend of Captain Jones* (1631), a burlesque about the adventures of a braggart sailor, which ran to several editions during his lifetime.

LLOYD, DAVID (1752–1838), poet. Born near Llanbister, Rads., he had little formal schooling but prepared himself for Holy Orders and became curate of Putley, Herefs., in 1785. Five years later he was given the living of Llanbister, where he remained until his death. Besides composing music, including the march 'The Loyal Cambrian Volunteers', he published a long poem entitled *The Voyage of Life* (1792) of which an enlarged edition, *Characteristics of Men, Manners and Sentiments or The Voyage of Life*, appeared in 1812.

Lloyd, David (1912–69), singer. Born at Trelogan, Flints., a miner's son, he left school at the age of fourteen and was apprenticed to a carpenter, but entered the Guildhall School of Music in 1933. As a professional singer he was renowned in the concert halls of Europe for his interpretation of the music of Verdi and Mozart. He was also immensely popular in Wales, delighting audiences with his repertoire of hymns and ballads from the nineteenth century.

LLOYD, DAVID MYRDDIN (1909–81), scholar, literary critic and editor. Born at Fforest Fach, Glam., and educated at University College, Swansea, and at the University of Ireland, Dublin, he worked in the *National Library of Wales before his appointment to the staff of the National Library of Scotland, where he became Keeper of the Department of Printed Books. He was the author of *Beirniadaeth Lenyddol* (1962), an essay on Emrys ap Iwan (Robert Ambrose *Jones) in the *Writers of Wales* series (1974) and *Rhai agweddau ar Ddysg y Gogynfeirdd* (1977), and he translated W. J. *Gruffydd's *Hen Atgofion* as *The Years of the Locust* (1976); he was also co-translator (with Tomás O Cléirigh) of *Ystorïau Byr o'r Wyddeleg* (1934), a volume of stories by

Pádraic Ó Conaire. Among the books he edited were *Erthyglau Emrys ap Iwan* (3 vols., 1937, 1939, 1940), *Seiliau Hanesyddol Cenedlaetholdeb Cymru/The Historical Basis of Welsh Nationalism* (1950), *Atgofion am Sirhywi a'r Cylch* (1951), *A *Book of Wales* (1953), *A Reader's Guide to Scotland* (1968) and *O Erddi Eraill* (1981), an anthology of verse translated from eighteen languages into Welsh.

There is an appreciation of D. Myrddin Lloyd's work by B. G. Owens in *Taliesin* (vol. 44, 1982).

LLOYD, DAVID TECWYN (E. H. **Francis Thomas**; 1914–), editor, essayist and critic, was born at Glanyrafon, near Corwen, Mer., and educated at the University College of North Wales, Bangor. From 1938 to 1946 he worked for the Workers' Education Association and from 1946 to 1955 as a lecturer and librarian at *Coleg Harlech. He was a director of the publishing company *Hughes a'i Fab* (see under HUGHES, RICHARD, 1794–1871) and deputy editor of *Y *Cymro* from 1956 to 1961. He then joined the staff of the Extra-Mural Department of the University College of Wales, Aberystwyth, a post in which he remained until his retirement. Editor of the magazine *Taliesin* since 1965, D. Tecwyn Lloyd is a perceptive, witty social commentator and a staunch ally in his editorials of contemporary protest movements. He has published a volume of literary criticism, *Erthyglau Beirniadol* (1946), and has co-edited (with Gwilym Rees *Hughes) a volume of essays on the life and work of Saunders *Lewis (1975). His collections of essays, *Safle'r Gerbydres* (1970), *Lady Gwladys a Phobl Eraill* (1971) and *Bore Da, Lloyd* (1980), express a wide-ranging curiosity, an idiosyncratic sense of humour and a passionate love of Welsh rural culture. Under his pseudonym, D. Tecwyn Lloyd has published two collections of short stories, *Rhyw Ystyr Hud* (1944) and *Hyd Eithaf y Ddaear* (1972).

LLOYD, ELLIS (1879–1939), journalist and novelist. Born in Newport, Mon., he was orphaned at the age of nine and brought up by relatives in Bridgend, Glam. He began his career in a solicitor's office but soon turned to journalism, spending some years on the *Glamorgan Gazette* and, from 1905, working for the *South Wales News and Echo*. During the latter period he published three novels, *Love and the Agitator* (1911), *Scarlet Nest* (1919) and *A Master of Dreams* (1921). The success of these books encouraged him to resign from his newspaper post early in 1924 in order to write, to study law and to work for the Labour Party. No more novels resulted, but he was called to the Bar at Gray's Inn in 1926 and was elected as Member of Parliament for the Llandaff and Barry constituency in 1929, only to lose his seat in the Labour defeat two years later. Appointed coroner for the manor of Ogmore in 1933, he held that post until his death.

All his novels, set in the mixed rural and industrial areas of upland Glamorgan, attempt seriously and without irony to describe Welsh life and tradition, with which he was familiar. In *Scarlet Nest* he outlines with some perspicacity the contest between the unattached (though not apparently unionized) colliers and the older Liberal, chapel-going element of the working-class population. A plausible central plot, however, is spoiled by the presence of an impossible heroine—a 'liberated' actress whose mind is nevertheless riddled with rural superstition—and a Socialist didacticism conveyed in long speeches by Owen John, the collier. For these reasons the novel becomes little more than a romantic confection.

LLOYD, EVAN (1734–76), satirist. Born near Bala, Mer., and educated at Jesus College, Oxford, he was the absentee vicar of Llanfair Dyffryn Clwyd, Denbs., from 1763 until his death. Besides *An Epistle to David Garrick* (1773), he published a number of verse satires which include *The Powers of the Pen* (1766), *The Curate* (1766), *The Methodist* (1766) and *Conversation* (1767) and, in turn, he was abused by *Scriblerius Flagellarius*, the anonymous author of *A Whipping for the Welsh Parson* (1773).

For further details see Cecil J. L. Price, *A Man of Genius and a Welch Man* (1963).

LLOYD, HENRY (*c.*1720–1783), soldier and military writer, of Cwmbychan in the parish of Llanbedr, Mer. Of Jacobite sympathies, he went to France in the hope of obtaining a commission in the French army but, failing in that aim, he taught the military arts to officers of the Irish Brigade. He took part in the battle of Fontenoy (1745) and, during the Jacobite Rising of the same year, he was employed as a secret agent with orders to maintain contact with sympathizers in Wales (see under JACOBITISM). Towards the end of his life he made his peace with the British Government which, despite his service with the Prussian, Austrian and Russian armies, granted him a pension. His principal literary works were *A Political and Military Rhapsody on the Defence of Great Britain* (1779) and *The History of the late war in Germany between the King of Prussia and the Empress of Germany and her allies* (*c.*1776). The latter, which includes his reflections on military strategy, won him a European reputation and is believed to have had an influence on Napoleon.

There is an account of the Llwyd family of Cwmbychan in Thomas Pennant's *Tours in Wales* (1781), including a memorable pen-portrait of Evan Llwyd, a splendid example of the Welsh mountain squire whose type was fast dying out in Pennant's day.

Lloyd, Herbert (1720–69), the infamous squire of Peterwell, a mansion near Lampeter, Cards., was regarded by his contemporaries and later generations as the very epitome of evil. Edu-cated at Jesus College, Oxford, and at the Middle Temple, he lived for a while at Foelallt near Llanddewibrefi, moving to Peterwell in 1755 after inheriting the estate from his brother. The lawlessness for which he was to become notorious in the county began in 1753 when, acting as the agent of his brother-in-law, William Powell of *Nanteos, he led an armed mob to the Esgair Mwyn lead-mines and assaulted the Crown representative, Lewis *Morris, the antiquary. Removed from his office as Justice of the Peace, he then embarked on a political career and—by various forms of chicanery and violence—became the Member of Parliament for Cardigan Boroughs in 1761. He was created baronet by George III two years later.

One of the many tales in which Sir Herbert figures as a rogue and tyrant concerns a poor freeholder named Siôn Philip who owned a field which was coveted by the squire. It was alleged that a black ram was lowered down the chimney of this man's cottage by two of the Peterwell servants who then summoned the local constable. Siôn Philip, found guilty of sheep-stealing, was duly hanged. This incident was used by the composer Ian Parrott as the basis for his opera, *The Black Ram* (1957).

Hated for his arrogance and corruption by both the peasantry and his fellow-gentry, Sir Herbert was defeated in the general election of 1768 by a coalition consisting of the families of Trawsgoed, *Gogerddan and Nanteos, and he was soon afterwards deprived of all public office in the county. It was said at the time of his death that he had shot himself in the garden of a London gambling club and that, on its return to Peterwell, his corpse was impounded by bailiffs until his debts had been paid. His death and the subsequent demise of Peterwell (which no longer exists) were attributed in the popular view to Rhys *Prichard's curse on *Maesyfelin, an estate which had belonged to the Lloyd family.

The reputation of Sir Herbert Lloyd and the history of his family are examined by Bethan Phillips in her book, *Peterwell* (1983).

LLOYD, IORWERTH HEFIN (Talfryn; 1920–), poet, was born near Llanrhaeadr-ym-Mochnant, Denbs. He left school at the age of fourteen to work on his father's farm and was appointed to the staff of Merionethshire's mobile library in 1955. Well known for his witty *englynion*, he has published two volumes of verse, *Cerddi'r Mynydd* (1960) and *Cerddi Talfryn* (1980).

Lloyd, John (1630?–79), Catholic martyr. A native of Brecon, he studied at the English College in Valladolid and was ordained priest there in 1653. Little is known of his ministry in south Wales until his arrest in 1678 during the agitation caused by rumours of the Popish Plot. With Philip *Evans, he was butchered with particular ferocity at Cardiff Castle on 22 July 1679. He was canonized by Pope Paul VI in 1970 as one of the *Forty Martyrs of England and Wales.

Lloyd, John (Silver John; c.1740–1814?), bone-setter, was the most famous of the Lloyds who are still known in Radnorshire and Herefordshire for the charmer's skills. It is believed that he was murdered for the pieces of silver on his coat which he took for his services instead of money. His body was found under the frozen surface of Llyn Heilyn, near New Radnor, 'in the year of the Great Frost' (1814?), and the lake was later thought to be haunted by his spirit. At the spot where he was buried in Radnor Forest the grass is said to be always luxuriantly green. The well-known verse which commemorates his death became a jibe against the people of New Radnor:

> Silver John is dead and gone
> So they came home a-singing,
> Radnor boys pulled out his eyes
> And set the bells a-ringing.

LLOYD, JOHN (1797–1875), poet, was born at Brecon and educated at Christ College in the town, at Eton and at Balliol College, Oxford. A classical scholar, he inherited his father's East India Company wealth and built, a mile outside Brecon, the mansion of Dinas; the house was demolished to make way for a bypass in 1980. It was his success with a poem in English at the Cardiff Eisteddfod of 1834 which prompted him to begin writing more seriously. Unusually for a member of the squirearchy of his day, Lloyd considered himself to be a Welsh patriot, writing of the glories of Welsh arms in the royal service. The Welsh language, however, he believed was a source of confusion which would be better abandoned. His admiration for John Hampden and the Parliamentarians prevented adulation of Queen Victoria but *Owain Glyndŵr, *Llywelyn ap Gruffudd and other Welsh heroes jostled in his mind with English imperial concerns. The literary talent displayed in his first collection, *Poems* (1847), was modest, but rhythmic competence and an occasionally felicitous turn of phrase illumine his comments on the local scene, as on Llanfaes in decay, Brecon Castle ever more ruinous and the murder in Cwmdŵr of the higgler, David Lewis. His second volume of verse, surprisingly entitled *The English Country Gentleman* (1849), begins by celebrating Eton but soon returns, by way of sport, to Y Farteg, Cwmtyleri and the valleys of south Wales.

The poet's son, also named **John Lloyd** (1833–1915), was a prominent barrister and public figure in London and in his native county where he campaigned for the abolition of turnpike gates and supported commoners' rights in the Great Forest of Brecknock. His interests were antiquarian and he published much record material in his three principal works, *Historical Memoranda of Breconshire* (2 vols., 1903, 1904), *The Great Forest of Brecknock* (1905) and *The Early History of the Old South Wales Ironworks* (1906).

For further details see Edwin Poole, *The Illustrated History and Biography of Brecknockshire* (1886) and the article by Roland Mathias, 'Poets of Breconshire' in *Brycheiniog* (vol. XIX, 1980–81).

Lloyd, John Ambrose (1815–74), composer. Born at Mold, Flints., and brought up in Liverpool, he was a teacher by profession but also worked as a commercial representative in north Wales. He published two collections of hymn-tunes and anthems, *Casgliad o Donau* (1843) and *Aberth Moliant* (1870), the latter including many of the compositions for which he is still remembered among Welsh congregations, such as '*Wyddgrug*', '*Alun*', '*Whitford*', '*Wynnstay*' and especially the anthem *'Teyrnasoedd y Ddaear'*.

LLOYD, JOHN EDWARD (1861–1947), historian. Born in Liverpool of Welsh parents, he was educated at the University College of Wales, Aberystwyth, and Lincoln College, Oxford. He began his academic career in 1885 as a lecturer in Welsh and History at Aberystwyth but, in 1892, was appointed Registrar and Lecturer in Welsh History at the University College of North Wales, Bangor, and Professor of History in the same College seven years later.

It was at Bangor that he earned his reputation as a scholar, his particular interest being the history of early and medieval Wales. The centrepiece of his life's work was *A History of Wales to the Edwardian Conquest* (2 vols., 1911), the first comprehensive survey to be successfully undertaken. These books, the product of meticulous, critical research into historical sources, and written with impeccable style, were counterparts to the contribution made by John *Morris-Jones to the study of the Welsh language. J. E. Lloyd was knighted in 1934.

Of J. E. Lloyd's later works, *Owen Glendower* (1931) is the most important. His lecture, *The Welsh Chronicles* (1930), his many contributions to the *Dictionary of Welsh Biography* (of which he was Consultant Editor), and his editorship of *The History of Carmarthenshire* (2 vols., 1935) are also highly regarded. In a powerful elegy for the historian, Saunders *Lewis referred to him as '*hen ddewin Bangor*' ('the old magician of Bangor') and '*goleuwr lampau holl ganrifoedd*' ('the lamplighter of all the centuries').

For further details see the article by John Rowlands on Saunders Lewis's elegy for Sir John Edward Lloyd in *Bardos* (ed. R. Geraint Gruffydd, 1982); see also the obituary of J. E. Lloyd by J. G. Edwards in the *Proceedings* of the British Academy (vol. XLI, 1953).

LLOYD, JOHN SELWYN (1931–   ), children's author, was born at Tal-y-sarn, Caerns., and educated at the Normal College, Bangor; he is a schoolmaster at Corwen. His adventure novels, which are mostly set in foreign countries, include *Llygad y Daran* (1974), *Esgyrn Sychion* (1977), *Trysor Bryniau Caspar* (1979), *Drwy'r Awyr Wenfflam* (1979), *Mae Torch yn Llosgi* (1980), *Croes Bren yn Norwy* (1982), *Brenin y Paith* (1982), *Wrth Draed y Meirw* (1982), *Cysgod Rhyfel* (1983), *Saethau ar y Paith* (1983), *Gwaed ar y Dagrau* (1983) and *Y Dylluan Wen* (1984). J. Selwyn Lloyd won the Drama Medal at the National Eisteddfod in 1979 and has been awarded the Tir na n-Og Prize on two occasions (see under CHILDREN'S LITERATURE).

LLOYD, LUDOVIC (*fl.* 1573–1610), poet, a descendant of the Blainey family of Gregynog, Mont., was a courtier of both Elizabeth I and James I. His works, such as *The Pilgrimage of Princes* (1573), are compilations of material from biblical, classical and British sources but they also include verses of his own composition, some of which are to be found in contemporary collections.

Lloyd, Meredith (*c.* 1620–1695), antiquary, a native of Welshpool, Mont., specialized in the collection of manuscripts relating to Welsh law. He boasted of his manuscripts in 1664 that they were 'more in number and more choise than any studie in Northwales contaynes'—this from a scholar who knew of the Hengwrt collection because he was related to Robert *Vaughan. From Thomas *Vaughan, the brother of Henry *Vaughan, he may have learned some chemistry and John Aubrey (see under AUBREY, WILLIAM), who relied heavily on him for information about Wales, referred to him as 'the chymist'. Lloyd corresponded over many years with Robert Vaughan and William *Maurice, and he visited John *Jones of Gellilyfdy in the Fleet prison. He was an important link between their generation and the scholars of the late seventeenth and early eighteenth century such as Edward *Lhuyd.

Further details will be found in the article by Nesta Lloyd in the *Journal* of the Welsh Bibliographical Society (vol. XI, 1975–6).

LLOYD, OWEN MORGAN (1910–79), poet. Born at Blaenau Ffestiniog, Mer., he was an Independent minister, latterly at Dolgellau. He was a master of *cynghanedd and a prominent figure in literary competitions at the *National Eisteddfod and on radio. O. M. Lloyd's verse is to be found in the volume *O Em i Em* (1978), which was presented to him on the occasion of his retirement by *Cymdeithas Cerdd Dafod, a society of which he was a prominent member, and in *Barddoniaeth O. M. Lloyd* (1981), published posthumously.

LLOYD, RICHARD LLEWELLYN (**Richard Llewellyn**; 1906–83), novelist. He was born at St. David's, Pembs., but his early immersion in the totally Welsh environment of his grandfather's household was lost by his subsequent education in Cardiff, London and Venice, where he studied hotel management. After some years in the catering trade, he sought a new career as a writer of film-scripts and stageplays, more than one novel remaining uncompleted during this period. A few months spent as a collier in Gilfach Goch, in preparation for the writing of his first published novel, *How Green was my Valley* (1939), added realism to the strongly emotional charge which he gave to the ethos of that book, and it rapidly became a bestseller in many parts of the world.

Back in his native country when he wrote *A Few Flowers for Shiner* (1950), he still possessed some of the poetic drive which made his first book so memorable, but although he subsequently published another two dozen novels, none matched the reputation of *How Green was my Valley*, despite their commercial success. The best of them include *None but the Lonely Heart* (1943), *A Man in a Mirror* (1961), *Up, Into the Singing Mountain* (1963), *Sweet Morn of Judas' Day* (1964), *Down Where the Moon is Small* (1966), *At Sunrise, the Rough Music* (1976) and *A Night of Bright Stars* (1979). Indeed, after the first few they rank as 'entertainments', the subjectmatter and lack of authorial involvement combining to create an impression of slickness. Among Richard Llewellyn's other writings are several books for children and a few plays, including *Poison Pen* (1937), *Norse* (1947), *The Scarlet Suit* (1962), *Ecce!* (1974) and *Hat!* (1974).

For further details see the article by Mick Felton in *Dictionary of Literary Biography: British Novelists, 1930–1959* (1983).

Lloyd, Robert (**Llwyd o'r Bryn**; 1888–1961), adjudicator and *eisteddfodwr*, of Cefnddwysarn, Mer. Born near Llandderfel, he began working on his father's farm at the age of thirteen. He is remembered on account of his prodigious zeal for Welsh culture, especially as manifested at the *National Eisteddfod, where his gifts as a public speaker entertained audiences throughout Wales. It was he who coined the phrase *Y Pethe* (lit. 'The Things') to denote that amalgam of values and interests which make up traditional Welsh culture and of which he was a brilliant exemplar. He published a volume of his writings, *Y Pethe* (1955), and a selection of his numerous letters (which virtually constitute his autobiography) was edited by his nephew, Trebor Lloyd *Evans, under the title *Diddordebau Llwyd o'r Bryn* (1967). His daughter, Dwysan Rowlands, has edited a collection of her father's work under the title *Adlodd Llwyd o'r Bryn* (1983).

Lloyd, William (1627–1717), bishop and controversialist. A grandson of Dafydd Llwyd of Henblas, he was born at Sonning, Berks., and was reputed to have graduated at Jesus College,

Oxford, at the age of fifteen. During the Commonwealth he proceeded to ordination but tutored privately, latterly at Oxford, which he had to leave hurriedly as the consequence of some anti-royalist buffoonery. His anti-Catholic pamphlets after the Restoration brought him a succession of offices and in 1680 he became Bishop of *St. Asaph. Although probably not Welsh-speaking, he was learned in Welsh history and resisted Anglicization in his diocese by ensuring the appointment of Welshmen. A good administrator, he was distinguished by his public disputations with leading Dissenters, answering attacks on the episcopacy in his *History of the Government of the Church* (1684). An aggressive Protestant and later a supporter of 'the Glorious Revolution', Lloyd was one of the seven bishops who petitioned James II against the second Declaration of Indulgence (intended for Catholics) and led the deputation to the King. Interested in Welsh history and tradition, he was also widely learned. Bishop Wilkins said of him that he had 'more learning in ready cash' than any man he ever knew.

Lloyd George, David (1863–1945), politician and world statesman, was born in Manchester and brought up by his widowed mother and his uncle at Llanystumdwy, Caerns. Established at Cricieth as a solicitor in 1885, he became involved in local Radical causes and was narrowly elected Member of Parliament for Caernarfon Boroughs at the by-election of 1890. At Westminster he became a prominent spokesman for Nonconformist grievances (notably over *Disestablishment) and the leading proponent of the rising Welsh political *Nationalism of the 1890s. After the failure of *Cymru Fydd, he identified himself less with Welsh affairs and more with general British Radical issues, his opposition to the Boer War winning him both hatred and renown. In Wales, where he enjoyed great popularity, he was a familiar figure at the *National Eisteddfod, delighting audiences with his oratory and wit. He was also prominent in leading the revolt of the Welsh County Councils against the Education Act of 1902.

Appointed President of the Board of Trade in 1905, he proved an energetic minister with a remarkable ability in handling complex industrial matters. As Chancellor of the Exchequer from 1908 to 1915, he sought to use the Treasury to further schemes of social welfare, including old age pensions and national health insurance. His 'People's Budget' of 1909 aimed at financing social reform through large increases in taxation. The House of Lords, incensed by the new taxes on land values, rejected the budget in an unprecedented vote, giving Lloyd George the opportunity of attacking the peerage with vituperation. The Parliament Act of 1911 was the result. His National Insurance Act of 1911, the cause of

further controversy, particularly among doctors, was a cornerstone of the British Welfare State.

The declaration of war by Britain in August 1914 caused Lloyd George great agony of mind but, once convinced of its necessity, he became committed to unconditional victory over Germany and critical of Asquith's apparent equivocation. Minister of Munitions from 1915 to 1916 and Minister of War in the period from July to December 1916, he came to symbolize the British determination to wage total war. Elevated to the Premiership in December 1916 in circumstances which caused deep divisions within the Liberal Party, he created new instruments of government which gave him, as Prime Minister, extensive powers and allowed him to counter the ambitions of the generals. He was hailed as 'the Man who won the War' and 'the Welsh Wizard', his coalition with the Conservatives winning an overwhelming victory in the General Election of 1918. A leading figure in the peace negotiations of 1919, he sought to mediate between Clemenceau's vengefulness and Woodrow Wilson's idealism, and he continued the attempt to revise the peace treaties for the next three years. At the same time, his Government's handling of the miners' demand for nationalization caused lasting bitterness in the coalfield of south Wales, as did its deployment of the Black and Tans in Ireland. Faced with intransigence in Ireland, north and south, Lloyd George's ultimatum to the Irish leaders in 1921 led to the division of Ireland and to the establishment of the Irish Free State.

By 1922 his premiership was increasingly under attack: unfulfilled promises of 'a country fit for heroes' brought disillusionment, his involvement in the sale of honours led to scandal, his Near Eastern policies in favour of the Greeks caused alarm and his plans for a Centre Party dismayed Tory loyalists. In October 1922 Conservative Members of Parliament voted to withdraw from the Coalition and in the General Election which followed Lloyd George was left with only fifty-nine 'National Liberal' supporters. Thereafter he never held office, although he was ceaseless in his efforts to return to power. Elected leader of the reunited Liberal Party in 1926, he fought the General Election of 1929 on Keynesian policies designed to revive the British economy and to reduce unemployment. He failed to regain power and was prevented by illness from playing a direct part in the political crisis of 1931, his parliamentary supporters in the General Election of that year being reduced to four. In 1935 he campaigned vigorously but in vain for his Council of Action for Peace and Reconstruction. His last major intervention in public life was his dramatic speech in May 1940 demanding Chamberlain's resignation. On ceasing to represent Caernarfon Boroughs in January 1945, he was elevated to the peerage as Earl Lloyd-George of Dwyfor but died two months later. He was buried near the river Dwyfor at Llanystumdwy.

Lloyd George has remained since his death, as throughout his political career, a deeply controversial man. He seemed to his contemporaries a volatile and erratic politician, especially in relation to the established world of party politics. Many held him to be uniquely responsible for the downfall of the Liberal Party, although from the 1960s onwards a more positive view began to emerge among historians. For all that, he was a creative and dynamic figure whose impact upon modern British history was immense. Before 1914 he was the main architect of new programmes of social welfare and during the First World War he was an incomparable leader. After the war he was far from a total failure as a peacemaker and in the inter-war years he remained a fount of new ideas on both economic and foreign policy. In relation to Wales, he did more than perhaps any other political spokesman to give it a new political status as a nation and to make it something of a political reality, so that he may be regarded as a leading representative of the modern sense of Welsh identity.

Among the numerous books about Lloyd George the following are the most useful: Thomas Jones, *Lloyd George* (1951), A. J. P. Taylor (ed.), *Lloyd George: Twelve Essays* (1971), *Lloyd George: a Diary* by Frances Stevenson (1971), John Grigg, *The Young Lloyd George* (1973), Kenneth O. Morgan (ed.), *Lloyd George: Family Letters* (1973) and *Lloyd George* (1974), John Campbell, *The Goat in the Wilderness* (1977), John Grigg, *The People's Champion* (1977), Kenneth O. Morgan, *Consensus and Disunity* (1979), W. R. P. George, *Lloyd George: Backbencher* (1983) and Cyril Parry, *David Lloyd George* (1984); see also *Lloyd George was my Father* (1985) by Olwen Carey-Evans, the politician's daughter.

LLOYD-JONES, DAVID MARTYN (1899–1981), preacher and author, was born in Cardiff but spent his formative years at Llangeitho, Cards. After his conversion, he exchanged a brilliant medical career for the pastorate of a small Calvinistic Methodist Forward Movement church at Aberafan, Glam., where he remained from 1927 until 1938. Thereafter he ministered at Westminster Chapel, London, well known as a brilliant preacher, but resigned in 1968 in order to devote himself to a wider preaching ministry and the preparation of his sermons for the press. Evangelical and antiecumenical in his convictions and teaching, he emphasized the centrality of expository preaching, the need for revival, reformed theology and the necessity for church discipline. His most influential works were *Studies in the Sermon on the Mount* (1959–60) and *Spiritual Depression: its Causes and Cures* (1965).

For an account of his life and work see Iain H. Murray, *David Martyn Lloyd-Jones: the First Forty Years, 1899–1939* (1982), Bethan Lloyd-Jones, *Memories of Sandfields, 1927–1938* (1983) and Frederick and Elizabeth Catherwood, *Martyn Lloyd-Jones: the Man and His Books* (1982); see also the commemorative issues of *The Evangelical Magazine of Wales* (1981) and *Y Cylchgrawn Efengylaidd* (1981); the last-named contains a bibliography of his publications.

LLOYD-JONES, JOHN (1885–1965), poet and scholar, was born at Dolwyddelan, Caerns, and educated at the University College of North Wales, Bangor, where he was taught by John *Morris-Jones, and at Jesus College, Oxford. Appointed to a lectureship in Welsh and Celtic at University College, Dublin, he spent more than forty years in Ireland; among the young students who worked under his supervision there were T. J. *Morgan, D. Myrddin *Lloyd, Melville *Richards, Idris *Foster, Brinley Rees, J. E. Caerwyn *Williams and R. M. *Jones (Bobi Jones). He won the *Chair at the National Eisteddfod of 1922 for his '*Awdl y Gaeaf*', one of the finest *awdlau* of the century, but he wrote very little poetry thereafter. His publications include a study of the place-names of Caernarfonshire (1928) and *The Court Poets of the Welsh Princes* (The John Rhŷs Lecture, 1928), but his most important work was *Geirfa Barddoniaeth Gynnar Gymraeg* (1931–63), a study of the vocabulary of early Welsh poetry.

Lloyd Price, Richard John (1843–1923), the squire of Rhiwlas, Llanfor, Mer. His schemes for the employment of local labour included the building of a distillery for the making of Welsh whisky in the village of Frongoch, near Bala. The enterprise flourished for a few years, despite opposition from the chapels, but did not survive the First World War. After the Easter Rising of 1916 the buildings were used as a camp for the internment of Irish Republicans, among whom was Michael Collins. R. J. Lloyd Price was a sportsman and the author of several books about the keeping of animals on a commercial basis and of another on the history of his district (1899). He is often credited with having devised the sport of sheep-dog trials. The inscription over the family vault in Llanfor churchyard is to the memory of Bendigo, a racehorse with which he won the Derby.

Lluagor, see under TRIOEDD Y MEIRCH.

Lludd and Llefelys, see under CYFRANC LLUDD A LLEFELYS.

LLWYD, ALAN (1948–), poet, editor and critic. Born at Dolgellau, Mer., but brought up on a farm at Cilan, Caerns., he was educated at the University College of North Wales, Bangor. He has worked as the manager of a bookshop in Bala, as editor for the publishing firm of Christopher Davies (see under LLYFRAU'R

Dryw) and as an editorial officer with the *Welsh Joint Education Committee.

He began writing verse in *cynghanedd* as a schoolboy and soon mastered its intricacies, eventually emulating the feat of T. H. *Parry-Williams by winning both *Crown and *Chair at the *National Eisteddfod on two occasions (in 1973 and 1976). His first volume of poetry, *Y March Hud* (1971), was published under his original name, Alan Lloyd Roberts, and has been followed by seven others: *Gwyfyn y Gaeaf* (1975), *Edrych Drwy Wydrau Lledrith* (1975), *Rhwng Pen Llŷn a Phenllyn* (1976), *Cerddi'r Cyfannu a Cherddi Eraill* (1980), *Yn Nydd yr Anghenfil* (1982), *Marwnad o Dirdeunaw* (1983) and *Einioes ar ei Hanner* (1984). The most prolific poet of his generation and perhaps the most accomplished, he has written poems in both strict and free forms which are characterized by a brilliant use of *cynghanedd* and by exciting imagery. His earlier work, imbued with a love for Wales, records the decay of the rural community and the passing of its colourful characters, as well as celebrating Nature and the seasons. Latterly, as a husband and father, he has pondered on mortality and the fate of Mankind.

No less industrious as an editor, Alan Llwyd has edited a volume comprising fifty *cywyddau* by *Dafydd ap Gwilym (1980) and initiated several major series of anthologies and critical studies, for some of which, namely *Y Flodeugerdd Englynion* (1978), *Y Flodeugerdd Sonedau* (1980), *Cerddi'r Prifeirdd 1* (1977) and *Cyfres y Meistri: R. Williams Parry* (1979), he took editorial responsibility while working for Christopher Davies. For the same company he co-edited the monthly magazine *Barn* for a year and also translated a collection of Christmas stories for children (1977) and an illustrated edition of the Bible (1978). This editorial work has continued with the publication of *Barddoniaeth O. M. Lloyd* (1981), an anthology, *Llywelyn y Beirdd* (1984), a collection of essays on the present state of Welsh poetic art, *Trafod Cerdd Dafod y Dydd* (1984) and *Y Flodeugerdd Epigramau* (1985). Alan Llwyd is a perceptive critic, although the first part of his exegesis on the work of Euros *Bowen (1977) did not please that poet. He has also written monographs on the poetry of Gwyn *Thomas (1984) and R. Williams *Parry (1984). Perhaps his most valuable contribution as a critic was his editorship of the poetry column of *Y *Cymro* (1974) during which he did a great deal to rekindle interest in *cynghanedd*. He had already published a student's guide to the medium, *Anghenion y Gynghanedd* (1973), and it was he who suggested forming *Cymdeithas Cerdd Dafod*, the society for poets writing in the traditional metres. Together with Gerallt Lloyd *Owen, he has edited the society's monthly magazine *Barddas* from its inception in 1976 and he was appointed the Society's first full-time organizer in 1983.

For further details see the reviews of the poet's books in *Barddas* (nos. 7, 1977; 46, 1980; 68, 1982; 72, 1983 and 91, 1984); see also the interview given to John Rowlands in *Llais Llyfrau* (Autumn, 1980), the note by the same author in *Profiles* (1980) and the article by Derwyn Jones in *Trafod Cerdd Dafod y Dydd* (ed. Alan Llwyd, 1984).

LLWYD, ANGHARAD (1780–1866), antiquary, was born at Caerwys, Flints., the daughter of the John Lloyd (1733–93), also an antiquary, who accompanied Thomas *Pennant on his tour of Wales. A member of the Honourable Society of *Cymmrodorion, she won numerous prizes at eisteddfodau for her essays on genealogy and other historical subjects. She also edited and published a new edition of Sir John *Wynn's *The History of the Gwydir Family* (1827). But her most important work was *The History of the Island of Mona* (1832). A voluminous collection of her manuscripts is kept in the National Library of Wales.

LLWYD or **LHUYD, HUMPHREY** (c. 1527–1568), antiquary and map-maker, was born at Denbigh and educated at the University of Oxford. It was formerly believed that he qualified as a doctor and was the author of books on medicinal subjects but it now seems that he may have been confused with a contemporary of the same name. Among his publications are *De Mona Druidium Insula* (1568), a letter addressed to Abraham Ortelius, the Dutch geographer, which was included in the latter's atlas, *Theatrum Orbis Terrarum* (1570); *Commentarioli Descriptionis Britannicae Fragmentum* (1572), translated into English by Thomas Twyne as *The Breuiary of Britayne* (1573); a version of a tract by Sir John *Price entitled *The Description of Cambria* and an English translation of the chronicle attributed to *Caradog of Llancarfan, both of which became the main sources for David *Powel's *The Historie of Cambria* (1584). Llwyd, whose motto was 'Hwy pery klod na golyd' ('Fame lasts longer than wealth'), also prepared maps which were the first of Wales, and of Wales and England, to be published separately (1573).

Further details will be found in the articles by I. M. Williams in *Llên Cymru* (vol. II, 1952) and R. Geraint Gruffydd in *Efrydiau Athronyddol* (vol. XXXIII, 1970).

LLWYD, HUW (1568?–1630?), poet and soldier, of Cynfal Fawr in the parish of Maentwrog, Mer., belonged to the same family as that of Morgan *Llwyd but their precise relationship is not known. A gentleman of comfortable means, he fought under Sir Roger *Williams against the armies of Spain in France and the Low Countries. He was not a professional poet but composed verse in the strict and free metres, some of which reflects his interest in hunting, chess and medicine. According to tradition, he practised magic and a rock near the river Cynfal, known as Huw Llwyd's Pulpit, is said to be the place where he meditated.

LLWYD, MORGAN (1619–59), Puritan author. He was born at Cynfal Fawr, Maentwrog, Mer., into the same family as that of Huw *Llwyd. After his father's death in 1629 he was taken by his mother, Mari Wyn of Hendremur, to be educated in Wrexham, where, in 1635, he was converted by listening to Walter *Cradock, then serving as a curate in that town. Llwyd joined Cradock at Llanfair Waterdine, Salop, and later moved with him to Llanfaches, Mon., where the first 'gathered church' in Wales was founded in 1639. It was at Llanfaches, where he remained for nearly three years, that he met and married his wife, Ann Herbert, who bore him at least eleven children. At the outbreak of the *Civil War, the Llanfaches congregation dispersed and fled, some first to Bristol and then, in July 1642, to London. Having sent his wife and children home to his mother at Cynfal, Llwyd joined the Parliamentary army as a chaplain and saw action in southern England. In 1644 he was sent by Parliament to north Wales as an itinerant preacher, settling eventually in Wrexham at Brynffynnon, which he rented from his friend, Colonel John *Jones of Maesygarnedd. From 1650 till 1653 he was an Approver under the Act for the *Propagation of the Gospel in Wales, charged with finding fit replacements for ejected ministers. In 1656, under the State Church set up during the Commonwealth, he was settled as minister of Wrexham parish church, having already been ministering for some nine years to the influential Independent 'church' in the town. There are hints in his correspondence that his final years were touched by personal tragedy.

Llwyd published eleven works in all, of which three were in English and eight in Welsh. They are *Llythur ir Cymru cariadus (1653), Gwaedd ynghymru yn wyneb pob cydwybod (1653), Dirgelwch i rai iw ddeall Ac i eraill iw wattwar . . . Neu arwydd i annerch y Cymru (1653), An Honest Discourse between Three Neighbours (1655), Lazarus and his Sisters Discoursing of Paradise (1655), Where is Christ? (1655), Gair o'r Gair (1656), Yr Ymroddiad (a translation of Of true Resignation, John Sparrow's version of part of Der Weg zu Christo by Jakob Böhme, 1657), Y Disgybl ai Athraw o newydd (a translation of Of the supersensual life . . . in a dialogue between a scholar and his master, Sparrow's version of another part of Der Weg zu Christo, 1657), Cyfarwyddid ir Cymru (1657) and Gwyddor vchod (1657), an astrological tract in verse. In addition several fragmentary prose works and a considerable number of his poems survive in manuscript.

The three books published in 1653 (of which the most notable is the Arwydd, generally known as *Llyfr y Tri Aderyn) are clarion calls to the Welsh to prepare themselves in spirit for the imminent coming of Christ to reign as King on earth. By contrast, those published in 1655 (all in English) are more controversial and seek to define Llwyd's position as contrasted both with that of *Fifth Monarchism, whose adherents wished to prepare for Christ's reign by political means, and with that of *Quakerism, of which the emphasis on the Inner Light led to disregard of both historical fact and external authority. The three works published in 1656 and 1657 seek to expound Llwyd's system of thought, which was deeply indebted to the writings of the Lutheran mystic Jakob Böhme; indeed, Llwyd appears to have reckoned his meeting with Böhme's mind in 1651 as a second conversion. Böhme offered Llwyd an alternative to the radical *Puritanism which he had received from Cradock and allowed him to emphasize (doubtless in accordance with his own deepest inclinations) experience at the expense of orthodoxy: God spoke in each man's heart and a man had only to listen and obey. But he was sufficiently grounded in the Bible and in Calvinist theology to avoid becoming an out-and-out heresiarch.

There is evidence that Llwyd was a remarkably eloquent preacher in both Welsh and English. His Welsh books, particularly the three published in 1653, capture the rhythms of exalted pulpit speech. His style is highly rhetorical and makes glowing use of sometimes esoteric imagery, for he was a disciple not only of Böhme but also of the whole Platonic and Hermetic tradition. But his chief debt is to the Welsh *Bible, to the Welsh religious prose classics of the Elizabethan and early Stuart periods and to the great Welsh late medieval poetic tradition of which Huw Llwyd, possibly his father, had been a minor devotee. It was not for nothing that he had been baptized, in all probability, by Edmund *Prys and catechized by Hugh *Lewis. Welsh proverbs flow as easily from his pen as do verses from the Bible and passages of rich metaphysical image-making. He possessed a profound knowledge of the Welsh language and its literature, a lofty if obscure metaphysic, burning conviction and literary genius of a high order. At its best, his prose is unequalled in Welsh; he was also, spasmodically, a fine poet.

Morgan Llwyd's works were edited by T. E. Ellis (2 vols., 1899) and J. H. Davies (1908). A volume of his shorter writings has been edited by Patrick Donovan under the title Ysgrifeniadau Byrion Morgan Llwyd (1985). Important historical and critical monographs on Llwyd have been published by E. Lewis Evans (1930) and Hugh Bevan (1954). See also the article by E. Lewis Evans in Y Traddodiad Rhyddiaith (ed. Geraint Bowen, 1970), the essays by Saunders Lewis in Meistri'r Canrifoedd (ed. R. Geraint Gruffydd, 1973), the article by John Davies on Morgan Llwyd's English works in The Anglo-Welsh Review (vol. 23, no. 51, 1974), R. Tudur Jones in Reformation, Conformity and Dissent (ed. R. Buick Knox, 1977), and the monograph by M. Wynn Thomas in the series Writers of Wales (1984).

LLWYD, RICHARD (**Bard of Snowdon**; 1752–1835), poet and antiquary, was born at Beaumaris, Ang. His father's sudden death from smallpox meant that he was raised in extreme poverty and had no more than nine months at the Beaumaris Free School. After a period in service with the Morgans of Henblas, Ang., and other families, he became in 1780 estate agent and clerk to Griffith of Caerhun, near Conwy, remaining there until his master's death. A man of notable frugality, friendliness and zest for research, Llwyd became an authority on Welsh genealogy and heraldry. Received with affection and respect in many aristocratic households, he was able to obtain grants from the Royal Literary Fund for Dic Aberdaron (Richard Robert *Jones), Dafydd Ddu Eryri (David *Thomas) and others. After 1807 he lived in Chester.

His long poem, *Beaumaris Bay* (1800), is a topographical palimpsest with notes which are twice as long as the text. The extent of his acquaintance with great houses is revealed in *Poems, Tales, Odes, Sonnets, Translations from the British* (1804). His research at the British Museum in 1808 was intended to result in a book on the Royal and Patrician Tribes of Wales, but Llwyd failed to find patronage sufficient to allow him to continue with it. A memoir by Edward Parry and a number of Llwyd's poems not previously published are included in his *Poetical Works* (1837). Llwyd was a fervent Welsh patriot and from 1824 a member of the Honourable Society of *Cymmrodorion. He wrote in English less defensively than was the fashion, lauding the Welsh heritage and calling for unity against Napoleon. Nowhere worse than competent, his verse is allusive, well-turned and witty.

The only published source for the life of Llwyd is the memoir by Edward Parry which precedes his *Poetical Works* (1837).

LLWYD, YR USTUS (*fl.* 14th cent.), a low-class poet, perhaps a native of Powys, who wrote verse which is coarse and abusive; almost nothing is known about him.

Llwyd fab Cil Coed. a magician in the Third Branch of *Pedair Cainc y Mabinogi. He avenges the maltreatment which his friend, Gwawl fab Clud, has received at the hands of *Pwyll in the First Branch by placing a spell over Dyfed and by imprisoning *Pryderi and *Rhiannon in *Annwfn. His courtiers, transformed into mice, are sent to destroy *Manawydan's corn but one of them, Llwyd's pregnant wife, is captured and condemned to be hanged. Llwyd attempts to secure her release by appearing in the semblance of a scholar, a priest and a bishop, offering to buy her freedom. The price demanded by Manawydan is the release of Pryderi and Rhiannon and Llwyd's promise never to seek revenge again.

Llwyd o'r Bryn, see LLOYD, ROBERT (1888–1961).

Llwydiarth, a mansion in the parish of Llanerchymedd, Ang., was well known for its owners' patronage of itinerant poets on the island. Poetry addressed to the heads of the family over six generations has survived, from the time of *Dafydd ab Ieuan who received *Dafydd ab Edmwnd and *Guto'r Glyn in the fifteenth century to the time of Rhys Wyn (d. 1581), the sixth and last to maintain the tradition. See also the next entry.

Llwydiarth, a mansion in the parish of Llanfihangel yng Ngwynfa, Mont., the home of one of the Vaughans, who as a family were among the most important patrons of poets in the county. The house was built by Gruffudd ap Siencyn, a supporter of *Owain Glyndŵr. Eight more generations maintained the tradition, most notably in the time of John Vaughan (d. 1599), to whom much poetry was dedicated, and of his son Owen, but patronage had ceased by the middle of the seventeenth century. See also the previous entry.

Llwyfenydd, a territory which belonged to the kingdom of *Urien Rheged in the sixth century, is mentioned four times in *Taliesin's poems to him. In 'Dadolwch Urien' there are references to the wealth, courtesy and bounteousness of the region and in 'Marwnad Owain' the son of Urien is described as '*udd Llwyfenydd llathraid*' ('the lord of splendid Llwyfenydd'). Its location is uncertain but both Leeming, south of Catterick, Yorks., and the river Lyvennet, may preserve the name.

Llwyn, a mansion near Dolgellau, Mer., famous for its patronage to itinerant poets, was the home of Lewis Owen and his son, Siôn Lewis Owain, in the sixteenth century. The death of the father, who was murdered by the Red Bandits of Mawddwy (*Gwylliaid Cochion Mawddwy) in 1555, was mourned in several poems which refer to his literary interests. *Owain Gwynedd is the poet most frequently associated with the son, who was one of the Commissioners of the eisteddfod held at *Caerwys in 1567.

'Llwyn Onn' (lit. 'The ash grove'), a harp-tune first published by Edward *Jones (Bardd y Brenin) in *The Bardic Museum* (1802). A tune entitled 'Constant Billy', to which the first part is similar, is found in *The Beggar's Opera* (1728) by John Gay. Words have been written to the tune in Welsh and English, none more popular than '*Gogoniant i Gymru*' by John *Jones (Talhaiarn), which were published with the air in 1860.

Llyfr y Tri Aderyn (lit. 'The book of the three birds'; 1653), the longest of three works published by Morgan *Llwyd in the year 1653 in order to prepare his compatriots for the coming of Christ to rule on earth, an event of which he believed the Saints' Parliament (5 July–12 Dec. 1653) to be the harbinger (see under FIFTH MONARCHISM); the two other works were *Llythur ir Cymru cariadus and Gwaedd ynghymru yn wyneb pob Cydwybod. Its full title in translation is 'A mystery for some to understand and for others to mock at, that is, three birds talking, the Eagle, and the Dove, and the Raven. Or a sign with which to confront the Welsh. In the year one thousand six hundred and fifty-three, before the coming of 666'. Here the Eagle represents the civil power, the Dove the Puritans and the Raven the Royalists; at a deeper level, the Eagle is the seeker for salvation, the Dove is the saint and the Raven the reprobate. In the first third of the book the dialogue is mostly between the Eagle and the Raven concerning the signs of the times and their interpretations. The Raven then departs and the Eagle and Dove go on to discuss the mysteries of the Spiritual Life and the necessity for the Welsh to possess that Life before Christ appears. At the end of the book Llwyd permits the reader an indirect glimpse of his own spiritual pilgrimage. Although the work has been criticized because of its somewhat incoherent structure, its style is characterized by great richness of both imagery and rhythm.

For further details see the article by W. J. Gruffydd in Y Cofiadur (1925) and those by T. Williams in Y Traethodydd (1949).

Llyfrau Ab Owen (lit. 'Ab Owen's books'), a series of books published by Owen M. *Edwards during the years from 1906 to 1914. Seventeen volumes in all were included, some describing the life and work of eminent Welshmen such as Robert *Owen (1907, 1910) and William *Owen Pughe (1914), others original works by contemporary writers, among them *Clych Atgof (1906), Tro trwy'r Gogledd (1907) and Tro i'r De (1907) by Owen M. Edwards. The books (which, the publisher made clear, were not originally intended as a series) were very similar in format and design to those in *Cyfres y Fil, with which they are sometimes confused.

Llyfrau Deunaw (lit. 'Eighteen pence books'), a series of books published by the University of Wales Press during the years from 1948 to 1957. It consisted of nineteen volumes, each with its own editor and presenting a selection from the work of a significant writer or a small anthology by various hands. Originally priced at a shilling and six pence each, the booklets were suggested to the Press by R. T. *Jenkins and W. J. *Gruffydd. Among the classics included in the series were extracts from the works of David *Owen (Brutus), Samuel *Roberts, William *Thomas (Islwyn), Thomas *Edwards (Twm o'r Nant), Jeremy *Owen and Evan *Jones (Ieuan Gwynedd).

Llyfrau Pawb (lit. 'Everyone's books'), a series of thirty-five booklets published by Gwasg Gee during the years from 1943 to 1948. The publisher's aim was to provide Welsh readers with a variety of reasonably priced volumes of contemporary literature and the series included novels, poetry, short stories, translations and memoirs. Some of these works, such as Gweddw'r Dafarn by Gwilym R. *Jones, had been successful at the *National Eisteddfod. Among others who contributed to the series were Elizabeth Mary *Jones (Moelona), T. E. *Nicholas, Aneirin Talfan *Davies and R. Bryn *Williams.

Llyfrau'r Dryw (lit. 'The wren's books'), a series of forty-four booklets on a variety of subjects, was edited and published by Aneirin Talfan *Davies and his brother Alun Talfan Davies during the years from 1940 to 1952. One of the most successful initiatives in the history of Welsh publishing, the series gave fresh hope to the book trade in Wales by finding new readers for the work of such writers as T. Gwynn *Jones, Ifor *Williams, Ambrose *Bebb and E. Tegla *Davies. The name Llyfrau'r Dryw was subsequently given to the publishing company which later became Christopher Davies Ltd. of Llandybie and Swansea. This firm made an important contribution to Welsh letters up to the mid-1970s by publishing a large number of books, including the series *Cyfres Crwydro Cymru, as well as the magazines *Barn and *Poetry Wales, but its output as a publisher declined thereafter.

Llyfrau'r Ford Gron (lit. 'The books of the round table'), a series of twenty booklets presenting selections from Welsh classics, published by Hughes a'i Fab (see under HUGHES, RICHARD, 1794–1871) in 1931 and 1932. Edited by John Tudor *Jones (John Eilian), it included extracts from the works of William *Williams (Pantycelyn), Goronwy *Owen, *Dafydd ap Gwilym, Morgan *Llwyd, Elis *Wynne, Theophilus *Evans, John *Morris-Jones and Owen M. *Edwards. The series was reprinted in 1977. See also FORD GRON.

Llyfrbryf, see FOULKES, ISAAC (1836–1904).

LLYGAD GŴR (fl. 1268), a court poet who was associated by *Gwilym Ddu o Arfon with Hendwr, Llandrillo, Mer. His poems fall into two groups: the first is in praise of minor princes in northern *Powys who are commended for defending the border with England, and the second, by far the more important, consists of five awdlau to *Llywelyn ap Gruffudd, the last independent Prince of Wales. They express the short-lived euphoria during the years when the Prince was at the peak of his power, from the Treaty of *Montgomery (1267) to the disas-

ter of *Aberconwy (1277), a period when he was
the supreme lord of *Gwynedd, Powys and
*Deheubarth. Llywelyn, who is compared with
the heroes of the *Old North, is said to be in
conflict 'rhag estrawn genedl anghyfiaith' ('with an
alien nation of different speech') and the poet
calls for the loyalty of every Cymro (Welshman),
a word he uses several times with great pride. Of
all the court poets it was Llygad Gŵr who was
the most unambiguous in his view of Wales as a
national entity and his was the most patriotic
poetry in Welsh until the time of *Owain
Glyndŵr.

Llymru or **Flummery**, a traditional dish consisting of oatbread steeped in cold water and
buttermilk, boiled until it thickens and served
cool with milk or treacle; the pottage was known
as sucan (E. sowans) in south-west Wales.
Similar foods popular in rural areas were oatmeal porridge and gruel. See also BRWES and
SIOT.

Llŷn, a cantref of *Gwynedd and a peninsula
which, under the provisions of the Statute of
*Rhuddlan (1284), became part of the county of
Caernarfon, is one of the most cherished heartlands of Welsh culture.

Llyn Cwm Llwch, a lake below the northern
face of the Brecon Beacons, was once believed to
have a secret door which opened every *May
Day into Fairyland. A folk-tale relates how the
inhabitants of Brecon tried to drain the lake in
order to discover its treasure, but were foiled by
a giant who emerged from its waters and
threatened to drown the town.

Llyn Lliwan, a lake near the Severn estuary, is
described in the episode of the hunt for the
*Twrch Trwyth in the tale of *Culhwch and
Olwen. Its characteristics, listed among the
*Mirabilia Britanniae at the end of *Nennius's
*Historia Brittonum, were that when the tide
flowed up the Severn, water entered the lake
without touching the banks; with the ebb, it
poured out and the water rose like a mountain,
flooding the surrounding land. If an army of
men stood facing the water they were engulfed
by it, but they were in no danger whatsoever if
they turned their backs on it.

Llyn Syfaddan, a lake near Llan-gors, Brecs.,
with which two folk-tales are associated. One,
on the theme of the palace or town which is
drowned because of the wickedness of the prince
and his subjects, is also associated with other
lakes in Wales, such as Llyn Tegid, near Bala,
Mer. According to the other, a tale told by
*Gerald de Barri (Giraldus Cambrensis), the
Birds of Syfaddan would sing only at the command of the true Prince of south Wales. Some
time during the reign of Henry I, when the

Normans had conquered almost the whole of the
area, Gruffudd ap Rhys, Prince of *Deheubarth,
was riding by the lake in the company of two
Norman lords. The birds refused to sing when
ordered to do so by the Normans, but rose from
the water and sang loudly for the rightful Prince.

Llyn Wyth Eidion, a lake in the parish of
Llaneugrad, Ang., is associated with a folk-tale
about the farm servant of Nant Uchaf beating his
eight oxen with a stick studded with nails
because he could not plough in a straight line.
The beasts rushed into the lake, dragging the
man with them, and drowned. The staff with
which he tried to save himself grew into an ash-
tree, the leaves of which were said to droop in
mourning for the animals.

Llyn y Fan Fach, a lake near Llanddeusant,
Carms., with which one of the best-known of all
Welsh folk-tales is associated. The son of Blaen
Sawdde, a farm in the district, falls in love with a
beautiful maiden who lives in the lake. After
being offered three kinds of bread, she agrees to
marry him but warns that she will leave him if he
strikes her 'three causeless blows'. They live
happily for many years at Esgair Llaethdy and
have three sons, but after the husband accidentally strikes his wife on three occasions she
returns to the lake, calling all her cattle to follow
her. She later appears to her three sons at places
now called Pant y Meddygon and Llidiart y
Meddygon, where she reveals to them the medicinal qualities of plants and herbs. Rhiwallon,
the eldest son, and his three sons, became physicians to *Rhys Gryg and thus established the
famous line known as the Physicians of
*Myddfai.
    This tale is believed to have its roots in the
folk-memory of a people who lived in a crannog
or primitive lake-dwelling. The descriptions of
the cattle are similar to those which existed in
Britain between the Iron Age and the Dark
Ages. It is possible that the original tale was
linked to the much later account of the Physicians of Myddfai because of the reference, in the
wife's call to her cattle, to the 'white bull from
the King's court' (a descendant of the early urus),
which became connected in the popular mind
with the white cattle of the royal court of
*Dinefwr.
For further details see John Rhŷs, Celtic Folklore: Welsh
and Manx (1901).

Llyn y Morwynion, a lake near Blaenau
Ffestiniog, Mer., is associated with the tradition
that the young men of Dyffryn Ardudwy used
to go to Dyffryn Clwyd to look for wives. When
they were killed by their rivals, the men of
Dyffryn Clwyd, the maidens were broken-
hearted and jumped into the lake and drowned.
It is said that the women may sometimes be seen
at the lake-side, combing their hair. In the

Fourth Branch of *Pedair Cainc y Mabinogi, *Blodeuwedd's maidens fall into the lake and are drowned.

Llŷr, the father of *Manawydan, Bendigeidfran (*Brân) and *Branwen, in the Second Branch of *Pedair Cainc y Mabinogi. It has been suggested that the name Manawydan fab Llŷr is a borrowing from the name of the sea-god in Irish mythology, Manannan mac Lir. In Welsh, examples occur of '*llŷr' meaning 'sea', as of '*ler' (gen. '*lir') in Irish. Llŷr is often referred to as Llŷr Llediaith ('half-language'), possibly an indication of his foreign origin. There are instances of the interchange of the forms Llŷr and Lludd, and the names Llŷr Lluyddawg, Llŷr Llurygawg and Llŷr Marini also occur. Shakespeare's Lear was derived from Raphael Holinshed's *Chronicles* (1577) which drew in turn on John Hooker's translation of *Gerald de Barri's work and on *Geoffrey of Monmouth's *Historia Regum Britanniae* in which the name Leir is found.

Llythur ir Cymru cariadus (lit. 'A letter to the loving Welshmen'; 1653), the earliest and shortest of three works published by Morgan *Llwyd in 1653 in order to prepare his compatriots for the coming of Christ to rule on earth (see under FIFTH MONARCHISM); the two other works were *Gwaedd ynghymru yn wyneb pob Cydwybod* and *Llyfr y Tri Aderyn*. It is likely that the *Llythur* was printed in Dublin by William Bladen and under the supervision of Colonel John *Jones of Maesygarnedd. At the beginning of the work Llwyd describes the spiritual life as contrasted with Man's life according to the flesh, thence proceeding to portray Christ's coming as King and Judge and exhorting the Welsh to prepare themselves. In spite of the occasional obscurities of the teaching, Llwyd's brilliant use of imagery and his haunting prose-rhythms (borrowed, it may be assumed, from pulpit oratory) have ensured that the *Llythur* is regarded as a point of new departure in the history of Welsh prose.

Llythurau 'Rhen Ffarmwr (lit. 'Letters of the old farmer'; 1878), a series of fictional letters by William *Rees (Gwilym Hiraethog), was first published sporadically in the periodical *Yr *Amserau* between 1846 and 1851. The letters deal with topics of the day such as high rents, landowners' rights, the tithe, the Poor Law, emigration to America and the franchise; some are addressed to Lord John Russell, others to the Pope and John Bull. One of the writer's aims was to persuade farmers to organize themselves in a trade union or guild. The Old Farmer is a fiery Welsh patriot and his letters, written in the dialect of the Hiraethog district, are full of rich rural idioms and enhanced by the lilt and balance of pulpit Welsh.

Llythyfnwg, a commot of southern *Powys, was known from the late eleventh century as the lordship of Radnor (Maesyfed). Seized by Philip de Braose in 1095, it passed in 1230 to the Mortimer family who thereafter resisted all attempts to include it within the county of Hereford. With the rest of the Mortimer inheritance, it was held by the English Crown from 1460 and it became part of the county of Radnor in 1536.

Llyw Olaf, Y, see LLYWELYN AP GRUFFUDD (c.1225–1282).

LLYWARCH AP LLYWELYN (Prydydd y Moch; *fl.* 1173–1220), one of the greatest of the Poets of the Princes, was probably a native of Rhos Is-Dulas, Denbs. He flourished during the reigns of *Dafydd ab Owain Gwynedd and *Llywelyn ap Iorwerth (Llywelyn Fawr). An enthusiastic supporter of the latter's policy of uniting Wales, he referred to himself as Llywelyn's man even in a number of poems to lesser princes such as *Rhys Gryg of *Deheubarth. Unlike some poets of his day who were critical of the aggressive policy pursued by the House of *Gwynedd, Llywarch saw the need for securing '*cadr heddwch*' ('a strong peace') by recognition of *Aberffraw's claims over all Wales, and he supported whoever ruled from that seat. In a powerful poem to Dafydd ab Owain Gwynedd he calls him '*prifdeyrn canhwynawl*' ('the chief ruler by inherent right'), but reminds the Prince that it was not love which had brought him to power but his success in bloody battle. Fratricidal war between the Princes was rife during Llywarch's lifetime and there is a reference to Cain and Abel in his ode to *Rhodri ab Owain Gwynedd. Praising Llywelyn, he emphasizes his ancestry in *Powys as well as in Gwynedd, stressing the bond between Prince and country in terms of the *Hero's Marriage with Sovereignty.

The poem by Llywarch known as 'Y *Canu Mawr' was written in support of Llywelyn's advance to Powys, while in 'Y *Canu Bychan' he expressed his jubilation at the Prince's success. In the *Hendregadredd Manuscript a series of awdlau to God is attributed to Llywarch, but from internal evidence the ascription in *The Myvyrian Archaiology* (1801–07) and in *The *Red Book of Hergest* to *Cynddelw Brydydd Mawr seems more probable because the bellicose sentiments are more typical of that poet. Some of Llywarch's love-poetry is extant, but far more memorable is the *awdl* in which, facing trial by ordeal for the alleged murder of a certain Madog, he appeals to God and the Apostles for mercy. It is not known how he acquired his nickname ('Poet of the Pigs') but a reference in one of his poems to swine may account for it. *Dafydd Benfras, his successor at Llywelyn's court, may have been his son.

For further details see the article by G. R. J. Jones 'The Tribal System in Wales' in *The Welsh History Review* (vol. I, no. 2, 1961) and that by Melville Richards in the *Transactions* of the Denbighshire Historical Society (vol. XI).

Llywarch Hen, see under CANU LLYWARCH HEN (9th or 10th cent.).

LLYWARCH LLAETY or **LLYWARCH Y NAM** (*fl.* 1140–60), a court poet to whom is ascribed a series of *englynion* to Llywelyn ap Madog ap Maredudd of *Powys, composed during the Prince's lifetime. Although in the form of *englynion unodl union*, they show some of the features and much of the spirit of the older poetry of Powys which is to be found in **Canu Llywarch Hen*.

Llywelyn ap Gruffudd (*c*.1225–1282), known as **Y Llyw Olaf** ('The Last Prince'), was the grandson of *Llywelyn ap Iorwerth (Llywelyn Fawr). On the death of his uncle Dafydd in 1245, Llywelyn and his elder brother Owain became joint rulers of *Gwynedd. The hostility of the English Crown having caused the downfall of the polity created by Llywelyn Fawr and by the Treaty of Woodstock (1247), Owain and Llywelyn were restricted to Gwynedd west of the Conwy, which they were to hold from Henry III in return for military service. But in 1255 Llywelyn embarked upon a career which closely resembled that of his grandfather. Depriving Owain and a younger brother, *Dafydd ap Gruffudd, of authority in Gwynedd, he attacked the English castles in Wales which Henry III had granted to his son Edward. By 1257 Llywelyn had regained Gwynedd east of the Conwy, captured the English strongholds in *Ceredigion and overrun the Marcher lordships in central and south-west Wales. The Welsh rulers of *Deheubarth and northern *Powys recognized him as overlord and when, in 1257, Gruffudd ap Gwenwynwyn of southern Powys refused to do so, Llywelyn deprived him of his lands. He assumed the title of Prince of Wales in the following year. While Henry III was embroiled in the struggle with his barons, led by Simon de Montfort, the Prince, in alliance with de Montfort, seized a chain of lordships along the eastern March which extended his rule to the borders of Gwent and Glamorgan. Although de Montfort was killed in 1265, instability in England prevented Henry III from coercing Llywelyn and, at the Treaty of *Montgomery (1267), the King confirmed him and his heirs in the title of Prince of Wales. Llywelyn was to retain his conquests and the lesser rulers of Wales were to pay homage to him, he in turn paying homage to the English Crown.

In the years following 1267, Llywelyn sought to consolidate his realm by developing its administration and fiscal system. Until the death of Henry III in 1272, his relations with the English Crown were cordial, although Llywelyn's pressure upon the King's vassals in south-east Wales caused difficulties, his success in winning the allegiance of the Welsh of northern Glamorgan causing the lord of that region to build the great castle at *Caerphilly. With the accession of Edward I, demands that Llywelyn should scrupulously fulfil his obligations under the Treaty of Montgomery became more insistent. Llywelyn, complaining that Edward was harbouring his enemies—his brother Dafydd and Gruffudd ap Gwenwynwyn—ceased paying tribute to the King, delayed in paying him homage, absented himself from his coronation and persisted in his intention of marrying Eleanor, the daughter of Simon de Montfort. In 1276, Edward, with England united behind him, attacked Llywelyn, whose united Wales was a recent and fragile construction. Under attack, that construction collapsed and the Treaty of *Aberconwy (1277) stripped Llywelyn of his conquests and allowed him to retain only Gwynedd west of the Conwy.

After 1277 Llywelyn behaved with circumspection towards the King, despite the fact that Edward's actions gave him cause for grievance. On the other hand, Llywelyn's brother Dafydd, who had been granted lands in north-east Wales in 1277 and who also had cause for dissatisfaction with the Crown, attacked the castle of *Hawarden on Palm Sunday 1282. In the subsequent conflagration, Llywelyn was unable to stand aside. The Welsh resistance to the subsequent English invasion achieved a degree of success until, on 11 December 1282, Llywelyn, who was rallying his forces in the middle March, was killed by English troops at a bridge over the Irfon, west of Builth. His head was sent for exhibition in London and his body buried at the abbey of *Cwm Hir.

Although resistance continued under Dafydd for a few months, Llywelyn's death marked the end of the House of Gwynedd and the collapse of the embryonic Welsh state which he had created. This national disaster inspired a number of poets to sing laments for Llywelyn, the greatest and most famous of which is the elegy by *Gruffudd ab yr Ynad Coch. The memorial to Llywelyn ap Gruffudd near the village of Cilmeri, Brecs., some hundreds of yards from the spot where he is said to have been killed, has become one of the principal rallying-places of the Welsh Nationalist movement since its erection in 1956. The seventh centenary of the Prince's death was commemorated at the spot in 1982. See also LLYWELYN'S CAVE.

For further details see J. E. Lloyd, *A History of Wales* (1911), T. D. Williams, *The Last Welsh Prince* (1970), A. D. Carr, *Llywelyn ap Gruffydd* (1982), David Stephenson, *The Last Prince of Wales* (1983) and *The*

Governance of Gwynedd (1984), and J. Beverley Smith, *Llywelyn ap Gruffudd, Tywysog Cymru* (1985); see also the article by Llinos Beverley Smith, 'The Death of Llywelyn ap Gruffudd: the Narratives Reconsidered', in *The Welsh History Review* (vol. 9, 1982). A bibliography of publications relating to Llywelyn ap Gruffudd and his times was compiled for the Gwynedd County Council Library Service in 1982.

Llywelyn ap Gruffudd (Llywelyn Bren; d. 1317), the lord of *Senghennydd and *Miskin, was the great-grandson of Ifor Bach (*Ifor ap Cadifor or Ifor Meurig). On good terms with Gilbert de Clare, under whom Senghennydd had been ruled since 1256, he was one of the many Welshmen who fell foul of Gilbert's successor, Pain de Turberville, the lord of Coety. After an unsympathetic hearing of his grievances by Edward II in 1316, he led the Welsh of upland Glamorgan in a brief uprising against the Marcher lords De Bohun and Mortimer, but was crushed by superior forces. He was imprisoned in the Tower of London and executed at Cardiff. A man of culture, he won the admiration of his captors and a contemporary English chronicler described him as 'a great man and powerful in his own country'. Records show that he was the owner of a manuscript of the French verse romance, the *Roman de la Rose*, as well as of Welsh manuscripts.

LLYWELYN AP GUTUN AP IEUAN LYDAN (*fl.* 1480), poet. About twenty of his *cywyddau* are preserved in manuscript; they include poems of disputation with *Guto'r Glyn, *Dafydd Llwyd of Mathafarn and *Lewys Môn, an elegy for his son, several request-poems and a lampoon on the dean of Bangor who had had a hand in his imprisonment.

Llywelyn ap Iorwerth (1173–1240), known as **Llywelyn Fawr** ('Llywelyn the Great'), was the greatest of the rulers of medieval Wales. After the death of his grandfather, *Owain Gwynedd, in 1170, the principality of *Gwynedd had been ruled by the half-brothers of Llywelyn's father and their sons, but by skilfully exploiting the quarrels among them Llywelyn had become master of Gwynedd east of the Conwy by 1194 and, by 1202, had won control of the whole of Gwynedd west of the Conwy. With the death of the Lord Rhys (*Rhys ap Gruffudd) of *Deheubarth in 1197, he was by far the most powerful of the Welsh rulers. Embarking on a campaign of expansion, he detached *Penllyn from *Powys in 1204. Three years later he took possession of southern Powys, the patrimony of his rival, Gwenwynwyn ab Owain Cyfeiliog, and divided *Ceredigion among the descendants of the Lord Rhys, acting as if he were overlord of Deheubarth. King John of England, who had sought to exploit the rivalry between Llywelyn and Gwenwynwyn, came to favour Llywelyn, who in 1205 married the King's natural daughter, Joan (*Siwan), and in 1209 accompanied his father-in-law on an expedition against King William of Scotland.

In 1210, however, their cordial relations came to an end. John invaded Gwynedd and Llywelyn was obliged to yield his conquests, retaining only (through the mediation of his wife) Gwynedd west of the Conwy. In 1212, with the King in conflict with the Pope and challenged by his own barons, Llywelyn, with Papal encouragement, recovered the lands he had lost and, in alliance with Gwenwynwyn and the lords of Deheubarth, challenged the hold of the English Crown upon Wales. With the struggle between John and his barons raging in England, Llywelyn joined the King's opponents and the *Magna Carta* of 1215 contained clauses granting the Welshman significant concessions. In 1216 Llywelyn presided at Aberdyfi over what was virtually a Welsh Parliament and there he arbitrated between the claimants to the land taken from the English and was acknowledged as the effective overlord of all other native rulers of Wales. His position was largely recognized by John's successor, Henry III, at the Peace of Worcester in 1218.

Although in 1223 Llywelyn's power was contested in south-west Wales by William Marshal, Earl of Pembroke, attempts in 1228 by Hubert de Burgh to undermine his position in southern Powys met with failure. So powerful was Llywelyn that in 1230 he could with impunity hang the leading Marcher Lord, William de Braose, as punishment for intrigue and suspected adultery with his wife, Joan (Siwan). During the 1230s Llywelyn, who by then was styling himself Prince of *Aberffraw and Lord of Snowdonia, devoted his energies to ensuring that his *Principality should pass in its entirety to his son Dafydd, rather than be divided, according to Welsh custom, among all his male heirs.

Llywelyn Fawr was a generous patron of monasticism and he died in the habit of a monk of the monastery at *Aberconwy. His work inspired a revision of the *Laws of Hywel Dda and his achievements were widely celebrated by the poets, most notably by *Dafydd Benfras. In seeking to establish a strong feudal state, he achieved remarkable success, expanding his territories, winning the allegiance of the lesser lords of Wales, creating new administrative machinery, maintaining cordial relations with the Church and leaving a peaceful and prosperous realm to his son.

For further details see J. E. Lloyd, *A History of Wales* (1911) and J. G. Edwards (ed.), *A Calendar of Ancient Correspondence concerning Wales* (1935); see also the plays by Thomas Parry, *Llywelyn Fawr* (1954) and Saunders Lewis, *Siwan* (1956; trans. *The King of England's Daughter*, 1985).

LLYWELYN AP MOEL Y PANTRI (d. 1440), poet, was the son of a poet nicknamed

Moel y Pantri and the father of the poet *Owain ap Llywelyn ab y Moel. He had connections with Llanwnnog and Meifod, Mont., but it is not certain in which of these two places he was born or brought up. Two of his poems about the outlaws of Coed y Graig suggest that he shared their life and in all likelihood he took part in the fighting towards the end of *Owain Glyndŵr's rising. In one poem he satirizes himself fleeing from battle, but in another he refers exultantly to an outlaw's life in the forest, returning to this subject in a cywydd which is a dialogue between the poet and his empty purse. Among his praise-poems are those to Dafydd Llwyd of Newtown, Huw Sae of Welshpool and Meredudd ab Ifan of Ystumcegid in Eifionydd; he also composed a few love-poems addressed to a girl named Euron. He took part in bardic contentions with *Rhys Goch Eryri, the first resulting from the latter's elegy for Gruffudd Llwyd and the second from another poem of his sending a red dragon to Sir William Thomas of Raglan. Towards the end of his life he turned to religion and was buried in the monastery of *Strata Marcella. *Guto'r Glyn and Rhys Goch Eryri were the poets who composed his elegies.

The work of Llywelyn ap Moel y Pantri has been edited by Ifor Williams in Cywyddau Iolo Goch ac eraill (1925); see also the article by Enid P. Roberts in the Bulletin of the Board of Celtic Studies (vol. XVII, 1957) and that by Bobi Jones, 'Pwnc mawr beirniadaeth lenyddol Gymraeg', in Ysgrifau Beirniadol III (ed. J. E. Caerwyn Williams, 1967).

LLYWELYN AP RHISIART or **LEWYS MORGANNWG** (fl. 1520–65), one of the greatest poets in the history of Glamorgan, was a native of *Tir Iarll but lived at either Cowbridge or Llanilltud Fawr. He was instructed in the craft of poetry by his father, Rhisiart ap Rhys, and by *Iorwerth Fynglwyd; *Tudur Aled was his bardic master and Sir Edward *Stradling of St. Donats in the Vale of Glamorgan his first patron. The greater part of Llywelyn's life was spent in bardic itinerancy in both south and north Wales. He won fame in the homes of the Gwynedd gentry, coming to be regarded as the head of the *Bardic Order between 1530 and 1560.

More than a hundred of his cywyddau and awdlau are preserved in manuscript. His devotional poems are of special interest for the reason that he was one of the last, or perhaps even the last, of the *Poets of the Gentry who professed the Catholic faith. An authority on Welsh prosody, he addressed in his youth an awdl to Lleision, the abbot of Neath, which contained all the *Twenty-four Metres and gave a vivid portrait of monastic life as it existed in his day. As the family poet to the Herberts, many of whom had been given posts under the new dispensation, he reflected in his work the attraction which the court in London held for the Welsh gentry after the *Act of Union (1536), but in his elegy for Rhys ap Siôn of Glyn Neath there is a note of

disapproval of the English influences which were gradually coming to be felt in Glamorgan and Gwent.

For further details see G. J. Williams, Traddodiad Llenyddol Morgannwg (1948) and Ceri W. Lewis, 'The Literary Tradition of Morgannwg down to the middle of the sixteenth century' in Glamorgan County History (vol. III, ed. T. B. Pugh, 1971).

Llywelyn Bren, see LLYWELYN AP GRUFFUDD (d. 1317).

LLYWELYN FARDD (fl. 1150–1175), poet, is called the son of Cywryd in The *Red Book of Hergest and he was probably a native of Merioneth. He claimed to have fought for *Madog ap Maredudd (d. 1160) and in a series of englynion to Madog's son, Owain Fychan, whom he had offended, he stated that he was senior to that Prince. The best of his poems is his awdl to *Cadfan and the church of Tywyn, Mer., its traditions and the religious life under its abbot, Morfran. From another poem on the Signs before the Day of Judgement (see under ENGLYNION DYDD BRAWD) it seems that Llywelyn was familiar with the popular eschatology of his day.

Llywelyn Fawr (The Great), see LLYWELYN AP IORWERTH (1173–1240).

LLYWELYN GOCH AP MEURIG HEN (fl. 1350–90), one of the last of the *Gogynfeirdd, between whom and the cywyddwyr he occupied an intermediate position, was of the stock of *Nannau. In the older manner he wrote poems in praise of his patrons, such as Hopcyn ap Tomas of Ynystawe and the families of Uwch-Aeron, Abermarlais and Penmynydd, and to the abbot of *Strata Florida. These poems, for the most part, laud his patrons' prowess in the French Wars and the good living to be had in the great houses. In spite of their elegance and dignity, however, Llywelyn became far better known for his cywyddau, and particularly for his superb elegy to *Lleucu Llwyd. With the latter he began a tradition lasting well into the seventeenth century by adapting the convention of the serenade and addressing his beloved from the threshold of the grave.

His cywyddau also include a debate between the poet and a skull, a lively poem to the coal-tit and another on the snow, in which the poet, kept indoors by the weather, enjoys a festive board, poetry, song, and the reading of law-books and the Brut. In his magnificent poem to God, contrasting the glorious works of the Deity with his own misdeeds, he ends by pleading for God's friendship. *Iolo Goch, who wrote Llywelyn's elegy, claiming to have been as close to him as *Amlyn was to Amig, assumed that God's pardon would be granted and that in heaven David the Prophet, who had himself been a poet, unchaste, repentant and forgiven, would delight in the poem to Lleucu and intervene on Llywelyn's behalf.

The poems of Llywelyn Goch ap Meurig Hen are included in the volume *Cywyddau Dafydd ap Gwilym a'i Gyfoeswyr* (ed. Ifor Williams and Thomas Roberts, 1914).

LLYWELYN GOCH Y DANT (*fl.* 1470), poet, one of the professional poets of Glamorgan, supported the men of *Tir Iarll in a controversy caused by *Hywel ap Dafydd ap Ieuan ap Rhys's elegy for *Ieuan ap Hywel Swrdwal (*c.* 1470). Among the few of his poems which have been preserved there is an elegy for Sir Roger *Vaughan of Tretower, executed by order of Jasper Tudor in 1471. In a *cywydd* by Ieuan Du'r Bilwg (*fl.* 1470) addressed to Llywelyn, the latter is described as '*pencerdd*' and '*pen prydydd*' ('chief of poets') but these claims remain unsubstantiated.

For further details see G. J. Williams, *Traddodiad Llenyddol Morgannwg* (1948) and Ceri W. Lewis, 'The Literary Tradition of Morgannwg down to the middle of the Sixteenth Century', in *Glamorgan County History* (vol. III, ed. T. B. Pugh, 1971).

Llywelyn Offeiriad (*fl.* 1350), see under CHWEDLAU SAITH DDOETHION RHUFAIN.

LLYWELYN SIÔN (1540–1615?), poet and copyist, was born at Llangewydd in Laleston, near Bridgend, Glam. His bardic teacher, according to one of his *cywyddau*, was Tomas *Llywelyn of Rhigos and he was probably initiated into the craft by contact with a select circle of literary-minded gentlemen and clerics. Only about fourteen poems, including *awdlau* and *cywyddau*, have been attributed to him, and they share the same weaknesses as are to be found in the work of his contemporaries in Glamorgan in a period when the poets no longer had complete mastery of their craft.

As a professional copyist, however, Llywelyn Siôn was one of the most influential figures in the literary history of his county. Commissioned by the landed gentry to transcribe collections of poetry and prose, he left thirteen manuscripts in all. The most important are *Llyfr Hir Amwythig* ('The Long Book of Shrewsbury'), *Llyfr Hir Llywarch Reynolds* ('The Long Book of Llywarch Reynolds') and *Llyfr Hir Llanharan* ('The Long Book of Llanharan'), three works thus named on account of the long, narrow books in which they were copied, as well as the only complete copy of Gruffydd *Robert's *Y Drych Cristnogol* and the only Welsh copy of the *Gesta Romanorum*. Furthermore, Llywelyn's industry preserved much of the verse written by the minor poets of Glamorgan during the second half of the sixteenth century and it is in his hand that the most complete collection of *carols and *cwndidau has survived. It was partly in recognition of Llywelyn's endeavours to save Welsh manuscripts from oblivion that Iolo Morganwg

(Edward *Williams) claimed that it was he who arranged in systematic form the 'Mysteries of the Bards of the Isle of Britain', but this claim was yet another figment of Iolo's imagination.

For further details see G. J. Williams, *Traddodiad Llenyddol Morgannwg* (1948) and Ceri W. Lewis, 'The Literary History of Glamorgan from 1550 to 1770', in *Glamorgan County History* (vol. IV, ed. Glanmor Williams, 1974).

Llywelyn y Glyn, see LEWYS GLYN COTHI (*c.* 1420–89).

LLYWELYN, TOMAS or **TOMAS AP LLYWELYN AP DAFYDD AP HYWEL** (*fl.* 1580–1610), poet, of Rhigos, Glam., was bardic tutor to *Llywelyn Siôn and one of the poets of *Tir Iarll. A gentleman poet for whom the craft was a pleasurable pastime, he wrote love-poems and nature-poems in his youth, but to his later years, when he had become blind, belong the *cwndidau for which he is remembered. It was Iolo Morganwg (Edward *Williams) who first insisted that Tomas was an early Nonconformist, that he had translated the English Bible into Welsh and had established Puritan congregations in the uplands of Glamorgan; these claims, as far as is known, are without foundation.

For further details see G. J. Williams, *Traddodiad Llenyddol Morgannwg* (1948) and Ceri W. Lewis, 'The Literary History of Glamorgan from 1550 to 1770' in *Glamorgan County History* (vol. IV, ed. Glanmor Williams, 1974).

Llywelyn's Cave, near Aberedw, Rads., the spot where *Llywelyn ap Gruffudd is said to have sought refuge shortly before his death in 1282. According to traditional belief, the Prince, after leaving the cave, had a local blacksmith named Madog Goch reverse the shoes of his own horse and that of his squire in order to mislead his pursuers. He then rode off to Builth. A Norman-led party seeking him tortured Madog, who was afterwards known as Min Mawr ('Big Mouth'), and obtained the information they wanted, but it was too late to catch Llywelyn on the north bank of the river. The story does not rank as history, but '*bradwyr Aberedw*' ('Aberedw traitors') persisted for long afterwards as a jibe against the people of the district. See also BUELLT.

LLYWELYN-WILLIAMS, ALUN (1913–), poet and critic. Born in Cardiff, a doctor's son, he was educated at University College, Cardiff, where he graduated in Welsh and History. His first job was as a temporary announcer and talks-producer with the BBC, prior to his appointment to the staff of the *National Library of Wales in 1936. During the Second World War he served in the Royal Welsh Fusiliers and afterwards returned to the BBC as a radio producer. Appointed in 1948 Director of Extra-Mural

Studies at the University College of North Wales, Bangor, he held a personal chair at that College from 1975 until his retirement. From 1935 to 1939 he was the editor of the magazine *Tir Newydd.

The poems in his first volume, *Cerddi 1934–42* (1944), are meditative, tightly wrought and deal in the main with the sadness of war but also, in a personal and analytical way, with the *Depression of the 1930s. There followed a more substantial collection, *Pont y Caniedydd* (1956), which showed him to be a poet acutely aware of the social movements of his time and who was able to express in his work what he saw as the increasingly complex barbarities of modern life. It was his later work, included in his collected poems, *Y Golau yn y Gwyll* (1974), which established his reputation as a perceptive, disciplined poet with a coherent personal philosophy, catholic in spirit, scholarly and humane.

His critical works include a study of the Welsh Romantics during the period from 1890 to 1914, *Y Nos, y Niwl a'r Ynys* (1960), as well as *Nes na'r Hanesydd?* (1968), a collection of essays on literary themes. He is also the author of two volumes in the *Crwydro Cymru series, on Arfon (1959) and Breconshire (1964). His *BBC Wales Lecture for 1966 was published under the title *Y Llenor a'i Gymdeithas* and he contributed an essay on R. T. *Jenkins to the *Writers of Wales series (1977). The first volume of his autobiography was published under the title *Gwanwyn yn y Ddinas* (1975).

There is an interview with Alun Llywelyn-Williams in *Ysgrifau Beirniadol I* (ed. J. E. Caerwyn Williams, 1965) and an autobiographical essay in the volume *Artists in Wales* (ed. Meic Stephens, 1973); see also the interview he gave to the magazine *Mabon* (ed. Gwyn Thomas, 1971), the note by John Rowlands in *Profiles* (1980) and the article by Dafydd Glyn Jones in *Poetry Wales* (vol. 7, no. 1, 1971).

LOCKLEY, RONALD MATHIAS (1903–   ), naturalist and writer. Born in Cardiff, he described his boyhood and his early passion for natural history in *The Way to an Island* (1941), rewritten under the title *Myself When Young* (1979). From 1927 to 1949 he farmed on Skokholm and at Dinas Cross, Pembs., and from 1954 to 1963 he lived at Orielton, near Pembroke. His career as a naturalist, especially his love of islands, is the subject of about forty of his books, including *Island Days* (1934), *I Know an Island* (1938) and *Letters from Skokholm* (1947). During his years at Orielton, which he described in *Orielton: the Human and Natural History of a Welsh Manor* (1977), he launched the journal *Nature in Wales*, under the auspices of the West Wales Naturalist Trust (formerly the West Wales Field Society), of which he was the founder. His best-known work is *The Private Life of the Rabbit* (1965) which, like all his books, communicates his own enthusiasm and sense of wonder, but without anthropomorphism or sentimentality. In the literature of natural history it is a classic study on which the English writer Richard Adams drew when writing *Watership Down* (1972). R. M. Lockley is also the author of several novels, including *The Island Dweller* (1932), *The Sea's a Thief* (1936) and *Seal Woman* (1974). He left Wales in 1970 to live with his daughters in New Zealand. Since then he has published several books about the wild life of the southern hemisphere, and a further volume of autobiography, *The House above the Sea* (1980).

Locrinus, see under CAMBER and DOLFORWYN.

Logan Stone, The, see MAEN LLOG.

Lolfa, Y (lit. 'The lounge' or 'The place of nonsense'), a publishing company established in 1966 by Robat Gruffudd at Tal-y-bont, Cards. It specializes in the production of books and other printed material deemed to be too politically extreme, or too bawdy, by the more orthodox commercial publishers of Wales, but also publishes works of a more serious or popular nature, such as *Cyfres y Beirdd Answyddogol*, a series devoted to the work of young poets. The firm's most notorious publication is the annual magazine *Lol*, perhaps a Welsh counterpart of *Private Eye*, which carries satirical, and sometimes scurrilous, stories about members of the Welsh Establishment.

Lôn Goed, Y, a tree-lined road in *Eifionydd, Caerns., runs from the estuary at Afon Wen northwards as far as Mynydd y Cennin. It was designed by an Englishman named John Maughan, shortly after he had become agent to the Plas-hen estate in 1817, in order to serve the remote farms in the district; it is also known as Ffordd Môn, a corruption of its builder's name. The quiet beauty of its four-and-a-half miles was celebrated by R. Williams *Parry in his famous poem, 'Eifionydd'.

Lôn Wen, Y (lit. 'The white road'; 1960), a volume of autobiography by Kate *Roberts. The road which 'crosses Moel Smatho to Waunfawr and to heaven' is the white road of the title, and in many respects this book is a history of the author's native district rather than her autobiography. Apart from the portraits of herself as a child and young girl in the opening and closing chapters, there is little here about Kate Roberts. The rest of the book is important for its description of her family and the community to which she belonged.

London Welsh, The, the oldest and largest community of Welsh expatriates. Welshmen were first attracted to the city during the Middle Ages as soldiers, administrators, lawyers and merchants. After Henry *Tudor's accession to the English throne in 1485, considerable numbers of Welsh gentry were established at court and in the city. The scale of Welsh emigration was to increase steadily over the next two hundred years and by the middle of the eighteenth century London had become the Mecca for Welsh writers and antiquaries. Foremost among the patriotic societies which led the revival of interest in the history and culture of Wales were the Honourable Society of *Cymmrodorion and the *Gwyneddigion Society, founded in London in 1751 and 1770 respectively. The city, which was the centre of Welsh publishing, drew many of the most illustrious Welshmen of the day, including Richard, one of the *Morris Brothers of Llanfihangel tre'r Beirdd, Goronwy *Owen, Owen *Jones (Owain Myfyr), Edward *Williams (Iolo Morganwg) and William *Owen Pughe. It was in London, which he saw as the heart of the old Brythonic world, that Iolo Morganwg chose to hold the first meeting of *Gorsedd Beirdd Ynys Prydain.

But by the late eighteenth century this institutionalized London Welsh milieu was largely out of touch with Wales itself. Predominantly 'north Wales and Church' (Iolo Morganwg was an untypical intruder), it both defended the ancient tradition of historical Wales and sought to explain it, in English, to an unheeding capital. The implication of its bilingualism, while devoted to Welsh antiquities, was that such glories must be preserved most of all because they were over and past. None of this had much meaning for the new lumpen Wales of the Methodist Revival, taught in Welsh from the Bible and knowing little else. Indeed, at the very time when expatriate Welshmen were treating London as the capital of Wales, the newer, younger Wales was turning away and looking inward to the Nonconformist society created by the Circulating Schools and *Sunday Schools and by the enthusiasm of a fresh generation of preachers. The early decades of the nineteenth century were characterized, therefore, by a kind of disjunction, and it was not until 1850 and later, when substantial numbers of Welsh emigrants from the seriously over-populated rural counties of west Wales, especially Cardiganshire, began to reach London that London Welsh society began once more to reflect more closely the essential character of the homeland.

There had always been a strong contingent of *drovers, temporarily resident in the capital in order to attend fairs, and they were now joined by dairymen, eager to seize their opportunities in a trade they knew something about, and by drapers, some of whose shops became the large departmental stores which are among the household names of today. In the 1880s there were almost six hundred Welsh dairymen in the metropolitan area. It was this influx of men from west Wales with an experience of grinding poverty that not merely altered the balance of London Welsh society but probably gave rise to the stories of *Cardi meanness, which reflected both some social resentment and a recognition of the tight-fistedness of those who had been the rural poor. Gradually, throughout the nineteenth century, the tavern life of the London Welsh of earlier generations gave way to a Nonconformist respectability more characteristic of Wales itself and dominated by the chapels built in the city by every denomination. As among the *Liverpool Welsh, the main medium for the religious life of the London Welsh was the Welsh language, and many spoke it at home, but the language of commercial and social success was necessarily English. The more numerous emigrants of the later nineteenth century, however, were less interested in a Welsh past of which they were largely ignorant and much more concerned about the poor and under-privileged Wales of their own time. The revitalized Cymmrodorion Society therefore provided an impetus for the establishment of such institutions as the *University of Wales, the *National Library and the *National Museum. The Society pressed for reform of secondary education in Wales and its members played a part in the formation of *Cymdeithas yr Iaith Gymraeg in 1885. The *National Eisteddfod was held in London in 1887 and again in 1909.

The *Depression of the years between the World Wars caused a massive influx of Welsh people into England, for reasons similar to those which had obtained in the nineteenth century. Many were teachers but most were industrial workers in search of jobs: women, too, had to leave Wales for domestic or hotel service. The majority of these had been forced out of the depressed industrial south-east and the resulting society in London was markedly less Welsh in speech than its predecessors. The Sunday evenings, however, which brought young people in great numbers first to hear such as Elfed (Howell Elvet *Lewis) preach and then to assemble at Hyde Park Corner and in Oxford Street, virtually ended with the advent of the Second World War.

Since that time London Welsh society has been much less cohesive. Emigration from Wales continues, but on a reduced scale: it is estimated that there are about a hundred thousand people who were born in Wales living in London today. It is not known how many are able to speak Welsh because the Census does not enumerate Welsh-speakers outside Wales. There has been a sharp decrease in chapel membership since 1945 and some congregations have been dispersed. Many arrivals from Wales in recent decades have not associated themselves with any London Welsh institution and have disappeared without trace into metropolitan society. The London Welsh Association, the London Welsh Rugby club and the county societies, however, remain centres for many and there is a primary school at Willesden Green at which Welsh is the language of instruction. The Cymmrodorion

Society continues to represent the more scholarly aspects of Welsh culture.

During the 1930s and 1940s a number of Welsh writers lived for periods in London, including Dylan *Thomas, Idris *Davies, Aneirin Talfan *Davies and Caradoc Evans (David *Evans), but only a few, such as Rhys *Davies, Keidrych *Rhys, Ll. Wyn *Griffith and Caradog *Prichard, made their permanent homes there. One of the meeting-places favoured by Welsh writers was Griff's Bookshop in Cecil Court off Charing Cross Road. More recently, in the 1960s, a group of expatriates formed a branch of the Guild of Welsh Writers: amongst them were Bryn *Griffiths, John *Tripp, Sally Roberts *Jones and Tom *Earley, some of whom have since returned to Wales. London continues to attract many Welsh people, especially in the spheres of law, medicine, government, teaching and broadcasting, and a number of prominent Welshmen still live there for professional reasons, but there is no longer any sense in which London Welsh society concentrates or leads the aspirations of Wales. Since the 1960s career opportunities at home, the growth of native institutions, the advent of the *Welsh Office and the increasing volatility of domestic politics have all combined to minimize emigration and create a de facto, as well as a de jure, capital in Cardiff.

For further details see R. T. Jenkins and Helen W. Ramage, History of the Honourable Society of Cymmrodorion (1951), Glanmor Williams, 'The Welsh in Tudor England' in Religion, Language and Nationality in Wales (1979) and Emrys Jones, 'The Welsh in London in the Seventeenth and Eighteenth Centuries' in The Welsh History Review (vol. 10, no. 4, 1981).

London Welshman, The, a periodical founded in 1894 by Thomas John Evans; it merged with a rival in the following year to become The London Welshman and Celt and later The Kelt, a bilingual weekly newspaper which survived until the advent of the First World War. During the 1920s and 1930s it was known as Y Ddolen and from 1945 to 1959 as Y Ddinas. Published by the London Welsh Association and counting among its several editors the writer Caradog *Prichard, it was mainly a vehicle for news about the religious, sporting and social life of the *London Welsh. The magazine became a monthly and took the title The London Welshman in 1959 when Tudor David became its editor and when its scope was widened to include not only news of the Association's activities but also articles about the cultural and political life of Wales, as well as verse, short stories and reviews of books. In particular it carried contributions by some of the Anglo-Welsh poets who emerged during the 1960s, especially those such as Bryn *Griffiths, Tom *Earley, Sally Roberts *Jones and John *Tripp, who lived in London at the time and belonged to the Guild of Welsh Writers. By 1970, however, the monthly had become a

quarterly and three years later Tudor David resigned from the editorship, leaving the publication to continue irregularly as a tabloid newspaper in its former role as a mirror of London Welsh life.

LOOMIS, ROGER SHERMAN (1887–1966), American scholar, was Professor of English at Columbia University and a cofounder of the International Arthurian Society (1930). His interest in the figure of *Arthur was first awakened by a study of medieval art and his earliest publications were on Arthurian iconography. This work led him to an intensive study of Arthurian literature in a number of European languages and to an interest in the question of origins. Throughout his life he laid emphasis on his belief that the traditions of the Celtic peoples had played a major part in the growth of the Arthurian legend. Unfortunately, his understanding of early Celtic literature fell far short of his enthusiasm, and he had little or no knowledge of either Welsh or Irish. Strongly influenced by the mythological studies of John *Rhŷs, he expressed out-dated views on 'Celtic myth' and paid little attention to the advances in scholarship made in Celtic countries during the twentieth century.

His principal publications include Celtic Myth and Arthurian Romance (1927), Arthurian Tradition and Chrétien de Troyes (1949) and The Grail: from Celtic Myth to Christian Symbol (1963). He was the editor of Arthurian Literature in the Middle Ages (1959), a compendium to which scholars from many countries contributed and which remains an indispensable work of reference. A collection of R. S. Loomis's articles was published in the volume Wales and the Arthurian Legend (1965).

Lord Cutglass, the recluse in Dylan *Thomas's *Under Milk Wood (1954), lives alone with his sixty-six clocks, 'one for each year of his loony age', all of which are set at different times. It is said that the nickname was given to the poet himself after his father had made him take elocution lessons, 'cut-glass' being an adjective sometimes used to describe an affected or overrefined English accent.

Lord Herbert of Cherbury, see HERBERT, EDWARD (1583–1648).

Lord Rhys, The, see RHYS AP GRUFFUDD (1132–97).

LORT, ROGER (1608–64), poet, was born at Stackpole Court, Pembs., and lived there all his life. The eldest of three brothers who all 'trimmed' during the first *Civil War, Roger was the only one of them to hold the King's Commission. By 1645 he and his brother Sampson were members of the Parliamentary 'Association' of

West Wales and at enmity with John *Poyer, whose imprisonment of them in 1647 helped to precipitate the second Civil War. He was made a baronet in 1662. Neither Royalists nor Parliamentarians thought highly of Roger Lort and an anonymous comment survives that he was willing to embrace any belief as long as it would make him wealthy. His Latin verse consists mainly of epigrams.

LOTH, JOSEPH (1847–1934), Celtic scholar. A Breton, he studied the Celtic languages under Gaidoz, d'Arbois de Jubainville and others, and was placed in charge of the course on Celtic Philology at the University of Rennes. He was later appointed a Professor at the Collège de France, Paris, where he remained until his retirement in 1930. In 1886 he established the periodical *Annales de Bretagne* and in 1911 he became editor of *Revue Celtique*. Among his publications were *Vocabulaire Vieux-breton* (1884), *L'Emigration Bretonne en Armorique* (1885), *Les Mabinogion* (1889), *Les Mots Latins dans les Langues Brittoniques* (1892) and *La Métrique Galloise* (1900–02). He discussed various aspects of the Arthurian legend concerning *Arthur in articles published in *Revue Celtique* (vols. 30–37, 1909–19).

For further information see the obituary article by J. Vendryes in *Revue Celtique* (vol. 51, 1934).

Love-messenger, see LLATAI.

Love Spoon, a wooden spoon carved by a young man and presented to his sweetheart as a token of his affection. The earliest surviving specimen is dated 1667 but the custom was widespread in Wales before that date. The spoon may be plain or so intricately decorated with symbols such as wheels, vines, birds, hearts, anchors and chains, that it hardly resembles a spoon. The precise origins of the custom are not clear: whether it denoted the declaration of love, the commencement of courtship or a more formal engagement may well have varied according to period, place and personal taste. In parts of south Wales the Welsh word '*sponer*', still used for a girl's sweetheart, is derived from the English word 'spooner'.

For further details see Trefor M. Owen, *Welsh Folk Customs* (1959); see also Jen Evans, *The Lore of the Love Spoon* (1971).

Lowland Hundred, The, see CANTRE'R GWAELOD.

Luned, a handmaiden in the romance of *Owain* or *The Lady of the Fountain* (see under TAIR RHAMANT). She first appears when Owain is trapped between the portcullis and inner door of the *Black Knight's castle. Given by Luned a ring which makes him invisible, Owain escapes when the doors are opened. Concealing him in a chamber, she intercedes with her lady on Owain's behalf and succeeds in arranging a marriage between them, although it is he who has killed the lady's husband in a tournament. Towards the end of the tale Owain discovers Luned imprisoned in a stone vessel by two of the lady's chamberlains because she had defended him when the servants called him a deceiver. The following day the two try to burn her, but they are slain by the lion which assists Owain. It is generally thought that the name Luned is a Welsh borrowing from the French form Lunette, despite the suggestion that it may only be a shortened form of Eluned.

Lyra Celtica (lit. 'The Celtic lyre'; 1896), an anthology of poetry edited by Elizabeth Sharp. It includes a number of English translations of poems from the earlier periods of all six Celtic literatures but the modern period is represented almost entirely by original poems in English, mainly from Ireland and Scotland. Among the Welsh poets are *Aneirin, *Taliesin and *Dafydd ap Gwilym. The contemporary poetry of Wales is represented by the so-called 'Anglo-Celtic poets', George Meredith, Sebastian Evans, Ebenezer *Jones, Emily Davis (Emily Jane *Pfeiffer) and Ernest *Rhys. The anthology's compiler was heavily influenced by Matthew *Arnold and, in her predilection for 'the Celtic twilight' of which her husband, William Sharp (Fiona Macleod; 1855–1905), was a leading practitioner, she was typical of her time.

M

Mab Cernyw, see MATHEWS, JOHN HOBSON (1858–1914).

Mab Darogan, Y, see under VATICINATION.

'Mab y Bwthyn' (lit. 'Son of the cottage'), a *pryddest* by Albert *Evans-Jones (Cynan), with which he won the *Crown at the *National Eisteddfod in 1921. New and challenging in its day, it remains one of the few poems which attempt to explore the subject of the First World War from a specifically Welsh point of view. The chief character, torn from his rural community, is seared by guilt as he tastes the pleasures of the wider world. Sentimental at times and reminiscent of such works as John Masefield's *The Everlasting Mercy* (1911), it is, nevertheless, among the best of Cynan's poems. Written in a lively metre and in vivid language, it achieved immediate popularity.

Mabinogion, The, the title used by Charlotte *Guest for her translations of twelve medieval Welsh tales, namely *Pwyll, *Branwen, *Manawydan, *Math, *Culhwch and Olwen, The Dream of *Macsen Wledig, Lludd and Llefelys (*Cyfranc Lludd a Llefelys*), The Dream of Rhonabwy (*Breuddwyd Rhonabwy*), Peredur, Owain, Geraint and Enid (see under TAIR RHAMANT) and the story of *Taliesin, which were published in three volumes between 1838 and 1849. The form 'mabinogion' occurs only once in a medieval Welsh text, at the end of the tale of Pwyll, where it is clearly a ghost-word influenced by the form 'dyledogyon' which precedes it by a short space in the text. The first four of the twelve tales had previously been known as *Pedair Cainc y Mabinogi and this name had not been applied to any of the others. In the modern period, however, there has been a tendency to follow Charlotte Guest and to use the word Mabinogion, particularly in English, as a convenient term for all the tales, but as a rule omitting Hanes Taliesin. The magisterial translation published by Gwyn *Jones and Thomas *Jones (1910–72) in 1948 gave a wider currency to this usage.

Mabon, the son of *Modron, was one of the Three Exalted Prisoners of the Isle of Britain, according to the Triads. In the tale of *Culhwch and Olwen, one of the tasks set for the hero by the giant, Ysbaddaden Bencawr, is to rescue Mabon who had been stolen from his mother's bed when only three days old. With the aid of the *Oldest Animals he is discovered in a prison at Gloucester and is freed by *Arthur and his men. During the hunting of the *Twrch Trwyth, Mabon succeeds in snatching the razor from behind the ear of the beast when it is chased into the river Severn. Mabon is also named as one of Arthur's followers and he is described as *Uthr Bendragon's servant in the poem, 'Pa ŵr yw'r Porthor?' in The *Black Book of Carmarthen. His name is derived from Mapon-os (-us) which belonged to a Celtic god to whom inscriptions have been discovered in northern England and who is commemorated by several place-names in Scotland. The name also occurred in Gaul and the Romans identified him with Apollo. But in the Celtic pantheon Maponos was the son-god and his mother Matrona (giving Modron in Welsh) was the mother-goddess. In his analysis of *Pedair Cainc y Mabinogi, W. J. *Gruffydd (1881–1954) argued in favour of identifying, or at least paralleling, Mabon with *Pryderi or Gwair (Gwri).

Mabon, see ABRAHAM, WILLIAM (1842–1922).

Mabon, a magazine published by the North Wales Arts Association between 1969 and 1976. Its aim was to stimulate an interest in creative writing among young people living in the region and to provide a platform for their literary work, as well as for contributions by older writers. Gwyn *Thomas (1936–) and Alun R. Jones of the University College of North Wales, Bangor, were the editors of the Welsh and English editions respectively and the contributors included R. S. *Thomas, Euros *Bowen and Anthony *Conran. The Welsh edition was distinguished by an important series of interviews with writers, among whom were Kate *Roberts, Islwyn Ffowc *Elis, John Gwilym *Jones, Alun *Llywelyn-Williams and T. Glynne *Davies. But the magazine did not discover any young writers who went on to publish more of their work, with the possible exception of Einir *Jones.

Mabsant, a festival associated with the patron saint of the parish church. An important social occasion, it often lasted a whole week and people would return to their native parishes in order to take part. The patronal feast lost much of its religious significance after the Reformation and by the beginning of the nineteenth century it had become a mainly secular festival with an emphasis on games, dancing, drinking and fighting. Fairs were often linked with the festivals and they continued to flourish after the religious significance had waned. Many of the fairs and wakes kept to the old calendar long after it was changed in 1752 and in Glamorgan the *Mabsant* tended to be confused with the *Taplas which was held weekly during the summer.

For further details see the article by G. J. Williams, 'Glamorgan Customs in the Eighteenth Century', in *Gwerin* (vol. 1, 1957).

MAC CANA, PROINSIAS (1926–   ), Celtic scholar. Born in Belfast, he was educated at Queen's University in that city and was appointed to a post in its Celtic Department in 1951. He became Lecturer in Irish in the Welsh Department at the University College of Wales, Aberystwyth, in 1955. Returning to the Dublin Institute for Advanced Studies in 1961, he was appointed to the Chair of Welsh at University College, Dublin, two years later and to the Chair of Early Irish in 1971.

Much of his work has been on the nature and tradition of the early Irish tales, some of which he has translated into Modern Irish and published in *Scéalaíocht na Rithe* (1956); his study of the tales appeared in the volume *The Medieval Irish Story-teller* (1980). His examination of the composition of the Second Branch of *Pedair Cainc y Mabinogi*, and of the Irish influences on it, was published as *Branwen Daughter of Llŷr* (1958) and he has contributed an essay on the *Mabinogi* to the *Writers of Wales* series (1977). His book *Celtic Mythology* (1970) is a standard study of ancient Celtic religion. In addition to his work on the tales, he has written many articles on the syntax of Welsh and Irish and on early Welsh poetry.

MACDONALD, TOM (1900–80), novelist. Born at Llandre, Cards., of Irish tinker parents, he was educated at the University College of Wales, Aberystwyth, and then worked as a journalist and newspaper editor in England, China, Australia and, for thirty years, in South Africa until his retirement and return to Wales in 1965. He published six novels in English: *Gareth the Ploughman* (1939), *The Peak* (1941), *Gate of Gold* (1946), *The Black Rabbit* (1948), *How Soon Hath Time* (1950) and *The Song of the Valley* (1951), all of which are set in Wales. He also wrote two novels in Welsh, *Y Nos Na Fu* (1974) and *Gwanwyn Serch* (1982) which was published posthumously, and two volumes of reminiscences, *Y Tincer Tlawd* (1971) and *The White Lanes of Summer* (1975). The last-named is a highly evocative account of his growing up in west Wales in the years before the First World War, and perhaps his finest work.

Machafwy, The Battle of (1198), see under AFALLENNAU.

Machen, Arthur, see JONES, ARTHUR (1863–1947).

Mackworth, Humphrey (1657–1727), industrialist, was a native of Shropshire who settled in Wales on his marriage to the daughter of Sir Herbert Evans of The Gnoll, Neath, Glam., in 1686. His wife's inheritance included leases of land rich in coal and the monopoly of copper-smelting in the district, both of which he exploited. Extending his interests to the estate of *Gogerddan, Cards., he began developing mineral deposits there in 1698. He was elected as the Tory Member of Parliament for the county in 1701 and knighted in 1683. In spite of his great wealth and dubious financial methods, he was known for his piety and charitable disposition, being one of the four laymen who helped Thomas Bray in the founding of the *Society for Promoting Christian Knowledge in 1699. He was also the author of several religious works.

A full account of Mackworth will be found in Gareth Elwyn Jones, *Modern Wales: A Concise History 1485–1979* (1984).

Macsen Wledig (d. 388), Emperor of Rome in *Breuddwyd Macsen* ('The Dream of Macsen Wledig'), one of the two historical tales in *The *Mabinogion*, may be identified with Magnus Maximus, a Spaniard by birth who—as commander of the Roman army in Britain—decided in AD 383 to dispossess the feeble Gratian of the imperial throne. Taking most of his army with him to Rome, he made himself Emperor but was put to death by Theodosius at Aquileia five years later. His fame in British annals is believed to have arisen from his treaty with the tribes known as the Votadini (see under GODODDIN) and the Dumnonii, whom he made *foederati* to hold the lands to the north of Hadrian's Wall, and from his marriage to Elen of the Hosts (*Elen Luyddog), a princess of Segontium (*Caernarfon).

In *Breuddwyd Macsen* he is already Emperor when he finds his way to Elen. On waking from his dream, he seeks her again, marries her and learns that the imperial throne has been usurped in his absence. He then sets off with Elen's brothers, Cynan and Gadeon, and the men of Segontium, to retake Rome but fails to capture the city until his brothers-in-law take it for him by cunning. The ridicule excited by this part of the tale has diminished since the discovery of the *Notitia Dignitatum* (AD 429) revealed the existence of a legion called the *Segontienses* serving in the Balkans early in the fifth century. Some historians also now believe, as 'The Dream' relates, that Cynan and his men, after long service, occupied lands granted them by the Emperor near Nantes, thus becoming the first

Britons to settle in Armorica, later known as Brittany.

For further details see M. P. Charlesworth, *The Lost Province* (The Gregynog Lectures, 1948, 1949) and the article by J. F. Matthews in *The Welsh History Review* (vol. 11, no. 4, 1983); see also Gwynfor Evans, *Magnus Maximus and the Birth of Wales the Nation* (1983).

Macwyaid, Y, see under BORD GRON CERIDWEN.

Madam Wen, see under OWEN, WILLIAM DAVID (1874–1925).

Maddocks, Ann (**The Maid of Cefn Ydfa**; 1704–27), tragic heroine, was the daughter of William Thomas of Cefn Ydfa, a house near Llangynwyd, Glam. At the age of twenty-one she married Anthony Maddocks and from this recorded fact there has been spun a romantic tale for which there is little or no foundation. Ann, whose father is known to have died when she was two years old, is said to have been married to Maddocks, her guardian's son and a rich lawyer, against her wish. She was in love, so the story goes, with a young poet named Wil Hopcyn, who composed the verses '*Bugeilio'r Gwenith Gwyn*' for her, and soon after her marriage to Maddocks she is said to have died of a broken heart.

It was Iolo Morganwg (Edward *Williams) who first stated that Wil Hopcyn was the author of the verses and his son, Taliesin ab Iolo (Taliesin *Williams), who began connecting them with the traditional belief. In the opinion of Griffith John *Williams, Iolo's son found the words of the poem among his father's manuscripts and gave them to Maria Jane Williams who published them in her *Ancient National Airs of Gwent and Morgannwg* (1844). The story found a champion in Mary Pendrill Llewelyn (1811–74), the wife of Llangynwyd's vicar. It was embroidered with maudlin details by Isaac Craigfryn *Hughes in his novel, *Y Ferch o Gefn Ydfa* (1881: also published as *The Maid of Cefn Ydfa*, 1881) and retold by Thomas Christopher *Evans (Cadrawd), a protégé of Mrs. Llewelyn, in his *History of the Parish of Llangynwyd* (1887). While it is true that a poet named Wiliam Hopcyn (1700–41) lived in the district of Llangynwyd, there is no evidence whatsoever to suggest that he was in love with Ann or that he wrote the words of the song. An opera based on the story, with English libretto by Joseph Bennet, was written by Joseph *Parry (1902).

For further details see the article on Wil Hopcyn and the Maid of Cefn Ydfa by G. J. Williams in *Glamorgan Historian* (ed. Stewart Williams, 1969) and the book by Brinley Richards, *Wil Hopcyn a'r Ferch o Gefn Ydfa* (1977).

Maddocks, William Alexander (1773–1828), industrialist and philanthropist. Born at Fron Iw, Denbs., and educated at Jesus College, Oxford, he later became a Member of Parliament and a leading advocate of parliamentary reform, but abandoned his political career in order to bring prosperity to a part of north-west Wales of which the scenic beauty had won his romantic heart. He spent his energies and fortune on the construction of a road from London to Holyhead, built the town of Tremadoc and much of Porthmadog, Caerns., which were named after him, and during the years from 1808 to 1811 (assisted by his remarkable agent, John Williams) completed the embankment later known as the Cob across Traeth Mawr, the delta of the Glaslyn river. This last enterprise caused his ruin and he left Wales for Paris, where he was to die.

For a detailed account of his life and work see Elizabeth Beazley, *Madocks and the Wonder of Wales* (1967).

'*Madog*' (1918), a long poem by T. Gwynn *Jones, was first published in the magazine *Y *Beirniad* and later in the author's volume, *Caniadau* (1926). Written in *cynghanedd* but without rhyme, on a metrical pattern of his own devising, the poem has four cantos and is one of the poet's greatest works. It deals with the lesser-known traditional tale about *Madog ab Owain Gwynedd, not his alleged discovery of America but the story of how his ship, the *Gwennan Gorn*, which was made of whale bone or stags' horns, was wrecked in a storm.

The Prince questions his old tutor, the monk Mabon, about the existence of God and the sins of men. As they converse, they see the fleet of *Hywel ab Owain Gwynedd, Madog's brother, setting sail against one of their other brothers, *Dafydd ab Owain Gwynedd, who has usurped Hywel's lands and wealth. Hywel is killed before their eyes by one of Dafydd's archers, at which Madog is cast down. After Mabon has declared that men are often victims of their own passions, Madog condemns the lust, malice, greed and oppression which he sees in the world. He asks his old teacher whether there is not somewhere a better land where such horrible deeds are unknown. The monk answers that *Brân and Osian, Gofran ab Aeddan and *Myrddin, all dreamed in their day of a land where there was neither pain nor treachery. Thereupon Madog sets out on a great adventure to find such a land but is caught in a terrible storm and his boat wrecked by the furious sea as he kneels to receive Mabon's blessing.

For further details see the article by D. J. Bowen in *Llên Cymru* (vol. VI, 1960).

Madog ab Owain Gwynedd (*fl.* 1170), prince and explorer. Disgusted at the strife which followed the death of his father, *Owain ap Gruffudd (Owain Gwynedd), he is reputed to have sailed with eight ships and his brother Rhiryd, from Abercerrig, near Abergele, in search of a new land to the west, making landfall in what is now called Mobile Bay in 1169 or the year following. Leaving Rhiryd and most of the party there, he returned to Wales for reinforcements and sailed again from Lundy Island in 1171. He was never again heard of in Wales and whether he ever rejoined the first group is arguable. Spanish evidence (through Cortes from Montezuma) suggested that Madog may have been the white leader from the east who brought an American tribe south to found the kingdom of Mexico, a theme developed by Robert Southey in his long poem, 'Madoc' (1805). More northerly sources, however, had the Welsh party travelling up the Alabama river, harried and finally defeated by the Iroquois at Muscle Shoals on the Ohio. The remnant marched away westward and were not heard of again until they were identified at the end of the eighteenth century as the Mandan Indians, living west of the Missouri in what is now North Dakota. The Mandans were virtually wiped out by smallpox in 1838 and the few survivors dispersed among other tribes.

In the sixteenth century, John *Dee was the first to claim the New World for the Queen of England on the strength of Madog's voyage, and in the centuries following a spate of stories about 'the Welsh Indians', most of them locationally impossible, flowed through the American colonies and back to Britain. These stories created a myth which, after the American Revolution, kindled fresh interest among Welsh Radicals. It caught the public imagination when the historian John Williams published an account of the Madog story in 1790 and, encouraged by the fabrication of Iolo Morganwg (Edward *Williams), it became a powerful incentive for emigration to America from a desperately poor, radical and newly nationalistic Wales. One of the most zealous victims of this 'Madog fever' was the Baptist leader Morgan John *Rhys. The whole affair, in the opinion of Gwyn A. *Williams, was part of a crisis of modernization in Welsh society and the dream of finding the Welsh Indians similar to attempts at recreating Druidism or the Patriarchal Language. It may be compared with the myth of the free-born Saxons living under the Norman yoke in England.

Most modern historians of the last hundred and fifty years have followed Thomas *Stephens, in his essay of 1858, and given small credence to the story of Madog, the discoverer of America, arguing that it was a sixteenth-century imperialist fiction and that John *Evans's denial of Mandan Welshness in his letter of 1797 to the *Cymmrodorion Society is conclusive. There are respects, however, in which this dismissal goes too far. Evans had become a Spanish agent and could scarcely have reported differently. Moreover, to disprove the existence of the Welsh Indians is not to discredit Madog's voyages, for which there is early evidence in Welsh poetry, in the account of Willem the Minstrel

and in Spanish maps. There is no longer any serious navigational argument against their possibility. Madog, it should be noted, may not have been a son of Owain Gwynedd: one fragmented document listing ships lost in 1171 refers to Rhiryd (in the *San Pedr*) as 'Prince' but gives Madog (in the *Gwennan Gorn*) no such title. See also MADOG (1918).

For a full discussion of the subject see Richard Deacon, *Madog and the Discovery of America* (1967) and Gwyn A. Williams, *Madoc, the Making of a Myth* (1979).

Madog ap Gruffudd (d. 1236), the ruler, from 1191 until his death, of the region of northern *Powys which was known as Powys Fadog after him. He was usually an ally of his cousin, *Llywelyn ap Iorwerth (Llywelyn Fawr), but he supported the English king between 1211 and 1215, when Llywelyn's fortunes were at a low ebb. It was Madog who founded the Cistercian abbey of *Valle Crucis in 1201 and he was buried there. Probably, too, the nearby castle of *Dinas Brân was built at his command. Among the poets who composed poems in his honour was *Llywarch ap Llywelyn (Prydydd y Moch). After Madog's death the unity of Powys Fadog was disrupted and the territory shared by his five sons.

MADOG AP GWALLTER (*fl.* second half of the 13th cent.?), poet and friar, was probably a native of Llanfihangel Glyn Myfyr, Denbs. He wrote an *awdl* to God and a sequence of *englynion* to Michael, the patron saint of his parish, and is believed to have been the *Frater Wallensis Madocus Edeirnianensis* who claimed to be the author of a series of Latin leonine hexameters of a patriotic nature. But he is chiefly remembered for his famous poem on the Nativity, '*Geni Crist*', sometimes said to be the first Christmas carol extant in Welsh, a poem which shares the fresh and simple vision of the early Franciscan world.

Madog ap Llywelyn (*fl.* 1294), see under WELSH REVOLT (1294–95).

Madog ap Maredudd (d. 1160), the last King of *Powys which, under him, had a prominent place in the history of Wales. *Breuddwyd Rhonabwy* is set in his kingdom and opens with a reference to his power. During the reign of the English king, Stephen, Madog took advantage of the prevailing anarchy by extending the boundaries of Powys eastwards, capturing Oswestry in 1149, but at the same time losing territory in the Vale of Clwyd to *Owain ap Gruffudd (Owain Gwynedd). In his resistance to the growing power of the House of *Gwynedd he sought the support of Henry II, whom he joined in the attack upon Owain in 1157. Madog was a generous patron of poets and some of the finest eulogies of the twelfth century were written in praise of him by such poets as *Gwalchmai ap Meilyr and *Cynddelw Brydydd Mawr. The latter's elegy for Madog lamented, in particular, the loss of unity in Powys which, after his death, was shared among the king's sons and nephews.

MADOG AP SELYF (*fl.* pre-1282), translator. Nothing is known of him except that he translated into Welsh the *Turpini Historia*, a Latin chronicle which claims to tell the story of Charlemagne. The work was done at the request of Gruffudd ap Maredudd ab Owain ap Gruffudd ap Rhys, the great-great-grandson of *Rhys ap Gruffudd (The Lord Rhys), the Prince of *Deheubarth. An uncertain reference in *The White Book of Rhydderch* seems to attribute the Welsh translation of the *Transitus Mariae* to the same translator and the same patron. It was for Gruffudd's sister, Efa, that *Gruffudd Bola translated the Athanasian Creed. Madog is perhaps correctly associated with *Strata Florida but, in view of his patron's connection with *Llanbadarn, it may have been there that he worked.

For further details see the introduction by Stephen J. Williams to his edition of *Ystoria de Carolo Magno* (1931) and Nora K. Chadwick, *Studies in the Early British Church* (1958).

MADOG BENFRAS (*fl.* 1320–60), poet, was a contemporary and friend of *Dafydd ap Gwilym; each wrote an elegy for the other during their lifetimes. Madog was the son of Gruffudd ab Iorwerth, the Lord of Sonlli in *Maelor. There is no evidence to support the assertion by Iolo Morganwg (Edward *Williams) that the poet, together with two of his brothers, competed at three eisteddfodau held during the reign of Edward III, nor for Iolo's claim that Llywelyn ap Gwilym of *Emlyn was their bardic teacher. Madog owned land in the district of Wrexham and he is named in the court records of that town. About a dozen of the *cywyddau* attributed to him have been preserved in manuscript, most of them love-poems in the style of Dafydd ap Gwilym.

MADOG DWYGRAIG (*fl.* 1370–80), one of the last of the *Gogynfeirdd. Eighteen of his *awdlau* are preserved in The *Red Book of Hergest*; most of them are satirical, but they also include three religious poems, two elegies for Gruffudd ap Madog of Llechwedd Ystrad in *Penllyn, a poem in praise of Hopcyn ap Tomas of Ynys Dawe and another addressed to Morgan ap Dafydd of Rhydodyn who held offices under the Crown between 1375 and 1381. See also HYWEL YSTORM (14th cent.).

Mae Rose Cottage, the nubile girl in Dylan *Thomas's *Under Milk Wood* (1954) who, 'raw as an onion', waits for Mr. Right and daydreams of sinning.

Maelgwn Gwynedd (d. 547), King of *Gwynedd, was the great-grandson of *Cunedda and had his court at *Degannwy. Tradition maintains that he came to power as a result of a contest with his rivals against the incoming tide, winning it by use of a floating chair so that his feet remained dry while those of his rivals were immersed in the sea. Widely condemned in the *Lives of the Saints for his equivocal attitude towards monasticism, Maelgwn was denounced for his many transgressions by *Gildas who suspected him of Pelagianism and perhaps of British nationalism, calling him '*Maglocunus, draig yr ynys*' ('Maglocunus, dragon of the island') and claiming that he had murdered his wife and his nephew whose widow he then married. The same traditions hint at Maelgwn's repentance and his patronage of poets and monasteries. No doubt a strong but wayward ruler, he is said to have died from plague which he caught by peering out through the key-hole of a church-door behind which he had taken refuge.

Maelienydd, a cantref of southern *Powys, was the patrimony of the line of Elystan Glodrydd, traditionally considered to be the fifth of the Royal Tribes of Wales. Its rulers were under constant pressure from the Mortimer family of Wigmore who after 1276 secured possession of it themselves, although their control was largely restricted to the district around the seignorial castle and borough of Cefnllys. Maelienydd, with the rest of the Mortimer lordships, came into the hands of the English Crown in 1460 and was incorporated into the county of Radnor in 1536.

Maelor, two commots of *Powys. Maelor Gymraeg (Welsh Maelor) became part of the *gwlad* of Powys Fadog (see under MADOG AP GRUFFUDD) at the division of Powys after the death of *Madog ap Maredudd in 1160. It was linked with *Yale (Iâl) from the lordship of Bromfield and Yale in 1282 and became part of the county of Denbigh in 1536. Maelor Saesneg (English Maelor) became a detached part of the county of Flint under the provisions of the Statute of *Rhuddlan (1284). Both commots now belong to the district of Maelor-Wrexham in the county of Clwyd.

Maen Llog, Y (lit. 'The logan stone'), the central stone from which the Archdruid conducts the open-air ceremonies of *Gorsedd Beirdd Ynys Prydain*, was a concept invented by Iolo Morganwg (Edward *Williams).

Maenan, see under ABERCONWY.

Maes Garmon, The Battle of (430), see under GARMON (c.378–448).

Maes-glas, a monastery near Holywell, Flints., with which is associated a folk-tale based on the theme of the strange passing of time. A monk goes into a wood in order to listen to the song of a nightingale but, on returning to the monastery, he finds it in ruins and no one remembers him. The theme also occurs in an anonymous poem about the Old Man of the Woods which includes the well-known verse beginning, '*Dwedai hen ŵr llwyd o'r gornel*' ('Said an old grey man from the corner').

Maes Gwenllian, The Battle of (1136), see under GWENLLIAN (d. 1136) and KIDWELLY.

Maes Meidog, The Battle of (1295), see under WELSH REVOLT (1294–95).

Maesyfelin, a mansion which once stood near Lampeter, Cards. It is said that Ellen, the only daughter of the house, was engaged to be married to Samuel Prichard, the son of Rhys *Prichard. According to the traditional tale, her four brothers did not want to have to share their inheritance with the young man, so they tied him to a horse, which dragged him from Lampeter to Llandovery, and then threw his corpse into the river Tywi. Ellen, in her grief, went mad and died. The Vicar Prichard is supposed to have pronounced a curse on Maesyfelin for, a few months afterwards, the mansion was burned to the ground and the eldest son murdered his brothers and hanged himself. There seems to be no factual basis whatsoever for this tale, which is now thought to have been made up by the people of the district in an attempt to explain the ruins of Maesyfelin. See also LLOYD, HERBERT (1720–69).

Magician, see DYN HYSBYS.

Magna Carta (lit. 'Great charter'; 1215), granted by King John under pressure from the barons of England, illustrates in its Welsh clauses the way in which *Llywelyn ap Iorwerth (Llywelyn Fawr) exploited the constitutional struggle in England in order to strengthen his own position within Wales. In alliance with dissident English barons, Llywelyn and the Welsh lords were threatening royal strongholds in Wales. By the Charter all lands in England and Wales lost by Welshmen were to be returned to them, local circumstances were to determine whether Welsh, English or Marcher law should apply in disputes, and Welsh hostages, including Llywelyn's son, Gruffudd, were to be released. Relations between the English barons and Llywelyn, on the one hand, and King John on the other, deteriorated further after the signing of the Charter. Llywelyn led a successful military campaign in south Wales and a number of castles, including those at *Cardigan, *Carmarthen and *Kidwelly, were captured. The Prince's position was further strengthened in the years which followed, as reflected in the poetry

of *Elidir Sais, *Llywarch ap Llywelyn (Prydydd y Moch) and *Dafydd Benfras.

Magnus Maximus, see MACSEN WLEDIG (d. 388).

Maid of Cefn Ydfa, The, see MADDOCKS, ANN (1704–27).

Maid of Sker, The, see WILLIAMS, ELIZABETH (c.1747–76).

MALKIN, BENJAMIN HEATH (1769–1842), antiquary and author. Born in London, he was headmaster of Bury St. Edmunds School from 1809 to 1828 and later Professor of History at London University. His wife, born Charlotte Williams, was the daughter of the headmaster of Cowbridge School and, from about 1830, Malkin lived at the Old Hall in that town, pursuing there his antiquarian interests in the life of Glamorgan. Malkin's best-known work is an account of his travels in south Wales in 1803, published as *The Scenery, Antiquities, and Biography of South Wales* (1804), which was described by R. T. *Jenkins as 'by far the best of the old travel books on South Wales—acute and interesting in its observation, usually tolerant in its judgements, with a substantial knowledge of Welsh history and (up to a point) of Welsh literature'.

Manawydan, the son of *Llŷr, is the chief character in the Third Branch of *Pedair Cainc y Mabinogi. Accompanying his brother Bendigeidfran (*Brân) on the campaign to avenge his sister *Branwen in Ireland, he is one of the seven who return from the expedition. Having no wish to contend with his cousin Caswallon for the sovereignty of the Island of the Mighty (Britain), he accepts *Pryderi's invitation to go with him to *Dyfed. There, Pryderi gives him his mother, *Rhiannon, to be his wife, and places him in authority over the seven cantrefi. Soon afterwards an enchantment falls on Dyfed and the kingdom is emptied of its people, except for Manawydan and Rhiannon, and Pryderi and his wife, Cigfa. The four leave for England, where Manawydan and Pryderi earn their living by practising the crafts of the saddler, the shield-maker and the cobbler. Wherever they go the local craftsmen are hostile towards them and they have to move on. Returning to Dyfed, Pryderi and Rhiannon are imprisoned in a magic fortress, which then vanishes, leaving Manawydan and Cigfa to live together, innocently, for two years. The Branch ends with the famous story about the mice in the wheat which tells how Manawydan, by cunning, succeeds in releasing Rhiannon and Pryderi from their imprisonment in *Annwn (see under LLWYD FAB CIL COED).

References to Manawydan also occur in *The *Book of Taliesin* and *The *Black Book of Carmar-*

then, as well as in the Triads. The relationship between Manawydan and Manannán mac Lir, the Irish sea-god, is problematic. The two names partially correspond with each other and both may be associated with the place-name, Manaw. But very different characteristics are attributed to Manannán and Manawydan: the former is a deceitful wizard who enchants men and women to their destruction, while the latter is pure, gentle, long-suffering and resourceful. In the Triads and in the Third Branch of the *Mabinogi*, Manawydan is called one of the Three Prostrate Chieftains of the Isle of Britain. If he was of Irish origin, as some believe, then his character must have been transformed in Welsh in order to fit within the framework of the theme of the Gentle Nobleman, or the Eustace Legend, in which a good man is put to many tests but eventually restored to his former happiness. In the Third Branch the theme is combined with Celtic traditions about the relationship between the human world and the powers of Annwn.

For detailed discussion of Manawydan see W. J. Gruffydd, *Rhiannon* (1953) and Rachel Bromwich, *Trioedd Ynys Prydein* (1961).

Manion (lit. 'Trifles'; 1932), a volume of poems by T. Gwynn *Jones, consists mainly of lyrics, sonnets, epigrams, adaptations and translations from German, Irish, Italian and Latin. Also included are his Welsh versions of Poe's 'The Raven' (1845) and Gray's 'Elegy written in a Country Churchyard' (1750). One of the most important poems in the collection is '*Y Nef a fu*', the longest of his poems in free verse, in which much of the poet's philosophy is expressed. T. Gwynn Jones was taken to task, on the book's appearance, by David Miall *Edwards, who accused the poet in *Y *Llenor* (Spring, 1933) of agnosticism and a bleak materialism. To this charge the poet replied in the introduction to his next volume, *Caniadau* (1934).

Mantle of Invisibility, The, a popular motif in many literatures, including Welsh. In the tale of *Culhwch and Olwen, *Arthur names his mantle, together with his ship, sword, spear, shield, dagger and wife, as being among his most precious possessions and those which Culhwch may not have. The mantle is described in greater detail in *Breuddwyd Rhonabwy: it is of ribbed, brocaded silk and 'no colour would ever abide on it save its own colour', which may have been white, since the name given to it is *Gwen* ('white' or 'fair'). For the distinctive quality of rendering its wearer invisible it is listed among the Thirteen Treasures of the Isle of Britain (*Tri Thlws ar Ddeg Ynys Prydain*). *Caswallon wears a similar garment in the story of *Branwen. With the invisibility it bestows he overthrows six of the seven lords who have been appointed to rule the Island of the Mighty (Britain) during *Brân's absence in Ireland. The sight of a sword, apparently without human aid, slaying

his companions, and the impossibility of identifying the killer, causes *Caradog, the son of Brân, the surviving lord, to die of terror. The theme also occurs in the story of *Jack the Giant-killer.

MAP or **MAHAP** or **MAPES, WALTER** (*c.*1140–*c.*1209), Latin author, sometimes said to have been a Welshman, was probably a native of Herefordshire, perhaps of *Erging. The assumption that he was Welsh is partly based on his own reference to '*compatriotae nostre Walenses*' but by this he may have meant 'our Welsh neighbours' rather than 'our Welsh compatriots'. Of noble stock and a friend of *Gerald de Barri (Giraldus Cambrensis), he was educated in Paris and had a successful career as a cleric and diplomat. He became Archdeacon of Oxford in 1197.

Although Map was famous in his day as a writer and wit, the only work which can be attributed to him with certainty is *De Nugis Curialium* (lit. 'Courtiers' trifles'), a collection of anecdotes and tales composed between 1180 and 1193 which is preserved in a manuscript dating from the fourteenth century. This work is a mixture of history, romance and gossip which was described by Map's editor as 'the untidy product of an untidy mind . . . a rough inventory of the mental furniture of a learned and witty twelfth-century clerk, a marvellous guide to a fascinating lumber room'. Some of the tales Map had to tell are of specifically Welsh interest, while others have significance for the student of folklore, but there is so much prejudice and caricature in his portrayal of contemporary persons and events that the work is far from reliable as a historical account.

For further details see the edition of *De Nugis Curialium* prepared by M. R. James for *Anecdota Oxoniensis* (1914) and his translation of the work which was published in the *Cymmrodorion Record Series* in 1923. The edition, together with the translation, was revised by C. N. L. Brooke and R. A. B. Mynors and republished in 1983; see also the article by R. T. Jenkins, '*Llygad yr Esgob*' in *Y Llenor* (vol. X, 1931). The Latin poems edited by Thomas Wright in 1841 are no longer thought to be the work of Walter Map.

Map of Love, The (1939), Dylan *Thomas's third volume, contains sixteen poems and seven short stories, all of which had been previously published in periodicals. Despite their characteristic themes of religion, sex and the creative artist, in a Welsh rural setting, the stories are in marked contrast to the comic realism of those in *Portrait of the Artist as a Young Dog* (1940). These earlier tales take a dream-like, mythic form and are governed by a surrealistic fantasy. As for the poems, although eight of them had their source in early notebooks kept between 1930 and 1933, the volume has a transitional quality about it. The poems often remain difficult in Thomas's early manner, with an emphasis on textural and syntactic density, but several of them, such as 'The spire cranes', 'Once it was the colour of saying' and 'On no work of words', are directly concerned with the theme of writing poetry, in a way which offers insights into the poet's need for a change of direction in style and idiom. The subjects of several others, moreover, are people distinct from the poet himself, in contrast to the total self-absorption of the poems in his two earlier volumes; the outstanding example is the poem *'After the Funeral'. This move towards the figures and experiences of a relatively more objective world was consolidated in the poet's next volume of verse, *Deaths and Entrances (1946), by which time he had sold his early notebooks to the library of an American university and had broken away from his dependence upon them.

March ap Meirchion or **March Amheirchion**, an early legendary hero, is named in the Triads as one of the Three Seafarers of the Isle of Britain. There are also allusions to him in *Breuddwyd Rhonabwy, in *Englynion y Beddau and in a poem in The *Black Book of Carmarthen. From references in the work of *Cynddelw Brydydd Mawr it seems that the historical March may have been the son of a king of Glamorgan who granted lands to *Illtud. In the legend of *Tristan and Iseult he is the King of Cornwall. A more recent tale, a Welsh version of an international motif, is associated with Castell March in Llŷn, Caerns., and relates how March kept secret the fact that he had horse's ears by growing his hair long and having his barbers killed and buried in a bog.

Marchog Crwydrad, Y (lit. 'The wandering knight'; c.1585), an ethical work (the earliest text is in Llanstephan MS 178) which is an anonymous prose translation of William Goodyear's The Voyage of the Wandering Knight (1581). The English version was derived from Le Voyage du Chevalier Errant, a medieval romance about human vanity written by Jean de Carthenay in the thirteenth century.

Marchog Glas o Went, Y, see WILIAM AP TOMAS (fl. 1406–46).

MAREDUDD AP RHYS (fl. 1440–83), poet. About forty of his cywyddau have been preserved in manuscript, some of which complain that the *vaticinations of his fellow-poets were lies. He also wrote religious poems and an elegy for Edward IV in 1483.

Margam, a *Cistercian abbey in Glamorgan, was built on the site of an earlier monastery by order of Robert Consul, Earl of Gloucester, in 1147. *Gerald de Barri (Giraldus Cambrensis) referred to the abbey's reputation for generous hospitality during his tour of Wales. Poems written by the abbot Walter about 1219 have been lost. During the thirteenth century the Annales Margam, which traces the abbey's history from 1066 to 1232 and which is a valuable source for the history of Glamorgan after 1185, was written here. The *Book of Taliesin may have been copied at the abbey about 1275. Margam is mentioned in the first poem known to have been written by a Glamorgan poet, namely *Casnodyn's elegy on the death of Madog Fychan about 1330. A lesser poet, known as Y Nant, requested a gown from the abbot, Wiliam Corntwn (fl. 1468–86), and *Lewys Glyn Cothi (Llywelyn y Glyn) composed the abbot's elegy. According to Thomas Wilkins of Llanfair, the history of Ifor Bach (*Ifor ap Cadifor) and his family was authorized in Wiliam's hand, an assertion from which it has been concluded that this abbot was one of Glamorgan's historians. Lewys Glyn Cothi is thought to have copied The *White Book of Hergest at Margam.

During the abbacy of Dafydd ap Tomas ap Hywel (c.1500–17) poets flocked to the abbey. The abbot belonged to a family of poets living in *Tir Iarll, two of whom, Rhisiart Brydydd and Siôn ap Hywel Gwyn, wrote poems in his praise, the latter in a bardic contest with *Iorwerth Fynglwyd. Wiliam Egwad also exchanged poems with Iorwerth Fynglwyd, both being concerned that the rhymester Siôn Lleision was usurping their patronage at Margam. Despite his popularity, Dafydd ap Tomas ap Hywel was replaced by Lleision Tomas, the abbot of Neath, for having made over some of the abbey's lands to members of his own family and for having sired several illegitimate children. Another of the poets of Tir Iarll, *Tomas ab Ieuan ap Rhys, wrote in praise of the last abbot of Margam, Lewis Tomas (c.1529–36). The abbey had appropriated Llangynwyd church about 1353 and pilgrims thronged to pay homage to the rood there during the late Middle Ages; Rhys Brydydd (or Ieuan Gethin) and *Gwilym Tew were among the poets who praised it. The englynion, attributed to Lleision Cradock, on the dissolution of Margam in 1536, are no longer accepted as authentic.

For further details see the histories of Margam abbey by Walter de Gray Birch (1897) and Arthur Leslie Evans (1958).

Marged uch Ifan, see EVANS, MARGARET (1695–1801?).

Mari Lwyd, a horse's skull covered with a white sheet and decorated with coloured ribbons. Carried on a pole by a man who crouched beneath the sheet and operated the jaw, it was led from house to house during the hours of darkness in the Christmas season. As the party (which included characters known as Sergeant, Merryman, Punch and Judy) approached the door, verses were sung in which the bearers asked for admittance. The people inside the house would reply in verse, pretending to refuse entry. There followed a contest in impromptu verse between the two sides until the callers, who were always better prepared, were allowed into the house. Once inside, the *Mari* chased the young women of the family and then, the horse-play over, the revellers would be given food and drink. The custom, a form of *wassailing, flourished during the mid-nineteenth century, especially in Glamorgan and Monmouthshire, but has now disappeared in its primitive form except in a few districts such as Llangynwyd and Maesteg. The poet Vernon *Watkins, whose family had connections with Taff's Well, Glam., where the tradition also survived into the twentieth century, used it as the basis for his long poem, *Ballad of the Mari Lwyd (1941). Examples of the horse's skull are exhibited in the galleries of the *Welsh Folk Museum and tape-recordings of verses associated with the custom are preserved in the Museum's archives.

The ritual and significance of the Mari Lwyd are discussed in Dora Polk, *Vernon Watkins and the Spring of Vision* (1977); see also Trefor M. Owen, *Welsh Folk Customs* (1959).

MARO, JUDITH (1927–), novelist, was born and educated in Jerusalem. She married Jonah *Jones in 1947 and has lived in Wales, mostly near Penrhyndeudraeth, Mer., since 1949. She writes in English but chooses, as a sign of identification with Wales, to have her works translated and published in Welsh. They include *Atgofion Haganah* (1973), a memoir of the time she spent as a member of the Zionist Movement during the British Mandate in Palestine (1939–48), a volume of essays about Wales and Israel entitled *Hen Wlad Newydd* (1974), and a novel set against the background of the struggle for the establishment of the state of Israel, *Y Porth nid â'n Anghof* (1974), which was later published in English under the title *The Remembered Gate* (1975).

MARSDEN, THOMAS (1802–49), cleric and author, was born at Lampeter, Cards. Educated at St. David's College, Lampeter, he was ordained in 1827 and held livings at Llan-y-crwys, Carms. (1827–29; 1831–38) and Tir-abad, Brecs. (1829–31). From 1838 until his resignation in 1840 he was vicar of Brymbo, Denbs., and from 1843 until his death, rector of Llanfrothen, Mer. Besides two collections of sermons in Welsh (1838 and 1843), he published a volume of hymns (1848) and his poems appeared under the title *The Poet's Orchard* (1848).

Martha'r Mynydd (*fl.* 1770), an old woman of Llanllyfni, Caerns., who claimed to be acquainted with a wealthy but invisible family by the name of Ingram who lived, she said, in a magnificent mansion in the district. Many were taken in by her fraud and seances were held in her cottage at which Mr. Ingram and his daughter were supposed to have appeared. Eventually, Martha gave up her deception and towards the end of her life she joined the Methodist cause in the village, as was recorded by Robert *Jones of Rhos-lan in his *Drych yr Amseroedd* (1820).

Martin Marprelate, see under PENRY, JOHN (1563–93).

Marvels of Britain, The, see MIRABILIA BRITANNIAE.

Marxism, a political philosophy founded by Karl Marx and Friedrich Engels and developed by V. I. Lenin, forms the theoretical foundation of Communism. Although Marx and Engels were interested in aspects of Welsh history, their ideas had virtually no influence in Wales during their lifetimes. Marxism began to take root only in the early twentieth century, as an outgrowth of Syndicalist trends among some of the miners of south Wales. These activists were trained at the Central Labour College and their organizations were the Unofficial Reform Committee and, later, the South Wales Socialist Society. Many joined the Communist Party of Great Britain on its formation in 1920 and in 1921 the *South Wales Miners' Federation declared itself in favour of joining the Communist International. For the next fifty years Marxism and the Communist Party were almost synonymous, with militant miners forming the Party's core.

The Communist Party played a key role in the *General Strike of 1926, but its subsequent growth was short-lived and its successes in the 1930s were better founded. Marxists in the National Unemployed Workers' Movement, such as Lewis *Jones (1897–1939), were instrumental in organizing the *Hunger Marches and were at the centre of the mass-protests against the Means test. Communist miners were to the forefront in the struggle to rebuild the South Wales Miners' Federation after 1926 and Arthur *Horner, a prominent Communist, was elected its President in 1936. As the Party was seen to be playing a leading role, its membership increased substantially and by 1935 it had sixteen members on local councils. Some villages, such as Maerdy in the *Rhondda Valley, were known as Little Moscow on account of their political complexion between the World Wars. Of the 174 Welshmen who fought in defence of the Republic during the Spanish Civil War, the great majority were Communist Party members or sympathizers.

The Party also became genuinely attentive to the claims of Wales as a nation. In 1937 a small North Wales District was established and T. E. *Nicholas began publishing his newspaper, *Llais y Werin*. In 1938 a bilingual pamphlet, published during the *National Eisteddfod at Cardiff, called for unity between Socialists, Communists, Liberals and Nationalists against Fascism. In 1939 the Communist Party of Great Britain recognized the principle of Welsh self-determination and during the next decade the Party in Wales published more than twenty pamphlets, seven bilingual or in Welsh only. *Devolution was advocated from 1943 and in 1945 the Communist Party held its first all-Wales Congress, at which nearly half the delegates were Welsh-speaking. Since 1969 a bilingual magazine, Cyffro (later entitled Moving Left) has been published occasionally. The Communist Party in Wales, however, has had, in the last three decades, far less of a distinctive identity and its fortunes have generally followed those of the Communist Party of Great Britain. It still has a significant industrial base, particularly among miners. Communists, especially Dai Francis, played a leading role in establishing the Wales Trades Union Council (1973) and one of the Party's best-known councillors, Annie Powell, has served as Mayor of Rhondda. By today the Communist Party and Marxism are no longer synonymous. The Party's membership has fallen steadily in Wales while Marxist-orientated groups have developed in and around the Labour Party (see under SOCIALISM) and *Plaid Cymru. See also REPUBLICANISM.

For further details see the autobiographies of Arthur Horner, Incorrigible Rebel (1960), and Will Paynter, My Generation (1972); see also the article by David Egan, 'The Swansea Conference of the British Council of Soldiers' and Workers' Delegates, July 1917: reaction to the Russian Revolution of 1917 and the anti-war movement in south Wales' in Llafur (vol. 1, no. 4, 1975). An account of Welsh participation in the Spanish Civil war will be found in Hywel Francis, Miners against Fascism (1984).

Mary Ann Sailors, the landlady of the Sailors Arms in Dylan *Thomas's *Under Milk Wood (1954). In her eighty-fifth year, she is still in love with life in Llareggub and 'praises the lord who made porridge'. Her son, Sinbad Sailors, yearns for Gossamer Beynon and in the Sailors Arms it is always opening-time.

Massacre of the Bards, The, a traditional tale found in Thomas Carte's History of England (1747–55), is believed to have had its origins in Welsh fables about the burning of Welsh books in London which were confused with the claim that the poets, too, had been proscribed. Edward I was said to have ordered the slaughter of the Welsh poets, an influential class, after his conquest of Wales in 1282. This may have been an exaggeration of the fact that kings of medieval England had been known to license Welsh poets because they caused discord by their *vaticinations. The story was given wider currency by Thomas Gray's Pindaric ode, 'The Bard' (1757), in which the last survivor of the massacre curses the English king and foretells the disasters await-

ing his descendants, the fulfilment of *Taliesin's prophecy and the advent of the *Tudor dynasty. Gray, who found the story in Carte's book, was inspired by the playing of the blind harpist John *Parry, but he did not believe that the story was literally true. There is also an account of the massacre in Sir John *Wynn's History of the Gwydir Family (1770), rationalized in an attempt to explain why his ancestors in *Eifionydd had had no household poet, on the unpublished manuscript of which Carte is believed to have drawn. The theme was taken up by writers outside Wales, most notably by the Hungarian poet János Árány (1817–82), whose poem 'A Welski Bárdok' ('The Welsh Bards'), is among the greatest of patriotic poems in Magyar and in which Edward I appears like a Habsburg emperor entering the Balkans. Among the painters who took the massacre as their subject were Paul Sandby, Philip de Loutherbourg, Fuseli, John Martin and Thomas *Jones of Pencerrig.

For further details see F. I. McCarthy, 'The Bard of Thomas Gray and its importance and use by painters' in the Journal of the National Library of Wales (1965), A. Johnston, Thomas Gray and the Bard (1966) and Prys Morgan, 'From a Death to a View: the hunt for the Welsh past in the Romantic period' in The Invention of Tradition (ed. Eric Hobsbawm and Terence Ranger, 1983); see also the article by Neville Masterman in The Welsh Review (vol. 7, no. 1, Spring, 1948).

Massacre of the Druids, The, see under DRUIDS, MONA ANTIQUA RESTAURATA (1723) and ORDOVICES.

Massacre of the Saints, The, see under CHESTER, THE BATTLE OF (c.613–16).

Matchless Orinda, The, see PHILIPPS, KATHERINE (1631–64).

Math fab Mathonwy, magician and King of *Gwynedd in the Fourth Branch of *Pedair Cainc y Mabinogi. He is said to be unable to live unless his feet are in the fold of a maiden's lap, except when this position is prevented by war. At the beginning of the Fourth Branch his foot-bearer is Goewin ferch Pebin and when Gilfaethwy fab Dôn falls in love with her, his brother *Gwydion plots a war between Gwynedd and *Deheubarth so that Math will leave his court in Caer Dathl. During the fighting Goewin is put in Math's bed, where she is raped by Gilfaethwy. Having returned to his court and heard about the rape, Math makes recompense to Goewin by taking her for his wife and punishes Gwydion and Gilfaethwy by turning them into animals, causing them to produce offspring by each other over a period of three years. Math is also mentioned in the ancient mythological poetry in The *Book of Taliesin where it is claimed that Math had created *Taliesin by magic.

For further details see W. J. Gruffydd, Math vab Mathonwy (1928) and Rachel Bromwich, Trioedd Ynys Prydein (1961).

Mathago or **Mathau Goch**, see GOUGH, MATHEW (1396–1450).

MATHERS, ZECHARIAH (**Zachary Mather**; 1843–1934), prose-writer. Born at Efail y Waun, Denbs., he was for many years a Congregational minister at Barmouth, Mer. He published *The Wonderful Story of Agnes and the White Dove* (1903) and *Tales from the Welsh Hills* (1909), the latter including the three short stories for which, on the adjudication of Sir Lewis *Morris, he won first prize at the *National Eisteddfod of 1902. In Welsh he wrote several biographies and a number of books for children, among which *Teulu Bronygraig* (n.d.) and *Llwyfan y Plant* (1922) are the most memorable.

Mathetes, see JONES, JOHN (1821–78).

MATHEW, DAVID (1902–76), historian and novelist. Descended from the Mathew family of Radyr and Castell y Mynach, Pentyrch, Glam., he was educated at Osborne and Dartmouth, becoming a midshipman in the Navy for a year before going on to Balliol College, Oxford, in 1919. Ordained to the Catholic priesthood in 1929, he was assistant priest at St. David's Cathedral in Cardiff from 1930 to 1934, before taking up a series of university chaplaincies and an appointment in 1938 as Bishop Auxiliary of Westminster. His despatch as Apostolic Visitor to Ethiopia in 1945 began a long association with Africa which culminated in his appointment in 1963 as Archbishop of Apamea.

At different times Ford Lecturer in English History at Oxford and Ballard Mathews Lecturer at the *University of Wales, he was, for a historian, a prolific writer. His first book, *The Celtic Peoples and Renaissance Europe* (1933), describes in some detail the Wales and the March of Sir Gelly *Meyrick. Namier-like and anti-Statistical in its approach to his chosen period, the sixteenth and the seventeenth centuries, his work is distinguished by his interest in *Roman Catholicism in high places and by a polished prose style. Of the sixteen historical works which he published, *The Jacobean Age* (1938), *The Age of Charles I* (1951), *James I* (1967), *Lord Acton and his Times* (1968), and perhaps his homage to an ancestor, *Sir Tobie Mathew* (1951), are the finest. He was also the author of four novels, *Steam Packet* (1936) and a trilogy entitled *In Vallombrosa* (1950–53).

MATHEWS, ABRAHAM (1832–99), minister, pioneer and writer. Born at Llanidloes, Mont., and educated at the Independent College, Bala, under Michael D. *Jones, he was a Congregational minister at Aberdare, Glam., until 1865 when he went with the first settlers to *Patagonia, where he worked as a minister and farmer for the rest of his life. His book, *Hanes y Wladfa Gymreig* (1894), is the most reliable on the early history of the colony.

MATHEWS, JOHN HOBSON (**Mab Cernyw**; 1858–1914), historian, was a Cornishman's son who practised as a solicitor in Cardiff for many years. Received into the Roman Catholic faith in 1877, he learned Cornish and Welsh and then devoted himself to the study of Cornish history and of the Catholic faith in Wales. It was he who first drew attention to the carols of Richard *Gwyn. He was the author of *The Life and Memorials of Saint Teilo* (1893), *The Vaughans of Courtfield* (1912) and, as archivist to the Cardiff Corporation, the editor of six volumes of *Cardiff Records* (1898–1911). His continuation of Duncumb's *History of Herefordshire* (1804–12) is particularly valuable for the district of Archenfield (formerly *Erging).

MATHIAS, ROLAND (1915–), poet, editor and critic, was born at Talybont-on-Usk, Brecs. His father, an army chaplain, served in Germany after the First World War and he was educated at British military schools in that country and at Caterham School and Jesus College, Oxford, where he read Modern History. Both his parents were Welsh but only his father was Welsh-speaking and the language of his home and education was English. He first became emotionally aware of his Welsh heritage, he records, at the age of nine when he read *Lone Tree Lode* (1913), a novel by Owen Rhoscomyl (Robert Scourfield *Mills), and his subsequent career has been one of increasing identification with Wales and a deepening interest in its culture and history. After teaching for a while in England he returned to Wales as headmaster of Pembroke Dock Grammar School in 1948, a post he held until 1958 when he was appointed headmaster of The Herbert Strutt School, Belper, Derby. He resigned from the headmastership of King Edward's Five Ways School, Birmingham, in 1969 in order to devote himself to writing and lecturing, and settled in Brecon. From 1969 to 1979 he was a member of the *Welsh Arts Council's Literature Committee and its Chairman for three years. He also served as Chairman of the English-language section of Yr *Academi Gymreig from 1975 to 1978.

In 1949 Roland Mathias was one of the founders of the magazine *Dock Leaves* (later *The *Anglo-Welsh Review*) and between 1961 and 1976 he was its editor, contributing a large number of poems, reviews, articles and substantial editorials. His first collection of poetry, *Break in Harvest* (1946), was followed by *The Roses of Tretower* (1952), *The Flooded Valley* (1960), *Absalom in the Tree* (1971) and *Snipe's Castle* (1979); his selected poems appeared under the title *Burning Brambles* in 1983. He is also the author of prose works which include a volume of short stories, *The Eleven Men of Eppynt* (1956), a historical monograph, *Whitsun Riot* (1963), an essay on Vernon *Watkins in the *Writers of Wales* series (1974) and a study of the poetry of

John Cowper *Powys, *The Hollowed-Out Elder Stalk* (1979). The editor of a volume of essays on David *Jones as writer and artist (1976), he has co-edited with Sam *Adams a selection of short stories by Anglo-Welsh writers, *The Shining Pyramid* (1970), and the collected stories of Geraint *Goodwin (1976). With Raymond *Garlick he was the co-editor of the anthology *Anglo-Welsh Poetry 1480–1980* (1984).

The contribution of Roland Mathias to *Anglo-Welsh literature has been varied and extensive, his work on the origins and development of writing in English in Wales deriving substance and accuracy from his training as a historian. Among his most important writings on this subject are his long essays 'Thin Spring and Tributary' in *Anatomy of Wales* (ed. R. Brinley Jones, 1972), 'The Welsh Language and the English Language' in *The Welsh Language Today* (ed. Meic Stephens, 1973) and 'Literature in English' in *The Arts in Wales 1950–75* (ed. Meic Stephens, 1979). His literary criticism, of which there is a great deal, is characterized by breadth of outlook, high seriousness and a concern with issues rather than with personalities. A selection of his writings on Anglo-Welsh literature was published under the title *A Ride Through the Wood* in 1985. Very much to do with Wales and its history, with specific Welsh places, and with Welsh characters known and unknown, his poetry is also highly personal, following no fashion, and in texture and vocabulary shows no dramatic change over the thirty years of its production. Its occasional difficulty, usually a matter of allusion or erudition, is compensated for by its honesty, vivid language and scrupulous craftsmanship.

There is an autobiographical essay by Roland Mathias in *Artists in Wales* (ed. Meic Stephens, 1971); see also the articles by Jeremy Hooker in *Poetry Wales* (vol. 7, no. 1, 1971 vol. no. 1, 1985), the interview in *Poetry Wales* (vol. 18, no. 4, 1983) and the critical assessment by Michael J. Collins in *Dictionary of Literary Biography: British Poets since World War II* (1984).

Matholwch, the King of Ireland in the Second Branch of *Pedair Cainc y Mabinogi*. At the beginning of the tale he arrives in Harlech with thirteen ships to seek the hand of *Branwen, the sister of Bendigeidfran (*Brân), with a view to forming an alliance with the Isle of Britain. His request is granted, but when *Efnysien insults him by disfiguring his men's horses Matholwch returns in anger to his fleet. Pacified by the gifts of new horses and the *Cauldron of Rebirth, he is entertained at a feast given by Bendigeidfran and later marries Branwen. During the first year of their reign a son, named Gwern, is born to Branwen, but soon afterwards Matholwch is obliged to yield to his people's fervent request that he take revenge on his wife for the insult which the Irish had suffered in Wales, and she is banished to work in the kitchen. Branwen sends a message to her brother by means of a starling,

acquainting him of her fate. Three years later, when Bendigeidfran and his host come to avenge Branwen, Matholwch offers to abdicate in favour of Gwern but Brân is not satisfied and there occurs a final clash between the Irish and the Welsh.

It has been suggested that the name Matholwch derives from the Irish form *Milscothach*, but it should be noted that the earliest Welsh form of the name is probably Mallolwch. The Triads name a Matholwch Wyddel ('Irishman') and the Life of *Collen refers to Vathylwch, Lord of Ireland. *Iolo Goch calls Ireland 'the land of Matholwch' and in a sixteenth-century text 'Matholwch the Irishman' is named as one of the four *penceirddiaid* who were consulted during the formulation of the *Twenty-four Metres of Welsh prosody.

Further details about Matholwch will be found in Ifor Williams, *Pedeir Keinc y Mabinogi* (1930), P. Mac Cana, *Branwen Daughter of Llŷr* (1958), Rachel Bromwich, *Trioedd Ynys Prydein* (1961) and in the article by Eurys Rowlands in *Llên Cymru* (vol. VI, 1961).

Mathrafal, the principal court of the rulers of *Powys and the most important church in that kingdom until the thirteenth century, was situated near Meifod, Mont. It was to Powys what *Aberffraw was to *Gwynedd and *Dinefwr to *Deheubarth. The name was later given to one of the three bardic provinces of Wales. John Cowper *Powys makes psychic and reverential use of the site in his novel *Owen Glendower* (1940), particularly in the consciousness of Broch o'Meifod, who is represented as a survivor of the pre-Celtic inhabitants of Wales.

Matter of Britain, The (F. *Matière de Bretagne*), together with *Matière de Rome* and the *Matière de France*, constituted the three principal categories of medieval French literature. It covered a field co-extensive with that of the legends concerning *Arthur in so far as the latter denoted literary material based on or derived from Celtic or Welsh traditions about the Arthurian period in Britain. The fact that *Bretagne* was also the name of Brittany, a country which acquired its own Arthurian associations, added a new dimension to the title. The Welsh or British material was of varied character; some of it was semi-historical but it mostly took the form of folklore or primitive legend. The oldest Arthurian literary tale is that of *Culhwch and Olwen, probably composed about 1100, in which a vast quantity of ancient folklore tradition has been fitted into an Arthurian framework.

Several channels apparently served for the transmission of the content of the *Matter of Britain* to continental Europe. One was *Geoffrey of Monmouth's *Historia Regum Britanniae* (1136), which portrayed Arthur as a feudal emperor and provided a political setting for the lengthy romances recounting the adventures of the knights of his court. Views differ as to the other channels. Some scholars have stressed the importance of contact between Welsh professional story-tellers and Norman minstrels in the years following the settlement of the Normans in parts of south Wales in the early twelfth century. Others have argued that the most important channel was supplied by the Breton *conteurs* who accompanied the Norman conquerors, not only in Wales but also in England. In the second half of the twelfth century Chrétien de Troyes composed his narrative poems *Erec*, *Yvain* and *Perceval*, which correspond with the Welsh prose romances of *Geraint*, *Owain* and *Peredur* respectively, though the nature of the relationship has been disputed (see under TAIR RHAMANT). The *lais* of Marie de France, which belong to the same period, have Breton associations. A subsequent development was the composition of prose romances, such as *Lancelot*, the *Queste del Saint Graal* and the *Mort Artu*. The legend of *Tristan and Iseult, which had its roots in Irish, Welsh, Cornish and Breton tradition, is found in a number of verse and prose forms.

Themes deriving from the *Matter of Britain* were used by writers in many languages other than French, such as Wolfram von Eschenbach and Gottfried von Strassburg in German in the early thirteenth century and Malory in English in the fifteenth century. Arthurian literature in general contains material derived from many sources other than the *Matter of Britain*, of course. Some American and European scholars such as Tatlock and Faral have tended to minimize the 'British' element, while others such as R. S. *Loomis and Frappier have in varying degrees stressed its importance.

The *Matter of Britain* is discussed in the following works: R. S. Loomis (ed.), *Arthurian Literature in the Middle Ages* (1959), E. K. Chambers, *Arthur of Britain* (1927, 1964) and P. B. Grout, R. A. Lodge, C. E. Pickford and E. K. C. Varty (ed.), *The Legend of Arthur in the Middle Ages* (1983); see also Cedric E. Pickford and Rex Last, *The Arthurian Bibliography, Part I* (1981) and the annual *Bibliographical Bulletin of the International Arthurian Society*.

MATTHEWS, EDWARD (1813–92), preacher and author. Born near St. Athan, Glam., he became a collier in Hirwaun at the age of fourteen and, in 1841, after a short course of education at Trefeca College, he was ordained by the Calvinistic Methodists. He ministered at Pontypridd, Glam., but settled later at Ewenni, near Bridgend, in the Vale of Glamorgan. Matthews Ewenni, as he was generally known thereafter, first achieved fame as a preacher who delighted his congregations by his droll use of the Glamorgan dialect, his dramatic delivery and his loud exclamations from the pulpit.

His very popular biography, *Hanes Bywyd Siencyn Penhydd* (1850), is a portrait of an old, unlearned but saintly Methodist exhorter named Jenkin Thomas of Pen-hydd, Glam. Written in an amusing style, it presents a type of preacher distinguished by an eccentricity which was greatly admired by the common people of his day. First published in the magazine *Y *Traethodydd*, the work ran to six editions between 1850 and 1867. A similar book, *George Heycock a'i Amserau* (1867), is more tedious. Matthews also published a more ambitious work, a biography of the Calvinistic Methodist preacher, Thomas Richard (1863), and he was a frequent contributor to the periodicals *Y Cylchgrawn*, which he edited, *Y Traethodydd* and *Y Drysorfa*.

A collection of his essays was edited by W. Llywel Morgan in 1911 and a volume of his sermons by D. M. Phillips in 1927. Memoirs of Matthews Ewenni were written by D. G. Jones (1893) and J. J. Morgan (1922); see also *Morgannwg Matthews Ewenni* (1953) by Henry Lewis.

Maude or **Matilda de St. Valerie (Mol Walbee**; d. 1210), the wife of *William de Braose, Lord of Painscastle, Rads., is remembered in local tradition as a witch, murderess and bogey to frighten children. It is said, for example, that she built Hay Castle in one night, carrying the stones in her apron, and that the wailing of the river Wye at midnight is caused by the cries of those whom she drowned in its waters. Although praised by *Gerald de Barri (Giraldus Cambrensis) for her godliness and household skills, she was described by William Camden (c.1585) as 'a very shrewd, stout and malapert, stomachful woman'. Mol Walbee met her end as a result of her slander of King John. Fleeing from his wrath, she and her young son were captured and imprisoned at Windsor Castle, where they were both starved to death.

Maurice, Godfrey, see JONES, JOHN or GRIFFITH (1559–98).

MAURICE, HUGH (1755?–1825), copyist and poet, was born in the parish of Llanfihangel Glyn Myfyr, Denbs., a nephew of Owen *Jones (Owain Myfyr). As a young man he went to work in his uncle's skin and fur business in London where, under Owain Myfyr's guidance, he excelled as a copyist of Welsh manuscripts. One of his early transcripts, an *awdl* by *Gwalchmai ap Meilyr, was written in the bardic alphabet known as *Coelbren y Beirdd and several others he decorated in water-colours. His contribution to *The Myvyrian Archaiology* (1801) is acknowledged in the preface to that work. A prominent member of the *Gwyneddigion Society, he was denied its medal for poetry in 1805 because he had failed to reveal his real name within the set period and the prize went instead to David *Owen (Dewi Wyn o Eifion).

The children of Hugh Maurice were brought up to take an interest in literature. His elder son, **Rowland Jones Maurice**, translated *Nennius's *Historia Brittonum* into English and his younger son, **Peter Maurice** (1803–78), who became chaplain of New College and All Souls College, Oxford, wrote anti-Catholic pamphlets and edited several English hymnals, including *The Choral Hymn Book* (1861). Their sister, **Jane Maurice** (b. 1812), wrote hymns and it was she who in 1899 presented to the British Museum the Caerhun Manuscripts, a collection of forty-nine volumes of Welsh manuscripts copied by her father and Owain Myfyr. Other manuscripts by Hugh Maurice are preserved in the *National Library of Wales.

MAURICE, WILLIAM (d. 1680), antiquary, belonged to the family of Moeliwrch, Llansilin, Denbs., but his name is usually associated with Cefn-y-braich in the same district. An assiduous collector of manuscripts, he worked mainly for his friend, Robert *Vaughan of Hengwrt, whom he regarded as his Gamaliel. But he had sufficient means to form his own collection, which was so extensive that he is said to have built a three-storey edifice, known locally as *Y Study*, for the purpose of housing it. After his death, his daughter inherited the library and sold it to Sir William Williams of Llanforda in 1682. The manuscripts were transferred to Wynnstay (see under WILLIAMS-WYNN FAMILY) in 1771 but most were lost in a fire at that house in 1858. Fortunately, some were on loan to Aneirin *Owen at the time and they survived.

They include some poetry and a copy of the Chirk extent, an essay by Maurice against altars and a copy of a letter from him to Robert Vaughan which attempts to set out part of the history of the *Celts and to defend *Geoffrey of Monmouth by reconciling his 'history' of Brennus with the classical evidence concerning Brennius the Gaul. Although the last-named thesis, like his notes on the chronology of the *Brut* in the same manuscript, is not without value, Maurice's most significant manuscripts are his *Corpus Hoelianum* or *Deddfgrawn* (Wynnstay MS 37–38) which he compiled between 1660 and 1663. Here, chiefly on the basis of the Hengwrt Manuscripts, is the first attempt to classify the texts of the *Laws of Hywel Dda. Maurice's work was to form the basis for the classification which Aneirin Owen adopted in his edition of the Laws in *Ancient Laws and Institutes of Wales* (1841).

Mawddwy, a commot of *Powys. After the death of Gruffudd ap Gwenwynwyn in 1286, it was held by the line of Gwilym ap Gruffudd and, unlike the rest of Powys Wenwynwyn, it never reverted to the senior line represented by Owain ap Gruffudd and his descendants. In 1536, perhaps because of its reputation for lawlessness (see under GWYLLIAID COCHION MAWDDWY), the commot was attached to the old-established county of Merioneth.

May Day, the beginning of summer in the Celtic calendar. The festival began on the previous evening (30 April), one of the three spirit-nights when ghosts were said to wander through the countryside and when, as on Winter's Eve, it was thought possible to foretell the future by divination. The lighting of bonfires was once typical of May Eve but that custom had been discontinued by the first half of the nineteenth century. May Day (1 May) was associated above all with courtship, the open air and the regeneration of nature, themes also found in the work of such poets as *Dafydd ap Gwilym. Flowers and branches were brought in to decorate the house. To this time also belonged the customs of the *Summer Birch and summer dancing, in which the *Cadi Haf figured so prominently; the summer carols associated with the day were a relatively late development. The significance of May Day has always been pagan and secular, despite the efforts of the Church to associate it with St. Philip and St. James. The date was thus quite naturally adopted in many countries as a Festival of Labour during the nineteenth century.

For accounts of May Day celebrations in Wales see T. Gwynn Jones, *Welsh Folklore and Folk-Custom* (1930), Alwyn and Brinley Rees, *Celtic Heritage* (1961) and Trefor M. Owen, *Welsh Folk Customs* (1959).

Mead, a drink made from honey, hops, yeast and water. In *Aneirin's poem 'Y *Gododdin' the phrase 'talu medd' ('to merit mead') refers to the traditional relationship between the warrior and his lord (see under HEROIC IDEAL); 'gobrynu gwin' ('to deserve one's wine') has a similar meaning, namely that the warrior deserves sustenance from his master by fighting valiantly in his battle and, if necessary, laying down his life. Mead was still drunk in Wales as late as the eighteenth century but was thereafter replaced by ale made from barley.

Mechain, a cantref of *Powys. At the division of the kingdom after the death of *Madog ap Maredudd in 1160 it became the patrimony of the line of Owain ap Madog, but by the 1280s it was in the hands of the lords of Pole, descendants of Owain ap Madog's cousin, Owain Cyfeiliog (*Owain ap Gruffudd ap Maredudd). In the fourteenth century the possession of Mechain was disputed between John Charlton and Gruffydd de la Pole.

Meddwl Modern, Y (lit. 'Modern thought'), a series of monographs on great thinkers and writers of the modern world, is published by *Gwasg Gee* under the editorship of Dafydd Glyn Jones and W. Gareth Jones. It was launched in 1980 and eighteen titles had appeared by 1985. The series includes studies of Marx, Wittgenstein, Toynbee, Malraux, Lenin, Bonhoeffer, Darwin, Freud, T. S. Eliot, Evans-Pritchard, Weber, Hegel, Durkheim, Hume, Bultmann, Fromm, Brecht and Jung.

Medr fab Medredydd, a character named in the list of *Arthur's retinue in the tale of *Culhwch and Olwen. It is said that from *Celli Wig in Cornwall he could shoot a wren on Esgeir Oerfel in Ireland and hit it between the legs. He may be compared with Drem fab Dremhidydd who could see, from Celli Wig, a fly rising on Pen Blathon in Scotland, or with Clust fab Clustfeinad who, were he to be buried seven fathoms under the earth, could hear an ant stirring from its nest fifty miles away. Apart from the humorous significance of these characters, their function was to help Culhwch in the accomplishment of the tasks set by Ysbaddaden Bencawr as conditions for the winning of Olwen.

Medrod, a traditional hero who, according to *Annales Cambriae*, fell with *Arthur at the battle of *Camlan. Whether the two men were allies or enemies is not clear. It was *Geoffrey of Monmouth who portrayed Medrod as a betrayer of Arthur but for the poets he was a standard of bravery. Medraut and Mordred are alternative forms of his name.

Meibion Glyndŵr (lit. 'Sons of Glyndŵr'), a clandestine Nationalist group which, since 1980, has claimed responsibility for carrying out a campaign of arson against property owned by English people in Welsh-speaking districts of north and west Wales. Its communiqués are usually signed Rhys Gethin, the name of one of *Owain Glyndŵr's captains. See also FREE WALES ARMY and MUDIAD AMDDIFFYN CYMRU.

Meic Myngfras (6th cent.), the traditional ancestor of the rulers of *Glyndyfrdwy in northern *Powys, according to the genealogies. *Iolo Goch referred to *Owain Glyndŵr as belonging to the stock of Meic Myngfras and he may have been a brother of the Brochfael Ysgithrog whose pursuit of a hare was foiled by *Melangell. His name is thought to be preserved in that of Meigen, the district lying around Cefn Digoll (Long Mountain), to the east of Welshpool, Mont., through which now runs the border with England. Owain Glyndŵr's claim in the Tripartite Indenture that the borders of Wales extended as far as 'Onennau Meigion' was taken by J. E. *Lloyd to refer to the ash-trees of Meigion, once a well-known landmark near the village now known as Six Ashes, on the road between Bridgnorth, Salop., and Stourbridge. The place-name Meigen also occurs in a sequence of *englynion* (9th or 10th cent.) which list the victories of *Cadwallon ap Cadfan over the English. In the *Annales Cambriae* Meigen is wrongly identified with Heathfield (probably Hatfield Chase, Yorks.) where Edwin of Northumbria was defeated and killed by Cadwallon and Penda in the year 632.

Meigan, the name given by the editors of The *Myvyrian Archaiology* (1801) to the author of '*Marwnad Cynddylan*', an early poem preserved in late manuscripts, and one other poem besides. He is also mentioned by Iolo Morganwg (Edward *Williams) who may have derived the form from the name Maugantius, assumed by Leland to have been an early British poet. There is no reliable evidence that a poet of this name ever existed and so he is listed here as a fictitious character.

Meigen, The Battle of (632), see under CADWALLON AP CADFAN (d. 633) and MEIC MYNGFRAS (6th cent.).

Meikle, Clive, see BROOKS, JEREMY (1926–   ).

MEILYR AP GWALCHMAI (*fl.* second half of the 12th cent.), poet. Little is known about him but he was probably the son of *Gwalchmai ap Meilyr and the brother of *Einion ap Gwalchmai and, perhaps, of *Elidir Sais. All his extant work consists of religious *awdlau* which are the simple expression of the piety of his age but none of these refers to any event which would help to give a precise date for his birth or death. He was the grandson of *Meilyr Brydydd.

MEILYR BRYDYDD (*fl.* 1100–37), the earliest of the *Gogynfeirdd* and the chief poet to *Gruffudd ap Cynan, whose elegy he composed. With his son, *Gwalchmai ap Meilyr, and his grandsons *Meilyr ap Gwalchmai and *Einion ap Gwalchmai, he belonged to a line of hereditary poets who held land in return for their eulogies, a tradition commemorated by the place-names Trefeilyr and Trewalchmai in Anglesey. The elegiac *awdl* written by Meilyr, consisting of four sequences each with different end-rhymes and in lines of nine syllables, marks (as far as can be judged from extant texts) the beginning of the bardic revival which accompanied the restoration of a powerful *Gwynedd through the successes of Gruffudd ap Cynan and his descendants. It is very consciously in the *Cynfeirdd* tradition of *Taliesin and *Aneirin and the Prince is placed in the succession of *Urien.

The similarities between the *Gogynfeirdd* and their predecessors are many: not only are the same descriptions found and archaic words employed but the poet's struggle is the same, namely 'to relieve the Christian world' as if the enemy still worshipped Thor and Wodin. The two main differences are the growth of the concept of a Wales united from Anglesey to Gwent and a much more prominent Christian element, features which persisted throughout the period of the Princes. Meilyr the *pencerdd* maintained that he knew more than did the '*manfeirdd*' ('petty poets'). At court he was to be found near his Prince, he fought alongside him, went on his errands, received his gifts, and sang of his valour and generosity; the bond between them was to be broken only by death.

Of the other two poems ascribed in the manuscripts to Meilyr, probably only the death-couch poem is his. It is the most intensely felt and the tenderest of the few extant poems of its kind. In fluid lines the poet pleads for God's mercy, confessing his burden of sins and his slackness in pursuit of true religion. He refers to gifts received from earthly rulers as rewards for the 'energy' of his muse and expresses his yearning to be laid in the churchyard on Ynys Enlli (*Bardsey), there to await the coming of Saint Peter.

For further details see the article by J. E. Caerwyn Williams, 'Beirdd y Tywysogion, Arolwg', in Llên Cymru (vol. XI, nos. 1 and 2, 1970).

Meini Gwagedd (lit. 'Stones of emptiness'; 1944), a verse-drama by J. Kitchener *Davies, takes its title from a description of waste land in the Old Testament (Isaiah 34:11). The characters are ghosts who have left their graves on St. Michael's Eve to haunt the ruins of Glangorsfach, a croft in Cors Caron, the bog near Tregaron, Cards. They belong to two generations; the Three (the croft's owner and his two daughters Mari and Siani) and the Four (the two brothers Ifan and Rhys and the two sisters Elen and Sal). The relationships of the Three are poisoned by oppression, treachery and guilt, while for the Four life is a curse. The evil prevalent is attributed to the marshland, a symbol of disillusionment after the dream of the 'gwyn-fan-draw' ('the blessedness yonder'), which produces the bickering, the vindictiveness and the penance without end. An experimental work, the play enjoyed a succès d'estime at the time of its first production and was praised for its attempt to create in Welsh a poetic language for the purposes of the theatre.

Meirionnydd, a cantref lying between the rivers Mawddach and Dyfi, was named, according to tradition, after Meriaun, the grandson of *Cunedda. It had its own dynasty until the ninth century but thereafter, until the death of *Gruffudd ap Llywelyn in 1063, it was absorbed into *Gwynedd. In 1063 it came under the aegis of the rulers of *Powys but was reconquered by the House of Gwynedd in 1123. From 1147 it was held as an apanage by Cynan ab Owain Gwynedd and his descendants but it came under the direct rule of *Llywelyn ap Gruffudd in 1256 when Llywelyn ap Maredudd (the father of Madog ap Llywelyn, the leader of the *Welsh Revolt of 1294) was driven from the cantref. The county of Meirionnydd was created under the provisions of the Statute of *Rhuddlan (1284) and it consisted of the cantrefi of Meirionnydd and *Penllyn together with *Ardudwy and *Edeirnion. The commot of Mawddwy was added to the county in 1536. The district of Meirionnydd, established in 1974, embraces the whole of the ancient county except for Edeirnion.

Meistri'r Canrifoedd (lit. 'Masters of the centuries'; 1973), a volume of essays on the history of Welsh literature by Saunders *Lewis. Having first appeared in various journals between 1925 and 1970, the essays were collected, under the editorship of R. Geraint *Gruffydd, to mark the occasion of the author's eightieth birthday. Of the thirty-seven essays, twelve deal with the medieval period and the remainder with the three-and-a-half centuries between the *Act of Union (1536) and the end of the nineteenth century. The book may therefore be thought of as taking the place of the author's projected second volume of *Braslun o Hanes Llenyddiaeth Gymraeg (1932). It includes important essays on *Pedair Cainc y Mabinogi, *Dafydd ap Gwilym, *Dafydd Nanmor, *Tudur Aled, the 'Protestant Ecclesiastical Theory', Charles *Edwards, the Welsh translations of À Kempis, Ann *Griffiths, the *biography in Welsh and Islwyn (William *Thomas). A companion volume appeared under the title Meistri a'u Crefft (ed. Gwynn ap Gwilym) in 1981.

Melai, a mansion in the parish of Llanfair Talhaearn, Denbs., was the home of the Wyn family which extended patronage to poets for at least six generations. The family, as an independent branch, was established there by Wiliam ap Maredudd (d. 1570) but the house may have belonged to his grandfather, Dafydd ab Einion Fychan of Fronheulog, in the same parish, for whom *Tudur Aled wrote. Siôn Wyn (d. 1629/30) and Wiliam Wyn (d. 1643) were the last to receive poets at Melai, although poems dedicated to other branches of the family have survived, a fact which suggests that a similar tradition was maintained at Fronheulog.

Melangell (6th cent.), a princess who, according to tradition, came to Wales from Ireland to avoid marriage to a warrior whom her father had chosen for her. It is said that she hid a hare beneath her robes in order to save it from the hounds of Brochfael Ysgithrog, Prince of *Powys. The huntsmen dared not approach the gentle girl, such was her sanctity. The prince gave her the lands around what later became the hamlet of Pennant Melangell, Mont., and she founded a community of nuns where the church, built in the twelfth century, stands today. Melangell (L. Monacella) later became the patron saint of all small creatures and for centuries afterwards the hare, known in the district as 'oen bach Melangell' ('Melangell's little lamb'), was never hunted.

Melissa, see BRERETON, JANE (1685–1740).

Melwas, the abductor of *Gwenhwyfar, *Arthur's queen, according to a traditional account in the Life of *Gildas by *Caradog of Llancarfan. From references in the work of several poets it seems that an older Welsh tale, in which Melwas had a more honourable role, was displaced when the story about him was drawn into the Arthurian cycle.

Member for Wales, The, see RENDEL, STUART (1834–1913) and RICHARD, HENRY (1812–88).

Men who possessed Adam's Qualities, a group of traditional heroes who are listed at the head of *Trioedd Ynys Prydain* in *The *Red Book of Hergest*. Three possessed Adam's strength (Hercules, Hector and Samson), three his beauty (Absalom, Jason and Paris) and three his wisdom (Cato the Old, Bede and the Wise Sibyl). The first two Triads combine a biblical name with two derived from Classical sources, and this was originally the case with the third, since a version of the three Triads quoted by the poets *Gwilym Ryfel and *Llywarch ap Llywelyn (Prydydd y Moch) gives Selef (Solomon) in place of Bede. The most probable source for the Classical names is *Dares Phrygius*, which was translated into Welsh during the first half of the fourteenth century, but which was evidently known to the poets in its Latin form some two centuries earlier. The names of Echdor (Hector), Ercwlf (Hercules) and other Classical heroes are not infrequently cited in eulogies by the *Gogynfeirdd* as patterns of the traditional qualities. Late in the fourteenth century, *Gruffudd Llwyd ap Dafydd ab Einion Llygliw quoted the three Triads in an elegy in which he attributed all three of Adam's Qualities to his subject, *Rhydderch ab Ieuan Llwyd.

Menevia, see ST. DAVID'S.

Menw fab Teirgwaedd, a wizard in the tale of *Culhwch and Olwen. He has the gift of invisibility and other powers, using them at the court of Ysbaddaden Bencawr in the service of Culhwch. In the hunting of the *Twrch Trwyth he is sent by *Arthur to Esgeir Oerfel in Ireland to make sure that the treasures sought are to be found between the beast's ears. He flies to its lair in the form of a bird. Menw is also named in the Triads as one of the Three Enchanters of the Isle of Britain.

Merch Gwern Hywel (lit. 'The daughter of Gwern Hywel'; 1964), a historical romance by Saunders *Lewis. The heroine, Sarah Jones (who was the author's great-grandmother), elopes with William Roberts, a young Methodist preacher from Anglesey. Their marriage is more than the union of two attractive and intelligent people, for it represents also the reconciliation of an old élite with a new, the landed Anglican class of the eighteenth century with the Methodist merchant class of the early nineteenth century. The latter, it is suggested, will thereafter lack neither the social graces of the former,

nor its sense of history, nor its awareness of the importance of theological continuity. Both the characterization and the dialogue in this short novel display the author's powers at their greatest. The theme is further explored by Saunders Lewis in his study of the marriage of John *Elias and Ann Bulkeley in the television play, *Dwy Briodas Ann* (1975).

For critical discussions of this novel see the articles by Bedwyr Lewis Jones in *Barn* (no. 23, Sept., 1964), Pennar Davies in *Barn* (no. 51, Jan., 1967) and Dafydd Glyn Jones in *Barn* (no. 56, June, 1967). An English translation by Joseph Clancy appeared under the title *The Daughter of Gwern Hywel* in 1985.

MERCHANT, MOELWYN (1913–), poet and critic. Born in Port Talbot, Glam., he became a Lecturer in English at University College, Cardiff, in 1940 and from 1961 to 1974 was Professor of English at the University of Exeter. He then returned to Wales as vicar of Llanddewibrefi, Cards., but now lives in England. Besides writing for radio, he is the author of three critical studies, *Wordsworth* (1955), *Shakespeare and the Artist* (1959) and *Creed and Drama* (1965), an essay on R. S. *Thomas in the *Writers of Wales* series (1979), and libretti for Alun Hoddinott's operas, *The Race of Adam* (1961) and *The Tree of Life* (1971). He has published two volumes of verse, *Breaking the Code* (1975) and *No Dark Glass* (1979).

Merched y Gerddi (lit. 'The garden girls'), young women of mid-Wales who, in the eighteenth century and at the beginning of the nineteenth, walked to London (often in the company of *drovers) to find work in the public gardens of the city. One of the best-known was Ruth Watcyn, a girl from Abergwesyn, Brecs., who became a maid in the service of Lady Goodrich.

The only authoritative account of these women is the article by John Williams-Davies, 'Merched y Gerddi: a seasonal migration of female labour from rural Wales' in *Folk Life* (vol. 15, 1977).

Merched y Mera (lit. 'The Mera girls'), women belonging to a tribe of tinkers, so called because they lived in a part of Neath known as the Mera. They were to be seen in the streets of Glamorgan during the nineteenth century and were remarkable for the style in which they carried their wares on their heads.

Merched y Wawr (lit. 'Daughters of the dawn'), a women's organization founded in 1967 at Parc, near Bala, Mer., in response to a refusal by the National Federation of Women's Institutes to allow the official use of Welsh at its branch meetings in the village. It has no political affiliations, works entirely through the medium of the Welsh language, publishes a magazine, *Y Wawr*, and has branches in most parts of Wales.

Merlin, see MYRDDIN.

MERRICK, RICE or **RHYS MEURIG** or **RHYS AMHEURUG** (*c*.1520–1586/7), genealogist and historian, was of Cottrell in the parish of St. Nicholas, Glam. His main interest was in the history of his native county and his principal work, *Morganiae Archaiographia: a Booke of Glamorganshire Antiquities*, written between 1578 and 1584, is among the most important of the older histories, not only for its description of Glamorgan in Norman times but also for its picture of the county in the author's own day. Merrick is believed to have compiled other works, including a history of Wales, a history of Glamorgan (lost when Thomas *Johnes's Hafod was destroyed by fire in 1807), a history of the bishopric of *Llandaf and a collection of manuscripts known as the Cottrell Book, but no copy of any of these has survived. The poets *Dafydd Benwyn and Silas ap Siôn composed elegies in memory of their patron.

A new edition of *Morganiae Archaiographia* has been edited by B. Ll. James (1983); see also G. J. Williams, *Traddodiad Llenyddol Morgannwg* (1948), the article by T. J. Hopkins in *Morgannwg* (vol. VIII, 1964) and the chapter by Ceri W. Lewis, 'The Literary History of Glamorgan from 1550 to 1770' in *Glamorgan County History* (vol. IV, 1974).

Merthyr Rising, The (1831), a popular rebellion which grew into an armed insurrection, was the result of workers' grievances over wages, municipal administration and parliamentary reform. The depression of 1829, with its wage-cuts and unemployment, created substantial debts among the working population of Merthyr Tydfil, Glam., which precipitated a credit crisis among shopkeepers and led the Court of Requests (the debtors' court) into widespread confiscation of the property of the poor. During the crisis, local Unitarian radicals in the Jacobin tradition took over the town in alliance with William *Crawshay II, who shielded his workers and preached a democratic, if idiosyncratic, *Radicalism. Into this disturbed community came the flood of specifically working-class political literature unleashed by the crisis of 1830. The middle-class radicals formed a Political Union and launched a series of campaigns in alliance with Crawshay, culminating in the general election over the first *Reform Bill in May 1831, when the ironmaster committed himself and his men in the election at Brecon.

Crowds began roaming the streets of Merthyr and demonstrating in favour of Reform. Prisoners were set free in a riot led by Thomas Llewelyn, a Cyfarthfa miner, and public order broke down. From 2 May workers formed political unions of their own and held three mass-meetings. At the height of the excitement, Crawshay was forced to cut the wages of his ironstone miners and to dismiss eighty-four puddlers. The climax was a Reform rally held at the Waun Fair above the town on 30 May, where delegates appeared from a new colliers' union affiliated to the Owenite National Association for the Protection of Labour (see under OWEN, ROBERT, 1771–1858). Over the next two days, while Llewelyn led a march to Aberdare for the equalization of wages, a natural justice rebellion broke out at Hirwaun as a result of the seizure of a trunk belonging to Lewis Lewis (1793–1848), a haulier and horse-breaker from Penderyn who was known as Lewsyn yr Heliwr ('The Huntsman'). Led by Lewis, a charismatic man, literate in both Welsh and English, with a gift of plain oratory, the miners David Jones (Dai Solomon) and David Hughes, the puddlers David Thomas (Dai Llaw Haearn) and William Williams, the rioters raised the Red Flag, the first time it was so used in Britain, and impaled a loaf of bread on the staff. On 2 June they marched on Merthyr, raided shops and houses, took goods confiscated by the Court and restored them to their original owners, drove off magistrates and special constables in defiance of the Riot Act, and burned the Court itself.

Overnight, some eighty soldiers of the Argyll and Sutherland Highlanders marched into the town from Brecon. Outside the Castle Inn, where magistrates, masters and shopkeepers who were special constables were concentrated, they were confronted by a crowd of between seven and ten thousand people. The tense, hour-long dialogue which followed the reading of the Riot Act broke down in an explosion of anger from Crawshay and, exhorted by Lewis Lewis, the crowd attacked the soldiers and tried to disarm them. After a furious hand-to-hand struggle, the troops inside the inn opened fire and kept on firing for some ten minutes. Hundreds of men returned to attack the Inn and Lewis Lewis rallied stragglers to fire back with captured weapons. Sixteen soldiers were wounded, at least two dozen workers killed and over seventy wounded. The military were forced to retreat to Penydarren House.

The whole district then rose in rebellion. At Hirwaun, men sacrificed a calf and washed a sheet in its blood, again for use as a Red Flag. There were raids for arms all over north Glamorgan and delegates were sent into Monmouthshire. Thousands of men and women, including a body of Irishmen carrying clubs, rallied around a core of some four hundred armed men who set up camp, with a signalling system, on the Brecon Road near Cefn Coed and on the Swansea Road above the town. They beat back an ammunition convoy from Brecon, ambushed and disarmed a contingent of the Swansea Yeomanry, and staged a demonstration in front of Penydarren House. The magistrates, in a series of deputations, succeeded in dividing the men. The last effort of the rebels came on 6 June, when a crowd of between twelve and twenty thousand men and women, marching from Gwent to join those already in revolt, were faced by the levelled muskets of soldiery at Dowlais. On 7 June the Merthyr Rising collapsed.

Within two weeks of the revolt the first Union lodges affiliated to a national organization appeared in south Wales. They spread rapidly and gripped the entire coalfield from Pontypool to Swansea, but were broken during the supreme crisis of the Reform Bill in November, in a lock-out of six weeks when the men were starved into renouncing their Union. The Home Secretary, Lord Melbourne, and the Merthyr magistrates broke the law to achieve their end, while the men became affiliated to the National Union of the Working Classes in London and sent delegates to Carmarthen.

Retribution for the revolt was exacted at the July Assizes in Cardiff, where twenty-eight scapegoats, mostly ironstone miners and puddlers but including two women, one aged sixty-two, were put on trial. Several were sentenced to terms of imprisonment and four to transportation for fourteen years or life. Lewis Lewis, under sentence of death, was reprieved and transported to Australia for life, but Richard Lewis, a twenty-three-year-old miner known as Dic Penderyn, was found guilty of wounding a soldier named Donald Black. Despite widespread belief in his innocence and a vigorous campaign to save his life, Dic was hanged at Cardiff on 13 August 1831. It is said that his last words from the scaffold were 'O Arglwydd, dyma gamwedd!' ('O Lord, this is a great wrong!'). Forty years later, another man, living in America, confessed to the crime for which Lewis had been executed. Dic Penderyn is generally held to be the first martyr of the Welsh working-class and the Merthyr Rising is in the history of Wales what the Peterloo Massacre (1819) is in that of England.

For detailed accounts see David Jones, *Before Rebecca* (1973), Gwyn A. Williams, *The Merthyr Rising* (1978) and 'The Merthyr Election of 1835' in *The Welsh in their History* (1982); the novels *All Things Betray Thee* (1949) by Gwyn Thomas and *The Fire People* (1972) by Alexander Cordell are set against the events of 1831.

Methodism, a religious movement which grew under the influence of Pietism, Moravianism and some elements in the Puritan tradition. The Evangelical Revival of the eighteenth century is also called 'the Methodist Revival'. The name Methodist was originally one of the contemptuous nicknames given to the 'Holy Club' which gathered around the Wesley brothers in Oxford, but with the work of Howel *Harris and Daniel *Rowland the Revival began in Wales before the Wesleys had experienced their conversions. It was organized through a network of societies, each led by an exhorter who was appointed by the Association, a gathering of the leaders.

The term Methodist is also applied to the theological emphasis and moral self-discipline which developed in the Methodist bodies and, in Wales especially, among the Calvinistic Methodists, a religious tradition portrayed in the novels of Daniel *Owen. This denomination is called today the Presbyterian Church of Wales and is popularly known as '*Yr Hen Gorff*' ('The Old Body'). The largest of the Nonconformist bodies in Wales, it has been particularly strong in the northern counties, as *Independency and *Baptists have flourished especially in the south. The Calvinistic Methodists in Wales separated from the Church of England in 1811 under the leadership of Thomas *Charles and others. The theology of the movement is based on the teaching of Calvin, with much emphasis on the sovereignty of God and his grace in Christ and on the election of the saints.

John *Elias carried the doctrine of predestination to extremes, maintaining a 'limited Atonement' and opposing the more moderate views of Thomas *Jones of Denbigh and John *Jones of Tal-y-sarn. Elias also opposed the Radical tendencies in *Nonconformity, but a later generation (under the leadership of Thomas *Gee) championed political and religious reforms. From the eighteenth century on there arose among the Welsh Calvinistic Methodists a number of outstanding writers, including William *Williams (Pantycelyn), Ann *Griffiths, Lewis *Edwards, William *Thomas (Islwyn), Daniel Owen, Robert Ambrose *Jones (Emrys ap Iwan), Gwenallt (David James *Jones) and Kate *Roberts. Although Saunders *Lewis is a convert to *Roman Catholicism, he owes much to his Methodist roots. The playwright John Gwilym *Jones exemplifies the sceptical turn of mind which, in some writers, has weakened the Calvinist heritage in Wales. Emyr *Humphreys's *Outside the House of Baal* (1965) is a more regretful view of the decline of *Yr Hen Gorff*.

Further details will be found in D. D. Williams, *Llawlyfr Hanes Cyfundeb y Methodistiaid Calfinaidd* (1927), R. E. Davies and G. E. Rupp, *A History of the Methodist Church of Great Britain* (1965) and Gomer M. Roberts (ed.), *Hanes Methodistiaeth Galfinaidd* (vol. 1, 1973, vol. 2, 1978).

Methodist Pope, The, see ELIAS, JOHN (1774–1841).

Meudwy Môn, see JONES, OWEN (1806–89).

MEURIG (*fl.* 1210), poet. According to *Gerald de Barri (Giraldus Cambrensis) in his *De Principis Instructione*, Meurig was a native of Glamorgan and a brother of Clement, the abbot of Neath. Bale's *Index Britanniae Scriptorum* also refers to Meurig as *Mauricius Morganensis*, attributing to him a volume of Latin epigrams and several volumes in Welsh, from which it has been concluded that he was the Meurig who was in Gerald's time the treasurer of the diocese of *Llandaf. There is a reference to this Meurig in the manuscripts of Iolo Morganwg (Edward

*Williams) as the author of *Y *Cwta Cyfarwydd*, presumed to be the prototype of the work written by *Gwilym Tew in 1445. Also attributed to him are a history of Britain, a book of proverbs, works on Welsh prosody and theology, and a translation from the Latin Gospel of St. John, but these claims should be treated with caution.

MEURIG AB IORWERTH (*fl.* 1320–70), one of the last of the *Gogynfeirdd, wrote verses in praise of Hopcyn ap Tomas of Ynys Dawe, near Swansea, depicting his patron as the ideal Welsh gentleman, skilful in battle, owner of proud horses, learned in the law and all things French, but above all '*yn dad y gerddwriaeth fad fawr*' ('a father of the poetic art').

Meuryn, see ROWLANDS, ROBERT JOHN (1880–1967).

'***Mewn Dau Gae***' (lit. 'In two fields'; 1956), one of Waldo *Williams's greatest poems, was written at a time when the poet was refusing to pay income-tax as a protest against weapons of war, and belongs to the same period as his address '*Brenhiniaeth a Brawdoliaeth*' ('Sovereignty and Brotherhood'). The fruit of his long and profound meditation on the pacifist philosophy, in which he was influenced by Berdyaev, the poem is more specifically an expression of the deeply personal religious experience which the poet had had some forty years previously in two fields known as Weun Parc y Blawd and Parc y Blawd, on a neighbour's farm, during which he had suddenly realized that men and women are, above all else, brothers and sisters. The poem ends with a powerful vision of '*Y Brenin Alltud*' ('The Exiled King') who comes to reclaim His kingdom, the rushes of the fields parting where He treads.

The merits of the poem are discussed by Bedwyr Lewis Jones in *Llên Ddoe a Heddiw* (ed. J. E. Caerwyn Williams, 1964).

Meyrick, Gelly (*c.*1556–1601), soldier, was born at Gelliswick, Pembs., but brought up at Lamphey in the service of Sir George Devereux and as companion to his nephew, the second Earl of Essex, to whose ambitions he devoted his life. After some years in the Low Countries he became Essex's steward about 1587 and from 1592 was unquestionably his right-hand man, applying himself—in the intervals of service at Cadiz in 1596, where his master knighted him, and in Ireland in 1599—to the creation of a power-base for the Earl in the Marches of Wales. From his houses at Wigmore, Herefs., and Llanelwedd, Rads., he engineered a loose coalition of Puritans and Catholic Recusants. Sheriffs were often his nominees, the courts were bribed to acquit Recusants (for a consideration paid to him afterwards) and for a decade Sir Gelly's writ was more powerful in and out of the Devereux lands than that of the Court of the

Marches. But his endeavours came to nothing, for in the Essex revolt of 1601, the London part of which he stage-managed, no worthwhile help came from Wales, although it is said that he bribed the Globe Theatre players to perform *Richard the Second* on the eve of the revolt. Saturnine to the last, he was the first of the rebels to be executed for treason, even silencing the pleas of his companion on the scaffold. The Essex connection, however, was important in securing Pembrokeshire for Parliament in the First *Civil War.

The best single account of Meyrick is to be found in David Mathew, *The Celtic Peoples and Renaissance Europe* (1933).

MEYRICK, SAMUEL RUSH (1783–1848), antiquary, was born in London, educated at Queen's College, Oxford, and qualified as a lawyer, practising in the ecclesiastical and admiralty courts. Married in 1803 to the daughter of James Parry of Llwyn Hywel, Cards., he built the mansion known as Goodrich Court near Ross-on-Wye, Herefs. He was the author of works of antiquarian and armorial interest, some of which, such as *History and Antiquities of the County of Cardigan* (1809–10) and *Costume of the Original Inhabitants of the British Islands* (1815), pertain to Wales. But his most important contribution was his editing of Lewys *Dwnn's *Heraldic Visitations of Wales and Part of the Marches* (2 vols., 1846), which was the result of work he had undertaken in 1840 for the Society for the Publication of Ancient Welsh Manuscripts (The *Welsh Manuscripts Society). With the aid of W. W. E. *Wynne of Peniarth, who made extensive annotations, the work was edited in large quarto volumes. Despite its deficiencies, it is still regarded as an essential reference book for students of Welsh genealogy and heraldry.

MIDLETON, WILLIAM or **GWILYM GANOLDREF** (*fl.* 1550–*c.*1600), poet and privateer. Born at Llansannan, Denbs., a district rich in literary tradition and scholarship, he may well have inherited from his family an interest in *Cerdd Dafod. Nothing is known of his early education though it seems that he was proficient in Latin and other languages and had a knowledge of Rhetoric. He may have gone to Oxford University; certainly he was by 1575 a member of the household of Henry Herbert, Earl of Pembroke, where Welsh letters were held in high regard. The Earl's third wife was Sir Philip Sidney's sister, so Midleton found himself in the midst of active humanist study. In the mid-1580s he became an adventurer on land and sea, travelling to the Netherlands, Portugal and the West Indies, and as a privateer he was sponsored by his cousin, Thomas Midleton. Nothing is known of him after 1596; he may have died on the way home from the West Indies.

The literary activity of William Midleton is

significant in the context of Welsh humanism. His elementary treatise on the poetic art, *Bardhoniaeth, neu brydydhiaeth* (1593), reprinted in 1930 with an appendix including examples of Midleton's poetry, explains the technicalities of the art but was intended for the cultured gentleman, clergyman, lawyer or courtier rather than for the poet or scholar. Midleton's most important work was his setting of the Psalms, completed in the West Indies in 1595/6 and published posthumously by Thomas Salisbury under the title *Psalmae y Brenhinol Brophwyd Dafydh* (1603); an earlier selection had been published before Midleton sailed for the West Indies. There is something of a virtuoso quality in his use of the traditional measures. From a literary point of view, the work is not to be compared with the version of Edmund *Prys but it nevertheless represents an important contribution to the humanist ideal of the cultured gentleman.

Midleton's principal work, *Bardhoniaeth, neu brydydhiaeth*, together with a selection of his poetry, was edited by G. J. Williams (1930); see also the article by Gruffydd Aled Williams in the *Transactions* of the Denbighshire Historical Society (vol. XXIV, 1975).

Mighty Atom, The, see WILDE, JIMMY (1892–1969).

MILES, GARETH (1938–   ), short-story writer and playwright, was born in Caernarfon and educated at the University College of North Wales, Bangor. Formerly a teacher of English at Amlwch, Wrexham and Dyffryn Nantlle, and the Organizer of the teachers' union, *Undeb Cenedlaethol Athrawon Cymru*, he became a freelance writer in 1982. He has published two volumes of short stories, *Cymru ar Wasgar* (1974) and *Treffin* (1979), and three plays, *Trotsci* (1973), *Diwedd y Saithdegau* (1982) and *Unwaith Eto, 'Nghymru Annwyl* (1984). With Robert Griffiths, he wrote the manifesto of the Welsh Republican Movement, *Socialism for the Welsh People* (1980), but later joined the Welsh Communist Party.

Miles, John (1621–83), leader of the Particular or Strict Baptists, was born at Clifford, Herefs., some five miles beyond the extent of the Welsh-speaking districts of that time, and educated at Brasenose College, Oxford. In 1649 he was sent to Wales by the Glass House Church in Broad Street, London, to preach the Christian gospel in its Antipaedobaptist form, that is to say in the belief that baptism must be for adults only and by total immersion. His English-speaking Church at Ilston, Gower, developed powerful axes, the most important connecting it with the Olchon/Hay Church in his native district. A gifted organizer and an inflexible propagandist, Miles became one of the Approvers under the Act for the *Propagation of the Gospel in Wales (1650). Proof against all the ideological excesses of Commonwealth sectarians, he refused to join

Vavasor *Powell's 'A Word for God' protest against Cromwell in 1655, but his acceptance of a State living meant his certain ejection at the Restoration. By 1663 he was in Massachusetts, organizing a Baptist church at Rehoboth, but on encountering opposition there from other sects he founded his own settlement in the same State in 1667 and called it Swanzey.

MILLS, JOHN (Ieuan Glan Alarch; 1812–73), musician and author, was a native of Llanidloes, Mont. Educated locally, he began work in his father's wool-factory when he was thirteen years old. He became a minister at Ruthin in 1841, moving five years later to London, where he became a missionary to the Jewish community and an authority on the Jewish faith. His numerous books on musical subjects include *Gramadeg Cerddoriaeth* (1838), *Y Cerddor Eglwysig* (1846), *Elfennau Cerddorol* (1848) and *Y Cerddor Dirwestol* (1855). He also wrote about British Jewry in such books as *Iddewon Prydain* (1852) and *British Jews* (1853). Mills founded a magazine entitled *Y Beirniadur Cymreig* in 1845, was a frequent contributor to the Welsh periodical press and did much to improve the common people's knowledge of music and singing.

MILLS, ROBERT SCOURFIELD (Arthur Owen Vaughan, Owen Rhoscomyl; 1863–1919), adventurer and writer, was born in Southport, Merseyside, but brought up by his maternal grandmother at Tremeirchion, Flints. He adopted the name Arthur Owen Vaughan in later life and devised a literary pseudonym from the first letters of *Rhobert Scourfield Mylne* (the Middle English form of 'mill'). Having run away to sea as a boy, he worked in many countries and won fame in the Boer War as the commander of a cavalry troop.

His first book, *The Jewel of Ynys Galon* (1895), a story for boys, was followed by *The White Rose of Arno* (1897), *Old Fireproof* (1906), *Vronina* (1907), *Lone Tree Lode* (1913), and at least three other books. His boys' stories are well constructed and exciting but in some of his novels the technical excellence of the writing does not sufficiently compensate for the high romanticism of the theme. After his return to Wales he immersed himself passionately in his country's history. His *Flamebearers of Welsh History* (1905) was an influential book which went into several school editions but, like *The Matter of Wales* (1913), it did not find favour with professional historians because Owen Rhoscomyl was the first Anglo-Welsh writer of modern times who deliberately tried to stir up Nationalist feeling.

Miners' Next Step, The (1912), see under ABLETT, NOAH (1883–1935) and COOK, ARTHUR JAMES (1884–1931).

'Minister, The' (1953), a narrative poem for

four voices by R. S. *Thomas, was commissioned by Aneirin Talfan *Davies and first broadcast in the Welsh Home Service on 18 September 1952, in a series of poems called 'Radio Odes'. Like An *Acre of Land (1952), it was published by Marcele Karczewski at the Montgomeryshire Printing Company, Newtown, in the following year. The author's longest work (nearly 500 lines), it developed from a never-completed poem about the Reverend Elias Morgan and charts a Nonconformist pastor's ministry to his sour, unresponsive people in the hill country of mid-Wales. The poem was reprinted, with small textual revisions, in the author's volume, Song at the Year's Turning (1955).

Miölnir Nanteos, see POWELL, GEORGE (1842–82).

Mirabilia Britanniae (lit. 'The marvels of Britain'), the title of a tract which is appended to texts of the Cambridge recension of the *Historia Brittonum, attributed to *Nennius. It describes a series of remarkable natural phenomena to be seen in England, Scotland, Wales and Ireland. Since ten of the twenty Marvels are located in south-east Wales and the Border country it may be concluded that the author probably belonged to that region and that he is to be identified with Nennius himself, the 'editor' of the Historia. Two of the Marvels are associated with 'Arthurus miles' ('Arthur the soldier', i.e. King *Arthur): the footprint of his 'hound' (recte 'horse'?), Cafall, impressed upon a stone on the summit of Carn Cafall, Rads., during Arthur's hunt of 'the boar Troynt' (*Twrch Trwyth) described in the tale of *Culhwch and Olwen, and the grave of an otherwise unrecorded son of Arthur which was to be seen at Gamber Head, Herefs. From these Mirabilia *Geoffrey of Monmouth abstracted an account of the sixty islands containing eagles' nests on Loch Lomond, together with an account of the Severn Bore.

A Welsh version of the Mirabilia, differing widely from that of Nennius, is appended to *Enwau Ynys Prydein in The *Red Book of Hergest where the Marvels are said to number thirty-four, though only twenty-seven are given in the text. Variant versions appear in a number of later manuscripts and English renderings were made by Ranulf Higden and John of Trevisa in the fourteenth century.

For further details see T. H. Parry-Williams (ed.), *Rhyddiaith Gymraeg 1488–1609* (vol. 1, 1954) and Rachel Bromwich, *Trioedd Ynys Prydein* (1961).

Misfortunes of Elphin, The (1829), a historical romance by the English writer Thomas Love *Peacock. Set in Wales in the sixth century, it is derived from two Welsh legends: the drowning of *Cantre'r Gwaelod through the negligence of Seithenyn, and the story of *Taliesin. Both these characters are larger than life, Taliesin having supernatural powers over events and Seithenyn a sublime indifference to them. Elphin, whose misfortunes give the book its title, is the mere mortal who suffers events as they occur (see ELFFIN AP GWYDDNO). The legends are combined through Taliesin's marriage to Elphin's daughter, Melanghel, which is not found in the Welsh originals. The scope of the romance is enlarged to include King *Arthur in a rich admixture of poetry, satire and adventure which has led some critics to the judgement that the work is among the few masterpieces in English which sprang from 'the Celtic revival' of the nineteenth century.

Since Peacock's sources included The *Cambro-Briton, The Myvyrian Archaiology (1801), which is largely in Welsh, and *Pedair Cainc y Mabinogi (not translated into English at that time), it is assumed that he was assisted by his Welsh wife in the preparation for writing his book. When it appeared, The *Cambrian Quarterly Magazine described the work as 'the most entertaining book, if not the best, that has yet been published on the ancient customs and traditions of Wales'. Its author was known to be proud that Welsh antiquaries treated it as a serious and valuable addition to the study of Welsh history. Modern critics have mostly concentrated on the Gargantuan character of Prince Seithenyn ap Seithyn Saidi (to give him his full name) whom David Garnett called 'one of the immortal drunkards in the literature of the world' and to whom J. B. Priestley devoted a whole chapter in his English Comic Characters (1925).

For details about the sources of this novel see the article by Jenny Rowland in *The Anglo-Welsh Review* (vol. 26, no. 57, 1976); see also David Gallon, 'Thomas Love Peacock and Wales' in *The Anglo-Welsh Review* (vol. 17, no. 39, 1968).

Miskin or **Meisgyn**, a commot of the cantref of Penychen in *Morgannwg, lay along the west bank of the river Taff. After the collapse of the kingdom of Morgannwg it was ruled by Maredudd, the grandson of *Iestyn ap Gwrgant, the last King of Morgannwg. In 1228 Maredudd's son Hywel added *Glynrhondda to his possessions. In 1246 Richard de Clare, Lord of Glamorgan, brought all Hywel's territories under his own direct rule, administering them from the castle which he had had built at Llantrisant. By the early fourteenth century the lowland portions of the commot had been organized into the manors of Pentyrch and Clun, later considered to be a separate lordship. The hundred of Miskin (including Glynrhondda), created in 1536, ensured a degree of administrative cohesion for the early industrial community in the Cynon valley and the Constable of Miskin Higher held an important office at Aberdare in the early nineteenth century.

MITCHELL, RONALD ELWY (1905–   ),

dramatist and novelist, was born in London and educated at King's College. He is best known as a writer of one-act plays, of which he has published more than twenty. Most are comedies of rural life in north Wales and are set in the fictitious village of Pentrebychan; they include *A Handful of Sheep* (1935), *A Husband for Breakfast* (1937) and *At the Sitting Hen* (1957). A few of his short plays, however, depart from this norm and are more serious or set elsewhere, but some still have a number of Welsh characters. Mitchell has spent part of his life in the USA and one of his novels, *Design for November* (1947), is set there. His other novels, *Deep Waters* (1937), *Dan Owen and the Angel Joe* (1948) and *Three Men went to Mow* (1951), are set in north Wales, although the last-named, again making use of Pentrebychan, deals humorously with the return to the village of three expatriate Welshmen.

Mochnant, a commot of *Powys, was divided in 1166 between Owain ap Madog and Owain Cyfeiliog (*Owain ap Gruffudd ap Maredudd) when Mochnant Uwch Rhaeadr became part of Powys Wenwynwyn and Mochnant Is Rhaeadr part of Powys Fadog. The division along the river Rhaeadr proved to be permanent: from 1536 it marked the boundary between Denbighshire and Montgomeryshire and, since 1974, that between Clwyd and Powys. Pistyll Rhaeadr, a waterfall on the river, is one of the *Seven Wonders of Wales.

'Mochyn Du, Y' (lit. 'The black pig'; *c*.1854), a ballad written by a farm-servant named John Owen (1836–1915) while he was in the employment of Thomas James of Felin Wrdan, Eglwyswrw, Pembs. It is believed that the words were first published by his master's wife, without the author's knowledge. All the characters mentioned in the song, which is usually sung to the air *'Lili Lon'*, were recognizable and well known in the Eglwyswrw district at the time; the greatly lamented pig belonged to David Thomas of Parcymaes, Brynberian. Although John Owen, who later became a minister with the Calvinistic Methodists, remained deeply ashamed of the ballad until the end of his days, it became extremely popular and was sung at fairs throughout south Wales by men such as Levi *Gibbon, who is reputed to have added a few verses of his own. Later its tune achieved greater fame as the tune to which English words were composed on the subject of Crawshay *Bailey's engine.

Modern Welsh Poetry (1944), an anthology edited by Keidrych *Rhys. Among its thirty-seven contributors were most of the Anglo-Welsh poets writing at the time of its compilation, especially younger writers such as Dylan *Thomas, Nigel *Heseltine, Alun *Lewis, Davies Aberpennar (Pennar *Davies) and Lynette *Roberts who were associated with the magazine *Wales, together with a number of older poets like Glyn *Jones, Huw Menai (Huw Owen *Williams), Idris *Davies and Vernon *Watkins. A number of other poets were represented who did not go on to consolidate their reputations while a few who were not then well known, such as David *Jones, R. S. *Thomas, Emyr *Humphreys and Ormond Thomas (John *Ormond), were also included. The anthology was, for the most part, aggressively 'modern' in the fashion (much favoured by the editor) of English poetry in the 1930s. But those poets whose work was to survive the passing of the decade gave the collection a significance which compensated for its deficiencies. Only the second anthology of Anglo-Welsh poetry ever to appear, it continued to be a landmark until 'the second flowering' of the 1960s and the publication of *The *Lilting House* (ed. John Stuart Williams and Meic Stephens, 1969).

Modron, the mother of *Mabon in the tale of *Culhwch and Olwen and, according to one of the Triads, of *Owain ab Urien. Her name is derived from that of Matrona, the *Mother Goddess of Celtic mythology. The incident of Mabon's removal from his mother's bed when three nights old may be a vestige of the myth of the Great Prisoner, son of the Great Mother, who is carried off by the powers of *Annwfn. The *Peniarth Manuscripts contain a folk-tale relating how *Urien Rheged meets a washer-woman at a ford called Rhyd y Gyfarthfa. Although she is not named, it is clear that this woman is Modron for she declares herself to be the daughter of the King of Annwfn and later bears Urien a son, Owain, and a daughter, Morfudd.

Moelona, see JONES, ELIZABETH MARY (1878–1953).

Mog Edwards, 'a draper mad with love' in Dylan *Thomas's *Under Milk Wood* (1954), writes passionate letters to Myfanwy Price, but loves his money more.

'Moliant Cadwallon' (lit. 'The praise of Cadwallon'; 7th cent.), a poem surviving imperfectly in a manuscript of the seventeenth century. The author may have been *Afan Ferddig who was remembered in later tradition as the poet of *Cadwallon ap Cadfan. Although the text is allusive and problematic, the reference to Cadwallon's battles can be related to early historical accounts of his career. If the poem is correctly dated, it contains the earliest known use of the word *Cymry* (lit. 'fellow-countrymen', later 'the Welsh') and the first allusion outside Y *Gododdin to the battle of Catraeth (*c*.600). The poem has been edited by R. Geraint Gruffydd in

Astudiaethau ar yr Hengerdd / Studies in Old Welsh Poetry (ed. R. Bromwich and R. Brinley Jones, 1978).

Mona Antiqua Restaurata (lit. 'Ancient Anglesey restored'; 1723), a volume consisting of two essays on the history of his native county by Henry *Rowlands. The author had several of the talents of the geographer, the antiquary, the archaeologist and the historian but his book is marred by his own idiosyncracies, such as his belief in the close relationship between Welsh and Hebrew. Rowlands also held the view that the *Druids had had their base in Anglesey. In his 'druidomania' he saw every cromlech and stone-circle as evidence of their cult and explained place-names in the same light. His vivid description of the Massacre of the Druids revived an interest in the traditional tale. The book had some influence on English antiquaries and, in Wales, on Theophilus *Evans and Iolo Morganwg (Edward *Williams).

For further details see the article by C. L. Hulbert-Powell in the *Transactions* of the Anglesey Antiquarian and Field Society (1953).

Monica (1930), a short novel by Saunders *Lewis. Dedicated to the memory of William *Williams (Pantycelyn), it is an imaginative development of that writer's portrayal of the woman dominated by lust in his *Ductor Nuptiarum* (1777). Monica—ironically named after St. Augustine's mother—is the daughter of a Cardiff shopkeeper and his bedridden wife. Denied a normal adolescence and young womanhood by the need to look after her mother, she retreats into sexual fantasy. Eventually she captivates her sister's fiancé, marries him and goes to live in a suburb of Swansea. For some years she is able to exercise sexual domination over her husband, but pregnancy intervenes and she becomes aware that her spell is broken. Her life then loses all its purpose. She relapses into slovenly, hostile inactivity until her husband rebels and spends a night with a prostitute. Although unsuspecting, Monica is roused from her stupor and agrees to see a doctor whose suggestion that her life is in danger coincides with her discovery that her husband has contracted venereal disease. She sets out to track him down but collapses (whether dead or not is left unstated) outside a surgery from which her husband is just emerging after receiving medical treatment.

The novel is a carefully constructed and forcefully written indictment of the notion that sexual passion alone is an adequate foundation for marriage. More generally, it condemns the kind of rootless, suburban existence in which satisfaction of the appetites and social advancement are the dominant motives, unenobled by intellectual, let alone spiritual, aspirations. In spite of the reticence and delicacy of its writing, the public's reaction to the novel was almost uniformly hostile and twenty years were to pass

before it began to receive the critical attention which it deserves.

For discussion of the novel see the article by Kate Roberts in *Saunders Lewis: ei feddwl a'i waith* (ed. Pennar Davies, 1950) and that by John Rowlands in *Ysgrifau Beirniadol V* (ed. J. E. Caerwyn Williams, 1970).

Monmouthshire, The Status of, see under SHIRING OF WALES.

Montgomery, a castle constructed by command of Henry III in 1223 on a site about a mile to the south of the first Norman motte-and-bailey castle known as Hen Domen or Old Montgomery. That fortress, built by order of Roger de Montgomery, Earl of Shrewsbury, about 1075, had been destroyed in 1095 by *Cadwgan ap Bleddyn of the royal house of *Powys. Rebuilt and granted to Baldwin de Bollers in 1102, it had remained in the possession of his family for the next hundred years. New Montgomery, completed in 1224, was granted in 1228 to Hubert de Burgh, Justiciar of England, and in the same year the garrison survived a siege mounted by Welsh forces. The castle was surrendered to *Llywelyn ap Gruffudd in 1265 but was not included among his possessions listed in the Treaty of Montgomery (1267) which recognized him as Prince of Wales and confirmed his territorial gains in the March. During the *Wars of Welsh Independence (1276–77, 1282–83), and again during the *Welsh Revolt (1294–95), Montgomery was one of the main military bases used by the royal army. The castle was held during the later Middle Ages by the Earls of the March and Richard, Duke of York, resided there as constable of the castle in 1446. In 1510 the castle was granted by Henry VIII to Sir Richard Herbert of Coldbrook, near Abergavenny, Mon., and his descendant, Edward, the first Lord *Herbert of Cherbury, held it during the *Civil War. The castle was surrendered to Parliamentary forces in 1644 and dismantled five years later.

For further details see the articles by G. T. Clark and C. J. Spurgeon in *Montgomeryshire Collections* (vols. X, 1877 and LIX, 1965–66).

Morfa Rhuddlan, The Battle of (796), was fought on the banks of the river Clwyd. According to tradition (for which there is no historical evidence), Caradog, King of *Gwynedd, was killed with all his men by the forces of Offa, the aged King of Mercia, during this battle. The sombre air known as '*Morfa Rhuddlan*' is said to commemorate the massacre but the music is obviously Purcellian.

Morfran, see under TALIESIN (*fl.* 6th cent.).

Morfudd, the principal sweetheart of *Dafydd ap Gwilym, if the evidence of his poems is accepted. On balance it seems more probable that she was a girl who really existed, rather than that her name is a pseudonym for any blonde girl whom the poet admired, as was widely believed at one time. Her father's name is given once as Madawg Lawgam, though it is possible that this is no more than a name invented for the purpose of *cynghanedd. She appears to have belonged to a family of good standing. The suggestion that she was related to the Vaughans of *Nannau, Mer., rests on the identification of the Ynyr from whom a single poem alleges her descent with Ynyr Nannau, the founder of the family, but this is far from reliable. What is certain is that every geographical indication given in Dafydd's *cywyddau* places her home, like the poet's, within the hundred of Uwch Aeron, which surrounds Aberystwyth, and that Morfudd is never specifically named in *cywyddau* relating to girls from other parts of Wales. She is 'Seren Nant-y-seri' ('the star of Nant-y-seri'), a place which has been identified with Cwmseiri, about four miles from Aberystwyth. The poet, in imagination, sends the wind as *llatai (love-messenger) to her in Uwch Aeron, he beseeches the wave on the river Dyfi not to prevent him from crossing southwards to meet her at *Llanbadarn, and he lists a series of still identifiable places within the triangle bounded by Aberystwyth, Tal-y-bont and Ponterwyd which he claims to have traversed while courting her.

Fair-haired with dark brows, Morfudd had for the poet an attraction as of magic, but she continually eluded him and rarely granted him her favours. She was exasperating in her persistent trickery and faithlessness which culminated in her ultimate betrayal of her husband, a man nicknamed Y Bwa Bach ('Little Bow' or 'Little Hunchback'). The authentic existence of this man is confirmed by the inclusion of Ebowa baghan (sic) in a list of witnesses in an Assize Roll for 1344 at Aberystwyth. Even after she had become a wife and mother Dafydd continued to woo Morfudd. Indeed, two poets of the late fifteenth century, Ifan Môn and *Llywelyn ap Gutun ap Ieuan Lydan, allude to a tradition that the men of Glamorgan paid a fine to her husband after Dafydd had eloped with her. This tradition, which was also known to William *Owen Pughe, gains some slight support from aspersions made by *Gruffudd Gryg in his bardic contention with Dafydd. Morfudd is occasionally given the epithet Llwyd and this, whatever may be its significance, has been related to the fact that Dafydd himself bears it in the heading to his poem to the Cross at Chester.

The thirty *cywyddau* which name Morfudd may be classified as follows: a small group expressing a lyrical and unembittered love, a larger number of poems of entreaty, grief and exasperation at Morfudd's fickleness and failure to reward the poet for his verses, several bitter poems relating to her marriage, and poems of the *fabliau* type concerning the poet's frustrated attempts to meet Morfudd or to gain access to her home. It may be safely assumed that she is also the unnamed subject of many more *cywyddau* by Dafydd ap Gwilym. See also DYDDGU.

For further details see Ifor Williams, Dafydd ap Gwilym a'i Gyfoeswyr (1935), Thomas Parry, Gwaith Dafydd ap Gwilym (1952), the articles by D. J. Bowen in Llên Cymru (1960, 1965), the articles by Eurys Rowlands in Y Traethodydd (1960, 1967) and by John Rowlands in Ysgrifau Beirniadol VI (ed. J. E. Caerwyn Williams, 1971).

Morgan, see PELAGIUS (fl. 350–418).

Morgan (6th cent.), one of the four kings of the *Old North who, according to the Saxon Genealogies incorporated in *Nennius's *Historia Brittonum*, resisted the Anglian king Hussa. The entry in the text (in which his name occurs as Morcant) adds that, impelled by jealousy, he plotted the death of *Urien Rheged while the latter was besieging the Angles in Lindisfarne. In the cycle of poems known as *'Canu Llywarch Hen' an *englyn* refers to Morgan(t) as an enemy and describes him contemptuously as 'llyg a grafai wrth glegyr' ('a shrew scratching at a rock'). In the Life of St. Kentigern (12th cent.) by Jocelin of Furness, the saint is said to have been persecuted and his work hindered by a tyrannical king called Morken; it is possible, though not certain, that this is a reference to the same person. See also PELAGIUS (fl. 350–418).

MORGAN AP HUW LEWYS (fl. 1550–1600), poet, of Hafod-y-wern in the parish of Llanwnda, Caerns., belonged to the minor gentry and was the son of Huw Lewys of Tryfan, High Constable of the commot of Uwch Gwyrfai in 1548. An amateur, writing at a time when there were few poets in the district, he composed poems on moral and religious subjects. It is possible that his literary connections were with the family of *Glynllifon.

MORGAN ELFAEL (fl. 1528–41), a poet about whose life little is known. He addressed poems to members of the landed families of south Wales, including Sir John Mathew of Radyr, near Cardiff, Sioned, the daughter of Sir Thomas *Philipps of Picton Castle, Pembs., Lewis Gwynn of Bishton, Mon., and Gruffudd Dwn of Ystradmerthyr, Carms.

Morgan Hen (d. 1001), King of *Morgannwg, which in his time included *Gwent, succeeded his father, Owain ab Hywel ap Rhys, about 930. He remained on good terms with the court of Wessex until after the death of *Hywel Dda and at his death was said to be 129 years old.

Morgan Tud, see under EDERN.

Morgan family, The, of Tredegar Park, Mon., claimed descent from Cadifor Fawr, Lord of Cilsant in the eleventh century. A descendant of his, Llywelyn ab Ifor, married the heiress of the Tredegar estates near Newport and one of their heirs was Ifor Hael (*Ifor ap Llywelyn), head of the branch family at Gwern-y-Glepa, Bassaleg, and the chief patron of *Dafydd ap Gwilym. Many other branch families emerged in Gwent, including those at Langstone, Llantarnam and St. Pierre, and they were staunch patrons of the Welsh poets. Despite enormous fines for Recusancy, the Llantarnam branch of the family was drawn further into the Catholic camp by intermarriage with the Somerset family of *Raglan and is believed to have been instrumental in establishing the Jesuit College of St. Xavier at The Cwm, Llanrothal, in the Monnow valley. In the view of Leland the Morgans were one of only three families in the whole of Wales who qualified, by English standards, for the name of gentry. Sir John Morgan supported Henry *Tudor and held the stewardship of Machen and other offices, his descendants at Machen and Tredegar serving as prominent local administrators until the early nineteenth century. Branches of the family also emerged at Rhymney, Llanfedw, Penllwynsarth and Y Dderw, Brecs. The Llantarnam estates were sequestrated after the *Civil War and not discharged until 1653, when Sir Edward Morgan, the heir, became a Protestant. The buccaneer Henry *Morgan married into and the poet Evan Frederick *Morgan belonged to the Machen and Tredegar Park family.

MORGAN, ALISON (1930–), children's author. Born in Kent but brought up at Llangasty, Brecs., she was educated at Somerville College, Oxford, and the University of London. Her family had been domiciled in Breconshire since the early nineteenth century and she returned to Wales to teach at Newtown, Mont., in 1954, moving to Llanafan, Builth, after her marriage in 1960. Her first two books, *Fish* (1971) and *Pete* (1972), deal mainly with the adventures of young boys in the fictitious village of Llanwern, while *Ruth Crane* (1973), concerned with a slightly older age group, describes a young American girl adjusting to life in her new home in the village. *At Willie Tucker's Place* (1975) tells the story of Dan, the younger brother of one of the main characters in *Fish*, and his passion for all things military. The Llanwern stories are distinguished by their author's ability to make a gripping narrative out of everyday events, but also by her convincing presentation of young people learning to communicate with each other and with the world around them. Among her other novels are *Leaving Home* (1979) and its sequel, *Paul's Kite* (1981), in which a country boy, uprooted from his familiar world by the death of his grandfather, learns to come to terms with a new life with relatives. For younger readers Alison Morgan has written *Brighteye* (1984) and *Christabel* (1984).

Morgan, Charles (1575?–1643), soldier, was of Pencarn, Mon., the nephew of Sir Thomas *Morgan (The Warrior) and the last but one of the county's great commanders in the Protestant cause abroad. His wife, Elizabeth van Marnix van Ste. Aldegonde, whom he married in 1606/7, was the daughter of the nobleman said to be the author of the Dutch national anthem. She died in childbirth in 1608 and the elaborate tomb to her memory in the Oude Kerke at Delft was erected at the expense of her husband in 1611, when he was described as colonel in the Army of the Dutch Republic and Governor of Bergen-op-Zoom. Back in England in 1620, Morgan joined the volunteer Netherlands force of Sir Horace Vere, commanded the British contingent at Bergen and was at the defence of Breda in 1625. In the following year, Charles I's foreign policy proving as indecisive as his father's, Morgan commanded a force of some six thousand men (paid for with money raised by Sir Thomas *Myddleton and others) sent to aid the King of Denmark on the lower Elbe, but despite naval assistance from Sir Sackville Trevor of Trefalun and considerable feats of improvisation, he was starved out and had to yield Staden to Tilly in 1628. The debts from this expedition pursued him back to the Netherlands, where in 1637 he assisted in the siege of Breda and became once again governor of Bergen-op-Zoom. This 'honest and brave captain', as Essex called him, was buried at Delft.

Further details will be found in J. A. Bradney, *History of Monmouthshire* (vol. 1, 1904).

Morgan, David Thomas (c.1695–1746), lawyer and Jacobite, was of Pen-y-Graig above Quaker's Yard, Glam. Descended through his mother from the Mathew and *Stradling families, he was a High Churchman, a barrister in London and a member of a London Jacobite club. He also wrote verse and perhaps practised on the Brecknock Circuit. In November 1745 he rode from south Wales, accompanied only by the Catholic William Vaughan of Courtfield, Mon., to join the Young Pretender at Preston (see under JACOBITISM). He helped to form the Manchester Regiment and his legal knowledge often gave him the Prince's ear. But his advice that the Jacobite army should march westward to Wales (from which Sir Watkin Williams *Wynn and his Circle of the White Rose had made no answer to letters) was overruled by the Council of War. When the Pretender began his retreat, Morgan told Vaughan, 'I had rather be hanged than go to Scotland to starve', left the army and rode homeward. Arrested at Stone, he was imprisoned in Newgate and was tried, convicted and executed in July 1746. Vaughan fought at Culloden and escaped abroad, where he became a general in the Spanish army.

For further details see the article by Peter D. G. Thomas, 'Jacobitism in Wales', in *The Welsh History Review* (vol. 1, no. 3, 1962).

MORGAN, DEREC LLWYD (1943–), critic and poet, was born at Cefnbrynbrain, Carms., and educated at the University College of North Wales, Bangor, and at Jesus College, Oxford. Formerly a Lecturer in Welsh at the University College of Wales, Aberystwyth, he became Reader in Welsh at Bangor in 1983.

He has published critical works such as *Y Soned Gymraeg* (1967), studies of T. Gwynn *Jones (1972), Kate *Roberts (1974), Daniel *Owen (1977), Islwyn *Williams (1980) and books on the history of *Methodism, among which are *Taith i Langeitho* (1976), *Y Diwygiad Mawr* (1981) and a monograph on William *Williams (Pantycelyn) in the series *Llên y Llenor* (1983). His three collections of poems are *Y Tân Melys* (1966), *Pryderi* (1970) and *Gwna yn Llawen, Wr Ieuanc* (1978); he has also written an arrangement for radio of Homer's *Iliad* (1976). He was the editor of *Cerddi* (1975), *Adnabod Deg* (1977), *Bro a Bywyd Kate Roberts* (1981), *Cerddi J. W. Llannerch y Medd* (1983) and (with Bedwyr Lewis *Jones) of *Bro'r Eisteddfod: Ynys Môn* (1983). A frequent broadcaster, Derec Llwyd Morgan was Chairman of the Council of the *National Eisteddfod from 1979 to 1982. He is the husband of Jane *Edwards, the novelist.

For further details see the profile by Marged Pritchard in *Portreadau'r Faner* (1976), the article in *Barddas* (no. 46, 1980) and the note by John Rowlands in *Profiles* (1980).

MORGAN, DYFNALLT (1917–), writer, critic and translator. Born at Dowlais, Merthyr Tydfil, Glam., he was a forestry worker, hospital orderly and BBC producer before his appointment in 1964 as a Lecturer in the Department of Extra-Mural Studies at the University College of North Wales, Bangor. The author of a volume of verse, *Y Llen a Myfyrdodau Eraill* (1967), an essay on Gwenallt (David James *Jones) in the *Writers of Wales* series (1972) and critical studies of T. H. *Parry-Williams (1971) and Waldo *Williams (1975), he has also written plays for radio and edited three volumes of literary criticism, *Gwŷr Llên y Ddeunawfed Ganrif* (1966), *Gwŷr Llên y Bedwaredd Ganrif ar Bymtheg* (1968) and *Y Ferch o Ddolwar Fach* (1977); the last-named deals with the life and work of Ann *Griffiths. Among the plays he has translated into Welsh are *Sadwrn fel Pob Sadwrn* (Vaclav Cibula, 1968) and, with Eleri Eirug Morgan, *Chwe Chymeriad* (Pirandello, 1980). He has also translated the libretti of musical works, including *Y Deyrnas* (Elgar, 1971), *Rhyw Fab o'n Hoes Ni* (Tippett, 1972), *Mam yr Iesu* (Pergolesi, 1973), *Offeren yn D Leiaf* (Haydn, 1974), *Gloria* (Poulenc, 1976), *Molawd* (Verdi, 1976), *Offeren*

(Beethoven, 1977), *Gwledd Belsassar* (Walton, 1978), *Ffantasi i Gôr* (Beethoven, 1979), *Mam yr Iesu* (Dvořák, 1980) and *Nabucco* (1982). His reminiscences have been published under the title *Y Wlad sydd Well* (1984).

There is an article on Dyfnallt Morgan's poetry by D. Tecwyn Lloyd in *Taliesin* (vol. 24, 1972).

MORGAN, ELAINE (1920–), television playwright and author, was born at Pontypridd, Glam., the daughter of a colliery pumpsman, and educated at Lady Margaret Hall, Oxford, where she read English. She was a Lecturer for the Workers' Education Association until her marriage in 1945 and became a free-lance writer in the early 1950s. As a writer for television she has specialized in serials, documentaries and adaptations. Among her most memorable successes were Richard Llewellyn's *How Green Was My Valley* (1976), Jack *Jones's *Off to Philadelphia in the Morning* (1978) and *The Life and Times of Lloyd George* (1980), all of which were made for BBC Wales. She has also published *The Descent of Woman* (1972), a feminist view of evolution which was an international best-seller, *Falling Apart: the Rise and Decline of Urban Civilisation* (1976) and *The Aquatic Ape* (1982), a theory of human evolution.

MORGAN, ELENA PUW (1900–73), novelist, was born at Corwen, Mer., where after her marriage in 1931 her home became a centre of Welsh culture; among her neighbours and friends was John Cowper *Powys. She was the author of three novels for adults, namely *Nansi Lovell* (1933), which is cast in the form of an old gypsy's reminiscences, *Y Wisg Sidan* (1939) and *Y Graith* (1943); with the last-named she won the *Prose Medal at the National Eisteddfod in 1938. Among her lesser works are three children's stories: *Angel y Llongau Hedd* (1931), *Tan y Castell* (1937) and *Kitty Cordelia* which was published in *Cymru'r Plant* in 1930. Her earlier works tended to be sentimental and melodramatic but *Y Graith*, her best novel, has a maturity which is significant in the development of the *novel in Welsh. Elena Puw Morgan gave up writing in 1939 in order to look after relatives suffering from ill health.

MORGAN, ELUNED (1870–1938), writer. A daughter of Lewis *Jones (1836–1904), she was born on board the *Myfanwy* during a voyage to *Patagonia and was christened Morgan ('seaborn'). After elementary education in the Welsh colony under R. J. Berwyn, she became a pupil at Dr. Williams's School, Dolgellau, Mer. For a while she took charge of a residential school for girls at Trelew and edited *Y *Drafod*, the colony's newspaper. During her stay in Wales between 1903 and 1909, when she came under the influence of the religious revival associated with Evan *Roberts, she worked in Cardiff

Library. In 1918 she returned finally to Patagonia, emerging as an energetic leader in the colony's religious and cultural life.

Her career as a writer began when she submitted essays to eisteddfod competitions in Patagonia and contributed articles to *Cymru, the periodical edited by Owen M. *Edwards, a man whom she greatly admired. She published four books: *Dringo'r Andes* (1904), *Gwymon y Môr* (1909), the story of a voyage during which she was tied to a mast to witness the fury of the sea, *Ar Dir a Môr* (1913), an account of her visit to Palestine, and *Plant yr Haul* (1915), the story of the Incas of Peru. These works, reflecting a lively romanticism, are full of detailed descriptions of nature and vivid cameos of the Patagonian adventure, but she has been criticized for exaggerating some aspects of the life of the colony and for excessive moralizing. Her literary style, in all its intimacy and detail, has been compared with that of an accomplished letter-writer. During the last years of her life, under the Pietistic influence of the Keswick Movement, she forsook her literary pursuits and channelled her gifts as a writer into her letters to friends in Wales.

Selections of her letters have appeared in the volume *Gyfaill Hoff* (ed. W. R. P. George, 1972) and *Tyred Drosodd* (ed. Dafydd Ifans, 1977). A biography of Eluned Morgan, together with selections of her work, was written by R. Bryn Williams (1945). See also the essay on Eluned Morgan as a children's writer in *Dewiniaid Difyr* (ed. Mairwen and Gwynn Jones, 1983).

MORGAN, EVAN FREDERIC (1893–1949), poet. Born into the *Morgan family which traced its descent from Ifor Hael (*Ifor ap Llywelyn), he was educated at Eton and Christ Church, Oxford, where he was among the founders of the Celtic Society. After the First World War, as the second Viscount Tredegar, he became a patron of several philanthropic organizations in Wales. A painter whose work was exhibited at the *Salon de Paris*, he also published a novel, *Trial by Ordeal* (1921), and seven volumes of verse, much of the material in which reflects his conversion to the Roman Catholic faith as a young man. The volumes are *Fragments* (1916), *Gold and Ochre* (1917), *Psyche* (1920), *A Sequence of Seven Sonnets* (1920), *At Dawn* (1924), *The Eel* (1926) and *The City of Canals* (1929).

Morgan, George Osborne (1826–97), politician, was born of a Swedish mother at Gothenburg, where his father was a chaplain. Educated at Friar's School, Bangor, and at Shrewsbury and Oxford, he was called to the Bar in 1853 and took silk in 1869. He was one of the first group of Liberal Members of Parliament returned to Westminster from Wales in 1868. The other Member for East Denbighshire was Sir Watkin Williams *Wynn, the Tory whom he

defeated in 1885, thus ending the Wynn hegemony of 169 years. Re-elected in 1886 and 1892, Morgan was twice a Government minister, in 1880 as Judge Advocate-General (when he abolished flogging in the Army) and in 1886, when as Parliamentary Under-Secretary for the Colonies he took a particular interest in *Patagonia.

His importance to Wales, however, was much more considerable. In 1880, after ten years of trying, he secured the passage of a Burials Act, which permitted Nonconformists to perform burial in parish churchyards with their own form of service. A strong supporter of the Welsh Sunday Closing Act of 1881 (see under TEMPERANCE), he declared in the House that 'people should understand that in dealing with Wales you are dealing with an entirely distinct nationality'. In 1870 he seconded the motion for the *Disestablishment of the Church in Wales, which Gladstone resisted, and was prominent in support of the Bills of 1893 and 1895 which received first readings. His other important interest was in education. Appointed joint secretary with Hugh *Owen in 1863 to promote the idea of a national *University for Wales, he and Henry *Richard, in May 1870, tried unsuccessfully to persuade Gladstone to finance a first University College at Aberystwyth. Ten years later he was concerned, with Stuart *Rendel, to move the subsidization of Aberystwyth (thus far supported by public subscription) as a third University College of Wales, and in 1890 its status as the equal of Cardiff and Bangor was agreed by the Government. Morgan refused office in 1892, the year in which he was made a baronet.

For further details see Kenneth O. Morgan, *Wales in British Politics 1868–1922* (1963).

MORGAN, GERALD (1935–), author and editor. Born in Brighton, Sussex, of Welsh parents, he was educated at Selwyn College, Cambridge, and Jesus College, Oxford, where he learned Welsh. Formerly an English teacher at Mold and Cardigan, he worked as a tutor-librarian in the Faculty of Education at the University College of Wales, Aberystwyth, where he wrote the pamphlet, *English Literature in the Schools of Wales* (1967), and was later appointed headmaster of Llangefni School. He became headmaster of the bilingual comprehensive school Ysgol Penweddig, Aberystwyth, in 1973. His publications include a pamphlet, *Y Tair Rhamant* (1965), a travel-book about Libya, *Yr Afal Aur* (1965), a study of the Welsh language in public life, *The Dragon's Tongue* (1966), an account of the life and work of the printer John Jones (1790–1855) of Llanrwst, *Y Dyn a Wnaeth Argraff* (1982), and a selection of verse and prose, *Gwyn Fyd* (with A. K. Morris, 1978). He was briefly, in 1968, the editor of *Poetry Wales* and he also edited an anthology of Anglo-Welsh poetry, *This World of Wales* (1968).

Morgan, Griffith (Guto Nyth Bran; 1700–37), champion runner, of Nyth Bran, a farm in the parish of Llanwynno, Glam. Few facts about him are known but the many stories told about his feats were given wider currency by William *Thomas (Glanffrwd) in his history of the parish (1888). It is said that, having won a twelve-mile race against an Englishman named Prince in fifty-three minutes, Guto was slapped on the back by a woman supporter known as Siani'r Siop, and forthwith dropped dead. Ballads about Guto Nyth Bran have been written by I. D. *Hooson and Harri *Webb.

Morgan, Henry (1635?–88), buccaneer. A native of Monmouthshire, possibly of Llangattock Lingoed, he was connected by marriage with the *Morgan family of Tredegar. He emigrated to Barbados as a bond-servant in 1658 and, after serving a three-year indenture, became first a pirate and then a privateer in the West Indies. Among his most famous exploits against the Spaniards in the service of Jamaica's Governor were the sacking of Porto Bello in 1668 and his march on and capture of Panama in 1671. He was knighted by Charles II in 1674 and made Deputy-Governor of Jamaica, where he named his estates Lanrumney and Pencarn, the first after his wife's old home and the latter in commemoration of his alleged connection with that branch of the Morgan family to which Thomas *Morgan (The Dwarf) also belonged.

There is a full account of his life in *Harry Morgan's Way* (1977) by Dudley Pope; see also Rosita Forbes, *Sir Henry Morgan, Pirate and Pioneer* (1948) and Alexander Winston, *No Purchase, no Pay: Morgan, Kidd and Woodes Rogers in the Great Age of Privateers and Pirates 1665–1715* (1970).

MORGAN, JOHN (1688–1733), scholar and poet, was born at Llangelynin, Mer., and educated at Jesus College, Oxford, where he became acquainted with Edward *Lhuyd. He held the curacies of Llandegfan, Ang., and Llanfyllin, Mont., before moving in 1713 to Matchin, Essex; it is with the last-named parish that he is usually associated. The author of carols, love-songs and moral verses, he is thought to have gone to Essex in order to participate in the literary life of the *London Welsh. His most important prose-work is *Myfyrdodau Bucheddol ar y Pedwar Peth Diweddaf* (1714), dedicated to his former parishioners in Llanfyllin, which also includes *englynion* in memory of Edward Lhuyd. Perhaps because it demonstrated the influence of Latin writers, it became something of a minor classic. John Morgan also copied and collected manuscripts, corresponded with Moses *Williams and published, with a preface written in his peculiar style, a Welsh translation of Tertullian's letter to Scapula (1716).

Morgan, John or **Edward** (d. 1835), see under SCOTCH CATTLE.

MORGAN, JOHN (1827–1903), clergyman and author, was born at Newport, Pembs., and was the rector of Llanilid and Llanharan, Glam., from 1875 until his death. As well as sermons in Welsh and English, he published two volumes of verse, *My Welsh Home* (1870) and *A Trip to Fairyland or Happy Wedlock* (1896). He also translated some of the hymns of William *Williams (Pantycelyn) into English and was among the staunchest defenders of the Established Church in Wales.

MORGAN, JOHN JAMES (1870–1954), biographer and Calvinistic Methodist minister. He wrote *Hanes Dafydd Morgan, Ysbyty, a Diwygiad '59* (1906), *Cofiant Edward Matthews* (1922), *Cofiant Evan Phillips* (1930) and *Hanes Daniel Owen* (1936). His most engaging work and the one which best shows the purity and vigour of his Welsh prose style is his autobiography, *A Welais ac a Glywais* (3 vols., 1948, 1949, 1953).

MORGAN, JOHN VYRNWY (1861–1925), biographer and controversialist, was born at Cwmafan, Glam. Although he was trained for the Congregational ministry at the Memorial College, Brecon, he later became a Baptist and ultimately joined the Church of England. His literary work belongs to this later period, beginning with biographies such as those of James Rhys (Kilsby) *Jones (1896) and Edward Roberts of Cwmafan (1904), which were published in both Welsh and English versions. His two best-known books are the reference works, *Welsh Religious Leaders in the Victorian Era* (1905) and *Welsh Political and Educational Leaders in the Victorian Era* (1908). He turned to more controversial aspects of Welsh culture in such books as *The Philosophy of Welsh History* (1914) and *The Welsh Mind in Evolution* (1925), in which he expressed his distrust of traditional Welsh values and achievements, but his work as a historian has little merit.

MORGAN, KENNETH OWEN (1934–), historian, was born in Wood Green, Middlesex, to a family whose origins were in north Cardiganshire and Merionethshire. He was educated at Oriel College, Oxford. After lecturing in the History Department at University College, Swansea, he was elected a Fellow of The Queens' College, Oxford, in 1966. He has written extensively on Radical movements in Britain during the nineteenth and early twentieth centuries and is an authority on the structure of modern British party politics and the career of David *Lloyd George. His writings on the political history of Wales in the same period are equally authoritative. Among the fourteen books which he has published are *David Lloyd*

George: Welsh Radical as World Statesman (1963), *Wales in British Politics 1868–1922* (1963), *The Age of Lloyd George* (1971), *Keir Hardie* (1975), *Consensus and Disunity* (1979), *Rebirth of a Nation: Wales 1880–1980* (1981) and *Labour in Power 1945–1951* (1984). Since 1965 K. O. Morgan has been the editor of *The *Welsh History Review* and he was elected a Fellow of the British Academy in 1983.

MORGAN, MAURICE (c.1725–1802), political writer and critic, was descended from the ancient family of Morgan of Blaenbylan in the parish of Clydey, Pembs. He spent many years in north America and was secretary to the Governor of New York in 1782. The author of several pamphlets on political and social subjects, he is mostly remembered for his *Essay on the Dramatic Character of Sir John Falstaff* (1777).

MORGAN, OWEN (**Morien**; 1836?–1921), journalist and local historian. He never revealed the year of his birth but is believed to have been born in the parish of Ystradyfodwg, Rhondda, the son of a miner from Dinas. A journalist with the **Western Mail* between 1870 and 1899, he wrote—under the influence of the fictions of Iolo Morganwg (Edward *Williams) and Myfyr Morganwg (Evan *Davies)—a number of books which include *Pabell Dafydd* (1889), which is about the *Druids, *Kimmerian Discoveries* (n.d.), on the alleged Chaldean origins of the Welsh, *A Guide to the Gorsedd* (n.d.) and *A History of Pontypridd and the Rhondda Valleys* (1903). The last-named, although described by R. T. *Jenkins as 'an odd jumble of Druidism, mythology, topography, local history and biography', is of interest for its account of the industrial valleys of Glamorgan during the nineteenth century.

MORGAN, PRYS (1937–), writer and historian. Born in Cardiff, a son of Thomas John *Morgan, he was educated at St. John's College, Oxford. He has been a member of the staff of the History Department of University College, Swansea, since 1964. A prolific broadcaster and contributor to periodicals on literary and historical subjects, he was the deputy editor of **Barn* from 1966 to 1973 and is the editor of the *Transactions of the Honourable Society of *Cymmrodorion. His published works include *Background to Wales* (1968), a novel, *I'r Bur Hoff Bau* (1968), a volume of poetry, *Trugareddau* (1973), a study of the work of Iolo Morganwg (Edward *Williams) in the **Writers of Wales* series (1975), and two books on subjects of Welsh history, *The Eighteenth Century Renaissance* (1981) in the series *A New History of Wales*, and (with David Thomas), *Wales: the shaping of a Nation* (1984). He has also edited *Writers of the West* (1974), translated Camus's play *Caligula* into Welsh (1978) and contributed a chapter to

The Invention of Tradition (ed. Eric Hobsbawm and Terence Ranger, 1983). With his father, he is co-author of *Welsh Surnames* (1985), an authoritative study. From 1980 to 1983 he was the Chairman of the *Welsh Arts Council's Literature Committee.

MORGAN, RHYS (c.1700–c.1775), poet, of Cadoxton in the Vale of Neath, Glam., was the bardic pupil of Edward *Dafydd (c.1600–78) of Margam. He is significant in the literary history of the county not so much on account of his own verse, which is mediocre, but because—under the influence of men such as Edward *Lhuyd and John *Roderick—he helped to bring about a cultural revival in the uplands of Glamorgan during the first half of the eighteenth century, mainly by holding eisteddfodau on the pattern of those which had become popular in north Wales. According to Iolo Morganwg (Edward *Williams), Morgan was a carpenter, weaver and harpist who was renowned for his knowledge of the bardic grammars.

MORGAN, ROBERT (1921–), poet. Born at Penrhiwceiber, Glam., a miner's son, he left school at the age of fourteen to work with his father in the local colliery. In 1947, having won the short-story competition for two consecutive years at the South Wales Miners' Eisteddfod, he obtained a place at Fircroft College, Birmingham, and in 1953 qualified as a teacher at Bognor Regis College of Education. For many years a teacher of retarded and maladjusted boys at a school in Portsmouth, Hants., he retired in 1981 to become a full-time writer. Among his publications are five volumes of poems, *The Night's Prison* (1967), *The Storm* (1974), *On the Banks of the Cynon* (1975), *The Pass* (1976) and *Poems and Drawings* (1983), as well as a verse-play, *Voices in the Dark* (1976), and a volume of autobiography, *My Lamp Still Burns* (1981). Almost all his writing, like his painting, is concerned with his experiences as collier and teacher.

Morgan, Thomas (**The Warrior**; c.1542–95), soldier, was a younger son of William Morgan of Pencarn, Mon. He first made his name in 1572 as the musterer and commander of the first levy from England, some three hundred strong, to serve in the Netherlands against the Spaniards. The inexperience of the English and Dutch forces was bitterly exposed by the Spaniards and Morgan, back in England in 1573 to raise more men, found his most important function as an instructor in the arts of war. He was the first to train English soldiers in the use of the musket and to school officers, among them Sir Roger *Williams, in the technicalities of their profession. The largely unsuccessful fighting of the years from 1572 to 1574, described in the manuscripts of Walter Morgan and in Roger Williams's *The Actions of the Lowe Countries* (1618), was succeeded, for Morgan, by a brief period in Ireland. But he returned to the Netherlands in 1578 and remained there for the next fifteen years, fighting in countless actions, succeeding Sir Humphrey Gilbert as colonel of the regiment of English volunteers and serving as Governor of Flushing and Bergen-op-Zoom. He was knighted by Queen Elizabeth in 1587. His nephews, Sir Mathew Morgan and Sir Charles *Morgan, both commanders abroad, were inspired by his example. Lord Willoughby, a later commander-in-chief and no friend of Morgan's, thought him 'a very sufficient gallant gentleman' but 'unfurnished of language'.

For further details see Duncan Caldecott-Baird, *The Expedition in Holland 1572–1574* (1976).

Morgan, Thomas (1543–*c*.1611), Catholic conspirator. Probably a member of either the Llantarnam family or that of Machen, Mon., he dedicated himself from 1569 to the service of Mary, Queen of Scots, and was involved in several conspiracies to place her on the English throne, among them the Ridolfi Plot (1572) and the Babington Plot (1586). As one of the Welsh faction among exiled Catholics, he opposed the pro-Spanish policy of the English Jesuits who in turn accused him of being Elizabeth's secret agent working to secure Mary's execution. He wrote, with Gilbert Gifford and Edward Gratley, a work urging English Catholics to reject the ideas of the *Society of Jesus and he was believed to have been the chief author of *Leycester's Commonwealth* (1584), an anonymous libel on Elizabeth's Protestant advisers.

Morgan, Thomas (The Dwarf; 1604–79), the last of the great Gwent captains in the royal service abroad, was born at Llangattock Lingoed, Mon., probably into the same family as that to which Henry *Morgan, the buccaneer, belonged. A Welsh-speaker and never literate in English, he joined Sir Horace Vere's volunteers at the age of sixteen and saw service in the Thirty Years War until 1643, acquiring a European reputation in the conduct of siege operations. His alignment with the forces of the Parliament on his return to England marks the end of that fighting Royalist tradition among the gentry of Gwent which had been continuous since the reign of Edward III. Governor of Gloucester for the Parliament in 1645, Morgan helped reduce Chepstow and Hereford and was one of three victors over Astley at Stow-on-the-Wold in 1646. In May of that year he appeared before *Raglan Castle as commander-in-chief and his mining operations settled the fate of that last significant Royalist stronghold. After serving in Scotland for six years from 1651, most of them as major-general, he was commander at the Battle of the Dunes in the campaign to aid the French in Flanders and was knighted by Richard

Cromwell. As one of General Monck's aides he played a part in the Restoration and spent the last fourteen years of his life as Governor of Jersey. John Aubrey, William *Aubrey's great-grandson, was told Morgan was 'a little man, not many degrees above a dwarfe'.

For further details see J. A. Bradney, *History of Monmouthshire* (vol. 1, 1904) and J. R. Phillips, *Memoirs of the Civil War in Wales and the Marches* (vol. 1, 1874).

MORGAN, THOMAS JOHN (1907–), scholar and essayist, was born in the village of Glais, near Swansea, and educated at University College, Swansea, and University College, Dublin. He began his academic career as a Lecturer in the Department of Welsh at University College, Cardiff, and, after a period as a civil servant during the Second World War, he became Registrar of the *University of Wales in 1951. Returning to Swansea as Professor of Welsh Language and Literature in 1961, he remained in that post until his retirement. Prys *Morgan is one of his sons.

T. J. Morgan's most important work of scholarship is the magisterial volume on the mutation system in Welsh, *Y Treigladau a'u Cystrawen* (1952). As an essayist he is fond of returning to the Swansea Valley, in the dialect, humour and popular culture of which he is deeply interested. His first volumes of essays, *Dal Llygoden* (1937), *Trwm ac Ysgafn* (1945) and *Cynefin* (1948), are redolent of the wit which was to become typical of his work, and his contribution to the *essay form was enlarged by three more collections, *Amryw Flawd* (1966), *Dydd y Farn* (1969) and *Hirfelyn Tesog* (1969). His volume of literary criticism, *Ysgrifau Llenyddol* (1951), displays the same wide interests, light-hearted wit and catholic sensibility shown in the more personal essays, while the volume *Diwylliant Gwerin* (1972) brilliantly reflects his interest in folk-custom. The co-editor, and later editor, of the magazine Y *Llenor, T. J. Morgan has contributed an essay on W. J. *Gruffydd to the *Writers of Wales series (1970) and many essays on literary subjects to volumes such as *Ysgrifau Beirniadol* (ed. J. E. Caerwyn Williams). With Prys Morgan, he is the co-author of the authoritative study, *Welsh Surnames* (1985). From 1967 to 1972 he was Chairman of the Literature Committee of the *Welsh Arts Council.

For a bibliography of his writings and further details of his career see the volume of *Ysgrifau Beirniadol X* (ed. J. E. Caerwyn Williams, 1979) which was published in his honour.

MORGAN, WILLIAM (1545–1604), bishop and translator of the *Bible into Welsh. As the son of a tenant on the estate, he was educated at Gwydir (see under WYNN FAMILY), and from there went on in 1565 to Cambridge University, where he studied Latin, Greek and Hebrew, the original languages of the Bible, graduating in

1571 and taking the degree of Doctor of Divinity in 1583. He was at the University during the years of controversy over *Puritanism and seems to have sided with the conservatives. Some of his closest friends in Cambridge were Welshmen: Edmund *Prys, Richard *Vaughan, Gabriel *Goodman, William Hughes (d. 1600), Hugh Bellot and others. Morgan was made deacon and priest in the cathedral church of Ely in 1568. Four years later he was appointed vicar of *Llanbadarn Fawr (where he came into contact with Richard *Davies, the translator of the New Testament) and was presented to the living of Llanrhaeadr ym Mochnant, Denbs., together with Llanarmon Mynydd Mawr, in 1578. In Llanrhaeadr he met his wife, Catherine ferch George, who was one of the causes of his quarrel with Ifan Maredudd of Lloran Uchaf which was taken to the Court of Star Chamber.

Despite this litigation, it was in Llanrhaeadr that William Morgan undertook the translation of the Bible into Welsh, a dauntingly difficult task for a man far from libraries, short of money and in the midst of enemies. Had he not won the staunch support of Archbishop Whitgift, Morgan—on his own admission—would have been disheartened and would have published the *Pentateuch* only. In 1587, however, Whitgift urged him to come to London, to Gabriel Goodman's house, in order to finish the translation and publish it in the following year. The Archbishop, who saw the work as a reply to John *Penry, very probably bore the main costs of publishing this Bible. In Morgan's view it was an answer to those who argued that the remedy for ignorance of God's Word among the Welsh was to compel them to learn English and not to translate the Bible into their language: his chief aim was to save his fellow-countrymen from spiritual death and eternal punishment. By September 1588 the Welsh Bible was ready for distribution to the parishes, with a command from the Privy Council that they should buy it before Christmas. In his dedication Morgan praised the Queen and the Archbishop warmly and thanked his friends for their help.

The most striking achievements of William Morgan's Bible were the inclusion of the Old Testament, his skilful handling of the original texts, the elimination of William *Salesbury's literary quirks, the artistic, sensitive and contemporaneous nature of the translation and, most of all, the revelation of Morgan as a great writer and scholar who had a sure and intuitive grasp of the resources of the Welsh language. His work was ecstatically received by poets and writers such as *Siôn Tudur, Ieuan Tew, Thomas Jones, Siôn Dafydd *Rhys, Hugh *Lewis and others. Morris *Kyffin wrote of it in his *Deffynniad Ffydd Eglwys Loegr* (1594) that it was 'a necessary, excellent, choice and learned work, for which Wales can never repay or thank him as much as he deserves'. At the very time

when the *Bardic Order was facing extinction, it was Morgan who ensured that the purity, accuracy and strength of the poetic vocabulary should live on. His Bible had far-reaching influences on the religion, language, literature and nationhood of Wales. More than anything else, it rooted the reforming faith among the Welsh and did much to save the language from degenerating into a bundle of dialects or even dying out altogether. His work was the foundation and example for all the literature written in Welsh after the end of the sixteenth century and it helped to create a consciousness of national identity over the centuries which followed. The Bible of 1588 was as influential in keeping alive the idea of an independent Wales as the defeat of the Armada (1588) was in maintaining English independence.

In 1595 William Morgan was appointed Bishop of *Llandaf, a poor diocese, containing many Recusants, where he continued with his literary work, revised his translation of the New Testament and also published a new edition of the Prayer Book, the first to be published in accordance with the text of Morgan's Bible and probably prepared for the press by him. He also encouraged other authors such as John *Davies of Mallwyd, who was to be responsible for the Bible of 1620, Edward *James, the translator of *The Book of Homilies*, and James *Parry, who rendered some of the Psalms into Welsh. In 1601 Morgan was moved to *St. Asaph, another poor diocese, where he renovated the roof of the cathedral church at his own cost and began the repair of the bishop's palace. He frequently welcomed poets to his residence and in 1603 completed another version of his New Testament. The manuscript of the latter work was lost when Thomas Salisbury fled from the plague in London in 1603. William Morgan may also have compiled a Welsh dictionary, mentioned by John Davies of Mallwyd, but no trace of it has survived. At St. Asaph he was involved in bitter quarrels with David Holland of Teirdan, from which Sir John *Wynn had to rescue him. Then he fell out with Sir John over the living of Llanrwst. The latter insisted, among other things, that Morgan had promised him the patronage of Llanrwst, but the bishop maintained that he ought not to repay him favours at the expense of the interests of the Church. Before they could be reconciled Morgan died, a poor man whose goods were worth only a little more than a hundred pounds and who was in debt to the Crown on account of some of his clergy. The place of his burial at St. Asaph is not marked by any stone but outside the cathedral stands a memorial to the translators of the Welsh Bible; Morgan is placed at its centre, an honour which he richly deserves for there is none to whom the Welsh nation owes a greater debt.

Biographies of William Morgan have been written by Charles Ashton (1891), W. Hughes (1891), T. Evan

Jacob (1891), G. J. Roberts (1955) and R. T. Edwards (1968); see also the chapter by R. Geraint Gruffydd in *Y Traddodiad Rhyddiaith* (ed. Geraint Bowen, 1970).

MORGAN, WILLIAM (Gwilym Gellideg; 1808–78)

MORGAN, WILLIAM (Gwilym Gellideg; 1808–78), poet and musician, was a Carmarthen man who spent most of his life in Gellideg, near Merthyr Tydfil, Glam., where he worked as a miner. A poor but cultured man, he won prizes for poetry in the strict and free metres, a selection of which was published in the volume *Cerbyd yr Awen* (1846). He is remembered as the author of the well-known ballad, 'P'le byddaf 'mhen can mlynedd?'.

Morgannwg, the name loosely applied in the early Middle Ages to most of south-east Wales. After the *Norman Conquest it denoted more precisely the Marcher lordship situated between the rivers Nedd and Taf. The *Act of Union (1536) added *Gower to create the new shire of Glamorgan, which remained the unit of local government until 1974 when the county was subdivided into West, Mid and South Glamorgan. Rice *Merrick in his *Booke of Glamorganshire Antiquities* (1578) claimed that Glamorgan originally included only that part of Morgannwg on the coastland between the rivers Ogwr and Ely, that is to say, *Bro Morgannwg* or the Vale of Glamorgan.

From the fourteenth century Morgannwg had its own lively literary tradition. It decayed in the late sixteenth century but began to recover in the *Blaenau* (Uplands) in the eighteenth century and took on a new brilliance in the work of Iolo Morganwg (Edward *Williams). One of the districts most renowned for its poets was that of *Tir Iarll. During the twentieth century the greater part of *Anglo-Welsh literature has been written by writers from the industrial valleys of Glamorgan, so much so that, for many English readers, Glamorgan has seemed to typify Wales itself.

The literature of the region up to the time of Iolo Morganwg was analysed by G. J. Williams in his magisterial work, *Traddodiad Llenyddol Morgannwg* (1948); see also J. S. Corbett, *Glamorgan* (1925), T. B. Pugh (ed.), *Glamorgan County History* (1971), G. Williams, *Glamorgan County History* (1974) and Rice Merrick, *Morganiae Archaiographia* (ed. B. Ll. James, 1983).

Morien, see MORGAN, OWEN (1836?–1921).

MORRIS BROTHERS, THE, antiquaries and writers, were brought up at Pentre-eiriannell, Penrhosllugwy, Ang. The eldest, Lewis *Morris (1701–65), was the most gifted of the four. The second brother, **Richard Morris** (1703–79), while still a boy, made a collection of the traditional songs and verses of Anglesey which is an invaluable source of information about Welsh folk-literature; it was edited by T. H. *Parry-Williams in 1931. At the age of eighteen, Richard went to London, where he

was to spend the rest of his life, for much of the time as a clerk in the Navy Office. It was he, more than anyone else, who was responsible for the founding of the Honourable Society of *Cymmrodorion in 1751. He supervised new editions of the Welsh Book of Common Prayer (1746, 1752, 1768 and 1770) and of the Bible (1746 and 1752). The third brother, **William Morris** (1705–63), stayed in Anglesey, where he was employed as Collector of Customs at Holyhead. Like his brothers, he collected Welsh manuscripts, but his main interest was in his garden and his unique collection of plants. The youngest of the four, **John Morris** (1706–40), joined the Navy and died during the attack on Cartagena in Spain, but he too shared his brothers' interest in folklore and literature.

The brothers were in regular correspondence with one another and about a thousand of their letters, written in Welsh and in English, have been preserved, some four hundred of which are in the hand of William writing from Holyhead. The letters, from one brother to another and to others of the Morris Circle, are an especially rich source of material about literary and cultural matters in the Wales of their day and parts of them have considerable literary merit. All four brothers, together with their nephew, **John Owen** (d. 1759), the son of their sister Ellen, had creative talent and a splendid command of colloquial and literary Welsh.

The letters have been edited by J. H. Davies, *The Letters of Lewis, Richard, William and John Morris* (2 vols., 1907 and 1909) and by Hugh Owen, *Additional Letters of the Morrises of Anglesey* (2 vols., 1947 and 1949). For further details see Saunders Lewis, *A School of Welsh Augustans* (1924), the monograph by W. J. Gruffydd in the *St. David's Day* series (1939), R. T. Jenkins and Helen M. Ramage, *A History of the Honourable Society of Cymmrodorion* (1951), and the article by Bedwyr Lewis Jones on the prose-writings of the Morris Brothers in *Y Traddodiad Rhyddiaith* (ed. Geraint Bowen, 1970).

MORRIS, BRIAN (1930–), poet and critic. Born in Cardiff and educated at Worcester College, Oxford, he was Professor of English Literature at Sheffield University from 1971 until his appointment as Principal of St. David's University College, Lampeter, in 1980. The general editor of the New Mermaid Drama series and the New Arden Shakespeare, he is the author of two volumes of poetry, *Tide Race* (1976) and *Stones in the Brook* (1978), and a frequent broadcaster on literary topics.

MORRIS, DAVID or **DAFYDD** (1744–91), hymn-writer and preacher with the Calvinistic Methodists. Born at Lledrod, Cards., he was a *drover in his younger days, but settled at Twr-gwyn in the parish of Troed-yr-aur, Cards., in 1774. Of his hymns, collected under the title *Cân y Pererinion Cystuddiedig* (1773), the finest is 'N'ad im fodloni ar ryw rith o grefydd heb ei grym', which is included in many contemporary collections.

MORRIS, EDWARD (1607–89), poet, was born at Perthllwydion, Cerrig-y-Drudion, Denbs., and was by trade a *drover. Calling himself 'The Poet of Gloddaeth', he wrote a great deal for the *Mostyn family but also composed elegies for Sir John Owen of Clenennau, Gabriel *Goodman and Rowland *Vaughan of Caergai. He died while on a cattle-drive into England and was buried somewhere in Essex. Huw *Morys was among the five friends who wrote elegies for him.

The love-songs of Edward Morris are simple, tender and melodious, among the best of their kind, and like those of Huw Morys, were meant to be sung to popular contemporary airs. He was a master of the *tri-thrawiad* metre, with its intricate rhyme-scheme and *cynghanedd* in the second and fourth lines. Among his best-known poems are 'Carol Ciwpyd' and 'Carol yn gyrru'r Haf at ei gariad', the first of which is a dialogue between the poet and Cupid, who visits him in a dream, and the second a poem in which he sends Summer as a messenger to his sweetheart. Although composed for the common people's pleasure, these poems are as intricate as if they had been written in traditional *cynghanedd*. Morris also composed many *awdlau* and *cywyddau* on the pattern set by the poets of the classical period, but he avoided their obscure terminology and the Anglicized forms which are found in the work of some of his contemporaries.

Steeped in the Scriptures, Morris also wrote Christmas carols and poems warning against drunkenness, covetousness and foul language, but he did not enter into religious or political controversy. His concern for the moral state of the common people led him, at the instigation of Margaret Vaughan of *Llwydiarth (Mont.), to undertake the translation of John Rawlet's *The Christian Monitor* into Welsh and it was published at her expense as *Y Rhybuddiwr Christ'nogawl* (1689).

For further details see the selection of Edward Morris's work edited by Owen M. Edwards in the series *Cyfres y Fil* (1904) and the article by D. Eifion Evans in *Yr Haul* (April–July, 1947).

MORRIS, JAN formerly **JAMES** (1926–   ), travel-writer and historian, was born at Clevedon, Somerset, and educated at Lancing and Christ Church, Oxford. As James Morris he joined the editorial staff of *The Times* in 1951 and moved to *The Guardian* in 1957. His earlier books grew out of his work as a journalist and traveller. Combining an understanding of current events with an appreciation of the deeper stresses of history and a delight in new places, they include *Sultan in Oman* (1957), *Venice* (1960), *The Presence of Spain* (1964), *Oxford* (1965) and five books of travel essays. He also published a trilogy about the British Empire, *Pax Britannica* (1968), *Heaven's Command* (1974) and *Farewell the Trumpets* (1978). The first book

she wrote as Jan Morris, *Conundrum* (1974), describes her lifelong trans-sexual dilemma and its eventual solution. The increasing importance of her Welsh identity has been emphasized in her two anthologies, *My Favourite Stories of Wales* (1980) and *Wales* (1982), in her extended essay, *Wales, the First Place* (1982) and in *The Matter of Wales: Epic Views of a Small Country* (1984).

MORRIS, KENNETH VENNOR (Cenydd Morus; 1879–1937), writer of fantasy. Born at Ammanford, Carms., he was taken to live in London at the age of six. After leaving school in 1896 he spent several years in Dublin, where he became a close friend of the writer A.E. (George Russell). A lifelong Theosophist, adhering to the faction led by Katherine Tingley, he lived for many years in the community founded by her at Point Loma in California. After returning to Wales in 1930, he published from his home in Ferndale, Rhondda, the monthly magazine *Y Fforum Theosophaid*. His first work of fiction, *The Fates of the Princes of Dyfed* (1913), published under his pseudonym, is a retelling of parts of *Pedair Cainc y Mabinogi*. In *The Secret Mountain* (1926), a collection of short stories, he expanded his interest in myth to include tales from several other countries, notably India and China. But his reputation among *aficionados* of modern fantasy is based on his last major work, *Book of the Three Dragons* (1930), in which he returned to themes from the Mabinogion. He also collaborated with Cyril *Hodges in the writing of *China Speaks* (1941), a sequence of prose translations.

MORRIS, LEWIS (Llewelyn Ddu o Fôn; 1701–65), scholar, poet and cartographer, was the eldest of the four *Morris Brothers of Anglesey. He was born in the parish of Llanfihangel Tre'r-beirdd (either at Tyddyn-melys or at Fferam) and grew up at Pentre-eiriannell, Penrhosllugwy, on the other side of Bodafon mountain. Little is known of his early life, but he mastered the rudiments of land-surveying and in 1724 was employed by Owen Meyrick of Bodorgan to survey the estate's scattered lands in Anglesey. In 1729 he was appointed searcher at the custom-house of Holyhead and Beaumaris. His contact with mariners convinced him of the need for a properly surveyed chart of the Welsh coastline, a project on which he embarked single-handed in 1737. It led to two cartographical publications in 1748, namely a chart of the coast from the Orme to Milford Haven and an atlas, *Plans of Harbours, Bars, Bays and Roads in St. George's Channel*, containing twenty-five detailed maps. A second enlarged edition of the *Plans*, edited by his son William Morris, was published in 1801.

His cartographic work took Lewis Morris to Aberystwyth about 1742 and there his interest was aroused in the lead-mining industry of that area. He never returned to live in Anglesey but found employment as a collector of customs at Aberdyfi. In 1744 he was commissioned to survey the Crown manor of Perfedd between the rivers Clarach and Rheidol, which led to his appointment in 1746 as Deputy-Steward of the Crown manors in Cardiganshire. In his official capacity he became involved in ceaseless litigation between the Crown grantees of lead-mining rights and the local gentry, including Herbert *Lloyd of Peterwell, who persistently challenged the Crown's right to mine for lead. Morris made his position more difficult by engaging in prospecting ventures of his own and by responding to all criticism with characteristic haughtiness, so that his years in Cardiganshire were marked by controversy and acrimony on all sides. From 1746 until 1757 he made his home at Galltfadog, near Capel Dewi, and he died at Pen-bryn, Goginan.

One of Lewis Morris's anxieties, even as a young man, was that the traditional patrons of Welsh literature were being attracted more and more by English books and English culture, and in order to counter this tendency he resolved to produce an entertaining body of writing in Welsh. He began by publishing, from his own printing-press at Holyhead, the first part of *Tlysau yr Hen Oesoedd* (1735), a selection of light-hearted verse and prose in Welsh. He also composed, especially between 1730 and 1750, a considerable number of short prose works and poems, mostly in Welsh, for circulation among friends such as William Vaughan, the squire of *Nannau and *Corsygedol. These works include satirical letters from 'the world of the stars' and from Purgatory, and some draw on writing in English by Tom Brown, Swift and L'Estrange. Morris also wrote poems in the strict and free metres, often bawdy and almost always humorous. A selection of the less indecent of the poems was included in *Y Diddanwch Teuluaidd* (1763). A further aspect of Lewis Morris's concern for reviving Welsh literature was the constant support which he gave to younger poets, such as Goronwy *Owen, Ieuan Fardd (Evan *Evans) and Edward *Richard, all of whom he tutored in poetry. Towards the end of his life he was regarded as an authority on the Welsh language in both Wales and England.

History and antiquities, and especially the early history of Wales, were among Lewis Morris's principal interests. He took it upon himself to defend the Welsh nation's reputation by sending information concerning its history to foreign scholars and by seeking to defend the authenticity of *Brut Tysilio*. His dictionary of personal names and place-names referred to in Welsh tradition, entitled *Celtic Remains*, was published in part in 1878 under the editorship of Daniel Silvan *Evans. Morris had other ambitious plans, including a new, expanded edition of the dictionary of John *Davies of Mallwyd, a large

volume on the antiquities and natural history of Anglesey, an edition of *Dafydd ap Gwilym's poems and a collection of Welsh proverbs. Although he did not find the time to complete any of these projects, he left behind him a large body of manuscripts which helped to preserve Welsh learning and literature at a time when there was no institution to undertake that responsibility. He was, undoubtedly, the prime mover in the classical revival of Welsh learning and writing during the eighteenth century and he was also a more important poet and prose-writer than has hitherto been acknowledged.

For further details see Saunders Lewis, *A School of Welsh Augustans* (1924), R. T. Jenkins and Helen M. Ramage, *A History of the Honourable Society of Cymmrodorion* (1951), Hugh Owen (ed.), *The Life and Works of Lewis Morris* (1951), A. O. H. Jarman, 'Lewis Morris a Brut Tysilio' in *Llên Cymru* (vol. II, 1952–53) and the book by Tegwyn Jones, *Y Llew a'i Deulu* (1982).

MORRIS, LEWIS (1833–1907), poet. Born at Carmarthen, the son of the town clerk and a great-grandson of Lewis *Morris (Llewelyn Ddu o Fôn), he was educated at the Queen Elizabeth Grammar School there, at Cowbridge School, Sherborne and Jesus College, Oxford. Called to the Bar, he embarked on a career which in its later stages was distinguished by his zeal for the fostering of higher education in Wales and the establishment of a national *University. From 1878 to 1896 he was joint-secretary and subsequently joint-treasurer of the University College of Wales, Aberystwyth, and thereafter its Vice-President until his death. A Liberal in politics, he sought election as a Member of Parliament on several occasions, but without success.

Three years after Tennyson's death in 1892, Lewis Morris was knighted and began to entertain hopes of becoming Poet Laureate. But the offer was withdrawn, it is thought, as a result of Queen Victoria's disapproval when she learned that he had a common-law wife and three children, a fact which he had hitherto managed to conceal from the world. It was during the delay over this appointment that, having complained to Oscar Wilde that there seemed to be a conspiracy of silence against him, he asked, 'What shall I do?', and drew the famous reply, 'Join it'.

He was a prolific and popular poet who wrote a number of poems based on incidents in Welsh history and mythology, some of them patriotic. Besides *The *Epic of Hades* (1876–77), his best-known work, he published among other volumes *Songs of Two Worlds* (3 vols., 1872, 1874, 1875), *Gwen* (1880), *The Ode of Life* (1880), *Songs Unsung* (1883) and *Songs of Britain* (1887). Unfortunately, he was an imitator of his friend, Alfred, Lord Tennyson, but lacked his genius. His verse now seems grandiose or vapid in both style and content and almost totally lacking in inspiration, yet his *Collected Works* sold many thousands of copies and enjoyed much public acclaim.

Morris's most interesting poem is '*Gwen*', set in the parish of Llangunnor, near Carmarthen, where he lived and was buried. The story of the love of a young aristocrat for a vicar's daughter, it consists of a series of lyrical monologues tracing the course of the doomed courtship. Its involvement with the lovers' plight makes it the most moving of Morris's long poems and it seems to reflect aspects of his own secretive love-life. The poem also contains some effective descriptions of the Towy valley, as does 'The Physicians of *Myddfai'. It is this ability to capture the spirit of place which marks some of Morris's best work and is now most likely to afford the reader pleasure.

One of the paradoxes of Morris's life was that, although he was a man of deep feeling and occasionally impulsive action, his verse, in general, lacks a sense of compulsion. For the most part, a technical facility combines with a superficial treatment of theme. Ironically, his most committed writing is to be found in his collection of essays, *The New Rambler* (1905), where he condemns blood sports and writes on a number of other topics with a vigour which most of his verse lacks.

There is an essay on Sir Lewis Morris by Douglas Phillips in the *Writers of Wales* series (1981).

MORRIS, ROGER (*fl.* 1580–1607), copyist, of Coedytalwrn, Llanfair Dyffryn Clwyd, Denbs. The manuscripts in his hand which are extant, and which now belong to the *Llanstephan, Mostyn and *Peniarth collections, reveal the breadth of his interests: they include poetry, *Lives of the Saints, heraldry, history, genealogy, romances, grammars and botany. He had access to manuscripts such as The *Black Book of Carmarthen and The *White Book of Rhydderch, and he copied parts of them. Some of his manuscripts were by 1607 in the possession of Thomas *Evans (Thomas ab Ifan) of Hendreforfudd.

MORRIS, WILLIAM (1889–1979), poet, a native of Blaenau Ffestiniog, Mer., was educated at Bala Theological College and served as a Calvinistic Methodist minister in Anglesey and Caernarfonshire. He won the *Chair at the National Eisteddfod in 1934 for his awdl, '*Ogof Arthur*', and was Archdruid from 1957 to 1959. His volumes of poetry include *Clychau Gwynedd* (1946), *Sgwrs a Phennill* (1950), *Atgof a Phrofiad* (1961), *Oriau Difyr a Dwys* (1963), *Cwmni'r Pererin* (1967), *Hedd Wyn* (1969) and *Crist y Bardd* (1975). A collection of his poems was edited by his daughter, Glennys Roberts, under the title *Canu Oes* (1981).

MORRIS-JONES, JOHN (1864–1929), scholar, poet and critic. Born at Trefor, Llandry-garn, Ang., but brought up at Llanfair-pwll, he was educated at Christ College, Brecon, and Jesus College, Oxford, where he graduated in Mathematics. His interest in Welsh studies was awakened by Sir John *Rhŷs, Professor of Celtic at Oxford, under whom he studied for a while, and he was one of the founder members of *Cymdeithas Dafydd ap Gwilym in 1886. In 1889 he was appointed Lecturer in Welsh at the University College of North Wales, Bangor, becoming Professor of Welsh six years later. He was knighted in 1918.

One of a new generation of scholars associated with the *University of Wales at the turn of the century, John Morris-Jones was determined to set studies of the Welsh language and its literature on a firm academic foundation. He published, jointly with John Rhŷs, an edition of The *Book of the Anchorite (1894) and edited a diplomatic edition of *Gweledigaetheu y Bardd Cwsc (1896), the introduction to which was important not only for its study of Ellis *Wynne's sources, but also for its discussion of style. By demonstrating the splendour and purity of the language used in Y Bardd Cwsc he found it possible to denounce the alien forms which had crept into Welsh as a result of the baneful influence of William *Owen Pughe and others in the nineteenth century. Such zeal for the purity of the language was to become the paramount concern of his life's work. His volume, *A Welsh Grammar, Historical and Comparative* (1913), placed him—despite some weaknesses—in the company of Gruffydd *Robert and John *Davies of Mallwyd as one of the three great grammarians of the Welsh language, a reputation consolidated by his *Welsh Syntax* (1931), published posthumously.

A pioneer in the movement for a revised *Orthography of Welsh, he served as secretary of a committee set up in 1885 by *Cymdeithas yr Iaith Gymraeg (The Society for the Utilization of the Welsh Language) which published the fruits of its discussions in the volumes *Welsh Orthography* (1893) and *Orgraff yr Iaith Gymraeg* (1928), still regarded as authoritative works on the subject. He made a similar contribution to the study of Welsh prosody with *Cerdd Dafod* (1925) in which the system of *cynghanedd and the strict metres was described and analysed. The scientific detail and regard for symmetry which characterize his analyses of language and metrics owe much to his study of Mathematics. Another of his important works was *Taliesin*, a study of the poems addressed to *Urien Rheged and *Owain ab Urien found in The *Book of Taliesin, which was published in the journal, Y Cymmrodor (vol. XXVIII), although this work has since been largely supplanted by that of Ifor *Williams.

As an eisteddfod critic who legislated on language and metrics, John Morris-Jones was highly regarded and his influence was, for the most part, extremely beneficial. Many decades were to pass before his critical standards and etymological theories were called into question. He was among the first to doubt the authenticity of *Gorsedd Beirdd Ynys Prydain* and in a series of five articles in the magazine *Cymru*, published in 1896, he came to the conclusion that its ceremonies had been invented by Glamorgan poets in the seventeenth century. In this he was incorrect but no other conclusion was possible from the evidence known to him at that time. An account of his subsequent research is found in his preface to G. J. Williams's *Iolo Morganwg a Chywyddau'r Ychwanegiad* (1926).

John Morris-Jones published only one volume of poetry, *Caniadau* (1907), which includes his two famous awdlau, '*Cymru Fu: Cymru Fydd*' and '*Salm i Famon*', as well as a number of skilful, charming lyrics. Whereas the awdlau are given to political exhortation and satire in a polished, vigorous style, the lyrics abound in a Romanticism which is too sentimental for modern taste. In the same volume are to be found a number of his translations from Heine and Omar Khayyám. The linguistic elegance of these translations was intended to be a model for other poets and the pagan sensuousness of Omar's verses was badly needed in Welsh poetry after the heavy philosophizing of the *Bardd Newydd*. Although he does not rank as a major poet, John Morris-Jones's influence on the development of Welsh poetry during the first years of the twentieth century was unique.

For further details see the essay by Thomas Parry in the *St. David's Day* series (1958), the articles by J. E. Caerwyn Williams in the *Transactions of the Honourable Society of Cymmrodorion* (1965 and 1966), the chapter by Geraint Bowen in *Y Traddodiad Rhyddiaith yn yr Ugeinfed Ganrif* (ed. Geraint Bowen, 1976), the critical article by John Gwilym Jones in *Swyddogaeth Beirniadaeth* (1977) and the chapter by Bedwyr Lewis Jones in *Gwŷr Môn* (1979); see also Dafydd Glyn Jones, 'Criticism in Welsh', in *Poetry Wales* (vol. 15, no. 3, Winter, 1979).

Mortimer's Cross, The Battle of (1461), one of the major confrontations in the Wars of the Roses. The defeat of the Lancastrian forces at a site near Leominster was followed by the execution of Owain *Tudor, the accession to the English throne of Edward IV and the elevation to the peerage, as Lord Herbert, of Sir William *Herbert (d. 1469) of Raglan. *Lewys Glyn Cothi (Llywelyn y Glyn), an associate of the sons of Gruffudd ap Nicholas of *Dinefwr, was involved in the campaign which led to the battle. He celebrated the Yorkist ascendancy in an awdl which praised both the new king and Lord Herbert and in another he praised Sir Richard Herbert, Lord Herbert's brother.

MORUS AP DAFYDD AB IFAN AB EINION (**Morus Dwyfech**; *fl.* 1523–90), poet, was a native of *Eifionydd who took his bardic

name from the river Dwyfech (now called Dwyfach) near Cricieth. A graduate of the *Caerwys Eisteddfod of 1523, he wrote poems in praise of most of the landed families of *Gwynedd, especially those of Talhenbont and *Cefnamwlch, whose household poet he was. His work includes religious and satirical poems and a series of *englynion* pleading the cause of the Llŷn gentry imprisoned in London for their opposition to the schemes of the Earl of Leicester in the Forest of Snowdon.

Morus Cyfannedd, see JONES, MORUS (1895–1982).

Morus Dwyfech, see MORUS AP DAFYDD AB IFAN AB EINION (*fl.* 1523–90).

Morus, Cenydd, see MORRIS, KENNETH VENNOR (1879–1937).

MORYS, HUW (**Eos Ceiriog**; 1622–1709), the most prolific and gifted Welsh poet of the seventeenth century, was probably born in the commot of Hafodgynfor in the parish of Llangollen, Denbs. His father, Morris ap Siôn ap Ednyfed, and his family, moved to Pontymeibion in Dyffryn Ceiriog about 1647. Huw may have attended either the Free Grammar School in Oswestry or Ruthin Grammar School. In one of his poems he complained that he had spent seven years as an apprentice tanner at Overton, Flints., but he does not appear to have followed this trade, for there is evidence which shows that he spent all his adult life, unmarried, helping his father, and later his brother, to farm Pontymeibion. The family was moderately affluent, owning its own land, and socially acceptable among the squireens of Dyffryn Ceiriog. Among his patrons were Sir William Williams of Glascoed, William Owen of *Brogyntyn, Sir Thomas *Mostyn of Gloddaeth and Sir Thomas *Myddleton of Chirk Castle.

A devout Churchman and an uncompromising Royalist, Huw Morys lived through the *Civil War and the Commonwealth, witnessing the Roundheads' desecration of the parish church of Llansilin, where he was warden. In his view, Cromwell's success was to be deplored: his political poems are highly critical of the Puritans for overthrowing the established order and for their expulsion of licensed clergymen who were replaced, Morys complained, by ignorant laymen. The opinions of the leading Welsh Puritans, Walter *Cradock, William *Erbery, Morgan *Llwyd and Vavasor *Powell, he thought were highly dangerous. The religious and social reformers of his day left him unmoved and he continued to believe in the Divine Right of Kings and in the merits of a stable, conservative society. Unlike Rowland *Vaughan of Caer-gai and William Phylip of Hendre Fechan, Ardudwy, however, Huw

Morys prudently refrained from openly slandering the Roundheads, preferring instead the use of allegory, and thus he avoided the persecution meted out to Cromwell's critics. He wrote two interludes on the subjects of the Civil War and the Prodigal Son, both of which, like his political poems, vividly reflect the social life of his time but which also abound with his political prejudices.

It was as a poet that Huw Morys excelled. Although he composed in the strict traditional metres, the diction and craft of his *cywyddau* cannot be compared with the work of the great masters of the fifteenth century. His unique contribution to Welsh prosody was that he developed, or perhaps invented, a new verse-form based on the traditional accented metre but embellished with *cynghanedd*, which was more closely related to the strict metres peculiar to *Cerdd Dafod* than to the traditional accented free verse; at the same time he sought to maintain the standards of the *cywyddwyr*. The types of *cynghanedd* which lent themselves to this metrical form are based either on internal rhyme or a combination of rhyme and alliteration. The diction contains a fair proportion of colloquial forms and English borrowings, which made it easier to set the verse to well-known airs. Besides poems requesting gifts, love-poems, elegies and Christmas carols, he also composed a large number of *May Day and *Summer Carols. Although the metres are generally of English origin, by his deft use of *cynghanedd* he adapted them and gave them peculiarly Welsh forms.

Just as *Dafydd ap Gwilym had established the pre-eminence of the *cywydd*, so Huw Morys founded a new school of poets who excelled in composing his type of poetry. His great achievement was the blending of words to music, thus giving his poems an aesthetic rather than an intellectual appeal. A good deal of his poetry is of social importance and provides an insight into the daily life and customs of the common people who were his contemporaries. Of the eighteen elegies composed by him in free verse, four—including that for *Barbara Miltwn (Middleton)—are in the form of a dialogue between the living and the dead.

An edition of Huw Morys's poems was published by Walter Davies (Gwallter Mechain) under the title *Eos Ceiriog, sef casgliad o bêr ganiadau Huw Morys* (2 vols., 1823) and a small selection was made by Owen M. Edwards for the series *Cyfres y Fil* (1902); a biography of the poet was published by T. R. Roberts (Asaph) in 1902.

Mostyn family, The, of Mostyn Hall, Flints., was descended from Ieuan Fychan, poet and kinsman of the *Tudors of Penmynydd, and his wife Angharad, the heiress of Hywel ap Tudur of Mostyn. Their son Howel married Margaret, the heiress of Gloddaeth, Caerns., an estate which included much of the land upon which the town of Llandudno was later built. Howel's son, Richard ap Howel (d. 1539), fought for Henry Tudor at the battle of *Bosworth (1485) but refused to follow the King to London, making the well-known declaration, 'I dwell among my own people'. He was president of the first *Caerwys Eisteddfod (1523) and the family tradition of patronage of the poets was continued by his son, Thomas (d. 1558), the first of the family to assume the surname of Mostyn and whose younger son, Piers, was the ancestor of the Mostyns of Talacre. Piers's great-great-grandson, Edward, was created a baronet in 1670; his descendants included eleven successors to the title as well as Francis Edward Mostyn (1860–1929), the son of the eighth baronet and the first Roman Catholic archbishop of Cardiff.

Thomas's elder son, William (d. 1576), initiated the long association between the Mostyns and the Parliamentary representation of Flintshire, and was one of the Commissioners appointed to hold the second Caerwys Eisteddfod (1567). William's son, Thomas (d. 1618), a member of the Council of Wales, founded the famous Mostyn library. Thomas's great-grandson, Roger (1623–90), who was the foremost defender of the Royalist cause in north-east Wales, was said to have spent some sixty thousand pounds in the interests of the king (for which he was made a baronet in 1660); he was also active in exploiting the coal and lead resources of his estate. His son, Thomas (1651–1700?), the second baronet, greatly expanded the family library and was an authority on Welsh genealogy. The third and fourth baronets, Roger (1673–1734) and Thomas (1704–58), maintained the family's interest in literature. To the former George Farquhar dedicated *The Constant Couple* (1700); the latter added to the family's collection of manuscripts. Roger (1734–96), the fifth baronet, was a Vice-President of the Welsh Charity School in London and Evan *Evans (Ieuan Fardd) dedicated his book, *Some Specimens of the Poetry of the Antient Welsh Bards* (1764), to him. With Roger's son, Thomas (1776–1831), the direct line came to an end. Mostyn and Gloddaeth passed to his sister's son, Edward Lloyd (1795–1884), whose father, Edward Price Lloyd (1768–1854), had been elevated to the peerage as Lord Mostyn in 1831. Edward, the second baron, took the surname Mostyn. Owner of some five thousand acres in Flintshire and two thousand in Caernarfonshire, he obtained in 1854 an Act of Parliament authorizing the laying out of Llandudno. His son, Llywelyn (1859–1929), the third baron, was President of the Honourable Society of *Cymmrodorion.

The collection known as the Mostyn Manuscripts, established at the family's home and in the libraries of several other houses inherited by marriage, such as *Corsygedol, Gloddaeth, Bodysgallen, *Bodidris, Plas-hên and Pengwern, was presented to the *National Library of Wales in 1918 by Llywelyn, the third Baron Mostyn. Additional items, together with a large number of the family's papers, were deposited at the library of the University College of North Wales, Bangor, in the early 1960s. The collection, an important source for scholars, contains many manuscripts of great value, including the poetry of Tomos *Prys of Plas Iolyn in the hand of Wiliam *Cynwal. Among other valuable items are *The White Book of Cors-y-Gedol*, which contains the bardic contention between Edmund *Prys and Wiliam Cynwal, *The Red Book of Nannau* which contains a large collection of *englynion* in the hand of John *Jones of Gelli-lyfdy, and *The White Book of Perth Ddu*. But the most interesting works are a history of England and Wales by Elis *Gruffydd, copies of *Dares Phrygius*, *Brut y Tywysogyon* and *Brut y Brenhinedd* by *Geoffrey of Monmouth, and a version of the Legend of the Holy Grail, written towards the end of the fifteenth century.

The history of the Mostyn family was compiled by the third baron and T. Allen Glenn under the title *History of the Family of Mostyn of Mostyn* (1925).

Mother Goddesses, a feature of pagan Celtic religion in Britain and Ireland, which recognized a Divine Mother who was the mother of the gods themselves, the *Tuatha Dé Danann* ('Tribes of the Goddess Danu'). The Irish Danu (or Anu) has her counterpart in the Welsh *Dôn of *Pedair Cainc y Mabinogi* and also in *Modron ('The Great Mother'), who was commemorated as the river-goddess of the Marne and whose son was Maponos or *Mabon ('The Great or Divine Son'). Evidence from Ireland and ancient Gaul emphasizes the intimate territorial association of Celtic goddesses and in both countries they were closely linked with such natural features as mountains, rivers and springs. Goddesses were representatives of fertility, both of the land and its produce, and of human fertility in motherhood. Some, however, presided over warfare, as is the case with the Irish goddess of war, the Morrígan ('Queen of Phantoms') and the female warrior, Scathach ('the Shadowy One'), who instructed Cú Chulainn in arms. Her Welsh equivalent is found in the Nine Witches of Gloucester who gave similar instructions to the hero Peredur (see under TAIR RHAMANT). Goddesses frequently took the forms of animals and birds: the Gaulish goddess Epona had her counterpart in *Rhiannon and in the Irish Macha. They frequently appeared in triple forms, such as the Morrígan, Badb and Macha (cf. perhaps the Triad of the three *Gwenhwyfars who were *Arthur's queens). This may account for the plural form *Matres* or *Matronae* in numerous Roman dedications in Gaul and Britain. The name *Bendith y Mamau* ('Blessing of the Mothers'), found in some parts of Wales for the

Tylwyth Teg, seems to reflect a remote memory of the Mother Goddesses.

For further details see Edward Anwyl, *Celtic Religion in Pre-Christian Times* (1906), Anne Ross, *Pagan Celtic Britain* (1967) and *Everyday Life of the Pagan Celts* (1970), Proinsias Mac Cana, *Celtic Mythology* (1970) and Barry Cunliffe, *The Celtic World* (1979).

Mother of Wales, The, see CATRIN OF BERAIN (1534/5–91).

MOTLEY, JAMES (1809–59), poet, was born at Osmondthorpe Hall, near Leeds, the son of a wool-stapler. Educated at St. John's College, Cambridge, he became a civil engineer, mainly with a view to supervising his father's ironworks at Maesteg and coalmines in the district of Llangynwyd, Glam. An ardent naturalist and a Romantic who had read widely about Wales, especially in the works of such authors as Edmund *Jones, he published only one volume, *Tales of the Cymry* (1848), which contains six long narrative poems, each based on folk-tales of west Glamorgan. In the same year as the book's publication he went prospecting for coal in Borneo and there, a decade later, he was killed during a tribal uprising.

Moulded in Earth (1951), a novel by Richard Vaughan (Ernest Lewis *Thomas), was the first in a trilogy which also includes *Who Rideth so Wild* (1952) and *Son of Justin* (1955). Set among the farming communities of the Carmarthenshire-Breconshire border, especially around the author's native village of Llanddeusant, near the Carmarthenshire Fannau (Vans or Black Mountain), it tells the story of a bitter feud between two families which reaches its climax when Edwin Peele, the narrator and younger son of one family, falls in love with Grett Ellis, the beautiful daughter of the other. Despite the recognizable location of all three novels, the author maintained that place was incidental to his primary concern, which was the portrayal of people who 'live close to the earth, whose concepts of birth, death, love, hatred, and the will to wrest a living from the soil, are the same the world over'. This aim he achieved in all three novels by employing permutations of the most traditional romantic themes.

Mr Pugh, the schoolmaster in Dylan *Thomas's *Under Milk Wood* (1954) who, henpecked by his wife, finds solace in fantasies about poisoning her.

Mrs Ogmore-Pritchard, the landlady of the Bay View guest-house in Dylan *Thomas's *Under Milk Wood* (1954). House-proud and domineering, she bullies the ghosts of her two husbands, Mr Ogmore and Mr Pritchard, to whom she gives the order, 'And before you let the sun in, mind it wipes its shoes'.

Mrs Thrale, see under PIOZZI, HESTER LYNCH (1741–1821).

Mudiad Amddiffyn Cymru (lit. 'Movement for the defence of Wales'), a Nationalist group which caused explosions in several parts of Wales during the late 1960s, mainly in protest against the investiture of the Prince of Wales. Among the buildings damaged was the Temple of Peace in Cathays Park, Cardiff. In 1969 two members of the organization, now known as the *Abergele Martyrs, were accidentally killed by their own explosive devices. In the following year a sergeant in the Royal Army Dental Corps, John Jenkins, was sentenced to ten years' imprisonment for his part in the campaign and another man was given a lesser sentence. John Jenkins was imprisoned again in 1983 for harbouring a Welsh Republican found guilty of taking part in a second campaign involving the use of explosives. See also FREE WALES ARMY and MEIBION GLYNDŴR.

Mudiad Cymreig, Y, see under BEBB, WILLIAM AMBROSE (1894–1955).

My People (1915), a volume of short stories by Caradoc Evans (David *Evans), was the author's first, most famous and most influential book. It presents a coherent and unsparing picture of a brutish peasantry, a debased religion and a grudging soil, in which the mainsprings of action are greed, hypocrisy and lust, and their consequences pain, misery and death. The fifteen stories are told with hypnotic and sometimes oppressive power in an intensely disciplined, highly wrought and, on the surface, not infrequently grotesque prose style which had been perfected by the author from personal, biblical, Welsh, and often 'Welshified' elements, an amalgam uniquely suited to their substance. Both style and content gave immediate and lasting offence to many Welsh readers who judged them wantonly defamatory of their most cherished conceptions of the Welsh character and way of life, while less implicated readers praised so original a *tour de force*. Including as it does such classic tales as 'The Way of the Earth', 'A Just Man in Sodom' and 'Lamentations', and the two masterpieces, 'A Father in Sion' and 'Be This Her Memorial', the book is probably the most powerful and unforgettable, as it was certainly the most notorious, collection of stories so far written by an Anglo-Welsh author.

Myddfai, The Physicians of, a family of country doctors who lived in the parish of Myddfai, Carms. Their origins are associated with a story preserved in a series of medieval medical texts (the oldest of which is BL Add. 14912) which mentions one Rhiwallon Feddyg and his sons, Cadwgan, Gruffudd and Einion, who were doctors to *Rhys Gryg, lord of *Dinefwr in the thirteenth century. Myddfai was one of the free manors of *Cantref Bychan, the territory of *Rhys ap Gruffudd (The Lord Rhys),

and with the demise of the native Welsh Princes it became part of the lordship of Llandovery. According to a thirteenth-century extent of that lordship, the lord of Llandovery had the right to call to his service a doctor from among the freeholders of Myddfai.

There is evidence that some kind of medical succession continued in Myddfai until the eighteenth century. The Physicians of Myddfai are mentioned in the letters of Lewis *Morris, the antiquary, and the gravestones of the last of their line, David Jones (d. 1719) and John Jones (d. 1739), are still to be seen in the church there. Such a succession in educated, professional families was a characteristic of Celtic society and similar examples are known to have existed in Scotland and Ireland. During the last two hundred years the traditions concerning the ability of the Physicians have become associated with a folk-tale about *Llyn y Fan Fach.

The manuscripts of the Physicians of Myddfai contain collections of medical material of a type common to the whole of Europe in the Middle Ages, aimed at giving instructions for diagnosis, prognosis, treatment by surgery, by drugs, by letting blood and by cauterizing. The instructions are recorded either in the form of short tractates or in the form of lists of recipes using herbs, animals and minerals. Some are translations of short works emanating from the Classical period, while others reflect medical movements of the Middle Ages, such as the Salerno and Chartres movements. The philosophical basis of the instructions is that of the humours inherited from the Classical period and expressed in the work of Galen and Hippocrates. The colophon to the medical texts emphasizes the connection between Rhiwallon and his sons and the tradition of writing medical texts. The justification for this emphasis is given in a sentence which echoes a principle expressed in the work of Galen himself, 'And this is the reason they caused their knowledge to be written in this way: lest there be no-one who would know as much as they knew after them'.

For further details see *The Physicians of Myddfai* (ed. John Williams, trans. John Pughe, 1861) and the article by Morfydd E. Owen, '*Meddygon Myddfai*: a preliminary survey of some medieval medical writing in Welsh' in *Studia Celtica* (vols. X/XI, 1975–76); see also Nesta Lloyd and Morfydd E. Owen, *Drych yr Oesoedd Canol* (1985).

Myddleton family, The, of Chirk Castle, Denbs., was descended from Rhirid ap Dafydd (*fl.* late 14th cent.) who adopted the surname of Myddleton on marrying the daughter of Sir Alexander Myddleton of Myddleton, Salop. His descendant, Richard (*c.* 1508–75), was Member of Parliament for the county and active in building up an estate which, by the nineteenth century, extended over some eight thousand acres. Richard had nine sons of whom the fourth, Thomas (1550–1631) and the ninth, Hugh

(1560–1631), distinguished themselves in the commercial life of London. Thomas, one of the original shareholders in the East India Company, was the Lord Mayor of London in 1613 and represented the city in the Parliaments of 1624 and 1626. He retained close links with the gentry of north Wales and in 1595 bought the castle and lordship of *Chirk. A devout Puritan, he contributed, with Rowland *Heilyn, towards the cost of publishing the first pocket edition of the Welsh *Bible, *Y Beibl Bach* (1630). His brother Hugh, a goldsmith, established the New River Company which was the first to provide London with water, and successfully exploited the silver-lead deposits of Cardiganshire. Hugh was created baronet in 1622, a title held by his descendants until his line died out in 1828.

Thomas's son, Thomas (1586–1667), lord of Chirk, was also a Puritan and the chief supporter of the Parliamentary cause in north Wales. Appointed Serjeant-General of North Wales by Parliament in 1643, he captured *Montgomery Castle and was zealous in ejecting Royalist clergy. Disillusioned by the King's execution and the Protectorate, he proclaimed Charles II king in Wrexham in August 1659 and was elected to the Convention Parliament of 1660. His son, Thomas (c.1624–63), was closely involved in the restoration of Charles II and was made a baronet in 1660.

Under the later Stuarts the Myddletons established a hegemony over the parliamentary representation of Denbighshire, Richard (1654–1716), the fourth baronet, being returned in thirteen successive elections between 1685 and 1715. In the eighteenth century the county became the Tory preserve of Watkin Williams *Wynn of Wynnstay but the Myddletons represented the boroughs as Whigs. On the death of Richard Myddleton, unmarried, in 1796, the estates were divided among his sisters. The Ruthin Castle estate, which the family had acquired in 1677, became the property of the Cornwallis-West family, the descendants of Maria, while Chirk went to Charlotte and her husband, Robert Biddulph. The Myddleton-Biddulphs were prominent in the public life of Denbighshire in the nineteenth century and the family still lives at Chirk Castle.

For further details see Margaret Mahler, *Chirk Castle and Chirkland* (1912), G. C. Berry, 'Sir Hugh Myddleton and the New River' in the *Transactions of the Honourable Society of Cymmrodorion* (1956) and G. M. Griffiths, 'Chirk Castle election activities 1600–1750' in the *Journal* of the National Library of Wales (vol. XI, 1957–58); see also Samuel Smiles, *Lives of the Engineers* (vol. I, 1874) for a full account of Hugh Myddleton's career.

'*Myfanwy Fychan*', a love-poem by John Ceiriog *Hughes, was written for the Eisteddfod held at Llangollen in 1858 but first published in his volume *Oriau'r Hwyr* (1860). Although set in the fourteenth century, the poem reflects the moral standards of the Victorian era in the story of how the heroine, the virtuous Myfanwy Fychan, falls in love with the poet Hywel ab Einion. Written as an attempt to disprove the allegations of the *Blue Books Commissioners about the immorality of the Welsh, the poem proved to be extremely popular and remained a model for love-poetry in Welsh for the rest of the nineteenth century.

Myfyr Morganwg, see DAVIES, EVAN (1801–88).

Myfyrian, a mansion in the parish of Llanidan, Ang., was a famous resort for poets on the island. Poetry written for three generations of the family has survived, from the time of Rhydderch ap Dafydd (d. 1561/2), his son, Rhisiart ap Rhydderch (d. 1576), who maintained *Lewis Menai as household poet, and Rhydderch ap Rhisiart who was himself a poet.

Mynachdy, a mansion in the parish of Bleddfa, Rads., was the home of the Prices, an influential family who extended patronage to poets during the sixteenth century. The works of poets such as Siôn Ceri (fl. 1500?–1530?), *Bedo Hafesp and Lewys *Dwnn are eulogies to the patrons, James Price (fl. 1550), John Price (fl. 1573), and another John Price towards the end of the century, after whose time the tradition waned.

Mynydd Carn, The Battle of (1081), see under TRAHAEARN AP CARADOG (d. 1081).

Mynyddawg Mwynfawr, see under GODODDIN (c.600).

Mynyddog, see DAVIES, RICHARD (1833–77).

Myrddin or **Merlin**, a fictional poet and prophet. With him have been associated a number of poems which include the *'*Afallennau*', the '*Hoianau*', *'*Cyfoesi Myrddin a Gwenddydd ei Chwaer*', '*Gwasgargerdd Fyrddin yn y Bedd*' and '*Peirian Faban*'. As far as may be gathered from these difficult texts, he was a member of the court of *Gwenddolau fab Ceido, who was believed to have been killed in the battle of Arfderydd in 573. As a result of a terrifying vision which he saw during that battle, Myrddin lost his reason and fled to Celyddon Wood where he lived as a wild man, communing with the animals and living in fear of Rhydderch, Gwenddolau's enemy. In his madness he received the gift of prophecy.

It appears that this tale is part of the fictional material dealing with the battle of Arfderydd, remains of which are preserved in the poems, together with prophecies about battles between the Welsh and the Normans. The detail of the wild man is connected in some way with the poem about Suibhne Geilt in Irish and the character called Lailoken in the story of St. Kentigern, and it is these, together with the fairly complete version given by *Geoffrey of Monmouth in his *Vita Merlini*, which make possible a reconstruction of the tale. According to the most commonly accepted thesis, Myrddin is a fictional character from the *Old North whose tale was relocated in Wales and who was given a new name from the place-name Caerfyrddin (Carmarthen), rather than a historical early poet who turned into a prophet, as did *Taliesin. The two are associated with each other in the poem *'Ymddiddan Myrddin a Thaliesin', as well as in *Vita Merlini*. In the latter, Myrddin is king of south Wales, which was Geoffrey's attempt to connect the traditional prophet with the character previously described by him in his *Historia Regum Britanniae* (1136). This Myrddin, the son of a nun from Carmarthen and an incubus, the 'fatherless child' whose blood had to be sprinkled on the foundations of the fortress which Gwrtheyrn (*Vortigern) was trying to build, was Geoffrey's invention. The detail of Myrddin the knowledgeable boy he borrowed from the story of Ambrosius in *Nennius's *Historia Brittonum*. The seventh Book of the *Historia*, in which the author purports to explain the significance of the battle between the red dragon and the white dragon, and foretells the course of British history until the end of time, is a masterly concoction of Welsh prophecies, apocalyptic literature, history and imagination. In the *Historia* it is Myrddin who causes the great stones to be brought from Ireland for the building of Stonehenge and it is he who facilitates *Uthr Bendragon's sleeping with Igerna (*Eigr) in the form of her husband, with the result that *Arthur is conceived. The Myrddin of the *Historia* is so different from the prophet of tradition that it must be assumed that Geoffrey knew nothing more of Myrddin than his name at that time, but that he had acquainted himself with the authentic tradition by the time he came to write the *Vita*.

*Gerald de Barri (Giraldus Cambrensis) noticed the difference between the versions and concluded that there were two Myrddins, Geoffrey's *Merlinus Ambrosius*, and the *Merlinus Silvestris* of the Welsh prophecies. The poem *'Armes Prydein' (c.930) demonstrates that Myrddin's popularity was on the increase in the tenth century, and throughout the Middle Ages references to him occur which show that there were other elements in the tale about him, for example the threefold manner of his death, his house of glass and his courtships. The Latin form of his name, *Merlinus*, is the work of Geoffrey of Monmouth, and under that form (*ang.* Merlin) and through his connection with Arthur he became one of the chief characters in the Continental Arthurian legend.

A full discussion of the complexities of the tale may be found in A. O. H. Jarman, *The Legend of Merlin* (1960),

and in his chapter in *Arthurian Literature in the Middle Ages* (ed. R. S. Loomis, 1959); see also Basil Clarke, *Life of Merlin* (1973) and N. Tolstoy, *Quest for Merlin* (1985).

Myrddin Fardd, see JONES, JOHN (1836–1921).

Mystic Mark, The, see NOD CYFRIN.

Mysticism, the experience in prayer and meditation of the nearness of God or even of union with God, and the quest for such experience, is found in many religions and has taken various forms among Christians. The type which emphasizes the divine transcendence goes back to the Pseudo-Dionysius (c.AD 500) who points to the way of 'unknowing' and the light of the Divine Darkness. The Christ-mysticism found in Anselm and Bernard of Clairvaux influenced *Cysegrlan Fuchedd*, a medieval tract on holy living, and seems also to have promoted the religious application of the *Grail romances.

The light-darkness paradox is one of the influences on the mysticism of Henry *Vaughan while that of Thomas Traherne, though touched by Neo-Platonism, is essentially pantheistic. The movement in Roman Catholic mysticism which led to the controversial phenomenon of Quietism is exemplified temperately in David *Baker, who knew something of 'the Dark Night of the Soul' and spoke of the ethical implications of the love of Christ. The thought of Böhme fertilized the Puritan spirituality of Morgan *Llwyd. Biblical imagery, Methodist fervour and a mysticism centred in the Incarnation came together in the unique devotion of Ann *Griffiths, which differs from the warm Christ-mysticism of William *Williams (Pantycelyn). Nature-mysticism was one of the aspects of the Romantic experience and coloured the other-worldly longings of William *Thomas (Islwyn).

For further details see J. Dyfnallt Owen, *Neges Cyfriniaeth Morgan Llwyd* (1925), T. Hywel Hughes, *The Philosophical Basis of Mysticism* (1937), F. C. Happold, *Mysticism* (1964), J. R. Jones, *Ac Onide* (1970) and Pennar Davies, *Y Brenin Alltud* (1974).

Myth of Descent, The, the subject of debate regarding the origins of the Welsh or British people, can be traced to *Geoffrey of Monmouth's *Historia Regum Britanniae* (1136) which presented a version of the history of Britain from the time of *Brutus (11th cent. BC) to that of *Cadwaladr Fendigaid (AD 7th cent.). During the Roman occupation of Britain, Geoffrey maintained, the Britons had prospered but, with the legions' departure in the fifth century, Saxon conquest forced them to yield their sovereignty of the Island. This claim, in the furtherance of which Geoffrey's prime motive was to present to the Norman conquerors an image of British grandeur, was introduced as 'the *Matter of Britain' into the literary world of Europe.

The validity of Geoffrey's interpretation was hotly disputed by scholars such as the English chronicler William of Newburgh and, in the sixteenth century, the Italian historian Polydore Vergil and the English antiquary William Camden (see under BRITANNIA) both rejected his version. But in spite of the adverse cultural effects of *Tudor policy on Wales, the century saw the emergence of humanist writing which was intended to preserve Welsh national identity and to uphold the claim of antiquity which Geoffrey had championed. Among the Welsh scholars who defended his view were Richard *Davies in *Epistol at y Cembru (1567), Sir John *Price in *Historiae Britannicae Defensio (1573) and Humphrey *Llwyd in Commentarioli Descriptionis Britannicae Fragmentum (1572). English scholars joined with them in the belief that the ascent of Henry Tudor to the throne in 1485 had implied that the English, as well as the Welsh, were co-inheritors of the illustrious British tradition. For example, John Leland, Thomas Churchyard, Michael Drayton (see under POLYOLBION) and Percy *Enderbie believed that the Britons were a much older and more renowned people than even the Romans, and Bishop Richard *Davies (who had corresponded with Archbishop Matthew Parker on these matters) based much of his Protestant Church Theory on Geoffrey's Historia.

In the seventeenth century the British 'myth' was supported by writers such as Rowland *Vaughan of Caer-gai in his preface to Yr Ymarfer o Dduwioldeb (1630), Charles *Edwards in Hanes y Ffydd Ddiffuant (1667) and Robert *Vaughan of Hengwrt. The tradition was maintained in the eighteenth century, principally by Theophilus *Evans in Drych y Prif Oesoedd (1716) and by the literary circle associated with the *Morris Brothers. Lewis *Morris believed that the Historia was a medieval version of an original produced by *Tysilio in the sixth century. In the eighteenth and nineteenth centuries Welsh antiquaries and historians such as Edward *Williams (Iolo Morganwg), Thomas *Price (Carnhuanawc) and Robert John *Pryse (Gweirydd ap Rhys) accepted the basis of the Galfridian tradition.

Several modern critical studies have attempted to place Geoffrey, and the debate which he created, in their proper historical context; see, for example, T. D. Kendrick, British Antiquity (1950).

Mytton, John (1796–1834), eccentric, was born at Halston Hall, Salop, a mile or two from the Welsh Border. Expelled from school at Westminster and Harrow, he began his career in 1816 with the rank of cornet in the 7th Hussars. Elected Member of Parliament for Shrewsbury in 1819, he attended the House of Commons only once, and then only for half an hour. Having inherited an estate at Dinas Mawddwy, Mer., he indulged in many extravagances, such as the over-generous payment of village children for rolling down the side of Moel Dinas. A memoir of his life, which ended in a debtors' prison, was published by C. J. *Apperley (Nimrod) in 1837.

For further details see Jean Holdsworth, Mango: The Life and Times of John Mytton of Halston (1972).

Myvyrian Archaiology, The (1801, 1807), see under JONES, OWEN (1741–1814).

N

Nanheudwy, a commot of *Powys Fadog in the valley of the Dee, was divided in 1282 between the lordship of *Chirk and Chirkland and the lordship of Bromfield and *Yale.

Nannau or **Nanney family, The**, of Nannau, Mer., claimed descent from the kings of *Powys through Ynyr Hen (*fl.* early 13th cent.). Huw Nannau in the late sixteenth century held lands which his ancestors had acquired in the district of Dolgellau. The family were patrons of poets; Siôn Dafydd Las (John *Davies), who sang their praises, was among the last of the household poets. Huw Nannau's grandson, Hugh Nanney (d. 1701), Member of Parliament for the county from 1695 to 1701, left a daughter, Janet, who married Robert Vaughan of Hengwrt, the great-grandson of his namesake, the antiquary. Their son, Robert Vaughan (1723–92) of Hengwrt and Nannau, was created a baronet in 1791. His son, Robert (1768–1843), the second baronet, rebuilt Nannau and represented Merioneth in Parliament for forty-four years. It was Robert (1803–59), the third baronet, the last of his line, who bequeathed the Hengwrt library to W. W. E. *Wynne of Peniarth; his estates, which extended over some sixteen thousand acres, went eventually to his kinsman, John Vaughan (1829–1900) of Dolmelynllyn, the Tory opponent of T. E. *Ellis in the election of 1886. John Vaughan's son, Major-General John Vaughan (1871–1950), was the author of *My Cavalry and Sporting Memories* (1955).

For further details see E. D. Jones, 'The family of Nannau of Nannau' in the *Journal* of the Merioneth Historical and Record Society (1953).

Nansi'r Nant, see under GWEN TOMOS (1894).

Nant Gwrtheyrn, a village on the northern coast of the Llŷn peninsula, which acquired its name, according to tradition, because *Vortigern (Gwrtheyrn) took refuge there after fleeing from Dinas Emrys. The village is associated with the tale of Rhys and Meinir which was recorded by Glasynys (Owen Wynne *Jones) and included in the anthology *Cymru Fu* (1862–64). Meinir, on the morning of her wedding to her childhood sweetheart, is said to have challenged Rhys's family (as was the local custom, see under PWNCO) by hiding in a hollow tree. The wedding guests failed to find her, however, and she was trapped in her hiding-place. Many years later, the tree was struck by lightning and

her skeleton, still wearing a bridal gown, was discovered. The tale is the subject of a ballad by Cynan (Albert *Evans-Jones), '*Baled y Ceubren Crin*'. With the decline of its quarry, the village of Nant Gwrtheyrn was abandoned by its inhabitants in the 1950s but was renovated in the 1970s as a centre for the teaching of the Welsh language to adults.

Nant Teyrnon, see LLANTARNAM.

Nanteos, a mansion near Aberystwyth, Cards., built in the mid-eighteenth century at the expense of the Powell family, is famous on account of its associations with the Nanteos Cup. This wooden vessel, reputedly brought to Glastonbury by Joseph of Arimathea from the Holy Land, thence to *Strata Florida and eventually to Nanteos, was thought to have great healing powers but, used excessively and reinforced with a silver rim, it lost this quality. The tradition that Wagner stayed at Nanteos and was inspired by the presence of the Cup to begin work on his opera *Parsifal* must be put down to the enthusiasm for Wagner's work shown by George *Powell, a member of the family. There is no reliable evidence that Wagner was ever at Nanteos and the opera's plot was conceived some ten years before the composer's visit to Britain in 1855.

Nantlais, see WILLIAMS, WILLIAM NANTLAIS (1874–1959).

Nash, Richard (**Beau Nash**; 1674–1761), 'the King of Bath', was born in Swansea of Pembrokeshire parents; his mother was a niece of John *Poyer. Educated at Queen Elizabeth Grammar School, Carmarthen, and Jesus College, Oxford, where he did not take a degree, he first tried the Army (which proved too expensive and demanding) and then reverted to the Law, becoming a student of the Inner Temple in 1693. He did little work but mysteriously contrived to live a gay life on small means. In 1695 his organization of the pageant at the Middle Temple so pleased King William that he was offered a knighthood but, for lack of means to support a title, he refused it; thereafter he lived by gaming and making extravagant wagers.

In 1705 he was attracted to Bath, where he first organized a band, took a lease of rooms for assembly and in 1706 raised the sum of £18,000 by subscription for the improvement of the roads thereabout. He drew up rules against the wearing of swords, duelling, informal dress, promiscuous smoking and the cheating of chairmen and lodging-house keepers, and proceeded to enforce them autocratically against the noble as well as the insignificant. In 1738 he welcomed the Prince of Wales to Bath and set up an obelisk, inscribed by Alexander Pope, to mark his visit, but the tighter laws against gaming introduced in 1740 and 1745 reduced his income greatly and his influence gradually waned. When he was eighty-two years old the Corporation voted him an allowance of ten pounds a month. Large and clumsy in person, with harsh, irregular features, Beau Nash nevertheless had conversation as fine and distinctive as his clothes, and his vanity was matched by his generosity.

NASH-WILLIAMS, VICTOR ERLE (1897–1955), archaeologist and author. Born at Fleur-de-Lys, Mon., he was educated at University College, Cardiff, and became Assistant Keeper of Archaeology at the *National Museum of Wales in 1924 and Keeper two years later. Besides his numerous contributions to learned journals, especially to *Archaeologia Cambrensis*, which he edited for the *Cambrian Archaeological Association from 1950 to 1955, he wrote a monograph, *The Roman Fortress at Caerleon* (1940), and two major works, *The Early Christian Monuments of Wales* (1950) and *The Roman Frontier in Wales* (1954).

National Eisteddfod, The, the principal cultural festival of the Welsh people, is held annually during the first week of August, the venue alternating between north and south Wales. After a period of decline during the eighteenth century, when it degenerated into an occasion for disputation between poets meeting in taverns, the *eisteddfod was revived in the nineteenth century under the auspices of the *Gwyneddigion Society. It was not until 1860, however, at an eisteddfod held in Denbigh, that the concept of a national festival won general approval. The first National Eisteddfod was held at Aberdare, Glam., in the following year and such an event was organized annually thereafter until 1868, when the series was abandoned as the result of a financial crisis in the festival's affairs. The eisteddfodau held in north Wales during the 1870s were national in name only. In 1880, however, Hugh *Owen succeeded in establishing the National Eisteddfod Association under the aegis of the Honourable Society of *Cymmrodorion and the first National Eisteddfod to be held under the Society's patronage was held at Merthyr Tydfil in 1881. Since then a National Eisteddfod has been held annually, except in 1914 and 1940 when it was prevented by wartime conditions; in the latter case a 'radio eisteddfod' was broadcast by the BBC.

The Eisteddfod was essentially a literary and musical festival, but between 1862 and 1868 an attempt was made to establish a 'Social Science Section' in order to discuss and encourage social, commercial, industrial and scientific enterprises in Wales. The project never took root, however, and it was soon abandoned. A more congenial development was the prominence given to music towards the end of the nineteenth century: the choral competitions were enthusiastically patronized, even by English choirs, and the evening concerts featured artistes of international renown and presented large-scale works by the masters, with an occasional oratorio by a Welshman, such as David *Jenkins's *Dewi Sant*. In this way the Eisteddfod contributed substantially to the musical education of the common people.

The relationship between the National Eisteddfod Association and *Gorsedd Beirdd Ynys Prydain* was not entirely satisfactory in the early years but in 1937 the two bodies agreed to the formation of the National Eisteddfod Council. A new constitution introduced in 1952 established the Court of the National Eisteddfod as the governing body, membership of which is by subscription or by membership of the *Gorsedd*, and the Council became the executive body functioning through its specialist committees. In 1959 two full-time Organisers were appointed and a full-time Director, with an office in Cardiff, in 1978. The cost of mounting the National Eisteddfod is defrayed by grants from local and central government and from such sources as industry and the broadcasting authorities, but also by the raising of funds in the district where the festival is to be held. The preparation of the site (often of about seventy acres) and the erection of the main pavilion (with seating for about five thousand spectators) are major elements in the Eisteddfod's annual budget of approximately a million pounds, but the advantages of a peripatetic Eisteddfod have been deemed to outweigh those of a permanent, central site.

The frequent use of English in the proceedings of the National Eisteddfod used to cause controversy, which continued even after 1937 when Welsh was declared the official language, for English was still heard on the stage as late as the 1950s. The new constitution of 1952 re-asserted the view that the official language of the National Eisteddfod is Welsh and this ruling is now unequivocally observed. The 'Welsh Rule' has ensured the essential nature of the festival as a unique institution devoted to the fostering of the *Welsh language and its culture. Although some local authorities in the English-speaking parts of Wales have cited the rule as a reason for refusing their financial contribution, it has a wide measure of public support. In 1967, for example, a number of prominent Anglo-Welsh writers signed a petition calling on the Court to maintain the rule.

Attracting an attendance of about a hundred and fifty thousand, the National Eisteddfod has become a major rallying-point for all those concerned with the culture of Wales. The festival's heart is the main pavilion where the musical competitions and concerts are held and the ceremonies of Gorsedd Beirdd Ynys Prydain, including those of the *Chair and *Crown, take place. But on the periphery of the Eisteddfod Field there are scores of smaller stands at which a great variety of societies, institutions and commercial companies is represented. Practitioners of the visual arts, crafts, music and theatre have their own pavilions, while the main gathering place for writers is Y Babell Lên ('The Literature Tent'), where adjudications and lectures are delivered and poetry contests are held. The week of the National Eisteddfod is an important date in the calendar of Welsh publishers and the annual volume, Cyfansoddiadau a Beirniadaethau, which contains the prize-winning entries and adjudications, is eagerly bought and read. Although the National Eisteddfod has produced, in the twentieth century, work of lasting merit, it is generally recognized that not all the entries in any given year are likely to be of the highest standard. Nevertheless, it is not by the number of masterpieces it has produced that the festival should be judged, but rather by the opportunity it affords the eisteddfodwr of enriching his appreciation of literature, whether as writer or reader. In this, as in other respects, the National Eisteddfod is a great popular festival which combines the best of the professional and amateur traditions of Wales.

The full history of the National Eisteddfod has not yet been written but the following are among the most important accounts of its development: R. T. Jenkins, 'Hanes Cymdeithas yr Eisteddfod Genedlaethol' in the Transactions of the Honourable Society of Cymmrodorion (1933–35), Idris Foster (ed.), Twf yr Eisteddfod (1968), Hywel Teifi Edwards, Yr Eisteddfod (1976) and Gŵyl Gwalia: Yr Eisteddfod yn Oes Aur Victoria 1858–1868 (1980), and Dilwyn Miles, The Royal National Eisteddfod of Wales (1978); for personal accounts of what the Eisteddfod means to selected individuals see the series Eisteddfota (3 vols., 1978, 1979, 1980). A list of articles pertaining to the Eisteddfod and Gorsedd Beirdd Ynys Prydain will be found in Thomas Parry and Merfyn Morgan (ed.), Llyfryddiaeth Llenyddiaeth Gymraeg (1976).

National Library of Wales, The, together with its sister institution, the *National Museum of Wales, was granted its royal charter on 19 March 1907, after a campaign which was launched in the National Eisteddfod held at Mold in 1873. The support of the University College of Wales, Aberystwyth, was of vital significance in the campaign and among those who played a leading part were Thomas Edward *Ellis, Sir John Herbert Lewis and Sir John *Williams (1840–1926). The Library opened its doors to readers in the Old Assembly Rooms at Laura Place, Aberystwyth, on 1 January 1909.

Two years later building began on the Grogythan site above the town, on land which had been purchased by Lord *Rendel in 1897 and to the design of Sidney Kyffin Greenslade; the Library moved there in 1916.

The National Library is charged by its charter not only to collect all material—whether in printed, manuscript or graphic form—relating to Wales and the other Celtic countries, but also to build as comprehensive a general research collection as possible. To the latter end it has had since 1912 the right to claim free of charge one copy of nearly every book published in the United Kingdom. By today the Library houses some three million books and journals, some forty thousand manuscript volumes, about four million deeds and documents and a vast collection of maps, prints, drawings, paintings, photographs, gramophone records, audiotapes, video-tapes and films. Its collections include virtually all books published in Welsh or relating to Wales (its collection of journals and newspapers is more patchy), and perhaps as large a proportion as seventy per cent of all Welsh literary manuscripts, including such famous medieval codices as The *Black Book of Carmarthen, The *White Book of Rhydderch, The *Black Book of Chirk, The *Book of Taliesin and the *Hendregadredd Manuscript. Since 1939 the Library has published its own journal and has also issued catalogues and monographs of a high scholarly standard.

In its building works, which have never ceased, the Library has been supported not only by Government funds but also (especially in the early years) by donations from the public, including many small sums from the people of Wales. Its general running costs (now amounting to some two million pounds) were borne by the Treasury until 1965 and thereafter by the *Welsh Office. In 1984 its staff, employed in three main Departments—Printed Books, Manuscripts and Records, and Prints, Drawings and Maps—numbered about 148. The Library is governed by a Council of some thirty-five members who are elected, for the most part, by a Court of about 165 persons. There have been seven Librarians: John *Ballinger (1909–30), William Llewelyn Davies (1930–52), Thomas *Parry (1953–58), E. D. *Jones (1958–69), David *Jenkins (1969–79), R. Geraint *Gruffydd (1980–85) and Brynley F. *Roberts (1985–).

For accounts of the Library's history see W. Ll. Davies, The National Library of Wales (1937), David Jenkins, 'A National Library for Wales: The Prologue' in the Transactions of the Honourable Society of Cymmrodorion (1982), and the booklets published by the Library in Welsh and English in 1974 and 1982.

National Museum of Wales, The, which was granted a royal charter in 1907, opened its galleries in Cathays Park, Cardiff, in 1922. It is now, after the British Museum, one of the largest of the national museums funded by the Government, with a staff numbering more than four hundred and an annual budget of some six million pounds. The Museum's reputation and its contribution to scholarship depend on its six Departments: Archaeology and Numismatics, Art, Botany, Geology, Industry and Zoology. But the Museum also presents scholarship with a common touch by means of publications, exhibitions, public lectures and projects for children. Among the best-known works in the Art Department's collection are the paintings, mostly French, which were bequeathed by Gwendoline and Margaret Davies, the granddaughters of David *Davies of Llandinam, in 1951 and 1963. The Museum has had a pioneering role in the field of education through its services to the secondary schools of Wales. Its first Director was W. Evans Hoyle (1908–24), who was followed by Mortimer Wheeler (1925–26), Cyril Fox (1926–48), D. Dilwyn John (1948–68) and G. O. *Jones (1968–77); Douglas A. Bassett was appointed in 1977. The *Welsh Folk Museum at St. Fagans near Cardiff and the *Welsh Industrial and Maritime Museum in Butetown, Cardiff, are integral parts of the National Museum of Wales, as are several smaller specialist museums in other parts of the country.

Further information about the history of the National Museum will be found in the brochure The National Museum of Wales (1977), the lectures by Glanmor Williams, Wales and the Past: a Consort of Voices (1983), and the articles, 'The Making of a National Museum' by Douglas Bassett in the Transactions of the Honourable Society of Cymmrodorion (1982, 1983 and 1984); see also the Bulletin of the National Museum which appeared between 1969 and 1976, the Annual Reports and the catalogue of the Museum's publications compiled by Hywel G. Rees (1982; supplement, 1984).

National Society, The, formed in 1811 with the aim of establishing elementary schools for the education of the poor in the principles of the Established Church, opened its first schools in Wales in 1812 at Penley, Flints., and Bridgend, Glam. It received the financial support of many landowners and leaders of industry and trade who were members of the Church and, from 1833, also accepted grants from Government sources on a pound-for-pound basis. The school at Abergwili, Carms., was probably the first in Wales to receive a grant (of £84), in 1843. By these means Church schools were opened in most parts of Wales, particularly along the coastal lowlands. There followed an acrimonious rivalry between the National Society and the *British and Foreign School Society (formed by Dissenting interests to promote a non-doctrinal education) over the building of schools. A Welsh Education Committee was formed in 1846 as an auxiliary branch of the National Society with a view to giving special attention to Wales. During the next three years it collected money to encourage the establishment of schools and the founding of a teachers' training college at Carmarthen in 1848. In Caernarfon the National School had already participated in the training of teachers and in 1849 this initiative led to the creation of another training college in the town. By the time the Education Act of 1870 had been passed, the National Society had been successful in founding some five hundred National Schools in Wales. Unlike the schools of the British Society, they were not transferred to the School Boards, with which there was keen competition for the rest of the century.

For further details see Frank Smith, A History of English Elementary Education 1700–1902 (1931), Jac L. Williams, Addysg i Gymru (1966), J. R. Webster, Dyheadau'r Bedwaredd Ganrif ar Bymtheg (1966) and The History of Education in Wales (vol. 1, ed. Jac L. Williams and Gwilym Rees Hughes, 1978).

National Winner (1971), a novel by Emyr *Humphreys, was the first to appear of a quartet (later a sextet) of novels intended to examine, over a period of several generations, the means by which 'good' (or conscience) is transmitted in a society with the traditional values of Wales: the novel is, nevertheless, the last in narrative sequence of the original quartet. It depicts the children of the dead John Cilydd More, poet, Nationalist and homosexual, and his widow Amy, now Lady Brangor, who has become an Anglicized snob. The children themselves are a diversity: the youngest, Peredur, a university lecturer in England, is the uninformed pilgrim in search of his dead father's spirit; the eldest, Bedwyr, a successful architect, is not involved in the matter of moral values—it is his wife Siân who reintroduces to the family the essential 'goodness' which the author seeks to identify; Gwydion is a film producer and rogue after the type of Roger Allendale in *Hear and Forgive (1952). The conscience of John Cilydd, then, is weakened and dissipated in his children, though one of them may find a way back by his own efforts. Modern Wales, the novel suggests, is a dilution of a once-strong principle of responsibility and mutual concern.

Nationalism, a term denoting a wide spectrum of beliefs and ideas, has been one of the most powerful forces in the shaping of the modern world. Loosely defined, it can mean a warm feeling of attachment to a nation's language, land, history, literature and art—the sentiment often called Cultural Nationalism. More strictly defined, it is the term for that political theory which argues that each nation should constitute a state and that a vigorous national community is the essential precondition for the fulfilment of individual aspirations. Nationalism in this sense refers to a movement with a coherent body of ideas which seeks to maintain or to achieve self-government for a group which conceives of itself as possessing, or as being capable of attaining, the characteristics of a nation. It is a theory which developed in the wake of the French Revolution (1789) and has been interpreted as constituting the defensive reaction of ethnic groups in the face of social or intellectual crisis, especially when such groups are confronted with rapid change and by the tension created by modernization. The word 'nationalism' was first used in English in 1844 and in Welsh ('cenedlaetholdeb') in 1858.

Patriotism, or a sense of nationhood, has a long history among the Welsh. The adoption of the name Cymry (from the Brythonic Cambrogi, 'fellow-countrymen'), probably in the late sixth century, indicates an early consciousness that the Welsh were to each other what they were not to anyone else. The poem *'Armes Prydein' is infused with Welsh racial pride and *Gerald de Barri (Giraldus Cambrensis), in his description of the Welsh, provides a remarkable definition of the essentials of a nation. The legal code associated with the name of *Hywel Dda was a vital component of the Welsh people's awareness of their identity in the early Middle Ages and that awareness can also be discerned as a political motive in the statecraft of *Llywelyn ap Iorwerth and *Llywelyn ap Gruffudd. A much more general patriotism fuelled the flames of *Owain Glyndŵr's rising and provided the impetus for the cultural achievements of the sixteenth-century Welsh humanists and their successors.

Nationalism strictly defined, however, cannot be considered to be a significant force in Wales until the second half of the nineteenth century when, encouraged by the example of Ireland and by the writings of continental Nationalists, Welsh Nationalism was vigorously advocated in particular by Michael D. *Jones and Robert Ambrose *Jones (Emrys ap Iwan). Between 1886 and 1896 members of *Cymru Fydd were active in seeking a measure of self-government for Wales. By the later nineteenth century the ideal of a Wales in control of its own destiny and holding its historic culture in high esteem seized the imagination of young intellectuals such as T. E. *Ellis, Owen M. *Edwards, J. Edward *Lloyd and John *Morris-Jones and was the inspiration of much of the passionate oratory of the young David *Lloyd George. It was this wave of Nationalist fervour which led to the founding of such institutions as the *University of Wales, the *National Library and the *National Museum of Wales.

Nationalism has been a vigorous factor in the life of Wales during the twentieth century, but it has not proved to be as dominant a force among the Welsh as it has been among the Irish and among some of the peoples of eastern Europe. Although the policy of self-government for Wales has found fitful expression in the thinking of the *Liberal and *Labour Parties, it was not until 1925, with the founding of *Plaid Cymru,

that Welsh Nationalism was given overt political expression. Whereas the term 'Nationalist' had been used in a highly indiscriminate fashion in early twentieth-century Wales, its use after 1925 became restricted to the activities and to the members of Plaid Cymru. Saunders *Lewis, the party's first President, sought to provide Wales with a rigorously Nationalist doctrine which placed the safeguarding of Welsh-speaking communities at the forefront of the party's aims. In the inter-war years Plaid Cymru attracted the support of perhaps the majority of Welsh-language writers and other intellectuals but it proved unable to win a mass following. After the war, it shed some of the more rigorous doctrines of Saunders Lewis and under the leadership of Gwynfor *Evans (President 1945–81), it had a degree of success in attracting electoral support. During the upsurge in Nationalist feeling in the 1960s and 1970s (manifested in particular by Gwynfor Evans's victory in the Carmarthen by-election of 1966), a number of new Nationalist movements came into existence, among which the most active is *Cymdeithas yr Iaith Gymraeg.

For studies of Welsh Nationalism see The Historical Basis of Welsh Nationalism (ed. D. Myrddin Lloyd, 1950), Reginald Coupland, Welsh and Scottish Nationalism (1954), the chapter by Ioan Rhys (Ioan Bowen Rees) in Celtic Nationalism (1968), Gwynfor Evans, Land of my Fathers (1974), R. Tudur Jones, The Desire of Nations (1974), Alan Butt Philip, The Welsh Question: Nationalism in Welsh Politics 1945–70 (1975) and Michael Hechter, Internal Colonialism: the Celtic Fringe in British National Development 1536–1966 (1975); see also John Osmond (ed.), The National Question Again (1985).

Nationalist, The, a magazine published between 1907 and 1912 under the editorship of Thomas Marchant *Williams. A lively journal which could be scathing and controversial in its remarks about some of the foremost Welshmen of the day, it reacted fiercely when the editor's favourite institutions, such as *Gorsedd Beirdd Ynys Prydain, were attacked, and it was particularly severe on O. M. *Edwards and John *Morris-Jones. Of the latter's volume, Caniadau (1907), T. Marchant Williams commented, 'Machine-made poetry on hand-made paper'. The magazine published several important articles on literary topics by writers such as W. J. *Gruffydd, T. Gwynn *Jones, J. Gwenogvryn *Evans and John Glyn *Davies, as well as translations of Welsh poetry by H. Idris *Bell.

For further details see the article by J. E. Caerwyn Williams in Ysgrifau Beirniadol IX (1976).

Naw Helwriaeth, Y (lit. 'The nine kinds of hunting'), a treatise attributed to *Gruffudd ap Cynan, although internal evidence proves it to be of much later date. Four manuscript copies of the text are extant, the oldest of which (Peniarth MS 155, 1561–62) is in the hand of Richard Philipps of Picton. The work is in three parts: a list of the nine kinds of hunting, the nine animals of the hunt and the three types of hunt; a list of the customs of the hunt; and a list of the three things which excite the hounds while they are hunting. The text may be dated firmly, in one respect, because the third list is a translation of part of *The Boke of St. Albans* (1486), a hunting handbook; the first and second are based on rules found in the Welsh law-books. The text is often associated with that of *Y Pedwar Camp ar Hugain* (lit. 'The Twenty-four Feats') and its Welsh nature is reflected in its triadic arrangement. The work was probably inspired, however, by the fashion for hunting books which was at its peak in England during the later Middle Ages.

For further details see the articles by I. C. Peate and W. Linnard in the *Bulletin* of the Board of Celtic Studies (1933 and 1984).

Neath, an abbey in Glamorgan which was founded about 1129 as a daughter-house of the Order of Savigny by Richard de Granville and affiliated to the *Cistercian Order in 1147, took its name from the river Nedd. During the fifteenth century *The Register of Neath*, a manuscript lost about 1725, was written at the abbey. The manuscript known as *Y *Cwta Cyfarwydd* may have belonged to Neath's scriptorium and the lost manuscript of *The *White Book of Hergest* was copied either there or at *Margam. Griffith John *Williams suggested that *The *Red Book of Hergest*, too, was copied at Neath about 1400. It was he who showed that the claim by Iolo Morganwg (Edward *Williams) that Ieuan Du'r Bilwg wrote his poem requesting the *Llyfr y Greal* from the abbot of Glyn Neath is without foundation. During the later fifteenth century *Llywelyn Goch y Dant eulogized the abbot Siôn and Lewys Morganwg (*Llywelyn ap Rhisiart) paid tribute in a masterly *awdl* to the last abbot, Lleision Tomas, an influential reformer within the Cistercian Order, referring especially to his great scholarship. The abbey was dissolved in 1539.

The history of Neath abbey was written by Walter de Gray Birch (1902); see also the chapter by Glanmor Williams in *Neath and District* (ed. E. Jenkins, 1974).

Nedw (1922), a collection of short stories by E. Tegla *Davies. Although the eponymous hero is about the same age as the boy in *Hunangofiant Tomi* (1912), he is even more mischievous. It is he, often in collaboration with his cousin Wmffre, who plans the hilarious adventures which usually turn into disasters. The best-known tale is '*Gwneud Zebras*', in which the boys paint stripes on a donkey named Spargo, but several others are equally inventive. Nedw narrates the stories in the dialect of Iâl (*Yale) and the dialogue is often scintillating.

Dyddgu Owen discusses E. Tegla Davies as a children's author in *Edward Tegla Davies, Llenor a Phroffwyd* (ed. Islwyn Ffowc Elis, 1956); see also the article by the same author in *Dewiniaid Difyr* (ed. Mairwen and Gwynn Jones, 1983).

'Nefoedd, Y' (lit. 'The heavens'), a sacred song by T. Osborne Roberts (1879–1948), is a setting of words by John *Roberts (Ieuan Gwyllt). Originally published by Leila Megane, the composer's wife, under the pseudonym Gerald Orme, the song was immortalized by her rendering of it. Ieuan Gwyllt is reputed to have written the words under emotional strain while his younger brother Isaac was dying from consumption.

NEIRIN, see ANEIRIN (*fl.* the latter part of the 6th cent.).

NENNIUS (*fl.* 800), the name traditionally given to the author of the work entitled *Historia Brittonum*, which purports to give the history of Britain from the time of Julius Caesar down to the end of the seventh century. He says of himself that he was a pupil of bishop Elbodugus (*Elfodd) of Gwynedd, but neither the author's name nor the identification occurs in the older manuscripts. The usual assumption is that he was a monk and some historians have thought that he came from *Erging. In a manuscript written in 817 and now in the Bodleian Library at Oxford it is stated that *Nemnivus* fabricated a set of characters to represent the letters of the Welsh alphabet because a mocking Englishman had said that the Welsh possessed no alphabet. The *Historia* contains some fanciful material, but it is important for the study of the origins of the legend concerning *Arthur.

For further details see David N. Dumville, 'Nennius and the *Historia Brittonum*' in *Studia Celtica* (vols. X/XI, 1975–76).

Neo-Classicism, a term applied to a literary movement which, especially in the 1930s and 1940s, reacted against *Romanticism and advocated anew some of the principles of *Classicism, especially the conception of the artist as a craftsman, the emphasis on cerebration rather than on a naïve emotionalism and the idea that the best literature is a contribution to a majestic tradition. The movement was influenced by Aestheticism and French Symbolism, and some of its representatives, such as T. S. Eliot and Ezra Pound, used the techniques of literary Modernism. In some of its exemplars Neo-Classicism is associated with *Roman Catholicism, or Anglo-Catholicism, as well as with political and social attitudes which emphasize stability, obedience and the responsibilities of class or privilege or leadership.

In Wales the Neo-Classical movement includes Saunders *Lewis, Gwenallt (David James *Jones), Aneirin Talfan *Davies and Euros *Bowen. Among the influences upon these writers were Mallarmé, Laforgue, T. S. Eliot and Charles Williams. Eric Gill, particularly in his Catholicism and his promotion of religious craftsmanship, influenced David *Jones, Aneirin Talfan Davies and Dafydd

*Jenkins, although his dictum 'All art is propaganda' affected not only Neo-Classicists but the group known as *Cylch Cadwgan, among others.

NEPEAN, EDITH (c.1890–1969), romantic novelist, was born at Llandudno, Caerns., but later moved to London where, by marriage to Molyneux Nepean, she became a member of the English gentry. The first of her thirty-five novels was *Gwyneth of the Welsh Hills* (1917) and among the others were *Petals in the Wind* (1922), *Cambria's Fair Daughter* (1923) and *Sweetheart of the Valley* (1927). The background for all these was provided by Welsh life and gypsy-lore, but neither was treated with any depth. The plots and the characterization of all her stories have the melodramatic quality usual in romances of the time. The earlier novels deal with the Welsh peasantry and although she accused Caradoc Evans (David *Evans) of libelling her in *Wasps* (1933), her first novel shows the influence of his work. Her later books, in which there is a stronger element of romantic fantasy, have country-house settings and principal characters who are either aristocratic or artistic.

Nest (fl. 1100–1120), the daughter of Rhys ap Tewdwr, the last king of *Deheubarth, was renowned for her beauty. She was married to Gerald of Windsor about the year 1100 and among their descendants were *Gerald de Barri (Giraldus Cambrensis) and a number of the knights who accompanied Strongbow to Ireland. She was known as 'The Helen of Wales' on account of her abduction by *Owain ap Cadwgan in 1109. The scene of this incident is thought to have been *Cilgerran castle and Nest may well have been Owain's willing accomplice. She had many lovers, including Henry I, and is reputed to have borne at least seventeen children.

Newport Rising, The (1839), see under CHARTISM.

Nia Ben Aur, see under TIR NA N-OG (1916).

Nicander, see WILLIAMS, MORRIS (1809–74).

Nichol, William (d. 1558), one of the three Protestant martyrs burned in Wales during the reign of Mary Tudor, lived in Haverfordwest, Pembs., and it was there he met his death. The other two Marian martyrs of Wales were Robert *Ferrar and Rawlins *White.

NICHOLAS, JAMES (1928–), poet. Born at St. David's, Pembs., he was a mathematics teacher at Bala and Pembroke before his appointment as headmaster of *Ysgol y Preseli*, Crymych, in 1963 but joined Her Majesty's Inspectorate of Schools in 1975. He has

published two volumes of verse, *Olwynion* (1967) and *Cerddi'r Llanw* (1969), and a study of the work of his friend Waldo *Williams in the *Writers of Wales* series (1975); he also edited the volume published in commemoration of the poet in 1977. In 1979 he published a lecture on the poet T. E. *Nicholas entitled *Pan Oeddwn Grwt Diniwed yn y Wlad*. At the National Eisteddfod of 1969 he won the *Chair and he served as Archdruid from 1981 to 1984.

Nicholas, Jemima (d. 1832), a heroine who, according to tradition, helped to defeat the French at Strumble Head near Fishguard, Pembs., where the incident known as 'the Last Invasion of Britain' took place in 1797. A French expeditionary force, led by an American named Tate, had been sent up the Bristol Channel to start a peasants' revolt in England. Forced by the winds to land instead on the Welsh coast, they surrendered after a few days of looting to the Castlemartin Yeomanry under Lord Cawdor. In the popular view their capture was attributable to a crowd of local women, led by Jemima Nicholas and dressed in red shawls and tall, black hats, whom the French were said to have mistaken for soldiery. It was also said that Jemima Nicholas captured a number of Frenchmen with the aid of a pitchfork.

For further details see E. H. Stuart Jones, *The Last Invasion of Britain* (1950) and John Kinross, *Fishguard Fiasco* (1974).

NICHOLAS, THOMAS EVAN (**Niclas y Glais**; 1878–1971), poet, was born at Llanfyrnach, Pembs., where his family were farmers. Educated at the Gwynfryn Academy in Ammanford under the direction of Watcyn Wyn (Watkin Hezekiah *Williams) and Gwili (John *Jenkins), he was ordained at Llandeilo and served in the Congregational ministry in Dodgeville, USA (1903–04), at Glais in the Swansea Valley (1904–14), and at Llangybi and Llanddewibrefi, Cards. (1914–18). His political convictions developed through his association with the workers of Glais, his friendship with Keir *Hardie, and his reading of R. J. *Derfel and Robert *Owen, and were confirmed by the Bolshevik Revolution of October 1917.

He was the most eloquent spokesman for the Independent Labour Party in the Welsh language, edited the Welsh column of its newspaper, *The Merthyr Pioneer*, and stood as the party's candidate for Aberdare in the 'Khaki Election' of 1918. After suffering police harassment and recriminations from both political and religious opponents because of his opposition to the War, Nicholas and his wife trained as dentists and established practices first at Pontardawe and, in 1921, at Aberystwyth, where he remained until his death. Between 1917 and 1945 he delivered more than a thousand lectures on the Soviet Union and was a founder-member of the Communist Party of Great Britain, but he did not resume his role as political journalist until 1937, when his weekly contributions to *Y ★Cymro* began to appear under the title '*O Fyd y Werin*'. He also founded at this time, with J. Roose Williams, the short-lived newspaper, *Llais y Werin*. His pronouncements led ultimately to his detention for two months, on spurious charges, in Swansea and Brixton prisons but, with his son Islwyn he was released as a result of a vigorous campaign by the Labour movement. Acclaimed by Harry Pollitt in 1949 as 'Wales's greatest man', T. E. Nicholas was a unique apologist for the Welsh working class, combining a rigorous Marxist analysis of society with what he saw as most progressive within the Welsh Radical, Nonconformist tradition.

His prolific career as a poet can be divided into two periods. The volumes *Salmau'r Werin* (1909), *Cerddi Gwerin* (1912), *Cerddi Rhyddid* (1914) and *Dros Eich Gwlad* (1920) contain, for the most part, poems of political polemic, alternately vitriolic and apocalyptic, and most effective when the bludgeon of rhetoric is supplemented by the cutting edge of irony. In the later volumes, *Terfysgoedd Daear* (1939), *Llygad y Drws* (1940), *Canu'r Carchar* (1942), *Y Dyn a'r Gaib* (1944), *Dryllio'r Delwau* (1941) and '*Rwy'n Gweld o Bell* (1963), the influences of the earlier period were held in check by a greater economy of diction and control of form (the sonnet being especially favoured), though the war between Labour and international Capital remained his favourite subject. A volume of his poems in English translation appeared under the title *Prison Sonnets* (1948) and a bilingual selection of his political verse in the volume *Tros Ryddid Daear* (1981).

For further details about the poet's life and work see T. E. Nicholas, *Proffwyd Sosialaeth a Bardd Gwrthryfel* (ed. J. Roose Williams, 1971), the essay by D. Tecwyn Lloyd in *Gwŷr Llên* (ed. Aneirin Talfan Davies, 1948) and James Nicholas, *Pan Oeddwn Grwt Diniwed yn y Wlad* (1979).

NICHOLAS, WILLIAM RHYS (1914–), poet, hymn-writer and editor. Born at Tegryn, Llanfyrnach, Pembs., he was a Congregational minister, latterly at Porthcawl, Glam., until his retirement in 1983. He has published three volumes of poetry, *Cerdd a Charol* (1969), *Oedfa'r Ifanc* (1974) and *Cerddi Mawl* (1980), and a study of the ★*Bardd Gwlad* in the ★*Writers of Wales* series under the title *The Folk Poets* (1978); he was also the co-author of the volumes *Writers of the West* (1974) and *Dilyn Afon* (1977). His address to the Union of Welsh Independents was published as *Maen Prawf ein Cristionogaeth* (1982). From 1954 until the magazine's demise in 1980 he was co-editor (with Emlyn Evans) of *Y ★Genhinen* and he also edited the verse anthologies *Beirdd Penfro* (1961), *Cerddi '77* (1977) and *Triongl* (1977).

NICHOLL, THEODORE (1902–73), poet

and novelist. Born at Llanelli, Carms., the son of D. W. Nicholl, the rugby-player, he was a journalist in London for most of his adult life. He published four volumes of verse, *Sung before the Bridal* (1930), *Poems* (1934), *Wild Swans* (1939) and *The Immortal Ease* (1948) as well as a collection of short stories, *The Hostile Friends* (1925), and a novel, *The Luck of Wealth* (1926), which is set in a Welsh industrial town.

Niclas y Glais, see NICHOLAS, THOMAS EVAN (1878–1971).

NICOLAS, DAFYDD (1705?–74), poet, may have been born at Ystradyfodwg, Glam., but Thomas Christopher ★Evans (Cadrawd) maintained that he was a native of Llangynwyd. It is known that he kept a school in the latter parish. In his youth he was an itinerant schoolmaster in the uplands of Glamorgan but about 1745 he came to the attention of the Williams family of ★Aberpergwm and subsequently became the family's household poet and private tutor. He was reputed to be a classical scholar and to have translated a part of Homer's *Iliad* into Welsh. Iolo Morganwg (Edward ★Williams) referred to him as one of the greatest poets of his day. No examples of his work are extant, except for two lyrical poems in Maria Jane Williams's collection, *Ancient National Airs of Gwent and Morgannwg* (1844), namely '*Callyn Serchus*' and '*Ffanni Blodau'r Ffair*', although several others were fabricated and ascribed to him by Iolo Morganwg.

For further details see G. J. Williams, *Traddodiad Llenyddol Morgannwg* (1948).

Night Must Fall (1935), a play in three acts by Emlyn ★Williams, was the author's first commercial success. Running for more than four hundred performances on the London stage, it was a departure from conventional crime-and-detection drama in that it revealed the identity of the murderer in the prologue in order to concentrate on character, motive and the psychology of murder, a central theme of Emlyn Williams's later work. Dan, the chief character, is 'a bell-boy in a roadhouse who was once a seaman and a blackmailer and a ponce before he took to murder'. A servant who conceals hatred of his superiors under a boyish, whimsical charm, he takes revenge on them by murdering two rich, selfish women. He is a coldly proficient manipulator of emotions and takes a self-conscious delight in his own cleverness until neurosis overcomes his self-control. Under arrest and on trial, however, he regains his poise and goes to the gallows delighted by his own notoriety.

Nimrod, see APPERLEY, CHARLES JAMES (1779–1843).

Nine Men's Morris, a game which was particularly popular among farm-labourers in Wales during the latter part of the nineteenth century and the beginning of the twentieth century. A board game, also known as Crown, it was played by moving counters over a pattern of three concentric squares with the object of removing the opponent's counters. See also Fox and Geese and Gwyddbwyll.

Nine Witches of Gloucester, The, see under Mother Goddesses.

Ninian Park, the stadium of Cardiff City Football Club, a team known as the Bluebirds (from the colour of its jerseys) which won the Cup Final in 1927. The club's triumphs and star players, such as the captain Fred *Keenor, are recalled in the autobiographies and poetry of Dannie *Abse who remains one of the team's staunchest supporters.

NISBET, ROBERT (1941–   ), short-story writer, was born at Haverfordwest, Pembs., and educated at University College, Swansea, and the University of Essex. A teacher of English in Milford Haven, he is the author of four collections of stories, namely *Dreams and Dealings* (1973), *The Rainbow's End* (1979), *Sounds of the Town* (1982) and *Stories of Sheepskin* (1983), and a volume of verse, *Pastoral* (1983). He has also edited two anthologies of stories, *Dismays and Rainbows* (1979) and *Pieces of Eight* (1982).

Nod Cyfrin, Y (lit. 'The mystic mark') or **Nod Pelydr Goleuni** (lit. 'The mark of the shaft of light'), the symbol /|\ devised by Iolo Morganwg (Edward *Williams) to represent the attributes of Love, Justice and Truth in the ceremonies and regalia of *Gorsedd Beirdd Ynys Prydain.

Nogood Boyo, the layabout in Dylan *Thomas's *Under Milk Wood* (1954), looks up at the sky from his dinghy and remarks, 'I don't know who's up there and I don't care'. He carries on, in the wash-house, with Lily Smalls.

Non (fl. late 5th cent.), the mother of *Dewi Sant (St. David). According to *Bonedd y Saint*, she was the daughter of Cynyr of Caer Gawch in Mynyw and her mother was Anna, the daughter of *Uthr Bendragon, *Arthur's father. In *Rhygyfarch's Life of St. David, Non is said to have been a nun who, although violated by Sant, King of Ceredigion, remained chaste and after the birth of her son, Dewi Sant, lived on nothing but bread and water. There are in Wales five places bearing the name Llan Non, all in close proximity to churches dedicated to Dewi, and she is also commemorated in Cornwall, Devon and Brittany.

Non Con Quill, see Jones, John Cynddylan (1840–1930).

Nonconformity or **Dissent**, the position of Christians who choose not to conform to the doctrine and practice of an Established Church. The term is generally used in Britain with reference to early post-Reformation denominations such as the *Baptists and *Independency and, later, to *Methodism (Calvinistic and Wesleyan) and, among the less orthodox, to those who embraced *Quakerism and *Unitarianism. Nonconformists trace their spiritual lineage to the Early Church, but modern Nonconformity arose in the wake of the Reformation. As a result of the new freedom to read the Bible, not everyone was able to accept the religious compromise instituted by Elizabeth I who, for political reasons, chose the middle path between *Roman Catholicism and *Puritanism. Most of the early Puritans were concerned to move the doctrine and practice of the Church of England farther away from the Roman, but gradually separatists appeared, people who were convinced that further reform of the Church had become impossible. Their number was increased rather than diminished by the attempt of Archbishop Laud to re-Catholicize the Church and, although the main religious challenge came from the Presbyterians, who wished to establish an alternative State Church, it was ultimately Cromwell's Independents who triumphed in the *Civil War. The State Church established under the Commonwealth was Puritan but offered a wide measure of doctrinal toleration. On the restoration of the Monarchy in 1660 many Puritan ministers were ejected and some four thousand ministers of that Church left their parishes rather than conform to the Act of Uniformity (1662). They suffered no little persecution until the Act of Toleration (1689) which granted freedom of worship but allowed other penalties to remain.

The first Welshman to embrace Dissenting principles was John *Penry, martyred in 1593, but not until 1639—if the 'Dissenting' position of the *Celtic Church be disregarded—was the first church established, a 'gathered church' of Independents and Baptists, at Llanfaches, Mon. In the eighteenth century the influence of Methodism and a series of spiritual awakenings were responsible not only for the eventual addition of two Nonconformist denominations but also for reviving the fortunes of the older Dissenters. By 1851, seven out of ten places of worship in Wales belonged to the Nonconformists (compared with five out of ten in England) and the influence of Nonconformity, symbolized by the Chapel, penetrated deeply into every aspect of Welsh life. Dissenting worshippers (members and adherents) accounted for eight out of every ten in the population on a whole. Long after its golden age during the first half of the nineteenth century, the spiritual energy of Nonconformity and its emphasis on the upright 'character' of the individual continued to exert a powerful influence upon private, social and political morality. These elements found expression in the 'Nonconformist Conscience', the battle for religious and educational equality, missionary enterprise and the *Temperance movement. They were to be seen, too, in the increasing awareness in the nineteenth century that Nonconformity, in alliance with *Radicalism, had a political responsibility to lead the Welsh people, a role which could be filled through support for *Liberalism. Only after the First World War did it become obvious that this influence was on the wane, a trend first reflected in literature in the work of some Anglo-Welsh writers such as Caradoc Evans (David *Evans) and Rhys *Davies. By today Chapel membership and attendance have decreased in most parts of Wales to the point of crisis.

The history of literature in modern Wales cannot be understood without detailed attention to the contribution and influence of Nonconformity, and the reaction against it. In its own right it produced an enormous wealth of literature, including biblical commentaries, sermons, biographies (which portray the Nonconformist 'character' so accurately), doctrinal and controversial books, scriptural dictionaries and concordances, periodicals, historical works, poetry (especially hymns), moralistic novels and translations of Nonconformist writings in English. Through the medium of the chapels, and particularly the *Sunday Schools, the Welsh people learned to read and there too they became familiar with the classical language of the Welsh *Bible and with the experiential sublimity of the *hymn, both of which were to leave their mark on the spiritual consciousness and literary expression of many a generation. It is no doubt true that the literary horizons of Nonconformity were restricted, that it frowned for too long on the *novel, the *interlude, the theatre and the *eisteddfod, and that it produced much verse of an indifferent quality. But it is also true that Nonconformity gave rise to literature of the highest order in the works of such Welsh writers as Morgan *Llwyd, Charles *Edwards, William *Williams (Pantycelyn), Ann *Griffiths, Thomas *Jones of Denbigh, Islwyn (William *Thomas), Daniel *Owen and Gwenallt (David James *Jones) and that it has not been without its influence on some writers in English who include Glyn *Jones, Emyr *Humphreys and Roland *Mathias. It has been in essence a spiritual movement, but it has also created and sustained an articulate, literary and creative people, not the least of its achievements being that it has done so mainly through the medium of the Welsh language.

In addition to the various denominational histories, see T. Rees, *History of Protestant Nonconformity in Wales* (1861), *Dylanwad Ymneilltuaeth ar Fywyd y Genedl* (ed. James Evans, 1913), R. I. Parry, *Ymneilltuaeth* (1962) and R. M. Jones, *Llên Cymru a Chrefydd* (1977).

Norman Conquest of Wales, The. William the Conqueror, well aware of the problems of the Welsh Border, followed his victory at Hastings in 1066 by establishing three of his most trusted leaders to watch the Welsh—William Fitz Osbern at Hereford, Roger of Montgomery at Shrewsbury and Hugh of Avranches at Chester. The death of Fitz Osbern in Normandy in 1071, however, set back the advances already made south-westwards and the rise of an acknowledged Welsh leader, Rhys ap Tewdwr, with whom William could treat, delayed further serious operations for some twenty-five years. The first real penetrations of Wales, therefore, were made by the House of Montgomery advancing south-westwards through Cardigan to *Pembroke, where a castle was built in 1092. Thereafter, and particularly after the death of Rhys ap Tewdwr in battle in 1094, several Norman leaders established their own lordships in south Wales. These Marcher Lords, though holding their lands from the King, were effectively much more independent than the Earl of Chester (who ruled the only surviving Palatine Earldom), a fact which permitted *Gwynedd to persist under an independent Welsh prince. By 1135 lordships in the Border areas and along the southern coastal plain were firmly established and castles (with *Chepstow the first) had been built. In fertile and low-lying districts, where manors could be established according to the feudal custom, Englishries grew up. The uplands, by contrast, where Welsh life continued largely undisturbed, became known as Welshries, in which the native population lived according to their own customs and laws, paying annual tributes to their lord and acknowledging his authority.

During the first two centuries after the Normans' settlement of Wales the relationship between them and the Welsh fluctuated according to political circumstances. Gradually, however, social and cultural links were established through the use made of latimers in Norman and Welsh courts, and by inter-marriage. In the twelfth century the Normans became acquainted with themes, characters and tales derived from the Welsh narrative tradition. *Arthur, a central figure, was depicted by *Geoffrey of Monmouth in his *Historia Regum Britanniae (1136) in a Norman context and the portrayal of Arthur's court and knights was based on contemporary ideals of *Chivalry. The transmission of this narrative tradition may explain the similarities between the Welsh stories of Geraint, Owain and Peredur (see under TAIR RHAMANT) and the three Old French romances by Chrétien de Troyes. Long before the integration of the Normans with Welsh society had become clear, *Gerald de Barri, perhaps for reasons not entirely patriotic, called himself Cambrensis and identified himself with Welsh ecclesiastical interests. As the generations passed, families of Norman descent (though hardly ever descended from lords of the first rank, among whom the survival rate was low) made their mark in Wales —the Aubreys, the Walbeoffs, the Turbervilles, the Havards, the Delahays, the Devereux and the Scudamores were among the most prominent examples. The last two of these were to provide, respectively, an Earl of Essex who rebelled against Queen Elizabeth and one of *Owain Glyndŵr's most trusted field captains.

For further details see J. E. Lloyd, *A History of Wales from the earliest times to the Edwardian Conquest* (2nd edn., 1912) and D. Walker, *The Norman Conquerors* (1977).

Norris, Charles (1779–1858), painter, was an Englishman who lived and worked in Wales for nearly sixty years. He settled at Milford, Pembs., in 1800 but moved in 1810 to Tenby, and spent the rest of his life painting scenes in the county; he also published *A Historical Account of Tenby* (1818).

NORRIS, LESLIE (1921–   ), poet and short-story writer, was born on a farm near Merthyr Tydfil, Glam. Formerly a teacher, a headmaster and a college lecturer, he has earned his living since 1974 as a full-time writer. Especially popular in the USA where, like Vernon *Watkins before him, he earned a reputation as writer and lecturer at the University of Washington at Seattle, he travels extensively and has been Visiting Professor at many universities, including the Brigham Young University of Utah.

He has published nine volumes of poetry: *The Tongue of Beauty* (1941), *Poems* (1944), *The Loud Winter* (1967), *Finding Gold* (1967), *Ransoms* (1970), *Mountains Polecats Pheasants* (1974), *Islands off Maine* (1977), *Merlin and the Snake's Egg* (1978), a volume of poetry for children, and *Water Voices* (1980). His prose works include a collection of short stories, *Sliding* (1978), and an essay on Glyn *Jones in the *Writers of Wales* series (1973). The collected poems of Leslie Norris have been published in America under the title *Walking the White Fields* (1980).

The emotional basis of Leslie Norris's writing is linked very strongly with his childhood experiences. His home town (although, as he says, 'I live in England, seem English') has exercised a powerful influence on his imagination. The Merthyr in which he was brought up and went to school in the last phase of its 'metropolitan' vitality and in Leslie Norris's poems about boxers, horses, greyhounds, birds, as well as the colourful characters of the town, may be seen that integration of literary and physical life in the community which the Second World War was to terminate. He has, however, contrived to carry that vitality into the north Carmarthenshire scene where he has made a second home and *Sliding*, in particular, manifests moods more diverse and humorous than the poetry. The especial quality of his writing is, in prose, a remarkable felicity of style, an ability so to order syntax as to 'improve' material which might otherwise, on occasion, seem thin. This syntactical power is carried over into his poetry, too: fecund in images and often verbally ingenious, his poems are rarely allowed to lose emotional impact by the obscuring of the narrative line. His skill in avoiding sentimentality is not unconnected with the presence, beneath the surface, of a deep melancholy which is more obvious in his later work and gives an especial poignancy to the pastoral eclogues of childhood. It is almost as though he is aware that he himself is 'the last of the old Merthyr' and that the farther he fares the emptier seems the world. His experiences in America have made his poetry more diffuse and urbane—the emotional centre of the work is less visible and the emphasis more descriptive—but his contact with Wales has by no means diminished.

For further details see the articles by Sam Adams in *Poetry Wales* (vol. 7, no. 2, 1971) and Randal Jenkins in *The Anglo-Welsh Review* (vol. 20, no. 46, 1972), and the note by Glyn Jones in *Profiles* (1980).

North Wales Gazette, The (1808–25), a weekly newspaper published in Bangor, Caerns., took a Conservative, pro-Church of England stance, opposing all Radical tendencies such as the call for constitutional *Reform. It also carried articles dealing with various aspects of Welsh history and correspondence on Welsh affairs. Among its contributors were Dewi Wyn o Eifion (David *Owen), Robert ap Gwilym Ddu (Robert *Williams) and Twm o'r Nant (Thomas *Edwards) and there was a column devoted to 'British Poetry' under the editorship of Dafydd Ddu Eryri (David *Thomas). It was succeeded by *The North Wales Chronicle* which continues to be published as a weekly newspaper.

'Nos Galan' (lit. 'New Year's Eve'), an air with refrain first published as a dance-tune in the major key by John *Parry (1710?–82) in *A Collection of Welsh, English and Scotch Airs . . .* (1761). He later published, in *British Harmony* (1781), a version which is closer to the present form of the tune and which became very popular in Wales and abroad. Many *Hen Benillion with the refrain '*ffa la la*' were set to the tune but by the end of the nineteenth century the words most commonly associated with it were those by John Ceiriog *Hughes, '*Oer yw'r gŵr sy'n methu caru*'.

Noson Lawen (lit. 'A merry evening'), an informal entertainment around the hearth during the winter evenings when neighbours assembled after the day's work, corresponding to the *ceilidh* of Ireland and Scotland. An occasion for the recitation of tales and singing, it was often combined with work, as in the *noson wau* (*knitting night). By the twentieth century the term had come to mean a concert held in a public hall and it was also the title of a popular radio programme broadcast during the 1940s.

For further details see R. W. Jones, *Bywyd Cymdeithasol Cymru yn y Ddeunawfed Ganrif* (1931).

Novel in English, The, in spite of a comparatively early start with T. J. Ll. *Prichard's *The Adventures and Vagaries of * Twm Shôn Catti* (1828), was slow to get into its stride in Wales. Apart from Allen Raine (Anne Adaliza Beynon *Puddicombe), Joseph *Keating and a few others, all the most important novelists of the first generation immediately established the two main genres which have persisted, with only small alteration, to the present, namely the proletarian novel and the rural romance.

The early coalfield novels of Jack *Jones, Rhys *Davies, Gwyn *Jones and Richard Llewellyn (Richard Llewellyn *Lloyd) were written by first-hand witnesses of social hardship in the mining valleys before and during the *Depression, and they exhibit anger at the helplessness of ordinary people in the face of impersonal economic forces. The stark, documentary style in which poor living and working conditions are presented, set against the rough vitality and native intelligence of the miners and their families, serves to highlight the message of these writers—that the suffering is undeserved and ought not to be accepted willingly. Concerned as they are with the effect of external events on a community as a whole, these novels exhibit little psychological depth or sensitivity of character and their plots are usually loosely constructed family sagas extending over several decades. At their heart are often strong, vivacious mother-figures who lend a certainty to life in the midst of change and confusion. The proletarian family saga continued in the later novels of Jack Jones who, like Alexander Cordell (George Alexander *Graber), extended its historical range, but with little alteration of style or attitude. In the hands of other writers, however, the form has undergone radical changes. While moral anger mingles with anarchic humour in the work of Gwyn *Thomas, Ron *Berry and Alun *Richards, for example, the chief impression these writers give is of a hopeless, disintegrating society which lacks control over its own destiny.

The second principal genre, the rural romance, may be divided into two broad types. The first consists of the earlier novels of the Welsh Border as written by Hilda *Vaughan, Margiad Evans (Peggy Eileen *Whistler) and Geraint *Goodwin, the other of the later novels, set in rural, Welsh-speaking Wales, of Rhys Davies and Richard Vaughan (Ernest Lewis *Thomas). These novels are more inward-looking than the proletarian novel and more concerned with human relationships, especially love between men and women. They are more tightly plotted, with a simple story-line and a lyrical, passionate style. The central characters are more important than the community in which they are set and minor characters are often vividly depicted. Whereas the proletarian novel presents the danger to the Welsh community of outside forces in economic terms, the Border romances focus on the process of Anglicization and social tension between Welsh and English. They are rather limited, however, in their depiction of the social and cultural dichotomy of Wales because they are restricted to the subjective experience of their characters. A fuller, more objective approach is to be found in the work of Raymond *Williams and Emyr *Humphreys who clothe the proletarian novel's plain presentation of historical processes in the more sophisticated fictive techniques of the rural romance. Each, in his own way, has achieved a mature representation of human character and the human condition by combining the best qualities of the proletarian novel with those of the rural romance.

Fantasy and a child's-eye view are frequent elements of the Welsh novel in English. The former, at home in the subjective world of the romances, is obtrusive when it occurs in the proletarian novel, notably those of Richard Llewellyn and Alexander Cordell. These, authors, however, share with many other Anglo-Welsh novelists the power to exploit, without excessive sentimentality, the innocent view-point of the child. It is in the novels of Glyn *Jones that these two elements are most powerfully and movingly fused. Deriving from the historical reality of emigration as a result of industrial depression, rural depopulation and social ambition, departure from Wales is also a common element of the plots, while in later novels the return to Wales grows more frequent. Both have been used by Anglo-Welsh writers to explore their relationship with their social and cultural roots. Language is, inevitably, an essential aspect of such an exploration and, unlike the poets, the novelists have reflected the distinctive English of Anglicized areas of Wales in their dialogue and narrative. They have been less convincing in depicting Welsh-speaking communities and, with the notable exception of Emyr Humphreys, in their handling of the linguistic and psychological complexities of a bilingual society.

For further discussion of the Welsh novel in English see G. F. Adam, *Three Contemporary Anglo-Welsh Novelists* (1948), Glyn Jones, *The Dragon has Two Tongues* (1968), David Smith, 'Myth and Meaning in the Literature of the South Wales Coalfield—the 1930s', in *The Anglo-Welsh Review* (no. 56, Spring, 1976) and Raymond Williams, *The Welsh Industrial Novel* (The Gwyn Jones Lecture, 1978; reprinted in the author's book, *Problems in Materialism and Culture* (1980); for discussion of individual novelists see the *Writers of Wales* series.

Novel in Welsh, The, has its origins in the early nineteenth century. The first book with claims to belong to the genre was *Y Bardd, neu y Meudwy Cymreig* (1830) by William Ellis *Jones

(Cawrdaf), but it is little more than a shapeless, moralistic fantasy. Serial fiction, some examples of which were translations from the English, had begun to appear in periodicals from about 1822. Soon afterwards original fiction in Welsh began to appear in the form of love-stories, historical romances, novelettes preaching *Temperance and chastity, and thrillers, including some crude 'westerns'. Because Welsh readers, for the most part, were the products of the *Sunday School, the writers felt obliged to assert that their tales were educative or morally uplifting. The two most talented authors were William *Rees (Gwilym Hiraethog) and David *Owen (Brutus), the one a natural story-teller, the other a very gifted satirist, but the works of both lack the structure and unity of novels. Daniel *Owen was in the direct line of these tellers of tales and well acquainted with their work, but by reading the best English fiction he acquired a clearer vision of the nature of the novel. Despite some serious technical faults in his books, Daniel Owen had a rare natural gift which can only be called genius. He was a major influence on the writers who immediately succeeded him, such as W. Llewelyn *Williams and Annie Harriet *Hughes (Gwyneth Vaughan), although they are very pale shadows of the master.

Good novels in the years between the World Wars were few, yet this period was one of the most exciting in the history of Welsh-language fiction. The only full-length novel by E. Tegla *Davies, *Gŵr Pen y Bryn (1923), was the first to satisfy in both structure and content. It was followed by Saunders *Lewis's first short novel, *Monica (1930), of which the finely-wrought plot upset a conservative readership by its daring tale of suburban lust, *Plasau'r Brenin (1934) by Gwenallt (David James *Jones), set in an English prison, and Kate *Roberts's first novel, *Traed Mewn Cyffion (1936), which has become a classic. Another writer at the end of this period was Elena Puw *Morgan, whose two works, Y Wisg Sidan (1939) and Y Graith (1943), are, despite a laborious style, powerful evocations of rural life in the nineteenth century. The years after the Second World War saw the emergence of T. Rowland *Hughes who, with the skills of a professional novelist, portrayed his native slate-quarrying community with affection, celebrating the courage of the rock-men and their womenfolk.

In the 1950s and 1960s a new generation of gifted novelists included Islwyn Ffowc *Elis whose early romantic works won great critical acclaim, although they are not his best. Of the younger writers the ablest is John *Rowlands, who has shunned the conventional social novel to explore the 'inner hell' of deficient individuals in a claustrophobic environment, while Jane *Edwards and Eigra Lewis *Roberts examine the woman's role in a changing society. The story-lines of these young authors are tenuous, for they are mainly interested in recording thoughts and analysing emotions, and the meaninglessness of contemporary life can be sensed in their work. Most older authors have continued to write conventionally, the most productive being the fastidious craftsman, Selyf *Roberts. One notable exception is Pennar *Davies, whose books are experimental in form and content, affirming the Christian faith, without being openly propagandist, in an exalted prose style. Others who have published only one novel of distinction include Caradog *Prichard, author of *Un Nos Ola Leuad (1961), and T. Glynne *Davies whose Marged (1974) is the longest work of fiction in Welsh apart from the works of Daniel Owen. John Gwilym *Jones has crowned a fruitful life as a playwright by writing a masterly prose-work, Tri Diwrnod ac Angladd (1979), a critic's novel, with a skilful plot and carefully created characters, rich in symbolism and irony. Good as these writers are, however, the genius of Kate Roberts raises her above them all. Apart from her short stories, perhaps her greatest creations, the four novels which she published after the War, together with her superb Traed Mewn Cyffion, form a body of fictional prose which is second in importance only to that of Daniel Owen.

The most accomplished historical novel in Welsh was, for many years, R. T. *Jenkins's short masterpiece, *Orinda (1943), but historical novels increased in number during the 1960s and 1970s. The most successful in story-line, characterization and evocation of a historical period, as well as the most popular, is Y Stafell Ddirgel (1969) by Marion *Eames. The meticulous short historical novels of Rhiannon Davies *Jones are distinguished by the moving lyrical nature of their prose. Of war novels, rare in Welsh, by far the best is Gwaed y Gwirion (1965) by Emyr *Jones, which relates the experiences of a Welsh soldier in France during the First World War without sentimentality or melodrama. The majority of Welsh novels have a rural or industrial village setting, but some of the best, including three by Daniel Owen and three by Kate Roberts, are set in small towns. Several recent works have a newer background: school and university, the worlds of banking and fine art, trade unionism, modern industry and the law courts. There have been, too, a few serious attempts at writing science fiction, some excellent detective novels by John Ellis *Williams and the highly popular thrillers of T. Llew *Jones.

The future of the novel in Welsh, as in every language, is uncertain. But the number of new novels published annually in Welsh is comparatively high and the creative energy and inventiveness of some young writers now entering the field indicate that this art-form will continue for many years yet.

For discussion of the genre see Dafydd Jenkins, Y Nofel: datblygiad y nofel Gymraeg ar ol Daniel Owen

(1948) and Islwyn Ffowc Elis, *Themau yn y nofel Gymraeg* (1962) and 'The Modern Novel in Welsh' in *The Anglo-Welsh Review* (no. 36, 1966), the chapter by Kate Roberts in *Llên Ddoe a Heddiw* (ed. J. E. Caerwyn Williams, 1964); see also the essays by John Rowlands and Dafydd Ifans in *Ysgrifau Beirniadol IX* (ed. J. E. Caerwyn Williams, 1976) and by John Gwilym Jones in *Swyddogaeth Beirniadaeth* (1977); there is also a chapter by John Rowlands in *The Arts in Wales 1950–1975* (ed. Meic Stephens, 1979).

Novello, Ivor, see DAVIES, DAVID IVOR (1893–1951).

Nudd, the son of Senyllt and, according to the genealogy of *Bonedd y Saint*, a cousin to both *Rhydderch Hael and Mordaf Hael. Together with his two cousins, Nudd is cited in the Triads as one of the 'Three *Generous Men of the Isle of Britain'. Although the early genealogies treat him as a historical figure, his true origins may lie in the realms of Celtic mythology and with the Irish god, Nuada Argatlám. Nudd is generally taken by Welsh poets as a standard of generosity, though reference is also made to his courage in battle. Reference to his son, *Gwyn ap Nudd, in the story of *Culhwch and Olwen, suggests again the mythological status of father and son.

It is believed that the Nodens whose temple has been discovered near Lydney, Glos., and who was worshipped there in the second and third centuries AD can be identified with Nudd.

NUTTALL, GEOFFREY (1911–   ), scholar and historian of English Puritanism, was born at Colwyn Bay, Denbs., and educated at Balliol and Mansfield Colleges, Oxford. Ordained to the ministry at Warminster Congregational Church in 1938, he was, during the Second World War, successively Research Fellow and Lecturer at Woodbrooke College, Birmingham, and then, from 1945, Lecturer in Church History at New College, London. The author of numerous authoritative works, including *The Holy Spirit in Puritan Faith and Experience* (1946) and *Visible Saints: the Congregational Way, 1640–1660* (1957), he has also contributed to the history of Welsh *Puritanism in the seventeenth century and of Welsh *Methodism in the eighteenth century in his *The Welsh Saints, 1640–1660* (1957) and *Howel Harris 1714–1773: the Last Enthusiast* (1965).

Nynniaw and Peibiaw, see HORNED OXEN.

O

O Gors y Bryniau (lit. 'From the marsh of the hills'; 1925), the first published collection of short stories by Kate *Roberts. Dedicated to the memory of Richard Hughes *Williams (Dic Tryfan), a pioneer of the *short story in Welsh, the volume represents a leap forward in the development of the form. The nine stories, written between 1921 and 1924, have the slate-quarrying community of Caernarfonshire as their background, but two deal with people who have left that district. The predominant note struck throughout is one of sadness because the conditions in which the characters live are so relentlessly harsh. The most famous story in the volume, 'Henaint', is a subtle but excruciating presentation of an old woman's mental decline.

O Law i Law (lit. 'From hand to hand'; 1943), the first novel of T. Rowland *Hughes. The narrator is John Davies, a middle-aged bachelor, who on the death of his mother decides to move into lodgings. Loath to put his furniture up for auction, he sells it to relations and acquaintances, 'from hand to hand' as one of them says. Each chapter of the book, apart from the first and last, is concerned with one of the items sold in this manner—the mangle, the harmonium, the tea-service and so on—and each gives rise to a flood of memories, some sad and others humorous. The story does not follow a chronological sequence but moves backwards and forwards in time, the personality of the main character forging a link between the anecdotes.

The novel was translated into English by Richard Ruck under the title *From Hand to Hand* (1950). There is a discussion of the novel's themes by T. Emrys Parry in *Ysgrifau Beirniadol VI* (ed. J. E. Caerwyn Williams, 1971).

O Oes Gwrtheyrn Gwrthenau (lit. 'From the age of Vortigern'), a simple chronology of which about six manuscript copies are extant. The earliest version (in *Peniarth MS 32, c. 1404) was written by one of the copyists of The *Red Book of Hergest. The first part enumerates the years between one event and another but does not note the opening year: it begins (trans.) 'From the age of *Vortigern to the Battle of Baddon . . .' and, for the most part, follows the pattern of *Brut y Tywysogion, though with some additional entries. The *Red Book* version ends in 1210 but the Peniarth Manuscript proceeds to 1214, 'the winning of Pennard Dylavc', and continues with another series of dated entries which closes in 1307. This meagre text has no value as a historical source but, together with a number of other minor chronicles, it is a useful pointer to the sort of historical writing carried out in parallel to *Brut y Tywysogion* towards the end of the Middle Ages.

Observations on the River Wye (1782), a didactic and topographical work, was the product of two summers (1770 and 1782) spent on the Welsh Border by the English writer William Gilpin (1724–1804). Illustrated by a number of delicately mannered aquatints, the book went into five editions before 1800, in which year a French version was published in Breslau. Its main contention, delivered with 'a good-mannered eccentricity of style', was that the degree of beauty in a landscape is measurable by that landscape's suitability for painting. Gilpin praised the work of the Parliamentarians on *Raglan Castle for having broken up its straight lines and suggested that *Tintern Abbey, from the near view, might be improved with 'a mallet judiciously used', for, as it was, the 'cross isles (*sic*) confound the perspective'. This exposition of the picturesque brought many gentlemanly travellers to the Wye valley in the decades which followed, and the book became the aesthetic bible of a new cult. The invasion was on such a scale as to provide a subject for satire by the French-American Louis Simond, himself a Wye traveller, in 1811.

Offa's Dyke, an earthwork which runs, with interruptions, from the river Wye in the vicinity of Monmouth to a point just short of Prestatyn, Flints., was probably built in the eighth century by order of King Offa of Mercia as an agreed boundary between his territory and that of the Welsh. Although the dyke no longer coincides with the border between Wales and England, the term is often used with this meaning.

Offrwm (lit. 'Offering'), the money collected during a funeral service and presented to the parish priest. Before the Reformation its purpose was to pay the priest to say masses for the deceased but by the eighteenth century the money had come to be regarded as a gift to the officiating clergyman who might give it to the bereaved family, if they were in need. In the slate-quarrying districts of north Wales during the nineteenth century the custom of sending an offering to the home of the deceased became common: a sixpence or a shilling piece would be placed on a handkerchief laid out on a table to receive such gifts. A similar custom was the *arian rhaw* ('spade money') collected by the sexton to pay for his part in the funeral.

For further accounts of the custom see the articles by Gwynfryn Richards in the *Journal* of the Historical Society of the Church in Wales (vol. II, 1950) and F. P. Jones in *Gwerin* (vol. I, 1956); see also Trefor M. Owen, *Welsh Folk Customs* (1959).

Ogam, an alphabet containing twenty letters based on a pattern of straight lines and notches and devised to be carved on the edge of a piece of wood or stone. The letters were divided into four categories of five sounds, with the lines representing the consonants n, v, s, l, b; q, c, t, d, h; r, z, ng, g, m; the notches corresponded to the vowels i, e, u, o, a; the symbol ↑ for p was added on some British inscriptions.

Until recently all theories regarding the derivation of Ogam were nebulous, but it is now believed that it was invented for the Irish language and based on the Latin alphabet. In Ireland, throughout the Middle Ages, it was believed that knowledge of Ogam was an essential part of the poet's education. The letters were known by the names of trees such as *betha* (birch, W. *bedwen*), *luis* (elm, W. *llwyfen*) and *ninn* (ash, W. *onnen*). A number of Ogam inscriptions, including some three hundred examples carved in stone, have survived in Ireland, most of them in the counties of Waterford and Kerry.

There are about forty Ogam stones in Wales, mainly in districts which had strong Irish communities in the Dark Ages, namely the old counties of Pembrokeshire, Breconshire and Carmarthenshire. They are important because the majority are bilingual, with Brythonic-Latin and Irish usually appearing on the same stone, thus demonstrating the phonetic differences between the two languages. The stones are memorials bearing personal names in the genitive case, using the formula 'the stone of X MAQI (son of) / AVI (grandson of) MUCOI (descendant of) Z.' It is supposed that the inscriptions containing the word MUCOI represent a pagan era and that the name which follows refers to a pagan god who was considered to be the ancestor of the tribe. Because the people who are commemorated by the stones are otherwise unknown it is only possible to date them epigraphically in relation to the Latin-Brythonic inscriptions. The only exception among the Ogam stones of Wales is the inscription 'VOTECORIGAS (Ogam) / MEMORIA VOTEPORIGIS PROTICTOR' (Latin-Brythonic), now kept in Dwyran Church, Ang., which is believed to be a memorial to King Voteporius or Gwrthebyr who was rebuked by *Gildas in *De Excidio Britanniae*.

Further details will be found in John MacNeill, 'Notes on the Distribution, History, Grammar and Import of Irish Ogam Inscriptions' in the *Proceedings* of the Royal Irish Academy (vol. XXVII, 1909), K. H. Jackson, 'Notes on the Ogam Inscriptions of Southern Britain' in *The Early Cultures of North-west Europe* (ed. Cyril Fox and Bruce Dickens (1950), V. E. Nash-Williams, *The Early Christian Monuments of Wales* (1960) and Melville Richards, 'The Irish Settlements in South-west Wales' in the *Journal* of the Royal Society of Antiquaries of Ireland (vol. XC, 1960).

Ogmore or **Ogwr**, a mesne lordship of the lordship of Glamorgan. Like *Kidwelly, it was in the possession of the de Londres family, from whom it passed to the Chaworth family and then to the Duchy of Lancaster. Its archives are better preserved than are those of other lordships of the March and, in consequence, Ogmore provides the classic example of the division of Marcher territory into Englishries and Welshries.

Ogre of Abergavenny, The, see WILLIAM DE BRAOSE (*c.*1150–1211).

Old King Cole, see COEL HEN (5th cent.).

Old Man of Pencader, The, an anonymous Welshman who, according to *Gerald de Barri (Giraldus Cambrensis) in his *Descriptio Kambriae*, was questioned by Henry II during the king's progress through Wales in 1163 on whether he thought the Welsh would continue to resist the power of England. Speaking in Welsh, he gave this reply: 'This nation, O King, may now, as in former times, be harassed, and in a great measure weakened and destroyed by your and other powers, and it will often prevail by its laudable exertions, but it can never be totally subdued through the wrath of man, unless the wrath of God shall concur. Nor do I think that any other nation than this of Wales, or any other language, whatever may hereafter come to pass, shall on the day of severe examination before the Supreme Judge, answer for this corner of the earth'. The old man's defiant but dignified answer is one of the classic statements of Welsh nationhood. Pencader is a village north of Carmarthen where a plaque commemorating the incident was placed under the auspices of *Plaid Cymru in 1952.

Old North, The, the name given to the ancestral territories of the Britons, considerably greater than modern Wales, which lay to the south of a line from Stirling to Loch Lomond and extended southwards over Cumbria, much of Lancashire and Yorkshire, and eastwards to the Humber estuary. This was the old Cumbria, the land of the *Cumbri* or Cumbrenses, the 'fellow-countrymen' of the *Cymry* or *Cymru*, whose lands marched with Wales until the connection between them was severed by the Battle of *Chester in 615. Their language was Cumbric, a Brittonic dialect sufficiently close to

Welsh for the early poetry of *Aneirin and *Taliesin, which was originally composed in it, to have been transmitted down the ages as belonging to Wales.

During the fifth and sixth centuries this greater Cumbria was ruled by *Gwŷr y Gogledd* ('The Men of the North'), a group of related dynasties, many of the rulers of which bore names destined to become famous in history, literature and legend. Their ancestors had carved the kingdoms of Strathclyde, Rheged and *Gododdin— together with some smaller principalities, such as Elmet in what is now Yorkshire—out of the old Brittonic tribal territories of the Dumnonii, Novantai, Selgovai and Votadini in Scotland, and of the Brigantes to the south of Hadrian's Wall. This military activity may have been carried out under Roman encouragement, in order that these kingdoms might serve as buffer-states against the Picts from the north and the Scots from Ireland. Their rulers claimed descent from one or other of two ancestral stocks, being descendants either of *Coel Hen or of Dyfnwal Hen, grandson of Ceredig Wledig. This last progenitor has been identified with the *Coroticus* whom *Patrick denounced, in the mid-fifth century, in an indignant letter resulting from the murder by his soldiers of some Christians newly baptized by the saint; like Coel Hen, Coroticus may have been born near the end of the fourth century.

Strathclyde (the Cumbric *Strad Clud*) was broadly coterminous with the modern county, excluding the area north-west of the Clyde, but including part of Stirlingshire. Its capital was Din Alclud ('the Rock of the Clyde') at Dumbarton, and its ecclesiastical centre was at Glasgow, the foundation of St. Kentigern. In the south it bordered with *Urien's kingdom of Rheged, which bestrode the Solway estuary, probably had its capital at Carlisle and comprised the whole of the modern Cumbria, extending over the Pennines to Catterick. To the north it included Galloway and part of the old county of Ayrshire, though Ayrshire (or Aeron) seems to have been territory contested between Strathclyde and Rheged.

The principal kingdom on the east was Gododdin, which lay to the south of the Firth of Forth, with its capital at Din Eidyn, securely established upon the Rock of Edinburgh: from here the Gododdin force set out about the year 600 for their disastrous expedition against the Angles at Catterick. Originally the kingdom probably extended as far south as the Tyne. In its north-west corner lay the sub-province called Manaw Gododdin, the home from which *Cunedda and his sons departed in the mid-fifth century to expel the Irish from *Gwynedd, and to establish there a dynasty which was to rule for five centuries.

Edinburgh was besieged and captured by the Angles in 638 and with its loss the Gododdin kingdom perished. Very nearly at the same time the kingdom of Rheged also came to an end, but by more peaceful means, passing under Northumbrian rule about 635 by the marriage of the Northumbrian prince Oswiu with a great-granddaughter of Urien. Only Strathclyde retained its independence, with intermittent fortune, for nearly four more centuries, during which it became the principal centre in which the records of all the north-British kingdoms were brought together and preserved, and subsequently transmitted to Wales. This movement probably began about the ninth century and comprised both documentary material and orally preserved tales and poetry. By the twelfth century the Cumbric language had fallen into desuetude, except for the stray survival in some English country districts over many centuries of corrupt forms of the numerals which were used for counting sheep. With those exceptions, the language has left no traces apart from place-names, a few personal names in written sources and on inscriptions, and three isolated legal terms in an eleventh-century document known as the *Leges inter Brettos et Scottos*.

For further details see the introductions by Ifor Williams to his *Canu Aneirin* (1938) and *Canu Taliesin* (1960) and the article by the same author in *The Beginnings of Welsh Poetry* (ed. R. Bromwich, 1972); see also Kenneth H. Jackson, *The Gododdin: the Oldest Scottish Poem* (1969) and the monograph by A. O. H. Jarman on the *Cynfeirdd* in the *Writers of Wales* series (1981).

Old Wales, see under WILLIAMS, WILLIAM RETLAW JEFFERSON (1863–1944).

Oldest Animals, The, an international folk-tale probably originating in India, the most famous Welsh version of which is found in the story of *Culhwch and Olwen. The animals are the Blackbird of Cilgwri, the Stag of Rhedynfre, the Owl of Cwm Cowlyd, the Eagle of Gwernabwy, the Salmon of Llyn Llyw and the Toad of Cors Fochno. The tale's main feature is the eliciting of information from each animal in turn concerning the whereabouts of *Mabon fab Modron, until the oldest is eventually located. The medieval poets often refer to these animals, and the Triad, 'The Three Elders of the World', names the birds.

For further details see the articles by E. B. Cowell in *Y Cymmrodor* (vol. V, 1882), Thomas Jones in the *Journal* of the National Library of Wales (1951–52) and Dafydd Ifans in the *Bulletin* of the Board of Celtic Studies (1970–72).

OLIVERS, THOMAS (1725–99), early Methodist preacher and pamphleteer. Born at Tregynon, Mont., he had little formal education and was converted to the Wesleyan cause while working as a shoemaker. A blunt speaker of fiery temper but ever a diligent exhorter, he became an itinerant preacher in 1753 and a fierce polemicist against the Calvinistic view of predestination. Among his tracts were *A Scourge to Calumny* (1774) and *A Rod for a Reviler* (1777) but he is remembered more for two of his hymns, 'Come, Immortal King of Glory' and 'The God of Abraham praise'.

His autobiography, first published in *The Arminian Magazine* (1779), has been edited by Glyn Tegai Hughes and was reprinted by the Gregynog Press in 1979; see also the article by Richard Shindler in *The Red Dragon* (vol. 1, 1885).

Oll Synnwyr Pen Kembero Ygyd (lit. 'All the senses in a Welshman's head'; 1547), one of the earliest of Welsh printed books, consists of a collection of proverbs which William *Salesbury said he 'stole' from *Gruffudd Hiraethog. As part of the immense vogue achieved by Erasmus's *Adagia*, it became common to publish such anthologies in order to reveal the wealth of wisdom enshrined in European vernacular tongues. In his introduction, considered to be the first manifesto of Welsh Protestant human- ism, Salesbury appealed eloquently for the need to assemble all surviving Welsh manuscripts in order to facilitate the translation of the Scriptures into Welsh. This literary task he regarded as overriding all others in importance and the one most necessary to establish Welsh as a language of learning worthy to meet the challenges of the Renaissance and Reformation.

For further details see the edition of the work edited by J. Gwenogvryn Evans (1902) and the articles by Ifor Williams in *Y Traethodydd* (1946) and Saunders Lewis in *Efrydiau Catholig* (1948).

Olor Iscanus (lit. 'The swan of Usk'; 1651), Henry *Vaughan's second volume of poems and translations, was prefaced from Newton-by- Usk in December 1647 but not published until four years later. The lesser reason for the delay was the need to delete some of the war-poems, now lost, which were deemed impolitic, and the greater was that the poet's conversion and sub- sequent immersion in devotional poetry made him reluctant to admit to his previous secular work. The first part of *Silex Scintillans* (1650) therefore reached the public before *Olor Iscanus* and Thomas *Powell, it is believed, was the 'Friend' who saw the latter, described as 'For- merly written by Mr. Henry Vaughan Silurist', through the press. In the preface to the second edition of *Silex Scintillans* (1654), the author writes of having 'suppret my greatest follies' and let appear only those poems which are 'innoxious', but his wish would nevertheless be that 'none would read them'. *Olor Iscanus* includes the poems 'To the River Isca', 'The Charnel-House' and three others with war-settings, two of them elegies for friends.

Olwen, see CULHWCH AND OLWEN.

ONIONS, OLIVER (1873–1961), novelist.

Born in Bradford, Yorks., he was apprenticed as a boy to a printer, but his excellence as a draughtsman won him a scholarship to the Royal Academy of Art and he later became an illustrator with *The Daily Mail*. By 1900 he had published his first book, *The Compleat Bachelor*, a collection of sketches which became a best- seller; Yorkshire stories followed, but his bent became increasingly for the macabre. By 1909, when he married Berta *Ruck, he had already published ten books. Of the works he wrote before the First World War *Widdershins* (1911) and *In Accordance with the Evidence* (1915) were those most frequently reprinted; *The Tower of Oblivion* (1921) and *The Painted Face* (1929) were two of many which earned him the accolade of a volume of collected ghost-stories (1935). Although at this time no more than an occasional visitor to Wales (where his wife's parents lived), Onions was immediately attracted to Welsh folk-songs and one of these, '*Serch Hudol*' (the tune of which is now played as a processional in the ceremonies of *Gorsedd Beirdd Ynys Prydain) was the inspiration for one of his most famous ghost-stories, 'The Beckoning Fair One'.

With his wife, Onions came to live perma- nently at Aberdyfi, Mer., in 1939 and this move brought about a directional change in the writ- ing of one who was then approaching his seven- tieth birthday. He began to write historical novels which surpass in distinction even the best of his tales of the macabre: *The Story of Ragged Robyn* (1945), *Poor Man's Tapestry* (1946), *Arras of Youth* (1949) and *A Penny for the Harp* (1951). Of his forty books only *Poor Man's Tapestry* and *A Penny for the Harp* are localized in 'Gwlad', a frontier territory in east Montgomeryshire in the fifteenth century, but Gandelyn, the minstrel- secretary-spy and equivocal hero of these works appears also in *Arras of Youth* (which returns to the author's native county). The Middle Ages in which these books are set, although sometimes deliberately confused for the reader, are never romanticized except in terms, perhaps, of artisan standards and ideals. His best novel, *Poor Man's Tapestry*, has a narrator called Willie Mid- dlemiss, a Yorkshire metal-worker and engraver, whose political intelligence is not of the highest; if Willie's naïvety allows the plot another dimension, his encounters with tradesmen and artificers, the description of whose work is seldom found in fiction, offer the reader a rare experience.

Oppressions which came to this Island, Three, namely the *Coraniaid*, the *Gwyddyl Ffichti* (Picts) and the *Saeson* (English), a Triad reflecting a deep-seated tradition that the early history of *Britain consisted of successive in- vasions by alien peoples. As in the story known as *Cyfranc Lludd a Llefelys*, the supernatural people called the *Coraniaid* are presented as the earliest of these invaders. They may, however, have replaced the *Cesariaid* (Romans) in an earlier version and can be compared with the supernatural invaders of Ireland, the *Túatha Dé Danann* (lit. 'Tribes of the Goddess Danu'). It is not improbable that the tale of Lludd and Llefelys is itself a deliberate re-adaptation by a story-teller of the pre-existing Triad, in which the tradition of the legendary invasions has been partially obscured by the substitution of the folklore themes of dragons and rapacious giants —to be destroyed by the hero Lludd—in place of the invasions of Britain by the Picts and the Saxons.

Ordovex, see PARRY, JOHN HUMPHREYS (1786–1825).

Ordovices, The, one of the tribes of pre-Roman and Roman Wales noted by the Egyptian geographer Ptolemy (*fl.* 2nd cent.), occupied a territory which appears to have extended from Leintwardine, Herefs., in the south-east in a north-westerly swathe as far as and including Anglesey, between the lands of the Gangani in the Llŷn peninsula and those of the Deceangli, east of the Vale of Clwyd. The name Ordovices seems to mean 'hammer fighters' and the prehistoric stone-axe 'factory' at Graig Lwyd, near Penmaenmawr, Caerns., may be significant in that context. Modern Dinorwig and Rhyd Orddwy near Rhyl, Flints., are survivals of the tribal name.

What the focus of druidic observances on Anglesey meant to the Ordovices has not yet been evaluated. The decision of *Caratacus in AD 47 to march north to join them was probably dictated by Roman penetration of what later became Herefordshire and the final battle of his campaign was fought and lost in Ordovician territory, possibly near Caersws. The note by Tacitus that Caratacus was there 'joined by those who dreaded our (i.e. Roman) peace' has been taken by some historians to indicate that he had an understanding with the *Druids.

In AD 59 Suetonius Paulinus began a campaign against the Ordovices which culminated two years later with an attempt to cross the Menai Straits. Tacitus describes the scene vividly: 'Among the enemy were black-robed women with dishevelled hair like Furies, brandishing torches. Nearby stood the Druids raising their hands to heaven and screaming dreadful curses'. The Roman soldiers, at first overawed, eventually crossed the Straits, defeated the remaining Ordovices and destroyed 'the groves devoted to Mona's barbarous superstitions'. Paulinus, however, was recalled by the revolt of *Boudica before he could subdue Anglesey and it was AD 78 before Agricola, his attention drawn to the Ordovices by their annihilation of a cavalry squadron the year before, marched into north Wales and brought the whole of Ordovician

territory, Anglesey included, under Roman control.

The best single account of the Ordovices is that by Barry Cunliffe in *Iron Age Communities in Britain* (1974).

Organ Morgan, the husband of the groceress in Dylan *Thomas's *Under Milk Wood* (1954), is 'up every night until midnight playing the organ', causing his wife to complain, 'Oh, I'm a martyr to music'.

Orinda (1943), a short historical novel by R. T. *Jenkins. In his preface the author claims to have discovered a manuscript by the Reverend Richard Aubrey, a Fellow of Jesus College and a Royalist dismissed from Oxford by the Visitors of the Long Parliament in 1648. Through this fictional character we meet Katherine *Philipps, 'The Matchless Orinda', and her husband Sir James, a leading supporter of Cromwell. Having lost his Fellowship, Aubrey wanders fearfully until he comes to Cardigan Priory and is accepted by Orinda (a Royalist like himself) as her secretary and tutor, with the grudging consent of her Roundhead husband. The old Puritan butler, Timothy Benet, like Aubrey, worships 'the mistress' and this triangular relationship is the heart of the novel. As the author says, it has no story or plot, but it is skilfully constructed. The dialogue is in literary Welsh throughout, unnatural though this is, but each character speaks with a distinctive voice. Aubrey, the faint-hearted scholar with his amiable prejudices and stoical acceptance of hardship, is a memorable character, perhaps an intentional self-portrait of R. T. Jenkins.

Ormes Britanniae, see DE EXCIDIO BRITANNIAE (*c.*538).

ORMOND, JOHN (1923–), poet and film-maker. Born at Dunvant, near Swansea, and educated at University College, Swansea, he joined the staff of *Picture Post* in London in 1945. His early verse (under the name of Ormond Thomas) appeared in the volume *Indications* (1943) with that of James Kirkup and John Bayliss. Later, advised by Vernon *Watkins to publish no more verse until he was thirty, he did not foresee that this strategy would foster a self-awareness so critical that he would feel compelled to destroy most of what he wrote in his twenties and thirties, and eventually cease writing altogether for a time. In 1949 he returned to Swansea to work as a sub-editor and in 1957 began what was to become a distinguished career with BBC Wales as a director and producer of documentary films, which include studies of Welsh painters and writers such as Ceri *Richards, Dylan *Thomas, Alun *Lewis and R. S. *Thomas.

He resumed the writing of poetry in the mid-1960s, publishing it in *Poetry Wales*. His first major volume, *Requiem and Celebration* (1969), which collects work written over a period of twenty-five years, is uneven in quality but provides fascinating evidence of his struggle to find his own voice. It was followed by *Definition of a Waterfall* (1973), which established his reputation as a poet of assured maturity and one of the finest Anglo-Welsh poets of his generation. A significant number of his poems, many of them elegiac, probe his Welsh roots, demonstrating an abiding concern with family and locality. Others focus on particular aspects of the natural world, seeking to capture their elusive quiddities. Stylistically, they vary from the extremely plain to the highly-wrought; some are witty and ironic, paradoxical and conceited. Typically unsentimental, shapely and meticulously crafted, his are the poems of a sensibility which delights in explorations, probes complex themes and problematical areas of feeling, and refuses to settle for easy answers. The selection of John Ormond's work (with that of Emyr *Humphreys and John *Tripp) in *Penguin Modern Poets 27* (1978) includes eight uncollected poems.

There is an autobiographical essay by John Ormond in *Artists in Wales* (ed. Meic Stephens, 1973); see also the articles on his poetry by Randal Jenkins in *Poetry Wales* (vol. 8, no. 1, 1972), by Jeremy Hooker in *The Anglo-Welsh Review* (vol. 23, no. 51, 1974) and by Richard Poole and Michael Collins in *Poetry Wales* (vol. 16, no. 2, 1980).

Orpheus Junior, see VAUGHAN, WILLIAM (1575–1641).

Orthography of Welsh, The, was in great disarray at the beginning of the nineteenth century, mainly as a result of the false etymological theories propounded by William *Owen Pughe in his Dictionary and Grammar (1803). Despite attempts by such men as D. Silvan *Evans and Thomas Rowlands (1824–84), the spelling of Welsh remained unstandardized until 1859, when a committee, which met at the Eisteddfod held in Llangollen in the previous year, published *Orgraff yr Iaith Gymraeg* (1859), the work of two of the most eminent literary historians of the day, Gweirydd ap Rhys (Robert John *Pryse) and Thomas *Stephens. Even then some disapproved of the reforms recommended, most notably D. Silvan Evans in his *Llythyraeth yr Iaith Gymraeg* (1861). The subsequent work of such scholars as Zeuss, Pedersen, Strachan and, especially, John *Rhŷs in his *Lectures on Welsh Philology* (1877) brought hope of agreement.

After discussions held by *Cymdeithas Dafydd ap Gwilym at Oxford in 1888, new reliable criteria emerged and magazines such as *Cymru and Y *Traethodydd appeared in the agreed orthography. A more elaborate and official declaration of these recommendations appeared in *Welsh Orthography* (1893), the result of the deliberations of a joint-committee of *Cymdeithas yr Iaith Gymraeg (The Society for the Utilization of the Welsh Language) and scholars such as John Rhŷs, Thomas *Powel, J. E. *Lloyd and John *Morris-Jones. This report was given a lukewarm welcome but it sold sufficiently well to warrant a reprint in 1905. In 1928 the Language and Literature Committee of the *Board of Celtic Studies considered the subject and produced a report, *Orgraff yr Iaith Gymraeg*. This publication contains a detailed discussion of basic principles and a list of about fifteen hundred words of which the spelling may present difficulties. After a great deal of controversy and compromise, a system of Welsh orthography had at last been devised and generally approved, to an extent which has yet to be achieved in the other Celtic languages, and this agreement has continued to have beneficial consequences for the written word in Welsh down to the present.

OSMOND, JOHN (1946–   ), journalist and writer on political topics, was born at Abergavenny, Mon., and educated at the University of Bristol. Having worked for *Yorkshire Post Newspapers* and the *Western Mail, he edited the magazine *Arcade from 1980 to 1982 and then found work with HTV Wales. He has published three books on contemporary politics in Wales, *The Centralist Enemy* (1974), *Creative Conflict: the Politics of Welsh Devolution* (1978) and *Police Conspiracy?* (1984), and has edited a fourth, *The National Question Again: Welsh Political Identity in the 1980s* (1985).

Ossian Gwent, see DAVIES, JOHN (1839–92).

Otherworld, The, see ANNWN.

Our Saviour's Letter, a document printed in various Welsh and English versions during the eighteenth and nineteenth centuries. It was popularly reputed to have been written by Jesus Christ and to have been discovered under a large stone near the Cross. Containing religious and moral precepts, the letter was often used as a *charm against sickness and during childbirth.

Outside the House of Baal (1965), the ninth novel of Emyr *Humphreys, is his longest completed inquiry into 'the transmission of good' in society. Enlarged schematically to cover four generations, it is provided with an inter-cutting time-scheme, a single day in the present being interrupted by a past coming up rapidly to it. The book is a full-length portrait of J. T. Miles, a Calvinistic Methodist minister who is the very type of 'the good man', selfless, open-hearted, pacific, uneloquent, if also subject to human folly. The unfolded narrative shows him 'betraying' Argoed—here the symbol for the older Calvinistic Wales—by marrying the light-minded Lydia rather than her elder sister, Kate.

He fails to influence his wife and children, is responsible for the death of a comrade in the war and comes to the end of his life, disregarded by all but Kate (who none the less does not understand him), in a suburb opposite a new public house, a symbol of what he has always fought against. This powerful novel examines *agape*, again betrayed by *eros*, with a demanding rationality and finds it a failure, too quick to depart from tradition and too slow for the leaping vulgarities of the human mind. Goodness, the author concludes, cannot be seen to be transmitted; there is, perhaps, a space left for God.

There is a study of this novel by Jeremy Hooker in *Planet* (no. 39, 1977).

Owain ab Urien (6th cent.), a historical character who became a hero in the medieval romances concerning *Arthur. Reference is made to him in two poems attributed to *Taliesin and he can be placed among the Men of the *Old North in the sixth century. From the poem 'Gwaith *Argoed Llwyfain', in which he defies the demand of Fflamddwyn, the Saxon leader, to call a halt to the battle and surrender hostages, he appears to have been the leader of the army of Rheged. In 'Marwnad Owain', the oldest extant elegy in Welsh, it is said that he killed Fflamddwyn and that no man could compete with him in pursuance of the enemy. Owain is also mentioned several times in *'Canu Llywarch Hen' (9th cent.), in which he is referred to as Owain Rheged and emphasis placed on his leadership of the kingdom. According to an incomplete Life of Cyndeyrn (Kentigern), the patron saint of Glasgow, written in the twelfth century, Owain was the saint's father, but this statement is not generally given any credence.

By the twelfth century Owain had developed into a legendary character and taken his place in the Arthurian cycle. He is the hero of the tale of Owain and Luned, or the Lady of the Fountain (see under TAIR RHAMANT) which corresponds to the poem by Chrétien de Troyes, *Yvain* or *Le Chevalier au Lion* (c.1177–81). The connection between the two tales is not clear and theories exist for and against their derivation from a common but lost source. The nucleus of both stories is the killing by Owain of the guardian of the fountain and Owain's marriage to his widow. Owain also plays a major part in *Breuddwyd Rhonabwy* where Arthur and Owain play a board-game (see GWYDDBWYLL) and Owain's ravens fight with Arthur's men. It is very unlikely, however, that Owain was Arthur's contemporary. Frequent reference is made to Owain by the poets of the Middle Ages who sometimes addressed him as *Iarll y Cawg* ('The Knight of the Fountain').

For further details see Ifor Williams, *Canu Taliesin* (1960) and *The Poems of Taliesin* (1968), Rachel Bromwich, *Trioedd Ynys Prydein* (1961) and R. L. Thomson, *Owein* (1968).

Owain ap Cadwgan (d. 1116), Prince of the royal House of *Powys, was the abductor of *Nest. His grandfather, *Bleddyn ap Cynfyn, had established himself as ruler of Powys and *Gwynedd after the fall of his half-brother, *Gruffudd ap Llywelyn, in 1063 and the dynasty was to exercise power there as kings, lords and Lords Marcher until the sixteenth century. Owain's father, *Cadwgan ap Bleddyn, was the most powerful of the Welsh rulers in the early twelfth century, holding Powys and, after the collapse of *Deheubarth, *Ceredigion. In 1109 Owain carried away Nest, the wife of Gerald de Windsor, castellan of Pembroke, and the daughter of Rhys ap Tewdwr, from *Cilgerran Castle. After fleeing to Ireland, he returned to Wales and, in 1110, killed William of Brabant, a leader of the Flemish colony in Dyfed, whereupon Henry I deprived his father of Ceredigion and bestowed it upon the Clare family. On his father's death in 1111 Owain became ruler of Powys and won back the King's favour. Five years later he joined the Normans in resisting the resurgence of Deheubarth under Gruffudd ap Rhys ap Tewdwr and, in the ensuing struggle, he was killed by his ostensible allies, the Flemings and the forces of Gerald of Windsor.

Owain ap Gruffudd or **Owain Gwynedd** or **Owain Fawr** (c.1100–1170), King of *Gwynedd and the son of *Gruffudd ap Cynan, continued his father's efforts to establish Gwynedd as a defensible state. His policy was successful during the period of civil discord in England and by 1149 the boundaries of his kingdom extended from the river Dyfi to the outskirts of Chester. With the accession of Henry II to the English throne in 1154, the situation changed and Owain, after Henry's expedition to Gwynedd in 1157, recognized him as feudal overlord. Owain then abandoned the title of King but, unlike other Welsh rulers, styled himself Prince rather than lord. Consistent with his assertion that he was more than a tribal chieftain was his resistance to the attempts of the Archbishop of Canterbury to deprive him of his influence over the bishopric of *Bangor. That Gwynedd, unlike *Powys and *Deheubarth, did not disintegrate in the late twelfth century can, to a large measure, be attributed to the wise and patient statesmanship of Owain Fawr. He was widely and extravagantly praised by the poets, among whom was *Cynddelw Brydydd Mawr who wrote his elegy and a sequence of thirty-six *englynion* entitled 'Teulu Owain Gwynedd'. This sequence praised the courage of fallen warriors in a manner similar to that of *Englynion y Beddau and the cycle known as *'Canu Llywarch Hen'. By strengthening Gwynedd, Owain paved the way for its pre-eminence under his grandson *Llywelyn ap Iorwerth (Llywelyn Fawr) and his great-great-grandson *Llywelyn ap Gruffudd. See also OWAIN GWYNEDD (*c*.1545–1601).

For further details see Paul Barbier, *The Age of Owain Gwynedd* (1908), J. E. Lloyd, *A History of Wales* (1911) and the article by J. B. Smith in the *Transactions* of the Caernarfonshire Historical Society (1971).

OWAIN AP GRUFFUDD AP MARE-DUDD (*c*.1130–1197), Prince and poet, became known as **OWAIN CYFEILIOG** in 1149 when he was granted the commot of *Cyfeiliog, jointly with his brother Meurig, by his uncle *Madog ap Maredudd, Prince of *Powys. After the division of Powys upon Madog's death in 1160, Owain became its leading prince and ruled southern Powys, with his chief court probably at Welshpool. Although he was among the Welsh princes who assembled to oppose Henry II's expedition into Wales in 1165, he subsequently supported the English King. In 1188 he refused to meet Archbishop Baldwin and *Gerald de Barri (Giraldus Cambrensis) during their itinerary through Wales and was, as a result, excommunicated. Yet he was complimented by Gerald for his fluency of speech and good sense and was praised as one of three contemporary Welsh princes renowned for their 'equity, prudence and princely moderation'. In 1170 Owain had donated land for the establishment of *Strata Marcella abbey and, in 1195, after transferring power to his son, Gwenwynwyn, he entered the abbey as a monk; it was there that he died and was buried.

Only one poem can be ascribed with certainty to Owain, his *'*Hirlas Owain*', one of the finest poems of the period of the *Gogynfeirdd. In the *Hendregadredd Manuscript and *The *Red Book of Hergest* there are *englynion* which trace the progress of Owain's war-band as it makes a circuit of Powys and Gwynedd, but there is no evidence as to their authorship. Besides being a poet himself, Owain was also a patron of poets: *Cynddelw Brydydd Mawr served as his *pencerdd* and composed a long *awdl* praising his martial exploits and a series of *englynion* celebrating his court by the Severn. Owain, who often warred against his Norman neighbours, is portrayed in the Anglo-Norman romance '*Historie de Fouke Fitz Warin*' (13th cent.) as a knight who wounds Fulk *Fitzwarine with a spear, an incident inspired perhaps by the memory of his raids on the lordship of Caus where the Fitz Warin family held land. His name was also associated with one of the *Areithiau Pros, *Casbethau Owain Cyfeiliog*.

OWAIN AP LLYWELYN AB Y MOEL (*fl.* 1470–1500), poet, as was his father, *Llywelyn ap Moel y Pantri, and his grandfather, Moel y Pantri. It is believed that he lived in the vicinity of Welshpool and was related to the poet *Llywelyn ap Gutun ap Ieuan Lydan. Of the twenty-six *cywyddau* by Owain which are extant, most are eulogies and elegies. Although he wandered as far as Anglesey and visited Here-

fordshire, his poetry was mostly composed for patrons in the Border districts of north-east Wales. One of his principal patrons was Gruffudd ap Hywel of Brompton (Chirbury) and Bachelldref (Churchstoke), whose grandfather, Dafydd ap Cadwaladr, had been praised for his hospitality by the poets Dafydd Bach ap Madog Wladaidd and *Llywelyn Goch Amheurig Hen in the previous century. Owain's work is of historical interest as evidence that Welsh culture was flourishing among the gentry of the Border districts in his day. One of his poems makes a unique reference to a device at Oxford which is thought to have been a forerunner of the telescope.

For further details see the article by Eurys Rolant in *Ysgrifau Beirniadol IX* (ed. J. E. Caerwyn Williams, 1976) and the same author's edition of the poet's work (1984).

Owain ap Thomas ap Rhodri or **Owain Lawgoch** or **Yvain de Galles** (*c*.1300–1378), mercenary and claimant Prince of Wales, was a great-great-grandson of *Llywelyn ap Iorwerth (Llywelyn Fawr) and the great-nephew of *Llywelyn ap Gruffudd. A professional soldier, he spent most of his life in the service of the Kings of France and had an outstanding career as the leader of mercenary forces employed to fight against the English Crown. Although born in England, he was highly aware of his family's origins and ancestral rights, as Froissart records, and from 1363, when he was briefly in Wales to claim a patrimony in Montgomeryshire, he had propagandists there devoted to his proclamation as Prince of Wales. In 1372, when an English fleet had been defeated off La Rochelle, Owain obtained from the French King permission to detach a naval force for the conquest of Wales but he had done no more than take Guernsey when his master recalled him in order to invest La Rochelle and invade Poitou. Lawgoch, still more the soldier of fortune than prospective Prince, obeyed. But this episode was not forgotten. So greatly did England feel threatened by Owain that a Scottish traitor named John Lamb was hired to win his trust and murder him during the siege of Mortagne-sur-Mer. There are references to Owain in *vaticinatory poetry which appear to confuse him with *Arthur: like the latter, he sleeps in a cave with his followers and will rise, at a signal, to free Wales from English rule.

Owain Goch ap Gruffudd (d. 1282?), the eldest son of *Gruffudd ap Llywelyn. Imprisoned with his father in Cricieth castle in 1239, he accompanied him to England two years later but, at the death of his uncle, *Dafydd ap Llywelyn, in 1246, he returned to *Gwynedd to claim the succession, only to be persuaded to share it, under the terms of the Treaty of Woodstock (1247), with his brother Llywelyn. There was no room for two princes in Gwynedd and, in 1255, Owain was defeated by his brother at the battle of Bryn Derwin and incarcerated until 1277, for which Llywelyn was frequently rebuked by the poets of the day.

Owain Alaw, see OWEN, JOHN (1821–83).

Owain Cyfeiliog, see OWAIN AP GRUFFUDD AP MAREDUDD (c. 1130–97).

Owain Fawr, see OWAIN AP GRUFFUDD (c. 1100–70).

Owain Glyndŵr or **Owen Glendower** (c. 1354–c. 1416), Prince of Wales and national hero, was the descendant through his father of the rulers of *Powys and, on the distaff side, of the rulers of *Deheubarth. His connection with the House of *Gwynedd, though more remote, was sufficient to enable him to consider himself the successor of *Llywelyn ap Iorwerth (Llywelyn Fawr) and *Llywelyn ap Gruffudd, but he made no attempt to assert any lineal claims to power in Wales until 1400, by which time he was in middle age. As a youth he had spent some time at the Inns of Court and had rendered military service to the English Crown, participating in the invasion of Scotland in 1385. Until his late forties he had lived largely at his homes at Carrog in the valley of the Dyfrdwy (Dee) and at Sycharth, close to the Shropshire border. *Iolo Goch, writing in the 1380s, drew an idyllic picture of life at the latter place.

In 1400 Owain resorted to arms in a quarrel with his neighbour, Reginald Grey, Lord of Ruthin, one of King Henry IV's supporters, who had seized 'a peece of commons' claimed by Owain. The Welshman, who had reputedly had a legal decision in his favour during the previous reign, applied to the English Parliament for confirmation of his right, but the retort made by members to Siôn *Trefor, Bishop of St. Asaph, when he put the case, was 'What care we for the barefoot rascals?'. The King, likewise, had no thought of restraining Grey. Owain, incensed, attacked Ruthin and was proclaimed by his followers as Prince of Wales on 16 September 1400. The rising spread from the north-east and in 1401 the men of Deheubarth responded to its leader's call to 'free the Welsh people from the slavery of their English enemies'. By 1405, from his bases at the castles of Aberystwyth and *Harlech, Owain's power was evident along the length and breadth of Wales. He proved adept in exploiting English antagonism towards Henry IV, who had seized the English Crown in 1399, and he won the support of the Percy family of Northumberland and of the powerful Mortimers who had allied themselves to Glyndŵr through the marriage of Edmund Mortimer to Catherine, Owain's daughter. The Tripartite Indenture, which gave Glyndŵr Wales and a large tract of western England—the rest being divided between Percy and Mortimer—was signed in 1405. The extent of the lands in England to be given to Glyndŵr was determined, in part, according to bardic *vaticination.

An outstanding military leader, Glyndŵr also displayed gifts of statesmanship of a high order. He won the support of Robert III of Scotland and of Irish rulers, and he made a treaty with France. Parliaments were held at Machynlleth and Dolgellau and in March 1406 he summoned an assembly at Pennal near Machynlleth from which he despatched to Charles VI of France a letter (known as the *Pennal Policy) which contained proposals that the Welsh should recognize the Pope of Avignon on terms which would include the severance of the Welsh Church from Canterbury and the establishment of two universities in Wales.

By 1406, however, the military power of the English Crown was reasserting itself and, in 1408, when Glyndŵr lost the castles of Aberystwyth and Harlech, the rising was doomed. Much of upland Wales remained loyal to him, nevertheless, and it was not until 1413 that the rising was finally suppressed. By then the whereabouts of Owain Glyndŵr were unknown. He was never betrayed and no definite information about the place and manner of his death has come to light. It has been suggested that he spent his last years at his daughter's house in Monnington Straddel, Herefordshire, or at the home of his other daughter who was married to Sir John *Scudamore of Kentchurch Court. In a chronology written by *Gruffudd Hiraethog (Peniarth MS 135) the following entry is found for the year 1415 (trans.): 'Owain went into hiding on St. Matthew's Day in Harvest, and thereafter his hiding-place was unknown. Very many say that he died; the seers maintain that he did not'.

The name of Owain Glyndŵr inspired awe and admiration in both Wales and England. In Shakespeare's time there was still something of the supernatural about his reputation: in *Henry IV* (Part 1) Owain declares, 'At my birth / The front of heaven was full of fiery shapes . . . I am not in the roll of common men.' Glyndŵr's meteoric rise, his strenuous attempts to establish Welsh statehood and the visionary nature of his policies have been a powerful inspiration to Welsh patriots, especially to the advocates of political *Nationalism in modern times, and he is generally considered, as much as Llywelyn ap Gruffudd, to be the national hero of Wales.

The standard work is J. E. Lloyd, *Owen Glendower* (1931); see also Glanmor Williams, *Owen Glendower* (1966).

OWAIN GWYNEDD (c. 1545–1601), one of the last of the *Poets of the Gentry, was a main pillar of the *Bardic Order after the deaths of *Gruffudd Hiraethog and *Wiliam Llŷn. He was probably a son of the poet-cleric 'Sir Ifan' of

Carno in Montgomeryshire, and it was to the nobility of that district that he addressed most of his eulogies. For Siôn Lewys Owain of Dolgellau he wrote a *cywydd* which demonstrated his mastery of the craft when he graduated as a master-poet at the second *Caerwys Eisteddfod (1567). Like many of his fellow-poets, he had been a pupil of Gruffudd Hiraethog and he eventually became a bardic teacher in his own right.

Of his work five *awdlau*, ninety-six *cywyddau* and forty-six *englynion* have survived in manuscript. Besides poems of eulogy and elegy, most of his writing consists of poems of request, advice, meditation, satire, dialogue and challenge-and-response, while the *englynion* also cover a variety of topics. Observing all the conventions and showing little originality, almost every one of his *cywyddau* is devoted to the versification of pedigrees. The bulk of his imagery derives from the medieval concept of the Chain of Being, as well as from agriculture, the Scriptures and the mythology of Britain, Rome and Greece. His verse excels in aphoristic lines and couplets and he was a master of the art of expressing truisms in a memorable fashion. See also OWAIN AP GRUFFUDD (*c.*1100–1170).

For further details see the article by D. Roy Saer in *Llên Cymru* (no. 6, 1961).

Owain Lawgoch, see OWAIN AP THOMAS AP RHODRI (*c.*1330–78).

Owain Myfyr, see JONES, OWEN (1741–1814).

OWAIN, OWAIN LLEWELYN (1878–1956), journalist and author, was born at Tal-y-sarn, Caerns., one of eight children, all of whom inherited the talents of their father, Hugh Owen, a well-known musician. After a short period working in local quarries he joined the staff of Y *Genedl Gymreig* as a reporter and for a time was the editor. When the newspaper amalgamated with Yr *Herald Gymraeg* he remained on the staff as a sub-editor. He played an active part in the cultural life of his locality, as an eisteddfod adjudicator, music teacher, one of the pioneers of *Urdd Gobaith Cymru* in Caernarfon and one of the three founder-members of *Clwb Awen a Chân*, the society associated with R. D. *Rowland (Anthropos). Owning a good personal library, he wrote extensively in Y *Traethodydd* on the musicians of his native county and published a number of biographies, including those of Fanny Jones (1907), J. O. Jones (1912), Llew Llwyfo (Lewis Williams *Lewis, 1910) and T. E. *Ellis (1915). More important because of their entertaining portrayal of Caernarfon's literary life are his books *Anthropos a Chlwb Awen a Chân* (1946) and *Bywyd, Gwaith ac Arabedd Anthropos* (1953). His most ambitious work was *Hanes y Ddrama yng Nghymru, 1850–1943* (1948), a history of drama in Wales. O Llew

Owain represented the best traditions of the cultured amateur who serves his local community but who produces work of more general interest.

'Owdyl i Fair', see HYMN TO THE VIRGIN (*c.*1470).

Owen Glendower, see OWAIN GLYNDŴR (*c.*1354–*c.*1416).

Owen Glendower (1940), a long novel by John Cowper *Powys, set in parts of Wales and contiguous parts of England during the period 1400 to 1416, is based on the rising of *Owain Glyndŵr. In it the author maintains an intricate narrative, dramatizes contemporary ideas and beliefs, and vividly renders the period's material culture. Sub-titled 'an historical novel', it is, however, one of his major romances. The psychology of the large cast of characters, both historical and invented, is modern and he ascribes to Glyndŵr his own 'mythology of escape', depicting Wales as a source of spiritual forces won from political defeat. Owen is a figure of Powysian complexity, a self-projection of the author rather than an attempt at a historical portrait, though having many of the external trappings of the Prince. He is curiously passive, breaking his magic crystal at his coronation and so resigning himself to fate, but retaining an unusual way of drawing upon his own resources. Innocent of sustained political commitment, he acts more in accord with his 'life-illusion', finally becoming 'Prince of *Annwn' and thus 'the spirit of Wales' as Powys interpreted it.

Owen Gospiol, see GRIFFITH, OWEN (1803–68).

Owen Gwyrfai, see WILLIAMS, OWEN (1790–1874).

Owen Rhoscomyl, see MILLS, ROBERT SCOURFIELD (1863–1919).

OWEN, ALUN (1925–), dramatist, was born in Liverpool of Welsh-speaking parents. From 1942 to 1959 he worked in the theatre both as actor and director but his career was interrupted during the War when he served as a Bevin Boy in collieries in south Wales and as a seaman in the Merchant Navy. Besides playing Shakespearean parts with the Birmingham Repertory Company, the Old Vic and the English Stage Company, he has written many plays for the theatre, the cinema, radio and television, including *The Rough and Ready Lot* (1959), *Progress to the Park* (1959), *The Rose Affair* (1961), *A Little Winter Love* (1963), *Maggie May* (1964), *The Male of the Species* (1974), *Lucia* (1982) and *Norma* (1983). His screen-plays for the cinema include *A Hard Day's Night* (1964), which featured the Beatles pop-group. Many of his plays, some six of which have been written for television, are set in Liverpool and deal with the humour and harshness of life in that city. Those with Welsh settings, such as *After the Funeral* (1960), *A Little Winter Love* (1963) and *Dare to be a Daniel* (1965), tend to concentrate on the contrast between small-town values and the wider world beyond. The last-named is included, with *No Trams to Lime Street* (1959) and *Lena, Oh my Lena* (1960), in the volume *Three TV Plays* (1961) for which he won the Guild of Television Producers and Directors Award as the best television playwright of 1960. Alun Owen left Dublin to live in Cardiff in 1981.

OWEN, ANEURIN (1792–1851), scholar, was born in London, a son of William *Owen Pughe, but was reared in the parish of Nantglyn, Denbs., where his father had inherited an estate. For a while he was a pupil at Friars School, Bangor, but received most of his education from his father, who wished to impart to him all the knowledge of Welsh literature which he had acquired over many years. The son became very influential in his day as one of the Assistant Tithe Commissioners for England and Wales, as Assistant Poor Law Commissioner, as Commissioner for the Enclosure of Common Lands and in 1825, after the death of John Humphreys *Parry, as adviser to the Public Record Office concerning matters of Welsh interest.

The scholarship of Aneurin Owen was devoted to the *Laws of Hywel Dda and to *Brut y Tywysogyon. During the period from 1830 to 1840 he worked diligently on both, visiting many public and private libraries and accumulating a wealth of material. His edition of the Laws, entitled *Ancient Laws and Institutes of Wales*, appeared in 1841, but his work on the *Brut* was not published until nine years after his death, when it was edited by John *Williams (Ab Ithel) without acknowledgement of Owen's part in its preparation. These works are Owen's memorial, showing him to have been a skilful palaeographer and a perceptive, learned critic: he had his father's erudition but none of his eccentricities.

Owen, Bob (Croesor), see OWEN, ROBERT (1885–1962).

OWEN, DAFYDD (1919–), poet, a native of Rhiw, Bylchau, Denbs., was educated at the University College of North Wales, Bangor, and at Bala-Bangor Theological College. Formerly a Congregational minister and schoolmaster, he was a translator with Clwyd County Council until his retirement in 1984. He won the *Crown at the National Eisteddfod in 1943 for his *pryddest*, 'Rhosydd Moab', and the *Chair in 1972 for his *awdl*, 'Preselau'. His publications include *Cerddi* (1947), *Elfed a'i Waith* (1965), *Baledi* (1965), *Adrodd ac Adroddiadau* (1966), *Dal*

Pridd y Dail Pren (1972), *Crist Croes* (1977), *Cerddi Lôn Goch* (1983) and a monograph on Cynan (Albert *Evans-Jones) in the *Writers of Wales series (1979).

OWEN, DANIEL (1836–95), novelist, was born at Mold, Flints., the youngest of six children. When he was only a few months old his father and two of his brothers were drowned by water which broke into the Argoed coal-mine where they worked, and he was brought up in desperate poverty. He had very little schooling and when about twelve years old he was apprenticed to a tailor. Zealous in his attendance at Bethesda Chapel, he did not become a member of his favourite institution, the *Seiat* (Church Fellowship), until the age of twenty-three. Five years later, intending to enter the Calvinistic Methodist ministry, he went to Bala College where he spent many hours reading English literature, but after two and a half years he returned home to care for his mother and sister. He probably had a deeper reason for leaving the College, namely doubt about his own vocation for the ministry. Resuming work for his former master, he preached on Sundays and, in the company of his fellow-tailors, would read aloud the novels of Scott, Dickens, Thackeray and George Eliot. He also started his own draper's business with a partner, but at the age of forty his health broke down and he was ill for the rest of his life. Unexpectedly, in his very last year, he took up public work by serving as a member of the new Urban Council of his native town: he was appointed Chairman and, in that capacity, a magistrate, but died shortly afterwards. The bronze statue erected to his memory in Mold, the work of W. Goscombe *John, bears the novelist's own words, '*Nid i'r doeth a'r deallus yr ysgrifenais, ond i'r dyn cyffredin*' ('I wrote not for the wise and the learned, but for the common man').

Having tried his hand at writing since his early twenties, Daniel Owen had already had published, in the periodical *Charles o'r Bala*, a translation of an American novelette, *Ten Nights in a Barroom* (1854) by Timothy Shay Arthur. When his health failed, however, he was persuaded by his minister and friend, Roger *Edwards, to publish his sermons in *Y Drysorfa*, the Methodist monthly which Edwards edited. He went on to write a five-part story about the election of church elders in a small rural chapel, a simple tale but well constructed and with vivid characterization. The sermons and the story were published together in the volume *Offrymau Neillduaeth a Cymeriadau Methodistaidd* (1879). It was an instant success, and Edwards persuaded the author to write a novel. Not all would agree that *Y *Dreflan* (1881) satisfies that description, but Owen had made his first impressive attempt at full-length fiction and his characterization, dialogue and satire were highly promising.

His next book, *Rhys Lewis* (1885), which was first serialized over a period of three years in Y Drysorfa, is regarded as his most important novel. Its main characters are the people of the Seiat, but in his next book, *Enoc Huws* (1891), serialized by Isaac *Foulkes in Y Cymro (Liverpool), Owen turned to the motley characters on the fringes of that holy club. He had great difficulty in writing his last novel, *Gwen Tomos (1894), for throughout his adult life he had suffered from hypochondria and depression, and he was now very ill, dejected and short of money. Believing that it would be easier to ranslate Thomas Hardy's The Mayor of Casterb idge (1886), Owen asked his publisher to seek the author's permission, but Foulkes was determined to have another novel from him. Gwen Tomos is a better constructed book than the others and depicts the emergence of Calvinistic *Methodism in rural Flintshire before the author's own time. Towards the end of his life Owen also published a collection of his essays, Y Siswrn (1888) and, in the year of his death, *Straeon y Pentan (1895), a volume of short stories which had previously appeared in periodicals.

Daniel Owen had a great gift for creating memorable characters and portraying places and communities: he could fathom the depths of the human soul and devise social comedy at the same time, often by use of irony, satire, graphic similes and rich dialect. The major theme of his books is the duality between Man as he is and Man as he appears to others. It has been said that many of Owen's dialogues are set-pieces or debates on the model of discussions he had heard in the Seiat. But not only ideas clash in these dialogues: his characters are made of flesh and blood and they turn every argument into drama of a universal kind.

Nevertheless, although he could tell a story in a compelling way, Daniel Owen could not construct a novel. This inability worried him and he tried to decorate his works with what he considered to be the elements of plot. He maintained that there were no mysteries or unexpected coincidences in Gwen Tomos, but there are, in that novel as in all his works. The main mystery in Rhys Lewis is the identity of Rhys's father, in Enoc Huws it is that of Enoc's father and in Gwen Tomos that of Gwen's father. Owen did not remember his own father and the figure of the absent father held fascination for him. There are too many clumsy coincidences in all his books, which have delighted 'the common man' but have irritated some of his critics. Shapeless though his books are, they are given unity by the magnetism of their inner life and the completeness of the communities in which they are set. The fact that Owen did not succeed in writing a truly great novel has been blamed on his parochialism, the blinkers imposed by his denominational background, his lack of education and his limited culture. But the hindrance was more probably in his own temperament. He was a gentle man, lacking in passion, though he could be roused by hypocrisy, ostentation, avarice, tyranny and pride. There is much righteous indignation in his work towards these failings, but never the controlled passion and power which produce great art. Yet he had all the necessary skills of a great novelist and remains without equal in Welsh literature as an observer of character and society.

Brief biographies of Daniel Owen were written by his contemporaries John Owen (1899) and Isaac Foulkes (1903). For critical discussion see the short volumes by Saunders Lewis (1936) and John Gwilym Jones (1970), the biographical booklets by T. Gwynn Jones (1936), R. Gerallt Jones (1963) and T. Ceiriog Williams (1975) and the volume on his life and work in the series Cyfres y Meistri (ed. Urien Wiliam, 2 vols., 1982, 1983). A number of memorial lectures about the writer include those by John Gwilym Jones, The Novelist from Mold (1976), Derec Llwyd Morgan, Daniel Owen and Methodism (1977), Hywel Teifi Edwards, Daniel Owen and the 'Truth' (1978), E. G. Millward The Literary Relations of Daniel Owen (1979), R. Geraint Gruffydd, Daniel Owen and Preaching (1980) and Marion Eames, Women in the Novels of Daniel Owen (1984).

Owen, David (Dafydd y Garreg Wen; 1711/ 12–41), harpist, was popularly known by the name of his farm at Ynyscynhaearn, Caerns., and was famous for having composed, among other tunes, 'Codiad yr Ehedydd' and 'Dafydd y Garreg Wen'. Both tunes were first published by Edward *Jones (Bardd y Brenin) in Musical and Poetical Relicks of the Welsh Bards (1784). It was John Ceiriog *Hughes who, to the former tune, composed the words beginning 'Cwyd, cwyd, ehedydd cwyd', and who, in 1873, gave the poignant melody of the latter suitably touching words. The traditional belief persists, nevertheless, that Dafydd sang the latter on his death-bed.

OWEN, DAVID (Dewi Wyn o Eifion; 1784– 1841), poet, was born at Y Gaerwen, in the parish of Llanystumdwy, Caerns., where he remained for most of his life. Under the tuition of his bardic teacher and neighbour, Robert *Williams (Robert ap Gwilym Ddu), he became one of the best-known poets of his day. His awdl 'Elusengarwch' (1819), with its much-quoted couplet describing the honest Welsh peasant, and his chain of englynion to the Menai Bridge (1832) are among his most memorable works. Under the influence of Goronwy *Owen, Dewi Wyn had an ambition to produce a successful *epic in the Welsh language, on the pattern suggested by the master, and this accounts for the tiresome length of his poems. For 'Molawd Ynys Brydain' (1805) he was awarded the Medal of the *Gwyneddigion Society and in 1811 he won a prize at the Tremadog Eisteddfod with his 'Awdl i Amaethyddiaeth'. His mastery of *cynghanedd was of a very high order and his work left its mark on the development of the *awdl and the *englyn during the nineteenth century.

A selection of his verse, together with a biography by Edward Parry of Chester, was published as Blodau Arfon in 1842. A second edition with a supplement containing an article about the poet, some of his prose work and more of his poetry was edited by Robert *Ellis (Cynddelw) and published in 1869.

For further details see the article by W. J. Gruffydd in Y Llenor (vol. IV, 1925) and that by Stephen J. Williams in Gwŷr Llên y Bedwaredd Ganrif ar Bymtheg (ed. Dyfnallt Morgan, 1968).

OWEN, DAVID (Brutus; 1795–1866), preacher, schoolmaster and editor, was born at Llanpumsaint, Carms. He was brought up in the Independent cause but joined the *Baptists and began to preach and set up schools in several places in north Wales. Ordained a Baptist minister in Llŷn, he was dismissed for attempting to obtain money by fraud, and rejoined the Independents. He edited two unsuccessful journals before being appointed editor of the Anglican journal Yr Haul in 1835, after which he began to attend the services of the Church of England. He had returned by this time to his native county and was living at Pentre-tŷ-gwyn.

In the course of his life he published seventeen books, including biographies of Christmas *Evans and John *Elias. For Yr Haul he wrote four mock-biographies: Cofiant Wil Bach o'r Pwll-dŵr, Cofiant Siencyn Bach y Llwywr, Cofiant Dai Hunan-dyb (all under different pseudonyms) and *Wil Brydydd y Coed (1863–65) under the name Brutus. In the last three, especially, he chastised *Nonconformity and those he considered to be 'noisy, ill-mannered Jacks', its lay-preachers. As he himself had been a 'Jack' until 1835, his attacks are thought to have been motivated as much by disillusion as by a concern for religious standards. Nevertheless, he wrote eloquently in a colourful style and was an effective satirist, though he could not always distinguish between satire and querulous scolding.

For further details see Thomas Jones, Mân Us (1949) and the articles by D. Melvin Davies in The Journal of the Historical Society of the Church in Wales (1962, 1963, 1964, 1965).

Owen, Dickie, see OWEN, RICHARD MORGAN (1877–1932).

OWEN, DYDDGU (1906–   ), writer of children's books, was born at Pontrobert, Mont., and educated at the University College of Wales, Aberystwyth. A teacher and a lecturer at Trinity College, Carmarthen, until her retirement, she came to prominence in the 1950s as the author of three very successful adventure novels for older children, namely Cri'r Gwylanod (1953), Caseg y Ddrycin (1955) and Brain Borromeo (1958). She has also contributed stories for younger children

to the series Glöyn Byw, such as Mostyn y Mul (1961) and Modlen y Gath Fach Ddewr (1962). Besides two travel-books for adults, Bob yn Eilddydd (1968) and Ethiopia (1974), she has published Y Flwyddyn Honno (1978), a historical novel for young readers which describes the adventures of a family from Cwm Nantcol, Mer., during the *Civil Wars.

OWEN, ELIAS (1833–99), cleric and antiquary, was born at Llandysilio, Mont. Educated at Trinity College, Dublin, he became headmaster of the National School at Llanllechid, Caerns., and after his ordination in 1872 held curacies at Llanwnnog, Mont., and Oswestry, until his preferment to the living of Efenechtyd, near Ruthin, Denbs., in 1881. His publications include Arvona Antiqua (1886), The Old Stone Crosses of the Vales of Clwyd (1886) and Welsh Folklore (1896).

OWEN, ELLIS (1789–1868), poet and antiquary, was born at Cefnymeysydd, Ynyscynhaearn, Caerns. As a poet he was not distinguished; many of his englynion are epitaphs. He is remembered chiefly because of Cymdeithas Lenyddol Cefnymeysydd, a literary society which met at his home and over which he presided. It was Ellis Owen who drew attention to David *Owen (Dafydd y Garreg Wen) and who collected subscriptions for a new stone for the harpist's grave. A selection of his verse and prose was edited by R. J. *Jones (Alltud Eifion) and published posthumously under the title Cell Meudwy (1877).

OWEN, GEORGE (1552–1613), historian, antiquary and genealogist, of Henllys, Pembs., was the son of Willian *Owen by a niece of the first Earl of Pembroke. Educated locally, and briefly at Barnard's Inn, he became by marriage an ally of the Phillips-Stepney faction which resisted Sir John *Perrot's dominance over Pembrokeshire. Later in life the most influential squire in the north of the county, Owen responded strongly to the contemporary awakening of interest in Welsh antiquities, corresponding with William Camden, Lewys *Dwnn and Thomas *Jones (Twm Shon Catti) of Tregaron, gathering round him antiquaries such as George Owen *Harry, Robert *Holland and George William Griffith (1584–1655?) of Penybenglog, Pembs., and offering patronage to poets.

His most important work is The Description of Penbrokeshire (1603), of which only the first volume was published. He also wrote A Dialogue of the present Government of Wales (1594) and A Description of Wales (1602), but the greater part of his work remains in manuscript. Camden used Owen's map of Pembrokeshire (1602) in the sixth edition of his *Britannia (1586). Constantly involved in litigation and as factious as any of his contemporaries, Owen was sheriff of the county in 1587 and 1602 and, as Vice-

Admiral, Deputy-Lieutenant and Justice of the Peace, frequently represented to London the dangers of Spanish invasion and the need for the fortification of Milford Haven. He was also an admirer of Humphrey *Llwyd, David *Powel and Sir John *Price and a cartographer, genealogist, antiquary and progressive agriculturist of unquestionable importance, but his comments on changes in public order and attitudes of mind are markedly those of an interested party.

There is a full account of Owen's life and work in B. G. Charles, *George Owen of Henllys, a Welsh Elizabethan* (1973).

OWEN, GEORGE, see HARRY, GEORGE OWEN (*c*.1553–*c*.1614).

OWEN, GERAINT DYFNALLT (1908–), historian and novelist, was born at Pontypridd, Glam., the son of John Dyfnallt *Owen, and educated at the University College of Wales, Aberystwyth, and at Oxford, where he had a brilliant academic career. He was for some years a member of the staff of the BBC and then worked for the Historical Manuscripts Commission. As a historian he has published *Ysgolion a Cholegau'r Annibynwyr* (1939), *Elizabethan Wales* (1963) and *Tomos Glyn Cothi* (The Dyfnallt Memorial Lecture, 1964). The books *Helynt y Pibydd* (1932) and *Y Blaidd Hud* (1941) are translations, from Breton and Romanian respectively, while *Y Machlud* (1936) is a volume of his short stories. His novels include *Aeddan Hopcyn* (1942), *Cefn Ydfa* (1948), which recounts the romantic tale of Ann *Maddocks, *Nest* (1949) and *Dyddiau'r Gofid* (1950), the last two of which tell the story of *Nest, the wife of Gerald de Windsor. He has also published a war-diary, *Aeth Deugain Mlynedd Heibio* (1985).

OWEN, GERALLT LLOYD (1944–), poet. Born and brought up at Y Sarnau, Mer., he was educated at Bangor Normal College and later spent five years as a teacher at Trawsfynydd and in Bridgend, Glam. In 1972 he established his own printing and publishing company, *Gwasg Gwynedd*, which he developed into one of the most prolific and enterprising in Wales. He mastered the rules of *cynghanedd at an early age and published his first volume of poetry, *Ugain Oed a'i Ganiadau*, in 1966, but it was with the collection entitled *Cerddi'r Cywilydd* (1972) that he won a reputation as an accomplished poet. Many of the poems in the latter volume were written during the time of the investiture of the Prince of Wales in 1969 (see under PRINCIPALITY) and they express, in rich and vivid language, the Nationalist attitude to that event. He won the *Chair at the National Eisteddfod in 1975 and 1982 and he is well known as an adjudicator in bardic contests at the Eisteddfod and on radio. Two selections of poetry written for radio have appeared under his editorship, both entitled *Talwrn y Beirdd* (1981, 1984). From 1976 to 1983

he was co-editor with Alan *Llwyd of *Barddas*, the magazine of *Cymdeithas Cerdd Dafod*. The puckish humour of Gerallt Lloyd Owen as an adjudicator and broadcaster contrasts with the sadness of his poetry, which expresses a profound sense of loss at the decline of the Welsh-speaking community of the poet's youth.

For further details see the interview with the poet in *Barddas* (no. 67, Dec., 1982) and the article by Branwen Jarvis in *Trafod Cerdd Dafod y Dydd* (ed. Alan Llwyd, 1984).

OWEN, GORONWY (**Goronwy Ddu o Fôn**; 1723–69), poet, was born in the parish of Llanfair Mathafarn Eithaf, Ang., the son of Owen Gronw who belonged to a family of tinkers from Tafarn Goch. Both his father and grandfather were able to compose *englynion* and he was brought up in what remained of the bardic tradition. At Friars School, Bangor, he learned Latin with the intention of becoming a priest and later studied briefly at Jesus College, Oxford. After a period as an assistant teacher at schools in Pwllheli (1742–44) and Denbigh (1745), he was ordained deacon in 1746 and served in his native parish. But he was obliged to leave within the year. Thereafter he led a wandering existence, living in the constant hope that he would be given a parish in Wales instead of having to suffer the poverty of a curate's life. The opportunity never arose and, on being offered a teaching post at the grammar school connected with William and Mary College in Williamsburg, Virginia, he promptly accepted it. He sailed from London in November 1757 with his wife and three children, but she and their youngest child died during the voyage. Owen married again in America, but his second wife, too, died not long afterwards. He then turned to alcohol and prodigal living, as a consequence of which he lost his job. The last nine years of his life were spent as vicar of a parish in St. Andrew's, Brunswick County, in the heart of Virginia, where he also became a tobacco planter and married for the third time. He was buried on his plantation near Dolphin, to the north of Lawrenceville.

As a young man Goronwy Owen had engaged in poetic exercises in both Welsh and Latin and he returned to the writing of poetry, under the encouragement of Lewis *Morris, the antiquary, towards the end of 1751. The task which he set himself was no less than the revival of Welsh poetry, by raising it from the nadir to which it had fallen and giving it a new function: instead of praising patrons, he would write *awdlau* and *cywyddau* in the manner of Horace, expressing a Christian classicist's reflections on the nature of 'the good life'. His letters to the *Morris Brothers are full of his plans for the writing of an *epic on Miltonic lines, but he had left for Virginia before he could realize them. The composition of such an epic became the ambition of generations of Welsh poets and, to a great extent, the *Crown and *Chair competitions in the *eisteddfodau* of the nineteenth century were intended to produce a poem such as that on which Goronwy Owen had set his heart.

By then he had become a hero in the eyes of many Welsh poets and his verse, published in the anthology *Diddanwch Teuluaidd* (1763, 1817), was widely imitated. His letters, published in the periodical press, were accepted as canons of literary criticism to a degree which was to make him a baneful influence on the course of Welsh letters. Nevertheless, his work has real and lasting merits. His letters, for example, contain passages of excellent prose, particularly in his descriptions of his loneliness in Virginia. Among his finest poems are 'Awdl Gofuned', *'Cywydd y Farn Fawr', 'Cywydd y Gem neu'r Maen Gwerthfawr', 'Cywydd y Gwahodd'* and *'Cywydd yn ateb Huw'r Bardd Coch o Fôn'*, all written before his departure for America. The last-named, a reply to Hugh *Hughes (1693–1773), is a most eloquent expression of his *hiraeth for Anglesey in which he expressed simple truths succinctly and memorably.

A selection of Goronwy Owen's work was published in the series *Cyfres y Fil* (ed. O. M. Edwards, 2 vols., 1902) and his letters were edited by J. H. Davies (1924); see also *The Poetical Works of the Rev. Goronwy Owen with his Life and Correspondence* (ed. Robert Jones, 2 vols., 1951). There is a monograph on the writer by W. D. Williams in the *St. David's Day* series (1951); see also the article by Bobi Jones in *Gwŷr Llên y Ddeunawfed Ganrif* (ed. Dyfnallt Morgan, 1966), that by Bedwyr Lewis Jones in the *Transactions* of the Honourable Society of Cymmrodorion (1971) and another by Saunders Lewis collected in the volume *Meistri'r Canrifoedd* (ed. R. Geraint Gruffydd, 1973); see also *A School of Welsh Augustans* (1924) by Saunders Lewis.

Owen, Herbert Isambard (1850–1927), pioneer of the *University of Wales, was a doctor by profession. Born at Chepstow, Mon., the son of an engineer who had been a pupil of Isambard Brunel, he was educated at the University of Cambridge and later studied medicine. Deeply involved in the life of the *London Welsh, he played a prominent part in reviving the Honourable Society of *Cymmrodorion in 1873 and, as a member of *Cymdeithas yr Iaith Gymraeg and a friend of its secretary, Dan Isaac *Davies, in furthering the cause of the Welsh language in the intermediate schools. It was he who drafted, in 1891 and the following year, a scheme for the establishment of the University of Wales and, when the University was founded two years later, he became its first Deputy-Chancellor.

OWEN, HUGH (1575?–1642), translator and Recusant, of Gwenynog, Ang., left his native county in 1621 as a result of persecution and went to London where he found employment as secretary to Henry Somerset, the Lord Herbert. He removed to *Raglan Castle with his master in 1627 and died at his home near Tintern Abbey

after some twenty years as estate manager to the Somerset family. Owen is remembered for his translation into Welsh of *De Imitatione Christi* by Thomas à Kempis, which he made between 1615 and 1642 and which was published in 1684 by his son, also named Hugh Owen, under the title *Dilyniad Christ*. A second version of this work was made by an anonymous W.M. (perhaps William Meyrick) under the title *Pattrwm y Gwir Gristion* (1723). Part of a manuscript of the father's translation of *The Book of Resolution* by Robert Parsons, which was bequeathed to his son, is preserved in transcript at the Cardiff Free Library.

Hugh Owen the younger (1615–86) entered the English College in Rome as a student in 1636, was ordained priest in 1640/41, joined the *Society of Jesus in 1648, becoming known as Father John Hughes, and spent the rest of his life as a missionary in Wales and the Marches. His sole literary work was *Allwydd neu Agoriad Paradwys i'r Cymry* (1670), a rendering into fine Welsh of extracts from the Gospels and Catholic catechisms.

For further details see the articles by Geraint Bowen in the *Journal* of the Welsh Bibliographical Society (vol. VII, 1953), *Y Genhinen* (vol. 5, 1955) and the *Journal* of the National Library of Wales (vol. XI, 1956).

Owen, Hugh (1804–81), civil servant and educationist, was a native of Llangeinwen, Ang. He first came to the attention of the public in 1843 when he published an open letter which was intended to be a clarion call to the Welsh people on the subject of elementary education, in particular on the need for the establishment of schools under the aegis of the *British and Foreign Schools Society. A man of great influence in his day, he played a prominent part in the affairs of the *National Eisteddfod and the Honourable Society of *Cymmrodorion. Among the institutions with which he was associated was the Normal College, Bangor, established in 1858, which became the first college in Wales to admit the sons of Nonconformist parents. A college for the training of women teachers was opened in Swansea in 1871 largely as a result of his initiative. From 1854 he led the movement to establish the *University of Wales and it was his zeal which led to the founding of the University College at Aberystwyth in 1872.

Having resigned from his post with the Poor Law Commission in order to devote himself more fully to the task of creating a complete education system for Wales, Hugh Owen went on to press for an investigation into the state of intermediate education. His efforts paved the way for the passing of the Welsh Intermediate Education Act in 1889 and the subsequent provision of secondary schools throughout the country. Despite his distinguished service, in recognition of which he was knighted in 1881, some historians have been critical of Hugh

Owen's motives, which were fairly typical of the Anglicized middle classes of Victorian Wales, and of his failure to devise a system of education more suited to the needs of Wales. Particularly is this criticism made in the matter of the teaching of the Welsh language, which always had a low priority in his schemes.

For accounts of Hugh Owen's life and work see the biography by W. E. Davies (1885) and the bilingual monograph by B. L. Davies in the *St. David's Day* series (1977); his influence on the growth of the National Eisteddfod is described by Hywel Teifi Edwards in *Gŵyl Gwalia* (1980).

OWEN, JEREMY (*fl.* 1704–44), controversialist, followed his father in 1711 as the pastor of the Calvinistic Methodist congregation at Henllan Amgoed, Carms. He was educated in the Academy at Shrewsbury kept by his uncle, James Owen, where he was trained in Classics and in moderate Calvinism. The Nonconformist churches of south Wales, especially the *Baptists, were plagued in Owen's day by bitter disputes between moderate and hyper-Calvinists and, organizationally, between Methodists and Independents. There was a strong party of hyper-Calvinists in Henllan Amgoed led by Lewis Thomas (*fl.* 1706–45) of Bwlch-y-sais and when he and his followers were excommunicated they founded a church at Rhyd-y-ceisiaid. Further contention arose in the years from 1707 to 1709 and another party seceded to Rhyd-y-ceisiaid under the leadership of the Independents Mathias Maurice (1684–1738) and Henry Palmer (1679–1742). Maurice published a *Brief History* (1727), relating the troubles at Henllan, which so disturbed Owen that he published a rejoinder entitled *Golwg ar y Beiau* (1732–33), in which Maurice was severely castigated. This pamphlet was reprinted under the editorship of R. T. *Jenkins (1950), not for the sake of its contents but for its vigorous Welsh style. Owen's use of strong, precise language is also clearly seen in his *Y Dyledswydd Fawr Efangylaidd o Weddio dros Weinidogion* (1733).

There is an essay on Jeremy Owen by Saunders Lewis in the volume *Meistri'r Canrifoedd* (ed. R. Geraint Gruffydd, 1973).

OWEN, JOHN (**The British Martial**; 1564?–1628?), epigrammatist. Born at Plas-du, Llanarmon, Caerns., he was educated at Winchester and New College, Oxford. He was schoolmaster at Trelech, Mon., until 1595, then became headmaster of Warwick School, after which nothing more is known about his life. A man of lively and generous mind, a wit, a scholar and a satirist, he enjoyed great popularity in his day on account of the eleven books of Latin epigrams which he published between 1606 and 1613. There are frequent allusions to Wales in his work and, in the book which he dedicated to Henry, Prince of Wales (the elder son of James I), he described himself as 'a Cambro-Briton'. The

range of his epigrams was wide and they include lines addressed to Lady Mary Neville, Sir Philip Sidney and Sir Francis Drake; a number are virulently anti-Catholic. Although put on the *Index Expurgatorius*, they were very popular in England and, translated into French, German and Spanish, proved equally so elsewhere in Europe, particularly in Germany where Owen had a considerable influence on the development of the genre.

His collected works were published as *Epigrams* (trans. T. Vicars, 1619) and *Epigrammata* (ed. A. A. Renouard, 1794). For further details see the article by J. Henry Jones in the *Transactions* of the Honourable Society of Cymmrodorion (1940).

Owen, John (1600–66), see under CIVIL WARS (1642–48) and DALAR HIR (1648).

OWEN, JOHN (1757–1829), poet, of Machynlleth, Mont., was a Calvinistic Methodist who wrote *Troedigaeth Atheos* (1788), an epic poem modelled on *Bywyd a Marwolaeth Theomemphus* (1764) by William *Williams (Pantycelyn). His pamphlet *Golygiad ar Achosion ag Effeithiau'r Cyfnewidiad yn Ffrainc* (1797) is a declaration of the political views of some Methodists of the period and his poem, *Golygiad ar Adfywiad Crefydd yn yr Eglwys Sefydledig yng Nghymru* (1818), is of great interest to historians of *Methodism.

Owen, John (**Owain Alaw**; 1821–83), musician, a native of Chester, was a vocalist, accompanist and composer who won many prizes at eisteddfodau. He published a famous collection entitled *Gems of Welsh Melodies* (1860) and an oratorio, *Jeremiah* (1878), which was perhaps his greatest work, as well as numerous popular anthems. Much in demand as an adjudicator, he also performed in musical concerts with John *Jones (Talhaiarn) who wrote the words for some of his compositions.

Owen, John (1854–1926), Bishop of *St. David's and one of those who worked hardest for *Disestablishment and the creation of the Church in Wales, was born of Nonconformist parents at Llanengan, Caerns. He was Professor of Welsh at St. David's College, Lampeter (1879–85), Warden of Llandovery College (1885–89), Dean of *St. Asaph (1889–92), Principal of St. David's College (1892–97) and Bishop of St. David's from 1897 until his death. A vigorous champion of denominational education and of the Church Established, he sought the best possible terms for the Welsh Church under the Disestablishment Act of 1914. Dismayed by the gulf between the Anglican Church and Welsh culture, he was a supporter of the *National Eisteddfod and chairman of the committee which produced the report *Welsh in Education and Life* (1927).

OWEN, JOHN DYFNALLT (**Dyfnallt**; 1873–1956), poet and prose writer, was born at

Rhiw-fawr in the parish of Llangiwg, Glam. Educated at the University College of North Wales, Bangor, and at Bala-Bangor Theological College, he became a Congregational minister and was editor of the denominational weekly newspaper Y *Tyst from 1927 to 1956. Geraint Dyfnallt *Owen is his son.

Dyfnallt won the *Crown at the National Eisteddfod of 1907 for a long poem on the Holy Grail, later published in the volume Y Greal a Cherddi Eraill (1946) together with numerous lyrics and a remarkable ballad, 'Baled Ysbryd Coed-y-Deri'. Among his special interests was the culture of the other Celtic nations and his book on Brittany, O Ben Tir Llydaw (1934), merits comparison with the writings of Owen M. *Edwards and Ambrose *Bebb on that country. His essays were collected in the volumes Rhamant a Rhyddid (1952) and Ar y Tŵr (1953). It was as editor of Y Tyst, however, that he exerted most influence, particularly in his emphasis on the importance of Christian *Nationalism and Internationalism. Dyfnallt is remembered, in the words of R. Tudur *Jones, for 'his exceptionally broad culture, his tolerant nature, and his complete mastery of a strong and colourful Welsh style'.

His life and work are described in Bywyd a Gwaith John Dyfnallt Owen (1976) by Geraint Elfyn Jones; see also the chapter by Emrys Jones in Adnabod Deg (ed. Derec Llwyd Morgan, 1977).

Owen, Lewis (d. 1555), see under GWYLLIAID COCHION MAWDDWY.

OWEN, LEWIS (1572–1633), spy and anti-Roman propagandist, of family uncertain but unquestionably of Merioneth, matriculated at Christ Church, Oxford, in 1590 but left without a degree to travel on the Continent. Anthony à Wood, in his Athenae Oxonienses, asserts that Owen entered the *Society of Jesus and was enrolled at the College of Valladolid but observed after a while that the Society's intrigues 'tended to worldly policy rather than true religion'. This account telescopes Owen's career, however, for, after publishing A Key to the Spanish Tongue (1605), he translated from the French and published in 1609 Catholique Traditions: A Treatise of the Beliefe of the Christians of Asia, Europa and Africa, a fact which suggests that at that date his alienation from the Catholic cause was not complete. In 1611 he was sent, on the Secretary of State's behalf, to Rome to watch Hugh O'Neill, Earl of Tyrone, and for the next dozen years, in various disguises, he travelled to and through many European countries. In 1626 he published The Running Register, recording a True Relation of the English Colledges, Seminaries and Cloysters in all Forraine Parts, a deadly exposé, with names, of Catholics operating or training abroad. After two more years as a spy, he published The Unmasking of all Popish Monks,

Friars and Jesuits (1628) and Speculum Jesuiticum, or the Iesuites Looking-Glasse (1629).

The best single source for Owen's career is W. Llewelyn Williams, 'Welsh Catholics on the Continent', in the Transactions of the Honourable Society of Cymmrodorion (1901–02).

OWEN, MARY (1796–1875), hymn-writer, was born at Ynysymaerdy, Briton Ferry, Glam. Her hymns were published, on the recommendation of William *Williams (Caledfryn), under the title Hymnau ar Amryw Destunau (1839) and some, such as 'Caed modd i faddau beiau' and 'Dyma gariad, pwy a'i traetha', are still in vogue.

OWEN, MATTHEW (1631–79), poet, of Llangar in *Edeirnion, Mer., wrote poems in the style of Huw *Morys, together with englynion, cywyddau and at least one awdl. His work suggests that he spent some time in Oxford and there his Carol o Gyngor (1658) was published. A number of his dyriau appear in Carolau a Dyriau Duwiol (1686) and three others in Blodeu Gerdd Cymry (1779). He also wrote an elegy for Sir John Owen of Clenennau and a poem to Richard Hughes, the vicar of Gwytherin.

Owen, Morfydd Llwyn (1891–1918), musician. Born at Treforest, Glam., she had a brilliant career at the Royal Academy of Music before winning fame as a singer and composer of orchestral and choral works, hymn tunes, chamber music and piano solos, many of which were inspired by the folk songs and literature of Wales. In 1917 she married the psychoanalyst Ernest *Jones but the marriage was marred by the tension between her religious faith and his atheism. Her death from a chest complaint in the following year robbed Welsh music of one of its most versatile geniuses. On her gravestone at Oystermouth, Glam., is carved a quotation from Goethe: 'Das unbeschreibliche, hier ist es gethan' ('Here the indescribable consequences [of love] have been fulfilled').

Owen, Nicholas (d. 1606), martyr, was the eldest son of a Welsh Catholic family established at Oxford in the reign of Mary. Of his three brothers, two became priests and one a Catholic printer. He was known as Little John because of his diminutive stature and has often been mistakenly called John Owen for that reason, as in Waldo *Williams's poem 'Wedi'r Canrifoedd Mudan', where he appears as 'John Owen y Saer' ('the Carpenter'). Nicholas entered the *Society of Jesus in 1579 as a lay coadjutor and by 1590 had made his profession as a full member. From 1587 he was the principal maker of priest-holes in England and his ingenuity as architect and carpenter saved the lives of many priests and preserved the estates of many laymen which might have been forfeit. The 'servant' in turn of Fathers Campion, Gerard and Garnet, he was several times imprisoned and tortured but confessed nothing. In 1597 he planned and effected the escape of Father Gerard from the Tower of London. In 1606, however, in the aftermath of the Gunpowder Plot, Hindlip Hall, Worcs., which Owen had fitted up as a meeting-place for priests, was searched by a posse commanded by Sir Henry Bromley, the County Sheriff. Eleven priest-holes were found but no priests. After four days, Owen walked out of his hiding-place to draw off the search for Fathers Garnet and Oldcorne, but Bromley, possessed of 'information', persisted and on the eighth day the two priests were captured. Owen, although ruptured (which by custom should have exempted him) was repeatedly racked in the Tower but once more he revealed nothing. Despite the iron plate with which they girded him, 'his bowels gushed out' and the death of Little John, 'lame, ingenious, silent', was reported as suicide.

OWEN, OWEN GRIFFITH (Alafon; 1847–1916), poet, was a native of *Eifionydd and in his youth a farm labourer, quarryman and clerk in a local quarry. Educated later at Bala College and Edinburgh University, he began preaching for the Calvinistic Methodists in 1876. His only pastorate was at Clwt-y-bont, Caerns., where he remained until his death. Besides editing *Y Drysorfa* for a few years, he published a volume of poetry, *Cathlau Bore a Nawn* (1912), and a collection of essays, *Ceinion y Gynghanedd* (1915). As a poet he excelled in writing simple, pensive lyrics but his *englynion* are also memorable. His translation of Richard Mant's hymn, 'Round the Lord in glory seated', *'Glân geriwbiaid a seraffiaid'*, sung to the tune *'Sanctus'*, is still very popular.

Owen, Richard Morgan (Dickie Owen; 1877–1932), one of the great Welsh rugby-players of the early twentieth century. Small, tough and, as a half-back, a master of tactics around the scrummage, he was capped for Wales thirty-five times between 1901 and 1910.

OWEN, ROBERT (1771–1858), factory reformer, Utopian Socialist and writer, was born at Newtown, Mont., the son of a saddler-ironmonger. At the age of ten he was apprenticed to a Scottish draper at Stamford, Lincs., in whose shop he began to doubt all existing religions because of their contradictions. It was there, too, that he first postulated the idea that Man's character was formed by his environment with the dictum, 'Nature gave the qualities and Society directed them'. This belief, as it grew, gave him 'illimitable charity' towards his fellows. After a brief period as a draper's assistant in London, he went to Manchester in 1788 to seek his fortune. Several abortive enterprises in machine-making and spinning were followed by his appointment, at the age of twenty, to manage a spinning-mill with a work-force of some five hundred, and four years later he became the managing partner in the Chorlton Twist Company which, in 1799, bought the New Lanark Mills, where his experiments were to make his name.

Broadly, Owen's intention was to make his work-people 'rational' by improving factory conditions, shortening hours of work, educating factory children and inducing the harmony which he remembered from the rural community of his native Montgomeryshire. His outstanding success at New Lanark led him to advocate a national system of education and the provision of state-aided unemployment relief by the establishment of 'villages of co-operation', communities in which the co-operative life was gradually to become, for him, an end in itself. He spent some forty thousand pounds on a co-operative experiment at New Harmony, Indiana, between 1824 and the project's collapse four years later. Rejected by Radicals for seeking to control the poor as well as to assist them, and disliked by the religious, he nevertheless became the titular head of many popular movements, especially in America, all of them anti-capitalist and many millenarian. But, insufficiently educated and repeating himself more and more, he retreated in his last years into self-justification and an Owenite 'religion' with its own hymns. He returned to Newtown to die. The Robert Owen wing of the Newtown Public Library was built at the expense of the Cooperative Union in 1903 and the statue in the town's centre was erected in 1956. A museum devoted to his memory was opened in Newtown in 1983.

Owen's best-known work, *A New View of Society or Essays on the Formation of Human Character* (1813), dedicated to William Wilberforce, was the last influential statement of a rationalist doctrine to be published in England and his *Report to the County of Lanark* (1821) a reply to an attack in *The Edinburgh Review* on his 'villages of co-operation'. His autobiography, *The Life of Robert Owen by Himself* (1857), is valuable for its history of working-class movements. Owen's basic belief was in the rationality of Man, of his perfectibility by pragmatic means without either doctrinaire or violent change. Nevertheless, although praised by Karl Marx, the benevolently patriarchal Owen underestimated the bitterness of the class-struggle. His influence played its part in the development of modern *Socialism and of experiments in co-operative economy, however. Among his disciples in Wales was R. J. *Derfel and his teaching—without the rationalistic, optimistic view of human nature—may have had some effect on the early outlook of *Plaid Cymru.

For further details see *The Life of Robert Owen by Himself* (1857), F. Podmore, *Robert Owen: A Biography* (1906) and G. D. H. Cole, *Robert Owen* (1925); there is a useful introduction by V. A. C. Gatrell to the Penguin edition (1969) of *Report to the County of Lanark* and *A New View of Society*.

OWEN, ROBERT (1820–1902), poet, was born at Dolgellau, Mer., was ordained in 1843 and lived for many years at Barmouth in the same county. A fervent Anglo-Catholic, he supported the *Disestablishment of the Church of England in Wales from a conviction that this would enable it to preserve its Catholicism. Among the books he published were a volume of verse, *The Pilgrimage to Rome* (1863), and *The Kymry, their Origin, History and International Relations* (1891).

Owen, Robert (Bob Owen Croesor; 1885–1962), antiquary and book-collector, was a native of Llanfrothen, Mer. He was employed in his youth as a farm labourer and shepherd, but later became a clerk in the Parc and Croesor Slate Quarry, an organizer of a rural community service and a lecturer with the Workers' Educational Association. His chief interests lay in Welsh genealogy, the collecting of rare Welsh books and the copying of parish records, all of which made him not only a well-known 'character' but also an authority on the history of *Quakerism and Welsh Quaker families. At his home in Croesor, near Llanfrothen, he amassed a huge library of books, papers and manuscripts, most of them relating to emigration, into which he carried out meticulous research. His knowledge was much in demand among Americans of Welsh extraction and his genealogical expertise extended to the historic families of Wales, especially those of his native county. A popular lecturer, famous for his eloquence, infectious enthusiasm and abrasive manner, he was a unique figure in Welsh life. His contribution was recognized by the *University of Wales when it conferred an honorary degree upon him. The society for book-collectors, *Cymdeithas Bob Owen*, is named after him.

Bob Owen is one of the three men celebrated by Robin Williams in *Y Tri Bob* (1970) and his biography was written by Dyfed Evans (1977); there is a chapter devoted to this extraordinary man in Philip O'Connor's *Living in Croesor* (1962).

OWEN, WILLIAM (1488–1574), lawyer and author, of Henllys, Pembs., was the son of a freeholder from the north of the county. He studied at the Middle Temple, where he 'wrote out' for Anthony Fitzherbert the latter's *Graunde Abridgement* (1514) of the laws of the realm. A much smaller volume, his own *Bregement de toutes les estatuts* (1521), was the first book by a Welshman to be printed in Britain. His legal activities in Pembroke, where he became mayor in 1527, in Bristol and in London, culminated in 1543 in the outright purchase from Lord Audley of the barony of *Cemais, which had been in mortgage to him for nineteen years. He died at Henllys and the poets *Huw Llŷn and Morus

Llwyd Wiliam wrote elegies for him. George *Owen, the antiquary, was his son.

OWEN, WILLIAM (1890–1964), novelist, was born at Bangor, Caerns., but spent most of his life in the wholesale grocery business in England. His novels include *Rhaff* (1947), *Bore Gwlyb* (1956), *Amos Beri* (1958), *Pen y Dalar* (1960), *Chwedlau Pen Deitsh* (1961) and *Bu farw Ezra Bebb* (1963). He won the *Prose Medal at the National Eisteddfod in 1959 and 1962.

OWEN, WILLIAM DAVID (1874–1925), novelist, was a native of Bodedern, Ang. A barrister until obliged to retire owing to ill health, he worked towards the end of his life as a solicitor in Rhosneigr. Two of his novels first appeared in serial form in *Y *Genedl Gymreig*, namely *Elin Cadwaladr* (1914) and *Madam Wen* (1914–17). The latter, first published in book form in 1925, is a popular romance about a female Robin Hood. It is not known for certain whether there is any historical basis for this story (interest in which was revived by a television film in 1982) but recent research has tended to confirm the traditional belief that the novel's Einir Wyn, alias Madam Wen, may have been based on an actual person, Margaret Wynne, the wife of Robert Williams, squire of *Chwaen Wen in the mid-eighteenth century.

There is an essay on W. D. Owen by Mairwen Gwynn Jones in *Dewiniaid Difyr* (1983).

OWEN PUGHE, WILLIAM (1759–1835), lexicographer, was born William Owen at Llanfihangel-y-Pennant, Mer., but adopted the surname Pughe out of gratitude to a distant relative, Rice Pughe, vicar of Nantglyn, near Denbigh, who left him an estate in 1806. Brought up at Egryn Ardudwy, where he was immersed in a rich cultural heritage, he went to London in 1776 and lived there until 1825. He was introduced to the *Gwyneddigion Society in 1782 and became an active member of the societies of the *London Welsh. With Owain Myfyr (Owen *Jones), he helped to produce the volumes *Barddoniaeth Dafydd ap Gwilym* (1789) and *The Myvyrian Archaiology of Wales* (1801–07). Industrious, erudite, kind-hearted but also gullible, he was persuaded by Iolo Morganwg (Edward *Williams) into publishing some of Iolo's pastiches of *Dafydd ap Gwilym in his edition of that poet's work; some of Iolo's fabrications also appeared in the *Myvyrian Archaiology*. One of the more eccentric aspects of Owen Pughe's character was his devotion to Joanna Southcott, the prophetess from Devon, whose factotum he was from about 1803 until her death in 1814. Aneurin *Owen, the editor of *Ancient Laws and Institutes of Wales* (1841) was his son.

Pughe was the author of *The Heroic Elegies of Llywarch Hen* (1792–94), *The Cambrian Biography* (1803), *A Grammar of the Welsh Language* (1803) and *Cadwedigaeth yr Iaith Gymraeg* (1808), and he edited *The *Cambrian Register* for a while. His feeble attempts at poetry are to be found in *Coll Gwynfa* (1819), the translation he made of Milton's *Paradise Lost*, and in his *cywydd* on the subject of *Hu Gadarn (1882). But his best-known work was *Geiriadur Cymraeg a Saesneg* or *A Welsh and English Dictionary* which was published in two large volumes in 1803. It was unpopular from the outset because of its unfamiliar orthography and Pughe's erroneous etymology. Many of the words included were his own inventions, an attempt to illustrate the diversity of Welsh compound nouns and adjectives, and some of his ideas were based on the spurious bardic alphabet known as *Coelbren y Beirdd*. He also tinkered with the orthography in order to render it more 'rational', with every sound represented by a single letter. So enamoured was he of all things Welsh that he believed that an analysis of the language would yield the secrets of the primeval language of Mankind. In the words of Prys *Morgan, 'He wished to recreate modern Welsh as if it were the unchanged language of the patriarchs and he made a language which was as solid and sublime as a neo-classical mausoleum'.

Although Pughe's idiosyncrasies are very apparent in his dictionary, it is less commonly acknowledged that he had a profound knowledge of early and medieval Welsh texts from which he quoted abundantly in order to illustrate the vocabulary he provided, including many words which had been ignored by earlier lexicographers. It is nevertheless true that his erroneous ideas on etymology and his orthographical experiments did a great deal of harm. It may be added, in mitigation, that to a large extent he merely applied the general theories of his age to the Welsh language and that his ideas were far less fantastic than those of grammarians such as Rowland *Jones. More positively, Pughe contributed—despite his idiosyncrasies—to the work of saving much of early Welsh literature for posterity. Fortunately, the Anglican clerics (see under HEN BERSONIAID LLENGAR) resisted any attempt to depart from the language of the Welsh *Bible of 1588 and so Pughisms were restricted to grammar and style. At the same time, many Welshmen were attracted to Pughe's notions of the language's purity, the patriarchal tradition and the 'infinite copiousness' which he tried to demonstrate. It was Pughe who revealed to them that Welsh was 'the language of Heaven', an assertion which by today has become a cliché.

The most authoritative study of William Owen Pughe is that by Glenda Carr (1983); see also the biography by T. Mordaf Pierce (1914) and the articles by Glenda Parry Williams, 'Yr Ysgolhaig a'r Broffwydes' in *Y*

Traethodydd (vol. CXXI, no. 518, 1966), G. J. Williams in *Agweddau ar Hanes Dysg Gymraeg* (ed. Aneirin Lewis, 1969), Arthur Johnston in the *Journal* of the National Library of Wales (vol. X, 1957–58) and Glenda Carr in the *Transactions* of the Honourable Society of Cymmrodorion (1982).

OWENS, PHILIP (1947–), poet, was born at Wrexham, Denbs., and educated at the University College of North Wales, Bangor, and Wells Theological College. An Anglican priest in Suffolk, he is the author of three volumes of verse, *To Hymn the Miracle* (1977), *The Hard Seed* (1978) and *Look, Christ* (1979), all of which reflect the tribulations and blessings of his pastoral work.

Owl of Cwm Cowlyd, The, see under OLDEST ANIMALS.

Owredd, Yr, a mansion in *Maelor Saesneg, Flints., was the main home of the Hanmers, an immigrant family which first settled in the county as administrators for Edward I but which, through marriage, later became thoroughly Welsh. Some of the Hanmers supported *Owain Glyndŵr, whose wife was the daughter of Sir David Hanmer, and from Sir David's time on (*fl.* 1380–90) until that of John Hanmer (d. 1604) they were bardic patrons. The poetry addressed to the Hanmers refers frequently to their military activities. Other branches of the family lived at Halton, Fens, Y Bryn and Pentre-pant, and they too maintained the tradition.

Oxford Book of Welsh Verse, The (1962), an anthology of poetry from the early period to the middle of the twentieth century, compiled by Thomas *Parry. The editor's preface discusses the tradition of Welsh poetry and emphasizes the importance of the strict metres in its development. Although the free metres, such as the hymn and the lyric, are represented among the 370 poems included in the book, pride of place is given to verse in the classical strict metres. This anthology, the first attempt in modern times to present Welsh poetry from its beginnings to the present day, was criticized by Gwenallt (David James *Jones) because, in his opinion, it did not sufficiently represent the Christian element in Welsh poetry, which he considered to be one of the most Christian in Europe. Be that as it may, the work reflects the wide learning and catholic taste of the editor and its authority has not yet been replaced by that of any other anthology. An eighth edition, with revisions and additions, appeared in 1983.

Oxford Glosses, The, a number of notes made by Welshmen in the margin of Latin texts during the period of Old Welsh (8th–11th cent.) when knowledge of Latin was failing. Four collections of these notes have been preserved, two in

Oxford and two in Cambridge. They are found in a Latin manuscript (Aust. MS F4 32, c.820) containing miscellaneous material which is known as *Oxoniensis Prior* (Ox. 1) and in another designated as *Oxoniensis Posterior* (Ox. 2. Bodleian MS 572). These glosses have been studied by scholars such as Ifor *Williams, Henry *Lewis and Kenneth H. *Jackson because of the importance of the evidence about the early history of the Welsh language which they contain.

For further details see Kenneth H. Jackson, *Language and History in Early Britain* (1953) and D. Simon Evans, *Llafar a Llyfr yn yr Hen Gyfnod* (1982).

Oxford Movement, The, within the Church of England, sought to defend it against liberalizing tendencies which were considered a threat to its spiritual purity and to its freedom from State control. The main purpose was to emphasize the authority of the Anglican Church as the guardian of the faith, the validity of the apostolic succession, and the importance of the Book of Common Prayer and of ritual in worship. These principles may be traced back to the High Church Party of the seventeenth century, but they were promoted in the nineteenth by a *Romanticism which became increasingly interested in the Middle Ages. The leaders of the Movement in England were J. H. Newman, E. B. Pusey, John Keble and Isaac *Williams and a sermon preached by Keble at Oxford in 1833 signalled its emergence. After the publication of the first of its *Tracts for the Times* in the same year, it was also known as the Tractarian Movement.

It inclined towards the Roman Catholic Church in emphasizing frequent communion, the confession of sins, the monastic life and the importance of ceremonial. Newman was received into the Roman Catholic Church in 1845.

It was in the diocese of *Bangor that the impact of the Oxford Movement was felt most strongly in Wales. One of its leaders was Morris *Williams (Nicander) but other prominent Tractarians were John *Williams (Ab Ithel), Owen Wynne *Jones (Glasynys) and Robert *Roberts (Y Sgolor Mawr). A Tractarian periodical, *Baner y Groes*, was published between 1854 and 1858, and St. Michael's College, Llandaf, was established for the training of priests largely as an expression of Tractarian ideals. It was in its effects on Welsh *Nonconformity, however, that the movement had its most important consequences. Reacting against its spiritual leanings towards Rome and its political inclination towards extreme Toryism, the Methodists were driven increasingly to make common cause with other Nonconformist sects and adopted an even more hostile attitude towards the Established Church. The movement to defend the Church of England thus had, as one of its long-term results, the *Disestablishment of that Church in Wales.

The history of the Oxford Movement in Wales is traced by D. E. Evans in the *Journal* of the Historical Society of the Church in Wales (vol. IV, 1954, vol. VI, 1956, vol. VIII, 1958, vol. X, 1960) and by A. Tudno Williams in *Mudiad Rhydychen a Chymru* (1983).

Oxoniensis (T. H. Parry-Williams; 1887–1975), see under BORD GRON CERIDWEN.

P

Pacifism, the conviction that it is wrong to take part in war. It is often confused with pacificism, a concern to prevent war while accepting that the controlled use of armed force may be necessary. While the latter is a political idea, the former is a moral creed. There is a long tradition of pacificism in the Christian Church and in many ethical movements, but Pacifism as a coherent doctrine is essentially a twentieth-century phenomenon; the word dates from 1907 and its Welsh equivalent, *Heddychiaeth*, was first recorded in 1947. The Society of Friends (see under QUAKERISM), almost from its inception, advocated non-resistance, but it was not until 1816, with the establishment in London of the Peace Society, that the advocacy of peace became a proselytizing movement rather than a creed confined to static, self-contained sects. The first Chairman of the Society was Joseph Tregelles *Price, a Quaker and the owner of the Neath Abbey Ironworks. In the following decades such advocacy won extensive support as religious, utilitarian and ethical considerations caused suspicion of warmongering to become an integral part of British Liberal, Protestant, political culture. This was especially true in Wales where William *Rees (Gwilym Hiraethog) and Samuel *Roberts were prominent in the opposition to all forms of bellicosity. The tradition was continued by Henry *Richard, Secretary of the Peace Society from 1848 to 1885, who, because of his tireless championship of international arbitration, became revered as 'The Apostle of Peace'.

Twentieth-century Pacifism is the legacy of the First World War. Although the vast majority of the people of Wales supported David *Lloyd George's call for total victory, some adherents to the Christian and to the Socialist traditions felt grave misgivings. A number of Welsh Nonconformists, George M. Ll. *Davies the most influential amongst them, joined the Fellowship of Reconciliation, founded in 1914. The monthly journal Y *Deyrnas*, published from 1916 to 1919 and edited by Thomas Rees of Bangor, became the focus of Welsh anti-war sentiment, a sentiment which was fuelled by Liberal repugnance toward military conscription. The left wing of the Labour movement, while not pacifist, won increasing support for its view that the War was wholly inimical to the interests of the working class and by 1917 thousands were attending anti-war meetings in the south Wales coalfield.

In the General Election of 1918, Lloyd George's pugnacious British patriotism was endorsed by the majority of the Welsh electorate but reaction was not long in coming: in 1923 George M. Ll. Davies was elected as the Christian Pacifist Member of Parliament for the *University of Wales. *Plaid Cymru, established in 1925, had from the beginning a strong pacifist streak and the *Penyberth episode was, in part, a pacifist protest. Among the party's members was D. Gwenallt Jones (David James *Jones), whose recollections of his imprisonment in Dartmoor as a conscientious objector provided the basis for his novel, *Plasau'r Brenin (1934). Widespread support was accorded to the Welsh Council of the League of Nations. Founded in 1922, under the patronage of Lord Davies of Llandinam, the Council was energetically led by Gwilym *Davies, who in 1923 launched the Goodwill Message of the Children of Wales. The Union achieved remarkable success in 1934 and the year following when it persuaded sixty-two per cent of the adult population of Wales to participate in the Peace Ballot, the results of which indicated that Christian Pacifism enjoyed more extensive support in Wales than in other parts of the United Kingdom. Welsh pacifists were prominent in the Peace Pledge Union, founded in 1936, and Cymdeithas Heddychwyr Cymru was established in 1937 with George M. Ll. Davies as President and Gwynfor *Evans as Secretary.

By 1939, however, the Nazi threat had rehabilitated warfare. The pacifists of Wales continued their operations throughout the war and conscientious objectors in Wales were proportionately more numerous than they were elsewhere, but they constituted only a tiny fraction of those who were called up for military service. After the war there were protests, especially from members of Plaid Cymru, against the continuance of military conscription in peacetime and in 1960–61 Waldo *Williams was twice imprisoned for refusing to pay taxes which might finance the war machine. Non-violent resistance in the Gandhian mould influenced the actions of *Cymdeithas yr Iaith Gymraeg and Welsh pacifists have been prominent in the anti-nuclear movement: C.N.D. Cymru played a part in the campaign which resulted in the declaration that Wales is a nuclear-free country and the Greenham Common camp was set up after a march initiated in Cardiff.

For further details see E. H. Griffiths, *Heddychwyr Mawr Cymru* (1967–68), G. J. Jones, *Wales and the Quest for Peace* (1969), M. Ceadel, *Pacifism in Britain, 1914–1945* (1980), and K. O. Morgan, 'Peace movements in Wales, 1899–1945' in *The Welsh History Review* (vol. 10, no. 3, 1981).

Padarn (mid-6th cent.), a saint who was probably a contemporary of *Dewi Sant and *Teilo, with whom, according to the Lives, he went on a pilgrimage to Jerusalem. The Life of Padarn, composed in the twelfth century, has little historical value, although it may reflect some genuine traditions about his conflicts with *Maelgwn Gwynedd and *Arthur. Because there was more than one saint bearing the name *Paternus*, it may be that this work is a conflation of two Lives, one Breton and the other Welsh. Padarn is said to have been a native of Letavia, probably not Brittany (W. *Llydaw*) but a district in south-east Wales. His preaching centre was *Llanbadarn Fawr, near what is today Aberystwyth, and from there his cult spread throughout *Ceredigion and beyond. The *clas*, or community, at Llanbadarn Fawr survived for a long time after Padarn's day but his cult was eventually absorbed by that of Dewi.

Pais (lit. 'Petticoat'), a monthly magazine for women, the first number of which appeared in 1978 under the editorship of Annes Glynn and Eleri Llewelyn Morris. Like its predecessor, *Hon* (1963–65), it publishes—besides articles of special interest to women—a variety of features of more general cultural appeal, including book reviews, poetry and short stories.

'Pais Dinogad' (lit. 'Dinogad's coat'), a mother's lullaby for her child in the form of a hunting-song. Its seventeen lines are found interpolated in 'Y *Gododdin' (*c.*600) and refer to the feats performed by Dinogad's father in pursuit of fish, fowl and beast. The reference to eight slaves and the waterfall of Derwent suggests that it reflects the life of an early community, possibly within Gododdin territory. Its content has nothing to do with the theme of *Aneirin's poem but its inclusion in the text may be due to the sanguinary nature of its subject-matter, as well as to the elegiac overtones which at least one scholar has detected in it.

For further details see Ifor Williams, *Canu Aneirin* (1938), Kenneth Jackson, *The Gododdin* (1969), and R. L. Thomson, '*Amser ac Agwedd yn y Cynfeirdd*' in *Astudiaethau ar yr Hengerdd/Studies in Old Welsh Poetry* (ed. R. Bromwich and R. Brinley Jones, 1978).

PALMER, ALFRED NEOBARD (Robert Rees; 1847–1915), local historian, was born in Suffolk but lived at Wrexham, Denbs., from 1880 until his death. Soon after settling in Wales he began to take an interest in local history and learned Welsh in order to conduct his research. His most distinguished work is the essay, *A History of Ancient Tenures of Land in the Marches of North Wales* (1885). He also wrote, under the pseudonym Robert Rees, a novel about Welsh life entitled *Owen Tanat* (1897), which was not well received but which is not without literary merit.

Palug's Cat, see under POWERFUL SWINEHERDS.

Pant y Groes Hen, see VALLE CRUCIS.

Panton, Paul (1727–97), patron and antiquary, was born at Bagillt, Holywell, Flints. Educated at Trinity Hall, Cambridge, and at Lincoln's Inn, he was called to the Bar in 1749 and was prominent in the public life both of Anglesey, where Plas Gwyn was his home, and of his native county. Like his friend Thomas *Pennant, he travelled widely throughout the countries of Great Britain in search of manuscripts and antiquities and, despite his inability to speak Welsh, he was knowledgeable about the literary traditions of Wales. Many of the papers of the *Wynn family of Gwydir came into his possession and, in return for his patronage of Evan *Evans (Ieuan Fardd), he acquired that scholar's manuscripts in 1788. With his son, also named Paul Panton (1758–1822), he was a patron of David *Thomas (Dafydd Ddu Eryri) and facilitated the publication of *The Myvyrian Archaiology* (1801–07) by allowing the editors, Owen *Jones (Owain Myfyr) and William *Owen Pughe, to consult the Plas Gwyn library. The Panton manuscripts were purchased by the *National Library of Wales in 1914.

Pantycelyn, see WILLIAMS, WILLIAM (1717–91).

Pantyfedwen Foundations, The, see under JAMES, DAVID (1887–1967).

Papur Pawb (lit. 'Everybody's paper'; 1893–1917, 1922–55), a weekly newspaper edited in turn by Daniel Rees, Picton Davies and Evan Abbott for F. Coolestone, the owner of the *Herald* newspapers in Caernarfon. Popular and entertaining, it carried short stories and extracts from novels, as well as humorous material. Among its contributors were T. Gwynn *Jones and Richard Hughes *Williams (Dic Tryfan), who developed their skills as story-tellers in its columns; J. R. Lloyd Hughes produced many of its cartoons. The circulation gradually declined during the First World War and the paper ceased publication in 1917. Revived in 1922, it continued until 1937 when it merged with *Y *Werin a'r Eco* to form *Papur Pawb a'r Werin a'r Eco*, until that publication came to an end in 1955.

Papurau Bro (lit. 'Neighbourhood or community newspapers'), periodicals with a local or regional appeal, first appeared during the 1970s.

The aim of their promoters was to halt the decline in the reading of Welsh by providing news and features through the medium of the language, a role often ignored by newspapers with wider circulations. The first, *Y Dinesydd*, was launched by Welsh-speakers in Cardiff in 1973 and still flourishes. Most have enjoyed a certain success, although several have failed, and by 1984 it was estimated that about fifty were selling, between them, approximately seventy thousand copies monthly. The majority are published with the support of *Welsh Office grants administered by the Regional Arts Associations, but more vital to their survival is the enthusiasm of their editorial teams, amateurs all. Some have become the focus for other cultural initiatives such as drama festivals and the publishing of books with local appeal.

Parcrhydderch, a house in the parish of Llangeitho, Cards., later known as **Glyn Aeron**, was the home of a family which had an important place in the literary history of the county during the fourteenth and fifteenth centuries. Many poets enjoyed the patronage of Ieuan ap Gruffudd Foel (*fl.* 1340), of his son, Ieuan Llwyd, and of his grandson, *Rhydderch ab Ieuan Llwyd. Poetry dedicated to Ieuan ap Gruffudd ab Ieuan Llwyd, presumably Rhydderch's nephew, is to be found in the *Hendregadredd Manuscript. *Dafydd ap Gwilym addressed poems to Angharad, the wife of Ieuan Llwyd, and other poems composed for her are included in The *Red Book of Hergest*, as well as in the Llanstephan 3 and Peniarth 20 copies of the Grammar of *Einion Offeiriad. Rhydderch ab Ieuan Llwyd, who held offices under the Crown and was reputed to be an authority on the Welsh Laws, was also a patron of *Iolo Goch, *Dafydd y Coed and others. The *White Book of Rhydderch either belonged to him or he was the patron of the scribes who compiled it; he was also the father of Ieuan ap Rhydderch (*fl.* 1430–70), the poet. The descendants of this family received poets at houses in many other parts of the county for at least three more generations.

PARKER, JOHN (1922–82), novelist. Born in Cardiff and of Irish descent, he was a feature-writer with the *Western Mail and news-editor of The South Wales Echo before joining the staff of the Central Office of Information in London. He later worked in the *Welsh Office, at the United Nations Organisation in New York and latterly as the Deputy Director of Information at the Home Office in London. One of his two novels, *Iron in the Valleys* (1959), is set in Merthyr Tydfil during the early nineteenth century, and the other, *The Alien Land* (1961), is the story of an Italian café-owner and his family in the industrial valleys of south Wales in the years before and during the Second World War.

Parliament for Wales Campaign, The, launched in 1951 on an all-party basis under the chairmanship of Megan Lloyd George, the Liberal Member of Parliament for Anglesey. A petition, carrying the signatures of about a quarter of a million persons who declared themselves in favour of an elected, legislative Parliament for Wales, was presented at Westminster six years later by Goronwy Roberts, the Labour Member of Parliament for Caernarfon. In addition a bill setting up such a Parliament was introduced in the House of Commons by S. O. Davies (1883–1972), the Labour Member of Parliament for Merthyr Tydfil, in March 1955. The initiative failed, largely because, of the thirty-six Members of Parliament representing constituencies in Wales, only six supported it (including five Labour members in opposition to their party's policy), and because the British political system cannot be changed by means of petition alone. The campaign drew from Saunders *Lewis one of his most pungent shorter poems.

There is an account of the campaign in the biography, *S.O. Davies, a Socialist Faith* (1983) by Robert Griffiths; see also Alan Butt Philip, *The Welsh Question, Nationalism in Welsh Politics 1945–70* (1975) and the chapter by Elwyn Roberts in *Cymru'n Deffro* (ed. John Davies, 1981).

PARRI, DAFYDD (1926–   ), children's author and short-story writer. Born at Rowen in Dyffryn Conwy, Caerns., and educated at the Normal College, Bangor, he was a teacher at Llanrwst, in his native county, before becoming a full-time writer. He is the author of a very popular series of twenty-five novels for children, *Cyfres y Llewod* (1975–80), which has won many young readers. Besides two volumes of short stories for adults, *Nos Lun a Storïau Eraill* (1976) and *Bwrw Hiraeth* (1981), he has also published the first titles in a new series for children about the adventures of a sheep-dog named Cailo. These books have established his reputation as one of the most prolific and successful children's writers in the Welsh language.

Parry, Blanche (1508?–90), lady-in-waiting to Elizabeth I, was born at New Court in the Golden Valley, on the border between Breconshire and Herefordshire. In 1565 she was appointed 'Chief Gentlewoman of the Queen's most honourable Privy Chamber and Keeper of her Majesty's Jewels', an office which, though not 'noble', was both profitable and influential. Catholic, unmarried and blind in her last years, she owned extensive lands in her native district. James Parry of Poston, Master of the Buckhounds, was a distant cousin and Rowland *Vaughan of New Court, another courtier, her nephew by marriage. William Cecil, Lord Burleigh, whom she called kinsman, drew up her will and was her executor.

For further details see C. A. Bradford, *Blanche Parry,*

Queen Elizabeth's Gentlewoman (1935) and Theophilus Jones, *History of Brecknock* (3rd edn., 1930).

PARRY, EDWARD (1723–86), hymn-writer, was a native of Llansannan, Denbs. Except for six published at Trefeca in 1774, most of his hymns were printed posthumously in a small collection shared with William Evans of Bala under the title *Ychydig o Emynau* (1789). His best hymn, '*Caned nef a daear lawr*', is still in vogue.

For further details see the article by Morris Davies in *Y Traethodydd* (1874) and T. Brynmor Davies in *Llawlyfrau Llansannan* (1945).

PARRY, GEORGE (1613?–78), see under PARRY, JAMES RHYS (*c.*1570?–1625?).

PARRY, GWENLYN (1932–), playwright, was born at Deiniolen, Caerns., and educated at the Normal College, Bangor. He discovered an interest in the theatre while working as a teacher in London, where Ryan *Davies and Rhydderch *Jones were among his friends. After returning to Wales to become a teacher at Bethesda, Caerns., he earned a reputation as a writer of promise by winning prizes at the *National Eisteddfod. In 1966 he was appointed to a post with BBC Wales, later becoming Senior Script Editor. He has written a good deal for television and has produced a number of popular programmes such as *Fo a Fe* and *Pobol y Cwm*.

Although the one-act plays in his volume *Tair Drama* (1965) show remarkable vitality, it is in Gwenlyn Parry's full-length plays that his unique style is fully demonstrated. The first of these, *Saer Doliau* (1966), puzzled its first audiences because it lacked a clear story-line and was capable of more than one interpretation, for which reasons he was labelled a playwright of the Absurd. In his subsequent plays, which include *Tŷ ar y Tywod* (1968), *Y Ffin* (1973) and *Y Tŵr* (1978), he has made even fuller use of the anti-naturalistic techniques of the post-war theatre and demonstrated a gift for devising imaginative and highly theatrical situations. Although his style is unliterary, in comparison with that of some contemporary Welsh playwrights, he has an excellent ear for dialogue and the subtleties of dialect. His most recent play, *Sâl* (1982), based on the story of Sarah *Jacob, suggests that he is still searching for new methods of expression.

A book-length study of the ideas in Gwenlyn Parry's work has been written by Dewi Z. Phillips (1982); see also the note about him by John Rowlands in *Profiles* (1980).

PARRY, HENRY, see PERRI, HENRY (1560/1–1617).

PARRY, JAMES RHYS (Eos Eyas; *c.*1570–1625), poet, the author of a Welsh metrical version of the Psalms, was descended from the Parrys of Poston, Herefs. He is remembered for having presented his manuscripts to William *Morgan, Bishop of Llandaf, who showed them to Edmund *Prys before the latter's more famous *Salmau Cân* were published in 1621. Parry's son, **George Parry** (1613?–78), who became vicar of Cheriton and Llanmadoc, Gower, about 1649, also made a version of the Psalms, in both free and traditional metres, adding to each a parallel version in Latin.

Parry, John (**The Blind Harpist**; 1710?–82), musician, born at Nefyn, Caerns., was employed as a harpist at Wynnstay, the home of the *Williams Wynn family. One of the most brilliant harpists of his day, he played at concerts in London, Oxford and Dublin. His most important contributions to Welsh culture were his three publications, *Antient British Music* (1742), *A Collection of Welsh, English, and Scotch Airs* (1761) and *British Harmony, being a Collection of Antient Welsh Airs* (1781).

For further details see the account of John Parry's life by Huw Williams (1983).

PARRY, JOHN (1775–1846), editor, was a native of Llandwrog, Caerns., but from 1806 until his death he lived in Chester, where he kept a bookshop and founded his own press. In 1818 he began publishing the magazine *Goleuad Gwynedd* (afterwards *Goleuad Cymru*) and was the editor of *Y Drysorfa* from 1831 onwards. Ordained in 1814, he had a hand in the drafting of the Confession of Faith adopted by the Calvinistic Methodists in 1823, but is remembered primarily as the author of *Rhodd Mam* (1811), a catechism for children which, for more than a century, remained the denomination's primer of systematic religious instruction.

PARRY, JOHN HUMPHREYS or **HUMFFREYS** (**Ordovex**; 1786–1825), editor, was born at Mold, Flints. He went to London in 1807 and was called to the Bar four years later, but neglected his practice, fell into debt and turned to journalism, writing under a pseudonym. He became a member of the *Gwyneddigion Society and was among those who revived the Honourable Society of *Cymmrodorion in 1820. In 1819 he founded the magazine *The *Cambro-Briton* and was editor until it ceased publication three years later. He also compiled a biographical dictionary, *The Cambrian Plutarch* (1824). Described by a contemporary as 'a generally intelligent man, though somewhat hasty and overbearing', he was killed in an incident near the Prince of Wales tavern in Pentonville.

Parry, Joseph (1841–1903), composer and musician. Born in Merthyr Tydfil, Glam., and a collier-boy at the age of nine, he emigrated with his family to the USA in 1854 and worked in the steel-works at Dannville, Pennsylvania, until

1865, studying music in his spare time. After he had won competitions at the *National Eisteddfod in 1863, a public fund was opened to enable him to study at the Royal Academy of Music in London. He became, in 1874, the first Professor of Music at the University College of Wales, Aberystwyth, but later taught at Swansea and Cardiff. Much in demand as adjudicator and conductor, he also composed a large number of musical works, including the opera *Blodwen (1880) and the hymn-tune *'Aberystwyth'. His romantic career, distinguished by a fluent talent and prodigious energy, is the subject of the novel *Off to Philadelphia in the Morning* (1947) by Jack *Jones, in which there is a wholly fictitious account of how Parry came to write another of his famous tunes, '*Myfanwy*'.

A biography of Joseph Parry was written by E. Keri Evans (1921); see also the bilingual monograph by Owain T. Edwards in the *St. David's Day* series (1970).

PARRY, RICHARD (1560–1623), bishop and biblical scholar, was born at Pwllhalog, Flints., and educated at Christ Church, Oxford. Ordained deacon in 1584, he was appointed Master of Ruthin Free School, remaining there until he became in 1592 Chancellor of *Bangor. He was appointed Rector of Gresford in 1593 and of Cilcain in 1596, and Dean of Bangor in 1599; he succeeded William *Morgan as Bishop of *St. Asaph in 1604. The revised editions of the Welsh *Bible published in 1620 and of the Book of Common Prayer (1621) were partly Parry's work, although it was to his brother-in-law, John *Davies of Mallwyd, that the greater credit was due.

There is a study of Richard Parry and John Davies by R. Geraint Gruffydd in *Y Traddodiad Rhyddiaith* (ed. Geraint Bowen, 1970); see also the article by J. G. Jones in the *Transactions* of the Denbighshire Historical Society (1974).

PARRY, ROBERT (*fl.* 1540?–1612?), author, a cousin of *Catrin of Berain (for whom he wrote an elegy in English), was born at Tywysog in the parish of Henllan, Denbs. He kept a diary which is regarded as a valuable source-book for the history of north Wales families, and published a prose work of fiction entitled *Moderatus, the most delectable and famous Historie of the Black Knight* (1595).

PARRY, ROBERT WILLIAMS (1884–1956), poet. Born at Tal-y-sarn, Dyffryn Nantlle, Caerns., he was related through his father to both T. H. *Parry-Williams and Thomas *Parry. He spent two years at the University College of Wales, Aberystwyth, but left in 1904 without a degree and for the next three years he taught at elementary schools in Wales and England. Resuming his studies in 1907 under John *Morris-Jones at Bangor, he graduated there in 1908 and subsequently taught Welsh and English at Brynrefail in his native county.

He came to public notice as a poet when, in 1910, he won the *Chair at the *National Eisteddfod with his *awdl*, 'Yr *Haf'. This poem, with its euphony, rich vocabulary and emphasis on the beauty of the moment, was acclaimed as one of the most important works of the 'new school' of poets, among whom T. Gwynn *Jones and W. J. *Gruffydd were also numbered, and Williams Parry was subsequently known as '*Bardd yr Haf*' ('The poet of summer'). At about the same time he began publishing essays on the nature of poetry and working, for a master's degree, on a thesis on the relationship between Welsh and Breton. After spending a year as headmaster of a small rural school at Cefnddwysarn (Sarnau), Mer., he became a teacher at secondary schools in Barry and Cardiff. In November 1916 he was called up for military service and spent the following two years at camps in England. Although lonely and unhappy during this period of his life, he wrote a number of fine sonnets, including '*Gadael Tir*' and '*Cysur Henaint*', as well as the famous *englynion* in memory of Hedd Wyn (Ellis Humphrey *Evans). He returned to Cardiff as a teacher in 1919 and then, two years later, took the post of Headmaster of Oakley Park School, near Llanidloes, Mont. He remained there only a few months, however, before being appointed to the staff of his old College at Bangor, where he became a Lecturer partly in the Welsh Department and partly to extra-mural classes. Marrying in 1923, he settled at Bethesda where he spent the rest of his life.

During the 1920s, a happy period for him, R. Williams Parry published a number of literary essays in periodicals, was active as an adjudicator at eisteddfodau and established himself as an important poet with the publication of a volume of his collected poems, *Yr Haf a Cherddi Eraill* (1924), which includes some of his most mature work. Then, between 1929 and 1933, his happiness was clouded by a misunderstanding which arose over the terms of his employment as a lecturer. Dejected by the belief that he was being treated unfairly because he was a writer rather than a scholar, as he claimed in his poem '*Chwilota*', he took umbrage and went on a kind of literary strike, ceasing to publish his poetry, refusing to allow the *Gregynog Press to bring out a volume of his work and turning instead to the writing of linguistic notes on Welsh and Breton. This period of his life came to an abrupt end, however, in September 1936 with the incident at the bombing school at *Penyberth on the Llŷn peninsula. The poet was incensed by the subsequent dismissal of Saunders *Lewis from the staff of University College, Swansea, and it spurred him to campaign on his behalf. When it became clear that Lewis was not going to be reinstated, the poet took up the most effective weapon within his reach and began writing poems of political satire, among them the vitri-olic '*J.S.L.*' and '*Y Gwrthodedig*'. This pro-ductive disturbance of his equilibrium continued into the time of his great sonnets of the late 1930s. Retiring in 1944, he was troubled by poor health and aged prematurely. He had to rely on the help of friends for the preparation of his second and last volume of poetry, *Cerddi'r Gaeaf* (1952).

R. Williams Parry's total poetic output was comparatively small, filling only two volumes, but it includes some fifty poems of permanent value: the early romantic sonnets, the *englynion* in memory of friends who died in the First World War, the nature lyrics of the 1920s which convey in an exquisitely sensuous manner the wonder of Creation and the transience of things, poems about growing old and the ravages of time, and the sonnets of the late 1930s which are both compassionate and scathingly critical of man's pettiness and self-satisfaction.

A selection of the poet's literary criticism is to be found in *Rhyddiaith R. Williams Parry* (ed. Bedwyr Lewis Jones, 1974), and his additional poems were collected at the end of T. Emrys Parry's study, *Barddoniaeth Robert Williams Parry* (1973). There is an essay on the poet by Bedwyr Lewis Jones in the *Writers of Wales* series (1972) and another by Alan Llwyd in the *Llên y Llenor* series (1984); the latter has also edited a volume of critical essays in the series, *Cyfres y Meistri* (1979). A limited edition of R. Williams Parry's poems, edited by Thomas Parry, was published by *Gwasg Gregynog* in 1981.

PARRY, THOMAS (1904–85), scholar, critic and editor. Born at Carmel, Caerns., he gradu-ated in Welsh at the University College of North Wales, Bangor, in 1926, and was appointed Lecturer in Welsh and Latin at University Col-lege, Cardiff, in the same year. Returning to his old College as a Lecturer in 1929, he became Professor of Welsh at Bangor in 1947 and Librarian of the *National Library of Wales in 1953. From 1958 until his retirement in 1969 he was Principal of the University College of Wales, Aberystwyth; he was knighted in 1978.

Thomas Parry's major contribution to Welsh scholarship was made over a period of some fifty years. He began by publishing a modern inter-pretation of the story of the Holy Grail, *Saint Greal* (1933), then turned from Arthurian legend to a study of the balladry of the eighteenth century in *Baledi'r Ddeunawfed Ganrif* (1935). But his greatest achievement was his comprehensive survey of the whole field of Welsh literature to 1900, entitled *Hanes Llenyddiaeth Gymraeg* (1945). This work, informed not only by vast erudition but also by the author's typically forth-right literary judgements, was translated by H. Idris *Bell and published as *A History of Welsh Literature* (1955); an appendix, *Llenyddiaeth Cymru, 1900–1945*, appeared in 1945.

Even more important from the scholarly point of view was Thomas Parry's definitive edition of the poetry of *Dafydd ap Gwilym (1952), a landmark in modern Welsh scholar-ship, in which the canon of that poet's work was established for the first time by reference to all the available manuscript evidence, a mammoth task carried out with rare assurance. There were also several notable by-products of this great work in the form of scholarly articles on various aspects of Dafydd ap Gwilym's art.

Although Thomas Parry was best known for his scholarship, he was also a writer who came within an ace of winning the *Chair at the *National Eisteddfod with his *awdl*, '*Y Fam*', in 1925. He translated T. S. Eliot's *Murder in the Cathedral* (1935) into Welsh under the title *Lladd Wrth yr Allor* (1949) and he was the author of a verse-play, *Llywelyn Fawr* (1954). His anthology, *The *Oxford Book of Welsh Verse* (1962), rapidly won its place as the most authoritative selection of Welsh poetry available to the general reader. He also compiled (with Merfyn Morgan) a standard bibliography of writings about Welsh literature, *Llyfryddiaeth i Lenyddiaeth Gymraeg* (1976).

For further details, including a bibliography of Thomas Parry's writings, see *Ysgrifau Beirniadol X* (ed. J. E. Caerwyn Williams, 1977); there is an interview with Thomas Parry in vol. IX (1976) of the same series; see also the article by Huw Llew Williams in *Dyrnaid o Awduron Cyfoes* (ed. D. Ben Rees, 1975).

PARRY, WILLIAM (**Gwilym Pant Tâf**; 1836–1903), poet, was born at Nelson, Glam., and became a Baptist minister at Penarth and Ynysybwl in the same county. He published three volumes of verse, namely *The Cymanfa* (1892), *The Old Evangelist* (1893) and *Welsh Hill-side Saints* (1896).

Parry, William John (1842–1927), quarry-workers' leader. Born at Bethesda, Caerns., he took a prominent part in the creation of the North Wales Quarrymen's Union in 1874, later serving as its first Secretary and President, and throughout his life he was active in the Liberal and Independent causes. He published several works in Welsh and English dealing with the quarrying industry, including *The Penrhyn Lock-out* (1901) and *The Cry of the People* (1906), and was a frequent contributor to the periodical press on labour problems, *Home Rule, the Welsh language and local government; he was also one of the founders of the newspaper *Y *Werin* in 1885.

An account of W. J. Parry's life and work is to be found in *Quarryman's Champion* (1978) by J. Roose Williams.

PARRY-JONES, DANIEL (1891–1981), author. Born at Llangeler, Carms., and educated at St. David's College, Lampeter, he was or-dained a clergyman of the Church of England at Pontypridd, Glam., in 1914 and thereafter served in parishes in Glamorgan and Breconshire, becoming Rural Dean of Crickhowell in 1957 and Honorary Canon of Brecon Cathedral two years later. He published four volumes of autobiography: *Welsh Country Upbringing* (1948), *Welsh Country Characters* (1952), *My Own Folk* (1972) and *A Welsh Country Parson* (1975). Written partly for the sake of his children and grandchildren, and partly out of dissatisfaction with the portrayal of Welsh life to be found in the work of such writers as Caradoc Evans (David *Evans), they are of interest chiefly for their sympathetic description of the Welsh-speaking, rural society in which the author was brought up and, more specifically, for their detailed accounts of agricultural methods and customs which have now almost entirely disappeared. D. Parry-Jones also published *Welsh Legends and Fairy Lore* (1953) and *Welsh Children's Games and Pastimes* (1964), of which the latter is generally considered to be a valuable contribution to the study of its subject.

PARRY-WILLIAMS, THOMAS HERBERT (1887–1975), poet, essayist and scholar. Born at Rhyd-ddu, Caerns., where his father was schoolmaster, he was educated at the University College of Wales, Aberystwyth, graduating in Welsh in 1908 and in Latin in 1909, and at Jesus College, Oxford; he later studied Comparative Linguistics at the Universities of Freiburg and Paris. In 1912, while still a student, T. H. Parry-Williams won both the *Chair and the *Crown at the National Eisteddfod, a triumph he was to repeat three years later. In 1914 he was appointed to an assistant lectureship in the Welsh Department at Aberystwyth but, as a result of dissension in 1919 caused by a recommendation that he be appointed Professor (some held the view that priority should be given to ex-soldiers) he turned his back on Celtic Studies and enrolled as a medical student. The following year, however, saw his appointment to the Chair of Welsh at Aberystwyth, a post in which he was to remain until his retirement in 1952.

The distinguished contribution of T. H. Parry-Williams to Welsh scholarship began with his first publication, *The English Element in Welsh* (1923), and continued with several studies of poetry in the free metres, such as *Carolau Richard White* (1931), *Canu Rhydd Cynnar* (1932) and *Hen Benillion* (1940), in addition to a treatise on the nature of poetry, *Elfennau Barddoniaeth* (1935). Concurrently he was publishing volumes of creative work, usually a combination of prose and verse, which established him as a major writer who was an innovator in both style and theme. These books include *Ysgrifau* (1928), *Cerddi* (1931), *Olion* (1935), *Ugain o Gerddi* (1949), *Myfyrdodau* (1957) and *Pensynnu* (1966); a collection of his essays appeared posthumously under the title *Casgliad o Ysgrifau* in 1984. To these he added translations into Welsh of opera libretti and did a great deal of work on behalf of such bodies as the *National Eisteddfod and the

*National Library of Wales. He became a prominent figure in the public life of Wales and was knighted in 1958.

As a writer, T. H. Parry-Williams chose two genres which had not previously been vehicles for serious literary expression in Welsh, and gave a new dignity to a third, by virtually limiting his creative work to essays, poems in rhyming couplets and sonnets. In the *essay, or personal discourse, he created a finely-wrought medium in which his questing, analytical mind combined with his intuitive sense of the mysteries of the universe in a series of philosophical contemplations which often had the intensity of the prose-poem. In the rhyming couplet, commonly used for light-hearted versifying in Welsh, he was able by employing a subtle interplay of rhythms, and by avoiding the over-rich in vocabulary, to develop a medium which allowed him to comment on a variety of subjects with critical irony. But his basic philosophy was reserved for the sonnet and it was he, together with his kinsman, Robert Williams *Parry, who made the most powerful use of that form in the Welsh language.

In his essays, couplets and sonnets alike, the themes are both consistent and complete, and his style direct. Among his central concerns were his own neighbourhood, his family background, his relationship with the mountains of *Eryri (Snowdonia), and the ways in which natural environment moulds human personality. In many essays, such as 'Bro', 'Oerddwr' and 'Y Lon Ucha', in couplet poems such as 'Hon', 'Bro', 'I'm Hynafiaid', and especially in the sonnets, 'Moelni', 'Ty'r Ysgol', 'Gweddill', 'Llyn y Gadair' and 'Tynfa', he returns time and again to these themes. 'Bro' ('neighbourhood' or 'community') is the title of the concluding poem in his last collection of poems and of the last essay in his final volume of essays. The work of T. H. Parry-Williams developed from a consideration of the significance of family and locality to a philosophical contemplation of the nature of life itself, especially in sonnets such as 'Dychwelyd' and 'Ymwacâd' and in couplet-sequences such as 'Yr Esgyrn Hyn' and 'Celwydd'.

It often seemed as if he rejected any attempt to give absolute meaning to life, and death often figures in his poems, but his method of investigation was not (as some have claimed) a coldly analytical observation of scientific phenomena. He was certainly consumed by a keen curiosity, as his essays show, but the mystery of life is ever present in his thoughts and this dimension to his sensibilities is clear enough in essays such as 'Yr Ias', 'Cydwybod' and 'Dieithrwch', and in very many of his poems. Although his philosophy was complex and sometimes ambiguous, he employed a precise, detached and courageous intelligence, together with a mastery of language, to explore an existence which was, for him, inexplicable. This combination of searching intelligence, linguistic directness and mystical sensibility was revolutionary in its time and remains a unique contribution to Welsh literature.

A full bibliography of the work of T. H. Parry-Williams is to be found in the volume edited in his honour by Idris Foster (1967); see also the supplement in the memorial number of *Y Traethodydd* (Autumn, 1975). A special number of *Poetry Wales* (Summer, 1974) was devoted to his work. Dyfnallt Morgan has written a study of the writer, *Rhyw Hanner Ieuenctid* (1971), and there is an essay on him by R. Gerallt Jones in the *Writers of Wales* series (1978); see also the photographic study in the *Bro a Bywyd* series (ed. Ifor Rees, 1981) and the obituary by J. E. Caerwyn Williams in *Studia Celtica* (vols. XII/XIII, 1977–78).

Pastai, see BID ALE.

Patagonia, a province of Argentina where a Welsh colony was established in 1865. Poverty, religious oppression and landlordism were mainly responsible for emigration from Wales during the eighteenth and nineteenth centuries, thousands leaving for North America in the hope of finding freedom to maintain their language and culture, only to become absorbed into American society and see their children lose the language and their nationality. The idea of establishing a colony in Patagonia stemmed from the desire of Welsh Americans to channel this emigration to a country which offered more favourable conditions and, at that time, Argentina was anxious to attract immigrants from Europe who would settle in its remote southern territories.

The first group of Welsh settlers, about 160 in all, mostly from the industrial valleys of south Wales but almost all born in rural districts, set sail from Liverpool on 31 May 1865 on a small ship, *The Mimosa*. Edwin Roberts of Wisconsin and Lewis *Jones (1836–1904) led the expedition, but it was Michael D. *Jones who provided the political vision and the finance for the enterprise. The party landed on the desolate beach at Porth Madryn on 28 July 1865, celebrated to this day as the Festival of the Landing, and spent several weeks in the shelter of caves. Bitterly disappointed by the wild desert of the Camwy Valley, they endured many years of terrible hardship and would have perished without the practical help in the early days of the Argentinian Government, which sent them food, and of a local tribe of Indians, the Tuelche, who taught them how to hunt. In 1885 a number of families crossed four hundred miles of desert to establish another settlement in Cwm Hyfryd at the foot of the Andes. By the end of the century the settlers had succeeded in controlling the waters of the river Camwy and the valley prospered. Emigration from Wales continued, mostly from the valleys of the south, until 1914.

At the turn of the century Welsh was the language of the colony (known in Welsh as *Y Wladfa*) and all its institutions. Welsh bank-notes were printed, Welsh textbooks were published and Welsh was the language of the courts. Chapels were built, forming the heart of the colony's cultural life with their prayer-meetings and singing-festivals, and several Welsh newspapers were published, such as *Y Brut* and *Y *Drafod*. An annual eisteddfod was held, its competitions giving prominence to the history of the colony, especially as recorded in the diaries describing the pioneers' journey into the heartland. Welsh cultural life began to decline, however, during the first decades of the twentieth century when immigrants from Spain and Italy, attracted by the colony's economic success, began arriving in the province. Contacts with Wales were severed at the start of the Second World War but were restored in 1965 when the colony celebrated its centenary and since then they have continued in a spirit of mutual interest and respect. Only a few of the colony's Welsh-speakers (often bilingual in Welsh and Spanish) have settled in Wales but a number of young Patagonians have spent periods as students in Wales. Even so, Welsh is dying in Patagonia and it is estimated that by today only some five thousand people still speak the language, most of them old or middle-aged. The colony has produced two important Welsh writers, namely Eluned *Morgan and R. Bryn *Williams, and its foremost Welsh poet among the living is Irma Hughes de Jones, a granddaughter of Gwyneth Vaughan (Annie Harriet *Hughes).

Several writers have published books about the colony, including Abraham Mathews, *Hanes y Wladfa Gymreig* (1894), Lewis Jones, *Ymfidiaeth y Cymry* (1895) and *Y Wladfa Gymraeg* (1898), W.M. Hughes, *Ar Lannau'r Camwy* (1927), R. Bryn Williams, *Crwydro Patagonia* (1960) and *Y Wladfa* (1962), Glyn Williams, *The Desert and the Dream* (1975), Gareth Alban Davies, *Tan Tro Nesaf* (1976) and *Atgofion o'r Wladfa* (ed. R. Bryn Williams, 1981).

Paternostering, see under WAKE.

Patrick or **Patricius** or **Padrig** (*c*.385–*c*.460), the patron saint of Ireland, was of Romano-Brythonic stock, having been born in *Bannavem Taberniae* (Banwen, perhaps) in the western regions of Britain. He was the grandson of a priest named Potitus and the son of a deacon, Calpurnius, who was also a local magistrate. When he was sixteen years old Patrick was abducted by Irish raiders and sold as a slave in Ireland, where he worked as a shepherd and grew in Christian devotion. Escaping after six years, he received religious instruction in Gaul, possibly under the care of Germanus (*Garmon) in Auxerre, or in Britain. About the year 432 he felt a call to evangelize in Ireland, where there were some Christians already, and probably made his headquarters at Armagh. Confusion between him and Palladius, who was appointed bishop in Ireland in 431, seems to have been responsible for an old supposition that there were two Patricks. Besides his confessions in Latin, the saint wrote *Epistula ad Coroticum*, a letter addressed to Ceredig, a Brythonic chieftain whose men had attacked a gathering of Patrick's people. A *Lorica* praying for divine protection is also attributed to Patrick. His acceptance as patron saint of all Ireland (much of which he never visited) is now believed to be the result of the political dominance of the northern dynasty of the Ui Neill.

*Rhygyfarch, in his Life of St. David (*Dewi Sant), tells of Patrick, 'polished with Roman learning and teeming with excellences, having been made a bishop', coming to Vallis Rosina (i.e. Glyn Rhosyn, *St. David's) and vowing to serve God faithfully there. But he was warned in a dream that the place was reserved for one not due to be born for another thirty years. Angry, he went up to the rock which is called (says the narrative) 'The seat of Patrick', where an angel showed him Ireland in the distance, the land which was to be his for evangelization. This story is probably apocryphal and intended to show Patrick's British origin, to trade on his considerable reputation and to demonstrate the importance of St. David's to both Patrick and Dewi, an argument current in Rhygyfarch's day.

The *Works of St. Patrick* were edited by L. Bieler (1952, 1953) and A. B. E. Hood (1978). The historical background and the problems of interpreting the Lives are discussed by D. A. Binchy in *Studia Hibernica* (vol. II, 1962); see also James Carney, *The Problem of St. Patrick* (1961) and R. P. C. Hanson, *St. Patrick, his Origins and Career* (1968).

Patripassianism, see under SABELLIANISM.

Patti, Adelina (The Queen of Song; 1843–1919), opera singer. Born in Madrid of Italian parents and brought up in New York, she was at the height of her career as a prima donna when, in 1878, on the advice of Lord Swansea, she bought the castle and estate of Craig-y-nos, Brecs., as a refuge from the fashionable world. To Craig-y-nos, built in 1842 and 'improved' in the Scottish baronial style, this wealthy, world-famous soprano—whom Verdi considered to be the greatest of her day—returned by special train after each triumphant tour. After her death the castle's winter gardens were re-erected in Victoria Park, Swansea, where they are still known as the Patti Pavilion.

For further details see the account by Froom Tyler in *Glamorgan Historian* (ed. Stewart Williams, 1967).

PAYNE, FFRANSIS GEORGE (1900–   ), folk historian, was born at Kington, Herefs., and educated at University College, Cardiff. He was appointed to the staff of the Folk Life Department at the *National Museum of Wales in 1936 and in 1962 became Head of the Department of Material Culture at the *Welsh Folk Museum. Besides a classic study of early agri-

culture in Wales, *Yr Aradr Gymreig* (1954), and the booklet *Welsh Peasant Costume* (first printed in *Folk Life* in 1964), he has written on the former county of Radnorshire in the series *Cyfres Crwydro Cymru* (2 vols., 1966, 1968). A selection of his essays, including some from his earlier volume, *Y Chwaryddion Crwydrol* (1943), was published in 1980 under the title *Cwysau*, a book in which his elegant style is to be seen at its most polished.

Pea Sunday, see under LENT.

Peace of Worcester, The (1218), see under LLYWELYN AP IORWERTH (1173–1240).

PEACOCK, THOMAS LOVE (1785–1866), English novelist. Born at Weymouth, Dorset, and employed for most of his life by the East India Company, he was attracted as a young man to the folklore and mythology of Wales, as one of his earliest poems, 'The Genius of the Thames' (1810), testifies. He first visited Wales in 1810, staying at Tremadoc, Caerns., where he saw William *Maddocks's embankment in the course of construction, a scene described in his first prose work, *Headlong Hall* (1816). Then he moved to nearby Maentwrog, living in the village for about a year: there he met Jane Gryffydh, a daughter of the local parson, who was later to become his wife. He visited Wales again three years later but made no attempt to see Jane. It was not until 1818, without any intervening meeting, that he wrote to her proposing marriage and another two years went by before they became husband and wife. By that time Peacock had become the close friend and confidant of the poet Shelley, who described Jane as 'the white Snowdonian antelope' in his 'Letter to Maria Gisborne' (1820). He had also consolidated his reputation as a writer with *Melincourt* (3 vols., 1817) and *Nightmare Abbey* (1818). In the year after their marriage, which took place at Eglwys-fach, Cards., in 1820, Jane gave birth to a daughter, named Mary Ellen, who was to become the first wife of the writer George Meredith.

The attraction to Wales felt by Peacock was essentially Romantic; unlike George *Borrow, he was inspired by its mountains but rarely noticed the people who lived among them. Yet he hoped to do for Wales what Sir Walter Scott had done for Scotland. He gave fullest expression to his passion for the Welsh past in *The *Misfortunes of Elphin* (1829), but his fame rests more on those of his works with English settings: *Maid Marian* (1822), *Crotchet Castle* (1831) and *Gryll Grange* (1860–61), his last and best work. In these books the plots are tenuous and the most important feature is the brilliant talk of the characters, who are satirical representations of various contemporary types; the action is usually farcical. Peacock's wit succeeds in always presenting his own conservative viewpoint as the most reasonable, namely that the 'progress' of the present with all its corruption is to be contrasted unfavourably with the old, hierarchical, rural society which he saw fast disappearing about him.

Among the numerous critical studies of Thomas Love Peacock those by A.M. Freeman (1911), J.I.M. Stewart (1963), David Garnett (1963), H. Mills (1969), Felix Felton (1973) and Bryan Burns (1984) are especially recommended. See also the article 'Thomas Love Peacock and Wales' by David Gallon in The Anglo-Welsh Review (vol. 17, no. 39, 1968) and that by Lionel Madden in Planet (no. 31, March, 1976).

PEATE, IORWERTH CYFEILIOG (1901–82), poet and scholar. Born at Pandy Rhiwsaeson in the parish of Llanbrynmair, Mont., the son of a craftsman-carpenter, he was educated at the University College of Wales, Aberystwyth, where he studied under T. Gwynn *Jones and H. J. Fleure. Having specialized in Celtic archaeology, he wrote Gyda'r Wawr (1923), an account of the prehistory of Wales planned in conjunction with a team of young scholars and published under Fleure's editorship. In 1927 he was appointed Assistant Keeper in the Department of Archaeology at the *National Museum of Wales and, in 1932, was promoted Head of the Sub-Department of Welsh Folk Culture and Industry. There he began to realize his dream of establishing in Wales a Folk Museum on the same lines as those in Scandinavia. When, at last, after the Second World War, the *Welsh Folk Museum was established at St. Fagans, on the outskirts of Cardiff, Iorwerth Peate became its first Curator, a post which he held until his retirement in 1971.

Throughout his life Iorwerth Peate engaged in literary activity, chiefly as an exponent of the Nonconformist, Radical folk culture (sometimes called the Llanbrynmair Tradition) into which he had been born. His work falls into three categories: scholarly writing, prose essays and poetry. He wrote a great deal on the material culture of Wales and on the rich heritage of its rural crafts, a field in which he was a pioneer. Among his most important books are Cymru a'i Phobl (1931), Y Crefftwr yng Nghymru (1933), Diwylliant Gwerin Cymru (1942) and Amgueddfeydd Cymru (1948). He also edited a number of publications concerned with his spiritual and ideological heritage, such as Hen Gapel Llanbrynmair (1939), Ysgrifau John Breese Davies (1949) and Cilhaul ac Ysgrifau Eraill gan S.R. (1961). His most important book in English is The Welsh House (1940) but he also published A Guide to Welsh Bygones (1929), Welsh Folk Crafts (1935), Clock and Watch Makers in Wales (1945), Tradition and Folk Life: A Welsh View (1972) and others.

A man of strong convictions and forthright manner, Peate was an uncompromising pacifist who suffered severe persecution during the Second World War. On the issue of the Welsh language he did not believe that there could be a future for it in a bilingual society and he condemned the Anglicization of contemporary Wales by contrasting it with what he saw as the wholesome stability of the monoglot, rural society of his youth. In his four volumes of essays, Sylfeini (1938), Ym Mhob Pen (1948), Syniadau (1969) and Personau (1982), he expressed such opinions unequivocally and sometimes caustically, in a muscular and flowing style. His own account of his life is given in a volume of autobiography, Rhwng Dau Fyd (1976), and in the collection of autobiographical essays, Personau.

As a poet, Iorwerth Peate was a conservative, although he did not use the strict metres. A writer of sensitive lyrics, he made great play of double-rhymes, especially in his early poems, and for that he incurred the displeasure of some critics. His main theme was the inevitable passage of time, but his love for his wife, for nature, and for the old rural life were constant sources of inspiration, as was also his love of certain places, whether his native district or the vanished glories of the Vale of Glamorgan on the borders of which he lived for most of his life. Some of his poems, such as 'Ronsyfál', 'Men Ychen' and 'Awyrblandy Sain Tathan', are among the finest poems of this century, and they have immense charm and melodiousness. They are to be found in his collections of verse, Y Cawg Aur (1928), Plu'r Gweunydd (1933), Y Deyrnas Goll (1947) and in a volume of his selected poems, Canu Chwarter Canrif (1957). A volume of his later verse, Cerddi Diweddar (1982), was published shortly after his death.

A bibliography of Iorwerth Peate's writings down to 1966 is included in Studies in Folk Life (1969), a volume of essays in his honour which was edited by Geraint Jenkins; a fuller bibliography has been compiled by Emrys Bennett Owen (1981). Iorwerth Peate's contribution to Folk Studies is discussed by Trefor M. Owen in Folk Life (no. 21, 1983); the latter also wrote an obituary in The Welsh History Review (vol. 11, no. 4, 1983); see also the article by Dewi Eurig Davies in Y Traethodydd (Jan., 1983).

Pebidiog, see DEWISLAND.

Pedair Cainc y Mabinogi (lit. 'The four branches of the Mabinogi'), the title of four distinct, but linked, medieval Welsh tales, preserved in two complete texts found in The *White Book of Rhydderch (c.1300) and The *Red Book of Hergest (c.1400); two fragments of the texts are also found in *Peniarth Manuscript 6 (c.1225/35). It is probable that all these texts derive from an earlier written common source and that the Four Branches existed in manuscript shortly after, or possibly before, the year 1200. A date around 1060 was suggested by Ifor *Williams as the date of their composition, but many scholars would prefer a less precise dating in the latter half of the eleventh century. It is uncertain whether they were originally composed in written form, or were first transmitted orally over a period of unknown duration. Many of their raw materials and constituent elements, however, belonged to the traditional repertoire of the professional story-tellers whose function from early times had been to provide entertainment at the royal courts, and a lengthy period of oral transmission may be presumed to have preceded the final composition of the tales, as we now have them, in the eleventh century. The term *mabinogi* originally meant 'youth', then 'a tale of youth', and finally 'a tale'. The tales in the Four Branches are tales of wonder and magic, and the customs portrayed are those of the court, such as hunting and feasting, one marvellous event following swiftly upon another. There is general agreement that they were the work of a single author of genius and that the *Mabinogi* is the Welsh people's greatest contribution to the literature of Europe.

The First Branch, *Pwyll Pendefig Dyfed* ('Pwyll Prince of Dyfed'), deals mainly with the marriage of *Pwyll and *Rhiannon and the boyhood of their son, *Pryderi. The Second Branch, *Branwen ferch Llŷr* ('Branwen daughter of Llŷr'), relates the tale of *Branwen and the consequences of her subsequent marriage to *Matholwch. In the Third Branch, *Manawydan fab Llŷr* ('Manawydan son of Llŷr'), is found the story of the manhood of Pryderi and Rhiannon's marriage to *Manawydan. The Fourth Branch, *Math fab Mathonwy* ('Math son of Mathonwy'), tells the story of *Math, *Gwydion, *Blodeuwedd and *Lleu Llawgyffes.

It is believed that many of the principal characters of these tales, such as Rhiannon, *Teyrnon, *Brân, Manawydan, Gwydion and Lleu, were originally Celtic deities. In the human form which they have assumed in later story they retain many magical and superhuman powers from an earlier period. Some characters, such as Brân, Manawydan and Lleu, have Irish affinities, and it is virtually certain that a large part of the subject-matter of the Four Branches is derived from the traditional folklore of the early Goidelic (or Gwyddel) immigrants into *Gwynedd and *Dyfed, where most of the action of the tales occurs.

In a series of studies published between 1897 and 1901 Edward *Anwyl emphasized the central position of Pryderi in the Four Branches, the original nucleus of which, he argued, consisted of accounts of Pryderi's birth and disappearance, his imprisonment, and finally his death brought about by Gwydion. To this hero-tale two other sagas were later attached, recounting the adventures of the families of *Llŷr and *Dôn, in the Second and Fourth Branches respectively. Anwyl's view was confirmed by Ifor Williams in his standard edition of the text (1930), in which he explained the term *Mabinogi* as meaning 'a tale of a hero's youth'. The study

of the Pryderi theme was further pursued in much detail in a number of articles and books by W.J. *Gruffydd, who argued that the Four Branches reflect an original tale in which the hero's life-story was divided into four main episodes: his conception and birth, his rape or imprisonment, his youthful exploits and his death. The addition to this basic narrative sequence of further stories incorporating such themes as the *Calumniated Wife (*Pwyll*, *Branwen*), the Eustace Legend (*Manawydan*) and the *Unfaithful Wife (*Math*), with the resultant displacement and realignment of much of the content, ultimately produced the final version of the Four Branches. Some recent critics, notably Proinsias *Mac Cana and Kenneth H. *Jackson, have tended to discount the organic historical development of the tales, to which Gruffydd attached such importance, and have stressed the final redactor's borrowings from Irish sources and his use of international popular themes.

Criticism of the Four Branches from a synchronic viewpoint would, of course, stress the obvious fact that their final 'author' was unaware of the stages through which the material of which he was the inheritor had passed, his sole interest being the welding of it into coherent narrative. His perceptive delineation of character has been much remarked, as well as his skill in the construction of passages of conversation. The simplicity and directness of his style match the urbanity and moderation of his attitude towards the social life and human activities he depicts. J.K. Bollard has cogently argued that he deliberately develops three functional themes, 'Friendship, Marriage and Feuds', in a juxtaposed, interlacing structure.

Translations of the text in English have been published in Lady Charlotte Guest's *Mabinogion* (1838–49) and *The Mabinogion* (1949) by Thomas Jones and Gwyn Jones. A version in Modern Welsh appeared in *Y Mabinogion* (1980) by Rhiannon and Dafydd Ifans, where it is explained in the introduction that the word *Mabinogion* is an Anglicized form of *Mabinogi* and refers to other medieval Welsh tales such as Culhwch and Olwen, whereas the term *Mabinogi* applies only to the Four Branches. A full bibliography of studies of the *Mabinogi* up to 1974 is to be found in *Y Traddodiad Rhyddiaith yn yr Oesau Canol* (ed. Geraint Bowen, 1974); see also W.J. Gruffydd, *Folklore and Myth in the Mabinogion* (1958), and Alwyn D. Rees and Brinley Rees, *Celtic Heritage* (1961). Proinsias Mac Cana has contributed an essay on the *Mabinogi* to the *Writers of Wales* series (1977).

Pedair Colofn Gwladwriaeth (lit. 'The four pillars of State'; 1786), an *interlude by Twm o'r Nant (Thomas *Edwards), consists of a series of dialogues and a flimsy plot. The four pillars are the King to wage war, the Judge to see that the law is kept, the Bishop to evangelize, and the Husbandman to provide food. The link between the characters is Syr Rhys y Geiriau Duon but the Husbandman, named Arthur Drafferthus, has the largest part in the action and, although the other three pillars offer their *apologiae*, it is around him, cast as a miser, that the story revolves.

Pedair Morwyn y Drindod (lit. 'The four maidens of the Trinity'), a popular allegory in the Middle Ages, is based on Psalm 85, verse 10: 'Mercy and truth are met together: righteousness and peace have kissed each other'. Here Righteousness and Truth argue with Mercy and Peace about Adam's fate. The only prose version in Welsh, in the hand of John *Jones of Gelli-lyfdy, is unfortunately incomplete, ending after a fruitless search by Righteousness for a worthy sacrifice to atone for Adam's sin. But there are other versions of the allegory in *cywyddau* by *Dafydd ab Edmwnd, Wiliam *Cynwal and Edmund *Prys.

Pedestrian Tour through North Wales, A (1795), by the English writer Joseph Hucks (b. 1772), is an account of a journey he made in 1794 in the company of a fellow-undergraduate later to make his name, the poet Coleridge. Not the record of the first of the *Tours of Wales, but characteristic of its period in its sympathy for the Welsh, its quest for 'nature unmechanised by the ingenuity of man' and its literary references, the book (in the form of seven letters) has a pleasant freshness of observation and a balanced description of people and scenery. Some incidents on the journey were also described by Coleridge in his own letters, including a political brawl in an inn at Bala, the playing of a flautist in the ruins of *Denbigh castle and a parched descent from Penmaenmawr to which the poet later attributed the 'grinning for joy', at discovering water, in *The Rhyme of the Ancient Mariner* (1798).

A new edition of the *Tour* was edited with an introduction by Alun R. Jones and William Tydeman in 1979.

Pedr Fardd, see JONES, PETER (1775–1845).

Pedrog, see WILLIAMS, JOHN OWEN (1853–1932).

Pedwar Ansawdd ar Hugain, Y (lit. 'The twenty-four qualities', the name Iolo Morganwg (Edward *Williams) gave to his collection of poetic measures, some of which were of his own invention. In Iolo's book, *Cyfrinach y Beirdd* (1829), which his son, Taliesin *Williams, innocently explained was the first printed edition of a genuine extant Glamorgan manuscript (but which was in fact one of Iolo's fabrications), the county was said to have had its unique poetic tradition independent of the rest of Wales. The Qualities derived from that tradition were recognized by Iolo's followers at the Dyfed Eisteddfod which was held in Carmarthen in 1819 as genuine and worthy measures to be used in eisteddfodau side by side with the *Twenty-

four Metres of *Dafydd ab Edmwnd. Other names were given to the collection, such as '*Hen Ddosbarth*' ('Old Classification') and '*Mesurau Morgannwg*' ('Glamorgan Measures').

The principles adopted by Linnaeus to classify and identify plants are discernible in Iolo's analysis of the measures. He claimed that his system consisted of the measures used by the poets of the Isle of Britain in ancient times and he argued that, on grounds of antiquity, it should have a more privileged place than that of Dafydd ab Edmwnd. In his ignorance, Gwallter Mechain (Walter *Davies) did not doubt the authenticity of Iolo's claims and he won a prize at the Carmarthen Eisteddfod for an essay demonstrating the superiority of the Qualities. Although Cynddelw (Robert *Ellis) gave them considerable publicity in *Tafol y Beirdd* (1853), they were hardly ever used by other poets and they were eventually exposed as a deception by Dafydd Ddu Eryri (David *Thomas) and Bardd Nantglyn (Robert *Davies).

There is a discussion of Iolo Morganwg's *Dosbarth* by John Morris-Jones in *Cerdd Dafod* (1925).

Pedwar Marchog ar Hugain, Y (lit. 'The twenty-four knights'), a group of eight Triads which accompanies *Trioedd Ynys Prydain in a number of manuscripts of the sixteenth and seventeenth centuries. The framework of these recalls the *'Arthur's Court' framework which replaces the older 'Isle of Britain' framework in some versions of the Triads. The oldest manuscript (Llanstephan 28) is in the hand of *Gutun Owain and, although this is evidently a copy, it is not likely that the tract itself is older than the mid-fifteenth century. The number twenty-four is a significantly symbolic number of which there are other examples in medieval Welsh, such as the *Twenty-four Metres, the Twenty-four Officers of the Court in the *Laws of Hywel Dda, the Twenty-four Marvels of the Isle of Britain (see MIRABILIA BRITANNIAE) and the Twenty-four Kings 'who were adjudged to be the Mightiest'.

The eight Triads list the twenty-four names of the knights under the following epithets: '*Tri Marchog Eurdafodiog*' ('Golden-tongued Knights'), '*Tri Marchog Gwyryf*' ('Virgin Knights'), '*Tri Chadfarchog*' ('Knights of Battle'), '*Tri Marchog Lledrithiol*' ('Enchanter Knights'), '*Tri Marchog Brenhinol*' ('Royal Knights'), '*Tri Marchog Cyfiawn*' ('Just Knights'), '*Tri Marchog Diwrthwyneb*' ('Unopposable Knights'), a version of the three men who escaped from the Battle of Camlan in the tale of *Culhwch, and '*Tri Marchog Cynghoriad*' ('Counsellor Knights'). Two-thirds of the names of the characters included belong essentially to the native Welsh narrative tradition, while the others are names adapted from *Geoffrey of Monmouth's *Historia Regum Britanniae*, *Y Seint Greal* and the French 'Vulgate' cycle of Arthurian prose romances dating from the thirteenth century. These names provide some evidence that there may once have existed Welsh versions of parts of the French romances, in addition to the *Grail Romances which have not survived. It seems that the romances of the 'Vulgate Cycle' were as popular in Wales during the fifteenth century as they were in England, where they form the basis of Malory's *Morte d'Arthur* (1485). A precedent for the number twenty-four as that of Arthur's knights is to be found in the tale of Peredur in Y * *Tair Rhamant*. It occurs also in an English poem of the fifteenth century and it also happens to be that of the number of seats allotted to Arthur's knights at the Round Table.

Further details will be found in Rachel Bromwich, *Trioedd Ynys Prydein* (1961).

Peerless Jim, see DRISCOLL, JAMES (1880–1925).

PELAGIUS (*fl.* 350–418), a theologian who was of British origin, has sometimes, especially in Wales, been called **MORGAN**, a name understood as meaning 'sea-born' and so the Welsh equivalent of Pelagius. An opponent of the Augustinian doctrine of irresistible grace, he taught in his *De Natura* and *De Libero Arbitrio* that God's grace has given men the *posse* or possibility of living sinlessly and that Christ's example helps them so to live. Traditionally regarded as a heresiarch, he has been interpreted by some modern scholars as a thinker of evangelical piety or one concerned for social righteousness. Germanus (*Garmon) was said to have visited Britain to combat widespread Pelagianism after the Briton's teaching had been condemned by Rome in the year 418. But a century and more later *Maelgwn Gwynedd was reputed to have been a Pelagian and the conference at Llanddewi Brefi to which *Dewi Sant was summoned to condemn the heresy seems to have been called because of widespread concern among the hierarchy of the *Celtic Church that Pelagianism still had a strong foothold in Wales.

Pembroke, a fortress built on a rocky promontory by order of Arnulf de Montgomery, the younger son of the Earl of Shrewsbury. After the rebellion and defeat of Robert of Bellême, Arnulf's elder brother, King Henry I obtained possession of it and appointed Gerald de Windsor, grandfather of *Gerald de Barri (Giraldus Cambrensis), to be his castellan. About 1108 the northern parts of the lordship of Pembroke were subjected to extensive Flemish settlement and, as Welsh attempts to dislodge the colonists failed, the social character of the area was changed. The Earldom of Pembroke was held in later reigns by the powerful barons, Richard de Clare (Strongbow), William Marshal and William and Aymer de Valence. The castle escaped damage during the rising of *Owain Glyndŵr. In the fifteenth century Jasper Tudor, younger son of Owain Tudor and Catherine de Valois, held the Earldom and it was in Pembroke castle in 1457 that his nephew, Henry *Tudor, was born. There, too, the boy spent his first fourteen years. During the first *Civil War Pembroke was the only fortress in Wales consistently held for the Parliament and Rowland *Laugharne always had the option, during the two campaigns when he was confronted by Gerard, of retreating to it for safety. Four years later John *Poyer, who had first declared Pembroke for the Parliament, refused to hand over the castle to Colonel Fleming, Fairfax's representative, and began to negotiate with the Royalists. But after the defeat of Laugharne and Rice *Powell at the battle of St. Fagans, Cromwell advanced into Wales and invested Pembroke. At the end of June 1648, after a six-week siege marked by the bravery of the defenders, town and castle surrendered when the Parliament's heavy guns arrived and defence was no longer possible.

For further details see the articles by G.T. Clark and D.J.C. King in *Archaeologia Cambrensis* (1859–61 and 1978); see also A.L. Leach, *The Civil War in Pembrokeshire* (1937).

Penal Laws (1401–02), a series of restrictive laws against the Welsh introduced by Parliament after the rebellion of *Owain Glyndŵr, included the provision that poets should be restrained. The poets, who had welcomed the appearance of a comet in the year 1402 as an omen signifying liberation for the Welsh, were described as 'wasters, rhymers, minstrels and other vagabonds'. The influence of the poets, who viewed Glyndŵr as the fulfilment of ancient prophecies (see under VATICINATION), was illustrated during the rebellion. In his letters seeking the support of the King of Scotland and the lords of Ireland Glyndŵr revealed his awareness of the prophecy that national freedom was to be achieved through the assistance of the other Celtic countries. The ancient claim to lands in western England, an essential feature of the prophetic tradition, explains the territorial provisions of the Tripartite Indenture (1405) and the *Pennal Policy (1406).

Pencerdd, see under BARDIC ORDER.

Pencerdd Gwalia, see THOMAS, JOHN (1826–1913).

Penelope, a beautiful fairy who was given work as a maid at Ystrad farm, Betws Garmon, Caerns. According to the folk-tale, she agreed to marry the son of the house because he succeeded in discovering her name, but she disappeared when he struck her with a horse's bridle. It was believed that a prosperous family who lived in the district during the nineteenth century, the Pellings, were their descendants. In other versions of the tale the girl is called Penloi, Belene or Bela. See also TYLWYTH TEG.

Pengwern, see under ERYR PENGWERN and POWYS.

Penhesgin, a house at Penmynydd, Ang., the heir to which is said to have gone to live in England in order to escape the fate prophesied by a magician that he would be killed by a winged viper which had been seen in the district. According to tradition, the snake was eventually killed and, on his return, the young man kicked the brass pan in which the carcass was kept. This vengeful gesture proved fatal, for his foot was poisoned and he died immediately.

Peniarth Manuscripts, The, the most important single collection of Welsh manuscripts, was formed by Robert *Vaughan of Hengwrt, Mer. It contains more than five hundred manuscripts in Welsh, English, Latin, French and Cornish, and almost every aspect of Medieval and Renaissance Welsh literature is represented. Among its treasures are The *Black Book of Carmarthen, The *Book of Taliesin, the awdlau of *Cynddelw Brydydd Mawr, fragments of *Pedair Cainc y Mabinogi, the romance of *Geraint fab Erbin, a version of the *Grail Romances in Welsh, two early manuscripts of the *Laws of Hywel Dda, two Latin manuscripts of *Geoffrey of Monmouth's *Historia Regum Britanniae and a copy of *Brut y Tywysogyon. Besides many manuscripts by the *Poets of the Gentry, the collection also includes those of John *Jones of Gellilyfdy and some formerly owned by Sir Thomas *Wiliems, together with a copy of Bede's Ecclesiastica Historia Gentis Anglorum and the manuscript of Chaucer's Canterbury Tales which had belonged to Andrew Botrefon of Llanfair Isgaer. The manuscripts, which became the property of W.R.M. *Wynne of Peniarth, were bought by Sir John *Williams in 1905 and the collection is now housed at the *National Library of Wales.

For further details see J. Gwenogvryn Evans, Report on Manuscripts in the Welsh Language (vol. I, parts II and III, 1899 and 1905) and A Handlist of Manuscripts in the National Library of Wales (vol. I, part I, 1940).

Penllyn, the district around Llyn Tegid, near Bala, Mer., is famous for its literary and cultural traditions, which are among the richest in Wales. The five parishes of Penllyn are Llandderfel, Llanfor, Llangywair, Llanuwchllyn and Llanycil. Among the poets who were associated with the district in medieval times were *Tudur Penllyn and his son *Ieuan ap Tudur Penllyn, *Huw Cae Llwyd, *Bedo Aeddren and John *Davies (Siôn Dafydd Las). The district was also the birthplace, in the nineteenth century, of four leading figures in Welsh life: Michael D. *Jones, R. J. *Derfel, T. E. *Ellis and Owen M. *Edwards. The writers associated with Penllyn during the twentieth century include Ifan *Rowlands and his son, R.J. *Rowlands (1915–), Gerallt Lloyd *Owen and Euros *Bowen; the

last-named was the vicar of Llangywair from 1939 to 1973.

A description of the district's cultural heritage will be found in Geraint Bowen, Penllyn (1967), and a selection of verse by poets associated with the district in Blodeugerdd Penllyn (ed. Elwyn Edwards, 1983).

Penllyn Manuscript, The, see under ROBERT AP HUW (1580–1665).

Penmon, a priory on the island of Anglesey. In the sixth century *Seiriol founded a church on the site and another on the adjacent island of Priestholm (Ynys Seiriol). During the thirteenth century the monks adopted the rule of the Order of *Augustinian Canons. The poet *Tudur Aled wrote in praise of the prior, Sir Siôn Ingram (c.1487–97). The priory was dissolved about 1537 but the church, part of the ruins, the fishpond and the well are still to be seen. Among later poets inspired by the place's charm was T. Gwynn *Jones.

Pennal Policy, The, the name usually given to a long official document, accompanied by a letter, which was sent by *Owain Glyndŵr to the French king, Charles VI, after an assembly held at Pennal, Machynlleth, in 1406. Its conditions for Welsh recognition of the Avignon Pope, Benedict XIII, which Charles had requested, included the acceptance of *St. David's as a metropolitan church, with authority over both the Welsh dioceses and the sees of Exeter, Bath, Hereford, Worcester and Lichfield. Furthermore, the appropriation of Welsh churches by English monasteries was to be annulled, only Welsh-speakers were to be appointed to ecclesiastical offices within Wales and two universities were to be established, one in the north and the other in south Wales. This policy document, drawn up by Gruffudd Young (c.1370–c.1435), Owain's chancellor, also made a proposal for the training of administrators for the independent Welsh State which Glyndŵr had in mind. The claim for influence outside the traditional boundaries of Wales was based on the precedent of the Tripartite Indenture (1405), but military reverses eventually prevented the realization of both aims. The document is preserved in the Archives Nationales in Paris.

For further details see T. Matthews (ed.), Welsh Records in Paris (1910), J.E. Lloyd, Owen Glendower (1931) and Glanmor Williams, The Welsh Church from Conquest to Reformation (1962).

PENNANT, THOMAS (1726–98), naturalist and antiquary, was born at Downing, a house in the parish of Whiteford, Flints., which was destroyed by fire in 1922. He was educated at Wrexham, in London and at The Queen's College, Oxford, but left without taking a degree. A book lent him when he was twelve years old by his relative, John Salusbury of *Bachegraig, stimulated his interest in natural history and a visit to Cornwall in 1746/7 created in him a strong liking for geology. He later travelled widely, in Ireland, Scotland and the Hebrides, the Isle of Man and north Wales, keeping a record of his journeys and observations.

Of the works Pennant completed only four were published during his lifetime: *British Zoology* (4 vols., 1761–77), *Tours in Wales* (2 vols., 1778 and 1781), a history of Whiteford and Holywell (1796) and *The Literary Life of the Late Thomas Pennant Esq. by Himself* (1793). An account of his continental travels, the manuscript of which is kept in the *National Library of Wales, was not published until 1948 and there are twenty-two manuscript volumes of his ambitious *Outlines of the Globe* (only four of which have been published) in the National Maritime Museum at Greenwich. His accounts of his travels in Scotland and of the zoology of India and the Arctic also remain in manuscript.

The correspondent of Linnaeus, Le Comte de Buffon, Gilbert White and the *Morris Brothers of Anglesey, amongst others, Pennant became a man of distinction in his own day. His *Tours of Wales*, which cover only the northern parts of the country and on which he was accompanied by John Lloyd (1733–93), the rector of Caerwys, have a well-written and clearly-illustrated text (the drawings were by his servant, Moses *Griffith) which make them, among detailed surveys, the best as well as the earliest of their kind. Only the *Tours* in south Wales of Benjamin *Malkin, more than twenty years later, offer serious rivalry.

For further details see the article by the Countess of Denbigh in *The British Review* (vol. 2, 1913), that by Cecil Price in *The Welsh Anvil* (vol. VIII, 1958), that by Eiluned Rees and G. Walters in the *Journal* of the National Library of Wales (vol. 15, 1968) and another by Geraint Vaughan Jones in *Taliesin* (vol. 24, 1972).

PENNAR, MEIRION (1944–), poet. Born in Cardiff, a son of Pennar *Davies, he was educated at University College, Swansea, and at Jesus College, Oxford. Formerly a research assistant with the Schools Council and a lecturer at University College, Dublin, he was appointed to a lectureship in Welsh at St. David's University College, Lampeter, in 1975. He has published two volumes of poetry, *Syndod y Sêr* (1972) and *Pair Dadeni* (1978), as well as two long poems, *Saga* (1972) and *Y Gadwyn* (1976), all of which reflect his interest in the literary Modernism of certain German and French poets during the years between the World Wars. His wife, Carmel Gahan (1954–), is the author of a volume of poetry, *Lodes Fach Neis* (1980).

PENNY, ANNE (*fl.* 1729–80), poet. Born Anne Hughes at Bangor, Caerns., where her father later became vicar, she lived in London after her marriage. Her published works were *Anningait and Ajutt* (1761), a tale of Greenland which she dedicated to Samuel Johnson, *Select*

Poems from Mr. Gesner's Pastorals (1762), *Poems with a Dramatic Entertainment* (1771; reprinted as *Poems* in 1780) and *A Pastoral Elegy* (1773).

Penpingion, a comic character in the tale of *Culhwch and Olwen. A servant of *Glewlyd Gafaelfawr, the gate-keeper of *Arthur's court, he was remarkable in that he was said to go about his duties on his head, in order to save his feet. He was killed during the hunt for *Twrch Trwyth.

Penrhyn, a commot of *Cantref Gwarthaf in Dyfed, between the estuaries of the rivers Tywi and Taf, was coterminous with the lordship of Llanstephan and was held by the Camville family.

Penrhyn Blathaon, Penrhyn Penwaedd and **Penrhyn Rhionedd**, see under ENWAU YNYS PRYDAIN.

Penrhyn Lock-outs, The (1896–97, 1900–03), a major dispute in the slate-quarrying industry of north Wales, were essentially one struggle with a three-year truce between the first encounter and the final, tragic confrontation. Some three thousand men, mostly monoglot Welsh-speakers, worked in the quarries owned by Lord Penrhyn (1836–1907). Their long and bitter struggle had a profound and permanent effect on the communities around Bethesda in Dyffryn Ogwen, Caerns. It also constituted a crucial period in the history of the county, in the economic fortunes of the slate industry, and in the development of the Labour movement.

The central issue was 'the right of combination' which was claimed by the quarrymen who belonged to the North Wales Quarrymen's Union. The Penrhyn workers had exercised this right from 1874, when they had emerged victorious from another lock-out, until 1885. But the new Lord Penrhyn, a staunch Anglican and Conservative, refused to tolerate his father's concessions and determined to remove the influence of the trades unions from his quarries. Union activists were victimized and the management attempted to abolish the old system under which the men 'bargained' monthly for their wages. This change was crucial to the quarryman's consciousness of himself as a skilled worker and it was Lord Penrhyn's attack on the men's status as craftsmen which led directly to the lock-outs. The local political context of a relentless battle between an aggressive Welsh *Radicalism and the landed Conservative interest ensured, moreover, a vitriolic atmosphere in Bethesda. The community was divided into irreconcilable factions: the majority, largely Nonconformist, was dispersed, many moving to south Wales in search of work, while the minority who took the owner's side moved into closely adjacent streets from which they could be escorted to work by police and soldiers. The famous statement, '*Nid oes bradwr yn y tŷ hwn*' ('There is no traitor in this house'), put up on doors and windows by those loyal to the Union, dates from this time.

The intervention of soldiers and of the Government in the dispute, together with its sheer scale and duration, ensured that the Penrhyn Lock-outs assumed great importance in the British politics of the day. The quarrymen and their families were sustained by money donated by workers in other industries and areas. Their defeat in 1903 had catastrophic consequences: a third of the work-force never returned to the district and the community was divided against itself, with results which linger to the present day. The Welsh slate industry, having reached peak production in 1899, could not survive the closure of one of its main units and the spiral of its decline began soon afterwards.

For a full account of the Penrhyn Lock-outs see R. Merfyn Jones, *The North Wales Quarrymen 1874–1922* (1981); the lock-outs provide the background for T. Rowland Hughes's novel, *Chwalfa* (1946).

PENRY, JOHN (1563–93), Puritan pamphleteer and martyr, was born at Cefn-brith, a farm near Llangammarch, Brecs., on the northern slope of Mynydd Eppynt. Graduating from Peterhouse, Cambridge, which university was then a hotbed of *Puritanism, he demonstrated his concern for the lack of preaching ministers in Wales by having presented to Parliament in 1587 *A Treatise containing the Aequity of an Humble Supplication*, an initiative which brought about his arrest and appearance before the Court of High Commission. Released, he began his association with Robert Waldegrave's clandestine printing-press, which published his *Exhortation unto the Governours and people of Hir Maiesties countrie of Wales* (1588). From this press, which was constantly on the move, also came the Martin Marprelate tracts (1588–89) directed against the institution of episcopacy, and the official hunt for it became intense. The aim of the tracts was to make fun of the foibles and corruption of the bishops of the Church of England, which they did in colloquial language and with pungent satire.

The press also published Penry's *Supplication unto the High Court of Parliament* (1589), again about Wales, but shortly afterwards, its master-printer having been arrested, Penry fled to Scotland, where he remained until 1592 and where three more of his pamphlets were published. In the following year he was betrayed and seized in London and indicted before the King's Bench under the Act of Uniformity, which, oddly for the result, did not provide for the death penalty. While in prison he wrote his *Declaration of Faith and Allegiance*. Despite a last-minute appeal to his countryman, Burleigh, Penry was condemned

to death and executed. The fury of the bishops against him was doubtless because he was believed to be Martin Marprelate, though this was never alleged and certainly proved. A recent word-count by computer suggests that the real Marprelate was not Penry but Job Throckmorton, the Member of Parliament for Warwickshire.

For further details see David Williams (ed.), *Three Treatises Concerning Wales* (1960), Donald J. MacGinn, *John Penry and the Marprelate Controversy* (1966) and the article by Glanmor Williams, 'John Penry—Marprelate and Patriot?' in *The Welsh History Review* (vol. 3, no. 4, 1967); the fullest account is provided in Thomas Pierce, *John Penry, His Life, Times and Writings* (1923).

Pentraeth, The Battle of (1170), see under PERYF AP CEDIFOR WYDDEL (*fl.* 1170).

Pentre Ifan, a burial chamber, one of the finest megalithic monuments in Britain, is situated near Nevern (Nanhyfer), Pembs. Erected about four thousand years ago, the cromlech consists of a capstone supported by three standing stones. The site was excavated in 1936. See also BRYN-CELLI-DDU.

Pentref Gwyn, Y (lit. 'The white or fair village'; 1909), an account of his childhood by R.D. *Rowland (Anthropos) in the village of Tŷ'n-y-Cefn, near Corwen, Mer. Written in a lively style, it deals with life in rural Wales before the days of 'what is called etiquette', with much emphasis on the role of traditional craftsmen and customs.

Penweddig, the only cantref of *Ceredigion of which the name and location are known, embraced the commots of Genau'r Glyn, Perfedd and *Creuddyn. The name had long passed into disuse when it was revived in 1973 as the title of the Welsh-medium secondary school at Aberystwyth.

Penyberth, a farmhouse near Penrhos, Pwllheli, Caerns., is associated with a famous protest which took place on its lands in 1936. The Government's decision to establish a bombing-school at Penyberth, a place of some significance in the Welsh cultural tradition in that it was the home of a Recusant family (see GWYN, ROBERT) in the late sixteenth and early seventeenth centuries, caused widespread opposition in Wales, which turned into bitterness when similar protests against the siting of the school in various parts of England met with success on ecological grounds.

The campaign led by *Plaid Cymru culminated in the early hours of 8 September 1936 when three prominent party members—Saunders *Lewis, Lewis Valentine and D.J. *Williams—set fire to hutments and contractors' materials on the site and then reported their symbolic action to the police. The three were tried at Caernarfon

Assizes in the following October before an English-speaking judge and a Welsh-speaking jury which, to the delight of large crowds gathered outside the court and to the satisfaction of a wide spectrum of public opinion, failed to agree on a verdict. The judge then ordered the case to be re-tried at the next Assizes in Caernarfon but the trial was moved to London and, at the Old Bailey on 9 January 1937, the three arsonists were convicted; each was sentenced to nine months' imprisonment. D. J. Williams was allowed to address the jury in Welsh because it could not be proved that he was able to speak English. Saunders Lewis, whose speech from the dock at Caernarfon and subsequent pamphlet, *Why we burnt the Bombing School* (1937), are among the finest of his political utterances, was dismissed from his lectureship at University College, Swansea. The incident had a powerful influence on many Welsh intellectuals and writers, including R. Williams *Parry.

A full account is to be found in Dafydd Jenkins, *Tân yn Llŷn* (1937); see also D. Hywel Davies, *The Welsh Nationalist Party 1925–1945* (1983) and the article by Emyr Humphreys, 'The Night of the Fire', in *Planet* (nos. 49/50, Jan., 1980).

Pêr Ganiedydd, Y, see WILLIAMS, WILLIAM (1717–91).

Perchentyaeth (lit. "Privilege of ownership'), an old Welsh principle which was codified in the *Laws of Hywel Dda, where it is linked with the individual's duties towards his family, neighbourhood and nation. The hospitality associated with these traditional responsibilities is described by *Gerald de Barri (Giraldus Cambrensis) and in the work of medieval poets. The term, originally referring to the role of the nobleman in the Middle Ages, was redefined by Saunders *Lewis, notably in an essay on *Dafydd Nanmor in the magazine Y *Llenor in 1925, in which he adapted it for his own religious, political, economic and philosophical purposes. Among the influences on his thinking at that time were de Tocqueville, the neo-Thomists and the encyclical of Pope Leo XIII, *Rerum Novarum* (1891). Lewis's aim was, in essence, to preserve the stabilizing aspects of medieval life which would help keep the latter-day Welsh from being polarized by either collectivism or excessive individualism. *Perchentyaeth*, for him, stressed the need for co-operation but also implied a veneration for the old nobility and for an aristocratic way of life. This attempt to restore the concept was related to those movements in the 1930s which espoused medievalism and a return to the land. At the same time, the principle was in tune with the traditional Welsh dislike of the leasehold system.

Peredur, see under TAIR RHAMANT.

Pererindod Siarlymaen (lit. 'The pilgrimage of

Charlemagne'), a story belonging to the cycle of Charlemagne tales, is found complete in *The *White Book of Rhydderch* (Peniarth 5) and *The *Red Book of Hergest*, and in part in other manuscripts of the fourteenth and fifteenth centuries. The work, a translation into Welsh of *Pèlerinage de Charlemagne* or *Voyage à Jérusalem*, was put together some time after 1109. It has been edited by Stephen J. *Williams under the title *Ystorya de Carolo Magno* (1930).

Perfeddwlad, also known as the Four Cantrefi or Gwynedd Is Conwy (see under GWYNEDD), consisted of the cantrefi of *Rhos, *Rhufoniog, Dyffryn Clwyd and Tegeingl (*Englefield). Its history often followed a different course from that of Gwynedd Uwch Conwy because it had fewer natural defences and was therefore more frequently subject to English aggression. With Powys Fadog and *Edeirnion, it is now part of the county of Clwyd.

Perfidious Welshman, The (1910), a satire on the Welsh people written by Arthur Tyssilio Johnson (d. 1956) under the pseudonym Draig Glas ('Blue Dragon'), was prompted by the author's desire to outrage Welsh opinion and play on the chauvinism of English readers at the time of the *Home Rule campaign. The book sold well enough, however, to suggest the viability of an equally flippant reply, *The Welshman's Reputation* (1911), again by Johnson under the pseudonym 'An Englishman', which purported to defend the Welsh from the slanders of Draig Glas. A more serious, perhaps over-earnest, defence was published in the same year by an anonymous writer calling himself Fluellyn. The controversy engendered by Johnson's book, and by a similar work, T. W. H. Crosland's *Taffy was a Welshman* (1912), did not pass unnoticed by Caradoc Evans (David *Evans).

Perllan (lit. 'Orchard'), a small tray or board decorated with an apple, leaves and a bird, was carried from house to house as part of the *Wassailing ceremony on New Year's Day in some parts of Carmarthenshire. There are references to the custom in wassail songs of other districts and in some of the verses associated with the *Mari Lwyd. The ornate lids of the famous wassail bowls made in the potteries at Ewenni, Glam., may have been influenced by the motifs with which the *perllan* was decorated.

For further details see Trefor M. Owen, *Welsh Folk Customs* (1959).

PERRI or **PARRY, HENRY** (1560/1–1617), clergyman and scholar, was a native of Maesglas, Flints. He travelled extensively before settling in Anglesey as chaplain to Sir Richard Bulkeley and holding the livings of Rhoscolyn (1601), Trefdraeth (1606) and Llanfachreth (1613); he was elevated to the canonry of

*Bangor cathedral in 1612. His only work, *Eglvryn Phraethineb sebh Dosparth ar Retoreg* (1595), made use of William *Salesbury's book on rhetoric but Perri's is more detailed and many of his examples were derived from medieval Welsh poetry. His praise of the art of rhetoric was characteristic of Renaissance scholarship.

For further details see the edition of *Eglvryn Phraethineb* prepared by G. J. Williams (1930).

Perrot, John (1530–92), politician and Lord Deputy of Ireland, was popularly believed to be Henry VIII's illegitimate son by Mary Berkeley, who was married off to Sir Thomas Perrot of Haroldston, Pembs. The boy, probably born there, grew up to be a big, brawling fellow with an arbitrary temper who made the most of the covert recognition given him by the *Tudor monarchs, but his convinced anti-Catholicism earned him a short spell in the Fleet prison under Queen Mary and a longer period abroad.

In 1562 he became Vice-Admiral of the South Wales Coast and in 1563 Member of Parliament for Pembrokeshire, the latter event inaugurating a long, complicated and violent story of political intrigue in west Wales. Queen Elizabeth appointed Sir John President of Munster in 1571 and by 1573 he had successfully suppressed the rebellion of James Fitzmaurice. Between 1575, when he was appointed Chief Commissioner for the suppression of piracy round the county's shores, and 1579, when he was given a squadron of five ships to intercept Spanish vessels putting into Ireland's west coast, the number of Sir John's enemies greatly increased. Appointed Lord Deputy of Ireland by Elizabeth in 1584, he spent there four years which were dogged by quarrels until, ill and bitter, he asked to be recalled. Shortly afterwards the whispers of his enemies in Ireland had him removed to the Tower and tried for treason but, condemned to death, he died before sentence could be carried out. His real fault was almost certainly not treason but a rough tongue and a capacity to arouse antagonism wherever he went. Sir James Perrot (1571–1636), his illegitimate son by Sibil Jones of Radnorshire, was the most able and anti-Catholic Member from Wales during the Parliaments of James I and Charles I.

A full account of Sir John in Ireland will be found in Richard Rawlinson, *The History of Sir John Perrott* (1728) and J. E. Neale gives a detailed account of Perrot in the Haverfordwest election of 1571 in *The Elizabethan House of Commons* (1949).

PERRY, ALAN (1942–), poet and short-story writer, was born in Swansea, where he is an art teacher. He has published five volumes of poetry: *Characters* (1969), *Live Wires* (1970), *Black Milk* (1974), *Fires on the Common* (1975) and *Winter Bathing* (1980). His pamphlets of stories are entitled *Road Up* (1977) and *55999 and Other Stories* (1979).

PERYF AP CEDIFOR WYDDEL (*fl.* 1170), a poet who composed two poignant elegies for *Hywel ab Owain Gwynedd and his foster-brothers, Peryf's own brothers, killed in battle against Dafydd and Rhodri, the sons of Owain Gwynedd (*Owain ap Gruffudd), 'in the hollow above Pentraeth' in Anglesey in 1170. Peryf states that there were originally seven brave brothers, but that only three survived. It is probable that Brochfael, Iddon, Aerddur and Caradog were the brothers who fell 'near their foster-brother', Hywel, while Ithel ap Cedifor Wyddel, lamented by *Cynddelw Brydydd Mawr, had been killed previously at Rhuddlan.

PETER, JOHN (**Ioan Pedr**; 1833–77), Independent minister and scholar, was born at Bala, Mer., and worked as a boy in his father's flour-mill. Having taught himself geology and several foreign languages, he entered the Independent College at Bala at the age of twenty-two and was appointed to a tutor's post there in 1869. He resigned from his pastorate of the churches of Bala and Ty'n-y-bont in 1870 as the result of a disagreement with Michael D. *Jones over the question of the 'New Constitution', but retained his appointment in the College until his premature death.

In his study of comparative philology John Peter adopted the methods of the German school and began publishing the fruits of his research in *Certain Peculiarities of Celtic Grammar* (1867). He went on to write a major review of Ebel's edition of Zeuss's *Grammatica Celtica* (1871), as well as articles on Welsh phonology in *Revue Celtique* (vol. I) and on Welsh particles in *Y Cymmrodor* (vol. I). A pioneer in his field and a copious writer on general subjects, he might, had he lived, have made a contribution to Welsh scholarship comparable with that of Sir John *Rhŷs.

For further details see the essay by R. T. Jenkins in the *Journal* of the Welsh Bibliographical Society (vol. IV, 1933).

Peterwell, see under LLOYD, HERBERT (1720–69).

PFEIFFER, EMILY JANE (1827–90), poet, was born into a family named Davis which had connections with Montgomeryshire. Deprived by straitened circumstances of a formal education, she was nevertheless encouraged by her father to practise and study painting and poetry. She published during her lifetime six volumes of verse which included *Glan Alarch* (1877), *Sonnets and Songs* (1880) and *Under the Aspens* (1882). She has been described, not unjustly, as a lesser Elizabeth Barrett Browning, equally fluent and moral in tone but with less technical ability. Married to a German merchant resident in London in 1853, she was much concerned for the social status and education of women. After her death, a donation was made from her estate to

Aberdare Hall, the residence for women students at University College, Cardiff.

For further details see A. H. Mills, *The Poets and Poetry of the Century* (vol. VII, 1891–97).

Philipps family, The, of Picton Castle, in the parish of Slebech, Pembs., was descended from Sir Thomas Philipps of Cilsant (d. *c.*1520) and Joan, the heiress of the Dwnns of Kidwelly and the Wogans of Picton. Sir Thomas, who held many offices in west Wales, was a patron of *Lewys Glyn Cothi. His son, John (d. 1551), greatly benefited from the fall of *Rhys ap Gruffydd of Dinefwr in 1531. John's brother, Owen, was the founder of the Philipps family of Cardigan Priory, and his great-great-grandson, James Philipps, married Katherine Fowler (The Matchless Orinda; see next entry). John's great-grandson, also named John (d. 1629), was created a baronet in 1621. His son, Richard (d. 1648), a rather uncertain Parliamentarian, defended Picton Castle briefly against the Royalists. The third baronet was Sir Erasmus Philipps, a Commissioner under the Act for the *Propagation of the Gospel in Wales. His grandson, John (1666?–1737), the fourth baronet, was one of the greatest religious and educational reformers of his day. The leading figure in the *Society for Promoting Christian Knowledge and a friend of Wesley and Whitefield, he was the chief patron of Griffith *Jones of Llanddowror, the pioneer of Circulating Schools. Of his sisters, Margaret married Griffith Jones and Elizabeth became mother-in-law to Robert Walpole. John was succeeded by his son, Erasmus (1700–43), a distinguished economist, who was succeeded by his brother, John (1701–64), a prominent Jacobite and member of the Society of Sea Serjeants (see under JACOBITISM), a club founded about 1725 at Tenby, Pembs. John's son, Richard (1742–1823), the seventh baronet, was created Lord Milford in 1776.

On his death, childless, the barony became extinct and the baronetcy passed to Rowland Philipps (d. 1832), a descendant of the first baronet, and then to Rowland's brother, William (d. 1840). William's descendants included John Wynford Philipps (1860–1938), the thirteenth baronet, Chairman of the Welsh National Liberal Council and a close associate of David *Lloyd George, and his brother Lawrence, the founder of the Welsh Plant Breeding Station, who was created Baron Milford in 1939. The estate, however, had passed in 1823 to Richard Philipps Grant (1801–57), the great-grandson of Bulkeley, the youngest son of the fourth baronet, and then to Richard's half-brother, Gwyther Philipps (d. 1875), whose great-grandson now lives at Picton Castle, making the Philippses one of the very few great landowning families of Wales still to occupy the ancestral seat.

For further details see M. M. Philipps, *The History of Philipps of Picton* (1906) and Mary Clement, *The S.P.C.K. and Wales 1699–1740* (1954); see also the short novel by R. T. Jenkins, *Orinda* (1943).

PHILIPPS, KATHERINE (The Matchless Orinda; 1631–64), poet. She was born Katherine Fowler in London, where her precocity as a poet excited attention, and in 1647 she married James Philipps of Cardigan Priory (see previous entry), the son of her mother's second husband, Hector Philipps of Porth Eynon. She lived thereafter partly in London and partly in Wales, where she maintained by correspondence the coterie of literary and philosophical friends, on the French model, which she had first established in London. Her verse is somewhat artificial and mainly platonic, though certain of her addresses to Welsh friends and relatives sound a warm, personal note. Poems such as that to Henry *Vaughan and her mildly heroic couplets on the Welsh language show a fond affinity with Wales, but despite these and some poems to her friend Lucasia (Anne Owen), she was in general a pleasing metrist and charming person (despite John Aubrey's report of her that she had 'a red spotty face') rather than a poet of any stature. It has been claimed for her, at least, that she was the first woman writer in Britain to win professional and public recognition in her own right. Orinda was her *nom-de-coterie*, as Antenor was her affectionate husband's, while 'the Matchless' came from her admiring friends and literary panegyrists.

Her verse was collected under the title *Poems by the incomparable Mrs K(atherine) P(hilips)* (1664), a volume of which an authorized edition appeared three years later. The standard modern edition is found in Saintsbury's *Minor Poets of the Caroline Period* (vol. 3, 1905). The short novel *Orinda* (1943) by R. T. *Jenkins is based on her life and times.

For further details see the article by Patrick Thomas in *The Anglo-Welsh Review* (vol. 26, no. 57, Autumn, 1976) and Lucy Brashear, 'The Forgotten Legacy of the Matchless Orinda' in *The Anglo-Welsh Review* (no. 65, 1979).

PHILLIMORE, EGERTON GRENVILLE BAGOT (1856–1937), antiquary, was an Englishman who, about 1903, settled at Corris, Mer., and lived there for the rest of his life. He had begun to learn Welsh while a student at Christ Church, Oxford, and counted a number of young Welsh and Celtic scholars among his friends. Able to read and write the language fluently, he spoke the classical Welsh of the *Bible and had an extensive knowledge of the dialects. Early Welsh history, topography and place-names were his chief interests and he found a place in scholarly circles about 1886 when he published in *Y Cymmrodor*, which he edited from 1889 until 1891, extracts from the poetry of Iaco ap Dewi (James *Davies), Triads, poems and other parts of the *Hengwrt Manuscript* (see under VAUGHAN, ROBERT), especially the *Annales Cambriae* and the genealogies from the Harleian Manuscript. The high point of this activity was his critical article entitled 'The Publication of Welsh Historical Records' which appeared in *Y Cymmrodor* (vol. XI). It was once thought that Phillimore had published a collection of pornographic literature in Welsh, but it has been shown (in *Studia Celtica*, VI) that this was, in fact, his article 'Welsh Aedoeology' which appeared in the journal *KΡΥΠΤ'ΑΔΙΑ* in 1884. His detailed footnotes about place-names, mythology and Welsh traditions were published in Henry Owen's edition of George *Owen's *Description of Penbrockshire* in the *Cymmrodorion Record Series* (4 vols., 1892–1936). Phillimore owned a splendid library which included a number of rare books. His manuscripts were sold to Sir John *Williams in 1894 and are now kept, with his notebooks, in the *National Library of Wales.

Further details will be found in the article by R. J. Thomas in *Baner ac Amserau Cymru* (Jan., 1941).

PHILLIPS, DOUGLAS (1929–), poet. Born at Carmarthen and educated at Wadham College, Oxford, he was a journalist with newspapers in Wales and Manchester between 1953 and 1962, when he became a teacher. He was appointed Lecturer in English at the Derbyshire College of Higher Education in 1968. He has published two volumes of poems, *Merlin's Town* (1965) and *Beyond the Frontier* (1972), and is the author of an essay on Sir Lewis *Morris in the *Writers of Wales* series (1981).

PHILLIPS, EDGAR (**Trefin**; 1889–1962), poet. A native of Tre-fin, Pembs., and a tailor by trade, he was seriously wounded during the First World War and later became a teacher of Welsh at Blackwood, Mon. He was a prominent member of *Gorsedd Beirdd Ynys Prydain, serving as Keeper of the Great Sword from 1947 to 1960 and as Archdruid from 1960 to 1962. A master of *cynghanedd, he won the *Chair at the National Eisteddfod in 1933 for his awdl, 'Harlech'. Besides four volumes of verse for children, collectively entitled *Trysor o Gân* (1930–36), he published only one collection of poems, *Caniadau Trefin* (1950), almost all of which are in the strict metres.

His wife, **Maxwell Fraser** (1902–80), who was born in London of Scottish-American parentage, wrote several books of Welsh interest, including the guidebooks *Wales* (1952), *West of Offa's Dyke* (1958), *Welsh Border Country* (1972) and *Gwynedd* (1978), and edited the anthology *In Praise of Wales* (1950). Her extensive research on Augusta Waddington *Hall (Lady Llanover) and related topics appeared in the *Journal* of the National Library of Wales between 1960 and 1970 and in the *Transactions* of

the Honourable Society of *Cymmrodorion (1963, 1964).

PHILLIPS, ELUNED (1915?–), poet and biographer, was born at Cenarth, Cards. Her studies at the University of London were interrupted by the Second World War and thereafter she earned a living as a freelance writer for English magazines. She came to public attention after winning the *Crown at the National Eisteddfod in 1967, a feat repeated in 1983 with her *pryddest*, 'Clymau', which is about the Falkland Islands campaign. Her biography of Dewi Emrys (David Emrys *James) appeared in 1971 and a collection of her poems, *Cerddi Glyn-y-Mêl*, in 1985.

Phillips, John (1810–67), see under BRITISH AND FOREIGN SCHOOLS SOCIETY.

PHILLIPS, THOMAS (1801–67), author. Born in the parish of Llanelli, Brecs., but brought up at Trosnant, near Pontypool, Mon., he became Mayor of Newport in 1838 and was wounded in the rioting of the Chartists outside the Westgate Hotel in the following year (see under CHARTISM). A successful barrister in London, and a colliery owner, he wrote a biography of James Davies (1765–1849), the pedlar schoolmaster of Devauden, Mon., as well as *Wales, the Language, Social Conditions, Moral Character, and Religious Opinions of the People considered in their relation to Education* (1849). The latter is a masterly refutation of the aspersions cast by the *Blue Book Commissioners of 1847.

PHYLIP FAMILY, THE, of *Ardudwy, a group of poets who, during a period of cultural decline, continued to go on itinerary in the traditional manner. According to Lewys *Dwnn, their ancestry could be traced to Catrin, the daughter of John Palgus, and to Ieuan de Colier, members of families which had settled in the district of Ardudwy, Mer., at the time of the Edwardian Conquest of Wales. The work of these poets is significant as a mirror of the political and social changes which were taking place in Wales during the late sixteenth century and the first half of the seventeenth century.

The two brothers Rhisiart and Siôn Phylip span the period from the early part of Elizabeth's reign almost to the Civil War. **Rhisiart** (d. 1641) composed more than two hundred *cywyddau* and *awdlau* and a number of *englynion*, including some anti-Catholic verses about a Spanish ship wrecked in the mouth of the Dyfi in 1597. **Siôn** (c.1543–1620), who was the more prolific of the two, earned a living partly by farming Mochres and partly by performing as a minstrel. His patrons were the Wynns of Gwydir and the *Nannau family, although it was Rhisiart who was the latter's household poet. Siôn graduated at the second *Caerwys Eisteddfod (1567), competed with Edmund *Prys, Tomos *Prys and *Siôn Tudur in the writing of *cywyddau* and composed an elegy for Wiliam Thomas, who died with Sir Philip Sidney in the Netherlands. His verse displayed the new learning of his day and in an elegy for Elizabeth I he boasted that she was an heir of '*brenhinwaed bro hen Wynedd*' ('the royal blood of the land of old Gwynedd'). Siôn died by drowning while on his way home from one of his itineraries.

Gruffudd (d. 1666) and **Phylip Siôn Phylip** were Siôn's sons. Phylip did not perform as a minstrel but was educated in the strict metres, most probably by his father, and four elegiac *cywyddau* of his have survived. About sixty of Gruffudd's *cywyddau* have been preserved, together with a number of poems in the free metres and a few *englynion*. His circuit was smaller than his father's or his uncle's and he wrote chiefly for the families of *Eifionydd and Ardudwy, including those of *Corsygedol, Ystumllyn and Bronyfoel. With his death the tradition of the itinerant poet came to an end in Wales.

It is not known whether or how **Wiliam Phylip** (1579–1669) of Hendrefechan was related to the family of Siôn Phylip. Although, on his own testimony, he was the son of parents who had arrived in Ardudwy from Corwen, it is usual to include him as one of the group. A gentleman who wrote for his own amusement, Wiliam Phylip left verse which is largely personal in content and composed in the free metres. He was a Churchman who hated both *Roman Catholicism and *Puritanism and his work reflects the misfortunes he had suffered, as in the *englynion* on parting with his home, Hendrefechan. An ardent Royalist, he composed an elegy for Charles I and warmly congratulated Charles II on his accession to the throne in 1660. When he died, poor and without an heir, his estate became the property of the Crown. His elegy was written by Phylip Siôn Phylip.

There are articles on the Phylips of Ardudwy by William Davies in *Y Beirniad* (vol. III, 1913) and a survey of their work in English in *Y Cymmrodor* (vol. XLII).

PHYLIP BRYDYDD (*fl.* 1222), poet. A native of *Ceredigion, he wrote in praise of *Rhys Gryg, the son of *Rhys ap Gruffudd (The Lord Rhys), of Rhys Gryg's nephew, Rhys Ieuanc (Rhys ap Gruffudd, d. 1222), and of *Llywelyn ap Iorwerth (Llywelyn Fawr). He complained that the high-ranking poets had to compete for attention in some of the courts of south Wales with poets of lower grades. In a series of intercessionary *englynion* he reassured his patron that, although he had addressed poems to another Prince, he was still loyal to Rhys Gryg. Phylip's verse is significant mainly for these two valuable glimpses into the relationship between poet and patron.

Phylip Dorddu (early 14th cent.), nobleman, of *Maelienydd in what later became Radnorshire, was a descendant of Elystan Glodrydd (*c.*940–1010), king of the lands *Rhwng Gwy a Hafren ('between Wye and Severn') before the *Norman Conquest. The houses of Phylip Dorddu's sons were praised by *Iolo Goch in a *cywydd* describing the poet's itinerary through Wales. The family, which had numerous branches, continued to be important bardic patrons until the end of the fifteenth century.

Pibgorn, a horn pipe or primitive shawm, a traditional musical instrument. Although it never enjoyed the status of the *harp or the *crwth (no wind instrument was recognized by the rules of *Cerdd Dant), the *pibgorn*, in one form or another, remained popular in Wales for several centuries. Edward *Jones (Bardd y Brenin) claimed at the end of the eighteenth century that it was confined, in his day, to Anglesey shepherds but a simpler form may have been in use in northern Pembrokeshire about a hundred years later. Each of the three examples in the collection of the *Welsh Folk Museum, all belonging to the eighteenth century, has an animal-horn at either end and the pipe is made of wood or bone, with seven holes and a single reed.

For further details see the article by Malcolm Siôr Defus in *Welsh Music* (vol. IV, part 1, Spring, 1972) and the entry by Joan Rimmer in *The New Grove Dictionary of Musical Instruments* (ed. Stanley Sadie, 1985).

Picton, Bernard, see KNIGHT, BERNARD (1931–).

Picton, Thomas (1758–1815), soldier, was born at Poyston, Pembs. An ensign in his uncle's regiment before his fourteenth birthday, he was promoted lieutenant five years later. Having sailed for the West Indies in 1794 without orders and pressed his services upon Sir John Vaughan, he was soon promoted in recognition of successful actions there. When Trinidad was taken in 1797, he was appointed Governor and for nine years he held the island with few men, little money, frequent threats, some corruption and an alliance with French émigré planters against constant invasion plans by French and Spaniards. Later colonists from England resented his rule and in 1806 he was brought to trial in London on a variety of charges, including the torture of a slave. All these charges were dismissed, the last on appeal.

Governor of Flushing in 1809, Picton afterwards joined the Peninsular Army, where his bravery and the exploits of his division at the battles of Badajos, Vittoria and Ciudad Rodrigo made him a popular hero. Wellington, however, disliked his familiarity with his officers and thought him 'a rough foul-mouthed devil as ever lived' and on his return home Picton was the only general not to be made a peer. Knighted in 1815, he was seriously wounded in the same year at the battle of Quatre Bras, where 'the thin red line' held, but he concealed the fact and died in action at Waterloo, shortly after the repulse of a French charge. Captain Rees Howell *Gronow, to whom Picton in 1815 had promised a place as aide-de-camp, described him as 'a stern-looking, strong-built man, about the middle height'.

For further details see Rees Howell Gronow, *The Reminiscences and Recollections of Captain Gronow* (1862–66; reprinted 1892; abridged edn., 1964) and H. B. Robinson, *Memoir of Sir Thomas Picton* (1835); for an account of Picton in Trinidad see V. S. Naipaul, *The Loss of Eldorado* (1969).

Picws mali, see SIOT.

PIERCE, ELLIS (Elis o'r Nant; 1841–1912), novelist, was born in the parish of Dolwyddelan, Caerns. He earned a living as a bookseller and between 1865 and 1900 wrote a large number of articles for *Baner ac Amserau Cymru on topics relating to social reform and local history. His books, some of which are historical romances, include *Nanws ach Robert* (1880), *Yr Ymfudwr Cymreig* (1883), *Rhamant Hanesyddol: Gruffydd ab Cynan* (1885), *Gwilym Morgan: neu gyfieithydd cyntaf yr Hen Destament i'r Gymraeg* (1890), *Syr Williams o Benamnen* (1894), *Teulu'r Gilfach, neu Robert Siôn* (1897) and *Dafydd ab Siencyn yr Herwr a Rhys yr Arian Daear* (1905).

PIERCE, THOMAS JONES (1905–64), historian, was born in Liverpool and educated at the University in that city. As a tutor in the Extra-Mural Department and Assistant Lecturer in the Department of History at the University College of North Wales, Bangor, he pioneered research into the structure of medieval Welsh society, both urban and rural. He contributed papers on the *Laws of Hywel Dda, the kindred system and land tenure, and the organization of early human settlements, especially in *Gwynedd, and published extensively on the government of that kingdom and on the transition from medieval to modern agrarian conditions in Wales. In 1945 he was appointed (jointly by the University College of Wales, Aberystwyth, and the *National Library of Wales) to the post of Special Lecturer in Medieval Welsh History and three years later he was given a personal chair in the subject. The first editor of the Caernarfonshire Historical Society's *Transactions*, he was elected the Society's Chairman in 1962 and President of the *Cambrian Archaeological Association in 1964. A collection of his most important writings appeared in the volume *Medieval Welsh Society* (ed. J. Beverley Smith, 1972).

Pilleth, The Battle of (1402), was fought at Bryn Glas, Rads., during the rising of *Owain Glyndŵr. In Shakespeare's *Henry IV* the Earl of Westmorland reports with alarm the English defeat under Mortimer at the hands of the 'wild and irregular Glendower'. The king's reluctance to ransom Mortimer, who was captured during the battle, caused the latter to throw in his lot with Owain Glyndŵr, marry his daughter and make possible the Tripartite Indenture.

Pilnos, see under KNITTING NIGHT.

PIOZZI, HESTER LYNCH (1741–1821), author. She was born at *Bodfel, near Pwllheli, Caerns., the only child of John Salusbury of *Bachegraig, Flints. At the age of twenty-two she married Henry Thrale, a wealthy London brewer, through whom she became acquainted with many prominent figures of the day, including Oliver Goldsmith, David Garrick, Joshua Reynolds and Samuel Johnson. To the captivation of the last-named her subsequent fame was largely attributable. Johnson accompanied the Thrales on a two-month journey to north Wales in 1774, for which she wrote a *Diary* (1816), and to France in the following year. Thrale died in 1781 and three years later—much to the Doctor's disapproval—his widow married an Italian music-teacher, Gabriele Piozzi. From 1795 the Piozzis lived at Bachegraig, near Tremeirchion, her father's old home, and at Brynbella, a house they built near by.

Besides her correspondence with Dr Johnson and her reminiscences of their friendship, Mrs Piozzi published a number of books, amongst them *British Synonymy or an attempt at regulating the choice of words in familiar conversation* (1794), *Three Warnings to John Bull before he dies, by an old acquaintance of the Public* (1798) and *Retrospection* (1801), a survey of civilization since the time of Jesus Christ. A pretty, vivacious woman who was a compulsive conversationalist and inordinately proud of her Welsh heritage, she corresponded with a wide circle of distinguished people in Wales and England. Her letters now form collections of Piozziana and Thraliana in several libraries, including the *National Library of Wales. Among her friends in Wales were Thomas *Pennant and the Ladies of Llangollen (Eleanor *Butler and Sarah Ponsonby). Her last years, after her second husband's death in 1809, were spent at Bath but she was buried, according to her expressed wish, at Tremeirchion.

The career of Hester Lynch Piozzi has been described by several authors, including Colwyn Edward Vulliamy (1936) and James L. Clifford (1941); see also A. M. Broadley, *Doctor Johnson and Mrs Thrale* (1910). The collections of Thraliana have been edited by K. C. Balderson (2 vols., 1942 and 1951).

Plaid Cymru (lit. 'The party of Wales'), a political party founded in 1925, was first known as *Plaid Genedlaethol Cymru* ('The National Party of Wales'). Created largely as the result of the efforts of Hugh Robert *Jones to link groups such as Y *Gymdeithas Genedlaethol Gymreig in north Wales with others in the south, it had among its earliest members Griffith John *Williams, Saunders *Lewis and Ambrose *Bebb. The last-named became editor of the party's monthly newspaper, *Y Ddraig Goch*, in 1926. The party adopted the aim of Dominion Status for Wales and fought its first election in 1929 when Lewis Valentine, its President, polled 609 votes in Caernarfonshire. Its Secretary from 1930 to 1962 was J. E. Jones (1905–70), who described its early years in his autobiography, *Tros Gymru* (1970). During the presidency of Saunders Lewis (1926–39), when it attracted mainly intellectuals, the party's fortunes were ¨mpaired by its opponents' detection of Fascist r¨ndencies in its *Nationalism and *Pacifism, and it made little electoral progress, although its leaders' symbolic act at *Penyberth in 1936 won widespread sympathy.

After 1945, when Gwynfor *Evans became President, the party's membership and influence grew steadily and, at the time of the flooding of the *Tryweryn valley, it began winning seats at local elections in several parts of the country. During the 1960s it took a significant share of the Labour and Liberal votes, especially after Gwynfor Evans was elected as Member of Parliament for Carmarthenshire at a by-election in 1966. Since then the party has won and held the constituencies of Arfon and Meirionydd Nant Conwy. It has also led several successful campaigns such as that for a television service in the Welsh language. Now firmly established in the political life of Wales, the party is devoted to constitutional methods of achieving self-government and has its own Radical policies for the Welsh economy deriving from its commitment to decentralized *Socialism. In the cultural sphere the influence of *Plaid Cymru* has been profound. The writers who have been active members (besides those mentioned above) include Kate *Roberts, D. J. *Williams, Gwenallt (David James *Jones), J. Kitchener *Davies, Waldo *Williams, Bobi Jones (R. M. *Jones), R. S. *Thomas, Emyr *Humphreys, Harri *Webb and many others. See also NATIONALISM.

The history of *Plaid Cymru* is given in the volume *Cymru'n Deffro* (ed. John Davies, 1981); see also the chapter by Ioan Rhys (Ioan Bowen Rees) in *Celtic Nationalism* (1968), Alan Butt Philip, *The Welsh Question: Nationalism in Welsh Politics 1945–70* (1975) and D. Hywel Davies, *The Welsh Nationalist Party 1925–1945* (1983). There are essays on some of the party's early leaders in *Adnabod Deg* (ed. Derec Llwyd Morgan, 1973) and its recent history is discussed in John Osmond (ed.), *The National Question Again* (1985).

Planet, a magazine launched in 1970, was edited and published six times a year by Ned Thomas (Edward Morley *Thomas) and his wife, Sara Erskine, from their home at Llangeitho, Cards.; the editorial team included Tudor David, Harri *Webb and John *Tripp. The magazine's viewpoint was left-wing and Nationalist, with a strong interest in European minorities, sociology, ecology and politics; in 1977 it took the

subtitle *The Welsh Internationalist*. During its first two years its campaigns in favour of such causes as broadcasting in Welsh, the language's legal status and *Devolution for Wales and Scotland, were publicly condemned by certain Labour Members of Parliament, but as the views it propagated became more widely accepted the magazine grew less controversial. In literature its preference was for socially orientated, realist prose and 'public poetry', with prominence given to essays, short stories and poems by Anglo-Welsh writers, to book-reviews and graphics, and to translations of verse and prose from Welsh and other languages. The magazine ceased publication in 1979, with its fiftieth number, as a result of the editors' decision not to continue with the work, but was revived in 1985, again under the editorship of Ned Thomas.

An index to the magazine's first fifty numbers was compiled by G. M. Madden (1980).

Plant y Cedyrn, see under ANATIOMAROS (1925).

Plas Iolyn, a mansion in the parish of Pentrefoelas, Denbs., was the home of one of the most prominent families of north Wales. The first important member of this family, Maredudd ap Tudur (*fl.* 1450), who managed the extensive lands of the abbey of *Aberconwy and other lands in Dôl Gynwal, gained royal favour by his adherence to the Lancastrian cause. It was his son, Rhys ap Maredudd (Rhys Fawr; *fl.* 1510), who first patronized poets at the original home, Bryn Gwyn, at which *Tudur Aled is believed to have been entertained. Rhys added to the family's wealth and had two sons, Morys and Robert; the former established a branch of the family at Foelas and Cernioge. Robert (d. 1534), who founded the Plas Iolyn branch, was a learned man in Holy Orders who had great influence in the district as a legal administrator; Tudur Aled and *Lewys Môn were among the poets who praised him as a patron. After his day Plas Iolyn passed to Elis *Prys (Y Doctor Coch); his son, Tomos *Prys, inherited a smaller estate and the family began to lose interest in the poets after his time.

Plas Newydd, Ang., see under BAYLY, LEWIS (d. 1631); **Plas Newydd, Denbs.**, see under BUTLER, ELEANOR (1739–1829).

Plasau'r Brenin (lit. 'The king's mansions'; 1934), a novel by Gwenallt (David James *Jones), was based on his experience of imprisonment as a conscientious objector in Wormwood Scrubs and Dartmoor during the years from 1917 to 1919. There is a striking similarity between Myrddin Tomos, the novel's main character, and Gwenallt himself, which led at least one critic, Saunders *Lewis, to the view that the book is not a novel but 'a profound part of a poet's autobiography'. An essential key to Gwenallt's poetry, its strength lies not in the portrayal of prison life but rather in the author's reminiscences of rural Carmarthenshire and in the light it sheds on the growth of his political convictions.

Platonism, the doctrine of the Forms as the perfect and eternal elements, the only true reality, was the legacy of Plato (c.427–348 BC). From it there developed as a dualistic view of man as body and soul and as a concept of an unseen world of which the visible world is only a pale copy. Philosophy elevates Man, so the argument goes, from the sensuous world of flux, of becoming, to the world of being, of essences, of which alone he can have knowledge. Thus it is the philosopher who is best able to judge what is good for the individual and the community. Saunders *Lewis argued that late medieval Welsh praise-poetry derived from Platonism in that a poet's praise of lord or lady was praise of the ideal form, and that this belief is succinctly portrayed in *Einion Offeiriad's Grammar.

The step from Plato's theories to *Mysticism was not abrupt and was accomplished in the third century in what has come to be called Neo-Platonism, particularly by its chief representative, Plotinus. In him there is a development of the hierarchy of Creation, culminating in the perfect good, the One; the Self attempts to attain unity with the One through the Beatific Vision. One of the fruits of this mystical tradition in medieval Wales was Y Cysegrlan Fuchedd, a medieval tract on holy living. The development from hierarchical order to the doctrine of the Great Chain of Being finds an echo in Ellis *Wynne's *Gweledigaetheu'r Bardd Cwsc (1703) and later in the work of William *Williams (Pantycelyn).

The great revival of Platonism in the fifteenth century, with Florence as its centre, had little direct influence in Wales, though Gruffydd *Robert justified the dialogue form of his Dosparth Byrr by reference to Plato. Rowland *Vaughan of Caer-gai in Yr Ymarfer o Dduwioldeb referred to John *Davies of Mallwyd as 'yr unig Plato ardderchawg o'n hiaith ni' ('the only excellent Plato of our tongue'). Indirectly, the Platonic revival reached Wales fitfully through the Cambridge Platonists and Jacob Böhme. The Platonists strove to unite religion and philosophy, to reaffirm the oneness of a divine world, experienced as a continuing ecstasy. Morgan *Llwyd came into contact with them mainly through his friendship with Peter Sterry, Cromwell's chaplain. Through Böhme it was the mystic, hermetic, visionary aspect which influenced Llwyd and in places the Platonic element reveals itself very clearly: 'O Eryr, deall nad yw'r byd a welir ond cysgod o'r byd nis gwelir' ('O

Eagle, know that the visible world is but a shadow of the invisible world').

In the nineteenth century Platonic elements entered the poetry of Islwyn (William *Thomas) through Shelley and Wordsworth and, particularly, Emerson. In 1897 Tafolog (Richard Davies, 1830–1904) insisted, 'What are seen in the world of the senses are only shadows or appearances; the real substances are all invisible and the secret of secrets is God', and went on to suggest that the *Bardd Newydd would express this. But the New Poet, alas, could not distinguish between the significant and the high-sounding. Satisfactory translations of some of Plato's works into Welsh by D. Emrys *Evans first began to appear in the 1930s. Among Anglo-Welsh writers, Henry *Vaughan most shows his debt to the Cambridge Platonists, though it is worth noting that Traherne has been called their Poet Laureate. In the twentieth century neo-Platonic thought and symbol are also evident in the poems of Vernon *Watkins, who first encountered Plotinus in the poetry of Yeats.

For discussion of Platonism in Welsh literature see Saunders Lewis, Braslun o Hanes Llenyddiaeth Gymraeg (1932), the article by Pennar Davies, 'Cysylltiad Crefyddol Cymru ac Ewrop oddi ar adeg y Dadeni Dysg' in Efrydiau Athronyddol (vol. XXVII, 1964) and that by O. R. Jones, 'Platon: Damcaniaeth y Ffurfiau' in Efrydiau Athronyddol (vol. XLIV, 1981).

Plygain, a carol service held in the parish church between the hours of three and six on Christmas morning; the word is derived from the Latin pulli cantio ('cock crow'). The service developed from the midnight mass of the pre-Reformation period and became an important part of the Christmas celebrations. Churches were decorated with candles and their light was thought to have a symbolic significance. The plygain began with an abbreviated service of morning prayer which was followed by the singing of carols set to the old measures. Many hundreds of plygain carols have survived from the seventeenth, eighteenth and nineteenth centuries. Their poetry, religious and doctrinal in content, was characterized by the intricate style and metrical form of the popular *ballad tunes of the day. More recently, plygain services have been held in the evening between the middle of December and the middle of January, especially in northern Montgomeryshire.

A selection of plygain carols, together with texts, will be found in the series of recordings Welsh Folk Heritage (1977); see also J. Fisher, 'Two Welsh-Manx Christmas Customs' in Archaeologia Cambrensis (1929), Gwynfryn Richards, 'Y Plygain' in the Journal of the Historical Society of the Church in Wales (vol. I, 1947), Enid Pierce Roberts, 'Hen Garolau Plygain' in the Transactions of the Honourable Society of Cymmrodorion (1954) and D. Roy Saer, 'The Christmas Carol-Singing Tradition in the Tanad Valley' in Folk Life (vol. 7, 1969).

Poems, a series of anthologies of contemporary

Anglo-Welsh poetry, published annually during the years from 1969 to 1974 and thereafter alternately with its Welsh counterpart, *Cerddi*, until 1979, when the series ended. Intended to present a selection of the verse published during the previous year, each volume had a different editor. Among the editors were John Stuart *Williams (1969), Jeremy *Hooker (1971), John Ackerman *Jones (1972) and Glyn *Jones (1976). Among the poets and critics who edited *Cerddi* were Gwilym Rees *Hughes (1969), James *Nicholas (1971), J. Eirian *Davies (1972), Derec Llwyd *Morgan (1975) and T. Llew *Jones (1979). The last-named caused controversy by limiting his choice for *Cerddi '79* mainly to poems in the traditional metres and by excluding what he considered to be 'difficult' verse.

Poet Jones, see JONES, JOHN (1788–1858).

Poet of Mount Pleasant, The, see WILLIAMS, WILLIAM (1850–1917).

Poetry Wales, a magazine first published at Merthyr Tydfil in 1965 by the Triskel Press, was founded and edited until 1973 by Meic *Stephens; three numbers were edited by Gerald *Morgan (1967–68) and Gwilym Rees *Hughes served as Welsh-language editor from 1967 to 1975. The magazine was issued as a quarterly by Christopher Davies Ltd. of Swansea (see LLYFRAU'R DRYW) from 1967 to 1980 and it is now published by the Poetry Wales Press in Bridgend.

Under the editorship of Meic Stephens *Poetry Wales* was national in outlook, but not narrowly so. Among its concerns was the fostering of mutual interest between writers in the two languages of Wales. It published new poems in Welsh, translations from the Welsh and articles in English about modern Welsh poetry, as well as reviews of new books from Wales and elsewhere. The magazine's principal success was in the discovery and encouragement of the work of Anglo-Welsh poets and it was largely responsible for what Meic Stephens called 'the second flowering' of Anglo-Welsh poetry which took place during the 1960s. Among regular contributors were John *Ormond, Harri *Webb, John *Tripp, Raymond *Garlick, Roland *Mathias, Leslie *Norris and Gillian *Clarke, for whom the magazine served as a stimulus and rallying-point.

The editorial policy established by the magazine's founder was maintained by Sam *Adams, its editor from 1973 to 1975. J. P. *Ward, the editor from 1975 to 1980, gave the magazine a more academic attitude but Cary Archard, the present editor and publisher, is more concerned with Welsh contemporary realism. All four editors developed the magazine's role by attracting new contributors and editing special numbers devoted to the work of some of the more important poets of Wales, both Welsh and Anglo-Welsh.

For accounts of the magazine's early years see the article entitled 'The Second Flowering' by Meic Stephens in the Winter 1967–68 number and the letters from some of its principal contributors in the twenty-first number (vol. 8, no. 3, Winter, 1971); an index to the first fourteen volumes of *Poetry Wales* (1965–79) has been compiled by D. Hywel E. Roberts (1980) for the Welsh Library Association.

Poets of the Gentry, The, or **Beirdd yr Uchelwyr**, came into their own after the downfall of *Llywelyn ap Gruffudd in 1282, with whose death ended the last possibility of bardic patronage by the Princes. The tradition was continued by the gentry who assumed new, if more circumscribed, powers of administration. From about 1330 onwards, for three hundred years or more, a new class of poet flourished under the aegis of these landed families. A large part of the output of these poets (the work of about a hundred and fifty has survived) was concerned with praise of the patron, his lineage, his wife, his house, his hearth and his hospitality. The *cywydd* was their favourite form but the *awdl* was also popular. One of the most strikingly sustained of the *cywyddau* is *Iolo Goch's description of Sycharth, the home of *Owain Glyndŵr. In general, the more accomplished the poet, the higher the social status of the family whose patronage he enjoyed. Many of the poets came from the same social class as the families for whom they wrote their eulogies and they were well acquainted with the refinements of food, wine, clothes and architecture which they described with such relish. Their poems, often sung to the accompaniment of a *harp, were social, learned, technically accomplished and grounded in Christianity. Typical of their art was the composition of a *cywydd* requesting a gift, such as a horse, followed by another thanking the donor. These poets belonged to a professional guild, the rules of which were reviewed and amended from time to time as in the Statute associated with *Gruffudd ap Cynan. Among the most distinguished were Iolo Goch, *Dafydd ap Gwilym, *Siôn Cent, *Gutun Owain, *Guto'r Glyn, *Dafydd Nanmor, *Lewys Glyn Cothi, *Dafydd ab Edmwnd, *Tudur Aled, *Gruffudd Hiraethog, Lewys Morgannwg (*Llywelyn ap Rhisiart), *Wiliam Llŷn and *Simwnt Fychan.

There is a full critical discussion of these poets in D. J. Bowen, *Barddoniaeth yr Uchelwyr* (1957); the same author has also published important articles in the *Transactions* of the Honourable Society of Cymmrodorion (1970), in *Ysgrifau Beirniadol VII* (ed. J. E. Caerwyn Williams, 1971) and in *Llên Cymru* (vol. IX). For further discussion see Saunders Lewis, *Braslun o Hanes Llenyddiaeth Gymraeg* (1931), Thomas Parry, *A History of Welsh Literature* (1955) and Gwyn Thomas, *Y Traddodiad Barddol* (1976); see also the essay by R. M. Jones in *Ysgrifau Beirniadol VIII* (ed. J. E. Caerwyn Williams, 1974), the chapter by Rachel Bromwich in *A Guide to Welsh Literature* (vol. II, ed. A. O. H. Jarman and G. R. Hughes, 1979) and the article by Eurys Rowlands in *Llên Cymru* (vol. II). A selection of poems by these poets will be found in English translation by Joseph P. Clancy in the volume *Medieval Welsh Lyrics* (1965).

Poets of the Princes, The, see GOGYNFEIRDD.

Pola or **Pool**, see STRATA MARCELLA.

Polly Garter, the wanton girl in Dylan *Thomas's *Under Milk Wood* (1954) who scrubs the steps of the Welfare Hall, has babies by her several lovers and remarks, 'Oh isn't life a terrible thing, thank God?'

Polyolbion (1622), a topographical poem by the English poet Michael Drayton (1563–1631), consists of thirty 'Songs', each of between three hundred and five hundred lines in hexameter couplets. It was intended to awaken English readers to the beauties of Britain and 'Poly-Olbion', the form of the title used for the first edition, is Greek for 'having many blessings'. From his preface it is evident that Drayton was encouraged to visit Wales by the 'much loved, the learned Humphrey Floyd' (i.e. Humphrey *Llwyd) and by another friend, John Williams (*c.*1584–1627?), the King's goldsmith. In his poem he describes, or enumerates, the principal topographical features encountered during his journey through south and north Wales, gives some account of Welsh legends, interspersed with fragments of history, and indulges his passion for flora and fauna. Wales, for him, was still the Land of High Romance: it is Merlin (*Myrddin) and the Princes of *Gwynedd who are invoked. Drayton had the advantage over Thomas Churchyard of being able to consult Speed's maps of Wales (1610) and his work is far superior to The *Worthines of Wales* (1587), which is confined to Gwent and the Marches.

POOK, JOHN (1942–   ), poet, was born at Neath, Glam., and educated at Queen's College, Cambridge, and the University College of North Wales, Bangor. A teacher of English at Ruthin, Denbs., he is the author of one collection of verse, *That Cornish Facing Door* (1975), a quiet, introspective volume which makes powerful use of irony and understatement.

POOLE, EDWIN (1851–95), journalist, printer and county historian, was born in Oswestry but at the age of seventeen he obtained a post in the office of *The Brecon County Times*. He wrote and published *A History of the Breconshire Charities* (1880), *Military Annals of the County of Brecknock* (1885), *The Illustrated History and Biography of Brecknockshire* (1886) and a life of John *Penry (1893); he also brought out *Old Brecon Chips* (1886–88), a short-lived but valuable antiquarian journal. In 1889 he set up *The Brecon and Radnor Express* (which still survives)

and became its first editor. His history of the county is a useful corrective to that of his predecessor, Theophilus *Jones, who omitted virtually all reference to *Nonconformity, and its section on the biographies of local worthies and on books written by Breconshire writers breaks ground which has been little tilled since.

POOLE, RICHARD (1945–   ), poet and critic, was born in Bradford, Yorks., and educated at the University College of North Wales, Bangor. Tutor in Literature at *Coleg Harlech since 1971, he is the author of two collections of verse, *Goings and Other Poems* (1978) and *Words Before Midnight* (1981), which display a metaphysical delight in paradox and in the marriage of sensuality and intellect. An authority on the work of Richard *Hughes, he has edited the writer's early stories under the title *In the Lap of Atlas* (1979) and a selection of his literary writings in the volume *Fiction as Truth* (1983).

Porius (1951), a novel by John Cowper *Powys. Sub-titled 'A Romance of the Dark Ages', its time is one week in October 499 and its setting the valley of Edeirnion, Mer. The action, centred on the House of *Cunedda, involves personal, political, racial and religious conflicts, and there are aboriginal giants among its characters. Concerned with the power of imagination and the relation of the individual psyche to planetary forces, the action of the book reflects the modern situation of contending beliefs and ideas rather than the emergency of the historical setting. Powys reduced its size before publication, altering his original conception, but it is still his third longest novel and the most complete imaginative expression of his personal vision.

Porkington, see BROGYNTYN.

Porthamal, a mansion in the parish of Llanidan, Ang., was a famous resort for poets in medieval times. From the time of Maredudd ap Thomas, for six generations poets wrote for members of the family: Maredudd's tradition was continued by his son, Owain, by his granddaughter and heiress, Elin, who married William Bulkeley of Beaumaris, and by three more generations of their descendants until the middle of the sixteenth century.

Portmeirion, see under WILLIAMS-ELLIS, CLOUGH (1883–1978).

Portrait of the Artist as a Young Dog (1940), a collection of autobiographical short stories by Dylan *Thomas. While the title echoes that of James Joyce's novel, *A Portrait of the Artist as a Young Man* (1916), the real comparison is with Joyce's evocation of his background in *Dubliners* (1914). Thomas, however, remains a character in all the stories of his collection, as a small boy and a young man up to the age of twenty, when he first left Swansea for London. In a different medium, his unfinished novel *Adventures in the Skin Trade* (1955) sought to continue the autobiography into his early experience of London. The *Portrait* contains ten stories. The first two, 'The Peaches' and 'A Visit to Grandpa's', concern the young boy's holiday experiences in rural Carmarthenshire; 'The Peaches' is a comic-realistic evocation of the farm which in the later poem *'Fern Hill'* receives a more romantic treatment. The allocation of the other eight stories to Swansea experiences underlines the fact that Thomas's background was there, deeply though often only indirectly registered in his poetry. Generally regarded as being among the best of his prose works, the book is a lively fusion of imagination and reportage. What comes through very strongly is the essentially suburban nature of the poet's upbringing—comfortable, half-loved and half-lamented—against which the aspirations of the young writer are given an engaging, mock-heroic flavour.

POVEY, MICHAEL (1950–), script-writer, was born at Tremadog, Caerns. Formerly employed on the staff of BBC Wales, he is now an actor and freelance writer for television. Besides a novel, *Mae'r Sgwâr yn Wâg* (1974), he has written the following plays: *Yr Aderyn* (1972), *Terfyn* (1978), *Dim ond Heddiw* (1978), *Y Cadfridog* (1979), *Cofiant y Cymro Olaf* (1980), *Nos Sadwrn Bach* (1980), *Aelwyd Gartrefol* (1982), *Meistres y Chwarae* (1983) and *Chwara Plant* (1983); he also wrote the scripts for the television series *Glas y Dorlan* (1976–83) and for *Taff Acre* (1981).

POWEL, DAVID (1552–98), historian and humanist scholar, was a native of Bryneglwys, Denbs. It is believed that he was the first student to graduate at Jesus College, Oxford, which he did in March 1572/73; he added a doctorate in divinity in 1583. He was vicar of Rhiwabon (1570) and Llanfyllin (1571) before he had even graduated, but in 1579 he exchanged Llanfyllin for Meifod and in 1588 secured the sinecure rectory of Llansantffraid-ym-Mechain. At the request of Sir Henry Sidney, he prepared the translation by Humphrey *Llwyd of *Brut y Tywysogion* for publication, adding to the text the essay by Sir Edward *Stradling on the *Norman Conquest of Glamorgan, a work given to Powel by Blanche *Parry. In this essay there appears, for the first time in print, what purports to be an account of the conquest of Glamorgan, in 1090, by Robert Fitzhamo and his Twelve Knights.

In preparation for the writing of his *Historie of Cambria, now called Wales* (1584), Powel obtained Lord Burghley's permission to search official records and, in his introduction, he included Llwyd's translation of Sir John *Price's treatise on the provincial divisions of Wales. The *Historie* is of prime importance, not only because it reflects the *Tudor interpretation of history but also because it was the standard work on the history of Wales down to 1282 before John Edward *Lloyd published his *History of Wales* (1911).

William Wynne (1617–1704) published an adaptation of the *Historie* in his *History of Wales* (1697), which was reprinted several times between 1697 and 1832, and the work had an immense influence on later historians such as Charles *Edwards and Theophilus *Evans.

Further details will be found in the article by I. M. Williams in *Llên Cymru* (vol. II, 1952) and in Ceri Davies, *Rhagymadroddion a Chyflwyniadau Lladin 1551–1632* (1980) and *Latin Writers of the Renaissance* (1981).

POWEL, THOMAS (1845–1922), scholar, was born at Llanwrtyd, Brecs., and educated at Jesus College, Oxford, where he graduated with Honours in Classics in 1872. When University College, Cardiff, was established in 1883 he was appointed to its staff and in the following year he was promoted to the Chair of Celtic, the first in Wales and a post in which he remained until his retirement. Besides editing *Y Cymmrodor* (1880–86), he edited *Ystorya de Carolo Magno* (1883) from The *Red Book of Hergest*, Thomas *Stephens's *The Gododdin of Aneirin Gwawdrydd* (1888) on behalf of the Honourable Society of *Cymmrodorion, and a reprint (1896–97) of William *Morgan's *Psalmau Dafydd* (1588).

POWELL, GEORGE (**Miölnir Nanteos**; 1842–82), poet, was born at *Nanteos, Cards., and educated at Eton and Brasenose College, Oxford. A misfit among the squirearchy, he had published three books of verse, *Quod Libet* (1860), *Poems First Series* (1860) and *Poems Second Series* (1861), before he was twenty years old. For the second and third of these books he used the pseudonym Miölnir Nanteos, evidence of his already deep interest in Iceland, its culture and struggle for independence. Although structurally competent, his verse is sometimes feebly jocular and his prefaces show him aware of his limitations as a poet; indeed, he wrote no more verse after 1861.

In the following year he met the scholar Eirikr Magnusson, with whom he collaborated in the translating of *The Legends of Iceland* (1864, 1866), and subsequent travels on the Continent turned his attention to music. A devotee of Wagner, he also gave generous support to other contemporary composers. He first made the acquaintance of Swinburne, with whom he shared an interest in the works of the Marquis de Sade, in 1866 and their eccentricities brought Maupassant to visit their villa on the Normandy coast in 1868; the result was a short story entitled '*L'Anglais d'Étretat*'. Always at odds with his father, Powell did not succeed to the Nanteos estate until four years before his premature death.

For further details see the article by David Lewis Jones in *The Anglo-Welsh Review* (vol. 19, no. 44, 1971), that by Richard Brinkley in *The Anglo-Welsh Review* (vol. 22, no. 48, 1972) and another by R. J. Colyer in *The Welsh History Review* (vol. 10, no. 4, 1981).

Powell, Philip (1594–1646), Catholic martyr. Born at Trallong, Brecs., he was recommended by Morgan Lewis, Headmaster of Abergavenny Grammar School and later the father of David *Lewis (Charles Baker), to Dom Augustine Baker (David *Baker) who paid for his law studies and education at the University of Louvain. Ordained priest in 1618, he became a Benedictine monk in the following year and, having studied under John *Jones (Leander), was sent on the English mission in 1622. He served as chaplain to families in Devon and Somerset for the next twenty years but was arrested during the Civil War while making his way across the Bristol Channel to Monmouth, and was later executed at Tyburn on account of his priesthood.

Powell, Rees or **Rice** (*fl.* 1638–65), Parliamentary commander, was described in 1638 as being of Jeffreyston, Pembs. An officer in Ormonde's army in Ireland, he deserted in September 1643 to help his Parliamentarian friends in *Pembroke. He shared the triumphs and setbacks of the campaigns led by Rowland *Laugharne and John *Poyer in 1644, and his defiance of Gerard at *Cardigan castle was a spectacular success. When Laugharne was totally routed by Gerard before Newcastle Emlyn, in April 1645, Powell fired the castle and took his men back to Pembroke by sea. In April of the following year, hostilities over, he became Governor of Tenby and early in 1648, while Laugharne was absent in London, Powell was in command of Parliamentary forces in west Wales. The order to disband supernumeraries, with arrears of pay outstanding, aroused great discontent and he joined Poyer in refusing to obey and, later, in negotiating with the King. He assembled his men at Carmarthen, beat off Colonels Horton and Fleming commanding troops loyal to Parliament, took Swansea and Neath and advanced towards Cardiff. Horton, making a forced march from Brecon, intercepted him at St. Fagans where, on 11 May 1648, Powell and Laugharne were defeated. Powell fell back on Tenby, where he held out till 31 May. Courtmartialled, he was sentenced to death but was later reprieved by Cromwell.

The military activities of Powell are outlined in J. R. Phillips, *Memoirs of the Civil War in Wales and the Marches* (2 vols., 1874) and in A. L. Leach, *The History of the Civil War in Pembrokeshire* (1937); the only evidence of his family and pedigree so far discovered is to be found in the article by Francis Green, 'Cuny of Welston and Golden', in *West Wales Historical Records* (vol. XII).

POWELL, THOMAS (1608?–60), cleric and writer, was born at Cantref, Brecs., and became successively Scholar and Fellow of Jesus College, Oxford. It was probably while he was a Fellow in residence there in 1638 that his acquaintance with Thomas and Henry *Vaughan, then undergraduates, began. Rector of Cantref from 1635 (though not in immediate succession to his father), he was deprived of the living under the Commonwealth in 1650. He is believed to have been the 'Friend' who published Henry Vaughan's *Olor Iscanus* in 1651. In the Spring of 1654 he attempted to obtain from Jenkin *Jones a licence to preach again, but the refusal sent him overseas. His only Welsh book, *Cerbyd Iechydwriaeth* (1657), reflects his bitterness.

Powell translated from the Italian Malvezzi's *Christian Politician*, an achievement celebrated by Vaughan in *Olor Iscanus* and that part of the same author's *Stoa Triumphans* (1651) which was entitled 'The Praise of Banishment'. Among his other works were *Elementae Opticae* (1651) and the posthumous *Humane Industry* (1661) which contains translations by Henry Vaughan. His unpublished manuscripts, including 'A Short Account of the Lives, Manners and Religion of the British Druids and Bards', were left with Vaughan who nevertheless seemed ignorant of their contents in writing to John Aubrey (see under AUBREY, WILLIAM) in 1694.

There is some account of Thomas Powell in Theophilus Jones, *A History of Brecknock* (vol. IV, 1909); other references will be found in L. C. Martin's edition (1914) of Henry Vaughan's *Poems* and in F. E. Hutchinson, *Henry Vaughan: A Life and an Interpretation* (1947).

POWELL, VAVASOR (1617–70), Puritan preacher and author, was born at Cnwclas (Knucklas), Rads. After spending some years as a schoolmaster at Clun, he was converted to Puritan views (see under PURITANISM) by reading the sermons of Richard Sibbes and hearing Walter *Cradock preach. He became a Puritan preacher, fought in the *Civil War and flung himself with enthusiasm into the task of evangelizing Wales by the use of itinerant preachers under the Act for the *Propagation of the Gospel in Wales (1650). His Calvinism was 'higher' than that favoured by some other Welsh Puritan Radicals but it was accompanied by expectations usually associated with *Fifth Monarchism. Such convictions made him a daring opponent of Cromwell against whose rule he organized Welsh opposition in his manifesto, *A Word for God* (1655). After the Restoration he suffered arrests and imprisonments, dying in the Fleet prison. His works include *The Scriptures Concord* (1646), *God the Father Glorified* (1649), *Christ and Moses Excellency* (1650), *Saving Faith* (1651), *Christ Exalted* (1651), *Common-Prayer-*

Book No Divine Service (1660), *The Bird in the Cage Chirping* (1661), *The Sufferers Catechism* (1664), *Divine Love* (1677) and an autobiography.

An account of Vavasor Powell's life has been written by R. Tudur Jones (1971); see also G. F. Nuttall, *The Welsh Saints* (1957). Thomas Carlyle, in his *Oliver Cromwell's Letters and Speeches* (1845), has some lively paragraphs about Powell, who was plainly one of his favourite characters.

Powerful Swineherds of the Isle of Britain, Three, a Triad naming *Pryderi ap Pwyll Pen Annwfn, Drystan ap Tallwch and Coll ap Collfrewi, is the longest and most informative of *Trioedd Ynys Prydain*, since to each of the three names is appended a brief narrative. They appear to have their origin in the story-material of south Wales rather than of the north. The first gives a slightly variant account from that found in the tale of *Math concerning the introduction of the swine from *Annwfn into south Wales and it may derive from an older, pre-literary version. The second, alluding to Drystan (*Tristan) and his love for Esyllt (Isolt or Iseult), the wife of *March ap Meirchion, is a typical precursor of the recurrent narratives of stolen meetings between the lovers which characterize the Old French romances of Tristan and Yseult. They are only sparsely indicated in the survivals of this story which have come down in Welsh, though there is reason to believe that it was in south Wales that the story developed its characteristic features. Coll ap Collfrewi, unknown outside this Triad, figures here as the swineherd in charge of the magical sow Henwen which he is said to have pursued from Cornwall through Gwent and Dyfed to Gwynedd. As she passed from south to north Wales this beast bestowed the benefits of wheat, barley and bees upon the fertile south, but in the north she gave birth only to a wolf, an eagle and the savage cat-monster known as *Cath Palug* (Palug's Cat), one of the 'three scourges of Anglesey'. The story, as John *Rhŷs commented, is remarkable for giving to south Wales the credit for certain resources, but to north Wales that for pests and scourges.

Powis or **Powys**, a castle near Welshpool, Mont., was an early fortification begun by order of *Cadwgan ap Bleddyn about 1109 and completed during the time of Gwenwynwyn ab Owain Cyfeiliog (d. 1216). It was replaced by the present building in the early thirteenth century and from then on its fortunes were linked with those of the Princes of south *Powys. The son of Gruffudd ap Gwenwynwyn, Owen de la Pole, lived in the castle and it remained in the family's possession until the marriage of his daughter Hawys to Sir John Charleton in 1309. Their descendants held it until 1421 when it passed to the family of Henry Grey, the grandson of Edward de Charleton. In 1587 the castle was purchased by Sir Edward Herbert, a younger son of the Earl of Pembroke, who added the famous Long Gallery. His son, William *Herbert (1580–1630), created Baron Powys in 1629, garrisoned the castle for the Crown during the first *Civil War but, badly damaged, it was taken by Parliament in 1644. After 1667 his grandson, the third Baron Powys, restored the castle and it was probably he who added substantially to the fabric, including the State bedroom and Grand Staircase. Powis Castle is remarkable in that, unlike other Welsh castles of the thirteenth century, it was the residence of the Earls of Powys over many centuries. The valuable collection of Herbert papers, previously housed in the castle, is now in the *National Library of Wales.

For further details see Richard Haslam, *Powys* (1979).

Powys, a kingdom which had its origins in the period which followed the departure of the Romans, extended over much of what is today Shropshire as well as a large part of mid-Wales. The traditions dealing with the early history of the dynasty are far from clear and there is uncertainty with regard to the site of the royal seat of Pengwern. Wroxeter (*Viroconium*) was the tribal capital of the Cornovii, who in Roman and post-Roman times occupied the area westwards from Lichfield well into what is now called Wales, and the name Powys, according to some, derives from *Pagenses*, a Roman term for the rural parts of that area, which, if true, must have become applicable while *Romanitas* was still strong. Lichfield and the fertile lands of the later Shropshire were conquered by the Mercians from 655 onwards and the court at Pengwern (whether that should be equated with Wroxeter or with a later seat at Shrewsbury) was abandoned. The two cycles of *englynion* in *Canu Llywarch Hen* and *Canu Heledd* are thought to belong to the restricted Powys of the Welsh borderlands, and Llywarch Hen, who belonged to the *Old North in the ninth century, perhaps coming to Powys in a period of new oppression, identified his tale with the epic of the territory's troubled past. The *awdl* to *Cynan Garwyn and the elegy to Cynddylan, king of the lost kingdom, belong to the same time.

By the twelfth century, when its boundaries had been affected by Saxon settlement and the *Norman Conquest, the kingdom was partly restored by a royal line whose efforts reached a climax during the reign of *Madog ap Maredudd. A new royal seat was established at *Mathrafal castle, near Meifod, with *Aberffraw in *Gwynedd and *Dinefwr in *Deheubarth one of the three chief courts of Wales. The glory of Powys under the authority of Madog ap Maredudd is reflected in the poetry of *Cynddelw Brydydd Mawr who also conveys the change which occurred in the kingdom when the heir, Llywelyn ap Madog, was killed early in the merciless contention during the years after the king's death.

No member of the royal lineage managed to win complete supremacy, however, and a compromise was reached which was to leave Powys divided for ever. Apart from *Edeirnion and *Mechain, two main lordships were established. Owain Cyfeiliog (*Owain ap Gruffudd ap Maredudd), son of Madog ap Maredudd's brother, established in the southern parts an authority which is reflected both in his own poetry, such as *'Hirlas Owain', and in that of Cynddelw Brydydd Mawr. He was succeeded by his son Gwenwynwyn (d. 1216) and it was by that name that this lordship, with its centre at Welshpool, came to be known. He, in turn, was succeeded by his son Gruffudd ap Gwenwynwyn (d. 1286) and the stormy relationship between the lords of Powys Wenwynwyn and *Llywelyn ap Iorwerth (Llywelyn Fawr) and *Llywelyn ap Gruffudd was an important factor in Welsh politics of the thirteenth century. In the northerly parts of Powys, a lordship known as Powys Fadog, so named after *Madog ap Gruffudd, the grandson of Madog ap Maredudd, was established with its centre at *Dinas Brân. The work of poets such as *Llywarch ap Llywelyn (Prydydd y Moch) and *Llygad Gŵr in praise of Madog ap Gruffudd and his son Gruffudd ap Madog (d. 1269) is significant in that it reflects the values of a royal lineage during an important period in the history of Wales. Powys is also the background against which the romance *Breuddwyd Rhonabwy is set but the Dream was composed after the kingdom had been shattered.

Powys Fadog was broken up after the death of Gruffudd ap Madog and by 1282, apart from the lordship of *Glyndyfrdwy which eventually became the inheritance of *Owain Glyndŵr, its lands fell to the lords of the Border to form the lordship of *Chirk. Powys Wenwynwyn remained intact in the hands of the royal line, but as its members married into other families this, too, became a Border lordship.

The modern county of Powys dates from 1974 and was created by the amalgamation of the previous shires of Brecon, Radnor and Montgomery. The resulting administrative unit, very thinly populated, extends from Llanfyllin in the north and Machynlleth in the west as far south as Ystradgynlais in the Swansea Valley, embracing a great deal of territory which has no connection with medieval Powys, the southernmost extremity of which (and that dubious) was the commot of *Elfael.

For the history of Powys see J. E. Lloyd, *A History of Wales* (1911) and Wendy Davies, *Wales in the Early Middle Ages* (1982); there is a survey of the Welsh literature of Powys in Enid P. Roberts, *Braslun o Hanes Llên Powys* (1965).

POWYS, JOHN COWPER (1872–1963), novelist. His father, the Reverend C. F. Powys,

claimed descent from a Welsh lord of the seventeenth century and his mother counted the English poets Cowper and Donne among her ancestors; both were descended, more immediately, from generations of English parsons. John, who was born at Shirley, Derby., was the eldest of their eleven children and one of three notable writers among them, the others being T. F. Powys (1875–1953) and Llywelyn Powys (1884–1939). The family moved to Dorchester, Dorset, in 1879 and to Montacute, Som., in 1886, and John spent his most formative years in those counties. From an early age he was hypersensitive and self-tormenting, but with a large capacity for enjoying books and nature. These factors, together with his membership of a close-knit, highly individual family, his pride in his Welsh ancestry and his love of the West Country, stimulated the development of his romantic individualism and were the main influences in the development of his imagination.

Educated at Sherborne School and, from 1891 to 1894, at Corpus Christi College, Cambridge, Powys studied History. But Literature was his main subject when, after graduating, he became a visiting teacher to girls' schools in Sussex and then, from 1898, an itinerant lecturer for the University Extension Movement. He married in 1896 and had one son, but was later separated from his wife. Having lectured widely in England and on the Continent, he undertook his first American lecture tour in 1905. From 1910 until his retirement in 1932 he did all his lecturing in America, where he visited almost every State and where he became widely known as an inspiring orator and an imaginative interpreter of literature and philosophy. He returned to Dorset in 1934, moved to Corwen, Mer., in the following year and then to Blaenau Ffestiniog, Mer., in 1955. There he lived in a small quarryman's house, with a simplicity which was always his ideal and on a frugal diet which his state of health (he had been tormented by gastric ulcers all his adult life) had long necessitated, but his pleasure in the elements and his great physical and mental energy continued almost until his death. He acquired a good reading knowledge of Welsh and extended his study of Welsh history and mythology. As a young man he had been acquainted with Thomas Hardy and in Wales, as in America, some of the leading writers of the day were among the many friends attracted by his magnetic and generous personality. He had devoted readers scattered throughout the world, but enjoyed no fashionable reputation nor much serious critical attention during his lifetime.

Powys's maturing process as a writer, which lasted until his late fifties, encompassed *Odes and Other Poems* (1896) and *Poems* (1899), three more books of poems published between 1916 and 1922, his first three novels, *Wood and Stone* (1915), *Rodmoor* (1916) and *Ducdame* (1925), his first philosophical work, *The Complex Vision*

(1920), and other philosophical, autobiographical and critical writings. His first major phase of creative writing began with his fifth novel, *Wolf Solent* (1929), and continued with his other important 'Wessex romances', *A Glastonbury Romance* (1932), *Weymouth Sands* (1934) and *Maiden Castle* (1936). In the same period he wrote an autobiography (1934) and works of non-fiction, *The Meaning of Culture* (1929), *In Defence of Sensuality* (1930) and *A Philosophy of Solitude* (1933). His second major phase of writing occurred in Wales, where he wrote his Welsh historical romances, *Owen Glendower* (1940) and *Porius* (1951), as well as some of his most notable literary criticism, *The Pleasures of Literature* (1938), *Dostoievsky* (1946) and *Rabelais* (1948), several other novels and more critical and philosophical writings. Towards the end of his life his fiction became increasingly fantastic; of his books published posthumously it is the numerous collections of letters which reveal his genius most fully. Among Welsh writers acquainted with Powys was Iorwerth C. *Peate who edited a volume of letters received by the writer during the years from 1937 to 1954 (1974). A selection of Powys's essays on Welsh themes appeared under the title *Obstinate Cymric* (1947).

A prolific writer in several forms, Powys was at his best as autobiographer and novelist. His massive novels are structured after the fashion of Thomas Hardy and Walter Scott and comprise inter-connected stories, a large variety of character and incident, suspense, rich period detail and a vivid sense of place. They are modern, not in form, but in their philosophy and psychology and the means by which these elements are embodied. Powys's use of Celtic mythology and of natural settings and symbols to explore his characters' psyches contributes to the original poetic quality of his fiction, while his passages of platform oratory and general literariness work against it. He arrived at his philosophy and psychology through a long and painful process of self-understanding and in reaction against the theory and practice of mechanistic world-views. In their private myths, the sustenance they draw from nature and their return to personal quest for liberation, each of his long novels is a multiverse in which creatures and things are as alive and, frequently, as conscious as human beings, and inhabit their own peculiar worlds. They are transformers and often, like Powys, enemies of 'reality' conceived as external, single and absolute. He stresses the power of imagination, evokes elemental forces, creates subhuman and superhuman beings and has a remarkable insight into sexual relationships and the processes of consciousness. The reconciliation of contraries and the inter-penetration of sex and religion are among his major themes. Like Jung and W. B. Yeats, he was one of the great late Romantics among modern thinkers and writers.

Glen Cavaliero's *John Cowper Powys: Novelist* (1973) is a full treatment of the novels; see also *Essays on John Cowper Powys* (ed. Belinda Humfrey, 1972), Jeremy Hooker's essay in the *Writers of Wales* series (1973) and a study of Powys as poet by Roland Mathias, *The Hollowed-Out Elder Stalk* (1979). A selection of Powys's poems was edited by Kenneth Hopkins (1964). Morine Krissdottir's *John Cowper Powys and the Magical Quest* (1980) is a detailed treatment of his 'mythology' and *Recollections of the Powys Brothers* (ed. Belinda Humfrey, 1980) contains numerous reminiscences of John Cowper Powys. The magazine *The Powys Review*, founded in 1977 under the auspices of the Powys Society and edited by Belinda Humfrey, is devoted to the study of the Powys family. See also C. A. Coates, *John Cowper Powys in Search of a Landscape* (1982) and Richard Perceval Graves, *The Brothers Powys* (1983).

Poyer, John (d. 1649), merchant and military commander, committed *Pembroke to the Parliamentary cause when the *Civil War broke out in 1642. In all Wales only Tenby made a similar declaration. Again, it was Poyer's acceptance of Prince Charles's commission in 1647 that began the Second Civil War. Politically a rabid anti-Catholic but probably a Churchman rather than a Separatist, he had, before the conflict began, repeatedly warned Parliament of the dangers of invasion from Ireland. In 1642, as a former mayor of Pembroke and captain of the trained bands, he usurped the mayoral authority, seized several ships in the Cleddau estuary and prepared the castle for defence. His dour posture in Pembroke in the difficult first year of the war was crucial and, with Rowland *Laugharne and Rees *Powell, he took part in the rout of the Royalists in the Spring of 1644. It was, however, his capture of *Carew Castle that offensive which proved his ultimate downfall. Impulsive and short of gentlemanly status, he aroused the animosity of a group of turncoat Royalists, led by Roger *Lort and John Elyot, whose successful intrigues in London were to undo both him and Laugharne, his leader in the field. Poyer's retention of the Carew lands (necessary, he argued, to defray his expenses) met with hostility from the County Committee and when he was ordered in 1647 to disband his supernumeraries and surrender Pembroke Castle, his paranoia was such that he refused all terms, declaring that he had been traduced. Widespread opposition to disbandment followed, Royalist agents took a hand and in April 1648 Laugharne and Powell joined Poyer in open resistance to the Parliament. But defeat at the battle of St. Fagans and the fall of Pembroke Castle to Cromwell in July ended the prowess of the new Royalists. Laugharne, Powell and Poyer were all condemned to death, but Cromwell decided to execute only one. The lot fell upon Poyer, who was shot at Covent Garden on the morning of 25 April 1649. He died, Clarendon testifies, 'with singular courage'.

The best single source for Poyer's career is A. L. Leach, *The History of the Civil War in Pembrokeshire* (1937).

Prayer Book, The (1567), was published in Welsh as the result of the Act of 1563. Although William *Salesbury had translated the Epistles and Gospels of the First Prayer Book in his *Kynniver Llith a Ban* (1551), no complete translation of the Prayer Book appeared before 1567. It was long supposed that Richard *Davies (1501?–81) was responsible, but it is now recognized that Salesbury undertook the work. The Scriptural passages were translated from the original texts but the rest of the work was translated from English. This first edition, like that of 1586, is marked by all Salesbury's particular linguistic idiosyncrasies and therefore was less valuable than it might have been. The 1599 edition of the Prayer Book was the first to make use of William *Morgan's work and it was he who revised his original translation of the *Bible and prepared it for this new version. After John *Davies of Mallwyd undertook the revision of the translation of the Bible for the Authorized Version of 1620, published by Bishop Richard *Parry, a new edition of the Prayer Book containing his translations appeared in 1621.

For further details see Isaac Thomas, *Y Testament Newydd Cymraeg* (1976), the article by R. Geraint Gruffydd in *Y Traddodiad Rhyddiaith* (ed. Geraint Bowen, 1970) and Melville Richards and Glanmor Williams, *Llyfr Gweddi Gyffredin 1567* (1965).

'Preiddiau Annwfn' (lit. 'The spoils of Annwfn'), a poem in *The *Book of Taliesin*. Despite the title of the manuscript in which it is contained, it cannot be the work of the historic poet *Taliesin who, according to *Nennius's *Historia Brittonum*, flourished in the sixth century. It is, however, pre-Norman, the language and technique being comparable with those of *'Armes Prydein' (c.930). *Annwfn, the Otherworld, is depicted here as a four-cornered glass fortress standing on an island. It has a silent sentinel, a wonderful fountain, a doleful prisoner and ever-youthful inhabitants much occupied with feasting. The poem tells of one of *Arthur's expeditions to Annwfn, in his ship *Prydwen, in order to capture the cauldron of the chief of Annwfn. This cauldron, the rim of which is decorated with pearls, is heated by the breath of nine maidens and will not boil the food of a coward. The expedition is a disaster and each stanza ends with the words, '*nam(yn) saith ny dyrreith o gaer (sidi)*', ('save seven, none returned'). The expedition may be compared with an episode in the tale of *Culhwch and Olwen in which the hero has to procure, among other things, the cauldron of *Diwrnach Wyddel, the steward of Odgar, King of Ireland.

For a full discussion of the poem see the chapter by R. S. Loomis in *Wales and the Arthurian Legend* (1956).

Presaeddfed, see under BODEON and BODYCHEN.

Presbyterian Church of Wales, The, see under METHODISM.

Price, Herbert (*fl.* 1615–65), the great-grandson of Sir John *Price, was, like his ancestor, of the Priory, Brecon, where in 1645 he entertained King Charles I. The Member of Parliament for Brecknock in both the Short and the Long Parliaments, he was an extreme or Divine Right Royalist, possibly the only one among Welsh members. Henry *Vaughan, whose friend and patron he became, served in his troop of cavalry in 1645, when the Royalist cause was almost lost. Sir Herbert's friendship with George Digby, later the second Earl of Bristol, took him to Coleshill Manor, Warwicks., the home of the elder line of the Digbys, and he married Goditha Arden of nearby Park Hall, Castle Bromwich. This marriage in turn brought about that of Henry Vaughan to Catherine Wise of Gylsdon Hall, near Coleshill, to whom he first declared his love in the Priory Grove at Brecon. Sir Herbert was also the patron of Rowland *Watkyns, who called him 'a walking library' and his 'tutelary angel'.

Price, Hugh (1495?–1574), the founder of Jesus College, Oxford, was born at Brecon. He became a doctor of canon law at Oxford in 1525. Little is known of his career except that he was appointed first prebendary of Rochester in 1541, treasurer of *St. David's cathedral in 1571 and bailiff (or mayor) of Brecon in 1572; he was buried in the Priory in his native town. Late in life he set about the founding of a college at Oxford for Welsh students, whose main congregation until then had been at Oriel. In 1571 he petitioned Elizabeth I and letters patent of that year incorporated the first society to become a College since the Reformation. The charter named the Queen as founder (a tradition still maintained in the customs of the College's undergraduates) but Hugh Price, called therein 'Benefactor', made it clear in his will that he regarded himself as founder. He reputedly spent some fifteen hundred pounds in erecting buildings and left another three hundred pounds for their completion. Of the sixty pounds a year he willed to the College for its upkeep, part has been identified as rent from Pwll Llaca, a holding in Llanfihangel Nant Bran, Brecs. Jesus College has maintained its close associations with Wales: nearly all its endowments have been provided by Welshmen and many eminent Welshmen have been educated there.

For further details about Hugh Price see Theophilus Jones, *A History of Brecknock* (vol. II, 1909); see also R. Brinley Jones, *Prifysgol Rhydychen a'i Chysylltiadau Cymreig* (1983).

PRICE, JOHN (1502–55), gentleman, royal

administrator and scholar, was a native of Brecon who graduated in law at Oxford and entered the Middle Temple in 1523. Appointed about 1530 to the service of Thomas Cromwell, he held the important offices of Public Notary, Chief Registrar of the Crown in matters ecclesiastical and Secretary of the Council in the Marches of Wales. He took a leading part in administering the measures necessary to annul papal power in England and visited monasteries to arrange for their dissolution. For his services he was granted privileges in land, such as the lease of Brecon Priory. After purchasing St. Guthlac Priory, Hereford, he settled there but continued to hold a number of offices relating to local government in south Wales. Sir John took a keen interest in the history and literature of Wales, collecting manuscripts relating to the humanistic activity of his age. It was he who published the first book in Welsh, *Yn y lhyvyr hwnn (1546); he also defended *Geoffrey of Monmouth against the strictures of Polydore Vergil. His *Historiae Britannicae Defensio (1573) was published posthumously. Price was a worthy representative of early Protestant scholarship in Wales: one of his objectives was to ensure that essential parts of the Scriptures were made available in Welsh. Sir Herbert *Price was his great-grandson.

Further details will be found in the article by N. R. Ker in Library (vol. V, 1955) and in Ceri Davies, Rhagymadroddion a Chyflwyniadau Lladin 1551–1632 (1980); see also F. C. Morgan, 'The Will of Sir John Price of Hereford, 1555', in the Journal of the National Library of Wales (vol. IX, no. 2, Winter, 1955).

Price, Joseph Tregelles (1784–1854), Quaker, ironmaster and philanthropist. By birth a Cornishman, he came to Wales at the age of fifteen when his father was appointed manager of the Neath Abbey Iron Works. Both his parents, who were Quakers, were noted for their *Pacifism. Their son became managing director of the works in 1818 and won for it a pre-eminent reputation for the manufacture of all kinds of machinery, never once relaxing his rule that no cannon, shot or gun was to be made there. He took a leading part in the formation of the first Peace Society, founded in London in 1816, and became its president; he was also a patron of the Anti-Slavery Movement. It was he who succeeded in winning a reprieve, if only of ten days, for Dic Penderyn (Richard Lewis) while the latter was under sentence of death in Cardiff gaol for his alleged part in the *Merthyr Rising of 1831. Price remained convinced of Dic's innocence.

PRICE, RICHARD (1723–91), Dissenting minister, philosopher and actuary, was born at Llangeinor, Glam. Educated under Samuel Jones (c.1715–64) at Pen-twyn, at Vavasor Griffiths's Academy at Chancefield, Talgarth, and at the Academy in Tenter Alley, Moorfields,

London, he began his ministry as family chaplain to George Streatfield at Stoke Newington. After his patron's death in 1757 he officiated at meeting-houses in London and its environs for the rest of his career, principally at Newington Green (1758–83) and at the Gravel Pit Meeting House at Hackney (1770–91).

His first publication and main contribution to philosophical thought was A Review of the Principal Questions and Difficulties in Morals (1758), a work which still commands attention as a classic statement of rational intuitionism in ethics. It was followed by Four Dissertations (1767), a series of essays in theology and divinity which brought him to the attention of the Earl of Shelburne, to whom he remained a lifelong friend and adviser. In 1756 Price was elected to a fellowship of the Royal Society, largely in recognition of his work in editing Thomas Bayes's celebrated essay on the theory of probability, 'An essay towards solving a problem in the doctrine of chances', published in the Philosophical Transactions of the Royal Society in 1763. His expertise in mathematics led him to advise the newly founded Equitable Assurance Society on actuarial and demographic matters, an involvement which in turn led to the publication of his standard work in the field, Observations on Reversionary Payments (1771). In An Appeal to the Public (1772) he drew attention to what he regarded as a great evil, the existence of a National Debt so large that it threatened national bankruptcy and ruin, and he advocated sinking fund procedures for its redemption. His persistent advocacy of this measure had a considerable influence upon the financial policies of Shelburne and William Pitt, and particularly upon the formulation of the Sinking Fund Act of 1786.

The fame of Richard Price became more generally established with the publication of his pamphlets in defence of the American rebels, Observations on the Nature of Civil Liberty (1776), Additional Observations (1777) and Two Tracts (1778). These three works advocated the federal principle of government and raised the argument between Britain and the rebellious colonies from the level of mutual vituperation to that of philosophical principle. His view was that every community conscious of itself had the right to govern itself and that the authority vested in government derived solely from the consent of the governed. In propounding this view Price appeared to be taking the side of the colonies, but his real hope was that within unity there could be autonomy, that the Empire could become a voluntary confederation of self-governing communities. Events, however, had gone too far for any such solution. Faced with opprobrium in England, Price never flinched from his view that the colonies had an absolute right to oppose the demands of the British Parliament. For his contribution in raising the level of debate about the colonies he was widely honoured, receiving the freedom of London in 1776 and, alone with George Washington, an honorary degree from the University of Yale in 1781. He did not, however, accept the invitation to become an American citizen, though he continued to take a keen interest in American affairs and the publication of his *Observations on the Importance of the American Revolution* (1784), in which he advocated the creation of a strong Federal authority, was warmly received. Price is now best remembered for *A Discourse on the Love of our Country* (1789), a sermon in which he greeted with ecstatic enthusiasm the opening events of the French Revolution, thereby provoking Edmund Burke into writing *Reflections on the Revolution in France* (1790).

For accounts of Price's life and work see Roland Thomas, *Richard Price* (1924), Carl B. Cone, *Torchbearer of Freedom* (1952), Henri Laboucheix, *Richard Price* (1970; English trans. by Sylvia and David Raphael, 1982), D. O. Thomas, *The Honest Mind* (1977), Bernard Peach, *Richard Price and the Ethical Foundations of the American Revolution* (1979) and *The Correspondence of Richard Price* (vol. I, ed. D.O. Thomas and W. B. Peach, 1983). See also the *Price-Priestley Newsletter* (1977–80) and its successor, the journal *Enlightenment and Dissent* (1982–   ).

PRICE, ROBERT HOLLAND (*fl.* 1770–1804?), gentleman and poet, of Llangollen, Denbs. He was the author of *The Horrors of Invasion* (2nd edn., 1804), a poem addressed to 'The Chirk Hundred Volunteers and all Welshmen' and dedicated to Eleanor *Butler and Sarah Ponsonby (The Ladies of Llangollen). This poem rehearses the warrior spirit of ancient Wales as it was exhibited against the Saxons and the early Norman kings and then, without a hint of incongruity, calls on all Welshmen to defend the British realm against Bonaparte. Its theme links the poem with the Welsh celebration of *Tudor success rather than with any Anglo-Welsh writing for a century and a half before it.

PRICE, THOMAS (Carnhuanawc; 1787–1848), antiquary, was born in the parish of Llanfihangel Bryn Pabuan, Brecs., and educated at Christ College, Brecon. Ordained priest in the Church of England in 1812, he held the curacies of Llanfihangel Helygen and of Crickhowell, Brecs., before his preferment to the living of Llanfihangel Cwm Du, Brecs., in 1825. His main interest was in the antiquities of the Celtic countries and he won several prizes for his historical essays at provincial eisteddfodau.

Besides the numerous articles which he published in Welsh journals, his principal works were *An Essay on the Physiognomy and Physiology of the Present Inhabitants of Britain* (1829), *Hanes Cymru a Chenedl y Cymry o'r Cynoesoedd hyd at Farwolaeth Llywelyn ap Gruffydd* (1836–42) and *The Geographical Progress of Empire and Civilization* (1847). He did much to foster relations between Wales and Brittany, learned Breton and

sponsored Le Gonidec's translation of the Bible into that language. The establishment of Welsh literary societies in Brecon (1823) and Abergavenny (1833) owed much to his efforts and, as one of *Yr *Hen Bersoniaid Llengar* ('The Old Literary Clerics'), he was exceptional for his passionate interest in Welsh culture. He was among those who helped Lady Charlotte *Guest in the translation of *The *Mabinogion* and he was one of the founders of the *Cambrian Quarterly Magazine*. Price was also an ardent advocate of education through the medium of the Welsh language and he founded a school for this purpose at Gelli Felen. He attacked the Established Church for condoning the use of English in its services and for the appointment of clerics who knew no Welsh. Although he enjoyed the esteem of the gentry who supported the eisteddfodau of his day, he always expressed his admiration for the way in which the common people cherished their cultural heritage. He was particularly active on behalf of the Welsh Minstrelsy Society, supporting a school for blind harpists, and he participated in the work of the *Welsh Manuscripts Society, for which, after the death of Taliesin *Williams, he edited *The Iolo Manuscripts*. Some of his later writings, which are not based on the best historical sources, appeared in a volume of his *Literary Remains* (1854–55) to which Jane *Williams (Ysgafell) added a biography.

For further details see the articles by T. Gwynn Jones in *Welsh Outlook* (vol. X, 1923), Stephen J. Williams in the *Transactions* of the Honourable Society of Cymmrodorion (1954), and Mary Ellis in *Yr Haul* (Winter, 1974) and *The Brecon and Radnor Express* (14 Feb.–30 May, 1974).

Price, William (1800–93), doctor, Chartist and pioneer of cremation. He was a familiar figure in the district of Pontypridd, Glam., where, dressed in a white tunic, scarlet waistcoat, green trousers and a fox-skin hat, he would perform druidic rites at the Rocking Stone on the Common, and he won a wider reputation as a physician and surgeon. His notoriety was caused as much by his advocacy of free love, vegetarianism and cremation as by his eloquent denunciation of vaccination, vivisection, orthodox religion, the ironmasters and the law. After the Chartist march on Newport in 1839 (see under CHARTISM), he fled to France disguised as a woman and in Paris he became acquainted with the poet Heine. Of the many lawsuits in which he delighted the most important was his trial at Cardiff Assizes in 1884 when he was accused of having tried to burn the corpse of his infant son, whom he had named Iesu Grist (Jesus Christ). His acquittal established the legality of cremation in British law and paved the way for the passing of the first comprehensive Cremation Act in 1902. Huge crowds attended the doctor's funeral at Caerlan Fields, Llantrisant, when his

body was cremated in accordance with his detailed instructions.

For further details see Islwyn ap Nicholas, *A Welsh Heretic* (1973), and the chapter by Brian Davies in *A People and a Proletariat* (ed. David Smith, 1980).

PRICHARD, CARADOG (1904–80), poet and novelist. A native of Bethesda, Caerns., he was a journalist with newspapers in Caernarfon, Llanrwst, Cardiff and finally London, where he spent the greater part of his life working on the staff of *The News Chronicle* and, later, of *The Daily Telegraph*. He was only twenty-three years of age when he won his first *Crown at the *National Eisteddfod and he accomplished the remarkable feat of winning the prize in three successive years.

Although the three poems were composed for the purposes of competition, there is a strong autobiographical element in them. In the first, '*Y *Briodas*' (1927), a woman swears an oath of fidelity to her dead husband and gradually deteriorates into insanity. The poet's father had died when he was a few months old and one of the most bitter experiences of his life was having to commit his mother to a mental hospital. In the second poem, '*Penyd*' (1928), which is almost a sequel, the widow, by now in hospital, expresses her emotions in a series of lyrics. The third poem, '*Y Gân Ni Chanwyd*' (1929), does not follow the same theme but strikes the same note of hopelessness and suffering. The subject of his unsuccessful poem '*Terfysgoedd Daear*' (1939) is suicide and its composition, on the poet's own testimony, was a catharsis for him. He also won the *Chair at the National Eisteddfod for his awdl '*Llef Un yn Llefain*' (1962). The poetry of Caradog Prichard was published in the volumes *Canu Cynnar* (1937), *Tantalus* (1957) and *Llef Un yn Llefain* (1963); a collected edition of his work appeared in 1979.

Amongst his other works are an unusual and important novel, *Un Nos Ola Leuad* (1961), which is also a study of insanity, and a collection of short stories, *Y Genod yn ein Bywyd* (1964). His frank autobiography, *Afal Drwg Adda* (1973), is essential for a full understanding of this enigmatic author.

For critical discussion of Caradog Prichard's work see R. M. Jones, *Llenyddiaeth Gymraeg 1936–1972* (1975) and the article by Dafydd Glyn Jones in *Dyrnaid o Awduron Cyfoes* (ed. D. Ben Rees, 1975); see also the note by John Rowlands in *Profiles* (1980).

PRICHARD, CATHERINE (Buddug; 1842–1909), see under PRYSE, ROBERT JOHN (1807–89).

PRICHARD, EVAN (Ieuan Lleyn; 1769–1832), poet and schoolmaster of Bryncroes, Caerns., was the founder and editor of the literary magazine *Greal, neu Eurgrawn: sef Trysorfa Gwybodaeth* (1800). He composed a few hymns, among which '*Tosturi dwyfol fawr*' and '*Teg arnom wawriodd ddydd*' are still in vogue. His verse was edited by John *Jones (Myrddin Fardd) and published under the title *Caniadau Ieuan Lleyn* (1878).

PRICHARD, RHYS (Yr Hen Ficer; 1579–1644), clergyman and poet, was born at Llandovery, Carms. Very little is known of his early life and education, but he entered Jesus College, Oxford, in 1597. After ministering for a very short time in Essex, he obtained the living of Llandovery in 1602 and lived there until 1614, when he became chaplain to Robert, Earl of Essex. He became prebendary of Christ College, Brecon, and Chancellor and later Canon of St. David's. Puritanically inclined, he preached widely in west Wales (as was the custom of those bearing the Puritan message) but he drew back from rebelling against the King in 1642 and seems to have taken no part for either side in the *Civil War. In his will he provided for the establishment of a free school at Llandovery. Also concerned about the moral condition of his monoglot parishioners, *Yr Hen Ficer* ('The Old Vicar'), as he was commonly known, composed a large number of homely, didactic stanzas on the Christian life which were published by Stephen *Hughes in 1659, 1660 and 1672, and collected under the title *Canwyll y Cymru* in 1681. This volume came to occupy a place in the history of the common people equal to that of *Taith y Pererin*, the Welsh translation of Bunyan's *Pilgrim's Progress*. See also MAESYFELIN.

The verse of Rhys Prichard was edited by Owen M. Edwards in the series *Cyfres y Fil* (1908); for a discussion of his work see the studies by John Jenkins (1913) and D. Gwenallt Jones (1946) and the article by John Ballinger in *Y Cymmrodor* (vol. XIII, 1900).

PRICHARD, THOMAS JEFFERY LLEWELYN (1790–1862), writer, was born at Builth, Brecs. The circumstances of his upbringing are uncertain but, by his own account, he left Wales in his boyhood. He contributed to *The *Cambro-Briton in 1820, when it seems likely that he was living as an actor in London, and three years later he published by subscription a collection of naïve and mostly lamentable poems entitled *Welsh Minstrelsy* (1823). Having returned to Wales to sell his book, he probably settled for a time in Aberystwyth. In January 1826, however, he married Naomi James of Builth and for some years he lived in that town as a bookseller. It was at this time that he put together an anthology of poems by English writers on Welsh historical subjects, together with translations by Welsh writers from the work of such poets as *Taliesin, *Aneirin and *Dafydd ap Gwilym, and published them under the title *The Cambrian Wreath* (1828). The first and, in stylistic and narrative terms, the crudest version of his book *The Adventures and Vagaries of Twm Shon Catti, descriptive of Life in Wales* (1828) appeared two years later (see under Twm Shon Catti). The success and public recognition of this work, 'the first Welsh novel', encouraged him to revise and enlarge it, new editions coming out in 1839 and, posthumously, in 1873.

After 1839 he seems to have returned to the life of a strolling player, until he suffered the misfortune of having his nose cut off in a fencing accident. It is said that he later found employment at Llanover, cataloguing books in the library there for Benjamin and Augusta *Hall. He invested many years of research in *Heroines of Welsh History* (1854), an idiosyncratic view of characters and events, turgid and splenetic by turns, but this book failed to find a public. By this time he was living alone in Swansea. Reduced to penury, he was saved from destitution by the proceeds of a fund organized on his behalf by the newspaper, *The *Cambrian*, only to die shortly afterwards of burns received when he fell into his own fire.

For further details see the articles by Sam Adams in *The Anglo-Welsh Review* (vol. 24, no. 52, 1974) and in *Brycheiniog* (vol. XXI, 1985).

Prifardd Pendant, see ROBERTS, WILLIAM JOHN (1828–1904).

Principality of Wales, The, a term originally applied to the lands claimed by Edward I after he had defeated *Llywelyn ap Gruffudd of the House of *Gwynedd in 1282. In 1301 Edward gave these lands as a Principality to his son, afterwards King Edward II, and they were divided into two administrative units with centres at *Caernarfon and *Carmarthen. Throughout the two centuries following the territory was by custom an appanage granted to the eldest son of the English King. The Principality was thus only a part of Wales and did not include the Marcher lordships in the east and south of the country, but it survived as a fiscal unit in government until the later eighteenth century. The *Acts of Union of 1536 and 1542 removed the primary distinction between the Principality and the Marches (see PURA WALLIA) and after 1542 the expression 'Principality of Wales' was used in a much less precise way, the title of Prince of Wales coming to be applied to the whole country.

The motto of the Prince of Wales, '*Ich Dien*' (G. 'I serve'), is said to have been adopted by Edward the Black Prince, together with the three white ostrich feathers which form the Prince's insignia, after he had defeated King John of Bohemia at the battle of Poitiers in 1356. Tradition also has it that Edward I, having promised the Welsh a Prince who could speak no word of English, presented his infant son at Caernarfon castle in 1284 with the words, '*Eich dyn*' ('Your man'). Both these traditions are without foundation in historical fact and the second is almost certainly a misinterpretation of the first. It is more likely that the Black Prince

took the insignia because they belonged to the House of Hainault, of which his mother, Queen Philippa, was a member. Nevertheless, the motto and the feathers were displayed in the ceremonies of the *Ancient Britons in order to remind the Hanoverians that the Welsh were loyal, unlike the rebellious Irish and Scots. Adopted by the Honourable Society of *Cymmrodorion in 1751, the feathers were not displaced by the *Red Dragon until the twentieth century. The motto is now considered obsequious by Nationalists and Socialists in Wales but, with the ostrich plumes, it still adorns the badge of the Welsh Rugby Union.

The title of Prince of Wales has been conferred a total of twenty-one times but there have been only twelve formal investitures, ten of which were parliamentary occasions in London. The first investiture to be held in Wales was that of Albert Edward at Caernarfon castle in 1911, a picturesque ceremony devised by David *Lloyd George and A. G. Edwards, who later became Archbishop of Wales. It was this member of the royal family, destined to become King Edward VIII, who, during a visit to south Wales in November 1936, was so shocked by the plight of the unemployed at Dowlais, Merthyr Tydfil, that he was moved to utter the famous, if belated, remark, 'Something must be done. I will do all I can to assist you', thus raising hopes which were dashed by his abdication only a few weeks later.

The investiture of Charles, the eldest son of Queen Elizabeth II, again at Caernarfon, on 1 July 1969, was an occasion which was marked by popular festivities as well as by bitter controversy, much satire (as in the songs of Dafydd *Iwan) and vigorous protests by Nationalist groups such as the *Free Wales Army and *Cymdeithas yr Iaith Gymraeg, which saw in the symbolism of the event 'the grotesque celebration of the conquest of Wales'. *Plaid Cymru, on the other hand, refused to declare either its support or its opposition, preferring to concentrate on what it saw as more important issues. The general mood of the time, however, was deferential towards the institution of the monarchy and affectionate towards the person of the young Prince, especially after it had been announced that he was to spend a term as a student at the University College of Wales, Aberystwyth, where he would learn something of the language, literature and history of Wales. Unlike the politicians of Wales, many Welsh writers—in so far as they saw any political significance in the event at all—shared the view of the philosopher J. R. *Jones, who commented that the investiture of 1969 revealed the extent of the devastation which had been wrought on the Welsh people's sense of their national identity.

For further details see Francis Jones, *The Princes and Principality of Wales* (1969), Ralph A. Griffiths, *The Principality of Wales in the later Middle Ages* (1972) and

Wynford Vaughan-Thomas, *The Princes of Wales* (1982).

Printing and Publishing. The first book to be printed in Welsh, *Yn y lhyvyr hwnn by Sir John *Price of Brecon, was published in 1546, almost a century after the invention of printing. For the next hundred years, until 1660, the printing of books was confined to London, Oxford and Cambridge, and during this period only about a hundred books were published in the Welsh language. During the reign of Elizabeth I Catholics were forbidden the right to publish in England, which is why Morys *Clynnog had his *Athravaeth Gristnogawl* printed in Milan in 1568. For the same reason the first part of Robert *Gwyn's *Y Drych Cristionogawl* was produced on a secret press in a cave at Rhiwledyn, near Llandudno, Caerns, during the winter of 1586/87. There is also evidence of at least one other clandestine press operated by Catholics, at the home of Sion Dafydd *Rhys outside Brecon. In 1567 there appeared William *Salesbury's Welsh translation of the New Testament and the Book of Common Prayer, for which he and Bishop Richard *Davies were responsible, and William *Morgan's translation of the complete *Bible was published in 1588.

The law relating to the licensing of printing was relaxed in 1695 and, thus encouraged, Thomas *Jones (1648?–1713) moved his press from London to Shrewsbury. Equally successful as a book-distributor, Jones inaugurated a new era in the history of the Welsh book trade. About 1674, in order to provide religious literature for the common people, Thomas Gouge formed the *Welsh Trust, with the co-operation of Stephen *Hughes and Charles *Edwards. Later, in 1699, encouraged by Sir John Phillipps and Sir Humphrey *Mackworth, and with the support of Moses *Williams and Griffith *Jones, the *Society for Promoting Christian Knowledge extended its activities to Wales. The total number of Welsh books published between 1546 and 1660 was 108, but after the Restoration there was a significant increase to about 545 titles for the period from 1660 to 1729. The trade's main problems had to do with patronage and distribution. Scholars such as Moses Williams sought in vain for financial backing sufficient to enable them to publish old Welsh texts and when David *Jones of Trefriw was about to publish his anthology, *Blodeugerdd Cymry*, in 1759, he had to travel throughout Wales in order to collect subscriptions. Nevertheless, the success of Thomas Jones inspired others and for nearly seventy years the centre of the Welsh book trade was Shrewsbury and, to a lesser extent, other Border towns such as Chester, Oswestry, Hereford and Bristol. The first publishing press to be set up legally in Wales was that of Isaac *Carter, established first at Atpar, near Newcastle Emlyn, Cards., in 1718 and transferred seven

years later to Carmarthen where Nicholas Thomas had already opened a printing-office. Gradually, printing-offices were established in other market towns, but the standard of their craftsmanship was generally poor.

The growth of *Nonconformity during the nineteenth century, coupled with the success of the *Sunday School movement, created an enormous demand for books, periodicals and weekly newspapers in Welsh, so that the period from 1850 to 1890 may properly be considered as 'the golden age' of Welsh publishing. The *Industrial Revolution provided another important stimulus in that it brought substantial communities of monoglot but literate Welsh-speakers from rural areas to the valleys of Glamorgan and Monmouthshire, with the result that there appeared a steady flow of religious, historical, literary and musical works. The most prolific publisher of the century was Thomas *Gee but equally important was the firm of *Hughes a'i Fab* (see under HUGHES, RICHARD, 1794–1871); at the turn of the century a unique contribution was made by Owen M. *Edwards. The Welsh book trade was so buoyant during this period that it attracted some of the leading English and Scottish publishers of the day.

By the end of the nineteenth century, however, the number of titles published annually in Welsh had fallen to about a hundred and it was to remain at this level until about 1965. The only successful initiative in Welsh publishing during the years between the World Wars (notwithstanding the exceptional case of the *Gregynog Press) was that of E. Prosser *Rhys, whose Welsh Books Club was active between 1937 and 1952. Despite a shortage of paper and a dearth of popular reading material, several other commercial publishers made valiant efforts during the 1940s to bring out booklets in serial form, most notably *Llyfrau'r Dryw*. By 1950 the situation had become critical: the number of Welsh titles published in that year had fallen to about fifty. The Home Office was then persuaded to appoint a committee to examine the state of publishing in the Welsh language. Two years later, the Ready Report recommended that a Welsh Books Foundation be established and that it should derive its income partly from local government and partly from central government sources. Thus was initiated a system of Government subsidy for Welsh books which has continued on an increasing scale down to the present. In 1951 the Librarian for Cardiganshire, Alun R. Edwards, persuaded his council to spend £2,000 a year 'to encourage the writing, illustrating and publishing of Welsh books for children'. This scheme soon won the support of seven of the Welsh counties and in 1968 it was adopted by the *Welsh Joint Education Committee.

But the most important milestone in the history of the Welsh book trade since the second

World War was undoubtedly the creation of the *Welsh Books Council in 1961 and its subsequent development, mainly by means of grants from the *Welsh Arts Council, during the 1970s. Under the Books Council's supervision, the provision of public funds (notably those provided by the *Welsh Office) has rejuvenated a sector of Welsh culture which seemed to be in danger of collapse. The number of Welsh-language titles has increased steadily from 109 in 1963 to 364 in 1984—the largest number published in any minority language in western Europe with the exception of Catalan. Although produced in comparatively small print-runs (usually of about a thousand copies), Welsh books are now designed and printed to a higher standard, and published in greater variety, than ever before. The old problems to do with distribution and sales have not been entirely solved but the Books Council provides a reliable service which has no equivalent in England while, at the same time, it strives to stimulate publishers and booksellers to improve their resources and take initiatives of their own. Books produced by Welsh publishers in English, on the other hand, present even more difficult problems; they are fewer in number (perhaps a hundred titles a year), they receive no subsidy from public funds unless they are published with the financial support of the Welsh Arts Council, their sales in Wales generally compare unfavourably with the sales of books in Welsh and no commercial Welsh publisher has yet succeeded in reaching the English-language market outside Wales. The Books Council works in association with the Welsh Union of Publishers and Booksellers.

Further details will be found in Ifano Jones, *A History of Printing and Printers in Wales to 1810* (1925), R. Geraint Gruffydd, *Argraffwyr Cyntaf Cymru* (1972), Geraint H. Jenkins, *Literature, Religion and Society in Wales 1660–1730* (1978) and Alun R. Edwards, *Yr Hedyn Mwstard* (1980); see also the chapter by R. Gerallt Jones, 'The Welsh Writer and his Books' in *The Welsh Language Today* (ed. Meic Stephens, 1973), the report of the Council for Wales and Monmouthshire, *The Welsh Language Today* (1963), the report of the Council for the Welsh Language, *Publishing in the Welsh Language* (1978), the Annual Reports of the Welsh Books Council and occasional articles in the Books Council's trade-journal, *Llais Llyfrau/Book News from Wales*.

PRITCHARD, MARGED (1919–), novelist and short-story writer. Born at Tregaron, Cards., she was educated at the University College of North Wales, Bangor, and later taught French at schools in Tywyn and Porthmadog. She has published several novels and volumes of short stories which have a rural, or seaside, background, but with some emphasis on contemporary problems. They include *Cregyn ar y Traeth* (1974), *Gwylanod y Mynydd* (1975), *Cysgodion ar yr Haul* (1977), *Breuddwydion* (1978) and *Enfys y Bore* (1980). Her novel, *Nid Mudan Mo'r Môr* (1976), won the *Prose Medal at the

*National Eisteddfod in the year of its publication. In *Portreadau'r Faner* (1976) she published a series of profiles of contemporary Welsh writers which first appeared in *Baner ac Amserau Cymru*.

Private Adventure Schools, in early nineteenth-century Wales, were run by individuals, mostly unqualified, as a way of earning their living. Some of these men were remarkable for their good work: James Davies (1765–1829), for example, a former weaver and pedlar, was respected as the schoolmaster of Devauden, Mon., because he kept a schoolhouse there during the years from 1815 to 1848, devoting himself to the religious and educational welfare of the district. But many were incompetent and this type was depicted in Daniel *Owen's novel *Rhys Lewis* (1885) in the character of the peg-legged scoundrel, Robyn y Sowldiwr.

Propagation of the Gospel in Wales, The Act for the (1650), delegated the religious authority of Cromwell's government in Wales to Colonel Thomas Harrison and seventy other Commissioners, among whom the most prominent Welshmen were Colonel Philip *Jones of Llangyfelach, Colonel John *Jones and Sir Erasmus *Philipps of Picton. Their task was to examine ministers of religion and, if they deemed it necessary, to eject them from their livings. The reasons for dismissal included pluralism, inability to preach in Welsh, use of the Book of Common Prayer and scandal in private life. By the time the Act lapsed in 1653 a total of 278 incumbents had been dismissed in this way. The Act also nominated twenty-five Approvers to appoint successors to the ejected ministers and among these 'godly and painful men' were Oliver Thomas, Walter *Cradock, Jenkin *Jones, John *Miles, Morgan *Llwyd and Vavasor *Powell. By the terms of the Act free schools were to be provided for both sexes and in Wales about sixty such schools were established in predominantly Puritan areas.

Prophetiae Merlini (lit. 'The prophecies of Merlin'), the title of the seventh chapter of *Geoffrey of Monmouth's *Historia Regum Britanniae*, contains the prophecies of the boy *Myrddin (Merlin) before King *Vortigern. It is believed that Geoffrey published them as an independent work a year or two before the remainder of the *Historia* appeared. At the beginning of the chapter he claims that Alexander, Bishop of Lincoln, had urged him to publish the prophecies and, in a letter presenting them to the Bishop, he refers to them as a translation from Welsh into Latin. They can hardly be associated with any known early Welsh *vaticinations, but it must be inferred that Geoffrey had some acquaintance with the nature of the Welsh prophetic tradition and that he used it as a pattern for his own purposes. The *Prophetiae* open by referring to the contest between the Red Dragon and the White Dragon before Vortigern (see under EMRYS WLEDIG) and then the coming of *Arthur, called '*Baedd Cernyw*' ('The Boar of Cornwall'), who will free the Britons from their Saxon oppressors, is prophesied; there follow references to events between Arthur's time and the Norman period. The prophecies become more open to various interpretations as the chapter progresses until they reach a point where they depend completely on animal symbolism and astrological references.

For further details see the chapter by J. J. Parry and R. A. Caldwell in R. S. Loomis (ed.), *Arthurian Literature in the Middle Ages* (1959), Lewis Thorpe, *Geoffrey of Monmouth: The History of the Kings of Britain* (1966) and the same author's article in the *Bibliographical Bulletin of the International Arthurian Society* (1977); see also the articles by Brynley F. Roberts in the *Journal of the National Library of Wales* (Summer, 1977) and by Bernard Meehan in the *Bulletin* of the Board of Celtic Studies (1978).

Prose Medal, The, one of the principal prizes at the *National Eisteddfod since 1937, is awarded for a *novel, a volume of *short stories or *essays or any other writing in the prose genres which are set for the purposes of the competition. Among the winners have been John Gwilym *Jones (1939), Islwyn Ffowc *Elis (1951), Eigra Lewis *Roberts (1968), Dafydd *Rowlands (1972), Dafydd *Ifans (1974), Marged *Pritchard (1976) and R. Gerallt *Jones (1977). The Medal, presented to the winner in a ceremony held during the Eisteddfod, is accompanied by a monetary award (£300 in 1985) and is generally regarded as being equal in prestige to the *Chair and *Crown for poetry.

Prostrate Chieftains of the Isle of Britain, Three, a Triad which names Llywarch Hen ab Elidir Llydanwen, Manawydan ap Llŷr Llediaith and Gwgon Gwron ap Peredur ab Elidir Gosgorddfawr. All were men who did not uphold their hereditary claims to territory. In *Pedair Cainc y Mabinogi *Pryderi quotes the Triad to *Manawydan in admonition of him.

Protestantism, the kind of Christian dogma and practice which sprang from the Reformation associated with the work of Luther, Zwingli, Calvin and others. The word comes from the *Protestatio* made by the Lutherans in the Diet of the Holy Roman Empire held at Speier in 1529. Although it means primarily 'declaration', the word carries with it an element of 'protest' against the policy of those who sought to check the spread of the Reformation. It has mostly been used as the opposite of *Roman Catholicism, but sometimes in a way which would exclude the Anabaptists and other sectarian Puritans and which appears to emphasize the necessity of State establishment in religion.

Among the basic principles of Protestantism are God's sovereign grace, justification by faith, the priesthood of all believers and the authority of the Bible as God's Word, but some would claim that Protestantism has also promoted the right of private judgement and has led to a proliferation of sects and theological movements. In *Anglicanism today there is a 'Protestant' party which is opposed to Anglo-Catholic tendencies.

Protestantism was not at first accepted in Wales with any great enthusiasm, but in ignorance and indifference the Welsh shortly came to submit to the established Church of England. The superficiality of the conversion is perhaps best exemplified by the fact that in the reign of Catholic Mary Wales produced only three Protestant martyrs, one of them Bishop Robert *Ferrar himself. The Protestant settlement under Elizabeth, though slow to be accepted, was greatly helped by the translation of the *Bible and *Prayer Book into Welsh (1586) and, at a higher intellectual level, by the 'Protestant theory' of the nature of the primitive Welsh Church advanced by William *Salesbury, Richard *Davies and Humphrey *Llwyd. Before long, *Puritanism, a more extreme form of Protestantism, had claimed its first Welsh martyr in John *Penry. Among Welsh translators who promoted Protestantism as upheld by the Established Church in the sixteenth and seventeenth centuries were Morris *Kyffin, Hugh *Lewis, Edward *James, Rowland *Vaughan of Caer-gai (who translated Lewis *Bayly) and John *Davies of Mallwyd. Types of Protestantism—Anglicanism, Puritanism, *Independency, *Methodism and other movements—have played important parts in the religious and social life of Wales. Protestant prejudices long hindered a just appreciation of the Welsh literature of the Middle Ages.

In the twentieth century many Welsh people have turned to secularism and humanism and a small but influential minority to Roman or Anglican Catholicism. The old Protestant patterns of thought have become more and more unfashionable in intellectual circles, although Protestantism has been more open than Roman Catholicism to theological *Liberalism. Some have sought to rebuild Protestantism on a Fundamentalist basis. A Protestant emphasis in the novels of Emyr *Humphreys has been contrasted with the Catholic emphasis of Graham Greene, while Saunders *Lewis has suggested that Pennar *Davies offers a new opportunity for Protestantism in Man's present predicament.

Further details will be found in S. O. Tudor, *Protestaniaeth* (1940), J. S. Whale, *The Protestant Tradition* (1955) and Glanmor Williams, *Welsh Reformation Essays* (1967).

Protheroe, Daniel (1866–1934), musician. Born at Ystradgynlais, Brecs., he emigrated to Scranton, Pennsylvania, in 1885 and there won fame as a conductor of choirs. A frequent visitor to the *National Eisteddfod, he composed numerous hymn-tunes, including 'Jesu, Lover of my soul', and an arrangement of *Bryn Calfaria entitled 'Laudamus', both of which are still popular.

Proverb, a short traditional saying which embodies a common belief or truism. Since the period of the *Cynfeirdd Welsh poets have coined proverbs or included familiar ones in their work. In some medieval manuscripts such as The *Red Book of Hergest are found collections of proverbs associated with the name of the Hen Cyrys (or Bach Buddugre) of Yale (12th cent.), about whom nothing is known. Several Renaissance scholars took an interest in the genre. *Gruffudd Hiraethog made a collection which William *Salesbury published under the title *Oll Synnwyr Pen Kembero Ygyd (1547) and Thomas *Wiliems of Trefriw collected more than three thousand proverbs, following the example of Erasmus. At the close of the eighteenth century Iolo Morganwg (Edward *Williams) fabricated hundreds of sayings which resembled proverbs and passed them on to Owain Myfyr (Owen *Jones) for inclusion in The Myvyrian Archaiology (1801). The practice of collecting proverbs continued throughout the nineteenth century and persists to the present day.

One of the most valuable collections is Gemmau Doethineb (1714) by Rhys Prydderch (c.1620–99) and among the best modern collections are those made by William Hay (1955) and J. J. Evans (1965); for discussion of the form see the article by R. M. Jones in Y Traethodydd (Oct., 1976).

Pryddest, a long poem not written in a set metrical pattern, may be in blank verse or in *cynghanedd, but not in one of the traditional *Twenty-four Metres. The earliest form of the word (the root of which is 'prydu', 'to compose verse'), is found in the Dictionary published by John *Davies of Mallwyd in 1632. Although William *Williams (Pantycelyn) composed long poems in free forms, they were not called pryddestau. But William *Williams (Caledfryn) in his Drych Barddonol (1839) alludes to long poems, 'heb un odl, ac eraill yn odli heb gynghanedd' ('without a single rhyme, and others rhyming without cynghanedd') as pryddestau, adding that there was much opposition to poems of this kind from those who worshipped the strict metres, while Gutyn Peris (Griffith *Williams) used the word pryddestau for his long poems in blank verse. By 1834 the term pryddest had become acceptable in eisteddfodic circles: at the Eisteddfod held in Cardiff in that year a competition called for a pryddest diodl ('without rhyme') which would take the form of an elegy for Archdeacon Beynon, and in the Eisteddfod held by the *Cymreigyddion Society in London in 1841 a prize was offered for a pryddest on *Temperance. At the Rhuddlan Eisteddfod of 1850 the pryddest composed by Ieuan Glan Geirionydd (Evan *Evans) was awarded the first prize, while an *awdl by Caledfryn was placed second. It was at the Ruthin Eisteddfod of 1860 that the custom of awarding a *Crown for a pryddest and a *Chair for an awdl was introduced, a tradition which has continued, with some amendment, to the present day. Some of the pryddestau awarded the Crown are among the finest long poems written in Welsh during the twentieth century; they include *'Mab y Bwthyn' (1921) and 'Y *Dyrfa' (1931) by Cynan (Albert *Evans-Jones) and 'Y *Briodas' (1927) by Caradog *Prichard.

A selection of prize-winning poems in this form, together with a useful introduction, will be found in Pryddestau Eisteddfodol Detholedig (ed. E. G. Millward, 1973).

Pryderi, the only character mentioned by name in all Four Branches of *Pedair Cainc y Mabinogi, may have been the central character in the original form of that work. He is not one of the most important characters in any of the Four Branches as they have come down, but he has an essential part in the development of some of the stories.

In the First Branch he is born to *Pwyll and *Rhiannon but he disappears immediately after his birth and is taken by some mysterious power to the court of *Teyrnon Twrf Liant, where he is named Gwri Wallt Eurin ('Gwri Golden Hair') and nurtured for four years. He is as strong at two years as a boy of six and at four he begins to attend to the horses. But when Teyrnon and his wife understand that Gwri is the boy who was lost from the court of *Dyfed, they take him back to his parents. Henceforth he is called Pryderi from the words spoken by Rhiannon when she hears that her son has been restored to her: 'Oedd esgor fy mhryder im, pe gwir hynny!' ('I should be delivered of my anxiety if that were true!'). In Dyfed Pryderi is raised with care until he is 'the most gallant youth and the handsomest and the best skilled in every good pursuit' in the kingdom, and in time he succeeds to the throne. Before long he adds the three cantrefi of *Ystrad Tywi and the four hundreds of *Ceredigion to the seven of Dyfed, and he takes a wife, Cigfa, the daughter of Gwyn Gohoyw.

In the Second Branch, Pryderi is mentioned as the first of the seven who return from the expedition led by *Brân (Bendigeidfran) to Ireland and with *Manawydan he appears at the beginning of the Third Branch. The two return to Dyfed and there Pryderi gives his mother, Rhiannon, in marriage to Manawydan. After paying homage to Caswallon in Oxford, he is next seen, in the middle of a feast, ascending Gorsedd *Arberth with the other three, Manawydan, Rhiannon and Cigfa. A magical mist then descends upon Dyfed and turns the land barren. The four go to England, maintaining themselves by various crafts until the local craftsmen drive them out and they return to Dyfed. There Pryderi and

Rhiannon are imprisoned in a magical fort which disappears with both of them inside, but they are eventually rescued from their prison in *Annwfn by Manawydan.

The Fourth Branch contains a short, complete tale about the way in which Pryderi is killed. He is tricked by *Gwydion, the magician, into leaving the pigs he has received as a present from *Arawn, the King of Annwfn, in exchange for horses and hunting dogs which prove to be illusory. When he sees that Gwydion has tricked him thus, he pursues the magician to Gwynedd and challenges him to fight. In the ensuing battle Pryderi is killed. The emphasis in this story is on the valour of Pryderi: he can be defeated only by means of magic.

There is now a consensus among scholars that the story of Pryderi was the basic theme around which the Four Branches were constructed—his conception, his disappearance, his feats and his death—and that to the stories which related these events were added tales about the children of *Llŷr and *Dôn, which tended in due course to displace Pryderi from the mainstream of the story.

There is further discussion by W. J. Gruffydd in *Math Vab Mathonwy* (1928) and *Rhiannon* (1953) and by Ifor Williams in *Pedeir Keinc y Mabinogi* (1951).

Prydwen, the ship of King *Arthur. In the poem *'Preiddiau Annwfn'* it is stated that 'three (ship) loads of Prydwen' sailed to Caer Sidi and in the tale of *Culhwch and Olwen there are three references to Arthur's voyages in the ship. But in *Geoffrey of Monmouth's *Historia Regum Britanniae*, Arthur's sword is called Prydwen and the image of the Virgin Mary is said to be emblazoned thereon.

PRYDYDD BYCHAN, Y (*fl.* 1220–70), poet, was probably the Gwilym named by *Gwilym Ddu o Arfon, together with *Phylip Brydydd, as one of two poets from *Ceredigion. The twenty series of *englynion* by him which are extant are addressed mostly to minor princes (but including *Rhys Gryg and *Owain Goch ap Gruffudd) from south-west Wales, among them the descendants of *Rhys ap Gruffudd (The Lord Rhys). All his references to the English are disparaging. In an elegiac *englyn* to Owain ap Gruffudd (d. 1236) he summed up the relationship between patron and poet in a single line, '*Fy llyw oedd fur glyw a gwledd*' ('My leader was a wall of protection to heroes and feastings').

Prydydd y Moch, see LLYWARCH AP LLYWELYN (*fl.* 1173–1220).

PRYS, EDMUND (1543/4–1623), poet and humanist, was a native of Llanrwst, Denbs., and a kinsman of William *Salesbury. Like William *Morgan, the translator of the *Bible into Welsh, he may have received tuition at the *Wynne mansion of Gwydir and in 1565, with Morgan, he entered St. John's College, Cambridge, where one of the Wynnes had been a Fellow. At Cambridge, where he was elected Fellow of his College in 1570 and University Preacher about five years later, he learned eight languages, including Hebrew, which he studied under the renowned French Hebraist, Antoine Chevallier. Intent on an ecclesiastical career, he was appointed rector of Ffestiniog and Maentwrog, Mer., in 1573, and rector of Ludlow and archdeacon of Merioneth in 1576, but he probably continued to reside mainly at Cambridge until 1577. After resigning from his Ludlow living in 1579, he lived wholly at Y Tyddyn Du in Maentwrog, obtaining the additional living of Llanenddwyn and Llanddwywe in 1580. Prys combined his ecclesiastical duties with the life of a minor country gentleman, acquiring land in Ffestiniog and Maentwrog (which led to allegations against him in the Court of Star Chamber) and serving as a Justice of the Peace. He married twice and two of his sons, John and Foulk, also wrote poetry.

A prolific poet, Prys composed in both the strict and the free metres and some sixty-five *cywyddau*, two *awdlau* and more than a hundred of his *englynion* have survived. His *englynion* include a number written in Latin and he also wrote a poem in Latin hexameters which prefaced the Grammar (1621) of John *Davies of Mallwyd. Two-thirds of his *cywyddau* are poems belonging to his famous debate with Wiliam *Cynwal, in which he urged Welsh poets to adopt humanistic standards (see under BARDIC CONTROVERSY). He also debated with Siôn Phylip (see under PHYLIP FAMILY), Huw Machno and Tomos *Prys of Plas Iolyn, and wrote *cywyddau* and *awdlau* on religious and moral themes. Among his liveliest secular poems are a *cywydd* describing a game of football in Cambridge, a *cywydd* addressed to *Siôn Tudur begging the gift of a bardic grammar and a collection of bardic prognostications, a *cywydd* of thanks for the gift of a gun-barrel at the time of the Armada, and a famous allegorical *cywydd* on 'The Misrule of the Mighty' which was inspired by the controversy over the Forest of Snowdonia during the 1590s. He composed three elegiac *cywyddau*, for Wiliam Cynwal at the end of their debate, for Richard Vaughan, Bishop of London, his contemporary at Cambridge, and for Siôn Phylip, his closest companion among the poets of Ardudwy. As well as his poems in the traditional strict metres, Prys composed a ballad about Spring in the metre of the English song 'About the Bank of Helicon', one of the earliest examples of tune-metre *cynghanedd* poetry. Despite his extensive poetry in the strict metres Prys is chiefly remembered for his metrical Psalms, published as an appendix to the Welsh Book of Common Prayer (1621). These psalms, known in Welsh as *'Salmau Cân', were virtually the only hymnal used in Wales until the eighteenth century and they still have a place in some churches.

Edmund Prys was a unique figure among Welsh poets of his period, being steeped in both the humanistic learning of the Renaissance and the traditional culture of his native land. Much of his work, especially his metrical Psalms and his debate with Cynwal, reflects the values of contemporary Protestant humanism. Apart from his general learning, he wrote copious Welsh and technically he was the equal of any professional poet among his contemporaries, especially in the combination of intellectual energy and verbal felicity found in his work.

For further details see A. Owen Evans, *The Life and Work of Edmund Prys* (1923) and the articles by Gruffydd Aled Williams in the *Transactions* of the Denbighshire Historical Society (vol. XXIII, 1974), the *Journal* of the Merioneth Historical and Records Society (vol. VIII, 1980) and the *Journal* of the National Library of Wales (vol. XXII, 1982).

Prys, Elis (Y Doctor Coch; 1512?–94?), of Plas Iolyn, Ysbyty Ifan, Denbs., was educated at the University of Cambridge and was known as '*Y Doctor Coch*' ('The Red Doctor') from the colour of his gown. In 1535 Cromwell appointed him as one of the visitors of monasteries in Wales, in arranging for the dissolution of which Prys showed exceptional zeal. During the reigns of Mary and Elizabeth he was engaged in civil administration, as Member of Parliament for Merioneth and as Sheriff of Merioneth, Denbighshire, Anglesey and Caernarfonshire, and as a member of the Council of the Marches. A friend of Robert Dudley, he was described by Thomas *Pennant as 'a creature of the Earl of Leicester and devoted to all his bad designs', but allowance should be made for Pennant's prejudice against him. Prys, as a patron of Welsh poets, was associated with the *Caerwys Eisteddfod of 1567 and Tomos *Prys was his son.

PRYS, TOMOS (*c*.1564–1634), poet and soldier, was the son of Elis *Prys of Plas Iolyn, Denbs. He went to Flanders as a soldier in 1585 and afterwards took part in the campaigns in Germany, France, Spain and Scotland. At Tilbury as one of the defenders against the Armada in 1588, he also fought in Ireland in 1594, but after his father's death in 1596 he settled at Plas Iolyn. He later became a pirate off the coasts of Spain and Ireland. With William *Midleton, he was reputed to have been the first to smoke tobacco in public in London.

A friend of several poets such as Rhys Wyn (*fl.* 1600), *Rhys Cain, Edward Prys and Edmund *Prys, he composed many conventional poems, *cywyddau* of request, thanks, praise and dispute. Some of his elegies, such as those to his young sons and to Pyrs Gruffudd, are among his best poems. But he also composed verse on new themes springing from the venturesome society in which he lived, referring to his experiences as a soldier, sailor and pirate, and to his extravagant losses by litigation. He was fond of joking and satire, intermingling the classical language of the Welsh poets with English naval slang, as in his poem describing a battle at sea. Although not in the front rank of the Welsh poets of his age, Tomos Prys was certainly one of the most amusing and original.

There is an account of his life and work by William Rowland in the *St. David's Day* series (1964); see also the article by Enid P. Roberts in the *Transactions* of the Denbighshire Historical Society (vol. XIII, 1964).

PRYSE, ROBERT JOHN (Gweirydd ap Rhys; 1807–89), writer and historian, was born at Llanbadrig, Ang. Orphaned by the age of eleven, he had only four days' schooling but later learned to read and write Welsh while working as a farm labourer. From 1828 to 1857 he kept a shop in Llanrhuddlad, Ang., producing very fine work as a weaver and continuing to educate himself by learning Latin, Greek and English. In 1857 he moved to Denbigh in order to work on *Y *Gwyddoniadur Cymreig*, to which he made a substantial contribution, and on *Y Geiriadur Cynraniadol*. About five years later he moved again, this time to Bangor and in the hope of earning his living as a journalist, but the newspaper which he edited, *Papur y Cymry*, soon ceased publication.

He suffered great poverty for a while but, in 1870, advance payment for his *Hanes y Brytaniaid a'r Cymry* (1872–74) helped to improve his circumstances and he later obtained a Civil List pension. At the Eisteddfod held in Cardiff in 1883 he won prizes for his *Hanes Llenyddiaeth Gymreig, 1300–1650* (1885) and for an essay on Welsh *proverbs. He also prepared editions of *The Myvyrian Archaiology* (1870) and the Welsh Bible (1876). Acknowledged in his day as an authority on the Welsh language and its literature, he was an industrious writer whose work is still valuable for the independence of its judgement. The poets **Golyddan (John Robert Pryse**, 1840–62) and **Buddug (Catherine Prichard**, 1842–1909) were his children.

For further details see the extracts from the diary of Gweirydd ap Rhys edited by Enid P. Roberts (1949); see also *Y Traethodydd* (1947).

PRYS-JONES, ARTHUR GLYN (1888–), poet. He was born at Denbigh, but his family moved to Pontypridd, Glam., when he was nine years old. Educated at Llandovery College and Jesus College, Oxford, he began his career as a teacher of History and English at Macclesfield and Walsall Grammar Schools, and at Dulwich College, London, before becoming one of His Majesty's Inspectors of Schools in west Wales and Glamorgan. In 1919 he was appointed Staff Inspector for Secondary Education in Wales. During his long residence in Cardiff he was among the founders of the Little Theatre and served as Secretary of the Welsh Committee of the Festival of Britain in 1951.

Besides editing the first anthology of Anglo-Welsh poetry, *Welsh Poets (1917), A. G. Prys-Jones has published six volumes of his own verse: Poems of Wales (1923), Green Places (1948), A Little Nonsense (1954), High Heritage (1969), Valedictory Verses (1978) and More Nonsense (1984). For the most part, his poems are on patriotic themes and concerned with the history and landscape of Wales: he may be regarded as the first Anglo-Welsh poet of the twentieth century for whom the Welsh nation was consistently a source of pride and inspiration. Usually intended to be read aloud or sung by young people, his poems are written in the simpler metrical and alliterative styles of Welsh lyrical poetry. He is among the few Anglo-Welsh poets to have excelled at writing funny poems. Among his other books are Gerald of Wales (1955) and The Story of Carmarthenshire (2 vols., 1959, 1972); he was also the literary editor of The National Songs of Wales (1959). A resident of Kingston-upon-Thames for the last years of his life, A. G. Prys-Jones is the doyen of Anglo-Welsh writers and was elected President of the English-language section of Yr *Academi Gymreig in 1970.

PRYSE, JOHN ROBERT (Golyddan; 1840-62), see under PRYSE, ROBERT JOHN (1807-89).

**PUDDICOMBE, ANNE ADALIZA BEYNON (Allen Raine; 1836-1908), romantic novelist, was born at Newcastle Emlyn, Cards., the eldest child of a solicitor named Evans. She was sent at the age of thirteen, with her sister, to live in Cheltenham and Wandsworth with the family of a Mr. Solly, Unitarian minister and friend of Charles Dickens. In 1856 she returned to Wales, living in Newcastle Emlyn and the coastal village of Tresaith until 1872 when she married Beynon Puddicombe, a banker, with whom she settled in London. After her husband had suffered a mental breakdown in 1900 they moved back to Tresaith and it was there that they both died.

Having won a prize at the *National Eisteddfod of 1894 for a story depicting Welsh life, she published her first novel, A Welsh Singer (1896), and during the next twelve years she produced another ten, the best of which are Torn Sails (1898), By Berwen Banks (1899), On the Wings of the Wind (1903) and Hearts of Wales (1905), as well as a volume of short stories, All in a Month (1908). Her novels are all set, at least partly, in small coastal villages in west Wales and her principal characters are usually the ordinary people of these districts, though they make occasional journeys to Glamorgan or London. The books are romances, developed with a narrative skill which made their author one of the four most popular best-sellers of her day. The plots

may be love-stories, with all the standard attributes of the genre, but they have an unusual depth of character and feeling, and the social background against which they are set is drawn with understanding and humour. Her early novels tend towards the melodramatic but she later proved herself capable of handling such difficult themes as social pretensions in Garthowen (1900) and A Welsh Witch (1902), and the effects of religious fervour in Queen of the Rushes (1906). Although more sophisticated and more charitable than Caradoc Evans (David *Evans), she was nearer in her attitude to Welsh life to the bleak conclusions of *My People (1915) than to the golden age of *How Green Was My Valley (1939) and her work was not without influence on later Anglo-Welsh writers, including Emlyn *Williams.

An essay by Sally Roberts Jones on the life and work of Allen Raine is included in the Writers of Wales series (1979).

**PUGH, EDWARD (c. 1761-1813), painter and topographical writer, was born at Ruthin, Denbs. He exhibited twenty-three pictures, including a portrait of Twm o'r Nant (Thomas *Edwards), at the Royal Academy between 1793 and 1808, while probably working mainly in London, though his address in 1800 was Chester. He illustrated Modern London (1805) but his chief work was his own Cambria Depicta: a Tour through North Wales (1816), an account accompanied by seventy of his own engraved drawings of outstanding vitality and variety. In his vigorous, discursive narrative of a journey from Chester to Shrewsbury, he exploits nine years (1804-13) of travel on foot over his native country and his intimacy with its language, people and customs. His literary concern, however, was predominantly with painting and painters. Like many an English author, he supports topographical description with quotations from poetry and also corrects his predecessors, chiefly Thomas *Pennant and Warner, as when, for example, he disagrees with the latter's view that Gray in The Bard (1757) inaccurately described the river Conwy as 'foaming'.

**PUGH, SHEENAGH (1950-), poet, was born in Birmingham and educated at Bristol University; she moved to Wales in 1971. Her three volumes of verse are Crowded by Shadows (1977), What a Place to Grow Flowers (1980) and Earth Studies and Other Voyages (1983). Her work derives much of its subject-matter from history, mythology and the author's own travels, particularly to Iceland, and employs a wide range of mainly traditional forms with economy and discipline. She has also published a volume of verse translations from the French and German, Prisoners of Transience (1985).

PUGHE, WILLIAM OWEN, see OWEN PUGHE, WILLIAM (1759-1835).

Puleston family, see under EMRAL.

Pum Breuddwyd Gwenddydd (lit. 'The five dreams of Gwenddydd'), a series of dreams in conversation form, found in *The *Red Book of Hergest*. Gwenddydd describes her dreams and *Myrddin (Merlin) interprets them and comforts her. The content is remarkably similar to that of the visions of Piers Plowman by William Langland and to the ideas expressed in *Iolo Goch's poem, '*Cywydd y Llafurwr*'.

Pura Wallia (lit. 'Wales proper'), a term which was used during the Middle Ages to denote the north and west of the country as distinct from the semi-feudal, Normanized, Marcher lordships in south and east Wales. The distinction was swept away by the *Acts of Union (1536–42) when the whole of Wales came under English law and the legal and administrative distinctions disappeared. The expression was revived by Welsh geographers in the twentieth century who found it a useful term to distinguish the areas of north and west Wales where Welsh is still the language of the majority from those areas, mostly in the south and east, which are more susceptible to English influences.

Puritanism, a religious attitude, increasingly held during the reigns of Elizabeth I, James I and Charles I, which sought to purify the Church of England from all that savoured of *Roman Catholicism, to promote evangelical preaching and a life of moral and religious dedication and even to reform the organization of the Church on the foundation of the New Testament. It found varied expression at the time of the Puritan Commonwealth and the Cromwellian Protectorate and continued to influence *Nonconformity after 1662. Some would distinguish between Puritans who sought to purify the Church from within and Separatists who worshipped outside the Establishment, but it is customary to use the word Puritanism to include almost all the movements which defied Anglican uniformity. The term Puritan is often used in the present to imply a repressive attitude to the pleasures of life and the appreciation of beauty, but such a charge cannot be brought against all aspects of historical Puritanism.

There were Puritan tendencies in some of those who sought to further the Protestant cause in Wales under Elizabeth I, such as Richard *Davies. John *Penry's Puritanism was much more daring and he became a Separatist before the end of his short life. In the seventeenth century the most prominent Welsh Puritans, Walter *Cradock, William *Erbery, Vavasor *Powell and Morgan *Llwyd, who are grouped with the Independents (although Llwyd was a mystic, Erbery an unclassifiable Seeker and Powell a free Baptist), were more radical in theology or politics than most, whereas others

such as Philip Henry and Christopher Love had Presbyterian tendencies. It was *Quakerism which, in Wales, reaped the harvest sown by the radicals. Others, however, such as Charles *Edwards and Stephen *Hughes, are sometimes called 'later Puritans', and not without good reason; their work can be regarded as similar in its aims to that of the Pietists in Germany.

Further details will be found in Thomas Richards, *The Puritan Movement in Wales* (1920), G. F. Nuttall, *The Holy Spirit in Puritan Faith and Experience* (1946) and Owen C. Watkins, *The Puritan Experience* (1972); see also R. Geraint Gruffydd, *In that Gentile Country* (1976) and Noel H. Gibbard, *Elusen i'r Enaid* (1979).

PUW, GWILYM (*c*.1618–*c*.1689), poet, of Penrhyn Creuddyn, Caerns. A captain in the army of Charles I, he later entered the Benedictine Order at St. Edmund's, Paris, after several years of wandering on the Continent. He spent seven years at the college of Valladolid (1670–77) before returning to Wales, where he found refuge in the Catholic house of Blackbrook, Mon. In the two manuscripts of his which have survived and which can be dated 1674 and 1676, there are a number of Catholic poems in the strict and free metres, as well as Welsh versions of *Sallwyr Iesu* and *Littaniav Evraid*. He also composed a Welsh and Latin catechism for children, *Eglvrhad Helaeth-lawn* (1681).

Puw, Huw (1663–1743), athlete, born in the parish of Tal-y-llyn, Mer., was by calling a priest but he became famous as a jumper, wrestler and hurler of stones. Many stories are told of his feats: it is said, for example, that he leaped over the heads of his parents one Sunday morning as they walked to church, causing his mother to die of fright. A monument to Puw, who was educated at Jesus College, Oxford, was erected at the Ashmolean Museum and verses were composed about him in Latin, Welsh and English.

Pwll Melyn, The Battle of (1405), see under DAFYDD GAM (d. 1415).

Pwnco, a custom associated with weddings, was especially popular in west Wales. The bridegroom would send a party of 'seek-outs' to escort the bride from her home to the church. The group was obliged to compete in impromptu verse at the bride's door before gaining admittance, her family replying to each verse with various excuses for refusing entry. As in the ceremonies associated with the *Mari Lwyd, both sides would secure the services of local poets to compete on their behalf. Once inside, the 'seek-outs' had to search for the bride throughout the house until her hiding-place was discovered. Known in some districts as the Quintain, the custom was based on the traditional practice of placing ritual obstacles in the bridegroom's way, in pretence of opposing the marriage, vestiges of which can still be observed at weddings of the present day.

For further accounts see Trefor M. Owen, *Welsh Folk Customs* (1959) and Rhiannon Ifans, *Sêrs a Rybana* (1983).

Pwyll, Prince of Dyfed, the main character in the First Branch of *Pedair Cainc y Mabinogi*, returns to Dyfed after spending a year as King of *Annwfn in place of *Arawn, whose appearance he has assumed. He marries *Rhiannon and a son is born to them, but the child disappears immediately after his birth and Rhiannon is falsely accused of infanticide. Although Pwyll is urged to divorce his wife, he refuses to do so but is content for her to suffer penance. The child is later restored to his parents by *Teyrnon Twrf Liant and named *Pryderi. Pwyll continues to rule over Dyfed and is succeeded, in the fullness of time, by his son.

At the end of the introductory section of the tale, Pwyll is given the title '*Pen Annwfn*' ('Head of Annwfn'), from which it is supposed that in the original form of the story he was the King of Annwfn. In the early poem *'*Preiddiau Annwfn*' there is a reference to the '*ebostol*' ('story') of Pwyll and Pryderi, which was probably the name of that original form. But if Pwyll was a character whose origins lay in the myths behind the *Mabinogi*, he is portrayed as a fallible human being by the author of the First Branch: faithful, dependable but occasionally foolish, he is subservient to the will of his domineering wife at the most critical moment in the narrative.

Further details about Pwyll will be found in Ifor Williams, *Pedeir Keinc y Mabinogi* (1930), W. J. Gruffydd, *Rhiannon* (1953), R. L. Thomson, *Pwyll Pendevic Dyvet* (1956) and the article by Saunders Lewis in *Meistri'r Canrifoedd* (1973).

Pŷr (6th cent.), abbot. The island of Caldey, off the south-west coast of Wales, was first named after *Illtud but it later became known as Ynys Bŷr. The abbot is reputed to have died after falling, while drunk, into a well. Samson, elected abbot in his place, found the young monks were ungovernable, because Pŷr's rule had been so lax, and he resigned the abbacy in disgust. The castle of Manorbier, near Pembroke, called Maenor Bŷr in Welsh, was the birthplace of *Gerald de Barri (Giraldus Cambrensis) who described it as 'the pleasantest spot in Wales'.

Q

Quakerism, a term applied to the beliefs and practices of the Quakers, also known as the Religious Society of Friends. The nickname Quakers was given to them either because they trembled in worship or bade others tremble before God. The movement was founded in England by George Fox who began to preach in 1647, but it was largely a product of the Anti-nomianism which sprang from Reformation emphases on justification by faith and the inner testimony of the Spirit. The Inner Light, which for the Quakers was the indispensable authority, meant spiritual illumination, for which reason the early Quakers were known as 'The Children of the Light' and 'The Friends of Truth'. Their belief involved a rejection of externals in worship and by this they meant sacred buildings, liturgies, ordained ministries and even the 'letter' of Scripture.

The nature of Welsh *Puritanism seems to have prepared the way for the spread of Quakerism in Wales. One of Fox's earliest disciples was the Baptist Rice Jones in the Nottingham area. The pioneering Welsh-speaking Quaker was *John ap John who had once been a disciple of Morgan *Llwyd. In Merioneth and Montgomeryshire some who had been influenced by Llwyd and Vavasor *Powell embraced the teachings of the Friends. Among notable Welsh converts were Richard *Davies of Cloddiau Cochion, Charles Lloyd and Thomas Lloyd (see under LLOYD FAMILY of Dolobran), Rowland *Ellis and Ellis Pugh (1656–1718). Some of these were among the many Welsh Quakers who, under persecution, went out to found a colony in the New World in accordance with the plan of William Penn (who tended to claim Welsh descent). The territory which grew into the State of Pennsylvania was originally to have been called New Wales, but although Thomas Lloyd was Deputy-Governor to Penn until 1693, the hope of a Welsh-speaking community there did not come to fruition. The fortunes of these Welsh Quakers provide the background for some of the novels of Marion *Eames.

Welsh-speaking Quakerism languished in Wales after this migration but English-speaking fellowships maintained their witness especially in Cardiff, Swansea, Neath and Pontymoel. In Wales, as in England, Quakers often succeeded in the world of finance and industry. The banking firm of Lloyds was founded by a descendant of Charles Lloyd of Dolobran. Influential Quaker ironmasters settled at Neath and one of them, Joseph Tregelles *Price, founded the Peace Society in London. His nephew, Elijah *Waring, befriended Iolo Morganwg (Edward *Williams) and wrote a biography of him. The humanitarian and pacific interests of the Friends have brought them into association with those of like mind, such as the poet Waldo *Williams who became a Quaker. The Society founded an education settlement at Maes-yr-Haf, Trealaw, Rhondda, and George M. Ll. *Davies gave fruitful service there and at Brynmawr; he also supported Tom Nefyn, whose dissident fellowship at Llain-y-Delyn was set up under Quaker patronage.

Further details will be found in J. M. Rees, *History of the Quakers in Wales* (1925), Richard Jones, *Crynwyr Bore Cymru* (1931), H. Barbour, *The Quakers in Puritan England* (1964) and Harold Loukes, *The Quaker Contribution* (1965); see also Geraint H. Jenkins, 'Quaker and Anti-Quaker Literature in Welsh from the Restoration to Methodism' in *The Welsh History Review* (vol. 7, no. 4, 1975).

Queen of Song, The, see PATTI, ADELINA (1843–1919).

Question Test, The, a common theme in folk-literature: unless the hero does the one compulsory thing, misfortune ensues. In the tale of *Peredur (see under TAIR RHAMANT), he omits to ask the meaning of the strange sights in the Castle of Wonders, with the result that the owner of the castle is not healed.

Quintain, The, see PWNCO.

Quoits, a game played by throwing a flat metal ring over an agreed distance at a prescribed target, usually a peg secured in clay. A similar game was known during Roman times and its popularity continued throughout the Middle Ages, despite prohibition in several royal statutes on the grounds that it distracted young men from more military pursuits. The game is still played in Wales and it is encouraged at both local and international level by the Welsh Quoiting Board. See also KAYLES.

R

'*Rachie*', a popular hymn-tune composed by Caradog *Roberts for the hymnal *Y Caniedydd Cynulleidfaol Newydd* (1921) to the words, '*I bob un sydd ffyddlon*' by Henry Lloyd (Ap Hefin; 1870–1946). In some English hymnals it is set to the words 'Who is on the Lord's side?'.

Radicalism. The adjective 'Radical' was first used by the Tories as an offensive nickname for revolutionary democrats at the beginning of the nineteenth century. The earliest Radicals of Wales belonged to the Deist and Unitarian traditions but in the 1830s, with the struggle for Parliamentary Reform and the agitation against the Church Tithe, leading Congregationalists and Baptists embraced Radical ideas. The concept of Radicalism contained many strands, among them agrarian Radicalism (at once reactionary and revolutionary), Byronic Radicalism (pessimistic, romantic and aristocratic) and Benthamite Radicalism (respectable, middle-class, prosaic and calculating). All these were woven into Welsh Radicalism which was not, in consequence, a wholly consistent body of doctrine. Characteristic of Welsh Radicalism of the mid-nineteenth century was 'the Llanbrynmair Tradition' associated with Samuel *Roberts, which was concerned with public witness by the individual conscience, with peace, free trade and the limitation of the role of the State. Early Radicals tended to be associated both with the Whigs and the Tories but by the late nineteenth century they had been incorporated into the left wing of the Liberal Party. In the course of the century Radicals shed their more extreme individualism and men such as Michael D. *Jones warmed to collective ideas, both Socialist and Nationalist.

By the early twentieth century the outstanding Welsh Radical was David *Lloyd George who, as his welfare legislation shows, had a positive view of the role of the State. After the first World War, the confrontation between Capital and Labour tended to squeeze Radicalism out of industrial Wales, but it survived as a rallying-cry, especially in *Plaid Cymru* and the Labour Party, and it remains a convenient term for suggesting militancy without dogma.

For discussion of the concept see Cyril Parry, *The Radical Tradition in Welsh Politics: a study of Liberal and Labour Politics in Gwynedd 1900–1920* (1970) and Frank Price Jones, *Radicaliaeth a'r Werin Gymreig yn y Bedwaredd Ganrif ar Bymtheg* (1977).

Radio and Television, Writing for. The first radio play by a British writer to exploit the new medium's imaginative potential was Richard *Hughes's *Danger*, broadcast from London in 1924 and set in the darkness of a coal-mine, its characters as unseeing as the listening audience. A landmark of comparable significance in Welsh was *Buchedd Garmon*, a verse-play by Saunders *Lewis which was broadcast by the newly created Welsh Region of the BBC in 1937. There followed, especially in 'the golden age of Welsh radio' from 1945 to 1960, a large number of plays, documentaries and feature programmes of which the literary significance has yet to be fully measured. Many writers of the post-War years wrote for radio. Among regular contributors in English were Gwyn *Thomas (1913–81), Glyn *Jones, Dylan *Thomas and Emyr *Humphreys while, in Welsh, Kate *Roberts, Islwyn *Williams, John Ellis *Williams and Islwyn Ffowc *Elis were among those whose work was frequently broadcast. These writers were encouraged by sympathetic producers such as T. Rowland *Hughes, Alun *Llywelyn-Williams, John Gwilym *Jones and Aneirin Talfan *Davies.

The outstanding literary productions of this period included R. S. *Thomas's *The *Minister* and J. Kitchener *Davies's *'Sŵn y Gwynt sy'n Chwythu*', both broadcast in the *Radio Ode* series of 1952, and *Gazooka*, Gwyn Thomas's evocation of the *Rhondda Valley which was broadcast in 1956. A short-list of excellence hardly does justice, however, to the rich variety of creative writing for Welsh radio during the 1950s for it included, on the one hand, the erudite but entertaining talks of Ifor *Williams and, on the other, Eynon *Evans's comedy-scripts based on the character of *Tommy Trouble. The tradition of the eisteddfod was fostered by the radio *Noson Lawen, developed by Sam Jones in Bangor, and by competitions between teams of local poets. The increasing appeal of television in the early 1960s and the launching of BBC Wales Television in 1964 caused a decline in public interest in radio which has only recently been arrested with the advent of Radio Wales in 1978 and of *Radio Cymru* in 1979. Programmes of literary interest continue to be broadcast on radio from time to time, sometimes with the financial support of the *Welsh Arts Council, but they are not as regular as they used to be and the opportunities for hearing new work by contemporary writers have diminished.

Faced with the dilemma of serving two language communities, the broadcasting authorities in Wales have tended to make more strenuous efforts in the provision of programmes in the Welsh language, which is their unique responsibility, than they have done for the English-speaking majority. For several years after its inception in 1964, BBC Wales Television produced a number of plays for the British network, but little was done in English specifically for Wales, which is why such writers as Elaine *Morgan, Elwyn *Jones, Alun *Richards and Ewart *Alexander found their main markets in London. A series of films made in Cardiff by John *Ormond did much to bring the work of such poets as Vernon *Watkins and Alun *Lewis to the attention of a wider audience. Writing for television in Welsh, on the other hand, flourished increasingly during the 1970s under the aegis of both the BBC and the commercial companies such as HTV. Plays by Saunders Lewis, John Gwilym *Jones, Gwenlyn *Parry, Huw Lloyd *Edwards and Emyr Humphreys were broadcast and there were successful adaptations of novels by Daniel *Owen, Marion *Eames and Eigra Lewis *Roberts. At a more popular level the soap-opera *Pobol y Cwm* (said to be the Welsh equivalent of *Coronation Street*) and the situation comedy *Fo a Fe*, with both of which Gwenlyn Parry was associated, provided new opportunities for writers in Welsh.

Throughout the 1970s the structure of television in Wales was the subject of vigorous debate, Government reports and direct action by *Cymdeithas yr Iaith Gymraeg. A campaign during which scores of young people were imprisoned and hundreds fined for the non-payment of television licences also brought the participation of writers. In 1979 Pennar *Davies, Meredydd Evans and Ned Thomas (Edward Morley *Thomas) symbolically switched off the Pencarreg transmitter in Dyfed. A year later, under the pressure of a threatened hunger-strike by the President of *Plaid Cymru, Gwynfor *Evans, the Government agreed to fulfil its promise of a Welsh-language television channel, which came on the air in 1982 as *Sianel Pedwar Cymru (S4C)*, broadcasting some twenty-three hours per week in peak hours. The advent of the new channel not only increased the production of television but extended the spectrum, particularly in respect of children's programmes, documentaries, current affairs, situation comedy and television plays. It is now possible for at least a few writers in Welsh to make a living from their craft alone, although it has meant working in teams and under pressure which may not always favour the highest literary standards. At the same time, there has been a small expansion of programmes in English for Wales, but the English-language writer in Wales still has fewer opportunities in television than his Welsh-speaking compatriot. Despite the cost and range of the radio and television produced in Wales, the standard of public discussion is low. There is no longer any equivalent of *Llafar*, the broadcasting year-book edited by Aneirin Talfan Davies between 1951 and 1956, while television critics in Y *Cymro, *Barn and Y Faner (*Baner ac Amserau Cymru) cover a wide range of programmes in no more than a cursory manner. The *S4C* programme journal *Sbec*, although more widely distributed than any periodical ever has been in the Welsh language, is very limited in its editorial content.

For discussions of broadcasting in Wales see Alwyn D. Rees, *Dear Sir Harry Pilkington* (1969), *Broadcasting in Wales* (1971) and the same author's contribution to *The Welsh Language Today* (ed. Meic Stephens, 1973); see also Aneirin Talfan Davies, *Darlledu a'r Genedl* (1972) and Hywel Davies, *The Role of the Regions in British Broadcasting* (1965). A wealth of information will be found in the Annual Reports of the Broadcasting Council for Wales and in those of the commercial companies TWW and HTV. The principal reports published by H.M.S.O. are *Report of the Committee on Broadcasting Coverage* (*The Crawford Report*, 1974), *Report of the Working-Party on a Fourth Television Service for Wales* (*The Siberry Report*, 1975), *Report of the Committee on the Future of Broadcasting* (*The Annan Report*, 1977) and *Report of the Working-Party on the Welsh Television Fourth Channel Project* (1978). An account of the growth of broadcasting by the BBC in Wales from 1923 to 1973 has been written by Rowland Lucas, *The Voice of a Nation?* (1981).

Raglan, a castle situated between Monmouth and Usk, Mon., was built by order of Sir *Wiliam ap Thomas. His eldest son, also named Wiliam, was elevated to the peerage as Lord Herbert after the battle of *Mortimer's Cross (1461), a victory on which he and his brother, Sir Richard Herbert, were complimented by *Lewys Glyn Cothi in *awdlau* commemorating the Yorkist ascendancy. In 1468 Lord Herbert led the successful attack on *Harlech castle, after which he was reminded by *Guto'r Glyn of his responsibilities to his fellow-Welshmen. Granted the earldom of *Pembroke, he then set out on the campaign which was to end in his defeat and death at the battle of *Banbury (1469); Guto'r Glyn composed his elegy. The earl was a renowned patron of poets, including *Ieuan Deulwyn, *Siôn Cent and Hywel Dafi (c. 1450–80). Raglan, which had passed to the Somersets, Earls of Worcester, by a marriage with the Herbert heiress, was a Royalist stronghold during the *Civil War but, after a siege of three months, surrendered in August 1646 in face of the mining operations of Sir Thomas *Morgan (The Dwarf), and was dismantled soon afterwards.

For further details see A. J. Taylor, *Raglan Castle* (1950) and A. Clark, *Raglan Castle and the Civil War in Monmouthshire* (1953).

Raiders' Dawn (1942), the first collection of

poems by Alun *Lewis, was written in 1940 and 1941, while he was undergoing initial army training at Bordon Camp. There are signs of immaturity, or haste, or lack of critical judgement, in some poems and the burden of ideas and emotional intensity sometimes overwhelms the poet's technical control. Consistent antitheses of thought and imagery, however, become obvious, in particular the tension between personal involvement and detached observation, between love and hate, life and death, nature's beauty and its indifference, Man's dignity and his baseness, creation and waste. The allusions are, in the main, drawn from the Bible and Greek mythology and the poet's method tends to parable or allegory, often presented in lyrical form. The better known poems, including 'All Day It Has Rained' and 'To Edward Thomas', testify to Lewis's descriptive and reflective skills.

Raine, Allen, see PUDDICOMBE, ANNE ADALIZA BEYNON (1836–1908).

Rebecca, a magazine published in Cardiff at irregular intervals between 1973 and 1982 under the editorship of Paddy French, took its title from the *Rebecca Riots. It had a reputation for investigative journalism, especially into alleged corruption in the public life of south Wales, several of its numbers leading to the prosecution of those whose affairs it examined. After reorganizing itself on co-operative lines and becoming a monthly in September 1981, the magazine found its circulation falling and it was obliged to cease publication ten months later.

Rebecca Riots, The, a major social disturbance in west Wales during the second quarter of the nineteenth century, took the form of attacks on toll-gates belonging to road trusts which had been established late in the previous century. The initiative at first rested with farmers aggravated at the heavy cost of the tolls on transporting lime, but later the many other victims of discriminatory pressures extended the violence. The first attack occurred at Efail-wen, near the border between Pembrokeshire and Carmarthenshire, on 13 May 1839 and the initial phase culminated in the destruction of the Water Street gate at Carmarthen thirteen days later. More severe riots broke out in the winter of 1842 and, by the autumn of the following year, toll-gates had been destroyed in all three counties of south-west Wales as well as in Radnorshire, Breconshire and Glamorgan. The rioters took their text from a verse in the Book of Genesis 24: 60: 'And they blessed Rebekah and said unto her, Let thy seed possess the gates of those which hate thee'. Each band of rioters had its Rebecca, its leader for the occasion, a man who was often disguised as a woman, but although a number have been identified, it has proved impossible to identify any overall leader.

The roots of the protest lay in the dislocation caused to a traditional community by the over-rapid growth of population and the imposition of a money economy while outmoded systems of government and administration were still in operation. While attacks upon toll-gates were the most common form of protest, vengeance was also wreaked upon the new workhouses, unpopular magistrates, extortionate tithe-owners and the builders of weirs, all tangible symbols of an oppressive order. A few of the rioters were arrested but, because of the widespread support they enjoyed, evidence sufficient to convict them was not available. As the result of a Commission of Inquiry, road boards were set up to take over all the trusts in the counties of south Wales and tolls were reduced and simplified. The Rebecca Riots have been seen as a remarkable example of the crowd in action, the one successful uprising since the Great Rebellion (1642–48). The disturbance attracted the attention of *The Times*, which published valuable evidence of social conditions in south-west Wales at a crucial period in its history. See also REES, THOMAS (1806?–76).

The standard work on the subject is David Williams, *The Rebecca Riots: A Study in Agrarian Discontent* (1955); see also Pat Molloy, *And they blessed Rebecca* (1983).

RECORDE, ROBERT (d. 1558), mathematician, physician and writer, was born at Tenby, Pembs. A Fellow of All Souls College, Oxford, by 1531, he proceeded to further study of mathematics and medicine at Cambridge, becoming a Doctor of Medicine in 1545. After a brief period as a teacher at Oxford, he settled in London to practise medicine and is said to have been physician to both Edward VI and Queen Mary. In 1549 he became Comptroller of the Mint at Bristol and, in 1551, Surveyor of the Mines and Monies of Ireland (including the Irish Mint), from which post he was removed on charges of incompetence and dishonesty. He died in the King's Bench Prison, confined there either for debt or because of his alleged misconduct in Ireland. The evidence for the charges against him is inconclusive, but he is believed to have been an ardent Protestant.

His earliest work, *The Grounde of Artes* (1540), was the first sound arithmetic textbook for the unacademic reader, the first in English and the first based on Arabic numbers. Couched in dialogue form, it was later augmented by John *Dee and went through twenty-six editions before 1662. It was the standard textbook of its time and the 'equals' sign (=), which it contained, was Recorde's own invention. His next work, *The Urinal of Physics* (1547), dealt with urine diagnosis for surgeons. With *The Pathway to Knowledge* (1551), a textbook of geometry and astronomy, he met the needs of practical men even better than in his first book; useful for navigation, the book also adopted Copernicus's explanations of eclipses of the sun and moon. Recorde's *The Whetstone of Witte* (1557), a textbook of algebra, completed the trio intended for the unlearned reader. Recorde was the foremost scientific teacher and writer of his day, his Renaissance emphasis on progress seeing the vernacular as its necessary medium.

For further details see the article by Samuel Lilley in the journal published at the University of Nottingham, *Renaissance and Modern Studies* (vol. II, ed. V. S. de Pinto, 1958).

Recusancy, see under COUNTER-REFORMATION.

Red Bandits of Mawddwy, The, see GWYLL-IAID COCHION MAWDDWY.

Red Book of Asaph, The, see under ST. ASAPH.

Red Book of Hergest, The, or *Llyfr Coch Hergest*, one of the most important Welsh manuscripts of the Middle Ages, contains examples of almost every kind of Welsh literature of the period. The contents are so organized as to suggest that it was designed as an entity rather than that it grew haphazardly. It opens with all the principal prose texts: the traditional historical Welsh texts, *Ystorya Dared*, the *Brut* of *Geoffrey of Monmouth and *Brut y Tywysogyon* come first, then *Chwedlau Saith Ddoethion Rhufain*, *Breuddwyd Rhonabwy* and a series of Triads, followed by the tales which are now called *The *Mabinogion*, then *Ystorya Bown o Hamtwn*, the manuscripts of the *Myddfai Physicians and others which include *Amlyn ac Amig*, a grammar and a collection of proverbs. The rest of the work comprises poetry by the Poets of the Princes and the later *Gogynfeirdd*, which makes this collection, together with the *Hendregadredd Manuscript*, the main medieval source for the work of these poets. It does not contain any religious texts or versions of the *Laws, but these are the only important omissions. The apparent deficiency was probably intentional, since this comprehensive, authoritative manuscript was intended for a specific nobleman.

The copy of *Brut y Tywysogyon* ends in 1382 and as the same hand is evident in Peniarth Manuscript 32, which contains the date 1404, the *Red Book* can be dated to some time between 1382 and 1410. Although some pieces are written in other hands, the manuscript is mainly the work of one man, a consistent and intelligent copyist whose hand is evident in a number of other manuscripts, in particular Peniarth 32 (the Laws), Llanstephan 27 (*The Red Book of Talgarth* and religious texts), Peniarth 11 (*Y Seint Greal*) and Philadelphia Pub. Lib. 86800, in the last of which he identifies himself as Hywel Fychan fab Hywel Goch o Fuellt and refers to his master, Hopcyn ap Tomas ab Einion (*c.*1330–*post* 1403) of Ynys Dawe, whose brother Rhys is named in Llanstephan 27.

The manuscript probably became the property of the Vaughans of Tretower (see under VAUGHAN, JOHN, d. 1471) when Hopcyn ap Tomas lost his possessions in 1465, and it then passed to another branch of the family at *Hergest, a mansion in Herefordshire, where it remained until the beginning of the seventeenth century. By 1634 it was back in Glamorgan with Sir Lewis Mansel of Margam. Edward *Lhuyd saw it in 1697 when it was with Thomas Wilkins of Llanfair yn y Fro (although he was not its owner) and in 1701 the latter's son gave the manuscript to Jesus College, Oxford; it is now kept in the Bodleian Library. See also WHITE BOOK OF HERGEST.

For further details see B. F. Roberts, '*Un o Lawysgrifau Hopcyn ap Tomos*' in the Bulletin of the Board of Celtic Studies (vol. XXII, 1967); see also the article by Prys Morgan in *Morgannwg* (1978), that by Ceri W. Lewis in *Glamorgan County History III* and G. J. Williams, *Traddodiad Llenyddol Morgannwg* (1948).

Red Book of Nannau, The, see under MOSTYN FAMILY.

Red Book of Talgarth, The, see under LLAN-STEPHAN MANUSCRIPTS.

Red Dogs of Morfa, The, apparitions which were said to have run through the streets of Aberafan, Glam., on the eve of an explosion at Morfa colliery on 10 March 1890. Among other premonitions of the disaster were the scent of roses, *corpse candles, the ghosts of dead colliers and white horses drawing trams. Almost half the miners on the morning shift stayed home in fear and, later in the day, eighty-seven others lost their lives in the disaster.

Red Dragon, The (W. *Y Ddraig Goch*), the heraldic symbol of Wales as incorporated in the national flag, where it is set thus: '*perfesse argent and vert a dragon passant gules*'. The earliest references to a red dragon representing the British or Welsh are found in *Nennius's *Historia Brittonum*, in which *Emrys Wledig (Ambrosius) solves the mystery of *Vortigern's collapsing fortress, in *Cyfranc Lludd a Llefelys, in a version of the same tale by *Geoffrey of Monmouth and in vaticinatory poems of the medieval period. According to tradition, the red dragon appeared on a crest borne by *Arthur, whose father, *Uthr Bendragon, had seen a dragon in the sky foretelling that he would be king.

Probably introduced into Britain by the Roman legions, the dragon was often used by Welsh poets in similes praising the bravery of their leaders. *Meilyr Brydydd referred to *Gruffudd ap Cynan as 'the dragon of Gwynedd', Prydydd y Moch (*Llywarch ap Llywelyn) bestowed the epithet '*bendragon*' ('chief dragon') on *Llywelyn ap Iorwerth (Llywelyn Fawr) and *Gruffudd ab yr Ynad Coch said of *Llywelyn ap Gruffudd, '*Pen dragon, pen draig oedd arnaw*' ('A dragon's head he had'). The forces of *Owain Glyndŵr were said to have marched under a banner bearing a golden dragon (or wyvern) on a white field during their attack on *Caernarfon castle in 1401. The symbol (in its rampant form) was given a wider currency between 1485 and 1603 as part of the arms of the *Tudor dynasty where it was probably meant to represent their descent from *Cadwaladr Fendigaid and their claim to the overlordship of Britain, but it was removed from the royal coat of arms by order of James I and replaced by a unicorn.

The Red Dragon made its reappearance as the royal badge for Wales in 1807. Thereafter it was frequently seen in the regalia of Welsh patriotic societies and slowly came to vie with the three white ostrich feathers as a symbol for the *Principality of Wales. Officially recognized by the Queen in 1959, at the suggestion of *Gorsedd Beirdd Ynys Prydain, the Red Dragon is now widely used as the national flag and is seen flying from public and private buildings throughout Wales. The motto '*Y Ddraig Goch ddyry cychwyn*' ('The red dragon will show the way'), which was added to the royal badge in 1953, is taken from a poem by *Deio ab Ieuan Du thanking Siôn ap Rhys of Glyn-nedd for the gift of a bull.

Red Dragon, The, a magazine created and edited by Charles *Wilkins and published monthly in Cardiff between 1882 and 1887. The only magazine in English of its time and the first such with a south Wales emphasis, it attempted an ethos more decidedly Anglo-Welsh than that of *The Cambrian Journal*. The editor's interest lay less in the Welsh literary heritage, though there were regular translations from Welsh poetry, and more in the recent history of Wales. Each number began with an account of a historical figure, on a range from Daniel *Rowland to William *Crawshay and Miss Williams of *Aberpergwm, and the editor provided studies of writers in English from Wales such as Henry *Vaughan, James *Howell and Lewis *Morris. Longer fictions, serialized and either devoid of Welsh interest or pseudonymous, vied for the body of the magazine with sketches living on the credit of the early *Tours of Wales. Much of the verse, often by Welsh expatriates, dramatized incidents in Welsh history; the remainder was sentimental and undistinguished, with only a few writers, among them H. Elvet *Lewis and Arthur Mee, regularly willing to admit authorship. The editor, nevertheless, writing some of each issue himself, was making a brave attempt to create a relatively cultured reading public in English where none sufficient as yet existed. At the end of 1885 Charles Wilkins gave way as editor to James Harris of Cardiff, under whom the emphasis of *The Red Dragon* returned

markedly to the antiquarian, the Notes and Queries section engrossing the bulk of its pages.

Red Lady of Paviland, The, a human skeleton discovered in 1823 by the pioneer archaeologist Dean Buckland at Goat's Hole, a cave on the coast of Gower, Glam. Later research proved that the headless remains, which were stained with red ochre, dated from the Cro-Magnon period and were those of a young man, who had perhaps been killed in a primitive form of religious ritual.

REES, ALWYN DAVID (1911–74), editor, writer and sociologist. A miner's son, he was born at Gorseinon, near Swansea, and educated at the University College of Wales, Aberystwyth. A Tutor in the Extra-Mural Department of the same College from 1936 to 1946, he was appointed its Director in 1949, a post which he held until his death. From the outset he was interested in the social life of Welsh-speaking Wales and, as a committed patriot, he saw clearly the threat posed in the modern world to the survival of minority cultures. A keen observer and powerful debater, he was unstinting in his support of Welsh cultural and linguistic movements, including *Cymdeithas yr Iaith Gymraeg during its most controversial phase. His most important contribution to Welsh letters was his encouragement of writers of all kinds during his term as editor of the magazine *Barn (1966–1974); he also edited Yr Einion (*The *Welsh Anvil*) from 1949 to 1958. He published Life in a Welsh Countryside (1950), co-edited Welsh Rural Communities (1961) and, with his brother Brinley Rees, wrote Celtic Heritage (1961).

A selection of his articles and a full bibliography will be found in *Ym Marn Alwyn D. Rees* (ed. Bobi Jones, 1976).

REES, DANIEL (1855–1931), journalist and translator. Born at Whitchurch-in-Cemais, Pembs., he devoted his early career to journalism, mainly as the editor of Yr *Herald Cymraeg and the Carnarvon and Denbigh Herald. An uncompromising Liberal, he wielded a powerful if sometimes unpopular influence in north Wales as a staunch supporter of David *Lloyd George in his early parliamentary election campaigns. One of his major achievements was the foundation in 1893 of the weekly newspaper *Papur Pawb. But his principal claim to fame rests on his Dwyfol Gân Dante (1903), a selection from La Divina Commedia (c.1314), with an introduction by his colleague, T. Gwynn *Jones. Relying on their mutual friendship and a common interest in Dante, they collaborated in the writing of a play in English, Dante and Beatrice (1903). In 1907 Rees joined the staff of the Board of Trade in London and spent the rest of his life in England.

REES, DAVID (1801–69), minister, printer and editor, was born in the parish of Tre-lech, Carms. Educated at home and in *Sunday School, he later attended the Grammar School in Carmarthen and the Independent Academy at Newtown, Mont., where his encounters with Samuel *Roberts (S.R.) influenced his outlook. Ordained as a Congregational minister in 1829, he served at Capel Als, Llanelli, for the rest of his life, and it is with that chapel that his name is usually associated. A born leader, of strong and uncompromising principles, he was one of the pillars of his denomination in the town of Llanelli, and a popular preacher. His appointment as the first editor of the journal *Y Diwygiwr* in 1835, a post in which he remained until 1865, was a milestone in the history of Welsh Congregationalism, for in its pages he brought a Radical influence to bear on the *Nonconformity of his day. Known as '*Y Cynhyrfwr*' ('The Agitator') on account of his admiration for Daniel O'Connell, Rees was a brilliant propagandist against the Established Church and a ferocious opponent of Brutus (David *Owen) who taunted him in *Yr Haul*. His literary style (a conscious rejection of the high writing of Welsh tradition) was inclined to be hurried and careless, but he could be explosively effective when dealing with causes close to his heart.

An account of his life and work will be found in Iorwerth Jones, *David Rees y Cynhyrfwr* (1971); a selection of his work was edited by Glanmor Williams in 1950.

Rees, Dilwyn, see DANIEL, GLYN EDMUND (1914–).

REES, EVAN (Dyfed; 1850–1923), poet, was born at Puncheston, Pembs., but brought up in Aberdare, Glam., where he started work as a collier-boy. Ordained in 1884, he later moved to Cardiff but never held a pastorate. Between 1881 and 1901 he won the *Chair at the National Eisteddfod four times and with his *awdl*, 'Iesu o Nazareth', the Chair at the World Fair Eisteddfod held in Chicago in 1893. His published works, *Caniadau Dyfedfab* (1875), *Gwaith Barddonol Dyfed* (n.d.), *Gwlad yr Addewid a Iesu o Nazareth* (1894) and *Oriau gydag Islwyn* (n.d.), were typical of their time and are no longer held in high esteem. From 1905 to 1923 Dyfed served *Gorsedd Beirdd Ynys Prydain as Archdruid.

REES, GORONWY (1909–79), journalist, academic and author. Born at Aberystwyth, Cards., the son of a minister of the Presbyterian Church in Wales, he was educated at the High School for Boys, Cardiff, after his father's appointment as Superintendent of the Presbyterian Forward Movement, and subsequently at New College, Oxford. He became a Fellow of All Souls in 1931 and in the following year he was appointed leader-writer with *The Manchester Guardian*; he became Assistant Editor of *The Spectator* in 1936.

After the Second World War, in which he served as a gunner with the Royal Artillery and as an officer in the Royal Welsh Fusiliers, he worked in industry but returned to academic life in 1951 as Estates Bursar of All Souls. From 1953 to 1957 he was Principal of the University College of Wales, Aberystwyth, but resigned in circumstances marked by acrimony on both sides, and for the rest of his life he lived in England.

During his time at Oxford Goronwy Rees, a Marxist, was a close friend of Guy Burgess, the spy who was to defect to the Soviet Union in 1951. Shortly before his death, when he made this fact public, speculation arose as to why he had made no earlier disclosure and how much he had known about the defection at the time.

His childhood in Aberystwyth, which was happy, and in Cardiff, which he found uncongenial, his years at Oxford in the 1930s, his experience in Germany both before and after the War, and his subsequent career, including the controversial period spent at Aberystwyth, are all described with sophistication and percipience in his two volumes of autobiographical sketches, *A Bundle of Sensations* (1960) and *A Chapter of Accidents* (1972). Both volumes, which are among the best of his writing, reveal how Goronwy Rees, while engaged in English life, was also able to preserve a certain detachment from it, partly by virtue of his Welsh identity, which made him feel an outsider, and partly of the European, particularly German, culture with which he was deeply imbued.

He also published three novels, *A Summer Flood* (1932), *A Bridge to Divide Them* (1937), both of which are set partly in Wales, and *Where no Wounds Were* (1950); he also wrote *The Rhine* (1967). Among his other books are *The Multimillionaires: six studies in wealth* (1961), *St. Michael: a history of Marks & Spencer* (1969), *The Great Slump: Capitalism in Crisis 1929–33* (1970), and the translations *Danton's Death* (1939) and *Conversations with Kafka* (1939), both done in collaboration with the English writer Stephen Spender. A selection of the long essays on political, social and literary subjects of the day which he wrote between 1966 and 1973 for the magazine *Encounter* was republished in the volume *Brief Encounters* (1974).

Rees, Henry (1798–1869), religious leader, was born in the parish of Llansannan, Denbs. His devotion to a ministerial vocation with the Calvinistic Methodists was much more single-minded than that of his younger brother among the Independents, William *Rees (Gwilym Hiraethog). Beginning to preach in 1818, he showed gifts of a rare excellence and his preaching inspired John *Jones of Tal-y-sarn to enter the ministry. He became the first Moderator of the General Assembly of the Calvinistic Methodists in 1864. Besides contributions to religious periodicals, he published two volumes of sermons which reflect his debt to Puritan divines, especially John Owen (1616–83).

REES, IOAN BOWEN (1929–), author. Born at Dolgellau, Mer., he read Modern History at The Queen's College, Oxford. He was appointed Chief Executive of Gwynedd County Council in 1980. Among his publications are a number of legal studies of the Welsh language and several pamphlets on political subjects, including The Welsh Political Tradition (1961), his contribution (as Ioan Rhys) to the volume Celtic Nationalism (1968) and Government by Community (1971). His more literary essays, on mountains and climbing, have been published in three volumes, Galwad y Mynydd (1961), Dringo Mynyddoedd Cymru (1965) and Mynyddoedd (1975). His wife, Margaret Bowen Rees (1935–), has published some of her poems under the title Cerddi Cegin (1972).

REES, JOHN FREDERICK (1883–1967), historian, was born at Milford Haven, Pembs. Educated at the University College, Cardiff, and Lincoln College, Oxford, he was a lecturer at Bangor, Belfast and Edinburgh Universities before his appointment as Principal of his old College in 1929, a post which he held until his retirement; he was knighted in 1945. He took a keen interest in the history of Wales and among his publications were Studies in Welsh History (1947), The Story of Milford (1954) and The Problem of Wales and Other Essays (1963).

REES, JOHN RODERICK (1920–), poet, was born at Penuwch, Cards., where he still lives. Educated at the University College of Wales, Aberystwyth, he was a schoolmaster in his native county for twenty years before returning to full-time farming in 1981. He has published two volumes of verse, Cerddi'r Ymylon (1959) and Cerddi (1984). At the *National Eisteddfod in 1984 he won the *Crown for a pryddest entitled 'Llygaid' and again in 1985 with 'Glannau'.

REES, MARGARET BOWEN (1935–), see under REES, IOAN BOWEN (1929–).

Rees, Robert, see PALMER, ALFRED NEOBARD (1847–1915).

REES, SARAH JANE (Cranogwen; 1839–1916), poet and editor, was a native of Llangrannog, Cards., and a schoolmistress by profession. She was the editor of Y Frythones (1878–91), a magazine for women, and the founder of the Temperance Union of the Women of South Wales. A collection of her poetry was published in the volume Caniadau Cranogwen (1870).

A study of her life and work is to be found in D. G. Jones, Cofiant Cranogwen (n.d.) and in Cranogwen: Portread Newydd (1981) by Gerallt Jones.

Rees, Thomas (Twm Carnabwth; 1806?–76), pugilist, acquired his sobriquet from the name of his farm near Mynachlog-ddu, Pembs. According to local tradition, he took part in an attack on the toll-gate at Efail-wen in 1839 and, from then on, his name was inseparably associated with the *Rebecca Riots.

REES, THOMAS (1815–85), historian, was born at Llanfynydd, Carms. He received little formal education, but opened a school at Aberdare, Glam., in 1835 and later became an Independent minister renowned for his powerful preaching, at Llanelli, Beaufort and Swansea. With A History of Protestant Nonconformity in Wales (1861) he prepared the way for his more important work, Hanes Eglwysi Annibynol Cymru (1875), which he wrote in collaboration with John *Thomas (1821–92) of Liverpool. Rees demonstrated some pro-denominational bias and many of his transcripts of source material were inaccurate, but his assiduous research established him as the earliest authority on the history of his denomination.

REES, THOMAS IFOR (1890–1977), translator. Born at Bow Street, Cards., and educated at the University College of Wales, Aberystwyth, he spent most of his life in the Civil Service, retiring as British Ambassador to Bolivia in 1949. His publications include In and around the Valley of Mexico (1953), Sajama (1960) and Illimani (1964); he also made Welsh translations of novels by René Bazin (1933), Xavier de Maistre (1944), J. R. Jiminez (1961), Henri Troyat (1967) and C. F. Ramuz (1968), and of 'The Rubáiyát' of Omar Khayyám (1939) and of Gray's 'Elegy written in a Country Churchyard' (1949).

REES, WILLIAM (Gwilym Hiraethog; 1802–83), editor and writer. A farmer's son, born at Llansannan, Denbs., he became a Congregational minister, an influential Radical leader and a prolific writer. His publications include the substantial volume Gweithiau Barddonol (1855) and his vast epic *Emmanuel (1861, 1867), which runs to more than twenty thousand lines. But, with the exception of a few hymns, his verse is uninspired and less lively than his prose.

The most striking features of Gwilym Hiraethog's life were his great industry and his passion for social justice. Although he wished to be remembered as a poet rather than as a writer of prose, the standard of Welsh poetry in his time was low, despite its abundance, and his fictional and journalistic writings are now regarded as his most important contributions to Welsh literature. He made Yr *Amserau, which he edited from 1843 to 1859, into an influential Radical weekly and it was in that newspaper he published his *Llythurau 'Rhen Ffarmwr (1878). His adaptation of Harriet Beecher Stowe's Uncle

Tom's Cabin (1851) in *Yr Amserau*, under the title *Aelwyd F'Ewythr Robert* (1852), did much to make Welsh readers aware of the evils of slavery. Among other Radical causes espoused by Rees were the new national movements on the Continent: he met and corresponded with Garibaldi and supported the campaign of Kossuth in Hungary. His *Helyntion Bywyd Hen Deiliwr* (1877) was an attempt to write a novel which would also be an important social document; he also wrote a play, *Y Dydd Hwnnw*, and a number of religious books. The first to be awarded the Medal of the Honourable Society of *Cymmrodorion, he died before it could be presented to him.

For further details see the article by J. Cadvan Davies in *Y Geninen* (vol. 25, 1907) and the introduction by Dafydd Jenkins to his edition of *Helyntion Bywyd Hen Deiliwr* (1940).

Rees, William (1808–73), printer and publisher, was a native of Tonn, near Llandovery, Carms., where in 1829 he set up a press which was to become one of the most celebrated in Wales. There he printed the journals *Y Cylchgrawn* (1834–35) and *Yr Haul*, as well as the three volumes of Charlotte *Guest's *The Mabinogion* (1838–49), the publications of the *Welsh Manuscripts Society, and a host of other important titles. The Tonn Manuscripts are now housed in Cardiff City Library.

REES, WILLIAM (1887–1978), historian, was born at Aberyscir, Brecs., brought up at Abercynrig Mill, near Brecon, and educated at University College, Cardiff. He became a lecturer at his old College in 1920 and published some of the research done during ten years in London in the volume *South Wales and the March 1284–1415: a Social and Agrarian Study* (1924). His interest in historical geography was already demonstrated by *The Making of Europe* (1919) and he went on to produce his unique map of *South Wales and the Border in the Fourteenth Century* (1933), his most significant work and the precursor to *An Historical Atlas of Wales* (1951). In 1930 he was appointed Professor of Welsh History at Cardiff and in 1935 accepted responsibility for the Department of History as well, in which double capacity he continued until his retirement in 1953. Abstemious, patient, tireless, he was the last survivor of the first generation of major Welsh historians. Late in life, he edited the *Survey of the Duchy of Lancaster Lordships* (1953), published his massive *Industry before the Industrial Revolution* (2 vols., 1968) and edited the *Calendar of Ancient Petitions relating to Wales* (1975). He also wrote *A History of Cardiff* (1962) and *A History of the Order of St. John of Jerusalem in Wales* (1947).

There is an obituary of William Rees by Gwynedd O. Pierce in *The Welsh History Review* (vol. 9, no. 4, 1979); see also *An Address presented to William Rees by the* *Brecknock Society* (1968) in which there is a long essay by Ceri W. Lewis and a full bibliography.

REES, WILLIAM JENKINS (1772–1855), antiquary and cleric, was born at Llandovery, Carms., and educated at Wadham College, Oxford. He held curacies in Herefordshire and became vicar of Cascob and Heyop, Rads., in 1806. Made prebendary of Christ College, Brecon, in 1820, he continued to live at Cascob until his death. His published works and voluminous correspondence are deposited in the Cardiff City Library. As one of *Yr *Hen Bersoniaid Llengar* ('The Old Literary Clerics'), W. J. Rees was enthusiastically involved in the *Eisteddfod and the Honourable Society of *Cymmrodorion, and he was active with the *Welsh Manuscripts Society. He completed an edition of the *Liber Landavensis* (1840), prepared by his nephew, Rice Rees (1804–39), and published his own edition of *The Lives of the Cambro-British Saints* (1853), but these works were unsatisfactory.

For further details see the articles by Mary Ellis in the *Transactions* of the Radnorshire Society (1969–72).

Reform Bills, The (1832, 1867, 1884, 1918), four legislative measures which were designed to improve the distribution of Members of Parliament and to extend the franchise.

The first, passed in 1832, abolished a great many 'rotten' and 'pocket' boroughs, 143 seats in all, and allocated them to counties and large towns where there had been substantial increases in the population. In Wales the counties of Glamorgan, Carmarthen and Denbigh were thus given an additional member and Merthyr Tydfil (where the *Merthyr Rising had taken place the previous year) acquired a member of its own. The Glamorgan boroughs were divided into two constituencies, with Cardiff and Swansea as their centres. As a result, Wales was represented by thirty-two Members of Parliament. The changes in the franchise were not far-reaching, however, and the Act did little to break the landowners' stranglehold in the shires.

The Act of 1867 brought small alteration to the number of constituencies in Wales, although Merthyr Tydfil was given an additional member. The most significant change was in the extension of the franchise: in the boroughs every male householder worth ten pounds a year was given the vote and, in the counties, every male householder worth twelve pounds a year. At the election held in the following year, three Nonconformists—Henry *Richard, Richard Davies and E. M. Richards—were returned as Liberals representing constituencies in Wales; Liberals captured twenty-one seats in all and twelve were held by Tories. In retribution, some landlords evicted their tenant-farmers who had voted against Tory candidates, which led Henry Richard and others to secure the passing of the Ballot Act of 1872.

The third Act, passed in 1884, led to very

many changes in Wales. The constituencies of Beaumaris, Brecon, Cardigan, Haverfordwest and Radnor were abolished and the franchise was transferred to the counties. Swansea and Monmouthshire were given an additional member and Denbighshire was divided into two single-member constituencies. The county representation in Glamorgan increased from two to five and included south, east, west and mid-Glamorgan as well as the Rhondda. The franchise was enormously widened: every male householder—if British, in his right mind, over twenty-one years of age, and neither a peer nor a felon—was given the vote. After the election of 1885 the Conservatives kept only four of the thirty-four seats in Wales: the 1884 Act had finally brought to an end the power of the landlord, which gave way to that of *Liberalism and the subsequent election of members such as T. E. *Ellis in 1886 and David *Lloyd George in 1890. The 1918 Reform Act gave Welsh women over thirty the vote—as it enfranchised all others in the same category in Britain—and allotted a seat to the *University of Wales.

For further details see David Williams, *Modern Wales* (1950) and K. O. Morgan, *Wales in British Politics 1868–1922* (1963).

Religious Census, The (1851), the only official count of places available for, and attendance at, religious worship ever taken in England and Wales, was a part of the decennial Census, and enumeration took place on the last Sunday in March 1851. By it Wales was revealed as much more 'religious' than England, more than two-thirds of the people attending in all parts except for the new urban centres. There were 898,442 seats in 3,883 places of worship for a total population of 1,188,914.

The provision varied from district to district, from a plethora in Haverfordwest (Baptist) and Llanfyllin (Calvinistic Methodist) to a dearth in Merthyr Tydfil, where *Nonconformity had not yet arrived in strength. In the country as a whole some three-quarters of the attenders were found in Nonconformist chapels, but the Church of England was the strongest single denomination in Wrexham, Montgomery, Chepstow, Monmouth, Hay, Brecon and Pembroke, all Border areas or districts long affected by the English language. In north Wales, especially the north-west, Calvinistic Methodists were far and away the most numerous, but not in south Wales, save for Cardiff and Cardiganshire as far south as Tregaron and Aberaeron. *Baptists comprised the largest single denomination in Cardigan, Haverfordwest, Llanelli, Abergavenny, Pontypool and Newport, while *Independency was strongest in Newcastle Emlyn, Lampeter, Narberth, Llandeilo, Llandovery, Builth, Crickhowell, Bridgend, Neath and Swansea. Wesleyan *Methodism was surprisingly strong in north Wales, probably as a result

of the revived mission of 1801. Church people were recorded as turning out well for morning service, but evening services were overwhelmingly Nonconformist, many of the attenders doubtless being adherents rather than members.

The Census became almost immediately a key element in the controversy between Nonconformity and *Anglicanism and effective use was soon made of it by Nonconformists such as Henry *Richard and the *Liberation Society in the campaign for *Disestablishment of the Church of England in Wales.

For further details see Ieuan Gwynedd Jones, *The Religious Census of 1851* (2 vols., 1976, 1981); see also E. T. Davies, *Religion and Society in the Nineteenth Century* (1981) and the chapter entitled '*Crefydda mewn Llan a Chapel*' in *Grym Tafodau Tân* (1984) by Glanmor Williams.

RENAN, ERNEST (1823–92), French philosopher and Orientalist. Born at Tréguier in Brittany and educated for the priesthood, he later abandoned orthodox Christianity, as is evinced in his most celebrated work, *La Vie de Jésus* (1863). His theories concerning certain distinctive characteristics possessed in common by the various Celtic peoples are developed in his *Essai sur la Poésie des Races Celtiques* (1854; revised edn., 1859), a survey of recently published translations from Welsh and Breton, in which he gives pride of place to Lady Charlotte *Guest's *The Mabinogion* (1849) and to the works of La *Villemarqué, but also considers Welsh, Breton and Irish hagiography. Renan's study influenced Matthew *Arnold, who found in it the germ of each of the three distinguishing characteristics which he divined in the literature of the Celtic peoples. Renan wrote primarily of the Breton people among whom he had passed his childhood, but his definitions are intended to apply equally to the Irish, Scots and Welsh. In his view the Celtic nature was reserved, inward-looking, lacking in initiative or political aptitude, fatalistic and given to defending lost causes, yet redeemed by a sensitivity and deep feeling for nature and all living creatures, exhibited in Brittany by the cult of forests, springs and wells. He emphasized the close bonds of blood-relationship which are manifested among all the Celtic peoples and expressed in their 'backward look' —their faithfulness to their past and to the memory of their dead. He described *The Mabinogion* as 'the real expression of the Celtic genius' and regarded it, with the legend of *Arthur, as the source of all the romantic creations which in the twelfth century had 'changed the direction of the European imagination'. In spite of the threat of modern industrialized civilization, Renan believed firmly that the Celtic peoples had not yet 'said their last word' but might still have a mature and unique contribution to make to European life and culture.

For further details see H. Psichari, *Œuvres complètes de*

Ernest Renan, tome II, Essais de morale et de critique (1948); the translation by W. G. Hutchison, *Poetry of the Celtic Races and Other Essays by Ernest Renan* (1896) and R. M. Galand, *L'âme celtique de Renan* (1959).

Rendel, Stuart (1834–1913), politician and philanthropist. Born in Plymouth and educated at Oriel College, Oxford, he entered Parliament as Liberal member for Montgomeryshire in 1880, breaking a Conservative predominance in that county which had lasted for more than eighty years. He soon became the leader of the Welsh contingent at Westminster and was popularly known as 'the Member for Wales'. On intimate terms with W. E. Gladstone, he took a keen interest in promoting Welsh affairs, especially education and proposals for the *Dis-establishment of the Church. To Rendel belongs most of the credit for the passing of the Inter-mediate Education Act of 1889 which em-powered the county councils of Wales to raise a halfpenny rate for the purpose of developing a system of secondary education; the funds thus created were to be matched from Government sources. By 1902, when the system adopted in Wales was also applied to England, a total of ninety-five intermediate schools had been established under the supervision of the Central Welsh Board, created in 1896. A benefactor of the University College of Wales, Aberystwyth, where the Chair of English was named after him, Rendel also presented land at Penglais in that town as the site for the *National Library of Wales.

Republicanism, the principle or theory which advocates a form of government in which supreme power is invested in the people and in which the head of state is not a monarch but an elected president. In Wales early Radicals such as Richard *Price and David *Williams defended American independence and hailed the French Revolution of 1789. Although British in political outlook, these Jacobins—together with Thomas *Evans (Tomos Glyn Cothi), Edward *Wil-liams (Iolo Morganwg) and John *Jones (Jac Glan-y-gors)—also championed Radical causes in their own country. During the first decades of the twentieth century there was a strong anti-monarchist tendency in the thinking of Keir *Hardie who attacked the institution of the Crown with egalitarian and Republican argu-ments, most notably in his newspaper, *The Merthyr Pioneer*; he boycotted the investiture of the Prince of Wales in 1911 (see under PRINCIPALITY OF WALES). T. E. *Nicholas was among the most consistent opponents of the monarchy among Welsh writers during the inter-War years.

The Welsh Republican Movement which flourished briefly during the 1950s grew out of disaffection among some members of *Plaid Cymru with the party's leadership and its refusal to adopt a Republican platform at its annual conference in 1949. It never had more than a hundred adherents and put up a candidate at a general election only once, at Ogmore in 1950. It published a lively newspaper, *Welsh Republican* (1950–57), of which Harri *Webb was an editor, and it caused uproar at many a public meeting with its left-wing, anti-English views. But it made little impression on the course of politics in Wales and ceased to exist during the late 1950s, when its few remaining members decided to resume working within the parties of their former allegiance, the Labour Party and *Plaid Cymru*. One prominent former member, Gwilym Prys Davies, was made a peer in 1983.

There were Welsh Republican protests against the investiture of the Prince of Wales in 1969. The movement was revived among Nationalists and Socialists in 1980 after the publication of the pamphlets *Sosialaeth i'r Cymry* (1979) and *Social-ism for the Welsh People* (1980) by Robert Griffiths and Gareth *Miles, and began publishing two newspapers, *Y Faner Goch* and *Welsh Republic*, in which it argued in favour of Welsh independence from English rule on Socialist and anti-British grounds. Several of its members were arrested (two were subsequently gaoled and five acquitted) after a group known as the Workers' Army of the Welsh Republic was alleged to have been involved in planting explosive devices in 1981.

For further details see Alan Butt Philip, *The Welsh Question: Nationalism in Welsh Politics* (1973).

Revival of 1859, The, a movement of extra-ordinary spiritual activity affecting every reli-gious denomination in Wales, was initiated by Humphrey Rowland Jones at his native Tre'r Ddôl, Cards., and led by the Calvinistic Methodist preacher, Dafydd Morgan of Ysbyty Ystwyth in the same county. The Revival's chief characteristics were powerful preaching, a pro-fusion of prayer-meetings, a great influx into the chapels and a spontaneous, widespread aware-ness of spiritual issues. After 1860 the Revival waned, but more than twenty thousand mem-bers had been won, with the result that fresh impetus was given to the work of the Bible Society and to missionary and *Temperance movements. It had profoundly influenced moral attitudes and elevated the literary and educa-tional consciousness of a whole generation.

For accounts of the Revival see J. J. Morgan, *Hanes Dafydd Morgan Ysbyty a Diwygiad '59* (1906) and *The '59 Revival in Wales* (1909); Evan Esaac, *Humphrey Jones a Diwygiad 1859* (1930); J. Edwin Orr, *The Second Evangelical Awakening in Britain* (1949); Eifion Evans, *When He is Come* (1959) and *Humphrey Jones a Diwygiad 1859* (1981).

Revue Celtique (lit. 'Celtic review'), the first of the great scholarly periodicals in Celtic Studies, was founded in Paris in 1870 by Henri Gaidoz, then Professor of Geography and Ethnography at the *École des Sciences Politiques*. It had a comprehensive brief, encompassing every facet of Celtic scholarship, and a list of contributors which included all the great names in the pantheon of Celtic Studies. In 1886 Gaidoz was succeeded in the editorship by H. d'Arbois de Jubainville and he, in turn, was followed by Joseph *Loth, with Ernault, Dottin, Joseph *Vendryes and M. L. Sjoestedt-Jonval also involved in the work. In 1936, after a brilliant run of sixty-four years, the *Revue* ceased publication, leaving a gap which was eventually filled by *Études Celtiques*.

Rhahawd eil Morgant, see under FRIVOLOUS POETS.

Rhedegydd, Y (lit. 'The courier'), a Radical weekly newspaper established by the partners William J. Roberts and Lewis Davies in Blaenau Ffestiniog, Mer., in 1878. By 1903 Davies had also begun publishing *Y Gloch* and the two papers were then merged until 1918. Robert Owen Hughes (Elfyn), J. D. Davies and John Ellis *Williams were among its editors. With its circulation in decline, *Y Rhedegydd* was taken over by *Y *Cymro* in 1951.

Rheinallt ap Gruffudd ap Bleddyn (c.1438–65/6), soldier and gentleman, of Y Tŵr ym Mron-coed, Mold, Flints. According to tradition, he took the Mayor of Chester prisoner in 1464 and hanged him from a pillar. There is some corroboration of this incident in two *cywyddau* by *Hywel Cilan who called him '*fraw'r Mars*' ('the terror of the March') and described how he cut a swathe through the ranks of his enemies. *Tudur Penllyn and *Gutun Owain also wrote in his praise and *Ieuan ap Tudur Penllyn wrote his elegy.

Rhiannon, one of the main characters in the First and Third Branches of *Pedair Cainc y Mabinogi*. Despite her love for *Pwyll, the lord of *Dyfed, she is betrothed to Gwawl, the son of Clud, but eventually she marries Pwyll. After a prosperous period as Queen of Dyfed, she bears a son but the child disappears the night after his birth and his mother is accused of killing him. She is proved innocent four years later when *Teyrnon Twrf Liant, the King of Gwent Is Coed, brings the boy, named *Pryderi, back to the court of Dyfed. In the Third Branch many years have passed, Pwyll has died and Pryderi is King of Dyfed. On his return from the attack on Ireland, Pryderi gives his mother, Rhiannon, as a wife to his companion, *Manawydan. A magical mist then suddenly descends on Dyfed and none but Pryderi and his wife, and Manawydan and Rhiannon, are left. Later, Pryderi and Rhiannon disappear inside a faery fortress and are held captive in *Annwfn but they are eventually freed by Manawydan. It was Llwyd fab Cil Coed who had imprisoned them and caused a

mist to fall over Dyfed, in order to avenge the harm which Gwawl had suffered in the First Branch by the loss of Rhiannon.

It is thought that Rhiannon was originally the Celtic goddess Rigantona, the 'Queen-goddess', and an element of magic surrounds her in the *Mabinogi*. She has also been identified with Epona the 'horse-goddess' and on several occasions Rhiannon is connected with horses in the course of the tale. In the Second Branch the Birds of Rhiannon are said to sing over the sea near *Harlech and in the tale of *Culhwch and Olwen they wake the dead and send the living to sleep.

The mythological themes connected with Rhiannon have been examined in a book by W.J. Gruffydd, *Rhiannon* (1953).

Rhigymau (lit. 'Rhymes'), impromptu verses composed by the common people, have been part of the folk tradition of Wales for many centuries. They refer mainly to everyday life and are especially popular among children at play, but many reflect the adult world, often humorously, as in those expressing animosity between the religious denominations or parodying well-known hymns. Others derive from superstitions and folk customs, or are meant to entertain by referring to extraordinary events and people, particularly in the form of epitaphs and false elegies. The authorship of even the most famous rhymes is no longer known, but some of those dating from the nineteenth century were composed by local poets such as John Jenkins, the author of *Cerddi Cerngoch* (1904). Earlier, such verses had been disparaged by professional poets as '*rhigymau pen pastwn*' ('staff-head rhymes') because those who sang or recited them, having no musical instrument, were obliged to accompany the words with the beating of a staff. Very few had the literary merit of *Hen Benillion (harp-stanzas) or the *Triban and for this reason they were often associated with rhymesters such as Y Bardd Cocos (John *Evans). During the twentieth century, however, some of the features of the '*rhigwm*' such as repetition and an emphasis on the rhythms of the spoken language, have been used to serious effect by Welsh poets such as T. H. *Parry-Williams and Gwyn *Thomas (1936–). Many examples are to be found scattered in manuscripts, periodicals and books, but no comprehensive collection has so far been published.

Rhirid Flaidd (*fl.* 1160), see under BARDIC ORDER and CYNDDELW BRYDYDD MAWR (*fl.* 1155–1200).

RHISIERDYN (*fl.* late 14th cent.), poet, was probably an Anglesey man. He is thought to have been the author of *awdlau* to *Hywel ap Gruffudd (Hywel y Fwyall) and to Goronwy ap Tudur of Penmynydd. These patrons were descendants of *Ednyfed Fychan ap Cynwrig, seneschal to *Llywelyn ap Iorwerth (Llywelyn Fawr), who had made their peace with the English Crown, had been prominent in the French wars and had been rewarded with important offices, but who remained enthusiastic supporters of Welsh culture in their native districts. Rhisierdyn's function was to offer them dignified, grandiloquent praise for their leadership and patronage. Although he belonged to the first phase of the period when the *cywydd was in vogue, he held to the old style and metres.

Rhita Gawr, a giant who, according to tradition, wore the beards of the many kings he had killed. There is an onomastic folk-tale which relates how he was killed by *Arthur who commanded his men to place stones on the giant's body, thus forming Yr Wyddfa, a mountain formerly called Gwyddfa Rhita ('Rhita's cairn') and known in English as Snowdon (*Eryri).

Rhiwallon, see under MYDDFAI, THE PHYSICIANS OF.

Rhiwedog, a house in the parish of Llanfor, Mer., was the home of a family who were prominent bardic patrons for more than two centuries. Elisau ap Wiliam Llwyd (d. 1583) was the most notable but his father and grandfather also extended a welcome to poets, among whom was *Tudur Aled. A number of poems to Elisau have survived which testify to his literary interests, including some by *Owain Gwynedd, *Wiliam Llŷn, Wiliam *Cynwal and *Gruffudd Hiraethog. Elisau's nephew John (d. 1646) and his wife Margaret maintained Rhisiart *Cynwal as their household poet and the tradition was kept for another four generations.

Rhiwlas, a house in the parish of Llanfor, Mer., at which itinerant poets, including *Gruffudd Hiraethog, were welcome from the time there of Cadwaladr ap Robert (d. 1554). His descendant, Siôn Wyn (d. 1589), maintained the custom but the latter's son, Cadwaladr (d. 1606), is said to have squandered much of the family's wealth. By the beginning of the seventeenth century the tradition had waned. See also LLOYD PRICE, RICHARD JOHN (1843–1923).

Rhiwsaeson, a house in the parish of Llanbrynmair, Mont., was often visited by itinerant poets during the sixteenth and seventeenth centuries. Patronage was extended without interruption by seven generations of the family but the most notable period was that of Rhisiart Morys (d. 1598).

Rhodd Mam, see under PARRY, JOHN (1775–1846).

Rhodri ab Owain Gwynedd (d. 1195), one of the sons of Owain Gwynedd (*Owain ap Gruffudd) by his second wife, Cristin. With his brother *Dafydd ab Owain Gwynedd as his ally, he defeated his half-brothers at the battle of Pentraeth (1170), but in 1175 Dafydd was driven out of *Gwynedd west of the river Conwy and the kingdom was henceforth divided between them. When Archbishop Baldwin preached the crusade in Anglesey in 1188, Rhodri and his retinue refused to take the Cross and *Gerald de Barri (Giraldus Cambrensis) suggested that his subsequent misfortunes were a divine judgement on him. Expelled from Anglesey by his nephews, the sons of Cynan ab Owain Gwynedd, about the year 1190, he returned with Manx assistance in 1193, an episode remembered in Welsh tradition as 'Haf y Gwyddyl' ('the Irish summer').

Rhodri Mawr (d. 877), the son of Merfyn Frych, became King of *Gwynedd after his father's death in 844, of *Powys at the death of his uncle in 855 and of *Seisyllwg (*Ceredigion and *Ystrad Tywi) after the death of his brother-in-law in 872. He was a resolute defender of his realm against the Danes and the English, resisting the ravages of the former upon Anglesey and dying in battle against the latter. His subsequent reputation was such that to be of the line of Rhodri Mawr was, in succeeding centuries, the first qualification for rulers in both north and south Wales. The union of three of the principal kingdoms of Wales under one ruler, although it did not survive Rhodri, set an example which was emulated by his grandson *Hywel Dda, by Maredudd ab Owain (d. 1072) and by *Gruffudd ap Llywelyn.

Rhonabwy, see under BREUDDWYD RHONABWY.

Rhondda, The, the name of two valleys (Rhondda Fach and Rhondda Fawr) which became synonymous with the heyday of the Welsh coal industry in the period from 1860 to 1920 and with the radical politics and proletarian culture which the industry shaped between 1910 and 1950. These once remote and sylvan valleys, lying to the north-west of Pontypridd, Glam., praised for their picturesque qualities by John Leland, Benjamin Heath *Malkin and many another visitor to south Wales during the early nineteenth century, were opened up during the 1850s by the rapid development of the steam coal trade and, in the following decade, by the mining of deeper seams. As in the neighbouring valleys of the Cynon and Taff, the rate of growth was dramatic as the Rhondda's population of less than a thousand in 1851 increased to more than 150,000 by 1911. In 1913, fifty-three large collieries employed 42,000 men to dig nine-and-a-half million tons of coal, or one-sixth of the maximum output of the South Wales coalfield, and townships such as Porth, Tonypandy,

Treorci, Ferndale and Maerdy were famous as mining communities. After the First World War a brief respite from economic crisis saw the population reach its highest total of 169,000 but an economy based on coal (with two-thirds of the work-force engaged in mining) could not withstand the *Depression of the inter-War years. The unemployment rate was among the highest in western Europe for more than a decade, poverty was rife, the population drained away and, despite some diversification of industry in the post-War years, it continues to do so.

By the 1980s the Rhondda had some 80,000 inhabitants, only one pit was still working and the two valleys now symbolize the decay of the older industrial areas of south Wales. None the less, the valleys remain emblematic of a once-vibrant culture which attempted, by political means rooted in a sense of community, to give direction to the lives of their people beyond the imperatives of wages and work. The manifestation of this rich and variegated culture was to be found in brass bands, male voice choirs, singing festivals, *Sunday School outings, trade union lodges, the Labour Party, chapels, boxing booths, football matches, *jazz bands and *hunger marches, to such an extent that the ethos of the Rhondda called forth a cornucopia of clichés and literary melodrama, not the least example of which was the novel *How Green was my Valley (1939) by Richard Llewellyn (Richard Llewellyn *Lloyd). The experience of the Rhondda is best recaptured in the novels, plays and short stories of Rhys *Davies, Jack *Jones, J. Kitchener *Davies, Lewis *Jones (1897–1934) and Ron *Berry, in the poetry of Idris *Davies and in the autobiographies of miners' leaders such as Arthur *Horner and Will Paynter. See also TONYPANDY RIOTS.

For discussion of various aspects of life in the valleys see E. D. Lewis, *Rhondda Valleys* (1959) and K. S. Hopkins (ed.), *Rhondda Past and Future* (1974).

Rhondda Roundabout (1934), the first of Jack *Jones's novels to be published, is set in the *Rhondda Valley during the early 1930s and tells of the love of Dan Price, the new minister of Beulah Chapel, for Lucy Meredith, a beautiful shop girl. But the novel's real interest lies in its gallery of colourful characters such as the minister's Uncle Shoni and Auntie Emily Lloyd, Big Mog the bookmaker, the Captain and Llew Rhondda the conductor. Religion, politics, music and sport are all encompassed in this lively, engaging novel which was later turned into a successful play.

Rhongomiant, *Arthur's spear in the legend of *Culhwch and Olwen.

Rhonwen, see ALICE ROWENA (mid-5th cent.).

Rhos, an early lordship, with its centre at *Deganwy, was the stronghold of *Maelgwn Gwynedd and later a cantref of *Gwynedd Is Conwy. In 1277 *Llywelyn ap Gruffudd was deprived of Rhos by Edward I and in 1282 the cantref (with the exception of the commot of *Creuddyn, which was attached to Caernarfon-shire) became part of the honour of Denbigh and was granted to the Earl of Lincoln.

'Rhosymedre', a hymn-tune by John David Edwards (1805–85), a native of Cardiganshire who spent more than forty years as an Anglican priest at Rhosymedre, Denbs. The tune first appeared under the title 'Lovely' in *Y Drysorfa* (May, 1838) to the words '*Mae'r wawr yn torri draw, / A'r twllwch yn ysgoi*' by John Phillips (Tegidon; 1810–77). It has found a place in all the Welsh hymnals and is now usually sung to the words '*O! Nefol addfwyn Oen*' by William *Williams (Pantycelyn) and '*Dewch, hen ac ieuanc, dewch*' by Morgan *Rhys. The English composer Ralph Vaughan Williams used it as one of the melodies on which he based his *Three Preludes on Welsh Hymn Tunes for Organ* (1920).

Rhuddlan, the site of castles built successively by the Welsh, the Normans and Edward I at strategic points overlooking the estuary of the river Clwyd. In this district, at *Morfa Rhuddlan, in 796, was fought an important battle at which King Offa of Mercia was killed. The castle built by order of Llywelyn ap Seisyllt about 1015 was used by his son, Gruffudd ap Llywelyn, as a royal residence. He was driven from Rhuddlan in 1063 by Earl Harold and in 1073, possibly on the same site, a motte and bailey castle was built by order of Robert of Rhuddlan. From this base the Normans expanded westwards into *Gwynedd, control of the castle and its associated borough fluctuating throughout the twelfth and thirteenth centuries (see under NORMAN CONQUEST). During the first *War of Independence (1276–77) the English army marched on Rhuddlan from Chester and in 1277 Edward I embarked upon the construction of a new castle and borough to the north of the Norman edifice. Rhuddlan was again an important military base during the second War of Independence (1282–83) and, after the defeat of *Llywelyn ap Gruffudd, it became the head-quarters of the Edwardian administration.

It was from Rhuddlan in 1284 that the English king proclaimed the Statute of Wales (or Statute of Rhuddlan) which outlined the arrangements for the government of the territory conquered by the royal armies. The hundred of Tegeingl (*Englefield) became the shire of Flint and was to be administered by the Justice of Chester. The three shires of Anglesey, Caernarfon and Merioneth, created in Gwynedd to the west of the river Conwy, were placed under the authority of the Justice of North Wales based in Caernarfon castle. In west Wales the existing counties of

Cardigan and Carmarthen were extended and administered by the Justice of West Wales based in Carmarthen castle. A sheriff was appointed in each shire, a system of courts was established and English criminal law replaced Welsh procedures. The use of Welsh law in civil actions was allowed to continue but alternative English procedures were explained in detail and some of these became popular in the fourteenth century. The administrative and legal provisions of the Statute of Rhuddlan were accompanied by the construction of castles and the foundation of boroughs in several parts of Wales (see under SHIRING OF WALES).

For further details see C. R. Williams, *The History of Flintshire* (1961) and A. J. Taylor, *Rhuddlan Castle* (1982); for a study of the Statute of Rhuddlan see Llinos Beverley Smith, 'The Statute of Wales 1284' in *The Welsh History Review* (vol. 10, 1980–81).

Rhufawn, see under CYNDDILIG (1935) and DWYMYN (1944).

Rhufawn Befyr ap Dewrarth Wledig, see under FAIR PRINCES.

Rhufoniog, a cantref of *Gwynedd Is Conwy, was named, according to tradition, after Rumaun, one of the sons of *Cunedda. With its centre at *Denbigh, it was granted to *Dafydd ap Gruffudd in 1277 and five years later it became part of the honour of Denbigh granted to Henry Lacy, Earl of Lincoln.

Rhun ap Maelgwn Gwynedd (*fl.* 550), King of *Gwynedd. In a text found among the Laws of Gwynedd a story entitled '*Breiniau Gwŷr Arfon*' ('The privileges of the men of Arfon') relates how the men of north Wales, campaigning in Gwynedd to avenge the killing of Elidir Mwynfawr, are checked by Rhun's forces. According to more recent traditions preserved by Thomas *Wiliems and Robert *Vaughan of Hengwrt, the cause of the trouble was an attempt by Elidir Mwynfawr to dethrone Rhun on the grounds that he was the illegitimate son of *Maelgwn Gwynedd. In the Triads Rhun is listed as one of the Three Blessed Rulers of the Isle of Britain. *Cynddelw Brydydd Mawr referred to Gwynedd as '*gwlad Rhun*' ('the land of Rhun') and its kings as '*hil Rhun*' ('the progeny of Rhun') and '*Rhun blant*' ('Rhun's children'). It is possible that Rhun is remembered in the placename Caerhun in Dyffryn Conwy.

Rhupunt Byr and **Rhupunt Hir**, see under TWENTY-FOUR METRES.

Rhwng Gwy a Hafren, the name given to the cantrefi and commots lying between the rivers Wye and Severn. The region, which never had cohesion as a lordship, included *Buellt, Cwmwd Deuddwr, *Elfael, *Gwrtheyrnion and *Maelienydd, and may be more properly considered as a lost province of *Powys.

Rhydderch Hen or **Rhydderch Hael** (6th cent.), one of the four kings of the *Old North who, according to the Saxon genealogies incorporated in *Nennius's *Historia Brittonum, resisted the Anglian king Hussa. An early reference to him is found in Adamnán's Life (7th cent.) of St. Columba which shows that he ruled in Strathclyde and was a contemporary of the saint, who died in 597. In the Triads he is listed as one of the Three *Generous Men of the Isle of Britain. He became associated with the legend of *Myrddin at an early stage in its development and there are several references in the Myrddin poems which suggest that he fought at the battle of Arfderydd in 573. In *Geoffrey of Monmouth's *Vita Merlini (*c.*1148), a poem drawing on Welsh sources, Rhydderch appears as Rodarchus, King of the Cumbri, who defeats Guonnolous (*Gwenddolau) and his supporter Merlinus (Myrddin) in battle. In the Life of St. Kentigern by Jocelyn of Furness (12th cent.) Rhydderch is praised for his generosity and portrayed as a patron of the Church.

Rhydderch, Siôn, see RODERICK, JOHN (1673–1735).

Rhyd-y-gloch, a ford on the river Taff near Pontypridd, Glam., is associated with an onomastic folk-tale about the traditional rivalry between the inhabitants of the contiguous parishes of Llanfabon and Llanwynno. It is said that the men of Llanfabon crossed the river one dark night with the intention of stealing the silver-tongued bell of Llanwynno's church. On the way back across the ford, with the bell wrapped in straw on their shoulders, they were startled when a full moon suddenly appeared from behind a cloud. The bell was dropped, its loud chiming awoke the people of Llanwynno and the marauders fled back to Llanfabon. Ever after the spot was called 'the ford of the bell' and, in that part of the valley, the full moon was known as '*haul Llanfabon*' ('the sun of Llanfabon').

Rhyd-y-Groes, The Battle of (1039), was fought at an unidentified place on the river Severn where the forces of *Gruffudd ap Llywelyn defeated those of Mercia. The battle was important because it enabled Gruffudd, who was made King of *Gwynedd and *Powys in the same year, to protect his eastern boundary and go on to defeat the kingdom of *Deheubarth in 1055.

'Rhydygroes', a well-known hymn-tune by Thomas David Edwards (1875–1930). Composed in 1902, it became popular after its appearance in the hymnals *Attodiad Llawlyfr Moliant* (1908) and *Cân a Moliant* (1916), and later in the composer's arrangement for male voices. It is usually sung to the words '*Duw mawr* *y rhyfeddodau maith'*, a translation by J. R. *Jones of Ramoth of a hymn by Samuel Davies (1818–91). Another hymn-tune, entitled '*Tuba Mirum*', which is very similar, appeared in *Llyfr Tonau ac Emynau y Wesleyaid* (1904) and there was controversy over its authorship.

Rhyfel y Sais Bach (lit. 'The war of the little Englishman'; 1820–26), was caused by a wealthy, young English gentleman named Augustus Brackenbury. Having bought 850 acres of land on Mynydd Bach near Llangwyryfon, Cards., he proceeded to enclose them and to build a house with the intention of establishing himself as a landowner in the district. The local inhabitants, fearing the loss of pasture for their sheep, destroyed Brackenbury's first house but, undaunted, he set about rebuilding it under the protection of hired troops. When the second building was set on fire by men disguised as women, he sought legal redress but, despite his offer of a reward, the identity of the culprits was never revealed. It is said that the men who pulled down the cottages on Brackenbury's land by night were those whom he employed as builders by day. After the destruction of his third house, in 1826, by a crowd of some six hundred men, one of their leaders—a blacksmith named David Jones—was brought to trial but acquitted by a local jury. Brackenbury, at last dispirited, decided to sell the land to his tenants and, leaving the district for the last time, went to London where he died, in his seventies, in 1874. The 'war' is the background of the long poem by Jeremy *Hooker which gives its title to his collection, *Englishman's Road* (1980).

There is a full account of the incident in David Jones, *Before Rebecca: Popular Protests in Wales 1793–1835* (1973).

'Rhyfelgyrch Capten Morgan' (lit. 'The war song of Captain Morgan'), a famous marching-song of which the music was first published by Edward *Jones (Bardd y Brenin) in his *Musical and Poetical Relicks of the Welsh Bards* (1784). According to Jones, it commemorates the exploits of the Morgan (ap Maredudd?) who led the men of Glamorgan during the *Welsh Revolt of Madog ap Llywelyn in 1294, but this claim is dubious. The song may refer to the buccaneer Henry *Morgan, or to some other man of the same name. The tune is also known in Brittany, where there is a traditional belief, recorded by Theodore Hersart de la *Villemarqué in *Barzaz Breiz* (1839), that Breton and Welsh soldiers, fighting in the French and English armies at the battle of Saint Cast (1758), recognized the tune as it was played on both sides and refused to fight their Celtic brothers until forced to do so by their officers. The words beginning '*Rhwym wrth dy wregys*', which are often sung to the tune, were composed by J. Ceiriog *Hughes and first published by Brinley Richards (1817–85) in *Songs of Wales* (1873). The version by Cynan (Albert *Evans-Jones), beginning '*Henffych i'n Prifardd*', is sung during the *Chair ceremony at the *National Eisteddfod.

'Rhyfelgyrch Gwŷr Harlech' (lit. 'The war song of the men of Harlech'), a famous marching-song first published by Edward *Jones (Bardd y Brenin) in his *Musical and Poetical Relicks of the Welsh Bards* (1784). The song, which has long been very popular, is usually sung to the words '*Wele goelcerth wen yn fflamio*' by J. Ceiriog *Hughes or '*Henffych well i wlad fy nghalon*' by John *Jones (Talhaiarn), but several parodies with English words are equally well known.

RHYGYFARCH or **RICEMARCHUS** (1056?–99), the son of *Sulien, was the most outstanding member of the *clas* at *Llanbadarn Fawr. The Latin manuscript known as *The Ricemarch Psalter* (now kept at Trinity College, Dublin), which is his work, includes a martyrology by Jerome and a translation by Rhygyfarch of the Hebrew Psalter, together with verses of his own composition. In Insular script, with illuminated initials, the Psalter was copied by a scribe named Ithael and the illumination was done by *Ieuan ab Sulien, one of Rhygyfarch's brothers, probably at Llanbadarn about 1079. The manuscript is of particular interest in that it is one of the few surviving examples of the work of the only identifiable scriptorium in the Wales of its period. Rhygyfarch's metrical ability is also demonstrated in his Lamentation, a poem written about 1094, which displays a knowledge of classical Latin learning. It is a profound, patriotic poem about the wretchedness of the land of *Ceredigion under attacks from the Normans. The other work attributed to Rhygyfarch is the *Vita Davidis* (a Life of St. David or *Dewi Sant) which he composed about 1094 as part of the campaign to defend the independence of the bishopric of *St. David's.

For further details see the article by Michael Lapidge in *Studia Celtica* (vols. VIII-IX, 1973–74).

Rhymi, a bitch hunted by *Arthur in the tale of *Culhwch and Olwen. Arriving at Tringad's house at Aberdaugleddyf, he hears that the animal, in the form of a she-wolf, has been roaming the district in pursuit of prey and is lurking, with her cubs, in a nearby cave. Surrounded by Arthur's men, Rhymi is revealed in human shape as a woman who had been transformed by God into a beast as punishment for some misdeed.

Rhys ap Gruffudd (The Lord Rhys; 1132–97), the last Welsh ruler of *Deheubarth to enjoy a wide degree of power, was the grandson of Rhys ap Tewdwr and also, through his mother *Nest, of *Gruffudd ap Cynan, King of *Gwynedd. During the anarchy of Stephen's reign in England, he joined his elder brothers in seeking to destroy Norman authority in south-west Wales and, on the death of his brother Maredudd in 1155, he became the sole lord of those parts of Deheubarth still acknowledging Welsh rule. On the accession of Henry II in 1157, he was deprived of most of his conquests but was confirmed as lord of *Cantref Mawr. He protested in arms in 1159, 1162 and 1164, his third revolt bringing the English king to Deheubarth, there to hear the prophecy of the *Old Man of Pencader recorded by *Gerald de Barri (Giraldus Cambrensis). In 1166, taking advantage of the King's failure to invade Gwynedd, Rhys recaptured the lands he had lost and, in 1171, with Henry by then gravely weakened and fearful of the power of his Norman vassals in Deheubarth, he was appointed Justiciar of South Wales.

Thereafter, until his death, Rhys was secure in his hold on most of Deheubarth and, with the House of Gwynedd temporarily in eclipse, he was acknowledged as the most powerful of the Welsh rulers. His office gave him authority over the lesser Welsh rulers of south Wales, many of whom, such as Ifor Bach (*Ifor ap Cadifor), were related to him by marriage. He remained loyal to the English Crown until Henry II's death in 1189 but in the last years of his life he resumed his opposition to Royal and Marcher authority in south-west Wales. After his death, his unruly sons (including *Rhys Gryg) tore apart the kingdom which he had created.

Rhys was a generous patron of the Church: he endowed the monastery of *Whitland, the mother-house of the Welsh *Cistercians, he was the main benefactor of the monastery of *Strata Florida, the necropolis of the House of Deheubarth, and he founded a house of Premonstratensian Canons at Talyllychau (*Talley). See also DINEFWR.

For further details see J. E. Lloyd, *A History of Wales* (1911), William Rees, *An Historical Atlas of Wales* (1951) and Gwynfor Evans, *Yr Arglwydd Rhys, Tywysog Deheubarth* (1982).

Rhys ap Thomas (1449–1525), see under BOSWORTH, THE BATTLE OF (1485), CAREW, CARMARTHEN CASTLE and CARREG CENNEN.

Rhys Amheurig or **Rhys Meurig**, see MERRICK, RICE (c. 1520–1586/7).

RHYS CAIN (d. 1614), poet and herald, was a native of Oswestry but adopted the name of the river Cain which runs through Mechain Iscoed; his son, *Siôn Cain, was also a poet and herald. Rhys addressed cywyddau in the traditional style to prominent families in north Wales. Much of his poetry, together with pedigrees, was destroyed by a fire at Wynnstay (see under WILLIAMS-WYNN FAMILY) in 1859, but another collection, written between 1574 and 1590, has been preserved, together with an account-book which is an important source of information about the practice of bardic itinerancy. His elegy for *Wiliam Llŷn, who was his bardic teacher, is his most famous poem and takes the form of a dialogue between the living and the dead, a form made popular by his master. There is some evidence to suggest that Rhys Cain was also a painter but none of his work has survived. He inherited Wiliam Llŷn's library and in, turn, influenced Robert *Vaughan of Hengwrt, the antiquary.

RHYS FARDD (**Y Bardd Bach**, **Bardd Cwsg**; *fl.* 1460–80), see under CWTA CYFARWYDD (c. 1425–c. 1456).

Rhys Goch ap Rhiccert, whose name is found only in pedigrees, was the ancestor of the poets Rhys Brydydd and Lewys Morgannwg (*Llywelyn ap Rhisiart). It was Iolo Morganwg (Edward *Williams) who composed the body of verse which he attributed to Rhys, in an attempt to demonstrate that, under Norman influence, there existed in Glamorgan during the twelfth century a school of Welsh troubadours.

For further details see the article by G. J. Williams in *Y Beirniad* (vol. VIII, 1919).

RHYS GOCH ERYRI (*fl.* 1385–1448), poet, was a native of Beddgelert, Caerns. For his bardic teacher, *Gruffudd Llwyd ap Dafydd ab Einion Llygliw, he wrote an elegy in which *Llywelyn ap Moel y Pantri thought he detected a slur on *Powys. Later, however, Rhys honoured Llywelyn with an elegy containing references to an eclipse of the sun at the time of his death, which suggests that his fellow-poet died in 1440. An elegy written for Maredudd ap Cynwrig, who died about 1448, is also attributed to Rhys. According to tradition, he spent his life at Hafod Garegog and was buried at Beddgelert.

Among his cywyddau on traditional themes is one dealing with the lineage of Wiliam Fychan ap Gwilym of Penrhyn. He also wrote a eulogy and an elegy for Wiliam's father, Gwilym ap Gruffudd, as well as poems addressed to Robert ap Maredudd, Saint *Beuno and Sir Gruffudd Fychan. Although no poem of his addressed to *Owain Glyndŵr has survived, references in the Penrhyn poems suggest that the poet's sympathies were on the Welsh side. He is perhaps best remembered as a participant in the *bardic controversy with Llywelyn ap Moel y Pantri and *Siôn Cent which was instigated by the comment on Powys in his elegy for Gruffudd Llwyd. The debate assumed greater relevance than the merely personal and eventually resulted in an exchange of ideas and a re-examination of the basic principles of the poetic art in general.

A selection of the work of Rhys Goch Eryri is to be found in the volume *Cywyddau Iolo Goch ac Eraill* (ed. Henry Lewis, Thomas Roberts, Ifor Williams, 1925); see also Saunders Lewis, *Braslun o Hanes Llenyddiaeth Gymraeg* (1932) and Bobi Jones, 'Pwnc Mawr

Beirniadaeth Lenyddol Gymraeg' in *Ysgrifau Beirniadol III* (ed. J. E. Caerwyn Williams, 1967).

Rhys Gryg (d. 1234), the son of *Rhys ap Gruffudd (The Lord Rhys), took part in the struggle for supremacy in *Deheubarth which began after his father's death in 1197. He held the throne of *Dinefwr and the province of the Vale of Tywi, and was confirmed in his possession of this territory when the lands of Deheubarth were distributed at a meeting held in the presence of *Llywelyn ap Iorwerth in 1216. The lands he had won in battle were added and, when peace was restored, he was forced to accept these conditions, although he was reluctant to pay homage to the king. It may have been at this time, in an attempt to reconcile the two, that Prydydd y Moch (*Llywarch ap Llywelyn) composed an *awdl* to commemorate Rhys Gryg's military feats. Rhys was also the subject of a eulogy and an elegy by *Phylip Brydydd. After his death from a wound received in battle, the Vale of Tywi was divided between his sons, Rhys Mechyll and Maredudd ap Rhys.

Rhys Lewis (1885), Daniel *Owen's second novel, was first published in monthly parts in the magazine *Y Drysorfa* (1882–84). The author chose the autobiographical form to tell the story of the fictitious Rhys Lewis, minister of Bethel, partly because such novels were popular in English, but mainly because the 'true' biography was far more acceptable to Welsh readers than the *novel. The search after form reflects the central problem of this novel: how 'true' are biographies which claim to tell the truth and how fully can 'the truth' be known about anyone? In the preface the eponymous hero reminds himself, 'Remember to tell the truth', but he does not always do so. Such was Daniel Owen's fascination with community that the book, rather than amounting to an exhaustive study of Rhys's own spiritual experience, becomes a gallery of the best-known characters in Welsh-language fiction: Mari Lewis, Rhys's mother, and his elder brother Bob, the pious Abel Hughes, kind old Thomas Bartley and Wil Bryan, Rhys's *alter ego*, the man whom Rhys would have been but for the grace of God. Daniel Owen's most Methodist novel and the most serious in intent, *Rhys Lewis* was, despite its loose structure and technical weaknesses, the greatest single step forward in the history of the Welsh-language novel.

An inept English translation by James Harris was published in 1888–89 and a revised edition in modern Welsh orthography, edited by Thomas Parry, in 1948. There are studies of the novel by R. Gerallt Jones in *Ansawdd y Seiliau* (1972) and by Hugh Bevan in *Beirniadaeth Lenyddol* (ed. Brynley F. Roberts, 1982); see also the article by T. R. Chapman in *Taliesin* (no. 46, 1983).

RHYS MEIGEN (14th cent.), a poet about whom *Dafydd ap Gwilym composed a satirical *awdl*. According to tradition, Rhys died on hearing the poem recited in reply to one of his own satirical *englynion* about Dafydd's mother. There are other references to him in the work of Dafydd ap Gwilym but hardly any of his work has survived. Nothing else is known about him and, though he may have been a man from Meigen, a district to the east of Welshpool, Mont., that is no more than conjecture.

RHYS NANMOR (*fl.* 1485–1513), the family poet of Sir Rhys ap Thomas, was the son of Maredudd ab Ieuan and Nest, the daughter of Owen ap Iorwerth of Merioneth. His best-known poem is '*Yr Awdl Fraith*' which is not an *awdl by modern standards but a *pryddest of ninety-nine lines, each beginning with the letter c and ending with the rhyme *-og*. The poem, in which twenty-six different animals are named, was composed as a prophetic eulogy of Henry VII, but none of the people to whom it alludes can now be identified. Rhys also wrote an elegy for Arthur, the King's eldest son, who died in 1502. Very different from *Dafydd Nanmor, his bardic teacher, in his style and vocabulary, Rhys Nanmor delighted in a profusion of archaic words, high-sounding phrases and a complex scheme of *cynghanedd. He was a friend of *Tudur Aled, with whom he exchanged *englynion*, and his elegy was written by his friend *Lewys Môn.

RHYS, EDWARD PROSSER (1901–45), editor and poet, was born at Bethel, Mynydd Bach, Cards. Owing to ill health, he left school at the age of sixteen and found work on *The Welsh Gazette*, embarking on a journalist's career which included the editorship of *Baner ac Amserau Cymru, a post in which he remained from 1923 until his death.

The publication of a volume of E. Prosser Rhys's lyrical poetry, *Gwaed Ifanc (1923), written in collaboration with John Tudor *Jones (John Eilian), was followed a year later by his winning the *Crown at the National Eisteddfod for his *pryddest*, '*Atgof*. Because this poem described a young man's homosexual feelings it caused controversy and the consternation of some critics prevented them from reaching a full appreciation of its literary merit. The reaction in some circles to '*Atgof* was partly responsible for the fact that no other volume of the author's work appeared until the publication of his collected poems in 1950, five years after his death. He continued, however, to encourage other writers in his capacity as editor of *Baner ac Amserau Cymru* and, from 1928 onwards, he was responsible for publishing many of their books at *Gwasg Aberystwyth, the press he founded. His diligence as a publisher and his indifferent health were among the factors which prevented him from maturing fully as a poet, but at least one of his poems, 'Cymru', is among the finest patriotic poems of the twentieth century.

A biography of E. Prosser Rhys has been written by Rhisiart Hincks (1980); see also the article by Gwyn Williams in Y Traethodydd (Oct., 1977).

RHYS, ERNEST (1859–1946), poet, novelist and editor. Born in Islington, London, the son of a Carmarthen man and an English mother, he spent six years of his childhood in his father's home town. He began his career as a mining engineer in the north of England but turned to writing novels, the first of which was The Fiddler of Carne (1896). By then he had become a well-known participant in the literary life of London, having founded the society known as the Rhymers' Club with W. B. Yeats and T. W. Rolleston in 1891.

It is chiefly for his editorship of Dent's Everyman Library that Ernest Rhys is remembered today. He was appointed to this post in 1906, after working as editor for a Tyneside publisher, and he it was who chose the name of the series and served as general editor of the 983 titles published before he died. This was the largest library of cheaply-priced books in the history of publishing before the advent of Penguin Books and Rhys became known as 'Mr. Everyman', on account of his editorship. In the judgement of his friend, Ezra Pound, he sacrificed a talent for spinning 'Welsh gold' by having to undertake 'much editing and hack-work'.

Rhys was, however, a poet and prose-writer who was held in high esteem during his own lifetime. His books include four volumes of verse, A London Rose (1894), Welsh Ballads (1898), Rhymes for Everyman (1933) and Song of the Sun (1937), none of which has great literary merit, and four more novels, The Whistling Maid (1900), The Man at Odds (1904), both of which are set in Wales, The Leaf Burners (1918) and Black Horse Pit (1925), and two volumes of autobiography, Everyman Remembers (1931) and Wales England Wed (1940). He also published two textbooks for schools, Readings in Welsh Literature (1924) and Readings in Welsh History (1927), translated a number of Welsh poems into English and was among the contributors to *Welsh Poets (ed. A. G. Prys-Jones, 1917). His wife, Grace Rhys (d. 1929), was also a novelist, and the editor of A *Celtic Anthology (1927). Ernest Rhys was a leading figure in the 'Celtic Twilight' movement of the 1890s but that he was considered in England as the chief representative Welsh poet of his day is a sad comment on the state of Anglo-Welsh literature at the turn of the century and on England's acquaintance with literature written in Welsh.

There is a study of the life and work of Ernest Rhys by J. K. Roberts in the Writers of Wales series (1983); see also the essay by Anthony Conran in The Cost of Strangeness (1982).

RHŶS, JOHN (1840–1915), Celtic scholar, was born near Ponterwyd, Cards. After training to be a teacher at the Normal College, Bangor, and teaching for a time at Rhos-y-bol, Ang., he entered Jesus College, Oxford, where he graduated with honours in Classics in 1869; in the same year he was elected a Fellow of Merton College. He spent his summer vacations studying at the Universities of Paris, Heidelberg, Leipzig and Göttingen. Appointed Inspector of Schools for Flintshire and Denbighshire in 1871, he became the first Professor of Celtic in the University of Oxford in 1877 and Principal of Jesus College in 1895. He was the first President of *Cymdeithas Dafydd ap Gwilym, a society formed in 1886. Prominent in Welsh public life, he received many honours: he was made a Fellow of the British Academy, received the Medal of the Honourable Society of *Cymmrodorion, was knighted in 1907, was elected a member of the Privy Council and received honorary degrees from the Universities of Edinburgh and Wales.

Primarily a philologist, John Rhŷs published a number of important articles on topics related to Celtic Philology. His first book, Lectures on Welsh Philology (1877), was in many respects his most valuable work. He was the first to use the methods of Comparative Philology in a study of the development of Welsh from Brythonic inscriptions to the language of his own time, placing it in context both with other Celtic languages and with some of the other Indo-European languages. He also published The Outlines of the Phonology of Manx Gaelic (1894), at a time when Manx was still a living language. His other main philological interest was in inscriptions, especially of European Celtic, on which he read several papers to the British Academy. He edited, with J. Gwenogvryn *Evans, The Text of the Mabinogion from the Red Book of Hergest (1887), The Text of the Bruts from the Red Book of Hergest (1890) and The Text of the Book of Llan Dâv (1893), and with John *Morris-Jones, The Elucidarium . . . from Llyvyr Agkyr Llanddewivrevi (1894).

He also developed his interest in archaeology, mythology, folk-literature and ethnology, publishing many books and articles on these subjects. Some of the more important include Celtic Britain (1882), Lectures on the Origin and Growth of Religion as illustrated by Celtic Heathendom (The Hibbert Lectures, 1888), Studies in the Arthurian Legend (1891), The Welsh People (with D. Brynmor Jones, 1900) and Celtic Folklore, Welsh and Manx (2 vols., 1901). Although from a modern viewpoint many of these works are unsatisfactory, John Rhŷs was the first and most important of the pioneers in these fields during the nineteenth century.

For further details about the life and work of Sir John Rhŷs, see the account by John Morris-Jones in the Proceedings of the British Academy (vol. XI, 1924–25);

see also the study by T. H. Parry-Williams in the *St. David's Day* series (1954).

RHYS, KEIDRYCH (1915–), editor and poet, was born William Ronald Rees Jones at Bethlehem, near Llandeilo, Carms., but later changed his name. He began his career as a literary journalist in London in 1937 and in that year founded the periodical *Wales which remained entirely identified with him throughout its existence. After serving in the Army with the Ministry of Information (1939–45), he returned to live in Wales at Llanybri, Carms., and set up the Druid Press in Carmarthen; from 1939 to 1948 he was married to the writer Lynette *Roberts. Returning to London in 1950, he worked in journalism and public relations, as a columnist for *The People* (1954–60) and as London editor of *Poetry London–New York* (1956–60).

Keidrych Rhys was highly influential in the development of Anglo-Welsh writing during the 1930s and 1940s, principally as an impresario and editor with a keen eye for new talent. He had an ebullient personality which delighted in controversy and literary anecdote. Among the anthologies he edited were *Poems from the Forces* (1941), *More Poems from the Forces* (1943) and *Modern Welsh Poetry* (1944). A selection of his own verse was published under the title *The Van Pool* (1942), but it was as an editor that his most important contribution was made. The largely autobiographical volume by Glyn *Jones, *The *Dragon has Two Tongues* (1968), opens with a letter to Keidrych Rhys.

RHYS, MORGAN (1716–79), hymn-writer, was born at Cil-y-cwm, Carms. Little is known of his early life, but he worked as a teacher in the Circulating Schools of Griffith *Jones between 1757 and 1775; several testimonies to his labours were published in *Welch Piety*, the Schools' annual report. From the evidence of two of Rhys's letters (1757–58) copied into the diary of his friend, John Thomas of Tre-main, it is clear that he had been fired by the spirit of the Methodist awakening which had swept through his native district.

He is remembered today as one of the most important Welsh hymn-writers of the eighteenth century. His hymns were first published in the volume *Golwg o Ben Nebo* (1755), a title he gave to two more volumes published in 1764 and 1775, and in a number of smaller collections including *Cascliad o Hymnau* (1757), *Casgliad o Hymnau* (1760), *Golwg ar Ddull y Byd Hwn* (1767), *Golwg ar Ddinas Noddfa* (1770), *Griddfannau'r Credadyn* (c.1773) and *Y Frwydr Ysprydol* (c.1774); the last-named includes hymns written by Thomas *Dafydd. Rhys also published elegies, in the style of William *Williams (Pantycelyn), in memory of Griffith Jones, Lewis Lewis of Llanddeiniol, Howel Davies of Pembrokeshire, William Richards of Llanddewibrefi, Siôn Parry of Talyllychau and Morgan Nathan of Llandeilo. He was not a prolific hymn-writer, but the spiritual worth of his work is equal to that of the best hymns composed during the golden age of Welsh hymnology and a good selection is found in all contemporary hymnals.

An account of the life and work of Morgan Rhys has been published by Gomer M. Roberts (1951); see also *Gwaith Morgan Rhys. Rhan 1* (ed. H. Elvet Lewis, 1910), the essay by G. O. Williams in *Gwŷr Llên y Ddeunawfed Ganrif* (ed. Dyfnallt Morgan, 1966) and the essay by D. Simon Evans in *Ysgrifau Beirniadol XI* (ed. J. E. Caerwyn Williams, 1979). A selection of his hymns is to be found in *Pedwar Emynydd* (ed. Bobi Jones, 1970).

Rhys, Morgan John (1760–1804), minister and political propagandist. Born at Llanbradach, Glam., he became a Baptist minister at Penygarn, near Pontypool, Mon. A lover of Liberty who saw in the French Revolution of 1789 the dawn of a New Age, he preached against the slave trade and advocated parliamentary reform in *Y *Cylch-grawn Cynmraeg*, a monthly magazine which he launched at Trefeca in 1793 but which ran for only five numbers. In 1794, disgusted with the anti-*Liberalism characteristic of the political and religious life of the day, and to avoid arrest for his remarks on what he considered to be the tyranny of the Government, he crossed the Atlantic to prepare a place in America for a free Welsh settlement. Four years later, in the Allegheny Mountains of western Pennsylvania, he purchased a tract of land which he called Cambria and which he intended to be 'the home of a free and enlightened people when the old Cambria is neglected and despised'. The settlement's principal town was called Beulah and it attracted many immigrants from Wales. There Rhys published a newspaper, *The Western Sky*, founded a new denomination known as the Church of Christ, and established a missionary society for the Red Indians. His involvement in the community of Beulah, where the settlers encountered great natural difficulties, was short-lived, and in 1799 he moved to Somerset County, where for the last four years of his life he was a prominent public figure.

For further details see J. J. Evans, *Morgan John Rhys a'i Amserau* (1935) and Gwyn A. Williams, *The Search for Beulah Land* (1980); the novel by Emyr Humphreys, *The Anchor Tree* (1980), is symbolically concerned with Beulah.

RHYS, SIÔN DAFYDD (1534–c.1619), doctor of medicine and scholar, known as **John Davies** to his contemporaries, was born in the parish of Llanfaethlu, Âng., a nephew of Bishop Richard *Davies. He was educated at Christ Church, Oxford, and travelled extensively on the Continent, graduating Master of Divinity at the University of Siena in 1567. On his return to Wales in 1574 he was appointed headmaster of Friars School, Bangor, but later practised medicine in Cardiff and at Clun Hir, his home in

Cwm Llwch, near Brecon. Although he had been at one time a Protestant and had assisted with the translation of the Scriptures into Welsh, he returned, after a few years back in Wales, to that Roman Catholic faith which had attracted him in Italy.

While he was abroad he published three books: one was a Greek grammar written in Latin, of which no copy has survived; the second was a guide to Latin or Italian pronunciation (1569). His most notable work, however, was *Cambrobrytannicae Cymraecaeve Linguae Institutiones et Rudimenta* (1592), a grammar of the Welsh language together with material relating to Welsh prosody. Rhys's gifts as a grammarian were far inferior to those of Gruffydd *Robert and John *Davies of Mallwyd, for he forced Welsh into a Latin structure entirely inappropriate to it, but he rendered valuable service by publicizing the rules of *Cerdd Dafod, which the poets tended to keep secret. As one of the foremost Renaissance scholars in the Wales of his day, he strove to present to the world, in the Latin language, some idea of the wealth of the Welsh language and its literature, and he was a master of Welsh prose. He also wrote an essay, preserved in manuscript, as part of the controversy concerning Polydore Vergil's criticism of *Geoffrey of Monmouth (see under MYTH OF DESCENT). Also preserved in manuscript is his famous letter to the poets in which he praises their craftsmanship and advises them to adopt contemporary humanistic standards.

For further details see the articles by Thomas Parry in *Y Llenor* (vols. IX and X, 1930, 1931), and in the *Bulletin* of the Board of Celtic Studies (vol. VI). Of special importance is R. Geraint Gruffydd's article, 'The Life of Dr. John Davies of Brecon', in the *Transactions* of the Honourable Society of Cymmrodorion (1971, part ii). The letter to the poets was published in *Rhyddiaith Gymraeg II* (ed. Thomas Jones, 1956) and is discussed by Branwen Jarvis in *Llên Cymru* (vol. XII, 1972).

Ricemarchus, see RHYGYFARCH (1056?–99).

RICHARD, EDWARD (1714–77), poet, was born and brought up at Ystradmeurig, Cards. He received lessons in Greek and Latin from his brother Abraham before attending the Queen Elizabeth Grammar School in Carmarthen. Returning to Ystradmeurig about 1735 to keep the village school, he spent the rest of his life there. Among his pupils were David *Richards (Dafydd Ionawr) and Evan *Evans (Ieuan Brydydd Hir) who were later to become poets. Owen M. *Edwards recalled in one of his essays how Richard once closed the school for a whole year because his conscience told him he should learn more if he was to be a worthy teacher. Only a little of his verse survives: two pastoral poems, two songs about Pontrhydfendigaid, a hymn, a translation of John Gay's ballad ''Twas when the seas were roaring', and the well-known '*In Sepulchrum Infantoli*'. It is for his two

pastoral poems that he is remembered today. The first, written about 1765 on the occasion of his mother's death, strikes a note of profound grief, while the second, which was published in 1776, combines the personal with the social in a particularly charming way.

For further details see *Gwaith Edward Richard* (ed. O. M. Edwards, 1912) and the essay by John Gwilym Jones in *Gwŷr Llên y Ddeunawfed Ganrif* (ed. Dyfnallt Morgan, 1966); there is an article on Edward Richard and Ieuan Fardd by Aneirin Lewis in *Ysgrifau Beirniadol* X (ed. J. E. Caerwyn Williams, 1977).

Richard, Henry (1812–88), political reformer and idealist, was born at Tregaron, Cards. A Congregational minister in London from 1835 to 1850, he first came to prominence in 1848 as Secretary of the Peace Society and, in that office, 'The Apostle of Peace', as he was known in Wales, became friendly with Richard Cobden, travelled a good deal in Europe and was active in attempting to promote arbitration in international disputes. In the crucial Parliamentary election of 1868 he was returned as Liberal member for Merthyr Tydfil, a result which for the first time gave a voice to Welsh *Nonconformity in the House of Commons. Despite the many years he spent in England, he was keenly interested in Welsh education, *Land Reform, *Disestablishment of the Church and the Welsh language, and generally in the presentation of Welsh interests to a wider audience. For these reasons he was known in political circles as 'The Member for Wales' (but see also RENDEL, STUART).

He wrote powerfully and lucidly in both languages, but chiefly in English, as evidenced by his many pamphlets, by his *Letters on the Social and Political Condition of Wales* (1866), and by the diaries of his European tours. Although he was not a politician of the first rank, few commanded such widespread respect and his reputation did much for the image of Welsh Nonconformist *Radicalism. His practical, social and international achievements were in the long run not very great, but in Wales a remarkable romantic aura was for long associated with his name.

For further details see Charles S. Miall, *Henry Richard M.P.* (1889), Eleazar Roberts, *Bywyd a Gwaith y diweddar Henry Richard* (1907); see also the references in Ieuan Gwynedd Jones, *Explorations and Explanations* (1981).

RICHARDS, ALUN (1929–   ), playwright and novelist, was born in Pontypridd, Glam., and educated at the Monmouthshire Training College, Caerleon, and at University College, Swansea. Drawing on his experiences as probation officer, hospital patient, sailor and teacher for the material of his writing, he rejects the portrayal of a romanticized Welsh past of anecdote and myth and is more concerned with the contemporary Wales of *rugby, beauty queens, television, the language question and the valleys of Glamorgan in industrial and spiritual decline.

His view is warm, sharply observed, deeply understanding, and often very funny, and it encompasses an unusually wide range of social classes.

He has published six novels: *The Elephant you Gave Me* (1963), *The Home Patch* (1966), *A Woman of Experience* (1969), *Home to an Empty House* (1973), *Ennal's Point* (1977) and *Barque Whisper* (1979); the last two are the first parts of a trilogy about the sea. His two collections of short stories are entitled *Dai Country* (1973) and *The Former Miss Merthyr Tydfil* (1976). Besides editing *The Penguin Book of Welsh Short Stories* (1976) and two anthologies of sea-stories, he has written a book about Welsh rugby, *A Touch of Glory* (1980), a memoir of Carwyn James (1984) and many plays and adaptations for television, notably *The Onedin Line*. Four of his stage plays, three of which are set in Wales, have been published in the volume *Plays for Players* (1975).

There is an autobiographical essay by Alun Richards in the volume *Artists in Wales* (ed. Meic Stephens, 1971); see also the note by Glyn Jones in *Profiles* (1980) and the article by Shaun McCarthy, 'Home from the Sea: Tradition and Innovation in the Novels of Alun Richards', in *The Anglo-Welsh Review* (no. 78, 1985).

RICHARDS, BRINLEY (1904–81), poet, was born and lived all his life in the Llynfi Valley, Glam., where he practised as a solicitor. He won the *Chair at the National Eisteddfod in 1951 with his poem '*Y Dyffryn*' and, as Brinli, he served as Archdruid from 1972 to 1974. Besides a volume of verse, *Cerddi'r Dyffryn* (1967), he published a biography of Edgar *Phillips, *Cofiant Trefin* (1961), a collection of essays, *Hamddena* (1972), a book in defence of the story of Wil Hopcyn and Ann *Maddocks (1977) and *A History of the Llynfi Valley* (1982) which was published posthumously. His study of Edward *Williams, *Golwg Newydd ar Iolo Morganwg* (1979), is regarded as unreliable.

A selection of his essays and poems, together with a bibliography and articles about him by some of his friends, will be found in the memorial volume, *Brinli: Cyfreithiwr, Bardd, Archdderwydd* (ed. Huw Walters and W. Rhys Nicholas, 1984).

Richards, Ceri (1903–71), painter, was born at Dunvant, Swansea. His early work showed the influence of Matisse but he became a member of the British Surrealist Group in 1936. Among works which won him an international reputation as one of the most important British painters of the twentieth century was a series of paintings based on the poetry of Dylan *Thomas and Vernon *Watkins.

A study of the relationship between his painting and the poetry of Dylan Thomas is to be found in Richard Burns, *Keys to Transformation* (1981).

RICHARDS, DAVID (**Dafydd Ionawr**; 1751–1827), poet, was born near Tywyn, Mer., and educated at Edward *Richard's school at Ystradmeurig. By profession he was a schoolmaster and he ended his career at Dolgellau. Most of his verse is Scriptural in inspiration and written in the strict metres. His poem, '*Cywydd y Drindod*' (1793), which comprises about 13,000 lines, is one of the longest in the Welsh language, but that is its only distinction. Besides a few flyting poems in the free metres, which are livelier than his more serious work, he published the volumes *Y Mil-Blynyddau* (1799), *Gwaith Prydyddawl* (1803), *Joseph, Llywodraethwr yr Aipht* (1809), *Barddoniaeth Gristianogawl* (1815) and *Cywydd y Diluw* (1821); his collected works were edited by Morris *Williams (Nicander) in 1851.

RICHARDS, MELVILLE (1910–73), scholar, was born at Ffair-fach, Llandeilo, Carms., and educated at University College, Swansea. He completed his studies of Old Irish in Dublin and of Indo-European in Paris before returning to Swansea as a lecturer in 1936, by which time he had published a handbook of Old Irish for students. He moved to Liverpool University in 1948 as a Lecturer, and later Reader, in the Department of Celtic, and he was appointed Professor of Welsh at the University College of North Wales, Bangor, in 1965. His first research studies were into Welsh syntax in the Middle Ages and they later developed into an interest in the history of the institutions of medieval Welsh society and the *Laws of Hywel Dda. He published *Cystrawen y Frawddeg Gymraeg* (1938), the text of *Breuddwyd Rhonabwy (1948), an English translation of one of the Hywelian law books (1954), the text of another (1957), and the volume *Welsh Administrative and Territorial Units: Medieval and Modern* (1969). His intention was to produce a historical dictionary of Welsh place-names, but he died before he could convert his enormous collection into an onomasticon. He also published a spy novel, *Y Gelyn Mewnol* (1946), in which he drew on his experiences in the Secret Service during the Second World War.

For further details see the obituary of Melville Richards by Idris Foster in *Studia Celtica* (vols. X/XI, 1975–76).

RICHARDS, RICHARD (*fl.* 1838–68), poet and journalist, was a native of the Oswestry district, possibly of Llanymynech, Mont. About 1854 he moved to Bangor as a journalist with *The North Wales Chronicle*, to which he contributed, over a number of years, two sets of letters, one from 'A Welsh Girl' and the other signed 'Old Mountaineer'. Flippant and mildly satirical, these letters were anti-Dissent (*Nonconformity) but forward-looking in trade and technical matters. The second set was plainly a Churchman's response, in English, to *Llythurau 'Rhen Ffarmwr (1878) by Gwilym Hiraethog (William *Rees). Richards's first volume of verse (1854) circulated only in the neighbourhoods of Oswestry and Wrexham; his second, *Miscellaneous Poems and Pen-and-Ink Sketches* (1868), prints a selection from the verse and the letters, together with more straightforward accounts of scenery, slate-quarries and railway enterprises. The prose is only occasionally lively, while the verse is fluent, correct and conventional.

RICHARDS, THOMAS (1878–1962), historian and essayist, was born at Talybont, Cards., and educated at the University College of North Wales, Bangor. He began his career as a teacher of History but in 1926 was appointed Librarian at his old College, a post in which he remained until his retirement in 1946. It was he who, by continuing the work of collecting and cataloguing books and periodicals which had been begun by Thomas *Shankland, made the College's library into one of the foremost centres of learning in Wales. He was the author of eight books, including *A History of the Puritan Movement in Wales, 1639–53* (1920), *Religious Developments in Wales, 1654–62* (1923), *Wales under the Penal Code, 1662–87* (1925), *Wales under the Indulgence, 1672–75* (1928) and *Cymru a'r Uchel Gomisiwn* (1929). His two volumes of autobiography, *Atgofion Cardi* (1960) and *Rhagor o Atgofion Cardi* (1963), together with the essays and radio talks in *Rhwng y Silffoedd* (1978), make some of the liveliest reading in the Welsh language.

RICHARDS, THOMAS (1883–1958), poet. Born at Trawsfynydd, Mer., he worked in the gold-mines at Gwynfynydd before emigrating to America but, on his return, he settled as a farmer in Llanfrothen. In the company of local poets, he learned to write *englynion* and won prizes with them at the *National Eisteddfod. He is remembered chiefly for his famous *englyn* to a sheep-dog which gave the title to his only collection of verse, *Y Ci Defaid a Cherddi Eraill* (1964).

RICHARDS, THOMAS (1909–   ), playwright, a native of Tywyn, Mer., worked as a journalist from 1927 to 1942, first with *The Cambrian News* in Aberystwyth and later with the *Western Mail. From 1945 until his retirement in 1969 he was employed by the BBC, of which he was the principal officer in Swansea. His plays include *Y Carnifal* (1939), *Y Cymro Cyffredin* (1960), *Eisteddfa Gwatwarwyr* (1982) and *Mi Glywaf Dyner Lais* (1982). Like his only novel, *Mae'r Oll yn Gysegredig* (1966), his plays are satirical and they are among the funniest written in Welsh since the Second World War.

RICHARDS, WILLIAM LESLIE (1916–   ), poet and novelist, was born at Capel Isaac, near Llandeilo, Carms., and educated at the University College of Wales, Aberystwyth. By profession a schoolmaster, he was Deputy Head-master of Llandeilo Comprehensive School from 1975 until his retirement in 1981. He is the author of several novels, including *Yr Etifeddion* (1956), *Llanw a Thrai* (1958) and *Cynffon o Wellt* (1960), and of four volumes of verse, namely *Telyn Teilo* (1957), *Bro a Bryniau* (1963), *Dail yr Hydref* (1968) and *Adlodd* (1973). He has edited the works of Dafydd Llwyd of Mathafarn (*Dafydd Llwyd ap Llywelyn ap Gruffudd) and, with D. H. Culpitt, published a volume about D. J. *Williams, *Y Cawr o Rydcymerau* (1970).

Riddles. There is evidence that the *Celts, seen in their Continental domicile two or more centuries before Christ, brought riddles and ambiguities regularly into their behaviour. In the military context—the one in which they were most frequently observed—these riddles were linked with the boasting and threatening practices which preceded battles. The Greek historian Diodorus Siculus, probably relying on the much earlier evidence of Posidonius, reported that 'in conversation . . . they use few words and speak in riddles, for the most part hinting at things and leaving a great deal to be understood'. A more political or distant example of this practice is found in the *Dream* of *Macsen Wledig when Maximus, receiving an unfinished threat—'If ever thou come to Rome'—replies with another, 'And if I go to Rome, and if I go'.

Riddles in the form of questions intended to test the wit of the listener have come down in the Welsh folk-tradition and have been popular, especially among children, for many centuries. Although transmitted orally, often in the form of *rhigymau or in *dialect, they are also to be found in Welsh poetry, as in some early poems which describe objects without actually naming them. The most famous example, perhaps, is the poem in The *Book of Taliesin which describes the wind. The more recent use of simile, as found in the work of the *Poets of the Gentry, is believed to have grown out of this riddle poetry. In the work of the *Gogynfeirdd an object is described in terms of a girl's body, or a nobleman's house, by the listing of a large number of short similes and ending with the name of the thing itself, as in *Dafydd ap Gwilym's poem to the mist and *Dafydd Nanmor's to Llio's hair.

For a study of the form see Vernon E. Hull and Archer Taylor, *A Collection of Welsh Riddles* (1942).

River Out of Eden (1951), a novel by Jack *Jones about the growth of Cardiff, traces the fortunes of the Regan family, of which the head is Dan Regan, an immigrant Irish labourer. With the increase of the city's wealth and importance, the Regans prosper and Dan's grandson Tirso is the aged Lord Pantmawr with whom the novel opens and closes.

ROBERT AB IFAN or **ROBERT AB IEUAN** or **ROBERT IFANS** (*fl.* 1572–1603), poet and gentleman of Brynsiencyn, Ang. His verse, composed after the second *Caerwys Eisteddfod (1567), was mostly addressed to local gentry, but he also wrote a series of *englynion* on various topics, including one dated 26 February 1575 on the occasion of an earth tremor. He made a copy for himself of a bardic grammar (1587) and compiled a history of the *Bardic Order in which he testified to the disrespect shown towards the poet's profession in his own day.

Robert ap Gwilym Ddu, see WILLIAMS, ROBERT (1766–1850).

Robert ap Huw (1580–1665), musician, was descended from the *Tudor family of Penmynydd, Ang. Harpist to King James I, he was the author or copyist of a manuscript (now in the British Library) which is virtually the only guide to Welsh harp music in medieval times. It dates from about 1613 but was copied, in part at least, from another manuscript belonging to the poet Wiliam Penllyn (*fl.* 1550–70). The manuscript contains pieces for the harp, among which are several apparently intended to accompany singing or recitation. Also known as the Penllyn Manuscript, it has been the subject of intense study and curiosity since the mid-eighteenth century but all attempts to transcribe the music into modern notation have so far been thwarted.

The manuscript was edited by Henry Lewis in 1936. The fullest account of Robert ap Huw's life is that by Dafydd Wyn Wiliam (1975).

ROBERT, GRUFFYDD (pre-1532 – post-1598), humanist, grammarian and the first master of Ciceronian prose in the Welsh language, was a native of Llŷn or *Eifionydd, Caerns. Educated at Christ Church, Oxford, he became Archdeacon of Anglesey in 1558 but left for the Continent in the following year after the passing of the Acts of Supremacy and Uniformity. He spent several years in Rome with his friend, Morys *Clynnog, but moved in the 1560s to Milan, where he was to remain for the rest of his life as Canon Theologian at the Duomo and confessor to the Archbishop, Cardinal (later Saint) Carlo Borromeo. The first part of Robert's Welsh Grammar, *Dosparth Byrr ar y rhann gyntaf i ramadeg Cymraeg* (1567), was published in Milan; the remaining parts were probably all composed after Borromeo's death in 1584. If Gruffydd Robert was the 'Dr. Griffith' who was confessor to a nunnery at Milan in 1605, he survived into the seventeenth century; the identification is not certain but he was acting as ecclesiastical censor there as late as 1598.

That the vernacular could be raised to the dignity of a great literary language like Latin or Greek—provided learned men could be persuaded to cultivate it and give it the genres already possessed by the classical languages—was a doctrine frequently reiterated by the major figures of Italian humanism and it is the basis of Gruffydd Robert's Grammar. Like Bembo's *Prose della volgar lingua*, this work is a dialogue on the author's own language and was intended to persuade the learned among his compatriots to develop its literary potential and to demonstrate what a fine medium for literature it could become. Offered to other writers as an aid to perfecting their style, it is so well written as to have become one of the classics of the literature which it sought to promote. Robert differs from Bembo, however, in showing greater respect for spoken usage, perhaps as a result of his acquaintance with the theories of Tolomei and other philologists from Siena, with whom Siôn Dafydd *Rhys may have provided a link, and his interest in orthographical reform certainly suggests a knowledge of their work. Robert's Grammar, which includes a discussion of Welsh metrics and a small anthology of Welsh poetry, is followed by his translation of part of Cicero's *De senectute*. Here, as in the Grammar itself, he provided a model in Welsh of Ciceronian prose and thus introduced to Welsh literature the doctrines and style favoured by the major authors of the Italian Renaissance.

The Grammar of Gruffydd Robert was edited with an introduction by G. J. Williams (1939). For further details of his life and work see the account by D. Rhys Phillips, *Dr. Griffith Roberts: Canon of Milan* (1922); see also the essay by Saunders Lewis in *Ysgrifau Dydd Mercher* (1945), the article by T. Gwynfor Griffiths, 'Italian Humanism and Welsh Prose' in *Yorkshire Celtic Studies* (vol. VI, 1953–58) and the same author's *Avventure Linguistiche del Cinquecento* (1961).

ROBERTS, ABSALOM (1780?–1864), poet, a native of Trefriw, Caerns., was a travelling shoemaker who settled at Eglwys-bach, Denbs., and later at Llanrwst. He delighted in collecting *Hen Benillion* (harp-stanzas) and published a selection of them in the volume *Lloches Mwyneidd-dra* (1845). The style of these verses is to be seen in his own poems, for example, in 'Trawsfynydd', which W. J. *Gruffydd included in his anthology *Y Flodeugerdd Gymraeg* (1937).

Roberts, Bartholomew (Barti Ddu or Black Bart; 1682?–1722), sailor. A Pembrokeshire man, he was second mate on *The Princess* when, in 1718, it was captured by the pirate Howel Davis (Hywel Dafydd). On his captor's death he turned pirate himself and won a brief notoriety in the Caribbean until his ship, *The Royal Fortune*, was attacked by British naval vessels off Cape Lopez and he was killed. Barti Ddu, '*y morwr tal â'r chwerthiniad iach*' ('the tall sailor with the hearty laugh'), is the subject of a famous ballad by I. D. *Hooson.

ROBERTS, BRYNLEY FRANCIS (1931–), scholar. A native of Aberdare, Glam., he was educated at the University College of Wales, Aberystwyth, and after lecturing in Welsh at his old College, became Professor of Welsh Language and Literature at University College, Swansea, in 1978. His main academic interests are in medieval Welsh prose and his publications include *Gwasanaeth Meir* (1961), *Brut y Brenhinedd* (1971), *Cyfranc Lludd a Llefelys* (1975), *Brut Tysilio* (1980), *Edward Lhuyd, the Making of a Scientist* (1980), and an essay on *Gerald de Barri (Giraldus Cambrensis) in the *Writers of Wales* series (1982). He was appointed Librarian of the *National Library of Wales in 1985.

Roberts, Caradog (1878–1935), musician. Born at Rhosllannerchrugog, Denbs., he was apprenticed to a carpenter but devoted himself to the study of music from an early age, taking an Oxford degree in the subject in 1905. Much in demand as organist, adjudicator and conductor, he edited the Independent hymnals, *Y Caniedydd Cynulleidfaol* (1921) and *Caniedydd Newydd yr Ysgol Sul* (1930), and composed a number of hymn-tunes, the most famous of which is perhaps *'Rachie'*.

ROBERTS, DAVID (Dewi Havhesp; 1831–84), poet, took his bardic name from a stream near his home at Llanfor, near Bala, Mer. A tailor by trade, he spent most of his life in Llandderfel. His only collection of verse was the very popular book, *Oriau'r Awen* (1876). Only four of his *englynion* appear in *Y Flodeugerdd Englynion* (1978), however, because the editor, Alan *Llwyd, agreed with Gwenallt (David James *Jones), that Dewi Havhesp, like Trebor Mai (Robert *Williams), was responsible for reducing the artistic integrity of the *englyn* by his habit of composing the last line first.

ROBERTS, EDWARD (Iorwerth Glan Aled; 1819–67), poet, a native of Llansannan, Denbs., was a shopkeeper in Rhuddlan and Denbigh before becoming a Baptist minister and serving in Liverpool and Rhymney, Mon. He was notable only for his attempts to compose in Welsh a biblical *epic which would be comparable with Milton's *Paradise Lost* (1667). However, his *pryddestau*, 'Y Tŵr' and 'Palestina' (1851), like all other attempts to master the genre in Welsh, were over-long, inflated and structurally deficient. His nephew, Edward Jones, collected his poetical works (1890) and Gwenallt (David James *Jones) edited a selection of his shorter poems in the *Llyfrau Deunaw* series (1955).

For further details see the two articles by Derwyn Jones in the *Transactions* of the Welsh Baptist Historical Society (1956, 1957).

ROBERTS, EIGRA LEWIS (1939–), novelist, short-story writer and playwright, was born at Blaenau Ffestiniog, Mer., and educated at the University College of North Wales, Bangor. Formerly a teacher, she is a full-time writer and lives at Dolwyddelan, Caerns. She first came to prominence with her novel *Bryn-hyfryd* (1959) which was highly praised as a young woman's vivid response to 'the generation gap' in Wales during the years after the Second World War. Concentrating mainly on the everyday problems of the individual, particularly from a woman's point of view, she explored similar themes in two more novels, *Tŷ ar y Graig* (1966) and *Digon i'r Diwrnod* (1974), and in several collections of short stories, including *Y Drych Creulon* (1968), *Cudynnau* (1970) and *Fe Ddaw Eto* (1976). As well as writing for the stage, radio and television, she has published a play based on the life of Ann *Griffiths and a collection of essays about famous Welshwomen, *Siwgwr a Sbeis* (1975); her play, *Byd o Amser* (1976), won the Drama Medal at the National Eisteddfod in 1974. She has also published, under the title *Plentyn yr Haul* (1981), a recreation of the life of Katherine Mansfield, and has edited a volume, *Merch yr Oriau Mawr* (1981), dealing with the life and work of Dilys *Cadwaladr. Some critics saw the influence of Kate *Roberts on her early work, mainly because she was a woman writer and came from a similar background. But it was soon realized that Eigra Lewis Roberts belonged to a different generation and when her novel *Mis o Fehefin* was published in 1980, it was generally recognized that hers was a mature, independent talent which places her among the most distinguished Welsh novelists of the twentieth century. A fifth novel, *Ha' Bach*, appeared in 1985.

The author discusses her own writing in an article entitled 'Words that Burn' in *The Powys Review* (no. 14, 1984).

ROBERTS, ELEAZAR (1825–1912), musician and author. Born at Pwllheli, Caerns., he was brought up in Liverpool and worked from the age of thirteen at various clerical jobs in the legal profession. A pioneer of the tonic sol-fa system in Wales, he published several textbooks in Welsh and a novel, *Owen Rees* (1894), written in English, which is notable for its portrayal of the life of the *Liverpool Welsh during the heyday of that expatriate community.

ROBERTS, ELIS (Y Cowper; d. 1789), poet and writer of *interludes, was a native of Bala, Mer. He lived at Llanddoged, Denbs., and earned a living as a cooper. One of his interludes, *Pedwar Chwarter y Flwyddyn* (1787), contains some social criticism, but he was more concerned with moral issues: *Gras a Natur* (1769) is an allegory, *Cristion a Drygddyn* (1788) deals with religious controversy and the horror of the American War of Independence is realistically described in *Y Ddau Gyfamod* (1777). Although scorned by Goronwy *Owen and the *Morris Brothers, Roberts was as popular in his day as Twm o'r Nant (Thomas *Edwards). His interludes are a valuable mirror of their age and some of them still make amusing reading.

ROBERTS, ELLIS (**Elis Wyn o Wyrfai**; 1827–95), poet and editor. Born at Llandwrog, Caerns., he attended the school kept by Eben Fardd (Ebenezer *Thomas), became a schoolmaster and was later ordained. While vicar of Llangwm, Denbs., in 1872, he witnessed some of the most vicious incidents in the *Tithe War. As editor of the Church periodical, *Yr Haul*, he was widely respected for his trenchant but balanced editorials condemning violence. The most notable of his prose writings, *Llan Cwm Awen*, is a story of Church life in the diocese of Bangor during the 1830s. His *Hymnau yr Eglwys* (1893) contains some hymns of his own and some translated from the English. He was also the author of a historical work, *Hanes y Cymry* (1853), the poems '*Awdl y Sabboth*' (*c.*1856), '*Awdl Maes Bosworth*' (1858), '*Awdl Farwnad Ab Ithel*' (*c.*1878) and '*Buddugoliaeth y Groes*' (1880), and two works in English, *The Wreck of the London* (1865) and *The Massacre of the Monks of Bangor Iscoed* (1876). His long-winded *awdlau* and *pryddestau* may daunt the modern reader but he wrote some charming nature poetry.

ROBERTS, EMRYS (1929–), poet, was born in Liverpool and reared at Penrhyndeudraeth, Mer., but was evacuated to the district of *Penllyn, Mer., at the beginning of the Second World War. Educated at the Normal College, Bangor, he has been a teacher at various primary schools in Anglesey, Oswestry and Montgomeryshire. He won the *Chair at the National Eisteddfod for his *awdl* '*Y Gwyddonydd*' in 1967, and again in 1971 for '*Y Chwarelwr*'. His five volumes of poetry are *Gwaed y Gwanwyn* (1970), *Lleu* (1974), *Y Gair yn y Glaw* (1978), *Pwerau* (1981) and *Pennill o Ddyffryn Banw* (1984). A master of the strict metres, he has combined *cynghanedd* with the writing of verse in the free metres. He has published three collections of stories for children, *Siani Rhuban* (1973), *Siarc* (1976) and *Achub* (1982), and was also the editor of *Byd y Beirdd* (1983), a selection of verse which appeared in *Y *Cymro*.

ROBERTS, ENID (1917–), scholar, was born at Llangadfan, Mont., and educated at the University College of North Wales, Bangor. Having spent some time as a school teacher, she was appointed in 1947 Lecturer in Welsh at her old College. She has written extensively, particularly in the *Transactions* of the Denbighshire Historical Society, on the social life of the Welsh gentry of the sixteenth and seventeenth centuries, and on some of the poets who sang their praises, such as Wiliam *Cynwal and Dafydd *Llwyd ap Llywelyn ap Gruffudd of Mathafarn. Among her other publications are an edition of the autobiography of Gweirydd ap Rhys (Robert John *Pryse), published in 1949, and a work of literary history, *Braslun o Hanes Llên Powys* (1965). Her edition of the work of *Siôn

Tudur (1980) is a monumental achievement and a model of informed and judicious editing.

Roberts, Evan (1878–1951), evangelist, was leader of a religious revival which swept through Wales in 1904 and the year following. He worked in a coalmine and as a blacksmith's apprentice before training for the ministry with the Calvinistic Methodists. After undergoing an intense religious experience at Blaenannerch in 1904, he became the focus of a spiritual awakening at his home church, Moriah, in Loughor, Glam. The revival spread rapidly in the valleys of Glamorgan, in Liverpool and in parts of north Wales but its enthusiasm died away in the winter of 1905–6, during which its leader suffered a mental breakdown. No intellectual and a poor orator, he has been criticized for an overemphasis on emotional conversions. Unlike many revivalists, however, he cared little for wealth or fame and his example is still revered in Evangelical circles in Wales. See also WITHERED ROOT (1927).

For further details see D. M. Phillips, *Evan Roberts, the Great Welsh Revivalist, and his Work* (1923) and *Evan Roberts a'i Waith* (1924); C. R. Williams, 'The Welsh Religious Revival 1904–5' in *The British Journal of Sociology* (1952); Sidney Evans and Gomer M. Roberts (ed.), *Cyfrol Goffa Diwygiad 1904–1905* (1954) and R. Tudur Jones, *Ffydd ac Argyfwng Cenedl* (2 vols., 1981, 1982).

ROBERTS, GLYN (1904–62), historian, was born at Bangor, Caerns., and educated at the University College of North Wales in that city. He became Registrar of his old College in 1946 and was appointed to the Chair of Welsh History, as successor to R. T. *Jenkins, in 1949. Exceptionally gifted as an administrator, he served on many public bodies representing historical interests in Wales. He published a study of the municipal growth of Swansea in 1940 and wrote the chapter on Carmarthenshire politics in J. E. *Lloyd's second volume on the history of that county which appeared in 1939. Interested in the sixteenth century, and especially in the later Middle Ages, he analysed the social origins of the Welsh nobility in a study of the growth of the *Tudor family of Penmynydd in Anglesey, and explored the interrelationships between the Welsh and the English after 1284. He also examined in detail the poetry of the *cywyddwyr*, thus contributing substantially to the historian's understanding of the foundations of Welsh society and national feeling in medieval times. Glyn Roberts's principal writings were collected in the volume *Aspects of Welsh History* (1969).

There is an obituary of Glyn Roberts by A. H. Dodd in *The Welsh History Review* (vol. 1, no. 4, 1963).

ROBERTS, GOMER MORGAN (1904–), minister and historian, was born at Llandybie, Carms., and became a coalminer at the age of thirteen. After studying in evening classes, he was awarded a scholarship to Fircroft, one of the Selly Oak Colleges in Birmingham, and later completed courses at Trefeca College and the Theological College, Aberystwyth, entering the Calvinistic Methodist ministry in 1930. A prolific writer, mainly in Welsh, his most popular publications include a volume on upland Glamorgan in the series *Cyfres Crwydro Cymru (1962) and two volumes of essays, *Cloc y Capel* (1973) and *Crogi Dic Penderyn* (1977). An authority on hymnology and the history of his denomination, he was the editor of the Calvinistic Methodist historical magazine from 1948 to 1977. His chief publications are *Hanes Plwyf Llandybie* (1939), *Bywyd a Gwaith Peter Williams* (1943), *Y Pêr Ganiedydd* (2 vols., 1949, 1958), *Selected Trevecka Letters, 1747–1794* (1962), *Y Can Mlynedd Hyn, 1864–1964* (1964), *Portread o Ddiwygiwr* (1969) and *Hanes Methodistiaeth Galfinaidd Cymru* (2 vols., 1973, 1978).

For a full bibliography of Gomer M. Roberts's writings see the volume edited in his honour by J. E. Wynne Davies, *Gwanwyn Duw* (1982).

ROBERTS, GRIFFITH JOHN (1912–69), poet. Born at Afonwen, Caerns., and educated at the University College of North Wales, Bangor, where he was briefly a lecturer, he spent the rest of his life as a priest in the Church of Wales, latterly at Conwy. He won the *Crown at the National Eisteddfod in 1947, contributed extensively to the periodical press and published three volumes of poetry, namely *Coed Celyddon* (1945), *Cerddi* (1954) and *Awdl Goffa R. Williams Parry* (1967).

Roberts, John (1576–1610), Catholic martyr. Born at Trawsfynydd, Mer., and educated at St. John's College, Oxford, he became a convert to *Roman Catholicism during a visit to Paris and joined the Benedictine Order in 1598, taking the name Juan de Mervinia in honour of his native county. After studying at Salamanca, he was ordained priest in 1602 and joined the English mission in the following year. A pioneer of the Benedictine revival in England, he was one of the founders and the first prior of St. Gregory's College, Douai. He also served the victims of the London plagues in the years from 1603 to 1610. Arrested and exiled several times, once on suspicion of involvement in the Gunpowder Plot of 1605, he was ultimately found guilty of high treason and executed at Tyburn on 10 December 1610. On the night before his execution a Spanish lady named Luisa de Carvajal paid for a great feast to be held in his honour at Newgate prison. John Roberts was canonized by Pope Paul VI in 1970 as one of the *Forty Martyrs of England and Wales.

ROBERTS, JOHN (Siôn Robert Lewis; 1731–1806), hymn-writer and compiler of *almanacs, was a native of Holyhead, Ang. He

published his hymns in three collections, *Rhai Hymnau* (1760), *Hymnau neu Ganiadau* (1767) and *Hymnau Preswylwyr y Llwch* (1778); his most famous verse begins, 'Braint, braint yw cael cymdeithas gyda'r saint'. Among his other publications were *Rhyfyddeg neu Arithmetic* (1768), the first book on the subject of arithmetic in Welsh, *Geirlyfr Ysgrythurol* (1773), the first Welsh biblical concordance and *Yr Athrofa Rad* (1788), a spelling-book. He is chiefly remembered for his almanacs, which he published between 1761 and the year of his death.

ROBERTS, JOHN (J.R.; 1804–84), see under ROBERTS, SAMUEL (1800–85).

ROBERTS, JOHN (Ieuan Gwyllt; 1822–77), musician, editor and minister, was born near Aberystwyth, Cards. After working as a clerk and a schoolmaster, he became sub-editor of *Yr *Amserau* in Liverpool in 1852 and editor of *Y *Gwladgarwr* at Aberdare in 1858; he also served as a Calvinistic Methodist minister at Merthyr Tydfil (1859–65) and Llanberis (1865–69). Among the periodicals which he established were *Telyn y Plant* (the precursor of *Trysorfa'r Plant*) in 1859, *Y Cerddor Cymreig* in 1861 and *Cerddor y Tonic Solffa* in 1869; he also edited *Y Goleuad* (1871–72). His *Llyfr Tonau Cynulleidfaol* (1859) was a landmark in the development of congregational hymn-singing in Welsh and his *Sŵn y Jiwbili* (1874), a collection of tunes by Sankey and Moody with words in Welsh, was extremely popular. Of his own hymn-tunes the best-known are 'Ardudwy', 'Esther', 'Liverpool' and 'Moab'.

ROBERTS, JOHN JOHN (Iolo Carnarvon; 1840–1914), poet, was born at Llanllyfni, Caerns., and educated at Bala Theological College. He was a minister with the Calvinistic Methodists at Trefriw, Caerns., until 1879 and thereafter at Porthmadog, Caerns., where he had a reputation for eloquence. The winner of the *Crown at the National Eisteddfod on three occasions (1890, 1891, 1892), he was one of the most prolific of the *Bardd Newydd school. He published seven books: *Oriau yng Ngwlad Hud a Lledrith* (1891), *Ymsonau* (1895), *Myfyrion* (1901), *Breuddwydion y Dydd* (1904), *Cofiannau Cyfiawnion* (1906), *Crefydd a Chymeriad* (1910) and *Cofiant Dr. Owen Thomas* (1912).

ROBERTS, KATE (1891–1985), novelist, short-story writer and literary journalist, is generally regarded as the twentieth century's most distinguished prose-writer in Welsh. She was born and brought up in the quarrying village of Rhosgadfan, near Caernarfon, at a time when the slate industry was at its peak, employing some seventeen thousand men and supporting an exclusively Welsh-speaking culture. Her hold on a rich and lively dialect remained with her all her life, but it was combined with a thorough education in literary Welsh when she studied at the University College of North Wales, Bangor, under John *Morris-Jones and Ifor *Williams. She later taught Welsh at schools in Ystalyfera, Glam. (1915–17), where Gwenallt (David James *Jones) was her pupil, and in Aberdare, Glam., (1917–28). In 1928 she married Morris T. Williams and, after a period in Cardiff and Tonypandy (1929–35), the couple bought *Gwasg Gee*, the publishers of the newspaper **Baner ac Amserau Cymru*, and settled in Denbigh. When her husband died in 1946 Kate Roberts ran the business alone for a further ten years. Not only did she publish *Y Faner* but she was a regular contributor to its columns, writing on a variety of subjects, literary, political and domestic. In her later years she received numerous honours from the *University of Wales, the Honourable Society of *Cymmrodorion and the *Welsh Arts Council, and in 1983 a national testimonial was organized for her benefit.

The creative work of Kate Roberts falls into two distinct periods, the first running from *O Gors y Bryniau* (1925) through **Deian a Loli* (1927), *Rhigolau Bywyd* (1929), *Laura Jones* (1930) and **Traed Mewn Cyffion* (1936) to **Ffair Gaeaf* (1937). There followed a break of twelve years in her creative writing before **Stryd y Glep* (1949), *Y *Byw Sy'n Cysgu* (1956), **Te yn y Grug* (1959), *Y *Lôn Wen* (1960), **Tywyll Heno* (1962), *Hyn o Fyd* (1964), **Tegwch y Bore* (1967), *Prynu Dol* (1969), *Gobaith* (1972), *Yr Wylan Deg* (1976) and *Haul a Drycin* (1981).

The impulse which led to each of the phases of her creative writing seems to have been a personal loss. According to her own testimony, it was the First World War, which killed one of her brothers and broke the health of another, that first drove her to write as a kind of therapeutic necessity, to rid herself of a burden. The short novel *Traed Mewn Cyffion* deals with a quarrying family during the First World War and manages to suggest the epic proportions of the suffering of Welsh working-people who, in addition to all their other hardships, also lost their menfolk in the slaughter. The conclusion of one of the main characters at the end of the book—that there has been enough mute suffering and that the time has come to act—may be seen as reflecting Kate Roberts's own decision to enter polemical journalism and politics. She was a member of the Welsh Nationalist Party (later *Plaid Cymru) from its earliest days and contributed extensively to the party's newspaper, *Y Ddraig Goch*.

Although few of Kate Roberts's works have public themes, they reflect a society which shapes and often constrains the destinies of its members. She often portrays life in a domestic setting, from within women's experience, but always in the earlier work there is the tramp of men on their way to and from the quarry, the news of accidents at work and the slow agony of

death on the hearth. The thin soil and rocky landscape of Arfon become both scene and symbol of an austere but homely life lived in the face of necessity. Though not a religious writer, Kate Roberts perceived the strengths of the Puritan culture of her childhood, above all its high seriousness before the great questions of life, but she could also depict the full tragedy which is entailed in its repression of emotion. In one of her best short stories, '*Y Condemniedig*', for example, a quarryman lies at home dying. Under the pressure of work and the repression of emotion (itself a response to life's hardship), he has never come to know his wife closely, but now he has leisure to observe her making bread and to talk to her. Soon he is too weak to do even that: '*Pan oedd ar fin colli peth, dechreuodd ei fwynhau*' ('When he was about to lose something he began to enjoy it'). In that phrase may be seen in miniature the strong formal sense holding in deep emotion which is so characteristic of Kate Roberts's work.

It was after the death of her husband in 1946 that she returned to creative writing. Her later work often deals with women or old people living alone in an outwardly much more comfortable period which yet cannot provide the social support she knew in former times. The harsh landscape and Puritan culture of her youth now become a kind of inner standard, sometimes used to judge the trivial world of mass communication, package holidays and easy divorce, but sometimes subjected to questioning in the light of these changes. As a character in one of her later stories, who is himself a writer, puts it: '*Yr oedd wedi sgrifennu am bobl a chanddynt asgwrn cefn, ac wedi cyrraedd oes pan oedd sliwod yn ceisio dal y byd i fyny: ac eto, yr oedd lle i sliwod mewn bywyd ac mewn llenyddiaeth*' ('He had written about people with backbone, and had survived into an age when eels were trying to hold up the world: and yet there was a place for eels in life and in literature').

A more smiling side of Kate Roberts's work is seen in her books for and about children, namely *Deian a Loli*, *Laura Jones* and *Te yn y Grug*. The last-named is a small masterpiece which catches the freshness of childhood without a hint of sentimentality and with sharp social observation. But there is a life and a verve even in her darker stories, deriving in great measure from the tightness of form and style which are analogues for a plucky stoicism. In the short story, a form which seemed to express her essential cast of mind, Kate Roberts's masters were Chekhov, Maupassant, Strindberg and Katherine Mansfield. Her colloquial dialogue is embedded in a carefully formed narrative style which holds and distances the emotions but can then open out, in a paragraph or two, those great human questions which are often associated with Russian literature but which here are set in the Welsh society of a generation or two ago.

A selection of short stories in English translation from Kate Roberts's earlier period was published under the title *A Summer Day and Other Stories* (1946). A representative selection of her literary journalism will be found in *Erthyglau ac Ysgrifau Llenyddol* (ed. David Jenkins, 1978). For studies of her work see *Enaid Clwyfus* (1976) by John Emyr and a monograph in the *Writers of Wales* series (1974) by Derec Llwyd Morgan. See also *Kate Roberts: Cyfrol Deyrnged* (ed. Bobi Jones, 1969), *Bro a Bywyd Kate Roberts* (ed. Derec Llwyd Morgan, 1981) and *Kate Roberts a'i Gwaith* (ed. Rhydwen Williams, 1983).

ROBERTS, LEWIS (1596–1640), merchant and author. Born into a wealthy family who lived at Beaumaris, Ang., he served in the East India Company (of which he later became a governor) and was widely travelled. His book, *The Merchantes Mappe of Commerce* (1638), a guide-book for traders, is full of detail about the geography, currencies and products of the countries with which he was familiar. It also contains a number of verses by his friend Izaak Walton and others by his son Gabriel, who was nine years old in the year of its publication. In *The Treasure of Trafficke* (1640), Roberts turned to the theory of political economy, advocating Government control of commerce and what amounted to the nationalization of insurance.

For further details see the article by G. Milwyn Griffiths, 'A Seventeenth Century Welshman Abroad', in the *Journal* of the National Library of Wales (vol. XVII, no. 4, 1972).

ROBERTS, LYNETTE (1909–   ), poet, was born in Buenos Aires of parents whose origins were partly Welsh but who had emigrated to Argentina from Australia. Educated in the country of her birth and in England, she married Keidrych *Rhys in 1939 and made a home at Llanybri, Carms., but they were divorced in 1948. The poetry in a packed and quizzical style which she began writing in the late 1930s claimed the attention of T. S. Eliot who published two volumes of her work, *Poems* (1944) and *Gods with Stainless Ears* (1951). She also wrote *Village Dialect* (1944), a collection of monologues inspired by Llanybri, and *The Endeavour* (1954), a journal about one of Captain Cook's journeys, but she gave up writing in 1956 on becoming a Jehovah's Witness.

There is an essay on the poetry of Lynette Roberts by Anthony Conran in *The Cost of Strangeness* (1982); see also the number of *Poetry Wales* (vol. 19, no. 2, 1983) which is devoted to a study of her work.

ROBERTS, ROBERT (Y Sgolor Mawr; 1834–85), cleric and scholar, was born at Llanddewi, Denbs. Ordained as an Anglican priest in 1860, he was obliged to give up his curacy and emigrate to Australia a year later. Returning to Wales in 1875, he found work as a private tutor at Betws, near Abergele, Denbs., where, because of his erudition, he earned a formidable reputation. In his autobiography, which was

written in Australia and subsequently edited by J. H. *Davies under the title *The Life and Opinions of Robert Roberts, a Wandering Scholar, as told by himself* (1923), he drew a vivid picture of religious life, both Anglican and Nonconformist, in the Wales of his time.

For further details see the account of Robert Roberts's life by T. O. Phillips (1957); see also the edition of Roberts's *Life and Opinions* edited by John Burnett (1984).

Roberts, Robert (Bob Tai'r Felin; 1870–1951), folk-singer, was a farmer at Cwm-tir-mynach, near Bala, Mer. A star at many a *noson lawen*, he was one of the best-loved 'characters' associated with that traditional form of entertainment and some of the lustier songs in his repertoire have been immortalized by his rendering of them. He is one of the three examples of the cultured countryman commemorated by Robin *Williams in his lectures, *Y Tri Bob* (1970).

ROBERTS, ROBERT (Silyn; 1871–1930), poet, a native of Llanllyfni, Caerns., was a prominent figure in the literary revival which occurred during the first years of the twentieth century. After working as a quarryman, he was educated at the University College of North Wales, Bangor, and at the Methodist Theological College, Bala. A Socialist by conviction, he published a Welsh pamphlet on the Independent Labour Party (1908) and, in 1925, established the North Wales Branch of the Workers' Education Association. As a poet, he is always associated with W. J. *Gruffydd, with whom he published a volume of poetry, *Telynegion* (1900). At the National Eisteddfod of 1902 he won the *Crown for a *pryddest* which was later published in his volume, *Trystan ac Esyllt a Chaniadau Eraill* (1904). He later published two translations, *Gwyntoedd Croesion* (J. O. Francis, 1924) and *Bugail Geifr Lorraine* (Souvestre, 1925). A selection of his verse was published posthumously under the title *Cofarwydd* (1930), as was the novel *Llio Plas y Nos* (1945).

For further details see the account of his life and work by David Thomas (1956).

ROBERTS, ROBERT MEIRION (1906–67), poet, was born at Llandrillo, Mer., and educated at the University College of North Wales, Bangor, and at the Theological Colleges of Aberystwyth and Bala. Ordained a minister with the Calvinistic Methodists in 1933, he was a tutor at *Coleg Harlech, an army chaplain and a Presbyterian minister in Scotland. He published two volumes of verse, *Plant y Llawr* (1946) and *Amryw Ganu* (1965).

ROBERTS, SAMUEL (S.R.; 1800–85), minister, writer and Radical, was born at Llanbrynmair, Mont. Educated at his father's school, then in Shrewsbury and, under George *Lewis, at the Independent Academy at Llanfyllin, he joined his father as co-pastor of Yr Hen Gapel at Llanbrynmair in 1827; a younger brother, John (J.R.; 1804–84) shared their work for a while.

Through his journal, Y *Cronicl, launched in 1843, Roberts wielded great influence and enjoyed widespread respect among Noncon-formists in Wales. His brother, who was the editor from 1857 until his death, also contributed frequently to this publication. The progressive political views of S.R., as he was generally known, led him to oppose the intervention of the State in education and to protest against the reports of the *Blue Books in 1847. He denounced slavery, English imperialism, the war in the Crimea and capital punishment, while advocating universal suffrage, including votes for women, and supporting the cause of *Temperance and the building of railways. A staunch Independent, he carried on a public debate with Lewis *Edwards concerning the freedom of congregations from centralized authority. His zeal for the rights of the individual led him to oppose not only landlordism, from which his own family had suffered, but also the establishment of the Union of Welsh In-dependents in 1872 and the advent of unionism in industry. In order to escape the hostility of the steward of the Wynnstay estate (see under WIL-LIAMS-WYNN), to which his farm belonged, Roberts emigrated to the USA in 1857, to settle, in company with other natives of Llanbrynmair, a tract of a hundred thousand acres of land he had bought in Tennessee. Deceived by the vendors and deserted by some of the emigrants who found themselves far from other Welsh settle-ments, he was also caught up in the American Civil War, in which his pacifist sentiments caused him to be misunderstood by both sides. Vilified even in the Welsh press, he returned to Wales for good in 1867.

S.R.'s most important publications were Caniadau (1830), Cofiant John Roberts (1837), Diosg Farm (1854), Gweithiau (1856), Pregethau a Darlithiau (1865), Detholion (1867), Crynodeb o Helyntion ei Fywyd (1875), Farmer Careful (1881), Pleadings for Reform (1881) and Hunan-amddiff-yniad S.R. (1882); the volumes Caniadau Byrion a Cilhaul (1906) and Heddwch a Rhyfel (n.d.) were published posthumously.

For an account of his life and work see Glanmor Williams, Samuel Roberts, Llanbrynmair (1950).

ROBERTS, SELYF (1912–), novelist and short-story writer, was born at Corwen, Mer., a minister's son who followed a career in banking. He first came to public notice by winning the *Prose Medal at the National Eisteddfod for a collection of essays, subsequently published under the title Deg o'r Diwedd (1955). Since then he has published seven novels; Cysgod yr Arian (1959), Helynt yr Hoelion (1960), A Eilw ar Ddyfnder (1962), Wythnos o Hydref (1965),

Ymweled ag Anwiredd (1976), Iach o'r Cadwynau (1978) and Tebyg Nid Oes (1981). He has to his name two collections of short stories, Mesur Byr (1977) and Hel Meddyliau (1982), and a volume of memoirs about his experiences as a prisoner of war, Tocyn Dwyffordd (1984). He has also translated Lewis Carroll's Alice's Adventures in Wonderland (1865) into Welsh under the title Anturiaethau Alys yng Ngwlad Hud (1982) and Through the Looking-glass (1872) as Trwy'r Drych a'r Hyn a Welodd Alys Yno (1984).

ROBERTS, THOMAS (1765/6–1841), pam-phleteer, was born at Llwyn'rhudol, Abererch, Caerns. A goldsmith by trade, and a Quaker holding Radical views, he was one of the founders of the *Cymreigyddion Society in London and an active member of the *Gwyneddigion. In his famous pamphlet, Cwyn yn erbyn Gorthrymder (1798), written under the influence of the French Revolution of 1789, he attacked the Established Church in Wales and its tithes, as well as lawyers, doctors and the Methodists. He also wrote a pamphlet (1806) in defence of the Methodists, under the pseudonym Arvonius, in answer to a libellous pamphlet (1797) by Edward *Charles (Siamas Gwynedd). His An English and Welsh Vocabulary (1827) and The Welsh Interpreter (1831) were intended to help tourists who flocked to see the new suspension bridge over the Menai Straits. He also published Y Ffordd i Gaffael Cyfoeth (1839), based on Benjamin Franklin's Poor Richard's Almanack (1733–58).

ROBERTS, WILLIAM JOHN (Gwilym Cowlyd; 1828–1904), poet, was born at Tre-friw, Caerns., where he earned a living as a printer and bookseller. His verse, published in the volume Y Murmuron (1868), includes the poem 'Mynyddoedd Eryri' with which he won the *Chair at the Conwy Eisteddfod of 1861, but he wrote little of lasting significance. A nephew of Ieuan Glan Geirionydd (Evan *Evans), he published the life and works of his uncle under the title Geirionydd (1862) and a collection of harp-stanzas entitled Diliau'r Delyn (n.d.). His chief claim to fame was his attempt to found a bardic institution as a rival to *Gorsedd Beirdd Ynys Prydain, which he accused of having an Anglicizing influence on the literary life of Wales. He called his assembly Arwest Glan Geirionydd and it met annually between 1865 and 1890 on the shores of Llyn Geirionydd, Caerns., the lake near the reputed birth-place of *Taliesin. The festival, which was organized according to the letter of the Statute of *Gruffudd ap Cynan, placed an emphasis on learning, morality, reli-gion and the exclusive use of the Welsh langu-age. Despite its initial success, the event was in a sorry state by the end of Gwilym Cowlyd's life, especially after the 'Prifardd Pendant' ('Chief Poet Positive'), as he styled himself, was declared bankrupt and came to be regarded as highly eccentric.

For an account of Gwilym Cowlyd's life see the study by G. Gerallt Davies (1976).

ROBIN CLIDRO (*fl.* 1545–80), poet and parodist, believed to have lived in or near Ruthin, Denbs., was one of those against whom the professional poets intended to legislate at the *Caerwys Eisteddfod of 1523. A butt for the scorn of his contemporaries, he was notorious as an incompetent versifier until well into the eighteenth century. An itinerant poet, or *clerwr*, he wrote on humorous topics and his narrative poems, such as his elegy for a cat and his picaresque account of a journey to Ludlow, were meant to be recited in public and to cause laughter. Some of his poems are parodies of the professional poets and of the tradition of writing pedigrees, eulogies and elegies. In several of his *cywyddau* he satirized *Cerdd Dafod itself by means of consistently defective patterns of *cynghanedd. He was credited with having devised the metre known as '*mesur Clidro*'.

Some of Robin Clidro's verse has been published in the pamphlet *Llên Cymru* (ed. T. Gwynn Jones, 1926), in *Cerddi Rhydd Cynnar* (ed. David Lloyd Jenkins, 1931) and in *Canu Rhydd Cynnar* (ed. T. H. Parry-Williams, 1932).

ROBIN DDU AP SIENCYN BLEDRYDD (*fl.* 1450), poet, was a native of Anglesey, but almost nothing else is known about him. Among the *cywyddau* ascribed to him, about ninety in all, there are several vaticinatory poems but some also bear the name of *Dafydd Llwyd ap Llywelyn ap Gruffudd, who suggested in a *cywydd* that there had been a disagreement between them over the interpretation of certain ancient prophecies. Robin Ddu addressed poems to the *Griffith family of Penrhyn. He was a supporter of the *Tudors and wrote an epitaph in memory of Owain Tudur, the grandfather of Henry VII. Also known as Robin Ddu Ddewin, he had a reputation as a wizard and several traditional tales are told about him.

RODERICK, JOHN (**Siôn Rhydderch**; 1673–1735), grammarian and publisher, was probably a native of Cemais, Mont. He published a grammar entitled *Grammadeg Cymraeg* (1728) and many *almanacs, mostly at Shrewsbury. The first edition of his *English and Welch Dictionary* (1725) was compiled in collaboration with John Williams, a Shropshire man.

ROGER OF CONWAY or **ROGER CAMBRENSIS** (d. 1360), friar. Born probably at Conwy, Caerns., and educated at the University of Oxford, he acquired influence in the Order of Grey Friars (see under FRANCISCANS), becoming its Provincial Minister in England in 1355. His defence of the mendicant orders, *Defensio Mendi-*

cantium (1357), was written in reply to the strictures of Richard FitzRalph, Archbishop of Armagh, who had condemned their cult of poverty and their custom of begging.

ROGERS, NATHAN (b. 1639), topographical writer. Born at Llanfaches, Mon., the son of a colonel in Cromwell's army, he published only one book, the extremely rare volume entitled *Memoirs of Monmouth-Shire* (1708; new edn., 1984). Apart from its description of history and scenery, the book is chiefly remarkable for its appendix, in which the author's purpose was to incite the county's leading men to claim the restitution of their rights in the forest of Wentwood which, he argued, had been wrested from them by the Marquis of Worcester and his descendant, the Duke of Beaufort. For his spirited invective against 'the Tory High-flying Party' Rogers was sentenced to a term of imprisonment.

Rolant o Fôn, see JONES, ROWLAND (1909–62).

Rolls, Anthony, see VULLIAMY, COLWYN EDWARD (1886–1971).

Roman Catholicism, that part of the Christian Church which accepts the primacy of the Bishop of Rome (the Pope) and regards the Sacrifice of the Mass as the focus of its worship. It was the ruling tradition in Wales from the country's first Christianization until the sixteenth century, although it was affected from the end of the sixth century to the middle of the eighth by controversy regarding Easter and other matters. The earliest Welsh literature, although the product of a heroic ethos, reflects clearly the tenets of this tradition. During the Middle Ages much of the literature written in Wales was explicitly religious and most of the rest assumed without question the verity of Catholic dogma. Three notable religious poets were *Einion ap Gwalchmai, *Madog ap Gwallter and *Siôn Cent; the most interesting of the prose-writers was the anonymous author of *Cysegrlan Fuchedd*. With the advent of *Protestantism in its Anglican form, Roman Catholicism was proscribed, but until the Titus Oates Plot (1678–81) the Catholics in the Marches maintained a stubborn, if secret, resistance; in Wales further west there was not the same conviction. This resistance bore some literary fruit (see under COUNTER-REFORMATION). But by the eighteenth century Roman Catholicism throughout Wales was weak. The most notable Catholic author of this period was David Powell (Dewi Nantbrân) of Abergavenny, a Franciscan and the author of three books. During the nineteenth century, particularly from about 1850 onwards, there was substantial immigration from Ireland to the industrial areas of Wales, and Catholicism revived as a result. In 1850 two Welsh dioceses were established (although including initially parts of England as well): these have now become the Archdiocese of Cardiff and the Diocese of Menevia. Side by side with this working-class Catholicism, the Church also received more aristocratic converts, who were attracted mainly by the historical aspects of the Faith, such as H. W. Lloyd and J. Y. W. ('Chevalier') Lloyd; in spite of his penury, William Owen ('Y Pab') belongs to their number rather than to the immigrant labourers from Ireland. Gerard Manley *Hopkins spent three years at Tremeirchion during the 1870s: he had little immediate effect on Wales, but Wales and its literature had a revolutionary effect on him. Wales's greatest Catholic author of the twentieth century is Saunders *Lewis: by means of his extraordinary literary gifts, as well as his profound Catholicism, he has presented the Old Faith anew to his fellow-countrymen and has tried to persuade them to give it serious consideration for the first time for four centuries. He founded the society known as *Y Cylch Catholig* which published the journals *Efrydiau Catholig* and *Ysgrifau Catholig*. Several writers of ability belonged to this society, which was patronized by such Church dignitaries as Archbishop Michael McGrath and Canon John Bassett Davies.

For further details see Donald Attwater, *The Catholic Church in Modern Wales* (1935), Emyr Gwynne Jones, *Cymru a'r Hen Fydd* (1951), Glanmor Williams, *The Welsh Church from Conquest to Reformation* (1962), Roland Mathias, *Whitsun Riot* (1963) and Siân Victory, *The Celtic Church in Wales* (1977).

Roman Conquest of Britain, The, due to last for nearly four centuries, is sometimes said to date from Julius Caesar's landings in Britain in 55 and 54 BC. But those expeditions were prompted mainly by his annoyance at the help given by the Belgae in the south-east of the Island to their fellow-tribesmen in Gaul in their resistance to the Romans. On his second and more significant landing in 54 BC, Caesar encountered serious opposition from the Catuvellauni under their king, Cassivellaunus. After taking their water-dyked camp near Wheathampstead, he exacted an annual tribute, probably unleviable, and retired to Gaul. Owing to civil wars and internal problems in Rome, Caesar's initiative was not followed up by his successors, Augustus, Tiberius and Caligula. In AD 43 the emperor Claudius despatched a force of four legions and auxiliaries, amounting to some fifty thousand men, under his general, Aulus Plautius. The Catuvellauni, then politically dominant, had attempted to coerce the pro-Roman Belgae of the south and south-east into a military alliance. At the Battle of the Medway the forces of Togodumnus and *Caratacus, the sons of Cunobelin, the aged Catuvellaunian king, were broken and forced back. The sub-

mission of the Cantiaci, the Catuvellauni, the Trinovantes (with their capital at Camelodunum), the Iceni of what is now Norfolk and perhaps the Coritani followed in due course, and the Belgic kingdoms of the south offered no resistance.

Caratacus (Caradoc), however, fled westwards, avoiding the probable treacheries of the nearer Belgae, and took refuge with the *Silures on the northern bank of the Severn in and near Wentwood. For several years he waged a successful guerrilla war against Roman forces established by AD 47 on the line of the Fosse Way, but the establishment of a fort at Kingsholm, near Gloucester, and the probable occupation by the Romans of the lands north of the Forest of Dean, forced him to abandon his customary sorties and march on a wide curve west and north to join the *Ordovices in mid- and north-west Wales. On a hill-top, probably near Caersws, Mont., and not at any of the hills listed on the map as Caer Caradoc, he was brought to bay by Ostorius Scapula and his smaller force defeated after a hard struggle. Caradoc escaped, but only to the court of Cartimandua, Queen of the Brigantes, who, already subject to Roman pressure, surrendered him to the Roman governor. So ended the pan-Celtic hope which Caradoc had learned at the Catuvellaunian court.

The Silures, however, were by no means cowed. The harassment of Roman working-parties, continuous guerrilla warfare and the defeat of a Roman legion in a pitched battle, all characterized the attempt of the conquerors to occupy Silurian territory. The struggle came to an end only when, at some date before AD 75, the main camp of the Silures at Llanmelin Wood had been outflanked and a fortress established at Isca (*Caerleon). The Silurian camps were forcibly evacuated and the disarmed tribesmen re-located in a civilian town at Caerwent. Long before this the south-west of Britain had been subdued by *Legio II* under the future emperor Vespasian, and in AD 61 Suetonius Paulinus crossed to Anglesey and crushed the resistance of the Ordovices. He was compelled to return rapidly eastwards, however, by the rebellion of the Iceni under their formidable queen, *Boudica. After yielding Londinium to the rebels, he finally defeated them, with much slaughter, at an unidentified place in the south Midlands.

The subsequent stages of the Conquest, despite some sabre-rattling from Venutius, Cartimandua's ex-consort, were largely a matter of consolidation and political pressure. No serious attempt was made to move north of the Brigantian kingdom and into what was later Scotland until the time of the Roman general Agricola, whose campaigns were written up by his son-in-law, Tacitus. Beginning his northward advance in AD 78 he established forts as he went and in AD 83 had reached his most northerly point where, in the Grampian Hills, he defeated the army of the Caledonian (Pictish) league. His recall to Rome in AD 84 brought consistent campaigning to an end. The subsequent building of Hadrian's Wall and the Antonine Wall are less the outcome of conquest than of imperial decisions of a later date which reflected the army strength to be allocated to Britain and the success or failure of the alignment of frontier tribes.

Roman Britain, once the main campaigns were over, was divided broadly into two parts. The lands south and east of a line from Isca, the base of *Legio II Augusta*, to Deva (Chester), where *Legio XX Valeria Victrix* was stationed, and across to Eboracum (York), the base of *Legio IX Hispana*, were regarded as fully pacified and in them towns and Roman villas grew plentiful; the lands north and west of that line, though for the most part peaceful, were regarded as frontier regions which required a continuous military presence. From AD 367 the military position of the Roman Empire began to decline. Magnus Maximus (*Macsen Wledig) was the first of four usurper Emperors, all Governors of Britain, whose actions accelerated that decline. The last of these, Constantine III, took with him almost all army units remaining in the island and in AD 410 the Emperor Honorius responded to British appeals for help with a declaration that Britain must now be responsible for its own defence. The evidence of coins found on Hadrian's Wall, however, suggests that auxiliary units, possibly officered by Romans, were being paid from Rome as late as AD 429.

For further details see V. E. Nash-Williams, *The Roman Frontier in Wales* (1954), Peter Salway, *Roman Britain* (1981) and Graham Webster, *Rome against Caratacus* (1981).

Romanticism, a movement in European literature (but affecting also music, art, philosophy and theology) which flourished especially in the late eighteenth and early nineteenth centuries and which emphasized the role of feeling, imagination and self-expression rather than the adherence to traditional rules favoured by *Classicism.

Jean-Jacques Rousseau is sometimes regarded as the movement's founder, but there are touches of Romantic individualism in the work of earlier writers. A measure of pre-Romantic nostalgia has been detected in the personal, elegiac note struck by such poets as Ieuan Fardd (Evan *Evans) and his friend, Thomas Gray. The emphasis on feeling, imagination and the soul is found in a different form in the Evangelical Revival of the eighteenth century and William *Williams (Pantycelyn), who shared with Rousseau an interest in psychology, was regarded by Saunders *Lewis as the first poet of the Romantic Movement. The tendency to literary forgery, as found in such writers as Thomas Chatterton and James Macpherson, may be con-

sidered a symptom of Romanticism and, in this respect, Iolo Morganwg (Edward *Williams), whose fertile imagination left permanent monuments, both tangible and intangible, in the culture of Wales, can be seen as one of Romanticism's precursors.

Nevertheless, except for the special cases of Pantycelyn and Iolo Morganwg, Welsh literature was not affected by the Romantic Revival at the time of its greatest vitality in England, France and Germany. It was not until much later, in the nineteenth century, that the Romantic sensibility could be clearly identified, when it appeared in the work of such poets as Eben Fardd (Ebenezer *Thomas), Alun (John *Blackwell), Islwyn (William *Thomas), Ceiriog (John Ceiriog *Hughes), Talhaiarn (John *Jones) and Elfed (Howell Elvet *Lewis). The full impact of Romanticism came belatedly but excitingly in the poetry of T. Gwynn *Jones, W. J. *Gruffydd, R. Williams *Parry and, to a lesser extent, Elphin (Robert Arthur *Griffiths), but by then it was mingled with aestheticism and was soon challenged by *Neo-Classicism and realism.

For fuller accounts see Saunders Lewis, *Williams Pantycelyn* (1927), Mario Praz, *The Romantic Agony* (1933), Huw Llewelyn Williams, *Safonau Beirniadu Barddoniaeth* (1941), C. M. Bowra, *The Romantic Imagination* (1950) and Alun Llywelyn-Williams, *Y Nos, y Niwl a'r Ynys* (1960).

Roos, William (1808–78), painter, was born at Amlwch, Ang. Among examples of his work kept at the National Library of Wales are portraits of Christmas *Evans, Thomas *Charles and John *Jones (Talhaiarn).

ROOSE-EVANS, JAMES (1927–   ), author, was born of Welsh and English parents in London and educated at St. Benet's Hall, Oxford; he now lives in Powys. His career has been mainly in the theatre, as director and lecturer, and he founded the Hampstead Theatre in 1959. In 1971 he began writing a heptology of adventure stories for younger children about Elsewhere the Clown and Odd the Bear, a saga using themes from Arthurian lore and set in Wales and London. They are *The Adventures of Odd and Elsewhere* (1971), *The Secret of the Seven Bright Shiners* (1972), *Odd and the Great Bear* (1973), *Elsewhere and the Gathering of the Clowns* (1974), *The Return of the Great Bear* (1975), *The Secret of Tippity-Witchit* (1975) and *The Lost Treasure of Wales* (1977); some of these have been published as paperbacks under different titles. He has also written for broadcasting and published several books on the theatre which include *Directing a Play* (1968), *Experimental Theatre* (1970) and *London Theatre* (1977).

ROSCOE, THOMAS (1791–1871), writer and translator, was born at Toxteth Park, Liverpool, and educated privately. His first published work was *Gonzalo the Traitor: A Tragedy* (1820) and of his next two fictions, both published anonymously, the earlier was *Owain Goch: A Tale of the Revolution* (3 vols., 1827). The first of his travel-books, *The Tourist in Switzerland and Italy*, appeared in 1830 and of the eight similar volumes which followed two were about Wales, *Wanderings and Excursions in North Wales* (1836) and its like-titled sequel on south Wales (1837). A latecomer among travellers, Roscoe keeps his history to a manageable minimum, and his liveliest descriptions well justify the successive editions of his books. Among his many other works may be noted a *Life of William the Conqueror* (1846), a volume of poems, *The Last of the Abencerages* (1850), a long list of translations, beginning with *The Memoirs of Benvenuto Cellini* (1822), and editions of the works of Fielding, Smollett and Swift.

Rothesay Castle, The, a steam-packet wrecked in the bay of Beaumaris, Ang., on the night of 17 August 1831, was one of the earliest passenger steamers plying between Liverpool and north Wales. Of 114 people aboard, ninety-three lost their lives. The disaster was the subject of an *awdl* by William *Williams (Caledfryn) with which he won the *Chair at the Beaumaris Eisteddfod of 1832.

Round Table, The, see under ARTHUR (late 5th cent. – early 6th cent.).

Rowland, Daniel (1713–90), Methodist leader, was the son of the incumbent of the parishes of Nantcwnlle and Llangeitho, Cards. Ordained priest in 1735, he served in these parishes as curate to his brother and afterwards to his own son, but was converted to *Methodism after undergoing a deep religious experience, the result of a sermon preached by Griffith *Jones. Rowland met Howel *Harris in 1737 and they became joint leaders of the Methodist Revival in Wales. But disagreement at length arose between them and Rowland rebuked Harris in his *Ymddiddan rhwng Methodist Uniongred ac un Cyfeiliornus* (lit. 'Discourse between an orthodox Methodist and a heretical one'; 1749), the two afterwards going their separate ways in 1752. Like William *Williams (Pantycelyn) and almost all other Welsh Methodists, he followed the Calvinism of Whitefield rather than the Arminianism of Wesley: Harris's attempts to bridge the gap produced strained relations and when the latter showed Patripassian tendencies and fell under the spell of Madam Sidney Griffith, the breach was complete. Rowland built a chapel for himself in Llangeitho which became the mecca of Welsh Methodism, and it was he who, in 1762, led the Revival associated with that village. Avoiding Harris's tendency to Patripassianism, he excelled as a preacher and thousands came from all parts of Wales to hear him. Several of his sermons were published in the volumes *Pum Pregeth* (1772) and *Tair Pregeth* (1775). He was also a pioneer of the *hymn in Welsh and translated a number of books, including Bunyan's *Holy War* (1744).

For further details see the biography by D. J. Odwyn Jones (1938) and Gomer M. Roberts (ed.), *Hanes Methodistiaeth Galfinaidd Cymru* (vol. 1, 1973, vol. 2, 1978).

ROWLAND, ROBERT DAVID (Anthropos; 1853?–1944), minister, journalist and poet, was brought up at Tŷ'n-y-Cefn, near Corwen, Mer., and was later, in *Y *Pentref Gwyn* (1909), to write a vivid account of his childhood there. Educated at the Calvinistic Methodist Theological College, Bala, he found work as a journalist with *Yr *Herald Cymraeg* at Caernarfon in 1879 and edited *Y *Genedl Gymreig* between 1881 and 1884. From 1890 until his retirement in 1933 he served as minister of Beulah Presbyterian Church, Caernarfon. Besides editing the literary column of *Baner ac Amserau Cymru* (1904–14), he contributed numerous articles to a variety of periodicals, including *Y Drysorfa*, *Y *Geninen* and *Y *Traethodydd*, and wrote weekly articles for *Y Dinesydd* (1925–28) and *Yr Herald Cymraeg* (1929–44). He was the author of some two dozen books, the most important of which are *Caneuon Anthropos* (1904), *Y Ffenestri Aur* (1907) and *Oriau gydag Enwogion* (1909); he also wrote stories and verse for children and was editor of *Trysorfa'r Plant* (1912–32). A man renowned for his wit and conviviality, he was the founder of *Clwb Awen a Chân* and its president from 1908 to 1932.

For further details of the life of Anthropos and his famous club see the accounts by O. Llew Owain (1953 and 1967); there is a discussion of him as a children's writer by Glenys Howells in *Dewiniaid Difyr* (ed. Mairwen and Gwynn Jones, 1983).

ROWLANDS, DAFYDD (1931–), poet and prose-writer. Born at Pontardawe, Glam., and educated at University College, Swansea, and the Presbyterian College, Carmarthen, he was a minister at Brynaman and a schoolmaster in Glamorgan before becoming a Lecturer in Welsh at Trinity College, Carmarthen, in 1968; he became a full-time writer in 1983. He first came to prominence by winning the *Crown at the National Eisteddfod in 1969 with a sequence of poems entitled '*I Gwestiynau fy Mab*', a feat which he repeated three years later with his *pryddest*, '*Dadeni*'; he also won the *Prose Medal in 1972 with his volume of essays, *Ysgrifau yr Hanner Bardd* (1972). Since then he has published two collections of poems, *Meini* (1972) and *Yr Wythfed Dydd* (1975), as well as a pamphlet of prose-poems, *Paragraffau o Serbia* (1980). In his experimental 'novel/poem', *Mae Theomemphus yn Hen* (1977), the author explores his relationship with his father, achieving a work of profound and uncompromising self-examination of a kind which is rare in modern Welsh prose. He has also published a lecture on Gwenallt (David James *Jones), *Gwenallt a Chwm Tawe* (1973), and edited the volume on that poet in the *Bro a Bywyd* series (1982).

There is a profile of Dafydd Rowlands in *Portreadau'r Faner* (1976) by Marged Pritchard.

ROWLANDS, EURYS (1926–   ), scholar, was born in Caernarfon, the son of Meuryn (Robert John *Rowlands), and educated at the University College of North Wales, Bangor. He has held lectureships in the University of Glasgow and at the University Colleges of Cardiff and Dublin. His publications include editions of the work of *Lewys Môn (1975), *Iorwerth Fynglwyd (1975), Rhys Brydydd and Rhisiart ap Rhys (1976) and Owain ap Llywelyn ab y Moel (1984), *Poems of the Cywyddwyr* (1976) and a number of important articles on the period of the *cywyddwyr*.

ROWLANDS, HENRY (1655–1723), antiquary, was a native of Llanidan, Ang., and spent his life as an Anglican priest in his native county. Deeply interested in the history and antiquities of the island, he wrote his *Idea Agriculturae* (1764) in 1709. His most famous work, *Mona Antiqua Restaurata* (1723), surveys the antiquities of Anglesey and attempts to prove that the *Druids had originated there. An earlier work of his, *Antiquitates Parochiales* (1710), noted the county's main archaeological sites. A correspondent of Edward *Lhuyd, but without that scholar's insight into the antiquities of Wales, he preserved details of some archaeological remains which have now disappeared, but his theories were generally fanciful and many of his statements groundless.

For further details see the articles by J. Gareth Thomas in the *Transactions* of the Anglesey Historical Society (1958) and in the *Transactions* of the Anglesey Antiquarian and Field Society (1958), and that by Brynley F. Roberts in *Gwŷr Môn* (ed. Bedwyr Lewis Jones, 1979).

ROWLANDS, IFAN (1879–1977), poet, of Y Gistfaen, Llandderfel, Mer., where he worked a smallholding, was born in Cwm Celyn and spent his last years at Llandrillo-yn-Edeirnion, Mer. He won the *Chair at the National Eisteddfod in 1927 with his *awdl*, 'Y Tyddynnwr', and was the author of several famous *englynion*; a collection of his verse was published in the volume *O'r Gist* (1974). Robert John *Rowlands (1915–   ) is his son.

ROWLANDS, JOHN (1938–   ), novelist, was born at Trawsfynydd, Mer., and educated at the University College of North Wales, Bangor, and Jesus College, Oxford. Formerly a tutor in the Extra-Mural Department at University College, Swansea, and a lecturer at Trinity College, Carmarthen, and St. David's University College, Lampeter, he was appointed Lec-turer in the Department of Welsh at the University College of Wales, Aberystwyth, in 1975, and is now Senior Lecturer there.

The subject of his academic research has been the poetry of *Dafydd ap Gwilym and he edited the volume *Dafydd ap Gwilym a Chanu Serch yr Oesoedd Canol* (1975). He has published numerous critical studies of modern Welsh literature in *Ysgrifau Beirniadol (ed. J. E. Caerwyn Williams) and contributed an important summary of the subject to *The Arts in Wales 1950–75* (ed. Meic Stephens, 1979). He has also published an essay on T. Rowland *Hughes in the *Writers of Wales* series (1975) and a volume of biographical essays, *Profiles* (with Glyn *Jones, 1981).

He is the author of seven novels. With *Lle Bo'r Gwenyn* (1960), *Yn Ôl i'w Teyrnasoedd* (1963), *Ieuenctid yw Mhechod* (1965; trans. *A Taste of Apples*, 1966), *Llawer Is na'r Angylion* (1968) and *Bydded Tywyllwch* (1969), he won a reputation for the explicit description of sexual scenes and the exploration of the psychology of young people. A more complex theme is handled in *Arch ym Mhrag* (1972), which is about the political dilemmas of young people in the Czechoslovakia of 1968, a country he was visiting at the time of the Russian intervention. His latest novel, *Tician Tician* (1978), which presents a provocative picture of life in a Welsh university town, is perhaps the most mature of all his works and suggests that he is gradually moving in new directions.

ROWLANDS, ROBERT JOHN (Meuryn; 1880–1967), poet and journalist, was born at Abergwyngregin, Caerns. He began his career as a journalist with *Y *Cymro in Liverpool but later moved to Caernarfon where he worked as editor of *Yr *Herald Cymraeg* from 1921 until his retirement in 1954. With his *awdl*, 'Ar y Traeth', adjudicated by R. Williams *Parry, he won the *Chair at the National Eisteddfod in 1919, a feat he repeated in 1921 with his *awdl*, 'Min y Môr'. Besides three volumes of poetry, *Swynion Serch* (1906), *Y Barcud Olaf* (1944) and *Chwedlau'r Meini* (1946), he published a number of very popular children's books which include *Ar Lwybrau Antur* (1926), *Dirgelwch Hendre Galed* (1944), *Y Gelli Bant* (1946) and *Dirgelwch Plas y Coed* (1948). Famous for his part in the BBC programme *Ymryson y Beirdd*, he is remembered in the title now given to an adjudicator in such contests, namely 'meurynnwr'. The scholar Eurys *Rowlands is his son.

There is an essay on Meuryn as a children's writer in *Dewiniaid Difyr* (ed. Mairwen and Gwynn Jones, 1983).

ROWLANDS, ROBERT JOHN (1915–   ), poet, was born at Y Gistfaen, Llandderfel, Mer., the son of Ifan *Rowlands. He worked as a draper in Bala but retired in 1975 in order to give more time to his writing. A selection of his work was published in the *Beirdd Bro* series in 1976.

ROWLANDS, WILLIAM (Gwilym Lleyn; 1802–65), bibliographer and editor. A native of Bryncroes, Caerns., he was ordained a Wesleyan minister and served in various parts of Wales between 1828 and 1864. Besides editing *Yr ∗Eurgrawn Wesleyaidd* (1842–45, 1852–56), he was a pioneer in the collecting and cataloguing of Welsh books. His most important compilation was *The Cambrian Bibliography* (1869), a volume edited by D. Silvan ∗Evans, which gives an account of the Welsh books and books dealing with Wales published between 1546 and 1800. The work leaves gaps, and mistakes are many, but it proved valuable to later students of Welsh literature.

Royal Charter, The, a sailing vessel wrecked by a storm on the rocks of Porth Helaeth, near Moelfre, Ang., on 26 October 1859. One of the finest emigrant ships in trade between Liverpool and Australia, it went down with the loss of more than four hundred lives and a cargo of bullion. The desperate attempts by the people of Moelfre to rescue survivors (and their search for gold) made the shipwreck one of the most famous in the maritime history of north Wales. The part played by Stephen Roose Hughes, the rector of Llaneugrad and Llanallgo, in burying the victims and helping their relatives, is mentioned in several contemporary accounts, the best-known of which is found in *The Uncommercial Traveller* (1861) by Charles Dickens, who visited the village two months after the disaster. Subsequent accounts include those by Alexander McKee in *The Golden Wreck* (1961) and T. Llew ∗Jones in *Ofnadwy Nos* (1971). In the latter is reproduced a ballad by Ywain Meirion (Owen ∗Griffith), one of the many written about the shipwreck.

RUBENS, BERNICE (1927–), novelist, was born in Cardiff and educated at the University College in the city; she lives in London. Her novels are *Set on Edge* (1960), *Madame Sousatzka* (1962), *Mate in Three* (1966), *The Elected Member* (1969), *Sunday Best* (1971), *Go tell the Lemming* (1973), *I sent a Letter to my Love* (1975), *The Ponsonby Post* (1977), *A Five Year Sentence* (1978), *Spring Sonata* (1979), *Birds of Passage* (1982) and *Brothers* (1983). Of these only one, *I sent a Letter to my Love*, is wholly set in Wales, although the last-named has some Welsh characters.

RUCK, BERTA (1878–1978), romantic novelist. Born in India, she received her early education at Bangor and later studied art in Paris and at the Slade School, London, where she met Oliver ∗Onions, whom she married in 1909; from 1939 she lived at Aberdyfi, Mer. Among her novels, about forty in all, those which are set partly or wholly in Wales are *The Lap of Luxury* (1931), *A*

Star in Love (1935), *Out to Marry Money* (1940), *Intruder Marriage* (1945), *Surprise Engagement* (1947) and *Tomboy in Lace* (1947). None is of any lasting merit and her four volumes of autobiography, *A Story-teller Tells the Truth* (1935), *A Smile for the Past* (1959), *A Trickle of Welsh Blood* (1967) and *An Asset to Wales* (1970), are distinguished only by their author's zest for life.

Her brother, **Richard Ruck** (1887–1973), who was born in Caernarfon and who retired from the Indian Army to live in Machynlleth, Mont., in 1939, is remembered as the translator of the five novels of T. Rowland ∗Hughes.

RUDDOCK, GILBERT (1938–), poet. Having learned the language at Cathays High School, Cardiff, he graduated in Welsh and was appointed Lecturer in the Welsh Department of University College, Cardiff, in 1969. His three volumes of verse are *Y Funud Hon* (1967), *Cwysi* (1973) and *Hyn o Iachawdwriaeth* (1985).

Rug, Y, a mansion in the parish of Corwen, Mer., which played a prominent part in the tradition of patronage to itinerant poets in the county. Robert Salusbury (d. 1550) was the most important patron, but some poetry to his father, Piers, and to others of his ancestors has survived. His son, John, and his grandson, Robert (d. 1599), also maintained the tradition. Two more generations welcomed poets at the house but very little of the poetry composed during this later period has been preserved.

Rugby, a game which is generally considered to be the national sport of Wales and, by some, an expression of the Welsh identity. Of English provenance, it was first played in Wales during the 1870s but was confined to the coastal towns and the educated middle class. From about 1881, however, when the Welsh Football Union was formed, the game gained in popularity, especially in the industrial valleys of Glamorgan. It soon came to be regarded as a typically Welsh game as local clubs fostered communal pride and, after 1893, the national side began to defeat the socially superior teams of England, Scotland and Ireland. The 'golden eras' of Welsh rugby were the years from 1900 to 1911 (when six Triple Crowns were won) and from 1970 to 1979. Some players in both periods became household names and were revered for their prowess on the field. The establishment of a National Ground (formerly the Cardiff Arms Park) during the 1970s provided an arena in which the theatricality of Welsh rugby continues to attract huge crowds on the days of international matches. The game has been devotedly served by journalists such as W. J. T. ∗Collins, Clem Thomas and J. B. G. Thomas. The writers Islwyn ∗Williams and Alun ∗Richards are among those who have examined its social ramifications, while the singer Max ∗Boyce has expressed something of the fervour which the game generates.

For further details see Alun Richards, *A Touch of Glory* (1980) and David Smith and Gareth Williams, *Fields of Praise: the Official History of the Welsh Rugby Union 1881–1981* (1980).

RUMSEY, WALTER (1584–1660), judge and author, was born at Llanover, Mon., but belonged to a family resident near Crickhowell, Brecs. A gentleman commoner at Gloucester Hall, Oxford, he left without taking a degree and studied law at Gray's Inn. Called to the Bar in 1608 and most successful thereafter in practice, he was appointed Puisne Judge on the Brecon Circuit of the Great Sessions of Wales in 1635 and, two years later, Chief Justice. Elected Member of Parliament for Monmouthshire to the Short Parliament in 1640, he refused re-election to its successor and, as a Royalist, was removed from judicial office in 1647. The resulting leisure he devoted to his hobbies of music, tree-grafting and the construction of fishponds. His chief claim to fame was his development of the provang (or probang), a whalebone with a piece of sponge on the end, which was designed to clean the larynx and thorax of phlegm. He publicized the instrument in his book, *Organon Salutis* (1657), to which was added a pamphlet entitled *Divers new experiments of the virtue of tobacco and coffee*.

Ruthin, a lordship which, after 1282, embraced the territory previously known as the cantref of Dyffryn Clwyd. It was a dispute with Reginald Grey, lord of Ruthin, which sparked off the rising of *Owain Glyndŵr in 1400. The Grey family, Earls of Kent, sold Ruthin to the English Crown in 1508. Ruthin was the only lordship of the March of which the court rolls have survived, for which reason the history of its administration is unusually well documented. The name should not be confused with that of Rhuthin, a lordship of Glamorgan.

S

Sabellianism, an attempt to reconcile the doctrine that there is but one God with the doctrine that there are three Persons in the Godhead. The solution offered by the Roman writer Sabellius, in the early third century, was that the Son and the Holy Spirit were merely modes or aspects of God, manifestations of the one Divine Essence, rather than distinct and real Persons, a view for which he was excommunicated. Because of the primacy given to the Father in this teaching, it is sometimes called Modalistic Monarchism and its corollary is Patripassianism, namely the belief that the Father himself suffered in the death of the Son.

Elements of both doctrines may be seen in the teaching of Howel *Harris, and they were partly responsible for the rift between him and other Methodist leaders, such as Daniel *Rowland. The most notable example of Sabellianism in Wales, however, was that of Peter *Williams, whom the Calvinistic Methodist Association, meeting at Llandeilo in 1791, excommunicated, with the result that two prominent hymn-writers, Thomas *William of Bethesda'r Fro and John *Williams of St. Athan, left the Methodists and joined the Independents. This controversy had reverberations among the Independents of Glamorgan, while the publication of *Dialogus* (1778) by Nathaniel *Williams caused heated debates on the subject among *Baptists. In the twentieth century, Sabellian tendencies were detected in *Cenadwri'r Eglwys a Phroblemau'r Dydd* (1923) by Thomas Rees (1869–1926) and *Bannau'r Ffydd* (1929) by D. Miall *Edwards.

For a full discussion of the subject see J. Gwili Jenkins, *Hanfod Duw a Pherson Crist* (1931).

Sabrina, see under DOLFORWYN.

Sacred Animals, Birds and Trees, a feature of pagan Celtic religion manifested zoomorphically in the iconography of Britain and the Continent. The most prominent cult-animals appear to have been the bull, boar, horse and stag, but representations of the ram, dog and serpent also occur. Among divine animals are found *Epona* (the horse-goddess), *Moccus* (the divine boar) and *Deiotarus* (the divine bull). Carved human figures with the heads, horns and ears of animals are also found, the most famous being *Cernunnos* (the horned god) who appears as 'lord of the animals' on the Gundestrup Cauldron. Significant survivals of all these zoomorphic elements have come down in the vernacular literature of Wales and Ireland: *Cernunnos* (the herdsman god) reappears as the Giant Herdsman in the tales of *Culhwch and of Owain (see under TAIR RHAMANT), while *Rhiannon and Macha are the Welsh and Irish equivalents of the horse-goddess, *Epona*. Traditions about the hunt of a monstrous, savage boar are found in both countries: in Wales the *Twrch Trwyth (the boar Troit of the *Mirabilia Britanniae) is a transformed human being and another mythical hunt for a magic sow is recorded in the Triad of the *Powerful Swineherds. Both literatures provide numerous examples of human transformations into animals and birds, while the motif of congenital animal companions appears in the horses associated at birth with the heroes Cú Chulainn and *Pryderi. The words for 'horse', 'hound' and 'bear' (in Welsh also for 'wolf') are frequent elements in personal names, while Cú Chulainn's taboo against eating dog-flesh is a reminder of the dog-totem enshrined in his name.

Sacred birds were a significant aspect of pagan Celtic symbolism in early Welsh and Irish literature. They are portrayed in Continental zoography in striking detail, the swan, the raven, the eagle, the owl and the crane appearing most frequently. In the literatures, the swan possesses connotations of beauty and love, while the raven has warlike, sinister associations and is a harbinger of doom. *Badhbh* ('raven') was a name for the Irish war-goddess and the *Branhes Owain* (whether warriors or birds) were the supporters of this hero in battle. The genus of the famous Birds of Rhiannon is not specified, but such magical birds as hers are a recurrent feature of *Annwn: their marvellous singing could drown sorrow and lull those who heard them to sleep. Gods and goddesses had the ability to take on bird-form, apparently at will, and when thus transformed they were linked in pairs by gold or silver chains. Wisdom, prophetic powers and great age have always been associated with birds. The *Druids are said to have divined future events by their flight and in Wales an owl and a blackbird were traditionally among the *Oldest Animals.

The veneration of sacred trees was also a feature of pagan Celtic religion. The oak is believed to have been held by the Druids as particularly sacred. Early Irish tradition preserves the memory of certain sacred trees, such as the ash, the yew and the oak, and there is evidence that tribal inauguration ceremonies were held under them. Vestigial survivals in Welsh may be the *afallen peren* ('sweet apple-tree') in Coed Celyddon (see under AFALLENNAU) which is associated in an early poem with *Myrddin, and 'Merlin's Oak' at Carmarthen, whose continued existence was believed to ensure the town's survival. Early Irish personal names meaning 'son of holly' and 'son of yew' are found and may be paralleled in Welsh by Gwyddien (*Guidgen*, 'tree-born') and Gwernen (*Guerngen*, 'alder-born'). The tree imagery which is a feature of Irish and Gaelic praise-poetry from the earliest times may represent an ultimate survival of this pagan tree-cult. Such imagery also recurs in Welsh, though at a later date, in those *cywyddau* in which a family is portrayed as a spreading tree of which the children are the branches.

For further details see Edward Anwyl, *Celtic Religion in Pre-Christian Times* (1906), M. L. Sjoestedt (trans. Myles Dillon), *Gods and Heroes of the Celts* (1949), Anne Ross, *Pagan Celtic Britain* (1967) and Proinsias Mac Cana, *Celtic Mythology* (1970).

Sadrach Danyrefail, the most fully presented and frequently deployed character in the 'stories of the peasantry of West Wales' written by Caradoc Evans (David *Evans). His hypocrisy, selfishness and amorality, assisted by a command of Scripture and distorted theology, make him the foremost of his unpleasant kind. The central figure and driving-force of the story 'A Father in Sion' in *My People* (1915), he is also the main instrument of evil in 'A Just Man in Sodom' and the main contributor to the tragedy of Nanni in 'Be This Her Memorial'. He is at times the adjutant in wickedness of the Respected Josiah Bryn-Bevan, but most memorably a monster when most fully himself.

Saer Doliau (lit. 'The carpenter of dolls'; 1966), a play by Gwenlyn *Parry, broke new ground in the Welsh theatre by means of allegory and ambiguity. Some critics saw in it the influence of Beckett, Pinter and the Theatre of the Absurd, and it certainly created a great deal of disagreement among its first audiences. A 'progressive' young couple challenge the 'naïve' belief of the Carpenter that the Gaffer (perhaps God) is at the other end of the telephone; what causes most argument is that, at the end of the play, the telephone rings across an empty stage.

For a discussion of the play's merits see the essay by Dewi Z. Phillips in *Ysgrifau Beirniadol IV* (ed. J. E. Caerwyn Williams, 1969) and the same author's book, *Dramâu Gwenlyn Parry* (1982).

Saethon, a mansion in the parish of Llanfihangel Bachellaeth, Caerns., which was a well-known resort for poets in *Llŷn. Patronage was extended there by at least seven generations of the family. Wiliam *Cynwal eulogized Ieuan ap Robert ap Hywel in a tradition established by his father and grandfather. Ieuan was followed by his son, Robert, but the most notable period was that of his grandson, Ifan (d. 1538). The tradition waned over the next two generations and the last patron was Ifan ap Robert Wyn who died in 1683.

St. Asaph or **Llanelwy**, a cathedral and diocese in north-east Wales. The original manuscript of *The Red Book of Asaph* was lost during the *Civil War but the four incomplete copies made by Robert *Vaughan, and others, reveal that it was a collection of legal documents, in both Latin and Welsh, which related to the history and administration of the diocese in the thirteenth and fourteenth centuries. The traditional belief that St. Kentigern (*fl.* 6th cent.) founded a monastery at St. Asaph and received privileges from *Maelgwn Gwynedd, as related in the *Red Book*, is no longer accepted. *Geoffrey of Monmouth became Bishop of St. Asaph in 1151, but did not, apparently, visit his diocese. During the episcopate of Anian (d. 1293) the cathedral was burned and again in 1402 during the rising of *Owain Glyndŵr. Many others among its bishops and canons were praised by the poets: *Iolo Goch addressed poems to Dafydd ap Bleddyn, (Bishop, 1314–46), Ieuan Trefor II (Bishop, 1395–1411), Hywel Kyffin (Dean, 1385–97) and Ithel ap Robert (Archdeacon, 1375–82); *Tudur Aled wrote for Dafydd ab Owain (Bishop, 1503–12) and Ffoulke Salisbury (Dean, 1515–43), and *Wiliam Llŷn for William Hughes (Bishop, 1573–1600). William *Morgan, translator of the *Bible, was Bishop of St. Asaph from 1601 to 1604 and John *Davies of Mallwyd was chaplain to Richard *Parry (Bishop, 1604–23). Notable amongst later Bishops of the diocese was William Lloyd (1680–92).

In 1838 an attempt was made by the Anglican hierarchy in England to amalgamate the diocese of St. Asaph with that of *Bangor, in order to apply the St. Asaph revenues to a new diocese in Manchester, but this was stoutly and successfully resisted by Welsh clergy and laymen, particularly Rowland *Williams (Goronva Camlann) and Arthur James *Johnes.

St. David's or **Tŷ Ddewi**, a cathedral and diocese in Pembrokeshire, was known during the Middle Ages as Menevia and Manor Fynyw. According to tradition, *Dewi Sant (St. David), the patron saint of Wales, was born in the vicinity and he is believed to have founded a cell there in the sixth century. The earliest evidence for the existence of a monastery on the site is found, however, in Irish documents of the eighth and ninth centuries. The monasticism professed by the saint was ascetic but it was as a centre of learning that Menevia afterwards gained renown. From there King Alfred summoned *Asser to assist him in the re-establishment of Christian learning in Wessex. At

Menevia was kept the Latin chronicle, now lost, which underlies both the *Annales Cambriae and *Brut y Tywysogyon. There were frequent attacks by *Vikings in the tenth and eleventh centuries, two of which resulted in the death of Bishops, that of Morgenau in 999 and that of Abraham in 1080; the gravestone of Hedd and Isaac, Abraham's sons, is preserved in the cathedral. In 1073 *Sulien became Bishop and, according to *Historia Gruffudd vab Kenan, it was he who, in 1081, arranged a meeting at Menevia between *Gruffudd ap Cynan and Rhys ap Tewdwr before the battle of Mynydd Carn. Sulien's son, *Rhygyfarch, wrote a Latin Life of St. David (c. 1090), using older sources which he had found at the saint's own monastery, together with legendary material. The Welsh Life by the Anchorite of Llanddewibrefi was not composed until 1346 (see BOOK OF THE ANCHORITE).

The succession of Welsh bishops of St. David's was broken by the appointment of a Norman named Bernard in 1115 and the subsequent heroic efforts of *Gerald de Barri (Giraldus Cambrensis) to restore Menevia's privileges and independence were unsuccessful. It was Gerald who wrote the Lives of St. David and St. Caradog, a hermit who was buried in the cathedral in 1124, and it was in his time that Bishop Peter de Leia began the construction of the present building. Pope Calixtus II (1119–24) secured the status of Menevia as a centre for pilgrimage by granting it a *privilegium*, to which the rhyme refers: *Roma semel quantum/Bis dat Menevia tantum.* ('Two visits to Menevia have the same value as one to Rome').

Among the Kings of England who made the journey to Menevia were William the Conqueror (1081), Henry II (1171) and Edward I (1284). *Gwynfardd Brycheiniog eulogized Dewi, his relics and his privileges, as did Ieuan ap Rhydderch ap Ieuan Llwyd and *Lewys Glyn Cothi (Llywelyn y Glyn), though the latter associated him with *Elfael. According to *Lewys Môn, it was at Menevia that *Rhys Nanmor lived. *Dafydd Llwyd ap Llywelyn ap Gruffudd and Rhys Fardd refer in their vaticinatory poetry both to Menevia and to its patron saint. Bishop John Morgan (d. 1504) and the image of the Blessed Virgin Mary at Menevia were praised by *Ieuan Deulwyn and *Hywel Swrdwal respectively.

After the Reformation several changes took place at St. David's. Bishop William Barlow (1499?–1568) seized the saint's relics and Bishop Robert *Ferrar and Chantor Thomas Huett (d. 1591) destroyed the medieval service books. The body of Edmund Tudor (1430–56) was moved, at the Dissolution in 1539, from the church of the Greyfriars at Carmarthen to the cathedral where many Welsh princes were already buried, including *Rhys ap Gruffudd (The Lord Rhys), his son *Rhys Gryg and, perhaps, his grand-

father Rhys ap Tewdwr (d. 1093). Richard *Davies became Bishop of St. David's in 1561.

George *Owen is believed to have been the author of the anonymous account of St. David's used by Browne Willis in his *Survey of the Cathedral Church of St. David's* (1717). William Laud was bishop from 1621 to 1626 and Rhys *Prichard was Chancellor from 1626 to 1644. The cathedral library, together with the organ, bells and windows, suffered damage at the hands of Parliamentarian troops during the *Civil War; only one volume survives, a copy of the *Annales Cambriae* written in the thirteenth century. *The *Black Book of St. David's*, an extent of episcopal lands made in 1326, survives in a sixteenth-century copy. An account of the cathedral and its dignitaries by Edward Yardley (1698–1770), Archdeacon of Cardigan, survives in manuscript, as does another by Archdeacon H. T. Payne (1759–1832). Connop *Thirlwall was bishop when W. Basil Jones (1822–97) and E. A. Freeman published *The History and Antiquities of St. David's* (1856), a work which roused the authorities to commission Sir Gilbert Scott to restore the cathedral. The diocese of St. David's continued to extend over the whole of south and mid-Wales (except for the area episcopally ruled from Llandaf in the south-east) until 1923, when a new diocese of Swansea and Brecon was carved out of it. See also ABERGWILI.

For further details see the article by Glanmor Williams, 'The diocese of St. David's from the end of the Middle Ages to the Methodist Revival' in the *Journal* of the Historical Society of the Church in Wales (vol. XXV, 1976); see also Wyn Evans and Roger Worsley, *St. David's Cathedral 1181–1981* (1981), and David W. James, *St. David's and Dewisland, a social history* (1981).

St. David's Day Series, see CYFRES GWYL DDEWI.

St. Fagans, The Battle of (1648), see under POWELL, REES or RICE (*fl.* 1638–65) and POYER, JOHN (d. 1649).

St. John's Day, the religious feast of St. John the Baptist, which falls on 24 June, three days after the longest day (Alban Hefin), was celebrated by several folk-customs commemorating midsummer. The Eve of St. John was marked by the lighting of bonfires and various forms of divination, particularly those relating to love, as celebrated in the play by Saunders *Lewis, *The *Eve of St. John* (1921). The traditions of the *Summer Birch and dancing were associated with this feast and with May Day. By the middle of the nineteenth century most of these customs had begun to die out but Owen Wyn *Jones (Glasynys) wrote a popular pastoral poem about them, 'Nos Wyl Ifan' (1860). The well-known verses beginning 'Awn allan, fwyn forynion, fe ddaeth Gwyl Ifan ddoeth' are a translation and refer not to Welsh but to Spanish customs.

Saintly Lineages of the Isle of Britain, Three, a Triad in the original version of which the three families of saints were named as those of *Brychan Brycheiniog, *Cunedda Wledig and Caw o Brydyn (Pictland); thus, one belonged to south Wales, one to north Wales and one to north Britain, the *Old North of Welsh tradition. The numerous saintly descendants of Brychan, who included St. *Cadog, are listed in *De Situ Brycheiniog* (11th cent.), while the equally numerous saints said to have been descended from Cunedda, including *Dewi Sant (St. David), are listed in *Bonedd y Saint* (13th cent.). The dedications of churches bear witness to the significant part played by ecclesiastical founders claiming allegiance to one or other of these families as pioneers of Christianity in Wales.

In comparison, little is known of the saintly descendants of Caw of Pictland, with the exception of their most famous member, the polemicist *Gildas. The medieval sources indicate that traditions of Caw and his descendants had become largely obliterated by the time that these came to be recorded in writing and therefore it is the less surprising that a later version of the Triad (in Peniarth 50) substituted the name of the legendary Grail hero, Joseph of Arimathea, for that of Caw. Iolo Morganwg (Edward *Williams) tampered still further with the Triad by substituting for this name that of *Brân ap Llŷr (Bendigeidfran) in *The Myvyrian Archaiology* (1801), in order to give prominence to the fiction, devised by himself, concerning the introduction of Christianity into Britain by Brân and his son *Caradog.

Salem, a small Baptist chapel in Cwm Nantcol, near Llanbedr, Mer., was immortalized by the English painter Curnow Vosper (1866–1942), whose study of an old lady in traditional dress making her way down the aisle is commonly to be seen on the walls of Welsh homes. The portrait, hung in the Royal Academy in 1909, was reproduced and widely distributed as an advertisement for a brand of soap and it is now kept in the Lady Lever Art Gallery, Port Sunlight. Part of the painting's sentimental appeal is explained by the fact that it has acquired a folklore of its own: Siân Owen of Ty'n-y-fawnog, who posed for the painter, is said to have been notoriously vain and that is why a devil's face is discernible in the folds of her magnificent shawl. Vosper, however, denied that this effect was deliberate and always maintained that the shawl had been borrowed from the wife of Harlech's vicar. Most of the other figures in the picture are recognizable as those of actual people from the district. The scene, so evocative of a sunlit morning in a country chapel, is the subject of a well-known poem by T. Rowland *Hughes who admired its rustic simplicity and calm. Siân Owen is featured again in Vosper's painting 'Market Day', which is only slightly less popular and which, in turn, inspired the poet in the writing of his poem '*Steil*'.

Salesbury or **Salusbury** or **Salisbury** or **Salbri family, The**, of Llewenni in the Vale of Clwyd, Denbs., prospered during the time of the *Tudors. The John Salusbury who died in 1566 was the first husband of *Catrin of Berain; their elder son, Thomas Salusbury, was executed in 1586 for his part in the Babington Plot which sought to put Mary, Queen of Scots, on the English throne. Their younger son, John Salusbury (1567–1612), became the companion and patron of a circle of free-thinking intellectuals who gathered around Sir Walter Raleigh. It has been suggested that Shakespeare, in *Love's Labour's Lost* (c.1594), satirized the group (who included Marlowe, Chapman and possibly the young Edward *Herbert of Cherbury) as 'The School of Night'. At that time there was bitter rivalry between the Salusburys of Llewenni and another branch of the family, the Salesburys of Y *Rug who supported the Earl of Essex in opposition to Raleigh.

Further details about John Salusbury will be found in Carleton Brown, *Poems by Sir John Salusbury and Robert Chester* (1914) and in M. C. Bradbrook, *The School of Night* (1936).

SALESBURY, WILLIAM (c.1520–1584?), scholar and translator of the New Testament into Welsh, was born in the parish of Llansannan, Denbs., into a cadet branch of the *Salesbury family of Llewenni which had been founded by his grandfather. He was educated at the University of Oxford, where he first came into contact with the ideas associated with the Reformation and Renaissance, and possibly at one of the Inns of Court.

Between 1547 and 1552 he was astonishingly prolific and versatile in his literary work, publishing *A Dictionary in Englyshe and Welshe* (1547), *Oll Synnwyr Pen Kembero Ygyd* (1547), *A Brief and Playne Introduction* (1550) and two polemical works against Papists, *Ban wedy i dynnu . . . o hen gyfreith Howel Dda* (1550) and *The Baterie of the Popes Botereulx* (1550). His translation of a work on astronomy, *The Description of the Sphere . . . of the World* (1550), was followed by a Welsh translation of the Epistles and Gospels of the Book of Common Prayer, *Kynniver Llith a Bann* (1551); he also wrote a version of *The Book of Rhetoric* (1552) which remains in manuscript.

The frequency and number of these publications suggest that he spent much of his time in London and may have envisaged a career as a professional writer. The contents reveal his appreciation of the importance of the printing-press for Welsh and English, his admiration for the English language, his intense love and knowledge of Welsh and its literary tradition and his profound concern that they should successfully rise to the challenge posed to their existence by the spread of Renaissance ideas, Reformation doctrine and the influence of English. His most important book, *Kynniver Llith a Bann*, though it shows unmistakable signs of his eccentric views on language and spelling, was nevertheless much the most extensive Biblical translation undertaken in Welsh and, despite its unfortunate quirks of orthography and mutation, set a very high standard.

During the reign of Mary I (1553–58) all this publishing activity ceased and Salesbury is reputed to have gone into hiding at Cae Du, his father's house, where he may secretly have continued his translations. After the accession of Elizabeth, Salesbury quickly became friendly with Bishop Richard *Davies with whom, it seems probable, he was responsible for bringing about the Act of Parliament of 1563 for the translation of the *Bible into Welsh. Shortly afterwards, he joined Davies at *Abergwili, where they cooperated in translating into Welsh the Book of Common Prayer and the New Testament, both of which were published in 1567. No outward indication of the authorship of the Prayer Book appears but, from the internal evidence of style and orthography, it seems that Salesbury was responsible for translating the whole of it. He also translated all the New Testament, except for five epistles translated by Davies and Thomas Huet's work (see under BIBLE) on the Book of Revelation. Although an impressive achievement, these translations were markedly less successful than they might have been. They were greatly impaired by Salesbury's linguistic oddities, particularly his tendency to use Latinized spellings, to ignore nasal mutations, to employ many archaisms and to overlook inconsistencies; he knew beforehand of serious objections to these peculiarities but stubbornly refused to make any changes. In 1567 he and Davies intended to publish a translation of the Old Testament but they never did so, having, according to Sir John *Wynn, quarrelled irreconcilably over one word. Possibly because of this dispute and the opposition to his translation, Salesbury published nothing after 1567. He was, however, at work on a medicinal herbal, *Llysieulyfr Meddyginiaethol*, between 1568 and 1574, and he left it in manuscript.

William Salesbury, despite his shortcomings, is a seminal figure in the literary history of Wales. To his perception of his country's needs and his efforts to meet them, more than to almost anyone else's, are owed the survival and renewal of the language and literature of Wales from the sixteenth century onwards. The most learned Renaissance scholar in the Wales of his day, he was also steeped in the knowledge of earlier Welsh poetry and prose. He saw the need for a Welsh Bible, did much to bring it about and was the most important pioneer of the printed book in Welsh. William *Morgan's Bible of 1588 took over a large part of Salesbury's version of the New Testament, and that Bible, in an age when the *Bardic Order was in rapid decline, was the main bulwark of the language and literature, as well as the foundation of religious belief, in modern Wales.

For further details see D. R. Thomas, *The Life and Work of Bishop Davies and William Salesbury* (1902) and Isaac Thomas, *William Salesbury a'i Destament* (1967) and *Y Testament Newydd Cymraeg 1551–1620* (1976); see also the two chapters by W. Alun Mathias in *Y Traddodiad Rhyddiaith* (ed. Geraint Bowen, 1970).

Salmau Cân (lit. 'Psalms'; 1621), the most important of Welsh metrical Psalters, was the work of Edmund *Prys. Originally bound together with the Welsh Book of Common Prayer (1621) and entitled *Llyfr y Psalmau, wedi eu cyfieithu a'i cyfansoddi ar fesur cerdd yn Gymraeg*, it was intended for congregational singing and was accompanied by twelve tunes, the first music to appear in a Welsh printed book. Although he was an accomplished poet in the strict metres, Prys chose to compose his Psalms in free metre, explaining in a foreword that he wished to be true to the Scriptural text. He also referred to the unsuitability of the strict metres for congregational singing and to the ease with which the common people could learn simple free-metre verses. All but four of his Psalms were composed in what became known as *Mesur Salm*, the old *carol metre adapted by extending the first and third lines by one syllable, so that a line of eight syllables was followed by a line of seven. A skilled Hebraist, Prys succeeded in respecting the integrity of the originals without sacrificing literary quality and his work is notable for its richness and dignity of expression. His Psalms were the main texts for congregational singing in Welsh until the advent of *Methodism and some of them, after more than a hundred editions, are still sung today.

Salmon Llwyd, see JONES, OWEN WYNNE (1828–70).

Salmon of Llyn Llyw, The, see under OLDEST ANIMALS.

SALUSBURY, THOMAS (1612–43), poet, a member of the *Salesbury family, was born at *Chirk and lived at Llewenni, Denbs. A man of sophisticated tastes and literary interests, he was knighted in 1632, fought in the *Civil War on the Royalist side, and served as Member of Parliament for the County during the last three years of his short life. Although he wrote a good deal, he published only one long poem, *The History of Joseph* (1636), which was intended to restore the reputation of the Puritan *Myddletons, of whom his mother was one. The full range and facility of his writing can be seen in the fashionable English poems, translations, plays and masques which were performed at Chirk Castle and the manuscripts of which are now kept in the *National Library of Wales. In the aftermath of the bardic tradition, Salusbury fostered Sidneyan and Jonsonian ideas about literature in his community and something of the vigour of Welsh life in the early seventeenth century appears in his work.

SAMUEL, EDWARD (1674–1748), poet and translator, was born at Penmorfa, Caerns., and educated at Oriel College, Oxford. The rector of Betws Gwerful Goch, Mer., from 1702 to 1721, and thereafter of Llangar, Mer., he was the grandfather of David *Samwell. His verse, in the strict and free metres, includes light and humorous cywyddau, an elegy to Huw *Morys, many englynion (most of which remain in manuscript) and a number of carols, some of which appear in the anthologies Blodeu-gerdd Cymry (1759), Llu o Ganiadau (1798) and Beirdd y Berwyn (1902). Besides an original work entitled Buchedda'r Apostolion a'r Efengylwyr (1704), Samuel translated into Welsh books by such authors as Hugo Grotius, Richard Allestree and William Beveridge; his translation, Holl Ddyledswydd Dyn (1718), is considered superior to that of John *Langford (1672). Samuel's classic work, in which his mastery of prose style is amply demonstrated, is Gwirionedd y Grefydd Grist'nogol (1716).

SAMWELL, DAVID (Dafydd Ddu Feddyg; 1751–98), doctor and author, was born at Nantglyn, Denbs., a grandson of Edward *Samuel, the rector of Llangar. He was a surgeon on board The Discovery during Captain Cook's expedition in search of the North-West Passage (1776–78) and on the next voyage was an eye-witness of Cook's death at the hands of natives in Hawaii, circumstances which he described in A Narrative of the Death of Captain James Cook (1786). His journal, 'Some Account of a Voyage to South Seas 1776–1777–1778' (deposited in the British Museum and the National Library of Wales) is a pioneering work of social anthropology. Samwell played an active part in the society and in the literary life of the *London Welsh: he was a founder-member of the *Gwyneddigion Society and a member of the *Caradogion. He was acquainted with Gwallter Mechain (Walter *Davies) and Iolo Morganwg (Edward *Williams) and he was among those who helped in the creation of *Gorsedd Beirdd Ynys Prydain. His interest in the legend of *Madog ab Owain Gwynedd's discovery of America is reflected in his poem 'The Padouca Hunt' (1799).

There is an account of David Samwell's life by E. G. Bowen in the St. David's Day series (1974); see also the essay by Elis Wynne Williams in Portreadau Enwogion 1500–1800 (1976). Samwell's narrative about Cook's death was republished under the title Captain Cook and Hawaii in 1957.

'Sanctus', a very well-known, powerful hymn-tune by John Richards (Isalaw; 1843–1901), to which are set the words 'Glan geriwbiaid a seraffiaid', a translation by Owen Griffith *Owen (Alafon) of a hymn by Richard Mant. It first appeared in the second appendix to Llyfr Tonau Cynulleidfaol (1890) under the editorship of Ieuan Gwyllt (John *Roberts).

Sandde Bryd Angel, a young man among those present at *Arthur's court in the tale of *Culhwch and Olwen, of whom it is said that he received no blow at the battle of *Camlan because he was so beautiful.

Sangiad, a term in *Cerdd Dafod denoting an interference with the normal run of syntax by a word or phrase interpolated into the line. The use of highly appropriate sangiadau was regarded as an essential part of the professional poet's skill in medieval times and it is still a feature of poetry in the strict metres. See also DYFALU.

Sarn Helen, see under ELEN LUYDDOG (4th cent.).

Sarnicol, see THOMAS, THOMAS JACOB (1873–1945).

SAUNDERS, ERASMUS (1670–1724), priest and author, was born in the parish of Clydey, Pembs., and educated at Jesus College, Oxford. From 1705 until his death he was rector of Blockley, Worcs., and of Helmdon, Northants. He supported the *Society for Promoting Christian Knowledge in its provision of Welsh Bibles but is remembered chiefly as the author of A View of the State of Religion in the Diocese of St. Davids (1721), a primary source for the religious history of the eighteenth century in Wales. The work of a devoted Churchman, this book draws a dark picture of ruined churches, absenteeism and pluralism amongst the clergy and ignorance amongst curates, but the work also pays an eloquent tribute to the common people's devotion to *Anglicanism.

Scholarship (Linguistic and Literary) in Welsh. After the decline of the *Bardic Order in the sixteenth century, the study of Welsh was carried out by amateurs. The court poets of medieval Wales and the *Poets of the Gentry who succeeded them were professional writers trained within a school system where the curriculum included metrics, vocabulary, grammar, the Welsh poetic tradition and native learning of myth, onomastics, history, *genealogies and heraldry. This learned class assured the preservation and transmission of accepted standards and a common literary language. The school environment was lost as the change in social structures in the sixteenth and seventeenth centuries led to the Anglicization of the gentry and to a decline in patronage, and there was a danger that an emerging popular literature would not inherit established standards. In Wales, however, the humanists, though inspired by European ideals and educated in the Classics, never lost sight of the antiquity of their own tradition. Welsh, for them, had been the language and literature of kings, the noble history of whose ancestors *Geoffrey of Monmouth had portrayed, while contemporary views claimed that the native poets were the descendants of Caesar's learned *Druids. The mantle of the poets as guardians of a standard language and native learning was taken up by humanists such as William *Salesbury, Thomas *Wiliems, Henry Salesbury and John *Davies of Mallwyd, who produced dictionaries, and those such as Gruffydd *Robert, Siôn Dafydd *Rhys and John Davies who produced grammars. The Welsh *Bible of 1588, revised by John Davies in 1620, ensured that the language of the poets became the basis of modern literary Welsh.

Contemporary opinion claimed that Welsh was one of the original or 'mother tongues' and throughout the seventeenth and eighteenth centuries Celtomania was adversely to affect the quality of work on Welsh grammar and lexicography. The sane voice of Edward *Lhuyd was silenced by his early death in 1709 before he could fully instruct his students in his attitudes and methods. His influence remained in Welsh *antiquarianism, topographical studies and the will to publish historical records, but none understood his linguistics. The leaders of the cultural revival of the eighteenth century were scribes, literary historians and antiquaries: Lewis *Morris, Evan *Evans (Ieuan Fardd), Edward *Richard and the immensely learned but wayward genius Iolo Morganwg (Edward *Williams). These men and others associated with them, by collecting and transcribing manuscripts, by their own enquiries, and more especially by their founding of literary societies in London such as the Honourable Society of *Cymmrodorion and the *Gwyneddigion, were able to inspire and organize research which led to the publication of two important collections of medieval Welsh literature, Barddoniaeth Dafydd ap Gwilym (1789) and The Myfyrian Archaiology of Wales (1801), mainly at the expense of Owen *Jones (Owain Myfyr).

Many of these scholarly functions were continued during the nineteenth century by Yr *Hen Bersoniaid Llengar ('The Old Literary Clerics') and by the provincial eisteddfodau which paved the way for the revival of modern Welsh scholarship. There was much false scholarship in the nineteenth century (see, for example, the entry on William *Owen Pughe) but Evan Evans's Some Specimens of the Poetry of the Antient Welsh Bards (1764) was to be followed by the rational attitudes of Thomas *Stephens and his important book, The Literature of the Kymry (1849). D. Silvan *Evans, one of the literary clerics, was to be the last of the old school and the first of the new. John *Peter, Llywarch Reynolds, Robert *Jones of Rotherhithe, Robert *Williams (1810–81) and others began to find scholarly guidance among the new Celtic linguists of France and Germany, while the diplomatic editions of J. Gwenogvryn *Evans provided a fresh view of the raw materials of research.

The appointment in 1877 of John *Rhŷs, a product of the London and German philological schools, as the first occupant of the Chair of Celtic at Oxford University, was to prove of crucial significance. He was able to attract to Oxford scores of eager and able young Welshmen, some of whom attended his lectures though formally studying other subjects, but all of whom profited from the discussions of *Cymdeithas Dafydd ap Gwilym on subjects such as orthographic reform. The leavening effect of Oxford education, formal and informal, on Welsh scholarship and writing at the turn of the century cannot be overemphasized for, had it not been for John Rhŷs's enthusiastic teaching, the Welsh Departments of the *University of Wales would not have been as well fitted as they were for their task. There had been provision for the teaching of Welsh at St. David's College, Lampeter, from its establishment in 1827, but not until the setting up of the colleges of the future University of Wales at Aberystwyth (1872), Cardiff (1883) and Bangor (1884), each with its Chair of Welsh, can it be said that Welsh studies gained the benefits of a university environment. Although excellent work had previously been done by the Guild of Graduates and the Bangor Manuscripts Society, it was with the establishment of the University's *Board of Celtic Studies in 1919 and its Press Board three years later, that it became possible for the first time to initiate and co-ordinate research on a wide scale and to ensure its publication. The first Professors of Welsh—Edward *Anwyl at Aberystwyth, Thomas *Powel at Cardiff and John *Morris-Jones at Bangor—were graduates in other disciplines who had come to the study of Welsh by the path of the native tradition in literature and antiquarianism and, more significantly, by the formal study of Welsh historical linguistics and medieval literature under John Rhŷs.

With the exception of W. J. *Gruffydd, the second generation of modern Welsh scholars, including Ifor *Williams, G. J. *Williams, J. *Lloyd-Jones, Henry *Lewis, T. H. *Parry-Williams and Timothy *Lewis, were the first to graduate in Welsh. The lack of published primary material and of research aids was the fundamental problem facing Welsh studies in the early years of the twentieth century. The *National Eisteddfod had nurtured aspects of the study of Welsh literary history by setting ambitious essay subjects, but though such competitions produced good work by Charles *Ashton, Thomas *Richards, and others, they could not support the level of research needed. The provision of this support was to be the function of the University of Wales and its Board of Celtic Studies whose *Bulletin* soon became an indispensable medium of publication. John Lloyd-Jones began producing his lexicon of early Welsh poetry in 1931 (it was left unfinished upon his death in 1963) and the first fascicule of the University of Wales Dictionary of the Welsh Language, initiated in 1920, appeared in 1951. Henry Lewis and T. H. Parry-Williams published pioneer studies of Old Welsh, syntax, historical linguistics, borrowings and free-metre poetry, but in sheer volume and variety, Ifor Williams's work was of outstanding importance. His editions of the *Hengerdd*, medieval prose, the poetry of the *cywyddwyr* and Old Welsh texts opened up an immensely rich field, while his notes on place-names and individual words form a lexicon of Middle Welsh. In the field of literary history one of the seminal works was G. J. Williams's *Iolo Morganwg a Chywyddau'r Ychwanegiad* (1926), an authoritative linguistic and stylistic analysis which revealed many of Iolo's *cywyddau* to be fabrications. Even more significantly, the book was evidence that both the discipline and the material for a strictly academic study of the history of Welsh literature were becoming available. This work was the first in a series of magisterial examinations by G. J. Williams which were to map out the nature of Renaissance and modern Welsh literary history and scholarship, and of Glamorgan's literary tradition in particular. The publication of an increasing number of books and articles enabled Thomas *Parry to produce his lively but sound synthesis, *Hanes Llenyddiaeth Gymraeg*, in 1948. His edition of the work of *Dafydd ap Gwilym (1952) allowed readers to approach this corpus of poetry confidently for the first time. By the 1950s a great deal of leeway was being made up with the publication of grammars, dictionaries, editions and monographs, with the result that recent Welsh literary scholarship is now less linguistically orientated, while linguistic studies have become more synchronic than diachronic. Scholarship, too, has achieved a broader base, being confined not solely to the University of Wales or indeed to Wales, but attracting a growing number of scholars in the other Celtic countries, elsewhere in Europe and in the USA.

For fuller treatment of this subject see G. J. Williams, *Agweddau ar Hanes Dysg Gymraeg* (1969) and the same author's article, 'The History of Welsh Scholarship' in *Studia Celtica* (vols. VIII/IX, 1973–74); see also the volume *Celtic Studies in Wales* (ed. Elwyn Davies, 1963).

SCHREIBER, CHARLOTTE, see GUEST, CHARLOTTE (1812–95).

Scotch Cattle, the name given to bands of workers who, in the valleys of south-east Wales during the years from 1820 to 1835, attacked those against whom they had grievances or amongst whom they were determined to enforce solidarity. The area in which they had their strongholds was known as the Black Domain and included those industrial districts of Monmouthshire, Breconshire and Glamorganshire which extended from Rhymney to Abergavenny and from Llangynidr to Caerphilly.

The name of this illegal organization, which took a red bull's head as its symbol, may have derived from the skins worn by its members as a disguise; or, because they were black-faced, it may have referred to their ferocious appearance; they were also said to 'scotch' their victims. The leader, known as *Tarw Scotch* ('Scotch Bull'), whose identity was never revealed, was reputed to be an Englishman by the name of Lolly and nicknamed Ned, perhaps an allusion to the Ned Ludd who had given his name to the Luddites in England a few years previously. Most of those who took part in the Scotch Cattle's activities were young, Welsh-speaking colliers such as William Jenkins (Wil Aberhonddu) and John James (Shoni Coal Tar) who, in their daily lives, had been incensed by wage-reductions, the truck-system and other harsh conditions. Among their practices were the holding of open-air meetings at night to the accompaniment of horns, drums and gunfire, the sending of warning notes to blacklegs and informers, and the organizing of attacks on the owners' property and of midnight visits to the homes of fellow-workers whom they wanted to intimidate.

These events reached their climax in 1835 when a young miner named John (or Edward) Morgan was tried for his part in the killing of a woman during a raid on a house at Bedwellty, Mon. He was found guilty but, because he had not fired the fatal shot, the jury recommended mercy. The authorities, however, were in no mood to heed the plea and, on 6 April 1835, Morgan was hanged at Monmouth, dying what was to become in the popular view a martyr's death second only to that of Richard Lewis (Dic Penderyn) after the *Merthyr Rising of 1831.

For a full account of the Scotch Cattle's activities, see David Jones, *Before Rebecca: Popular Protests in Wales 1793–1835* (1973).

SCOTT-ELLIS, THOMAS EVELYN (Lord Howard de Walden; 1880–1946), patron and author, was born in London into a family whose origins were Welsh. In 1912 he settled at *Chirk Castle, Denbs., learning Welsh and encouraging its study; a keen sportsman and antiquary, he was also deeply interested in the theatre. His operatic trilogy, *The Cauldron of Annwn* (1922), was based on *Pedair Cainc y Mabinogi*, but he is more often remembered for his part in the development of amateur drama in

Wales. A keen advocate of the establishment of a Welsh National Drama Company (see under DRAMA), to perform in both Welsh and English, he was involved in several attempts to start such a venture, none of which met with any success. His generous patronage of writers helped, among others, J. O. *Francis, R. G. *Berry and Dylan *Thomas.

SCOURFIELD, JOHN (1808–76), author, was born John Philipps but took the surname of his mother's family when he inherited the estate of Moat and Robeston Hall, Pembs., in 1862. Educated at Oriel College, Oxford, he was the Member of Parliament for Haverfordwest from 1852 to 1868 and for the County from 1868 until 1876; he was knighted in 1862 and made a baronet by Disraeli in the year of his death. Among his published works were *Lyrics and Philippics* (1859), *The Grand Serio-Comic Opera of Lord Bateman and his Sophia* (1863) and *The Mayor's Tale: a Tragic and a Diabolic Opera* (post-1862).

Scudamore, John (*fl.* 1360–1420?), gentleman, of Kentchurch, came of a Norman family settled in the *Ewias district of *Erging since the twelfth century, one of whose scions had married the heiress of Troy, near Monmouth, and acquired other property in the lordship of Abergavenny. Sir John, an *uchelwr* of Welsh-speaking Archenfield (Erging), was in 1403 an esquire in the King's service and custodian of *Carreg Cennen castle, which he held against the forces of *Owain Glyndŵr. But, unlike *Dafydd Gam and other men of the old Siluria, he found means of changing sides, mainly because he had married Alice, Glyndŵr's daughter, in 1414. The later attitude of the Scudamores is best demonstrated by John's brother, Philip Scudamore of Troy, one of Glyndŵr's diehard captains, who was captured and executed at Shrewsbury in 1410. It was widely suspected that the fugitive Glyndŵr was hidden between 1415 and his death (*c.*1416) in one or other of Sir John's houses, either at Monnington Straddel in the Golden Valley or at Kentchurch Court, which possesses a secret room to this day. That no Welshman offered information about Glyndŵr's whereabouts is a measure both of the emergence of a new patriotism and of Sir John's standing among his people. But, accused of treason, he was deprived of his estates.

Second Aeon, a magazine which was published and edited by Peter *Finch in Cardiff between 1966 and 1974; twenty-one numbers (including the final, triple number) were issued. It began as a cyclostyled pamphlet of verse by young poets associated with No Walls, a group which met for the reading of its members' work, but from its fifth issue it gradually extended its purview to include poetry and prose by a large number of writers, many from outside Wales. The Anglo-Welsh poets who were among its contributors included John *Tripp, John *Ormond, Dannie *Abse, Herbert *Williams and J. P. *Ward. Devoted to the Anglo-American avant-garde and to foreign poetry in translation, the magazine gave prominence to experimental work, including sound and concrete poetry, and to graphics; it also carried information about 'the small press scene' in Europe and the USA. By the time it ceased publication in the year of Peter Finch's appointment as the manager of the *Welsh Arts Council's bookshop at Oriel in Cardiff, it had a circulation of some two thousand copies, a remarkable achievement for a 'little magazine'.

Segontium, see CAERNARFON.

Seiriol (6th cent.), a saint who, according to the *Lives of the Saints, was the son of Owain Danwyn, whose father, Einion Yrth, had been the son of *Cunedda Wledig. He is thought to have founded the church at *Penmon in the south-east corner of Anglesey, where the remains of his settlement are still to be seen. On the nearby island known as Ynys Lannog or Ynys Seiriol (Puffin Island), where the saint settled, there lived hermits in the time of *Gerald de Barri (Giraldus Cambrensis). With his companion, *Cybi, Seiriol was the most important of Anglesey's saints but his cult was confined to the island. His feast-day is 1 February.

SEISYLL BRYFFWRCH (*fl.* 1155–75), a poet whose *bardic contention with *Cynddelw Brydydd Mawr for the office of *pencerdd* at the court of *Madog ap Maredudd, Prince of Powys, is the earliest extant example of its kind. Boasting of his descent from a poet called Culfardd, he taunted Cynddelw for his lack of bardic pedigree, but to no avail. Among his patrons were the Lord Rhys (*Rhys ap Gruffudd), *Owain Gwynedd and Iorwerth Drwyndwn.

Seisyllwg, a *gwlad* of early Wales, was created about 730 when Seisyll ap Clydog, King of *Ceredigion, annexed *Ystrad Tywi. The marriage of Angharad, the great-great-granddaughter of Seisyll, to Rhodri ap Merfyn (*Rhodri Mawr) led to the unification of Seisyllwg and *Gwynedd in 871. Seisyllwg was again an independent kingdom under Cadell ap Rhodri but the name fell into disuse when, as a result of *Hywel Dda's annexation of Dyfed, Seisyllwg became part of the wider kingdom of *Deheubarth.

Seithenyn, see under CANTRE'R GWAELOD and MISFORTUNES OF ELPHIN (1829).

Selyf (d. *c.*615), King of *Powys, the son of *Cynan Garwyn and a grandson of Brochfael

Ysgithrog, was killed by the Northumbrians under Ethelfrith at the battle of Chester. A poem attributed to *Taliesin describes him as very belligerent and records that none from outside Powys came to his aid. Yet he remained a hero, for *Cynddelw Brydydd Mawr referred to the young warriors of Powys in his day as '*cenawon Selyf* ('Selyf's whelps').

Senghennydd, a cantref of *Morgannwg lying between the rivers Taf and Rhymni. By the mid-twelfth century the two northernmost commots of the cantref, Is and Uwch Caeach, were ruled by *Ifor ap Meurig (Ifor Bach), the brother-in-law of *Rhys ap Gruffudd (The Lord Rhys) of *Deheubarth. Gruffudd ap Rhys, a great-grandson of Ifor, became an ally of *Llewelyn ap Gruffudd and the threat that the alliance represented to the lordship of Glamorgan caused Gilbert de Clare in 1268 to begin the building of the great castle of *Caerphilly. By 1272 Gilbert had dispossessed Gruffudd and had incorporated Senghennydd Is and Uwch Caeach into his demesne.

Senghennydd Explosion, The, one of the worst disasters in the annals of British mining, occurred on 14 October 1913 at the Lancaster Pit of the Universal Colliery in Senghennydd, a village near Caerphilly, Glam. A total of 439 men were killed.

A full account of the explosion is given in John H. Brown, *The Valley of the Shadow* (1981).

Seren, Y (lit. 'The star'; 1885–1974), a weekly Radical newspaper established by the partners Robert John Davies and Robert Evans at Bala, Mer. After the death of Davies in 1906, the name of their press was changed to *Gwasg y Bala* and by 1921 it had become the property of Robert Evans's son, Robert Stanley Evans, who bought another newspaper, *Yr Wythnos a'r Eryr*, and in the same year incorporated it with *Y Seren*. The press belonged to the firm of A. J. Chapple until 1968 when the copyright of *Y Seren* was bought by *Gwasg y Cyfnod*, Bala.

Seren Cymru (lit. 'Star of Wales'), a newspaper established in 1851 at Carmarthen by Samuel Evans (Gomerydd) after he had quarrelled with the owner of *Seren Gomer, of which he had been editor. The venture was a failure and publication ceased in December 1852, only to be restarted in 1856 under the editorship of J. Emlyn Jones. The newspaper continued to appear fortnightly until 1863, when it became a weekly. Although it had been re-established as an Independent periodical and the personal property of W. Morgan Evans, its printer, it was sold to a group of *Baptists in 1880 and since 1936 it has belonged to the Welsh Baptists' Union, which continues to publish it. A number of prominent Baptists have been among its editors, including Benjamin Thomas (Myfyr Emlyn), John *Jenkins (Gwili) and D. Eirwyn Morgan. In its early days the paper carried foreign, national and local news and its viewpoint was Radical, but it is now almost entirely devoted to the affairs of its denomination.

Seren Gomer (lit. 'Star of Gomer'; 1814–1983), the first newspaper in the Welsh language, was established by Joseph *Harris (Gomer) as a 'General Weekly Informant for the whole of the Principality of Wales'. Published by David Jenkin in Swansea, it carried foreign and national news, reports of fairs and markets, news of ships' movements, a poetry section and letters. Although it had a comparatively wide circulation, being sold in about fifty places throughout Wales, Harris found that the Government stamp duty and a dearth of advertisers were major obstacles to his newspaper's success and it ceased publication with its eighty-fifth number. It was revived, however, in 1818 and ran for another four years, when it was sold after Gomer's death to a publisher in Carmarthen. As a quarterly magazine, published by the *Baptists, *Seren Gomer* survived until 1983.

Seren y Dwyrain, see under UNDEB Y CYMRY AR WASGAR.

Seven Wonders of Wales, The, an anonymous rhyme of which the best-known version runs as follows:

> Pistyll Rhaeadr and Wrexham steeple,
> Snowdon's mountain without its people,
> Overton yew-trees, St. Winifred wells,
> Llangollen bridge and Gresford bells.

The lines are presumed to date from the late eighteenth or the early nineteenth century and probably reflect the interest of English visitors in the scenery of north Wales (see under TOURS OF WALES).

Sgilti Ysgafndroed, a character in the tale of *Culhwch and Olwen who is among those present at *Arthur's court. It is said of him that he is so light of foot that, when bearing a message on his lord's behalf, he never follows a road but, in a forest, walks along the top of the trees and, on a mountain, of the reeds. The name Sgilti may have been derived from Caolite, the name of a famous runner in the legends of Ireland.

Sgolor Mawr, Y, see ROBERTS, ROBERT (1834–85).

SHADRACH, AZARIAH (1774–1844), devotional writer, was born at Llanfair, near Fishguard, Pembs. He kept schools in various parts of north Wales and was ordained a minister with the Independents at Llanrwst, Denbs. He later ministered at Tal-y-bont and Llanbadarn Fawr, Cards., and in 1819 he founded Seion Church (later Baker Street and now Seion again) in Aberystwyth. During a period of fervent theological debate he earned a reputation as 'the Bunyan of Wales' by writing twenty-four books of a devotional or expository nature, including one in English, *Meditations on Jewels* (1833) and another, *Rhosyn Saron* (1816), in which he argued keenly in favour of Calvinism against the assertions of the Arminians. His most popular works were *Allwedd Myfyrdod* (1801) and *Tabernacl Newydd* (1821); *A Looking Glass: neu Ddrych Cywir* (1807) was translated into English by Edward S. Byam under the title *The Backslider's Mirror* (1845).

A biography of Azariah Shadrach was written by Josiah Jones (1863).

SHANKLAND, THOMAS (1858–1927), librarian and historian, was born at St. Clears, Carms., and served the Baptist ministry at Mold and Rhyl, Flints. In 1905 he was appointed Assistant Librarian at the University College of North Wales, Bangor. By his zeal in collecting rare books and filling gaps in the runs of old periodicals, he greatly added to the wealth of material in the College library during the twenty years before his health broke down in 1925. As a historian he was interested in the religious movements of the seventeenth and eighteenth centuries, especially the work of such men as John *Miles, Stephen *Hughes and *John ap John. He also wrote on hymns and hymn-tunes. The sum of his work was immense, but it is scattered in periodicals and remains uncollected.

A bibliography of his writings appeared in the *Transactions of Cymdeithas Hanes Bedyddwyr Cymru* (1926–27).

Shemi Wâd, see WADE, JAMES (d. 1887).

Shepherd's Hey (1953), a collection of short stories by Gwyn *Jones. All seven are melodramatic tales of passion, deceit, struggle and sacrifice, occasionally erupting into violence, but they contain remarkable studies of men and women who are frail, in one way or another doomed to loss, some of them momentarily touched with noble qualities. The delineation of these characters and their relationships is perhaps the author's finest achievement in fiction.

Shimli, a gathering held in a kiln while corn was dried before being ground. The damp climate of west Wales, where the custom was especially popular, sometimes necessitated the harvesting of corn before it had fully ripened and so it was dried slowly over a period of some thirty-six hours. The kiln provided a warm meeting-place for young people who took this opportunity of entertaining themselves with songs and recitations. See also STABLE LOFT SINGING.

For further details see the article by Elfyn Scourfield in *The Carmarthenshire Antiquary* (no. 8, 1972).

Shiring of Wales, The (1284, 1536, 1542, 1972), began after Edward I's victory over *Llywelyn ap Gruffudd: the Statute of Wales (1284) converted the Prince's former territory into the shires of Anglesey, Caernarfon and Merioneth, while out of lands in the south-west, already for forty years in the King's direct holding, the shires of Cardigan and Carmarthen were formed. To Flint, separate from the royal Earldom of Chester but judicially dependent upon it, was added—because it was the Queen's possession—the geographically detached region of *Maelor Saesneg, the eastern part of which was demonstrably English, and this curiosity still persists. Thus the whole of north Wales, except the Marcher holding of *Perfeddwlad and the more northerly lands of *Powys, was directly ruled by the English Crown from 1284.

By the *Act of Union of 1536 all the surviving Marcher lordships became shire ground. Mawddwy was added to the existing county of Merioneth, Cardigan and Carmarthen were much enlarged, and Pembroke and Glamorgan, which had become Crown lordships, were augmented when they were granted shire status. Four other shires—two in the south (Brecknock and Radnor) and two in the north (Denbigh and Montgomery)—brought the total to eleven. Flint was included in 1536 among those shires instructed to appoint Justices of the Peace and the revisionary Act of 1542 associated it with Denbigh and Montgomery in one of four Welsh circuits of the Court of Great Sessions. There were thus twelve shires in Wales. A thirteenth was prevented by a new anomaly: the subjection of the new shire of Monmouth (created from the ancient tribal territory of the *Silures) to the Courts of Westminster, though ecclesiastically it remained part of the diocese of *Llandaf. It was this separation which necessitated in many subsequent Acts of Parliament the use of the phrase 'Wales and Monmouthshire'. The reasons for this decision can only be guessed at, for if a 'tidy dozen' was the aim, Flint was much the more anomalous. George *Owen thought Monmouthshire became 'odd shire out' because it was the nearest to Westminster. Others have suspected that greater wealth among the gentry and their tradition of leadership on the battlefield made the detachment of Monmouthshire from Wales the more desirable of the two possibilities.

The Act of 1536 also conveyed to English shires some strongly Welsh portions of Marcher lordships. Oswestry and its region (in marked contrast with Maelor Saesneg) became part of Shropshire, as did a large tract of land east of the upper reaches of the Teme; Archenfield—probably for reasons identical with those for Monmouthshire—was attached to Herefordshire, though still ecclesiastically subject to the diocese of *St. David's. Monmouthshire's reward for detachment was to obtain two knights of the shire in Parliament. All other

Welsh shires had one, with a burgess from each 'shire town' (except Merioneth, whose shire town, Harlech, was too poor to afford its member). This representative quota, while only half of that allotted to shires in England, was probably a concession to the poverty of Wales rather than unjust discrimination, for the expense of attending in London was considerable and not readily to be borne by 'mountain squires'. Welsh Members of Parliament were paid, at a time when their English counterparts were ceasing to be, and after 1543 a system of contributory boroughs was set up within Welsh shires, whereby the elected burgess should be both voted for and supported financially by boroughs other than the 'shire town'.

The Act of 1972, drawn up in the belief that larger administrative units would be cheaper to operate, reduced the thirteen shires of Wales to eight, with effect from 1974. Anglesey, Caernarfon and Merioneth were amalgamated in the new county of Gwynedd, Denbigh and Flint in that of Clwyd, Brecknock, Radnor and Montgomery in that of Powys, and Cardigan, Pembroke and Carmarthen in that of Dyfed. Monmouthshire, slightly enlarged, was re-named Gwent, and Glamorgan was divided into the three counties of West Glamorgan, Mid-Glamorgan and South Glamorgan. The eight County councils of Wales are elected bodies which enjoy a large measure of autonomy. It is nevertheless true that, for most Welsh people, the counties created in 1974 are so large and of such recent provenance that it is still to the older, smaller counties that reference is usually made, especially as several of the names of the former shires survived as electoral constituencies after the alterations made in 1983.

Shoni Onions or **Sioni Nionod**, see JOHNNY ONIONS.

Shoni Sgubor Fawr, see JONES, JOHN (1811–58).

Short Story in English, The. That the short story has been more characteristic of the work of Welsh writers in English than has the *novel is probably the result, in the main, of two factors. First, it was, even in its heyday in the 1930s and 1940s, the natural product, like the poem, of a still-poor society in which the writer was necessarily amateur, writing for brief periods in such time as he had. Second, it was a vehicle, again like the poem, which could carry the exuberant rhetoric and the sheer delight in language which marked a particular generation which, with the tradition of eloquence in Welsh still half-sounding in its ears, plunged into the sea of English with the zest of explorers. The success of the genre was, however, short-lived, owing to the rapid disappearance of the distinctive linguistic and social pattern in which writers were

nurtured and to the consequent fall in the market valuation which had been set in London upon the airing of this distinctiveness. Furthermore, the tradition of Anglo-Welsh writing inherited from the nineteenth century was markedly unconfident and the short story, even in its flowering, was a fine burst of words rather than writing socially mature enough to include satire. It was generally anecdotal, lyrical or comic (and sometimes all three), verbally rebellious or extravagant but non-revolutionary, and frequently projected as the vision of a child.

The defensive complex engendered in such Welsh writers in English as can be discovered in the nineteenth century, taunted as they constantly were with the inferiority of the Celts, can best be seen in the poets Rowland *Williams (Goronva Camlann) and Ivan *Hues. Prose-writers, perhaps taking courage from the friendly sketches of Welsh rural life by the incomer Anne *Beale, saw the sketch as their natural form. In the pages of Charles *Wilkins's periodical, The *Red Dragon, during the 1880s, for example, there are numerous pieces timidly evoking the antiquarian, quaint and pastoral aspects of Welsh society. By the end of the century some of the bolder spirits, such as Alfred Thomas, David *Davies (1849–1926), Bertha Thomas and Zachary Mather (Zechariah *Mathers), had begun to publish collections of stories in book form. Rarely, however, did they escape the sentimental or transform the sketch into something structurally more dramatic and assured.

It is customary, therefore, to date the emergence of the Anglo-Welsh short story from the appearance of *My People (1915) by Caradoc Evans (David *Evans). This judgement can be justified broadly on three grounds: the overwhelming contrast seen in its attitude to Wales, the market it obtained, and the confidence it eventually created. Caradoc Evans's hate-writing, however, was not well enough observed to be termed satire: it projected the vices of greed, lust and religious hypocrisy, unmitigated, to create an atmosphere of such strangeness as almost to seem allegory. But the novelty (as well as the archaic quality) of its language announced that a writer from Wales could be something other than an approval-seeker: there was, after all, a way of being different and successful. Those who followed, twenty years later—Glyn *Jones and Dylan *Thomas in particular—also concentrated on a new language, a lyricism in prose which was poetic and unabashed. Without the hatred, they were conscious of the market among London publishers for the eccentricities and curiosities, the sheer strangeness, of Welsh life.

Even then, however, the true gold was melting out of the alloy: the Welshness and the difference were disappearing from the community around them and their realization of this process is demonstrated most of all in the prevalence in their stories of the child-narrator. In the stories of Rhys *Davies, Wales is the country of his adolescence because he left it for London in his early twenties, while in those of Glyn Jones, Gwyn *Jones and Dylan Thomas there is no permanent removal but a greater consciousness of loss. The tendency to hark back to the 'different' in a search for material made a reliance on childhood memory likely. It is also possible that a lack of life-view, as of confidence, amid changing conditions affected Dylan Thomas sufficiently to create a preference for the child-narrator as ultimately non-responsible and unassailable.

Of them all Arthur Machen (Arthur *Jones), Geraint *Goodwin and Alun *Lewis are least true to type because they spent much of their writing lives away from Wales. The first, despite the use of antiquated models, is unique in evoking the spirit of his native landscape of Gwent and in peopling it with ancient terror and superstition. The second, influenced by D. H. Lawrence (as were Glyn Jones, Rhys Davies and Alun Lewis) came back to his native Montgomeryshire to write adult-centred stories robust enough to avoid sentiment and, on occasion, to achieve a memorable pathos. Alun Lewis, who was never 'inside' working-class Wales, wrote his few Welsh stories about a holiday countryside from which he had been parted by war.

Not one of the writers so far mentioned attempted stories about religious principle (as distinct from unworthy religious practice), class conflict, crime or deviant sex. For all but the first the society they knew offered little evidence. The upper classes, the stories of Nigel *Heseltine apart, were left unmolested and linguistic and national issues were largely a matter for nostalgia. Gwyn *Thomas (1913–81), who broke new ground with a concern for *Socialism, was influenced by European Absurdists sufficiently to cancel his 'revolution' by the play of wit and the development of such farce as renders his philosophers part of an Absurdist community and incapable of altering it. The presence of wit and humour, indeed, aerates even the most lyrical of Anglo-Welsh stories of the time. Dylan Thomas, the most memorable of all these writers, succeeds supremely because his humour is adolescent and basic enough to uninhibit even the most prudish reader.

By about 1950, however, the market in England for Welsh buffooneries was disappearing and publishers had begun to convince themselves that short stories of any kind were an uncommercial risk. In this opinion they have continued and in recent decades only Emyr *Humphreys and Alun *Richards, assisted by their reputations as novelists, and Leslie *Norris, a stylist so assured that he can often dare to discard structure and return to the sketch or the anecdote, have had significant collections of stories published. But even Leslie Norris relies greatly on the 'different' Wales of his youth. The elements of the typical Anglo-Welsh short story of the period from 1930 to 1950 no longer approximate even faintly to the observable facts of contemporary society and new writers of quality, when they appear, will have to vitalize in other ways their experience of a now seriously Anglicized society. Among younger writers who have published collections of short stories are Robert *Nisbet and Peter *Finch.

Short stories by Welsh writers in English are to be found in the following anthologies: *Welsh Short Stories* (1937), *Welsh Short Stories* (ed. Gwyn Jones, 1940), *Welsh Short Stories* (ed. Gwyn Jones, 1956), *Welsh Short Stories* (ed. George Ewart Evans, 1959), *The Shining Pyramid* (ed. Sam Adams and Roland Mathias, 1970), *Twenty-five Welsh Short Stories* (ed. Gwyn Jones and Islwyn Ffowc Elis, 1971), *The Penguin Book of Welsh Short Stories* (ed. Alun Richards, 1976) and *Pieces of Eight* (ed. Robert Nisbet, 1982).

Short Story in Welsh, The. The raconteur has always been a figure of importance in Welsh society, losing none of his influence whatever the changes in his material and mode of address. After the period of *Pedair Cainc y Mabinogi* there came other tellers and other tales, less epic but almost as spellbinding, tales like those recreated in the stories of Owen Wynne *Jones (Glasynys) in the nineteenth century and retold in the twentieth in Evan Isaac's *Coelion Cymru* (1938). But *Methodism had arrived with its sobering influence and it was that influence which crushed the Catholic and miraculous elements out of the folk-tale. Anecdotes of the strong and the crafty, practical jokes, blunders and coincidences, storms, ghosts and witty characters—these became the material of oral tales in Welsh-speaking communities until the early years of the twentieth century.

It was to be expected that some of the early short-story writers would adopt some of these oral tales and invent similar ones. Daniel *Owen did so in *Straeon y Pentan* (1895), R. Dewi *Williams in *Clawdd Terfyn* (1912), J. J. *Williams in *Straeon y Gilfach Ddu* (1931) and D. J. *Williams in *Storïau'r Tir Glas* (1936). But when the story 'Clawdd Terfyn' appeared in Y *Beirniad in 1911, it was seen to be more than a raw anecdote. So too were the short stories of Richard Hughes *Williams (Dic Tryfan), which first appeared in O. M. *Edwards's *Cymru, and Kate *Roberts's *O Gors y Bryniau, published in 1925. Here, at last, were short-story writers who had read Continental masters such as Maupassant and Chekhov and studied their craft. They had discovered that the short story could depict an uneventful day in the life of an insignificant individual, the story's sole distinction lying in its structure and in the way it is told. In his introduction to the first selection of short stories published in Welsh, *Ystorïau Heddiw* (1938),

T. H. *Parry-Williams quoted some definitions of the short story which may well have influenced these authors: Princess Bibesco's 'shooting star of literature' (Kate Roberts's favourite definition), 'a day in the pilgrim's progress' and 'a slice of life artistically presented to entertain'.

When it is remembered that the short story in Welsh had not been born in 1910, its development seems astonishingly rapid, particularly during the 1920s and 1930s. Collections of stories by several authors were published between 1921 and 1936, when the first volume of D. J. Williams's stories appeared. Most of these writers found a wealth of material within their own communities: R. Dewi Williams and D. J. Williams in their agricultural neighbourhoods, Richard Hughes Williams and Kate Roberts among the quarrymen of Rhosgadfan and the surrounding district, although the latter also included stories about coalminers and their families, using her experience of living in the industrial valleys of south Wales.

As well as making the greatest individual contribution to the short story in Welsh, publishing ten collections between 1925 and 1981, Kate Roberts was also the greatest influence on the genre in the language. Although it may not be quite accurate to speak of a 'Kate Roberts school' of short-story writers, a number of authors have obviously tried to emulate her in both subject-matter and treatment, some more successfully than others. The characteristic story in this mould is very short, often of no more than two thousand words. A character is selected and observed at a certain point in time; he or she may be at a crossroads, or merely trudging along the same interminable road; there is no preamble. In two or three economical paragraphs the reader is made aware of the character's age, environment, work—or lack of it—and physical condition, likes and dislikes, and that mainly by suggestion or implication rather than by plain statement of fact. He or she may be carrying a weight of worry, hardship or illness, indulging in nostalgia or daydreams, facing a momentary choice or contemplating a possible change. A nice balance is struck in the writing between narrative and dialogue, the one as sparse and telling as the other. There is usually a second character and sometimes a third, or even a fourth. The reader may be viewing a relationship at a crucial point, a love-affair, perhaps, or a marriage. At the end of the story the situation may have changed somewhat, or not at all. But the reader has been made aware of a little world whose two or three characters represent many in the same predicament. Despite the gloom which often overhangs such stories, the principal character usually has a dogged heroism which gives a hint of hope.

The stories of D. J. Williams are quite different—especially his early ones, which are strikingly longer, more loquacious and buoyant—but it was he who coined the expression 'the square mile' for his childhood locality, an expression which fits many of the most important short stories written in Welsh. Like the northern authors, it was in their own warm coalmining communities that J. J. Williams first, and then Islwyn *Williams, found their material. Of the two, it was Islwyn Williams who could manipulate his dialect the better; it was he, too, who trod more securely the tightrope between pathos and sentimentality, and he did so by virtue of humour, his own and that of his people.

Humour is the distinguishing mark of another category of story-tellers who have written richly of their own square mile: the comic writers. At the beginning of the century the stories of Winnie Parry, who was censured by unenlightened critics for writing her narrative as well as her dialogue in dialect, were a *tour-de-force*. The best-known of the comic writers was W. J. *Griffith of Henllys Fawr, who imagined his irrepressible grocer, 'my friend Williams', in a fictional Aberffraw. It was obviously in the same Anglesey village that Tom Parri *Jones's *Teisennau Berffro* (1958) was located. There have been other gifted humorists, among them J. O. *Williams, William *Owen, W. S. *Jones and Gruffudd Parry, and the prolific Harri Parri, who sets his folk in his own square mile of Llŷn. These authors' works are generally in the line of the oral anecdote, their characters often distinguished by their wit or gaucherie. But as their works are skilfully constructed and well told, they must be included in any review of the genre.

Among the literary square miles must be placed the mid-Ceredigion of T. Hughes Jones and the Blaenau Ffestiniog of Eigra Lewis *Roberts, an author in the lineage of Kate Roberts by virtue of her talent as well as the local nature of her material. Marged *Pritchard's square mile is more extended and more difficult to locate. Some story-writers, however, have wandered far beyond the confines of their own localities, and indeed beyond the borders of common experience. R. G. *Berry's characters are mostly eccentrics. E. Tegla *Davies tried to write stories in the manner of Kate Roberts but failed, because the form cramped his rich inventiveness; he turned powerfully to prehistory and myth and religious experiences. Some of Alun T. *Lewis's best works are incident stories rather than character portraits, especially those with a war background. Roger Boore has ventured into the future, Harri Pritchard *Jones, most convincingly, into the complex life of cities and Islwyn Ffowc *Elis into the absurd and the paranormal. The world is the parish of Bobi Jones (R. M. *Jones) in his experimental stories and Pennar *Davies explores ideas and experiences in the realm of learning and culture. But the revolutionary figure of the Welsh-language short story is undoubtedly John Gwilym *Jones. His collection Y *Goeden Eirin (1946) contains only six stories. The stream-of-consciousness narrative has never been used more successfully than in this little volume, nor have the layers of consciousness been more searchingly probed but this pioneer's example has not been followed by any other Welsh writer.

Very many authors in Welsh have portrayed their childhood in autobiographies and volumes of reminiscences. It is therefore surprising to find so few short stories about childhood. Apart from the three memorable collections *Te yn y Grug (1959) by Kate Roberts, Gwared y Gwirion (1966) by R. Gerallt *Jones and Tyfu (1973) by Jane *Edwards there are only a few stories about childhood. Short-story writers in Welsh have preferred to examine the darker world of adults, its poverty and bigotry yesterday, its affluence, alcoholism and broken marriages today. It is likely, the world being as it is, that the paths of tomorrow's writers of fiction in Welsh will lie very much in the same direction.

A selection of Welsh short stories will be found in Ystoriau Heddiw (ed. T. H. Parry-Williams, 1938), Storïau'r Deffro (ed. Islwyn Ffowc Elis, 1959), Storïau'r Dydd (ed. Islwyn Jones and Gwilym Rees Hughes, 1968) and Storïau Awr Hamdden (ed. Urien Wiliam, 5 vols., 1974–79). For critical discussion of the form see Dafydd Jenkins, Y Stori Fer Gymraeg (1966), the essay by Kate Roberts in Ysgrifau Beirniadol IV (ed. J. E. Caerwyn Williams, 1969), the chapter by Derec Llwyd Morgan in Y Traddodiad Rhyddiaith yn yr Ugeinfed Ganrif (ed. Geraint Bowen, 1976), the essay by John Gwilym Jones in Swyddogaeth Beirniadaeth (1977) and John Jenkins (ed.), Y Stori Fer: Seren Wib Llenyddiaeth (1979). Short stories translated from the Welsh can be found in the following anthologies: Welsh Short Stories (1937), Welsh Short Stories (ed. Gwyn Jones, 1940), Welsh Short Stories (ed. Gwyn Jones, 1956), Welsh Short Stories (ed. George Ewart Evans, 1959), Twenty-Five Welsh Short Stories (ed. Gwyn Jones and Islwyn Ffowc Elis, 1971) and The Penguin Book of Welsh Short Stories (ed. Alun Richards, 1976).

Siamas Gwynedd, see CHARLES, EDWARD (1757–1828).

Siân Owen, Ty'n-y-fawnog, see under SALEM.

SICILIAN BRITON, THE (fl. 410), an unnamed young man, British but living in Sicily, who, after the capture of Rome by the Goths in 410, wrote the daring tract known as De Divitiis. This work postulates, on behalf of a radical group among the adherents of *Pelagius (Morgan), a levelling doctrine of 'socialistic' implications, with the slogan 'Tolle divitem' ('Down with the rich man').

Siddons, Sarah (1755–1831), actress. Born at The Shoulder of Mutton Inn in Brecon, she was the daughter of Roger Kemble and Sarah Ward, players in the travelling company of her grandfather John Ward, and sister of the poet Julia Ann *Hatton. Both her first stage appearance and the crisis caused by her love for her fellow-player, William Siddons, took place in Brecon. During a highly successful career on the English stage, she maintained her contacts with Wales by occasional visits to Brynbella, the home of her friend, Hester Lynch *Piozzi (Mrs Thrale).

The first biography of Sarah Siddons was written by Thomas Campbell (1839); see also Yvonne Ffrench, Mrs Siddons: Tragic Actress (1936) and Cecil Price, The English Theatre in Wales (1948).

Silex Scintillans (lit. 'Sparkling rock'; 1650), sub-titled 'Sacred Poems and Private Eiaculations', is the work on which the fame of Henry *Vaughan chiefly rests. It was the product of the poet's 'conversion', the causes of which have been conjectured variously as the death of his brother William in 1648, his reading of George *Herbert's The Temple (by which his writing was undoubtedly influenced), and a new and serious study of the Bible. In his 'Dedication', a poem three times as long in the second edition (1655), he writes, 'Some drops of thy all-quickning bloud/Fell on my heart' and 'ground' that was 'curs'd and void of store' began to nourish life. The lengthy preface to the second edition decries the 'Wits' who write 'wilfully-published vanities' (of whom he acknowledges he has in the past been one) and argues that 'the more acute the Author, there is so much the more danger and death in the work'. His previous follies, he hopes, will not be read. George Herbert, he asserts, was the first to seek to divert 'this foul and overflowing stream' and he, in his turn, will devote his 'poor Talent to the Church'. Most of Vaughan's best-known poems appear in the first edition but those entitled 'Ascension-day', 'They are all gone into the world of light!', 'Cock-Crowing', 'Childe-hood' and 'The Night' were added in 1655. The poet apologizes for the near-death tone of some of the late poems: 'I was nigh unto death', he writes, 'and am still at too great distance from it'. The appellation 'Silurist', first made public on the title-page of Silex Scintillans, Vaughan had in fact already used on that of the long-delayed *Olor Iscanus (1651).

Silures, The, a Celtic tribe whose 'swarthy faces' and 'the tendency of their hair to curl' was noted by Tacitus, although his suggestion that their origin was in Spain was supported with faulty geography. These references were used during the nineteenth century to bear out the argument, now rejected, that the Silures were Iberians, the pre-Celtic inhabitants of south-east Wales, and that, despite military subjugation, they had afterwards remained dominant in blood and physique.

The Silures are now believed to have been Iron Age 'provincials' (that is, they practised an undeveloped Hallstatt Culture) who entered Wales by way of Cornwall from Armorica or western Gaul early in the second century before Christ. Their first landings were on the shore of the river Severn, at Sudbrook and Caldicot and, possibly, further west at Coygen, in Carmarthenshire. Their main camp, nearly two hundred years later, was at Llanmelin Wood, the residual artefacts of which do not differ significantly from those of the Dobunni on the other side of the Severn. The military temper of the two tribes was, however, very different and it must have been the reputation of the Silures as fighters which in AD 43 attracted to them the defeated *Caratacus who became their leader in a series of lightning raids across the lightly-defended Fosse Way into Roman-occupied territory.

After the defeat of Caratacus, in mid-Wales, the Silures continued their struggle against the Romans, reputedly defeating the Second Legion in a pitched battle in AD 52 or 53. The only Celtic tribe continuing to resist Roman arms, they were ultimately defeated at some time after AD 58 and settled in Venta Silurum (Caerwent), the only town in Wales to be recognized as *civitas*. Disarmed, they flourished: their tribal area expanded to Pencraig in the east and to Moccas in the north, reaching within four miles of Hereford. Thus, in struggles against the Mercians and Saxons, was created the kingdom of *Erging, with its own version of the Welsh language and its elaborately named hamlets such as Llanfihangel vibon Awel, Llanvihangel ystern Llewern and the like. The westerly boundaries of the Silures are much less certain, as is the claim that as early as AD 156 Lucius, the King of the Silures, sent to Rome asking for Christian baptism.

The military prowess of the tribe persisted. The number of castles on the rivers Usk, Monnow and Wye indicates the difficulty which the Normans encountered in subjugating them. *Gerald de Barri (Giraldus Cambrensis) recounts Norman stories of their devastating use of the longbow and, at the battles of *Crécy (1346) and Poitiers (1356), Silurian bowmen, especially those from Archenfield and Crickhowell, brought victory for the King of England. In the greater prosperity of Elizabethan times the military tradition became more gentlemanly: a succession of royal commanders on the Continent, from Sir Roger *Williams to Sir Thomas *Morgan (The Dwarf), epitomized the particular flair and bravery inherited from their Silurian forefathers.

Silurist, The, see VAUGHAN, HENRY (1621–95).

Silver John, see LLOYD, JOHN (*c.*1740–1814?).

Silyn, see ROBERTS, ROBERT (1871–1930).

SIMON, BEN (*c.*1703–93), poet and antiquary, was a native of Abergwili, Carms. A diligent copyist, he wrote his most important manuscript, *Tlysau'r Beirdd*, between 1747 and 1751 and made his collection of the work of *Dafydd ap Gwilym in 1754. His poetry was influenced by Griffith *Jones of Llanddowror, whose elegy he composed, and his most famous ballad is that on the death of seventeen colliers at Wern Fraith, near Neath, Glam., in 1758.

SIMON OF CARMARTHEN (*fl.* 1250), poet, the author of religious poems in Norman French, was a member of the order of *Augustinian Canons in the priory of *Carmarthen. Two poems of his are extant, one on the way of penitence, '*De un chemin plus large asset*', and the other on deliverance from sin, '*Par la prïere du vn men compaignon*'.

SIMWNT FYCHAN (*c.*1530–1606), poet and genealogist. His home was in the parish of Llanfair Dyffryn Clwyd, Denbs. A pupil of *Gruffudd Hiraethog, he graduated as *pencerdd* in the second *Caerwys Eisteddfod (1567). He wrote many eulogies and elegies in the traditional manner and some love-poems, but they have not been edited. He is remembered for his *Pum Llyfr Cerddwriaeth* (*c.*1570), in which he brought together and classified the instructions given by the master poets to their pupils in the bardic schools. The contents are as follows: letters and syllables; the parts of speech and syntax; the metres; the *cynganeddion*; the forbidden errors, and instructions in the principles of eulogy. Little, if any, of this material can be regarded as being Simwnt's original work and Gruffudd Hiraethog may well have been the author of parts of it. Nevertheless, the discussion is more detailed than anything found in the books of other bardic teachers of the fifteenth century. There still exist several manuscripts containing pedigrees in Simwnt's hand, *genealogy being one of the chief interests of the *pencerddiaid* of the age.

Further details will be found in G. J. Williams and E. J. Jones, *Gramadegau'r Penceirddiaid* (1934); see also the articles by E. D. Jones in the *Bulletin* of the Board of Celtic Studies (1926–27, 1933–35).

Singing to Oxen, a folk-custom which survived in Wales until the second half of the nineteenth century. The ploughman would sing to the oxen as he walked in front of the team in the traditional manner. It was said that the beasts would not work unless they were thus encouraged and named in the songs. The tradition was particularly strong in Glamorgan where many *tribannau* referring to the custom have been collected. The most famous song associated with the ploughing is the one beginning, 'O Mari, Mari, cwyn'.

For further details see Ffransis G. Payne, *Yr Aradr Gymreig* (1975) and Tegwyn Jones, *Tribannau Morgannwg* (1976).

SIÔN AP HYWEL AP LLYWELYN FYCHAN (*fl.* 1530), poet, of Holywell, Flints., was a pupil of *Tudur Aled, for whom he composed an elegy. He wrote on a variety of subjects, addressing poems to patrons such as the abbot of Glyn Conwy and Sir Hywel of Whitford, and some to St. Catherine and *Gwenffrewi; he wrote others about the games of dice and cards. It is believed that he was the author of the cywydd to the mist which is no longer accepted as belonging to the canon of *Dafydd ap Gwilym's work.

SIÔN BRWYNOG (d. 1567?), poet, a native of Llanfflewyn, Ang., addressed poems in the traditional metres to gentry families of north Wales. A fervent Roman Catholic, he hated the new *Protestantism and composed a well-known cywydd to the two faiths, pointing the contrast in favour of his own.

For further details see the article by R. M. Kerr in Ysgrifau Catholig (vol. II, 1963).

SIÔN CAIN (c. 1575–c. 1650), herald poet, the son of *Rhys Cain who probably taught him the poetic craft, was born at Mechain Iscoed shortly before his father settled in Oswestry. The last herald poet to travel through north Wales, he composed many genealogical poems, mainly in the period from 1607 to 1648, for the gentry who were his patrons. All his manuscripts were preserved by Robert *Vaughan of Hengwrt, who had corresponded with him. In a famous letter written to Wiliam Bodwrda in 1647, Siôn complained that the practice of the poetic craft had declined, a view borne out by a comparison of his work with that of his father.

SIÔN CENT (c. 1400–30/45), poet. Despite the uncertainty about the dates of his birth and death and confusion regarding the canon of his work, he is one of the few important cywyddwyr of his period whose work has survived. He may have been a native of Breconshire or perhaps was domiciled there, for he wrote several cywyddau in praise of that county. The painting which is kept in the mansion of Llangain, Herefs., is thought to be a portrait of him. On the evidence of his verse, it seems that he had lived a sinful life before experiencing a religious conversion.

Although some scholars contest it, the view of Saunders *Lewis was that Siôn had studied at Oxford, where his ideas had been transformed by Roger Bacon's new scientific philosophy, Scientia Experimentalis. It is this, Lewis argued, that caused him, when contending with *Rhys Goch Eryri, to denounce the Welsh bardic tradition in his 'Cywydd Dychan i'r Awen Gelwyddog', condemning the Platonic foundation of praise and its extremes of falsehood as derived not from Christ but 'o ffwrn natur uffernawl' ('from the oven of hellish nature'). According to Siôn Cent, the purpose of poetry was to depict Man in his true or eternal nature and the form he chose was satire. His most famous cywydd of this type is 'I

Wagedd ac Oferedd y Byd', in which he turns from the world of fact and matter to embrace Christianity and its vision of Heaven. Other critics have maintained that Siôn Cent, as regards the substance of his poems and certain prosodical features too, was merely following a fashion which was popular in the England of his day. This argument is strengthened by the fact that he is always associated with the Marches.

The essence of much of Siôn Cent's work is the belief that worldly reality is transient and, illustrating the terrors of the grave and of the soul in Hell or Purgatory, he stresses the need for men to repent before the Day of Judgement. In this he reflects the religious climate of his age: the poet becomes a preacher. Foreign and native elements are blended in his work, including an erotic sensibility, the whole expressed in a simple style of great power. He was especially fond of word-play, antithesis and the coining of *proverbs. One of his most famous lines is 'Gobeithiaw a ddaw ydd wyf' ('My hope lies in what is to come'). The first poet to divide the cywydd into sections, each with a refrain, he composed at least four poems of this kind. Siôn Cent's influence on his contemporaries and on later poets, especially his preaching style, was to be profound and longlasting.

A selection of Siôn Cent's poems is to be found in Cywyddau Iolo Goch ac eraill (ed. Henry Lewis, Thomas Roberts, Ifor Williams, 1925). There are critical discussions of his poetry by Gilbert Ruddock in A Guide to Welsh Literature (ed. A. O. H. Jarman and Gwilym Rees Hughes, 1979) and by Saunders Lewis in Meistri a'u Crefft (ed. Gwynn ap Gwilym, 1981); see also the article by Dafydd Densil Morgan in Y Traethodydd (Jan., 1983).

Siôn Ceryn Bach, see JONES, JOHN PRITCHARD (d. 1927).

Siôn Cwilt (fl. 18th cent.), a smuggler, so called on account of the colourful patches on his coat. He lived in a tŷ unnos (a house built in one night) on the high moorland between Post Bach and Cross Hands, Cards., a district known to this day as Banc Siôn Cwilt. It is said that he stored his contraband in sea-caves and sold them to the local gentry at exorbitant prices.

Siôn Dafi (fl. 1441–68), gentleman, of Cemais in Cyfeiliog, Mont. Like so many Welshmen of the period, he fought in France and later served in the army of Richard, Duke of York, at the battle of *Mortimer's Cross (1461); he was a favourite of Edward, Earl of March, the duke's son, who became king, as Edward IV, soon after that battle. In 1462 Siôn's hand was cut off for striking a man in the presence of the judges in Westminster Hall and he received a silver hand in its place, an incident recorded in a cywydd by *Guto'r Glyn.

For further details see Gwaith Guto'r Glyn (ed. J. Ll. Williams and Ifor Williams, 1939, 1961).

Siôn Dafydd or **Siôn Dafydd Las**, see DAVIES, JOHN (d. 1694).

Siôn Eos (*fl.* second half of the 15th cent.), harpist. Having killed a man in a brawl, he was found guilty by a Chirkland jury and was hanged in accordance with English law. In an elegy for him, *Dafydd ab Edmwnd maintained that the killing had been accidental and that Siôn's execution compounded the moral evil. The poem expresses anger that the jurors had employed 'the law of London' rather than 'the law of Hywel' with its more humane punishment, the payment of compensation by the offender and his kin. In Marcher lordships such as *Chirk judgement according to the *Laws of Hywel Dda was not uncommon but the jurymen had rejected this option, despite the fact that compensation money was already promised. The poet goes on to lament the loss caused to the musical art by the death of Siôn Eos, warns the jurymen that they will have to appear before God the Judge, and forecasts eternal life for the harpist. Dafydd's *cywydd*, at once passionate, reflective and artistically brilliant, with its poignant indictment of 'judicial murder', is one of the great poems of its period.

SIÔN MAWDDWY (*c.*1575–1613), poet, a native of Mawddwy, Mer., addressed poems in the traditional metres to gentry throughout Wales, making frequent use of the *llatai (love-messenger) in his eulogies. Some of his poems reflect anxiety about the lack of patronage and he requested of George *Owen of Henllys that an eisteddfod be held for the professional poets. He took part in a *bardic contention with Meurig *Dafydd about the privileges of Gwent poets and complained, in a letter which is an important source for a study of the decline of the *Bardic Order in their day, that Meurig—despite the loan of a bardic grammar—had not mastered the poetic craft.

Siôn Robert Lewis, see ROBERTS, JOHN (1731–1806).

SIÔN TUDUR (*c.*1522–1602), one of the last of the *Poets of the Gentry, was related to several of the most eminent families of north Wales, including the *Mostyns and the Trefors. A landed gentleman, he kept a house at Wicwair, St. Asaph, Flints., although much of his early life was spent in London as one of the Yeomen of the Guard and of the even more select Yeomen of the Crown. The duty of these bodies was to wait on members of the royal family and Siôn Tudur served Prince Edward in this capacity before and after that monarch's accession to the throne in 1547. He also served Elizabeth during the early years of her reign.

On his return to Wales, after a dispute the nature of which is no longer known, Siôn Tudur was both poet and patron, enjoying the hospitality of his fellow-gentry and welcoming other poets to Wicwair. A bardic disciple of *Gruffudd Hiraethog, he graduated at the second *Caerwys Eisteddfod in 1567. The comparatively large number of his extant poems, mostly composed after 1566, includes more than a hundred eulogies and elegies addressed to some sixty families in north Wales, but satire is the most distinctive element in his work. Disillusioned with life at court in London, he found much (despite its delights) to criticize and mock at in the fashionable life of his day, while his scathing comments on Welsh poets reveal his realization of the deterioration which the *Bardic Order was suffering in its last phases. Nevertheless, Siôn Tudur was admired for his mastery of the craft and eight poets composed elegies for him.

The standard edition of Siôn Tudur's work is that edited by Enid Pierce Roberts (1978).

Siôn Wyn o Eifion, see THOMAS, JOHN (1786–1859).

Siôn y Gof (d. 1719), blacksmith and murderer, was believed to have been a Cardiganshire man who had found work in the lead-mines at Dylife, Mont. He killed his wife and two children by throwing them down a mineshaft, in the belief that the end of the world was imminent, and was hanged for the crime. His body was gibbeted and his skull, which was discovered in 1938 still encased in an iron frame, is now preserved at the *Welsh Folk Museum. The murder became the subject of several ballads, fragments of which are still sung.

Sioronwy (**Evan George Jones**; 1892–1953), see under CILIE FAMILY.

Siot, a traditional dish popular in the rural districts of north Wales, consisted of crushed oatbread and buttermilk; served as a light snack with afternoon tea, it was also known as *picws mali*. See also BRWES and LLYMRU.

Siwan or **Joan** (1195–1237), the natural daughter of King John and the wife of *Llywelyn ap Iorwerth (Llywelyn Fawr). The agreement of 1204, whereby Llywelyn acknowledged John as overlord and the English King recognized Llywelyn's territorial conquests, included a settlement of marriage between Llywelyn and Siwan, which took place in 1205. She proved an able counsellor to Llywelyn, interceding with John on his behalf in 1211 and negotiating with her half-brother, Henry III, in 1225 and again in 1228 and 1232. Her brief affair with the young Marcher lord, William de Braose, perhaps as an act of revolt against a marriage of convenience, led to his death by hanging in 1230 and to her temporary imprisonment. By the time of her death, however, Llywelyn was wholly reconciled to her and established at Llanfaes, Ang., where she was buried, a house of Franciscan friars to pray for her soul; her tomb and effigy are still to be seen there.

The episode of Siwan's adultery with William de Braose (Gwilym Brewys) inspired a verse-play by Saunders *Lewis entitled *Siwan* (1955). The play follows the historical facts closely but develops the characters of Siwan and Llywelyn in psychological terms. The mood changes quickly from the magical evocation of sexual attraction, tinged with foreboding, in the first act, through the excruciating tension of the second (in which the execution of Gwilym Brewys is described to Siwan, manacled to a wall, by her maid from a vantage-point by the window), to the profound serenity of the third act in which the value of human relationships, especially marriage, is asserted in spite of their imperfections and transience. In the final act, with *Gwynedd in peril as a result of the ex-ecution, Llywelyn and Siwan are partially reconciled and she discovers that her husband has always loved her deeply, although he had been too inhibited to say so: the hanging had been a perverse expression of that love. Siwan will return to Llywelyn's bed but, in death, will lie alone in Llanfaes Priory. The verse in this play is written with complete mastery and some critics have considered it Saunders Lewis's finest work.

For a critical discussion of the play see the essays by Alun Llywelyn-Williams in *Y Traethodydd* (1956), Geraint Wyn Jones in *Taliesin* (1963), R. Gerallt Jones in *Ansawdd y Seiliau* (1972) and by John Rowlands in *Ysgrifau Beirniadol VIII* (ed. J. E. Caerwyn Williams, 1974). A translation of the play by Emyr Humphreys will be found in *Presenting Saunders Lewis* (ed. Alun R. Jones and Gwyn Thomas, 1973) and another, by Joseph Clancy, under the title *The King of England's Daughter* (1985).

SKENE, WILLIAM FORBES (1809–92), see under FOUR ANCIENT BOOKS OF WALES (1868).

Sleeping Lord, The (1974), David *Jones's third major poetic work, consists of nine 'fragments' which are, in fact, carefully wrought, formally various and innovatory poems with an overall thematic unity. Their main concern is the ten-sion between the forces of uniformity, on the one hand, and cultural diversity on the other, represented by the Roman Empire in relation to Palestine at the time of Christ, and Arthurian Wales. The title poem and 'The Tutelar of the Place', which are commemorative and cel-ebratory poems with the latter setting, sustain some of the author's most rhythmically exciting and sensuous writing, while 'The Tribune's Visitation' depicts the imperial idea with an equally effective linguistic austerity. Outstand-ing dramatic and visionary qualities characterize the whole collection.

SMART, CHRISTOPHER (1722–71), English poet, was the son of Peter Smart of the County Palatine of Durham and Winifred Grif-fiths, a Radnorshire woman. Born prematurely at Shipbourne, Kent, where his father was steward to Viscount Vane, the boy was of a delicate constitution and precocious mind. By the age of thirteen he was already turning out verse, some of it amatory, and at a still tender age was said to have attempted a runaway match with the even younger Anne Vane. Some years later her aunt, the Duchess of Cleveland, made him an allowance of forty pounds a year, which allowed him to enter Pembroke Hall, Cam-bridge, in 1739, and there he remained for ten years as sizar, scholar, and (after 1745) as Fellow. His classical studies prospered, he wrote skilful minor verse in various modes, translated and 'imitated', and began that course of debt, drunkenness and folly which he pursued after his departure for London in 1749.

In London he set up as a man of letters, with the encouragement of John Newbery, book-seller and purveyor of patent medicines, did a good deal of hack-work and fell into several degrading literary quarrels. He published his *Poems on Several Occasions* (1752) as though to demonstrate his versatility, his metrical skill, his determination to be fashionable and his lack of any worthwhile literary purpose. Married to Newbery's stepdaughter, Anna Maria Carnan, in 1753, he forfeited his stipend and soon after-wards his mind began to give way. The bent of his mania was religious, its most impressive manifestation being that of vociferous and often public prayer. He entered St. Luke's Hospital in 1757, was restored to his family in the following year, was committed again in 1759, presumably the year in which he began to write his *Jubilate Agno* or *Rejoice in the Lamb* (c.1760), and was taken to Bethlehem Hospital (Bedlam) on a date unknown. Released yet again, probably in 1763, he went to live with a family near St. James's Park, neither much mad nor wholly sane, his own family being domiciled elsewhere. 'Shivers of genius' continued to shake him. For a while his friends and well-wishers saved him from indigence and he worked hard and to noble purpose: he finished *A Song to David* and *Jubilate Agno* and published the *Psalms* and the *Hymns for the Festivals of the Church of England* in 1765; the little-known but delightful *Hymns for the Amuse-ment of Children* was announced in 1770, although no copy of the first two editions seems to have survived. But there were more quarrels and further debts and the poet was confined within the rules of the King's Bench Prison for the last two years of his life.

Smart's connections with Wales were well known to his contemporaries. It is possible that he spoke Welsh, for in *The Old Woman's Dunciad* (1751) his Grub Street enemy William Kenrick refers to *Cambria*, a eulogium on the Welsh language, in which Mrs Midnight, alias Kit Smart, proposes to improve the English language by selecting 'several thousands of the most curious and copious in the Gomerian or *Welsh* Tongue, which will far exceed any Embellishment whatsoever drawn from the *Greek* and *Latin*'. In 1753, 'an Address to his Royal Highness The Prince of Wales, to be presented to him by the Lord Bishop of Peterborough (his Highness's Preceptor) in the Name of the Society of *Ancient Britons, on St. David's Day next' was drawn up in English and sent to Goronwy *Owen for translation into Welsh, and to Smart (referred to by Goronwy in his letter to William *Morris as 'some young Cymro in Cambridge') for translation into Latin. The synthesis of sycophancy and patriotism in Smart's poem is not a little absurd. However, both Owen's Welsh and Smart's Latin were included in *Diddanwch Teuluaidd* under the auspices of the Honourable Society of *Cymmrodorion in 1763. Smart occasionally satirized certain aspects of the Welsh character: the obsession with genealogy in his 'Epilogue' to *The Conscious Lovers*, the irritability in 'To the Rev. Mr P(owel)l on the non-performance of a promise he made the author of a hare', the garrulity in an advertisement for the pseudonymous *History of Jack the Giant Killer* and the love of patriotic revelry in *Mother Midnight's Comical Pocket-Book*. But that he was proud of his Welshness is shown in the poem he wrote while confined for madness and in *Jubilate Agno* he wrote, 'For I am the seed of the Welch Woman and speak the truth from my heart'. For long a poet neglected by readers and critics alike, Christopher Smart is only now receiving the attention he deserves.

A good modern edition of Smart's work is that by N. Callan (2 vols., 1949), although *Jubilate Agno* is best read in the edition by W. H. Bond (1954). Detailed accounts are to be found in E. G. Ainsworth and C. E. Noyes, *Christopher Smart, a Biographical and Critical Study* (1943), Arthur Sherbo, *Christopher Smart, Scholar of the University* (1967), and Moira Dearnley, *The Poetry of Christopher Smart* (1969); see also Marcus Walsh and Karina Williamson, *The Poetical Works of Christopher Smart* (vol. II, 1984).

SMITH, DAVID (1945–), historian and critic, was born at Tonypandy in the Rhondda Valley and educated at Balliol College, Oxford, Columbia University, New York, and University College, Swansea. Formerly a Lecturer in History at the University of Lancaster and at University College, Swansea, he is now Senior Lecturer in the History of Wales at University College, Cardiff. He is the co-author (with Hywel Francis) of *The Fed: A History of the South Wales Miners in the Twentieth Century* (1980) and (with Gareth Williams) of *Fields of Praise: The*

Official History of the Welsh Rugby Union 1881–1981 (1980); he has also contributed a monograph on Lewis *Jones (1897–1939) to the *Writers of Wales* series (1982). The joint editor of *Llafur*, the journal of the Society for the Study of Welsh Labour History, from 1975 to 1981, he edited *A People and a Proletariat: Essays in the History of Wales 1780–1980* (1980). His book *Wales! Wales?* (1984) is an extended treatment of the issues explored in a series of television programmes which he made for the BBC.

SMYTH, ROGER (1541–1625), Catholic priest and translator, was a native of St. Asaph, Flints. Having fled to the English College at Douai about 1573, he joined the Jesuit College in Rome before 1579 but was dismissed after a dispute between the Welsh and English students there and because he had refused to take holy orders and conduct his missionary activities in England. Three books of his were published in Paris, namely *Crynnodeb o addysc Cristnogawl* (1609), a translation of parts of St. Petrus Canisius's catechism, *Summa Doctrinae Christianae* (1611), a full translation of that catechism, and *Theater dv Mond sef ivv. Gorsedd y Byd* (1615; ed. Thomas Parry, 1930), a translation of Pierre Boaistuau's work on the misery and redemption of Man. Although Smyth's literary works were inferior to those of other Welsh translators of his period, they are important for the author's views concerning liberty of conscience.

For further details see the introduction to Thomas Parry's edition of *Gorsedd y Byd* (1930); see also W. Llewelyn Williams, 'Welsh Catholics on the Continent' in the *Transactions* of the Honourable Society of Cymmrodorion (1901–02).

Snowdon (Yr Wyddfa), see under ERYRI and RHITA GAWR.

Socialism, a political philosophy opposed to the exploitation and inequality which are inherent in the economic system based on Capitalism. As an alternative to Capitalism, Socialists wish to establish a classless society in which there is common ownership of the means of production and planning of the economy for the benefit of all. Historically, the Socialist movement has been divided between revolutionary Socialists, who have advocated insurrection, and democratic Socialists who have sought to bring about gradual change by popular consent. In Wales, as in England, the Communist Party (see under MARXISM) has been the principal advocate of the revolutionary road to Socialism, while the tradition of democratic Socialism and gradual reform has been upheld by the Labour Party.

During the nineteenth century, Socialist ideas had only a limited influence upon Welsh workers and it was not until the early years of the twentieth century that Socialism began to win mass support. Until 1914 the foremost Socialist group presenting a challenge to the Liberal-Labour consensus of Edwardian Wales was the Independent Labour Party. Imbued with a strong ethical commitment to democratic Socialism and linked closely with the Trade Union movement under the umbrella of the Labour Party, the Independent Labour Party campaigned for greater industrial militancy and working-class representation at all levels of government. Within the newly-formed *South Wales Miners' Federation, members of the Independent Labour Party were persistent critics of 'Lib-Lab' leaders such as William *Abraham (Mabon) until they themselves assumed positions of responsibility.

To achieve significant independent working-class representation in local and, especially, central government, proved to be difficult, but after a decade or so of sporadic electoral gains, Labour as a separate party came into its own in south Wales. The first Socialist elected to represent a Welsh constituency at Westminster was Keir *Hardie, who was returned in 1900. In the wake of the First World War, increasing numbers of working people were elected to local authorities and the Labour Party won control of dozens of councils across the coalfield. During the 1920s the party also made spectacular advances in parliamentary elections and by 1930 twenty-five of the thirty-six Members of Parliament representing constituencies in Wales were Labour. Most were trades unionists, often with experience of local government, and many, including Aneurin *Bevan, had received their education through the institutions of the Labour movement. After the Second World War, the Labour Party maintained its hegemony in industrial Wales and extended its influence to rural areas. At the General Election of 1966 it won thirty-two of the thirty-six seats. Since then, the fortunes of the party have declined, mainly under challenge from *Plaid Cymru and the Conservative Party, but even after the General Election of 1983, when it held nineteen of the thirty-eight seats, the Labour Party could still claim to be the dominant force in the political life of Wales. See also REPUBLICANISM.

For further details of Socialism in Wales see James Griffiths, *Pages from Memory* (1969), Michael Foot, *Aneurin Bevan* (2 vols., 1962 and 1973), the article by Peter Stead, 'Working-class Leadership in South Wales 1900–1920' in *The Welsh History Review* (vol. 6, no. 3, June, 1973), Kenneth O. Morgan, *Rebirth of a Nation: Wales 1800–1980* (1981) and Robert Griffiths, *S. O. Davies: a Socialist Faith* (1983); see also John Osmond (ed.), *The National Question Again* (1985).

Society for Promoting Christian Knowledge, The, founded in London in 1699 with the twofold intention of spreading the Gospel in foreign lands and establishing charity schools in England and Wales, was the result of an initiative by a group of philanthropists among whom the most prominent was Thomas Bray (1656–1730). Associated with him in the Society's early years were Sir Humphrey *Mackworth of Neath and

Sir John Philipps of Picton Castle, Pembs. (see under PHILIPPS FAMILY of Picton). From the outset the S.P.C.K., as it was known, had close connections with Wales and these men were very aware of the fact that they were continuing the work of Thomas Gouge and the *Welsh Trust. Nevertheless, unlike that body, the Society confined its membership to the Established Church.

Most active during the early years of the eighteenth century, the Society distributed, either free or cheaply, thousands of devotional books and pamphlets in Welsh and English, and sponsored two editions of the Welsh Bible. Of greater importance was the foundation, before 1739, of ninety-five Charity Schools, in addition to twenty-nine others which were privately endowed. Apart from Sir John Philipps, the best-known patrons of the Society in Wales were Dr John Jones, the Dean of Bangor, and Edmund Meyricke, the treasurer of *St. David's. With their financial support, the Society paid the salaries of its teachers, bought books and even food and clothing for the more needy children. The main aim of the schools, which were usually held in churches, was to teach boys to read and write and the girls to knit and sew. The children also learned the catechism and the formularies of the Established Church for at least two days a week. The schoolmasters, as a rule, were curates, of whom Griffith *Jones of Llanddowror later became the best-known. After the death of Queen Anne, in 1714, the number of schools declined and there is no record of a school being opened after 1727. The Society's flagging efforts were absorbed into the work of the Circulating Schools of Griffith Jones, whose diplomacy with the S.P.C.K. in London ensured that the progress of education in Wales was not barred by ill-will.

For a full account see R. T. Jenkins, *Hanes Cymru yn y Ddeunawfed Ganrif* (1928), M. G. Jones, *The Charity School Movement* (1938), David Williams, *Modern Wales* (1950), Mary Clement, *The S.P.C.K. and Wales* (1954), Idris Jones, *Modern Welsh History* (1960) and Jac L. Williams and Gwilym Rees Hughes (ed.), *The History of Education in Wales* (1978).

Society for the Utilization of the Welsh Language, The, see CYMDEITHAS YR IAITH GYMRAEG (1885).

Society of Friends, The, see under QUAKERISM.

Society of Jesus, The, founded in Paris in 1534 by Ignatius Loyola and approved by Pope Paul III in 1540, took as its mission the defence of the *Roman Catholic faith against the claims of the Protestant Reformation. That defence included attack. It involved the Society in attempts to overthrow Protestant monarchs and necessitated the placing of the claims of Catholicism above those of nationality. Quarrels in the

English College at Rome during the rule of Morys *Clynnog there caused such hatred of the Society in the hearts of almost all Welshmen training to be priests that, with the exception of Robert *Jones, no Welshman of any great ability became a Jesuit during the period from about 1579 to 1610. Many, like David *Baker, avoided the controversy by entering the Benedictine Order, but secular priests in general remained hostile to the Society and instilled into many faithful Catholics in Wales their deep distrust of measures which involved disloyalty to the Crown and the State. This situation did not alter until the drive of the *Counter-Reformation had spent itself: by the twenties of the seventeenth century it was plain that Wales would not emerge as another Ireland. Apolitical works by Jesuits, such as Robert Parsons's *A Book of Christian Exercise, appertaining to Resolusion,* nevertheless had their influence in Wales; the translation of it by John *Davies of Mallwyd was entitled *Llyfr y Resolution* (1632). Richard Vaughan of Bodeiliog translated Robert Bellarmino's *Dichiarazione piu copiosa della dottrina Cristiana* (1598) in his *Eglurhad helaethlawn o'r Athrawaeth Gristnogawl* (1618).

It was Salusbury who established headquarters for the Jesuits at Cwm in the parish of Llanrothal (Llanrhyddol) on the Monmouthshire border, where a Jesuit College, St. Xavier's, was founded. Among the College's Welsh-speaking members was John Hughes (1615–1686), the son of Hugh *Owen, who printed his father's translation into Welsh of the *Imitatio* of Thomas à Kempis and who was himself the author of *Allwydd neu Agoriad Paradwys i'r Cymry* (1670). In 1678 Bishop Croft of Hereford, whose intention it was to purge his diocese, found a large number of books by learned Jesuits at Cwm and, in the following year, two Welsh Jesuits, Philip *Evans and David *Lewis, were martyred on account of their faith.

For further details about the Jesuits in Wales see the article by Geraint Bowen in *Y Faner* (29 Aug., 1951) and the book by Emyr Gwynne Jones, *Cymru a'r Hen Ffydd* (1957); for a discussion of the alienation of Welsh Catholics from the Jesuits see Roland Mathias, *Whitsun Riot* (1963).

Society of Sea Serjeants, The, see under JACOBITISM.

Soldier of Calais, The, see GRUFFYDD, ELIS (c. 1490–c. 1552).

Some Trust in Chariots (1948), a novel by Jack *Jones, deals with three generations of the Tewdwr family and with the history of their town, 'Pontyglo' (Pontypridd), between 1882 and 1945. As the coalmining industry of the area is developed, so the haulage business of the numerous Tewdwrs prospers. Another of Jack Jones's matriarchs appears here in the person of Elizabeth Tewdwr. Her son, Rhys, and his nephew, Harry, are prominent among the novel's many colourful characters. The author intended this novel to be an epic about south Wales and it succeeds in presenting, in his inimitable way, much of the social and political upheaval of the period. The title is taken from the Bible (Ps. 20:7): 'Some trust in chariots, and some in horses: but we will remember the name of the Lord our God'.

'Sosban Fach' (lit. 'Little saucepan'), a rugbysong usually associated with the town of Llanelli, Carms., of which the utensil has become the civic emblem. The first verse was written by Richard *Davies (Mynyddog) as part of his poem, 'Rheolau yr Aelwyd' (1873). It was Talog Williams, an accountant from Dowlais, Glam., who altered it and added four verses and the chorus, all of which may have been intended as a parody of a nursery-rhyme or, more probably, as a nonsense song. It is, to say the least, unclear what the relationship may be between the characters mentioned in the song—Meri Ann, Dafydd the servant, Joni Bach and Dai Bach the soldier—and the significance of the boiling saucepan and the crying baby remains a mystery, despite some ingenious attempts to explain it. The tune, of uncertain origin, is reminiscent of a Welsh hymn (even in its 'Russian' version) and it is perhaps the most popular of all those sung at international rugby-matches.

South Wales Miners' Federation, The, was founded in 1898, largely as a consequence of a stoppage in the coalfield in that year and in an attempt, after decades of discontent, to forge a new unity among workers in the industry. By the end of 1899, when it was admitted to the Miners' Federation of Great Britain, its membership stood at more than a hundred thousand, but it subsequently had difficulty in organizing its adherents. Its first President was William *Abraham (Mabon), with William Brace as Vice-President and Tom Richards as General Secretary (1898–1931). By 1914 the 'Lib-Lab' policies of both Abraham and Brace were out of favour with the younger, militant men, some of whom supported the Independent Labour Party and others of whom, the Syndicalist element, were calling for the centralization of the South Wales Miners' Federation as a means to more decision-making by its rank-and-file members. The pre-war debate about democracy within the 'Fed', as it was commonly known in south Wales, continued through the industrial strife of the 1920s. Re-organization, however, came only in 1934, in the wake of the defeat suffered in the *General Strike of 1926 and the subsequent reduction of membership to less than half those in employment. Under the youthful presidency of James *Griffiths and then of Arthur L. *Horner (1936–47), the 'Fed' won back its membership by 1939 and became the catalyst for political and social initiative in Wales down to the end of the Second World War. In 1944 it became the South Wales Area of the newly-formed National Union of Mineworkers, but retained its autonomy and its progressive stance into the 1970s.

The history of the organization has been written by David Smith and Hywel Francis, *The Fed* (1980).

South Wales Voice, see under LLAIS LLAFUR.

SOUTHALL, JOHN EDWARD (1855–1928), printer and author. Born at Leominster, Herefs., he settled as a printer in Newport, Mon., in 1879 and continued in business there until his retirement in 1924. Having learned Welsh as a young man, he made a special study of the problems of teaching the language and several of the books he wrote were on this subject. They include *Wales and her language considered from a historical, educational, and social standpoint* (1892), *The Welsh Language Census of 1891* (1895), *Preserving and Teaching the Welsh Language in English speaking Districts* (1899) and *The Welsh Language Census of 1901* (1904). The first of these books affords valuable information about the locational strength or weakness of the Welsh language at points in the southern March, together with the state of opinion about it. Southall also wrote a number of bilingual text-books for use in the schools of Wales.

Sowans or **Sucan**, see LLYMRU.

Spade money, see under OFFRWM.

SPRING, HOWARD (1889–1965), novelist. Born in Cardiff, one of a gardener's nine children, he first described his childhood in a public lecture which was delivered in his native city and later published as the delightfully evocative *Heaven Lies About Us* (1939). He left school at the age of twelve and, after attending evening classes and working as a messenger-boy for *The South Wales Daily News*, became a reporter with *The Yorkshire Observer* and *The Manchester Standard*. A selection of his journalistic writing, done between 1911 and 1931, when he succeeded Arnold Bennett as book critic on *The Evening Standard* in London, was republished in the volume *Book Parade* (1938).

His first book was a collection of short stories for children, *Darkie and Co* (1932), which was followed by a novel, *Shabby Tiger* (1934), and its sequel, *Rachel Rosing* (1935). After the appearance of his best-selling novels, *O Absalom!* (1938; republished as *My Son, my Son*, 1938) and *Fame is the Spur* (1940), he went to live in Cornwall, the setting for most of his later fiction. During the Second World War he accompanied Winston Churchill, as one of two civilians in the delegation, on the voyage to meet President Roosevelt which resulted in the Atlantic Charter.

Among Howard Spring's other works were the novels *Hard Facts* (1944), *The Houses in Between* (1951), *These Lovers Fled Away* (1955) and *I Met a Lady* (1961), and a play, *Jinny Morgan* (1952), which is set in the *Rhondda Valley. They are, for the most part, leisurely chronicles teeming with characters in the manner of Dickens, whom the author greatly admired. It is not the plot which carries the reader on so much as human life itself, rolling along with its even tenor broken by humour and pathos. His solidly traditional style is also to be found in two further volumes of autobiography, *In the Meantime* (1942) and *And Another Thing* (1946).

Spurrell, William (1813–89), printer and publisher. He established the firm which bore his family's name at Carmarthen in 1840, developing it as an imprint for a wide range of religious, literary and topographical works. After his death, his son Walter Spurrell (1858–1934) enhanced the firm's reputation by printing to a high standard for such institutions as the *National Library of Wales and the *University of Wales, and by publishing several editions of his father's Welsh dictionaries as revised by J. Bodfan Anwyl (see under ANWYL, EDWARD). The firm declined rapidly as a publishing house after the Second World War and it was bought in 1957 by H. G. Walters Ltd. of Narberth, a company now known as The Five Arches Press, Tenby.

S.R., see ROBERTS, SAMUEL (1800–85).

Stable Loft Singing, a folk custom which flourished in north and west Wales during the eighteenth and nineteenth centuries. It was usual for unmarried male servants to sleep above the stable or in some other outhouse, rather than in the farmhouse itself. Despite the cold in winter, the men enjoyed the independence which went with this arrangement, being able to entertain themselves and their friends without interference from their employers. The songs they sang were of the kind associated less with the chapel and school and more with the public house and fair, but they expressed a wide range of emotions and reflected events from both far and near. Ballads were popular and verses were recited to the accompaniment of the Jew's harp and the accordion. Like the *Shimli, the stable loft provided a means by which folklore was transmitted from generation to generation.

A selection of stable loft songs from the Llŷn peninsula, together with texts, is featured in the *Welsh Folk Heritage* series (1980) published by the Welsh Folk Museum.

Stafell (lit. 'Room'), a folk custom associated with weddings, flourished in west Wales during the nineteenth century. The bride's dowry, consisting of furniture and other household items, together with gifts presented by relatives and neighbours, was arranged in a ritual manner on the night before the wedding, under the supervision of the mothers of the bride and groom. The ceremony varied in its detail according to district but it usually took place in the presence of women only. See also BIDDING.

'*Stafell Cynddylan*', see under CANU HELEDD (9th or 10th cent.).

Stag of Rhedynfre, The, see under OLDEST ANIMALS.

STANLEY, HENRY MORTON (1841–1904), explorer and writer, was born John Rowlands at Denbigh. He was an illegitimate child and, after his father's death and his mother's flight to London, he spent most of his childhood in the workhouse at St. Asaph. After escaping from that institution, he worked his passage to the USA and, while at sea, was adopted by one Henry Stanley, from whom he took his name. He had a variety of jobs in America, but it was as a journalist that he set out in search of David Livingstone in 1871 and crossed the continent of Africa three years later. During the first of three expeditions, at Ujiji on 10 November 1871, he is reputed to have uttered the famous words, 'Dr Livingstone, I presume?'. Stanley's travels are recounted in *How I Found Livingstone* (1872), *Through the Dark Continent* (1878) and *In Darkest Africa* (1890). He received the Grand Cross of the Bath in 1899 in recognition of his services as an explorer.

For further details see Richard Hall, *Stanley: an Adventure Explored* (1974); his *Autobiography* (1909), and the biography in Welsh (1890) generally believed to be the work of Thomas Gee, give accounts of Stanley's youth in Wales; see also Lucy M. Jones and Ivor Wynne Jones, *H. M. Stanley and Wales* (1972). The volume *The Exploration Diaries of H. M. Stanley* (1961) was edited by Richard Stanley and Alan Neame.

Stanton, Charles Butt (1873–1946), trade union leader and politician, was the key figure in the conversion of the industrial valleys of south Wales from *Liberalism to *Socialism. A native of Aberaman, near Aberdare, Glam., he played an important part in the miners' strike of 1898, founded a branch of the Independent Labour Party in 1900 and was instrumental in inviting Keir *Hardie to stand for the Merthyr Tydfil seat. A vehemently eloquent speaker, Stanton succeeded Hardie as the ILP member for Merthyr in 1915 and was elected to represent Aberdare, where he was opposed by T. E. *Nicholas, three years later. Defeated in 1922 by the Labour candidate, he retired from public life, joined the Liberals and went to live in London, where he later found employment as an actor in the film industry, usually taking aristocratic and clerical parts.

Statute of Wales, The (1284), see under RHUDDLAN and SHIRING OF WALES.

STEPHENS, MEIC (1938–), poet and editor. Born at Treforest, near Pontypridd, Glam., he was educated at the University College of Wales, Aberystwyth, and at the University of Rennes. From 1962 to 1966, when he taught French at Ebbw Vale, Mon., he lived in Merthyr Tydfil where he founded the Triskel Press and *Poetry Wales. He edited the magazine from 1965 until 1973. In 1967, after nearly a year on the staff of the *Western Mail in Cardiff, he was appointed to the post of Literature Director for the *Welsh Arts Council. With those of Harri *Webb and Peter Griffith (Peter *Gruffydd), his early poems were published in *Triad* (1963) and he contributed a booklet, *Exiles All* (1973), to the *Triskel Poets* series. He has also written topical songs and ballads. His book *Linguistic Minorities in Western Europe* (1976) is a study of the interaction between culture and politics in sixteen states. Among the works he has edited, besides this *Companion*, are an anthology of Anglo-Welsh poetry, *The *Lilting House* (with John Stuart *Williams, 1969), *Artists in Wales* (3 vols., 1971, 1973, 1977), *The Welsh Language Today* (1973), *A Reader's Guide to Wales* (1973), the *Writers of Wales* series (with R. Brinley Jones, 1970–), the anthology *Green Horse* (with Peter *Finch, 1978) and *The Arts in Wales 1950–75* (1979). For the *Gregynog Press he has made a selection from the diary of Francis *Kilvert, *The Curate of Clyro* (1983).

STEPHENS, THOMAS (1821–75), antiquary and literary critic. He was born, a cobbler's son, at Pont Nedd Fechan, Glam., and received little formal education (except in Latin) before being apprenticed, at Merthyr Tydfil in 1835, to a chemist whose business he carried on, after qualifying, for the rest of his life. About 1840 he began winning prizes at eisteddfodau for essays on historical and literary subjects. At the Abergavenny Eisteddfod of 1848 he was awarded the Prince of Wales Prize for an essay on 'The Literature of Wales during the Twelfth and Succeeding Centuries', and it was this work which later appeared as *The Literature of the Kymry* (1849). A second edition of this, the author's most important book, was edited by D. Silvan *Evans in 1876. On its publication Thomas Stephens was recognized by philologists in Wales and abroad as an authority on Welsh antiquities, especially on the poetry of the *Gogynfeirdd.

Prominent in public life, Thomas Stephens enjoyed the encouragement and friendship of Lord Aberdare (H. A. Bruce), the Member of Parliament for Merthyr Tydfil from 1851 to 1868, and of Sir Josiah John Guest, the iron-master, and his wife, Lady Charlotte *Guest. He was among those who sponsored various schemes for the improvement of the town's sanitary, welfare and educational facilities, including a Temperance Hall, a Board of Health and a public library; he also helped to organize the Gethin Relief Fund for the families of pit explosions. Appointed High Constable of Merthyr in 1858 and manager of *The Merthyr Express* in 1864, he was of an industrious, generous, amiable and strongly independent character and a staunch Unitarian.

Among Thomas Stephens's other books in English was *Madoc: an Essay on the Discovery of America by Madoc ap Owen Gwynedd in the Twelfth Century* (1893) which examined and ultimately refuted the widely cherished notion that America had been reached by the Welsh before the time of Columbus (see under MADOG AB OWAIN GWYNEDD). The essay was acknowledged as the outstanding entry in the competition at the Eisteddfod which was held at Llangollen in 1858 but the adjudicators, although convinced by the author's arguments, were loath to relinquish the old claim. Led by John *Williams (Ab Ithel), they decided to withhold the prize and, in disgust, Thomas Stephens never took part as a competitor in the Eisteddfod again. He continued with his literary and philological studies, however, and in collaboration with Gweirydd ap Rhys (Robert John *Pryse), he wrote an orthography of the Welsh language, *Orgraff yr Iaith Gymraeg* (1859), and contributed articles to *Y *Beirniad* and *Archaeologia Cambrensis*, the journal of the *Cambrian Archaeological Association.

In all his writings Thomas Stephens was a stern champion of historical truth, patriotic in his love for the language and literature of Wales but yielding to no prejudice and seeking always to reveal the falsity which national pride can sometimes perpetuate. He is generally considered to have been the first Welsh literary critic to adopt a scientific method and to have done more, as an adjudicator, to raise the standards of the National Eisteddfod and to win for it the confidence of scholars, than any other Welshman of his time.

For further details see the article by J. Ll. Thomas marking the centenary of Thomas Stephens's birth in *Y Geninen* (vol. XXIX, 1921), the article by Havard Walters on *The Literature of the Kymry* in *Llên Cymru* (vol. X, 1969) and the article by Stephen J. Williams in *Gwŷr Llên y Bedwaredd Ganrif ar Bymtheg* (ed. Dyfnallt Morgan, 1969). For a less favourable view of Thomas Stephens see Emyr Humphreys, *The Taliesin Tradition* (1983).

STEPNEY, GEORGE (1663–1707), poet and diplomat, was born in London into a family whose home was at Prendergast, Haverfordwest., Pembs. Educated at Trinity College, Cambridge, he owed his promotion in the diplomatic service to his friend Charles Montagu (later Earl of Halifax) and was sent as envoy to the courts of Germany. More distinguished as a man of affairs than as a poet, he nevertheless contributed a translation of Ovid to Dryden's *Miscellany Poems* (1684) and some of his work was included in Chalmers's *English Poets* and other collections. He also wrote *An Epistle to Charles Montagu Esq. on his Majesty's Voyage to Holland* (1691) and *A Poem addressed to the Blessed Memory of her late Gracious Majesty Queen Mary* (1695). Despite Stepney's gift as a linguist, Samuel Johnson described him as 'a very licentious translator' who did not 'recompense his neglect of the author by beauties of his own'. There is an extensive collection of his letters in the British Library and in the Public Record Office.

Stocsio, see under EASTER.

Stonehenge, see under DRUIDS.

Stones of the Field, The (1946), R. S. *Thomas's first volume of poems, was published by Keidrych *Rhys at the Druid Press in Carmarthen. It contains fifty-seven poems written between 1941 and 1946, some having previously appeared in periodicals. The title quotes the Book of Job (5: 23): 'For thou shalt be in league with the stones of the field: and the beasts of the field shall be at peace with thee'. The collection 'seeks to reaffirm man's affinity with the age-old realities of stone, field, and tree'. Some of the poet's best-known poems, such as 'A Peasant', 'A Priest to his People' and 'The Airy Tomb', are included here but eighteen were never reprinted.

Storïau'r Tir (lit. 'Stories of the land'; 1966), a selection of short stories by D. J. *Williams from three earlier volumes, namely *Storïau'r Tir Glas* (1936), *Storïau'r Tir Coch* (1941) and *Storïau'r Tir Du* (1949). Although several have an urban setting, most draw on the author's rural background and the main theme is loyalty to community. The principal virtue of the technique employed is a cunning simplicity, perhaps seen at its best in the story '*Blwyddyn Lwyddiannus*', in which a farmer buys a calf and wins a wife at the same time. The mood of the stories varies from volume to volume but the third, consisting mainly of stories set in the years of the Second World War, is on the whole more sombre. The stories '*Pwll yr Onnen*' and '*Yr Eunuch*' are small masterpieces, unusual in that they are based on farce. When the author's gift for humour turns to satire, as in '*Meca'r Genedl*', it wears a more serious guise, but without losing its keen powers of observation.

'*Storm, Y*' (lit. 'The storm'; 1854–56), the title of two long poems written by William *Thomas (Islwyn) after the sudden death of Anne Bowen, the young woman to whom he was engaged to be married. The failure by Owen M. *Edwards, in his edition of Islwyn's work (1897), to distinguish between the two poems, and his rearrangement of the original texts, were major factors in the debate among literary critics as to the significance of 'Y Storm', but it is now generally acknowledged that they include some of the greatest Welsh poetry of the nineteenth century.

The first poem, comprising some six thousand lines and written between the end of 1854 and the beginning of 1856, describes storms both natural and figurative, and reflects the passionate nature of a young man in love with life. By contrast, the second poem (about as long and written in mid-1856) consists of a series of metaphysical meditations which were inspired by Edward Young's *Night Thoughts* (1742–45). The soul's pilgrimage and its triumph over the storm of life constitute the epic's central theme. Both poems gave expression to Islwyn's Romantic and mystical tendencies and they contain his most innovative and sublime poetry.

The poems are discussed in D. Gwenallt Jones, *Y Storm: Dwy gerdd gan Islwyn* (1954); other critical works include contributions by Meurig Walters to *Ysgrifau Beirniadol* (ed. J. E. Caerwyn Williams, 1965, 1966, 1967), and articles by Saunders Lewis in *Llên Cymru* (vol. IV, 1956–57) and W. J. Gruffydd in *Y Llenor* (vol. II, 1923). The full text of the earlier poem has been edited by Meurig Walters (1980).

Stradling family, The, of St. Donat's, Glam., was in residence at the castle in the late thirteenth century. Edward Stradling (*fl.* 1316–52), active in public affairs in the County, was one of the chief patrons of *Neath abbey. His great-grandson, Sir Edward Stradling, was a close associate of the House of Lancaster and with his wife Jane, the daughter of Cardinal Beaufort, he held numerous offices in south Wales.

The family were prominent as patrons of the poets and Lewys Morgannwg (*Llywelyn ap Rhisiart) considered himself the family poet of Sir Edward Stradling II (d. 1535). Sir Edward's grandson, also named Edward Stradling (1529–1609), was a scholar and antiquary, who collected a fine library at St. Donat's and paid for the publication of Siôn Dafydd *Rhys's Welsh Grammar (1592). His account of the Norman invasion of Glamorgan gave currency to the Myth of the Twelve Knights and was included in David *Powel's *Historie of Cambria* (1584). He was described by Thomas *Wiliems as 'the chief cherisher of our Welsh language in south Wales'. On Edward's death, St. Donat's passed to his second cousin, John (d. 1637), the founder of Cowbridge Grammar School. John Stradling, who spoke no Welsh, wrote a number of books and treatises, including *Beati Pacifici: a divine poem* (1623), *Divine Poems* (1625) and *The Storie of the Lower Borowes of Merthyrmawr*, which was published in 1932. John's son, Edward (1601–44), raised troops for the Crown in Glamorgan and was taken prisoner at the battle of Edgehill (1642); his wife gave refuge to Archbishop Ussher of Armagh.

The last of the Stradlings of St. Donat's was Thomas (1710–38), the seventh baronet, who died in a skirmish at Montpellier. The family properties were then divided and St. Donat's came into the possession of the Tyrwhit-Drakes and later of the Nicholl-Carne families. In the 1930s the castle was owned by the American newspaper proprietor William Randolph Hearst ('Citizen Kane') and since 1962 it has been the home of the United World College of the Atlantic.

For further details of the family see the article by Glanmor Williams in *Vale of History* (ed. Stewart Williams, 1961) and his chapter in *The Story of St. Donat's Castle and Atlantic College* (ed. Roy Denning, 1983); see also R. A. Griffiths, 'The rise of the Stradlings of St. Donat's Castle' in *Morgannwg* (vol. VII, 1963).

Straeon y Pentan (lit. 'Tales of the hearth'; 1895), Daniel *Owen's last book, is a collection of stories narrated by the author through a fictitious character called Uncle Edward. Previously published in periodicals, they are not short stories in the modern sense, but rather anecdotes which Daniel Owen claimed were 'true'. Several are constructed around remarkable coincidences and, since the author was fascinated by the spine-chilling and the calamitous, two are ghost stories and some are accounts of disasters. One or two tales illustrating the moral that Providence punishes cruelty and rewards the godly with material prosperity are among the least inspired pieces he ever wrote, but several are skilfully written and Daniel Owen's genius for character portrayal is abundantly evident here.

Strata Florida or **Ystrad Fflur**, an abbey near Pontrhydfendigaid, Cards. The house was first established in 1164 by Robert Fitzstephen on the banks of the river Fflur in the upper reaches of the Teifi Valley, as a daughter-house of the Cistercian abbey of *Whitland. Later, *Rhys ap Gruffudd (The Lord Rhys) bestowed his patronage upon it and the abbey was relocated at Ystrad Fflur. Daughter-houses were founded at *Llantarnam, *Aberconwy and *Llanllŷr, and the monastery became (in the words of J. E. *Lloyd) 'the premier abbey of Wales'. A number of Welsh princes, including Cadell ap Gruffudd (1175), Rhys Ieuanc (1222) and Maelgwn ap Rhys (c. 1230), were buried in its grounds. *Llywelyn ap Iorwerth (Llywelyn Fawr) recognized the abbey's pre-eminence in 1238 when he assembled there all the princes of Wales to swear allegiance to his son and heir, Dafydd. It has been suggested that both *Madog ap Selyf and *Gruffudd Bola, translator of the Athanasian Creed from Latin into Welsh, were monks at Strata Florida. The lost Latin version of *Brut y Tywysogyon was probably written at the abbey towards the end of the thirteenth century. Some scholars maintain that *The White Book of Rhydderch* and *The *Red Book of Hergest* also belonged to Strata Florida's scriptorium. *Llywelyn Goch ap Meurig Hen greeted the abbot, Llywelyn Fychan ap Llywelyn (*fl.* 1360–80), in an *awdl*. It is believed that *Dafydd ap Gwilym was buried in the abbey's graveyard, a claim based on a poem by *Gruffudd Gryg which suggests that the poet's remains lie under a yew tree in the churchyard (but see the entry for TALLEY abbey).

The monastery was sacked during the rising of *Owain Glyndŵr and again in 1427–28 when the abbot of Aberconwy came to plunder its possessions. The next abbot, Rhys (1430–41), inherited a despoiled building but was praised by Guto ap Siencyn and *Guto'r Glyn for his hospitality in terms which belie the state of disarray prevailing during his time. Rhys died in the debtors' prison at Carmarthen, having lavished a fortune on the abbey's repair. *Dafydd Nanmor, who eulogized the abbot Morgan, mentioned 'a great roll' kept at the monastery but it is not known to what this was a reference. *Ieuan Deulwyn visited the abbey to pay tribute in verse to the abbot Dafydd ab Owain who was also, in his time, abbot of *Strata Marcella and Aberconwy, and Bishop of St. Asaph. The abbey of Strata Florida, of which the grange lands extended over great parts of mid-Wales, as far as the valleys of the Wye and the Irfon, was dissolved in 1539.

For further details see Stephen W. Williams, *The Cistercian Abbey of Strata Florida* (1889), the articles by T. Jones Pierce and E. G. Bowen in *Ceredigion* (vol. I, 1950–51), Glanmor Williams, *The Welsh Church from Conquest to Reformation* (1962), D. H. Williams, *The Cistercians in Wales* (1969) and F. G. Cowley, *The Monastic Order in South Wales 1066–1349* (1977).

Strata Marcella or **Ystrad Marchell**, an abbey near Welshpool, Mont., affiliated to the *Cistercian Order, was founded about 1170 by Owain Cyfeiliog (*Owain ap Gruffudd Maredudd) as a daughter-house of *Whitland; it was also known as **Pola** or **Pool**. The abbey's early years were clouded by a scandal involving the first abbot, Enoch, and a nun from Llansant-ffraid-yn-Elfael, Rads., but daughter-houses were established at *Valle Crucis and *Llanllu-gan in due course. Many princes, including Owain Cyfeiliog and Gruffudd Maelor II, were buried in the abbey's grounds but *Cynddelw Brydydd Mawr refused a burial place there and composed a satirical *englyn* to Strata Marcella. Towards the end of the fifteenth century the poets *Tudur Aled, *Gruffudd ap Llywelyn Fychan and *Bedo Brwynllys wrote poems requesting gifts from the abbot, Dafydd ab Owain, and *Guto'r Glyn and Tudur Aled eulo-gized him. The last abbot, Siôn ap Robert ap Rhys, a member of the *Plas Iolyn family, was among those from whom Huw *Llwyd requested oxen. The abbey was dissolved in 1536.

For further details see the article by E. Owen in *Y Cymmrodor* (vol. XXIX, 1919) and that by J. Conway Davies in *Montgomeryshire Collections* (1949–50); see also Glanmor Williams, *The Welsh Church from Conquest to Reformation* (1962) and D. H. Williams, *The Cistercians in Wales* (1969).

Strigoil, see CHEPSTOW.

Stryd y Glep (lit. 'Gossip row'; 1949), a novel by Kate *Roberts, the first work written during her Denbigh period, after the death of her husband, when she began to focus on problems of a per-sonal nature. The book takes the form of a diary, with the main character, a bedridden spinster named Ffebi Beca, pouring her anxieties into it. It contains few incidents but is filled with details of day-to-day life in a small town. Searching for a reason for her existence, Ffebi ends by quoting a line from *Siôn Cent: '*Gobeithiaw a ddaw ydd wyf*' ('My hope lies in what is to come').

The novel's merits are discussed by Hugh Bevan in an essay in *Beirniadaethau Llenyddol* (ed. Brynley F. Roberts, 1982).

Studia Celtica (lit. 'Celtic studies'), a periodical which first appeared in 1966 under the editorship of J. E. Caerwyn *Williams, was launched on the initiative of the Language and Literature Committee of the *Board of Celtic Studies of the University of Wales. The journal was an immediate success, attracting contributions from some of the leading specialists in Indo-European, Continental and Insular Celtic, and has continued to play an important role in the fields of dialectology and linguistics. Still under the direction of its first editor, it has a valuable section on *nécrologie*, carries reviews and biblio-graphies of recent publications relating to the Celtic languages, and more recent volumes con-tain bibliographical lists of research-theses on Celtic subjects.

STYLES, FRANK SHOWELL (Glyn Carr; 1908–), novelist and topographical writer, was born at Four Oaks, Warwicks. His nine years as a bank clerk were followed by freelance writing, war service in the Navy, leadership of climbing and surveying expeditions to Arctic Norway (1952 and 1953) and the Himalayas (1954), and a Fellowship of the Royal Geo-graphical Society. Many visits to north Wales resulted in his settling there in 1946, at Borth-y-gest, Caerns., and beginning to write in earnest; he married a Welshwoman in 1954 and lived at Croesor for fifteen years before returning to Borth-y-gest. Among the books he has published, more than a hundred in all, fifteen appeared under his pseudonym and seven of these are set in Snowdonia: *Death on a Milestone Buttress* (1951), *Death under Snowdon* (1954), *Murder of an Owl* (1956), *Swing Away Climber* (1959), *Death Finds a Foothold* (1962), *Death of a Weirdy* (1965) and *Fat Man's Agony* (1969). Another seventeen, published under his own name, have Welsh settings; they include *Traitor's Mountain* (1946), *A Climber in Wales* (1948), *The Rising of the Lark*

(1948), *Welsh Walks and Legends* (1972), *The Mountains of North Wales* (1973), *Welsh Tales for Children* (1974) and *Legends of North Wales* (1975).

Suffering Queen, The, see CALUMNIATED WIFE.

Sulien (*c.* 1010–91), a cleric who was twice bishop of *St. David's but who was chiefly associated with the cloister of *Llanbadarn Fawr. It may have been he who established at Llanbadarn a centre of learning which was maintained by his four sons, *Rhygyfarch, Daniel, Ieuan and Arthen, and by their sons, Sulien, Cydifor and Henry. Among the manuscripts connected with the cloister is St. Augustine's *De Trinitate*, in Ieuan's hand, which has an *englyn* written in the margin, of which the subject is the Curwen, *Padarn's pastoral staff. The chief literary work of the cloister, apart from that of Rhygyfarch, is a Latin poem by Ieuan to his father (in Corpus Christi MS 199), a poem which is the main source of knowledge about Sulien. According to this poem, Sulien was of noble lineage and attended schools in Britain, but received much of his education in Ireland, where he spent thirteen years. He was called from Llanbadarn to St. David's twice (1073–78, 1080–85) and, according to *Brut y Tywysogyon*, it was there that he died, widely known for his learning. The style of the poem is rather laborious and uneven and contains no real mastery of Latin grammar or versification, and that is also true of the *invocatio* and the *disticha* composed by Ieuan in the same manuscript.

Summer Birch, The, a fertility symbol, was cut down early on *May Day and erected at some central spot where it was decorated for the festival associated with the coming of summer. There is an early reference to this custom, said to have been practised at Llanidloes, Mont., in a *cywydd* by *Gruffudd ab Adda ab Dafydd. The 'raising of the birch' was prohibited in 1644 but after the Restoration the custom was revived, especially in north-east Wales, in the form of 'the Summer Branch' which was carried from house to house by parties of dancers. In Glamorgan and Gwent the Summer Birch, also known as the Summer Pole, was associated with *St. John's Day and the *Taplas*: it was customary for villagers to try to steal each other's tree, as described by William Thomas (1727–95), the diarist from St. Fagan's, Glam. The tradition also flourished at Tenby, Pembs., until the middle of the nineteenth century but, apart from occasional attempts to revive it, is no longer carried on. See also the next entry.

For further details see Trefor M. Owen, *Welsh Folk Customs* (1959).

Summer Carols, sung early on *May Day and throughout the month, were religious in nature and frequently referred to the events of the previous twelve months and to the fertility expected through God's generosity during the forthcoming summer. Skilful and lyrical descriptions of the beauties of nature were set to the complicated metres of the 'summer singing', as exemplified in the work of such masters as Huw *Morys. The Church authorities placed special emphasis on this religious verse during the seventeenth century in an attempt to counteract the secular and pagan tendencies of the celebration of May Day.

Sunday Schools, founded in Wales during the last decade of the eighteenth century, were primarily intended for the religious instruction of the common people. Their precursors had been the schools of the *Welsh Trust and the *Society for Promoting Christian Knowledge and the Circulating Schools of Griffith *Jones, but it was the work of Robert Raikes (1736–1811) of Gloucester and the establishment of a Sunday School Society in London in 1785 which provided the impetus for the movement in Wales. Under the leadership of Thomas *Charles of Bala the schools spread rapidly, first among the Methodists (see under METHODISM) and then among the *Baptists and Congregationalists (see under INDEPENDENCY).

The Sunday Schools were popular on account of their comprehensive character: they were free, they embraced all classes in the community, they were attended by young and old, by male and female, and they were adaptable to meet the needs and abilities of all. The very young had Bible stories, the young and illiterate had reading lessons, and for the adult and more able members there were lively discussion groups. Attention was given to the reciting and memorizing of long portions of the Scriptures, to competitions and examinations in religious knowledge, as well as to the catechizing of the young and old. A large proportion of the common people of Wales thus became literate in Welsh, acquiring in their discussions a grasp of democratic principles and the skills of self-expression, a process which helped to encourage the growth of *Temperance, *Radicalism and *Nonconformity during the latter half of the nineteenth century. The marginal activities of the Sunday Schools were also of social significance: they brought colour to the otherwise drab lives of the people: tea-parties, parades, lending libraries, savings-banks and outings to the seaside and countryside were regularly organized. For more than a century, and certainly at the height of their influence between 1870 and 1920, the Sunday Schools were a vital source of religious, intellectual and social vigour in the life of Wales, and many owed a great deal to their teaching and stimulus.

For further details see David Evans, *The Sunday Schools*

in Wales (1883), R. T. Jenkins, *Hanes Cymru yn y Ddeunawfed Ganrif* (1928), Mary Clement, *Dechrau Addysgu'r Werin* (1966), W. Llywelyn Jones, *A History of the Sunday Schools in Wales* (1967), Jac L. Williams, *Addysg i Gymru* (1966), and Jac L. Williams and Gwilym Rees Hughes (ed.), *The History of Education in Wales* (1978).

'Suo Gân' (lit. 'A soothing song'), a lullaby first published in its present form by Robert *Bryan in *Alawon y Celt* (1905); an earlier version was published by Edward *Jones (Bardd y Brenin) in *Musical and Poetical Relicks of the Welsh Bards* (1794), with the note that it was a song 'which the Welsh nurses sing to compose the children to sleep'. It was Bryan who wrote the two verses which are usually sung to the tune, including the better-known verse, '*Huna blentyn ar fy mynwes*'.

Surexit Memorandum, The, see under BOOK OF ST. CHAD.

Surnames, unknown among the Welsh (except in immigrant families and those of mixed blood) until the great social changes of the sixteenth century, were largely the result of innovations in the country's administration which followed the passing of the *Act of Union (1536). The Welsh had used up to then a patronymic system by which, for example, Gruffudd, the son of Llywelyn, was known as Gruffudd ap Llywelyn and his son, Rhys, was known as Rhys ap Gruffudd, and so on, the second element changing with the generation; the particle *ap*, or *ab* before a vowel, was an abbreviated form of *mab* (son). This traditional method was abandoned, at least for administrative purposes, as the forces of Anglicization spread throughout the country. In the first place, the spelling of Welsh baptismal names was Anglicized and old names such as Meilir, Llywarch and Gwalchmai were discouraged; in their place came biblical or royal names such as John, David, Richard and Henry. Furthermore, the Welsh were obliged to adopt a system of permanent fixed surnames to be transmitted from generation to generation, as in England. If a man's name, at the moment when he faced officialdom for the first time, happened to be Rhisiart ab Ifan, he was recorded as Richard Jones or Evans or Bevan; if it was Siôn ap Dafydd he became John Davies. He was then expected to pass his new surname to all his family and descendants. The old English way of turning a personal name into a surname was by adding an -s, so that John became Jones and William, Williams.

The very period when the choice of baptismal names had become severely limited was also the time when most Welshmen adopted fixed surnames, with the result that many families were thereafter called Evans, Jones, Davies, Thomas, Rees, Roberts and so on. A change which was slightly more Welsh than the adding of the English -s, was to keep the last letter of the word *ap* or *ab* so that, for example, ap Rhys, ap Hywel and ab Owen would become Price, Powell and Bowen. The gentry of north Wales in the sixteenth century made surnames out of the names of their homes or localities, a few of which, such as Mostyn and Nanney, have survived. Another method of early Welsh nomenclature was to add an adjective to the name, such as Dafydd Llwyd (Grey), which by the process of Anglicization became David Lloyd. The adjective '*Fychan*' ('junior'), added to the name of a son who had the same name as his father, became the surname Vaughan. The names Hywel, sometimes abbreviated to Huw, and Llywelyn to Lewys, lie at the root of the common surnames Hughes and Lewis. The Welsh were also fond of using pet-names or hypocoristic forms such as Guto or Gutyn for Gruffudd and Bedo for Maredudd, forms which gave Gittoes, Gittins and Beddoes. The name Iorwerth was Anglicized to Yorath, but was often thought to approximate to the name Edward, which explains the popularity of the surname Edwards in Wales. At the same time as this process was becoming widespread, the Protestant Reformation was responsible for introducing names from the Old Testament, with the result that many families acquired surnames such as Samuel, Isaac, Levi and Abraham.

The dearth of genuinely Welsh surnames since the eighteenth century is partly the reason why so many eminent Welshmen have been known by their place of origin or residence, such as Williams Pantycelyn (William *Williams). It also contributed to the development of the Welsh genius for coining nicknames and, especially in the nineteenth century, to the widespread use of bardic names such as Ieuan Glan Geirionydd (Evan *Evans): by such means a man could be distinguished from his fellows of the same name. Among the first to revert to the old patronymic system, at least partially, was Owen M. *Edwards who gave to his son the name Ifan ab Owen *Edwards in 1895. Since the Second World War there has been a growing trend among young Welsh people, mainly for patriotic reasons, to change their names by deed poll either to the original Welsh spelling (e.g. Rhys for Rees) or according to the patronymic principle, or merely to drop the Anglicized surname altogether. Rather more, however, consistently use *ap* or *ab* without having officially changed their names, and most keep the second element over several generations as if it were a surname. The incongruity of naming daughters in this way has not deterred some parents, though the use of *ferch* (or *ach*, 'daughter') is extremely rare.

Further details will be found in Peter Bartrum, *Welsh Genealogies* (2 vols., 1974, 1983); see also Prys Morgan and David Thomas, *Wales: the Shaping of a Nation*

(1984). The most authoritative account is that by T. J. Morgan and Prys Morgan, *Welsh Surnames* (1985).

Swan of Usk, The, see OLOR ISCANUS (1651).

'Swn y Gwynt sy'n Chwythu' (lit. 'The sound of the wind that blows'; 1952), a long *pryddest* for radio by J. Kitchener *Davies, was commissioned by Aneirin Talfan *Davies for the BBC in 1952 and broadcast a day or two before the author died of cancer. It was subsequently published as a booklet with a foreword by Gwenallt (David James *Jones), who expressed the view that it was 'one of the greatest poems written in Welsh in the twentieth century'.

A poem in free verse specifically intended to be spoken, it takes the form of a dramatic monologue describing the poet's spiritual and earthly pilgrimage, from his childhood and youth in the Cardiganshire countryside to the industrial desert of the *Rhondda Valley during the *Depression of the 1930s. Kitchener Davies was a Christian and a Welsh Nationalist who longed to see the industrial valleys of south Wales restored to their cultural inheritance and he devoted his energies to the cause of *Plaid Cymru in an attempt to stem the tide of Anglicization and materialism which he abhorred. The wind that blows throughout the earlier parts of the poem symbolizes the hostile, destructive powers which the poet had sought to defy and to master. What gives special force to the expression of his experience is the pitiless honesty of his self-questioning and the trenchant examination of his own motives.

The influence of William *Williams (Pantycelyn)—especially his *Theomemphus*—is evident throughout the poem and the brutal self-analysis reveals in the end that the poet's pilgrimage leads inevitably to a spiritual conversion more potent than his longing for the security of family and tradition, because salvation demands the total surrender of self. The wind that blows with such power in the final parts of the poem is the Holy Spirit which sweeps the poet, despite himself, to the path of sainthood. The agony of soul apparent in the prayer of the final section is one of the most impressive examples of confessional verse in Welsh since the days of the great hymn-writers of the eighteenth century. The poem not only presents a moving personal confession of faith but also expresses the crisis of a whole generation whose politics were an integral part of their religion.

An English translation of the poem will be found in Joseph P. Clancy, *Twentieth Century Welsh Poems* (1982); for critical discussion see the monograph on Kitchener Davies by Ioan Williams in the series *Llên y Llenor* (1984).

Sycharth, see under OWAIN GLYNDŵR (*c*.1354–*c*.1416).

SYPYN CYFEILIOG (*fl.* latter half of the 14th cent.), poet. It is difficult to tell from the manuscripts which verses are his and whether certain nicknames refer to him or to others. He was certainly not the Cnepyn Gwerthryniawn mentioned in the work of *Trahaearn Brydydd Mawr. It appears that several poets, such as Y Sypyn, Y Cnepyn and Bach Buddugre received their nicknames on account of their small physical stature and that these names caused them to be confused one with another. Of all the poems attributed to Sypyn, Ifor *Williams in his *Cywyddau Iolo Goch ac Eraill* (1925) accepted as certain only two *cywyddau* to girls, both attractively fresh and clear in their imagery. If, as is claimed, Dafydd Bach ap Madog Wladaidd was the same poet, it was he who composed a short but very warm-hearted *awdl* of invitation to Dafydd ap Cadwaladr of Bachelldre, near Church Stoke, Mont., which ends with the words, '*Dyred pan fynnych, cymer a welych, a gwedy delych, tra fynnych trig*' ('Come when you wish, take whatever you like and, after coming, stay as long as you like'). These words, often quoted, have become a traditional expression of hospitality.

Syr Meurig Grynswth, see under BARDD A'R CERDDOR (1863) and GOHEBIAETHAU SYR MEURIG GRYNSWTH (1856–58).

T

Tad a'r Mab, Y (lit. 'The father and the son'; 1963), a play by John Gwilym *Jones, was first performed by the Drama Company of the University College of North Wales, Bangor, in 1959. Like the author's earlier plays, it is about family relationships but, unlike *Lle Mynno'r Gwynt* and *Gŵr Llonydd* (1958), it has only a few characters and the dialogue is more authentic and less consciously literary. Gwyn, an intelligent lad, is shielded jealously and then tyrannically by his father, Richard Owen, but attempts to break away by associating with Pegi, a young girl less privileged and less cultured than he. The father is unable to accept this threat to his relationship with his son and his obsessional love has terrible consequences.

Tad y Tlodion, see LEWIS, DAVID (1617–79).

Taffy, a nickname for a Welshman, is derived from the common Welsh Christian name Dafydd (E. David). It is used by the English both good-humouredly and pejoratively (cf. Jock and Paddy for the Scots and the Irish) and is perhaps best known from the rhyme which begins,

> Taffy was a Welshman, Taffy was a thief,
> Taffy came to my house and stole a leg of beef.

In a version slightly different from others which have since been current, this rhyme was first published in *Nancy Cook's Pretty Song Book* about 1780. It may not have been in its original form an allusion to the cattle-raiding Welsh, as is sometimes claimed, but a corruption of an anti-clerical squib brought to west Wales by Flemish settlers in the twelfth century (see under ANGLIA TRANSWALLINA). The sobriquet survives most persistently in the armed forces, where it is usually abbreviated to Taff (the Anglicized form of the name of the river on which Cardiff stands), and the name Taffy is traditionally given to the white *goats which are the mascots of the Royal Welch Fusiliers and the Royal Regiment of Wales. The neologism Taphydom, for Wales or the Welsh in general, dates from the seventeenth century and has now been replaced in journalese by Taffia (cf. Maffia), a word which refers to the alleged influence of Welshmen in high places.

Taffy (1923), a satirical comedy by Caradoc Evans (David *Evans), was first presented at the Prince of Wales Theatre, London, on 26 February 1923 and subsequently at the Quarry Theatre, Aberystwyth, by Oliver Sandys, the author's wife. The première was marked by the vociferous protests of the *London Welsh in the audience, who were insulted by the play's theme of avarice, unremittingly displayed. Few observed that the love of the younger characters, Spurgeon and Marged (the latter part played by Edith Evans), shows more human warmth than is usual for Caradoc Evans and the play contributed immensely to the author's reputation as 'the most hated man in Wales'.

Taffy was a Welshman (1912), a book by the English writer T. W. H. Crosland (1865–1924), has for its central theme the take-over of England by the Welsh. This coup has been preceded by the retreat of the Scots, in whose dishonour the same author wrote *The Unspeakable Scot* (1902). Davy Bach, a thin disguise for David *Lloyd George, is said to be shackling England, the home of a distinctly hierarchical freedom, to the anarchical democracy of Wales in the name of *Liberalism. Other targets include Lord Howard de Walden (Thomas Evelyn *Scott-Ellis) and Theodore Watts-Dunton, the author of the allegedly ill-written novel, *Aylwin* (1878). Unlike Arthur Tyssilio Johnson, the author of *The *Perfidious Welshman* (1910), Crosland does not slander the individual Welshman but, after a token show of fair-mindedness, proceeds to denigrate in a heavy-handed and uninformed manner the history, literature and music of Wales, reserving his most disparaging remarks for the *National Eisteddfod, *Nonconformity and Radical newspapers.

Taffydeis, The (1747), sub-titled 'a humorous heroic poem in honour of St. David and the Leek', was written under the pseudonym Hywgi ap Englyn Morganwc by an author who remains anonymous. The story turns on the heroine's announcement to her suitors that she will choose him who 'honours best St. David's Day'. There follows a series of mock battles between the English and the Welsh in which the latter are eventually victorious. The poem provides opportunities for the usual comic references to national character but is among the more entertaining of its kind.

Tafod y Ddraig, see under CYMDEITHAS YR IAITH GYMRAEG (1962).

Tair Rhamant, Y (lit. 'The three romances'),

namely *Iarlles y Ffynnon* (or *Owain*), *Geraint* and *Peredur*, survive wholly or partly in *The *White Book of Rhydderch* and *The *Red Book of Hergest*; the last two occur fragmentarily in other early manuscripts, while the first is also well represented in later manuscripts of the sixteenth to the eighteenth centuries. The Romances are couched in similar language to **Pedair Cainc y Mabinogi* and the native tales, with the same objectivity and concentration on the story, the same extensive use of direct speech, the same revelation of character through action and speech, and the same restraint in regard to description. They differ from the Four Branches, however, in having an Arthurian setting, in being less clearly localized in Wales, and in having as their heroes characters who, in name at least, are historical personages of the British Heroic Age of the sixth century or thereabouts, whereas the chief characters of the Four Branches are in origin members of the Celtic pantheon.

It is doubtful whether the three should be regarded as a group, except in being the only tales of their kind extant in Welsh, and certain that they cannot have the same author. Despite the general similarity of language, which they owe to traditional narrative method, there are differences in their orthography in the *White Book*, which show that they were not transmitted as a group. They exhibit very different degrees of skill in construction, *Geraint* and *Owain* being in this respect much superior to *Peredur* and, in the use of clusters of compound adjectives for rhetorical effect, *Geraint* and *Peredur* stand apart from the undecorated language of the other.

As regards subject-matter, on the other hand, the Romances have a good deal in common, for all are tales of **Chivalry* in a world which is peopled with villains and monsters of various kinds. In each the hero has lessons to learn about himself and his relations with others and all three could be said to be concerned with the education of the perfect knight. In *Peredur* a start is made with very raw material indeed, namely a lad of noble birth who, for his own safety, has been kept in ignorance of the knightly way of life. In *Owain*, the protagonist of the first adventure, Cynon, sets out full of youthful arrogance and comes to grief, but Owain, who repeats the expedition more successfully, and Geraint, are both experienced and prudent men by the time they first appear. Their lessons are contrasted in several respects. Owain has won himself a domain by his valour and the intelligent devotion of **Luned, but when allowed a three-month leave of absence to return to **Arthur's court, he forgets his wife and his responsibilities for three years until she repudiates him. Driven mad by remorse, he has to undergo a period of privation and to fight his way back to health and self-esteem before he can return to her. Geraint also

wins himself a wife, rescuing her from genteel poverty, but his attention is too uxoriously engaged so that his subjects are provoked to censure his conduct. He misinterprets his wife's grief as desire for another man and tests her faithfulness by taking her on an expedition during which he forbids her to speak to him. She remains remarkably loyal, however, repeatedly warning him of approaching dangers which include two attempts on his life, and they are eventually reconciled.

There is much less unity to *Peredur*. This Romance falls into three parts, beginning with the training of the hero as a knight and his early adventures up to his winning of Angharad (though his marital status is ambiguous throughout), a sequence which takes up more than half the tale. A second part relates a series of adventures culminating in a fourteen-year sojourn with the Empress of Constantinople. In the third part Peredur is back with Arthur and goes in search of information about the head on the salver and the dripping spear which he saw at his uncle's court in the first part. The mystery is cleared up in a rather offhand way and Peredur fulfils the duty of vengeance imposed on him by killing, with Arthur's help, the Witches of Gloucester, his tutors in the martial arts.

Among the tales composed in French verse by Chrétien de Troyes in the second half of the twelfth century are three which correspond to some extent to the Three Romances: *Erec* to *Geraint*, *Yvain* to *Owain* and *Perceval* (which he left unfinished) to *Peredur*, where the resemblance is less close. Some or all of these also spread to Germany, Scandinavia and England but, except for the English *Syr Percyvelle*, they are all closely based on Chrétien and, with some Scandinavian exceptions, are also in verse. The relationship of the Welsh tales to Chrétien's has been much disputed. Before the date of the *Red Book* was known they were assumed to be the basis of the French poems but when it appeared that there was no manuscript evidence for them earlier than Chrétien's time they were taken to be prose abridgements of his work. But analysis now points to the Celtic origins of the principal characters. There are also many Celtic parallels, in Irish as well as in Welsh, to incidents in these tales, and their similarity to native Welsh storytelling in language and technique (often recognizably distinct from the alien style of translation literature) proves that the Romances are not adaptations of Chrétien. The Welsh and French versions are now seen as the end-products of a common source and were probably produced in a bilingual district or situation. They are of mainly Celtic inspiration but have grown apart with the passage of time, the Welsh remaining more conservative in content, the French sometimes preserving elements, including proper names, which the Welsh tales have lost. To the evolving French versions Chrétien added his own interpretation and treatment, always emphasizing the existence of inferior sources for his work; he thus produced the versions the excellence of which eclipsed their predecessors.

The Romance of *Peredur* has been edited by K. Meyer (1884) and by G. W. Goetinck, *Historia Peredur vab Efrawc* (1976) and that of *Owain* by R. L. Thomson (1968). Diplomatic texts can be found in John Rhŷs and J. Gwenogvryn Evans, *The Text of the Mabinogion from the Red Book of Hergest* (1887) and J. Gwenogvryn Evans, *The White Book Mabinogion* (1907); the former is modernized by R. M. Jones in *Y Tair Rhamant* (1960). The text and translation of a later version of *Owain* (Llanstephan 58) appear in *Studia Celtica* (vol. VI, 1971). Translations were made by Charlotte Guest, T. P. Ellis and John Lloyd, Gwyn Jones and Thomas Jones, and by Jeffrey Gantz. The works are discussed in *Arthurian Literature in the Middle Ages* (ed. R. S. Loomis, 1959), in *Y Traddodiad Rhyddiaith yn yr Oesau Canol* (ed. Geraint Bowen, 1974), and in *A Guide to Welsh Literature* (ed. A. O. Jarman and Gwilym Rees Hughes, 1976). There are further comments by Proinsias Mac Cana, *The Mabinogi* in the *Writers of Wales* series (1977) and by Brynley F. Roberts in *Ysgrifau Beirniadol X* (ed. J. E. Caerwyn Williams, 1977).

Tâl Moelfre, The Battle of (1157), was fought on the coast of Anglesey between the forces of Owain Gwynedd (*Owain ap Gruffudd) and those of Henry II. Engaged in heavy fighting in Tegeingl (*Englefield) throughout the previous summer, the English pushed forward as far as the river Clwyd and a contingent of Henry's men landed on Anglesey, plundering the countryside and desecrating the churches of Llanbedr-goch and Llanfair Mathafarn Eithaf. During the furious battle which ensued at Tâl Moelfre Henry's half-brother, his father's son by the Princess *Nest, was among the English knights who were killed. The incident is recounted in a medieval chronicle, *O Oes Gwrtheyrn Gwrtheneu, and in poetry composed by *Gwalchmai ap Meilyr for the victorious Owain Gwynedd.

Talfryn, see LLOYD, IORWERTH HEFIN (1920–).

Talgarth, a cantref of *Brycheiniog, was coterminous with the Marcher lordship of Blaenllyfni which, after the division of the lands of Bernard of Neufmarché in 1143, came into the possession of the Fitz Herbert family. By the late fourteenth century it had become part of the extensive territories of the Mortimers.

TALHAEARN TAD AWEN (*fl.* 6th cent.), one of five *Cynfeirdd who are listed by *Nennius in the *Historia Brittonum as having flourished in the *Old North during the sixth century. His name, together with the epithet *Tad Awen* ('Father of the Muse'), is also mentioned in a poem in The *Book of Taliesin, but none of his work has survived.

Talhaiarn, see JONES, JOHN (1810–69).

TALIESIN (*fl.* late 6th cent.), a poet named with *Aneirin in a famous passage in *Nennius's *Historia Brittonum which lists the poets who once flourished in the *Old North of Britain. In The *Book of Taliesin there is a group of twelve poems believed to represent his authentic work, together with a much larger number of religious, scriptural, prophetic and legendary poems which were once supposed to be by him but cannot possibly be so. In language, style, technique and metrical features the poems in the early group resemble Aneirin's 'Y *Gododdin'. Six are eulogies addressed to Urien ap Cynfarch (*Urien Rheged) and to his son *Owain ab Urien, and these include the earliest extant example of a *dadolwch* ('intercession') by the poet after a period of estrangement from his patron. Two other poems present graphic accounts of battles fought by Urien and Owain against Angle invaders from the east and against Picts from the north. Two more are praise-poems addressed to a certain Gwallog, who may have ruled over the little kingdom of Elmet which lay in the area around what is now Leeds, and one is in praise of *Cynan Garwyn, a ruler in *Powys. The *dadolwch* offers an indication that the poet came only as a visitor to the court of Urien. It was the opinion of Ifor *Williams that Taliesin may have been a native of Powys, since the poem which is probably the earliest in the group is in praise of Cynan Garwyn. If this is the case, it would not only bear witness to the wide area covered by a poet in this early period during his travels between one patron and another—journeys matched at a later date by those of the *Gogynfeirdd within Wales—but it would also be consistent with the Powysian origin attributed to Taliesin in *Hanes Taliesin*.

A folk-tale with a highly mythological content, *Hanes Taliesin* has at its theme the origin of poetic inspiration. By a complicated process of reincarnation, it presents Taliesin as the child of the goddess Ceridwen who lives at Bala with her husband Tegid Foel, after whom Llyn Tegid (Bala Lake) was named. Ceridwen brews a magic cauldron from the contents of which she intends that her own son, Morfran, shall drink and by so doing become imbued with the gift of poetry. Instead, it is her servant, Gwion Bach, who swallows drops from the cauldron and thus acquires the gift. When pursued by Ceridwen both he and she pass through a series of metamorphoses until he is eventually swallowed as a grain of wheat by Ceridwen in the form of a hen. He is reborn from her womb in a form of such great beauty that she refrains from killing him, but instead casts him adrift on the sea, to be discovered and adopted by *Elffin ap Gwyddno Garanhir, who renames him Taliesin. When he grows older the boy Taliesin accompanies Elffin to the court of *Maelgwn Gwynedd at *Degannwy (this association cannot possibly be historical), where he successfully silences the poets of Maelgwn's household by his magic and a demonstration of his superior poetic powers.

Ifor *Williams believed that *Hanes Taliesin* developed in north Wales during the ninth or tenth century. Its existence in some form at that date is substantiated by a number of allusions to it, with other mythological adventures attributed to the poet, in the verse which was brought together under his name in *The Book of Taliesin* (14th cent.). But it is extant in its full form, in interspersed prose and verse, only from the sixteenth century, in the long chronicle of Elis *Gruffydd. Several poets of the twelfth century allude to the story of Taliesin's contention with Maelgwn's poets; others, however, such as *Cynddelw Brydydd Mawr, give evidence of their knowledge that the historic Taliesin lived in the Old North and was associated with Urien Rheged and Owain ab Urien. Although the spurious tradition of Taliesin and Elffin and the poets of Maelgwn was evidently the more popular among later poets, both *Dafydd ap Gwilym and *Guto'r Glyn show that they knew of Taliesin correctly as Urien's poet.

There is other evidence that Taliesin was featured in stories of a semi-mythical character at an early date. In the story of *Branwen he is named among the seven men who escaped from Ireland after the death of Bendigeidfran (*Brân), an episode which may be related to the incident of a raid upon *Annwn outlined in the poem *'Preiddiau Annwfn' in *The Book of Taliesin*. Between the eleventh and thirteenth centuries Taliesin's reputation as an omniscient prophet appears to have been on the increase, as borne out by a number of vaticinatory poems foretelling victory against the Saxons, and later the Normans, in which his name is frequently coupled with that of *Myrddin (Merlin) to give authority to the prophecies. Occult knowledge of this kind was an essential aspect of the omniscience accredited to poets in early Celtic society, both in Ireland and in Wales. There is an early dialogue poem in *The *Black Book of Carmarthen* which presents Myrddin and Taliesin as prophesying together the battle of Arfderydd. A knowledge of this poem seems to be reflected in a long Latin poem by *Geoffrey of Monmouth called the * *Vita Merlini* in which *Telgesinus* discourses with *Merlinus* about geography and natural phenomena. Evidently Geoffrey had obtained some information concerning the current medieval conception of Taliesin's omniscience as this is reflected in the Welsh poems. Throughout the Middle Ages the *Gogynfeirdd* and the *cywyddwyr* referred to Myrddin and Taliesin as the two great and authoritative poets who stood together at the very beginning of the Welsh poetic tradition.

For a study of the early poems attributed to the poet see the edition *Canu Taliesin* (1960) by Ifor Williams; the same author's *Chwedlau Taliesin* (1957) discusses the origin and growth of the folk-tale relating to Taliesin's life. J. E. Caerwyn Williams has made an English translation, *The Poems of Taliesin* (1968). The late version of the folk-tale by Elis Gruffydd is translated by P. K. Ford in *The Mabinogi and Other Medieval Welsh Tales* (1977).

Taliesin (1859–61), a quarterly magazine edited by John *Williams (Ab Ithel), of which eight numbers appeared, was published under the auspices of the provincial literary societies of Wales. Besides prose and poetry which had won prizes at the eisteddfodau, it carried essays which are now a valuable source for the study of the literature and thought of the period. It was in this magazine that J. Ceiriog *Hughes's poem *'Myfanwy Fychan' and the *awdl* by Eben Fardd (Ebenezer *Thomas) on the subject of the battle of *Bosworth first appeared.

Taliesin, the literary magazine of Yr *Academi Gymreig, first appeared under the editorship of Gwenallt (David James *Jones) in 1961. Among its earliest contributors were E. Tegla *Davies, T. H. *Parry-Williams, D. J. *Williams and Iorwerth C. *Peate. In 1965, after the publication of nine numbers, the editor resigned and D. Tecwyn *Lloyd was appointed in his place; he was assisted by Islwyn Ffowc *Elis for two years. Under the sole editorship of D. Tecwyn Lloyd, the magazine was published twice a year until 1984, when it became a quarterly. It carries poems, stories, essays, reviews and translations from foreign literature into Welsh. The magazine's contributors, who are not drawn exclusively from the *Academi*'s membership, include almost all the important writers of the day and, as a platform for their work, it has a place with the most illustrious of Welsh literary journals.

An index to the magazine's contents (1961–79) was compiled for the Welsh Library Association by D. Hywel E. Roberts and Elinor Thomas (1982).

Taliesin ab Iolo, see WILLIAMS, TALIESIN (1787–1847).

Talley or **Talyllychau**, an abbey near Llandeilo, Carms., was founded by *Rhys ap Gruffudd (The Lord Rhys) about 1197 and was affiliated to the Premonstratensian Order. Although the canons were drawn from the native population and the abbey was on the route of itinerant poets, there has survived only one poem which can be associated with Talley, a *cywydd* by *Ieuan Deulwyn requesting a goshawk of the abbot. The abbey was dissolved in 1536.

There has persisted a local tradition that Talley, rather than *Strata Florida, was the burial-place of *Dafydd ap Gwilym. Some scholars, notably Rachel *Bromwich, are of the opinion that the claim of Strata Florida is based on a misunderstanding of the *cywydd* by *Gruffudd Gryg which seems to suggest that the poet was buried in the grounds of that abbey. They believe that this poem belongs to the tradition of the *marwnad ffug*, or mock-elegy, a form of witty address or rejoinder sometimes exchanged by poets in the medieval period, and that Gruffudd Gryg's poem merely speculates as to the place of Dafydd's burial, probably well before the event. The tradition of the poet's burial at Talley is first recorded in a list of the burial-places of famous poets which was compiled by Thomas *Wiliems of Trefriw about 1600 and this tradition was later espoused by Iolo Morganwg (Edward *Williams). Those who believe that the poet was buried at Talley argue that the critical assessment of Iolo Morganwg's literary forgeries made by Griffith John *Williams was largely responsible for the virtual suppression of the Talley tradition, except in the abbey's immediate neighbourhood, but that this tradition long antedates Iolo's day. A memorial stone to the poet was erected in the churchyard at Talley in September 1984.

For further details of the rival claims see the articles by W. Leslie Richards in *Barn* (Aug., 1984) and those in *Barddas* (nos. 87–89, 1984).

Tanner, Phil (1862–1950), folk-singer, of Llangennith, Gower, belonged to a family of weavers who were renowned for their songs and traditional dances. Much in demand as a bidder at weddings, he had perfect pitch and a repertoire of several hundred songs which ranged from fifteenth-century ballads to the favourites of the Victorian music-hall. Some he had learned at singing concerts in the West Country but others, such as the *Gower Wassail Song* and the *Gower Reel*, a jig in the mouth-music tradition, belonged to his native district.

Tanwedd, a premonition of death said to take the form of a fiery streak of brilliant light moving slowly in a low, straight, long line across the sky at night. See also CORPSE BIRD, CORPSE CANDLE and TOILI.

Taplas, a musical gathering held on Saturday nights between Easter Monday and Winter's Eve. In addition to dancing and the singing of verses to the accompaniment of *crwth and *harp, games were played, including roof-ball, football and jumping. The custom was associated with the *Summer Birch and *St. John's Day and, during the nineteenth century, it was often confused with *Mabsant; in north Wales it was known as *Twmpath Chwarae*.

Tarian y Gweithiwr (lit. 'The worker's shield'; 1875–1934), a weekly Radical newspaper launched by John Mills, Francis Lynch and Caradoc Davies at Aberdare, Glam. As well as reports of industrial and political events in Wales, it carried features of literary interest and foreign news. Lynch was replaced in 1889 by G. M. Evans who, after 1895, became the sole publisher. In 1911 the newspaper was bought by the proprietors of *The Aberdare Leader* and three years later its name was changed to *Y Darian*. The leader writers were Edward Davies of Rhymney, John Morgan Jones, D. Silyn Evans and J. Tywi Jones, the last of whom also edited the paper.

Unlike *Y *Gwladgarwr* (1848–54), *Y Darian* strove to protect Welsh workers against exploitation by the coal-owners and attacked landlordism, Toryism and the Established Church. It appealed especially to workers in the coal, iron and tin plate industries of south Wales, blending local news with a review of international politics and enjoying a weekly sale of some fifteen thousand copies. Under the editorship of J. Tywi Jones the paper's literary content was increased with accounts of eisteddfodau, lessons in Welsh grammar and *cynghanedd, a poetry column and stories in serial form. Among regular contributors were such writers as J. Dyfnallt *Owen, John *Morris-Jones and Saunders *Lewis. Its popularity waned during the 1920s, however, partly because of the editor's pacifism and partly as a result of the decline in the use of the Welsh language and the poverty caused by the economic *Depression in south Wales. J. Tywi Jones continued as editor until March 1934, when he was succeeded by Henry Lloyd (Ap Hefin; 1870–1946) but the paper survived only for another six months.

Tavern Eisteddfodau, see under ALMANAC.

Tawddgyrch Cadwynog, see under TWENTY-FOUR METRES.

TAYLOR, MARGARET STEWART (1902–), author. Born in Coventry, War., she was Chief Librarian at Merthyr Tydfil, Glam., from 1939 until her retirement in 1967. Her thirteen novels include *Another Door Opened* (1963) and *The Link was Strong* (1964), both of which are set in Merthyr, and *Marian's Daughter* (1967) which is about Adelina *Patti; she also wrote a family biography, *The Crawshays of Cyfarthfa Castle* (1967).

Te yn y Grug (lit. 'Tea in the heather'; 1959), a volume of short stories by Kate *Roberts. The central character, Begw, is a young girl whose gradual awakening to a realization of the pain and the pleasure of life forms the book's main theme. Her two friends are Mair, the somewhat haughty daughter of the manse, and Winni Ffinni Hadog, a black sheep, always outspoken and impudent. Winni is the most amusing of all the author's characters and the vein of humour running through this book sets it apart from her other works.

For critical discussion of these stories see the articles by Hugh Bevan in *Yr Arloeswr* (1960), John Rowlands in the volume edited by Bobi Jones in honour of Kate Roberts (1969) and John Gwilym Jones in *Crefft y Llenor* (1977). An English translation entitled *Tea in the Heather* (1968) was made by Ll. Wyn Griffith.

Tegau Eurfron, the wife of *Caradog Freich-fras, was regarded as a standard of chastity by Welsh poets of the medieval period. According to tradition, she rescued her lover from a poisonous snake but, in doing so, was bitten in the breast which, because her life was threatened, had to be removed and replaced by another made of gold. Her cloak, listed as one of the *Tri Thlws ar Ddeg Ynys Prydain*, was said not to fit any woman who had broken her marriage vows.

Tegeingl, see ENGLEFIELD.

Tegid, see JONES, JOHN (1792–1852).

Tegla, see DAVIES, EDWARD TEGLA (1880–1967).

Tegwch y Bore (lit. 'Fair weather in the morning'; 1967), a novel by Kate *Roberts, was first published in weekly instalments in *Baner ac Amserau Cymru* in 1957 and the year following. Unlike the other novels of her Denbigh period, it is set during the years of the First World War, as if it were an attempt to rewrite the ending of *Traed Mewn Cyffion* (1936). It describes the relationship of a young teacher, Ann Owen, with her family and with her brother in particular, and her love-affair with Richard Edmwnd. Despite the great sadness which weighs heavily on the writing, the novel ends by striking a note of confidence and anticipation.

For further details see the article by Dafydd Glyn Jones in the volume edited by Bobi Jones in honour of Kate Roberts (1969) and that by John Rowlands in *Kate Roberts: ei Meddwl a'i Gwaith* (ed. Rhydwen Williams, 1983).

Teilo (6th cent.), saint. The churches, chapels and wells which bear his name (a hypocoristic form of Eludd) are to be found, in the main, in those parts of south-west Wales which were not thoroughly Romanized, but also in Gwent. He and *Dewi Sant, who seems to have been a contemporary of his, belonged to the same missionary movement, which was characterized by zeal and asceticism. The centre of Teilo's cult was at *Llandeilo Fawr, Carms., where *The *Book of St. Chad* was kept in the eighth century.

The Life of Teilo, written in the twelfth century, is associated with Geoffrey (d. 1133), the brother of Urban, Bishop of *Llandaf, and it exists in two versions. The earlier is preserved in the Cotton Vespasian Manuscript and the other, with additions, is found in *The Book of Llandâv*. The latter names the saint as the second bishop of the see, in succession to *Dyfrig, and claims Penalun (Penally), Pembs., as his birthplace. With *Padarn and Dewi, Teilo is said to have gone on a pilgrimage to Jerusalem and, on his return, to have fled from Wales to escape the yellow plague. After spending seven years and seven months in Brittany, he came back and died in his monastery on the banks of the Tywi. His corpse was claimed by Penalun, Llandeilo and Llandaf and these churches had their requests granted, for his body was miraculously transformed so that it could be seen in all three places at once. Remains of Teilo's cult are to be found in Brittany but *Geoffrey of Monmouth's assertion that he was appointed Archbishop of Dol, in succession to Samson, can be discounted.

Teirtu, in the tale of *Culhwch and Olwen, owns a magic harp which, at his command, plays without having its strings plucked. One of the tasks which Ysbaddaden Bencawr sets Culhwch is to procure the instrument for his entertainment at the wedding-feast of his daughter.

Teithi Hen, the son of Gwynnan, is named in the tale of *Culhwch and Olwen as one of those present at *Arthur's court; it is said that the sea had flooded his kingdom. A Latin Triad, not found among *Trioedd Ynys Prydain*, corroborates this story and adds that Teithi Hen's island lay between Menevia (*St. David's) and Ireland. It has been suggested that the name is a corruption of Seithennin and that the references are to a version of the legend about the drowning of *Cantre'r Gwaelod.

Temperance, in its general sense meaning self-discipline against excess, but in a special sense the exercise of restraint in the taking of alcoholic drinks, is for many synonymous with total abstention. The Temperance Movement developed in the eighteenth and nineteenth centuries, especially in the USA and England, in response to social conditions in which drunkenness, poverty and crime seemed to be inseparably linked. In Wales, the first to advocate total abstinence, or 'tee-totalism', as it came to be known, is thought to have been Evan Davies (Eta Delta; 1794–1855), an Independent minister.

The movement gained ground in Wales throughout the first half of the nineteenth century, despite opposition from men such as John *Jones (Talhaiarn). Fellowships, *Friendly Societies, hospitals and hotels were established on a Temperance basis, and there were *Bands of Hope for children. Hymns with a Temperance message were written, the best known being 'I bob un sy'n ffyddlon' by Henry Lloyd (Ap Hefin; 1870–1946); there were, too, novels, such as *Llywelyn Parri* (1855) by Llew Llwyfo (Lewis William *Lewis), *Jeffrey Jarman* (1855) by Gruffydd Rhisiart (Richard Roberts 1810–83) and *Arthur Llwyd y Felin* (1879) by John *Thomas (1821–92). The first literary venture of Daniel *Owen was a translation of an American Temperance novelette, *Ten Nights in a Barroom* (1854) by Timothy Shay Arthur.

The Sunday Closing Act of 1881, the first example of special legislation for Wales, was passed as the result of a combination of Sabbatarianism and Temperance. For the next eighty years the whole of Wales, including Monmouthshire after 1921, remained 'dry', or, as the song 'Cosher Bailey's Engine' (see under BAILEY, CRAWSHAY) puts it, 'if you wanted drink on Sunday, you had to wait till Monday'. In 1960, however, the Licensing Act gave the counties of Wales the right to open or to close public houses on Sundays on the basis of a referendum to be held every seven years. Since then the cause of Sunday closing has declined in further local polls (held in 1968, 1975 and 1982) and public houses are now closed on Sundays only in two small districts of Dwyfor and Ceredigion.

For further details see W. R. Lambert, *Drink and Sobriety in Victorian Wales* (1983) and the same author's article, 'The Welsh Sunday Closing Act, 1881' in *The Welsh History Review* (vol. 6, no. 2, 1972); see also H. Carter and J. S. Thomas, 'The Referendum on the Sunday Opening of Licensed Premises in Wales as a Criterion of a Culture Region' in *Regional Studies* (vol. 3, 1969).

Tewdrig (5th–6th cent.), prince and saint. All that is known about him is found in *The Book of Llandâv* (*Llandaf) where it is said that he abdicated in favour of his son Meurig and became a hermit at *Tintern. Called once more to lead the people of Glamorgan against Saxon invaders, he put the enemy to flight but was mortally wounded by a lance. He was buried at Mathern, formerly Merthyr Tewdrig, near Chepstow. Francis Godwin, Bishop of Llandaf from 1601 to 1617, discovered in the church at Mathern a stone coffin containing the saint's skeleton, which had a fractured skull.

'Teyrnasoedd y Ddaear' (lit. 'The kingdoms of the earth'; 1852), an anthem for solo bass, quartet, trio and mixed choir, was composed by John Ambrose Lloyd (1815–74) for the Eisteddfod held at Bethesda, Caerns., in 1852. Based on Psalm 68: 32; 'Sing unto God, ye kingdoms of the earth; O sing praises unto the Lord', the work was sometimes said to be the 'Hallelujah Chorus' of the Welsh and was frequently performed at eisteddfodau in the nineteenth century. Joseph *Parry thought it the best anthem ever written in Wales.

Teyrnon Twrf Liant, the lord of Gwent-is-Coed in the First Branch of *Pedair Cainc y Mabinogi, finds the son of *Pwyll and *Rhiannon while rescuing a foal from the attack of a monster. Not knowing whose child he is and unaware that he has been taken from his mother's bed, Teyrnon and his wife decide to bring him up as their own and they give him the name Gwri. When the boy is in his fourth year, his resemblance to Pwyll becomes evident and he is restored to his parents, who rename him

Pryderi. Pwyll offers the foster-parents a reward for rearing the child but none is accepted. The church of Llantarnam, Mon., formerly Nant Teyrnon, commemorates Teyrnon and the epithet Twrf Liant (lit. 'the roar of the sea') may be connected with the sound of the incoming tide in the rivers Wye and Severn at certain times of the year. It is possible that the name is derived from the Brythonic *Tigernonos* ('the great king'), the mythological partner of *Rigantona* ('the great queen') or Rhiannon.

Thalia Rediviva (lit. 'The muse of comic poetry renewed'; 1678), subtitled 'The Pass-Times and Diversions of a Countrey-Muse in Choice Poems on several Occasions', was the last published work of Henry *Vaughan. The title-page does not carry the Silurist's name, though commendatory poems by his deceased friends Katherine *Philipps (The Matchless Orinda) and Thomas *Powell, with others by the editor and his brother, are found at the head of the collection. Vaughan's motive in agreeing to publish again was to honour his dead twin-brother Thomas *Vaughan, some of whose Latin poems are included, but the elegiac eclogue 'Daphnis', though obviously written partly for Thomas, presents difficulties, for much of it may have already been written after the death of Henry's younger brother William in 1648. Thomas, however, in his *Lumen de Lumine*, discovers Thalia, one of the nine Muses, as the spirit who, dressed all in green, affords him a vision of the *prima materia* and, herself the creative force of Nature, becomes the Muse of his alchemy. The book's title, therefore, is both commemorative and confirmatory. No more than half a dozen poems can be dated later than 1655: the commendatory poems make plain that some of those which follow were excluded from *Olor Iscanus (1651) and the Etesia poems were probably disqualified from the volume of 1646. The latest poems of firm date in *Thalia Rediviva* are the elegy for Judge Trevor (1666) and the address 'To the editor of the matchless Orinda' (1667). Thereafter Henry Vaughan seems to have been immersed in his medical practice.

THELWALL, JOHN (1764–1834), poet, was born in London into a branch of the family whose home was Plas y Ward, Denbs. A friend of the English writers Southey, Hazlitt, Coleridge and Lamb, he was influenced by the democratic ideals of the French Revolution (1789) and became a member of the Society of the Friends of the People. He was imprisoned in 1794 for his extreme Radical beliefs but was later acquitted, describing his experience in *Poems written in Close Confinement in the Tower and Newgate* (1795). Besides editing *The Biographical and Imperial Magazine*, he published two other volumes of verse, *Poems upon various subjects* (1787) and *Poems chiefly written in retirement*

(1801); the latter includes a memoir and a number of poems on Welsh subjects. He was also the author of several books on the art of public speaking and others on political topics.

Theomemphus, see BYWYD A MARWOLAETH THEOMEMPHUS (1764).

Theophilus and Eusebius, see under DRWS Y SOCIETY PROFIAD (1777).

'There Were Three Jovial Welshmen', a song of fools. One of the earliest versions is found in a broadside ballad of 1632 in which three men of Gotham, a village in Nottinghamshire renowned for its folly of its inhabitants, go hunting on St. David's Day (1 March). The song turned into raillery about the Welsh when it appeared in sheet music form under the title 'The Pursuit of Reynard' in 1725. Another version in Lancashire dialect, 'The Three Jovial Huntsmen', was popularized by Randolph Caldecott's illustrations, which were published in 1880.

Thesbiad, Y, see ELIAS, JOHN ROOSE (1819–81).

Thirlwall, Connop (1797–1875), Bishop of ★St. David's, belonged to the long line of '*Esgyb Eingl*' ('English-speaking bishops') whose appointment was widely and bitterly criticized in Wales during the eighteenth and nineteenth centuries. An Englishman, he countered the charge that he knew no Welsh, made in the Church magazine *Yr Haul* and elsewhere, by quickly learning the language well enough to use it in religious services, albeit incomprehensibly for some among his congregations. Bishop from 1840 to 1874, he was noted for his charitable works and his zeal in visiting all parts of his large diocese. He encouraged the restoration of churches, many of which had fallen into a sorry state of disrepair, as well as the building of schools and the establishment of a teachers' training college at Carmarthen. He was bitterly indicted, however, by Lord Llanover (see under HALL, AUGUSTA WADDINGTON) for his diversion of the revenues of Christ College, Brecon, which in 1851 had become near-derelict. Thirlwall was, in any case, too reserved to be popular among the Welsh and he became more and more estranged from his own clergy.

Thirteen Treasures of the Isle of Britain, The, see TRI THLWS AR DDEG YNYS PRYDAIN.

This World of Wales (1968), an anthology of Anglo-Welsh poetry from the seventeenth to the twentieth century, edited by Gerald ★Morgan. Dedicated to Raymond ★Garlick, it was the first serious attempt to present a historical survey of the poetry written in Wales in the English language and, like The ★Lilting House (1969), an important milestone in the development of Anglo-Welsh literary studies. It includes several poems by each of these poets: Henry ★Vaughan, John ★Dyer, Evan ★Lloyd, Gerard Manley ★Hopkins, W. H. ★Davies, Edward ★Thomas, David ★Jones, Idris ★Davies, Glyn ★Jones, Vernon ★Watkins, R. S. ★Thomas, Dylan ★Thomas and Alun ★Lewis. Represented by one poem each are a number of lesser poets such as Sir Lewis ★Morris and A. G. ★Prys-Jones, as well as some of the younger poets of the twentieth century, including Brenda ★Chamberlain, Leslie ★Norris, T. H. ★Jones, Anthony ★Conran and Meic ★Stephens. The anthology's title is taken from the sonnet 'In the Valley of the Elwy' by Gerard Manley Hopkins:

Lovely the woods, waters, meadows, combes, vales,
All the air things wear that build this world of Wales.

THOMAS (*fl.* 1160), a poet who wrote in the dialect of Norman French which was spoken in England and Wales during the twelfth century. His *Roman de Tristan* (*c.*1160), only parts of which are extant, is a romance written probably for Eleanor of Aquitaine, the wife of Henry II. Although the poem praises London and was designed to entertain Henry's court, the German name given to the author, Thomas von Britanje, suggests that he was of Breton or Welsh background.

For him, Breri (★Bledri ap Cydifor, almost certainly) was the authoritative source for the story of ★Tristan and Iseult. Thomas's poem is probably the oldest surviving written form of the tale, although Béroul's more sensuous poem in the Normandy dialect was composed about the same time. Thomas handles his material didactically, making Tristan the joyous lover and Iseult a timid or pitiful lady and some of the proper names such as Brangwain and Cariado are thought to reflect a Welsh background. Thomas's poem was the model for Gottfried von Strassburg and for the authors of many other versions of the story.

It has been suggested that Thomas and the author of *Horn*, which combines Viking material with an interest in Celtic lands such as Brittany, Devon and Ireland, were one and the same man. Furthermore, the author of *Tristan* may possibly be identified with the Thomas of Kent who wrote *Le Roman de Toute Chevalerie*, which treats of the life of Alexander the Great, for the name Kent was not used exclusively for that part of south-east England represented by the modern county but referred also to several other areas, including Gwent.

For further details see Joseph Bédier (ed.), *Le Roman de Tristan* (1905), Jessie Crossland, *Medieval French Literature* (1956) and Sigmund Eisner, *The Tristan Legend* (1969).

Thomas ab Ifan, see EVANS, THOMAS (*fl.* 1596–1633).

Thomas ap Roger Vaughan (d. 1469), gentleman, of *Hergest, Herefs., was the son of Sir Roger *Vaughan of Tretwr (Tretower) and Gwladus, the daughter of Sir *Dafydd Gam. With his half-brothers, the Herberts, he took a prominent part on the Yorkist side in the Wars of the Roses. They were together at the disastrous battle of Banbury (1469), when a certain Welshman distinguished himself by fighting his way twice through the enemy's ranks, leaving two rows of dead. According to the English chroniclers, this man was Sir Richard Herbert, but there is reason to believe that it was Thomas ap Roger Vaughan, not his half-brother, who performed this extraordinary feat, only to be killed shortly afterwards. *Lewys Glyn Cothi, who composed his elegy, described in another poem the tomb and effigies which his widow, Ellen Gethin, caused to be erected in the church at Kington.

Thomas Bartley, see under RHYS LEWIS (1885).

THOMAS OF MONMOUTH or **THOMAS MONUMENTENSIS** (fl. 1146–72), monk and Latin author. He probably spent some time in the Benedictine monastery at Monmouth before moving to England, perhaps as a protégé of *Geoffrey of Monmouth; he was received into the Order's house in Norwich between 1146 and 1150. Despite his learning, he became involved in the cult of the 'martyr' and 'saint', William of Norwich, a child who was said to have been crucified by Jews during the Passover of 1144. The claim was without foundation but gave rise to the persistent charge of ritual murder brought against the Jews in medieval England. While it was not Thomas who invented the story, he accepted it and welcomed supplementary stories of 'miracles' in connection with the cult. The only authority for these incidents is his book, *De Vita et Passione Sancti Willelmi Martyris Norwicensis*, known in English as *The Life and Miracles of Saint William of Norwich*.

THOMAS WALLENSIS or **THOMAS WALEYS** (d. c.1350), Dominican friar, theologian and Latin author, was of Welsh origin and was educated at the Universities of Oxford and Paris. He is remembered chiefly for having defied the authority of Pope John XXII at Avignon in 1333 by maintaining before the cardinals that the saints receive the Beatific Vision (the vision of God which is the goal of salvation) without having to wait for the Resurrection of the Dead and the Last Judgement. The Pope had tried to check the spread of this heresy, Papal orthodoxy holding that before the Resurrection the saints in heaven see only the humanity of Christ. Thomas was imprisoned by the Inquisition and afterwards transferred to a place of captivity under Papal control. However, his views were championed in the University of

Paris and the Pope wavered: the next Pope, the reforming Benedict XII, ruled that the souls of the Just behold the Vision immediately after departing this life. Eventually Thomas was released from prison, a broken old man, paralysed and destitute, but one who had played a decisive part in the significant modification of eschatological doctrine. Among his writings are listed a commentary on Augustine's *De Civitate Dei*, a collection of tracts by doctors of the Church called *Campus Florum* and a treatise on preaching written after his release entitled *De Arte Praedicandi* or *De Modo Componendi Sermones*.

For further details see G. Hartwell Jones, *Celtic Britain and the Pilgrim Movement* (1912) and G. R. Owst, *Medieval Preaching in England* (1926).

Thomas, Daniel (**Daniel y Pant**; 1851–1930), a man noted for his *white lie tales, lived at a farm known as Y Pant at Dinas, Pembs., and during the latter part of his life at Y Parrog, Newport, in the same county. There is a portrait of him and an example of one of his most famous stories—about what happened when he gave his sow Siwsan too much home-made beer—in the volume *Wês Wês* (ed. John Phillips and Gwyn Griffiths, 1976).

THOMAS, DAVID (**Dafydd Ddu Eryri**; 1759–1822), poet and bardic teacher, was born at Waun-fawr, Caerns., a weaver's son, and later became a schoolmaster. The only formal schooling he ever received was a few months with a local clergyman but he was taught the rules of *Cerdd Dafod by friends and neighbours. His own poetry has little merit, yet he won prizes at eisteddfodau held under the auspices of the *Gwyneddigion Society in 1790 and 1791. He later fell out with the Society because of the members' Radical sentiments and William *Owen Pughe's strange ideas about the Welsh language.

In 1783 Dafydd Ddu began to establish literary societies in Arfon and these gave him the opportunity of teaching the poetic art to his fellow-poets. Known as 'Cywion Dafydd Ddu' ('Dafydd Ddu's chicks'), they included William Williams (Gwilym Peris, 1769–1847), Griffith *Williams (Gutyn Peris), Richard Jones (Gwyndaf Eryri, 1785–1848), Owen *Williams (Owen Gwyrfai) and John Roberts (Siôn Lleyn, 1749–1817). By this teaching Dafydd Ddu was able to exercise a beneficial influence on the writing of poetry in the traditional metres and to help others to withstand the more outlandish theories of Iolo Morganwg (Edward *Williams) and Owen Pughe. He published the work of his pupils in the volume *Corph y Gaingc* (1810), together with a selection of his own verse.

A lecture on Dafydd Ddu Eryri by Cynan (Albert Evans-Jones) was published in the *Transactions* of the Honourable Society of Cymmrodorion (1970) and another by Thomas Parry in the *Transactions* of the Caernarfonshire Historical Society (1980).

Thomas, David (1794–1882), 'the father of the American anthracite iron idustry', was born at Tŷ-llwyd, a farm in the parish of Cadoxton, near Neath, Glam. In 1812 he found employment at the Neath Abbey Ironworks and, five years later, was engaged as supervisor of the blast furnaces at the Ynyscedwyn Ironworks in the Swansea Valley. During the next twenty-two years he experimented in smelting with anthracite coal, a mineral which had been regarded as ineffective because it could not be converted to coke. After visiting James Neilson, the inventor of the raw-coal-heated 'hot blast', in Glasgow in 1837, Thomas completed his own 'hot blast' process using anthracite coal. The results were immediate and the anthracite area of west Wales was quickly industrialized. In 1839 Thomas was induced by the Lehigh Coal and Navigation Company of Pennsylvania to superintend their anthracite smelting works. There followed a new and massive emigration to that State, mainly from west Wales, which resulted in the chief towns of Scranton and Wilkes Barre becoming largely Welsh in character. The expansion of Pennsylvania's iron and coal industries was one of the main reasons why the industrial output of the USA had surpassed that of Britain by the time of David Thomas's death.

For further details see the article by Edward Roberts in the 'Notable Men of Wales' series in *The Red Dragon* (vol. 4, no. 4, Oct., 1883).

THOMAS, DAVID (Dewi Hefin; 1828–1909), poet, was born at Llanwennog, Cards., and kept schools in the County until 1883. He wrote a great deal for the periodicals *Seren Gomer and Yr Ymofynydd and published four volumes of verse, namely Y Blodau (1854), Blodau Hefin (1859), Blodau'r Awen (1866) and Blodau Hefin (1883).

THOMAS, DAVID (1880–1967), historian, born in the parish of Llanfechain, Mont., was a schoolteacher at Rhostryfan, Tal-y-sarn and Bangor, Caerns., for most of his life. His chief publications were Y Werin a'i Theyrnas (1910), Y Cynganeddion Cymreig (1923), Y Ddinasyddaeth Fawr (1938), Hen Longau a Llongwyr Cymru (1949), Cau'r Tiroedd Comin (1952), Hen Longau Sir Gaernarfon (1952), Silyn (1956) and Ann Griffiths a'i Theulu (1963). A Socialist by conviction, he established the periodical *Lleufer in 1944 and continued as editor until 1965.

Thomas, David Alfred (1856–1918), industrialist and politician. Born at Aberdare, Glam., he was educated at Gonville and Caius College, Cambridge, and at the age of twenty-three went to work in his family's colliery at Clydach Vale. He began his political career as the

Liberal member for Merthyr Tydfil but after 1906 he redirected his energies into the Cambrian Combine, amassing a fortune and at the same time making enemies among the leaders of the *South Wales Miners' Federation. Besides his major influence on the development of the mining industry in south Wales, he made an important contribution to British life as the first Viscount Rhondda and in the post of Food Controller during the later years of the First World War.

Thomas, David Vaughan (1873–1934), composer, was born at Ystalyfera, Glam. Many of his musical works had their inspiration in Welsh literature and were based on folk-tales like those about *Llyn y Fan and Tir na n-Óg (see under YNYS AFALLON). He also made vocal settings of the *cywyddau* of such poets as Dafydd Ionawr (David *Richards), Emrys (William *Ambrose), Cynddelw (Robert *Ellis) and others, which were published as *Saith o Ganeuon* (1923). He was the father of Wynford *Vaughan-Thomas.

For further details see the biography by Emrys Cleaver published in 1964.

THOMAS, DYLAN (1914–53), poet and prose-writer. He was born in Swansea, Glam., to parents whose family roots were in rural, Welsh-speaking Carmarthenshire and Cardiganshire, places to which the poet returned in life and art after the early shaping years in Swansea. His father, a nephew of Gwilym Marles (William *Thomas), was English master at Swansea Grammar School, where Dylan Thomas was a pupil between 1925 and 1931. He had no other period of formal education and the fifteen months he spent as a junior reporter on *The South Wales Daily Post*, after leaving school, were to be his only term of full-time employment.

His passion for English poetry, fostered early by his father's more than professional interest, had already manifested itself in four notebooks in which schoolboy verse suddenly matured into original poems between 1930 and 1934. These notebooks remained the major source of his output to the end of the 1930s, feeding his first three published volumes, *18 Poems* (1934), *Twenty-five Poems* (1936) and *The *Map of Love* (1939). This prolonged mining of early material accounts for the intensity of the sexually assertive themes and the atmosphere of adolescence now so much associated with Dylan Thomas's work. The originality of these early poems, on the other hand, lay in their conflation of the processes of the human body with those of the natural world. Drawing on the notebooks for so long was also made necessary because of the slowness with which the complicated structural forms of his verse allowed new work to be written. Some striking single poems published in London periodicals in 1933 and 1934 led to his first volume, to his first move to London in November 1934, and to invitations to review books for leading periodicals such as *New Verse* and *The Adelphi*. The pattern whereby literary-social life in London alternated with more creative periods in Wales was to continue throughout his career. The liveliness of the young poet's personality and literary interests as they must have struck Swansea and London society in the 1930s is reflected in the earlier part of his *Selected Letters* (1966) and in *Letters to Vernon Watkins* (1957).

In 1937 Dylan Thomas married Caitlin Macnamara and, in May of the following year, moved for the first time to live in Laugharne, Carms., the village now most closely identified with his name and a profound influence on the atmosphere of his last poems. Even in 1938 and the following year his childhood and holiday memories of the Carmarthenshire countryside were added to the urban and suburban experience of Swansea in the autobiographical short stories published as ★*Portrait of the Artist as a Young Dog* (1940). Their comic realism marked a decisive shift away from the dark, surrealistic imaginings of his earlier short stories, collected posthumously in *A Prospect of the Sea* (1955) and in *Dylan Thomas: Early Prose Writings* (ed. Walford Davies, 1971). About 1938 some of the new poems, too, expressed the need to break out from their private, verbally autonomous world.

The writing of poetry was interrupted during the period of the Second World War, when Dylan Thomas started to write radio scripts and to take part in broadcast talks and readings for the BBC. He remained a popular, prolific and professionally effective broadcaster to the end of his life; some of his best work for this medium is found in the volume *Quite Early One Morning* (1954). As an impressive reader of his own and of other poets' work, he was to be a significant influence on the growth in popularity of live and recorded readings of poetry. From 1942 to the end of the War he was also employed as a scriptwriter for Strand Films in London; *The Doctor and the Devils* (1953) is probably the best example of several scripts and scenarios later published in book form.

Towards the end of the War, Wales again became his principal home: at Llan-gain, Carms., and New Quay, Cards., in 1944–45, a new period of poetic creativity started, the most productive since the early notebooks, which made possible his fourth volume of poetry, ★*Deaths and Entrances* (1946). Work for films and radio, however, once again made proximity to London necessary and between 1946 and 1949 the poet lived in or near Oxford. It was in May 1949 that he moved to live in the Boat House at Laugharne, now a Dylan Thomas museum. By this time the father of three children, he planned to make Laugharne his permanent home. His growing reputation in the USA made lecturing

visits to that country appear a new and profitable source of income. An American tour (Feb.–June 1950) was followed by three more in 1952 and 1953. Most of his attention from 1950 onwards was given to the 'play for voices', ★*Under Milk Wood* (1954), which drew on his experience of New Quay as well as of Laugharne. But new poems were also written in this last creative phase, poems of place celebrating emblems of life and death in the landscapes and seascapes of Laugharne. Although he did not complete a plan to link some of these poems in a composite structure to be called 'In Country Heaven', they made possible his last individual volume of poems, published during his second American tour, and in America only, as *In Country Sleep* (1952). This book was added to his four earlier volumes of poetry to make up the *Collected Poems 1934–1952* (1952), for which Dylan Thomas was awarded Foyle's Poetry Prize. But heavy drinking and his irresponsibility in financial matters also brought their problems. He died in New York, after a bout of excessive drinking, on 9 November 1953. His body was brought back for burial in the churchyard at Laugharne. A memorial stone in his honour was placed in Poets' Corner at Westminster Abbey in 1982.

The standing of Dylan Thomas as one of the most important and challenging of twentieth-century poets in English is assured. The meticulous craftsmanship of his work shows a delight in firmly achieved structures and an unembarrassed belief in the emotional power of the musical resources of language. A reaction against that emotional power was provoked to some degree by the ballyhoo which marked his premature death and the subsequent growth of legends concerning his bohemian way of life, but some critical reservations had been made about his writing even before then. The generation of poets who either survived or succeeded him felt that they needed to escape from the kind of verbal archness which, whether or not it derived from his direct influence, tended to be concomitant with his powerful reputation. The English poets who came to prominence in the 1950s and 1960s reacted by turning to the more sober strategies of restrained diction, irony and understatement, and to less obviously 'poetic' themes. But Dylan Thomas himself already represented one side of a similar split between intellect and emotion. In the work of his two great predecessors, namely W. B. Yeats and T. S. Eliot, these qualities had been more comprehensively unified. The Yeatsian ideal of 'blood, imagination, intellect, running together' had diverged during the 1930s into W. H. Auden's emphasis on ideas and beliefs and, on the other hand, into Thomas's emphasis on more instinctive, elemental themes. Certainly, part of the Welshman's significance is the uncompromising way in which he stood out against the intellectualization of poetry and any thinning of its textural and musical delights. In terms more specifically of Anglo-Welsh writing, a particular power in his poetry derives from the unresolved tensions which come from living imaginatively on the blurred edge between two cultures. Although English was his only language, the different linguistic instincts of Wales, no less than its society and topography, run deep in his poetry, where the Welshness of his materials is less self-consciously capitalized upon than in his prose. But with respect to the prose and poetry alike, renewed interest in the regional forces shaping British literature in English continues to enrich their appeal.

The bibliography of works relating to Dylan Thomas is by now enormous. A full list to the year of publication is to be found in R. N. Maud, *Dylan Thomas in Print* (1972). Biographies of the writer have been published by J. M. Brinnin (1955), John Ackerman Jones (1964, 1979), Constantine FitzGibbon (1965) and Paul Ferris (1977); FitzGibbon also edited his selected letters (1966) and Ferris his *Collected Letters* (1985). Among critical studies the most perceptive are E. W. Tedlock, *Dylan Thomas: The Legend of the Poet* (1960), T. H. Jones, *Dylan Thomas* (1963), R. N. Maud, *Entrances to Dylan Thomas's Poetry* (1963) and Aneirin Talfan Davies, *Dylan: Druid of the Broken Body* (1964). There is an essay on Dylan Thomas in the *Writers of Wales* series by Walford Davies (1972) who has also edited *Dylan Thomas: New Critical Essays* (1972). The collected stories of Dylan Thomas were published under the editorship of Leslie Norris in 1983.

THOMAS, EBENEZER (Eben Fardd; 1802–63), poet and critic, was born in the parish of Llanarmon, Caerns., a weaver's son. Owing to the family's poverty and his mother's death in 1821, he was deprived of an education, took to a wanton, drunken life and, on his own testimony, lost his religious faith. Eventually, however, he settled at Clynnog Fawr, Caerns., and there he was to spend the rest of his life, initially as a schoolmaster and later as a grocer. In 1839 he rejoined the Calvinistic Methodists and his school became a preparatory school for the training of candidates for the ministry. His last years were unhappy, his wife, son and two of his daughters dying before him.

Eben Fardd, who chose to be known as Cybi o Eifion in his youth, learned the art of prosody from the poets of *Eifionydd, his native district. Siôn Wyn o Eifion (John *Thomas) was an early friend and Dewi Wyn o Eifion (David *Owen) his first bardic teacher. The young poet came to prominence by winning the *Chair at the Powys Eisteddfod of 1824 for his *awdl*, *'Dinystr Jerusalem'*, an epic poem in the style of *'Cywydd y Farn Fawr'* by Goronwy *Owen. He won two other Chairs, at Liverpool in 1840 for 'Cystudd, Amynedd ac Adferiad Job', and at Llangollen in 1858 for 'Brwydr Maes Bosworth'; it was upon the former occasion that he assumed the bardic name with which he was to become famous. His most bitter disappointment was in not winning

the Chair at Rhuddlan in 1850 for his epic, *'Yr Atgyfodiad'*, and he failed again at Caernarfon in 1862 with 'Y Flwyddyn'.

The work of Eben Fardd does not represent merely the demise of the Classical movement, as is sometimes claimed. Although they did not always win him prizes at eisteddfodau, his poems heralded the golden age of the *epic in Welsh and are the highest achievements of the Romantic literature of this period. In his last *awdl*, 'Y Flwyddyn', and in some of his short poems and hymns, there is an authentic emotional note which had for long been absent from Welsh poetry. As a critic, Eben Fardd improved the standard of literary criticism at the Eisteddfod beyond the formal and trivial by welcoming imagination and invention and by emphasizing that a poem's form should be decided by a consideration of what the poet had to say.

An unsatisfactory volume of Eben Fardd's works appeared under the title *Gweithiau Barddonol* (c.1873). For more authoritative accounts of his work see *Detholion o Ddyddiadur Eben Fardd* (ed. E. G. Millward, 1968) and articles by E. G. Millward in *Llên Cymru* (vols. III, 1954–55; IV, 1956–57; V, 1958–59) and by W. J. Gruffydd in *Y Llenor* (vol. V, 1926).

THOMAS, EDWARD (1878–1917), poet and prose-writer, was born at Lambeth in London. His father was a civil servant from Tredegar, Mon., who had roots farther west, and his mother, less Welsh in blood, was brought up in Newport, Mon. Edward, whose childhood was spent in various London suburbs, was educated at St. Paul's School and Lincoln College, Oxford, where he read History under Owen M. *Edwards. His connection with Wales, however, seems to have been stimulated less by this than by holiday visits to his father's relatives in the Hendy-Pontarddulais region of Carmarthenshire, which he continued into maturity, making of Gwili (John Gwili *Jenkins) a particular friend. Unquestionably, Thomas as a full-time writer, which he became from the moment of his leaving university, was the celebrator of that 'South Country' of England (in the phrase he took from Belloc), the Kent and Hampshire in which he lived, together with the Wiltshire of his mentor Richard Jefferies and the Sussex, Surrey, Berkshire and eastern Somerset in which he walked incessantly and alone. The especial burden of his many works of rural observation —such as *The Heart of England* (1906) and *The Icknield Way* (1913)—like that of the poetry which began to flow from him in 1914 after his meeting with Robert Frost the year previous, was a melancholy and regret at the disappearance of the old rural way of life which Thomas Hardy before him had clung to and celebrated.

His relationship with Wales, however, is more difficult to interpret. *Beautiful Wales*, which he wrote in 1905, misses the opportunity to describe and understand the semi-rural mining communities to which he had social entry.

Instead, while hating 'ostentation, snobbery, hypocrisy, affectation and sentimentality'—the words of his wife Helen in her introduction to *The South Country* (1909)—he involves himself in contradictions: while hard on Ossianic Kensington-based Celt-lovers, he nevertheless evades the impact of a true Welsh-speaking community, sentimentalizes Wales by approaching it through Arthurian romance and makes vaguely patriotic statements whose application is never revealed. *Beautiful Wales* is an oddly unsatisfactory book, frequently over-written, empty of named persons and real places and memorable only for the witty negativity of its opening and a very few 'portraits', the later of which become versions of the mind of Edward Thomas. The cloying nature of much of the writing and the inability to go far beyond personal experience also affect *The Happy-Go-Lucky Morgans* (1913), a novel of suburban life with Welsh overtones. In a letter of 1900 he made the claim that in Wales, 'I always feel, in the profoundest sense, at home', and his poem 'Words' recognizes the contribution of 'some sweetness / From Wales' to the music of his medium. But his prose writing rarely convinces the reader of this feeling: descriptions of landscape in *Beautiful Wales*, for instance, more than occasionally contain regrets for 'the South Country'. When he is pressed to the positive the model that emerges is usually the peace and the nucleation of the English village.

On the other hand, the 'Englishness' for which Thomas's poetry is renowned has been enriched by his Welsh perspective. Calling himself Welsh, he had that sense of being an outsider in his favoured landscape, a spirit endlessly searching for something that he could call 'home'. He declared that he had forgotten all the history he learned or that it was present in him 'in a form which defies evocation and analysis': he preferred a country church to a cathedral and 'Sumer is icumen' in' to Beethoven: always his instinct was for the residual, for man in landscape and for the landscape which has responded to man. Of his beloved 'South Country' he wrote, 'The people are not hospitable, but the land is'. Undoubtedly it was at the level of the residual that he approached Wales too. He was deeply interested in folk-songs and folk-tales. His wife Helen, inclined perhaps to make of him the family man that he rarely was, writes of him sitting 'with a child on each knee, reading aloud Chaucer, or singing some of his native Welsh songs till bedtime came', and in *Beautiful Wales* he included a number of Carmarthenshire folksongs, or poems by Watcyn Wyn (Watkin Hezekiah *Williams), which he probably Englished himself. In its pages, too, he acknowledges that he was amongst the few in the inn who drove out the English-speakers who would not listen to the harper as he played his old Welsh airs.

Edward Thomas's attitude to Wales and the emphases with which he wrote of it are, of course, no measure of his stature as a writer, least of all of his achievement as a poet. When his poems appeared under the pseudonym of Edward Eastaway in 1917, some months after his death at Arras, it could be seen that he had cleared away most of the poeticisms and all the over-writing: instead, his poems were marked by a sustained attempt to use the rhythms of common speech, occasionally with a close dialectic and sometimes by the repeated use of a small clique of words. Experimental, many of them, they carried a high risk of failure. That a method of this sort could support the melancholic passion of his material is perhaps the chief reason why, of all the poets of the Georgian era, Edward Thomas has been the one whose posthumous influence has been the most evident, especially upon the poets of 'The Movement' and scarcely less so to this day. His faith that the language of poetry could be 'worn new' has been amply justified. F. R. Leavis rightly said of him that he had a 'distinctively modern sensibility'.

Edward Thomas's *Collected Poems* have been printed in a number of editions and impressions since 1920. *Poems* (1917) and *Last Poems* (1918) were combined in the 1920 edition, together with one additional poem. An annotated text of *Poems* and *Last Poems* is available (ed. Edna Longley, 1973). Several further poems were added to the *Collected Poems* up to R. George Thomas's definitive and scholarly edition (1978). Biographical and critical studies include: John Moore, *The Life and Letters of Edward Thomas* (1939), H. Coombes, *Edward Thomas* (1956), Eleanor Farjeon, *Edward Thomas: The Last Four Years* (1958) and William Cooke, *Edward Thomas: A Critical Biography* (1970). R. George Thomas has contributed a monograph on the poet to the *Writers of Wales* series (1972) and he is the author of the biography *Edward Thomas: A Portrait* (1985). The two books by the poet's widow, Helen Thomas, *As it Was* (1926) and *World Without End* (1931), contain much detail about his life after their marriage.

THOMAS, EDWARD MORLEY, commonly known as **NED THOMAS** (1936–), critic and editor. Born at Little Lever, Lancs., of Welsh parents, he spent his boyhood in various places in England, Germany, Switzerland and mid-Wales and was educated at New College, Oxford. He worked as a journalist with Times Newspapers, as the editor of *Angliya*, the British Government's Russian-language magazine, and as a lecturer at the Universities of Moscow and Salamanca before his return to Wales in 1969. Appointed to a Lectureship in the English Department at the University College of Wales, Aberystwyth, in 1970, he inaugurated an English-medium course in the literature of twentieth-century Wales and a Welsh-medium course in the literature of the Third World. He has published two volumes of criticism, *George Orwell* (1965) and *The Welsh Extremist* (1971). The latter, a political and literary study of contemporary Wales, with special reference to

Welsh and Anglo-Welsh writers, broadcasting and the status of the Welsh language, was an influential work which did much to popularize a left-wing view of Welsh *Nationalism, particularly as manifested in the campaigns of *Cymdeithas yr Iaith Gymraeg. His interest in cultural minorities was reflected in *Planet, the magazine which he founded in 1970. Ned Thomas is also the author of Poet of the Islands (1980), a study of the Caribbean writer Derek Walcott, the winner of the *Welsh Arts Council's International Writer's Prize in 1980, and also of a monograph on Waldo *Williams in the series Llên y Llenor (1985).

Thomas, E. H. Francis, see LLOYD, DAVID TECWYN (1914–).

THOMAS, ERNEST LEWIS (Richard Vaughan; 1904–83), novelist. Born at Llanddeusant, Carms., and educated at West Monmouth School, Pontypool, he worked as a bank clerk in Merthyr Tydfil and London from 1921 to 1932 but then found employment as a free-lance journalist in the metropolis. After the Second World War, in which he served for four years, he trained as a teacher and later taught English and Religious Studies in schools in London. He retired in 1961 and returned to Wales, living on a small farm at Talyllychau, Carms., until his wife's death in 1978, after which he went to live in a nursing home in Bristol, where he died.

His first novel, *Moulded in Earth (1951), had an immediate success among English critics, including C. P. Snow, and was translated into several languages. It was followed by two more in what came to be known as the Black Mountain trilogy, namely Who Rideth So Wild (1952) and Son of Justin (1955). He also wrote All Through the Night (1957), the autobiographical There is a River (1961), a play entitled Dewin y Daran (1974) and All the Moon Long (1974), the last-named being his least successful work. His novels are set in the farming communities on the border between Carmarthenshire and Breconshire during the latter part of the nineteenth century and the first decades of the twentieth. Their principal characters have passionate natures and are involved in turbulent events which are described in an unforced, lyrical style which sometimes achieves moments of great beauty.

There is a monograph on Richard Vaughan by Tony Bianchi in the Writers of Wales series (1984).

THOMAS, FRANCES (1943–), writer of books for children. Born at Aberdare, Glam., she was educated at Queen Mary's College, University of London. She won the Tir na nOg Prize (see under CHILDREN'S LITERATURE) with her first novel, The Blindfold Track (1980); like its sequel, A Knot of Spells (1983), it deals with the story of *Taliesin in the context of post-Roman Britain. Among her other books are Secrets (1982), Dear Comrade (1983) and Zak (1984).

Thomas, Frederick Hall (Freddie Welsh; 1886–1927), boxer. Born at Pontypridd, Glam., he became the first winner of the Lonsdale Belt in 1909 and, five years later, the lightweight champion of the world.

THOMAS, GEORGE (c.1791–c.1872), poet. Born at Newtown, Mont., he ran a corngrinding business in Welshpool but, in 1826, settled in Llandysil, in the same county, as a schoolmaster. He wrote mock-heroic and satirical verse dealing mainly with local events, as well as epitaphs and epigrams. His publications include the books The Otter Hunt and the Death of Roman (1817), The Welsh Flannel (n.d.), History of the Chartists and the Bloodless Wars of Montgomeryshire (1840), The Death of Rowton (n.d.) and The Extinction of the Mormons (n.d.).

THOMAS, GRAHAM (1944–), poet, was born at Abertillery, Mon., and educated at the University College of Wales, Aberystwyth. He is a chemistry teacher at Nantyglo in his native county. Many of the poems in his first collection, The One Place (1983), take a sympathetic but unsentimental view of social decay in the valleys of south Wales.

THOMAS, GWYN (1913–81), novelist, shortstory writer and playwright. Born at Porth in the *Rhondda Valley, Glam., the youngest of the twelve children of an often unemployed miner, he won a scholarship to St. Edmund Hall, Oxford, to read Modern Languages. After working in adult education in England and Wales from 1940 to 1942, he taught French at Cardigan Grammar School for two years and subsequently Spanish at Barry Grammar School, Glam., but abandoned teaching in 1962 to become a full-time writer.

He was the author of nine novels: The Dark Philosophers (1946), The *Alone to the Alone (1947), *All Things Betray Thee (1949), The World Cannot Hear You (1951), Now Lead Us Home (1952), A Frost on my Frolic (1953), The Stranger at my Side (1954), A Point of Order (1956) and The Love Man (1958). His collections of short stories are Where did I put my Pity? (1946), Gazooka (1957), Ring Delirium 123 (1960) and The Lust Lobby (1971); a volume of his selected stories appeared in 1984. He also wrote six stage-plays, a great many talks, plays and features for radio and television, two volumes of essays, namely A Welsh Eye (1964) and A Hatful of Humours (1965), and an autobiography, A Few Selected Exits (1968).

Much of his work deals with working-class life in the mining valleys of Glamorgan in the first half of the twentieth century. His material is often fundamentally grim but he treats it with wit, eloquence and a humour which can at times become farcical. He identified closely with the community he described, with the aspirations, the suffering and even the absurdities of his characters, and his compassion saves his writing from the charge of buffoonery. His novels are usually narrated in the first person singular and the narrator is frequently one of a small group of friends, unemployed young men living in one of the poverty-stricken areas which the author calls Meadow Prospect or Mynydd Coch. Articulate, funny and well-meaning, they are likely to become involved in the schemes of rich, powerful or upper-class characters such as August Slezacher the arms dealer, Shadrach Sims the business tycoon or Sylvester Strang the idealistic landowner. Plot is usually of less importance than the array of characters, the hilarious episodes and the verbal wit. All who appear in the novels—be they ordinary people (Gwyn Thomas's 'elements' or 'voters'), or Spanish grandees, or Welsh schoolboys, or American millionaires, or nineteenth century turnkeys— all tend to express themselves in a characteristically colourful idiom, used by Thomas for dialogue and narration alike. It has been suggested that this style owes something to modern American humorists like Perelman and Damon Runyon, whose work he admired.

In the 1950s Gwyn Thomas began to turn his attention to writing for the theatre. His stage plays are *The Keep* (1962), *Jackie the Jumper* (1963), *The Loot* (1965), *Loud Organs* (first performed in 1962), *Sap* (first performed in 1974) and *The Breakers* (first performed in 1976); the last three remain unpublished. *The Keep*, perhaps his most popular play, deals naturalistically with the various conflicts arising in a family of five sons in the south Wales of the 1950s. *Jackie the Jumper* takes as its theme the *Merthyr Rising of 1831, which he had already treated in one of his most successful novels, *All Things Betray Thee*. Later, in such plays as *Sap*, he moved in the direction of greater technical flexibility and used lighting and cutting from one part of the stage to another to indicate changes of time and location. But his ability to use vivid, rich and witty language remained undiminished in whatever medium he chose to express his response to the suffering and absurdity he saw in the life around him.

There is an autobiographical essay by Gwyn Thomas in the volume *Artists in Wales* (ed. Meic Stephens, 1971) and a monograph on the writer's work by Ian Michael in the *Writers of Wales* series (1977); for critical discussion see the article, 'Absurdity in the Novels of Gwyn Thomas' by Roger Stephens Jones in *The Anglo-Welsh Review* (vol. 25, no. 56, 1976) and the lecture by Glyn Jones, *Random Entrances to Gwyn Thomas* (1982); see also the article by Belinda Humfrey in *Dictionary of Literary Biography: British Novelists, 1930–1959* (1983).

THOMAS, GWYN (1936–), poet and scholar, was born at Tanygrisiau and brought up at Blaenau Ffestiniog, Mer. Educated at the University College of North Wales, Bangor, and Jesus College, Oxford, he was appointed Lecturer in the Welsh Department at Bangor in 1961 and was given a personal Chair in 1980.

His most important scholarly work is the major study of Ellis *Wynne, *Y Bardd Cwsg a'i Gefndir* (1971), but he has also shown an interest in the historical background to Welsh literature, as in his monograph on the *Caerwys Eisteddfodau* (1968). He has also been concerned to make the Welsh poetic tradition more easily available to the modern reader and *Yr Aelwyd Hon* (1970), a selection of the earliest Welsh poetry, *Y Traddodiad Barddol* (1976) and *Gruffydd ab yr Ynad Coch* (1982), all pursue this aim, while his *Ymarfer Ysgrifennu* (1977) is a valuable guide to the craft of writing. In co-editing the volume *Presenting Saunders Lewis* (1973) he shows a concern for presenting contemporary writers to a wider readership and as editor of the series *Dramau'r Byd* (which includes his own translation of Beckett's *Fin de Partie*) he has contributed substantially to an understanding of the European dramatic tradition. He has also translated, with Kevin Crossley-Holland, *The Mabinogion* (1984) in an edition for children.

The concern for communication and contemporaneity which informs so much of his scholarly work is central to Gwyn Thomas's own creative activity. Although primarily a poet, he has shown a lively interest in all the media of creative communication. He has published two stage plays, *Lliw'r Delyn* (1969) and *Amser Dyn* (1972), and written dramatic poems for television and radio, including his long poem for radio, 'Blaenau', and the radio satire on commercial advertising, *Cysgodion*. But perhaps his most effective venture into this field was *Cadwynau yn y Meddwl* (1976), a tribute to Martin Luther King which was written specifically for television and conceived as an amalgam of words and visual images.

Gwyn Thomas's first volume of poetry was *Chwerwder yn y Ffynhonnau* (1962). The implications of that title ('Bitterness in the wells') indicated the nature of his critical response to the impersonal forces of modern life. This awareness was even more evident in his second volume, *Y Weledigaeth Haearn* (1965), and in his mature synthesis of scholarship and contemporaneity in the richly crafted poems of his third book, *Ysgyrion Gwaed* (1968). In these early volumes, which represent a gradual development to full maturity, the most telling aspects of his verse are his capacity to harness images from Welsh legend and early Welsh poetry to a truly modern response to the complexities of contemporary life.

In his later poetry, included in the volumes *Enw'r Gair* (1972), *Y Pethau Diwethaf a Phethau Eraill* (1975), *Croesi Traeth* (1978), *Symud y*

Lliwiau (1981) and *Wmgawa* (1984), he has begun to assume a colloquial and sometimes jocular stance which offers a subtle and flexible vehicle for his imaginative powers. It is especially suitable for his numerous studies of the child's idiosyncratic view of life, most brilliantly explored in *Enw'r Gair*. Probably unique among living Welsh poets in his capacity to use the broken constructions and halting, often Anglicized, vocabulary of modern colloquial Welsh, he has also been remarkably successful in making his poetry available to a wide readership. His comment is direct, often earthy and sometimes hilarious, but in his last two volumes his response to life has once more become more contemplative and reflects his own awareness of the passing of the years.

A selection of Gwyn Thomas's poems has been edited and presented by Joseph P. Clancy under the title *Living a Life* (1982). For a critical discussion of the poet's work see the monograph by Alan Llwyd in the series *Llên y Llenor* (1984); see also the author's autobiographical lecture, *Yn Blentyn yn y Blaenau* (1981) and the interview published in *Y Traethodydd* (Autumn, 1984).

Thomas, Idris, see JENKINS, ROBERT THOMAS (1881–1969).

THOMAS, JENNIE (1898–1979), children's author, was born in Birkenhead of Welsh parents and educated at Liverpool University. She taught for many years at Bethesda, Caerns., before her appointment as Language Organizer for the County, a post she held until her retirement. She is remembered as the joint author, with J. O. *Williams, of *Llyfr Mawr y Plant* (1931), a delightful book which contained stories, poems, songs, sketches and games for young readers. Its two main characters, Siôn Blewyn Coch and Wil Cwac Cwac, are as familiar to Welsh children as Mickey Mouse and Donald Duck. Further volumes appeared under the same title in 1939, 1949 and 1975 and the book has kept its appeal for later generations.

There is an article on Jennie Thomas in *Dewiniaid Difyr* (ed. Mairwen and Gwynn Jones, 1983).

THOMAS, JOHN (1730–1804?), hymn-writer. Born in the parish of Myddfai, Carms., he was for two years a manservant to Griffith *Jones of Llanddowror. Howel *Harris arranged for him to have free tuition at Trefeca and he became an itinerant schoolmaster and an exhorter with the Methodists; but in 1767 he was ordained a Congregational minister at Rhayader, Rads. His chief literary work was *Rhad Ras* (1810), an account of his spiritual pilgrimage which has been called 'the first Welsh autobiography'. As well as elegies for Harris and Dafydd *Jones of Caeo, he published his hymns in several volumes under the title *Caniadau Seion* (1759–86) and later as one collection in 1788.

THOMAS, JOHN (Siôn Wyn o Eifion; 1786–1859), poet and hymn-writer, a native of Chwilog, Caerns., was educated at Llanarmon, Caerns., where he was a fellow-pupil of David *Owen (Dewi Wyn o Eifion). Confined to his bed from the age of twelve as the result of a serious illness, he read extensively and enjoyed the friendship of many poets who came to keep him company; the Nanney (*Nannau) family of Gwynfryn and the poet Dafydd Ddu Eryri (David *Thomas) were especially kind to him. He wrote *awdlau* and *pryddestau* for eisteddfodau (but was never a successful competitor), as well as poems in the strict and free metres to greet his friends. The volume entitled *Gwaith Barddonol Siôn Wyn o Eifion* (1861) is a collection of his verse and contains a biography by his nephew, William Jones (Bleddyn).

THOMAS, JOHN (Ieuan Ddu; 1795–1871), musician and poet, was born at Pibwrlwyd, near Carmarthen, and for most of his life was a teacher at Merthyr Tydfil and Treforest, near Pontypridd, Glam. Noted for his bass voice, he trained many other eminent musicians of his day and, a pioneer conductor, led his choir to victory several times in the Eisteddfodau held at Abergavenny in the years between 1838 and 1845. His book, *Y Caniedydd Cymreig* (1845), is a collection of more than a hundred Welsh airs with words in Welsh and English, together with some compositions of his own.

His disillusionment as an adjudicator at eisteddfodau is revealed in *Cambria upon Two Sticks*, the volume of poems he published in 1867. The title-poem rehearses the resilience of the Welsh language, fed by Vicar Prichard (Rhys *Prichard) and a host of others, and reminds the English that they, too, had resisted the Normans in defence of their language. The second long poem in the book, 'The Eisteddfod', is mainly descriptive but castigates the praise-seekers of low standard and the prize-donors who favoured their own friends. The third long poem, 'Harry Vaughan', is of interest mainly for its digressions, intended to praise the author's native county and to demonstrate his lack of reverence for contemporary English poets. Ieuan Ddu, combative if not always clear, was not especially gifted as a versifier, but this book is a valuable statement from a patriotic Welshman of the mid-nineteenth century who felt free to criticize both the patronizing attitude of the English (and their Welsh adherents) and the venal practices found in Welsh institutions.

For further details see the lecture by Roland Mathias in the volume *Dathlu* (ed. R. Gerallt Jones, 1985).

THOMAS, JOHN (1821–92), preacher and writer, was born at Holyhead, Ang., a brother to Owen *Thomas. Brought up a Methodist, he became a Congregational minister at Bwlchnewydd, Carms., at Glyn Neath, Glam., and in Liverpool. A prominent member of his denomination, he was editor in turn of the journals *Y Gwerinwr*, *Yr Annibynwr*, and *Y *Tyst*. He published a volume of essays and sermons in 1864 and a number of biographies and works on the history of Congregationalism (*Independency) in Wales, but he is noted here as the author of a *Temperance novel, *Arthur Llwyd y Felin* (1879).

Thomas, John (**Pencerdd Gwalia**; 1826–1913), harpist. Born at Bridgend, Glam., he studied at the Royal Academy of Music, was appointed harpist to Queen Victoria in 1871 and, in 1882, became a teacher of the *harp at both the Royal College and the Guildhall School of Music in London. He played for many of the royal courts of Europe and composed a great deal of instrumental music, especially for the harp. A collection of his work was published under the title *Welsh Melodies* (4 vols., 1862, 1870, 1874), for which the words were written by Talhaiarn (John *Jones), Mynyddog (Richard *Davies) and John Ceiriog *Hughes.

THOMAS, JOHN (**Eifionydd**; 1848–1922), journalist and editor, was born at Penmorfa, Caerns. As a boy of nine still unable to read, he became an apprentice in the offices of *Y Brython* in Tremadog and learned the printer's craft. He began to preach with the Independents and spent two years as a theological student at Brecon Memorial College, but left to take up journalism. Among the periodicals he edited were *Y *Genedl Gymreig* and *Y *Werin* and he produced two popular anthologies of verse under the title *Pigion Englynion fy Ngwlad* (1881–82); but his most important contribution to Welsh letters was his editorship of *Y *Geninen*, which he founded in 1883 and edited until his death. This magazine is an invaluable source of information about the cultural life of Wales in its period and Eifionydd was one of the most distinguished of editors.

For further details see the article by E. Morgan Humphreys in *Gwŷr Enwog Gynt* (2nd series, 1953).

THOMAS, LESLIE (1931–), novelist. He was born in Newport, Mon., but spent much of his adolescence after the age of twelve at a Dr. Barnardo's Home in Kingston, Surrey, a phase of his life which he described in his autobiographical work, *This Time Next Week* (1964). His novel *Virgin Soldiers* (1966), based on the experience of national servicemen in Malaya, was followed by *Onward Virgin Soldiers* (1971), *Stand Up Virgin Soldiers* (1975), *Dangerous Davies* (1976), *The Magic Army* (1982) and others in the same mode, all of which are characterized by a vivid prose style and authentic dialogue. He has continued his autobiography with the publication of the volume *In my Wildest Dreams* (1984).

Thomas, Llywelyn (**Llywelyn Fawr o Fawddwy**; d. 1807), a man famous for his great physical strength, lived at Ty'n Llwyn, Llanymawddwy, Mer. Tales are still told of his feats and he is remembered in the well-known rhyme which begins, '*Llywelyn Fawr o Fawddwy a aeth i foddi cath*' ('Big Llywelyn of Fawddwy who went to drown a cat'). It should be noted, however, that this rhyme is also associated with other folk-heroes such as the Red Cobbler of Rhuddlan and Jenkin John of Hengoed.

Thomas, Lucy (1781–1847), 'the mother of the Welsh coal trade'. She is remembered for having opened in 1828 at Waunwyllt, Abercanaid, near Merthyr Tydfil, Glam., the first level for the mining of coal for household, rather than smelting, purposes.

THOMAS, NED, see THOMAS, EDWARD MORLEY (1936–).

THOMAS, OLIVER (*c.*1598–1652), Puritan clergyman and author, was a Montgomeryshire man who settled at West Felton, near Oswestry, Salop. In 1650 he was appointed an Approver under the Act for the *Propagation of the Gospel in Wales and was given the living of Llanrhaeadr-ym-Mochnant, Denbs. Like other Puritans of his day, he played a part in providing a number of religious books in the Welsh language, including the catechism, *Car-wr y Cymru yn anfon ychydig gymmorth i bôb Tad a mam sy'n ewyllysio bod eu plant yn blant i Dduw hefyd* (1630), *Car-wr y Cymru yn annog ei genedl anwyl . . . i chwilio yr Scrythyrau* (1631), *Sail Crefydd Ghristnogol* (*c.*1640), of which Evan Roberts of Llanbadarn was co-author, and *Drych i Dri Math o Bobl* (*c.*1647).

For further details see the edition of *Car-wr y Cymru* prepared by John Ballinger (1930); see also Merfyn Morgan (ed.), *Gweithiau Oliver Thomas ac Evan Roberts* (1981).

Thomas, Ormond, see ORMOND, JOHN (1923–).

THOMAS, OWEN (1812–91), biographer. Born at Holyhead, Ang., a brother of John *Thomas (1821–92), he worked as a stonemason until he began preaching with the Calvinistic Methodists in 1834. Educated at Bala Theological College and the University of Edinburgh, he became one of the most powerful and erudite preachers of his day. Lewis *Edwards depended on him during the early years of *Y *Traethodydd*, both as contributor and co-editor. His greatest literary work, an account of the life of John *Jones of Tal-y-sarn (1874), was a milestone in the history of *biography in Welsh. It not only describes its subject's career, but includes two long chapters on theological controversies during the period from 1701 to 1841 and a study of Calvinistic Methodist preaching and preachers. Owen Thomas also published a memoir of Henry *Rees (1890).

J. J. Roberts (Iolo Carnarvon) wrote Owen Thomas's biography (1912), but the study by D. Ben Rees, *Pregethwr y Bobl* (1979), is more satisfactory.

Thomas, Richard (1838–1916), industrialist, was born at Bridgwater, Som., but entered the tin plate trade at Margam, Glam., as a young man. By 1863 he was already clerk in charge of the building of the Melincryddan works near Neath and in 1865 he began his career as an employer by borrowing the capital necessary to buy the Lydbrook tin plate works and colliery. In 1884 he formed the private company of Richard Thomas and Sons and thereafter made a steady series of acquisitions: the Melingriffith iron and tin plate works near Cardiff (1888), and works at Aberdare (1890), Abercarn (1895), Cwmfelin (1896), Llanelli and Burry Port (1898), Cwmbwrla (1898) and elsewhere. In 1918 Thomas's sons re-formed the private company as a public one which bought the steelworks at Ebbw Vale, Mon., in 1935. When, in 1945, the firm merged with another large combine, Baldwin's, they controlled between them some two-thirds of the five hundred pack-mills in south Wales. In 1947 the giant Steel Company of Wales was formed (as a result of a merger between Richard Thomas and Baldwin, Guest Keen and others) and a period of prosperity followed for the electrolytic tinning lines at Ebbw Vale. Towards the end of the same buoyant period, in 1962, a new strip-mill, the third largest in Wales, was opened. But the gradual fall in demand for steel and tin plate, unchecked by the nationalization of the industry in 1951, its de-nationalization in 1953 and its re-nationalization in 1965, brought about the closure of the Ebbw Vale works in 1976. Llanwern, with a much reduced labour force, survives so far.

THOMAS, RICHARD JAMES (1908–76), lexicographer, was born in Cardiff and educated at the University College in that city. In 1937 he joined the staff of *Geiriadur Prifysgol Cymru* (The University of Wales Dictionary) as reader and, in 1947, was appointed its first editor, a post he held until his retirement in 1975. His main interest outside the field of lexicography was the study of Welsh place-names, as demonstrated in his book *Enwau Afonydd a Nentydd Cymru* (1938), which remains the standard work on the names of rivers and streams in Wales. It was R. J. Thomas who, in 1960, purchased Yr Hen Gapel, Tre'r-ddol, Cards., and adapted it as a Methodist and local museum.

THOMAS, ROBERT (**Ap Vychan**; 1809–80), theologian and writer, was born at Llanuwchllyn, Mer. Having learned the rules of *Cerdd Dafod* from his father, he was made a member of the local *Cymreigyddion Society when he was only fourteen years old. Apprenticed to a local blacksmith, he afterwards moved about the country, plying his trade in various places, until in 1830 a longer stay in Oswestry made him acquainted with the English language and the theological writing available in it. In 1835 he was ordained a Congregational minister. Of a genial disposition and a popular preacher, he was appointed Professor of Divinity at Bala Independent College in 1873. He was co-editor of the magazine *Y Dysgedydd* for fifteen years, wrote a biography of his father (1863) and another of Cadwaladr Jones of Dolgellau; he also won the *Chair at the National Eisteddfod in 1864 and 1866. His autobiography, edited by W. Lliedi Williams in the series *Llyfrau Deunaw (1948), is important for an understanding of the suffering caused by landlordism in Wales during the nineteenth century.

A selection of Ap Vychan's theological essays was edited by Michael D. Jones and D. V. Thomas, and an anthology of his work was included by O. M. Edwards in the series *Cyfres y Fil* (1903).

THOMAS, RONALD STUART (1913–), poet. He was born in Cardiff but his father served in the Merchant Navy and the family moved from place to place before settling at Holyhead, Ang., in 1918. Educated at the University College of North Wales, Bangor, where he read Classics, he received his theological training at St. Michael's College, Llandaf, Cardiff. After ordination in 1936 he held two curacies in the Marches, at Chirk, Denbs. (1936–40), where he met and married the painter Mildred E. Eldridge, and at Hanmer, Flints. (1940–42). He became rector of Manafon, Mont., in 1942, and it was at this time that he began seriously to learn the Welsh language. At Manafon he wrote nearly all the poems which were published in his first three volumes, *The *Stones of the Field* (1946), *An *Acre of Land* (1952) and *The *Minister* (1955), and later collected in *Song at the Year's Turning* (1955). Some of these early poems, such as 'Out of the Hills', 'A Labourer', 'A Peasant', 'The Welsh Hill Country' and 'Cynddylan on a Tractor', show a developed philosophy of nature and a concern with the geography and history, as with the farmers and farm-labourers, of the hill-country. As an epitome of these people he created the character of the peasant Iago Prytherch, who appears in about twenty poems written during the period from 1946 to 1970, developing into a complex *persona* for the poet, as spokesman, opponent, friend and even *alter ego*.

R. S. Thomas was alienated from much of Welsh country life by his status as a priest in the Church in Wales. He felt the exclusion keenly, saying once that an Anglicized upbringing like his 'prevents one from ever feeling a hundred per cent at home in Welsh Wales'. Partly to draw closer to Welsh-speaking Wales, he moved in 1954 to become vicar of Eglwys-fach, Cards., and stayed there until 1967, although English settlers proved to be more numerous than natives among his parishioners. To this period belong four volumes of poems, namely *Poetry for Supper* (1958), *Tares* (1961), *The Bread of Truth* (1965) and *Pietà* (1966). The debate with Iago Prytherch continues, but there are new characters such as Walter Llywarch, Job Davies and Rhodri Theophilus Owen. Two particular themes stand out: a deepening concern with the nature of God, in such poems as 'The Journey' and 'Dialectic', and an increasingly powerful Welsh *Nationalism. The volume *Tares* contains many patriotic poems, but the most fiercely nationalistic are in *The Bread of Truth*, especially the final poem, 'Looking at Sheep'. *Pietà*, however, moderates the patriotic ferocity and is characterized by the austere religious exploration typified by the title-poem with its startling image of the empty cross. This is the new direction in R. S. Thomas's work, which grows increasingly religious but less and less orthodox.

When he became vicar of Aberdaron, Caerns., in 1967, he at last found himself in a community whose primary language was Welsh. But apart from a grimly light-hearted little volume, *What is a Welshman?* (1974), he has written virtually nothing further about Wales. His poetry is essentially a poetry of search and once he had found the Wales he had been seeking he did not need to write about it. The volume *Not that He Brought Flowers* (1968) is transitional, including both satires such as 'Welcome to Wales' and intense meditations like 'The Priest', in which he at last makes peace with his vocation; but the key image comes in 'Kneeling', where the poet kneels before an altar, 'waiting for the God / To speak'. This poem is prophetic of the line of development in *H'm* (1972), *Laboratories of the Spirit* (1975), *The Way of It* (1977) and *Frequencies* (1978). The waiting, the search for the *deus absconditus*, is typified by the poem 'Via Negativa' which refers to God as 'that great absence / In our lives'. In *Frequencies* he approaches the limits of Christian orthodoxy and the imagery of all these later volumes is scientific and technological. Having retired from the priesthood of the Church in Wales at Easter 1978, R. S. Thomas went to live at Y Rhiw, near Aberdaron. The first volume of his retirement, *Between Here and Now* (1981), is like none of his previous collections in that half the poems are meditations on Impressionist paintings in the Louvre; many of the others continue to ask the question, 'How far is it to God?'. A second volume of poems exploring the relationship between painting and poetry appeared in 1985 under the title *Ingrowing Thoughts*.

The occasional prose writings of R. S. Thomas include reviews and articles in periodicals such as *Wales, Dock Leaves* (The *Anglo-Welsh Review*) *Y *Fflam* and *Baner ac Amserau Cymru*, and more formal meditations on the writer's art in *Words and the Poet* (The W. D. Thomas Memorial Lecture, 1964), *Abercuawg* (The Annual Literary Lecture of the National Eisteddfod, 1976) and *The Creative Writer's Suicide*, a lecture delivered at the University College of Wales, Aberystwyth, which was published in Welsh in *Taliesin*, (Dec., 1977) and in English in *Planet* (Jan., 1978). He has also edited *The Batsford Book of Country Verse* (1961), *The Penguin Book of Religious Verse* (1963), *Edward Thomas: Selected Poems* (1964), *A Choice of George Herbert's Verse* (1967) and *A Choice of Wordsworth's Verse* (1971). The introductions to these anthologies are important for an understanding of his own poetic development. A selection of his prose writings (including some translated from the Welsh) has been edited by Sandra Anstey (1983).

The reputation now accorded to R. S. Thomas, both in Wales and England, counterbalances that of Dylan *Thomas in the 1950s and 1960s, replacing it with an intellectual rigour absent from those earlier decades. Much of his later poetry embodies the quest for God, the God of the interstices—a quest which is circular, the tale that of 'a traveller . . . who has arrived / after long journeying where he / began' and of bafflements arranged by the enemy Time. The philosophical and scientific concepts in terms of which the quest is described mark this poetry as essentially modern.

For critical discussions of R. S. Thomas's poetry see the essay by R. George Thomas in the *Writers and their Work* series (1964), the special number of *Poetry Wales* (Spring, 1972), the essay by W. Moelwyn Merchant in the *Writers of Wales* series (1979), the volume *Critical Writing on R. S. Thomas* (ed. Sandra Anstey, 1982), A. E. Dyson, *Yeats, Eliot and R. S. Thomas* (1981) and the chapter by C. B. Cox on R. S. Thomas and Dylan Thomas in *The New Pelican Guide to English Literature* (vol. 8, 1983).

Thomas, Sidney Gilchrist (1850–85), inventor. Born in London of Cardiganshire parents, he was first employed as a teacher and then, for many years, as clerk to police courts in the City. Between 1870 and 1878 he devoted his energies to the search for a method of de-phosphorizing the pig-iron used in the manufacture of steel, a process the secret of which had for long eluded Sir Henry Bessemer. Thomas eventually succeeded in his experiments, assisted by his cousin Percy Gilchrist, a chemist at an ironworks in Blaenavon, Mon. The discovery resulted in a great increase in steel production in Britain and abroad. From the patent, and from the production of basic slag which could be used as a soil fertilizer, Thomas became very rich but found that his health had been ruined by his labours. He died and was buried in Paris, leaving his fortune to be used for philanthropic purposes by Lilian Gilchrist Thompson, who published a biography of her brother in 1940.

THOMAS, THOMAS JACOB (**Sarnicol**; 1873–1945), poet, was a native of Capel Cynon, near Llandysul, Cards. Educated at the University College of Wales, Aberystwyth, he later taught in schools at Southampton, Abergele and Abertillery; he was appointed Headmaster of Quakers' Yard Secondary School, near Merthyr Tydfil, in 1922. He won the *Chair at the National Eisteddfod in 1913 with his *awdl*, 'Aelwyd y Cymro', and between 1898 and 1944 he published ten volumes of poetry and prose which were popular because of their local appeal and lively wit. As a writer, Sarnicol's milieu was Banc *Siôn Cwilt and in his observation of its people he moved with ease from the lyrical to the satirical; some of his epigrams are memorable. The best of his work will be found in the volumes *Stori Shaci'r Gwas* (1906), *Odlau Môr a Mynydd* (1912), *Blodau Drain Duon* (1935) and *Ar Fanc Siôn Cwilt* (ed. J. Tysul Jones, 1972).

THOMAS, TREVOR CYRIL (1896–), playwright. Born at Merthyr Tydfil, Glam., he became a teacher in Brecon where he was closely connected with the town's Little Theatre, and particularly for his own company, The Llynsafaddan Players, for which he wrote a number of light comedies. Several deal with the adventures of a signalman, such as *Davy Jones's Dinner* (1955) and *Davy Jones's Locker* (1956), both one-act plays. T. C. Thomas wrote for radio, published short stories and had a general interest in the fostering of amateur *drama in Wales.

Thomas, Watcyn (1906–78), a rugby forward who played for Llanelli, Swansea and Wales. A hard, fearless player, he won fourteen caps between 1927 and 1933 and captained the national team on three occasions, including a famous Welsh victory at Twickenham in the year last mentioned.

THOMAS, WILLIAM (**Islwyn**; 1832–78), poet. Born near Ynysddu, Mon., the youngest of ten children, he was a frail and pampered child who was never to enjoy good health. Well educated at the expense of parents in comfortable circumstances and advanced years, he was intended to become a surveyor, but the course of his life was altered when he was still a young man. Under the influence of Daniel Jenkyns, his minister and brother-in-law, he discovered a profound religious faith and a passionate interest in Welsh poetry. Still more decisive was the sudden death in 1853 of Anne Bowen, a young woman from Swansea to whom he was engaged to be married. It was in response to this tragedy that he wrote two long poems bearing the same title, *Y *Storm*, on which his reputation rests. Soon afterwards he applied for the Calvinistic Methodist ministry and was ordained in 1859, remaining in his native district as a preacher but declining to take charge of a church. In 1864 he

married Martha Davies, also of Swansea, but their childless marriage was haunted by the shadow of Anne Bowen from the very beginning; Anne's mother had meanwhile married Martha's father. Islwyn's dying words, according to one witness, were '*Diolch i ti, Martha, am y cyfan a wnest i mi. Buost yn garedig iawn. 'Rwyf yn mynd at Anne 'nawr*' ('Thank you, Martha, for all you did for me. You have been very kind. I am going to Anne now'). A museum to the poet's memory is housed at Babell chapel, near Ynysddu, under the auspices of the Islwyn Memorial Society.

Although the crucial tension in Islwyn's life was between his love for the dead Anne and his marriage to Martha, there were also unresolved problems arising from the discrepancies between his Anglicized upbringing and his deep interest in Welsh poetry, between the melancholic and the light-hearted in his personality, and between the demands made upon him by his work as both preacher and poet. There is a fundamental dichotomy between the content and form of the two poems known as '*Y Storm*', and between those poems and his other writings. Besides those major poems, Islwyn published only two volumes of verse, *Barddoniaeth* (1854) and *Caniadau* (1867). Thereafter, he tended to write either poetry in the strict metres for eisteddfodau, or else elegies of little distinction. His many attempts at winning the *Chair at the National Eisteddfod were all unsuccessful. As adjudicator and poetry editor of various periodicals, he greatly encouraged the growth of the lyric in Welsh but his own inspiration came to be much more classical. Although he was claimed as the progenitor of Y *Bardd Newydd, he was reluctant to recognize his progeny. There was tension, too, between the daring mysticism of some of his poetry and the orthodoxy of his calling, between the pressures of religious duty and his natural inertia, between his allegiance to old doctrines and his acceptance of advanced theological ideas. Even in his physical appearance there was something paradoxical, for he had a small body and a huge head. Nevertheless, it was undoubtedly the spiritual, emotional, psychological and mental storm which he experienced in the wake of Anne Bowen's death which was responsible not only for many of these enigmas but also for his greatest contribution to Welsh poetry, '*Y Storm*'.

Selections of Islwyn's verse were edited by O. M. Edwards in 1897, by J. T. Jones in 1932 and by T. H. Parry-Williams in 1948. For critical discussion see the studies by W. J. Gruffydd (1942), D. Gwenallt Jones (1948) and Hugh Bevan (1965); see also *Islwyn: Man of the Mountain* (1983) by Meurig Walters, who has also edited '*Y Storm*' (1980).

THOMAS, WILLIAM (**Gwilym Marles**; 1834–79), poet and Radical leader. Born at Llanybydder, Carms., he was educated at the University of Glasgow and became known as a champion of the people against landlordism. A Unitarian minister, he wrote lyrical poetry, much of it diffuse and melancholy, which was published in the volume *Prydyddiaeth* (1859), as well as short stories with moralistic plots. For four months he was a private tutor to Islwyn (William *Thomas) and he kept a school at Llandysul for the last twenty years of his life. It was in honour of Gwilym Marles, his father's uncle, that Dylan *Thomas was given his second name, Marlais; some have seen in the effusions of the Reverend *Eli Jenkins, in *Under Milk Wood* (1954), a resemblance to the verse of Gwilym Marles.

For further details see the biography of Gwilym Marles by Nansi Martin (1979).

THOMAS, WILLIAM (Glanffrwd; 1843–90), local historian, was born at Ynysybwl, Glam., a woodcutter's son. After working as a sawyer, and for four years as a schoolmaster, he was briefly pastor of a Calvinistic Methodist chapel at Pontypridd before being ordained as an Anglican priest. His subsequent incumbencies were all in the diocese of *St. Asaph. He was the author of a volume of poems, *Sisialon y Ffrwd* (1874), but is remembered chiefly for his *Plwyf Llanwynno* (1888), a history of the parish which lies between the rivers Rhondda Fach and Taff, which first appeared in *Tarian y Gweithiwr*. He wrote charmingly, in a manner reminiscent of Francis *Kilvert, about the people of his native parish and the old way of life during a period when this upland part of Glamorgan was mostly Welsh-speaking.

There is an article on the preface to *Plwyf Llanwynno* by Morfydd E. Owen in *Ysgrifau Beirniadol VI* (ed. J. E. Caerwyn Williams, 1971). A reprint of Glanffrwd's book was published under the editorship of Henry Lewis in 1949 and the English translation by Thomas Evans (1950); see also Trefor M. Owen, *Llanwyno a Phortreadau Bro* (1982).

THOMAS, WILLIAM JENKYN (1870–1959), editor and folklorist; the exact place of his birth in Caernarfonshire is not known. Educated at Trinity College, Cambridge, he became a Lecturer in Classics at the University College of North Wales, Bangor, and in 1896 the Headmaster of the first Intermediate School in Wales at Aberdare, Glam. He left Wales in 1905, however, to take up an appointment as Headmaster of a school in London. He edited a volume of Welsh poetry, *Penillion Telyn* (1894), and two school readers, *Cambrensia* (1894) and *Heroes of Wales* (1896), as well as a number of classical texts. His most important works were *The Welsh Fairy Book* (1907) and *More Welsh Fairy and Folk Tales* (1958), both of which have literary merit.

Three Elders of the World, The, see OLDEST ANIMALS.

Tiger Bay, a sobriquet for the docklands of Cardiff, especially the district off Bute Street. It is believed that the name was derived from a popular song which was current in the 1870s. Once a fashionable quarter, it earned its notoriety as a ghetto and slum, also known as Hell's Acre, in the years when the city was a major port. In 1919 it was the setting for the first race-riot in modern Britain. Although the area has been redeveloped, the community of Tiger Bay still strikes the visitor as closely-knit and under-privileged and its exotic character has caught the imagination of many journalists. Among its more famous residents were the boxer Joe Erskine and Shirley Bassey, the torch-singer.

TILSLEY, GWILYM RICHARD (Tilsli; 1911–), poet, was born at Ty-llwyd, near Llanidloes, Mont., and educated at the University College of Wales, Aberystwyth, and at Wesley House, Cambridge. His experiences as a Wesleyan minister in north and south Wales went into the writing of two *awdlau* which brought him into prominence: he won the *Chair at the National Eisteddfod in 1950 with the *awdl* 'Moliant y Glöwr' and again in 1957 with 'Cwm Carnedd'. Both became extremely popular as poems for recitation and musical accompaniment, each reflecting its author's compassion for industrial workers, the one for the miners of south Wales and the other for the quarrymen of the north. His poems in the free metres are to be found in the volume *Y Glöwr a Cherddi Eraill* (1958). As Tilsli, he served as Archdruid of *Gorsedd Beirdd Ynys Prydain between 1969 and 1972 and he was the editor of *Yr *Eurgrawn*, the Wesleyan magazine, from 1966 until it was merged with others to form *Cristion* in 1983.

Times Like These (1936), a novel by Gwyn *Jones which describes the humdrum life of Jenkinstown, a fictitious community in the valleys of south Wales, during the years from 1924 to 1932. The industrial and social history of the coalfield provides the framework within which Oliver Biesty, a collier distinguished only by his ordinariness, his semi-invalid wife and their son and daughter, portray the virtues, the suffering and the aspirations of the working class. The trials of Luke, the son, are central to the narrative, for he is one of the downtrodden, a bemused, hopeless victim of circumstances. The views of managers and men, including the politically active, are represented and there are rousing set-piece descriptions to change the pace and lift the gloom, but the novel remains notable chiefly for its understatement and its vivid evocation of the commonplace.

Tintern, an abbey on the bank of the river Wye near Chepstow, Mon., was first established in 1131 by *Cistercian monks from Normandy under the patronage of Walter de Clare, Earl of

Casgwent. The fame of a painting of the Virgin Mary attracted pilgrims to the abbey during the fifteenth century but the house was dissolved in 1536. Among the first English painters to find a subject in the ruins were Samuel and Nathaniel Buck in 1732 and Paul Sandby in 1773; they were followed by others like Girtin, Turner and Palmer. The Wye valley in which Tintern is set was visited by many literary tourists, among the earliest of whom were Thomas Gray and William Gilpin. The latter's *Observations on the River Wye* (1782) was carried by Dorothy and William Wordsworth during their visit to Tintern in 1798 and the poet drew on Gilpin's work when writing his 'Lines composed a few miles above Tintern Abbey' (1798), the most famous poem of all those inspired by the ruins and surrounding countryside. Some Tourists (see under TOURS OF WALES), such as Grose, disliked the abbey, but others were inspired by its Gothic qualities—like Joseph Cottle, for example, who was a visitor with Coleridge and Southey in 1795. There were more modest responses to Tintern in Robert Bloomfield's 'The *Banks of Wye' (1811) and in Edward *Davies's poem, 'Chepstow' (1811). Francis *Kilvert, who visited the abbey in July 1875, thought it 'almost too perfect to be entirely picturesque'.

Tir Iarll (lit. 'The earl's land'), a district in Glamorgan (including the parishes of Llangynwyd, Betws, Cynffig and Margam), was so called because it came into the possession of the Earl of Gloucester after the *Norman Conquest. Its literary traditions can be traced from the fifteenth century to the time of Iolo Morganwg (Edward *Williams), whose sometimes extravagant claims on its behalf should not be allowed to obscure its very considerable contribution to Welsh culture. Among the poets associated with the district, which was famous for its *cwndidau and *tribannau, were Siôn *Bradford, Rhys Brydydd and Dafydd *Benwyn. Iolo's assertion that *Cadair Tir Iarll* was the Chair of King *Arthur's Round Table, brought to Llangynwyd from *Caerleon, is without foundation. The later associations of Llangynwyd, known as 'Yr Hen Blwyf' ('The old parish'), are numerous and rich: the *Mari Lwyd once flourished there and the story of Ann *Maddocks, 'The Maid of Cefn Ydfa', is set in the vicinity.

For further details see G. J. Williams, *Traddodiad Llenyddol Morgannwg* (1948).

'Tir na n-Óg' (Irish, lit. 'The land of the young ones'; 1916), a lyrical *awdl by T. Gwynn *Jones, is based on a folk-tradition (see under YNYS AFALLON) associated with the Isle of Rathlin. The poem tells of how the poet Osian falls in love with Nia Ben Aur, the daughter of the king of Tir na n-Óg, and follows her to her father's kingdom. He remains there for three hundred years, knowing no sadness and seeing no death,

but eventually he yearns for Ireland and his friends. Nia warns him that if he sets foot on Irish soil he will grow old and die, but nevertheless accepts the fact of his homesickness and allows him to leave *Tir na n-Óg*. Arriving at his old home on horseback, Osian recognizes nobody but, seeing masons trying to place an enormous stone in the wall of a fort, he offers to help them in return for food and drink. As he does so, the girth-band of his saddle snaps, he falls to the ground and is transformed into a blind old man. He pleads in song with Nia to call him back to *Tir na n-Óg* but it is in vain and he dies.

Tir Newydd (lit. 'New ground'), a quarterly magazine edited in Cardiff by Alun *Llywelyn-Williams, assisted by D. Llewelyn Walters; seventeen numbers were published between 1935 and 1939. Taking English periodicals such as *New Verse* as models, and initially supported by students of University College, Cardiff, the editor was of the opinion that Welsh culture and the journals of the day were too rural in character, too restricted in their purview and lacking interest in contemporary world affairs. His intention was to reflect the urban, left-wing Welshman's view of Wales and the world and to provide a forum in which young artists of every kind—architects, painters, musicians, theatre and cinema people as well as poets and writers—could express their ideas and discuss their special interests. But, although it published articles on the arts, together with poems and short stories, the magazine was mainly concerned with literary criticism and radical politics. Among the special numbers published were those devoted to *Drama (Summer, 1936), W. J. *Gruffydd (May, 1938), Freedom (Nov., 1938) and David Vaughan *Thomas (June, 1939). By the editor's own admission, *Tir Newydd* did not discover many young writers of note (although it published early work by several) and his ambition to create a new awareness of the arts in Wales was only partly realized when the outbreak of the Second World War obliged him to cease publication.

A fuller account of the magazine's brief but lively history is given in Alun Llywelyn-Williams's autobiography, *Gwanwyn yn y Ddinas* (1975); see also *Pair* (no. 1, Summer, 1972).

Tithe War, The, which began in Wales during the late 1880s, was caused by long years of economic depression aggravated by social and sectarian bitterness between landlord and tenant. Disturbances spread to nearly every county in Wales but the Vale of Clwyd was the chief centre of unrest. Thomas *Gee, founder of the Welsh Land League in 1886, was a major figure in the anti-Tithe movement and the young David *Lloyd George was active in Caernarfonshire. Led by Nonconformist tenant farmers who refused to pay tithes to the Established Church, the 'War' erupted most notably at Llanarmon, Denbs., in 1886, at Llangwm and Mochdre in the following year, when several farmers were injured during confrontations with police, and at Llanefydd in 1888. These riots drew attention to the political problems posed both by *Land Reform and the *Disestablishment of the Anglican Church. After much parliamentary debate from 1887 onwards, they led to the Tithe Act of 1891, which defused some of the anger by merging tithe with rent and making it payable by the owner rather than the occupier of land. After 1892, the tithe troubles petered out, although disturbances took place in Cardiganshire and Pembrokeshire during the rest of the decade.

For further details see R. E. Prothero, *The Anti-Tithe Agitation in Wales* (1889) and Elwyn L. Jones, *Gwaedu Gwerin* (1983). The novel *Gŵr Pen y Bryn* (1923) by E. Tegla Davies is set against the background of the Tithe War. See also J. P. D. Dunbabin, *Rural Discontent in Nineteenth Century Britain* (1974) and, for a Welsh study which argues that landlords were unfairly castigated, David W. Howell, *Land and People in Nineteenth Century Wales* (1977).

Toad of Cors Fochno, The, see under OLDEST ANIMALS.

Toddaid, see under TWENTY-FOUR METRES.

Toili, a dialect form of the word '*teulu*' (family), used especially in west Wales to denote the phantom funeral said to appear, like the *Corpse Candle, as a premonition of death. According to the traditional belief, a supernatural procession would set out from the home where a bereavement was to take place and proceed to the spot in the churchyard where the grave was to be dug, lingering there until after the body had been committed to the earth.

TOMAS AB IEUAN AP RHYS (*c.*1510–*c.*1560), poet, of Tythegston, Glam. One of the first poets to write *cwndidau, he has a special place in the history of free-metre poetry for, as the grandson of Rhys Brydydd and a cousin of Lewys Morgannwg (*Llywelyn ap Rhisiart), he belonged to the foremost family of traditional poets in the district of *Tir Iarll. Yet his technique was faulty and his diction that of the *clêr: he employed defective imitations of the recognized measures such as the *cyhydedd nawban and the *cyhydedd hir (see under TWENTY-FOUR METRES). As a professional poet he was unique in his use of the *cwndid measures for the purpose of singing eulogies and elegies for the gentry families of the county and he was the author of the earliest surviving examples of the *Triban Morgannwg. Fond of references to the Scriptures, he wrote one *cwndid which is a metrical version of the Parable of the Sower; personal and social problems are also reflected in his work. It was his reputation as a prognosticator which led Iolo Morganwg (Edward *Williams) to invent fic-titious tales about him. A *cwndid in his memory was written by his pupil and friend, Hopcyn Tomas Phylip.

For further details see G. J. Williams, *Traddodiad Llenyddol Morgannwg* (1948).

Tomas ap Llywelyn ap Dafydd ap Hywel, see LLYWELYN, TOMAS (*fl.* 1580–1610).

Tomas Siôn Dafydd Madoc, see JONES or JOHNS, THOMAS (*c.*1530–1609).

Tommy Trouble, a character created in a series of radio sketches by E. Eynon *Evans. His adventures, in which innocence and homespun wit always triumphed, delighted listeners to the BBC Welsh Home Service during the years from 1945 to 1953, and some of his catch-phrases were current for long afterwards.

Tomos Glyn Cothi, see EVANS, THOMAS (1764–1833).

Tonn Manuscripts, The, see under REES, WILLIAM (1808–73).

Tonypandy Riots, The, perhaps the most famous civil disturbance in the history of south Wales after the *Merthyr Rising of 1831, occurred on 8 November 1910 when shops in the high street of the *Rhondda township were wrecked by striking colliers and their families. The previous night, policemen concentrated at the Glamorgan Colliery, north of Tonypandy, had fought fiercely with the crowd demonstrating for its closure. The workers had already kept out blackleg labour at all other pits in the Cambrian Combine group with which they were locked in a dispute over piecework payments. The management, under David Alfred *Thomas and his general manager, Leonard Llewellyn, was determined not to accede to demands for extra payment for work in difficult conditions underground. It was their determination to use blackleg labour, under heavy police guard, which caused the bitterness among the twelve thousand men affected. The fierce clash between about seven thousand miners and a hundred policemen protecting the colliery produced a frustration which boiled over in the attack on the shopkeepers. At a more profound level this violence was indicative of the long-existing tensions within the community.

The controversial part attributed to Winston Churchill, Home Secretary at the time, has obscured to some extent the significance of the Riots. Having halted the movement of troops requested by local magistrates on 7 November and deployed the foot and mounted police in their stead, Churchill was correctly believed (after the second clash between strikers and police) to have ordered troops to be sent from Cardiff to supplement the police forces. The troops, though used circumspectly, acted with vigour and caused Churchill to be seen thereafter as the villain of the affair. This allegation became part of the folklore of south Wales and is still current. Be that as it may, the presence of large numbers of troops in the district until well into 1911 was a vital factor in the collapse of the Cambrian Strike from August of that year. Eventually, in 1912, there was some compensation for the miners as a result of their partially successful strike for a minimum wage and many local leaders who had supported the Cambrian Combine Strike rose to positions of influence as a result. The name of Tonypandy has remained a byword for the industrial militancy of south Wales. See also GENERAL STRIKE.

For further details see L. J. Williams, 'The Road to Tonypandy', in *Llafur* (vol. 1, no. 2, 1973) and David Smith, 'Tonypandy, 1910: Definitions of Community' in *Past and Present* (no. 83, 1980) and the chapter 'A Place in South Wales' in the same author's *Wales! Wales?* (1984).

Top Sawyer, see DAVIES, DAVID (1818–90).

TORRANCE, CHRIS (1941–), poet, was born in Edinburgh and settled in Wales in 1970. A full-time writer, he has published eight collections of poetry, including *Green Orange Purple Red* (1968) and *Aries under Saturn and Beyond* (1969). His long poem, *The Magic Door*, of which four parts have so far appeared—*The Magic Door* (1975), *Citrinas* (1977), *The Diary of Palug's Cat* (1980) and *The Book of Brychan* (1982)—employs 'open field' techniques to explore themes of geography, history and myth associated with the locality of Pontneddfechan, near Glyn Neath, where he lives.

Tour round North Wales, A (1800), by the English writer William Bingley (1774–1823), is the account of an undergraduate's holiday excursion from Cambridge in 1798. Believing himself to be a pioneer in describing such tours, with only Thomas *Pennant to guide him, Bingley gives advice to tourists on routes and means of travel which is not only shrewd and careful but is interspersed with entertaining anecdotes about his experiences, such as his taking a dangerous path up Snowdon in search of plants. A Fellow of the Linnean Society, he had a keen eye for botanical detail. His book, vigorously written, is generally informative and its descriptions of scenery vivid, but these merits are secondary to his interest in Welsh people encountered during his itinerary. After a second visit to north Wales in 1801, he published *North Wales Delineated from Two Excursions* (1804), as well as a work of musical interest, *Sixty of the Most Admired Welsh Airs* (1803, 1810).

Tour throughout South Wales and Monmouthshire, A (1803), by the English writer J. T. Barber, is the genuine narrative of his travels in that he admits his difficulties and omissions—his hurried visit to Thomas *Johnes's Hafod, for example, or his failure to find *Strata Florida— and he does not use other tourists' accounts to supplement his own. The book has a lively, conversational style, is full of detail, particularly about scenery, and the author attempts to involve the reader in his adventures, whether he is describing the 'terrors' of Devil's Bridge, Cards., or his subsequent drying out with the aid of mutton chops and a peat fire at the Hafod Arms. He also complains about the 'sloppy ride' to Tregaron and the 'lumpy hills' near Carmarthen, enthuses about the Towy Valley with quotations from John *Dyer and delights in escaping from the sooty blacksmith sent to shave him at *Tintern.

Tours of Wales. The practice of travelling in Wales and either then or subsequently writing an account of the sites visited and the mountains traversed became suddenly popular during the last three decades of the eighteenth century and continued into the first half of the nineteenth. This new development owed something to the increasing difficulty and expense of undertaking the Grand Tour of a war-torn Europe; perhaps it was encouraged even more by the spread of Romantic attitudes which had parted company entirely from that of Daniel Defoe, for whom (in his *Tours* of 1724–26) the mountains of Breconshire and Radnorshire seemed as bad or worse than the Alps because the elevation of the Welsh mountains in one perspective from the valley bottom to the peak 'makes the height look horrid and frightful, even worse than those mountains abroad'. A particular direction was afforded to Romanticism, early on, by William Gilpin's *Observations on the River Wye*, the result of a tour made in 1770, which suggested that beauty in landscape should properly be identified with the degree to which it could satisfactorily be painted. It may be that such a guideline was more honoured in the creation of a tourist locality on the lower Wye than in the recognition of beauty in Wales's extremities. Louis Simond, a French-American who was in Wales in 1811, found on the Wye between Ross and Chepstow a fully organized tourist industry, with all facilities easily available: 'Wales and the Wye', he commented caustically, 'are visited by all tourists; we are precisely in the tract, and meet them at all the inns—stalking round every ruin of castle or abbey—and climbing every high rock for a prospect; each with his Gilpin or his Cambrian Guide in hand, and each, no doubt, writing a journal. This is rather ridiculous and discouraging'. But such doubts did not prevent him from accepting Gilpin's thesis about *Raglan Castle and other ruins.

More than a hundred *Tours* of Wales were published within the period indicated, though perhaps no more than a dozen show any originality of material or viewpoint. The more serious among the tourists quoted from *Gerald de Barri's *Itinerarium Kambriae* (available in Sir Richard Colt Hoare's translation from 1806), Thomas Churchyard's topographical verse guide to Monmouthshire and the March, *The *Worthines of Wales* (1587), Michael Drayton's *Polyolbion* (1613) and William Camden's *Britannia* (first Englished in 1610). Colt Hoare, indeed, much influenced by the *Tour through Monmouthshire and Wales* (1781) of his fellow-Wiltshireman Henry Penruddocke Wyndham, pressed the genre of topographical writing some distance towards the genuinely historical: his *Journeys* (1793–1810), and especially those of his protégé, Archdeacon William *Coxe, afford a proportion of useful source material. Meanwhile, Welsh antiquarian scholarship was developing concurrently but largely in a different locale: Thomas *Pennant's *Tours* (1778–84), concerned not merely with topography but with antiquities and natural history, limited themselves to north Wales. Richard *Fenton, on the other hand, both acknowledged the encouragement of Colt Hoare and confined his *Tour* of Pembrokeshire (1810) to material more strictly historical. Probably the most valuable *Tour* of south Wales, in terms of its observation and the quality of the information amassed, was that of Benjamin Heath *Malkin (1804), who was married to a Welshwoman and was to become, like Camden, a headmaster and, later, a Professor of History.

Amongst those who were travellers without prior acquaintance with Wales there are a few worthy of remark: J. T. Barber (1803) occasionally made social observations which are still of interest and Edward Donovan (1805) used his scientific training wherever it was appropriate. The clergyman Richard Warner, one of those who set a new fashion by actually walking through Wales—his second *Tour* of 1798 is perhaps particularly valuable—did more than describe closely, for he was also one of those who best explains a common aim of the Romantic quest: in searching for the ideal historical identity, he declares that he will 'breathe the inspiring air where liberty made her last stand in these kingdoms, against the strides of Roman power, under the gallant Silurian and Ordovician chieftains'. Donovan widens this by explaining that he is concerned with 'the manners of a people who have retained the language, the custom, habits and opinions of our hardy ancestors, the early Britons'.

Wales also attracted some of the Romantic poets. The first to come was Wordsworth: a pedestrian tour of north Wales (1791) produced the dedication to his *Descriptive Sketches* (1793) and the revelatory ascent of Snowdon in Book XIV of *The Prelude* (1799–1805, though it was not published till 1850). Incidents during his tours of the Wye Valley in 1793 and 1798

inspired the poems 'We Are Seven', 'Peter Bell' and 'Tintern Abbey', and a further tour in 1824 some less memorable sonnets. Coleridge made tours in 1794, 1795 and 1802 which are recorded both in his own letters and in *A *Pedestrian Tour through North Wales in a Series of Letters* (1795) by his companion Joseph Hucks; these experiences are thought to have had some later, subtle results in his poems. Walter Savage Landor in 1798 and Shelley in 1811, both of them expelled from Oxford, went to live amid the scenery of Wales, Landor to Swansea, where he wrote 'Rose Aylmer' and other poems, and later to Llanthony, Mon., Shelley to the Elan Valley. De Quincey made his first long tour of north Wales after running away from his school in Manchester in 1802, a journey later recorded in his *Confessions* (1822). Another who lived in rather than visited north Wales was Thomas Love *Peacock: some of his novels were nominally located there and in the end he made use of his knowledge of Welsh literary tradition by writing *The *Misfortunes of Elphin* (1829).

Some of the more individual tourists were late on the scene. One was Michael Faraday the scientist, whose tours of 1819 and 1822 are chiefly memorable for the attention he gave to the limestone formations of the Hepste and Mellte, to the copperworks of Swansea and to the primitive mining conditions in the Parys copper mountain in Anglesey. Another was Thomas *Roscoe, whose *Wanderings in South Wales* (1837) and its companion volume of 1844 cover old ground with a new liveliness of style and interest. The last to make his mark before relatively modern tourists like A. G. Bradley was George *Borrow, who brought to his tours (1854–67) a knowledge of the Welsh language, an unusual reverence for Wales's bardic tradition and an array of unconventional prejudices: his *Wild Wales* (1862) was the shaped experience of a creative writer.

Toy Epic, A (1958), the seventh published novel of Emyr *Humphreys, was (in its first draft) his first novelistic writing. Its theme, like that of *The *Little Kingdom* (1946), is an attack on that innate sense of leadership which goes on to ambition and betrayal, with Wales as the symbolic sacrifice. The story is that of three boys, Albie, Iorwerth and Michael, each of whom represents a facet of the socially and linguistically divided north-east Wales of the author's birth. They become friends at grammar school: Albie, the bus-driver's son, belies his early academic promise and turns to Communism; Iorwerth, the religious, Welsh-speaking farmer's son, feels betrayed by his beloved father's death and Michael's easy capture of his girl-friend; Michael succeeds academically, if against expectations, and becomes a Welsh Nationalist, although he shares few of the traditions and beliefs of his countrymen. A short work, ending where schooldays end, the novel is full of the raw poetry of a youth soon to be shattered on the stone walls of reality. It was awarded the Hawthornden Prize in 1959 and also appeared in a Welsh version as *Y Tri Llais* (1958).

Tractarianism, see OXFORD MOVEMENT.

Traed mewn Cyffion (lit. 'Feet in fetters'; 1936), a novel by Kate *Roberts. The story, set in the years between 1880 and 1914, is about one family but reflects the history of a whole society, that of the slate-quarrying districts of the author's native county. The chief character, Jane Gruffydd, has her roots in Llŷn and, with six children, she has to learn a harder way of life than that to which she is accustomed. There is little joy in her life and, despite deep sensitivity, she accepts that there is scant hope of casting off her fetters.

A translation of the novel by Idwal Walters and John Idris Jones was published under the title *Feet in Chains* (1977).

Traethodl, a series of couplets of seven-syllable lines, without any restrictions on the accentuation of the rhymes. This measure, refined with certain technical requirements including *cynghanedd, developed into the *cywydd. The *traethodl* persisted into the sixteenth century in folk-poetry and was occasionally used for light verse by the *Poets of the Gentry.

Traethodydd, Y (lit. 'The essayist'), a quarterly magazine first published by Thomas *Gee the younger at Denbigh in 1845, was launched under the editorship of Lewis *Edwards and Roger *Edwards. It was intended as a Welsh counterpart to such periodicals as *The Edinburgh Review* and *Blackwood's Magazine* but it placed a greater emphasis on theology, philosophy and education while also devoting space to essays and book reviews. Always an influential journal, not only did it lead public opinion on religious questions but it also introduced to its Welsh readers contemporary scholarship from England, Germany and France. From 1854, when Lewis Edwards was succeeded by Owen *Thomas of Liverpool, until 1904, the publisher was P. M. Evans of Holywell, Flints. Daniel Rowlands of Bangor was its editor from 1862 to 1898. Although its aim was to be an interdenominational magazine, *Y Traethodydd* found the larger part of its readership among Methodists and from 1913 to the present it has been published by the Calvinistic Methodist Press (*Gwasg Pantycelyn*) at Caernarfon. During the twentieth century the magazine's editors have included Ifor *Williams, J. R. *Jones (1911–70), Harri *Williams and J. E. Caerwyn *Williams; the last-named was appointed in 1965. After the demise of Y *Beirniad and Y *Llenor, Y *Traethodydd* became more of a literary magazine, regularly carrying poetry, essays and criticism, but it still tends to favour contributions of a philosophical or theological nature. The writers to whom special numbers have been devoted include T. Gwynn *Jones, Gwenallt (David James *Jones), Waldo *Williams and T. H. *Parry-Williams.

An index to the contents of *Y Traethodydd*, compiled by W. Phillips, has been published by the Welsh Library Association (2 vols., part 1, 1845–95, 1976, 1978; part 2, 1896–1957, 1980). The history of the magazine is traced in an article by J. E. Caerwyn Williams in *Y Traethodydd* (Jan., 1981) and by the same author in *Llên Cymru* (vol. XIV, nos. 1 and 2, 1981–82).

'Trafferth mewn Tafarn' (lit. 'Trouble at an inn'), one of *Dafydd ap Gwilym's funniest and most celebrated *cywyddau*, describes the poet's arrival at 'a choice city' (perhaps Rhosyr in Newborough, Ang.) and his meeting there with a pretty girl whom he entertains with food and wine. In an abrupt and jerky style, with frequent use of *sangiad, the poet then relates the misfortune which befalls him as he tries to reach the girl in her bed. Stumbling over a stool and upsetting a brass bowl, he wakes up three English tinkers, Hickin, Jenkin and Jack, who raise the alarm in the belief that their merchandise is being stolen. During the subsequent commotion, the poet finds his way back to his own bed. The narration of the incident, whether real or imaginary, may owe something to Dafydd's acquaintance with the popular French *fabliaux*, episodic, usually ribald poems which were internationally current in his day. But it is characteristic of him that he is the protagonist here, describing the incident in the first person, and that the laughter is at his own expense. The poem is rich in innuendo and allows interpretation on more than one level.

There is a discussion of the poem and its background in the article by D. J. Bowen in *Ysgrifau Beirniadol XII* (ed. J. E. Caerwyn Williams, 1982).

Trahaearn ab Ieuan ap Meurig (fl. 1450–63), gentleman and patron, of Penrhosfwrdios, Mon., was one of the early Welsh supporters of Edward IV. He was closely associated with the Lord Herbert, acting on his behalf in the lordship of Pembroke. *Dafydd ab Edmwnd addressed a *cywydd* to him asking for the gift of a cloak, and his praise was also sung by *Lewys Glyn Cothi. But he is remembered chiefly as the owner of a copy of the *Seint Greal*, the loan of which was requested in a poem by *Guto'r Glyn on behalf of Dafydd, the Abbot of *Valle Crucis.

Trahaearn ap Caradog (d. 1081), King of *Gwynedd. By hereditary right the ruler of *Arwystli, he extended his dominion over large parts of north Wales and invaded the south until, challenged by *Gruffudd ap Cynan and Rhys ap Tewdwr, he was defeated at the battle of Mynydd Carn in 1081.

TRAHAEARN BRYDYDD MAWR (fl. first

half of the 14th cent.), poet, was a native of Merioneth and a son of Goronwy ap Rotbert ap Bledri. He belonged to the period which followed the fall of the House of *Gwynedd, and *Gwilym Ddu o Arfon, who composed his elegy, placed him in the succession of the learned court poets of a former age. Of Trahaearn's work there are extant a panegyric awdl addressed to Hywel of Llandingad in the Tywi Valley, another in praise of God and a number of satirical englynion of the scatological type common in his day. From several pejorative and satirical references it may be concluded that he was not only large of physical stature but also proud, which may be why he was accorded the sarcastic epithet meaning 'Great Poet'.

TRAHERNE, JOHN MONTGOMERY (1788–1860), antiquary, of Coedrhiglan, near Cardiff, was educated at Oriel College, Oxford. He was ordained a priest in 1813 but never held a living. About 1823 he demolished the family home and built near by the house known as Coedrhydyglyn which is still owned by the Trahernes. His wide scientific and antiquarian interests were acknowledged by his election to the Linnean Society in 1813, the Royal Society in 1823 and the Society of Antiquaries in 1838. Deeply interested in the history of Glamorgan, he published numerous essays and articles, many anonymously or pseudonymously. Among the works which he edited the most important is the volume entitled Stradling Correspondence (1870).

Translators, The, a group of writers, mostly anonymous and clerical, who were responsible for translating a variety of material from Latin, French and English into Welsh prose during the later Middle Ages. Although few have been identified, it is likely that those whose names have survived in the manuscripts, such as *Gruffudd Bola and *Madog ap Selyf, were clerics; some worked for patrons like Gruffudd ab Maredudd and Hopcyn ap Thomas. From the mid-thirteenth century onwards, at a time when new native Welsh prose was rare, a corpus of very varied texts emerged. It included devotional literature, parts of the Scriptures translated from Latin, Welsh versions of texts of a practical nature, such as Walter of Henly's English treatise on husbandry, as well as literature for entertainment, like the tales of Charlemagne and *Arthur which were translated from French. Although the translators, in dealing with religious texts, kept very close to their sources, they tended to adapt the secular tales for the new audiences, fitting them to native narrative tradition and adopting the style and techniques of earlier Welsh prose, such as *Pedair Cainc y Mabinogi. It is unlikely that a school of translators ever existed, but as individuals they succeeded in broadening the range and developing the style of Welsh prose.

For further details see the article by Stephen J. Williams in Y Traddodiad Rhyddiaith yn yr Oesau Canol (ed. Geraint Bowen, 1974) and another by Morfydd E. Owen in A Guide to Welsh Literature (ed. A. O. H. Jarman and Gwilym Rees Hughes, 1979).

Treachery of the Long Knives, The, a legendary incident first related by *Nennius, who added to the work of *Gildas the story of the love of the British king *Vortigern for *Alice Rowena, the daughter of the Saxon leader, Hengist. It was Nennius who described how the Saxons invited Vortigern and the British leaders to a banquet and, at a pre-arranged signal, 'Nemet eour saxes!' ('Grab your knives!'), slaughtered three hundred of the British with their long knives, after which Vortigern was forced to yield the whole of southern Britain; only one British lord, Eidol, the Earl of Gloucester, survived the massacre. The tale was elaborated by *Geoffrey of Monmouth and given a new currency in the eighteenth century by Theophilus *Evans and others. It was illustrated by Romantic artists such as Henry Fuseli and Angelica Kauffmann in the 1770s. The legend was so well known that it was possible, in 1854, for R. J. *Derfel to satirize the *Blue Books on Wales as 'The Treachery of the Blue Books', in the full knowledge that all would understand the reference. It should be noted that the story of the Long Knives is also known in Germany, where a similar tale occurs in Widukind's chronicle of the early Saxons and where, in 1934, the Roehm purge by Hitler was called 'The Night of the Long Knives'.

For further details see the article by Prys Morgan, 'From Long Knives to Blue Books', in Welsh Society and Nationhood (ed. R. R. Davies, Ralph A. Griffiths, Ieuan Gwynedd Jones and Kenneth O. Morgan, 1984).

Treaty of Gloucester, The (1240), see under DAFYDD AP LLYWELYN (d. 1246).

Trebor Mai, see WILLIAMS, ROBERT (1830–77).

Trefeca, see under HARRIS, HOWEL (1714–73).

Trefin, see PHILLIPS, EDGAR (1889–1962).

TREFOR, DAFYDD or **DAFYDD AP HYWEL AB IEUAN AB IORWERTH** (d. 1528?), poet, was priest of Llaneugrad and Llanallgo, Ang. Some thirty of his cywyddau are extant, among them nine request poems and several on religious themes. They also include one requesting a concubine and a harp, eulogies to the saints *Deiniol and *Dwynwen, an elegy for Henry VII and a cywydd to the Menai ferryboat which provoked a dispute between the poet and Gruffudd ap Tudur ap Hywel. Dafydd wrote two cywyddau in a bid to reconcile William Glyn and Sir Richard Bulkeley, who were bitter rivals in Church administration. One of his finest elegies, composed in memory of Owain ap

Maredudd ap Thomas, describes Death leading a *danse macabre*. His work is of interest in that it reflects the world of a cultured Welsh priest on the eve of the Protestant Reformation.

For discussion of the poet's work see the articles by I. George in the *Transactions* of the Anglesey Antiquarian and Field Society (1934, 1935, 1936).

TREFOR, SIÔN (d. 1410), Bishop of *St. Asaph and author, was probably a native of Trefor, near Llangollen, Denbs. He came to prominence in the service of Richard II and was sent on a mission to Scotland, a journey which is the theme of a poem by *Iolo Goch. A member of the parliamentary commission which pronounced the sentence of deposition on Richard, he lent his support to *Owain Glyndŵr after 1404 and worked to promote the Welsh cause. After warning the House of Commons in 1400 against rejection of Glyndŵr's claim to the 'peece of commons' disputed with Lord Grey, he was shouted down with the cry, 'What care we for the barefoot rascals?' One scholar has argued that Siôn Trefor was the author of a heraldic work called *Tractatus de Armis*, which he translated into Welsh under the title *Llyfr Arveu*; it has also been claimed that he wrote a Life of St. Martin.

For further details see E. J. Jones, *Medieval Heraldry* (1943) and the article by Ifor Williams in the *Bulletin* of the Board of Celtic Studies (vol. V, 1929).

Trevithick, Richard (1771–1833), engineer. A Cornishman, he found employment with Samuel *Homfray, master of the Penydarren ironworks at Merthyr Tydfil, Glam., in 1803. With the aid of local workers, he built a steam locomotive (his third model, its predecessors having run on the road) to carry iron from the works down the Taff Valley, thus avoiding the use of the canal which was controlled by Homfray's rival, Richard *Crawshay. The first official journey of 'the tram waggon', which ran on rails from Penydarren to Navigation (opposite Abercynon), a distance of nine miles, at a speed of five miles an hour, was witnessed by a large and admiring crowd on 21 February 1804.

Trew, William John (1878–1926), rugby-player. A centre three-quarter who began his career with Swansea, he was first capped for Wales in 1900 and subsequently appeared in twenty-nine international games, often as captain.

Tri Brenin o Gwlen, Y (lit. 'The three kings from Cologne'; 16th cent.), one of only two Welsh miracle plays to have survived from the Middle Ages; the other is *Y Dioddefaint a'r Atgyfodiad*. A verse drama which first appears in manuscripts of the sixteenth century, *Y Tri Brenin o Gwlen* was probably composed not much earlier and its language suggests that it originally belonged to *Powys. The work depicts the exchanges between the Three Kings and Herod, the visit to the infant Jesus, the Flight into Egypt and the Massacre of the Innocents.

For further details see Gwenan Jones, *A Study of Three Welsh Religious Plays* (1918).

Tri Chof, Y (lit. 'The three records of memorials'), a tract dealing with the *Bardic Order which is preserved in the hand of John *Jones of Gellilyfdy (Llanstephan MS 144). The text, written in English, lists the 'Three Records of Memorialls' which should be kept by the poets, namely the history of the notable acts of the Kings of 'Bruttaen and Cambria', the language of the 'Bruttons', and the genealogies of the nobility and the divisions of the land. It is thought that the precedents of the material listed in this tract are much older than the seventeenth century and that it reflects the fields of medieval bardic learning, as confirmed by contemporary poetry and by the bardic grammars. The subjects listed as part of the bardic heritage correspond closely to what is known of the training given in the bardic schools of medieval Ireland.

Tri Chryfion Byd (lit. 'The three mighty ones of the world'; 1789), the best and most famous of the interludes of Twm o'r Nant (Thomas *Edwards). A silent reading of the text affords little impression of its power, but in public performance it captivates the audience with the music of its verse and its dramatic impact. The character linking the episodes is Syr Tom Tell Truth who opens the proceedings with an oration calling for silence. A narrator then outlines the story and enumerates the characters, who include personifications of 'the Three Mighty Ones': Poverty, Love and Death. It is Syr Tom's function to encourage Rheinallt the Miser (whose part the author was fond of playing), Lowri Lew, Evan Offeiriad and others to expatiate on their lot in life. Bristling with satire, the work remains, despite its comic effects, a sober sermon on the responsibilities of Life and the inevitability of Death.

The interlude is still performed from time to time and has been published in modern editions, most recently under the editorship of Norah Isaac (1975) with introductory notes by Saunders Lewis, T. Gwynn Jones, Thomas Parry and Bobi Jones.

Tri Thlws ar Ddeg Ynys Prydain (lit. 'The thirteen treasures of the Isle of Britain'), a document listing thirteen precious objects which served as magical talismans and were said to have belonged to traditional Welsh heroes. Like *Y *Pedwar Marchog ar Hugain* ('The Twenty-four Knights of Arthur's Court'), the manuscript dates from the latter half of the fifteenth century and exists in a number of variant copies made in the sixteenth and seventeenth centuries; the text frequently accompanies *Trioedd Ynys Prydain*.

The Treasures include the sword of *Rhydd-erch Hen, the horn of Brân Galed, the chess-board of *Gwenddolau, the hamper of *Gwydd-no Garanhir and the cauldron of *Diwrnach the Giant. In some versions, two items from popular romances, namely the mantle of *Tegau Eurfron and the stone and ring of Eluned (see under TAIR RHAMANT), have supplanted others, but the number of the Treasures never exceeds thirteen. All are magical talismans and about half are objects which can satisfy human wishes, especially with regard to food and drink, while others serve to give invisibility, to distinguish between the brave and the cowardly or the noble and the base born, and one is a chastity test. Some, such as the hamper of Gwyddno and the cauldron of Diwrnach, which are listed among the things (*Anoethau) to be obtained by *Culhwch in his quest for Olwen, are derived from much older sources. The food-producing horns, cups and vats have parallels in Irish literature where certain magical treasures are said to have been brought home by Irish kings on their return from the Otherworld. It seems probable that the Welsh treasures may have had a similar mythological origin: they may have been the subject of lost stories which told how they were either won or given as gifts by the inhabitants of *Annwn to heroes who made visits there. Most of such names as are ident-ifiable among the owners of the Treasures are heroes of the *Old North and their association with stories belonging to that territory is con-firmed both by the titles in some of the versions and by a gloss on the name Brân Galed in a manuscript from the sixteenth century.

Although the Treasures are not mentioned in poetry before the fifteenth century, numerous allusions are made to them by the cywyddwyr, both individually and collectively. The earliest reference, by *Guto'r Glyn, bears out the north-ern associations of the stories about the Treasures by commenting on Brân Galed that he belonged to the nobility of the Old North and that *Taliesin, 'no mean magician', transformed him into one better than the Three *Generous Men of the Isle of Britain. This tradition, which gives credit for winning the Treasures to Taliesin rather than to *Myrddin, may possibly be the older of the two and it is corroborated by several of the titles in the manuscripts. References by the cywyddwyr indicate that the association of the Treasures with Myrddin is likely to have been influenced by accounts of the incarceration of the Arthurian Merlin at the hands of his lover, Vivianne, a story evidently well known to them. There was, however, a late tradition according to which Myrddin was buried on the island of *Bardsey.

For further details see Rachel Bromwich, Trioedd Ynys Prydein (1961); see also the articles by P. C. Bartrum in Études Celtiques (vol. X, 1963) and Eurys Rowlands in Llên Cymru (vol. V, 1959).

Triads, see under TRIOEDD Y MEIRCH and TRI-OEDD YNYS PRYDAIN.

Triban, one of the metres used by the non-professional poets, the minstrels or the *Clêr. It consists of two seven-syllable lines, followed by a third line of seven or eight syllables which rhymes with the caesura of the fourth line; the fourth line ends with an unaccented syllable rhyming with the first two lines. Here is an example in English:

> Three things I cannot relish:
> A woman who is peevish,
> To meet a parson without wit
> And Llantwit's broken English.

The development of the Triban from the *Englyn Cyrch is not easily traced because the unofficial free-metre poetry, which existed side by side with the official strict metres, was not recorded until the sixteenth century. Welsh manuscripts after that date, however, demon-strate that it was a highly popular metre and one which was common to all parts of Wales. The free metres were more commonly used in Glamorgan, where the Triban was also an integral part of several customs peculiar to the County, such as the practice of *singing to oxen and that of the *Mari Lwyd. For these and other reasons, the metre came to be associated with this part of Wales at an early date and the Triban-nau are characterized by the dialect of Glamorgan, its place-names, its way of life and its customs.

The name Triban is also applied to the badge and symbol of *Plaid Cymru, which takes the form of three green triangles representing the mountains of Wales.

For further details and a collection of some seven hundred examples see Tribannau Morgannwg (ed. Teg-wyn Jones, 1976).

Trioedd y Meirch (lit. 'Triads of horses'), a list of the names of the horses of traditional heroes, together with the names of their owners, forms a distinctive subsidiary in the manuscripts of *Trioedd Ynys Prydain and is the earliest of these to be recorded in writing as a group.

A fragment of four Triads of Horses has been preserved in The *Black Book of Carmarthen and, in addition, there is in The *Book of Taliesin a poem, 'Canu'r Meirch' (10th or 11th cent.), which reproduces a number of the same names, both of the horses and of their owners, as are found in the later manuscripts. The variation in these names throughout the different versions suggests that a period of oral transmission underlies the texts as they have come down. As preserved in the 'Early Version' (Peniarth 16) of the Triads, the Triads of Horses are grouped under the following headings: Three Bestowed Horses of the Isle of Britain, Three Chief Steeds, Three Plundered Horses, Three Lovers' Horses, Three Lively Steeds, Three Pack Horses, and

Three Horses which carried the Three Horse Burdens; there are also the Three Prominent Oxen and the Three Prominent Cows. The horses' names are descriptive—'Long Tongue', 'Huge Yellow', 'Grey Fetlock' and the like—and include fabulous characteristics: some are cloven-hoofed, one is horned, others can carry superhuman burdens. The only one of these Triads which appends brief narrative details to the three names is that of the 'Three Horses which carried the Three Horse Burdens' and only one, concerning the traditions of the Battle of Arfderydd, can be partially elucidated from any other source.

Nor do the Welsh tales provide more than minimal information concerning the role played by these horses in the native tradition: one or two are named in the tale of *Culhwch and Olwen and one in the *englynion* of *'Canu Llywarch Hen'*. This dearth of information gives the greater interest to the fact that the names of two of these horses, together with those of their original owners, were preserved in the romances about *Arthur written by the French poet Chrétien de Troyes and his successors. These are Ceingaled ('hard-backed'), the horse of Gwalchmai, which reappears in French as *le Guingalet*, the horse of the knight Gauvain, and Lluagor ('host-splitter'), the horse of *Caradog Freichfras, which becomes *Lorzagor* and belongs to Carados Briebras. These names, which must have entered French sources through unrecorded oral channels, are more likely to be derived from the lost stories on which the Triads of Horses are based than on the Triads themselves, since the repertoire of the Welsh *cyfarwydd (story-teller) was mainly transmitted by word of mouth and only very rarely committed to writing.

For further details see Rachel Bromwich, *Trioedd Ynys Prydein* (1961) and A. O. H. Jarman, *Llyfr Du Caerfyrddin* (1982).

Trioedd Ynys Prydain (lit. 'The triads of the Isle of Britain'), a collection or index of legendary characters, arranged in groups of three, demonstrates that fondness for triple groupings which appears from the earliest times as a characteristic feature of the Celtic cultural tradition in Britain and Ireland. In medieval Wales, a society in which oral instruction was the chief means of conserving and transmitting the learned tradition, Triads served as a mnemonic device for cataloguing a variety of facts and precepts imparted by teachers of all branches of the native learning to their pupils and, with the *Trioedd Cerdd ('Triads of the Poetic Art'), *Trioedd Ynys Prydain* formed an essential element in bardic lore. Collections of Triads also occur in the *Laws of Hywel Dda and in the medical treatises where they originally had a similar didactic purpose. The texts of *Trioedd Ynys Prydain* are frequently accompanied in the manuscripts by lists of proverbial and gnomic Triads of a kind similar to those preserved abundantly in the old three-line *englyn, a verse-form which is in itself an outstanding example of the medieval Welsh predilection for Triadic utterance. By far the most extensive of the medieval collections, *Trioedd Ynys Prydain* commemorates a number of the heroes and heroines of the native tales. Brief outlines of stories are sometimes attached to the names, as in *Tri Gwrddfeichiad Ynys Prydain* ('The Three *Powerful Swineherds') and *Tri Chudd a Thri Datgudd Ynys Prydain* ('The Three Concealments and Three Disclosures').

The collections are preserved in a number of manuscripts from the thirteenth and fourteenth centuries. Since the earliest of these are themselves copies, it seems likely that the Triad collections were first brought together during the twelfth century, the earliest extant collection being the fragmentary *Trioedd y Meirch ('Triads of Horses') in *The Black Book of Carmarthen*. Some individual Triads, however, appear much earlier: a few are cited in 'Y *Gododdin' and in *The *Book of Taliesin*. The medieval collections have come down in two main recensions known as the 'Early Version' (Peniarth MSS 16 and 45) and the 'WR Version' (from *The *White Book of Rhydderch* and *The *Red Book of Hergest*). A comparison of the names in the Triads with the allusions made in poetry by the *Gogynfeirdd indicates that the 'Early Version' comprises the field of reference to such of the legendary heroes as were known to the poets down to about 1200. The 'WR Version' gives the older Triads in a different order and sometimes in variant forms, and adds a number of new ones, in some instances substituting in the titles 'of Arthur's Court' for the older formula 'of the Isle of Britain'. The additions include material from *Brut y Brenhinedd which is unknown in the 'Early Version'. Later manuscripts add further Triads to the series, some of which are derived from additional literary and romance material, though others appear to be ancient and traditional.

The sequences of Triads which are concerned with each of the various branches of native learning display certain common stylistic features, such as the fondness for groups of Triads with the same caption being paralleled by others in the Blegywryd text of the Laws and in antithetical pairs. Each of these characteristics is displayed also in a series of Irish Triads—geographical, legal and sententious, rather than legendary—which has come down from the ninth century and the very existence of which emphasizes the antiquity of the common Celtic tradition to which the formation of Triads belongs. They also corroborate the rhetorical value of Triads for the dramatic emphasis and epigrammatic brevity which are apparent in the Welsh Triads: it is the final entry in a Triad which is usually the one on which the emphasis falls, this being equally true of the third line in the old type of *englyn*. The rhetorical potential of Triads is illustrated by the eloquent manner in which *Trioedd Ynys Prydain* are cited in a number of instances in the *Pedair Cainc y Mabinogi*.

References made by the poets from the fourteenth to the seventeenth centuries to the characters named in the Triads indicate that the *Trioedd* retained their value as a repository of exemplary names, since unremarkable characters are only exceptionally mentioned by the poets long after the actual stories attached to these names had been forgotten. This diminishing knowledge on the part of the poets did not, however, mean that the Triads themselves were forgotten, since from the sixteenth century there was a steadily increasing interest in them among scholars and antiquaries. Not only did the early manuscripts continue to be copied, but the year 1567 saw the appearance of the first printed text of *Trioedd Ynys Prydain* in *Y Diarebion Camberäec*, the second edition of William *Salesbury's *Oll Synnwyr Pen* (1547). This book, which now exists only in a single mutilated copy in the British Library, was known to William Camden, who quoted three of the Triads from it in his *Britannia* (1586), an eloquent witness to the fact that wherever the Triads were known they were regarded as an ancient and authoritative source for the early history and antiquities of Britain.

This reverence for their authority explains the activities of three scholars who made extensive collections of Triads from older but mainly identifiable sources. The most important was Robert *Vaughan of Hengwrt, since his collection (made in 1652) became the basis for the first of the three series of *Trioedd Ynys Prydain* in the *Myvyrian Archaiology of Wales* (1801). The second series of Triads in this book reproduces those from *The Red Book of Hergest* and the much discussed third series is the work of Iolo Morganwg (Edward *Williams) who, about 1791, rewrote a number of the older Triads in a peculiarly inflated style and in a curious form of language. Of the 126 Triads in the third series, exactly two-thirds are expansions of Triads contained in the first series, while the remaining third are Iolo's own creations and have no identifiable source other than manuscripts in his own handwriting. Fortunately, these manuscripts include his own English translations of his Triads, which is a very necessary aid to their interpretation. It was not until Thomas *Stephens launched a detailed and percipient attack on Iolo's third series in *The Cambrian Journal* and in *Y *Beirniad* in the 1850s and 1860s that the authority of Iolo's work became thoroughly discredited. Inevitably, however, the recognition of the value of the authentic medieval Triads in the two earlier series in *The Myvyrian Archaiology* has to some extent suffered in the intervening years by this eclipse.

The text of *Trioedd Ynys Prydain* has been edited with a translation, introduction and commentary by Rachel Bromwich (1961; 2nd edn., 1978); for the history of the Triads see the same author's '*Trioedd Ynys Prydain*' in *Welsh Literature and Scholarship* (The G. J. Williams Memorial Lecture, 1969). Iolo Morganwg's own translation of his Triads is to be found in the *Transactions* of the Honourable Society of Cymmrodorion (1969, 1970). For a discussion of Triads in Celtic mythology see J. Vendryes, '*L'Unité en Trois Personnes chez les Celtes*' in his *Choix d'Études Linguistiques et Celtiques* (1952).

TRIPP, JOHN (1927–), poet, was born at Bargoed, Glam., and brought up, a farrier's son, in Whitchurch, Cardiff. After working as a journalist in London, where he was a member of the Guild of Welsh Writers, he returned to Wales in 1969 and since then has lived as a free-lance writer.

His early poems appeared in *Poetry Wales and The *London Welshman* and in his booklet *Diesel to Yesterday* (1966) in the *Triskel Poets* series. Since then he has published six volumes of poetry: *The Loss of Ancestry* (1969), *The Province of Belief* (1971), *Bute Park* (1971), *The Inheritance File* (1973), *For King and Country* (1980) and *Passing Through* (1984). A selection of his verse appeared in the *Penguin Modern Poets* series (1979) and his *Collected Poems 1958–78* was published in 1978. From 1973 until it suspended publication in 1979 John Tripp was the literary editor of *Planet.

The principal subjects of John Tripp's work are the history of Wales and the present condition of its people. An English-speaking Welshman with left-wing and pacifist convictions, he is concerned not only with his own roots, his family and friends, but with what he denounces as the shoddy materialism which has severed the Welsh people's links with their own past. He employs a contemporary vocabulary and a vigorous style, sometimes prone to overstatement, to describe what fascinates him most—the spectacle of the once great and famous now fallen on harder times. A laconic eye is often turned on himself as poet-observer, grizzled by suburban living but still capable of humour, anger and compassion.

For a critical discussion of John Tripp's poetry see the review-article by Richard Poole in *Poetry Wales* (vol. 14, no. 4, 1979); see also the article by Jeremy Hooker in *The Anglo-Welsh Review* (no. 65, 1979) and the note by Glyn Jones in *Profiles* (1980). There is an interview with the poet in the volume *Common Ground: Poets in a Welsh Landscape* (ed. Susan Butler, 1985).

Triskel Press, The, see under STEPHENS, MEIC (1938–).

Tristan and Iseult, lovers, the tale of whose passion and destruction is told in several medieval romances which became linked to the Arthurian Cycle. In some versions of their story Tristan is said to be *Arthur's nephew. There is disagreement as to the sources of the legend but it seems to have developed among the Celtic peoples. Some scholars take the view that Tristan was Pictish and that its origins therefore lie in north Britain, while others postulate Irish sources on the grounds that Iseult's home was in Ireland and that a very similar story of unhappy lovers is told in the tale of Diarmuit and Gráinne. The place-names and other references in French texts of Anglo-Norman origin, however, point to close links with Cornwall.

During a sea voyage from Ireland to Cornwall, where Iseult is to marry King Mark, she and Tristan drink a potion prepared by Iseult's mother for her daughter's wedding and the two immediately fall irrevocably in love. With the help of the maid Brangwen (Brangien or Brengain in Continental versions), who has administered the love-potion, the lovers meet secretly and succeed in deceiving Mark for a while, despite gossip at court, but are obliged to flee into the forest of Brocéliande after the king discovers their liaison. Tristan marries another Iseult, from Brittany, but their marriage is not consummated and the love between him and the first Iseult deepens. He meets his death after being wounded by Mark in battle: Iseult is summoned to his death-bed but arrives too late and the lovers are united only in death.

Although references to the tragic lovers in *Trioedd Ynys Prydain* and in the poetry of the *Gogynfeirdd* and the *cywyddwyr* attest to the theme's popularity in Wales, no medieval Welsh text is extant which tells the full story of Tristan and Esyllt, as she is known in Welsh. A poem in The *Black Book of Carmarthen* recounts part of the tale, but it is obscure in passages. More detail is provided in *Ystorya Trystan*, a composite text of prose interspersed with *englynion*, but in its present form it does not pre-date the sixteenth century and is far from complete. Fuller texts are found in French and German literature from the twelfth century onwards, such as the romances attributed to Béroul, *Thomas and Gottfried von Strassburg. The Welsh texts contain some material in common with the Continental romances but they are of native inspiration and have not been influenced by the latter. From the various versions extant the French scholar Joseph Bédier succeeded in 1910 in re-creating the complete story of Tristan and Iseult, which by then had achieved renown as the subject of Wagner's opera, *Tristan und Isolde* (1865).

For further details see R. S. Loomis (ed.), *Arthurian Literature in the Middle Ages* (1959), Renee L. Curtis, *Tristan Studies* (1965), Joyce Hill (ed.), *The Tristan Legend: Texts from Northern and Eastern Europe in modern English translation* (1977), Sigmund Eisner, *The Tristan Legend, a Study in Sources* (1969) and Denis de Rougemont, *L'Amour et l'Occident* (1939; trans. *Passion and Society*, 1940).

TRISTFARDD (*fl.* 6th cent.), the poet of *Urien Rheged, named in a Triad as one of the Three Red-Speared Poets of the Isle of Britain, is reported to have had a liaison with Urien's wife. The late manuscript in which this story is found contains a dialogue in the form of *englynion*, some of which have older sources, telling how Urien slew his poet at a ford, subsequently called Rhyd Tristfardd, in *Powys.

Troelus a Chresyd (lit. 'Troilus and Cressida'; *c.*1600), a tragedy and the earliest full-length play in Welsh, is largely (apart from the first two scenes) an abbreviated and dramatized translation of Chaucer's *Troylus and Cryseyde* (*c.*1372–86) and Henryson's *Testament of Cresseid* (1593). With the exception of the prose description of the assembling of the gods in the thirteenth scene, the play is in verse and employs five different metres, of which only one (in the first two scenes) belongs to Welsh prosody. The verse lacks polish and the soliloquies are overlong. The play's virtues lie in its unified presentation of a Tragedy of Fortune, established in the opening two scenes but culminating in the fall of Cresyd. Although the Chorus directs the audience's attention to the contrast between the faithful love of Troelus and the faithless love of Cresyd, the play has another, more profound theme, namely the thwarting of the human will by Fate, which it presents in a ritualistic manner.

Neither the date of the play's composition nor the name of its author is known, although most critics agree that it was written during the first years of the seventeenth century. The dialect forms used suggest an author who was a native of Denbighshire or Flintshire and who had a command of English which was superior to that commonly found in the England of the period. There is no record of a performance of the play prior to 1954, when it was presented at the *National Eisteddfod, although it was clearly the author's intention that his work should be staged.

Two editions of the text are available, a scholarly one edited by W. Beynon Davies (1976) and a modernized version edited by Gwyn Williams (1976). The earliest substantial consideration of the play is J. S. P. Tatlock's article, 'The Welsh *Troilus and Cressida* and its Relation to the Elizabethan Drama' in *Modern Language Review* (vol. X, 1915). See also the articles by Gwyn Williams in the *Transactions of the Honourable Society of Cymmrodorion* (1957) and by Roger Stephens Jones in the *Bulletin* of the Board of Celtic Studies (May, 1976, Nov., 1977 and May, 1979); the latter proposes a composition date in the 1560s and offers evidence in support of Humphrey Llwyd as the play's author.

Trysorfa'r Plant, see under LEVI, THOMAS (1825–1916).

Tryweryn, a valley near Bala, Mer., which, with the village of Capel Celyn, was drowned in the early 1960s to make a reservoir, now called Llyn Celyn, for the supply of water to Liverpool. Like the proposal to build a bombing-school at *Penyberth in 1936, the scheme was unanimously opposed by public opinion in

Wales but the Members of Parliament representing Welsh constituencies were overruled at Westminster by a Conservative Government which pushed through a private bill sponsored by Liverpool City Council. The affair sparked off a campaign of direct action by Welsh Nationalists, which included sabotage, and also marked a new phase in the growth of support for *Plaid Cymru*. Ever since, the use and cost of water collected in Wales has been one of the most controversial issues in Welsh affairs.

For a detailed account see Alan Butt Philip, *The Welsh Question* (1975); see also Gwynfor Evans, *Save Cwm Tryweryn for Wales* (1956) and *We Learn from Tryweryn* (1957).

TUCKER, NORMAN (1894–1971), historian, novelist and poet, born in Swansea, Glam., belonged to a family with roots in Gower. By profession he was a journalist and contributed frequently to the *North Wales Weekly News*. The author of many articles and books on historical subjects, he wrote a dozen novels, mainly historical, eight of which are set in north Wales: *Castle of Care* (1937), *Ride Gloriously* (1944), *Gay Salute* (1946), *Minions of the Moon* (1946), *No Coward Soul* (1947), *Master of the Field* (1949), *Restless We Roam* (1950) and *The Rising Gull* (1952). He also published several volumes of verse, including *Maple and Oak* (1953) and *Rhymes of the Countryside* (1959).

Tudful or **Tydfil** (late 5th cent.), saint, was one of the daughters of *Brychan Brycheiniog. Almost nothing is known about her, but a story was told by Iolo Morganwg (Edward *Williams) in the Llanover Manuscripts of how she was killed by pagans while visiting her father. She is remembered in the name of Merthyr Tydfil, Glam., but there 'merthyr' has the meaning 'memorial', not 'martyr' (cf. Merthyr Cynog, Brecs.); a well in the town also bears her name. The tradition relating to her martyrdom is late and may be an onomastic interpretation of a place-name. According to Charles *Wilkins in his *Tales and Sketches of Wales* (1879), Tydfil was killed by Picts while returning from a visit to Tangwystl, Brychan's favourite daughter, who is said to have lived about five miles from where the town of Merthyr Tydfil is now situated, but this assertion relies on T. J. Ll. *Prichard's *Heroines of Welsh History* (1854).

Tudor or **Tudur family, The**, the holders of the English throne from 1485 to 1603, were descended from *Ednyfed Fychan, seneschal of *Llywelyn ap Iorwerth (Llywelyn Fawr). Tudur ap Goronwy ap Tudur ap Goronwy ap Ednyfed Fychan (d. 1367), who owned lands in Caernarfonshire and Anglesey, including those of Penmynydd, was considered to be the founder of the Tudor line and he was a patron of poets, including *Iolo Goch and *Gruffudd ap Maredudd ap Dafydd. His sons Rhys and Goronwy were close associates of *Owain Glyndŵr and the former was executed for his part in the rising of 1400. The family's estate at Penmynydd was later repossessed by the descendants of Goronwy ap Tudur (d. 1382). They took the name of Theodore and constituted an undistinguished line of Anglesey squires until the early eighteenth century when Penmynydd was absorbed by the Baron Hill estate of the *Bulkeley family.

Maredudd, the brother of Rhys and Goronwy, is a shadowy figure but his son, Owain Tudur (c.1400–61), held minor offices at the court of Henry V. After that king's death, his widow, Catherine de Valois, daughter of the King of France, fell in love with her handsome Gentleman of the Bedchamber and, contrary to custom, married him secretly in 1429. Owain, no longer protected after Catherine's death in 1436, incurred the animosity of the Regent, the Duke of Gloucester, and was deprived of the custody of his children. The accession of Henry VI, however, brought her stepfather back to favour and Owain was loyal to the Lancastrian cause until his capture at the battle of *Mortimer's Cross and subsequent execution at Hereford.

Of Owain's five children, Edmund Tudor (c.1430–56), Earl of Richmond, the father of the future King Henry VII, and his brother Jasper Tudor (c.1431–95), Earl of Pembroke and Duke of Bedford, played a significant part in the events to follow. Edmund married Margaret Beaufort, a descendant of John of Gaunt, and after the death of Henry VI in 1471 she was the main Lancastrian claimant to the English throne. Their son, Henry Tudor (1457–1509), exiled in Brittany from 1471, sailed to Wales in 1485 and, after defeating Richard III at the battle of *Bosworth, was crowned King of England. He married Elizabeth, the daughter of Edward IV and a descendant of the Mortimers and of *Gwladus Ddu, the daughter of Llywelyn Fawr. With Henry's accession to the throne, there was a belief among the Welsh that 'the Crown of Britain' had been restored to them, in accordance with the *vaticination of the poets. King Henry made much use of bardic propaganda but during his reign Wales was inevitably drawn more closely into the orbit of English government.

Further details about the Welsh connections of the Tudors will be found in H. T. Evans, *Wales and the Wars of the Roses* (1915), W. Garmon Jones, 'Welsh Nationalism and Henry Tudor' in the *Transactions of the Honourable Society of Cymmrodorion* (1917–18), R. T. Jenkins, *Yr Apêl at Hanes* (1930). W. Ambrose Bebb, *Cyfnod y Tuduriaid* (1939), J. F. Rees, *Studies in Welsh History* (1947), Glyn Roberts, *Aspects of Welsh History* (1969), S. B. Chrimes, *The Reign of Henry VII* (1974), Penry Williams, *The Tudor Regime* (1979) and the monograph on Henry Tudor by Glanmor Williams in the *St. David's Day* series (1985).

TUDUR ALED (*c*.1465–*c*.1525), one of the greatest among the *Poets of the Gentry, was born in the parish of Llansannan, Denbs. According to his own testimony, his bardic teacher was his uncle, *Dafydd ab Edmwnd, and he adds that Ieuan ap Llywelyn ab Ieuan ap Dafydd was another. In his elegy for Ieuan ap Dafydd ab Ithel Fychan of Tegeingl, he states that it was at a wedding-feast held in his patron's house that he first graduated as a poet. He was one of the commissioners of the *Caerwys Eisteddfod of 1523. Many poets, in their elegies for Tudur Aled, refer to him as '*bardd cadeiriog*' ('chaired poet'), and *Siôn ap Hywel ap Llywelyn Fychan and *Lewys Daron both mention his '*cadair arian*' ('silver chair'). Furthermore, Lewys Daron calls him '*bencerdd y ddwy gerdd*' ('a master craftsman of the two crafts') and *Lewys Môn refers to him as '*fardd dwbl*' ('a double poet'). It is not clear what precisely these epithets signify. T. Gwynn *Jones thought that 'a master craftsman of the two crafts' meant that Tudur Aled was an instructor in both the poet's and the musician's craft, but recent research has shown that this explanation is hardly feasible.

From the nine elegies composed on his death, which testify to the high esteem in which he was held by his fellow-poets, a clear picture of Tudur Aled emerges. He is portrayed as a well-dressed gentleman, physically strong, a good horseman and an athlete. During his last illness he retreated to the Franciscan monastery of Carmarthen, where his body was later buried. Since he did not compose an elegy on the death of his patron, Sir Rhys ap Thomas of *Dinefwr, in 1525, it is probable that he did not die later than that year. A persistent tradition which circulated after his death is that, in conversation with Tomos Pennant, Abbot of *Basingwerk, Tudur Aled admitted that Dafydd ab Edmwnd was the best at composing an *awdl*, *Guto'r Glyn at a praise-*cywydd* and *Dafydd ap Gwilym at a love-*cywydd*, but that he then went on to boast that he had composed *awdlau* and *cywyddau* of these types which had not been surpassed by any of the other three poets.

A great deal of his poetry is extant, including about a hundred and twenty-five *cywyddau*, some eighty-five of which are praise-poems. His poems contain more references to genealogy than those of almost any other poet of his period. He wrote in praise not only of native Welsh families but also of families of Norman or English origin which had become integrated into the Welsh society of Dyffryn Clwyd and Tegeingl (*Englefield). His chief patrons were the *Salesburys of Lleweni, near Llansannan. The Church has a central place in many of his poems, and about twenty are addressed to clerics such as Robert ap Rhys of Dôl Cynwal, who was a chaplain to Cardinal Wolsey.

The bardic tradition of the Middle Ages reached its climax in the poetry of Tudur Aled. A master of *Cerdd Dafod, he used imagery both traditional and daringly new, and in his mature work there are many glimpses of a dignified and compassionate personality. His work also reflects the changes taking place in Welsh society at the beginning of the sixteenth century. After his death there was a rapid deterioration in Welsh culture and especially in the bardic craft.

The standard edition of Tudur Aled's work is the one edited by T. Gwynn Jones (2 vols., 1926). For further details see the essay by Saunders Lewis in *Meistri'r Canrifoedd* (ed. R. Geraint Gruffydd, 1973) and the chapter by Eurys Rowlands in *A Guide to Welsh Literature* (ed. A. O. H. Jarman and Gwilym Rees Hughes, 1979). See also John Morris-Jones's remarks on the poet's craftsmanship in the *Transactions* of the Honourable Society of Cymmrodorion (1908–09).

TUDUR PENLLYN (*c*.1420–*c*.1485), poet and gentleman, of Caer-gai in the parish of Llanuwchllyn, Mer. He traded in wool and it was probably on visits to the homes of his fellow-gentry, rather than on bardic circuits, that he wrote praise-poems for some of the most eminent families of north Wales. Of the thirty-five poems attributed to him some are eulogies and elegies of a traditional kind, but he also wrote several poems of greeting, solicitation and reconciliation, as well as a few pungently satirical *englynion*. It is doubtful whether he was the author of a very funny *cywydd* to a Flint piper but it was certainly he who wrote a macaronic poem in the form of a dialogue with a girl, the poet pleading for her favours in Welsh and she refusing them in Middle English according to the rules of *cynghanedd. Tudur Penllyn was a supporter of the Lancastrians during the Wars of the Roses but he also composed poetry eulogizing members of the Yorkist faction. His wife, Gwerful Fychan, wrote verse and their son, *Ieuan ap Tudur Penllyn, was the author of fourteen *cywyddau* and a few *englynion*.

Further details about father and son will be found in *Gwaith Tudur Penllyn ac Ieuan ap Tudur Penllyn* (ed. Thomas Roberts, 1958).

Twenty-four Knights, The, see PEDWAR MARCHOG AR HUGAIN.

Twenty-four Metres, The, a classification of poetic metres originating in the first half of the fourteenth century, is usually attributed to *Einion Offeiriad but sometimes to *Dafydd Ddu Athro o Hiraddug. It consists of eight types of *englyn, four types of *cywydd and twelve others. Three of the others were Einion's own inventions, which suggests that the classification was a purely arbitrary one and not a faithful description of bardic practice. This view is strengthened by the classification's tendency to regard all the metres as stanzas, consisting of a specified number of lines, which was quite alien to the Welsh metrical tradition in which the only stanza was the *englyn* in its various forms. Nevertheless, the classification won respect and authority, and whatever changes were made subsequently, the number of twenty-four was never changed, although during the fifteenth century one *englyn* was discarded and one other admitted. At the Eisteddfod held in Carmarthen about the year 1450, *Dafydd ab Edmwnd rejected two other *englynion* in order to make room for two new metres of extreme complexity which he had himself devised. The classification was largely theoretical, because poets used only a small number of the metres, except on the rare occasions when they composed an exemplary *awdl* to demonstrate the use of all twenty-four. The only time the classification was put to practical use was at the first *Caerwys Eisteddfod (1523), when the metres which the bardic disciples were expected to master were stipulated, but it is not known to what extent these rules were implemented.

The Twenty-four Metres are known by the following names: *Gorchest y Beirdd, Cadwynfyr, Englyn Unodl Union, Englyn Unodl Crwca, Englyn Cyrch, Englyn Proest Cyfnewidiog, Englyn Proest Cadwynog, Awdl-gywydd, Cywydd Deuair Hirion, Cywydd Deuair Fyrion, Cywydd Llosgyrnog, Rhupynt Byr, Rhupynt Hir, Cyhydedd Fer, Byr-a-thoddaid, Clogyrnach, Cyhydedd Naw Ban, Cyhydedd Hir, Toddaid, Gwawdodyn, Gwawdodyn Hir, Hir-a-thoddaid, Cyrch-a-chwta, Tawddgyrch Cadwynog, Gorchest y Beirdd* and *Cadwynfyr.*

For a detailed account of the Twenty-four Metres see John Morris-Jones, *Cerdd Dafod* (1925).

Twenty-four Qualities, The, see Pedwar Ansawdd ar Hugain.

Twm Carnabwth, see Rees, Thomas (1806?–76).

Twm Chwarae Teg, see Williams, Thomas (1737–1802).

Twm o'r Nant, see Edwards, Thomas (1738–1810).

Twm Shon Catti (1828), sometimes called 'the first Welsh novel in English', has as its full title, *The Adventures and Vagaries of Twm Shon Catti, descriptive of Life in Wales*, and was published privately by its author, T. J. Llewelyn *Prichard. The book's hero is the legendary figure said to be the Welsh equivalent of the English Robin Hood or the Scottish Rob Roy, whose exploits were supposedly based upon incidents in the early life of Thomas *Jones (c.1530–1609) of Tregaron, landowner, antiquary, genealogist and minor poet. Although there had been at least one earlier English account of 'Tomshone Catty's Tricks' in a pamphlet printed by John Ross of Carmarthen in 1763, Prichard's was the first book-length celebration of this hero.

In its first state, the book was a crudely shaped narrative employing traditional material which retains the pleasing freshness and simplicity of folk-tale. Twm's courage and guile are put to the test in a number of picaresque episodes which still have the merit of being entertaining. Other characters are, at best, comic grotesques and descriptive passages are generally naïve, though Twm's cave near Rhandirmwyn is described vividly enough to suggest that the author knew the locality well. The book was presumably intended to appeal to Welshmen, as Prichard is openly critical of the English Tourists (see under Tours of Wales) and there is in it an element of blatant anti-English feeling.

Encouraged by the serious consideration given to his tale by critics such as William *Owen Pughe and David *Owen (Brutus), and by the public's response in terms of copies sold, Prichard brought out a much enlarged second edition in 1839. This version is structurally far more sophisticated but the additions of character and incident are almost without exception derivative and, for the most part, stylistically coarse and turgid. A slightly expanded third edition appeared after the author's death, in 1873, and since then there have been numerous retellings of Twm's adventures, mainly for children, of which the most recent is the novel by Lynn Hughes, *Hawkmoor* (1977), republished as *Twm Sion Catti's Men* (1983).

For further details see the article by Gerald Morgan in *The Anglo-Welsh Review* (vol. 17, no. 39, 1968).

Twm Siambar Wen (*fl.* 18th cent.), a witty old man from the district of Pen-y-bont-fawr, Mont., who was employed by the Wynnstay family (see under Williams-Wynn) as an entertainer and fool. Some of the stories still told about him are also attributed to Twm o'r Nant (Thomas *Edwards).

Twm Siôn Cati, see Jones, Thomas (c.1530–1609).

Twm Teg, see Vulliamy, Colwyn Edward (1886–1971).

Twmi Nathaniel, see under Williams, Nathaniel (1742–1826).

Twmpath, a spot, usually on common land, where young people gathered during the summer months to dance, sing and perform physical feats such as jumping and wrestling. Like many other manifestations of the old rural culture, the custom had lapsed by the middle of the nineteenth century. See also Taplas.

Twrch Trwyth, a ferocious wild boar the hunting of which is described in the tale of *Culhwch and Olwen. There are two references to the beast in early sources: in the poem '*Gorchan Cynfelyn*' which is found in *The Book of Aneirin* (see under GODODDIN) and among the *Mirabilia Britanniae* at the end of Nennius's *Historia Brittonum*. In the latter there is an account of *Arthur's hunting the boar in the vicinity of Builth during which his dog Cafall leaves the imprint of its foot on a stone.

One of the tasks set Culhwch is to acquire the comb and shears which lie between the ears of Twrch Trwyth in order to trim the hair of Ysbaddaden Bencawr in readiness for the wedding of the giant's daughter. The boar lives, with its seven offspring, at Esgair Oerfel in Ireland, and there the hunt begins. Arthur and his men pursue it for nine days and nine nights but succeed only in killing one of its piglets. When Arthur is asked about the origins of the boar he replies that it was once a king who had been transformed by God in punishment for his sins, a popular motif in medieval Welsh and Irish tales. He tries to parley with it but is told that the treasures between its ears can be obtained only by force. Twrch Trwyth then crosses from Ireland to Wales, landing at Porth Clais in Dyfed, and is pursued as far as the river Severn, and thence to Cornwall where it is driven into the sea and disappears. In the fighting it loses its other six piglets and many of Arthur's men are killed, but the treasures are eventually snatched from its ears. It is thought that the episode concerning Y Sgithrwyn Pen Beidd ('Sgithrwyn Chief Boar') in the tale of Culhwch and Olwen is a duplication of this story of hunting Twrch Trwyth.

For further details see John Rhŷs, *Celtic Folklore, Welsh and Manx* (vol. 2, 1901) and the same author's article in the *Transactions* of the Honourable Society of Cymmrodorion (1894–95); see also the article by Ruth Roberts in the *Bibliographical Bulletin* of the International Arthurian Society (1962).

Twyn Barlwm, a hill near Risca, Mon., on which a fierce battle is said to have been waged between bees and wasps, their humming filling the air for miles around like the loud music of an organ. On its summit, according to tradition, the *Druids held their courts, hurling the bodies of law-breakers into the valley still known as Dyffryn y Gladdfa. It is also said that the hill was one of the mounds thrown up by *Arthur as a look-out post for his soldiers. Twyn Barlwm was a key-point in the landscape of Arthur Machen (Arthur *Jones) who, in *Far Off Things (1922), referred to it as 'that mystic tumulus, the memorial of peoples that dwelt in that region before the Celts left the Land of Summer'.

Tŷ Gwyn, Y, see WHITLAND.

Ty unnos, see under ENCLOSURES.

'Tydi a Roddaist' (lit. 'Thou who gavest'), a well-known hymn-tune by Arwel Hughes (1909–   ), which he composed as a setting of the words '*Tydi a roddaist liw i'r wawr*' by T. Rowland *Hughes. The composer and author, who were colleagues on the staff of the BBC in Cardiff, collaborated in the writing of a verse play for radio which was broadcast on St. David's Day in 1938. The tune, composed as a finale for the programme, was written during the small hours in a waiting-room at Shrewsbury station while Arwel Hughes was on a rail-journey from Bangor to Cardiff. Subsequently included in the repertoires of many singing festivals and in hymnals, it is one of the few tunes composed during the twentieth century which is widely sung and it is especially popular in the composer's arrangement for male voices.

Tydu (John Jones; 1883–1968), see under CILIE FAMILY.

Tylorstown Terror, The, see WILDE, JIMMY (1892–1969).

Tylwyth Teg, Y (lit. 'The fair folk'), the name used in Wales for the small creatures (the counterpart of the English fairies) who are ruled over by *Gwyn ap Nudd. Although legends about them were recorded as early as the twelfth century by *Gerald de Barri (Giraldus Cambrensis), the name first appears in a *cywydd* to the mist by an unknown poet of the late fifteenth century. It is also included in William *Salesbury's *Dictionary in Englyshe and Welshe* (1547), but is given in error as synonymous with the English word 'fairies' (a word derived from the Old French *faerie*, meaning 'magic' or 'supernatural', rather than 'fair').

Many of the tales about the *Tylwyth Teg*, especially the earliest examples, are connected with lakes, such as *Llyn y Fan Fach. They are thought to have been based on a folk-memory of small people who lived in crannogs—primitive dwellings built in the middle of lakes before the beginning of the Dark Ages. Also connected with lakes were the magic cattle belonging to the *Tylwyth Teg*, such as the Speckled Cow of Hiraethog. The commonest theme in these tales is that of a young man's quest to marry one of the beautiful daughters of the *Tylwyth Teg*. The girl agrees but only on condition that he does not strike her with iron, or with 'three unnecessary blows'. These stories originate, it has been suggested, from an identification of the *Tylwyth Teg* with the earlier inhabitants of Britain, a people short of stature and dark-complexioned, who retired to remote districts before the advance of taller, more warlike invaders during the Iron Age. The *Tylwyth Teg* were said to emerge at night in search of food and water and it used to be the custom in some districts to leave victuals and a wash-bowl on the kitchen table before retiring to bed. Moralistic elements were later added to these traditions: maidens could expect silver from the *Tylwyth Teg* if they were kind to them and kept the house clean. At night, especially under a full moon, the *Tylwyth Teg* were to be seen dancing and singing in their rings, green patches which, if ploughed, would bring bad luck. Some tales, based on the theme of the magical passage of time, tell of young men being enticed into joining the dance and visiting the land of the *Tylwyth Teg* 'for a year and a day'. Another condition sometimes imposed by the *Tylwyth Teg* was that a young man had first to discover the name of the girl he wished to marry, a reference perhaps to the ancient belief that knowing a person's name gives power over the soul.

The *Tylwyth Teg* were usually assumed to be of a kindly disposition, unlike the pixies in England, and although some were mischievous few were malevolent. There are, however, tales about goblins exchanging children with mortals, as in that associated with the house known as Twt y Cwmrws in Trefeglwys, Mont., and others about their seeking the services of human midwives for fairy births. Both of these have been explained by anthropologists as attempts to improve the physical stock of the hidden people to the point at which they could take their place in the overt world and 'disappear'. Some tales illustrate the fragility of life and a fear of the unknown. It was believed important, for example, to consecrate a child through baptism as soon as possible after birth in case the *Tylwyth Teg* should steal it. If a baby was physically frail, it was said to be one of the *Tylwyth Teg*'s children and, because they were believed to fear iron, it was usual to place a poker or tongs across the cradle to protect the child until it could be baptized. The belief in the *Tylwyth Teg* survived in many parts of Wales until the end of the nineteenth century, despite opposition from the religious authorities and writers such as Charles *Edwards, Ellis *Wynne, Edmund *Jones and William Roberts (Nefydd). Other names by which they were known are *Jili Frwtan, Sili-go-dwt, Gwarwyn a Throt, Trwtyn Tratyn, Penelope, Dynion Bach Teg* and, in Glamorgan, *Bendith y Mamau*.

For further details see John Rhŷs, *Celtic Folklore, Welsh and Manx* (1901), T. Gwynn Jones, *Welsh Folklore and Folk-custom* (1979) and Hugh Evans, *Y Tylwyth Teg* (1935).

Tynged yr Iaith (lit. 'The fate of the language'; 1962), a lecture by Saunders *Lewis which was commissioned, broadcast and published as one of the *BBC Wales Annual Lectures, presents an analysis of the British Government's negative attitude towards the Welsh language since the *Act of Union (1536), an attitude adopted also by the Welsh themselves (with a few notable exceptions) until the twentieth century. The only hope for the language, the lecture argues, is to ensure that the administration for both local and central government in the Welsh-speaking areas is carried on through the medium of Welsh. The methods recommended by Saunders Lewis are those used by the Beasley family of Llangennech, near Llanelli, Carms., during the 1950s, namely civil disobedience and the challenging of the law. Within the genre of political pamphleteering the lecture is an indubitable classic. Although its message was addressed to members of *Plaid Cymru* in Welsh-speaking areas, it led to the formation of *Cymdeithas yr Iaith Gymraeg* later in the same year.

A recording of the author reading the lecture in Welsh has been published (1983); English versions of the text are to be found in *Planet* (no. 4, 1971) and in *Presenting Saunders Lewis* (ed. Gwyn Thomas and Alun R. Jones, 1973).

Tyno Helyg, see under CANTRE'R GWAELOD.

Tysilio (7th cent.), saint. According to the *Lives of the Saints, he was the son of Brochfael Ysgithrog, Prince of *Powys, and a brother to *Cynan Garwyn whose praises were sung by *Taliesin. He is the subject of a poem by *Cynddelw Brydydd Mawr and is mentioned in the Life of *Beuno as having lived with that saint at Meifod for forty days. He seems to have become confused with the Breton saint Suliac, and some of the traditions associated with him were incorporated in the latter's Life. This work attributes to him the desire, at an early age, to lead a religious life, despite his father's disapproval. He fled to Meifod and was taught there by an abbot named Gwyddfarch. Settling later on the banks of the Menai, Tysilio founded the church of Llandysilio. He remained there for seven years, but returned to Meifod and succeeded Gwyddfarch as abbot. According to the Breton Life, he suffered many tribulations caused by his sister-in-law's attempts to find him a wife and make him a prince, to escape from which he fled to Brittany where he founded the church of St. Suliac on the river Rance. The contents of the Suliac Life apart, the distribution of the churches which bear Tysilio's name seems to accord with the traditions associated with the saint, for there is evidence of his cult in south Cardiganshire and in Anglesey as well as in many parts of Powys, but it is unlikely that he went to Brittany, although his cult was later to spread there.

The text known as *Brut Tysilio*, a version of *Geoffrey of Monmouth's *Historia Regum Britanniae* which belongs to the fifteenth century, has no connection whatsoever with the saint.

Tyst, Y (lit. 'The witness'; 1867–   ), a weekly

newspaper first published in Liverpool as *Y Tyst Cymreig* under the editorship of John *Thomas (1821–92), who was assisted by a group of Independent ministers. In 1871 it was amalgamated with *Y Dydd* to continue as *Y Tyst a'r Dydd* until 1891 when the two went their separate ways. After the death of the first editor in 1892, the editorship passed to various Congregational ministers who included John Thomas of Merthyr Tydfil and Job Miles of Aberystwyth, a partnership which lasted until the former's death in 1911; H. M. Hughes of Cardiff was then appointed editor. From 1923, under the editorship of Beriah Gwynfe *Evans, an experienced journalist, the paper's circulation was doubled, but before long its frequent coverage of controversial issues caused its readership to decline. John Dyfnallt *Owen was appointed editor in 1927 and he was the most successful in that post in the paper's history. *Y Tyst* became the property of the Welsh Independents in 1936 and is still published by the Union. Among recent editors were E. Lewis Evans and Iorwerth Jones. Like other denominational newspapers, *Y Tyst* used to carry foreign, national and local news, all presented from a Radical viewpoint, but now it is confined to denominational affairs.

Tywyll Heno (lit. 'Dark tonight'; 1962), a novella by Kate *Roberts. The chief character is Bet Jones, a minister's wife who is in a mental hospital after losing her religious faith. Tracing the course of her insanity and her eventual recovery, the novel places an emphasis more on Bet's thoughts and emotions than on external events and yet, in a very subtle way, it comments on the crisis of faith in the modern world. Bet Jones conquers her illness and is determined to face the future boldly, having learnt to accept life in all its complexity. The title is taken from the famous *englynion* about the hall of Cynddylan in the *Canu Llywarch Hen* cycle.

For a critical discussion of this novel see the article by Geraint Wyn Jones in *Ysgrifau Beirniadol VII* (ed. J. E. Caerwyn Williams, 1972) and that by John Gwilym Jones in *Swyddogaeth Beirniadaeth* (1977).

U

Ugeined, see under BOWEN, EUROS (1904–   ).

Un Nos Ola Leuad (lit. 'One moonlit night'; 1961), a novel by Caradog *Prichard. Written in the first person singular, in the dialect of Bethesda, Caerns., the author's native district, and in a style resembling at times 'the stream of consciousness', it appears to have little or no form, but the terror and madness in the narrator's reminiscences are mixed with a measure of humour in proportions not entirely fortuitous. The narrator's mother enters an asylum, as the author's own mother did, and what follows in this powerful and moving work, one of the most impressive novels to be published in Welsh since the Second World War, is largely autobiographical.

The novel was translated into English by Menna Gallie as *Full Moon* (1973).

Undeb Awduron Cymru (lit. 'The union of the writers of Wales'), a union of writers in the Welsh language, was founded in 1973. It has campaigned on behalf of its seventy members in such areas as publicity, reviews, contracts and fees, and has served as a forum for public discussion and as a consultative body. See also WELSH UNION OF WRITERS.

Undeb Cymru Fydd (lit. 'The union of the Wales of the future'), an organization known in English as **The New Wales Union**, was founded in 1941 when *Undeb Cenedlaethol y Cymdeithasau Cymraeg* ('The national union of Welsh societies') joined with another group, *Pwyllgor Amddiffyn Diwylliant Cymru* ('The Committee for the Defence of the Culture of Wales'). With T. I. *Ellis as its Secretary from its inception until 1967, the organization brought together virtually every prominent Welshman who was committed to the cause of the Welsh language and its culture. Throughout the 1940s it made representations to the British Government on such questions of national importance as broadcasting, education and the acquisition of land in Wales for military purposes, some of which met with success. Among its publications were *Yr Athro*, a magazine for teachers, *Cofion Cymru*, a monthly newsletter for Welsh people serving in the armed forces, and *Llythyr Ceridwen*, a journal for women. Perhaps its most important single act was its decision in 1950 to call a conference which led to the launching of the *Parliament for Wales Campaign. After a period of stagnation, it became in 1966 an educational charity with the intention of creating a network of classes for the teaching of Welsh to adults, but it decided to suspend all activity three years later in the belief that, with the advent of other organizations such as *Cymdeithas yr Iaith Gymraeg*, it no longer had a role to play. See also CYMRU FYDD.

For details of the history of the organization see T. I. Ellis, *Undeb Cymru Fydd* (1960) and R. Gerallt Jones, *A Bid for Unity* (1971).

Undeb y Cymry ar Wasgar (lit. 'The union of Welsh people in dispersion'), an organization known in English since 1969 as **Wales International**, was founded in 1948 for the purpose of fostering cultural links between Wales and Welsh expatriates or people of Welsh descent living in other countries. Its founders were a small group of servicemen who, during the Second World War, had felt the need for a society of this kind. The first President of the Union was H. Elvet *Lewis (Elfed) and among those prominent in its creation were Ifan ab Owen *Edwards, T. I. *Ellis, R. E. Griffith and T. Elwyn Griffiths. The last-named, who was editor of *Seren y Dwyrain*, a magazine published in Cairo during the War which was read by Welsh men and women serving in the Middle East, became editor of the society's journal, *Yr Enfys*. The Union, which has a membership of about four thousand, is responsible for staging at the *National Eisteddfod the annual ceremony in which Welsh people living overseas, or people of Welsh extraction, are welcomed as visitors to Wales. The ceremony, which tends to be emotional, has been criticized for being irrelevant to the ethos of contemporary Wales, but, like the Union itself, it provides a symbolic link with the homeland for many who cherish the connection. See also UNWAITH ETO'N NGHYMRU ANNWYL.

Under Milk Wood (1954), a 'play for voices' by Dylan *Thomas and his most famous prose work. Published in book form after the author's death, it had first appeared in 1952 as parts of a work-in-progress in *Botteghe Oscure*, a periodical edited in Rome, under the title 'Llareggub (A Piece for Radio Perhaps)'. Solo readings and cast performances had taken place during Thomas's third visit to America (April–June, 1953). Although stylistically and imaginatively indebted to many of the writer's earlier works, especially his film-scripts of the 1940s, the play's most obvious predecessor was the radio script, *Quite Early One Morning*, which had been written in 1944.

The setting, the fictional seaside town of Llareggub (the spelling of this palingram was altered, after the author's death, to the more delicate Llaregyb), is an evocation mainly of Laugharne, Carms., where Dylan Thomas lived for the last four years of his life. He described the play's structure as 'an interweaving of many voices, with the strong central voice of a narrator to supply the unities of time, place and situation'. The narrator was finally split into a First Voice and a Second Voice, alternating for the sake of variety. Together they set the scene and select the characters to be described and overheard in the town's cyclical progress through the space of a single spring day, first in their dreams and then in their activities and relationships during the waking day until night comes again. There are more than sixty characters, many of whom, despite the sketchiness of their portrayal, have become household names, but an extra element is provided by the relatively greater attention paid to three of them: *Captain Cat, the Reverend *Eli Jenkins and *Polly Garter. The natural sexuality of the last-named contrasts with the repressions and neuroses of some of the other characters and was doubtless intended to be taken as a norm in the celebration of Llareggub as 'this place of love'.

The play's low-key comic tone is determined not so much by dramatic or sociological considerations as by the writer's delight in human eccentricity and, above all, in the evocative power of its language. It is significant that he abandoned an earlier plan (under the title *The Town that was Mad*) of using a more formally structured plot in which the town would be put on trial for being 'an insane area' but would choose in the end its own isolation and eccentricity as being morally superior to the 'sanity' of the outside world. *Under Milk Wood* in its final form makes a philosophical point less directly, with a Chaucerian relish for life in the face of time's passing and the inevitability of death. Although it has been successfully performed on the stage and on television, the play is essentially a product of the auditory imagination, blending narrative, dream-sequences, monologues, dialogues, songs and children's games. It afforded the ultimate opportunity for Dylan Thomas's lyrical impulse but its gusto is tempered by a strong element of satire and self-parody.

For discussion of the play's merits see the article by R. Williams in *Critical Quarterly* (Spring, 1959), Douglas Cleverdon, *The Growth of Milk Wood* (1969) and L. Lerner, 'Sex in Arcadia', in Walford Davies (ed.), *Dylan Thomas: New Critical Essays* (1972).

Unfaithful Wife, The, a popular theme in folk-literature, in which the wife lures her husband to his death by discovering the secret of his vulnerability, is represented in Welsh literature by the story of *Blodeuwedd, who becomes the wife of *Lleu Llawgyffes. There is a variation of this tale in a *cywydd* to the owl, once wrongly attributed to *Dafydd ap Gwilym, in which the story is essentially the same except that Blodeuwedd is said to be the daughter of a lord of Anglesey rather than a woman made by magic from flowers.

For a detailed discussion of the theme see W. J. Gruffydd, *Math vab Mathonwy* (1928).

Unfinished Journey (1937), the first of the autobiographies of Jack *Jones, is an account of the first fifty-two years of his colourful life, from his birth and childhood in a Merthyr Tydfil slum to his early days of authorship in Rhiwbina, Cardiff. A work of great vividness and engaging candour, some of its chapters, including those dealing with his childhood and his life as a collier, rank with the finest and most moving of the author's writings.

Unitarianism, a religious belief which denies the doctrine of the Trinity and the deity of Jesus Christ. Opposition in the Early Church to the orthodox doctrines had arisen in the form of *Sabellianism and Arianism, which held that Christ had not co-existed with the Father from eternity and was therefore God only in a subordinate sense. During the Reformation, Socinianism went a step further in teaching that Christ had no existence before he was born of the Virgin Mary and that his essential humanity was intended to demonstrate the efficacy of repentance without atonement and the certainty of resurrection on the Last Day. Unitarianism, under the leadership of Joseph Priestley and others in the second half of the eighteenth century, went on to reject both the miraculous conception and the worship of Christ. In its modern creed it emphasizes the unity of the Godhead, the example of Christ and the goodness and brotherhood of Man; it opposes formal creeds and actively supports religious and political liberty.

During the eighteenth century Arianism was espoused by such Welshmen as David Lloyd (1724–79), David *Davis of Castell Hywel, Abraham Rees (1743–1825) and Richard *Price. The Presbyterian College at Carmarthen served to propagate its principles, thus preparing the way for more explicitly Unitarian beliefs. Thomas *Evans (Tomos Glyn Cothi) founded the first Unitarian meeting-house in Wales (*c.*1794) and the Unitarian Association of South Wales was established in 1802. Among its members were William *Owen Pughe, Edward *Williams (Iolo Morganwg) and his son Taliesin *Williams, together with several former General Baptist ministers. Through the influence of William *Thomas (Gwilym Marles), biblical criticism came to exert a still greater hold over Unitarian thinking.

Formal Unitarianism has had little success in Wales as a whole, however. Only twenty-seven meeting-houses belonged to the movement in 1851 and the same number in 1979. It has been strongest in south Cardiganshire and north Carmarthenshire, an area known to the orthodox denominations as 'The Black Spot', but many individuals have embraced Unitarian teachings without ever belonging to a Unitarian church. Some have made important contributions to Welsh literature: in addition to those already named, notable examples are Thomas *Stephens, J. Gwenogvryn *Evans, George Eyre Evans (1857–1939) and D. Jacob Davies (1916–74). The movement's theological tenets were opposed in the work of such men as William *Williams (Pantycelyn), Peter *Williams, Christmas *Evans and Joseph *Harris (Gomer).

For a discussion of Unitarianism in Wales see J. G. Jenkins, *Hanfod Duw a Pherson Crist* (1931), T. Oswald Williams, *Undodiaeth a Rhyddid Meddwl* (1962) and D. E. Davies, *Y Smotiau Duon* (1981) and *They Thought for Themselves* (1982); see also the Unitarian magazine *Yr Ymofynnydd*.

University of Wales, The. By the middle of the nineteenth century Wales had in St. David's College, Lampeter (founded in 1822), a college which granted degrees to candidates for the Anglican ministry, but the need was felt for a non-denominational, national University. Public discussion about the future shape of higher education in Wales was led, in particular, by Hugh *Owen, who canvassed among the *London Welsh the idea of a University for Wales. In due course it was accepted but the aim was modified in favour of a College which would prepare students for examinations under the aegis of London University, a common procedure in England at the time. In 1869 a building intended as a hotel was bought at Aberystwyth and, three years later, it opened as a University College with twenty-six students and Thomas Charles Edwards (1837–1900), the son of Lewis *Edwards, as its Principal.

There was, at first, no formal link between the University College at Aberystwyth and the Colleges which were established at Cardiff in 1883 and Bangor in 1884 as a result of a recommendation by a Departmental Committee, appointed by Gladstone's Government, under the chairmanship of Lord Aberdare. The initial progress of the three Colleges was slow, partly because there were few secondary schools to prepare pupils for higher education, but after the passing of the Welsh Intermediate Education Act in 1889 there was an improvement in numbers attending. The three Colleges were brought together under a Royal Charter in 1893 as a federal University with power to grant its own degrees.

The prime mover of the new institution was Herbert Isambard *Owen.

The University had three official bodies—the Court, the Senate (consisting of the Professors of the three Colleges) and the Guild of Graduates—but there was dissatisfaction with these arrangements and a Royal Commission, chaired by Lord Haldane, recommended in 1918 the creation of an enlarged Court, a new executive body to be known as the Council, and an Academic Board to take over the duties of the Old Senate. This constitution has survived to the present day. The officers of the University are the Chancellor (a member of the royal family), the Pro-Chancellor (a prominent Welshman), the Vice-Chancellor (the Principals of the Colleges in turn), the Warden of the Guild of Graduates, the Secretary of the Council and the Registrar. The University's headquarters are in Cathays Park, Cardiff, its motto is '*Scientia Ingenium Artes*' ('Science, Engineering, Arts') and it has about eighteen thousand full-time students.

To the three Colleges which constituted the University of Wales in 1918 were added University College, Swansea, in 1920, the Welsh National School of Medicine in 1931, the Institute of Science and Technology in 1967 and St. David's University College in 1971. In 1964 a committee was appointed to consider defederalization and the establishment of four independent Universities but its subsequent advocacy of such a course was rejected by the Court. Among those who vigorously defended the University's federal structure were Alwyn D. *Rees and Jac L. *Williams. Each of the seven institutions enjoys a high degree of autonomy and the University has the responsibility for providing the means by which the Colleges may co-operate on central boards, most notably the Academic Board, the *Board of Celtic Studies and the University of Wales Press Board. The Press, which was established in 1922, has made an enormous contribution to the publication of scholarly works in several fields, but especially in the study of the history, language and literature of Wales. The University is also the owner of Gregynog Hall, near Newtown in Powys, where a variety of committees, seminars and conferences are held and where the *Gregynog Press is housed.

The contribution of the University to *scholarship in Wales has been of the utmost importance. Welsh was recognized as a subject from the beginning only at Cardiff, with the appointment of Thomas *Powel to a lectureship, a post which was elevated to a professorship in 1884. Three years elapsed between the opening of the College at Aberystwyth and the appointment of Daniel Silvan *Evans as part-time Professor in 1875 and five years before John *Morris-Jones was made Professor of Welsh at Bangor in 1889. There are now Welsh Departments in all five University Colleges and there has been progress in the provision of courses taught through the medium of Welsh since the 1960s. English Departments, on the other hand, have been much slower to accord critical recognition to Anglo-Welsh literature and the initiative in this respect has come mostly from universities in England, Canada and the USA.

Further details will be found in D. Emrys Evans, *The University of Wales, A Historical Sketch* (1953), E. L. Ellis, *The University College of Wales Aberystwyth 1872–1972* (1972), D. T. W. Price, *A History of St. David's College* (vol. 1, 1977), Gwyn Jones and Michael Quinn (ed.), *Fountains of Praise: University College, Cardiff 1883–1983* (1983) and J. Gwynn Williams, *The University College of North Wales: Foundations* (1985).

University of Wales Review, The, see WELSH ANVIL.

Unrestrained Ravagings of the Isle of Britain, Three, a Triad listing three royal courts which were devastated and all their resources consumed. *Medrod ravaged *Arthur's court, at Celli-wig in Cornwall, dragged *Gwenhwyfar from her chair and slapped her, Arthur reciprocated by devastating Medrod's court at a place not named and Aeddan Fradog devastated the court of *Rhydderch Hael at Alclud (Dumbarton). The Triad of Harmful Blows and the account of Medrod's liaison with Gwenhwyfar in *Brut y Brenhinedd* can be compared with the first of these. No account of Arthur's raid has been preserved. The third alludes to hostility between Rhydderch and Aeddan, the rulers of Strathclyde and Dal Riada, the contiguous kingdoms of the Britons and the Scots respectively, which lay in the *Old North.

'Unwaith Eto'n Nghymru Annwyl' (lit. 'Once again in dear Wales'), a song originally composed as a soprano/tenor solo which is sung every year at the *National Eisteddfod during the ceremony of welcome to Welsh expatriates; some find it lachrymose and it is often ridiculed (see under UNDEB Y CYMRY AR WASGAR). The tune and words are of uncertain origin but are probably the work of Dyfed Lewis (1855–1927), a native of Llan-crwys, Carms.

Urdd Gobaith Cymru (lit. 'The league of the hope of Wales'), known in English as **The Welsh League of Youth**, a movement for children and young people, was founded by Ifan ab Owen *Edwards, who first invited his readers to join the new organization through the pages of his magazine *Cymru'r Plant* in January 1922. Based on the principles of fidelity to Wales, Mankind and Christ, it has always maintained a non-political, non-sectarian stance. Its internationalist outlook was acquired during the 1920s when, with the League of Nations Union, it began to sponsor the annual Goodwill Message of the Children of Wales to the Children of

the World (see under DAVIES, GWILYM). During the inter-War years it held athletic meetings, dressed its members in uniforms and generally endeavoured to make Welsh culture more attractive to the young. Among its contributions to the wider cultural life of Wales was the support it lent to the establishment of the first Welsh-medium primary school, opened at Aberystwyth in 1939, and to the foundation in 1943 of the Union of Welsh Publishers and Booksellers. Today, as part of the British Government's youth service, it includes in its programme a wide variety of educational, cultural and recreational activity. For example, from its headquarters at Aberystwyth the *Urdd* publishes four magazines, runs two residential centres and an annual Eisteddfod, and administers the work of more than a thousand branches in all parts of Wales. Its role as a bastion of Welsh national consciousness among the young continues to be of the first importance.

The history of the movement has been written in Welsh by R. E. Griffith (3 vols., 1971, 1972, 1973); an English version was published in one volume in 1973.

Urien Rheged (6th cent.), a king of the *Old North, is named in *Achau'r Saeson*, a work included in *Nennius's *Historia Brittonum*, as one of the four kings who opposed the infiltration of the Angles into the Brythonic territories; the other three were *Rhydderch Hen (or Hael), *Gwallog and *Morgan. It is said that Urien was killed by an agent of Morgan's while he was besieging the enemy in their last stronghold on Ynys Medgawdd, the island of Lindisfarne off the coast of Northumberland. Urien's court may have been at Carlisle and his authority as King of Rheged may once have extended as far as Catterick, Yorks. Nine *awdlau* to him, all the work of *Taliesin, have been preserved and that poet's description of him may be considered as the corner-stone of traditional Welsh praise-poetry. The two principal themes in these poems are the King's generosity at court and his ferocity on the battlefield. In peacetime a just and responsible ruler and a generous patron, he protected the kingdom in time of war by defeating his enemies and driving them far from his lands. No elegy to Urien by Taliesin has been preserved, although *The *Book of Taliesin* contains an elegy to his son, *Owain ab Urien. Traditions about him occur in mythological form in *'Canu Llywarch Hen', including an elegy recited by Llywarch who, according to ancient genealogies, was Urien's cousin.

Uthr Bendragon, the son of Constantine II and the father of King *Arthur according to *Geoffrey of Monmouth's *Historia Regum Britanniae*, which states that he was brought up in Brittany in order to avoid the hostility of *Vortigern. After engaging in war against Vortigern, together with his brother Ambrosius (*Emrys Wledig), he succeeds the latter to the throne of

Britain. He begets Arthur on Ygerna (*Eigr), the wife of Gorlois, Duke of Cornwall, with the help of *Myrddin (Merlin), who uses his magic powers to transform him into the likeness of the Duke. Shortly afterwards Gorlois is killed and Uthr marries Ygerna, but the king meets his death by poison and Arthur then inherits the throne.

Uthr was known in Welsh tradition before Geoffrey's time. An old poem in *The *Black Book of Carmarthen* states that *Mabon, the son of Modron, was one of Uthr's servants. According to the poem entitled *'Ymddiddan Arthur a'r Eryr'*, Arthur had a nephew called Eliwlad, who was the son of Madog mab Uthr. It is therefore probable that an old tradition made Arthur a brother of Madog and a son of Uthr, and that this tradition was used by Geoffrey. In the Triad of the Three Principal Enchantments of the Isle of Britain Uthr is said to have taught magic to *Menw mab Teirgwaedd, a character in the tale of *Culhwch and Olwen who possessed magical powers. The epithet 'Pendragon', which signified 'chief leader' or 'warrior', was explained by Geoffrey as 'dragon's head'. The writer associated it with a ball of fire in the form of a dragon attached to a brilliant star which was supposed to have appeared in the heavens at the time of Ambrosius's death.

For further details see Rachel Bromwich, *Trioedd Ynys Prydein* (1961).

Utilitarianism, the teaching that Man's good should be happiness and that his conduct should be directed towards securing the greatest good of the greatest number. The principle was systematized in England by Jeremy Bentham, James Mill and John Stuart Mill, the last-named complicating the doctrine by his assertion that the value of any happiness must be estimated according to its quality as well as its extent. Utilitarianism was associated with the ideas of Progress and political *Radicalism during the nineteenth century. Some protested against the doctrine on the grounds that it bred a materialistic outlook and tended to promote a mechanical uniformity. Its effect was certainly to depreciate minorities and, in Wales, it helped to bring about an attitude which regarded the Welsh language and its culture as comparatively unimportant or even as an obstacle to worldly success. It can be argued that men such as Hugh *Owen and Kilsby Jones (James Rhys *Jones), for example, were engaged not so much in enriching the distinctive culture of Wales as in seeking to foster a middle-class respectability and efficiency on what they took to be English lines. The Utilitarian movement, beginning with Robert *Owen, who was a friend of Bentham, prepared the way for *Socialism, a political creed which called for more drastic changes than the older Radicalism had contemplated, including the concept of the Welfare State.

V

Valiant Welshman, The (1615), a play attributed to the English writer Robert Armin (*fl.* 1610), purports to describe 'the true chronicle of the life and valiant deeds of Caradoc the Great, King of Cambria, now called Wales'. Its interest is as much comic as historical, deriving its humour from the wit of Morgan, Earl of Anglesey, and his son Morion.

Valle Crucis, an abbey founded in 1201 by the *Cistercian Order as a daughter-house of *Strata Marcella, under the patronage of *Madog ap Gruffudd, Prince of Powys. Situated on the banks of the river Eglwyseg in the commot of ᴬYale (Iâl), it was known in Welsh as Llynegwestl, Glynegwestl, Llanegwestl, Glyn y Groes and Pant y Groes Hen. Siôn ap Rhisiart, Abbot from about 1450 to about 1480, was a member of the Trefor family and an uncle to the poet *Gutun Owain. The close relationship between them is reflected in the latter's five eulogies, a poem requesting a horse and an elegy upon his patron's death. *Dafydd ab Edmwnd sang the Abbot's praises, an unknown poet asked him for the gift of a horse and Rhys o Garno and *Guto'r Glyn were among the poets who debated the merits of the Abbot's court; all these poems emphasize the delightful life to be had at the abbey. To another Abbot, Dafydd ab Ieuan ab Iorwerth (*c.*1480–1500), also a generous patron, Gutun Owain dedicated eight poems and *Tudur Aled wrote a satirical poem on the Abbot's behalf. Guto'r Glyn, who referred to himself as '*prydydd Arglwydd Dafydd Dda*' ('the good Lord Dafydd's poet'), addressed eleven poems to him, one of which requested the loan of *Llyfr y Greal*. It seems from his *cywydd*, '*Cysur Henaint*', that Guto spent his last years, old and blind, under his patron's protection at the monastery. Dafydd ab Ieuan later became Bishop of *St. Asaph (*c.*1503–27) where *Lewys Môn, Tudur Aled, Gruffudd ab Ieuan ap Llywelyn Fychan and Dafydd Cowper wrote poems in his praise. According to tradition, Lewys Môn died at the abbey in 1527. The Abbot Robert Salbri (*c.*1528–35) was one of those from whom the poet Huw *Llwyd requested oxen. He was, however, removed from office by Lleision Tomas, Abbot of Neath, on suspicion of minting money and of being a highway robber, and was later imprisoned in the Tower of London. The abbey was dissolved in 1536. *Owain Gwynedd, describing the ruins of the monastery in an *englyn*, declared that its destruction was due to God's wrath at the monks' sinful lives.

It was the Abbot of Valle Crucis who, according to a manuscript in the hand of Elis *Gruffydd, the chronicler, was met by *Owain Glyndŵr while out walking early in the Berwyn hills. 'You have risen early, Master Abbot', said the Prince, to which the Abbot replied, 'Nay, sire, it is you who have risen early, a hundred years before your time'.

For further details see G. Vernon Price, *Valle Crucis Abbey* (1952), Glanmor Williams, *The Welsh Church from Conquest to Reformation* (1962) and Derrick Pratt, *The Dissolution of Valle Crucis Abbey* (1982).

Valley, The City, The Village, The (1956), Glyn *Jones's first novel, is the most memorable in detail although not the best constructed. Trystan Morgan, brought up in poverty by his grandmother, who wants him to be a preacher, gradually grows aware of his own ambition to become an artist. While he is at university, his grandmother's death frees him from the restraint of her love and, in terms of the book's structure, removes the necessary tension from the theme. The third section, set in 'Llansant' (probably Llanstephan, Carms.), the village with which Trystan has family connections, is a long interior monologue in which he imagines a Judgement Day for himself, his relations and his friends, with his grandmother as judge. Amusing as this is, it is no more than a buttress to the novel's theme and the work is most remarkable on account of its language and marvellous descriptions, especially of the gallery of characters who are so superbly portrayed in it.

Vaticination, the prediction of events in the future, has its origins in witchcraft and magic. Among the earliest examples of vaticinatory poetry in Welsh is *'*Armes Prydein*' (*c.*930), in which it was prophesied that *Cynan and *Cadwaladr would restore the ancient glory of the British people and drive the Saxons into the sea. Other early examples are the verses known as 'Yr *Afallennau, 'Hoianau' and 'Gwasgargerdd Myrddin yn y Bedd'. Several are preserved in the *Historia Brittonum of *Nennius and in *Geoffrey of Monmouth's *Historia Regum Britanniae, while others were falsely attributed to *Myrddin (Merlin) and *Taliesin. In the thirteenth and fourteenth centuries much verse of a vaticinatory nature was written by such poets as

*Adda Fras, Y *Bergam and Rhys Fardd (*fl.* 1460–80), and a number of anonymous prose prophecies are extant in both Welsh and Latin. The essence of almost all these vaticinations is the same: the Welsh will regain sovereignty over the Isle of Britain under the leadership of a messiah, known as *Y Mab Darogan* ('The Son of Destiny'), who is often *Arthur or some other national hero, and the English will be defeated for all time.

The tradition reached its peak during the Wars of the Roses in the work of such poets as *Lewys Glyn Cothi (Llywelyn y Glyn) and *Dafydd Llwyd ap Llywelyn ap Gruffudd of Mathafarn who regarded William *Herbert, and later Owain Tudur (see under TUDOR FAMILY), as the deliverer of the Welsh. The symbols used to represent the nation's hero, his allies and his enemies, were mostly derived from Geoffrey of Monmouth and were usually animals or birds —the raven for Sir Rhys ap Thomas, the ox for Jasper Tudor, the swallow for Owain Tudur, the mole for Richard III, the bear for the Earl of Warwick, and so on—and there was a variety of metaphors for the destruction of the English. Among other poets who wrote vaticinatory verse were *Dafydd Gorlech, *Gruffudd ap Dafydd Fychan and *Robin Ddu ap Siencyn Bledrydd. The truth of these prophecies was regarded as having been fulfilled at the battle of *Bosworth (1485), after which Henry Tudor ascended the English throne: a Welshman had won the Crown of Britain, a victory which was interpreted as heralding a new dawn of national freedom for the Welsh.

For further details see M. E. Griffiths, *Early Vaticination in Welsh with English Parallels* (1937), Glanmor Williams, 'Prophecy, Poetry and Politics in Medieval and Tudor Wales' in *British Government and Administration* (ed. H. Hearder and H. R. Loyn, 1974) and the chapter by R. Wallis Evans in *A Guide to Welsh Literature* (ed. A. O. H. Jarman and Gwilym Rees Hughes, 1979).

VAUGHAN, ALED (1920–   ), prose writer. Born at Glyndyfrdwy, Mer., he left school at the age of thirteen, worked as a journalist in London after being invalided out of the RAF in 1944, and joined the staff of the BBC as a radio producer in 1952. From 1960 until 1967 he worked as a television director and producer, mainly in current affairs, but then left the BBC to help establish Harlech Television (HTV) as Programme Controller. Besides short stories, including the much admired 'The White Dove', he has published a novel, *The Seduction* (1968), and a biography, *Beyond the Old Bone Trail* (1958); he also edited the anthology *Celtic Story* (1946).

There is an autobiographical essay by Aled Vaughan in *Artists in Wales* (ed. Meic Stephens, 1973).

Vaughan, Arthur Owen, see MILLS, ROBERT SCOURFIELD (1863–1919).

Vaughan, Gruffudd (*fl.* 1417–47), gentleman, of Guilsfield, Mont., was among those who imprisoned Sir John Oldcastle in Broniarth, where in 1417 the latter was hiding as a Lollard with a price on his head. He then fought in France and, according to a *cywydd* which may have been written by *Llywelyn ap Moel y Pantri, he was knighted in a town beyond Rouen, perhaps in 1440. For having killed his master, Sir Christopher Talbot, the most famous jouster of his day, in a tournament at Cawres Castle in 1443, he was deprived of the defence of the law and he became an outlaw. He avoided capture until July 1447 when, invited to Castell Coch in Powys, he was caught and executed. *Lewys Glyn Cothi (Llywelyn y Glyn) and *Dafydd ap Llywelyn ap Gruffudd composed elegies for him.

Vaughan, Gwyneth, see HUGHES, ANNIE HARRIET (1852–1910).

VAUGHAN, HENRY (1621–95), poet and physician, was born at Newton, Scethrog, in the vale of Usk, and was a grandson of William Vaughan of Tretower, Brecs. His father's circumstances had been much improved by marriage to the daughter of David Morgan David Howel of Newton, who was an important influence on her son's religious development. The boy, with his twin brother Thomas *Vaughan, was educated at Llangattock by Matthew Herbert, the rector there and a distant relative. Academically clever, they acquired a sound classical education and perhaps an introduction to Hermetic philosophy and science. In 1638 the twins enrolled at Jesus College, Oxford, but Henry seems to have stayed only two years, without taking a degree, before going to study law in London, his father deeming it necessary for the heir to Newton to be qualified for legal office within the County. At the outbreak of the *Civil War, Henry was called home and served for a while as clerk to Sir Marmaduke Lloyd, Chief Justice of the Brecon Circuit. Responding to the King's desperate plight in 1645, the brothers saw action with Sir Herbert *Price's troop at the battle of Rowton Heath, near Chester, and at Beeston Castle, both scenes of Royalist defeats, after which Henry probably returned to Newton.

In 1646 there appeared his first volume, entitled simply *Poems*. Most of its contents are dedicated to his *Amoret, the Catherine Wise of Coleshill, Warwicks., to whom he had become engaged in the Priory Grove at Brecon, but two poems recall his London days and one his intemperate Royalism; also included is a translation of Juvenal's *Tenth Satire*. Two years later, either as a result of his brother William's death or his reading of George *Herbert's *The Temple*, or perhaps both, he had an intense religious experience which was to produce the remarkable poetry of the first part of *Silex Scintillans (1650). As a result, the contents of the earlier collection *Olor Iscanus (1651) might have been suppressed but for the efforts of a friend, probably Thomas *Powell, who arranged for their publication. These poems, though secular, were in no sense degenerate: a few were written in recollection of friends, some as dedications to other authors, and others are translations; the opening poem, 'To the River Isca', is the one which justifies the book's title. Several illnesses helped to maintain Henry Vaughan's high spiritual tension, though the additional poems published as Silex Scintillans II (1655) demonstrate a quieter manner, attention to biblical topics and a recurrence of political bitterness; there are also two elegies, probably for his wife Catherine.

Between 1650 and 1655 Vaughan devoted himself to the writing of prose works and translations, including Of the Benefit Wee may get by our Enemies (1651), translated from a Latin version by Reynolds of the Greek of Plutarchus Chaeronensis, Of the Diseases of the Mind and Body (1651), translated by the same means from the Greek of Maximus Tirius, and The Praise and Happiness of the Countrie-Life (1651), from the Spanish of Antonio de Guevara. They were followed by Man in Glory (1652), a translation from the Latin of Anselm, Archbishop of Canterbury, and by a prose work very indicative of Vaughan's thinking entitled The Mount of Olives or Solitary Devotions (1652). More substantial translations were to follow under the titles of Flores Solitudinis (1654), which consisted of two discourses on Temperance and Patience and Life and Death by the Jesuit Johannis Eusebius Nierembergius, The World Condemned by Eucherius, Bishop of Lyons, and The Life of Paulinus, Bishop of Nola; these pieces were described by Vaughan as 'Collected in his Sickness and Retirement'. Both Eucherius and Paulinus were Gaulish Celts of the early fifth century, the former a conspicuous example of contemptus mundi, the latter a religious poet and bishop.

There had already been indications of Vaughan's growing interest in medicine and in 1655 he published Hermetical Physick, or The Right Way to preserve, and to restore Health, a translation from the Latin of Henry Nollius. It was probably in the same year that he began to practise as a physician, though no university enrolment has so far been discovered to justify the M.D. engraved on his tombstone. Thereafter, he seems to have abandoned authorship. His one remaining work, *Thalia Rediviva (1678), was ready, it appears, in 1673 and consists mainly of poems dating from some ten years earlier still, together with a few excluded from Olor Iscanus. One of the impulses to publish is shown by the inclusion of some 'Learned Remains' of his dead brother Thomas, 'the Eminent Eugenius Philalethes'. Henry's few

late letters to John Aubrey (see under AUBREY, WILLIAM) and Anthony à Wood (all that survive of his correspondence) show signs of weariness and lack of enthusiasm for any further literary task.

Henry Vaughan was a man of unyielding temper. Consistently unaccommodating to his religious and political opponents, he likened them to the Jews who had crucified Jesus. He saw society as reaching the end of its appointed time and in Silex Scintillans there is a remarkable sense of his own, occasionally transfigured, spirit alone in the midst of a worshipping Nature. He prayed that this intransigence might not involve violence, but it led to litigation by and against his children and it was perhaps the main reason why, in intermittent penitence, he asked to be buried outside the church of Llansantffraid, prescribing for his tombstone the words, 'Servus Inutilis: Peccator Maximus Hic Iaceo: Gloria Miserere'.

One of the great Metaphysical Poets, Vaughan paraphrased widely from the Bible and other revered texts such as those of his 'cousin', George Herbert, as was the custom in his day. But his best poetry, while occasionally short of the argumentative organization of Herbert's, contrives a mutability of rhythm and stress within the fixed form which resembles the speaking voice. Some of his poems pile up short, descriptive phrases (a technique likened by some to the Welsh technique of *dyfalu) and his sense of movement in Nature and the Hermetic perfectibility of its components is unrivalled in English poetry. The meditative night watches and the agonizing of Silex Scintillans, on which his reputation mainly rests, have too readily been taken as typical of his entire work. Most of his early poems, and a few late ones, possess the wit and some of the conceits of his period.

His adoption of the title 'Silurist' (first seen in Olor Iscanus) is puzzling. It is unlikely either to reflect the fighting prowess of the *Silures or to proffer an alternative to 'Welsh' and, although he was Welsh-speaking, his familiarity with the poetic tradition of his country has been overstated. His poem 'To the River Isca', written before the 'doom' of Silex Scintillans, makes it reasonably plain that, while he loved and celebrated his native valley, he regarded himself not as a successor in the Welsh tradition but as the first poet of a 'civilizing' poetry in English.

The best general account of Henry Vaughan's life and work is that by F. E. Hutchinson (1947); see also the monograph by Alan Rudrum in the Writers of Wales series (1981). There have been several editions of Vaughan's works since his rediscovery by H. F. Lyte in the mid-nineteenth century, the most complete of which is still that by L. C. Martin (2 vols., 1914); the most recent was edited by Alan Rudrum (1976). See also the special number of Poetry Wales (Autumn, 1975) and the article by Evelyn Simpson, 'The Local Setting of Henry Vaughan's Poetry' in The Anglo-Welsh Review (vol. 21, no. 47, 1972).

VAUGHAN, HERBERT MILLING-CHAMP (1870–1948), author, was born at Llangoedmor, Cards., and educated at Clifton and Keble College, Oxford. His private means enabled him to devote himself entirely to literary and historical pursuits. A keen contributor to many of the antiquarian journals of the day, he also published more than a dozen books, including *Essays on the Welsh Church* (1908), *Meleager: A Fantasy* (1916), *The Dial of Ahaz* (1919), *Sonnets from Italy* (1919), *The South Wales Squires* (1926) and *Nepheloccygia: or Letters from Paradise* (1929). Shortly before his death he wrote an autobiography, 'Memoirs of a Literary Bloke', the unpublished manuscript of which is kept at the *National Library of Wales.

VAUGHAN, HILDA (1892–), novelist. She was born at Builth, Brecs., although her father's appointment as Clerk of Radnorshire County Council may have been the cause of her closer identification, as a writer, with that County. Educated privately, she served during the First World War in a Red Cross hospital and as Organising Secretary of the Women's Land Army in Breconshire and Radnorshire. It was while taking a writing course at Bedford College, London, that she met and, in 1923, married Charles Morgan, then the drama critic of *The Times*, who was later to become a novelist of repute. Their shared ambition to become writers undoubtedly drew them together, as her husband's letters reveal.

Her first published novel, *The Battle to the Weak* (1925), set in the main near Builth, is a didactic work which exploits to the full her knowledge of the speech, topography and atmosphere of Radnorshire, but also reflects obliquely the author's own struggle to achieve maturity and independence. By comparison, *Here Are Lovers* (1926) is a failure, because of its naïvety and artificiality, but with *The Invader* (1928), a comedy which is the most authentically Welsh of her books, and *Her Father's House* (1930), she again makes use of her native ground. Her most successful novel, *The Soldier and the Gentlewoman* (1932), a new departure into ironic tragedy, is set in Carmarthenshire and refines the theme of *The Invader*. The novels *The Curtain Rises* (1935), *Harvest Home* (1936), *Pardon and Peace* (1945), *Iron and Gold* (1948) and *The Candle and the Light* (1954), if less memorable, exemplify their author's unwillingness merely to repeat a formula or two. In collaboration with Laurier Lister, Hilda Vaughan also wrote two plays, *She Too was Young* (1938), performed in London concurrently with her husband's play *The Flashing Stream*, and *Forsaking All Other* (1950). Her last novel, *Recovered Greenness*, was never completed. Perhaps her most exquisite writing is found in the novella *A Thing of Nought* (1934), a tale of star-crossed love in which the background of *The Battle to the Weak* is used again with greater economy.

The reputation of Hilda Vaughan since 1950 does her less than justice. The compassion at the heart of her work is free, in her best novels, from all sentimentality, the structure of her stories is often sharp and the quality of her writing, especially about Radnorshire, matches it.

For further details see the essay on Hilda Vaughan by Christopher W. Newman in the *Writers of Wales* series (1981) and G. F. Adam, *Three Contemporary Anglo-Welsh Novelists* (1948). Hilda Vaughan's two autobiographical essays were reprinted in the *Transactions* of the Radnorshire Society (vol. LII, 1983).

Vaughan, John (1603–74), lawyer, was a member of the Vaughan family which had held land at Trawsgoed, Cards., since the early thirteenth century. He distinguished himself in the Court of the Star Chamber in the 1630s and was elected Member of Parliament for Cardigan Boroughs in 1640. A constitutional critic of royal policy, he was alarmed at the last moment by the prospect of outright rebellion and decided to support the King. He subsequently commanded the militia and other Royalist forces in Cardiganshire but saw little action. He was elected Member of Parliament for Cardiganshire in 1661 and became a leading figure in the 'country' party. Appointed Chief Justice of the Court of Common Pleas in 1667, he is remembered for his ruling that a jury should not be punished for reaching a verdict which runs counter to the judge's directive. He was influential in safeguarding the Welsh judiciary and showed an enlightened interest in Welsh history and antiquities. Under him the Trawsgoed estate, which extended over forty thousand acres by the nineteenth century, was greatly augmented and provided the territorial justification for the elevation of his grandson to the Viscountcy (later Earldom) of Lisburne.

VAUGHAN, RICHARD (fl. 1585–1624), translator, Recusant and gentleman, of Bodeiliog, Henllan, near Denbigh. It was he, according to his co-religionist Gwilym *Puw of Penrhyn, who was responsible for translating the catechism *Dottrina Christiana* (1603) by Roberto Bellarmino from Italian into Welsh. On the title-page of his Welsh version, *Eglvrhad Helaeth-lawn o'r Athrawaeth Gristnogawl* (1618), are the initials of his name printed in reverse order. Bibliographers once attributed the translation to John Salisbury of Y *Rug, head of the Jesuit mission in Wales at that time, on the evidence of an entry in a manuscript dated 1632 which is kept in the English College at Rome. It is probable that Salisbury arranged for the publication of the translation. An English translation of the catechism by Richard Hadock, entitled *An Ample Declaration of the Chris(t)ian Doctrine*, had appeared in 1604, but there is evidence to suggest that Vaughan's is a version from the Italian, as the wording of the title-page claims.

For further details see the articles by Geraint Bowen in the *Journal* of the National Library of Wales (vol. VIII, no. 4, 1954 and vol. XII, no. 1, 1961).

Vaughan, Richard, see THOMAS, ERNEST LEWIS (1904–83).

VAUGHAN, ROBERT (*c*.1592–1667), antiquary, was the son of Hywel Fychan of Gwengraig, Dolgellau, Mer. He entered Oriel College, Oxford, in 1612 but left without taking a degree and, after his marriage to the daughter of Griffith *Nanney, he made his home at Hengwrt in Llanelltyd, Mer. A Justice of the Peace and a man of influence in the district, he seems to have been untouched by the *Civil War and its aftermath. His main interests were in antiquities, genealogy and the collection of manuscripts and books; he corresponded with a wide circle of eminent men of similar tastes in both Wales and England, including *Rhys Cain, *Siôn Cain, John *Davies of Mallwyd and John *Jones of Gellilyfdy. The library of Hengwrt contained the finest collection of Welsh manuscripts ever assembled by one man. Bought by W. R. M. *Wynne of Peniarth, Mer., in 1859 and sold to Sir John *Williams in 1905, the collection is now known as the *Peniarth Manuscripts and is housed in the *National Library of Wales. It includes The *Black Book of Carmarthen, The *White Book of Rhydderch and The *Book of Taliesin, among many others.

Robert Vaughan's only published work is a refutation of the claim of Thomas Canon that Cadell was the son of *Rhodri Mawr and that, subsequently, the Princes of *Deheubarth had superiority over those of *Gwynedd. Other works of his remain in manuscript, including an English translation of *Brut y Tywysogyon, a collection of Welsh *proverbs with an English translation and a study of *Trioedd Ynys Prydain.

For further details see the articles by E. D. Jones in the *Journal* of the Merioneth History and Records Society (vols. I and VIII).

Vaughan, Roger (d. 1471), gentleman, of Tretwr (Tretower), Brecs., was related to William *Herbert, the first Earl of Pembroke, who may well have given him the house. A zealous Yorkist who took part in the victory of Mortimer's Cross (1461), it was he who led Owain Tudur (see under TUDOR FAMILY) to his death, a service for which he was rewarded with offices and lands by Edward IV. When William Herbert and his brother were killed in the battle of Banbury (1469), *Lewys Glyn Cothi (Llywelyn y Glyn) urged Vaughan and his son Watkin to avenge him. After the battle of Tewkesbury (1471), Sir Roger was captured by Jasper Tudor and executed in vengeance for his father's death.

VAUGHAN, ROWLAND (*c*.1587–1667),

poet and translator, was the son of the lesser gentry family of Caer-gai, near Llanuwchllyn, Mer. He studied at the University of Oxford but there is no record of his having taken a degree there. A staunch Churchman and Royalist who became High Sheriff of the County in 1642, he is believed to have taken part in the battle of Naseby (1645), when the New Model Army under Cromwell and Fairfax routed the Royalist forces. In 1645 Caer-gai was burned to the ground by Parliamentarian soldiers, Vaughan took refuge at Cil-gellan on the slopes of Aran Benllyn and the Parliament gave his estate to his nephew. Imprisoned at Chester in 1650, Vaughan eventually regained his property and built a new home at Caer-gai.

A poet who composed in both the strict and free metres, he was a good example of the nonprofessional poet who nevertheless wrote poetry of good quality in the traditional manner. Among his poems in the strict metres are some addressed to his relations and friends, and a few *cywyddau* requesting such gifts as a stallion, a mare, a hawk and items of clothing. The personal note in many of his verses reflects his status as a member of the gentry who was on equal terms with those to whom he addressed his poems. His religious and political views were expressed in poems written in the free metres which were published in the volume *Carolau a Dyriau Duwiol* (1729).

It is, however, as a translator that Rowland Vaughan is remembered today, in particular for his *Yr Ymarfer o Dduwioldeb* (1630), a translation of Lewis *Bayly's The Practice of Piety (1611), which demonstrates his mastery over Welsh prose style. It was followed by *Eikon Basilike* (*c*.1650), *Yr Arfer o Weddi yr Arglwydd* (1658), *Pregeth yn erbyn Schism* (1658), *Prifannau Sanctaidd neu Lawlyfr o Weddïau* (1658), *Ymddiffyniad Rhag Pla o Schism* (1658), *Y Llwybreidd-fodd Byrr o Gristnogawl Grefydd* (1658) and *Evochologia: neu Yr Athrawiaeth i arferol weddïo* (*c*.1660), most of which are works of religion.

Further details will be found in the edition of *Yr Ymarfer o Dduwioldeb* prepared by John Ballinger (1930) and in the article by Gwyn Thomas in *Y Traddodiad Rhyddiaith* (ed. Geraint Bowen, 1970).

Vaughan, Rowland (d. 1629), gentleman, of New Court in the Golden Valley, Herefs., which he called 'Paradice of the backside of the Principallitie', was a grand-nephew of Blanche *Parry, under whose patronage he spent some years at court. It was her 'careful, though crabbed, authority', which drove him to the Irish wars but, afflicted by what he called 'the country-disease', he came home and married. Thereafter it was boredom, he claimed, which drove him to try irrigating his lands by having dug a 'trench-royall', some three miles long, which resembled 'the River Nilus' drowning 'Aegipt from the Abissine Mountaines'.

His book, *Most Approved and Long experienced Waterworks containing the Manner of Winter and Summer-drowning of Medow and Pasture*, published in 1610 but dictated in 1604, is remarkable not only for irrelevance and sardonic exaggeration but also for its novel attempt to raise money: a bond on the book's last page binds the author and his heirs to pay the owner after five years the sum of forty shillings. The watercourse he dug followed the hill contour from the Trenant brook by Whitehouse (where he seems to have lived) to work the New Court mill and water the fields below, but the community of four thousand 'mechanicalls' with which he intended to relieve local poverty never materialized. John *Davies of Hereford, whose commendatory 'Panegyricke' is signed 'Your poore kinsman', uses only the future tense for these *Jovialists* in their 'Scarlet Cappes'. Rowland Vaughan, it seems, never made any money, his talk was always bigger than himself and towards the end of his life he was virtually ruined.

VAUGHAN, THOMAS (1621–66), alchemist and poet, was the younger twin brother of Henry *Vaughan and enjoyed the same upbringing and education. But, unlike his brother, he remained at Jesus College for ten or twelve years, latterly as a Fellow. He was appointed rector of his native parish of Llansantffraid, Brecs., about 1645. With his brother, he took part in the brief military excursion under Colonel Herbert *Price which ended at Beeston Castle in 1645, and probably returned to Oxford afterwards. In 1650 he was ejected from his living under the Act for the *Propagation of the Gospel in Wales on the charge that, amongst other things, he was 'a common drunkard' and had been 'in armes personally against the Parliament'. He then went to London, was briefly married and thereafter threw himself into alchemical experiments and the writing of treatises. His unpublished notebook refers to the discovery, on the very day of his wife's death in 1658, of the secret of 'extracting the oyle of Hacali', perhaps his name for the *prima materia*, once hit upon previously when he was at 'the Pinner of Wakefield' and forgotten. In 1661 he secured the patronage of Sir Robert Moray, who was in charge of the King's laboratory at Whitehall, and when in 1665 the Court moved to Oxford to avoid the plague, Vaughan accompanied it. He died at Albury, near Oxford, perhaps of plague or as the result of a laboratory explosion: a late account by Anthony à Wood describes him as 'operating strong mercurie, some of which by chance getting up his nose marched him off'.

Probably the most important Hermetical philosopher of his day, Thomas Vaughan was not one of those 'who will hear of nothing but *Metalls*'. For him metaphysics and divinity went hand in hand and his search for the world's *prima materia* was a use of the language of physical alchemy to express the idea of the regeneration of Man: 'matter', for him, was 'the House of Light'. He wrote some eight treatises under the pseudonym of Eugenius Philalethes, the most easily dated of which are *Lumen de Lumine* and *Aula Lucis* (both 1651), and engaged in abusive controversy with the Cambridge Platonist, Henry More. Of his twenty-five Latin poems, twenty-four were included by his brother in *Thalia Rediviva* (1678); he also wrote six or seven in English, either commendatory verses for friends or prefaces for his own treatises.

The standard edition of the writer's works is that edited by Alan Rudrum (1984). A useful short assessment of Vaughan's attitude and spirit will be found in the article by Eluned Crawshaw in *The Anglo-Welsh Review* (vol. 18, no. 42, 1970).

VAUGHAN, WILLIAM (1575–1641), colonial pioneer and writer, of Golden Grove, Carms., was educated at Jesus College, Oxford, and became Sheriff of his County in 1616. In the following year, depressed by the poverty of his native district, he bought land in Newfoundland and, at his own expense, sent settlers there two years later; the name Cambriol was given to the settlement. The venture foundered after more than a dozen years, mainly owing to harsh weather conditions, and Sir William never visited Newfoundland. Among his publications were a commonplace book, *Golden Grove* (1600), a Latin poem in celebration of the marriage of Charles I, a compilation entitled *The Golden Fleece* (1626), which bears the pseudonym Orpheus Junior, and a volume of verse entitled *The Church Militant* (1640). The last-named includes verse in both Latin and English as well as arguments in favour of colonization, particularly in Newfoundland.

VAUGHAN-THOMAS, WYNFORD (1908–), writer and broadcaster. Born in Swansea, a son of David Vaughan *Thomas, and educated at Exeter College, Oxford, he joined the staff of the BBC in 1937 and thereafter made his career in broadcasting, first as a war correspondent (he was awarded the *Croix de Guerre* in 1945) and later as Director of Programmes with HTV. The author of much humorous verse, which remains uncollected, he has also written *Anzio* (1962), *Madly in all Directions* (1967), *The Shell Guide to Wales* (with Alun *Llewellyn, 1969), *The Splendour Falls* (1973), *Portrait of Gower* (1975) and *Wales* (1981); all except the first are about the history and topography of Wales. Among his later books are *The Countryside Companion* (1979), a volume of autobiography, *Trust to Talk* (1980), in which his gifts as a raconteur are fully demonstrated, *The Princes of Wales* (1982) and *Wales: a History* (1985).

VENDRYES, JOSEPH (1875–1960), Celtic scholar, was born in Paris, where he studied under the most eminent authorities of the late nineteenth century. He began teaching Comparative Grammar in Paris in 1907 and was appointed Professor of Philology in 1923; he also taught General Linguistics at the *École Normale Supérieure* from 1920 onwards. Elected as successor to Henry Gaidoz in 1925, he lectured in Celtic at the *École des Hautes Études*, but lost his post for a time during the Second World War.

A scholar of balanced judgement, with a wide spectrum of interests, he published a host of important works in the field of linguistic studies, especially in that part of it concerned with historical and comparative philology. He worked most diligently on the Celtic languages, editing and interpreting Gaelic, Irish, Breton and Welsh texts, and revealed a gift for discussing various aspects of the literary traditions of the Celtic countries, especially those of Ireland and Wales. His chief contributions to the study of the Welsh literary tradition were his Zaharoff Lecture, *La Poésie galloise des XIe et XIIe siècles dans sa rapport avec la langue* (1930), and his discussions of more than twenty *awdlau* by the *Gogynfeirdd*, in which he explained the language, metrics and historical background of these poems. He also published important works on the religion of the Celts and the mythology which grew around the *Matter of Britain and its Celtic sources. For many years he was co-editor of *Revue Celtique* and founded *Études Celtiques* in 1936.

Vengeance Quest, The, a common theme in folk-literature. The hero undertakes a quest to avenge his king or father, or to fulfil a promise. In *Pedair Cainc y Mabinogi*, Bendigeidfran (*Brân) seeks vengeance on *Matholwch, King of Ireland, for the wrong done to his sister *Branwen, *Llwyd fab Cilcoed casts enchantment over the seven cantrefi of *Dyfed in order to avenge his friend Gwawl fab Clud who had been robbed of his bride by *Pwyll, and *Lleu seeks vengeance on his wife *Blodeuwedd, and on her lover, for plotting his death. The classic example of a whole tale based on this theme is that of Peredur (see under TAIR RHAMANT) in which the hero sets out to regain the sovereignty which was lost on the death of his father and to wreak revenge on his enemies.

Vicar Prichard, The, see PRICHARD, RHYS (1579–1644).

Viking Raids, The, which spread from Scandinavia across Europe in the early ninth century and later through the western isles into the Irish Sea, began to affect Wales seriously about 850. From that date, with a respite between 918 and 952, a period which coincides with the reign of *Hywel Dda, the raids were incessant until the end of the tenth century.

Other names by which the Vikings were known included the Black Gentiles, the Black Host and the Black Pagans. Apart from the obvious intent to loot churches and monasteries (the cathedral church of *St. David's suffered many times), the Norsemen had in mind the capture of slaves, whom they regularly sold in the slave-markets of Dublin and Scandinavia. From 1000 to 1150 the raids gradually diminished: Welsh–Norse treaties grew more frequent and the interest of the Vikings, then coming under Christian influence, was more commonly directed towards trade. In this later stage there were Viking trading stations along the south and west coasts of Wales from Fishguard to Cardiff and they almost certainly exacted tribute from areas farther inland. The names of all the islands off the Welsh coast, from Anglesey to Steepholm, have Norse suffixes, not because they were settled but because they constituted sailors' bearings, and older Welsh names such as *Gwales (Grassholm) and Ynys *Pyr (Caldey) were ousted. Swansea, Haverford and Fishguard are all names Norse in origin and in the late twelfth century there was a remarkable coincidence of names among the burgesses of Cardiff and Dublin (then a Norse city). Despite all this, however, and the survival of a few Norse surnames among the population of Dyfed, no permanent Viking settlement can be pointed to with certainty, and Welsh literature carries no trace of the Scandinavian presence.

For further details see B. G. Charles, *Old Norse Relations with Wales* (1934), P. H. Sawyer, *The Age of the Vikings* (2nd edn., 1971), A. P. Smyth, *Scandinavian York and Dublin* (2 vols., 1975, 1979) and the general work by Wendy Davies, *Wales in the Early Middle Ages* (1982); see also Proinsias Mac Cana, 'The Influence of the Vikings on Celtic Literature' in Brian Ó Cuív (ed.), *The Impact of the Scandinavian Invasions on the Celtic-Speaking Peoples* (1975).

VILLEMARQUÉ, THEODORE HERSART DE LA (1815–95), Breton nobleman and writer. It was he who originated the Romantic movement in Brittany with his book *Barzaz Breiz: Chants Populaires de la Bretagne* (1839), allegedly based on traditional ballads. He supplied Lady Charlotte *Guest with a translation of *Yvain où le Chevalier au Lion* which she published as an appendix to the romance of *The Lady of the Fountain* (see under TAIR RHAMANT) in the first edition of her book *The Mabinogion* (1838). Charged by the French Ministry of Public Instruction to make a report on Welsh manuscripts of Breton interest, Villemarqué visited Wales and Oxford in 1838 and the following year. Under the auspices of Carnhuanawc (Thomas *Price), he was welcomed at the Abergavenny Eisteddfod, where he made a speech emphasizing the unity between the Bretons and the Welsh. In his subsequent report to the Ministry he noted the debt of Old French literature to Welsh sources and strove to minimize all differences between the current spoken languages of Wales and Brittany. Relations with Lady Guest became strained, however, when Villemarqué attempted to anticipate the publication of her translation of *Peredur* by publishing a French translation based on hers, which he had seen on a visit to Dowlais; in this he was unsuccessful, and her translation appeared before the end of 1839. In his *Contes Populaires des Anciens Bretons* (1842), Villemarqué subsequently published French versions, based on those of Lady Guest but without acknowledgement, of the three romances included in her book.

For further details see Carrington Bolton, *Breton Ballads from the Barzaz Breiz* (1886), W. Ambrose Bebb, *Pererindodau* (1941), F. Gourvil, *Theodore Hersart de la Villemarqué et le 'Varzaz Breiz'* (1960) and David Greene, *Makers and Forgers* (1975).

Viscount Rhondda, see THOMAS, DAVID ALFRED (1856–1918).

Vision-producing Sleep, The, an international motif in folk-literature which has many variations, including the love-dream, the adventure-dream, the prophetic dream and the vision of heaven and hell. A common version embodies a dream in which a man falls in love with an unknown girl and sets out on a quest for her, as in the story of *Macsen Wledig. A less romantic version of the motif is contained in *Breuddwyd Rhonabwy* and there is an example of the prophetic dream in the tale of *Amlyn and Amig. The dream genre is not confined to prose, however. *Dafydd ap Gwilym used it in a poem about a clock which wakes him from a pleasant vision of himself in the company of a beautiful maiden, and in another in which he recalls a vision of himself hunting a white doe in the forest. Dream poetry survived as a literary genre into the sixteenth century, when its themes were mainly those of love, contention, adventure, heaven and hell. The best-known work in Welsh embodying this theme is *Gweledigaetheu y Bardd Cwsc* (1703) by Ellis *Wynne.

'Vita Merlini' (lit. 'The life of Merlin'; *c.*1148), a poem in hexameters of some fifteen hundred lines, the last work of *Geoffrey of Monmouth. It has survived in only one manuscript and does not appear to have been well known. Although the Merlin (*Myrddin) of the poem resembles the character of the same name created in the author's *Historia Regum Britanniae* the likelihood is that Geoffrey had realized how contrary to the Welsh tradition his Merlin really was. He had learned meanwhile the native version of the story and it is that version which appears in this poem, which takes the form of a dialogue between Merlin and *Taliesin. Besides the narrative of the *Vita*, it includes Merlin's prophecies about the history of Britain and the restoration to the Britons of the whole island, while Taliesin

voices much contemporary 'scientific' knowledge. The same drawing together of traditional sources, international learning, pseudo-history and contemporary longings, creates here a literary composition similar to that of the *Historia*.

There is an edition and translation of the poem by Basil Clarke, *Life of Merlin* (1973).

Vivian family, The, originally from Cornwall, the pioneers of the copper-smelting industry in and around Swansea. John Henry Vivian, the Member of Parliament for Swansea from 1822 to 1855, leased land at Hafod in 1810 and developed his company until it became a major business; he was also responsible for improving local harbours. Much of the Llansamlet area was polluted by the copper-smelting of the Vivians, a fact remarked upon by many visitors, including Michael Faraday. After J. H. Vivian's death in 1855 the control of Hafod passed to his son, Henry Hussey Vivian (1821–94), who took out patents to develop a wide range of by-products. The Member of Parliament for Glamorgan (1857–59) and for Swansea (1885–93), he was created Baron Swansea in 1893 and was the first Chairman of Glamorgan County Council in 1889. Among the family's memorials are Singleton Abbey (now U. C. Swansea) and the Glynn Vivian Art Gallery.

For further details see Averil Stewart, *Family Tapestry* (1961).

Voluntaryism, see under BRITISH AND FOREIGN SCHOOLS SOCIETY.

Vortigern (*fl.* early 5th cent.), one of the Brythonic kings, is known in Welsh tradition as **Gwrtheyrn**. Little historical evidence about him exists but he was mentioned by Bede in his *Historia*, in the poem *'Armes Prydein' and by *Nennius in the *Historia Brittonum. *Gildas, writing about the year 547, referred to '*superbus tyrannus*' ('a proud ruler', perhaps from the Welsh '*gor*' + '*teyrn*') who gave land to the Saxons in payment for their military support. For this reason Gwrtheyrn is remembered in Welsh tradition as an arch-traitor, although it may be that he was merely following the old Roman policy of according the status of *foederati* to the Saxons in return for their assistance in the defence of his kingdom. It is believed that Vortigern was over-king of the Britons, which may account for his involvement in Kent as well as with what seems to have been his native kingdom of *Powys. According to the *Historia Brittonum*, Vortigern fell in love with *Alice Rowena, the daughter of Hengist; it was also he who sent for the boy Ambrosius (*Emrys Wledig) during his attempts to build a fortress in Snowdonia. Later, at Caer Wrtheyrn in Dyfed, he was consumed by fire from heaven while fleeing from *Garmon. In another version of the traditional tale, Vortigern spent the rest of his life wandering the earth, and in *Englynion y Beddau* there is an allusion to his grave as '*y bedd yn Ystyfachau, y mae pawb yn ei amau*' ('the grave in Ystyfachau which everyone doubts'). See also TREACHERY OF THE LONG KNIVES.

For further details see the articles by Ifor Williams in the *Transactions* of the Honourable Society of Cymmrodorion (1946–47), H. M. and N. K. Chadwick in *Studies in Early British History* (1959) and D. P. Kirby in the *Bulletin* of the Board of Celtic Studies (vol. XXIII, 1968); see also Rachel Bromwich, *Trioedd Ynys Prydein* (1961) and Stephen Johnson, *Later Roman Britain* (1982).

VULLIAMY, COLWYN EDWARD (Anthony Rolls, Twm Teg; 1886–1971), writer, was born into a Welsh gentry family at Glasbury, Rads.; the surname derives from an Italian ancestor who settled in Wales in the seventeenth century. An extraordinarily prolific and versatile writer who excelled in several fields, both scholarly and creative, he first attracted serious attention during the 1920s with books dealing with aspects of anthropology and archaeology, such as *Our Prehistoric Forerunners* (1925), *Immortal Man* (1926), a study of funeral customs, and his influential *Archaeology of Middlesex and London* (1930). His interest in modern history was revealed at about the same time in two books concerning contemporary Russia, *The Letters of the Tsar to the Tsaritsa, 1914–1917* (1929) and *The Red Archives: Russian State Papers* (1929), both of which he edited. His translation of a selection of Voltaire's poetry and prose appeared as *The White Bull* (1929); it was followed in 1930 by his biography of the French writer and, over the next decade, by his biographical studies of Jean-Jacques Rousseau (1931), John Wesley (1931), James Boswell (1932), William Penn (1933), Hester Lynch *Piozzi (1936), Samuel Johnson (1946) and Lord Byron (1948). He also published four novels under the pen-name Anthony Rolls, and two more historical studies, *Outlanders* (1938), which is about South Africa, and *Crimea: the Campaign of 1854–56* (1939).

It was with the publication of his mock-edition of *Judas Maccabaeus* (1934) that Vulliamy was recognized as a descendant of the Augustan satirists, and the appearance of his autobiographical book *Calico Pie* (1940) confirmed the satirical talent for which he is best known. His gift is seen at its wittiest in the 'biographies' and 'memoirs' of imaginary characters which he wrote during the 1940s, including *A Short History of the Montagu-Puffins* (1941), *The Polderoy Papers* (1943), *Doctor Philligo* (1944), *Edwin and Eleanor* (1945) and *Henry Plumdew* (1950). After the Second World War he assembled a comprehensive anthology of satirical prose and verse, *The Anatomy of Satire* (1950), but also wrote a serious topical treatise, *Man and the Atom* (1947). Most of the books written during the last twenty years of his life were novels, although of various kinds. The satirical thriller *Don among the Dead Men* (1952), established him as a writer of murder and mystery stories; his distinctive brand of comic horror is evident in, for example, *Justice for Judy* (1960) and *Floral Tribute* (1963). On the other hand, *Jones, A Gentleman of Wales* (1954), which he published under the name of Twm Teg, is a comic novel of Welsh village life, while *The Proud Walkers* (1955), issued under his own name, also has a Welsh setting. During these years he wrote, too, about national characteristics and idiosyncrasies, as in *Rocking Horse Journey* (1953) and *Little Arthur's Guide to Humbug* (1960).

W

Wade, James (**Shemi Wâd**; d. 1887), a man famous for his *white-lie tales, many of which are still told in his native Pembrokeshire. One relates how he fell asleep in the barrel of a cannon at Milford Haven and was shot through the air, landing near his home in Goodwick, some twenty-five miles away. There is a description of Shemi Wâd in the volume *Ysgrifau* (1937) by Dewi Emrys (David Emrys *James).

WADE-EVANS, ARTHUR (1875–1964), historian, was born at Fishguard, Pembs., and educated at Jesus College, Oxford. Ordained a priest of the Anglican Church in 1898, he spent most of his life in England as vicar of parishes in Gloucestershire and Northamptonshire and later as rector of Wrabness, Essex. His special interest was in the history of early Britain and he spent many years in the study of the Welsh *Laws, research which culminated in his book, *Welsh Medieval Law* (1909), a transcript with notes and a translation of one of the Harleian Manuscripts. He also published *Lives of the Saints and genealogies, including *The Life of Saint David* (1923) and *Vitae Sanctorum Britanniae et Genealogie* (1944).

In his books *Nennius's 'History of the Britons'* (1938) and *Coll Prydain* (1950) he expressed his fervently held conviction that *Gildas's *De Excidio Britanniae* had been misinterpreted by Welsh historians and, reacting against the pro-Saxon approach in the teaching of early history at Oxford in his student days, he denounced the accepted view of an Anglo-Saxon conquest of that part of Britain later called England. He believed that the Welsh were not Britons who had been forced to flee into what later became Wales, as Bede had claimed, but that Roman culture or *Romanitas* had been maintained in the material and spiritual traditions of Wales, while *Barbaritas* had triumphed in the cities of what was to become England, such as Bath, overrun by the invaders in 443. This theory was expounded in his books *Welsh Christian Origins* (1934) and *The Emergence of England and Wales* (1959).

For further details see the article by H. D. Emanuel in the *Transactions* of the Honourable Society of Cymmrodorion (1965).

Wake, an informal religious meeting held on the eve of a funeral in the deceased person's home, was known throughout Wales in the eighteenth and nineteenth centuries. The corpse was usually placed in a coffin laid across two chairs and the room lit by three candles. Parts of the burial service were read by the sexton and the *paternoster* was recited by all who called at the house. Besides the religious nature of this 'paternostering', as it was sometimes known, there were secular customs associated with the wake such as the telling of traditional tales, but by the end of the eighteenth century they had been largely displaced by sermons. There is no evidence to suggest that the more convivial customs of the Irish wake, such as singing and drinking, were observed in Wales.

Wales, the country of the Welsh people. In Old English the noun '*walh*' or '*wealh*' (meaning a native Briton as distinct from an Anglo-Saxon) had the plural forms '*walas*' or '*wealas*', which closely resemble the modern 'Wales'. Like the adjective '*welisc*' or '*waelisc*' (from which 'Welsh' is derived), these words probably date from the earliest years of the Anglo-Saxon invasion of Britain. But the words '*brittas*' and '*brittisc*' were also used by the Anglo-Saxons to describe the Britons or Welsh, as were the mixed forms '*bretwalas*' and '*bretwielisc*'. In the same period the Welsh called themselves not only '*Cymry*' but also '*Brythoniaid*'. Even before their arrival in the Island the Anglo-Saxons would have been familiar with the words '*walh*' and '*walas*', for they were used by Germanic peoples to denote those foreigners who spoke Celtic languages but who had become Romanized and to some extent were Latin-speaking. Although later applied by Germanic peoples to Celts in general, the word appears originally to have been a version of the name of one of the largest Celtic tribes, the Volcae. The form '*welsch*' is still the colloquial German word for Italian and the same word lies behind the names of the Belgian Walloons and the Romanian-speaking Wallachians. The forms 'British' and 'Welsh' (often spelled 'Welch') were used interchangeably for the Welsh and their language until the later eighteenth century. The spelling 'Welch' survives in some regimental names, as in that of the Royal Welch Fusiliers, officially approved by the Army Council in 1919, but which until then had been a defiantly cherished peculiarity. The origin of the verb 'to welsh' (meaning 'to swindle a person out of money laid as a bet') is unknown. See also BRITAIN and CYMRU.

Wales, a monthly magazine edited by Owen M. *Edwards between May 1894 and December 1897. The editor's aim was to elicit the interest of the English-speaking Welsh in the cultural history of Wales by introducing them to Welsh literature. The magazine carried translations, including one of Daniel *Owen's novel *Enoc Huws* (1891), and articles on the history, literature and famous men of Wales, as well as on science and the fine arts; photographs and illustrations played an important part in its appeal. Nevertheless, public response to the editor's initiative was poor and the magazine ceased publication for lack of support. See also CYMRU (1891–1927) and the next two entries.

An index to the contents of the magazine, compiled by Joan M. Thomas, was published by the Welsh Library Association in 1979.

Wales, a monthly magazine which appeared between 1911 and 1914 under the editorship of J. Hugh *Edwards, who had also edited *Young Wales*, the journal of *Cymru Fydd*. A lively periodical, it reflected the aspirations of that movement, especially in the fields of education, religion and local government, but its success was short-lived and, like the magazine of the same title edited by Owen M. *Edwards (see previous entry), it ceased publication for want of subscribers. See also the next entry.

Wales, a magazine founded and edited by Keidrych *Rhys, set out to be 'an independent pamphlet of creative work by the younger progressive Welsh writers', on whose behalf it claimed that 'though we write in English, we are rooted in Wales'.

Among contributors to the first series (11 nos., Summer, 1937 to Winter, 1939/40), published in Carmarthen, were Dylan *Thomas (who co-edited two numbers in March, 1939 with Nigel *Heseltine), Glyn *Jones, Idris *Davies, Vernon *Watkins, Rhys *Davies and Caradoc Evans (David *Evans). The second series (18 nos., July, 1943 to October, 1949), published in London, was less avant-garde in literary terms and included more comment on topics of the day. The editorial style of Keidrych Rhys, whose ebullient personality was stamped on every number of his magazine, was always pungent and generally iconoclastic. His deadliest darts were reserved for what he considered to be the Welsh Establishment but the magazine attacked all conservative, provincial attitudes, calling for change in the cultural and political life of Wales. The magazine's most important achievement, however, was the discovery and promotion of new writers. It published the early work of Gwyn *Williams, Davies Aberpennar (Pennar *Davies), R. S. *Thomas and Roland *Mathias, and that of younger writers such as Emyr *Humphreys, Leslie *Norris and Harri *Webb, among others. Translations from the Welsh and reviews were regular features and a

questionnaire about writers' attitudes to Wales and their writing elicited a number of valuable replies.

The third series (13 nos., September, 1958 to New Year, 1960), also published in London, was more glossily produced than its predecessors, and even more of a general review of Welsh affairs, but it continued to carry poems, stories and articles by new writers such as Alun *Richards. The magazine's demise, which was unannounced, was caused by the strain imposed on the editor's finances by the rising cost of publication and the failure to sell a minimum of a thousand copies. See also the previous two entries.

Wales International, see UNDEB Y CYMRU AR WASGAR.

Walk through Wales, A (1798), a book by the English writer Richard Warner (1763–1857), describes in a series of letters a journey from Bath to Holyhead, Ang. The author's chief interests were in the history, scenery and industry of Wales, especially the processes and economics of mining, and his main sources were the *Itinerary of John Leland*, Camden's *Britannia* and Thomas *Pennant. A visit to the last-named at Downing is recorded in a second volume with the same title which Warner published in 1799. The sentiments of the books are commonplace, but their style is jocular and the author's anecdotes about people and places encountered on the way are most entertaining. See also TOURS OF WALES.

WALLACE, ALFRED RUSSEL (1823–1913), naturalist and author. Born at Usk, Mon., he trained as a surveyor but, in 1848, discovered his life's work when he went on his first expedition to the Amazon. He later visited the Malay Archipelago, where he established the dividing line, now known as Wallace's Line, between the Asian and the Australian sections of the islands' flora and fauna. While in Borneo he wrote an essay in which he independently formulated the principle of 'the survival of the fittest', on which Charles Darwin had also been working. He sent his essay to Darwin and they collaborated in a joint paper read before the Linnean Society in 1858. Wallace's principal works are *Contributions to the Theory of Natural Selection* (1870), *The Geographical Distribution of Animals* (1876), *Darwinism* (1889), *Studies Scientific and Social* (1900), *Man's Place in the Universe* (1903) and an autobiography, *My Life* (1905).

Walter, Lucy (1630?–58), the mistress of King Charles II, was related to the families of Laugharne, Philipps and the Vaughans of Golden Grove. Her father, of Roch Castle, Pembs., alleged losses of some three thousand pounds in the *Civil War and took his family to

London in pursuit of the claim. How Lucy met the young Prince of Wales or how, at the age of eighteen, she found her way to the exiled English court at The Hague, is not known, but in 1649 she gave birth to a son, James, of whom Prince Charles acknowledged he was the father; she also bore him a daughter, named Mary, at The Hague in 1651. Attempts were made during the agitation over the Exclusion Bill (1679–81) to argue that Charles had made Lucy his wife and that James, created Duke of Monmouth and seen as the Protestant champion against the Catholic James II, was the rightful heir to the English throne, but Monmouth's cause ultimately failed at the battle of Sedgemoor in 1685. Lucy Walter died in Paris before the Restoration.

WALTER, ROWLAND (Ionoron Glan Dwyryd; 1819–84), poet, a native of Blaenau Ffestiniog, Mer., was a quarryman who emigrated to the USA in 1852, remaining there until his death. Two volumes of his poetry were published, one, *Lloffion y Gweithiwr* (1852), in Wales and the other, *Caniadau Ionoron* (1872), in Utica.

WALTERS, JOHN (1721–97), lexicographer, a native of Llanedi, Carms., was educated at Cowbridge Grammar School and then became a schoolmaster at Margam, Glam. Ordained priest in 1750, he served as a curate until appointed Rector of Llandough, near Cowbridge. Besides publishing *A Dissertation on the Welsh Language* (1771) and *Dwy Bregeth* (1772), he compiled an English-Welsh Dictionary, for which work alone he is remembered. It was printed at Cowbridge in fourteen parts between 1770 and 1783 by Rhys Thomas; Owain Myfyr (Owen *Jones) arranged for the remainder to be printed in London in 1794. The dictionary was based on the manuscript of William *Gambold but Walters added to it and included many neologisms of his own which have since found a place in the Welsh language. Two further editions, on which D. Silvan *Evans drew heavily, appeared in 1815 and 1828.

His son, also named **John Walters** (1760–89), was a poet who wrote in English. Educated at Cowbridge Grammar School, of which he later became Headmaster, and at Jesus College, Oxford, he was regarded by *London Welshmen as one of the most promising young scholars of his day and his premature death was keenly lamented. He published a number of works which include *Poems with Notes* (1780) and *Translated Specimens of Welsh Poetry* (1782). Some of his English versions of *'Canu Llywarch Hen' appeared in William *Warrington's *The History of Wales* (1788). Walters also provided Edward *Jones (Bardd y Brenin) with notes for inclusion in his *Musical and Poetical Relicks of the Welsh Bards* (1784).

WALTERS, MEURIG (1915–), novelist

and poet. Born at Cwm-gors, Glam., and educated at University College, Cardiff, and the Presbyterian Colleges at Aberystwyth and Bala, he was a minister at Aberkenfig, Glam., until his retirement in 1980. The author of three novels, *Cymylau Amser* (1955), *Diogel y Daw* (1956) and *Tu ôl i'r Llenni* (1967), he has also edited the first of the two poems entitled '*Y *Storm*' by Islwyn (William *Thomas). A later essay, *Islwyn, Man of the Mountain*, was published in 1983. He was one of the Welsh poets who contributed verse in English to Keidrych *Rhys's magazine, **Wales*.

WALTON, ROBERT (1948–), poet, was born in Cardiff and educated at the University of Exeter. A teacher of English in Bristol, he won the *Welsh Arts Council's New Poets Competition in 1978 with his collection, *Workings* (1979).

WARD, JOHN POWELL (1937–), poet and critic, was born in Suffolk and educated at the Universities of Toronto, Cambridge and Wales; he has been a lecturer in the Education Department at University College, Swansea, since 1963. The author of five volumes of poetry, *The Other Man* (1968), *The Line of Knowledge* (1972), *From Alphabet to Logos* (1972), *To Get Clear* (1981) and *The Clearing* (1984), he has also published an essay on Raymond *Williams in the *Writers of Wales series (1981), and two critical studies entitled *Poetry and the Sociological Idea* (1981) and *Wordsworth's Language of Men* (1984). From 1975 to 1980 J. P. Ward was editor of the magazine *Poetry Wales*.

WARING, ELIJAH (*c.*1788–1857), journalist, was the editor of *The Cambrian Visitor*, a magazine which he founded in Swansea in 1813, about three years after he had settled in Wales from his native Hampshire. The journal, which was intended to enlighten English readers about the history of Wales, lasted for less than a year, but his own interest in Welsh affairs proved more durable. Making his home at Neath, Glam., he became a Wesleyan and campaigned for parliamentary reform, writing a number of leading articles on that subject for *The *Cambrian*. A friend of Iolo Morganwg (Edward *Williams), he published an amusing but unreliable biography of that writer entitled *Recollections and Anecdotes of Edward Williams, the Bard of Glamorgan* (1850). His daughter, **Anna Letitia Waring** (1823–1910), was a hymn-writer.

WARNER, RICHARD (1763–1857), see under WALK THROUGH WALES (1798).

WARREN, SAMUEL (1807–77), novelist, was born near Wrexham, Denbs. Besides numerous legal works, he wrote two books which were immensely popular in their day, namely *Passages from the Diary of a Late Physician* (1838) and *Ten Thousand a Year* (1839). The latter is the story of a Mr Tittlebat Titmouse and his fraudulent rise to power and wealth.

WARRINGTON, WILLIAM (*fl.* 1780–90), historian and chaplain to the Earl of Bessborough. His compilation, *The History of Wales* (2 vols., 1786), deals, in the first volume, with the period from the withdrawal of the Romans to the *Act of Union (1536); the second volume contains a summary of bardic and ecclesiastical traditions, together with an appendix of transcribed documents. Warrington wrote his *History* as an Englishman making 'a voluntary tribute of justice and humanity to the cause of injured liberty'.

Warrior, The, see MORGAN, THOMAS (*c.*1542–95).

Wars of the Roses, The, see under BANBURY, THE BATTLE OF (1469) and BOSWORTH, THE BATTLE OF (1485).

Wars of Welsh Independence, The (1276–77 and 1282–83), were fought between the forces of *Llywelyn ap Gruffudd and those of Edward I. The first war broke out after both rulers had claimed that the terms of the Treaty of *Montgomery had been ignored. There were preliminary skirmishes in the autumn of 1276; with the royal army based upon Chester, Montgomery and *Carmarthen, *Dinefwr and *Carreg Cennen fell to the supporters of the King. In the summer of 1277 Edward's army advanced from Chester to *Rhuddlan and *Degannwy, troops were sent to Anglesey to turn Llywelyn's defensive bastion at Penmaenmawr and the Welsh, shocked by the loss of '*Môn, mam Cymru*' ('Anglesey, the mother of Wales'), surrendered. New royal castles were built at Aberystwyth and Builth. As a result of these military defeats, Llywelyn ap Gruffudd was confined to *Eryri (Snowdonia). In November 1277 he concluded the Treaty of *Aberconwy with Edward, who was anxious to avoid a winter campaign in north Wales.

The second war began with an attack on *Hawarden castle by *Dafydd ap Gruffudd, Llywelyn's brother, on 21 March 1282. There were risings in other parts of Wales as a result of popular discontent. Edward adopted a strategy similar to that of 1277, again operating from the bases of Chester, Montgomery and Carmarthen. This time, however, Llywelyn and his followers did not succumb to the loss of Anglesey: an attack across the bridge of boats built at Moel-y-Don on the Menai Straits was beaten back with great loss of life to the attackers. But Llywelyn, knowing that he must somehow escape from the encirclement and divert the King's attention from Gwynedd, rode southwards to rouse the men of the Wye Valley, only to be killed after a skirmish near Cilmeri, west of Builth, on 11 December 1282. His brother Dafydd took Llywelyn's place as leader of the Welsh forces but he was captured and executed in 1283. Several of the Welsh lords were imprisoned for their part in the campaign and new administrative arrangements for the territories conquered by the English were set out in the Statute of Rhuddlan (1284).

Further details will be found in J. E. Morris, *The Welsh Wars of Edward I* (1901), J. E. Lloyd, *A History of Wales* (vol. II, 1911), Michael Prestwich, *War, Politics and Finance under Edward I* (1972) and the article by R. F. Walker, 'Edward I and the Organisation of War' in *The Welsh History Review* (vol. VII, 1975).

'War-Song of Dinas Vawr, The', a poem in *The *Misfortunes of Elphin* (1829), a novel by the English writer Thomas Love *Peacock. *Taliesin hears it sung by the warriors of King Melvas at the castle on the river Towy which they have captured. Described sardonically by its author as 'the quintessence of all the warsongs that ever were written', it commemorates a raid on the territory of 'Ednyfed, king of Dyfed' and begins with the famous lines:

> The mountain sheep are sweeter,
> But the valley sheep are fatter;
> We therefore deemed it meeter
> To carry off the latter.

Wassailing, a folk-custom which had its origins in the fertility-cult of pagan tradition. Revellers, calling at their neighbours' homes to wish them good health, would drink from a wassail bowl which they carried from house to house in the expectation that it would be replenished by their hosts. The ritual drinking was followed by dancing and refreshments until, having received gifts of money for relieving each household of anxiety about the prosperity of farm and family for another year, the callers took their leave. The custom was associated with holidays such as Christmas, the New Year, Twelfth Night, the Feast of Mary of the Candles and *May Day. Similar traditions were the *Calennig, *Hunting the Wren, the *Mari Lwyd and the singing of *Summer Carols. The terms '*canu gwirod*' ('liquor singing'), '*canu yn drws*' ('singing at the door') and '*canu dan bared*' ('singing under the wall') refer to various forms of Wassailing, an essential part of which was a contest in verse between the revellers outside and the head of the household from within. Each side tried to outdo the other by singing from a repertoire of puzzlesongs and accumulative songs, until the visitors, who were always better prepared, were victorious and invited into the house.

Further details will be found in Rhiannon Ifans, *Sêrs a Rybana* (1983).

Watcyn Wyn, see WILLIAMS, WATKIN HEZEKIAH (1844–1905).

Water Music, The (1944), Glyn *Jones's second

collection of short stories, greatly enlarged the achievement of his earlier book, *The ★Blue Bed* (1937). It has its quota of allegories in 'The Apple-Tree', 'The Saviour', 'The Wanderer' and 'The Four-Loaded Man', but the author's essential quality emerges much more clearly in the lyrical evocation of boyhood in the title-story. In something of the same vein is 'Bowen, Morgan and Williams' and in 'Price-Parry' the pride of the central character is matched by a marvellous ice-pack of words. This collection established Glyn Jones as a very distinctive voice in the field of the ★short story.

WATERS, IVOR (1907–   ), poet and local historian, was born at Chepstow, Mon., and most of his work as writer, lecturer and publisher is related to the history of his native town and County. Among his books are *Chepstow Parish Records* (1955), *Chepstow Miscellany* (1958), *Folklore and Dialect of the Lower Wye Valley* (1973), *Chepstow Printers and Newspapers* (1981) and *Chepstow Packets* (1983). He has written two biographies, *The Unfortunate Valentine Morris* (1964) and *Henry Martin and the Long Parliament* (1973), and three volumes of verse, *Looking Back to the Present* (1969), *Impressions and Versions* (1973) and *Sunlight and Scarlet* (1973); the last-named is a collection of translations from the work of Antonio Machado and other Spanish poets. His *Collected Verse* appeared in 1977. Honorary Curator of the Chepstow Museum from 1948 to 1963, Ivor Walters is also a printer and the owner of the Moss Rose Press.

WATKIN, MORGAN (1878–1970), scholar, was a native of Clydach, Glam., where he began work as a stonemason. Educated at University College, Cardiff, and at the Universities of Paris and Zurich, he later became Professor of French and Romance Philology at University College, Cardiff. He published a number of articles on the influence of Norman-French culture on medieval Wales and the Welsh language. They include 'The French Linguistic Influence in Mediaeval Wales' (1918–19), 'The Chronology of the *Annales Cambriae* and the *Liber Landavensis*' (1960), 'The Chronology of *The White Book of Rhydderch*' (1964), '*The Book of Aneirin*, its Old French Remaniements' (1965), 'The Chronology of *The Black Book of Carmarthen*' (1965), '*The Black Book of Chirk* and the Orthographia of Carmarthen' (1966) and *La Civilisation Française dans les Mabinogion* (1962). Although many of his theories on the nature and extent of French influence on Welsh literature are no longer accepted, he was the first to draw attention to this aspect of the subject. He also edited ★*Ystorya Bown o Hamtwn* (1958).

WATKINS, VERNON (1906–67), poet. He was born at Maesteg, Glam., but the frequent postings of his father, who was a bank manager, took the family to live at Bridgend and Llanelli before they settled, in 1913, in Swansea. Ten years later they moved out to Redcliffe, Caswell Bay and finally, in 1931, on his father's retirement, to Heatherslade on Pennard Cliffs. It was the shoreline of Gower, which he knew as a resident from the age of seventeen and had often visited previously, which was to provide the illustrative material of Vernon Watkins's poetry, the more nostalgically because, after a year at Swansea Grammar School, he was despatched first to Tyttenhanger Lodge, Seaford, Sussex, and then to Repton School in Derbyshire. Both his parents were Welsh-speaking but Vernon, a victim of that contemporary parental belief that it was necessary to escape from the parochiality of Wales, never spoke or learned the language. The only Welsh source he was able later to use in his poetry was the story of ★Taliesin, of which his beloved Gower provided a variant.

At Magdalene College, Cambridge, where he read French and German, he found the course's emphasis on criticism to be uncongenial and, despite satisfactory examination results at the end of his first year, he decided to abandon Cambridge and tried to persuade his father to allow him to travel to Italy in order to acquire experience for the poetry to which he was already committed. His father's response was unsympathetic; in the autumn of 1925 Vernon Watkins became a junior clerk in the Butetown branch of Lloyds Bank in Cardiff. Associating poetry with the idyllic experience of his last eighteen months at Repton—retrospectively a golden and heroic society—and desperate at both the need to grow up and the glum reality of a working life, he suffered a nervous breakdown which necessitated his removal, after six months' absence, to the branch at Lloyds Bank at St. Helen's, Swansea, so that he could live and be cared for at home. He remained in that employment, except for military service during the Second World War, until his retirement and he lived the rest of his life at Pennard. He always spoke of his nervous breakdown as 'a revolution of sensibility': his poetry, when it came, was to be devoted to 'the conquest of time', by which he meant, at first, the immortalization of the Eden-like memories of youth and the validation of all that he had known and loved. The 'grief' he felt was the genesis of all that followed. Gradually the paganism of the Romantic poets who had nourished him (despite the Christian background of his home) gave way to Neo-Platonism (with the idea of the replica and the moment which is all moments) and that to a more Christian, if always unorthodox, view of life. The defeat of time was integral, in his view, to the function of the poet.

His first volume of poetry, ★*Ballad of the Mari Lwyd* (1941), appeared after he had left the bombed town of Swansea for service in the RAF Police: the title-poem is a striking adaptation of

the familiar Welsh folk-ceremony to the validation of the dead (see under MARI LWYD). *The
Lamp and the Veil* (1945) consists of three long
poems (one to his sister Dorothy) and was succeeded by *Selected Poems* (1948), *The North Sea*
(translations from Heine, 1951) and two collections which are his most successful, *The *Lady
with the Unicorn* (1948) and *The *Death Bell*
(1954), the title-poem of which commemorates
his father. He also published *Cypress and Acacia*
(1959) and *Affinities* (1962); *Fidelities* (1968)
appeared posthumously, although the selection
was made by the poet himself.

Although a meticulous craftsman and as much
a master of poetic form as Dylan *Thomas, by
whom he was for long overshadowed, Vernon
Watkins became nevertheless a very different
kind of poet—a modern metaphysical, whose
insight-symbols from the Gower shoreline carried his 'grief' towards an immortality which, in
Christianizing itself, gradually calmed the original impetus. His later poetry maintained its
formal excellence but the weakening of the emotional impulse, a tendency to short-cut the metaphysical argument and an increasing emphasis
on the centrality of the poet's role make it both
less accessible and less attractive. His best work
was mostly done by 1960 but its achievement
throughout a lifetime of 'toil' makes him one of
the greatest of Welsh poets in English as well as
one of the most unusual. At the time of his death
in Seattle, during a second visit as Professor of
Poetry at the University of Washington, his
name was being canvassed, with others, for the
Poet Laureateship. After his death, *Uncollected
Poems* (1969), *Selected Verse Translations* (1977),
The Breaking of the Wave (1979) and *The Ballad of
the Outer Dark* (1979) were all put together from
a mass of unpublished material, while *I That Was
Born in Wales* (1976) and *Unity of the Stream*
(1978) were selections made from his published
works.

Further details will be found in the Vernon Watkins
memorial volume edited by Leslie Norris (1970), the
essay by Roland Mathias in the *Writers of Wales* series
(1974), Dora Polk, *Vernon Watkins and the Spring of
Vision* (1977) and the special number of *Poetry Wales*
(Spring, 1977). See also *Vernon Watkins and the Elegiac
Muse* (The W. D. Thomas Memorial lecture, 1973) by
the poet's widow, Gwen Watkins, who describes his
relationship with Dylan Thomas in *Portrait of a Friend*
(1983).

WATKYNS, ROWLAND (d. 1663?), poet,
was born at Longtown, Herefs., at that time in
the diocese of *St. David's, and became vicar of
Llanfrynach, Brecs., in 1635. Deprived of his
living between 1648 and the Restoration, he
spent this period in straitened circumstances and
in writing many of the poems included in his
only book, *Flamma sine Fumo: or Poems without
Fictions* (1662). Little is known of the details of
his life but the values in which he believed can be
easily discerned from his verse. Most of his
poems are intended to express religious truths,
often in the form of proverbs, and many are on
the themes of the world's vanity and the virtue of
moderation in all things. They are almost all
orthodox in the doctrines which they uphold. A
number of classical metres are employed in his
Latin poems and his several styles include the
satirical. When not explicitly religious, the
poems are addressed to various eminent people
in the Border counties, while others reflect the
author's loyalty to Church and Crown.

For further details see the edition of *Flamma sine Fumo*
introduced by Paul C. Davies (1968); see also the same
author's article in *The Anglo-Welsh Review* (vol. 16, no.
38, 1967).

WATSON, ROBERT (1947–), novelist,
was born at Newbridge, Mon., and educated at
the London School of Film Technique and the
University of Sussex. A teacher in Suffolk, he is
the author of two novels, *Events Beyond the
Heartlands* (1980) and *Rumours of Fulfilment*
(1982), both of which are concerned with contemporary Wales.

WEBB, HARRI (1920–), poet. He was born
in Swansea of a family whose roots were in
Gower and was educated at Magdalen College,
Oxford, where he read Romance Languages.
After serving as an interpreter in the Navy during the Second World War, he worked with
Keidrych *Rhys at the Druid Press in Carmarthen, as a bookseller in Cardiff and as a librarian,
first at Dowlais in Merthyr Tydfil and, until his
retirement in 1974, at Mountain Ash, Glam.
Formerly a member of the Welsh Republican
Movement (see under REPUBLICANISM) and
editor of its newspaper, he was active from 1959
on behalf of *Plaid Cymru, mainly in the
industrial valleys of south-east Wales. While
living in Merthyr Tydfil he was associated with
Meic *Stephens in the launching of *Poetry Wales
and they shared an interest in the writing of
topical songs and patriotic ballads.

A prolific journalist, public speaker and
pamphleteer, Harri Webb has published two
essays, *Dic Penderyn and the Merthyr Rising of
1831* (1956) and *Our National Anthem* (1964). His
early poems appeared with those of Meic
Stephens and Peter M. Griffith (Peter *Gruffydd) in the volume *Triad* (1963). He has described himself as 'a poet with only one theme,
one preoccupation', whose work is 'unrepen-
tantly nationalistic'. Most of the poems in his
first collection, *The Green Desert* (1969), are
about the history and social condition of Wales.
His mordant wit is to be savoured in such well-
known poems as 'Our Budgie', 'Synopsis of the
Great Welsh Novel', 'Local Boy Makes Good'
and 'Ode to the Severn Bridge', and in as many
in his second volume, *A Crown for Branwen*
(1974). The latter includes one of his poems in
Welsh, now widely known and sung as 'Colli
Iaith'.

During the 1970s Harri Webb began writing scripts for television; they include *The Green Desert* (1971), *How Green Was my Father* (1976), *Song of the River* (1978), *Fishermen of Milford* (1978) and *Memoirs of a Pit Orchestra* (1979). He has also published a collection of songs and ballads dealing with the more light-hearted sides of Welsh history, entitled *Rampage and Revel* (1977); a second collection, in the same vein, *Poems and Points*, appeared in 1983. His adaptations for children of stories from the *Mabinogion* were published as *Tales from Wales* (1984).

There are autobiographical essays by Harri Webb in *Planet* (no. 30, Jan., 1976) and in *Artists in Wales* (ed. Meic Stephens, 1977). For a critical discussion of his poetry see the article by Belinda Humfrey in *The Anglo-Welsh Review* (vol. 21, 1972); see also the note on Harri Webb by Glyn Jones in *Profiles* (1980) and the article by Chris O'Neill in *The Anglo-Welsh Review* (no. 65, 1979).

Welch, Ronald, see FELTON, RONALD OLIVER (1909–82).

Welch Piety, see under JONES, GRIFFITH (1683–1761).

'We'll Keep a Welcome', a song first published in 1949, was originally associated with the Lyrian Singers in the radio series 'Welsh Rarebit'. The words were written by Lyn Joshua and James Harper and the tune by Mai Jones (1899–1960). Made famous by the rendering of Harry Secombe, the song is a good example of Welsh schmaltz.

WELLS, NIGEL (1944–), poet, was born in Northampton and educated at the University College of Wales, Aberystwyth; he lives near Machynlleth, Mont. He is the author of two collections of verse, *Venturing out from Trees* (1970) and *The Winter Festivals* (1980); the latter is an original and powerfully rhythmic reworking of mythic themes.

Welsh, Freddie, see THOMAS, FREDERICK HALL (1886–1927).

Welsh Academy, The, see ACADEMI GYMREIG.

Welsh Anvil, The, sub-titled **Yr Einion** (lit. 'The anvil'), the annual journal of the Guild of Graduates of the *University of Wales, was edited at Aberystwyth by Alwyn D. *Rees between 1949 and 1958. Mainly in English, it was intended to be 'a forum for the expression of informed opinion in Wales upon intellectual and social questions', by means of articles on religion, education, the arts, science, broadcasting, language, tourism, industry and other topics of the day. Among contributions of literary interest were those by Gwyn *Jones, Aneirin Talfan *Davies, Alun *Llywelyn-Williams, Ioan Bowen *Rees, J. E. Caerwyn *Williams, Raymond *Garlick, Waldo *Williams and Bobi Jones (Robert Maynard *Jones). The journal was revived briefly in 1964 under the title *The University of Wales Review*, primarily for the purpose of defending the decision by the Court of the University to remain a single, federal, national institution.

Welsh Arts Council, The, a constituent but largely autonomous committee of the Arts Council of Great Britain, assumed its role as the Government's principal agent for the patronage of the arts in Wales in 1967, before which time it had been only a Welsh Committee of the parent body. Its Chairmen from that year until 1985 were Gwyn *Jones, Sir William Crawshay, the Marchioness of Anglesey and Sir Hywel Evans, and its Director Aneurin M. Thomas; Thomas Arfon Owen was appointed Director in 1984. Dispensing its funds (some seven million pounds in 1985/86) on the recommendation of specialist committees, the Council offers subsidy across a wide spectrum of the arts, including music and opera, the visual arts, literature, *drama, dance, film and crafts, and thus plays a major part in the provision of cultural amenities and the encouragement of professional standards. Three Regional Arts Associations were established, with similar objectives, in the north, west and south-east of Wales in 1967, 1971 and 1973 respectively, each depending on funds from the Council and local authorities. The Council has a staff of sixty-seven and its offices are in Cardiff.

The Literature Department was established in 1967 with the appointment of Meic *Stephens as Literature Director. Many writers, critics and editors have served as co-opted members of the Literature Committee under the chairmanship of T. J. *Morgan, Glyn Tegai Hughes, Roland *Mathias, Prys *Morgan and Walford *Davies. Among the recipients of grant-aid recommended by the Literature Committee (£550,000 in 1985–86) are the *Welsh Books Council, Yr *Academi Gymreig, the principal publishers and their magazines, *Cymdeithas Cerdd Dafod and the *Welsh National Centre for Children's Literature. The Council has also made awards to writers in the form of prizes and bursaries, and it administers directly the Oriel Bookshop and Gallery in Cardiff.

Further details of the Council's work will be found in its Annual Reports; see also *The Arts in Wales 1950–75* (ed. Meic Stephens, 1979).

Welsh Books Council, The, a public body founded in 1961 as a result of co-operation between the Union of Welsh Book Societies and a number of local authorities. Established in order to promote the writing and marketing of popular books for adults in the Welsh language, it began by implementing a scheme for the payment of grants to authors, by publishing books for libraries only, by introducing book-tokens for Welsh books and by developing a wholesale distribution centre. Under its Director Alun Creunant Davies its responsibilities have grown to encompass all aspects of publishing in Wales, in both Welsh and English. This growth was largely the result of a decision by the *Welsh Arts Council, in the early 1970s, to enable the Books Council to establish four Departments offering a central service to authors, publishers and booksellers in the fields of editing, design, publicity and marketing. The Books Council's offices are situated at Castell Brychan in Aberystwyth and the Books Centre is at Llanbadarn, on the outskirts of the town. In 1979 the Council was charged with responsibility for administering the Government grant for Welsh-language books and periodicals (a total of £345,000 in 1985/86). It also runs a children's book club and publishes catalogues and a bilingual trade-journal, *Llais Llyfrau/Book News from Wales*. See also PRINTING AND PUBLISHING.

The early history of the Welsh Books Council is described by Alun R. Edwards in his autobiography, *Yr Hedyn Mwstard* (1980); further details of the Council's work will be found in its Annual Reports.

Welsh Costume, The, was the product of the imagination and idealism of the nineteenth century which, in Wales as in many other parts of Europe, sought to elevate the everyday dress of the common people to the status of a national costume. The petticoat, apron, bedgown and tall black hat had for long been prominent features of the dress worn by women in some parts of Wales, but they were common to both Wales and England in the seventeenth century. Their use had survived unselfconsciously among the poor of some mountainous districts of Wales until the end of the eighteenth century or later, so that the first English Tourists (see under TOURS OF WALES) to visit the country could not fail to note them. Some of the regional variations described by such writers as T. J. Llewelyn *Prichard were the fruit of *Romanticism and some, as illustrated by the artist J. C. Rowlands (1848), became part of what visitors expected to see during their holidays in Wales.

The idea of a distinct national costume was first advocated by Lady Llanover (Augusta Waddington *Hall) in an essay which won a prize at the Cardiff Royal Eisteddfod of 1834. Her original intention was to persuade the women of Wales to wear local tweeds in preference to cotton or calico and she offered prizes for collections of traditional designs. But within a few years, out of a characteristic zeal for all things Welsh, she had become interested in the possibility of creating a homogenized national costume which would appeal to painters and tourists. The 'Welsh costume' as it is known today, consisting of a red cloak worn over a petticoat and bedgown, together with a tall black hat

similar to that of Mother Goose, was first seen in the processions organized by Lady Llanover at the eisteddfodau held in Abergavenny under the auspices of the *Cymreigyddion Society during the mid-nineteenth century. She also invented a costume for the male servants at Llanover Court but this fancy dress proved to have no wider appeal for those who were not obliged to wear it. The female version of the 'Welsh costume' soon became a national caricature, as in the figure of *Dame Wales, and this despite the fact that, in Lady Llanover's day, the old native styles in all their local variety were being abandoned as Wales became one of the most industrialized countries in Europe. The *National Eisteddfod and the revival of folk-dancing in the twentieth century gave further impetus to the survival of an artificial form of 'Welsh costume', but it is now worn only on ceremonial and patriotic occasions, particularly by schoolchildren on St. David's Day (1 March), and for the purposes of tourism.

For further details see M. Ellis, *Welsh Costumes and Customs* (1951), Ken Etheridge, *Welsh Costume* (1958), F. G. Payne, *Welsh Peasant Costume* (1964) and Ilid E. Anthony, *Costumes of the Welsh People* (1975); see also the chapter by Prys Morgan, 'From a Death to a View: The Hunt for the Welsh Past in the Romantic Period', in *The Invention of Tradition* (ed. E. Hobsbawm and Terence Ranger, 1983).

Welsh Fasting Girl, The, see JACOB, SARAH (1857–69).

Welsh Folk Museum, The, a part of the *National Museum of Wales, was opened in 1948 at St. Fagans Castle, near Cardiff, a building which was the gift of the third Earl of Plymouth. Its first Curator was Iorwerth C. *Peate, formerly Keeper of the Folk Life Department at the National Museum, and his successor, Trefor M. *Owen, was appointed in 1976. The institution was modelled on the major folk museums of Scandinavia. The first examples of traditional buildings were re-erected in the grounds of the castle in 1951. The Folk Museum's purpose is to record and study the culture of Wales, including its crafts, architecture, costume, agriculture, folklore and dialects, from the sixteenth century to the present. See also WELSH INDUSTRIAL AND MARITIME MUSEUM.

Welsh History Review, The, a magazine which first appeared in 1960 under the editorship of Glanmor *Williams, is published by the University of Wales Press under the auspices of the History and Law Committee of the *Board of Celtic Studies. The journal is the only major scholarly periodical which covers the whole of Welsh history, medieval and modern, political, social, economic, religious, linguistic and sociological. It has devoted special numbers to the Welsh *Laws (1963), to the career of David *Williams (1967) and to Welsh Labour History

(1973); a twenty-first anniversary number was published in June 1981 (vol. 10, no. 3). Comparable in stature with its counterparts in England, Scotland and Ireland, the magazine has played a vital part in the revival of the study of Welsh history. Since 1965 it has been edited by Kenneth O. *Morgan, who was formerly its assistant editor.

Welsh Indians, see under EVANS, JOHN (1770–99) and MADOG AB OWAIN GWYNEDD (*fl.* 1170).

Welsh Industrial and Maritime Museum, The, a part of the *National Museum of Wales, was opened in 1977 in Bute Street, Cardiff. It grew out of the Department of Industry at the National Museum and its first Curator was D. Morgan Rees. The exhibits, many of substantial size, include a working replica of the famous locomotive invented by Richard *Trevithick. The Museum, of which the Curator is J. Geraint *Jenkins, complements the *Welsh Folk Museum in presenting the industrial history of Wales since the *Industrial Revolution.

Welsh Joint Education Committee, The, a body established by the British Government in 1948 to represent all the Local Education Authorities of Wales, together with the teaching profession, is recognized as the official spokesman for Wales on educational matters. In 1949 it assumed responsibility for the examinations formerly conducted by the Central Welsh Board and since then it has operated as an examining board for Wales. The Committee has an important cultural role in its administration of schemes for the publication of books in Welsh for children. It does not act as a publisher but is responsible for two schemes to promote publication, one for reading books and the other for textbooks. Both schemes are supported by the Local Education Authorities so that about forty titles enjoy guaranteed minimum sales every year. In recent years, mainly owing to finance made available through the specific grant proposals of the Education Act of 1980, there has been an expansion of work in the field of Welsh textbooks. Competitions are also organized regularly to stimulate the production of children's books in Welsh and, with the *Welsh Arts Council, the Committee contributes to the funding of the Tir na n-Óg Prizes. See also CHILDREN'S LITERATURE.

Welsh Language, The, a sister language of Cornish and Breton, belongs to the Brythonic branch of the Celtic family of Indo-European languages; Irish, Scots Gaelic and Manx belong to the Goidelic branch. The vocabulary of Welsh is basically Celtic but it has borrowed at various periods in its history from Latin, Irish, Norse, Norman French and particularly from English. Welsh shares with other Celtic languages features such as the mutation of initial consonants and the fusing of personal pronouns with some prepositions to produce systematic conjugational paradigms. There is considerable complexity in the structure of the sentence in respect of word-order and the rules of concord. The verb normally stands at the beginning of the sentence, followed by the subject when such is expressed, followed by the object and then the remainder of the predicate. There is no indefinite article, nouns have two numbers (singular and plural) and two genders (masculine and feminine). The attributive adjective normally follows the noun it qualifies and the numeral, when it is used adjectivally, normally precedes the noun, which remains singular. The accent usually falls on the penultimate syllable.

By the second half of the sixth century the parent Brythonic language had registered changes sufficiently marked to justify its being regarded as the period in which Early Welsh, Early Cornish and Early Breton were born. Scholars refer to Early or Primitive Welsh as the language of the period from the middle of the sixth century to the late eighth century. Evidence for this period is sparse and based mainly on inscriptions, such as the personal names in early inscriptions found in Anglesey, and on examples in Latin texts. Welsh poetry attributed to the early part of the period, as in *The Book of Aneirin* (see under GODODDIN), and attested in manuscripts dating from the thirteenth century, has its locale in the regions known today as the south of Scotland and the north-west of England, the *Old North of Welsh tradition. In the period of Old Welsh, although the evidence is still scanty, there are textual examples such as the Welsh glosses contained in a Latin paraphrase of the Gospels by *Juvencus. Middle Welsh is seen as the language of the period from the mid-twelfth century to the end of the fourteenth century or the middle of the fifteenth century, a period when it was exposed to external influences and was rich in prose (see PEDAIR CAINC Y MABINOGI) and verse material. In the period which follows, as far as the end of the sixteenth century, the language is usually described, for study purposes, as Early Modern, and from then onwards to the present day as Late Modern.

In independent Wales the poets and prose-writers were the custodians of the language but the *Acts of Union (1536 and 1542) proscribed its use for official purposes and deprived it of prestige and authority. The *Tudors, while taking full advantage of their Welsh connection, were anxious to ensure uniformity throughout the realm and the English language was one way of providing such uniformity. In contrast with the situation in Brittany and Ireland, however, the translation of the Scriptures in the sixteenth century, particularly in William *Morgan's translation of the *Bible in 1588, together with the publication of books in Welsh from 1547, gave the language credibility and a standard of usage. The emergence of popular religious movements in the seventeenth and eighteenth centuries, the Circulating Schools of Griffith *Jones and the importance of the *Sunday Schools in the heyday of *Nonconformity, all contributed to its survival by ensuring that large numbers of the population became literate in Welsh.

The *Industrial Revolution, although it kept Welsh people at home, imported its managerial class from England and its manpower from all parts of Britain and Ireland. It is estimated that during the first quarter of the nineteenth century some eighty per cent of the population was Welsh-speaking. English was confined to a small upper class, to those who had received a formal education, to the larger towns, to places along the Border with England and to parts of south-west Wales, such as *Gower and southern Pembrokeshire. Formal education did nothing to encourage the preservation of Welsh and the *Welsh Not was a token of the disrespect in which the language was held. By 1901 the proportion of Welsh-speakers had decreased to about fifty per cent and there has been a further decline at every Census since then: 43.5% spoke Welsh in 1911, 37.1% in 1921, 36.8% in 1931, 28.9% in 1951, 26% in 1961, 20.8% in 1971 and 18.9%, or 503,549 persons over the age of three, in 1981. Today the western counties of Gwynedd (63%) and Dyfed (47%) have the highest proportion of Welsh-speakers. It is not known how many Welsh-speakers live outside Wales because the Census does not enumerate them. Among factors which have contributed to the decline of the Welsh language are the economic deterioration and depopulation of the rural areas, emigration (particularly during the *Depression of the inter-War years), rapidly increasing facilities for transport and communication, tourism, radio and television, advertising, the periodical and daily press, the afforestation of agricultural land, military service, marriages between Welsh-speakers and English-speakers, immigration, holiday-homes, the decline of Nonconformity and the apathy of many Welsh-speakers themselves, conditioned as they are by the social pressures usually exerted on speakers of minority languages.

As early as the sixteenth century there were those who saw that the Welsh language needed cultivation and patronage, prominent among whom were William *Salesbury, Gruffydd *Robert and Siôn Dafydd *Rhys. The recall to a distinguished literary past, then as later, was one of the language's greatest supports. By the later part of the nineteenth century Welsh national consciousness was growing; the language was gaining new prestige from the distinguished philological studies of John *Rhŷs and later of John *Morris-Jones and a new impetus from a renaissance in Welsh literature and the emergence of political concern. Writers and educationalists such as Emrys ap Iwan (Robert Ambrose *Jones), Dan Isaac *Davies, Thomas *Gee and Owen M. *Edwards were to assert the right of a people to the dignity of their own language. In the twentieth century the Welsh Departments of the *University of Wales have contributed substantially to a remarkable period in Welsh *scholarship.

Various investigations, studies and recommendations concerning the language have appeared. The report entitled *Welsh in Education and Life* (1927) was the result of an inquiry into the position occupied by the language and its literature in the educational system of Wales and into the ways in which its study might best be promoted; a further report, *The Place of Welsh and English in the Schools of Wales*, appeared in 1953. Saunders *Lewis's radio lecture *Tynged yr Iaith* (1962) resulted in the formation of *Cymdeithas yr Iaith Gymraeg* which calls for action to save the language. The Hughes-Parry Report, *The Legal Status of the Welsh Language* (1956), recommended the adoption of the principle of the equal validity of Welsh and English, its recommendations being implemented by the Welsh Language Act (1967) which made special reference to the use of Welsh in legal proceedings and on official forms. The Gittins Report, *Primary Education in Wales* (1967), recommended that 'every child should be given sufficient opportunity to become reasonably bilingual by the end of the primary stage'. A further substantial report, *A Future for the Welsh Language* (1978), was presented to the Secretary of State for Wales by the Council for the Welsh Language; among its recommendations, so far not implemented, was the creation of a permanent body to promote the language. Principles have been converted into practice in some spheres: bilingual road-signs, nursery schools, bilingual schools and adult learners' classes have been set up and some Colleges and University Departments provide for teaching through the medium of Welsh. Books in Welsh are now more numerous (about four hundred new titles are published every year), produced to a higher standard and of more varied interest than ever before (see under PRINTING AND PUBLISHING). Welsh scholarship flourishes and is producing reliable texts and critical studies; the University of Wales *Board of Celtic Studies is preparing a major standard dictionary of the language, parts of which have already appeared. There is substantial support from public bodies such as the *National Eisteddfod, *Urdd Gobaith Cymru, the *Welsh Arts Council, the *Welsh Office, the BBC, HTV (see under RADIO AND TELEVISION) and most recently *Sianel Pedwar Cymru (S4C)*, the fourth television channel established in 1982, which broadcasts about twenty-three hours a week in the Welsh language. Since the 1960s there has been a renaissance of interest in the language, among the younger generation in particular, many of whom have asserted themselves as Welsh-speakers. The migration from the Welsh heartlands has led to an impoverishment of the traditional bastions of the language and its idiom but the new awareness of Welsh identity in general has resulted in a positive and active programme of effort to save and encourage the use of the vernacular in Wales.

For further details see Henry Lewis, *Datblygiad yr Iaith Gymraeg* (1946), K. Jackson, *Language and History in Early Britain* (1953), Ceri W. Lewis, 'The Welsh Language' in *The Cardiff Region* (ed. J. F. Rees, 1960), Gerald Morgan, *The Dragon's Tongue* (1966), R. Brinley Jones, *The Old British Tongue: the Vernacular in Wales 1540–1640* (1970), D. Ellis Evans, 'The Language and Literature of Wales' in *Anatomy of Wales* (ed. R. Brinley Jones, 1972), Meic Stephens (ed.), *The Welsh Language Today* (1973), Clive Betts, *Culture in Crisis: the future of the Welsh language* (1976), Morris Jones and Alan R. Thomas, *The Welsh Language: studies in its syntax and semantics* (1977) and J. W. Aitchison and H. Carter, *The Welsh Language 1961–1981: an Interpretative Atlas* (1985).

Welsh Language Society, The, see CYM-DEITHAS YR IAITH GYMRAEG (1962).

Welsh League of Youth, The, see URDD GOBAITH CYMRU.

Welsh Manuscripts Society, The, was founded in 1836 by six prominent members of the *Cymreigyddion Society of Abergavenny. Its first publication, *Liber Landavensis* (1840), was edited by W. J. *Rees of Cascob but the most important was Lewys *Dwnn's *Heraldic Visitations* (ed. Samuel Rush Meyrick, 2 vols., 1846). The Society also published *The Iolo Manuscripts* (1848), a volume edited by Taliesin *Williams and Carnhuanawc (Thomas *Price), and W. J. Rees completed *Lives of the Cambro-British Saints*, a work which had been begun by his nephew, Rice Rees. The Society was thereafter taken over by John *Williams (Ab Ithel) and it was he who edited, quite unscientifically, the remainder of the Society's publications, namely *Dosparth Edeyrn Davod Aur* (1856), *Annales Cambriae* and *The Chronicle of the Princes* (1860), *The Physicians of Myddfai* (1861) and *Barddas* (1862).

Welsh National Centre for Children's Literature, The, established in 1979 and situated in Aberystwyth, was created on the initiative of the *Welsh Arts Council and in response to a growth of public interest in the genre which it now exists to foster. The Centre houses a collection of some six thousand items, including books, periodicals, manuscripts, illustrations and other related audio-visual material, in both Welsh and English, and it administers a programme of events designed to promote *Children's Literature in Wales.

Welsh Nationalist Party, The, see PLAID CYMRU.

Welsh Nightingale, The, see WYNNE, EDITH (1842–97).

Welsh Not, The, a piece of wood or slate with the letters w.n. cut into it, was used in some schools during the eighteenth and nineteenth centuries for the purpose of discouraging children from speaking their native language. It was hung around the neck of a pupil caught speaking Welsh until he or she, in turn, could pass it on to another, the pupil wearing it at the end of the day being punished by the teacher. This infamous practice became widespread after the publication of the *Blue Books in 1847. A description of the Welsh Not, as used in Llanuwchllyn in the 1860s, will be found in Owen M. *Edwards's book *Clych Atgof* (1906).

For further details see the article by E. G. Millward, '*Yr Hen Gyfundrefn Felltigedig*', in *Barn* (April/May, 1980).

Welsh Office, The, the headquarters of the British Government in Wales, was established in 1965 and is housed in the Crown Offices in Cathays Park, Cardiff. Whereas in its early days it dealt only with roads, housing and local government, by today—as the result of a gradual process of devolution from Whitehall in London to Wales—the Welsh Office (with a staff of 2,300 civil servants) also has responsibility for such areas as agriculture, forestry, water, land use, education (except the *University of Wales), health, social services, environmental protection, industrial development, economic planning, ancient monuments and historic buildings. The office of Secretary of State for Wales, a post of Cabinet rank, has been held by James *Griffiths (1965–66), Cledwyn Hughes (1966–68), George Thomas (1968–70), Peter Thomas (1970–74), John Morris (1974–79) and Nicholas Edwards (1979–   ). With the exception of the fourth, all these were Members of Parliament for constituencies in Wales.

The Government's support for activity in the Welsh language, in the form of Welsh Office grants, amounted to some two-and-a-half million pounds in 1985/86. Under the terms of the Education Act of 1980 it dispenses funds to a variety of projects in the field of bilingual education from the pre-school stage to tertiary level, including grants for the preparation of Welsh-language teaching materials such as the textbooks produced under the auspices of the *Welsh Joint Education Committee. The Council for the Welsh Language, appointed by the Secretary of State for Wales in 1973, was charged with responsibility for advising on the social factors affecting the use and welfare of Welsh. It published a number of reports on such topics as nursery education, television broadcasting, publishing and the teaching of Welsh to adults, concluding its work in 1978 with the publication of *A Future for the Welsh Language*. The Government grant (£345,000 in 1985/86) for the purpose of publishing books and periodicals in the Welsh language for adults and children, was introduced by the Welsh Office in 1956 and has been administered by the *Welsh Books Council since 1979.

Among other cultural organizations in receipt of Welsh Office grants are the *National Eisteddfod, Yr *Academi Gymreig, Bwrdd Ffilmiau Cymraeg (The Welsh Films Board) and *Urdd Gobaith Cymru. This expenditure is in addition to that of the *Welsh Arts Council which, as a constituent committee of the Arts Council of Great Britain (a body with its own royal charter), is not placed under the aegis of the Welsh Office.

Welsh Outlook, The, a monthly magazine devoted to the discussion of Welsh affairs, was launched in 1914 under the sponsorship of the coalowner Lord Davies of Llandinam, and the editorship of Thomas *Jones. Styling itself a 'journal of national social progress' and speaking on behalf of a nationality which it saw as threatened by an increasingly uniform culture, it ventured with missionary zeal into a wide area of concerns, including *Nationalism at home and abroad, education, literature, industry and labour problems, and the Welsh language. Although it carried material by a variety of contributors, the magazine's philosophy reflected the intellectual bent of its founders: Liberal, internationalist, moderately decentralist, but often rigidly conservative over ideological questions. Among Thomas Jones's successors as editor were Edgar L. *Chappell, Robert *Roberts (Silyn), Thomas Huws Davies and Elias Henry *Jones. Lord Davies withdrew his financial support in 1927 and thereafter the periodical gradually declined in popularity, ceasing publication at the end of 1933.
For details of the part played by Thomas Jones in fostering *The Welsh Outlook* see the article by Trevor L. Williams in *The Anglo-Welsh Review* (no. 64, 1979); see also Roland Mathias: *The Lonely Editor: A Glance at Anglo-Welsh Magazines* (The Gwyn Jones Lecture, 1984).

Welsh Poetry Old and New (1912), an anthology of translations by the Anglo-Irish writer Alfred Perceval Graves (1843–1931). All periods are represented, from the earliest times to the beginning of the twentieth century and among the contemporary poets included are H. Elvet *Lewis (Elfed), John *Morris-Jones, Eifion Wyn (Eliseus *Williams), T. Gwynn *Jones and W. J. *Gruffydd. The translations are typical of their period in the flowery archaism of the language and the translator's attempts to render the originals in traditional English metres. Graves, who took a leading part in the Irish literary and musical revivals, was also an enthusiast for the music and literature of Wales, a keen *eisteddfodwr*

and a founder member of the Welsh Folk Song Society. But his knowledge of Welsh was incomplete and in the task of translation he relied heavily on the work of other translators such as Edmund O. *Jones and H. Idris *Bell, and on the advice of scholars and poets, including John Morris-Jones and T. Gwynn Jones, with whom he was acquainted.

He published two other books which are of Welsh interest, namely *Welsh Melodies* (1907) and *English Verse Translations of the Welsh Poems of Ceiriog Hughes* (1926). His son, the English poet Robert Graves, recalls with affection in his autobiography, *Goodbye to All That* (1929), the house near Harlech, Mer., where the family often spent the summer.

Welsh Poets (1917), the first anthology devoted exclusively to Anglo-Welsh poetry, was edited by A. G. *Prys-Jones. Its aim was 'to give collective utterance to the English-speaking poets of modern Wales', of whom twenty-two are represented. Besides translations from the Welsh by H. Idris *Bell and poems in English by T. Gwynn *Jones and Robert *Roberts (Silyn), the anthology consists of poems by poets who, with the exception of W. H. *Davies, Ernest *Rhys, the editor and a few others, are no longer considered important. The book was, nevertheless, a milestone in the development of Anglo-Welsh poetry and the editor's initiative in compiling the work was to be recognized by later editors and critics. A. G. Prys-Jones described his motives in compiling the anthology, not the least of which was to express his 'contempt and loathing' for *My People* (1915) by Caradoc Evans (David *Evans), in an article published in *The *London Welshman* in 1964.

Welsh Rabbit, a dish consisting of cheese melted with milk, eggs or butter and served on toast. The name, first recorded in 1725, is not a corruption of 'rarebit', as is commonly supposed, but is thought to refer to the frugal diet of the upland Welsh. The Welsh fondness for cheese was noted by the English poet John Skelton (*c.*1460–1529), who used it as a gibe against the many Welshmen who had flocked to the *Tudor court after 1485. It was he who recorded the story in which St. Peter, tired of the clamour of Welshmen for all the best jobs in Heaven, arranged for an angel to shout '*Caws pobi!*' ('Toasted cheese!') outside, whereupon the Welsh rushed out and the gates were slammed behind them. The dish now known as Welsh Rabbit is still popular in all parts of Wales. See also LAVERBREAD.

Welsh Review, The, a magazine published monthly by Penmark Press under the editorship of Gwyn *Jones between February and November 1939 and, after a suspension of publication during the Second World War, as a quarterly from March 1944 to December 1948; thirty numbers in all were issued. It was announced as 'a journal for the English-speaking Welshman which though conducted in English will recognise and champion the unique importance of the Welsh language and the distinctive national culture inseparable from it'. The magazine published creative work by Anglo-Welsh writers and translations from the Welsh, as well as wide-ranging comment on matters of Welsh interest such as history, education and politics. Among contributors to the pre-War numbers were all those Anglo-Welsh writers whose reputations had been made or consolidated during the 1930s.

Despite a new format, *The Welsh Review*, revived, was recognizably the same journal, informed with the same editorial intention and carrying poetry, short stories, articles and reviews as before. Caradoc Evans (David *Evans) and Alun *Lewis became regular contributors. The number of expository articles on Welsh-language literature was increased and a series of anonymous but highly percipient profiles of distinguished Welshmen was among the magazine's most notable features. Contributors from outside Wales included T. S. Eliot, H. E. Bates, J. R. R. Tolkien and A. L. Rowse. Like *Wales (ed. Keidrych *Rhys), *The Welsh Review* was a major platform for Anglo-Welsh writers during the 1940s and it provided a valuable forum for the public discussion of Welsh affairs through the medium of English. But it enjoyed no subsidy and, under the increasing burden of editing and publishing, Gwyn Jones decided in 1948 to cease publication of his magazine.

Welsh Revolt, The (1294–95), an episode which had among its immediate causes the English Crown's imposition of a tax on movable goods and the compulsory enlistment of soldiers for the campaign in Gascony. It was also a reaction against the terms of the Statute of *Rhuddlan (1284) and the Edwardian settlement of Wales: there was widespread resentment at the financial and legal implications of conquest. Castles, the symbols of the new order, were attacked in west and mid-Wales, and also in the lordships of Brecon and Glamorgan. The revolt's leader was Madog ap Llywelyn, a kinsman of the royal House of *Gwynedd who—despite his earlier antipathy to *Llywelyn ap Gruffudd—now assumed the title of Prince of Wales. Madog's forces launched an attack on the castle and borough of Caernarfon and extensive damage was also caused in the lordship of Denbigh. Edward I then led an army into north Wales and, after being besieged in *Conwy castle, succeeded in reasserting his authority. Madog ap Llywelyn, marching into Powys, was defeated by the Earl of Warwick at the battle of Maes Meidog (1295) in Caereinion: he surrendered later in the same year and, although he was not executed, his subsequent fate is

unknown. In order to strengthen his hold on north-west Wales, Edward I authorized the construction of a castle and the establishment of a borough at *Beaumaris.

Further details will be found in J. E. Morris, *The Welsh Wars of Edward I* (1901), J. G. Edwards, 'The Battle of Maes Meidog and the Welsh Campaign of 1294–95' in *The English Historical Review* (vol. XXXIX, 1924), J. Griffiths, 'The Revolt of Madog ap Llywelyn' in the *Transactions* of the Caernarfonshire Historical Society (1955) and Michael Prestwich, 'A new account of the Welsh Campaign of 1294–95' in *The Welsh History Review* (vol. 6, 1972).

Welsh Theatre Company, see under DRAMA.

Welsh Tract, The, a parcel of land to the north-west of Philadelphia which was promised by William Penn to Welsh Quaker immigrants, to be independently governed by 'officers, magistrates, juries of our own language'. It included what became the townships of Upper Meirion, Lower Meirion, Haverford, Radnor, Tredyffrin, East and West Whiteland, East and West Goshen, Willistown, East Town and part of West Town. The first Welshmen, including Edward Jones of Bala, reached the Delaware on 13 August 1682. In the following year Thomas Lloyd of Dolobran (see under LLOYD FAMILY) became Deputy Governor to Penn, but differences had already become evident between Penn and the Welsh Quakers, who considered that he had betrayed his original promises when their land was divided between two counties and interspersed with that of other settlers. Prominent among the first settlers was Rowland *Ellis, the name of whose old home at Bryn Mawr, Dolgellau, was given to his new home, near which was founded the college of Bryn Mawr, Philadelphia. Among others were Ellis Pugh (1656–1718), author of *Annerch i'r Cymry* (1721), the first Welsh book to be printed in America, and David Lloyd of Manafon, Mont., who succeeded Thomas Lloyd as Deputy Governor. The novel *Y Rhandir Mwyn* (1972) by Marion *Eames is set in the Welsh Tract. See also QUAKERISM.

For further details see Richard Jones, *Crynwyr Bore Cymru* (1931), David Williams, *Cymry ac America* (1946) and J. Gwynn Williams, 'The Quakers of Merioneth during the Seventeenth Century' in the *Journal* of the Merioneth Record Society (1979).

Welsh Trust, The, a fund established in 1674 by the English Nonconformist divine and philanthropist, Thomas Gouge (1605?–81). Its purpose was to provide elementary schools in Wales in which children would be taught to read and write English. In co-operation with Stephen *Hughes and Charles *Edwards, Gouge also endeavoured to supply adults with devotional books in Welsh and in 1677 they published a new edition of the Welsh Bible. After the founder's death, the schools, of which there were some three hundred, were closed and the Trust dissolved, but the work of distributing books continued. The money left in the fund was used to found charity schools in London which became the pattern for the education of the poor in the eighteenth century. The Trust's example helped to pave the way for its more effective successor, the *Society for Promoting Christian Knowledge.

Welsh Union of Writers, The, was established in 1982 with the aim of representing authors in their dealings with publishers, broadcasting companies and other public bodies. It also campaigns for greater recognition of contemporary literature in the field of education, monitors the interest shown by the media in cultural matters and seeks to nurture the relationship between writers and such bodies as the *Welsh Arts Council, the *Welsh Books Council and the Regional Arts Associations. The Union, which has a membership of about two hundred, published in 1983 a pilot-number of a new magazine entitled *New Wales*, but it failed to attract subsidy from the Welsh Arts Council. See also ACADEMI GYMREIG and UNDEB AWDURON CYMRU.

Welsh Voices (1967), an anthology of English-language poetry edited by Bryn *Griffiths. Besides older living poets such as A. G. *Prys-Jones, David *Jones, R. S. *Thomas, Glyn *Jones and Vernon *Watkins, most of the other fourteen contributors were poets born in the years between the World Wars and some, such as Leslie *Norris and Harri *Webb, had made their names more recently in the pages of the magazine *Poetry Wales*. The anthology was in some respects unsatisfactory and was shortly to be superseded by The *Lilting House (ed. John Stuart Williams and Meic Stephens, 1969), but it served the valuable purpose of presenting to a wider audience a selection of the work of those poets who had contributed to 'the second flowering' of Anglo-Welsh poetry in the 1960s. The first anthology of Anglo-Welsh poetry since *Modern Welsh Poetry (ed. Keidrych Rhys, 1944), it was for several years the only book of its kind used as a textbook in the schools of Wales.

Welsh Way, The, see under DROVERS.

Welsh Wizard, The, see LLOYD GEORGE, DAVID (1863–1945).

Welshman, The (1832), a weekly Radical newspaper established in Carmarthen by a group which included John Lewis Brigstocke and John Palmer, the latter a mathematics teacher at the Presbyterian College in the town. Sold to C. W. Wisley and Joseph Spawforth in 1842 and to William James Morgan and Howell Davies in 1862, it was published between 1880 and Davies's death in 1888 by Morgan alone. Among its editors were Hugh Carleton Tierney, S. W. Shearman and H. L. Lewis. The newspaper was bought by the owners of The *Carmarthen Journal towards the end of the 1940s and its publication was discontinued in 1984.

'Welshman's Public Recantation, The' (1642), an anonymous song, printed in London, which mocks the deaths of many Welsh soldiers who fought on the Royalist side at the battle of Edgehill in 1642. Under the command of Colonel Salesbury, Sir Edward Stradling and John Owen of Clenennau, the Welsh were described thus in one of the Harleian Manuscripts: 'Arms were the great deficiency, and the men stood in the same garments in which they left their native fields; and with scythes, pitchforks, and even sickles in their hands, they cheerfully took the field, and literally like reapers descended to that harvest of death'. Here, as at Tewkesbury and Cirencester, there was great loss of Welsh life because the Welsh, 'as usual', were placed to the fore. With its refrain, 'O Taffy, poor Taffy!', the song acknowledges the valour of the Welshman (referred to throughout as 'her') but also makes stock jokes about cheese, goats and sheep.

Werin, Y (lit. 'The common people'), a weekly newspaper established in 1885 by the Welsh National Press Company at Caernarfon, was edited in turn by some of the best-known figures in Welsh journalism, including Beriah Gwynfe *Evans, John *Thomas (Eifionydd) and E. Morgan *Humphreys. Owing to a shortage of paper in the months prior to the First World War, the paper was amalgamated with Yr Eco Cymreig to form Y Werin a'r Eco in 1914 and was merged with *Papur Pawb in 1937.

Wesleyanism, or **Wesleyan Methodism** (see under METHODISM), a generic term describing the doctrine and organization of the Methodist Church established by John Wesley, who visited and preached in Wales many times between 1739 and 1790. After the rift with the Calvinists, however, Wesleyanism flourished only in those areas where English was widely spoken, such as east Breconshire, south Pembrokeshire and the Cardiff region. In Brecon town a Wesleyan Methodist Society was formed before 1756 and the Connexion always had there, until the later nineteenth century, more than its fair share of support from persons of social weight. It was Thomas *Coke, who had first heard Wesley preach in Brecon when he was a schoolboy, who, on becoming Wesleyanism's chief administrator, persuaded the British Conference to correct its almost total failure in Welsh-speaking regions by sending in 1800 two 'missionaries'—Owen Davies (1752–1830) and John Hughes of Brecon (1776–1843)—to north-east

Wales. The work there developed in some districts only and became very successful in no more than a few, amongst which Coedpoeth, Denbs., Llanrhaeadr-ym-Mochnant, Denbs., and Tregarth, Caerns., were notable. By the time of the *Religious Census (1851), however, there was very considerable Wesleyan strength in Holywell and Llanfyllin, and in other regions in the north-east, and Welsh Wesleyanism had re-entered some parts of south Wales. Methodism was originally intended only to revitalize the faith and practice of the Church of England, but from 1771 Wesleyan chapels were built in Wales. The breach with the Church took place between 1784 and 1795—earlier than in the case of the Calvinistic Methodists.

The effect of Wesleyanism on Welsh life and literature has been relatively marginal, partly because the itinerant tradition (that is, the transference of ministers from circuit to circuit by decision of the central hierarchy) prevented close identification with particular districts, and partly because its links with the British Conference remained so strong. Ministers have always received their theological education in England and, for many years, it was not uncommon for their sons to be educated at Kingswood School, Bath. Nevertheless, Wesleyanism has produced preachers of great power, notably John Evans (1840–97) of Eglwysbach in the nineteenth century, and D. Tecwyn Evans (1876–1957) and John Roger Jones in the years between the World Wars. Its chief historians have been Hugh Jones (1837–1919), David Young (1844–1913), Thomas Jones-Humphreys, A. H. Williams and Garfield H. Hughes (1912–69). The Connexion published extensively in the nineteenth century and among its periodical publications have been some of the most long-lived in the language: Yr *Eurgrawn (1809–1983), the children's monthlies Trysorfa'r Plant (1825–42) and Y Winllan (1848–1963), Y *Gwyliedydd (1877–1908), followed by Y Gwyliedydd Newydd (1910–), and the historical journal Bathafarn (1946–); the first Wesleyan hymn-book was Diferion y Cyssegr (1802).

No major hymn-writers have been produced but, in addition to John Bryan's translations of Charles Wesley, a few hymns by the following have some merit: J. Cadvan *Davies, William *Jones (Ehedydd Iâl) and John Hughes (Glanystwyth, 1842–1902). There have been notable antiquaries in John Hughes of Brecon, William *Rowlands (Gwilym Lleyn), Owen *Williams (Owen Gwyrfai) and Evan Isaac (1865–1738), and theologians and controversialists in Owen Davies, Samuel Davies (1788–1854), Thomas Aubrey (1808–67) and William Davies (1765–1851). The writer who best expresses the character of the Connexion in his work is E. Tegla *Davies, but the Wesleyan writers of Wales also include William Ellis *Jones (Cawrdaf), Lewis Meredith (Lewis Glyn Dyfi, 1826–91), John Wil-liams (Ioan Mai, 1823–87), Selyf *Roberts, R. J. *Rowlands (Meuryn) and two Archdruids, David Griffiths (Clwydfardd, 1800–94) and Gwilym R. *Tilsley.

For accounts of Wesleyanism in Wales see David Young, Origin and History of Methodism in Wales and the Borders (1893), T. Jones-Humphreys, Methodistiaeth Wesleyaidd Cymreig (1900), Hugh Jones, Hanes Wesleyaeth yng Nghymru (4 vols., 1911–13), A. H. Williams, Welsh Wesleyan Methodism 1800–1858 (1935) and the article by Garfield H. Hughes, 'Charles Wesley yn Gymraeg' in Yr Eurgrawn (vol. CLI, 1959).

Western, Barry, see EVANS, GWYNFIL (1898–1938).

Western Mail, a newspaper established in 1869 for the purpose of promoting the business and political interests of John Patrick Crichton Stuart, the third Marquess of *Bute. Its first Editor, C. W. Adams, left within three months of his appointment, but under his successor, Henry Lascelles Carr, a Yorkshireman who bought the paper in 1877, it became established as the foremost daily newspaper in Wales. A supporter of the Conservative Party from the outset, it competed with the Cardiff Times (founded in 1857) and the South Wales Daily News (founded in 1872), the Liberal papers of the Duncan family. By the end of the First World War the Western Mail had become the property of Allied Newspapers under the supervision of Seymour Berry (later Lord Camrose) and Sir Emsley Carr, nephew and son-in-law of Lascelles Carr and founder of the News of the World. In 1928 Allied Newspapers also purchased the Duncan company and the South Wales Daily News was then incorporated with the Western Mail. The latter remained a part of Allied Newspapers, later the Kemsley Group, until it was bought by Roy Thomson in 1959.

The Editor of the Western Mail from 1901 to 1931 was William Davies, who was influential in the public life of Wales by virtue of his distinguished journalistic and managerial skills. He was followed by J. A. Sandbrook (1931–42), David Prosser (1942–56), David Cole (1956–59), Don Rowlands (1959–64), John Gay Davies (1964), John Giddings (1964–73), Duncan Gardiner (1974–81) and John Rees, who was appointed editor in 1981. The newspaper's offices have been located since 1959 at Thomson House in Cardiff, where the South Wales Echo, an evening daily owned by the same company, is also published. The daily sales of the Western Mail are around a hundred thousand copies.

Under the editorship of William Davies the newspaper, although staunchly Tory, was sympathetic to the plight of Welsh workers, winning praise from William *Abraham (Mabon), the miners' leader, on more than one occasion. It was also complimented by Owen M. *Edwards for its attempts to foster interest in the history and literature of Wales, a policy which depended to some extent on the enthusiasm of its staff writers, notably D. Tudor Evans, James Harris and Edward Thomas (Idris Wyn), all of whom were knowledgeable in those subjects. During the 1930s, however, faced with hostility on the part of militant Socialists in industrial south Wales, to which its circulation was largely confined, the paper became more aggressively Conservative and antipathetic to the interests of the Welsh working class. Against Aneurin *Bevan in the 1940s it waged (in the words of Michael Foot) 'a vendetta of unexampled and occasionally brilliant virulence'.

During the late 1960s it began to develop a more independent position and—despite the fact that it is read mostly in the south and west of the country— to earn more serious attention as 'the national newspaper of Wales'. Since the time of David *Lloyd George, it had campaigned for the *Devolution of government from London to Cardiff and, unlike the South Wales Echo, it argued in favour of a Welsh Assembly prior to the referendum of 1979. There is much fulmination against the Western Mail among writers in Wales, mainly on account of its indifference to serious writing. Unfortunately, the space given to subjects of literary interest is now much less than it was under the editorship of Sir William Davies. There is no longer a Welsh column such as the one written for many years by Aneirin Talfan *Davies and complaints are often heard about the paper's failure even to carry reviews of new books by Welsh writers on a regular basis. Nevertheless, despite these and other shortcomings, in its coverage of Welsh affairs the Western Mail has no rival among the newspapers of Wales.

For further details about the newspaper's early years see the article by Geraint Talfan Davies, 'The Capital Makes News', in The Cardiff Book (vol. 2, ed. Stewart Williams, 1974); a discussion of its attitudes to Welsh affairs will be found in the article by Ned Thomas, 'The Western Mail—Everybody's Dilemma', in Planet (no. 9, Dec., 1971/Jan., 1972); see also Viscount Camrose, British Newspapers and their Controllers (1947).

WHISTLER, PEGGY EILEEN (Margiad Evans; 1909–58), novelist. Born in Uxbridge, London, to English parents whose forebears included a family from south Wales named Evans, she lived from about 1920 until 1936 at Bridstow, near Ross-on-Wye, Herefs. Her sister, **Nancy Esther** (1912–), wrote short stories under the pen-name Siân Evans. After her marriage in 1940, Peggy lived for eight years at Llangarron, near Ross, and later in Gloucestershire and Sussex, where her husband was a teacher. Having suffered from epilepsy from about 1950, she died of a brain tumour and was buried in the churchyard at Hartfield, Sussex.

Feeling herself to be essentially a Border woman, tied by birth to the English side but drawn to Wales by her imaginative affinities, Margiad Evans used this 'coincidence of blood and soil' to give more than narrative significance

to her first novel, Country Dance (1932). Ostensibly the diary of Ann Goodman, but presented with a strongly directive introduction by the editor-author, it is the story of a woman who has two suitors, one English and the other Welsh: the jealous and sullen Gabriel Ford and his rival, the violent Evan ap Evans. Her diary is written to appease Gabriel's fears that he may lose her to Evan, but it has the contrary effect. Ann is found dead in the river, Gabriel becomes a fugitive and Evan is driven by grief and the smirch of public opinion to leave his farm and his country for ever. These disasters are fused with the author's vision of all Border lands as places of torn allegiances and incessant strife.

The three novels which followed in quick succession, The Wooden Doctor (1933), Turf or Stone (1934) and Creed (1936), have much in common: vitality, evocative writing about love and sex, scenes of violence both physical and emotional, and far more of human misery than of splendour and joy. They are, for the most part, novels about suffering, and pain informs their imagery at both a literal and metaphorical level. The characters, anguished though they are, participate in their author's attempt to define Man's place in relation to God. They feel to excess and what they feel is bewilderment, grief, pain, resentment, lust and guilt. Among the agonies depicted there are some fine comic scenes, splendid dialogue and occasionally a visionary gleam.

The arrangement of Margiad Evans's journals and essays entitled Autobiography (1943) is the record of her perceptions rather than the facts of her life. Her short stories, a genre which includes some of her finest writing, were collected in the volume The Old and the Young (1948) and her verse, which achieves a poignant simplicity, in Poems from Obscurity (1947) and A Candle Ahead (1956). In her second autobiographical work, A Ray of Darkness (1952), she wrote movingly and with dignity about the onset of epilepsy and her search for God.

The best account of the life and work of Margiad Evans is the monograph by Moira Dearnley in the Writers of Wales series (1982); see also the article by Idris Parry, 'Margiad Evans and Tendencies in European Literature', in the Transactions of the Honourable Society of Cymmrodorion (1971).

White, Rawlins (1485?–1555), fisherman, was one of the three Marian martyrs of Wales; the other two were Robert *Ferrar and William *Nichol. Illiterate, he had learnt passages from the Bible by heart and, refusing to renounce the Protestant faith, was burned at the stake in his native Cardiff.

WHITE, RICHARD, see GWYN, RICHARD (c.1557–84).

White Book of Corsygedol, The and **White Book of Perth Ddu, The**, see under MOSTYN FAMILY.

White Book of Hergest, The, or **Llyfr Gwyn**

Hergest, a manuscript dating from the mid-fifteenth century which Robert *Vaughan believed had been copied by *Lewys Glyn Cothi. It is thought to have been destroyed by fire in 1810 while in the keeping of a bookbinder, or else accidentally burned in 1840 or 1858. The several descriptions of its contents which have survived suggest that this was a manuscript of some importance. Among its contents were a text of the *Laws of Hywel Dda, copies of the Statute of *Rhuddlan, *Y Bibyl Ynghymraec*, *Cysegrlan Fuchedd*, the *Elucidarium* and examples of poetry in the strict metres. A transcript of parts of the manuscript in the hand of Thomas *Wiliems and another in that of Evan *Evans (Ieuan Fardd) are preserved in the British Library and the *National Library of Wales respectively. See also RED BOOK OF HERGEST.

For further details see the articles by Thomas Jones and J. E. Caerwyn Williams respectively in the *Bulletin* of the Board of Celtic Studies (vol. X, 1939, and vol. X, 1940).

White Book of Rhydderch, The, or **Llyfr Gwyn Rhydderch**, a collection of passages of medieval Welsh prose, was written on parchment about the middle of the fourteenth century. Peniarth 4 contains the texts of the Mabinogion tales, including *Pedair Cainc y Mabinogi*, *Y *Tair Rhamant*, the Dream of *Macsen Wledig, Lludd and Llefelys (see under CYFRANC LLUDD A LLEFELYS) and *Culhwch and Olwen; it is not certain whether *Breuddwyd Rhonabwy* ever belonged to this group of manuscripts. Many of the texts in Peniarth 5 are of a religious nature and include Welsh versions of *Imago Mundi*, the Gospel of Nicodemus, the story of the Passion, the stories of Pilate and Judas, the Prophecy of Sybil, the Lives of the Blessed Virgin Mary and Saints Catherine and Margaret, the Apostles' Creed, Mary of Egypt, the Athanasian Creed, Patrick's Purgatory, the Charlemagne romances and Beves of Hampton.

The name of the transcriber is not known, but the nature of the dialect in the text suggests that he was from *Deheubarth and the palaeographical evidence suggests that he may have been connected with the monastery at *Strata Florida. By the end of the fourteenth century the manuscript was owned by Rhydderch ab Ieuan Llwyd of *Parc Rhydderch and, after his death, it passed to his daughter Tangwystl who married Einion ap Gruffudd of *Corsygedol in Ardudwy. Who owned the manuscript during the sixteenth and the early seventeenth century is not known but it was transcribed by Richard Langford (d. 1586) of Allington, Roger Morris (*fl.* 1590) of Coedytalwrn, Thomas *Wiliems, Jasper Gruffyth and John *Jones of Gellilyfdy, the Humanists of Dyffryn Clwyd. When the last-named died about 1658 the manuscript became part of Robert *Vaughan's library at Hengwrt and there it remained for two hundred years until it was transferred to the library of W. W. E. Wynne at Peniarth. The manuscript was rebound in the National Library of Wales in 1940, in two volumes with covers of white leather.

The text of Peniarth 4 was reproduced by J. Gwenogvryn Evans in 1907 and reprinted in 1973; see the same writer's *Report on Manuscripts in the Welsh Language* (vol. 1, part 2, 1899).

White Friars, see CISTERCIANS.

White Lie Tales, or tales which are obviously untrue, are part of the folk-tradition of Wales. Among the best-known exponents of the genre were James *Wade (Shemi Wâd), Daniel *Thomas (Daniel y Pant), Gruffydd *Jones (Y Deryn Mawr) and John *Pritchard (Siôn Ceryn Bach), men whose wit and narrative gifts provided entertainment for the communities in which they lived. Most of the tales belong to cycles of which the narrative is as preposterous as it is long. Some of the most common elements are the narrator's experiences in America, his adventures while being carried through the air on the wings of a great bird, his prowess at growing enormous vegetables or at shooting around corners, his ability to see over huge distances, and so on in great variety. The White Lie tradition survives in some districts and new episodes are still being added to the old stories.

White Mount, The, see under BRÂN.

WHITFORD, RICHARD (*fl.* 1495–1542), priest and devotional writer, was probably born at Whytford, near Holywell, Flints., where his family had property. He was educated at Queen's College, Cambridge. As chaplain to Lord Mountjoy, he travelled widely in Europe and became a friend of Erasmus, his patron's tutor, and of Sir Thomas More. From 1507 until its dissolution in 1539 he lived in the convent of Syon House in Isleworth, where he spent his time writing devotional works which, although primarily for the use of the nuns, won a wider readership. Among the books attributed to him are *A Dayly Exercyse and Experyence of Dethe* (1537), *The Martiloge in Englyshe* (1526), *Saint Augustin's Rule in English alone* (1525), *The Pomander of Prayer* (1532) and *A Treatise of Patience* (1540). His most important work was undoubtedly *The Following of Christ* (1556), based on the first three books of the *De Imitatione* of Thomas à Kempis made by William Atkinson in 1504. The translation has been described as the finest rendering into English of the famous original.

For further details see the article by Glanmor Williams, 'Two neglected London-Welsh clerics: Richard Whitford and Richard Gwent', in the *Transactions* of the Honourable Society of Cymmrodorion (1961), in which a case is made against Whitford's having been the translator of the *De Imitatione*.

Whitland, an abbey affiliated to the *Cistercian

Order, was founded near Haverfordwest, Pembs., as a daughter-house of Clairvaux, about 1140, but was moved some ten years later to a new site on the banks of the river Gronw near Whitland, Carms., under the patronage of John de Torrington; it was also known as Alba Landa, Blanchland and, in Welsh, as *Y Tŷ Gwyn* ('The White House'). The monastery became the mother-house of the Cistercian Order in Wales in the time of its patron *Rhys ap Gruff-ydd (The Lord Rhys); daughter-houses were founded at *Strata Florida, *Strata Marcella and *Cwm-hir. It has been suggested that one of its monks wrote the *Cronica de Wallia* (1190–1260) and, according to tradition, the poet *Dafydd Nanmor was buried in the abbey's grounds. *Lewys Glyn Cothi sang in praise of Morys ab Ieuan (c.1476–91) before that abbot was dismissed for '*criminibus enormibus casibus et delictis*'. Tomas ap Rhys, the next abbot (c.1491–c.1510), was eulogized by Ieuan Tew Brydydd Hen in a poem requesting the gift of a horse. The abbey was dissolved in 1539.

For further details see J. F. O'Sullivan, *Cistercian Settlements in Wales and Monmouthshire 1140–1540* (1947), Glanmor Williams, *The Welsh Church from Conquest to Reformation* (1962), D. H. Williams, *The Cistercians in Wales, Aspects of their Economic History* (1969) and F. G. Cowley, *The Monastic Order in South Wales 1066–1349* (1977).

Wil Bryan, see under RHYS LEWIS (1885).

Wil Brydydd y Coed (lit. 'Wil the rhymester of the woods'), a satirical tale by David *Owen (Brutus), first appeared occasionally in the Anglican magazine *Yr Haul* between 1863 and 1865. Wil, a village yokel, having gone off to learn English and find 'education', returns bearded and monstrously dressed to take up preaching. Helped by his scheming uncle, a deacon, he tries to oust the minister of his church. The plot fails and a 'split' church is founded in a barn, where a further split leads to the formation of yet another church in a stable loft. The author's intention was to satirize the 'Jacks'—the uneducated, unlicensed Nonconformist preachers of his time—and his methods are slapstick comedy and wild farce. At its best the satire is exquisite but all too often it degenerates into mere abuse. The prose style, on the other hand, is vivacious, spiced with dialect words and wholly authentic.

The full text, edited and introduced by Thomas Jones, was published in 1949; see also the same author's article in *Mân Us* (1949) and that by Glaswyn in the 'Notable Men of Wales' series in *The Red Dragon* (vol. 3, 1883).

Wil Cwch Angau, see ASHTON, GLYN MILLS (1910–).

Wil Ifan, see EVANS, WILLIAM (1882–1968).

Wil Ysgeifiog, see EDWARDS, WILLIAM (1790–1855).

Wild Man of the Woods, The, the theme underlying the legend of *Myrddin (Merlin) in early and medieval Welsh literature, is also found in the related Scottish and Irish legends of Lailoken and Suibhne Geilt respectively. Its literary forms portray an outcast from society leading a wild life in the forest, often with his reason impaired and partaking in some measure of the nature of the animals which are his daily companions. The earliest example of the theme is probably Nebuchadnezzar in the Book of Daniel and it often occurs in the art of the Middle Ages. Originally linked with the ancient legend of the hairy anchorite, which contained a strong religious element, it appears in varying forms in the Welsh, Scottish and Irish tales of the Wild Man. Myrddin, in particular, declares that he has been guilty of causing the death of the son of Gwenddydd and implores the Lord of Hosts to receive him into bliss.

Wild Wales (1862), a book by the English writer George *Borrow, is in essence the journal of a walking-tour which he made during 1854. Its title gave a wider currency to the lines, well known before Borrow's time,

> Eu ner a folant
> Eu hiaith a gadwant
> Eu tir a gollant
> Ond gwyllt Gwalia.

('Their lord they shall praise, / Their language they shall keep, / Their land they shall lose, / Except wild Wales'). These lines are found in prophetic verse of the late medieval period and are wrongly attributed to *Taliesin.

A late-comer among Tourists (see under TOURS OF WALES), Borrow was unique in that his primary interests were the Welsh language and the topography of Welsh literature. His enquiries after the homes or graves of Welsh writers, including Huw *Morys, Goronwy *Owen, Twm o'r Nant (Thomas *Edwards), *Dafydd ap Gwilym and many others, are almost comically reverential and his knowledge of Welsh history and philology (though in some respects outmoded now) was extraordinary for an Englishman. Although reasonably fluent in Welsh, he was often taken for a southerner in north Wales and as a northerner in the south; on one occasion, putting a question in Welsh, he was answered in Spanish.

Borrow was anything but a simple traveller, however: quirky and occasionally quarrelsome, he loved prolonging misunderstandings (especially about his origins), and his physique—he was tall, broad-shouldered and muscular, with a hand 'about the size of a shoulder of small Welsh mutton'—made him a man not to be trifled with. Unsympathetic to genteel Anglicizers, he was nevertheless a zealous Churchman, beating the anti-Popery drum whenever he encountered Irish itinerants and dismissing as 'bitter' those Methodists who dared to argue with him. His tongue was often in his cheek: at his journey's end he acknowledged that 'the worthiest creature I ever knew was a Welsh Methodist'—almost certainly John Jones, the weaver who was his guide in Llangollen.

Two factors limit the value of Borrow's account as a view of Wales. In the first place, meetings with pedlars, commercial travellers, innkeepers and their maids could not reveal overmuch of Welsh society or the use of the Welsh language within it. Second, the writing-up of the original journal—something only to be guessed at from the verbatim conversations and the supposedly off-the-cuff translations of Welsh verse—may well have altered the balance of events, especially if completed after a considerable interval. But the attitude of this traveller remains unparalleled and his information often irreplaceable.

He began his tour in July 1854, staying with his wife and stepdaughter at Llangollen, Denbs., until October, using it as a centre for daily expeditions and taking a long solo walk via Cerrigydrudion to Bangor and Holyhead and then returning by way of Beddgelert and Bala. Afterwards he set off alone for south Wales, travelling by Sychnant, Bala, Mallwyd, Machynlleth, Devil's Bridge, Tregaron, Llandovery, Gwter Fawr (Brynaman), Swansea, Neath, Merthyr Tydfil, Caerphilly and Newport, arriving at Chepstow nine days before Christmas. From Gwter Fawr onwards, however, his account is perfunctory: place-names have been forgotten, industrial Wales plainly horrified him and the only conversations hereabouts are with Irish wayfarers. The occasions which remain best in the memory from the whole journey are Borrow's encounter at Dyffryn Gaint, Ang., with the Man in Grey ('the greatest *prydydd* in the whole world'), his short wait in the Compting Room of the Potosi Mining Company in the hills south of Dyfi, and his formal tasting of the springs of Severn, Wye and Rheidol. It is characteristic of Borrow that he pronounces Llandovery 'about the pleasantest little town in which I have halted', largely because everyone he meets there knows about *Yr Hen Ficer* (Rhys *Prichard). It is this emphasis which gives *Wild Wales* its unique value.

For further details see the article by Angus M. Fraser, 'George Borrow's *Wild Wales*: Fact and Fabrication' in the *Transactions* of the Honourable Society of Cymmrodorion (1980).

Wilde, Jimmy (1892–1969), boxer, a native of Tylorstown, Rhondda, Glam., was the flyweight champion of the world from 1916 to 1923. Despite his small size, he was a formidable puncher and during a career which consisted of some eight hundred and fifty fights he was defeated on only four occasions. Among the nicknames by which he was widely known were 'The Mighty Atom' and 'The Tylorstown Terror' and he was often described as 'The Ghost with a Hammer in his Hand'.

Wiliam ap Siôn Edwart (*fl.* 1513), Constable of *Chirk Castle, was portrayed in a *cywydd* by *Tudur Aled as the epitome of the Welsh courtier and Renaissance gentleman. The poet extolled the several virtues of his patron: his prowess in hunting and fighting, his skill at playing musical instruments and his knowledge of genealogy. As an esquire of the body to Henry VIII, Wiliam distinguished himself at the siege of Tournai in 1513 and was given by the King the motto '*A fynno Duw derfydd*' ('Whom God wills shall perish').

Wiliam ap Tomas (*fl.* 1406–46), gentleman, was the son of Tomos ap Gwilym ap Siencyn of Berth-hir, Mon. He fought in France and was present at the battle of Agincourt (1415) when *Dafydd Gam and Sir Roger Vaughan of Tretower were killed. *Guto'r Glyn, in a *cywydd* addressed to him much later, referred to his mansions—Raglan, Gefenni, Llandeilo, Gresynni and Tre'r-twr. As the consequence of Wiliam's two marriages, his military earnings and influential connections had by that time brought him rich stewardships and he had come to prominence among the gentry of Gwent and Glamorgan, holding public office and earning respect as a skilled administrator. It was through marriage to his first wife, the widow of Sir James Berkeley, that he became owner of the manor of Raglan in 1406. Knighted in 1426, he was known as *Y Marchog Glas o Went* ('The Blue Knight of Gwent'). His second wife was the widow of Sir Roger Vaughan and the daughter of Dafydd Gam.

WILIAM LLŶN (1534/5–80), poet, was a native of *Llŷn, Caerns., and had a brother, *Huw Llŷn, who was also a poet. Wiliam lived in Oswestry for the last sixteen years of his life and was buried there. A pupil of *Gruffudd Hiraethog, some of whose manuscripts he inherited, he graduated at the second *Caerwys Eisteddfod (1567). Among the poets who were his pupils were *Rhys Cain and Siôn Phylip (see under PHYLIP FAMILY), both of whom wrote elegies in his memory; to the former Wiliam left all his manuscripts. Like many professional poets of his day, Wiliam Llŷn collected genealogies and coats of arms. Although he wrote at least one bardic grammar, no copy has survived, but a copy of Gruffudd Hiraethog's dictionary (kept in the Cardiff Library) contains two manuscript collections of Wiliam Llŷn's poems in his own hand.

An itinerant poet, he wrote for gentry in both north and south Wales, including those of Gwydir, Lleweni, Mostyn, Y Rug, Abermarlais, Golden Grove and Ystradmerthyr. A substantial proportion of his poetry remains in manuscript, of which nearly half is in his own hand. It includes twenty-five *awdlau*, among which are seventeen poems of praise, seven elegies, one exemplary *awdl* to a girl, and one hundred and fifty *cywyddau*, some fifty of which are poems of praise, another sixty elegies and the remainder poems of request, gratitude, reconciliation, debate and satire. A masterly religious *cywydd* and about a hundred *englynion* are also attributed to this poet.

Wiliam Llŷn belonged to the last generation of poets to enjoy the patronage of the native aristocracy. In a period of great social and religious upheaval, when the *Bardic Order was in decline, he clung to his craft of praising the hospitality of the noblemen who had sustained his kind since the death of *Llywelyn ap Gruffudd in 1282. Although the form of the elegy in his work is the same in essence as it had been for centuries, there are examples among his poems of the elegiac colloquy between the living and the dead. His verse has some features in common with the serenade, as in the elegies for Gruffudd Hiraethog and Owain ap Gwilym, the rector of Tal-y-llyn. Throughout his work are found turns of phrase and a quality of feeling which convey the poet's awareness of the frailty of life in a most memorable way.

A substantial collection of his work and the main facts of his life are to be found in *Barddoniaeth Wiliam Llŷn* (1908) by J. C. Morrice; most of the poems in this edition are reproduced in facsimile from the poet's own manuscript, but about half are love-poems wrongly attributed to him. Other examples of his work are included in *Cynfeirdd Llŷn 1500–1800* (ed. John Jones, 1905). For discussion of Wiliam Llŷn's poetry see the article by Ifan Wyn Williams in *Y Traethodydd* (vol. CXXXV, 1980) and the introduction to the selection of his work made by Roy Stephens (1980).

WILIAM, URIEN (1929–), novelist and playwright, was born in Swansea, Glam., a son of Stephen J. *Williams, and educated at University College, Swansea, and the University of Liverpool; he was a Senior Lecturer in Welsh at the Polytechnic of Wales until his retirement in 1981. His six novels are *Dirgelwch y Rocedi* (1968), *Pluen yn fy Het / Stafell Ddwbl* (1970), *Perygl o'r Sêr* (1972), *Tu Hwnt i'r Mynydd Du* (1975) and *Chwilio Gem* (1980). The winner of the Drama Medal at the National Eisteddfod in 1972 and 1973, he has published a number of plays, including *Y Pypedau/Y Llyw Olaf* (1976), and also writes for television.

WILIEMS, THOMAS (1545/6–1622), lexicographer and genealogist, was a native of Trefriw, Denbs., and a kinsman of the *Wynn family of Gwydir; it is believed that he studied at Brasenose College, Oxford. He was an industrious collector and copier of manuscripts, among them *Prif Achau Holl Gymru Benbaladr*, and of the Welsh Laws and *proverbs. His masterpiece, *Thesaurus Linguae Latinae et Cam-* *brobrytannicae*, was based on the *Dictionarium Linguae Latinae et Anglicanae* of Thomas Thomas, the first printer to Cambridge University; it was fifty years in preparation and reveals Wiliems's thorough knowledge of the bardic tradition. After his death the manuscript was given by Sir John Wynn of Gwydir to John *Davies of Mallwyd to be edited. It was not published separately but was used, in an abridged form, as the Latin–Welsh section of Davies's dictionary, *Antiquae Linguae Britannicae Dictionarium Duplex* (1632).

For further details see the article by J. E. Caerwyn Williams, 'Thomas Wiliems y Geiriadurwr', in *Studia Celtica* (vols. XVI/XVII, 1981–82).

WILKINS, CHARLES (1831–1913), journalist, editor and historian. Born at Stonehouse, Glos., he was the son of a bookseller who, having settled in Merthyr Tydfil, Glam., became the town's postmaster in 1851. He succeeded his father in the post in 1871 and held it until his retirement in 1898; he was also, from 1846 to 1866, the librarian of the local subscription library of which Thomas *Stephens was secretary. A prolific contributor to the weekly newspapers of Merthyr Tydfil and Cardiff, Charles Wilkins published a number of historical works, chief among which are *The History of Merthyr Tydfil* (1867), *The History of the Coal Trade in South Wales* (1888) and *The History of the Iron, Steel, Tinplate and other Trades of Wales* (1903). An incomer, he nevertheless acquired a strong local patriotism which became, in due course, an identification with Wales. His principal literary works were *The History of the Literature of Wales from 1300 to 1650* (1884), an enlargement of the essay for which he was awarded a prize at the *National Eisteddfod of 1880, and *Tales and Sketches of Wales* (1879). Charles Wilkins endeavoured, not least in the pages of *The *Red Dragon*, which he edited for three years, to create in the English language a readership with sympathies like his own, and for that attempt, some fifty years before it became feasible, he deserves to be remembered.

Wilkinson, John (1728–1808), 'the father of the iron trade', was the son of a Cumberland ironworker-turned-master who obtained the lease of the smelting furnace at Bersham, Wrexham, in 1753, and settled at Plas Grono, the ancient home of the Yales. The son developed the works by constructing plant for boring accurate cylinders which, from 1775, were used for James Watt's steam engine, and by manufacturing guns. A Radical in politics, he was accused of supplying the French with cannon during the Revolutionary War, but was never convicted. In 1792 he purchased the Brymbo Hall estate, where he set up blast furnaces and farmed the land on improved principles; it was he who used the first steam threshing-machine to be seen in north Wales. He was also a leading shareholder in the Ellesmere Canal Company and served as High Sheriff of the County. Dictatorial and unscrupulous, he was nevertheless said to be a good employer. After his death the family's fortune was squandered in litigation between his mistress and his nephew, and the Bersham works had become derelict by 1830.

William de Braose (*c*.1150–1211), one of the most notorious of the Marcher Lords. He is remembered in Welsh tradition for his treachery in 1175 in inviting Seisyll ap Dyfnwal, and others among his neighbours, to a banquet at Abergavenny, at which he ordered the massacre of his guests, a crime for which he became known as 'The Ogre of Abergavenny'. The Welsh of Gwent then rose against de Braose but he escaped. Another of the misdeeds attributed to him was the slaughter of some three thousand followers of Gwenwynwyn, Prince of Powys, at Painscastle, Rads., in 1198, an incident mentioned in The *Black Book of Carmarthen* and in Sir Walter Scott's novel, *The Betrothed* (1825). Like his wife, *Maude de St. Valerie (Mol Walbee), de Braose eventually incurred the displeasure of King John, who distrained his estates, and he died in exile in France. The William de Braose (Gwilym Brewys) who was hanged in 1230 for his alleged adultery with Joan (*Siwan), the wife of *Llywelyn ap Iorwerth (Llywelyn Fawr), was one of his grandsons.

WILLIAM, DAFYDD (1720/1–94), hymn-writer and preacher, was born in the parish of Llanedi, Carms., but lived for many years in the parish of Llandeilo-fach (also known as Llandeilo Tal-y-bont), now Pontarddulais. He taught in the Circulating Schools and was a Calvinistic Methodist exhorter. Later, in the 1770s, he settled at Peterston-super-Ely in the Vale of Glamorgan, and, after baptism in the river Ely, was received into the *Baptist denomination.

His first collection of hymns was published under the title *Gorfoledd ym Mhebyll Seion* (*c*.1762); three supplements appeared in 1777–78 and complete editions in 1782 and 1786. It was followed by an English edition of some of his hymns, *Joy in the Tents of Zion* (1779), and the volumes *Telynau i Blant yr Addewid* (1782), *Gwin i'r Diffygiol* (*c*.1785), *Hymnau Priodferch y Brenin Alpha* (*c*.1787), *Myfyrdod y Pererin* (1788?) and *Yr Udgorn Arian* (1789). He was the author of some one hundred and twenty Welsh hymns in all, most of which were based on Scriptural passages and imbued with a warm Evangelical fervour. Several are to be found in contemporary collections, the favourites being '*Yn y dyfroedd mawr a'r tonnau*', '*Anghrediniaeth, gad fi'n llonydd*' and '*O Arglwydd, dyro awel*'. He also published six booklets containing secular songs in the *ballad tradition and seventeen elegies in the style of William *Williams (Pantycelyn).

A study of Dafydd William's life, together with a bibliography, has been published by Gomer M. Roberts (1954); a selection of his hymns is to be found in *Pedwar Emynydd* (ed. Bobi Jones, 1970). For further details see the article by Ann Hughes in *Cylchgrawn Cymdeithas Hanes y Methodistiaid Calfinaidd* (1984).

WILLIAM, THOMAS (1761–1844), hymn-writer, was born at Trerhedyn, Pendeulwyn, Glam., but his name is always associated with Bethesda'r Fro, the Independent chapel in the Vale of Glamorgan where he was a minister for many years. He composed some of the best-known hymns in Welsh, such as '*O'th flaen, O Dduw, 'rwy'n dyfod*' which appeared in *Dyfroedd Bethesda* (1824), his principal collection. Two previous collections of his hymns were published under the titles *Llais y Durtur* (1812) and *Perl mewn Adfyd* (1814). His most popular hymn is '*Adenydd fel c'lomen pe cawn*'. He also wrote elegies, notably '*Llef Eliseus ar ôl Elias*', which was composed in memory of John *Williams of St. Athan. A collection of his hymns, together with a memoir, was edited by Thomas Rees in 1882.

William Jones (1944), the second novel of T. Rowland *Hughes, is a portrait of a man tormented by a harridan of a wife. The eponymous hero, a well-mannered quarryman, loses patience with his wife's slovenly ways and, refusing his supper with the famous remark, '*Cadw dy blydi chips!*' ('Keep your bloody chips!'), he leaves home to look for work in south Wales. Life in the mining villages of south Wales during the *Depression is not easy but William Jones finds work and even success as an actor in radio plays, much to his wife's chagrin as she listens at home in Caernarfonshire.

The novel was translated into English by Richard Ruck under the same title (1953).

WILLIAMS, ALICE MATILDA LANG-LAND (**Alis Mallt Williams**; 1867–1950), novelist, was born at Oystermouth, Glam., and spent her early years at Talybont-on-Usk, Brecs.; she lived later at Llanarthne, Carms., and St. Dogmael's, Pembs. With her sister **Gwenffreda** she wrote, under the pseudonym 'The Dau Wynne', two novels, *One of the Royal Celts* (1889) and *A Maid of Cymru* (1901). The latter, although unremarkable in literary terms, combines romanticism with a demanding Welsh patriotism and an outspokenness very uncommon at the time. A meeting at Llanover Court in 1899 between the two sisters and the Breton poets Abherv (François Vallée) and Taldir (François Jaffrennou) inspired the composition of the former's poem '*An Diou Vag*' and resulted in Mallt's lifelong enthusiasm for the cause of the Breton language. Of considerable private means and a pioneer feminist, she was also one of *Plaid Cymru's earliest and most generous supporters. A long article by Alis Mallt Williams, entitled

'Welsh Women's Mission in the Twentieth Century', will be found in the volume *Wales Today and Tomorrow* (ed. T. Stephens, 1907). The historian William Retlaw Jefferson *Williams was her elder brother.

WILLIAMS, ANNA (1706–83), poet. Born at Rosemarket, Pembs., the daughter of the inventor Zachariah Williams (1673–1755), she accompanied her father to London when she was about twenty-one years old and lived there for the rest of her life. She became blind after an operation on her eyes in 1752, by which time she had won the esteem and protection of Dr Samuel Johnson, who helped her in the composition of her *Miscellanies in Prose and Verse* (1766).

WILLIAMS, CHARLES HANBURY (1708–59), verse satirist. Born Charles Hanbury at Pontypool, Mon., the godson of Charles Williams of Caerleon who fled the country after killing his cousin in a duel, he eventually inherited the Williams estate and assumed his godfather's surname. After his marriage in 1732 he entered Parliament as a supporter of Sir Robert Walpole. Knighted in 1746, he served thereafter as Envoy to the courts of Saxony, Prussia, Poland and Russia. In 1757 his physical and mental health broke down and it is believed that he died by his own hand. Most of his poetry, collected in three volumes (1822), is skilled versifying in various modes, though the satirical, both political and personal, predominates.

For further details see the *Works* of Charles Hanbury Williams with notes by Horace Walpole (3 vols., 1822).

WILLIAMS, DAVID (1738–1816), philosopher, was born at Waun Waelod in the parish of Eglwysilan, near Caerphilly, Glam., and educated at the Carmarthen Academy. He became a minister with the Independents and held pastorates in Frome, Exeter and London, but abandoned the ministry in 1773, maintaining himself thereafter as a political pamphleteer, lecturer and schoolmaster. His *Treatise on Education* (1774) attracted the attention of Benjamin Franklin and together they founded the Thirteen Club, a group of deists for whom Williams wrote *A Liturgy on the Universal Principles of Religion and Morality* (1776), which was praised by Voltaire and Rousseau. Williams's reputation in France, where he was held in high esteem, was established by a French translation of his *Letters on Political Liberty* (1782), a defence of the American colonists which advocated radical reform. Ten years later, he was awarded the honorary citizenship of France and was invited to Paris to help draw up a constitution for the Girondists. He was also the author of a voluminous work, *The History of Monmouthshire* (1796), and an unpublished autobiography, the manuscript of which is kept at the Central Library, Cardiff.

His chief claim to literary fame lies ultimately in his establishment of the Royal Literary Fund in 1790. Williams had first canvassed the idea of a benevolent society for needy geniuses in 1773, but had met with no response. Among the Fund's earliest patrons was the Prince of Wales (later King George IV) who made generous contributions and granted its royal charter.

For further details see the biographies of David Williams by H. P. Richards (1980) and Peter France (1981).

WILLIAMS, DAVID (1900–78), historian, was a native of Llan-y-cefn, near Narberth, Pembs., and was educated at University College, Cardiff. After a period as a teacher, he was awarded a Rockefeller Scholarship in 1926 and later studied at the Universities of Columbia (New York), Paris and Berlin. Appointed to the staff of the History Department at Cardiff in 1930, he held the Sir John Williams Chair of Welsh History at the University College of Wales, Aberystwyth, from 1945 until 1967. His *History of Wales 1485–1931* (1934) and *A History of Modern Wales* (1950) proved to be indispensable textbooks for many generations of students, while his books *John Frost: a Study in Chartism* (1939) and *The Rebecca Riots: a Study in Agrarian Discontent* (1955) established him as the greatest authority on the social history of Wales in the nineteenth century. Among his other interests were early Welsh *Radicalism and Welsh emigration to the USA. He contributed many articles to historical journals on modern Welsh history and published other works such as *Wales and America* (1946), *John Penry: Three Treatises Concerning Wales* (1960) and *John Evans and the Legend of Madog, 1770–1799* (1963).

For further details see the obituary of David Williams by Richard Cobb in *The Welsh History Review* (vol. 9, no. 2, 1978).

WILLIAMS, DAVID JOHN (1885–1970), writer. He was born at Rhydcymerau, Carms., the countryside and inhabitants of which he immortalized in his autobiography *Hen Dŷ Ffarm* (1953) and *Yn Chwech ar Hugain Oed* (1959), but at the age of fifteen he found work in the *Rhondda Valley as a collier, an experience reflected in some of his short stories. After about four years in the pits, he attended in turn the Stephens School at Llanybydder, Carms., the school of the Old College, Carmarthen, then under the principalship of Joseph Harry, and went on to the University College of Wales, Aberystwyth, and finally to Jesus College, Oxford, at both of which he took degrees in English. He was then appointed an assistant master at The Lewis School, Pengam, and later at the Grammar School in Fishguard, Pembs., where he remained until his retirement in 1945. Among the founders of *Plaid Cymru (having previously supported the Labour movement), he took part with Saunders *Lewis and Lewis Valentine in the symbolic act of burning the sheds of the bombing school at *Penyberth in

1936, and spent nine months in Wormwood Scrubs as a consequence.

His earliest literary works—articles and short stories contributed to periodicals—were collected in *Y Gaseg Ddu* (ed. J. Gwyn Griffiths, 1970). The four short stories in that book are more romantic and idealistic in tone than those which later brought him acclaim, but they are not juvenilia. In them can be seen the lively interpretation of character, light-hearted verve and quick insight which are features of the best stories in his trilogy, *Storiau'r Tir* (1936, 1941, 1949). His two masterpieces are undoubtedly *Hen Dŷ Ffarm* and *Hen Wynebau* (1934), the latter a gallery of portraits of people and animals he had known and loved in his native district. Besides these books, D. J. Williams wrote a host of articles dealing with aspects of *Nationalism, including studies of Mazzini (1954) and George William Russell (1963), and a memoir of the early days of *Plaid Cymru* under the title *Codi'r Faner* (1968). In most of these works his fondness for portraying human character, especially that of men who incorporated ideals about nationhood and society, is always evident.

The vision which inspired D. J. Williams throughout his life and in all his writing was that of 'the square mile' around his birthplace, a small, close community where human values exalted the individual and the spirit of co-operation was a natural instinct. An ideological theme binds all his works together in an attractive unity. Among his chief characteristics as a writer are his kindly humour, his love of animals, especially of horses, his readiness to digress freely and yet to cunning effect, a gift for satire which is more conspicuous in his later stories, and a style both sophisticated and true to the idiom of his native district. D.J., as he was known throughout Wales, was a man who won the affection of his contemporaries by both the quality of his writing and the example of his devotion to Welsh culture in all its forms.

Studies of his work are to be found in the volume edited in his honour by J. Gwyn Griffiths (1965); the bibliography by David Jenkins in that work has been supplemented by Gareth Watts in *Y Gaseg Ddu* (1970); see also the essay on D. J. Williams by Dafydd Jenkins in the *Writers of Wales* series (1973) and a photographic record of his life in the *Bro a Bywyd* series (ed. J. Gwyn Griffiths, 1983). A collection of poems in the writer's memory was published in the volume *Y Cawr o Rydcymerau* (ed. D. H. Culpitt and W. Leslie Richards, 1970).

WILLIAMS, DAVID JOHN (1896–1950), children's writer, born at Corris, Mer., was a village schoolmaster in his native county. It was he, more than any other teacher, who took up the challenge of preparing reading material in Welsh for schoolchildren as recommended in the report *Welsh in Education and Life* (1927). Besides editing five textbooks between 1926 and 1941, he was the author of *Hen Chwedlau Groeg* (1922),

Plant Gwledydd Pell (1926) and *Dyddgwaith Iesu Grist* (1948). But he is mostly remembered as the founder of *Hwyl*, a Welsh comic which he launched in 1949 and which continues to be published.

WILLIAMS, DAVID MATTHEW (Ieuan Griffiths; 1900–70), playwright, was born at Cellan Court, Cards., a blacksmith's son and the younger brother of Griffith John *Williams. Educated at the University College of Wales, Aberystwyth, where he graduated in Chemistry, he was for a time a schoolmaster at Ebbw Vale, Mon., before returning to his old College as a lecturer. He was later appointed to Her Majesty's Inspectorate of Schools, a post he held until his retirement.

Most of his plays, which were written under his pseudonym, became very popular and were frequently performed by amateur groups. They include the full-length plays *Dirgel Ffyrdd* (1933), *Awel Dro* (1934), *Yr Oruwchwyliaeth Newydd* (1937), *Dau Dylwyth* (1938), *Tarfu'r Clomennod* (1947) and *Y Fflam Leilac* (1952), the short plays *Lluest y Bwci* (1931), *Y Ciwrad yn y Pair* (1932), *Neithior* (1947) and *Ted* (1952), and three plays for children, *Ddoe a Heddiw* (1954), *Gwragedd Arberth* (1954) and *Peredur* (1954).

WILLIAMS, EDWARD (Iolo Morganwg; 1747–1826), poet and antiquary, was born at Llancarfan, Glam., and worked for most of his life as a stonemason in his native county and in England. As a youth he came into contact with lexicographers such as Thomas *Richards and John *Walters, and with many of the poets of the Glamorgan uplands. While still young he began taking the drug laudanum (a tincture of opium), to which he was addicted for the rest of his life, and it is believed that this habit affected his mental condition. Deeply influenced by the cultural and antiquarian revival in Wales during the eighteenth century (see under Antiquarianism), he became a poet in both Welsh and English, an avid copyist, a knowledgeable collector of manuscripts and an antiquary of renown.

He worked in and around London during the 1770s and 1790s, becoming acquainted with the life of the *London Welsh community at meetings of the *Gwyneddigion Society. A friend of English writers such as Robert Southey, he also frequented Radical circles and at this time began calling himself 'The Bard of Liberty'. It was in London, in 1792, that he organized the first public meeting of *Gorsedd Beirdd Ynys Prydain, thereby introducing the Welsh to the arcana of neo-Druidism. He participated fully in most of the enthusiasms of his day such as the Madoc fever (see under Madog ab Owain Gwynedd) and in 1802 he was one of the main founders of the Unitarian Society in south Wales (see under Unitarianism). All his business ventures were failures: he was declared bankrupt and spent some time in Cardiff Gaol, where it is said that his son, Taliesin *Williams, who became a pupil of his father's and the editor of some of his works, was born. His greatest moment was when, late in life, he succeeded in introducing the *Gorsedd*, which was his own invention, as a preliminary to the *Eisteddfod at the famous meeting held in the Ivy Bush tavern at Carmarthen in 1819. The last years of his life were spent in preparing literary, historical and neo-Druidical material for the press, works which were published only after his death. He died at the cottage where he had lived for most of his life, at Flemingston in the Vale of Glamorgan.

The first major work by Iolo Morganwg to be published during his lifetime was the collection of poems which he claimed were by *Dafydd ap Gwilym but which were, in fact, his own. This volume appeared under the auspices of the Gwyneddigion Society in 1789. His English poetry was published under the title *Poems Lyric and Pastoral* (2 vols., 1794). He was one of the editors of the three volumes of *The Myvyrian Archaiology* (1801–7), published at the expense of Owen *Jones (Owain Myfyr), and his Welsh Unitarian hymnody (a vast collection of hymns all written by himself) appeared in 1812. After his death there appeared his treatise on Welsh metrics, *Cyfrinach Beirdd Ynys Prydain* (1829), and his collection of miscellaneous prose and verse in a bewildering variety of styles, the *Iolo Manuscripts* (1848). Other volumes comprising material from Iolo's huge archive appeared during the nineteenth century, including *Coelbren y Beirdd* (1840), *Dosparth Edeyrn Dafod Aur* (ed. John Williams, 1856) and *Barddas* (ed. John Williams, 2 vols., 1862, 1874).

Iolo Morganwg is without doubt a controversial figure in Welsh letters. The most brilliant child of the antiquarian revival, he was the greatest interpreter of Romantic enthusiasm in Wales and, although a Unitarian and a political Radical, one of the greatest influences on Welsh letters and culture in his day. Historian, poet and visionary, he strove in all his work to demonstrate that the history and literature of Glamorgan, unworthy though it seemed to many, had been central to the cultural tradition of Wales and that the bardic tradition was an essential part of that literature. Furthermore, he believed that the Welsh were the most important people of the Isle of Britain and that Welsh tradition could be traced back without break to the *Druids, the earliest defenders of Celtic civilization against Saxon invaders. In furtherance of these claims he was prepared to exercise a fertile imagination and his considerable literary gifts, even to falsify the sources of Welsh history and to mislead his contemporaries about the nature, especially the antiquity, of the Welsh literary tradition, with the result that many scholars laboured throughout the nineteenth century under misapprehensions for which Iolo had been responsible.

Despite the reputation enjoyed by Iolo Morganwg during his lifetime and for a hundred years after his death, his vision of Wales was so different from the known historical evidence that by the 1890s much of his work, especially that part relating to neo-Druidism, had become suspect in the eyes of scholars such as John *Morris-Jones. In 1916, Iolo's manuscript archive having passed from Llanover Court to the *National Library of Wales, Griffith John *Williams began the formidable task of studying the writer's work. The first-fruits of his research was *Iolo Morganwg a Chywyddau'r Ychwanegiad* (1926), an examination of Iolo's contributions to the volume purporting to be by Dafydd ap Gwilym which had been published in 1789. Although G. J. Williams succeeded in exposing Iolo as a fabricator or forger, he also rehabilitated him as a brilliant scholar and a most charming Romantic poet. He went on to complete a study of the literary tradition of Glamorgan, *Traddodiad Llenyddol Morgannwg* (1948), as a background to Iolo's work, but lived only to complete one volume of his projected biography.

Iolo has been the subject of a number of other biographies and there is still academic argument about his life and work. Although not reliable accounts, Elijah Waring's *Recollections and Anecdotes of Edward Williams* (1850) and T. D. Thomas's biography (1857) are highly entertaining. The work of G. J. Williams is the most authoritative account in Welsh. The study by Brinley Richards, *Golwg Newydd ar Iolo Morganwg* (1979), has been discounted by Thomas Parry. Prys Morgan has contributed a monograph on Iolo Morganwg to the *Writers of Wales* series (1975) in which further bibliographical details will be found. A selection of Iolo's verse in the free metres has been edited by P. J. Donovan (1980).

WILLIAMS, ELIEZER (1754–1820), poet. Born at Pibwr-lwyd, near Carmarthen, the eldest son of Peter *Williams, he was educated at Jesus College, Oxford, and for the last fifteen years of his life was vicar of Lampeter, where he opened a school. He published one volume of verse during his lifetime, *Nautical Odes, or Poetical Sketches designed to commemorate the Achievement of the British Navy* (1801), the result of his service as chaplain on the warship *Cambridge*. After his death there appeared his *English Works* (1840), the bulk of which consisted of a *History of the Britons*, with a memoir by his son, St. George Armstrong Williams.

WILLIAMS, ELISEUS (Eifion Wyn: 1867–1926), poet, was born at Porthmadog, Caerns. He had little formal education except at Sunday School, but became a teacher in his home town and later at Pentrefoelas. From 1896 until his death he was clerk and accountant to the North Wales Slate Company. His reputation as a lyricist was established by the volume *Telynegion Maes a Môr* (1906), which contains a number of poems still famous as recitation pieces. Among his other collections are *Ieuenctid y Dydd* (1894), *Y Bugail* (*c.*1900) and the posthumous volumes *Caniadau'r Allt* (1927) and *O Drum i Draeth* (1929). For the most part, his poems are simple in structure and undemanding in content. Eifion Wyn could write with facility and there is at times a note of insincerity in his work. Some of his hymns remain popular.

For further details see the biography by the poet's son, Peredur Wyn Williams, *Cofiant Eifion Wyn* (1980).

Williams, Elizabeth (**The Maid of Sker**; *c.*1747–76), tragic heroine, was the daughter of Sker House, near Porthcawl, Glam. According to tradition, she fell in love with a harper named Thomas Evans who is supposed to have composed the song '*Y Ferch o'r Sger*' for her. After being obliged by her father to marry Thomas Kirkhouse, a rich but dull industrialist, she was said to have followed the harper about the countryside and to have died of a broken heart. This story, first recorded in 1806, was elaborated by Jane *Williams (Ysgafell) in 1838 and given its full form by Llyfnwy (Thomas Morgan of Maesteg) in his book *The Cupid* (1869); it was also the basis of a novel by Isaac Craigfryn *Hughes, published in English translation in 1902. The tale's similarity to others such as that of Ann *Maddocks (The Maid of Cefn Ydfa) has led most historians to reject it, but there is evidence to suggest that, in April 1768, shortly before marrying Kirkhouse, Elizabeth Williams was indeed engaged to another man. It was probably the memory of this romance, compounded by local traditions, which formed the essence of the tale. The novel by R. D. *Blackmore, *The Maid of Sker* (1872), has nothing whatsoever to do with the story of Elizabeth Williams.

For further details see A. Leslie Evans, *The Story of Sker House* (1956).

WILLIAMS, ELIZABETH (1862–1953), prose writer, began writing at the age of eighty-nine and was the author of memoirs about her childhood and youth in the district of Llanrwst, Denbs. Her three books, *Brethyn Cartref* (1951), *Siaced Fraith* (1952) and *Dirwyn Edafedd* (1953), are remarkable for their vigorous style and vivid recollection of rural life. Her brother, **John Lloyd Williams** (1854–1945), who was Professor of Botany at the University College of Wales, Aberystwyth, also wrote memoirs.

WILLIAMS, EMLYN (1905–   ), playwright. Born at Pen-y-ffordd, Mostyn, Flints., he was educated at Holywell County School and won an open scholarship to Christ Church, Oxford, in 1923. While recovering from a nervous breakdown in 1926 he wrote *Full Moon* (1927), his first play to be professionally produced. In the same year he began his career as an actor in the West End, returning briefly to Oxford to complete his degree, and he has lived ever since as a man of the theatre.

He is the author of some thirty plays in all. Among his early successes were *Glamour* (1928), *The Late Christopher Bean* (1933) and *Night Must Fall* (1935), his first exploration of the psychology of murder. His most important later works are *The *Corn is Green* (1938), *Pen Don* (1943), *The *Druid's Rest* (1944), *The *Wind of Heaven* (1945) and *The Power of Dawn* (1976), a television drama about the dying Tolstoy. He has also written eight film-scripts, including *The Last Days of Dolwyn* (1949), *Beyond Belief* (1967), a study of 'the Moors Murders', and a novel entitled *Headlong* (1980).

Like G. B. Shaw, Emlyn Williams prepared his plays as carefully for reading as for performance, but he avoided trying to educate or elevate his audiences, preferring to tell an entertaining story. Uninfluenced by the avant-garde or the West End stereotype of the 1930s, he wrote naturalistic plays about ordinary people, combining realism with an effective lyricism. An optimistic philosophy made him essentially a comic writer, but his plays evoke most emotions except the genuinely tragic. His great achievement was to bring to the English stage the first authentic re-creation of Welsh village life in a language based, like that of J. M. Synge, on the presence and overtones of an older tongue which was his first language. The conventional English prose of his two volumes of autobiography, *George* (1961) and *Emlyn* (1973), has great sensitivity and evocative power. His main weaknesses are the exaggeration of true feeling into sentimentality or melodrama, an excessive fondness for eccentricity of character and an indulgence in theatrical ingenuities for their own sake.

The two best studies of Emlyn Williams are those by Richard Findlater (1956) and Don Dale-Jones, the latter in the *Writers of Wales* series (1979); a bibliography of his writings compiled by Sandra Henderson was published by the Welsh Library Association in 1985.

WILLIAMS, ERNI LLWYD (1906–60), poet, was brought up at Efail-wen, near Crymych, Pembs. After a brief career as a chemist he was ordained and served as an Independent minister at Maesteg and Ammanford. His publications include *Rhamant Rhydychen* (1939), *Hen Ddwylo* (1941), *Tua'r Cyfnos* (1943), *Cofiant Thomas Phillips* (1946), *Tir Hela* (1957), and two volumes on his native county in the series *Cyfres Crwydro Cymru* (1958, 1960). With Waldo *Williams he wrote a collection of poems for children, *Cerddi'r Plant* (1936). He won the *Chair at the National Eisteddfod in 1953 for his *awdl*, '*Y Ffordd*', and the *Crown for a *pryddest*, '*Y Bannau*', in the following year.

WILLIAMS, FRED (1907–72), poet. Born at Cwmtudu, Cards., the son of Marged, the eldest daughter of the *Cilie family, he spent several years in Australia and America before settling in his native district, where, in the family tradition, he served the local community as *bardd gwlad*. After his death, his cousin Gerallt *Jones edited a collection of his poems, *Codi'r Wal* (1974).

WILLIAMS, GLANMOR (1920–), historian. Born at Dowlais, Merthyr Tydfil, Glam., and educated at the University College of Wales, Aberystwyth, he was appointed Lecturer in History at University College, Swansea, in 1945 and was Professor of History in the same College from 1957 until his retirement in 1982. His main researches have been into the Protestant establishment in Wales during the Reformation, his articles on this subject being published in his volume *Welsh Reformation Essays* (1966). The chief authority on early modern Wales, he is the author of *The Welsh Church from Conquest to Reformation* (1962), a much acclaimed study of the medieval Church. He has also published works on the nineteenth century and is the general editor of the *Glamorgan County History*. His book *Language, Religion and Nationality in Wales* (1979) draws on a number of themes and sources ranging over the whole span of Welsh history and, like all his writings, is characterized by lucidity, percipience and an erudite interpretation of Welsh literature. A collection of his essays in Welsh on the religion and culture of Wales appeared under the title *Grym Tafodau Tân* in 1984. His other main works are *Bywyd ac Amserau'r Esgob Richard Davies* (1953), *Dadeni, Diwygiad a Diwylliant Cymru* (1964), *Owen Glendower* (1966) and *Reformation Views of Church History* (1970).

A full bibliography of Glanmor Williams's publications will be found in *Welsh Society and Nationhood* (ed. R. R. Davies *et al*, 1984), a volume of essays presented to him to mark the occasion of his retirement.

Williams, Grace (1906–77), composer, was born at Barry, Glam., and educated at University College, Cardiff, and at the Royal College of Music. From 1931 she worked in London as a teacher and later joined the BBC, but returned to live in her native town in 1947. Among her best-known works are *Fantasia on Welsh Nursery Tunes* (1940) and *Sea Sketches* (1944), but with *Penillion* (1955) her music began to show the stylistic maturity developed in her later works. They include an opera, *The Parlour* (1966), a setting of the Latin mass written in collaboration with Saunders *Lewis, *Missa Cambrensis* (1971), and other choral and solo vocal compositions, several of which are settings of Welsh and English poems.

WILLIAMS, GRIFFITH (**Gutyn Peris**; 1769–1838), poet, was born at Waunfawr, Caerns., but lived most of his life at Llandygái, employed as a quarryman. In an unusual *cywydd* addressed to his friend Gwilym Peris (William Williams), he describes their boyhood at Llanberis, recalling Abraham Williams, their first instructor

in poetry, and Dafydd Ddu Eryri (David *Thomas), of whom Gutyn Peris was the foremost disciple. Both took part in a bardic ceremony organized by Iolo Morganwg (Edward *Williams) during an eisteddfod held at Dinorwic in 1799, but Gutyn Peris had a low opinion of Iolo as a poet. He championed *cynghanedd against the arguments of Ieuan Glan Geirionydd (Evan *Evans) in *Y *Gwyliedydd* and his poetry was collected in the volume *Ffrwyth Awen* (1816).

WILLIAMS, GRIFFITH JOHN (1892–1963), literary historian and perhaps the most versatile Welsh scholar of all time. Born at Cellan, Cards., a blacksmith's son, he was educated at the University College of Wales, Aberystwyth. Thereafter he taught at schools in Porth, Glam., and Dolgellau, Mer., before being appointed to a lectureship in Welsh at University College, Cardiff, in 1921. He succeeded W. J. *Gruffydd to the Chair in Welsh in 1947 and remained there until his retirement in 1957.

The course of his career was decided in 1916 when he began to examine the manuscripts of Iolo Morganwg (Edward *Williams) which had recently been acquired by the *National Library of Wales. He spent virtually the rest of his life in mastering the complexities of this archive and the fruits of his research, the volume *Iolo Morganwg a Chywyddau'r Ychwanegiad* (1926), demonstrated how Iolo had written the *cywyddau* which had been added to the edition of the works of *Dafydd ap Gwilym published by the *Gwyneddigion Society in 1789. His last major work was the first volume of his projected biography of Iolo Morganwg (1956), in which he presented the poet as a romantic visionary rather than a forger. Between these two volumes he wrote authoritative introductions to the Grammars of the *Penceirddiaid* (1934) and to the *Grammar* of Gruffydd *Robert (1939), a magisterial volume on the literary tradition of Glamorgan entitled *Traddodiad Llenyddol Morgannwg* (1948), and a host of important articles and reviews, as well as a little poetry. G. J. Williams founded the scholarly magazine *Llên Cymru* in 1950 and was its editor until his death. He was the first President of *Yr *Academi Gymreig, which awards an annual prize in his memory.

A list of publications by G. J. Williams will be found in *Agweddau ar Hanes Dysg Cymraeg* (ed. Aneirin Lewis, 1969). There is an article on this scholar by Saunders Lewis in *Meistri a'u Crefft* (ed. Gwynn ap Gwilym, 1981); see also the note by Morlais Jones in *Deri o'n Daear Ni* (ed. D. J. Goronwy Evans, 1984).

WILLIAMS, GWYN (1904–), poet and translator. Born at Port Talbot, Glam., he was educated at the University College of Wales, Aberystwyth, and Jesus College, Oxford. From 1935 until his retirement in 1969 he taught at the Universities of Cairo, Alexandria, Libya and Istanbul, latterly as Professor of English

Literature. On his return to Wales he settled at Trefenter, Cards., his father's old home, but moved to Aberystwyth in 1983.

During the years spent in the Near East he began translating Welsh poetry into English and it was as a translator and critic that he made his first reputation with the publication of *The Rent that's Due to Love* (1950), *An Introduction to Welsh Poetry* (1953), *The Burning Tree* (1956; reprinted as *Welsh Poems, sixth century to 1600*, 1973) and *Presenting Welsh Poetry* (1959). His translations, for long considered to be the best available, were collected in the volume *To Look for a Word* in 1976.

A prolific writer in both Welsh and English, Gwyn Williams has published *Against Women* (1953), a translation of an anonymous Welsh poem, and *In Defence of Woman* (1958), a translation of a poem by Wiliam *Cynwal. His three novels are *This Way to Lethe* (1962), *The Avocet* (1970) and *Y Cloc Tywod* (1984) which are set in Cyrenaica and Thrace. Of his four travel-books about Cyrenaica and Turkey, one is in Welsh. He has also published four volumes of his own poetry, *Inns of Love* (1970), *Foundation Stock* (1974), *Choose Your Stranger* (1979) and *Y Ddefod Goll* (1980), a pair of novellas, *Two Sketches of Womanhood* (1975), an adaptation of the tragedy *Troelus a Chresyd* (1976), a history of Wales entitled *The Land Remembers* (1977) and *An Introduction to Welsh Literature* in the *Writers of Wales* series (1978). A collection of his Shakespearean studies was published under the title *Person and Persona* in 1981.

A fascinating account of this highly distinctive writer's life, especially in relation to the places in which he has lived, is to be found in his autobiographical volume *ABC of (D)GW* (1981), which explores the personality and opinions of a Welsh patriot whose culture is at once intensely local and yet richly cosmopolitan, qualities with which his poetry is also informed.

There is an autobiographical essay by Gwyn Williams in the volume *Artists in Wales* (ed. Meic Stephens, 1971) and a note on him by Glyn Jones in *Profiles* (1980); see also an account of Gwyn Williams as translator by Anthony Conran in *The Cost of Strangeness* (1982).

WILLIAMS, GWYN ALFRED (1925–), historian, was born at Dowlais, Merthyr Tydfil, Glam., and educated at the University College of Wales, Aberystwyth, where he was appointed Lecturer in Welsh History in 1954. He became Reader and then Professor of History at York University in 1965 and, in 1974, Professor of History at University College, Cardiff, a post from which he retired in 1983. An authority on modern *Socialism and *Marxism, he has made a major contribution to the history of Wales, especially in respect of its urban and Radical traditions in the eighteenth and nineteenth centuries. His books are characterized by passion, a colourful style and wide erudition, qualities

which have made him one of the most recognizably individual public speakers in contemporary Wales. He has seen himself as 'a people's remembrancer', attempting to influence contemporary opinion in Wales by a dramatic presentation of Welsh history. More than anyone of his generation Gwyn A. Williams has infused scholarly history with immediate concerns and his books, in range and content, reflect both his rooted particularity and his international perspective. They include *Medieval London: from Commune to Capital* (1963), *Artisans and Sansculottes* (1968), *Proletarian Order: Antonio Gramsci, Factory Councils and the Origins of Communism in Italy, 1911–1921* (1975), a translation of Paolo Spriano's *Occupation of the Factories: Italy 1920* (1975) and *Goya and the Impossible Revolution* (1976). His books on specifically Welsh subjects are *The Merthyr Rising* (1978), *Madoc: the Making of a Myth* (1979), *The Search for Beulah Land* (1980), *The Welsh in their History* (1982), and *When was Wales?* (1985). On the last-named was based his part in the making of the television series, *The Dragon has Two Tongues*, written in association with Wynford *Vaughan-Thomas and broadcast in 1985.

WILLIAMS, GWYNNE (1937–), poet. Born at Ponciau, near Rhosllannerchrugog, Denbs., he is a teacher of Welsh at Llangollen and the author of two volumes of verse, *Rhwng Gewyn ac Asgwrn* (1969) and *Gwreichion* (1973).

WILLIAMS, HARRI (1913–83), scholar, theologian and novelist, was born in Liverpool but spent part of his childhood in Anglesey, where his family had its roots. Educated at Oxford and Bala Theological College, he became a Presbyterian minister at Tywyn, Mer., and later at Waunfawr and Bangor, Caerns., before his appointment as Professor at the Theological College, Aberystwyth. He won the *Prose Medal at the National Eisteddfod in 1978 with a novel, *Y Ddaeargryn Fawr* (1978), a fictitious autobiography based on the life and work of Søren Kierkegaard. A man of wide culture, he was a prolific author on a variety of subjects, including music, and contributed regularly to the Welsh periodical press. Besides travel books and many theological works, he published four more novels, *Ward 8* (1963), *Rhyfel yn Syria* (1972), *Deunydd Dwbl* (1982) and *Mam a Fi* (1983); the third of these is based on the life of Dostoyevsky.

For further details see the articles by Islwyn Ffowc Elis and E. R. Lloyd-Jones in *Y Traethodydd* (Oct., 1984).

Williams, Henry (1624–84), Puritan preacher, of Ysgafell, a farm in the parish of Llanllwchaearn, Mont., was a disciple of Vavasor *Powell. After the Restoration of the Monarchy in 1660, he and his family were persecuted on account of their Baptist faith. At the height of their suffering, a field amongst the lands of Ysgafell suddenly yielded a crop of excellent wheat, thus saving them from starvation. The quasi-miraculous qualities of this field, known as Cae'r Fendith ('Field of the Blessing') were described by William Richards (1749–1818) in his Cambro-British Biography (1798) and by David *Davies (1849–1926) in his biography of Vavasor Powell (1896). The name of the farm is commemorated in the pen-name of the historian Janc *Williams (Ysgafell), who was a distant relative of the family.

WILLIAMS, HERBERT LLOYD (1932–), writer. Born at Aberystwyth, Cards., he is a freelance journalist and radio producer. He has published three volumes of poetry, *Too Wet for the Devil* (1963), *The Dinosaurs* (1966) and *The Trophy* (1967), a verse-play, *A Lethal Kind of Love* (1968), and four books on historical subjects, *Battles in Wales* (1975), *Come Out, Wherever You Are* (1976), *Stage Coaches in Wales* (1977) and *Railways in Wales* (1981).

Williams, Hugh (1796–1874), political agitator. Born near Machynlleth, Mont., he practised as a solicitor in Carmarthenshire from 1822 until his death. He is thought by some to have master-minded the *Rebecca Riots and was also involved with *Chartism, defending some activists in court. The collection of Radical poems which he compiled, *National Songs and Poetical Pieces, dedicated to the Queen and Countrywomen* (1839/40), contains several which are his own work.

WILLIAMS, HUGH (1843–1911), Church historian, a native of Menai Bridge, Ang., was educated at Bala College, where he became Professor of Greek and Mathematics in 1875. Ordained by the Calvinistic Methodists in 1873, in 1891 he was appointed Professor of Church History and later became Vice-Principal. His edition and translation of *Gildas's *De Excidio Britanniae* which were published in the *Cymmrodorion Record Series* (1899–1901), have not been superseded and his *Christianity in Early Britain* (1912) is still useful in spite of new historical interpretations. There is a profile of Hugh Williams by R. T. *Jenkins in the latter's essay, 'Rabbi Saunderson', in *Y *Llenor* (1930).

WILLIAMS, HUW OWEN (**Huw Menai**; 1888–1961), poet, was born at Caernarfon, the son of a miner who worked in south Wales. He left school at the age of twelve and had a variety of jobs before finding employment as a weigher near Merthyr Tydfil, Glam., in 1906. There he became a political agitator and left-wing journalist in English, the language of his wide reading, although his mother-tongue was Welsh. During the First World War he turned to the writing of poetry. He published four volumes of verse,

namely *Through the Upcast Shaft* (1920), *The Passing of Guto* (1929), which includes an autobiographical note, *Back in the Return* (1933) and *The Simple Vision* (1945), the last of which has an introduction by his friend, John Cowper *Powys. Huw Menai lived most of his life in the industrial valleys of south Wales and wrote from time to time about the miner's life, but his work is in large measure that of a nature poet in the tradition of Wordsworth, the poet whom he admired most.

For further details see Glyn Jones, *The Dragon has Two Tongues* (1968), and Anthony Conran, *The Cost of Strangeness* (1982).

WILLIAMS, IFOR (1881–1965), scholar, was a native of Tre-garth, near Bethesda, Caerns. He was educated at the University College of North Wales, Bangor, where he graduated in Greek and Welsh, and where he taught until his retirement in 1947. Granted a personal Chair in 1920, he became Head of the Welsh Department in 1929; he was knighted in 1947.

His life's work was the editing of Early Welsh poetry, a field which he transformed with his numerous publications. They include the following books: *Canu Llywarch Hen* (1935), *Canu Aneirin* (1938), *Armes Prydain* (1955; English version, ed. Rachel Bromwich, 1972), *Canu Taliesin* (1960; English version, ed. J. E. Caerwyn Williams, 1968), *The Poems of Llywarch Hen* (The Sir John Rhŷs Memorial Lecture, 1932), *Lectures on Early Welsh Poetry* (1944), *Chwedl Taliesin* (The O'Donnell Lecture, 1957), *Breuddwyd Maxen* (1908, 1920, 1927), *Cyfranc Lludd a Llevelys* (1910), *Chwedlau Odo* (1926) and, most important of all, *Pedeir Keinc y Mabinogi* (1930).

He also published texts of the poetry of a number of the *Poets of the Gentry, including *Ieuan Deulwyn (1909), *Dafydd ap Gwilym (1914, 1921, 1935), *Dafydd Nanmor (with Thomas Roberts, 1923), some of *Iolo Goch's contemporaries (1925, 1937) and *Guto'r Glyn (1939). Of his numerous articles, essays, notes and reviews, many appeared in the *Bulletin* of the *Board of Celtic Studies; he edited the Language and Literature section of that periodical from 1921 and was its general editor from 1937 until 1948. He also edited *Y *Traethodydd* from 1939 to 1964 and was advisory editor to the University of Wales Dictionary.

Some of his broadcast talks and essays were collected in *Meddwn i* (1946), *I Ddifyrru'r Amser* (1959) and *Meddai Syr Ifor* (ed. Melville Richards, 1968). As popular, but no less authoritative, were his study of Welsh place-names, *Enwau Lleoedd* (1945), and his radio lecture, *Cymraeg Byw* (1960). A selection of his most important scholarly articles on Early Welsh poetry was edited by Rachel *Bromwich in the volume *The Beginnings of Welsh Poetry* (1972).

For further details see the index to Ifor Williams's works compiled by Thomas Parry (1939) and the complete bibliography by Alun Eirug Davies in *Studia Celtica* (vol. IV, 1969); see also the memorial number of *Y Traethodydd* (April, 1966) and the article by J. E. Caerwyn Williams in the same magazine (Oct., 1981). There is a tribute to Ifor Williams by Idris Ll. Foster in the *Proceedings* of the British Academy (1953) and an essay by Thomas Jones in *Gwŷr Llên* (ed. Aneirin Talfan Davies, 1948).

WILLIAMS, IOLO ANEURIN (1890–1962), journalist and author, was born in Middlesborough, Yorks., a great-great-grandson of Iolo Morganwg (Edward *Williams) and the son of Aneurin Williams (1859–1924), the Liberal politician. He published two volumes of verse, *Poems* (1915) and *New Poems* (1919), as well as *English Folk Song and Dance* (1935), *Flowers of Marsh and Stream* (1946) and *Early English Water-Colours* (1952). Among his other works, *Points in Eighteenth Century Verse* (1934) became a standard bibliographical reference book. His brother, **Orlando Cyprian Williams** (1883–1967), was also a literary critic and the author of several works on the history of the House of Commons, where he was employed as a civil servant.

WILLIAMS, ISAAC (1802–65), poet, was born at Cwmcynfelin, Llangorwen, Cards., and educated at Harrow and Trinity College, Oxford. As an undergraduate he was influenced by John Keble and, already Vice-President of his old College, he was in 1841 already seen as the favoured candidate to succeed him as Professor of Poetry. He was by then the author of two volumes of poetry, *The Cathedral* (1838) and *Thoughts in Past Years* (1838), and was known as a contributor to *Lyra Apostolica* (1836), a collection of devotional verse by some of the early Tractarians. It was also known, however, that Williams had written the particularly notorious *Tract 80* and such was the hostility generated by this fact towards the *Oxford Movement that he was obliged to withdraw his name a few days before the election. He left Oxford and took a curacy under Keble's brother at Bisley, Yorks., where he continued to write poetry, frequently on Welsh subjects, but was also a frequent visitor to Llangorwen where his brother owned land.

As a poet, Isaac Williams was a disciple of Wordsworth, and his own poetry, especially in the early volumes, belongs to the Romantic school. His later poetry is more explicitly devotional: *The Baptistery* (1842) is a meditation on baptism and *The Altar* (1842) a commentary on the Holy Sacrament. He never forgot that he was a country clergyman and, like George *Herbert, his compatriot and forerunner in the priesthood, he used the humble material of his poems as the basis of religious instruction for his parishioners.

For a critical discussion of Isaac Williams's poetry see the article by Barbara Dennis in *The Anglo-Welsh Review* (no. 65, 1979); the Oxford Poetry Election of 1841 is described by Raymond Chapman in *Oxford* (vol. 35, no. 2, 1983). The poet's autobiography was edited by his brother-in-law, Sir George Prevost, and published in 1892. See also Geoffrey Faber, *Oxford Apostles* (1933), Owen Chadwick, *The Victorian Church* (vol. 1, 1966), O. W. Jones, *Isaac Williams and his Circle* (1971), and the article by A. Tudno Williams in *Taliesin* (no. 46, 1983).

WILLIAMS, ISLWYN (1903–57), short-story writer, was born at Ystalyfera and educated at Trinity College, Carmarthen. He is remembered as the author of two volumes of short stories, *Cap Wil Tomos* (1946) and *Storïau a Phortreadau* (1954). Most of his work is written in the dialect of the Swansea Valley and set in chapel, colliery, trade union, choir, eisteddfod, fair and rugby match. He created a gallery of colourful characters and wrote some of the funniest and most moving stories in Welsh.

For further details see Derec Llwyd Morgan, *Islwyn Williams a'i Gymdeithas* (1980); see also Saunders Lewis, *Crefft y Stori Fer* (1949), the tribute by Alun Oldfield-Davies in *Y Dysgedydd* (1957), the essay by T. J. Morgan in *Amryw Flawd* (1966) and the article by Kate Roberts in *Ysgrifau Beirniadol VI* (ed. J. E. Caerwyn Williams, 1971).

WILLIAMS, JAC LEWIS (1918–77), scholar and short-story writer, was born at Aber-arth, Cards., and educated at the University College of Wales, Aberystwyth, and the University of London. From 1945 until 1956 he was a lecturer at Trinity College, Carmarthen, and was appointed Professor of Education at Aberystwyth in 1960. He was widely recognized as an authority in the field of bilingual education. A prolific contributor to magazines, particularly *Barn, on topics relating to the Welsh language, he was a champion of the federal structure of the *University of Wales and a keen supporter of the Welsh Schools Movement. He was also among those Welsh-speakers keenly interested in contemporary Anglo-Welsh literature and the culture of English-speaking Wales. Of an independent mind and strongly opposed to the principle of a Welsh television channel, mainly on the grounds that it would isolate Welsh culture from the English-speaking Welsh, he was almost alone in arguing long and consistently against it. Besides editing a number of important literary pamphlets, a series of spoken-word records, *Cyfres yr Ysgol a'r Aelwyd*, and a dictionary of technical terms, *Geiriadur Termau* (1973), Jac L. Williams wrote two volumes of short stories and essays, *Straeon y Meirw* (1947) and *Trioedd* (1973), and after his death there appeared a third volume of stories, *Straeon Jac L* (1981).

WILLIAMS, JANE (**Ysgafell**; 1806–85), writer, was born in London, a descendant of the Puritan preacher Henry *Williams of Ysgafell, Mont., but spent the early part of her life at Talgarth, Brecs. There, after making the acquaintance of Lady Llanover (Augusta Waddington *Hall), she discovered an interest in

Welsh literature and learned the language. She published a number of books, the most noteworthy of which are *Miscellaneous Poems* (1824), *The Literary Women of England* (1861), *Celtic Fables, Fairy Tales and Legends* (1862) and *A History of Wales derived from Authentic Sources* (1869); the last-named is generally considered to be the best book on its subject before the publication of Sir John Edward *Lloyd's work. She also wrote a biography of Beti Cadwaladr (Elizabeth *Davies) and edited the *Literary Remains* (1854–55) of Thomas *Price (Carnhuanawc).

Williams, John (1582–1650), archbishop, was born at Conwy, Caerns., a descendant of the Cochwillan and Gwydir families (see under WYNN FAMILY) and the godson of Sir John Wynn. Rapidly promoted under James I, he was by 1620 Dean of Westminster, Bishop of Lincoln and Keeper of the Great Seal. On the Accession of Charles I in 1625 he lost the Keepership and the hostility of Laud led to his imprisonment in the Tower of London, but he was released in 1640 at the behest of the House of Lords. Appointed Archbishop of York in 1641, he joined the King when hostilities broke out in the following year and was active in seeking cohesion among the supporters of the Crown. He spent his own fortune in fortifying *Conwy Castle but in 1645 he was deprived of his command there and, disillusioned, he assisted the Parliamentarians in their attack on the castle in 1646. A man of great wealth and influence, he was generous to the sons of Welsh families who sought his patronage. A moderate, he found his advice consistently disregarded: the historian Gardiner thought that, had it been otherwise, the *Civil War might have been avoided.

For details about John Williams as bishop and politician see H. R. Trevor-Roper, *Archbishop Laud 1573–1645* (1940) and G. E. Aylmer, *The Civil Service of Charles I 1625–42* (1961); for his part in military operations see Norman Tucker, *North Wales in the Civil War* (1958).

WILLIAMS, JOHN (c.1728–1806), hymnwriter, a native of Llandyfaelog, Carms., who settled at St. Athan in the Vale of Glamorgan, was one of the founders of the chapel known as Bethesda'r Fro and a staunch supporter of Thomas *William, its first minister. Some of his hymns, such as '*Pwy welaf o Edom yn dod*' and '*Pa feddwl, pa 'madrodd, pa ddawn*', are still in vogue. His verse was collected in the volume *Cân Diddarfod* (1793).

WILLIAMS, JOHN (Ab Ithel; 1811–62), antiquary and editor, was born at Llangynhafal, Denbs., and educated at Jesus College, Oxford. For many years the rector of Llanymawddwy, Mer., he was one of *Yr *Hen Bersoniaid Llengar* ('The Old Literary Clerics') whose patriotic zeal played an important part in the fostering of Welsh culture during the first half of the nineteenth century. Industrious and amiable, he was a prolific contributor to the periodical press on many aspects of Welsh history but, a Tractarian (see under OXFORD MOVEMENT) and a disciple of Iolo Morganwg (Edward *Williams), he was quite uncritical of the Established Church and lacking in scholarship. His chief contribution was his achievement in organizing the Eisteddfod held at Llangollen in 1858, an occasion which may be regarded as the forerunner of the *National Eisteddfod. The event was also memorable for the controversy caused by the adjudicators' decision to deny Thomas *Stephens the prize for his essay on *Madog ap Gwynedd: Ab Ithel prevented Stephens from defending his thesis by ordering the band to strike up and he was later accused of nepotism in the award of other prizes.

He founded and edited the magazine *The Cambrian Journal* in 1853, launched *Baner y Groes* in 1854 and *Taliesin* in 1859, and edited *Archaeologia Cambrensis*, the journal of the *Cambrian Archaeological Association, from 1846 to 1853. Among the texts he edited for the *Welsh Manuscripts Society were *Y *Gododdin* (1852), *Dosparth Edeyrn Davod Aur* (1856), *Brut y Tywysogyon* (1860), *Annales Cambriae* (1860), *Meddygon Myddfai* (1861) and *Barddas* (1862). None of these editions is of any permanent value, however. His translations of Latin hymns are included in the volume *Emynau'r Eglwys* (1941).

For further details see the articles by G. J. Jones in *Y Traethodydd* (1968) and Mary Ellis in *Yr Haul* (Spring, 1983); see also James Kenward, *Ab Ithel* (1871).

Williams, John (1840–1926), the principal benefactor of the *National Library of Wales, was born at Gwynfe, Carms. He had a distinguished career as a surgeon at University College Hospital, London, during the course of which he was appointed physician to Queen Victoria, who made him a baronet in 1894. Returning in 1903 to live at Plas Llanstephan in his native county, in order to remain in contact with the Welsh cultural movements to which he was devoted, he continued to add to the collection of manuscripts which he had begun to put together when he was in practice in Swansea (before going to London).

The nucleus of this collection, now known as the Llanstephan Manuscripts (formerly the Shirburn Castle Manuscripts), had been formed between 1690 and 1742 by Samuel *Williams and his son Moses *Williams. It had been supplemented by manuscripts from other sources, including the collections of Walter *Davies (Gwallter Mechain), Lewis *Morris the antiquary and Sir Thomas Phillips. An important source for medieval and Renaissance literature, it includes items in the hands of *Gutun Owain, *Siôn Brwynog, *Morgan Elfael, Siôn Dafydd *Rhys and Edward *Lhuyd. Perhaps the most valuable manuscript is *The Red Book of Talgarth*, written about 1400 by Hywel Fychan ap Hywel Goch of Builth. The collection also includes the work of *Dafydd ap Gwilym, *Lewys Glyn Cothi, *Guto'r Glyn and *Tudur Aled.

Sir John, who had also bought the *Peniarth Manuscripts in 1898, was from 1909 resident in Aberystwyth; there he was closely associated with the Welsh Library Committee at the University College of Wales which worked for the establishment of a National Library and a *National Museum. It was he, it is said, who was mainly responsible for the decision to locate the National Library of Wales at Aberystwyth, the gift of his entire collection being made on that condition.

For further details see the monograph on Sir John Williams by Ruth Evans in the St. David's Day series (1952), John Cule, Wales and Medicine (1973) and David Jenkins, 'The National Library of Wales', in the Transactions of the Honourable Society of Cymmrodorion (1982).

WILLIAMS, JOHN ELLIS (1901–75), dramatist, novelist and writer of children's books, was born at Penmachno, Caerns., and educated at the Normal College, Bangor. He taught at schools in Manchester, Llanfrothen and Blaenau Ffestiniog. After retiring in 1960, he moved to Llanbedr, Ardudwy, Mer., and later to Gaerwen, Ang. A prolific writer, he published more than seventy books, including eleven for children and the adventure novel Drwy Ddŵr a Thân (1957). He wrote two series of detective novels, the Hopkyn series (1958–61) and the Parri series (1965–67), as well as some thirty original plays and translations. Among his other volumes are Sglodion (1932), Y Gŵr Drws Nesaf (1946), Whilmentan (1961), Tri Dramaydd Cyfoes (1961), Inc yn fy Ngwaed (1963), Dychangerddi (1967), Glywsoch chi hon? (1968) and Moi Plas (1969).

For further details see Meredydd Evans (ed.), Gŵr wrth Grefft (1974) and Mairwen and Gwynn Jones (ed.), Dewiniaid Difyr (1983).

WILLIAMS, JOHN ELLIS CAERWYN (1912–), scholar and editor, was born at Gwauncaegurwen, Glam., and educated at the University College of North Wales, Bangor, at University College and Trinity College, Dublin, and at the Presbyterian Theological Colleges of Aberystwyth and Bala. After joining the staff of the Welsh Department at Bangor in 1945, he was in 1953 appointed to the Professorship, a post in which he remained until 1965, when he moved to Aberystwyth as Professor of Irish. After his retirement in 1979 he was appointed Director of the Centre for Welsh and Celtic Studies.

A leading authority on the civilization of the Celtic world, he has written prolifically on the literary traditions of Wales and Ireland. He has also been very active as an editor of scholarly periodicals and other publications. Amongst the latter are a volume of translations into Welsh of the stories and essays of Padraic Ó Conaire (1947), a collection of stories translated from Irish, Yr Ebol Glas (1954), and three studies of Irish literature, Traddodiad Llenyddol Iwerddon (1958), Y Storïwr Gwyddeleg a'i Chwedlau (1972) and The Court Poet in Medieval Ireland (1972). His studies of Welsh literature include Edward Jones, Maes-y-Plwm (1963), Beirdd y Tywysogion (1973), Canu Crefyddol y Gogynfeirdd (1977), The Poets of the Welsh Princes (1978) in the *Writers of Wales series and Geiriadurwyr y Gymraeg yng Nghyfnod y Dadeni (1983). He was the compiler of the symposia Llên a Llafar Môn (1963), Llên Doe a Heddiw (1964) and Literature in Celtic Countries (1971), and is the editor of a series of critical essays *Ysgrifau Beirniadol, the scholarly journal *Studia Celtica, and the magazine Y *Traethodydd. The contribution of J. E. Caerwyn Williams has been that of a meticulous scholar, but one whose literary judgements have been consistently informed by a sensitive and wide-ranging critical faculty.

A full bibliography of his writings is included in the volume Bardos (1982) which was edited in his honour by R. Geraint Gruffydd.

WILLIAMS, JOHN GRIFFITH (1915–), prose-writer, was born at Llangwnadl, Caerns. He left school at the age of fifteen to work as a carpenter on the Gwynfryn and Talhenbont estate, and later became a teacher of woodwork. His first book, a very fine autobiography entitled Pigau'r Ser (1969), describes life on the estate and his early years in *Llŷn and *Eifionydd. The sequel, Maes Mihangel (1974), takes his story to the outbreak of the Second World War, during which he was imprisoned for 'refusing to recognise the right of the English Government to impose military service on Wales'. He has also published a historical novel dealing with the rising of *Owain Glyndŵr, Betws Hirfaen (1978), and a study of the Rubáiyát of Omar Khayyám, Omar (1981).

WILLIAMS, JOHN JAMES (1869–1954), short-story writer and poet, was born near Tal-y-bont, Cards. Having worked as a collier at Ynysybwl, Glam., he was educated at the Brecon Memorial College and became a Congregational minister in south Wales. He is remembered as the author of a volume of stories, Straeon y Gilfach Ddu (1931), which displays a delight in the people and speech of industrial Glamorgan. He won the *Chair at the National Eisteddfod on two occasions, in 1906 for his poem 'Y Lloer' and in 1908 with 'Ceiriog'. Archdruid from 1936 to 1939, he also published a collection of poems entitled Y Lloer (1936).

WILLIAMS, JOHN LLOYD (1854–1945), see under WILLIAM, ELIZABETH (1862–1953).

WILLIAMS, JOHN OWEN (**Pedrog**; 1853–1932), poet. An orphan, he was brought up by an aunt at Llanbedrog, Caerns., and worked as a gardener. In 1878, when he had been in Liverpool for two years working for a firm of provision merchants, he began to preach for the Wesleyans but four years later joined Kensington Congregational Church whose minister, after ordination, he remained from 1884 to 1930. Archdruid from 1928 to 1932, Chairman of the Union of Welsh Independents in 1927 and editor of *Y Dysgedydd* from 1922 to 1928, Pedrog was a prolific contributor to the periodical press and won more prizes at eisteddfodau than any other poet before or since his day. No collection of his verse has been published but he left an account of his life, entitled *Stori 'Mywyd* (1932).

WILLIAMS, JOHN OWEN (1892–1973), children's writer, was born at Bethesda, Caerns., and educated at the University College of North Wales, Bangor. He published a number of short stories in *Y *Llenor*, but is remembered chiefly for his collaboration with Jennie *Thomas in the writing of *Llyfr Mawr y Plant* (4 vols., 1931, 1939, 1949 and 1975), a book which, in its early editions, delighted children at a time when there was a dearth of reading material in Welsh. He also published a novel, *Trysor yr Incas* (1970), and two volumes of essays, of which *Corlannau* (1957) is the more interesting.

WILLIAMS, JOHN RICHARD (J. R. Try-fanwy; 1867–1924), poet, was born at Rhostryfan, Caerns. An illness during childhood left him blind and dumb and, after the death of his parents, he lived with an aunt at Porthmadog, where he enjoyed the friendship of Eifion Wyn (Eliseus *Williams). He published two volumes of verse, *Lloffion yr Amddifad* (1892) and *Ar Fin y Traeth* (1910).

WILLIAMS, JOHN ROBERTS (John Aelod Jones; 1914–), journalist, broadcaster and short-story writer. Born at Llangybi, Caerns., he was educated at the University College of North Wales, Bangor, before embarking on a career which culminated in his appointment as editor of *Y *Cymro* in 1945. A lively and perceptive editor, he brought a sense of contemporaneity and professionalism to the newspaper, contributing a witty column under the pseudonym by which he is well known. He left *Y Cymro* in 1962 and in the following year joined BBC Wales as editor of the television newsmagazine programme *Heddiw*; he was appointed Head of the BBC's North Wales Department at Bangor in 1970. Besides a volume of essays, *Annwyl Gyfeillion* (1975), and a selection of his radio talks, *Tros fy Sbectol* (1984), he has published a collection of short stories, *Arch Noa* (1977). The humour of his writing, in which some detect the influence of Damon Runyon, is deeply rooted in the rich dialect and colourful characters of the town of Caernarfon. He has

been editor of *Y Casglwr*, the magazine of *Cymdeithas Bob Owen*, since its inception in 1976.

WILLIAMS, JOHN STUART (1920–), poet and critic. Born at Mountain Ash, Glam., he began his career as an English teacher at Whitchurch Grammar School, Cardiff, before becoming Head of the Department of English and Drama at the City of Cardiff College of Education in 1956. A critic with a special interest in modern Anglo-Welsh literature, he has edited three anthologies: *Dragons and Daffodils* (with Richard Milner, 1960), *Poems '69* (1969) and *The *Lilting House* (with Meic *Stephens, 1969). Four volumes of his own poetry have been published, namely *Last Fall* (1962), *Green Rain* (1967), *Dic Penderyn* (1970) and *Banna Strand* (1975); the penultimate collection includes the poem for voices about the *Merthyr Rising of 1831 which was broadcast by BBC Wales in 1968.

Williams, Maria Jane (Llinos; 1795–1873), see under ABERPERGWM.

WILLIAMS, MORRIS (Nicander; 1809–74), hymn-writer, a native of Llangybi, Caerns., was employed in his youth as a carpenter by a friend of Ieuan Glan Geirionydd (Evan *Evans) but later entered King's School, Chester, and Jesus College, Oxford, where he graduated in 1835. He became curate of Holywell, Flints., and then of Bangor, Caerns., and from 1859 until his death he held the living of Llanrhuddlad, Ang.

Zealous in the cause of the *Oxford Movement during the early years of his ministry, he wrote books such as *Y Flwyddyn Eglwysig* (1843), which was based on Keble's *The Christian Year* (1827), as well as producing a new edition of *Llyfr yr Homiliau* (1847) and a metrical version of the Psalter (1850), in which he paraphrased the Psalms. His aim was to provide hymns for the use of Anglican congregations in Wales and he still has more hymns in the Church hymnal than any other hymn-writer except William *Williams (Pantycelyn). He acquired the name Nicander from his pseudonym at the Eisteddfod held at Aberffraw in 1849 when he won the *Chair for his *awdl*, 'Greadigaeth'; the decision caused controversy because Eben Fardd (Ebenezer *Thomas), one of the adjudicators, believed the *awdl* by Emrys (William *Ambrose) to be the better composition. Nicander's adaptations of the fables of La Fontaine were edited by his son W. Glynn Williams under the title *Damhegion Esop ar Gân* (1901).

For further details see the series of articles by D. Eifion Evans in *Yr Haul* (1955–56).

WILLIAMS, MOSES (1685–1742), antiquary, was born the son of Samuel *Williams at Glaslwyn, Llandysul, Cards., and educated at University College, Oxford. After working as a librarian at the Ashmolean Museum, where he was taught by Edward *Lhuyd, he was ordained priest in 1714 and in the following year accepted the living of Llanwenog, Cards. In 1732 he exchanged the living of Defynnog, Brecs., for the rectorship of Bridgwater, Som., where he spent the remainder of his life.

Like his father, Moses Williams was a translator and by 1715 he had published several translations into Welsh of English devotional works. But his main interest was in antiquities, partly as a result of his acquaintance with Edward Lhuyd, and he travelled throughout Wales in search of manuscripts. His intention was to publish a Welsh Dictionary, an extension of the one compiled by John *Davies of Mallwyd, but this work was never published. It was he who translated from the French the Breton grammar which was published in Edward Lhuyd's *Archaeologia Britannica (1707). His collection of Triads, a catalogue of the contents of the Bodleian Library and a survey of translations of the Scriptures into Welsh also remain in manuscript.

In 1717 he published a bibliography, Cofrestr o'r Holl Lyfrau Printiedig, which formed the basis for Llyfryddiaeth y Cymry by William *Rowlands (Gwilym Lleyn), and in 1726 there appeared his Latin index to the Welsh poets. By this time he was also assisting William Wotton in the preparation of his comprehensive edition of the Welsh *Laws. Although Leges Wallicae (1730), published after Wotton's death, appears under the name of William Clarke, much of the credit for the work is due to Moses Williams. He was also responsible for editions of the Bible (1718) and the Welsh Book of Common Prayer (1727). His collection of old Welsh books and manuscripts passed into the possession of the Earl of Macclesfield and the Shirburn Castle library and was later acquired by the *National Library of Wales from Sir John *Williams.

For an account of his life and a complete catalogue of his work see John Davies, Bywyd a Gwaith Moses Williams (1937).

WILLIAMS, NATHANIEL (1742–1826), Baptist minister and hymn-writer. A native of Llanwinio, Carms., he edited a book containing one of George Whitefield's sermons (1770) and a few of his own hymns, and published a controversial work entitled Dialogue (1778), which was a defence of Peter *Williams. A selection of his hymns appeared in the volume Ychydig o Hymnau Newyddion (1787). Two in particular, namely 'O! Iachadwriaeth fawr' and 'O! rhwyga'r tew gymylau duon', are still sung. Nathaniel Williams was also interested in medicine and was the author of Darllen Dwfr a Meddyginiaeth (1785) and Pharmacopoeia (1796). His theological views, especially his disagreement with the Athanasian theory of the Trinity, caused much contention, but, although for long a colourful personality,

he died in obscurity. His son, known as Twmi Nathaniel, was a ballad-singer.

WILLIAMS, ORLANDO CYPRIAN (1883–1967), see under WILLIAMS, IOLO ANEURIN (1890–1962).

WILLIAMS, OWEN (Owen Gwyrfai; 1790–1874), poet, was a native of Waunfawr, Caerns., and a cooper by trade. A pupil of Dafydd Ddu Eryri (David *Thomas), he composed many elegies and epitaphs, copied Welsh poetry and collected genealogies. Four parts of his Y Drysorfa Hynafiaethol (1839) were published and he worked for many years on a dictionary, Y Geirlyfr Cymraeg. His son, Thomas Williams, published a memoir of him, together with some of his poetry, in Gemau Gwyrfai (1904), and another posthumous selection of his work appeared in Gemau Môn ac Arfon (1911).

WILLIAMS, PETER (1723–96), Methodist clergyman and biblical commentator, was born at Llansadyrnin, Carms. Converted in 1743 by George Whitefield's preaching, he took deacon's orders two years later and served the Anglican Church as a curate in several parishes in south Wales. Refused priest's orders because of his Methodist inclinations, he joined the Methodists in 1747 and spent the rest of his life as an itinerant preacher.

He was the author of about twenty books and booklets which include hymns, children's books, elegies and works of a religious nature. The most important among them are Blodau i Blant (1758), Galwad gan Wyr Eglwysig (1781), Cydymaith mewn Cystudd (1782), Yr Hyfforddwr Cymreigaidd (1784), Y Briodas Ysbrydol (1784) and Ymddygiad Cristionogol (1784). His hymns are to be found in Rhai Hymnau ac Odlau Ysprydol (1759) and Hymns on Various Subjects (1771). But he is remembered best for his annotated edition of the Welsh *Bible, which was published by John Ross in Carmarthen in 1770. This was the first edition of the Welsh Bible to be printed in Wales and it was frequently reprinted thereafter. Many homes in Wales owned a copy of 'Peter Williams's Bible' and it was popular throughout the nineteenth century. He also published a biblical concordance (1773) and a pocket Bible (1790) with notes by John Canne. Suspected of *Sabellianism on account of some of his expositions, he was excommunicated by the Methodists in 1791 and spent the last years of his life in bitter controversy.

His son, **Peter Bailey Williams** (1763–1836), was an antiquary and translator. He was associated with the editors of The Myvyrian Archaiology (1801) and he translated two of Richard Baxter's books under the titles Tragwyddol Orphwysfa'r Saint (1825) and Galwad i'r Annychweledig (1825). Among his publications in English was A Tourist's Guide through the County of Caernarvon (1821).

A study of Peter Williams's life and work was published by Gomer M. Roberts in 1943; see also the article by Derec Llwyd Morgan in *Y Traethodydd* (Oct., 1972). A short autobiography of Peter Williams is included as an appendix in *The English Works* of his son, Eliezer Williams, published in 1840.

WILLIAMS, RAYMOND (1921–), social historian, critic and novelist, was born at Pandy, Mon., where his father was a railway signalman. After attending King Henry VIII Grammar School, Abergavenny, he went to Trinity College, Cambridge, in 1939 to begin a student career interrupted by war service, which included involvement in the Normandy landings and the Arnhem operations. After the war he returned to Cambridge and was later appointed Staff Tutor with the Oxford University Extra-Mural Delegacy. In 1961 he was elected Fellow of Jesus College, Cambridge. The publication of his books *Culture and Society* (1958) and *The Long Revolution* (1966) brought him the recognition as a cultural historian which he has enjoyed ever since. He has been engaged in political activity all his life. Always his own man, he is closest to the 'New Left' position in Britain, having resigned from the Labour Party in 1966. This political attitude is a constant if implicit theme in all his literary and cultural writings. In 1974 he was appointed Professor of Drama at Cambridge, a post from which he retired in 1983.

The work of Raymond Williams displays an unceasing concern to elucidate the modern concept of 'culture' as the expression, in both high and popular modes, of life in contemporary Britain. Within that field the press and television, the traditional forms of novel and drama, speech, language, education and political discourse have all received his thorough attention. His first widely known book, *Culture and Society*, traced the idea of 'culture' from its origins in the nineteenth century to the present time when, he argues, it must accept the addition of working-class culture. *The Long Revolution* traces such cultural forms as education, the growth of the press and of the reading public from their beginnings to the time of the far-reaching cultural revolution which is now under way. These interests were continued in *Communications* (1962) and *Television: Technology and Cultural Form* (1974). Two specialist but unusual books on traditional drama, a study of the English novel, the explicitly Radical *May Day Manifesto* (1968), a monograph on George Orwell (1970) and the influential work *The Country and the City* (1973) are among the other books, more than twenty in all, which Raymond Williams has written. His later work has returned to the conceptual investigation of culture, but from a much more Marxist standpoint. The definitive work among his later books is *Marxism and Literature* (1977), preceded by *Keywords* (1976), an original and successful study of social and cultural terms important in contemporary use, and followed by *Politics and Letters* (1979), a collection of interviews about his life and work by the staff of the journal *New Left Review* to which he has been a frequent contributor. He has also published *Problems in Materialism and Culture* (1980), *Culture* (1980), *Towards 2000* (1983) and *Writing in Society* (1983).

Many who do not share the politics of Raymond Williams have been influenced by the scope and originality of his investigations. Sometimes criticized for obscurity and over-abstraction, he has, nevertheless, by such methods, looked with great consistency at complex issues over many years. In even his theoretical writings there is a strong autobiographical note, further underlined in his important trilogy of novels, *Border Country (1960), Second Generation (1964) and The Fight for Manod (1979), which are set largely in Wales. His growing identification with Wales and the newly emerging Welsh consciousness of the 1960s has coincided with the appearance of these books, especially the third. His novels *The Volunteers* (1978) and *Loyalties* (1985) also have Welsh settings.

There is a monograph on Raymond Williams by J. P. Ward in the *Writers of Wales* series (1981) which contains a bibliography of critical articles; see also the chapters on Raymond Williams in Terry Eagleton, *Criticism and Ideology* (1976) and Lesley Johnson, *The Cultural Critics* (1979).

WILLIAMS, RHYDWEN (1916–), poet and novelist. Born at Pentre in the Rhondda Valley, he was reared in a Welsh-speaking home and attended a Welsh chapel, but his family moved to Chester on his fifteenth birthday, an uprooting which marred his adolescence. He found work as a gardener and in various shops and offices before becoming a student at the University Colleges of Swansea and Bangor. At the outbreak of war he registered as a conscientious objector on Welsh Nationalist grounds and served with an ambulance unit. Returning to the Rhondda, he became a Baptist minister at Ynyshir, a friend of Kitchener *Davies and a member of the circle known as *Cylch Cadwgan. He held pastorates in Resolven and Pont-lliw before being appointed to a post in commercial television; since then he has lived by his writing and as an actor.

He won the *Crown at the National Eisteddfod on two occasions, with 'Yr Arloeswr' in 1946 and 'Y Ffynhonnau' in 1964. A prolific writer, he has published five volumes of poetry, namely *Barddoniaeth* (1964), *Y Ffynhonnau* (1970), *Y Chwyldro Gwyrdd* (1972), *Ystlumod* (1977), which is a poem written for television, and *Dei Gratia* (1984). His novels include *Arswyd y Byd* (1949), *Mentra Gwen* (1953) and *Cwm Hiraeth*, which was published in three volumes, *Y Briodas* (1969), *Y Siôl Wen* (1970) and *Dyddiau Dyn*

(1973). This trilogy, which is considered to be his main achievement as a novelist, depicts life in the mining valleys of south Wales. Among his other novels are *Breuddwyd Rhonabwy Jones* (1972), which satirizes *Gorsedd Beirdd Ynys Prydain, Apolo* (1975), which is set in the world of television, and *Adar y Gwanwyn* (1972), a mischievous reply to Pennar *Davies's *Meibion Darogan* (1968) which he thought to contain a portrait of himself. He has also published a novel in English, *The Angry Vineyard* (1975). Rhydwen Williams became editor of the magazine *Barn* in 1981.

For further details see J. Gwyn Griffiths, *I Ganol y Frwydr* (1970), R. M. Jones, *Llenyddiaeth Gymraeg 1936–1972* (1975) and Glyn Jones and John Rowlands, *Profiles* (1980); see also the author's volume of autobiography, *Gorwelion* (1984), and the interview he gave to the magazine *Barddas* (nos. 82 and 87–88, Feb. and July–August, 1984).

WILLIAMS, RICHARD (Dic Dywyll, Bardd Gwagedd; *c.*1790–1862?), balladeer. Born either in Anglesey or Caernarfonshire, he won his reputation as 'the king of all the balladsingers' in south Wales. Blind, and described by contemporaries as a short, fat man, he used to put his little finger in the corner of his eye when singing his ballads. Little is known about his life, but he witnessed the *Merthyr Rising (1831) and sang about the *Rebecca Riots (1839–43). According to tradition, it was his ballad '*Cân ar Ddull y Gyfraith Newydd*' which caused such excitement among the inhabitants of Merthyr Tydfil that the building of a workhouse in the town was delayed for some twenty years. Of Dic's ballads, seventy-three survive in print and others are preserved in manuscript at the *National Library of Wales. Many are satirical or comic in tone but he was also capable of writing more delicate verse, as in '*Lliw gwyn, rhosyn yr haf*'.

WILLIAMS, RICHARD (Gwydderig; 1842–1917), poet, a native of Brynaman, Carms., was one of the circle of country poets in that neighbourhood which included Watcyn Wyn (Watkin Hezekiah *Williams), to whom he was related. As a young man he emigrated to the USA, working as a miner in Pennsylvania, but returned to spend the last years of his life in his native district. A keen competitor at eisteddfodau, he excelled at the *englyn and won more prizes at the *National Eisteddfod for poems in that form than any other poet except Eifion Wyn (Eliseus *Williams). A selection of his poetry was edited by J. Lloyd Thomas in the volume *Detholion o Waith Gwydderig* (1959).

WILLIAMS, RICHARD BRYN (1902–81), poet, prose writer, playwright and historian of the Welsh settlement in *Patagonia. Born at Blaenau Ffestiniog, Mer., he was taken by his parents to Trelew, Chubut, when he was seven

years old and there he grew up. Returning to Wales in 1923, he studied at the University College of North Wales, Bangor, and the Theological College at Aberystwyth. From 1932 to 1952 he served as a Welsh Presbyterian minister and thereafter was a member of staff of the Celtic Department of the *National Library of Wales. He won the *Chair at the National Eisteddfod of 1964 with his *awdl*, '*Patagonia*', and again in 1968 with '*Y Morwr*'. He was Archdruid from 1973 to 1976.

Much of his writing was devoted to portraying the life of the Welsh settlement in Patagonia which he knew intimately and of which he became the chief interpreter. He published novels and stories for children about the prairie, including *Y March Coch* (1954), *Bandit yr Andes* (1956), *Croesi'r Paith* (1958), *Yn Nwylo'r Eirth* (1967), *Y Rebel* (1969), *Agar* (1973) and *Y Gwylliaid* (1976). Many of the poems in his volumes *Pentewynion* (1949), *Patagonia* (1965) and *O'r Tir Pell* (1972) refer to the Welsh life of the colony. He also published collections of prose and poetry written by the settlers, including *Straeon Patagonia* (1944), *Lloffion o'r Wladfa* (1944), *Rhyddiaith y Wladfa* (1946), *Awen Ariannin* (1960) and *Canu'r Wladfa* (1965), and contributed a travelbook about Patagonia to the series *Cyfres Crwydro Cymru* (1960). But his most important studies were the historical sketch *Cymry Patagonia* (1942) and the magisterial history, *Y Wladfa* (1962); they were followed by *Gwladfa Patagonia 1865–1965* (1965) and a volume of reminiscences by some living Welsh Patagonians, *Atgofion o Batagonia* (1980). R. Bryn Williams also wrote a biography of Eluned *Morgan (1945), three plays, *Pedrito* (1947), *Cariad Creulon* (1970) and *Dafydd Dywysog* (1975), two travel books, *Taith i Sbaen* (1949) and *Teithiau Tramor* (1970), and a volume of autobiography, *Prydydd y Paith* (1983). His translation of Garcia Lorca's play *Bodas de Sangre* appeared under the title *Priodas Waed* in 1977.

For further details see Saunders Lewis, *Ysgrifau Dydd Mercher* (1945) and the profile by Aneurin O. Edwards in *Atgofion am bymtheg o wŷr llên yr ugeinfed ganrif* (1975).

WILLIAMS, RICHARD HUGHES (Dic Tryfan; 1878?–1919), journalist and short-story writer, was born at Rhosgadfan, Caerns. After a period as a quarryman he went to Liverpool and London, but returned to Wales to work on newspapers in Caernarfon, Aberystwyth and Llanelli. During the First World War his health was ruined by work in the munitions factory at Pembrey, Carms., and he died soon afterwards. His ambition was to be a novelist but, according to his friend T. Gwynn *Jones, he wrote some hundreds of stories in both Welsh and English. Most of his published stories are about quarrymen and, because of their preoccupation with poverty and death, they have been described as morbid. Some, nevertheless, like

'*Twmi*', show a remarkable economy in narrative and dialogue and are among the best ever written in Welsh. Two volumes of his stories appeared during his lifetime, *Straeon y Chwarel* (n.d.) and *Tair Stori Fer* (1916), and a selection entitled *Storiau gan Richard Hughes Williams* was published posthumously in 1919.

For further details about Richard Hughes Williams see the introduction by E. Morgan Humphreys to his collected stories which were published in 1932, the article by T. Gwynn Jones in *Cymeriadau* (1933), the lecture by Kate Roberts, '*Dau Lenor o Ochr Moeltryfan* (1970), and the same author's article in *Taliesin* (vol. 5, 1962).

WILLIAMS, ROBERT (1744–1815), poet, lived at Pandy Isaf, Rhiwaedog, near Bala, Mer. He wrote *cywyddau*, but after his religious conversion his work consisted mainly of carols and moral effusions. Most of his verse remains in manuscript but selections have been published in the anthology *Beirdd y Bala* (1911) and in some periodicals. He is remembered mainly for his famous line, '*Beibl i bawb o bobl y byd*' ('A Bible for everyone in the world'), which occurs in one of his *englynion*, but which is sometimes attributed to Robert *Davies (Bardd Nantglyn).

WILLIAMS, ROBERT (Robert ap Gwilym Ddu; 1766–1850), poet and hymn-writer, was a farmer in the parish of Llanystumdwy, Caerns. He learned the craft of poetry from the poets of *Eifionydd and in his turn became bardic instructor to Dewi Wyn o Eifion (David *Owen) and others.

His work is notable in that, spurning the mock-heroic poetry fashionable in his time, he concentrated on writing about the everyday events of his neighbourhood, and about his family and friends. For example, the elegy which he wrote on the death of his only daughter, who died in 1834 at the age of seventeen, is one of the most moving in the Welsh language. Under the influence of Goronwy *Owen's meditative classicism and the tradition of poetry in the strict metres, he was a master of the concise couplet and the memorable line, especially when expressing his religious faith. Because he chose not to write in the popular eisteddfodic style, he received little attention as a poet during his lifetime, but the quality of his best verse, to be found in the volume *Gardd Eifion* (1841), is now generally recognized. He was a close friend of John Richard *Jones (1765–1822) of Ramoth whom he helped in the publishing of hymns and there are twenty hymns by Robert ap Gwilym Ddu in the third part of J. R. Jones's collection, *Aleluia neu Ganiadau Cristionogol* (1822). His most famous hymn, '*Mae'r gwaed a redodd ar y Groes*', first appeared in the periodical *Seren Gomer in 1824.

For further details see the study of Robert ap Gwilym Ddu, together with a selection of his writings, edited by Stephen J. Williams (1948); see also the article by

Saunders Lewis in *Meistri'r Canrifoedd* (ed. R. Geraint Gruffydd, 1973).

WILLIAMS, ROBERT (1810–81), lexicographer, a native of Conwy, Caerns., was educated at Christ Church, Oxford. An Anglican priest, he held livings in Wales and Herefordshire and for the last nine years of his life was an honorary canon of *St. Asaph. He compiled the volumes *Enwogion Cymru: a Biographical Dictionary of Eminent Welshmen* (1852) and *Lexicon Cornu-Britannicum* (1865), a study of the Cornish language, and also published numerous scholarly studies on aspects of Welsh history, including *The History and Antiquities of the Town of Aberconwy* (1835) and *Selections from the Hengwrt Manuscripts* (1876). It was he who translated *The *Book of Taliesin* for W. F. Skene's *The *Four Ancient Books of Wales* (1868).

WILLIAMS, ROBERT (Trebor Mai; 1830–77), poet, was born at Llanrhychwyn, Caerns., the son of a tailor who belonged to a family of country poets, and he followed his father's trade at Llanrwst, Denbs., where Caledfryn (William *Williams) was his mentor in poetry. He wrote much verse of an indifferent quality and is remembered only for his numerous *englynion*, some of which are excellent. Two volumes of his work were published, namely *Fy Noswyl* (1861) and *Y Geninen* (1869), and Isaac *Foulkes edited a posthumous collection which appeared in 1883 under the title *Gwaith Barddonol Prif Englyniwr Cymru*. One of the more curious poems composed by Trebor Mai (his bardic name reads 'I am Robert' in reverse) is a eulogy of his fellow-poets which has rhyming lines set in the shape of an oak-tree.

WILLIAMS, ROBERT DEWI (1874–1958), short-story writer, was born near Pandytudur, Denbs. After leaving school he worked at home on the farm for five years and was given private tuition by his uncle, Robert *Roberts (Y Sgolor Mawr). Having attended the University College of Wales, Aberystwyth, and the University of Oxford, he became a minister in the Presbyterian Church. He spent twenty-two years as headmaster of his denomination's preparatory school at Clynnog and later at Rhyl. A volume of his stories, *Clawdd Terfyn* (1912), was very well received when first published, but the humour now seems forced and dependent on puns. A volume of his reminiscences entitled *Dyddiau Mawr Mebyd* was published posthumously in 1973.

WILLIAMS, ROBIN (1923–), essayist and travel-writer, was born at Penycaerau, Caerns., and educated at the University College of North Wales, Bangor, and the Theological Colleges at Aberystwyth and Bala. He is a Presbyterian minister and free-lance broadcaster. Among his collections of essays and travel-books are *Basged *y Saer* (1969), *Y Tri Bob* (1970), *Wrthi* (1971), *Esgyrn Eira* (1972), *Blynyddoedd Gleision* (1973), *Mêl Gwyllt* (1976), *Cracio Concrit* (1979), *Lliw Haul* (1980) and *Llongau'r Nos* (1983).

WILLIAMS, ROGER (1540?–95), soldier and author. A member of the Williams family of Penrhos, Mon., he became a soldier at the age of seventeen. Famed for his bravery in action and an expert in the art of warfare, he spent the greater part of his life in Europe, most notably fighting with the Dutch against the armies of Spain. He wrote three books on military subjects: *A Brief Discourse of War* (1590), *Newes from Sir Roger Williams* (1591) and the posthumous *Actions of the Low Countries* (1618). A favourite with Queen Elizabeth, he may well have been the man on whom Shakespeare drew in *Henry V* (1599) for the character of the brave, choleric and pedantic Welsh officer, Fluellen. He was also among those suspected of being the author of the Marprelate Tracts (see under PENRY, JOHN).

The works of Sir Roger Williams have been edited by John X. Evans (1972); for further details see the article by Amos C. Miller in the *Transactions* of the Honourable Society of Cymmrodorion (1971).

WILLIAMS, ROWLAND (Goronva Camlann; 1817–70), theologian and poet, was born at Halkyn, Flints., where his father was vicar, but spent seventeen of his first nineteen years at Meifod, Mont., in the vicarage there. Educated at Eton and King's College, Cambridge, he was, for a short time, a master at Eton, but became Classical Fellow of his old College (1842–50) and an ordained priest (1843). In 1846, under the pseudonym Goronva Camlann, he published *Lays from the Cimbric Lyre* which, though undistinguished as verse, is remarkable for its open displays of anger at the patronizing sneers suffered by the Welsh and its resurrection of the theme of Welsh seniority in the British partnership. With the Welsh heritage in full display, the book offers a useful insight into one strand of 'Anglo-Welsh' opinion on contemporary subjects.

In 1850 Williams was appointed Vice-Principal and Professor of Hebrew at St. David's College, Lampeter, and for twelve years strove to reform an institution which had defeated the previous bishop. But a sermon on 'Rational Godliness' which he preached at Cambridge in 1854 disquieted Evangelicals and opposition to him at Lampeter was intensified by the apparent unorthodoxies which his survey of recent biblical criticism revealed in *Essays and Reviews* (1860). Virtually ostracized, he abandoned Lampeter in 1862 for the living of Broad Chalke, Wilts., the parish in which John Aubrey (see under AUBREY, WILLIAM) was born, and eight years later he was buried there. A theologian of stature, he always argued, despite the Oxford Declaration prepared by Pusey and signed by four thousand others, that his tenets were absolutely consistent with the doctrine of the Church of England. His most important theological work was *Christianity and Hinduism* (1856). As Goronva Camlann he also published *Orestes and the Avengers: An Hellenic Mystery* (1859) and *Owen Glendower: A Dramatic Biography, with other Poems* (1870) was in the press when he died.

A memoir was written by Rowland Williams's widow in 1874; see also the articles by Owain W. Jones in *Trivium 6* (1971) and the *Journal* of the History Society of the Church in Wales (1965), and that by A. Tudno Williams in *Taliesin* (no. 50, 1984).

WILLIAMS, ROWLAND (Hwfa Môn; 1823–1905), poet, was a native of Trefdraeth, Ang., but was brought up at Rhos-tre-Hwfa, near Llangefni. Ordained a minister with the Independents in 1851, he held pastorates in various parts of Wales and in London and became minister of Llannerch-y-medd in his native county in 1881. Although he won both the *Chair and the *Crown at the National Eisteddfod, there was little permanent merit in his work, as his two volumes, both published under the title *Gwaith Barddonol* (1883, 1903), amply demonstrate. He is remembered only as Archdruid, an office to which he was elected in 1895, and in which he remained until his death.

WILLIAMS, SAMUEL (c. 1660–c. 1722), copyist, was rector of Llandyfriog and Llangynllo, Cards. Most of the *halsingod which he wrote for the enlightenment of his parishioners remain in manuscript, but some were collected in the volume *Pedwar o Ganuau* (1718). These verses, which expound the orthodox Christian faith, may have been used by William *Williams (Pantycelyn) as patterns for his hymns. Samuel Williams's most important work, in an age when it was still the only means of making literature available, was to collect and copy Welsh manuscripts. He copied the *Psalmae* (1696) of William *Midleton and specimens of the work of the *cywyddwyr*, some of which exist in no other copy. In this task he was helped by his son Moses *Williams, who also assisted in the copying of *Dafydd ap Gwilym's poems. Many of their manuscripts later belonged to John *Williams whose collection, known as the Llanstephan Manuscripts, is now housed in the *National Library of Wales. Samuel Williams, in addition, translated devotional books, not all of which were published, and an example of his dignified prose is to be found in *Amser a Diwedd Amser* (1707), a translation of a book by John Fox.

For further details see John Davies, *Bywyd a Gwaith Moses Williams* (1937), and the article by Geraint Bowen, 'Yr Halsingod', in the *Transactions* of the Honourable Society of Cymmrodorion (1946).

WILLIAMS, STEPHEN JOSEPH (1896–), scholar. Born near Ystradgynlais, Brecs., he was educated at University College, Cardiff, but shortly after the outbreak of the First World War he joined the Army and served in India. After graduating in Welsh in 1921, he became a schoolmaster at Aberaeron and Llandeilo and in 1927 was appointed Lecturer in Welsh at University College, Swansea, where he succeeded Henry *Lewis as Professor in 1954. Urien *Wiliam is one of his sons.

Among Stephen J. Williams's publications are *Ffordd y Brawd Odrig* (1929) and an annotated edition of the Welsh versions of the tales of Charlemagne, *Ystorya de Carolo Magno* (1930). With J. Enoch Powell (the Unionist Member of Parliament for South Down) he edited *Llyfr Blegywryd* (1942), the first modern edition of the *Laws of Hywel Dda. He also edited (1948) the works of Robert ap Gwilym Ddu (Robert *Williams) and studied the writings of Ifor Ceri (John *Jenkins), Carnhuanawc (Thomas *Price), Thomas *Stephens, Gweirydd ap Rhys (Robert John *Pryse) and T. Gwynn *Jones. A descriptive grammarian, he is the author of *Beginner's Welsh* (1934), *Elfennau Gramadeg Cymraeg* (1959) and *A Welsh Grammar* (1980), all of which are authoritative. A devoted *eisteddfodwr*, he was elected a Fellow of the *National Eisteddfod in 1975 and a selection of his articles was published under the title *Beirdd ac Eisteddfodwyr* (ed. Brynley F. Roberts) in 1981.

WILLIAMS, TALIESIN (Taliesin ab Iolo; 1787–1847), poet. The son of Iolo Morganwg (Edward *Williams), he was said to have been born in Cardiff Gaol where his father was serving a sentence for bankruptcy. He received a little education in a school at Cowbridge, Glam., before joining his father as a stonemason, and later he kept schools at Gileston, Neath and Merthyr Tydfil, at the last of which places he served for thirty-one years until his death. It was through his connections with the Provincial Welsh Societies and the associates of his father that he came to prominence in the literary life of Wales about 1820. He assisted Iolo in the preparation of *Cyfrinach Beirdd Ynys Prydain* (1829) and worked thereafter on his father's manuscripts, preparing them for publication by the *Welsh Manuscripts Society in 1848. Like many of his contemporaries, he believed implicitly Iolo's claims about the antiquity of *Gorsedd Beirdd Ynys Prydain and actively encouraged the acceptance of all his father's theories. In this he was naïve but innocent, for Iolo had not shared the secret of his fabrications with his son. Taliesin ab Iolo published two long English poems of his own, *Cardiff Castle* (1827) and *The Doom of Colyn Dolphyn* (1837). He won the *Chair at the Eisteddfod held in Cardiff in 1834 with his *awdl*, 'Y Derwyddon', and a prize at the Abergavenny Eisteddfod of 1838 for an essay on *Coelbren y Beirdd.

Williams, Thomas (Twm Chwarae Teg; 1737–1802), industrialist, of Llanidan, Ang., began by working the Roman coppermines on Parys Mountain near Amlwch and, by the end of his career, controlled half the copper production of Britain. He earned his sobriquet ('Tom Fair Play') on account of his honest dealings with his workers and competitors.

WILLIAMS, THOMAS (Eos Gwynfa, Eos y Mynydd; c.1769–1848), poet, a native of Llanfyllin or perhaps Llanfihangel-yng-Ngwynfa, Mont., was a weaver by trade. A prolific writer, he published a large number of *carols and songs for Christmas matins, the most notable of which are to be found in the volumes *Telyn Dafydd* (1820), *Ychydig o Ganiadau Buddiol* (1824), *Newyddion Gabriel* (1825), *Manna'r Anialwch* (1831) and *Mer Awen* (1844).

WILLIAMS, THOMAS (Gwilym Morgannwg; 1778–1835), poet, was born at Llanddeti, Brecs., but was taken three years later to live at Cefncoedycymer, near Merthyr Tydfil, Glam. During his later years he settled in Pontypool, Mon., where he kept a tavern and was prominent in the literary life of the district. With John Jenkins (1779–1853) of Hengoed, he wrote the first version of a geographical work entitled *Y Parthsyllydd* (1815–16). Examples of his verse were published in the anthologies *Llais Awen Gwent a Morgannwg* (ed. John Davies, 1824) and *Awenyddion Morgannwg neu Farddoniaeth Cadair a Gorsedd Pendefigaeth Morgannwg a Gwent* (1826). In 1814 he was initiated into the arcana of neo-Druidism, in the company of Taliesin ab Iolo (Taliesin *Williams), by the latter's father, Iolo Morganwg (Edward *Williams). His poetical works were collected in the volume *Awen y Maen Chwyf* (1890) and published at his son's expense; they include an admirable *cywydd* in memory of Iolo Morganwg.

WILLIAMS, THOMAS (Brynfab; 1848–1927), poet, was born at Cwmaman, Aberdare, Glam., and was a farmer in the parish of Eglwys Ilan, on the hillside above Pontypridd, for most of his life. A well-known literary figure, especially as a member of *Clic y Bont, he edited the poetry column in *Tarian y Gweithiwr for many years, was a frequent contributor to periodicals and a keen *eisteddfodwr*. His verse has not been collected but his novel, *Pan oedd Rhondda'n bur* (1912), gives a lively account of life in the *Rhondda Valley before industrialization.

WILLIAMS, THOMAS ARFON (1935–), poet, was born at Treherbert in the Rhondda Valley, Glam. He trained as a dentist at King's College Hospital, London, and became a Dental Officer at the *Welsh Office in Cardiff in 1970. Discovering an interest in *cynghanedd in 1974, he quickly established a reputation as a writer of *englynion* and became a prominent member of **Cymdeithas Cerdd Dafod*. He has published two collections of poems in his favourite form, namely *Englynion Arfon* (1978) and *Annus Mirabilis* (1984), and has edited a symposium about the poetic craft, *Ynglŷn â Chrefft Englyna* (1981). A gifted *cynganeddwr*, he excels in the writing of the **englyn* which consists of a single, uninterrupted sentence.

WILLIAMS, THOMAS MARCHANT (The Acid Drop; 1845–1914), editor and writer. Born at Aberdare, Glam., a miner's son, he trained as a teacher at the Normal College, Bangor, and after spending some years at schools in Wales and Yorkshire he was among the first students to enrol at the University College of Wales, Aberystwyth. He later became an Inspector of Schools in London, where he took an active part in the revival of the Honourable Society of **Cymmrodorion* and in the establishment of the National Eisteddfod Society, of which he became Chairman. Abandoning his career in education, he was called to the Bar in 1885 and appointed Stipendiary Magistrate of Merthyr Tydfil in 1900, a position he held until his death.

A Liberal in politics and a prolific contributor to the press on topics of the day, T. Marchant Williams was the author of a satirical novel, *Land of my Fathers* (1889), a series of critical sketches, with caricatures, entitled *The Welsh Members of Parliament* (1894) and a volume of poems, *Odlau Serch a Bywyd* (1907). He was knighted in 1904 for his services to the **University of Wales* and the **National Eisteddfod*. His most important literary work was done as editor of the magazine *The *Nationalist*, his caustic wit and critical view of Welsh political and religious leaders earning him the sobriquet by which he was widely known.

For further details see the obituary of T. Marchant Williams by Vincent Evans in the *Transactions* of the Honourable Society of Cymmrodorion (1913–14) and the same writer's article in *Y Geninen* (March, 1915).

WILLIAMS, WALDO (1904–71), poet, was born the son of a schoolmaster at Haverfordwest, Pembs. The home was English-speaking and he was seven before he learned Welsh from the children of Mynachlogddu, in the north of the county, where the family had moved. It was a remarkable household, influenced on the one hand by the Baptist chapel, on the other by the most radical ideas of the day. Among his father's heroes were Edward Carpenter, Tolstoy, Whitman, Keir **Hardie* and Shelley. On more than one occasion in his adolescence Waldo had mystical experiences, involving feelings of unity with nature and of universal brotherhood, which were related to the First World War (both his parents were pacifists) and which were to be reflected in the poetry he wrote under the stress of the Second World War and the war in Korea.

In 1915, when the family had moved a few miles to Llandysilio, his elder sister Morfydd died and this bereavement was to inform a much later poem.

Leaving Narberth Grammar School for the University College of Wales, Aberystwyth, in 1923, he read English. During his undergraduate years he developed, in collaboration with Idwal **Jones*, a talent for the writing of light verse in Welsh and discovered an interest in the English Romantic poets which was to remain with him for the rest of his life. His earliest poetry appeared during the 1930s in *Y *Ford Gron* and was, by turns, humorous, satirical and sentimental. One of his best-known poems, 'Cofio', written at this time, won immediate acclaim, though his later development now makes it appear an immature work. However, whereas other Welsh poets of his generation rejected **Romanticism* entirely, Waldo Williams deepened his understanding of its philosophical roots.

The Second World War and its aftermath challenged his belief in Man's essential goodness and also brought personal suffering. His wife Linda died in 1943, scarcely more than a year after their marriage, and in 1944 he left Wales to teach in Huntingdon and Wiltshire. The years following the explosion of atomic bombs over Hiroshima and Nagasaki produced some of his most anguished poetry. It was while he was living in England that he wrote a small group of immensely powerful poems about Welsh nationhood which include 'Preseli', 'Cymru'n Un' and 'Cymru a Chymraeg'. The immediate occasion for these poems was the threat to the communities of the Preseli Hills caused by an announcement that the armed forces were to use some sixteen thousand acres as an artillery range. The will to resist which was manifested in Waldo's poetry at this time exerted a political influence twenty years later, and more immediately carried him into conventional politics. He stood as the **Plaid Cymru* candidate in the General Election of 1959 but he was not by nature a politician and his instinct was to distrust the State, as can be seen from his lecture 'Brenhiniaeth a Brawdoliaeth', which shows the influence of Berdyaev's thought.

After his return to Wales in 1950 Waldo announced, in a personal response to the Korean war, that he would withhold his income tax. He maintained that words without action were not enough and only when he had taken this decision was he persuaded to publish *Dail Pren* (1956). This small volume is his only book, apart from a collection of poems for children, *Cerddi'r Plant* (1970), which he produced in collaboration with E. Llwyd **Williams*. He spent six weeks in prison for non-payment of tax in 1960 and served a second sentence in 1961. The affection and admiration in which he was generally held depended not only on his poetry but also on his genial personality, his single-minded commitment to *Pacifism and the cause of *Plaid Cymru*, on his complete lack of self-assertion and on a lively wit which often found expression in *englynion*.

His book *Dail Pren* contains an immense range of poetry, but perhaps he is best seen as a great Romantic poet in the earliest sense of that word. The unity of Man with the natural world is memorably expressed in the tree-and-fountain image of *'Mewn Dau Gae'*, generally considered to be his finest poem. But the expanded consciousness of the individual as he looks back to prehistory or out to the furthest stars is balanced in Waldo's work by a social sense which often finds expression in visionary and apocalyptic imagery, as in Blake: in his poems about Wales he perceives his own identity in terms of place and people, not as an abstraction. The will to resist is forcefully articulated in the emotional intonations of his verse, but where much patriotic poetry in Welsh is defensive and traditionalist, his takes a forward-looking, universalist form. The brotherhood of all men was for him a practical principle embedded in his experience of neighbourhood and community. For these reasons Waldo Williams is considered by many to be the twentieth century's most astonishingly original poet in the Welsh language.

For studies of the writer and his work see Dafydd Owen, *Dal Bridd y Dail Pren* (1972), the monograph by James Nicholas in the *Writers of Wales* series (1975) and that by Ned Thomas in the series *Llên y Llenor* (1985). The volume *Waldo: Teyrnged* (ed. James Nicholas, 1977) gathers together biographical and critical essays about the poet, three of his prose pieces and an extensive bibliography. The volume on Waldo Williams in the series *Cyfres y Meistri* (ed. Robert Rhys, 1981) brings together the great bulk of critical writing about the poet up to that date. See also Dyfnallt Morgan, *Waldo Williams: thema yn ei waith* (1974), the memorial number of *Y Traethodydd* (1971), the article by Saunders Lewis in *Meistri a'u Crefft* (ed. Gwynn ap Gwilym, 1981) and that by John Rowlands in *Ysgrifau Beirniadol IV* (ed. J. E. Caerwyn Williams, 1969); the poet's article on War and the State, first published in *Y Faner* in 1956, was translated by Ned Thomas and published in *Planet* (nos. 37/38, 1977).

WILLIAMS, WATKIN HEZEKIAH (Watcyn Wyn; 1844–1905), poet and teacher, a native of Brynaman, Carms., began working underground at the age of eight but, in 1874, entered the Presbyterian College, Carmarthen, to prepare for the Congregational ministry. He was never in charge of a specific congregation but became famous and widely respected as the Principal of *Ysgol y Gwynfryn*, Ammanford, a school where young men were prepared for the Nonconformist ministry. His publications include several volumes of poetry, notably *Caneuon* (1871), *Hwyr Ddifyrion* (1883) and *Cân a Thelyn* (1895), his translation into Welsh of the hymns of Sankey and Moody, *Odlau'r Efengyl* (1883), and two novels written in collaboration

with Elwyn Thomas, *Irfon Meredydd* (1907) and *Nansi, Merch y Pregethwr Dall* (1906). The most famous of his hymns is the one beginning '*Rwy'n gweld o bell y dydd yn dod*'. He shared a prize with Islwyn (William *Thomas) at an Eisteddfod in 1875 and won both the *Crown (1881) and the *Chair (1885). Two or three of his poems, translated, were introduced into the text of Edward *Thomas's *Beautiful Wales* (1905).

Watcyn Wyn's memoirs were edited by Gwili (John Jenkins) in 1907 and his biography was written by Pennar Griffiths (1915); see also the critical study by Bryan Martin Davies, *Rwy'n gweld o bell* (1980).

WILLIAMS, WILLIAM (Williams Pantycelyn or **Pantycelyn**; 1717–91), hymn-writer, poet and prose writer, was born at Cefn-coed in the parish of Llanfair-ar-y-bryn, Carms. His father, a farmer and elder of Cefnarthen Independent Church, was sixty-one years old when William was born, and his mother, the daughter of Pantycelyn, a neighbouring farm, was twenty-eight. On her husband's death in 1742 his widow moved to Pantycelyn, which she had inherited five years previously, and lived there until her death in 1784. The boy was educated locally and at Chancefield Nonconformist Academy near Talgarth, Brecs., under the exacting but stimulating tutelage of Vavasor Griffiths (1698?–1741). His original intention was to become a physician but, about 1737, soon after joining the Academy, he was converted by the preaching of Howel *Harris at Talgarth. He took deacon's orders in 1740 and was appointed curate to Theophilus *Evans at Llanwrtyd, Llanfihangel Abergwesyn and Llanddewi Abergwesyn, Brecs. In 1743, however, he was refused priest's orders because of his extra-parochial Methodist activities, and thereafter he devoted himself entirely to the work of the burgeoning Methodist movement. He spent the rest of his life as an itinerant preacher, a founder and overseer of Methodist societies (a field in which he was peculiarly talented) and, with Harris and Daniel *Rowland, was acknowledged as one of the three leaders of Welsh *Methodism. About 1748 he married Mary Francis of Llansawel, who also owned land in Llanfynydd, and they settled at Pantycelyn. Eight children were born to them, of whom the second son, John (1754–1828), was active in the Methodist movement. Williams's income as a farmer, minor landlord, publisher and perhaps tea-merchant, kept the family in reasonable comfort.

The career of William Williams as an author began with the publication of the first part of *Aleluia* (1744), a collection of hymns; five other parts appeared before 1747 and the six parts were issued in one volume in 1749. There followed *Hosanna i Fab Dafydd* in two parts (1751 and 1754), *Rhai Hymnau a Chaniadau Duwiol* (1759), *Caniadau y rhai sydd ar y Môr o Wydr* (1762, with further edns. in 1763, 1764 and 1773), *Ffarwel

Weledig, Groesaw Anweledig Bethau (1763, with two further parts in 1766 and 1769), *Gloria in Excelsis* (1771, with a further part in 1772), *Ychydig Hymnau* (1774) and *Rhai Hymnau Newyddion* (in three parts, 1781, 1782 and 1787). Williams also published two English collections, *Hosannah to the Son of David* (1759) and *Gloria in Excelsis* (1772). He is undoubtedly Wales's most important hymn-writer and is regarded by some as the country's most important poet. Although woefully uneven and often deliberately slipshod in his use of language, at his best he conveys religious passion with a rare immediacy and symbolic richness. It is fitting that, by common assent, Williams is known in Welsh as 'Y Pêr Ganiedydd' ('The Sweet Singer').

He did not confine himself to the writing of hymns. His long poem, *Golwg ar Deyrnas Crist* (1756, revised edn. 1764), portrays Christ's dominion in the Created Order, in Providence and in Grace; an important source was the work of William Durham (1637–1735). A second long poem, *Bywyd a Marwolaeth Theomemphus* (1764), traced the progress of the individual soul from reprobation to redemption and was, the author claimed, a work without exact precedent in poetry. He also wrote a number of shorter poems on religious themes, of which the most notable are '*Y Gân Benrhydd*' (1762) and '*Y Gerdd Newydd am Briodas*' (1762), and some thirty elegies upon the deaths of fellow-Methodists.

Pantycelyn was also a prose writer of distinction. His most ambitious work, *Pantheologia neu Hanes holl Grefyddau'r Byd* (1762, 1779), consisted largely of translated extracts from such authors as Paul Ricaut, Thomas Salmon and Hadrian Reland. More significant, although far shorter, are his original works, *Llythyr Martha Philopur* (1762), *Ateb Philo-Evangelius* (1763), *Crocodil Afon yr Aifft* (1767), *Hanes Bywyd a Marwolaeth Tri Wŷr o Sodom a'r Aifft* (1768), *Aurora Borealis* (1774), *Ductor Nuptiarum neu Gyfarwyddwr Priodas* (1777) and *Drws y Society Profiad* (1777); all of these were designed to further the spiritual growth of the converts of the Methodist Revival. Williams published nearly ninety books and pamphlets during his lifetime.

The major study of the writer published by Saunders *Lewis in the volume *Williams Pantycelyn* (1927) attempts to interpret his life and work in the light of medieval and *Counter-Reformation Catholic mysticism and modern studies in religious psychology. Lewis saw him as the total negation of the prevailing classical aesthetic of the medieval period in Wales and as the earliest exponent of *Romanticism in European literature. He traced Williams's spiritual development through his work, discerning in it vestiges of St. Bonaventure's Threefold Way. As Williams achieved spiritual maturity, Lewis observed in him a shifting of emphasis from the individual to the social, the

emergence of a new classical synthesis in which the earlier Romanticism is embraced and contained. Whatever may be thought of some of Lewis's premises and conclusions, his study revealed for the first time, and in the most brilliant fashion, Williams's stature as a major author and profound thinker.

The poetry of Williams Pantycelyn was collected by his son John in 1811, his poetry and prose by J. Kilsby Jones in 1867 and, in two volumes, by Nathaniel Cynhafal Jones (1887, 1891). The Board of Celtic Studies has embarked on a new collected edition of his works, of which the long poems (ed. Gomer M. Roberts, 1964) and the original prose works (ed. Garfield H. Hughes, 1967) have appeared so far. There are book-length studies of the writer by Gomer M. Roberts (1949, 1958) and John Gwilym Jones (1969); see also the essay by Glyn Tegai Hughes in the *Writers of Wales* series (1983), another by Derec Llwyd Morgan in the series *Llên y Llenor* (1983) and the article by Wyn Roberts, 'Saunders Lewis and Williams Pantycelyn: Notes for a Revaluation', in *The Anglo-Welsh Review* (vol. 15, no. 35, Summer, 1965), in which Lewis's arguments are castigated.

Williams, William (1781–1840), reckoned, with John *Elias and Christmas *Evans, one of the three outstanding preachers of his age, was born at Cwm-hyswn-ganol in the parish of Llanfachreth, Mer. Stirred in his thirteenth year by the preaching of the eccentric Rhys Davies (1772–1847), he became a member with the Independents and, after entering the Academy at Wrexham, developed into a preacher of charm, eloquence, imagination and warmth. At Wern and Harwd, near Wrexham, Denbs., from 1808 to 1836, he was a vigorous minister, founding new chapels and attracting many by his pulpit oratory and genial personality. Like others of the 'New System' among the Independents, he favoured a moderate type of Calvinism and became one of the leaders of his denomination.

Williams, William (1788–1865), industrialist and politician, was a native of Llanpumsaint, Carms. He amassed a great fortune in the cotton trade and, as Member of Parliament for Coventry from 1835 to 1847 and later for Lambeth from 1850 to 1865, became one of the foremost Radicals of his day, advocating the secret ballot, the extension of the franchise and other reforms. A self-made man and an indefatigable reformer and believer in progress, he wished all Welshmen to get on in the world but felt that they were held back for lack of English. It was his proposal made in the House of Commons in 1846 which led to the setting up of the Commission to enquire into the state of education in Wales, the reports of which became notorious as the *Blue Books* (1847). He published two pamphlets on educational matters (1848), for which he was attacked by Ieuan Gwynedd (Evan *Jones), and in 1863 he played a prominent part in the movement to establish the *University of Wales.

WILLIAMS, WILLIAM (Caledfryn; 1801–69), poet and critic, was born into a weaver's family at Bryn y Ffynnon, Denbigh. After a short period at Rotherham College he was ordained as an Independent minister in 1829 and, during the last forty years of his life, held the pastorate of Groes-wen, Glam. He was the author of five books: *Grawn Awen* (1826), *Drych Barddonol* (1839), *Grammadeg Cymreig* (1851), *Caniadau Caledfryn* (1856) and an autobiography (ed. Thomas Roberts, 1877) which also contains some of his verse and prose. As well as editing the works of Robert ap Gwilym Ddu (Robert *Williams) and Eos Gwynedd (John Thomas, 1742–1818), he was for many years the editor of several journals. A Liberal in politics, he supported Radical causes such as the Anti-Corn Law League, the Peace Society and the *Liberation Society, and gave evidence on behalf of Nonconformists to the Commissioners whose reports were subsequently published as the *Blue Books* (1847). But it was as an adjudicator at eisteddfodau that he achieved the greatest prominence. A severe critic, and sometimes scathing in his adjudication, he did much to improve the standards of poetry in his day by urging simplicity and directness. In his own work, his aim was to write objective poetry and with an *awdl* on the sinking of the *Rothesay Castle* he won the *Chair at the Beaumaris Eisteddfod of 1832.

A selection of Caledfryn's work was published by Owen M. Edwards in the series *Cyfres y Fil* (1913); for further details see the article by Gwilym Rees Hughes in *Llên Cymru* (vol. XII, nos. 1 and 2, 1972).

WILLIAMS, WILLIAM (Gwilym Cyfeiliog; 1801–76), poet, was born at Llanbrynmair, Mont., where he later kept a wool shop. A keen competitor at eisteddfodau, he wrote verse in the strict metres and was a master of the *englyn. He was the author of the well-known hymn which begins 'Caed trefn i faddau pechod'. His poems were collected posthumously in the volume *Caniadau Cyfeiliog* (1878). His son, **Richard Williams** (1835–1906), was the author of *Montgomeryshire Worthies* (1884) and the editor of a second edition of Philip *Yorke's *Royal Tribes of Wales* (1887).

WILLIAMS, WILLIAM (Carw Coch; 1808–72), see under CYMREIGYDDION Y CARW COCH.

WILLIAMS, WILLIAM (Creuddynfab; 1814–69), critic, was born at Creuddyn, Llandudno, Caerns. A stonemason's son, he had little formal education and began work as a farm labourer. From 1845 until 1862 he was employed as a railwayman in the Pennines, where he became a friend of John Ceiriog *Hughes. Returning to Wales as the first Secretary of the *National Eisteddfod Association, he remained in that post for less than two years, owing to poor health. He was considered in his day to be a progressive critic; he took issue in his sole published volume, *Y *Barddoniadur Cymmreig* (1855), with the *Neo-Classicism of poets such as Caledfryn (William *Williams), and encouraged young poets to write in the free metres, especially the lyric.

WILLIAMS, WILLIAM (Y Lefiad; *fl.* 1853), translator and author. His dates are not known although he was certainly living in Ystradgynlais, Brecs., in 1853. His translation of Harriet Beecher Stowe's *Uncle Tom's Cabin*, *Caban 'Newyrth Tom* (1853), and his book against the Mormons, *Dynoethiad Mormoniaeth . . . o enau tystion* (1853), brought him into prominence in his day.

WILLIAMS, WILLIAM (1850–1917), poet, was born at Abersychan, Mon., and was employed as a clerk for nearly fifty years by the Great Western Railway at Pontypool. A learned, saintly man and a keen *eisteddfodwr*, he was known as 'The Poet of Mount Pleasant' from his life-long adherence to the Congregational chapel of that name in Pontypool. One of his poems describes the massacre of Seisyll ap Dyfnwal and his men by the hirelings of *William de Braose; it is included, with poems on other Welsh themes, in the poet's only volume, *Songs of Siluria* (1916).

WILLIAMS, WILLIAM CRWYS (Crwys; 1875–1968), poet, was born at Craig-cefn-parc, Glam., and spent his life as a Congregational minister. He began writing poetry at an early age and was influenced more by the culture of his native district than by any writer, except perhaps John *Morris-Jones. His early poems tended to be versified sermons, although he avoided the worst excesses of the *Bardd Newydd and achieved a simplicity of expression and lyrical style in his more mature work. Archdruid from 1939 to 1947, he won the *Crown at the National Eisteddfod on three occasions: in 1910 for 'Ednyfed Fychan', in 1911 for 'Gwerin Cymru' and in 1919 for 'Morgan Llwyd o Wynedd'. He published four volumes of his verse, namely *Cerddi Crwys* (1920), *Cerddi Newydd Crwys* (1924), *Trydydd Cerddi Crwys* (1935) and *Cerddi Crwys: y pedwerydd llyfr* (1944). Some of his shorter lyrics, such as 'Dysgub y Dail', are among the best-known poems in the Welsh language.

WILLIAMS, WILLIAM DAVID (1900–85), poet, was born at Llawr y Betws, near Corwen, Mer., and educated at the University College of North Wales, Bangor. He was a teacher at Barmouth until his retirement in 1961. Among his published works are *Adlais Odlau* (1939), *Cerddi'r Hogiau* (1941), *Cân ac Englyn* (1951), *Camp a Rhemp* (1960) and *Rhyw Bwt o Lawr y Betws* (1975). A master of *cynghanedd, W. D. Williams won the *Chair at the National Eistedddfod in 1965 and was prominent among the poets who founded *Cymdeithas Cerdd Dafod in 1976. His most famous *englyn is the one beginning 'O Dad, yn deulu dedwydd', which is frequently heard recited as a grace before a meal.

WILLIAMS, WILLIAM LLEWELYN

(1867–1922), journalist, politician and historian, was born at Brownhill, Llansadwrn, Carms. Educated at Llandovery College and Brasenose College, Oxford, he became the first editor of The South Wales Post, the new Radical newspaper at Swansea, but abandoned journalism for the law in 1897. His heart had for long been in history, *Nationalism and Liberal politics and, after several attempts, he was elected Member of Parliament in 1906 for Carmarthen Boroughs, a seat he held until its abolition in 1918. In 1912 he took silk, became 'leader' of the South Wales Circuit and successively Recorder of Swansea (1914–15) and of Cardiff (1915–22). As a journalist he had campaigned against monoglot English judges in Wales and later he was a strong advocate of *Disestablishment of the Church and of *Home Rule. A pacifist who was cajoled to support the War in 1914, he became increasingly uneasy and finally broke with David *Lloyd George and the Liberal Party; he stood against the official Liberal for the Cardiganshire seat in 1921 and lost narrowly.

His writing in Welsh was unpretentious: he published Gwilym a Benni Bach (1897), Gŵr y Dolau (1899) and 'Slawer Dydd (1918), the last of which had become very popular in serial form in Y *Beirniad. His main historical interest lay in the *Tudor period, essays upon which, appearing first in the Transactions of the Honourable Society of *Cymmrodorion, were collected in The Making of Modern Wales (1919). His thesis that schisms in the English College at Rome were the root cause of the failure of the Counter-Reformation in Wales is the most stimulating and enduring of these writings.

WILLIAMS, WILLIAM NANTLAIS

(Nantlais; 1874–1959), poet and hymn-writer, was born at Pencader, Carms., and later became a minister with the Calvinistic Methodists. Besides editing the periodicals Yr Efengylydd, Y Lladmerydd and Trysorfa'r Plant, he published two volumes of lyrics, Murmuron y Nant (1898) and Murmuron Newydd (1926). His best hymns for adults are to be found in the hymnals of the two Methodist Churches and in his collection Emynau'r Daith (1949). Among his most familiar hymns are 'Plant bach Iesu Grist ydym ni bob un', 'Draw draw yn China' and 'Uno wnawn â'r nefol gôr'. Part of his important correspondence with Eluned *Morgan between 1924 and 1938, as well as an account of his visit to *Patagonia, have been published in Tyred Drosodd (ed. Dafydd Ifans, 1977).

There is an account of his life in his autobiography, O

Gopa Bryn Nebo (1967); see also the article by D. Eirwyn Morgan in the Bulletin of Cymdeithas Emynau Cymru (vol. 1, 1968), John Thickens, Emynau a'u Hawduriaid (1961) and H. Turner Evans, A Bibliography of Welsh Hymnology to 1960 (1977).

WILLIAMS, WILLIAM RETLAW JEFFERSON

(1863–1944), historian and editor, was born at Brecon, an elder brother of Alice Matilda Langland *Williams, and was educated as a day-boy at Cheltenham College. He trained as a lawyer but, having broken down in his first case, he lived thereafter at Talybont-on-Usk, Brecs., as a virtual recluse. Uncreative but industrious, he bought and copied Army and Navy Lists as well as Calendars of State Papers, and employed agents in London to copy records which he could not himself reach. His book The Parliamentary History of the Principality of Wales 1541–1895 (1895) is a useful work of reference. It was followed by Parliamentary histories of Worcester (1897), Gloucester (1898), and Oxford (1899), and by The History of the Great Sessions of Wales 1542–1830, together with the Lives of the Welsh Judges (1899) and Official Lists of the Duchy and County of Lancaster (1901), all of which were published in Brecon at his own expense. Between 1905 and 1907 he produced Old Wales, a journal modelled upon Notes and Queries, to which he had been a contributor, but by this time he had exhausted his share of the family wealth. In 1911 he had to sell much of his valuable library in order to finance his last work, which was to have been a complete list of officers who had served in the British Army. This list never appeared and his papers, deposited with a Cambridge College, have been lost.

WILLIAMS-ELLIS, CLOUGH

(1883–1978), architect and author. Born at Gayton, Northants., of Welsh parents, and educated at Trinity College, Cambridge, he served with the Welsh Guards in Flanders during the First World War. In 1925 he became the owner of the old mansion known as Aber Ia, near Penrhyndeudraeth, Mer., and transformed it into the focal point of an Italianate dream-village, now famous as Portmeirion, which has been called 'the Xanadu of Wales'. The estate, with its delightful eclecticism of styles, has often been used as a film set and Noël Coward is said to have written Blithe Spirit while staying there in 1940. Its creator, knighted in 1972, was a distinguished member of his profession and the author of numerous books on architecture. He also wrote two volumes of autobiography, Architect Errant (1971) and Around the World in Ninety Years (1978), and Portmeirion, the Place and its Meaning (1963).

His wife, Amabel Williams-Ellis (1894–1984), was born in Surrey, a sister of Lytton Strachey. Among her publications are An Anatomy of Poetry (1922), a collection of short stories entitled Volcano (1931), the novels Noah's

Ark (1926), *To Tell the Truth* (1933), *The Big Firm* (1938) and *Learn to Love First* (1939). She collaborated with her husband in the writing of a short novel, *Headlong down the Years* (1951), which was intended to combat what they considered to be the despoliation of the countryside of north Wales by the building of a hydro-electric power station. A volume of her autobiography, *All Stracheys are Cousins*, appeared in 1983.

Williams-Wynn family, The, of Wynnstay, Ruabon, Denbs., was by the nineteenth century the greatest landed family in Wales, owning 150,000 acres in Denbighshire, Merioneth and Montgomeryshire. Like the Habsburgs, they married their way to territorial power. William Williams (1634–1700), whose father was rector of Llantrisant, Ang., became Speaker of the House of Commons and Attorney General. He bought the Llanforda estate, near Oswestry, in 1675, married the heiress of the Glascoed estate, Denbs., and was created a baronet in 1688. His son, also named William Williams (d. 1740), the second baronet, married Jane Thelwall, the heiress of the Plas y Ward estate and the granddaughter of Sir John Wynn (1553–1627), the first baronet of Gwydir (see under WYNN FAMILY). This marriage also brought to the family the estates which Sir John Wynn (d. 1719), the last baronet of Gwydir, had acquired through his marriage with the heiress of Eyton Evans of Wattstay, Denbs. William Williams's son, Watkin Williams (1693–1749), the third baronet, married the heiress of the Llwydiarth estate, Mont. A leading Jacobite and persecutor of the Methodists, he took the surname Wynn and changed the house's name from Wattstay to Wynnstay.

Thereafter one Watkin Williams Wynn followed another in a long succession. The fourth baronet (1748–96), who acquired the Mathafarn estate, Mont., and was the friend of Handel and Joshua Reynolds, was President of the Honourable Society of *Cymmrodorion, an office also held by his son, the fifth baronet (1772–1840). From 1716 to 1885 Denbighshire was represented in Parliament by an almost unbroken line of Wynns, but after the division of the constituency in 1885 the seventh baronet was defeated in East Denbighshire by the Liberal candidate, George Osborne *Morgan. The family also enjoyed extensive political influence in Montgomeryshire, which was represented from 1799 to 1850 by the fifth baronet's brother, Charles, one of the three Welsh Members of Parliament to reach Cabinet rank during the nineteenth century. The Wynns were enlightened landlords and their territorial influence was such that successive Sir Watkins were known as the 'Uncrowned Kings of North Wales'. The family retains extensive land holdings but after the death of the tenth baronet (1904–51), their mansion at Glanllyn,

near Bala, Mer., became a centre for *Urdd Gobaith Cymru and Wynnstay now houses Lindisfarne College.

For further details see Askew Roberts, *Wynnstay and the Wynns* (1876), P. D. G. Thomas, 'Parliamentary elections in Denbighshire 1716–1741' in the *Journal* of the National Library of Wales (vol. XI, 1959) and Jane Morgan, 'Denbighshire's *Annus Mirabilis*' in *The Welsh History Review* (1974).

WILSON, JOHN (1626–*c*.1695), playwright, was born in London of Welsh parents and was called to the Bar in 1652. A fervent Royalist, he became Recorder of Londonderry about 1681. He was the author of two political essays, *A Discourse of Monarchy* (1684) and *Jus Regium Coronae* (1686?), but was best known in his day for two comedies, *The Cheats* (1662) and *The Projectors* (1665), and two tragedies, *Andronicus Commenius* (1664) and *Belphegor* (1690). The first of his comedies contains many references to the Welsh and was played on the London stage to the end of the century.

Wilson, Richard (1713–82), landscape painter, was born at Penegoes, near Machynlleth, Mont., and brought up at Mold, Flints.; he was a kinsman of Thomas *Pennant. Primarily a portrait painter until 1750, he spent seven years thereafter in Italy, where he trained himself to become a landscape artist in the Continental Grand Style. His painting 'The Destruction of the Children of Niobe' was exhibited to critical acclaim in London in 1760. The combination of classical idealism and topographical realism was a hallmark of his style, many of his subjects deriving from antique literature. Besides Italian views, he painted English and Welsh landscapes such as those of Snowdon and *Cadair Idris, many of which brought him financial security. But his career foundered in the early 1770s, mainly as the result of an irascible temper, alcoholism and chronically bad health, and during his last years he was almost completely forgotten. Returning to Wales shortly before his death, he was buried at Mold. He is now generally regarded as the father of British landscape painting.

For an account of his life and work see the catalogue by David H. Solkin to the exhibition of Richard Wilson's paintings held at the Tate Gallery in 1982; see also the study by W. G. Constable (1953).

Wind of Heaven, The (1945), a play in six scenes by Emlyn *Williams—his best and profoundest play—was inspired by a wartime visit to Palestine, where the singing of Arab peasants reminded him of Welsh miners singing at Pen-y-Maes, Glanrafon, and suggested a vision of Wales as Holy Land. Set in the village of Blestin in 1856, the play tells of the redemption accomplished by the latter-day Christ-child, Gwyn, a servant's illegitimate son. He brings back happiness and song to the bereaved villagers, faith to the materialistic expatriate Ambrose Ellis and the embittered Dilys Parry, and reunites the lovers Menna and Islwyn by bringing the last-named and other victims of the Crimean typhus back to life. The sacrifice which Gwyn has to pay is his own death in agony. The play, mysterious and deeply moving, is distinctively Welsh in setting, in its evocation of community and in the use of the Welsh language and of song. G. Wilson Knight pointed out that it belongs to a tradition which can be traced to the Middle Ages.

Winni Finni Hadog, see under TE YN Y GRUG (1959).

Winter's Eve, see HOLLANTIDE.

Winwaed Field, The Battle of (654), was fought on the banks of an unidentified river near Leeds, Yorks., between the Bernicians under King Oswy and a composite force of Mercians led by King Penda, who was killed there, and of Britons under a number of their princes. The Bernician victory made permanent the separation of the Britons of Wales from their allies in Strathclyde which had been effected by the battle of Chester (615).

Witches, old women who were believed to have the power of casting spells over people and animals, were found in Wales until the late nineteenth century. Many place-names refer to the superstitious belief in witches and many traditional stories about them are recorded in books and manuscripts. Some of the most famous witches were Sal Fawr of Clydau, Pembs., Yr Hen Jem of Penderyn, Brecs., Beti Ty'n Twll of Capel Celyn, Mer., and Mari Berllan Piter of Aberarth, Cards. Others belonged to specific families and districts, such as the Witches of Llanddona, Ang., of whom Lisi Blac and Bela Fawr were the most notorious. Among the powers popularly attributed to witches were the ability to ride a broomstick through the air, to tell fortunes and to heal and cause diseases by means of charms. The evil they caused could be undone only by Y *Dyn Hysbys. It was said that they were able to take the form of a hare and that only a silver bullet could kill them. During the Middle Ages the right to punish witches belonged to the lord of the manor and to the Church but between 1563 and 1736, when the law was amended, they were persecuted in the courts, although few in Wales were sentenced to death. There were, however, unofficial methods of ascertaining whether a woman was a witch, as is vividly illustrated by the description of the drowning of Betsan in the river Wnion in the novel Y Stafell Ddirgel (1969) by Marion *Eames.

For further details see Eirlys Gruffydd, *Gwrachod Cymru* (1980).

Withered Root, The (1927), the first novel of Rhys *Davies. Like Evan *Roberts, the leader of the religious revival of 1904–05, its hero Reuben Daniels is a handsome young Welsh-speaking collier. He leaves the pit and, joining a revivalist sect known as the Corinthians, preaches throughout Wales at large and emotional meetings. Eventually, however, sick and disillusioned, he returns to his mother's home to die, the conflict between spirit, mind and flesh having brought about his destruction.

Wizard, see DYN HYSBYS.

Wladfa, Y, see under PATAGONIA.

Wogan, Thomas (*fl.* 1648–69), colonel and regicide, was the third son of John Wogan of Wiston, Pembs., who represented the County in every Parliament from 1614 until his death in 1644 and was one of the two 'fathers' of the Parliamentary cause in west Wales. Unlike his brothers, Thomas did not serve in Pembrokeshire during the first *Civil War, but in 1648 he was ordered to Wales by Cromwell and earned special commendation from Colonel Horton at the battle of St. Fagans, where one of his brothers, fighting on the Royalist side, was captured. Member of Parliament for Cardigan from 1646, he sat again in the recalled Rump Parliament of 1659. He was one of the judges who tried Charles I in January 1649 and one of two Welshmen who signed the King's death-warrant. Put on trial in his absence at the Restoration and excepted from the Act of Oblivion, he surrendered in 1664, was clapped into the Tower of London, but escaped a month later and was known to be in Utrecht in 1666 and still alive three years later.

Women of Mumbles Head, The, see ACE, MAGGIE (b. 1854) and JESSIE (b. 1861).

Women who possessed Eve's Beauty, Three, a Triad which names Helen of Troy, Polixena the daughter of Priam, and Diadema (Dido), the lover of Aeneas. In The *Red Book of Hergest and in some other manuscripts this Triad is appended to that of the *Men who Possessed Adam's Qualities. It has the distinction of having been quoted in full by *Dafydd ap Gwilym, who added his sweetheart (an unnamed girl from Gwynedd) as a fourth woman. A similar comparison was made later by *Gutun Owain.

Wondrous Child, The, an international folk-narrative. The child, often after an extraordinary conception and birth, demonstrates his heroic virtues through feats of strength, wisdom or bravery. He may grow to the size of a boy twice or three times his age, as do *Pryderi and *Lleu Llawgyffes, or he may demonstrate great fleetness as does Peredur (see under TAIR RHAMANT) when he herds two wild hinds along with his goats. *Myrddin (Merlin) displays his precocity in wisdom and prophecy when, sought out by *Vortigern as a fatherless child, he astonishes the king's magicians with his accurate disclosure of the red and white dragons (see under EMRYS WLEDIG). The infant *Taliesin, after his transmogrification from the shape-shifting Gwion Bach, speaks verses of comfort to his rescuer, *Elffin ap Gwyddno, and as a youth defeats the poets of *Maelgwn Gwynedd in competition. The deeds of such secular heroes are paralleled by those in the *Lives of the Saints, for many of whom it was claimed that, while still children, they had learned to read in a single day, mastered Scripture and argued theology with their elders.

Wood family, The, the principal family of Welsh gypsies. Its founder was Abram Wood (1699?–1799), who migrated from England to Wales with his wife Sarah in the eighteenth century. He was mentioned by Twm o'r Nant (Thomas *Edwards) in his interlude *Pleser a Gofid* (1787), and his descendants became known in Welsh as '*Teulu Abram Wood*' ('Abram Wood's Family'), a name later used for gypsies in general. Among the Woods were numbered many colourful characters such as Ellen Ddu, Albaina, Sylvaina and Saiforella, all celebrated practitioners of the arts of magic and fortune-telling. Many of the family had musical gifts and more than a score of Welsh harpists were descendants of Abram Wood. They included John Wood Jones (1800–44), the harpist employed by Lady Llanover (Augusta Waddington *Hall), Jeremiah Wood (c.1778–1867), the harpist at *Gogerddan, Cards., and John Roberts (1816–94), whose mother was Abram Wood's granddaughter. Ellen Ddu is reputed to have been able to recite some three hundred folk-tales from memory, many of which were recorded from the lips of her grandson Mathew by John Sampson and Dora Yeats. Sampson also compiled a grammar of the Romany language as spoken by the Woods, including in it a voluminous collection of their traditional sayings.

For further details see Eldra Jarman and A. O. H. Jarman, *Y Sipsiwn Cymreig* (1979); see also John Sampson (ed.), *Gypsy Folk Tales* (1933).

Worthines of Wales, The (1587), a topographical morality in verse by the English poet Thomas Churchyard (1520?–1604), a native of Shrewsbury and for forty years a soldier. Disillusioned, he saw Wales as 'the soundest state', possessed of the positive values he cherished, namely loyalty to the Queen, concord, courtesy, hospitality and obedience to the law. The poem purports to describe a journey (the account is, in fact, based on the notes of many journeys) to Monmouthshire and Breconshire, back to Ludlow and Shrewsbury, then into Denbighshire and Flintshire. Accurate observation is supported by a strong sense of the grandeur and simplicity of country life, a morality shed by mountains, while the interspersed discussion of antiquities is chiefly Arthurian. Churchyard insists that Shropshire was once part of Wales.

For further details see the article by Barbara Dennis in *The Anglo-Welsh Review* (vol. 18, no. 42, 1975).

Writers of Wales, a series of monographs on the lives and works of the more important Welsh and Anglo-Welsh writers, was launched in 1970. Published in an elegant format by the *University of Wales Press on the *Welsh Arts Council's behalf, it is edited by Meic *Stephens and R. Brinley Jones. Besides essays on individual writers, the series includes critical studies of the *Cynfeirdd, the *Gogynfeirdd, *Pedair Cainc y Mabinogi, Latin writers of the Renaissance and the *Bardd Gwlad. With a total of sixty-two titles published (1985) and with at least a further thirty titles commissioned, the series is unique in presenting an introduction to the literature of Wales through the medium of English.

Wrnach, a giant named in the legend of *Culhwch and Olwen. One of the tasks set by Ysbaddaden Bencawr as a condition for winning his daughter is that Culhwch must acquire the giant's sword. This feat is accomplished by *Cai who then decapitates Wrnach with the weapon. It has been suggested that the episode is concerned not merely with the acquisition of the sword but with an old mythical tradition about the hero's campaign against the King of *Annwfn.

Wroth, William (1576?–1641), Puritan leader, was born near Abergavenny, Mon., and educated at Oxford, from which he returned to hold the living of Llanfaches in his native county. Among those who came under his influence were Walter *Cradock and William *Erbery. The first 'gathered church' in Wales was established at Llanfaches in 1638 under Wroth's leadership; it consisted at first of Independents and Baptists in near-equal numbers, but later it developed as in Independent cause. A few examples of Wroth's poetry have been preserved, including two *Tribannau* which were included by R. Geraint *Gruffydd in the volume *In That Gentile Country* (1976).

Wynn family, The, of Gwydir, Caerns., claimed descent from *Owain Gwynedd. In the early fourteenth century Dafydd ap Gruffydd of Nantconwy married Efa, the heiress of Gruffydd Fychan, who owned estates in *Eifionydd. Among their descendants, a quarrelsome and land-hungry clan, was Maredudd ab Ieuan of Y Gesail Gyfarch in Eifionydd, who bought the Gwydir estate in the Conwy Valley about 1500. His son, John Wyn ap Maredudd (d. 1559), rebuilt Gwydir and was involved in the suppression of the bandits known as *Gwylliaid

Cochion Mawddwy. The son of John Wyn ap Maredudd, Morus or Maurice (d. 1580), adopted the surname Wynn and, like his father, represented Caernarfonshire in Parliament.

Maurice's son, Sir John Wynn (1553–1627), was a splendid example of the rumbustious, grasping, litigious gentry of early modern Wales. Educated at All Souls College, Oxford, and at the Inner Temple, he dominated the politics of Caernarfonshire for nearly half a century and was involved in numerous commercial enterprises for the development of his estates. A scholar and a patron of poets, he was imbued with a Renaissance love of beauty. To stress the distinction of his lineage, he wrote *The History of the Gwydir Family* (not, after all, published until 1770), in which he noted what 'a great temporal blessing it is . . . to a man to find that he is well descended'. He also corresponded with John *Davies of Mallwyd about the publication of Sir Thomas *Wiliems's Latin–Welsh dictionary.

Of Sir John's ten sons, the second, Richard (1588–1649), succeeded to the baronetcy. Treasurer to Queen Henrietta Maria, Richard Wynn avoided involvement in the *Civil War, as did his brother Owen (1592–1660), the third baronet, but Owen's son, Richard (c. 1625–74), the fourth baronet, was imprisoned for his part in the Royalist rising of 1659. On his death, the baronetcy was inherited by John Wynn (1628–1719), the son of Henry, the tenth son of the first baronet. Dying childless, John Wynn was the last baronet of Gwydir and the estate then passed to the fourth baronet's daughter, Mary, who married Lord Willoughby d'Eresby (1660–1723), who later became the Duke of Ancaster. Their granddaughter, Priscilla (1761–1828), married Peter Burrell (1779–1820) who was created Baron Gwydir in 1796, and their great-grandson, Lord Willoughby d'Eresby (1830–1910), who was created Earl of Ancaster in 1892, began to dispose of the Gwydir estate, some thirty thousand acres in all, during the 1890s.

For further details see John Ballinger (ed.), *The History of the Gwydir family* (1927), the *Calendar of the Wynn papers 1515–1690* published by the National Library of Wales in 1926, E. G. Jones, 'County Politics and Electioneering 1558–1625' in the *Transactions of the Caernarfonshire Historical Society* (1939), W. O. Williams, *Tudor Gwynedd* (1958), J. K. Gruenfelder, 'The Wynns of Gwydir and Parliamentary Elections in Wales 1604–40' in *The Welsh History Review* (vol. 9, no. 2, 1978) and J. G. Jones, 'Sir John Wynn of Gwydir and his tenants' in *The Welsh History Review* (vol. 11, no. 1, 1982).

Wynne family, The, of Peniarth, Mer., was descended from Robert Wynn (d. 1670) of Glyncywarch, Mer., whose eldest son, Owen Wynn, was the ancestor of the Ormsby-Gore family, later the Lords Harlech. Robert's fourth son, William Wynne I (d. 1700), married Elizabeth, the heiress of the Joneses of Wern, Mer. Thereafter William Wynnes followed in a long succession. William Wynne IV (1745–96) married Jane, the heiress of Lewis Owen of Peniarth. Their grandson, William Watkin Edward Wynne (1801–80), was a distinguished antiquary, genealogist and historian. It was he who became owner, through the will of Sir Robert Vaughan (d. 1859), of Hengwrt and *Nannau and of the great library collected at Hengwrt by Robert *Vaughan (1592–1667). He was President of the *Cambrian Archaeological Association and contributed a large number of articles on Welsh history and antiquities to *Archaeologia Cambrensis* and other journals. A supporter of the *Oxford Movement, he gave the living of Llanegryn to Griffith Arthur Jones (1827–1906), who later became the leader of the High Church Movement in Cardiff. Elected Member of Parliament for the County in 1852, he found his tractarian sympathies an issue in the General Election of 1859 when he was challenged by a Nonconformist candidate, David Williams of Castell Deudraeth. After Wynne's narrow victory, a number of Liberal voters and abstainers were victimized by Tory landowners. His son, William Wynne VII (1840–1909), the owner of estates in north-west Wales, was elected Member of Parliament for Merioneth in 1865 but his withdrawal from the contest in 1868 allowed David Williams to be elected unopposed, thus initiating Liberal hegemony over the seat. It was William Wynne VII, dying childless, who sold the Hengwrt-Peniarth library to Sir *John Williams in 1898. See also PENIARTH MANUSCRIPTS.

For further details see W. W. E. Wynne, *A History of the Parish of Llanegryn* (1879) and G. Tibbot, 'W. W. E. Wynne of Peniarth' in the *Journal* of the Merioneth Historical and Record Society (1952).

Wynne, Edith (1842–97), singer, born at Northop, Flints., was a great favourite as a soloist at the *National Eisteddfod and the first Welsh singer to win fame in the USA, where she was known as 'The Welsh Nightingale'.

WYNNE, ELLIS (1671–1734), devotional writer, was born at Y Lasynys, a substantial farmhouse between Talsarnau and Harlech, Mer., the son of Edward Wynne of the Glyncywarch family (see under WYNNE FAMILY). Educated at Jesus College, Oxford, where he may have been associated with Edward *Lhuyd, he was ordained an Anglican priest in 1704 and presented to the rectorship of Llanbedr and Llandanwg in his native district. In 1711 he moved to nearby Llanfair, remaining there until his death. He is remembered as the author of *Gweledigaetheu y Bardd Cwsc* (1703), a work written from the standpoint of a Welsh Churchman and Royalist, but he also published *Rheol Buchedd Sanctaidd* (1701), a translation of the eighteenth edition of Jeremy Taylor's *The Rule and Exercises of Holy Living* (1650), in which he captured the original's refinement of expression.

Wynne also produced an edition of the Welsh Book of Common Prayer (1710). After his death, his son Edward published *Prif Addysc y Cristion* (1755), which includes a short explanation of the Catechism, together with a number of prayers, hymns and carols composed by Ellis Wynne.

For a detailed discussion of Wynne's work see Gwyn Thomas, *Y Bardd Cwsg a'i Gefndir* (1971) and the same author's monograph in the *Writers of Wales* series (1984); see also the chapter by D. Tecwyn Lloyd in *Y Traddodiad Rhyddiaith* (ed. Geraint Bowen, 1970).

Wynnstay, see under WILLIAMS-WYNN FAMILY.

Wythnos yng Nghymru Fydd (lit. 'A week in the Wales of the future'; 1957), a science-fiction novel by Islwyn Ffowc *Elis, tells how Ifan Powell is projected into two possible futures for a Wales which might exist in the year 2033. The greater part of the story deals with his transference under the supervision of Dr Heinkel, a scientist well versed in the mysteries of time-space, the fourth dimension and psychological suggestion, with the welcome he receives from Dr Llywarch and with his subsequent experiences.

The first future is one of prosperity and happiness for a pacifist and Welsh patriot: Ifan rejoices as he sees and hears the Welsh language, learns that Wales enjoys self-government and has taken its place among the peace-loving nations of the world, and appreciates that Welsh Christians are at last united. The government is in the hands of the Co-operative Party, but the enemies of Welsh freedom are still plotting and Ifan is abducted by a group known as the Purple Shirts. He escapes and returns to the Wales of the 1950s but, drawn back by the memory of Dr Llywarch's daughter, arranges to be sent into the future once more. On his second visit he finds an entirely different country, a Wales which has lost its language and identity, a province now called Western England. Among the more memorable scenes is the one in which Ifan, during a visit to Bala, is taken to see a deranged old woman who is said to speak sometimes in a language which no one else can understand. He persuades her to join him in reciting the words of the twenty-third Psalm but, her memory of the language almost extinguished, she reverts to muttering in English, whereupon he realizes that he has seen with his own eyes the death of the Welsh language. This novel, not the best of the author's works, marred as it is by propaganda, was nevertheless one of the first examples of science fiction in Welsh, a genre to which Islwyn Ffowc Elis was later to make an important contribution.

YZ

Yale or **Iâl**, a commot of *Powys Fadog. In 1282 it was linked with *Maelor Gymraeg to form the lordship of Bromfield and Yale which was granted to John Warenne, Earl of Surrey. Bromfield and Yale passed by marriage to the Fitzalan family in 1347 and to the Mowbray family in 1415. After the death of the Duke of York, the husband of Anne Mowbray, in 1483, it was granted to Sir William Stanley, but became the property of the Crown after the attainder of Stanley in 1495 and was incorporated into the county of Denbigh in 1536. The attempt to grant the lordship to William Bentinck, Duke of Portland, in 1695, led to strenuous and successful opposition in Parliament. Among the members of the Yale family of Plas yn Iâl was Elihu Yale (1649–1721), whose grants to the college at New Haven, Connecticut, induced the college to adopt the name of Yale.

'Ymadawiad Arthur' (lit. 'The passing of Arthur'), an *awdl* by T. Gwynn *Jones with which he won the *Chair at the National Eisteddfod of 1902. *Arthur, severely wounded in battle and left in the care of *Bedwyr, orders him to throw his sword *Caledfwlch into a nearby lake, to watch what happens and to bring him a detailed account. The knight considers hiding the intricately fashioned sword because he believes it to be the only weapon which will defend the nation, but eventually, rather than invoke Arthur's wrath, he hurls it high above the lake. As it falls, a strong arm grasps the hilt and draws it under the water. After relating what he has seen, Bedwyr is commanded to carry the king to the shore of the lake, whereupon a barge appears to carry Arthur to *Ynys Afallon. Saddened, Bedwyr is left to return alone to the battlefield.

Although T. Gwynn Jones was indebted to Tennyson's '*Morte d'Arthur*' (1842) for both the plan and sequence of events in his poem, it is structurally the superior composition. The elegant language and brilliant style which are among the poem's qualities were revolutionary in their day and the poem contains some of the best-known descriptive passages in the Welsh language. It marked a turning-point in the poet's own creative work and also provided impetus for the renaissance in Welsh literature which was under way at the turn of the century.

The *awdl* was included in the volume *Ymadawiad Arthur a Chaniadau Eraill* (1926) and in *Caniadau* (1934); each version differs slightly from that published in 1902. For critical discussion see the adjudication by John Morris-Jones (under the pseudonym Tir na n-Og) in *Y Cymro* (18 Sept., 1902), the article by R. A. Griffiths in *Y Cymmrodor* (vol. XVI, 1903), the article by D. Myrddin Lloyd in *Yr Athro* (vol. VII, 1934), the notes by Thomas Parry in *Y Llenor* (vol. XXVIII, 1949) and the article by Saunders Lewis in *Y Traethodydd* (vol. CXXVI, 1971).

Ymborth yr Eneit (lit. 'The food of the soul'; 1346), a religious work (the earliest text is in Jesus College MS 2), is the third and only surviving part of a larger work, *Cysegrlan Fuchedd*, a medieval tract on holy living. Concerned particularly with spirituality and mysticism, it is not a translation, but the original writing of an anonymous Dominican friar who was a master of the theology and prose of his day.

'Ymddiddan Arthur a'r Eryr' (lit. 'The colloquy of Arthur and the eagle'), a dramatic dialogue of some fifty *englynion* spoken by *Arthur and his nephew Eliwlad, who has been transformed (like *Lleu Llawgyffes) into an eagle. The religious content of the poem indicates that it was composed by a monk or a hermit not later than 1150. It conforms with the older genre of the *ymddiddan cyfarch*, a poem of greeting between two interlocutors, of whom one is unknown to the other until, in the course of the dialogue, mutual identification is established. Other examples are the verse dialogues between Gwalchmai and Drystan, *Taliesin and Ugnach, *Gwenhwyfar and Melwas. All these poems are composed in the old type of three-line *englyn milwr* and share metrical and linguistic features which point to an original date of composition prior to 1100. Their narrative context seems to have been explained by a prose accompaniment which has been lost. The scene of this colloquy is set in Cornwall and Arthur is portrayed as a semi-pagan ruler more closely akin to the Arthur in the tale of *Culhwch and Olwen than to the imperial ruler of *Geoffrey of Monmouth's *Historia Regum Britanniae*. Once Arthur has discovered his nephew's identity, he enquires of the eagle whether war could free him from his enchantment, but the eagle replies, after giving other spiritual advice, that death is the ultimate fate of all Mankind and that opposition to God is in vain.

For further details see the article by Ifor Williams in the *Bulletin* of the Board of Celtic Studies (vol. II, 1925) and another by T. Gwynn Jones in *Aberystwyth Studies* (vol. VIII, 1926). For Eliwlod see Rachel Bromwich, *Trioedd Ynys Prydein* (1961) and for '*ymddiddan*' as a technical term for a verse dialogue see the article by Brynley F. Roberts in *Astudiaethau ar yr Hengerdd* (ed. Rachel Bromwich and R. Brinley Jones, 1978).

'Ymddiddan Llywelyn a Gwrnerth' (lit. 'The colloquy of Llywelyn and Gwrnerth'), a series of *englynion* of the old type which is found in *The *Red Book of Hergest*. In the first part Gwrnerth, addressed by Llywelyn, replies that he is on the verge of death and begs to be given the last rites. Gwrnerth, in the second part, addresses Llywelyn but the latter does not recognize him. It is possible that there once existed a piece of prose linking the two parts, but it has not survived.

'Ymddiddan Myrddin a Thaliesin' (lit. 'The colloquy of Merlin and Taliesin'), a poem in *The *Black Book of Carmarthen* which brings together the prophet *Myrddin and the supernatural poet *Taliesin to impart their arcane knowledge to each other. The poem's interest is mainly historical in that it records details of early battles and their participants, particularly the fateful battle of Arfderydd and an attack on Dyfed by *Maelgwn Gwynedd. The poem, which has been dated to the second half of the eleventh century, seems to have inspired the dialogue between *Telgesinus* and *Merlinus* in *Geoffrey of Monmouth's **'Vita Merlini'*, although the subject-matter of the conversation there is very different.

The text was edited by A. O. H. Jarman (1951).

'Ymddiddan y Corff a'r Enaid' (lit. 'The colloquy between the body and the spirit'), a poem of some hundred and sixty lines preserved in *The *Black Book of Carmarthen*, is thought to have been written before 1100. It consists of a short introduction and three speeches, two by the Soul and one by the Body. The Soul criticizes the Body for its attachment to worldly riches, its devotion to lust and its neglect of religious duties. In its answer the Body excuses itself by referring to its worldly descent and claims that it was created out of seven elements: fire, earth, wind, mist, flowers and two others which are missing from the text. In its second speech the Soul declares its hope that both Body and Soul will be delivered on the Day of Judgement.

Other examples of Welsh poems on this subject, which was popular during the Middle Ages, are found in *The Red Book of Talgarth* and in Peniarth Manuscript 50. There is also extant a Welsh prose version, attributed to *Iolo Goch, of a Latin poem thought to be the work of Walter *Map, '*Dialogus Inter Corpus et Animam*'.

For further details see the article by Bobi Jones in *Ysgrifau Beirniadol V* (ed. J. E. Caerwyn Williams, 1970).

Yn Chwech ar Hugain Oed (lit. 'Twenty-six years old'; 1959), the second part of D. J. *Williams's autobiography, encompasses twenty years of his life and opens with a picture of Abernant, the house to which the family moved from Penrhiw, the 'Old Farmhouse' of the first volume, *Hen Dŷ Ffarm* (1953). A whole society is portrayed here, including the affairs of school, chapel and tavern. The author describes his life as a collier in the valleys of the *Rhondda, Aman and Dulais and, by the end of the book, looks forward to a career at the University College of Wales, Aberystwyth. More personal than its predecessor, the book is also more entertaining, especially in its vivacious portraits of people. It includes forthright discussion of religious, political and emotional matters, as well as an earnest account of the author's experiences as a pupil-teacher at Llandrillo: bitterly disappointed in a love-affair, D. J. Williams contemplated suicide, but then came an illuminating religious experience which brought him great joy.

Yn ôl i Leifior (1956), see under CYSGOD Y CRYMAN (1953).

'Yn wyneb haul, llygad goleuni' (lit. 'In the face of the sun, the eye of light'), one of the mottoes devised by Iolo Morganwg (Edward *Williams) which are inscribed on the regalia of *Gorsedd Beirdd Ynys Prydain.

Yn y llyvyr hwnn (lit. 'In this book'; 1546), believed to be the first book to be published in the Welsh language, was written by John *Price of Brecon. Generally known by its opening words, it contains the alphabet, a calendar, the Creed, the Lord's Prayer, the Ten Commandments, the Seven Virtues of the Church, the Seven Deadly Sins, as well as instructions on how to read Welsh and advice for farmers during each month of the year. The author, one of the earliest Protestant Humanists in Wales, was acutely aware of the ignorance and apathy which existed among his countrymen in religious and moral affairs. Anxious to improve their spiritual condition, mainly by translating parts of the Scriptures into Welsh, he was also aware of the shortcomings of a Church until very recently Roman Catholic and of the lack of enthusiasm among its clergy. The book was intended to instruct the common people in the principles of the Christian faith, especially the tenets most necessary for the good of the soul.

The work was reprinted with an introduction by J. H. Davies in 1902. For further details see the article by R. Geraint Gruffydd, '*Yny Lhyvyr Hwn* (1546): the earliest Welsh printed book', in the *Bulletin* of the Board of Celtic Studies (vol. XXIII, 1969).

Yniwl Iarll, the father of Enid in the romance of *Geraint fab Erbin, lives in an old ruined court not far from the town of Caerdyf (Cardiff), having been dispossessed of his fortress by a nephew. He and his wife make Geraint welcome and support him in his successful contest with

*Edern fab Nudd for a sparrowhawk. After Enid is given to Geraint in marriage, Yniwl's property is restored to him.

Ynyr Hen (*fl.* early 13th cent.), see under NAN-NAU FAMILY.

Ynys Afallon, the magic island in the western ocean to which *Arthur was carried after being mortally wounded in battle. The name derives from the '*insula Avallonis*' of *Geoffrey of Monmouth's **Historia Regum Britanniae* but the island is described more fully in the *'*Vita Merlini*' where it is called '*insula pomorum que fortunata vocatur*' (lit. 'the island of apples which is called happy'). It is depicted as a land of perpetual youth, fertility, feasting and every kind of sensuous pleasure, including magical birds which sing enchanting songs, and Morgen is the chief of nine sisters who rule there. This account corresponds in every detail with the descriptions given in early Irish sources of the island which was the pagan Celtic Otherworld (see under ANNWFN) situated somewhere in the western seas and ruled over by women. It is known in Irish by various names such as *Tir na nÓg* ('The land of the young ones') and *Tir inna mBéo* ('The land of the living ones'). The earliest account is that given in the tale of *The Voyage of Brân* (8th cent.). Ynys Afallon thus portrays one of the two contrasting concepts of the Celtic Otherworld which are common to the Welsh and the Irish.

All the Welsh versions of **Brut y Brenhinedd* render Geoffrey's '*insula Avallonis*' by '*Ynys Afallach*', implying that the name contains the word '*afall*' ('apple-tree(s)'). The supposed meaning 'place of apples' gained some support from *Avallon*, the name of a town in Burgundy which derives from Gaulish *Aballone* or *Avallone* ('apple-place'). But '*ynys Afallach*' is the form preserved consistently in the *Brut* as well as in certain other medieval Welsh sources and it seems far more likely that the name derived from that of *Aballac(h)* or *Afallach who appears in several early Welsh genealogies as an ancestor-deity from whom a number of ruling dynasties in Wales and the *Old North claimed descent. This name is presumably the original of William of Malmesbury's Avalloc who, according to his *De Antiquitate Glastoniensis*, ruled over an island-kingdom inhabited by his daughters. The identification of '*insula Avallonis*' with Glastonbury is due to William of Malmesbury and to *Gerald de Barri (Giraldus Cambrensis) who followed William's account in his *Speculum Ecclesiae*.

For further details see Kuno Meyer, *The Voyage of Brân son of Febal* (1895), R. S. Loomis, *Arthurian Literature in the Middle Ages* (1959), R. Bromwich, *Trioedd Ynys Prydein* (1961), B. F. Roberts, *Brut y Brenhinedd* (1971), Basil Clarke, *Geoffrey of Monmouth's Vita Merlini* (1973) and Lewis Thorpe, *Gerald of Wales, the Itinerary through Wales and the Description of Wales* (1978).

Ynys Bŷr (**Caldey**), see under PŶR (6th cent.).

Ynys Enlli, see BARDSEY.

Ynys yr Hud (lit. 'The island of magic'; 1923), a collection of thirty-four poems by W. J. *Gruffydd. It includes a longish poem on *Rhys ap Gruffudd (The Lord Rhys), another on Goronwy *Owen's farewell to Wales, with which the author won the *Crown at the National Eisteddfod held in London in 1910, as well as some of the poet's best-known shorter poems, such as '*Ywen Llanddeiniolen*', '*Gwladys Rhys*' and '*Thomas Morgan yr Ironmonger*'. Others express his strong antipathy for those in positions of authority who had sent young men to be slaughtered in the First World War. The title-poem was inspired by a legend incorporated in the early Irish tale, *The Voyage of Brân*, and which is also reflected in **Pedair Cainc y Mabinogi* in the tale of *Branwen. It tells how a dozen sailors from the banks of the Menai discover an island in the South Seas where they lead a lotus-eating life beyond the bounds of time. Eventually, the magic spent, they obey the call of their homeland but, on returning to Wales, discover that three generations separate them from the age in which they had lived and that they have been forgotten.

Ynysarwed, a mansion in the parish of Lower Neath, Glam., was the home of a family which patronized poets for at least four generations. Tomas ap Siancyn, the first known patron, was followed by his son Richard and his grandsons Rhys and Thomas; Thomas, the son of Rhys, maintained the tradition for another generation. The family owned a number of important manuscripts, including Y *Cwta Cyfarwydd.

Ynysmaengwyn, a mansion near Tywyn, Mer., has a prominent place in the history of bardic patronage in the county. Poets visited the house from the time of Hywel ap Siancyn (d. 1494), the first known patron. In the time of his son Humphrey *Tudur Aled and *Gruffudd Hiraethog were among the poets who received a welcome there. Patronage was intermittent after their day, but poems addressed to John Wynn, Humphrey's son, and Humphrey Wynn, his heir, have survived. The tradition was maintained until the eighteenth century by Vincent Corbet (d. 1723/4) and his daughter Ann (d. 1760).

YORKE, PHILIP (1743–1804), gentleman and antiquary, of Erddig, near Wrexham, Denbs., was educated at the University of Cambridge and at Lincoln's Inn. He was elected to the Society of Antiquaries in 1768, a year after his succession to the Erddig estate, to the improvement of which he was devoted. After his marriage in 1782 to the daughter of Piers Wynn of

Dyffryn Aled, he became interested in her descent from Marchudd, lord of Uwchdulas, and from this research grew his book *Tracts of Powys* (1795), which was based on the available printed sources and on correspondence with Welsh scholars. The work, which includes a refutation of Polydore Vergil's opinions as well as notes on Crown lordships in *Powys, was enlarged and published as his authoritative book, *Royal Tribes of Wales* (1799). Its erudition contrasts oddly with Yorke's extraordinary gifts as a writer of doggerel, as demonstrated in his collection *Crude Ditties*, which was published in 1914. The house of Erddig, built for Joshua Edisbury in 1683, now belongs to the National Trust.

There is a vivid portrait of Philip Yorke in C. J. Apperley's *My Life and Times* (1927) and an evocative account of the family in Albinia Cust, *Chronicles of Erthig on the Dyke* (1914); see also Merlin Waterson, *The Servants' Hall* (1980).

Young, Jubilee (1887–1962), preacher, was born near Maenclochog, Pembs., in the year of Queen Victoria's Golden Jubilee. He worked in a draper's shop in the Rhondda Valley before entering the Presbyterian College, Carmarthen, to prepare for the Baptist ministry. After holding pastorates in his native county and in the Rhondda, he became famous during his ministry at Seion, Llanelli, in the years from 1931 to 1957. He was a most eloquent preacher, a master of illustration and application, and a virtuoso in the modulation of his voice for the purposes of that combination of fervour and dramatic effect known in Welsh as '*hwyl*'. Some who heard him have doubted whether preaching can preserve its purity when it becomes entertainment of such a deliberate kind.

Young Wales, see Cymru Fydd.

Ysbaddaden Bencawr, see under Culhwch and Olwen.

Ysgafell, see under Williams, Henry (1624–84) and Williams, Jane (1806–85).

Ysgolan, the subject of a tale of which traces occur in a poem in *The *Black Book of Carmarthen*. To him are attributed the burning of a church, the killing of a cow and the drowning of a book which he had received as a gift. His name occurs later in vaticinatory verse in which he is accused of burning Welsh books in the Tower of London. A similar story about a man of the same name was current in Brittany in the nineteenth century.

For further details see the article by A. O. H. Jarman in *Ysgrifau Beirniadol X* (ed. J. E. Caerwyn Williams, 1977).

Ysgrifau Beirniadol (lit. 'Critical essays'), a series, published by *Gwasg Gee*, devoted to literary criticism and related topics, which has been edited since its inception in 1965 by J. E. Caerwyn *Williams. Among the contributors are most of the members of the Welsh Departments of the University of Wales, together with a number of other scholars, critics and writers. Four of the thirteen volumes which had appeared by 1985 were *Festschriften* in honour of eminent writers: John Gwilym *Jones (1971), Thomas *Parry (1977), T. J. *Morgan (1979) and Rachel *Bromwich (1985).

'**Ystoria Ysgan ab Asgo**', a story of an attempt by the lord of Bodeugan, Denbs., to flee from Death. No other example of the motif is recorded in Welsh, although certain elements in the story are quite common in other literatures. There is only one copy extant and that is in the hand of John *Jones of Gellilyfdy and dated December 1608. The fact that the copyist revealed nothing about his sources, and also that the setting of the story is near his home, suggest that the work may have been based on a local oral tradition. On the other hand, the language and style reflect medieval Welsh prose at its most traditional, which suggests a literary exemplar.

'**Ystorya Adaf ac Eua y Wreic**' a translation of one of the various forms of the tale *Vita Adae et Euae* which was translated into most of the languages of western Europe. There are eight copies of the tale in Welsh manuscripts dating from about 1350 to the end of the nineteenth century, but they are all derived from the oldest extant copy which is in The *White Book of Rhydderch* (Peniarth MS 5). The work tells of the wanderings and penance of Adam and Eve after their banishment from Paradise.

'**Ystorya Bown de Hamtwn**', a prose translation of a lost Anglo-Norman poem, '*La Geste de Boun de Hantone*'. The oldest copy is in The *White Book of Rhydderch* (*c*.1350) but the work may have been translated before 1300. The structure of the romance is episodic but its language is masterly. The hero, Befus or Bown, is sold as a slave to the King of Egypt but is offered the hand of the princess Iosian in marriage. Foiled in his first attempts to convert her to Christianity, he is imprisoned for seven years by another of the girl's suitors, Bradmwnd. Iosian marries Ifor, King of Mobrant, and later the earl Milys, whom she strangles on their wedding-night. After many adventures, Bown is reunited with her and they return to Egypt. His name appears in *cywyddau* of the medieval period as an example of courage and Christian endeavour.

The text has been edited with an introduction by Morgan Watkin (1958).

Ystorya Dared, one of the three great historical texts of medieval Wales, is often associated in the

manuscripts with the other two, *Brut y Brenhinedd* and *Brut y Tywysogion*. It is a translation
of a sixth-century Latin text entitled *Historia
Daretis Phrygii de Excidio Troiae* which was
famous during the Middle Ages as evidence for
the traditional belief that the nations which grew
out of the Roman Empire were descended
through Aeneas from the Trojans. Almost
certainly first translated about 1300 under the
influence of *Geoffrey of Monmouth, it was
intended as an introduction to *Brut y Brenhinedd*.

Ystorya de Carolo Magno, see PERERINDOD
SIARLYMAEN.

Ystrad Fflur, see STRATA FLORIDA.

Ystrad Marchell, see STRATA MARCELLA.

Ystrad Tywi, a *gwlad* of early Wales, of which
the dynastic history is obscure. It appears to have
been conquered by Seisyll, King of *Ceredigion,
about 730, after which the joint kingdom of
Ceredigion and Ystrad Tywi was known as
*Seisyllwg.

Yvain de Galles, see OWAIN AP THOMAS AP
RHODRI (*c.*1330–78).

Ywain Meirion, see GRIFFITH, OWEN
(1803–68).

Zeitschrift für Celtische Philologie (lit. 'Journal
for Celtic philology'), the oldest journal devoted
to Celtic studies, was founded in 1896 by Kuno
Meyer, then Professor of German at the University of Liverpool, and Ludwig Ch. Stern. Before
the creation of the *Bulletin* of the *Board of
Celtic Studies in 1921, it was a major vehicle for
the publication of specifically Welsh scholarship.
After Meyer's death in 1919 the journal was
edited by a succession of eminent scholars,
among them Julius Pokorny, Rudolf Thurneysen
and Ludwig Muelhausen; its present editors are
Heinrich Wagner and Karl Horst Schmidt. Besides contributions of philological interest, it
carries articles in both German and English on
other aspects of Celtic civilization, including
archaeology. It was in this journal that John
*Morris-Jones's classification of the *cyngan-
eddion* first appeared.

A CHRONOLOGY OF THE HISTORY OF WALES

AD 43   The beginning of the Roman Conquest of Britain.

47–51   Caratacus and the Silures resist the Romans.

61   The massacre of the Druids of Anglesey by the troops of Suetonius.

74–75   The Roman victory over the Silures and the founding of Isca (Caerleon).

78   Agricola defeats the Ordovices in north Wales.

383   The Roman legions leave Britain with Macsen Wledig (Magnus Maximus) who seeks to become Emperor.

c.400   Cunedda moves from Manaw Gododdin to Gwynedd to eject the Gwyddel (Irish).

c.410   The first British settlement of Armorica (Brittany).

429   Garmon (Germanus) visits Britain.

c.440   The reign of Gwrtheyrn (Vortigern) and the arrival of the Jutes Hengist and Horsa and their mercenary band.

c.505   The death of Dyfrig (Dubricius), the first Welsh saint.

c.519   The battle of Mount Badon, a British victory traditionally associated with Arthur.

c.539   The battle of Camlan, in which Arthur is killed.

c.547   Gildas writes his *De Excidio Britanniae*. The death of Maelgwn Gwynedd.

c.550   Old Welsh emerges from the British language.

577   The battle of Dyrham (Deorham), after which the Welsh lose contact with the Britons of Devon and Cornwall. Urien Rheged, patron of Taliesin, has the Angles at bay on Lindisfarne.

c.589   The death of Dewi Sant.

c.595   The battle of Catraeth, commemorated by Aneirin in '*Y Gododdin*'.

c.615   The battle of Chester and the massacre of the monks of Bangor Iscoed, after which the Welsh begin to lose contact with the Britons of 'the Old North'.

632   Cadwallon of Gwynedd, in alliance with Penda of Mercia, defeats Edwin of Northumbria at the battle of Meigen (Heathfield).

c.635   The word *Cymry* is used to denote the Welsh.

c.638   The territory of the Gododdin is overrun by the Angles.

c.642   The Mercians attack the kingdom of Powys.

654   The battle of Winwaed Field and the final separation of the Welsh from their compatriots in 'the Old North'.

664   The death of Cadwaladr, the last Welsh 'King of Britain'.

c.767   Bishop Elfodd and the Welsh Church accept the Roman date for Easter.

c.784   Offa of Mercia constructs the earthwork known as Offa's Dyke.

c.800   Nennius compiles his *Historia Brittonum*.

844–77   The reign of Rhodri Mawr, King of Wales.

c.850   Viking attacks on Wales begin.

855   The ancient House of Powys becomes extinct. The cycle known as 'Canu Heledd' is written.

c.890   Welsh rulers acknowledge the overlordship of Alfred of Wessex.

c.900–50   The reign of Hywel Dda, King of Wales.

904   The extinction of the ancient line of Irish rulers in Dyfed.

928   Hywel Dda goes on pilgrimage to Rome.

c.945   The Welsh Laws are codified under Hywel Dda.

c.960   The *Annales Cambriae* are written.

1018   The extinction of the British kingdom of Strathclyde.

1039–63   Gruffudd ap Llywelyn unites Wales under his rule.

1067   The Normans begin to penetrate Wales and the lordships of the March are created.

c.1070   The beginnings of Latin monasticism in Wales.

1075–93   Rhys ap Tewdwr rules over Deheubarth.

1090   The Normans begin to conquer south and west Wales.

c.1108   Henry I settles Flemings around the estuary of the Cleddau.

1115   The Normans take control of the dioceses of St. David's and Llandaf.

1118   The House of Gwynedd begins to expand under Gruffudd ap Cynan.

1120   Dewi Sant is canonized by Rome as Saint David.

1136   Geoffrey of Monmouth writes his *Historia Regum Britanniae*.

1137–70   The reign of Owain Gwynedd.

1140   The foundation of Whitland Abbey, the mother-house of Cistercianism in *Pura Wallia*.

1160   The death of Madog ap Maredudd, the last ruler of a united Powys.

1165   The Welsh under Owain Gwynedd resist Henry II's attempt to subdue Wales.

1170–97   Rhys ap Gruffudd (The Lord Rhys) rules south Wales.

1176   An 'eisteddfod' is held at Cardigan Castle.

1188   Gerald de Barri (Giraldus Cambrensis) accompanies Archbishop Baldwin on his journey through Wales.

1196–1240   The reign of Llywelyn ap Iorwerth (Llywelyn Fawr), latterly recognized as Prince of Wales.

1246–82   The reign of Llywelyn ap Gruffudd of the House of Gwynedd.

1267   The Treaty of Montgomery recognizes Llywelyn as Prince of Wales.

1276–77   The first War of Welsh Independence, after which Llywelyn's authority is restricted to Gwynedd.

1282–83   The second War of Welsh Independence and the death of Llywelyn ap Gruffudd (The Last Prince) near Cilmeri.

1283   Edward I orders the building of castles in Wales.

1284   The Statute of Rhuddlan.

1294–96	The Welsh under Madog ap Llywelyn revolt against English occupation.
1301	Edward I proclaims his seventeen-year-old son as Prince of Wales.
1316	The revolt of Llywelyn Bren.
c.1330	Einion Offeiriad writes his Grammar.
c.1320–70	The age of Dafydd ap Gwilym.
1348–50	The Black Death ravages Wales.
1369–77	Owain Lawgoch threatens English rule.
1400	The rising of Owain Glyndŵr.
1402	The English Parliament passes Penal Laws against the Welsh.
1404–06	Owain Glyndŵr holds Parliaments at Machynlleth and Pennal, and offers his allegiance to the Pope of Avignon, proposing an archbishopric and two universities for Wales.
c.1415	The disappearance of Owain Glyndŵr.
c.1451	An eisteddfod is held at Carmarthen Castle under the patronage of Gruffudd ap Nicolas.
1461	Welsh forces take part in the battle of Mortimer's Cross, a major engagement in the Wars of the Roses and a Yorkist victory.
1471	The Yorkist King Edward IV establishes at Ludlow the Council in the Marches of Wales.
1485	Henry Tudor lands near Milford Haven and marches through Wales to defeat Richard III at Bosworth.
1523	An eisteddfod is held at Caerwys.
1531	The execution of Rhys ap Gruffudd and the fall of the House of Dinefwr.
1534	Rowland Lee, Bishop of Lichfield, is appointed President of the Council in the Marches.
1536–39	The dissolution of the monasteries.
1536 and 1542	The Acts of Union which annex Wales to England.
1547	The publication of Sir John Price's *Yn y Lhyvyr Hwnn*, the first printed book in Welsh.
1562	An Act of Parliament authorizes the creation of a Protestant liturgy in Welsh.
1567	The publication of the New Testament and the Book of Common Prayer in Welsh. A second eisteddfod is held at Caerwys.
1571	The foundation of Jesus College, Oxford.
1573	The publication of Humphrey Llwyd's map of Wales and Sir John Price's *Historiae Britannicae Defensio*.
1584	The martyrdom of the Catholic Richard Gwyn. The publication of David Powel's *Historie of Cambria*.
1585	The publication of *Y Drych Cristianogawl*, the first book to be printed in Wales.
1588	William Morgan's translation of the complete Bible is published.
1593	The martyrdom of the Puritan John Penry.
1617–32	William Vaughan seeks to establish Cambriol, a Welsh colony in Newfoundland, but ultimately fails.
1621	The publication of John Davies's Welsh Grammar and of Edmund Prys's metrical psalms.

1630   *Y Beibl Bach*, a popular edition of the Bible, is published.

1632   The publication of John Davies's Welsh-Latin Dictionary.

1639   The first 'gathered' Church (of Independents and Baptists) is founded at Llanfaches.

1642   John Poyer commits Pembroke to the cause of the Parliament; in royalist Wales only Tenby makes a similar declaration.

1645   King Charles in Wales, raising troops for a last effort.

1648   The second Civil War, begun by John Poyer. The battle of St. Fagans. Cromwell in Wales.

1650–53   The Act for the Propagation of the Gospel operating in Wales.

1650   Henry Vaughan publishes *Silex Scintillans*.

1653   The publication of Morgan Llwyd's *Llyfr y Tri Aderyn*.

1659–72   Stephen Hughes publishes Rhys Prichard's *Cannwyll y Cymry*.

1660   The restoration of the Council of Wales.

1660–62   The ejection of Puritan ministers.

1674   The Welsh Trust opens schools in Wales.

1678   The Popish Plot and the discovery of a Jesuit College in the Monnow Valley.

1682   Welsh Quakers migrate to Pennsylvania.

1689   The abolition of the Council of Wales.

1694   The death of Siôn Dafydd Las, the last of the household poets.

1699   The establishment of the Society for Promoting Christian Knowledge.

1704   Ellis Wynne's *Gweledigaetheu y Bardd Cwsc* is published.

1707   The publication of Edward Lhuyd's *Archaeologia Britannica*.

1715   The establishment of the Society of Ancient Britons, the first society of the London Welsh.

1716   Theophilus Evans's *Drych y Prif Oesoedd* is published.

1718   Isaac Carter establishes the first permanent printing-press in Wales at Atpar, Cards.

1731   The first Circulating School is opened by Griffith Jones of Llanddowror.

1733   The passage of the first Enclosure Act relating to Wales.

1735   The conversion of Howel Harris.

1742   The first meeting of a Methodist Association in Wales.

1744   William Williams (Pantycelyn) publishes his first collection of hymns.

1751   The foundation of the Honourable Society of Cymmrodorion in London.

1752   Howel Harris establishes the Trefeca 'family'.

1759   John Guest begins to develop the ironworks at Merthyr Tydfil. The publication of the first of the works of Goronwy Owen.

1771   The Gwyneddigion Society is founded in London.

1776   The publication of Richard Price's *Observations on the nature of Civil Liberty*.

1782   The slate industry of north-west Wales is launched by Lord Penrhyn.

1789 Thomas Charles of Bala opens his first Sunday School.

1792 Edward Williams (Iolo Morganwg) holds the first session of *Gorsedd Beirdd Ynys Prydain* on Primrose Hill in London.

1793 The launching of the periodical *Y Cylchgrawn Cynmraeg* by Morgan John Rhys.

1797 A French revolutionary fleet lands a force at Fishguard.

1801 The first official Census records that the population of Wales is 587,000 and that Merthyr Tydfil, with 7,705 inhabitants, is the largest town in Wales.

1804 The foundation of the British and Foreign Bible Society. Richard Trevithick experiments with a steam locomotive at Merthyr Tydfil. The first weekly newspaper in Wales, *The Cambrian*, is launched in Swansea.

1805 The publication of the hymns of Ann Griffiths.

1811 The separation of Welsh Methodists from the Church of England.

1814 The launching of *Seren Gomer*, the first monthly newspaper in Welsh.

1819 An eisteddfod is held at the Ivy Bush tavern, Carmarthen, in association with *Gorsedd Beirdd Ynys Prydain*.

1822 The foundation of St. David's College, Lampeter.

1826 The opening of Telford's bridge across the Menai Straits.

1831 The workers' rising at Merthyr Tydfil.

1832–40 The Scotch Cattle are active in south-east Wales.

1838–49 The publication of Lady Charlotte Guest's translation, *The Mabinogion*.

1839 The Chartists march on Newport. The opening of the Bute Dock at Cardiff.

1839–44 The Rebecca Riots.

1841 The opening of the Taff Vale Railway. The death of the preacher John Elias, called 'The Methodist Pope'.

1846 The establishment of the Cambrian Archaeological Association.

1847 The publication of the Blue Book reports on the state of education in Wales.

1851 The religious Census shows a huge majority of Nonconformists in Wales.

1854 The publication of the first part of the encyclopaedia *Y Gwyddoniadur Cymreig*.

1855 The first coal-pit is sunk in the Rhondda Valley.

1856 Evan James and James James of Pontypridd compose '*Hen Wlad fy Nhadau*', later adopted as the Welsh national anthem.

1858 The Eisteddfod held at Llangollen begins a pattern of annual gatherings.

1859 Liberal victories at General Elections and the eviction of tenants. A religious revival sweeps Wales. The establishment of the newspaper *Baner ac Amserau Cymru* by Thomas Gee.

1862 The foundation of Bangor Normal College.

1863 A campaign is launched for the establishment of a Welsh National University.

1865 A Welsh colony is founded in Patagonia.

1868 Liberal victories at 'the Great Election'.

1872 The University College of Wales opens at Aberystwyth.

1874 The establishment of the North Wales Quarrymen's Union.

1877 The foundation of the Chair of Celtic at the University of Oxford.

1881 The establishment of the Welsh Rugby Union. The Welsh Sunday Closing Act is passed.

1883 A University College is opened in Cardiff. The magazine *Y Geninen* is launched.

1884 A University College is opened at Bangor.

1885 The first Welsh Language Society is launched.

1886 The Tithe War begins. The establishment of the *Cymru Fydd* (Young Wales) movement and, at Oxford, of the Dafydd ap Gwilym Society.

1889 The Welsh Intermediate Schools Act. The opening of Barry Docks by David Davies.

1890 The election of David Lloyd George as a member for Caernarfon Boroughs. T. E. Ellis advocates Home Rule for Wales.

1891 Owen M. Edwards launches his magazine *Cymru*.

1893 The University of Wales is granted a charter as a federal institution. The Royal Commission on land in Wales holds its first sessions.

1896 The collapse of the *Cymru Fydd* movement. The first stoppage at the Penrhyn Quarries. The establishment of the Central Welsh Board of Education.

1898 The establishment of the South Wales Miners' Federation.

1900 Keir Hardie, the first Independent Labour Member of Parliament, is elected at Merthyr Tydfil. The Penrhyn Quarry Strike.

1904 Evan Roberts leads a religious revival.

1907 The foundation of the National Museum of Wales, the National Library of Wales and the Welsh Department of the Board of Education.

1910 The Tonypandy Riots.

1911 The Census enumerates the population of Wales as 2,400,000, of whom almost a million are Welsh-speakers. The investiture of Edward as Prince of Wales at Caernarfon Castle.

1912 The publication of *The Miners' Next Step*.

1913 The Senghennydd Disaster. John Morris-Jones publishes his *Welsh Grammar*.

1914–18 The First World War.

1915 The publication of Caradoc Evans's collection of short stories, *My People*.

1916 Lloyd George becomes Prime Minister.

1920 The Disestablishment of the Anglican Church in Wales. A University College is opened at Swansea.

1921 The Census shows the population of Wales to have increased to 2,656,000.

1922 The Labour Party wins half of the parliamentary seats in Wales. The foundation of *Urdd Gobaith Cymru* (The Welsh League of Youth). W. J. Gruffydd launches his magazine *Y Llenor*.

1925 The establishment of *Plaid Genedlaethol Cymru* (The Welsh Nationalist Party).

1926 The General Strike.

1929 Aneurin Bevan is elected as the Labour Member of Parliament for Ebbw Vale.

1931 The Census reveals a decrease in the population of Wales, down to 2,593,000.

1932 Unemployment in Wales among the male population reaches thirty-eight per cent.

1934 The Gresford Disaster.

1936 Welsh Nationalists burn materials at the bombing school in the Llŷn peninsula.

1937 The BBC Welsh Region is opened in Cardiff. Keidrych Rhys launches his magazine *Wales*.

1939 Emigration from Wales since 1921 is estimated at 450,000. Gwyn Jones launches his magazine *The Welsh Review*. The first Welsh-medium primary school opens at Aberystwyth.

1939–45 The Second World War.

1941 The foundation of *Undeb Cymru Fydd* (The New Wales Union).

1942 The Welsh Courts Act.

1945 The publication of Thomas Parry's *Hanes Llenyddiaeth Gymraeg*.

1946 St. Fagans Castle is designated as the Welsh Folk Museum.

1947 The nationalization of the coal industry. The International Musical Eisteddfod is founded at Llangollen.

1948 The Council for Wales and Monmouthshire is established and the Welsh Joint Education Committee founded.

1949 The magazine *Dock Leaves* (later *The Anglo-Welsh Review*) is launched.

1951 The creation of the Ministry for Welsh Affairs. The Parliament for Wales campaign is launched.

1953 The publication of *Y Bywgraffiadur Cymreig hyd 1940 (The Dictionary of Welsh Biography down to 1940)* under the auspices of the Honourable Society of Cymmrodorion.

1955 Cardiff is officially declared the capital of Wales.

1958 The launching of the first independent television company in Wales, Television Wales and the West (TWW).

1959 The establishment of *Yr Academi Gymreig*.

1961 The Census shows the population of Wales to be still below the total for 1921, at 2,653,000. The creation of the Welsh Books Council.

1962 The creation of *Cymdeithas yr Iaith Gymraeg* (The Welsh Language Society). The launching of the monthly magazine *Barn*. The publication of *The Oxford Book of Welsh Verse*, edited by Thomas Parry.

1964 The establishment of the Welsh Office and the appointment of James Griffiths as the first Secretary of State for Wales.

1965 The launching of the magazine *Poetry Wales* by Meic Stephens.

1966 Gwynfor Evans, President of *Plaid Cymru*, is elected Member of Parliament at a by-election in Carmarthenshire. The Aberfan Disaster. The foundation of the women's organization *Merched y Wawr*.

1967   The Welsh Committee of the Arts Council of Great Britain becomes the Welsh Arts Council and the Council's Literature Department is established. The Welsh Language Act is passed.

1968   The creation of an English-language section of *Yr Academi Gymreig*.

1969   The investiture of the Prince of Wales at Caernarfon Castle.

1970   Ned Thomas launches his magazine *Planet*.

1971   The foundation of *Mudiad Ysgolion Meithrin* (The Welsh Nursery Schools Movement).

1973   The Kilbrandon Commission recommends an elected Assembly for Wales. The foundation of the Wales Trades Union Council.

1974   The reorganization of local government reduces the number of county authorities in Wales from thirteen to eight.

1976   The establishment of *Cymdeithas Cerdd Dafod*, the society for poets in the traditional metres.

1979   In a referendum on Devolution for Wales the Government's proposals for an elected Assembly are defeated.

1981   The Census enumerates the population of Wales as 2,749,400, of whom 503,549 are Welsh-speakers.

1982   The opening of *Sianel Pedwar Cymru (S4C)*, the fourth television channel broadcasting partly in Welsh.

1983   At the General Election the Conservative Party takes fifteen of the seats in Wales (the largest number held in the twentieth century); the Labour Party's representation is reduced to nineteen seats, and the Liberals and *Plaid Cymru* win two seats each.

1984–85   The miners' strike.